09-AIC-68

THIS BIBLE BELONGS TO

_____

IT IS A GIFT FROM

_____

ON THIS SPECIAL DAY,

_____

DATE

_____

"Don't let anyone think less of you because you are young. Be an example to all believers in what you say, in the way you live, in your love, your faith, and your purity."

1 Timothy 4:12

GUYS LIFE APPLICATION STUDY BIBLE

Guys LIFE® APPLICATION STUDY BIBLE

New Living Translation®

SECOND EDITION

Tyndale House Publishers, Inc.
Carol Stream, Illinois

Visit Tyndale online at www.newlivingtranslation.com and www.tyndale.com.

Features and Bible helps copyright © 2007 by Tyndale House Publishers, Inc., Carol Stream, IL 60188. All rights reserved.

Cover and interior illustrations copyright © 2007 by Juan Alvarez. All rights reserved.

Guys Life Application Study Bible is an edition of the *Holy Bible,* New Living Translation.

Holy Bible, New Living Translation, copyright © 1996, 2004, 2007 by Tyndale House Foundation. All rights reserved.

The text of the *Holy Bible,* New Living Translation, may be quoted in any form (written, visual, electronic, or audio) up to and inclusive of five hundred (500) verses without express written permission of the publisher, provided that the verses quoted do not account for more than 25 percent of the work in which they are quoted, and provided that a complete book of the Bible is not quoted.

When the *Holy Bible,* New Living Translation, is quoted, one of the following credit lines must appear on the copyright page or title page of the work:

> Scripture quotations are taken from the *Holy Bible,* New Living Translation, copyright © 1996, 2004, 2007 by Tyndale House Foundation. Used by permission of Tyndale House Publishers, Inc., Carol Stream, Illinois 60188. All rights reserved.

> Unless otherwise indicated, all Scripture quotations are taken from the *Holy Bible,* New Living Translation, copyright © 1996, 2004, 2007 by Tyndale House Foundation. Used by permission of Tyndale House Publishers, Inc., Carol Stream, Illinois 60188. All rights reserved.

> Scripture quotations marked *NLT* are taken from the *Holy Bible,* New Living Translation, copyright © 1996, 2004, 2007 by Tyndale House Foundation. Used by permission of Tyndale House Publishers, Inc., Carol Stream, Illinois 60188. All rights reserved.

When quotations from the NLT text are used in nonsalable media, such as church bulletins, orders of service, newsletters, transparencies, or similar media, a complete copyright notice is not required, but the initials *NLT* must appear at the end of each quotation.

Quotations in excess of five hundred (500) verses or 25 percent of the work, or other permission requests, must be approved in writing by Tyndale House Publishers, Inc. Send requests by e-mail to: permission@tyndale.com or call 630-668-8300, ext. 8817.

Publication of any commentary or other Bible reference work produced for commercial sale that uses the New Living Translation requires written permission for use of the NLT text.

This Bible is typeset in the typeface *Lucerna,* designed by Brian Sooy & Co. exclusively for Tyndale House Publishers, Inc. All rights reserved.

TYNDALE, New Living Translation, NLT, the New Living Translation logo, *Life Application,* and *LeatherLike* are registered trademarks of Tyndale House Publishers, Inc. *The Truth Made Clear* is a trademark of Tyndale House Publishers, Inc.

For manufacturing information regarding this product, please call 1-800-323-9400.

ISBN 978-1-4143-1597-3 Hardcover
ISBN 978-1-4143-1598-0 Softcover
ISBN 978-1-4143-1599-7 LeatherLike Onyx

Printed in China

17 16 15 14 13 12 11
9 8 7 6 5 4 3

Tyndale House Publishers and Wycliffe Bible Translators share the vision for an understandable, accurate translation of the Bible for every person in the world. Each sale of the *Holy Bible,* New Living Translation, benefits Wycliffe Bible Translators. Wycliffe is working with partners around the world to accomplish Vision 2025—an initiative to start a Bible translation program in every language group that needs it by the year 2025.

ACKNOWLEDGMENTS

CONCEPT DEVELOPMENT TEAM
Dr. Bruce B. Barton
Kim Johnson
Doug Knox
Jaqueline L. Nuñez
Mark Norton
Betsy Todt Schmitt
Dr. Mary Manz Simon
Jeff Smith
Linda Chaffee Taylor
David R. Veerman
Linda Washington
Tim Willms

SENIOR EDITOR
Betsy Todt Schmitt

TYNDALE HOUSE EDITORS
Leanne Rolland
Betty Free Swanberg

PROJECT CONSULTANT
Dr. Mary Manz Simon

GRAPHIC DESIGN
Jacqueline L. Nuñez

INTERIOR ILLUSTRATIONS
Juan Alvarez

TYNDALE HOUSE PRODUCTION TEAM
Tim Bensen
Gwen Elliott

CHART ILLUSTRATIONS
Jenny Swanson

NOTES AND FEATURES
What Now?
Jeanette Dall
Leanne Rolland

I'm Not the Only One!
Jennifer Karrer

Amazing Facts
Carol Smith

Is It OK?
Paige Drygas

Freeze Frame
John Perrodin

Bible Book Introductions
Carol Smith

Memory Verses
Allison B. Schmitt

History Remix
Carol Smith

Indexes
Phoebe Blaustein
Madeleine Garber
Jennifer Karrer

I Survived!
Shelley Kimmons Bacote
Katherine Cloyd
Jack Crabtree
Mary Ann Lackland
Jonathan R. McKee
Len Woods
Walter Woods

With assistance from the following senior high students: Brianna Lafleur, Kimmy Anderson, Taryn Erdvig, Alex Mohring, Alyssa Flores, Mark Johnston, Alec McKee, Shawna Reilly, and Jason Fullmore, Orangevale, CA; Breanne Becker, Laura Englehardt, Brittany Williams, Christian Jones, Jarred Anton, John Leon, Andrew Yenchko, and Ivanna Young, Long Island, NY; Ben Kirby, Matthew Kirby, Matthew Moore, Shekinah Siegmund, Ashley Binns, Brett Pettijohn, Brian Garcia, Kade McDonald, Blair McDonald, and Aaron Jones, Rushton, LA; Whitney Walling and Ginnie Snead, Waco, TX; Hannah Bridges, Isaac Bridges, Cristin Beverley, Karlie Tedford, and Megan Lansford, Tyler, TX; Ashley N. Hart, Abilene, TX; Daniel Lichtenberger and Andria Lawson, Phoenix, AZ; Angela Marcinkowski, Jackson, TN; Bryan Wood, Alicia Rhyner, and the Senior High Youth Group at Grace Chapel, Oshkosh, WI; the Bellevue Baptist Church Teen Sunday school class, Chicago, IL; the South Shore Baptist Church Youth Group, Chicago, IL.

With special thanks to moms Christine Erickson and Margaret Henry.

contents

The Books of the Bible A8
The Books of the Bible in Alphabetical Order . . . A9
User's Guide to the Features A10
Quick-Answers Index A12
A Note to Parents A26
Introduction to the NLT A27
NLT Bible Translation Team A35
Old Testament. 1
New Testament 1089
The Greatest Stories Reading Plan 1477
God's Gift to You. 1485
How to Read the Bible 1487
"I Survived!" Index 1489
"Is It OK?" Index 1490
"Freeze Frame" Index. 1491
"What Now?" Index. 1492
"I'm Not the Only One!" Index 1494
"Amazing Facts" Index 1495
"Memory Verse" Index 1498
Index to Charts and Maps 1501
"Where to Find It" Index 1502

THE BOOKS

OF THE BIBLE

The Old Testament

3 Genesis
65 Exodus
115 Leviticus
151 Numbers
203 Deuteronomy
245 Joshua
275 Judges
303 Ruth
309 1 Samuel
347 2 Samuel
377 1 Kings
413 2 Kings
449 1 Chronicles
485 2 Chronicles
527 Ezra
541 Nehemiah
561 Esther
573 Job
611 Psalms
711 Proverbs
749 Ecclesiastes
761 Song of Songs
771 Isaiah
849 Jeremiah
919 Lamentations
929 Ezekiel
987 Daniel
1007 Hosea
1021 Joel
1027 Amos
1037 Obadiah
1041 Jonah
1045 Micah
1053 Nahum
1057 Habakkuk
1061 Zephaniah
1067 Haggai
1071 Zechariah
1083 Malachi

The New Testament

1091 Matthew
1135 Mark
1165 Luke
1211 John
1245 Acts
1289 Romans
1311 1 Corinthians
1329 2 Corinthians
1343 Galatians
1353 Ephesians
1361 Philippians
1369 Colossians
1377 1 Thessalonians
1383 2 Thessalonians
1387 1 Timothy
1395 2 Timothy
1401 Titus
1405 Philemon
1407 Hebrews
1423 James
1431 1 Peter
1439 2 Peter
1443 1 John
1449 2 John
1451 3 John
1453 Jude
1455 Revelation

THE BOOKS

OF THE BIBLE IN ALPHABETICAL ORDER

1245 Acts
1027 Amos
449 1 Chronicles
485 2 Chronicles
1369 Colossians
1311 1 Corinthians
1329 2 Corinthians
987 Daniel
203 Deuteronomy
749 Ecclesiastes
1353 Ephesians
561 Esther
65 Exodus
929 Ezekiel
527 Ezra
1343 Galatians
3 Genesis
1057 Habakkuk
1067 Haggai
1407 Hebrews
1007 Hosea
771 Isaiah
1423 James
849 Jeremiah
573 Job
1021 Joel
1211 John
1443 1 John
1449 2 John
1451 3 John
1041 Jonah
245 Joshua
1453 Jude
275 Judges
377 1 Kings
413 2 Kings
919 Lamentations
115 Leviticus
1165 Luke
1083 Malachi
1135 Mark
1091 Matthew
1045 Micah
1053 Nahum
541 Nehemiah
151 Numbers
1037 Obadiah
1431 1 Peter
1439 2 Peter
1405 Philemon
1361 Philippians
711 Proverbs
611 Psalms
1455 Revelation
1289 Romans
303 Ruth
309 1 Samuel
347 2 Samuel
761 Song of Songs
1377 1 Thessalonians
1383 2 Thessalonians
1387 1 Timothy
1395 2 Timothy
1401 Titus
1071 Zechariah
1061 Zephaniah

How to Use
Your Guys Life Application Study Bible

God's Word is meant for you. Whatever your life situation is right now, and whatever situations you may encounter in the future, God's Word is here to guide you, counsel you, encourage you, and help you through those circumstances. The features in this Bible are designed to help you connect God's Word with your life in a way that is meaningful, fresh, and fun! So get ready for the adventure that will last a lifetime. Here's what to look for in your *Guys Life Application Study Bible*.

I was angry and ready to fight. I had just broken up with my girlfriend. Then I found out she was planning to go out with one of my closest friends. He was the friend who for the past couple months had been telling me that I shouldn't be wasting my time with this girl.

Now the truth was out. He had wanted to go out with my girlfriend the whole time he was advising me to break up with her.

I wanted to give him a good pounding. But I never did fight him. I knew that fighting would have hurt my relationship with God. Jesus told his disciples in Matthew 5:38–42 that revenge is not the way to settle a problem. God helped me see that even though I was hurt and angry about what my friend and ex-girlfriend had done, what was done to me was over. I couldn't go back and change what had happened. The only choice I had was how I would respond to what they had done. I chose not to make it worse by starting a fight with this guy, who had been my close friend.

I sent him an IM one day and told him how angry I was about what he had done. But I said that I didn't want to fight about it. He understood and said he would feel the same way. We decided that this was a great opportunity for both of us to get our focus back on God.

One more thing . . . my friend never did go out with my ex-girlfriend. And I saved my friendship with this guy by forgiving him for what he had planned to do.

Check out what God has to say about revenge in Matthew 5:38–42. Also check out Leviticus 19:18; Psalm 37:8; Proverbs 29:22; and Romans 12:18–21.

I Survived! As you encounter new experiences, feelings, and situations, it helps to know that someone else has made it through those very same circumstances—and survived! Collected from older teens from across the country, these are their personal survival stories about how they made it through the situations that you face right now.

What Now? Ever wonder what to do when life gets sticky and you are faced with making difficult decisions? These notes will take you through a variety of real-life situations, pointing you to Scripture, so you can learn how to make good choices in tough times.

THE PHONE FIB

"What a day! Everything went wrong at work and the boss is mad," Spencer's dad said at dinner. Spencer's mom mentioned that the pastor was going to call later to talk about the church budget. "Not tonight," said Dad. "No more problems today." As soon as Dad sat down, the phone rang. Spencer answered the phone, "Hello, Pastor Ted." In the background Spencer's dad shook his head no. "Dad? Well . . ." Spencer didn't know what to do. He didn't want to lie, but he didn't want to get his dad upset. What should Spencer do? Read Acts 5:29 for a clue.

History Remix. Take a visual tour through these fun full-color pages to see what life was like in biblical times. See how transportation, occupations, battles, weapons, and other areas of life were strikingly different from today.

JESUS AND WOMEN

In first-century Jewish culture, women were usually treated as second-class citizens and had few of the rights men had. But Jesus crossed those barriers, and Luke showed the special care Jesus had for women. Jesus treated all people with equal respect. Here are some of his encounters with women.

Jesus raises a widow's son from the dead Luke 7:11–17
A sinful woman anoints Jesus' feet Luke 7:36–50
Jesus forgives an unfaithful wife John 8:1–11
A group of women travels with Jesus Luke 8:1–3
Jesus visits Mary and Martha Luke 10:38–42
Jesus heals a handicapped woman Luke 13:10–17
Jesus heals the daughter of a Gentile woman Mark 7:24–30
Weeping women follow Jesus on his way to the cross Luke 23:27–31
Jesus' mother and other women gather at the cross John 19:25–27
Jesus appears to Mary Magdalene Mark 16:9–11
Jesus appears to other women after his resurrection Matthew 28:8–10

Charts and Maps. Scattered throughout the Bible are special maps to help you locate key Bible places, as well as charts that help break down big ideas into bite-sized bits of information.

Why do I have to be so careful about what I say?

A small rudder makes a huge ship turn. . . . In the same way, the tongue is a small thing that makes grand speeches. But a tiny spark can set a great forest on fire. JAMES 3:4-5

IS IT OK?

IS IT OK TO LEAVE OUT SOMEONE WHO'S NOT COOL?

Zacchaeus was *not cool*. He was super-short. He had no friends. He collected taxes for the Romans and then cheated his own people. Nobody wanted to hang out with him. What's surprising is that Jesus went out of his way to find Zacchaeus and go with him to his house. Zacchaeus changed into a pretty cool follower of Jesus after that. (You can read about it in Luke 19:1–10). Jesus did miracles, gave mind-boggling speeches, and had crowds following him everywhere—he was really *cool*. But he didn't let that stop him from hanging out with a guy who truly *needed* a friend. So be like Jesus and try to include others. You never know what might happen!

Is it OK? So, is it OK to think that church is boring? Is it OK not to like your life? What about getting a tattoo or dating? These notes are designed to give you a reality check on what the Bible has to say about the questions that are really on your mind. Check it out.

JOSHUA

I wandered with my people in the desert for 40 years. Yesterday we reached the flooding waters of the Jordan River. God promised a miracle. I told the people the Lord would lead us and get us all safely across, even though I didn't know how. Then I had the priests step into the river. I'm sure they were afraid. But they obeyed. The moment their toes touched the river, the water stopped. Everyone scrambled to the other side. Thousands of us.

Then I had twelve men run back and each grab a rock from the river bed. With those stones we built an altar. A reminder that God keeps his promises.

Joshua's story is told in the book of Joshua.

Amazing Facts. Think that the Bible is just a bunch of boring stories that you have heard since you started going to Sunday school? Well, take another look. This feature points out some of the more offbeat and surprising bits of information that you just might have missed. Check out these incredible facts. (And remember, they're all true!)

AMAZING FACTS

Jack hammers. Bulldozers. Shouting people. Which tore down city walls? It was those loud Israelites, yelling just like God told them to!

JOSHUA 6:20

Freeze Frame. Hear from a variety of Bible men and boys about their personal faith journeys and how God worked through a specific moment in their lives to shape them and teach them. You may discover that God is teaching you the very same lesson.

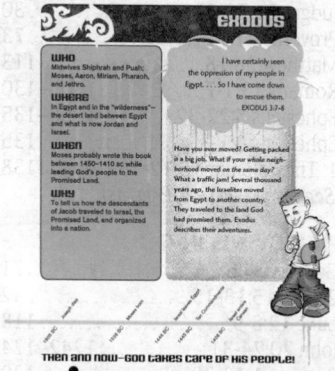

I'm Not the Only One! Did you ever have one of those "this-is-so-embarrassing-I-hope-no-one-saw-that" moments? Well guess what—you're not the only one! And to prove it, these stories have been collected from real teens and adults to help you see the lighter side of those embarrassing situations. Hopefully, you will see through these short, funny notes that God's plan for us includes the ability to lighten up and laugh at ourselves.

Book Introductions. These brief overviews will give you a snapshot of what you will read in each Bible book and the main theme of each book.

I'M NOT THE ONLY ONE!

I WAS IN THE audience with my family for a concert at school. It was just beginning—the lights had dimmed, the audience had quieted, and the first performer was onstage. At that exact instant I was overcome with a loud, uncontrollable hiccup, which erupted during that moment of total silence. Several people in the audience nearby laughed, and others turned to look at me. I buried my head in embarrassment.

Lighten Up!

Memory Verses. What do you do when you're feeling lonely? Does God really listen to your prayers? These questions and many more point to the answers that lie in key Scripture verses throughout the Bible. Use these questions to help identify and memorize those verses that can guide you and encourage you through whatever you are facing.

QUICK ANSWERS

INDEX

Need answers to nagging questions?
Check out the Scripture under each topic.

ABILITIES
Matthew 25:14-30 1127–1128
Luke 12:48 1190
1 Corinthians 12 1322–1324
1 Timothy 4:14-16 1390
(See also POTENTIAL)

ADVICE
Psalm 16:7-8 618
Psalm 25:4-7 625
Psalm 119:105 693
Proverbs 3 714–716
Proverbs 13:10, 13 ..... 725, 726
(See also BELIEVING IN GOD, FUTURE, GOD'S WILL, PRAYER)

ANGELS
Matthew 18:10 1117
Acts 12:5-7 1262

ANGER
Numbers 22:29 184
1 Kings 21:4-10 408–409
Proverbs 12:16 725
Mark 3:5-6 1139
John 2:13-17 1213
Romans 1:18-32 1290
James 3:5-6 1425
(See also HATRED, REVENGE)

APPEARANCE
Proverbs 19:22 733
Matthew 6:25-34 1101
Matthew 22:11-12 1123
1 Timothy 2:8-10 1388
1 Peter 3:1-5 1434

APPROVAL
Joshua 23:12-14 271
Matthew 10:32-33 1107
John 5:41-42 1218
John 7:18 1222
Acts 5:29 1251–1252

ATTITUDES
Exodus 14:11-14 81–82
Numbers 13:25–14:38 168–172
Numbers 16:41-50 177
Proverbs 15:13-15 728
Matthew 5:3-12 1095–1098
(See also THANKFULNESS)

AUTHORITY
Judges 21:23-25 302
Proverbs 21:1 735
Matthew 28:18 1134
Romans 13:1-7 1303–1304
Ephesians 5:22-32 1358–1359
Ephesians 6:1-3 1359
1 Thessalonians 5:12-13 1382
(See also MARRIAGE, PARENTS)

BELIEVING IN GOD
Genesis 15:6 19
2 Kings 5:13-15 420
Luke 12:8-9 1189
John 20:24-31 1242–1243
Romans 1:18-20 1290
Romans 10:9-10 1300
(See also ADVICE, BIBLE, ETERNAL LIFE/SALVATION, GOD'S WILL, OBEDIENCE, PRAYER, TIME WITH GOD)

BIBLE
Deuteronomy 17:18-20 224
2 Kings 22 443
Psalm 119 689–695
Matthew 4:1-11 1094–1095
John 20:30-31 1243
Romans 1:16-17 1290

2 Timothy 2:15 1398
2 Peter 1:16-21 1440
1 John 2:1-17 1444–1445
Revelation 22:18-19 1476
(See also Advice, God's Will, Time with God)

BLAME
(See Criticism, Excuses)

BLESSINGS
2 Samuel 7:18-27 354–355
2 Samuel 22:47-51 373
1 Chronicles 4:9-10 453
Psalm 95:2 674
Psalm 103 678–679
(See also Thankfulness)

BRAGGING
Genesis 37:5 45–46
Proverbs 27:2 742
Isaiah 10:15 783

CALLING
1 Samuel 10:21-22 319
Psalm 37:23 635

CHANGE
Genesis 6:3 9
Exodus 32:9-14 104
Psalm 103:15-18 679
James 1:17 1424

CHARACTER
(See Integrity, Values)

CHEATING
Proverbs 11:1 723
Amos 8:4-7 1034–1035
Malachi 3:8-10 1087

CHOICES
Genesis 3:1-11 6–7
Deuteronomy 30:15-20 237
Joshua 24:14-28 272–273
Proverbs 8:1-21 719–720
Matthew 12:30 1109
Matthew 13:47-52 1112
Luke 6:12-16 1175
James 1:5 1424
(See also Freedom)

CHORES
Nehemiah 13:31 559
2 Thessalonians 3:10 1385

CHURCH
Luke 4:16 1172
Acts 2:1-47 1246–1248
Romans 12:3-21 1303
1 Corinthians 12 1322–1324

COMMITMENT
Psalm 37:1-11 634–635
Matthew 10:32-33 1107
Matthew 13:18-23 1111
Matthew 28:19-20 1134
Acts 24:16 1282
(See also Marriage)

COMMUNICATION
Deuteronomy 5:1 210
Proverbs 10:8; 13:18 ..... 721, 726
Proverbs 11:13 723
Ephesians 4:32 1357
James 1:19 1424
James 3:1-18 1425–1426
(See also Criticism, Gossip, Talking about God)

COMMUNION
Matthew 26:26-30 1129
Mark 14:22-26 1158

COMPARISONS
Matthew 25:31-46 1128–1129
Luke 13:18-20 1191
2 Corinthians 10:12 1337
Galatians 6:4 1350
Philippians 2:5-11 1363
(See also Jealousy, Pride)

COMPASSION
Genesis 16:7-14 20
Genesis 21:8-21 25
Exodus 33:19 105
Psalm 51:1-12 644–645
Matthew 9:36-38 1106
Mark 3:1-6 1139
Luke 10:25-37 1185
Acts 9:36-42 1258–1259
(See also Serving God and Others)

COMPLAINING
Exodus 16:1–17:7 83–85
Numbers 12 167–168

Matthew 20:1-16 1120
Philippians 2:14-16 1363
(See also Contentment)

CONFESSION

Psalm 51 644–645
Psalm 66:13-20 653
Luke 3:4-18 1170–1171
James 5:16 1429
1 John 1:8-10 1444
(See also Forgiveness)

CONFIDENCE

2 Kings 18:5-6 437
Proverbs 3:26 714
Acts 5:19-32 1251–1252

CONFORMITY

Exodus 32:1-10 103–104
Leviticus 18:3 136
Daniel 6 997–998
1 Peter 1:13-14 1432
(See also Peer Pressure, Popularity)

CONSCIENCE

Job 27:6 596
Romans 1:18-25 1290
1 Timothy 1:18-20 1388
1 Peter 3:15-16 1434

CONSEQUENCES

Genesis 3:14-19 7
Exodus 34:7 106
Leviticus 26:14-33 147–148
Deuteronomy 27:15-26 233
1 Samuel 2:23-25 312
2 Samuel 11:1–12:18 357–359
Matthew 10:32-33 1107
2 Corinthians 5:10 1333

CONTENTMENT

Genesis 3:1-10 6
Psalm 17:15 620
Psalm 131 698
Matthew 6:25 1101
Philippians 4:10-14 1366–1367
(See also Greed)

COURAGE

Exodus 6:9 72
Esther 4:14-16 567
Daniel 3:17 993

CREATION

Genesis 1 3–5
Genesis 5:1-2 8
Psalm 8:4-5 615
Psalm 33:4-11 631

CRITICISM

Genesis 16:1-6 19–20
1 Samuel 1:6-28 310–311
Psalm 141:5 705
Proverbs 9:7-9 721
Zechariah 7:9 1075
Matthew 7:1-5 1101
(See also Communication, Excuses)

CROSS

John 19:17-18 1241

DATING

2 Corinthians 6:14-18 1334
James 1:5 1424

DEATH

1 Corinthians 15 1326–1328
2 Corinthians 5:8 1333
Philippians 1:21-24 1362
1 Thessalonians 4:13-14 1381
Hebrews 9:27 1417
1 John 4:17 1447
Revelation 20:14 1474

DECISIONS

(See Choices, Freedom)

DEPRESSION

1 Kings 19 405–406
Job 3:1-26 575–576
Psalm 119:25 690
Proverbs 15:13 728
Proverbs 17:22 731
2 Timothy 2:3-13 1398
(See also Suffering, Troubles)

DISCIPLINE (PUNISHMENT)

Deuteronomy 25:1-3 231
Proverbs 13:24 726
Matthew 7:22-23 1103
Hebrews 12:5-7 1421
(See also Consequences)

DISCIPLINE (SELF-CONTROL; TRAINING)

Luke 14:25-33 1192–1193
1 Corinthians 9:24-27 1320

DISCOURAGEMENT
Psalm 23 624
Psalm 42:5-11 639
Isaiah 40:28-31 815
John 16:33 1234–1236
Romans 8:35-39 1298
Galatians 6:9-10 1351

DIVORCE
Psalm 27:10 627
Malachi 2:16 1087

DOING RIGHT
Proverbs 1:1-3 711
Amos 5:24 1032
Mark 7:19 1145–1146
John 8:12 1223
1 Timothy 4:12 1390
2 Timothy 3:16-17 1399

DOUBTS
Genesis 17:15-21 21
Matthew 11:1-6 1107–1108
John 20:24-31 1242–1243
James 1:5-8 1424
(See also Faith, Trust)

DRINKING
Genesis 19:31-33 24
Esther 1:10–2:1 562
Proverbs 23:29-35 738
Proverbs 31:4-6 747
Romans 13:11-14 1304
Ephesians 5:18 1358
(See also Partying)

DRUGS
Proverbs 1:7-19 712
Proverbs 2 713–714
1 Corinthians 6:19-20 1316
(See also Partying)

ENEMIES
Psalm 3:1-8 612–613
Psalm 23:4-5 624
Psalm 31:4 628
Proverbs 16:7 730
Micah 7:1-7 1051
Matthew 5:43-48 1100
Luke 6:27-31 1176
Romans 5:10 1294
(See also Hatred)

ENTHUSIASM
Jeremiah 20:9 875
Philippians 4:13 1366
Revelation 3:15-16 1459

ETERNAL LIFE/SALVATION
Matthew 7:13-14 1102
John 3:16 1214
Ephesians 2:8-10 1354
Romans 5–6 1294–1296
Revelation 3:5 1458
(See also Faith, Forgiveness, Future, Heaven)

EVANGELISM
Psalm 78:5-6 662
Matthew 5:13 1098
Matthew 28:19-20 1134
Acts 1:8 1246
Romans 10:15 1300
2 Corinthians 3:3 1331
Philemon 1:13 1406

EVIL
Genesis 3:1 6
2 Kings 21:1-2 442
Psalm 101:2-3 677
Isaiah 14:12 787

EXCUSES
Genesis 3:8-13 6–7
Luke 14:16-24 1192
Romans 1:20 1290
James 1:13-16 1424
(See also Criticism)

FAILURE
(See Depression, Making Mistakes)

FAIRNESS
Psalm 58 649
Proverbs 16:11 730
Ecclesiastes 9:11 757
Isaiah 3:1-26 774–775

FAITH
Genesis 15:6 19
Matthew 8:5-13 1103
Matthew 9:18-30 1105
Luke 17:6 1195–1196
Luke 18:35-43 1198
Romans 4:3-5 1293

Hebrews 11 1419–1420
(See also Doubts, Trust)

FAITHFULNESS
Isaiah 50:7 828–829
Daniel 6:4 997
Revelation 3:15-16 1459

FAKING IT (HYPOCRISY)
Matthew 7:1-5 1101
Matthew 7:21-23 1102–1103
Matthew 23 1124–1125
Luke 12:1-5 1188
1 Peter 2:1 1432

FALSE TEACHING
Deuteronomy 18:20-22 225
Jeremiah 23:9-10 878
Ezekiel 13:1-9 943–944
Matthew 7:15 1102
1 Thessalonians 5:21-23 1382
2 Timothy 3:6-7 1398
1 John 4:1-6 1447
2 John 1:1-13 1449–1450
(See also Believing in God, Bible)

FAMILY
Proverbs 5:15-17 717
Proverbs 11:29 724
John 1:12 1212
John 7:1-10 1221–1222
1 Corinthians 1:10-13 1312
1 Timothy 5:8 1392
2 Timothy 1:5-8 1395–1396
(See also Marriage, Parents)

FEAR
Genesis 15:1 19
Joshua 1:6-9 246
Psalm 25:12-14 626
Psalm 27:1-14 626–627
Psalm 46:1-11 641
Proverbs 29:25 745
(See also Worry)

FOLLOWING GOD/JESUS
Exodus 40:36 114
Psalm 23:1-4 624
John 8:12 1223
John 10:27 1227
Acts 4:37 1251
Romans 1:18-19 1290
Romans 9:21 1299
1 Corinthians 10:13 1320
Galatians 1:6-7 1344
Ephesians 3:20 1356
Colossians 2:7 1372
2 Peter 1:3 1439–1440

FORGIVENESS
Isaiah 1:18 772
Ezekiel 36:25-27 971
Matthew 18:15-35 1117–1118
Luke 3:3 1170
Acts 13:38-39 1266
Romans 10:9-10 1300
Hebrews 9:22-28 1417
1 John 1:8-9 1444
(See also Confession)

FREEDOM
John 8:30-36 1224
Romans 8:1-11 1296–1297
Romans 14:1-16 1304
Galatians 5:1-6 1348
(See also Choices)

FRIENDSHIP
Exodus 33:11 105
Ruth 1:6-22 303–305
1 Samuel 18:1-4 331
Proverbs 11:9-10 723
Proverbs 17:17 731
Proverbs 18:24 732
Proverbs 19:22 733
Proverbs 27:6 742
John 15:11-17 1233
Acts 9:26-29 1258
(See also Peer Pressure, Popularity)

FUN FACTS
Exodus 16:14 84
Leviticus 11:21-22 126
Nehemiah 8:10 550
Nehemiah 13:31 559
Psalm 50:10-11 643
Daniel 1:12 988
Mark 7:19 1145–1146
Acts 12:23 1262
Revelation 3:15-16 1459

FUTURE
Psalm 31:15 630
Proverbs 24:14 738–739
Jeremiah 29:11 885

John 3:16 1214
2 Timothy 2:11-13 1398
(See also Advice, Eternal Life/Salvation)

GIFTS

(See Abilities)

GIVING

Genesis 4:4 7
Deuteronomy 14:22-23 221
Deuteronomy 15:7-11 222
Nehemiah 7:70-72 550
Proverbs 22:9 736
Malachi 3:8-10 1087
2 Corinthians 8–9 1335–1337
(See also God's Will)

GOALS

Psalm 20:4 622
Psalm 37:5 634
Psalm 97:10 676
Ecclesiastes 12:13-14 759
Philippians 3:12-20 1365
James 4:13-16 1428
(See also Success)

GOD'S COMMANDS

Exodus 20:3-17 89
Leviticus 11:21-22 126
Deuteronomy 5:19 210
Deuteronomy 6:4-9 212
Deuteronomy 15:11 222
Deuteronomy 19:14 226
Deuteronomy 26:16-18 232
Proverbs 6:20-21 718
2 John 1:6 1450

GOD'S CREATION

Genesis 1:1 3
Genesis 1:27 4
Job 12:7-9 584
Psalm 8:4-5 615
Psalm 50:10-11 643
Psalm 139:13-14 703
Jeremiah 1:5 850
Galatians 3:28 1346

GOD'S DISCIPLINE

Judges 2:3 277
Proverbs 1:1-3 711
Amos 3:6-7 1030
Zephaniah 2:2 1063
Acts 12:23 1262

GOD'S FAMILY

1 Chronicles 1:1-4 449
Isaiah 43:1 818
John 19:17-18 1241
1 Corinthians 12:12 1322
Galatians 3:28 1346
Ephesians 1:5 1354
Hebrews 13:3 1422
1 John 5:18 1448
Revelation 21:7 1474

GOD'S LOVE

Exodus 28:29 99
Psalm 17:8 620
Psalm 27:10 627
Psalm 56:8 648
Psalm 127:3 697
Psalm 136:1 701
Psalm 139:13-17 703–704
Isaiah 43:1 818
Isaiah 49:1 827
Jeremiah 1:5 850
Lamentations 4:2 925
Jonah 3:10 1044
Malachi 3:17-18 1088
Matthew 10:30 1107
Matthew 18:10 1117
John 3:14-16 1214
John 19:17-18 1241
Acts 14:21-22 1267–1268
Romans 5:8 1294
Titus 3:4-5 1403
Philemon 1:15 1406

GOD'S PLANS

Genesis 50:20 63
1 Samuel 10:21-22 319
Esther 4:14 567
Esther 8:1-2 569
Psalm 37:23 635
Jeremiah 29:11 885
Romans 8:28 1298
Romans 9:21 1299
Ephesians 1:5 1354

GOD'S POWER

Joshua 3:15-16 248
1 Kings 17:14-16 403
Job 12:7-9 584
Psalm 104 679–680
Isaiah 40:31 815
Zechariah 4:6 1073

Luke 24:5-6 1208
John 15:5 1233
Acts 1:8 1246
Ephesians 3:20 1356

GOD'S PROTECTION

Genesis 7:18 10
Exodus 2:3 66
Exodus 16:14 84
2 Samuel 22:29 373
1 Chronicles 14:10 466
Esther 8:1-2 569
Psalm 18:30 621
Psalm 23:1-4 624
Psalm 62:6-7 651
Hosea 11:4 1016
Nahum 1:7 1054
Matthew 11:28-29 1108

GOD'S VOICE

Exodus 3:4 68
Mark 1:10-11 1136
John 10:27 1227
Romans 1:18-19 1290

GOD'S WILL

Exodus 20 88–89
Micah 6:8 1050
Matthew 22:37-40 1124
1 Peter 4:1-3 1436
(See also Believing in God, Bible, Advice, Prayer)

GOSSIP

Exodus 23:1 92
Leviticus 19:16 138
Proverbs 11:13 723
Proverbs 25:9-10 740
1 Timothy 5:13 1392
Titus 3:2 1403
(See also Communication, Honesty, Lying)

GRATITUDE

(See Thankfulness)

GREED

Numbers 16:8-10 175
Proverbs 28:22, 25 744
Isaiah 56:9-12 836
Luke 12:15 1189
Ephesians 5:5 1358
(See also Giving, Money and Possessions)

GROWING AS A CHRISTIAN

(See Spiritual Growth)

GUIDANCE

(See Advice)

GUILT

Leviticus 4:3 117
Psalm 19:12-13 622
Psalm 51 644–645
John 15:21-22 1233
Acts 13:38-39 1266
Romans 3:21-24 1293
(See also Confession, Forgiveness)

HANDICAPS

2 Samuel 4:4 351
Philippians 4:13 1366

HATRED

Genesis 37 45–47
Leviticus 19:17 138
Esther 5:9-14 567
Psalm 139:21-24 704
Proverbs 6:16-19 718
Proverbs 10:12 721
Ecclesiastes 3:8 751
John 15:18-25 1233–1234
(See also Anger, Enemies, Revenge)

HEALING

Matthew 8:8-9 1103
Matthew 17:20 1117
James 5:14-15 1429

HEAVEN

Isaiah 25:8 797
Matthew 5:18-20 1098
Matthew 7:13-14 1102
Luke 13:29 1191
John 14:1-7 1232
Colossians 3:1-6 1373
Revelation 21–22 1474–1476
(See also Eternal Life/Salvation)

HELL

Matthew 7:13-14 1102
Luke 16:19-31 1194–1195
John 14:6 1232
Romans 2:1-9 1291
2 Thessalonians 1:7-9 1384
Revelation 1:17-18 1456
Revelation 20:14 1474

HELPFULNESS
Judges 5:16-18 281
Nehemiah 13:31 559
Mark 9:41 1150
Galatians 2:10 1345
Galatians 6:2 1350

HOLY SPIRIT
Judges 3:10 278
1 Samuel 16:13 328
Matthew 12:31-32 1109
John 3:6-8 1214
John 14:26 1232
John 16:5-15 1234
Acts 2:1-4 1246
Romans 8:2 1296
2 Corinthians 5:16-17 1333

HONESTY
Psalm 24:1-6 624–625
Proverbs 6:16-17 718
Proverbs 19:1 732
Proverbs 28:6 743
Romans 12:3 1303
(See also Integrity, Lying)

HONOR (RESPECT OR PRAISE)
Deuteronomy 5:16 210
Ezra 7:27-28 534–535
Psalm 29:1-2 627
Romans 12:10 1303
1 Thessalonians 5:12-13 1382

HOPE
Psalm 42:5-11 639
1 Corinthians 15:51-58 ... 1327–1328
Revelation 22:12-21 1476
(See also Faith)

HUMILITY
Psalm 131 698
Proverbs 11:2 723
Matthew 20:20-28 1121
Luke 14:7-11 1192
Philippians 2:5-11 1363
James 4:10 1428
1 Peter 5:5 1437

INFERIORITY
Psalm 139:13-18 703–704
Matthew 10:29-30 1107
Mark 8:37 1148
Philippians 3:12-14 1365
(See also Self-Worth)

INTEGRITY
Psalm 101:3-8 677
Psalm 119:113-117 693–694
Proverbs 3:1-4 714
Proverbs 20:11 734
Matthew 5:33-37 1100
Matthew 6:1-4 1100
Romans 5:3-4 1294
Philippians 3:17 1365
James 5:12 1428–1429
(See also Honesty, Leadership, Lying)

JEALOUSY
Genesis 37 45–47
Proverbs 14:30 727
Song of Songs 8:6 768
2 Corinthians 11:1-2 1338
Galatians 5:19-20 1350
(See also Comparisons)

JESUS' DEATH
Leviticus 1:4 115
Leviticus 16:10 133
John 19:17-18 1241
Romans 5:8 1294

JESUS, GOD'S SON
Mark 1:10 1136
John 1:14 1212
John 3:14-16 1214
John 5:18 1217
John 14:6 1232
1 John 5:18 1448

JESUS' LIFE
Matthew 4:10-11 1095
Matthew 8:8-9 1103
Matthew 18:21-22 1118
Mark 1:10 1136
Mark 11:8-9 1153
Mark 12:10 1154
Luke 4:17-19 1172
Luke 9:62 1184
Luke 17:15-17 1196
Luke 18:16 1197
Luke 24:5-6 1208
John 1:14 1212
John 4:17-18 1216
John 6:9 1218
John 6:48 1221
John 8:12 1223
John 15:5 1233

JESUS' RESURRECTION
Luke 24:5-6 1208

JESUS' RETURN
1 Corinthians 15:52 1327
1 Thessalonians 4:16-17 1381
2 Peter 3:8-9 1442
Revelation 22:13 1476

JOY
Nehemiah 8:10 550
Psalm 1:1-3 611–612
Habakkuk 3:17-18 1060
Luke 10:21 1185
2 Corinthians 4:17-18 1332

JUDGING OTHERS
(See Criticism)

JUSTICE
Amos 5:24 1032

KIDS
Luke 10:21 1185
Luke 18:16 1197
1 Timothy 4:12 1390

KINDNESS
Deuteronomy 15:11 222
2 Kings 7:9-10 422
John 6:9 1218
Acts 4:37 1251
Galatians 2:10 1345
Galatians 6:2 1350
1 Peter 3:8-9 1434
3 John 1:5 1452
Jude 1:22 1454

LAZINESS
Proverbs 6:6-11 717
Proverbs 10:4-5 721
Proverbs 12:24 725
Proverbs 28:19 743
2 Thessalonians 3:6-15 1385

LEADERSHIP
Exodus 3:1–4:17 68–70
Jeremiah 17:7-8 872
Matthew 20:20-28 1121
John 13:1-17 1231
Romans 12:8 1303
1 Timothy 3 1389–1390
Titus 1:7-9 1402

LONELINESS
Exodus 2:21-25 68
Psalm 68:6 654
Psalm 71:5 657
Proverbs 18:24 732
Hebrews 13:5 1422

LOVE
Jeremiah 31:3 887
Matthew 5:43-48 1100
Matthew 22:37-40 1124
John 3:16 1214
Romans 8:31-39 1298
Romans 12:9-21 1303
1 Corinthians 13:4-7 1324

LYING
Genesis 12:11-20 16–17
Exodus 20:16 89
Proverbs 6:12-19 717–718
Matthew 15:16-20 1114
(See also Communication, Honesty, Integrity)

MAKING MISTAKES (FAILURE, SIN)
Genesis 3 6–7
Genesis 4:3-12 7–8
Joshua 7 252–253
Judges 2:17-19 277
1 Kings 11:1-11 394
Psalm 119:11 690
Matthew 25:45-46 1129
Luke 22:55-62 1205
Romans 3:23 1293
Romans 5:8-21 1294–1295
Romans 6:23 1296
Romans 7:15-25 1296
James 4:17 1428
(See also Conscience, Consequences, Excuses, Temptation)

MANNERS
Leviticus 19:32 139

MARRIAGE
Genesis 2:18-24 5–6
Proverbs 31:10-31 747
1 Corinthians 7 1316–1318
2 Corinthians 11:2 1338
Ephesians 5:21-24 1358
Ephesians 5:25-30 1358–1359
(See also Family)

MATERIALISM
(See Greed, Money and Possessions)

MEANING
Ecclesiastes 1 749–750
Ecclesiastes 2 750–751
John 10:10 1226
Galatians 3:28-29 1346
Galatians 5:13 1348
1 Thessalonians 2:4 1378

MONEY AND POSSESSIONS
Deuteronomy 8:11-20 215–216
1 Chronicles 29:10-17 483
Proverbs 15:27 728
Matthew 6:19-24 1101
Matthew 19:16-30 1119–1120
Mark 10:17-31 1151–1152
Luke 12:13-34 1189
Acts 2:42-47 1248
1 Timothy 6:9-19 1392–1393
James 2:1-9 1424
(See also Greed)

OBEDIENCE
Genesis 6:9-22 10
Exodus 23:13 93
Psalm 119:115 693–694
Proverbs 28:7 743
John 15:9-17 1233
Romans 13:1 1303
Hebrews 13:17 1422
1 Peter 1:14 1432
1 John 2:3-11 1444–1445
(See also Authority, Believing in God)

OCCULT, THE
Leviticus 19:26 139
Leviticus 20:6-8 139–140
Deuteronomy 18:9-14 225
1 Samuel 28:3-19 343–344
Jeremiah 10:2-3 863
Acts 19:11-20 1275
(See also False Teaching)

PARENTS
Exodus 20:12 89
Leviticus 20:9 140
Proverbs 13:1 725
Proverbs 15:5 727
Ephesians 6:1-4 1359
(See also Authority, Honor)

PARTYING
Proverbs 5:21 717
Romans 13:13-14 1304
1 Corinthians 10:31 1320
Galatians 5:19-21 1350
1 Peter 4:1-3 1436
(See also Drinking, Peer Pressure)

PATIENCE
1 Samuel 13:8-14 322–323
Galatians 5:22-23 1350
Colossians 3:12 1373
James 5:10-11 1428
2 Peter 1:5-9 1440

PEACE
Psalm 29:11 628
John 14:27 1232
Romans 5:1 1294
Romans 12:18 1303
Galatians 5:22-23 1350
Philippians 4:6-7 1366
Colossians 3:15 1373

PEER PRESSURE
Psalm 119:143 694
Proverbs 18:24 732
Luke 6:22-23 1176
Romans 12:1-2 1302–1303
Colossians 2:23 1373
James 1:2-4 1423–1424
(See also Conformity, Popularity, Temptation)

PERSECUTION
(See Suffering, Troubles)

PERSEVERANCE
1 Corinthians 9:24-27 1320
Galatians 6:9-10 1351
Philippians 3:12-14 1365
Colossians 4:2 1374
1 Thessalonians 5:16-18 1382
1 Peter 5:10 1437
2 Peter 1:5-9 1440
(See also Potential, Prayer)

PLEASING GOD
Numbers 6:25 159
1 Samuel 2:26 312
Psalm 1:1-3 611–612
Psalm 95:8 674
Psalm 101:2-3 677
Matthew 6:20 1101

Romans 12:2 1302–1303
2 Peter 1:3 1439–1440

POPULARITY
Ecclesiastes 4:13-16 754
Mark 8:36-38 1148
John 15:18-25 1233–1234
James 4:4 1426
1 John 2:15-17 1445
(See also Conformity, Peer Pressure)

POSSESSIONS
(See Greed, Money and Possessions)

POTENTIAL
Judges 13:2–16:22 292–297
1 Samuel 16:7 328
Philippians 1:6 1362
Philippians 4:13 1366
(See also Abilities)

POVERTY
Deuteronomy 15:11 222
Galatians 2:10 1345

PRAISE
2 Samuel 6:16 353
1 Chronicles 16:33 469
Nehemiah 8:10 550
Mark 11:8-10 1153
Luke 17:15-17 1196

PRAYER
Psalm 3:1-8 612–613
Psalm 4:3 613
Matthew 7:7-12 1102
Matthew 21:21-22 1122
Luke 11:1-13 1186
1 Thessalonians 5:16-18 1382
James 5:16-18 1429
(See also Advice, Choices)

PREJUDICE
Esther 3:1-6 564
Mark 6:1-6 1143
Luke 10:25-37 1185
Acts 10:34-43 1260
Galatians 3:28-29 1346
Ephesians 2:11-16 1354–1355
(See also Hatred)

PRIDE
Proverbs 6:16-17 718
Proverbs 11:2 723
Proverbs 13:10 725
Proverbs 18:12 732
Proverbs 29:23 745
1 Corinthians 3:20-21 1314
(See also Comparisons, Humility)

PRIORITIES
(See Values)

PRISON
Isaiah 42:3 817
Isaiah 61:1 842
Hebrews 13:3 1422

PROBLEMS
(See Suffering, Troubles)

PROMISES IN GOD'S WORD
Genesis 9:13-16 14
Exodus 12:13 78
Joshua 1:8 246
Psalm 91:1 672
Psalm 121:5-6 695
Isaiah 40:31 815
Isaiah 43:25 820
Romans 8:28 1298
1 Corinthians 10:13 1320
1 Thessalonians 4:16-17 1381
James 5:14-15 1429
2 Peter 1:3 1439–1440
Revelation 7:17 1462

PURITY
Psalm 1:1-3 611–612
Psalm 86:11 668
Psalm 119:9-20 690
Matthew 5:27-30 1100
John 17:17 1236
2 Corinthians 7:1 1334
Philippians 3:7-11 1365
(See also Marriage)

PURPOSE
Psalm 139:13-14 703
Jeremiah 1:5 850

RACE
Esther 3:6 564
Galatians 3:28 1346

REJECTION
Judges 11:1-2 290
Psalm 27:10 627
Psalm 94:14 674

Isaiah 53 831–832
Matthew 13:53-58 1112
Luke 10:16 1185

REPENTING
Joel 2:12 1023
Zephaniah 2:2 1063
2 Peter 3:8-9 1442
1 John 1:9 1444

REPUTATION
(See Integrity)

RESPECT FOR GOD
Ecclesiastes 12:1 758
Jeremiah 18:5-6 873
Haggai 1:8 1068
John 1:14 1212

RESPECT FOR OTHERS
Leviticus 19:32 139
Deuteronomy 19:14 226
Esther 3:5-6 564
Proverbs 12:18 725
Proverbs 15:28 728
Matthew 7:4 1101
1 Timothy 2:2 1388
James 3:5 1425

RESPONSIBILITY
Matthew 5:13-16 1098
Matthew 25:14-30 1127–1130
Romans 14 1304–1306
1 Timothy 3 1389–1390

REVENGE
Leviticus 19:18 138
1 Samuel 25:23-33 340–341
Psalm 35:1-10 632–633
Matthew 5:38-48 1100
Mark 11:25 1153
Romans 12:17-18 1303
(See also Anger, Hatred)

SACRIFICE
Leviticus 1:4 115
Leviticus 16:10 133
Hebrews 9:14 1416–1417

SALVATION
(See Believing in God, Eternal Life, Faith, Forgiveness)

SELF-WORTH
Genesis 1:26-27 4
Psalm 8:3-5 615
Luke 12:7 1189
John 3:16 1214
Romans 8:35-39 1298
(See also Inferiority)

SERVING GOD AND OTHERS
Joshua 24:14 272
Matthew 20:28 1121
Luke 10:25-37 1185
John 13:1-17 1231
1 Corinthians 7:35 1318
Galatians 5:13 1348
(See also Compassion)

SIN
Leviticus 1:4 115
Isaiah 1:18 772
Isaiah 43:1 818
Isaiah 43:25 820
Isaiah 61:1 842
Zephaniah 2:2 1063
Zechariah 3:3-4 1073
Matthew 7:4 1101
John 3:14-16 1214
John 19:17-18 1241
Romans 1:18-19 1290
1 Thessalonians 5:1 1381
Hebrews 9:14 1416–1417
1 Peter 4:8 1436
1 John 1:9 1444
1 John 5:18 1448

SPIRITUAL GROWTH
Deuteronomy 11:16-21 218
Proverbs 13:14 726
Lamentations 3:27-33 924
John 15:1-27 1233–1234
Colossians 2:7 1372
1 Peter 2:2 1432
2 Peter 3:18 1442
(See also Bible, Discipline)

STEALING
Exodus 20:15 89
Leviticus 19:11 138
Malachi 3:8-10 1087
Ephesians 4:28 1357

STRESS
(See Suffering, Troubles, Worry)

SUCCESS
Genesis 11:1-9 15
Proverbs 15:22 728
Proverbs 16:3 728
Proverbs 22:4 736
Proverbs 28:13 743
2 Corinthians 3:5 1331
(See also Goals, Thankfulness)

SUICIDE
(See Depression)

SUFFERING
Job 16:1-6 588
Psalm 3:1-8 612–613
Matthew 11:28-30 1108
John 16:33 1234–1236
Romans 8:28 1298
Philippians 1:29-30 1362–1363
Philippians 3:7-11 1365
1 Peter 4:1-2 1436
1 Peter 5:10 1437
(See also Depression, Discouragement)

TALKING ABOUT GOD
Matthew 5:14-16 1098
Matthew 28:19-20 1134
Mark 16:15 1163
John 14:26 1232
Romans 1:16 1290
1 Corinthians 9:22 1319-1320
2 Timothy 4:1-8 1399–1400
(See also Communication, Believing in God)

TEAMWORK
Ecclesiastes 4:9 752
Isaiah 10:15 783
1 Corinthians 12:12 1322

TELEVISION
Psalm 101:2-3 677
Romans 12:2 1302–1303

TEMPTATION
Psalm 19:13 622
Proverbs 7:1-5 719
Matthew 4:1-11 1094–1095
1 Corinthians 10:13 1320
2 Timothy 2:22 1398
Hebrews 2:16-18 1409
Hebrews 4:14-16 1412
James 1:12-16 1424
(See also Making Mistakes)

THANKFULNESS
Psalm 100 677
Mark 8:6 1146
Luke 17:11-19 1196
Ephesians 2:4-10 1354
Colossians 3:16-17 1373
1 Thessalonians 5:18 1382
(See also Blessings)

THOUGHTS
Romans 12:2 1302–1303
Hebrews 4:12 1412

TIME WITH GOD
Psalm 63 651–652
Mark 1:35 1136
John 15:7 1233

TROUBLES
Exodus 5:13 71
Exodus 6:9 72
1 Samuel 17:48-49 330
Psalm 18:30 621
Psalm 23:1-4 624
Psalm 91:1 672
Daniel 3:17 993
Nahum 1:7 1054
Matthew 11:28-29 1108
Matthew 17:20 1117
Acts 14:21-22 1267–1268
2 Corinthians 4:17-18 1332
Galatians 6:2 1350

TRUST
1 Samuel 17:34-37 330
Psalm 34:4 631
Psalm 56:3-4, 11 648
John 20:24-31 1242–1243
1 John 4:16 1447
(See also Doubts, Faith)

TRUTH
Proverbs 8:1 719
Luke 10:21 1185
John 4:17-18 1216
John 14:6 1232
Romans 1:18-19 1290
Galatians 1:6-7 1344
Colossians 2:7 1372
2 Timothy 2:15 1398
2 Timothy 3:16-17 1399
Hebrews 4:12 1412

VALUES

Psalm 119:111, 162 ..... 693, 695
Matthew 6:21 1101
Matthew 13:45-46 1112
(See also Choices)

WISDOM

1 Kings 3:3-14 383
Psalm 119:98-104 693
Proverbs 2–4; 8 ... 713–716, 719–720
Proverbs 19:8 732
James 1:5-8 1424

WITNESSING

(See Talking about God)

WORK

Proverbs 26:13-14 741
1 Corinthians 12:12 1322
2 Thessalonians 3:10 1385
2 Timothy 2:15 1398

WORRY

Matthew 6:25-34 1101
Matthew 10:19-20 1106
Luke 12:22-34 1189
Philippians 4:6-19 1366–1367
(See also Fear, Suffering, Troubles)

WORSHIP

Exodus 20:3-5 89
Psalm 29:1-2 627
Psalm 150 709
Matthew 15:9 1114
Matthew 15:25 1114
Ephesians 5:19-20 1358
Revelation 14:3-7 1468
(See also Believing in God, Honor, Thankfulness)

A NOTE TO PARENTS FROM THE PUBLISHERS OF THE NEW LIVING TRANSLATION

The *Holy Bible,* New Living Translation, was first published in 1996. It quickly became one of the most popular Bible translations in the English-speaking world. While the NLT's influence was rapidly growing, the Bible Translation Committee determined that an additional investment in scholarly review and text refinement could make it even better. So shortly after its initial publication, the committee began an eight-year process with the purpose of increasing the level of the NLT's precision without sacrificing its easy-to-understand quality. This second-generation text was completed in 2004, with minor changes subsequently introduced in 2007.

The goal of any Bible translation is to convey the meaning and content of the ancient Hebrew and Greek texts as accurately as possible to contemporary readers. The challenge for our translators was to create a text that would communicate as clearly and powerfully to today's readers as the original texts did to readers and listeners in the ancient biblical world. The resulting translation is easy to read and understand, while also accurately communicating the meaning and content of the original biblical texts. The NLT is a general-purpose text especially good for study, devotional reading, and reading aloud in worship services.

We believe that the New Living Translation—which combines the latest biblical scholarship with a clear, dynamic writing style—will communicate God's word powerfully to all who read it. We publish it with the prayer that God will use it to speak his timeless truth to the church and the world in a fresh, new way.

The Publishers
October 2007

INTRODUCTION TO THE NEW LIVING TRANSLATION

Translation Philosophy and Methodology

English Bible translations tend to be governed by one of two general translation theories. The first theory has been called "formal-equivalence," "literal," or "word-for-word" translation. According to this theory, the translator attempts to render each word of the original language into English and seeks to preserve the original syntax and sentence structure as much as possible in translation. The second theory has been called "dynamic-equivalence," "functional-equivalence," or "thought-for-thought" translation. The goal of this translation theory is to produce in English the closest natural equivalent of the message expressed by the original-language text, both in meaning and in style.

Both of these translation theories have their strengths. A formal-equivalence translation preserves aspects of the original text—including ancient idioms, term consistency, and original-language syntax—that are valuable for scholars and professional study. It allows a reader to trace formal elements of the original-language text through the English translation. A dynamic-equivalence translation, on the other hand, focuses on translating the message of the original-language text. It ensures that the meaning of the text is readily apparent to the contemporary reader. This allows the message to come through with immediacy, without requiring the reader to struggle with foreign idioms and awkward syntax. It also facilitates serious study of the text's message and clarity in both devotional and public reading.

The pure application of either of these translation philosophies would create translations at opposite ends of the translation spectrum. But in reality, all translations contain a mixture of these two philosophies. A purely formal-equivalence translation would be unintelligible in English, and a purely dynamic-equivalence translation would risk being unfaithful to the original. That is why translations shaped by dynamic-equivalence theory are usually quite literal when the original text is relatively clear, and the translations shaped by formal-equivalence theory are sometimes quite dynamic when the original text is obscure.

The translators of the New Living Translation set out to render the message of the original texts of Scripture into clear, contemporary English. As they did so, they kept the concerns of both formal-equivalence and dynamic-equivalence in mind. On the one hand, they translated as simply and literally as possible when that approach yielded an accurate, clear, and natural English text. Many words and phrases were rendered literally and consistently into English, preserving essential literary and rhetorical devices, ancient metaphors, and word choices that give structure to the text and provide echoes of meaning from one passage to the next.

On the other hand, the translators rendered the message more dynamically when the literal rendering was hard to understand, was misleading, or yielded archaic or foreign wording. They clarified difficult metaphors and terms to aid in the reader's understanding. The translators first struggled with the meaning of the words and phrases in the ancient context; then they rendered the message into clear, natural English. Their goal was to be both faithful to the ancient texts and eminently readable. The result is a translation that is both exegetically accurate and idiomatically powerful.

Translation Process and Team

To produce an accurate translation of the Bible into contemporary English, the translation team needed the skills necessary to enter into the thought patterns of the ancient authors and then to render their ideas, connotations, and effects into clear, contemporary English. To begin this process, qualified biblical scholars were needed to interpret the meaning of the original text and to check it against our base English translation. In order to guard against personal and theological biases, the scholars needed to represent a diverse group of Evangelicals who would employ the best exegetical tools. Then to work alongside the scholars, skilled English stylists were needed to shape the text into clear, contemporary English.

With these concerns in mind, the Bible Translation Committee recruited teams of scholars that represented a broad spectrum of denominations, theological perspectives, and backgrounds within the worldwide Evangelical community. (These scholars are listed at the end of this introduction.) Each book of the Bible was assigned to three different scholars with proven expertise in the book or group of books to be reviewed. Each of these scholars made a thorough review of a base translation and submitted suggested revisions to the appropriate Senior Translator. The Senior Translator then reviewed and summarized these suggestions and proposed a first-draft revision of the base text. This draft served as the basis for several additional phases of exegetical and stylistic committee review. Then the Bible Translation Committee jointly reviewed and approved every verse of the final translation.

Throughout the translation and editing process, the Senior Translators and their scholar teams were given a chance to review the editing done by the team of stylists. This ensured that exegetical errors would not be introduced late in the process and that the entire Bible Translation Committee was happy with the final result. By choosing a team of qualified scholars and skilled stylists and by setting up a process that allowed their interaction throughout the process, the New Living Translation has been refined to preserve the essential formal elements of the original biblical texts, while also creating a clear, understandable English text.

The New Living Translation was first published in 1996. Shortly after its initial publication, the Bible Translation Committee began a process of further committee review and translation refinement. The purpose of this continued revision was to increase the level of precision without sacrificing the text's easy-to-understand quality. This second-edition text was completed in 2004, and an additional update with minor changes was subsequently introduced in 2007. This printing of the New Living Translation reflects the updated 2007 text.

Written to Be Read Aloud

It is evident in Scripture that the biblical documents were written to be read aloud, often in public worship (see Nehemiah 8; Luke 4:16-20; 1 Timothy 4:13; Revelation 1:3). It is still the case today that more people will hear the Bible read aloud in church than are likely to read it for themselves. Therefore, a new translation must communicate with clarity and power when it is read publicly. Clarity was a primary goal for the NLT translators, not only to facilitate private reading and understanding, but also to ensure that it would be excellent for public reading and make an immediate and powerful impact on any listener.

The Texts behind the New Living Translation

The Old Testament translators used the Masoretic Text of the Hebrew Bible as represented in *Biblia Hebraica Stuttgartensia* (1977), with its extensive system of textual notes; this is an update of Rudolf Kittel's *Biblia Hebraica* (Stuttgart, 1937). The translators also further compared the Dead Sea Scrolls, the Septuagint and other Greek manuscripts, the Samaritan Pentateuch, the Syriac Peshitta, the Latin Vulgate, and any other versions or manuscripts that shed light on the meaning of difficult passages.

The New Testament translators used the two standard editions of the Greek New Testament: the *Greek New Testament*, published by the United Bible Societies (UBS, fourth revised edition, 1993), and *Novum Testamentum Graece*, edited by Nestle and Aland (NA, twenty-seventh edition, 1993). These two editions, which have the same text but differ in punctuation and textual notes, represent, for the most part, the best in modern textual scholarship. However, in cases where strong textual or other scholarly evidence supported the decision, the translators sometimes chose to differ from the UBS and NA Greek texts and followed variant readings found in other ancient witnesses. Significant textual variants of this sort are always noted in the textual notes of the New Living Translation.

Translation Issues

The translators have made a conscious effort to provide a text that can be easily understood by the typical reader of modern English. To this end, we sought to use only vocabulary and language structures in common use today. We avoided using language likely to become quickly dated or that reflects only a narrow subdialect of English, with the goal of making the New Living Translation as broadly useful and timeless as possible.

But our concern for readability goes beyond the concerns of vocabulary and sentence structure. We are also concerned about historical and cultural barriers to understanding the Bible, and we have sought to translate terms shrouded in history and culture in ways that can be immediately understood. To this end:

- We have converted ancient weights and measures (for example, "ephah" [a unit of dry volume] or "cubit" [a unit of length]) to modern English (American) equivalents, since the ancient measures are not generally meaningful to today's readers. Then in the textual footnotes we offer the literal Hebrew, Aramaic, or Greek measures, along with modern metric equivalents.
- Instead of translating ancient currency values literally, we have expressed them in common terms that communicate the message. For example, in the Old Testament, "ten shekels of silver" becomes "ten pieces of silver" to convey the intended message. In the New Testament, we have often translated the "denarius" as "the normal daily wage" to facilitate understanding. Then a footnote offers: "Greek *a denarius,* the payment for a full day's wage." In general, we give a clear English rendering and then state the literal Hebrew, Aramaic, or Greek in a textual footnote.
- Since the names of Hebrew months are unknown to most contemporary readers, and since the Hebrew lunar calendar fluctuates from year to year in relation to the solar calendar used today, we have looked for clear ways to communicate the time of year the Hebrew months (such as Abib) refer to. When an expanded or interpretive rendering is given in the text, a textual note gives the literal rendering. Where it is possible to define a specific ancient date in terms of our modern calendar, we use modern dates in the text. A textual footnote then gives the literal Hebrew date and states the rationale for our rendering. For example, Ezra 6:15 pinpoints the date when the postexilic Temple was completed in Jerusalem: "the third day of the month Adar." This was during the sixth year of King Darius's reign (that is, 515 B.C.). We have translated that date as March 12, with a footnote giving the Hebrew and identifying the year as 515 B.C.
- Since ancient references to the time of day differ from our modern methods of denoting time, we have used renderings that are instantly understandable to the modern reader. Accordingly, we have rendered specific times of day by using approximate equivalents in terms of our common "o'clock" system. On occasion, translations such as "at dawn the next morning" or "as the sun was setting" have been used when the biblical reference is more general.
- When the meaning of a proper name (or a wordplay inherent in a proper name) is relevant to the message of the text, its meaning is often illuminated with a textual footnote. For example, in Exodus 2:10 the text reads: "The princess named him Moses, for she explained, 'I lifted him out of the water.' " The accompanying footnote reads: "*Moses* sounds like a Hebrew term that means 'to lift out.' "

Sometimes, when the actual meaning of a name is clear, that meaning is included in parentheses within the text itself. For example, the text at Genesis 16:11 reads: "You are to name him Ishmael (*which means 'God hears'*), for the LORD has heard your cry of distress." Since the original hearers and readers would have instantly understood the meaning of the name "Ishmael," we have provided modern readers with the same information so they can experience the text in a similar way.

- Many words and phrases carry a great deal of cultural meaning that was obvious to the original readers but needs explanation in our own culture. For example, the phrase "they beat their breasts" (Luke 23:48) in ancient times meant that people were very upset, often in mourning. In our translation we chose to translate this phrase dynamically for clarity: "They went home *in deep sorrow*." Then we included a footnote with the literal Greek, which reads: "Greek *went home beating their breasts*." In other similar cases, however, we have sometimes chosen to illuminate the existing literal expression to make it immediately understandable. For example, here we might have expanded the literal Greek phrase to read: "They went home beating their breasts *in sorrow*." If we had done this, we would not have included a textual footnote, since the literal Greek clearly appears in translation.
- Metaphorical language is sometimes difficult for contemporary readers to understand, so at times we have chosen to translate or illuminate the meaning of a metaphor. For example, the ancient poet writes, "Your neck is *like* the tower of David" (Song of Songs 4:4). We have rendered it "Your neck is *as beautiful as* the tower of David" to clarify the intended positive meaning of the simile. Another example comes in Ecclesiastes 12:3, which can be literally rendered: "Remember him . . . when the grinding women cease because they are few, and the women who look through the windows see dimly." We have rendered it: "Remember him before your teeth—your few remaining servants—stop grinding; and before your eyes—the women looking through the windows—see dimly." We clarified such metaphors only when we believed a typical reader might be confused by the literal text.
- When the content of the original language text is poetic in character, we have rendered it in English poetic form. We sought to break lines in ways that clarify and highlight the relationships between phrases of the text. Hebrew poetry often uses parallelism, a literary form where a second phrase (or in some instances a third or fourth) echoes the initial phrase in some way. In Hebrew parallelism, the subsequent parallel phrases continue, while also furthering and sharpening, the thought expressed in the initial line or phrase. Whenever possible, we sought to represent these parallel phrases in natural poetic English.
- The Greek term *hoi Ioudaioi* is literally translated "the Jews" in many English translations. In the Gospel of John, however, this term doesn't always refer to the Jewish people generally. In some contexts, it refers more particularly to the Jewish religious leaders. We have attempted to capture the meaning in these different contexts by using terms such as "the people" (with a footnote: Greek *the Jewish people*) or "the religious leaders," where appropriate.
- One challenge we faced was how to translate accurately the ancient biblical text that was originally written in a context where male-oriented terms were used to refer to humanity generally. We needed to respect the nature of the ancient context while also trying to make the translation clear to a modern audience that tends to read male-oriented language as applying only to males. Often the original text, though using masculine nouns and pronouns, clearly intends that the message be applied to both men and women. A typical example is found in the New Testament letters, where the believers are called "brothers" (*adelphoi*). Yet it is clear from the content of these letters that they were addressed to all the believers—male and female. Thus, we have usually translated this Greek word as "brothers and sisters" in order to represent the historical situation more accurately.

We have also been sensitive to passages where the text applies generally to human beings or to the human condition. In some instances we have used plural pronouns (they, them) in place of the masculine singular (he, him). For example, a traditional rendering of Proverbs

22:6 is: "Train up a child in the way he should go, and when he is old he will not turn from it." We have rendered it: "Direct your children onto the right path, and when they are older, they will not leave it." At times, we have also replaced third person pronouns with the second person to ensure clarity. A traditional rendering of Proverbs 26:27 is: "He who digs a pit will fall into it, and he who rolls a stone, it will come back on him." We have rendered it: "If you set a trap for others, you will get caught in it yourself. If you roll a boulder down on others, it will crush you instead."

We should emphasize, however, that all masculine nouns and pronouns used to represent God (for example, "Father") have been maintained without exception. All decisions of this kind have been driven by the concern to reflect accurately the intended meaning of the original texts of Scripture.

Lexical Consistency in Terminology

For the sake of clarity, we have translated certain original-language terms consistently, especially within synoptic passages and for commonly repeated rhetorical phrases, and within certain word categories such as divine names and non-theological technical terminology (e.g., liturgical, legal, cultural, zoological, and botanical terms). For theological terms, we have allowed a greater semantic range of acceptable English words or phrases for a single Hebrew or Greek word. We have avoided some theological terms that are not readily understood by many modern readers. For example, we avoided using words such as "justification" and "sanctification," which are carryovers from Latin translations. In place of these words, we have provided renderings such as "made right with God" and "made holy."

The Spelling of Proper Names

Many individuals in the Bible, especially the Old Testament, are known by more than one name (e.g., Uzziah/Azariah). For the sake of clarity, we have tried to use a single spelling for any one individual, footnoting the literal spelling whenever we differ from it. This is especially helpful in delineating the kings of Israel and Judah. King Joash/Jehoash of Israel has been consistently called Jehoash, while King Joash/Jehoash of Judah is called Joash. A similar distinction has been used to distinguish between Joram/Jehoram of Israel and Joram/Jehoram of Judah. All such decisions were made with the goal of clarifying the text for the reader. When the ancient biblical writers clearly had a theological purpose in their choice of a variant name (e.g., Esh-baal/Ishbosheth), the different names have been maintained with an explanatory footnote.

For the names Jacob and Israel, which are used interchangeably for both the individual patriarch and the nation, we generally render it "Israel" when it refers to the nation and "Jacob" when it refers to the individual. When our rendering of the name differs from the underlying Hebrew text, we provide a textual footnote, which includes this explanation: "The names 'Jacob' and 'Israel' are often interchanged throughout the Old Testament, referring sometimes to the individual patriarch and sometimes to the nation."

The Rendering of Divine Names

All appearances of *'el, 'elohim,* or *'eloah* have been translated "God," except where the context demands the translation "god(s)." We have generally rendered the tetragrammaton (*YHWH*) consistently as "the LORD," utilizing a form with small capitals that is common among English translations. This will distinguish it from the name *'adonai,* which we render "Lord." When *'adonai* and *YHWH* appear together, we have rendered it "Sovereign LORD." This also distinguishes *'adonai YHWH* from cases where *YHWH* appears with *'elohim,* which is rendered "LORD God." When *YH* (the short form of *YHWH*) and *YHWH* appear together, we have rendered it "LORD GOD." When *YHWH* appears with the term *tseba'oth,* we have rendered it "LORD of Heaven's Armies" to translate the meaning of the name. In a few cases, we have utilized the transliteration, *Yahweh,* when the personal character of the name is being invoked in contrast to another divine name or the name of some other god (for example, see Exodus 3:15; 6:2-3).

In the New Testament, the Greek word *christos* has been translated as "Messiah" when the context assumes a Jewish audience. When a Gentile audience can be assumed, *christos* has been translated as "Christ." The Greek word *kurios* is consistently translated "Lord," except that it is translated "LORD" wherever the New Testament text explicitly quotes from the Old Testament, and the text there has it in small capitals.

Textual Footnotes

The New Living Translation provides several kinds of textual footnotes, all designated in the text with an asterisk:

- When for the sake of clarity the NLT renders a difficult or potentially confusing phrase dynamically, we generally give the literal rendering in a textual footnote. This allows the reader to see the literal source of our dynamic rendering and how our translation relates to other more literal translations. These notes are prefaced with "Hebrew," "Aramaic," or "Greek," identifying the language of the underlying source text. For example, in Acts 2:42 we translated the literal "breaking of bread" (from the Greek) as "the Lord's Supper" to clarify that this verse refers to the ceremonial practice of the church rather than just an ordinary meal. Then we attached a footnote to "the Lord's Supper," which reads: "Greek *the breaking of bread*."
- Textual footnotes are also used to show alternative renderings, prefaced with the word "Or." These normally occur for passages where an aspect of the meaning is debated. On occasion, we also provide notes on words or phrases that represent a departure from long-standing tradition. These notes are prefaced with "Traditionally rendered." For example, the footnote to the translation "serious skin disease" at Leviticus 13:2 says: "Traditionally rendered *leprosy*. The Hebrew word used throughout this passage is used to describe various skin diseases."
- When our translators follow a textual variant that differs significantly from our standard Hebrew or Greek texts (listed earlier), we document that difference with a footnote. We also footnote cases when the NLT excludes a passage that is included in the Greek text known as the *Textus Receptus* (and familiar to readers through its translation in the King James Version). In such cases, we offer a translation of the excluded text in a footnote, even though it is generally recognized as a later addition to the Greek text and not part of the original Greek New Testament.
- All Old Testament passages that are quoted in the New Testament are identified by a textual footnote at the New Testament location. When the New Testament clearly quotes from the Greek translation of the Old Testament, and when it differs significantly in wording from the Hebrew text, we also place a textual footnote at the Old Testament location. This note includes a rendering of the Greek version, along with a cross-reference to the New Testament passage(s) where it is cited (for example, see notes on Psalms 8:2; 53:3; Proverbs 3:12).
- Some textual footnotes provide cultural and historical information on places, things, and people in the Bible that are probably obscure to modern readers. Such notes should aid the reader in understanding the message of the text. For example, in Acts 12:1, "King Herod" is named in this translation as "King Herod Agrippa" and is identified in a footnote as being "the nephew of Herod Antipas and a grandson of Herod the Great."
- When the meaning of a proper name (or a wordplay inherent in a proper name) is relevant to the meaning of the text, it is either illuminated with a textual footnote or included within parentheses in the text itself. For example, the footnote concerning the name "Eve" at Genesis 3:20 reads: "*Eve* sounds like a Hebrew term that means 'to give life.' " This wordplay in the Hebrew illuminates the meaning of the text, which goes on to say that Eve "would be the mother of all who live."

As we submit this translation for publication, we recognize that any translation of the Scriptures is subject to limitations and imperfections. Anyone who has attempted to communicate the richness of God's Word into another language will realize it is impossible to make a perfect translation. Recognizing these limitations, we sought God's guidance and wisdom throughout this project. Now we pray that he will accept our efforts and use this translation for the benefit of the church and of all people.

We pray that the New Living Translation will overcome some of the barriers of history, culture, and language that have kept people from reading and understanding God's Word. We hope that readers unfamiliar with the Bible will find the words clear and easy to understand and that readers well versed in the Scriptures will gain a fresh perspective. We pray that readers will gain insight and wisdom for living, but most of all that they will meet the God of the Bible and be forever changed by knowing him.

The Bible Translation Committee
October 2007

BIBLE TRANSLATION TEAM
HOLY BIBLE, NEW LIVING TRANSLATION

PENTATEUCH
Daniel I. Block, Senior Translator
Wheaton College

GENESIS
Allen Ross, *Beeson Divinity School, Samford University*
Gordon Wenham, *Trinity Theological College, Bristol*

EXODUS
Robert Bergen, *Hannibal-LaGrange College*
Daniel I. Block, *Wheaton College*
Eugene Carpenter, *Bethel College, Mishawaka, Indiana*

LEVITICUS
David Baker, *Ashland Theological Seminary*
Victor Hamilton, *Asbury College*
Kenneth Mathews, *Beeson Divinity School, Samford University*

NUMBERS
Dale A. Brueggemann, *Assemblies of God Division of Foreign Missions*
R. K. Harrison (deceased), *Wycliffe College*
Paul R. House, *Beeson Divinity School, Samford University*
Gerald L. Mattingly, *Johnson Bible College*

DEUTERONOMY
J. Gordon McConville, *University of Gloucester*
Eugene H. Merrill, *Dallas Theological Seminary*
John A. Thompson (deceased), *University of Melbourne*

HISTORICAL BOOKS
Barry J. Beitzel, Senior Translator
Trinity Evangelical Divinity School

JOSHUA, JUDGES
Carl E. Armerding, *Schloss Mittersill Study Centre*
Barry J. Beitzel, *Trinity Evangelical Divinity School*
Lawson Stone, *Asbury Theological Seminary*

1 & 2 SAMUEL
Robert Gordon, *Cambridge University*
V. Philips Long, *Regent College*
J. Robert Vannoy, *Biblical Theological Seminary*

1 & 2 KINGS
Bill T. Arnold, *Asbury Theological Seminary*
William H. Barnes, *North Central University*
Frederic W. Bush, *Fuller Theological Seminary*

1 & 2 CHRONICLES
Raymond B. Dillard (deceased), *Westminster Theological Seminary*
David A. Dorsey, *Evangelical School of Theology*
Terry Eves, *Erskine College*

RUTH, EZRA—ESTHER
William C. Williams, *Vanguard University*
H. G. M. Williamson, *Oxford University*

WISDOM BOOKS
Tremper Longman III, Senior Translator
Westmont College

JOB
August Konkel, *Providence Theological Seminary*
Tremper Longman III, *Westmont College*
Al Wolters, *Redeemer College*

PSALMS 1–75
Mark D. Futato, *Reformed Theological Seminary*
Douglas Green, *Westminster Theological Seminary*
Richard Pratt, *Reformed Theological Seminary*

PSALMS 76–150
David M. Howard Jr., *Bethel Theological Seminary*
Raymond C. Ortlund Jr., *Immanuel Church, Nashville, Tennessee*
Willem VanGemeren, *Trinity Evangelical Divinity School*

PROVERBS
Ted Hildebrandt, *Gordon College*
Richard Schultz, *Wheaton College*
Raymond C. Van Leeuwen, *Eastern College*

ECCLESIASTES, SONG OF SONGS
Daniel C. Fredericks, *Belhaven College*
David Hubbard (deceased), *Fuller Theological Seminary*
Tremper Longman III, *Westmont College*

PROPHETS
John N. Oswalt, Senior Translator
Asbury Theological Seminary

ISAIAH
John N. Oswalt, *Asbury Theological Seminary*
Gary Smith, *Union University*
John Walton, *Wheaton College*

JEREMIAH, LAMENTATIONS
G. Herbert Livingston, *Asbury Theological Seminary*
Elmer A. Martens, *Mennonite Brethren Biblical Seminary*

EZEKIEL
Daniel I. Block, *Wheaton College*
David H. Engelhard, *Calvin Theological Seminary*
David Thompson, *Asbury Theological Seminary*

DANIEL, HAGGAI—MALACHI
Joyce Baldwin Caine (deceased), *Trinity College, Bristol*
Douglas Gropp, *Catholic University of America*
Roy Hayden, *Oral Roberts School of Theology*
Andrew Hill, *Wheaton College*
Tremper Longman III, *Westmont College*

HOSEA—ZEPHANIAH
Joseph Coleson, *Nazarene Theological Seminary*
Roy Hayden, *Oral Roberts School of Theology*
Andrew Hill, *Wheaton College*
Richard Patterson, *Liberty University*

GOSPELS AND ACTS
Grant R. Osborne, Senior Translator
Trinity Evangelical Divinity School

MATTHEW
Craig Blomberg, *Denver Seminary*
Donald A. Hagner, *Fuller Theological Seminary*
David Turner, *Grand Rapids Baptist Seminary*

MARK
Robert Guelich (deceased), *Fuller Theological Seminary*
George Guthrie, *Union University*
Grant R. Osborne, *Trinity Evangelical Divinity School*

LUKE
Darrell Bock, *Dallas Theological Seminary*
Scot McKnight, *North Park University*
Robert Stein, *The Southern Baptist Theological Seminary*

JOHN
Gary M. Burge, *Wheaton College*
Philip W. Comfort, *Coastal Carolina University*
Marianne Meye Thompson, *Fuller Theological Seminary*

ACTS
D. A. Carson, *Trinity Evangelical Divinity School*
William J. Larkin, *Columbia International University*
Roger Mohrlang, *Whitworth University*

LETTERS AND REVELATION
Norman R. Ericson, Senior Translator
Wheaton College

ROMANS, GALATIANS
Gerald Borchert, *Northern Baptist Theological Seminary*
Douglas J. Moo, *Wheaton College*
Thomas R. Schreiner, *The Southern Baptist Theological Seminary*

1 & 2 CORINTHIANS
Joseph Alexanian, *Trinity International University*
Linda Belleville, *Bethel College, Mishawaka, Indiana*
Douglas A. Oss, *Central Bible College*
Robert Sloan, *Houston Baptist University*

EPHESIANS—PHILEMON
Harold W. Hoehner (deceased), *Dallas Theological Seminary*
Moises Silva, *Gordon-Conwell Theological Seminary*
Klyne Snodgrass, *North Park Theological Seminary*

HEBREWS, JAMES, 1 & 2 PETER, JUDE
Peter Davids, *St. Stephen's University*
Norman R. Ericson, *Wheaton College*
William Lane (deceased), *Seattle Pacific University*
J. Ramsey Michaels, *S. W. Missouri State University*

1–3 JOHN, REVELATION
Greg Beale, *Westminster Theological Seminary*
Robert Mounce, *Whitworth University*
M. Robert Mulholland Jr., *Asbury Theological Seminary*

SPECIAL REVIEWERS
F. F. Bruce (deceased), *University of Manchester*
Kenneth N. Taylor (deceased), *Translator,* The Living Bible

COORDINATING TEAM
Mark D. Taylor, *Director and Chief Stylist*
Ronald A. Beers, *Executive Director and Stylist*
Mark R. Norton, *Managing Editor and O.T. Coordinating Editor*
Philip W. Comfort, *N.T. Coordinating Editor*
Daniel W. Taylor, *Bethel University, Senior Stylist*

OLD TESTAMENT

Genesis

WHO
Adam, Eve, Cain, Abel, Noah, Abraham, Sarah, Isaac, Lot, Melchizedek, Jacob, Esau, Joseph, and many others.

WHERE
Genesis begins with the story of Adam and Eve. Their story takes place in the Garden of Eden. Other stories in Genesis take place in the parts of the world that today are called Iraq, Israel, and Egypt.

WHEN
Moses probably wrote this book between 1450–1410 BC., while leading God's people to the Promised Land of Israel.

WHY
To tell about God's creation of the world and to show that God wants people to worship and obey him.

Then God looked over all he had made, and he saw that it was very good!
GENESIS 1:31

Genesis answers questions like . . . Where do animals come from? Why do people hurt each other? Where did different languages get started?

You'll learn a lot here about God, his creation, and the beginning of the human race.

Creation	Noah	Abram born	Isaac born	Jacob and Esau born	Joseph born	Joseph rules Egypt
Undated	2166 BC	2066 BC	2006 BC	1915 BC	1885 BC	

THIS IS WHERE GOD'S STORY BEGINS!

CHAPTER 1

The Account of Creation

In the beginning God created the heavens
and the earth.* [2]The earth was formless
and empty, and darkness covered the deep
waters. And the Spirit of God was hovering
over the surface of the waters.
[3]Then God said, "Let there be light," and there
was light. [4]And God saw that the light was
good. Then he separated the light from the
darkness. [5]God called the light "day" and the
darkness "night."

And evening passed and morning came,
marking the first day.

1:1 Or *In the beginning when God created the heavens and the earth, . . .* Or *When God began to create the heavens and the earth, . . .*

6 Then God said, "Let there be a space between
the waters, to separate the waters of the
heavens from the waters of the earth."
7 And that is what happened. God made this
space to separate the waters of the earth
from the waters of the heavens. 8 God
called the space "sky."
And evening passed and morning
came, marking the second day.

9 Then God said, "Let the waters beneath the
sky flow together into one place, so dry
ground may appear." And that is what
happened. 10 God called the dry ground
"land" and the waters "seas." And God saw
that it was good. 11 Then God said, "Let the
land sprout with vegetation—every sort of
seed-bearing plant, and trees that grow
seed-bearing fruit. These seeds will then
produce the kinds of plants and trees
from which they came." And that is
what happened. 12 The land produced
vegetation—all sorts of seed-bearing
plants, and trees with seed-bearing fruit.
Their seeds produced plants and trees of
the same kind. And God saw that it was
good.
13 And evening passed and morning
came, marking the third day.

Why should I treat people with respect if they don't deserve it?

So God created human beings in his own image. GENESIS 1:27

14 Then God said, "Let lights appear in the
sky to separate the day from the night.
Let them be signs to mark the seasons,
days, and years. 15 Let these lights in the
sky shine down on the earth." And that is
what happened. 16 God made two great
lights—the larger one to govern the day,
and the smaller one to govern the night.
He also made the stars. 17 God set these
lights in the sky to light the earth, 18 to
govern the day and night, and to separate
the light from the darkness. And God saw
that it was good.
19 And evening passed and morning
came, marking the fourth day.

20 Then God said, "Let the waters swarm with
fish and other life. Let the skies be filled
with birds of every kind." 21 So God
created great sea creatures and every
living thing that scurries and swarms in
the water, and every sort of bird—each
producing offspring of the same kind.
And God saw that it was good. 22 Then God
blessed them, saying, "Be fruitful and
multiply. Let the fish fill the seas, and let
the birds multiply on the earth."
23 And evening passed and morning
came, marking the fifth day.

24 Then God said, "Let the earth produce
every sort of animal, each producing
offspring of the same kind—livestock,
small animals that scurry along the
ground, and wild animals." And that is
what happened. 25 God made all sorts of
wild animals, livestock, and small animals,
each able to produce offspring of the
same kind. And God saw that it was good.
26 Then God said, "Let us make human
beings* in our image, to be like us. They
will reign over the fish in the sea, the
birds in the sky, the livestock, all the
wild animals on the earth, and the small
animals that scurry along the ground."

27 So God created human beings* in his
own image.
In the image of God he created them;
male and female he created them.

28 Then God blessed them and said, "Be
fruitful and multiply. Fill the earth and
govern it. Reign over the fish in the sea,
the birds in the sky, and all the animals
that scurry along the ground."
29 Then God said, "Look! I have given
you every seed-bearing plant throughout
the earth and all the fruit trees for your
food. 30 And I have given every green plant
as food for all the wild animals, the birds
in the sky, and the small animals that

1:26 Or *man;* Hebrew reads *adam.* **1:27** Or *the man;* Hebrew reads *ha-adam.*

scurry along the ground—everything that has life." And that is what happened.
31 Then God looked over all he had made, and he saw that it was very good!
And evening passed and morning came, marking the sixth day.

CHAPTER 2

So the creation of the heavens and the earth and everything in them was completed.
2 On the seventh day God had finished his work of creation, so he rested* from all his work. 3 And God blessed the seventh day and declared it holy, because it was the day when he rested from all his work of creation.

4 This is the account of the creation of the heavens and the earth.

The Man and Woman in Eden

When the LORD God made the earth and the heavens, 5 neither wild plants nor grains were growing on the earth. For the LORD God had not yet sent rain to water the earth, and there were no people to cultivate the soil. 6 Instead, springs* came up from the ground and watered all the land. 7 Then the LORD God formed the man from the dust of the ground. He breathed the breath of life into the man's nostrils, and the man became a living person.

2:2 Or *ceased;* also in 2:3. 2:6 Or *mist.*

8 Then the LORD God planted a garden in Eden in the east, and there he placed the man he had made. 9 The LORD God made all sorts of trees grow up from the ground—trees that were beautiful and that produced delicious fruit. In the middle of the garden he placed the tree of life and the tree of the knowledge of good and evil.

10 A river flowed from the land of Eden, watering the garden and then dividing into four branches. 11 The first branch, called the Pishon, flowed around the entire land of Havilah, where gold is found. 12 The gold of that land is exceptionally pure; aromatic resin and onyx stone are also found there. 13 The second branch, called the Gihon, flowed around the entire land of Cush. 14 The third branch, called the Tigris, flowed east of the land of Asshur. The fourth branch is called the Euphrates.

15 The LORD God placed the man in the Garden of Eden to tend and watch over it. 16 But the LORD God warned him, "You may freely eat the fruit of every tree in the garden—17 except the tree of the knowledge of good and evil. If you eat its fruit, you are sure to die."

18 Then the LORD God said, "It is not good for the man to be alone. I will make a helper who is just right for him." 19 So the LORD God formed from the ground all the wild animals and all the birds of the sky. He brought them

DAYS OF CREATION

First Day
Light (so there was light and darkness)

Second Day
Sky and water

Third Day
Seas and land

Fourth Day
Sun, moon, and stars

Fifth Day
Fish and birds

Sixth Day
Animals,
Man and woman

Seventh Day
God rested and was pleased

to the man* to see what he would call them,
and the man chose a name for each one. [20]He
gave names to all the livestock, all the birds of
the sky, and all the wild animals. But still there
was no helper just right for him.

[21]So the LORD God caused the man to fall
into a deep sleep. While the man slept, the
LORD God took out one of the man's ribs* and
closed up the opening. [22]Then the LORD God
made a woman from the rib, and he brought
her to the man.

[23]"At last!" the man exclaimed.

"This one is bone from my bone,
and flesh from my flesh!
She will be called 'woman,'
because she was taken from 'man.'"

[24]This explains why a man leaves his father
and mother and is joined to his wife, and the
two are united into one.

[25]Now the man and his wife were both na-
ked, but they felt no shame.

CHAPTER 3

The Man and Woman Sin

The serpent was the shrewdest of all the wild
animals the LORD God had made. One day he
asked the woman, "Did God really say you
must not eat the fruit from any of the trees in
the garden?"

[2]"Of course we may eat fruit from the trees
in the garden," the woman replied. [3]"It's only
the fruit from the tree in the middle of the
garden that we are not allowed to eat. God
said, 'You must not eat it or even touch it; if
you do, you will die.'"

[4]"You won't die!" the serpent replied to the
woman. [5]"God knows that your eyes will be
opened as soon as you eat it, and you will be
like God, knowing both good and evil."

[6]The woman was convinced. She saw that
the tree was beautiful and its fruit looked deli-
cious, and she wanted the wisdom it would
give her. So she took some of the fruit and ate
it. Then she gave some to her husband, who
was with her, and he ate it, too. [7]At that mo-
ment their eyes were opened, and they sud-
denly felt shame at their nakedness. So they
sewed fig leaves together to cover themselves.

[8]When the cool evening breezes were blow-
ing, the man* and his wife heard the LORD God
walking about in the garden. So they hid from
the LORD God among the trees. [9]Then the LORD
God called to the man, "Where are you?"

[10]He replied, "I heard you walking in the
garden, so I hid. I was afraid because I was
naked."

[11]"Who told you that you were naked?" the
LORD God asked. "Have you eaten from the

The Video Game

Mitchell had invited his friends to stay for a night in the basement family room. After Mitchell's parents went to bed, Peter said, "Hey, I brought a video game to play." Mitchell looked at the game. "This is rated *M*." Peter answered, "Oh, come on. My older brother said it's awesome!" *Well,* Mitchell thought, *It does look pretty cool.* The other guys were up for it, and Mitchell didn't want them to think he was a wimp. His parents would never know.

What would you do? Check out Genesis 3:1-7.

2:19 Or *Adam,* and so throughout the chapter. **2:21** Or *took a part of the man's side.* **3:8** Or *Adam,* and so throughout the chapter.

tree whose fruit I commanded you not to eat?"

12 The man replied, "It was the woman you gave me who gave me the fruit, and I ate it."

13 Then the LORD God asked the woman, "What have you done?"

"The serpent deceived me," she replied. "That's why I ate it."

14 Then the LORD God said to the serpent,

"Because you have done this, you are cursed
more than all animals, domestic
and wild.
You will crawl on your belly,
groveling in the dust as long as you live.
15 And I will cause hostility between you
and the woman,
and between your offspring and
her offspring.
He will strike* your head,
and you will strike his heel."

16 Then he said to the woman,

"I will sharpen the pain of your pregnancy,
and in pain you will give birth.
And you will desire to control your
husband,
but he will rule over you.*"

17 And to the man he said,

"Since you listened to your wife and ate
from the tree
whose fruit I commanded you not
to eat,
the ground is cursed because of you.
All your life you will struggle to scratch
a living from it.
18 It will grow thorns and thistles for you,
though you will eat of its grains.
19 By the sweat of your brow
will you have food to eat
until you return to the ground
from which you were made.
For you were made from dust,
and to dust you will return."

Paradise Lost: God's Judgment

20 Then the man—Adam—named his wife Eve, because she would be the mother of all who live.* 21 And the LORD God made clothing from animal skins for Adam and his wife.

22 Then the LORD God said, "Look, the human beings* have become like us, knowing both good and evil. What if they reach out, take fruit from the tree of life, and eat it? Then they will live forever!" 23 So the LORD God banished them from the Garden of Eden, and he sent Adam out to cultivate the ground from which he had been made. 24 After sending them out, the LORD God stationed mighty cherubim to the east of the Garden of Eden. And he placed a flaming sword that flashed back and forth to guard the way to the tree of life.

CHAPTER 4

Cain and Abel

Now Adam* had sexual relations with his wife, Eve, and she became pregnant. When she gave birth to Cain, she said, "With the LORD's help, I have produced* a man!" 2 Later she gave birth to his brother and named him Abel.

When they grew up, Abel became a shepherd, while Cain cultivated the ground. 3 When it was time for the harvest, Cain presented some of his crops as a gift to the LORD. 4 Abel also brought a gift—the best of the firstborn lambs from his flock. The LORD accepted Abel and his gift, 5 but he did not accept Cain and his gift. This made Cain very angry, and he looked dejected.

6 "Why are you so angry?" the LORD asked Cain. "Why do you look so dejected? 7 You will be accepted if you do what is right. But if you refuse to do what is right, then watch out! Sin is crouching at the door, eager to control you. But you must subdue it and be its master."

8 One day Cain suggested to his brother, "Let's go out into the fields."* And while they were in the field, Cain attacked his brother, Abel, and killed him.

9 Afterward the LORD asked Cain, "Where is your brother? Where is Abel?"

"I don't know," Cain responded. "Am I my brother's guardian?"

10 But the LORD said, "What have you done? Listen! Your brother's blood cries out to me from the ground! 11 Now you are cursed and banished from the ground, which has

3:15 Or *bruise;* also in 3:15b. **3:16** Or *And though you will have desire for your husband, / he will rule over you.* **3:20** *Eve* sounds like a Hebrew term that means "to give life." **3:22** Or *the man;* Hebrew reads *ha-adam.* **4:1a** Or *the man;* also in 4:25. **4:1b** Or *I have acquired. Cain* sounds like a Hebrew term that can mean "produce" or "acquire." **4:8** As in Samaritan Pentateuch, Greek and Syriac versions, and Latin Vulgate; Masoretic Text lacks *"Let's go out into the fields."*

swallowed your brother's blood. [12]No longer will the ground yield good crops for you, no matter how hard you work! From now on you will be a homeless wanderer on the earth."

[13]Cain replied to the LORD, "My punishment* is too great for me to bear! [14]You have banished me from the land and from your presence; you have made me a homeless wanderer. Anyone who finds me will kill me!"

[15]The LORD replied, "No, for I will give a sevenfold punishment to anyone who kills you." Then the LORD put a mark on Cain to warn anyone who might try to kill him. [16]So Cain left the LORD's presence and settled in the land of Nod,* east of Eden.

The Descendants of Cain

[17]Cain had sexual relations with his wife, and she became pregnant and gave birth to Enoch. Then Cain founded a city, which he named Enoch, after his son. [18]Enoch had a son named Irad. Irad became the father of* Mehujael. Mehujael became the father of Methushael. Methushael became the father of Lamech.

[19]Lamech married two women. The first was named Adah, and the second was Zillah. [20]Adah gave birth to Jabal, who was the first of those who raise livestock and live in tents. [21]His brother's name was Jubal, the first of all who play the harp and flute. [22]Lamech's other wife, Zillah, gave birth to a son named Tubal-cain. He became an expert in forging tools of bronze and iron. Tubal-cain had a sister named Naamah. [23]One day Lamech said to his wives,

"Adah and Zillah, hear my voice;
listen to me, you wives of Lamech.
I have killed a man who attacked me,
a young man who wounded me.
[24] If someone who kills Cain is punished
seven times,
then the one who kills me will be
punished seventy-seven times!"

The Birth of Seth

[25]Adam had sexual relations with his wife again, and she gave birth to another son. She named him Seth,* for she said, "God has granted me another son in place of Abel, whom Cain killed." [26]When Seth grew up, he had a son and named him Enosh. At that time people first began to worship the LORD by name.

CHAPTER 5

The Descendants of Adam

This is the written account of the descendants of Adam. When God created human beings,* he made them to be like himself. [2]He created them male and female, and he blessed them and called them "human."

[3]When Adam was 130 years old, he became the father of a son who was just like him—in his very image. He named his son Seth. [4]After the birth of Seth, Adam lived another 800 years, and he had other sons and daughters. [5]Adam lived 930 years, and then he died.

[6]When Seth was 105 years old, he became the father of* Enosh. [7]After the birth of*

4:13 Or *My sin.* **4:16** *Nod* means "wandering." **4:18** Or *the ancestor of,* and so throughout the verse. **4:25** *Seth* probably means "granted"; the name may also mean "appointed." **5:1** Or *man;* Hebrew reads *adam;* similarly in 5:2. **5:6** Or *the ancestor of;* also in 5:9, 12, 15, 18, 21, 25. **5:7** Or *the birth of this ancestor of;* also in 5:10, 13, 16, 19, 22, 26.

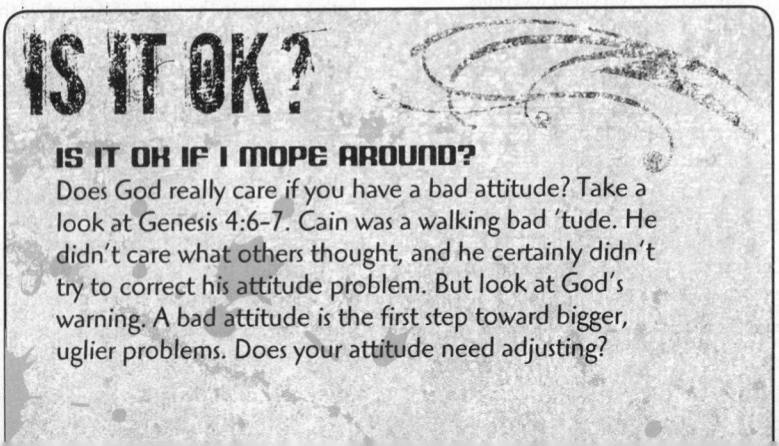

Enosh, Seth lived another 807 years, and
he had other sons and daughters. [8]Seth
lived 912 years, and then he died.
[9]When Enosh was 90 years old, he became
the father of Kenan. [10]After the birth of
Kenan, Enosh lived another 815 years,
and he had other sons and daughters.
[11]Enosh lived 905 years, and then he died.
[12]When Kenan was 70 years old, he became
the father of Mahalalel. [13]After the birth
of Mahalalel, Kenan lived another
840 years, and he had other sons and
daughters. [14]Kenan lived 910 years, and
then he died.
[15]When Mahalalel was 65 years old, he
became the father of Jared. [16]After the
birth of Jared, Mahalalel lived another
830 years, and he had other sons and
daughters. [17]Mahalalel lived 895 years,
and then he died.
[18]When Jared was 162 years old, he became
the father of Enoch. [19]After the birth of
Enoch, Jared lived another 800 years, and
he had other sons and daughters. [20]Jared
lived 962 years, and then he died.
[21]When Enoch was 65 years old, he became
the father of Methuselah. [22]After the birth
of Methuselah, Enoch lived in close
fellowship with God for another
300 years, and he had other sons and
daughters. [23]Enoch lived 365 years,
[24]walking in close fellowship with God.
Then one day he disappeared, because
God took him.
[25]When Methuselah was 187 years old, he
became the father of Lamech. [26]After
the birth of Lamech, Methuselah lived
another 782 years, and he had other
sons and daughters. [27]Methuselah lived
969 years, and then he died.
[28]When Lamech was 182 years old, he
became the father of a son. [29]Lamech
named his son Noah, for he said, "May he
bring us relief* from our work and the
painful labor of farming this ground that
the LORD has cursed." [30]After the birth of
Noah, Lamech lived another 595 years,
and he had other sons and daughters.
[31]Lamech lived 777 years, and then he
died.
[32]By the time Noah was 500 years old, he was
the father of Shem, Ham, and Japheth.

CHAPTER 6

A World Gone Wrong

Then the people began to multiply on the
earth, and daughters were born to them. [2]The
sons of God saw the beautiful women* and
took any they wanted as their wives. [3]Then
the LORD said, "My Spirit will not put up with*
humans for such a long time, for they are only
mortal flesh. In the future, their normal life-
span will be no more than 120 years."
[4]In those days, and for some time after, gi-
ant Nephilites lived on the earth, for whenever
the sons of God had intercourse with women,
they gave birth to children who became the
heroes and famous warriors of ancient times.

AMAZING FACTS

Methuselah lived to be 969! Noah was 950. Now that's old!

GENESIS 5:27; 9:29

[5]The LORD observed the extent of human
wickedness on the earth, and he saw that
everything they thought or imagined was con-
sistently and totally evil. [6]So the LORD was
sorry he had ever made them and put them on
the earth. It broke his heart. [7]And the LORD
said, "I will wipe this human race I have cre-
ated from the face of the earth. Yes, and I will
destroy every living thing—all the people, the
large animals, the small animals that scurry
along the ground, and even the birds of the
sky. I am sorry I ever made them." [8]But Noah
found favor with the LORD.

5:29 *Noah* sounds like a Hebrew term that can mean "relief" or "comfort." **6:2** Hebrew *daughters of men;* also in 6:4. **6:3** Greek version reads *will not remain in.*

The Story of Noah

9 This is the account of Noah and his family.
Noah was a righteous man, the only blameless
person living on earth at the time, and he
walked in close fellowship with God. 10 Noah
was the father of three sons: Shem, Ham, and
Japheth.

11 Now God saw that the earth had become
corrupt and was filled with violence. 12 God
observed all this corruption in the world, for
everyone on earth was corrupt. 13 So God said
to Noah, "I have decided to destroy all living
creatures, for they have filled the earth with
violence. Yes, I will wipe them all out along
with the earth!

14 "Build a large boat* from cypress wood*
and waterproof it with tar, inside and out.
Then construct decks and stalls throughout
its interior. 15 Make the boat 450 feet long,
75 feet wide, and 45 feet high.* 16 Leave an
18-inch opening* below the roof all the way
around the boat. Put the door on the side, and
build three decks inside the boat—lower,
middle, and upper.

17 "Look! I am about to cover the earth with a
flood that will destroy every living thing that
breathes. Everything on earth will die. 18 But I
will confirm my covenant with you. So enter
the boat—you and your wife and your sons and
their wives. 19 Bring a pair of every kind of ani-
mal—a male and a female—into the boat with
you to keep them alive during the flood. 20 Pairs
of every kind of bird, and every kind of animal,
and every kind of small animal that scurries
along the ground, will come to you to be kept
alive. 21 And be sure to take on board enough
food for your family and for all the animals."

22 So Noah did everything exactly as God
had commanded him.

CHAPTER 7

The Flood Covers the Earth

When everything was ready, the LORD said to
Noah, "Go into the boat with all your family,
for among all the people of the earth, I can see
that you alone are righteous. 2 Take with you
seven pairs—male and female—of each ani-
mal I have approved for eating and for sacri-
fice,* and take one pair of each of the others.
3 Also take seven pairs of every kind of bird.
There must be a male and a female in each
pair to ensure that all life will survive on the
earth after the flood. 4 Seven days from now I
will make the rains pour down on the earth.
And it will rain for forty days and forty nights,
until I have wiped from the earth all the living
things I have created."

5 So Noah did everything as the LORD com-
manded him.

6 Noah was 600 years old when the flood
covered the earth. 7 He went on board the boat
to escape the flood—he and his wife and his
sons and their wives. 8 With them were all the
various kinds of animals—those approved for
eating and for sacrifice and those that were
not—along with all the birds and the small an-
imals that scurry along the ground. 9 They en-
tered the boat in pairs, male and female, just
as God had commanded Noah. 10 After seven
days, the waters of the flood came and cov-
ered the earth.

11 When Noah was 600 years old, on the
seventeenth day of the second month, all the
underground waters erupted from the earth,
and the rain fell in mighty torrents from the
sky. 12 The rain continued to fall for forty days
and forty nights.

13 That very day Noah had gone into the
boat with his wife and his sons—Shem, Ham,
and Japheth—and their wives. 14 With them in
the boat were pairs of every kind of animal—
domestic and wild, large and small—along
with birds of every kind. 15 Two by two they
came into the boat, representing every living
thing that breathes. 16 A male and female of
each kind entered, just as God had com-
manded Noah. Then the LORD closed the door
behind them.

17 For forty days the floodwaters grew
deeper, covering the ground and lifting the
boat high above the earth. 18 As the waters
rose higher and higher above the ground, the
boat floated safely on the surface. 19 Finally,
the water covered even the highest moun-
tains on the earth, 20 rising more than twenty-
two feet* above the highest peaks. 21 All the
living things on earth died—birds, domestic
animals, wild animals, small animals that
scurry along the ground, and all the people.
22 Everything that breathed and lived on dry

6:14a Traditionally rendered *an ark.* **6:14b** Or *gopher wood.* **6:15** Hebrew *300 cubits* [138 meters] *long, 50 cubits* [23 meters] *wide, and 30 cubits* [13.8 meters] *high.* **6:16** Hebrew *an opening of 1 cubit* [46 centimeters]. **7:2** Hebrew *of each clean animal;* similarly in 7:8. **7:20** Hebrew *15 cubits* [6.9 meters].

land died. [23]God wiped out every living thing on the earth—people, livestock, small animals that scurry along the ground, and the birds of the sky. All were destroyed. The only people who survived were Noah and those with him in the boat. [24]And the floodwaters covered the earth for 150 days.

CHAPTER 8

The Flood Recedes

But God remembered Noah and all the wild animals and livestock with him in the boat. He sent a wind to blow across the earth, and the floodwaters began to recede. [2]The underground waters stopped flowing, and the torrential rains from the sky were stopped. [3]So the floodwaters gradually receded from the earth. After 150 days, [4]exactly five months from the time the flood began,* the boat came to rest on the mountains of Ararat. [5]Two and a half months later,* as the waters continued to go down, other mountain peaks became visible.

[6]After another forty days, Noah opened the window he had made in the boat [7]and released a raven. The bird flew back and forth until the floodwaters on the earth had dried up. [8]He also released a dove to see if the water had receded and it could find dry ground. [9]But the dove could find no place to land because the water still covered the ground. So it returned to the boat, and Noah held out his hand and drew the dove back inside. [10]After waiting another seven days, Noah released the dove again. [11]This time the dove returned to him in the evening with a fresh olive leaf in its beak. Then Noah knew that the floodwaters were almost gone. [12]He waited another seven days and then released the dove again. This time it did not come back.

[13]Noah was now 601 years old. On the first day of the new year, ten and a half months after the flood began,* the floodwaters had almost dried up from the earth. Noah lifted back the covering of the boat and saw that the surface of the ground was drying. [14]Two more months went by,* and at last the earth was dry!

[15]Then God said to Noah, [16]"Leave the boat, all of you—you and your wife, and your sons and their wives. [17]Release all the animals—the birds, the livestock, and the small animals that scurry along the ground—so they can be fruitful and multiply throughout the earth."

[18]So Noah, his wife, and his sons and their wives left the boat. [19]And all of the large and small animals and birds came out of the boat, pair by pair.

[20]Then Noah built an altar to the LORD, and there he sacrificed as burnt offerings the animals and birds that had been approved for that purpose.* [21]And the LORD was pleased with the aroma of the sacrifice and said to himself, "I will never again curse the ground because of the human race, even though everything they think or imagine is bent toward evil from childhood. I will never again destroy all living things. [22]As long as the earth remains, there will be planting and harvest, cold and heat, summer and winter, day and night."

CHAPTER 9

God Confirms His Covenant

Then God blessed Noah and his sons and told them, "Be fruitful and multiply. Fill the earth. [2]All the animals of the earth, all the birds of the sky, all the small animals that scurry along the ground, and all the fish in the sea will look on you with fear and terror. I have placed them in your power. [3]I have given them to you for food, just as I have given you grain and vegetables. [4]But you must never eat any meat that still has the lifeblood in it.

[5]"And I will require the blood of anyone who takes another person's life. If a wild animal kills a person, it must die. And anyone who murders a fellow human must die. [6]If anyone takes a human life, that person's life will also be taken by human hands. For God made human beings* in his own image. [7]Now be fruitful and multiply, and repopulate the earth."

[8]Then God told Noah and his sons, [9]"I hereby confirm my covenant with you and your descendants, [10]and with all the animals that were on the boat with you—the birds, the livestock, and all the wild animals—every living creature on earth. [11]Yes, I am confirming my

8:4 Hebrew *on the seventeenth day of the seventh month;* see 7:11. **8:5** Hebrew *On the first day of the tenth month;* see 7:11 and note on 8:4. **8:13** Hebrew *On the first day of the first month;* see 7:11. **8:14** Hebrew *The twenty-seventh day of the second month arrived;* see note on 8:13. **8:20** Hebrew *every clean animal and every clean bird.* **9:6** Or *man;* Hebrew reads *ha-adam.*

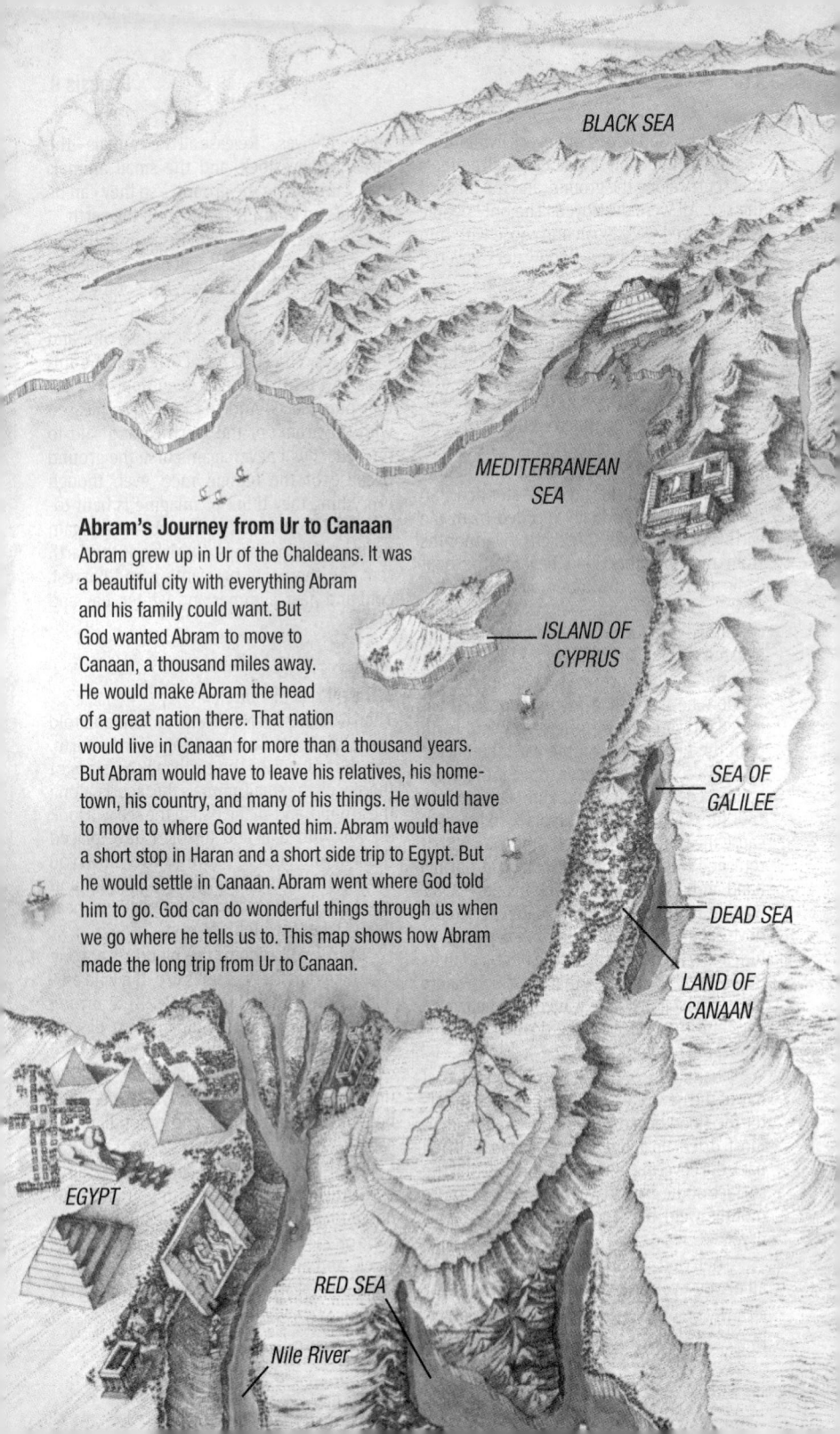

Abram's Journey from Ur to Canaan

Abram grew up in Ur of the Chaldeans. It was a beautiful city with everything Abram and his family could want. But God wanted Abram to move to Canaan, a thousand miles away. He would make Abram the head of a great nation there. That nation would live in Canaan for more than a thousand years. But Abram would have to leave his relatives, his hometown, his country, and many of his things. He would have to move to where God wanted him. Abram would have a short stop in Haran and a short side trip to Egypt. But he would settle in Canaan. Abram went where God told him to go. God can do wonderful things through us when we go where he tells us to. This map shows how Abram made the long trip from Ur to Canaan.

CASPIAN SEA
Haran
Tigris River
Euphrates River
Babylon
(Babel)
PERSIAN
GULF
ARABIAN
DESERT
Ur of the Chaldeans

covenant with you. Never again will flood-
waters kill all living creatures; never again will
a flood destroy the earth."
12 Then God said, "I am giving you a sign of
my covenant with you and with all living cre-
atures, for all generations to come. 13 I have
placed my rainbow in the clouds. It is the sign
of my covenant with you and with all the earth.
14 When I send clouds over the earth, the rain-
bow will appear in the clouds, 15 and I will re-
member my covenant with you and with all
living creatures. Never again will the flood-
waters destroy all life. 16 When I see the rain-
bow in the clouds, I will remember the eternal
covenant between God and every living cre-
ature on earth." 17 Then God said to Noah, "Yes,
this rainbow is the sign of the covenant I am
confirming with all the creatures on earth."

Noah's Sons

18 The sons of Noah who came out of the boat
with their father were Shem, Ham, and Ja-
pheth. (Ham is the father of Canaan.) 19 From
these three sons of Noah came all the people
who now populate the earth.
20 After the flood, Noah began to cultivate
the ground, and he planted a vineyard. 21 One
day he drank some wine he had made, and he
became drunk and lay naked inside his tent.
22 Ham, the father of Canaan, saw that his
father was naked and went outside and told
his brothers. 23 Then Shem and Japheth took a
robe, held it over their shoulders, and backed
into the tent to cover their father. As they did
this, they looked the other way so they would
not see him naked.
24 When Noah woke up from his stupor, he
learned what Ham, his youngest son, had done.
25 Then he cursed Canaan, the son of Ham:

"May Canaan be cursed!
May he be the lowest of servants
to his relatives."

26 Then Noah said,

"May the LORD, the God of Shem, be blessed,
and may Canaan be his servant!
27 May God expand the territory of Japheth!
May Japheth share the prosperity of Shem,*
and may Canaan be his servant."

28 Noah lived another 350 years after the
great flood. 29 He lived 950 years, and then he
died.

CHAPTER 10

This is the account of the families of Shem,
Ham, and Japheth, the three sons of Noah.
Many children were born to them after the
great flood.

Descendants of Japheth

2 The descendants of Japheth were Gomer,
Magog, Madai, Javan, Tubal, Meshech, and
Tiras.
3 The descendants of Gomer were Ashkenaz,
Riphath, and Togarmah.
4 The descendants of Javan were Elishah,
Tarshish, Kittim, and Rodanim.* 5 Their
descendants became the seafaring
peoples that spread out to various lands,
each identified by its own language, clan,
and national identity.

Descendants of Ham

6 The descendants of Ham were Cush,
Mizraim, Put, and Canaan.
7 The descendants of Cush were Seba,
Havilah, Sabtah, Raamah, and Sabteca.
The descendants of Raamah were Sheba
and Dedan.
8 Cush was also the ancestor of Nimrod,
who was the first heroic warrior on earth.
9 Since he was the greatest hunter in the
world,* his name became proverbial.
People would say, "This man is like
Nimrod, the greatest hunter in the world."
10 He built his kingdom in the land of
Babylonia,* with the cities of Babylon,
Erech, Akkad, and Calneh. 11 From there
he expanded his territory to Assyria,*
building the cities of Nineveh, Rehoboth-
ir, Calah, 12 and Resen (the great city
located between Nineveh and Calah).
13 Mizraim was the ancestor of the Ludites,
Anamites, Lehabites, Naphtuhites,
14 Pathrusites, Casluhites, and the Caph-
torites, from whom the Philistines came.*
15 Canaan's oldest son was Sidon, the ancestor
of the Sidonians. Canaan was also the

9:27 Hebrew *May he live in the tents of Shem.* **10:4** As in some Hebrew manuscripts and Greek version (see also 1 Chr 1:7); most Hebrew manuscripts read *Dodanim.* **10:9** Hebrew *a great hunter before the LORD;* also in 10:9b. **10:10** Hebrew *Shinar.* **10:11** Or *From that land Assyria went out.* **10:14** Hebrew *Casluhites, from whom the Philistines came, and Caphtorites.* Compare Jer 47:4; Amos 9:7.

ancestor of the Hittites,* [16]Jebusites,
Amorites, Girgashites, [17]Hivites, Arkites,
Sinites, [18]Arvadites, Zemarites, and
Hamathites. The Canaanite clans
eventually spread out, [19]and the territory
of Canaan extended from Sidon in the
north to Gerar and Gaza in the south, and
east as far as Sodom, Gomorrah, Admah,
and Zeboiim, near Lasha.
[20]These were the descendants of Ham, identified by clan, language, territory, and national identity.

Descendants of Shem

[21]Sons were also born to Shem, the older
brother of Japheth.* Shem was the
ancestor of all the descendants of Eber.
[22]The descendants of Shem were Elam,
Asshur, Arphaxad, Lud, and Aram.
[23]The descendants of Aram were Uz, Hul,
Gether, and Mash.
[24]Arphaxad was the father of Shelah,* and
Shelah was the father of Eber.
[25]Eber had two sons. The first was named
Peleg (which means "division"), for during
his lifetime the people of the world were
divided into different language groups.
His brother's name was Joktan.
[26]Joktan was the ancestor of Almodad,
Sheleph, Hazarmaveth, Jerah, [27]Hadoram,
Uzal, Diklah, [28]Obal, Abimael, Sheba,
[29]Ophir, Havilah, and Jobab. All these were
descendants of Joktan. [30]The territory they
occupied extended from Mesha all the
way to Sephar in the eastern mountains.
[31]These were the descendants of Shem, identified by clan, language, territory, and national identity.

Conclusion

[32]These are the clans that descended from Noah's sons, arranged by nation according to their lines of descent. All the nations of the earth descended from these clans after the great flood.

CHAPTER 11

The Tower of Babel

At one time all the people of the world spoke the same language and used the same words.
[2]As the people migrated to the east, they found a plain in the land of Babylonia* and settled there.
[3]They began saying to each other, "Let's make bricks and harden them with fire." (In this region bricks were used instead of stone, and tar was used for mortar.) [4]Then they said, "Come, let's build a great city for ourselves with a tower that reaches into the sky. This will make us famous and keep us from being scattered all over the world."
[5]But the LORD came down to look at the city and the tower the people were building. [6]"Look!" he said. "The people are united, and they all speak the same language. After this, nothing they set out to do will be impossible for them! [7]Come, let's go down and confuse the people with different languages. Then they won't be able to understand each other."

AMAZING FACTS

The world's first skyscraper was made of mud and straw and may have been almost 300 feet tall.

GENESIS 11:1-9

[8]In that way, the LORD scattered them all over the world, and they stopped building the city. [9]That is why the city was called Babel,* because that is where the LORD confused the people with different languages. In this way he scattered them all over the world.

The Line of Descent from Shem to Abram

[10]This is the account of Shem's family.
Two years after the great flood, when
Shem was 100 years old, he became the
father of* Arphaxad. [11]After the birth

10:15 Hebrew *ancestor of Heth* **10:21** Or *Shem, whose older brother was Japheth.* **10:24** Greek version reads *Arphaxad was the father of Cainan, Cainan was the father of Shelah.* Compare Luke 3:36. **11:2** Hebrew *Shinar.* **11:9** Or *Babylon. Babel* sounds like a Hebrew term that means "confusion." **11:10** Or *the ancestor of;* also in 11:12, 14, 16, 18, 20, 22, 24.

of* Arphaxad, Shem lived another
500 years and had other sons and
daughters.
12 When Arphaxad was 35 years old, he
became the father of Shelah. 13 After the
birth of Shelah, Arphaxad lived another
403 years and had other sons and
daughters.*
14 When Shelah was 30 years old, he became
the father of Eber. 15 After the birth of
Eber, Shelah lived another 403 years and
had other sons and daughters.
16 When Eber was 34 years old, he became
the father of Peleg. 17 After the birth of
Peleg, Eber lived another 430 years and
had other sons and daughters.
18 When Peleg was 30 years old, he became
the father of Reu. 19 After the birth of Reu,
Peleg lived another 209 years and had
other sons and daughters.
20 When Reu was 32 years old, he became the
father of Serug. 21 After the birth of Serug,
Reu lived another 207 years and had
other sons and daughters.
22 When Serug was 30 years old, he became
the father of Nahor. 23 After the birth of
Nahor, Serug lived another 200 years and
had other sons and daughters.
24 When Nahor was 29 years old, he became
the father of Terah. 25 After the birth of
Terah, Nahor lived another 119 years and
had other sons and daughters.
26 After Terah was 70 years old, he became
the father of Abram, Nahor, and Haran.

The Family of Terah

27 This is the account of Terah's family. Terah
was the father of Abram, Nahor, and Haran;
and Haran was the father of Lot. 28 But Haran
died in Ur of the Chaldeans, the land of his
birth, while his father, Terah, was still living.
29 Meanwhile, Abram and Nahor both mar-
ried. The name of Abram's wife was Sarai,
and the name of Nahor's wife was Milcah.
(Milcah and her sister Iscah were daughters
of Nahor's brother Haran.) 30 But Sarai was
unable to become pregnant and had no
children.

31 One day Terah took his son Abram, his
daughter-in-law Sarai (his son Abram's wife),
and his grandson Lot (his son Haran's child)
and moved away from Ur of the Chaldeans.
He was headed for the land of Canaan, but
they stopped at Haran and settled there. 32 Te-
rah lived for 205 years* and died while still
in Haran.

CHAPTER 12

The Call of Abram

The LORD had said to Abram, "Leave your na-
tive country, your relatives, and your father's
family, and go to the land that I will show you.
2 I will make you into a great nation. I will bless
you and make you famous, and you will be
a blessing to others. 3 I will bless those who
bless you and curse those who treat you with
contempt. All the families on earth will be
blessed through you."

4 So Abram departed as the LORD had in-
structed, and Lot went with him. Abram was
seventy-five years old when he left Haran. 5 He
took his wife, Sarai, his nephew Lot, and all his
wealth—his livestock and all the people he
had taken into his household at Haran—and
headed for the land of Canaan. When they ar-
rived in Canaan, 6 Abram traveled through the
land as far as Shechem. There he set up camp
beside the oak of Moreh. At that time, the
area was inhabited by Canaanites.

7 Then the LORD appeared to Abram and
said, "I will give this land to your descen-
dants.*" And Abram built an altar there and
dedicated it to the LORD, who had appeared to
him. 8 After that, Abram traveled south and set
up camp in the hill country, with Bethel to the
west and Ai to the east. There he built another
altar and dedicated it to the LORD, and he wor-
shiped the LORD. 9 Then Abram continued
traveling south by stages toward the Negev.

Abram and Sarai in Egypt

10 At that time a severe famine struck the land
of Canaan, forcing Abram to go down to
Egypt, where he lived as a foreigner. 11 As he
was approaching the border of Egypt, Abram
said to his wife, Sarai, "Look, you are a very
beautiful woman. 12 When the Egyptians see
you, they will say, 'This is his wife. Let's kill

11:11 Or *the birth of this ancestor of;* also in 11:13, 15, 17, 19, 21, 23, 25. **11:12-13** Greek version reads 12 *When Arphaxad was 135 years old, he became the father of Cainan.* 13 *After the birth of Cainan, Arphaxad lived another 430 years and had other sons and daughters, and then he died. When Cainan was 130 years old, he became the father of Shelah. After the birth of Shelah, Cainan lived another 330 years and had other sons and daughters, and then he died.* Compare Luke 3:35-36. **11:32** Some ancient versions read *145 years;* compare 11:26 and 12:4. **12:7** Hebrew *seed.*

him; then we can have her!' [13]So please tell them you are my sister. Then they will spare my life and treat me well because of their interest in you."

[14]And sure enough, when Abram arrived in Egypt, everyone noticed Sarai's beauty. [15]When the palace officials saw her, they sang her praises to Pharaoh, their king, and Sarai was taken into his palace. [16]Then Pharaoh gave Abram many gifts because of her—sheep, goats, cattle, male and female donkeys, male and female servants, and camels.

[17]But the LORD sent terrible plagues upon Pharaoh and his household because of Sarai, Abram's wife. [18]So Pharaoh summoned Abram and accused him sharply. "What have you done to me?" he demanded. "Why didn't you tell me she was your wife? [19]Why did you say, 'She is my sister,' and allow me to take her as my wife? Now then, here is your wife. Take her and get out of here!" [20]Pharaoh ordered some of his men to escort them, and he sent Abram out of the country, along with his wife and all his possessions.

CHAPTER 13

Abram and Lot Separate

So Abram left Egypt and traveled north into the Negev, along with his wife and Lot and all that they owned. [2](Abram was very rich in livestock, silver, and gold.) [3]From the Negev, they continued traveling by stages toward Bethel, and they pitched their tents between Bethel and Ai, where they had camped before. [4]This was the same place where Abram had built the altar, and there he worshiped the LORD again.

[5]Lot, who was traveling with Abram, had also become very wealthy with flocks of sheep and goats, herds of cattle, and many tents. [6]But the land could not support both Abram and Lot with all their flocks and herds living so close together. [7]So disputes broke out between the herdsmen of Abram and Lot. (At that time Canaanites and Perizzites were also living in the land.)

[8]Finally Abram said to Lot, "Let's not allow this conflict to come between us or our herdsmen. After all, we are close relatives! [9]The whole countryside is open to you. Take your choice of any section of the land you want, and we will separate. If you want the land to the left, then I'll take the land on the right. If you prefer the land on the right, then I'll go to the left."

[10]Lot took a long look at the fertile plains of the Jordan Valley in the direction of Zoar. The whole area was well watered everywhere, like the garden of the LORD or the beautiful land of Egypt. (This was before the LORD destroyed

Making a Good Impression

On a recent camping trip, Connor and some new friends were talking about their families. It seemed like all the guys had something really great to tell about their families. Connor liked his family, but to be truthful, they weren't really that impressive. Still, Connor wanted to impress his new friends. Should Connor make up a great story? Or should he just say nothing? Or should he be honest and say he has no story?

What would you do? Genesis 12:10-20 tells how Abraham solved a similar problem. Was it a good solution or not?

Sodom and Gomorrah.) [11]Lot chose for himself the whole Jordan Valley to the east of them. He went there with his flocks and servants and parted company with his uncle Abram. [12]So Abram settled in the land of Canaan, and Lot moved his tents to a place near Sodom and settled among the cities of the plain. [13]But the people of this area were extremely wicked and constantly sinned against the LORD.

[14]After Lot had gone, the LORD said to Abram, "Look as far as you can see in every direction—north and south, east and west. [15]I am giving all this land, as far as you can see, to you and your descendants* as a permanent possession. [16]And I will give you so many descendants that, like the dust of the earth, they cannot be counted! [17]Go and walk through the land in every direction, for I am giving it to you."

[18]So Abram moved his camp to Hebron and settled near the oak grove belonging to Mamre. There he built another altar to the LORD.

CHAPTER 14

Abram Rescues Lot

About this time war broke out in the region. King Amraphel of Babylonia,* King Arioch of Ellasar, King Kedorlaomer of Elam, and King Tidal of Goiim [2]fought against King Bera of Sodom, King Birsha of Gomorrah, King Shinab of Admah, King Shemeber of Zeboiim, and the king of Bela (also called Zoar).

[3]This second group of kings joined forces in Siddim Valley (that is, the valley of the Dead Sea*). [4]For twelve years they had been subject to King Kedorlaomer, but in the thirteenth year they rebelled against him.

[5]One year later Kedorlaomer and his allies arrived and defeated the Rephaites at Ashteroth-karnaim, the Zuzites at Ham, the Emites at Shaveh-kiriathaim, [6]and the Horites at Mount Seir, as far as El-paran at the edge of the wilderness. [7]Then they turned back and came to En-mishpat (now called Kadesh) and conquered all the territory of the Amalekites, and also the Amorites living in Hazazon-tamar.

[8]Then the rebel kings of Sodom, Gomorrah, Admah, Zeboiim, and Bela (also called Zoar) prepared for battle in the valley of the Dead Sea.* [9]They fought against King Kedorlaomer of Elam, King Tidal of Goiim, King Amraphel of Babylonia, and King Arioch of Ellasar—four kings against five. [10]As it happened, the valley of the Dead Sea was filled with tar pits. And as the army of the kings of Sodom and Gomorrah fled, some fell into the tar pits, while the rest escaped into the mountains. [11]The victorious invaders then plundered Sodom and Gomorrah and headed for home, taking with them all the spoils of war and the food supplies. [12]They also captured Lot—Abram's nephew who lived in Sodom—and carried off everything he owned.

[13]But one of Lot's men escaped and reported everything to Abram the Hebrew, who was living near the oak grove belonging to Mamre the Amorite. Mamre and his relatives, Eshcol and Aner, were Abram's allies.

[14]When Abram heard that his nephew Lot had been captured, he mobilized the 318 trained men who had been born into his household. Then he pursued Kedorlaomer's army until he caught up with them at Dan. [15]There he divided his men and attacked during the night. Kedorlaomer's army fled, but Abram chased them as far as Hobah, north of Damascus. [16]Abram recovered all the goods that had been taken, and he brought back his nephew Lot with his possessions and all the women and other captives.

Melchizedek Blesses Abram

[17]After Abram returned from his victory over Kedorlaomer and all his allies, the king of Sodom went out to meet him in the valley of Shaveh (that is, the King's Valley).

[18]And Melchizedek, the king of Salem and a priest of God Most High,* brought Abram some bread and wine. [19]Melchizedek blessed Abram with this blessing:

"Blessed be Abram by God Most High,
Creator of heaven and earth.
[20] And blessed be God Most High,
who has defeated your enemies
for you."

Then Abram gave Melchizedek a tenth of all the goods he had recovered.

[21]The king of Sodom said to Abram, "Give

13:15 Hebrew *seed;* also in 13:16. **14:1** Hebrew *Shinar;* also in 14:9. **14:3** Hebrew *Salt Sea.* **14:8** Hebrew *Siddim Valley* (see 14:3); also in 14:10. **14:18** Hebrew *El-Elyon;* also in 14:19, 20, 22.

back my people who were captured. But you may keep for yourself all the goods you have recovered."

[22]Abram replied to the king of Sodom, "I solemnly swear to the LORD, God Most High, Creator of heaven and earth, [23]that I will not take so much as a single thread or sandal thong from what belongs to you. Otherwise you might say, 'I am the one who made Abram rich.' [24]I will accept only what my young warriors have already eaten, and I request that you give a fair share of the goods to my allies—Aner, Eshcol, and Mamre."

CHAPTER 15

The LORD's Covenant Promise to Abram

Some time later, the LORD spoke to Abram in a vision and said to him, "Do not be afraid, Abram, for I will protect you, and your reward will be great."

What should I do when I'm feeling afraid and insecure?

Do not be afraid, Abram, for I will protect you. GENESIS 15:1

[2]But Abram replied, "O Sovereign LORD, what good are all your blessings when I don't even have a son? Since you've given me no children, Eliezer of Damascus, a servant in my household, will inherit all my wealth. [3]You have given me no descendants of my own, so one of my servants will be my heir."

[4]Then the LORD said to him, "No, your servant will not be your heir, for you will have a son of your own who will be your heir." [5]Then the LORD took Abram outside and said to him, "Look up into the sky and count the stars if you can. That's how many descendants you will have!"

[6]And Abram believed the LORD, and the LORD counted him as righteous because of his faith.

[7]Then the LORD told him, "I am the LORD who brought you out of Ur of the Chaldeans to give you this land as your possession."

[8]But Abram replied, "O Sovereign LORD, how can I be sure that I will actually possess it?"

[9]The LORD told him, "Bring me a three-year-old heifer, a three-year-old female goat, a three-year-old ram, a turtledove, and a young pigeon." [10]So Abram presented all these to him and killed them. Then he cut each animal down the middle and laid the halves side by side; he did not, however, cut the birds in half. [11]Some vultures swooped down to eat the carcasses, but Abram chased them away.

[12]As the sun was going down, Abram fell into a deep sleep, and a terrifying darkness came down over him. [13]Then the LORD said to Abram, "You can be sure that your descendants will be strangers in a foreign land, where they will be oppressed as slaves for 400 years. [14]But I will punish the nation that enslaves them, and in the end they will come away with great wealth. [15](As for you, you will die in peace and be buried at a ripe old age.) [16]After four generations your descendants will return here to this land, for the sins of the Amorites do not yet warrant their destruction."

[17]After the sun went down and darkness fell, Abram saw a smoking firepot and a flaming torch pass between the halves of the carcasses. [18]So the LORD made a covenant with Abram that day and said, "I have given this land to your descendants, all the way from the border of Egypt* to the great Euphrates River—[19]the land now occupied by the Kenites, Kenizzites, Kadmonites, [20]Hittites, Perizzites, Rephaites, [21]Amorites, Canaanites, Girgashites, and Jebusites."

CHAPTER 16

The Birth of Ishmael

Now Sarai, Abram's wife, had not been able to bear children for him. But she had an Egyptian servant named Hagar. [2]So Sarai said to Abram, "The LORD has prevented me from having children. Go and sleep with my servant. Perhaps I can have children through her." And Abram agreed with Sarai's proposal. [3]So Sarai, Abram's wife, took Hagar the Egyptian servant and gave her to Abram as a

15:18 Hebrew *the river of Egypt*, referring either to an eastern branch of the Nile River or to the Brook of Egypt in the Sinai (see Num 34:5).

Abraham

Those dusty hills over there look just like the hills we saw hours ago. I'll let Sarah think I know where I'm going. But what's important is that you know the way . . . don't you, God? I know you do.

You told us to pack up everything and leave home. So we did. You also said I'd have a family larger than the number of stars in the sky. That was a promise. But Sarah and I don't even have one child.

Yet I believe what you say, God. Sometimes I don't understand, but I still trust that your promises will come true.

Read all about Abraham's life in Genesis 11–25.

wife. (This happened ten years after Abram had settled in the land of Canaan.)

4 So Abram had sexual relations with Hagar,
and she became pregnant. But when Hagar
knew she was pregnant, she began to treat her
mistress, Sarai, with contempt. 5 Then Sarai
said to Abram, "This is all your fault! I put my
servant into your arms, but now that she's
pregnant she treats me with contempt. The
Lord will show who's wrong—you or me!"

6 Abram replied, "Look, she is your servant,
so deal with her as you see fit." Then Sarai
treated Hagar so harshly that she finally ran
away.

7 The angel of the Lord found Hagar beside
a spring of water in the wilderness, along the
road to Shur. 8 The angel said to her, "Hagar,
Sarai's servant, where have you come from,
and where are you going?"

"I'm running away from my mistress, Sarai," she replied.

9 The angel of the Lord said to her, "Return
to your mistress, and submit to her authority." 10 Then he added, "I will give you more descendants than you can count."

11 And the angel also said, "You are now
pregnant and will give birth to a son. You are
to name him Ishmael (which means 'God
hears'), for the Lord has heard your cry of distress. 12 This son of yours will be a wild man, as
untamed as a wild donkey! He will raise his
fist against everyone, and everyone will be
against him. Yes, he will live in open hostility
against all his relatives."

13 Thereafter, Hagar used another name to
refer to the Lord, who had spoken to her. She
said, "You are the God who sees me."* She
also said, "Have I truly seen the One who sees
me?" 14 So that well was named Beer-lahai-roi
(which means "well of the Living One who
sees me"). It can still be found between Kadesh and Bered.

15 So Hagar gave Abram a son, and Abram
named him Ishmael. 16 Abram was eighty-six
years old when Ishmael was born.

CHAPTER 17

Abram Is Named Abraham

When Abram was ninety-nine years old, the
Lord appeared to him and said, "I am El-
Shaddai—'God Almighty.' Serve me faithfully
and live a blameless life. 2 I will make a covenant with you, by which I will guarantee to
give you countless descendants."

3 At this, Abram fell face down on the
ground. Then God said to him, 4 "This is my
covenant with you: I will make you the father
of a multitude of nations! 5 What's more, I am
changing your name. It will no longer be
Abram. Instead, you will be called Abraham,*
for you will be the father of many nations. 6 I
will make you extremely fruitful. Your de-

16:13 Hebrew *El-roi*. **17:5** *Abram* means "exalted father"; *Abraham* sounds like a Hebrew term that means "father of many."

scendants will become many nations, and kings will be among them!

7"I will confirm my covenant with you and your descendants* after you, from generation to generation. This is the everlasting covenant: I will always be your God and the God of your descendants after you. 8And I will give the entire land of Canaan, where you now live as a foreigner, to you and your descendants. It will be their possession forever, and I will be their God."

The Mark of the Covenant

9Then God said to Abraham, "Your responsibility is to obey the terms of the covenant. You and all your descendants have this continual responsibility. 10This is the covenant that you and your descendants must keep: Each male among you must be circumcised. 11You must cut off the flesh of your foreskin as a sign of the covenant between me and you. 12From generation to generation, every male child must be circumcised on the eighth day after his birth. This applies not only to members of your family but also to the servants born in your household and the foreign-born servants whom you have purchased. 13All must be circumcised. Your bodies will bear the mark of my everlasting covenant. 14Any male who fails to be circumcised will be cut off from the covenant family for breaking the covenant."

Sarai Is Named Sarah

15Then God said to Abraham, "Regarding Sa-rai, your wife—her name will no longer be Sarai. From now on her name will be Sarah.* 16And I will bless her and give you a son from her! Yes, I will bless her richly, and she will become the mother of many nations. Kings of nations will be among her descendants."

17Then Abraham bowed down to the ground, but he laughed to himself in disbelief. "How could I become a father at the age of 100?" he thought. "And how can Sarah have a baby when she is ninety years old?" 18So Abraham said to God, "May Ishmael live under your special blessing!"

19But God replied, "No—Sarah, your wife, will give birth to a son for you. You will name him Isaac,* and I will confirm my covenant with him and his descendants as an everlasting covenant. 20As for Ishmael, I will bless him also, just as you have asked. I will make him extremely fruitful and multiply his descendants. He will become the father of twelve princes, and I will make him a great nation. 21But my covenant will be confirmed with Isaac, who will be born to you and Sarah about this time next year." 22When God had finished speaking, he left Abraham.

23On that very day Abraham took his son, Ishmael, and every male in his household, including those born there and those he had bought. Then he circumcised them, cutting off their foreskins, just as God had told him. 24Abraham was ninety-nine years old when he was circumcised, 25and Ishmael, his son, was thirteen. 26Both Abraham and his son, Ishmael, were circumcised on that same day, 27along with all the other men and boys of the household, whether they were born there or bought as servants. All were circumcised with him.

CHAPTER 18

A Son Is Promised to Sarah

The LORD appeared again to Abraham near the oak grove belonging to Mamre. One day Abraham was sitting at the entrance to his tent during the hottest part of the day. 2He looked up and noticed three men standing nearby. When he saw them, he ran to meet them and welcomed them, bowing low to the ground.

3"My lord," he said, "if it pleases you, stop here for a while. 4Rest in the shade of this tree while water is brought to wash your feet. 5And since you've honored your servant with this visit, let me prepare some food to refresh you before you continue on your journey."

"All right," they said. "Do as you have said."

6So Abraham ran back to the tent and said to Sarah, "Hurry! Get three large measures* of your best flour, knead it into dough, and bake some bread." 7Then Abraham ran out to the herd and chose a tender calf and gave it to his servant, who quickly prepared it. 8When the food was ready, Abraham took some yogurt and milk and the roasted meat, and he served it to the men. As they ate, Abraham waited on them in the shade of the trees.

17:7 Hebrew *seed;* also in 17:7b, 8, 9, 10, 19. **17:15** *Sarai* and *Sarah* both mean "princess"; the change in spelling may reflect the difference in dialect between Ur and Canaan. **17:19** *Isaac* means "he laughs." **18:6** Hebrew *3 seahs,* about 15 quarts or 14 liters.

[9]"Where is Sarah, your wife?" the visitors asked.

"She's inside the tent," Abraham replied.

[10]Then one of them said, "I will return to you about this time next year, and your wife, Sarah, will have a son!"

Sarah was listening to this conversation from the tent. [11]Abraham and Sarah were both very old by this time, and Sarah was long past the age of having children. [12]So she laughed silently to herself and said, "How could a worn-out woman like me enjoy such pleasure, especially when my master—my husband—is also so old?"

[13]Then the LORD said to Abraham, "Why did Sarah laugh? Why did she say, 'Can an old woman like me have a baby?' [14]Is anything too hard for the LORD? I will return about this time next year, and Sarah will have a son."

[15]Sarah was afraid, so she denied it, saying, "I didn't laugh."

But the LORD said, "No, you did laugh."

Abraham Intercedes for Sodom

[16]Then the men got up from their meal and looked out toward Sodom. As they left, Abraham went with them to send them on their way.

[17]"Should I hide my plan from Abraham?" the LORD asked. [18]"For Abraham will certainly become a great and mighty nation, and all the nations of the earth will be blessed through him. [19]I have singled him out so that he will direct his sons and their families to keep the way of the LORD by doing what is right and just. Then I will do for Abraham all that I have promised."

[20]So the LORD told Abraham, "I have heard a great outcry from Sodom and Gomorrah, because their sin is so flagrant. [21]I am going down to see if their actions are as wicked as I have heard. If not, I want to know."

[22]The other men turned and headed toward Sodom, but the LORD remained with Abraham. [23]Abraham approached him and said, "Will you sweep away both the righteous and the wicked? [24]Suppose you find fifty righteous people living there in the city—will you still sweep it away and not spare it for their sakes? [25]Surely you wouldn't do such a thing, destroying the righteous along with the wicked. Why, you would be treating the righteous and the wicked exactly the same! Surely you wouldn't do that! Should not the Judge of all the earth do what is right?"

[26]And the LORD replied, "If I find fifty righteous people in Sodom, I will spare the entire city for their sake."

[27]Then Abraham spoke again. "Since I have begun, let me speak further to my Lord, even though I am but dust and ashes. [28]Suppose there are only forty-five righteous people rather than fifty? Will you destroy the whole city for lack of five?"

And the LORD said, "I will not destroy it if I find forty-five righteous people there."

[29]Then Abraham pressed his request further. "Suppose there are only forty?"

And the LORD replied, "I will not destroy it for the sake of the forty."

[30]"Please don't be angry, my Lord," Abraham pleaded. "Let me speak—suppose only thirty righteous people are found?"

And the LORD replied, "I will not destroy it if I find thirty."

[31]Then Abraham said, "Since I have dared to speak to the Lord, let me continue—suppose there are only twenty?"

And the LORD replied, "Then I will not destroy it for the sake of the twenty."

[32]Finally, Abraham said, "Lord, please don't be angry with me if I speak one more time. Suppose only ten are found there?"

And the LORD replied, "Then I will not destroy it for the sake of the ten."

[33]When the LORD had finished his conversation with Abraham, he went on his way, and Abraham returned to his tent.

CHAPTER 19

Sodom and Gomorrah Destroyed

That evening the two angels came to the entrance of the city of Sodom. Lot was sitting there, and when he saw them, he stood up to meet them. Then he welcomed them and bowed with his face to the ground. [2]"My lords," he said, "come to my home to wash your feet, and be my guests for the night. You may then get up early in the morning and be on your way again."

"Oh no," they replied. "We'll just spend the night out here in the city square."

[3]But Lot insisted, so at last they went home

with him. Lot prepared a feast for them, complete with fresh bread made without yeast, and they ate. [4]But before they retired for the night, all the men of Sodom, young and old, came from all over the city and surrounded the house. [5]They shouted to Lot, "Where are the men who came to spend the night with you? Bring them out to us so we can have sex with them!"

[6]So Lot stepped outside to talk to them, shutting the door behind him. [7]"Please, my brothers," he begged, "don't do such a wicked thing. [8]Look, I have two virgin daughters. Let me bring them out to you, and you can do with them as you wish. But please, leave these men alone, for they are my guests and are under my protection."

[9]"Stand back!" they shouted. "This fellow came to town as an outsider, and now he's acting like our judge! We'll treat you far worse than those other men!" And they lunged toward Lot to break down the door.

[10]But the two angels* reached out, pulled Lot into the house, and bolted the door. [11]Then they blinded all the men, young and old, who were at the door of the house, so they gave up trying to get inside.

[12]Meanwhile, the angels questioned Lot. "Do you have any other relatives here in the city?" they asked. "Get them out of this place—your sons-in-law, sons, daughters, or anyone else. [13]For we are about to destroy this city completely. The outcry against this place is so great it has reached the LORD, and he has sent us to destroy it."

[14]So Lot rushed out to tell his daughters' fiancés, "Quick, get out of the city! The LORD is about to destroy it." But the young men thought he was only joking.

[15]At dawn the next morning the angels became insistent. "Hurry," they said to Lot. "Take your wife and your two daughters who are here. Get out right now, or you will be swept away in the destruction of the city!"

[16]When Lot still hesitated, the angels seized his hand and the hands of his wife and two daughters and rushed them to safety outside the city, for the LORD was merciful. [17]When they were safely out of the city, one of the angels ordered, "Run for your lives! And don't look back or stop anywhere in the valley! Escape to the mountains, or you will be swept away!"

[18]"Oh no, my lord!" Lot begged. [19]"You have been so gracious to me and saved my life, and you have shown such great kindness. But I cannot go to the mountains. Disaster would catch up to me there, and I would soon die. [20]See, there is a small village nearby. Please let me go there instead; don't you see how small it is? Then my life will be saved."

[21]"All right," the angel said, "I will grant your request. I will not destroy the little village. [22]But hurry! Escape to it, for I can do nothing until you arrive there." (This explains why that village was known as Zoar, which means "little place.")

AMAZING FACTS

After one wishful look back, Lot's wife was salt.
GENESIS 19:26

[23]Lot reached the village just as the sun was rising over the horizon. [24]Then the LORD rained down fire and burning sulfur from the sky on Sodom and Gomorrah. [25]He utterly destroyed them, along with the other cities and villages of the plain, wiping out all the people and every bit of vegetation. [26]But Lot's wife looked back as she was following behind him, and she turned into a pillar of salt.

[27]Abraham got up early that morning and hurried out to the place where he had stood in the LORD's presence. [28]He looked out across the plain toward Sodom and Gomorrah and watched as columns of smoke rose from the cities like smoke from a furnace.

19:10 Hebrew *men;* also in 19:12, 16.

[29]But God had listened to Abraham's request and kept Lot safe, removing him from the disaster that engulfed the cities on the plain.

Lot and His Daughters

[30]Afterward Lot left Zoar because he was afraid of the people there, and he went to live in a cave in the mountains with his two daughters. [31]One day the older daughter said to her sister, "There are no men left anywhere in this entire area, so we can't get married like everyone else. And our father will soon be too old to have children. [32]Come, let's get him drunk with wine, and then we will have sex with him. That way we will preserve our family line through our father."

[33]So that night they got him drunk with wine, and the older daughter went in and had intercourse with her father. He was unaware of her lying down or getting up again.

[34]The next morning the older daughter said to her younger sister, "I had sex with our father last night. Let's get him drunk with wine again tonight, and you go in and have sex with him. That way we will preserve our family line through our father." [35]So that night they got him drunk with wine again, and the younger daughter went in and had intercourse with him. As before, he was unaware of her lying down or getting up again.

[36]As a result, both of Lot's daughters became pregnant by their own father. [37]When the older daughter gave birth to a son, she named him Moab.* He became the ancestor of the nation now known as the Moabites. [38]When the younger daughter gave birth to a son, she named him Ben-ammi.* He became the ancestor of the nation now known as the Ammonites.

CHAPTER 20

Abraham Deceives Abimelech

Abraham moved south to the Negev and lived for a while between Kadesh and Shur, and then he moved on to Gerar. While living there as a foreigner, [2]Abraham introduced his wife, Sarah, by saying, "She is my sister." So King Abimelech of Gerar sent for Sarah and had her brought to him at his palace.

[3]But that night God came to Abimelech in a dream and told him, "You are a dead man, for that woman you have taken is already married!"

[4]But Abimelech had not slept with her yet, so he said, "Lord, will you destroy an innocent nation? [5]Didn't Abraham tell me, 'She is my sister'? And she herself said, 'Yes, he is my brother.' I acted in complete innocence! My hands are clean."

[6]In the dream God responded, "Yes, I know you are innocent. That's why I kept you from sinning against me, and why I did not let you touch her. [7]Now return the woman to her husband, and he will pray for you, for he is a prophet. Then you will live. But if you don't return her to him, you can be sure that you and all your people will die."

[8]Abimelech got up early the next morning and quickly called all his servants together. When he told them what had happened, his men were terrified. [9]Then Abimelech called for Abraham. "What have you done to us?" he demanded. "What crime have I committed that deserves treatment like this, making me and my kingdom guilty of this great sin? No one should ever do what you have done! [10]Whatever possessed you to do such a thing?"

[11]Abraham replied, "I thought, 'This is a godless place. They will want my wife and will kill me to get her.' [12]And she really is my sister, for we both have the same father, but different mothers. And I married her. [13]When God called me to leave my father's home and to travel from place to place, I told her, 'Do me a favor. Wherever we go, tell the people that I am your brother.'"

[14]Then Abimelech took some of his sheep and goats, cattle, and male and female servants, and he presented them to Abraham. He also returned his wife, Sarah, to him. [15]Then Abimelech said, "Look over my land and choose any place where you would like to live." [16]And he said to Sarah, "Look, I am giving your 'brother' 1,000 pieces of silver* in the presence of all these witnesses. This is to compensate you for any wrong I may have done to you. This will settle any claim against me, and your reputation is cleared."

[17]Then Abraham prayed to God, and God

19:37 *Moab* sounds like a Hebrew term that means "from father." **19:38** *Ben-ammi* means "son of my kinsman." **20:16** Hebrew *1,000 [shekels] of silver*, about 25 pounds or 11.4 kilograms in weight.

healed Abimelech, his wife, and his female servants, so they could have children. [18]For the LORD had caused all the women to be infertile because of what happened with Abraham's wife, Sarah.

CHAPTER 21

The Birth of Isaac

The LORD kept his word and did for Sarah exactly what he had promised. [2]She became pregnant, and she gave birth to a son for Abraham in his old age. This happened at just the time God had said it would. [3]And Abraham named their son Isaac. [4]Eight days after Isaac was born, Abraham circumcised him as God had commanded. [5]Abraham was 100 years old when Isaac was born.

[6]And Sarah declared, "God has brought me laughter.* All who hear about this will laugh with me. [7]Who would have said to Abraham that Sarah would nurse a baby? Yet I have given Abraham a son in his old age!"

Hagar and Ishmael Are Sent Away

[8]When Isaac grew up and was about to be weaned, Abraham prepared a huge feast to celebrate the occasion. [9]But Sarah saw Ishmael—the son of Abraham and her Egyptian servant Hagar—making fun of her son, Isaac.* [10]So she turned to Abraham and demanded, "Get rid of that slave woman and her son. He is not going to share the inheritance with my son, Isaac. I won't have it!"

[11]This upset Abraham very much because Ishmael was his son. [12]But God told Abraham, "Do not be upset over the boy and your servant. Do whatever Sarah tells you, for Isaac is the son through whom your descendants will be counted. [13]But I will also make a nation of the descendants of Hagar's son because he is your son, too."

[14]So Abraham got up early the next morning, prepared food and a container of water, and strapped them on Hagar's shoulders. Then he sent her away with their son, and she wandered aimlessly in the wilderness of Beersheba.

[15]When the water was gone, she put the boy in the shade of a bush. [16]Then she went and sat down by herself about a hundred yards* away. "I don't want to watch the boy die," she said, as she burst into tears.

[17]But God heard the boy crying, and the angel of God called to Hagar from heaven, "Hagar, what's wrong? Do not be afraid! God has heard the boy crying as he lies there. [18]Go to him and comfort him, for I will make a great nation from his descendants."

[19]Then God opened Hagar's eyes, and she saw a well full of water. She quickly filled her water container and gave the boy a drink.

[20]And God was with the boy as he grew up in the wilderness. He became a skillful archer, [21]and he settled in the wilderness of Paran. His mother arranged for him to marry a woman from the land of Egypt.

Abraham's Covenant with Abimelech

[22]About this time, Abimelech came with Phicol, his army commander, to visit Abraham. "God is obviously with you, helping you in everything you do," Abimelech said. [23]"Swear to me in God's name that you will never deceive me, my children, or any of my descendants. I have been loyal to you, so now swear that you will be loyal to me and to this country where you are living as a foreigner."

[24]Abraham replied, "Yes, I swear to it!" [25]Then Abraham complained to Abimelech about a well that Abimelech's servants had taken by force from Abraham's servants.

[26]"This is the first I've heard of it," Abimelech answered. "I have no idea who is responsible. You have never complained about this before."

[27]Abraham then gave some of his sheep, goats, and cattle to Abimelech, and they made a treaty. [28]But Abraham also took seven additional female lambs and set them off by themselves. [29]Abimelech asked, "Why have you set these seven apart from the others?"

[30]Abraham replied, "Please accept these seven lambs to show your agreement that I dug this well." [31]Then he named the place Beersheba (which means "well of the oath"), because that was where they had sworn the oath.

[32]After making their covenant at Beersheba, Abimelech left with Phicol, the commander of his army, and they returned home to the land of the Philistines. [33]Then Abraham planted a

21:6 The name *Isaac* means "he laughs." **21:9** As in Greek version and Latin Vulgate; Hebrew lacks *of her son, Isaac.*
21:16 Hebrew *a bowshot.*

tamarisk tree at Beersheba, and there he worshiped the LORD, the Eternal God.* 34And Abraham lived as a foreigner in Philistine country for a long time.

CHAPTER 22

Abraham's Faith Tested

Some time later, God tested Abraham's faith. "Abraham!" God called.

"Yes," he replied. "Here I am."

2"Take your son, your only son—yes, Isaac, whom you love so much—and go to the land of Moriah. Go and sacrifice him as a burnt offering on one of the mountains, which I will show you."

3The next morning Abraham got up early. He saddled his donkey and took two of his servants with him, along with his son, Isaac. Then he chopped wood for a fire for a burnt offering and set out for the place God had told him about. 4On the third day of their journey, Abraham looked up and saw the place in the distance. 5"Stay here with the donkey," Abraham told the servants. "The boy and I will travel a little farther. We will worship there, and then we will come right back."

6So Abraham placed the wood for the burnt offering on Isaac's shoulders, while he himself carried the fire and the knife. As the two of them walked on together, 7Isaac turned to Abraham and said, "Father?"

"Yes, my son?" Abraham replied.

"We have the fire and the wood," the boy said, "but where is the sheep for the burnt offering?"

8"God will provide a sheep for the burnt offering, my son," Abraham answered. And they both walked on together.

9When they arrived at the place where God had told him to go, Abraham built an altar and arranged the wood on it. Then he tied his son, Isaac, and laid him on the altar on top of the wood. 10And Abraham picked up the knife to kill his son as a sacrifice. 11At that moment the angel of the LORD called to him from heaven, "Abraham! Abraham!"

"Yes," Abraham replied. "Here I am!"

12"Don't lay a hand on the boy!" the angel said. "Do not hurt him in any way, for now I know that you truly fear God. You have not withheld from me even your son, your only son."

13Then Abraham looked up and saw a ram caught by its horns in a thicket. So he took the ram and sacrificed it as a burnt offering in place of his son. 14Abraham named the place Yahweh-Yireh (which means "the LORD will provide"). To this day, people still use that name as a proverb: "On the mountain of the LORD it will be provided."

15Then the angel of the LORD called again to Abraham from heaven. 16"This is what the LORD says: Because you have obeyed me and have not withheld even your son, your only son, I swear by my own name that 17I will certainly bless you. I will multiply your descendants* beyond number, like the stars in the sky and the sand on the seashore. Your descendants will conquer the cities of their enemies. 18And through your descendants all the nations of the earth will be blessed—all because you have obeyed me."

19Then they returned to the servants and traveled back to Beersheba, where Abraham continued to live.

20Soon after this, Abraham heard that Milcah, his brother Nahor's wife, had borne Nahor eight sons. 21The oldest was named Uz, the next oldest was Buz, followed by Kemuel (the ancestor of the Arameans), 22Kesed, Hazo, Pildash, Jidlaph, and Bethuel. 23(Bethuel became the father of Rebekah.) In addition to these eight sons from Milcah, 24Nahor had four other children from his concubine Reumah. Their names were Tebah, Gaham, Tahash, and Maacah.

CHAPTER 23

The Burial of Sarah

When Sarah was 127 years old, 2she died at Kiriath-arba (now called Hebron) in the land of Canaan. There Abraham mourned and wept for her.

3Then, leaving her body, he said to the Hittite elders, 4"Here I am, a stranger and a foreigner among you. Please sell me a piece of land so I can give my wife a proper burial."

5The Hittites replied to Abraham, 6"Listen, my lord, you are an honored prince among us. Choose the finest of our tombs and bury her

21:33 Hebrew *El-Olam.* **22:17** Hebrew *seed;* also in 22:17b, 18.

there. No one here will refuse to help you in this way."

7Then Abraham bowed low before the Hittites 8and said, "Since you are willing to help me in this way, be so kind as to ask Ephron son of Zohar 9to let me buy his cave at Machpelah, down at the end of his field. I will pay the full price in the presence of witnesses, so I will have a permanent burial place for my family."

10Ephron was sitting there among the others, and he answered Abraham as the others listened, speaking publicly before all the Hittite elders of the town. 11"No, my lord," he said to Abraham, "please listen to me. I will give you the field and the cave. Here in the presence of my people, I give it to you. Go and bury your dead."

12Abraham again bowed low before the citizens of the land, 13and he replied to Ephron as everyone listened. "No, listen to me. I will buy it from you. Let me pay the full price for the field so I can bury my dead there."

14Ephron answered Abraham, 15"My lord, please listen to me. The land is worth 400 pieces* of silver, but what is that between friends? Go ahead and bury your dead."

16So Abraham agreed to Ephron's price and paid the amount he had suggested—400 pieces of silver, weighed according to the market standard. The Hittite elders witnessed the transaction.

17So Abraham bought the plot of land belonging to Ephron at Machpelah, near Mamre. This included the field itself, the cave that was in it, and all the surrounding trees. 18It was transferred to Abraham as his permanent possession in the presence of the Hittite elders at the city gate. 19Then Abraham buried his wife, Sarah, there in Canaan, in the cave of Machpelah, near Mamre (also called Hebron). 20So the field and the cave were transferred from the Hittites to Abraham for use as a permanent burial place.

CHAPTER 24

A Wife for Isaac

Abraham was now a very old man, and the LORD had blessed him in every way. 2One day Abraham said to his oldest servant, the man in charge of his household, "Take an oath by putting your hand under my thigh. 3Swear by the LORD, the God of heaven and earth, that you will not allow my son to marry one of these local Canaanite women. 4Go instead to my homeland, to my relatives, and find a wife there for my son Isaac."

5The servant asked, "But what if I can't find a young woman who is willing to travel so far from home? Should I then take Isaac there to live among your relatives in the land you came from?"

6"No!" Abraham responded. "Be careful never to take my son there. 7For the LORD, the God of heaven, who took me from my father's house and my native land, solemnly promised to give this land to my descendants.* He will send his angel ahead of you, and he will see to it that you find a wife there for my son. 8If she is unwilling to come back with you, then you are free from this oath of mine. But under no circumstances are you to take my son there."

9So the servant took an oath by putting his hand under the thigh of his master, Abraham. He swore to follow Abraham's instructions. 10Then he loaded ten of Abraham's camels with all kinds of expensive gifts from his master, and he traveled to distant Aram-naharaim. There he went to the town where Abraham's brother Nahor had settled. 11He made the camels kneel beside a well just outside the town. It was evening, and the women were coming out to draw water.

12"O LORD, God of my master, Abraham," he prayed. "Please give me success today, and show unfailing love to my master, Abraham. 13See, I am standing here beside this spring, and the young women of the town are coming out to draw water. 14This is my request. I will ask one of them, 'Please give me a drink from your jug.' If she says, 'Yes, have a drink, and I will water your camels, too!'—let her be the one you have selected as Isaac's wife. This is how I will know that you have shown unfailing love to my master."

15Before he had finished praying, he saw a young woman named Rebekah coming out with her water jug on her shoulder. She was the daughter of Bethuel, who was the son of Abraham's brother Nahor and his wife, Milcah. 16Rebekah was very beautiful and old

23:15 Hebrew *400 shekels*, about 10 pounds or 4.6 kilograms in weight; also in 23:16. **24:7** Hebrew *seed;* also in 24:60.

enough to be married, but she was still a virgin. She went down to the spring, filled her jug, and came up again. 17Running over to her, the servant said, "Please give me a little drink of water from your jug."

18"Yes, my lord," she answered, "have a drink." And she quickly lowered her jug from her shoulder and gave him a drink. 19When she had given him a drink, she said, "I'll draw water for your camels, too, until they have had enough to drink." 20So she quickly emptied her jug into the watering trough and ran back to the well to draw water for all his camels.

21The servant watched her in silence, wondering whether or not the LORD had given him success in his mission. 22Then at last, when the camels had finished drinking, he took out a gold ring for her nose and two large gold bracelets* for her wrists.

23"Whose daughter are you?" he asked. "And please tell me, would your father have any room to put us up for the night?"

24"I am the daughter of Bethuel," she replied. "My grandparents are Nahor and Milcah. 25Yes, we have plenty of straw and feed for the camels, and we have room for guests."

26The man bowed low and worshiped the LORD. 27"Praise the LORD, the God of my master, Abraham," he said. "The LORD has shown unfailing love and faithfulness to my master, for he has led me straight to my master's relatives."

28The young woman ran home to tell her family everything that had happened. 29Now Rebekah had a brother named Laban, who ran out to meet the man at the spring. 30He had seen the nose-ring and the bracelets on his sister's wrists, and had heard Rebekah tell what the man had said. So he rushed out to the spring, where the man was still standing beside his camels. 31Laban said to him, "Come and stay with us, you who are blessed by the LORD! Why are you standing here outside the town when I have a room all ready for you and a place prepared for the camels?"

32So the man went home with Laban, and Laban unloaded the camels, gave him straw for their bedding, fed them, and provided water for the man and the camel drivers to wash their feet. 33Then food was served. But Abraham's servant said, "I don't want to eat until I have told you why I have come."

"All right," Laban said, "tell us."

34"I am Abraham's servant," he explained. 35"And the LORD has greatly blessed my master; he has become a wealthy man. The LORD has given him flocks of sheep and goats, herds of cattle, a fortune in silver and gold, and many male and female servants and camels and donkeys.

36"When Sarah, my master's wife, was very old, she gave birth to my master's son, and my master has given him everything he owns. 37And my master made me take an oath. He said, 'Do not allow my son to marry one of these local Canaanite women. 38Go instead to my father's house, to my relatives, and find a wife there for my son.'

39"But I said to my master, 'What if I can't find a young woman who is willing to go back with me?' 40He responded, 'The LORD, in whose presence I have lived, will send his angel with you and will make your mission successful. Yes, you must find a wife for my son from among my relatives, from my father's family. 41Then you will have fulfilled your obligation. But if you go to my relatives and they refuse to let her go with you, you will be free from my oath.'

42"So today when I came to the spring, I prayed this prayer: 'O LORD, God of my master, Abraham, please give me success on this mission. 43See, I am standing here beside this spring. This is my request. When a young woman comes to draw water, I will say to her, "Please give me a little drink of water from your jug." 44If she says, "Yes, have a drink, and I will draw water for your camels, too," let her be the one you have selected to be the wife of my master's son.'

45"Before I had finished praying in my heart, I saw Rebekah coming out with her water jug on her shoulder. She went down to the spring and drew water. So I said to her, 'Please give me a drink.' 46She quickly lowered her jug from her shoulder and said, 'Yes, have a drink, and I will water your camels, too!' So I drank, and then she watered the camels.

47"Then I asked, 'Whose daughter are you?' She replied, 'I am the daughter of Bethuel, and my grandparents are Nahor and

24:22 Hebrew *a gold nose-ring weighing a half shekel* [0.2 ounces or 6 grams] *and two gold bracelets weighing 10 shekels* [4 ounces or 114 grams].

Milcah.' So I put the ring on her nose, and the bracelets on her wrists.

48"Then I bowed low and worshiped the LORD. I praised the LORD, the God of my master, Abraham, because he had led me straight to my master's niece to be his son's wife. 49So tell me—will you or won't you show unfailing love and faithfulness to my master? Please tell me yes or no, and then I'll know what to do next."

50Then Laban and Bethuel replied, "The LORD has obviously brought you here, so there is nothing we can say. 51Here is Rebekah; take her and go. Yes, let her be the wife of your master's son, as the LORD has directed."

52When Abraham's servant heard their answer, he bowed down to the ground and worshiped the LORD. 53Then he brought out silver and gold jewelry and clothing and presented them to Rebekah. He also gave expensive presents to her brother and mother. 54Then they ate their meal, and the servant and the men with him stayed there overnight.

But early the next morning, Abraham's servant said, "Send me back to my master."

55"But we want Rebekah to stay with us at least ten days," her brother and mother said. "Then she can go."

56But he said, "Don't delay me. The LORD has made my mission successful; now send me back so I can return to my master."

57"Well," they said, "we'll call Rebekah and ask her what she thinks." 58So they called Rebekah. "Are you willing to go with this man?" they asked her.

And she replied, "Yes, I will go."

59So they said good-bye to Rebekah and sent her away with Abraham's servant and his men. The woman who had been Rebekah's childhood nurse went along with her. 60They gave her this blessing as she parted:

"Our sister, may you become
the mother of many millions!
May your descendants be strong
and conquer the cities of their
enemies."

61Then Rebekah and her servant girls mounted the camels and followed the man. So Abraham's servant took Rebekah and went on his way.

62Meanwhile, Isaac, whose home was in the Negev, had returned from Beer-lahai-roi. 63One evening as he was walking and meditating in the fields, he looked up and saw the camels coming. 64When Rebekah looked up and saw Isaac, she quickly dismounted from her camel. 65"Who is that man walking through the fields to meet us?" she asked the servant.

And he replied, "It is my master." So Rebekah covered her face with her veil. 66Then the servant told Isaac everything he had done.

67And Isaac brought Rebekah into his mother Sarah's tent, and she became his wife. He loved her deeply, and she was a special comfort to him after the death of his mother.

CHAPTER 25

The Death of Abraham

Abraham married another wife, whose name was Keturah. 2She gave birth to Zimran, Jokshan, Medan, Midian, Ishbak, and Shuah. 3Jokshan was the father of Sheba and Dedan. Dedan's descendants were the Asshurites, Letushites, and Leummites. 4Midian's sons were Ephah, Epher, Hanoch, Abida, and Eldaah. These were all descendants of Abraham through Keturah.

5Abraham gave everything he owned to his son Isaac. 6But before he died, he gave gifts to the sons of his concubines and sent them off to a land in the east, away from Isaac.

7Abraham lived for 175 years, 8and he died at a ripe old age, having lived a long and satisfying life. He breathed his last and joined his ancestors in death. 9His sons Isaac and Ishmael buried him in the cave of Machpelah, near Mamre, in the field of Ephron son of Zohar the Hittite. 10This was the field Abraham had purchased from the Hittites and where he had buried his wife Sarah. 11After Abraham's death, God blessed his son Isaac, who settled near Beer-lahai-roi in the Negev.

Ishmael's Descendants

12This is the account of the family of Ishmael, the son of Abraham through Hagar, Sarah's Egyptian servant. 13Here is a list, by their names and clans, of Ishmael's descendants: The oldest was Nebaioth, followed by Kedar, Adbeel, Mibsam, 14Mishma, Dumah, Massa, 15Hadad, Tema, Jetur, Naphish, and Kedemah. 16These twelve sons of Ishmael became the founders of twelve tribes named after them, listed according to the places they settled and camped. [17]Ishmael lived for 137 years. Then he breathed his last and joined his ancestors in death. [18]Ishmael's descendants occupied the region from Havilah to Shur, which is east of Egypt in the direction of Asshur. There they lived in open hostility toward all their relatives.*

The Births of Esau and Jacob

[19]This is the account of the family of Isaac, the son of Abraham. [20]When Isaac was forty years old, he married Rebekah, the daughter of Bethuel the Aramean from Paddan-aram and the sister of Laban the Aramean.

[21]Isaac pleaded with the LORD on behalf of his wife, because she was unable to have children. The LORD answered Isaac's prayer, and Rebekah became pregnant with twins. [22]But the two children struggled with each other in her womb. So she went to ask the LORD about it. "Why is this happening to me?" she asked.

[23]And the LORD told her, "The sons in your womb will be come two nations. From the very beginning, the two nations will be rivals. One nation will be stronger than the other; and your older son will serve your younger son."

[24]And when the time came to give birth, Rebekah discovered that she did indeed have twins! [25]The first one was very red at birth and covered with thick hair like a fur coat. So they named him Esau.* [26]Then the other twin was born with his hand grasping Esau's heel. So they named him Jacob.* Isaac was sixty years old when the twins were born.

Esau Sells His Birthright

[27]As the boys grew up, Esau became a skillful hunter. He was an outdoorsman, but Jacob had a quiet temperament, preferring to stay at home. [28]Isaac loved Esau because he enjoyed eating the wild game Esau brought home, but Rebekah loved Jacob.

[29]One day when Jacob was cooking some stew, Esau arrived home from the wilderness exhausted and hungry. [30]Esau said to Jacob, "I'm starved! Give me some of that red stew!" (This is how Esau got his other name, Edom, which means "red.")

[31]"All right," Jacob replied, "but trade me your rights as the firstborn son."

[32]"Look, I'm dying of starvation!" said Esau. "What good is my birthright to me now?"

[33]But Jacob said, "First you must swear that your birthright is mine." So Esau swore an oath, thereby selling all his rights as the firstborn to his brother, Jacob.

[34]Then Jacob gave Esau some bread and lentil stew. Esau ate the meal, then got up and left. He showed contempt for his rights as the firstborn.

CHAPTER 26

Isaac Deceives Abimelech

A severe famine now struck the land, as had happened before in Abraham's time. So Isaac moved to Gerar, where Abimelech, king of the Philistines, lived.

[2]The LORD appeared to Isaac and said, "Do not go down to Egypt, but do as I tell you. [3]Live here as a foreigner in this land, and I will be with you and bless you. I hereby confirm that I will give all these lands to you and your descendants,* just as I solemnly promised Abraham, your father. [4]I will cause your descendants to become as numerous as the stars of the sky, and I will give them all these lands. And through your descendants all the nations of the earth will be blessed. [5]I will do this because Abraham listened to me and obeyed all my requirements, commands, decrees, and instructions." [6]So Isaac stayed in Gerar.

[7]When the men who lived there asked Isaac about his wife, Rebekah, he said, "She is my sister." He was afraid to say, "She is my wife." He thought, "They will kill me to get her, because she is so beautiful." [8]But some time later, Abimelech, king of the Philistines, looked out his window and saw Isaac caressing Rebekah.

[9]Immediately, Abimelech called for Isaac and exclaimed, "She is obviously your wife! Why did you say, 'She is my sister'?"

"Because I was afraid someone would kill me to get her from me," Isaac replied.

[10]"How could you do this to us?" Abimelech exclaimed. "One of my people might easily have taken your wife and slept with her,

25:18 The meaning of the Hebrew is uncertain. **25:25** *Esau* sounds like a Hebrew term that means "hair." **25:26** *Jacob* sounds like the Hebrew words for "heel" and "deceiver." **26:3** Hebrew *seed;* also in 26:4, 24.

Isaac

For three hot days we traveled into the mountains. We have moved one heavy stone after another to make an altar. Father sure is quiet. Wonder what's wrong.

I joke about there being no sacrifice. Dad doesn't laugh. He points at me. I don't understand, but I agree. My father places me on the altar and lifts the knife. I close my eyes and hear a loud voice calling, "Abraham! Abraham!" It's for you, Dad!

An angel speaks. Then Dad spots a ram with horns caught in a bush nearby, and it takes my place. I can breathe again. Thank you, Lord.

Isaac's story is in Genesis 17:15–35:29 and Hebrews 11:17-19.

and you would have made us guilty of great sin."

[11]Then Abimelech issued a public proclamation: "Anyone who touches this man or his wife will be put to death!"

Conflict over Water Rights

[12]When Isaac planted his crops that year, he harvested a hundred times more grain than he planted, for the Lord blessed him. [13]He became a very rich man, and his wealth continued to grow. [14]He acquired so many flocks of sheep and goats, herds of cattle, and servants that the Philistines became jealous of him. [15]So the Philistines filled up all of Isaac's wells with dirt. These were the wells that had been dug by the servants of his father, Abraham.

[16]Finally, Abimelech ordered Isaac to leave the country. "Go somewhere else," he said, "for you have become too powerful for us."

[17]So Isaac moved away to the Gerar Valley, where he set up their tents and settled down. [18]He reopened the wells his father had dug, which the Philistines had filled in after Abraham's death. Isaac also restored the names Abraham had given them.

[19]Isaac's servants also dug in the Gerar Valley and discovered a well of fresh water. [20]But then the shepherds from Gerar came and claimed the spring. "This is our water," they said, and they argued over it with Isaac's herdsmen. So Isaac named the well Esek (which means "argument"). [21]Isaac's men then dug another well, but again there was a dispute over it. So Isaac named it Sitnah (which means "hostility"). [22]Abandoning that one, Isaac moved on and dug another well. This time there was no dispute over it, so Isaac named the place Rehoboth (which means "open space"), for he said, "At last the Lord has created enough space for us to prosper in this land."

[23]From there Isaac moved to Beersheba, [24]where the Lord appeared to him on the night of his arrival. "I am the God of your father, Abraham," he said. "Do not be afraid, for I am with you and will bless you. I will multiply your descendants, and they will become a great nation. I will do this because of my promise to Abraham, my servant." [25]Then Isaac built an altar there and worshiped the Lord. He set up his camp at that place, and his servants dug another well.

Isaac's Covenant with Abimelech

[26]One day King Abimelech came from Gerar with his adviser, Ahuzzath, and also Phicol, his army commander. [27]"Why have you come here?" Isaac asked. "You obviously hate me, since you kicked me off your land."

[28]They replied, "We can plainly see that the Lord is with you. So we want to enter into a sworn treaty with you. Let's make a covenant. [29]Swear that you will not harm us, just as we have never troubled you. We have always treated you well, and we sent you away from us in peace. And now look how the Lord has blessed you!"

30So Isaac prepared a covenant feast to celebrate the treaty, and they ate and drank together. 31Early the next morning, they each took a solemn oath not to interfere with each other. Then Isaac sent them home again, and they left him in peace.

32That very day Isaac's servants came and told him about a new well they had dug. "We've found water!" they exclaimed. 33So Isaac named the well Shibah (which means "oath"). And to this day the town that grew up there is called Beersheba (which means "well of the oath").

34At the age of forty, Esau married two Hittite wives: Judith, the daughter of Beeri, and Basemath, the daughter of Elon. 35But Esau's wives made life miserable for Isaac and Rebekah.

CHAPTER 27

Jacob Steals Esau's Blessing

One day when Isaac was old and turning blind, he called for Esau, his older son, and said, "My son."

"Yes, Father?" Esau replied.

2"I am an old man now," Isaac said, "and I don't know when I may die. 3Take your bow and a quiver full of arrows, and go out into the open country to hunt some wild game for me. 4Prepare my favorite dish, and bring it here for me to eat. Then I will pronounce the blessing that belongs to you, my firstborn son, before I die."

5But Rebekah overheard what Isaac had said to his son Esau. So when Esau left to hunt for the wild game, 6she said to her son Jacob, "Listen. I overheard your father say to Esau, 7'Bring me some wild game and prepare me a delicious meal. Then I will bless you in the LORD's presence before I die.' 8Now, my son, listen to me. Do exactly as I tell you. 9Go out to the flocks, and bring me two fine young goats. I'll use them to prepare your father's favorite dish. 10Then take the food to your father so he can eat it and bless you before he dies."

11"But look," Jacob replied to Rebekah, "my brother, Esau, is a hairy man, and my skin is smooth. 12What if my father touches me? He'll see that I'm trying to trick him, and then he'll curse me instead of blessing me."

13But his mother replied, "Then let the curse fall on me, my son! Just do what I tell you. Go out and get the goats for me!"

14So Jacob went out and got the young goats for his mother. Rebekah took them and prepared a delicious meal, just the way Isaac liked it. 15Then she took Esau's favorite clothes, which were there in the house, and gave them to her younger son, Jacob. 16She covered his arms and the smooth part of his neck with the skin of the young goats. 17Then she gave Jacob the delicious meal, including freshly baked bread.

18So Jacob took the food to his father. "My father?" he said.

"Yes, my son," Isaac answered. "Who are you—Esau or Jacob?"

19Jacob replied, "It's Esau, your firstborn son. I've done as you told me. Here is the wild game. Now sit up and eat it so you can give me your blessing."

20Isaac asked, "How did you find it so quickly, my son?"

"The LORD your God put it in my path!" Jacob replied.

21Then Isaac said to Jacob, "Come closer so I can touch you and make sure that you really are Esau." 22So Jacob went closer to his father, and Isaac touched him. "The voice is Jacob's, but the hands are Esau's," Isaac said. 23But he did not recognize Jacob, because Jacob's hands felt hairy just like Esau's. So Isaac prepared to bless Jacob. 24"But are you really my son Esau?" he asked.

"Yes, I am," Jacob replied.

25Then Isaac said, "Now, my son, bring me the wild game. Let me eat it, and then I will give you my blessing." So Jacob took the food to his father, and Isaac ate it. He also drank the wine that Jacob served him. 26Then Isaac said to Jacob, "Please come a little closer and kiss me, my son."

27So Jacob went over and kissed him. And when Isaac caught the smell of his clothes, he was finally convinced, and he blessed his son. He said, "Ah! The smell of my son is like the smell of the outdoors, which the LORD has blessed!

28 "From the dew of heaven
and the richness of the earth,
may God always give you abundant
harvests of grain
and bountiful new wine.

29 May many nations become your servants,
and may they bow down to you.
May you be the master over your
brothers,
and may your mother's sons bow
down to you.
All who curse you will be cursed,
and all who bless you will be
blessed."

30 As soon as Isaac had finished blessing Jacob, and almost before Jacob had left his father, Esau returned from his hunt. 31 Esau prepared a delicious meal and brought it to his father. Then he said, "Sit up, my father, and eat my wild game so you can give me your blessing."

32 But Isaac asked him, "Who are you?"

Esau replied, "It's your son, your firstborn son, Esau."

33 Isaac began to tremble uncontrollably and said, "Then who just served me wild game? I have already eaten it, and I blessed him just before you came. And yes, that blessing must stand!"

34 When Esau heard his father's words, he let out a loud and bitter cry. "Oh my father, what about me? Bless me, too!" he begged.

35 But Isaac said, "Your brother was here, and he tricked me. He has taken away your blessing."

36 Esau exclaimed, "No wonder his name is Jacob, for now he has cheated me twice.* First he took my rights as the firstborn, and now he has stolen my blessing. Oh, haven't you saved even one blessing for me?"

37 Isaac said to Esau, "I have made Jacob your master and have declared that all his brothers will be his servants. I have guaranteed him an abundance of grain and wine—what is left for me to give you, my son?"

38 Esau pleaded, "But do you have only one blessing? Oh my father, bless me, too!" Then Esau broke down and wept.

39 Finally, his father, Isaac, said to him,

"You will live away from the richness of
the earth,
and away from the dew of the heaven
above.
40 You will live by your sword,
and you will serve your brother.
But when you decide to break free,
you will shake his yoke from your
neck."

Jacob Flees to Paddan-Aram

41 From that time on, Esau hated Jacob because their father had given Jacob the blessing. And Esau began to scheme: "I will soon be mourning my father's death. Then I will kill my brother, Jacob."

42 But Rebekah heard about Esau's plans. So she sent for Jacob and told him, "Listen, Esau is consoling himself by plotting to kill you. 43 So listen carefully, my son. Get ready and flee to my brother, Laban, in Haran. 44 Stay there with him until your brother cools off. 45 When he calms down and forgets what you have done to him, I will send for you to come back. Why should I lose both of you in one day?"

46 Then Rebekah said to Isaac, "I'm sick and tired of these local Hittite women! I would rather die than see Jacob marry one of them."

CHAPTER 28

So Isaac called for Jacob, blessed him, and said, "You must not marry any of these Canaanite women. 2 Instead, go at once to Paddan-aram, to the house of your grandfather Bethuel, and marry one of your uncle Laban's daughters. 3 May God Almighty* bless you and give you many children. And may your descendants multiply and become many nations! 4 May God pass on to you and your descendants* the blessings he promised to Abraham. May you own this land where you are now living as a foreigner, for God gave this land to Abraham."

5 So Isaac sent Jacob away, and he went to Paddan-aram to stay with his uncle Laban, his mother's brother, the son of Bethuel the Aramean.

6 Esau knew that his father, Isaac, had blessed Jacob and sent him to Paddan-aram to find a wife, and that he had warned Jacob, "You must not marry a Canaanite woman." 7 He also knew that Jacob had obeyed his parents and gone to Paddan-aram. 8 It was now very clear to Esau that his father did not like the local Canaanite women. 9 So Esau visited his uncle Ishmael's family and married one of Ishmael's daughters, in addition to the wives he already had. His new wife's name was

27:36 *Jacob* sounds like the Hebrew words for "heel" and "deceiver." **28:3** Hebrew *El-Shaddai*. **28:4** Hebrew *seed;* also in 28:13, 14.

ALL ALONE

The classes were tough at Troy's new school, but fitting in was even tougher. Most of the kids were interested in the "right" clothes, cool vacations, and the hottest stuff. That didn't mean much to Troy. He just wanted to find a friend who enjoyed the same things he did—touch football, fishing, and listening to good music. As Troy got off the bus and walked home after school, he felt alone and discouraged.

What would you tell Troy to help in this situation? Read Genesis 28:15 to see how God comforted Jacob when he felt alone.

Mahalath. She was the sister of Nebaioth and the daughter of Ishmael, Abraham's son.

Jacob's Dream at Bethel

[10]Meanwhile, Jacob left Beersheba and traveled toward Haran. [11]At sundown he arrived at a good place to set up camp and stopped there for the night. Jacob found a stone to rest his head against and lay down to sleep. [12]As he slept, he dreamed of a stairway that reached from the earth up to heaven. And he saw the angels of God going up and down the stairway.

[13]At the top of the stairway stood the LORD, and he said, "I am the LORD, the God of your grandfather Abraham, and the God of your father, Isaac. The ground you are lying on belongs to you. I am giving it to you and your descendants. [14]Your descendants will be as numerous as the dust of the earth! They will spread out in all directions—to the west and the east, to the north and the south. And all the families of the earth will be blessed through you and your descendants. [15]What's more, I am with you, and I will protect you wherever you go. One day I will bring you back to this land. I will not leave you until I have finished giving you everything I have promised you."

[16]Then Jacob awoke from his sleep and said, "Surely the LORD is in this place, and I wasn't even aware of it!" [17]But he was also afraid and said, "What an awesome place this is! It is none other than the house of God, the very gateway to heaven!"

[18]The next morning Jacob got up very early. He took the stone he had rested his head against, and he set it upright as a memorial pillar. Then he poured olive oil over it. [19]He named that place Bethel (which means "house of God"), although it was previously called Luz.

[20]Then Jacob made this vow: "If God will indeed be with me and protect me on this journey, and if he will provide me with food and clothing, [21]and if I return safely to my father's home, then the LORD will certainly be my God. [22]And this memorial pillar I have set up will become a place for worshiping God, and I will present to God a tenth of everything he gives me."

CHAPTER 29

Jacob Arrives at Paddan-Aram

Then Jacob hurried on, finally arriving in the land of the east. [2]He saw a well in the distance. Three flocks of sheep and goats lay in an open field beside it, waiting to be watered. But a heavy stone covered the mouth of the well.

[3]It was the custom there to wait for all the

flocks to arrive before removing the stone and watering the animals. Afterward the stone would be placed back over the mouth of the well. [4]Jacob went over to the shepherds and asked, "Where are you from, my friends?"

"We are from Haran," they answered.

[5]"Do you know a man there named Laban, the grandson of Nahor?" he asked.

"Yes, we do," they replied.

[6]"Is he doing well?" Jacob asked.

"Yes, he's well," they answered. "Look, here comes his daughter Rachel with the flock now."

[7]Jacob said, "Look, it's still broad daylight—too early to round up the animals. Why don't you water the sheep and goats so they can get back out to pasture?"

[8]"We can't water the animals until all the flocks have arrived," they replied. "Then the shepherds move the stone from the mouth of the well, and we water all the sheep and goats."

Sometimes I feel that nobody cares and that I'm all alone.

[The Lord says,] "What's more, I am with you, and I will protect you wherever you go."

GENESIS 28:15

[9]Jacob was still talking with them when Rachel arrived with her father's flock, for she was a shepherd. [10]And because Rachel was his cousin—the daughter of Laban, his mother's brother—and because the sheep and goats belonged to his uncle Laban, Jacob went over to the well and moved the stone from its mouth and watered his uncle's flock. [11]Then Jacob kissed Rachel, and he wept aloud. [12]He explained to Rachel that he was her cousin on her father's side—the son of her aunt Rebekah. So Rachel quickly ran and told her father, Laban.

[13]As soon as Laban heard that his nephew Jacob had arrived, he ran out to meet him. He embraced and kissed him and brought him home. When Jacob had told him his story, [14]Laban exclaimed, "You really are my own flesh and blood!"

Jacob Marries Leah and Rachel

After Jacob had stayed with Laban for about a month, [15]Laban said to him, "You shouldn't work for me without pay just because we are relatives. Tell me how much your wages should be."

[16]Now Laban had two daughters. The older daughter was named Leah, and the younger one was Rachel. [17]There was no sparkle in Leah's eyes,* but Rachel had a beautiful figure and a lovely face. [18]Since Jacob was in love with Rachel, he told her father, "I'll work for you for seven years if you'll give me Rachel, your younger daughter, as my wife."

[19]"Agreed!" Laban replied. "I'd rather give her to you than to anyone else. Stay and work with me." [20]So Jacob worked seven years to pay for Rachel. But his love for her was so strong that it seemed to him but a few days.

[21]Finally, the time came for him to marry her. "I have fulfilled my agreement," Jacob said to Laban. "Now give me my wife so I can sleep with her."

[22]So Laban invited everyone in the neighborhood and prepared a wedding feast. [23]But that night, when it was dark, Laban took Leah to Jacob, and he slept with her. [24](Laban had given Leah a servant, Zilpah, to be her maid.)

[25]But when Jacob woke up in the morning—it was Leah! "What have you done to me?" Jacob raged at Laban. "I worked seven years for Rachel! Why have you tricked me?"

[26]"It's not our custom here to marry off a younger daughter ahead of the firstborn," Laban replied. [27]"But wait until the bridal week is over, then we'll give you Rachel, too—provided you promise to work another seven years for me."

[28]So Jacob agreed to work seven more years. A week after Jacob had married Leah, Laban gave him Rachel, too. [29](Laban gave Rachel a servant, Bilhah, to be her maid.) [30]So Jacob slept with Rachel, too, and he loved her much more than Leah. He then stayed and worked for Laban the additional seven years.

29:17 Or *Leah had dull eyes*, or *Leah had soft eyes*. The meaning of the Hebrew is uncertain.

JACOB

I'm tired of this old tent and tired of Uncle Laban. I want to head home. After all, I've worked hard, and Laban is a rich man, thanks to me. But he doesn't want my family to go. My trick will set us free, though Laban thinks he's getting the better deal.

My fee? I get to keep every black lamb and every spotted or speckled goat. He gets the rest.

Here's the trick: I will help only *my* animals get stronger. Laban's flock will dwindle—mine will grow. Sure, it's sneaky. I know how to get my way.

Check out Jacob's story in Genesis 25–50.

Jacob's Many Children

31When the LORD saw that Leah was unloved, he enabled her to have children, but Rachel could not conceive. 32So Leah became pregnant and gave birth to a son. She named him Reuben,* for she said, "The LORD has noticed my misery, and now my husband will love me."

33She soon became pregnant again and gave birth to another son. She named him Simeon,* for she said, "The LORD heard that I was unloved and has given me another son."

34Then she became pregnant a third time and gave birth to another son. She named him Levi,* for she said, "Surely this time my husband will feel affection for me, since I have given him three sons!"

35Once again Leah became pregnant and gave birth to another son. She named him Judah,* for she said, "Now I will praise the LORD!" And then she stopped having children.

CHAPTER 30

When Rachel saw that she wasn't having any children for Jacob, she became jealous of her sister. She pleaded with Jacob, "Give me children, or I'll die!"

2Then Jacob became furious with Rachel. "Am I God?" he asked. "He's the one who has kept you from having children!"

3Then Rachel told him, "Take my maid, Bilhah, and sleep with her. She will bear children for me,* and through her I can have a family, too." 4So Rachel gave her servant, Bilhah, to Jacob as a wife, and he slept with her. 5Bilhah became pregnant and presented him with a son. 6Rachel named him Dan,* for she said, "God has vindicated me! He has heard my request and given me a son." 7Then Bilhah became pregnant again and gave Jacob a second son. 8Rachel named him Naphtali,* for she said, "I have struggled hard with my sister, and I'm winning!"

9Meanwhile, Leah realized that she wasn't getting pregnant anymore, so she took her servant, Zilpah, and gave her to Jacob as a wife. 10Soon Zilpah presented him with a son. 11Leah named him Gad,* for she said, "How fortunate I am!" 12Then Zilpah gave Jacob a second son. 13And Leah named him Asher,* for she said, "What joy is mine! Now the other women will celebrate with me."

14One day during the wheat harvest, Reuben found some mandrakes growing in a field and brought them to his mother, Leah. Rachel begged Leah, "Please give me some of your son's mandrakes."

15But Leah angrily replied, "Wasn't it

29:32 *Reuben* means "Look, a son!" It also sounds like the Hebrew for "He has seen my misery." **29:33** *Simeon* probably means "one who hears." **29:34** *Levi* sounds like a Hebrew term that means "being attached" or "feeling affection for." **29:35** *Judah* is related to the Hebrew term for "praise." **30:3** Hebrew *bear children on my knees.* **30:6** *Dan* means "he judged" or "he vindicated." **30:8** *Naphtali* means "my struggle." **30:11** *Gad* means "good fortune." **30:13** *Asher* means "happy."

enough that you stole my husband? Now will you steal my son's mandrakes, too?"

Rachel answered, "I will let Jacob sleep with you tonight if you give me some of the mandrakes."

[16]So that evening, as Jacob was coming home from the fields, Leah went out to meet him. "You must come and sleep with me tonight!" she said. "I have paid for you with some mandrakes that my son found." So that night he slept with Leah. [17]And God answered Leah's prayers. She became pregnant again and gave birth to a fifth son for Jacob. [18]She named him Issachar,* for she said, "God has rewarded me for giving my servant to my husband as a wife." [19]Then Leah became pregnant again and gave birth to a sixth son for Jacob. [20]She named him Zebulun,* for she said, "God has given me a good reward. Now my husband will treat me with respect, for I have given him six sons." [21]Later she gave birth to a daughter and named her Dinah.

[22]Then God remembered Rachel's plight and answered her prayers by enabling her to have children. [23]She became pregnant and gave birth to a son. "God has removed my disgrace," she said. [24]And she named him Joseph,* for she said, "May the LORD add yet another son to my family."

Jacob's Wealth Increases

[25]Soon after Rachel had given birth to Joseph, Jacob said to Laban, "Please release me so I can go home to my own country. [26]Let me take my wives and children, for I have earned them by serving you, and let me be on my way. You certainly know how hard I have worked for you."

[27]"Please listen to me," Laban replied. "I have become wealthy, for* the LORD has blessed me because of you. [28]Tell me how much I owe you. Whatever it is, I'll pay it."

[29]Jacob replied, "You know how hard I've worked for you, and how your flocks and herds have grown under my care. [30]You had little indeed before I came, but your wealth has increased enormously. The LORD has blessed you through everything I've done. But now, what about me? When can I start providing for my own family?"

[31]"What wages do you want?" Laban asked again.

Jacob replied, "Don't give me anything. Just do this one thing, and I'll continue to tend and watch over your flocks. [32]Let me inspect your flocks today and remove all the sheep and goats that are speckled or spotted, along with all the black sheep. Give these to me as my wages. [33]In the future, when you check on the animals you have given me as my wages, you'll see that I have been honest. If you find in my flock any goats without speckles or spots, or any sheep that are not black, you will know that I have stolen them from you."

[34]"All right," Laban replied. "It will be as you say." [35]But that very day Laban went out and removed the male goats that were streaked and spotted, all the female goats that were speckled and spotted or had white patches, and all the black sheep. He placed them in the care of his own sons, [36]who took them a three-days' journey from where Jacob was. Meanwhile, Jacob stayed and cared for the rest of Laban's flock.

[37]Then Jacob took some fresh branches from poplar, almond, and plane trees and peeled off strips of bark, making white streaks on them. [38]Then he placed these peeled branches in the watering troughs where the flocks came to drink, for that was where they mated. [39]And when they mated in front of the white-streaked branches, they gave birth to young that were streaked, speckled, and spotted. [40]Jacob separated those lambs from Laban's flock. And at mating time he turned the flock to face Laban's animals that were streaked or black. This is how he built his own flock instead of increasing Laban's.

[41]Whenever the stronger females were ready to mate, Jacob would place the peeled branches in the watering troughs in front of them. Then they would mate in front of the branches. [42]But he didn't do this with the weaker ones, so the weaker lambs belonged to Laban, and the stronger ones were Jacob's. [43]As a result, Jacob became very wealthy, with large flocks of sheep and goats, female and male servants, and many camels and donkeys.

CHAPTER 31

Jacob Flees from Laban

But Jacob soon learned that Laban's sons were grumbling about him. "Jacob has robbed

30:18 *Issachar* sounds like a Hebrew term that means "reward." **30:20** *Zebulun* probably means "honor." **30:24** *Joseph* means "may he add." **30:27** Or *I have learned by divination that.*

our father of everything!" they said. "He has gained all his wealth at our father's expense."
[2]And Jacob began to notice a change in Laban's attitude toward him.

[3]Then the LORD said to Jacob, "Return to the land of your father and grandfather and to your relatives there, and I will be with you."

[4]So Jacob called Rachel and Leah out to the field where he was watching his flock. [5]He said to them, "I have noticed that your father's attitude toward me has changed. But the God of my father has been with me. [6]You know how hard I have worked for your father, [7]but he has cheated me, changing my wages ten times. But God has not allowed him to do me any harm. [8]For if he said, 'The speckled animals will be your wages,' the whole flock began to produce speckled young. And when he changed his mind and said, 'The striped animals will be your wages,' then the whole flock produced striped young. [9]In this way, God has taken your father's animals and given them to me.

[10]"One time during the mating season, I had a dream and saw that the male goats mating with the females were streaked, speckled, and spotted. [11]Then in my dream, the angel of God said to me, 'Jacob!' And I replied, 'Yes, here I am.'

[12]"The angel said, 'Look up, and you will see that only the streaked, speckled, and spotted males are mating with the females of your flock. For I have seen how Laban has treated you. [13]I am the God who appeared to you at Bethel,* the place where you anointed the pillar of stone and made your vow to me. Now get ready and leave this country and return to the land of your birth.'"

[14]Rachel and Leah responded, "That's fine with us! We won't inherit any of our father's wealth anyway. [15]He has reduced our rights to those of foreign women. And after he sold us, he wasted the money you paid him for us. [16]All the wealth God has given you from our father legally belongs to us and our children. So go ahead and do whatever God has told you."

[17]So Jacob put his wives and children on camels, [18]and he drove all his livestock in front of him. He packed all the belongings he had acquired in Paddan-aram and set out for the land of Canaan, where his father, Isaac, lived. [19]At the time they left, Laban was some distance away, shearing his sheep. Rachel stole her father's household idols and took them with her. [20]Jacob outwitted Laban the Aramean, for they set out secretly and never told Laban they were leaving. [21]So Jacob took all his possessions with him and crossed the Euphrates River,* heading for the hill country of Gilead.

Laban Pursues Jacob

[22]Three days later, Laban was told that Jacob had fled. [23]So he gathered a group of his relatives and set out in hot pursuit. He caught up with Jacob seven days later in the hill country of Gilead. [24]But the previous night God had appeared to Laban the Aramean in a dream and told him, "I'm warning you—leave Jacob alone!"

[25]Laban caught up with Jacob as he was camped in the hill country of Gilead, and he set up his camp not far from Jacob's. [26]"What do you mean by deceiving me like this?" Laban demanded. "How dare you drag my daughters away like prisoners of war? [27]Why did you slip away secretly? Why did you deceive me? And why didn't you say you wanted to leave? I would have given you a farewell

31:13 As in Greek version and an Aramaic Targum; Hebrew reads *the God of Bethel.* **31:21** Hebrew *the river.*

IS IT OK?

IS IT OK TO SPEND TIME JUST CHILLIN'?

There's nothing wrong with taking time to relax. Even God took a break after he created the world (see Genesis 2:2). But it's best to finish your work first. God honors hard work. Jacob worked for years with little reward. But God was pleased. And that's what matters.

feast, with singing and music, accompanied
by tambourines and harps. [28]Why didn't you
let me kiss my daughters and grandchildren
and tell them good-bye? You have acted very
foolishly! [29]I could destroy you, but the God of
your father appeared to me last night and
warned me, 'Leave Jacob alone!' [30]I can under-
stand your feeling that you must go, and your
intense longing for your father's home. But
why have you stolen my gods?"

[31]"I rushed away because I was afraid," Ja-
cob answered. "I thought you would take your
daughters from me by force. [32]But as for your
gods, see if you can find them, and let the per-
son who has taken them die! And if you find
anything else that belongs to you, identify it
before all these relatives of ours, and I will
give it back!" But Jacob did not know that Ra-
chel had stolen the household idols.

[33]Laban went first into Jacob's tent to search
there, then into Leah's, and then the tents of
the two servant wives—but he found nothing.
Finally, he went into Rachel's tent. [34]But Rachel
had taken the household idols and hidden
them in her camel saddle, and now she was sit-
ting on them. When Laban had thoroughly
searched her tent without finding them, [35]she
said to her father, "Please, sir, forgive me if I
don't get up for you. I'm having my monthly
period." So Laban continued his search, but he
could not find the household idols.

[36]Then Jacob became very angry, and he
challenged Laban. "What's my crime?" he de-
manded. "What have I done wrong to make
you chase after me as though I were a crimi-
nal? [37]You have rummaged through every-
thing I own. Now show me what you found
that belongs to you! Set it out here in front of
us, before our relatives, for all to see. Let them
judge between us!

[38]"For twenty years I have been with you,
caring for your flocks. In all that time your
sheep and goats never miscarried. In all those
years I never used a single ram of yours for
food. [39]If any were attacked and killed by wild
animals, I never showed you the carcass and
asked you to reduce the count of your flock.
No, I took the loss myself! You made me pay
for every stolen animal, whether it was taken
in broad daylight or in the dark of night.

[40]"I worked for you through the scorching
heat of the day and through cold and sleep-
less nights. [41]Yes, for twenty years I slaved in
your house! I worked for fourteen years earn-
ing your two daughters, and then six more
years for your flock. And you changed my
wages ten times! [42]In fact, if the God of my fa-
ther had not been on my side—the God of
Abraham and the fearsome God of Isaac*—
you would have sent me away empty-handed.
But God has seen your abuse and my hard
work. That is why he appeared to you last
night and rebuked you!"

Jacob's Treaty with Laban

[43]Then Laban replied to Jacob, "These
women are my daughters, these children are
my grandchildren, and these flocks are my
flocks—in fact, everything you see is mine.
But what can I do now about my daughters
and their children? [44]So come, let's make a
covenant, you and I, and it will be a witness to
our commitment."

[45]So Jacob took a stone and set it up as a
monument. [46]Then he told his family mem-
bers, "Gather some stones." So they gathered
stones and piled them in a heap. Then Jacob
and Laban sat down beside the pile of stones
to eat a covenant meal. [47]To commemorate
the event, Laban called the place Jegar-
sahadutha (which means "witness pile" in Ar-
amaic), and Jacob called it Galeed (which
means "witness pile" in Hebrew).

[48]Then Laban declared, "This pile of stones
will stand as a witness to remind us of the cov-
enant we have made today." This explains
why it was called Galeed—"Witness Pile."
[49]But it was also called Mizpah (which means
"watchtower"), for Laban said, "May the LORD
keep watch between us to make sure that we
keep this covenant when we are out of each
other's sight. [50]If you mistreat my daughters
or if you marry other wives, God will see it
even if no one else does. He is a witness to this
covenant between us.

[51]"See this pile of stones," Laban continued,
"and see this monument I have set between
us. [52]They stand between us as witnesses of
our vows. I will never pass this pile of stones to
harm you, and you must never pass these
stones or this monument to harm me. [53]I call
on the God of our ancestors—the God of your

31:42 Or *and the Fear of Isaac.*

grandfather Abraham and the God of my grandfather Nahor—to serve as a judge between us."

So Jacob took an oath before the fearsome God of his father, Isaac,* to respect the boundary line. [54]Then Jacob offered a sacrifice to God there on the mountain and invited everyone to a covenant feast. After they had eaten, they spent the night on the mountain.

[55]*Laban got up early the next morning, and he kissed his grandchildren and his daughters and blessed them. Then he left and returned home.

CHAPTER 32

[1]*As Jacob started on his way again, angels of God came to meet him. [2]When Jacob saw them, he exclaimed, "This is God's camp!" So he named the place Mahanaim.*

Jacob Sends Gifts to Esau

[3]Then Jacob sent messengers ahead to his brother, Esau, who was living in the region of Seir in the land of Edom. [4]He told them, "Give this message to my master Esau: 'Humble greetings from your servant Jacob. Until now I have been living with Uncle Laban, [5]and now I own cattle, donkeys, flocks of sheep and goats, and many servants, both men and women. I have sent these messengers to inform my lord of my coming, hoping that you will be friendly to me.'"

AMAZING FACTS

Jacob wrestled with God—in the form of an angel—and won! He got a blessing, too!

GENESIS 32:24-28

[6]After delivering the message, the messengers returned to Jacob and reported, "We met your brother, Esau, and he is already on his way to meet you—with an army of 400 men!" [7]Jacob was terrified at the news. He divided his household, along with the flocks and herds and camels, into two groups. [8]He thought, "If Esau meets one group and attacks it, perhaps the other group can escape."

[9]Then Jacob prayed, "O God of my grandfather Abraham, and God of my father, Isaac—O LORD, you told me, 'Return to your own land and to your relatives.' And you promised me, 'I will treat you kindly.' [10]I am not worthy of all the unfailing love and faithfulness you have shown to me, your servant. When I left home and crossed the Jordan River, I owned nothing except a walking stick. Now my household fills two large camps! [11]O LORD, please rescue me from the hand of my brother, Esau. I am afraid that he is coming to attack me, along with my wives and children. [12]But you promised me, 'I will surely treat you kindly, and I will multiply your descendants until they become as numerous as the sands along the seashore—too many to count.'"

[13]Jacob stayed where he was for the night. Then he selected these gifts from his possessions to present to his brother, Esau: [14]200 female goats, 20 male goats, 200 ewes, 20 rams, [15]30 female camels with their young, 40 cows, 10 bulls, 20 female donkeys, and 10 male donkeys. [16]He divided these animals into herds and assigned each to different servants. Then he told his servants, "Go ahead of me with the animals, but keep some distance between the herds."

[17]He gave these instructions to the men leading the first group: "When my brother, Esau, meets you, he will ask, 'Whose servants are you? Where are you going? Who owns these animals?' [18]You must reply, 'They belong to your servant Jacob, but they are a gift for his master Esau. Look, he is coming right behind us.'"

[19]Jacob gave the same instructions to the second and third herdsmen and to all who followed behind the herds: "You must say the same thing to Esau when you meet him. [20]And be sure to say, 'Look, your servant Jacob is right behind us.'"

31:53 Or *the Fear of his father, Isaac.* **31:55** Verse31:55 is numbered 32:1 in Hebrew text. **32:1** Verses 32:1-32 are numbered 32:2-33 in Hebrew text. **32:2** *Mahanaim* means "two camps."

Jacob thought, "I will try to appease him by sending gifts ahead of me. When I see him in person, perhaps he will be friendly to me." [21]So the gifts were sent on ahead, while Jacob himself spent that night in the camp.

Jacob Wrestles with God

[22]During the night Jacob got up and took his two wives, his two servant wives, and his eleven sons and crossed the Jabbok River with them. [23]After taking them to the other side, he sent over all his possessions.

[24]This left Jacob all alone in the camp, and a man came and wrestled with him until the dawn began to break. [25]When the man saw that he would not win the match, he touched Jacob's hip and wrenched it out of its socket. [26]Then the man said, "Let me go, for the dawn is breaking!"

But Jacob said, "I will not let you go unless you bless me."

[27]"What is your name?" the man asked.

He replied, "Jacob."

[28]"Your name will no longer be Jacob," the man told him. "From now on you will be called Israel,* because you have fought with God and with men and have won."

[29]"Please tell me your name," Jacob said.

"Why do you want to know my name?" the man replied. Then he blessed Jacob there.

[30]Jacob named the place Peniel (which means "face of God"), for he said, "I have seen God face to face, yet my life has been spared." [31]The sun was rising as Jacob left Peniel,* and he was limping because of the injury to his hip. [32](Even today the people of Israel don't eat the tendon near the hip socket because of what happened that night when the man strained the tendon of Jacob's hip.)

CHAPTER 33

Jacob and Esau Make Peace

Then Jacob looked up and saw Esau coming with his 400 men. So he divided the children among Leah, Rachel, and his two servant wives. [2]He put the servant wives and their children at the front, Leah and her children next, and Rachel and Joseph last. [3]Then Jacob went on ahead. As he approached his brother, he bowed to the ground seven times before him. [4]Then Esau ran to meet him and embraced him, threw his arms around his neck, and kissed him. And they both wept.

[5]Then Esau looked at the women and children and asked, "Who are these people with you?"

"These are the children God has graciously given to me, your servant," Jacob replied. [6]Then the servant wives came forward with their children and bowed before him. [7]Next came Leah with her children, and they bowed before him. Finally, Joseph and Rachel came forward and bowed before him.

[8]"And what were all the flocks and herds I met as I came?" Esau asked.

Jacob replied, "They are a gift, my lord, to ensure your friendship."

[9]"My brother, I have plenty," Esau answered. "Keep what you have for yourself."

[10]But Jacob insisted, "No, if I have found favor with you, please accept this gift from me. And what a relief to see your friendly smile. It is like seeing the face of God! [11]Please take this gift I have brought you, for God has been very gracious to me. I have more than enough." And because Jacob insisted, Esau finally accepted the gift.

[12]"Well," Esau said, "let's be going. I will lead the way."

[13]But Jacob replied, "You can see, my lord, that some of the children are very young, and the flocks and herds have their young, too. If they are driven too hard, even for one day, all the animals could die. [14]Please, my lord, go ahead of your servant. We will follow slowly, at a pace that is comfortable for the livestock and the children. I will meet you at Seir."

[15]"All right," Esau said, "but at least let me assign some of my men to guide and protect you."

Jacob responded, "That's not necessary. It's enough that you've received me warmly, my lord!"

[16]So Esau turned around and started back to Seir that same day. [17]Jacob, on the other hand, traveled on to Succoth. There he built himself a house and made shelters for his livestock. That is why the place was named Succoth (which means "shelters").

[18]Later, having traveled all the way from Paddan-aram, Jacob arrived safely at the town of Shechem, in the land of Canaan. There he

32:28 *Jacob* sounds like the Hebrew words for "heel" and "deceiver." *Israel* means "God fights." **32:31** Hebrew *Penuel*, a variant spelling of Peniel.

set up camp outside the town. [19]Jacob bought the plot of land where he camped from the family of Hamor, the father of Shechem, for 100 pieces of silver.* [20]And there he built an altar and named it El-Elohe-Israel.*

CHAPTER 34

Revenge against Shechem

One day Dinah, the daughter of Jacob and Leah, went to visit some of the young women who lived in the area. [2]But when the local prince, Shechem son of Hamor the Hivite, saw Dinah, he seized her and raped her. [3]But then he fell in love with her, and he tried to win her affection with tender words. [4]He said to his father, Hamor, "Get me this young girl. I want to marry her."

[5]Soon Jacob heard that Shechem had defiled his daughter, Dinah. But since his sons were out in the fields herding his livestock, he said nothing until they returned. [6]Hamor, Shechem's father, came to discuss the matter with Jacob. [7]Meanwhile, Jacob's sons had come in from the field as soon as they heard what had happened. They were shocked and furious that their sister had been raped. Shechem had done a disgraceful thing against Jacob's family,* something that should never be done.

[8]Hamor tried to speak with Jacob and his sons. "My son Shechem is truly in love with your daughter," he said. "Please let him marry her. [9]In fact, let's arrange other marriages, too. You give us your daughters for our sons, and we will give you our daughters for your sons. [10]And you may live among us; the land is open to you! Settle here and trade with us. And feel free to buy property in the area."

[11]Then Shechem himself spoke to Dinah's father and brothers. "Please be kind to me, and let me marry her," he begged. "I will give you whatever you ask. [12]No matter what dowry or gift you demand, I will gladly pay it—just give me the girl as my wife."

[13]But since Shechem had defiled their sister, Dinah, Jacob's sons responded deceitfully to Shechem and his father, Hamor. [14]They said to them, "We couldn't possibly allow this, because you're not circumcised. It would be a disgrace for our sister to marry a man like you! [15]But here is a solution. If every man among you will be circumcised like we are, [16]then we will give you our daughters, and we'll take your daughters for ourselves. We will live among you and become one people. [17]But if you don't agree to be circumcised, we will take her and be on our way."

[18]Hamor and his son Shechem agreed to their proposal. [19]Shechem wasted no time in acting on this request, for he wanted Jacob's daughter desperately. Shechem was a highly respected member of his family, [20]and he went with his father, Hamor, to present this proposal to the leaders at the town gate.

[21]"These men are our friends," they said. "Let's invite them to live here among us and trade freely. Look, the land is large enough to hold them. We can take their daughters as wives and let them marry ours. [22]But they will consider staying here and becoming one people with us only if all of our men are circumcised, just as they are. [23]But if we do this, all their livestock and possessions will eventually be ours. Come, let's agree to their terms and let them settle here among us."

[24]So all the men in the town council agreed with Hamor and Shechem, and every male in the town was circumcised. [25]But three days later, when their wounds were still sore, two of Jacob's sons, Simeon and Levi, who were Dinah's full brothers, took their swords and entered the town without opposition. Then they slaughtered every male there, [26]including Hamor and his son Shechem. They killed them with their swords, then took Dinah from Shechem's house and returned to their camp.

[27]Meanwhile, the rest of Jacob's sons arrived. Finding the men slaughtered, they plundered the town because their sister had been defiled there. [28]They seized all the flocks and herds and donkeys—everything they could lay their hands on, both inside the town and outside in the fields. [29]They looted all their wealth and plundered their houses. They also took all their little children and wives and led them away as captives.

[30]Afterward Jacob said to Simeon and Levi, "You have ruined me! You've made me stink among all the people of this land—among all the Canaanites and Perizzites. We are so few that they will join forces and crush us. I will

33:19 Hebrew *100 kesitahs;* the value or weight of the kesitah is no longer known. **33:20** *El-Elohe-Israel* means "God, the God of Israel." **34:7** Hebrew *a disgraceful thing in Israel.*

be ruined, and my entire household will be wiped out!"

31"But why should we let him treat our sister like a prostitute?" they retorted angrily.

CHAPTER 35

Jacob's Return to Bethel

Then God said to Jacob, "Get ready and move to Bethel and settle there. Build an altar there to the God who appeared to you when you fled from your brother, Esau."

2So Jacob told everyone in his household, "Get rid of all your pagan idols, purify yourselves, and put on clean clothing. 3We are now going to Bethel, where I will build an altar to the God who answered my prayers when I was in distress. He has been with me wherever I have gone."

4So they gave Jacob all their pagan idols and earrings, and he buried them under the great tree near Shechem. 5As they set out, a terror from God spread over the people in all the towns of that area, so no one attacked Jacob's family.

6Eventually, Jacob and his household arrived at Luz (also called Bethel) in Canaan. 7Jacob built an altar there and named the place El-bethel (which means "God of Bethel"), because God had appeared to him there when he was fleeing from his brother, Esau.

8Soon after this, Rebekah's old nurse, Deborah, died. She was buried beneath the oak tree in the valley below Bethel. Ever since, the tree has been called Allon-bacuth (which means "oak of weeping").

9Now that Jacob had returned from Paddan-aram, God appeared to him again at Bethel. God blessed him, 10saying, "Your name is Jacob, but you will not be called Jacob any longer. From now on your name will be Israel."* So God renamed him Israel.

11Then God said, "I am El-Shaddai—'God Almighty.' Be fruitful and multiply. You will become a great nation, even many nations. Kings will be among your descendants! 12And I will give you the land I once gave to Abraham and Isaac. Yes, I will give it to you and your descendants after you." 13Then God went up from the place where he had spoken to Jacob.

14Jacob set up a stone pillar to mark the place where God had spoken to him. Then he poured wine over it as an offering to God and anointed the pillar with olive oil. 15And Jacob named the place Bethel (which means "house of God"), because God had spoken to him there.

Esau

Enough is enough. My brother, Jacob, fled years ago because he was afraid of my anger. Now he's back with a huge parade of animals and people. Still trying to impress, to weasel out of trouble. But I've got a surprise for him.

I may look tough and I'm surrounded by an army of men, but I've had it with being bitter. I'm going to put an end to it. When I finally see Jacob, I have a plan for welcoming him home that he will never expect. I'm giving him a big hug!

I think it's time we started acting like a family again.

Read about Esau in Genesis 25–36.

35:10 *Jacob* sounds like the Hebrew words for "heel" and "deceiver." *Israel* means "God fights."

The Deaths of Rachel and Isaac

16 Leaving Bethel, Jacob and his clan moved on
toward Ephrath. But Rachel went into labor
while they were still some distance away. Her
labor pains were intense. 17 After a very hard
delivery, the midwife finally exclaimed, "Don't
be afraid—you have another son!" 18 Rachel
was about to die, but with her last breath she
named the baby Ben-oni (which means "son
of my sorrow"). The baby's father, however,
called him Benjamin (which means "son of my
right hand"). 19 So Rachel died and was buried
on the way to Ephrath (that is, Bethlehem).
20 Jacob set up a stone monument over Rachel's
grave, and it can be seen there to this day.

21 Then Jacob* traveled on and camped be-
yond Migdal-eder. 22 While he was living
there, Reuben had intercourse with Bilhah,
his father's concubine, and Jacob soon heard
about it.

These are the names of the twelve sons of
Jacob:

23 The sons of Leah were Reuben (Jacob's
oldest son), Simeon, Levi, Judah, Issachar,
and Zebulun.
24 The sons of Rachel were Joseph and
Benjamin.
25 The sons of Bilhah, Rachel's servant, were
Dan and Naphtali.
26 The sons of Zilpah, Leah's servant, were
Gad and Asher.

These are the names of the sons who were
born to Jacob at Paddan-aram.

27 So Jacob returned to his father, Isaac, in
Mamre, which is near Kiriath-arba (now called
Hebron), where Abraham and Isaac had both
lived as foreigners. 28 Isaac lived for 180 years.
29 Then he breathed his last and died at a ripe
old age, joining his ancestors in death. And his
sons, Esau and Jacob, buried him.

CHAPTER 36

Descendants of Esau

This is the account of the descendants of
Esau (also known as Edom). 2 Esau married
two young women from Canaan: Adah, the
daughter of Elon the Hittite; and Oholiba-
mah, the daughter of Anah and grand-
daughter of Zibeon the Hivite. 3 He also
married his cousin Basemath, who was the
daughter of Ishmael and the sister of Neba-
ioth. 4 Adah gave birth to a son named Eliphaz
for Esau. Basemath gave birth to a son named
Reuel. 5 Oholibamah gave birth to sons named
Jeush, Jalam, and Korah. All these sons were
born to Esau in the land of Canaan.

6 Esau took his wives, his children, and his
entire household, along with his livestock and
cattle—all the wealth he had acquired in the
land of Canaan—and moved away from his
brother, Jacob. 7 There was not enough land
to support them both because of all the live-
stock and possessions they had acquired. 8 So
Esau (also known as Edom) settled in the hill
country of Seir.

9 This is the account of Esau's descendants,
the Edomites, who lived in the hill country of
Seir.

10 These are the names of Esau's sons:
Eliphaz, the son of Esau's wife Adah; and
Reuel, the son of Esau's wife Basemath.
11 The descendants of Eliphaz were Teman,
Omar, Zepho, Gatam, and Kenaz. 12 Timna,
the concubine of Esau's son Eliphaz,
gave birth to a son named Amalek. These
are the descendants of Esau's wife
Adah.
13 The descendants of Reuel were Nahath,
Zerah, Shammah, and Mizzah. These are
the descendants of Esau's wife Basemath.
14 Esau also had sons through Oholibamah,
the daughter of Anah and granddaughter
of Zibeon. Their names were Jeush, Jalam,
and Korah.

15 These are the descendants of Esau who be-
came the leaders of various clans:

The descendants of Esau's oldest son, Eliphaz,
became the leaders of the clans of Teman,
Omar, Zepho, Kenaz, 16 Korah, Gatam, and
Amalek. These are the clan leaders in the
land of Edom who descended from
Eliphaz. All these were descendants of
Esau's wife Adah.
17 The descendants of Esau's son Reuel
became the leaders of the clans of
Nahath, Zerah, Shammah, and Mizzah.
These are the clan leaders in the land of
Edom who descended from Reuel. All
these were descendants of Esau's wife
Basemath.

35:21 Hebrew *Israel;* also in 35:22a. The names "Jacob" and "Israel" are often interchanged throughout the Old Testament, referring sometimes to the individual patriarch and sometimes to the nation.

[18]The descendants of Esau and his wife
Oholibamah became the leaders of the
clans of Jeush, Jalam, and Korah. These
are the clan leaders who descended from
Esau's wife Oholibamah, the daughter of
Anah.
[19]These are the clans descended from Esau
(also known as Edom), identified by their clan
leaders.

Original Peoples of Edom

[20]These are the names of the tribes that descended from Seir the Horite. They lived in the land of Edom: Lotan, Shobal, Zibeon, Anah, [21]Dishon, Ezer, and Dishan. These were the Horite clan leaders, the descendants of Seir, who lived in the land of Edom.

[22]The descendants of Lotan were Hori and
Hemam. Lotan's sister was named
Timna.
[23]The descendants of Shobal were Alvan,
Manahath, Ebal, Shepho, and Onam.
[24]The descendants of Zibeon were Aiah and
Anah. (This is the Anah who discovered
the hot springs in the wilderness while he
was grazing his father's donkeys.)
[25]The descendants of Anah were his son,
Dishon, and his daughter, Oholibamah.
[26]The descendants of Dishon* were
Hemdan, Eshban, Ithran, and Keran.
[27]The descendants of Ezer were Bilhan,
Zaavan, and Akan.
[28]The descendants of Dishan were Uz and
Aran.
[29]So these were the leaders of the Horite
clans: Lotan, Shobal, Zibeon, Anah, [30]Dishon,
Ezer, and Dishan. The Horite clans are named
after their clan leaders, who lived in the land
of Seir.

Rulers of Edom

[31]These are the kings who ruled in the land of Edom before any king ruled over the Israelites*:

[32]Bela son of Beor, who ruled in Edom from
his city of Dinhabah.
[33]When Bela died, Jobab son of Zerah from
Bozrah became king in his place.
[34]When Jobab died, Husham from the land of
the Temanites became king in his place.
[35]When Husham died, Hadad son of Bedad
became king in his place and ruled from
the city of Avith. He was the one who
defeated the Midianites in the land of
Moab.
[36]When Hadad died, Samlah from the city
of Masrekah became king in his place.
[37]When Samlah died, Shaul from the city of
Rehoboth-on-the-River became king in
his place.
[38]When Shaul died, Baal-hanan son of Acbor
became king in his place.
[39]When Baal-hanan son of Acbor died,
Hadad* became king in his place and
ruled from the city of Pau. His wife was
Mehetabel, the daughter of Matred and
granddaughter of Me-zahab.

[40]These are the names of the leaders of the clans descended from Esau, who lived in the places named for them: Timna, Alvah, Jetheth, [41]Oholibamah, Elah, Pinon, [42]Kenaz, Teman, Mibzar, [43]Magdiel, and Iram. These are the leaders of the clans of Edom, listed according to their settlements in the land they occupied. They all descended from Esau, the ancestor of the Edomites.

CHAPTER 37

Joseph's Dreams

So Jacob settled again in the land of Canaan, where his father had lived as a foreigner.

[2]This is the account of Jacob and his family. When Joseph was seventeen years old, he often tended his father's flocks. He worked for his half brothers, the sons of his father's wives Bilhah and Zilpah. But Joseph reported to his father some of the bad things his brothers were doing.

[3]Jacob* loved Joseph more than any of his other children because Joseph had been born to him in his old age. So one day Jacob had a special gift made for Joseph—a beautiful robe.* [4]But his brothers hated Joseph because their father loved him more than the rest of them. They couldn't say a kind word to him.

[5]One night Joseph had a dream, and when he told his brothers about it, they hated him

36:26 Hebrew *Dishan*, a variant spelling of Dishon; compare 36:21, 28. **36:31** Or *before an Israelite king ruled over them*. **36:39** As in some Hebrew manuscripts, Samaritan Pentateuch, and Syriac version (see also 1 Chr 1:50); most Hebrew manuscripts read *Hadar*. **37:3a** Hebrew *Israel*; also in 37:13. See note on 35:21. **37:3b** Traditionally rendered *a coat of many colors*. The exact meaning of the Hebrew is uncertain.

more than ever. 6"Listen to this dream," he
said. 7"We were out in the field, tying up bun-
dles of grain. Suddenly my bundle stood up,
and your bundles all gathered around and
bowed low before mine!"

8His brothers responded, "So you think you
will be our king, do you? Do you actually think
you will reign over us?" And they hated him all
the more because of his dreams and the way
he talked about them.

9Soon Joseph had another dream, and
again he told his brothers about it. "Listen, I
have had another dream," he said. "The sun,
moon, and eleven stars bowed low before
me!"

10This time he told the dream to his father
as well as to his brothers, but his father scolded
him. "What kind of dream is that?" he asked.
"Will your mother and I and your brothers
actually come and bow to the ground before
you?" 11But while his brothers were jealous of
Joseph, his father wondered what the dreams
meant.

12Soon after this, Joseph's brothers went to
pasture their father's flocks at Shechem.
13When they had been gone for some time,
Jacob said to Joseph, "Your brothers are pas-
turing the sheep at Shechem. Get ready, and I
will send you to them."

"I'm ready to go," Joseph replied.

14"Go and see how your brothers and the
flocks are getting along," Jacob said. "Then
come back and bring me a report." So Jacob
sent him on his way, and Joseph traveled to
Shechem from their home in the valley of He-
bron.

15When he arrived there, a man from the
area noticed him wandering around the
countryside. "What are you looking for?" he
asked.

16"I'm looking for my brothers," Joseph re-
plied. "Do you know where they are pasturing
their sheep?"

17"Yes," the man told him. "They have
moved on from here, but I heard them say,
'Let's go on to Dothan.'" So Joseph followed
his brothers to Dothan and found them there.

Joseph Sold into Slavery

18When Joseph's brothers saw him coming,
they recognized him in the distance. As he
approached, they made plans to kill him.
19"Here comes the dreamer!" they said.
20"Come on, let's kill him and throw him into
one of these cisterns. We can tell our father,
'A wild animal has eaten him.' Then we'll see
what becomes of his dreams!"

21But when Reuben heard of their scheme,
he came to Joseph's rescue. "Let's not kill
him," he said. 22"Why should we shed any
blood? Let's just throw him into this empty
cistern here in the wilderness. Then he'll die
without our laying a hand on him." Reuben
was secretly planning to rescue Joseph and
return him to his father.

23So when Joseph arrived, his brothers
ripped off the beautiful robe he was wearing.
24Then they grabbed him and threw him into
the cistern. Now the cistern was empty; there
was no water in it. 25Then, just as they were
sitting down to eat, they looked up and saw a
caravan of camels in the distance coming to-
ward them. It was a group of Ishmaelite trad-
ers taking a load of gum, balm, and aromatic
resin from Gilead down to Egypt.

26Judah said to his brothers, "What will we
gain by killing our brother? We'd have to
cover up the crime.* 27Instead of hurting him,
let's sell him to those Ishmaelite traders. After
all, he is our brother—our own flesh and
blood!" And his brothers agreed. 28So when
the Ishmaelites, who were Midianite traders,
came by, Joseph's brothers pulled him out of
the cistern and sold him to them for twenty
pieces* of silver. And the traders took him to
Egypt.

29Some time later, Reuben returned to get
Joseph out of the cistern. When he discov-
ered that Joseph was missing, he tore his
clothes in grief. 30Then he went back to his
brothers and lamented, "The boy is gone!
What will I do now?"

31Then the brothers killed a young goat and
dipped Joseph's robe in its blood. 32They sent
the beautiful robe to their father with this mes-
sage: "Look at what we found. Doesn't this robe
belong to your son?"

33Their father recognized it immediately.
"Yes," he said, "it is my son's robe. A wild ani-
mal must have eaten him. Joseph has clearly
been torn to pieces!" 34Then Jacob tore his
clothes and dressed himself in burlap. He

37:26 Hebrew *cover his blood.* **37:28** Hebrew *20 shekels,* about 8 ounces or 228 grams in weight.

mourned deeply for his son for a long time.
35His family all tried to comfort him, but he refused to be comforted. "I will go to my grave* mourning for my son," he would say, and then he would weep.

36Meanwhile, the Midianite traders* arrived in Egypt, where they sold Joseph to Potiphar, an officer of Pharaoh, the king of Egypt. Potiphar was captain of the palace guard.

CHAPTER 38

Judah and Tamar

About this time, Judah left home and moved to Adullam, where he stayed with a man named Hirah. 2There he saw a Canaanite woman, the daughter of Shua, and he married her. When he slept with her, 3she became pregnant and gave birth to a son, and he named the boy Er. 4Then she became pregnant again and gave birth to another son, and she named him Onan. 5And when she gave birth to a third son, she named him Shelah. At the time of Shelah's birth, they were living at Kezib.

6In the course of time, Judah arranged for his firstborn son, Er, to marry a young woman named Tamar. 7But Er was a wicked man in the LORD's sight, so the LORD took his life. 8Then Judah said to Er's brother Onan, "Go and marry Tamar, as our law requires of the brother of a man who has died. You must produce an heir for your brother."

9But Onan was not willing to have a child who would not be his own heir. So whenever he had intercourse with his brother's wife, he spilled the semen on the ground. This prevented her from having a child who would belong to his brother. 10But the LORD considered it evil for Onan to deny a child to his dead brother. So the LORD took Onan's life, too.

11Then Judah said to Tamar, his daughter-in-law, "Go back to your parents' home and remain a widow until my son Shelah is old enough to marry you." (But Judah didn't really intend to do this because he was afraid Shelah would also die, like his two brothers.) So Tamar went back to live in her father's home.

12Some years later Judah's wife died. After the time of mourning was over, Judah and his friend Hirah the Adullamite went up to Timnah to supervise the shearing of his sheep.
13Someone told Tamar, "Look, your father-in-law is going up to Timnah to shear his sheep."

14Tamar was aware that Shelah had grown up, but no arrangements had been made for her to come and marry him. So she changed out of her widow's clothing and covered herself with a veil to disguise herself. Then she sat beside the road at the entrance to the village of Enaim, which is on the road to Timnah. 15Judah noticed her and thought she was a prostitute, since she had covered her face. 16So he stopped and propositioned her. "Let me have sex with you," he said, not realizing that she was his own daughter-in-law.

"How much will you pay to have sex with me?" Tamar asked.

17"I'll send you a young goat from my flock," Judah promised.

"But what will you give me to guarantee that you will send the goat?" she asked.

18"What kind of guarantee do you want?" he replied.

She answered, "Leave me your identification seal and its cord and the walking stick you are carrying." So Judah gave them to her. Then he had intercourse with her, and she became pregnant. 19Afterward she went back home, took off her veil, and put on her widow's clothing as usual.

20Later Judah asked his friend Hirah the Adullamite to take the young goat to the woman and to pick up the things he had given her as his guarantee. But Hirah couldn't find her. 21So he asked the men who lived there, "Where can I find the shrine prostitute who was sitting beside the road at the entrance to Enaim?"

"We've never had a shrine prostitute here," they replied.

22So Hirah returned to Judah and told him, "I couldn't find her anywhere, and the men of the village claim they've never had a shrine prostitute there."

23"Then let her keep the things I gave her," Judah said. "I sent the young goat as we agreed, but you couldn't find her. We'd be the laughingstock of the village if we went back again to look for her."

24About three months later, Judah was told, "Tamar, your daughter-in-law, has acted like a prostitute. And now, because of this, she's pregnant."

37:35 Hebrew *go down to Sheol*. **37:36** Hebrew *the Medanites*. The relationship between the Midianites and Medanites is unclear; compare 37:28. See also 25:2.

"Bring her out, and let her be burned!" Judah demanded.

25 But as they were taking her out to kill her, she sent this message to her father-in-law: "The man who owns these things made me pregnant. Look closely. Whose seal and cord and walking stick are these?"

26 Judah recognized them immediately and said, "She is more righteous than I am, because I didn't arrange for her to marry my son Shelah." And Judah never slept with Tamar again.

27 When the time came for Tamar to give birth, it was discovered that she was carrying twins. 28 While she was in labor, one of the babies reached out his hand. The midwife grabbed it and tied a scarlet string around the child's wrist, announcing, "This one came out first." 29 But then he pulled back his hand, and out came his brother! "What!" the midwife exclaimed. "How did you break out first?" So he was named Perez.* 30 Then the baby with the scarlet string on his wrist was born, and he was named Zerah.*

CHAPTER 39

Joseph in Potiphar's House

When Joseph was taken to Egypt by the Ishmaelite traders, he was purchased by Potiphar, an Egyptian officer. Potiphar was captain of the guard for Pharaoh, the king of Egypt.

2 The LORD was with Joseph, so he succeeded in everything he did as he served in the home of his Egyptian master. 3 Potiphar noticed this and realized that the LORD was with Joseph, giving him success in everything he did. 4 This pleased Potiphar, so he soon made Joseph his personal attendant. He put him in charge of his entire household and everything he owned. 5 From the day Joseph was put in charge of his master's household and property, the LORD began to bless Potiphar's household for Joseph's sake. All his household affairs ran smoothly, and his crops and livestock flourished. 6 So Potiphar gave Joseph complete administrative responsibility over everything he owned. With Joseph there, he didn't worry about a thing—except what kind of food to eat!

Joseph was a very handsome and well-built young man, 7 and Potiphar's wife soon began to look at him lustfully. "Come and sleep with me," she demanded.

8 But Joseph refused. "Look," he told her, "my master trusts me with everything in his entire household. 9 No one here has more authority than I do. He has held back nothing from me except you, because you are his wife. How could I do such a wicked thing? It would be a great sin against God."

SETBACKS

Taylor and Cody spent weeks working on their English project. Finally, they pulled everything together and made what Taylor thought was a fantastic poster. When Taylor walked into English class on their presentation day, he couldn't believe his eyes! He thought Cody looked awful. "My little brother got into my room and 'colored' the poster," Cody whispered. "I'm sorry." Taylor was about to panic. He thought, *We can't turn in a scribbled-up poster!*

What do you think Taylor should do? Genesis 39:19-23 tells how Joseph handled setbacks.

38:29 *Perez* means "breaking out." **38:30** *Zerah* means "scarlet" or "brightness."

JOSEPH

Two frightened men sit with me in this smelly prison cell. They've been having bad dreams and have asked me to figure out what their dreams mean.

One man was the pharaoh's protector. He tasted whatever the king ate or drank to make sure it wasn't poisoned. He dreamed of a grapevine with three strong branches. That means in three days he'll be back on the job. Great news!

But the baker saw three full baskets on his head. Birds swooped in to snatch the baked goods. How do I tell him that he'll die in three days? Sometimes this gift God has given me is tough to use.

Joseph's story is told in Genesis 37–50.

10She kept putting pressure on Joseph day
after day, but he refused to sleep with her,
and he kept out of her way as much as possi-
ble. 11One day, however, no one else was
around when he went in to do his work. 12She
came and grabbed him by his cloak, demand-
ing, "Come on, sleep with me!" Joseph tore
himself away, but he left his cloak in her hand
as he ran from the house.

13When she saw that she was holding his
cloak and he had fled, 14she called out to
her servants. Soon all the men came running.
"Look!" she said. "My husband has brought
this Hebrew slave here to make fools of us!
He came into my room to rape me, but I
screamed. 15When he heard me scream, he
ran outside and got away, but he left his cloak
behind with me."

16She kept the cloak with her until her hus-
band came home. 17Then she told him her
story. "That Hebrew slave you've brought into
our house tried to come in and fool around
with me," she said. 18"But when I screamed,
he ran outside, leaving his cloak with me!"

Joseph Put in Prison

19Potiphar was furious when he heard his
wife's story about how Joseph had treated her.
20So he took Joseph and threw him into the
prison where the king's prisoners were held,
and there he remained. 21But the LORD was
with Joseph in the prison and showed him his
faithful love. And the LORD made Joseph a fa-
vorite with the prison warden. 22Before long,
the warden put Joseph in charge of all the
other prisoners and over everything that hap-
pened in the prison. 23The warden had no
more worries, because Joseph took care of
everything. The LORD was with him and
caused everything he did to succeed.

CHAPTER 40

Joseph Interprets Two Dreams

Some time later, Pharaoh's chief cup-bearer
and chief baker offended their royal master.
2Pharaoh became angry with these two
officials, 3and he put them in the prison
where Joseph was, in the palace of the cap-
tain of the guard. 4They remained in prison
for quite some time, and the captain of the
guard assigned them to Joseph, who looked
after them.

5While they were in prison, Pharaoh's cup-
bearer and baker each had a dream one night,
and each dream had its own meaning. 6When
Joseph saw them the next morning, he no-
ticed that they both looked upset. 7"Why do
you look so worried today?" he asked them.

8And they replied, "We both had dreams
last night, but no one can tell us what they
mean."

"Interpreting dreams is God's business,"
Joseph replied. "Go ahead and tell me your
dreams."

9So the chief cup-bearer told Joseph his

dream first. "In my dream," he said, "I saw a grapevine in front of me. [10]The vine had three branches that began to bud and blossom, and soon it produced clusters of ripe grapes. [11]I was holding Pharaoh's wine cup in my hand, so I took a cluster of grapes and squeezed the juice into the cup. Then I placed the cup in Pharaoh's hand."

[12]"This is what the dream means," Joseph said. "The three branches represent three days. [13]Within three days Pharaoh will lift you up and restore you to your position as his chief cup-bearer. [14]And please remember me and do me a favor when things go well for you. Mention me to Pharaoh, so he might let me out of this place. [15]For I was kidnapped from my homeland, the land of the Hebrews, and now I'm here in prison, but I did nothing to deserve it."

[16]When the chief baker saw that Joseph had given the first dream such a positive interpretation, he said to Joseph, "I had a dream, too. In my dream there were three baskets of white pastries stacked on my head. [17]The top basket contained all kinds of pastries for Pharaoh, but the birds came and ate them from the basket on my head."

[18]"This is what the dream means," Joseph told him. "The three baskets also represent three days. [19]Three days from now Pharaoh will lift you up and impale your body on a pole. Then birds will come and peck away at your flesh."

[20]Pharaoh's birthday came three days later, and he prepared a banquet for all his officials and staff. He summoned* his chief cup-bearer and chief baker to join the other officials. [21]He then restored the chief cup-bearer to his former position, so he could again hand Pharaoh his cup. [22]But Pharaoh impaled the chief baker, just as Joseph had predicted when he interpreted his dream. [23]Pharaoh's chief cup-bearer, however, forgot all about Joseph, never giving him another thought.

CHAPTER 41

Pharaoh's Dreams

Two full years later, Pharaoh dreamed that he was standing on the bank of the Nile River. [2]In his dream he saw seven fat, healthy cows come up out of the river and begin grazing in the marsh grass. [3]Then he saw seven more cows come up behind them from the Nile, but these were scrawny and thin. These cows stood beside the fat cows on the riverbank. [4]Then the scrawny, thin cows ate the seven healthy, fat cows! At this point in the dream, Pharaoh woke up.

[5]But he fell asleep again and had a second dream. This time he saw seven heads of grain, plump and beautiful, growing on a single stalk. [6]Then seven more heads of grain appeared, but these were shriveled and withered by the east wind. [7]And these thin heads swallowed up the seven plump, well-formed heads! Then Pharaoh woke up again and realized it was a dream.

AMAZING FACTS

What slave was thrown into prison in a foreign country, only to become second-in-command of that country? Joseph, of course!

GENESIS 41:1-46

[8]The next morning Pharaoh was very disturbed by the dreams. So he called for all the magicians and wise men of Egypt. When Pharaoh told them his dreams, not one of them could tell him what they meant.

[9]Finally, the king's chief cup-bearer spoke up. "Today I have been reminded of my failure," he told Pharaoh. [10]"Some time ago, you were angry with the chief baker and me, and you imprisoned us in the palace of the captain of the guard. [11]One night the chief baker and I each had a dream, and each dream had its own meaning. [12]There was a young Hebrew man with us in the prison who was a slave of the captain of the guard. We told him our dreams, and he told us what each of our dreams

40:20 Hebrew *He lifted up the head of.*

meant. [13]And everything happened just as he had predicted. I was restored to my position as cup-bearer, and the chief baker was executed and impaled on a pole."

[14]Pharaoh sent for Joseph at once, and he was quickly brought from the prison. After he shaved and changed his clothes, he went in and stood before Pharaoh. [15]Then Pharaoh said to Joseph, "I had a dream last night, and no one here can tell me what it means. But I have heard that when you hear about a dream you can interpret it."

[16]"It is beyond my power to do this," Joseph replied. "But God can tell you what it means and set you at ease."

[17]So Pharaoh told Joseph his dream. "In my dream," he said, "I was standing on the bank of the Nile River, [18]and I saw seven fat, healthy cows come up out of the river and begin grazing in the marsh grass. [19]But then I saw seven sick-looking cows, scrawny and thin, come up after them. I've never seen such sorry-looking animals in all the land of Egypt. [20]These thin, scrawny cows ate the seven fat cows. [21]But afterward you wouldn't have known it, for they were still as thin and scrawny as before! Then I woke up.

Some days I feel like I can't do anything right.

"It is beyond my power to do this," Joseph replied. "But God can tell you what it means and set you at ease." GENESIS 41:16

[22]"Then I fell asleep again, and I had another dream. This time I saw seven heads of grain, full and beautiful, growing on a single stalk. [23]Then seven more heads of grain appeared, but these were blighted, shriveled, and withered by the east wind. [24]And the shriveled heads swallowed the seven healthy heads. I told these dreams to the magicians, but no one could tell me what they mean."

[25]Joseph responded, "Both of Pharaoh's dreams mean the same thing. God is telling Pharaoh in advance what he is about to do. [26]The seven healthy cows and the seven healthy heads of grain both represent seven years of prosperity. [27]The seven thin, scrawny cows that came up later and the seven thin heads of grain, withered by the east wind, represent seven years of famine.

[28]"This will happen just as I have described it, for God has revealed to Pharaoh in advance what he is about to do. [29]The next seven years will be a period of great prosperity throughout the land of Egypt. [30]But afterward there will be seven years of famine so great that all the prosperity will be forgotten in Egypt. Famine will destroy the land. [31]This famine will be so severe that even the memory of the good years will be erased. [32]As for having two similar dreams, it means that these events have been decreed by God, and he will soon make them happen.

[33]"Therefore, Pharaoh should find an intelligent and wise man and put him in charge of the entire land of Egypt. [34]Then Pharaoh should appoint supervisors over the land and let them collect one-fifth of all the crops during the seven good years. [35]Have them gather all the food produced in the good years that are just ahead and bring it to Pharaoh's storehouses. Store it away, and guard it so there will be food in the cities. [36]That way there will be enough to eat when the seven years of famine come to the land of Egypt. Otherwise this famine will destroy the land."

Joseph Made Ruler of Egypt

[37]Joseph's suggestions were well received by Pharaoh and his officials. [38]So Pharaoh asked his officials, "Can we find anyone else like this man so obviously filled with the spirit of God?" [39]Then Pharaoh said to Joseph, "Since God has revealed the meaning of the dreams to you, clearly no one else is as intelligent or wise as you are. [40]You will be in charge of my court, and all my people will take orders from you. Only I, sitting on my throne, will have a rank higher than yours."

[41]Pharaoh said to Joseph, "I hereby put you in charge of the entire land of Egypt." [42]Then Pharaoh removed his signet ring from his hand and placed it on Joseph's finger. He dressed him in fine linen clothing and hung a gold chain around his neck. [43]Then he had

Joseph ride in the chariot reserved for his second-in-command. And wherever Joseph went, the command was shouted, "Kneel down!" So Pharaoh put Joseph in charge of all Egypt. [44]And Pharaoh said to him, "I am Pharaoh, but no one will lift a hand or foot in the entire land of Egypt without your approval."

[45]Then Pharaoh gave Joseph a new Egyptian name, Zaphenath-paneah.* He also gave him a wife, whose name was Asenath. She was the daughter of Potiphera, the priest of On.* So Joseph took charge of the entire land of Egypt. [46]He was thirty years old when he began serving in the court of Pharaoh, the king of Egypt. And when Joseph left Pharaoh's presence, he inspected the entire land of Egypt.

[47]As predicted, for seven years the land produced bumper crops. [48]During those years, Joseph gathered all the crops grown in Egypt and stored the grain from the surrounding fields in the cities. [49]He piled up huge amounts of grain like sand on the seashore. Finally, he stopped keeping records because there was too much to measure.

[50]During this time, before the first of the famine years, two sons were born to Joseph and his wife, Asenath, the daughter of Potiphera, the priest of On. [51]Joseph named his older son Manasseh,* for he said, "God has made me forget all my troubles and everyone in my father's family." [52]Joseph named his second son Ephraim,* for he said, "God has made me fruitful in this land of my grief."

[53]At last the seven years of bumper crops throughout the land of Egypt came to an end. [54]Then the seven years of famine began, just as Joseph had predicted. The famine also struck all the surrounding countries, but throughout Egypt there was plenty of food. [55]Eventually, however, the famine spread throughout the land of Egypt as well. And when the people cried out to Pharaoh for food, he told them, "Go to Joseph, and do whatever he tells you." [56]So with severe famine everywhere, Joseph opened up the storehouses and distributed grain to the Egyptians, for the famine was severe throughout the land of Egypt. [57]And people from all around came to Egypt to buy grain from Joseph because the famine was severe throughout the world.

CHAPTER 42

Joseph's Brothers Go to Egypt

When Jacob heard that grain was available in Egypt, he said to his sons, "Why are you standing around looking at one another? [2]I have heard there is grain in Egypt. Go down there, and buy enough grain to keep us alive. Otherwise we'll die."

[3]So Joseph's ten older brothers went down to Egypt to buy grain. [4]But Jacob wouldn't let Joseph's younger brother, Benjamin, go with them, for fear some harm might come to him. [5]So Jacob's* sons arrived in Egypt along with others to buy food, for the famine was in Canaan as well.

[6]Since Joseph was governor of all Egypt and in charge of selling grain to all the people, it was to him that his brothers came. When they arrived, they bowed before him with their faces to the ground. [7]Joseph recognized his brothers instantly, but he pretended to be a stranger and spoke harshly to them. "Where are you from?" he demanded.

"From the land of Canaan," they replied. "We have come to buy food."

[8]Although Joseph recognized his brothers, they didn't recognize him. [9]And he remembered the dreams he'd had about them many years before. He said to them, "You are spies! You have come to see how vulnerable our land has become."

[10]"No, my lord!" they exclaimed. "Your servants have simply come to buy food. [11]We are all brothers—members of the same family. We are honest men, sir! We are not spies!"

[12]"Yes, you are!" Joseph insisted. "You have come to see how vulnerable our land has become."

[13]"Sir," they said, "there are actually twelve of us. We, your servants, are all brothers, sons of a man living in the land of Canaan. Our youngest brother is back there with our father right now, and one of our brothers is no longer with us."

[14]But Joseph insisted, "As I said, you are spies! [15]This is how I will test your story. I swear by the life of Pharaoh that you will never leave Egypt unless your youngest brother comes here! [16]One of you must go and get your brother. I'll keep the rest of you here in prison.

41:45a *Zaphenath-paneah* probably means "God speaks and lives." **41:45b** Greek version reads *of Heliopolis;* also in 41:50. **41:51** *Manasseh* sounds like a Hebrew term that means "causing to forget." **41:52** *Ephraim* sounds like a Hebrew term that means "fruitful." **42:5** Hebrew *Israel's.* See note on 35:21.

Then we'll find out whether or not your story is true. By the life of Pharaoh, if it turns out that you don't have a younger brother, then I'll know you are spies."

17 So Joseph put them all in prison for three days. 18 On the third day Joseph said to them, "I am a God-fearing man. If you do as I say, you will live. 19 If you really are honest men, choose one of your brothers to remain in prison. The rest of you may go home with grain for your starving families. 20 But you must bring your youngest brother back to me. This will prove that you are telling the truth, and you will not die." To this they agreed.

21 Speaking among themselves, they said, "Clearly we are being punished because of what we did to Joseph long ago. We saw his anguish when he pleaded for his life, but we wouldn't listen. That's why we're in this trouble."

22 "Didn't I tell you not to sin against the boy?" Reuben asked. "But you wouldn't listen. And now we have to answer for his blood!"

23 Of course, they didn't know that Joseph understood them, for he had been speaking to them through an interpreter. 24 Now he turned away from them and began to weep. When he regained his composure, he spoke to them again. Then he chose Simeon from among them and had him tied up right before their eyes.

25 Joseph then ordered his servants to fill the men's sacks with grain, but he also gave secret instructions to return each brother's payment at the top of his sack. He also gave them supplies for their journey home. 26 So the brothers loaded their donkeys with the grain and headed for home.

27 But when they stopped for the night and one of them opened his sack to get grain for his donkey, he found his money in the top of his sack. 28 "Look!" he exclaimed to his brothers. "My money has been returned; it's here in my sack!" Then their hearts sank. Trembling, they said to each other, "What has God done to us?"

29 When the brothers came to their father, Jacob, in the land of Canaan, they told him everything that had happened to them. 30 "The man who is governor of the land spoke very harshly to us," they told him. "He accused us of being spies scouting the land. 31 But we said, 'We are honest men, not spies. 32 We are twelve brothers, sons of one father. One brother is no longer with us, and the youngest is at home with our father in the land of Canaan.'

33 "Then the man who is governor of the land told us, 'This is how I will find out if you are honest men. Leave one of your brothers here with me, and take grain for your starving families and go on home. 34 But you must bring your youngest brother back to me. Then I will know you are honest men and not spies. Then I will give you back your brother, and you may trade freely in the land.'"

35 As they emptied out their sacks, there in each man's sack was the bag of money he had paid for the grain! The brothers and their father were terrified when they saw the bags of money. 36 Jacob exclaimed, "You are robbing me of my children! Joseph is gone! Simeon is gone! And now you want to take Benjamin, too. Everything is going against me!"

37 Then Reuben said to his father, "You may kill my two sons if I don't bring Benjamin back to you. I'll be responsible for him, and I promise to bring him back."

38 But Jacob replied, "My son will not go down with you. His brother Joseph is dead, and he is all I have left. If anything should happen to him on your journey, you would send this grieving, white-haired man to his grave.*"

CHAPTER 43

The Brothers Return to Egypt

But the famine continued to ravage the land of Canaan. 2 When the grain they had brought from Egypt was almost gone, Jacob said to his sons, "Go back and buy us a little more food."

3 But Judah said, "The man was serious when he warned us, 'You won't see my face again unless your brother is with you.' 4 If you send Benjamin with us, we will go down and buy more food. 5 But if you don't let Benjamin go, we won't go either. Remember, the man said, 'You won't see my face again unless your brother is with you.'"

6 "Why were you so cruel to me?" Jacob* moaned. "Why did you tell him you had another brother?"

7 "The man kept asking us questions about our family," they replied. "He asked, 'Is your

42:38 Hebrew *to Sheol.* **43:6** Hebrew *Israel;* also in 43:11. See note on 35:21.

father still alive? Do you have another brother?' So we answered his questions. How could we know he would say, 'Bring your brother down here'?"

[8]Judah said to his father, "Send the boy with me, and we will be on our way. Otherwise we will all die of starvation—and not only we, but you and our little ones. [9]I personally guarantee his safety. You may hold me responsible if I don't bring him back to you. Then let me bear the blame forever. [10]If we hadn't wasted all this time, we could have gone and returned twice by now."

[11]So their father, Jacob, finally said to them, "If it can't be avoided, then at least do this. Pack your bags with the best products of this land. Take them down to the man as gifts—balm, honey, gum, aromatic resin, pistachio nuts, and almonds. [12]Also take double the money that was put back in your sacks, as it was probably someone's mistake. [13]Then take your brother, and go back to the man. [14]May God Almighty* give you mercy as you go before the man, so that he will release Simeon and let Benjamin return. But if I must lose my children, so be it."

[15]So the men packed Jacob's gifts and double the money and headed off with Benjamin. They finally arrived in Egypt and presented themselves to Joseph. [16]When Joseph saw Benjamin with them, he said to the manager of his household, "These men will eat with me this noon. Take them inside the palace. Then go slaughter an animal, and prepare a big feast." [17]So the man did as Joseph told him and took them into Joseph's palace.

[18]The brothers were terrified when they saw that they were being taken into Joseph's house. "It's because of the money someone put in our sacks last time we were here," they said. "He plans to pretend that we stole it. Then he will seize us, make us slaves, and take our donkeys."

A Feast at Joseph's Palace

[19]The brothers approached the manager of Joseph's household and spoke to him at the entrance to the palace. [20]"Sir," they said, "we came to Egypt once before to buy food. [21]But as we were returning home, we stopped for the night and opened our sacks. Then we discovered that each man's money—the exact amount paid—was in the top of his sack! Here it is; we have brought it back with us. [22]We also have additional money to buy more food. We have no idea who put our money in our sacks."

[23]"Relax. Don't be afraid," the household manager told them. "Your God, the God of your father, must have put this treasure into your sacks. I know I received your payment." Then he released Simeon and brought him out to them.

[24]The manager then led the men into Joseph's palace. He gave them water to wash their feet and provided food for their donkeys. [25]They were told they would be eating there, so they prepared their gifts for Joseph's arrival at noon.

[26]When Joseph came home, they gave him the gifts they had brought him, then bowed low to the ground before him. [27]After greeting

43:14 Hebrew *El-Shaddai.*

them, he asked, "How is your father, the old man you spoke about? Is he still alive?"

[28]"Yes," they replied. "Our father, your servant, is alive and well." And they bowed low again.

[29]Then Joseph looked at his brother Benjamin, the son of his own mother. "Is this your youngest brother, the one you told me about?" Joseph asked. "May God be gracious to you, my son." [30]Then Joseph hurried from the room because he was overcome with emotion for his brother. He went into his private room, where he broke down and wept. [31]After washing his face, he came back out, keeping himself under control. Then he ordered, "Bring out the food!"

[32]The waiters served Joseph at his own table, and his brothers were served at a separate table. The Egyptians who ate with Joseph sat at their own table, because Egyptians despise Hebrews and refuse to eat with them. [33]Joseph told each of his brothers where to sit, and to their amazement, he seated them according to age, from oldest to youngest. [34]And Joseph filled their plates with food from his own table, giving Benjamin five times as much as he gave the others. So they feasted and drank freely with him.

CHAPTER 44

Joseph's Silver Cup

When his brothers were ready to leave, Joseph gave these instructions to his palace manager: "Fill each of their sacks with as much grain as they can carry, and put each man's money back into his sack. [2]Then put my personal silver cup at the top of the youngest brother's sack, along with the money for his grain." So the manager did as Joseph instructed him.

[3]The brothers were up at dawn and were sent on their journey with their loaded donkeys. [4]But when they had gone only a short distance and were barely out of the city, Joseph said to his palace manager, "Chase after them and stop them. When you catch up with them, ask them, 'Why have you repaid my kindness with such evil? [5]Why have you stolen my master's silver cup,* which he uses to predict the future? What a wicked thing you have done!'"

[6]When the palace manager caught up with the men, he spoke to them as he had been instructed.

[7]"What are you talking about?" the brothers responded. "We are your servants and would never do such a thing! [8]Didn't we return the money we found in our sacks? We brought it back all the way from the land of Canaan. Why would we steal silver or gold from your master's house? [9]If you find his cup with any one of us, let that man die. And all the rest of us, my lord, will be your slaves."

[10]"That's fair," the man replied. "But only the one who stole the cup will be my slave. The rest of you may go free."

[11]They all quickly took their sacks from the backs of their donkeys and opened them. [12]The palace manager searched the brothers' sacks, from the oldest to the youngest. And the cup was found in Benjamin's sack! [13]When the brothers saw this, they tore their clothing in despair. Then they loaded their donkeys again and returned to the city.

[14]Joseph was still in his palace when Judah and his brothers arrived, and they fell to the ground before him. [15]"What have you done?" Joseph demanded. "Don't you know that a man like me can predict the future?"

[16]Judah answered, "Oh, my lord, what can we say to you? How can we explain this? How can we prove our innocence? God is punishing us for our sins. My lord, we have all returned to be your slaves—all of us, not just our brother who had your cup in his sack."

[17]"No," Joseph said. "I would never do such a thing! Only the man who stole the cup will be my slave. The rest of you may go back to your father in peace."

Judah Speaks for His Brothers

[18]Then Judah stepped forward and said, "Please, my lord, let your servant say just one word to you. Please, do not be angry with me, even though you are as powerful as Pharaoh himself.

[19]"My lord, previously you asked us, your servants, 'Do you have a father or a brother?' [20]And we responded, 'Yes, my lord, we have a father who is an old man, and his youngest son is a child of his old age. His full brother is

44:5 As in Greek version; Hebrew lacks this phrase.

dead, and he alone is left of his mother's children, and his father loves him very much.'

[21]"And you said to us, 'Bring him here so I can see him with my own eyes.' [22]But we said to you, 'My lord, the boy cannot leave his father, for his father would die.' [23]But you told us, 'Unless your youngest brother comes with you, you will never see my face again.'

[24]"So we returned to your servant, our father, and told him what you had said. [25]Later, when he said, 'Go back again and buy us more food,' [26]we replied, 'We can't go unless you let our youngest brother go with us. We'll never get to see the man's face unless our youngest brother is with us.'

[27]"Then my father said to us, 'As you know, my wife had two sons, [28]and one of them went away and never returned. Doubtless he was torn to pieces by some wild animal. I have never seen him since. [29]Now if you take his brother away from me, and any harm comes to him, you will send this grieving, white-haired man to his grave.*'

[30]"And now, my lord, I cannot go back to my father without the boy. Our father's life is bound up in the boy's life. [31]If he sees that the boy is not with us, our father will die. We, your servants, will indeed be responsible for sending that grieving, white-haired man to his grave. [32]My lord, I guaranteed to my father that I would take care of the boy. I told him, 'If I don't bring him back to you, I will bear the blame forever.'

[33]"So please, my lord, let me stay here as a slave instead of the boy, and let the boy return with his brothers. [34]For how can I return to my father if the boy is not with me? I couldn't bear to see the anguish this would cause my father!"

CHAPTER 45

Joseph Reveals His Identity

Joseph could stand it no longer. There were many people in the room, and he said to his attendants, "Out, all of you!" So he was alone with his brothers when he told them who he was. [2]Then he broke down and wept. He wept so loudly the Egyptians could hear him, and word of it quickly carried to Pharaoh's palace.

[3]"I am Joseph!" he said to his brothers. "Is my father still alive?" But his brothers were speechless! They were stunned to realize that Joseph was standing there in front of them. [4]"Please, come closer," he said to them. So they came closer. And he said again, "I am Joseph, your brother, whom you sold into slavery in Egypt. [5]But don't be upset, and don't be angry with yourselves for selling me to this place. It was God who sent me here ahead of you to preserve your lives. [6]This famine that has ravaged the land for two years will last five more years, and there will be neither plowing nor harvesting. [7]God has sent me ahead of you to keep you and your families alive and to preserve many survivors.* [8]So it was God who sent me here, not you! And he is the one who made me an adviser* to Pharaoh—the manager of his entire palace and the governor of all Egypt.

[9]"Now hurry back to my father and tell him, 'This is what your son Joseph says: God has made me master over all the land of Egypt. So come down to me immediately! [10]You can live in the region of Goshen, where you can be near me with all your children and grandchildren, your flocks and herds, and everything you own. [11]I will take care of you there, for there are still five years of famine ahead of us. Otherwise you, your household, and all your animals will starve.'"

[12]Then Joseph added, "Look! You can see for yourselves, and so can my brother Benjamin, that I really am Joseph! [13]Go tell my father of my honored position here in Egypt. Describe for him everything you have seen, and then bring my father here quickly." [14]Weeping with joy, he embraced Benjamin, and Benjamin did the same. [15]Then Joseph kissed each of his brothers and wept over them, and after that they began talking freely with him.

Pharaoh Invites Jacob to Egypt

[16]The news soon reached Pharaoh's palace: "Joseph's brothers have arrived!" Pharaoh and his officials were all delighted to hear this.

[17]Pharaoh said to Joseph, "Tell your brothers, 'This is what you must do: Load your pack animals, and hurry back to the land of Canaan. [18]Then get your father and all of your families, and return here to me. I will give you

44:29 Hebrew *to Sheol;* also in 44:31. **45:7** Or *and to save you with an extraordinary rescue.* The meaning of the Hebrew is uncertain. **45:8** Hebrew *a father.*

REVENGE?

Max was always picking on Justin—and for no good reason. He pushed Justin around and made fun of him every chance he got.

Walking home from school one day, Justin saw Max's backpack by the sidewalk. No one was around. Whoa! Now was Justin's chance to get back at Max. Maybe he could give the backpack a little kick. Or maybe he could toss it into the bushes. That would serve Max right.

How would you handle this temptation? Read Genesis 45:1-18 to find out how Joseph treated his mean brothers.

the very best land in Egypt, and you will eat from the best that the land produces.'"

[19]Then Pharaoh said to Joseph, "Tell your brothers, 'Take wagons from the land of Egypt to carry your little children and your wives, and bring your father here. [20]Don't worry about your personal belongings, for the best of all the land of Egypt is yours.'"

[21]So the sons of Jacob* did as they were told. Joseph provided them with wagons, as Pharaoh had commanded, and he gave them supplies for the journey. [22]And he gave each of them new clothes—but to Benjamin he gave five changes of clothes and 300 pieces* of silver. [23]He also sent his father ten male donkeys loaded with the finest products of Egypt, and ten female donkeys loaded with grain and bread and other supplies he would need on his journey.

[24]So Joseph sent his brothers off, and as they left, he called after them, "Don't quarrel about all this along the way!" [25]And they left Egypt and returned to their father, Jacob, in the land of Canaan.

[26]"Joseph is still alive!" they told him. "And he is governor of all the land of Egypt!" Jacob was stunned at the news—he couldn't believe it. [27]But when they repeated to Jacob everything Joseph had told them, and when he saw the wagons Joseph had sent to carry him, their father's spirits revived.

[28]Then Jacob exclaimed, "It must be true! My son Joseph is alive! I must go and see him before I die."

CHAPTER 46

Jacob's Journey to Egypt

So Jacob* set out for Egypt with all his possessions. And when he came to Beersheba, he offered sacrifices to the God of his father, Isaac. [2]During the night God spoke to him in a vision. "Jacob! Jacob!" he called.

"Here I am," Jacob replied.

[3]"I am God,* the God of your father," the voice said. "Do not be afraid to go down to Egypt, for there I will make your family into a great nation. [4]I will go with you down to Egypt, and I will bring you back again. You will die in Egypt, but Joseph will be with you to close your eyes."

[5]So Jacob left Beersheba, and his sons took him to Egypt. They carried him and their little ones and their wives in the wagons Pharaoh had provided for them. [6]They also took all their livestock and all the personal belongings they had acquired in the land of Canaan. So Jacob and his entire family went to Egypt—[7]sons and grandsons, daughters and granddaughters—all his descendants.

[8]These are the names of the descendants

45:21 Hebrew *Israel;* also in 45:28. See note on 35:21. **45:22** Hebrew *300 shekels,* about 7.5 pounds or 3.4 kilograms in weight. **46:1** Hebrew *Israel;* also in 46:29, 30. See note on 35:21. **46:3** Hebrew *I am El.*

of Israel—the sons of Jacob—who went to Egypt:

Reuben was Jacob's oldest son. [9]The sons of Reuben were Hanoch, Pallu, Hezron, and Carmi.
[10]The sons of Simeon were Jemuel, Jamin, Ohad, Jakin, Zohar, and Shaul. (Shaul's mother was a Canaanite woman.)
[11]The sons of Levi were Gershon, Kohath, and Merari.
[12]The sons of Judah were Er, Onan, Shelah, Perez, and Zerah (though Er and Onan had died in the land of Canaan). The sons of Perez were Hezron and Hamul.
[13]The sons of Issachar were Tola, Puah,* Jashub,* and Shimron.
[14]The sons of Zebulun were Sered, Elon, and Jahleel.
[15]These were the sons of Leah and Jacob who were born in Paddan-aram, in addition to their daughter, Dinah. The number of Jacob's descendants (male and female) through Leah was thirty-three.

[16]The sons of Gad were Zephon,* Haggi, Shuni, Ezbon, Eri, Arodi, and Areli.
[17]The sons of Asher were Imnah, Ishvah, Ishvi, and Beriah. Their sister was Serah. Beriah's sons were Heber and Malkiel.
[18]These were the sons of Zilpah, the servant given to Leah by her father, Laban. The number of Jacob's descendants through Zilpah was sixteen.

[19]The sons of Jacob's wife Rachel were Joseph and Benjamin.
[20]Joseph's sons, born in the land of Egypt, were Manasseh and Ephraim. Their mother was Asenath, daughter of Potiphera, the priest of On.*
[21]Benjamin's sons were Bela, Beker, Ashbel, Gera, Naaman, Ehi, Rosh, Muppim, Huppim, and Ard.
[22]These were the sons of Rachel and Jacob. The number of Jacob's descendants through Rachel was fourteen.

[23]The son of Dan was Hushim.
[24]The sons of Naphtali were Jahzeel, Guni, Jezer, and Shillem.
[25]These were the sons of Bilhah, the servant given to Rachel by her father, Laban. The number of Jacob's descendants through Bilhah was seven.

[26]The total number of Jacob's direct descendants who went with him to Egypt, not counting his sons' wives, was sixty-six. [27]In addition, Joseph had two sons* who were born in Egypt. So altogether, there were seventy* members of Jacob's family in the land of Egypt.

Jacob's Family Arrives in Goshen

[28]As they neared their destination, Jacob sent Judah ahead to meet Joseph and get directions to the region of Goshen. And when they finally arrived there, [29]Joseph prepared his chariot and traveled to Goshen to meet his father, Jacob. When Joseph arrived, he embraced his father and wept, holding him for a long time. [30]Finally, Jacob said to Joseph, "Now I am ready to die, since I have seen your face again and know you are still alive."

[31]And Joseph said to his brothers and to his father's entire family, "I will go to Pharaoh and tell him, 'My brothers and my father's entire family have come to me from the land of Canaan. [32]These men are shepherds, and they raise livestock. They have brought with them their flocks and herds and everything they own.'"

[33]Then he said, "When Pharaoh calls for you and asks you about your occupation, [34]you must tell him, 'We, your servants, have raised livestock all our lives, as our ancestors have always done.' When you tell him this, he will let you live here in the region of Goshen, for the Egyptians despise shepherds."

CHAPTER 47

Jacob Blesses Pharaoh

Then Joseph went to see Pharaoh and told him, "My father and my brothers have arrived from the land of Canaan. They have come with all their flocks and herds and possessions, and they are now in the region of Goshen."

[2]Joseph took five of his brothers with him

46:13a As in Syriac version and Samaritan Pentateuch (see also 1 Chr 7:1); Hebrew reads *Puvah*. **46:13b** As in some Greek manuscripts and Samaritan Pentateuch (see also Num 26:24; 1 Chr 7:1); Hebrew reads *Job*. **46:16** As in Greek version and Samaritan Pentateuch (see also Num 26:15); Hebrew reads *Ziphion*. **46:20** Greek version reads *of Heliopolis*. **46:27a** Greek version reads *nine sons*, probably including Joseph's grandsons through Ephraim and Manasseh (see 1 Chr 7:14-20). **46:27b** Greek version reads *seventy-five*; see note on Exod 1:5.

and presented them to Pharaoh. [3]And Pharaoh asked the brothers, "What is your occupation?"

They replied, "We, your servants, are shepherds, just like our ancestors. [4]We have come to live here in Egypt for a while, for there is no pasture for our flocks in Canaan. The famine is very severe there. So please, we request permission to live in the region of Goshen."

[5]Then Pharaoh said to Joseph, "Now that your father and brothers have joined you here, [6]choose any place in the entire land of Egypt for them to live. Give them the best land of Egypt. Let them live in the region of Goshen. And if any of them have special skills, put them in charge of my livestock, too."

[7]Then Joseph brought in his father, Jacob, and presented him to Pharaoh. And Jacob blessed Pharaoh.

[8]"How old are you?" Pharaoh asked him.

[9]Jacob replied, "I have traveled this earth for 130 hard years. But my life has been short compared to the lives of my ancestors." [10]Then Jacob blessed Pharaoh again before leaving his court.

[11]So Joseph assigned the best land of Egypt—the region of Rameses—to his father and his brothers, and he settled them there, just as Pharaoh had commanded. [12]And Joseph provided food for his father and his brothers in amounts appropriate to the number of their dependents, including the smallest children.

Joseph's Leadership in the Famine

[13]Meanwhile, the famine became so severe that all the food was used up, and people were starving throughout the lands of Egypt and Canaan. [14]By selling grain to the people, Joseph eventually collected all the money in Egypt and Canaan, and he put the money in Pharaoh's treasury. [15]When the people of Egypt and Canaan ran out of money, all the Egyptians came to Joseph. "Our money is gone!" they cried. "But please give us food, or we will die before your very eyes!"

[16]Joseph replied, "Since your money is gone, bring me your livestock. I will give you food in exchange for your livestock." [17]So they brought their livestock to Joseph in exchange for food. In exchange for their horses, flocks of sheep and goats, herds of cattle, and donkeys, Joseph provided them with food for another year.

[18]But that year ended, and the next year they came again and said, "We cannot hide the truth from you, my lord. Our money is gone, and all our livestock and cattle are yours. We have nothing left to give but our bodies and our land. [19]Why should we die before your very eyes? Buy us and our land in exchange for food; we offer our land and ourselves as slaves for Pharaoh. Just give us grain so we may live and not die, and so the land does not become empty and desolate."

[20]So Joseph bought all the land of Egypt for Pharaoh. All the Egyptians sold him their fields because the famine was so severe, and soon all the land belonged to Pharaoh. [21]As for the people, he made them all slaves,* from one end of Egypt to the other. [22]The only land he did not buy was the land belonging to the priests. They received an allotment of food directly from Pharaoh, so they didn't need to sell their land.

[23]Then Joseph said to the people, "Look, today I have bought you and your land for Pharaoh. I will provide you with seed so you can plant the fields. [24]Then when you harvest it, one-fifth of your crop will belong to Pharaoh. You may keep the remaining four-fifths as seed for your fields and as food for you, your households, and your little ones."

[25]"You have saved our lives!" they exclaimed. "May it please you, my lord, to let us be Pharaoh's servants." [26]Joseph then issued a decree still in effect in the land of Egypt, that Pharaoh should receive one-fifth of all the crops grown on his land. Only the land belonging to the priests was not given to Pharaoh.

[27]Meanwhile, the people of Israel settled in the region of Goshen in Egypt. There they acquired property, and they were fruitful, and their population grew rapidly. [28]Jacob lived for seventeen years after his arrival in Egypt, so he lived 147 years in all.

[29]As the time of his death drew near, Jacob* called for his son Joseph and said to him, "Please do me this favor. Put your hand under my thigh and swear that you will treat me with unfailing love by honoring this last request: Do not bury me in Egypt. [30]When I die, please

47:21 As in Greek version and Samaritan Pentateuch; Hebrew reads *he moved them all into the towns.* **47:29** Hebrew *Israel;* also in 47:31b. See note on 35:21.

take my body out of Egypt and bury me with
my ancestors."
So Joseph promised, "I will do as you ask."
31"Swear that you will do it," Jacob insisted.
So Joseph gave his oath, and Jacob bowed
humbly at the head of his bed.*

CHAPTER 48

Jacob Blesses Manasseh and Ephraim

One day not long after this, word came to Joseph, "Your father is failing rapidly." So Joseph went to visit his father, and he took with him his two sons, Manasseh and Ephraim.
2When Joseph arrived, Jacob was told, "Your son Joseph has come to see you." So Jacob* gathered his strength and sat up in his bed.
3Jacob said to Joseph, "God Almighty* appeared to me at Luz in the land of Canaan and blessed me. 4He said to me, 'I will make you fruitful, and I will multiply your descendants. I will make you a multitude of nations. And I will give this land of Canaan to your descendants* after you as an everlasting possession.'
5"Now I am claiming as my own sons these two boys of yours, Ephraim and Manasseh, who were born here in the land of Egypt before I arrived. They will be my sons, just as Reuben and Simeon are. 6But any children born to you in the future will be your own, and they will inherit land within the territories of their brothers Ephraim and Manasseh.
7"Long ago, as I was returning from Paddan-aram, Rachel died in the land of Canaan. We were still on the way, some distance from Ephrath (that is, Bethlehem). So with great sorrow I buried her there beside the road to Ephrath."
8Then Jacob looked over at the two boys. "Are these your sons?" he asked.
9"Yes," Joseph told him, "these are the sons God has given me here in Egypt."
And Jacob said, "Bring them closer to me, so I can bless them."
10Jacob was half blind because of his age and could hardly see. So Joseph brought the boys close to him, and Jacob kissed and embraced them. 11Then Jacob said to Joseph, "I never thought I would see your face again, but now God has let me see your children, too!"
12Joseph moved the boys, who were at their grandfather's knees, and he bowed with his face to the ground. 13Then he positioned the boys in front of Jacob. With his right hand he directed Ephraim toward Jacob's left hand, and with his left hand he put Manasseh at Jacob's right hand. 14But Jacob crossed his arms as he reached out to lay his hands on the boys' heads. He put his right hand on the head of Ephraim, though he was the younger boy, and his left hand on the head of Manasseh, though he was the firstborn. 15Then he blessed Joseph and said,

"May the God before whom my
grandfather Abraham
and my father, Isaac, walked—
the God who has been my shepherd
all my life, to this very day,
16 the Angel who has redeemed me from
all harm—
may he bless these boys.
May they preserve my name
and the names of Abraham and Isaac.
And may their descendants multiply
greatly
throughout the earth."

17But Joseph was upset when he saw that his father placed his right hand on Ephraim's head. So Joseph lifted it to move it from Ephraim's head to Manasseh's head. 18"No, my father," he said. "This one is the firstborn. Put your right hand on his head."
19But his father refused. "I know, my son; I know," he replied. "Manasseh will also become a great people, but his younger brother will become even greater. And his descendants will become a multitude of nations."
20So Jacob blessed the boys that day with this blessing: "The people of Israel will use your names when they give a blessing. They will say, 'May God make you as prosperous as Ephraim and Manasseh.'" In this way, Jacob put Ephraim ahead of Manasseh.
21Then Jacob said to Joseph, "Look, I am about to die, but God will be with you and will take you back to Canaan, the land of your ancestors. 22And beyond what I have given your brothers, I am giving you an extra portion of the land* that I took from the Amorites with my sword and bow."

47:31 Greek version reads *and Israel bowed in worship as he leaned on his staff.* Compare Heb 11:21. **48:2** Hebrew *Israel;* also in 48:8, 10, 11, 13, 14, 21. See note on 35:21. **48:3** Hebrew *El-Shaddai.* **48:4** Hebrew *seed;* also in 48:19. **48:22** Or *an extra ridge of land.* The meaning of the Hebrew is uncertain.

CHAPTER 49

Jacob's Last Words to His Sons

Then Jacob called together all his sons and said, "Gather around me, and I will tell you what will happen to each of you in the days to come.

2 "Come and listen, you sons of Jacob;
listen to Israel, your father.

3 "Reuben, you are my firstborn, my strength,
the child of my vigorous youth.
You are first in rank and first in power.
4 But you are as unruly as a flood,
and you will be first no longer.
For you went to bed with my wife;
you defiled my marriage couch.

5 "Simeon and Levi are two of a kind;
their weapons are instruments of violence.
6 May I never join in their meetings;
may I never be a party to their plans.
For in their anger they murdered men,
and they crippled oxen just for sport.
7 A curse on their anger, for it is fierce;
a curse on their wrath, for it is cruel.
I will scatter them among the descendants of Jacob;
I will disperse them throughout Israel.

8 "Judah, your brothers will praise you.
You will grasp your enemies by the neck.
All your relatives will bow before you.
9 Judah, my son, is a young lion
that has finished eating its prey.
Like a lion he crouches and lies down;
like a lioness—who dares to rouse him?
10 The scepter will not depart from Judah,
nor the ruler's staff from his descendants,*
until the coming of the one to whom it belongs,*
the one whom all nations will honor.
11 He ties his foal to a grapevine,
the colt of his donkey to a choice vine.
He washes his clothes in wine,
his robes in the blood of grapes.
12 His eyes are darker than wine,
and his teeth are whiter than milk.

13 "Zebulun will settle by the seashore
and will be a harbor for ships;
his borders will extend to Sidon.

14 "Issachar is a sturdy donkey,
resting between two saddlepacks.*
15 When he sees how good the countryside is
and how pleasant the land,
he will bend his shoulder to the load
and submit himself to hard labor.

16 "Dan will govern his people,
like any other tribe in Israel.
17 Dan will be a snake beside the road,
a poisonous viper along the path
that bites the horse's hooves
so its rider is thrown off.
18 I trust in you for salvation, O LORD!

19 "Gad will be attacked by marauding bands,
but he will attack them when they retreat.

20 "Asher will dine on rich foods
and produce food fit for kings.

21 "Naphtali is a doe set free
that bears beautiful fawns.

22 "Joseph is the foal of a wild donkey,
the foal of a wild donkey at a spring—
one of the wild donkeys on the ridge.*
23 Archers attacked him savagely;
they shot at him and harassed him.
24 But his bow remained taut,
and his arms were strengthened
by the hands of the Mighty One of Jacob,
by the Shepherd, the Rock of Israel.
25 May the God of your father help you;
may the Almighty bless you
with the blessings of the heavens above,
and blessings of the watery depths below,
and blessings of the breasts and womb.
26 May the blessings of your father
surpass the blessings of the ancient mountains,*

49:10a Hebrew *from between his feet.* **49:10b** Or *until tribute is brought to him and the peoples obey;* traditionally rendered *until Shiloh comes.* **49:14** Or *sheepfolds,* or *hearths.* **49:22** Or *Joseph is a fruitful tree, / a fruitful tree beside a spring. / His branches reach over the wall.* The meaning of the Hebrew is uncertain. **49:26** Or *of my ancestors.*

reaching to the heights of the eternal hills.
May these blessings rest on the head of Joseph,
who is a prince among his brothers.

27 "Benjamin is a ravenous wolf,
devouring his enemies in the morning
and dividing his plunder in the evening."

28 These are the twelve tribes of Israel, and this is what their father said as he told his sons good-bye. He blessed each one with an appropriate message.

I am feeling overwhelmed. Where can I get some help?

May the God of your father help you. GENESIS 49:25

Jacob's Death and Burial

29 Then Jacob instructed them, "Soon I will die and join my ancestors. Bury me with my father and grandfather in the cave in the field of Ephron the Hittite. 30 This is the cave in the field of Machpelah, near Mamre in Canaan, that Abraham bought from Ephron the Hittite as a permanent burial site. 31 There Abraham and his wife Sarah are buried. There Isaac and his wife, Rebekah, are buried. And there I buried Leah. 32 It is the plot of land and the cave that my grandfather Abraham bought from the Hittites."

33 When Jacob had finished this charge to his sons, he drew his feet into the bed, breathed his last, and joined his ancestors in death.

CHAPTER 50

Joseph threw himself on his father and wept over him and kissed him. 2 Then Joseph told the physicians who served him to embalm his father's body; so Jacob* was embalmed. 3 The embalming process took the usual forty days. And the Egyptians mourned his death for seventy days.

4 When the period of mourning was over, Joseph approached Pharaoh's advisers and said, "Please do me this favor and speak to Pharaoh on my behalf. 5 Tell him that my father made me swear an oath. He said to me, 'Listen, I am about to die. Take my body back to the land of Canaan, and bury me in the tomb I prepared for myself.' So please allow me to go and bury my father. After his burial, I will return without delay."

6 Pharaoh agreed to Joseph's request. "Go and bury your father, as he made you promise," he said. 7 So Joseph went up to bury his father. He was accompanied by all of Pharaoh's officials, all the senior members of Pharaoh's household, and all the senior officers of Egypt. 8 Joseph also took his entire household and his brothers and their households. But they left their little children and flocks and herds in the land of Goshen. 9 A great number of chariots and charioteers accompanied Joseph.

10 When they arrived at the threshing floor of Atad, near the Jordan River, they held a very great and solemn memorial service, with a seven-day period of mourning for Joseph's father. 11 The local residents, the Canaanites, watched them mourning at the threshing floor of Atad. Then they renamed that place (which is near the Jordan) Abel-mizraim,* for they said, "This is a place of deep mourning for these Egyptians."

12 So Jacob's sons did as he had commanded them. 13 They carried his body to the land of Canaan and buried him in the cave in the field of Machpelah, near Mamre. This is the cave that Abraham had bought as a permanent burial site from Ephron the Hittite.

Joseph Reassures His Brothers

14 After burying Jacob, Joseph returned to Egypt with his brothers and all who had accompanied him to his father's burial. 15 But now that their father was dead, Joseph's brothers became fearful. "Now Joseph will show his anger and pay us back for all the wrong we did to him," they said.

16 So they sent this message to Joseph: "Be-

50:2 Hebrew *Israel*. See note on 35:21. **50:11** *Abel-mizraim* means "mourning of the Egyptians."

fore your father died, he instructed us [17]to say to you: 'Please forgive your brothers for the great wrong they did to you—for their sin in treating you so cruelly.' So we, the servants of the God of your father, beg you to forgive our sin." When Joseph received the message, he broke down and wept. [18]Then his brothers came and threw themselves down before Joseph. "Look, we are your slaves!" they said.

[19]But Joseph replied, "Don't be afraid of me. Am I God, that I can punish you? [20]You intended to harm me, but God intended it all for good. He brought me to this position so I could save the lives of many people. [21]No, don't be afraid. I will continue to take care of you and your children." So he reassured them by speaking kindly to them.

50:23 Hebrew *who were born on Joseph's knees.*

The Death of Joseph

[22]So Joseph and his brothers and their families continued to live in Egypt. Joseph lived to the age of 110. [23]He lived to see three generations of descendants of his son Ephraim, and he lived to see the birth of the children of Manasseh's son Makir, whom he claimed as his own.*

[24]"Soon I will die," Joseph told his brothers, "but God will surely come to help you and lead you out of this land of Egypt. He will bring you back to the land he solemnly promised to give to Abraham, to Isaac, and to Jacob."

[25]Then Joseph made the sons of Israel swear an oath, and he said, "When God comes to help you and lead you back, you must take my bones with you." [26]So Joseph died at the age of 110. The Egyptians embalmed him, and his body was placed in a coffin in Egypt.

EXODUS

WHO
Midwives Shiphrah and Puah; Moses, Aaron, Miriam, Pharaoh, and Jethro.

WHERE
In Egypt and in the "wilderness"—the desert land between Egypt and what is now Jordan and Israel.

WHEN
Moses probably wrote this book between 1450–1410 BC while leading God's people to the Promised Land.

WHY
To tell us how the descendants of Jacob traveled to Israel, the Promised Land, and organized into a nation.

I have certainly seen the oppression of my people in Egypt. . . . So I have come down to rescue them.
EXODUS 3:7-8

Have you ever moved? Getting packed is a big job. What if your *whole neighborhood* moved *on the same day?* What a traffic jam! Several thousand years ago, the Israelites moved from Egypt to another country. They traveled to the land God had promised them. Exodus describes their adventures.

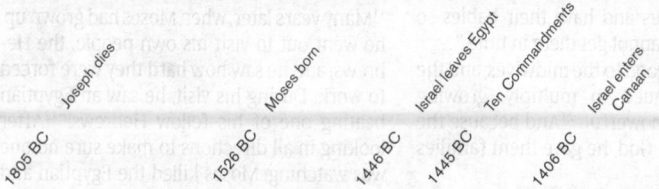

THEN AND NOW—GOD TAKES CARE OF HIS PEOPLE!

CHAPTER 1

The Israelites in Egypt

These are the names of the sons of Israel (that is, Jacob) who moved to Egypt with their father, each with his family: [2]Reuben, Simeon, Levi, Judah, [3]Issachar, Zebulun, Benjamin, [4]Dan, Naphtali, Gad, and Asher. [5]In all, Jacob had seventy* descendants in Egypt, including Joseph, who was already there.

[6]In time, Joseph and all of his brothers died, ending that entire generation. [7]But their descendants, the Israelites, had many children and grandchildren. In fact, they multiplied so greatly that they became extremely powerful and filled the land.

[8]Eventually, a new king came to power in Egypt who knew nothing about Joseph or what he had done. [9]He said to his people, "Look, the

1:5 Dead Sea Scrolls and Greek version read *seventy-five;* see notes on Gen 46:27.

people of Israel now outnumber us and are stronger than we are. [10]We must make a plan to keep them from growing even more. If we don't, and if war breaks out, they will join our enemies and fight against us. Then they will escape from the country.*"

[11]So the Egyptians made the Israelites their slaves. They appointed brutal slave drivers over them, hoping to wear them down with crushing labor. They forced them to build the cities of Pithom and Rameses as supply centers for the king. [12]But the more the Egyptians oppressed them, the more the Israelites multiplied and spread, and the more alarmed the Egyptians became. [13]So the Egyptians worked the people of Israel without mercy. [14]They made their lives bitter, forcing them to mix mortar and make bricks and do all the work in the fields. They were ruthless in all their demands.

[15]Then Pharaoh, the king of Egypt, gave this order to the Hebrew midwives, Shiphrah and Puah: [16]"When you help the Hebrew women as they give birth, watch as they deliver.* If the baby is a boy, kill him; if it is a girl, let her live." [17]But because the midwives feared God, they refused to obey the king's orders. They allowed the boys to live, too.

[18]So the king of Egypt called for the midwives. "Why have you done this?" he demanded. "Why have you allowed the boys to live?"

[19]"The Hebrew women are not like the Egyptian women," the midwives replied. "They are more vigorous and have their babies so quickly that we cannot get there in time."

[20]So God was good to the midwives, and the Israelites continued to multiply, growing more and more powerful. [21]And because the midwives feared God, he gave them families of their own.

[22]Then Pharaoh gave this order to all his people: "Throw every newborn Hebrew boy into the Nile River. But you may let the girls live."

CHAPTER 2

The Birth of Moses

About this time, a man and woman from the tribe of Levi got married. [2]The woman became pregnant and gave birth to a son. She saw that he was a special baby and kept him hidden for three months. [3]But when she could no longer hide him, she got a basket made of papyrus reeds and waterproofed it with tar and pitch. She put the baby in the basket and laid it among the reeds along the bank of the Nile River. [4]The baby's sister then stood at a distance, watching to see what would happen to him.

[5]Soon Pharaoh's daughter came down to bathe in the river, and her attendants walked along the riverbank. When the princess saw the basket among the reeds, she sent her maid to get it for her. [6]When the princess opened it, she saw the baby. The little boy was crying, and she felt sorry for him. "This must be one of the Hebrew children," she said.

[7]Then the baby's sister approached the princess. "Should I go and find one of the Hebrew women to nurse the baby for you?" she asked.

[8]"Yes, do!" the princess replied. So the girl went and called the baby's mother.

[9]"Take this baby and nurse him for me," the princess told the baby's mother. "I will pay you for your help." So the woman took her baby home and nursed him.

[10]Later, when the boy was older, his mother brought him back to Pharaoh's daughter, who adopted him as her own son. The princess named him Moses,* for she explained, "I lifted him out of the water."

Moses Escapes to Midian

[11]Many years later, when Moses had grown up, he went out to visit his own people, the Hebrews, and he saw how hard they were forced to work. During his visit, he saw an Egyptian beating one of his fellow Hebrews. [12]After looking in all directions to make sure no one was watching, Moses killed the Egyptian and hid the body in the sand.

[13]The next day, when Moses went out to visit his people again, he saw two Hebrew men fighting. "Why are you beating up your friend?" Moses said to the one who had started the fight.

[14]The man replied, "Who appointed you to be our prince and judge? Are you going to kill me as you killed that Egyptian yesterday?"

Then Moses was afraid, thinking, "Everyone

1:10 Or *will take the country.* **1:16** Hebrew *look upon the two stones;* perhaps the reference is to a birthstool. **2:10** *Moses* sounds like a Hebrew term that means "to lift out."

My parents divorced when I was pretty young. In eighth grade, I moved from my mom's house into my dad's house—something I'd wanted to do for as long as I could remember. However, that meant I had to change schools and leave a place I loved. My new school was far from anything I'd ever experienced. I'm not exaggerating when I say the kids were different from my old friends. Many were involved in gangs. There were problems all the time with fights, drugs, smoking, cussing, and kids being expelled. I was hesitant to even try and make new friends.

I basically put myself on autopilot the entire school year, just doing my work and stepping outside of my comfort zone as little as possible. Looking back, I wish I had made a conscious effort to get to know more people. Rather than complain about my loneliness, I could have shared Jesus' love, and I could have looked for kids who would have made good friends.

If you've ever moved, you know how hard it is to be the new kid. However, it is also the perfect opportunity to meet people and even tell them about Jesus just because you're new and different.

I definitely did not make the most of my time at that school. If I could do it again, I would not complain so much, blaming God for placing me in a difficult situation. Instead, I would focus on making the most of the opportunity God had given me.

Check out Exodus 2:7-8 to see how the baby Moses' sister, Miriam, made the most of an opportunity God gave to her. For other verses on this topic, look up Philippians 2:14-15 and Colossians 4:5-6.

moses

I'm a Hebrew. I let my anger get the best of me and killed an Egyptian I saw beating up another Hebrew. The next day I tried to stop two Hebrews from fighting. One asked, "Are you going to kill me like you did that Egyptian yesterday?"

I escaped to the desert, where I ran into more bullies at a well. They were picking on seven sisters. After I rescued them, their father invited me to stay at their home, but I never forgot my Hebrew people, who were slaves in Egypt. God never forgot either. He decided to send someone—me—to free them from Pharaoh.

You can read about Moses in the books of Exodus through Deuteronomy.

knows what I did." [15]And sure enough, Pharaoh heard what had happened, and he tried to kill Moses. But Moses fled from Pharaoh and went to live in the land of Midian.

When Moses arrived in Midian, he sat down beside a well. [16]Now the priest of Midian had seven daughters who came as usual to draw water and fill the water troughs for their father's flocks. [17]But some other shepherds came and chased them away. So Moses jumped up and rescued the girls from the shepherds. Then he drew water for their flocks.

[18]When the girls returned to Reuel, their father, he asked, "Why are you back so soon today?"

[19]"An Egyptian rescued us from the shepherds," they answered. "And then he drew water for us and watered our flocks."

[20]"Then where is he?" their father asked. "Why did you leave him there? Invite him to come and eat with us."

[21]Moses accepted the invitation, and he settled there with him. In time, Reuel gave Moses his daughter Zipporah to be his wife. [22]Later she gave birth to a son, and Moses named him Gershom,* for he explained, "I have been a foreigner in a foreign land."

[23]Years passed, and the king of Egypt died. But the Israelites continued to groan under their burden of slavery. They cried out for help, and their cry rose up to God. [24]God heard their groaning, and he remembered his covenant promise to Abraham, Isaac, and Jacob. [25]He looked down on the people of Israel and knew it was time to act.*

CHAPTER 3

Moses and the Burning Bush

One day Moses was tending the flock of his father-in-law, Jethro,* the priest of Midian. He led the flock far into the wilderness and came to Sinai,* the mountain of God. [2]There the angel of the LORD appeared to him in a blazing fire from the middle of a bush. Moses stared in amazement. Though the bush was engulfed in flames, it didn't burn up. [3]"This is amazing," Moses said to himself. "Why isn't that bush burning up? I must go see it."

[4]When the LORD saw Moses coming to take a closer look, God called to him from the middle of the bush, "Moses! Moses!"

"Here I am!" Moses replied.

[5]"Do not come any closer," the LORD warned. "Take off your sandals, for you are standing on holy ground. [6]I am the God of your father*—the God of Abraham, the God of Isaac, and the God of Jacob." When Moses

2:22 *Gershom* sounds like a Hebrew term that means "a foreigner there." **2:25** Or *and acknowledged his obligation to help them.* **3:1a** Moses' father-in-law went by two names, Jethro and Reuel. **3:1b** Hebrew *Horeb*, another name for Sinai. **3:6** Greek version reads *your fathers.*

heard this, he covered his face because he was afraid to look at God.

7Then the LORD told him, "I have certainly seen the oppression of my people in Egypt. I have heard their cries of distress because of their harsh slave drivers. Yes, I am aware of their suffering. 8So I have come down to rescue them from the power of the Egyptians and lead them out of Egypt into their own fertile and spacious land. It is a land flowing with milk and honey—the land where the Canaanites, Hittites, Amorites, Perizzites, Hivites, and Jebusites now live. 9Look! The cry of the people of Israel has reached me, and I have seen how harshly the Egyptians abuse them. 10Now go, for I am sending you to Pharaoh. You must lead my people Israel out of Egypt."

Who is worthy of my respect? ✱ **The LORD warned, "Take off your sandals, for you are standing on holy ground."** EXODUS 3:5

11But Moses protested to God, "Who am I to appear before Pharaoh? Who am I to lead the people of Israel out of Egypt?"

12God answered, "I will be with you. And this is your sign that I am the one who has sent you: When you have brought the people out of Egypt, you will worship God at this very mountain."

13But Moses protested, "If I go to the people of Israel and tell them, 'The God of your ancestors has sent me to you,' they will ask me, 'What is his name?' Then what should I tell them?"

14God replied to Moses, "I AM WHO I AM.* Say this to the people of Israel: I AM has sent me to you." 15God also said to Moses, "Say this to the people of Israel: Yahweh,* the God of your ancestors—the God of Abraham, the God of Isaac, and the God of Jacob—has sent me to you.

This is my eternal name,
my name to remember for all
generations.

16"Now go and call together all the elders of Israel. Tell them, 'The LORD, the God of your ancestors—the God of Abraham, Isaac, and Jacob—has appeared to me. He told me, "I have been watching closely, and I see how the Egyptians are treating you. 17I have promised to rescue you from your oppression in Egypt. I will lead you to a land flowing with milk and honey—the land where the Canaanites, Hittites, Amorites, Perizzites, Hivites, and Jebusites now live."'

18"The elders of Israel will accept your message. Then you and the elders must go to the king of Egypt and tell him, 'The LORD, the God of the Hebrews, has met with us. So please let us take a three-day journey into the wilderness to offer sacrifices to the LORD, our God.'

19"But I know that the king of Egypt will not let you go unless a mighty hand forces him.* 20So I will raise my hand and strike the Egyptians, performing all kinds of miracles among them. Then at last he will let you go. 21And I will cause the Egyptians to look favorably on you. They will give you gifts when you go so you will not leave empty-handed. 22Every Israelite woman will ask for articles of silver and gold and fine clothing from her Egyptian neighbors and from the foreign women in their houses. You will dress your sons and daughters with these, stripping the Egyptians of their wealth."

CHAPTER 4

Signs of the LORD's Power

But Moses protested again, "What if they won't believe me or listen to me? What if they say, 'The LORD never appeared to you'?"

2Then the LORD asked him, "What is that in your hand?"

"A shepherd's staff," Moses replied.

3"Throw it down on the ground," the LORD told him. So Moses threw down the staff, and it turned into a snake! Moses jumped back.

4Then the LORD told him, "Reach out and grab its tail." So Moses reached out and grabbed it, and it turned back into a shepherd's staff in his hand.

3:14 Or *I WILL BE WHAT I WILL BE.* **3:15** *Yahweh* is a transliteration of the proper name *YHWH* that is sometimes rendered "Jehovah"; in this translation it is usually rendered "the LORD" (note the use of small capitals). **3:19** As in Greek and Latin versions; Hebrew reads *will not let you go, not by a mighty hand.*

5"Perform this sign," the LORD told him. "Then they will believe that the LORD, the God of their ancestors—the God of Abraham, the God of Isaac, and the God of Jacob—really has appeared to you."

6Then the LORD said to Moses, "Now put your hand inside your cloak." So Moses put his hand inside his cloak, and when he took it out again, his hand was white as snow with a severe skin disease.* 7"Now put your hand back into your cloak," the LORD said. So Moses put his hand back in, and when he took it out again, it was as healthy as the rest of his body.

8The LORD said to Moses, "If they do not believe you and are not convinced by the first miraculous sign, they will be convinced by the second sign. 9And if they don't believe you or listen to you even after these two signs, then take some water from the Nile River and pour it out on the dry ground. When you do, the water from the Nile will turn to blood on the ground."

10But Moses pleaded with the LORD, "O Lord, I'm not very good with words. I never have been, and I'm not now, even though you have spoken to me. I get tongue-tied, and my words get tangled."

11Then the LORD asked Moses, "Who makes a person's mouth? Who decides whether people speak or do not speak, hear or do not hear, see or do not see? Is it not I, the LORD? 12Now go! I will be with you as you speak, and I will instruct you in what to say."

13But Moses again pleaded, "Lord, please! Send anyone else."

14Then the LORD became angry with Moses. "All right," he said. "What about your brother, Aaron the Levite? I know he speaks well. And look! He is on his way to meet you now. He will be delighted to see you. 15Talk to him, and put the words in his mouth. I will be with both of you as you speak, and I will instruct you both in what to do. 16Aaron will be your spokesman to the people. He will be your mouthpiece, and you will stand in the place of God for him, telling him what to say. 17And take your shepherd's staff with you, and use it to perform the miraculous signs I have shown you."

Moses Returns to Egypt

18So Moses went back home to Jethro, his father-in-law. "Please let me return to my relatives in Egypt," Moses said. "I don't even know if they are still alive."

"Go in peace," Jethro replied.

19Before Moses left Midian, the LORD said to him, "Return to Egypt, for all those who wanted to kill you have died."

20So Moses took his wife and sons, put them on a donkey, and headed back to the land of Egypt. In his hand he carried the staff of God.

21And the LORD told Moses, "When you arrive back in Egypt, go to Pharaoh and perform all the miracles I have empowered you to do. But I will harden his heart so he will refuse to let the people go. 22Then you will tell him, 'This is what the LORD says: Israel is my firstborn son. 23I commanded you, "Let my son go, so he can worship me." But since you have refused, I will now kill your firstborn son!'"

24On the way to Egypt, at a place where Moses and his family had stopped for the night, the LORD confronted him and was about to kill him. 25But Moses' wife, Zipporah, took a flint knife and circumcised her son. She touched his feet* with the foreskin and said, "Now you are a bridegroom of blood to me." 26(When she said "a bridegroom of blood," she was referring to the circumcision.) After that, the LORD left him alone.

27Now the LORD had said to Aaron, "Go out into the wilderness to meet Moses." So Aaron went and met Moses at the mountain of God, and he embraced him. 28Moses then told Aaron everything the LORD had commanded him to say. And he told him about the miraculous signs the LORD had commanded him to perform.

29Then Moses and Aaron returned to Egypt and called all the elders of Israel together. 30Aaron told them everything the LORD had told Moses, and Moses performed the miraculous signs as they watched. 31Then the people of Israel were convinced that the LORD had sent Moses and Aaron. When they heard that the LORD was concerned about them and had seen their misery, they bowed down and worshiped.

4:6 Or *with leprosy*. The Hebrew word used here can describe various skin diseases. **4:25** The Hebrew word for "feet" may refer here to the male sex organ.

CHAPTER 5

Moses and Aaron Speak to Pharaoh

After this presentation to Israel's leaders, Moses and Aaron went and spoke to Pharaoh. They told him, "This is what the LORD, the God of Israel, says: Let my people go so they may hold a festival in my honor in the wilderness."

[2]"Is that so?" retorted Pharaoh. "And who is the LORD? Why should I listen to him and let Israel go? I don't know the LORD, and I will not let Israel go."

[3]But Aaron and Moses persisted. "The God of the Hebrews has met with us," they declared. "So let us take a three-day journey into the wilderness so we can offer sacrifices to the LORD our God. If we don't, he will kill us with a plague or with the sword."

[4]Pharaoh replied, "Moses and Aaron, why are you distracting the people from their tasks? Get back to work! [5]Look, there are many of your people in the land, and you are stopping them from their work."

Making Bricks without Straw

[6]That same day Pharaoh sent this order to the Egyptian slave drivers and the Israelite foremen: [7]"Do not supply any more straw for making bricks. Make the people get it themselves! [8]But still require them to make the same number of bricks as before. Don't reduce the quota. They are lazy. That's why they are crying out, 'Let us go and offer sacrifices to our God.' [9]Load them down with more work. Make them sweat! That will teach them to listen to lies!"

[10]So the slave drivers and foremen went out and told the people: "This is what Pharaoh says: I will not provide any more straw for you. [11]Go and get it yourselves. Find it wherever you can. But you must produce just as many bricks as before!" [12]So the people scattered throughout the land of Egypt in search of stubble to use as straw.

[13]Meanwhile, the Egyptian slave drivers continued to push hard. "Meet your daily quota of bricks, just as you did when we provided you with straw!" they demanded. [14]Then they whipped the Israelite foremen they had put in charge of the work crews. "Why haven't you met your quotas either yesterday or today?" they demanded.

[15]So the Israelite foremen went to Pharaoh and pleaded with him. "Please don't treat your servants like this," they begged. [16]"We are given no straw, but the slave drivers still demand, 'Make bricks!' We are being beaten, but it isn't our fault! Your own people are to blame!"

[17]But Pharaoh shouted, "You're just lazy! Lazy! That's why you're saying, 'Let us go and offer sacrifices to the LORD.' [18]Now get back to work! No straw will be given to you, but you must still produce the full quota of bricks."

[19]The Israelite foremen could see that they were in serious trouble when they were told, "You must not reduce the number of bricks you make each day." [20]As they left Pharaoh's court, they confronted Moses and Aaron, who were waiting outside for them. [21]The foremen said to them, "May the LORD judge and punish you for making us stink before Pharaoh and his officials. You have put a sword into their hands, an excuse to kill us!"

[22]Then Moses went back to the LORD and protested, "Why have you brought all this trouble on your own people, Lord? Why did you send me? [23]Ever since I came to Pharaoh as your spokesman, he has been even more brutal to your people. And you have done nothing to rescue them!"

CHAPTER 6

Promises of Deliverance

Then the LORD told Moses, "Now you will see what I will do to Pharaoh. When he feels the force of my strong hand, he will let the people go. In fact, he will force them to leave his land!"

[2]And God said to Moses, "I am Yahweh—'the LORD.'* [3]I appeared to Abraham, to Isaac, and to Jacob as El-Shaddai—'God Almighty'*—but I did not reveal my name, Yahweh, to them. [4]And I reaffirmed my covenant with them. Under its terms, I promised to give them the land of Canaan, where they were living as foreigners. [5]You can be sure that I have heard the groans of the people of Israel, who are now slaves to the Egyptians. And I am well aware of my covenant with them.

6:2 *Yahweh* is a transliteration of the proper name *YHWH* that is sometimes rendered "Jehovah"; in this translation it is usually rendered "the LORD" (note the use of small capitals). **6:3** *El-Shaddai*, which means "God Almighty," is the name for God used in Gen 17:1; 28:3; 35:11; 43:14; 48:3.

[6]"Therefore, say to the people of Israel: 'I am the LORD. I will free you from your oppression and will rescue you from your slavery in Egypt. I will redeem you with a powerful arm and great acts of judgment. [7]I will claim you as my own people, and I will be your God. Then you will know that I am the LORD your God who has freed you from your oppression in Egypt. [8]I will bring you into the land I swore to give to Abraham, Isaac, and Jacob. I will give it to you as your very own possession. I am the LORD!'"

[9]So Moses told the people of Israel what the LORD had said, but they refused to listen anymore. They had become too discouraged by the brutality of their slavery.

[10]Then the LORD said to Moses, [11]"Go back to Pharaoh, the king of Egypt, and tell him to let the people of Israel leave his country."

[12]"But LORD!" Moses objected. "My own people won't listen to me anymore. How can I expect Pharaoh to listen? I'm such a clumsy speaker!*"

[13]But the LORD spoke to Moses and Aaron and gave them orders for the Israelites and for Pharaoh, the king of Egypt. The LORD commanded Moses and Aaron to lead the people of Israel out of Egypt.

The Ancestors of Moses and Aaron

[14]These are the ancestors of some of the clans of Israel:

The sons of Reuben, Israel's oldest son, were Hanoch, Pallu, Hezron, and Carmi. Their descendants became the clans of Reuben.

[15]The sons of Simeon were Jemuel, Jamin, Ohad, Jakin, Zohar, and Shaul. (Shaul's mother was a Canaanite woman.) Their descendants became the clans of Simeon.

[16]These are the descendants of Levi, as listed in their family records: The sons of Levi were Gershon, Kohath, and Merari. (Levi lived to be 137 years old.)

[17]The descendants of Gershon included Libni and Shimei, each of whom became the ancestor of a clan.

[18]The descendants of Kohath included Amram, Izhar, Hebron, and Uzziel. (Kohath lived to be 133 years old.)

[19]The descendants of Merari included Mahli and Mushi.

These are the clans of the Levites, as listed in their family records.

[20]Amram married his father's sister Jochebed, and she gave birth to his sons, Aaron and Moses. (Amram lived to be 137 years old.)

[21]The sons of Izhar were Korah, Nepheg, and Zicri.

[22]The sons of Uzziel were Mishael, Elzaphan, and Sithri.

[23]Aaron married Elisheba, the daughter of Amminadab and sister of Nahshon, and she gave birth to his sons, Nadab, Abihu, Eleazar, and Ithamar.

[24]The sons of Korah were Assir, Elkanah, and Abiasaph. Their descendants became the clans of Korah.

[25]Eleazar son of Aaron married one of the daughters of Putiel, and she gave birth to his son, Phinehas.

These are the ancestors of the Levite families, listed according to their clans.

[26]The Aaron and Moses named in this list are the same ones to whom the LORD said, "Lead the people of Israel out of the land of Egypt like an army." [27]It was Moses and Aaron who spoke to Pharaoh, the king of Egypt, about leading the people of Israel out of Egypt.

[28]When the LORD spoke to Moses in the land of Egypt, [29]he said to him, "I am the LORD! Tell Pharaoh, the king of Egypt, everything I am telling you." [30]But Moses argued with the LORD, saying, "I can't do it! I'm such a clumsy speaker! Why should Pharaoh listen to me?"

CHAPTER 7

Aaron's Staff Becomes a Serpent

Then the LORD said to Moses, "Pay close attention to this. I will make you seem like God to Pharaoh, and your brother, Aaron, will be your prophet. [2]Tell Aaron everything I command you, and Aaron must command Pharaoh to let the people of Israel leave his country. [3]But I will make Pharaoh's heart stubborn so I can multiply my miraculous signs and wonders in the land of Egypt. [4]Even then Pharaoh will refuse to listen to you. So I will bring down my fist on Egypt. Then I will rescue my forces—my people, the Israelites—from the land of Egypt with great acts of judgment. [5]When I

6:12 Hebrew *I have uncircumcised lips;* also in 6:30.

raise my powerful hand and bring out the Israelites, the Egyptians will know that I am the LORD."

6So Moses and Aaron did just as the LORD had commanded them. 7Moses was eighty years old, and Aaron was eighty-three when they made their demands to Pharaoh.

8Then the LORD said to Moses and Aaron, 9"Pharaoh will demand, 'Show me a miracle.' When he does this, say to Aaron, 'Take your staff and throw it down in front of Pharaoh, and it will become a serpent.*'"

10So Moses and Aaron went to Pharaoh and did what the LORD had commanded them. Aaron threw down his staff before Pharaoh and his officials, and it became a serpent! 11Then Pharaoh called in his own wise men and sorcerers, and these Egyptian magicians did the same thing with their magic. 12They threw down their staffs, which also became serpents! But then Aaron's staff swallowed up their staffs. 13Pharaoh's heart, however, remained hard. He still refused to listen, just as the LORD had predicted.

A Plague of Blood

14Then the LORD said to Moses, "Pharaoh's heart is stubborn,* and he still refuses to let the people go. 15So go to Pharaoh in the morning as he goes down to the river. Stand on the bank of the Nile and meet him there. Be sure to take along the staff that turned into a snake. 16Then announce to him, 'The LORD, the God of the Hebrews, has sent me to tell you, "Let my people go, so they can worship me in the wilderness." Until now, you have refused to listen to him. 17So this is what the LORD says: "I will show you that I am the LORD." Look! I will strike the water of the Nile with this staff in my hand, and the river will turn to blood. 18The fish in it will die, and the river will stink. The Egyptians will not be able to drink any water from the Nile.'"

19Then the LORD said to Moses: "Tell Aaron, 'Take your staff and raise your hand over the waters of Egypt—all its rivers, canals, ponds, and all the reservoirs. Turn all the water to blood. Everywhere in Egypt the water will turn to blood, even the water stored in wooden bowls and stone pots.'"

20So Moses and Aaron did just as the LORD commanded them. As Pharaoh and all of his officials watched, Aaron raised his staff and struck the water of the Nile. Suddenly, the whole river turned to blood! 21The fish in the river died, and the water became so foul that the Egyptians couldn't drink it. There was blood everywhere throughout the land of Egypt. 22But again the magicians of Egypt used their magic, and they, too, turned water into blood. So Pharaoh's heart remained hard. He refused to listen to Moses and Aaron, just as the LORD had predicted. 23Pharaoh returned to his palace and put the whole thing out of his mind. 24Then all the Egyptians dug along the riverbank to find drinking water, for they couldn't drink the water from the Nile.

25Seven days passed from the time the LORD struck the Nile.

AMAZING FACTS

There were frogs, gnats, flies, and locusts everywhere, but they weren't just pests. God used them to free the Israelites!

EXODUS 7:15–11:10

CHAPTER 8

A Plague of Frogs

1*Then the LORD said to Moses, "Go back to Pharaoh and announce to him, 'This is what the LORD says: Let my people go, so they can worship me. 2If you refuse to let them go, I will send a plague of frogs across your entire land. 3The Nile River will swarm with frogs. They will come up out of the river and into your palace, even into your bedroom and onto your bed! They will enter the houses of your officials and your people. They will even

7:9 Hebrew *tannin*, which elsewhere refers to a sea monster. Greek version translates it "dragon." **7:14** Hebrew *heavy*. **8:1** Verses 8:1-4 are numbered 7:26-29 in Hebrew text.

jump into your ovens and your kneading
bowls. [4]Frogs will jump on you, your people,
and all your officials.'"

[5]*Then the LORD said to Moses, "Tell
Aaron, 'Raise the staff in your hand over all
the rivers, canals, and ponds of Egypt, and
bring up frogs over all the land.'" [6]So Aaron
raised his hand over the waters of Egypt, and
frogs came up and covered the whole land!
[7]But the magicians were able to do the same
thing with their magic. They, too, caused
frogs to come up on the land of Egypt.

[8]Then Pharaoh summoned Moses and
Aaron and begged, "Plead with the LORD to
take the frogs away from me and my people. I
will let your people go, so they can offer sacri-
fices to the LORD."

[9]"You set the time!" Moses replied. "Tell
me when you want me to pray for you, your
officials, and your people. Then you and your
houses will be rid of the frogs. They will re-
main only in the Nile River."

[10]"Do it tomorrow," Pharaoh said.

"All right," Moses replied, "it will be as you
have said. Then you will know that there is no
one like the LORD our God. [11]The frogs will
leave you and your houses, your officials, and
your people. They will remain only in the Nile
River."

[12]So Moses and Aaron left Pharaoh's palace,
and Moses cried out to the LORD about the
frogs he had inflicted on Pharaoh. [13]And the
LORD did just what Moses had predicted.
The frogs in the houses, the courtyards, and the
fields all died. [14]The Egyptians piled them into
great heaps, and a terrible stench filled the
land. [15]But when Pharaoh saw that relief had
come, he became stubborn.* He refused to lis-
ten to Moses and Aaron, just as the LORD had
predicted.

A Plague of Gnats

[16]So the LORD said to Moses, "Tell Aaron,
'Raise your staff and strike the ground. The
dust will turn into swarms of gnats through-
out the land of Egypt.'" [17]So Moses and Aaron
did just as the LORD had commanded them.
When Aaron raised his hand and struck the
ground with his staff, gnats infested the en-
tire land, covering the Egyptians and their an-
imals. All the dust in the land of Egypt turned
into gnats. [18]Pharaoh's magicians tried to do
the same thing with their secret arts, but this
time they failed. And the gnats covered every-
one, people and animals alike.

[19]"This is the finger of God!" the magicians
exclaimed to Pharaoh. But Pharaoh's heart
remained hard. He wouldn't listen to them,
just as the LORD had predicted.

A Plague of Flies

[20]Then the LORD told Moses, "Get up early in
the morning and stand in Pharaoh's way as he
goes down to the river. Say to him, 'This is
what the LORD says: Let my people go, so they
can worship me. [21]If you refuse, then I will
send swarms of flies on you, your officials,
your people, and all the houses. The Egyptian
homes will be filled with flies, and the ground
will be covered with them. [22]But this time I
will spare the region of Goshen, where my
people live. No flies will be found there. Then
you will know that I am the LORD and that I am
present even in the heart of your land. [23]I will
make a clear distinction between* my people
and your people. This miraculous sign will
happen tomorrow.'"

[24]And the LORD did just as he had said. A
thick swarm of flies filled Pharaoh's palace
and the houses of his officials. The whole
land of Egypt was thrown into chaos by the
flies.

[25]Pharaoh called for Moses and Aaron. "All
right! Go ahead and offer sacrifices to your
God," he said. "But do it here in this land."

[26]But Moses replied, "That wouldn't be
right. The Egyptians detest the sacrifices that
we offer to the LORD our God. Look, if we of-
fer our sacrifices here where the Egyptians
can see us, they will stone us. [27]We must take
a three-day trip into the wilderness to offer
sacrifices to the LORD our God, just as he has
commanded us."

[28]"All right, go ahead," Pharaoh replied. "I
will let you go into the wilderness to offer sac-
rifices to the LORD your God. But don't go too
far away. Now hurry and pray for me."

[29]Moses answered, "As soon as I leave you, I
will pray to the LORD, and tomorrow the
swarms of flies will disappear from you and
your officials and all your people. But I am
warning you, Pharaoh, don't lie to us again

8:5 Verses 8:5-32 are numbered 8:1-28 in Hebrew text. **8:15** Hebrew *made his heart heavy;* also in 8:32. **8:23** As in Greek and Latin versions; Hebrew reads *I will set redemption between.*

and refuse to let the people go to sacrifice to the LORD."

30So Moses left Pharaoh's palace and pleaded with the LORD to remove all the flies. 31And the LORD did as Moses asked and caused the swarms of flies to disappear from Pharaoh, his officials, and his people. Not a single fly remained. 32But Pharaoh again became stubborn and refused to let the people go.

CHAPTER 9

A Plague against Livestock

"Go back to Pharaoh," the LORD commanded Moses. "Tell him, 'This is what the LORD, the God of the Hebrews, says: Let my people go, so they can worship me. 2If you continue to hold them and refuse to let them go, 3the hand of the LORD will strike all your livestock—your horses, donkeys, camels, cattle, sheep, and goats—with a deadly plague. 4But the LORD will again make a distinction between the livestock of the Israelites and that of the Egyptians. Not a single one of Israel's animals will die! 5The LORD has already set the time for the plague to begin. He has declared that he will strike the land tomorrow.'"

6And the LORD did just as he had said. The next morning all the livestock of the Egyptians died, but the Israelites didn't lose a single animal. 7Pharaoh sent his officials to investigate, and they discovered that the Israelites had not lost a single animal! But even so, Pharaoh's heart remained stubborn,* and he still refused to let the people go.

A Plague of Festering Boils

8Then the LORD said to Moses and Aaron, "Take handfuls of soot from a brick kiln, and have Moses toss it into the air while Pharaoh watches. 9The ashes will spread like fine dust over the whole land of Egypt, causing festering boils to break out on people and animals throughout the land."

10So they took soot from a brick kiln and went and stood before Pharaoh. As Pharaoh watched, Moses threw the soot into the air, and boils broke out on people and animals alike. 11Even the magicians were unable to stand before Moses, because the boils had broken out on them and all the Egyptians. 12But the LORD hardened Pharaoh's heart, and just as the LORD had predicted to Moses, Pharaoh refused to listen.

A Plague of Hail

13Then the LORD said to Moses, "Get up early in the morning and stand before Pharaoh. Tell him, 'This is what the LORD, the God of the Hebrews, says: Let my people go, so they can worship me. 14If you don't, I will send more plagues on you* and your officials and your people. Then you will know that there is no one like me in all the earth. 15By now I could have lifted my hand and struck you and your people with a plague to wipe you off the face of the earth. 16But I have spared you for a purpose—to show you my power* and to spread my fame throughout the earth. 17But you still lord it over my people and refuse to let them go. 18So tomorrow at this time I will send a hailstorm more devastating than any in all the history of Egypt. 19Quick! Order your livestock and servants to come in from the fields to find shelter. Any person or animal left outside will die when the hail falls.'"

20Some of Pharaoh's officials were afraid because of what the LORD had said. They quickly brought their servants and livestock in from the fields. 21But those who paid no attention to the word of the LORD left theirs out in the open.

22Then the LORD said to Moses, "Lift your hand toward the sky so hail may fall on the people, the livestock, and all the plants throughout the land of Egypt."

23So Moses lifted his staff toward the sky, and the LORD sent thunder and hail, and lightning flashed toward the earth. The LORD sent a tremendous hailstorm against all the land of Egypt. 24Never in all the history of Egypt had there been a storm like that, with such devastating hail and continuous lightning. 25It left all of Egypt in ruins. The hail struck down everything in the open field—people, animals, and plants alike. Even the trees were destroyed. 26The only place without hail was the region of Goshen, where the people of Israel lived.

27Then Pharaoh quickly summoned Moses and Aaron. "This time I have sinned," he confessed. "The LORD is the righteous one, and my people and I are wrong. 28Please beg the

9:7 Hebrew *heavy*. **9:14** Hebrew *on your heart*. **9:16** Greek version reads *to display my power in you;* compare Rom 9:17.

LORD to end this terrifying thunder and hail. We've had enough. I will let you go; you don't need to stay any longer."

29"All right," Moses replied. "As soon as I leave the city, I will lift my hands and pray to the LORD. Then the thunder and hail will stop, and you will know that the earth belongs to the LORD. 30But I know that you and your officials still do not fear the LORD God."

31(All the flax and barley were ruined by the hail, because the barley had formed heads and the flax was budding. 32But the wheat and the emmer wheat were spared, because they had not yet sprouted from the ground.)

33So Moses left Pharaoh's court and went out of the city. When he lifted his hands to the LORD, the thunder and hail stopped, and the downpour ceased. 34But when Pharaoh saw that the rain, hail, and thunder had stopped, he and his officials sinned again, and Pharaoh again became stubborn.* 35Because his heart was hard, Pharaoh refused to let the people leave, just as the LORD had predicted through Moses.

CHAPTER 10

A Plague of Locusts

Then the LORD said to Moses, "Return to Pharaoh and make your demands again. I have made him and his officials stubborn* so I can display my miraculous signs among them. 2I've also done it so you can tell your children and grandchildren about how I made a mockery of the Egyptians and about the signs I displayed among them—and so you will know that I am the LORD."

3So Moses and Aaron went to Pharaoh and said, "This is what the LORD, the God of the Hebrews, says: How long will you refuse to submit to me? Let my people go, so they can worship me. 4If you refuse, watch out! For tomorrow I will bring a swarm of locusts on your country. 5They will cover the land so that you won't be able to see the ground. They will devour what little is left of your crops after the hailstorm, including all the trees growing in the fields. 6They will overrun your palaces and the homes of your officials and all the houses in Egypt. Never in the history of Egypt have your ancestors seen a plague like this one!" And with that, Moses turned and left Pharaoh.

7Pharaoh's officials now came to Pharaoh and appealed to him. "How long will you let this man hold us hostage? Let the men go to worship the LORD their God! Don't you realize that Egypt lies in ruins?"

8So Moses and Aaron were brought back to Pharaoh. "All right," he told them, "go and worship the LORD your God. But who exactly will be going with you?"

9Moses replied, "We will all go—young and old, our sons and daughters, and our flocks and herds. We must all join together in celebrating a festival to the LORD."

10Pharaoh retorted, "The LORD will certainly need to be with you if I let you take your little ones! I can see through your evil plan. 11Never! Only the men may go and worship the LORD, since that is what you requested." And Pharaoh threw them out of the palace.

12Then the LORD said to Moses, "Raise your hand over the land of Egypt to bring on the locusts. Let them cover the land and devour every plant that survived the hailstorm."

13So Moses raised his staff over Egypt, and the LORD caused an east wind to blow over the land all that day and through the night. When morning arrived, the east wind had brought the locusts. 14And the locusts swarmed over the whole land of Egypt, settling in dense swarms from one end of the country to the other. It was the worst locust plague in Egyptian history, and there has never been another one like it. 15For the locusts covered the whole country and darkened the land. They devoured every plant in the fields and all the fruit on the trees that had survived the hailstorm. Not a single leaf was left on the trees and plants throughout the land of Egypt.

16Pharaoh quickly summoned Moses and Aaron. "I have sinned against the LORD your God and against you," he confessed. 17"Forgive my sin, just this once, and plead with the LORD your God to take away this death from me."

18So Moses left Pharaoh's court and pleaded with the LORD. 19The LORD responded by shifting the wind, and the strong west wind blew the locusts into the Red Sea.* Not a single locust remained in all the land of Egypt.

9:34 Hebrew *made his heart heavy.* **10:1** Hebrew *have made his heart and his officials' hearts heavy.* **10:19** Hebrew *sea of reeds.*

[20]But the LORD hardened Pharaoh's heart
again, so he refused to let the people go.

A Plague of Darkness

[21]Then the LORD said to Moses, "Lift your
hand toward heaven, and the land of Egypt
will be covered with a darkness so thick you
can feel it." [22]So Moses lifted his hand to the
sky, and a deep darkness covered the entire
land of Egypt for three days. [23]During all that
time the people could not see each other, and
no one moved. But there was light as usual
where the people of Israel lived.

[24]Finally, Pharaoh called for Moses. "Go
and worship the LORD," he said. "But leave
your flocks and herds here. You may even
take your little ones with you."

[25]"No," Moses said, "you must provide us
with animals for sacrifices and burnt offer-
ings to the LORD our God. [26]All our livestock
must go with us, too; not a hoof can be left be-
hind. We must choose our sacrifices for the

THE PLAGUES
What Happened/Result

BLOOD	God turns water into blood/Pharaoh's magicians also turn water into blood 7:14-24
FROGS	Frogs cover the land/Pharaoh's magicians also make frogs appear 8:1-15
GNATS	All the dust of Egypt turns into gnats/Magicians say it is the "finger of God," but Pharaoh's heart is still hard and stubborn 8:16-19
FLIES	Swarms of flies cover the land/Pharaoh promises to let the Hebrews go, but then hardens his heart 8:20-32
LIVESTOCK	All the Egyptians' livestock die—but none of Israel's are even sick/Pharaoh still refuses to let the people go 9:1-7
BOILS	Horrible boils break out on everyone/Magicians cannot do anything because they have boils too 9:8-12
HAIL	Hailstorms kill all the slaves and animals left outside/Pharaoh refuses to let the people go 9:13-35
LOCUSTS	Locusts cover Egypt and eat everything/Everyone advises Pharaoh to let the Hebrews go, but he refuses 10:1-20
DARKNESS	Total darkness covers Egypt for three days, but the Hebrews still have light/Pharaoh promises to let Israel go, but changes his mind 10:21-29
DEATH OF FIRSTBORN	The firstborn of all the people and livestock of Egypt die/Pharaoh makes Israel leave, but changes his mind and chases after them 11:1–12:33

LORD our God from among these animals. And we won't know how we are to worship the LORD until we get there."

27But the LORD hardened Pharaoh's heart once more, and he would not let them go. 28"Get out of here!" Pharaoh shouted at Moses. "I'm warning you. Never come back to see me again! The day you see my face, you will die!"

29"Very well," Moses replied. "I will never see your face again."

CHAPTER 11

Death for Egypt's Firstborn

Then the LORD said to Moses, "I will strike Pharaoh and the land of Egypt with one more blow. After that, Pharaoh will let you leave this country. In fact, he will be so eager to get rid of you that he will force you all to leave. 2Tell all the Israelite men and women to ask their Egyptian neighbors for articles of silver and gold." 3(Now the LORD had caused the Egyptians to look favorably on the people of Israel. And Moses was considered a very great man in the land of Egypt, respected by Pharaoh's officials and the Egyptian people alike.)

4Moses had announced to Pharaoh, "This is what the LORD says: At midnight tonight I will pass through the heart of Egypt. 5All the firstborn sons will die in every family in Egypt, from the oldest son of Pharaoh, who sits on his throne, to the oldest son of his lowliest servant girl who grinds the flour. Even the firstborn of all the livestock will die. 6Then a loud wail will rise throughout the land of Egypt, a wail like no one has heard before or will ever hear again. 7But among the Israelites it will be so peaceful that not even a dog will bark. Then you will know that the LORD makes a distinction between the Egyptians and the Israelites. 8All the officials of Egypt will run to me and fall to the ground before me. 'Please leave!' they will beg. 'Hurry! And take all your followers with you.' Only then will I go!" Then, burning with anger, Moses left Pharaoh.

9Now the LORD had told Moses earlier, "Pharaoh will not listen to you, but then I will do even more mighty miracles in the land of Egypt." 10Moses and Aaron performed these miracles in Pharaoh's presence, but the LORD hardened Pharaoh's heart, and he wouldn't let the Israelites leave the country.

CHAPTER 12

The First Passover

While the Israelites were still in the land of Egypt, the LORD gave the following instructions to Moses and Aaron: 2"From now on, this month will be the first month of the year for you. 3Announce to the whole community of Israel that on the tenth day of this month each family must choose a lamb or a young goat for a sacrifice, one animal for each household. 4If a family is too small to eat a whole animal, let them share with another family in the neighborhood. Divide the animal according to the size of each family and how much they can eat. 5The animal you select must be a one-year-old male, either a sheep or a goat, with no defects.

6"Take special care of this chosen animal until the evening of the fourteenth day of this first month. Then the whole assembly of the community of Israel must slaughter their lamb or young goat at twilight. 7They are to take some of the blood and smear it on the sides and top of the doorframes of the houses where they eat the animal. 8That same night they must roast the meat over a fire and eat it along with bitter salad greens and bread made without yeast. 9Do not eat any of the meat raw or boiled in water. The whole animal—including the head, legs, and internal organs—must be roasted over a fire. 10Do not leave any of it until the next morning. Burn whatever is not eaten before morning.

11"These are your instructions for eating this meal: Be fully dressed,* wear your sandals, and carry your walking stick in your hand. Eat the meal with urgency, for this is the LORD's Passover. 12On that night I will pass through the land of Egypt and strike down every firstborn son and firstborn male animal in the land of Egypt. I will execute judgment against all the gods of Egypt, for I am the LORD! 13But the blood on your doorposts will serve as a sign, marking the houses where you are staying. When I see the blood, I will pass over you. This plague of death will not touch you when I strike the land of Egypt.

12:11 Hebrew *Bind up your loins.*

[14]"This is a day to remember. Each year, from generation to generation, you must celebrate it as a special festival to the LORD. This is a law for all time. [15]For seven days the bread you eat must be made without yeast. On the first day of the festival, remove every trace of yeast from your homes. Anyone who eats bread made with yeast during the seven days of the festival will be cut off from the community of Israel. [16]On the first day of the festival and again on the seventh day, all the people must observe an official day for holy assembly. No work of any kind may be done on these days except in the preparation of food.

[17]"Celebrate this Festival of Unleavened Bread, for it will remind you that I brought your forces out of the land of Egypt on this very day. This festival will be a permanent law for you; celebrate this day from generation to generation. [18]The bread you eat must be made without yeast from the evening of the fourteenth day of the first month until the evening of the twenty-first day of that month. [19]During those seven days, there must be no trace of yeast in your homes. Anyone who eats anything made with yeast during this week will be cut off from the community of Israel. These regulations apply both to the foreigners living among you and to the native-born Israelites. [20]During those days you must not eat anything made with yeast. Wherever you live, eat only bread made without yeast."

[21]Then Moses called all the elders of Israel together and said to them, "Go, pick out a lamb or young goat for each of your families, and slaughter the Passover animal. [22]Drain the blood into a basin. Then take a bundle of hyssop branches and dip it into the blood. Brush the hyssop across the top and sides of the doorframes of your houses. And no one may go out through the door until morning. [23]For the LORD will pass through the land to strike down the Egyptians. But when he sees the blood on the top and sides of the doorframe, the LORD will pass over your home. He will not permit his death angel to enter your house and strike you down.

[24]"Remember, these instructions are a permanent law that you and your descendants must observe forever. [25]When you enter the land the LORD has promised to give you, you will continue to observe this ceremony. [26]Then your children will ask, 'What does this ceremony mean?' [27]And you will reply, 'It is the Passover sacrifice to the LORD, for he passed over the houses of the Israelites in Egypt. And though he struck the Egyptians, he spared our families.'" When Moses had finished speaking, all the people bowed down to the ground and worshiped.

[28]So the people of Israel did just as the LORD had commanded through Moses and Aaron. [29]And that night at midnight, the LORD struck down all the firstborn sons in the land of Egypt, from the firstborn son of Pharaoh, who sat on his throne, to the firstborn son of the prisoner in the dungeon. Even the firstborn of their livestock were killed. [30]Pharaoh and all his officials and all the people of Egypt woke up during the night, and loud wailing was heard throughout the land of Egypt. There was not a single house where someone had not died.

Israel's Exodus from Egypt

[31]Pharaoh sent for Moses and Aaron during the night. "Get out!" he ordered. "Leave my people—and take the rest of the Israelites with you! Go and worship the LORD as you have requested. [32]Take your flocks and herds, as you said, and be gone. Go, but bless me as you leave." [33]All the Egyptians urged the people of Israel to get out of the land as quickly as possible, for they thought, "We will all die!"

[34]The Israelites took their bread dough before yeast was added. They wrapped their kneading boards in their cloaks and carried them on their shoulders. [35]And the people of Israel did as Moses had instructed; they asked the Egyptians for clothing and articles of silver and gold. [36]The LORD caused the Egyptians to look favorably on the Israelites, and they gave the Israelites whatever they asked for. So they stripped the Egyptians of their wealth!

[37]That night the people of Israel left Rameses and started for Succoth. There were about 600,000 men,* plus all the women and children. [38]A rabble of non-Israelites went with them, along with great flocks and herds of livestock. [39]For bread they baked flat cakes from the dough without yeast they had brought

12:37 Or *fighting men;* Hebrew reads *men on foot.*

from Egypt. It was made without yeast because the people were driven out of Egypt in such a hurry that they had no time to prepare the bread or other food.

40The people of Israel had lived in Egypt* for 430 years. 41In fact, it was on the last day of the 430th year that all the LORD's forces left the land. 42On this night the LORD kept his promise to bring his people out of the land of Egypt. So this night belongs to him, and it must be commemorated every year by all the Israelites, from generation to generation.

Instructions for the Passover

43Then the LORD said to Moses and Aaron, "These are the instructions for the festival of Passover. No outsiders are allowed to eat the Passover meal. 44But any slave who has been purchased may eat it if he has been circumcised. 45Temporary residents and hired servants may not eat it. 46Each Passover lamb must be eaten in one house. Do not carry any of its meat outside, and do not break any of its bones. 47The whole community of Israel must celebrate this Passover festival.

48"If there are foreigners living among you who want to celebrate the LORD's Passover, let all their males be circumcised. Only then may they celebrate the Passover with you like any native-born Israelite. But no uncircumcised male may ever eat the Passover meal. 49This instruction applies to everyone, whether a native-born Israelite or a foreigner living among you."

50So all the people of Israel followed all the LORD's commands to Moses and Aaron. 51On that very day the LORD brought the people of Israel out of the land of Egypt like an army.

CHAPTER 13

Dedication of the Firstborn

Then the LORD said to Moses, 2"Dedicate to me every firstborn among the Israelites. The first offspring to be born, of both humans and animals, belongs to me."

3So Moses said to the people, "This is a day to remember forever—the day you left Egypt, the place of your slavery. Today the LORD has brought you out by the power of his mighty hand. (Remember, eat no food containing yeast.) 4On this day in early spring, in the month of Abib,* you have been set free. 5You must celebrate this event in this month each year after the LORD brings you into the land of the Canaanites, Hittites, Amorites, Hivites, and Jebusites. (He swore to your ancestors that he would give you this land—a land flowing with milk and honey.) 6For seven days the bread you eat must be made without yeast. Then on the seventh day, celebrate a feast to the LORD. 7Eat bread without yeast during those seven days. In fact, there must be no yeast bread or any yeast at all found within the borders of your land during this time.

8"On the seventh day you must explain to your children, 'I am celebrating what the LORD did for me when I left Egypt.' 9This annual festival will be a visible sign to you, like a mark branded on your hand or your forehead. Let it remind you always to recite this teaching of the LORD: 'With a strong hand, the LORD rescued you from Egypt.'* 10So observe the decree of this festival at the appointed time each year.

11"This is what you must do when the LORD fulfills the promise he swore to you and to your ancestors. When he gives you the land where the Canaanites now live, 12you must present all firstborn sons and firstborn male animals to the LORD, for they belong to him. 13A firstborn donkey may be bought back from the LORD by presenting a lamb or young goat in its place. But if you do not buy it back, you must break its neck. However, you must buy back every firstborn son.

14"And in the future, your children will ask you, 'What does all this mean?' Then you will tell them, 'With the power of his mighty hand, the LORD brought us out of Egypt, the place of our slavery. 15Pharaoh stubbornly refused to let us go, so the LORD killed all the firstborn males throughout the land of Egypt, both people and animals. That is why I now sacrifice all the firstborn males to the LORD—except that the firstborn sons are always bought back.' 16This ceremony will be like a mark branded on your hand or your forehead. It is a reminder that the power of the LORD's mighty hand brought us out of Egypt."

12:40 Samaritan Pentateuch reads *in Canaan and Egypt;* Greek version reads *in Egypt and Canaan.* **13:4** Hebrew *On this day in the month of Abib.* This first month of the ancient Hebrew lunar calendar usually occurs within the months of March and April. **13:9** Or *Let it remind you always to keep the instructions of the LORD on the tip of your tongue, because with a strong hand, the LORD rescued you from Egypt.*

Israel's Wilderness Detour

[17]When Pharaoh finally let the people go, God did not lead them along the main road that runs through Philistine territory, even though that was the shortest route to the Promised Land. God said, "If the people are faced with a battle, they might change their minds and return to Egypt." [18]So God led them in a roundabout way through the wilderness toward the Red Sea.* Thus the Israelites left Egypt like an army ready for battle.*

[19]Moses took the bones of Joseph with him, for Joseph had made the sons of Israel swear to do this. He said, "God will certainly come to help you. When he does, you must take my bones with you from this place."

[20]The Israelites left Succoth and camped at Etham on the edge of the wilderness. [21]The LORD went ahead of them. He guided them during the day with a pillar of cloud, and he provided light at night with a pillar of fire. This allowed them to travel by day or by night. [22]And the LORD did not remove the pillar of cloud or pillar of fire from its place in front of the people.

CHAPTER 14

Then the LORD gave these instructions to Moses: [2]"Order the Israelites to turn back and camp by Pi-hahiroth between Migdol and the sea. Camp there along the shore, across from Baal-zephon. [3]Then Pharaoh will think, 'The Israelites are confused. They are trapped in the wilderness!' [4]And once again I will harden Pharaoh's heart, and he will chase after you.* I have planned this in order to display my glory through Pharaoh and his whole army. After this the Egyptians will know that I am the LORD!" So the Israelites camped there as they were told.

The Egyptians Pursue Israel

[5]When word reached the king of Egypt that the Israelites had fled, Pharaoh and his officials changed their minds. "What have we done, letting all those Israelite slaves get away?" they asked. [6]So Pharaoh harnessed his chariot and called up his troops. [7]He took with him 600 of Egypt's best chariots, along with the rest of the chariots of Egypt, each with its commander. [8]The LORD hardened the heart of Pharaoh, the king of Egypt, so he chased after the people of Israel, who had left with fists raised in defiance. [9]The Egyptians chased after them with all the forces in Pharaoh's army—all his horses and chariots, his charioteers, and his troops. The Egyptians caught up with the people of Israel as they were camped beside the shore near Pi-hahiroth, across from Baal-zephon.

[10]As Pharaoh approached, the people of Israel looked up and panicked when they saw the Egyptians overtaking them. They cried out to the LORD, [11]and they said to Moses, "Why did you bring us out here to die in the wilderness? Weren't there enough graves for

13:18a Hebrew *sea of reeds.* **13:18b** Greek version reads *left Egypt in the fifth generation.* **14:4** Hebrew *after them.*

DOUBTERS IN THE BIBLE

Doubter	*Doubtful Moment*	*Reference*
Abraham	When God told him he would be a father	Genesis 17:17
Sarah	When she heard she would be a mother	Genesis 18:12
Moses	When God told him to return to Egypt to lead the people	Exodus 3:10-15
Israelites	Whenever they faced hard times in the wilderness	Exodus 16:1-3
Gideon	When God told him he would lead his people	Judges 6:14-23
Zechariah	When God told him he would be a father	Luke 1:18
Thomas	When his friends told him that Jesus had risen	John 20:24-25

Many of the people God used to accomplish great things started out as real doubters.

us in Egypt? What have you done to us? Why did you make us leave Egypt? [12]Didn't we tell you this would happen while we were still in Egypt? We said, 'Leave us alone! Let us be slaves to the Egyptians. It's better to be a slave in Egypt than a corpse in the wilderness!'"

[13]But Moses told the people, "Don't be afraid. Just stand still and watch the LORD rescue you today. The Egyptians you see today will never be seen again. [14]The LORD himself will fight for you. Just stay calm."

Escape through the Red Sea

[15]Then the LORD said to Moses, "Why are you crying out to me? Tell the people to get moving! [16]Pick up your staff and raise your hand over the sea. Divide the water so the Israelites can walk through the middle of the sea on dry ground. [17]And I will harden the hearts of the Egyptians, and they will charge in after the Israelites. My great glory will be displayed through Pharaoh and his troops, his chariots, and his charioteers. [18]When my glory is displayed through them, all Egypt will see my glory and know that I am the LORD!"

[19]Then the angel of God, who had been leading the people of Israel, moved to the rear of the camp. The pillar of cloud also moved from the front and stood behind them. [20]The cloud settled between the Egyptian and Israelite camps. As darkness fell, the cloud turned to fire, lighting up the night. But the Egyptians and Israelites did not approach each other all night.

[21]Then Moses raised his hand over the sea, and the LORD opened up a path through the water with a strong east wind. The wind blew all that night, turning the seabed into dry land. [22]So the people of Israel walked through the middle of the sea on dry ground, with walls of water on each side!

[23]Then the Egyptians—all of Pharaoh's horses, chariots, and charioteers—chased them into the middle of the sea. [24]But just before dawn the LORD looked down on the Egyptian army from the pillar of fire and cloud, and he threw their forces into total confusion. [25]He twisted* their chariot wheels, making their chariots difficult to drive. "Let's get out of here—away from these Israelites!" the Egyptians shouted. "The LORD is fighting for them against Egypt!"

[26]When all the Israelites had reached the other side, the LORD said to Moses, "Raise your hand over the sea again. Then the waters will rush back and cover the Egyptians and their chariots and charioteers." [27]So as the sun began to rise, Moses raised his hand over the sea, and the water rushed back into its usual place. The Egyptians tried to escape, but the LORD swept them into the sea. [28]Then the waters returned and covered all the chariots and charioteers—the entire army of Pharaoh. Of all the Egyptians who had chased the Israelites into the sea, not a single one survived.

[29]But the people of Israel had walked through the middle of the sea on dry ground, as the water stood up like a wall on both sides. [30]That is how the LORD rescued Israel from the hand of the Egyptians that day. And the Israelites saw the bodies of the Egyptians washed up on the seashore. [31]When the people of Israel saw the mighty power that the LORD had unleashed against the Egyptians, they were filled with awe before him. They put their faith in the LORD and in his servant Moses.

CHAPTER 15

A Song of Deliverance

Then Moses and the people of Israel sang this song to the LORD:

"I will sing to the LORD,
for he has triumphed gloriously;
he has hurled both horse and rider
into the sea.
[2] The LORD is my strength and my song;
he has given me victory.
This is my God, and I will praise him—
my father's God, and I will exalt him!
[3] The LORD is a warrior;
Yahweh* is his name!
[4] Pharaoh's chariots and army
he has hurled into the sea.
The finest of Pharaoh's officers
are drowned in the Red Sea.*
[5] The deep waters gushed over them;
they sank to the bottom like a stone.

[6] "Your right hand, O LORD,
is glorious in power.

14:25 As in Greek version, Samaritan Pentateuch, and Syriac version; Hebrew reads *He removed.* **15:3** *Yahweh* is a transliteration of the proper name *YHWH* that is sometimes rendered "Jehovah"; in this translation it is usually rendered "the LORD" (note the use of small capitals). **15:4** Hebrew *sea of reeds;* also in 15:22.

Your right hand, O LORD,
smashes the enemy.
7 In the greatness of your majesty,
you overthrow those who rise against you.
You unleash your blazing fury;
it consumes them like straw.
8 At the blast of your breath,
the waters piled up!
The surging waters stood straight like a wall;
in the heart of the sea the deep waters became hard.

9 "The enemy boasted, 'I will chase them
and catch up with them.
I will plunder them
and consume them.
I will flash my sword;
my powerful hand will destroy them.'
10 But you blew with your breath,
and the sea covered them.
They sank like lead
in the mighty waters.

11 "Who is like you among the gods, O LORD—
glorious in holiness,
awesome in splendor,
performing great wonders?
12 You raised your right hand,
and the earth swallowed our enemies.

13 "With your unfailing love you lead
the people you have redeemed.
In your might, you guide them
to your sacred home.
14 The peoples hear and tremble;
anguish grips those who live in Philistia.
15 The leaders of Edom are terrified;
the nobles of Moab tremble.
All who live in Canaan melt away;
16 terror and dread fall upon them.
The power of your arm
makes them lifeless as stone
until your people pass by, O LORD,
until the people you purchased pass by.
17 You will bring them in and plant them on your own mountain—
the place, O LORD, reserved for your own dwelling,
the sanctuary, O Lord, that your hands have established.
18 The LORD will reign forever and ever!"

19 When Pharaoh's horses, chariots, and charioteers rushed into the sea, the LORD brought the water crashing down on them. But the people of Israel had walked through the middle of the sea on dry ground!

20 Then Miriam the prophet, Aaron's sister, took a tambourine and led all the women as they played their tambourines and danced. 21 And Miriam sang this song:

"Sing to the LORD,
for he has triumphed gloriously;
he has hurled both horse and rider
into the sea."

Bitter Water at Marah

22 Then Moses led the people of Israel away from the Red Sea, and they moved out into the desert of Shur. They traveled in this desert for three days without finding any water. 23 When they came to the oasis of Marah, the water was too bitter to drink. So they called the place Marah (which means "bitter").

24 Then the people complained and turned against Moses. "What are we going to drink?" they demanded. 25 So Moses cried out to the LORD for help, and the LORD showed him a piece of wood. Moses threw it into the water, and this made the water good to drink.

It was there at Marah that the LORD set before them the following decree as a standard to test their faithfulness to him. 26 He said, "If you will listen carefully to the voice of the LORD your God and do what is right in his sight, obeying his commands and keeping all his decrees, then I will not make you suffer any of the diseases I sent on the Egyptians; for I am the LORD who heals you."

27 After leaving Marah, the Israelites traveled on to the oasis of Elim, where they found twelve springs and seventy palm trees. They camped there beside the water.

CHAPTER 16

Manna and Quail from Heaven

Then the whole community of Israel set out from Elim and journeyed into the wilderness of Sin,* between Elim and Mount Sinai. They

16:1a The geographical name *Sin* is related to *Sinai* and should not be confused with the English word *sin*.

arrived there on the fifteenth day of the second month, one month after leaving the land of Egypt.* [2]There, too, the whole community of Israel complained about Moses and Aaron.

[3]"If only the LORD had killed us back in Egypt," they moaned. "There we sat around pots filled with meat and ate all the bread we wanted. But now you have brought us into this wilderness to starve us all to death."

[4]Then the LORD said to Moses, "Look, I'm going to rain down food from heaven for you. Each day the people can go out and pick up as much food as they need for that day. I will test them in this to see whether or not they will follow my instructions. [5]On the sixth day they will gather food, and when they prepare it, there will be twice as much as usual."

[6]So Moses and Aaron said to all the people of Israel, "By evening you will realize it was the LORD who brought you out of the land of Egypt. [7]In the morning you will see the glory of the LORD, because he has heard your complaints, which are against him, not against us. What have we done that you should complain about us?" [8]Then Moses added, "The LORD will give you meat to eat in the evening and bread to satisfy you in the morning, for he has heard all your complaints against him. What have we done? Yes, your complaints are against the LORD, not against us."

[9]Then Moses said to Aaron, "Announce this to the entire community of Israel: 'Present yourselves before the LORD, for he has heard your complaining.'" [10]And as Aaron spoke to the whole community of Israel, they looked out toward the wilderness. There they could see the awesome glory of the LORD in the cloud.

[11]Then the LORD said to Moses, [12]"I have heard the Israelites' complaints. Now tell them, 'In the evening you will have meat to eat, and in the morning you will have all the bread you want. Then you will know that I am the LORD your God.'"

[13]That evening vast numbers of quail flew in and covered the camp. And the next morning the area around the camp was wet with dew. [14]When the dew evaporated, a flaky substance as fine as frost blanketed the ground. [15]The Israelites were puzzled when they saw it. "What is it?" they asked each other. They had no idea what it was.

And Moses told them, "It is the food the LORD has given you to eat. [16]These are the LORD's instructions: Each household should gather as much as it needs. Pick up two quarts* for each person in your tent."

[17]So the people of Israel did as they were told. Some gathered a lot, some only a little. [18]But when they measured it out,* everyone had just enough. Those who gathered a lot had nothing left over, and those who gathered only a little had enough. Each family had just what it needed.

[19]Then Moses told them, "Do not keep any of it until morning." [20]But some of them didn't listen and kept some of it until morning. But by then it was full of maggots and had a terrible smell. Moses was very angry with them.

[21]After this the people gathered the food morning by morning, each family according to its need. And as the sun became hot, the flakes they had not picked up melted and disappeared. [22]On the sixth day, they gathered twice as much as usual—four quarts* for each person instead of two. Then all the leaders of the community came and asked Moses for an explanation. [23]He told them, "This is what the LORD commanded: Tomorrow will be a day of complete rest, a holy Sabbath day set apart for the LORD. So bake or boil as much as you want today, and set aside what is left for tomorrow."

[24]So they put some aside until morning, just as Moses had commanded. And in the morning the leftover food was wholesome and good, without maggots or odor. [25]Moses said, "Eat this food today, for today is a Sabbath day dedicated to the LORD. There will be no food on the ground today. [26]You may gather the food for six days, but the seventh day is the Sabbath. There will be no food on the ground that day."

[27]Some of the people went out anyway on the seventh day, but they found no food. [28]The LORD asked Moses, "How long will these people refuse to obey my commands and instructions? [29]They must realize that the Sabbath is the LORD's gift to you. That is why he gives you a two-day supply on the sixth day, so

16:1b The Exodus had occurred on the fifteenth day of the first month (see Num 33:3). **16:16** Hebrew *1 omer* [2 liters]; also in 16:32, 33. **16:18** Hebrew *measured it with an omer*. **16:22** Hebrew *2 omers* [4 liters].

there will be enough for two days. On the Sabbath day you must each stay in your place. Do not go out to pick up food on the seventh day." [30]So the people did not gather any food on the seventh day.

[31]The Israelites called the food manna.* It was white like coriander seed, and it tasted like honey wafers.

[32]Then Moses said, "This is what the LORD has commanded: Fill a two-quart container with manna to preserve it for your descendants. Then later generations will be able to see the food I gave you in the wilderness when I set you free from Egypt."

[33]Moses said to Aaron, "Get a jar and fill it with two quarts of manna. Then put it in a sacred place before the LORD to preserve it for all future generations." [34]Aaron did just as the LORD had commanded Moses. He eventually placed it in the Ark of the Covenant—in front of the stone tablets inscribed with the terms of the covenant.* [35]So the people of Israel ate manna for forty years until they arrived at the land where they would settle. They ate manna until they came to the border of the land of Canaan.

[36]The container used to measure the manna was an omer, which was one-tenth of an ephah; it held about two quarts.*

CHAPTER 17

Water from the Rock

At the LORD's command, the whole community of Israel left the wilderness of Sin* and moved from place to place. Eventually they camped at Rephidim, but there was no water there for the people to drink. [2]So once more the people complained against Moses. "Give us water to drink!" they demanded.

"Quiet!" Moses replied. "Why are you complaining against me? And why are you testing the LORD?"

[3]But tormented by thirst, they continued to argue with Moses. "Why did you bring us out of Egypt? Are you trying to kill us, our children, and our livestock with thirst?"

[4]Then Moses cried out to the LORD, "What should I do with these people? They are ready to stone me!"

[5]The LORD said to Moses, "Walk out in front of the people. Take your staff, the one you used when you struck the water of the Nile, and call some of the elders of Israel to join you. [6]I will stand before you on the rock at Mount Sinai.* Strike the rock, and water will come gushing out. Then the people will be able to drink." So Moses struck the rock as he was told, and water gushed out as the elders looked on.

[7]Moses named the place Massah (which means "test") and Meribah (which means "arguing") because the people of Israel argued with Moses and tested the LORD by saying, "Is the LORD here with us or not?"

Israel Defeats the Amalekites

[8]While the people of Israel were still at Rephidim, the warriors of Amalek attacked them. [9]Moses commanded Joshua, "Choose some men to go out and fight the army of Amalek for us. Tomorrow, I will stand at the top of the hill, holding the staff of God in my hand."

AMAZING FACTS

God's people needed water, but they only had rocks. So guess what? Water came from a rock!

EXODUS 17:1-7

[10]So Joshua did what Moses had commanded and fought the army of Amalek. Meanwhile, Moses, Aaron, and Hur climbed to the top of a nearby hill. [11]As long as Moses held up the staff in his hand, the Israelites had the advantage. But whenever he dropped his hand, the Amalekites gained the advantage. [12]Moses' arms soon became so tired he could no longer hold them up. So Aaron and Hur

16:31 *Manna* means "What is it?" See 16:15. **16:34** Hebrew *He placed it in front of the Testimony;* see note on 25:16. **16:36** Hebrew *An omer is one-tenth of an ephah.* **17:1** The geographical name *Sin* is related to *Sinai* and should not be confused with the English word *sin.* **17:6** Hebrew *Horeb,* another name for Sinai.

found a stone for him to sit on. Then they stood on each side of Moses, holding up his hands. So his hands held steady until sunset. [13]As a result, Joshua overwhelmed the army of Amalek in battle.

[14]After the victory, the LORD instructed Moses, "Write this down on a scroll as a permanent reminder, and read it aloud to Joshua: I will erase the memory of Amalek from under heaven." [15]Moses built an altar there and named it Yahweh-Nissi (which means "the LORD is my banner"). [16]He said, "They have raised their fist against the LORD's throne, so now* the LORD will be at war with Amalek generation after generation."

CHAPTER 18

Jethro's Visit to Moses

Moses' father-in-law, Jethro, the priest of Midian, heard about everything God had done for Moses and his people, the Israelites. He heard especially about how the LORD had rescued them from Egypt.

[2]Earlier, Moses had sent his wife, Zipporah, and his two sons back to Jethro, who had taken them in. [3](Moses' first son was named Gershom,* for Moses had said when the boy was born, "I have been a foreigner in a foreign land." [4]His second son was named Eliezer,* for Moses had said, "The God of my ancestors was my helper; he rescued me from the sword of Pharaoh.") [5]Jethro, Moses' father-in-law, now came to visit Moses in the wilderness. He brought Moses' wife and two sons with him, and they arrived while Moses and the people were camped near the mountain of God. [6]Jethro had sent a message to Moses, saying, "I, Jethro, your father-in-law, am coming to see you with your wife and your two sons."

[7]So Moses went out to meet his father-in-law. He bowed low and kissed him. They asked about each other's welfare and then went into Moses' tent. [8]Moses told his father-in-law everything the LORD had done to Pharaoh and Egypt on behalf of Israel. He also told about all the hardships they had experienced along the way and how the LORD had rescued his people from all their troubles. [9]Jethro was delighted when he heard about all the good things the LORD had done for Israel as he rescued them from the hand of the Egyptians.

THE POOL PARTY

While attending a conference, Mason's youth group was staying in a hotel that had a pool. Mason and his friends were busy with conference events throughout the first day and evening. By the time the guys returned to their room, it was already 10:30 P.M. "Lights out" was coming up soon—11:00 P.M. Kevin, though, had other plans. He said, "Time to get crazy and party! Let's make a splash in the pool." The pool sounded inviting, and Mason wanted to swim. It couldn't hurt to take a quick dip.

What should Mason do? Read Exodus 18:19-20.

[10]"Praise the LORD," Jethro said, "for he has rescued you from the Egyptians and from Pharaoh. Yes, he has rescued Israel from the powerful hand of Egypt! [11]I know now that the LORD is greater than all other gods, because he rescued his people from the oppression of the proud Egyptians."

17:16 Or *Hands have been lifted up to the LORD's throne, and now there.* **18:4** *Eliezer* means "God is my helper." **18:3** *Gershom* sounds like a Hebrew term that means "a foreigner

[12]Then Jethro, Moses' father-in-law, brought
a burnt offering and sacrifices to God. Aaron
and all the elders of Israel came out and joined
him in a sacrificial meal in God's presence.

Jethro's Wise Advice

[13]The next day, Moses took his seat to hear
the people's disputes against each other.
They waited before him from morning till
evening.

[14]When Moses' father-in-law saw all that
Moses was doing for the people, he asked,
"What are you really accomplishing here?
Why are you trying to do all this alone while
everyone stands around you from morning
till evening?"

[15]Moses replied, "Because the people come
to me to get a ruling from God. [16]When a dis-
pute arises, they come to me, and I am the one
who settles the case between the quarreling
parties. I inform the people of God's decrees
and give them his instructions."

[17]"This is not good!" Moses' father-in-law
exclaimed. [18]"You're going to wear yourself
out—and the people, too. This job is too heavy
a burden for you to handle all by yourself.
[19]Now listen to me, and let me give you a word
of advice, and may God be with you. You
should continue to be the people's represen-
tative before God, bringing their disputes to
him. [20]Teach them God's decrees, and give
them his instructions. Show them how to
conduct their lives. [21]But select from all the
people some capable, honest men who fear
God and hate bribes. Appoint them as leaders
over groups of one thousand, one hundred,
fifty, and ten. [22]They should always be avail-
able to solve the people's common disputes,
but have them bring the major cases to you.
Let the leaders decide the smaller matters
themselves. They will help you carry the load,
making the task easier for you. [23]If you follow
this advice, and if God commands you to do
so, then you will be able to endure the pres-
sures, and all these people will go home in
peace."

[24]Moses listened to his father-in-law's ad-
vice and followed his suggestions. [25]He chose
capable men from all over Israel and ap-
pointed them as leaders over the people. He
put them in charge of groups of one thousand,
one hundred, fifty, and ten. [26]These men were
always available to solve the people's common
disputes. They brought the major cases to
Moses, but they took care of the smaller mat-
ters themselves.

[27]Soon after this, Moses said good-bye to
his father-in-law, who returned to his own
land.

CHAPTER 19

The Lord Reveals Himself at Sinai

Exactly two months after the Israelites left
Egypt,* they arrived in the wilderness of Si-
nai. [2]After breaking camp at Rephidim, they
came to the wilderness of Sinai and set up
camp there at the base of Mount Sinai.

[3]Then Moses climbed the mountain to ap-
pear before God. The Lord called to him
from the mountain and said, "Give these in-
structions to the family of Jacob; announce it
to the descendants of Israel: "You have seen
what I did to the Egyptians. You know how I
carried you on eagles' wings and brought you
to myself. [5]Now if you will obey me and keep
my covenant, you will be my own special trea-
sure from among all the peoples on earth; for
all the earth belongs to me. [6]And you will be
my kingdom of priests, my holy nation.' This
is the message you must give to the people of
Israel."

[7]So Moses returned from the mountain
and called together the elders of the people
and told them everything the Lord had com-
manded him. [8]And all the people responded
together, "We will do everything the Lord has
commanded." So Moses brought the people's
answer back to the Lord.

[9]Then the Lord said to Moses, "I will come
to you in a thick cloud, Moses, so the people
themselves can hear me when I speak with
you. Then they will always trust you."

Moses told the Lord what the people had
said. [10]Then the Lord told Moses, "Go down
and prepare the people for my arrival. Conse-
crate them today and tomorrow, and have
them wash their clothing. [11]Be sure they are
ready on the third day, for on that day the
Lord will come down on Mount Sinai as all
the people watch. [12]Mark off a boundary all
around the mountain. Warn the people, 'Be
careful! Do not go up on the mountain or even

19:1 Hebrew *In the third month after the Israelites left Egypt, on the very day,* i.e., two lunar months to the day after leaving Egypt. Compare Num 33:3.

touch its boundaries. Anyone who touches
the mountain will certainly be put to death.
[13]No hand may touch the person or animal
that crosses the boundary; instead, stone
them or shoot them with arrows. They must
be put to death.' However, when the ram's
horn sounds a long blast, then the people may
go up on the mountain.*"

[14]So Moses went down to the people. He
consecrated them for worship, and they
washed their clothes. [15]He told them, "Get
ready for the third day, and until then abstain
from having sexual intercourse."

[16]On the morning of the third day, thun-
der roared and lightning flashed, and a
dense cloud came down on the mountain.
There was a long, loud blast from a ram's
horn, and all the people trembled. [17]Moses
led them out from the camp to meet with
God, and they stood at the foot of the moun-
tain. [18]All of Mount Sinai was covered with
smoke because the LORD had descended on
it in the form of fire. The smoke billowed
into the sky like smoke from a brick kiln, and
the whole mountain shook violently. [19]As the
blast of the ram's horn grew louder and
louder, Moses spoke, and God thundered his
reply. [20]The LORD came down on the top of
Mount Sinai and called Moses to the top of
the mountain. So Moses climbed the moun-
tain.

[21]Then the LORD told Moses, "Go back
down and warn the people not to break
through the boundaries to see the LORD, or
they will die. [22]Even the priests who regularly
come near to the LORD must purify them-
selves so that the LORD does not break out
and destroy them."

[23]"But LORD," Moses protested, "the people
cannot come up to Mount Sinai. You already
warned us. You told me, 'Mark off a bound-
ary all around the mountain to set it apart as
holy.'"

[24]But the LORD said, "Go down and bring
Aaron back up with you. In the meantime, do
not let the priests or the people break
through to approach the LORD, or he will
break out and destroy them."

[25]So Moses went down to the people and
told them what the LORD had said.

CHAPTER 20

Ten Commandments for the Covenant Community

Then God gave the people all these instruc-
tions*:

19:13 Or *up to the mountain.* **20:1** Hebrew *all these words.*

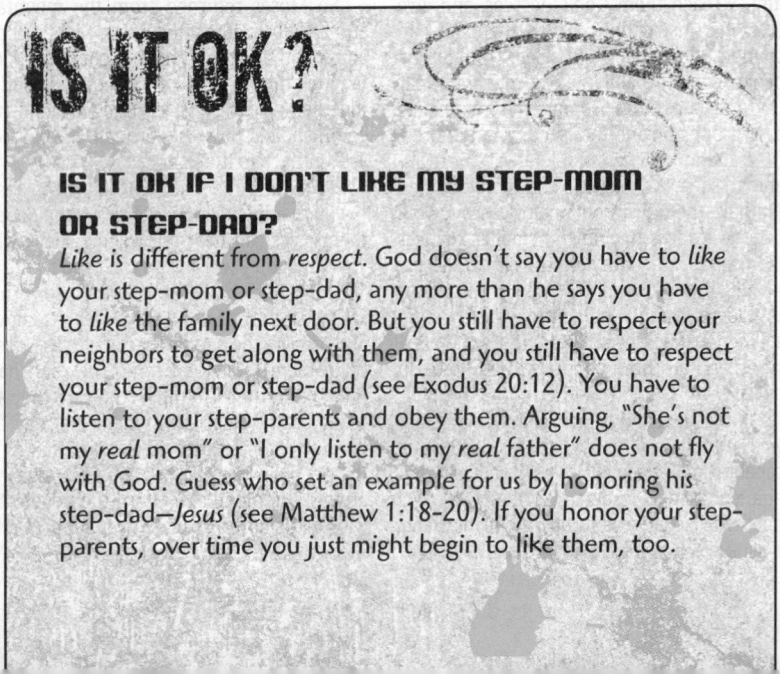

2"I am the LORD your God, who rescued you
from the land of Egypt, the place of your
slavery.
3"You must not have any other god but me.
4"You must not make for yourself an idol of
any kind or an image of anything in the
heavens or on the earth or in the sea. 5You
must not bow down to them or worship
them, for I, the LORD your God, am a
jealous God who will not tolerate your
affection for any other gods. I lay the sins
of the parents upon their children; the
entire family is affected—even children in
the third and fourth generations of those
who reject me. 6But I lavish unfailing love
for a thousand generations on those* who
love me and obey my commands.

Do I have to do everything my parents tell me?

Honor your father and mother. Then you will live a long, full life.
EXODUS 20:12

7"You must not misuse the name of the LORD
your God. The LORD will not let you go
unpunished if you misuse his name.
8"Remember to observe the Sabbath day by
keeping it holy. 9You have six days each
week for your ordinary work, 10but the
seventh day is a Sabbath day of rest
dedicated to the LORD your God. On that
day no one in your household may do any
work. This includes you, your sons and
daughters, your male and female servants,
your livestock, and any foreigners living
among you. 11For in six days the LORD
made the heavens, the earth, the sea, and
everything in them; but on the seventh
day he rested. That is why the LORD
blessed the Sabbath day and set it apart
as holy.
12"Honor your father and mother. Then you
will live a long, full life in the land the
LORD your God is giving you.
13"You must not murder.
14"You must not commit adultery.
15"You must not steal.
16"You must not testify falsely against your
neighbor.
17"You must not covet your neighbor's
house. You must not covet your
neighbor's wife, male or female servant,
ox or donkey, or anything else that
belongs to your neighbor."

18When the people heard the thunder and
the loud blast of the ram's horn, and when
they saw the flashes of lightning and the
smoke billowing from the mountain, they
stood at a distance, trembling with fear.
19And they said to Moses, "You speak to us,
and we will listen. But don't let God speak di-
rectly to us, or we will die!"
20"Don't be afraid," Moses answered them,
"for God has come in this way to test you, and
so that your fear of him will keep you from
sinning!"
21As the people stood in the distance, Moses
approached the dark cloud where God was.

Proper Use of Altars

22And the LORD said to Moses, "Say this to the
people of Israel: You saw for yourselves that I
spoke to you from heaven. 23Remember, you
must not make any idols of silver or gold to ri-
val me.
24"Build for me an altar made of earth, and
offer your sacrifices to me—your burnt offer-
ings and peace offerings, your sheep and
goats, and your cattle. Build my altar wher-
ever I cause my name to be remembered, and
I will come to you and bless you. 25If you use
stones to build my altar, use only natural, un-
cut stones. Do not shape the stones with a
tool, for that would make the altar unfit for
holy use. 26And do not approach my altar by
going up steps. If you do, someone might look
up under your clothing and see your naked-
ness.

CHAPTER 21

Fair Treatment of Slaves

"These are the regulations you must present
to Israel.
2"If you buy a Hebrew slave, he may serve
for no more than six years. Set him free in the
seventh year, and he will owe you nothing for
his freedom. 3If he was single when he

20:6 Hebrew *for thousands of those.*

THE KETCHUP CAPER

Cesar accidentally squirted ketchup on the wall in the kitchen, but his mom didn't see who did it. When Mom saw it, she immediately blamed Cesar's little brother for the mess. Mom made Luis clean up the sticky red wall. "And no TV for two days," Mom told Luis. Cesar knew it was wrong for Luis to get punished for something he didn't do, but he sure didn't want to get punished either.

What would you say to Cesar, or how would you react? Check out Exodus 20:16 for help in deciding what you should do.

became your slave, he shall leave single. But if he was married before he became a slave, then his wife must be freed with him.

4"If his master gave him a wife while he was a slave and they had sons or daughters, then only the man will be free in the seventh year, but his wife and children will still belong to his master. 5But the slave may declare, 'I love my master, my wife, and my children. I don't want to go free.' 6If he does this, his master must present him before God.* Then his master must take him to the door or doorpost and publicly pierce his ear with an awl. After that, the slave will serve his master for life.

7"When a man sells his daughter as a slave, she will not be freed at the end of six years as the men are. 8If she does not satisfy her owner, he must allow her to be bought back again. But he is not allowed to sell her to foreigners, since he is the one who broke the contract with her. 9But if the slave's owner arranges for her to marry his son, he may no longer treat her as a slave but as a daughter.

10"If a man who has married a slave wife takes another wife for himself, he must not neglect the rights of the first wife to food, clothing, and sexual intimacy. 11If he fails in any of these three obligations, she may leave as a free woman without making any payment.

Cases of Personal Injury

12"Anyone who assaults and kills another person must be put to death. 13But if it was simply an accident permitted by God, I will appoint a place of refuge where the slayer can run for safety. 14However, if someone deliberately kills another person, then the slayer must be dragged even from my altar and be put to death.

15"Anyone who strikes father or mother must be put to death.

16"Kidnappers must be put to death, whether they are caught in possession of their victims or have already sold them as slaves.

17"Anyone who dishonors* father or mother must be put to death.

18"Now suppose two men quarrel, and one hits the other with a stone or fist, and the injured person does not die but is confined to bed. 19If he is later able to walk outside again, even with a crutch, the assailant will not be punished but must compensate his victim for lost wages and provide for his full recovery.

20"If a man beats his male or female slave with a club and the slave dies as a result, the owner must be punished. 21But if the slave recovers within a day or two, then the owner shall not be punished, since the slave is his property.

21:6 Or *before the judges.* **21:17** Greek version reads *Anyone who speaks disrespectfully of.* Compare Matt 15:4; Mark 7:10.

22"Now suppose two men are fighting, and in the process they accidentally strike a pregnant woman so she gives birth prematurely.* If no further injury results, the man who struck the woman must pay the amount of compensation the woman's husband demands and the judges approve. 23But if there is further injury, the punishment must match the injury: a life for a life, 24an eye for an eye, a tooth for a tooth, a hand for a hand, a foot for a foot, 25a burn for a burn, a wound for a wound, a bruise for a bruise.

26"If a man hits his male or female slave in the eye and the eye is blinded, he must let the slave go free to compensate for the eye. 27And if a man knocks out the tooth of his male or female slave, he must let the slave go free to compensate for the tooth.

28"If an ox* gores a man or woman to death, the ox must be stoned, and its flesh may not be eaten. In such a case, however, the owner will not be held liable. 29But suppose the ox had a reputation for goring, and the owner had been informed but failed to keep it under control. If the ox then kills someone, it must be stoned, and the owner must also be put to death. 30However, the dead person's relatives may accept payment to compensate for the loss of life. The owner of the ox may redeem his life by paying whatever is demanded.

31"The same regulation applies if the ox gores a boy or a girl. 32But if the ox gores a slave, either male or female, the animal's owner must pay the slave's owner thirty silver coins,* and the ox must be stoned.

33"Suppose someone digs or uncovers a pit and fails to cover it, and then an ox or a donkey falls into it. 34The owner of the pit must pay full compensation to the owner of the animal, but then he gets to keep the dead animal.

35"If someone's ox injures a neighbor's ox and the injured ox dies, then the two owners must sell the live ox and divide the price equally between them. They must also divide the dead animal. 36But if the ox had a reputation for goring, yet its owner failed to keep it under control, he must pay full compensation—a live ox for the dead one—but he may keep the dead ox.

CHAPTER 22

Protection of Property

1*"If someone steals an ox* or sheep and then kills or sells it, the thief must pay back five oxen for each ox stolen, and four sheep for each sheep stolen.

2*"If a thief is caught in the act of breaking into a house and is struck and killed in the process, the person who killed the thief is not guilty of murder. 3But if it happens in daylight, the one who killed the thief is guilty of murder.

"A thief who is caught must pay in full for everything he stole. If he cannot pay, he must be sold as a slave to pay for his theft. 4If someone steals an ox or a donkey or a sheep and it is found in the thief's possession, then the thief must pay double the value of the stolen animal.

5"If an animal is grazing in a field or vineyard and the owner lets it stray into someone else's field to graze, then the animal's owner must pay compensation from the best of his own grain or grapes.

6"If you are burning thornbushes and the fire gets out of control and spreads into another person's field, destroying the sheaves or the uncut grain or the whole crop, the one who started the fire must pay for the lost crop.

7"Suppose someone leaves money or goods with a neighbor for safekeeping, and they are stolen from the neighbor's house. If the thief is caught, the compensation is double the value of what was stolen. 8But if the thief is not caught, the neighbor must appear before God,* who will determine if he stole the property.

9"Suppose there is a dispute between two people who both claim to own a particular ox, donkey, sheep, article of clothing, or any lost property. Both parties must come before God, and the person whom God declares* guilty must pay double compensation to the other.

10"Now suppose someone leaves a donkey, ox, sheep, or any other animal with a neighbor for safekeeping, but it dies or is injured or gets away, and no one sees what happened. 11The neighbor must then take an oath in the presence of the LORD. If the LORD confirms

21:22 Or *so she has a miscarriage;* Hebrew reads *so her children come out.* **21:28** Or *bull,* or *cow;* also in 21:29-36. **21:32** Hebrew *30 shekels of silver,* about 12 ounces or 342 grams in weight. **22:1a** Verse 22:1 is numbered 21:37 in Hebrew text. **22:1b** Or *bull,* or *cow;* also in 22:4, 9, 10. **22:2** Verses 22:2-31 are numbered 22:1-30 in Hebrew text. **22:8** Or *before the judges.* **22:9** Or *before the judges, and the person whom the judges declare.*

that the neighbor did not steal the property, the owner must accept the verdict, and no payment will be required. 12But if the animal was indeed stolen, the guilty person must pay compensation to the owner. 13If it was torn to pieces by a wild animal, the remains of the carcass must be shown as evidence, and no compensation will be required.

14"If someone borrows an animal from a neighbor and it is injured or dies when the owner is absent, the person who borrowed it must pay full compensation. 15But if the owner was present, no compensation is required. And no compensation is required if the animal was rented, for this loss is covered by the rental fee.

Social Responsibility

16"If a man seduces a virgin who is not engaged to anyone and has sex with her, he must pay the customary bride price and marry her. 17But if her father refuses to let him marry her, the man must still pay him an amount equal to the bride price of a virgin.

18"You must not allow a sorceress to live.

19"Anyone who has sexual relations with an animal must certainly be put to death.

20"Anyone who sacrifices to any god other than the LORD must be destroyed.*

21"You must not mistreat or oppress foreigners in any way. Remember, you yourselves were once foreigners in the land of Egypt.

22"You must not exploit a widow or an orphan. 23If you exploit them in any way and they cry out to me, then I will certainly hear their cry. 24My anger will blaze against you, and I will kill you with the sword. Then your wives will be widows and your children fatherless.

25"If you lend money to any of my people who are in need, do not charge interest as a money lender would. 26If you take your neighbor's cloak as security for a loan, you must return it before sunset. 27This coat may be the only blanket your neighbor has. How can a person sleep without it? If you do not return it and your neighbor cries out to me for help, then I will hear, for I am merciful.

28"You must not dishonor God or curse any of your rulers.

29"You must not hold anything back when you give me offerings from your crops and your wine.

"You must give me your firstborn sons.

30"You must also give me the firstborn of your cattle, sheep, and goats. But leave the newborn animal with its mother for seven days; then give it to me on the eighth day.

31"You must be my holy people. Therefore, do not eat any animal that has been torn up and killed by wild animals. Throw it to the dogs.

CHAPTER 23

A Call for Justice

"You must not pass along false rumors. You must not cooperate with evil people by lying on the witness stand.

2"You must not follow the crowd in doing wrong. When you are called to testify in a dispute, do not be swayed by the crowd to twist justice. 3And do not slant your testimony in favor of a person just because that person is poor.

4"If you come upon your enemy's ox or donkey that has strayed away, take it back to its owner. 5If you see that the donkey of someone who hates you has collapsed under its load, do not walk by. Instead, stop and help.

6"In a lawsuit, you must not deny justice to the poor.

7"Be sure never to charge anyone falsely with evil. Never sentence an innocent or blameless person to death, for I never declare a guilty person to be innocent.

8"Take no bribes, for a bribe makes you ignore something that you clearly see. A bribe makes even a righteous person twist the truth.

9"You must not oppress foreigners. You know what it's like to be a foreigner, for you yourselves were once foreigners in the land of Egypt.

10"Plant and harvest your crops for six years, 11but let the land be renewed and lie uncultivated during the seventh year. Then let the poor among you harvest whatever grows on its own. Leave the rest for wild animals to eat. The same applies to your vineyards and olive groves.

12"You have six days each week for your ordinary work, but on the seventh day you must stop working. This gives your ox and your

22:20 The Hebrew term used here refers to the complete consecration of things or people to the LORD, either by destroying them or by giving them as an offering.

FUN AT THE WATER PARK

Austin and some church friends went to a really cool water park. When they arrived, their youth leader said, "Enjoy the water park; just meet back at the bus by 3:45." Austin and his friends tried everything—they had an absolute blast! Around 3:40, one of Austin's friends yelled, "Let's go on the tube slide again." When Austin saw the huge line by the slide he said, "There's no way. We'll never get through in time." His friends urged him to stay.

What do you think Austin should do? For help read Exodus 23:2.

donkey a chance to rest. It also allows your slaves and the foreigners living among you to be refreshed.

13"Pay close attention to all my instructions. You must not call on the name of any other gods. Do not even speak their names.

Three Annual Festivals

14"Each year you must celebrate three festivals in my honor. 15First, celebrate the Festival of Unleavened Bread. For seven days the bread you eat must be made without yeast, just as I commanded you. Celebrate this festival annually at the appointed time in early spring, in the month of Abib,* for that is the anniversary of your departure from Egypt. No one may appear before me without an offering.

16"Second, celebrate the Festival of Harvest,* when you bring me the first crops of your harvest.

"Finally, celebrate the Festival of the Final Harvest* at the end of the harvest season, when you have harvested all the crops from your fields. 17At these three times each year, every man in Israel must appear before the Sovereign, the LORD.

18"You must not offer the blood of my sacrificial offerings together with any baked goods containing yeast. And do not leave the fat from the festival offerings until the next morning.

19"As you harvest your crops, bring the very best of the first harvest to the house of the LORD your God.

"You must not cook a young goat in its mother's milk.

A Promise of the LORD's Presence

20"See, I am sending an angel before you to protect you on your journey and lead you safely to the place I have prepared for you. 21Pay close attention to him, and obey his instructions. Do not rebel against him, for he is my representative, and he will not forgive your rebellion. 22But if you are careful to obey him, following all my instructions, then I will be an enemy to your enemies, and I will oppose those who oppose you. 23For my angel will go before you and bring you into the land of the Amorites, Hittites, Perizzites, Canaanites, Hivites, and Jebusites, so you may live there. And I will destroy them completely. 24You must not worship the gods of these nations or serve them in any way or imitate their evil practices. Instead, you must utterly destroy them and smash their sacred pillars.

23:15 Hebrew *appointed time in the month of Abib*. This first month of the ancient Hebrew lunar calendar usually occurs within the months of March and April. **23:16a** Or *Festival of Weeks*. This was later called the Festival of Pentecost (see Acts 2:1). It is celebrated today as Shavuot (or Shabuoth). **23:16b** Or *Festival of Ingathering*. This was later called the Festival of Shelters or Festival of Tabernacles (see Lev 23:33-36). It is celebrated today as Sukkot (or Succoth).

[25]"You must serve only the LORD your God. If you do, I* will bless you with food and water, and I will protect you from illness. [26]There will be no miscarriages or infertility in your land, and I will give you long, full lives.

[27]"I will send my terror ahead of you and create panic among all the people whose lands you invade. I will make all your enemies turn and run. [28]I will send terror* ahead of you to drive out the Hivites, Canaanites, and Hittites. [29]But I will not drive them out in a single year, because the land would become desolate and the wild animals would multiply and threaten you. [30]I will drive them out a little at a time until your population has increased enough to take possession of the land. [31]And I will fix your boundaries from the Red Sea to the Mediterranean Sea,* and from the eastern wilderness to the Euphrates River.* I will hand over to you the people now living in the land, and you will drive them out ahead of you.

[32]"Make no treaties with them or their gods. [33]They must not live in your land, or they will cause you to sin against me. If you serve their gods, you will be caught in the trap of idolatry."

CHAPTER 24

Israel Accepts the LORD's Covenant

Then the LORD instructed Moses: "Come up here to me, and bring along Aaron, Nadab, Abihu, and seventy of Israel's elders. All of you must worship from a distance. [2]Only Moses is allowed to come near to the LORD. The others must not come near, and none of the other people are allowed to climb up the mountain with him."

[3]Then Moses went down to the people and repeated all the instructions and regulations the LORD had given him. All the people answered with one voice, "We will do everything the LORD has commanded."

[4]Then Moses carefully wrote down all the LORD's instructions. Early the next morning Moses got up and built an altar at the foot of the mountain. He also set up twelve pillars, one for each of the twelve tribes of Israel. [5]Then he sent some of the young Israelite men to present burnt offerings and to sacrifice bulls as peace offerings to the LORD. [6]Moses drained half the blood from these animals into basins. The other half he splattered against the altar.

[7]Then he took the Book of the Covenant and read it aloud to the people. Again they all responded, "We will do everything the LORD has commanded. We will obey."

[8]Then Moses took the blood from the basins and splattered it over the people, declaring, "Look, this blood confirms the covenant the LORD has made with you in giving you these instructions."

[9]Then Moses, Aaron, Nadab, Abihu, and the seventy elders of Israel climbed up the mountain. [10]There they saw the God of Israel. Under his feet there seemed to be a surface of brilliant blue lapis lazuli, as clear as the sky itself. [11]And though these nobles of Israel gazed upon God, he did not destroy them. In fact, they ate a covenant meal, eating and drinking in his presence!

[12]Then the LORD said to Moses, "Come up to me on the mountain. Stay there, and I will give you the tablets of stone on which I have inscribed the instructions and commands so you can teach the people." [13]So Moses and his assistant Joshua set out, and Moses climbed up the mountain of God.

[14]Moses told the elders, "Stay here and wait for us until we come back. Aaron and Hur are here with you. If anyone has a dispute while I am gone, consult with them."

[15]Then Moses climbed up the mountain, and the cloud covered it. [16]And the glory of the LORD settled down on Mount Sinai, and the cloud covered it for six days. On the seventh day the LORD called to Moses from inside the cloud. [17]To the Israelites at the foot of the mountain, the glory of the LORD appeared at the summit like a consuming fire. [18]Then Moses disappeared into the cloud as he climbed higher up the mountain. He remained on the mountain forty days and forty nights.

CHAPTER 25

Offerings for the Tabernacle

The LORD said to Moses, [2]"Tell the people of Israel to bring me their sacred offerings. Accept the contributions from all whose hearts

23:25 As in Greek and Latin versions; Hebrew reads *he*. **23:28** Often rendered *the hornet*. The meaning of the Hebrew is uncertain. **23:31a** Hebrew *from the sea of reeds to the sea of the Philistines*. **23:31b** Hebrew *from the wilderness to the river*.

are moved to offer them. [3]Here is a list of sacred offerings you may accept from them:

gold, silver, and bronze;
[4] blue, purple, and scarlet thread;
fine linen and goat hair for cloth;
[5] tanned ram skins and fine goatskin leather;
acacia wood;
[6] olive oil for the lamps;
spices for the anointing oil and the fragrant incense;
[7] onyx stones, and other gemstones to be set in the ephod and the priest's chestpiece.

[8]"Have the people of Israel build me a holy sanctuary so I can live among them. [9]You must build this Tabernacle and its furnishings exactly according to the pattern I will show you.

Plans for the Ark of the Covenant

[10]"Have the people make an Ark of acacia wood—a sacred chest 45 inches long, 27 inches wide, and 27 inches high.* [11]Overlay it inside and outside with pure gold, and run a molding of gold all around it. [12]Cast four gold rings and attach them to its four feet, two rings on each side. [13]Make poles from acacia wood, and overlay them with gold. [14]Insert the poles into the rings at the sides of the Ark to carry it. [15]These carrying poles must stay inside the rings; never remove them. [16]When the Ark is finished, place inside it the stone tablets inscribed with the terms of the covenant,* which I will give to you.

[17]"Then make the Ark's cover—the place of atonement—from pure gold. It must be 45 inches long and 27 inches wide.* [18]Then make two cherubim from hammered gold, and place them on the two ends of the atonement cover. [19]Mold the cherubim on each end of the atonement cover, making it all of one piece of gold. [20]The cherubim will face each other and look down on the atonement cover. With their wings spread above it, they will protect it. [21]Place inside the Ark the stone tablets inscribed with the terms of the covenant, which I will give to you. Then put the atonement cover on top of the Ark. [22]I will meet with you there and talk to you from above the atonement cover between the gold cherubim that hover over the Ark of the Covenant.* From there I will give you my commands for the people of Israel.

Plans for the Table

[23]"Then make a table of acacia wood, 36 inches long, 18 inches wide, and 27 inches high.* [24]Overlay it with pure gold and run a gold molding around the edge. [25]Decorate it with a 3-inch border* all around, and run a gold molding along the border. [26]Make four gold rings for the table and attach them at the four corners next to the four legs. [27]Attach the rings near the border to hold the poles that are used to carry the table. [28]Make these poles from acacia wood, and overlay them with gold. [29]Make special containers of pure gold for the table—bowls, pans, pitchers, and jars—to be used in pouring out liquid offerings. [30]Place the Bread of the Presence on the table to remain before me at all times.

Plans for the Lampstand

[31]"Make a lampstand of pure, hammered gold. Make the entire lampstand and its decorations of one piece—the base, center stem, lamp cups, buds, and petals. [32]Make it with six branches going out from the center stem, three on each side. [33]Each of the six branches will have three lamp cups shaped like almond blossoms, complete with buds and petals. [34]Craft the center stem of the lampstand with four lamp cups shaped like almond blossoms, complete with buds and petals. [35]There will also be an almond bud beneath each pair of branches where the six branches extend from the center stem. [36]The almond buds and branches must all be of one piece with the center stem, and they must be hammered from pure gold. [37]Then make the seven lamps for the lampstand, and set them so they reflect their light forward. [38]The lamp snuffers and trays must also be made of pure gold. [39]You will need seventy-five pounds* of pure gold for the lampstand and its accessories.

25:10 Hebrew *2.5 cubits* [115 centimeters] *long, 1.5 cubits* [69 centimeters] *wide, and 1.5 cubits high.* **25:16** Hebrew *Place inside the Ark the Testimony;* similarly in 25:21. The Hebrew word for "testimony" refers to the terms of the LORD's covenant with Israel as written on stone tablets, and also to the covenant itself. **25:17** Hebrew *2.5 cubits* [115 centimeters] *long and 1.5 cubits* [69 centimeters] *wide.* **25:22** Or *Ark of the Testimony.* **25:23** Hebrew *2 cubits* [92 centimeters] *long, 1 cubit* [46 centimeters] *wide, and 1.5 cubits* [69 centimeters] *high.* **25:25** Hebrew *a border of a handbreadth* [8 centimeters]. **25:39** Hebrew *1 talent* [34 kilograms].

[40]"Be sure that you make everything according to the pattern I have shown you here on the mountain.

CHAPTER 26

Plans for the Tabernacle

"Make the Tabernacle from ten curtains of finely woven linen. Decorate the curtains with blue, purple, and scarlet thread and with skillfully embroidered cherubim. [2]These ten curtains must all be exactly the same size—42 feet long and 6 feet wide.* [3]Join five of these curtains together to make one long curtain, then join the other five into a second long curtain. [4]Put loops of blue yarn along the edge of the last curtain in each set. [5]The fifty loops along the edge of one curtain are to match the fifty loops along the edge of the other curtain. [6]Then make fifty gold clasps and fasten the long curtains together with the clasps. In this way, the Tabernacle will be made of one continuous piece.

[7]"Make eleven curtains of goat-hair cloth to serve as a tent covering for the Tabernacle. [8]These eleven curtains must all be exactly the same size—45 feet long and 6 feet wide.* [9]Join five of these curtains together to make one long curtain, and join the other six into a second long curtain. Allow 3 feet of material from the second set of curtains to hang over the front* of the sacred tent. [10]Make fifty loops for one edge of each large curtain. [11]Then make fifty bronze clasps, and fasten the loops of the long curtains with the clasps. In this way, the tent covering will be made of one continuous piece. [12]The remaining 3 feet* of this tent covering will be left to hang over the back of the Tabernacle. [13]Allow 18 inches* of remaining material to hang down over each side, so the Tabernacle is completely covered. [14]Complete the tent covering with a protective layer of tanned ram skins and a layer of fine goatskin leather.

[15]"For the framework of the Tabernacle, construct frames of acacia wood. [16]Each frame must be 15 feet high and 27 inches wide,* [17]with two pegs under each frame. Make all the frames identical. [18]Make twenty of these frames to support the curtains on the south side of the Tabernacle. [19]Also make forty silver bases—two bases under each frame, with the pegs fitting securely into the bases. [20]For the north side of the Tabernacle, make another twenty frames, [21]with their forty silver bases, two bases under each frame. [22]Make six frames for the rear—the west side of the Tabernacle—[23]along with two additional frames to reinforce the rear corners of the Tabernacle. [24]These corner frames will be matched at the bottom and firmly attached at the top with a single ring, forming a single corner unit. Make both of these corner units the same way. [25]So there will be eight frames at the rear of the Tabernacle, set in sixteen silver bases—two bases under each frame.

[26]"Make crossbars of acacia wood to link the frames, five crossbars for the north side of the Tabernacle [27]and five for the south side. Also make five crossbars for the rear of the Tabernacle, which will face west. [28]The middle crossbar, attached halfway up the frames, will run all the way from one end of the Tabernacle to the other. [29]Overlay the frames with gold, and make gold rings to hold the crossbars. Overlay the crossbars with gold as well.

[30]"Set up this Tabernacle according to the pattern you were shown on the mountain.

[31]"For the inside of the Tabernacle, make a special curtain of finely woven linen. Decorate it with blue, purple, and scarlet thread and with skillfully embroidered cherubim. [32]Hang this curtain on gold hooks attached to four posts of acacia wood. Overlay the posts with gold, and set them in four silver bases. [33]Hang the inner curtain from clasps, and put the Ark of the Covenant* in the room behind it. This curtain will separate the Holy Place from the Most Holy Place.

[34]"Then put the Ark's cover—the place of atonement—on top of the Ark of the Covenant inside the Most Holy Place. [35]Place the table outside the inner curtain on the north side of the Tabernacle, and place the lampstand across the room on the south side.

[36]"Make another curtain for the entrance to the sacred tent. Make it of finely woven linen and embroider it with exquisite designs, using blue, purple, and scarlet thread. [37]Craft

26:2 Hebrew *28 cubits* [12.9 meters] *long and 4 cubits* [1.8 meters] *wide.* **26:8** Hebrew *30 cubits* [13.8 meters] *long and 4 cubits* [1.8 meters] *wide.* **26:9** Hebrew *Double over the sixth sheet at the front.* **26:12** Hebrew *The half sheet that is left over.* **26:13** Hebrew *1 cubit* [46 centimeters]. **26:16** Hebrew *10 cubits* [4.6 meters] *high and 1.5 cubits* [69 centimeters] *wide.* **26:33** Or *Ark of the Testimony;* also in 26:34.

JESUS AND THE TEN COMMANDMENTS

The Ten Commandments said . . .	Jesus said . . .
"You must not have any other god but me." Exodus 20:3	*"You must worship the LORD your God and serve only him."* Matthew 4:10
"You must not make for yourself an idol of any kind." Exodus 20:4	*"No one can serve two masters."* Luke 16:13
"You must not misuse the name of the LORD your God." Exodus 20:7	*"Do not make any vows! Do not say, 'By heaven!' because heaven is God's throne."* Matthew 5:34
"Remember to observe the Sabbath day by keeping it holy." Exodus 20:8	*"The Sabbath was made to meet the needs of people, and not people to meet the requirements of the Sabbath. So the Son of Man is Lord, even over the Sabbath!"* Mark 2:27-28
"Honor your father and mother." Exodus 20:12	*"If you love your father or mother more than you love me, you are not worthy of being mine."* Matthew 10:37
"You must not murder." Exodus 20:13	*"If you are even angry with someone, you are subject to judgment!"* Matthew 5:22
"You must not commit adultery." Exodus 20:14	*"Anyone who even looks at a woman with lust has already committed adultery with her in his heart."* Matthew 5:28
"You must not steal." Exodus 20:15	*"If . . . your shirt is taken from you, give your coat, too."* Matthew 5:40
"You must not testify falsely against your neighbor." Exodus 20:16	*"You must give an account on judgment day for every idle word you speak."* Matthew 12:36
"You must not covet." Exodus 20:17	*"Beware! Guard against every kind of greed."* Luke 12:15

five posts from acacia wood. Overlay them with gold, and hang the curtain from them with gold hooks. Cast five bronze bases for the posts.

CHAPTER 27

Plans for the Altar of Burnt Offering

"Using acacia wood, construct a square altar 7½ feet wide, 7½ feet long, and 4½ feet high.* [2]Make horns for each of its four corners so that the horns and altar are all one piece. Overlay the altar with bronze. [3]Make ash buckets, shovels, basins, meat forks, and firepans, all of bronze. [4]Make a bronze grating for it, and attach four bronze rings at its four corners. [5]Install the grating halfway down the side of the altar, under the ledge. [6]For carrying the altar, make poles from acacia wood, and overlay them with bronze. [7]Insert the poles through the rings on the two sides of the altar. [8]The altar must be hollow, made from planks. Build it just as you were shown on the mountain.

Plans for the Courtyard

[9]"Then make the courtyard for the Tabernacle, enclosed with curtains made of finely woven linen. On the south side, make the curtains 150 feet long.* [10]They will be held up by twenty posts set securely in twenty bronze bases. Hang the curtains with silver hooks and rings. [11]Make the curtains the same on the north side—150 feet of curtains held up by twenty posts set securely in bronze bases. Hang the curtains with silver hooks and rings. [12]The curtains on the west end of the courtyard will be 75 feet long,* supported by ten posts set into ten bases. [13]The east end of the courtyard, the front, will also be 75 feet long. [14]The courtyard entrance will be on the east end, flanked by two curtains. The curtain on the right side will be 22½ feet long,* supported by three posts set into three bases. [15]The curtain on the left side will also be 22½ feet long, supported by three posts set into three bases.

[16]"For the entrance to the courtyard, make a curtain that is 30 feet long.* Make it from finely woven linen, and decorate it with beautiful embroidery in blue, purple, and scarlet thread. Support it with four posts, each securely set in its own base. [17]All the posts around the courtyard must have silver rings and hooks and bronze bases. [18]So the entire courtyard will be 150 feet long and 75 feet wide, with curtain walls 7½ feet high,* made from finely woven linen. The bases for the posts will be made of bronze.

[19]"All the articles used in the rituals of the Tabernacle, including all the tent pegs used to support the Tabernacle and the courtyard curtains, must be made of bronze.

Light for the Tabernacle

[20]"Command the people of Israel to bring you pure oil of pressed olives for the light, to keep the lamps burning continually. [21]The lampstand will stand in the Tabernacle, in front of the inner curtain that shields the Ark of the Covenant.* Aaron and his sons must keep the lamps burning in the LORD's presence all night. This is a permanent law for the people of Israel, and it must be observed from generation to generation.

CHAPTER 28

Clothing for the Priests

"Call for your brother, Aaron, and his sons, Nadab, Abihu, Eleazar, and Ithamar. Set them apart from the rest of the people of Israel so they may minister to me and be my priests. [2]Make sacred garments for Aaron that are glorious and beautiful. [3]Instruct all the skilled craftsmen whom I have filled with the spirit of wisdom. Have them make garments for Aaron that will distinguish him as a priest set apart for my service. [4]These are the garments they are to make: a chestpiece, an ephod, a robe, a patterned tunic, a turban, and a sash. They are to make these sacred garments for your brother, Aaron, and his sons to wear when they serve me as priests. [5]So give them fine linen cloth, gold thread, and blue, purple, and scarlet thread.

Design of the Ephod

[6]"The craftsmen must make the ephod of finely woven linen and skillfully embroider it with gold and with blue, purple, and scarlet thread. [7]It will consist of two pieces, front and back, joined at the shoulders with two

27:1 Hebrew *5 cubits* [2.3 meters] *wide, 5 cubits long, a square, and 3 cubits* [1.4 meters] *high.* **27:9** Hebrew *100 cubits* [46 meters]; also in 27:11. **27:12** Hebrew *50 cubits* [23 meters]; also in 27:13. **27:14** Hebrew *15 cubits* [6.9 meters]; also in 27:15. **27:16** Hebrew *20 cubits* [9.2 meters]. **27:18** Hebrew *100 cubits* [46 meters] *long and 50 by 50* [23 meters] *wide and 5 cubits* [2.3 meters] *high.* **27:21** Hebrew *in the Tent of Meeting, outside the inner curtain that is in front of the Testimony.* See note on 25:16.

shoulder-pieces. [8]The decorative sash will be made of the same materials: finely woven linen embroidered with gold and with blue, purple, and scarlet thread.

[9]"Take two onyx stones, and engrave on them the names of the tribes of Israel. [10]Six names will be on each stone, arranged in the order of the births of the original sons of Israel. [11]Engrave these names on the two stones in the same way a jeweler engraves a seal. Then mount the stones in settings of gold filigree. [12]Fasten the two stones on the shoulder-pieces of the ephod as a reminder that Aaron represents the people of Israel. Aaron will carry these names on his shoulders as a constant reminder whenever he goes before the LORD. [13]Make the settings of gold filigree, [14]then braid two cords of pure gold and attach them to the filigree settings on the shoulders of the ephod.

Design of the Chestpiece

[15]"Then, with great skill and care, make a chestpiece to be worn for seeking a decision from God.* Make it to match the ephod, using finely woven linen embroidered with gold and with blue, purple, and scarlet thread. [16]Make the chestpiece of a single piece of cloth folded to form a pouch nine inches* square. [17]Mount four rows of gemstones* on it. The first row will contain a red carnelian, a pale-green peridot, and an emerald. [18]The second row will contain a turquoise, a blue lapis lazuli, and a white moonstone. [19]The third row will contain an orange jacinth, an agate, and a purple amethyst. [20]The fourth row will contain a blue-green beryl, an onyx, and a green jasper. All these stones will be set in gold filigree. [21]Each stone will represent one of the twelve sons of Israel, and the name of that tribe will be engraved on it like a seal.

[22]"To attach the chestpiece to the ephod, make braided cords of pure gold thread. [23]Then make two gold rings and attach them to the top corners of the chestpiece. [24]Tie the two gold cords to the two rings on the chestpiece. [25]Tie the other ends of the cords to the gold settings on the shoulder-pieces of the ephod. [26]Then make two more gold rings and attach them to the inside edges of the chestpiece next to the ephod. [27]And make two more gold rings and attach them to the front of the ephod, below the shoulder-pieces, just above the knot where the decorative sash is fastened to the ephod. [28]Then attach the bottom rings of the chestpiece to the rings on the ephod with blue cords. This will hold the chestpiece securely to the ephod above the decorative sash.

[29]"In this way, Aaron will carry the names of the tribes of Israel on the sacred chestpiece* over his heart when he goes into the Holy Place. This will be a continual reminder that he represents the people when he comes before the LORD. [30]Insert the Urim and Thummim into the sacred chestpiece so they will be carried over Aaron's heart when he goes into the LORD's presence. In this way, Aaron will always carry over his heart the objects used to determine the LORD's will for his people whenever he goes in before the LORD.

Additional Clothing for the Priests

[31]"Make the robe that is worn with the ephod from a single piece of blue cloth, [32]with an opening for Aaron's head in the middle of it. Reinforce the opening with a woven collar* so it will not tear. [33]Make pomegranates out of blue, purple, and scarlet yarn, and attach them to the hem of the robe, with gold bells between them. [34]The gold bells and pomegranates are to alternate all around the hem. [35]Aaron will wear this robe whenever he ministers before the LORD, and the bells will tinkle as he goes in and out of the LORD's presence in the Holy Place. If he wears it, he will not die.

[36]"Next make a medallion of pure gold, and engrave it like a seal with these words: HOLY TO THE LORD. [37]Attach the medallion with a blue cord to the front of Aaron's turban, where it must remain. [38]Aaron must wear it on his forehead so he may take on himself any guilt of the people of Israel when they consecrate their sacred offerings. He must always wear it on his forehead so the LORD will accept the people.

[39]"Weave Aaron's patterned tunic from fine linen cloth. Fashion the turban from this linen as well. Also make a sash, and decorate it with colorful embroidery.

[40]"For Aaron's sons, make tunics, sashes, and

28:15 Hebrew *a chestpiece for decision.* **28:16** Hebrew *1 span* [23 centimeters]. **28:17** The identification of some of these gemstones is uncertain. **28:29** Hebrew *the chestpiece for decision;* also in 28:30. See 28:15. **28:32** The meaning of the Hebrew is uncertain.

special head coverings that are glorious and beautiful. [41]Clothe your brother, Aaron, and his sons with these garments, and then anoint and ordain them. Consecrate them so they can serve as my priests. [42]Also make linen undergarments for them, to be worn next to their bodies, reaching from their hips to their thighs. [43]These must be worn whenever Aaron and his sons enter the Tabernacle* or approach the altar in the Holy Place to perform their priestly duties. Then they will not incur guilt and die. This is a permanent law for Aaron and all his descendants after him.

CHAPTER 29

Dedication of the Priests

"This is the ceremony you must follow when you consecrate Aaron and his sons to serve me as priests: Take a young bull and two rams with no defects. [2]Then, using choice wheat flour and no yeast, make loaves of bread, thin cakes mixed with olive oil, and wafers spread with oil. [3]Place them all in a single basket, and present them at the entrance of the Tabernacle, along with the young bull and the two rams.

[4]"Present Aaron and his sons at the entrance of the Tabernacle,* and wash them with water. [5]Dress Aaron in his priestly garments—the tunic, the robe worn with the ephod, the ephod itself, and the chestpiece. Then wrap the decorative sash of the ephod around him. [6]Place the turban on his head, and fasten the sacred medallion to the turban. [7]Then anoint him by pouring the anointing oil over his head. [8]Next present his sons, and dress them in their tunics. [9]Wrap the sashes around the waists of Aaron and his sons, and put their special head coverings on them. Then the right to the priesthood will be theirs by law forever. In this way, you will ordain Aaron and his sons.

[10]"Bring the young bull to the entrance of the Tabernacle, where Aaron and his sons will lay their hands on its head. [11]Then slaughter the bull in the LORD's presence at the entrance of the Tabernacle. [12]Put some of its blood on the horns of the altar with your finger, and pour out the rest at the base of the altar. [13]Take all the fat around the internal organs, the long lobe of the liver, and the two kidneys and the fat around them, and burn it all on the altar. [14]Then take the rest of the bull, including its hide, meat, and dung, and burn it outside the camp as a sin offering.

[15]"Next Aaron and his sons must lay their hands on the head of one of the rams. [16]Then slaughter the ram, and splatter its blood against all sides of the altar. [17]Cut the ram into pieces, and wash off the internal organs and the legs. Set them alongside the head and the other pieces of the body, [18]then burn the entire animal on the altar. This is a burnt offering to the LORD; it is a pleasing aroma, a special gift presented to the LORD.

[19]"Now take the other ram, and have Aaron and his sons lay their hands on its head. [20]Then slaughter it, and apply some of its blood to the right earlobes of Aaron and his sons. Also put it on the thumbs of their right hands and the big toes of their right feet. Splatter the rest of the blood against all sides of the altar. [21]Then take some of the blood from the altar and some of the anointing oil, and sprinkle it on Aaron and his sons and on their garments. In this way, they and their garments will be set apart as holy.

[22]"Since this is the ram for the ordination of Aaron and his sons, take the fat of the ram, including the fat of the broad tail, the fat around the internal organs, the long lobe of the liver, and the two kidneys and the fat around them, along with the right thigh. [23]Then take one round loaf of bread, one thin cake mixed with olive oil, and one wafer from the basket of bread without yeast that was placed in the LORD's presence. [24]Put all these in the hands of Aaron and his sons to be lifted up as a special offering to the LORD. [25]Afterward take the various breads from their hands, and burn them on the altar along with the burnt offering. It is a pleasing aroma to the LORD, a special gift for him. [26]Then take the breast of Aaron's ordination ram, and lift it up in the LORD's presence as a special offering to him. Then keep it as your own portion.

[27]"Set aside the portions of the ordination ram that belong to Aaron and his sons. This includes the breast and the thigh that were lifted up before the LORD as a special offering. [28]In the future, whenever the people of Israel lift up a peace offering, a portion of it must be set aside for Aaron and his descen-

28:43 Hebrew *Tent of Meeting*. **29:4** Hebrew *Tent of Meeting;* also in 29:10, 11, 30, 32, 42, 44.

dants. This is their permanent right, and it is a sacred offering from the Israelites to the LORD.

29"Aaron's sacred garments must be preserved for his descendants who succeed him, and they will wear them when they are anointed and ordained. 30The descendant who succeeds him as high priest will wear these clothes for seven days as he ministers in the Tabernacle and the Holy Place.

31"Take the ram used in the ordination ceremony, and boil its meat in a sacred place. 32Then Aaron and his sons will eat this meat, along with the bread in the basket, at the Tabernacle entrance. 33They alone may eat the meat and bread used for their purification* in the ordination ceremony. No one else may eat them, for these things are set apart and holy. 34If any of the ordination meat or bread remains until the morning, it must be burned. It may not be eaten, for it is holy.

35"This is how you will ordain Aaron and his sons to their offices, just as I have commanded you. The ordination ceremony will go on for seven days. 36Each day you must sacrifice a young bull as a sin offering to purify them, making them right with the LORD.* Afterward, cleanse the altar by purifying it*; make it holy by anointing it with oil. 37Purify the altar, and consecrate it every day for seven days. After that, the altar will be absolutely holy, and whatever touches it will become holy.

38"These are the sacrifices you are to offer regularly on the altar. Each day, offer two lambs that are a year old, 39one in the morning and the other in the evening. 40With one of them, offer two quarts of choice flour mixed with one quart of pure oil of pressed olives; also, offer one quart of wine* as a liquid offering. 41Offer the other lamb in the evening, along with the same offerings of flour and wine as in the morning. It will be a pleasing aroma, a special gift presented to the LORD.

42"These burnt offerings are to be made each day from generation to generation. Offer them in the LORD's presence at the Tabernacle entrance; there I will meet with you and speak with you. 43I will meet the people of Israel there, in the place made holy by my glorious presence. 44Yes, I will consecrate the Tabernacle and the altar, and I will consecrate Aaron and his sons to serve me as priests. 45Then I will live among the people of Israel and be their God, 46and they will know that I am the LORD their God. I am the one who brought them out of the land of Egypt so that I could live among them. I am the LORD their God.

CHAPTER 30

Plans for the Incense Altar

"Then make another altar of acacia wood for burning incense. 2Make it 18 inches square and 36 inches high,* with horns at the corners carved from the same piece of wood as the altar itself. 3Overlay the top, sides, and horns of the altar with pure gold, and run a gold molding around the entire altar. 4Make two gold rings, and attach them on opposite sides of the altar below the gold molding to hold the carrying poles. 5Make the poles of acacia wood and overlay them with gold. 6Place the incense altar just outside the inner curtain that shields the Ark of the Covenant,* in front of the Ark's cover—the place of atonement—that covers the tablets inscribed with the terms of the covenant.* I will meet with you there.

7"Every morning when Aaron maintains the lamps, he must burn fragrant incense on the altar. 8And each evening when he lights the lamps, he must again burn incense in the LORD's presence. This must be done from generation to generation. 9Do not offer any unholy incense on this altar, or any burnt offerings, grain offerings, or liquid offerings.

10"Once a year Aaron must purify* the altar by smearing its horns with blood from the offering made to purify the people from their sin. This will be a regular, annual event from generation to generation, for this is the LORD's most holy altar."

Money for the Tabernacle

11Then the LORD said to Moses, 12"Whenever you take a census of the people of Israel, each man who is counted must pay a ransom for himself to the LORD. Then no plague will strike the people as you count them. 13Each

29:33 Or *their atonement.* **29:36a** Or *to make atonement.* **29:36b** Or *by making atonement for it;* similarly in 29:37.
29:40 Hebrew *1/10 of an ephah* [2.2 liters] *of choice flour . . . 1/4 of a hin* [1 liter] *of pure oil . . . 1/4 of a hin of wine.* **30:2** Hebrew *1 cubit* [46 centimeters] *long and 1 cubit wide, a square, and 2 cubits* [92 centimeters] *high.* **30:6a** Or *Ark of the Testimony;* also in 30:26.
30:6b Hebrew *that covers the Testimony;* see note on 25:16. **30:10** Or *make atonement for;* also in 30:10b.

person who is counted must give a small
piece of silver as a sacred offering to the
LORD. (This payment is half a shekel,* based
on the sanctuary shekel, which equals twenty
gerahs.) 14All who have reached their twenti-
eth birthday must give this sacred offering to
the LORD. 15When this offering is given to the
LORD to purify your lives, making you right
with him,* the rich must not give more than
the specified amount, and the poor must not
give less. 16Receive this ransom money from
the Israelites, and use it for the care of the
Tabernacle.* It will bring the Israelites to the
LORD's attention, and it will purify your lives."

Plans for the Washbasin

17Then the LORD said to Moses, 18"Make a
bronze washbasin with a bronze stand. Place
it between the Tabernacle and the altar, and
fill it with water. 19Aaron and his sons will
wash their hands and feet there. 20They must
wash with water whenever they go into the
Tabernacle to appear before the LORD and
when they approach the altar to burn up their
special gifts to the LORD—or they will die!
21They must always wash their hands and feet,
or they will die. This is a permanent law for
Aaron and his descendants, to be observed
from generation to generation."

The Anointing Oil

22Then the LORD said to Moses, 23"Collect
choice spices—12½ pounds of pure myrrh,
6¼ pounds of fragrant cinnamon, 6¼ pounds
of fragrant calamus,* 24and 12½ pounds of
cassia*—as measured by the weight of the
sanctuary shekel. Also get one gallon of olive
oil.* 25Like a skilled incense maker, blend
these ingredients to make a holy anointing
oil. 26Use this sacred oil to anoint the Taber-
nacle, the Ark of the Covenant, 27the table and
all its utensils, the lampstand and all its acces-
sories, the incense altar, 28the altar of burnt
offering and all its utensils, and the wash-
basin with its stand. 29Consecrate them to
make them absolutely holy. After this, what-
ever touches them will also become holy.

30"Anoint Aaron and his sons also, conse-
crating them to serve me as priests. 31And say
to the people of Israel, 'This holy anointing oil
is reserved for me from generation to genera-
tion. 32It must never be used to anoint anyone
else, and you must never make any blend like
it for yourselves. It is holy, and you must treat
it as holy. 33Anyone who makes a blend like it
or anoints someone other than a priest will be
cut off from the community.'"

The Incense

34Then the LORD said to Moses, "Gather fra-
grant spices—resin droplets, mollusk shell,
and galbanum—and mix these fragrant spices
with pure frankincense, weighed out in equal
amounts. 35Using the usual techniques of the
incense maker, blend the spices together and
sprinkle them with salt to produce a pure and
holy incense. 36Grind some of the mixture into
a very fine powder and put it in front of the
Ark of the Covenant,* where I will meet with
you in the Tabernacle. You must treat this in-
cense as most holy. 37Never use this formula to
make this incense for yourselves. It is reserved
for the LORD, and you must treat it as holy.
38Anyone who makes incense like this for per-
sonal use will be cut off from the community."

CHAPTER 31

Craftsmen: Bezalel and Oholiab

Then the LORD said to Moses, 2"Look, I have
specifically chosen Bezalel son of Uri, grand-
son of Hur, of the tribe of Judah. 3I have filled
him with the Spirit of God, giving him great
wisdom, ability, and expertise in all kinds
of crafts. 4He is a master craftsman, expert in
working with gold, silver, and bronze. 5He is
skilled in engraving and mounting gemstones
and in carving wood. He is a master at every
craft!

6"And I have personally appointed Oholiab
son of Ahisamach, of the tribe of Dan, to be
his assistant. Moreover, I have given special
skill to all the gifted craftsmen so they can
make all the things I have commanded you to
make:

7 the Tabernacle;*
the Ark of the Covenant;*
the Ark's cover—the place of atonement;

30:13 Or *0.2 ounces,* or *6 grams.* **30:15** Or *to make atonement for your lives;* similarly in 30:16. **30:16** Hebrew *Tent of Meeting;* also in 30:18, 20, 26, 36. **30:23** Hebrew *500 shekels* [5.7 kilograms] *of pure myrrh, 250 shekels* [2.9 kilograms] *of fragrant cinnamon, 250 shekels of fragrant calamus.* **30:24a** Hebrew *500 shekels* [5.7 kilograms] *of cassia.* **30:24b** Hebrew *1 hin* [3.8 liters] *of olive oil.* **30:36** Hebrew *in front of the Testimony;* see note on 25:16. **31:7a** Hebrew *the Tent of Meeting.* **31:7b** Hebrew *the Ark of the Testimony.*

all the furnishings of the Tabernacle;
8 the table and its utensils;
the pure gold lampstand with all its accessories;
the incense altar;
9 the altar of burnt offering with all its utensils;
the washbasin with its stand;
10 the beautifully stitched garments—the sacred garments for Aaron the priest, and the garments for his sons to wear as they minister as priests;
11 the anointing oil;
the fragrant incense for the Holy Place.

The craftsmen must make everything as I have commanded you."

Instructions for the Sabbath

12The LORD then gave these instructions to Moses: 13"Tell the people of Israel: 'Be careful to keep my Sabbath day, for the Sabbath is a sign of the covenant between me and you from generation to generation. It is given so you may know that I am the LORD, who makes you holy. 14You must keep the Sabbath day, for it is a holy day for you. Anyone who desecrates it must be put to death; anyone who works on that day will be cut off from the community. 15You have six days each week for your ordinary work, but the seventh day must be a Sabbath day of complete rest, a holy day dedicated to the LORD. Anyone who works on the Sabbath must be put to death. 16The people of Israel must keep the Sabbath day by observing it from generation to generation. This is a covenant obligation for all time. 17It is a permanent sign of my covenant with the people of Israel. For in six days the LORD made heaven and earth, but on the seventh day he stopped working and was refreshed.'"

18When the LORD finished speaking with Moses on Mount Sinai, he gave him the two stone tablets inscribed with the terms of the covenant,* written by the finger of God.

CHAPTER 32

The Gold Calf

When the people saw how long it was taking Moses to come back down the mountain, they gathered around Aaron. "Come on," they said, "make us some gods who can lead us. We don't know what happened to this fellow Moses, who brought us here from the land of Egypt."

2So Aaron said, "Take the gold rings from the ears of your wives and sons and daughters, and bring them to me."

3All the people took the gold rings from their ears and brought them to Aaron. 4Then Aaron took the gold, melted it down, and molded it into the shape of a calf. When the people saw it, they exclaimed, "O Israel, these are the gods who brought you out of the land of Egypt!"

5Aaron saw how excited the people were, so he built an altar in front of the calf. Then he announced, "Tomorrow will be a festival to the LORD!"

AMAZING FACTS

While God wrote the Ten Commandments, did the Israelites worship him? No. They made and worshiped a gold calf. Arrgh!

EXODUS 32:1-20

6The people got up early the next morning to sacrifice burnt offerings and peace offerings. After this, they celebrated with feasting and drinking, and they indulged in pagan revelry.

7The LORD told Moses, "Quick! Go down the mountain! Your people whom you brought from the land of Egypt have corrupted themselves. 8How quickly they have turned away from the way I commanded them to live! They have melted down gold and made a calf, and they have bowed down and sacrificed to it. They are saying, 'These are your gods, O Israel, who brought you out of the land of Egypt.'"

31:18 Hebrew *the two tablets of the Testimony;* see note on 25:16.

[9]Then the LORD said, "I have seen how stubborn and rebellious these people are. [10]Now leave me alone so my fierce anger can blaze against them, and I will destroy them. Then I will make you, Moses, into a great nation."

[11]But Moses tried to pacify the LORD his God. "O LORD!" he said. "Why are you so angry with your own people whom you brought from the land of Egypt with such great power and such a strong hand? [12]Why let the Egyptians say, 'Their God rescued them with the evil intention of slaughtering them in the mountains and wiping them from the face of the earth'? Turn away from your fierce anger. Change your mind about this terrible disaster you have threatened against your people! [13]Remember your servants Abraham, Isaac, and Jacob.* You bound yourself with an oath to them, saying, 'I will make your descendants as numerous as the stars of heaven. And I will give them all of this land that I have promised to your descendants, and they will possess it forever.'"

[14]So the LORD changed his mind about the terrible disaster he had threatened to bring on his people.

[15]Then Moses turned and went down the mountain. He held in his hands the two stone tablets inscribed with the terms of the covenant.* They were inscribed on both sides, front and back. [16]These tablets were God's work; the words on them were written by God himself.

[17]When Joshua heard the boisterous noise of the people shouting below them, he exclaimed to Moses, "It sounds like war in the camp!"

[18]But Moses replied, "No, it's not a shout of victory nor the wailing of defeat. I hear the sound of a celebration."

[19]When they came near the camp, Moses saw the calf and the dancing, and he burned with anger. He threw the stone tablets to the ground, smashing them at the foot of the mountain. [20]He took the calf they had made and burned it. Then he ground it into powder, threw it into the water, and forced the people to drink it.

[21]Finally, he turned to Aaron and demanded, "What did these people do to you to make you bring such terrible sin upon them?"

[22]"Don't get so upset, my lord," Aaron replied. "You yourself know how evil these people are. [23]They said to me, 'Make us gods who will lead us. We don't know what happened to this fellow Moses, who brought us here from the land of Egypt.' [24]So I told them, 'Whoever has gold jewelry, take it off.' When they brought it to me, I simply threw it into the fire—and out came this calf!"

[25]Moses saw that Aaron had let the people get completely out of control, much to the amusement of their enemies.* [26]So he stood at the entrance to the camp and shouted, "All of you who are on the LORD's side, come here and join me." And all the Levites gathered around him.

[27]Moses told them, "This is what the LORD, the God of Israel, says: Each of you, take your swords and go back and forth from one end of the camp to the other. Kill everyone—even your brothers, friends, and neighbors." [28]The Levites obeyed Moses' command, and about 3,000 people died that day.

[29]Then Moses told the Levites, "Today you have ordained yourselves* for the service of the LORD, for you obeyed him even though it meant killing your own sons and brothers. Today you have earned a blessing."

Moses Intercedes for Israel

[30]The next day Moses said to the people, "You have committed a terrible sin, but I will go back up to the LORD on the mountain. Perhaps I will be able to obtain forgiveness* for your sin."

[31]So Moses returned to the LORD and said, "Oh, what a terrible sin these people have committed. They have made gods of gold for themselves. [32]But now, if you will only forgive their sin—but if not, erase my name from the record you have written!"

[33]But the LORD replied to Moses, "No, I will erase the name of everyone who has sinned against me. [34]Now go, lead the people to the place I told you about. Look! My angel will lead the way before you. And when I come to call the people to account, I will certainly hold them responsible for their sins."

32:13 Hebrew *Israel*. The names "Jacob" and "Israel" are often interchanged throughout the Old Testament, referring sometimes to the individual patriarch and sometimes to the nation. **32:15** Hebrew *the two tablets of the Testimony;* see note on 25:16. **32:25** Or *out of control, and they mocked anyone who opposed them.* The meaning of the Hebrew is unclear. **32:29** As in Greek and Latin versions; Hebrew reads *Today ordain yourselves.* **32:30** Or *to make atonement.*

[35]Then the LORD sent a great plague upon the people because they had worshiped the calf Aaron had made.

CHAPTER 33

The LORD said to Moses, "Get going, you and the people you brought up from the land of Egypt. Go up to the land I swore to give to Abraham, Isaac, and Jacob. I told them, 'I will give this land to your descendants.' [2]And I will send an angel before you to drive out the Canaanites, Amorites, Hittites, Perizzites, Hivites, and Jebusites. [3]Go up to this land that flows with milk and honey. But I will not travel among you, for you are a stubborn and rebellious people. If I did, I would surely destroy you along the way."

[4]When the people heard these stern words, they went into mourning and stopped wearing their jewelry and fine clothes. [5]For the LORD had told Moses to tell them, "You are a stubborn and rebellious people. If I were to travel with you for even a moment, I would destroy you. Remove your jewelry and fine clothes while I decide what to do with you." [6]So from the time they left Mount Sinai,* the Israelites wore no more jewelry or fine clothes.

[7]It was Moses' practice to take the Tent of Meeting* and set it up some distance from the camp. Everyone who wanted to make a request of the LORD would go to the Tent of Meeting outside the camp.

[8]Whenever Moses went out to the Tent of Meeting, all the people would get up and stand in the entrances of their own tents. They would all watch Moses until he disappeared inside. [9]As he went into the tent, the pillar of cloud would come down and hover at its entrance while the LORD spoke with Moses. [10]When the people saw the cloud standing at the entrance of the tent, they would stand and bow down in front of their own tents. [11]Inside the Tent of Meeting, the LORD would speak to Moses face to face, as one speaks to a friend. Afterward Moses would return to the camp, but the young man who assisted him, Joshua son of Nun, would remain behind in the Tent of Meeting.

Moses Sees the LORD's Glory

[12]One day Moses said to the LORD, "You have been telling me, 'Take these people up to the Promised Land.' But you haven't told me whom you will send with me. You have told me, 'I know you by name, and I look favorably on you.' [13]If it is true that you look favorably on me, let me know your ways so I may understand you more fully and continue to enjoy your favor. And remember that this nation is your very own people."

[14]The LORD replied, "I will personally go with you, Moses, and I will give you rest—everything will be fine for you."

[15]Then Moses said, "If you don't personally go with us, don't make us leave this place. [16]How will anyone know that you look favorably on me—on me and on your people—if you don't go with us? For your presence among us sets your people and me apart from all other people on the earth."

[17]The LORD replied to Moses, "I will indeed do what you have asked, for I look favorably on you, and I know you by name."

[18]Moses responded, "Then show me your glorious presence."

[19]The LORD replied, "I will make all my goodness pass before you, and I will call out my name, Yahweh,* before you. For I will show mercy to anyone I choose, and I will show compassion to anyone I choose. [20]But you may not look directly at my face, for no one may see me and live." [21]The LORD continued, "Look, stand near me on this rock. [22]As my glorious presence passes by, I will hide you in the crevice of the rock and cover you with my hand until I have passed by. [23]Then I will remove my hand and let you see me from behind. But my face will not be seen."

CHAPTER 34

A New Copy of the Covenant

Then the LORD told Moses, "Chisel out two stone tablets like the first ones. I will write on them the same words that were on the tablets you smashed. [2]Be ready in the morning to climb up Mount Sinai and present yourself to me on the top of the mountain. [3]No one else may come with you. In fact, no one is to appear anywhere on the mountain. Do not even

33:6 Hebrew *Horeb*, another name for Sinai. **33:7** This "Tent of Meeting" is different from the Tabernacle described in chapters 26 and 36. **33:19** *Yahweh* is a transliteration of the proper name *YHWH* that is sometimes rendered "Jehovah"; in this translation it is usually rendered "the LORD" (note the use of small capitals).

let the flocks or herds graze near the mountain."

4So Moses chiseled out two tablets of stone like the first ones. Early in the morning he climbed Mount Sinai as the LORD had commanded him, and he carried the two stone tablets in his hands.

5Then the LORD came down in a cloud and stood there with him; and he called out his own name, Yahweh.* 6The LORD passed in front of Moses, calling out,

"Yahweh!* The LORD!
The God of compassion and mercy!
I am slow to anger
and filled with unfailing love and faithfulness.
7 I lavish unfailing love to a thousand generations.*
I forgive iniquity, rebellion, and sin.
But I do not excuse the guilty.
I lay the sins of the parents upon their children and grandchildren;
the entire family is affected—
even children in the third and fourth generations."

8Moses immediately threw himself to the ground and worshiped. 9And he said, "O Lord, if it is true that I have found favor with you, then please travel with us. Yes, this is a stubborn and rebellious people, but please forgive our iniquity and our sins. Claim us as your own special possession."

10The LORD replied, "Listen, I am making a covenant with you in the presence of all your people. I will perform miracles that have never been performed anywhere in all the earth or in any nation. And all the people around you will see the power of the LORD—the awesome power I will display for you. 11But listen carefully to everything I command you today. Then I will go ahead of you and drive out the Amorites, Canaanites, Hittites, Perizzites, Hivites, and Jebusites.

12"Be very careful never to make a treaty with the people who live in the land where you are going. If you do, you will follow their evil ways and be trapped. 13Instead, you must break down their pagan altars, smash their sacred pillars, and cut down their Asherah poles. 14You must worship no other gods, for the LORD, whose very name is Jealous, is a God who is jealous about his relationship with you.

Does God ever get angry at us?

[I am] the God of compassion and mercy! I am slow to anger and filled with unfailing love and faithfulness.

EXODUS 34:6

15"You must not make a treaty of any kind with the people living in the land. They lust after their gods, offering sacrifices to them. They will invite you to join them in their sacrificial meals, and you will go with them. 16Then you will accept their daughters, who sacrifice to other gods, as wives for your sons. And they will seduce your sons to commit adultery against me by worshiping other gods. 17You must not make any gods of molten metal for yourselves.

18"You must celebrate the Festival of Unleavened Bread. For seven days the bread you eat must be made without yeast, just as I commanded you. Celebrate this festival annually at the appointed time in early spring, in the month of Abib,* for that is the anniversary of your departure from Egypt.

19"The firstborn of every animal belongs to me, including the firstborn males from your herds of cattle and your flocks of sheep and goats. 20A firstborn donkey may be bought back from the LORD by presenting a lamb or young goat in its place. But if you do not buy it back, you must break its neck. However, you must buy back every firstborn son.

"No one may appear before me without an offering.

21"You have six days each week for your ordinary work, but on the seventh day you must stop working, even during the seasons of plowing and harvest.

34:5 *Yahweh* is a transliteration of the proper name *YHWH* that is sometimes rendered "Jehovah"; in this translation it is usually rendered "the LORD" (note the use of small capitals). **34:6** See note on 34:5. **34:7** Hebrew *for thousands.* **34:18** Hebrew *appointed time in the month of Abib.* This first month of the ancient Hebrew lunar calendar usually occurs within the months of March and April.

22"You must celebrate the Festival of Harvest* with the first crop of the wheat harvest,
and celebrate the Festival of the Final Harvest* at the end of the harvest season. 23Three
times each year every man in Israel must appear before the Sovereign, the LORD, the God
of Israel. 24I will drive out the other nations ahead of you and expand your territory, so no
one will covet and conquer your land while you appear before the LORD your God three
times each year.

25"You must not offer the blood of my sacrificial offerings together with any baked
goods containing yeast. And none of the meat of the Passover sacrifice may be kept over until the next morning.

26"As you harvest your crops, bring the very best of the first harvest to the house of the
LORD your God.

"You must not cook a young goat in its mother's milk."

27Then the LORD said to Moses, "Write down all these instructions, for they represent the terms of the covenant I am making with you and with Israel."

28Moses remained there on the mountain with the LORD forty days and forty nights. In all that time he ate no bread and drank no water. And the LORD* wrote the terms of the covenant—the Ten Commandments*—on the stone tablets.

29When Moses came down Mount Sinai carrying the two stone tablets inscribed with the terms of the covenant,* he wasn't aware that his face had become radiant because he had spoken to the LORD. 30So when Aaron and the people of Israel saw the radiance of Moses' face, they were afraid to come near him.

31But Moses called out to them and asked Aaron and all the leaders of the community to come over, and he talked with them. 32Then all the people of Israel approached him, and Moses gave them all the instructions the LORD had given him on Mount Sinai. 33When Moses finished speaking with them, he covered his face with a veil. 34But whenever he went into the Tent of Meeting to speak with the LORD, he would remove the veil until he came out again. Then he would give the people whatever instructions the LORD had given him, 35and the people of Israel would see the radiant glow of his face. So he would put the veil over his face until he returned to speak with the LORD.

CHAPTER 35

Instructions for the Sabbath

Then Moses called together the whole community of Israel and told them, "These are the instructions the LORD has commanded you to follow. 2You have six days each week for your ordinary work, but the seventh day must be a Sabbath day of complete rest, a holy day dedicated to the LORD. Anyone who works on that day must be put to death. 3You must not even light a fire in any of your homes on the Sabbath."

Offerings for the Tabernacle

4Then Moses said to the whole community of Israel, "This is what the LORD has commanded: 5Take a sacred offering for the LORD. Let those with generous hearts present the following gifts to the LORD:

gold, silver, and bronze;
6 blue, purple, and scarlet thread;
fine linen and goat hair for cloth;
7 tanned ram skins and fine goatskin leather;
acacia wood;
8 olive oil for the lamps;
spices for the anointing oil and the fragrant incense;
9 onyx stones, and other gemstones to be set in the ephod and the priest's chestpiece.

10"Come, all of you who are gifted craftsmen. Construct everything that the LORD has commanded:

11 the Tabernacle and its sacred tent, its covering, clasps, frames, crossbars, posts, and bases;
12 the Ark and its carrying poles;
the Ark's cover—the place of atonement;
the inner curtain to shield the Ark;
13 the table, its carrying poles, and all its utensils;
the Bread of the Presence;

34:22a Hebrew *Festival of Weeks;* compare 23:16. This was later called the Festival of Pentecost. It is celebrated today as Shavuot (or Shabuoth). **34:22b** Or *Festival of Ingathering*. This was later called the Festival of Shelters or Festival of Tabernacles (see Lev 23:33-36). It is celebrated today as Sukkot (or Succoth). **34:28a** Hebrew *he*. **34:28b** Hebrew *the ten words*. **34:29** Hebrew *the two tablets of the Testimony;* see note on 25:16.

14 for light, the lampstand, its accessories,
the lamp cups, and the olive oil for
lighting;
15 the incense altar and its carrying poles;
the anointing oil and fragrant incense;
the curtain for the entrance of the
Tabernacle;
16 the altar of burnt offering;
the bronze grating of the altar and its
carrying poles and utensils;
the washbasin with its stand;
17 the curtains for the walls of the courtyard;
the posts and their bases;
the curtain for the entrance to the
courtyard;
18 the tent pegs of the Tabernacle and
courtyard and their ropes;
19 the beautifully stitched garments for the
priests to wear while ministering in the
Holy Place—the sacred garments for
Aaron the priest, and the garments for
his sons to wear as they minister as
priests."

20 So the whole community of Israel left Moses and returned to their tents. 21 All whose hearts were stirred and whose spirits were moved came and brought their sacred offerings to the LORD. They brought all the materials needed for the Tabernacle,* for the performance of its rituals, and for the sacred garments. 22 Both men and women came, all whose hearts were willing. They brought to the LORD their offerings of gold—brooches, earrings, rings from their fingers, and necklaces. They presented gold objects of every kind as a special offering to the LORD. 23 All those who owned the following items willingly brought them: blue, purple, and scarlet thread; fine linen and goat hair for cloth; and tanned ram skins and fine goatskin leather. 24 And all who had silver and bronze objects gave them as a sacred offering to the LORD. And those who had acacia wood brought it for use in the project.

25 All the women who were skilled in sewing and spinning prepared blue, purple, and scarlet thread, and fine linen cloth. 26 All the women who were willing used their skills to spin the goat hair into yarn. 27 The leaders brought onyx stones and the special gemstones to be set in the ephod and the priest's chestpiece. 28 They also brought spices and olive oil for the light, the anointing oil, and the fragrant incense. 29 So the people of Israel—every man and woman who was eager to help in the work the LORD had given them through Moses—brought their gifts and gave them freely to the LORD.

30 Then Moses told the people of Israel, "The LORD has specifically chosen Bezalel son of Uri, grandson of Hur, of the tribe of Judah. 31 The LORD has filled Bezalel with the Spirit of God, giving him great wisdom, ability, and expertise in all kinds of crafts. 32 He is a master craftsman, expert in working with gold, silver, and bronze. 33 He is skilled in engraving and mounting gemstones and in carving wood. He is a master at every craft. 34 And the LORD has given both him and Oholiab son of Ahisamach, of the tribe of Dan, the ability to teach their skills to others. 35 The LORD has given them special skills as engravers, designers, embroiderers in blue, purple, and scarlet thread on fine linen cloth, and weavers. They excel as craftsmen and as designers.

CHAPTER 36

"The LORD has gifted Bezalel, Oholiab, and the other skilled craftsmen with wisdom and ability to perform any task involved in building the sanctuary. Let them construct and furnish the Tabernacle, just as the LORD has commanded."

2 So Moses summoned Bezalel and Oholiab and all the others who were specially gifted by the LORD and were eager to get to work. 3 Moses gave them the materials donated by the people of Israel as sacred offerings for the completion of the sanctuary. But the people continued to bring additional gifts each morning. 4 Finally the craftsmen who were working on the sanctuary left their work. 5 They went to Moses and reported, "The people have given more than enough materials to complete the job the LORD has commanded us to do!"

6 So Moses gave the command, and this message was sent throughout the camp: "Men and women, don't prepare any more gifts for the sanctuary. We have enough!" So the people stopped bringing their sacred offerings. 7 Their contributions were more than enough to complete the whole project.

35:21 Hebrew *Tent of Meeting*.

Building the Tabernacle

8The skilled craftsmen made ten curtains of finely woven linen for the Tabernacle. Then Bezalel* decorated the curtains with blue, purple, and scarlet thread and with skillfully embroidered cherubim. 9All ten curtains were exactly the same size—42 feet long and 6 feet wide.* 10Five of these curtains were joined together to make one long curtain, and the other five were joined to make a second long curtain. 11He made fifty loops of blue yarn and put them along the edge of the last curtain in each set. 12The fifty loops along the edge of one curtain matched the fifty loops along the edge of the other curtain. 13Then he made fifty gold clasps and fastened the long curtains together with the clasps. In this way, the Tabernacle was made of one continuous piece.

14He made eleven curtains of goat-hair cloth to serve as a tent covering for the Tabernacle. 15These eleven curtains were all exactly the same size—45 feet long and 6 feet wide.* 16Bezalel joined five of these curtains together to make one long curtain, and the other six were joined to make a second long curtain. 17He made fifty loops for the edge of each large curtain. 18He also made fifty bronze clasps to fasten the long curtains together. In this way, the tent covering was made of one continuous piece. 19He completed the tent covering with a layer of tanned ram skins and a layer of fine goatskin leather.

20For the framework of the Tabernacle, Bezalel constructed frames of acacia wood. 21Each frame was 15 feet high and 27 inches wide,* 22with two pegs under each frame. All the frames were identical. 23He made twenty of these frames to support the curtains on the south side of the Tabernacle. 24He also made forty silver bases—two bases under each frame, with the pegs fitting securely into the bases. 25For the north side of the Tabernacle, he made another twenty frames, 26with their forty silver bases, two bases under each frame. 27He made six frames for the rear—the west side of the Tabernacle—28along with two additional frames to reinforce the rear corners of the Tabernacle. 29These corner frames were matched at the bottom and firmly attached at the top with a single ring, forming a single corner unit. Both of these corner units were made the same way. 30So there were eight frames at the rear of the Tabernacle, set in sixteen silver bases—two bases under each frame.

31Then he made crossbars of acacia wood to link the frames, five crossbars for the north side of the Tabernacle 32and five for the south side. He also made five crossbars for the rear of the Tabernacle, which faced west. 33He made the middle crossbar to attach halfway up the frames; it ran all the way from one end of the Tabernacle to the other. 34He overlaid the frames with gold and made gold rings to hold the crossbars. Then he overlaid the crossbars with gold as well.

35For the inside of the Tabernacle, Bezalel made a special curtain of finely woven linen. He decorated it with blue, purple, and scarlet thread and with skillfully embroidered cherubim. 36For the curtain, he made four posts of acacia wood and four gold hooks. He overlaid the posts with gold and set them in four silver bases.

37Then he made another curtain for the entrance to the sacred tent. He made it of finely woven linen and embroidered it with exquisite designs using blue, purple, and scarlet thread. 38This curtain was hung on gold hooks attached to five posts. The posts with their decorated tops and hooks were overlaid with gold, and the five bases were cast from bronze.

CHAPTER 37

Building the Ark of the Covenant

Next Bezalel made the Ark of acacia wood—a sacred chest 45 inches long, 27 inches wide, and 27 inches high.* 2He overlaid it inside and outside with pure gold, and he ran a molding of gold all around it. 3He cast four gold rings and attached them to its four feet, two rings on each side. 4Then he made poles from acacia wood and overlaid them with gold. 5He inserted the poles into the rings at the sides of the Ark to carry it.

6Then he made the Ark's cover—the place of atonement—from pure gold. It was 45 inches long and 27 inches wide.* 7He made two cherubim from hammered gold and placed them on the two ends of the

36:8 Hebrew *he;* also in 36:16, 20, 35. See 37:1. **36:9** Hebrew *28 cubits* [12.9 meters] *long and 4 cubits* [1.8 meters] *wide.* **36:15** Hebrew *30 cubits* [13.8 meters] *long and 4 cubits* [1.8 meters] *wide.* **36:21** Hebrew *10 cubits* [4.6 meters] *high and 1.5 cubits* [69 centimeters] *wide.* **37:1** Hebrew *2.5 cubits* [115 centimeters] *long, 1.5 cubits* [69 centimeters] *wide, and 1.5 cubits high.* **37:6** Hebrew *2.5 cubits* [115 centimeters] *long and 1.5 cubits* [69 centimeters] *wide.*

atonement cover. [8]He molded the cherubim on each end of the atonement cover, making it all of one piece of gold. [9]The cherubim faced each other and looked down on the atonement cover. With their wings spread above it, they protected it.

Building the Table

[10]Then Bezalel* made the table of acacia wood, 36 inches long, 18 inches wide, and 27 inches high.* [11]He overlaid it with pure gold and ran a gold molding around the edge. [12]He decorated it with a 3-inch border* all around, and he ran a gold molding along the border. [13]Then he cast four gold rings for the table and attached them at the four corners next to the four legs. [14]The rings were attached near the border to hold the poles that were used to carry the table. [15]He made these poles from acacia wood and overlaid them with gold. [16]Then he made special containers of pure gold for the table—bowls, pans, jars, and pitchers—to be used in pouring out liquid offerings.

Building the Lampstand

[17]Then Bezalel made the lampstand of pure, hammered gold. He made the entire lampstand and its decorations of one piece—the base, center stem, lamp cups, buds, and petals. [18]The lampstand had six branches going out from the center stem, three on each side. [19]Each of the six branches had three lamp cups shaped like almond blossoms, complete with buds and petals. [20]The center stem of the lampstand was crafted with four lamp cups shaped like almond blossoms, complete with buds and petals. [21]There was an almond bud beneath each pair of branches where the six branches extended from the center stem, all made of one piece. [22]The almond buds and branches were all of one piece with the center stem, and they were hammered from pure gold.

[23]He also made seven lamps for the lampstand, lamp snuffers, and trays, all of pure gold. [24]The entire lampstand, along with its accessories, was made from seventy-five pounds* of pure gold.

Building the Incense Altar

[25]Then Bezalel made the incense altar of acacia wood. It was 18 inches square and 36 inches high,* with horns at the corners carved from the same piece of wood as the altar itself. [26]He overlaid the top, sides, and horns of the altar with pure gold, and he ran a gold molding around the entire altar. [27]He made two gold rings and attached them on opposite sides of the altar below the gold molding to hold the carrying poles. [28]He made the poles of acacia wood and overlaid them with gold.

[29]Then he made the sacred anointing oil and the fragrant incense, using the techniques of a skilled incense maker.

CHAPTER 38

Building the Altar of Burnt Offering

Next Bezalel* used acacia wood to construct the square altar of burnt offering. It was 7½ feet wide, 7½ feet long, and 4½ feet high.* [2]He made horns for each of its four corners so that the horns and altar were all one piece. He overlaid the altar with bronze. [3]Then he made all the altar utensils of bronze—the ash buckets, shovels, basins, meat forks, and firepans. [4]Next he made a bronze grating and installed it halfway down the side of the altar, under the ledge. [5]He cast four rings and attached them to the corners of the bronze grating to hold the carrying poles. [6]He made the poles from acacia wood and overlaid them with bronze. [7]He inserted the poles through the rings on the sides of the altar. The altar was hollow and was made from planks.

Building the Washbasin

[8]Bezalel made the bronze washbasin and its bronze stand from bronze mirrors donated by the women who served at the entrance of the Tabernacle.*

Building the Courtyard

[9]Then Bezalel made the courtyard, which was enclosed with curtains made of finely woven linen. On the south side the curtains were 150 feet long.* [10]They were held up by twenty

37:10a Hebrew *he;* also in 37:17, 25. **37:10b** Hebrew *2 cubits* [92 centimeters] *long, 1 cubit* [46 centimeters] *wide, and 1.5 cubits* [69 centimeters] *high.* **37:12** Hebrew *a border of a handbreadth* [8 centimeters]. **37:24** Hebrew *1 talent* [34 kilograms]. **37:25** Hebrew *1 cubit* [46 centimeters] *long and 1 cubit wide, a square, and 2 cubits* [92 centimeters] *high.* **38:1a** Hebrew *he;* also in 38:8, 9. **38:1b** Hebrew *5 cubits* [2.3 meters] *wide, 5 cubits long, a square, and 3 cubits* [1.4 meters] *high.* **38:8** Hebrew *Tent of Meeting;* also in 38:30. **38:9** Hebrew *100 cubits* [46 meters]; also in 38:11.

posts set securely in twenty bronze bases. He hung the curtains with silver hooks and rings. [11]He made a similar set of curtains for the north side—150 feet of curtains held up by twenty posts set securely in bronze bases. He hung the curtains with silver hooks and rings. [12]The curtains on the west end of the courtyard were 75 feet long,* hung with silver hooks and rings and supported by ten posts set into ten bases. [13]The east end, the front, was also 75 feet long.

[14]The courtyard entrance was on the east end, flanked by two curtains. The curtain on the right side was 22½ feet long* and was supported by three posts set into three bases. [15]The curtain on the left side was also 22½ feet long and was supported by three posts set into three bases. [16]All the curtains used in the courtyard were made of finely woven linen. [17]Each post had a bronze base, and all the hooks and rings were silver. The tops of the posts of the courtyard were overlaid with silver, and the rings to hold up the curtains were made of silver.

[18]He made the curtain for the entrance to the courtyard of finely woven linen, and he decorated it with beautiful embroidery in blue, purple, and scarlet thread. It was 30 feet long, and its height was 7½ feet,* just like the curtains of the courtyard walls. [19]It was supported by four posts, each set securely in its own bronze base. The tops of the posts were overlaid with silver, and the hooks and rings were also made of silver.

[20]All the tent pegs used in the Tabernacle and courtyard were made of bronze.

Inventory of Materials

[21]This is an inventory of the materials used in building the Tabernacle of the Covenant.* The Levites compiled the figures, as Moses directed, and Ithamar son of Aaron the priest served as recorder. [22]Bezalel son of Uri, grandson of Hur, of the tribe of Judah, made everything just as the LORD had commanded Moses. [23]He was assisted by Oholiab son of Ahisamach, of the tribe of Dan, a craftsman expert at engraving, designing, and embroidering with blue, purple, and scarlet thread on fine linen cloth.

[24]The people brought special offerings of gold totaling 2,193 pounds,* as measured by the weight of the sanctuary shekel. This gold was used throughout the Tabernacle.

[25]The whole community of Israel gave 7,545 pounds* of silver, as measured by the weight of the sanctuary shekel. [26]This silver came from the tax collected from each man registered in the census. (The tax is one beka, which is half a shekel,* based on the sanctuary shekel.) The tax was collected from 603,550 men who had reached their twentieth birthday. [27]The hundred bases for the frames of the sanctuary walls and for the posts supporting the inner curtain required 7,500 pounds of silver, about 75 pounds for each base.* [28]The remaining 45 pounds* of silver was used to make the hooks and rings and to overlay the tops of the posts.

[29]The people also brought as special offerings 5,310 pounds* of bronze, [30]which was used for casting the bases for the posts at the entrance to the Tabernacle, and for the bronze altar with its bronze grating and all the altar utensils. [31]Bronze was also used to make the bases for the posts that supported the curtains around the courtyard, the bases for the curtain at the entrance of the courtyard, and all the tent pegs for the Tabernacle and the courtyard.

CHAPTER 39

Clothing for the Priests

The craftsmen made beautiful sacred garments of blue, purple, and scarlet cloth—clothing for Aaron to wear while ministering in the Holy Place, just as the LORD had commanded Moses.

Making the Ephod

[2]Bezalel* made the ephod of finely woven linen and embroidered it with gold and with blue, purple, and scarlet thread. [3]He made gold thread by hammering out thin sheets of gold and cutting it into fine strands. With great skill and care, he worked it into the fine linen with the blue, purple, and scarlet thread.

38:12 Hebrew *50 cubits* [23 meters]; also in 38:13. **38:14** Hebrew *15 cubits* [6.9 meters]; also in 38:15. **38:18** Hebrew *20 cubits* [9.2 meters] *long and 5 cubits* [2.3 meters] *high.* **38:21** Hebrew *the Tabernacle, the Tabernacle of the Testimony.* **38:24** Hebrew *29 talents and 730 shekels* [994 kilograms]. Each shekel weighed about 0.4 ounces. **38:25** Hebrew *100 talents and 1,775 shekels* [3,420 kilograms]. **38:26** Or *0.2 ounces,* or *6 grams.* **38:27** Hebrew *100 talents* [3,400 kilograms] *of silver, 1 talent* [34 kilograms] *for each base.* **38:28** Hebrew *1,775 shekels* [20.2 kilograms]. **38:29** Hebrew *70 talents and 2,400 shekels* [2,407 kilograms]. **39:2** Hebrew *He;* also in 39:8, 22.

[4]The ephod consisted of two pieces, front and back, joined at the shoulders with two shoulder-pieces. [5]The decorative sash was made of the same materials: finely woven linen embroidered with gold and with blue, purple, and scarlet thread, just as the LORD had commanded Moses. [6]They mounted the two onyx stones in settings of gold filigree. The stones were engraved with the names of the tribes of Israel, just as a seal is engraved. [7]He fastened these stones on the shoulder-pieces of the ephod as a reminder that the priest represents the people of Israel. All this was done just as the LORD had commanded Moses.

Making the Chestpiece

[8]Bezalel made the chestpiece with great skill and care. He made it to match the ephod, using finely woven linen embroidered with gold and with blue, purple, and scarlet thread. [9]He made the chestpiece of a single piece of cloth folded to form a pouch nine inches* square. [10]They mounted four rows of gemstones* on it. The first row contained a red carnelian, a pale-green peridot, and an emerald. [11]The second row contained a turquoise, a blue lapis lazuli, and a white moonstone. [12]The third row contained an orange jacinth, an agate, and a purple amethyst. [13]The fourth row contained a blue-green beryl, an onyx, and a green jasper. All these stones were set in gold filigree. [14]Each stone represented one of the twelve sons of Israel, and the name of that tribe was engraved on it like a seal.

[15]To attach the chestpiece to the ephod, they made braided cords of pure gold thread. [16]They also made two settings of gold filigree and two gold rings and attached them to the top corners of the chestpiece. [17]They tied the two gold cords to the rings on the chestpiece. [18]They tied the other ends of the cords to the gold settings on the shoulder-pieces of the ephod. [19]Then they made two more gold rings and attached them to the inside edges of the chestpiece next to the ephod. [20]Then they made two more gold rings and attached them to the front of the ephod, below the shoulder-pieces, just above the knot where the decorative sash was fastened to the ephod. [21]They attached the bottom rings of the chestpiece to the rings on the ephod with blue cords. In this way, the chestpiece was held securely to the ephod above the decorative sash. All this was done just as the LORD had commanded Moses.

Additional Clothing for the Priests

[22]Bezalel made the robe that is worn with the ephod from a single piece of blue woven cloth, [23]with an opening for Aaron's head in the middle of it. The opening was reinforced with a woven collar* so it would not tear. [24]They made pomegranates of blue, purple, and scarlet yarn, and attached them to the hem of the robe. [25]They also made bells of pure gold and placed them between the pomegranates along the hem of the robe, [26]with bells and pomegranates alternating all around the hem. This robe was to be worn whenever the priest ministered before the LORD, just as the LORD had commanded Moses.

[27]They made tunics for Aaron and his sons from fine linen cloth. [28]The turban and the special head coverings were made of fine linen, and the undergarments were also made of finely woven linen. [29]The sashes were made of finely woven linen and embroidered with blue, purple, and scarlet thread, just as the LORD had commanded Moses.

[30]Finally, they made the sacred medallion—the badge of holiness—of pure gold. They engraved it like a seal with these words: HOLY TO THE LORD. [31]They attached the medallion with a blue cord to Aaron's turban, just as the LORD had commanded Moses.

Moses Inspects the Work

[32]And so at last the Tabernacle* was finished. The Israelites had done everything just as the LORD had commanded Moses. [33]And they brought the entire Tabernacle to Moses:

the sacred tent with all its furnishings, clasps, frames, crossbars, posts, and bases;
[34] the tent coverings of tanned ram skins and fine goatskin leather;
the inner curtain to shield the Ark;
[35] the Ark of the Covenant* and its carrying poles;
the Ark's cover—the place of atonement;

39:9 Hebrew *1 span* [23 centimeters]. **39:10** The identification of some of these gemstones is uncertain. **39:23** The meaning of the Hebrew is uncertain. **39:32** Hebrew *the Tabernacle, the Tent of Meeting;* also in 39:40. **39:35** Or *Ark of the Testimony.*

36 the table and all its utensils;
the Bread of the Presence;
37 the pure gold lampstand with its
symmetrical lamp cups, all its
accessories, and the olive oil for
lighting;
38 the gold altar;
the anointing oil and fragrant incense;
the curtain for the entrance of the sacred
tent;
39 the bronze altar;
the bronze grating and its carrying poles
and utensils;
the washbasin with its stand;
40 the curtains for the walls of the courtyard;
the posts and their bases;
the curtain for the entrance to the
courtyard;
the ropes and tent pegs;
all the furnishings to be used in worship
at the Tabernacle;
41 the beautifully stitched garments for the
priests to wear while ministering in the
Holy Place—the sacred garments for
Aaron the priest, and the garments for
his sons to wear as they minister as
priests.

42So the people of Israel followed all of the
LORD's instructions to Moses. 43Then Moses
inspected all their work. When he found it
had been done just as the LORD had com-
manded him, he blessed them.

CHAPTER 40

The Tabernacle Completed

Then the LORD said to Moses, 2"Set up the
Tabernacle* on the first day of the new year.*
3Place the Ark of the Covenant* inside, and
install the inner curtain to enclose the Ark
within the Most Holy Place. 4Then bring in
the table, and arrange the utensils on it. And
bring in the lampstand, and set up the lamps.

5"Place the gold incense altar in front of
the Ark of the Covenant. Then hang the cur-
tain at the entrance of the Tabernacle. 6Place
the altar of burnt offering in front of the Tab-
ernacle entrance. 7Set the washbasin be-
tween the Tabernacle* and the altar, and fill it
with water. 8Then set up the courtyard
around the outside of the tent, and hang the
curtain for the courtyard entrance.

9"Take the anointing oil and anoint the
Tabernacle and all its furnishings to conse-
crate them and make them holy. 10Anoint the
altar of burnt offering and its utensils to con-
secrate them. Then the altar will become ab-
solutely holy. 11Next anoint the washbasin
and its stand to consecrate them.

12"Present Aaron and his sons at the en-
trance of the Tabernacle, and wash them with
water. 13Dress Aaron with the sacred gar-
ments and anoint him, consecrating him to
serve me as a priest. 14Then present his sons
and dress them in their tunics. 15Anoint them
as you did their father, so they may also serve
me as priests. With their anointing, Aaron's
descendants are set apart for the priesthood
forever, from generation to generation."

16Moses proceeded to do everything just as
the LORD had commanded him. 17So the Tab-
ernacle was set up on the first day of the first
month of the second year. 18Moses erected
the Tabernacle by setting down its bases,
inserting the frames, attaching the crossbars,
and setting up the posts. 19Then he spread
the coverings over the Tabernacle framework
and put on the protective layers, just as the
LORD had commanded him.

20He took the stone tablets inscribed with
the terms of the covenant and placed them*
inside the Ark. Then he attached the carrying
poles to the Ark, and he set the Ark's cover—
the place of atonement—on top of it. 21Then
he brought the Ark of the Covenant into the
Tabernacle and hung the inner curtain to
shield it from view, just as the LORD had com-
manded him.

22Next Moses placed the table in the Taber-
nacle, along the north side of the Holy Place,
just outside the inner curtain. 23And he ar-
ranged the Bread of the Presence on the table
before the LORD, just as the LORD had com-
manded him.

24He set the lampstand in the Tabernacle
across from the table on the south side of the
Holy Place. 25Then he lit the lamps in the
LORD's presence, just as the LORD had com-
manded him. 26He also placed the gold in-
cense altar in the Tabernacle, in the Holy

40:2a Hebrew *the Tabernacle, the Tent of Meeting;* also in 40:6, 29. **40:2b** Hebrew *the first day of the first month.* This day of the ancient Hebrew lunar calendar occurred in March or April. **40:3** Or *Ark of the Testimony;* also in 40:5, 21. **40:7** Hebrew *Tent of Meeting;* also in 40:12, 22, 24, 26, 30, 32, 34, 35. **40:20** Hebrew *He placed the Testimony;* see note on 25:16.

Place in front of the inner curtain. [27]On it he burned the fragrant incense, just as the LORD had commanded him.

[28]He hung the curtain at the entrance of the Tabernacle, [29]and he placed the altar of burnt offering near the Tabernacle entrance. On it he offered a burnt offering and a grain offering, just as the LORD had commanded him.

[30]Next Moses placed the washbasin between the Tabernacle and the altar. He filled it with water so the priests could wash themselves. [31]Moses and Aaron and Aaron's sons used water from it to wash their hands and feet. [32]Whenever they approached the altar and entered the Tabernacle, they washed themselves, just as the LORD had commanded Moses.

[33]Then he hung the curtains forming the courtyard around the Tabernacle and the altar. And he set up the curtain at the entrance of the courtyard. So at last Moses finished the work.

The LORD's Glory Fills the Tabernacle

[34]Then the cloud covered the Tabernacle, and the glory of the LORD filled the Tabernacle. [35]Moses could no longer enter the Tabernacle because the cloud had settled down over it, and the glory of the LORD filled the Tabernacle.

[36]Now whenever the cloud lifted from the Tabernacle, the people of Israel would set out on their journey, following it. [37]But if the cloud did not rise, they remained where they were until it lifted. [38]The cloud of the LORD hovered over the Tabernacle during the day, and at night fire glowed inside the cloud so the whole family of Israel could see it. This continued throughout all their journeys.

Leviticus

WHO
Moses, Aaron, Nadab, Abihu, Eleazar, and Ithamar.

WHERE
Mount Sinai, in the wilderness between Egypt and the Promised Land.

WHEN
Moses probably wrote this book between 1445–1444 BC while he was leading his people to the Promised Land.

WHY
To help the Israelites survive as a nation and worship God in the right way.

Do not use dishonest standards when measuring length, weight, or volume. Your scales and weights must be accurate.
LEVITICUS 19:35-36

The only person who knows *everything* about you is God. He knew everything about the Israelites, too. So, he knew the best way for them to live. Because God loved them and wanted them to be safe, he gave them laws to obey that would protect them.

Joseph dies — 1805 BC
Slavery in Egypt — 1446 BC
Israel leaves Egypt — 1445 BC
Ten Commandments — 1444 BC
Israel camps at Mount Sinai

THEN AND NOW—GOD'S LAWS ARE WORTH KEEPING!

CHAPTER 1

Procedures for the Burnt Offering

The LORD called to Moses from the Tabernacle* and said to him, [2]"Give the following instructions to the people of Israel. When you present an animal as an offering to the LORD, you may take it from your herd of cattle or your flock of sheep and goats.

[3]"If the animal you present as a burnt offering is from the herd, it must be a male with no defects. Bring it to the entrance of the Tabernacle so you* may be accepted by the LORD. [4]Lay your hand on the animal's head, and the LORD will accept its death in your place to purify you, making you right with him.* [5]Then slaughter the young bull in the LORD's presence, and Aaron's sons, the priests, will present the animal's blood by splattering it against all

1:1 Hebrew *Tent of Meeting;* also in 1:3, 5. **1:3** Or *it.* **1:4** Or *to make atonement for you.*

sides of the altar that stands at the entrance to the Tabernacle. 6Then skin the animal and cut it into pieces. 7The sons of Aaron the priest will build a wood fire on the altar. 8They will arrange the pieces of the offering, including the head and fat, on the wood burning on the altar. 9But the internal organs and the legs must first be washed with water. Then the priest will burn the entire sacrifice on the altar as a burnt offering. It is a special gift, a pleasing aroma to the LORD.

10"If the animal you present as a burnt offering is from the flock, it may be either a sheep or a goat, but it must be a male with no defects. 11Slaughter the animal on the north side of the altar in the LORD's presence, and Aaron's sons, the priests, will splatter its blood against all sides of the altar. 12Then cut the animal in pieces, and the priests will arrange the pieces of the offering, including the head and fat, on the wood burning on the altar. 13But the internal organs and the legs must first be washed with water. Then the priest will burn the entire sacrifice on the altar as a burnt offering. It is a special gift, a pleasing aroma to the LORD.

14"If you present a bird as a burnt offering to the LORD, choose either a turtledove or a young pigeon. 15The priest will take the bird to the altar, wring off its head, and burn it on the altar. But first he must drain its blood against the side of the altar. 16The priest must also remove the crop and the feathers* and throw them in the ashes on the east side of the altar. 17Then, grasping the bird by its wings, the priest will tear the bird open, but without tearing it apart. Then he will burn it as a burnt offering on the wood burning on the altar. It is a special gift, a pleasing aroma to the LORD.

CHAPTER 2

Procedures for the Grain Offering

"When you present grain as an offering to the LORD, the offering must consist of choice flour. You are to pour olive oil on it, sprinkle it with frankincense, 2and bring it to Aaron's sons, the priests. The priest will scoop out a handful of the flour moistened with oil, together with all the frankincense, and burn this representative portion on the altar. It is a special gift, a pleasing aroma to the LORD. 3The rest of the grain offering will then be given to Aaron and his sons. This offering will be considered a most holy part of the special gifts presented to the LORD.

4"If your offering is a grain offering baked in an oven, it must be made of choice flour, but without any yeast. It may be presented in the form of thin cakes mixed with olive oil or wafers spread with olive oil. 5If your grain offering is cooked on a griddle, it must be made of choice flour mixed with olive oil but without any yeast. 6Break it in pieces and pour olive oil on it; it is a grain offering. 7If your grain offering is prepared in a pan, it must be made of choice flour and olive oil.

8"No matter how a grain offering for the LORD has been prepared, bring it to the priest, who will present it at the altar. 9The priest will take a representative portion of the grain offering and burn it on the altar. It is a special gift, a pleasing aroma to the LORD. 10The rest of the grain offering will then be given to Aaron and his sons as their food. This offering will be considered a most holy part of the special gifts presented to the LORD.

11"Do not use yeast in preparing any of the grain offerings you present to the LORD, because no yeast or honey may be burned as a special gift presented to the LORD. 12You may add yeast and honey to an offering of the first crops of your harvest, but these must never be offered on the altar as a pleasing aroma to the LORD. 13Season all your grain offerings with salt to remind you of God's eternal covenant. Never forget to add salt to your grain offerings.

14"If you present a grain offering to the LORD from the first portion of your harvest, bring fresh grain that is coarsely ground and roasted on a fire. 15Put olive oil on this grain offering, and sprinkle it with frankincense. 16The priest will take a representative portion of the grain moistened with oil, together with all the frankincense, and burn it as a special gift presented to the LORD.

CHAPTER 3

Procedures for the Peace Offering

"If you present an animal from the herd as a peace offering to the LORD, it may be a male or a female, but it must have no defects. 2Lay your hand on the animal's head, and slaughter

1:16 Or *the crop and its contents.* The meaning of the Hebrew is uncertain.

it at the entrance of the Tabernacle.* Then Aaron's sons, the priests, will splatter its blood against all sides of the altar. [3]The priest must present part of this peace offering as a special gift to the LORD. This includes all the fat around the internal organs, [4]the two kidneys and the fat around them near the loins, and the long lobe of the liver. These must be removed with the kidneys, [5]and Aaron's sons will burn them on top of the burnt offering on the wood burning on the altar. It is a special gift, a pleasing aroma to the LORD.

[6]"If you present an animal from the flock as a peace offering to the LORD, it may be a male or a female, but it must have no defects. [7]If you present a sheep as your offering, bring it to the LORD, [8]lay your hand on its head, and slaughter it in front of the Tabernacle. Aaron's sons will then splatter the sheep's blood against all sides of the altar. [9]The priest must present the fat of this peace offering as a special gift to the LORD. This includes the fat of the broad tail cut off near the backbone, all the fat around the internal organs, [10]the two kidneys and the fat around them near the loins, and the long lobe of the liver. These must be removed with the kidneys, [11]and the priest will burn them on the altar. It is a special gift of food presented to the LORD.

[12]"If you present a goat as your offering, bring it to the LORD, [13]lay your hand on its head, and slaughter it in front of the Tabernacle. Aaron's sons will then splatter the goat's blood against all sides of the altar. [14]The priest must present part of this offering as a special gift to the LORD. This includes all the fat around the internal organs, [15]the two kidneys and the fat around them near the loins, and the long lobe of the liver. These must be removed with the kidneys, [16]and the priest will burn them on the altar. It is a special gift of food, a pleasing aroma to the LORD. All the fat belongs to the LORD.

[17]"You must never eat any fat or blood. This is a permanent law for you, and it must be observed from generation to generation, wherever you live."

CHAPTER 4

Procedures for the Sin Offering

Then the LORD said to Moses, [2]"Give the following instructions to the people of Israel. This is how you are to deal with those who sin unintentionally by doing anything that violates one of the LORD's commands.

[3]"If the high priest* sins, bringing guilt upon the entire community, he must give a sin offering for the sin he has committed. He must present to the LORD a young bull with no defects. [4]He must bring the bull to the LORD at the entrance of the Tabernacle,* lay his hand on the bull's head, and slaughter it before the LORD. [5]The high priest will then take some of the bull's blood into the Tabernacle, [6]dip his finger in the blood, and sprinkle it seven times before the LORD in front of the inner curtain of the sanctuary. [7]The priest will then put some of the blood on the horns of the altar for fragrant incense that stands in the LORD's presence inside the Tabernacle. He will pour out the rest of the bull's blood at the base of the altar for burnt offerings at the entrance of the Tabernacle. [8]Then the priest must remove all the fat of the bull to be offered as a sin offering. This includes all the fat around the internal organs, [9]the two kidneys and the fat around them near the loins, and the long lobe of the liver. He must remove these along with the kidneys, [10]just as he does with cattle offered as a peace offering, and burn them on the altar of burnt offerings. [11]But he must take whatever is left of the bull—its hide, meat, head, legs, internal organs, and dung—[12]and carry it away to a place outside the camp that is ceremonially clean, the place where the ashes are dumped. There, on the ash heap, he will burn it on a wood fire.

[13]"If the entire Israelite community sins by violating one of the LORD's commands, but the people don't realize it, they are still guilty. [14]When they become aware of their sin, the people must bring a young bull as an offering for their sin and present it before the Tabernacle. [15]The elders of the community must then lay their hands on the bull's head and slaughter it before the LORD. [16]The high priest will then take some of the bull's blood into the Tabernacle, [17]dip his finger in the blood, and sprinkle it seven times before the LORD in front of the inner curtain. [18]He will then put some of the blood on the horns of the altar for fragrant incense that stands in the LORD's presence inside the Tabernacle. He will pour out the rest of the

3:2 Hebrew *Tent of Meeting;* also in 3:8, 13. **4:3** Hebrew *the anointed priest;* also in 4:5, 16. **4:4** Hebrew *Tent of Meeting;* also in 4:5, 7, 14, 16, 18.

blood at the base of the altar for burnt offerings at the entrance of the Tabernacle. [19]Then the priest must remove all the animal's fat and burn it on the altar, [20]just as he does with the bull offered as a sin offering for the high priest. Through this process, the priest will purify the people, making them right with the LORD,* and they will be forgiven. [21]Then the priest must take what is left of the bull and carry it outside the camp and burn it there, just as is done with the sin offering for the high priest. This offering is for the sin of the entire congregation of Israel.

[22]"If one of Israel's leaders sins by violating one of the commands of the LORD his God but doesn't realize it, he is still guilty. [23]When he becomes aware of his sin, he must bring as his offering a male goat with no defects. [24]He must lay his hand on the goat's head and slaughter it at the place where burnt offerings are slaughtered before the LORD. This is an offering for his sin. [25]Then the priest will dip his finger in the blood of the sin offering and put it on the horns of the altar for burnt offerings. He will pour out the rest of the blood at the base of the altar. [26]Then he must burn all the goat's fat on the altar, just as he does with the peace offering. Through this process, the priest will purify the leader from his sin, making him right with the LORD, and he will be forgiven.

[27]"If any of the common people sin by violating one of the LORD's commands, but they don't realize it, they are still guilty. [28]When they become aware of their sin, they must bring as an offering for their sin a female goat with no defects. [29]They must lay a hand on the head of the sin offering and slaughter it at the place where burnt offerings are slaughtered. [30]Then the priest will dip his finger in the blood and put it on the horns of the altar for burnt offerings. He will pour out the rest of the blood at the base of the altar. [31]Then he must remove all the goat's fat, just as he does with the fat of the peace offering. He will burn the fat on the altar, and it will be a pleasing aroma to the LORD. Through this process, the priest will purify the people, making them right with the LORD, and they will be forgiven.

[32]"If the people bring a sheep as their sin offering, it must be a female with no defects. [33]They must lay a hand on the head of the sin offering and slaughter it at the place where burnt offerings are slaughtered. [34]Then the priest will dip his finger in the blood of the sin offering and put it on the horns of the altar for burnt offerings. He will pour out the rest of the blood at the base of the altar. [35]Then he must remove all the sheep's fat, just as he does with the fat of a sheep presented as a peace offering. He will burn the fat on the altar on top of the special gifts presented to the LORD. Through this process, the priest will purify the people from their sin, making them right with the LORD, and they will be forgiven.

CHAPTER 5

Sins Requiring a Sin Offering

"If you are called to testify about something you have seen or that you know about, it is sinful to refuse to testify, and you will be punished for your sin.

[2]"Or suppose you unknowingly touch something that is ceremonially unclean, such as the carcass of an unclean animal. When you realize what you have done, you must admit your defilement and your guilt. This is true whether it is a wild animal, a domestic animal, or an animal that scurries along the ground.

[3]"Or suppose you unknowingly touch something that makes a person unclean. When you realize what you have done, you must admit your guilt.

[4]"Or suppose you make a foolish vow of any kind, whether its purpose is for good or for bad. When you realize its foolishness, you must admit your guilt.

[5]"When you become aware of your guilt in any of these ways, you must confess your sin. [6]Then you must bring to the LORD as the penalty for your sin a female from the flock, either a sheep or a goat. This is a sin offering with which the priest will purify you from your sin, making you right with the LORD.*

[7]"But if you cannot afford to bring a sheep, you may bring to the LORD two turtledoves or two young pigeons as the penalty for your sin. One of the birds will be for a sin offering, and the other for a burnt offering. [8]You must bring them to the priest, who will present the first bird as the sin offering. He will wring its

4:20 Or *will make atonement for the people;* similarly in 4:26, 31, 35. **5:6** Or *will make atonement for you for your sin;* similarly in 5:10, 13, 16, 18.

SERVES HIM RIGHT!

Jeff can't stand Eric, who is the biggest bully in school. He always picks on smaller kids. One day someone smashed a window during the lunch hour. "I bet Eric did it," yelled Leo, a kid whom Eric bullied constantly. But Jeff knew Eric didn't do it. He saw Eric on the other side of the lunchroom when the window crashed. Other kids knew that too, but they figured that Eric deserved to be punished just for being a bully.

Should Jeff explain to the teacher what he saw? Or should he stay silent too? Leviticus 5:1 has the answer.

neck but without severing its head from the body. [9]Then he will sprinkle some of the blood of the sin offering against the sides of the altar, and the rest of the blood will be drained out at the base of the altar. This is an offering for sin. [10]The priest will then prepare the second bird as a burnt offering, following all the procedures that have been prescribed. Through this process the priest will purify you from your sin, making you right with the LORD, and you will be forgiven.

[11]"If you cannot afford to bring two turtledoves or two young pigeons, you may bring two quarts* of choice flour for your sin offering. Since it is an offering for sin, you must not moisten it with olive oil or put any frankincense on it. [12]Take the flour to the priest, who will scoop out a handful as a representative portion. He will burn it on the altar on top of the special gifts presented to the LORD. It is an offering for sin. [13]Through this process, the priest will purify those who are guilty of any of these sins, making them right with the LORD, and they will be forgiven. The rest of the flour will belong to the priest, just as with the grain offering."

Procedures for the Guilt Offering

[14]Then the LORD said to Moses, [15]"If one of you commits a sin by unintentionally defiling the LORD's sacred property, you must bring a guilt offering to the LORD. The offering must be your own ram with no defects, or you may buy one of equal value with silver, as measured by the weight of the sanctuary shekel.* [16]You must make restitution for the sacred property you have harmed by paying for the loss, plus an additional 20 percent. When you give the payment to the priest, he will purify you with the ram sacrificed as a guilt offering, making you right with the LORD, and you will be forgiven.

[17]"Suppose you sin by violating one of the LORD's commands. Even if you are unaware of what you have done, you are guilty and will be punished for your sin. [18]For a guilt offering, you must bring to the priest your own ram with no defects, or you may buy one of equal value. Through this process the priest will purify you from your unintentional sin, making you right with the LORD, and you will be forgiven. [19]This is a guilt offering, for you have been guilty of an offense against the LORD."

CHAPTER 6

Sins Requiring a Guilt Offering

[1]*Then the LORD said to Moses, [2]"Suppose one of you sins against your associate and is

5:11 Hebrew *1/10 of an ephah* (2.2 liters). **5:15** Each shekel was about 0.4 ounces or 11 grams in weight. **6:1** Verses 6:1-7 are numbered 5:20-26 in Hebrew text.

unfaithful to the LORD. Suppose you cheat in
a deal involving a security deposit, or you steal
or commit fraud, [3]or you find lost property
and lie about it, or you lie while swearing to
tell the truth, or you commit any other such
sin. [4]If you have sinned in any of these ways,
you are guilty. You must give back whatever
you stole, or the money you took by extortion,
or the security deposit, or the lost property
you found, [5]or anything obtained by swearing
falsely. You must make restitution by paying
the full price plus an additional 20 percent to
the person you have harmed. On the same day
you must present a guilt offering. [6]As a guilt
offering to the LORD, you must bring to the
priest your own ram with no defects, or you
may buy one of equal value. [7]Through this
process, the priest will purify you before the
LORD, making you right with him,* and you
will be forgiven for any of these sins you have
committed."

Further Instructions for the Burnt Offering

[8]*Then the LORD said to Moses, [9]"Give Aaron
and his sons the following instructions regarding the burnt offering. The burnt offering must be left on top of the altar until the
next morning, and the fire on the altar must
be kept burning all night. [10]In the morning, after the priest on duty has put on his official
linen clothing and linen undergarments, he
must clean out the ashes of the burnt offering
and put them beside the altar. [11]Then he must
take off these garments, change back into his
regular clothes, and carry the ashes outside
the camp to a place that is ceremonially clean.
[12]Meanwhile, the fire on the altar must be kept
burning; it must never go out. Each morning
the priest will add fresh wood to the fire and
arrange the burnt offering on it. He will then
burn the fat of the peace offerings on it.
[13]Remember, the fire must be kept burning on
the altar at all times. It must never go out.

Further Instructions for the Grain Offering

[14]"These are the instructions regarding the
grain offering. Aaron's sons must present this
offering to the LORD in front of the altar.
[15]The priest on duty will take from the
grain offering a handful of the choice flour
moistened with olive oil, together with all the
frankincense. He will burn this representative portion on the altar as a pleasing aroma to
the LORD. [16]Aaron and his sons may eat the
rest of the flour, but it must be baked without
yeast and eaten in a sacred place within the
courtyard of the Tabernacle.* [17]Remember, it
must never be prepared with yeast. I have
given it to the priests as their share of the special gifts presented to me. Like the sin offering and the guilt offering, it is most holy.
[18]Any of Aaron's male descendants may eat
from the special gifts presented to the LORD.
This is their permanent right from generation to generation. Anyone or anything that
touches these offerings will become holy."

Procedures for the Ordination Offering

[19]Then the LORD said to Moses, [20]"On the day
Aaron and his sons are anointed, they must
present to the LORD a grain offering of two
quarts* of choice flour, half to be offered in
the morning and half to be offered in the evening. [21]It must be carefully mixed with olive
oil and cooked on a griddle. Then slice* this
grain offering and present it as a pleasing
aroma to the LORD. [22]In each generation, the
high priest* who succeeds Aaron must prepare this same offering. It belongs to the
LORD and must be burned up completely.
This is a permanent law. [23]All such grain offerings of a priest must be burned up entirely.
None of it may be eaten."

Further Instructions for the Sin Offering

[24]Then the LORD said to Moses, [25]"Give Aaron
and his sons the following instructions regarding the sin offering. The animal given as an offering for sin is a most holy offering, and it
must be slaughtered in the LORD's presence
at the place where the burnt offerings are
slaughtered. [26]The priest who offers the sacrifice as a sin offering must eat his portion in a
sacred place within the courtyard of the Tabernacle. [27]Anyone or anything that touches the
sacrificial meat will become holy. If any of the
sacrificial blood spatters on a person's clothing, the soiled garment must be washed in a

6:7 Or *will make atonement for you before the* LORD. **6:8** Verses 6:8-30 are numbered 6:1-23 in Hebrew text. **6:16** Hebrew *Tent of Meeting;* also in 6:26, 30. **6:20** Hebrew *1/10 of an ephah* [2.2 liters]. **6:21** The meaning of this Hebrew term is uncertain. **6:22** Hebrew *the anointed priest.*

sacred place. [28]If a clay pot is used to boil the sacrificial meat, it must then be broken. If a bronze pot is used, it must be scoured and thoroughly rinsed with water. [29]Any male from a priest's family may eat from this offering; it is most holy. [30]But the offering for sin may not be eaten if its blood was brought into the Tabernacle as an offering for purification* in the Holy Place. It must be completely burned with fire.

CHAPTER 7

Further Instructions for the Guilt Offering

"These are the instructions for the guilt offering. It is most holy. [2]The animal sacrificed as a guilt offering must be slaughtered at the place where the burnt offerings are slaughtered, and its blood must be splattered against all sides of the altar. [3]The priest will then offer all its fat on the altar, including the fat of the broad tail, the fat around the internal organs, [4]the two kidneys and the fat around them near the loins, and the long lobe of the liver. These are to be removed with the kidneys, [5]and the priests will burn them on the altar as a special gift presented to the LORD. This is the guilt offering. [6]Any male from a priest's family may eat the meat. It must be eaten in a sacred place, for it is most holy.

[7]"The same instructions apply to both the guilt offering and the sin offering. Both belong to the priest who uses them to purify someone, making that person right with the LORD.* [8]In the case of the burnt offering, the priest may keep the hide of the sacrificed animal. [9]Any grain offering that has been baked in an oven, prepared in a pan, or cooked on a griddle belongs to the priest who presents it. [10]All other grain offerings, whether made of dry flour or flour moistened with olive oil, are to be shared equally among all the priests, the descendants of Aaron.

Further Instructions for the Peace Offering

[11]"These are the instructions regarding the different kinds of peace offerings that may be presented to the LORD. [12]If you present your peace offering as an expression of thanksgiving, the usual animal sacrifice must be accompanied by various kinds of bread made without yeast—thin cakes mixed with olive oil, wafers spread with oil, and cakes made of choice flour mixed with olive oil. [13]This peace offering of thanksgiving must also be accompanied by loaves of bread made with yeast. [14]One of each kind of bread must be presented as a gift to the LORD. It will then belong to the priest who splatters the blood of the peace offering against the altar. [15]The meat of the peace offering of thanksgiving must be eaten on the same day it is offered. None of it may be saved for the next morning.

[16]"If you bring an offering to fulfill a vow or as a voluntary offering, the meat must be eaten on the same day the sacrifice is offered, but whatever is left over may be eaten on the second day. [17]Any meat left over until the third day must be completely burned up. [18]If any of the meat from the peace offering is eaten on the third day, the person who presented it will not be accepted by the LORD. You will receive no credit for offering it. By then the meat will be contaminated; if you eat it, you will be punished for your sin.

[19]"Meat that touches anything ceremonially unclean may not be eaten; it must be completely burned up. The rest of the meat may be eaten, but only by people who are ceremonially clean. [20]If you are ceremonially unclean and you eat meat from a peace offering that was presented to the LORD, you will be cut off from the community. [21]If you touch anything that is unclean (whether it is human defilement or an unclean animal or any other unclean, detestable thing) and then eat meat from a peace offering presented to the LORD, you will be cut off from the community."

The Forbidden Blood and Fat

[22]Then the LORD said to Moses, [23]"Give the following instructions to the people of Israel. You must never eat fat, whether from cattle, sheep, or goats. [24]The fat of an animal found dead or torn to pieces by wild animals must never be eaten, though it may be used for any other purpose. [25]Anyone who eats fat from an animal presented as a special gift to the LORD will be cut off from the community. [26]No matter where you live, you must never consume the blood of any bird or animal. [27]Anyone who consumes blood will be cut off from the community."

6:30 Or *an offering to make atonement.* 7:7 Or *to make atonement.*

A Portion for the Priests

28Then the LORD said to Moses, 29"Give the following instructions to the people of Israel. When you present a peace offering to the LORD, bring part of it as a gift to the LORD. 30Present it to the LORD with your own hands as a special gift to the LORD. Bring the fat of the animal, together with the breast, and lift up the breast as a special offering to the LORD. 31Then the priest will burn the fat on the altar, but the breast will belong to Aaron and his descendants. 32Give the right thigh of your peace offering to the priest as a gift. 33The right thigh must always be given to the priest who offers the blood and the fat of the peace offering. 34For I have reserved the breast of the special offering and the right thigh of the sacred offering for the priests. It is the permanent right of Aaron and his descendants to share in the peace offerings brought by the people of Israel. 35This is their rightful share. The special gifts presented to the LORD have been reserved for Aaron and his descendants from the time they were set apart to serve the LORD as priests. 36On the day they were anointed, the LORD commanded the Israelites to give these portions to the priests as their permanent share from generation to generation."

37These are the instructions for the burnt offering, the grain offering, the sin offering, and the guilt offering, as well as the ordination offering and the peace offering. 38The LORD gave these instructions to Moses on Mount Sinai when he commanded the Israelites to present their offerings to the LORD in the wilderness of Sinai.

CHAPTER 8

Ordination of the Priests

Then the LORD said to Moses, 2"Bring Aaron and his sons, along with their sacred garments, the anointing oil, the bull for the sin offering, the two rams, and the basket of bread made without yeast, 3and call the entire community of Israel together at the entrance of the Tabernacle.*"

4So Moses followed the LORD's instructions, and the whole community assembled at the Tabernacle entrance. 5Moses announced to them, "This is what the LORD has commanded us to do!" 6Then he presented Aaron and his sons and washed them with water. 7He put the official tunic on Aaron and tied the sash around his waist. He dressed him in the robe, placed the ephod on him, and attached the ephod securely with its decorative sash. 8Then Moses placed the chestpiece on Aaron and put the Urim and the Thummim inside it. 9He placed the turban on Aaron's head and attached the gold medallion—the badge of holiness—to the front of the turban, just as the LORD had commanded him.

10Then Moses took the anointing oil and anointed the Tabernacle and everything in it, making them holy. 11He sprinkled the oil on the altar seven times, anointing it and all its utensils, as well as the washbasin and its stand, making them holy. 12Then he poured some of the anointing oil on Aaron's head, anointing him and making him holy for his work. 13Next Moses presented Aaron's sons. He clothed them in their tunics, tied their sashes around them, and put their special head coverings on them, just as the LORD had commanded him.

14Then Moses presented the bull for the sin offering. Aaron and his sons laid their hands on the bull's head, 15and Moses slaughtered it. Moses took some of the blood, and with his finger he put it on the four horns of the altar to purify it. He poured out the rest of the blood at the base of the altar. Through this process, he made the altar holy by purifying it.* 16Then Moses took all the fat around the internal organs, the long lobe of the liver, and the two kidneys and the fat around them, and he burned it all on the altar. 17He took the rest of the bull, including its hide, meat, and dung, and burned it on a fire outside the camp, just as the LORD had commanded him.

18Then Moses presented the ram for the burnt offering. Aaron and his sons laid their hands on the ram's head, 19and Moses slaughtered it. Then Moses took the ram's blood and splattered it against all sides of the altar. 20Then he cut the ram into pieces, and he burned the head, some of its pieces, and the fat on the altar. 21After washing the internal organs and the legs with water, Moses burned the entire ram on the altar as a burnt offering. It was a pleasing aroma, a special gift pre-

8:3 Hebrew *Tent of Meeting;* also in 8:4, 31, 33, 35. **8:15** Or *by making atonement for it,* or *that offerings for purification might be made on it.*

sented to the LORD, just as the LORD had commanded him.

22Then Moses presented the other ram, which was the ram of ordination. Aaron and his sons laid their hands on the ram's head, 23and Moses slaughtered it. Then Moses took some of its blood and applied it to the lobe of Aaron's right ear, the thumb of his right hand, and the big toe of his right foot. 24Next Moses presented Aaron's sons and applied some of the blood to the lobes of their right ears, the thumbs of their right hands, and the big toes of their right feet. He then splattered the rest of the blood against all sides of the altar.

25Next Moses took the fat, including the fat of the broad tail, the fat around the internal organs, the long lobe of the liver, and the two kidneys and the fat around them, along with the right thigh. 26On top of these he placed a thin cake of bread made without yeast, a cake of bread mixed with olive oil, and a wafer spread with olive oil. All these were taken from the basket of bread made without yeast that was placed in the LORD's presence. 27He put all these in the hands of Aaron and his sons, and he lifted them up as a special offering to the LORD. 28Moses then took all the offerings back from them and burned them on the altar on top of the burnt offering. This was the ordination offering. It was a pleasing aroma, a special gift presented to the LORD. 29Then Moses took the breast and lifted it up as a special offering to the LORD. This was Moses' portion of the ram of ordination, just as the LORD had commanded him.

30Next Moses took some of the anointing oil and some of the blood that was on the altar, and he sprinkled them on Aaron and his garments and on his sons and their garments. In this way, he made Aaron and his sons and their garments holy.

31Then Moses said to Aaron and his sons, "Boil the remaining meat of the offerings at the Tabernacle entrance, and eat it there, along with the bread that is in the basket of offerings for the ordination, just as I commanded when I said, 'Aaron and his sons will eat it.' 32Any meat or bread that is left over must then be burned up. 33You must not leave the Tabernacle entrance for seven days, for that is when the ordination ceremony will be completed. 34Everything we have done today was commanded by the LORD in order to purify you, making you right with him.* 35Now stay at the entrance of the Tabernacle day and night for seven days, and do everything the LORD requires. If you fail to do this, you will die, for this is what the LORD has commanded." 36So Aaron and his sons did everything the LORD had commanded through Moses.

CHAPTER 9

The Priests Begin Their Work

After the ordination ceremony, on the eighth day, Moses called together Aaron and his sons and the elders of Israel. 2He said to Aaron, "Take a young bull for a sin offering and a ram for a burnt offering, both without defects, and present them to the LORD. 3Then tell the Israelites, 'Take a male goat for a sin offering, and take a calf and a lamb, both a year old and without defects, for a burnt offering. 4Also take a bull* and a ram for a peace offering and flour moistened with olive oil for a grain offering. Present all these offerings to the LORD because the LORD will appear to you today.'"

5So the people presented all these things at the entrance of the Tabernacle,* just as Moses had commanded. Then the whole community came forward and stood before the LORD. 6And Moses said, "This is what the LORD has commanded you to do so that the glory of the LORD may appear to you."

7Then Moses said to Aaron, "Come to the altar and sacrifice your sin offering and your burnt offering to purify yourself and the people. Then present the offerings of the people to purify them, making them right with the LORD,* just as he has commanded."

8So Aaron went to the altar and slaughtered the calf as a sin offering for himself. 9His sons brought him the blood, and he dipped his finger in it and put it on the horns of the altar. He poured out the rest of the blood at the base of the altar. 10Then he burned on the altar the fat, the kidneys, and the long lobe of the liver from the sin offering, just as the LORD had commanded Moses. 11The meat and the hide, however, he burned outside the camp.

12Next Aaron slaughtered the animal for

8:34 Or *to make atonement for you.* **9:4** Or *cow;* also in 9:18, 19. **9:5** Hebrew *Tent of Meeting;* also in 9:23. **9:7** Or *to make atonement for them.*

the burnt offering. His sons brought him the blood, and he splattered it against all sides of the altar. [13]Then they handed him each piece of the burnt offering, including the head, and he burned them on the altar. [14]Then he washed the internal organs and the legs and burned them on the altar along with the rest of the burnt offering.

AMAZING FACTS

How did God show he was pleased with the offerings of his people? He sent fire from heaven!

LEVITICUS 9:24

[15]Next Aaron presented the offerings of the people. He slaughtered the people's goat and presented it as an offering for their sin, just as he had first done with the offering for his own sin. [16]Then he presented the burnt offering and sacrificed it in the prescribed way. [17]He also presented the grain offering, burning a handful of the flour mixture on the altar, in addition to the regular burnt offering for the morning.

[18]Then Aaron slaughtered the bull and the ram for the people's peace offering. His sons brought him the blood, and he splattered it against all sides of the altar. [19]Then he took the fat of the bull and the ram—the fat of the broad tail and from around the internal organs—along with the kidneys and the long lobes of the livers. [20]He placed these fat portions on top of the breasts of these animals and burned them on the altar. [21]Aaron then lifted up the breasts and right thighs as a special offering to the LORD, just as Moses had commanded.

[22]After that, Aaron raised his hands toward the people and blessed them. Then, after presenting the sin offering, the burnt offering, and the peace offering, he stepped down from the altar. [23]Then Moses and Aaron went into the Tabernacle, and when they came back out, they blessed the people again, and the glory of the LORD appeared to the whole community. [24]Fire blazed forth from the LORD's presence and consumed the burnt offering and the fat on the altar. When the people saw this, they shouted with joy and fell face down on the ground.

CHAPTER 10

The Sin of Nadab and Abihu

Aaron's sons Nadab and Abihu put coals of fire in their incense burners and sprinkled incense over them. In this way, they disobeyed the LORD by burning before him the wrong kind of fire, different than he had commanded. [2]So fire blazed forth from the LORD's presence and burned them up, and they died there before the LORD.

[3]Then Moses said to Aaron, "This is what the LORD meant when he said,

'I will display my holiness
through those who come near me.
I will display my glory
before all the people.'"

And Aaron was silent.

[4]Then Moses called for Mishael and Elzaphan, Aaron's cousins, the sons of Aaron's uncle Uzziel. He said to them, "Come forward and carry away the bodies of your relatives from in front of the sanctuary to a place outside the camp." [5]So they came forward and picked them up by their garments and carried them out of the camp, just as Moses had commanded.

[6]Then Moses said to Aaron and his sons Eleazar and Ithamar, "Do not show grief by leaving your hair uncombed* or by tearing your clothes. If you do, you will die, and the LORD's anger will strike the whole community of Israel. However, the rest of the Israelites, your relatives, may mourn because of the LORD's fiery destruction of Nadab and Abihu. [7]But you must not leave the entrance of the Tabernacle* or you will die, for you have been anointed

10:6 Or *by uncovering your heads.* **10:7** Hebrew *Tent of Meeting;* also in 10:9.

with the LORD's anointing oil." So they did as Moses commanded.

Instructions for Priestly Conduct

[8]Then the LORD said to Aaron, [9]"You and your descendants must never drink wine or any other alcoholic drink before going into the Tabernacle. If you do, you will die. This is a permanent law for you, and it must be observed from generation to generation. [10]You must distinguish between what is sacred and what is common, between what is ceremonially unclean and what is clean. [11]And you must teach the Israelites all the decrees that the LORD has given them through Moses."

[12]Then Moses said to Aaron and his remaining sons, Eleazar and Ithamar, "Take what is left of the grain offering after a portion has been presented as a special gift to the LORD, and eat it beside the altar. Make sure it contains no yeast, for it is most holy. [13]You must eat it in a sacred place, for it has been given to you and your descendants as your portion of the special gifts presented to the LORD. These are the commands I have been given. [14]But the breast and thigh that were lifted up as a special offering may be eaten in any place that is ceremonially clean. These parts have been given to you and your descendants as your portion of the peace offerings presented by the people of Israel. [15]You must lift up the thigh and breast as a special offering to the LORD, along with the fat of the special gifts. These parts will belong to you and your descendants as your permanent right, just as the LORD has commanded."

[16]Moses then asked them what had happened to the goat of the sin offering. When he discovered it had been burned up, he became very angry with Eleazar and Ithamar, Aaron's remaining sons. [17]"Why didn't you eat the sin offering in the sacred area?" he demanded. "It is a holy offering! The LORD has given it to you to remove the guilt of the community and to purify the people, making them right with the LORD.* [18]Since the animal's blood was not brought into the Holy Place, you should have eaten the meat in the sacred area as I ordered you."

[19]Then Aaron answered Moses, "Today my sons presented both their sin offering and their burnt offering to the LORD. And yet this tragedy has happened to me. If I had eaten the people's sin offering on such a tragic day as this, would the LORD have been pleased?" [20]And when Moses heard this, he was satisfied.

CHAPTER 11

Ceremonially Clean and Unclean Animals

Then the LORD said to Moses and Aaron, [2]"Give the following instructions to the people of Israel.

"Of all the land animals, these are the ones you may use for food. [3]You may eat any animal that has completely split hooves and chews the cud. [4]You may not, however, eat the following animals* that have split hooves or that chew the cud, but not both. The camel chews the cud but does not have split hooves, so it is ceremonially unclean for you. [5]The hyrax* chews the cud but does not have split hooves, so it is unclean. [6]The hare chews the cud but does not have split hooves, so it is unclean. [7]The pig has evenly split hooves but does not chew the cud, so it is unclean. [8]You may not eat the meat of these animals or even touch their carcasses. They are ceremonially unclean for you.

[9]"Of all the marine animals, these are ones you may use for food. You may eat anything from the water if it has both fins and scales, whether taken from salt water or from streams. [10]But you must never eat animals from the sea or from rivers that do not have both fins and scales. They are detestable to you. This applies both to little creatures that live in shallow water and to all creatures that live in deep water. [11]They will always be detestable to you. You must never eat their meat or even touch their dead bodies. [12]Any marine animal that does not have both fins and scales is detestable to you.

[13]"These are the birds that are detestable to you. You must never eat them: the griffon vulture, the bearded vulture, the black vulture, [14]the kite, falcons of all kinds, [15]ravens of all kinds, [16]the eagle owl, the short-eared owl, the seagull, hawks of all kinds, [17]the little owl, the cormorant, the great owl, [18]the barn owl, the desert owl, the Egyptian

10:17 Or *to make atonement for the people before the LORD.* **11:4** The identification of some of the animals, birds, and insects in this chapter is uncertain. **11:5** Or *coney*, or *rock badger*.

vulture, [19]the stork, herons of all kinds, the hoopoe, and the bat.

[20]"You must not eat winged insects that walk along the ground; they are detestable to you. [21]You may, however, eat winged insects that walk along the ground and have jointed legs so they can jump. [22]The insects you are permitted to eat include all kinds of locusts, bald locusts, crickets, and grasshoppers. [23]All other winged insects that walk along the ground are detestable to you.

[24]"The following creatures will make you ceremonially unclean. If any of you touch their carcasses, you will be defiled until evening. [25]If you pick up their carcasses, you must wash your clothes, and you will remain defiled until evening.

[26]"Any animal that has split hooves that are not evenly divided or that does not chew the cud is unclean for you. If you touch the carcass of such an animal, you will be defiled. [27]Of the animals that walk on all fours, those that have paws are unclean. If you touch the carcass of such an animal, you will be defiled until evening. [28]If you pick up its carcass, you must wash your clothes, and you will remain defiled until evening. These animals are unclean for you.

[29]"Of the small animals that scurry along the ground, these are unclean for you: the mole rat, the rat, large lizards of all kinds, [30]the gecko, the monitor lizard, the common lizard, the sand lizard, and the chameleon. [31]All these small animals are unclean for you. If any of you touch the dead body of such an animal, you will be defiled until evening. [32]If such an animal dies and falls on something, that object will be unclean. This is true whether the object is made of wood, cloth, leather, or burlap. Whatever its use, you must dip it in water, and it will remain defiled until evening. After that, it will be ceremonially clean and may be used again.

[33]"If such an animal falls into a clay pot, everything in the pot will be defiled, and the pot must be smashed. [34]If the water from such a container spills on any food, the food will be defiled. And any beverage in such a container will be defiled. [35]Any object on which the carcass of such an animal falls will be defiled. If it is an oven or hearth, it must be destroyed, for it is defiled, and you must treat it accordingly.

[36]"However, if the carcass of such an animal falls into a spring or a cistern, the water will still be clean. But anyone who touches the carcass will be defiled. [37]If the carcass falls on seed grain to be planted in the field, the seed will still be considered clean. [38]But if the seed is wet when the carcass falls on it, the seed will be defiled.

[39]"If an animal you are permitted to eat dies and you touch its carcass, you will be defiled until evening. [40]If you eat any of its meat

IS IT OK?

IS IT OK TO TRY SMOKING?

Want some good reasons *not* to try smoking? (1) It's illegal—and God wants you to obey the law. (2) It's bad for your health—and God wants you to take care of your body. (3) It's a sign that you're blending in with everyone else—and God wants you to stand out. Have you ever thought about the third reason? See, God tells us that he wants us to be holy (check out Leviticus 11:44). *Holy* means "set apart," which basically means "different." We're supposed to be different, because God is different. So if your friends try smoking and you wonder if you should join in, try standing out instead.

or carry away its carcass, you must wash your clothes, and you will remain defiled until evening.

41"All small animals that scurry along the ground are detestable, and you must never eat them. 42This includes all animals that slither along on their bellies, as well as those with four legs and those with many feet. All such animals that scurry along the ground are detestable, and you must never eat them. 43Do not defile yourselves by touching them. You must not make yourselves ceremonially unclean because of them. 44For I am the LORD your God. You must consecrate yourselves and be holy, because I am holy. So do not defile yourselves with any of these small animals that scurry along the ground. 45For I, the LORD, am the one who brought you up from the land of Egypt, that I might be your God. Therefore, you must be holy because I am holy.

Why is it so important to live a clean life?

I am the LORD your God. You must . . . be holy, because I am holy.
LEVITICUS 11:44

46"These are the instructions regarding land animals, birds, marine creatures, and animals that scurry along the ground. 47By these instructions you will know what is unclean and clean, and which animals may be eaten and which may not be eaten."

CHAPTER 12

Purification after Childbirth

The LORD said to Moses, 2"Give the following instructions to the people of Israel. If a woman becomes pregnant and gives birth to a son, she will be ceremonially unclean for seven days, just as she is unclean during her menstrual period. 3On the eighth day the boy's foreskin must be circumcised. 4After waiting thirty-three days, she will be purified from the bleeding of childbirth. During this time of purification, she must not touch anything that is set apart as holy. And she must not enter the sanctuary until her time of purification is over. 5If a woman gives birth to a daughter, she will be ceremonially unclean for two weeks, just as she is unclean during her menstrual period. After waiting sixty-six days, she will be purified from the bleeding of childbirth.

6"When the time of purification is completed for either a son or a daughter, the woman must bring a one-year-old lamb for a burnt offering and a young pigeon or turtledove for a purification offering. She must bring her offerings to the priest at the entrance of the Tabernacle.* 7The priest will then present them to the LORD to purify her.* Then she will be ceremonially clean again after her bleeding at childbirth. These are the instructions for a woman after the birth of a son or a daughter.

8"If a woman cannot afford to bring a lamb, she must bring two turtledoves or two young pigeons. One will be for the burnt offering and the other for the purification offering. The priest will sacrifice them to purify her, and she will be ceremonially clean."

CHAPTER 13

Serious Skin Diseases

The LORD said to Moses and Aaron, 2"If anyone has a swelling or a rash or discolored skin that might develop into a serious skin disease,* that person must be brought to Aaron the priest or to one of his sons.* 3The priest will examine the affected area of the skin. If the hair in the affected area has turned white and the problem appears to be more than skin-deep, it is a serious skin disease, and the priest who examines it must pronounce the person ceremonially unclean.

4"But if the affected area of the skin is only a white discoloration and does not appear to be more than skin-deep, and if the hair on the spot has not turned white, the priest will quarantine the person for seven days. 5On the seventh day the priest will make another examination. If he finds the affected area has not changed and the problem has not spread on the skin, the priest will quarantine the person for seven more days. 6On the seventh day the priest will make another examination. If he finds the affected area has faded and has not

12:6 Hebrew *Tent of Meeting*. **12:7** Or *to make atonement for her;* also in 12:8. **13:2a** Traditionally rendered *leprosy*. The Hebrew word used throughout this passage is used to describe various skin diseases. **13:2b** Or *one of his descendants*.

spread, the priest will pronounce the person ceremonially clean. It was only a rash. The person's clothing must be washed, and the person will be ceremonially clean. [7]But if the rash continues to spread after the person has been examined by the priest and has been pronounced clean, the infected person must return to be examined again. [8]If the priest finds that the rash has spread, he must pronounce the person ceremonially unclean, for it is indeed a skin disease.

[9]"Anyone who develops a serious skin disease must go to the priest for an examination. [10]If the priest finds a white swelling on the skin, and some hair on the spot has turned white, and there is an open sore in the affected area, [11]it is a chronic skin disease, and the priest must pronounce the person ceremonially unclean. In such cases the person need not be quarantined, for it is obvious that the skin is defiled by the disease.

[12]"Now suppose the disease has spread all over the person's skin, covering the body from head to foot. [13]When the priest examines the infected person and finds that the disease covers the entire body, he will pronounce the person ceremonially clean. Since the skin has turned completely white, the person is clean. [14]But if any open sores appear, the infected person will be pronounced ceremonially unclean. [15]The priest must make this pronouncement as soon as he sees an open sore, since open sores indicate the presence of a skin disease. [16]However, if the open sores heal and turn white like the rest of the skin, the person must return to the priest [17]for another examination. If the affected areas have indeed turned white, the priest will then pronounce the person ceremonially clean by declaring, 'You are clean!'

[18]"If anyone has a boil on the skin that has started to heal, [19]but a white swelling or a reddish white spot develops in its place, that person must go to the priest to be examined. [20]If the priest examines it and finds it to be more than skin-deep, and if the hair in the affected area has turned white, the priest must pronounce the person ceremonially unclean. The boil has become a serious skin disease. [21]But if the priest finds no white hair on the affected area and the problem appears to be no more than skin-deep and has faded, the priest must quarantine the person for seven days. [22]If during that time the affected area spreads on the skin, the priest must pronounce the person ceremonially unclean, because it is a serious disease. [23]But if the area grows no larger and does not spread, it is merely the scar from the boil, and the priest will pronounce the person ceremonially clean.

[24]"If anyone has suffered a burn on the skin and the burned area changes color, becoming either reddish white or shiny white, [25]the priest must examine it. If he finds that the hair in the affected area has turned white and the problem appears to be more than skin-deep, a skin disease has broken out in the burn. The priest must then pronounce the person ceremonially unclean, for it is clearly a serious skin disease. [26]But if the priest finds no white hair on the affected area and the problem appears to be no more than skin-deep and has faded, the priest must quarantine the infected person for seven days. [27]On the seventh day the priest must examine the person again. If the affected area has spread on the skin, the priest must pronounce that person ceremonially unclean, for it is clearly a serious skin disease. [28]But if the affected area has not changed or spread on the skin and has faded, it is simply a swelling from the burn. The priest will then pronounce the person ceremonially clean, for it is only the scar from the burn.

[29]"If anyone, either a man or woman, has a sore on the head or chin, [30]the priest must examine it. If he finds it is more than skin-deep and has fine yellow hair on it, the priest must pronounce the person ceremonially unclean. It is a scabby sore of the head or chin. [31]If the priest examines the scabby sore and finds that it is only skin-deep but there is no black hair on it, he must quarantine the person for seven days. [32]On the seventh day the priest must examine the sore again. If he finds that the scabby sore has not spread, and there is no yellow hair on it, and it appears to be only skin-deep, [33]the person must shave off all hair except the hair on the affected area. Then the priest must quarantine the person for another seven days. [34]On the seventh day he will examine the sore again. If it has not spread and appears to be no more than skin-deep, the priest will pronounce the person ceremonially clean. The person's clothing

must be washed, and the person will be ceremonially clean. [35]But if the scabby sore begins to spread after the person is pronounced clean, [36]the priest must do another examination. If he finds that the sore has spread, the priest does not need to look for yellow hair. The infected person is ceremonially unclean. [37]But if the color of the scabby sore does not change and black hair has grown on it, it has healed. The priest will then pronounce the person ceremonially clean.

[38]"If anyone, either a man or woman, has shiny white patches on the skin, [39]the priest must examine the affected area. If he finds that the shiny patches are only pale white, this is a harmless skin rash, and the person is ceremonially clean.

[40]"If a man loses his hair and his head becomes bald, he is still ceremonially clean. [41]And if he loses hair on his forehead, he simply has a bald forehead; he is still clean. [42]However, if a reddish white sore appears on the bald area at the top or back of his head, this is a skin disease. [43]The priest must examine him, and if he finds swelling around the reddish white sore anywhere on the man's head and it looks like a skin disease, [44]the man is indeed infected with a skin disease and is unclean. The priest must pronounce him ceremonially unclean because of the sore on his head.

[45]"Those who suffer from a serious skin disease must tear their clothing and leave their hair uncombed.* They must cover their mouth and call out, 'Unclean! Unclean!' [46]As long as the serious disease lasts, they will be ceremonially unclean. They must live in isolation in their place outside the camp.

Treatment of Contaminated Clothing

[47]"Now suppose mildew* contaminates some woolen or linen clothing, [48]woolen or linen fabric, the hide of an animal, or anything made of leather. [49]If the contaminated area in the clothing, the animal hide, the fabric, or the leather article has turned greenish or reddish, it is contaminated with mildew and must be shown to the priest. [50]After examining the affected spot, the priest will put the article in quarantine for seven days. [51]On the seventh day the priest must inspect it again. If the contaminated area has spread, the clothing or fabric or leather is clearly contaminated by a serious mildew and is ceremonially unclean. [52]The priest must burn the item—the clothing, the woolen or linen fabric, or piece of leather—for it has been

13:45 Or *and uncover their heads.* **13:47** Traditionally rendered *leprosy*. The Hebrew term used throughout this passage is the same term used for the various skin diseases described in 13:1-46.

IS IT OK?

IS IT OK TO BE MESSY?

If you have candy wrappers and piles of clothes on the floor, can you still be admitted into heaven? Nowhere in the Ten Commandments does God say, "Thou shalt clean thy room." But before you celebrate and throw another wrapper on your floor, notice that God *does* give pages of specific instructions on the topic of cleanliness. (For an example, read Leviticus 13:47-52.) Apparently, being clean is important to God. He wanted his people to keep their clothes, houses, and bodies clean so they'd be healthy and safe. It doesn't make you righteous or guarantee you a place in heaven, but it does keep you clean. So quit tripping over that pizza box and clean up a little!

contaminated by a serious mildew. It must be completely destroyed by fire.

53"But if the priest examines it and finds that the contaminated area has not spread in the clothing, the fabric, or the leather, 54the priest will order the object to be washed and then quarantined for seven more days. 55Then the priest must examine the object again. If he finds that the contaminated area has not changed color after being washed, even if it did not spread, the object is defiled. It must be completely burned up, whether the contaminated spot* is on the inside or outside. 56But if the priest examines it and finds that the contaminated area has faded after being washed, he must cut the spot from the clothing, the fabric, or the leather. 57If the spot later reappears on the clothing, the fabric, or the leather article, the mildew is clearly spreading, and the contaminated object must be burned up. 58But if the spot disappears from the clothing, the fabric, or the leather article after it has been washed, it must be washed again; then it will be ceremonially clean.

59"These are the instructions for dealing with mildew that contaminates woolen or linen clothing or fabric or anything made of leather. This is how the priest will determine whether these items are ceremonially clean or unclean."

CHAPTER 14

Cleansing from Skin Diseases

And the LORD said to Moses, 2"The following instructions are for those seeking ceremonial purification from a skin disease.* Those who have been healed must be brought to the priest, 3who will examine them at a place outside the camp. If the priest finds that someone has been healed of a serious skin disease, 4he will perform a purification ceremony, using two live birds that are ceremonially clean, a stick of cedar,* some scarlet yarn, and a hyssop branch. 5The priest will order that one bird be slaughtered over a clay pot filled with fresh water. 6He will take the live bird, the cedar stick, the scarlet yarn, and the hyssop branch, and dip them into the blood of the bird that was slaughtered over the fresh water. 7The priest will then sprinkle the blood of the dead bird seven times on the person being purified of the skin disease. When the priest has purified the person, he will release the live bird in the open field to fly away.

8"The persons being purified must then wash their clothes, shave off all their hair, and bathe themselves in water. Then they will be ceremonially clean and may return to the camp. However, they must remain outside their tents for seven days. 9On the seventh day they must again shave all the hair from their heads, including the hair of the beard and eyebrows. They must also wash their clothes and bathe themselves in water. Then they will be ceremonially clean.

10"On the eighth day each person being purified must bring two male lambs and a one-year-old female lamb, all with no defects, along with a grain offering of six quarts* of choice flour moistened with olive oil, and a cup* of olive oil. 11Then the officiating priest will present that person for purification, along with the offerings, before the LORD at the entrance of the Tabernacle.* 12The priest will take one of the male lambs and the olive oil and present them as a guilt offering, lifting them up as a special offering before the LORD. 13He will then slaughter the male lamb in the sacred area where sin offerings and burnt offerings are slaughtered. As with the sin offering, the guilt offering belongs to the priest. It is a most holy offering. 14The priest will then take some of the blood of the guilt offering and apply it to the lobe of the right ear, the thumb of the right hand, and the big toe of the right foot of the person being purified.

15"Then the priest will pour some of the olive oil into the palm of his own left hand. 16He will dip his right finger into the oil in his palm and sprinkle some of it with his finger seven times before the LORD. 17The priest will then apply some of the oil in his palm over the blood from the guilt offering that is on the lobe of the right ear, the thumb of the right hand, and the big toe of the right foot of the person being purified. 18The priest will apply the oil remaining in his hand to the head of the person being purified. Through this pro-

13:55 The meaning of the Hebrew is uncertain. **14:2** Traditionally rendered *leprosy;* see note on 13:2a. **14:4** Or *juniper;* also in 14:6, 49, 51. **14:10a** Hebrew *3/10 of an ephah* [6.6 liters]. **14:10b** Hebrew *1 log* [0.3 liters]; also in 14:21. **14:11** Hebrew *Tent of Meeting;* also in 14:23.

cess, the priest will purify* the person before the LORD.

19"Then the priest must present the sin offering to purify the person who was cured of the skin disease. After that, the priest will slaughter the burnt offering 20and offer it on the altar along with the grain offering. Through this process, the priest will purify the person who was healed, and the person will be ceremonially clean.

21"But anyone who is too poor and cannot afford these offerings may bring one male lamb for a guilt offering, to be lifted up as a special offering for purification. The person must also bring two quarts* of choice flour moistened with olive oil for the grain offering and a cup of olive oil. 22The offering must also include two turtledoves or two young pigeons, whichever the person can afford. One of the pair must be used for the sin offering and the other for a burnt offering. 23On the eighth day of the purification ceremony, the person being purified must bring the offerings to the priest in the LORD's presence at the entrance of the Tabernacle. 24The priest will take the lamb for the guilt offering, along with the olive oil, and lift them up as a special offering to the LORD. 25Then the priest will slaughter the lamb for the guilt offering. He will take some of its blood and apply it to the lobe of the right ear, the thumb of the right hand, and the big toe of the right foot of the person being purified.

26"The priest will also pour some of the olive oil into the palm of his own left hand. 27He will dip his right finger into the oil in his palm and sprinkle some of it seven times before the LORD. 28The priest will then apply some of the oil in his palm over the blood from the guilt offering that is on the lobe of the right ear, the thumb of the right hand, and the big toe of the right foot of the person being purified. 29The priest will apply the oil remaining in his hand to the head of the person being purified. Through this process, the priest will purify the person before the LORD.

30"Then the priest will offer the two turtledoves or the two young pigeons, whichever the person can afford. 31One of them is for a sin offering and the other for a burnt offering, to be presented along with the grain offering. Through this process, the priest will purify the person before the LORD. 32These are the instructions for purification for those who have recovered from a serious skin disease but who cannot afford to bring the offerings normally required for the ceremony of purification."

Treatment of Contaminated Houses

33Then the LORD said to Moses and Aaron, 34"When you arrive in Canaan, the land I am giving you as your own possession, I may contaminate some of the houses in your land with mildew.* 35The owner of such a house must then go to the priest and say, 'It appears that my house has some kind of mildew.' 36Before the priest goes in to inspect the house, he must have the house emptied so nothing inside will be pronounced ceremonially unclean. 37Then the priest will go in and examine the mildew on the walls. If he finds greenish or reddish streaks and the contamination appears to go deeper than the wall's surface, 38the priest will step outside the door and put the house in quarantine for seven days. 39On the seventh day the priest must return for another inspection. If he finds that the mildew on the walls of the house has spread, 40the priest must order that the stones from those areas be removed. The contaminated material will then be taken outside the town to an area designated as ceremonially unclean. 41Next the inside walls of the entire house must be scraped thoroughly and the scrapings dumped in the unclean place outside the town. 42Other stones will be brought in to replace the ones that were removed, and the walls will be replastered.

43"But if the mildew reappears after all the stones have been replaced and the house has been scraped and replastered, 44the priest must return and inspect the house again. If he finds that the mildew has spread, the walls are clearly contaminated with a serious mildew, and the house is defiled. 45It must be torn down, and all its stones, timbers, and plaster must be carried out of town to the place designated as ceremonially unclean. 46Those who enter the house during the period of quarantine will be ceremonially unclean until evening, 47and all who sleep or eat in the house must wash their clothing.

48"But if the priest returns for his inspection

14:18 Or *will make atonement for;* similarly in 14:19, 20, 21, 29, 31, 53. **14:21** Hebrew *1/10 of an ephah* [2.2 liters].
14:34 Traditionally rendered *leprosy;* see note on 13:47.

and finds that the mildew has not reappeared
in the house after the fresh plastering, he will
pronounce it clean because the mildew is
clearly gone. [49]To purify the house the priest
must take two birds, a stick of cedar, some
scarlet yarn, and a hyssop branch. [50]He will
slaughter one of the birds over a clay pot filled
with fresh water. [51]He will take the cedar stick,
the hyssop branch, the scarlet yarn, and the
live bird, and dip them into the blood of the
slaughtered bird and into the fresh water.
Then he will sprinkle the house seven times.
[52]When the priest has purified the house in
exactly this way, [53]he will release the live bird
in the open fields outside the town. Through
this process, the priest will purify the house,
and it will be ceremonially clean.

[54]"These are the instructions for dealing
with serious skin diseases,* including scabby
sores; [55]and mildew,* whether on clothing or
in a house; [56]and a swelling on the skin, a rash,
or discolored skin. [57]This procedure will determine whether a person or object is ceremonially clean or unclean.

"These are the instructions regarding skin
diseases and mildew."

CHAPTER 15

Bodily Discharges

The LORD said to Moses and Aaron, [2]"Give the
following instructions to the people of Israel.

"Any man who has a bodily discharge is ceremonially unclean. [3]This defilement is caused
by his discharge, whether the discharge continues or stops. In either case the man is unclean. [4]Any bed on which the man with the
discharge lies and anything on which he sits
will be ceremonially unclean. [5]So if you touch
the man's bed, you must wash your clothes and
bathe yourself in water, and you will remain
unclean until evening. [6]If you sit where the
man with the discharge has sat, you must wash
your clothes and bathe yourself in water, and
you will remain unclean until evening. [7]If you
touch the man with the discharge, you must
wash your clothes and bathe yourself in water,
and you will remain unclean until evening. [8]If
the man spits on you, you must wash your
clothes and bathe yourself in water, and you
will remain unclean until evening. [9]Any saddle
blanket on which the man rides will be ceremonially unclean. [10]If you touch anything that
was under the man, you will be unclean until
evening. You must wash your clothes and
bathe yourself in water, and you will remain
unclean until evening. [11]If the man touches
you without first rinsing his hands, you must
wash your clothes and bathe yourself in water,
and you will remain unclean until evening.
[12]Any clay pot the man touches must be broken, and any wooden utensil he touches must
be rinsed with water.

[13]"When the man with the discharge is
healed, he must count off seven days for the
period of purification. Then he must wash his
clothes and bathe himself in fresh water, and
he will be ceremonially clean. [14]On the eighth
day he must get two turtledoves or two young
pigeons and come before the LORD at the entrance of the Tabernacle* and give his offerings to the priest. [15]The priest will offer one
bird for a sin offering and the other for a burnt
offering. Through this process, the priest will
purify* the man before the LORD for his discharge.

[16]"Whenever a man has an emission of semen, he must bathe his entire body in water,
and he will remain ceremonially unclean until
the next evening.* [17]Any clothing or leather
with semen on it must be washed in water, and
it will remain unclean until evening. [18]After a
man and a woman have sexual intercourse,
they must each bathe in water, and they will
remain unclean until the next evening.

[19]"Whenever a woman has her menstrual
period, she will be ceremonially unclean for
seven days. Anyone who touches her during
that time will be unclean until evening.
[20]Anything on which the woman lies or sits
during the time of her period will be unclean. [21]If any of you touch her bed, you must
wash your clothes and bathe yourself in
water, and you will remain unclean until evening. [22]If you touch any object she has sat on,
you must wash your clothes and bathe yourself in water, and you will remain unclean until evening. [23]This includes her bed or any
other object she has sat on; you will be unclean until evening if you touch it. [24]If a man
has sexual intercourse with her and her
blood touches him, her menstrual impurity
will be transmitted to him. He will remain

14:54 Traditionally rendered *leprosy;* see note on 13:2a. **14:55** Traditionally rendered *leprosy;* see note on 13:47. **15:14** Hebrew *Tent of Meeting;* also in 15:29. **15:15** Or *will make atonement for;* also in 15:30. **15:16** Hebrew *until evening;* also in 15:18.

unclean for seven days, and any bed on which
he lies will be unclean.
25"If a woman has a flow of blood for many
days that is unrelated to her menstrual period, or if the blood continues beyond the
normal period, she is ceremonially unclean.
As during her menstrual period, the woman
will be unclean as long as the discharge continues. 26Any bed she lies on and any object
she sits on during that time will be unclean,
just as during her normal menstrual period.
27If any of you touch these things, you will be
ceremonially unclean. You must wash your
clothes and bathe yourself in water, and you
will remain unclean until evening.
28"When the woman's bleeding stops, she
must count off seven days. Then she will be
ceremonially clean. 29On the eighth day she
must bring two turtledoves or two young pigeons and present them to the priest at the
entrance of the Tabernacle. 30The priest will
offer one for a sin offering and the other for a
burnt offering. Through this process, the
priest will purify her before the LORD for the
ceremonial impurity caused by her bleeding.
31"This is how you will guard the people of
Israel from ceremonial uncleanness. Otherwise they would die, for their impurity would
defile my Tabernacle that stands among
them. 32These are the instructions for dealing
with anyone who has a bodily discharge—a
man who is unclean because of an emission
of semen 33or a woman during her menstrual
period. It applies to any man or woman who
has a bodily discharge, and to a man who has
sexual intercourse with a woman who is ceremonially unclean."

CHAPTER 16

The Day of Atonement

The LORD spoke to Moses after the death of
Aaron's two sons, who died after they entered the LORD's presence and burned the
wrong kind of fire before him. 2The LORD
said to Moses, "Warn your brother, Aaron,
not to enter the Most Holy Place behind the
inner curtain whenever he chooses; if he
does, he will die. For the Ark's cover—the
place of atonement—is there, and I myself
am present in the cloud above the atonement cover.
3"When Aaron enters the sanctuary area, he
must follow these instructions fully. He must
bring a young bull for a sin offering and a ram
for a burnt offering. 4He must put on his linen
tunic and the linen undergarments worn next
to his body. He must tie the linen sash around
his waist and put the linen turban on his head.
These are sacred garments, so he must bathe
himself in water before he puts them on.
5Aaron must take from the community of Israel two male goats for a sin offering and a ram
for a burnt offering.
6"Aaron will present his own bull as a sin offering to purify himself and his family, making

AMAZING FACTS

The first scapegoat was a real goat! It was sent into the wilderness and represented taking away the people's sins.
LEVITICUS 16:9-10, 20-22

them right with the LORD.* 7Then he must take
the two male goats and present them to the
LORD at the entrance of the Tabernacle.* 8He is
to cast sacred lots to determine which goat will
be reserved as an offering to the LORD and
which will carry the sins of the people to the
wilderness of Azazel. 9Aaron will then present
as a sin offering the goat chosen by lot for the
LORD. 10The other goat, the scapegoat chosen
by lot to be sent away, will be kept alive, standing before the LORD. When it is sent away to
Azazel in the wilderness, the people will be purified and made right with the LORD.*
11"Aaron will present his own bull as a sin
offering to purify himself and his family,
making them right with the LORD. After he has
slaughtered the bull as a sin offering, 12he will

16:6 Or *to make atonement for himself and his family;* similarly in 16:11, 17b, 24, 34. **16:7** Hebrew *Tent of Meeting;* also in 16:16, 17, 20, 23, 33. **16:10** Or *wilderness, it will make atonement for the people.*

fill an incense burner with burning coals from the altar that stands before the LORD. Then he will take two handfuls of fragrant powdered incense and will carry the burner and the incense behind the inner curtain. [13]There in the LORD's presence he will put the incense on the burning coals so that a cloud of incense will rise over the Ark's cover—the place of atonement—that rests on the Ark of the Covenant.* If he follows these instructions, he will not die. [14]Then he must take some of the blood of the bull, dip his finger in it, and sprinkle it on the east side of the atonement cover. He must sprinkle blood seven times with his finger in front of the atonement cover.

[15]"Then Aaron must slaughter the first goat as a sin offering for the people and carry its blood behind the inner curtain. There he will sprinkle the goat's blood over the atonement cover and in front of it, just as he did with the bull's blood. [16]Through this process, he will purify* the Most Holy Place, and he will do the same for the entire Tabernacle, because of the defiling sin and rebellion of the Israelites. [17]No one else is allowed inside the Tabernacle when Aaron enters it for the purification ceremony in the Most Holy Place. No one may enter until he comes out again after purifying himself, his family, and all the congregation of Israel, making them right with the LORD.

[18]"Then Aaron will come out to purify the altar that stands before the LORD. He will do this by taking some of the blood from the bull and the goat and putting it on each of the horns of the altar. [19]Then he must sprinkle the blood with his finger seven times over the altar. In this way, he will cleanse it from Israel's defilement and make it holy.

[20]"When Aaron has finished purifying the Most Holy Place and the Tabernacle and the altar, he must present the live goat. [21]He will lay both of his hands on the goat's head and confess over it all the wickedness, rebellion, and sins of the people of Israel. In this way, he will transfer the people's sins to the head of the goat. Then a man specially chosen for the task will drive the goat into the wilderness. [22]As the goat goes into the wilderness, it will carry all the people's sins upon itself into a desolate land.

[23]"When Aaron goes back into the Tabernacle, he must take off the linen garments he was wearing when he entered the Most Holy Place, and he must leave the garments there. [24]Then he must bathe himself with water in a sacred place, put on his regular garments, and go out to sacrifice a burnt offering for himself and a burnt offering for the people. Through this process, he will purify himself and the people, making them right with the LORD. [25]He must then burn all the fat of the sin offering on the altar.

[26]"The man chosen to drive the scapegoat into the wilderness of Azazel must wash his clothes and bathe himself in water. Then he may return to the camp.

[27]"The bull and the goat presented as sin offerings, whose blood Aaron takes into the Most Holy Place for the purification ceremony, will be carried outside the camp. The animals' hides, internal organs, and dung are all to be burned. [28]The man who burns them must wash his clothes and bathe himself in water before returning to the camp.

[29]"On the tenth day of the appointed month in early autumn,* you must deny yourselves.* Neither native-born Israelites nor foreigners living among you may do any kind of work. This is a permanent law for you. [30]On that day offerings of purification will be made for you,* and you will be purified in the LORD's presence from all your sins. [31]It will be a Sabbath day of complete rest for you, and you must deny yourselves. This is a permanent law for you. [32]In future generations, the purification* ceremony will be performed by the priest who has been anointed and ordained to serve as high priest in place of his ancestor Aaron. He will put on the holy linen garments [33]and purify the Most Holy Place, the Tabernacle, the altar, the priests, and the entire congregation. [34]This is a permanent law for you, to purify the people of Israel from their sins, making them right with the LORD once each year."

Moses followed all these instructions exactly as the LORD had commanded him.

16:13 Hebrew *that is above the Testimony.* The Hebrew word for "testimony" refers to the terms of the LORD's covenant with Israel as written on stone tablets, which were kept in the Ark, and also to the covenant itself. **16:16** Or *make atonement for;* similarly in 16:17a, 18, 20, 27, 33. **16:29a** Hebrew *On the tenth day of the seventh month.* This day in the ancient Hebrew lunar calendar occurred in September or October. **16:29b** Or *must fast;* also in 16:31. **16:30** Or *atonement will be made for you, to purify you.* **16:32** Or *atonement.*

My two "best friends" in junior high weren't Christians. Whenever I spent time with them, I knew we'd end up going to houses we shouldn't go to, meet up with older guys we shouldn't meet, and do things that my parents told me not to do.

I thought of them as friends at the time, but I've since learned that their idea of friendship was just having someone to party with, and they wouldn't give up until I gave in.

Looking back, I don't think they even liked me that much. They knew I didn't drink alcohol, but they drank around me anyway. And one time they put vodka in my water glass when I wasn't looking. Nice, huh? The worst time was when everyone started passing around chocolate candy with weed in it.

"Come on, try it," my friends begged.

They just cracked up, laughing at me when I refused. Not knowing how else to react, I laughed along. But it wasn't funny. I was scared. I wanted to go home. I wanted to call my mom. I learned that partying can get you in over your head. I had been desperate enough to consider these girls my friends, but I would have been better off without their friendship.

If you find yourself where I've been, my advice is that you don't need so-called friends like these. You know how your parents always say, "Call me if you need me to come get you"? Don't be "too cool" to call. Going home is the best thing you can do. Take it from me—I wish I hadn't tried to be so cool.

Check out Leviticus 18:3-5 to see how God wants us to act around people who don't follow him. Read these other verses on how partying with friends can be a real downer: Proverbs 12:26 and Romans 13:13.

CHAPTER 17

Prohibitions against Eating Blood

Then the LORD said to Moses, 2"Give the following instructions to Aaron and his sons and all the people of Israel. This is what the LORD has commanded.

3"If any native Israelite sacrifices a bull* or a lamb or a goat anywhere inside or outside the camp 4instead of bringing it to the entrance of the Tabernacle* to present it as an offering to the LORD, that person will be as guilty as a murderer.* Such a person has shed blood and will be cut off from the community. 5The purpose of this rule is to stop the Israelites from sacrificing animals in the open fields. It will ensure that they bring their sacrifices to the priest at the entrance of the Tabernacle, so he can present them to the LORD as peace offerings. 6Then the priest will be able to splatter the blood against the LORD's altar at the entrance of the Tabernacle, and he will burn the fat as a pleasing aroma to the LORD. 7The people must no longer be unfaithful to the LORD by offering sacrifices to the goat idols.* This is a permanent law for them, to be observed from generation to generation.

8"Give them this command as well. If any native Israelite or foreigner living among you offers a burnt offering or a sacrifice 9but does not bring it to the entrance of the Tabernacle to offer it to the LORD, that person will be cut off from the community.

10"And if any native Israelite or foreigner living among you eats or drinks blood in any form, I will turn against that person and cut him off from the community of your people, 11for the life of the body is in its blood. I have given you the blood on the altar to purify you, making you right with the LORD.* It is the blood, given in exchange for a life, that makes purification possible. 12That is why I have said to the people of Israel, 'You must never eat or drink blood—neither you nor the foreigners living among you.'

13"And if any native Israelite or foreigner living among you goes hunting and kills an animal or bird that is approved for eating, he must drain its blood and cover it with earth. 14The life of every creature is in its blood. That is why I have said to the people of Israel, 'You must never eat or drink blood, for the life of any creature is in its blood.' So whoever consumes blood will be cut off from the community.

15"And if any native-born Israelites or foreigners eat the meat of an animal that died naturally or was torn up by wild animals, they must wash their clothes and bathe themselves in water. They will remain ceremonially unclean until evening, but then they will be clean. 16But if they do not wash their clothes and bathe themselves, they will be punished for their sin."

CHAPTER 18

Forbidden Sexual Practices

Then the LORD said to Moses, 2"Give the following instructions to the people of Israel. I am the LORD your God. 3So do not act like the people in Egypt, where you used to live, or like the people of Canaan, where I am taking you. You must not imitate their way of life. 4You must obey all my regulations and be careful to obey my decrees, for I am the LORD your God. 5If you obey my decrees and my regulations, you will find life through them. I am the LORD.

6"You must never have sexual relations with a close relative, for I am the LORD.

7"Do not violate your father by having sexual relations with your mother. She is your mother; you must not have sexual relations with her.

8"Do not have sexual relations with any of your father's wives, for this would violate your father.

9"Do not have sexual relations with your sister or half sister, whether she is your father's daughter or your mother's daughter, whether she was born into your household or someone else's.

10"Do not have sexual relations with your granddaughter, whether she is your son's daughter or your daughter's daughter, for this would violate yourself.

11"Do not have sexual relations with your stepsister, the daughter of any of your father's wives, for she is your sister.

12"Do not have sexual relations with your father's sister, for she is your father's close relative.

13"Do not have sexual relations with your

17:3 Or *cow*. **17:4a** Hebrew *Tent of Meeting;* also in 17:5, 6, 9. **17:4b** Hebrew *will be guilty of blood*. **17:7** Or *goat demons*. **17:11** Or *to make atonement for you*.

mother's sister, for she is your mother's close relative.

[14]"Do not violate your uncle, your father's brother, by having sexual relations with his wife, for she is your aunt.

[15]"Do not have sexual relations with your daughter-in-law; she is your son's wife, so you must not have sexual relations with her.

[16]"Do not have sexual relations with your brother's wife, for this would violate your brother.

[17]"Do not have sexual relations with both a woman and her daughter. And do not take* her granddaughter, whether her son's daughter or her daughter's daughter, and have sexual relations with her. They are close relatives, and this would be a wicked act.

[18]"While your wife is living, do not marry her sister and have sexual relations with her, for they would be rivals.

[19]"Do not have sexual relations with a woman during her period of menstrual impurity.

[20]"Do not defile yourself by having sexual intercourse with your neighbor's wife.

[21]"Do not permit any of your children to be offered as a sacrifice to Molech, for you must not bring shame on the name of your God. I am the LORD.

18:17 Or *do not marry.*

[22]"Do not practice homosexuality, having sex with another man as with a woman. It is a detestable sin.

[23]"A man must not defile himself by having sex with an animal. And a woman must not offer herself to a male animal to have intercourse with it. This is a perverse act.

[24]"Do not defile yourselves in any of these ways, for the people I am driving out before you have defiled themselves in all these ways. [25]Because the entire land has become defiled, I am punishing the people who live there. I will cause the land to vomit them out. [26]You must obey all my decrees and regulations. You must not commit any of these detestable sins. This applies both to native-born Israelites and to the foreigners living among you.

[27]"All these detestable activities are practiced by the people of the land where I am taking you, and this is how the land has become defiled. [28]So do not defile the land and give it a reason to vomit you out, as it will vomit out the people who live there now. [29]Whoever commits any of these detestable sins will be cut off from the community of Israel. [30]So obey my instructions, and do not defile yourselves by committing any of these detestable practices that were committed by

IS IT OK?

IS IT OK IF SOMEONE'S GAY?

Some people say that because God loves everyone, he doesn't care if someone's gay. The first part of that statement is true, but the second part is false. Yes, God does love everyone, even gay people. But (and that's a big *but*), God also cares if someone's gay. Check it out for yourself in Leviticus 18:22. Homosexuality is absolutely *forbidden,* for it is an *enormous* sin. This doesn't mean that God won't help or forgive a person who practices homosexuality, or that we shouldn't love that person. However, it does mean that if we agree with God, we will agree that it's not OK to live a gay lifestyle.

Stolen Goods

During lunch, Jared overheard a boy bragging to his friends, "Guess what? I just got some 'free' candy from the snack bar." Jared didn't really believe the kid, but then the guy handed out candy bars to his friends. They laughed as they enjoyed their stolen treats. Jared looked around the lunchroom and saw the principal on the other side.

Should Jared tell the principal what he saw and heard? Tell the kid to stop stealing? Or ask for a "free" candy bar? Leviticus 19:11 can guide Jared.

the people who lived in the land before you. I am the Lord your God."

CHAPTER 19

Holiness in Personal Conduct

The Lord also said to Moses, 2"Give the following instructions to the entire community of Israel. You must be holy because I, the Lord your God, am holy.

3"Each of you must show great respect for your mother and father, and you must always observe my Sabbath days of rest. I am the Lord your God.

4"Do not put your trust in idols or make metal images of gods for yourselves. I am the Lord your God.

5"When you sacrifice a peace offering to the Lord, offer it properly so you* will be accepted by God. 6The sacrifice must be eaten on the same day you offer it or on the next day. Whatever is left over until the third day must be completely burned up. 7If any of the sacrifice is eaten on the third day, it will be contaminated, and I will not accept it. 8Anyone who eats it on the third day will be punished for defiling what is holy to the Lord and will be cut off from the community.

9"When you harvest the crops of your land, do not harvest the grain along the edges of your fields, and do not pick up what the harvesters drop. 10It is the same with your grape crop—do not strip every last bunch of grapes from the vines, and do not pick up the grapes that fall to the ground. Leave them for the poor and the foreigners living among you. I am the Lord your God.

11"Do not steal.

"Do not deceive or cheat one another.

12"Do not bring shame on the name of your God by using it to swear falsely. I am the Lord.

13"Do not defraud or rob your neighbor.

"Do not make your hired workers wait until the next day to receive their pay.

14"Do not insult the deaf or cause the blind to stumble. You must fear your God; I am the Lord.

15"Do not twist justice in legal matters by favoring the poor or being partial to the rich and powerful. Always judge people fairly.

16"Do not spread slanderous gossip among your people.*

"Do not stand idly by when your neighbor's life is threatened. I am the Lord.

17"Do not nurse hatred in your heart for any of your relatives.* Confront people directly so you will not be held guilty for their sin.

18"Do not seek revenge or bear a grudge against a fellow Israelite, but love your neighbor as yourself. I am the Lord.

19"You must obey all my decrees.

19:5 Or *it*. **19:16** Hebrew *Do not act as a merchant toward your own people.* **19:17** Hebrew *for your brother*.

"Do not mate two different kinds of animals. Do not plant your field with two different kinds of seed. Do not wear clothing woven from two different kinds of thread.

Is it OK to tell just a little lie if it won't hurt anyone?

Do not deceive or cheat one another. LEVITICUS 19:11

[20]"If a man has sex with a slave girl whose freedom has never been purchased but who is committed to become another man's wife, he must pay full compensation to her master. But since she is not a free woman, neither the man nor the woman will be put to death. [21]The man, however, must bring a ram as a guilt offering and present it to the LORD at the entrance of the Tabernacle.* [22]The priest will then purify him* before the LORD with the ram of the guilt offering, and the man's sin will be forgiven.

[23]"When you enter the land and plant fruit trees, leave the fruit unharvested for the first three years and consider it forbidden.* Do not eat it. [24]In the fourth year the entire crop must be consecrated to the LORD as a celebration of praise. [25]Finally, in the fifth year you may eat the fruit. If you follow this pattern, your harvest will increase. I am the LORD your God.

[26]"Do not eat meat that has not been drained of its blood.

"Do not practice fortune-telling or witchcraft.

[27]"Do not trim off the hair on your temples or trim your beards.

[28]"Do not cut your bodies for the dead, and do not mark your skin with tattoos. I am the LORD.

[29]"Do not defile your daughter by making her a prostitute, or the land will be filled with prostitution and wickedness.

[30]"Keep my Sabbath days of rest, and show reverence toward my sanctuary. I am the LORD.

[31]"Do not defile yourselves by turning to mediums or to those who consult the spirits of the dead. I am the LORD your God.

[32]"Stand up in the presence of the elderly, and show respect for the aged. Fear your God. I am the LORD.

[33]"Do not take advantage of foreigners who live among you in your land. [34]Treat them like native-born Israelites, and love them as you love yourself. Remember that you were once foreigners living in the land of Egypt. I am the LORD your God.

[35]"Do not use dishonest standards when measuring length, weight, or volume. [36]Your scales and weights must be accurate. Your containers for measuring dry materials or liquids must be accurate.* I am the LORD your God who brought you out of the land of Egypt.

[37]"You must be careful to keep all of my decrees and regulations by putting them into practice. I am the LORD."

CHAPTER 20

Punishments for Disobedience

The LORD said to Moses, [2]"Give the people of Israel these instructions, which apply both to native Israelites and to the foreigners living in Israel.

"If any of them offer their children as a sacrifice to Molech, they must be put to death. The people of the community must stone them to death. [3]I myself will turn against them and cut them off from the community, because they have defiled my sanctuary and brought shame on my holy name by offering their children to Molech. [4]And if the people of the community ignore those who offer their children to Molech and refuse to execute them, [5]I myself will turn against them and their families and will cut them off from the community. This will happen to all who commit spiritual prostitution by worshiping Molech.

[6]"I will also turn against those who commit spiritual prostitution by putting their trust in mediums or in those who consult the spirits

19:21 Hebrew *Tent of Meeting.* **19:22** Or *make atonement for him.* **19:23** Hebrew *consider it uncircumcised.* **19:36** Hebrew *Use an honest ephah* [a dry measure] *and an honest hin* [a liquid measure].

of the dead. I will cut them off from the community. [7]So set yourselves apart to be holy, for I am the LORD your God. [8]Keep all my decrees by putting them into practice, for I am the LORD who makes you holy.

[9]"Anyone who dishonors* father or mother must be put to death. Such a person is guilty of a capital offense.

[10]"If a man commits adultery with his neighbor's wife, both the man and the woman who have committed adultery must be put to death.

[11]"If a man violates his father by having sex with one of his father's wives, both the man and the woman must be put to death, for they are guilty of a capital offense.

[12]"If a man has sex with his daughter-in-law, both must be put to death. They have committed a perverse act and are guilty of a capital offense.

[13]"If a man practices homosexuality, having sex with another man as with a woman, both men have committed a detestable act. They must both be put to death, for they are guilty of a capital offense.

[14]"If a man marries both a woman and her mother, he has committed a wicked act. The man and both women must be burned to death to wipe out such wickedness from among you.

[15]"If a man has sex with an animal, he must be put to death, and the animal must be killed.

[16]"If a woman presents herself to a male animal to have intercourse with it, she and the animal must both be put to death. You must kill both, for they are guilty of a capital offense.

[17]"If a man marries his sister, the daughter of either his father or his mother, and they have sexual relations, it is a shameful disgrace. They must be publicly cut off from the community. Since the man has violated his sister, he will be punished for his sin.

[18]"If a man has sexual relations with a woman during her menstrual period, both of them must be cut off from the community, for together they have exposed the source of her blood flow.

[19]"Do not have sexual relations with your aunt, whether your mother's sister or your father's sister. This would dishonor a close relative. Both parties are guilty and will be punished for their sin.

[20]"If a man has sex with his uncle's wife, he has violated his uncle. Both the man and woman will be punished for their sin, and they will die childless.

[21]"If a man marries his brother's wife, it is an act of impurity. He has violated his brother, and the guilty couple will remain childless.

[22]"You must keep all my decrees and regulations by putting them into practice; otherwise the land to which I am bringing you as your new home will vomit you out. [23]Do not live according to the customs of the people I am driving out before you. It is because they do these shameful things that I detest them. [24]But I have promised you, 'You will possess their land because I will give it to you as your possession—a land flowing with milk and honey.' I am the LORD your God, who has set you apart from all other people.

[25]"You must therefore make a distinction between ceremonially clean and unclean animals, and between clean and unclean birds. You must not defile yourselves by eating any unclean animal or bird or creature that scurries along the ground. I have identified them as being unclean for you. [26]You must be holy because I, the LORD, am holy. I have set you apart from all other people to be my very own.

[27]"Men and women among you who act as mediums or who consult the spirits of the dead must be put to death by stoning. They are guilty of a capital offense."

CHAPTER 21

Instructions for the Priests

The LORD said to Moses, "Give the following instructions to the priests, the descendants of Aaron.

"A priest must not make himself ceremonially unclean by touching the dead body of a relative. [2]The only exceptions are his closest relatives—his mother or father, son or daughter, brother, [3]or his virgin sister who depends on him because she has no husband. [4]But a priest must not defile himself and make himself unclean for someone who is related to him only by marriage.

[5]"The priests must not shave their heads or

20:9 Greek version reads *Anyone who speaks disrespectfully of*. Compare Matt 15:4; Mark 7:10.

trim their beards or cut their bodies. [6]They must be set apart as holy to their God and must never bring shame on the name of God. They must be holy, for they are the ones who present the special gifts to the LORD, gifts of food for their God.

[7]"Priests may not marry a woman defiled by prostitution, and they may not marry a woman who is divorced from her husband, for the priests are set apart as holy to their God. [8]You must treat them as holy because they offer up food to your God. You must consider them holy because I, the LORD, am holy, and I make you holy.

[9]"If a priest's daughter defiles herself by becoming a prostitute, she also defiles her father's holiness, and she must be burned to death.

[10]"The high priest has the highest rank of all the priests. The anointing oil has been poured on his head, and he has been ordained to wear the priestly garments. He must never leave his hair uncombed* or tear his clothing. [11]He must not defile himself by going near a dead body. He may not make himself ceremonially unclean even for his father or mother. [12]He must not defile the sanctuary of his God by leaving it to attend to a dead person, for he has been made holy by the anointing oil of his God. I am the LORD.

[13]"The high priest may marry only a virgin. [14]He may not marry a widow, a woman who is divorced, or a woman who has defiled herself by prostitution. She must be a virgin from his own clan, [15]so that he will not dishonor his descendants among his clan, for I am the LORD who makes him holy."

[16]Then the LORD said to Moses, [17]"Give the following instructions to Aaron: In all future generations, none of your descendants who has any defect will qualify to offer food to his God. [18]No one who has a defect qualifies, whether he is blind, lame, disfigured, deformed, [19]or has a broken foot or arm, [20]or is hunchbacked or dwarfed, or has a defective eye, or skin sores or scabs, or damaged testicles. [21]No descendant of Aaron who has a defect may approach the altar to present special gifts to the LORD. Since he has a defect, he may not approach the altar to offer food to his God. [22]However, he may eat from the food offered to God, including the holy offerings and the most holy offerings. [23]Yet because of his physical defect, he may not enter the room behind the inner curtain or approach the altar, for this would defile my holy places. I am the LORD who makes them holy."

[24]So Moses gave these instructions to Aaron and his sons and to all the Israelites.

CHAPTER 22

The LORD said to Moses, [2]"Tell Aaron and his sons to be very careful with the sacred gifts that the Israelites set apart for me, so they do not bring shame on my holy name. I am the LORD. [3]Give them the following instructions.

"In all future generations, if any of your descendants is ceremonially unclean when he approaches the sacred offerings that the people of Israel consecrate to the LORD, he must be cut off from my presence. I am the LORD.

[4]"If any of Aaron's descendants has a skin disease* or any kind of discharge that makes him ceremonially unclean, he may not eat from the sacred offerings until he has been pronounced clean. He also becomes unclean by touching a corpse, or by having an emission of semen, [5]or by touching a small animal that is unclean, or by touching someone who is ceremonially unclean for any reason. [6]The man who is defiled in any of these ways will remain unclean until evening. He may not eat from the sacred offerings until he has bathed himself in water. [7]When the sun goes down, he will be ceremonially clean again and may eat from the sacred offerings, for this is his food. [8]He may not eat an animal that has died a natural death or has been torn apart by wild animals, for this would defile him. I am the LORD.

[9]"The priests must follow my instructions carefully. Otherwise they will be punished for their sin and will die for violating my instructions. I am the LORD who makes them holy.

[10]"No one outside a priest's family may eat the sacred offerings. Even guests and hired workers in a priest's home are not allowed to eat them. [11]However, if the priest buys a slave for himself, the slave may eat from the sacred offerings. And if his slaves have children, they

21:10 Or *never uncover his head.* **22:4** Traditionally rendered *leprosy;* see note on 13:2a.

also may share his food. [12]If a priest's daughter marries someone outside the priestly family, she may no longer eat the sacred offerings. [13]But if she becomes a widow or is divorced and has no children to support her, and she returns to live in her father's home as in her youth, she may eat her father's food again. Otherwise, no one outside a priest's family may eat the sacred offerings.

[14]"Any such person who eats the sacred offerings without realizing it must pay the priest for the amount eaten, plus an additional 20 percent. [15]The priests must not let the Israelites defile the sacred offerings brought to the LORD [16]by allowing unauthorized people to eat them. This would bring guilt upon them and require them to pay compensation. I am the LORD who makes them holy."

Worthy and Unworthy Offerings

[17]And the LORD said to Moses, [18]"Give Aaron and his sons and all the Israelites these instructions, which apply both to native Israelites and to the foreigners living among you.

"If you present a gift as a burnt offering to the LORD, whether it is to fulfill a vow or is a voluntary offering, [19]you* will be accepted only if your offering is a male animal with no defects. It may be a bull, a ram, or a male goat. [20]Do not present an animal with defects, because the LORD will not accept it on your behalf.

[21]"If you present a peace offering to the LORD from the herd or the flock, whether it is to fulfill a vow or is a voluntary offering, you must offer a perfect animal. It may have no defect of any kind. [22]You must not offer an animal that is blind, crippled, or injured, or that has a wart, a skin sore, or scabs. Such animals must never be offered on the altar as special gifts to the LORD. [23]If a bull* or lamb has a leg that is too long or too short, it may be offered as a voluntary offering, but it may not be offered to fulfill a vow. [24]If an animal has damaged testicles or is castrated, you may not offer it to the LORD. You must never do this in your own land, [25]and you must not accept such an animal from foreigners and then offer it as a sacrifice to your God. Such animals will not be accepted on your behalf, for they are mutilated or defective."

[26]And the LORD said to Moses, [27]"When a calf or lamb or goat is born, it must be left with its mother for seven days. From the eighth day on, it will be acceptable as a special gift to the LORD. [28]But you must not slaughter a mother animal and her offspring on the same day, whether from the herd or the flock. [29]When you bring a thanksgiving offering to the LORD, sacrifice it properly so you will be accepted. [30]Eat the entire sacrificial animal on the day it is presented. Do not leave any of it until the next morning. I am the LORD.

[31]"You must faithfully keep all my commands by putting them into practice, for I am the LORD. [32]Do not bring shame on my holy name, for I will display my holiness among the people of Israel. I am the LORD who makes you holy. [33]It was I who rescued you from the land of Egypt, that I might be your God. I am the LORD."

CHAPTER 23

The Appointed Festivals

The LORD said to Moses, [2]"Give the following instructions to the people of Israel. These are the LORD's appointed festivals, which you are to proclaim as official days for holy assembly.

[3]"You have six days each week for your ordinary work, but the seventh day is a Sabbath day of complete rest, an official day for holy assembly. It is the LORD's Sabbath day, and it must be observed wherever you live.

[4]"In addition to the Sabbath, these are the LORD's appointed festivals, the official days for holy assembly that are to be celebrated at their proper times each year.

Passover and the Festival of Unleavened Bread

[5]"The LORD's Passover begins at sundown on the fourteenth day of the first month.* [6]On the next day, the fifteenth day of the month, you must begin celebrating the Festival of Unleavened Bread. This festival to the LORD continues for seven days, and during that time the bread you eat must be made without yeast. [7]On the first day of the festival, all the people must stop their ordinary work and observe an official day for holy assembly. [8]For seven days you must present special gifts to the LORD. On the seventh day the people must

22:19 Or *it*. **22:23** Or *cow*. **23:5** This day in the ancient Hebrew lunar calendar occurred in late March, April, or early May.

again stop all their ordinary work to observe
an official day for holy assembly."

Celebration of First Harvest

9 Then the LORD said to Moses, 10 "Give the fol-
lowing instructions to the people of Israel.
When you enter the land I am giving you and
you harvest its first crops, bring the priest a
bundle of grain from the first cutting of your
grain harvest. 11 On the day after the Sabbath,
the priest will lift it up before the LORD so it
may be accepted on your behalf. 12 On that
same day you must sacrifice a one-year-old
male lamb with no defects as a burnt offering
to the LORD. 13 With it you must present a
grain offering consisting of four quarts* of
choice flour moistened with olive oil. It will
be a special gift, a pleasing aroma to the LORD.
You must also offer one quart* of wine as a
liquid offering. 14 Do not eat any bread or
roasted grain or fresh kernels on that day un-
til you bring this offering to your God. This is
a permanent law for you, and it must be ob-
served from generation to generation wher-
ever you live.

The Festival of Harvest

15 "From the day after the Sabbath—the day
you bring the bundle of grain to be lifted up
as a special offering—count off seven full
weeks. 16 Keep counting until the day after the
seventh Sabbath, fifty days later. Then pre-
sent an offering of new grain to the LORD.
17 From wherever you live, bring two loaves of
bread to be lifted up before the LORD as a spe-
cial offering. Make these loaves from four
quarts of choice flour, and bake them with
yeast. They will be an offering to the LORD
from the first of your crops. 18 Along with the
bread, present seven one-year-old male
lambs with no defects, one young bull, and
two rams as burnt offerings to the LORD.
These burnt offerings, together with the
grain offerings and liquid offerings, will be
a special gift, a pleasing aroma to the LORD.
19 Then you must offer one male goat as a sin
offering and two one-year-old male lambs as
a peace offering.
20 "The priest will lift up the two lambs as a
special offering to the LORD, together with
the loaves representing the first of your
crops. These offerings, which are holy to the
LORD, belong to the priests. 21 That same day
will be proclaimed an official day for holy as-
sembly, a day on which you do no ordinary
work. This is a permanent law for you, and it
must be observed from generation to genera-
tion wherever you live.*
22 "When you harvest the crops of your
land, do not harvest the grain along the edges
of your fields, and do not pick up what the
harvesters drop. Leave it for the poor and the
foreigners living among you. I am the LORD
your God."

The Festival of Trumpets

23 The LORD said to Moses, 24 "Give the follow-
ing instructions to the people of Israel. On the
first day of the appointed month in early au-
tumn,* you are to observe a day of complete
rest. It will be an official day for holy assem-
bly, a day commemorated with loud blasts of
a trumpet. 25 You must do no ordinary work
on that day. Instead, you are to present special
gifts to the LORD."

The Day of Atonement

26 Then the LORD said to Moses, 27 "Be careful
to celebrate the Day of Atonement on the
tenth day of that same month—nine days af-
ter the Festival of Trumpets.* You must ob-
serve it as an official day for holy assembly, a
day to deny yourselves* and present special
gifts to the LORD. 28 Do no work during that
entire day because it is the Day of Atonement,
when offerings of purification are made for
you, making you right with* the LORD your
God. 29 All who do not deny themselves that
day will be cut off from God's people. 30 And I
will destroy anyone among you who does any
work on that day. 31 You must not do any work
at all! This is a permanent law for you, and it
must be observed from generation to genera-
tion wherever you live. 32 This will be a Sab-
bath day of complete rest for you, and on that
day you must deny yourselves. This day of rest

23:13a Hebrew *2/10 of an ephah* [4.4 liters]; also in 23:17. **23:13b** Hebrew *1/4 of a hin* [1 liter]. **23:21** This celebration, called the Festival of Harvest or the Festival of Weeks, was later called the Festival of Pentecost (see Acts 2:1). It is celebrated today as Shavuot (or Shabuoth). **23:24** Hebrew *On the first day of the seventh month.* This day in the ancient Hebrew lunar calendar occurred in September or October. This festival is celebrated today as Rosh Hashanah, the Jewish new year. **23:27a** Hebrew *on the tenth day of the seventh month;* see 23:24 and the note there. This day in the ancient Hebrew lunar calendar occurred in September or October. It is celebrated today as Yom Kippur. **23:27b** Or *to fast;* similarly in 23:29, 32. **23:28** Or *when atonement is made for you before.*

will begin at sundown on the ninth day of the month and extend until sundown on the tenth day."

The Festival of Shelters

33And the LORD said to Moses, 34"Give the following instructions to the people of Israel. Begin celebrating the Festival of Shelters* on the fifteenth day of the appointed month—five days after the Day of Atonement.* This festival to the LORD will last for seven days. 35On the first day of the festival you must proclaim an official day for holy assembly, when you do no ordinary work. 36For seven days you must present special gifts to the LORD. The eighth day is another holy day on which you present your special gifts to the LORD. This will be a solemn occasion, and no ordinary work may be done that day.

37("These are the LORD's appointed festivals. Celebrate them each year as official days for holy assembly by presenting special gifts to the LORD—burnt offerings, grain offerings, sacrifices, and liquid offerings—each on its proper day. 38These festivals must be observed in addition to the LORD's regular Sabbath days, and the offerings are in addition to your personal gifts, the offerings you give to fulfill your vows, and the voluntary offerings you present to the LORD.)

39"Remember that this seven-day festival to the LORD—the Festival of Shelters—begins on the fifteenth day of the appointed month,* after you have harvested all the produce of the land. The first day and the eighth day of the festival will be days of complete rest. 40On the first day gather branches from magnificent trees*—palm fronds, boughs from leafy trees, and willows that grow by the streams. Then celebrate with joy before the LORD your God for seven days. 41You must observe this festival to the LORD for seven days every year. This is a permanent law for you, and it must be observed in the appointed month* from generation to generation. 42For seven days you must live outside in little shelters. All native-born Israelites must live in shelters. 43This will remind each new generation of Israelites that I made their ancestors live in shelters when I rescued them from the land of Egypt. I am the LORD your God."

44So Moses gave the Israelites these instructions regarding the annual festivals of the LORD.

CHAPTER 24

Pure Oil and Holy Bread

The LORD said to Moses, 2"Command the people of Israel to bring you pure oil of pressed olives for the light, to keep the lamps burning continually. 3This is the lampstand that stands in the Tabernacle, in front of the inner curtain that shields the Ark of the Covenant.* Aaron must keep the lamps burning in the LORD's presence all night. This is a permanent law for you, and it must be observed from generation to generation. 4Aaron and the priests must tend the lamps on the pure gold lampstand continually in the LORD's presence.

5"You must bake twelve loaves of bread from choice flour, using four quarts* of flour for each loaf. 6Place the bread before the LORD on the pure gold table, and arrange the loaves in two rows, with six loaves in each row. 7Put some pure frankincense near each row to serve as a representative offering, a special gift presented to the LORD. 8Every Sabbath day this bread must be laid out before the LORD. The bread is to be received from the people of Israel as a requirement of the eternal covenant. 9The loaves of bread will belong to Aaron and his descendants, who must eat them in a sacred place, for they are most holy. It is the permanent right of the priests to claim this portion of the special gifts presented to the LORD."

An Example of Just Punishment

10One day a man who had an Israelite mother and an Egyptian father came out of his tent and got into a fight with one of the Israelite men. 11During the fight, this son of an Israelite woman blasphemed the Name of the LORD* with a curse. So the man was brought to Moses for judgment. His mother was Shelomith, the daughter of Dibri of the tribe of Dan. 12They kept the man in custody until the

23:34a Or *Festival of Booths*, or *Festival of Tabernacles*. This was earlier called the Festival of the Final Harvest or Festival of Ingathering (see Exod 23:16b). It is celebrated today as Sukkot (or Succoth). **23:34b** Hebrew *on the fifteenth day of the seventh month;* see 23:27a and the note there. **23:39** Hebrew *on the fifteenth day of the seventh month*. **23:40** Or *gather fruit from majestic trees*. **23:41** Hebrew *the seventh month*. **24:3** Hebrew *in the Tent of Meeting, outside the inner curtain of the Testimony;* see note on 16:13. **24:5** Hebrew *2/10 of an ephah* [4.4 liters]. **24:11** Hebrew *the Name;* also in 24:16b.

LORD's will in the matter should become clear to them.

[13]Then the LORD said to Moses, [14]"Take the blasphemer outside the camp, and tell all those who heard the curse to lay their hands on his head. Then let the entire community stone him to death. [15]Say to the people of Israel: Those who curse their God will be punished for their sin. [16]Anyone who blasphemes the Name of the LORD must be stoned to death by the whole community of Israel. Any native-born Israelite or foreigner among you who blasphemes the Name of the LORD must be put to death.

[17]"Anyone who takes another person's life must be put to death.

[18]"Anyone who kills another person's animal must pay for it in full—a live animal for the animal that was killed.

[19]"Anyone who injures another person must be dealt with according to the injury inflicted—[20]a fracture for a fracture, an eye for an eye, a tooth for a tooth. Whatever anyone does to injure another person must be paid back in kind.

[21]"Whoever kills an animal must pay for it in full, but whoever kills another person must be put to death.

[22]"This same standard applies both to native-born Israelites and to the foreigners living among you. I am the LORD your God."

[23]After Moses gave all these instructions to the Israelites, they took the blasphemer outside the camp and stoned him to death. The Israelites did just as the LORD had commanded Moses.

CHAPTER 25

The Sabbath Year

While Moses was on Mount Sinai, the LORD said to him, [2]"Give the following instructions to the people of Israel. When you have entered the land I am giving you, the land itself must observe a Sabbath rest before the LORD every seventh year. [3]For six years you may plant your fields and prune your vineyards and harvest your crops, [4]but during the seventh year the land must have a Sabbath year of complete rest. It is the LORD's Sabbath. Do not plant your fields or prune your vineyards during that year. [5]And don't store away the crops that grow on their own or gather the grapes from your unpruned vines. The land must have a year of complete rest. [6]But you may eat whatever the land produces on its own during its Sabbath. This applies to you, your male and female servants, your hired workers, and the temporary residents who live with you. [7]Your livestock and the wild animals in your land will also be allowed to eat what the land produces.

The Year of Jubilee

[8]"In addition, you must count off seven Sabbath years, seven sets of seven years, adding up to forty-nine years in all. [9]Then on the Day of Atonement in the fiftieth year,* blow the ram's horn loud and long throughout the land. [10]Set this year apart as holy, a time to proclaim freedom throughout the land for all who live there. It will be a jubilee year for you, when each of you may return to the land that belonged to

25:9 Hebrew *on the tenth day of the seventh month, on the Day of Atonement;* see 23:27a and the note there.

your ancestors and return to your own clan.
[11]This fiftieth year will be a jubilee for you.
During that year you must not plant your fields
or store away any of the crops that grow on
their own, and don't gather the grapes from
your unpruned vines. [12]It will be a jubilee year
for you, and you must keep it holy. But you may
eat whatever the land produces on its own. [13]In
the Year of Jubilee each of you may return to
the land that belonged to your ancestors.

[14]"When you make an agreement with your
neighbor to buy or sell property, you must not
take advantage of each other. [15]When you buy
land from your neighbor, the price you pay
must be based on the number of years since
the last jubilee. The seller must set the price by
taking into account the number of years re-
maining until the next Year of Jubilee. [16]The
more years until the next jubilee, the higher
the price; the fewer years, the lower the price.
After all, the person selling the land is actually
selling you a certain number of harvests.
[17]Show your fear of God by not taking advan-
tage of each other. I am the LORD your God.

[18]"If you want to live securely in the land,
follow my decrees and obey my regulations.
[19]Then the land will yield large crops, and
you will eat your fill and live securely in it.
[20]But you might ask, 'What will we eat during
the seventh year, since we are not allowed to
plant or harvest crops that year?' [21]Be assured
that I will send my blessing for you in the
sixth year, so the land will produce a crop
large enough for three years. [22]When you
plant your fields in the eighth year, you will
still be eating from the large crop of the sixth
year. In fact, you will still be eating from that
large crop when the new crop is harvested in
the ninth year.

Redemption of Property

[23]"The land must never be sold on a perma-
nent basis, for the land belongs to me. You are
only foreigners and tenant farmers working
for me.

[24]"With every purchase of land you must
grant the seller the right to buy it back. [25]If
one of your fellow Israelites falls into poverty
and is forced to sell some family land, then a
close relative should buy it back for him. [26]If
there is no close relative to buy the land, but
the person who sold it gets enough money to
buy it back, [27]he then has the right to redeem
it from the one who bought it. The price of
the land will be discounted according to the
number of years until the next Year of Jubi-
lee. In this way the original owner can then re-
turn to the land. [28]But if the original owner
cannot afford to buy back the land, it will re-
main with the new owner until the next Year
of Jubilee. In the jubilee year, the land must
be returned to the original owners so they can
return to their family land.

[29]"Anyone who sells a house inside a
walled town has the right to buy it back for
a full year after its sale. During that year, the
seller retains the right to buy it back. [30]But if
it is not bought back within a year, the sale of
the house within the walled town cannot
be reversed. It will become the permanent
property of the buyer. It will not be returned
to the original owner in the Year of Jubilee.
[31]But a house in a village—a settlement with-
out fortified walls—will be treated like prop-
erty in the countryside. Such a house may
be bought back at any time, and it must be
returned to the original owner in the Year of
Jubilee.

[32]"The Levites always have the right to buy
back a house they have sold within the towns
allotted to them. [33]And any property that is
sold by the Levites—all houses within the
Levitical towns—must be returned in the Year
of Jubilee. After all, the houses in the towns
reserved for the Levites are the only property
they own in all Israel. [34]The open pastureland
around the Levitical towns may never be sold.
It is their permanent possession.

Redemption of the Poor and Enslaved

[35]"If one of your fellow Israelites falls into pov-
erty and cannot support himself, support him
as you would a foreigner or a temporary resi-
dent and allow him to live with you. [36]Do not
charge interest or make a profit at his expense.
Instead, show your fear of God by letting him
live with you as your relative. [37]Remember, do
not charge interest on money you lend him or
make a profit on food you sell him. [38]I am the
LORD your God, who brought you out of the
land of Egypt to give you the land of Canaan
and to be your God.

[39]"If one of your fellow Israelites falls into
poverty and is forced to sell himself to you,
do not treat him as a slave. [40]Treat him in-

stead as a hired worker or as a temporary
resident who lives with you, and he will serve
you only until the Year of Jubilee. [41]At that
time he and his children will no longer be
obligated to you, and they will return to their
clans and go back to the land originally allot-
ted to their ancestors. [42]The people of Israel
are my servants, whom I brought out of the
land of Egypt, so they must never be sold as
slaves. [43]Show your fear of God by not treat-
ing them harshly.

[44]"However, you may purchase male and
female slaves from among the nations
around you. [45]You may also purchase the
children of temporary residents who live
among you, including those who have been
born in your land. You may treat them as your
property, [46]passing them on to your children
as a permanent inheritance. You may treat
them as slaves, but you must never treat your
fellow Israelites this way.

[47]"Suppose a foreigner or temporary resi-
dent becomes rich while living among you. If
any of your fellow Israelites fall into poverty
and are forced to sell themselves to such a for-
eigner or to a member of his family, [48]they still
retain the right to be bought back, even after
they have been purchased. They may be
bought back by a brother, [49]an uncle, or a
cousin. In fact, anyone from the extended fam-
ily may buy them back. They may also redeem
themselves if they have prospered. [50]They will
negotiate the price of their freedom with the
person who bought them. The price will be
based on the number of years from the time
they were sold until the next Year of Jubilee—
whatever it would cost to hire a worker for that
period of time. [51]If many years still remain until
the jubilee, they will repay the proper propor-
tion of what they received when they sold
themselves. [52]If only a few years remain until
the Year of Jubilee, they will repay a small
amount for their redemption. [53]The foreigner
must treat them as workers hired on a yearly
basis. You must not allow a foreigner to treat
any of your fellow Israelites harshly. [54]If any Is-
raelites have not been bought back by the time
the Year of Jubilee arrives, they and their chil-
dren must be set free at that time. [55]For the
people of Israel belong to me. They are my ser-
vants, whom I brought out of the land of Egypt.
I am the LORD your God.

CHAPTER 26

Blessings for Obedience

"Do not make idols or set up carved images, or
sacred pillars, or sculptured stones in your
land so you may worship them. I am the LORD
your God. [2]You must keep my Sabbath days
of rest and show reverence for my sanctuary.
I am the LORD.

[3]"If you follow my decrees and are careful
to obey my commands, [4]I will send you the
seasonal rains. The land will then yield its
crops, and the trees of the field will produce
their fruit. [5]Your threshing season will over-
lap with the grape harvest, and your grape
harvest will overlap with the season of plant-
ing grain. You will eat your fill and live se-
curely in your own land.

[6]"I will give you peace in the land, and you
will be able to sleep with no cause for fear. I
will rid the land of wild animals and keep
your enemies out of your land. [7]In fact, you
will chase down your enemies and slaughter
them with your swords. [8]Five of you will chase
a hundred, and a hundred of you will chase ten
thousand! All your enemies will fall beneath
your sword.

[9]"I will look favorably upon you, making you
fertile and multiplying your people. And I will
fulfill my covenant with you. [10]You will have
such a surplus of crops that you will need to
clear out the old grain to make room for the
new harvest! [11]I will live among you, and I will
not despise you. [12]I will walk among you; I will
be your God, and you will be my people. [13]I am
the LORD your God, who brought you out of the
land of Egypt so you would no longer be their
slaves. I broke the yoke of slavery from your
neck so you can walk with your heads held
high.

Punishments for Disobedience

[14]"However, if you do not listen to me or obey
all these commands, [15]and if you break my
covenant by rejecting my decrees, treating my
regulations with contempt, and refusing to
obey my commands, [16]I will punish you. I will
bring sudden terrors upon you—wasting dis-
eases and burning fevers that will cause your
eyes to fail and your life to ebb away. You will
plant your crops in vain because your ene-
mies will eat them. [17]I will turn against you,
and you will be defeated by your enemies.

Those who hate you will rule over you, and
you will run even when no one is chasing you!
18"And if, in spite of all this, you still dis-
obey me, I will punish you seven times over
for your sins. 19I will break your proud spirit
by making the skies as unyielding as iron and
the earth as hard as bronze. 20All your work
will be for nothing, for your land will yield no
crops, and your trees will bear no fruit.
21"If even then you remain hostile toward
me and refuse to obey me, I will inflict disas-
ter on you seven times over for your sins. 22I
will send wild animals that will rob you of
your children and destroy your livestock.
Your numbers will dwindle, and your roads
will be deserted.
23"And if you fail to learn the lesson and
continue your hostility toward me, 24then I
myself will be hostile toward you. I will per-
sonally strike you with calamity seven times
over for your sins. 25I will send armies against
you to carry out the curse of the covenant you
have broken. When you run to your towns for
safety, I will send a plague to destroy you
there, and you will be handed over to your en-
emies. 26I will destroy your food supply, so
that ten women will need only one oven to
bake bread for their families. They will ration
your food by weight, and though you have
food to eat, you will not be satisfied.
27"If in spite of all this you still refuse to lis-
ten and still remain hostile toward me, 28then
I will give full vent to my hostility. I myself will
punish you seven times over for your sins.
29Then you will eat the flesh of your own sons
and daughters. 30I will destroy your pagan
shrines and knock down your places of wor-
ship. I will leave your lifeless corpses piled on
top of your lifeless idols,* and I will despise
you. 31I will make your cities desolate and de-
stroy your places of pagan worship. I will take
no pleasure in your offerings that should be a
pleasing aroma to me. 32Yes, I myself will dev-
astate your land, and your enemies who come
to occupy it will be appalled at what they see.
33I will scatter you among the nations and
bring out my sword against you. Your land
will become desolate, and your cities will lie
in ruins. 34Then at last the land will enjoy its
neglected Sabbath years as it lies desolate
while you are in exile in the land of your ene-
mies. Then the land will finally rest and enjoy
the Sabbaths it missed. 35As long as the land
lies in ruins, it will enjoy the rest you never al-
lowed it to take every seventh year while you
lived in it.
36"And for those of you who survive, I will
demoralize you in the land of your enemies.
You will live in such fear that the sound of a
leaf driven by the wind will send you fleeing.
You will run as though fleeing from a sword,
and you will fall even when no one pursues
you. 37Though no one is chasing you, you will
stumble over each other as though fleeing
from a sword. You will have no power to stand
up against your enemies. 38You will die among
the foreign nations and be devoured in the
land of your enemies. 39Those of you who
survive will waste away in your enemies' lands
because of their sins and the sins of their
ancestors.
40"But at last my people will confess their
sins and the sins of their ancestors for betray-
ing me and being hostile toward me. 41When I
have turned their hostility back on them and
brought them to the land of their enemies,
then at last their stubborn hearts will be hum-
bled, and they will pay for their sins. 42Then I
will remember my covenant with Jacob and
my covenant with Isaac and my covenant with
Abraham, and I will remember the land. 43For
the land must be abandoned to enjoy its years
of Sabbath rest as it lies deserted. At last the
people will pay for their sins, for they have
continually rejected my regulations and de-
spised my decrees.
44"But despite all this, I will not utterly re-
ject or despise them while they are in exile in
the land of their enemies. I will not cancel my
covenant with them by wiping them out, for I
am the LORD their God. 45For their sakes I will
remember my ancient covenant with their an-
cestors, whom I brought out of the land of
Egypt in the sight of all the nations, that I
might be their God. I am the LORD."
46These are the decrees, regulations, and
instructions that the LORD gave through Moses
on Mount Sinai as evidence of the relation-
ship between himself and the Israelites.

CHAPTER 27

Redemption of Gifts Offered to the LORD

The LORD said to Moses, 2"Give the following
instructions to the people of Israel. If anyone

26:30 The Hebrew term (literally *round things*) probably alludes to dung.

makes a special vow to dedicate someone to
the LORD by paying the value of that person,
3here is the scale of values to be used. A man
between the ages of twenty and sixty is valued
at fifty shekels* of silver, as measured by the
sanctuary shekel. 4A woman of that age is
valued at thirty shekels* of silver. 5A boy be-
tween the ages of five and twenty is valued at
twenty shekels of silver; a girl of that age is
valued at ten shekels* of silver. 6A boy be-
tween the ages of one month and five years is
valued at five shekels of silver; a girl of that
age is valued at three shekels* of silver. 7A
man older than sixty is valued at fifteen shek-
els of silver; a woman of that age is valued at
ten shekels* of silver. 8If you desire to make
such a vow but cannot afford to pay the re-
quired amount, take the person to the priest.
He will determine the amount for you to pay
based on what you can afford.

9"If your vow involves giving an animal that
is acceptable as an offering to the LORD, any
gift to the LORD will be considered holy. 10You
may not exchange or substitute it for another
animal—neither a good animal for a bad one
nor a bad animal for a good one. But if you do
exchange one animal for another, then both
the original animal and its substitute will be
considered holy. 11If your vow involves an un-
clean animal—one that is not acceptable as an
offering to the LORD—then you must bring
the animal to the priest. 12He will assess its
value, and his assessment will be final,
whether high or low. 13If you want to buy back
the animal, you must pay the value set by the
priest, plus 20 percent.

14"If someone dedicates a house to the
LORD, the priest will come to assess its value.
The priest's assessment will be final, whether
high or low. 15If the person who dedicated the
house wants to buy it back, he must pay the
value set by the priest, plus 20 percent. Then
the house will again be his.

16"If someone dedicates to the LORD a
piece of his family property, its value will be
assessed according to the amount of seed re-
quired to plant it—fifty shekels of silver for
a field planted with five bushels of barley
seed.* 17If the field is dedicated to the LORD
in the Year of Jubilee, then the entire assess-
ment will apply. 18But if the field is dedicated
after the Year of Jubilee, the priest will assess
the land's value in proportion to the number
of years left until the next Year of Jubilee. Its
assessed value is reduced each year. 19If the
person who dedicated the field wants to buy
it back, he must pay the value set by the priest,
plus 20 percent. Then the field will again be
legally his. 20But if he does not want to buy it
back, and it is sold to someone else, the field
can no longer be bought back. 21When the
field is released in the Year of Jubilee, it will
be holy, a field specially set apart* for the
LORD. It will become the property of the
priests.

22"If someone dedicates to the LORD a field
he has purchased but which is not part of his
family property, 23the priest will assess its
value based on the number of years left until
the next Year of Jubilee. On that day he must
give the assessed value of the land as a sacred
donation to the LORD. 24In the Year of Jubilee
the field must be returned to the person from
whom he purchased it, the one who inherited
it as family property. 25(All the payments
must be measured by the weight of the sanc-
tuary shekel,* which equals twenty gerahs.)

26"You may not dedicate a firstborn animal
to the LORD, for the firstborn of your cattle,
sheep, and goats already belong to him. 27How-
ever, you may buy back the firstborn of a cere-
monially unclean animal by paying the
priest's assessment of its worth, plus 20 per-
cent. If you do not buy it back, the priest will
sell it at its assessed value.

28"However, anything specially set apart
for the LORD—whether a person, an animal,
or family property—must never be sold or
bought back. Anything devoted in this way
has been set apart as holy, and it belongs to
the LORD. 29No person specially set apart for
destruction may be bought back. Such a per-
son must be put to death.

30"One-tenth of the produce of the land,
whether grain from the fields or fruit from
the trees, belongs to the LORD and must be set
apart to him as holy. 31If you want to buy back
the LORD's tenth of the grain or fruit, you

27:3 Or *20 ounces* [570 grams]. **27:4** Or *12 ounces* [342 grams]. **27:5** Or *A boy . . . 8 ounces* [228 grams] *of silver; a girl . . . 4 ounces* [114 grams]. **27:6** Or *A boy . . . 2 ounces* [57 grams] *of silver; a girl . . . 1.2 ounces* [34 grams]. **27:7** Or *A man . . . 6 ounces* [171 grams] *of silver; a woman . . . 4 ounces* [114 grams]. **27:16** Hebrew *50 shekels* [20 ounces, or 570 grams] *of silver for a homer* [182 liters] *of barley seed.* **27:21** The Hebrew term used here refers to the complete consecration of things or people to the LORD, either by destroying them or by giving them as an offering; also in 27:28, 29. **27:25** Each shekel was about 0.4 ounces [11 grams] in weight.

must pay its value, plus 20 percent. [32]Count off every tenth animal from your herds and flocks and set them apart for the LORD as holy. [33]You may not pick and choose between good and bad animals, and you may not substitute one for another. But if you do exchange one animal for another, then both the original animal and its substitute will be considered holy and cannot be bought back."

[34]These are the commands that the LORD gave through Moses on Mount Sinai for the Israelites.

NUMBERS

WHO
Moses, Aaron, Miriam, Joshua, Caleb, Eleazar, Korah, and Balaam.

WHERE
The desert wilderness between Egypt and the Promised Land.

WHEN
Moses probably wrote this book between 1450–1410 BC while leading God's people to the Promised Land.

WHY
Numbers tells the story of how Israel prepared to enter the new land, how they sinned and were punished, and how they *again* prepared to enter years later.

You must wander in the wilderness for forty years . . . suffering the consequences of your sins.
NUMBERS 14:34

Getting lost is a terrible feeling! You can wander around for hours, afraid and worried. Imagine the whole nation of Israel being lost for years. God was there to help them find their way, but they didn't always listen. They didn't follow his directions. The book of Numbers tells their story.

1805 BC Joseph dies
Slavery in Egypt
1446 BC Exodus from Egypt
1443 BC First spy mission
Wilderness Wanderings
1406 BC Joshua appointed
1375 BC Judges begin to rule

DON'T GET LOST! LISTEN TO GOD'S DIRECTIONS.

CHAPTER 1

Registration of Israel's Troops

A year after Israel's departure from Egypt, the LORD spoke to Moses in the Tabernacle* in
the wilderness of Sinai. On the first day of the
second month* of that year he said, [2]"From
the whole community of Israel, record the
names of all the warriors by their clans and
families. List all the men [3]twenty years old or
older who are able to go to war. You and Aaron
must register the troops, [4]and you will be as-
sisted by one family leader from each tribe.
[5]"These are the tribes and the names of the
leaders who will assist you:

1:1a Hebrew *the Tent of Meeting*. **1:1b** This day in the ancient Hebrew lunar calendar occurred in April or May.

	Tribe	*Leader*
	Reuben	Elizur son of Shedeur
6	Simeon	Shelumiel son of Zurishaddai
7	Judah	Nahshon son of Amminadab
8	Issachar	Nethanel son of Zuar
9	Zebulun	Eliab son of Helon
10	Ephraim son of Joseph	Elishama son of Ammihud
	Manasseh son of Joseph	Gamaliel son of Pedahzur
11	Benjamin	Abidan son of Gideoni
12	Dan	Ahiezer son of Ammishaddai
13	Asher	Pagiel son of Ocran
14	Gad	Eliasaph son of Deuel
15	Naphtali	Ahira son of Enan

16These are the chosen leaders of the community, the leaders of their ancestral tribes, the heads of the clans of Israel."

17So Moses and Aaron called together these chosen leaders, 18and they assembled the whole community of Israel on that very day.* All the people were registered according to their ancestry by their clans and families. The men of Israel who were twenty years old or older were listed one by one, 19just as the LORD had commanded Moses. So Moses recorded their names in the wilderness of Sinai.

20-21This is the number of men twenty years old or older who were able to go to war, as their names were listed in the records of their clans and families*:

	Tribe	*Number*
	Reuben (Jacob's* oldest son)	46,500
22-23	Simeon	59,300
24-25	Gad	45,650
26-27	Judah	74,600
28-29	Issachar	54,400
30-31	Zebulun	57,400
32-33	Ephraim son of Joseph	40,500
34-35	Manasseh son of Joseph	32,200
36-37	Benjamin	35,400
38-39	Dan	62,700
40-41	Asher	41,500
42-43	Naphtali	53,400

44These were the men registered by Moses and Aaron and the twelve leaders of Israel, all listed according to their ancestral descent. 45They were registered by families—all the men of Israel who were twenty years old or older and able to go to war. 46The total number was 603,550.

47But this total did not include the Levites. 48For the LORD had said to Moses, 49"Do not include the tribe of Levi in the registration; do not count them with the rest of the Israelites. 50Put the Levites in charge of the Tabernacle of the Covenant,* along with all its furnishings and equipment. They must carry the Tabernacle and all its furnishings as you travel, and they must take care of it and camp around it. 51Whenever it is time for the Tabernacle to move, the Levites will take it down. And when it is time to stop, they will set it up again. But any unauthorized person who goes too near the Tabernacle must be put to death. 52Each tribe of Israel will camp in a designated area with its own family banner. 53But the Levites will camp around the Tabernacle of the Covenant to protect the community of Israel from the LORD's anger. The Levites are responsible to stand guard around the Tabernacle."

54So the Israelites did everything just as the LORD had commanded Moses.

CHAPTER 2

Organization for Israel's Camp

Then the LORD gave these instructions to Moses and Aaron: 2"When the Israelites set up camp, each tribe will be assigned its own area. The tribal divisions will camp beneath their family banners on all four sides of the Tabernacle,* but at some distance from it.

3-4"The divisions of Judah, Issachar, and Zebulun are to camp toward the sunrise on the east side of the Tabernacle, beneath their family banners. These are the names of the tribes, their leaders, and the numbers of their registered troops:

	Tribe	*Leader*	*Number*
	Judah	Nahshon son of Amminadab	74,600
5-6	Issachar	Nethanel son of Zuar	54,400
7-8	Zebulun	Eliab son of Helon	57,400

9So the total of all the troops on Judah's side of the camp is 186,400. These three tribes

1:18 Hebrew *on the first day of the second month;* see 1:1. **1:20-21a** In the Hebrew text, this sentence (*This is the number of men twenty years old or older who were able to go to war, as their names were listed in the records of their clans and families*) is repeated in 1:22, 24, 26, 28, 30, 32, 34, 36, 38, 40, 42. **1:20-21b** Hebrew *Israel's.* The names "Jacob" and "Israel" are often interchanged throughout the Old Testament, referring sometimes to the individual patriarch and sometimes to the nation. **1:50** Or *Tabernacle of the Testimony;* also in 1:53. **2:2** Hebrew *the Tent of Meeting;* also in 2:17.

are to lead the way whenever the Israelites travel to a new campsite.

10-11"The divisions of Reuben, Simeon, and Gad are to camp on the south side of the Tabernacle, beneath their family banners. These are the names of the tribes, their leaders, and the numbers of their registered troops:

Tribe	*Leader*	*Number*
Reuben	Elizur son of Shedeur	46,500
12-13Simeon	Shelumiel son of Zurishaddai	59,300
14-15Gad	Eliasaph son of Deuel*	45,650

16So the total of all the troops on Reuben's side of the camp is 151,450. These three tribes will be second in line whenever the Israelites travel.

17"Then the Tabernacle, carried by the Levites, will set out from the middle of the camp. All the tribes are to travel in the same order that they camp, each in position under the appropriate family banner.

18-19"The divisions of Ephraim, Manasseh, and Benjamin are to camp on the west side of the Tabernacle, beneath their family banners. These are the names of the tribes, their leaders, and the numbers of their registered troops:

Tribe	*Leader*	*Number*
Ephraim	Elishama son of Ammihud	40,500
20-21Manasseh	Gamaliel son of Pedahzur	32,200
22-23Benjamin	Abidan son of Gideoni	35,400

24So the total of all the troops on Ephraim's side of the camp is 108,100. These three tribes will be third in line whenever the Israelites travel.

25-26"The divisions of Dan, Asher, and Naphtali are to camp on the north side of the Tabernacle, beneath their family banners. These are the names of the tribes, their leaders, and the numbers of their registered troops:

Tribe	*Leader*	*Number*
Dan	Ahiezer son of Ammishaddai	62,700
27-28Asher	Pagiel son of Ocran	41,500
29-30Naphtali	Ahira son of Enan	53,400

31So the total of all the troops on Dan's side of the camp is 157,600. These three tribes will be last, marching under their banners whenever the Israelites travel."

32In summary, the troops of Israel listed by their families totaled 603,550. 33But as the LORD had commanded, the Levites were not

2:14-15 As in many Hebrew manuscripts, Samaritan Pentateuch, and Latin Vulgate (see also 1:14); most Hebrew manuscripts read *son of Reuel.*

ARRANGEMENT OF TRIBES AROUND THE TABERNACLE WHILE IN THE WILDERNESS

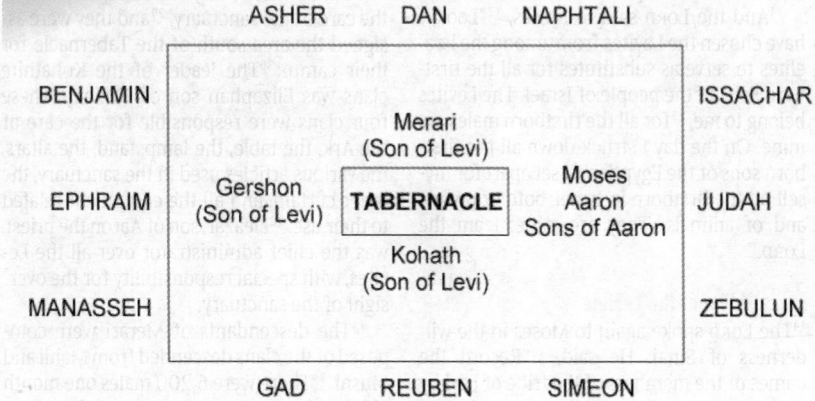

included in this registration. [34]So the people of Israel did everything as the LORD had commanded Moses. Each clan and family set up camp and marched under their banners exactly as the LORD had instructed them.

CHAPTER 3

Levites Appointed for Service

This is the family line of Aaron and Moses as it was recorded when the LORD spoke to Moses on Mount Sinai: [2]The names of Aaron's sons were Nadab (the oldest), Abihu, Eleazar, and Ithamar. [3]These sons of Aaron were anointed and ordained to minister as priests. [4]But Nadab and Abihu died in the LORD's presence in the wilderness of Sinai when they burned before the LORD the wrong kind of fire, different than he had commanded. Since they had no sons, this left only Eleazar and Ithamar to serve as priests with their father, Aaron.

[5]Then the LORD said to Moses, [6]"Call forward the tribe of Levi, and present them to Aaron the priest to serve as his assistants. [7]They will serve Aaron and the whole community, performing their sacred duties in and around the Tabernacle.* [8]They will also maintain all the furnishings of the sacred tent,* serving in the Tabernacle on behalf of all the Israelites. [9]Assign the Levites to Aaron and his sons. They have been given from among all the people of Israel to serve as their assistants. [10]Appoint Aaron and his sons to carry out the duties of the priesthood. But any unauthorized person who goes too near the sanctuary must be put to death."

[11]And the LORD said to Moses, [12]"Look, I have chosen the Levites from among the Israelites to serve as substitutes for all the firstborn sons of the people of Israel. The Levites belong to me, [13]for all the firstborn males are mine. On the day I struck down all the firstborn sons of the Egyptians, I set apart for myself all the firstborn in Israel, both of people and of animals. They are mine; I am the LORD."

Registration of the Levites

[14]The LORD spoke again to Moses in the wilderness of Sinai. He said, [15]"Record the names of the members of the tribe of Levi by their families and clans. List every male who is one month old or older." [16]So Moses listed them, just as the LORD had commanded.

[17]Levi had three sons, whose names were Gershon, Kohath, and Merari.
[18]The clans descended from Gershon were named after two of his descendants, Libni and Shimei.
[19]The clans descended from Kohath were named after four of his descendants, Amram, Izhar, Hebron, and Uzziel.
[20]The clans descended from Merari were named after two of his descendants, Mahli and Mushi.

These were the Levite clans, listed according to their family groups.

[21]The descendants of Gershon were composed of the clans descended from Libni and Shimei. [22]There were 7,500 males one month old or older among these Gershonite clans. [23]They were assigned the area to the west of the Tabernacle for their camp. [24]The leader of the Gershonite clans was Eliasaph son of Lael. [25]These two clans were responsible to care for the Tabernacle, including the sacred tent with its layers of coverings, the curtain at its entrance, [26]the curtains of the courtyard that surrounded the Tabernacle and altar, the curtain at the courtyard entrance, the ropes, and all the equipment related to their use.

[27]The descendants of Kohath were composed of the clans descended from Amram, Izhar, Hebron, and Uzziel. [28]There were 8,600* males one month old or older among these Kohathite clans. They were responsible for the care of the sanctuary, [29]and they were assigned the area south of the Tabernacle for their camp. [30]The leader of the Kohathite clans was Elizaphan son of Uzziel. [31]These four clans were responsible for the care of the Ark, the table, the lampstand, the altars, the various articles used in the sanctuary, the inner curtain, and all the equipment related to their use. [32]Eleazar, son of Aaron the priest, was the chief administrator over all the Levites, with special responsibility for the oversight of the sanctuary.

[33]The descendants of Merari were composed of the clans descended from Mahli and Mushi. [34]There were 6,200 males one month old or older among these Merarite clans.

3:7 Hebrew *around the Tent of Meeting, doing service at the Tabernacle.* **3:8** Hebrew *the Tent of Meeting;* also in 3:25. **3:28** Some Greek manuscripts read *8,300;* see total in 3:39.

35 They were assigned the area north of the
Tabernacle for their camp. The leader of the
Merarite clans was Zuriel son of Abihail.
36 These two clans were responsible for the
care of the frames supporting the Taberna-
cle, the crossbars, the pillars, the bases, and all
the equipment related to their use. 37 They
were also responsible for the posts of the
courtyard and all their bases, pegs, and ropes.

38 The area in front of the Tabernacle, in the
east toward the sunrise,* was reserved for the
tents of Moses and of Aaron and his sons, who
had the final responsibility for the sanctuary
on behalf of the people of Israel. Anyone
other than a priest or Levite who went too
near the sanctuary was to be put to death.

39 When Moses and Aaron counted the Le-
vite clans at the LORD's command, the total
number was 22,000 males one month old or
older.

Redeeming the Firstborn Sons

40 Then the LORD said to Moses, "Now count all
the firstborn sons in Israel who are one month
old or older, and make a list of their names.
41 The Levites must be reserved for me as sub-
stitutes for the firstborn sons of Israel; I am
the LORD. And the Levites' livestock must be
reserved for me as substitutes for the first-
born livestock of the whole nation of Israel."

42 So Moses counted the firstborn sons of
the people of Israel, just as the LORD had com-
manded. 43 The number of firstborn sons who
were one month old or older was 22,273.

44 Then the LORD said to Moses, 45 "Take the
Levites as substitutes for the firstborn sons
of the people of Israel. And take the livestock
of the Levites as substitutes for the firstborn
livestock of the people of Israel. The Levites
belong to me; I am the LORD. 46 There are 273
more firstborn sons of Israel than there are
Levites. To redeem these extra firstborn sons,
47 collect five pieces of silver* for each of them
(each piece weighing the same as the sanctu-
ary shekel, which equals twenty gerahs). 48 Give
the silver to Aaron and his sons as the redemp-
tion price for the extra firstborn sons."

49 So Moses collected the silver for redeem-
ing the firstborn sons of Israel who exceeded
the number of Levites. 50 He collected 1,365
pieces of silver* on behalf of these firstborn
sons of Israel (each piece weighing the same
as the sanctuary shekel). 51 And Moses gave
the silver for the redemption to Aaron and his
sons, just as the LORD had commanded.

CHAPTER 4

Duties of the Kohathite Clan

Then the LORD said to Moses and Aaron, 2 "Re-
cord the names of the members of the clans
and families of the Kohathite division of the
tribe of Levi. 3 List all the men between the
ages of thirty and fifty who are eligible to
serve in the Tabernacle.*

4 "The duties of the Kohathites at the Tab-
ernacle will relate to the most sacred objects.
5 When the camp moves, Aaron and his sons
must enter the Tabernacle first to take down
the inner curtain and cover the Ark of the
Covenant* with it. 6 Then they must cover the
inner curtain with fine goatskin leather and
spread over that a single piece of blue cloth.
Finally, they must put the carrying poles of
the Ark in place.

7 "Next they must spread a blue cloth over
the table where the Bread of the Presence is
displayed, and on the cloth they will place
the bowls, pans, jars, pitchers, and the special
bread. 8 They must spread a scarlet cloth over
all of this, and finally a covering of fine goat-
skin leather on top of the scarlet cloth. Then
they must insert the carrying poles into the
table.

9 "Next they must cover the lampstand with
a blue cloth, along with its lamps, lamp snuf-
fers, trays, and special jars of olive oil. 10 Then
they must cover the lampstand and its acces-
sories with fine goatskin leather and place
the bundle on a carrying frame.

11 "Next they must spread a blue cloth over
the gold incense altar and cover this cloth
with fine goatskin leather. Then they must at-
tach the carrying poles to the altar. 12 They
must take all the remaining furnishings of
the sanctuary and wrap them in a blue cloth,
cover them with fine goatskin leather, and
place them on the carrying frame.

13 "They must remove the ashes from the
altar for sacrifices and cover the altar with
a purple cloth. 14 All the altar utensils—the

3:38 Hebrew *toward the sunrise, in front of the Tent of Meeting.* **3:47** Hebrew *5 shekels* [2 ounces or 57 grams]. **3:50** Hebrew *1,365 shekels* [34 pounds or 15.5 kilograms]. **4:3** Hebrew *the Tent of Meeting;* also in 4:4, 15, 23, 25, 28, 30, 31, 33, 35, 37, 39, 41, 43, 47. **4:5** Or *Ark of the Testimony.*

firepans, meat forks, shovels, basins, and all the containers—must be placed on the cloth, and a covering of fine goatskin leather must be spread over them. Finally, they must put the carrying poles in place. [15]The camp will be ready to move when Aaron and his sons have finished covering the sanctuary and all the sacred articles. The Kohathites will come and carry these things to the next destination. But they must not touch the sacred objects, or they will die. So these are the things from the Tabernacle that the Kohathites must carry.

[16]"Eleazar son of Aaron the priest will be responsible for the oil of the lampstand, the fragrant incense, the daily grain offering, and the anointing oil. In fact, Eleazar will be responsible for the entire Tabernacle and everything in it, including the sanctuary and its furnishings."

[17]Then the LORD said to Moses and Aaron, [18]"Do not let the Kohathite clans be destroyed from among the Levites! [19]This is what you must do so they will live and not die when they approach the most sacred objects. Aaron and his sons must always go in with them and assign a specific duty or load to each person. [20]The Kohathites must never enter the sanctuary to look at the sacred objects for even a moment, or they will die."

Duties of the Gershonite Clan

[21]And the LORD said to Moses, [22]"Record the names of the members of the clans and families of the Gershonite division of the tribe of Levi. [23]List all the men between the ages of thirty and fifty who are eligible to serve in the Tabernacle.

[24]"These Gershonite clans will be responsible for general service and carrying loads. [25]They must carry the curtains of the Tabernacle, the Tabernacle itself with its coverings, the outer covering of fine goatskin leather, and the curtain for the Tabernacle entrance. [26]They are also to carry the curtains for the courtyard walls that surround the Tabernacle and altar, the curtain across the courtyard entrance, the ropes, and all the equipment related to their use. The Gershonites are responsible for all these items. [27]Aaron and his sons will direct the Gershonites regarding all their duties, whether it involves moving the equipment or doing other work. They must assign the Gershonites responsibility for the loads they are to carry. [28]So these are the duties assigned to the Gershonite clans at the Tabernacle. They will be directly responsible to Ithamar son of Aaron the priest.

Duties of the Merarite Clan

[29]"Now record the names of the members of the clans and families of the Merarite division of the tribe of Levi. [30]List all the men between the ages of thirty and fifty who are eligible to serve in the Tabernacle.

[31]"Their only duty at the Tabernacle will be to carry loads. They will carry the frames of the Tabernacle, the crossbars, the posts, and the bases; [32]also the posts for the courtyard walls with their bases, pegs, and ropes; and all the accessories and everything else related to their use. Assign the various loads to each man by name. [33]So these are the duties of the Merarite clans at the Tabernacle. They are directly responsible to Ithamar son of Aaron the priest."

Summary of the Registration

[34]So Moses, Aaron, and the other leaders of the community listed the members of the Kohathite division by their clans and families. [35]The list included all the men between thirty and fifty years of age who were eligible for service in the Tabernacle, [36]and the total number came to 2,750. [37]So this was the total of all those from the Kohathite clans who were eligible to serve at the Tabernacle. Moses and Aaron listed them, just as the LORD had commanded through Moses.

[38]The Gershonite division was also listed by its clans and families. [39]The list included all the men between thirty and fifty years of age who were eligible for service in the Tabernacle, [40]and the total number came to 2,630. [41]So this was the total of all those from the Gershonite clans who were eligible to serve at the Tabernacle. Moses and Aaron listed them, just as the LORD had commanded.

[42]The Merarite division was also listed by its clans and families. [43]The list included all the men between thirty and fifty years of age who were eligible for service in the Tabernacle, [44]and the total number came to 3,200. [45]So this was the total of all those from the Merarite clans who were eligible for service.

Moses and Aaron listed them, just as the LORD had commanded through Moses.

46 So Moses, Aaron, and the leaders of Israel listed all the Levites by their clans and families. 47 All the men between thirty and fifty years of age who were eligible for service in the Tabernacle and for its transportation 48 numbered 8,580. 49 When their names were recorded, as the LORD had commanded through Moses, each man was assigned his task and told what to carry.

And so the registration was completed, just as the LORD had commanded Moses.

CHAPTER 5

Purity in Israel's Camp

The LORD gave these instructions to Moses: 2 "Command the people of Israel to remove from the camp anyone who has a skin disease* or a discharge, or who has become ceremonially unclean by touching a dead person. 3 This command applies to men and women alike. Remove them so they will not defile the camp in which I live among them." 4 So the Israelites did as the LORD had commanded Moses and removed such people from the camp.

5 Then the LORD said to Moses, 6 "Give the following instructions to the people of Israel: If any of the people—men or women—betray the LORD by doing wrong to another person, they are guilty. 7 They must confess their sin and make full restitution for what they have done, adding an additional 20 percent and returning it to the person who was wronged. 8 But if the person who was wronged is dead, and there are no near relatives to whom restitution can be made, the payment belongs to the LORD and must be given to the priest. Those who are guilty must also bring a ram as a sacrifice, and they will be purified and made right with the LORD.* 9 All the sacred offerings that the Israelites bring to a priest will belong to him. 10 Each priest may keep all the sacred donations that he receives."

Protecting Marital Faithfulness

11 And the LORD said to Moses, 12 "Give the following instructions to the people of Israel.

"Suppose a man's wife goes astray, and she is unfaithful to her husband 13 and has sex with another man, but neither her husband nor anyone else knows about it. She has defiled herself, even though there was no witness and she was not caught in the act. 14 If her husband becomes jealous and is suspicious of his wife and needs to know whether or not she has defiled herself, 15 the husband must bring his wife to the priest. He must also bring an offering of two quarts* of barley flour to be presented on her behalf. Do not mix it with olive oil or frankincense, for it is a jealousy offering—an offering to prove whether or not she is guilty.

16 "The priest will then present her to stand trial before the LORD. 17 He must take some holy water in a clay jar and pour into it dust he has taken from the Tabernacle floor. 18 When the priest has presented the woman before the LORD, he must unbind her hair and place in her hands the offering of proof—the jealousy offering to determine whether her husband's suspicions are justified. The priest will stand before her, holding the jar of bitter water that brings a curse to those who are guilty. 19 The priest will then put the woman under oath and say to her, 'If no other man has had sex with you, and you have not gone astray and defiled yourself while under your husband's authority, may you be immune from the effects of this bitter water that brings on the curse. 20 But if you have gone astray by being unfaithful to your husband, and have defiled yourself by having sex with another man—'

21 "At this point the priest must put the woman under oath by saying, 'May the people know that the LORD's curse is upon you when he makes you infertile, causing your womb to shrivel* and your abdomen to swell. 22 Now may this water that brings the curse enter your body and cause your abdomen to swell and your womb to shrivel.*' And the woman will be required to say, 'Yes, let it be so.' 23 And the priest will write these curses on a piece of leather and wash them off into the bitter water. 24 He will make the woman drink the bitter water that brings on the curse. When the water enters her body, it will cause bitter suffering if she is guilty.

25 "The priest will take the jealousy offering from the woman's hand, lift it up before the

5:2 Traditionally rendered *leprosy*. The Hebrew word used here describes various skin diseases. **5:8** Or *bring a ram for atonement, which will make atonement for them*. **5:15** Hebrew *1/10 of an ephah* [2.2 liters]. **5:21** Hebrew *when he causes your thigh to waste away*. **5:22** Hebrew *and your thigh to waste away*.

LORD, and carry it to the altar. [26]He will take a
handful of the flour as a token portion and
burn it on the altar, and he will require the
woman to drink the water. [27]If she has defiled
herself by being unfaithful to her husband,
the water that brings on the curse will cause
bitter suffering. Her abdomen will swell and
her womb will shrink,* and her name will be-
come a curse among her people. [28]But if she
has not defiled herself and is pure, then she
will be unharmed and will still be able to have
children.

[29]"This is the ritual law for dealing with
suspicion. If a woman goes astray and defiles
herself while under her husband's authority,
[30]or if a man becomes jealous and is suspi-
cious that his wife has been unfaithful, the
husband must present his wife before the
LORD, and the priest will apply this entire rit-
ual law to her. [31]The husband will be innocent
of any guilt in this matter, but his wife will be
held accountable for her sin."

CHAPTER 6

Nazirite Laws

Then the LORD said to Moses, [2]"Give the fol-
lowing instructions to the people of Israel.

"If any of the people, either men or women,
take the special vow of a Nazirite, setting
themselves apart to the LORD in a special way,
[3]they must give up wine and other alcoholic
drinks. They must not use vinegar made from
wine or from other alcoholic drinks, they must
not drink fresh grape juice, and they must not
eat grapes or raisins. [4]As long as they are
bound by their Nazirite vow, they are not
allowed to eat or drink anything that comes
from a grapevine—not even the grape seeds or
skins.

[5]"They must never cut their hair through-
out the time of their vow, for they are holy and
set apart to the LORD. Until the time of their
vow has been fulfilled, they must let their hair
grow long. [6]And they must not go near a dead
body during the entire period of their vow to
the LORD. [7]Even if the dead person is their
own father, mother, brother, or sister, they
must not defile themselves, for the hair on
their head is the symbol of their separation to
God. [8]This requirement applies as long as
they are set apart to the LORD.

[9]"If someone falls dead beside them, the
hair they have dedicated will be defiled. They
must wait for seven days and then shave their
heads. Then they will be cleansed from their
defilement. [10]On the eighth day they must
bring two turtledoves or two young pigeons to
the priest at the entrance of the Tabernacle.*
[11]The priest will offer one of the birds for a
sin offering and the other for a burnt offer-
ing. In this way, he will purify them* from the
guilt they incurred through contact with the
dead body. Then they must reaffirm their
commitment and let their hair begin to grow
again. [12]The days of their vow that were
completed before their defilement no longer
count. They must rededicate themselves to
the LORD as a Nazirite for the full term of their
vow, and each must bring a one-year-old male
lamb for a guilt offering.

[13]"This is the ritual law for Nazirites. At the
conclusion of their time of separation as Naz-
irites, they must each go to the entrance of
the Tabernacle [14]and offer their sacrifices to
the LORD: a one-year-old male lamb without
defect for a burnt offering, a one-year-old fe-
male lamb without defect for a sin offering, a
ram without defect for a peace offering, [15]a
basket of bread made without yeast—cakes
of choice flour mixed with olive oil and wa-
fers spread with olive oil—along with their
prescribed grain offerings and liquid offer-
ings. [16]The priest will present these offerings
before the LORD: first the sin offering and the
burnt offering; [17]then the ram for a peace of-
fering, along with the basket of bread made
without yeast. The priest must also present
the prescribed grain offering and liquid of-
fering to the LORD.

[18]"Then the Nazirites will shave their heads
at the entrance of the Tabernacle. They will
take the hair that had been dedicated and
place it on the fire beneath the peace-offering
sacrifice. [19]After the Nazirite's head has been
shaved, the priest will take for each of them
the boiled shoulder of the ram, and he will
take from the basket a cake and a wafer made
without yeast. He will put them all into the
Nazirite's hands. [20]Then the priest will lift
them up as a special offering before the LORD.
These are holy portions for the priest, along
with the breast of the special offering and the

5:27 Hebrew *and her thigh will waste away.* **6:10** Hebrew *the Tent of Meeting;* also in 6:13, 18. **6:11** Or *make atonement for them.*

thigh of the sacred offering that are lifted up
before the LORD. After this ceremony the Naz-
irites may again drink wine.
21"This is the ritual law of the Nazirites,
who vow to bring these offerings to the LORD.
They may also bring additional offerings if
they can afford it. And they must be careful to
do whatever they vowed when they set them-
selves apart as Nazirites."

The Priestly Blessing

22Then the LORD said to Moses, 23"Tell Aaron
and his sons to bless the people of Israel with
this special blessing:

24 'May the LORD bless you
and protect you.
25 May the LORD smile on you
and be gracious to you.
26 May the LORD show you his favor
and give you his peace.'

27Whenever Aaron and his sons bless the
people of Israel in my name, I myself will
bless them."

gave two wagons and four oxen to the Ger-
shonite division for their work, 8and he gave
four wagons and eight oxen to the Merarite di-
vision for their work. All their work was done
under the leadership of Ithamar son of Aaron
the priest. 9But he gave none of the wagons or
oxen to the Kohathite division, since they were
required to carry the sacred objects of the Tab-
ernacle on their shoulders.

10The leaders also presented dedication
gifts for the altar at the time it was anointed.
They each placed their gifts before the altar.
11The LORD said to Moses, "Let one leader
bring his gift each day for the dedication of
the altar."

12On the first day Nahshon son of Ammina-
dab, leader of the tribe of Judah, presented
his offering.

13His offering consisted of a silver platter
weighing 3¼ pounds and a silver basin
weighing 1¾ pounds* (as measured by
the weight of the sanctuary shekel). These
were both filled with grain offerings of

How can I calm myself down when I'm nervous?

May the LORD show you his favor and give you his peace.
NUMBERS 6:26

CHAPTER 7

Offerings of Dedication

On the day Moses set up the Tabernacle, he
anointed it and set it apart as holy. He also
anointed and set apart all its furnishings and
the altar with its utensils. 2Then the leaders of
Israel—the tribal leaders who had registered
the troops—came and brought their offer-
ings. 3Together they brought six large wagons
and twelve oxen. There was a wagon for every
two leaders and an ox for each leader. They
presented these to the LORD in front of the
Tabernacle.

4Then the LORD said to Moses, 5"Receive
their gifts, and use these oxen and wagons for
transporting the Tabernacle.* Distribute them
among the Levites according to the work they
have to do." 6So Moses took the wagons and
oxen and presented them to the Levites. 7He

choice flour moistened with olive oil. 14He
also brought a gold container weighing
four ounces,* which was filled with
incense. 15He brought a young bull, a ram,
and a one-year-old male lamb for a burnt
offering, 16and a male goat for a sin
offering. 17For a peace offering he
brought two bulls, five rams, five male
goats, and five one-year-old male lambs.
This was the offering brought by Nahshon
son of Amminadab.

18On the second day Nethanel son of Zuar,
leader of the tribe of Issachar, presented his
offering.

19His offering consisted of a silver platter
weighing 3¼ pounds and a silver basin
weighing 1¾ pounds (as measured by the
weight of the sanctuary shekel). These

7:5 Hebrew *the Tent of Meeting;* also in 7:89. **7:13** Hebrew *silver platter weighing 130 shekels* [1.5 kilograms] *and a silver basin weighing 70 shekels* [800 grams]; also in 7:19, 25, 31, 37, 43, 49, 55, 61, 67, 73, 79, 85. **7:14** Hebrew *10 shekels* [114 grams]; also in 7:20, 26, 32, 38, 44, 50, 56, 62, 68, 74, 80, 86.

were both filled with grain offerings of
choice flour moistened with olive oil. [20]He
also brought a gold container weighing
four ounces, which was filled with
incense. [21]He brought a young bull, a ram,
and a one-year-old male lamb for a burnt
offering, [22]and a male goat for a sin
offering. [23]For a peace offering he
brought two bulls, five rams, five male
goats, and five one-year-old male lambs.
This was the offering brought by
Nethanel son of Zuar.

[24]On the third day Eliab son of Helon, leader of the tribe of Zebulun, presented his offering.

[25]His offering consisted of a silver platter
weighing 3¼ pounds and a silver basin
weighing 1¾ pounds (as measured by the
weight of the sanctuary shekel). These
were both filled with grain offerings of
choice flour moistened with olive oil. [26]He
also brought a gold container weighing
four ounces, which was filled with
incense. [27]He brought a young bull, a ram,
and a one-year-old male lamb for a burnt
offering, [28]and a male goat for a sin
offering. [29]For a peace offering he
brought two bulls, five rams, five male
goats, and five one-year-old male lambs.
This was the offering brought by Eliab
son of Helon.

[30]On the fourth day Elizur son of Shedeur, leader of the tribe of Reuben, presented his offering.

[31]His offering consisted of a silver platter
weighing 3¼ pounds and a silver basin
weighing 1¾ pounds (as measured by the
weight of the sanctuary shekel). These
were both filled with grain offerings of
choice flour moistened with olive oil. [32]He
also brought a gold container weighing
four ounces, which was filled with
incense. [33]He brought a young bull, a ram,
and a one-year-old male lamb for a burnt
offering, [34]and a male goat for a sin
offering. [35]For a peace offering he
brought two bulls, five rams, five male
goats, and five one-year-old male lambs.
This was the offering brought by Elizur
son of Shedeur.

[36]On the fifth day Shelumiel son of Zurishaddai, leader of the tribe of Simeon, presented his offering.

[37]His offering consisted of a silver platter
weighing 3¼ pounds and a silver basin
weighing 1¾ pounds (as measured by the
weight of the sanctuary shekel). These
were both filled with grain offerings of
choice flour moistened with olive oil. [38]He
also brought a gold container weighing
four ounces, which was filled with
incense. [39]He brought a young bull, a ram,
and a one-year-old male lamb for a burnt
offering, [40]and a male goat for a sin
offering. [41]For a peace offering he
brought two bulls, five rams, five male
goats, and five one-year-old male lambs.
This was the offering brought by
Shelumiel son of Zurishaddai.

[42]On the sixth day Eliasaph son of Deuel, leader of the tribe of Gad, presented his offering.

[43]His offering consisted of a silver platter
weighing 3¼ pounds and a silver basin
weighing 1¾ pounds (as measured by the
weight of the sanctuary shekel). These
were both filled with grain offerings of
choice flour moistened with olive oil. [44]He
also brought a gold container weighing
four ounces, which was filled with
incense. [45]He brought a young bull, a ram,
and a one-year-old male lamb for a burnt
offering, [46]and a male goat for a sin
offering. [47]For a peace offering he
brought two bulls, five rams, five male
goats, and five one-year-old male lambs.
This was the offering brought by Eliasaph
son of Deuel.

[48]On the seventh day Elishama son of Ammihud, leader of the tribe of Ephraim, presented his offering.

[49]His offering consisted of a silver platter
weighing 3¼ pounds and a silver basin
weighing 1¾ pounds (as measured by the
weight of the sanctuary shekel). These
were both filled with grain offerings of
choice flour moistened with olive oil. [50]He
also brought a gold container weighing
four ounces, which was filled with
incense. [51]He brought a young bull, a ram,
and a one-year-old male lamb for a burnt
offering, [52]and a male goat for a sin

offering. [53]For a peace offering he
brought two bulls, five rams, five male
goats, and five one-year-old male lambs.
This was the offering brought by
Elishama son of Ammihud.

[54]On the eighth day Gamaliel son of Pedah-
zur, leader of the tribe of Manasseh, pre-
sented his offering.
[55]His offering consisted of a silver platter
weighing 3¼ pounds and a silver basin
weighing 1¾ pounds (as measured by the
weight of the sanctuary shekel). These
were both filled with grain offerings of
choice flour moistened with olive oil. [56]He
also brought a gold container weighing
four ounces, which was filled with
incense. [57]He brought a young bull, a ram,
and a one-year-old male lamb for a burnt
offering, [58]and a male goat for a sin
offering. [59]For a peace offering he
brought two bulls, five rams, five male
goats, and five one-year-old male lambs.
This was the offering brought by Gamaliel
son of Pedahzur.

[60]On the ninth day Abidan son of Gideoni,
leader of the tribe of Benjamin, presented his
offering.
[61]His offering consisted of a silver platter
weighing 3¼ pounds and a silver basin
weighing 1¾ pounds (as measured by the
weight of the sanctuary shekel). These
were both filled with grain offerings of
choice flour moistened with olive oil. [62]He
also brought a gold container weighing
four ounces, which was filled with
incense. [63]He brought a young bull, a ram,
and a one-year-old male lamb for a burnt
offering, [64]and a male goat for a sin
offering. [65]For a peace offering he
brought two bulls, five rams, five male
goats, and five one-year-old male lambs.
This was the offering brought by Abidan
son of Gideoni.

[66]On the tenth day Ahiezer son of Ammishad-
dai, leader of the tribe of Dan, presented his
offering.
[67]His offering consisted of a silver platter
weighing 3¼ pounds and a silver basin
weighing 1¾ pounds (as measured by the
weight of the sanctuary shekel). These
were both filled with grain offerings of
choice flour moistened with olive oil. [68]He
also brought a gold container weighing
four ounces, which was filled with
incense. [69]He brought a young bull, a ram,
and a one-year-old male lamb for a burnt
offering, [70]and a male goat for a sin
offering. [71]For a peace offering he
brought two bulls, five rams, five male
goats, and five one-year-old male lambs.
This was the offering brought by Ahiezer
son of Ammishaddai.

[72]On the eleventh day Pagiel son of Ocran,
leader of the tribe of Asher, presented his of-
fering.
[73]His offering consisted of a silver platter
weighing 3¼ pounds and a silver basin
weighing 1¾ pounds (as measured by the
weight of the sanctuary shekel). These
were both filled with grain offerings of
choice flour moistened with olive oil. [74]He
also brought a gold container weighing
four ounces, which was filled with
incense. [75]He brought a young bull, a ram,
and a one-year-old male lamb for a burnt
offering, [76]and a male goat for a sin
offering. [77]For a peace offering he
brought two bulls, five rams, five male
goats, and five one-year-old male lambs.
This was the offering brought by Pagiel
son of Ocran.

[78]On the twelfth day Ahira son of Enan, leader
of the tribe of Naphtali, presented his offer-
ing.
[79]His offering consisted of a silver platter
weighing 3¼ pounds and a silver basin
weighing 1¾ pounds (as measured by the
weight of the sanctuary shekel). These
were both filled with grain offerings of
choice flour moistened with olive oil. [80]He
also brought a gold container weighing
four ounces, which was filled with
incense. [81]He brought a young bull, a ram,
and a one-year-old male lamb for a burnt
offering, [82]and a male goat for a sin
offering. [83]For a peace offering he
brought two bulls, five rams, five male
goats, and five one-year-old male lambs.
This was the offering brought by Ahira
son of Enan.

[84]So this was the dedication offering brought
by the leaders of Israel at the time the altar was

anointed: twelve silver platters, twelve silver basins, and twelve gold incense containers. 85Each silver platter weighed 3¼ pounds, and each silver basin weighed 1¾ pounds. The total weight of the silver was 60 pounds* (as measured by the weight of the sanctuary shekel). 86Each of the twelve gold containers that was filled with incense weighed four ounces (as measured by the weight of the sanctuary shekel). The total weight of the gold was three pounds.* 87Twelve young bulls, twelve rams, and twelve one-year-old male lambs were donated for the burnt offerings, along with their prescribed grain offerings. Twelve male goats were brought for the sin offerings. 88Twenty-four bulls, sixty rams, sixty male goats, and sixty one-year-old male lambs were donated for the peace offerings. This was the dedication offering for the altar after it was anointed.

89Whenever Moses went into the Tabernacle to speak with the LORD, he heard the voice speaking to him from between the two cherubim above the Ark's cover—the place of atonement—that rests on the Ark of the Covenant.* The LORD spoke to him from there.

CHAPTER 8

Preparing the Lamps

The LORD said to Moses, 2"Give Aaron the following instructions: When you set up the seven lamps in the lampstand, place them so their light shines forward in front of the lampstand." 3So Aaron did this. He set up the seven lamps so they reflected their light forward, just as the LORD had commanded Moses. 4The entire lampstand, from its base to its decorative blossoms, was made of beaten gold. It was built according to the exact design the LORD had shown Moses.

The Levites Dedicated

5Then the LORD said to Moses, 6"Now set the Levites apart from the rest of the people of Israel and make them ceremonially clean. 7Do this by sprinkling them with the water of purification, and have them shave their entire body and wash their clothing. Then they will be ceremonially clean. 8Have them bring a young bull and a grain offering of choice flour moistened with olive oil, along with a second young bull for a sin offering. 9Then assemble the whole community of Israel, and present the Levites at the entrance of the Tabernacle.* 10When you present the Levites before the LORD, the people of Israel must lay their hands on them. 11Raising his hands, Aaron must then present the Levites to the LORD as a special offering from the people of Israel, thus dedicating them to the LORD's service.

12"Next the Levites will lay their hands on the heads of the young bulls. Present one as a sin offering and the other as a burnt offering to the LORD, to purify the Levites and make them right with the LORD.* 13Then have the Levites stand in front of Aaron and his sons, and raise your hands and present them as a special offering to the LORD. 14In this way, you will set the Levites apart from the rest of the people of Israel, and the Levites will belong to me. 15After this, they may go into the Tabernacle to do their work, because you have purified them and presented them as a special offering.

16"Of all the people of Israel, the Levites are reserved for me. I have claimed them for myself in place of all the firstborn sons of the Israelites; I have taken the Levites as their substitutes. 17For all the firstborn males among the people of Israel are mine, both of people and of animals. I set them apart for myself on the day I struck down all the firstborn sons of the Egyptians. 18Yes, I have claimed the Levites in place of all the firstborn sons of Israel. 19And of all the Israelites, I have assigned the Levites to Aaron and his sons. They will serve in the Tabernacle on behalf of the Israelites and make sacrifices to purify* the people so no plague will strike them when they approach the sanctuary."

20So Moses, Aaron, and the whole community of Israel dedicated the Levites, carefully following all the LORD's instructions to Moses. 21The Levites purified themselves from sin and washed their clothes, and Aaron lifted them up and presented them to the LORD as a special offering. He then offered a sacrifice to purify them and make them right with the LORD.* 22After that the Levites went into the Tabernacle to perform their duties, assisting

7:85 Hebrew *2,400 shekels* [27.6 kilograms]. **7:86** Hebrew *120 shekels* [1.4 kilograms]. **7:89** Or *Ark of the Testimony*. **8:9** Hebrew *the Tent of Meeting*; also in 8:15, 19, 22, 24, 26. **8:12** Or *to make atonement for the Levites*. **8:19** Or *make atonement for*. **8:21** Or *then made atonement for them to purify them*.

Aaron and his sons. So they carried out all the commands that the LORD gave Moses concerning the Levites.

[23]The LORD also instructed Moses, [24]"This is the rule the Levites must follow: They must begin serving in the Tabernacle at the age of twenty-five, [25]and they must retire at the age of fifty. [26]After retirement they may assist their fellow Levites by serving as guards at the Tabernacle, but they may not officiate in the service. This is how you must assign duties to the Levites."

CHAPTER 9

The Second Passover

A year after Israel's departure from Egypt, the LORD spoke to Moses in the wilderness of Sinai. In the first month* of that year he said, [2]"Tell the Israelites to celebrate the Passover at the prescribed time, [3]at twilight on the fourteenth day of the first month.* Be sure to follow all my decrees and regulations concerning this celebration."

[4]So Moses told the people to celebrate the Passover [5]in the wilderness of Sinai as twilight fell on the fourteenth day of the month. And they celebrated the festival there, just as the LORD had commanded Moses. [6]But some of the men had been ceremonially defiled by touching a dead body, so they could not celebrate the Passover that day. They came to Moses and Aaron that day [7]and said, "We have become ceremonially unclean by touching a dead body. But why should we be prevented from presenting the LORD's offering at the proper time with the rest of the Israelites?"

[8]Moses answered, "Wait here until I have received instructions for you from the LORD."

[9]This was the LORD's reply to Moses. [10]"Give the following instructions to the people of Israel: If any of the people now or in future generations are ceremonially unclean at Passover time because of touching a dead body, or if they are on a journey and cannot be present at the ceremony, they may still celebrate the LORD's Passover. [11]They must offer the Passover sacrifice one month later, at twilight on the fourteenth day of the second month.* They must eat the Passover lamb at that time with bitter salad greens and bread made without yeast. [12]They must not leave any of the lamb until the next morning, and they must not break any of its bones. They must follow all the normal regulations concerning the Passover.

[13]"But those who neglect to celebrate the Passover at the regular time, even though they are ceremonially clean and not away on a trip, will be cut off from the community of Israel. If they fail to present the LORD's offering at the proper time, they will suffer the consequences of their guilt. [14]And if foreigners living among you want to celebrate the Passover to the LORD, they must follow these same decrees and regulations. The same laws apply both to native-born Israelites and to the foreigners living among you."

The Fiery Cloud

[15]On the day the Tabernacle was set up, the cloud covered it.* But from evening until morning the cloud over the Tabernacle looked like a pillar of fire. [16]This was the regular pattern—at night the cloud that covered the Tabernacle had the appearance of fire. [17]Whenever the cloud lifted from over the sacred tent, the people of Israel would break camp and follow it. And wherever the cloud settled, the people of Israel would set up camp. [18]In this way, they traveled and camped at the LORD's command wherever he told them to go. Then they remained in their camp as long as the cloud stayed over the Tabernacle. [19]If the cloud remained over the Tabernacle for a long time, the Israelites stayed and performed their duty to the LORD. [20]Sometimes the cloud would stay over the Tabernacle for only a few days, so the people would stay for only a few days, as the LORD commanded. Then at the LORD's command they would break camp and move on. [21]Sometimes the cloud stayed only overnight and lifted the next morning. But day or night, when the cloud lifted, the people broke camp and moved on. [22]Whether the cloud stayed above the Tabernacle for two days, a month, or a year, the people of Israel stayed in camp and did not move on. But as soon as it lifted, they broke camp and moved on. [23]So they camped

9:1 The first month of the ancient Hebrew lunar calendar usually occurs within the months of March and April. **9:3** This day in the ancient Hebrew lunar calendar occurred in late March, April, or early May. **9:11** This day in the ancient Hebrew lunar calendar occurred in late April, May, or early June. **9:15** Hebrew *covered the Tabernacle, the Tent of the Testimony.*

or traveled at the LORD's command, and they did whatever the LORD told them through Moses.

CHAPTER 10

The Silver Trumpets

Now the LORD said to Moses, [2]"Make two trumpets of hammered silver for calling the community to assemble and for signaling the breaking of camp. [3]When both trumpets are blown, everyone must gather before you at the entrance of the Tabernacle.* [4]But if only one trumpet is blown, then only the leaders—the heads of the clans of Israel—must present themselves to you.

[5]"When you sound the signal to move on, the tribes camped on the east side of the Tabernacle must break camp and move forward. [6]When you sound the signal a second time, the tribes camped on the south will follow. You must sound short blasts as the signal for moving on. [7]But when you call the people to an assembly, blow the trumpets with a different signal. [8]Only the priests, Aaron's descendants, are allowed to blow the trumpets. This is a permanent law for you, to be observed from generation to generation.

[9]"When you arrive in your own land and go to war against your enemies who attack you, sound the alarm with the trumpets. Then the LORD your God will remember you and rescue you from your enemies. [10]Blow the trumpets in times of gladness, too, sounding them at your annual festivals and at the beginning of each month. And blow the trumpets over your burnt offerings and peace offerings. The trumpets will remind the LORD your God of his covenant with you. I am the LORD your God."

The Israelites Leave Sinai

[11]In the second year after Israel's departure from Egypt—on the twentieth day of the second month*—the cloud lifted from the Tabernacle of the Covenant.* [12]So the Israelites set out from the wilderness of Sinai and traveled on from place to place until the cloud stopped in the wilderness of Paran.

[13]When the people set out for the first time, following the instructions the LORD had given through Moses, [14]Judah's troops led the way. They marched behind their banner, and their leader was Nahshon son of Amminadab. [15]They were joined by the troops of the tribe of Issachar, led by Nethanel son of Zuar, [16]and the troops of the tribe of Zebulun, led by Eliab son of Helon.

[17]Then the Tabernacle was taken down, and the Gershonite and Merarite divisions of the Levites were next in the line of march, carrying the Tabernacle with them. [18]Reuben's troops went next, marching behind their banner. Their leader was Elizur son of Shedeur. [19]They were joined by the troops of the tribe of Simeon, led by Shelumiel son of Zurishaddai, [20]and the troops of the tribe of Gad, led by Eliasaph son of Deuel.

[21]Next came the Kohathite division of the Levites, carrying the sacred objects from the Tabernacle. Before they arrived at the next camp, the Tabernacle would already be set up at its new location. [22]Ephraim's troops went next, marching behind their banner. Their leader was Elishama son of Ammihud. [23]They were joined by the troops of the tribe of Manasseh, led by Gamaliel son of Pedahzur, [24]and the troops of the tribe of Benjamin, led by Abidan son of Gideoni.

[25]Dan's troops went last, marching behind their banner and serving as the rear guard for all the tribal camps. Their leader was Ahiezer son of Ammishaddai. [26]They were joined by the troops of the tribe of Asher, led by Pagiel son of Ocran, [27]and the troops of the tribe of Naphtali, led by Ahira son of Enan.

[28]This was the order in which the Israelites marched, division by division.

[29]One day Moses said to his brother-in-law, Hobab son of Reuel the Midianite, "We are on our way to the place the LORD promised us, for he said, 'I will give it to you.' Come with us and we will treat you well, for the LORD has promised wonderful blessings for Israel!"

[30]But Hobab replied, "No, I will not go. I must return to my own land and family."

[31]"Please don't leave us," Moses pleaded. "You know the places in the wilderness where we should camp. Come, be our guide. [32]If you do, we'll share with you all the blessings the LORD gives us."

[33]They marched for three days after leaving the mountain of the LORD, with the Ark of

10:3 Hebrew *Tent of Meeting*. **10:11a** This day in the ancient Hebrew lunar calendar occurred in late April, May, or early June.
10:11b Or *Tabernacle of the Testimony*.

Be honest. Do you complain and moan a lot? Do you ever grumble and whine? Do you talk about how terrible your life is? Believe me, I can relate. I do.

If I don't watch myself, I can easily fall into the bad habit of complaining . . . a lot . . . and usually over stupid stuff. Like when my parents tell me to do some little thing that will take me all of five minutes—you know, like doing the dishes or taking out the garbage.

Think about how simple this is. The Bible tells us not to complain. Philippians 2:14 says, "Do everything without complaining and arguing." Notice it doesn't say "do *some* things" but "do *everything*."

I've learned that many people on the other side of the world don't complain when they have no food to eat, and I complain when I have to eat something I don't like. They don't complain about not having the basic necessities of life, and I complain when I don't get the luxuries I want.

My dad just got back from a mission trip to Africa, and you should see the video. The people he went to work with are grateful for any little thing; and even when they have nothing, they are still joyful and smiling.

My parents encourage me to think about what I'm saying when I complain, and I'm trying to break the habit. Now, when I start to complain, I usually catch myself. It didn't take long for me to get into this bad habit. Getting out of it is taking much longer, but I am determined to get out.

Look at Numbers 11 to see how awful it looks when people grumble and complain—and how much God hates it when we do that.

the LORD's Covenant moving ahead of them to
show them where to stop and rest. [34]As they
moved on each day, the cloud of the LORD
hovered over them. [35]And whenever the Ark
set out, Moses would shout, "Arise, O LORD,
and let your enemies be scattered! Let them
flee before you!" [36]And when the Ark was set
down, he would say, "Return, O LORD, to the
countless thousands of Israel!"

CHAPTER 11

The People Complain to Moses

Soon the people began to complain about
their hardship, and the LORD heard every-
thing they said. Then the LORD's anger blazed
against them, and he sent a fire to rage among
them, and he destroyed some of the people in
the outskirts of the camp. [2]Then the people
screamed to Moses for help, and when he
prayed to the LORD, the fire stopped. [3]After
that, the area was known as Taberah (which
means "the place of burning"), because fire
from the LORD had burned among them
there.

[4]Then the foreign rabble who were travel-
ing with the Israelites began to crave the good
things of Egypt. And the people of Israel also
began to complain. "Oh, for some meat!" they
exclaimed. [5]"We remember the fish we used
to eat for free in Egypt. And we had all the cu-
cumbers, melons, leeks, onions, and garlic we
wanted. [6]But now our appetites are gone. All
we ever see is this manna!"

[7]The manna looked like small coriander
seeds, and it was pale yellow like gum resin.
[8]The people would go out and gather it from
the ground. They made flour by grinding it
with hand mills or pounding it in mortars.
Then they boiled it in a pot and made it into
flat cakes. These cakes tasted like pastries
baked with olive oil. [9]The manna came
down on the camp with the dew during the
night.

[10]Moses heard all the families standing in
the doorways of their tents whining, and the
LORD became extremely angry. Moses was
also very aggravated. [11]And Moses said to the
LORD, "Why are you treating me, your servant,
so harshly? Have mercy on me! What did I do
to deserve the burden of all these people?
[12]Did I give birth to them? Did I bring them
into the world? Why did you tell me to carry
them in my arms like a mother carries a nurs-
ing baby? How can I carry them to the land
you swore to give their ancestors? [13]Where
am I supposed to get meat for all these peo-
ple? They keep whining to me, saying, 'Give us
meat to eat!' [14]I can't carry all these people by
myself! The load is far too heavy! [15]If this is
how you intend to treat me, just go ahead
and kill me. Do me a favor and spare me this
misery!"

Moses Chooses Seventy Leaders

[16]Then the LORD said to Moses, "Gather be-
fore me seventy men who are recognized as
elders and leaders of Israel. Bring them to the
Tabernacle* to stand there with you. [17]I will
come down and talk to you there. I will take
some of the Spirit that is upon you, and I will
put the Spirit upon them also. They will bear
the burden of the people along with you, so
you will not have to carry it alone.

[18]"And say to the people, 'Purify yourselves,
for tomorrow you will have meat to eat. You
were whining, and the LORD heard you when
you cried, "Oh, for some meat! We were
better off in Egypt!" Now the LORD will give
you meat, and you will have to eat it. [19]And it
won't be for just a day or two, or for five or ten
or even twenty. [20]You will eat it for a whole
month until you gag and are sick of it. For you
have rejected the LORD, who is here among
you, and you have whined to him, saying,
"Why did we ever leave Egypt?"'"

[21]But Moses responded to the LORD, "There
are 600,000 foot soldiers here with me, and
yet you say, 'I will give them meat for a whole
month!' [22]Even if we butchered all our flocks
and herds, would that satisfy them? Even if
we caught all the fish in the sea, would that be
enough?"

[23]Then the LORD said to Moses, "Has my
arm lost its power? Now you will see whether
or not my word comes true!"

[24]So Moses went out and reported the
LORD's words to the people. He gathered the
seventy elders and stationed them around
the Tabernacle.* [25]And the LORD came down
in the cloud and spoke to Moses. Then he
gave the seventy elders the same Spirit that
was upon Moses. And when the Spirit rested

11:16 Hebrew *the Tent of Meeting.* **11:24** Hebrew *the tent;* also in 11:26.

upon them, they prophesied. But this never happened again.

[26]Two men, Eldad and Medad, had stayed behind in the camp. They were listed among the elders, but they had not gone out to the Tabernacle. Yet the Spirit rested upon them as well, so they prophesied there in the camp. [27]A young man ran and reported to Moses, "Eldad and Medad are prophesying in the camp!"

[28]Joshua son of Nun, who had been Moses' assistant since his youth, protested, "Moses, my master, make them stop!"

[29]But Moses replied, "Are you jealous for my sake? I wish that all the LORD's people were prophets and that the LORD would put his Spirit upon them all!" [30]Then Moses returned to the camp with the elders of Israel.

The LORD Sends Quail

[31]Now the LORD sent a wind that brought quail from the sea and let them fall all around the camp. For miles in every direction there were quail flying about three feet above the ground.* [32]So the people went out and caught quail all that day and throughout the night and all the next day, too. No one gathered less than fifty bushels*! They spread the quail all around the camp to dry. [33]But while they were gorging themselves on the meat—while it was still in their mouths—the anger of the LORD blazed against the people, and he struck them with a severe plague. [34]So that place was called Kibroth-hattaavah (which means "graves of gluttony") because there they buried the people who had craved meat from Egypt. [35]From Kibroth-hattaavah the Israelites traveled to Hazeroth, where they stayed for some time.

CHAPTER 12

The Complaints of Miriam and Aaron

While they were at Hazeroth, Miriam and Aaron criticized Moses because he had married a Cushite woman. [2]They said, "Has the LORD spoken only through Moses? Hasn't he spoken through us, too?" But the LORD heard them. [3](Now Moses was very humble—more humble than any other person on earth.)

[4]So immediately the LORD called to Moses, Aaron, and Miriam and said, "Go out to the Tabernacle,* all three of you!" So the three of them went to the Tabernacle. [5]Then the LORD descended in the pillar of cloud and stood at the entrance of the Tabernacle.* "Aaron and Miriam!" he called, and they stepped forward. [6]And the LORD said to them, "Now listen to what I say:

11:31 Or *there were quail 3 feet* [2 cubits or 92 centimeters] *deep on the ground.* **11:32** Hebrew *10 homers* [1.8 kiloliters]. **12:4** Hebrew *the Tent of Meeting.* **12:5** Hebrew *the tent;* also in 12:10.

IS IT OK?

IS IT OK TO BE JEALOUS OF MY BROTHER OR SISTER?

It's easy to feel jealous—especially if your brother or sister is the star basketball player, the person with the lead role in a musical, the beauty queen, or the student every teacher loves. *Gag!* Coming in second or third gets old really fast. That's how Miriam and Aaron felt. Moses got a lot of attention. So they said mean things about him and tried to steal the spotlight. That did *not* go over well with God! In fact, Miriam got leprosy, a disease that eats your skin (Numbers 12:1-16). Jealousy is a lot like leprosy—it eats away at you. Don't let it eat you up.

"If there were prophets among you,
I, the LORD, would reveal myself
in visions.
I would speak to them in dreams.
7 But not with my servant Moses.
Of all my house, he is the one I trust.
8 I speak to him face to face,
clearly, and not in riddles!
He sees the LORD as he is.
So why were you not afraid
to criticize my servant Moses?"

9 The LORD was very angry with them, and he departed. 10 As the cloud moved from above the Tabernacle, there stood Miriam, her skin as white as snow from leprosy.* When Aaron saw what had happened to her, 11 he cried out to Moses, "Oh, my master! Please don't punish us for this sin we have so foolishly committed. 12 Don't let her be like a stillborn baby, already decayed at birth."

13 So Moses cried out to the LORD, "O God, I beg you, please heal her!"

14 But the LORD said to Moses, "If her father had done nothing more than spit in her face, wouldn't she be defiled for seven days? So keep her outside the camp for seven days, and after that she may be accepted back."

15 So Miriam was kept outside the camp for seven days, and the people waited until she was brought back before they traveled again. 16 Then they left Hazeroth and camped in the wilderness of Paran.

CHAPTER 13

Twelve Scouts Explore Canaan

The LORD now said to Moses, 2 "Send out men to explore the land of Canaan, the land I am giving to the Israelites. Send one leader from each of the twelve ancestral tribes." 3 So Moses did as the LORD commanded him. He sent out twelve men, all tribal leaders of Israel, from their camp in the wilderness of Paran. 4 These were the tribes and the names of their leaders:

	Tribe	*Leader*
	Reuben	Shammua son of Zaccur
5	Simeon	Shaphat son of Hori
6	Judah	Caleb son of Jephunneh
7	Issachar	Igal son of Joseph
8	Ephraim	Hoshea son of Nun
9	Benjamin	Palti son of Raphu
10	Zebulun	Gaddiel son of Sodi
11	Manasseh son of Joseph	Gaddi son of Susi
12	Dan	Ammiel son of Gemalli
13	Asher	Sethur son of Michael
14	Naphtali	Nahbi son of Vophsi
15	Gad	Geuel son of Maki

16 These are the names of the men Moses sent out to explore the land. (Moses called Hoshea son of Nun by the name Joshua.)

17 Moses gave the men these instructions as he sent them out to explore the land: "Go north through the Negev into the hill country. 18 See what the land is like, and find out whether the people living there are strong or weak, few or many. 19 See what kind of land they live in. Is it good or bad? Do their towns have walls, or are they unprotected like open camps? 20 Is the soil fertile or poor? Are there many trees? Do your best to bring back samples of the crops you see." (It happened to be the season for harvesting the first ripe grapes.)

21 So they went up and explored the land from the wilderness of Zin as far as Rehob, near Lebo-hamath. 22 Going north, they passed through the Negev and arrived at Hebron, where Ahiman, Sheshai, and Talmai—all descendants of Anak—lived. (The ancient town of Hebron was founded seven years before the Egyptian city of Zoan.) 23 When they came to the valley of Eshcol, they cut down a branch with a single cluster of grapes so large that it took two of them to carry it on a pole between them! They also brought back samples of the pomegranates and figs. 24 That place was called the valley of Eshcol (which means "cluster"), because of the cluster of grapes the Israelite men cut there.

The Scouting Report

25 After exploring the land for forty days, the men returned 26 to Moses, Aaron, and the whole community of Israel at Kadesh in the wilderness of Paran. They reported to the whole community what they had seen and showed them the fruit they had taken from the land. 27 This was their report to Moses: "We entered the land you sent us to explore, and it is indeed a bountiful country—a land flowing with milk and honey. Here is the kind of fruit it produces. 28 But the people liv-

12:10 Or *with a skin disease*. The Hebrew word used here can describe various skin diseases.

ing there are powerful, and their towns are large and fortified. We even saw giants there, the descendants of Anak! [29]The Amalekites live in the Negev, and the Hittites, Jebusites, and Amorites live in the hill country. The Canaanites live along the coast of the Mediterranean Sea* and along the Jordan Valley."

[30]But Caleb tried to quiet the people as they stood before Moses. "Let's go at once to take the land," he said. "We can certainly conquer it!"

[31]But the other men who had explored the land with him disagreed. "We can't go up against them! They are stronger than we are!" [32]So they spread this bad report about the land among the Israelites: "The land we traveled through and explored will devour anyone who goes to live there. All the people we saw were huge. [33]We even saw giants* there, the descendants of Anak. Next to them we felt like grasshoppers, and that's what they thought, too!"

CHAPTER 14

The People Rebel

Then the whole community began weeping aloud, and they cried all night. [2]Their voices rose in a great chorus of protest against Moses and Aaron. "If only we had died in Egypt, or even here in the wilderness!" they complained. [3]"Why is the LORD taking us to this country only to have us die in battle? Our wives and our little ones will be carried off as plunder! Wouldn't it be better for us to return to Egypt?" [4]Then they plotted among themselves, "Let's choose a new leader and go back to Egypt!"

[5]Then Moses and Aaron fell face down on the ground before the whole community of Israel. [6]Two of the men who had explored the land, Joshua son of Nun and Caleb son of Jephunneh, tore their clothing. [7]They said to all the people of Israel, "The land we traveled through and explored is a wonderful land! [8]And if the LORD is pleased with us, he will bring us safely into that land and give it to us. It is a rich land flowing with milk and honey. [9]Do not rebel against the LORD, and don't be afraid of the people of the land. They are only helpless prey to us! They have no protection, but the LORD is with us! Don't be afraid of them!"

[10]But the whole community began to talk about stoning Joshua and Caleb. Then the glorious presence of the LORD appeared to all the Israelites at the Tabernacle.* [11]And the LORD said to Moses, "How long will these people treat me with contempt? Will they never believe me, even after all the miraculous signs I have done among them? [12]I will disown them and destroy them with a plague. Then I will make you into a nation greater and mightier than they are!"

AMAZING FACTS

The warriors in the Promised Land were so big that the Israelite soldiers felt like grasshoppers next to them!

NUMBERS 13:33

Moses Intercedes for the People

[13]But Moses objected. "What will the Egyptians think when they hear about it?" he asked the LORD. "They know full well the power you displayed in rescuing your people from Egypt. [14]Now if you destroy them, the Egyptians will send a report to the inhabitants of this land, who have already heard that you live among your people. They know, LORD, that you have appeared to your people face to face and that your pillar of cloud hovers over them. They know that you go before them in the pillar of cloud by day and the pillar of fire by night. [15]Now if you slaughter all these people with a single blow, the nations that have heard of your fame will say, [16]'The LORD was not able to bring them into the land he swore to give them, so he killed them in the wilderness.'

[17]"Please, Lord, prove that your power is as great as you have claimed. For you said, [18]'The

13:29 Hebrew *the sea.* 13:33 Hebrew *nephilim.* 14:10 Hebrew *the Tent of Meeting.*

The Exodus and 40 Years in the Wilderness

The people of Israel were slaves in Egypt. They had been there 400 years. It must have seemed as if God had forgotten them. But he hadn't. God had plans for them in Canaan. He would lead them there and would make them a great nation.

Why didn't the people of Israel go straight from Egypt to Canaan? God knew they were not ready to fight the enemies along that route. Instead he would lead them through the wilderness where he would help them become an army. At Mount Sinai, God would give them his laws. There he would show them how to make his house, the Tabernacle. The Israelites could not become a great nation without God's laws and God's house.

Sometimes it may seem that the way we are going is the hard way. But if God is leading us, we are going the right way. God's way is always the right way!

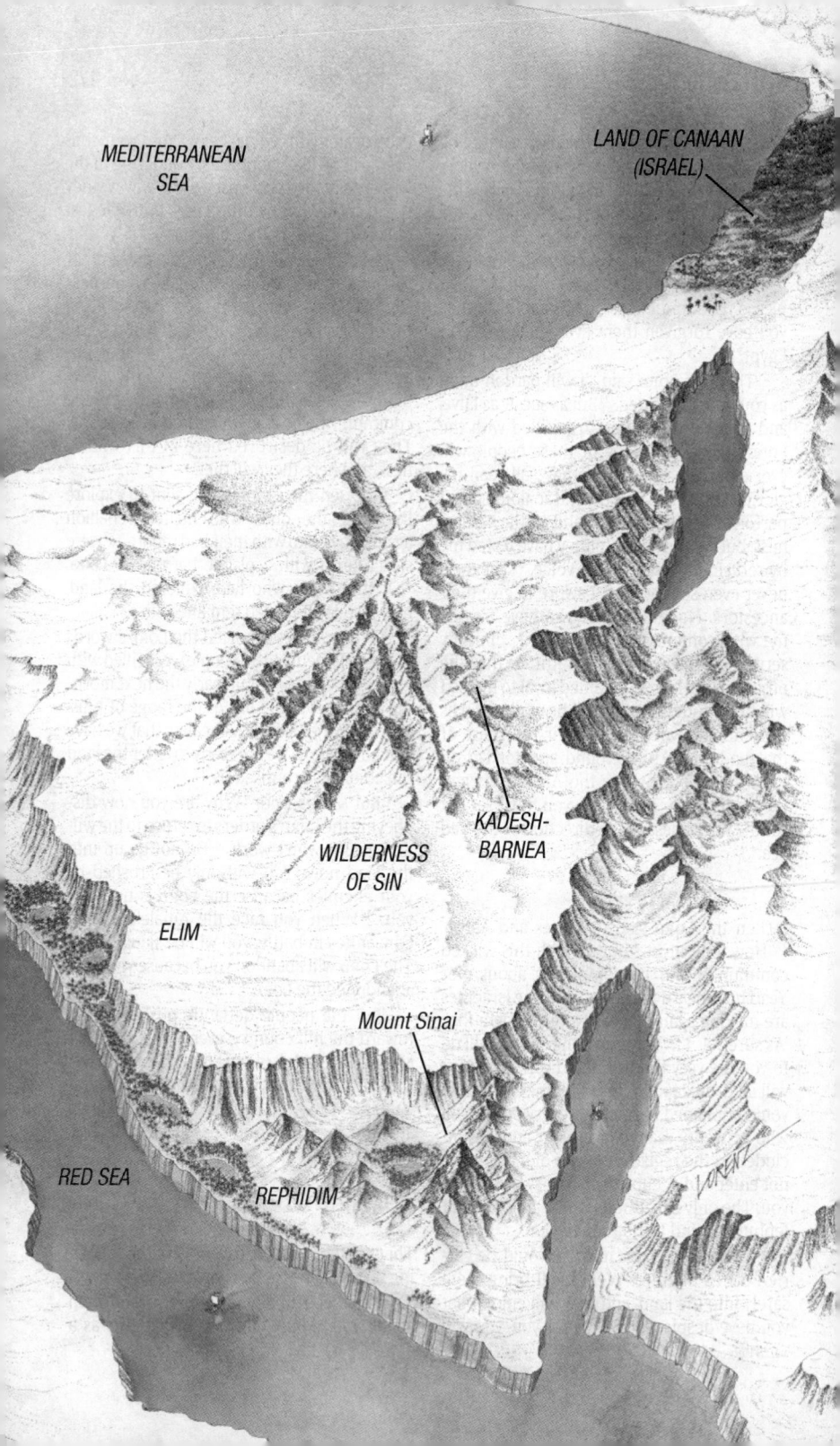
MEDITERRANEAN SEA
LAND OF CANAAN (ISRAEL)
KADESH-BARNEA
WILDERNESS OF SIN
ELIM
Mount Sinai
RED SEA
REPHIDIM
LORENZ

LORD is slow to anger and filled with unfailing
love, forgiving every kind of sin and rebellion.
But he does not excuse the guilty. He lays the
sins of the parents upon their children; the
entire family is affected—even children in
the third and fourth generations.' [19]In keep-
ing with your magnificent, unfailing love,
please pardon the sins of this people, just as
you have forgiven them ever since they left
Egypt."

[20]Then the LORD said, "I will pardon them
as you have requested. [21]But as surely as I live,
and as surely as the earth is filled with the
LORD's glory, [22]not one of these people will
ever enter that land. They have all seen my
glorious presence and the miraculous signs I
performed both in Egypt and in the wilder-
ness, but again and again they have tested me
by refusing to listen to my voice. [23]They will
never even see the land I swore to give their
ancestors. None of those who have treated
me with contempt will ever see it. [24]But my
servant Caleb has a different attitude than the
others have. He has remained loyal to me, so I
will bring him into the land he explored. His
descendants will possess their full share of
that land. [25]Now turn around, and don't go on
toward the land where the Amalekites and
Canaanites live. Tomorrow you must set out
for the wilderness in the direction of the Red
Sea.*"

The LORD Punishes the Israelites

[26]Then the LORD said to Moses and Aaron,
[27]"How long must I put up with this wicked
community and its complaints about me?
Yes, I have heard the complaints the Israelites
are making against me. [28]Now tell them this:
'As surely as I live, declares the LORD, I will do
to you the very things I heard you say. [29]You
will all drop dead in this wilderness! Because
you complained against me, every one of you
who is twenty years old or older and was in-
cluded in the registration will die. [30]You will
not enter and occupy the land I swore to give
you. The only exceptions will be Caleb son of
Jephunneh and Joshua son of Nun.

[31]" 'You said your children would be car-
ried off as plunder. Well, I will bring them
safely into the land, and they will enjoy what
you have despised. [32]But as for you, you will
drop dead in this wilderness. [33]And your chil-
dren will be like shepherds, wandering in the
wilderness for forty years. In this way, they
will pay for your faithlessness, until the last
of you lies dead in the wilderness.

[34]"'Because your men explored the land for
forty days, you must wander in the wilderness
for forty years—a year for each day, suffering
the consequences of your sins. Then you will
discover what it is like to have me for an en-
emy.' [35]I, the LORD, have spoken! I will cer-
tainly do these things to every member of the
community who has conspired against me.
They will be destroyed here in this wilder-
ness, and here they will die!"

[36]The ten men Moses had sent to explore
the land—the ones who incited rebellion
against the LORD with their bad report—[37]were
struck dead with a plague before the LORD.
[38]Of the twelve who had explored the land,
only Joshua and Caleb remained alive.

[39]When Moses reported the LORD's words
to all the Israelites, the people were filled with
grief. [40]Then they got up early the next morn-
ing and went to the top of the range of hills.
"Let's go," they said. "We realize that we have
sinned, but now we are ready to enter the land
the LORD has promised us."

[41]But Moses said, "Why are you now dis-
obeying the LORD's orders to return to the wil-
derness? It won't work. [42]Do not go up into
the land now. You will only be crushed by
your enemies because the LORD is not with
you. [43]When you face the Amalekites and
Canaanites in battle, you will be slaughtered.
The LORD will abandon you because you have
abandoned the LORD."

[44]But the people defiantly pushed ahead
toward the hill country, even though neither
Moses nor the Ark of the LORD's Covenant left
the camp. [45]Then the Amalekites and the Ca-
naanites who lived in those hills came down
and attacked them and chased them back as
far as Hormah.

CHAPTER 15

Laws concerning Offerings

Then the LORD told Moses, [2]"Give the follow-
ing instructions to the people of Israel.

"When you finally settle in the land I am
giving you, [3]you will offer special gifts as a

14:25 Hebrew *sea of reeds.*

Two weeks after I made the school volleyball team, I learned the coaches had accepted too many girls onto the team, and they would have to cut four of us. But during our practices before the start of the season, we'd already grown so close. I thought about how much I'd miss those girls when four were gone.

I never dreamed I would be one of the four! I was devastated. I still remember having to turn in my brand new volleyball uniform. They didn't ask any of the four to be team managers, second stringers, or even mascots—it was just over! At first, I went through all the natural reactions anyone would have. The coaches had hurt my feelings so much. Not to mention how embarrassing it was to tell the same story over and over again to my friends who wanted to know why I wasn't on the team anymore.

But I learned a great lesson about the power of a person's attitude. Instead of criticizing the coaches, burying my head in embarrassment, or boycotting the games, I decided to make the best of it. In fact, I supported my former teammates and cheered them on at all their games.

Several of my friends told me later how much they admired how I handled the situation. It wasn't easy, but instead of focusing on my disappointment, I tried contributing my talents in other ways and making new friends. Now I love playing on the basketball team for my school. What I thought was the worst thing that could happen actually turned out to be best!

Read Numbers 13:25-30 and discover what a difference dwelling on the positives can have on our attitude. Check out these verses to see the importance of our attitude: Romans 14:8; Ephesians 4:23.

pleasing aroma to the LORD. These gifts may take the form of a burnt offering, a sacrifice to fulfill a vow, a voluntary offering, or an offering at any of your annual festivals, and they may be taken from your herds of cattle or your flocks of sheep and goats. 4When you present these offerings, you must also give the LORD a grain offering of two quarts* of choice flour mixed with one quart* of olive oil. 5For each lamb offered as a burnt offering or a special sacrifice, you must also present one quart of wine as a liquid offering.

6"If the sacrifice is a ram, give a grain offering of four quarts* of choice flour mixed with a third of a gallon* of olive oil, 7and give a third of a gallon of wine as a liquid offering. This will be a pleasing aroma to the LORD.

8"When you present a young bull as a burnt offering or as a sacrifice to fulfill a vow or as a peace offering to the LORD, 9you must also give a grain offering of six quarts* of choice flour mixed with two quarts* of olive oil, 10and give two quarts of wine as a liquid offering. This will be a special gift, a pleasing aroma to the LORD.

11"Each sacrifice of a bull, ram, lamb, or young goat should be prepared in this way. 12Follow these instructions with each offering you present. 13All of you native-born Israelites must follow these instructions when you offer a special gift as a pleasing aroma to the LORD. 14And if any foreigners visit you or live among you and want to present a special gift as a pleasing aroma to the LORD, they must follow these same procedures. 15Native-born Israelites and foreigners are equal before the LORD and are subject to the same decrees. This is a permanent law for you, to be observed from generation to generation. 16The same instructions and regulations will apply both to you and to the foreigners living among you."

17Then the LORD said to Moses, 18"Give the following instructions to the people of Israel.

"When you arrive in the land where I am taking you, 19and you eat the crops that grow there, you must set some aside as a sacred offering to the LORD. 20Present a cake from the first of the flour you grind, and set it aside as a sacred offering, as you do with the first grain from the threshing floor. 21Throughout the generations to come, you are to present a sacred offering to the LORD each year from the first of your ground flour.

22"But suppose you unintentionally fail to carry out all these commands that the LORD has given you through Moses. 23And suppose your descendants in the future fail to do everything the LORD has commanded through Moses. 24If the mistake was made unintentionally, and the community was unaware of it, the whole community must present a young bull for a burnt offering as a pleasing aroma to the LORD. It must be offered along with its prescribed grain offering and liquid offering and with one male goat for a sin offering. 25With it the priest will purify the whole community of Israel, making them right with the LORD,* and they will be forgiven. For it was an unintentional sin, and they have corrected it with their offerings to the LORD—the special gift and the sin offering. 26The whole community of Israel will be forgiven, including the foreigners living among you, for all the people were involved in the sin.

27"If one individual commits an unintentional sin, the guilty person must bring a one-year-old female goat for a sin offering. 28The priest will sacrifice it to purify* the guilty person before the LORD, and that person will be forgiven. 29These same instructions apply both to native-born Israelites and to the foreigners living among you.

30"But those who brazenly violate the LORD's will, whether native-born Israelites or foreigners, have blasphemed the LORD, and they must be cut off from the community. 31Since they have treated the LORD's word with contempt and deliberately disobeyed his command, they must be completely cut off and suffer the punishment for their guilt."

Penalty for Breaking the Sabbath

32One day while the people of Israel were in the wilderness, they discovered a man gathering wood on the Sabbath day. 33The people who found him doing this took him before Moses, Aaron, and the rest of the community. 34They held him in custody because they did not know what to do with him. 35Then the

15:4a Hebrew *1/10 of an ephah* [2.2 liters]. **15:4b** Hebrew *1/4 of a hin* [1 liter]; also in 15:5. **15:6a** Hebrew *2/10 of an ephah* [4.4 liters]. **15:6b** Hebrew *1/3 of a hin* [1.3 liters]; also in 15:7. **15:9a** Hebrew *3/10 of an ephah* [6.6 liters]. **15:9b** Hebrew *1/2 of a hin* [2 liters]; also in 15:10. **15:25** Or *will make atonement for the whole community of Israel.* **15:28** Or *to make atonement for.*

LORD said to Moses, "The man must be put to death! The whole community must stone him outside the camp." [36]So the whole community took the man outside the camp and stoned him to death, just as the LORD had commanded Moses.

Tassels on Clothing

[37]Then the LORD said to Moses, [38]"Give the following instructions to the people of Israel: Throughout the generations to come you must make tassels for the hems of your clothing and attach them with a blue cord. [39]When you see the tassels, you will remember and obey all the commands of the LORD instead of following your own desires and defiling yourselves, as you are prone to do. [40]The tassels will help you remember that you must obey all my commands and be holy to your God. [41]I am the LORD your God who brought you out of the land of Egypt that I might be your God. I am the LORD your God!"

CHAPTER 16

Korah's Rebellion

One day Korah son of Izhar, a descendant of Kohath son of Levi, conspired with Dathan and Abiram, the sons of Eliab, and On son of Peleth, from the tribe of Reuben. [2]They incited a rebellion against Moses, along with 250 other leaders of the community, all prominent members of the assembly. [3]They united against Moses and Aaron and said, "You have gone too far! The whole community of Israel has been set apart by the LORD, and he is with all of us. What right do you have to act as though you are greater than the rest of the LORD's people?"

[4]When Moses heard what they were saying, he fell face down on the ground. [5]Then he said to Korah and his followers, "Tomorrow morning the LORD will show us who belongs to him* and who is holy. The LORD will allow only those whom he selects to enter his own presence. [6]Korah, you and all your followers must prepare your incense burners. [7]Light fires in them tomorrow, and burn incense before the LORD. Then we will see whom the LORD chooses as his holy one. You Levites are the ones who have gone too far!"

[8]Then Moses spoke again to Korah: "Now listen, you Levites! [9]Does it seem insignificant to you that the God of Israel has chosen you from among all the community of Israel to be near him so you can serve in the LORD's Tabernacle and stand before the people to minister to them? [10]Korah, he has already given this special ministry to you and your fellow Levites. Are you now demanding the priesthood as well? [11]The LORD is the one you and your

Aaron

Some of my fellow Israelites live to whine. They complain about Moses, me (Moses' brother), the food . . . everything. God told Moses to take twelve walking sticks, each marked with the name of a tribe's leader. One had "Aaron" carved into it. I represent the tribe of Levi. The Lord said he'd make one of these dead sticks sprout and grow. Moses went into the Tabernacle. He tossed out stick after stick. Finally, he brought out the last one—mine. It had done more than sprout. It had buds, blossoms, and delicious almonds!

Read more about Aaron in Exodus 4:14—Deuteronomy 10:6 .

16:5 Greek version reads *God has visited and knows those who are his.* Compare 2 Tim 2:19.

followers are really revolting against! For who is Aaron that you are complaining about him?"

12 Then Moses summoned Dathan and Abiram, the sons of Eliab, but they replied, "We refuse to come before you! 13 Isn't it enough that you brought us out of Egypt, a land flowing with milk and honey, to kill us here in this wilderness, and that you now treat us like your subjects? 14 What's more, you haven't brought us into another land flowing with milk and honey. You haven't given us a new homeland with fields and vineyards. Are you trying to fool these men?* We will not come."

15 Then Moses became very angry and said to the LORD, "Do not accept their grain offerings! I have not taken so much as a donkey from them, and I have never hurt a single one of them." 16 And Moses said to Korah, "You and all your followers must come here tomorrow and present yourselves before the LORD. Aaron will also be here. 17 You and each of your 250 followers must prepare an incense burner and put incense on it, so you can all present them before the LORD. Aaron will also bring his incense burner."

18 So each of these men prepared an incense burner, lit the fire, and placed incense on it. Then they all stood at the entrance of the Tabernacle* with Moses and Aaron. 19 Meanwhile, Korah had stirred up the entire community against Moses and Aaron, and they all gathered at the Tabernacle entrance. Then the glorious presence of the LORD appeared to the whole community, 20 and the LORD said to Moses and Aaron, 21 "Get away from all these people so that I may instantly destroy them!"

22 But Moses and Aaron fell face down on the ground. "O God," they pleaded, "you are the God who gives breath to all creatures. Must you be angry with all the people when only one man sins?"

23 And the LORD said to Moses, 24 "Then tell all the people to get away from the tents of Korah, Dathan, and Abiram."

25 So Moses got up and rushed over to the tents of Dathan and Abiram, followed by the elders of Israel. 26 "Quick!" he told the people. "Get away from the tents of these wicked men, and don't touch anything that belongs to them. If you do, you will be destroyed for their sins." 27 So all the people stood back from the tents of Korah, Dathan, and Abiram. Then Dathan and Abiram came out and stood at the entrances of their tents, together with their wives and children and little ones.

28 And Moses said, "This is how you will know that the LORD has sent me to do all these things that I have done—for I have not done them on my own. 29 If these men die a natural death, or if nothing unusual happens, then the LORD has not sent me. 30 But if the LORD does something entirely new and the ground opens its mouth and swallows them and all their belongings, and they go down alive into the grave,* then you will know that these men have shown contempt for the LORD."

31 He had hardly finished speaking the words when the ground suddenly split open beneath them. 32 The earth opened its mouth and swallowed the men, along with their households and all their followers who were standing with them, and everything they owned. 33 So they went down alive into the grave, along with all their belongings. The earth closed over them, and they all vanished from among the people of Israel. 34 All the people around them fled when they heard their screams. "The earth will swallow us, too!" they cried. 35 Then fire blazed forth from the LORD and burned up the 250 men who were offering incense.

36* And the LORD said to Moses, 37 "Tell Eleazar son of Aaron the priest to pull all the incense burners from the fire, for they are holy. Also tell him to scatter the burning coals. 38 Take the incense burners of these men who have sinned at the cost of their lives, and hammer the metal into a thin sheet to overlay the altar. Since these burners were used in the LORD's presence, they have become holy. Let them serve as a warning to the people of Israel."

39 So Eleazar the priest collected the 250 bronze incense burners that had been used by the men who died in the fire, and he hammered them into a thin sheet to overlay the altar. 40 This would warn the Israelites that no unauthorized person—no one who was not a descendant of Aaron—should ever enter the LORD's presence to burn incense. If anyone did, the same thing would happen to him as

16:14 Hebrew *Are you trying to put out the eyes of these men?* **16:18** Hebrew *the Tent of Meeting;* also in 16:19, 42, 43, 50.
16:30 Hebrew *into Sheol;* also in 16:33. **16:36** Verses 16:36-50 are numbered 17:1-15 in Hebrew text.

happened to Korah and his followers. So the LORD's instructions to Moses were carried out.

41But the very next morning the whole community of Israel began muttering again against Moses and Aaron, saying, "You have killed the LORD's people!" 42As the community gathered to protest against Moses and Aaron, they turned toward the Tabernacle and saw that the cloud had covered it, and the glorious presence of the LORD appeared.

43Moses and Aaron came and stood in front of the Tabernacle, 44and the LORD said to Moses, 45"Get away from all these people so that I can instantly destroy them!" But Moses and Aaron fell face down on the ground.

46And Moses said to Aaron, "Quick, take an incense burner and place burning coals on it from the altar. Lay incense on it, and carry it out among the people to purify them and make them right with the LORD.* The LORD's anger is blazing against them—the plague has already begun."

47Aaron did as Moses told him and ran out among the people. The plague had already begun to strike down the people, but Aaron burned the incense and purified* the people. 48He stood between the dead and the living, and the plague stopped. 49But 14,700 people died in that plague, in addition to those who had died in the affair involving Korah. 50Then because the plague had stopped, Aaron returned to Moses at the entrance of the Tabernacle.

CHAPTER 17

The Budding of Aaron's Staff

1*Then the LORD said to Moses, 2"Tell the people of Israel to bring you twelve wooden staffs, one from each leader of Israel's ancestral tribes, and inscribe each leader's name on his staff. 3Inscribe Aaron's name on the staff of the tribe of Levi, for there must be one staff for the leader of each ancestral tribe. 4Place these staffs in the Tabernacle in front of the Ark containing the tablets of the Covenant,* where I meet with you. 5Buds will sprout on the staff belonging to the man I choose. Then I will finally put an end to the people's murmuring and complaining against you."

6So Moses gave the instructions to the people of Israel, and each of the twelve tribal leaders, including Aaron, brought Moses a staff. 7Moses placed the staffs in the LORD's presence in the Tabernacle of the Covenant.* 8When he went into the Tabernacle of the Covenant the next day, he found that Aaron's staff, representing the tribe of Levi, had sprouted, budded, blossomed, and produced ripe almonds!

9When Moses brought all the staffs out from the LORD's presence, he showed them to the people. Each man claimed his own staff. 10And the LORD said to Moses: "Place Aaron's staff permanently before the Ark of the Covenant* to serve as a warning to rebels. This should put an end to their complaints against me and prevent any further deaths." 11So Moses did as the LORD commanded him.

12Then the people of Israel said to Moses, "Look, we are doomed! We are dead! We are ruined! 13Everyone who even comes close to the Tabernacle of the LORD dies. Are we all doomed to die?"

CHAPTER 18

Duties of Priests and Levites

Then the LORD said to Aaron: "You, your sons, and your relatives from the tribe of Levi will be held responsible for any offenses related to the sanctuary. But you and your sons alone will be held responsible for violations connected with the priesthood.

2"Bring your relatives of the tribe of Levi—your ancestral tribe—to assist you and your sons as you perform the sacred duties in front of the Tabernacle of the Covenant.* 3But as the Levites go about all their assigned duties at the Tabernacle, they must be careful not to go near any of the sacred objects or the altar. If they do, both you and they will die. 4The Levites must join you in fulfilling their responsibilities for the care and maintenance of the Tabernacle,* but no unauthorized person may assist you.

5"You yourselves must perform the sacred duties inside the sanctuary and at the altar. If

16:46 Or *to make atonement for them.* **16:47** Or *and made atonement for.* **17:1** Verses 17:1-13 are numbered 17:16-28 in Hebrew text. **17:4** Hebrew *in the Tent of Meeting before the Testimony.* The Hebrew word for "testimony" refers to the terms of the LORD's covenant with Israel as written on stone tablets, which were kept in the Ark, and also to the covenant itself. **17:7** Or *Tabernacle of the Testimony;* also in 17:8. **17:10** Hebrew *before the Testimony;* see note on 17:4. **18:2** Or *Tabernacle of the Testimony.* **18:4** Hebrew *the Tent of Meeting;* also in 18:6, 21, 22, 23, 31.

you follow these instructions, the LORD's anger will never again blaze against the people of Israel. [6]I myself have chosen your fellow Levites from among the Israelites to be your special assistants. They are a gift to you, dedicated to the LORD for service in the Tabernacle. [7]But you and your sons, the priests, must personally handle all the priestly rituals associated with the altar and with everything behind the inner curtain. I am giving you the priesthood as your special privilege of service. Any unauthorized person who comes too near the sanctuary will be put to death."

Support for the Priests and Levites

[8]The LORD gave these further instructions to Aaron: "I myself have put you in charge of all the holy offerings that are brought to me by the people of Israel. I have given all these consecrated offerings to you and your sons as your permanent share. [9]You are allotted the portion of the most holy offerings that is not burned on the fire. This portion of all the most holy offerings—including the grain offerings, sin offerings, and guilt offerings—will be most holy, and it belongs to you and your sons. [10]You must eat it as a most holy offering. All the males may eat of it, and you must treat it as most holy.

[11]"All the sacred offerings and special offerings presented to me when the Israelites lift them up before the altar also belong to you. I have given them to you and to your sons and daughters as your permanent share. Any member of your family who is ceremonially clean may eat of these offerings.

[12]"I also give you the harvest gifts brought by the people as offerings to the LORD—the best of the olive oil, new wine, and grain. [13]All the first crops of their land that the people present to the LORD belong to you. Any member of your family who is ceremonially clean may eat this food.

[14]"Everything in Israel that is specially set apart for the LORD* also belongs to you.

[15]"The firstborn of every mother, whether human or animal, that is offered to the LORD will be yours. But you must always redeem your firstborn sons and the firstborn of ceremonially unclean animals. [16]Redeem them when they are one month old. The redemption price is five pieces of silver* (as measured by the weight of the sanctuary shèkel, which equals twenty gerahs).

[17]"However, you may not redeem the firstborn of cattle, sheep, or goats. They are holy and have been set apart for the LORD. Sprinkle their blood on the altar, and burn their fat as a special gift, a pleasing aroma to the LORD. [18]The meat of these animals will be yours, just like the breast and right thigh that are presented by lifting them up as a special offering before the altar. [19]Yes, I am giving you all these holy offerings that the people of Israel bring to the LORD. They are for you and your sons and daughters, to be eaten as your permanent share. This is an eternal and unbreakable covenant* between the LORD and you, and it also applies to your descendants."

[20]And the LORD said to Aaron, "You priests will receive no allotment of land or share of property among the people of Israel. I am your share and your allotment. [21]As for the tribe of Levi, your relatives, I will compensate them for their service in the Tabernacle. Instead of an allotment of land, I will give them the tithes from the entire land of Israel.

[22]"From now on, no Israelites except priests or Levites may approach the Tabernacle. If they come too near, they will be judged guilty and will die. [23]Only the Levites may serve at the Tabernacle, and they will be held responsible for any offenses against it. This is a permanent law for you, to be observed from generation to generation. The Levites will receive no allotment of land among the Israelites, [24]because I have given them the Israelites' tithes, which have been presented as sacred offerings to the LORD. This will be the Levites' share. That is why I said they would receive no allotment of land among the Israelites."

[25]The LORD also told Moses, [26]"Give these instructions to the Levites: When you receive from the people of Israel the tithes I have assigned as your allotment, give a tenth of the tithes you receive—a tithe of the tithe—to the LORD as a sacred offering. [27]The LORD will consider this offering to be your harvest offering, as though it were the first grain from your own threshing floor or wine from your own winepress. [28]You must present one-tenth of the tithe received from the Israelites

18:14 The Hebrew term used here refers to the complete consecration of things or people to the LORD, either by destroying them or by giving them as an offering. **18:16** Hebrew *5 shekels* [2 ounces or 57 grams] *of silver*. **18:19** Hebrew *a covenant of salt*.

as a sacred offering to the LORD. This is the LORD's sacred portion, and you must present it to Aaron the priest. [29]Be sure to give to the LORD the best portions of the gifts given to you.

Is it OK to give God what's left over of my money and my time?

Be sure to give to the LORD the best portions of the gifts given to you. NUMBERS 18:29

[30]"Also, give these instructions to the Levites: When you present the best part as your offering, it will be considered as though it came from your own threshing floor or winepress. [31]You Levites and your families may eat this food anywhere you wish, for it is your compensation for serving in the Tabernacle. [32]You will not be considered guilty for accepting the LORD's tithes if you give the best portion to the priests. But be careful not to treat the holy gifts of the people of Israel as though they were common. If you do, you will die."

CHAPTER 19

The Water of Purification

The LORD said to Moses and Aaron, [2]"Here is another legal requirement commanded by the LORD: Tell the people of Israel to bring you a red heifer, a perfect animal that has no defects and has never been yoked to a plow. [3]Give it to Eleazar the priest, and it will be taken outside the camp and slaughtered in his presence. [4]Eleazar will take some of its blood on his finger and sprinkle it seven times toward the front of the Tabernacle.* [5]As Eleazar watches, the heifer must be burned—its hide, meat, blood, and dung. [6]Eleazar the priest must then take a stick of cedar,* a hyssop branch, and some scarlet yarn and throw them into the fire where the heifer is burning.

[7]"Then the priest must wash his clothes and bathe himself in water. Afterward he may return to the camp, though he will remain ceremonially unclean until evening. [8]The man who burns the animal must also wash his clothes and bathe himself in water, and he, too, will remain unclean until evening. [9]Then someone who is ceremonially clean will gather up the ashes of the heifer and deposit them in a purified place outside the camp. They will be kept there for the community of Israel to use in the water for the purification ceremony. This ceremony is performed for the removal of sin. [10]The man who gathers up the ashes of the heifer must also wash his clothes, and he will remain ceremonially unclean until evening. This is a permanent law for the people of Israel and any foreigners who live among them.

[11]"All those who touch a dead human body will be ceremonially unclean for seven days. [12]They must purify themselves on the third and seventh days with the water of purification; then they will be purified. But if they do not do this on the third and seventh days, they will continue to be unclean even after the seventh day. [13]All those who touch a dead body and do not purify themselves in the proper way defile the LORD's Tabernacle, and they will be cut off from the community of Israel. Since the water of purification was not sprinkled on them, their defilement continues.

[14]"This is the ritual law that applies when someone dies inside a tent: All those who enter that tent and those who were inside when the death occurred will be ceremonially unclean for seven days. [15]Any open container in the tent that was not covered with a lid is also defiled. [16]And if someone in an open field touches the corpse of someone who was killed with a sword or who died a natural death, or if someone touches a human bone or a grave, that person will be defiled for seven days.

[17]"To remove the defilement, put some of the ashes from the burnt purification offering in a jar, and pour fresh water over them.

19:4 Hebrew *the Tent of Meeting*. **19:6** Or *juniper*.

[18]Then someone who is ceremonially clean must take a hyssop branch and dip it into the water. That person must sprinkle the water on the tent, on all the furnishings in the tent, and on the people who were in the tent; also on the person who touched a human bone, or touched someone who was killed or who died naturally, or touched a grave. [19]On the third and seventh days the person who is ceremonially clean must sprinkle the water on those who are defiled. Then on the seventh day the people being cleansed must wash their clothes and bathe themselves, and that evening they will be cleansed of their defilement.

[20]"But those who become defiled and do not purify themselves will be cut off from the community, for they have defiled the sanctuary of the LORD. Since the water of purification has not been sprinkled on them, they remain defiled. [21]This is a permanent law for the people. Those who sprinkle the water of purification must afterward wash their clothes, and anyone who then touches the water used for purification will remain defiled until evening. [22]Anything and anyone that a defiled person touches will be ceremonially unclean until evening."

CHAPTER 20

Moses Strikes the Rock

In the first month of the year,* the whole community of Israel arrived in the wilderness of Zin and camped at Kadesh. While they were there, Miriam died and was buried.

[2]There was no water for the people to drink at that place, so they rebelled against Moses and Aaron. [3]The people blamed Moses and said, "If only we had died in the LORD's presence with our brothers! [4]Why have you brought the congregation of the LORD's people into this wilderness to die, along with all our livestock? [5]Why did you make us leave Egypt and bring us here to this terrible place? This land has no grain, no figs, no grapes, no pomegranates, and no water to drink!"

[6]Moses and Aaron turned away from the people and went to the entrance of the Tabernacle,* where they fell face down on the ground. Then the glorious presence of the LORD appeared to them, [7]and the LORD said to Moses, [8]"You and Aaron must take the staff and assemble the entire community. As the people watch, speak to the rock over there, and it will pour out its water. You will provide enough water from the rock to satisfy the whole community and their livestock."

[9]So Moses did as he was told. He took the staff from the place where it was kept before the LORD. [10]Then he and Aaron summoned the people to come and gather at the rock. "Listen, you rebels!" he shouted. "Must we bring you water from this rock?" [11]Then Moses raised his hand and struck the rock twice with the staff, and water gushed out. So the entire community and their livestock drank their fill.

[12]But the LORD said to Moses and Aaron, "Because you did not trust me enough to demonstrate my holiness to the people of Israel, you will not lead them into the land I am giving them!" [13]This place was known as the waters of Meribah (which means "arguing") because there the people of Israel argued with the LORD, and there he demonstrated his holiness among them.

Edom Refuses Israel Passage

[14]While Moses was at Kadesh, he sent ambassadors to the king of Edom with this message:

> "This is what your relatives, the people of Israel, say: You know all the hardships we have been through. [15]Our ancestors went down to Egypt, and we lived there a long time, and we and our ancestors were brutally mistreated by the Egyptians. [16]But when we cried out to the LORD, he heard us and sent an angel who brought us out of Egypt. Now we are camped at Kadesh, a town on the border of your land. [17]Please let us travel through your land. We will be careful not to go through your fields and vineyards. We won't even drink water from your wells. We will stay on the king's road and never leave it until we have passed through your territory."

[18]But the king of Edom said, "Stay out of my land, or I will meet you with an army!"

[19]The Israelites answered, "We will stay on the main road. If our livestock drink your water, we will pay for it. Just let us pass through your country. That's all we ask."

20:1 The first month of the ancient Hebrew lunar calendar usually occurs within the months of March and April. The number of years since leaving Egypt is not specified. **20:6** Hebrew *the Tent of Meeting*.

[20]But the king of Edom replied, "Stay out! You may not pass through our land." With that he mobilized his army and marched out against them with an imposing force. [21]Because Edom refused to allow Israel to pass through their country, Israel was forced to turn around.

The Death of Aaron

[22]The whole community of Israel left Kadesh and arrived at Mount Hor. [23]There, on the border of the land of Edom, the LORD said to Moses and Aaron, [24]"The time has come for Aaron to join his ancestors in death. He will not enter the land I am giving the people of Israel, because the two of you rebelled against my instructions concerning the water at Meribah. [25]Now take Aaron and his son Eleazar up Mount Hor. [26]There you will remove Aaron's priestly garments and put them on Eleazar, his son. Aaron will die there and join his ancestors."

[27]So Moses did as the LORD commanded. The three of them went up Mount Hor together as the whole community watched. [28]At the summit, Moses removed the priestly garments from Aaron and put them on Eleazar, Aaron's son. Then Aaron died there on top of the mountain, and Moses and Eleazar went back down. [29]When the people realized that Aaron had died, all Israel mourned for him thirty days.

CHAPTER 21

Victory over the Canaanites

The Canaanite king of Arad, who lived in the Negev, heard that the Israelites were approaching on the road through Atharim. So he attacked the Israelites and took some of them as prisoners. [2]Then the people of Israel made this vow to the LORD: "If you will hand these people over to us, we will completely destroy* all their towns." [3]The LORD heard the Israelites' request and gave them victory over the Canaanites. The Israelites completely destroyed them and their towns, and the place has been called Hormah* ever since.

The Bronze Snake

[4]Then the people of Israel set out from Mount Hor, taking the road to the Red Sea* to go around the land of Edom. But the people grew impatient with the long journey, [5]and they began to speak against God and Moses. "Why have you brought us out of Egypt to die here in the wilderness?" they complained. "There is nothing to eat here and nothing to drink. And we hate this horrible manna!"

AMAZING FACTS

God told the Israelites to form a bronze snake and put it on a pole. Why? It made a great snakebite kit!

NUMBERS 21:4-9

[6]So the LORD sent poisonous snakes among the people, and many were bitten and died. [7]Then the people came to Moses and cried out, "We have sinned by speaking against the LORD and against you. Pray that the LORD will take away the snakes." So Moses prayed for the people.

[8]Then the LORD told him, "Make a replica of a poisonous snake and attach it to a pole. All who are bitten will live if they simply look at it!" [9]So Moses made a snake out of bronze and attached it to a pole. Then anyone who was bitten by a snake could look at the bronze snake and be healed!

Israel's Journey to Moab

[10]The Israelites traveled next to Oboth and camped there. [11]Then they went on to Iyeabarim, in the wilderness on the eastern border of Moab. [12]From there they traveled to the valley of Zered Brook and set up camp. [13]Then they moved out and camped on the far side of the Arnon River, in the wilderness adjacent to the territory of the Amorites. The

21:2 The Hebrew term used here refers to the complete consecration of things or people to the LORD, either by destroying them or by giving them as an offering; also in 21:3. **21:3** *Hormah* means "destruction." **21:4** Hebrew *sea of reeds*.

Arnon is the boundary line between the
Moabites and the Amorites. [14]For this reason
The Book of the Wars of the LORD speaks of
"the town of Waheb in the area of Suphah,
and the ravines of the Arnon River, [15]and the
ravines that extend as far as the settlement of
Ar on the border of Moab."

[16]From there the Israelites traveled to
Beer,* which is the well where the LORD said
to Moses, "Assemble the people, and I will
give them water." [17]There the Israelites sang
this song:

"Spring up, O well!
Yes, sing its praises!
[18] Sing of this well,
which princes dug,
which great leaders hollowed out
with their scepters and staffs."

Then the Israelites left the wilderness and
proceeded on through Mattanah, [19]Nahaliel,
and Bamoth. [20]After that they went to the val-
ley in Moab where Pisgah Peak overlooks the
wasteland.*

Victory over Sihon and Og

[21]The Israelites sent ambassadors to King Si-
hon of the Amorites with this message:

[22]"Let us travel through your land. We will
be careful not to go through your fields
and vineyards. We won't even drink water
from your wells. We will stay on the king's
road until we have passed through your
territory."

[23]But King Sihon refused to let them cross
his territory. Instead, he mobilized his entire
army and attacked Israel in the wilderness,
engaging them in battle at Jahaz. [24]But the Is-
raelites slaughtered them with their swords
and occupied their land from the Arnon River
to the Jabbok River. They went only as far as
the Ammonite border because the boundary
of the Ammonites was fortified.*

[25]So Israel captured all the towns of the
Amorites and settled in them, including the
city of Heshbon and its surrounding villages.
[26]Heshbon had been the capital of King Sihon
of the Amorites. He had defeated a former
Moabite king and seized all his land as far as
the Arnon River. [27]Therefore, the ancient po-
ets wrote this about him:

"Come to Heshbon and let it be
rebuilt!
Let the city of Sihon be restored.
[28] A fire flamed forth from Heshbon,
a blaze from the city of Sihon.
It burned the city of Ar in Moab;
it destroyed the rulers of the Arnon
heights.
[29] What sorrow awaits you, O people of
Moab!
You are finished, O worshipers of
Chemosh!
Chemosh has left his sons as refugees,
his daughters as captives of Sihon, the
Amorite king.
[30] We have utterly destroyed them,
from Heshbon to Dibon.
We have completely wiped them out
as far away as Nophah and Medeba.*"

[31]So the people of Israel occupied the terri-
tory of the Amorites. [32]After Moses sent men
to explore the Jazer area, they captured all the
towns in the region and drove out the Amo-
rites who lived there. [33]Then they turned and
marched up the road to Bashan, but King Og
of Bashan and all his people attacked them at
Edrei. [34]The LORD said to Moses, "Do not be
afraid of him, for I have handed him over to
you, along with all his people and his land. Do
the same to him as you did to King Sihon of
the Amorites, who ruled in Heshbon." [35]And
Israel killed King Og, his sons, and all his sub-
jects; not a single survivor remained. Then Is-
rael occupied their land.

CHAPTER 22

Balak Sends for Balaam

Then the people of Israel traveled to the
plains of Moab and camped east of the Jordan
River, across from Jericho. [2]Balak son of Zip-
por, the Moabite king, had seen everything
the Israelites did to the Amorites. [3]And when
the people of Moab saw how many Israelites
there were, they were terrified. [4]The king of
Moab said to the elders of Midian, "This mob
will devour everything in sight, like an ox de-
vours grass in the field!"

21:16 *Beer* means "well." **21:20** Or *overlooks Jeshimon.* **21:24** Or *because the terrain of the Ammonite frontier was rugged;* Hebrew reads *because the boundary of the Ammonites was strong.* **21:30** Or *until fire spread to Medeba.* The meaning of the Hebrew is uncertain.

So Balak, king of Moab, [5]sent messengers
to call Balaam son of Beor, who was living in
his native land of Pethor* near the Euphrates
River.* His message said:

> "Look, a vast horde of people has arrived
> from Egypt. They cover the face of the
> earth and are threatening me. [6]Please
> come and curse these people for me
> because they are too powerful for me.
> Then perhaps I will be able to conquer
> them and drive them from the land. I
> know that blessings fall on any people
> you bless, and curses fall on people
> you curse."

[7]Balak's messengers, who were elders of
Moab and Midian, set out with money to pay
Balaam to place a curse upon Israel.* They
went to Balaam and delivered Balak's mes-
sage to him. [8]"Stay here overnight," Balaam
said. "In the morning I will tell you whatever
the LORD directs me to say." So the officials
from Moab stayed there with Balaam.

[9]That night God came to Balaam and asked
him, "Who are these men visiting you?"

[10]Balaam said to God, "Balak son of Zippor,
king of Moab, has sent me this message:
[11]'Look, a vast horde of people has arrived
from Egypt, and they cover the face of the
earth. Come and curse these people for me.
Then perhaps I will be able to stand up to
them and drive them from the land.'"

[12]But God told Balaam, "Do not go with
them. You are not to curse these people, for
they have been blessed!"

[13]The next morning Balaam got up and
told Balak's officials, "Go on home! The LORD
will not let me go with you."

[14]So the Moabite officials returned to King
Balak and reported, "Balaam refused to come
with us." [15]Then Balak tried again. This time
he sent a larger number of even more distin-
guished officials than those he had sent the
first time. [16]They went to Balaam and deliv-
ered this message to him:

> "This is what Balak son of Zippor says:
> Please don't let anything stop you from
> coming to help me. [17]I will pay you very
> well and do whatever you tell me. Just
> come and curse these people for me!"

THE PARTY POOPERS

Alvin and his friends went to a party at a classmate's house. They were having a good time, eating pizza and listening to music. Then Alvin said to his friends, "Hey, how about a little football?" Soon they were darting around the room, tossing the football. They knocked into people and almost broke a lamp. When some kids started yelling, the father came downstairs. He was really mad and said, "I want everyone to leave, *now!*"

One guy muttered, "What a jerk!" Alvin was totally humiliated and angry. What should Alvin do? Read Numbers 22:21-34.

[18]But Balaam responded to Balak's messen-
gers, "Even if Balak were to give me his palace
filled with silver and gold, I would be power-
less to do anything against the will of the LORD
my God. [19]But stay here one more night, and I
will see if the LORD has anything else to say
to me."

22:5a Or *who was at Pethor in the land of the Amavites.* **22:5b** Hebrew *the river.* **22:7** Hebrew *set out with the money of divination in their hand.*

[20]That night God came to Balaam and told him, "Since these men have come for you, get up and go with them. But do only what I tell you to do."

Balaam and His Donkey

[21]So the next morning Balaam got up, saddled his donkey, and started off with the Moabite officials. [22]But God was angry that Balaam was going, so he sent the angel of the LORD to stand in the road to block his way. As Balaam and two servants were riding along, [23]Balaam's donkey saw the angel of the LORD standing in the road with a drawn sword in his hand. The donkey bolted off the road into a field, but Balaam beat it and turned it back onto the road. [24]Then the angel of the LORD stood at a place where the road narrowed between two vineyard walls. [25]When the donkey saw the angel of the LORD, it tried to squeeze by and crushed Balaam's foot against the wall. So Balaam beat the donkey again. [26]Then the angel of the LORD moved farther down the road and stood in a place too narrow for the donkey to get by at all. [27]This time when the donkey saw the angel, it lay down under Balaam. In a fit of rage Balaam beat the animal again with his staff.

AMAZING FACTS

A prophet cursing. A donkey talking. An angel blocking the road. God can work through any person—or creature.

NUMBERS 22:21-34

[28]Then the LORD gave the donkey the ability to speak. "What have I done to you that deserves your beating me three times?" it asked Balaam.

[29]"You have made me look like a fool!" Balaam shouted. "If I had a sword with me, I would kill you!"

[30]"But I am the same donkey you have ridden all your life," the donkey answered. "Have I ever done anything like this before?"

"No," Balaam admitted.

[31]Then the LORD opened Balaam's eyes, and he saw the angel of the LORD standing in the roadway with a drawn sword in his hand. Balaam bowed his head and fell face down on the ground before him.

[32]"Why did you beat your donkey those three times?" the angel of the LORD demanded. "Look, I have come to block your way because you are stubbornly resisting me. [33]Three times the donkey saw me and shied away; otherwise, I would certainly have killed you by now and spared the donkey."

[34]Then Balaam confessed to the angel of the LORD, "I have sinned. I didn't realize you were standing in the road to block my way. I will return home if you are against my going."

[35]But the angel of the LORD told Balaam, "Go with these men, but say only what I tell you to say." So Balaam went on with Balak's officials. [36]When King Balak heard that Balaam was on the way, he went out to meet him at a Moabite town on the Arnon River at the farthest border of his land.

[37]"Didn't I send you an urgent invitation? Why didn't you come right away?" Balak asked Balaam. "Didn't you believe me when I said I would reward you richly?"

[38]Balaam replied, "Look, now I have come, but I have no power to say whatever I want. I will speak only the message that God puts in my mouth." [39]Then Balaam accompanied Balak to Kiriath-huzoth, [40]where the king sacrificed cattle and sheep. He sent portions of the meat to Balaam and the officials who were with him. [41]The next morning Balak took Balaam up to Bamoth-baal. From there he could see some of the people of Israel spread out below him.

CHAPTER 23

Balaam Blesses Israel

Then Balaam said to King Balak, "Build me seven altars here, and prepare seven young bulls and seven rams for me to sacrifice." [2]Balak followed his instructions, and the two of them sacrificed a young bull and a ram on each altar.

[3]Then Balaam said to Balak, "Stand here by

your burnt offerings, and I will go to see if the LORD will respond to me. Then I will tell you whatever he reveals to me." So Balaam went alone to the top of a bare hill, [4]and God met him there. Balaam said to him, "I have prepared seven altars and have sacrificed a young bull and a ram on each altar."

[5]The LORD gave Balaam a message for King Balak. Then he said, "Go back to Balak and give him my message."

[6]So Balaam returned and found the king standing beside his burnt offerings with all the officials of Moab. [7]This was the message Balaam delivered:

"Balak summoned me to come from
Aram;
the king of Moab brought me from the
eastern hills.
'Come,' he said, 'curse Jacob for me!
Come and announce Israel's doom.'
[8] But how can I curse those
whom God has not cursed?
How can I condemn those
whom the LORD has not condemned?
[9] I see them from the cliff tops;
I watch them from the hills.
I see a people who live by themselves,
set apart from other nations.
[10] Who can count Jacob's descendants, as
numerous as dust?
Who can count even a fourth of Israel's
people?
Let me die like the righteous;
let my life end like theirs."

[11]Then King Balak demanded of Balaam, "What have you done to me? I brought you to curse my enemies. Instead, you have blessed them!"

[12]But Balaam replied, "I will speak only the message that the LORD puts in my mouth."

Balaam's Second Message

[13]Then King Balak told him, "Come with me to another place. There you will see another part of the nation of Israel, but not all of them. Curse at least that many!" [14]So Balak took Balaam to the plateau of Zophim on Pisgah Peak. He built seven altars there and offered a young bull and a ram on each altar.

[15]Then Balaam said to the king, "Stand here by your burnt offerings while I go over there to meet the LORD."

[16]And the LORD met Balaam and gave him a message. Then he said, "Go back to Balak and give him my message."

[17]So Balaam returned and found the king standing beside his burnt offerings with all the officials of Moab. "What did the LORD say?" Balak asked eagerly.

[18]This was the message Balaam delivered:

"Rise up, Balak, and listen!
Hear me, son of Zippor.
[19] God is not a man, so he does not lie.
He is not human, so he does not change
his mind.
Has he ever spoken and failed to act?
Has he ever promised and not carried
it through?
[20] Listen, I received a command to bless;
God has blessed, and I cannot
reverse it!
[21] No misfortune is in his plan for Jacob;
no trouble is in store for Israel.
For the LORD their God is with them;
he has been proclaimed their king.
[22] God brought them out of Egypt;
for them he is as strong as a wild ox.
[23] No curse can touch Jacob;
no magic has any power against Israel.
For now it will be said of Jacob,
'What wonders God has done for
Israel!'
[24] These people rise up like a lioness,
like a majestic lion rousing itself.
They refuse to rest
until they have feasted on prey,
drinking the blood of the slaughtered!"

[25]Then Balak said to Balaam, "Fine, but if you won't curse them, at least don't bless them!"

[26]But Balaam replied to Balak, "Didn't I tell you that I can do only what the LORD tells me?"

Balaam's Third Message

[27]Then King Balak said to Balaam, "Come, I will take you to one more place. Perhaps it will please God to let you curse them from there."

[28]So Balak took Balaam to the top of Mount Peor, overlooking the wasteland.* [29]Balaam

23:28 Or *overlooking Jeshimon.*

again told Balak, "Build me seven altars, and
prepare seven young bulls and seven rams for
me to sacrifice." [30]So Balak did as Balaam or-
dered and offered a young bull and a ram on
each altar.

CHAPTER 24

By now Balaam realized that the LORD was de-
termined to bless Israel, so he did not resort to
divination as before. Instead, he turned and
looked out toward the wilderness, [2]where he
saw the people of Israel camped, tribe by
tribe. Then the Spirit of God came upon him,
[3]and this is the message he delivered:

"This is the message of Balaam son
of Beor,
the message of the man whose eyes
see clearly,
[4] the message of one who hears the words
of God,
who sees a vision from the Almighty,
who bows down with eyes wide open:
[5] How beautiful are your tents, O Jacob;
how lovely are your homes, O Israel!
[6] They spread before me like palm groves,*
like gardens by the riverside.
They are like tall trees planted by the
LORD,
like cedars beside the waters.
[7] Water will flow from their buckets;
their offspring have all they need.
Their king will be greater than Agag;
their kingdom will be exalted.
[8] God brought them out of Egypt;
for them he is as strong as a wild ox.
He devours all the nations that oppose
him,
breaking their bones in pieces,
shooting them with arrows.
[9] Like a lion, Israel crouches and lies down;
like a lioness, who dares to arouse her?
Blessed is everyone who blesses you,
O Israel,
and cursed is everyone who curses
you."

[10]King Balak flew into a rage against Ba-
laam. He angrily clapped his hands and
shouted, "I called you to curse my enemies!
Instead, you have blessed them three times.
[11]Now get out of here! Go back home! I prom-
ised to reward you richly, but the LORD has
kept you from your reward."

[12]Balaam told Balak, "Don't you remember
what I told your messengers? I said, [13]'Even if
Balak were to give me his palace filled with
silver and gold, I would be powerless to do
anything against the will of the LORD.' I told
you that I could say only what the LORD says!
[14]Now I am returning to my own people. But
first let me tell you what the Israelites will do
to your people in the future."

Balaam's Final Messages

[15]This is the message Balaam delivered:

"This is the message of Balaam son
of Beor,
the message of the man whose eyes
see clearly,
[16] the message of one who hears the words
of God,
who has knowledge from the Most
High,
who sees a vision from the Almighty,
who bows down with eyes wide open:
[17] I see him, but not here and now.
I perceive him, but far in the distant
future.
A star will rise from Jacob;
a scepter will emerge from Israel.
It will crush the foreheads of Moab's
people,
cracking the skulls of the people
of Sheth.
[18] Edom will be taken over,
and Seir, its enemy, will be conquered,
while Israel marches on in triumph.
[19] A ruler will rise in Jacob
who will destroy the survivors of Ir."

[20]Then Balaam looked over toward the people
of Amalek and delivered this message:

"Amalek was the greatest of nations,
but its destiny is destruction!"

[21]Then he looked over toward the Kenites and
delivered this message:

"Your home is secure;
your nest is set in the rocks.
[22] But the Kenites will be destroyed
when Assyria* takes you captive."

24:6 Or *like a majestic valley.* **24:22** Hebrew *Asshur;* also in 24:24.

[23]Balaam concluded his messages by saying:

"Alas, who can survive
unless God has willed it?
[24] Ships will come from the coasts
of Cyprus*;
they will oppress Assyria and afflict
Eber,
but they, too, will be utterly destroyed."

[25]Then Balaam and Balak returned to their homes.

CHAPTER 25

Moab Seduces Israel

While the Israelites were camped at Acacia Grove,* some of the men defiled themselves by having* sexual relations with local Moabite women. [2]These women invited them to attend sacrifices to their gods, so the Israelites feasted with them and worshiped the gods of Moab. [3]In this way, Israel joined in the worship of Baal of Peor, causing the LORD's anger to blaze against his people.

[4]The LORD issued the following command to Moses: "Seize all the ringleaders and execute them before the LORD in broad daylight, so his fierce anger will turn away from the people of Israel."

[5]So Moses ordered Israel's judges, "Each of you must put to death the men under your authority who have joined in worshiping Baal of Peor."

[6]Just then one of the Israelite men brought a Midianite woman into his tent, right before the eyes of Moses and all the people, as everyone was weeping at the entrance of the Tabernacle.* [7]When Phinehas son of Eleazar and grandson of Aaron the priest saw this, he jumped up and left the assembly. He took a spear [8]and rushed after the man into his tent. Phinehas thrust the spear all the way through the man's body and into the woman's stomach. So the plague against the Israelites was stopped, [9]but not before 24,000 people had died.

[10]Then the LORD said to Moses, [11]"Phinehas son of Eleazar and grandson of Aaron the priest has turned my anger away from the Israelites by being as zealous among them as I was. So I stopped destroying all Israel as I had intended to do in my zealous anger. [12]Now tell him that I am making my special covenant of peace with him. [13]In this covenant, I give him and his descendants a permanent right to the priesthood, for in his zeal for me, his God, he purified the people of Israel, making them right with me.*"

[14]The Israelite man killed with the Midianite woman was named Zimri son of Salu, the leader of a family from the tribe of Simeon. [15]The woman's name was Cozbi; she was the daughter of Zur, the leader of a Midianite clan.

[16]Then the LORD said to Moses, [17]"Attack the Midianites and destroy them, [18]because they assaulted you with deceit and tricked you into worshiping Baal of Peor, and because of Cozbi, the daughter of a Midianite leader, who was killed at the time of the plague because of what happened at Peor."

CHAPTER 26

The Second Registration of Israel's Troops

After the plague had ended, the LORD said to Moses and to Eleazar son of Aaron the priest, [2]"From the whole community of Israel, record the names of all the warriors by their families. List all the men twenty years old or older who are able to go to war."

[3]So there on the plains of Moab beside the Jordan River, across from Jericho, Moses and Eleazar the priest issued these instructions to the leaders of Israel: [4]"List all the men of Israel twenty years old and older, just as the LORD commanded Moses."

This is the record of all the descendants of Israel who came out of Egypt.

The Tribe of Reuben

[5]These were the clans descended from the sons of Reuben, Jacob's* oldest son:

The Hanochite clan, named after their ancestor Hanoch.
The Palluite clan, named after their ancestor Pallu.
[6] The Hezronite clan, named after their ancestor Hezron.
The Carmite clan, named after their ancestor Carmi.

[7]These were the clans of Reuben. Their registered troops numbered 43,730.

24:24 Hebrew *Kittim*. **25:1a** Hebrew *Shittim*. **25:1b** As in Greek version; Hebrew reads *some of the men began having*.
25:6 Hebrew *the Tent of Meeting*. **25:13** Or *he made atonement for the people of Israel*. **26:5** Hebrew *Israel's*; see note on 1:20-21b.

[8]Pallu was the ancestor of Eliab, [9]and Eliab was the father of Nemuel, Dathan, and Abiram. This Dathan and Abiram are the same community leaders who conspired with Korah against Moses and Aaron, rebelling against the LORD. [10]But the earth opened up its mouth and swallowed them with Korah, and fire devoured 250 of their followers. This served as a warning to the entire nation of Israel. [11]However, the sons of Korah did not die that day.

The Tribe of Simeon

[12]These were the clans descended from the sons of Simeon:

The Jemuelite clan, named after their ancestor Jemuel.*

The Jaminite clan, named after their ancestor Jamin.

The Jakinite clan, named after their ancestor Jakin.

[13] The Zoharite clan, named after their ancestor Zohar.*

The Shaulite clan, named after their ancestor Shaul.

[14]These were the clans of Simeon. Their registered troops numbered 22,200.

The Tribe of Gad

[15]These were the clans descended from the sons of Gad:

The Zephonite clan, named after their ancestor Zephon.

The Haggite clan, named after their ancestor Haggi.

The Shunite clan, named after their ancestor Shuni.

[16] The Oznite clan, named after their ancestor Ozni.

The Erite clan, named after their ancestor Eri.

[17] The Arodite clan, named after their ancestor Arodi.*

The Arelite clan, named after their ancestor Areli.

[18]These were the clans of Gad. Their registered troops numbered 40,500.

The Tribe of Judah

[19]Judah had two sons, Er and Onan, who had died in the land of Canaan. [20]These were the clans descended from Judah's surviving sons:

The Shelanite clan, named after their ancestor Shelah.

The Perezite clan, named after their ancestor Perez.

The Zerahite clan, named after their ancestor Zerah.

[21]These were the subclans descended from the Perezites:

The Hezronites, named after their ancestor Hezron.

The Hamulites, named after their ancestor Hamul.

[22]These were the clans of Judah. Their registered troops numbered 76,500.

The Tribe of Issachar

[23]These were the clans descended from the sons of Issachar:

The Tolaite clan, named after their ancestor Tola.

The Puite clan, named after their ancestor Puah.*

[24] The Jashubite clan, named after their ancestor Jashub.

The Shimronite clan, named after their ancestor Shimron.

[25]These were the clans of Issachar. Their registered troops numbered 64,300.

The Tribe of Zebulun

[26]These were the clans descended from the sons of Zebulun:

The Seredite clan, named after their ancestor Sered.

The Elonite clan, named after their ancestor Elon.

The Jahleelite clan, named after their ancestor Jahleel.

[27]These were the clans of Zebulun. Their registered troops numbered 60,500.

26:12 As in Syriac version (see also Gen 46:10; Exod 6:15); Hebrew reads *Nemuelite . . . Nemuel.* **26:13** As in parallel texts at Gen 46:10 and Exod 6:15; Hebrew reads *Zerahite . . . Zerah.* **26:17** As in Samaritan Pentateuch and Greek and Syriac versions (see also Gen 46:16); Hebrew reads *Arod.* **26:23** As in Samaritan Pentateuch, Greek and Syriac versions, and Latin Vulgate (see also 1 Chr 7:1); Hebrew reads *The Punite clan, named after its ancestor Puvah.*

The Tribe of Manasseh

28 Two clans were descended from Joseph
through Manasseh and Ephraim.

29 These were the clans descended from Ma-
nasseh:
The Makirite clan, named after their
ancestor Makir.
The Gileadite clan, named after their
ancestor Gilead, Makir's son.

30 These were the subclans descended from
the Gileadites:
The Iezerites, named after their ancestor
Iezer.
The Helekites, named after their ancestor
Helek.
31 The Asrielites, named after their ancestor
Asriel.
The Shechemites, named after their
ancestor Shechem.
32 The Shemidaites, named after their
ancestor Shemida.
The Hepherites, named after their
ancestor Hepher.
33 (One of Hepher's descendants,
Zelophehad, had no sons, but his
daughters' names were Mahlah, Noah,
Hoglah, Milcah, and Tirzah.)

34 These were the clans of Manasseh. Their
registered troops numbered 52,700.

The Tribe of Ephraim

35 These were the clans descended from the
sons of Ephraim:
The Shuthelahite clan, named after their
ancestor Shuthelah.
The Bekerite clan, named after their
ancestor Beker.
The Tahanite clan, named after their
ancestor Tahan.

36 This was the subclan descended from the
Shuthelahites:
The Eranites, named after their ancestor
Eran.

37 These were the clans of Ephraim. Their reg-
istered troops numbered 32,500.

These clans of Manasseh and Ephraim were
all descendants of Joseph.

The Tribe of Benjamin

38 These were the clans descended from the
sons of Benjamin:
The Belaite clan, named after their
ancestor Bela.
The Ashbelite clan, named after their
ancestor Ashbel.
The Ahiramite clan, named after their
ancestor Ahiram.
39 The Shuphamite clan, named after their
ancestor Shupham.*
The Huphamite clan, named after their
ancestor Hupham.

40 These were the subclans descended from
the Belaites:
The Ardites, named after their ancestor Ard.*
The Naamites, named after their ancestor
Naaman.

41 These were the clans of Benjamin. Their
registered troops numbered 45,600.

The Tribe of Dan

42 These were the clans descended from the
sons of Dan:
The Shuhamite clan, named after their
ancestor Shuham.

43 These were the Shuhamite clans of Dan.
Their registered troops numbered 64,400.

The Tribe of Asher

44 These were the clans descended from the
sons of Asher:
The Imnite clan, named after their
ancestor Imnah.
The Ishvite clan, named after their
ancestor Ishvi.
The Beriite clan, named after their
ancestor Beriah.

45 These were the subclans descended from
the Beriites:
The Heberites, named after their ancestor
Heber.
The Malkielites, named after their
ancestor Malkiel.

46 Asher also had a daughter named Serah.

47 These were the clans of Asher. Their regis-
tered troops numbered 53,400.

26:39 As in some Hebrew manuscripts, Samaritan Pentateuch, Greek and Syriac versions, and Latin Vulgate; most Hebrew manuscripts read *Shephupham*. **26:40** As in Samaritan Pentateuch, some Greek manuscripts, and Latin Vulgate; Hebrew lacks *named after their ancestor Ard*.

The Tribe of Naphtali

48 These were the clans descended from the
sons of Naphtali:
The Jahzeelite clan, named after their
ancestor Jahzeel.
The Gunite clan, named after their
ancestor Guni.
49 The Jezerite clan, named after their
ancestor Jezer.
The Shillemite clan, named after their
ancestor Shillem.

50 These were the clans of Naphtali. Their registered troops numbered 45,400.

Results of the Registration

51 In summary, the registered troops of all Israel numbered 601,730.

52 Then the LORD said to Moses, 53 "Divide the land among the tribes, and distribute the grants of land in proportion to the tribes' populations, as indicated by the number of names on the list. 54 Give the larger tribes more land and the smaller tribes less land, each group receiving a grant in proportion to the size of its population. 55 But you must assign the land by lot, and give land to each ancestral tribe according to the number of names on the list. 56 Each grant of land must be assigned by lot among the larger and smaller tribal groups."

The Tribe of Levi

57 This is the record of the Levites who were counted according to their clans:
The Gershonite clan, named after their
ancestor Gershon.
The Kohathite clan, named after their
ancestor Kohath.
The Merarite clan, named after their
ancestor Merari.

58 The Libnites, the Hebronites, the Mahlites, the Mushites, and the Korahites were all subclans of the Levites.

Now Kohath was the ancestor of Amram, 59 and Amram's wife was named Jochebed. She also was a descendant of Levi, born among the Levites in the land of Egypt. Amram and Jochebed became the parents of Aaron, Moses, and their sister, Miriam. 60 To Aaron were born Nadab, Abihu, Eleazar, and Ithamar. 61 But Nadab and Abihu died when they burned before the LORD the wrong kind of fire, different than he had commanded.

62 The men from the Levite clans who were one month old or older numbered 23,000. But the Levites were not included in the registration of the rest of the people of Israel because they were not given an allotment of land when it was divided among the Israelites.

63 So these are the results of the registration of the people of Israel as conducted by Moses and Eleazar the priest on the plains of Moab beside the Jordan River, across from Jericho. 64 Not one person on this list had been among those listed in the previous registration taken by Moses and Aaron in the wilderness of Sinai. 65 For the LORD had said of them, "They will all die in the wilderness." Not one of them survived except Caleb son of Jephunneh and Joshua son of Nun.

CHAPTER 27

The Daughters of Zelophehad

One day a petition was presented by the daughters of Zelophehad—Mahlah, Noah, Hoglah, Milcah, and Tirzah. Their father, Zelophehad, was a descendant of Hepher son of Gilead, son of Makir, son of Manasseh, son of Joseph. 2 These women stood before Moses, Eleazar the priest, the tribal leaders, and the entire community at the entrance of the Tabernacle.* 3 "Our father died in the wilderness," they said. "He was not among Korah's followers, who rebelled against the LORD; he died because of his own sin. But he had no sons. 4 Why should the name of our father disappear from his clan just because he had no sons? Give us property along with the rest of our relatives."

5 So Moses brought their case before the LORD. 6 And the LORD replied to Moses, 7 "The claim of the daughters of Zelophehad is legitimate. You must give them a grant of land along with their father's relatives. Assign them the property that would have been given to their father.

8 "And give the following instructions to the people of Israel: If a man dies and has no son, then give his inheritance to his daughters. 9 And if he has no daughter either, transfer his inheritance to his brothers. 10 If he has no brothers, give his inheritance to his father's brothers. 11 But if his father has no brothers, give his inheritance to the nearest relative in

27:2 Hebrew *the Tent of Meeting*.

his clan. This is a legal requirement for the people of Israel, just as the LORD commanded Moses."

Joshua Chosen to Lead Israel

12 One day the LORD said to Moses, "Climb one of the mountains east of the river,* and look out over the land I have given the people of Israel. 13 After you have seen it, you will die like your brother, Aaron, 14 for you both rebelled against my instructions in the wilderness of Zin. When the people of Israel rebelled, you failed to demonstrate my holiness to them at the waters." (These are the waters of Meribah at Kadesh* in the wilderness of Zin.)

Why do we need leaders? ✱ **Give them someone who will guide them . . . so the community of the LORD will not be like sheep without a shepherd.**
NUMBERS 27:17

15 Then Moses said to the LORD, 16 "O LORD, you are the God who gives breath to all creatures. Please appoint a new man as leader for the community. 17 Give them someone who will guide them wherever they go and will lead them into battle, so the community of the LORD will not be like sheep without a shepherd."

18 The LORD replied, "Take Joshua son of Nun, who has the Spirit in him, and lay your hands on him. 19 Present him to Eleazar the priest before the whole community, and publicly commission him to lead the people. 20 Transfer some of your authority to him so the whole community of Israel will obey him. 21 When direction from the LORD is needed, Joshua will stand before Eleazar the priest, who will use the Urim—one of the sacred lots cast before the LORD—to determine his will. This is how Joshua and the rest of the community of Israel will determine everything they should do."

22 So Moses did as the LORD commanded. He presented Joshua to Eleazar the priest and the whole community. 23 Moses laid his hands on him and commissioned him to lead the people, just as the LORD had commanded through Moses.

CHAPTER 28

The Daily Offerings

The LORD said to Moses, 2 "Give these instructions to the people of Israel: The offerings you present as special gifts are a pleasing aroma to me; they are my food. See to it that they are brought at the appointed times and offered according to my instructions.

3 "Say to the people: This is the special gift you must present to the LORD as your daily burnt offering. You must offer two one-year-old male lambs with no defects. 4 Sacrifice one lamb in the morning and the other in the evening. 5 With each lamb you must offer a grain offering of two quarts* of choice flour mixed with one quart* of pure oil of pressed olives. 6 This is the regular burnt offering instituted at Mount Sinai as a special gift, a pleasing aroma to the LORD. 7 Along with it you must present the proper liquid offering of one quart of alcoholic drink with each lamb, poured out in the Holy Place as an offering to the LORD. 8 Offer the second lamb in the evening with the same grain offering and liquid offering. It, too, is a special gift, a pleasing aroma to the LORD.

The Sabbath Offerings

9 "On the Sabbath day, sacrifice two one-year-old male lambs with no defects. They must be accompanied by a grain offering of four quarts* of choice flour moistened with olive oil, and a liquid offering. 10 This is the burnt offering to be presented each Sabbath day, in addition to the regular burnt offering and its accompanying liquid offering.

The Monthly Offerings

11 "On the first day of each month, present an extra burnt offering to the LORD of two young bulls, one ram, and seven one-year-old male lambs, all with no defects. 12 These must be accompanied by grain offerings of choice flour

27:12 Or *the mountains of Abarim.* **27:14** Hebrew *waters of Meribath-kadesh.* **28:5a** Hebrew *1/10 of an ephah* (2.2 liters); also in 28:13, 21, 29. **28:5b** Hebrew *1/4 of a hin* (1 liter); also in 28:7. **28:9** Hebrew *2/10 of an ephah* (4.4 liters); also in 28:12, 20, 28.

moistened with olive oil—six quarts* with each bull, four quarts with the ram, [13]and two quarts with each lamb. This burnt offering will be a special gift, a pleasing aroma to the LORD. [14]You must also present a liquid offering with each sacrifice: two quarts* of wine for each bull; a third of a gallon* for the ram, and one quart* for each lamb. Present this monthly burnt offering on the first day of each month throughout the year.

[15]"On the first day of each month, you must also offer one male goat for a sin offering to the LORD. This is in addition to the regular burnt offering and its accompanying liquid offering.

Offerings for the Passover

[16]"On the fourteenth day of the first month,* you must celebrate the LORD's Passover. [17]On the following day—the fifteenth day of the month—a joyous, seven-day festival will begin, but no bread made with yeast may be eaten. [18]The first day of the festival will be an official day for holy assembly, and no ordinary work may be done on that day. [19]As a special gift you must present a burnt offering to the LORD—two young bulls, one ram, and seven one-year-old male lambs, all with no defects. [20]These will be accompanied by grain offerings of choice flour moistened with olive oil—six quarts with each bull, four quarts with the ram, [21]and two quarts with each of the seven lambs. [22]You must also offer a male goat as a sin offering to purify yourselves and make yourselves right with the LORD.* [23]Present these offerings in addition to your regular morning burnt offering. [24]On each of the seven days of the festival, this is how you must prepare the food offering that is presented as a special gift, a pleasing aroma to the LORD. These will be offered in addition to the regular burnt offerings and liquid offerings. [25]The seventh day of the festival will be another official day for holy assembly, and no ordinary work may be done on that day.

Offerings for the Festival of Harvest

[26]"At the Festival of Harvest,* when you present the first of your new grain to the LORD, you must call an official day for holy assembly, and you may do no ordinary work on that day. [27]Present a special burnt offering on that day as a pleasing aroma to the LORD. It will consist of two young bulls, one ram, and seven one-year-old male lambs. [28]These will be accompanied by grain offerings of choice flour moistened with olive oil—six quarts with each bull, four quarts with the ram, [29]and two quarts with each of the seven lambs. [30]Also, offer one male goat to purify yourselves and make yourselves right with the LORD. [31]Prepare these special burnt offerings, along with their liquid offerings, in addition to the regular burnt offering and its accompanying grain offering. Be sure that all the animals you sacrifice have no defects.

CHAPTER 29

Offerings for the Festival of Trumpets

"Celebrate the Festival of Trumpets each year on the first day of the appointed month in early autumn.* You must call an official day for holy assembly, and you may do no ordinary work. [2]On that day you must present a burnt offering as a pleasing aroma to the LORD. It will consist of one young bull, one ram, and seven one-year-old male lambs, all with no defects. [3]These must be accompanied by grain offerings of choice flour moistened with olive oil—six quarts* with the bull, four quarts* with the ram, [4]and two quarts* with each of the seven lambs. [5]In addition, you must sacrifice a male goat as a sin offering to purify yourselves and make yourselves right with the LORD.* [6]These special sacrifices are in addition to your regular monthly and daily burnt offerings, and they must be given with their prescribed grain offerings and liquid offerings. These offerings are given as a special gift to the LORD, a pleasing aroma to him.

Offerings for the Day of Atonement

[7]"Ten days later, on the tenth day of the same month,* you must call another holy assembly. On that day, the Day of Atonement, the people

28:12 Hebrew *3/10 of an ephah* [6.6 liters]; also in 28:20, 28. **28:14a** Hebrew *1/2 of a hin* [2 liters]. **28:14b** Hebrew *1/3 of a hin* [1.3 liters]. **28:14c** Hebrew *1/4 of a hin* [1 liter]. **28:16** This day in the ancient Hebrew lunar calendar occurred in late March, April, or early May. **28:22** Or *to make atonement for yourselves;* also in 28:30. **28:26** Hebrew *Festival of Weeks.* This was later called the Festival of Pentecost (see Acts 2:1). It is celebrated today as Shavuot (or Shabuoth). **29:1** Hebrew *the first day of the seventh month.* This day in the ancient Hebrew lunar calendar occurred in September or October. This festival is celebrated today as Rosh Hashanah, the Jewish new year. **29:3a** Hebrew *3/10 of an ephah* [6.6 liters]; also in 29:9, 14. **29:3b** Hebrew *2/10 of an ephah* [4.4 liters]; also in 29:9, 14. **29:4** Hebrew *1/10 of an ephah* [2.2 liters]; also in 29:10, 15. **29:5** Or *to make atonement for yourselves.* **29:7** Hebrew *On the tenth day of the seventh month;* see 29:1 and the note there. This day in the ancient Hebrew lunar calendar occurred in September or October. It is celebrated today as Yom Kippur.

must go without food and must do no ordinary work. [8]You must present a burnt offering as a pleasing aroma to the LORD. It will consist of one young bull, one ram, and seven one-year-old male lambs, all with no defects. [9]These offerings must be accompanied by the prescribed grain offerings of choice flour moistened with olive oil—six quarts of choice flour with the bull, four quarts of choice flour with the ram, [10]and two quarts of choice flour with each of the seven lambs. [11]You must also sacrifice one male goat for a sin offering. This is in addition to the sin offering of atonement and the regular daily burnt offering with its grain offering, and their accompanying liquid offerings.

Offerings for the Festival of Shelters

[12]"Five days later, on the fifteenth day of the same month,* you must call another holy assembly of all the people, and you may do no ordinary work on that day. It is the beginning of the Festival of Shelters,* a seven-day festival to the LORD. [13]On the first day of the festival, you must present a burnt offering as a special gift, a pleasing aroma to the LORD. It will consist of thirteen young bulls, two rams, and fourteen one-year-old male lambs, all with no defects. [14]Each of these offerings must be accompanied by a grain offering of choice flour moistened with olive oil—six quarts for each of the thirteen bulls, four quarts for each of the two rams, [15]and two quarts for each of the fourteen lambs. [16]You must also sacrifice a male goat as a sin offering, in addition to the regular burnt offering with its accompanying grain offering and liquid offering.

[17]"On the second day of this seven-day festival, sacrifice twelve young bulls, two rams, and fourteen one-year-old male lambs, all with no defects. [18]Each of these offerings of bulls, rams, and lambs must be accompanied by its prescribed grain offering and liquid offering. [19]You must also sacrifice a male goat as a sin offering, in addition to the regular burnt offering with its accompanying grain offering and liquid offering.

[20]"On the third day of the festival, sacrifice eleven young bulls, two rams, and fourteen one-year-old male lambs, all with no defects. [21]Each of these offerings of bulls, rams, and lambs must be accompanied by its prescribed grain offering and liquid offering. [22]You must also sacrifice a male goat as a sin offering, in addition to the regular burnt offering with its accompanying grain offering and liquid offering.

[23]"On the fourth day of the festival, sacrifice ten young bulls, two rams, and fourteen one-year-old male lambs, all with no defects. [24]Each of these offerings of bulls, rams, and lambs must be accompanied by its prescribed grain offering and liquid offering. [25]You must also sacrifice a male goat as a sin offering, in addition to the regular burnt offering with its accompanying grain offering and liquid offering.

[26]"On the fifth day of the festival, sacrifice nine young bulls, two rams, and fourteen one-year-old male lambs, all with no defects. [27]Each of these offerings of bulls, rams, and lambs must be accompanied by its prescribed grain offering and liquid offering. [28]You must also sacrifice a male goat as a sin offering, in addition to the regular burnt offering with its accompanying grain offering and liquid offering.

[29]"On the sixth day of the festival, sacrifice eight young bulls, two rams, and fourteen one-year-old male lambs, all with no defects. [30]Each of these offerings of bulls, rams, and lambs must be accompanied by its prescribed grain offering and liquid offering. [31]You must also sacrifice a male goat as a sin offering, in addition to the regular burnt offering with its accompanying grain offering and liquid offering.

[32]"On the seventh day of the festival, sacrifice seven young bulls, two rams, and fourteen one-year-old male lambs, all with no defects. [33]Each of these offerings of bulls, rams, and lambs must be accompanied by its prescribed grain offering and liquid offering. [34]You must also sacrifice one male goat as a sin offering, in addition to the regular burnt offering with its accompanying grain offering and liquid offering.

[35]"On the eighth day of the festival, proclaim another holy day. You must do no ordinary work on that day. [36]You must present

29:12a Hebrew *On the fifteenth day of the seventh month;* see 29:1, 7 and the notes there. This day in the ancient Hebrew lunar calendar occurred in late September, October, or early November. **29:12b** Or *Festival of Booths,* or *Festival of Tabernacles.* This was earlier called the Festival of the Final Harvest or Festival of Ingathering (see Exod 23:16b). It is celebrated today as Sukkot (or Succoth).

a burnt offering as a special gift, a pleasing aroma to the LORD. It will consist of one young bull, one ram, and seven one-year-old male lambs, all with no defects. [37]Each of these offerings must be accompanied by its prescribed grain offering and liquid offering. [38]You must also sacrifice one male goat as a sin offering, in addition to the regular burnt offering with its accompanying grain offering and liquid offering.

[39]"You must present these offerings to the LORD at your annual festivals. These are in addition to the sacrifices and offerings you present in connection with vows, or as voluntary offerings, burnt offerings, grain offerings, liquid offerings, or peace offerings."

[40]*So Moses gave all of these instructions to the people of Israel as the LORD had commanded him.

CHAPTER 30

Laws concerning Vows

[1]*Then Moses summoned the leaders of the tribes of Israel and told them, "This is what the LORD has commanded: [2]A man who makes a vow to the LORD or makes a pledge under oath must never break it. He must do exactly what he said he would do.

[3]"If a young woman makes a vow to the LORD or a pledge under oath while she is still living at her father's home, [4]and her father hears of the vow or pledge and does not object to it, then all her vows and pledges will stand. [5]But if her father refuses to let her fulfill the vow or pledge on the day he hears of it, then all her vows and pledges will become invalid. The LORD will forgive her because her father would not let her fulfill them.

[6]"Now suppose a young woman makes a vow or binds herself with an impulsive pledge and later marries. [7]If her husband learns of her vow or pledge and does not object on the day he hears of it, her vows and pledges will stand. [8]But if her husband refuses to accept her vow or impulsive pledge on the day he hears of it, he nullifies her commitments, and the LORD will forgive her. [9]If, however, a woman is a widow or is divorced, she must fulfill all her vows and pledges.

[10]"But suppose a woman is married and living in her husband's home when she makes a vow or binds herself with a pledge. [11]If her husband hears of it and does not object to it, her vow or pledge will stand. [12]But if her husband refuses to accept it on the day he hears of it, her vow or pledge will be nullified, and the LORD will forgive her. [13]So her husband may either confirm or nullify any vows or pledges she makes to deny herself. [14]But if he does not object on the day he hears of it, then he is agreeing to all her vows and pledges. [15]If he waits more than a day and then tries to nullify a vow or pledge, he will be punished for her guilt."

[16]These are the regulations the LORD gave Moses concerning relationships between a man and his wife, and between a father and a young daughter who still lives at home.

CHAPTER 31

Conquest of the Midianites

Then the LORD said to Moses, [2]"On behalf of the people of Israel, take revenge on the Midianites for leading them into idolatry. After that, you will die and join your ancestors."

[3]So Moses said to the people, "Choose some men, and arm them to fight the LORD's war of revenge against Midian. [4]From each tribe of Israel, send 1,000 men into battle." [5]So they chose 1,000 men from each tribe of Israel, a total of 12,000 men armed for battle. [6]Then Moses sent them out, 1,000 men from each tribe, and Phinehas son of Eleazar the priest led them into battle. They carried along the holy objects of the sanctuary and the trumpets for sounding the charge. [7]They attacked Midian as the LORD had commanded Moses, and they killed all the men. [8]All five of the Midianite kings—Evi, Rekem, Zur, Hur, and Reba—died in the battle. They also killed Balaam son of Beor with the sword.

[9]Then the Israelite army captured the Midianite women and children and seized their cattle and flocks and all their wealth as plunder. [10]They burned all the towns and villages where the Midianites had lived. [11]After they had gathered the plunder and captives, both people and animals, [12]they brought them all to Moses and Eleazar the priest, and to the whole community of Israel, which was camped on the plains of Moab beside the Jordan River, across from Jericho. [13]Moses, Elea-

29:40 Verse 29:40 is numbered 30:1 in Hebrew text. **30:1** Verses 30:1-16 are numbered 30:2-17 in Hebrew text.

zar the priest, and all the leaders of the community went to meet them outside the camp.
14 But Moses was furious with all the generals
and captains* who had returned from the
battle.
15 "Why have you let all the women live?"
he demanded. 16 "These are the very ones who
followed Balaam's advice and caused the people of Israel to rebel against the LORD at
Mount Peor. They are the ones who caused
the plague to strike the LORD's people. 17 So
kill all the boys and all the women who have
had intercourse with a man. 18 Only the young
girls who are virgins may live; you may keep
them for yourselves. 19 And all of you who
have killed anyone or touched a dead body
must stay outside the camp for seven days.
You must purify yourselves and your captives
on the third and seventh days. 20 Purify all
your clothing, too, and everything made of
leather, goat hair, or wood."
21 Then Eleazar the priest said to the men
who were in the battle, "The LORD has given
Moses this legal requirement: 22 Anything
made of gold, silver, bronze, iron, tin, or
lead—23 that is, all metals that do not burn—
must be passed through fire in order to be
made ceremonially pure. These metal objects must then be further purified with the
water of purification. But everything that
burns must be purified by the water alone.
24 On the seventh day you must wash your
clothes and be purified. Then you may return to the camp."

Division of the Plunder

25 And the LORD said to Moses, 26 "You and Eleazar the priest and the family leaders of
each tribe are to make a list of all the plunder
taken in the battle, including the people and
animals. 27 Then divide the plunder into two
parts, and give half to the men who fought
the battle and half to the rest of the people.
28 From the army's portion, first give the LORD
his share of the plunder—one of every 500 of
the prisoners and of the cattle, donkeys,
sheep, and goats. 29 Give this share of the
army's half to Eleazar the priest as an offering to the LORD. 30 From the half that belongs
to the people of Israel, take one of every fifty
of the prisoners and of the cattle, donkeys,
sheep, goats, and other animals. Give this
share to the Levites, who are in charge of
maintaining the LORD's Tabernacle." 31 So
Moses and Eleazar the priest did as the LORD
commanded Moses.
32 The plunder remaining from everything
the fighting men had taken totaled 675,000
sheep and goats, 33 72,000 cattle, 34 61,000
donkeys, 35 and 32,000 virgin girls.
36 Half of the plunder was given to the
fighting men. It totaled 337,500 sheep and
goats, 37 of which 675 were the LORD's share;
38 36,000 cattle, of which 72 were the LORD's
share; 39 30,500 donkeys, of which 61 were
the LORD's share; 40 and 16,000 virgin girls,
of whom 32 were the LORD's share. 41 Moses
gave all the LORD's share to Eleazar the priest,
just as the LORD had directed him.
42 Half of the plunder belonged to the people of Israel, and Moses separated it from the
half belonging to the fighting men. 43 It totaled 337,500 sheep and goats, 44 36,000
cattle, 45 30,500 donkeys, 46 and 16,000 virgin
girls. 47 From the half-share given to the people, Moses took one of every fifty prisoners
and animals and gave them to the Levites,
who maintained the LORD's Tabernacle. All
this was done as the LORD had commanded
Moses.
48 Then all the generals and captains came
to Moses 49 and said, "We, your servants, have
accounted for all the men who went out to
battle under our command; not one of us is
missing! 50 So we are presenting the items of
gold we captured as an offering to the LORD
from our share of the plunder—armbands,
bracelets, rings, earrings, and necklaces. This
will purify our lives before the LORD and
make us right with him.*"
51 So Moses and Eleazar the priest received
the gold from all the military commanders—
all kinds of jewelry and crafted objects. 52 In all,
the gold that the generals and captains presented as a gift to the LORD weighed about
420 pounds.* 53 All the fighting men had taken
some of the plunder for themselves. 54 So
Moses and Eleazar the priest accepted the gifts
from the generals and captains and brought
the gold to the Tabernacle* as a reminder to
the LORD that the people of Israel belong to
him.

31:14 Hebrew *the commanders of thousands, and the commanders of hundreds;* also in 31:48, 52, 54. **31:50** Or *will make atonement for our lives before the LORD.* **31:52** Hebrew *16,750 shekels* [191 kilograms]. **31:54** Hebrew *the Tent of Meeting.*

Quitting Time

Dimitri and his younger brother were each responsible for raking one area of the yard. Dimitri felt lucky—his area had only two trees, but his brother's part had four trees. They started at the same time, but since Dimitri was older and had fewer leaves, he finished quickly. *Quitting time,* he thought. *Now I can shoot some hoops with the guys.* Then Dimitri saw his brother resting. He had raked less than half of his area. Poor guy—he had a lot of leaves left.

What should Dimitri do? Read Numbers 32:16-19.

CHAPTER 32

The Tribes East of the Jordan

The tribes of Reuben and Gad owned vast numbers of livestock. So when they saw that the lands of Jazer and Gilead were ideally suited for their flocks and herds, [2]they came to Moses, Eleazar the priest, and the other leaders of the community. They said, [3]"Notice the towns of Ataroth, Dibon, Jazer, Nimrah, Heshbon, Elealeh, Sibmah,* Nebo, and Beon. [4]The LORD has conquered this whole area for the community of Israel, and it is ideally suited for all our livestock. [5]If we have found favor with you, please let us have this land as our property instead of giving us land across the Jordan River."

[6]"Do you intend to stay here while your brothers go across and do all the fighting?" Moses asked the men of Gad and Reuben. [7]"Why do you want to discourage the rest of the people of Israel from going across to the land the LORD has given them? [8]Your ancestors did the same thing when I sent them from Kadesh-barnea to explore the land. [9]After they went up to the valley of Eshcol and explored the land, they discouraged the people of Israel from entering the land the LORD was giving them. [10]Then the LORD was very angry with them, and he vowed, [11]'Of all those I rescued from Egypt, no one who is twenty years old or older will ever see the land I swore to give to Abraham, Isaac, and Jacob, for they have not obeyed me wholeheartedly. [12]The only exceptions are Caleb son of Jephunneh the Kenizzite and Joshua son of Nun, for they have wholeheartedly followed the LORD.'

[13]"The LORD was angry with Israel and made them wander in the wilderness for forty years until the entire generation that sinned in the LORD's sight had died. [14]But here you are, a brood of sinners, doing exactly the same thing! You are making the LORD even angrier with Israel. [15]If you turn away from him like this and he abandons them again in the wilderness, you will be responsible for destroying this entire nation!"

[16]But they approached Moses and said, "We simply want to build pens for our livestock and fortified towns for our wives and children. [17]Then we will arm ourselves and lead our fellow Israelites into battle until we have brought them safely to their land. Meanwhile, our families will stay in the fortified towns we build here, so they will be safe from any attacks by the local people. [18]We will not return to our homes until all the people of Israel have received their portions of land. [19]But we do not claim any of the land on the other side of the Jordan. We would rather live

32:3 As in Samaritan Pentateuch and Greek version (see also 32:38); Hebrew reads *Sebam.*

here on the east side and accept this as our grant of land."

[20]Then Moses said, "If you keep your word and arm yourselves for the LORD's battles, [21]and if your troops cross the Jordan and keep fighting until the LORD has driven out his enemies, [22]then you may return when the LORD has conquered the land. You will have fulfilled your duty to the LORD and to the rest of the people of Israel. And the land on the east side of the Jordan will be your property from the LORD. [23]But if you fail to keep your word, then you will have sinned against the LORD, and you may be sure that your sin will find you out. [24]Go ahead and build towns for your families and pens for your flocks, but do everything you have promised."

[25]Then the men of Gad and Reuben replied, "We, your servants, will follow your instructions exactly. [26]Our children, wives, flocks, and cattle will stay here in the towns of Gilead. [27]But all who are able to bear arms will cross over to fight for the LORD, just as you have said."

[28]So Moses gave orders to Eleazar the priest, Joshua son of Nun, and the leaders of the clans of Israel. [29]He said, "The men of Gad and Reuben who are armed for battle must cross the Jordan with you to fight for the LORD. If they do, give them the land of Gilead as their property when the land is conquered. [30]But if they refuse to arm themselves and cross over with you, then they must accept land with the rest of you in the land of Canaan."

[31]The tribes of Gad and Reuben said again, "We are your servants, and we will do as the LORD has commanded! [32]We will cross the Jordan into Canaan fully armed to fight for the LORD, but our property will be here on this side of the Jordan."

[33]So Moses assigned land to the tribes of Gad, Reuben, and half the tribe of Manasseh son of Joseph. He gave them the territory of King Sihon of the Amorites and the land of King Og of Bashan—the whole land with its cities and surrounding lands.

[34]The descendants of Gad built the towns of Dibon, Ataroth, Aroer, [35]Atroth-shophan, Jazer, Jogbehah, [36]Beth-nimrah, and Beth-haran. These were all fortified towns with pens for their flocks.

[37]The descendants of Reuben built the towns of Heshbon, Elealeh, Kiriathaim, [38]Nebo, Baal-meon, and Sibmah. They changed the names of some of the towns they conquered and rebuilt.

[39]Then the descendants of Makir of the tribe of Manasseh went to Gilead and conquered it, and they drove out the Amorites living there. [40]So Moses gave Gilead to the Makirites, descendants of Manasseh, and they settled there. [41]The people of Jair, another clan of the tribe of Manasseh, captured many of the towns in Gilead and changed the name of that region to the Towns of Jair.* [42]Meanwhile, a man named Nobah captured the town of Kenath and its surrounding villages, and he renamed that area Nobah after himself.

CHAPTER 33

Remembering Israel's Journey

This is the route the Israelites followed as they marched out of Egypt under the leadership of Moses and Aaron. [2]At the LORD's direction, Moses kept a written record of their progress. These are the stages of their march, identified by the different places where they stopped along the way.

[3]They set out from the city of Rameses in early spring—on the fifteenth day of the first month*—on the morning after the first Passover celebration. The people of Israel left defiantly, in full view of all the Egyptians. [4]Meanwhile, the Egyptians were burying all their firstborn sons, whom the LORD had killed the night before. The LORD had defeated the gods of Egypt that night with great acts of judgment!

[5]After leaving Rameses, the Israelites set up camp at Succoth.
[6]Then they left Succoth and camped at Etham on the edge of the wilderness.
[7]They left Etham and turned back toward Pi-hahiroth, opposite Baal-zephon, and camped near Migdol.
[8]They left Pi-hahiroth and crossed the Red Sea* into the wilderness beyond. Then they traveled for three days into the Etham wilderness and camped at Marah.

32:41 Hebrew *Havvoth-jair*. **33:3** This day in the ancient Hebrew lunar calendar occurred in late March, April, or early May.
33:8 Hebrew *the sea*.

9 They left Marah and camped at Elim, where
there were twelve springs of water and
seventy palm trees.
10 They left Elim and camped beside the Red
Sea.*
11 They left the Red Sea and camped in the
wilderness of Sin.*
12 They left the wilderness of Sin and
camped at Dophkah.
13 They left Dophkah and camped at Alush.
14 They left Alush and camped at Rephidim,
where there was no water for the people
to drink.
15 They left Rephidim and camped in the
wilderness of Sinai.
16 They left the wilderness of Sinai and
camped at Kibroth-hattaavah.
17 They left Kibroth-hattaavah and camped
at Hazeroth.
18 They left Hazeroth and camped at
Rithmah.
19 They left Rithmah and camped at
Rimmon-perez.
20 They left Rimmon-perez and camped at
Libnah.
21 They left Libnah and camped at Rissah.
22 They left Rissah and camped at
Kehelathah.
23 They left Kehelathah and camped at
Mount Shepher.
24 They left Mount Shepher and camped at
Haradah.
25 They left Haradah and camped at
Makheloth.
26 They left Makheloth and camped at
Tahath.
27 They left Tahath and camped at Terah.
28 They left Terah and camped at Mithcah.
29 They left Mithcah and camped at
Hashmonah.
30 They left Hashmonah and camped at
Moseroth.
31 They left Moseroth and camped at Bene-
jaakan.
32 They left Bene-jaakan and camped at Hor-
haggidgad.
33 They left Hor-haggidgad and camped at
Jotbathah.
34 They left Jotbathah and camped at
Abronah.
35 They left Abronah and camped at Ezion-
geber.
36 They left Ezion-geber and camped at
Kadesh in the wilderness of Zin.
37 They left Kadesh and camped at Mount
Hor, at the border of Edom. 38 While
they were at the foot of Mount Hor,
Aaron the priest was directed by the
LORD to go up the mountain, and there
he died. This happened in midsummer,
on the first day of the fifth month*
of the fortieth year after Israel's
departure from Egypt. 39 Aaron was
123 years old when he died there on
Mount Hor.
40 At that time the Canaanite king of Arad,
who lived in the Negev in the land of
Canaan, heard that the people of Israel
were approaching his land.
41 Meanwhile, the Israelites left Mount Hor
and camped at Zalmonah.
42 Then they left Zalmonah and camped at
Punon.
43 They left Punon and camped at Oboth.
44 They left Oboth and camped at Iye-abarim
on the border of Moab.
45 They left Iye-abarim* and camped at
Dibon-gad.
46 They left Dibon-gad and camped at
Almon-diblathaim.
47 They left Almon-diblathaim and camped
in the mountains east of the river,* near
Mount Nebo.
48 They left the mountains east of the river
and camped on the plains of Moab beside
the Jordan River, across from Jericho.
49 Along the Jordan River they camped
from Beth-jeshimoth as far as the
meadows of Acacia* on the plains of
Moab.

50 While they were camped near the Jordan
River on the plains of Moab opposite Jericho,
the LORD said to Moses, 51 "Give the following
instructions to the people of Israel: When you
cross the Jordan River into the land of Ca-
naan, 52 you must drive out all the people liv-
ing there. You must destroy all their carved
and molten images and demolish all their
pagan shrines. 53 Take possession of the land
and settle in it, because I have given it to you

33:10 Hebrew *sea of reeds;* also in 33:11. **33:11** The geographical name *Sin* is related to *Sinai* and should not be confused with the English word *sin.* **33:38** This day in the ancient Hebrew lunar calendar occurred in July or August. **33:45** As in 33:44; Hebrew reads *Iyim,* another name for Iye-abarim. **33:47** Or *the mountains of Abarim;* also in 33:48. **33:49** Hebrew *as far as Abel-shittim.*

to occupy. 54You must distribute the land among the clans by sacred lot and in proportion to their size. A larger portion of land will be allotted to each of the larger clans, and a smaller portion will be allotted to each of the smaller clans. The decision of the sacred lot is final. In this way, the portions of land will be divided among your ancestral tribes. 55But if you fail to drive out the people who live in the land, those who remain will be like splinters in your eyes and thorns in your sides. They will harass you in the land where you live. 56And I will do to you what I had planned to do to them."

CHAPTER 34

Boundaries of the Land

Then the LORD said to Moses, 2"Give these instructions to the Israelites: When you come into the land of Canaan, which I am giving you as your special possession, these will be the boundaries. 3The southern portion of your country will extend from the wilderness of Zin, along the edge of Edom. The southern boundary will begin on the east at the Dead Sea.* 4It will then run south past Scorpion Pass* in the direction of Zin. Its southernmost point will be Kadesh-barnea, from which it will go to Hazar-addar, and on to Azmon. 5From Azmon the boundary will turn toward the Brook of Egypt and end at the Mediterranean Sea.*

6"Your western boundary will be the coastline of the Mediterranean Sea.

7"Your northern boundary will begin at the Mediterranean Sea and run east to Mount Hor, 8then to Lebo-hamath, and on through Zedad 9and Ziphron to Hazar-enan. This will be your northern boundary.

10"The eastern boundary will start at Hazar-enan and run south to Shepham, 11then down to Riblah on the east side of Ain. From there the boundary will run down along the eastern edge of the Sea of Galilee,* 12and then along the Jordan River to the Dead Sea. These are the boundaries of your land."

13Then Moses told the Israelites, "This territory is the homeland you are to divide among yourselves by sacred lot. The LORD has commanded that the land be divided among the nine and a half remaining tribes. 14The families of the tribes of Reuben, Gad, and half the tribe of Manasseh have already received their grants of land 15on the east side of the Jordan River, across from Jericho toward the sunrise."

Leaders to Divide the Land

16And the LORD said to Moses, 17"Eleazar the priest and Joshua son of Nun are the men designated to divide the grants of land among the people. 18Enlist one leader from each tribe to help them with the task. 19These are the tribes and the names of the leaders:

	Tribe	*Leader*
	Judah	Caleb son of Jephunneh
20	Simeon	Shemuel son of Ammihud
21	Benjamin	Elidad son of Kislon
22	Dan	Bukki son of Jogli
23	Manasseh son of Joseph	Hanniel son of Ephod

34:3 Hebrew *Salt Sea;* also in 34:12. **34:4** Or *the ascent of Akrabbim.* **34:5** Hebrew *the sea;* also in 34:6, 7. **34:11** Hebrew *Sea of Kinnereth.*

24 Ephraim son of Joseph . . . . . Kemuel son of Shiphtan
25 Zebulun . . . . . Elizaphan son of Parnach
26 Issachar . . . . . Paltiel son of Azzan
27 Asher . . . . . Ahihud son of Shelomi
28 Naphtali . . . . . Pedahel son of Ammihud

29 These are the men the LORD has appointed to divide the grants of land in Canaan among the Israelites."

CHAPTER 35

Towns for the Levites

While Israel was camped beside the Jordan on the plains of Moab across from Jericho, the LORD said to Moses, 2 "Command the people of Israel to give to the Levites from their property certain towns to live in, along with the surrounding pasturelands. 3 These towns will be for the Levites to live in, and the surrounding lands will provide pasture for their cattle, flocks, and other livestock. 4 The pastureland assigned to the Levites around these towns will extend 1,500 feet* from the town walls in every direction. 5 Measure off 3,000 feet* outside the town walls in every direction—east, south, west, north—with the town at the center. This area will serve as the larger pastureland for the towns.

6 "Six of the towns you give the Levites will be cities of refuge, where a person who has accidentally killed someone can flee for safety. In addition, give them forty-two other towns. 7 In all, forty-eight towns with the surrounding pastureland will be given to the Levites. 8 These towns will come from the property of the people of Israel. The larger tribes will give more towns to the Levites, while the smaller tribes will give fewer. Each tribe will give property in proportion to the size of its land."

Cities of Refuge

9 The LORD said to Moses, 10 "Give the following instructions to the people of Israel.

"When you cross the Jordan into the land of Canaan, 11 designate cities of refuge to which people can flee if they have killed someone accidentally. 12 These cities will be places of protection from a dead person's relatives who want to avenge the death. The slayer must not be put to death before being tried by the community. 13 Designate six cities of refuge for yourselves, 14 three on the east side of the Jordan River and three on the west in the land of Canaan. 15 These cities are for the protection of Israelites, foreigners living among you, and traveling merchants. Anyone who accidentally kills someone may flee there for safety.

16 "But if someone strikes and kills another person with a piece of iron, it is murder, and the murderer must be executed. 17 Or if someone with a stone in his hand strikes and kills another person, it is murder, and the murderer must be put to death. 18 Or if someone strikes and kills another person with a wooden object, it is murder, and the murderer must be put to death. 19 The victim's nearest relative is responsible for putting the murderer to death. When they meet, the avenger must put the murderer to death. 20 So if someone hates another person and pushes him or throws a dangerous object at him and he dies, it is murder. 21 Or if someone hates another person and hits him with a fist and he dies, it is murder. In such cases, the avenger must put the murderer to death when they meet.

22 "But suppose someone pushes another person without having shown previous hostility, or throws something that unintentionally hits another person, 23 or accidentally drops a huge stone on someone, though they were not enemies, and the person dies. 24 If this should happen, the community must follow these regulations in making a judgment between the slayer and the avenger, the victim's nearest relative: 25 The community must protect the slayer from the avenger and must escort the slayer back to live in the city of refuge to which he fled. There he must remain until the death of the high priest, who was anointed with the sacred oil.

26 "But if the slayer ever leaves the limits of the city of refuge, 27 and the avenger finds him outside the city and kills him, it will not be considered murder. 28 The slayer should have stayed inside the city of refuge until the death of the high priest. But after the death of the high priest, the slayer may return to his own property. 29 These are legal requirements for you to observe from generation to generation, wherever you may live.

35:4 Hebrew *1,000 cubits* [460 meters]. 35:5 Hebrew *2,000 cubits* [920 meters].

30"All murderers must be put to death, but only if evidence is presented by more than one witness. No one may be put to death on the testimony of only one witness. 31Also, you must never accept a ransom payment for the life of someone judged guilty of murder and subject to execution; murderers must always be put to death. 32And never accept a ransom payment from someone who has fled to a city of refuge, allowing a slayer to return to his property before the death of the high priest. 33This will ensure that the land where you live will not be polluted, for murder pollutes the land. And no sacrifice except the execution of the murderer can purify the land from murder.* 34You must not defile the land where you live, for I live there myself. I am the LORD, who lives among the people of Israel."

CHAPTER 36

Women Who Inherit Property

Then the heads of the clans of Gilead—descendants of Makir, son of Manasseh, son of Joseph—came to Moses and the family leaders of Israel with a petition. 2They said, "Sir, the LORD instructed you to divide the land by sacred lot among the people of Israel. You were told by the LORD to give the grant of land owned by our brother Zelophehad to his daughters. 3But if they marry men from another tribe, their grants of land will go with them to the tribe into which they marry. In this way, the total area of our tribal land will be reduced. 4Then when the Year of Jubilee comes, their portion of land will be added to that of the new tribe, causing it to be lost forever to our ancestral tribe."

5So Moses gave the Israelites this command from the LORD: "The claim of the men of the tribe of Joseph is legitimate. 6This is what the LORD commands concerning the daughters of Zelophehad: Let them marry anyone they like, as long as it is within their own ancestral tribe. 7None of the territorial land may pass from tribe to tribe, for all the land given to each tribe must remain within the tribe to which it was first allotted. 8The daughters throughout the tribes of Israel who are in line to inherit property must marry within their tribe, so that all the Israelites will keep their ancestral property. 9No grant of land may pass from one tribe to another; each tribe of Israel must keep its allotted portion of land."

10The daughters of Zelophehad did as the LORD commanded Moses. 11Mahlah, Tirzah, Hoglah, Milcah, and Noah all married cousins on their father's side. 12They married into the clans of Manasseh son of Joseph. Thus, their inheritance of land remained within their ancestral tribe.

13These are the commands and regulations that the LORD gave to the people of Israel through Moses while they were camped on the plains of Moab beside the Jordan River across from Jericho.

35:33 Or *can make atonement for murder.*

Deuteronomy

WHO
Moses, Joshua, and the Israelites.

WHERE
The east side of the Jordan River.

WHEN
Moses probably wrote this book around 1407 BC when God's people were close to the Promised Land.

WHY
To remind the nation of Israel what God had done for them, so they would keep their promise to obey him.

The LORD your God is indeed God. He is the faithful God.
DEUTERONOMY 7:9

When someone makes a promise, you expect that person to keep his or her word. If that doesn't happen, you are disappointed. God promised the people of Israel that he would take care of them. Israel promised to worship only God. Moses reminded his people that God had kept his promise. Would the people keep theirs?

Joseph dies — 1805 BC
Exodus from Egypt — 1446 BC
Ten Commandments given — 1445 BC
Moses' death — 1406 BC
Judges begin to rule — 1375 BC

God always keeps his promises. Do you keep your promises to him?

CHAPTER 1

Introduction to Moses' First Address

These are the words that Moses spoke to all the people of Israel while they were in the wilderness east of the Jordan River. They were camped in the Jordan Valley* near Suph, between Paran on one side and Tophel, Laban, Hazeroth, and Di-zahab on the other.

2 Normally it takes only eleven days to travel from Mount Sinai* to Kadesh-barnea, going by way of Mount Seir. 3 But forty years after the Israelites left Egypt, on the first day of the

1:1 Hebrew *the Arabah;* also in 1:7. **1:2** Hebrew *Horeb,* another name for Sinai; also in 1:6, 19.

The Class Picnic

Nathan was in charge of the class picnic. He announced a meeting after school for anyone who wanted to help. The kids quickly decided on food, games, and the date. When they talked about a place, Brett, who lived in the most expensive house in the neighborhood, offered, "We can have it at my house. I have a pool, deck, screened-in porch, and a huge yard." Rachel had another suggestion for the location. But the group loved Brett's idea and didn't even want to hear Rachel's suggestion.

Should Nathan listen to Rachel or ignore her? Read Deuteronomy 1:16-17.

eleventh month,* Moses addressed the people of Israel, telling them everything the LORD had commanded him to say. 4This took place after he had defeated King Sihon of the Amorites, who had ruled in Heshbon, and King Og of Bashan, who had ruled in Ashtaroth and Edrei.

5While the Israelites were in the land of Moab east of the Jordan River, Moses carefully explained the LORD's instructions as follows.

The Command to Leave Sinai

6"When we were at Mount Sinai, the LORD our God said to us, 'You have stayed at this mountain long enough. 7It is time to break camp and move on. Go to the hill country of the Amorites and to all the neighboring regions—the Jordan Valley, the hill country, the western foothills,* the Negev, and the coastal plain. Go to the land of the Canaanites and to Lebanon, and all the way to the great Euphrates River. 8Look, I am giving all this land to you! Go in and occupy it, for it is the land the LORD swore to give to your ancestors Abraham, Isaac, and Jacob, and to all their descendants.'"

Moses Appoints Leaders from Each Tribe

9Moses continued, "At that time I told you, 'You are too great a burden for me to carry all by myself. 10The LORD your God has increased your population, making you as numerous as the stars! 11And may the LORD, the God of your ancestors, multiply you a thousand times more and bless you as he promised! 12But you are such a heavy load to carry! How can I deal with all your problems and bickering? 13Choose some well-respected men from each tribe who are known for their wisdom and understanding, and I will appoint them as your leaders.'

14"Then you responded, 'Your plan is a good one.' 15So I took the wise and respected men you had selected from your tribes and appointed them to serve as judges and officials over you. Some were responsible for a thousand people, some for a hundred, some for fifty, and some for ten.

16"At that time I instructed the judges, 'You must hear the cases of your fellow Israelites and the foreigners living among you. Be perfectly fair in your decisions 17and impartial in your judgments. Hear the cases of those who are poor as well as those who are rich. Don't be afraid of anyone's anger, for the decision you make is God's decision. Bring me any cases

1:3 Hebrew *In the fortieth year, on the first day of the eleventh month.* This day in the ancient Hebrew lunar calendar occurred in January or February. **1:7** Hebrew *the Shephelah.*

that are too difficult for you, and I will handle them.'

18"At that time I gave you instructions about everything you were to do.

Scouts Explore the Land

19"Then, just as the LORD our God commanded us, we left Mount Sinai and traveled through the great and terrifying wilderness, as you yourselves remember, and headed toward the hill country of the Amorites. When we arrived at Kadesh-barnea, 20I said to you, 'You have now reached the hill country of the Amorites that the LORD our God is giving us. 21Look! He has placed the land in front of you. Go and occupy it as the LORD, the God of your ancestors, has promised you. Don't be afraid! Don't be discouraged!'

22"But you all came to me and said, 'First, let's send out scouts to explore the land for us. They will advise us on the best route to take and which towns we should enter.'

23"This seemed like a good idea to me, so I chose twelve scouts, one from each of your tribes. 24They headed for the hill country and came to the valley of Eshcol and explored it. 25They picked some of its fruit and brought it back to us. And they reported, 'The land the LORD our God has given us is indeed a good land.'

Israel's Rebellion against the LORD

26"But you rebelled against the command of the LORD your God and refused to go in. 27You complained in your tents and said, 'The LORD must hate us. That's why he has brought us here from Egypt—to hand us over to the Amorites to be slaughtered. 28Where can we go? Our brothers have demoralized us with their report. They tell us, "The people of the land are taller and more powerful than we are, and their towns are large, with walls rising high into the sky! We even saw giants there—the descendants of Anak!"'

29"But I said to you, 'Don't be shocked or afraid of them! 30The LORD your God is going ahead of you. He will fight for you, just as you saw him do in Egypt. 31And you saw how the LORD your God cared for you all along the way as you traveled through the wilderness, just as a father cares for his child. Now he has brought you to this place.'

32"But even after all he did, you refused to trust the LORD your God, 33who goes before you looking for the best places to camp, guiding you with a pillar of fire by night and a pillar of cloud by day.

34"When the LORD heard your complaining, he became very angry. So he solemnly swore, 35'Not one of you from this wicked generation will live to see the good land I swore to give your ancestors, 36except Caleb son of Jephunneh. He will see this land because he has followed the LORD completely. I will give to him and his descendants some of the very land he explored during his scouting mission.'

37"And the LORD was also angry with me because of you. He said to me, 'Moses, not even you will enter the Promised Land! 38Instead, your assistant, Joshua son of Nun, will lead the people into the land. Encourage him, for he will lead Israel as they take possession of it. 39I will give the land to your little ones—your innocent children. You were afraid they would be captured, but they will be the ones who occupy it. 40As for you, turn around now and go on back through the wilderness toward the Red Sea.*'

41"Then you confessed, 'We have sinned against the LORD! We will go into the land and fight for it, as the LORD our God has commanded us.' So your men strapped on their weapons, thinking it would be easy to attack the hill country.

42"But the LORD told me to tell you, 'Do not attack, for I am not with you. If you go ahead on your own, you will be crushed by your enemies.'

43"This is what I told you, but you would not listen. Instead, you again rebelled against the LORD's command and arrogantly went into the hill country to fight. 44But the Amorites who lived there came out against you like a swarm of bees. They chased and battered you all the way from Seir to Hormah. 45Then you returned and wept before the LORD, but he refused to listen. 46So you stayed there at Kadesh for a long time.

CHAPTER 2

Remembering Israel's Wanderings

"Then we turned around and headed back across the wilderness toward the Red Sea,*

1:40 Hebrew *sea of reeds.* **2:1** Hebrew *sea of reeds.*

just as the LORD had instructed me, and we wandered around in the region of Mount Seir for a long time.

2"Then at last the LORD said to me, 3'You have been wandering around in this hill country long enough; turn to the north. 4Give these orders to the people: "You will pass through the country belonging to your relatives the Edomites, the descendants of Esau, who live in Seir. The Edomites will feel threatened, so be careful. 5Do not bother them, for I have given them all the hill country around Mount Seir as their property, and I will not give you even one square foot of their land. 6If you need food to eat or water to drink, pay them for it. 7For the LORD your God has blessed you in everything you have done. He has watched your every step through this great wilderness. During these forty years, the LORD your God has been with you, and you have lacked nothing."'

8"So we bypassed the territory of our relatives, the descendants of Esau, who live in Seir. We avoided the road through the Arabah Valley that comes up from Elath and Ezion-geber.

"Then as we turned north along the desert route through Moab, 9the LORD warned us, 'Do not bother the Moabites, the descendants of Lot, or start a war with them. I have given them Ar as their property, and I will not give you any of their land.'"

10(A race of giants called the Emites had once lived in the area of Ar. They were as strong and numerous and tall as the Anakites, another race of giants. 11Both the Emites and the Anakites are also known as the Rephaites, though the Moabites call them Emites. 12In earlier times the Horites had lived in Seir, but they were driven out and displaced by the descendants of Esau, just as Israel drove out the people of Canaan when the LORD gave Israel their land.)

13Moses continued, "Then the LORD said to us, 'Get moving. Cross the Zered Brook.' So we crossed the brook.

14"Thirty-eight years passed from the time we first left Kadesh-barnea until we finally crossed the Zered Brook! By then, all the men old enough to fight in battle had died in the wilderness, as the LORD had vowed would happen. 15The LORD struck them down until they had all been eliminated from the community.

16"When all the men of fighting age had died, 17the LORD said to me, 18'Today you will cross the border of Moab at Ar 19and enter the land of the Ammonites, the descendants of Lot. But do not bother them or start a war with them. I have given the land of Ammon to them as their property, and I will not give you any of their land.'"

20(That area was once considered the land of the Rephaites, who had lived there, though the Ammonites call them Zamzummites. 21They were also as strong and numerous and tall as the Anakites. But the LORD destroyed them so the Ammonites could occupy their land. 22He had done the same for the descendants of Esau who lived in Seir, for he destroyed the Horites so they could settle there in their place. The descendants of Esau live there to this day. 23A similar thing happened when the Caphtorites from Crete* invaded and destroyed the Avvites, who had lived in villages in the area of Gaza.)

24Moses continued, "Then the LORD said, 'Now get moving! Cross the Arnon Gorge. Look, I will hand over to you Sihon the Amorite, king of Heshbon, and I will give you his land. Attack him and begin to occupy the land. 25Beginning today I will make people throughout the earth terrified because of you. When they hear reports about you, they will tremble with dread and fear.'"

Victory over Sihon of Heshbon

26Moses continued, "From the wilderness of Kedemoth I sent ambassadors to King Sihon of Heshbon with this proposal of peace:

> 27'Let us travel through your land. We will stay on the main road and won't turn off into the fields on either side. 28Sell us food to eat and water to drink, and we will pay for it. All we want is permission to pass through your land. 29The descendants of Esau who live in Seir allowed us to go through their country, and so did the Moabites, who live in Ar. Let us pass through until we cross the Jordan into the land the LORD our God is giving us.'

30"But King Sihon of Heshbon refused to allow us to pass through, because the LORD

2:23 Hebrew *from Caphtor*.

your God made Sihon stubborn and defiant so he could help you defeat him, as he has now done.

31"Then the LORD said to me, 'Look, I have begun to hand King Sihon and his land over to you. Begin now to conquer and occupy his land.'

32"Then King Sihon declared war on us and mobilized his forces at Jahaz. 33But the LORD our God handed him over to us, and we crushed him, his sons, and all his people. 34We conquered all his towns and completely destroyed* everyone—men, women, and children. Not a single person was spared. 35We took all the livestock as plunder for ourselves, along with anything of value from the towns we ransacked.

36"The LORD our God also helped us conquer Aroer on the edge of the Arnon Gorge, and the town in the gorge, and the whole area as far as Gilead. No town had walls too strong for us. 37However, we avoided the land of the Ammonites all along the Jabbok River and the towns in the hill country—all the places the LORD our God had commanded us to leave alone.

CHAPTER 3

Victory over Og of Bashan

"Next we turned and headed for the land of Bashan, where King Og and his entire army attacked us at Edrei. 2But the LORD told me, 'Do not be afraid of him, for I have given you victory over Og and his entire army, and I will give you all his land. Treat him just as you treated King Sihon of the Amorites, who ruled in Heshbon.'

3"So the LORD our God handed King Og and all his people over to us, and we killed them all. Not a single person survived. 4We conquered all sixty of his towns—the entire Argob region in his kingdom of Bashan. Not a single town escaped our conquest. 5These towns were all fortified with high walls and barred gates. We also took many unwalled villages at the same time. 6We completely destroyed* the kingdom of Bashan, just as we had destroyed King Sihon of Heshbon. We destroyed all the people in every town we conquered—men, women, and children alike. 7But we kept all the livestock for ourselves and took plunder from all the towns.

8"So we took the land of the two Amorite kings east of the Jordan River—all the way from the Arnon Gorge to Mount Hermon. 9(Mount Hermon is called Sirion by the Sidonians, and the Amorites call it Senir.) 10We had now conquered all the cities on the plateau and all Gilead and Bashan, as far as the towns of Salecah and Edrei, which were part of Og's kingdom in Bashan. 11(King Og of Bashan was the last survivor of the giant Rephaites. His bed was made of iron and was more than thirteen feet long and six feet wide.* It can still be seen in the Ammonite city of Rabbah.)

AMAZING FACTS

King Og's bed, which was made of iron, was 13 feet long and 6 feet wide! Now, that's a king-sized bed!

DEUTERONOMY 3:11

Land Division East of the Jordan

12"When we took possession of this land, I gave to the tribes of Reuben and Gad the territory beyond Aroer along the Arnon Gorge, plus half of the hill country of Gilead with its towns. 13Then I gave the rest of Gilead and all of Bashan—Og's former kingdom—to the half-tribe of Manasseh. (This entire Argob region of Bashan used to be known as the land of the Rephaites. 14Jair, a leader from the tribe of Manasseh, conquered the whole Argob region in Bashan, all the way to the border of the Geshurites and Maacathites. Jair renamed this region after himself, calling it the Towns

2:34 The Hebrew term used here refers to the complete consecration of things or people to the LORD, either by destroying them or by giving them as an offering. **3:6** The Hebrew term used here refers to the complete consecration of things or people to the LORD, either by destroying them or by giving them as an offering; also in 3:6b. **3:11** Hebrew *9 cubits* [4.1 meters] *long and 4 cubits* [1.8 meters] *wide*.

of Jair,* as it is still known today.) 15 I gave Gilead to the clan of Makir. 16 But I also gave part of Gilead to the tribes of Reuben and Gad. The area I gave them extended from the middle of the Arnon Gorge in the south to the Jabbok River on the Ammonite frontier. 17 They also received the Jordan Valley, all the way from the Sea of Galilee down to the Dead Sea,* with the Jordan River serving as the western boundary. To the east were the slopes of Pisgah.

18 "At that time I gave this command to the tribes that would live east of the Jordan: 'Although the LORD your God has given you this land as your property, all your fighting men must cross the Jordan ahead of your Israelite relatives, armed and ready to assist them. 19 Your wives, children, and numerous livestock, however, may stay behind in the towns I have given you. 20 When the LORD has given security to the rest of the Israelites, as he has to you, and when they occupy the land the LORD your God is giving them across the Jordan River, then you may all return here to the land I have given you.'

Moses Forbidden to Enter the Land

21 "At that time I gave Joshua this charge: 'You have seen for yourself everything the LORD your God has done to these two kings. He will do the same to all the kingdoms on the west side of the Jordan. 22 Do not be afraid of the nations there, for the LORD your God will fight for you.'

23 "At that time I pleaded with the LORD and said, 24 'O Sovereign LORD, you have only begun to show your greatness and the strength of your hand to me, your servant. Is there any god in heaven or on earth who can perform such great and mighty deeds as you do? 25 Please let me cross the Jordan to see the wonderful land on the other side, the beautiful hill country and the Lebanon mountains.'

26 "But the LORD was angry with me because of you, and he would not listen to me. 'That's enough!' he declared. 'Speak of it no more. 27 But go up to Pisgah Peak, and look over the land in every direction. Take a good look, but you may not cross the Jordan River. 28 Instead, commission Joshua and encourage and strengthen him, for he will lead the people across the Jordan. He will give them all the land you now see before you as their possession.' 29 So we stayed in the valley near Beth-peor.

CHAPTER 4

Moses Urges Israel to Obey

"And now, Israel, listen carefully to these decrees and regulations that I am about to teach you. Obey them so that you may live, so you may enter and occupy the land that the LORD, the God of your ancestors, is giving you. 2 Do not add to or subtract from these commands I am giving you. Just obey the commands of the LORD your God that I am giving you.

3 "You saw for yourself what the LORD did to you at Baal-peor. There the LORD your God destroyed everyone who had worshiped Baal, the god of Peor. 4 But all of you who were faithful to the LORD your God are still alive today—every one of you.

5 "Look, I now teach you these decrees and regulations just as the LORD my God commanded me, so that you may obey them in the land you are about to enter and occupy. 6 Obey them completely, and you will display your wisdom and intelligence among the surrounding nations. When they hear all these decrees, they will exclaim, 'How wise and prudent are the people of this great nation!' 7 For what great nation has a god as near to them as the LORD our God is near to us whenever we call on him? 8 And what great nation has decrees and regulations as righteous and fair as this body of instructions that I am giving you today?

9 "But watch out! Be careful never to forget what you yourself have seen. Do not let these memories escape from your mind as long as you live! And be sure to pass them on to your children and grandchildren. 10 Never forget the day when you stood before the LORD your God at Mount Sinai,* where he told me, 'Summon the people before me, and I will personally instruct them. Then they will learn to fear me as long as they live, and they will teach their children to fear me also.'

11 "You came near and stood at the foot of the mountain, while flames from the mountain shot into the sky. The mountain was shrouded in black clouds and deep darkness.

3:14 Hebrew *Havvoth-jair*. **3:17** Hebrew *from Kinnereth to the Sea of the Arabah, the Salt Sea*. **4:10** Hebrew *Horeb*, another name for Sinai; also in 4:15.

[12]And the LORD spoke to you from the heart of the fire. You heard the sound of his words but didn't see his form; there was only a voice. [13]He proclaimed his covenant—the Ten Commandments*—which he commanded you to keep, and which he wrote on two stone tablets. [14]It was at that time that the LORD commanded me to teach you his decrees and regulations so you would obey them in the land you are about to enter and occupy.

A Warning against Idolatry

[15]"But be very careful! You did not see the LORD's form on the day he spoke to you from the heart of the fire at Mount Sinai. [16]So do not corrupt yourselves by making an idol in any form—whether of a man or a woman, [17]an animal on the ground, a bird in the sky, [18]a small animal that scurries along the ground, or a fish in the deepest sea. [19]And when you look up into the sky and see the sun, moon, and stars—all the forces of heaven—don't be seduced into worshiping them. The LORD your God gave them to all the peoples of the earth. [20]Remember that the LORD rescued you from the iron-smelting furnace of Egypt in order to make you his very own people and his special possession, which is what you are today.

[21]"But the LORD was angry with me because of you. He vowed that I would not cross the Jordan River into the good land the LORD your God is giving you as your special possession. [22]You will cross the Jordan to occupy the land, but I will not. Instead, I will die here on the east side of the river. [23]So be careful not to break the covenant the LORD your God has made with you. Do not make idols of any shape or form, for the LORD your God has forbidden this. [24]The LORD your God is a devouring fire; he is a jealous God.

[25]"In the future, when you have children and grandchildren and have lived in the land a long time, do not corrupt yourselves by making idols of any kind. This is evil in the sight of the LORD your God and will arouse his anger.

[26]"Today I call on heaven and earth as witnesses against you. If you break my covenant, you will quickly disappear from the land you are crossing the Jordan to occupy. You will live there only a short time; then you will be utterly destroyed. [27]For the LORD will scatter you among the nations, where only a few of you will survive. [28]There, in a foreign land, you will worship idols made from wood and stone—gods that neither see nor hear nor eat nor smell. [29]But from there you will search again for the LORD your God. And if you search for him with all your heart and soul, you will find him.

[30]"In the distant future, when you are suffering all these things, you will finally return to the LORD your God and listen to what he tells you. [31]For the LORD your God is a merciful God; he will not abandon you or destroy you or forget the solemn covenant he made with your ancestors.

There Is Only One God

[32]"Now search all of history, from the time God created people on the earth until now, and search from one end of the heavens to the other. Has anything as great as this ever been seen or heard before? [33]Has any nation ever heard the voice of God* speaking from fire—as you did—and survived? [34]Has any other god dared to take a nation for himself out of another nation by means of trials, miraculous signs, wonders, war, a strong hand, a powerful arm, and terrifying acts? Yet that is what the LORD your God did for you in Egypt, right before your eyes.

[35]"He showed you these things so you would know that the LORD is God and there is no other. [36]He let you hear his voice from heaven so he could instruct you. He let you see his great fire here on earth so he could speak to you from it. [37]Because he loved your ancestors, he chose to bless their descendants, and he personally brought you out of Egypt with a great display of power. [38]He drove out nations far greater than you, so he could bring you in and give you their land as your special possession, as it is today.

[39]"So remember this and keep it firmly in mind: The LORD is God both in heaven and on earth, and there is no other. [40]If you obey all the decrees and commands I am giving you today, all will be well with you and your children. I am giving you these instructions so you will enjoy a long life in the land the LORD your God is giving you for all time."

4:13 Hebrew *the ten words.* **4:33** Or *voice of a god.*

Eastern Cities of Refuge

41Then Moses set apart three cities of refuge
east of the Jordan River. 42Anyone who killed
another person unintentionally, without pre-
vious hostility, could flee there to live in
safety. 43These were the cities: Bezer on the
wilderness plateau for the tribe of Reuben;
Ramoth in Gilead for the tribe of Gad; Golan
in Bashan for the tribe of Manasseh.

Introduction to Moses' Second Address

44This is the body of instruction that Moses
presented to the Israelites. 45These are the
laws, decrees, and regulations that Moses gave
to the people of Israel when they left Egypt,
46and as they camped in the valley near Beth-
peor east of the Jordan River. (This land was
formerly occupied by the Amorites under
King Sihon, who ruled from Heshbon. But
Moses and the Israelites destroyed him and his
people when they came up from Egypt. 47Israel
took possession of his land and that of King Og
of Bashan—the two Amorite kings east of the
Jordan. 48So Israel conquered the entire area
from Aroer at the edge of the Arnon Gorge all
the way to Mount Sirion,* also called Mount
Hermon. 49And they conquered the eastern
bank of the Jordan River as far south as the
Dead Sea,* below the slopes of Pisgah.)

CHAPTER 5

Ten Commandments for the Covenant Community

Moses called all the people of Israel together
and said, "Listen carefully, Israel. Hear the de-
crees and regulations I am giving you today,
so you may learn them and obey them!

2"The LORD our God made a covenant with
us at Mount Sinai.* 3The LORD did not make
this covenant with our ancestors, but with all
of us who are alive today. 4At the mountain the
LORD spoke to you face to face from the heart
of the fire. 5I stood as an intermediary be-
tween you and the LORD, for you were afraid of
the fire and did not want to approach the
mountain. He spoke to me, and I passed his
words on to you. This is what he said:

6"I am the LORD your God, who rescued you
from the land of Egypt, the place of your
slavery.

7"You must not have any other god but me.

8"You must not make for yourself an idol of
any kind, or an image of anything in the
heavens or on the earth or in the sea. 9You
must not bow down to them or worship
them, for I, the LORD your God, am a
jealous God who will not tolerate your
affection for any other gods. I lay the
sins of the parents upon their children;
the entire family is affected—even
children in the third and fourth
generations of those who reject me. 10But
I lavish unfailing love for a thousand
generations on those* who love me and
obey my commands.

11"You must not misuse the name of the
LORD your God. The LORD will not let you
go unpunished if you misuse his name.

12"Observe the Sabbath day by keeping it
holy, as the LORD your God has
commanded you. 13You have six days
each week for your ordinary work, 14but
the seventh day is a Sabbath day of rest
dedicated to the LORD your God. On that
day no one in your household may do any
work. This includes you, your sons and
daughters, your male and female servants,
your oxen and donkeys and other
livestock, and any foreigners living among
you. All your male and female servants
must rest as you do. 15Remember that you
were once slaves in Egypt, but the LORD
your God brought you out with his strong
hand and powerful arm. That is why the
LORD your God has commanded you to
rest on the Sabbath day.

16"Honor your father and mother, as the
LORD your God commanded you. Then
you will live a long, full life in the land the
LORD your God is giving you.

17"You must not murder.

18"You must not commit adultery.

19"You must not steal.

20"You must not testify falsely against your
neighbor.

21"You must not covet your neighbor's wife.
You must not covet your neighbor's house
or land, male or female servant, ox or
donkey, or anything else that belongs to
your neighbor.

4:48 As in Syriac version (see also 3:9); Hebrew reads *Mount Sion.* **4:49** Hebrew *took the Arabah on the east side of the Jordan as far as the sea of the Arabah.* **5:2** Hebrew *Horeb,* another name for Sinai. **5:10** Hebrew *for thousands of those.*

22"The LORD spoke these words to all of
you assembled there at the foot of the moun-
tain. He spoke with a loud voice from the
heart of the fire, surrounded by clouds and
deep darkness. This was all he said at that
time, and he wrote his words on two stone
tablets and gave them to me.
23"But when you heard the voice from the
heart of the darkness, while the mountain
was blazing with fire, all your tribal leaders
and elders came to me. 24They said, 'Look, the
LORD our God has shown us his glory and
greatness, and we have heard his voice from
the heart of the fire. Today we have seen that
God can speak to us humans, and yet we live!
25But now, why should we risk death again? If
the LORD our God speaks to us again, we will
certainly die and be consumed by this awe-
some fire. 26Can any living thing hear the
voice of the living God from the heart of the
fire as we did and yet survive? 27Go yourself
and listen to what the LORD our God says.
Then come and tell us everything he tells you,
and we will listen and obey.'
28"The LORD heard the request you made
to me. And he said, 'I have heard what the
people said to you, and they are right. 29Oh,
that they would always have hearts like this,
that they might fear me and obey all my com-
mands! If they did, they and their descen-
dants would prosper forever. 30Go and tell
them, "Return to your tents." 31But you stand
here with me so I can give you all my com-
mands, decrees, and regulations. You must
teach them to the people so they can obey
them in the land I am giving them as their
possession.'"
32So Moses told the people, "You must be
careful to obey all the commands of the LORD
your God, following his instructions in every
detail. 33Stay on the path that the LORD your
God has commanded you to follow. Then you
will live long and prosperous lives in the land
you are about to enter and occupy.

CHAPTER 6

A Call for Wholehearted Commitment

"These are the commands, decrees, and regu-
lations that the LORD your God commanded
me to teach you. You must obey them in the
land you are about to enter and occupy, 2and
you and your children and grandchildren
must fear the LORD your God as long as you
live. If you obey all his decrees and com-
mands, you will enjoy a long life. 3Listen
closely, Israel, and be careful to obey. Then all
will go well with you, and you will have many
children in the land flowing with milk and
honey, just as the LORD, the God of your an-
cestors, promised you.

IS IT OK?

IS IT OK TO WANT WHAT MY FRIENDS HAVE?

Maybe you wish you had your friend's parents because yours got divorced. Maybe you wish you had your friend's talent because you aren't that good at anything. Maybe you wish you had your friend's cool stuff because you don't have much money. God tells us not to want what others have (see Deuteronomy 5:21). He wants us to focus on what we *do* have instead of what we *don't* have. Having what your friend has doesn't guarantee happiness. But if you can learn to be content with what you have now, you'll be pleased to discover how happy you can be no matter what you have!

4"Listen, O Israel! The LORD is our God, the
LORD alone.* 5And you must love the LORD
your God with all your heart, all your soul, and
all your strength. 6And you must commit your-
selves wholeheartedly to these commands that
I am giving you today. 7Repeat them again and
again to your children. Talk about them when
you are at home and when you are on the road,
when you are going to bed and when you are
getting up. 8Tie them to your hands and wear
them on your forehead as reminders. 9Write
them on the doorposts of your house and on
your gates.

20"In the future your children will ask you,
'What is the meaning of these laws, decrees,
and regulations that the LORD our God has
commanded us to obey?'
21"Then you must tell them, 'We were Pha-
raoh's slaves in Egypt, but the LORD brought us
out of Egypt with his strong hand. 22The LORD
did miraculous signs and wonders before our
eyes, dealing terrifying blows against Egypt
and Pharaoh and all his people. 23He brought
us out of Egypt so he could give us this land he
had sworn to give our ancestors. 24And the
LORD our God commanded us to obey all these

How can I keep from doing wrong things?

Commit yourselves wholeheartedly to these commands that I am giving you today. Repeat them again and again. DEUTERONOMY 6:6-7

10"The LORD your God will soon bring you
into the land he swore to give you when he
made a vow to your ancestors Abraham, Isaac,
and Jacob. It is a land with large, prosperous
cities that you did not build. 11The houses will
be richly stocked with goods you did not pro-
duce. You will draw water from cisterns you
did not dig, and you will eat from vineyards
and olive trees you did not plant. When you
have eaten your fill in this land, 12be careful
not to forget the LORD, who rescued you from
slavery in the land of Egypt. 13You must fear
the LORD your God and serve him. When you
take an oath, you must use only his name.
14"You must not worship any of the gods of
neighboring nations, 15for the LORD your God,
who lives among you, is a jealous God. His an-
ger will flare up against you, and he will wipe
you from the face of the earth. 16You must not
test the LORD your God as you did when you
complained at Massah. 17You must diligently
obey the commands of the LORD your God—
all the laws and decrees he has given you. 18Do
what is right and good in the LORD's sight, so
all will go well with you. Then you will enter
and occupy the good land that the LORD
swore to give your ancestors. 19You will drive
out all the enemies living in the land, just as
the LORD said you would.

decrees and to fear him so he can continue to
bless us and preserve our lives, as he has done
to this day. 25For we will be counted as righ-
teous when we obey all the commands the
LORD our God has given us.'

CHAPTER 7

The Privilege of Holiness

"When the LORD your God brings you into the
land you are about to enter and occupy, he will
clear away many nations ahead of you: the
Hittites, Girgashites, Amorites, Canaanites,
Perizzites, Hivites, and Jebusites. These seven
nations are greater and more numerous than
you. 2When the LORD your God hands these
nations over to you and you conquer them,
you must completely destroy* them. Make no
treaties with them and show them no mercy.
3You must not intermarry with them. Do not
let your daughters and sons marry their sons
and daughters, 4for they will lead your chil-
dren away from me to worship other gods.
Then the anger of the LORD will burn against
you, and he will quickly destroy you. 5This is
what you must do. You must break down their
pagan altars and shatter their sacred pillars.
Cut down their Asherah poles and burn their
idols. 6For you are a holy people, who belong

6:4 Or *The LORD our God is one LORD;* or *The LORD our God, the LORD is one;* or *The LORD is our God, the LORD is one.* **7:2** The Hebrew term used here refers to the complete consecration of things or people to the LORD, either by destroying them or by giving them as an offering; also in 7:26.

Do you sometimes get the feeling that your parents are doing everything they can to mess up your life? I sure did.

I remember a time when I was younger and had been planning all week to go with some friends to see a movie. Everyone wanted to see this new movie, and I was really excited. When Friday finally came, I sort of announced to my parents that I was going to see this movie with my friends. I told them, "Everyone's going."

They asked, "What's the movie about?" And the next thing I knew, they were looking it up online at a screening Web site! After reading all about the movie, they told me I couldn't go to see it. I remember them saying that it had some questionable scenes and bad language in it. Talk about being disappointed and embarrassed! I felt so stupid. And I had to sit at home that night while my friends went to the movies.

Now that I'm a little bit older, I think I understand why my parents made their decision. There are things kids should not be exposed to until they are much older. I'm starting to see that lots of times when we think our parents are out looking for ways to keep us from having fun, they're really just trying to guard us from stuff that could hurt us.

The next time your parents make a rule, instead of seeing it as a form of punishment, try to see it as a form of protection. It just might help your outlook.

In Deuteronomy 6:1-9 we can read some very important instructions from God to our parents about how they are to teach us throughout the day—and our lives.

to the LORD your God. Of all the people on earth, the LORD your God has chosen you to be his own special treasure.

7"The LORD did not set his heart on you and choose you because you were more numerous than other nations, for you were the smallest of all nations! 8Rather, it was simply that the LORD loves you, and he was keeping the oath he had sworn to your ancestors. That is why the LORD rescued you with such a strong hand from your slavery and from the oppressive hand of Pharaoh, king of Egypt. 9Understand, therefore, that the LORD your God is indeed God. He is the faithful God who keeps his covenant for a thousand generations and lavishes his unfailing love on those who love him and obey his commands. 10But he does not hesitate to punish and destroy those who reject him. 11Therefore, you must obey all these commands, decrees, and regulations I am giving you today.

12"If you listen to these regulations and faithfully obey them, the LORD your God will keep his covenant of unfailing love with you, as he promised with an oath to your ancestors. 13He will love you and bless you, and he will give you many children. He will give fertility to your land and your animals. When you arrive in the land he swore to give your ancestors, you will have large harvests of grain, new wine, and olive oil, and great herds of cattle, sheep, and goats. 14You will be blessed above all the nations of the earth. None of your men or women will be childless, and all your livestock will bear young. 15And the LORD will protect you from all sickness. He will not let you suffer from the terrible diseases you knew in Egypt, but he will inflict them on all your enemies!

16"You must destroy all the nations the LORD your God hands over to you. Show them no mercy, and do not worship their gods, or they will trap you. 17Perhaps you will think to yourselves, 'How can we ever conquer these nations that are so much more powerful than we are?' 18But don't be afraid of them! Just remember what the LORD your God did to Pharaoh and to all the land of Egypt. 19Remember the great terrors the LORD your God sent against them. You saw it all with your own eyes! And remember the miraculous signs and wonders, and the strong hand and powerful arm with which he brought you out of Egypt. The LORD your God will use this same power against all the people you fear. 20And then the LORD your God will send terror* to drive out the few survivors still hiding from you!

21"No, do not be afraid of those nations, for the LORD your God is among you, and he is a great and awesome God. 22The LORD your God will drive those nations out ahead of you little by little. You will not clear them away all at once, otherwise the wild animals would multiply too quickly for you. 23But the LORD your God will hand them over to you. He will throw them into complete confusion until they are destroyed. 24He will put their kings in your power, and you will erase their names from the face of the earth. No one will be able to stand against you, and you will destroy them all.

25"You must burn their idols in fire, and you must not covet the silver or gold that covers them. You must not take it or it will become a trap to you, for it is detestable to the LORD your God. 26Do not bring any detestable objects into your home, for then you will be destroyed, just like them. You must utterly detest such things, for they are set apart for destruction.

CHAPTER 8

A Call to Remember and Obey

"Be careful to obey all the commands I am giving you today. Then you will live and multiply, and you will enter and occupy the land the LORD swore to give your ancestors. 2Remember how the LORD your God led you through the wilderness for these forty years, humbling you and testing you to prove your character, and to find out whether or not you would obey his commands. 3Yes, he humbled you by letting you go hungry and then feeding you with manna, a food previously unknown to you and your ancestors. He did it to teach you that people do not live by bread alone; rather, we live by every word that comes from the mouth of the LORD. 4For all these forty years your clothes didn't wear out, and your feet didn't blister or swell. 5Think about it: Just as a parent disciplines a child, the LORD your God disciplines you for your own good.

6"So obey the commands of the LORD your God by walking in his ways and fearing him. 7For the LORD your God is bringing you into a good land of flowing streams and pools of

7:20 Often rendered *the hornet*. The meaning of the Hebrew is uncertain.

water, with fountains and springs that gush
out in the valleys and hills. [8]It is a land of
wheat and barley; of grapevines, fig trees, and
pomegranates; of olive oil and honey. [9]It is a
land where food is plentiful and nothing is
lacking. It is a land where iron is as common
as stone, and copper is abundant in the hills.
[10]When you have eaten your fill, be sure to
praise the LORD your God for the good land he
has given you.

[11]"But that is the time to be careful! Beware
that in your plenty you do not forget the LORD
your God and disobey his commands, regula-
tions, and decrees that I am giving you today.
[12]For when you have become full and pros-
perous and have built fine homes to live in,
[13]and when your flocks and herds have
become very large and your silver and gold
have multiplied along with everything else, be
careful! [14]Do not become proud at that time
and forget the LORD your God, who rescued
you from slavery in the land of Egypt. [15]Do not
forget that he led you through the great and
terrifying wilderness with its poisonous
snakes and scorpions, where it was so hot and
dry. He gave you water from the rock! [16]He
fed you with manna in the wilderness, a food
unknown to your ancestors. He did this to
humble you and test you for your own good.
[17]He did all this so you would never say to

OBEDIENCE

Deuteronomy 8:1 tells us to obey God's commands. We do this by obeying God with . . .

OUR MIND	By learning about him and his Word, the Bible
OUR WILL	By committing ourselves completely to him
OUR BODY	By using our energy and talents according to his rules, not ours
OUR MONEY	By remembering that all the money and other nice things we have come from God and really belong to him, not us
OUR HEART	By loving him more than anything else
OUR FUTURE	By deciding to spend our lives doing things for God and other people

100%

yourself, 'I have achieved this wealth with my
own strength and energy.' [18]Remember the
LORD your God. He is the one who gives you
power to be successful, in order to fulfill the
covenant he confirmed to your ancestors
with an oath.

[19]"But I assure you of this: If you ever forget
the LORD your God and follow other gods,
worshiping and bowing down to them, you
will certainly be destroyed. [20]Just as the LORD
has destroyed other nations in your path, you
also will be destroyed if you refuse to obey the
LORD your God.

CHAPTER 9

Victory by God's Grace

"Listen, O Israel! Today you are about to cross
the Jordan River to take over the land belong-
ing to nations much greater and more power-
ful than you. They live in cities with walls that
reach to the sky! [2]The people are strong and
tall—descendants of the famous Anakite gi-
ants. You've heard the saying, 'Who can stand
up to the Anakites?' [3]But recognize today that
the LORD your God is the one who will cross
over ahead of you like a devouring fire to de-
stroy them. He will subdue them so that you
will quickly conquer them and drive them
out, just as the LORD has promised.

[4]"After the LORD your God has done this for
you, don't say in your hearts, 'The LORD has
given us this land because we are such good
people!' No, it is because of the wickedness of
the other nations that he is pushing them out
of your way. [5]It is not because you are so good
or have such integrity that you are about to
occupy their land. The LORD your God will
drive these nations out ahead of you only be-
cause of their wickedness, and to fulfill the
oath he swore to your ancestors Abraham,
Isaac, and Jacob. [6]You must recognize that
the LORD your God is not giving you this good
land because you are good, for you are not—
you are a stubborn people.

Remembering the Gold Calf

[7]"Remember and never forget how angry you
made the LORD your God out in the wilderness.
From the day you left Egypt until now, you have
been constantly rebelling against him. [8]Even at
Mount Sinai* you made the LORD so angry
he was ready to destroy you. [9]This happened
when I was on the mountain receiving the tab-
lets of stone inscribed with the words of the
covenant that the LORD had made with you. I
was there for forty days and forty nights, and
all that time I ate no food and drank no water.
[10]The LORD gave me the two tablets on which
God had written with his own finger all the
words he had spoken to you from the heart
of the fire when you were assembled at the
mountain.

[11]"At the end of the forty days and nights,
the LORD handed me the two stone tablets
inscribed with the words of the covenant.
[12]Then the LORD said to me, 'Get up! Go down
immediately, for the people you brought out
of Egypt have corrupted themselves. How
quickly they have turned away from the way I
commanded them to live! They have melted
gold and made an idol for themselves!'

[13]"The LORD also said to me, 'I have seen
how stubborn and rebellious these people are.
[14]Leave me alone so I may destroy them and
erase their name from under heaven. Then
I will make a mighty nation of your descen-
dants, a nation larger and more powerful than
they are.'

[15]"So while the mountain was blazing with
fire I turned and came down, holding in my
hands the two stone tablets inscribed with
the terms of the covenant. [16]There below me
I could see that you had sinned against the
LORD your God. You had melted gold and
made a calf idol for yourselves. How quickly
you had turned away from the path the LORD
had commanded you to follow! [17]So I took the
stone tablets and threw them to the ground,
smashing them before your eyes.

[18]"Then, as before, I threw myself down be-
fore the LORD for forty days and nights. I ate no
bread and drank no water because of the great
sin you had committed by doing what the
LORD hated, provoking him to anger. [19]I feared
that the furious anger of the LORD, which
turned him against you, would drive him to de-
stroy you. But again he listened to me. [20]The
LORD was so angry with Aaron that he wanted
to destroy him, too. But I prayed for Aaron, and
the LORD spared him. [21]I took your sin—the
calf you had made—and I melted it down in
the fire and ground it into fine dust. Then I
threw the dust into the stream that flows down
the mountain.

9:8 Hebrew *Horeb*, another name for Sinai.

22"You also made the LORD angry at Taberah,* Massah,* and Kibroth-hattaavah.*
23And at Kadesh-barnea the LORD sent you out
with this command: 'Go up and take over the
land I have given you.' But you rebelled against
the command of the LORD your God and re-
fused to put your trust in him or obey him.
24Yes, you have been rebelling against the
LORD as long as I have known you.

25"That is why I threw myself down before
the LORD for forty days and nights—for the
LORD said he would destroy you. 26I prayed to
the LORD and said, 'O Sovereign LORD, do not
destroy them. They are your own people.
They are your special possession, whom you
redeemed from Egypt by your mighty power
and your strong hand. 27Please overlook the
stubbornness and the awful sin of these peo-
ple, and remember instead your servants
Abraham, Isaac, and Jacob. 28If you destroy
these people, the Egyptians will say, "The Is-
raelites died because the LORD wasn't able to
bring them to the land he had promised to
give them." Or they might say, "He destroyed
them because he hated them; he deliberately
took them into the wilderness to slaughter
them." 29But they are your people and your
special possession, whom you brought out of
Egypt by your great strength and powerful
arm.'

CHAPTER 10

A New Copy of the Covenant

"At that time the LORD said to me, 'Chisel out
two stone tablets like the first ones. Also
make a wooden Ark—a sacred chest to store
them in. Come up to me on the mountain,
2and I will write on the tablets the same words
that were on the ones you smashed. Then
place the tablets in the Ark.'

3"So I made an Ark of acacia wood and cut
two stone tablets like the first two. Then I
went up the mountain with the tablets in my
hand. 4Once again the LORD wrote the Ten
Commandments* on the tablets and gave
them to me. They were the same words the
LORD had spoken to you from the heart of the
fire on the day you were assembled at the foot
of the mountain. 5Then I turned and came
down the mountain and placed the tablets in
the Ark of the Covenant, which I had made,
just as the LORD commanded me. And the tab-
lets are still there in the Ark."

6(The people of Israel set out from the
wells of the people of Jaakan* and traveled to
Moserah, where Aaron died and was buried.
His son Eleazar ministered as high priest in
his place. 7Then they journeyed to Gudgodah,
and from there to Jotbathah, a land with many
brooks and streams. 8At that time the LORD
set apart the tribe of Levi to carry the Ark
of the LORD's Covenant, and to stand before
the LORD as his ministers, and to pronounce
blessings in his name. These are their duties
to this day. 9That is why the Levites have no
share of property or possession of land
among the other Israelite tribes. The LORD
himself is their special possession, as the
LORD your God told them.)

10"As for me, I stayed on the mountain in
the LORD's presence for forty days and nights,
as I had done the first time. And once again
the LORD listened to my pleas and agreed not
to destroy you. 11Then the LORD said to me,
'Get up and resume the journey, and lead the
people to the land I swore to give to their an-
cestors, so they may take possession of it.'

A Call to Love and Obedience

12"And now, Israel, what does the LORD your
God require of you? He requires only that you
fear the LORD your God, and live in a way that
pleases him, and love him and serve him with
all your heart and soul. 13And you must always
obey the LORD's commands and decrees that
I am giving you today for your own good.

14"Look, the highest heavens and the earth
and everything in it all belong to the LORD
your God. 15Yet the LORD chose your ances-
tors as the objects of his love. And he chose
you, their descendants, above all other na-
tions, as is evident today. 16Therefore, change
your hearts* and stop being stubborn.

17"For the LORD your God is the God of gods
and Lord of lords. He is the great God, the
mighty and awesome God, who shows no par-
tiality and cannot be bribed. 18He ensures that
orphans and widows receive justice. He shows
love to the foreigners living among you and
gives them food and clothing. 19So you, too,

9:22a *Taberah* means "place of burning." See Num 11:1-3. **9:22b** *Massah* means "place of testing." See Exod 17:1-7. **9:22c** *Kibroth-hattaavah* means "graves of gluttony." See Num 11:31-34. **10:4** Hebrew *the ten words.* **10:6** Or *set out from Beeroth of Bene-jaakan.* **10:16** Hebrew *circumcise the foreskin of your hearts.*

must show love to foreigners, for you yourselves were once foreigners in the land of Egypt. [20]You must fear the LORD your God and worship him and cling to him. Your oaths must be in his name alone. [21]He alone is your God, the only one who is worthy of your praise, the one who has done these mighty miracles that you have seen with your own eyes. [22]When your ancestors went down into Egypt, there were only seventy of them. But now the LORD your God has made you as numerous as the stars in the sky!

CHAPTER 11

"You must love the LORD your God and obey all his requirements, decrees, regulations, and commands. [2]Keep in mind that I am not talking now to your children, who have never experienced the discipline of the LORD your God or seen his greatness and his strong hand and powerful arm. [3]They didn't see the miraculous signs and wonders he performed in Egypt against Pharaoh and all his land. [4]They didn't see what the LORD did to the armies of Egypt and to their horses and chariots—how he drowned them in the Red Sea* as they were chasing you. He destroyed them, and they have not recovered to this very day!

[5]"Your children didn't see how the LORD cared for you in the wilderness until you arrived here. [6]They didn't see what he did to Dathan and Abiram (the sons of Eliab, a descendant of Reuben) when the earth opened its mouth in the Israelite camp and swallowed them, along with their households and tents and every living thing that belonged to them. [7]But you have seen the LORD perform all these mighty deeds with your own eyes!

The Blessings of Obedience

[8]"Therefore, be careful to obey every command I am giving you today, so you may have strength to go in and take over the land you are about to enter. [9]If you obey, you will enjoy a long life in the land the LORD swore to give to your ancestors and to you, their descendants—a land flowing with milk and honey! [10]For the land you are about to enter and take over is not like the land of Egypt from which you came, where you planted your seed and made irrigation ditches with your foot as in a vegetable garden. [11]Rather, the land you will soon take over is a land of hills and valleys with plenty of rain—[12]a land that the LORD your God cares for. He watches over it through each season of the year!

[13]"If you carefully obey all the commands I am giving you today, and if you love the LORD your God and serve him with all your heart and soul, [14]then he will send the rains in their proper seasons—the early and late rains—so you can bring in your harvests of grain, new wine, and olive oil. [15]He will give you lush pastureland for your livestock, and you yourselves will have all you want to eat.

[16]"But be careful. Don't let your heart be deceived so that you turn away from the LORD and serve and worship other gods. [17]If you do, the LORD's anger will burn against you. He will shut up the sky and hold back the rain, and the ground will fail to produce its harvests. Then you will quickly die in that good land the LORD is giving you.

[18]"So commit yourselves wholeheartedly to these words of mine. Tie them to your hands and wear them on your forehead as reminders. [19]Teach them to your children. Talk about them when you are at home and when you are on the road, when you are going to bed and when you are getting up. [20]Write them on the doorposts of your house and on your gates, [21]so that as long as the sky remains above the earth, you and your children may flourish in the land the LORD swore to give your ancestors.

[22]"Be careful to obey all these commands I am giving you. Show love to the LORD your God by walking in his ways and holding tightly to him. [23]Then the LORD will drive out all the nations ahead of you, though they are much greater and stronger than you, and you will take over their land. [24]Wherever you set foot, that land will be yours. Your frontiers will stretch from the wilderness in the south to Lebanon in the north, and from the Euphrates River in the east to the Mediterranean Sea in the west.* [25]No one will be able to stand against you, for the LORD your God will cause the people to fear and dread you, as he promised, wherever you go in the whole land.

[26]"Look, today I am giving you the choice between a blessing and a curse! [27]You will be blessed if you obey the commands of the LORD your God that I am giving you today.

11:4 Hebrew *sea of reeds.* **11:24** Hebrew *to the western sea.*

[28]But you will be cursed if you reject the commands of the LORD your God and turn away from him and worship gods you have not known before.

[29]"When the LORD your God brings you into the land and helps you take possession of it, you must pronounce the blessing at Mount Gerizim and the curse at Mount Ebal. [30](These two mountains are west of the Jordan River in the land of the Canaanites who live in the Jordan Valley,* near the town of Gilgal, not far from the oaks of Moreh.) [31]For you are about to cross the Jordan River to take over the land the LORD your God is giving you. When you take that land and are living in it, [32]you must be careful to obey all the decrees and regulations I am giving you today.

CHAPTER 12

The LORD's Chosen Place for Worship

"These are the decrees and regulations you must be careful to obey when you live in the land that the LORD, the God of your ancestors, is giving you. You must obey them as long as you live.

[2]"When you drive out the nations that live there, you must destroy all the places where they worship their gods—high on the mountains, up on the hills, and under every green tree. [3]Break down their altars and smash their sacred pillars. Burn their Asherah poles and cut down their carved idols. Completely erase the names of their gods!

[4]"Do not worship the LORD your God in the way these pagan peoples worship their gods. [5]Rather, you must seek the LORD your God at the place of worship he himself will choose from among all the tribes—the place where his name will be honored. [6]There you will bring your burnt offerings, your sacrifices, your tithes, your sacred offerings, your offerings to fulfill a vow, your voluntary offerings, and your offerings of the firstborn animals of your herds and flocks. [7]There you and your families will feast in the presence of the LORD your God, and you will rejoice in all you have accomplished because the LORD your God has blessed you.

[8]"Your pattern of worship will change. Today all of you are doing as you please, [9]because you have not yet arrived at the place of rest, the land the LORD your God is giving you as your special possession. [10]But you will soon cross the Jordan River and live in the land the LORD your God is giving you. When he gives you rest from all your enemies and you're living safely in the land, [11]you must bring everything I command you—your burnt offerings, your sacrifices, your tithes, your sacred offerings, and your offerings to fulfill a vow—to the designated place of worship, the place the LORD your God chooses for his name to be honored.

[12]"You must celebrate there in the presence of the LORD your God with your sons and daughters and all your servants. And remember to include the Levites who live in your towns, for they will receive no allotment of land among you. [13]Be careful not to sacrifice your burnt offerings just anywhere you like. [14]You may do so only at the place the LORD will choose within one of your tribal territories. There you must offer your burnt offerings and do everything I command you.

11:30 Hebrew *the Arabah.*

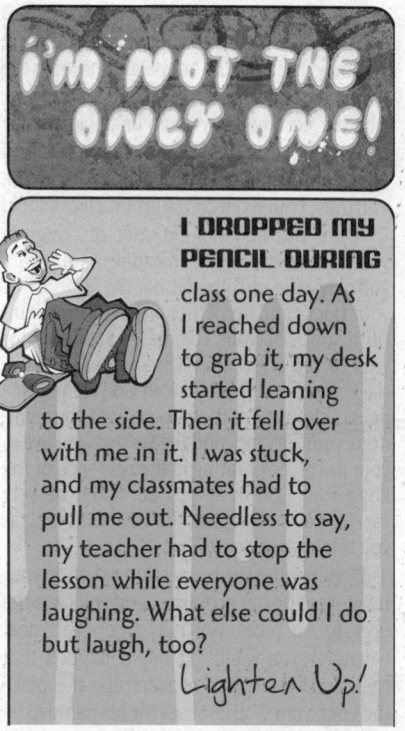

15"But you may butcher your animals and
eat their meat in any town whenever you want.
You may freely eat the animals with which the
LORD your God blesses you. All of you,
whether ceremonially clean or unclean, may
eat that meat, just as you now eat gazelle and
deer. 16But you must not consume the blood.
You must pour it out on the ground like water.

17"But you may not eat your offerings in
your hometown—neither the tithe of your grain
and new wine and olive oil, nor the firstborn of
your flocks and herds, nor any offering to ful-
fill a vow, nor your voluntary offerings, nor
your sacred offerings. 18You must eat these in
the presence of the LORD your God at the place
he will choose. Eat them there with your chil-
dren, your servants, and the Levites who live in
your towns, celebrating in the presence of the
LORD your God in all you do. 19And be very
careful never to neglect the Levites as long as
you live in your land.

20"When the LORD your God expands your
territory as he has promised, and you have the
urge to eat meat, you may freely eat meat
whenever you want. 21It might happen that
the designated place of worship—the place
the LORD your God chooses for his name to be
honored—is a long way from your home. If so,
you may butcher any of the cattle, sheep, or
goats the LORD has given you, and you may
freely eat the meat in your hometown, as I
have commanded you. 22Anyone, whether cer-
emonially clean or unclean, may eat that meat,
just as you do now with gazelle and deer. 23But
never consume the blood, for the blood is the
life, and you must not consume the lifeblood
with the meat. 24Instead, pour out the blood
on the ground like water. 25Do not consume
the blood, so that all may go well with you and
your children after you, because you will be
doing what pleases the LORD.

26"Take your sacred gifts and your offer-
ings given to fulfill a vow to the place the
LORD chooses. 27You must offer the meat and
blood of your burnt offerings on the altar of
the LORD your God. The blood of your other
sacrifices must be poured out on the altar of
the LORD your God, but you may eat the meat.
28Be careful to obey all my commands, so that
all will go well with you and your children af-
ter you, because you will be doing what is
good and pleasing to the LORD your God.

29"When the LORD your God goes ahead of
you and destroys the nations and you drive
them out and live in their land, 30do not fall
into the trap of following their customs and
worshiping their gods. Do not inquire about
their gods, saying, 'How do these nations wor-
ship their gods? I want to follow their exam-
ple.' 31You must not worship the LORD your
God the way the other nations worship their
gods, for they perform for their gods every
detestable act that the LORD hates. They even
burn their sons and daughters as sacrifices to
their gods.

32*"So be careful to obey all the commands
I give you. You must not add anything to them
or subtract anything from them.

CHAPTER 13

A Warning against Idolatry

1*"Suppose there are prophets among you or
those who dream dreams about the future,
and they promise you signs or miracles, 2and
the predicted signs or miracles occur. If they
then say, 'Come, let us worship other gods'—
gods you have not known before—3do not lis-
ten to them. The LORD your God is testing you
to see if you truly love him with all your heart
and soul. 4Serve only the LORD your God and
fear him alone. Obey his commands, listen to
his voice, and cling to him. 5The false prophets
or visionaries who try to lead you astray must
be put to death, for they encourage rebellion
against the LORD your God, who redeemed you
from slavery and brought you out of the land
of Egypt. Since they try to lead you astray from
the way the LORD your God commanded you to
live, you must put them to death. In this way
you will purge the evil from among you.

6"Suppose someone secretly entices you—
even your brother, your son or daughter, your
beloved wife, or your closest friend—and
says, 'Let us go worship other gods'—gods that
neither you nor your ancestors have known.
7They might suggest that you worship the
gods of peoples who live nearby or who come
from the ends of the earth. 8But do not give in
or listen. Have no pity, and do not spare or
protect them. 9You must put them to death!
Strike the first blow yourself, and then all the

12:32 Verse 12:32 is numbered 13:1 in Hebrew text. **13:1** Verses 13:1-18 are numbered 13:2-19 in Hebrew text.

people must join in. [10]Stone the guilty ones to death because they have tried to draw you away from the LORD your God, who rescued you from the land of Egypt, the place of slavery. [11]Then all Israel will hear about it and be afraid, and no one will act so wickedly again.

[12]"When you begin living in the towns the LORD your God is giving you, you may hear [13]that scoundrels among you are leading their fellow citizens astray by saying, 'Let us go worship other gods'—gods you have not known before. [14]In such cases, you must examine the facts carefully. If you find that the report is true and such a detestable act has been committed among you, [15]you must attack that town and completely destroy* all its inhabitants, as well as all the livestock. [16]Then you must pile all the plunder in the middle of the open square and burn it. Burn the entire town as a burnt offering to the LORD your God. That town must remain a ruin forever; it may never be rebuilt. [17]Keep none of the plunder that has been set apart for destruction. Then the LORD will turn from his fierce anger and be merciful to you. He will have compassion on you and make you a large nation, just as he swore to your ancestors.

[18]"The LORD your God will be merciful only if you listen to his voice and keep all his commands that I am giving you today, doing what pleases him.

CHAPTER 14

Ceremonially Clean and Unclean Animals

"Since you are the people of the LORD your God, never cut yourselves or shave the hair above your foreheads in mourning for the dead. [2]You have been set apart as holy to the LORD your God, and he has chosen you from all the nations of the earth to be his own special treasure.

[3]"You must not eat any detestable animals that are ceremonially unclean. [4]These are the animals* you may eat: the ox, the sheep, the goat, [5]the deer, the gazelle, the roe deer, the wild goat, the addax, the antelope, and the mountain sheep.

[6]"You may eat any animal that has completely split hooves and chews the cud, [7]but if the animal doesn't have both, it may not be eaten. So you may not eat the camel, the hare, or the hyrax.* They chew the cud but do not have split hooves, so they are ceremonially unclean for you. [8]And you may not eat the pig. It has split hooves but does not chew the cud, so it is ceremonially unclean for you. You may not eat the meat of these animals or even touch their carcasses.

[9]"Of all the marine animals, you may eat whatever has both fins and scales. [10]You may not, however, eat marine animals that do not have both fins and scales. They are ceremonially unclean for you.

[11]"You may eat any bird that is ceremonially clean. [12]These are the birds you may not eat: the griffon vulture, the bearded vulture, the black vulture, [13]the kite, the falcon, buzzards of all kinds, [14]ravens of all kinds, [15]the eagle owl, the short-eared owl, the seagull, hawks of all kinds, [16]the little owl, the great owl, the barn owl, [17]the desert owl, the Egyptian vulture, the cormorant, [18]the stork, herons of all kinds, the hoopoe, and the bat.

[19]"All winged insects that walk along the ground are ceremonially unclean for you and may not be eaten. [20]But you may eat any winged bird or insect that is ceremonially clean.

[21]"You must not eat anything that has died a natural death. You may give it to a foreigner living in your town, or you may sell it to a stranger. But do not eat it yourselves, for you are set apart as holy to the LORD your God.

"You must not cook a young goat in its mother's milk.

The Giving of Tithes

[22]"You must set aside a tithe of your crops—one-tenth of all the crops you harvest each year. [23]Bring this tithe to the designated place of worship—the place the LORD your God chooses for his name to be honored—and eat it there in his presence. This applies to your tithes of grain, new wine, olive oil, and the firstborn males of your flocks and herds. Doing this will teach you always to fear the LORD your God.

[24]"Now when the LORD your God blesses you with a good harvest, the place of worship he

13:15 The Hebrew term used here refers to the complete consecration of things or people to the LORD, either by destroying them or by giving them as an offering; similarly in 13:17. **14:4** The identification of some of the animals and birds listed in this chapter is uncertain. **14:7** Or *coney*, or *rock badger*.

chooses for his name to be honored might be too far for you to bring the tithe. [25]If so, you may sell the tithe portion of your crops and herds, put the money in a pouch, and go to the place the LORD your God has chosen. [26]When you arrive, you may use the money to buy any kind of food you want—cattle, sheep, goats, wine, or other alcoholic drink. Then feast there in the presence of the LORD your God and celebrate with your household. [27]And do not neglect the Levites in your town, for they will receive no allotment of land among you.

[28]"At the end of every third year, bring the entire tithe of that year's harvest and store it in the nearest town. [29]Give it to the Levites, who will receive no allotment of land among you, as well as to the foreigners living among you, the orphans, and the widows in your towns, so they can eat and be satisfied. Then the LORD your God will bless you in all your work.

CHAPTER 15

Release for Debtors

"At the end of every seventh year you must cancel the debts of everyone who owes you money. [2]This is how it must be done. Everyone must cancel the loans they have made to their fellow Israelites. They must not demand payment from their neighbors or relatives, for the LORD's time of release has arrived. [3]This release from debt, however, applies only to your fellow Israelites—not to the foreigners living among you.

[4]"There should be no poor among you, for the LORD your God will greatly bless you in the land he is giving you as a special possession. [5]You will receive this blessing if you are careful to obey all the commands of the LORD your God that I am giving you today. [6]The LORD your God will bless you as he has promised. You will lend money to many nations but will never need to borrow. You will rule many nations, but they will not rule over you.

[7]"But if there are any poor Israelites in your towns when you arrive in the land the LORD your God is giving you, do not be hard-hearted or tightfisted toward them. [8]Instead, be generous and lend them whatever they need. [9]Do not be mean-spirited and refuse someone a loan because the year for canceling debts is close at hand. If you refuse to make the loan and the needy person cries out to the LORD, you will be considered guilty of sin. [10]Give generously to the poor, not grudgingly, for the LORD your God will bless you in everything you do. [11]There will always be some in the land who are poor. That is why I am commanding you to share freely with the poor and with other Israelites in need.

Release for Hebrew Slaves

[12]"If a fellow Hebrew sells himself or herself to be your servant* and serves you for six years, in the seventh year you must set that servant free.

[13]"When you release a male servant, do not send him away empty-handed. [14]Give him a generous farewell gift from your flock, your threshing floor, and your winepress. Share with him some of the bounty with which the LORD your God has blessed you. [15]Remember that you were once slaves in the land of Egypt and the LORD your God redeemed you! That is why I am giving you this command.

[16]"But suppose your servant says, 'I will not leave you,' because he loves you and your family, and he has done well with you. [17]In that case, take an awl and push it through his earlobe into the door. After that, he will be your servant for life. And do the same for your female servants.

[18]"You must not consider it a hardship when you release your servants. Remember that for six years they have given you services worth double the wages of hired workers, and the LORD your God will bless you in all you do.

Sacrificing Firstborn Male Animals

[19]"You must set aside for the LORD your God all the firstborn males from your flocks and herds. Do not use the firstborn of your herds to work your fields, and do not shear the firstborn of your flocks. [20]Instead, you and your family must eat these animals in the presence of the LORD your God each year at the place he chooses. [21]But if this firstborn animal has any defect, such as lameness or blindness, or if anything else is wrong with it, you must not sacrifice it to the LORD your God. [22]Instead, use it for food for your family in your hometown. Anyone, whether ceremonially clean or unclean, may eat it, just as anyone may eat a gazelle or deer. [23]But you must not consume the blood. You must pour it out on the ground like water.

15:12 Or *If a Hebrew man or woman is sold to you.*

CHAPTER 16

Passover and the Festival of Unleavened Bread

"In honor of the LORD your God, celebrate the Passover each year in the early spring, in the month of Abib,* for that was the month in which the LORD your God brought you out of Egypt by night. [2]Your Passover sacrifice may be from either the flock or the herd, and it must be sacrificed to the LORD your God at the designated place of worship—the place he chooses for his name to be honored. [3]Eat it with bread made without yeast. For seven days the bread you eat must be made without yeast, as when you escaped from Egypt in such a hurry. Eat this bread—the bread of suffering—so that as long as you live you will remember the day you departed from Egypt. [4]Let no yeast be found in any house throughout your land for those seven days. And when you sacrifice the Passover lamb on the evening of the first day, do not let any of the meat remain until the next morning.

How much do I need to give to God?

All must give as they are able, according to the blessings given to them by the LORD your God.

DEUTERONOMY 16:17

[5]"You may not sacrifice the Passover in just any of the towns that the LORD your God is giving you. [6]You must offer it only at the designated place of worship—the place the LORD your God chooses for his name to be honored. Sacrifice it there in the evening as the sun goes down on the anniversary of your exodus from Egypt. [7]Roast the lamb and eat it in the place the LORD your God chooses. Then you may go back to your tents the next morning. [8]For the next six days you may not eat any bread made with yeast. On the seventh day proclaim another holy day in honor of the LORD your God, and no work may be done on that day.

The Festival of Harvest

[9]"Count off seven weeks from when you first begin to cut the grain at the time of harvest. [10]Then celebrate the Festival of Harvest* to honor the LORD your God. Bring him a voluntary offering in proportion to the blessings you have received from him. [11]This is a time to celebrate before the LORD your God at the designated place of worship he will choose for his name to be honored. Celebrate with your sons and daughters, your male and female servants, the Levites from your towns, and the foreigners, orphans, and widows who live among you. [12]Remember that you were once slaves in Egypt, so be careful to obey all these decrees.

The Festival of Shelters

[13]"You must observe the Festival of Shelters* for seven days at the end of the harvest season, after the grain has been threshed and the grapes have been pressed. [14]This festival will be a happy time of celebrating with your sons and daughters, your male and female servants, and the Levites, foreigners, orphans, and widows from your towns. [15]For seven days you must celebrate this festival to honor the LORD your God at the place he chooses, for it is he who blesses you with bountiful harvests and gives you success in all your work. This festival will be a time of great joy for all.

[16]"Each year every man in Israel must celebrate these three festivals: the Festival of Unleavened Bread, the Festival of Harvest, and the Festival of Shelters. On each of these occasions, all men must appear before the LORD your God at the place he chooses, but they must not appear before the LORD without a gift for him. [17]All must give as they are able, according to the blessings given to them by the LORD your God.

Justice for the People

[18]"Appoint judges and officials for yourselves from each of your tribes in all the towns the LORD your God is giving you. They must judge the people fairly. [19]You must never twist

16:1 Hebrew *Observe the month of Abib, and keep the Passover unto the LORD your God.* Abib, the first month of the ancient Hebrew lunar calendar, usually occurs within the months of March and April. **16:10** Hebrew *Festival of Weeks;* also in 16:16. This was later called the Festival of Pentecost (see Acts 2:1). It is celebrated today as Shavuot (or Shabuoth). **16:13** Or *Festival of Booths,* or *Festival of Tabernacles;* also in 16:16. This was earlier called the Festival of the Final Harvest or Festival of Ingathering (see Exod 23:16b). It is celebrated today as Sukkot (or Succoth).

justice or show partiality. Never accept a bribe,
for bribes blind the eyes of the wise and cor-
rupt the decisions of the godly. [20]Let true jus-
tice prevail, so you may live and occupy the
land that the LORD your God is giving you.

[21]"You must never set up a wooden Ashe-
rah pole beside the altar you build for the
LORD your God. [22]And never set up sacred pil-
lars for worship, for the LORD your God hates
them.

CHAPTER 17

"Never sacrifice sick or defective cattle,
sheep, or goats to the LORD your God, for he
detests such gifts.

[2]"When you begin living in the towns the
LORD your God is giving you, a man or woman
among you might do evil in the sight of the
LORD your God and violate the covenant. [3]For
instance, they might serve other gods or wor-
ship the sun, the moon, or any of the stars—the
forces of heaven—which I have strictly forbid-
den. [4]When you hear about it, investigate the
matter thoroughly. If it is true that this detest-
able thing has been done in Israel, [5]then the
man or woman who has committed such an
evil act must be taken to the gates of the town
and stoned to death. [6]But never put a person to
death on the testimony of only one witness.
There must always be two or three witnesses.
[7]The witnesses must throw the first stones,
and then all the people may join in. In this way,
you will purge the evil from among you.

[8]"Suppose a case arises in a local court that
is too hard for you to decide—for instance,
whether someone is guilty of murder or only
of manslaughter, or a difficult lawsuit, or a
case involving different kinds of assault. Take
such legal cases to the place the LORD your
God will choose, [9]and present them to the Le-
vitical priests or the judge on duty at that
time. They will hear the case and declare the
verdict. [10]You must carry out the verdict they
announce and the sentence they prescribe at
the place the LORD chooses. You must do ex-
actly what they say. [11]After they have inter-
preted the law and declared their verdict, the
sentence they impose must be fully executed;
do not modify it in any way. [12]Anyone arro-
gant enough to reject the verdict of the judge
or of the priest who represents the LORD your
God must die. In this way you will purge the
evil from Israel. [13]Then everyone else will
hear about it and be afraid to act so arro-
gantly.

Guidelines for a King

[14]"You are about to enter the land the LORD
your God is giving you. When you take it over
and settle there, you may think, 'We should
select a king to rule over us like the other na-
tions around us.' [15]If this happens, be sure to
select as king the man the LORD your God
chooses. You must appoint a fellow Israelite;
he may not be a foreigner.

[16]"The king must not build up a large sta-
ble of horses for himself or send his people to
Egypt to buy horses, for the LORD has told you,
'You must never return to Egypt.' [17]The king
must not take many wives for himself, be-
cause they will turn his heart away from the
LORD. And he must not accumulate large
amounts of wealth in silver and gold for him-
self.

[18]"When he sits on the throne as king, he
must copy for himself this body of instruc-
tion on a scroll in the presence of the Levitical
priests. [19]He must always keep that copy with
him and read it daily as long as he lives. That
way he will learn to fear the LORD his God by
obeying all the terms of these instructions
and decrees. [20]This regular reading will pre-
vent him from becoming proud and acting as
if he is above his fellow citizens. It will also
prevent him from turning away from these
commands in the smallest way. And it will en-
sure that he and his descendants will reign
for many generations in Israel.

CHAPTER 18

Gifts for the Priests and Levites

"Remember that the Levitical priests—that is,
the whole of the tribe of Levi—will receive no
allotment of land among the other tribes in
Israel. Instead, the priests and Levites will eat
from the special gifts given to the LORD, for
that is their share. [2]They will have no land of
their own among the Israelites. The LORD
himself is their special possession, just as he
promised them.

[3]"These are the parts the priests may claim
as their share from the cattle, sheep, and
goats that the people bring as offerings: the
shoulder, the cheeks, and the stomach. [4]You

must also give to the priests the first share of
the grain, the new wine, the olive oil, and the
wool at shearing time. [5]For the LORD your God
chose the tribe of Levi out of all your tribes to
minister in the LORD's name forever.

[6]"Suppose a Levite chooses to move from
his town in Israel, wherever he is living, to the
place the LORD chooses for worship. [7]He may
minister there in the name of the LORD his
God, just like all his fellow Levites who are
serving the LORD there. [8]He may eat his share
of the sacrifices and offerings, even if he also
receives support from his family.

A Call to Holy Living

[9]"When you enter the land the LORD your God
is giving you, be very careful not to imitate
the detestable customs of the nations living
there. [10]For example, never sacrifice your son
or daughter as a burnt offering.* And do not
let your people practice fortune-telling, or use
sorcery, or interpret omens, or engage in
witchcraft, [11]or cast spells, or function as me-
diums or psychics, or call forth the spirits of
the dead. [12]Anyone who does these things is
detestable to the LORD. It is because the other
nations have done these detestable things that
the LORD your God will drive them out ahead
of you. [13]But you must be blameless before the
LORD your God. [14]The nations you are about to
displace consult sorcerers and fortune-tellers,
but the LORD your God forbids you to do such
things."

True and False Prophets

[15]Moses continued, "The LORD your God will
raise up for you a prophet like me from
among your fellow Israelites. You must listen
to him. [16]For this is what you yourselves re-
quested of the LORD your God when you were
assembled at Mount Sinai.* You said, 'Don't
let us hear the voice of the LORD our God any-
more or see this blazing fire, for we will die.'

[17]"Then the LORD said to me, 'What they
have said is right. [18]I will raise up a prophet
like you from among their fellow Israelites. I
will put my words in his mouth, and he will
tell the people everything I command him. [19]I
will personally deal with anyone who will not
listen to the messages the prophet proclaims
on my behalf. [20]But any prophet who falsely
claims to speak in my name or who speaks in
the name of another god must die.'

[21]"But you may wonder, 'How will we know
whether or not a prophecy is from the LORD?'
[22]If the prophet speaks in the LORD's name
but his prediction does not happen or come
true, you will know that the LORD did not give
that message. That prophet has spoken with-
out my authority and need not be feared.

THE UNKNOWN FUTURE

Some of Patrick's friends usually got together after school to mess around with a Ouija board. He knew they were very curious about their future. Then one day Neil mentioned that there was a woman who lived a few blocks away who could tell the future by reading palms and tarot cards. He asked, "Does anybody want to go with me and see what our futures hold?"

Patrick was really curious and wondered what he should do. See Deuteronomy 4:19 and 18:10-12 for the answer.

18:10 Or *never make your son or daughter pass through the fire.* **18:16** Hebrew *Horeb*, another name for Sinai.

CHAPTER 19

Cities of Refuge

"When the LORD your God destroys the nations whose land he is giving you, you will take over their land and settle in their towns and homes. [2]Then you must set apart three cities of refuge in the land the LORD your God is giving you. [3]Survey the territory,* and divide the land the LORD your God is giving you into three districts, with one of these cities in each district. Then anyone who has killed someone can flee to one of the cities of refuge for safety.

[4]"If someone kills another person unintentionally, without previous hostility, the slayer may flee to any of these cities to live in safety. [5]For example, suppose someone goes into the forest with a neighbor to cut wood. And suppose one of them swings an ax to chop down a tree, and the ax head flies off the handle, killing the other person. In such cases, the slayer may flee to one of the cities of refuge to live in safety.

[6]"If the distance to the nearest city of refuge is too far, an enraged avenger might be able to chase down and kill the person who caused the death. Then the slayer would die unfairly, since he had never shown hostility toward the person who died. [7]That is why I am commanding you to set aside three cities of refuge.

[8]"And if the LORD your God enlarges your territory, as he swore to your ancestors, and gives you all the land he promised them, [9]you must designate three additional cities of refuge. (He will give you this land if you are careful to obey all the commands I have given you—if you always love the LORD your God and walk in his ways.) [10]That way you will prevent the death of innocent people in the land the LORD your God is giving you as your special possession. You will not be held responsible for the death of innocent people.

[11]"But suppose someone is hostile toward a neighbor and deliberately ambushes and murders him and then flees to one of the cities of refuge. [12]In that case, the elders of the murderer's hometown must send agents to the city of refuge to bring him back and hand him over to the dead person's avenger to be put to death. [13]Do not feel sorry for that murderer! Purge from Israel the guilt of murdering innocent people; then all will go well with you.

Concern for Justice

[14]"When you arrive in the land the LORD your God is giving you as your special possession, you must never steal anyone's land by moving the boundary markers your ancestors set up to mark their property.

[15]"You must not convict anyone of a crime on the testimony of only one witness. The facts of the case must be established by the testimony of two or three witnesses.

[16]"If a malicious witness comes forward and accuses someone of a crime, [17]then both the accuser and accused must appear before the LORD by coming to the priests and judges in office at that time. [18]The judges must investigate the case thoroughly. If the accuser has brought false charges against his fellow Israelite, [19]you must impose on the accuser the sentence he intended for the other person. In this way, you will purge such evil from among you. [20]Then the rest of the people will hear about it and be afraid to do such an evil thing. [21]You must show no pity for the guilty! Your rule should be life for life, eye for eye, tooth for tooth, hand for hand, foot for foot.

CHAPTER 20

Regulations concerning War

"When you go out to fight your enemies and you face horses and chariots and an army greater than your own, do not be afraid. The LORD your God, who brought you out of the land of Egypt, is with you! [2]When you prepare for battle, the priest must come forward to speak to the troops. [3]He will say to them, 'Listen to me, all you men of Israel! Do not be afraid as you go out to fight your enemies today! Do not lose heart or panic or tremble before them. [4]For the LORD your God is going with you! He will fight for you against your enemies, and he will give you victory!'

[5]"Then the officers of the army must address the troops and say, 'Has anyone here just built a new house but not yet dedicated it? If so, you may go home! You might be killed in the battle, and someone else would

19:3 Or *Keep the roads in good repair.*

dedicate your house. [6]Has anyone here just planted a vineyard but not yet eaten any of its fruit? If so, you may go home! You might die in battle, and someone else would eat the first fruit. [7]Has anyone here just become engaged to a woman but not yet married her? Well, you may go home and get married! You might die in the battle, and someone else would marry her.'

[8]"Then the officers will also say, 'Is anyone here afraid or worried? If you are, you may go home before you frighten anyone else.' [9]When the officers have finished speaking to their troops, they will appoint the unit commanders.

[10]"As you approach a town to attack it, you must first offer its people terms for peace. [11]If they accept your terms and open the gates to you, then all the people inside will serve you in forced labor. [12]But if they refuse to make peace and prepare to fight, you must attack the town. [13]When the LORD your God hands the town over to you, use your swords to kill every man in the town. [14]But you may keep for yourselves all the women, children, livestock, and other plunder. You may enjoy the plunder from your enemies that the LORD your God has given you.

[15]"But these instructions apply only to distant towns, not to the towns of the nations in the land you will enter. [16]In those towns that the LORD your God is giving you as a special possession, destroy every living thing. [17]You must completely destroy* the Hittites, Amorites, Canaanites, Perizzites, Hivites, and Jebusites, just as the LORD your God has commanded you. [18]This will prevent the people of the land from teaching you to imitate their detestable customs in the worship of their gods, which would cause you to sin deeply against the LORD your God.

[19]"When you are attacking a town and the war drags on, you must not cut down the trees with your axes. You may eat the fruit, but do not cut down the trees. Are the trees your enemies, that you should attack them? [20]You may only cut down trees that you know are not valuable for food. Use them to make the equipment you need to attack the enemy town until it falls.

CHAPTER 21

Cleansing for Unsolved Murder

"When you are in the land the LORD your God is giving you, someone may be found murdered in a field, and you don't know who committed the murder. [2]In such a case, your elders and judges must measure the distance from the site of the crime to the nearby towns. [3]When the nearest town has been determined, that town's elders must select from the herd a young cow that has never been trained or yoked to a plow. [4]They must lead it down to a valley that has not been plowed or planted and that has a stream running through it. There in the valley they must break the young cow's neck. [5]Then the Levitical priests must step forward, for the LORD your God has chosen them to minister before him and to pronounce blessings in the LORD's name. They are to decide all legal and criminal cases.

[6]"The elders of the town must wash their hands over the young cow whose neck was broken. [7]Then they must say, 'Our hands did not shed this person's blood, nor did we see it happen. [8]O LORD, forgive your people Israel whom you have redeemed. Do not charge your people with the guilt of murdering an innocent person.' Then they will be absolved of the guilt of this person's blood. [9]By following these instructions, you will do what is right in the LORD's sight and will cleanse the guilt of murder from your community.

Marriage to a Captive Woman

[10]"Suppose you go out to war against your enemies and the LORD your God hands them over to you, and you take some of them as captives. [11]And suppose you see among the captives a beautiful woman, and you are attracted to her and want to marry her. [12]If this happens, you may take her to your home, where she must shave her head, cut her nails, [13]and change the clothes she was wearing when she was captured. She will stay in your home, but let her mourn for her father and mother for a full month. Then you may marry her, and you will be her husband and she will be your wife. [14]But if you marry her and she does not please you, you must let her go free.

20:17 The Hebrew term used here refers to the complete consecration of things or people to the LORD, either by destroying them or by giving them as an offering.

You may not sell her or treat her as a slave, for you have humiliated her.

Rights of the Firstborn

15"Suppose a man has two wives, but he loves one and not the other, and both have given him sons. And suppose the firstborn son is the son of the wife he does not love. 16When the man divides his inheritance, he may not give the larger inheritance to his younger son, the son of the wife he loves, as if he were the firstborn son. 17He must recognize the rights of his oldest son, the son of the wife he does not love, by giving him a double portion. He is the first son of his father's virility, and the rights of the firstborn belong to him.

Dealing with a Rebellious Son

18"Suppose a man has a stubborn and rebellious son who will not obey his father or mother, even though they discipline him. 19In such a case, the father and mother must take the son to the elders as they hold court at the town gate. 20The parents must say to the elders, 'This son of ours is stubborn and rebellious and refuses to obey. He is a glutton and a drunkard.' 21Then all the men of his town must stone him to death. In this way, you will purge this evil from among you, and all Israel will hear about it and be afraid.

Various Regulations

22"If someone has committed a crime worthy of death and is executed and hung on a tree,* 23the body must not remain hanging from the tree overnight. You must bury the body that same day, for anyone who is hung* is cursed in the sight of God. In this way, you will prevent the defilement of the land the LORD your God is giving you as your special possession.

CHAPTER 22

"If you see your neighbor's ox or sheep or goat wandering away, don't ignore your responsibility.* Take it back to its owner. 2If its owner does not live nearby or you don't know who the owner is, take it to your place and keep it until the owner comes looking for it. Then you must return it. 3Do the same if you find your neighbor's donkey, clothing, or anything else your neighbor loses. Don't ignore your responsibility.

4"If you see that your neighbor's donkey or ox has collapsed on the road, do not look the other way. Go and help your neighbor get it back on its feet!

5"A woman must not put on men's clothing, and a man must not wear women's clothing. Anyone who does this is detestable in the sight of the LORD your God.

6"If you happen to find a bird's nest in a tree or on the ground, and there are young ones or eggs in it with the mother sitting in the nest, do not take the mother with the young. 7You may take the young, but let the mother go, so that you may prosper and enjoy a long life.

8"When you build a new house, you must build a railing around the edge of its flat roof. That way you will not be considered guilty of murder if someone falls from the roof.

9"You must not plant any other crop be-

21:22 Or *impaled on a pole;* similarly in 21:23. **21:23** Greek version reads *for everyone who is hung on a tree.* Compare Gal 3:13.
22:1 Hebrew *don't hide yourself;* similarly in 22:3.

tween the rows of your vineyard. If you do, you are forbidden to use either the grapes from the vineyard or the other crop.

10"You must not plow with an ox and a donkey harnessed together.

11"You must not wear clothing made of wool and linen woven together.

12"You must put four tassels on the hem of the cloak with which you cover yourself—on the front, back, and sides.

Regulations for Sexual Purity

13"Suppose a man marries a woman, but after sleeping with her, he turns against her 14and publicly accuses her of shameful conduct, saying, 'When I married this woman, I discovered she was not a virgin.' 15Then the woman's father and mother must bring the proof of her virginity to the elders as they hold court at the town gate. 16Her father must say to them, 'I gave my daughter to this man to be his wife, and now he has turned against her. 17He has accused her of shameful conduct, saying, "I discovered that your daughter was not a virgin." But here is the proof of my daughter's virginity.' Then they must spread her bed sheet before the elders. 18The elders must then take the man and punish him. 19They must also fine him 100 pieces of silver,* which he must pay to the woman's father because he publicly accused a virgin of Israel of shameful conduct. The woman will then remain the man's wife, and he may never divorce her.

20"But suppose the man's accusations are true, and he can show that she was not a virgin. 21The woman must be taken to the door of her father's home, and there the men of the town must stone her to death, for she has committed a disgraceful crime in Israel by being promiscuous while living in her parents' home. In this way, you will purge this evil from among you.

22"If a man is discovered committing adultery, both he and the woman must die. In this way, you will purge Israel of such evil.

23"Suppose a man meets a young woman, a virgin who is engaged to be married, and he has sexual intercourse with her. If this happens within a town, 24you must take both of them to the gates of that town and stone them to death. The woman is guilty because she did not scream for help. The man must die because he violated another man's wife. In this way, you will purge this evil from among you.

25"But if the man meets the engaged woman out in the country, and he rapes her, then only the man must die. 26Do nothing to the young woman; she has committed no crime worthy of death. She is as innocent as a murder victim. 27Since the man raped her out in the country, it must be assumed that she screamed, but there was no one to rescue her.

28"Suppose a man has intercourse with a young woman who is a virgin but is not engaged to be married. If they are discovered, 29he must pay her father fifty pieces of silver.* Then he must marry the young woman because he violated her, and he may never divorce her as long as he lives.

30*"A man must not marry his father's former wife, for this would violate his father.

CHAPTER 23

Regulations concerning Worship

1*"If a man's testicles are crushed or his penis is cut off, he may not be admitted to the assembly of the LORD.

2"If a person is illegitimate by birth, neither he nor his descendants for ten generations may be admitted to the assembly of the LORD.

3"No Ammonite or Moabite or any of their descendants for ten generations may be admitted to the assembly of the LORD. 4These nations did not welcome you with food and water when you came out of Egypt. Instead, they hired Balaam son of Beor from Pethor in distant Aram-naharaim to curse you. 5But the LORD your God refused to listen to Balaam. He turned the intended curse into a blessing because the LORD your God loves you. 6As long as you live, you must never promote the welfare and prosperity of the Ammonites or Moabites.

7"Do not detest the Edomites or the Egyptians, because the Edomites are your relatives and you lived as foreigners among the Egyptians. 8The third generation of Edomites and Egyptians may enter the assembly of the LORD.

22:19 Hebrew *100 shekels of silver*, about 2.5 pounds or 1.1 kilograms in weight. **22:29** Hebrew *50 shekels of silver*, about 1.25 pounds or 570 grams in weight. **22:30** Verse 22:30 is numbered 23:1 in Hebrew text. **23:1** Verses 23:1-25 are numbered 23:2-26 in Hebrew text.

Miscellaneous Regulations

9"When you go to war against your enemies,
be sure to stay away from anything that is im-
pure.
10"Any man who becomes ceremonially
defiled because of a nocturnal emission must
leave the camp and stay away all day.
11Toward evening he must bathe himself, and
at sunset he may return to the camp.
12"You must have a designated area out-
side the camp where you can go to relieve
yourself. 13Each of you must have a spade as
part of your equipment. Whenever you re-
lieve yourself, dig a hole with the spade and
cover the excrement. 14The camp must be
holy, for the LORD your God moves around in
your camp to protect you and to defeat your
enemies. He must not see any shameful thing
among you, or he will turn away from you.
15"If slaves should escape from their mas-
ters and take refuge with you, you must not
hand them over to their masters. 16Let them
live among you in any town they choose, and
do not oppress them.
17"No Israelite, whether man or woman,
may become a temple prostitute. 18When you
are bringing an offering to fulfill a vow, you
must not bring to the house of the LORD your
God any offering from the earnings of a pros-
titute, whether a man* or a woman, for both
are detestable to the LORD your God.
19"Do not charge interest on the loans you
make to a fellow Israelite, whether you loan
money, or food, or anything else. 20You may
charge interest to foreigners, but you may not
charge interest to Israelites, so that the LORD
your God may bless you in everything you do
in the land you are about to enter and occupy.
21"When you make a vow to the LORD your
God, be prompt in fulfilling whatever you
promised him. For the LORD your God de-
mands that you promptly fulfill all your vows,
or you will be guilty of sin. 22However, it is not
a sin to refrain from making a vow. 23But once
you have voluntarily made a vow, be careful to
fulfill your promise to the LORD your God.
24"When you enter your neighbor's vine-
yard, you may eat your fill of grapes, but you
must not carry any away in a basket. 25And
when you enter your neighbor's field of grain,
you may pluck the heads of grain with your
hand, but you must not harvest it with a
sickle.

CHAPTER 24

"Suppose a man marries a woman but she
does not please him. Having discovered
something wrong with her, he writes her a let-
ter of divorce, hands it to her, and sends her
away from his house. 2When she leaves his
house, she is free to marry another man. 3But
if the second husband also turns against her
and divorces her, or if he dies, 4the first hus-
band may not marry her again, for she has
been defiled. That would be detestable to the
LORD. You must not bring guilt upon the land
the LORD your God is giving you as a special
possession.
5"A newly married man must not be
drafted into the army or be given any other
official responsibilities. He must be free to
spend one year at home, bringing happiness
to the wife he has married.
6"It is wrong to take a set of millstones, or
even just the upper millstone, as security for a
loan, for the owner uses it to make a living.
7"If anyone kidnaps a fellow Israelite and
treats him as a slave or sells him, the kidnap-
per must die. In this way, you will purge the
evil from among you.
8"In all cases involving serious skin dis-
eases,* be careful to follow the instructions
of the Levitical priests; obey all the com-
mands I have given them. 9Remember what
the LORD your God did to Miriam as you were
coming from Egypt.
10"If you lend anything to your neighbor,
do not enter his house to pick up the item he
is giving as security. 11You must wait outside
while he goes in and brings it out to you. 12If
your neighbor is poor and gives you his cloak
as security for a loan, do not keep the cloak
overnight. 13Return the cloak to its owner by
sunset so he can stay warm through the night
and bless you, and the LORD your God will
count you as righteous.
14"Never take advantage of poor and desti-
tute laborers, whether they are fellow Israel-
ites or foreigners living in your towns. 15You
must pay them their wages each day before
sunset because they are poor and are count-
ing on it. If you don't, they might cry out to the

23:18 Hebrew *a dog*. **24:8** Traditionally rendered *leprosy*. The Hebrew word used here can describe various skin diseases.

LORD against you, and it would be counted against you as sin.

16"Parents must not be put to death for the sins of their children, nor children for the sins of their parents. Those deserving to die must be put to death for their own crimes.

17"True justice must be given to foreigners living among you and to orphans, and you must never accept a widow's garment as security for her debt. 18Always remember that you were slaves in Egypt and that the LORD your God redeemed you from your slavery. That is why I have given you this command.

19"When you are harvesting your crops and forget to bring in a bundle of grain from your field, don't go back to get it. Leave it for the foreigners, orphans, and widows. Then the LORD your God will bless you in all you do. 20When you beat the olives from your olive trees, don't go over the boughs twice. Leave the remaining olives for the foreigners, orphans, and widows. 21When you gather the grapes in your vineyard, don't glean the vines after they are picked. Leave the remaining grapes for the foreigners, orphans, and widows. 22Remember that you were slaves in the land of Egypt. That is why I am giving you this command.

CHAPTER 25

"Suppose two people take a dispute to court, and the judges declare that one is right and the other is wrong. 2If the person in the wrong is sentenced to be flogged, the judge must command him to lie down and be beaten in his presence with the number of lashes appropriate to the crime. 3But never give more than forty lashes; more than forty lashes would publicly humiliate your neighbor.

4"You must not muzzle an ox to keep it from eating as it treads out the grain.

5"If two brothers are living together on the same property and one of them dies without a son, his widow may not be married to anyone from outside the family. Instead, her husband's brother should marry her and have intercourse with her to fulfill the duties of a brother-in-law. 6The first son she bears to him will be considered the son of the dead brother, so that his name will not be forgotten in Israel.

7"But if the man refuses to marry his brother's widow, she must go to the town gate and say to the elders assembled there, 'My husband's brother refuses to preserve his brother's name in Israel—he refuses to fulfill the duties of a brother-in-law by marrying me.' 8The elders of the town will then summon him and talk with him. If he still refuses and says, 'I don't want to marry her,' 9the widow must walk over to him in the presence of the elders, pull his sandal from his foot, and spit in his face. Then she must declare, 'This is what happens to a man who refuses to provide his brother with children.' 10Ever afterward in Israel his family will be referred to as 'the family of the man whose sandal was pulled off'!

11"If two Israelite men get into a fight and the wife of one tries to rescue her husband by grabbing the testicles of the other man, 12you must cut off her hand. Show her no pity.

13"You must use accurate scales when you weigh out merchandise, 14and you must use full and honest measures. 15Yes, always use honest weights and measures, so that you may enjoy a long life in the land the LORD your God is giving you. 16All who cheat with dishonest weights and measures are detestable to the LORD your God.

17"Never forget what the Amalekites did to you as you came from Egypt. 18They attacked you when you were exhausted and weary, and they struck down those who were straggling behind. They had no fear of God. 19Therefore, when the LORD your God has given you rest from all your enemies in the land he is giving you as a special possession, you must destroy the Amalekites and erase their memory from under heaven. Never forget this!

CHAPTER 26

Harvest Offerings and Tithes

"When you enter the land the LORD your God is giving you as a special possession and you have conquered it and settled there, 2put some of the first produce from each crop you harvest into a basket and bring it to the designated place of worship—the place the LORD your God chooses for his name to be honored. 3Go to the priest in charge at that time and say to him, 'With this gift I acknowledge to the LORD your God that I have entered the land he swore to our ancestors he would give us.' 4The priest will then take the basket from your hand and set it before the altar of the LORD your God.

5"You must then say in the presence of the LORD your God, 'My ancestor Jacob was a wandering Aramean who went to live as a foreigner in Egypt. His family arrived few in number, but in Egypt they became a large and mighty nation. 6When the Egyptians oppressed and humiliated us by making us their slaves, 7we cried out to the LORD, the God of our ancestors. He heard our cries and saw our hardship, toil, and oppression. 8So the LORD brought us out of Egypt with a strong hand and powerful arm, with overwhelming terror, and with miraculous signs and wonders. 9He brought us to this place and gave us this land flowing with milk and honey! 10And now, O LORD, I have brought you the first portion of the harvest you have given me from the ground.' Then place the produce before the LORD your God, and bow to the ground in worship before him. 11Afterward you may go and celebrate because of all the good things the LORD your God has given to you and your household. Remember to include the Levites and the foreigners living among you in the celebration.

12"Every third year you must offer a special tithe of your crops. In this year of the special tithe you must give your tithes to the Levites, foreigners, orphans, and widows, so that they will have enough to eat in your towns. 13Then you must declare in the presence of the LORD your God, 'I have taken the sacred gift from my house and have given it to the Levites, foreigners, orphans, and widows, just as you commanded me. I have not violated or forgotten any of your commands. 14I have not eaten any of it while in mourning; I have not handled it while I was ceremonially unclean; and I have not offered any of it to the dead. I have obeyed the LORD my God and have done everything you commanded me. 15Now look down from your holy dwelling place in heaven and bless your people Israel and the land you swore to our ancestors to give us—a land flowing with milk and honey.'

A Call to Obey the LORD's Commands

16"Today the LORD your God has commanded you to obey all these decrees and regulations. So be careful to obey them wholeheartedly. 17You have declared today that the LORD is your God. And you have promised to walk in his ways, and to obey his decrees, commands, and regulations, and to do everything he tells you. 18The LORD has declared today that you are his people, his own special treasure, just as he promised, and that you must obey all his commands. 19And if you do, he will set you high above all the other nations he has made. Then you will receive praise, honor, and renown. You will be a nation that is holy to the LORD your God, just as he promised."

CHAPTER 27

The Altar on Mount Ebal

Then Moses and the leaders of Israel gave this charge to the people: "Obey all these commands that I am giving you today. 2When you cross the Jordan River and enter the land the LORD your God is giving you, set up some large stones and coat them with plaster. 3Write this whole body of instruction on them when you cross the river to enter the land the LORD your God is giving you—a land flowing with milk and honey, just as the LORD, the God of your ancestors, promised you. 4When you cross the Jordan, set up these stones at Mount Ebal and coat them with plaster, as I am commanding you today.

5"Then build an altar there to the LORD your God, using natural, uncut stones. You must not shape the stones with an iron tool. 6Build the altar of uncut stones, and use it to offer burnt offerings to the LORD your God. 7Also sacrifice peace offerings on it, and celebrate by feasting there before the LORD your God. 8You must clearly write all these instructions on the stones coated with plaster."

9Then Moses and the Levitical priests addressed all Israel as follows: "O Israel, be quiet and listen! Today you have become the people of the LORD your God. 10So you must obey the LORD your God by keeping all these commands and decrees that I am giving you today."

Curses from Mount Ebal

11That same day Moses also gave this charge to the people: 12"When you cross the Jordan River, the tribes of Simeon, Levi, Judah, Issachar, Joseph, and Benjamin must stand on Mount Gerizim to proclaim a blessing over the people. 13And the tribes of Reuben, Gad,

Asher, Zebulun, Dan, and Naphtali must stand on Mount Ebal to proclaim a curse.

14"Then the Levites will shout to all the people of Israel:

15'Cursed is anyone who carves or casts an idol and secretly sets it up. These idols, the work of craftsmen, are detestable to the LORD.'
And all the people will reply, 'Amen.'

16'Cursed is anyone who dishonors father or mother.'
And all the people will reply, 'Amen.'

17'Cursed is anyone who steals property from a neighbor by moving a boundary marker.'
And all the people will reply, 'Amen.'

18'Cursed is anyone who leads a blind person astray on the road.'
And all the people will reply, 'Amen.'

19'Cursed is anyone who denies justice to foreigners, orphans, or widows.'
And all the people will reply, 'Amen.'

20'Cursed is anyone who has sexual intercourse with one of his father's wives, for he has violated his father.'
And all the people will reply, 'Amen.'

21'Cursed is anyone who has sexual intercourse with an animal.'
And all the people will reply, 'Amen.'

22'Cursed is anyone who has sexual intercourse with his sister, whether she is the daughter of his father or his mother.'
And all the people will reply, 'Amen.'

23'Cursed is anyone who has sexual intercourse with his mother-in-law.'
And all the people will reply, 'Amen.'

24'Cursed is anyone who attacks a neighbor in secret.'
And all the people will reply, 'Amen.'

25'Cursed is anyone who accepts payment to kill an innocent person.'
And all the people will reply, 'Amen.'

26'Cursed is anyone who does not affirm and obey the terms of these instructions.'
And all the people will reply, 'Amen.'

AMAZING FACTS

Did you know that God commanded his worship leaders to stand in a valley and shout curses?

DEUTERONOMY 27:11-26

CHAPTER 28

Blessings for Obedience

"If you fully obey the LORD your God and carefully keep all his commands that I am giving you today, the LORD your God will set you high above all the nations of the world. 2You will experience all these blessings if you obey the LORD your God:

3 Your towns and your fields
will be blessed.
4 Your children and your crops
will be blessed.
The offspring of your herds and flocks
will be blessed.
5 Your fruit baskets and breadboards
will be blessed.
6 Wherever you go and whatever you do,
you will be blessed.

7"The LORD will conquer your enemies when they attack you. They will attack you from one direction, but they will scatter from you in seven!

8"The LORD will guarantee a blessing on everything you do and will fill your storehouses with grain. The LORD your God will bless you in the land he is giving you.

9"If you obey the commands of the LORD your God and walk in his ways, the LORD will establish you as his holy people as he swore he would do. 10Then all the nations of the world will see that you are a people claimed by the LORD, and they will stand in awe of you.

[11]"The LORD will give you prosperity in the land he swore to your ancestors to give you, blessing you with many children, numerous livestock, and abundant crops. [12]The LORD will send rain at the proper time from his rich treasury in the heavens and will bless all the work you do. You will lend to many nations, but you will never need to borrow from them. [13]If you listen to these commands of the LORD your God that I am giving you today, and if you carefully obey them, the LORD will make you the head and not the tail, and you will always be on top and never at the bottom. [14]You must not turn away from any of the commands I am giving you today, nor follow after other gods and worship them.

Curses for Disobedience

[15]"But if you refuse to listen to the LORD your God and do not obey all the commands and decrees I am giving you today, all these curses will come and overwhelm you:

[16] Your towns and your fields
will be cursed.
[17] Your fruit baskets and breadboards
will be cursed.
[18] Your children and your crops
will be cursed.
The offspring of your herds and flocks
will be cursed.
[19] Wherever you go and whatever you do,
you will be cursed.

[20]"The LORD himself will send on you curses, confusion, and frustration in everything you do, until at last you are completely destroyed for doing evil and abandoning me. [21]The LORD will afflict you with diseases until none of you are left in the land you are about to enter and occupy. [22]The LORD will strike you with wasting diseases, fever, and inflammation, with scorching heat and drought, and with blight and mildew. These disasters will pursue you until you die. [23]The skies above will be as unyielding as bronze, and the earth beneath will be as hard as iron. [24]The LORD will change the rain that falls on your land into powder, and dust will pour down from the sky until you are destroyed.

[25]"The LORD will cause you to be defeated by your enemies. You will attack your enemies from one direction, but you will scatter from them in seven! You will be an object of horror to all the kingdoms of the earth. [26]Your corpses will be food for all the scavenging birds and wild animals, and no one will be there to chase them away.

[27]"The LORD will afflict you with the boils of Egypt and with tumors, scurvy, and the itch, from which you cannot be cured. [28]The LORD will strike you with madness, blindness, and panic. [29]You will grope around in broad daylight like a blind person groping in the darkness, but you will not find your way. You will be oppressed and robbed continually, and no one will come to save you.

[30]"You will be engaged to a woman, but another man will sleep with her. You will build a house, but someone else will live in it. You will plant a vineyard, but you will never enjoy its fruit. [31]Your ox will be butchered before your eyes, but you will not eat a single bite of the meat. Your donkey will be taken from you, never to be returned. Your sheep and goats will be given to your enemies, and no one will be there to help you. [32]You will watch as your sons and daughters are taken away as slaves. Your heart will break for them, but you won't be able to help them. [33]A foreign nation you have never heard about will eat the crops you worked so hard to grow. You will suffer under constant oppression and harsh treatment. [34]You will go mad because of all the tragedy you see around you. [35]The LORD will cover your knees and legs with incurable boils. In fact, you will be covered from head to foot.

[36]"The LORD will exile you and your king to a nation unknown to you and your ancestors. There in exile you will worship gods of wood and stone! [37]You will become an object of horror, ridicule, and mockery among all the nations to which the LORD sends you.

[38]"You will plant much but harvest little, for locusts will eat your crops. [39]You will plant vineyards and care for them, but you will not drink the wine or eat the grapes, for worms will destroy the vines. [40]You will grow olive trees throughout your land, but you will never use the olive oil, for the fruit will drop before it ripens. [41]You will have sons and daughters, but you will lose them, for they will be led away into captivity. [42]Swarms of insects will destroy your trees and crops.

[43]"The foreigners living among you will be-

come stronger and stronger, while you
become weaker and weaker. [44]They will lend
money to you, but you will not lend to them.
They will be the head, and you will be the tail!

[45]"If you refuse to listen to the LORD your
God and to obey the commands and decrees
he has given you, all these curses will pursue
and overtake you until you are destroyed.
[46]These horrors will serve as a sign and warn-
ing among you and your descendants forever.
[47]If you do not serve the LORD your God with
joy and enthusiasm for the abundant benefits
you have received, [48]you will serve your ene-
mies whom the LORD will send against you.
You will be left hungry, thirsty, naked, and
lacking in everything. The LORD will put an
iron yoke on your neck, oppressing you
harshly until he has destroyed you.

[49]"The LORD will bring a distant nation
against you from the end of the earth, and it
will swoop down on you like a vulture. It is
a nation whose language you do not under-
stand, [50]a fierce and heartless nation that
shows no respect for the old and no pity for
the young. [51]Its armies will devour your live-
stock and crops, and you will be destroyed.
They will leave you no grain, new wine, olive
oil, calves, or lambs, and you will starve to
death. [52]They will attack your cities until all
the fortified walls in your land—the walls you
trusted to protect you—are knocked down.
They will attack all the towns in the land the
LORD your God has given you.

[53]"The siege and terrible distress of the en-
emy's attack will be so severe that you will eat
the flesh of your own sons and daughters,
whom the LORD your God has given you. [54]The
most tenderhearted man among you will have
no compassion for his own brother, his be-
loved wife, and his surviving children. [55]He
will refuse to share with them the flesh he is
devouring—the flesh of one of his own chil-
dren—because he has nothing else to eat dur-
ing the siege and terrible distress that your
enemy will inflict on all your towns. [56]The
most tender and delicate woman among
you—so delicate she would not so much as
touch the ground with her foot—will be self-
ish toward the husband she loves and toward
her own son or daughter. [57]She will hide from
them the afterbirth and the new baby she has
borne, so that she herself can secretly eat
them. She will have nothing else to eat during
the siege and terrible distress that your en-
emy will inflict on all your towns.

[58]"If you refuse to obey all the words of in-
struction that are written in this book, and if
you do not fear the glorious and awesome
name of the LORD your God, [59]then the LORD
will overwhelm you and your children with
indescribable plagues. These plagues will be
intense and without relief, making you miser-
able and unbearably sick. [60]He will afflict you
with all the diseases of Egypt that you feared
so much, and you will have no relief. [61]The
LORD will afflict you with every sickness and
plague there is, even those not mentioned
in this Book of Instruction, until you are de-
stroyed. [62]Though you become as numerous
as the stars in the sky, few of you will be left
because you would not listen to the LORD your
God.

[63]"Just as the LORD has found great plea-
sure in causing you to prosper and multiply,
the LORD will find pleasure in destroying
you. You will be torn from the land you are
about to enter and occupy. [64]For the LORD
will scatter you among all the nations from
one end of the earth to the other. There you
will worship foreign gods that neither you
nor your an-cestors have known, gods made
of wood and stone! [65]There among those na-
tions you will find no peace or place to rest.
And the LORD will cause your heart to trem-
ble, your eyesight to fail, and your soul to de-
spair. [66]Your life will constantly hang in the
balance. You will live night and day in fear,
unsure if you will survive. [67]In the morning
you will say, 'If only it were night!' And in the
evening you will say, 'If only it were morn-
ing!' For you will be terrified by the awful
horrors you see around you. [68]Then the LORD
will send you back to Egypt in ships, to a des-
tination I promised you would never see
again. There you will offer to sell yourselves
to your enemies as slaves, but no one will
buy you."

CHAPTER 29

[1a]*These are the terms of the covenant the
LORD commanded Moses to make with the Is-
raelites while they were in the land of Moab,

29:1a Verse 29:1 is numbered 28:69 in Hebrew text.

in addition to the covenant he had made with them at Mount Sinai.*

Moses Reviews the Covenant

2*Moses summoned all the Israelites and said to them, "You have seen with your own eyes everything the LORD did in the land of Egypt to Pharaoh and to all his servants and to his whole country—3all the great tests of strength, the miraculous signs, and the amazing wonders. 4But to this day the LORD has not given you minds that understand, nor eyes that see, nor ears that hear! 5For forty years I led you through the wilderness, yet your clothes and sandals did not wear out. 6You ate no bread and drank no wine or other alcoholic drink, but he gave you food so you would know that he is the LORD your God.

AMAZING FACTS

The Israelites went for *40 years* with the same sandals—and not one of those shoes wore out!

DEUTERONOMY 29:5

7"When we came here, King Sihon of Heshbon and King Og of Bashan came out to fight against us, but we defeated them. 8We took their land and gave it to the tribes of Reuben and Gad and to the half-tribe of Manasseh as their grant of land.

9"Therefore, obey the terms of this covenant so that you will prosper in everything you do. 10All of you—tribal leaders, elders, officers, all the men of Israel—are standing today in the presence of the LORD your God. 11Your little ones and your wives are with you, as well as the foreigners living among you who chop your wood and carry your water. 12You are standing here today to enter into the covenant of the LORD your God. The LORD is making this covenant, including the curses. 13By entering into the covenant today, he will establish you as his people and confirm that he is your God, just as he promised you and as he swore to your ancestors Abraham, Isaac, and Jacob.

14"But you are not the only ones with whom I am making this covenant with its curses. 15I am making this covenant both with you who stand here today in the presence of the LORD our God, and also with the future generations who are not standing here today.

16"You remember how we lived in the land of Egypt and how we traveled through the lands of enemy nations as we left. 17You have seen their detestable practices and their idols* made of wood, stone, silver, and gold. 18I am making this covenant with you so that no one among you—no man, woman, clan, or tribe—will turn away from the LORD our God to worship these gods of other nations, and so that no root among you bears bitter and poisonous fruit.

19"Those who hear the warnings of this curse should not congratulate themselves, thinking, 'I am safe, even though I am following the desires of my own stubborn heart.' This would lead to utter ruin! 20The LORD will never pardon such people. Instead his anger and jealousy will burn against them. All the curses written in this book will come down on them, and the LORD will erase their names from under heaven. 21The LORD will separate them from all the tribes of Israel, to pour out on them all the curses of the covenant recorded in this Book of Instruction.

22"Then the generations to come, both your own descendants and the foreigners who come from distant lands, will see the devastation of the land and the diseases the LORD inflicts on it. 23They will exclaim, 'The whole land is devastated by sulfur and salt. It is a wasteland with nothing planted and nothing growing, not even a blade of grass. It is like the cities of Sodom and Gomorrah, Admah and Zeboiim, which the LORD destroyed in his intense anger.'

24"And all the surrounding nations will ask,

29:1b Hebrew *Horeb*, another name for Sinai. **29:2** Verses 29:2-29 are numbered 29:1-28 in Hebrew text. **29:17** The Hebrew term (literally *round things*) probably alludes to dung.

'Why has the LORD done this to this land? Why was he so angry?'

[25]"And the answer will be, 'This happened because the people of the land abandoned the covenant that the LORD, the God of their ancestors, made with them when he brought them out of the land of Egypt. [26]Instead, they turned away to serve and worship gods they had not known before, gods that were not from the LORD. [27]That is why the LORD's anger has burned against this land, bringing down on it every curse recorded in this book. [28]In great anger and fury the LORD uprooted his people from their land and banished them to another land, where they still live today!'

[29]"The LORD our God has secrets known to no one. We are not accountable for them, but we and our children are accountable forever for all that he has revealed to us, so that we may obey all the terms of these instructions.

CHAPTER 30

A Call to Return to the LORD

"In the future, when you experience all these blessings and curses I have listed for you, and when you are living among the nations to which the LORD your God has exiled you, take to heart all these instructions. [2]If at that time you and your children return to the LORD your God, and if you obey with all your heart and all your soul all the commands I have given you today, [3]then the LORD your God will restore your fortunes. He will have mercy on you and gather you back from all the nations where he has scattered you. [4]Even though you are banished to the ends of the earth, the LORD your God will gather you from there and bring you back again. [5]The LORD your God will return you to the land that belonged to your ancestors, and you will possess that land again. Then he will make you even more prosperous and numerous than your ancestors!

[6]"The LORD your God will change your heart* and the hearts of all your descendants, so that you will love him with all your heart and soul and so you may live! [7]The LORD your God will inflict all these curses on your enemies and on those who hate and persecute you. [8]Then you will again obey the LORD and keep all his commands that I am giving you today.

[9]"The LORD your God will then make you successful in everything you do. He will give you many children and numerous livestock, and he will cause your fields to produce abundant harvests, for the LORD will again delight in being good to you as he was to your ancestors. [10]The LORD your God will delight in you if you obey his voice and keep the commands and decrees written in this Book of Instruction, and if you turn to the LORD your God with all your heart and soul.

The Choice of Life or Death

[11]"This command I am giving you today is not too difficult for you to understand, and it is not beyond your reach. [12]It is not kept in heaven, so distant that you must ask, 'Who will go up to heaven and bring it down so we can hear it and obey?' [13]It is not kept beyond the sea, so far away that you must ask, 'Who will cross the sea to bring it to us so we can hear it and obey?' [14]No, the message is very close at hand; it is on your lips and in your heart so that you can obey it.

[15]"Now listen! Today I am giving you a choice between life and death, between prosperity and disaster. [16]For I command you this day to love the LORD your God and to keep his commands, decrees, and regulations by walking in his ways. If you do this, you will live and multiply, and the LORD your God will bless you and the land you are about to enter and occupy.

[17]"But if your heart turns away and you refuse to listen, and if you are drawn away to serve and worship other gods, [18]then I warn you now that you will certainly be destroyed. You will not live a long, good life in the land you are crossing the Jordan to occupy.

[19]"Today I have given you the choice between life and death, between blessings and curses. Now I call on heaven and earth to witness the choice you make. Oh, that you would choose life, so that you and your descendants might live! [20]You can make this choice by loving the LORD your God, obeying him, and committing yourself firmly to him. This* is the key to your life. And if you love and obey the LORD, you will live long in the land the LORD swore to give your ancestors Abraham, Isaac, and Jacob."

30:6 Hebrew *circumcise your heart.* **30:20** Or *He.*

CHAPTER 31

Joshua Becomes Israel's Leader

When Moses had finished giving these instructions* to all the people of Israel, [2]he said, "I am now 120 years old, and I am no longer able to lead you. The LORD has told me, 'You will not cross the Jordan River.' [3]But the LORD your God himself will cross over ahead of you. He will destroy the nations living there, and you will take possession of their land. Joshua will lead you across the river, just as the LORD promised.

[4]"The LORD will destroy the nations living in the land, just as he destroyed Sihon and Og, the kings of the Amorites. [5]The LORD will hand over to you the people who live there, and you must deal with them as I have commanded you. [6]So be strong and courageous! Do not be afraid and do not panic before them. For the LORD your God will personally go ahead of you. He will neither fail you nor abandon you."

[7]Then Moses called for Joshua, and as all Israel watched, he said to him, "Be strong and courageous! For you will lead these people into the land that the LORD swore to their ancestors he would give them. You are the one who will divide it among them as their grants of land. [8]Do not be afraid or discouraged, for the LORD will personally go ahead of you. He will be with you; he will neither fail you nor abandon you."

What's the most important decision I'll ever have to make?

Choose life . . . by loving the LORD your God, obeying him, and committing yourself firmly to him. This is the key to your life.

DEUTERONOMY 30:19-20

Public Reading of the Book of Instruction

[9]So Moses wrote this entire body of instruction in a book and gave it to the priests, who carried the Ark of the LORD's Covenant, and to the elders of Israel. [10]Then Moses gave them this command: "At the end of every seventh year, the Year of Release, during the Festival of Shelters, [11]you must read this Book of Instruction to all the people of Israel when they assemble before the LORD your God at the place he chooses. [12]Call them all together—men, women, children, and the foreigners living in your towns—so they may hear this Book of Instruction and learn to fear the LORD your God and carefully obey all the terms of these instructions. [13]Do this so that your children who have not known these instructions will hear them and will learn to fear the LORD your God. Do this as long as you live in the land you are crossing the Jordan to occupy."

Israel's Disobedience Predicted

[14]Then the LORD said to Moses, "The time has come for you to die. Call Joshua and present yourselves at the Tabernacle,* so that I may commission him there." So Moses and Joshua went and presented themselves at the Tabernacle. [15]And the LORD appeared to them in a pillar of cloud that stood at the entrance to the sacred tent.

[16]The LORD said to Moses, "You are about to die and join your ancestors. After you are gone, these people will begin to worship foreign gods, the gods of the land where they are going. They will abandon me and break my covenant that I have made with them. [17]Then my anger will blaze forth against them. I will abandon them, hiding my face from them, and they will be devoured. Terrible trouble will come down on them, and on that day they will say, 'These disasters have come down on us because God is no longer among us!' [18]At that time I will hide my face from them on account of all the evil they commit by worshiping other gods.

[19]"So write down the words of this song, and teach it to the people of Israel. Help them learn it, so it may serve as a witness for me against them. [20]For I will bring them into the land I swore to give their ancestors—a land flowing with milk and honey. There they will become prosperous, eat all the food they want, and become fat. But they will begin to worship other gods; they will despise me and break my covenant. [21]And when great disasters come down

31:1 As in Dead Sea Scrolls and Greek version; Masoretic Text reads *Moses went and spoke.* **31:14** Hebrew *Tent of Meeting;* also in 31:14b.

on them, this song will stand as evidence against them, for it will never be forgotten by their descendants. I know the intentions of these people, even now before they have entered the land I swore to give them."

22 So that very day Moses wrote down the words of the song and taught it to the Israelites.

23 Then the LORD commissioned Joshua son of Nun with these words: "Be strong and courageous, for you must bring the people of Israel into the land I swore to give them. I will be with you."

24 When Moses had finished writing this entire body of instruction in a book, 25 he gave this command to the Levites who carried the Ark of the LORD's Covenant: 26 "Take this Book of Instruction and place it beside the Ark of the Covenant of the LORD your God, so it may remain there as a witness against the people of Israel. 27 For I know how rebellious and stubborn you are. Even now, while I am still alive and am here with you, you have rebelled against the LORD. How much more rebellious will you be after my death!

28 "Now summon all the elders and officials of your tribes, so that I can speak to them directly and call heaven and earth to witness against them. 29 I know that after my death you will become utterly corrupt and will turn from the way I have commanded you to follow. In the days to come, disaster will come down on you, for you will do what is evil in the LORD's sight, making him very angry with your actions."

The Song of Moses

30 So Moses recited this entire song publicly to the assembly of Israel:

CHAPTER 32

1 "Listen, O heavens, and I will speak!
Hear, O earth, the words that I say!
2 Let my teaching fall on you like rain;
let my speech settle like dew.
Let my words fall like rain on tender grass,
like gentle showers on young plants.
3 I will proclaim the name of the LORD;
how glorious is our God!
4 He is the Rock; his deeds are perfect.
Everything he does is just and fair.
He is a faithful God who does no wrong;
how just and upright he is!
5 "But they have acted corruptly toward him;
when they act so perversely,
are they really his children?*
They are a deceitful and twisted generation.
6 Is this the way you repay the LORD,
you foolish and senseless people?
Isn't he your Father who created you?
Has he not made you and established you?
7 Remember the days of long ago;
think about the generations past.
Ask your father, and he will inform you.
Inquire of your elders, and they will tell you.
8 When the Most High assigned lands to the nations,
when he divided up the human race,
he established the boundaries of the peoples
according to the number in his heavenly court.*
9 "For the people of Israel belong to the LORD;
Jacob is his special possession.
10 He found them in a desert land,
in an empty, howling wasteland.
He surrounded them and watched over them;
he guarded them as he would guard his own eyes.*
11 Like an eagle that rouses her chicks
and hovers over her young,
so he spread his wings to take them up
and carried them safely on his pinions.
12 The LORD alone guided them;
they followed no foreign gods.
13 He let them ride over the highlands
and feast on the crops of the fields.
He nourished them with honey from the rock
and olive oil from the stony ground.
14 He fed them yogurt from the herd
and milk from the flock,
together with the fat of lambs.
He gave them choice rams from Bashan,
and goats,

32:5 The meaning of the Hebrew is uncertain. **32:8** As in Dead Sea Scrolls, which read *the number of the sons of God*, and Greek version, which reads *the number of the angels of God;* Masoretic Text reads *the number of the sons of Israel.* **32:10** Hebrew *as the pupil of his eye.*

Science Fair?

The seventh graders were assigned a big science project that counted for over half of their grade. Dustin mentioned his project idea to Clay. "I saw a couple of library books that will help me in my research," he said. Later, when Dustin went to the library, he discovered that the books were already checked out. Someone else had chosen the same topic! The next day, Dustin noticed one of the checked-out books on Clay's desk. Clay had stolen his idea! Dustin was furious! He felt like hiding the books.

What do you think Dustin should do? Read Deuteronomy 32:34-35.

together with the choicest wheat.
You drank the finest wine,
made from the juice of grapes.

15 "But Israel* soon became fat and unruly;
the people grew heavy, plump, and stuffed!
Then they abandoned the God who had made them;
they made light of the Rock of their salvation.
16 They stirred up his jealousy by worshiping foreign gods;
they provoked his fury with detestable deeds.
17 They offered sacrifices to demons, which are not God,
to gods they had not known before,
to new gods only recently arrived,
to gods their ancestors had never feared.
18 You neglected the Rock who had fathered you;
you forgot the God who had given you birth.
19 "The LORD saw this and drew back,
provoked to anger by his own sons and daughters.
20 He said, 'I will abandon them;
then see what becomes of them.
For they are a twisted generation,
children without integrity.
21 They have roused my jealousy by worshiping things that are not God;
they have provoked my anger with their useless idols.
Now I will rouse their jealousy through people who are not even a people;
I will provoke their anger through the foolish Gentiles.
22 For my anger blazes forth like fire
and burns to the depths of the grave.*
It devours the earth and all its crops
and ignites the foundations of the mountains.
23 I will heap disasters upon them
and shoot them down with my arrows.
24 I will weaken them with famine,
burning fever, and deadly disease.
I will send the fangs of wild beasts
and poisonous snakes that glide in the dust.
25 Outside, the sword will bring death,
and inside, terror will strike
both young men and young women,
both infants and the aged.
26 I would have annihilated them,
wiping out even the memory of them.

32:15 Hebrew *Jeshurun*, a term of endearment for Israel. **32:22** Hebrew *of Sheol*.

27 But I feared the taunt of Israel's enemy,
who might misunderstand and say,
"Our own power has triumphed!
The LORD had nothing to do with this!"'

28 "But Israel is a senseless nation;
the people are foolish, without
understanding.
29 Oh, that they were wise and could
understand this!
Oh, that they might know their fate!
30 How could one person chase a thousand
of them,
and two people put ten thousand to
flight,
unless their Rock had sold them,
unless the LORD had given them up?
31 But the rock of our enemies is not
like our Rock,
as even they recognize.*
32 Their vine grows from the vine of Sodom,
from the vineyards of Gomorrah.
Their grapes are poison,
and their clusters are bitter.
33 Their wine is the venom of serpents,
the deadly poison of cobras.

34 "The LORD says, 'Am I not storing up these
things,
sealing them away in my treasury?
35 I will take revenge; I will pay them back.
In due time their feet will slip.
Their day of disaster will arrive,
and their destiny will overtake them.'

36 "Indeed, the LORD will give justice to his
people,
and he will change his mind about* his
servants,
when he sees their strength is gone
and no one is left, slave or free.
37 Then he will ask, 'Where are their gods,
the rocks they fled to for refuge?
38 Where now are those gods,
who ate the fat of their sacrifices
and drank the wine of their offerings?
Let those gods arise and help you!
Let them provide you with shelter!
39 Look now; I myself am he!
There is no other god but me!
I am the one who kills and gives life;
I am the one who wounds and heals;
no one can be rescued from my
powerful hand!
40 Now I raise my hand to heaven
and declare, "As surely as I live,
41 when I sharpen my flashing sword
and begin to carry out justice,

32:31 The meaning of the Hebrew is uncertain. Greek version reads *our enemies are fools.* **32:36** Or *will take revenge for.*

IS IT OK?

IS IT OK TO GET REVENGE?

In Deuteronomy 32:35, God says that taking revenge is his job—*not ours*. Want to know why? If you try to seek revenge against someone, you'll find out that hurting a person who hurt you doesn't make you feel any better. It makes you feel worse. Maybe you thought that getting back at someone would feel so good, but in the end there is just more hurt. You'll find out that seeking revenge hurts you and your relationship with God. Don't take over God's job. (He's good at his job!) Even though it's sometimes hard to do, leave the revenge to God. He'll make things right, and it'll work out way better than your revenge plan.

I will take revenge on my enemies
and repay those who reject me.
42 I will make my arrows drunk with blood,
and my sword will devour flesh—
the blood of the slaughtered and the captives,
and the heads of the enemy leaders."'

43 "Rejoice with him, you heavens,
and let all of God's angels worship him.*
Rejoice with his people, you nations,
and let all the angels be strengthened in him.*
For he will avenge the blood of his servants;
he will take revenge against his enemies.
He will repay those who hate him*
and cleanse the land for his people."

44 So Moses came with Joshua* son of Nun and recited all the words of this song to the people.
45 When Moses had finished reciting all these words to the people of Israel, 46 he added: "Take to heart all the words of warning I have given you today. Pass them on as a command to your children so they will obey every word of these instructions. 47 These instructions are not empty words—they are your life! By obeying them you will enjoy a long life in the land you will occupy when you cross the Jordan River."

Moses' Death Foretold

48 That same day the LORD said to Moses, 49 "Go to Moab, to the mountains east of the river,* and climb Mount Nebo, which is across from Jericho. Look out across the land of Canaan, the land I am giving to the people of Israel as their own special possession. 50 Then you will die there on the mountain. You will join your ancestors, just as Aaron, your brother, died on Mount Hor and joined his ancestors. 51 For both of you betrayed me with the Israelites at the waters of Meribah at Kadesh* in the wilderness of Zin. You failed to demonstrate my holiness to the people of Israel there. 52 So you will see the land from a distance, but you may not enter the land I am giving to the people of Israel."

CHAPTER 33

Moses Blesses the People

This is the blessing that Moses, the man of God, gave to the people of Israel before his death:

2 "The LORD came from Mount Sinai
and dawned upon us* from Mount Seir;
he shone forth from Mount Paran
and came from Meribah-kadesh
with flaming fire at his right hand.*
3 Indeed, he loves his people;*
all his holy ones are in his hands.
They follow in his steps
and accept his teaching.
4 Moses gave us the LORD's instruction,
the special possession of the people of Israel.*
5 The LORD became king in Israel*—
when the leaders of the people assembled,
when the tribes of Israel gathered as one."

6 Moses said this about the tribe of Reuben:*

"Let the tribe of Reuben live and not die out,
though they are few in number."

7 Moses said this about the tribe of Judah:

"O LORD, hear the cry of Judah
and bring them together as a people.
Give them strength to defend their cause;
help them against their enemies!"

8 Moses said this about the tribe of Levi:

"O LORD, you have given your Thummim and Urim—the sacred lots—
to your faithful servants the Levites.*
You put them to the test at Massah
and struggled with them at the waters of Meribah.

32:43a As in Dead Sea Scrolls and Greek version; Masoretic Text lacks the first two lines. Compare Heb 1:6. **32:43b** As in Greek version; Hebrew text lacks this line. **32:43c** As in Dead Sea Scrolls and Greek version; Masoretic Text lacks this line. **32:44** Hebrew *Hoshea*, a variant name for Joshua. **32:49** Hebrew *the mountains of Abarim*. **32:51** Hebrew *waters of Meribath-kadesh*. **33:2a** As in Greek and Syriac versions; Hebrew reads *upon them*. **33:2b** Or *came from myriads of holy ones, from the south, from his mountain slopes*. The meaning of the Hebrew is uncertain. **33:3** As in Greek version; Hebrew reads *Indeed, lover of the peoples*. **33:4** Hebrew *of Jacob*. The names "Jacob" and "Israel" are often interchanged throughout the Old Testament, referring sometimes to the individual patriarch and sometimes to the nation. **33:5** Hebrew *in Jeshurun*, a term of endearment for Israel. **33:6** Hebrew lacks *Moses said this about the tribe of Reuben*. **33:8** As in Greek version; Hebrew lacks *the Levites*.

9 The Levites obeyed your word
and guarded your covenant.
They were more loyal to you
than to their own parents.
They ignored their relatives
and did not acknowledge their own children.
10 They teach your regulations to Jacob;
they give your instructions to Israel.
They present incense before you
and offer whole burnt offerings on the altar.
11 Bless the ministry of the Levites, O LORD,
and accept all the work of their hands.
Hit their enemies where it hurts the most;
strike down their foes so they never rise again."

12 Moses said this about the tribe of Benjamin:

"The people of Benjamin are loved by the LORD
and live in safety beside him.
He surrounds them continuously
and preserves them from every harm."

13 Moses said this about the tribes of Joseph:

"May their land be blessed by the LORD
with the precious gift of dew from the heavens
and water from beneath the earth;
14 with the rich fruit that grows in the sun,
and the rich harvest produced each month;
15 with the finest crops of the ancient mountains,
and the abundance from the everlasting hills;
16 with the best gifts of the earth and its bounty,
and the favor of the one who appeared in the burning bush.
May these blessings rest on Joseph's head,
crowning the brow of the prince among his brothers.
17 Joseph has the majesty of a young bull;
he has the horns of a wild ox.
He will gore distant nations,
driving them to the ends of the earth.
This is my blessing for the multitudes of Ephraim
and the thousands of Manasseh."

18 Moses said this about the tribes of Zebulun and Issachar*:

"May the people of Zebulun prosper in their travels.
May the people of Issachar prosper at home in their tents.
19 They summon the people to the mountain
to offer proper sacrifices there.
They benefit from the riches of the sea
and the hidden treasures in the sand."

20 Moses said this about the tribe of Gad:

"Blessed is the one who enlarges Gad's territory!
Gad is poised there like a lion
to tear off an arm or a head.
21 The people of Gad took the best land for themselves;
a leader's share was assigned to them.
When the leaders of the people were assembled,
they carried out the LORD's justice
and obeyed his regulations for Israel."

22 Moses said this about the tribe of Dan:

"Dan is a lion's cub,
leaping out from Bashan."

23 Moses said this about the tribe of Naphtali:

"O Naphtali, you are rich in favor
and full of the LORD's blessings;
may you possess the west and the south."

24 Moses said this about the tribe of Asher:

"May Asher be blessed above other sons;
may he be esteemed by his brothers;
may he bathe his feet in olive oil.
25 May the bolts of your gates be of iron and bronze;
may you be secure all your days."

26 "There is no one like the God of Israel.*
He rides across the heavens to help you,
across the skies in majestic splendor.
27 The eternal God is your refuge,
and his everlasting arms are under you.
He drives out the enemy before you;
he cries out, 'Destroy them!'
28 So Israel will live in safety,
prosperous Jacob in security,

33:18 Hebrew lacks *and Issachar*. **33:26** Hebrew *of Jeshurun*, a term of endearment for Israel.

in a land of grain and new wine,
while the heavens drop down dew.
29 How blessed you are, O Israel!
Who else is like you, a people saved by
the LORD?
He is your protecting shield
and your triumphant sword!
Your enemies will cringe before you,
and you will stomp on their backs!"

CHAPTER 34

The Death of Moses

Then Moses went up to Mount Nebo from the plains of Moab and climbed Pisgah Peak, which is across from Jericho. And the LORD showed him the whole land, from Gilead as far as Dan; 2 all the land of Naphtali; the land of Ephraim and Manasseh; all the land of Judah, extending to the Mediterranean Sea*; 3 the Negev; the Jordan Valley with Jericho—the city of palms—as far as Zoar. 4 Then the LORD said to Moses, "This is the land I promised on oath to Abraham, Isaac, and Jacob when I said, 'I will give it to your descendants.' I have now allowed you to see it with your own eyes, but you will not enter the land."

5 So Moses, the servant of the LORD, died there in the land of Moab, just as the LORD had said. 6 The LORD buried him* in a valley near Beth-peor in Moab, but to this day no one knows the exact place. 7 Moses was 120 years old when he died, yet his eyesight was clear, and he was as strong as ever. 8 The people of Israel mourned for Moses on the plains of Moab for thirty days, until the customary period of mourning was over.

9 Now Joshua son of Nun was full of the spirit of wisdom, for Moses had laid his hands on him. So the people of Israel obeyed him, doing just as the LORD had commanded Moses.

10 There has never been another prophet in Israel like Moses, whom the LORD knew face to face. 11 The LORD sent him to perform all the miraculous signs and wonders in the land of Egypt against Pharaoh, and all his servants, and his entire land. 12 With mighty power, Moses performed terrifying acts in the sight of all Israel.

34:2 Hebrew *the western sea.* 34:6 Hebrew *He buried him;* Samaritan Pentateuch and some Greek manuscripts read *They buried him.*

JOSHUA

WHO
Joshua, Rahab, Achan, Phinehas, and Eleazar.

WHERE
Canaan, also known as the Promised Land. This is the same area where Israel is located today.

WHEN
Between 1375 BC and 1045 BC, after Israel had entered the new land.

WHY
To tell the story of the Israelites taking over the Promised Land.

In three days you will cross the Jordan River and take possession of the land the LORD your God is giving you.
JOSHUA 1:11

It's not easy to be a good leader. You have to know how to do what's best for the people who listen to you. After Moses died, Joshua became the leader for the Israelites. He was a good leader because he had the courage to do what was right according to God's laws.

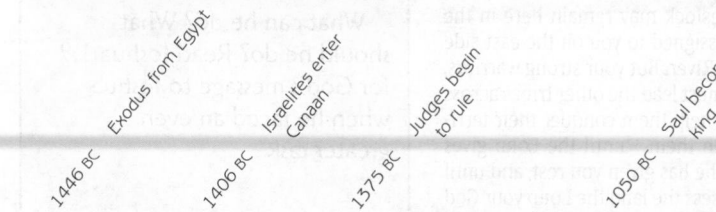

SEE WHAT YOU CAN LEARN ABOUT BEING A GOOD LEADER LIKE JOSHUA.

CHAPTER 1

The LORD's Charge to Joshua

After the death of Moses the LORD's servant, the LORD spoke to Joshua son of Nun, Moses' assistant. He said, [2]"Moses my servant is dead. Therefore, the time has come for you to lead these people, the Israelites, across the Jordan River into the land I am giving them. [3]I promise you what I promised Moses: 'Wherever you set foot, you will be on land I have given you—[4]from the Negev wilderness in the south to the Lebanon mountains in the north, from the Euphrates River in the east to the Mediterranean Sea* in the west, including all the land

1:4 Hebrew *the Great Sea.*

of the Hittites.' [5]No one will be able to stand against you as long as you live. For I will be with you as I was with Moses. I will not fail you or abandon you.

[6]"Be strong and courageous, for you are the one who will lead these people to possess all the land I swore to their ancestors I would give them. [7]Be strong and very courageous. Be careful to obey all the instructions Moses gave you. Do not deviate from them, turning either to the right or to the left. Then you will be successful in everything you do. [8]Study this Book of Instruction continually. Meditate on it day and night so you will be sure to obey everything written in it. Only then will you prosper and succeed in all you do. [9]This is my command—be strong and courageous! Do not be afraid or discouraged. For the LORD your God is with you wherever you go."

Joshua's Charge to the Israelites

[10]Joshua then commanded the officers of Israel, [11]"Go through the camp and tell the people to get their provisions ready. In three days you will cross the Jordan River and take possession of the land the LORD your God is giving you."

[12]Then Joshua called together the tribes of Reuben, Gad, and the half-tribe of Manasseh. He told them, [13]"Remember what Moses, the servant of the LORD, commanded you: 'The LORD your God is giving you a place of rest. He has given you this land.' [14]Your wives, children, and livestock may remain here in the land Moses assigned to you on the east side of the Jordan River. But your strong warriors, fully armed, must lead the other tribes across the Jordan to help them conquer their territory. Stay with them [15]until the LORD gives them rest, as he has given you rest, and until they, too, possess the land the LORD your God is giving them. Only then may you return and settle here on the east side of the Jordan River in the land that Moses, the servant of the LORD, assigned to you."

[16]They answered Joshua, "We will do whatever you command us, and we will go wherever you send us. [17]We will obey you just as we obeyed Moses. And may the LORD your God be with you as he was with Moses. [18]Anyone who rebels against your orders and does not obey your words and everything you command will be put to death. So be strong and courageous!"

SCARED SILLY

Two months ago, the music director at church asked Brad to sing a solo on one verse in the choir anthem. "That would be great," Brad said. From then on he practiced regularly with the choir. But during the last week before the big day, Brad became more and more nervous. He wished he had never agreed to sing. Each time he thought about it, he got a stomachache.

What can he do? What should he do? Read Joshua 1:9 for God's message to Joshua when he faced an even greater task.

CHAPTER 2

Rahab Protects the Spies

Then Joshua secretly sent out two spies from the Israelite camp at Acacia Grove.* He instructed them, "Scout out the land on the other side of the Jordan River, especially around Jericho." So the two men set out and

2:1 Hebrew *Shittim.*

came to the house of a prostitute named Rahab and stayed there that night.

2 But someone told the king of Jericho, "Some Israelites have come here tonight to spy out the land." 3 So the king of Jericho sent orders to Rahab: "Bring out the men who have come into your house, for they have come here to spy out the whole land."

4 Rahab had hidden the two men, but she replied, "Yes, the men were here earlier, but I didn't know where they were from. 5 They left the town at dusk, as the gates were about to close. I don't know where they went. If you hurry, you can probably catch up with them." 6 (Actually, she had taken them up to the roof and hidden them beneath bundles of flax she had laid out.) 7 So the king's men went looking for the spies along the road leading to the shallow crossings of the Jordan River. And as soon as the king's men had left, the gate of Jericho was shut.

What should I do when I'm afraid to try something new?

This is my command—be strong and courageous! Do not be afraid or discouraged. . . . God is with you wherever you go. JOSHUA 1:9

8 Before the spies went to sleep that night, Rahab went up on the roof to talk with them. 9 "I know the LORD has given you this land," she told them. "We are all afraid of you. Everyone in the land is living in terror. 10 For we have heard how the LORD made a dry path for you through the Red Sea* when you left Egypt. And we know what you did to Sihon and Og, the two Amorite kings east of the Jordan River, whose people you completely destroyed.* 11 No wonder our hearts have melted in fear! No one has the courage to fight after hearing such things. For the LORD your God is the supreme God of the heavens above and the earth below.

12 "Now swear to me by the LORD that you will be kind to me and my family since I have helped you. Give me some guarantee that 13 when Jericho is conquered, you will let me live, along with my father and mother, my brothers and sisters, and all their families."

14 "We offer our own lives as a guarantee for your safety," the men agreed. "If you don't betray us, we will keep our promise and be kind to you when the LORD gives us the land."

15 Then, since Rahab's house was built into the town wall, she let them down by a rope through the window. 16 "Escape to the hill country," she told them. "Hide there for three days from the men searching for you. Then, when they have returned, you can go on your way."

17 Before they left, the men told her, "We will be bound by the oath we have taken only if you follow these instructions. 18 When we come into the land, you must leave this scarlet rope hanging from the window through which you let us down. And all your family members—your father, mother, brothers, and all your relatives—must be here inside the house. 19 If they go out into the street and are killed, it will not be our fault. But if anyone lays a hand on people inside this house, we will accept the responsibility for their death. 20 If you betray us, however, we are not bound by this oath in any way."

21 "I accept your terms," she replied. And she sent them on their way, leaving the scarlet rope hanging from the window.

22 The spies went up into the hill country and stayed there three days. The men who were chasing them searched everywhere along the road, but they finally returned without success.

23 Then the two spies came down from the hill country, crossed the Jordan River, and reported to Joshua all that had happened to them. 24 "The LORD has given us the whole land," they said, "for all the people in the land are terrified of us."

CHAPTER 3

The Israelites Cross the Jordan

Early the next morning Joshua and all the Israelites left Acacia Grove* and arrived at the banks of the Jordan River, where they camped before crossing. 2 Three days later

2:10a Hebrew *sea of reeds*. **2:10b** The Hebrew term used here refers to the complete consecration of things or people to the LORD, either by destroying them or by giving them as an offering. **3:1** Hebrew *Shittim*.

the Israelite officers went through the camp,
3 giving these instructions to the people:
"When you see the Levitical priests carrying
the Ark of the Covenant of the LORD your
God, move out from your positions and fol-
low them. 4 Since you have never traveled this
way before, they will guide you. Stay about a
half mile* behind them, keeping a clear dis-
tance between you and the Ark. Make sure
you don't come any closer."

5 Then Joshua told the people, "Purify your-
selves, for tomorrow the LORD will do great
wonders among you."

6 In the morning Joshua said to the priests,
"Lift up the Ark of the Covenant and lead the
people across the river." And so they started
out and went ahead of the people.

7 The LORD told Joshua, "Today I will begin
to make you a great leader in the eyes of all
the Israelites. They will know that I am with
you, just as I was with Moses. 8 Give this com-
mand to the priests who carry the Ark of the
Covenant: 'When you reach the banks of the
Jordan River, take a few steps into the river
and stop there.'"

9 So Joshua told the Israelites, "Come and
listen to what the LORD your God says.
10 Today you will know that the living God is
among you. He will surely drive out the Ca-
naanites, Hittites, Hivites, Perizzites, Girga-
shites, Amorites, and Jebusites ahead of you.
11 Look, the Ark of the Covenant, which be-
longs to the Lord of the whole earth, will lead
you across the Jordan River! 12 Now choose
twelve men from the tribes of Israel, one
from each tribe. 13 The priests will carry the
Ark of the LORD, the Lord of all the earth. As
soon as their feet touch the water, the flow of
water will be cut off upstream, and the river
will stand up like a wall."

14 So the people left their camp to cross the
Jordan, and the priests who were carrying
the Ark of the Covenant went ahead of them.
15 It was the harvest season, and the Jordan
was overflowing its banks. But as soon as the
feet of the priests who were carrying the Ark
touched the water at the river's edge, 16 the
water above that point began backing up a
great distance away at a town called Adam,
which is near Zarethan. And the water below
that point flowed on to the Dead Sea* until
the riverbed was dry. Then all the people
crossed over near the town of Jericho.

17 Meanwhile, the priests who were carry-
ing the Ark of the LORD's Covenant stood on
dry ground in the middle of the riverbed as
the people passed by. They waited there un-
til the whole nation of Israel had crossed the
Jordan on dry ground.

CHAPTER 4

Memorials to the Jordan Crossing

When all the people had crossed the Jordan,
the LORD said to Joshua, 2 "Now choose
twelve men, one from each tribe. 3 Tell them,
'Take twelve stones from the very place
where the priests are standing in the middle
of the Jordan. Carry them out and pile them
up at the place where you will camp to-
night.'"

4 So Joshua called together the twelve men
he had chosen—one from each of the tribes
of Israel. 5 He told them, "Go into the middle
of the Jordan, in front of the Ark of the LORD
your God. Each of you must pick up one stone
and carry it out on your shoulder—twelve
stones in all, one for each of the twelve tribes
of Israel. 6 We will use these stones to build a
memorial. In the future your children will ask
you, 'What do these stones mean?' 7 Then you
can tell them, 'They remind us that the Jordan
River stopped flowing when the Ark of the
LORD's Covenant went across.' These stones
will stand as a memorial among the people of
Israel forever."

8 So the men did as Joshua had com-
manded them. They took twelve stones from
the middle of the Jordan River, one for each
tribe, just as the LORD had told Joshua. They
carried them to the place where they camped
for the night and constructed the memorial
there.

9 Joshua also set up another pile of twelve
stones in the middle of the Jordan, at the
place where the priests who carried the Ark
of the Covenant were standing. And they are
there to this day.

10 The priests who were carrying the Ark
stood in the middle of the river until all of the
LORD's commands that Moses had given to
Joshua were carried out. Meanwhile, the peo-
ple hurried across the riverbed. 11 And when

3:4 Hebrew *about 2,000 cubits* [920 meters]. **3:16** Hebrew *the sea of the Arabah, the Salt Sea.*

I SURVIVED

I've rarely told anyone this, but when I was ten years old, I was a victim of abuse. Because of this, my impression of boys and men got totally messed up. I feared they all had the potential—and maybe even the desire—to hurt me. I figured that if my own uncle would do this to me, how could I be sure someone else wouldn't try?

Thanks to the counsel I received over the next couple of years from the lady who works with my youth group, my fears slowly began slipping away. I even started feeling comfortable talking with a couple of guys from my church.

Then the leadership team announced they were going to take every graduating junior high student on a four-day trip—the girls and the guys. I wanted to go; but since I was nervous about being away from home, I told the lady who had counseled me that I couldn't go. The following Sunday she handed me a present—a little framed Scripture card with Joshua 1:9 embossed on it: *This is my command—be strong and courageous! Do not be afraid or discouraged. For the Lord your God is with you wherever you go.*

After reading it, I said nothing at first. When I did, the only thing I could say was, "Thank you." Her gift reminded me of the statement she'd made at the end of our sessions—"God is your protection."

I did go on that trip, and I had a great time. Since then I've misplaced the framed card, but the promise of the Scripture that was on it goes with me everywhere I go.

When you are facing fears, remember what God told Joshua in Joshua 1:9. For other verses that speak about God's protection, check out Psalms 9:9; 27:5; and 62:1-12.

JOSHUA

I wandered with my people in the desert for 40 years. Yesterday we reached the flooding waters of the Jordan River. God promised a miracle. I told the people the Lord would lead us and get us all safely across, even though I didn't know how. Then I had the priests step into the river. I'm sure they were afraid. But they obeyed. The moment their toes touched the river, the water stopped. Everyone scrambled to the other side. Thousands of us.

Then I had twelve men run back and each grab a rock from the river bed. With those stones we built an altar. A reminder that God keeps his promises.

Joshua's story is told in the book of Joshua.

everyone was safely on the other side, the priests crossed over with the Ark of the LORD as the people watched.

12 The armed warriors from the tribes of Reuben, Gad, and the half-tribe of Manasseh led the Israelites across the Jordan, just as Moses had directed. 13 These armed men—about 40,000 strong—were ready for battle, and the LORD was with them as they crossed over to the plains of Jericho.

14 That day the LORD made Joshua a great leader in the eyes of all the Israelites, and for the rest of his life they revered him as much as they had revered Moses.

15 The LORD had said to Joshua, 16 "Command the priests carrying the Ark of the Covenant* to come up out of the riverbed." 17 So Joshua gave the command. 18 As soon as the priests carrying the Ark of the LORD's Covenant came up out of the riverbed and their feet were on high ground, the water of the Jordan returned and overflowed its banks as before.

19 The people crossed the Jordan on the tenth day of the first month.* Then they camped at Gilgal, just east of Jericho. 20 It was there at Gilgal that Joshua piled up the twelve stones taken from the Jordan River.

21 Then Joshua said to the Israelites, "In the future your children will ask, 'What do these stones mean?' 22 Then you can tell them, 'This is where the Israelites crossed the Jordan on dry ground.' 23 For the LORD your God dried up the river right before your eyes, and he kept it dry until you were all across, just as he did at the Red Sea* when he dried it up until we had all crossed over. 24 He did this so all the nations of the earth might know that the LORD's hand is powerful, and so you might fear the LORD your God forever."

CHAPTER 5

When all the Amorite kings west of the Jordan and all the Canaanite kings who lived along the Mediterranean coast* heard how the LORD had dried up the Jordan River so the people of Israel could cross, they lost heart and were paralyzed with fear because of them.

Israel Reestablishes Covenant Ceremonies

2 At that time the LORD told Joshua, "Make flint knives and circumcise this second generation of Israelites.*" 3 So Joshua made flint knives and circumcised the entire male population of Israel at Gibeath-haaraloth.*

4 Joshua had to circumcise them because all the men who were old enough to fight in battle when they left Egypt had died in the wilderness. 5 Those who left Egypt had all been

4:16 Hebrew *Ark of the Testimony*. **4:19** This day in the ancient Hebrew lunar calendar occurred in late March, April, or early May. **4:23** Hebrew *sea of reeds*. **5:1** Hebrew *along the sea*. **5:2** Or *circumcise the Israelites a second time*. **5:3** *Gibeath-haaraloth* means "hill of foreskins."

circumcised, but none of those born after the Exodus, during the years in the wilderness, had been circumcised. [6]The Israelites had traveled in the wilderness for forty years until all the men who were old enough to fight in battle when they left Egypt had died. For they had disobeyed the LORD, and the LORD vowed he would not let them enter the land he had sworn to give us—a land flowing with milk and honey. [7]So Joshua circumcised their sons—those who had grown up to take their fathers' places—for they had not been circumcised on the way to the Promised Land. [8]After all the males had been circumcised, they rested in the camp until they were healed.

[9]Then the LORD said to Joshua, "Today I have rolled away the shame of your slavery in Egypt." So that place has been called Gilgal* to this day.

[10]While the Israelites were camped at Gilgal on the plains of Jericho, they celebrated Passover on the evening of the fourteenth day of the first month.* [11]The very next day they began to eat unleavened bread and roasted grain harvested from the land. [12]No manna appeared on the day they first ate from the crops of the land, and it was never seen again. So from that time on the Israelites ate from the crops of Canaan.

The LORD's Commander Confronts Joshua

[13]When Joshua was near the town of Jericho, he looked up and saw a man standing in front of him with sword in hand. Joshua went up to him and demanded, "Are you friend or foe?"

[14]"Neither one," he replied. "I am the commander of the LORD's army."

At this, Joshua fell with his face to the ground in reverence. "I am at your command," Joshua said. "What do you want your servant to do?"

[15]The commander of the LORD's army replied, "Take off your sandals, for the place where you are standing is holy." And Joshua did as he was told.

CHAPTER 6

The Fall of Jericho

Now the gates of Jericho were tightly shut because the people were afraid of the Israelites. No one was allowed to go out or in. [2]But the LORD said to Joshua, "I have given you Jericho, its king, and all its strong warriors. [3]You and your fighting men should march around the town once a day for six days. [4]Seven priests will walk ahead of the Ark, each carrying a ram's horn. On the seventh day you are to march around the town seven times, with the priests blowing the horns. [5]When you hear the priests give one long blast on the rams' horns, have all the people shout as loud as they can. Then the walls of the town will collapse, and the people can charge straight into the town."

[6]So Joshua called together the priests and said, "Take up the Ark of the LORD's Covenant, and assign seven priests to walk in front of it, each carrying a ram's horn." [7]Then he gave orders to the people: "March around the town, and the armed men will lead the way in front of the Ark of the LORD."

[8]After Joshua spoke to the people, the seven priests with the rams' horns started marching in the presence of the LORD, blowing the horns as they marched. And the Ark of the LORD's Covenant followed behind them. [9]Some of the armed men marched in front of the priests with the horns and some behind the Ark, with the priests continually blowing the horns. [10]"Do not shout; do not even talk," Joshua commanded. "Not a single word from any of you until I tell you to shout. Then shout!" [11]So the Ark of the LORD was carried around the town once that day, and then everyone returned to spend the night in the camp.

[12]Joshua got up early the next morning, and the priests again carried the Ark of the LORD. [13]The seven priests with the rams' horns marched in front of the Ark of the LORD, blowing their horns. Again the armed men marched both in front of the priests with the horns and behind the Ark of the LORD. All this time the priests were blowing their horns. [14]On the second day they again marched around the town once and returned to the camp. They followed this pattern for six days.

[15]On the seventh day the Israelites got up at dawn and marched around the town as they had done before. But this time they went around the town seven times. [16]The seventh time around, as the priests sounded the long

5:9 *Gilgal* sounds like the Hebrew word *galal*, meaning "to roll." **5:10** This day in the ancient Hebrew lunar calendar occurred in late March, April, or early May.

blast on their horns, Joshua commanded the people, "Shout! For the LORD has given you the town! [17]Jericho and everything in it must be completely destroyed* as an offering to the LORD. Only Rahab the prostitute and the others in her house will be spared, for she protected our spies.

[18]"Do not take any of the things set apart for destruction, or you yourselves will be completely destroyed, and you will bring trouble on the camp of Israel. [19]Everything made from silver, gold, bronze, or iron is sacred to the LORD and must be brought into his treasury."

[20]When the people heard the sound of the rams' horns, they shouted as loud as they could. Suddenly, the walls of Jericho collapsed, and the Israelites charged straight into the town and captured it. [21]They completely destroyed everything in it with their swords—men and women, young and old, cattle, sheep, goats, and donkeys.

AMAZING FACTS

Jack hammers. Bulldozers. Shouting people. Which tore down city walls? It was those loud Israelites, yelling just like God told them to!

JOSHUA 6:20

[22]Meanwhile, Joshua said to the two spies, "Keep your promise. Go to the prostitute's house and bring her out, along with all her family."

[23]The men who had been spies went in and brought out Rahab, her father, mother, brothers, and all the other relatives who were with her. They moved her whole family to a safe place near the camp of Israel.

[24]Then the Israelites burned the town and everything in it. Only the things made from silver, gold, bronze, or iron were kept for the treasury of the LORD's house. [25]So Joshua spared Rahab the prostitute and her relatives who were with her in the house, because she had hidden the spies Joshua sent to Jericho. And she lives among the Israelites to this day.

[26]At that time Joshua invoked this curse:

"May the curse of the LORD fall on anyone
who tries to rebuild the town of
Jericho.
At the cost of his firstborn son,
he will lay its foundation.
At the cost of his youngest son,
he will set up its gates."

[27]So the LORD was with Joshua, and his reputation spread throughout the land.

CHAPTER 7

Ai Defeats the Israelites

But Israel violated the instructions about the things set apart for the LORD.* A man named Achan had stolen some of these dedicated things, so the LORD was very angry with the Israelites. Achan was the son of Carmi, a descendant of Zimri* son of Zerah, of the tribe of Judah.

[2]Joshua sent some of his men from Jericho to spy out the town of Ai, east of Bethel, near Beth-aven. [3]When they returned, they told Joshua, "There's no need for all of us to go up there; it won't take more than two or three thousand men to attack Ai. Since there are so few of them, don't make all our people struggle to go up there."

[4]So approximately 3,000 warriors were sent, but they were soundly defeated. The men of Ai [5]chased the Israelites from the town gate as far as the quarries,* and they killed about thirty-six who were retreating down the slope. The Israelites were paralyzed with fear at this turn of events, and their courage melted away.

[6]Joshua and the elders of Israel tore their clothing in dismay, threw dust on their heads, and bowed face down to the ground before the Ark of the LORD until evening. [7]Then Joshua cried out, "Oh, Sovereign LORD,

6:17 The Hebrew term used here refers to the complete consecration of things or people to the LORD, either by destroying them or by giving them as an offering; similarly in 6:18, 21. **7:1a** The Hebrew term used here refers to the complete consecration of things or people to the LORD, either by destroying them or by giving them as an offering; similarly in 7:11, 12, 13, 15. **7:1b** As in parallel text at 1 Chr 2:6; Hebrew reads *Zabdi*. Also in 7:17, 18. **7:5** Or *as far as Shebarim*.

why did you bring us across the Jordan River if you are going to let the Amorites kill us? If only we had been content to stay on the other side! [8]Lord, what can I say now that Israel has fled from its enemies? [9]For when the Canaanites and all the other people living in the land hear about it, they will surround us and wipe our name off the face of the earth. And then what will happen to the honor of your great name?"

How can I be successful in what I do?

The LORD was with Joshua, and his reputation spread throughout the land. JOSHUA 6:27

[10]But the LORD said to Joshua, "Get up! Why are you lying on your face like this? [11]Israel has sinned and broken my covenant! They have stolen some of the things that I commanded must be set apart for me. And they have not only stolen them but have lied about it and hidden the things among their own belongings. [12]That is why the Israelites are running from their enemies in defeat. For now Israel itself has been set apart for destruction. I will not remain with you any longer unless you destroy the things among you that were set apart for destruction.

[13]"Get up! Command the people to purify themselves in preparation for tomorrow. For this is what the LORD, the God of Israel, says: Hidden among you, O Israel, are things set apart for the LORD. You will never defeat your enemies until you remove these things from among you.

[14]"In the morning you must present yourselves by tribes, and the LORD will point out the tribe to which the guilty man belongs. That tribe must come forward with its clans, and the LORD will point out the guilty clan. That clan will then come forward, and the LORD will point out the guilty family. Finally, each member of the guilty family must come forward one by one. [15]The one who has stolen what was set apart for destruction will himself be burned with fire, along with everything he has, for he has broken the covenant of the LORD and has done a horrible thing in Israel."

Achan's Sin

[16]Early the next morning Joshua brought the tribes of Israel before the LORD, and the tribe of Judah was singled out. [17]Then the clans of Judah came forward, and the clan of Zerah was singled out. Then the families of Zerah came forward, and the family of Zimri was singled out. [18]Every member of Zimri's family was brought forward person by person, and Achan was singled out.

[19]Then Joshua said to Achan, "My son, give glory to the LORD, the God of Israel, by telling the truth. Make your confession and tell me what you have done. Don't hide it from me."

[20]Achan replied, "It is true! I have sinned against the LORD, the God of Israel. [21]Among the plunder I saw a beautiful robe from Babylon,* 200 silver coins,* and a bar of gold weighing more than a pound.* I wanted them so much that I took them. They are hidden in the ground beneath my tent, with the silver buried deeper than the rest."

[22]So Joshua sent some men to make a search. They ran to the tent and found the stolen goods hidden there, just as Achan had said, with the silver buried beneath the rest. [23]They took the things from the tent and brought them to Joshua and all the Israelites. Then they laid them on the ground in the presence of the LORD.

[24]Then Joshua and all the Israelites took Achan, the silver, the robe, the bar of gold, his sons, daughters, cattle, donkeys, sheep, goats, tent, and everything he had, and they brought them to the valley of Achor. [25]Then Joshua said to Achan, "Why have you brought trouble on us? The LORD will now bring trouble on you." And all the Israelites stoned Achan and his family and burned their bodies. [26]They piled a great heap of stones over Achan, which remains to this day. That is why the place has been called the Valley of Trouble* ever since. So the LORD was no longer angry.

7:21a Hebrew *Shinar*. **7:21b** Hebrew *200 shekels of silver*, about 5 pounds or 2.3 kilograms in weight. **7:21c** Hebrew *50 shekels*, about 20 ounces or 570 grams in weight. **7:26** Hebrew *valley of Achor*.

CHAPTER 8

The Israelites Defeat Ai

Then the LORD said to Joshua, "Do not be afraid or discouraged. Take all your fighting men and attack Ai, for I have given you the king of Ai, his people, his town, and his land. [2]You will destroy them as you destroyed Jericho and its king. But this time you may keep the plunder and the livestock for yourselves. Set an ambush behind the town."

[3]So Joshua and all the fighting men set out to attack Ai. Joshua chose 30,000 of his best warriors and sent them out at night [4]with these orders: "Hide in ambush close behind the town and be ready for action. [5]When our main army attacks, the men of Ai will come out to fight as they did before, and we will run away from them. [6]We will let them chase us until we have drawn them away from the town. For they will say, 'The Israelites are running away from us as they did before.' Then, while we are running from them, [7]you will jump up from your ambush and take possession of the town, for the LORD your God will give it to you. [8]Set the town on fire, as the LORD has commanded. You have your orders."

[9]So they left and went to the place of ambush between Bethel and the west side of Ai. But Joshua remained among the people in the camp that night. [10]Early the next morning Joshua roused his men and started toward Ai, accompanied by the elders of Israel. [11]All the fighting men who were with Joshua marched in front of the town and camped on the north side of Ai, with a valley between them and the town. [12]That night Joshua sent 5,000 men to lie in ambush between Bethel and Ai, on the west side of the town. [13]So they stationed the main army north of the town and the ambush west of the town. Joshua himself spent that night in the valley.

[14]When the king of Ai saw the Israelites across the valley, he and all his army hurried out early in the morning and attacked the Israelites at a place overlooking the Jordan Valley.* But he didn't realize there was an ambush behind the town. [15]Joshua and the Israelite army fled toward the wilderness as though they were badly beaten. [16]Then all the men in the town were called out to chase after them. In this way, they were lured away from the town. [17]There was not a man left in Ai or Bethel* who did not chase after the Israelites, and the town was left wide open.

[18]Then the LORD said to Joshua, "Point the spear in your hand toward Ai, for I will hand the town over to you." Joshua did as he was commanded. [19]As soon as Joshua gave this signal, all the men in ambush jumped up from their position and poured into the town. They quickly captured it and set it on fire.

[20]When the men of Ai looked behind them, smoke from the town was filling the sky, and they had nowhere to go. For the Israelites who had fled in the direction of the wilderness now turned on their pursuers. [21]When Joshua and all the other Israelites saw that the ambush had succeeded and that smoke was rising from the town, they turned and attacked the men of Ai. [22]Meanwhile, the Israelites who were inside the town came out and attacked the enemy from the rear. So the men of Ai were caught in the middle, with Israelite fighters on both sides. Israel attacked them, and not a single person survived or escaped. [23]Only the king of Ai was taken alive and brought to Joshua.

[24]When the Israelite army finished chasing and killing all the men of Ai in the open fields, they went back and finished off everyone inside. [25]So the entire population of Ai, including men and women, was wiped out that day—12,000 in all. [26]For Joshua kept holding out his spear until everyone who had lived in Ai was completely destroyed.* [27]Only the livestock and the treasures of the town were not destroyed, for the Israelites kept these as plunder for themselves, as the LORD had commanded Joshua. [28]So Joshua burned the town of Ai,* and it became a permanent mound of ruins, desolate to this very day.

[29]Joshua impaled the king of Ai on a sharpened pole and left him there until evening. At sunset the Israelites took down the body, as Joshua commanded, and threw it in front of the town gate. They piled a great heap of stones over him that can still be seen today.

The LORD's Covenant Renewed

[30]Then Joshua built an altar to the LORD, the God of Israel, on Mount Ebal. [31]He followed the commands that Moses the LORD's servant had written in the Book of Instruction: "Make

8:14 Hebrew *the Arabah.* **8:17** Some manuscripts lack *or Bethel.* **8:26** The Hebrew term used here refers to the complete consecration of things or people to the LORD, either by destroying them or by giving them as an offering. **8:28** *Ai* means "ruin."

me an altar from stones that are uncut and
have not been shaped with iron tools."* Then
on the altar they presented burnt offerings
and peace offerings to the LORD. 32And as the
Israelites watched, Joshua copied onto the
stones of the altar* the instructions Moses had
given them.

33Then all the Israelites—foreigners and
native-born alike—along with the elders,
officers, and judges, were divided into two
groups. One group stood in front of Mount
Gerizim, the other in front of Mount Ebal.
Each group faced the other, and between
them stood the Levitical priests carrying the
Ark of the LORD's Covenant. This was all done
according to the commands that Moses, the
servant of the LORD, had previously given for
blessing the people of Israel.

34Joshua then read to them all the blessings
and curses Moses had written in the Book of
Instruction. 35Every word of every command
that Moses had ever given was read to the en-
tire assembly of Israel, including the women
and children and the foreigners who lived
among them.

CHAPTER 9

The Gibeonites Deceive Israel

Now all the kings west of the Jordan River
heard about what had happened. These were
the kings of the Hittites, Amorites, Canaan-
ites, Perizzites, Hivites, and Jebusites, who
lived in the hill country, in the western foot-
hills,* and along the coast of the Mediterra-
nean Sea* as far north as the Lebanon
mountains. 2These kings combined their ar-
mies to fight as one against Joshua and the Is-
raelites.

3But when the people of Gibeon heard what
Joshua had done to Jericho and Ai, 4they re-
sorted to deception to save themselves. They
sent ambassadors to Joshua, loading their
donkeys with weathered saddlebags and old,
patched wineskins. 5They put on worn-out,
patched sandals and ragged clothes. And the
bread they took with them was dry and moldy.
6When they arrived at the camp of Israel at
Gilgal, they told Joshua and the men of Israel,
"We have come from a distant land to ask you
to make a peace treaty with us."

7The Israelites replied to these Hivites,
"How do we know you don't live nearby? For
if you do, we cannot make a treaty with you."

8They replied, "We are your servants."

"But who are you?" Joshua demanded.
"Where do you come from?"

9They answered, "Your servants have come
from a very distant country. We have heard of
the might of the LORD your God and of all he
did in Egypt. 10We have also heard what he
did to the two Amorite kings east of the Jor-
dan River—King Sihon of Heshbon and King

8:31 Exod 20:25; Deut 27:5-6. **8:32** Hebrew *onto the stones.* **9:1a** Hebrew *the Shephelah.* **9:1b** Hebrew *the Great Sea.*

IS IT OK?

IS IT OK TO CHAT WITH STRANGERS ONLINE?

Joshua and the Israelite leaders fell for a scam (see Joshua 9:3-15). The Gibeonites had disguised themselves as worn-out travelers, and they tricked Joshua into making a peace treaty with them (which God had told the Israelites not to do). Unfortunately, there are a lot of people in this world like the Gibeonites—people who disguise themselves as good, honest, and even religious. They try to convince us that they're harmless, but they're not. If you meet a stranger online, be wise and protect yourself. Never give out any personal info or agree to meet a stranger. You just never know who might be hiding behind a disguise.

Og of Bashan (who lived in Ashtaroth). [11]So our elders and all our people instructed us, 'Take supplies for a long journey. Go meet with the people of Israel and tell them, "We are your servants; please make a treaty with us."'

[12]"This bread was hot from the ovens when we left our homes. But now, as you can see, it is dry and moldy. [13]These wineskins were new when we filled them, but now they are old and split open. And our clothing and sandals are worn out from our very long journey."

[14]So the Israelites examined their food, but they did not consult the LORD. [15]Then Joshua made a peace treaty with them and guaranteed their safety, and the leaders of the community ratified their agreement with a binding oath.

[16]Three days after making the treaty, they learned that these people actually lived nearby! [17]The Israelites set out at once to investigate and reached their towns in three days. The names of these towns were Gibeon, Kephirah, Beeroth, and Kiriath-jearim. [18]But the Israelites did not attack the towns, for the Israelite leaders had made a vow to them in the name of the LORD, the God of Israel.

The people of Israel grumbled against their leaders because of the treaty. [19]But the leaders replied, "Since we have sworn an oath in the presence of the LORD, the God of Israel, we cannot touch them. [20]This is what we must do. We must let them live, for divine anger would come upon us if we broke our oath. [21]Let them live." So they made them woodcutters and water carriers for the entire community, as the Israelite leaders directed.

[22]Joshua called together the Gibeonites and said, "Why did you lie to us? Why did you say that you live in a distant land when you live right here among us? [23]May you be cursed! From now on you will always be servants who cut wood and carry water for the house of my God."

[24]They replied, "We did it because we—your servants—were clearly told that the LORD your God commanded his servant Moses to give you this entire land and to destroy all the people living in it. So we feared greatly for our lives because of you. That is why we have done this. [25]Now we are at your mercy—do to us whatever you think is right."

[26]So Joshua did not allow the people of Israel to kill them. [27]But that day he made the Gibeonites the woodcutters and water carriers for the community of Israel and for the altar of the LORD—wherever the LORD would choose to build it. And that is what they do to this day.

CHAPTER 10

Israel Defeats the Southern Armies

Adoni-zedek, king of Jerusalem, heard that Joshua had captured and completely destroyed* Ai and killed its king, just as he had destroyed the town of Jericho and killed its king. He also learned that the Gibeonites had made peace with Israel and were now their allies. [2]He and his people became very afraid when they heard all this because Gibeon was a large town—as large as the royal cities and larger than Ai. And the Gibeonite men were strong warriors.

[3]So King Adoni-zedek of Jerusalem sent messengers to several other kings: Hoham of Hebron, Piram of Jarmuth, Japhia of Lachish, and Debir of Eglon. [4]"Come and help me destroy Gibeon," he urged them, "for they have made peace with Joshua and the people of Israel." [5]So these five Amorite kings combined their armies for a united attack. They moved all their troops into place and attacked Gibeon.

[6]The men of Gibeon quickly sent messengers to Joshua at his camp in Gilgal. "Don't abandon your servants now!" they pleaded. "Come at once! Save us! Help us! For all the Amorite kings who live in the hill country have joined forces to attack us."

[7]So Joshua and his entire army, including his best warriors, left Gilgal and set out for Gibeon. [8]"Do not be afraid of them," the LORD said to Joshua, "for I have given you victory over them. Not a single one of them will be able to stand up to you."

[9]Joshua traveled all night from Gilgal and took the Amorite armies by surprise. [10]The LORD threw them into a panic, and the Israelites slaughtered great numbers of them at Gibeon. Then the Israelites chased the enemy along the road to Beth-horon, killing them all along the way to Azekah and Makkedah. [11]As

10:1 The Hebrew term used here refers to the complete consecration of things or people to the LORD, either by destroying them or by giving them as an offering; also in 10:28, 35, 37, 39, 40.

the Amorites retreated down the road from Beth-horon, the LORD destroyed them with a terrible hailstorm from heaven that continued until they reached Azekah. The hail killed more of the enemy than the Israelites killed with the sword.

[12]On the day the LORD gave the Israelites victory over the Amorites, Joshua prayed to the LORD in front of all the people of Israel. He said,

"Let the sun stand still over Gibeon,
and the moon over the valley of
Aijalon."

[13]So the sun stood still and the moon stayed in place until the nation of Israel had defeated its enemies.

Is this event not recorded in *The Book of Jashar**? The sun stayed in the middle of the sky, and it did not set as on a normal day.* [14]There has never been a day like this one before or since, when the LORD answered such a prayer. Surely the LORD fought for Israel that day!

[15]Then Joshua and the Israelite army returned to their camp at Gilgal.

Joshua Kills the Five Southern Kings

[16]During the battle the five kings escaped and hid in a cave at Makkedah. [17]When Joshua heard that they had been found, [18]he issued this command: "Cover the opening of the cave with large rocks, and place guards at the entrance to keep the kings inside. [19]The rest of you continue chasing the enemy and cut them down from the rear. Don't give them a chance to get back to their towns, for the LORD your God has given you victory over them."

[20]So Joshua and the Israelite army continued the slaughter and completely crushed the enemy. They totally wiped out the five armies except for a tiny remnant that managed to reach their fortified towns. [21]Then the Israelites returned safely to Joshua in the camp at Makkedah. After that, no one dared to speak even a word against Israel.

[22]Then Joshua said, "Remove the rocks covering the opening of the cave, and bring the five kings to me." [23]So they brought the five kings out of the cave—the kings of Jerusalem, Hebron, Jarmuth, Lachish, and Eglon. [24]When they brought them out, Joshua told the commanders of his army, "Come and put your feet on the kings' necks." And they did as they were told.

[25]"Don't ever be afraid or discouraged," Joshua told his men. "Be strong and courageous, for the LORD is going to do this to all of your enemies." [26]Then Joshua killed each of the five kings and impaled them on five sharpened poles, where they hung until evening.

[27]As the sun was going down, Joshua gave instructions for the bodies of the kings to be taken down from the poles and thrown into the cave where they had been hiding. Then they covered the opening of the cave with a pile of large rocks, which remains to this very day.

AMAZING FACTS

Joshua needed extra time to win a battle, so he prayed for time to stand still. And it did—God stopped the sun!

JOSHUA 10:12-13

Israel Destroys the Southern Towns

[28]That same day Joshua captured and destroyed the town of Makkedah. He killed everyone in it, including the king, leaving no survivors. He destroyed them all, and he killed the king of Makkedah as he had killed the king of Jericho. [29]Then Joshua and the Israelites went to Libnah and attacked it. [30]There, too, the LORD gave them the town and its king. He killed everyone in it, leaving no survivors. Then Joshua killed the king of Libnah as he had killed the king of Jericho.

[31]From Libnah, Joshua and the Israelites

10:13a Or *The Book of the Upright*. **10:13b** Or *did not set for about a whole day*.

went to Lachish and attacked it. [32]Here again, the LORD gave them Lachish. Joshua took it on the second day and killed everyone in it, just as he had done at Libnah. [33]During the attack on Lachish, King Horam of Gezer arrived with his army to help defend the town. But Joshua's men killed him and his army, leaving no survivors.

[34]Then Joshua and the Israelite army went on to Eglon and attacked it. [35]They captured it that day and killed everyone in it. He completely destroyed everyone, just as he had done at Lachish. [36]From Eglon, Joshua and the Israelite army went up to Hebron and attacked it. [37]They captured the town and killed everyone in it, including its king, leaving no survivors. They did the same thing to all of its surrounding villages. And just as he had done at Eglon, he completely destroyed the entire population.

[38]Then Joshua and the Israelites turned back and attacked Debir. [39]He captured the town, its king, and all of its surrounding villages. He completely destroyed everyone in it, leaving no survivors. He did to Debir and its king just what he had done to Hebron and to Libnah and its king.

[40]So Joshua conquered the whole region—the kings and people of the hill country, the Negev, the western foothills,* and the mountain slopes. He completely destroyed everyone in the land, leaving no survivors, just as the LORD, the God of Israel, had commanded. [41]Joshua slaughtered them from Kadesh-barnea to Gaza and from the region around the town of Goshen up to Gibeon. [42]Joshua conquered all these kings and their land in a single campaign, for the LORD, the God of Israel, was fighting for his people.

[43]Then Joshua and the Israelite army returned to their camp at Gilgal.

CHAPTER 11

Israel Defeats the Northern Armies

When King Jabin of Hazor heard what had happened, he sent messages to the following kings: King Jobab of Madon; the king of Shimron; the king of Acshaph; [2]all the kings of the northern hill country; the kings in the Jordan Valley south of Galilee*; the kings in the Galilean foothills*; the kings of Naphoth-dor on the west; [3]the kings of Canaan, both east and west; the kings of the Amorites, the Hittites, the Perizzites, the Jebusites in the hill country, and the Hivites in the towns on the slopes of Mount Hermon in the land of Mizpah.

[4]All these kings came out to fight. Their combined armies formed a vast horde. And with all their horses and chariots, they covered the landscape like the sand on the seashore. [5]The kings joined forces and established their camp around the water near Merom to fight against Israel.

[6]Then the LORD said to Joshua, "Do not be afraid of them. By this time tomorrow I will hand all of them over to Israel as dead men. Then you must cripple their horses and burn their chariots."

[7]So Joshua and all his fighting men traveled to the water near Merom and attacked suddenly. [8]And the LORD gave them victory over their enemies. The Israelites chased them as far as Greater Sidon and Misrephoth-maim, and eastward into the valley of Mizpah, until not one enemy warrior was left alive. [9]Then Joshua crippled the horses and burned all the chariots, as the LORD had instructed.

[10]Joshua then turned back and captured Hazor and killed its king. (Hazor had at one time been the capital of all these kingdoms.) [11]The Israelites completely destroyed* every living thing in the city, leaving no survivors. Not a single person was spared. And then Joshua burned the city.

[12]Joshua slaughtered all the other kings and their people, completely destroying them, just as Moses, the servant of the LORD, had commanded. [13]But the Israelites did not burn any of the towns built on mounds except Hazor, which Joshua burned. [14]And the Israelites took all the plunder and livestock of the ravaged towns for themselves. But they killed all the people, leaving no survivors. [15]As the LORD had commanded his servant Moses, so Moses commanded Joshua. And Joshua did as he was told, carefully obeying all the commands that the LORD had given to Moses.

[16]So Joshua conquered the entire region—the hill country, the entire Negev, the whole area around the town of Goshen, the western

10:40 Hebrew *the Shephelah.* **11:2a** Hebrew *in the Arabah south of Kinnereth.* **11:2b** Hebrew *the Shephelah;* also in 11:16.
11:11 The Hebrew term used here refers to the complete consecration of things or people to the LORD, either by destroying them or by giving them as an offering; also in 11:12, 20, 21.

foothills, the Jordan Valley,* the mountains of Israel, and the Galilean foothills. [17]The Israelite territory now extended all the way from Mount Halak, which leads up to Seir in the south, as far north as Baal-gad at the foot of Mount Hermon in the valley of Lebanon. Joshua killed all the kings of those territories, [18]waging war for a long time to accomplish this. [19]No one in this region made peace with the Israelites except the Hivites of Gibeon. All the others were defeated. [20]For the LORD hardened their hearts and caused them to fight the Israelites. So they were completely destroyed without mercy, as the LORD had commanded Moses.

[21]During this period Joshua destroyed all the descendants of Anak, who lived in the hill country of Hebron, Debir, Anab, and the entire hill country of Judah and Israel. He killed them all and completely destroyed their towns. [22]None of the descendants of Anak were left in all the land of Israel, though some still remained in Gaza, Gath, and Ashdod.

[23]So Joshua took control of the entire land, just as the LORD had instructed Moses. He gave it to the people of Israel as their special possession, dividing the land among the tribes. So the land finally had rest from war.

CHAPTER 12

Kings Defeated East of the Jordan

These are the kings east of the Jordan River who had been killed by the Israelites and whose land was taken. Their territory extended from the Arnon Gorge to Mount Hermon and included all the land east of the Jordan Valley.*

[2]King Sihon of the Amorites, who lived in Heshbon, was defeated. His kingdom included Aroer, on the edge of the Arnon Gorge, and extended from the middle of the Arnon Gorge to the Jabbok River, which serves as a border for the Ammonites. This territory included the southern half of the territory of Gilead. [3]Sihon also controlled the Jordan Valley and regions to the east—from as far north as the Sea of Galilee to as far south as the Dead Sea,* including the road to Beth-jeshimoth and southward to the slopes of Pisgah.

[4]King Og of Bashan, the last of the Rephaites, lived at Ashtaroth and Edrei. [5]He ruled a territory stretching from Mount Hermon to Salecah in the north and to all of Bashan in the east, and westward to the borders of the kingdoms of Geshur and Maacah. This territory included the northern half of Gilead, as far as the boundary of King Sihon of Heshbon.

[6]Moses, the servant of the LORD, and the Israelites had destroyed the people of King Sihon and King Og. And Moses gave their land as a possession to the tribes of Reuben, Gad, and the half-tribe of Manasseh.

Kings Defeated West of the Jordan

[7]The following is a list of the kings that Joshua and the Israelite armies defeated on the west side of the Jordan, from Baal-gad in the valley of Lebanon to Mount Halak, which leads up to Seir. (Joshua gave this land to the tribes of Israel as their possession, [8]including the hill country, the western foothills,* the Jordan Valley, the mountain slopes, the Judean wilderness, and the Negev. The people who lived in this region were the Hittites, the Amorites, the Canaanites, the Perizzites, the Hivites, and the Jebusites.) These are the kings Israel defeated:

[9] The king of Jericho
The king of Ai, near Bethel
[10] The king of Jerusalem
The king of Hebron
[11] The king of Jarmuth
The king of Lachish
[12] The king of Eglon
The king of Gezer
[13] The king of Debir
The king of Geder
[14] The king of Hormah
The king of Arad
[15] The king of Libnah
The king of Adullam
[16] The king of Makkedah
The king of Bethel
[17] The king of Tappuah
The king of Hepher
[18] The king of Aphek
The king of Lasharon
[19] The king of Madon
The king of Hazor
[20] The king of Shimron-meron

11:16 Hebrew *the Shephelah, the Arabah.* **12:1** Hebrew *the Arabah;* also in 12:3, 8. **12:3** Hebrew *from the Sea of Kinnereth to the Sea of the Arabah, which is the Salt Sea.* **12:8** Hebrew *the Shephelah.*

The king of Acshaph
21 The king of Taanach
The king of Megiddo
22 The king of Kedesh
The king of Jokneam in Carmel
23 The king of Dor in the town of
Naphoth-dor*
The king of Goyim in Gilgal*
24 The king of Tirzah.

In all, thirty-one kings were defeated.

CHAPTER 13

The Land Yet to Be Conquered

When Joshua was an old man, the LORD said to him, "You are growing old, and much land remains to be conquered. 2This is the territory that remains: all the regions of the Philistines and the Geshurites, 3and the larger territory of the Canaanites, extending from the stream of Shihor on the border of Egypt, northward to the boundary of Ekron. It includes the territory of the five Philistine rulers of Gaza, Ashdod, Ashkelon, Gath, and Ekron. The land of the Avvites 4in the south also remains to be conquered. In the north, the following area has not yet been conquered: all the land of the Canaanites, including Mearah (which belongs to the Sidonians), stretching northward to Aphek on the border of the Amorites; 5the land of the Gebalites and all of the Lebanon mountain area to the east, from Baal-gad below Mount Hermon to Lebo-hamath; 6and all the hill country from Lebanon to Misrephothmaim, including all the land of the Sidonians.

"I myself will drive these people out of the land ahead of the Israelites. So be sure to give this land to Israel as a special possession, just as I have commanded you. 7Include all this territory as Israel's possession when you divide this land among the nine tribes and the half-tribe of Manasseh."

The Land Divided East of the Jordan

8Half the tribe of Manasseh and the tribes of Reuben and Gad had already received their grants of land on the east side of the Jordan, for Moses, the servant of the LORD, had previously assigned this land to them.

9Their territory extended from Aroer on the edge of the Arnon Gorge (including the town in the middle of the gorge) to the plain beyond Medeba, as far as Dibon. 10It also included all the towns of King Sihon of the Amorites, who had reigned in Heshbon, and extended as far as the borders of Ammon. 11It included Gilead, the territory of the kingdoms of Geshur and Maacah, all of Mount Hermon, all of Bashan as far as Salecah, 12and all the territory of King Og of Bashan, who had reigned in Ashtaroth and Edrei. King Og was the last of the Rephaites, for Moses had attacked them and driven them out. 13But the Israelites failed to drive out the people of Geshur and Maacah, so they continue to live among the Israelites to this day.

An Allotment for the Tribe of Levi

14Moses did not assign any allotment of land to the tribe of Levi. Instead, as the LORD had promised them, their allotment came from the offerings burned on the altar to the LORD, the God of Israel.

The Land Given to the Tribe of Reuben

15Moses had assigned the following area to the clans of the tribe of Reuben.

16Their territory extended from Aroer on the edge of the Arnon Gorge (including the town in the middle of the gorge) to the plain beyond Medeba. 17It included Heshbon and the other towns on the plain—Dibon, Bamoth-baal, Beth-baal-meon, 18Jahaz, Kedemoth, Mephaath, 19Kiriathaim, Sibmah, Zereth-shahar on the hill above the valley, 20Beth-peor, the slopes of Pisgah, and Beth-jeshimoth.

21The land of Reuben also included all the towns of the plain and the entire kingdom of Sihon. Sihon was the Amorite king who had reigned in Heshbon and was killed by Moses along with the leaders of Midian—Evi, Rekem, Zur, Hur, and Reba—princes living in the region who were allied with Sihon. 22The Israelites had also killed Balaam son of Beor, who used magic to tell the future. 23The Jordan River marked the western boundary for the tribe of Reuben. The towns and their surrounding villages in this area were

12:23a Hebrew *Naphath-dor*, a variant spelling of Naphoth-dor. **12:23b** Greek version reads *Goyim in Galilee*.

given as a homeland to the clans of the tribe of Reuben.

The Land Given to the Tribe of Gad

[24]Moses had assigned the following area to the clans of the tribe of Gad.

[25]Their territory included Jazer, all the towns of Gilead, and half of the land of Ammon, as far as the town of Aroer just west of* Rabbah. [26]It extended from Heshbon to Ramath-mizpeh and Betonim, and from Mahanaim to the territory of Lo-debar.* [27]In the valley were Beth-haram, Beth-nimrah, Succoth, Zaphon, and the rest of the kingdom of King Sihon of Heshbon. The western boundary ran along the Jordan River, extended as far north as the tip of the Sea of Galilee,* and then turned eastward. [28]The towns and their surrounding villages in this area were given as a homeland to the clans of the tribe of Gad.

The Land Given to the Half-Tribe of Manasseh

[29]Moses had assigned the following area to the clans of the half-tribe of Manasseh.

[30]Their territory extended from Mahanaim, including all of Bashan, all the former kingdom of King Og, and the sixty towns of Jair in Bashan. [31]It also included half of Gilead and King Og's royal cities of Ashtaroth and Edrei. All this was given to the clans of the descendants of Makir, who was Manasseh's son.

[32]These are the allotments Moses had made while he was on the plains of Moab, across the Jordan River, east of Jericho. [33]But Moses gave no allotment of land to the tribe of Levi, for the LORD, the God of Israel, had promised that he himself would be their allotment.

CHAPTER 14

The Land Divided West of the Jordan

The remaining tribes of Israel received land in Canaan as allotted by Eleazar the priest, Joshua son of Nun, and the tribal leaders. [2]These nine and a half tribes received their grants of land by means of sacred lots, in accordance with the LORD's command through Moses. [3]Moses had already given a grant of land to the two and a half tribes on the east side of the Jordan River, but he had given the Levites no such allotment. [4]The descendants of Joseph had become two separate tribes—Manasseh and Ephraim. And the Levites were given no land at all, only towns to live in with surrounding pasturelands for their livestock and all their possessions. [5]So the land was distributed in strict accordance with the LORD's commands to Moses.

Caleb Requests His Land

[6]A delegation from the tribe of Judah, led by Caleb son of Jephunneh the Kenizzite, came to Joshua at Gilgal. Caleb said to Joshua, "Remember what the LORD said to Moses, the man of God, about you and me when we were at Kadesh-barnea. [7]I was forty years old when Moses, the servant of the LORD, sent me from Kadesh-barnea to explore the land of Canaan. I returned and gave an honest report, [8]but my brothers who went with me frightened the people from entering the Promised Land. For my part, I wholeheartedly followed the LORD my God. [9]So that day Moses solemnly promised me, 'The land of Canaan on which you were just walking will be your grant of land and that of your descendants forever, because you wholeheartedly followed the LORD my God.'

[10]"Now, as you can see, the LORD has kept me alive and well as he promised for all these forty-five years since Moses made this promise—even while Israel wandered in the wilderness. Today I am eighty-five years old. [11]I am as strong now as I was when Moses sent me on that journey, and I can still travel and fight as well as I could then. [12]So give me the hill country that the LORD promised me. You will remember that as scouts we found the descendants of Anak living there in great, walled towns. But if the LORD is with me, I will drive them out of the land, just as the LORD said."

[13]So Joshua blessed Caleb son of Jephunneh and gave Hebron to him as his portion of land. [14]Hebron still belongs to the descendants of Caleb son of Jephunneh the Kenizzite because he wholeheartedly followed the

13:25 Hebrew *in front of*. **13:26** Hebrew *Li-debir*, apparently a variant spelling of Lo-debar (compare 2 Sam 9:4; 17:27; Amos 6:13).
13:27 Hebrew *Sea of Kinnereth*.

LORD, the God of Israel. [15](Previously Hebron had been called Kiriath-arba. It had been named after Arba, a great hero of the descendants of Anak.)

And the land had rest from war.

CHAPTER 15

The Land Given to the Tribe of Judah

The allotment for the clans of the tribe of Judah reached southward to the border of Edom, as far south as the wilderness of Zin.

[2]The southern boundary began at the south bay of the Dead Sea,* [3]ran south of Scorpion Pass* into the wilderness of Zin, and then went south of Kadesh-barnea to Hezron. Then it went up to Addar, where it turned toward Karka. [4]From there it passed to Azmon until it finally reached the Brook of Egypt, which it followed to the Mediterranean Sea.* This was their* southern boundary.

[5]The eastern boundary extended along the Dead Sea to the mouth of the Jordan River.

The northern boundary began at the bay where the Jordan River empties into the Dead Sea, [6]went up from there to Beth-hoglah, then proceeded north of Beth-arabah to the Stone of Bohan. (Bohan was Reuben's son.) [7]From that point it went through the valley of Achor to Debir, turning north toward Gilgal, which is across from the slopes of Adummim on the south side of the valley. From there the boundary extended to the springs at En-shemesh and on to En-rogel. [8]The boundary then passed through the valley of Ben-Hinnom, along the southern slopes of the Jebusites, where the city of Jerusalem is located. Then it went west to the top of the mountain above the valley of Hinnom, and on up to the northern end of the valley of Rephaim. [9]From there the boundary extended from the top of the mountain to the spring at the waters of Nephtoah,* and from there to the towns on Mount Ephron. Then it turned toward Baalah (that is, Kiriath-jearim). [10]The boundary circled west of Baalah to Mount Seir, passed along to the town of Kesalon on the northern slope of Mount Jearim, and went down to Beth-shemesh and on to Timnah. [11]The boundary then proceeded to the slope of the hill north of Ekron, where it turned toward Shikkeron and Mount Baalah. It passed Jabneel and ended at the Mediterranean Sea.

[12]The western boundary was the shoreline of the Mediterranean Sea.*

These are the boundaries for the clans of the tribe of Judah.

The Land Given to Caleb

[13]The LORD commanded Joshua to assign some of Judah's territory to Caleb son of Jephunneh. So Caleb was given the town of Kiriath-arba (that is, Hebron), which had been named after Anak's ancestor. [14]Caleb drove out the three groups of Anakites—the descendants of Sheshai, Ahiman, and Talmai, the sons of Anak.

[15]From there he went to fight against the

15:2 Hebrew *the Salt Sea;* also in 15:5. **15:3** Hebrew *Akrabbim.* **15:4a** Hebrew *the sea;* also in 15:11. **15:4b** Hebrew *your.* **15:9** Or *the spring at Me-nephtoah.* **15:12** Hebrew *the Great Sea;* also in 15:47.

people living in the town of Debir (formerly called Kiriath-sepher). [16]Caleb said, "I will give my daughter Acsah in marriage to the one who attacks and captures Kiriath-sepher." [17]Othniel, the son of Caleb's brother Kenaz, was the one who conquered it, so Acsah became Othniel's wife.

[18]When Acsah married Othniel, she urged him* to ask her father for a field. As she got down off her donkey, Caleb asked her, "What's the matter?"

[19]She said, "Give me another gift. You have already given me land in the Negev; now please give me springs of water, too." So Caleb gave her the upper and lower springs.

The Towns Allotted to Judah

[20]This was the homeland allocated to the clans of the tribe of Judah.

[21]The towns of Judah situated along the borders of Edom in the extreme south were Kabzeel, Eder, Jagur, [22]Kinah, Dimonah, Adadah, [23]Kedesh, Hazor, Ithnan, [24]Ziph, Telem, Bealoth, [25]Hazor-hadattah, Kerioth-hezron (that is, Hazor), [26]Amam, Shema, Moladah, [27]Hazar-gaddah, Heshmon, Beth-pelet, [28]Hazar-shual, Beersheba, Biziothiah, [29]Baalah, Iim, Ezem, [30]Eltolad, Kesil, Hormah, [31]Ziklag, Madmannah, Sansannah, [32]Lebaoth, Shilhim, Ain, and Rimmon—twenty-nine towns with their surrounding villages.

[33]The following towns situated in the western foothills* were also given to Judah: Eshtaol, Zorah, Ashnah, [34]Zanoah, En-gannim, Tappuah, Enam, [35]Jarmuth, Adullam, Socoh, Azekah, [36]Shaaraim, Adithaim, Gederah, and Gederothaim—fourteen towns with their surrounding villages.

[37]Also included were Zenan, Hadashah, Migdal-gad, [38]Dilean, Mizpeh, Joktheel, [39]Lachish, Bozkath, Eglon, [40]Cabbon, Lahmam, Kitlish, [41]Gederoth, Beth-dagon, Naamah, and Makkedah—sixteen towns with their surrounding villages.

[42]Besides these, there were Libnah, Ether, Ashan, [43]Iphtah, Ashnah, Nezib, [44]Keilah, Aczib, and Mareshah—nine towns with their surrounding villages.

[45]The territory of the tribe of Judah also included Ekron and its surrounding settlements and villages. [46]From Ekron the boundary extended west and included the towns near Ashdod with their surrounding villages. [47]It also included Ashdod with its surrounding settlements and villages and Gaza with its settlements and villages, as far as the Brook of Egypt and along the coast of the Mediterranean Sea.

[48]Judah also received the following towns in the hill country: Shamir, Jattir, Socoh, [49]Dannah, Kiriath-sannah (that is, Debir), [50]Anab, Eshtemoh, Anim, [51]Goshen, Holon, and Giloh—eleven towns with their surrounding villages.

[52]Also included were the towns of Arab, Dumah, Eshan, [53]Janim, Beth-tappuah, Aphekah, [54]Humtah, Kiriath-arba (that is, Hebron), and Zior—nine towns with their surrounding villages.

[55]Besides these, there were Maon, Carmel, Ziph, Juttah, [56]Jezreel, Jokdeam, Zanoah, [57]Kain, Gibeah, and Timnah—ten towns with their surrounding villages.

[58]In addition, there were Halhul, Beth-zur, Gedor, [59]Maarath, Beth-anoth, and Eltekon—six towns with their surrounding villages.

[60]There were also Kiriath-baal (that is, Kiriath-jearim) and Rabbah—two towns with their surrounding villages.

[61]In the wilderness there were the towns of Beth-arabah, Middin, Secacah, [62]Nibshan, the City of Salt, and En-gedi—six towns with their surrounding villages.

[63]But the tribe of Judah could not drive out the Jebusites, who lived in the city of Jerusalem, so the Jebusites live there among the people of Judah to this day.

CHAPTER 16

The Land Given to Ephraim and West Manasseh

The allotment for the descendants of Joseph extended from the Jordan River near Jericho, east of the springs of Jericho, through the wilderness and into the hill country of Bethel. [2]From Bethel (that is, Luz)* it ran

15:18 Some Greek manuscripts read *he urged her*. **15:33** Hebrew *the Shephelah*. **16:2** As in Greek version (also see 18:13); Hebrew reads *From Bethel to Luz*.

over to Ataroth in the territory of the
Arkites. [3]Then it descended westward to
the territory of the Japhletites as far as
Lower Beth-horon, then to Gezer and over
to the Mediterranean Sea.*

[4]This was the homeland allocated to the families of Joseph's sons, Manasseh and Ephraim.

The Land Given to Ephraim

[5]The following territory was given to the clans of the tribe of Ephraim.

The boundary of their homeland began at
Ataroth-addar in the east. From there it
ran to Upper Beth-horon, [6]then on to the
Mediterranean Sea. From Micmethath on
the north, the boundary curved eastward
past Taanath-shiloh to the east of Janoah.
[7]From Janoah it turned southward to
Ataroth and Naarah, touched Jericho, and
ended at the Jordan River. [8]From Tappuah
the boundary extended westward,
following the Kanah Ravine to the
Mediterranean Sea. This is the homeland
allocated to the clans of the tribe of
Ephraim.

[9]In addition, some towns with their
surrounding villages in the territory
allocated to the half-tribe of Manasseh
were set aside for the tribe of Ephraim.
[10]They did not drive the Canaanites out of
Gezer, however, so the people of Gezer
live as slaves among the people of
Ephraim to this day.

CHAPTER 17

The Land Given to West Manasseh

The next allotment of land was given to the half-tribe of Manasseh, the descendants of Joseph's older son. Makir, the firstborn son of Manasseh, was the father of Gilead. Because his descendants were experienced soldiers, the regions of Gilead and Bashan on the east side of the Jordan had already been given to them. [2]So the allotment on the west side of the Jordan was for the remaining families within the clans of the tribe of Manasseh: Abiezer, Helek, Asriel, Shechem, Hepher, and Shemida. These clans represent the male descendants of Manasseh son of Joseph.

[3]However, Zelophehad, a descendant of Hepher son of Gilead, son of Makir, son of Manasseh, had no sons. He had only daughters, whose names were Mahlah, Noah, Hoglah, Milcah, and Tirzah. [4]These women came to Eleazar the priest, Joshua son of Nun, and the Israelite leaders and said, "The LORD commanded Moses to give us a grant of land along with the men of our tribe."

So Joshua gave them a grant of land along with their uncles, as the LORD had commanded. [5]As a result, Manasseh's total allocation came to ten parcels of land, in addition to the land of Gilead and Bashan across the Jordan River, [6]because the female descendants of Manasseh received a grant of land along with the male descendants. (The land of Gilead was given to the rest of the male descendants of Manasseh.)

[7]The boundary of the tribe of Manasseh
extended from the border of Asher to
Micmethath, near Shechem. Then the
boundary went south from Micmethath
to the settlement near the spring of
Tappuah. [8]The land surrounding Tappuah
belonged to Manasseh, but the town
of Tappuah itself, on the border of
Manasseh's territory, belonged to the
tribe of Ephraim. [9]From the spring of
Tappuah, the boundary of Manasseh
followed the Kanah Ravine to the
Mediterranean Sea.* Several towns south
of the ravine were inside Manasseh's
territory, but they actually belonged to
the tribe of Ephraim. [10]In general,
however, the land south of the ravine
belonged to Ephraim, and the land north
of the ravine belonged to Manasseh.
Manasseh's boundary ran along the
northern side of the ravine and ended at
the Mediterranean Sea. North of Manasseh
was the territory of Asher, and to the east
was the territory of Issachar.

[11]The following towns within the
territory of Issachar and Asher, however,
were given to Manasseh: Beth-shan,*
Ibleam, Dor (that is, Naphoth-dor),*
Endor, Taanach, and Megiddo, each with
their surrounding settlements.

[12]But the descendants of Manasseh were
unable to occupy these towns. They could not

16:3 Hebrew *the sea;* also in 16:6, 8. **17:9** Hebrew *the sea;* also in 17:10. **17:11a** Hebrew *Beth-shean,* a variant spelling of Beth-shan; also in 17:16. **17:11b** The meaning of the Hebrew here is uncertain.

drive out the Canaanites who continued to
live there. [13]Later, however, when the Israel-
ites became strong enough, they forced the
Canaanites to work as slaves. But they did not
drive them out of the land.

[14]The descendants of Joseph came to Josh-
ua and asked, "Why have you given us only one
portion of land as our homeland when the
LORD has blessed us with so many people?"

[15]Joshua replied, "If there are so many of
you, and if the hill country of Ephraim is not
large enough for you, clear out land for your-
selves in the forest where the Perizzites and
Rephaites live."

[16]The descendants of Joseph responded,
"It's true that the hill country is not large
enough for us. But all the Canaanites in the
lowlands have iron chariots, both those in
Beth-shan and its surrounding settlements
and those in the valley of Jezreel. They are too
strong for us."

[17]Then Joshua said to the tribes of Ephraim
and Manasseh, the descendants of Joseph,
"Since you are so large and strong, you will be
given more than one portion. [18]The forests of
the hill country will be yours as well. Clear as
much of the land as you wish, and take pos-
session of its farthest corners. And you will
drive out the Canaanites from the valleys, too,
even though they are strong and have iron
chariots."

CHAPTER 18

The Allotments of the Remaining Land

Now that the land was under Israelite control,
the entire community of Israel gathered at
Shiloh and set up the Tabernacle.* [2]But there
remained seven tribes who had not yet been
allotted their grants of land.

[3]Then Joshua asked them, "How long are
you going to wait before taking possession of
the remaining land the LORD, the God of your
ancestors, has given to you? [4]Select three men
from each tribe, and I will send them out to
explore the land and map it out. They will
then return to me with a written report of
their proposed divisions of their new home-
land. [5]Let them divide the land into seven sec-
tions, excluding Judah's territory in the south
and Joseph's territory in the north. [6]And when
you record the seven divisions of the land and
bring them to me, I will cast sacred lots in the
presence of the LORD our God to assign land
to each tribe.

[7]"The Levites, however, will not receive any
allotment of land. Their role as priests of the
LORD is their allotment. And the tribes of Gad,
Reuben, and the half-tribe of Manasseh won't
receive any more land, for they have already
received their grant of land, which Moses, the
servant of the LORD, gave them on the east
side of the Jordan River."

[8]As the men started on their way to map out
the land, Joshua commanded them, "Go and
explore the land and write a description of it.
Then return to me, and I will assign the land
to the tribes by casting sacred lots here in the
presence of the LORD at Shiloh." [9]The men did
as they were told and mapped the entire terri-
tory into seven sections, listing the towns in
each section. They made a written record and
then returned to Joshua in the camp at Shiloh.
[10]And there at Shiloh, Joshua cast sacred lots in
the presence of the LORD to determine which
tribe should have each section.

The Land Given to Benjamin

[11]The first allotment of land went to the clans
of the tribe of Benjamin. It lay between the
territory assigned to the tribes of Judah and
Joseph.

[12]The northern boundary of Benjamin's
land began at the Jordan River, went north
of the slope of Jericho, then west through
the hill country and the wilderness of
Beth-aven. [13]From there the boundary
went south to Luz (that is, Bethel) and
proceeded down to Ataroth-addar on the
hill that lies south of Lower Beth-horon.

[14]The boundary then made a turn and
swung south along the western edge of
the hill facing Beth-horon, ending at the
village of Kiriath-baal (that is, Kiriath-
jearim), a town belonging to the tribe of
Judah. This was the western boundary.

[15]The southern boundary began at the
outskirts of Kiriath-jearim. From that
western point it ran* to the spring at the
waters of Nephtoah,* [16]and down to the
base of the mountain beside the valley of
Ben-Hinnom, at the northern end of the

18:1 Hebrew *Tent of Meeting*. **18:15a** Or *From there it went to Mozah*. The meaning of the Hebrew is uncertain. **18:15b** Or *the spring at Me-nephtoah*.

valley of Rephaim. From there it went
down the valley of Hinnom, crossing
south of the slope where the Jebusites
lived, and continued down to En-rogel.
17 From En-rogel the boundary proceeded
in a northerly direction and came to En-
shemesh and on to Geliloth (which is
across from the slopes of Adummim).
Then it went down to the Stone of Bohan.
(Bohan was Reuben's son.) 18 From there it
passed along the north side of the slope
overlooking the Jordan Valley.* The
border then went down into the valley,
19 ran past the north slope of Beth-hoglah,
and ended at the north bay of the Dead
Sea,* which is the southern end of the
Jordan River. This was the southern
boundary.
20 The eastern boundary was the Jordan
River.

These were the boundaries of the homeland allocated to the clans of the tribe of Benjamin.

The Towns Given to Benjamin

21 These were the towns given to the clans of the tribe of Benjamin.

Jericho, Beth-hoglah, Emek-keziz, 22 Beth-
arabah, Zemaraim, Bethel, 23 Avvim, Parah,
Ophrah, 24 Kephar-ammoni, Ophni, and
Geba—twelve towns with their
surrounding villages. 25 Also Gibeon,
Ramah, Beeroth, 26 Mizpah, Kephirah,
Mozah, 27 Rekem, Irpeel, Taralah, 28 Zela,
Haeleph, Jebus (that is, Jerusalem), Gibeah,
and Kiriath*—fourteen towns with their
surrounding villages.

This was the homeland allocated to the clans of the tribe of Benjamin.

CHAPTER 19

The Land Given to Simeon

The second allotment of land went to the clans of the tribe of Simeon. Their homeland was surrounded by Judah's territory.

2 Simeon's homeland included Beersheba,
Sheba, Moladah, 3 Hazar-shual, Balah,
Ezem, 4 Eltolad, Bethul, Hormah, 5 Ziklag,
Beth-marcaboth, Hazar-susah, 6 Beth-
lebaoth, and Sharuhen—thirteen towns
with their surrounding villages. 7 It also
included Ain, Rimmon, Ether, and
Ashan—four towns with their villages,
8 including all the surrounding villages as
far south as Baalath-beer (also known as
Ramah of the Negev).

This was the homeland allocated to the clans of the tribe of Simeon. 9 Their allocation of land came from part of what had been given to Judah because Judah's territory was too large for them. So the tribe of Simeon received an allocation within the territory of Judah.

The Land Given to Zebulun

10 The third allotment of land went to the clans of the tribe of Zebulun.

The boundary of Zebulun's homeland
started at Sarid. 11 From there it went west,
going past Maralah, touching Dabbesheth,
and proceeding to the brook east of
Jokneam. 12 In the other direction, the
boundary went east from Sarid to the
border of Kisloth-tabor, and from there
to Daberath and up to Japhia. 13 Then it
continued east to Gath-hepher, Eth-kazin,
and Rimmon and turned toward Neah.
14 The northern boundary of Zebulun
passed Hannathon and ended at the valley
of Iphtah-el. 15 The towns in these areas
included Kattath, Nahalal, Shimron,
Idalah, and Bethlehem—twelve towns
with their surrounding villages.

16 The homeland allocated to the clans of the tribe of Zebulun included these towns and their surrounding villages.

The Land Given to Issachar

17 The fourth allotment of land went to the clans of the tribe of Issachar.

18 Its boundaries included the following
towns: Jezreel, Kesulloth, Shunem,
19 Hapharaim, Shion, Anaharath,
20 Rabbith, Kishion, Ebez, 21 Remeth, En-
gannim, En-haddah, and Beth-pazzez.
22 The boundary also touched Tabor,
Shahazumah, and Beth-shemesh, ending
at the Jordan River—sixteen towns with
their surrounding villages.

18:18 Hebrew *overlooking the Arabah,* or *overlooking Beth-arabah.* **18:19** Hebrew *Salt Sea.* **18:28** Some Greek manuscripts read *Kiriath-jearim.*

[23]The homeland allocated to the clans of the tribe of Issachar included these towns and their surrounding villages.

The Land Given to Asher

[24]The fifth allotment of land went to the clans of the tribe of Asher.

[25]Its boundaries included these towns: Helkath, Hali, Beten, Acshaph, [26]Allammelech, Amad, and Mishal. The boundary on the west touched Carmel and Shihor-libnath, [27]then it turned east toward Beth-dagon, and ran as far as Zebulun in the valley of Iphtah-el, going north to Beth-emek and Neiel. It then continued north to Cabul, [28]Abdon,* Rehob, Hammon, Kanah, and as far as Greater Sidon. [29]Then the boundary turned toward Ramah and the fortress of Tyre, where it turned toward Hosah and came to the Mediterranean Sea.* The territory also included Mehebel, Aczib, [30]Ummah, Aphek, and Rehob—twenty-two towns with their surrounding villages.

[31]The homeland allocated to the clans of the tribe of Asher included these towns and their surrounding villages.

The Land Given to Naphtali

[32]The sixth allotment of land went to the clans of the tribe of Naphtali.

[33]Its boundary ran from Heleph, from the oak at Zaanannim, and extended across to Adami-nekeb, Jabneel, and as far as Lakkum, ending at the Jordan River. [34]The western boundary ran past Aznoth-tabor, then to Hukkok, and touched the border of Zebulun in the south, the border of Asher on the west, and the Jordan River* on the east. [35]The fortified towns included in this territory were Ziddim, Zer, Hammath, Rakkath, Kinnereth, [36]Adamah, Ramah, Hazor, [37]Kedesh, Edrei, En-hazor, [38]Yiron, Migdal-el, Horem, Beth-anath, and Beth-shemesh—nineteen towns with their surrounding villages.

[39]The homeland allocated to the clans of the tribe of Naphtali included these towns and their surrounding villages.

The Land Given to Dan

[40]The seventh allotment of land went to the clans of the tribe of Dan.

[41]The land allocated as their homeland included the following towns: Zorah, Eshtaol, Ir-shemesh, [42]Shaalabbin, Aijalon, Ithlah, [43]Elon, Timnah, Ekron, [44]Eltekeh, Gibbethon, Baalath, [45]Jehud, Bene-berak, Gath-rimmon, [46]Me-jarkon, Rakkon, and the territory across from Joppa.

[47]But the tribe of Dan had trouble taking possession of their land,* so they attacked the town of Laish.* They captured it, slaughtered its people, and settled there. They renamed the town Dan after their ancestor.

[48]The homeland allocated to the clans of the tribe of Dan included these towns and their surrounding villages.

The Land Given to Joshua

[49]After all the land was divided among the tribes, the Israelites gave a piece of land to Joshua as his allocation. [50]For the LORD had said he could have any town he wanted. He chose Timnath-serah in the hill country of Ephraim. He rebuilt the town and lived there.

[51]These are the territories that Eleazar the priest, Joshua son of Nun, and the tribal leaders allocated as grants of land to the tribes of Israel by casting sacred lots in the presence of the LORD at the entrance of the Tabernacle* at Shiloh. So the division of the land was completed.

CHAPTER 20

The Cities of Refuge

The LORD said to Joshua, [2]"Now tell the Israelites to designate the cities of refuge, as I instructed Moses. [3]Anyone who kills another person accidentally and unintentionally can run to one of these cities; they will be places of refuge from relatives seeking revenge for the person who was killed.

[4]"Upon reaching one of these cities, the one who caused the death will appear before

19:28 As in some Hebrew manuscripts (see also 21:30); most Hebrew manuscripts read *Ebron*. **19:29** Hebrew *the sea*. **19:34** Hebrew *and Judah at the Jordan River*. **19:47a** Or *had trouble holding on to their land*. **19:47b** Hebrew *Leshem*, a variant spelling of Laish. **19:51** Hebrew *Tent of Meeting*.

the elders at the city gate and present his case. They must allow him to enter the city and give him a place to live among them. [5]If the relatives of the victim come to avenge the killing, the leaders must not release the slayer to them, for he killed the other person unintentionally and without previous hostility. [6]But the slayer must stay in that city and be tried by the local assembly, which will render a judgment. And he must continue to live in that city until the death of the high priest who was in office at the time of the accident. After that, he is free to return to his own home in the town from which he fled."

[7]The following cities were designated as cities of refuge: Kedesh of Galilee, in the hill country of Naphtali; Shechem, in the hill country of Ephraim; and Kiriath-arba (that is, Hebron), in the hill country of Judah. [8]On the east side of the Jordan River, across from Jericho, the following cities were designated: Bezer, in the wilderness plain of the tribe of Reuben; Ramoth in Gilead, in the territory of the tribe of Gad; and Golan in Bashan, in the land of the tribe of Manasseh. [9]These cities were set apart for all the Israelites as well as the foreigners living among them. Anyone who accidentally killed another person could take refuge in one of these cities. In this way, they could escape being killed in revenge prior to standing trial before the local assembly.

CHAPTER 21

The Towns Given to the Levites

Then the leaders of the tribe of Levi came to consult with Eleazar the priest, Joshua son of Nun, and the leaders of the other tribes of Israel. [2]They came to them at Shiloh in the land of Canaan and said, "The LORD commanded Moses to give us towns to live in and pasturelands for our livestock." [3]So by the command of the LORD the people of Israel gave the Levites the following towns and pasturelands out of their own grants of land.

[4]The descendants of Aaron, who were members of the Kohathite clan within the tribe of Levi, were allotted thirteen towns that were originally assigned to the tribes of Judah, Simeon, and Benjamin. [5]The other families of the Kohathite clan were allotted ten towns from the tribes of Ephraim, Dan, and the half-tribe of Manasseh.

[6]The clan of Gershon was allotted thirteen towns from the tribes of Issachar, Asher, Naphtali, and the half-tribe of Manasseh in Bashan.

[7]The clan of Merari was allotted twelve towns from the tribes of Reuben, Gad, and Zebulun.

[8]So the Israelites obeyed the LORD's command to Moses and assigned these towns and pasturelands to the Levites by casting sacred lots.

[9]The Israelites gave the following towns from the tribes of Judah and Simeon [10]to the descendants of Aaron, who were members of the Kohathite clan within the tribe of Levi, since the sacred lot fell to them first: [11]Kiriath-arba (that is, Hebron), in the hill country of Judah, along with its surrounding pasturelands. (Arba was an ancestor of Anak.) [12]But the open fields beyond the town and the surrounding villages were given to Caleb son of Jephunneh as his possession.

[13]The following towns with their pasturelands were given to the descendants of Aaron the priest: Hebron (a city of refuge for those who accidentally killed someone), Libnah, [14]Jattir, Eshtemoa, [15]Holon, Debir, [16]Ain, Juttah, and Beth-shemesh—nine towns from these two tribes.

[17]From the tribe of Benjamin the priests were given the following towns with their pasturelands: Gibeon, Geba, [18]Anathoth, and Almon—four towns. [19]So in all, thirteen towns with their pasturelands were given to the priests, the descendants of Aaron.

[20]The rest of the Kohathite clan from the tribe of Levi was allotted the following towns and pasturelands from the tribe of Ephraim: [21]Shechem in the hill country of Ephraim (a city of refuge for those who accidentally killed someone), Gezer, [22]Kibzaim, and Beth-horon—four towns.

[23]The following towns and pasturelands were allotted to the priests from the tribe of Dan: Eltekeh, Gibbethon, [24]Aijalon, and Gath-rimmon—four towns.

[25]The half-tribe of Manasseh allotted the following towns with their pasturelands to the priests: Taanach and Gath-rimmon—two towns. [26]So in all, ten towns with their pasturelands were given to the rest of the Kohathite clan.

[27]The descendants of Gershon, another clan
within the tribe of Levi, received the following
towns with their pasturelands from the half-
tribe of Manasseh: Golan in Bashan (a city of
refuge for those who accidentally killed some-
one) and Be-eshterah—two towns.

[28]From the tribe of Issachar they received
the following towns with their pasturelands:
Kishion, Daberath, [29]Jarmuth, and En-gannim—
four towns.

[30]From the tribe of Asher they received
the following towns with their pasturelands:
Mishal, Abdon, [31]Helkath, and Rehob—four
towns.

[32]From the tribe of Naphtali they received
the following towns with their pasturelands:
Kedesh in Galilee (a city of refuge for those
who accidentally killed someone), Hammoth-
dor, and Kartan—three towns. [33]So in all, thir-
teen towns with their pasturelands were al-
lotted to the clan of Gershon.

[34]The rest of the Levites—the Merari clan—
were given the following towns with their
pasturelands from the tribe of Zebulun: Jok-
neam, Kartah, [35]Dimnah, and Nahalal—four
towns.

[36]From the tribe of Reuben they received
the following towns with their pasturelands:
Bezer, Jahaz,* [37]Kedemoth, and Mephaath—
four towns.

[38]From the tribe of Gad they received the
following towns with their pasturelands: Ra-
moth in Gilead (a city of refuge for those who
accidentally killed someone), Mahanaim,
[39]Heshbon, and Jazer—four towns. [40]So in all,
twelve towns were allotted to the clan of Me-
rari.

[41]The total number of towns and pastures-
lands within Israelite territory given to the Le-
vites came to forty-eight. [42]Every one of these
towns had pasturelands surrounding it.

[43]So the LORD gave to Israel all the land he
had sworn to give their ancestors, and they
took possession of it and settled there. [44]And
the LORD gave them rest on every side, just as
he had solemnly promised their ancestors.
None of their enemies could stand against
them, for the LORD helped them conquer all
their enemies. [45]Not a single one of all the
good promises the LORD had given to the fam-
ily of Israel was left unfulfilled; everything he
had spoken came true.

CHAPTER 22

The Eastern Tribes Return Home

Then Joshua called together the tribes of Reu-
ben, Gad, and the half-tribe of Manasseh. [2]He
told them, "You have done as Moses, the ser-
vant of the LORD, commanded you, and you
have obeyed every order I have given you.
[3]During all this time you have not deserted the
other tribes. You have been careful to obey the
commands of the LORD your God right up to
the present day. [4]And now the LORD your God
has given the other tribes rest, as he promised
them. So go back home to the land that Moses,
the servant of the LORD, gave you as your pos-
session on the east side of the Jordan River.
[5]But be very careful to obey all the commands
and the instructions that Moses gave to you.
Love the LORD your God, walk in all his ways,
obey his commands, hold firmly to him, and
serve him with all your heart and all your soul."
[6]So Joshua blessed them and sent them away,
and they went home.

[7]Moses had given the land of Bashan, east
of the Jordan River, to the half-tribe of Ma-
nasseh. (The other half of the tribe was given
land west of the Jordan.) As Joshua sent them
away and blessed them, [8]he said to them, "Go
back to your homes with the great wealth you
have taken from your enemies—the vast
herds of livestock, the silver, gold, bronze,
and iron, and the large supply of clothing.
Share the plunder with your relatives."

[9]So the men of Reuben, Gad, and the half-
tribe of Manasseh left the rest of Israel at Shi-
loh in the land of Canaan. They started the
journey back to their own land of Gilead, the
territory that belonged to them according to
the LORD's command through Moses.

The Eastern Tribes Build an Altar

[10]But while they were still in Canaan, and
when they came to a place called Geliloth*
near the Jordan River, the men of Reuben,
Gad, and the half-tribe of Manasseh stopped
to build a large and imposing altar.

[11]The rest of Israel heard that the people of
Reuben, Gad, and the half-tribe of Manasseh
had built an altar at Geliloth at the edge of the

21:36 Hebrew *Jahzah*, a variant spelling of Jahaz. **22:10** Or *to the circle of stones*; similarly in 22:11.

"I SPY"

Beau was helping his teacher clean out the cabinets for the summer. As they worked, another teacher came in and said, "An eighth grader was caught smoking outside the school." When the teacher saw Beau, he left. Beau was dying to know who the kid was. Later, while returning a box of supplies to the office, he saw a boy with the principal. It was Owen, an eighth grader who was always in trouble. He must have been the smoker! If he was, he wouldn't graduate! Beau had the hottest story in school. What should he do? Read Joshua 22:10-34.

land of Canaan, on the west side of the Jordan River. 12 So the whole community of Israel gathered at Shiloh and prepared to go to war against them. 13 First, however, they sent a delegation led by Phinehas son of Eleazar, the priest, to talk with the tribes of Reuben, Gad, and the half-tribe of Manasseh. 14 In this delegation were ten leaders of Israel, one from each of the ten tribes, and each the head of his family within the clans of Israel.

15 When they arrived in the land of Gilead, they said to the tribes of Reuben, Gad, and the half-tribe of Manasseh, 16 "The whole community of the LORD demands to know why you are betraying the God of Israel. How could you turn away from the LORD and build an altar for yourselves in rebellion against him? 17 Was our sin at Peor not enough? To this day we are not fully cleansed of it, even after the plague that struck the entire community of the LORD. 18 And yet today you are turning away from following the LORD. If you rebel against the LORD today, he will be angry with all of us tomorrow.

19 "If you need the altar because the land you possess is defiled, then join us in the LORD's land, where the Tabernacle of the LORD is situated, and share our land with us. But do not rebel against the LORD or against us by building an altar other than the one true altar of the LORD our God. 20 Didn't divine anger fall on the entire community of Israel when Achan, a member of the clan of Zerah, sinned by stealing the things set apart for the LORD*? He was not the only one who died because of his sin."

21 Then the people of Reuben, Gad, and the half-tribe of Manasseh answered the heads of the clans of Israel: 22 "The LORD, the Mighty One, is God! The LORD, the Mighty One, is God! He knows the truth, and may Israel know it, too! We have not built the altar in treacherous rebellion against the LORD. If we have done so, do not spare our lives this day. 23 If we have built an altar for ourselves to turn away from the LORD or to offer burnt offerings or grain offerings or peace offerings, may the LORD himself punish us.

24 "The truth is, we have built this altar because we fear that in the future your descendants will say to ours, 'What right do you have to worship the LORD, the God of Israel? 25 The LORD has placed the Jordan River as a barrier between our people and you people of Reuben and Gad. You have no claim to the LORD.' So your descendants may prevent our descendants from worshiping the LORD.

22:20 The Hebrew term used here refers to the complete consecration of things or people to the LORD, either by destroying them or by giving them as an offering.

[26]"So we decided to build the altar, not for burnt offerings or sacrifices, [27]but as a memorial. It will remind our descendants and your descendants that we, too, have the right to worship the LORD at his sanctuary with our burnt offerings, sacrifices, and peace offerings. Then your descendants will not be able to say to ours, 'You have no claim to the LORD.'

[28]"If they say this, our descendants can reply, 'Look at this copy of the LORD's altar that our ancestors made. It is not for burnt offerings or sacrifices; it is a reminder of the relationship both of us have with the LORD.' [29]Far be it from us to rebel against the LORD or turn away from him by building our own altar for burnt offerings, grain offerings, or sacrifices. Only the altar of the LORD our God that stands in front of the Tabernacle may be used for that purpose."

[30]When Phinehas the priest and the leaders of the community—the heads of the clans of Israel—heard this from the tribes of Reuben, Gad, and the half-tribe of Manasseh, they were satisfied. [31]Phinehas son of Eleazar, the priest, replied to them, "Today we know the LORD is among us because you have not committed this treachery against the LORD as we thought. Instead, you have rescued Israel from being destroyed by the hand of the LORD."

[32]Then Phinehas son of Eleazar, the priest, and the other leaders left the tribes of Reuben and Gad in Gilead and returned to the land of Canaan to tell the Israelites what had happened. [33]And all the Israelites were satisfied and praised God and spoke no more of war against Reuben and Gad.

[34]The people of Reuben and Gad named the altar "Witness,"* for they said, "It is a witness between us and them that the LORD is our God, too."

CHAPTER 23

Joshua's Final Words to Israel

The years passed, and the LORD had given the people of Israel rest from all their enemies. Joshua, who was now very old, [2]called together all the elders, leaders, judges, and officers of Israel. He said to them, "I am now a very old man. [3]You have seen everything the LORD your God has done for you during my lifetime. The LORD your God has fought for you against your enemies. [4]I have allotted to you as your homeland all the land of the nations yet unconquered, as well as the land of those we have already conquered—from the Jordan River to the Mediterranean Sea* in the west. [5]This land will be yours, for the LORD your God will himself drive out all the people living there now. You will take possession of their land, just as the LORD your God promised you.

[6]"So be very careful to follow everything Moses wrote in the Book of Instruction. Do not deviate from it, turning either to the right or to the left. [7]Make sure you do not associate with the other people still remaining in the land. Do not even mention the names of their gods, much less swear by them or serve them or worship them. [8]Rather, cling tightly to the LORD your God as you have done until now.

[9]"For the LORD has driven out great and powerful nations for you, and no one has yet been able to defeat you. [10]Each one of you will put to flight a thousand of the enemy, for the LORD your God fights for you, just as he has promised. [11]So be very careful to love the LORD your God.

[12]"But if you turn away from him and cling to the customs of the survivors of these nations remaining among you, and if you intermarry with them, [13]then know for certain that the LORD your God will no longer drive them out of your land. Instead, they will be a snare and a trap to you, a whip for your backs and thorny brambles in your eyes, and you will vanish from this good land the LORD your God has given you.

[14]"Soon I will die, going the way of everything on earth. Deep in your hearts you know that every promise of the LORD your God has come true. Not a single one has failed! [15]But as surely as the LORD your God has given you the good things he promised, he will also bring disaster on you if you disobey him. He will completely destroy you from this good land he has given you. [16]If you break the covenant of the LORD your God by worshiping and serving other gods, his anger will burn against you, and you will quickly vanish from the good land he has given you."

22:34 Some manuscripts lack this word. 23:4 Hebrew *the Great Sea.*

CHAPTER 24

The Lord's Covenant Renewed

Then Joshua summoned all the tribes of Israel to Shechem, including their elders, leaders, judges, and officers. So they came and presented themselves to God.

2 Joshua said to the people, "This is what the Lord, the God of Israel, says: Long ago your ancestors, including Terah, the father of Abraham and Nahor, lived beyond the Euphrates River,* and they worshiped other gods. 3 But I took your ancestor Abraham from the land beyond the Euphrates and led him into the land of Canaan. I gave him many descendants through his son Isaac. 4 To Isaac I gave Jacob and Esau. To Esau I gave the mountains of Seir, while Jacob and his children went down into Egypt.

5 "Then I sent Moses and Aaron, and I brought terrible plagues on Egypt; and afterward I brought you out as a free people. 6 But when your ancestors arrived at the Red Sea,* the Egyptians chased after you with chariots and charioteers. 7 When your ancestors cried out to the Lord, I put darkness between you and the Egyptians. I brought the sea crashing down on the Egyptians, drowning them. With your very own eyes you saw what I did. Then you lived in the wilderness for many years.

8 "Finally, I brought you into the land of the Amorites on the east side of the Jordan. They fought against you, but I destroyed them before you. I gave you victory over them, and you took possession of their land. 9 Then Balak son of Zippor, king of Moab, started a war against Israel. He summoned Balaam son of Beor to curse you, 10 but I would not listen to him. Instead, I made Balaam bless you, and so I rescued you from Balak.

11 "When you crossed the Jordan River and came to Jericho, the men of Jericho fought against you, as did the Amorites, the Perizzites, the Canaanites, the Hittites, the Girgashites, the Hivites, and the Jebusites. But I gave you victory over them. 12 And I sent terror* ahead of you to drive out the two kings of the Amorites. It was not your swords or bows that brought you victory. 13 I gave you land you had not worked on, and I gave you towns you did not build—the towns where you are now living. I gave you vineyards and olive groves for food, though you did not plant them.

14 "So fear the Lord and serve him wholeheartedly. Put away forever the idols your ancestors worshiped when they lived beyond the Euphrates River and in Egypt. Serve the Lord alone. 15 But if you refuse to serve the Lord, then choose today whom you will serve. Would you prefer the gods your ancestors served beyond the Euphrates? Or will it be the gods of the Amorites in whose land you now live? But as for me and my family, we will serve the Lord."

16 The people replied, "We would never abandon the Lord and serve other gods. 17 For the Lord our God is the one who rescued us and our ancestors from slavery in the land of Egypt. He performed mighty miracles before our very eyes. As we traveled through the wilderness among our enemies, he preserved us. 18 It was the Lord who drove out the Amorites and the other nations living here in the land. So we, too, will serve the Lord, for he alone is our God."

19 Then Joshua warned the people, "You are not able to serve the Lord, for he is a holy and jealous God. He will not forgive your rebellion and your sins. 20 If you abandon the Lord and serve other gods, he will turn against you and destroy you, even though he has been so good to you."

21 But the people answered Joshua, "No, we will serve the Lord!"

22 "You are a witness to your own decision," Joshua said. "You have chosen to serve the Lord."

"Yes," they replied, "we are witnesses to what we have said."

23 "All right then," Joshua said, "destroy the idols among you, and turn your hearts to the Lord, the God of Israel."

24 The people said to Joshua, "We will serve the Lord our God. We will obey him alone."

25 So Joshua made a covenant with the people that day at Shechem, committing them to follow the decrees and regulations of the Lord. 26 Joshua recorded these things in the Book of God's Instructions. As a reminder of their agreement, he took a huge stone and

24:2 Hebrew *the river;* also in 24:3, 14, 15. **24:6** Hebrew *sea of reeds.* **24:12** Often rendered *the hornet.* The meaning of the Hebrew is uncertain.

rolled it beneath the terebinth tree beside the Tabernacle of the LORD.

[27]Joshua said to all the people, "This stone has heard everything the LORD said to us. It will be a witness to testify against you if you go back on your word to God."

[28]Then Joshua sent all the people away to their own homelands.

Leaders Buried in the Promised Land

[29]After this, Joshua son of Nun, the servant of the LORD, died at the age of 110. [30]They buried him in the land he had been allocated, at Timnath-serah in the hill country of Ephraim, north of Mount Gaash.

[31]The people of Israel served the LORD throughout the lifetime of Joshua and of the elders who outlived him—those who had personally experienced all that the LORD had done for Israel.

[32]The bones of Joseph, which the Israelites had brought along with them when they left Egypt, were buried at Shechem, in the parcel of ground Jacob had bought from the sons of Hamor for 100 pieces of silver.* This land was located in the territory allotted to the descendants of Joseph.

[33]Eleazar son of Aaron also died. He was buried in the hill country of Ephraim, in the town of Gibeah, which had been given to his son Phinehas.

24:32 Hebrew *100 kesitahs;* the value or weight of the kesitah is no longer known.

JUDGES

WHO
Othniel, Ehud, Deborah, Barak, Jael, Gideon, Abimelech, Jephthah, Samson, and Delilah.

WHERE
Canaan (the Promised Land), later called Israel.

WHEN
About 1375–1050 BC, after Israel had come to live in the Promised Land.

WHY
The book of Judges shows that God punishes sin but forgives those who return to him.

In those days Israel had no king; all the people did whatever seemed right in their own eyes.
JUDGES 17:6

The Israelites forgot about God when things were going well. Then their enemies would move in, and (oh, no!) they would need help. God sent judges (leaders) to fight for the Israelites. For a while, the people would obey God—until they forgot again.

Exodus from Egypt	Israelites enter Canaan	Judges begin to rule	Deborah	Gideon	Samson	Saul becomes king	David becomes king
1446 BC	1406 BC	1375 BC	1209 BC	1162 BC	1075 BC	1050 BC	1010 BC

REMEMBER WHAT THE ISRAELITES FORGOT—TO TRUST AND OBEY GOD.

CHAPTER 1

Judah and Simeon Conquer the Land

After the death of Joshua, the Israelites asked the LORD, "Which tribe should go first to attack the Canaanites?"

2 The LORD answered, "Judah, for I have given them victory over the land."

3 The men of Judah said to their relatives from the tribe of Simeon, "Join with us to fight against the Canaanites living in the territory allotted to us. Then we will help you conquer your territory." So the men of Simeon went with Judah.

4 When the men of Judah attacked, the LORD gave them victory over the Canaanites and Perizzites, and they killed 10,000 enemy warriors

at the town of Bezek. [5]While at Bezek they encountered King Adoni-bezek and fought against him, and the Canaanites and Perizzites were defeated. [6]Adoni-bezek escaped, but the Israelites soon captured him and cut off his thumbs and big toes.

[7]Adoni-bezek said, "I once had seventy kings with their thumbs and big toes cut off, eating scraps from under my table. Now God has paid me back for what I did to them." They took him to Jerusalem, and he died there.

[8]The men of Judah attacked Jerusalem and captured it, killing all its people and setting the city on fire. [9]Then they went down to fight the Canaanites living in the hill country, the Negev, and the western foothills.* [10]Judah marched against the Canaanites in Hebron (formerly called Kiriath-arba), defeating the forces of Sheshai, Ahiman, and Talmai.

[11]From there they went to fight against the people living in the town of Debir (formerly called Kiriath-sepher). [12]Caleb said, "I will give my daughter Acsah in marriage to the one who attacks and captures Kiriath-sepher." [13]Othniel, the son of Caleb's younger brother, Kenaz, was the one who conquered it, so Acsah became Othniel's wife.

[14]When Acsah married Othniel, she urged him* to ask her father for a field. As she got down off her donkey, Caleb asked her, "What's the matter?"

[15]She said, "Let me have another gift. You have already given me land in the Negev; now please give me springs of water, too." So Caleb gave her the upper and lower springs.

[16]When the tribe of Judah left Jericho—the city of palms—the Kenites, who were descendants of Moses' father-in-law, traveled with them into the wilderness of Judah. They settled among the people there, near the town of Arad in the Negev.

[17]Then Judah joined with Simeon to fight against the Canaanites living in Zephath, and they completely destroyed* the town. So the town was named Hormah.* [18]In addition, Judah captured the towns of Gaza, Ashkelon, and Ekron, along with their surrounding territories.

Israel Fails to Conquer the Land

[19]The LORD was with the people of Judah, and they took possession of the hill country. But they failed to drive out the people living in the plains, who had iron chariots. [20]The town of Hebron was given to Caleb as Moses had promised. And Caleb drove out the people living there, who were descendants of the three sons of Anak.

[21]The tribe of Benjamin, however, failed to drive out the Jebusites, who were living in Jerusalem. So to this day the Jebusites live in Jerusalem among the people of Benjamin.

[22]The descendants of Joseph attacked the town of Bethel, and the LORD was with them. [23]They sent men to scout out Bethel (formerly known as Luz). [24]They confronted a man coming out of the town and said to him, "Show us a way into the town, and we will have mercy on you." [25]So he showed them a way in, and they killed everyone in the town except that man and his family. [26]Later the man moved to the land of the Hittites, where he built a town. He named it Luz, which is its name to this day.

[27]The tribe of Manasseh failed to drive out the people living in Beth-shan,* Taanach, Dor, Ibleam, Megiddo, and all their surrounding settlements, because the Canaanites were determined to stay in that region. [28]When the Israelites grew stronger, they forced the Canaanites to work as slaves, but they never did drive them completely out of the land.

[29]The tribe of Ephraim failed to drive out the Canaanites living in Gezer, so the Canaanites continued to live there among them.

[30]The tribe of Zebulun failed to drive out the residents of Kitron and Nahalol, so the Canaanites continued to live among them. But the Canaanites were forced to work as slaves for the people of Zebulun.

[31]The tribe of Asher failed to drive out the residents of Acco, Sidon, Ahlab, Aczib, Helbah, Aphik, and Rehob. [32]Instead, the people of Asher moved in among the Canaanites, who controlled the land, for they failed to drive them out.

[33]Likewise, the tribe of Naphtali failed to drive out the residents of Beth-shemesh and Beth-anath. Instead, they moved in among the

1:9 Hebrew *the Shephelah*. **1:14** Greek version and Latin Vulgate read *he urged her*. **1:17a** The Hebrew term used here refers to the complete consecration of things or people to the LORD, either by destroying them or by giving them as an offering. **1:17b** *Hormah* means "destruction." **1:27** Hebrew *Beth-shean*, a variant spelling of Beth-shan.

Canaanites, who controlled the land. Nevertheless, the people of Beth-shemesh and Beth-anath were forced to work as slaves for the people of Naphtali.

[34]As for the tribe of Dan, the Amorites forced them back into the hill country and would not let them come down into the plains. [35]The Amorites were determined to stay in Mount Heres, Aijalon, and Shaalbim, but when the descendants of Joseph became stronger, they forced the Amorites to work as slaves. [36]The boundary of the Amorites ran from Scorpion Pass* to Sela and continued upward from there.

CHAPTER 2

The LORD's Messenger Comes to Bokim

The angel of the LORD went up from Gilgal to Bokim and said to the Israelites, "I brought you out of Egypt into this land that I swore to give your ancestors, and I said I would never break my covenant with you. [2]For your part, you were not to make any covenants with the people living in this land; instead, you were to destroy their altars. But you disobeyed my command. Why did you do this? [3]So now I declare that I will no longer drive out the people living in your land. They will be thorns in your sides,* and their gods will be a constant temptation to you."

[4]When the angel of the LORD finished speaking to all the Israelites, the people wept loudly. [5]So they called the place Bokim (which means "weeping"), and they offered sacrifices there to the LORD.

The Death of Joshua

[6]After Joshua sent the people away, each of the tribes left to take possession of the land allotted to them. [7]And the Israelites served the LORD throughout the lifetime of Joshua and the leaders who outlived him—those who had seen all the great things the LORD had done for Israel.

[8]Joshua son of Nun, the servant of the LORD, died at the age of 110. [9]They buried him in the land he had been allocated, at Timnath-serah* in the hill country of Ephraim, north of Mount Gaash.

Israel Disobeys the LORD

[10]After that generation died, another generation grew up who did not acknowledge the LORD or remember the mighty things he had done for Israel.

[11]The Israelites did evil in the LORD's sight and served the images of Baal. [12]They abandoned the LORD, the God of their ancestors, who had brought them out of Egypt. They went after other gods, worshiping the gods of the people around them. And they angered the LORD. [13]They abandoned the LORD to serve Baal and the images of Ashtoreth. [14]This made the LORD burn with anger against Israel, so he handed them over to raiders who stole their possessions. He turned them over to their enemies all around, and they were no longer able to resist them. [15]Every time Israel went out to battle, the LORD fought against them, causing them to be defeated, just as he had warned. And the people were in great distress.

The LORD Rescues His People

[16]Then the LORD raised up judges to rescue the Israelites from their attackers. [17]Yet Israel did not listen to the judges but prostituted themselves by worshiping other gods. How quickly they turned away from the path of their ancestors, who had walked in obedience to the LORD's commands.

[18]Whenever the LORD raised up a judge over Israel, he was with that judge and rescued the people from their enemies throughout the judge's lifetime. For the LORD took pity on his people, who were burdened by oppression and suffering. [19]But when the judge died, the people returned to their corrupt ways, behaving worse than those who had lived before them. They went after other gods, serving and worshiping them. And they refused to give up their evil practices and stubborn ways.

[20]So the LORD burned with anger against Israel. He said, "Because these people have violated my covenant, which I made with their ancestors, and have ignored my commands, [21]I will no longer drive out the nations that Joshua left unconquered when he died. [22]I did this to test Israel—to see whether or not they would follow the ways of the LORD as their ancestors did." [23]That is why the LORD left those nations in place. He did not quickly drive them out or allow Joshua to conquer them all.

1:36 Hebrew *Akrabbim*. **2:3** Hebrew *They will be in your sides;* compare Num 33:55. **2:9** As in parallel text at Josh 24:30; Hebrew reads *Timnath-heres*, a variant spelling of Timnath-serah.

CHAPTER 3

The Nations Left in Canaan

These are the nations that the LORD left in the land to test those Israelites who had not experienced the wars of Canaan. [2]He did this to teach warfare to generations of Israelites who had no experience in battle. [3]These are the nations: the Philistines (those living under the five Philistine rulers), all the Canaanites, the Sidonians, and the Hivites living in the mountains of Lebanon from Mount Baal-hermon to Lebo-hamath. [4]These people were left to test the Israelites—to see whether they would obey the commands the LORD had given to their ancestors through Moses.

[5]So the people of Israel lived among the Canaanites, Hittites, Amorites, Perizzites, Hivites, and Jebusites, [6]and they intermarried with them. Israelite sons married their daughters, and Israelite daughters were given in marriage to their sons. And the Israelites served their gods.

Othniel Becomes Israel's Judge

[7]The Israelites did evil in the LORD's sight. They forgot about the LORD their God, and they served the images of Baal and the Asherah poles. [8]Then the LORD burned with anger against Israel, and he turned them over to King Cushan-rishathaim of Aram-naharaim.* And the Israelites served Cushan-rishathaim for eight years.

[9]But when the people of Israel cried out to the LORD for help, the LORD raised up a rescuer to save them. His name was Othniel, the son of Caleb's younger brother, Kenaz. [10]The Spirit of the LORD came upon him, and he became Israel's judge. He went to war against King Cushan-rishathaim of Aram, and the LORD gave Othniel victory over him. [11]So there was peace in the land for forty years. Then Othniel son of Kenaz died.

Ehud Becomes Israel's Judge

[12]Once again the Israelites did evil in the LORD's sight, and the LORD gave King Eglon of Moab control over Israel because of their evil. [13]Eglon enlisted the Ammonites and Amalekites as allies, and then he went out and defeated Israel, taking possession of Jericho, the city of palms. [14]And the Israelites served Eglon of Moab for eighteen years.

[15]But when the people of Israel cried out to the LORD for help, the LORD again raised up a rescuer to save them. His name was Ehud son of Gera, a left-handed man of the tribe of Benjamin. The Israelites sent Ehud to deliver

Best Friends?

Derek had church friends and school friends. He was close to his church friends because they were all Christians and wanted to live the right way. But most of those kids went to other schools, and Derek saw them only on Sundays. Derek's school friends were fun, and they liked him. The problem was that these friends weren't Christians. They said and did some things that Derek didn't agree with.

What should your *closest* friends be like? Judges 3:5-7 tells what happened when the Israelites let non-believing friends influence them.

3:8 *Aram-naharaim* means "Aram of the two rivers," thought to have been located between the Euphrates and Balih Rivers in northwestern Mesopotamia.

their tribute money to King Eglon of Moab.
16So Ehud made a double-edged dagger that
was about a foot* long, and he strapped it to
his right thigh, keeping it hidden under his
clothing. 17He brought the tribute money to
Eglon, who was very fat.

18After delivering the payment, Ehud
started home with those who had helped
carry the tribute. 19But when Ehud reached
the stone idols near Gilgal, he turned back.
He came to Eglon and said, "I have a secret
message for you."

So the king commanded his servants, "Be
quiet!" and he sent them all out of the room.

20Ehud walked over to Eglon, who was
sitting alone in a cool upstairs room. And
Ehud said, "I have a message from God for
you!" As King Eglon rose from his seat, 21Ehud
reached with his left hand, pulled out the
dagger strapped to his right thigh, and
plunged it into the king's belly. 22The dagger
went so deep that the handle disappeared be-
neath the king's fat. So Ehud did not pull out
the dagger, and the king's bowels emptied.*
23Then Ehud closed and locked the doors of
the room and escaped down the latrine.*

24After Ehud was gone, the king's servants
returned and found the doors to the upstairs
room locked. They thought he might be using
the latrine in the room, 25so they waited. But
when the king didn't come out after a long
delay, they became concerned and got a key.
And when they opened the doors, they found
their master dead on the floor.

26While the servants were waiting, Ehud es-
caped, passing the stone idols on his way to Se-
irah. 27When he arrived in the hill country of
Ephraim, Ehud sounded a call to arms. Then
he led a band of Israelites down from the hills.

28"Follow me," he said, "for the LORD has
given you victory over Moab your enemy." So
they followed him. And the Israelites took
control of the shallow crossings of the Jordan
River across from Moab, preventing anyone
from crossing.

29They attacked the Moabites and killed
about 10,000 of their strongest and most
able-bodied warriors. Not one of them es-
caped. 30So Moab was conquered by Israel
that day, and there was peace in the land for
eighty years.

Shamgar Becomes Israel's Judge

31After Ehud, Shamgar son of Anath rescued
Israel. He once killed 600 Philistines with an
ox goad.

CHAPTER 4

Deborah Becomes Israel's Judge

After Ehud's death, the Israelites again did evil
in the LORD's sight. 2So the LORD turned them
over to King Jabin of Hazor, a Canaanite king.
The commander of his army was Sisera, who
lived in Harosheth-haggoyim. 3Sisera, who
had 900 iron chariots, ruthlessly oppressed
the Israelites for twenty years. Then the people
of Israel cried out to the LORD for help.

4Deborah, the wife of Lappidoth, was a
prophet who was judging Israel at that time.
5She would sit under the Palm of Deborah, be-
tween Ramah and Bethel in the hill country of
Ephraim, and the Israelites would go to her for
judgment. 6One day she sent for Barak son of
Abinoam, who lived in Kedesh in the land of
Naphtali. She said to him, "This is what the
LORD, the God of Israel, commands you: Call
out 10,000 warriors from the tribes of Naph-
tali and Zebulun at Mount Tabor. 7And I will
call out Sisera, commander of Jabin's army,
along with his chariots and warriors, to the Ki-
shon River. There I will give you victory over
him."

8Barak told her, "I will go, but only if you go
with me."

9"Very well," she replied, "I will go with
you. But you will receive no honor in this ven-
ture, for the LORD's victory over Sisera will be
at the hands of a woman." So Deborah went
with Barak to Kedesh. 10At Kedesh, Barak
called together the tribes of Zebulun and
Naphtali, and 10,000 warriors went up with
him. Deborah also went with him.

11Now Heber the Kenite, a descendant of
Moses' brother-in-law* Hobab, had moved
away from the other members of his tribe and
pitched his tent by the oak of Zaanannim
near Kedesh.

12When Sisera was told that Barak son of
Abinoam had gone up to Mount Tabor, 13he
called for all 900 of his iron chariots and all
of his warriors, and they marched from
Harosheth-haggoyim to the Kishon River.

3:16 Hebrew *gomed*, the length of which is uncertain. **3:22** Or *and it came out behind*. **3:23** Or *and went out through the porch;* the meaning of the Hebrew is uncertain. **4:11** Or *father-in-law*.

[14]Then Deborah said to Barak, "Get ready!
This is the day the LORD will give you victory
over Sisera, for the LORD is marching ahead
of you." So Barak led his 10,000 warriors
down the slopes of Mount Tabor into battle.
[15]When Barak attacked, the LORD threw Sis-
era and all his chariots and warriors into a
panic. Sisera leaped down from his chariot
and escaped on foot. [16]Then Barak chased
the chariots and the enemy army all the way
to Harosheth-haggoyim, killing all of Sisera's
warriors. Not a single one was left alive.

[17]Meanwhile, Sisera ran to the tent of Jael,
the wife of Heber the Kenite, because Heber's
family was on friendly terms with King Jabin
of Hazor. [18]Jael went out to meet Sisera and
said to him, "Come into my tent, sir. Come in.
Don't be afraid." So he went into her tent, and
she covered him with a blanket.

[19]"Please give me some water," he said.
"I'm thirsty." So she gave him some milk from
a leather bag and covered him again.

[20]"Stand at the door of the tent," he told
her. "If anybody comes and asks you if there
is anyone here, say no."

[21]But when Sisera fell asleep from exhaus-
tion, Jael quietly crept up to him with a ham-
mer and tent peg in her hand. Then she drove
the tent peg through his temple and into the
ground, and so he died.

[22]When Barak came looking for Sisera, Jael
went out to meet him. She said, "Come, and I
will show you the man you are looking for." So
he followed her into the tent and found Sisera
lying there dead, with the tent peg through
his temple.

[23]So on that day Israel saw God defeat Jabin,
the Canaanite king. [24]And from that time on
Israel became stronger and stronger against
King Jabin until they finally destroyed him.

CHAPTER 5

The Song of Deborah

On that day Deborah and Barak son of Abino-
am sang this song:

2 "Israel's leaders took charge,
and the people gladly followed.
Praise the LORD!

3 "Listen, you kings!
Pay attention, you mighty rulers!

IS IT OK?

IS IT OK TO WANT TO BE THE PRESIDENT OR A FAMOUS SINGER?

When Deborah was young, do you think she dreamed of becoming a prophetess, warrior, and judge? She was a real superstar! We don't know what Deborah's dreams were. But it's fine to dream big, as long as your dreams are somewhat realistic. If you're shy, becoming President might be intimidating. If you hate singing in public, becoming a professional singer might be a stretch. (Of course, God can stretch us even beyond our dreams, but he usually works through the talents and skills he has already given us.) Whatever you become—the President, the President's speechwriter, a famous singer, or a famous singer's agent—remember that God can use you and your unique talents to make a difference.

For I will sing to the LORD.
I will make music to the LORD, the God
of Israel.

4 "LORD, when you set out from Seir
and marched across the fields of Edom,
the earth trembled,
and the cloudy skies poured down rain.

Who deserves our worship and praise? ✱ **Listen, you kings! Pay attention, you mighty rulers! For I will sing to the LORD. I will make music to the LORD, the God of Israel.** JUDGES 5:3

5 The mountains quaked in the presence
of the LORD,
the God of Mount Sinai—
in the presence of the LORD,
the God of Israel.

6 "In the days of Shamgar son of Anath,
and in the days of Jael,
people avoided the main roads,
and travelers stayed on winding
pathways.
7 There were few people left in the villages
of Israel*—
until Deborah arose as a mother
for Israel.
8 When Israel chose new gods,
war erupted at the city gates.
Yet not a shield or spear could be seen
among forty thousand warriors in
Israel!
9 My heart is with the commanders of
Israel,
with those who volunteered for war.
Praise the LORD!

10 "Consider this, you who ride on fine
donkeys,
you who sit on fancy saddle blankets,
and you who walk along the road.
11 Listen to the village musicians*
gathered at the watering holes.
They recount the righteous victories of
the LORD
and the victories of his villagers
in Israel.
Then the people of the LORD
marched down to the city gates.

12 "Wake up, Deborah, wake up!
Wake up, wake up, and sing a song!
Arise, Barak!
Lead your captives away, son of
Abinoam!

13 "Down from Tabor marched the few
against the nobles.
The people of the LORD marched down
against mighty warriors.
14 They came down from Ephraim—
a land that once belonged to the
Amalekites;
they followed you, Benjamin, with your
troops.
From Makir the commanders marched
down;
from Zebulun came those who carry
a commander's staff.
15 The princes of Issachar were with
Deborah and Barak.
They followed Barak, rushing into the
valley.
But in the tribe of Reuben
there was great indecision.
16 Why did you sit at home among the
sheepfolds—
to hear the shepherds whistle for
their flocks?
Yes, in the tribe of Reuben
there was great indecision.
17 Gilead remained east of the Jordan.
And why did Dan stay home?
Asher sat unmoved at the seashore,
remaining in his harbors.
18 But Zebulun risked his life,
as did Naphtali, on the heights
of the battlefield.

19 "The kings of Canaan came and fought,
at Taanach near Megiddo's springs,
but they carried off no silver treasures.
20 The stars fought from heaven.
The stars in their orbits fought against
Sisera.
21 The Kishon River swept them away—
that ancient torrent, the Kishon.

5:7 The meaning of the Hebrew is uncertain. **5:11** The meaning of the Hebrew is uncertain.

Barak

My name is Barak. I confess—I'm a coward. Deborah the prophet told me the Lord wanted me to lead 10,000 men to Mount Tabor. She promised I'd get to fight Sisera, a violent military man—and win—but I wasn't so sure. I told her I'd go only if she came along. A woman in battle? Never. But she said, "Sure." Deborah led the charge. She didn't seem nervous. She almost had to push me into battle. "Go!" she said. "God will give you victory!" She was right. There wasn't a single man left standing in Sisera's army. The Lord protected and saved us. All I had to do was obey.

Find out more about Barak in Judges 4–5.

March on with courage, my soul!
22 Then the horses' hooves hammered the ground,
the galloping, galloping of Sisera's mighty steeds.
23 'Let the people of Meroz be cursed,' said the angel of the LORD.
'Let them be utterly cursed,
because they did not come to help the LORD—
to help the LORD against the mighty warriors.'
24 "Most blessed among women is Jael,
the wife of Heber the Kenite.
May she be blessed above all women who live in tents.
25 Sisera asked for water,
and she gave him milk.
In a bowl fit for nobles,
she brought him yogurt.
26 Then with her left hand she reached for a tent peg,
and with her right hand for the workman's hammer.
She struck Sisera with the hammer, crushing his head.
With a shattering blow, she pierced his temples.
27 He sank, he fell,
he lay still at her feet.
And where he sank,
there he died.
28 "From the window Sisera's mother looked out.
Through the window she watched for his return, saying,
'Why is his chariot so long in coming?
Why don't we hear the sound of chariot wheels?'
29 "Her wise women answer,
and she repeats these words to herself:
30 'They must be dividing the captured plunder—
with a woman or two for every man.
There will be colorful robes for Sisera,
and colorful, embroidered robes for me.
Yes, the plunder will include colorful robes embroidered on both sides.'
31 "LORD, may all your enemies die like Sisera!
But may those who love you rise like the sun in all its power!"

Then there was peace in the land for forty years.

KINGS

At first Israel didn't have a king. God was their king, and he led them by working through religious leaders like Moses and his brother, Aaron, the High Priest. After the Israelites had settled in the Promised Land, people called judges ruled over them. But the people saw that the nations around them had kings! So the Israelites took a big step toward becoming like everyone else—by getting a king. Saul was their first king. David and his son Solomon were the second and third kings. Then Israel divided into two opposing nations. Many years (and many wicked kings) later, both nations were defeated by other countries. Whether you're talking about people or nations, your greatest strength comes from your spiritual health. Israel forgot that. They trusted kings—instead of God—to lead them.

KINGS OF ISRAEL
Saul
David
Solomon

Flip two pages to see more kings.

FEAST . . .	CELEBRATED . . .	WHEN . . .
Passover	Israel's deliverance from Egypt	14 Nisan
Unleavened Bread	40 years wandering in the wilderness	7 days after Passover
Weeks (Harvest/Pentecost)	the harvest	7 weeks after Passover
Trumpets (Rosh Hashanah)	God's creation, the New Year	1 Tishri
Day of Atonement (Yom Kippur)	national confession of sins	10 Tishri
Tabernacles (Booths)	journey from Egypt	15–21 Tishri
Lights	rededication of the Temple	25 Kislev
Purim	the deliverance of the Jews through Esther	13–15 Adar

FEASTS

Holidays (called feasts or festivals) for the Jews were a lot more than days off from work or school. They were reminders of Jewish history and God's faithfulness. Most of the holidays lasted one day, but some lasted longer. The Festival of Tabernacles lasted an entire week! Some of the activities at Jewish feasts were a lot like our holiday celebrations. Families kept various traditions, like gift-giving and having certain things to eat. They ate their meals together and went to church together.

MUSICAL INSTRUMENTS

Stringed instruments, like the lyre and harp, were made of cypress-wood boxes with strings of stretched sheep gut.

Wind instruments, like trumpets, were made from bronze and ram's horns, and a reeded pipe was carved out of wood or bone.

Percussion instruments, like drums, the player beat with sticks, and cymbals were made of copper.

David was not only a shepherd and king but a talented musician. He wrote many songs (psalms) and played a harp. David's harp was probably made from wood or animal bones. The strings may have been animal gut. Could those materials make beautiful music? They did!

WORSHIP AND HOLIDAYS

IDOLS

An idol was most often an object made of wood or metal that represented a false god the people worshiped. Baal, for instance, was usually represented by a bull. Even though they knew better, the Israelites made and bought some of their neighbors' idols–and actually worshiped them.

SACRIFICES

As gruesome as it sounds, animal offerings or sacrifices were a part of Old Testament worship. Yes, there was blood. That blood was a reminder that sin is serious. It kills. Jesus eventually gave up his life to be our sacrifice. Of course, he rose from the dead, and now we no longer need to offer sacrifices.

THE JEWISH CALENDAR

Shebat	Jan/Feb
Adar	Feb/Mar
Nisan	Mar/Apr
Ziv	Apr/May
Sivan	May/Jun
Tammuz	Jun/Jul
Ab	Jul/Aug
Elul	Aug/Sep
Ethanim (Tishri)	Sep/Oct
Bul (Marchesvan)	Oct/Nov
Kislev	Nov/Dec
Tebeth	Dec/Jan

NORTHERN KINGDOM: ISRAEL

Jeroboam I
Nadab
Baasha
Elah
Zimri
Tibni
Omri
Ahab
Ahaziah
Joram
Jehu
Jehoahaz
Jehoash
Jeroboam II
Zechariah
Shallum
Menahem
Pekahiah
Pekah
Hoshea

SOUTHERN KINGDOM: JUDAH

Rehoboam
Abijam
Asa
Jehoshaphat
Jehoram
Ahaziah
Athaliah (Queen)
Joash
Amaziah
Uzziah
Jotham
Ahaz
Hezekiah
Manasseh
Amon
Josiah
Jehoahaz
Jehoiakim
Jehoiachin
Zedekiah

CHAPTER 6

Gideon Becomes Israel's Judge

The Israelites did evil in the LORD's sight. So
the LORD handed them over to the Midian-
ites for seven years. [2]The Midianites were so
cruel that the Israelites made hiding places
for themselves in the mountains, caves,
and strongholds. [3]Whenever the Israelites
planted their crops, marauders from Midian,
Amalek, and the people of the east would
attack Israel, [4]camping in the land and de-
stroying crops as far away as Gaza. They left
the Israelites with nothing to eat, taking all
the sheep, goats, cattle, and donkeys. [5]These
enemy hordes, coming with their livestock
and tents, were as thick as locusts; they ar-
rived on droves of camels too numerous to
count. And they stayed until the land was
stripped bare. [6]So Israel was reduced to star-
vation by the Midianites. Then the Israelites
cried out to the LORD for help.

[7]When they cried out to the LORD because
of Midian, [8]the LORD sent a prophet to the
Israelites. He said, "This is what the LORD,
the God of Israel, says: I brought you up out
of slavery in Egypt. [9]I rescued you from the
Egyptians and from all who oppressed you. I
drove out your enemies and gave you their
land. [10]I told you, 'I am the LORD your God.
You must not worship the gods of the Amo-
rites, in whose land you now live.' But you
have not listened to me."

[11]Then the angel of the LORD came and sat
beneath the great tree at Ophrah, which be-
longed to Joash of the clan of Abiezer. Gideon
son of Joash was threshing wheat at the bot-
tom of a winepress to hide the grain from the
Midianites. [12]The angel of the LORD appeared
to him and said, "Mighty hero, the LORD is
with you!"

[13]"Sir," Gideon replied, "if the LORD is with
us, why has all this happened to us? And
where are all the miracles our ancestors told
us about? Didn't they say, 'The LORD brought
us up out of Egypt'? But now the LORD has
abandoned us and handed us over to the
Midianites."

[14]Then the LORD turned to him and said,
"Go with the strength you have, and rescue
Israel from the Midianites. I am sending
you!"

[15]"But Lord," Gideon replied, "how can I
rescue Israel? My clan is the weakest in the
whole tribe of Manasseh, and I am the least
in my entire family!"

[16]The LORD said to him, "I will be with you.
And you will destroy the Midianites as if you
were fighting against one man."

[17]Gideon replied, "If you are truly going
to help me, show me a sign to prove that it
is really the LORD speaking to me. [18]Don't go
away until I come back and bring my offering
to you."

He answered, "I will stay here until you re-
turn."

[19]Gideon hurried home. He cooked a young
goat, and with a basket* of flour he baked
some bread without yeast. Then, carrying the
meat in a basket and the broth in a pot, he
brought them out and presented them to the
angel, who was under the great tree.

[20]The angel of God said to him, "Place the
meat and the unleavened bread on this rock,
and pour the broth over it." And Gideon did as
he was told. [21]Then the angel of the LORD
touched the meat and bread with the tip of
the staff in his hand, and fire flamed up from
the rock and consumed all he had brought.
And the angel of the LORD disappeared.

[22]When Gideon realized that it was the an-
gel of the LORD, he cried out, "Oh, Sovereign
LORD, I'm doomed! I have seen the angel of
the LORD face to face!"

[23]"It is all right," the LORD replied. "Do not
be afraid. You will not die." [24]And Gideon
built an altar to the LORD there and named it
Yahweh-Shalom (which means "the LORD is
peace"). The altar remains in Ophrah in the
land of the clan of Abiezer to this day.

[25]That night the LORD said to Gideon,
"Take the second bull from your father's
herd, the one that is seven years old. Pull
down your father's altar to Baal, and cut down
the Asherah pole standing beside it. [26]Then
build an altar to the LORD your God here on
this hilltop sanctuary, laying the stones care-
fully. Sacrifice the bull as a burnt offering on
the altar, using as fuel the wood of the Ashe-
rah pole you cut down."

[27]So Gideon took ten of his servants and
did as the LORD had commanded. But he did it
at night because he was afraid of the other
members of his father's household and the
people of the town.

6:19 Hebrew *an ephah* [20 quarts or 22 liters].

[28]Early the next morning, as the people of the town began to stir, someone discovered that the altar of Baal had been broken down and that the Asherah pole beside it had been cut down. In their place a new altar had been built, and on it were the remains of the bull that had been sacrificed. [29]The people said to each other, "Who did this?" And after asking around and making a careful search, they learned that it was Gideon, the son of Joash.

AMAZING FACTS

How did God convince Gideon to be a leader? He made a piece of sheep's wool sopping wet one night, bone dry the next!

JUDGES 6:36-40

[30]"Bring out your son," the men of the town demanded of Joash. "He must die for destroying the altar of Baal and for cutting down the Asherah pole."

[31]But Joash shouted to the mob that confronted him, "Why are you defending Baal? Will you argue his case? Whoever pleads his case will be put to death by morning! If Baal truly is a god, let him defend himself and destroy the one who broke down his altar!" [32]From then on Gideon was called Jerub-baal, which means "Let Baal defend himself," because he broke down Baal's altar.

Gideon Asks for a Sign

[33]Soon afterward the armies of Midian, Amalek, and the people of the east formed an alliance against Israel and crossed the Jordan, camping in the valley of Jezreel. [34]Then the Spirit of the LORD took possession of Gideon. He blew a ram's horn as a call to arms, and the men of the clan of Abiezer came to him. [35]He also sent messengers throughout Manasseh, Asher, Zebulun, and Naphtali, summoning their warriors, and all of them responded.

[36]Then Gideon said to God, "If you are truly going to use me to rescue Israel as you promised, [37]prove it to me in this way. I will put a wool fleece on the threshing floor tonight. If the fleece is wet with dew in the morning but the ground is dry, then I will know that you are going to help me rescue Israel as you promised." [38]And that is just what happened. When Gideon got up early the next morning, he squeezed the fleece and wrung out a whole bowlful of water.

[39]Then Gideon said to God, "Please don't be angry with me, but let me make one more request. Let me use the fleece for one more test. This time let the fleece remain dry while the ground around it is wet with dew." [40]So that night God did as Gideon asked. The fleece was dry in the morning, but the ground was covered with dew.

CHAPTER 7

Gideon Defeats the Midianites

So Jerub-baal (that is, Gideon) and his army got up early and went as far as the spring of Harod. The armies of Midian were camped north of them in the valley near the hill of Moreh. [2]The LORD said to Gideon, "You have too many warriors with you. If I let all of you fight the Midianites, the Israelites will boast to me that they saved themselves by their own strength. [3]Therefore, tell the people, 'Whoever is timid or afraid may leave this mountain* and go home.'" So 22,000 of them went home, leaving only 10,000 who were willing to fight.

[4]But the LORD told Gideon, "There are still too many! Bring them down to the spring, and I will test them to determine who will go with you and who will not." [5]When Gideon took his warriors down to the water, the LORD told him, "Divide the men into two groups. In one group put all those who cup water in their hands and lap it up with their tongues like dogs. In the other group put all those who kneel down and drink with their mouths in the stream." [6]Only 300 of the men drank from their hands. All the others got down on

7:3 Hebrew *may leave Mount Gilead*. The identity of Mount Gilead is uncertain in this context. It is perhaps used here as another name for Mount Gilboa.

Gideon

When God told us to fight the mighty Midianites, I gathered more than 30,000 men. You won't believe what happened next. The Lord decided to send back anyone who was afraid. I did as he asked. That meant we lost 22,000 soldiers. We were down to only 10,000 men. From God's viewpoint, that was still too many. I took everyone to the water's edge. Some scooped up water into their hands and drank. Most simply put their faces into the water. Only 300 drank from their hands. God had me send the rest away. And guess what? With that small army we won the battle. It was a God thing.

Read about Gideon in Judges 6–8.

their knees and drank with their mouths in the stream.

7 The Lord told Gideon, "With these 300 men I will rescue you and give you victory over the Midianites. Send all the others home." 8 So Gideon collected the provisions and rams' horns of the other warriors and sent them home. But he kept the 300 men with him.

The Midianite camp was in the valley just below Gideon. 9 That night the Lord said, "Get up! Go down into the Midianite camp, for I have given you victory over them! 10 But if you are afraid to attack, go down to the camp with your servant Purah. 11 Listen to what the Midianites are saying, and you will be greatly encouraged. Then you will be eager to attack."

So Gideon took Purah and went down to the edge of the enemy camp. 12 The armies of Midian, Amalek, and the people of the east had settled in the valley like a swarm of locusts. Their camels were like grains of sand on the seashore—too many to count! 13 Gideon crept up just as a man was telling his companion about a dream. The man said, "I had this dream, and in my dream a loaf of barley bread came tumbling down into the Midianite camp. It hit a tent, turned it over, and knocked it flat!"

14 His companion answered, "Your dream can mean only one thing—God has given Gideon son of Joash, the Israelite, victory over Midian and all its allies!"

15 When Gideon heard the dream and its interpretation, he bowed in worship before the Lord.* Then he returned to the Israelite camp and shouted, "Get up! For the Lord has given you victory over the Midianite hordes!" 16 He divided the 300 men into three groups and gave each man a ram's horn and a clay jar with a torch in it.

17 Then he said to them, "Keep your eyes on me. When I come to the edge of the camp, do just as I do. 18 As soon as I and those with me blow the rams' horns, blow your horns, too, all around the entire camp, and shout, 'For the Lord and for Gideon!'"

19 It was just after midnight,* after the changing of the guard, when Gideon and the 100 men with him reached the edge of the Midianite camp. Suddenly, they blew the rams' horns and broke their clay jars. 20 Then all three groups blew their horns and broke their jars. They held the blazing torches in their left hands and the horns in their right hands, and they all shouted, "A sword for the Lord and for Gideon!"

21 Each man stood at his position around the camp and watched as all the Midianites rushed around in a panic, shouting as they ran to escape. 22 When the 300 Israelites blew

7:15 As in Greek version; Hebrew reads *he bowed.* **7:19** Hebrew *at the beginning of the second watch.*

their rams' horns, the LORD caused the warriors in the camp to fight against each other with their swords. Those who were not killed fled to places as far away as Beth-shittah near Zererah and to the border of Abel-meholah near Tabbath.

[23]Then Gideon sent for the warriors of Naphtali, Asher, and Manasseh, who joined in chasing the army of Midian. [24]Gideon also sent messengers throughout the hill country of Ephraim, saying, "Come down to attack the Midianites. Cut them off at the shallow crossings of the Jordan River at Beth-barah."

So all the men of Ephraim did as they were told. [25]They captured Oreb and Zeeb, the two Midianite commanders, killing Oreb at the rock of Oreb, and Zeeb at the winepress of Zeeb. And they continued to chase the Midianites. Afterward the Israelites brought the heads of Oreb and Zeeb to Gideon, who was by the Jordan River.

CHAPTER 8

Gideon Kills Zebah and Zalmunna

Then the people of Ephraim asked Gideon, "Why have you treated us this way? Why didn't you send for us when you first went out to fight the Midianites?" And they argued heatedly with Gideon.

[2]But Gideon replied, "What have I accomplished compared to you? Aren't even the leftover grapes of Ephraim's harvest better than the entire crop of my little clan of Abiezer? [3]God gave you victory over Oreb and Zeeb, the commanders of the Midianite army. What have I accomplished compared to that?" When the men of Ephraim heard Gideon's answer, their anger subsided.

[4]Gideon then crossed the Jordan River with his 300 men, and though exhausted, they continued to chase the enemy. [5]When they reached Succoth, Gideon asked the leaders of the town, "Please give my warriors some food. They are very tired. I am chasing Zebah and Zalmunna, the kings of Midian."

[6]But the officials of Succoth replied, "Catch Zebah and Zalmunna first, and then we will feed your army."

[7]So Gideon said, "After the LORD gives me victory over Zebah and Zalmunna, I will return and tear your flesh with the thorns and briers from the wilderness."

[8]From there Gideon went up to Peniel* and again asked for food, but he got the same answer. [9]So he said to the people of Peniel, "After I return in victory, I will tear down this tower."

[10]By this time Zebah and Zalmunna were in Karkor with 15,000 warriors—all that remained of the allied armies of the east, for 120,000 had already been killed. [11]Gideon circled around by the caravan route east of Nobah and Jogbehah, taking the Midianite army by surprise. [12]Zebah and Zalmunna, the two Midianite kings, fled, but Gideon chased them down and captured all their warriors.

[13]After this, Gideon returned from the battle by way of Heres Pass. [14]There he captured a young man from Succoth and demanded that he write down the names of all the seventy-seven officials and elders in the town. [15]Gideon then returned to Succoth and said to the leaders, "Here are Zebah and Zalmunna. When we were here before, you taunted me, saying, 'Catch Zebah and Zalmunna first, and then we will feed your exhausted army.'" [16]Then Gideon took the elders of the town and taught them a lesson, punishing them with thorns and briers from the wilderness. [17]He also tore down the tower of Peniel and killed all the men in the town.

[18]Then Gideon asked Zebah and Zalmunna, "The men you killed at Tabor—what were they like?"

"Like you," they replied. "They all had the look of a king's son."

[19]"They were my brothers, the sons of my own mother!" Gideon exclaimed. "As surely as the LORD lives, I wouldn't kill you if you hadn't killed them."

[20]Turning to Jether, his oldest son, he said, "Kill them!" But Jether did not draw his sword, for he was only a boy and was afraid.

[21]Then Zebah and Zalmunna said to Gideon, "Be a man! Kill us yourself!" So Gideon killed them both and took the royal ornaments from the necks of their camels.

Gideon's Sacred Ephod

[22]Then the Israelites said to Gideon, "Be our ruler! You and your son and your grandson

8:8 Hebrew *Penuel*, a variant spelling of Peniel; also in 8:9, 17.

will be our rulers, for you have rescued us from Midian."

23But Gideon replied, "I will not rule over you, nor will my son. The LORD will rule over you! 24However, I do have one request—that each of you give me an earring from the plunder you collected from your fallen enemies." (The enemies, being Ishmaelites, all wore gold earrings.)

25"Gladly!" they replied. They spread out a cloak, and each one threw in a gold earring he had gathered from the plunder. 26The weight of the gold earrings was forty-three pounds,* not including the royal ornaments and pendants, the purple clothing worn by the kings of Midian, or the chains around the necks of their camels.

27Gideon made a sacred ephod from the gold and put it in Ophrah, his hometown. But soon all the Israelites prostituted themselves by worshiping it, and it became a trap for Gideon and his family.

28That is the story of how the people of Israel defeated Midian, which never recovered. Throughout the rest of Gideon's lifetime—about forty years—there was peace in the land.

29Then Gideon* son of Joash returned home. 30He had seventy sons born to him, for he had many wives. 31He also had a concubine in Shechem, who gave birth to a son, whom he named Abimelech. 32Gideon died when he was very old, and he was buried in the grave of his father, Joash, at Ophrah in the land of the clan of Abiezer.

33As soon as Gideon died, the Israelites prostituted themselves by worshiping the images of Baal, making Baal-berith their god. 34They forgot the LORD their God, who had rescued them from all their enemies surrounding them. 35Nor did they show any loyalty to the family of Jerub-baal (that is, Gideon), despite all the good he had done for Israel.

CHAPTER 9

Abimelech Rules over Shechem

One day Gideon's* son Abimelech went to Shechem to visit his uncles—his mother's brothers. He said to them and to the rest of his mother's family, 2"Ask the leading citizens of Shechem whether they want to be ruled by all seventy of Gideon's sons or by one man. And remember that I am your own flesh and blood!"

3So Abimelech's uncles gave his message to all the citizens of Shechem on his behalf. And after listening to this proposal, the people of Shechem decided in favor of Abimelech because he was their relative. 4They gave him seventy silver coins from the temple of Baal-berith, which he used to hire some reckless troublemakers who agreed to follow him. 5He went to his father's home at Ophrah, and there, on one stone, they killed all seventy of his half brothers, the sons of Gideon.* But the youngest brother, Jotham, escaped and hid.

6Then all the leading citizens of Shechem and Beth-millo called a meeting under the oak beside the pillar* at Shechem and made Abimelech their king.

Jotham's Parable

7When Jotham heard about this, he climbed to the top of Mount Gerizim and shouted,

"Listen to me, citizens of Shechem!
Listen to me if you want God to listen
to you!
8 Once upon a time the trees decided
to choose a king.
First they said to the olive tree,
'Be our king!'
9 But the olive tree refused, saying,
'Should I quit producing the olive oil
that blesses both God and people,
just to wave back and forth over
the trees?'

10 "Then they said to the fig tree,
'You be our king!'
11 But the fig tree also refused, saying,
'Should I quit producing my sweet
fruit
just to wave back and forth over
the trees?'

12 "Then they said to the grapevine,
'You be our king!'
13 But the grapevine also refused, saying,
'Should I quit producing the wine
that cheers both God and people,
just to wave back and forth over
the trees?'

8:26 Hebrew *1,700 shekels* [19.4 kilograms]. **8:29** Hebrew *Jerub-baal;* see 6:32. **9:1** Hebrew *Jerub-baal's* (see 6:32); also in 9:2, 24. **9:5** Hebrew *Jerub-baal* (see 6:32); also in 9:16, 19, 28, 57. **9:6** The meaning of the Hebrew is uncertain.

14 "Then all the trees finally turned to the
thornbush and said,
'Come, you be our king!'
15 And the thornbush replied to the trees,
'If you truly want to make me your king,
come and take shelter in my shade.
If not, let fire come out from me
and devour the cedars of Lebanon.'"

16 Jotham continued, "Now make sure you have acted honorably and in good faith by making Abimelech your king, and that you have done right by Gideon and all of his descendants. Have you treated him with the honor he deserves for all he accomplished? 17 For he fought for you and risked his life when he rescued you from the Midianites. 18 But today you have revolted against my father and his descendants, killing his seventy sons on one stone. And you have chosen his slave woman's son, Abimelech, to be your king just because he is your relative.

19 "If you have acted honorably and in good faith toward Gideon and his descendants today, then may you find joy in Abimelech, and may he find joy in you. 20 But if you have not acted in good faith, then may fire come out from Abimelech and devour the leading citizens of Shechem and Beth-millo; and may fire come out from the citizens of Shechem and Beth-millo and devour Abimelech!"

21 Then Jotham escaped and lived in Beer because he was afraid of his brother Abimelech.

Shechem Rebels against Abimelech

22 After Abimelech had ruled over Israel for three years, 23 God sent a spirit that stirred up trouble between Abimelech and the leading citizens of Shechem, and they revolted. 24 God was punishing Abimelech for murdering Gideon's seventy sons, and the citizens of Shechem for supporting him in this treachery of murdering his brothers. 25 The citizens of Shechem set an ambush for Abimelech on the hilltops and robbed everyone who passed that way. But someone warned Abimelech about their plot.

26 One day Gaal son of Ebed moved to Shechem with his brothers and gained the confidence of the leading citizens of Shechem. 27 During the annual harvest festival at Shechem, held in the temple of the local god, the wine flowed freely, and everyone began cursing Abimelech. 28 "Who is Abimelech?" Gaal shouted. "He's not a true son of Shechem,* so why should we be his servants? He's merely the son of Gideon, and this Zebul is merely his deputy. Serve the true sons of Hamor, the founder of Shechem. Why should we serve Abimelech? 29 If I were in charge here, I would get rid of Abimelech. I would say* to him, 'Get some soldiers, and come out and fight!'"

30 But when Zebul, the leader of the city, heard what Gaal was saying, he was furious. 31 He sent messengers to Abimelech in Arumah,* telling him, "Gaal son of Ebed and his brothers have come to live in Shechem, and now they are inciting the city to rebel against you. 32 Come by night with an army and hide out in the fields. 33 In the morning, as soon as it is daylight, attack the city. When Gaal and those who are with him come out against you, you can do with them as you wish."

34 So Abimelech and all his men went by night and split into four groups, stationing themselves around Shechem. 35 Gaal was standing at the city gates when Abimelech and his army came out of hiding. 36 When Gaal saw them, he said to Zebul, "Look, there are people coming down from the hilltops!"

Zebul replied, "It's just the shadows on the hills that look like men."

37 But again Gaal said, "No, people are coming down from the hills.* And another group is coming down the road past the Diviners' Oak.*"

38 Then Zebul turned on him and asked, "Now where is that big mouth of yours? Wasn't it you that said, 'Who is Abimelech, and why should we be his servants?' The men you mocked are right outside the city! Go out and fight them!"

39 So Gaal led the leading citizens of Shechem into battle against Abimelech. 40 But Abimelech chased him, and many of Shechem's men were wounded and fell along the road as they retreated to the city gate. 41 Abimelech returned to Arumah, and Zebul drove Gaal and his brothers out of Shechem.

42 The next day the people of Shechem went out into the fields to battle. When

9:28 Hebrew *Who is Shechem?* **9:29** As in Greek version; Hebrew reads *And he said.* **9:31** Or *in secret;* Hebrew reads *in Tormah;* compare 9:41. **9:37a** Or *the center of the land.* **9:37b** Hebrew *Elon-meonenim.*

Abimelech heard about it, [43]he divided his men into three groups and set an ambush in the fields. When Abimelech saw the people coming out of the city, he and his men jumped up from their hiding places and attacked them. [44]Abimelech and his group stormed the city gate to keep the men of Shechem from getting back in, while Abimelech's other two groups cut them down in the fields. [45]The battle went on all day before Abimelech finally captured the city. He killed the people, leveled the city, and scattered salt all over the ground.

[46]When the leading citizens who lived in the tower of Shechem heard what had happened, they ran and hid in the temple of Baal-berith.* [47]Someone reported to Abimelech that the citizens had gathered in the temple, [48]so he led his forces to Mount Zalmon. He took an ax and chopped some branches from a tree, then put them on his shoulder. "Quick, do as I have done!" he told his men. [49]So each of them cut down some branches, following Abimelech's example. They piled the branches against the walls of the temple and set them on fire. So all the people who had lived in the tower of Shechem died—about 1,000 men and women.

[50]Then Abimelech attacked the town of Thebez and captured it. [51]But there was a strong tower inside the town, and all the men and women—the entire population—fled to it. They barricaded themselves in and climbed up to the roof of the tower. [52]Abimelech followed them to attack the tower. But as he prepared to set fire to the entrance, [53]a woman on the roof dropped a millstone that landed on Abimelech's head and crushed his skull.

[54]He quickly said to his young armor bearer, "Draw your sword and kill me! Don't let it be said that a woman killed Abimelech!" So the young man ran him through with his sword, and he died. [55]When Abimelech's men saw that he was dead, they disbanded and returned to their homes.

[56]In this way, God punished Abimelech for the evil he had done against his father by murdering his seventy brothers. [57]God also punished the men of Shechem for all their evil. So the curse of Jotham son of Gideon was fulfilled.

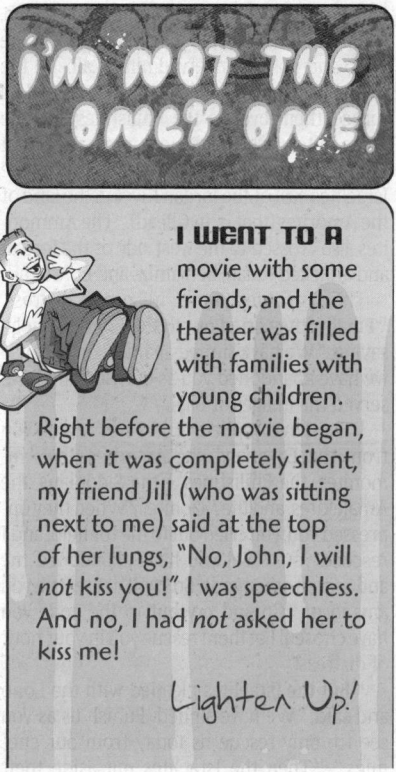

CHAPTER 10

Tola Becomes Israel's Judge

After Abimelech died, Tola son of Puah, son of Dodo, was the next person to rescue Israel. He was from the tribe of Issachar but lived in the town of Shamir in the hill country of Ephraim. [2]He judged Israel for twenty-three years. When he died, he was buried in Shamir.

Jair Becomes Israel's Judge

[3]After Tola died, Jair from Gilead judged Israel for twenty-two years. [4]His thirty sons rode around on thirty donkeys, and they owned thirty towns in the land of Gilead, which are still called the Towns of Jair.* [5]When Jair died, he was buried in Kamon.

The Ammonites Oppress Israel

[6]Again the Israelites did evil in the LORD's sight. They served the images of Baal and

9:46 Hebrew *El-berith*, another name for Baal-berith; compare 9:4. **10:4** Hebrew *Havvoth-jair*.

Ashtoreth, and the gods of Aram, Sidon, Moab, Ammon, and Philistia. They abandoned the LORD and no longer served him at all. 7 So the LORD burned with anger against Israel, and he turned them over to the Philistines and the Ammonites, 8 who began to oppress them that year. For eighteen years they oppressed all the Israelites east of the Jordan River in the land of the Amorites (that is, in Gilead). 9 The Ammonites also crossed to the west side of the Jordan and attacked Judah, Benjamin, and Ephraim.

The Israelites were in great distress. 10 Finally, they cried out to the LORD for help, saying, "We have sinned against you because we have abandoned you as our God and have served the images of Baal."

11 The LORD replied, "Did I not rescue you from the Egyptians, the Amorites, the Ammonites, the Philistines, 12 the Sidonians, the Amalekites, and the Maonites? When they oppressed you, you cried out to me for help, and I rescued you. 13 Yet you have abandoned me and served other gods. So I will not rescue you anymore. 14 Go and cry out to the gods you have chosen! Let them rescue you in your hour of distress!"

15 But the Israelites pleaded with the LORD and said, "We have sinned. Punish us as you see fit, only rescue us today from our enemies." 16 Then the Israelites put aside their foreign gods and served the LORD. And he was grieved by their misery.

17 At that time the armies of Ammon had gathered for war and were camped in Gilead, and the people of Israel assembled and camped at Mizpah. 18 The leaders of Gilead said to each other, "Whoever attacks the Ammonites first will become ruler over all the people of Gilead."

CHAPTER 11

Jephthah Becomes Israel's Judge

Now Jephthah of Gilead was a great warrior. He was the son of Gilead, but his mother was a prostitute. 2 Gilead's wife also had several sons, and when these half brothers grew up, they chased Jephthah off the land. "You will not get any of our father's inheritance," they said, "for you are the son of a prostitute." 3 So Jephthah fled from his brothers and lived in the land of Tob. Soon he had a band of worthless rebels following him.

4 At about this time, the Ammonites began their war against Israel. 5 When the Ammonites attacked, the elders of Gilead sent for Jephthah in the land of Tob. The elders said, 6 "Come and be our commander! Help us fight the Ammonites!"

7 But Jephthah said to them, "Aren't you the ones who hated me and drove me from my father's house? Why do you come to me now when you're in trouble?"

8 "Because we need you," the elders replied. "If you lead us in battle against the Ammonites, we will make you ruler over all the people of Gilead."

9 Jephthah said to the elders, "Let me get this straight. If I come with you and if the LORD gives me victory over the Ammonites, will you really make me ruler over all the people?"

10 "The LORD is our witness," the elders replied. "We promise to do whatever you say."

11 So Jephthah went with the elders of Gilead, and the people made him their ruler and commander of the army. At Mizpah, in the presence of the LORD, Jephthah repeated what he had said to the elders.

12 Then Jephthah sent messengers to the king of Ammon, asking, "Why have you come out to fight against my land?"

13 The king of Ammon answered Jephthah's messengers, "When the Israelites came out of Egypt, they stole my land from the Arnon River to the Jabbok River and all the way to the Jordan. Now then, give back the land peaceably."

14 Jephthah sent this message back to the Ammonite king:

> 15 "This is what Jephthah says: Israel did not steal any land from Moab or Ammon. 16 When the people of Israel arrived at Kadesh on their journey from Egypt after crossing the Red Sea,* 17 they sent messengers to the king of Edom asking for permission to pass through his land. But their request was denied. Then they asked the king of Moab for similar permission, but he wouldn't let them pass through either. So the people of Israel stayed in Kadesh.
>
> 18 "Finally, they went around Edom and Moab through the wilderness. They traveled along Moab's eastern border and camped on the other side of the Arnon

11:16 Hebrew *sea of reeds.*

River. But they never once crossed the
Arnon River into Moab, for the Arnon was
the border of Moab.

[19]"Then Israel sent messengers to
King Sihon of the Amorites, who ruled
from Heshbon, asking for permission to
cross through his land to get to their
destination. [20]But King Sihon didn't trust
Israel to pass through his land. Instead, he
mobilized his army at Jahaz and attacked
them. [21]But the LORD, the God of Israel,
gave his people victory over King Sihon.
So Israel took control of all the land of the
Amorites, who lived in that region, [22]from
the Arnon River to the Jabbok River, and
from the eastern wilderness to the Jordan.

[23]"So you see, it was the LORD, the God
of Israel, who took away the land from the
Amorites and gave it to Israel. Why, then,
should we give it back to you? [24]You keep
whatever your god Chemosh gives you,
and we will keep whatever the LORD our
God gives us. [25]Are you any better than
Balak son of Zippor, king of Moab? Did
he try to make a case against Israel for
disputed land? Did he go to war against
them?

[26]"Israel has been living here for
300 years, inhabiting Heshbon and its
surrounding settlements, all the way to
Aroer and its settlements, and in all the
towns along the Arnon River. Why have
you made no effort to recover it before
now? [27]Therefore, I have not sinned
against you. Rather, you have wronged me
by attacking me. Let the LORD, who is
judge, decide today which of us is right—
Israel or Ammon."

[28]But the king of Ammon paid no attention to
Jephthah's message.

Jephthah's Vow

[29]At that time the Spirit of the LORD came
upon Jephthah, and he went throughout the
land of Gilead and Manasseh, including
Mizpah in Gilead, and from there he led an
army against the Ammonites. [30]And Jephthah
made a vow to the LORD. He said, "If you give
me victory over the Ammonites, [31]I will give to
the LORD whatever comes out of my house to
meet me when I return in triumph. I will sac-
rifice it as a burnt offering."

[32]So Jephthah led his army against the Am-
monites, and the LORD gave him victory. [33]He
crushed the Ammonites, devastating about
twenty towns from Aroer to an area near
Minnith and as far away as Abel-keramim. In
this way Israel defeated the Ammonites.

[34]When Jephthah returned home to
Mizpah, his daughter came out to meet him,
playing on a tambourine and dancing for joy.
She was his one and only child; he had no
other sons or daughters. [35]When he saw her,
he tore his clothes in anguish. "Oh, my daugh-
ter!" he cried out. "You have completely de-
stroyed me! You've brought disaster on me!
For I have made a vow to the LORD, and I can-
not take it back."

[36]And she said, "Father, if you have made a
vow to the LORD, you must do to me what you
have vowed, for the LORD has given you a
great victory over your enemies, the Ammon-
ites. [37]But first let me do this one thing: Let
me go up and roam in the hills and weep with
my friends for two months, because I will die
a virgin."

[38]"You may go," Jephthah said. And he sent
her away for two months. She and her friends
went into the hills and wept because she
would never have children. [39]When she re-
turned home, her father kept the vow he had
made, and she died a virgin.

So it has become a custom in Israel [40]for
young Israelite women to go away for four
days each year to lament the fate of Jeph-
thah's daughter.

CHAPTER 12

Ephraim Fights with Jephthah

Then the people of Ephraim mobilized an
army and crossed over the Jordan River to Za-
phon. They sent this message to Jephthah:
"Why didn't you call for us to help you fight
against the Ammonites? We are going to burn
down your house with you in it!"

[2]Jephthah replied, "I summoned you at the
beginning of the dispute, but you refused to
come! You failed to help us in our struggle
against Ammon. [3]So when I realized you
weren't coming, I risked my life and went to
battle without you, and the LORD gave me
victory over the Ammonites. So why have you
now come to fight me?"

[4]The people of Ephraim responded, "You

men of Gilead are nothing more than fugitives from Ephraim and Manasseh." So Jephthah gathered all the men of Gilead and attacked the men of Ephraim and defeated them.

5 Jephthah captured the shallow crossings of the Jordan River, and whenever a fugitive from Ephraim tried to go back across, the men of Gilead would challenge him. "Are you a member of the tribe of Ephraim?" they would ask. If the man said, "No, I'm not," 6 they would tell him to say "Shibboleth." If he was from Ephraim, he would say "Sibboleth," because people from Ephraim cannot pronounce the word correctly. Then they would take him and kill him at the shallow crossings of the Jordan. In all, 42,000 Ephraimites were killed at that time.

7 Jephthah judged Israel for six years. When he died, he was buried in one of the towns of Gilead.

Ibzan Becomes Israel's Judge

8 After Jephthah died, Ibzan from Bethlehem judged Israel. 9 He had thirty sons and thirty daughters. He sent his daughters to marry men outside his clan, and he brought in thirty young women from outside his clan to marry his sons. Ibzan judged Israel for seven years. 10 When he died, he was buried at Bethlehem.

Elon Becomes Israel's Judge

11 After Ibzan died, Elon from the tribe of Zebulun judged Israel for ten years. 12 When he died, he was buried at Aijalon in Zebulun.

Abdon Becomes Israel's Judge

13 After Elon died, Abdon son of Hillel, from Pirathon, judged Israel. 14 He had forty sons and thirty grandsons, who rode on seventy donkeys. He judged Israel for eight years. 15 When he died, he was buried at Pirathon in Ephraim, in the hill country of the Amalekites.

CHAPTER 13

The Birth of Samson

Again the Israelites did evil in the LORD's sight, so the LORD handed them over to the Philistines, who oppressed them for forty years.

2 In those days a man named Manoah from the tribe of Dan lived in the town of Zorah. His wife was unable to become pregnant, and they had no children. 3 The angel of the LORD appeared to Manoah's wife and said, "Even though you have been unable to have children, you will soon become pregnant and give birth to a son. 4 So be careful; you must not drink wine or any other alcoholic drink nor eat any forbidden food.* 5 You will become pregnant and give birth to a son, and his hair must never be cut. For he will be dedicated to God as a Nazirite from birth. He will begin to rescue Israel from the Philistines."

6 The woman ran and told her husband, "A man of God appeared to me! He looked like one of God's angels, terrifying to see. I didn't ask where he was from, and he didn't tell me his name. 7 But he told me, 'You will become pregnant and give birth to a son. You must not drink wine or any other alcoholic drink nor eat any forbidden food. For your son will be dedicated to God as a Nazirite from the moment of his birth until the day of his death.'"

8 Then Manoah prayed to the LORD, saying, "Lord, please let the man of God come back to us again and give us more instructions about this son who is to be born."

9 God answered Manoah's prayer, and the angel of God appeared once again to his wife as she was sitting in the field. But her husband, Manoah, was not with her. 10 So she quickly ran and told her husband, "The man who appeared to me the other day is here again!"

11 Manoah ran back with his wife and asked, "Are you the man who spoke to my wife the other day?"

"Yes," he replied, "I am."

12 So Manoah asked him, "When your words come true, what kind of rules should govern the boy's life and work?"

13 The angel of the LORD replied, "Be sure your wife follows the instructions I gave her. 14 She must not eat grapes or raisins, drink wine or any other alcoholic drink, or eat any forbidden food."

15 Then Manoah said to the angel of the LORD, "Please stay here until we can prepare a young goat for you to eat."

16 "I will stay," the angel of the LORD replied, "but I will not eat anything. However, you may prepare a burnt offering as a sacrifice to the

13:4 Hebrew *any unclean thing;* also in 13:7, 14.

LORD." (Manoah didn't realize it was the angel of the LORD.)

17 Then Manoah asked the angel of the LORD, "What is your name? For when all this comes true, we want to honor you."

18 "Why do you ask my name?" the angel of the LORD replied. "It is too wonderful for you to understand."

19 Then Manoah took a young goat and a grain offering and offered it on a rock as a sacrifice to the LORD. And as Manoah and his wife watched, the LORD did an amazing thing. 20 As the flames from the altar shot up toward the sky, the angel of the LORD ascended in the fire. When Manoah and his wife saw this, they fell with their faces to the ground.

21 The angel did not appear again to Manoah and his wife. Manoah finally realized it was the angel of the LORD, 22 and he said to his wife, "We will certainly die, for we have seen God!"

23 But his wife said, "If the LORD were going to kill us, he wouldn't have accepted our burnt offering and grain offering. He wouldn't have appeared to us and told us this wonderful thing and done these miracles."

24 When her son was born, she named him Samson. And the LORD blessed him as he grew up. 25 And the Spirit of the LORD began to stir him while he lived in Mahaneh-dan, which is located between the towns of Zorah and Eshtaol.

CHAPTER 14

Samson's Riddle

One day when Samson was in Timnah, one of the Philistine women caught his eye. 2 When he returned home, he told his father and mother, "A young Philistine woman in Timnah caught my eye. I want to marry her. Get her for me."

3 His father and mother objected. "Isn't there even one woman in our tribe or among all the Israelites you could marry?" they asked. "Why must you go to the pagan Philistines to find a wife?"

But Samson told his father, "Get her for me! She looks good to me." 4 His father and mother didn't realize the LORD was at work in this, creating an opportunity to work against the Philistines, who ruled over Israel at that time.

14:11 Hebrew *they*.

5 As Samson and his parents were going down to Timnah, a young lion suddenly attacked Samson near the vineyards of Timnah. 6 At that moment the Spirit of the LORD came powerfully upon him, and he ripped the lion's jaws apart with his bare hands. He did it as easily as if it were a young goat. But he didn't tell his father or mother about it. 7 When Samson arrived in Timnah, he talked with the woman and was very pleased with her.

AMAZING FACTS

Samson killed a wild lion. Did he use a gun? bomb? bow? Nope—his bare hands!

JUDGES 14:6

8 Later, when he returned to Timnah for the wedding, he turned off the path to look at the carcass of the lion. And he found that a swarm of bees had made some honey in the carcass. 9 He scooped some of the honey into his hands and ate it along the way. He also gave some to his father and mother, and they ate it. But he didn't tell them he had taken the honey from the carcass of the lion.

10 As his father was making final arrangements for the marriage, Samson threw a party at Timnah, as was the custom for elite young men. 11 When the bride's parents* saw him, they selected thirty young men from the town to be his companions.

12 Samson said to them, "Let me tell you a riddle. If you solve my riddle during these seven days of the celebration, I will give you thirty fine linen robes and thirty sets of festive clothing. 13 But if you can't solve it, then you must give me thirty fine linen robes and thirty sets of festive clothing."

Trading Cards

Bryan had a big baseball card collection. "I'm going to trade one of my best cards for several cards that aren't as valuable," he told his dad. "I need them to complete some old-time team rosters." Bryan met a friend at Big Burger to make the trade. But before he could pick up his cards, his friend spilled his milkshake. The cards that Bryan had just traded for were covered with gooey, chocolate shake!

Should he call off the deal? Demand more cards? Or just wipe them off? Read Judges 15:7-11 to learn about the trouble Samson got into for taking revenge.

"All right," they agreed, "let's hear your riddle."

[14]So he said:

"Out of the one who eats came something
to eat;
out of the strong came something
sweet."

Three days later they were still trying to figure it out. [15]On the fourth* day they said to Samson's wife, "Entice your husband to explain the riddle for us, or we will burn down your father's house with you in it. Did you invite us to this party just to make us poor?"

[16]So Samson's wife came to him in tears and said, "You don't love me; you hate me! You have given my people a riddle, but you haven't told me the answer."

"I haven't even given the answer to my father or mother," he replied. "Why should I tell you?" [17]So she cried whenever she was with him and kept it up for the rest of the celebration. At last, on the seventh day he told her the answer because she was tormenting him with her nagging. Then she explained the riddle to the young men.

[18]So before sunset of the seventh day, the men of the town came to Samson with their answer:

"What is sweeter than honey?
What is stronger than a lion?"

Samson replied, "If you hadn't plowed with my heifer, you wouldn't have solved my riddle!"

[19]Then the Spirit of the LORD came powerfully upon him. He went down to the town of Ashkelon, killed thirty men, took their belongings, and gave their clothing to the men who had solved his riddle. But Samson was furious about what had happened, and he went back home to live with his father and mother. [20]So his wife was given in marriage to the man who had been Samson's best man at the wedding.

CHAPTER 15

Samson's Vengeance on the Philistines

Later on, during the wheat harvest, Samson took a young goat as a present to his wife. He said, "I'm going into my wife's room to sleep with her," but her father wouldn't let him in.

[2]"I truly thought you must hate her," her father explained, "so I gave her in marriage to your best man. But look, her younger sister is even more beautiful than she is. Marry her instead."

14:15 As in Greek version; Hebrew reads *seventh*.

[3]Samson said, "This time I cannot be blamed for everything I am going to do to you Philistines." [4]Then he went out and caught 300 foxes. He tied their tails together in pairs, and he fastened a torch to each pair of tails. [5]Then he lit the torches and let the foxes run through the grain fields of the Philistines. He burned all their grain to the ground, including the sheaves and the uncut grain. He also destroyed their vineyards and olive groves.

[6]"Who did this?" the Philistines demanded.

"Samson," was the reply, "because his father-in-law from Timnah gave Samson's wife to be married to his best man." So the Philistines went and got the woman and her father and burned them to death.

[7]"Because you did this," Samson vowed, "I won't rest until I take my revenge on you!" [8]So he attacked the Philistines with great fury and killed many of them. Then he went to live in a cave in the rock of Etam.

[9]The Philistines retaliated by setting up camp in Judah and spreading out near the town of Lehi. [10]The men of Judah asked the Philistines, "Why are you attacking us?"

The Philistines replied, "We've come to capture Samson. We've come to pay him back for what he did to us."

[11]So 3,000 men of Judah went down to get Samson at the cave in the rock of Etam. They said to Samson, "Don't you realize the Philistines rule over us? What are you doing to us?"

But Samson replied, "I only did to them what they did to me."

[12]But the men of Judah told him, "We have come to tie you up and hand you over to the Philistines."

"All right," Samson said. "But promise that you won't kill me yourselves."

[13]"We will only tie you up and hand you over to the Philistines," they replied. "We won't kill you." So they tied him up with two new ropes and brought him up from the rock.

[14]As Samson arrived at Lehi, the Philistines came shouting in triumph. But the Spirit of the LORD came powerfully upon Samson, and he snapped the ropes on his arms as if they were burnt strands of flax, and they fell from his wrists. [15]Then he found the jawbone of a recently killed donkey. He picked it up and killed 1,000 Philistines with it. [16]Then Samson said,

"With the jawbone of a donkey,
I've piled them in heaps!
With the jawbone of a donkey,
I've killed a thousand men!"

[17]When he finished his boasting, he threw away the jawbone; and the place was named Jawbone Hill.*

[18]Samson was now very thirsty, and he cried out to the LORD, "You have accomplished this great victory by the strength of your servant. Must I now die of thirst and fall into the hands of these pagans?" [19]So God caused water to gush out of a hollow in the ground at Lehi, and Samson was revived as he drank. Then he named that place "The Spring of the One Who Cried Out,"* and it is still in Lehi to this day.

[20]Samson judged Israel for twenty years during the period when the Philistines dominated the land.

CHAPTER 16

Samson Carries Away Gaza's Gates

One day Samson went to the Philistine town of Gaza and spent the night with a prostitute. [2]Word soon spread* that Samson was there, so the men of Gaza gathered together and waited all night at the town gates. They kept quiet during the night, saying to themselves, "When the light of morning comes, we will kill him."

[3]But Samson stayed in bed only until midnight. Then he got up, took hold of the doors of the town gate, including the two posts, and lifted them up, bar and all. He put them on his shoulders and carried them all the way to the top of the hill across from Hebron.

Samson and Delilah

[4]Some time later Samson fell in love with a woman named Delilah, who lived in the valley of Sorek. [5]The rulers of the Philistines went to her and said, "Entice Samson to tell you what makes him so strong and how he can be overpowered and tied up securely. Then each of us will give you 1,100 pieces* of silver."

[6]So Delilah said to Samson, "Please tell me what makes you so strong and what it would take to tie you up securely."

[7]Samson replied, "If I were tied up with

15:17 Hebrew *Ramath-lehi*. **15:19** Hebrew *En-hakkore*. **16:2** As in Greek and Syriac versions and Latin Vulgate; Hebrew lacks *Word soon spread*. **16:5** Hebrew *1,100 shekels*, about 28 pounds or 12.5 kilograms in weight.

seven new bowstrings that have not yet been dried, I would become as weak as anyone else."

[8]So the Philistine rulers brought Delilah seven new bowstrings, and she tied Samson up with them. [9]She had hidden some men in one of the inner rooms of her house, and she cried out, "Samson! The Philistines have come to capture you!" But Samson snapped the bowstrings as a piece of string snaps when it is burned by a fire. So the secret of his strength was not discovered.

[10]Afterward Delilah said to him, "You've been making fun of me and telling me lies! Now please tell me how you can be tied up securely."

[11]Samson replied, "If I were tied up with brand-new ropes that had never been used, I would become as weak as anyone else."

[12]So Delilah took new ropes and tied him up with them. The men were hiding in the inner room as before, and again Delilah cried out, "Samson! The Philistines have come to capture you!" But again Samson snapped the ropes from his arms as if they were thread.

[13]Then Delilah said, "You've been making fun of me and telling me lies! Now tell me how you can be tied up securely."

Samson replied, "If you were to weave the seven braids of my hair into the fabric on your loom and tighten it with the loom shuttle, I would become as weak as anyone else."

So while he slept, Delilah wove the seven braids of his hair into the fabric. [14]Then she tightened it with the loom shuttle.* Again she cried out, "Samson! The Philistines have come to capture you!" But Samson woke up, pulled back the loom shuttle, and yanked his hair away from the loom and the fabric.

[15]Then Delilah pouted, "How can you tell me, 'I love you,' when you don't share your secrets with me? You've made fun of me three times now, and you still haven't told me what makes you so strong!" [16]She tormented him with her nagging day after day until he was sick to death of it.

[17]Finally, Samson shared his secret with her. "My hair has never been cut," he confessed, "for I was dedicated to God as a Nazirite from birth. If my head were shaved, my strength would leave me, and I would become as weak as anyone else."

[18]Delilah realized he had finally told her the truth, so she sent for the Philistine rulers. "Come back one more time," she said, "for he has finally told me his secret." So the Philistine rulers returned with the money in their hands. [19]Delilah lulled Samson to sleep with his head in her lap, and then she called in a man to shave off the seven locks of his hair. In

samson

One day I saw a dead lion with bees and a honeycomb inside. At a party celebrating my wedding, I told my 30 guests a riddle about the lion and the honey. I promised a fine set of clothing to every guest if they could solve the riddle. My bride cried until I gave her the answer. She told, and I was so angry I killed 30 men for their clothes. I tied torches to the tails of 300 foxes that ran through fields, destroying my enemy's harvest. I killed 1,000 men with a donkey's jawbone. I am mighty and cannot be defeated. Right?

To find out what eventually happened to Samson and his pride, read his story in Judges 13–16.

16:13-14 As in Greek version and Latin Vulgate; Hebrew lacks *I would become as weak as anyone else. / So while he slept, Delilah wove the seven braids of his hair into the fabric.* [14]*Then she tightened it with the loom shuttle.*

this way she began to bring him down,* and his strength left him.

[20]Then she cried out, "Samson! The Philistines have come to capture you!"

When he woke up, he thought, "I will do as before and shake myself free." But he didn't realize the LORD had left him.

[21]So the Philistines captured him and gouged out his eyes. They took him to Gaza, where he was bound with bronze chains and forced to grind grain in the prison.

[22]But before long, his hair began to grow back.

Samson's Final Victory

[23]The Philistine rulers held a great festival, offering sacrifices and praising their god, Dagon. They said, "Our god has given us victory over our enemy Samson!"

[24]When the people saw him, they praised their god, saying, "Our god has delivered our enemy to us! The one who killed so many of us is now in our power!"

[25]Half drunk by now, the people demanded, "Bring out Samson so he can amuse us!" So he was brought from the prison to amuse them, and they had him stand between the pillars supporting the roof.

What happens when we live without God?

In those days Israel had no king; all the people did whatever seemed right in their own eyes.

JUDGES 17:6

[26]Samson said to the young servant who was leading him by the hand, "Place my hands against the pillars that hold up the temple. I want to rest against them." [27]Now the temple was completely filled with people. All the Philistine rulers were there, and there were about 3,000 men and women on the roof who were watching as Samson amused them.

[28]Then Samson prayed to the LORD, "Sovereign LORD, remember me again. O God, please strengthen me just one more time. With one blow let me pay back the Philistines for the loss of my two eyes." [29]Then Samson put his hands on the two center pillars that held up the temple. Pushing against them with both hands, [30]he prayed, "Let me die with the Philistines." And the temple crashed down on the Philistine rulers and all the people. So he killed more people when he died than he had during his entire lifetime.

[31]Later his brothers and other relatives went down to get his body. They took him back home and buried him between Zorah and Eshtaol, where his father, Manoah, was buried. Samson had judged Israel for twenty years.

CHAPTER 17

Micah's Idols

There was a man named Micah, who lived in the hill country of Ephraim. [2]One day he said to his mother, "I heard you place a curse on the person who stole 1,100 pieces* of silver from you. Well, I have the money. I was the one who took it."

"The LORD bless you for admitting it," his mother replied. [3]He returned the money to her, and she said, "I now dedicate these silver coins to the LORD. In honor of my son, I will have an image carved and an idol cast."

[4]So when he returned the money to his mother, she took 200 silver coins and gave them to a silversmith, who made them into an image and an idol. And these were placed in Micah's house. [5]Micah set up a shrine for the idol, and he made a sacred ephod and some household idols. Then he installed one of his sons as his personal priest.

[6]In those days Israel had no king; all the people did whatever seemed right in their own eyes.

[7]One day a young Levite, who had been living in Bethlehem in Judah, arrived in that area. [8]He had left Bethlehem in search of another place to live, and as he traveled, he came to the hill country of Ephraim. He happened to stop at Micah's house as he was traveling through. [9]"Where are you from?" Micah asked him.

16:19 Or *she began to torment him.* Greek version reads *He began to grow weak.* **17:2** Hebrew *1,100 shekels,* about 28 pounds or 12.5 kilograms in weight.

He replied, "I am a Levite from Bethlehem in Judah, and I am looking for a place to live."

[10]"Stay here with me," Micah said, "and you can be a father and priest to me. I will give you ten pieces* of silver a year, plus a change of clothes and your food." [11]The Levite agreed to this, and the young man became like one of Micah's sons.

[12]So Micah installed the Levite as his personal priest, and he lived in Micah's house. [13]"I know the LORD will bless me now," Micah said, "because I have a Levite serving as my priest."

CHAPTER 18

Idolatry in the Tribe of Dan

Now in those days Israel had no king. And the tribe of Dan was trying to find a place where they could settle, for they had not yet moved into the land assigned to them when the land was divided among the tribes of Israel. [2]So the men of Dan chose from their clans five capable warriors from the towns of Zorah and Eshtaol to scout out a land for them to settle in.

When these warriors arrived in the hill country of Ephraim, they came to Micah's house and spent the night there. [3]While at Micah's house, they recognized the young Levite's accent, so they went over and asked him, "Who brought you here, and what are you doing in this place? Why are you here?" [4]He told them about his agreement with Micah and that he had been hired as Micah's personal priest.

[5]Then they said, "Ask God whether or not our journey will be successful."

[6]"Go in peace," the priest replied. "For the LORD is watching over your journey."

[7]So the five men went on to the town of Laish, where they noticed the people living carefree lives, like the Sidonians; they were peaceful and secure.* The people were also wealthy because their land was very fertile. And they lived a great distance from Sidon and had no allies nearby.

[8]When the men returned to Zorah and Eshtaol, their relatives asked them, "What did you find?"

[9]The men replied, "Come on, let's attack them! We have seen the land, and it is very good. What are you waiting for? Don't hesitate to go and take possession of it. [10]When you get there, you will find the people living carefree lives. God has given us a spacious and fertile land, lacking in nothing!"

[11]So 600 men from the tribe of Dan, armed with weapons of war, set out from Zorah and Eshtaol. [12]They camped at a place west of Kiriath-jearim in Judah, which is called Mahaneh-dan* to this day. [13]Then they went on from there into the hill country of Ephraim and came to the house of Micah.

[14]The five men who had scouted out the land around Laish explained to the others, "These buildings contain a sacred ephod, as well as some household idols, a carved image, and a cast idol. What do you think you should do?" [15]Then the five men turned off the road and went over to Micah's house, where the young Levite lived, and greeted him kindly. [16]As the 600 armed warriors from the tribe of Dan stood at the entrance of the gate, [17]the five scouts entered the shrine and removed the carved image, the sacred ephod, the household idols, and the cast idol. Meanwhile, the priest was standing at the gate with the 600 armed warriors.

[18]When the priest saw the men carrying all the sacred objects out of Micah's shrine, he said, "What are you doing?"

[19]"Be quiet and come with us," they said. "Be a father and priest to all of us. Isn't it better to be a priest for an entire tribe and clan of Israel than for the household of just one man?"

[20]The young priest was quite happy to go with them, so he took along the sacred ephod, the household idols, and the carved image. [21]They turned and started on their way again, placing their children, livestock, and possessions in front of them.

[22]When the people from the tribe of Dan were quite a distance from Micah's house, the people who lived near Micah came chasing after them. [23]They were shouting as they caught up with them. The men of Dan turned around and said to Micah, "What's the matter? Why have you called these men together and chased after us like this?"

[24]"What do you mean, 'What's the matter?'" Micah replied. "You've taken away all

17:10 Hebrew *10 shekels*, about 4 ounces or 114 grams in weight. **18:7** The meaning of the Hebrew is uncertain. **18:12** *Mahaneh-dan* means "the camp of Dan."

the gods I have made, and my priest, and I have nothing left!"

[25]The men of Dan said, "Watch what you say! There are some short-tempered men around here who might get angry and kill you and your family." [26]So the men of Dan continued on their way. When Micah saw that there were too many of them for him to attack, he turned around and went home.

[27]Then, with Micah's idols and his priest, the men of Dan came to the town of Laish, whose people were peaceful and secure. They attacked with swords and burned the town to the ground. [28]There was no one to rescue the people, for they lived a great distance from Sidon and had no allies nearby. This happened in the valley near Beth-rehob.

Then the people of the tribe of Dan rebuilt the town and lived there. [29]They renamed the town Dan after their ancestor, Israel's son, but it had originally been called Laish.

[30]Then they set up the carved image, and they appointed Jonathan son of Gershom, son of Moses,* as their priest. This family continued as priests for the tribe of Dan until the Exile. [31]So Micah's carved image was worshiped by the tribe of Dan as long as the Tabernacle of God remained at Shiloh.

CHAPTER 19

The Levite and His Concubine

Now in those days Israel had no king. There was a man from the tribe of Levi living in a remote area of the hill country of Ephraim. One day he brought home a woman from Bethlehem in Judah to be his concubine. [2]But she became angry with him* and returned to her father's home in Bethlehem.

After about four months, [3]her husband set out for Bethlehem to speak personally to her and persuade her to come back. He took with him a servant and a pair of donkeys. When he arrived at* her father's house, her father saw him and welcomed him. [4]Her father urged him to stay awhile, so he stayed three days, eating, drinking, and sleeping there.

[5]On the fourth day the man was up early, ready to leave, but the woman's father said to his son-in-law, "Have something to eat before you go." [6]So the two men sat down together and had something to eat and drink. Then the woman's father said, "Please stay another night and enjoy yourself." [7]The man got up to leave, but his father-in-law kept urging him to stay, so he finally gave in and stayed the night.

[8]On the morning of the fifth day he was up early again, ready to leave, and again the woman's father said, "Have something to eat; then you can leave later this afternoon." So they had another day of feasting. [9]Later, as the man and his concubine and servant were preparing to leave, his father-in-law said, "Look, it's almost evening. Stay the night and enjoy yourself. Tomorrow you can get up early and be on your way."

[10]But this time the man was determined to leave. So he took his two saddled donkeys and his concubine and headed in the direction of Jebus (that is, Jerusalem). [11]It was late in the day when they neared Jebus, and the man's servant said to him, "Let's stop at this Jebusite town and spend the night there."

[12]"No," his master said, "we can't stay in this foreign town where there are no Israelites. Instead, we will go on to Gibeah. [13]Come on, let's try to get as far as Gibeah or Ramah, and we'll spend the night in one of those towns." [14]So they went on. The sun was setting as they came to Gibeah, a town in the land of Benjamin, [15]so they stopped there to spend the night. They rested in the town square, but no one took them in for the night.

[16]That evening an old man came home from his work in the fields. He was from the hill country of Ephraim, but he was living in Gibeah, where the people were from the tribe of Benjamin. [17]When he saw the travelers sitting in the town square, he asked them where they were from and where they were going.

[18]"We have been in Bethlehem in Judah," the man replied. "We are on our way to a remote area in the hill country of Ephraim, which is my home. I traveled to Bethlehem, and now I'm returning home.* But no one has taken us in for the night, [19]even though we have everything we need. We have straw and feed for our donkeys and plenty of bread and wine for ourselves."

[20]"You are welcome to stay with me," the old man said. "I will give you anything you might

18:30 As in an ancient Hebrew tradition, some Greek manuscripts, and Latin Vulgate; Masoretic Text reads *son of Manasseh*. **19:2** Or *she was unfaithful to him*. **19:3** As in Greek version; Hebrew reads *When she brought him to*. **19:18** As in Greek version (see also 19:29); Hebrew reads *now I'm going to the Tabernacle of the* LORD.

need. But whatever you do, don't spend the night in the square." [21]So he took them home with him and fed the donkeys. After they washed their feet, they ate and drank together.

[22]While they were enjoying themselves, a crowd of troublemakers from the town surrounded the house. They began beating at the door and shouting to the old man, "Bring out the man who is staying with you so we can have sex with him."

[23]The old man stepped outside to talk to them. "No, my brothers, don't do such an evil thing. For this man is a guest in my house, and such a thing would be shameful. [24]Here, take my virgin daughter and this man's concubine. I will bring them out to you, and you can abuse them and do whatever you like. But don't do such a shameful thing to this man."

[25]But they wouldn't listen to him. So the Levite took hold of his concubine and pushed her out the door. The men of the town abused her all night, taking turns raping her until morning. Finally, at dawn they let her go. [26]At daybreak the woman returned to the house where her husband was staying. She collapsed at the door of the house and lay there until it was light.

[27]When her husband opened the door to leave, there lay his concubine with her hands on the threshold. [28]He said, "Get up! Let's go!" But there was no answer.* So he put her body on his donkey and took her home.

[29]When he got home, he took a knife and cut his concubine's body into twelve pieces. Then he sent one piece to each tribe throughout all the territory of Israel.

[30]Everyone who saw it said, "Such a horrible crime has not been committed in all the time since Israel left Egypt. Think about it! What are we going to do? Who's going to speak up?"

CHAPTER 20

Israel's War with Benjamin

Then all the Israelites were united as one man, from Dan in the north to Beersheba in the south, including those from across the Jordan in the land of Gilead. The entire community assembled in the presence of the LORD at Mizpah. [2]The leaders of all the people and all the tribes of Israel—400,000 warriors armed with swords—took their positions in the assembly of the people of God. [3](Word soon reached the land of Benjamin that the other tribes had gone up to Mizpah.) The Israelites then asked how this terrible crime had happened.

[4]The Levite, the husband of the woman who had been murdered, said, "My concubine and I came to spend the night in Gibeah, a town that belongs to the people of Benjamin. [5]That night some of the leading citizens of Gibeah surrounded the house, planning to kill me, and they raped my concubine until she was dead. [6]So I cut her body into twelve pieces and sent the pieces throughout the territory assigned to Israel, for these men have committed a terrible and shameful crime. [7]Now then, all of you—the entire community of Israel—must decide here and now what should be done about this!"

[8]And all the people rose to their feet in unison and declared, "None of us will return home! No, not even one of us! [9]Instead, this is what we will do to Gibeah; we will draw lots to decide who will attack it. [10]One-tenth of the men* from each tribe will be chosen to supply the warriors with food, and the rest of us will take revenge on Gibeah* of Benjamin for this shameful thing they have done in Israel." [11]So all the Israelites were completely united, and they gathered together to attack the town.

[12]The Israelites sent messengers to the tribe of Benjamin, saying, "What a terrible thing has been done among you! [13]Give up those evil men, those troublemakers from Gibeah, so we can execute them and purge Israel of this evil."

But the people of Benjamin would not listen. [14]Instead, they came from their towns and gathered at Gibeah to fight the Israelites. [15]In all, 26,000 of their warriors armed with swords arrived in Gibeah to join the 700 elite troops who lived there. [16]Among Benjamin's elite troops, 700 were left-handed, and each of them could sling a rock and hit a target within a hairsbreadth without missing. [17]Israel had 400,000 experienced soldiers armed with swords, not counting Benjamin's warriors.

[18]Before the battle the Israelites went to Bethel and asked God, "Which tribe should go first to attack the people of Benjamin?"

19:28 Greek version adds *for she was dead.* **20:10a** Hebrew *10 men from every hundred, 100 men from every thousand, and 1,000 men from every 10,000.* **20:10b** Hebrew *Geba*, in this case a variant spelling of Gibeah; also in 20:33.

The LORD answered, "Judah is to go first."

[19]So the Israelites left early the next morning and camped near Gibeah. [20]Then they advanced toward Gibeah to attack the men of Benjamin. [21]But Benjamin's warriors, who were defending the town, came out and killed 22,000 Israelites on the battlefield that day.

[22]But the Israelites encouraged each other and took their positions again at the same place they had fought the previous day. [23]For they had gone up to Bethel and wept in the presence of the LORD until evening. They had asked the LORD, "Should we fight against our relatives from Benjamin again?"

And the LORD had said, "Go out and fight against them."

[24]So the next day they went out again to fight against the men of Benjamin, [25]but the men of Benjamin killed another 18,000 Israelites, all of whom were experienced with the sword.

[26]Then all the Israelites went up to Bethel and wept in the presence of the LORD and fasted until evening. They also brought burnt offerings and peace offerings to the LORD. [27]The Israelites went up seeking direction from the LORD. (In those days the Ark of the Covenant of God was in Bethel, [28]and Phinehas son of Eleazar and grandson of Aaron was the priest.) The Israelites asked the LORD, "Should we fight against our relatives from Benjamin again, or should we stop?"

The LORD said, "Go! Tomorrow I will hand them over to you."

[29]So the Israelites set an ambush all around Gibeah. [30]They went out on the third day and took their positions at the same place as before. [31]When the men of Benjamin came out to attack, they were drawn away from the town. And as they had done before, they began to kill the Israelites. About thirty Israelites died in the open fields and along the roads, one leading to Bethel and the other leading back to Gibeah.

[32]Then the warriors of Benjamin shouted, "We're defeating them as we did before!" But the Israelites had planned in advance to run away so that the men of Benjamin would chase them along the roads and be drawn away from the town.

[33]When the main group of Israelite warriors reached Baal-tamar, they turned and took up their positions. Meanwhile, the Israelites hiding in ambush to the west* of Gibeah jumped up to fight. [34]There were 10,000 elite Israelite troops who advanced against Gibeah. The fighting was so heavy that Benjamin didn't realize the impending disaster. [35]So the LORD helped Israel defeat Benjamin, and that day the Israelites killed 25,100 of Benjamin's warriors, all of whom were experienced swordsmen. [36]Then the men of Benjamin saw that they were beaten.

The Israelites had retreated from Benjamin's warriors in order to give those hiding in ambush more room to maneuver against Gibeah. [37]Then those who were hiding rushed in from all sides and killed everyone in the town. [38]They had arranged to send up a large cloud of smoke from the town as a signal. [39]When the Israelites saw the smoke, they turned and attacked Benjamin's warriors.

By that time Benjamin's warriors had killed about thirty Israelites, and they shouted, "We're defeating them as we did in the first battle!" [40]But when the warriors of Benjamin looked behind them and saw the smoke rising into the sky from every part of the town, [41]the men of Israel turned and attacked. At this point the men of Benjamin became terrified, because they realized disaster was close at hand. [42]So they turned around and fled before the Israelites toward the wilderness. But they couldn't escape the battle, and the people who came out of the nearby towns were also killed.* [43]The Israelites surrounded the men of Benjamin and chased them relentlessly, finally overtaking them east of Gibeah.* [44]That day 18,000 of Benjamin's strongest warriors died in battle. [45]The survivors fled into the wilderness toward the rock of Rimmon, but Israel killed 5,000 of them along the road. They continued the chase until they had killed another 2,000 near Gidom.

[46]So that day the tribe of Benjamin lost 25,000 strong warriors armed with swords, [47]leaving only 600 men who escaped to the rock of Rimmon, where they lived for four months. [48]And the Israelites returned and slaughtered every living thing in all the

20:33 As in Greek and Syriac versions and Latin Vulgate; Hebrew reads *hiding in the open space.* **20:42** Or *battle, for the people from the nearby towns also came out and killed them.* **20:43** The meaning of the Hebrew is uncertain.

towns—the people, the livestock, and everything they found. They also burned down all the towns they came to.

CHAPTER 21

Israel Provides Wives for Benjamin

The Israelites had vowed at Mizpah, "We will never give our daughters in marriage to a man from the tribe of Benjamin." [2]Now the people went to Bethel and sat in the presence of God until evening, weeping loudly and bitterly. [3]"O LORD, God of Israel," they cried out, "why has this happened in Israel? Now one of our tribes is missing from Israel!"

[4]Early the next morning the people built an altar and presented their burnt offerings and peace offerings on it. [5]Then they said, "Who among the tribes of Israel did not join us at Mizpah when we held our assembly in the presence of the LORD?" At that time they had taken a solemn oath in the LORD's presence, vowing that anyone who refused to come would be put to death.

[6]The Israelites felt sorry for their brother Benjamin and said, "Today one of the tribes of Israel has been cut off. [7]How can we find wives for the few who remain, since we have sworn by the LORD not to give them our daughters in marriage?"

[8]So they asked, "Who among the tribes of Israel did not join us at Mizpah when we assembled in the presence of the LORD?" And they discovered that no one from Jabesh-gilead had attended the assembly. [9]For after they counted all the people, no one from Jabesh-gilead was present.

[10]So the assembly sent 12,000 of their best warriors to Jabesh-gilead with orders to kill everyone there, including women and children. [11]"This is what you are to do," they said. "Completely destroy* all the males and every woman who is not a virgin." [12]Among the residents of Jabesh-gilead they found 400 young virgins who had never slept with a man, and they brought them to the camp at Shiloh in the land of Canaan.

[13]The Israelite assembly sent a peace delegation to the remaining people of Benjamin who were living at the rock of Rimmon. [14]Then the men of Benjamin returned to their homes, and the 400 women of Jabesh-gilead who had been spared were given to them as wives. But there were not enough women for all of them.

[15]The people felt sorry for Benjamin because the LORD had made this gap among the tribes of Israel. [16]So the elders of the assembly asked, "How can we find wives for the few who remain, since the women of the tribe of Benjamin are dead? [17]There must be heirs for the survivors so that an entire tribe of Israel is not wiped out. [18]But we cannot give them our own daughters in marriage because we have sworn with a solemn oath that anyone who does this will fall under God's curse."

[19]Then they thought of the annual festival of the LORD held in Shiloh, south of Lebonah and north of Bethel, along the east side of the road that goes from Bethel to Shechem. [20]They told the men of Benjamin who still needed wives, "Go and hide in the vineyards. [21]When you see the young women of Shiloh come out for their dances, rush out from the vineyards, and each of you can take one of them home to the land of Benjamin to be your wife! [22]And when their fathers and brothers come to us in protest, we will tell them, 'Please be sympathetic. Let them have your daughters, for we didn't find wives for all of them when we destroyed Jabesh-gilead. And you are not guilty of breaking the vow since you did not actually give your daughters to them in marriage.'"

[23]So the men of Benjamin did as they were told. Each man caught one of the women as she danced in the celebration and carried her off to be his wife. They returned to their own land, and they rebuilt their towns and lived in them.

[24]Then the people of Israel departed by tribes and families, and they returned to their own homes.

[25]In those days Israel had no king; all the people did whatever seemed right in their own eyes.

21:11 The Hebrew term used here refers to the complete consecration of things or people to the LORD, either by destroying them or by giving them as an offering.

RUTH

WHO
Ruth, Naomi, Boaz.

WHERE
The Promised Land, later called Israel.

WHEN
The story takes place during the time of the judges (1375–1050 BC) but was probably written sometime after that.

WHY
To show that people can keep their strong faith in God even when their circumstances are difficult.

Wherever you go, I will go; wherever you live, I will live. Your people will be my people, and your God will be my God.
RUTH 1:16

"They lived happily ever after!" That's how many stories end. But real-life stories can sometimes be very unhappy. People get sick and even die. The story of Ruth and her mother-in-law shows how God takes care of people who follow him during difficult times.

BE LOYAL LIKE RUTH AND DEPENDABLE LIKE NAOMI.

CHAPTER 1

Elimelech Moves His Family to Moab

In the days when the judges ruled in Israel, a severe famine came upon the land. So a man from Bethlehem in Judah left his home and went to live in the country of Moab, taking his wife and two sons with him. [2]The man's name was Elimelech, and his wife was Naomi. Their two sons were Mahlon and Kilion. They were Ephrathites from Bethlehem in the land of Judah. And when they reached Moab, they settled there.

[3]Then Elimelech died, and Naomi was left with her two sons. [4]The two sons married Moabite women. One married a woman named Orpah, and the other a woman named Ruth.

But about ten years later, [5]both Mahlon and Kilion died. This left Naomi alone, without her two sons or her husband.

Naomi and Ruth Return

[6]Then Naomi heard in Moab that the LORD had blessed his people in Judah by giving them good crops again. So Naomi and her daughters-in-law got ready to leave Moab to return to her homeland. [7]With her two daughters-in-law she set out from the place where she had been living, and they took the road that would lead them back to Judah.

[8]But on the way, Naomi said to her two daughters-in-law, "Go back to your mothers' homes. And may the LORD reward you for your kindness to your husbands and to me. [9]May the LORD bless you with the security of another marriage." Then she kissed them good-bye, and they all broke down and wept.

[10]"No," they said. "We want to go with you to your people."

[11]But Naomi replied, "Why should you go on with me? Can I still give birth to other sons who could grow up to be your husbands? [12]No, my daughters, return to your parents' homes, for I am too old to marry again. And even if it were possible, and I were to get married tonight and bear sons, then what? [13]Would you wait for them to grow up and refuse to marry someone else? No, of course not, my daughters! Things are far more bitter for me than for you, because the LORD himself has raised his fist against me."

[14]And again they wept together, and Orpah kissed her mother-in-law good-bye. But Ruth clung tightly to Naomi. [15]"Look," Naomi said to her, "your sister-in-law has gone back to her people and to her gods. You should do the same."

[16]But Ruth replied, "Don't ask me to leave you and turn back. Wherever you go, I will go; wherever you live, I will live. Your people will be my people, and your God will be my God. [17]Wherever you die, I will die, and there I will be buried. May the LORD punish me severely if I allow anything but death to separate us!" [18]When Naomi saw that Ruth was determined to go with her, she said nothing more.

[19]So the two of them continued on their journey. When they came to Bethlehem, the entire town was excited by their arrival. "Is it really Naomi?" the women asked.

[20]"Don't call me Naomi," she responded. "Instead, call me Mara,* for the Almighty has made life very bitter for me. [21]I went away full, but the LORD has brought me home empty. Why call me Naomi when the LORD has caused me to suffer* and the Almighty has sent such tragedy upon me?"

STICKING CLOSE

Ethan's best friend invited him to a party on Friday. He said yes and was looking forward to going. But the next day Luke said to Ethan, "The Cool Cats are having a concert on Friday. I have an extra ticket. I know you love their music. Can you go?"

Ethan doesn't want to miss a chance to hear his favorite group. But should he be loyal to his best friend and go to the party? Or should he explain the situation and have fun at the concert? Check out Ruth 1:16-18 for an example of true loyalty.

1:20 *Naomi* means "pleasant"; *Mara* means "bitter." **1:21** Or *has testified against me.*

[22]So Naomi returned from Moab, accompanied by her daughter-in-law Ruth, the young Moabite woman. They arrived in Bethlehem in late spring, at the beginning of the barley harvest.

CHAPTER 2

Ruth Works in Boaz's Field

Now there was a wealthy and influential man in Bethlehem named Boaz, who was a relative of Naomi's husband, Elimelech.

[2]One day Ruth the Moabite said to Naomi, "Let me go out into the harvest fields to pick up the stalks of grain left behind by anyone who is kind enough to let me do it."

Naomi replied, "All right, my daughter, go ahead." [3]So Ruth went out to gather grain behind the harvesters. And as it happened, she found herself working in a field that belonged to Boaz, the relative of her father-in-law, Elimelech.

[4]While she was there, Boaz arrived from Bethlehem and greeted the harvesters. "The LORD be with you!" he said.

"The LORD bless you!" the harvesters replied.

[5]Then Boaz asked his foreman, "Who is that young woman over there? Who does she belong to?"

[6]And the foreman replied, "She is the young woman from Moab who came back with Naomi. [7]She asked me this morning if she could gather grain behind the harvesters. She has been hard at work ever since, except for a few minutes' rest in the shelter."

[8]Boaz went over and said to Ruth, "Listen, my daughter. Stay right here with us when you gather grain; don't go to any other fields. Stay right behind the young women working in my field. [9]See which part of the field they are harvesting, and then follow them. I have warned the young men not to treat you roughly. And when you are thirsty, help yourself to the water they have drawn from the well."

[10]Ruth fell at his feet and thanked him warmly. "What have I done to deserve such kindness?" she asked. "I am only a foreigner."

[11]"Yes, I know," Boaz replied. "But I also know about everything you have done for your mother-in-law since the death of your husband. I have heard how you left your father and mother and your own land to live here among complete strangers. [12]May the LORD, the God of Israel, under whose wings you have come to take refuge, reward you fully for what you have done."

[13]"I hope I continue to please you, sir," she replied. "You have comforted me by speaking so kindly to me, even though I am not one of your workers."

[14]At mealtime Boaz called to her, "Come over here, and help yourself to some food. You can dip your bread in the sour wine." So she sat with his harvesters, and Boaz gave her some roasted grain to eat. She ate all she wanted and still had some left over.

[15]When Ruth went back to work again, Boaz ordered his young men, "Let her gather grain right among the sheaves without stopping her. [16]And pull out some heads of barley from the bundles and drop them on purpose for her. Let her pick them up, and don't give her a hard time!"

17 So Ruth gathered barley there all day, and
when she beat out the grain that evening, it
filled an entire basket.* 18 She carried it back
into town and showed it to her mother-in-
law. Ruth also gave her the roasted grain that
was left over from her meal.

19 "Where did you gather all this grain to-
day?" Naomi asked. "Where did you work?
May the LORD bless the one who helped you!"

So Ruth told her mother-in-law about the
man in whose field she had worked. She said,
"The man I worked with today is named
Boaz."

20 "May the LORD bless him!" Naomi told
her daughter-in-law. "He is showing his kind-
ness to us as well as to your dead husband.*
That man is one of our closest relatives, one
of our family redeemers."

21 Then Ruth* said, "What's more, Boaz even
told me to come back and stay with his har-
vesters until the entire harvest is completed."

22 "Good!" Naomi exclaimed. "Do as he said,
my daughter. Stay with his young women
right through the whole harvest. You might
be harassed in other fields, but you'll be safe
with him."

23 So Ruth worked alongside the women in
Boaz's fields and gathered grain with them
until the end of the barley harvest. Then she
continued working with them through the
wheat harvest in early summer. And all the
while she lived with her mother-in-law.

CHAPTER 3

Ruth at the Threshing Floor

One day Naomi said to Ruth, "My daughter,
it's time that I found a permanent home for
you, so that you will be provided for. 2 Boaz is a
close relative of ours, and he's been very kind
by letting you gather grain with his young
women. Tonight he will be winnowing barley
at the threshing floor. 3 Now do as I tell you—
take a bath and put on perfume and dress in
your nicest clothes. Then go to the threshing
floor, but don't let Boaz see you until he has
finished eating and drinking. 4 Be sure to no-
tice where he lies down; then go and uncover
his feet and lie down there. He will tell you
what to do."

5 "I will do everything you say," Ruth re-
plied. 6 So she went down to the threshing
floor that night and followed the instructions
of her mother-in-law.

7 After Boaz had finished eating and drink-
ing and was in good spirits, he lay down at the
far end of the pile of grain and went to sleep.
Then Ruth came quietly, uncovered his feet,
and lay down. 8 Around midnight Boaz sud-
denly woke up and turned over. He was sur-
prised to find a woman lying at his feet!
9 "Who are you?" he asked.

"I am your servant Ruth," she replied.
"Spread the corner of your covering over me,
for you are my family redeemer."

10 "The LORD bless you, my daughter!" Boaz
exclaimed. "You are showing even more fam-
ily loyalty now than you did before, for you
have not gone after a younger man, whether
rich or poor. 11 Now don't worry about a thing,
my daughter. I will do what is necessary, for
everyone in town knows you are a virtuous
woman. 12 But while it's true that I am one of
your family redeemers, there is another man
who is more closely related to you than I am.
13 Stay here tonight, and in the morning I will
talk to him. If he is willing to redeem you, very
well. Let him marry you. But if he is not will-
ing, then as surely as the LORD lives, I will
redeem you myself! Now lie down here until
morning."

14 So Ruth lay at Boaz's feet until the morn-
ing, but she got up before it was light enough
for people to recognize each other. For Boaz
had said, "No one must know that a woman
was here at the threshing floor." 15 Then Boaz
said to her, "Bring your cloak and spread it
out." He measured six scoops* of barley into
the cloak and placed it on her back. Then he*
returned to the town.

16 When Ruth went back to her mother-
in-law, Naomi asked, "What happened, my
daughter?"

Ruth told Naomi everything Boaz had done
for her, 17 and she added, "He gave me these
six scoops of barley and said, 'Don't go back
to your mother-in-law empty-handed.'"

18 Then Naomi said to her, "Just be patient,
my daughter, until we hear what happens.
The man won't rest until he has settled things
today."

2:17 Hebrew *it was about an ephah* [20 quarts or 22 liters]. **2:20** Hebrew *to the living and to the dead.* **2:21** Hebrew *Ruth the Moabite.* **3:15a** Hebrew *six measures,* an unknown quantity. **3:15b** Most Hebrew manuscripts read *he;* many Hebrew manuscripts, Syriac version, and Latin Vulgate read *she.*

BOAZ

I sleep on the floor to prevent thieves from stealing my grain. One night a woman came in and quietly lay down near my feet. I didn't even know she was there until I woke up around midnight.

I recognized Ruth. She had been picking up leftover grain in my fields. I knew that if I married Ruth, I could provide everything she and her mother-in-law, Naomi, needed. Thankfully another man gave up his claim to Ruth. He gave me his sandal. According to our custom, this showed that Ruth was mine to marry. Years later our great-grandson David was born and became king.

You can read Boaz's story in the book of Ruth.

CHAPTER 4

Boaz Marries Ruth

Boaz went to the town gate and took a seat there. Just then the family redeemer he had mentioned came by, so Boaz called out to him, "Come over here and sit down, friend. I want to talk to you." So they sat down together. [2]Then Boaz called ten leaders from the town and asked them to sit as witnesses. [3]And Boaz said to the family redeemer, "You know Naomi, who came back from Moab. She is selling the land that belonged to our relative Elimelech. [4]I thought I should speak to you about it so that you can redeem it if you wish. If you want the land, then buy it here in the presence of these witnesses. But if you don't want it, let me know right away, because I am next in line to redeem it after you."

The man replied, "All right, I'll redeem it."

[5]Then Boaz told him, "Of course, your purchase of the land from Naomi also requires that you marry Ruth, the Moabite widow. That way she can have children who will carry on her husband's name and keep the land in the family."

[6]"Then I can't redeem it," the family redeemer replied, "because this might endanger my own estate. You redeem the land; I cannot do it."

[7]Now in those days it was the custom in Israel for anyone transferring a right of purchase to remove his sandal and hand it to the other party. This publicly validated the transaction. [8]So the other family redeemer drew off his sandal as he said to Boaz, "You buy the land."

[9]Then Boaz said to the elders and to the crowd standing around, "You are witnesses that today I have bought from Naomi all the property of Elimelech, Kilion, and Mahlon. [10]And with the land I have acquired Ruth, the Moabite widow of Mahlon, to be my wife. This way she can have a son to carry on the family name of her dead husband and to inherit the family property here in his hometown. You are all witnesses today."

[11]Then the elders and all the people standing in the gate replied, "We are witnesses! May the LORD make this woman who is coming into your home like Rachel and Leah, from whom all the nation of Israel descended! May you prosper in Ephrathah and be famous in Bethlehem. [12]And may the LORD give you descendants by this young woman who will be like those of our ancestor Perez, the son of Tamar and Judah."

The Descendants of Boaz

[13]So Boaz took Ruth into his home, and she became his wife. When he slept with her, the LORD enabled her to become pregnant, and she gave birth to a son. [14]Then the women of

the town said to Naomi, "Praise the LORD, who
has now provided a redeemer for your family!
May this child be famous in Israel. 15 May he re-
store your youth and care for you in your old
age. For he is the son of your daughter-in-law
who loves you and has been better to you than
seven sons!"

16 Naomi took the baby and cuddled him to
her breast. And she cared for him as if he
were her own. 17 The neighbor women said,
"Now at last Naomi has a son again!" And they
named him Obed. He became the father of
Jesse and the grandfather of David.

18 This is the genealogical record of their
ancestor Perez:

Perez was the father of Hezron.
19 Hezron was the father of Ram.
Ram was the father of Amminadab.
20 Amminadab was the father of
Nahshon.
Nahshon was the father of Salmon.*
21 Salmon was the father of Boaz.
Boaz was the father of Obed.
22 Obed was the father of Jesse.
Jesse was the father of David.

4:20 As in some Greek manuscripts (see also 4:21); Hebrew reads *Salma*.

1 Samuel

WHO
Eli, Hannah, Samuel, Saul, Jonathan, David, Michal, and Abigail.

WHERE
Israel.

WHEN
This book was written after 930 BC, when David's reign had come to an end and Israel was divided into two kingdoms.

WHY
To tell us about the life of the judge Samuel, the king Saul, and David, who would be the next king.

It is me [the Lord] they are rejecting, not you. . . . Do as they ask, but solemnly warn them about the way a king will reign over them.
1 SAMUEL 8:7, 9

What if you were king for a week . . . would it be fun? What would be your first command? Saul was a king who did not always listen to God. So God chose David to be the next king because he did listen. The book of 1 Samuel tells their stories.

FOLLOW DAVID'S EXAMPLE: LISTEN AND OBEY GOD.

CHAPTER 1

Elkanah and His Family

There was a man named Elkanah who lived in Ramah in the region of Zuph* in the hill country of Ephraim. He was the son of Jeroham, son of Elihu, son of Tohu, son of Zuph, of Ephraim. [2]Elkanah had two wives, Hannah and Peninnah. Peninnah had children, but Hannah did not.

[3]Each year Elkanah would travel to Shiloh to worship and sacrifice to the LORD of Heaven's Armies at the Tabernacle. The priests of the LORD at that time were the two sons of Eli—Hophni and Phinehas. [4]On the days Elkanah presented his sacrifice, he would give portions of the meat to Peninnah and each of her children. [5]And though he loved Hannah, he would give her only one

1:1 As in Greek version; Hebrew reads *in Ramathaim-zophim;* compare 1:19.

UNJUST CRITICISM

Carson enjoyed music, practiced his clarinet faithfully, and never missed band rehearsal. However, the band director seemed to pick on him. Recently, the clarinet section had trouble playing a certain passage. Everyone could hear the clunkers. Mr. Parke yelled at them and then asked Carson to play the difficult passage. Carson knew the passage quite well, but Mr. Parke's fierce gaze made him nervous. Carson did his best, but it was a total disaster. The entire band laughed, and Carson felt utterly humiliated. What should he do? Read 1 Samuel 1:6-10.

choice portion* because the LORD had given
her no children. 6So Peninnah would taunt
Hannah and make fun of her because the
LORD had kept her from having children.
7Year after year it was the same—Peninnah
would taunt Hannah as they went to the Tab-
ernacle.* Each time, Hannah would be re-
duced to tears and would not even eat.
8"Why are you crying, Hannah?" Elkanah
would ask. "Why aren't you eating? Why be
downhearted just because you have no chil-
dren? You have me—isn't that better than
having ten sons?"

Hannah's Prayer for a Son

9Once after a sacrificial meal at Shiloh,
Hannah got up and went to pray. Eli the priest
was sitting at his customary place beside the
entrance of the Tabernacle.* 10Hannah was in
deep anguish, crying bitterly as she prayed to
the LORD. 11And she made this vow: "O LORD
of Heaven's Armies, if you will look upon my
sorrow and answer my prayer and give me a
son, then I will give him back to you. He will
be yours for his entire lifetime, and as a sign
that he has been dedicated to the LORD, his
hair will never be cut.*"
12As she was praying to the LORD, Eli
watched her. 13Seeing her lips moving but
hearing no sound, he thought she had been
drinking. 14"Must you come here drunk?" he
demanded. "Throw away your wine!"
15"Oh no, sir!" she replied. "I haven't been
drinking wine or anything stronger. But I am
very discouraged, and I was pouring out my
heart to the LORD. 16Don't think I am a wicked
woman! For I have been praying out of great
anguish and sorrow."
17"In that case," Eli said, "go in peace! May
the God of Israel grant the request you have
asked of him."
18"Oh, thank you, sir!" she exclaimed. Then
she went back and began to eat again, and she
was no longer sad.

Samuel's Birth and Dedication

19The entire family got up early the next
morning and went to worship the LORD once
more. Then they returned home to Ramah.
When Elkanah slept with Hannah, the LORD
remembered her plea, 20and in due time she
gave birth to a son. She named him Samuel,*
for she said, "I asked the LORD for him."
21The next year Elkanah and his family

1:5 Or *And because he loved Hannah, he would give her a choice portion.* The meaning of the Hebrew is uncertain. **1:7** Hebrew *the house of the LORD;* also in 1:24. **1:9** Hebrew *the Temple of the LORD.* **1:11** Some manuscripts add *He will drink neither wine nor intoxicants.* **1:20** *Samuel* sounds like the Hebrew term for "asked of God" or "heard by God."

went on their annual trip to offer a sacrifice to the LORD. 22But Hannah did not go. She told her husband, "Wait until the boy is weaned. Then I will take him to the Tabernacle and leave him there with the LORD permanently.*"

23"Whatever you think is best," Elkanah agreed. "Stay here for now, and may the LORD help you keep your promise." So she stayed home and nursed the boy until he was weaned.

24When the child was weaned, Hannah took him to the Tabernacle in Shiloh. They brought along a three-year-old bull* for the sacrifice and a basket* of flour and some wine. 25After sacrificing the bull, they brought the boy to Eli. 26"Sir, do you remember me?" Hannah asked. "I am the woman who stood here several years ago praying to the LORD. 27I asked the LORD to give me this boy, and he has granted my request. 28Now I am giving him to the LORD, and he will belong to the LORD his whole life." And they* worshiped the LORD there.

CHAPTER 2

Hannah's Prayer of Praise

Then Hannah prayed:

"My heart rejoices in the LORD!
The LORD has made me strong.*
Now I have an answer for my enemies;
I rejoice because you rescued me.

2 No one is holy like the LORD!
There is no one besides you;
there is no Rock like our God.

3 "Stop acting so proud and haughty!
Don't speak with such arrogance!
For the LORD is a God who knows what you have done;
he will judge your actions.

4 The bow of the mighty is now broken,
and those who stumbled are now strong.

5 Those who were well fed are now starving,
and those who were starving are now full.
The childless woman now has seven children,
and the woman with many children wastes away.

6 The LORD gives both death and life;
he brings some down to the grave* but raises others up.

7 The LORD makes some poor and others rich;
he brings some down and lifts others up.

8 He lifts the poor from the dust
and the needy from the garbage dump.
He sets them among princes,
placing them in seats of honor.
For all the earth is the LORD's,
and he has set the world in order.

9 "He will protect his faithful ones,
but the wicked will disappear in darkness.
No one will succeed by strength alone.

10 Those who fight against the LORD will be shattered.
He thunders against them from heaven;
the LORD judges throughout the earth.
He gives power to his king;
he increases the strength* of his anointed one."

11Then Elkanah returned home to Ramah without Samuel. And the boy served the LORD by assisting Eli the priest.

Eli's Wicked Sons

12Now the sons of Eli were scoundrels who had no respect for the LORD 13or for their duties as priests. Whenever anyone offered a sacrifice, Eli's sons would send over a servant

Sometimes life seems crazy and out of control. Is anyone really in control?

The LORD gives both death and life. . . . The LORD makes some poor and others rich; he brings some down and lifts others up. 1 SAMUEL 2:6-7

1:22 Some manuscripts add *I will offer him as a Nazirite for all time.* **1:24a** As in Dead Sea Scrolls, Greek and Syriac versions; Masoretic Text reads *three bulls.* **1:24b** Hebrew *and an ephah* [20 quarts or 22 liters]. **1:28** Hebrew *he.* **2:1** Hebrew *has exalted my horn.* **2:6** Hebrew *to Sheol.* **2:10** Hebrew *he exalts the horn.*

with a three-pronged fork. While the meat of the sacrificed animal was still boiling, [14]the servant would stick the fork into the pot and demand that whatever it brought up be given to Eli's sons. All the Israelites who came to worship at Shiloh were treated this way. [15]Sometimes the servant would come even before the animal's fat had been burned on the altar. He would demand raw meat before it had been boiled so that it could be used for roasting.

[16]The man offering the sacrifice might reply, "Take as much as you want, but the fat must be burned first." Then the servant would demand, "No, give it to me now, or I'll take it by force." [17]So the sin of these young men was very serious in the LORD's sight, for they treated the LORD's offerings with contempt.

[18]But Samuel, though he was only a boy, served the LORD. He wore a linen garment like that of a priest.* [19]Each year his mother made a small coat for him and brought it to him when she came with her husband for the sacrifice. [20]Before they returned home, Eli would bless Elkanah and his wife and say, "May the LORD give you other children to take the place of this one she gave to the LORD.*" [21]And the LORD gave Hannah three sons and two daughters. Meanwhile, Samuel grew up in the presence of the LORD.

[22]Now Eli was very old, but he was aware of what his sons were doing to the people of Israel. He knew, for instance, that his sons were seducing the young women who assisted at the entrance of the Tabernacle.* [23]Eli said to them, "I have been hearing reports from all the people about the wicked things you are doing. Why do you keep sinning? [24]You must stop, my sons! The reports I hear among the LORD's people are not good. [25]If someone sins against another person, God* can mediate for the guilty party. But if someone sins against the LORD, who can intercede?" But Eli's sons wouldn't listen to their father, for the LORD was already planning to put them to death.

[26]Meanwhile, the boy Samuel grew taller and grew in favor with the LORD and with the people.

A Warning for Eli's Family

[27]One day a man of God came to Eli and gave him this message from the LORD: "I revealed myself* to your ancestors when the people of Israel were slaves in Egypt. [28]I chose your ancestor Aaron* from among all the tribes of Israel to be my priest, to offer sacrifices on my altar, to burn incense, and to wear the priestly vest* as he served me. And I assigned the sacrificial offerings to you priests. [29]So why do you scorn my sacrifices and offerings? Why do you give your sons more honor than you give me—for you and they have become fat from the best offerings of my people Israel!

[30]"Therefore, the LORD, the God of Israel, says: I promised that your branch of the tribe of Levi* would always be my priests. But I will honor those who honor me, and I will despise those who think lightly of me. [31]The time is coming when I will put an end to your family, so it will no longer serve as my priests. All the members of your family will die before their time. None will reach old age. [32]You will watch with envy as I pour out prosperity on the people of Israel. But no members of your family will ever live out their days. [33]Those who survive will live in sadness and grief, and their children will die a violent death.* [34]And to prove that what I have said will come true, I will cause your two sons, Hophni and Phinehas, to die on the same day!

[35]"Then I will raise up a faithful priest who will serve me and do what I desire. I will establish his family, and they will be priests to my anointed kings forever. [36]Then all of your surviving family will bow before him, begging for money and food. 'Please,' they will say, 'give us jobs among the priests so we will have enough to eat.'"

CHAPTER 3

The LORD Speaks to Samuel

Meanwhile, the boy Samuel served the LORD by assisting Eli. Now in those days messages from the LORD were very rare, and visions were quite uncommon.

[2]One night Eli, who was almost blind by now, had gone to bed. [3]The lamp of God had not yet gone out, and Samuel was sleeping in

2:18 Hebrew *He wore a linen ephod.* **2:20** As in Dead Sea Scrolls and Greek version; Masoretic Text reads *this one he requested of the LORD.* **2:22** Hebrew *Tent of Meeting.* Some manuscripts lack this entire sentence. **2:25** Or *the judges.* **2:27** As in Greek and Syriac versions; Hebrew reads *Did I reveal myself.* **2:28a** Hebrew *your father.* **2:28b** Hebrew *an ephod.* **2:30** Hebrew *that your house and your father's house.* **2:33** As in Dead Sea Scrolls, which read *die by the sword;* Masoretic Text reads *die like mortals.*

SAMUEL

Ever since I was a young boy, I have devoted my life to serving God and his people as a judge and a prophet. I anointed two kings—first Saul and then David. King Saul was a big disappointment. I had told him exactly what the Lord demanded of him: Completely destroy the Amalekites and their possessions! But Saul allowed the king to live and took the best of what was left for himself. Saul claimed that he kept some of the animals to offer as sacrifices. Wrong answer! God loves obedience far better than sacrifice, I told him. He hadn't listened to God. That was a big mistake.

You will find the story of Samuel in 1 Samuel 1–28.

the Tabernacle* near the Ark of God.
4Suddenly the LORD called out, "Samuel!"

"Yes?" Samuel replied. "What is it?" 5He got up and ran to Eli. "Here I am. Did you call me?"

"I didn't call you," Eli replied. "Go back to bed." So he did.

6Then the LORD called out again, "Samuel!"

Again Samuel got up and went to Eli. "Here I am. Did you call me?"

"I didn't call you, my son," Eli said. "Go back to bed."

7Samuel did not yet know the LORD because he had never had a message from the LORD before. 8So the LORD called a third time, and once more Samuel got up and went to Eli. "Here I am. Did you call me?"

Then Eli realized it was the LORD who was calling the boy. 9So he said to Samuel, "Go and lie down again, and if someone calls again, say, 'Speak, LORD, your servant is listening.'" So Samuel went back to bed.

10And the LORD came and called as before, "Samuel! Samuel!"

And Samuel replied, "Speak, your servant is listening."

11Then the LORD said to Samuel, "I am about to do a shocking thing in Israel. 12I am going to carry out all my threats against Eli and his family, from beginning to end. 13I have warned him that judgment is coming upon his family forever, because his sons are blaspheming God* and he hasn't disciplined them. 14So I have vowed that the sins of Eli and his sons will never be forgiven by sacrifices or offerings."

Samuel Speaks for the LORD

15Samuel stayed in bed until morning, then got up and opened the doors of the Tabernacle* as usual. He was afraid to tell Eli what the LORD had said to him. 16But Eli called out to him, "Samuel, my son."

"Here I am," Samuel replied.

17"What did the LORD say to you? Tell me everything. And may God strike you and even kill you if you hide anything from me!" 18So Samuel told Eli everything; he didn't hold anything back. "It is the LORD's will," Eli replied. "Let him do what he thinks best."

19As Samuel grew up, the LORD was with him, and everything Samuel said proved to be reliable. 20And all Israel, from Dan in the north to Beersheba in the south, knew that Samuel was confirmed as a prophet of the LORD. 21The LORD continued to appear at Shiloh and gave messages to Samuel there at the Tabernacle. 4:1And Samuel's words went out to all the people of Israel.

3:3 Hebrew *the Temple of the LORD.* 3:13 As in Greek version; Hebrew reads *his sons have made themselves contemptible.*
3:15 Hebrew *the house of the LORD.*

CHAPTER 4

The Philistines Capture the Ark

At that time Israel was at war with the Philistines. The Israelite army was camped near Ebenezer, and the Philistines were at Aphek. [2]The Philistines attacked and defeated the army of Israel, killing 4,000 men. [3]After the battle was over, the troops retreated to their camp, and the elders of Israel asked, "Why did the LORD allow us to be defeated by the Philistines?" Then they said, "Let's bring the Ark of the Covenant of the LORD from Shiloh. If we carry it into battle with us, it* will save us from our enemies."

[4]So they sent men to Shiloh to bring the Ark of the Covenant of the LORD of Heaven's Armies, who is enthroned between the cherubim. Hophni and Phinehas, the sons of Eli, were also there with the Ark of the Covenant of God. [5]When all the Israelites saw the Ark of the Covenant of the LORD coming into the camp, their shout of joy was so loud it made the ground shake!

[6]"What's going on?" the Philistines asked. "What's all the shouting about in the Hebrew camp?" When they were told it was because the Ark of the LORD had arrived, [7]they panicked. "The gods have* come into their camp!" they cried. "This is a disaster! We have never had to face anything like this before! [8]Help! Who can save us from these mighty gods of Israel? They are the same gods who destroyed the Egyptians with plagues when Israel was in the wilderness. [9]Fight as never before, Philistines! If you don't, we will become the Hebrews' slaves just as they have been ours! Stand up like men and fight!"

[10]So the Philistines fought desperately, and Israel was defeated again. The slaughter was great; 30,000 Israelite soldiers died that day. The survivors turned and fled to their tents. [11]The Ark of God was captured, and Hophni and Phinehas, the two sons of Eli, were killed.

The Death of Eli

[12]A man from the tribe of Benjamin ran from the battlefield and arrived at Shiloh later that same day. He had torn his clothes and put dust on his head to show his grief. [13]Eli was waiting beside the road to hear the news of the battle, for his heart trembled for the safety of the Ark of God. When the messenger arrived and told what had happened, an outcry resounded throughout the town.

[14]"What is all the noise about?" Eli asked.

The messenger rushed over to Eli, [15]who was ninety-eight years old and blind. [16]He said to Eli, "I have just come from the battlefield—I was there this very day."

"What happened, my son?" Eli demanded.

[17]"Israel has been defeated by the Philistines," the messenger replied. "The people have been slaughtered, and your two sons, Hophni and Phinehas, were also killed. And the Ark of God has been captured."

[18]When the messenger mentioned what had happened to the Ark of God, Eli fell backward from his seat beside the gate. He broke his neck and died, for he was old and overweight. He had been Israel's judge for forty years.

[19]Eli's daughter-in-law, the wife of Phinehas, was pregnant and near her time of delivery. When she heard that the Ark of God had been captured and that her father-in-law and husband were dead, she went into labor and gave birth. [20]She died in childbirth, but before she passed away the midwives tried to encourage her. "Don't be afraid," they said. "You have a baby boy!" But she did not answer or pay attention to them.

[21]She named the child Ichabod (which means "Where is the glory?"), for she said, "Israel's glory is gone." She named him this because the Ark of God had been captured and because her father-in-law and husband were dead. [22]Then she said, "The glory has departed from Israel, for the Ark of God has been captured."

CHAPTER 5

The Ark in Philistia

After the Philistines captured the Ark of God, they took it from the battleground at Ebenezer to the town of Ashdod. [2]They carried the Ark of God into the temple of Dagon and placed it beside an idol of Dagon. [3]But when the citizens of Ashdod went to see it the next morning, Dagon had fallen with his face to the ground in front of the Ark of the LORD! So they took Dagon and put him in his place again. [4]But the next morning the same thing

4:3 Or *he*. **4:7** Or *A god has*.

happened—Dagon had fallen face down before the Ark of the LORD again. This time his head and hands had broken off and were lying in the doorway. Only the trunk of his body was left intact. [5]That is why to this day neither the priests of Dagon nor anyone who enters the temple of Dagon in Ashdod will step on its threshold.

[6]Then the LORD's heavy hand struck the people of Ashdod and the nearby villages with a plague of tumors.* [7]When the people realized what was happening, they cried out, "We can't keep the Ark of the God of Israel here any longer! He is against us! We will all be destroyed along with Dagon, our god." [8]So they called together the rulers of the Philistine towns and asked, "What should we do with the Ark of the God of Israel?"

The rulers discussed it and replied, "Move it to the town of Gath." So they moved the Ark of the God of Israel to Gath. [9]But when the Ark arrived at Gath, the LORD's heavy hand fell on its men, young and old; he struck them with a plague of tumors, and there was a great panic.

[10]So they sent the Ark of God to the town of Ekron, but when the people of Ekron saw it coming they cried out, "They are bringing the Ark of the God of Israel here to kill us, too!" [11]The people summoned the Philistine rulers again and begged them, "Please send the Ark of the God of Israel back to its own country, or it* will kill us all." For the deadly plague from God had already begun, and great fear was sweeping across the town. [12]Those who didn't die were afflicted with tumors; and the cry from the town rose to heaven.

CHAPTER 6

The Philistines Return the Ark

The Ark of the LORD remained in Philistine territory seven months in all. [2]Then the Philistines called in their priests and diviners and asked them, "What should we do about the Ark of the LORD? Tell us how to return it to its own country."

[3]"Send the Ark of the God of Israel back with a gift," they were told. "Send a guilt offering so the plague will stop. Then, if you are healed, you will know it was his hand that caused the plague."

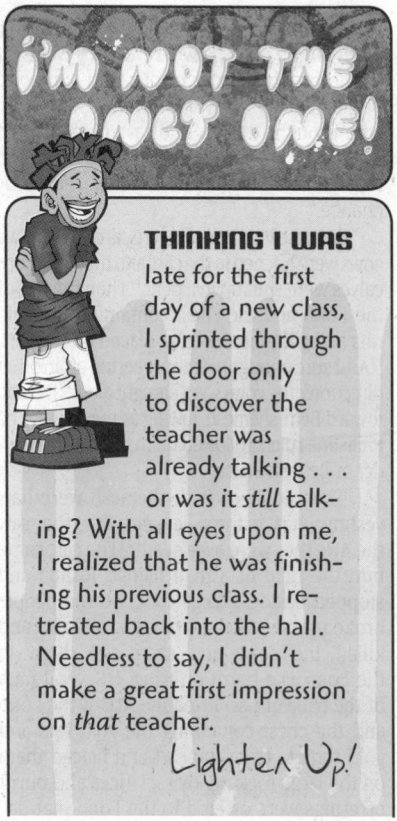

[4]"What sort of guilt offering should we send?" they asked.

And they were told, "Since the plague has struck both you and your five rulers, make five gold tumors and five gold rats, just like those that have ravaged your land. [5]Make these things to show honor to the God of Israel. Perhaps then he will stop afflicting you, your gods, and your land. [6]Don't be stubborn and rebellious as Pharaoh and the Egyptians were. By the time God was finished with them, they were eager to let Israel go.

[7]"Now build a new cart, and find two cows that have just given birth to calves. Make sure the cows have never been yoked to a cart. Hitch the cows to the cart, but shut their calves away from them in a pen. [8]Put the Ark of the LORD on the cart, and beside it place a chest containing the gold rats and gold

5:6 Greek version and Latin Vulgate read *tumors; and rats appeared in their land, and death and destruction were throughout the city.* **5:11** Or *he.*

tumors you are sending as a guilt offering. Then let the cows go wherever they want. [9]If they cross the border of our land and go to Beth-shemesh, we will know it was the LORD who brought this great disaster upon us. If they don't, we will know it was not his hand that caused the plague. It came simply by chance."

[10]So these instructions were carried out. Two cows were hitched to the cart, and their newborn calves were shut up in a pen. [11]Then the Ark of the LORD and the chest containing the gold rats and gold tumors were placed on the cart. [12]And sure enough, without veering off in other directions, the cows went straight along the road toward Beth-shemesh, lowing as they went. The Philistine rulers followed them as far as the border of Beth-shemesh.

[13]The people of Beth-shemesh were harvesting wheat in the valley, and when they saw the Ark, they were overjoyed! [14]The cart came into the field of a man named Joshua and stopped beside a large rock. So the people broke up the wood of the cart for a fire and killed the cows and sacrificed them to the LORD as a burnt offering. [15]Several men of the tribe of Levi lifted the Ark of the LORD and the chest containing the gold rats and gold tumors from the cart and placed them on the large rock. Many sacrifices and burnt offerings were offered to the LORD that day by the people of Beth-shemesh. [16]The five Philistine rulers watched all this and then returned to Ekron that same day.

[17]The five gold tumors sent by the Philistines as a guilt offering to the LORD were gifts from the rulers of Ashdod, Gaza, Ashkelon, Gath, and Ekron. [18]The five gold rats represented the five Philistine towns and their surrounding villages, which were controlled by the five rulers. The large rock at Beth-shemesh, where they set the Ark of the LORD, still stands in the field of Joshua as a witness to what happened there.

The Ark Moved to Kiriath-Jearim

[19]But the LORD killed seventy men* from Beth-shemesh because they looked into the Ark of the LORD. And the people mourned greatly because of what the LORD had done. [20]"Who is able to stand in the presence of the LORD, this holy God?" they cried out. "Where can we send the Ark from here?"

[21]So they sent messengers to the people at Kiriath-jearim and told them, "The Philistines have returned the Ark of the LORD. Come here and get it!"

CHAPTER 7

So the men of Kiriath-jearim came to get the Ark of the LORD. They took it to the hillside home of Abinadab and ordained Eleazar, his son, to be in charge of it. [2]The Ark remained in Kiriath-jearim for a long time—twenty years in all. During that time all Israel mourned because it seemed the LORD had abandoned them.

Samuel Leads Israel to Victory

[3]Then Samuel said to all the people of Israel, "If you are really serious about wanting to return to the LORD, get rid of your foreign gods and your images of Ashtoreth. Determine to obey only the LORD; then he will rescue you from the Philistines." [4]So the Israelites got rid of their images of Baal and Ashtoreth and worshiped only the LORD.

[5]Then Samuel told them, "Gather all of Israel to Mizpah, and I will pray to the LORD for you." [6]So they gathered at Mizpah and, in a great ceremony, drew water from a well and poured it out before the LORD. They also went without food all day and confessed that they had sinned against the LORD. (It was at Mizpah that Samuel became Israel's judge.)

[7]When the Philistine rulers heard that Israel had gathered at Mizpah, they mobilized their army and advanced. The Israelites were badly frightened when they learned that the Philistines were approaching. [8]"Don't stop pleading with the LORD our God to save us from the Philistines!" they begged Samuel. [9]So Samuel took a young lamb and offered it to the LORD as a whole burnt offering. He pleaded with the LORD to help Israel, and the LORD answered him.

[10]Just as Samuel was sacrificing the burnt offering, the Philistines arrived to attack Israel. But the LORD spoke with a mighty voice of thunder from heaven that day, and the Philistines were thrown into such confusion that the Israelites defeated them. [11]The men of Is-

6:19 As in a few Hebrew manuscripts; most Hebrew manuscripts read *70 men, 50,000 men*. Perhaps the text should be understood to read *the LORD killed 70 men and 50 oxen*.

rael chased them from Mizpah to a place below Beth-car, slaughtering them all along the way.

12 Samuel then took a large stone and placed it between the towns of Mizpah and Jeshanah.* He named it Ebenezer (which means "the stone of help"), for he said, "Up to this point the LORD has helped us!"

13 So the Philistines were subdued and didn't invade Israel again for some time. And throughout Samuel's lifetime, the LORD's powerful hand was raised against the Philistines. 14 The Israelite villages near Ekron and Gath that the Philistines had captured were restored to Israel, along with the rest of the territory that the Philistines had taken. And there was peace between Israel and the Amorites in those days.

15 Samuel continued as Israel's judge for the rest of his life. 16 Each year he traveled around, setting up his court first at Bethel, then at Gilgal, and then at Mizpah. He judged the people of Israel at each of these places. 17 Then he would return to his home at Ramah, and he would hear cases there, too. And Samuel built an altar to the LORD at Ramah.

CHAPTER 8

Israel Requests a King

As Samuel grew old, he appointed his sons to be judges over Israel. 2 Joel and Abijah, his oldest sons, held court in Beersheba. 3 But they were not like their father, for they were greedy for money. They accepted bribes and perverted justice.

4 Finally, all the elders of Israel met at Ramah to discuss the matter with Samuel. 5 "Look," they told him, "you are now old, and your sons are not like you. Give us a king to judge us like all the other nations have."

6 Samuel was displeased with their request and went to the LORD for guidance. 7 "Do everything they say to you," the LORD replied, "for it is me they are rejecting, not you. They don't want me to be their king any longer. 8 Ever since I brought them from Egypt they have continually abandoned me and followed other gods. And now they are giving you the same treatment. 9 Do as they ask, but solemnly warn them about the way a king will reign over them."

Samuel Warns against a Kingdom

10 So Samuel passed on the LORD's warning to the people who were asking him for a king. 11 "This is how a king will reign over you," Samuel said. "The king will draft your sons and assign them to his chariots and his charioteers, making them run before his chariots. 12 Some will be generals and captains in his army,* some will be forced to plow in his fields and harvest his crops, and some will make his weapons and chariot equipment. 13 The king will take your daughters from you and force them to cook and bake and make perfumes for him. 14 He will take away the best of your fields and vineyards and olive groves and give them to his own officials. 15 He will take a tenth of your grain and your grape harvest and distribute it among his officers and attendants. 16 He will take your male and female slaves and demand the finest of your cattle* and donkeys for his own use. 17 He will demand a tenth of your flocks, and you will be his slaves. 18 When that day comes, you will beg for relief from this king you are demanding, but then the LORD will not help you."

AMAZING FACTS

The Philistines once lost a battle to the Israelites because of . . . the sound of thunder?!?

1 SAMUEL 7:10

19 But the people refused to listen to Samuel's warning. "Even so, we still want a king," they said. 20 "We want to be like the nations around us. Our king will judge us and lead us into battle."

21 So Samuel repeated to the LORD what the

7:12 As in Greek and Syriac versions; Hebrew reads *Shen*. **8:12** Hebrew *commanders of thousands and commanders of fifties*. **8:16** As in Greek version; Hebrew reads *young men*.

people had said, [22]and the LORD replied, "Do as they say, and give them a king." Then Samuel agreed and sent the people home.

CHAPTER 9

Saul Meets Samuel

There was a wealthy, influential man named Kish from the tribe of Benjamin. He was the son of Abiel, son of Zeror, son of Becorath, son of Aphiah, of the tribe of Benjamin. [2]His son Saul was the most handsome man in Israel—head and shoulders taller than anyone else in the land.

[3]One day Kish's donkeys strayed away, and he told Saul, "Take a servant with you, and go look for the donkeys." [4]So Saul took one of the servants and traveled through the hill country of Ephraim, the land of Shalishah, the Shaalim area, and the entire land of Benjamin, but they couldn't find the donkeys anywhere.

[5]Finally, they entered the region of Zuph, and Saul said to his servant, "Let's go home. By now my father will be more worried about us than about the donkeys!"

[6]But the servant said, "I've just thought of something! There is a man of God who lives here in this town. He is held in high honor by all the people because everything he says comes true. Let's go find him. Perhaps he can tell us which way to go."

[7]"But we don't have anything to offer him," Saul replied. "Even our food is gone, and we don't have a thing to give him."

[8]"Well," the servant said, "I have one small silver piece.* We can at least offer it to the man of God and see what happens!" [9](In those days if people wanted a message from God, they would say, "Let's go and ask the seer," for prophets used to be called seers.)

[10]"All right," Saul agreed, "let's try it!" So they started into the town where the man of God lived.

[11]As they were climbing the hill to the town, they met some young women coming out to draw water. So Saul and his servant asked, "Is the seer here today?"

[12]"Yes," they replied. "Stay right on this road. He is at the town gates. He has just arrived to take part in a public sacrifice up at the place of worship. [13]Hurry and catch him before he goes up there to eat. The guests won't begin eating until he arrives to bless the food."

[14]So they entered the town, and as they passed through the gates, Samuel was coming out toward them to go up to the place of worship.

[15]Now the LORD had told Samuel the previous day, [16]"About this time tomorrow I will send you a man from the land of Benjamin. Anoint him to be the leader of my people, Israel. He will rescue them from the Philistines, for I have looked down on my people in mercy and have heard their cry."

[17]When Samuel saw Saul, the LORD said, "That's the man I told you about! He will rule my people."

[18]Just then Saul approached Samuel at the gateway and asked, "Can you please tell me where the seer's house is?"

[19]"I am the seer!" Samuel replied. "Go up to the place of worship ahead of me. We will eat there together, and in the morning I'll tell you what you want to know and send you on your way. [20]And don't worry about those donkeys that were lost three days ago, for they have been found. And I am here to tell you that you and your family are the focus of all Israel's hopes."

[21]Saul replied, "But I'm only from the tribe of Benjamin, the smallest tribe in Israel, and my family is the least important of all the families of that tribe! Why are you talking like this to me?"

[22]Then Samuel brought Saul and his servant into the hall and placed them at the head of the table, honoring them above the thirty special guests. [23]Samuel then instructed the cook to bring Saul the finest cut of meat, the piece that had been set aside for the guest of honor. [24]So the cook brought in the meat and placed it before Saul. "Go ahead and eat it," Samuel said. "I was saving it for you even before I invited these others!" So Saul ate with Samuel that day.

[25]When they came down from the place of worship and returned to town, Samuel took Saul up to the roof of the house and prepared a bed for him there.* [26]At daybreak the next morning, Samuel called to Saul, "Get up! It's time you were on your way." So Saul got ready,

9:8 Hebrew *¼ shekel of silver*, about 0.1 ounces or 3 grams in weight. **9:25** As in Greek version; Hebrew reads *and talked with him there.*

and he and Samuel left the house together.
[27] When they reached the edge of town, Samuel told Saul to send his servant on ahead. After the servant was gone, Samuel said, "Stay here, for I have received a special message for you from God."

CHAPTER 10

Samuel Anoints Saul as King

Then Samuel took a flask of olive oil and poured it over Saul's head. He kissed Saul and said, "I am doing this because the LORD has appointed you to be the ruler over Israel, his special possession.* [2] When you leave me today, you will see two men beside Rachel's tomb at Zelzah, on the border of Benjamin. They will tell you that the donkeys have been found and that your father has stopped worrying about them and is now worried about you. He is asking, 'Have you seen my son?'

[3] "When you get to the oak of Tabor, you will see three men coming toward you who are on their way to worship God at Bethel. One will be bringing three young goats, another will have three loaves of bread, and the third will be carrying a wineskin full of wine. [4] They will greet you and offer you two of the loaves, which you are to accept.

[5] "When you arrive at Gibeah of God,* where the garrison of the Philistines is located, you will meet a band of prophets coming down from the place of worship. They will be playing a harp, a tambourine, a flute, and a lyre, and they will be prophesying. [6] At that time the Spirit of the LORD will come powerfully upon you, and you will prophesy with them. You will be changed into a different person. [7] After these signs take place, do what must be done, for God is with you. [8] Then go down to Gilgal ahead of me. I will join you there to sacrifice burnt offerings and peace offerings. You must wait for seven days until I arrive and give you further instructions."

Samuel's Signs Are Fulfilled

[9] As Saul turned and started to leave, God gave him a new heart, and all Samuel's signs were fulfilled that day. [10] When Saul and his servant arrived at Gibeah, they saw a group of prophets coming toward them. Then the Spirit of God came powerfully upon Saul, and he, too, began to prophesy. [11] When those who knew Saul heard about it, they exclaimed, "What? Is even Saul a prophet? How did the son of Kish become a prophet?"

[12] And one of those standing there said, "Can anyone become a prophet, no matter who his father is?"* So that is the origin of the saying "Is even Saul a prophet?"

[13] When Saul had finished prophesying, he went up to the place of worship. [14] "Where have you been?" Saul's uncle asked him and his servant.

"We were looking for the donkeys," Saul replied, "but we couldn't find them. So we went to Samuel to ask him where they were."

[15] "Oh? And what did he say?" his uncle asked.

[16] "He told us that the donkeys had already been found," Saul replied. But Saul didn't tell his uncle what Samuel said about the kingdom.

Saul Is Acclaimed King

[17] Later Samuel called all the people of Israel to meet before the LORD at Mizpah. [18] And he said, "This is what the LORD, the God of Israel, has declared: I brought you from Egypt and rescued you from the Egyptians and from all of the nations that were oppressing you. [19] But though I have rescued you from your misery and distress, you have rejected your God today and have said, 'No, we want a king instead!' Now, therefore, present yourselves before the LORD by tribes and clans."

[20] So Samuel brought all the tribes of Israel before the LORD, and the tribe of Benjamin was chosen by lot. [21] Then he brought each family of the tribe of Benjamin before the LORD, and the family of the Matrites was chosen. And finally Saul son of Kish was chosen from among them. But when they looked for him, he had disappeared! [22] So they asked the LORD, "Where is he?"

And the LORD replied, "He is hiding among the baggage." [23] So they found him and brought him out, and he stood head and shoulders above anyone else.

[24] Then Samuel said to all the people, "This

10:1 Greek version reads *over Israel. And you will rule over the LORD's people and save them from their enemies around them. This will be the sign to you that the LORD has appointed you to be leader over his special possession.* **10:5** Hebrew *Gibeath-elohim.*
10:12 Hebrew *said, "Who is their father?"*

is the man the LORD has chosen as your king. No one in all Israel is like him!"

And all the people shouted, "Long live the king!"

[25]Then Samuel told the people what the rights and duties of a king were. He wrote them down on a scroll and placed it before the LORD. Then Samuel sent the people home again.

[26]When Saul returned to his home at Gibeah, a group of men whose hearts God had touched went with him. [27]But there were some scoundrels who complained, "How can this man save us?" And they scorned him and refused to bring him gifts. But Saul ignored them.

[Nahash, king of the Ammonites, had been grievously oppressing the people of Gad and Reuben who lived east of the Jordan River. He gouged out the right eye of each of the Israelites living there, and he didn't allow anyone to come and rescue them. In fact, of all the Israelites east of the Jordan, there wasn't a single one whose right eye Nahash had not gouged out. But there were 7,000 men who had escaped from the Ammonites, and they had settled in Jabesh-gilead.]*

CHAPTER 11

Saul Defeats the Ammonites

About a month later,* King Nahash of Ammon led his army against the Israelite town of Jabesh-gilead. But all the citizens of Jabesh asked for peace. "Make a treaty with us, and we will be your servants," they pleaded.

[2]"All right," Nahash said, "but only on one condition. I will gouge out the right eye of every one of you as a disgrace to all Israel!"

[3]"Give us seven days to send messengers throughout Israel!" replied the elders of Jabesh. "If no one comes to save us, we will agree to your terms."

[4]When the messengers came to Gibeah of Saul and told the people about their plight, everyone broke into tears. [5]Saul had been plowing a field with his oxen, and when he returned to town, he asked, "What's the matter? Why is everyone crying?" So they told him about the message from Jabesh.

[6]Then the Spirit of God came powerfully upon Saul, and he became very angry. [7]He took two oxen and cut them into pieces and sent the messengers to carry them throughout Israel with this message: "This is what will happen to the oxen of anyone who refuses to

10:27 This paragraph, which is not included in the Masoretic Text, is found in Dead Sea Scroll 4QSam[a]. **11:1** As in Greek version; Hebrew lacks *About a month later*.

IS IT OK?

IS IT OK IF I'M NOT THAT GOOD AT ANYTHING?

Do you ever feel like you're not that good at anything? That's how Saul felt. When the Israelites tried to make Saul king, he hid in a pile of luggage! He didn't think he was good enough for the job (see 1 Samuel 10:21-22). Most of us feel inadequate sometimes, too. If we're honest with ourselves, we have to admit we are average, not superstars. (If we were flavors of ice cream, we'd be chocolate or vanilla. *Maybe* strawberry.) And if that's OK with God, it should be OK with us. Remember, though, that there's something special and unique about *you*, and there is something only *you* can do. When your chance comes—and it *will* come—don't get caught hiding!

follow Saul and Samuel into battle!" And the LORD made the people afraid of Saul's anger, and all of them came out together as one. [8]When Saul mobilized them at Bezek, he found that there were 300,000 men from Israel and 30,000* men from Judah.

[9]So Saul sent the messengers back to Jabesh-gilead to say, "We will rescue you by noontime tomorrow!" There was great joy throughout the town when that message arrived!

[10]The men of Jabesh then told their enemies, "Tomorrow we will come out to you, and you can do to us whatever you wish." [11]But before dawn the next morning, Saul arrived, having divided his army into three detachments. He launched a surprise attack against the Ammonites and slaughtered them the whole morning. The remnant of their army was so badly scattered that no two of them were left together.

[12]Then the people exclaimed to Samuel, "Now where are those men who said, 'Why should Saul rule over us?' Bring them here, and we will kill them!"

[13]But Saul replied, "No one will be executed today, for today the LORD has rescued Israel!"

[14]Then Samuel said to the people, "Come, let us all go to Gilgal to renew the kingdom." [15]So they all went to Gilgal, and in a solemn ceremony before the LORD they made Saul king. Then they offered peace offerings to the LORD, and Saul and all the Israelites were filled with joy.

CHAPTER 12

Samuel's Farewell Address

Then Samuel addressed all Israel: "I have done as you asked and given you a king. [2]Your king is now your leader. I stand here before you—an old, gray-haired man—and my sons serve you. I have served as your leader from the time I was a boy to this very day. [3]Now testify against me in the presence of the LORD and before his anointed one. Whose ox or donkey have I stolen? Have I ever cheated any of you? Have I ever oppressed you? Have I ever taken a bribe and perverted justice? Tell me and I will make right whatever I have done wrong."

[4]"No," they replied, "you have never cheated or oppressed us, and you have never taken even a single bribe."

[5]"The LORD and his anointed one are my witnesses today," Samuel declared, "that my hands are clean."

"Yes, he is a witness," they replied.

[6]"It was the LORD who appointed Moses and Aaron," Samuel continued. "He brought your ancestors out of the land of Egypt. [7]Now stand here quietly before the LORD as I remind you of all the great things the LORD has done for you and your ancestors.

[8]"When the Israelites were* in Egypt and cried out to the LORD, he sent Moses and Aaron to rescue them from Egypt and to bring them into this land. [9]But the people soon forgot about the LORD their God, so he handed them over to Sisera, the commander of Hazor's army, and also to the Philistines and to the king of Moab, who fought against them.

[10]"Then they cried to the LORD again and confessed, 'We have sinned by turning away from the LORD and worshiping the images of Baal and Ashtoreth. But we will worship you and you alone if you will rescue us from our enemies.' [11]Then the LORD sent Gideon,* Bedan,* Jephthah, and Samuel* to save you, and you lived in safety.

[12]"But when you were afraid of Nahash, the king of Ammon, you came to me and said that you wanted a king to reign over you, even though the LORD your God was already your king. [13]All right, here is the king you have chosen. You asked for him, and the LORD has granted your request.

[14]"Now if you fear and worship the LORD and listen to his voice, and if you do not rebel against the LORD's commands, then both you and your king will show that you recognize the LORD as your God. [15]But if you rebel against the LORD's commands and refuse to listen to him, then his hand will be as heavy upon you as it was upon your ancestors.

[16]"Now stand here and see the great thing the LORD is about to do. [17]You know that it does not rain at this time of the year during the wheat harvest. I will ask the LORD to send thunder and rain today. Then you will realize

11:8 Dead Sea Scrolls and Greek version read *70,000*. **12:8** Hebrew *When Jacob was*. The names "Jacob" and "Israel" are often interchanged throughout the Old Testament, referring sometimes to the individual patriarch and sometimes to the nation. **12:11a** Hebrew *Jerub-baal*, another name for Gideon; see Judg 6:32. **12:11b** Greek and Syriac versions read *Barak*. **12:11c** Greek and Syriac versions read *Samson*.

how wicked you have been in asking the LORD
for a king!"
18 So Samuel called to the LORD, and the
LORD sent thunder and rain that day. And all
the people were terrified of the LORD and of
Samuel. 19 "Pray to the LORD your God for us,
or we will die!" they all said to Samuel. "For
now we have added to our sins by asking for a
king."
20 "Don't be afraid," Samuel reassured them.
"You have certainly done wrong, but make
sure now that you worship the LORD with all
your heart, and don't turn your back on him.
21 Don't go back to worshiping worthless idols
that cannot help or rescue you—they are to-
tally useless! 22 The LORD will not abandon his
people, because that would dishonor his great
name. For it has pleased the LORD to make you
his very own people.
23 "As for me, I will certainly not sin against
the LORD by ending my prayers for you. And I
will continue to teach you what is good and
right. 24 But be sure to fear the LORD and faith-
fully serve him. Think of all the wonderful
things he has done for you. 25 But if you con-
tinue to sin, you and your king will be swept
away."

How can I stop feeling sorry for myself?

Be sure to fear the LORD and faithfully serve him. Think of all the wonderful things he has done for you. 1 SAMUEL 12:24

CHAPTER 13

Continued War with Philistia

Saul was thirty* years old when he became
king, and he reigned for forty-two years.*
2 Saul selected 3,000 special troops from
the army of Israel and sent the rest of the men
home. He took 2,000 of the chosen men with
him to Micmash and the hill country of Beth-
el. The other 1,000 went with Saul's son Jona-
than to Gibeah in the land of Benjamin.
3 Soon after this, Jonathan attacked and de-
feated the garrison of Philistines at Geba. The
news spread quickly among the Philistines.
So Saul blew the ram's horn throughout the
land, saying, "Hebrews, hear this! Rise up in
revolt!" 4 All Israel heard the news that Saul
had destroyed the Philistine garrison at Geba
and that the Philistines now hated the Israel-
ites more than ever. So the entire Israelite
army was summoned to join Saul at Gilgal.
5 The Philistines mustered a mighty army
of 3,000* chariots, 6,000 charioteers, and as
many warriors as the grains of sand on the
seashore! They camped at Micmash east of
Beth-aven. 6 The men of Israel saw what a
tight spot they were in; and because they were
hard pressed by the enemy, they tried to hide
in caves, thickets, rocks, holes, and cisterns.
7 Some of them crossed the Jordan River and
escaped into the land of Gad and Gilead.

Saul's Disobedience and Samuel's Rebuke

Meanwhile, Saul stayed at Gilgal, and his men
were trembling with fear. 8 Saul waited there
seven days for Samuel, as Samuel had in-
structed him earlier, but Samuel still didn't
come. Saul realized that his troops were rap-
idly slipping away. 9 So he demanded, "Bring
me the burnt offering and the peace offer-
ings!" And Saul sacrificed the burnt offering
himself.
10 Just as Saul was finishing with the burnt
offering, Samuel arrived. Saul went out to
meet and welcome him, 11 but Samuel said,
"What is this you have done?"
Saul replied, "I saw my men scattering
from me, and you didn't arrive when you said
you would, and the Philistines are at Micmash
ready for battle. 12 So I said, 'The Philistines
are ready to march against us at Gilgal, and
I haven't even asked for the LORD's help!' So
I felt compelled to offer the burnt offering
myself before you came."
13 "How foolish!" Samuel exclaimed. "You
have not kept the command the LORD your
God gave you. Had you kept it, the LORD would
have established your kingdom over Israel
forever. 14 But now your kingdom must end,
for the LORD has sought out a man after his
own heart. The LORD has already appointed

13:1a As in a few Greek manuscripts; the number is missing in the Hebrew. **13:1b** Hebrew *reigned . . . and two;* the number is incomplete in the Hebrew. Compare Acts 13:21. **13:5** As in Greek and Syriac versions; Hebrew reads *30,000.*

him to be the leader of his people, because you have not kept the LORD's command."

Israel's Military Disadvantage

15 Samuel then left Gilgal and went on his way, but the rest of the troops went with Saul to meet the army. They went up from Gilgal to Gibeah in the land of Benjamin.* When Saul counted the men who were still with him, he found only 600 were left! 16 Saul and Jonathan and the troops with them were staying at Geba in the land of Benjamin. The Philistines set up their camp at Micmash. 17 Three raiding parties soon left the camp of the Philistines. One went north toward Ophrah in the land of Shual, 18 another went west to Bethhoron, and the third moved toward the border above the valley of Zeboim near the wilderness.

19 There were no blacksmiths in the land of Israel in those days. The Philistines wouldn't allow them for fear they would make swords and spears for the Hebrews. 20 So whenever the Israelites needed to sharpen their plowshares, picks, axes, or sickles,* they had to take them to a Philistine blacksmith. 21 (The charges were as follows: a quarter of an ounce of silver* for sharpening a plowshare or a pick, and an eighth of an ounce* for sharpening an ax, a sickle, or an ox goad.) 22 So on the day of the battle none of the people of Israel had a sword or spear, except for Saul and Jonathan.

23 The pass at Micmash had meanwhile been secured by a contingent of the Philistine army.

CHAPTER 14

Jonathan's Daring Plan

One day Jonathan said to his armor bearer, "Come on, let's go over to where the Philistines have their outpost." But Jonathan did not tell his father what he was doing.

2 Meanwhile, Saul and his 600 men were camped on the outskirts of Gibeah, around the pomegranate tree* at Migron. 3 Among Saul's men was Ahijah the priest, who was wearing the ephod, the priestly vest. Ahijah was the son of Ichabod's brother Ahitub, son of Phinehas, son of Eli, the priest of the LORD who had served at Shiloh.

No one realized that Jonathan had left the Israelite camp. 4 To reach the Philistine outpost, Jonathan had to go down between two rocky cliffs that were called Bozez and Seneh. 5 The cliff on the north was in front of Micmash, and the one on the south was in front of Geba. 6 "Let's go across to the outpost of those pagans," Jonathan said to his armor bearer. "Perhaps the LORD will help us, for nothing can hinder the LORD. He can win a battle whether he has many warriors or only a few!"

7 "Do what you think is best," the armor bearer replied. "I'm with you completely, whatever you decide."

8 "All right then," Jonathan told him. "We will cross over and let them see us. 9 If they say to us, 'Stay where you are or we'll kill you,' then we will stop and not go up to them. 10 But if they say, 'Come on up and fight,' then we will go up. That will be the LORD's sign that he will help us defeat them."

11 When the Philistines saw them coming, they shouted, "Look! The Hebrews are crawling out of their holes!" 12 Then the men from the outpost shouted to Jonathan, "Come on up here, and we'll teach you a lesson!"

"Come on, climb right behind me," Jonathan said to his armor bearer, "for the LORD will help us defeat them!"

13 So they climbed up using both hands and feet, and the Philistines fell before Jonathan, and his armor bearer killed those who came behind them. 14 They killed some twenty men in all, and their bodies were scattered over about half an acre.*

15 Suddenly, panic broke out in the Philistine army, both in the camp and in the field, including even the outposts and raiding parties. And just then an earthquake struck, and everyone was terrified.

Israel Defeats the Philistines

16 Saul's lookouts in Gibeah of Benjamin saw a strange sight—the vast army of Philistines began to melt away in every direction. 17 "Call the roll and find out who's missing," Saul ordered. And when they checked, they found

13:15 As in Greek version; Hebrew reads *Samuel then left Gilgal and went to Gibeah in the land of Benjamin.* **13:20** As in Greek version; Hebrew reads *or plowshares.* **13:21a** Hebrew *1 pim* [8 grams]. **13:21b** Hebrew *⅓ of a shekel* [4 grams]. **14:2** Or *around the rock of Rimmon;* compare Judg 20:45, 47; 21:13. **14:14** Hebrew *half a yoke;* a "yoke" was the amount of land plowed by a pair of yoked oxen in one day.

that Jonathan and his armor bearer were gone.

18 Then Saul shouted to Ahijah, "Bring the ephod here!" For at that time Ahijah was wearing the ephod in front of the Israelites.* 19 But while Saul was talking to the priest, the confusion in the Philistine camp grew louder and louder. So Saul said to the priest, "Never mind; let's get going!"*

20 Then Saul and all his men rushed out to the battle and found the Philistines killing each other. There was terrible confusion everywhere. 21 Even the Hebrews who had previously gone over to the Philistine army revolted and joined in with Saul, Jonathan, and the rest of the Israelites. 22 Likewise, the men of Israel who were hiding in the hill country of Ephraim joined the chase when they saw the Philistines running away. 23 So the LORD saved Israel that day, and the battle continued to rage even beyond Beth-aven.

AMAZING FACTS

Who got cursed for eating a little glob of honey? Why, no one but Jonathan—Saul's own son.

1 SAMUEL 14:24-29, 42-45

Saul's Foolish Oath

24 Now the men of Israel were pressed to exhaustion that day, because Saul had placed them under an oath, saying, "Let a curse fall on anyone who eats before evening—before I have full revenge on my enemies." So no one ate anything all day, 25 even though they had all found honeycomb on the ground in the forest. 26 They didn't dare touch the honey because they all feared the oath they had taken.

27 But Jonathan had not heard his father's command, and he dipped the end of his stick into a piece of honeycomb and ate the honey. After he had eaten it, he felt refreshed.* 28 But one of the men saw him and said, "Your father made the army take a strict oath that anyone who eats food today will be cursed. That is why everyone is weary and faint."

29 "My father has made trouble for us all!" Jonathan exclaimed. "A command like that only hurts us. See how refreshed I am now that I have eaten this little bit of honey. 30 If the men had been allowed to eat freely from the food they found among our enemies, think how many more Philistines we could have killed!"

31 They chased and killed the Philistines all day from Micmash to Aijalon, growing more and more faint. 32 That evening they rushed for the battle plunder and butchered the sheep, goats, cattle, and calves, but they ate them without draining the blood. 33 Someone reported to Saul, "Look, the men are sinning against the LORD by eating meat that still has blood in it."

"That is very wrong," Saul said. "Find a large stone and roll it over here. 34 Then go out among the troops and tell them, 'Bring the cattle, sheep, and goats here to me. Kill them here, and drain the blood before you eat them. Do not sin against the LORD by eating meat with the blood still in it.'"

So that night all the troops brought their animals and slaughtered them there. 35 Then Saul built an altar to the LORD; it was the first of the altars he built to the LORD.

36 Then Saul said, "Let's chase the Philistines all night and plunder them until sunrise. Let's destroy every last one of them."

His men replied, "We'll do whatever you think is best."

But the priest said, "Let's ask God first."

37 So Saul asked God, "Should we go after the Philistines? Will you help us defeat them?" But God made no reply that day.

38 Then Saul said to the leaders, "Something's wrong! I want all my army commanders to come here. We must find out what sin was committed today. 39 I vow by the name of the LORD who rescued Israel that the sinner will surely die, even if it is my own son Jonathan!"

14:18 As in some Greek manuscripts; Hebrew reads *"Bring the Ark of God." For at that time the Ark of God was with the Israelites.*
14:19 Hebrew *Withdraw your hand.* **14:27** Or *his eyes brightened;* similarly in 14:29.

We ruffled our bedsheets just in case Shanna's parents peeked in our room to check on us. Shanna even turned on the shower, closed the plastic curtain, and let the hot water run for a while, trying to make her parents think we were getting ready for bed. Then we opened the window and snuck out of the house! We had our excuse all planned out in case her parents busted us. We would simply make up a story about Shanna needing to talk about a problem to our coach, who happened to live down the street. The truth was that we were meeting up with some guys Shanna had flirted with earlier that night at the football game. They said they'd be waiting for us in the park around midnight.

I knew better. What I was doing wasn't really "me." I hated lying to my mom about my whereabouts whenever I spent the night at Shanna's. And I disliked deceiving Shanna's parents with our elaborate plan to sneak out.

But what was I supposed to do, bail on my friend? Tell her I really didn't want to hang out with guys I didn't know?

Looking back, that's exactly what I should have done. Shanna was a blast—even when we weren't getting into trouble, we still had fun.

I learned that our scheming came with a price. I paid it every time I lied to my parents and ignored my conscience.

King Saul learned the hard way that lying can lead to some serious consequences. Find out what happened in 1 Samuel 15:13-23 when Saul lied to Samuel.

But no one would tell him what the trouble was.

40Then Saul said, "Jonathan and I will stand over here, and all of you stand over there."

And the people responded to Saul, "Whatever you think is best."

41Then Saul prayed, "O LORD, God of Israel, please show us who is guilty and who is innocent.*" Then they cast sacred lots, and Jonathan and Saul were chosen as the guilty ones, and the people were declared innocent.

42Then Saul said, "Now cast lots again and choose between me and Jonathan." And Jonathan was shown to be the guilty one.

43"Tell me what you have done," Saul demanded of Jonathan.

"I tasted a little honey," Jonathan admitted. "It was only a little bit on the end of my stick. Does that deserve death?"

44"Yes, Jonathan," Saul said, "you must die! May God strike me and even kill me if you do not die for this."

45But the people broke in and said to Saul, "Jonathan has won this great victory for Israel. Should he die? Far from it! As surely as the LORD lives, not one hair on his head will be touched, for God helped him do a great deed today." So the people rescued Jonathan, and he was not put to death.

46Then Saul called back the army from chasing the Philistines, and the Philistines returned home.

Saul's Military Successes

47Now when Saul had secured his grasp on Israel's throne, he fought against his enemies in every direction—against Moab, Ammon, Edom, the kings of Zobah, and the Philistines. And wherever he turned, he was victorious.* 48He performed great deeds and conquered the Amalekites, saving Israel from all those who had plundered them.

49Saul's sons included Jonathan, Ishbosheth,* and Malkishua. He also had two daughters: Merab, who was older, and Michal. 50Saul's wife was Ahinoam, the daughter of Ahimaaz. The commander of Saul's army was Abner, the son of Saul's uncle Ner. 51Saul's father, Kish, and Abner's father, Ner, were both sons of Abiel.

52The Israelites fought constantly with the Philistines throughout Saul's lifetime. So whenever Saul observed a young man who was brave and strong, he drafted him into his army.

CHAPTER 15

Saul Destroys the Amalekites

One day Samuel said to Saul, "It was the LORD who told me to anoint you as king of his people, Israel. Now listen to this message from the LORD! 2This is what the LORD of Heaven's Armies has declared: I have decided to settle accounts with the nation of Amalek for opposing Israel when they came from Egypt. 3Now go and completely destroy* the entire Amalekite nation—men, women, children, babies, cattle, sheep, goats, camels, and donkeys."

4So Saul mobilized his army at Telaim. There were 200,000 soldiers from Israel and 10,000 men from Judah. 5Then Saul and his army went to a town of the Amalekites and lay in wait in the valley. 6Saul sent this warning to the Kenites: "Move away from where the Amalekites live, or you will die with them. For you showed kindness to all the people of Israel when they came up from Egypt." So the Kenites packed up and left.

7Then Saul slaughtered the Amalekites from Havilah all the way to Shur, east of Egypt. 8He captured Agag, the Amalekite king, but completely destroyed everyone else. 9Saul and his men spared Agag's life and kept the best of the sheep and goats, the cattle, the fat calves, and the lambs—everything, in fact, that appealed to them. They destroyed only what was worthless or of poor quality.

The LORD Rejects Saul

10Then the LORD said to Samuel, 11"I am sorry that I ever made Saul king, for he has not been loyal to me and has refused to obey my command." Samuel was so deeply moved when he heard this that he cried out to the LORD all night.

12Early the next morning Samuel went to find Saul. Someone told him, "Saul went to the town of Carmel to set up a monument to himself; then he went on to Gilgal."

14:41 Greek version adds *If the fault is with me or my son Jonathan, respond with Urim; but if the men of Israel are at fault, respond with Thummim.* **14:47** As in Greek version; Hebrew reads *he acted wickedly.* **14:49** Hebrew *Ishvi,* a variant name for Ishbosheth; also known as Esh-baal. **15:3** The Hebrew term used here refers to the complete consecration of things or people to the LORD, either by destroying them or by giving them as an offering; also in 15:8, 9, 15, 18, 20, 21.

[13]When Samuel finally found him, Saul greeted him cheerfully. "May the LORD bless you," he said. "I have carried out the LORD's command!"

[14]"Then what is all the bleating of sheep and goats and the lowing of cattle I hear?" Samuel demanded.

[15]"It's true that the army spared the best of the sheep, goats, and cattle," Saul admitted. "But they are going to sacrifice them to the LORD your God. We have destroyed everything else."

[16]Then Samuel said to Saul, "Stop! Listen to what the LORD told me last night!"

"What did he tell you?" Saul asked.

[17]And Samuel told him, "Although you may think little of yourself, are you not the leader of the tribes of Israel? The LORD has anointed you king of Israel. [18]And the LORD sent you on a mission and told you, 'Go and completely destroy the sinners, the Amalekites, until they are all dead.' [19]Why haven't you obeyed the LORD? Why did you rush for the plunder and do what was evil in the LORD's sight?"

[20]"But I did obey the LORD," Saul insisted. "I carried out the mission he gave me. I brought back King Agag, but I destroyed everyone else. [21]Then my troops brought in the best of the sheep, goats, cattle, and plunder to sacrifice to the LORD your God in Gilgal."

[22]But Samuel replied,

"What is more pleasing to the LORD:
your burnt offerings and sacrifices
or your obedience to his voice?
Listen! Obedience is better than sacrifice,
and submission is better than offering
the fat of rams.
[23] Rebellion is as sinful as witchcraft,
and stubbornness as bad as worshiping
idols.
So because you have rejected the
command of the LORD,
he has rejected you as king."

Saul Pleads for Forgiveness

[24]Then Saul admitted to Samuel, "Yes, I have sinned. I have disobeyed your instructions and the LORD's command, for I was afraid of the people and did what they demanded. [25]But now, please forgive my sin and come back with me so that I may worship the LORD."

[26]But Samuel replied, "I will not go back with you! Since you have rejected the LORD's command, he has rejected you as king of Israel."

[27]As Samuel turned to go, Saul tried to hold him back and tore the hem of his robe. [28]And Samuel said to him, "The LORD has torn the kingdom of Israel from you today and has given it to someone else—one who is better than you. [29]And he who is the Glory of Israel will not lie, nor will he change his mind, for he is not human that he should change his mind!"

[30]Then Saul pleaded again, "I know I have sinned. But please, at least honor me before the elders of my people and before Israel by coming back with me so that I may worship the LORD your God." [31]So Samuel finally agreed and went back with him, and Saul worshiped the LORD.

Samuel Executes King Agag

[32]Then Samuel said, "Bring King Agag to me." Agag arrived full of hope, for he thought, "Surely the worst is over, and I have been spared!"* [33]But Samuel said, "As your sword has killed the sons of many mothers, now your mother will be childless." And Samuel cut Agag to pieces before the LORD at Gilgal.

[34]Then Samuel went home to Ramah, and Saul returned to his house at Gibeah of Saul. [35]Samuel never went to meet with Saul again, but he mourned constantly for him. And the LORD was sorry he had ever made Saul king of Israel.

CHAPTER 16

Samuel Anoints David as King

Now the LORD said to Samuel, "You have mourned long enough for Saul. I have rejected him as king of Israel, so fill your flask with olive oil and go to Bethlehem. Find a man named Jesse who lives there, for I have selected one of his sons to be my king."

[2]But Samuel asked, "How can I do that? If Saul hears about it, he will kill me."

"Take a heifer with you," the LORD replied, "and say that you have come to make a sacrifice to the LORD. [3]Invite Jesse to the sacrifice, and I will show you which of his sons to anoint for me."

15:32 Dead Sea Scrolls and Greek version read *Agag arrived hesitantly, for he thought, "Surely this is the bitterness of death."*

[4]So Samuel did as the LORD instructed. When he arrived at Bethlehem, the elders of the town came trembling to meet him. "What's wrong?" they asked. "Do you come in peace?"

[5]"Yes," Samuel replied. "I have come to sacrifice to the LORD. Purify yourselves and come with me to the sacrifice." Then Samuel performed the purification rite for Jesse and his sons and invited them to the sacrifice, too.

[6]When they arrived, Samuel took one look at Eliab and thought, "Surely this is the LORD's anointed!"

[7]But the LORD said to Samuel, "Don't judge by his appearance or height, for I have rejected him. The LORD doesn't see things the way you see them. People judge by outward appearance, but the LORD looks at the heart."

[8]Then Jesse told his son Abinadab to step forward and walk in front of Samuel. But Samuel said, "This is not the one the LORD has chosen." [9]Next Jesse summoned Shimea,* but Samuel said, "Neither is this the one the LORD has chosen." [10]In the same way all seven of Jesse's sons were presented to Samuel. But Samuel said to Jesse, "The LORD has not chosen any of these." [11]Then Samuel asked, "Are these all the sons you have?"

"There is still the youngest," Jesse replied. "But he's out in the fields watching the sheep and goats."

"Send for him at once," Samuel said. "We will not sit down to eat until he arrives."

[12]So Jesse sent for him. He was dark and handsome, with beautiful eyes.

And the LORD said, "This is the one; anoint him."

[13]So as David stood there among his brothers, Samuel took the flask of olive oil he had brought and anointed David with the oil. And the Spirit of the LORD came powerfully upon David from that day on. Then Samuel returned to Ramah.

I'm tired of other kids making fun of the way I look.

* **People judge by outward appearance, but the LORD looks at the heart.** 1 SAMUEL 16:7

David Serves in Saul's Court

[14]Now the Spirit of the LORD had left Saul, and the LORD sent a tormenting spirit* that filled him with depression and fear.

[15]Some of Saul's servants said to him, "A tormenting spirit from God is troubling you. [16]Let us find a good musician to play the harp whenever the tormenting spirit troubles you. He will play soothing music, and you will soon be well again."

[17]"All right," Saul said. "Find me someone who plays well, and bring him here."

[18]One of the servants said to Saul, "One of Jesse's sons from Bethlehem is a talented harp player. Not only that—he is a brave warrior, a man of war, and has good judgment. He is also a fine-looking young man, and the LORD is with him."

[19]So Saul sent messengers to Jesse to say, "Send me your son David, the shepherd." [20]Jesse responded by sending David to Saul, along with a young goat, a donkey loaded with bread, and a wineskin full of wine.

[21]So David went to Saul and began serving him. Saul loved David very much, and David became his armor bearer.

[22]Then Saul sent word to Jesse asking, "Please let David remain in my service, for I am very pleased with him."

[23]And whenever the tormenting spirit from God troubled Saul, David would play the harp. Then Saul would feel better, and the tormenting spirit would go away.

CHAPTER 17

Goliath Challenges the Israelites

The Philistines now mustered their army for battle and camped between Socoh in Judah and Azekah at Ephes-dammim. [2]Saul countered by gathering his Israelite troops near the valley of Elah. [3]So the Philistines and Israelites faced each other on opposite hills, with the valley between them.

[4]Then Goliath, a Philistine champion from

16:9 Hebrew *Shammah*, a variant spelling of Shimea; compare 1 Chr 2:13; 20:7. **16:14** Or *an evil spirit;* also in 16:15, 16, 23.

LOOKING GOOD

Three candidates were running for class president. Denise was very smart, but plain looking, and her clothes were out of style. Vladimir was from another country and hadn't lived in the neighborhood very long, but he seemed to be nice; he was friendly, and he had good leadership skills. Chad was very good-looking, well dressed, and athletic. Most kids thought Chad would win easily. What do you think? How would you decide who to vote for? Read 1 Samuel 16:7 to see what the qualifications were for the king of Israel.

Gath, came out of the Philistine ranks to face the forces of Israel. He was over nine feet* tall! [5]He wore a bronze helmet, and his bronze coat of mail weighed 125 pounds.* [6]He also wore bronze leg armor, and he carried a bronze javelin on his shoulder. [7]The shaft of his spear was as heavy and thick as a weaver's beam, tipped with an iron spearhead that weighed 15 pounds.* His armor bearer walked ahead of him carrying a shield.

[8]Goliath stood and shouted a taunt across to the Israelites. "Why are you all coming out to fight?" he called. "I am the Philistine champion, but you are only the servants of Saul. Choose one man to come down here and fight me! [9]If he kills me, then we will be your slaves. But if I kill him, you will be our slaves! [10]I defy the armies of Israel today! Send me a man who will fight me!" [11]When Saul and the Israelites heard this, they were terrified and deeply shaken.

Jesse Sends David to Saul's Camp

[12]Now David was the son of a man named Jesse, an Ephrathite from Bethlehem in the land of Judah. Jesse was an old man at that time, and he had eight sons. [13]Jesse's three oldest sons—Eliab, Abinadab, and Shimea*—had already joined Saul's army to fight the Philistines. [14]David was the youngest son. David's three oldest brothers stayed with Saul's army, [15]but David went back and forth so he could help his father with the sheep in Bethlehem.

[16]For forty days, every morning and evening, the Philistine champion strutted in front of the Israelite army.

[17]One day Jesse said to David, "Take this basket* of roasted grain and these ten loaves of bread, and carry them quickly to your brothers. [18]And give these ten cuts of cheese to their captain. See how your brothers are getting along, and bring back a report on how they are doing.*" [19]David's brothers were with Saul and the Israelite army at the valley of Elah, fighting against the Philistines.

[20]So David left the sheep with another shepherd and set out early the next morning with the gifts, as Jesse had directed him. He arrived at the camp just as the Israelite army was leaving for the battlefield with shouts and battle cries. [21]Soon the Israelite and Philistine forces stood facing each other, army against army. [22]David left his things with the keeper of supplies and hurried out to the ranks to greet his brothers. [23]As he was talking with them, Goliath, the Philistine champion from

17:4 Hebrew *6 cubits and 1 span* [which totals about 9.75 feet or 3 meters]; Dead Sea Scrolls and Greek version read *4 cubits and 1 span* [which totals about 6.75 feet or 2 meters]. **17:5** Hebrew *5,000 shekels* [57 kilograms]. **17:7** Hebrew *600 shekels* [6.8 kilograms]. **17:13** Hebrew *Shammah*, a variant spelling of Shimea; compare 1 Chr 2:13; 20:7. **17:17** Hebrew *ephah* [20 quarts or 22 liters]. **17:18** Hebrew *and take their pledge*.

Gath, came out from the Philistine ranks. Then David heard him shout his usual taunt to the army of Israel.

24As soon as the Israelite army saw him, they began to run away in fright. 25"Have you seen the giant?" the men asked. "He comes out each day to defy Israel. The king has offered a huge reward to anyone who kills him. He will give that man one of his daughters for a wife, and the man's entire family will be exempted from paying taxes!"

26David asked the soldiers standing nearby, "What will a man get for killing this Philistine and ending his defiance of Israel? Who is this pagan Philistine anyway, that he is allowed to defy the armies of the living God?"

27And these men gave David the same reply. They said, "Yes, that is the reward for killing him."

28But when David's oldest brother, Eliab, heard David talking to the men, he was angry. "What are you doing around here anyway?" he demanded. "What about those few sheep you're supposed to be taking care of? I know about your pride and deceit. You just want to see the battle!"

29"What have I done now?" David replied. "I was only asking a question!" 30He walked over to some others and asked them the same thing and received the same answer. 31Then David's question was reported to King Saul, and the king sent for him.

David Kills Goliath

32"Don't worry about this Philistine," David told Saul. "I'll go fight him!"

33"Don't be ridiculous!" Saul replied. "There's no way you can fight this Philistine and possibly win! You're only a boy, and he's been a man of war since his youth."

34But David persisted. "I have been taking care of my father's sheep and goats," he said. "When a lion or a bear comes to steal a lamb from the flock, 35I go after it with a club and rescue the lamb from its mouth. If the animal turns on me, I catch it by the jaw and club it to death. 36I have done this to both lions and bears, and I'll do it to this pagan Philistine, too, for he has defied the armies of the living God! 37The LORD who rescued me from the claws of the lion and the bear will rescue me from this Philistine!"

Saul finally consented. "All right, go ahead," he said. "And may the LORD be with you!"

38Then Saul gave David his own armor—a bronze helmet and a coat of mail. 39David put it on, strapped the sword over it, and took a step or two to see what it was like, for he had never worn such things before.

"I can't go in these," he protested to Saul. "I'm not used to them." So David took them off again. 40He picked up five smooth stones from a stream and put them into his shepherd's bag. Then, armed only with his shepherd's staff and sling, he started across the valley to fight the Philistine.

41Goliath walked out toward David with his shield bearer ahead of him, 42sneering in contempt at this ruddy-faced boy. 43"Am I a dog," he roared at David, "that you come at me with a stick?" And he cursed David by the names of his gods. 44"Come over here, and I'll give your flesh to the birds and wild animals!" Goliath yelled.

45David replied to the Philistine, "You come to me with sword, spear, and javelin, but I come to you in the name of the LORD of Heaven's Armies—the God of the armies of Israel, whom you have defied. 46Today the LORD will conquer you, and I will kill you and cut off your head. And then I will give the dead bodies of your men to the birds and wild animals, and the whole world will know that there is a God in Israel! 47And everyone assembled here will know that the LORD rescues his people, but not with sword and spear. This is the LORD's battle, and he will give you to us!"

48As Goliath moved closer to attack, David quickly ran out to meet him. 49Reaching into his shepherd's bag and taking out a stone, he hurled it with his sling and hit the Philistine in the forehead. The stone sank in, and Goliath stumbled and fell face down on the ground.

50So David triumphed over the Philistine with only a sling and a stone, for he had no sword. 51Then David ran over and pulled Goliath's sword from its sheath. David used it to kill him and cut off his head.

Israel Routs the Philistines

When the Philistines saw that their champion was dead, they turned and ran. 52Then the men of Israel and Judah gave a great shout of triumph and rushed after the Philistines, chasing them as far as Gath* and the gates of Ekron. The bodies of the dead and wounded Philistines were strewn all along the road from Shaaraim, as far as Gath and Ekron. [53]Then the Israelite army returned and plundered the deserted Philistine camp. [54](David took the Philistine's head to Jerusalem, but he stored the man's armor in his own tent.)

[55]As Saul watched David go out to fight the Philistine, he asked Abner, the commander of his army, "Abner, whose son is this young man?"

"I really don't know," Abner declared.

[56]"Well, find out who he is!" the king told him.

[57]As soon as David returned from killing Goliath, Abner brought him to Saul with the Philistine's head still in his hand. [58]"Tell me about your father, young man," Saul said.

And David replied, "His name is Jesse, and we live in Bethlehem."

CHAPTER 18

Saul Becomes Jealous of David

After David had finished talking with Saul, he met Jonathan, the king's son. There was an immediate bond between them, for Jonathan loved David. [2]From that day on Saul kept David with him and wouldn't let him return home. [3]And Jonathan made a solemn pact with David, because he loved him as he loved himself. [4]Jonathan sealed the pact by taking off his robe and giving it to David, together with his tunic, sword, bow, and belt.

[5]Whatever Saul asked David to do, David did it successfully. So Saul made him a commander over the men of war, an appointment that was welcomed by the people and Saul's officers alike.

[6]When the victorious Israelite army was returning home after David had killed the Philistine, women from all the towns of Israel came out to meet King Saul. They sang and danced for joy with tambourines and cymbals.* [7]This was their song:

"Saul has killed his thousands,
and David his ten thousands!"

[8]This made Saul very angry. "What's this?" he said. "They credit David with ten thousands and me with only thousands. Next they'll be making him their king!" [9]So from that time on Saul kept a jealous eye on David.

[10]The very next day a tormenting spirit* from God overwhelmed Saul, and he began to rave in his house like a madman. David was playing the harp, as he did each day. But Saul had a spear in his hand, [11]and he suddenly hurled it at David, intending to pin him to the wall. But David escaped him twice.

[12]Saul was then afraid of David, for the LORD was with David and had turned away from Saul. [13]Finally, Saul sent him away and appointed him commander over 1,000 men, and David faithfully led his troops into battle.

[14]David continued to succeed in everything he did, for the LORD was with him. [15]When Saul recognized this, he became even more afraid of him. [16]But all Israel and Judah loved David because he was so successful at leading his troops into battle.

David Marries Saul's Daughter

[17]One day Saul said to David, "I am ready to give you my older daughter, Merab, as your wife. But first you must prove yourself to be a real warrior by fighting the LORD's battles." For Saul thought, "I'll send him out against the Philistines and let them kill him rather than doing it myself."

[18]"Who am I, and what is my family in Israel that I should be the king's son-in-law?" David exclaimed. "My father's family is nothing!" [19]So* when the time came for Saul to give his daughter Merab in marriage to David, he gave her instead to Adriel, a man from Meholah.

[20]In the meantime, Saul's daughter Michal had fallen in love with David, and Saul was delighted when he heard about it. [21]"Here's another chance to see him killed by the Philistines!" Saul said to himself. But to David he said, "Today you have a second chance to become my son-in-law!"

[22]Then Saul told his men to say to David, "The king really likes you, and so do we. Why don't you accept the king's offer and become his son-in-law?"

[23]When Saul's men said these things to David, he replied, "How can a poor man from a humble family afford the bride price for the daughter of a king?"

17:52 As in some Greek manuscripts; Hebrew reads *a valley*. **18:6** The type of instrument represented by the word *cymbals* is uncertain. **18:10** Or *an evil spirit*. **18:19** Or *But*.

[24]When Saul's men reported this back to the king, [25]he told them, "Tell David that all I want for the bride price is 100 Philistine foreskins! Vengeance on my enemies is all I really want." But what Saul had in mind was that David would be killed in the fight.

[26]David was delighted to accept the offer. Before the time limit expired, [27]he and his men went out and killed 200 Philistines. Then David fulfilled the king's requirement by presenting all their foreskins to him. So Saul gave his daughter Michal to David to be his wife.

[28]When Saul realized that the LORD was with David and how much his daughter Michal loved him, [29]Saul became even more afraid of him, and he remained David's enemy for the rest of his life.

[30]Every time the commanders of the Philistines attacked, David was more successful against them than all the rest of Saul's officers. So David's name became very famous.

CHAPTER 19

Saul Tries to Kill David

Saul now urged his servants and his son Jonathan to assassinate David. But Jonathan, because of his strong affection for David, [2]told him what his father was planning. "Tomorrow morning," he warned him, "you must find a hiding place out in the fields. [3]I'll ask my father to go out there with me, and I'll talk to him about you. Then I'll tell you everything I can find out."

[4]The next morning Jonathan spoke with his father about David, saying many good things about him. "The king must not sin against his servant David," Jonathan said. "He's never done anything to harm you. He has always helped you in any way he could. [5]Have you forgotten about the time he risked his life to kill the Philistine giant and how the LORD brought a great victory to all Israel as a result? You were certainly happy about it then. Why should you murder an innocent man like David? There is no reason for it at all!"

[6]So Saul listened to Jonathan and vowed, "As surely as the LORD lives, David will not be killed."

[7]Afterward Jonathan called David and told him what had happened. Then he brought David to Saul, and David served in the court as before.

[8]War broke out again after that, and David led his troops against the Philistines. He attacked them with such fury that they all ran away.

[9]But one day when Saul was sitting at

IS IT OK?

IS IT OK TO DISOBEY MY PARENTS . . . EVER?

Imagine being in a situation like this: Let's say your dad wants to kill your best friend, and he tells you to help him! (Couldn't happen, you say?) But it did—to Jonathan. His dad (King Saul) was trying to kill Jonathan's best friend (David). So what did Jonathan do? He disobeyed his dad, the king, and protected David. In this case, it was the right thing to do. (Check out 1 Samuel 19:1-3.) The *only* time it's ever OK to disobey your parents is if they ask you to do something that's against God's rules (like worshiping Buddha, lying to someone, or cheating on your math test). Remember, though, what God expects the other 99.9 percent of the time—*obedience.*

By the age of twelve, I had been winning talent competitions and playing for school programs for several years. So becoming the youngest musician to work with our church's teen choir seemed natural.

Since the choir often accompanied our pastor when he spoke at other churches, I knew that I would be around a lot of other musicians. I would have plenty of opportunities to show those older guys at the other churches how great I was.

Our first program was at a church on the other side of town. Several choirs had been invited to participate. The choirs were great—and so were their musicians. Much to my surprise, several of them came up to me after the program and said they enjoyed my playing.

I will never forget one guy in particular. He was more talented than I was, and not any older. When I complimented his musical ability, he downplayed it. He said, "I'm just happy God has blessed me in this way." Can you believe that? Rather than agree that he was a great musician (which is what I would have done), this guy gave God the credit! I had never thought of my talent as being a blessing from God . . . until then. The other guy's response really made me think about how I viewed myself—and others.

Now, when other musicians say to me, "Hey, I like what you did," I don't let their comments feed my ego. Instead, they are just one more reason to say thank you to the One who helps me play the way I do.

Take a look at 1 Samuel 18:18, 23 to see how David reacted to some good news. You can also read Philippians 2:1-9 and James 4:10 to see what else the Bible says about humility.

home, with spear in hand, the tormenting spirit* from the LORD suddenly came upon him again. As David played his harp, [10]Saul hurled his spear at David. But David dodged out of the way, and leaving the spear stuck in the wall, he fled and escaped into the night.

Michal Saves David's Life

[11]Then Saul sent troops to watch David's house. They were told to kill David when he came out the next morning. But Michal, David's wife, warned him, "If you don't escape tonight, you will be dead by morning." [12]So she helped him climb out through a window, and he fled and escaped. [13]Then she took an idol* and put it in his bed, covered it with blankets, and put a cushion of goat's hair at its head.

[14]When the troops came to arrest David, she told them he was sick and couldn't get out of bed.

[15]But Saul sent the troops back to get David. He ordered, "Bring him to me in his bed so I can kill him!" [16]But when they came to carry David out, they discovered that it was only an idol in the bed with a cushion of goat's hair at its head.

[17]"Why have you betrayed me like this and let my enemy escape?" Saul demanded of Michal.

"I had to," Michal replied. "He threatened to kill me if I didn't help him."

[18]So David escaped and went to Ramah to see Samuel, and he told him all that Saul had done to him. Then Samuel took David with him to live at Naioth. [19]When the report reached Saul that David was at Naioth in Ramah, [20]he sent troops to capture him. But when they arrived and saw Samuel leading a group of prophets who were prophesying, the Spirit of God came upon Saul's men, and they also began to prophesy. [21]When Saul heard what had happened, he sent other troops, but they, too, prophesied! The same thing happened a third time. [22]Finally, Saul himself went to Ramah and arrived at the great well in Secu. "Where are Samuel and David?" he demanded.

"They are at Naioth in Ramah," someone told him.

[23]But on the way to Naioth in Ramah the Spirit of God came even upon Saul, and he, too, began to prophesy all the way to Naioth! [24]He tore off his clothes and lay naked on the ground all day and all night, prophesying in the presence of Samuel. The people who were watching exclaimed, "What? Is even Saul a prophet?"

CHAPTER 20

Jonathan Helps David

David now fled from Naioth in Ramah and found Jonathan. "What have I done?" he exclaimed. "What is my crime? How have I offended your father that he is so determined to kill me?"

[2]"That's not true!" Jonathan protested. "You're not going to die. He always tells me everything he's going to do, even the little things. I know my father wouldn't hide something like this from me. It just isn't so!"

[3]Then David took an oath before Jonathan and said, "Your father knows perfectly well about our friendship, so he has said to himself, 'I won't tell Jonathan—why should I hurt him?' But I swear to you that I am only a step away from death! I swear it by the LORD and by your own soul!"

[4]"Tell me what I can do to help you," Jonathan exclaimed.

[5]David replied, "Tomorrow we celebrate the new moon festival. I've always eaten with the king on this occasion, but tomorrow I'll hide in the field and stay there until the evening of the third day. [6]If your father asks where I am, tell him I asked permission to go home to Bethlehem for an annual family sacrifice. [7]If he says, 'Fine!' you will know all is well. But if he is angry and loses his temper, you will know he is determined to kill me. [8]Show me this loyalty as my sworn friend—for we made a solemn pact before the LORD—or kill me yourself if I have sinned against your father. But please don't betray me to him!"

[9]"Never!" Jonathan exclaimed. "You know that if I had the slightest notion my father was planning to kill you, I would tell you at once."

[10]Then David asked, "How will I know whether or not your father is angry?"

[11]"Come out to the field with me," Jonathan replied. And they went out there together. [12]Then Jonathan told David, "I promise by the

19:9 Or *evil spirit*. **19:13** Hebrew *teraphim;* also in 19:16.

Jonathan

I wasn't supposed to be David's friend. He was poor; my dad was king. I didn't care, though. I liked David. He was strong, honest, and brave. My father was jealous of David for killing Goliath and getting all the attention. Plus, he knew that Samuel had anointed David as the next king over me. One night my father was outraged to find my friend missing from dinner. When he realized I was protecting David, my father threw a spear and tried to kill *me*. I knew I had to warn David to run away and never come back. Saying good-bye to my best friend was one of the hardest things I ever did.

Read about Jonathan's life in 1 Samuel 13–31.

LORD, the God of Israel, that by this time tomorrow, or the next day at the latest, I will talk to my father and let you know at once how he feels about you. If he speaks favorably about you, I will let you know. [13]But if he is angry and wants you killed, may the LORD strike me and even kill me if I don't warn you so you can escape and live. May the LORD be with you as he used to be with my father. [14]And may you treat me with the faithful love of the LORD as long as I live. But if I die, [15]treat my family with this faithful love, even when the LORD destroys all your enemies from the face of the earth."

[16]So Jonathan made a solemn pact with David,* saying, "May the LORD destroy all your enemies!" [17]And Jonathan made David reaffirm his vow of friendship again, for Jonathan loved David as he loved himself.

[18]Then Jonathan said, "Tomorrow we celebrate the new moon festival. You will be missed when your place at the table is empty. [19]The day after tomorrow, toward evening, go to the place where you hid before, and wait there by the stone pile.* [20]I will come out and shoot three arrows to the side of the stone pile as though I were shooting at a target. [21]Then I will send a boy to bring the arrows back. If you hear me tell him, 'They're on this side,' then you will know, as surely as the LORD lives, that all is well, and there is no trouble. [22]But if I tell him, 'Go farther—the arrows are still ahead of you,' then it will mean that you must leave immediately, for the LORD is sending you away. [23]And may the LORD make us keep our promises to each other, for he has witnessed them."

[24]So David hid himself in the field, and when the new moon festival began, the king sat down to eat. [25]He sat at his usual place against the wall, with Jonathan sitting opposite him* and Abner beside him. But David's place was empty. [26]Saul didn't say anything about it that day, for he said to himself, "Something must have made David ceremonially unclean." [27]But when David's place was empty again the next day, Saul asked Jonathan, "Why hasn't the son of Jesse been here for the meal either yesterday or today?"

[28]Jonathan replied, "David earnestly asked me if he could go to Bethlehem. [29]He said, 'Please let me go, for we are having a family sacrifice. My brother demanded that I be there. So please let me get away to see my brothers.' That's why he isn't here at the king's table."

[30]Saul boiled with rage at Jonathan. "You stupid son of a whore!"* he swore at him. "Do

20:16 Hebrew *with the house of David.* **20:19** Hebrew *the stone Ezel.* The meaning of the Hebrew is uncertain. **20:25** As in Greek version; Hebrew reads *with Jonathan standing.* **20:30** Hebrew *You son of a perverse and rebellious woman.*

you think I don't know that you want him to be king in your place, shaming yourself and your mother? 31As long as that son of Jesse is alive, you'll never be king. Now go and get him so I can kill him!"

32"But why should he be put to death?" Jonathan asked his father. "What has he done?" 33Then Saul hurled his spear at Jonathan, intending to kill him. So at last Jonathan realized that his father was really determined to kill David.

34Jonathan left the table in fierce anger and refused to eat on that second day of the festival, for he was crushed by his father's shameful behavior toward David.

35The next morning, as agreed, Jonathan went out into the field and took a young boy with him to gather his arrows. 36"Start running," he told the boy, "so you can find the arrows as I shoot them." So the boy ran, and Jonathan shot an arrow beyond him. 37When the boy had almost reached the arrow, Jonathan shouted, "The arrow is still ahead of you. 38Hurry, hurry, don't wait." So the boy quickly gathered up the arrows and ran back to his master. 39He, of course, suspected nothing; only Jonathan and David understood the signal. 40Then Jonathan gave his bow and arrows to the boy and told him to take them back to town.

41As soon as the boy was gone, David came out from where he had been hiding near the stone pile.* Then David bowed three times to Jonathan with his face to the ground. Both of them were in tears as they embraced each other and said good-bye, especially David.

CHAPTER 21

David Runs from Saul

1*David went to the town of Nob to see Ahimelech the priest. Ahimelech trembled when he saw him. "Why are you alone?" he asked. "Why is no one with you?"

2"The king has sent me on a private matter," David said. "He told me not to tell anyone why I am here. I have told my men where to meet me later. 3Now, what is there to eat? Give me five loaves of bread or anything else you have."

4"We don't have any regular bread," the priest replied. "But there is the holy bread, which you can have if your young men have not slept with any women recently."

5"Don't worry," David replied. "I never allow my men to be with women when they are on a campaign. And since they stay clean even on ordinary trips, how much more on this one!"

6Since there was no other food available, the priest gave him the holy bread—the Bread of the Presence that was placed before the LORD in the Tabernacle. It had just been replaced that day with fresh bread.

7Now Doeg the Edomite, Saul's chief herdsman, was there that day, having been detained before the LORD.*

8David asked Ahimelech, "Do you have a spear or sword? The king's business was so urgent that I didn't even have time to grab a weapon!"

9"I only have the sword of Goliath the Philistine, whom you killed in the valley of Elah," the priest replied. "It is wrapped in a cloth behind the ephod. Take that if you want it, for there is nothing else here."

How can I be a good friend?

Jonathan said to David, "Go in peace, for we have sworn loyalty to each other in the LORD'S name." 1 SAMUEL 20:42

42At last Jonathan said to David, "Go in peace, for we have sworn loyalty to each other in the LORD's name. The LORD is the witness of a bond between us and our children forever." Then David left, and Jonathan returned to the town.*

"There is nothing like it!" David replied. "Give it to me!"

10So David escaped from Saul and went to King Achish of Gath. 11But the officers of Achish were unhappy about his being there. "Isn't this David, the king of the land?" they

20:41 As in Greek version; Hebrew reads *near the south edge*. **20:42** This sentence is numbered 21:1 in Hebrew text. **21:1** Verses 21:1-15 are numbered 21:2-16 in Hebrew text. **21:7** The meaning of the Hebrew is uncertain.

asked. "Isn't he the one the people honor with dances, singing,

'Saul has killed his thousands,
and David his ten thousands'?"

[12]David heard these comments and was very afraid of what King Achish of Gath might do to him. [13]So he pretended to be insane, scratching on doors and drooling down his beard.

[14]Finally, King Achish said to his men, "Must you bring me a madman? [15]We already have enough of them around here! Why should I let someone like this be my guest?"

CHAPTER 22

David at the Cave of Adullam

So David left Gath and escaped to the cave of Adullam. Soon his brothers and all his other relatives joined him there. [2]Then others began coming—men who were in trouble or in debt or who were just discontented—until David was the captain of about 400 men.

[3]Later David went to Mizpeh in Moab, where he asked the king, "Please allow my father and mother to live here with you until I know what God is going to do for me." [4]So David's parents stayed in Moab with the king during the entire time David was living in his stronghold.

[5]One day the prophet Gad told David, "Leave the stronghold and return to the land of Judah." So David went to the forest of Hereth.

[6]The news of his arrival in Judah soon reached Saul. At the time, the king was sitting beneath the tamarisk tree on the hill at Gibeah, holding his spear and surrounded by his officers.

[7]"Listen here, you men of Benjamin!" Saul shouted to his officers when he heard the news. "Has that son of Jesse promised every one of you fields and vineyards? Has he promised to make you all generals and captains in his army?* [8]Is that why you have conspired against me? For not one of you told me when my own son made a solemn pact with the son of Jesse. You're not even sorry for me. Think of it! My own son—encouraging him to kill me, as he is trying to do this very day!"

[9]Then Doeg the Edomite, who was standing there with Saul's men, spoke up. "When I was at Nob," he said, "I saw the son of Jesse talking to the priest, Ahimelech son of Ahitub. [10]Ahimelech consulted the LORD for him. Then he gave him food and the sword of Goliath the Philistine."

The Slaughter of the Priests

[11]King Saul immediately sent for Ahimelech and all his family, who served as priests at Nob. [12]When they arrived, Saul shouted at him, "Listen to me, you son of Ahitub!"

"What is it, my king?" Ahimelech asked.

[13]"Why have you and the son of Jesse conspired against me?" Saul demanded. "Why did you give him food and a sword? Why have you consulted God for him? Why have you encouraged him to kill me, as he is trying to do this very day?"

[14]"But sir," Ahimelech replied, "is anyone among all your servants as faithful as David, your son-in-law? Why, he is the captain of your bodyguard and a highly honored member of your household! [15]This was certainly not the first time I had consulted God for him! May the king not accuse me and my family in this matter, for I knew nothing at all of any plot against you."

[16]"You will surely die, Ahimelech, along with your entire family!" the king shouted. [17]And he ordered his bodyguards, "Kill these priests of the LORD, for they are allies and conspirators with David! They knew he was running away from me, but they didn't tell me!" But Saul's men refused to kill the LORD's priests.

[18]Then the king said to Doeg, "You do it." So Doeg the Edomite turned on them and killed them that day, eighty-five priests in all, still wearing their priestly garments. [19]Then he went to Nob, the town of the priests, and killed the priests' families—men and women, children and babies—and all the cattle, donkeys, sheep, and goats.

[20]Only Abiathar, one of the sons of Ahimelech, escaped and fled to David. [21]When he told David that Saul had killed the priests of the LORD, [22]David exclaimed, "I knew it! When I saw Doeg the Edomite there that day, I knew he was sure to tell Saul. Now I have caused the death of all your father's family. [23]Stay here with me, and don't be afraid. I will protect you with my own life, for the same person wants to kill us both."

22:7 Hebrew *commanders of thousands and commanders of hundreds?*

CHAPTER 23

David Protects the Town of Keilah

One day news came to David that the Philistines were at Keilah stealing grain from the threshing floors. [2]David asked the LORD, "Should I go and attack them?"

"Yes, go and save Keilah," the LORD told him.

[3]But David's men said, "We're afraid even here in Judah. We certainly don't want to go to Keilah to fight the whole Philistine army!"

[4]So David asked the LORD again, and again the LORD replied, "Go down to Keilah, for I will help you conquer the Philistines."

[5]So David and his men went to Keilah. They slaughtered the Philistines and took all their livestock and rescued the people of Keilah. [6]Now when Abiathar son of Ahimelech fled to David at Keilah, he brought the ephod with him.

[7]Saul soon learned that David was at Keilah. "Good!" he exclaimed. "We've got him now! God has handed him over to me, for he has trapped himself in a walled town!" [8]So Saul mobilized his entire army to march to Keilah and besiege David and his men.

[9]But David learned of Saul's plan and told Abiathar the priest to bring the ephod and ask the LORD what he should do. [10]Then David prayed, "O LORD, God of Israel, I have heard that Saul is planning to come and destroy Keilah because I am here. [11]Will the leaders of Keilah betray me to him?* And will Saul actually come as I have heard? O LORD, God of Israel, please tell me."

And the LORD said, "He will come."

[12]Again David asked, "Will the leaders of Keilah betray me and my men to Saul?"

And the LORD replied, "Yes, they will betray you."

David Hides in the Wilderness

[13]So David and his men—about 600 of them now—left Keilah and began roaming the countryside. Word soon reached Saul that David had escaped, so he didn't go to Keilah after all. [14]David now stayed in the strongholds of the wilderness and in the hill country of Ziph. Saul hunted him day after day, but God didn't let Saul find him.

[15]One day near Horesh, David received the news that Saul was on the way to Ziph to search for him and kill him. [16]Jonathan went to find David and encouraged him to stay strong in his faith in God. [17]"Don't be afraid," Jonathan reassured him. "My father will never find you! You are going to be the king of Israel, and I will be next to you, as my father, Saul, is well

23:11 Some manuscripts lack the first sentence of 23:11.

MOVING UP

Nicolas and Andrea were in the same ice-skating class. Recently, the class had been invited to try out for a training class that prepared skaters to compete in the Junior Olympics. "Wow! What an honor to be asked!" Nicolas exclaimed. "I hope we both make it." After a long week, the list of names was posted. Andrea's name was right at the top, but Nicolas's name was nowhere on the list. Andrea made it, but Nicolas did not! How do you think Nicolas should react? Read 1 Samuel 23:16-18 to see how Jonathan handled being left out of the running.

aware." [18]So the two of them renewed their solemn pact before the LORD. Then Jonathan returned home, while David stayed at Horesh.

[19]But now the men of Ziph went to Saul in Gibeah and betrayed David to him. "We know where David is hiding," they said. "He is in the strongholds of Horesh on the hill of Hakilah, which is in the southern part of Jeshimon. [20]Come down whenever you're ready, O king, and we will catch him and hand him over to you!"

[21]"The LORD bless you," Saul said. "At last someone is concerned about me! [22]Go and check again to be sure of where he is staying and who has seen him there, for I know that he is very crafty. [23]Discover his hiding places, and come back when you are sure. Then I'll go with you. And if he is in the area at all, I'll track him down, even if I have to search every hiding place in Judah!" [24]So the men of Ziph returned home ahead of Saul.

Meanwhile, David and his men had moved into the wilderness of Maon in the Arabah Valley south of Jeshimon. [25]When David heard that Saul and his men were searching for him, he went even farther into the wilderness to the great rock, and he remained there in the wilderness of Maon. But Saul kept after him in the wilderness.

[26]Saul and David were now on opposite sides of a mountain. Just as Saul and his men began to close in on David and his men, [27]an urgent message reached Saul that the Philistines were raiding Israel again. [28]So Saul quit chasing David and returned to fight the Philistines. Ever since that time, the place where David was camped has been called the Rock of Escape.* [29]*David then went to live in the strongholds of En-gedi.

CHAPTER 24

David Spares Saul's Life

[1]*After Saul returned from fighting the Philistines, he was told that David had gone into the wilderness of En-gedi. [2]So Saul chose 3,000 elite troops from all Israel and went to search for David and his men near the rocks of the wild goats.

[3]At the place where the road passes some sheepfolds, Saul went into a cave to relieve himself. But as it happened, David and his men were hiding farther back in that very cave!

[4]"Now's your opportunity!" David's men whispered to him. "Today the LORD is telling you, 'I will certainly put your enemy into your power, to do with as you wish.' " So David crept forward and cut off a piece of the hem of Saul's robe.

[5]But then David's conscience began bothering him because he had cut Saul's robe. [6]"The LORD knows I shouldn't have done that to my lord the king," he said to his men. "The LORD forbid that I should do this to my lord the king and attack the LORD's anointed one, for the LORD himself has chosen him." [7]So David restrained his men and did not let them kill Saul.

After Saul had left the cave and gone on his way, [8]David came out and shouted after him, "My lord the king!" And when Saul looked around, David bowed low before him.

[9]Then he shouted to Saul, "Why do you listen to the people who say I am trying to harm you? [10]This very day you can see with your own eyes it isn't true. For the LORD placed you at my mercy back there in the cave. Some of my men told me to kill you, but I spared you. For I said, 'I will never harm the king—he is the LORD's anointed one.' [11]Look, my father, at what I have in my hand. It is a piece of the hem of your robe! I cut it off, but I didn't kill you. This proves that I am not trying to harm you and that I have not sinned against you, even though you have been hunting for me to kill me.

[12]"May the LORD judge between us. Perhaps the LORD will punish you for what you are trying to do to me, but I will never harm you. [13]As that old proverb says, 'From evil people come evil deeds.' So you can be sure I will never harm you. [14]Who is the king of Israel trying to catch anyway? Should he spend his time chasing one who is as worthless as a dead dog or a single flea? [15]May the LORD therefore judge which of us is right and punish the guilty one. He is my advocate, and he will rescue me from your power!"

[16]When David had finished speaking, Saul called back, "Is that really you, my son David?" Then he began to cry. [17]And he said to David, "You are a better man than I am, for you have

23:28 Hebrew *Sela-hammahlekoth*. **23:29** Verse 23:29 is numbered 24:1 in Hebrew text. **24:1** Verses 24:1-22 are numbered 24:2-23 in Hebrew text.

repaid me good for evil. [18]Yes, you have been
amazingly kind to me today, for when the
LORD put me in a place where you could have
killed me, you didn't do it. [19]Who else would
let his enemy get away when he had him in his
power? May the LORD reward you well for the
kindness you have shown me today. [20]And
now I realize that you are surely going to
be king, and that the kingdom of Israel will
flourish under your rule. [21]Now swear to me by
the LORD that when that happens you will not
kill my family and destroy my line of descen-
dants!"

[22]So David promised this to Saul with an
oath. Then Saul went home, but David and his
men went back to their stronghold.

CHAPTER 25

The Death of Samuel

Now Samuel died, and all Israel gathered for
his funeral. They buried him at his house in
Ramah.

Nabal Angers David

Then David moved down to the wilderness of
Maon.* [2]There was a wealthy man from Maon
who owned property near the town of Carmel.
He had 3,000 sheep and 1,000 goats, and it
was sheep-shearing time. [3]This man's name
was Nabal, and his wife, Abigail, was a sensible
and beautiful woman. But Nabal, a descendant
of Caleb, was crude and mean in all his deal-
ings.

[4]When David heard that Nabal was shear-
ing his sheep, [5]he sent ten of his young men
to Carmel with this message for Nabal:
[6]"Peace and prosperity to you, your family,
and everything you own! [7]I am told that it is
sheep-shearing time. While your shepherds
stayed among us near Carmel, we never
harmed them, and nothing was ever stolen
from them. [8]Ask your own men, and they will
tell you this is true. So would you be kind to
us, since we have come at a time of celebra-
tion? Please share any provisions you might
have on hand with us and with your friend
David." [9]David's young men gave this mes-
sage to Nabal in David's name, and they
waited for a reply.

[10]"Who is this fellow David?" Nabal
sneered to the young men. "Who does this
son of Jesse think he is? There are lots of ser-
vants these days who run away from their
masters. [11]Should I take my bread and my
water and my meat that I've slaughtered for
my shearers and give it to a band of outlaws
who come from who knows where?"

[12]So David's young men returned and told
him what Nabal had said. [13]"Get your swords!"
was David's reply as he strapped on his own.
Then 400 men started off with David, and
200 remained behind to guard their equip-
ment.

[14]Meanwhile, one of Nabal's servants went
to Abigail and told her, "David sent messen-
gers from the wilderness to greet our master,
but he screamed insults at them. [15]These men
have been very good to us, and we never suf-
fered any harm from them. Nothing was sto-
len from us the whole time they were with us.
[16]In fact, day and night they were like a wall of
protection to us and the sheep. [17]You need to
know this and figure out what to do, for there
is going to be trouble for our master and his
whole family. He's so ill-tempered that no one
can even talk to him!"

[18]Abigail wasted no time. She quickly gath-
ered 200 loaves of bread, two wineskins full of
wine, five sheep that had been slaughtered,
nearly a bushel* of roasted grain, 100 clusters
of raisins, and 200 fig cakes. She packed them
on donkeys [19]and said to her servants, "Go on
ahead. I will follow you shortly." But she didn't
tell her husband Nabal what she was doing.

[20]As she was riding her donkey into a
mountain ravine, she saw David and his men
coming toward her. [21]David had just been
saying, "A lot of good it did to help this fel-
low. We protected his flocks in the wilder-
ness, and nothing he owned was lost or
stolen. But he has repaid me evil for good.
[22]May God strike me and kill me* if even one
man of his household is still alive tomorrow
morning!"

Abigail Intercedes for Nabal

[23]When Abigail saw David, she quickly got
off her donkey and bowed low before him.
[24]She fell at his feet and said, "I accept all
blame in this matter, my lord. Please listen to
what I have to say. [25]I know Nabal is a wicked
and ill-tempered man; please don't pay any

25:1 As in Greek version (see also 25:2); Hebrew reads *Paran*. **25:18** Hebrew *5 seahs* [30 liters]. **25:22** As in Greek version; Hebrew reads *May God strike and kill the enemies of David*.

attention to him. He is a fool, just as his name suggests.* But I never even saw the young men you sent.

[26]"Now, my lord, as surely as the LORD lives and you yourself live, since the LORD has kept you from murdering and taking vengeance into your own hands, let all your enemies and those who try to harm you be as cursed as Nabal is. [27]And here is a present that I, your servant, have brought to you and your young men. [28]Please forgive me if I have offended you in any way. The LORD will surely reward you with a lasting dynasty, for you are fighting the LORD's battles. And you have not done wrong throughout your entire life.

[29]"Even when you are chased by those who seek to kill you, your life is safe in the care of the LORD your God, secure in his treasure pouch! But the lives of your enemies will disappear like stones shot from a sling! [30]When the LORD has done all he promised and has made you leader of Israel, [31]don't let this be a blemish on your record. Then your conscience won't have to bear the staggering burden of needless bloodshed and vengeance. And when the LORD has done these great things for you, please remember me, your servant!"

[32]David replied to Abigail, "Praise the LORD, the God of Israel, who has sent you to meet me today! [33]Thank God for your good sense! Bless you for keeping me from murder and from carrying out vengeance with my own hands. [34]For I swear by the LORD, the God of Israel, who has kept me from hurting you, that if you had not hurried out to meet me, not one of Nabal's men would still be alive tomorrow morning." [35]Then David accepted her present and told her, "Return home in peace. I have heard what you said. We will not kill your husband."

[36]When Abigail arrived home, she found that Nabal was throwing a big party and was celebrating like a king. He was very drunk, so she didn't tell him anything about her meeting with David until dawn the next day. [37]In the morning when Nabal was sober, his wife told him what had happened. As a result he had a stroke,* and he lay paralyzed on his bed like a stone. [38]About ten days later, the LORD struck him, and he died.

David Marries Abigail

[39]When David heard that Nabal was dead, he said, "Praise the LORD, who has avenged the insult I received from Nabal and has kept me from doing it myself. Nabal has received the punishment for his sin." Then David sent messengers to Abigail to ask her to become his wife.

[40]When the messengers arrived at Carmel, they told Abigail, "David has sent us to take you back to marry him."

[41]She bowed low to the ground and responded, "I, your servant, would be happy to marry David. I would even be willing to become a slave, washing the feet of his servants!" [42]Quickly getting ready, she took along five of her servant girls as attendants, mounted her donkey, and went with David's messengers. And so she became his wife. [43]David also married Ahinoam from Jezreel, making both of them his wives. [44]Saul, meanwhile, had given his daughter Michal, David's wife, to a man from Gallim named Palti son of Laish.

CHAPTER 26

David Spares Saul Again

Now some men from Ziph came to Saul at Gibeah to tell him, "David is hiding on the hill of Hakilah, which overlooks Jeshimon."

[2]So Saul took 3,000 of Israel's elite troops and went to hunt him down in the wilderness of Ziph. [3]Saul camped along the road beside the hill of Hakilah, near Jeshimon, where David was hiding. When David learned that Saul had come after him into the wilderness, [4]he sent out spies to verify the report of Saul's arrival.

[5]David slipped over to Saul's camp one night to look around. Saul and Abner son of Ner, the commander of his army, were sleeping inside a ring formed by the slumbering warriors. [6]"Who will volunteer to go in there with me?" David asked Ahimelech the Hittite and Abishai son of Zeruiah, Joab's brother.

"I'll go with you," Abishai replied. [7]So David and Abishai went right into Saul's camp and found him asleep, with his spear stuck in the ground beside his head. Abner and the soldiers were lying asleep around him.

[8]"God has surely handed your enemy over to you this time!" Abishai whispered to David. "Let me pin him to the ground with one thrust of the spear; I won't need to strike twice!"

25:25 The name *Nabal* means "fool." **25:37** Hebrew *his heart failed him.*

[9]"No!" David said. "Don't kill him. For who can remain innocent after attacking the LORD's anointed one? [10]Surely the LORD will strike Saul down someday, or he will die of old age or in battle. [11]The LORD forbid that I should kill the one he has anointed! But take his spear and that jug of water beside his head, and then let's get out of here!"

[12]So David took the spear and jug of water that were near Saul's head. Then he and Abishai got away without anyone seeing them or even waking up, because the LORD had put Saul's men into a deep sleep.

[13]David climbed the hill opposite the camp until he was at a safe distance. [14]Then he shouted down to the soldiers and to Abner son of Ner, "Wake up, Abner!"

"Who is it?" Abner demanded.

[15]"Well, Abner, you're a great man, aren't you?" David taunted. "Where in all Israel is there anyone as mighty? So why haven't you guarded your master the king when someone came to kill him? [16]This isn't good at all! I swear by the LORD that you and your men deserve to die, because you failed to protect your master, the LORD's anointed! Look around! Where are the king's spear and the jug of water that were beside his head?"

[17]Saul recognized David's voice and called out, "Is that you, my son David?"

And David replied, "Yes, my lord the king. [18]Why are you chasing me? What have I done? What is my crime? [19]But now let my lord the king listen to his servant. If the LORD has stirred you up against me, then let him accept my offering. But if this is simply a human scheme, then may those involved be cursed by the LORD. For they have driven me from my home, so I can no longer live among the LORD's people, and they have said, 'Go, worship pagan gods.' [20]Must I die on foreign soil, far from the presence of the LORD? Why has the king of Israel come out to search for a single flea? Why does he hunt me down like a partridge on the mountains?"

[21]Then Saul confessed, "I have sinned. Come back home, my son, and I will no longer try to harm you, for you valued my life today. I have been a fool and very, very wrong."

[22]"Here is your spear, O king," David replied. "Let one of your young men come over and get it. [23]The LORD gives his own reward for doing good and for being loyal, and I refused to kill you even when the LORD placed you in my power, for you are the LORD's anointed one. [24]Now may the LORD value my life, even as I have valued yours today. May he rescue me from all my troubles."

[25]And Saul said to David, "Blessings on you, my son David. You will do many heroic deeds, and you will surely succeed." Then David went away, and Saul returned home.

CHAPTER 27

David among the Philistines

But David kept thinking to himself, "Someday Saul is going to get me. The best thing I can do is escape to the Philistines. Then Saul will stop hunting for me in Israelite territory, and I will finally be safe."

[2]So David took his 600 men and went over and joined Achish son of Maoch, the king of Gath. [3]David and his men and their families settled there with Achish at Gath. David brought his two wives along with him—Ahinoam from Jezreel and Abigail, Nabal's widow from Carmel. [4]Word soon reached Saul that David had fled to Gath, so he stopped hunting for him.

[5]One day David said to Achish, "If it is all right with you, we would rather live in one of the country towns instead of here in the royal city."

[6]So Achish gave him the town of Ziklag (which still belongs to the kings of Judah to this day), [7]and they lived there among the Philistines for a year and four months.

[8]David and his men spent their time raiding the Geshurites, the Girzites, and the Amalekites—people who had lived near Shur, toward the land of Egypt, since ancient times. [9]David did not leave one person alive in the villages he attacked. He took the sheep, goats, cattle, donkeys, camels, and clothing before returning home to see King Achish.

[10]"Where did you make your raid today?" Achish would ask.

And David would reply, "Against the south of Judah, the Jerahmeelites, and the Kenites."

[11]No one was left alive to come to Gath and tell where he had really been. This happened again and again while he was living among the Philistines. [12]Achish believed David and thought to himself, "By now the people of Is-

SAUL

I have spent years trying to hunt David down and kill him. This time I was close on his trail. Night fell, and my men and I stopped for the night. We were all so tired that we quickly fell asleep. The next thing I knew I heard a voice calling out, "Wake up!" It was David. He had crept into my camp and had taken my spear and water jug. But even though he had the perfect opportunity, he didn't kill me. David spared my life! I knew then that I had been wrong and had been acting like a fool. It was time for me to go home.

Check out more about Saul in 1 Samuel 9–31.

rael must hate him bitterly. Now he will have to stay here and serve me forever!"

CHAPTER 28

Saul Consults a Medium

About that time the Philistines mustered their armies for another war with Israel. King Achish told David, "You and your men will be expected to join me in battle."

[2]"Very well!" David agreed. "Now you will see for yourself what we can do."

Then Achish told David, "I will make you my personal bodyguard for life."

[3]Meanwhile, Samuel had died, and all Israel had mourned for him. He was buried in Ramah, his hometown. And Saul had banned from the land of Israel all mediums and those who consult the spirits of the dead.

[4]The Philistines set up their camp at Shunem, and Saul gathered all the army of Israel and camped at Gilboa. [5]When Saul saw the vast Philistine army, he became frantic with fear. [6]He asked the LORD what he should do, but the LORD refused to answer him, either by dreams or by sacred lots* or by the prophets. [7]Saul then said to his advisers, "Find a woman who is a medium, so I can go and ask her what to do."

His advisers replied, "There is a medium at Endor."

[8]So Saul disguised himself by wearing ordinary clothing instead of his royal robes. Then he went to the woman's home at night, accompanied by two of his men.

"I have to talk to a man who has died," he said. "Will you call up his spirit for me?"

[9]"Are you trying to get me killed?" the woman demanded. "You know that Saul has outlawed all the mediums and all who consult the spirits of the dead. Why are you setting a trap for me?"

[10]But Saul took an oath in the name of the LORD and promised, "As surely as the LORD lives, nothing bad will happen to you for doing this."

[11]Finally, the woman said, "Well, whose spirit do you want me to call up?"

"Call up Samuel," Saul replied.

[12]When the woman saw Samuel, she screamed, "You've deceived me! You are Saul!"

[13]"Don't be afraid!" the king told her. "What do you see?"

"I see a god* coming up out of the earth," she said.

[14]"What does he look like?" Saul asked.

"He is an old man wrapped in a robe," she replied. Saul realized it was Samuel, and he fell to the ground before him.

28:6 Hebrew *by Urim.* **28:13** Or *gods.*

15"Why have you disturbed me by calling
me back?" Samuel asked Saul.
"Because I am in deep trouble," Saul re-
plied. "The Philistines are at war with me, and
God has left me and won't reply by prophets
or dreams. So I have called for you to tell me
what to do."
16But Samuel replied, "Why ask me, since
the LORD has left you and has become your
enemy? 17The LORD has done just as he said
he would. He has torn the kingdom from you
and given it to your rival, David. 18The LORD
has done this to you today because you re-
fused to carry out his fierce anger against the
Amalekites. 19What's more, the LORD will
hand you and the army of Israel over to the
Philistines tomorrow, and you and your sons
will be here with me. The LORD will bring
down the entire army of Israel in defeat."
20Saul fell full length on the ground, para-
lyzed with fright because of Samuel's words.
He was also faint with hunger, for he had
eaten nothing all day and all night.
21When the woman saw how distraught he
was, she said, "Sir, I obeyed your command at
the risk of my life. 22Now do what I say, and let
me give you a little something to eat so you
can regain your strength for the trip back."
23But Saul refused to eat anything. Then his
advisers joined the woman in urging him to
eat, so he finally yielded and got up from the
ground and sat on the couch.
24The woman had been fattening a calf, so
she hurried out and killed it. She took some
flour, kneaded it into dough and baked un-
leavened bread. 25She brought the meal to
Saul and his advisers, and they ate it. Then
they went out into the night.

SIMPLE OBJECTS

God often uses simple, ordinary objects to accomplish his tasks in the world. What do you have that God can use? Anything and everything is a possible "instrument" for him.

Object	Reference	Who used it?	How was it used?
a staff	Exodus 4:2-4	Moses	To work miracles before Pharaoh
horns	Joshua 6:3-5	Joshua	To flatten the walls of Jericho
a fleece	Judges 6:36-40	Gideon	To confirm God's will
horns, jars, and torches	Judges 7:19-22	Gideon	To defeat the Midianites
a jawbone	Judges 15:15	Samson	To kill 1,000 Philistines
a small stone	1 Samuel 17:40	David	To kill Goliath
oil	2 Kings 4:1-7	Elisha	To show God's power to provide
a river	2 Kings 5:9-14	Elisha	To heal a man of leprosy
a clay jar	Jeremiah 19:1-13	Jeremiah	To teach about God's anger at the people's sin
iron griddle, water, and food	Ezekiel 4:1-17	Ezekiel	To show how an enemy army would capture Jerusalem
five loaves of bread and two fish	Mark 6:30-44	Jesus	To feed a crowd of more than 5,000 people

CHAPTER 29

The Philistines Reject David

The entire Philistine army now mobilized
at Aphek, and the Israelites camped at the
spring in Jezreel. [2]As the Philistine rulers
were leading out their troops in groups of
hundreds and thousands, David and his men
marched at the rear with King Achish. [3]But
the Philistine commanders demanded,
"What are these Hebrews doing here?"

And Achish told them, "This is David, the
servant of King Saul of Israel. He's been with
me for years, and I've never found a single fault
in him from the day he arrived until today."

[4]But the Philistine commanders were angry.
"Send him back to the town you've given him!"
they demanded. "He can't go into the battle
with us. What if he turns against us in battle
and becomes our adversary? Is there any
better way for him to reconcile himself with
his master than by handing our heads over to
him? [5]Isn't this the same David about whom
the women of Israel sing in their dances,

'Saul has killed his thousands,
and David his ten thousands'?"

[6]So Achish finally summoned David and
said to him, "I swear by the LORD that you have
been a trustworthy ally. I think you should go
with me into battle, for I've never found a
single flaw in you from the day you arrived
until today. But the other Philistine rulers
won't hear of it. [7]Please don't upset them, but
go back quietly."

[8]"What have I done to deserve this treat-
ment?" David demanded. "What have you
ever found in your servant, that I can't go and
fight the enemies of my lord the king?"

[9]But Achish insisted, "As far as I'm con-
cerned, you're as perfect as an angel of God.
But the Philistine commanders are afraid to
have you with them in the battle. [10]Now get up
early in the morning, and leave with your men
as soon as it gets light."

[11]So David and his men headed back into
the land of the Philistines, while the Philistine
army went on to Jezreel.

CHAPTER 30

David Destroys the Amalekites

Three days later, when David and his men ar-
rived home at their town of Ziklag, they found
that the Amalekites had made a raid into the
Negev and Ziklag; they had crushed Ziklag
and burned it to the ground. [2]They had car-
ried off the women and children and every-
one else but without killing anyone.

[3]When David and his men saw the ruins
and realized what had happened to their fam-
ilies, [4]they wept until they could weep no
more. [5]David's two wives, Ahinoam from Jez-
reel and Abigail, the widow of Nabal from
Carmel, were among those captured. [6]David
was now in great danger because all his men
were very bitter about losing their sons and
daughters, and they began to talk of stoning
him. But David found strength in the LORD his
God.

[7]Then he said to Abiathar the priest, "Bring
me the ephod!" So Abiathar brought it. [8]Then
David asked the LORD, "Should I chase after
this band of raiders? Will I catch them?"

And the LORD told him, "Yes, go after them.
You will surely recover everything that was
taken from you!"

[9]So David and his 600 men set out, and
they came to the brook Besor. [10]But 200 of
the men were too exhausted to cross the
brook, so David continued the pursuit with
400 men.

[11]Along the way they found an Egyptian
man in a field and brought him to David. They
gave him some bread to eat and water to
drink. [12]They also gave him part of a fig cake
and two clusters of raisins, for he hadn't had
anything to eat or drink for three days and
nights. Before long his strength returned.

[13]"To whom do you belong, and where do
you come from?" David asked him.

"I am an Egyptian—the slave of an Amalek-
ite," he replied. "My master abandoned me
three days ago because I was sick. [14]We were
on our way back from raiding the Kerethites
in the Negev, the territory of Judah, and the
land of Caleb, and we had just burned Ziklag."

[15]"Will you lead me to this band of raid-
ers?" David asked.

The young man replied, "If you take an oath
in God's name that you will not kill me or give
me back to my master, then I will guide you to
them."

[16]So he led David to them, and they found
the Amalekites spread out across the fields,
eating and drinking and dancing with joy

because of the vast amount of plunder they had taken from the Philistines and the land of Judah. [17]David and his men rushed in among them and slaughtered them throughout that night and the entire next day until evening. None of the Amalekites escaped except 400 young men who fled on camels. [18]David got back everything the Amalekites had taken, and he rescued his two wives. [19]Nothing was missing: small or great, son or daughter, nor anything else that had been taken. David brought everything back. [20]He also recovered all the flocks and herds, and his men drove them ahead of the other livestock. "This plunder belongs to David!" they said.

[21]Then David returned to the brook Besor and met up with the 200 men who had been left behind because they were too exhausted to go with him. They went out to meet David and his men, and David greeted them joyfully. [22]But some evil troublemakers among David's men said, "They didn't go with us, so they can't have any of the plunder we recovered. Give them their wives and children, and tell them to be gone."

[23]But David said, "No, my brothers! Don't be selfish with what the LORD has given us. He has kept us safe and helped us defeat the band of raiders that attacked us. [24]Who will listen when you talk like this? We share and share alike—those who go to battle and those who guard the equipment." [25]From then on David made this a decree and regulation for Israel, and it is still followed today.

[26]When he arrived at Ziklag, David sent part of the plunder to the elders of Judah, who were his friends. "Here is a present for you, taken from the LORD's enemies," he said.

[27]The gifts were sent to the people of the following towns David had visited: Bethel, Ramoth-negev, Jattir, [28]Aroer, Siphmoth, Eshtemoa, [29]Racal,* the towns of the Jerahmeelites, the towns of the Kenites, [30]Hormah, Bor-ashan, Athach, [31]Hebron, and all the other places David and his men had visited.

30:29 Greek version reads *Carmel*.

CHAPTER 31

The Death of Saul

Now the Philistines attacked Israel, and the men of Israel fled before them. Many were slaughtered on the slopes of Mount Gilboa. [2]The Philistines closed in on Saul and his sons, and they killed three of his sons—Jonathan, Abinadab, and Malkishua. [3]The fighting grew very fierce around Saul, and the Philistine archers caught up with him and wounded him severely.

[4]Saul groaned to his armor bearer, "Take your sword and kill me before these pagan Philistines come to run me through and taunt and torture me."

But his armor bearer was afraid and would not do it. So Saul took his own sword and fell on it. [5]When his armor bearer realized that Saul was dead, he fell on his own sword and died beside the king. [6]So Saul, his three sons, his armor bearer, and his troops all died together that same day.

[7]When the Israelites on the other side of the Jezreel Valley and beyond the Jordan saw that the Israelite army had fled and that Saul and his sons were dead, they abandoned their towns and fled. So the Philistines moved in and occupied their towns.

[8]The next day, when the Philistines went out to strip the dead, they found the bodies of Saul and his three sons on Mount Gilboa. [9]So they cut off Saul's head and stripped off his armor. Then they proclaimed the good news of Saul's death in their pagan temple and to the people throughout the land of Philistia. [10]They placed his armor in the temple of the Ashtoreths, and they fastened his body to the wall of the city of Beth-shan.

[11]But when the people of Jabesh-gilead heard what the Philistines had done to Saul, [12]all their mighty warriors traveled through the night to Beth-shan and took the bodies of Saul and his sons down from the wall. They brought them to Jabesh, where they burned the bodies. [13]Then they took their bones and buried them beneath the tamarisk tree at Jabesh, and they fasted for seven days.

2 SAMUEL

WHO
David, Abner, Joab, Ishbosheth, Mephibosheth, Bathsheba, Nathan, and Absalom.

WHERE
Israel, when King David was king.

WHEN
This book was written after 930 BC, when David's reign had come to an end and Israel was divided into two kingdoms.

WHY
To record David's reign as king and to show the personal qualities that please God.

David realized that the LORD had confirmed him as king over Israel and had blessed his kingdom for the sake of his people Israel.
2 SAMUEL 5:12

Good friends are great to be with and to count on. God is our good friend, and we should be his. King David was a good friend to God because he tried to obey God. He sometimes did what was wrong, but he loved God, so he let God know how sorry he was.

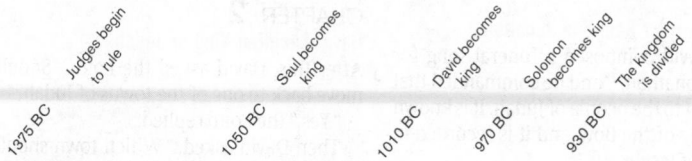

BE GOD'S FRIEND—LIKE DAVID.

CHAPTER 1

David Learns of Saul's Death

After the death of Saul, David returned from his victory over the Amalekites and spent two days in Ziklag. [2]On the third day a man arrived from Saul's army camp. He had torn his clothes and put dirt on his head to show that he was in mourning. He fell to the ground before David in deep respect.

[3]"Where have you come from?" David asked.

"I escaped from the Israelite camp," the man replied.

[4]"What happened?" David demanded. "Tell me how the battle went."

The man replied, "Our entire army fled from the battle. Many of the men are dead, and Saul and his son Jonathan are also dead."

5"How do you know Saul and Jonathan are dead?" David demanded of the young man.

6The man answered, "I happened to be on Mount Gilboa, and there was Saul leaning on his spear with the enemy chariots and chariot-eers closing in on him. 7When he turned and saw me, he cried out for me to come to him. 'How can I help?' I asked him.

8"He responded, 'Who are you?'

"'I am an Amalekite,' I told him.

9"Then he begged me, 'Come over here and put me out of my misery, for I am in terrible pain and want to die.'

10"So I killed him," the Amalekite told David, "for I knew he couldn't live. Then I took his crown and his armband, and I have brought them here to you, my lord."

11David and his men tore their clothes in sorrow when they heard the news. 12They mourned and wept and fasted all day for Saul and his son Jonathan, and for the LORD's army and the nation of Israel, because they had died by the sword that day.

13Then David said to the young man who had brought the news, "Where are you from?"

And he replied, "I am a foreigner, an Amalekite, who lives in your land."

14"Why were you not afraid to kill the LORD's anointed one?" David asked.

15Then David said to one of his men, "Kill him!" So the man thrust his sword into the Amalekite and killed him. 16"You have condemned yourself," David said, "for you yourself confessed that you killed the LORD's anointed one."

David's Song for Saul and Jonathan

17Then David composed a funeral song for Saul and Jonathan, 18and he commanded that it be taught to the people of Judah. It is known as the Song of the Bow, and it is recorded in *The Book of Jashar*.*

19 Your pride and joy, O Israel, lies dead on the hills!
Oh, how the mighty heroes have fallen!
20 Don't announce the news in Gath,
don't proclaim it in the streets of Ashkelon,
or the daughters of the Philistines will rejoice
and the pagans will laugh in triumph.
21 O mountains of Gilboa,
let there be no dew or rain upon you,
nor fruitful fields producing offerings of grain.*
For there the shield of the mighty heroes was defiled;
the shield of Saul will no longer be anointed with oil.
22 The bow of Jonathan was powerful,
and the sword of Saul did its mighty work.
They shed the blood of their enemies
and pierced the bodies of mighty heroes.
23 How beloved and gracious were Saul and Jonathan!
They were together in life and in death.
They were swifter than eagles,
stronger than lions.
24 O women of Israel, weep for Saul,
for he dressed you in luxurious scarlet clothing,
in garments decorated with gold.
25 Oh, how the mighty heroes have fallen in battle!
Jonathan lies dead on the hills.
26 How I weep for you, my brother Jonathan!
Oh, how much I loved you!
And your love for me was deep,
deeper than the love of women!
27 Oh, how the mighty heroes have fallen!
Stripped of their weapons, they lie dead.

CHAPTER 2

David Anointed King of Judah

After this, David asked the LORD, "Should I move back to one of the towns of Judah?"

"Yes," the LORD replied.

Then David asked, "Which town should I go to?"

"To Hebron," the LORD answered.

2David's two wives were Ahinoam from Jezreel and Abigail, the widow of Nabal from Carmel. So David and his wives 3and his men and their families all moved to Judah, and they settled in the villages near Hebron. 4Then the men of Judah came to David and anointed him king over the people of Judah.

When David heard that the men of Jabesh-

1:18 Or *The Book of the Upright*. **1:21** The meaning of the Hebrew is uncertain.

gilead had buried Saul, [5]he sent them this message: "May the LORD bless you for being so loyal to your master Saul and giving him a decent burial. [6]May the LORD be loyal to you in return and reward you with his unfailing love! And I, too, will reward you for what you have done. [7]Now that Saul is dead, I ask you to be my strong and loyal subjects like the people of Judah, who have anointed me as their new king."

Ishbosheth Proclaimed King of Israel

[8]But Abner son of Ner, the commander of Saul's army, had already gone to Mahanaim with Saul's son Ishbosheth.* [9]There he proclaimed Ishbosheth king over Gilead, Jezreel, Ephraim, Benjamin, the land of the Ashurites, and all the rest of Israel.

[10]Ishbosheth, Saul's son, was forty years old when he became king, and he ruled from Mahanaim for two years. Meanwhile, the people of Judah remained loyal to David. [11]David made Hebron his capital, and he ruled as king of Judah for seven and a half years.

War between Israel and Judah

[12]One day Abner led Ishbosheth's troops from Mahanaim to Gibeon. [13]About the same time, Joab son of Zeruiah led David's troops out and met them at the pool of Gibeon. The two groups sat down there, facing each other from opposite sides of the pool.

[14]Then Abner suggested to Joab, "Let's have a few of our warriors fight hand to hand here in front of us."

"All right," Joab agreed. [15]So twelve men were chosen to fight from each side—twelve men of Benjamin representing Ishbosheth son of Saul, and twelve representing David. [16]Each one grabbed his opponent by the hair and thrust his sword into the other's side so that all of them died. So this place at Gibeon has been known ever since as the Field of Swords.*

[17]A fierce battle followed that day, and Abner and the men of Israel were defeated by the forces of David.

The Death of Asahel

[18]Joab, Abishai, and Asahel—the three sons of Zeruiah—were among David's forces that day. Asahel could run like a gazelle, [19]and he began chasing Abner. He pursued him relentlessly, not stopping for anything. [20]When Abner looked back and saw him coming, he called out, "Is that you, Asahel?"

"Yes, it is," he replied.

[21]"Go fight someone else!" Abner warned. "Take on one of the younger men, and strip him of his weapons." But Asahel kept right on chasing Abner.

[22]Again Abner shouted to him, "Get away from here! I don't want to kill you. How could I ever face your brother Joab again?"

[23]But Asahel refused to turn back, so Abner thrust the butt end of his spear through Asahel's stomach, and the spear came out through his back. He stumbled to the ground and died there. And everyone who came by that spot stopped and stood still when they saw Asahel lying there.

[24]When Joab and Abishai found out what had happened, they set out after Abner. The sun was just going down as they arrived at the hill of Ammah near Giah, along the road to the wilderness of Gibeon. [25]Abner's troops from the tribe of Benjamin regrouped there at the top of the hill to take a stand.

[26]Abner shouted down to Joab, "Must we always be killing each other? Don't you realize that bitterness is the only result? When will you call off your men from chasing their Israelite brothers?"

[27]Then Joab said, "God only knows what would have happened if you hadn't spoken, for we would have chased you all night if necessary." [28]So Joab blew the ram's horn, and his men stopped chasing the troops of Israel.

[29]All that night Abner and his men retreated through the Jordan Valley.* They crossed the Jordan River, traveling all through the morning,* and didn't stop until they arrived at Mahanaim.

[30]Meanwhile, Joab and his men also returned home. When Joab counted his casualties, he discovered that only 19 men were missing in addition to Asahel. [31]But 360 of Abner's men had been killed, all from the tribe of Benjamin. [32]Joab and his men took Asahel's body to Bethlehem and buried him there in his father's tomb. Then they traveled all night and reached Hebron at daybreak.

2:8 *Ishbosheth* is another name for Esh-baal. **2:16** Hebrew *Helkath-hazzurim*. **2:29a** Hebrew *the Arabah*. **2:29b** Or *continued on through the Bithron*. The meaning of the Hebrew is uncertain.

CHAPTER 3

That was the beginning of a long war between those who were loyal to Saul and those loyal to David. As time passed David became stronger and stronger, while Saul's dynasty became weaker and weaker.

David's Sons Born in Hebron

2 These are the sons who were born to David in Hebron:

The oldest was Amnon, whose mother was Ahinoam from Jezreel.
3 The second was Daniel,* whose mother was Abigail, the widow of Nabal from Carmel.
The third was Absalom, whose mother was Maacah, the daughter of Talmai, king of Geshur.
4 The fourth was Adonijah, whose mother was Haggith.
The fifth was Shephatiah, whose mother was Abital.
5 The sixth was Ithream, whose mother was Eglah, David's wife.

These sons were all born to David in Hebron.

Abner Joins Forces with David

6 As the war between the house of Saul and the house of David went on, Abner became a powerful leader among those loyal to Saul. 7 One day Ishbosheth,* Saul's son, accused Abner of sleeping with one of his father's concubines, a woman named Rizpah, daughter of Aiah.

8 Abner was furious. "Am I some Judean dog to be kicked around like this?" he shouted. "After all I have done for your father, Saul, and his family and friends by not handing you over to David, is this my reward—that you find fault with me about this woman? 9 May God strike me and even kill me if I don't do everything I can to help David get what the LORD has promised him! 10 I'm going to take Saul's kingdom and give it to David. I will establish the throne of David over Israel as well as Judah, all the way from Dan in the north to Beersheba in the south." 11 Ishbosheth didn't dare say another word because he was afraid of what Abner might do.

12 Then Abner sent messengers to David, saying, "Doesn't the entire land belong to you? Make a solemn pact with me, and I will help turn over all of Israel to you."

13 "All right," David replied, "but I will not negotiate with you unless you bring back my wife Michal, Saul's daughter, when you come."

14 David then sent this message to Ishbosheth, Saul's son: "Give me back my wife Michal, for I bought her with the lives* of 100 Philistines."

15 So Ishbosheth took Michal away from her husband, Palti* son of Laish. 16 Palti followed along behind her as far as Bahurim, weeping as he went. Then Abner told him, "Go back home!" So Palti returned.

17 Meanwhile, Abner had consulted with the elders of Israel. "For some time now," he told them, "you have wanted to make David your king. 18 Now is the time! For the LORD has said, 'I have chosen David to save my people Israel from the hands of the Philistines and from all their other enemies.'" 19 Abner also spoke with the men of Benjamin. Then he went to Hebron to tell David that all the people of Israel and Benjamin had agreed to support him.

20 When Abner and twenty of his men came to Hebron, David entertained them with a great feast. 21 Then Abner said to David, "Let me go and call an assembly of all Israel to support my lord the king. They will make a covenant with you to make you their king, and you will rule over everything your heart desires." So David sent Abner safely on his way.

Joab Murders Abner

22 But just after David had sent Abner away in safety, Joab and some of David's troops returned from a raid, bringing much plunder with them. 23 When Joab arrived, he was told that Abner had just been there visiting the king and had been sent away in safety.

24 Joab rushed to the king and demanded, "What have you done? What do you mean by letting Abner get away? 25 You know perfectly well that he came to spy on you and find out everything you're doing!"

26 Joab then left David and sent messengers to catch up with Abner, asking him to return. They found him at the well of Sirah and

3:3 As in parallel text at 1 Chr 3:1 (see also Greek version, which reads *Daluia*, and Dead Sea Scrolls, which read *Dan[iel]*; Hebrew reads *Kileab*. **3:7** *Ishbosheth* is another name for Esh-baal. **3:14** Hebrew *the foreskins*. **3:15** As in 1 Sam 25:44; Hebrew reads *Paltiel*, a variant spelling of Palti.

brought him back, though David knew nothing about it. 27 When Abner arrived back at Hebron, Joab took him aside at the gateway as if to speak with him privately. But then he stabbed Abner in the stomach and killed him in revenge for killing his brother Asahel.

28 When David heard about it, he declared, "I vow by the LORD that I and my kingdom are forever innocent of this crime against Abner son of Ner. 29 Joab and his family are the guilty ones. May the family of Joab be cursed in every generation with a man who has open sores or leprosy* or who walks on crutches* or dies by the sword or begs for food!"

30 So Joab and his brother Abishai killed Abner because Abner had killed their brother Asahel at the battle of Gibeon.

David Mourns Abner's Death

31 Then David said to Joab and all those who were with him, "Tear your clothes and put on burlap. Mourn for Abner." And King David himself walked behind the procession to the grave. 32 They buried Abner in Hebron, and the king and all the people wept at his graveside. 33 Then the king sang this funeral song for Abner:

"Should Abner have died as fools die?
34 Your hands were not bound;
your feet were not chained.
No, you were murdered—
the victim of a wicked plot."

All the people wept again for Abner. 35 David had refused to eat anything on the day of the funeral, and now everyone begged him to eat. But David had made a vow, saying, "May God strike me and even kill me if I eat anything before sundown."

36 This pleased the people very much. In fact, everything the king did pleased them! 37 So everyone in Judah and all Israel understood that David was not responsible for Abner's murder.

38 Then King David said to his officials, "Don't you realize that a great commander has fallen today in Israel? 39 And even though I am the anointed king, these two sons of Zeruiah—Joab and Abishai—are too strong for me to control. So may the LORD repay these evil men for their evil deeds."

CHAPTER 4

The Murder of Ishbosheth

When Ishbosheth,* Saul's son, heard about Abner's death at Hebron, he lost all courage, and all Israel became paralyzed with fear. 2 Now there were two brothers, Baanah and Recab, who were captains of Ishbosheth's raiding parties. They were sons of Rimmon, a member of the tribe of Benjamin who lived in Beeroth. The town of Beeroth is now part of Benjamin's territory 3 because the original people of Beeroth fled to Gittaim, where they still live as foreigners.

4 (Saul's son Jonathan had a son named Mephibosheth,* who was crippled as a child. He was five years old when the report came from Jezreel that Saul and Jonathan had been killed in battle. When the child's nurse heard the news, she picked him up and fled. But as she hurried away, she dropped him, and he became crippled.)

5 One day Recab and Baanah, the sons of Rimmon from Beeroth, went to Ishbosheth's house around noon as he was taking his midday rest. 6 The doorkeeper, who had been sifting wheat, became drowsy and fell asleep. So Recab and Baanah slipped past her.* 7 They went into the house and found Ishbosheth sleeping on his bed. They struck and killed him and cut off his head. Then, taking his head with them, they fled across the Jordan Valley* through the night. 8 When they arrived at Hebron, they presented Ishbosheth's head to David. "Look!" they exclaimed to the king. "Here is the head of Ishbosheth, the son of your enemy Saul who tried to kill you. Today the LORD has given my lord the king revenge on Saul and his entire family!"

9 But David said to Recab and Baanah, "The LORD, who saves me from all my enemies, is my witness. 10 Someone once told me, 'Saul is dead,' thinking he was bringing me good news. But I seized him and killed him at Ziklag. That's the reward I gave him for his news! 11 How much more should I reward evil men who have killed an innocent man in his own house and on his own bed? Shouldn't I hold

3:29a Or *or a contagious skin disease.* The Hebrew word used here can describe various skin diseases. **3:29b** Or *who is effeminate;* Hebrew reads *who handles a spindle.* **4:1** *Ishbosheth* is another name for Esh-baal. **4:4** *Mephibosheth* is another name for Merib-baal. **4:6** As in Greek version; Hebrew reads *So they went into the house pretending to fetch wheat, but they stabbed him in the stomach. Then Recab and Baanah escaped.* **4:7** Hebrew *the Arabah.*

you responsible for his blood and rid the earth of you?"

12 So David ordered his young men to kill them, and they did. They cut off their hands and feet and hung their bodies beside the pool in Hebron. Then they took Ishbosheth's head and buried it in Abner's tomb in Hebron.

CHAPTER 5

David Becomes King of All Israel

Then all the tribes of Israel went to David at Hebron and told him, "We are your own flesh and blood. 2 In the past,* when Saul was our king, you were the one who really led the forces of Israel. And the LORD told you, 'You will be the shepherd of my people Israel. You will be Israel's leader.'"

3 So there at Hebron, King David made a covenant before the LORD with all the elders of Israel. And they anointed him king of Israel.

4 David was thirty years old when he began to reign, and he reigned forty years in all. 5 He had reigned over Judah from Hebron for seven years and six months, and from Jerusalem he reigned over all Israel and Judah for thirty-three years.

AMAZING FACTS

How did the Israelites know God was on his way to fight their enemy? They heard the sound of God's army marching in the treetops!

2 SAMUEL 5:22-25

David Captures Jerusalem

6 David then led his men to Jerusalem to fight against the Jebusites, the original inhabitants of the land who were living there. The Jebusites taunted David, saying, "You'll never get in here! Even the blind and lame could keep you out!" For the Jebusites thought they were safe. 7 But David captured the fortress of Zion, which is now called the City of David.

8 On the day of the attack, David said to his troops, "I hate those 'lame' and 'blind' Jebusites.* Whoever attacks them should strike by going into the city through the water tunnel.*" That is the origin of the saying, "The blind and the lame may not enter the house."*

9 So David made the fortress his home, and he called it the City of David. He extended the city, starting at the supporting terraces* and working inward. 10 And David became more and more powerful, because the LORD God of Heaven's Armies was with him.

11 Then King Hiram of Tyre sent messengers to David, along with cedar timber and carpenters and stonemasons, and they built David a palace. 12 And David realized that the LORD had confirmed him as king over Israel and had blessed his kingdom for the sake of his people Israel.

13 After moving from Hebron to Jerusalem, David married more concubines and wives, and they had more sons and daughters. 14 These are the names of David's sons who were born in Jerusalem: Shammua, Shobab, Nathan, Solomon, 15 Ibhar, Elishua, Nepheg, Japhia, 16 Elishama, Eliada, and Eliphelet.

David Conquers the Philistines

17 When the Philistines heard that David had been anointed king of Israel, they mobilized all their forces to capture him. But David was told they were coming, so he went into the stronghold. 18 The Philistines arrived and spread out across the valley of Rephaim. 19 So David asked the LORD, "Should I go out to fight the Philistines? Will you hand them over to me?"

The LORD replied to David, "Yes, go ahead. I will certainly hand them over to you."

20 So David went to Baal-perazim and defeated the Philistines there. "The LORD did it!" David exclaimed. "He burst through my enemies like a raging flood!" So he named that place Baal-perazim (which means "the Lord who bursts through"). 21 The Philistines had abandoned their idols there, so David and his men confiscated them.

5:2 Or *For some time.* **5:8a** Or *Those 'lame' and 'blind' Jebusites hate me.* **5:8b** Or *with scaling hooks.* The meaning of the Hebrew is uncertain. **5:8c** The meaning of this saying is uncertain. **5:9** Hebrew *the millo.* The meaning of the Hebrew is uncertain.

22 But after a while the Philistines returned
and again spread out across the valley of Reph-
aim. 23 And again David asked the LORD what to
do. "Do not attack them straight on," the LORD
replied. "Instead, circle around behind and at-
tack them near the poplar* trees. 24 When you
hear a sound like marching feet in the tops of
the poplar trees, be on the alert! That will be
the signal that the LORD is moving ahead of you
to strike down the Philistine army." 25 So David
did what the LORD commanded, and he struck
down the Philistines all the way from Gibeon*
to Gezer.

CHAPTER 6

Moving the Ark to Jerusalem

Then David again gathered all the elite troops
in Israel, 30,000 in all. 2 He led them to Baalah
of Judah* to bring back the Ark of God, which
bears the name of the LORD of Heaven's Ar-
mies,* who is enthroned between the cheru-
bim. 3 They placed the Ark of God on a new
cart and brought it from Abinadab's house,
which was on a hill. Uzzah and Ahio, Abina-
dab's sons, were guiding the cart as it left the
house, 4 carrying the Ark of God. Ahio walked
in front of the Ark. 5 David and all the people
of Israel were celebrating before the LORD,
singing songs* and playing all kinds of musi-
cal instruments—lyres, harps, tambourines,
castanets, and cymbals.

6 But when they arrived at the threshing
floor of Nacon, the oxen stumbled, and Uz-
zah reached out his hand and steadied the
Ark of God. 7 Then the LORD's anger was
aroused against Uzzah, and God struck him
dead because of this.* So Uzzah died right
there beside the Ark of God.

8 David was angry because the LORD's anger
had burst out against Uzzah. He named that
place Perez-uzzah (which means "to burst out
against Uzzah"), as it is still called today.

9 David was now afraid of the LORD, and he
asked, "How can I ever bring the Ark of the
LORD back into my care?" 10 So David decided
not to move the Ark of the LORD into the City
of David. Instead, he took it to the house of
Obed-edom of Gath. 11 The Ark of the LORD
remained there in Obed-edom's house for
three months, and the LORD blessed Obed-
edom and his entire household.

12 Then King David was told, "The LORD has
blessed Obed-edom's household and every-
thing he has because of the Ark of God." So
David went there and brought the Ark of God
from the house of Obed-edom to the City of
David with a great celebration. 13 After the
men who were carrying the Ark of the LORD
had gone six steps, David sacrificed a bull and
a fattened calf. 14 And David danced before the
LORD with all his might, wearing a priestly gar-
ment.* 15 So David and all the people of Israel
brought up the Ark of the LORD with shouts of
joy and the blowing of rams' horns.

Michal's Contempt for David

16 But as the Ark of the LORD entered the City
of David, Michal, the daughter of Saul, looked
down from her window. When she saw King
David leaping and dancing before the LORD,
she was filled with contempt for him.

17 They brought the Ark of the LORD and
set it in its place inside the special tent David
had prepared for it. And David sacrificed
burnt offerings and peace offerings to the
LORD. 18 When he had finished his sacrifices,
David blessed the people in the name of the
LORD of Heaven's Armies. 19 Then he gave to
every Israelite man and woman in the crowd
a loaf of bread, a cake of dates,* and a cake of
raisins. Then all the people returned to their
homes.

20 When David returned home to bless his
own family, Michal, the daughter of Saul, came
out to meet him. She said in disgust, "How dis-
tinguished the king of Israel looked today,
shamelessly exposing himself to the servant
girls like any vulgar person might do!"

21 David retorted to Michal, "I was dancing
before the LORD, who chose me above your fa-
ther and all his family! He appointed me as the
leader of Israel, the people of the LORD, so I cel-
ebrate before the LORD. 22 Yes, and I am willing
to look even more foolish than this, even to be
humiliated in my own eyes! But those servant
girls you mentioned will indeed think I am dis-
tinguished!" 23 So Michal, the daughter of Saul,
remained childless throughout her entire life.

5:23 Or *aspen*, or *balsam*; also in 5:24. The exact identification of this tree is uncertain. **5:25** As in Greek version (see also 1 Chr 14:16); Hebrew reads *Geba*. **6:2a** *Baalah of Judah* is another name for Kiriath-jearim; compare 1 Chr 13:6. **6:2b** Or *the Ark of God where the Name is proclaimed—the name of the LORD of Heaven's Armies*. **6:5** As in Dead Sea Scrolls and Greek version (see also 1 Chr 13:8); Masoretic Text reads *before the LORD with all manner of cypress wood*. **6:7** As in Dead Sea Scrolls; Masoretic Text reads *because of his irreverence*. **6:14** Hebrew *a linen ephod*. **6:19** Or *a portion of meat*. The meaning of the Hebrew is uncertain.

CHAPTER 7

The LORD's Covenant Promise to David

When King David was settled in his palace
and the LORD had given him rest from all the
surrounding enemies, [2]the king summoned
Nathan the prophet. "Look," David said, "I am
living in a beautiful cedar palace,* but the Ark
of God is out there in a tent!"
[3]Nathan replied to the king, "Go ahead and
do whatever you have in mind, for the LORD is
with you."
[4]But that same night the LORD said to Na-
than,

[5]"Go and tell my servant David, 'This is
what the LORD has declared: Are you the
one to build a house for me to live in? [6]I
have never lived in a house, from the day
I brought the Israelites out of Egypt until
this very day. I have always moved from
one place to another with a tent and a
Tabernacle as my dwelling. [7]Yet no matter
where I have gone with the Israelites, I have
never once complained to Israel's tribal
leaders, the shepherds of my people Israel.
I have never asked them, "Why haven't you
built me a beautiful cedar house?"'

[8]"Now go and say to my servant David,
'This is what the LORD of Heaven's Armies
has declared: I took you from tending
sheep in the pasture and selected you to
be the leader of my people Israel. [9]I have
been with you wherever you have gone,
and I have destroyed all your enemies
before your eyes. Now I will make your
name as famous as anyone who has ever
lived on the earth! [10]And I will provide a
homeland for my people Israel, planting
them in a secure place where they will
never be disturbed. Evil nations won't
oppress them as they've done in the past,
[11]starting from the time I appointed
judges to rule my people Israel. And I will
give you rest from all your enemies.

"'Furthermore, the LORD declares that
he will make a house for you—a dynasty of
kings! [12]For when you die and are buried
with your ancestors, I will raise up one of
your descendants, your own offspring, and
I will make his kingdom strong. [13]He is the
one who will build a house—a temple—for
my name. And I will secure his royal
throne forever. [14]I will be his father, and
he will be my son. If he sins, I will correct
and discipline him with the rod, like any
father would do. [15]But my favor will not be
taken from him as I took it from Saul,
whom I removed from your sight. [16]Your
house and your kingdom will continue
before me* for all time, and your throne
will be secure forever.'"

[17]So Nathan went back to David and told him
everything the LORD had said in this vision.

David's Prayer of Thanks

[18]Then King David went in and sat before the
LORD and prayed,

"Who am I, O Sovereign LORD, and what is
my family, that you have brought me this
far? [19]And now, Sovereign LORD, in
addition to everything else, you speak of
giving your servant a lasting dynasty! Do
you deal with everyone this way,
O Sovereign LORD?*

[20]"What more can I say to you? You
know what your servant is really like,
Sovereign LORD. [21]Because of your
promise and according to your will, you
have done all these great things and have
made them known to your servant.

[22]"How great you are, O Sovereign
LORD! There is no one like you. We have
never even heard of another God like you!
[23]What other nation on earth is like your
people Israel? What other nation, O God,
have you redeemed from slavery to be

Is there anyone else like God?

How great you are, O Sovereign LORD! There is no one like you. We have never even heard of another God like you! 2 SAMUEL 7:22

7:2 Hebrew *a house of cedar*. 7:16 As in Greek version and some Hebrew manuscripts; Masoretic Text reads *before you*. 7:19 Or *This is your instruction for all humanity, O Sovereign LORD*.

your own people? You made a great name
for yourself when you redeemed your
people from Egypt. You performed
awesome miracles and drove out the
nations and gods that stood in their way.*
24 You made Israel your very own people
forever, and you, O LORD, became their God.
25 "And now, O LORD God, I am your
servant; do as you have promised
concerning me and my family. Confirm it
as a promise that will last forever. 26 And
may your name be honored forever so
that everyone will say, 'The LORD of
Heaven's Armies is God over Israel!' And
may the house of your servant David
continue before you forever.
27 "O LORD of Heaven's Armies, God of
Israel, I have been bold enough to pray
this prayer to you because you have
revealed all this to your servant, saying,
'I will build a house for you—a dynasty of
kings!' 28 For you are God, O Sovereign
LORD. Your words are truth, and you have
promised these good things to your
servant. 29 And now, may it please you to
bless the house of your servant, so that it
may continue forever before you. For you
have spoken, and when you grant a
blessing to your servant, O Sovereign
LORD, it is an eternal blessing!"

CHAPTER 8

David's Military Victories

After this, David defeated and subdued the
Philistines by conquering Gath, their largest
town.* 2 David also conquered the land of
Moab. He made the people lie down on the
ground in a row, and he measured them off in
groups with a length of rope. He measured
off two groups to be executed for every one
group to be spared. The Moabites who were
spared became David's subjects and paid him
tribute money.
3 David also destroyed the forces of Hadad-
ezer son of Rehob, king of Zobah, when Had-
adezer marched out to strengthen his control
along the Euphrates River. 4 David captured
1,000 chariots, 7,000 charioteers,* and
20,000 foot soldiers. He crippled all the char-
iot horses except enough for 100 chariots.
5 When Arameans from Damascus arrived
to help King Hadadezer, David killed 22,000
of them. 6 Then he placed several army garri-
sons in Damascus, the Aramean capital, and
the Arameans became David's subjects and
paid him tribute money. So the LORD made
David victorious wherever he went.
7 David brought the gold shields of Hadade-
zer's officers to Jerusalem, 8 along with a large
amount of bronze from Hadadezer's towns of
Tebah* and Berothai.
9 When King Toi of Hamath heard that Da-
vid had destroyed the entire army of Hadade-
zer, 10 he sent his son Joram to congratulate
King David for his successful campaign. Had-
adezer and Toi had been enemies and were
often at war. Joram presented David with
many gifts of silver, gold, and bronze.
11 King David dedicated all these gifts to the
LORD, as he did with the silver and gold from
the other nations he had defeated—12 from
Edom,* Moab, Ammon, Philistia, and Ama-
lek—and from Hadadezer son of Rehob, king
of Zobah.
13 So David became even more famous when
he returned from destroying 18,000 Edom-
ites* in the Valley of Salt. 14 He placed army
garrisons throughout Edom, and all the Edom-
ites became David's subjects. In fact, the LORD
made David victorious wherever he went.
15 So David reigned over all Israel and did
what was just and right for all his people.
16 Joab son of Zeruiah was commander of the
army. Jehoshaphat son of Ahilud was the royal
historian. 17 Zadok son of Ahitub and Ahime-
lech son of Abiathar were the priests. Seraiah
was the court secretary. 18 Benaiah son of Je-
hoiada was captain of the king's bodyguard.*
And David's sons served as priestly leaders.*

CHAPTER 9

David's Kindness to Mephibosheth

One day David asked, "Is anyone in Saul's
family still alive—anyone to whom I can

7:23 As in Greek version (see also 1 Chr 17:21); Hebrew reads *You made a great name for yourself and performed awesome miracles for your land. You did this in the sight of your people, whom you redeemed from Egypt, from nations and their gods.* **8:1** Hebrew *by conquering Metheg-ammah*, a name that means "the bridle," possibly referring to the size of the town or the tribute money taken from it. Compare 1 Chr 18:1. **8:4** As in Dead Sea Scrolls and Greek version (see also 1 Chr 18:4); Masoretic Text reads *captured 1,700 charioteers.* **8:8** As in some Greek manuscripts (see also 1 Chr 18:8); Hebrew reads *Betah.* **8:12** As in a few Hebrew manuscripts and Greek and Syriac versions (see also 8:14; 1 Chr 18:11); most Hebrew manuscripts read *Aram.* **8:13** As in a few Hebrew manuscripts and Greek and Syriac versions (see also 8:14; 1 Chr 18:12); most Hebrew manuscripts read *Arameans.* **8:18a** Hebrew *of the Kerethites and Pelethites.* **8:18b** Hebrew *David's sons were priests;* compare parallel text at 1 Chr 18:17.

show kindness for Jonathan's sake?" [2]He summoned a man named Ziba, who had been one of Saul's servants. "Are you Ziba?" the king asked.

"Yes sir, I am," Ziba replied.

[3]The king then asked him, "Is anyone still alive from Saul's family? If so, I want to show God's kindness to them."

Ziba replied, "Yes, one of Jonathan's sons is still alive. He is crippled in both feet."

[4]"Where is he?" the king asked.

"In Lo-debar," Ziba told him, "at the home of Makir son of Ammiel."

[5]So David sent for him and brought him from Makir's home. [6]His name was Mephibosheth*; he was Jonathan's son and Saul's grandson. When he came to David, he bowed low to the ground in deep respect. David said, "Greetings, Mephibosheth."

Mephibosheth replied, "I am your servant."

[7]"Don't be afraid!" David said. "I intend to show kindness to you because of my promise to your father, Jonathan. I will give you all the property that once belonged to your grandfather Saul, and you will eat here with me at the king's table!"

[8]Mephibosheth bowed respectfully and exclaimed, "Who is your servant, that you should show such kindness to a dead dog like me?"

[9]Then the king summoned Saul's servant Ziba and said, "I have given your master's grandson everything that belonged to Saul and his family. [10]You and your sons and servants are to farm the land for him to produce food for your master's household.* But Mephibosheth, your master's grandson, will eat here at my table." (Ziba had fifteen sons and twenty servants.)

[11]Ziba replied, "Yes, my lord the king; I am your servant, and I will do all that you have commanded." And from that time on, Mephibosheth ate regularly at David's table,* like one of the king's own sons.

[12]Mephibosheth had a young son named Mica. From then on, all the members of Ziba's household were Mephibosheth's servants. [13]And Mephibosheth, who was crippled in both feet, lived in Jerusalem and ate regularly at the king's table.

CHAPTER 10

David Defeats the Ammonites

Some time after this, King Nahash* of the Ammonites died, and his son Hanun became king. [2]David said, "I am going to show loyalty to Hanun just as his father, Nahash, was always loyal to me." So David sent ambassadors to express sympathy to Hanun about his father's death.

But when David's ambassadors arrived in the land of Ammon, [3]the Ammonite commanders said to Hanun, their master, "Do you really think these men are coming here to honor your father? No! David has sent them to spy out the city so they can come in and conquer it!" [4]So Hanun seized David's ambassadors and shaved off half of each man's beard, cut off their robes at the buttocks, and sent them back to David in shame.

[5]When David heard what had happened, he sent messengers to tell the men, "Stay at Jericho until your beards grow out, and then come back." For they felt deep shame because of their appearance.

[6]When the people of Ammon realized how seriously they had angered David, they sent and hired 20,000 Aramean foot soldiers from the lands of Beth-rehob and Zobah, 1,000 from the king of Maacah, and 12,000 from the land of Tob. [7]When David heard about this, he sent Joab and all his warriors to fight them. [8]The Ammonite troops came out and drew up their battle lines at the entrance of the city gate, while the Arameans from Zobah and Rehob and the men from Tob and Maacah positioned themselves to fight in the open fields.

[9]When Joab saw that he would have to fight on both the front and the rear, he chose some of Israel's elite troops and placed them under his personal command to fight the Arameans in the fields. [10]He left the rest of the army under the command of his brother Abishai, who was to attack the Ammonites. [11]"If the Arameans are too strong for me, then come over and help me," Joab told his brother. "And if the Ammonites are too strong for you, I will come and help you. [12]Be courageous! Let us fight bravely for our people and the cities of our God. May the LORD's will be done."

[13]When Joab and his troops attacked, the

9:6 *Mephibosheth* is another name for Merib-baal. **9:10** As in Greek version; Hebrew reads *your master's grandson.* **9:11** As in Greek version; Hebrew reads *my table.* **10:1** As in parallel text at 1 Chr 19:1; Hebrew reads *the king.*

Arameans began to run away. [14]And when the Ammonites saw the Arameans running, they ran from Abishai and retreated into the city. After the battle was over, Joab returned to Jerusalem.

[15]The Arameans now realized that they were no match for Israel. So when they regrouped, [16]they were joined by additional Aramean troops summoned by Hadadezer from the other side of the Euphrates River.* These troops arrived at Helam under the command of Shobach, the commander of Hadadezer's forces.

[17]When David heard what was happening, he mobilized all Israel, crossed the Jordan River, and led the army to Helam. The Arameans positioned themselves in battle formation and fought against David. [18]But again the Arameans fled from the Israelites. This time David's forces killed 700 charioteers and 40,000 foot soldiers,* including Shobach, the commander of their army. [19]When all the kings allied with Hadadezer saw that they had been defeated by Israel, they surrendered to Israel and became their subjects. After that, the Arameans were afraid to help the Ammonites.

CHAPTER 11

David and Bathsheba

In the spring of the year,* when kings normally go out to war, David sent Joab and the Israelite army to fight the Ammonites. They destroyed the Ammonite army and laid siege to the city of Rabbah. However, David stayed behind in Jerusalem.

[2]Late one afternoon, after his midday rest, David got out of bed and was walking on the roof of the palace. As he looked out over the city, he noticed a woman of unusual beauty taking a bath. [3]He sent someone to find out who she was, and he was told, "She is Bathsheba, the daughter of Eliam and the wife of Uriah the Hittite." [4]Then David sent messengers to get her; and when she came to the palace, he slept with her. She had just completed the purification rites after having her menstrual period. Then she returned home. [5]Later, when Bathsheba discovered that she was pregnant, she sent David a message, saying, "I'm pregnant."

DAVID

I am now the King of Israel. Once I was just a young shepherd. Years ago my friend Jonathan saved my life. Now he is gone, but his son, Mephibosheth, still lives. I asked for him to be brought to the palace so I could show him kindness. When he came, he bowed down and promised to serve me. I knew he was afraid. I told him that many years ago his father and I had promised to take care of each other's families. Now was my chance. I gave Mephibosheth land that had belonged to his grandfather, King Saul, and I welcomed him at my table. It was the least I could do.

Read more about David in 1 Samuel 16–1 Kings 2.

[6]Then David sent word to Joab: "Send me Uriah the Hittite." So Joab sent him to David. [7]When Uriah arrived, David asked him how Joab and the army were getting along and how the war was progressing. [8]Then he told

10:16 Hebrew *the river*. **10:18** As in some Greek manuscripts (see also 1 Chr 19:18); Hebrew reads *charioteers*. **11:1** Hebrew *At the turn of the year*. The first day of the year in the ancient Hebrew lunar calendar occurred in March or April.

Uriah, "Go on home and relax.*" David even sent a gift to Uriah after he had left the palace. [9]But Uriah didn't go home. He slept that night at the palace entrance with the king's palace guard.

[10]When David heard that Uriah had not gone home, he summoned him and asked, "What's the matter? Why didn't you go home last night after being away for so long?"

[11]Uriah replied, "The Ark and the armies of Israel and Judah are living in tents,* and Joab and my master's men are camping in the open fields. How could I go home to wine and dine and sleep with my wife? I swear that I would never do such a thing."

[12]"Well, stay here today," David told him, "and tomorrow you may return to the army." So Uriah stayed in Jerusalem that day and the next. [13]Then David invited him to dinner and got him drunk. But even then he couldn't get Uriah to go home to his wife. Again he slept at the palace entrance with the king's palace guard.

David Arranges for Uriah's Death

[14]So the next morning David wrote a letter to Joab and gave it to Uriah to deliver. [15]The letter instructed Joab, "Station Uriah on the front lines where the battle is fiercest. Then pull back so that he will be killed." [16]So Joab assigned Uriah to a spot close to the city wall where he knew the enemy's strongest men were fighting. [17]And when the enemy soldiers came out of the city to fight, Uriah the Hittite was killed along with several other Israelite soldiers.

[18]Then Joab sent a battle report to David. [19]He told his messenger, "Report all the news of the battle to the king. [20]But he might get angry and ask, 'Why did the troops go so close to the city? Didn't they know there would be shooting from the walls? [21]Wasn't Abimelech son of Gideon* killed at Thebez by a woman who threw a millstone down on him from the wall? Why would you get so close to the wall?' Then tell him, 'Uriah the Hittite was killed, too.'"

[22]So the messenger went to Jerusalem and gave a complete report to David. [23]"The enemy came out against us in the open fields," he said. "And as we chased them back to the city gate, [24]the archers on the wall shot arrows at us. Some of the king's men were killed, including Uriah the Hittite."

[25]"Well, tell Joab not to be discouraged," David said. "The sword devours this one today and that one tomorrow! Fight harder next time, and conquer the city!"

[26]When Uriah's wife heard that her husband was dead, she mourned for him. [27]When the period of mourning was over, David sent for her and brought her to the palace, and she became one of his wives. Then she gave birth to a son. But the LORD was displeased with what David had done.

CHAPTER 12

Nathan Rebukes David

So the LORD sent Nathan the prophet to tell David this story: "There were two men in a certain town. One was rich, and one was poor. [2]The rich man owned a great many sheep and cattle. [3]The poor man owned nothing but one little lamb he had bought. He raised that little lamb, and it grew up with his children. It ate from the man's own plate and drank from his cup. He cuddled it in his arms like a baby daughter. [4]One day a guest arrived at the home of the rich man. But instead of killing an animal from his own flock or herd, he took the poor man's lamb and killed it and prepared it for his guest."

[5]David was furious. "As surely as the LORD lives," he vowed, "any man who would do such a thing deserves to die! [6]He must repay four lambs to the poor man for the one he stole and for having no pity."

[7]Then Nathan said to David, "You are that man! The LORD, the God of Israel, says: I anointed you king of Israel and saved you from the power of Saul. [8]I gave you your master's house and his wives and the kingdoms of Israel and Judah. And if that had not been enough, I would have given you much, much more. [9]Why, then, have you despised the word of the LORD and done this horrible deed? For you have murdered Uriah the Hittite with the sword of the Ammonites and stolen his wife. [10]From this time on, your family will live by the sword because you have de-

11:8 Hebrew *and wash your feet*, an expression that may also have a connotation of ritualistic washing. **11:11** Or *at Succoth*.
11:21 Hebrew *son of Jerub-besheth*. Jerub-besheth is a variation on the name Jerub-baal, which is another name for Gideon; see Judg 6:32.

The Truth Hurts

Andrew found some money on the floor in the school hallway—lots of money! Seventy-five dollars in a paper clip. Andrew picked it up and shoved it into his pocket. Later, the principal announced, "Some cafeteria money has been lost. If you found it, please bring it to the office." Andrew didn't say anything. But Andrew's friend said, "I was down the hall earlier today and saw you pick up something. Was it the money?" What should Andrew do? Read 2 Samuel 12:1-13 to see how David reacted when confronted by his friend.

spised me by taking Uriah's wife to be your own.

11"This is what the LORD says: Because of what you have done, I will cause your own household to rebel against you. I will give your wives to another man before your very eyes, and he will go to bed with them in public view. 12You did it secretly, but I will make this happen to you openly in the sight of all Israel."

David Confesses His Guilt

13Then David confessed to Nathan, "I have sinned against the LORD."

Nathan replied, "Yes, but the LORD has forgiven you, and you won't die for this sin. 14Nevertheless, because you have shown utter contempt for the LORD* by doing this, your child will die."

15After Nathan returned to his home, the LORD sent a deadly illness to the child of David and Uriah's wife. 16David begged God to spare the child. He went without food and lay all night on the bare ground. 17The elders of his household pleaded with him to get up and eat with them, but he refused.

18Then on the seventh day the child died. David's advisers were afraid to tell him. "He wouldn't listen to reason while the child was ill," they said. "What drastic thing will he do when we tell him the child is dead?"

19When David saw them whispering, he realized what had happened. "Is the child dead?" he asked.

"Yes," they replied, "he is dead."

20Then David got up from the ground, washed himself, put on lotions,* and changed his clothes. He went to the Tabernacle and worshiped the LORD. After that, he returned to the palace and was served food and ate.

21His advisers were amazed. "We don't understand you," they told him. "While the child was still living, you wept and refused to eat. But now that the child is dead, you have stopped your mourning and are eating again."

22David replied, "I fasted and wept while the child was alive, for I said, 'Perhaps the LORD will be gracious to me and let the child live.' 23But why should I fast when he is dead? Can I bring him back again? I will go to him one day, but he cannot return to me."

24Then David comforted Bathsheba, his wife, and slept with her. She became pregnant and gave birth to a son, and David* named him Solomon. The LORD loved the child 25and sent word through Nathan the prophet that they should name him Jedidiah (which means "beloved of the LORD"), as the LORD had commanded.*

12:14 As in Dead Sea Scrolls; Masoretic Text reads *the LORD's enemies.* **12:20** Hebrew *anointed himself.* **12:24** Hebrew *he;* an alternate Hebrew reading and some Hebrew manuscripts read *she.* **12:25** As in Greek version; Hebrew reads *because of the LORD.*

David Captures Rabbah

26 Meanwhile, Joab was fighting against Rab-
bah, the capital of Ammon, and he captured
the royal fortifications.* 27 Joab sent messen-
gers to tell David, "I have fought against Rab-
bah and captured its water supply.* 28 Now
bring the rest of the army and capture the
city. Otherwise, I will capture it and get credit
for the victory."

29 So David gathered the rest of the army
and went to Rabbah, and he fought against it
and captured it. 30 David removed the crown
from the king's head,* and it was placed on
his own head. The crown was made of gold
and set with gems, and it weighed seventy-
five pounds.* David took a vast amount of
plunder from the city. 31 He also made slaves
of the people of Rabbah and forced them to
labor with* saws, iron picks, and iron axes,
and to work in the brick kilns.* That is how he
dealt with the people of all the Ammonite
towns. Then David and all the army returned
to Jerusalem.

CHAPTER 13

The Rape of Tamar

Now David's son Absalom had a beautiful
sister named Tamar. And Amnon, her half
brother, fell desperately in love with her. 2 Am-
non became so obsessed with Tamar that
he became ill. She was a virgin, and Amnon
thought he could never have her.

3 But Amnon had a very crafty friend—his
cousin Jonadab. He was the son of David's
brother Shimea.* 4 One day Jonadab said to
Amnon, "What's the trouble? Why should the
son of a king look so dejected morning after
morning?"

So Amnon told him, "I am in love with Ta-
mar, my brother Absalom's sister."

5 "Well," Jonadab said, "I'll tell you what to
do. Go back to bed and pretend you are ill.
When your father comes to see you, ask him
to let Tamar come and prepare some food for
you. Tell him you'll feel better if she prepares
it as you watch and feeds you with her own
hands."

6 So Amnon lay down and pretended to be
sick. And when the king came to see him, Am-
non asked him, "Please let my sister Tamar
come and cook my favorite dish* as I watch.
Then I can eat it from her own hands." 7 So Da-
vid agreed and sent Tamar to Amnon's house
to prepare some food for him.

8 When Tamar arrived at Amnon's house,
she went to the place where he was lying
down so he could watch her mix some dough.
Then she baked his favorite dish for him. 9 But
when she set the serving tray before him, he
refused to eat. "Everyone get out of here,"
Amnon told his servants. So they all left.

10 Then he said to Tamar, "Now bring the
food into my bedroom and feed it to me here."
So Tamar took his favorite dish to him. 11 But as
she was feeding him, he grabbed her and de-
manded, "Come to bed with me, my darling
sister."

12 "No, my brother!" she cried. "Don't be
foolish! Don't do this to me! Such wicked
things aren't done in Israel. 13 Where could I go
in my shame? And you would be called one of
the greatest fools in Israel. Please, just speak to
the king about it, and he will let you marry me."

14 But Amnon wouldn't listen to her, and
since he was stronger than she was, he raped
her. 15 Then suddenly Amnon's love turned to
hate, and he hated her even more than he had
loved her. "Get out of here!" he snarled at her.

16 "No, no!" Tamar cried. "Sending me away
now is worse than what you've already done
to me."

But Amnon wouldn't listen to her. 17 He
shouted for his servant and demanded,
"Throw this woman out, and lock the door
behind her!"

18 So the servant put her out and locked the
door behind her. She was wearing a long,
beautiful robe,* as was the custom in those
days for the king's virgin daughters. 19 But now
Tamar tore her robe and put ashes on her
head. And then, with her face in her hands, she
went away crying.

20 Her brother Absalom saw her and asked,
"Is it true that Amnon has been with you?
Well, my sister, keep quiet for now, since
he's your brother. Don't you worry about it."
So Tamar lived as a desolate woman in her
brother Absalom's house.

12:26 Or *the royal city*. **12:27** Or *captured the city of water*. **12:30a** Or *from the head of Milcom* (as in Greek version). Milcom, also called Molech, was the god of the Ammonites. **12:30b** Hebrew *1 talent* [34 kilograms]. **12:31a** Or *He also brought out the people of Rabbah and put them under*. **12:31b** Or *and he made them pass through the brick kilns*. **13:3** Hebrew *Shimeah* (also in 13:32), a variant spelling of Shimea; compare 1 Chr 2:13. **13:6** Or *a couple of cakes*; also in 13:8, 10. **13:18** Or *a robe with sleeves*, or *an ornamented robe*. The meaning of the Hebrew is uncertain.

[21]When King David heard what had happened, he was very angry.* [22]And though Absalom never spoke to Amnon about this, he hated Amnon deeply because of what he had done to his sister.

Absalom's Revenge on Amnon

[23]Two years later, when Absalom's sheep were being sheared at Baal-hazor near Ephraim, Absalom invited all the king's sons to come to a feast. [24]He went to the king and said, "My sheep-shearers are now at work. Would the king and his servants please come to celebrate the occasion with me?"

[25]The king replied, "No, my son. If we all came, we would be too much of a burden on you." Absalom pressed him, but the king would not come, though he gave Absalom his blessing.

[26]"Well, then," Absalom said, "if you can't come, how about sending my brother Amnon with us?"

"Why Amnon?" the king asked. [27]But Absalom kept on pressing the king until he finally agreed to let all his sons attend, including Amnon. So Absalom prepared a feast fit for a king.*

[28]Absalom told his men, "Wait until Amnon gets drunk; then at my signal, kill him! Don't be afraid. I'm the one who has given the command. Take courage and do it!" [29]So at Absalom's signal they murdered Amnon. Then the other sons of the king jumped on their mules and fled.

[30]As they were on the way back to Jerusalem, this report reached David: "Absalom has killed all the king's sons; not one is left alive!" [31]The king got up, tore his robe, and threw himself on the ground. His advisers also tore their clothes in horror and sorrow.

[32]But just then Jonadab, the son of David's brother Shimea, arrived and said, "No, don't believe that all the king's sons have been killed! It was only Amnon! Absalom has been plotting this ever since Amnon raped his sister Tamar. [33]No, my lord the king, your sons aren't all dead! It was only Amnon." [34]Meanwhile Absalom escaped.

Then the watchman on the Jerusalem wall saw a great crowd coming down the hill on the road from the west. He ran to tell the king, "I see a crowd of people coming from the Horonaim road along the side of the hill."*

[35]"Look!" Jonadab told the king. "There they are now! The king's sons are coming, just as I said."

[36]They soon arrived, weeping and sobbing, and the king and all his servants wept bitterly with them. [37]And David mourned many days for his son Amnon.

Absalom fled to his grandfather, Talmai son of Ammihud, the king of Geshur. [38]He stayed there in Geshur for three years. [39]And King David,* now reconciled to Amnon's death, longed to be reunited with his son Absalom.*

CHAPTER 14

Joab Arranges for Absalom's Return

Joab realized how much the king longed to see Absalom. [2]So he sent for a woman from Tekoa who had a reputation for great wisdom. He said to her, "Pretend you are in mourning; wear mourning clothes and don't put on lotions.* Act like a woman who has been mourning for the dead for a long time. [3]Then go to the king and tell him the story I am about to tell you." Then Joab told her what to say.

[4]When the woman from Tekoa approached the king, she bowed with her face to the ground in deep respect and cried out, "O king! Help me!"

[5]"What's the trouble?" the king asked.

"Alas, I am a widow!" she replied. "My husband is dead. [6]My two sons had a fight out in the field. And since no one was there to stop it, one of them was killed. [7]Now the rest of the family is demanding, 'Let us have your son. We will execute him for murdering his brother. He doesn't deserve to inherit his family's property.' They want to extinguish the only coal I have left, and my husband's name and family will disappear from the face of the earth."

[8]"Leave it to me," the king told her. "Go home, and I'll see to it that no one touches him."

[9]"Oh, thank you, my lord the king," the woman from Tekoa replied. "If you are criticized for helping me, let the blame fall on me

13:21 Dead Sea Scrolls and Greek version add *But he did not punish his son Amnon, because he loved him, for he was his firstborn.* **13:27** As in Greek and Latin versions (compare also Dead Sea Scrolls); the Hebrew text lacks this sentence. **13:34** As in Greek version; Hebrew lacks this sentence. **13:39a** Dead Sea Scrolls and Greek version read *And the spirit of the king.* **13:39b** Or *no longer felt a need to go out after Absalom.* **14:2** Hebrew *don't anoint yourself with oil.*

and on my father's house, and let the king and his throne be innocent."

[10]"If anyone objects," the king said, "bring him to me. I can assure you he will never complain again!"

[11]Then she said, "Please swear to me by the LORD your God that you won't let anyone take vengeance against my son. I want no more bloodshed."

"As surely as the LORD lives," he replied, "not a hair on your son's head will be disturbed!"

[12]"Please allow me to ask one more thing of my lord the king," she said.

"Go ahead and speak," he responded.

[13]She replied, "Why don't you do as much for the people of God as you have promised to do for me? You have convicted yourself in making this decision, because you have refused to bring home your own banished son.

[14]All of us must die eventually. Our lives are like water spilled out on the ground, which cannot be gathered up again. But God does not just sweep life away; instead, he devises ways to bring us back when we have been separated from him.

[15]"I have come to plead with my lord the king because people have threatened me. I said to myself, 'Perhaps the king will listen to me [16]and rescue us from those who would cut us off from the inheritance* God has given us. [17]Yes, my lord the king will give us peace of mind again.' I know that you are like an angel of God in discerning good from evil. May the LORD your God be with you."

[18]"I must know one thing," the king replied, "and tell me the truth."

"Yes, my lord the king," she responded.

[19]"Did Joab put you up to this?"

And the woman replied, "My lord the king, how can I deny it? Nobody can hide anything from you. Yes, Joab sent me and told me what to say. [20]He did it to place the matter before you in a different light. But you are as wise as an angel of God, and you understand everything that happens among us!"

[21]So the king sent for Joab and told him, "All right, go and bring back the young man Absalom."

[22]Joab bowed with his face to the ground in deep respect and said, "At last I know that I have gained your approval, my lord the king, for you have granted me this request!"

[23]Then Joab went to Geshur and brought Absalom back to Jerusalem. [24]But the king gave this order: "Absalom may go to his own house, but he must never come into my presence." So Absalom did not see the king.

Absalom Reconciled to David

[25]Now Absalom was praised as the most handsome man in all Israel. He was flawless from head to foot. [26]He cut his hair only once a year, and then only because it was so heavy. When he weighed it out, it came to five pounds!* [27]He had three sons and one daughter. His daughter's name was Tamar, and she was very beautiful.

[28]Absalom lived in Jerusalem for two years, but he never got to see the king. [29]Then Absalom sent for Joab to ask him to intercede for him, but Joab refused to come. Absalom sent

14:16 Or *the property;* or *the people.* **14:26** Hebrew *200 shekels* [2.3 kilograms] *by the royal standard.*

for him a second time, but again Joab refused
to come. 30So Absalom said to his servants,
"Go and set fire to Joab's barley field, the field
next to mine." So they set his field on fire, as
Absalom had commanded.

31Then Joab came to Absalom at his house
and demanded, "Why did your servants set
my field on fire?"

32And Absalom replied, "Because I wanted
you to ask the king why he brought me back
from Geshur if he didn't intend to see me. I
might as well have stayed there. Let me see
the king; if he finds me guilty of anything,
then let him kill me."

33So Joab told the king what Absalom had
said. Then at last David summoned Absalom,
who came and bowed low before the king,
and the king kissed him.

CHAPTER 15

Absalom's Rebellion

After this, Absalom bought a chariot and
horses, and he hired fifty bodyguards to run
ahead of him. 2He got up early every morning
and went out to the gate of the city. When peo-
ple brought a case to the king for judgment,
Absalom would ask where in Israel they were
from, and they would tell him their tribe.
3Then Absalom would say, "You've really got a
strong case here! It's too bad the king doesn't
have anyone to hear it. 4I wish I were the judge.
Then everyone could bring their cases to me
for judgment, and I would give them justice!"

5When people tried to bow before him,
Absalom wouldn't let them. Instead, he took
them by the hand and kissed them. 6Absalom
did this with everyone who came to the king
for judgment, and so he stole the hearts of all
the people of Israel.

7After four years,* Absalom said to the
king, "Let me go to Hebron to offer a sacrifice
to the LORD and fulfill a vow I made to him.
8For while your servant was at Geshur in Aram,
I promised to sacrifice to the LORD in Hebron*
if he would bring me back to Jerusalem."

9"All right," the king told him. "Go and ful-
fill your vow."

So Absalom went to Hebron. 10But while he
was there, he sent secret messengers to all the
tribes of Israel to stir up a rebellion against
the king. "As soon as you hear the ram's horn,"
his message read, "you are to say, 'Absalom
has been crowned king in Hebron.'" 11He took
200 men from Jerusalem with him as guests,
but they knew nothing of his intentions.
12While Absalom was offering the sacrifices,
he sent for Ahithophel, one of David's coun-
selors who lived in Giloh. Soon many others
also joined Absalom, and the conspiracy
gained momentum.

David Escapes from Jerusalem

13A messenger soon arrived in Jerusalem to
tell David, "All Israel has joined Absalom in a
conspiracy against you!"

14"Then we must flee at once, or it will be
too late!" David urged his men. "Hurry! If we
get out of the city before Absalom arrives,
both we and the city of Jerusalem will be
spared from disaster."

15"We are with you," his advisers replied.
"Do what you think is best."

16So the king and all his household set out
at once. He left no one behind except ten
of his concubines to look after the palace.
17The king and all his people set out on foot,
pausing at the last house 18to let all the king's
men move past to lead the way. There were
600 men from Gath who had come with
David, along with the king's bodyguard.*

19Then the king turned and said to Ittai, a
leader of the men from Gath, "Why are you
coming with us? Go on back to King Absalom,
for you are a guest in Israel, a foreigner in exile.
20You arrived only recently, and should I force
you today to wander with us? I don't even
know where we will go. Go on back and take
your kinsmen with you, and may the LORD
show you his unfailing love and faithfulness.*"

21But Ittai said to the king, "I vow by the
LORD and by your own life that I will go wher-
ever my lord the king goes, no matter what
happens—whether it means life or death."

22David replied, "All right, come with us."
So Ittai and all his men and their families
went along.

23Everyone cried loudly as the king and his
followers passed by. They crossed the Kidron
Valley and then went out toward the wilder-
ness.

15:7 As in Greek and Syriac versions; Hebrew reads *forty years*. **15:8** As in some Greek manuscripts; Hebrew lacks *in Hebron*.
15:18 Hebrew *the Kerethites and Pelethites*. **15:20** As in Greek version; Hebrew reads *and may unfailing love and faithfulness go with you*.

[24]Zadok and all the Levites also came along, carrying the Ark of the Covenant of God. They set down the Ark of God, and Abiathar offered sacrifices* until everyone had passed out of the city.

[25]Then the king instructed Zadok to take the Ark of God back into the city. "If the LORD sees fit," David said, "he will bring me back to see the Ark and the Tabernacle* again. [26]But if he is through with me, then let him do what seems best to him."

[27]The king also told Zadok the priest, "Look,* here is my plan. You and Abiathar* should return quietly to the city with your son Ahimaaz and Abiathar's son Jonathan. [28]I will stop at the shallows of the Jordan River* and wait there for a report from you." [29]So Zadok and Abiathar took the Ark of God back to the city and stayed there.

[30]David walked up the road to the Mount of Olives, weeping as he went. His head was covered and his feet were bare as a sign of mourning. And the people who were with him covered their heads and wept as they climbed the hill. [31]When someone told David that his adviser Ahithophel was now backing Absalom, David prayed, "O LORD, let Ahithophel give Absalom foolish advice!"

[32]When David reached the summit of the Mount of Olives where people worshiped God, Hushai the Arkite was waiting there for him. Hushai had torn his clothing and put dirt on his head as a sign of mourning. [33]But David told him, "If you go with me, you will only be a burden. [34]Return to Jerusalem and tell Absalom, 'I will now be your adviser, O king, just as I was your father's adviser in the past.' Then you can frustrate and counter Ahithophel's advice. [35]Zadok and Abiathar, the priests, will be there. Tell them about the plans being made in the king's palace, [36]and they will send their sons Ahimaaz and Jonathan to tell me what is going on."

[37]So David's friend Hushai returned to Jerusalem, getting there just as Absalom arrived.

CHAPTER 16

David and Ziba

When David had gone a little beyond the summit of the Mount of Olives, Ziba, the servant of Mephibosheth,* was waiting there for him. He had two donkeys loaded with 200 loaves of bread, 100 clusters of raisins, 100 bunches of summer fruit, and a wineskin full of wine.

[2]"What are these for?" the king asked Ziba.

Ziba replied, "The donkeys are for the king's people to ride on, and the bread and summer fruit are for the young men to eat. The wine is for those who become exhausted in the wilderness."

[3]"And where is Mephibosheth, Saul's grandson?" the king asked him.

"He stayed in Jerusalem," Ziba replied. "He said, 'Today I will get back the kingdom of my grandfather Saul.'"

[4]"In that case," the king told Ziba, "I give you everything Mephibosheth owns."

"I bow before you," Ziba replied. "May I always be pleasing to you, my lord the king."

Shimei Curses David

[5]As King David came to Bahurim, a man came out of the village cursing them. It was Shimei son of Gera, from the same clan as Saul's family. [6]He threw stones at the king and the king's officers and all the mighty warriors who surrounded him. [7]"Get out of here, you murderer, you scoundrel!" he shouted at David. [8]"The LORD is paying you back for all the bloodshed in Saul's clan. You stole his throne, and now the LORD has given it to your son Absalom. At last you will taste some of your own medicine, for you are a murderer!"

[9]"Why should this dead dog curse my lord the king?" Abishai son of Zeruiah demanded. "Let me go over and cut off his head!"

[10]"No!" the king said. "Who asked your opinion, you sons of Zeruiah! If the LORD has told him to curse me, who are you to stop him?"

[11]Then David said to Abishai and to all his servants, "My own son is trying to kill me. Doesn't this relative of Saul* have even more reason to do so? Leave him alone and let him curse, for the LORD has told him to do it. [12]And perhaps the LORD will see that I am being wronged and will bless me because of these curses today." [13]So David and his men continued down the road, and Shimei kept pace with them on a nearby hillside, cursing as he went and throwing stones at David and tossing dust into the air.

15:24 Or *Abiathar went up.* **15:25** Hebrew *and his dwelling place.* **15:27a** As in Greek version; Hebrew reads *Are you a seer?* or *Do you see?* **15:27b** Hebrew lacks *and Abiathar;* compare 15:29. **15:28** Hebrew *at the crossing points of the wilderness.* **16:1** *Mephibosheth* is another name for Merib-baal. **16:11** Hebrew *this Benjaminite.*

[14]The king and all who were with him grew weary along the way, so they rested when they reached the Jordan River.*

Ahithophel Advises Absalom

[15]Meanwhile, Absalom and all the army of Israel arrived at Jerusalem, accompanied by Ahithophel. [16]When David's friend Hushai the Arkite arrived, he went immediately to see Absalom. "Long live the king!" he exclaimed. "Long live the king!"

[17]"Is this the way you treat your friend David?" Absalom asked him. "Why aren't you with him?"

[18]"I'm here because I belong to the man who is chosen by the LORD and by all the men of Israel," Hushai replied. [19]"And anyway, why shouldn't I serve you? Just as I was your father's adviser, now I will be your adviser!"

[20]Then Absalom turned to Ahithophel and asked him, "What should I do next?"

[21]Ahithophel told him, "Go and sleep with your father's concubines, for he has left them here to look after the palace. Then all Israel will know that you have insulted your father beyond hope of reconciliation, and they will throw their support to you." [22]So they set up a tent on the palace roof where everyone could see it, and Absalom went in and had sex with his father's concubines.

[23]Absalom followed Ahithophel's advice, just as David had done. For every word Ahithophel spoke seemed as wise as though it had come directly from the mouth of God.

CHAPTER 17

Now Ahithophel urged Absalom, "Let me choose 12,000 men to start out after David tonight. [2]I will catch up with him while he is weary and discouraged. He and his troops will panic, and everyone will run away. Then I will kill only the king, [3]and I will bring all the people back to you as a bride returns to her husband. After all, it is only one man's life that you seek.* Then you will be at peace with all the people." [4]This plan seemed good to Absalom and to all the elders of Israel.

Hushai Counters Ahithophel's Advice

[5]But then Absalom said, "Bring in Hushai the Arkite. Let's see what he thinks about this."

[6]When Hushai arrived, Absalom told him what Ahithophel had said. Then he asked, "What is your opinion? Should we follow Ahithophel's advice? If not, what do you suggest?"

[7]"Well," Hushai replied to Absalom, "this time Ahithophel has made a mistake. [8]You know your father and his men; they are mighty warriors. Right now they are as enraged as a mother bear who has been robbed of her cubs. And remember that your father is an experienced man of war. He won't be spending the night among the troops. [9]He has probably already hidden in some pit or cave. And when he comes out and attacks and a few of your men fall, there will be panic among your troops, and the word will spread that Absalom's men are being slaughtered. [10]Then even the bravest soldiers, though they have the heart of a lion, will be paralyzed with fear. For all Israel knows what a mighty warrior your father is and how courageous his men are.

[11]"I recommend that you mobilize the entire army of Israel, bringing them from as far away as Dan in the north and Beersheba in the south. That way you will have an army as numerous as the sand on the seashore. And I advise that you personally lead the troops. [12]When we find David, we'll fall on him like dew that falls on the ground. Then neither he nor any of his men will be left alive. [13]And if David were to escape into some town, you will have all Israel there at your command. Then we can take ropes and drag the walls of the town into the nearest valley until every stone is torn down."

[14]Then Absalom and all the men of Israel said, "Hushai's advice is better than Ahithophel's." For the LORD had determined to defeat the counsel of Ahithophel, which really was the better plan, so that he could bring disaster on Absalom!

Hushai Warns David to Escape

[15]Hushai told Zadok and Abiathar, the priests, what Ahithophel had said to Absalom and the elders of Israel and what he himself had advised instead. [16]"Quick!" he told them. "Find David and urge him not to stay at the shallows of the Jordan River* tonight. He must go across at once into the wilderness

16:14 As in Greek version (see also 17:16); Hebrew reads *when they reached their destination.* **17:3** As in Greek version; Hebrew reads *like the return of all is the man whom you seek.* **17:16** Hebrew *at the crossing points of the wilderness.*

beyond. Otherwise he will die and his entire army with him."

17 Jonathan and Ahimaaz had been staying at En-rogel so as not to be seen entering and leaving the city. Arrangements had been made for a servant girl to bring them the message they were to take to King David. 18 But a boy spotted them at En-rogel, and he told Absalom about it. So they quickly escaped to Bahurim, where a man hid them down inside a well in his courtyard. 19 The man's wife put a cloth over the top of the well and scattered grain on it to dry in the sun; so no one suspected they were there.

20 When Absalom's men arrived, they asked her, "Have you seen Ahimaaz and Jonathan?"

The woman replied, "They were here, but they crossed over the brook." Absalom's men looked for them without success and returned to Jerusalem.

21 Then the two men crawled out of the well and hurried on to King David. "Quick!" they told him, "cross the Jordan tonight!" And they told him how Ahithophel had advised that he be captured and killed. 22 So David and all the people with him went across the Jordan River during the night, and they were all on the other bank before dawn.

23 When Ahithophel realized that his advice had not been followed, he saddled his donkey, went to his hometown, set his affairs in order, and hanged himself. He died there and was buried in the family tomb.

24 David soon arrived at Mahanaim. By now, Absalom had mobilized the entire army of Israel and was leading his troops across the Jordan River. 25 Absalom had appointed Amasa as commander of his army, replacing Joab, who had been commander under David. (Amasa was Joab's cousin. His father was Jether,* an Ishmaelite.* His mother, Abigail daughter of Nahash, was the sister of Joab's mother, Zeruiah.) 26 Absalom and the Israelite army set up camp in the land of Gilead.

27 When David arrived at Mahanaim, he was warmly greeted by Shobi son of Nahash, who came from Rabbah of the Ammonites, and by Makir son of Ammiel from Lo-debar, and by Barzillai of Gilead from Rogelim. 28 They brought sleeping mats, cooking pots, serving bowls, wheat and barley, flour and roasted grain, beans, lentils, 29 honey, butter, sheep, goats, and cheese for David and those who were with him. For they said, "You must all be very hungry and tired and thirsty after your long march through the wilderness."

CHAPTER 18

Absalom's Defeat and Death

David now mustered the men who were with him and appointed generals and captains* to lead them. 2 He sent the troops out in three groups, placing one group under Joab, one under Joab's brother Abishai son of Zeruiah, and one under Ittai, the man from Gath. The king told his troops, "I am going out with you."

3 But his men objected strongly. "You must not go," they urged. "If we have to turn and run—and even if half of us die—it will make no difference to Absalom's troops; they will be looking only for you. You are worth 10,000 of us,* and it is better that you stay here in the town and send help if we need it."

4 "If you think that's the best plan, I'll do it," the king answered. So he stood alongside the gate of the town as all the troops marched out in groups of hundreds and of thousands.

5 And the king gave this command to Joab, Abishai, and Ittai: "For my sake, deal gently with young Absalom." And all the troops heard the king give this order to his commanders.

6 So the battle began in the forest of Ephraim, 7 and the Israelite troops were beaten back by David's men. There was a great slaughter that day, and 20,000 men laid down their lives. 8 The battle raged all across the countryside, and more men died because of the forest than were killed by the sword.

9 During the battle, Absalom happened to come upon some of David's men. He tried to escape on his mule, but as he rode beneath the thick branches of a great tree, his hair* got caught in the tree. His mule kept going and left him dangling in the air. 10 One of David's men saw what had happened and told Joab, "I saw Absalom dangling from a great tree."

11 "What?" Joab demanded. "You saw him there and didn't kill him? I would have re-

17:25a Hebrew *Ithra*, a variant spelling of Jether. **17:25b** As in some Greek manuscripts (see also 1 Chr 2:17); Hebrew reads *an Israelite*. **18:1** Hebrew *appointed commanders of thousands and commanders of hundreds*. **18:3** As in two Hebrew manuscripts and some Greek and Latin manuscripts; most Hebrew manuscripts read *Now there are 10,000 like us*. **18:9** Hebrew *his head*.

warded you with ten pieces of silver* and a hero's belt!"

12"I would not kill the king's son for even a thousand pieces of silver,*" the man replied to Joab. "We all heard the king say to you and Abishai and Ittai, 'For my sake, please spare young Absalom.' 13And if I had betrayed the king by killing his son—and the king would certainly find out who did it—you yourself would be the first to abandon me."

14"Enough of this nonsense," Joab said. Then he took three daggers and plunged them into Absalom's heart as he dangled, still alive, in the great tree. 15Ten of Joab's young armor bearers then surrounded Absalom and killed him.

16Then Joab blew the ram's horn, and his men returned from chasing the army of Israel. 17They threw Absalom's body into a deep pit in the forest and piled a great heap of stones over it. And all Israel fled to their homes.

18During his lifetime, Absalom had built a monument to himself in the King's Valley, for he said, "I have no son to carry on my name." He named the monument after himself, and it is known as Absalom's Monument to this day.

David Mourns Absalom's Death

19Then Zadok's son Ahimaaz said, "Let me run to the king with the good news that the LORD has rescued him from his enemies."

20"No," Joab told him, "it wouldn't be good news to the king that his son is dead. You can be my messenger another time, but not today."

21Then Joab said to a man from Ethiopia,* "Go tell the king what you have seen." The man bowed and ran off.

22But Ahimaaz continued to plead with Joab, "Whatever happens, please let me go, too."

"Why should you go, my son?" Joab replied. "There will be no reward for your news."

23"Yes, but let me go anyway," he begged.

Joab finally said, "All right, go ahead." So Ahimaaz took the less demanding route by way of the plain and ran to Mahanaim ahead of the Ethiopian.

24While David was sitting between the inner and outer gates of the town, the watchman climbed to the roof of the gateway by the wall. As he looked, he saw a lone man running toward them. 25He shouted the news down to David, and the king replied, "If he is alone, he has news."

As the messenger came closer, 26the

18:11 Hebrew *10 shekels of silver*, about 4 ounces or 114 grams in weight. **18:12** Hebrew *1,000 shekels*, about 25 pounds or 11.4 kilograms in weight. **18:21** Hebrew *from Cush;* similarly in 18:23, 31, 32.

IS IT OK?

IS IT OK TO HATE EVENTS IN MY LIFE?

Bad stuff happens to everyone. What has happened to you? Maybe someone you love died, your parents got divorced, or you failed fifth grade . . . *twice*. Does God expect you to be fake-happy and say, "I'm *so glad* all these lousy things happened to me"? No!

We learn in 2 Samuel 12:19 that King David's baby boy died, and in chapter 18 that his son Absalom was killed. David gives us a great example of how to respond to bad things in life: (1) Be honest with God, and tell him how you really feel. (2) Don't be afraid to let your emotions out. (3) And turn *to* God—not *away* from him—when you need him most.

watchman saw another man running toward them. He shouted down, "Here comes another one!"

The king replied, "He also will have news."

27"The first man runs like Ahimaaz son of Zadok," the watchman said.

"He is a good man and comes with good news," the king replied.

28Then Ahimaaz cried out to the king, "Everything is all right!" He bowed before the king with his face to the ground and said, "Praise to the LORD your God, who has handed over the rebels who dared to stand against my lord the king."

29"What about young Absalom?" the king demanded. "Is he all right?"

Ahimaaz replied, "When Joab told me to come, there was a lot of commotion. But I didn't know what was happening."

30"Wait here," the king told him. So Ahimaaz stepped aside.

31Then the man from Ethiopia arrived and said, "I have good news for my lord the king. Today the LORD has rescued you from all those who rebelled against you."

32"What about young Absalom?" the king demanded. "Is he all right?"

And the Ethiopian replied, "May all of your enemies, my lord the king, both now and in the future, share the fate of that young man!"

33*The king was overcome with emotion. He went up to the room over the gateway and burst into tears. And as he went, he cried, "O my son Absalom! My son, my son Absalom! If only I had died instead of you! O Absalom, my son, my son."

CHAPTER 19

Joab Rebukes the King

1*Word soon reached Joab that the king was weeping and mourning for Absalom. 2As all the people heard of the king's deep grief for his son, the joy of that day's victory was turned into deep sadness. 3They crept back into the town that day as though they were ashamed and had deserted in battle. 4The king covered his face with his hands and kept on crying, "O my son Absalom! O Absalom, my son, my son!"

5Then Joab went to the king's room and said to him, "We saved your life today and the lives of your sons, your daughters, and your wives and concubines. Yet you act like this, making us feel ashamed of ourselves. 6You seem to love those who hate you and hate those who love you. You have made it clear today that your commanders and troops mean nothing to you. It seems that if Absalom had lived and all of us had died, you would be pleased. 7Now go out there and congratulate your troops, for I swear by the LORD that if you don't go out, not a single one of them will remain here tonight. Then you will be worse off than ever before."

8So the king went out and took his seat at the town gate, and as the news spread throughout the town that he was there, everyone went to him.

Meanwhile, the Israelites who had supported Absalom fled to their homes. 9And throughout all the tribes of Israel there was much discussion and argument going on. The people were saying, "The king rescued us from our enemies and saved us from the Philistines, but Absalom chased him out of the country. 10Now Absalom, whom we anointed to rule over us, is dead. Why not ask David to come back and be our king again?"

11Then King David sent Zadok and Abiathar, the priests, to say to the elders of Judah, "Why are you the last ones to welcome back the king into his palace? For I have heard that all Israel is ready. 12You are my relatives, my own tribe, my own flesh and blood! So why are you the last ones to welcome back the king?" 13And David told them to tell Amasa, "Since you are my own flesh and blood, like Joab, may God strike me and even kill me if I do not appoint you as commander of my army in his place."

14Then Amasa* convinced all the men of Judah, and they responded unanimously. They sent word to the king, "Return to us, and bring back all who are with you."

David's Return to Jerusalem

15So the king started back to Jerusalem. And when he arrived at the Jordan River, the people of Judah came to Gilgal to meet him and escort him across the river. 16Shimei son of Gera, the man from Bahurim in Benjamin, hurried across with the men of Judah to welcome King

18:33 Verse 18:33 is numbered 19:1 in Hebrew text. **19:1** Verses 19:1-43 are numbered 19:2-44 in Hebrew text. **19:14** Or *David;* Hebrew reads *he.*

David. [17]A thousand other men from the tribe of Benjamin were with him, including Ziba, the chief servant of the house of Saul, and Ziba's fifteen sons and twenty servants. They rushed down to the Jordan to meet the king. [18]They crossed the shallows of the Jordan to bring the king's household across the river, helping him in every way they could.

David's Mercy to Shimei

As the king was about to cross the river, Shimei fell down before him. [19]"My lord the king, please forgive me," he pleaded. "Forget the terrible thing your servant did when you left Jerusalem. May the king put it out of his mind. [20]I know how much I sinned. That is why I have come here today, the very first person in all Israel* to greet my lord the king."

[21]Then Abishai son of Zeruiah said, "Shimei should die, for he cursed the LORD's anointed king!"

[22]"Who asked your opinion, you sons of Zeruiah!" David exclaimed. "Why have you become my adversary* today? This is not a day for execution but for celebration! Today I am once again the king of Israel!" [23]Then, turning to Shimei, David vowed, "Your life will be spared."

David's Kindness to Mephibosheth

[24]Now Mephibosheth,* Saul's grandson, came down from Jerusalem to meet the king. He had not cared for his feet, trimmed his beard, or washed his clothes since the day the king left Jerusalem. [25]"Why didn't you come with me, Mephibosheth?" the king asked him.

[26]Mephibosheth replied, "My lord the king, my servant Ziba deceived me. I told him, 'Saddle my donkey* so I can go with the king.' For as you know I am crippled. [27]Ziba has slandered me by saying that I refused to come. But I know that my lord the king is like an angel of God, so do what you think is best. [28]All my relatives and I could expect only death from you, my lord, but instead you have honored me by allowing me to eat at your own table! What more can I ask?"

[29]"You've said enough," David replied. "I've decided that you and Ziba will divide your land equally between you."

[30]"Give him all of it," Mephibosheth said. "I am content just to have you safely back again, my lord the king!"

David's Kindness to Barzillai

[31]Barzillai of Gilead had come down from Rogelim to escort the king across the Jordan. [32]He was very old, about eighty, and very wealthy. He was the one who had provided food for the king during his stay in Mahanaim. [33]"Come across with me and live in Jerusalem," the king said to Barzillai. "I will take care of you there."

[34]"No," he replied, "I am far too old to go with the king to Jerusalem. [35]I am eighty years old today, and I can no longer enjoy anything. Food and wine are no longer tasty, and I cannot hear the singers as they sing. I would only be a burden to my lord the king. [36]Just to go across the Jordan River with the king is all the honor I need! [37]Then let me return again to die in my own town, where my father and mother are buried. But here is your servant, my son Kimham. Let him go with my lord the king and receive whatever you want to give him."

[38]"Good," the king agreed. "Kimham will go with me, and I will help him in any way you would like. And I will do for you anything you want." [39]So all the people crossed the Jordan with the king. After David had blessed Barzillai and kissed him, Barzillai returned to his own home.

[40]The king then crossed over to Gilgal, taking Kimham with him. All the troops of Judah and half the troops of Israel escorted the king on his way.

An Argument over the King

[41]But all the men of Israel complained to the king, "The men of Judah stole the king and didn't give us the honor of helping take you, your household, and all your men across the Jordan."

[42]The men of Judah replied, "The king is one of our own kinsmen. Why should this make you angry? We haven't eaten any of the king's food or received any special favors!"

[43]"But there are ten tribes in Israel," the others replied. "So we have ten times as much right to the king as you do. What right do you

19:20 Hebrew *in the house of Joseph*. **19:22** Or *my prosecutor*. **19:24** *Mephibosheth* is another name for Merib-baal. **19:26** As in Greek, Syriac, and Latin versions; Hebrew reads *I will saddle a donkey for myself*.

have to treat us with such contempt? Weren't we the first to speak of bringing him back to be our king again?" The argument continued back and forth, and the men of Judah spoke even more harshly than the men of Israel.

CHAPTER 20

The Revolt of Sheba

There happened to be a troublemaker there named Sheba son of Bicri, a man from the tribe of Benjamin. Sheba blew a ram's horn and began to chant:

"Down with the dynasty of David!
We have no interest in the son of Jesse.
Come on, you men of Israel,
back to your homes!"

[2]So all the men of Israel deserted David and followed Sheba son of Bicri. But the men of Judah stayed with their king and escorted him from the Jordan River to Jerusalem.

[3]When David came to his palace in Jerusalem, he took the ten concubines he had left to look after the palace and placed them in seclusion. Their needs were provided for, but he no longer slept with them. So each of them lived like a widow until she died.

[4]Then the king told Amasa, "Mobilize the army of Judah within three days, and report back at that time." [5]So Amasa went out to notify Judah, but it took him longer than the time he had been given.

[6]Then David said to Abishai, "Sheba son of Bicri is going to hurt us more than Absalom did. Quick, take my troops and chase after him before he gets into a fortified town where we can't reach him."

[7]So Abishai and Joab,* together with the king's bodyguard* and all the mighty warriors, set out from Jerusalem to go after Sheba. [8]As they arrived at the great stone in Gibeon, Amasa met them. Joab was wearing his military tunic with a dagger strapped to his belt. As he stepped forward to greet Amasa, he slipped the dagger from its sheath.*

[9]"How are you, my cousin?" Joab said and took him by the beard with his right hand as though to kiss him. [10]Amasa didn't notice the dagger in his left hand, and Joab stabbed him in the stomach with it so that his insides gushed out onto the ground. Joab did not need to strike again, and Amasa soon died. Joab and his brother Abishai left him lying there and continued after Sheba.

[11]One of Joab's young men shouted to Amasa's troops, "If you are for Joab and David, come and follow Joab." [12]But Amasa lay in his blood in the middle of the road, and Joab's man saw that everyone was stopping to stare at him. So he pulled him off the road into a field and threw a cloak over him. [13]With Amasa's body out of the way, everyone went on with Joab to capture Sheba son of Bicri.

[14]Meanwhile, Sheba traveled through all the tribes of Israel and eventually came to the town of Abel-beth-maacah. All the members of his own clan, the Bicrites,* assembled for battle and followed him into the town. [15]When Joab's forces arrived, they attacked Abel-beth-maacah. They built a siege ramp against the town's fortifications and began battering down the wall. [16]But a wise woman in the town called out to Joab, "Listen to me, Joab. Come over here so I can talk to you." [17]As he approached, the woman asked, "Are you Joab?"

"I am," he replied.

So she said, "Listen carefully to your servant."

"I'm listening," he said.

[18]Then she continued, "There used to be a saying, 'If you want to settle an argument, ask advice at the town of Abel.' [19]I am one who is peace loving and faithful in Israel. But you are destroying an important town in Israel.* Why do you want to devour what belongs to the LORD?"

[20]And Joab replied, "Believe me, I don't want to devour or destroy your town! [21]That's not my purpose. All I want is a man named Sheba son of Bicri from the hill country of Ephraim, who has revolted against King David. If you hand over this one man to me, I will leave the town in peace."

"All right," the woman replied, "we will throw his head over the wall to you." [22]Then the woman went to all the people with her wise advice, and they cut off Sheba's head and threw it out to Joab. So he blew the ram's horn and called his troops back from the attack. They all returned to their homes, and Joab returned to the king at Jerusalem.

20:7a Hebrew *So Joab's men.* **20:7b** Hebrew *the Kerethites and Pelethites;* also in 20:23. **20:8** Hebrew *As he stepped forward, it fell out.* **20:14** As in Greek and Latin versions; Hebrew reads *All the Berites.* **20:19** Hebrew *a town that is a mother in Israel.*

[23]Now Joab was the commander of the
army of Israel. Benaiah son of Jehoiada was
captain of the king's bodyguard. [24]Adoni-
ram* was in charge of the labor force. Jehosh-
aphat son of Ahilud was the royal historian.
[25]Sheva was the court secretary. Zadok and
Abiathar were the priests. [26]And Ira, a descen-
dant of Jair, was David's personal priest.

AMAZING FACTS

A man named Sheba won't be a troublemaker anymore—the people from his town threw his head over a wall!

2 SAMUEL 20:20-22

CHAPTER 21

David Avenges the Gibeonites

There was a famine during David's reign that
lasted for three years, so David asked the
LORD about it. And the LORD said, "The fam-
ine has come because Saul and his family are
guilty of murdering the Gibeonites."

[2]So the king summoned the Gibeonites.
They were not part of Israel but were all that
was left of the nation of the Amorites. The
people of Israel had sworn not to kill them,
but Saul, in his zeal for Israel and Judah, had
tried to wipe them out. [3]David asked them,
"What can I do for you? How can I make
amends so that you will bless the LORD's peo-
ple again?"

[4]"Well, money can't settle this matter be-
tween us and the family of Saul," the Gibeon-
ites replied. "Neither can we demand the life
of anyone in Israel."

"What can I do then?" David asked. "Just
tell me and I will do it for you."

[5]Then they replied, "It was Saul who
planned to destroy us, to keep us from having
any place at all in the territory of Israel. [6]So let
seven of Saul's sons be handed over to us, and
we will execute them before the LORD at Gibe-
on, on the mountain of the LORD.*"

"All right," the king said, "I will do it." [7]The
king spared Jonathan's son Mephibosheth,*
who was Saul's grandson, because of the oath
David and Jonathan had sworn before the
LORD. [8]But he gave them Saul's two sons Ar-
moni and Mephibosheth, whose mother was
Rizpah daughter of Aiah. He also gave them
the five sons of Saul's daughter Merab,* the
wife of Adriel son of Barzillai from Meholah.
[9]The men of Gibeon executed them on the
mountain before the LORD. So all seven of
them died together at the beginning of the
barley harvest.

[10]Then Rizpah daughter of Aiah, the mother
of two of the men, spread burlap on a rock and
stayed there the entire harvest season. She
prevented the scavenger birds from tearing at
their bodies during the day and stopped wild
animals from eating them at night. [11]When
David learned what Rizpah, Saul's concubine,
had done, [12]he went to the people of Jabesh-
gilead and retrieved the bones of Saul and his
son Jonathan. (When the Philistines had killed
Saul and Jonathan on Mount Gilboa, the peo-
ple of Jabesh-gilead stole their bodies from the
public square of Beth-shan, where the Phi-
listines had hung them.) [13]So David obtained
the bones of Saul and Jonathan, as well as
the bones of the men the Gibeonites had exe-
cuted.

[14]Then the king ordered that they bury the
bones in the tomb of Kish, Saul's father, at the
town of Zela in the land of Benjamin. After
that, God ended the famine in the land.

Battles against Philistine Giants

[15]Once again the Philistines were at war with
Israel. And when David and his men were in
the thick of battle, David became weak and
exhausted. [16]Ishbi-benob was a descendant
of the giants*; his bronze spearhead weighed
more than seven pounds,* and he was armed
with a new sword. He had cornered David and
was about to kill him. [17]But Abishai son of
Zeruiah came to David's rescue and killed the

20:24 As in Greek version (see also 1 Kgs 4:6; 5:14); Hebrew reads *Adoram*. **21:6** As in Greek version (see also 21:9); Hebrew reads *at Gibeah of Saul, the chosen of the LORD*. **21:7** *Mephibosheth* is another name for Merib-baal. **21:8** As in a few Hebrew and Greek manuscripts and Syriac version (see also 1 Sam 18:19); most Hebrew manuscripts read *Michal*. **21:16a** Or *a descendant of the Rapha;* also in 21:18, 20, 22. **21:16b** Hebrew *300 shekels* [3.4 kilograms].

Philistine. Then David's men declared, "You are not going out to battle with us again! Why risk snuffing out the light of Israel?"

18 After this, there was another battle against the Philistines at Gob. As they fought, Sibbecai from Hushah killed Saph, another descendant of the giants.

19 During another battle at Gob, Elhanan son of Jair* from Bethlehem killed the brother of Goliath of Gath.* The handle of his spear was as thick as a weaver's beam!

20 In another battle with the Philistines at Gath, they encountered a huge man with six fingers on each hand and six toes on each foot, twenty-four in all, who was also a descendant of the giants. 21 But when he defied and taunted Israel, he was killed by Jonathan, the son of David's brother Shimea.*

AMAZING FACTS

David's nephew killed a giant who had 12 fingers and 12 toes!

2 SAMUEL 21:20-21

22 These four Philistines were descendants of the giants of Gath, but David and his warriors killed them.

CHAPTER 22

David's Song of Praise

David sang this song to the LORD on the day the LORD rescued him from all his enemies and from Saul. 2 He sang:

"The LORD is my rock, my fortress,
and my savior;
3 my God is my rock, in whom I find
protection.
He is my shield, the power that saves me,
and my place of safety.
He is my refuge, my savior,
the one who saves me from violence.
4 I called on the LORD, who is worthy
of praise,
and he saved me from my enemies.

5 "The waves of death overwhelmed me;
floods of destruction swept over me.
6 The grave* wrapped its ropes around me;
death laid a trap in my path.
7 But in my distress I cried out to the LORD;
yes, I cried to my God for help.
He heard me from his sanctuary;
my cry reached his ears.

8 "Then the earth quaked and trembled.
The foundations of the heavens shook;
they quaked because of his anger.
9 Smoke poured from his nostrils;
fierce flames leaped from his mouth.
Glowing coals blazed forth from him.
10 He opened the heavens and came down;
dark storm clouds were beneath
his feet.
11 Mounted on a mighty angelic being,*
he flew,
soaring* on the wings of the wind.
12 He shrouded himself in darkness,
veiling his approach with dense rain
clouds.
13 A great brightness shone around him,
and burning coals* blazed forth.
14 The LORD thundered from heaven;
the voice of the Most High resounded.
15 He shot arrows and scattered his
enemies;
his lightning flashed, and they were
confused.
16 Then at the command of the LORD,
at the blast of his breath,
the bottom of the sea could be seen,
and the foundations of the earth were
laid bare.

17 "He reached down from heaven and
rescued me;
he drew me out of deep waters.
18 He rescued me from my powerful
enemies,

21:19a As in parallel text at 1 Chr 20:5; Hebrew reads *son of Jaare-oregim*. **21:19b** As in parallel text at 1 Chr 20:5; Hebrew reads *killed Goliath of Gath*. **21:21** As in parallel text at 1 Chr 20:7; Hebrew reads *Shimei*, a variant spelling of Shimea. **22:6** Hebrew *Sheol*. **22:11a** Hebrew *a cherub*. **22:11b** As in some Hebrew manuscripts (see also Ps 18:10); other Hebrew manuscripts read *appearing*. **22:13** Or *and lightning bolts*.

from those who hated me and were too
strong for me.
19 They attacked me at a moment when
I was in distress,
but the LORD supported me.
20 He led me to a place of safety;
he rescued me because he delights
in me.
21 The LORD rewarded me for doing right;
he restored me because of my
innocence.
22 For I have kept the ways of the LORD;
I have not turned from my God to
follow evil.
23 I have followed all his regulations;
I have never abandoned his decrees.
24 I am blameless before God;
I have kept myself from sin.
25 The LORD rewarded me for doing right.
He has seen my innocence.

26 "To the faithful you show yourself faithful;
to those with integrity you show
integrity.
27 To the pure you show yourself pure,
but to the wicked you show yourself
hostile.
28 You rescue the humble,
but your eyes watch the proud and
humiliate them.
29 O LORD, you are my lamp.
The LORD lights up my darkness.
30 In your strength I can crush an army;
with my God I can scale any wall.

31 "God's way is perfect.
All the LORD's promises prove true.
He is a shield for all who look to him
for protection.
32 For who is God except the LORD?
Who but our God is a solid rock?
33 God is my strong fortress,
and he makes my way perfect.
34 He makes me as surefooted as a deer,
enabling me to stand on mountain
heights.
35 He trains my hands for battle;
he strengthens my arm to draw
a bronze bow.
36 You have given me your shield of victory;
your help* has made me great.
37 You have made a wide path for my feet
to keep them from slipping.

38 "I chased my enemies and destroyed
them;
I did not stop until they were conquered.
39 I consumed them;
I struck them down so they did not
get up;
they fell beneath my feet.
40 You have armed me with strength for the
battle;
you have subdued my enemies under
my feet.
41 You placed my foot on their necks.
I have destroyed all who hated me.
42 They looked for help, but no one came
to their rescue.
They even cried to the LORD, but he
refused to answer.
43 I ground them as fine as the dust of the
earth;
I trampled them* in the gutter like dirt.

44 "You gave me victory over my accusers.
You preserved me as the ruler over
nations;
people I don't even know now serve me.
45 Foreign nations cringe before me;
as soon as they hear of me, they submit.
46 They all lose their courage
and come trembling* from their
strongholds.

47 "The LORD lives! Praise to my Rock!
May God, the Rock of my salvation, be
exalted!
48 He is the God who pays back those who
harm me;
he brings down the nations under me
49 and delivers me from my enemies.
You hold me safe beyond the reach of my
enemies;
you save me from violent opponents.
50 For this, O LORD, I will praise you among
the nations;
I will sing praises to your name.
51 You give great victories to your king;
you show unfailing love to your
anointed,
to David and all his descendants
forever."

22:36 As in Dead Sea Scrolls (see also Ps 18:35); Masoretic Text reads *your answering*. **22:43** As in Dead Sea Scrolls (see also Ps 18:42); Masoretic Text reads *I crushed and trampled them*. **22:46** As in parallel text at Ps 18:45; Hebrew reads *come girding themselves*.

CHAPTER 23

David's Last Words

These are the last words of David:

"David, the son of Jesse, speaks—
David, the man who was raised
up so high,
David, the man anointed by the God
of Jacob,
David, the sweet psalmist of Israel.*

2 "The Spirit of the LORD speaks
through me;
his words are upon my tongue.
3 The God of Israel spoke.
The Rock of Israel said to me:
'The one who rules righteously,
who rules in the fear of God,
4 is like the light of morning at sunrise,
like a morning without clouds,
like the gleaming of the sun
on new grass after rain.'

5 "Is it not my family God has chosen?
Yes, he has made an everlasting
covenant with me.
His agreement is arranged and
guaranteed in every detail.

Can I really trust God to keep his promises?

Yes, he has made an everlasting covenant with me. His agreement is arranged and guaranteed in every detail. 2 SAMUEL 23:5

He will ensure my safety and success.
6 But the godless are like thorns to be
thrown away,
for they tear the hand that touches them.
7 One must use iron tools to chop them down;
they will be totally consumed by fire."

David's Mightiest Warriors

8 These are the names of David's mightiest warriors. The first was Jashobeam the Hacmonite,* who was leader of the Three*—the three mightiest warriors among David's men. He once used his spear to kill 800 enemy warriors in a single battle.*

9 Next in rank among the Three was Eleazar son of Dodai, a descendant of Ahoah. Once Eleazar and David stood together against the Philistines when the entire Israelite army had fled. 10 He killed Philistines until his hand was too tired to lift his sword, and the LORD gave him a great victory that day. The rest of the army did not return until it was time to collect the plunder!

11 Next in rank was Shammah son of Agee from Harar. One time the Philistines gathered at Lehi and attacked the Israelites in a field full of lentils. The Israelite army fled, 12 but Shammah* held his ground in the middle of the field and beat back the Philistines. So the LORD brought about a great victory.

13 Once during the harvest, when David was at the cave of Adullam, the Philistine army was camped in the valley of Rephaim. The Three (who were among the Thirty—an elite group among David's fighting men) went down to meet him there. 14 David was staying in the stronghold at the time, and a Philistine detachment had occupied the town of Bethlehem.

15 David remarked longingly to his men, "Oh, how I would love some of that good water from the well by the gate in Bethlehem." 16 So the Three broke through the Philistine lines, drew some water from the well by the gate in Bethlehem, and brought it back to David. But he refused to drink it. Instead, he poured it out as an offering to the LORD. 17 "The LORD forbid that I should drink this!" he exclaimed. "This water is as precious as the blood of these men* who risked their lives to bring it to me." So David did not drink it. These are examples of the exploits of the Three.

David's Thirty Mighty Men

18 Abishai son of Zeruiah, the brother of Joab, was the leader of the Thirty.* He once used his spear to kill 300 enemy warriors in a single battle. It was by such feats that he became

23:1 Or *the favorite subject of the songs of Israel;* or *the favorite of the Strong One of Israel.* **23:8a** As in parallel text at 1 Chr 11:11; Hebrew reads *Josheb-basshebeth the Tahkemonite.* **23:8b** As in Greek and Latin versions (see also 1 Chr 11:11); the meaning of the Hebrew is uncertain. **23:8c** As in some Greek manuscripts (see also 1 Chr 11:11); the meaning of the Hebrew is uncertain, though it might be rendered *the Three. It was Adino the Eznite who killed 800 men at one time.* **23:12** Hebrew *he.* **23:17** Hebrew *Shall I drink the blood of these men?* **23:18** As in a few Hebrew manuscripts and Syriac version; most Hebrew manuscripts read *the Three.*

as famous as the Three. [19]Abishai was the most famous of the Thirty* and was their commander, though he was not one of the Three.

[20]There was also Benaiah son of Jehoiada, a valiant warrior* from Kabzeel. He did many heroic deeds, which included killing two champions* of Moab. Another time, on a snowy day, he chased a lion down into a pit and killed it. [21]Once, armed only with a club, he killed a great Egyptian warrior who was armed with a spear. Benaiah wrenched the spear from the Egyptian's hand and killed him with it. [22]Deeds like these made Benaiah as famous as the Three mightiest warriors. [23]He was more honored than the other members of the Thirty, though he was not one of the Three. And David made him captain of his bodyguard.

[24]Other members of the Thirty included:

Asahel, Joab's brother;
Elhanan son of Dodo from Bethlehem;
[25] Shammah from Harod;
Elika from Harod;
[26] Helez from Pelon*;
Ira son of Ikkesh from Tekoa;
[27] Abiezer from Anathoth;
Sibbecai* from Hushah;
[28] Zalmon from Ahoah;
Maharai from Netophah;
[29] Heled* son of Baanah from Netophah;
Ithai* son of Ribai from Gibeah
(in the land of Benjamin);
[30] Benaiah from Pirathon;
Hurai* from Nahale-gaash*;
[31] Abi-albon from Arabah;
Azmaveth from Bahurim;
[32] Eliahba from Shaalbon;
the sons of Jashen;
Jonathan [33]son of Shagee* from Harar;
Ahiam son of Sharar from Harar;
[34] Eliphelet son of Ahasbai from Maacah;
Eliam son of Ahithophel from Giloh;
[35] Hezro from Carmel;
Paarai from Arba;
[36] Igal son of Nathan from Zobah;
Bani from Gad;
[37] Zelek from Ammon;
Naharai from Beeroth, Joab's armor
bearer;
[38] Ira from Jattir;
Gareb from Jattir;
[39] Uriah the Hittite.

There were thirty-seven in all.

CHAPTER 24

David Takes a Census

Once again the anger of the LORD burned against Israel, and he caused David to harm them by taking a census. "Go and count the people of Israel and Judah," the LORD told him.

[2]So the king said to Joab and the commanders* of the army, "Take a census of all the tribes of Israel—from Dan in the north to Beersheba in the south—so I may know how many people there are."

[3]But Joab replied to the king, "May the LORD your God let you live to see a hundred times as many people as there are now! But why, my lord the king, do you want to do this?"

[4]But the king insisted that they take the census, so Joab and the commanders of the army went out to count the people of Israel. [5]First they crossed the Jordan and camped at Aroer, south of the town in the valley, in the direction of Gad. Then they went on to Jazer, [6]then to Gilead in the land of Tahtim-hodshi* and to Dan-jaan and around to Sidon. [7]Then they came to the fortress of Tyre, and all the towns of the Hivites and Canaanites. Finally, they went south to Judah* as far as Beersheba.

[8]Having gone through the entire land for nine months and twenty days, they returned to Jerusalem. [9]Joab reported the number of people to the king. There were 800,000 capable warriors in Israel who could handle a sword, and 500,000 in Judah.

Judgment for David's Sin

[10]But after he had taken the census, David's conscience began to bother him. And he said to the LORD, "I have sinned greatly by taking

23:19 As in Syriac version; Hebrew reads *the Three*. **23:20a** Or *son of Jehoiada, son of Ish-hai*. **23:20b** Hebrew *two of Ariel*. **23:26** As in parallel text at 1 Chr 11:27 (see also 1 Chr 27:10); Hebrew reads *from Palti*. **23:27** As in some Greek manuscripts (see also 1 Chr 11:29); Hebrew reads *Mebunnai*. **23:29a** As in some Hebrew manuscripts (see also 1 Chr 11:30); most Hebrew manuscripts read *Heleb*. **23:29b** As in parallel text at 1 Chr 11:31; Hebrew reads *Ittai*. **23:30a** As in some Greek manuscripts (see also 1 Chr 11:32); Hebrew reads *Hiddai*. **23:30b** Or *from the ravines of Gaash*. **23:33** As in parallel text at 1 Chr 11:34; Hebrew reads *Jonathan, Shammah*; some Greek manuscripts read *Jonathan son of Shammah*. **24:2** As in Greek version (see also 24:4 and 1 Chr 21:2); Hebrew reads *Joab the commander*. **24:6** Greek version reads *to Gilead and to Kadesh in the land of the Hittites*. **24:7** Or *they went to the Negev of Judah*.

this census. Please forgive my guilt, LORD, for doing this foolish thing."

11 The next morning the word of the LORD came to the prophet Gad, who was David's seer. This was the message: 12 "Go and say to David, 'This is what the LORD says: I will give you three choices. Choose one of these punishments, and I will inflict it on you.'"

13 So Gad came to David and asked him, "Will you choose three* years of famine throughout your land, three months of fleeing from your enemies, or three days of severe plague throughout your land? Think this over and decide what answer I should give the LORD who sent me."

14 "I'm in a desperate situation!" David replied to Gad. "But let us fall into the hands of the LORD, for his mercy is great. Do not let me fall into human hands."

15 So the LORD sent a plague upon Israel that morning, and it lasted for three days.* A total of 70,000 people died throughout the nation, from Dan in the north to Beersheba in the south. 16 But as the angel was preparing to destroy Jerusalem, the LORD relented and said to the death angel, "Stop! That is enough!" At that moment the angel of the LORD was by the threshing floor of Araunah the Jebusite.

17 When David saw the angel, he said to the LORD, "I am the one who has sinned and done wrong! But these people are as innocent as sheep—what have they done? Let your anger fall against me and my family."

David Builds an Altar

18 That day Gad came to David and said to him, "Go up and build an altar to the LORD on the threshing floor of Araunah the Jebusite."

19 So David went up to do what the LORD had commanded him. 20 When Araunah saw the king and his men coming toward him, he came and bowed before the king with his face to the ground. 21 "Why have you come, my lord the king?" Araunah asked.

David replied, "I have come to buy your threshing floor and to build an altar to the LORD there, so that he will stop the plague."

22 "Take it, my lord the king, and use it as you wish," Araunah said to David. "Here are oxen for the burnt offering, and you can use the threshing boards and ox yokes for wood to build a fire on the altar. 23 I will give it all to you, Your Majesty, and may the LORD your God accept your sacrifice."

24 But the king replied to Araunah, "No, I insist on buying it, for I will not present burnt offerings to the LORD my God that have cost me nothing." So David paid him fifty pieces of silver* for the threshing floor and the oxen.

25 David built an altar there to the LORD and sacrificed burnt offerings and peace offerings. And the LORD answered his prayer for the land, and the plague on Israel was stopped.

24:13 As in Greek version (see also 1 Chr 21:12); Hebrew reads *seven*. **24:15** Hebrew *for the designated time*. **24:24** Hebrew *50 shekels of silver*, about 20 ounces or 570 grams in weight.

1 KINGS

WHO
David, Solomon, the queen of Sheba, Rehoboam, Jeroboam, Elijah, Ahab, and Jezebel.

WHERE
Israel and Judah.

WHEN
The stories of the kings were probably written down later—during the time of the prophets but before 539 BC when the Israelites returned to Jerusalem from Babylon.

WHY
To look at the kings of Israel and Judah, showing the difference between people who lived for God and those who didn't.

If you will follow me . . . as David your father did . . . then I will establish the throne of your dynasty over Israel forever.
1 KINGS 9:4-5

If you could have anything, what would you ask God for? Money? Happiness? Popularity? Good friends? Solomon asked God for wisdom so he could be a good king and rule the people well. Not only did he get wisdom, but he also got power, riches, and honor.

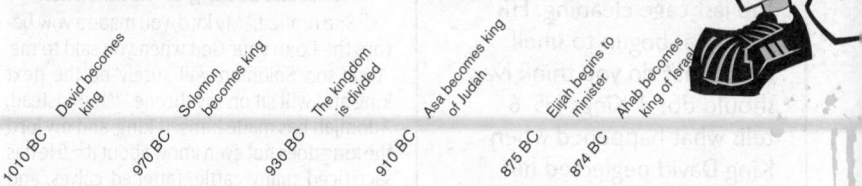

HOW CAN YOU BE WISE LIKE SOLOMON?

CHAPTER 1

David in His Old Age

King David was now very old, and no matter how many blankets covered him, he could not keep warm. [2]So his advisers told him, "Let us find a young virgin to wait on you and look after you, my lord. She will lie in your arms and keep you warm."

[3]So they searched throughout the land of Israel for a beautiful girl, and they found Abishag from Shunem and brought her to the king. [4]The girl was very beautiful, and she looked after the king and took care of him. But the king had no sexual relations with her.

Adonijah Claims the Throne

[5]About that time David's son Adonijah, whose mother was Haggith, began boasting, "I will

Pet Project

Ivan had a pet gerbil named Snickers. He had to feed and water Snickers each day. And the cage needed a weekly cleaning. Ivan followed through on his responsibilities for a while, and Snickers was happy. But then Ivan signed up on three different sports teams. All those practices made Ivan very tired. He still feeds Snickers each day, but three weeks have passed since the last cage cleaning. His room has begun to smell bad. What do you think Ivan should do? 1 Kings 1:5-6 tells what happened when King David neglected his responsibilities.

make myself king." So he provided himself with chariots and charioteers and recruited fifty men to run in front of him. 6Now his father, King David, had never disciplined him at any time, even by asking, "Why are you doing that?" Adonijah had been born next after Absalom, and he was very handsome.

7Adonijah took Joab son of Zeruiah and Abiathar the priest into his confidence, and they agreed to help him become king. 8But Zadok the priest, Benaiah son of Jehoiada, Nathan the prophet, Shimei, Rei, and David's personal bodyguard refused to support Adonijah.

9Adonijah went to the Stone of Zoheleth* near the spring of En-rogel, where he sacrificed sheep, cattle, and fattened calves. He invited all his brothers—the other sons of King David—and all the royal officials of Judah. 10But he did not invite Nathan the prophet or Benaiah or the king's bodyguard or his brother Solomon.

11Then Nathan went to Bathsheba, Solomon's mother, and asked her, "Haven't you heard that Haggith's son, Adonijah, has made himself king, and our lord David doesn't even know about it? 12If you want to save your own life and the life of your son Solomon, follow my advice. 13Go at once to King David and say to him, 'My lord the king, didn't you make a vow and say to me, "Your son Solomon will surely be the next king and will sit on my throne"? Why then has Adonijah become king?' 14And while you are still talking with him, I will come and confirm everything you have said."

15So Bathsheba went into the king's bedroom. (He was very old now, and Abishag was taking care of him.) 16Bathsheba bowed down before the king.

"What can I do for you?" he asked her.

17She replied, "My lord, you made a vow before the LORD your God when you said to me, 'Your son Solomon will surely be the next king and will sit on my throne.' 18But instead, Adonijah has made himself king, and my lord the king does not even know about it. 19He has sacrificed many cattle, fattened calves, and sheep, and he has invited all the king's sons to attend the celebration. He also invited Abiathar the priest and Joab, the commander of the army. But he did not invite your servant Solomon. 20And now, my lord the king, all Israel is waiting for you to announce who will become king after you. 21If you do not act, my son Solomon and I will be treated as criminals as soon as my lord the king has died."

22While she was still speaking with the king, Nathan the prophet arrived. 23The

1:9 Or *to the Serpent's Stone;* Greek version supports reading *Zoheleth* as a proper name.

I SURVIVED

I guess every kid has to face it in one form or another—you know, being disciplined or corrected. I am no exception. My parents have a system for disciplining my younger brothers, my sister, and me. When we break the rules, they don't let us get away with anything.

I remember that when I was little, my parents would do one of two things. They would either put us in "time out" (making us sit in the hall for a long time) or they would spank us. I have to admit that even though it was boring, I always wanted to sit in the hall rather than get spanked. But a lot of the time I did get spanked. Why? Because the Bible tells parents in Proverbs 23:13-14: "Don't fail to discipline your children. They won't die if you spank them. Physical discipline may well save them from death."

It's not complicated. If I didn't want to get in trouble, I knew I needed to obey my parents and follow what God wanted me to do—or face the consequences. I can definitely say I have learned some important lessons through being disciplined. I have learned that while my parents' correction makes me miserable for a short time, it makes my life better in the long run. I do realize they are trying to keep me out of trouble and show me the best way to live.

Now that I'm older, I don't get spanked anymore. But I still get disciplined. The consequences are stuff like having to do extra work around the house or losing special privileges. I still don't like it. But I realize that even though the consequences of wrongdoing never go away, there will be fewer of them if you learn both from your mistakes and from getting corrected.

Read 1 Kings 1:5-6 to see what happened when King David failed to discipline his own son. For more on the value of discipline, check out Proverbs 22:15 and Hebrews 12:5-11.

king's officials told him, "Nathan the prophet
is here to see you."

Nathan went in and bowed before the king
with his face to the ground. [24]Nathan asked,
"My lord the king, have you decided that
Adonijah will be the next king and that he will
sit on your throne? [25]Today he has sacrificed
many cattle, fattened calves, and sheep, and
he has invited all the king's sons to attend the
celebration. He also invited the commanders
of the army and Abiathar the priest. They are
feasting and drinking with him and shouting,
'Long live King Adonijah!' [26]But he did not in-
vite me or Zadok the priest or Benaiah or your
servant Solomon. [27]Has my lord the king real-
ly done this without letting any of his officials
know who should be the next king?"

David Makes Solomon King

[28]King David responded, "Call Bathsheba!" So
she came back in and stood before the king.
[29]And the king repeated his vow: "As surely as
the LORD lives, who has rescued me from
every danger, [30]your son Solomon will be the
next king and will sit on my throne this very
day, just as I vowed to you before the LORD,
the God of Israel."

[31]Then Bathsheba bowed down with her
face to the ground before the king and ex-
claimed, "May my lord King David live for-
ever!"

[32]Then King David ordered, "Call Zadok
the priest, Nathan the prophet, and Benaiah
son of Jehoiada." When they came into the
king's presence, [33]the king said to them,
"Take Solomon and my officials down to
Gihon Spring. Solomon is to ride on my own
mule. [34]There Zadok the priest and Nathan
the prophet are to anoint him king over Israel.
Blow the ram's horn and shout, 'Long live
King Solomon!' [35]Then escort him back here,
and he will sit on my throne. He will succeed
me as king, for I have appointed him to be
ruler over Israel and Judah."

[36]"Amen!" Benaiah son of Jehoiada replied.
"May the LORD, the God of my lord the king,
decree that it happen. [37]And may the LORD be
with Solomon as he has been with you, my
lord the king, and may he make Solomon's
reign even greater than yours!"

[38]So Zadok the priest, Nathan the prophet,
Benaiah son of Jehoiada, and the king's body-
guard* took Solomon down to Gihon Spring,
with Solomon riding on King David's own
mule. [39]There Zadok the priest took the flask
of olive oil from the sacred tent and anointed
Solomon with the oil. Then they sounded the
ram's horn and all the people shouted, "Long
live King Solomon!" [40]And all the people fol-
lowed Solomon into Jerusalem, playing flutes
and shouting for joy. The celebration was so
joyous and noisy that the earth shook with the
sound.

[41]Adonijah and his guests heard the cele-
brating and shouting just as they were finish-
ing their banquet. When Joab heard the
sound of the ram's horn, he asked, "What's
going on? Why is the city in such an uproar?"

[42]And while he was still speaking, Jonathan
son of Abiathar the priest arrived. "Come in,"
Adonijah said to him, "for you are a good
man. You must have good news."

[43]"Not at all!" Jonathan replied. "Our lord
King David has just declared Solomon king!
[44]The king sent him down to Gihon Spring
with Zadok the priest, Nathan the prophet,
and Benaiah son of Jehoiada, protected by
the king's bodyguard. They had him ride on
the king's own mule, [45]and Zadok and Na-
than have anointed him at Gihon Spring as
the new king. They have just returned, and
the whole city is celebrating and rejoicing.
That's what all the noise is about. [46]What's
more, Solomon is now sitting on the royal
throne as king. [47]And all the royal officials
have gone to King David and congratulated
him, saying, 'May your God make Solomon's
fame even greater than your own, and may
Solomon's reign be even greater than yours!'
Then the king bowed his head in worship as
he lay in his bed, [48]and he said, 'Praise the
LORD, the God of Israel, who today has cho-
sen a successor to sit on my throne while I am
still alive to see it.'"

[49]Then all of Adonijah's guests jumped up
in panic from the banquet table and quickly
scattered. [50]Adonijah was afraid of Solomon,
so he rushed to the sacred tent and grabbed
on to the horns of the altar. [51]Word soon
reached Solomon that Adonijah had seized
the horns of the altar in fear, and that he was

1:38 Hebrew *the Kerethites and Pelethites;* also in 1:44.

pleading, "Let King Solomon swear today that he will not kill me!"

52 Solomon replied, "If he proves himself to be loyal, not a hair on his head will be touched. But if he makes trouble, he will die." 53 So King Solomon summoned Adonijah, and they brought him down from the altar. He came and bowed respectfully before King Solomon, who dismissed him, saying, "Go on home."

CHAPTER 2

David's Final Instructions to Solomon

As the time of King David's death approached, he gave this charge to his son Solomon:

2 "I am going where everyone on earth must someday go. Take courage and be a man. 3 Observe the requirements of the LORD your God, and follow all his ways. Keep the decrees, commands, regulations, and laws written in the Law of Moses so that you will be successful in all you do and wherever you go. 4 If you do this, then the LORD will keep the promise he made to me. He told me, 'If your descendants live as they should and follow me faithfully with all their heart and soul, one of them will always sit on the throne of Israel.'

5 "And there is something else. You know what Joab son of Zeruiah did to me when he murdered my two army commanders, Abner son of Ner and Amasa son of Jether. He pretended that it was an act of war, but it was done in a time of peace,* staining his belt and sandals with innocent blood.* 6 Do with him what you think best, but don't let him grow old and go to his grave in peace.*

How can you repay those who have been kind to you?

Be kind. . . . Make them permanent guests at your table. 1 KINGS 2:7

7 "Be kind to the sons of Barzillai of Gilead. Make them permanent guests at your table, for they took care of me when I fled from your brother Absalom.

8 "And remember Shimei son of Gera, the man from Bahurim in Benjamin. He cursed me with a terrible curse as I was fleeing to Mahanaim. When he came down to meet me at the Jordan River, I swore by the LORD that I would not kill him. 9 But that oath does not make him innocent. You are a wise man, and you will know how to arrange a bloody death for him.*"

10 Then David died and was buried with his ancestors in the City of David. 11 David had reigned over Israel for forty years, seven of them in Hebron and thirty-three in Jerusalem. 12 Solomon became king and sat on the throne of David his father, and his kingdom was firmly established.

Solomon Establishes His Rule

13 One day Adonijah, whose mother was Haggith, came to see Bathsheba, Solomon's mother. "Have you come with peaceful intentions?" she asked him.

"Yes," he said, "I come in peace. 14 In fact, I have a favor to ask of you."

"What is it?" she asked.

15 He replied, "As you know, the kingdom was rightfully mine; all Israel wanted me to be the next king. But the tables were turned, and the kingdom went to my brother instead; for that is the way the LORD wanted it. 16 So now I have just one favor to ask of you. Please don't turn me down."

"What is it?" she asked.

17 He replied, "Speak to King Solomon on my behalf, for I know he will do anything you request. Ask him to let me marry Abishag, the girl from Shunem."

18 "All right," Bathsheba replied. "I will speak to the king for you."

19 So Bathsheba went to King Solomon to speak on Adonijah's behalf. The king rose from his throne to meet her, and he bowed down before her. When he sat down on his throne again, the king ordered that a throne be brought for his mother, and she sat at his right hand.

2:5a Or *He murdered them during a time of peace as revenge for deaths they had caused in time of war.* **2:5b** As in some Greek and Old Latin manuscripts; Hebrew reads *with the blood of war.* **2:6** Hebrew *don't let his white head go down to Sheol in peace.* **2:9** Hebrew *how to bring his white head down to Sheol in blood.*

[20]"I have one small request to make of you," she said. "I hope you won't turn me down."

"What is it, my mother?" he asked. "You know I won't refuse you."

[21]"Then let your brother Adonijah marry Abishag, the girl from Shunem," she replied.

[22]"How can you possibly ask me to give Abishag to Adonijah?" King Solomon demanded. "You might as well ask me to give him the kingdom! You know that he is my older brother, and that he has Abiathar the priest and Joab son of Zeruiah on his side."

[23]Then King Solomon made a vow before the LORD: "May God strike me and even kill me if Adonijah has not sealed his fate with this request. [24]The LORD has confirmed me and placed me on the throne of my father, David; he has established my dynasty as he promised. So as surely as the LORD lives, Adonijah will die this very day!" [25]So King Solomon ordered Benaiah son of Jehoiada to execute him, and Adonijah was put to death.

[26]Then the king said to Abiathar the priest, "Go back to your home in Anathoth. You deserve to die, but I will not kill you now, because you carried the Ark of the Sovereign LORD for David my father and you shared all his hardships." [27]So Solomon deposed Abiathar from his position as priest of the LORD, thereby fulfilling the prophecy the LORD had given at Shiloh concerning the descendants of Eli.

[28]Joab had not joined Absalom's earlier rebellion, but he had joined Adonijah's rebellion. So when Joab heard about Adonijah's death, he ran to the sacred tent of the LORD and grabbed on to the horns of the altar. [29]When this was reported to King Solomon, he sent Benaiah son of Jehoiada to execute him.

[30]Benaiah went to the sacred tent of the LORD and said to Joab, "The king orders you to come out!"

But Joab answered, "No, I will die here."

So Benaiah returned to the king and told him what Joab had said.

[31]"Do as he said," the king replied. "Kill him there beside the altar and bury him. This will remove the guilt of Joab's senseless murders from me and from my father's family. [32]The LORD will repay him* for the murders of two men who were more righteous and better than he. For my father knew nothing about the deaths of Abner son of Ner, commander of the army of Israel, and of Amasa son of Jether, commander of the army of Judah. [33]May their blood be on Joab and his descendants forever, and may the LORD grant peace forever to David, his descendants, his dynasty, and his throne."

[34]So Benaiah son of Jehoiada returned to the sacred tent and killed Joab, and he was buried at his home in the wilderness. [35]Then the king appointed Benaiah to command the army in place of Joab, and he installed Zadok the priest to take the place of Abiathar.

[36]The king then sent for Shimei and told him, "Build a house here in Jerusalem and live there. But don't step outside the city to go anywhere else. [37]On the day you so much as cross the Kidron Valley, you will surely die; and your blood will be on your own head."

[38]Shimei replied, "Your sentence is fair; I will do whatever my lord the king commands." So Shimei lived in Jerusalem for a long time.

[39]But three years later two of Shimei's slaves ran away to King Achish son of Maacah of Gath. When Shimei learned where they were, [40]he saddled his donkey and went to Gath to search for them. When he found them, he brought them back to Jerusalem.

[41]Solomon heard that Shimei had left Jerusalem and had gone to Gath and returned. [42]So the king sent for Shimei and demanded, "Didn't I make you swear by the LORD and warn you not to go anywhere else or you would surely die? And you replied, 'The sentence is fair; I will do as you say.' [43]Then why haven't you kept your oath to the LORD and obeyed my command?"

[44]The king also said to Shimei, "You certainly remember all the wicked things you did to my father, David. May the LORD now bring that evil on your own head. [45]But may I, King Solomon, receive the LORD's blessings, and may one of David's descendants always sit on this throne in the presence of the LORD." [46]Then, at the king's command, Benaiah son of Jehoiada took Shimei outside and killed him.

So the kingdom was now firmly in Solomon's grip.

2:32 Hebrew *will return his blood on his own head.*

CHAPTER 3

Solomon Asks for Wisdom

Solomon made an alliance with Pharaoh, the king of Egypt, and married one of his daughters. He brought her to live in the City of David until he could finish building his palace and the Temple of the LORD and the wall around the city. [2]At that time the people of Israel sacrificed their offerings at local places of worship, for a temple honoring the name of the LORD had not yet been built.

[3]Solomon loved the LORD and followed all the decrees of his father, David, except that Solomon, too, offered sacrifices and burned incense at the local places of worship. [4]The most important of these places of worship was at Gibeon, so the king went there and sacrificed 1,000 burnt offerings. [5]That night the LORD appeared to Solomon in a dream, and God said, "What do you want? Ask, and I will give it to you!"

[6]Solomon replied, "You showed faithful love to your servant my father, David, because he was honest and true and faithful to you. And you have continued your faithful love to him today by giving him a son to sit on his throne.

[7]"Now, O LORD my God, you have made me king instead of my father, David, but I am like a little child who doesn't know his way around. [8]And here I am in the midst of your own chosen people, a nation so great and numerous they cannot be counted! [9]Give me an understanding heart so that I can govern your people well and know the difference between right and wrong. For who by himself is able to govern this great people of yours?"

[10]The Lord was pleased that Solomon had asked for wisdom. [11]So God replied, "Because you have asked for wisdom in governing my people with justice and have not asked for a long life or wealth or the death of your enemies—[12]I will give you what you asked for! I will give you a wise and understanding heart such as no one else has had or ever will have! [13]And I will also give you what you did not ask for—riches and fame! No other king in all the world will be compared to you for the rest of your life! [14]And if you follow me and obey my decrees and my commands as your father, David, did, I will give you a long life."

[15]Then Solomon woke up and realized it had been a dream. He returned to Jerusalem and stood before the Ark of the Lord's Covenant, where he sacrificed burnt offerings and peace offerings. Then he invited all his officials to a great banquet.

Solomon Judges Wisely

[16]Some time later two prostitutes came to the king to have an argument settled. [17]"Please, my lord," one of them began, "this woman and I live in the same house. I gave birth to a baby while she was with me in the house. [18]Three days later this woman also had a baby. We were alone; there were only two of us in the house.

[19]"But her baby died during the night when she rolled over on it. [20]Then she got up in the night and took my son from beside me while I was asleep. She laid her dead child in my arms and took mine to sleep beside her. [21]And in the morning when I tried to nurse my son, he was dead! But when I looked more closely in the morning light, I saw that it wasn't my son at all."

[22]Then the other woman interrupted, "It certainly was your son, and the living child is mine."

"No," the first woman said, "the living child is mine, and the dead one is yours." And so they argued back and forth before the king.

[23]Then the king said, "Let's get the facts straight. Both of you claim the living child is yours, and each says that the dead one belongs to the other. [24]All right, bring me a sword." So a sword was brought to the king.

[25]Then he said, "Cut the living child in two, and give half to one woman and half to the other!"

[26]Then the woman who was the real mother of the living child, and who loved him very much, cried out, "Oh no, my lord! Give her the child—please do not kill him!"

But the other woman said, "All right, he will be neither yours nor mine; divide him between us!"

[27]Then the king said, "Do not kill the child, but give him to the woman who wants him to live, for she is his mother!"

[28]When all Israel heard the king's decision, the people were in awe of the king, for they saw the wisdom God had given him for rendering justice.

CHAPTER 4

Solomon's Officials and Governors

King Solomon now ruled over all Israel, [2]and
these were his high officials:

Azariah son of Zadok was the priest.
[3] Elihoreph and Ahijah, the sons of Shisha,
were court secretaries.
Jehoshaphat son of Ahilud was the royal
historian.
[4] Benaiah son of Jehoiada was commander
of the army.
Zadok and Abiathar were priests.
[5] Azariah son of Nathan was in charge of
the district governors.
Zabud son of Nathan, a priest, was a
trusted adviser to the king.
[6] Ahishar was manager of the palace
property.
Adoniram son of Abda was in charge of
the labor force.

[7]Solomon also had twelve district governors who were over all Israel. They were responsible for providing food for the king's household. Each of them arranged provisions for one month of the year. [8]These are the names of the twelve governors:

Ben-hur, in the hill country of Ephraim.
[9] Ben-deker, in Makaz, Shaalbim, Beth-
shemesh, and Elon-bethhanan.
[10] Ben-hesed, in Arubboth, including Socoh
and all the land of Hepher.
[11] Ben-abinadab, in all of Naphoth-dor.*
(He was married to Taphath, one of
Solomon's daughters.)
[12] Baana son of Ahilud, in Taanach and
Megiddo, all of Beth-shan* near
Zarethan below Jezreel, and all the
territory from Beth-shan to Abel-
meholah and over to Jokmeam.
[13] Ben-geber, in Ramoth-gilead, including
the Towns of Jair (named for Jair of the
tribe of Manasseh*) in Gilead, and in
the Argob region of Bashan, including
sixty large fortified towns with bronze
bars on their gates.
[14] Ahinadab son of Iddo, in Mahanaim.
[15] Ahimaaz, in Naphtali. (He was married to
Basemath, another of Solomon's
daughters.)
[16] Baana son of Hushai, in Asher and in
Aloth.
[17] Jehoshaphat son of Paruah, in Issachar.
[18] Shimei son of Ela, in Benjamin.
[19] Geber son of Uri, in the land of Gilead,*
including the territories of King Sihon
of the Amorites and King Og of Bashan.
There was also one governor over the land
of Judah.*

Solomon's Prosperity and Wisdom

[20]The people of Judah and Israel were as numerous as the sand on the seashore. They were very contented, with plenty to eat and drink. [21]*Solomon ruled over all the kingdoms from the Euphrates River* in the north to the land of the Philistines and the border of Egypt in the south. The conquered peoples of those lands sent tribute money to Solomon and continued to serve him throughout his lifetime.

[22]The daily food requirements for Solomon's palace were 150 bushels of choice flour and 300 bushels of meal*; [23]also 10 oxen from the fattening pens, 20 pasture-fed cattle, 100 sheep or goats, as well as deer, gazelles, roe deer, and choice poultry.*

[24]Solomon's dominion extended over all the kingdoms west of the Euphrates River, from Tiphsah to Gaza. And there was peace on all his borders. [25]During the lifetime of Solomon, all of Judah and Israel lived in peace and safety. And from Dan in the north to Beersheba in the south, each family had its own home and garden.*

[26]Solomon had 4,000* stalls for his chariot horses, and he had 12,000 horses.*

[27]The district governors faithfully provided food for King Solomon and his court; each made sure nothing was lacking during the month assigned to him. [28]They also brought the necessary barley and straw for the royal horses in the stables.

[29]God gave Solomon very great wisdom and understanding, and knowledge as vast as the sands of the seashore. [30]In fact, his wisdom ex-

4:11 Hebrew *Naphath-dor*, a variant spelling of Naphoth-dor. **4:12** Hebrew *Beth-shean*, a variant spelling of Beth-shan; also in 4:12b. **4:13** Hebrew *Jair son of Manasseh;* compare 1 Chr 2:22. **4:19a** Greek version reads *of Gad;* compare 4:13. **4:19b** As in some Greek manuscripts; Hebrew lacks *of Judah*. The meaning of the Hebrew is uncertain. **4:21a** Verses 4:21-34 are numbered 5:1-14 in Hebrew text. **4:21b** Hebrew *the river;* also in 4:24. **4:22** Hebrew *30 cors* [5.5 kiloliters] *of choice flour and 60 cors* [11 kiloliters] *of meal*. **4:23** Or *and fattened geese*. **4:25** Hebrew *each family lived under its own grapevine and under its own fig tree*. **4:26a** As in some Greek manuscripts (see also 2 Chr 9:25); Hebrew reads *40,000*. **4:26b** Or *12,000 charioteers*.

ceeded that of all the wise men of the East and the wise men of Egypt. [31]He was wiser than anyone else, including Ethan the Ezrahite and the sons of Mahol—Heman, Calcol, and Darda. His fame spread throughout all the surrounding nations. [32]He composed some 3,000 proverbs and wrote 1,005 songs. [33]He could speak with authority about all kinds of plants, from the great cedar of Lebanon to the tiny hyssop that grows from cracks in a wall. He could also speak about animals, birds, small creatures, and fish. [34]And kings from every nation sent their ambassadors to listen to the wisdom of Solomon.

CHAPTER 5

Preparations for Building the Temple

[1]*King Hiram of Tyre had always been a loyal friend of David. When Hiram learned that David's son Solomon was the new king of Israel, he sent ambassadors to congratulate him.

[2]Then Solomon sent this message back to Hiram:

> [3]"You know that my father, David, was not able to build a Temple to honor the name of the LORD his God because of the many wars waged against him by surrounding nations. He could not build until the LORD gave him victory over all his enemies. [4]But now the LORD my God has given me peace on every side; I have no enemies, and all is well. [5]So I am planning to build a Temple to honor the name of the LORD my God, just as he had instructed my father, David. For the LORD told him, 'Your son, whom I will place on your throne, will build the Temple to honor my name.'
>
> [6]"Therefore, please command that cedars from Lebanon be cut for me. Let my men work alongside yours, and I will pay your men whatever wages you ask. As you know, there is no one among us who can cut timber like you Sidonians!"

[7]When Hiram received Solomon's message, he was very pleased and said, "Praise the LORD today for giving David a wise son to be king of the great nation of Israel." [8]Then he sent this reply to Solomon:

> "I have received your message, and I will supply all the cedar and cypress timber you need. [9]My servants will bring the logs from the Lebanon mountains to the Mediterranean Sea* and make them into rafts and float them along the coast to whatever place you choose. Then we will break the rafts apart so you can carry the logs away. You can pay me by supplying me with food for my household."

[10]So Hiram supplied as much cedar and cypress timber as Solomon desired. [11]In return, Solomon sent him an annual payment of 100,000 bushels* of wheat for his household and 110,000 gallons* of pure olive oil. [12]So the LORD gave wisdom to Solomon, just as he had promised. And Hiram and Solomon made a formal alliance of peace.

[13]Then King Solomon conscripted a labor force of 30,000 men from all Israel. [14]He sent them to Lebanon in shifts, 10,000 every month, so that each man would be one month in Lebanon and two months at home. Adoniram was in charge of this labor force. [15]Solomon also had 70,000 common laborers, 80,000 quarry workers in the hill country, [16]and 3,600* foremen to supervise the work. [17]At the king's command, they quarried large blocks of high-quality stone and shaped them to make the foundation of the Temple. [18]Men from the city of Gebal helped Solomon's and Hiram's builders prepare the timber and stone for the Temple.

CHAPTER 6

Solomon Builds the Temple

It was in midspring, in the month of Ziv,* during the fourth year of Solomon's reign, that he began to construct the Temple of the LORD. This was 480 years after the people of Israel were rescued from their slavery in the land of Egypt.

[2]The Temple that King Solomon built for the LORD was 90 feet long, 30 feet wide, and 45 feet high.* [3]The entry room at the front of the Temple was 30 feet* wide, running across

5:1 Verses 5:1-18 are numbered 5:15-32 in Hebrew text. **5:9** Hebrew *the sea.* **5:11a** Hebrew *20,000 cors* [3,640 kiloliters]. **5:11b** As in Greek version, which reads *20,000 baths* [420 kiloliters] (see also 2 Chr 2:10); Hebrew reads *20 cors*, about 800 gallons or 3.6 kiloliters in volume. **5:16** As in some Greek manuscripts (see also 2 Chr 2:2, 18); Hebrew reads *3,300.* **6:1** Hebrew *It was in the month of Ziv, which is the second month.* This month of the ancient Hebrew lunar calendar usually occurs within the months of April and May. **6:2** Hebrew *60 cubits* [27.6 meters] *long, 20 cubits* [9.2 meters] *wide, and 30 cubits* [13.8 meters] *high.* **6:3a** Hebrew *20 cubits* [9.2 meters]; also in 6:16, 20.

the entire width of the Temple. It projected outward 15 feet* from the front of the Temple. [4]Solomon also made narrow recessed windows throughout the Temple.

[5]He built a complex of rooms against the outer walls of the Temple, all the way around the sides and rear of the building. [6]The complex was three stories high, the bottom floor being 7½ feet wide, the second floor 9 feet wide, and the top floor 10½ feet wide.* The rooms were connected to the walls of the Temple by beams resting on ledges built out from the wall. So the beams were not inserted into the walls themselves.

[7]The stones used in the construction of the Temple were finished at the quarry, so there was no sound of hammer, ax, or any other iron tool at the building site.

AMAZING FACTS

God's Temple was built in total silence—no sounds of a hammer, ax, or other iron tool.

1 KINGS 6:7

[8]The entrance to the bottom floor* was on the south side of the Temple. There were winding stairs going up to the second floor, and another flight of stairs between the second and third floors. [9]After completing the Temple structure, Solomon put in a ceiling made of cedar beams and planks. [10]As already stated, he built a complex of rooms on three sides of the building, attached to the Temple walls by cedar timbers. Each story of the complex was 7½ feet* high.

[11]Then the LORD gave this message to Solomon: [12]"Concerning this Temple you are building, if you keep all my decrees and regulations and obey all my commands, I will fulfill through you the promise I made to your father, David. [13]I will live among the Israelites and will never abandon my people Israel."

The Temple's Interior

[14]So Solomon finished building the Temple. [15]The entire inside, from floor to ceiling, was paneled with wood. He paneled the walls and ceilings with cedar, and he used planks of cypress for the floors. [16]He partitioned off an inner sanctuary—the Most Holy Place—at the far end of the Temple. It was 30 feet deep and was paneled with cedar from floor to ceiling. [17]The main room of the Temple, outside the Most Holy Place, was 60 feet* long. [18]Cedar paneling completely covered the stone walls throughout the Temple, and the paneling was decorated with carvings of gourds and open flowers.

[19]He prepared the inner sanctuary at the far end of the Temple, where the Ark of the LORD's Covenant would be placed. [20]This inner sanctuary was 30 feet long, 30 feet wide, and 30 feet high. He overlaid the inside with solid gold. He also overlaid the altar made of cedar.* [21]Then Solomon overlaid the rest of the Temple's interior with solid gold, and he made gold chains to protect the entrance* to the Most Holy Place. [22]So he finished overlaying the entire Temple with gold, including the altar that belonged to the Most Holy Place.

[23]He made two cherubim of wild olive* wood, each 15 feet* tall, and placed them in the inner sanctuary. [24]The wingspan of each of the cherubim was 15 feet, each wing being 7½ feet* long. [25]The two cherubim were identical in shape and size; [26]each was 15 feet tall. [27]He placed them side by side in the inner sanctuary of the Temple. Their outspread wings reached from wall to wall, while their inner wings touched at the center of the room. [28]He overlaid the two cherubim with gold.

[29]He decorated all the walls of the inner sanctuary and the main room with carvings of cherubim, palm trees, and open flowers. [30]He overlaid the floor in both rooms with gold.

6:3b Hebrew *10 cubits* [4.6 meters]. **6:6** Hebrew *the bottom floor being 5 cubits* [2.3 meters] *wide, the second floor 6 cubits* [2.8 meters] *wide, and the top floor 7 cubits* [3.2 meters] *wide*. **6:8** As in Greek version; Hebrew reads *middle floor*. **6:10** Hebrew *5 cubits* [2.3 meters]. **6:17** Hebrew *40 cubits* [18.4 meters]. **6:20** Or *overlaid the altar with cedar*. The meaning of the Hebrew is uncertain. **6:21** Or *to draw curtains across*. The meaning of the Hebrew is uncertain. **6:23a** Or *pine*; Hebrew reads *oil tree*; also in 6:31, 33. **6:23b** Hebrew *10 cubits* [4.6 meters]; also in 6:24, 25. **6:24** Hebrew *5 cubits* [2.3 meters].

31For the entrance to the inner sanctuary,
he made double doors of wild olive wood with
five-sided doorposts.* 32These double doors
were decorated with carvings of cherubim,
palm trees, and open flowers. The doors, in-
cluding the decorations of cherubim and
palm trees, were overlaid with gold.

33Then he made four-sided doorposts of
wild olive wood for the entrance to the Tem-
ple. 34There were two folding doors of cypress
wood, and each door was hinged to fold back
upon itself. 35These doors were decorated
with carvings of cherubim, palm trees, and
open flowers—all overlaid evenly with gold.

36The walls of the inner courtyard were built
so that there was one layer of cedar beams be-
tween every three layers of finished stone.

37The foundation of the LORD's Temple
was laid in midspring, in the month of Ziv,*
during the fourth year of Solomon's reign.
38The entire building was completed in every
detail by midautumn, in the month of Bul,*
during the eleventh year of his reign. So it
took seven years to build the Temple.

CHAPTER 7

Solomon Builds His Palace

Solomon also built a palace for himself, and it
took him thirteen years to complete the con-
struction.

2One of Solomon's buildings was called the
Palace of the Forest of Lebanon. It was
150 feet long, 75 feet wide, and 45 feet high.*
There were four rows of cedar pillars, and
great cedar beams rested on the pillars. 3The
hall had a cedar roof. Above the beams on the
pillars were forty-five side rooms,* arranged
in three tiers of fifteen each. 4On each end of
the long hall were three rows of windows fac-
ing each other. 5All the doorways and
doorposts* had rectangular frames and were
arranged in sets of three, facing each other.

6Solomon also built the Hall of Pillars,
which was 75 feet long and 45 feet wide.*
There was a porch in front, along with a can-
opy supported by pillars.

7Solomon also built the throne room,
known as the Hall of Justice, where he sat to
hear legal matters. It was paneled with cedar
from floor to ceiling.* 8Solomon's living
quarters surrounded a courtyard behind this
hall, and they were constructed the same way.
He also built similar living quarters for Pha-
raoh's daughter, whom he had married.

9From foundation to eaves, all these build-
ings were built from huge blocks of high-
quality stone, cut with saws and trimmed to
exact measure on all sides. 10Some of the huge
foundation stones were 15 feet long, and
some were 12 feet* long. 11The blocks of
high-quality stone used in the walls were also
cut to measure, and cedar beams were also
used. 12The walls of the great courtyard were
built so that there was one layer of cedar
beams between every three layers of finished
stone, just like the walls of the inner courtyard
of the LORD's Temple with its entry room.

Furnishings for the Temple

13King Solomon then asked for a man named
Huram* to come from Tyre. 14He was half Is-
raelite, since his mother was a widow from
the tribe of Naphtali, and his father had been
a craftsman in bronze from Tyre. Huram was
extremely skillful and talented in any work in
bronze, and he came to do all the metal work
for King Solomon.

15Huram cast two bronze pillars, each
27 feet tall and 18 feet in circumference.*
16For the tops of the pillars he cast bronze
capitals, each 7½ feet* tall. 17Each capital was
decorated with seven sets of latticework and
interwoven chains. 18He also encircled the
latticework with two rows of pomegranates to
decorate the capitals over the pillars. 19The
capitals on the columns inside the entry room
were shaped like water lilies, and they were six
feet* tall. 20The capitals on the two pillars had
200 pomegranates in two rows around them,
beside the rounded surface next to the lattice-
work. 21Huram set the pillars at the entrance
of the Temple, one toward the south and one

6:31 The meaning of the Hebrew is uncertain. **6:37** Hebrew *was laid in the month of Ziv.* This month of the ancient Hebrew lunar calendar usually occurs within the months of April and May. **6:38** Hebrew *by the month of Bul, which is the eighth month.* This month of the ancient Hebrew lunar calendar usually occurs within the months of October and November. **7:2** Hebrew *100 cubits* [46 meters] *long, 50 cubits* [23 meters] *wide, and 30 cubits* [13.5 meters] *high.* **7:3** Or *45 rafters,* or *45 beams,* or *45 pillars.* The architectural details in 7:2-6 can be interpreted in many different ways. **7:5** Greek version reads *windows.* **7:6** Hebrew *50 cubits* [23 meters] *long and 30 cubits* [13.8 meters] *wide.* **7:7** As in Syriac version and Latin Vulgate; Hebrew reads *from floor to floor.* **7:10** Hebrew *10 cubits* [4.6 meters] . . . *8 cubits* [3.7 meters]. **7:13** Hebrew *Hiram* (also in 7:40, 45); compare 2 Chr 2:13. This is not the same person mentioned in 5:1. **7:15** Hebrew *18 cubits* [8.3 meters] *tall and 12 cubits* [5.5 meters] *in circumference.* **7:16** Hebrew *5 cubits* [2.3 meters]. **7:19** Hebrew *4 cubits* [1.8 meters]; also in 7:38.

toward the north. He named the one on the
south Jakin, and the one on the north Boaz.*
22 The capitals on the pillars were shaped like
water lilies. And so the work on the pillars was
finished.

23 Then Huram cast a great round basin,
15 feet across from rim to rim, called the Sea.
It was 7½ feet deep and about 45 feet in cir-
cumference.* 24 It was encircled just below its
rim by two rows of decorative gourds. There
were about six gourds per foot* all the way
around, and they were cast as part of the basin.

25 The Sea was placed on a base of twelve
bronze oxen,* all facing outward. Three
faced north, three faced west, three faced
south, and three faced east, and the Sea rested
on them. 26 The walls of the Sea were about
three inches* thick, and its rim flared out like
a cup and resembled a water lily blossom. It
could hold about 11,000 gallons* of water.

27 Huram also made ten bronze water carts,
each 6 feet long, 6 feet wide, and 4½ feet
tall.* 28 They were constructed with side panels
braced with crossbars. 29 Both the panels and
the crossbars were decorated with carved
lions, oxen, and cherubim. Above and below
the lions and oxen were wreath decorations.
30 Each of these carts had four bronze wheels
and bronze axles. There were supporting
posts for the bronze basins at the corners of
the carts; these supports were decorated on
each side with carvings of wreaths. 31 The top
of each cart had a rounded frame for the ba-
sin. It projected 1½ feet* above the cart's top
like a round pedestal, and its opening was
2¼ feet* across; it was decorated on the out-
side with carvings of wreaths. The panels of
the carts were square, not round. 32 Under the
panels were four wheels that were connected
to axles that had been cast as one unit with
the cart. The wheels were 2¼ feet in diameter
33 and were similar to chariot wheels. The ax-
les, spokes, rims, and hubs were all cast from
molten bronze.

34 There were handles at each of the four
corners of the carts, and these, too, were cast
as one unit with the cart. 35 Around the top of
each cart was a rim nine inches wide.* The
corner supports and side panels were cast as
one unit with the cart. 36 Carvings of cheru-
bim, lions, and palm trees decorated the pan-
els and corner supports wherever there was
room, and there were wreaths all around.
37 All ten water carts were the same size and
were made alike, for each was cast from the
same mold.

38 Huram also made ten smaller bronze
basins, one for each cart. Each basin was six
feet across and could hold 220 gallons* of
water. 39 He set five water carts on the south
side of the Temple and five on the north side.
The great bronze basin called the Sea was
placed near the southeast corner of the Tem-
ple. 40 He also made the necessary washbasins,
shovels, and bowls.

So at last Huram completed everything
King Solomon had assigned him to make for
the Temple of the LORD:

41 the two pillars;
the two bowl-shaped capitals on top
of the pillars;
the two networks of interwoven chains
that decorated the capitals;
42 the 400 pomegranates that hung from
the chains on the capitals (two rows
of pomegranates for each of the chain
networks that decorated the capitals
on top of the pillars);
43 the ten water carts holding the ten basins;
44 the Sea and the twelve oxen under it;
45 the ash buckets, the shovels, and the
bowls.

Huram made all these things of burnished
bronze for the Temple of the LORD, just as
King Solomon had directed. 46 The king had
them cast in clay molds in the Jordan Valley
between Succoth and Zarethan. 47 Solomon
did not weigh all these things because there
were so many; the weight of the bronze could
not be measured.

48 Solomon also made all the furnishings of
the Temple of the LORD:

the gold altar;
the gold table for the Bread of
the Presence;

7:21 *Jakin* probably means "he establishes"; *Boaz* probably means "in him is strength." **7:23** Hebrew *10 cubits* [4.6 meters] *across. . . . 5 cubits* [2.3 meters] *deep and 30 cubits* [13.8 meters] *in circumference.* **7:24** Or *20 gourds per meter;* Hebrew reads *10 per cubit.* **7:25** Hebrew *12 oxen;* compare 2 Kgs 16:17, which specifies *bronze oxen.* **7:26a** Hebrew *a handbreadth* [8 centimeters]. **7:26b** Hebrew *2,000 baths* [42 kiloliters]. **7:27** Hebrew *4 cubits* [1.8 meters] *long, 4 cubits wide, and 3 cubits* [1.4 meters] *high.* **7:31a** Hebrew *a cubit* [46 centimeters]. **7:31b** Hebrew *1½ cubits* [69 centimeters]; also in 7:32. **7:35** Hebrew *half a cubit wide* [23 centimeters]. **7:38** Hebrew *40 baths* [840 liters].

49 the lampstands of solid gold, five on the
south and five on the north, in front of
the Most Holy Place;
the flower decorations, lamps, and
tongs—all of gold;
50 the small bowls, lamp snuffers, bowls,
dishes, and incense burners—all of
solid gold;
the doors for the entrances to the Most
Holy Place and the main room of the
Temple, with their fronts overlaid with
gold.

51 So King Solomon finished all his work on the Temple of the LORD. Then he brought all the gifts his father, David, had dedicated—the silver, the gold, and the various articles—and he stored them in the treasuries of the LORD's Temple.

CHAPTER 8

The Ark Brought to the Temple

Solomon then summoned to Jerusalem the elders of Israel and all the heads of the tribes—the leaders of the ancestral families of the Israelites. They were to bring the Ark of the LORD's Covenant to the Temple from its location in the City of David, also known as Zion. 2 So all the men of Israel assembled before King Solomon at the annual Festival of Shelters, which is held in early autumn in the month of Ethanim.*

3 When all the elders of Israel arrived, the priests picked up the Ark. 4 The priests and Levites brought up the Ark of the LORD along with the special tent* and all the sacred items that had been in it. 5 There, before the Ark, King Solomon and the entire community of Israel sacrificed so many sheep, goats, and cattle that no one could keep count!

6 Then the priests carried the Ark of the LORD's Covenant into the inner sanctuary of the Temple—the Most Holy Place—and placed it beneath the wings of the cherubim. 7 The cherubim spread their wings over the Ark, forming a canopy over the Ark and its carrying poles. 8 These poles were so long that their ends could be seen from the Temple's main room—the Holy Place—but not from the outside. They are still there to this day. 9 Nothing was in the Ark except the two stone tablets that Moses had placed in it at Mount Sinai,* where the LORD made a covenant with the people of Israel when they left the land of Egypt.

10 When the priests came out of the Holy Place, a thick cloud filled the Temple of the LORD. 11 The priests could not continue their service because of the cloud, for the glorious presence of the LORD filled the Temple.

Solomon Praises the LORD

12 Then Solomon prayed, "O LORD, you have said that you would live in a thick cloud of darkness. 13 Now I have built a glorious Temple for you, a place where you can live forever!*"

14 Then the king turned around to the entire community of Israel standing before him and gave this blessing: 15 "Praise the LORD, the God of Israel, who has kept the promise he made to my father, David. For he told my father, 16 'From the day I brought my people Israel out of Egypt, I have never chosen a city among any of the tribes of Israel as the place where a Temple should be built to honor my name. But I have chosen David to be king over my people Israel.'"

17 Then Solomon said, "My father, David, wanted to build this Temple to honor the name of the LORD, the God of Israel. 18 But the LORD told him, 'You wanted to build the Temple to honor my name. Your intention is good, 19 but you are not the one to do it. One of your own sons will build the Temple to honor me.'

20 "And now the LORD has fulfilled the promise he made, for I have become king in my father's place, and I now sit on the throne of Israel, just as the LORD promised. I have built this Temple to honor the name of the LORD, the God of Israel. 21 And I have prepared a place there for the Ark, which contains the covenant that the LORD made with our ancestors when he brought them out of Egypt."

Solomon's Prayer of Dedication

22 Then Solomon stood before the altar of the LORD in front of the entire community of Israel. He lifted his hands toward heaven, 23 and he prayed,

"O LORD, God of Israel, there is no God
like you in all of heaven above or on the

8:2 Hebrew *at the festival in the month Ethanim, which is the seventh month.* The Festival of Shelters began on the fifteenth day of the seventh month of the ancient Hebrew lunar calendar. This day occurred in late September, October, or early November. **8:4** Hebrew *the Tent of Meeting;* i.e., the tent mentioned in 2 Sam 6:17 and 1 Chr 16:1. **8:9** Hebrew *at Horeb,* another name for Sinai. **8:13** Some Greek texts add the line *Is this not written in the Book of Jashar?*

earth below. You keep your covenant and
show unfailing love to all who walk before
you in wholehearted devotion. [24]You have
kept your promise to your servant David,
my father. You made that promise with
your own mouth, and with your own
hands you have fulfilled it today.
[25]"And now, O LORD, God of Israel,
carry out the additional promise you
made to your servant David, my father.
For you said to him, 'If your descendants
guard their behavior and faithfully follow
me as you have done, one of them will
always sit on the throne of Israel.' [26]Now,
O God of Israel, fulfill this promise to
your servant David, my father.

Does God live in one place?

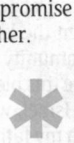

Will God really live on earth? Why, even the highest heavens cannot contain you. 1 KINGS 8:27

[27]"But will God really live on earth?
Why, even the highest heavens cannot
contain you. How much less this Temple
I have built! [28]Nevertheless, listen to my
prayer and my plea, O LORD my God. Hear
the cry and the prayer that your servant is
making to you today. [29]May you watch
over this Temple night and day, this place
where you have said, 'My name will be
there.' May you always hear the prayers I
make toward this place. [30]May you hear
the humble and earnest requests from
me and your people Israel when we pray
toward this place. Yes, hear us from heaven
where you live, and when you hear, forgive.
[31]"If someone wrongs another person
and is required to take an oath of innocence
in front of your altar in this Temple, [32]then
hear from heaven and judge between your
servants—the accuser and the accused.
Punish the guilty as they deserve. Acquit
the innocent because of their innocence.
[33]"If your people Israel are defeated by
their enemies because they have sinned
against you, and if they turn to you and
acknowledge your name and pray to you
here in this Temple, [34]then hear from
heaven and forgive the sin of your people
Israel and return them to this land you
gave their ancestors.
[35]"If the skies are shut up and there is
no rain because your people have sinned
against you, and if they pray toward this
Temple and acknowledge your name and
turn from their sins because you have
punished them, [36]then hear from heaven
and forgive the sins of your servants, your
people Israel. Teach them to follow the
right path, and send rain on your land that
you have given to your people as their
special possession.
[37]"If there is a famine in the land or a
plague or crop disease or attacks of
locusts or caterpillars, or if your people's
enemies are in the land besieging their
towns—whatever disaster or disease there
is—[38]and if your people Israel pray about
their troubles, raising their hands toward
this Temple, [39]then hear from heaven
where you live, and forgive. Give your
people what their actions deserve, for you
alone know each human heart. [40]Then
they will fear you as long as they live in
the land you gave to our ancestors.
[41]"In the future, foreigners who do not
belong to your people Israel will hear of
you. They will come from distant lands
because of your name, [42]for they will hear
of your great name and your strong hand
and your powerful arm. And when they
pray toward this Temple, [43]then hear
from heaven where you live, and grant
what they ask of you. In this way, all the
people of the earth will come to know and
fear you, just as your own people Israel
do. They, too, will know that this Temple I
have built honors your name.
[44]"If your people go out where you send
them to fight their enemies, and if they
pray to the LORD by turning toward this
city you have chosen and toward this
Temple I have built to honor your name,
[45]then hear their prayers from heaven and
uphold their cause.
[46]"If they sin against you—and who has
never sinned?—you might become angry
with them and let their enemies conquer
them and take them captive to their

land far away or near. [47]But in that land
of exile, they might turn to you in
repentance and pray, 'We have sinned,
done evil, and acted wickedly.' [48]If they
turn to you with their whole heart and
soul in the land of their enemies and
pray toward the land you gave to their
ancestors—toward this city you have
chosen, and toward this Temple I have
built to honor your name—[49]then hear
their prayers and their petition from
heaven where you live, and uphold their
cause. [50]Forgive your people who have
sinned against you. Forgive all the
offenses they have committed against
you. Make their captors merciful to them,
[51]for they are your people—your special
possession—whom you brought out of the
iron-smelting furnace of Egypt.

[52]"May your eyes be open to my
requests and to the requests of your
people Israel. May you hear and answer
them whenever they cry out to you. [53]For
when you brought our ancestors out of
Egypt, O Sovereign LORD, you told your
servant Moses that you had set Israel
apart from all the nations of the earth
to be your own special possession."

The Dedication of the Temple

[54]When Solomon finished making these
prayers and petitions to the LORD, he stood up
in front of the altar of the LORD, where he had
been kneeling with his hands raised toward
heaven. [55]He stood and in a loud voice blessed
the entire congregation of Israel:

[56]"Praise the LORD who has given rest to his
people Israel, just as he promised. Not one
word has failed of all the wonderful promises
he gave through his servant Moses. [57]May the
LORD our God be with us as he was with our an-
cestors; may he never leave us or abandon us.
[58]May he give us the desire to do his will in
everything and to obey all the commands, de-
crees, and regulations that he gave our ances-
tors. [59]And may these words that I have prayed
in the presence of the LORD be before him
constantly, day and night, so that the LORD our
God may give justice to me and to his people
Israel, according to each day's needs. [60]Then
people all over the earth will know that the
LORD alone is God and there is no other. [61]And
may you be completely faithful to the LORD
our God. May you always obey his decrees and
commands, just as you are doing today."

[62]Then the king and all Israel with him
offered sacrifices to the LORD. [63]Solomon
offered to the LORD a peace offering of
22,000 cattle and 120,000 sheep and goats.
And so the king and all the people of Israel
dedicated the Temple of the LORD.

[64]That same day the king consecrated the
central area of the courtyard in front of the
LORD's Temple. He offered burnt offerings,
grain offerings, and the fat of peace offerings
there, because the bronze altar in the LORD's
presence was too small to hold all the burnt
offerings, grain offerings, and the fat of the
peace offerings.

[65]Then Solomon and all Israel celebrated
the Festival of Shelters* in the presence of the
LORD our God. A large congregation had gath-
ered from as far away as Lebo-hamath in the
north and the Brook of Egypt in the south. The
celebration went on for fourteen days in all—
seven days for the dedication of the altar and
seven days for the Festival of Shelters.* [66]After
the festival was over,* Solomon sent the peo-
ple home. They blessed the king and went to
their homes joyful and glad because the LORD
had been good to his servant David and to his
people Israel.

CHAPTER 9

The LORD's Response to Solomon

So Solomon finished building the Temple of
the LORD, as well as the royal palace. He com-
pleted everything he had planned to do. [2]Then
the LORD appeared to Solomon a second time,
as he had done before at Gibeon. [3]The LORD
said to him,

"I have heard your prayer and your
petition. I have set this Temple apart to be
holy—this place you have built where my
name will be honored forever. I will always
watch over it, for it is dear to my heart.

[4]"As for you, if you will follow me with
integrity and godliness, as David your
father did, obeying all my commands,
decrees, and regulations, [5]then I will

8:65a Hebrew *the festival;* see note on 8:2. **8:65b** Hebrew *seven days and seven days, fourteen days;* compare parallel text at 2 Chr 7:8-10. **8:66** Hebrew *On the eighth day,* probably referring to the day following the seven-day Festival of Shelters; compare parallel text at 2 Chr 7:9-10.

establish the throne of your dynasty over
Israel forever. For I made this promise to
your father, David: 'One of your descen-
dants will always sit on the throne of Israel.'
6"But if you or your descendants
abandon me and disobey the commands
and decrees I have given you, and if you
serve and worship other gods, 7 then I will
uproot Israel from this land that I have
given them. I will reject this Temple that I
have made holy to honor my name. I will
make Israel an object of mockery and
ridicule among the nations. 8And though
this Temple is impressive now, all who
pass by will be appalled and will shake
their heads in amazement. They will ask,
'Why did the LORD do such terrible
things to this land and to this Temple?'
9"And the answer will be, 'Because his
people abandoned the LORD their God,
who brought their ancestors out of Egypt,
and they worshiped other gods instead
and bowed down to them. That is why the
LORD has brought all these disasters on
them.'"

Solomon's Agreement with Hiram

10It took Solomon twenty years to build the
LORD's Temple and his own royal palace. At
the end of that time, 11he gave twenty towns
in the land of Galilee to King Hiram of Tyre.
(Hiram had previously provided all the cedar
and cypress timber and gold that Solomon
had requested.) 12But when Hiram came from
Tyre to see the towns Solomon had given him,
he was not at all pleased with them. 13"What
kind of towns are these, my brother?" he
asked. So Hiram called that area Cabul (which
means "worthless"), as it is still known today.
14Nevertheless, Hiram paid* Solomon 9,000
pounds* of gold.

Solomon's Many Achievements

15This is the account of the forced labor that
King Solomon conscripted to build the LORD's
Temple, the royal palace, the supporting ter-
races,* the wall of Jerusalem, and the cities
of Hazor, Megiddo, and Gezer. 16(Pharaoh,
the king of Egypt, had attacked and captured
Gezer, killing the Canaanite population and
burning it down. He gave the city to his daugh-
ter as a wedding gift when she married Solo-
mon. 17So Solomon rebuilt the city of Gezer.)
He also built up the towns of Lower Beth-
horon, 18Baalath, and Tamar* in the wilder-
ness within his land. 19He built towns as sup-
ply centers and constructed towns where his
chariots and horses* could be stationed. He
built everything he desired in Jerusalem and
Lebanon and throughout his entire realm.
20There were still some people living in the
land who were not Israelites, including Amo-
rites, Hittites, Perizzites, Hivites, and Jebusites.
21These were descendants of the nations
whom the people of Israel had not completely
destroyed.* So Solomon conscripted them for
his labor force, and they serve in the labor
force to this day. 22But Solomon did not con-
script any of the Israelites for forced labor. In-
stead, he assigned them to serve as fighting
men, government officials, officers and cap-
tains in his army, commanders of his chariots,
and charioteers. 23Solomon appointed 550 of
them to supervise the people working on his
various projects.
24Solomon moved his wife, Pharaoh's
daughter, from the City of David to the new
palace he had built for her. Then he con-
structed the supporting terraces.
25Three times each year Solomon pre-
sented burnt offerings and peace offerings
on the altar he had built for the LORD. He also
burned incense to the LORD. And so he fin-
ished the work of building the Temple.
26King Solomon also built a fleet of ships at
Ezion-geber, a port near Elath* in the land of
Edom, along the shore of the Red Sea.* 27Hi-
ram sent experienced crews of sailors to sail
the ships with Solomon's men. 28They sailed
to Ophir and brought back to Solomon some
sixteen tons* of gold.

CHAPTER 10

Visit of the Queen of Sheba

When the queen of Sheba heard of Solomon's
fame, which brought honor to the name of the
LORD,* she came to test him with hard ques-

9:14a Or *For Hiram had paid.* **9:14b** Hebrew *120 talents* [4,000 kilograms]. **9:15** Hebrew *the millo;* also in 9:24. The meaning of the Hebrew is uncertain. **9:18** An alternate reading in the Masoretic Text reads *Tadmor.* **9:19** Or *and charioteers.* **9:21** The Hebrew term used here refers to the complete consecration of things or people to the LORD, either by destroying them or by giving them as an offering. **9:26a** As in Greek version (see also 2 Kgs 14:22; 16:6); Hebrew reads *Eloth,* a variant spelling of Elath. **9:26b** Hebrew *sea of reeds.* **9:28** Hebrew *420 talents* [14 metric tons]. **10:1** Or *which was due to the name of the LORD.* The meaning of the Hebrew is uncertain.

tions. [2]She arrived in Jerusalem with a large group of attendants and a great caravan of camels loaded with spices, large quantities of gold, and precious jewels. When she met with Solomon, she talked with him about everything she had on her mind. [3]Solomon had answers for all her questions; nothing was too hard for the king to explain to her. [4]When the queen of Sheba realized how very wise Solomon was, and when she saw the palace he had built, [5]she was overwhelmed. She was also amazed at the food on his tables, the organization of his officials and their splendid clothing, the cup-bearers, and the burnt offerings Solomon made at the Temple of the LORD.

[6]She exclaimed to the king, "Everything I heard in my country about your achievements* and wisdom is true! [7]I didn't believe what was said until I arrived here and saw it with my own eyes. In fact, I had not heard the half of it! Your wisdom and prosperity are far beyond what I was told. [8]How happy your people* must be! What a privilege for your officials to stand here day after day, listening to your wisdom! [9]Praise the LORD your God, who delights in you and has placed you on the throne of Israel. Because of the LORD's eternal love for Israel, he has made you king so you can rule with justice and righteousness."

[10]Then she gave the king a gift of 9,000 pounds* of gold, great quantities of spices, and precious jewels. Never again were so many spices brought in as those the queen of Sheba gave to King Solomon.

[11](In addition, Hiram's ships brought gold from Ophir, and they also brought rich cargoes of red sandalwood* and precious jewels. [12]The king used the sandalwood to make railings for the Temple of the LORD and the royal palace, and to construct lyres and harps for the musicians. Never before or since has there been such a supply of sandalwood.)

[13]King Solomon gave the queen of Sheba whatever she asked for, besides all the customary gifts he had so generously given. Then she and all her attendants returned to their own land.

Solomon's Wealth and Splendor

[14]Each year Solomon received about 25 tons* of gold. [15]This did not include the additional revenue he received from merchants and traders, all the kings of Arabia, and the governors of the land.

[16]King Solomon made 200 large shields of hammered gold, each weighing more than fifteen pounds.* [17]He also made 300 smaller shields of hammered gold, each weighing nearly four pounds.* The king placed these shields in the Palace of the Forest of Lebanon.

SOLOMON

I must be the richest king in the world. My throne is covered with gold and ivory. I drink only from golden cups. Merchants bring monkeys to entertain my many wives and children.

One day the queen of Sheba visited. She brought me spices, jewels, and of course . . . more gold. The queen had heard about me and wanted to see for herself what I was all about. Although she was impressed with my wealth, what she really wanted to know was if I was as wise as everyone said. So I let her ask me anything. I knew that nothing would be too hard for me to answer. Let's just say she went away more than satisfied.

Solomon's story is told in 2 Samuel 12:24–1 Kings 11:43.

10:6 Hebrew *your words.* **10:8** Greek and Syriac versions and Latin Vulgate read *your wives.* **10:10** Hebrew *120 talents* [4,000 kilograms]. **10:11** Hebrew *almug wood;* also in 10:12. **10:14** Hebrew *666 talents* [23 metric tons]. **10:16** Hebrew *600 [shekels] of gold* [6.8 kilograms]. **10:17** Hebrew *3 minas* [1.8 kilograms].

18 Then the king made a huge throne, decorated with ivory and overlaid with fine gold.
19 The throne had six steps and a rounded
back. There were armrests on both sides of
the seat, and the figure of a lion stood on each
side of the throne. 20 There were also twelve
other lions, one standing on each end of the
six steps. No other throne in all the world
could be compared with it!
21 All of King Solomon's drinking cups were
solid gold, as were all the utensils in the Pal-
ace of the Forest of Lebanon. They were not
made of silver, for silver was considered
worthless in Solomon's day!
22 The king had a fleet of trading ships* that
sailed with Hiram's fleet. Once every three
years the ships returned, loaded with gold,
silver, ivory, apes, and peacocks.*
23 So King Solomon became richer and
wiser than any other king on earth. 24 People
from every nation came to consult him and to
hear the wisdom God had given him. 25 Year
after year everyone who visited brought him
gifts of silver and gold, clothing, weapons,
spices, horses, and mules.
26 Solomon built up a huge force of chari-
ots and horses.* He had 1,400 chariots and
12,000 horses. He stationed some of them in
the chariot cities and some near him in Jeru-
salem. 27 The king made silver as plentiful in
Jerusalem as stone. And valuable cedar tim-
ber was as common as the sycamore-fig trees
that grow in the foothills of Judah.* 28 Solo-
mon's horses were imported from Egypt*
and from Cilicia*; the king's traders acquired
them from Cilicia at the standard price. 29 At
that time chariots from Egypt could be pur-
chased for 600 pieces of silver,* and horses
for 150 pieces of silver.* They were then ex-
ported to the kings of the Hittites and the
kings of Aram.

CHAPTER 11

Solomon's Many Wives

Now King Solomon loved many foreign
women. Besides Pharaoh's daughter, he mar-
ried women from Moab, Ammon, Edom, Si-
don, and from among the Hittites. 2 The LORD
had clearly instructed the people of Israel,
"You must not marry them, because they will
turn your hearts to their gods." Yet Solomon
insisted on loving them anyway. 3 He had
700 wives of royal birth and 300 concubines.
And in fact, they did turn his heart away from
the LORD.
4 In Solomon's old age, they turned his
heart to worship other gods instead of being
completely faithful to the LORD his God, as
his father, David, had been. 5 Solomon wor-
shiped Ashtoreth, the goddess of the Sidoni-
ans, and Molech,* the detestable god of the
Ammonites. 6 In this way, Solomon did what
was evil in the LORD's sight; he refused to fol-
low the LORD completely, as his father, David,
had done.
7 On the Mount of Olives, east of Jerusa-
lem,* he even built a pagan shrine for Che-
mosh, the detestable god of Moab, and
another for Molech, the detestable god of the
Ammonites. 8 Solomon built such shrines for
all his foreign wives to use for burning in-
cense and sacrificing to their gods.
9 The LORD was very angry with Solomon,
for his heart had turned away from the LORD,
the God of Israel, who had appeared to him
twice. 10 He had warned Solomon specifically
about worshiping other gods, but Solomon
did not listen to the LORD's command. 11 So
now the LORD said to him, "Since you have not
kept my covenant and have disobeyed my
decrees, I will surely tear the kingdom away
from you and give it to one of your servants.
12 But for the sake of your father, David, I will
not do this while you are still alive. I will take
the kingdom away from your son. 13 And even
so, I will not take away the entire kingdom; I
will let him be king of one tribe, for the sake
of my servant David and for the sake of Jeru-
salem, my chosen city."

Solomon's Adversaries

14 Then the LORD raised up Hadad the Edom-
ite, a member of Edom's royal family, to be
Solomon's adversary. 15 Years before, David
had defeated Edom. Joab, his army com-
mander, had stayed to bury some of the Isra-
elite soldiers who had died in battle. While
there, they killed every male in Edom. 16 Joab

10:22a Hebrew *fleet of ships of Tarshish*. **10:22b** Or *and baboons*. **10:26** Or *charioteers*; also in 10:26b. **10:27** Hebrew *the Shephelah*. **10:28a** Possibly *Muzur*, a district near Cilicia; also in 10:29. **10:28b** Hebrew *Kue*, probably another name for Cilicia. **10:29a** Hebrew *600 [shekels] of silver*, about 15 pounds or 6.8 kilograms in weight. **10:29b** Hebrew *150 [shekels]*, about 3.8 pounds or 1.7 kilograms in weight. **11:5** Hebrew *Milcom*, a variant spelling of Molech; also in 11:33. **11:7** Hebrew *On the mountain east of Jerusalem*.

and the army of Israel had stayed there for six months, killing them.

17 But Hadad and a few of his father's royal officials escaped and headed for Egypt. (Hadad was just a boy at the time.) 18 They set out from Midian and went to Paran, where others joined them. Then they traveled to Egypt and went to Pharaoh, who gave them a home, food, and some land. 19 Pharaoh grew very fond of Hadad, and he gave him his wife's sister in marriage—the sister of Queen Tahpenes. 20 She bore him a son named Genubath. Tahpenes raised him* in Pharaoh's palace among Pharaoh's own sons.

21 When the news reached Hadad in Egypt that David and his commander Joab were both dead, he said to Pharaoh, "Let me return to my own country."

22 "Why?" Pharaoh asked him. "What do you lack here that makes you want to go home?"

"Nothing," he replied. "But even so, please let me return home."

23 God also raised up Rezon son of Eliada as Solomon's adversary. Rezon had fled from his master, King Hadadezer of Zobah, 24 and had become the leader of a gang of rebels. After David conquered Hadadezer, Rezon and his men fled to Damascus, where he became king. 25 Rezon was Israel's bitter adversary for the rest of Solomon's reign, and he made trouble, just as Hadad did. Rezon hated Israel intensely and continued to reign in Aram.

Jeroboam Rebels against Solomon

26 Another rebel leader was Jeroboam son of Nebat, one of Solomon's own officials. He came from the town of Zeredah in Ephraim, and his mother was Zeruah, a widow.

27 This is the story behind his rebellion. Solomon was rebuilding the supporting terraces* and repairing the walls of the city of his father, David. 28 Jeroboam was a very capable young man, and when Solomon saw how industrious he was, he put him in charge of the labor force from the tribes of Ephraim and Manasseh, the descendants of Joseph.

29 One day as Jeroboam was leaving Jerusalem, the prophet Ahijah from Shiloh met him along the way. Ahijah was wearing a new cloak. The two of them were alone in a field, 30 and Ahijah took hold of the new cloak he was wearing and tore it into twelve pieces. 31 Then he said to Jeroboam, "Take ten of these pieces, for this is what the LORD, the God of Israel, says: 'I am about to tear the kingdom from the hand of Solomon, and I will give ten of the tribes to you! 32 But I will leave him one tribe for the sake of my servant David and for the sake of Jerusalem, which I have chosen out of all the tribes of Israel. 33 For Solomon has* abandoned me and worshiped Ashtoreth, the goddess of the Sidonians; Chemosh, the god of Moab; and Molech, the god of the Ammonites. He has not followed my ways and done what is pleasing in my sight. He has not obeyed my decrees and regulations as David his father did.

34 " 'But I will not take the entire kingdom from Solomon at this time. For the sake of my servant David, the one whom I chose and who obeyed my commands and decrees, I will keep Solomon as leader for the rest of his life. 35 But I will take the kingdom away from his son and give ten of the tribes to you. 36 His son will have one tribe so that the descendants of David my servant will continue to reign, shining like a lamp in Jerusalem, the city I have chosen to be the place for my name. 37 And I will place you on the throne of Israel, and you will rule over all that your heart desires. 38 If you listen to what I tell you and follow my ways and do whatever I consider to be right, and if you obey my decrees and commands, as my servant David did, then I will always be with you. I will establish an enduring dynasty for you as I did for David, and I will give Israel to you. 39 Because of Solomon's sin I will punish the descendants of David—though not forever.' "

40 Solomon tried to kill Jeroboam, but he fled to King Shishak of Egypt and stayed there until Solomon died.

Summary of Solomon's Reign

41 The rest of the events in Solomon's reign, including all his deeds and his wisdom, are recorded in *The Book of the Acts of Solomon*. 42 Solomon ruled in Jerusalem over all Israel for forty years. 43 When he died, he was buried in the City of David, named for his father. Then his son Rehoboam became the next king.

11:20 As in Greek version; Hebrew reads *weaned him*. **11:27** Hebrew *the millo*. The meaning of the Hebrew is uncertain. **11:33** As in Greek, Syriac, and Latin Vulgate; Hebrew reads *For they have*.

CHAPTER 12

The Northern Tribes Revolt

Rehoboam went to Shechem, where all Israel had gathered to make him king. [2]When Jeroboam son of Nebat heard of this, he returned from Egypt,* for he had fled to Egypt to escape from King Solomon. [3]The leaders of Israel summoned him, and Jeroboam and the whole assembly of Israel went to speak with Rehoboam. [4]"Your father was a hard master," they said. "Lighten the harsh labor demands and heavy taxes that your father imposed on us. Then we will be your loyal subjects."

[5]Rehoboam replied, "Give me three days to think this over. Then come back for my answer." So the people went away.

[6]Then King Rehoboam discussed the matter with the older men who had counseled his father, Solomon. "What is your advice?" he asked. "How should I answer these people?"

[7]The older counselors replied, "If you are willing to be a servant to these people today and give them a favorable answer, they will always be your loyal subjects."

[8]But Rehoboam rejected the advice of the older men and instead asked the opinion of the young men who had grown up with him and were now his advisers. [9]"What is your advice?" he asked them. "How should I answer these people who want me to lighten the burdens imposed by my father?"

[10]The young men replied, "This is what you should tell those complainers who want a lighter burden: 'My little finger is thicker than my father's waist! [11]Yes, my father laid heavy burdens on you, but I'm going to make them even heavier! My father beat you with whips, but I will beat you with scorpions!'"

[12]Three days later Jeroboam and all the people returned to hear Rehoboam's decision, just as the king had ordered. [13]But Rehoboam spoke harshly to the people, for he rejected the advice of the older counselors [14]and followed the counsel of his younger advisers. He told the people, "My father laid heavy burdens on you, but I'm going to make them even heavier! My father beat you with whips, but I will beat you with scorpions!"

[15]So the king paid no attention to the people. This turn of events was the will of the LORD, for it fulfilled the LORD's message to Jeroboam son of Nebat through the prophet Ahijah from Shiloh.

[16]When all Israel realized that the king had refused to listen to them, they responded,

GOOD ADVICE?

Timothy had an important decision to make. His parents advised him one way, and his friends gave him almost the opposite advice. Both answers made sense, but what Timothy's friends suggested sounded like a lot more fun. Timothy's parents said, "You can decide what to do." Whose advice do you think Timothy should follow?

Long ago, when Rehoboam was about to become king of Israel, he had two sets of advisers: older men who had counseled his father, and young friends from his neighborhood. Read 1 Kings 12:1-19 to see whose advice Rehoboam took—and what happened as a result!

12:2 As in Greek version and Latin Vulgate (see also 2 Chr 10:2); Hebrew reads *he lived in Egypt.*

"Down with the dynasty of David!
We have no interest in the son of Jesse.
Back to your homes, O Israel!
Look out for your own house, O David!"

So the people of Israel returned home. [17]But Rehoboam continued to rule over the Israelites who lived in the towns of Judah.

[18]King Rehoboam sent Adoniram,* who was in charge of the labor force, to restore order, but the people of Israel stoned him to death. When this news reached King Rehoboam, he quickly jumped into his chariot and fled to Jerusalem. [19]And to this day the northern tribes of Israel have refused to be ruled by a descendant of David.

[20]When the people of Israel learned of Jeroboam's return from Egypt, they called an assembly and made him king over all Israel. So only the tribe of Judah remained loyal to the family of David.

Shemaiah's Prophecy

[21]When Rehoboam arrived at Jerusalem, he mobilized the men of Judah and the tribe of Benjamin—180,000 select troops—to fight against the men of Israel and to restore the kingdom to himself.

[22]But God said to Shemaiah, the man of God, [23]"Say to Rehoboam son of Solomon, king of Judah, and to all the people of Judah and Benjamin, and to the rest of the people, [24]'This is what the LORD says: Do not fight against your relatives, the Israelites. Go back home, for what has happened is my doing!'" So they obeyed the message of the LORD and went home, as the LORD had commanded.

Jeroboam Makes Gold Calves

[25]Jeroboam then built up the city of Shechem in the hill country of Ephraim, and it became his capital. Later he went and built up the town of Peniel.*

[26]Jeroboam thought to himself, "Unless I am careful, the kingdom will return to the dynasty of David. [27]When these people go to Jerusalem to offer sacrifices at the Temple of the LORD, they will again give their allegiance to King Rehoboam of Judah. They will kill me and make him their king instead."

[28]So on the advice of his counselors, the king made two gold calves. He said to the people,* "It is too much trouble for you to worship in Jerusalem. Look, Israel, these are the gods who brought you out of Egypt!"

[29]He placed these calf idols in Bethel and in Dan—at either end of his kingdom. [30]But this became a great sin, for the people worshiped the idols, traveling as far north as Dan to worship the one there.

[31]Jeroboam also erected buildings at the pagan shrines and ordained priests from the common people—those who were not from the priestly tribe of Levi. [32]And Jeroboam instituted a religious festival in Bethel, held on the fifteenth day of the eighth month,* in imitation of the annual Festival of Shelters in Judah. There at Bethel he himself offered sacrifices to the calves he had made, and he appointed priests for the pagan shrines he had made. [33]So on the fifteenth day of the eighth month, a day that he himself had designated, Jeroboam offered sacrifices on the altar at Bethel. He instituted a religious festival for Israel, and he went up to the altar to burn incense.

CHAPTER 13

A Prophet Denounces Jeroboam

At the LORD's command, a man of God from Judah went to Bethel, arriving there just as Jeroboam was approaching the altar to burn incense. [2]Then at the LORD's command, he shouted, "O altar, altar! This is what the LORD says: A child named Josiah will be born into the dynasty of David. On you he will sacrifice the priests from the pagan shrines who come here to burn incense, and human bones will be burned on you." [3]That same day the man of God gave a sign to prove his message. He said, "The LORD has promised to give this sign: This altar will split apart, and its ashes will be poured out on the ground."

[4]When King Jeroboam heard the man of God speaking against the altar at Bethel, he pointed at him and shouted, "Seize that man!" But instantly the king's hand became paralyzed in that position, and he couldn't pull it back. [5]At the same time a wide crack appeared in the altar, and the ashes poured out,

12:18 As in some Greek manuscripts and Syriac version (see also 4:6; 5:14); Hebrew reads *Adoram*. **12:25** Hebrew *Penuel*, a variant spelling of Peniel. **12:28** Hebrew *to them*. **12:32** This day of the ancient Hebrew lunar calendar occurred in late October or early November, exactly one month after the annual Festival of Shelters in Judah (see Lev 23:34).

just as the man of God had predicted in his message from the LORD.

[6]The king cried out to the man of God, "Please ask the LORD your God to restore my hand again!" So the man of God prayed to the LORD, and the king's hand was restored and he could move it again.

[7]Then the king said to the man of God, "Come to the palace with me and have something to eat, and I will give you a gift."

[8]But the man of God said to the king, "Even if you gave me half of everything you own, I would not go with you. I would not eat or drink anything in this place. [9]For the LORD gave me this command: 'You must not eat or drink anything while you are there, and do not return to Judah by the same way you came.'" [10]So he left Bethel and went home another way.

[11]As it happened, there was an old prophet living in Bethel, and his sons* came home and told him what the man of God had done in Bethel that day. They also told their father what the man had said to the king. [12]The old prophet asked them, "Which way did he go?" So they showed their father* which road the man of God had taken. [13]"Quick, saddle the donkey," the old man said. So they saddled the donkey for him, and he mounted it.

[14]Then he rode after the man of God and found him sitting under a great tree. The old prophet asked him, "Are you the man of God who came from Judah?"

"Yes, I am," he replied.

[15]Then he said to the man of God, "Come home with me and eat some food."

[16]"No, I cannot," he replied. "I am not allowed to eat or drink anything here in this place. [17]For the LORD gave me this command: 'You must not eat or drink anything while you are there, and do not return to Judah by the same way you came.'"

[18]But the old prophet answered, "I am a prophet, too, just as you are. And an angel gave me this command from the LORD: 'Bring him home with you so he can have something to eat and drink.'" But the old man was lying to him. [19]So they went back together, and the man of God ate and drank at the prophet's home.

[20]Then while they were sitting at the table, a command from the LORD came to the old prophet. [21]He cried out to the man of God from Judah, "This is what the LORD says: You have defied the word of the LORD and have disobeyed the command the LORD your God gave you. [22]You came back to this place and ate and drank where he told you not to eat or drink. Because of this, your body will not be buried in the grave of your ancestors."

[23]After the man of God had finished eating and drinking, the old prophet saddled his own donkey for him, [24]and the man of God started off again. But as he was traveling along, a lion came out and killed him. His body lay there on the road, with the donkey and the lion standing beside it. [25]People who passed by saw the body lying in the road and the lion standing beside it, and they went and reported it in Bethel, where the old prophet lived.

[26]When the prophet heard the report, he said, "It is the man of God who disobeyed the LORD's command. The LORD has fulfilled his word by causing the lion to attack and kill him."

[27]Then the prophet said to his sons, "Saddle a donkey for me." So they saddled a donkey, [28]and he went out and found the body lying in the road. The donkey and lion were still standing there beside it, for the lion had not eaten the body nor attacked the donkey. [29]So the prophet laid the body of the man of God on the donkey and took it back to the town to mourn over him and bury him. [30]He laid the body in his own grave, crying out in grief, "Oh, my brother!"

[31]Afterward the prophet said to his sons, "When I die, bury me in the grave where the man of God is buried. Lay my bones beside his bones. [32]For the message the LORD told him to proclaim against the altar in Bethel and against the pagan shrines in the towns of Samaria will certainly come true."

[33]But even after this, Jeroboam did not turn from his evil ways. He continued to choose priests from the common people. He appointed anyone who wanted to become a priest for the pagan shrines. [34]This became a great sin and resulted in the utter destruction of Jeroboam's dynasty from the face of the earth.

13:11 As in Greek version; Hebrew reads *son*. **13:12** As in Greek version; Hebrew reads *They had seen*.

CHAPTER 14

Ahijah's Prophecy against Jeroboam

At that time Jeroboam's son Abijah became very sick. [2]So Jeroboam told his wife, "Disguise yourself so that no one will recognize you as my wife. Then go to the prophet Ahijah at Shiloh—the man who told me I would become king. [3]Take him a gift of ten loaves of bread, some cakes, and a jar of honey, and ask him what will happen to the boy."

[4]So Jeroboam's wife went to Ahijah's home at Shiloh. He was an old man now and could no longer see. [5]But the LORD had told Ahijah, "Jeroboam's wife will come here, pretending to be someone else. She will ask you about her son, for he is very sick. Give her the answer I give you."

[6]So when Ahijah heard her footsteps at the door, he called out, "Come in, wife of Jeroboam! Why are you pretending to be someone else?" Then he told her, "I have bad news for you. [7]Give your husband, Jeroboam, this message from the LORD, the God of Israel: 'I promoted you from the ranks of the common people and made you ruler over my people Israel. [8]I ripped the kingdom away from the family of David and gave it to you. But you have not been like my servant David, who obeyed my commands and followed me with all his heart and always did whatever I wanted. [9]You have done more evil than all who lived before you. You have made other gods for yourself and have made me furious with your gold calves. And since you have turned your back on me, [10]I will bring disaster on your dynasty and will destroy every one of your male descendants, slave and free alike, anywhere in Israel. I will burn up your royal dynasty as one burns up trash until it is all gone. [11]The members of Jeroboam's family who die in the city will be eaten by dogs, and those who die in the field will be eaten by vultures. I, the LORD, have spoken.'"

[12]Then Ahijah said to Jeroboam's wife, "Go on home, and when you enter the city, the child will die. [13]All Israel will mourn for him and bury him. He is the only member of your family who will have a proper burial, for this child is the only good thing that the LORD, the God of Israel, sees in the entire family of Jeroboam.

14:15 Hebrew *the river*.

[14]"In addition, the LORD will raise up a king over Israel who will destroy the family of Jeroboam. This will happen today, even now! [15]Then the LORD will shake Israel like a reed whipped about in a stream. He will uproot the people of Israel from this good land that he gave their ancestors and will scatter them beyond the Euphrates River,* for they have angered the LORD with the Asherah poles they have set up for worship. [16]He will abandon Israel because Jeroboam sinned and made Israel sin along with him."

[17]So Jeroboam's wife returned to Tirzah, and the child died just as she walked through the door of her home. [18]And all Israel buried him and mourned for him, as the LORD had promised through the prophet Ahijah.

[19]The rest of the events in Jeroboam's reign, including all his wars and how he ruled, are recorded in *The Book of the History of the Kings of Israel*. [20]Jeroboam reigned in Israel

twenty-two years. When Jeroboam died, his son Nadab became the next king.

Rehoboam Rules in Judah

21Meanwhile, Rehoboam son of Solomon was king in Judah. He was forty-one years old when he became king, and he reigned seventeen years in Jerusalem, the city the LORD had chosen from among all the tribes of Israel as the place to honor his name. Rehoboam's mother was Naamah, an Ammonite woman.

22During Rehoboam's reign, the people of Judah did what was evil in the LORD's sight, provoking his anger with their sin, for it was even worse than that of their ancestors. 23For they also built for themselves pagan shrines and set up sacred pillars and Asherah poles on every high hill and under every green tree. 24There were even male and female shrine prostitutes throughout the land. The people imitated the detestable practices of the pagan nations the LORD had driven from the land ahead of the Israelites.

25In the fifth year of King Rehoboam's reign, King Shishak of Egypt came up and attacked Jerusalem. 26He ransacked the treasuries of the LORD's Temple and the royal palace; he stole everything, including all the gold shields Solomon had made. 27King Rehoboam later replaced them with bronze shields as substitutes, and he entrusted them to the care of the commanders of the guard who protected the entrance to the royal palace. 28Whenever the king went to the Temple of the LORD, the guards would also take the shields and then return them to the guardroom.

29The rest of the events in Rehoboam's reign and everything he did are recorded in *The Book of the History of the Kings of Judah*. 30There was constant war between Rehoboam and Jeroboam. 31When Rehoboam died, he was buried among his ancestors in the City of David. His mother was Naamah, an Ammonite woman. Then his son Abijam* became the next king.

CHAPTER 15

Abijam Rules in Judah

Abijam* began to rule over Judah in the eighteenth year of Jeroboam's reign in Israel. 2He reigned in Jerusalem three years. His mother was Maacah, the daughter of Absalom.*

3He committed the same sins as his father before him, and he was not faithful to the LORD his God, as his ancestor David had been. 4But for David's sake, the LORD his God allowed his descendants to continue ruling, shining like a lamp, and he gave Abijam a son to rule after him in Jerusalem. 5For David had done what was pleasing in the LORD's sight and had obeyed the LORD's commands throughout his life, except in the affair concerning Uriah the Hittite.

6There was war between Abijam and Jeroboam* throughout Abijam's reign. 7The rest of the events in Abijam's reign and everything he did are recorded in *The Book of the History of the Kings of Judah*. There was constant war between Abijam and Jeroboam. 8When Abijam died, he was buried in the City of David. Then his son Asa became the next king.

Asa Rules in Judah

9Asa began to rule over Judah in the twentieth year of Jeroboam's reign in Israel. 10He reigned in Jerusalem forty-one years. His grandmother* was Maacah, the daughter of Absalom.

11Asa did what was pleasing in the LORD's sight, as his ancestor David had done. 12He banished the male and female shrine prostitutes from the land and got rid of all the idols* his ancestors had made. 13He even deposed his grandmother Maacah from her position as queen mother because she had made an obscene Asherah pole. He cut down her obscene pole and burned it in the Kidron Valley. 14Although the pagan shrines were not removed, Asa's heart remained completely faithful to the LORD throughout his life. 15He brought into the Temple of the LORD the silver and gold and the various items that he and his father had dedicated.

16There was constant war between King Asa of Judah and King Baasha of Israel. 17King Baasha of Israel invaded Judah and fortified Ramah in order to prevent anyone from entering or leaving King Asa's territory in Judah.

18Asa responded by removing all the silver and gold that was left in the treasuries of the

14:31 Also known as *Abijah*. **15:1** Also known as *Abijah*. **15:2** Hebrew *Abishalom* (also in 15:10), a variant spelling of Absalom; compare 2 Chr 11:20. **15:6** As in a few Hebrew and Greek manuscripts; most Hebrew manuscripts read *between Rehoboam and Jeroboam*. **15:10** Or *The queen mother*; Hebrew reads *His mother* (also in 15:13); compare 15:2. **15:12** The Hebrew term (literally *round things*) probably alludes to dung.

Temple of the LORD and the royal palace. He sent it with some of his officials to Ben-hadad son of Tabrimmon, son of Hezion, the king of Aram, who was ruling in Damascus, along with this message:

> [19]"Let there be a treaty* between you and me like the one between your father and my father. See, I am sending you a gift of silver and gold. Break your treaty with King Baasha of Israel so that he will leave me alone."

[20]Ben-hadad agreed to King Asa's request and sent the commanders of his army to attack the towns of Israel. They conquered the towns of Ijon, Dan, Abel-beth-maacah, and all Kinnereth, and all the land of Naphtali. [21]As soon as Baasha of Israel heard what was happening, he abandoned his project of fortifying Ramah and withdrew to Tirzah. [22]Then King Asa sent an order throughout Judah, requiring that everyone, without exception, help to carry away the building stones and timbers that Baasha had been using to fortify Ramah. Asa used these materials to fortify the town of Geba in Benjamin and the town of Mizpah.

[23]The rest of the events in Asa's reign—the extent of his power, everything he did, and the names of the cities he built—are recorded in *The Book of the History of the Kings of Judah*. In his old age his feet became diseased. [24]When Asa died, he was buried with his ancestors in the City of David.

Then Jehoshaphat, Asa's son, became the next king.

Nadab Rules in Israel

[25]Nadab son of Jeroboam began to rule over Israel in the second year of King Asa's reign in Judah. He reigned in Israel two years. [26]But he did what was evil in the LORD's sight and followed the example of his father, continuing the sins that Jeroboam had led Israel to commit.

[27]Then Baasha son of Ahijah, from the tribe of Issachar, plotted against Nadab and assassinated him while he and the Israelite army were laying siege to the Philistine town of Gibbethon. [28]Baasha killed Nadab in the third year of King Asa's reign in Judah, and he became the next king of Israel.

[29]He immediately slaughtered all the descendants of King Jeroboam, so that not one of the royal family was left, just as the LORD had promised concerning Jeroboam by the prophet Ahijah from Shiloh. [30]This was done because Jeroboam had provoked the anger of the LORD, the God of Israel, by the sins he had committed and the sins he had led Israel to commit.

[31]The rest of the events in Nadab's reign and everything he did are recorded in *The Book of the History of the Kings of Israel*.

Baasha Rules in Israel

[32]There was constant war between King Asa of Judah and King Baasha of Israel. [33]Baasha son of Ahijah began to rule over all Israel in the third year of King Asa's reign in Judah. Baasha reigned in Tirzah twenty-four years. [34]But he did what was evil in the LORD's sight and followed the example of Jeroboam, continuing the sins that Jeroboam had led Israel to commit.

CHAPTER 16

This message from the LORD was delivered to King Baasha by the prophet Jehu son of Hanani: [2]"I lifted you out of the dust to make you ruler of my people Israel, but you have followed the evil example of Jeroboam. You have provoked my anger by causing my people Israel to sin. [3]So now I will destroy you and your family, just as I destroyed the descendants of Jeroboam son of Nebat. [4]The members of Baasha's family who die in the city will be eaten by dogs, and those who die in the field will be eaten by vultures."

[5]The rest of the events in Baasha's reign and the extent of his power are recorded in *The Book of the History of the Kings of Israel*. [6]When Baasha died, he was buried in Tirzah. Then his son Elah became the next king.

[7]The message from the LORD against Baasha and his family came through the prophet Jehu son of Hanani. It was delivered because Baasha had done what was evil in the LORD's sight (just as the family of Jeroboam had done), and also because Baasha had destroyed the family of Jeroboam. The LORD's anger was provoked by Baasha's sins.

15:19 As in Greek version; Hebrew reads *There is a treaty*.

Elah Rules in Israel

8Elah son of Baasha began to rule over Israel
in the twenty-sixth year of King Asa's reign in
Judah. He reigned in the city of Tirzah for two
years.

9Then Zimri, who commanded half of the
royal chariots, made plans to kill him. One
day in Tirzah, Elah was getting drunk at the
home of Arza, the supervisor of the palace.
10Zimri walked in and struck him down and
killed him. This happened in the twenty-
seventh year of King Asa's reign in Judah.
Then Zimri became the next king.

11Zimri immediately killed the entire royal
family of Baasha, leaving him not even a sin-
gle male child. He even destroyed distant rel-
atives and friends. 12So Zimri destroyed the
dynasty of Baasha as the LORD had promised
through the prophet Jehu. 13This happened
because of all the sins Baasha and his son Elah
had committed, and because of the sins they
led Israel to commit. They provoked the an-
ger of the LORD, the God of Israel, with their
worthless idols.

14The rest of the events in Elah's reign and
everything he did are recorded in *The Book of
the History of the Kings of Israel.*

Zimri Rules in Israel

15Zimri began to rule over Israel in the
twenty-seventh year of King Asa's reign in Ju-
dah, but his reign in Tirzah lasted only seven
days. The army of Israel was then attacking
the Philistine town of Gibbethon. 16When
they heard that Zimri had committed treason
and had assassinated the king, that very day
they chose Omri, commander of the army, as
the new king of Israel. 17So Omri led the en-
tire army of Israel up from Gibbethon to at-
tack Tirzah, Israel's capital. 18When Zimri
saw that the city had been taken, he went into
the citadel of the palace and burned it down
over himself and died in the flames. 19For he,
too, had done what was evil in the LORD's
sight. He followed the example of Jeroboam
in all the sins he had committed and led Israel
to commit.

20The rest of the events in Zimri's reign and
his conspiracy are recorded in *The Book of the
History of the Kings of Israel.*

Omri Rules in Israel

21But now the people of Israel were split into
two factions. Half the people tried to make
Tibni son of Ginath their king, while the other
half supported Omri. 22But Omri's supporters
defeated the supporters of Tibni. So Tibni
was killed, and Omri became the next king.

23Omri began to rule over Israel in the
thirty-first year of King Asa's reign in Judah.
He reigned twelve years in all, six of them in
Tirzah. 24Then Omri bought the hill now
known as Samaria from its owner, Shemer, for
150 pounds of silver.* He built a city on it and
called the city Samaria in honor of Shemer.

25But Omri did what was evil in the LORD's
sight, even more than any of the kings before
him. 26He followed the example of Jeroboam
son of Nebat in all the sins he had committed
and led Israel to commit. The people pro-
voked the anger of the LORD, the God of Israel,
with their worthless idols.

27The rest of the events in Omri's reign, the
extent of his power, and everything he did are
recorded in *The Book of the History of the
Kings of Israel.* 28When Omri died, he was
buried in Samaria. Then his son Ahab be-
came the next king.

Ahab Rules in Israel

29Ahab son of Omri began to rule over Israel in
the thirty-eighth year of King Asa's reign in Ju-
dah. He reigned in Samaria twenty-two years.
30But Ahab son of Omri did what was evil in
the LORD's sight, even more than any of the
kings before him. 31And as though it were not
enough to follow the example of Jeroboam, he
married Jezebel, the daughter of King Ethbaal
of the Sidonians, and he began to bow down in
worship of Baal. 32First Ahab built a temple
and an altar for Baal in Samaria. 33Then he set
up an Asherah pole. He did more to provoke
the anger of the LORD, the God of Israel, than
any of the other kings of Israel before him.

34It was during his reign that Hiel, a man
from Bethel, rebuilt Jericho. When he laid its
foundations, it cost him the life of his oldest
son, Abiram. And when he completed it and
set up its gates, it cost him the life of his young-
est son, Segub.* This all happened accord-
ing to the message from the LORD concerning
Jericho spoken by Joshua son of Nun.

16:24 Hebrew *for 2 talents* (68 kilograms) *of silver.* **16:34** An ancient Hebrew scribal tradition reads *He killed his oldest son when he laid its foundations, and he killed his youngest son when he set up its gates.*

CHAPTER 17

Elijah Fed by Ravens

Now Elijah, who was from Tishbe in Gilead,
told King Ahab, "As surely as the LORD, the
God of Israel, lives—the God I serve—there
will be no dew or rain during the next few
years until I give the word!"
2 Then the LORD said to Elijah, 3 "Go to the
east and hide by Kerith Brook, near where it
enters the Jordan River. 4 Drink from the
brook and eat what the ravens bring you, for
I have commanded them to bring you
food."
5 So Elijah did as the LORD told him and
camped beside Kerith Brook, east of the Jor-
dan. 6 The ravens brought him bread and meat
each morning and evening, and he drank
from the brook. 7 But after a while the brook
dried up, for there was no rainfall anywhere
in the land.

The Widow at Zarephath

8 Then the LORD said to Elijah, 9 "Go and live in
the village of Zarephath, near the city of Si-
don. I have instructed a widow there to feed
you."
10 So he went to Zarephath. As he arrived at
the gates of the village, he saw a widow gath-
ering sticks, and he asked her, "Would you
please bring me a little water in a cup?" 11 As
she was going to get it, he called to her, "Bring
me a bite of bread, too."
12 But she said, "I swear by the LORD your
God that I don't have a single piece of bread in
the house. And I have only a handful of flour
left in the jar and a little cooking oil in the bot-
tom of the jug. I was just gathering a few
sticks to cook this last meal, and then my son
and I will die."
13 But Elijah said to her, "Don't be afraid!
Go ahead and do just what you've said, but
make a little bread for me first. Then use
what's left to prepare a meal for yourself and
your son. 14 For this is what the LORD, the God
of Israel, says: There will always be flour and
olive oil left in your containers until the time
when the LORD sends rain and the crops
grow again!"
15 So she did as Elijah said, and she and Eli-
jah and her family continued to eat for many
days. 16 There was always enough flour and ol-
ive oil left in the containers, just as the LORD
had promised through Elijah.
17 Some time later the woman's son be-
came sick. He grew worse and worse, and fi-
nally he died. 18 Then she said to Elijah,
"O man of God, what have you done to me?
Have you come here to point out my sins and
kill my son?"
19 But Elijah replied, "Give me your son."
And he took the child's body from her arms,
carried him up the stairs to the room where
he was staying, and laid the body on his bed.
20 Then Elijah cried out to the LORD, "O LORD
my God, why have you brought tragedy to this
widow who has opened her home to me, caus-
ing her son to die?"

AMAZING FACTS

Elijah prayed, and a dead boy came back to life. That's a powerful prayer—answered by our powerful God.

1 KINGS 17:17-22

21 And he stretched himself out over the
child three times and cried out to the LORD,
"O LORD my God, please let this child's life
return to him." 22 The LORD heard Elijah's
prayer, and the life of the child returned, and
he revived! 23 Then Elijah brought him down
from the upper room and gave him to his
mother. "Look!" he said. "Your son is alive!"
24 Then the woman told Elijah, "Now I know
for sure that you are a man of God, and that
the LORD truly speaks through you."

CHAPTER 18

The Contest on Mount Carmel

Later on, in the third year of the drought, the
LORD said to Elijah, "Go and present yourself
to King Ahab. Tell him that I will soon send
rain!" 2 So Elijah went to appear before Ahab.
Meanwhile, the famine had become very

severe in Samaria. [3]So Ahab summoned
Obadiah, who was in charge of the palace.
(Obadiah was a devoted follower of the
LORD. [4]Once when Jezebel had tried to kill all
the LORD's prophets, Obadiah had hidden
100 of them in two caves. He put fifty
prophets in each cave and supplied them
with food and water.) [5]Ahab said to Obadiah,
"We must check every spring and valley in
the land to see if we can find enough grass to
save at least some of my horses and mules."
[6]So they divided the land between them.
Ahab went one way by himself, and Obadiah
went another way by himself.

[7]As Obadiah was walking along, he sud-
denly saw Elijah coming toward him. Obadi-
ah recognized him at once and bowed low to
the ground before him. "Is it really you, my
lord Elijah?" he asked.

[8]"Yes, it is," Elijah replied. "Now go and tell
your master, 'Elijah is here.'"

[9]"Oh, sir," Obadiah protested, "what harm
have I done to you that you are sending me to
my death at the hands of Ahab? [10]For I swear
by the LORD your God that the king has
searched every nation and kingdom on earth
from end to end to find you. And each time he
was told, 'Elijah isn't here,' King Ahab forced
the king of that nation to swear to the truth of
his claim. [11]And now you say, 'Go and tell your
master, "Elijah is here."' [12]But as soon as I leave
you, the Spirit of the LORD will carry you away
to who knows where. When Ahab comes and
cannot find you, he will kill me. Yet I have
been a true servant of the LORD all my life.
[13]Has no one told you, my lord, about the time
when Jezebel was trying to kill the LORD's
prophets? I hid 100 of them in two caves and
supplied them with food and water. [14]And
now you say, 'Go and tell your master, "Elijah
is here."' Sir, if I do that, Ahab will certainly
kill me."

[15]But Elijah said, "I swear by the LORD Al-
mighty, in whose presence I stand, that I will
present myself to Ahab this very day."

[16]So Obadiah went to tell Ahab that Elijah
had come, and Ahab went out to meet Elijah.
[17]When Ahab saw him, he exclaimed, "So, is it
really you, you troublemaker of Israel?"

[18]"I have made no trouble for Israel," Elijah
replied. "You and your family are the trouble-
makers, for you have refused to obey the com-
mands of the LORD and have worshiped the
images of Baal instead. [19]Now summon all Is-
rael to join me at Mount Carmel, along with the
450 prophets of Baal and the 400 prophets of
Asherah who are supported by Jezebel.*"

[20]So Ahab summoned all the people of Is-
rael and the prophets to Mount Carmel.
[21]Then Elijah stood in front of them and said,
"How much longer will you waver, hobbling
between two opinions? If the LORD is God, fol-
low him! But if Baal is God, then follow him!"
But the people were completely silent.

[22]Then Elijah said to them, "I am the only
prophet of the LORD who is left, but Baal has
450 prophets. [23]Now bring two bulls. The
prophets of Baal may choose whichever one
they wish and cut it into pieces and lay it on
the wood of their altar, but without setting
fire to it. I will prepare the other bull and lay it
on the wood on the altar, but not set fire to it.
[24]Then call on the name of your god, and I will
call on the name of the LORD. The god who an-
swers by setting fire to the wood is the true
God!" And all the people agreed.

[25]Then Elijah said to the prophets of Baal,
"You go first, for there are many of you.
Choose one of the bulls, and prepare it and
call on the name of your god. But do not set
fire to the wood."

[26]So they prepared one of the bulls and
placed it on the altar. Then they called on the
name of Baal from morning until noontime,
shouting, "O Baal, answer us!" But there was
no reply of any kind. Then they danced, hob-
bling around the altar they had made.

[27]About noontime Elijah began mocking
them. "You'll have to shout louder," he
scoffed, "for surely he is a god! Perhaps he is
daydreaming, or is relieving himself.* Or may-
be he is away on a trip, or is asleep and needs
to be wakened!"

[28]So they shouted louder, and following
their normal custom, they cut themselves
with knives and swords until the blood
gushed out. [29]They raved all afternoon until
the time of the evening sacrifice, but still
there was no sound, no reply, no response.

[30]Then Elijah called to the people, "Come
over here!" They all crowded around him as
he repaired the altar of the LORD that had

18:19 Hebrew *who eat at Jezebel's table.* **18:27** Or *is busy somewhere else,* or *is engaged in business.*

been torn down. [31]He took twelve stones, one
to represent each of the tribes of Israel,*
[32]and he used the stones to rebuild the altar in
the name of the LORD. Then he dug a trench
around the altar large enough to hold about
three gallons.* [33]He piled wood on the altar,
cut the bull into pieces, and laid the pieces on
the wood.

Then he said, "Fill four large jars with water, and pour the water over the offering and the wood."

[34]After they had done this, he said, "Do the same thing again!" And when they were finished, he said, "Now do it a third time!" So they did as he said, [35]and the water ran around the altar and even filled the trench.

[36]At the usual time for offering the evening sacrifice, Elijah the prophet walked up to the altar and prayed, "O LORD, God of Abraham, Isaac, and Jacob,* prove today that you are God in Israel and that I am your servant. Prove that I have done all this at your command. [37]O LORD, answer me! Answer me so these people will know that you, O LORD, are God and that you have brought them back to yourself."

[38]Immediately the fire of the LORD flashed down from heaven and burned up the young bull, the wood, the stones, and the dust. It even licked up all the water in the trench! [39]And when all the people saw it, they fell face down on the ground and cried out, "The LORD—he is God! Yes, the LORD is God!"

[40]Then Elijah commanded, "Seize all the prophets of Baal. Don't let a single one escape!" So the people seized them all, and Elijah took them down to the Kishon Valley and killed them there.

Elijah Prays for Rain

[41]Then Elijah said to Ahab, "Go get something to eat and drink, for I hear a mighty rainstorm coming!"

[42]So Ahab went to eat and drink. But Elijah climbed to the top of Mount Carmel and bowed low to the ground and prayed with his face between his knees.

[43]Then he said to his servant, "Go and look out toward the sea."

The servant went and looked, then returned to Elijah and said, "I didn't see anything."

Seven times Elijah told him to go and look. [44]Finally the seventh time, his servant told him, "I saw a little cloud about the size of a man's hand rising from the sea."

Then Elijah shouted, "Hurry to Ahab and tell him, 'Climb into your chariot and go back home. If you don't hurry, the rain will stop you!'"

[45]And soon the sky was black with clouds. A heavy wind brought a terrific rainstorm, and Ahab left quickly for Jezreel. [46]Then the LORD gave special strength to Elijah. He tucked his cloak into his belt* and ran ahead of Ahab's chariot all the way to the entrance of Jezreel.

CHAPTER 19

Elijah Flees to Sinai

When Ahab got home, he told Jezebel everything Elijah had done, including the way he had killed all the prophets of Baal. [2]So Jezebel sent this message to Elijah: "May the gods strike me and even kill me if by this time tomorrow I have not killed you just as you killed them."

[3]Elijah was afraid and fled for his life. He went to Beersheba, a town in Judah, and he left his servant there. [4]Then he went on alone into the wilderness, traveling all day. He sat down under a solitary broom tree and prayed that he might die. "I have had enough, LORD," he said. "Take my life, for I am no better than my ancestors who have already died."

[5]Then he lay down and slept under the broom tree. But as he was sleeping, an angel touched him and told him, "Get up and eat!" [6]He looked around and there beside his head was some bread baked on hot stones and a jar of water! So he ate and drank and lay down again.

[7]Then the angel of the LORD came again and touched him and said, "Get up and eat some more, or the journey ahead will be too much for you."

[8]So he got up and ate and drank, and the food gave him enough strength to travel forty days and forty nights to Mount Sinai,* the

18:31 Hebrew *each of the tribes of the sons of Jacob to whom the LORD had said, "Your name will be Israel."* **18:32** Hebrew *2 seahs* [12 liters] *of seed.* **18:36** Hebrew *and Israel.* The names "Jacob" and "Israel" are often interchanged throughout the Old Testament, referring sometimes to the individual patriarch and sometimes to the nation. **18:46** Hebrew *He bound up his loins.* **19:8** Hebrew *to Horeb,* another name for Sinai.

mountain of God. [9]There he came to a cave, where he spent the night.

The Lord Speaks to Elijah

But the Lord said to him, "What are you doing here, Elijah?"

[10]Elijah replied, "I have zealously served the Lord God Almighty. But the people of Israel have broken their covenant with you, torn down your altars, and killed every one of your prophets. I am the only one left, and now they are trying to kill me, too."

[11]"Go out and stand before me on the mountain," the Lord told him. And as Elijah stood there, the Lord passed by, and a mighty windstorm hit the mountain. It was such a terrible blast that the rocks were torn loose, but the Lord was not in the wind. After the wind there was an earthquake, but the Lord was not in the earthquake. [12]And after the earthquake there was a fire, but the Lord was not in the fire. And after the fire there was the sound of a gentle whisper. [13]When Elijah heard it, he wrapped his face in his cloak and went out and stood at the entrance of the cave.

And a voice said, "What are you doing here, Elijah?"

[14]He replied again, "I have zealously served the Lord God Almighty. But the people of Israel have broken their covenant with you, torn down your altars, and killed every one of your prophets. I am the only one left, and now they are trying to kill me, too."

[15]Then the Lord told him, "Go back the same way you came, and travel to the wilderness of Damascus. When you arrive there, anoint Hazael to be king of Aram. [16]Then anoint Jehu grandson of Nimshi* to be king of Israel, and anoint Elisha son of Shaphat from the town of Abel-meholah to replace you as my prophet. [17]Anyone who escapes from Hazael will be killed by Jehu, and those who escape Jehu will be killed by Elisha! [18]Yet I will preserve 7,000 others in Israel who have never bowed down to Baal or kissed him!"

The Call of Elisha

[19]So Elijah went and found Elisha son of Shaphat plowing a field. There were twelve teams of oxen in the field, and Elisha was plowing with the twelfth team. Elijah went over to him and threw his cloak across his shoulders and then walked away. [20]Elisha left the oxen standing there, ran after Elijah, and said to him, "First let me go and kiss my father and mother good-bye, and then I will go with you!"

Elijah replied, "Go on back, but think about what I have done to you."

[21]So Elisha returned to his oxen and slaughtered them. He used the wood from the plow to build a fire to roast their flesh. He passed around the meat to the townspeople, and they all ate. Then he went with Elijah as his assistant.

CHAPTER 20

Ben-Hadad Attacks Samaria

About that time King Ben-hadad of Aram mobilized his army, supported by the chariots and horses of thirty-two allied kings. They went to besiege Samaria, the capital of Israel, and launched attacks against it. [2]Ben-hadad sent messengers into the city to relay this message to King Ahab of Israel: "This is what Ben-hadad says: [3]'Your silver and gold are mine, and so are your wives and the best of your children!'"

[4]"All right, my lord the king," Israel's king replied. "All that I have is yours!"

[5]Soon Ben-hadad's messengers returned again and said, "This is what Ben-hadad says: 'I have already demanded that you give me your silver, gold, wives, and children. [6]But about this time tomorrow I will send my officials to search your palace and the homes of your people. They will take away everything you consider valuable!'"

[7]Then Ahab summoned all the elders of the land and said to them, "Look how this man is stirring up trouble! I already agreed with his demand that I give him my wives and children and silver and gold."

[8]"Don't give in to any more demands," all the elders and the people advised.

[9]So Ahab told the messengers from Ben-hadad, "Say this to my lord the king: 'I will give you everything you asked for the first time, but I cannot accept this last demand of yours.'" So the messengers returned to Ben-hadad with that response.

[10]Then Ben-hadad sent this message to Ahab: "May the gods strike me and even kill

19:16 Hebrew *descendant of Nimshi;* compare 2 Kgs 9:2, 14.

AHAB

I'm a fussy king. What I want, I get. At least that's how it's supposed to work. One day I saw Naboth's vineyard and thought to myself, *Wouldn't it be nice to turn that into a garden? It's so close to the palace, I could have fresh vegetables whenever I want them.* So I offered to give Naboth better land. He refused. I sulked. I fussed and fumed and wouldn't eat. My wife, Queen Jezebel, asked what was wrong. She came up with a plan to get me what I wanted. First we would find two men to lie about Naboth, then we would have him killed.

Jezebel has some excellent ideas.

Check out the rest of Ahab's evil deeds in 1 Kings 16:28–22:40 and 2 Chronicles 18.

me if there remains enough dust from Samaria to provide even a handful for each of my soldiers."

[11]The king of Israel sent back this answer: "A warrior putting on his sword for battle should not boast like a warrior who has already won."

[12]Ahab's reply reached Ben-hadad and the other kings as they were drinking in their tents.* "Prepare to attack!" Ben-hadad commanded his officers. So they prepared to attack the city.

Ahab's Victory over Ben-Hadad

[13]Then a certain prophet came to see King Ahab of Israel and told him, "This is what the LORD says: Do you see all these enemy forces? Today I will hand them all over to you. Then you will know that I am the LORD."

[14]Ahab asked, "How will he do it?"

And the prophet replied, "This is what the LORD says: The troops of the provincial commanders will do it."

"Should we attack first?" Ahab asked.

"Yes," the prophet answered.

[15]So Ahab mustered the troops of the 232 provincial commanders. Then he called out the rest of the army of Israel, some 7,000 men. [16]About noontime, as Ben-hadad and the thirty-two allied kings were still in their tents drinking themselves into a stupor, [17]the troops of the provincial commanders marched out of the city as the first contingent.

As they approached, Ben-hadad's scouts reported to him, "Some troops are coming from Samaria."

[18]"Take them alive," Ben-hadad commanded, "whether they have come for peace or for war."

[19]But Ahab's provincial commanders and the entire army had now come out to fight. [20]Each Israelite soldier killed his Aramean opponent, and suddenly the entire Aramean army panicked and fled. The Israelites chased them, but King Ben-hadad and a few of his charioteers escaped on horses. [21]However, the king of Israel destroyed the other horses and chariots and slaughtered the Arameans.

[22]Afterward the prophet said to King Ahab, "Get ready for another attack. Begin making plans now, for the king of Aram will come back next spring.*"

Ben-Hadad's Second Attack

[23]After their defeat, Ben-hadad's officers said to him, "The Israelite gods are gods of the hills; that is why they won. But we can beat them easily on the plains. [24]Only this time replace the kings with field commanders! [25]Recruit another army like the one you lost.

20:12 Or *in Succoth;* also in 20:16. **20:22** Hebrew *at the turn of the year;* similarly in 20:26. The first day of the year in the ancient Hebrew lunar calendar occurred in March or April.

Give us the same number of horses, chariots, and men, and we will fight against them on the plains. There's no doubt that we will beat them." So King Ben-hadad did as they suggested.

[26]The following spring he called up the Aramean army and marched out against Israel, this time at Aphek. [27]Israel then mustered its army, set up supply lines, and marched out for battle. But the Israelite army looked like two little flocks of goats in comparison to the vast Aramean forces that filled the countryside!

[28]Then the man of God went to the king of Israel and said, "This is what the LORD says: The Arameans have said, 'The LORD is a god of the hills and not of the plains.' So I will defeat this vast army for you. Then you will know that I am the LORD."

[29]The two armies camped opposite each other for seven days, and on the seventh day the battle began. The Israelites killed 100,000 Aramean foot soldiers in one day. [30]The rest fled into the town of Aphek, but the wall fell on them and killed another 27,000. Ben-hadad fled into the town and hid in a secret room.

[31]Ben-hadad's officers said to him, "Sir, we have heard that the kings of Israel are merciful. So let's humble ourselves by wearing burlap around our waists and putting ropes on our heads, and surrender to the king of Israel. Then perhaps he will let you live."

[32]So they put on burlap and ropes, and they went to the king of Israel and begged, "Your servant Ben-hadad says, 'Please let me live!'"

The king of Israel responded, "Is he still alive? He is my brother!"

[33]The men took this as a good sign and quickly picked up on his words. "Yes," they said, "your brother Ben-hadad!"

"Go and get him," the king of Israel told them. And when Ben-hadad arrived, Ahab invited him up into his chariot.

[34]Ben-hadad told him, "I will give back the towns my father took from your father, and you may establish places of trade in Damascus, as my father did in Samaria."

Then Ahab said, "I will release you under these conditions." So they made a new treaty, and Ben-hadad was set free.

A Prophet Condemns Ahab

[35]Meanwhile, the LORD instructed one of the group of prophets to say to another man, "Hit me!" But the man refused to hit the prophet. [36]Then the prophet told him, "Because you have not obeyed the voice of the LORD, a lion will kill you as soon as you leave me." And when he had gone, a lion did attack and kill him.

[37]Then the prophet turned to another man and said, "Hit me!" So he struck the prophet and wounded him.

[38]The prophet placed a bandage over his eyes to disguise himself and then waited beside the road for the king. [39]As the king passed by, the prophet called out to him, "Sir, I was in the thick of battle, and suddenly a man brought me a prisoner. He said, 'Guard this man; if for any reason he gets away, you will either die or pay a fine of seventy-five pounds* of silver!' [40]But while I was busy doing something else, the prisoner disappeared!"

"Well, it's your own fault," the king replied. "You have brought the judgment on yourself."

[41]Then the prophet quickly pulled the bandage from his eyes, and the king of Israel recognized him as one of the prophets. [42]The prophet said to him, "This is what the LORD says: Because you have spared the man I said must be destroyed,* now you must die in his place, and your people will die instead of his people." [43]So the king of Israel went home to Samaria angry and sullen.

CHAPTER 21

Naboth's Vineyard

Now there was a man named Naboth, from Jezreel, who owned a vineyard in Jezreel beside the palace of King Ahab of Samaria. [2]One day Ahab said to Naboth, "Since your vineyard is so convenient to my palace, I would like to buy it to use as a vegetable garden. I will give you a better vineyard in exchange, or if you prefer, I will pay you for it."

[3]But Naboth replied, "The LORD forbid that I should give you the inheritance that was passed down by my ancestors."

[4]So Ahab went home angry and sullen because of Naboth's answer. The king went to bed with his face to the wall and refused to eat!

20:39 Hebrew *1 talent* [34 kilograms]. **20:42** The Hebrew term used here refers to the complete consecration of things or people to the LORD, either by destroying them or by giving them as an offering.

5"What's the matter?" his wife Jezebel asked him. "What's made you so upset that you're not eating?"

6"I asked Naboth to sell me his vineyard or trade it, but he refused!" Ahab told her.

7"Are you the king of Israel or not?" Jezebel demanded. "Get up and eat something, and don't worry about it. I'll get you Naboth's vineyard!"

8So she wrote letters in Ahab's name, sealed them with his seal, and sent them to the elders and other leaders of the town where Naboth lived. 9In her letters she commanded: "Call the citizens together for fasting and prayer, and give Naboth a place of honor. 10And then seat two scoundrels across from him who will accuse him of cursing God and the king. Then take him out and stone him to death."

11So the elders and other town leaders followed the instructions Jezebel had written in the letters. 12They called for a fast and put Naboth at a prominent place before the people. 13Then the two scoundrels came and sat down across from him. And they accused Naboth before all the people, saying, "He cursed God and the king." So he was dragged outside the town and stoned to death. 14The town leaders then sent word to Jezebel, "Naboth has been stoned to death."

15When Jezebel heard the news, she said to Ahab, "You know the vineyard Naboth wouldn't sell you? Well, you can have it now! He's dead!" 16So Ahab immediately went down to the vineyard of Naboth to claim it.

17But the LORD said to Elijah,* 18"Go down to meet King Ahab of Israel, who rules in Samaria. He will be at Naboth's vineyard in Jezreel, claiming it for himself. 19Give him this message: 'This is what the LORD says: Wasn't it enough that you killed Naboth? Must you rob him, too? Because you have done this, dogs will lick your blood at the very place where they licked the blood of Naboth!'"

20"So, my enemy, you have found me!" Ahab exclaimed to Elijah.

"Yes," Elijah answered, "I have come because you have sold yourself to what is evil in the LORD's sight. 21So now the LORD says, 'I will bring disaster on you and consume you. I will destroy every one of your male descendants, slave and free alike, anywhere in Israel! 22I am going to destroy your family as I did the family of Jeroboam son of Nebat and the family of Baasha son of Ahijah, for you have made me very angry and have led Israel into sin.'

23"And regarding Jezebel, the LORD says, 'Dogs will eat Jezebel's body at the plot of land in Jezreel.*'

24"The members of Ahab's family who die in the city will be eaten by dogs, and those who die in the field will be eaten by vultures."

25(No one else so completely sold himself to what was evil in the LORD's sight as Ahab did under the influence of his wife Jezebel. 26His worst outrage was worshiping idols* just as the Amorites had done—the people whom the LORD had driven out from the land ahead of the Israelites.)

27But when Ahab heard this message, he tore his clothing, dressed in burlap, and fasted. He even slept in burlap and went about in deep mourning.

28Then another message from the LORD came to Elijah: 29"Do you see how Ahab has humbled himself before me? Because he has done this, I will not do what I promised during his lifetime. It will happen to his sons; I will destroy his dynasty."

CHAPTER 22

Jehoshaphat and Ahab

For three years there was no war between Aram and Israel. 2Then during the third year, King Jehoshaphat of Judah went to visit King Ahab of Israel. 3During the visit, the king of Israel said to his officials, "Do you realize that the town of Ramoth-gilead belongs to us? And yet we've done nothing to recapture it from the king of Aram!"

4Then he turned to Jehoshaphat and asked, "Will you join me in battle to recover Ramoth-gilead?"

Jehoshaphat replied to the king of Israel, "Why, of course! You and I are as one. My troops are your troops, and my horses are your horses." 5Then Jehoshaphat added, "But first let's find out what the LORD says."

6So the king of Israel summoned the prophets, about 400 of them, and asked them, "Should I go to war against Ramoth-gilead, or should I hold back?"

21:17 Hebrew *Elijah the Tishbite;* also in 21:28. **21:23** As in several Hebrew manuscripts, Syriac, and Latin Vulgate (see also 2 Kgs 9:26, 36); most Hebrew manuscripts read *at the city wall.* **21:26** The Hebrew term (literally *round things*) probably alludes to dung.

They all replied, "Yes, go right ahead! The Lord will give the king victory."

7 But Jehoshaphat asked, "Is there not also a prophet of the LORD here? We should ask him the same question."

8 The king of Israel replied to Jehoshaphat, "There is one more man who could consult the LORD for us, but I hate him. He never prophesies anything but trouble for me! His name is Micaiah son of Imlah."

Jehoshaphat replied, "That's not the way a king should talk! Let's hear what he has to say."

9 So the king of Israel called one of his officials and said, "Quick! Bring Micaiah son of Imlah."

Micaiah Prophesies against Ahab

10 King Ahab of Israel and King Jehoshaphat of Judah, dressed in their royal robes, were sitting on thrones at the threshing floor near the gate of Samaria. All of Ahab's prophets were prophesying there in front of them. 11 One of them, Zedekiah son of Kenaanah, made some iron horns and proclaimed, "This is what the LORD says: With these horns you will gore the Arameans to death!"

12 All the other prophets agreed. "Yes," they said, "go up to Ramoth-gilead and be victorious, for the LORD will give the king victory!"

13 Meanwhile, the messenger who went to get Micaiah said to him, "Look, all the prophets are promising victory for the king. Be sure that you agree with them and promise success."

14 But Micaiah replied, "As surely as the LORD lives, I will say only what the LORD tells me to say."

15 When Micaiah arrived before the king, Ahab asked him, "Micaiah, should we go to war against Ramoth-gilead, or should we hold back?"

Micaiah replied sarcastically, "Yes, go up and be victorious, for the LORD will give the king victory!"

16 But the king replied sharply, "How many times must I demand that you speak only the truth to me when you speak for the LORD?"

17 Then Micaiah told him, "In a vision I saw all Israel scattered on the mountains, like sheep without a shepherd. And the LORD said, 'Their master has been killed.* Send them home in peace.'"

18 "Didn't I tell you?" the king of Israel exclaimed to Jehoshaphat. "He never prophesies anything but trouble for me."

19 Then Micaiah continued, "Listen to what the LORD says! I saw the LORD sitting on his throne with all the armies of heaven around him, on his right and on his left. 20 And the LORD said, 'Who can entice Ahab to go into battle against Ramoth-gilead so he can be killed?'

"There were many suggestions, 21 and finally a spirit approached the LORD and said, 'I can do it!'

22 "'How will you do this?' the LORD asked.

"And the spirit replied, 'I will go out and inspire all of Ahab's prophets to speak lies.'

"'You will succeed,' said the LORD. 'Go ahead and do it.'

23 "So you see, the LORD has put a lying spirit in the mouths of all your prophets. For the LORD has pronounced your doom."

24 Then Zedekiah son of Kenaanah walked up to Micaiah and slapped him across the face. "Since when did the Spirit of the LORD leave me to speak to you?" he demanded.

25 And Micaiah replied, "You will find out soon enough when you are trying to hide in some secret room!"

26 "Arrest him!" the king of Israel ordered. "Take him back to Amon, the governor of the city, and to my son Joash. 27 Give them this order from the king: 'Put this man in prison, and feed him nothing but bread and water until I return safely from the battle!'"

28 But Micaiah replied, "If you return safely, it will mean that the LORD has not spoken through me!" Then he added to those standing around, "Everyone mark my words!"

The Death of Ahab

29 So King Ahab of Israel and King Jehoshaphat of Judah led their armies against Ramoth-gilead. 30 The king of Israel said to Jehoshaphat, "As we go into battle, I will disguise myself so no one will recognize me, but you wear your royal robes." So the king of Israel disguised himself, and they went into battle.

31 Meanwhile, the king of Aram had issued these orders to his thirty-two chariot commanders: "Attack only the king of Israel. Don't

22:17 Hebrew *These people have no master.*

bother with anyone else!" [32]So when the Aramean chariot commanders saw Jehoshaphat in his royal robes, they went after him. "There is the king of Israel!" they shouted. But when Jehoshaphat called out, [33]the chariot commanders realized he was not the king of Israel, and they stopped chasing him.

[34]An Aramean soldier, however, randomly shot an arrow at the Israelite troops and hit the king of Israel between the joints of his armor. "Turn the horses* and get me out of here!" Ahab groaned to the driver of his chariot. "I'm badly wounded!"

[35]The battle raged all that day, and the king remained propped up in his chariot facing the Arameans. The blood from his wound ran down to the floor of his chariot, and as evening arrived he died. [36]Just as the sun was setting, the cry ran through his troops: "We're done for! Run for your lives!"

[37]So the king died, and his body was taken to Samaria and buried there. [38]Then his chariot was washed beside the pool of Samaria, and dogs came and licked his blood at the place where the prostitutes bathed,* just as the LORD had promised.

[39]The rest of the events in Ahab's reign and everything he did, including the story of the ivory palace and the towns he built, are recorded in *The Book of the History of the Kings of Israel.* [40]So Ahab died, and his son Ahaziah became the next king.

Jehoshaphat Rules in Judah

[41]Jehoshaphat son of Asa began to rule over Judah in the fourth year of King Ahab's reign in Israel. [42]Jehoshaphat was thirty-five years old when he became king, and he reigned in Jerusalem twenty-five years. His mother was Azubah, the daughter of Shilhi.

[43]Jehoshaphat was a good king, following the example of his father, Asa. He did what was pleasing in the LORD's sight. *During his reign, however, he failed to remove all the pagan shrines, and the people still offered sacrifices and burned incense there. [44]Jehoshaphat also made peace with the king of Israel.

[45]The rest of the events in Jehoshaphat's reign, the extent of his power, and the wars he waged are recorded in *The Book of the History of the Kings of Judah.* [46]He banished from the land the rest of the male and female shrine prostitutes, who still continued their practices from the days of his father, Asa.

[47](There was no king in Edom at that time, only a deputy.)

[48]Jehoshaphat also built a fleet of trading ships* to sail to Ophir for gold. But the ships never set sail, for they met with disaster in their home port of Ezion-geber. [49]At one time Ahaziah son of Ahab had proposed to Jehoshaphat, "Let my men sail with your men in the ships." But Jehoshaphat refused the request.

[50]When Jehoshaphat died, he was buried with his ancestors in the City of David. Then his son Jehoram became the next king.

Ahaziah Rules in Israel

[51]Ahaziah son of Ahab began to rule over Israel in the seventeenth year of King Jehoshaphat's reign in Judah. He reigned in Samaria two years. [52]But he did what was evil in the LORD's sight, following the example of his father and mother and the example of Jeroboam son of Nebat, who had led Israel to sin. [53]He served Baal and worshiped him, provoking the anger of the LORD, the God of Israel, just as his father had done.

22:34 Hebrew *Turn your hand.* **22:38** Or *his blood, and the prostitutes bathed (in it);* or *his blood, and they washed his armor.* **22:43** Verses 22:43b-53 are numbered 22:44-54 in Hebrew text. **22:48** Hebrew *fleet of ships of Tarshish.*

2 KINGS

WHO

Elijah, Elisha, Naaman, Naaman's servant girl, Jezebel, Jehu, Joash, Hezekiah, Sennacherib, Isaiah, Manasseh, Josiah, Jehoiakim, Zedekiah, and Nebuchadnezzar.

WHERE

Israel and Judah.

WHEN

The stories of the kings were probably written down later—during the time of the prophets but before 539 BC when the Israelites returned to Jerusalem from Babylon.

WHY

To show what happens to people who refuse to make God their true leader.

The LORD had sent his prophets and seers to warn both Israel and Judah: "Turn from all your evil ways." . . . But the Israelites would not listen. 2 KINGS 17:13-14

Ever wish you could see the future? *Prophets* knew what was going to happen because God told them. Elijah and Elisha were famous prophets. Even when it was hard, they told God's truth.

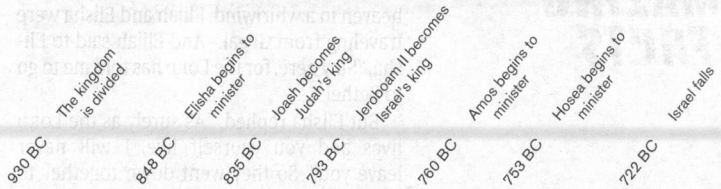

LEARN TO TELL GOD'S TRUTH, NO MATTER WHAT.

CHAPTER 1

Elijah Confronts King Ahaziah

After King Ahab's death, the land of Moab rebelled against Israel.

2 One day Israel's new king, Ahaziah, fell through the latticework of an upper room at his palace in Samaria and was seriously injured. So he sent messengers to the temple of Baal-zebub, the god of Ekron, to ask whether he would recover.

3 But the angel of the LORD told Elijah, who was from Tishbe, "Go and confront the messengers of the king of Samaria and ask them, 'Is there no God in Israel? Why are you going to Baal-zebub, the god of Ekron, to ask whether the king will recover? 4 Now, therefore, this is what the LORD says: You will never leave the bed you are lying on; you will surely die.'" So Elijah went to deliver the message.

5 When the messengers returned to the

king, he asked them, "Why have you returned so soon?"

[6]They replied, "A man came up to us and told us to go back to the king and give him this message. 'This is what the LORD says: Is there no God in Israel? Why are you sending men to Baal-zebub, the god of Ekron, to ask whether you will recover? Therefore, because you have done this, you will never leave the bed you are lying on; you will surely die.'"

[7]"What sort of man was he?" the king demanded. "What did he look like?"

[8]They replied, "He was a hairy man,* and he wore a leather belt around his waist."

"Elijah from Tishbe!" the king exclaimed.

[9]Then he sent an army captain with fifty soldiers to arrest him. They found him sitting on top of a hill. The captain said to him, "Man of God, the king has commanded you to come down with us."

[10]But Elijah replied to the captain, "If I am a man of God, let fire come down from heaven and destroy you and your fifty men!" Then fire fell from heaven and killed them all.

[11]So the king sent another captain with fifty men. The captain said to him, "Man of God, the king demands that you come down at once."

AMAZING FACTS

Elijah didn't die—
a chariot and horses of fire
came for him, and he rode
a whirlwind to heaven.
What a way to go!
2 KINGS 2:11

[12]Elijah replied, "If I am a man of God, let fire come down from heaven and destroy you and your fifty men!" And again the fire of God fell from heaven and killed them all.

[13]Once more the king sent a third captain with fifty men. But this time the captain went up the hill and fell to his knees before Elijah. He pleaded with him, "O man of God, please spare my life and the lives of these, your fifty servants. [14]See how the fire from heaven came down and destroyed the first two groups. But now please spare my life!"

[15]Then the angel of the LORD said to Elijah, "Go down with him, and don't be afraid of him." So Elijah got up and went with him to the king.

[16]And Elijah said to the king, "This is what the LORD says: Why did you send messengers to Baal-zebub, the god of Ekron, to ask whether you will recover? Is there no God in Israel to answer your question? Therefore, because you have done this, you will never leave the bed you are lying on; you will surely die."

[17]So Ahaziah died, just as the LORD had promised through Elijah. Since Ahaziah did not have a son to succeed him, his brother Joram* became the next king. This took place in the second year of the reign of Jehoram son of Jehoshaphat, king of Judah.

[18]The rest of the events in Ahaziah's reign are recorded in *The Book of the History of the Kings of Israel.*

CHAPTER 2

Elijah Taken into Heaven

When the LORD was about to take Elijah up to heaven in a whirlwind, Elijah and Elisha were traveling from Gilgal. [2]And Elijah said to Elisha, "Stay here, for the LORD has told me to go to Bethel."

But Elisha replied, "As surely as the LORD lives and you yourself live, I will never leave you!" So they went down together to Bethel.

[3]The group of prophets from Bethel came to Elisha and asked him, "Did you know that the LORD is going to take your master away from you today?"

"Of course I know," Elisha answered. "But be quiet about it."

[4]Then Elijah said to Elisha, "Stay here, for the LORD has told me to go to Jericho."

But Elisha replied again, "As surely as the LORD lives and you yourself live, I will never

1:8 Or *He was wearing clothing made of hair.* **1:17** Hebrew *Jehoram,* a variant spelling of Joram.

leave you." So they went on together to Jericho.

5 Then the group of prophets from Jericho
came to Elisha and asked him, "Did you know
that the LORD is going to take your master
away from you today?"

"Of course I know," Elisha answered. "But
be quiet about it."

6 Then Elijah said to Elisha, "Stay here, for
the LORD has told me to go to the Jordan River."

But again Elisha replied, "As surely as the
LORD lives and you yourself live, I will never
leave you." So they went on together.

7 Fifty men from the group of prophets
also went and watched from a distance as
Elijah and Elisha stopped beside the Jordan
River. 8 Then Elijah folded his cloak together
and struck the water with it. The river divided, and the two of them went across on
dry ground!

9 When they came to the other side, Elijah
said to Elisha, "Tell me what I can do for you
before I am taken away."

And Elisha replied, "Please let me inherit a
double share of your spirit and become your
successor."

10 "You have asked a difficult thing," Elijah
replied. "If you see me when I am taken from
you, then you will get your request. But if not,
then you won't."

11 As they were walking along and talking,
suddenly a chariot of fire appeared, drawn by
horses of fire. It drove between the two men,
separating them, and Elijah was carried by
a whirlwind into heaven. 12 Elisha saw it and
cried out, "My father! My father! I see the
chariots and charioteers of Israel!" And as
they disappeared from sight, Elisha tore his
clothes in distress.

13 Elisha picked up Elijah's cloak, which
had fallen when he was taken up. Then Elisha returned to the bank of the Jordan River.
14 He struck the water with Elijah's cloak and
cried out, "Where is the LORD, the God of Elijah?" Then the river divided, and Elisha went
across.

15 When the group of prophets from Jericho saw from a distance what happened, they
exclaimed, "Elijah's spirit rests upon Elisha!"
And they went to meet him and bowed to the
ground before him. 16 "Sir," they said, "just say
the word and fifty of our strongest men will
search the wilderness for your master. Perhaps the Spirit of the LORD has left him on
some mountain or in some valley."

"No," Elisha said, "don't send them." 17 But
they kept urging him until they shamed him
into agreeing, and he finally said, "All right,
send them." So fifty men searched for three
days but did not find Elijah. 18 Elisha was still

OLD AND FUNNY

Mr. Greaves had been at John's church for years and years. He knew the Bible backward and forward.

Mr. Greaves was very old and almost deaf. Because of his age and health problems, he walked slowly and with a strange twist. Because of his deafness, he often misunderstood what people said.

Before Sunday school, a couple of guys copied Mr. Greaves's actions and then laughed. John had to admit that they were very funny. What do you think? Was it OK to make fun of Mr. Greaves? Read 2 Kings 2:23-25 to read about a similar situation.

at Jericho when they returned. "Didn't I tell you not to go?" he asked.

Elisha's First Miracles

[19]One day the leaders of the town of Jericho visited Elisha. "We have a problem, my lord," they told him. "This town is located in pleasant surroundings, as you can see. But the water is bad, and the land is unproductive."

[20]Elisha said, "Bring me a new bowl with salt in it." So they brought it to him. [21]Then he went out to the spring that supplied the town with water and threw the salt into it. And he said, "This is what the LORD says: I have purified this water. It will no longer cause death or infertility.*" [22]And the water has remained pure ever since, just as Elisha said.

[23]Elisha left Jericho and went up to Bethel. As he was walking along the road, a group of boys from the town began mocking and making fun of him. "Go away, baldy!" they chanted. "Go away, baldy!" [24]Elisha turned around and looked at them, and he cursed them in the name of the LORD. Then two bears came out of the woods and mauled forty-two of them. [25]From there Elisha went to Mount Carmel and finally returned to Samaria.

CHAPTER 3

War between Israel and Moab

Ahab's son Joram* began to rule over Israel in the eighteenth year of King Jehoshaphat's reign in Judah. He reigned in Samaria twelve years. [2]He did what was evil in the LORD's sight, but not to the same extent as his father and mother. He at least tore down the sacred pillar of Baal that his father had set up. [3]Nevertheless, he continued in the sins that Jeroboam son of Nebat had committed and led the people of Israel to commit.

[4]King Mesha of Moab was a sheep breeder. He used to pay the king of Israel an annual tribute of 100,000 lambs and the wool of 100,000 rams. [5]But after Ahab's death, the king of Moab rebelled against the king of Israel. [6]So King Joram promptly mustered the army of Israel and marched from Samaria. [7]On the way, he sent this message to King Jehoshaphat of Judah: "The king of Moab has rebelled against me. Will you join me in battle against him?"

And Jehoshaphat replied, "Why, of course! You and I are as one. My troops are your troops, and my horses are your horses." [8]Then Jehoshaphat asked, "What route will we take?"

"We will attack from the wilderness of Edom," Joram replied.

[9]The king of Edom and his troops joined them, and all three armies traveled along a roundabout route through the wilderness for seven days. But there was no water for the men or their animals.

[10]"What should we do?" the king of Israel cried out. "The LORD has brought the three of us here to let the king of Moab defeat us."

[11]But King Jehoshaphat of Judah asked, "Is there no prophet of the LORD with us? If there is, we can ask the LORD what to do through him."

One of King Joram's officers replied, "Elisha son of Shaphat is here. He used to be Elijah's personal assistant.*"

[12]Jehoshaphat said, "Yes, the LORD speaks through him." So the kings of Israel, Judah, and Edom went to consult with Elisha.

[13]"Why are you coming to me?"* Elisha asked the king of Israel. "Go to the pagan prophets of your father and mother!"

But King Joram of Israel said, "No! For it was the LORD who called us three kings here—only to be defeated by the king of Moab!"

[14]Elisha replied, "As surely as the LORD Almighty lives, whom I serve, I wouldn't even bother with you except for my respect for King Jehoshaphat of Judah. [15]Now bring me someone who can play the harp."

While the harp was being played, the power* of the LORD came upon Elisha, [16]and he said, "This is what the LORD says: This dry valley will be filled with pools of water! [17]You will see neither wind nor rain, says the LORD, but this valley will be filled with water. You will have plenty for yourselves and your cattle and other animals. [18]But this is only a simple thing for the LORD, for he will make you victorious over the army of Moab! [19]You will conquer the best of their towns, even the fortified ones. You will cut down all their good trees,

2:21 Or *or make the land unproductive;* Hebrew reads *or barrenness.* 3:1 Hebrew *Jehoram,* a variant spelling of Joram; also in 3:6. 3:11 Hebrew *He used to pour water on the hands of Elijah.* 3:13 Hebrew *What is there in common between you and me?* 3:15 Hebrew *the hand.*

ELISHA

I enjoy helping people in need. A poor woman once came to me for help. Her husband had died with many debts. Unless she could pay off the debts, her two sons would be made slaves. I told her to borrow empty jars and fill them with oil from her jar. She looked at me like I was crazy but agreed to do it. She went home, closed the door, and started pouring out the remaining drops of olive oil from her own tiny jar. She filled many large containers. When the last jar was full, the oil stopped flowing. The woman sold the oil and paid all her debts. I'm glad that I could help and that God rewarded her faith.

Find out more about Elisha in 1 Kings 19:15—2 Kings 13:20.

stop up all their springs, and ruin all their good land with stones."

[20]The next day at about the time when the morning sacrifice was offered, water suddenly appeared! It was flowing from the direction of Edom, and soon there was water everywhere.

[21]Meanwhile, when the people of Moab heard about the three armies marching against them, they mobilized every man who was old enough to strap on a sword, and they stationed themselves along their border. [22]But when they got up the next morning, the sun was shining across the water, making it appear red to the Moabites—like blood. [23]"It's blood!" the Moabites exclaimed. "The three armies must have attacked and killed each other! Let's go, men of Moab, and collect the plunder!"

[24]But when the Moabites arrived at the Israelite camp, the army of Israel rushed out and attacked them until they turned and ran. The army of Israel chased them into the land of Moab, destroying everything as they went.* [25]They destroyed the towns, covered their good land with stones, stopped up all the springs, and cut down all the good trees. Finally, only Kir-hareseth and its stone walls were left, but men with slings surrounded and attacked it.

[26]When the king of Moab saw that he was losing the battle, he led 700 of his swordsmen in a desperate attempt to break through the enemy lines near the king of Edom, but they failed. [27]Then the king of Moab took his oldest son, who would have been the next king, and sacrificed him as a burnt offering on the wall. So there was great anger against Israel,* and the Israelites withdrew and returned to their own land.

CHAPTER 4

Elisha Helps a Poor Widow

One day the widow of a member of the group of prophets came to Elisha and cried out, "My husband who served you is dead, and you know how he feared the LORD. But now a creditor has come, threatening to take my two sons as slaves."

[2]"What can I do to help you?" Elisha asked. "Tell me, what do you have in the house?"

"Nothing at all, except a flask of olive oil," she replied.

[3]And Elisha said, "Borrow as many empty jars as you can from your friends and neighbors. [4]Then go into your house with your sons and shut the door behind you. Pour olive oil from your flask into the jars, setting each one aside when it is filled."

3:24 The meaning of the Hebrew is uncertain. **3:27** Or *So Israel's anger was great.* The meaning of the Hebrew is uncertain.

5 So she did as she was told. Her sons kept
bringing jars to her, and she filled one after
another. 6 Soon every container was full to the
brim!

"Bring me another jar," she said to one of
her sons.

"There aren't any more!" he told her. And
then the olive oil stopped flowing.

7 When she told the man of God what had
happened, he said to her, "Now sell the olive
oil and pay your debts, and you and your sons
can live on what is left over."

Elisha and the Woman from Shunem

8 One day Elisha went to the town of Shunem.
A wealthy woman lived there, and she urged
him to come to her home for a meal. After
that, whenever he passed that way, he would
stop there for something to eat.

9 She said to her husband, "I am sure this
man who stops in from time to time is a holy
man of God. 10 Let's build a small room for
him on the roof and furnish it with a bed, a
table, a chair, and a lamp. Then he will have a
place to stay whenever he comes by."

11 One day Elisha returned to Shunem, and
he went up to this upper room to rest. 12 He
said to his servant Gehazi, "Tell the woman
from Shunem I want to speak to her." When
she appeared, 13 Elisha said to Gehazi, "Tell
her, 'We appreciate the kind concern you
have shown us. What can we do for you? Can
we put in a good word for you to the king or to
the commander of the army?'"

"No," she replied, "my family takes good
care of me."

14 Later Elisha asked Gehazi, "What can we
do for her?"

Gehazi replied, "She doesn't have a son,
and her husband is an old man."

15 "Call her back again," Elisha told him.
When the woman returned, Elisha said to
her as she stood in the doorway, 16 "Next year
at this time you will be holding a son in your
arms!"

"No, my lord!" she cried. "O man of God,
don't deceive me and get my hopes up like
that."

17 But sure enough, the woman soon became pregnant. And at that time the following year she had a son, just as Elisha had said.

18 One day when her child was older, he
went out to help his father, who was working
with the harvesters. 19 Suddenly he cried out,
"My head hurts! My head hurts!"

His father said to one of the servants,
"Carry him home to his mother."

20 So the servant took him home, and his
mother held him on her lap. But around
noontime he died. 21 She carried him up and
laid him on the bed of the man of God, then
shut the door and left him there. 22 She sent a
message to her husband: "Send one of the
servants and a donkey so that I can hurry to
the man of God and come right back."

23 "Why go today?" he asked. "It is neither a
new moon festival nor a Sabbath."

But she said, "It will be all right."

24 So she saddled the donkey and said to the
servant, "Hurry! Don't slow down unless I tell
you to."

25 As she approached the man of God at
Mount Carmel, Elisha saw her in the distance.
He said to Gehazi, "Look, the woman from
Shunem is coming. 26 Run out to meet her and
ask her, 'Is everything all right with you, your
husband, and your child?'"

"Yes," the woman told Gehazi, "everything
is fine."

27 But when she came to the man of God at
the mountain, she fell to the ground before
him and caught hold of his feet. Gehazi began
to push her away, but the man of God said,
"Leave her alone. She is deeply troubled, but
the LORD has not told me what it is."

28 Then she said, "Did I ask you for a son, my
lord? And didn't I say, 'Don't deceive me and
get my hopes up'?"

29 Then Elisha said to Gehazi, "Get ready to
travel*; take my staff and go! Don't talk to
anyone along the way. Go quickly and lay the
staff on the child's face."

30 But the boy's mother said, "As surely as
the LORD lives and you yourself live, I won't go
home unless you go with me." So Elisha returned with her.

31 Gehazi hurried on ahead and laid the
staff on the child's face, but nothing happened. There was no sign of life. He returned
to meet Elisha and told him, "The child is still
dead."

32 When Elisha arrived, the child was in-

4:29 Hebrew *Bind up your loins.*

deed dead, lying there on the prophet's bed.
[33]He went in alone and shut the door behind
him and prayed to the LORD. [34]Then he lay
down on the child's body, placing his mouth
on the child's mouth, his eyes on the child's
eyes, and his hands on the child's hands. And
as he stretched out on him, the child's body
began to grow warm again! [35]Elisha got up,
walked back and forth across the room once,
and then stretched himself out again on the
child. This time the boy sneezed seven times
and opened his eyes!

[36]Then Elisha summoned Gehazi. "Call the
child's mother!" he said. And when she came
in, Elisha said, "Here, take your son!" [37]She fell
at his feet and bowed before him, over-
whelmed with gratitude. Then she took her
son in her arms and carried him downstairs.

Miracles during a Famine

[38]Elisha now returned to Gilgal, and there was
a famine in the land. One day as the group of
prophets was seated before him, he said to his
servant, "Put a large pot on the fire, and make
some stew for the rest of the group."

[39]One of the young men went out into the
field to gather herbs and came back with a
pocketful of wild gourds. He shredded them
and put them into the pot without realizing
they were poisonous. [40]Some of the stew was
served to the men. But after they had eaten a
bite or two they cried out, "Man of God,
there's poison in this stew!" So they would not
eat it.

[41]Elisha said, "Bring me some flour." Then
he threw it into the pot and said, "Now it's all
right; go ahead and eat." And then it did not
harm them.

[42]One day a man from Baal-shalishah
brought the man of God a sack of fresh grain
and twenty loaves of barley bread made from
the first grain of his harvest. Elisha said, "Give
it to the people so they can eat."

[43]"What?" his servant exclaimed. "Feed a
hundred people with only this?"

But Elisha repeated, "Give it to the people
so they can eat, for this is what the LORD says:
Everyone will eat, and there will even be some
left over!" [44]And when they gave it to the peo-
ple, there was plenty for all and some left
over, just as the LORD had promised.

CHAPTER 5

The Healing of Naaman

The king of Aram had great admiration for
Naaman, the commander of his army, be-
cause through him the LORD had given Aram
great victories. But though Naaman was a
mighty warrior, he suffered from leprosy.*

[2]At this time Aramean raiders had invaded
the land of Israel, and among their captives
was a young girl who had been given to Naa-
man's wife as a maid. [3]One day the girl said to
her mistress, "I wish my master would go to
see the prophet in Samaria. He would heal
him of his leprosy."

[4]So Naaman told the king what the young
girl from Israel had said. [5]"Go and visit the
prophet," the king of Aram told him. "I will
send a letter of introduction for you to take to
the king of Israel." So Naaman started out,
carrying as gifts 750 pounds of silver,
150 pounds of gold,* and ten sets of clothing.
[6]The letter to the king of Israel said: "With
this letter I present my servant Naaman. I
want you to heal him of his leprosy."

[7]When the king of Israel read the letter, he
tore his clothes in dismay and said, "This man
sends me a leper to heal! Am I God, that I can
give life and take it away? I can see that he's
just trying to pick a fight with me."

[8]But when Elisha, the man of God, heard
that the king of Israel had torn his clothes in
dismay, he sent this message to him: "Why
are you so upset? Send Naaman to me, and he
will learn that there is a true prophet here in
Israel."

[9]So Naaman went with his horses and
chariots and waited at the door of Elisha's
house. [10]But Elisha sent a messenger out to
him with this message: "Go and wash yourself
seven times in the Jordan River. Then your
skin will be restored, and you will be healed of
your leprosy."

[11]But Naaman became angry and stalked
away. "I thought he would certainly come out
to meet me!" he said. "I expected him to wave
his hand over the leprosy and call on the
name of the LORD his God and heal me!
[12]Aren't the rivers of Damascus, the Abana
and the Pharpar, better than any of the rivers
of Israel? Why shouldn't I wash in them and

5:1 Or *from a contagious skin disease.* The Hebrew word used here and throughout this passage can describe various skin diseases.
5:5 Hebrew *10 talents* [340 kilograms] *of silver, 6,000 shekels* [68 kilograms] *of gold.*

be healed?" So Naaman turned and went away in a rage.

13 But his officers tried to reason with him and said, "Sir,* if the prophet had told you to do something very difficult, wouldn't you have done it? So you should certainly obey him when he says simply, 'Go and wash and be cured!' " 14 So Naaman went down to the Jordan River and dipped himself seven times, as the man of God had instructed him. And his skin became as healthy as the skin of a young child's, and he was healed!

15 Then Naaman and his entire party went back to find the man of God. They stood before him, and Naaman said, "Now I know that there is no God in all the world except in Israel. So please accept a gift from your servant."

16 But Elisha replied, "As surely as the LORD lives, whom I serve, I will not accept any gifts." And though Naaman urged him to take the gift, Elisha refused.

17 Then Naaman said, "All right, but please allow me to load two of my mules with earth from this place, and I will take it back home with me. From now on I will never again offer burnt offerings or sacrifices to any other god except the LORD. 18 However, may the LORD pardon me in this one thing: When my master the king goes into the temple of the god Rimmon to worship there and leans on my arm, may the LORD pardon me when I bow, too."

19 "Go in peace," Elisha said. So Naaman started home again.

The Greed of Gehazi

20 But Gehazi, the servant of Elisha, the man of God, said to himself, "My master should not have let this Aramean get away without accepting any of his gifts. As surely as the LORD lives, I will chase after him and get something from him." 21 So Gehazi set off after Naaman.

When Naaman saw Gehazi running after him, he climbed down from his chariot and went to meet him. "Is everything all right?" Naaman asked.

22 "Yes," Gehazi said, "but my master has sent me to tell you that two young prophets from the hill country of Ephraim have just arrived. He would like 75 pounds* of silver and two sets of clothing to give to them."

23 "By all means, take twice as much* silver," Naaman insisted. He gave him two sets of clothing, tied up the money in two bags, and sent two of his servants to carry the gifts for Gehazi. 24 But when they arrived at the citadel,* Gehazi took the gifts from the servants and sent the men back. Then he went and hid the gifts inside the house.

25 When he went in to his master, Elisha asked him, "Where have you been, Gehazi?"

"I haven't been anywhere," he replied.

26 But Elisha asked him, "Don't you realize that I was there in spirit when Naaman stepped down from his chariot to meet you? Is this the time to receive money and clothing, olive groves and vineyards, sheep and cattle, and male and female servants? 27 Because you have done this, you and your descendants will suffer from Naaman's leprosy forever." When Gehazi left the room, he was covered with leprosy; his skin was white as snow.

CHAPTER 6

The Floating Ax Head

One day the group of prophets came to Elisha and told him, "As you can see, this place where we meet with you is too small. 2 Let's go down to the Jordan River, where there are plenty of logs. There we can build a new place for us to meet."

"All right," he told them, "go ahead."

3 "Please come with us," someone suggested.

"I will," he said. 4 So he went with them.

When they arrived at the Jordan, they began cutting down trees. 5 But as one of them was cutting a tree, his ax head fell into the river. "Oh, sir!" he cried. "It was a borrowed ax!"

6 "Where did it fall?" the man of God asked. When he showed him the place, Elisha cut a stick and threw it into the water at that spot. Then the ax head floated to the surface. 7 "Grab it," Elisha said. And the man reached out and grabbed it.

Elisha Traps the Arameans

8 When the king of Aram was at war with Israel, he would confer with his officers and say, "We will mobilize our forces at such and such a place."

5:13 Hebrew *My father*. 5:22 Hebrew *1 talent* [34 kilograms]. 5:23 Hebrew *take 2 talents* [68 kilograms]. 5:24 Hebrew *the Ophel*.

[9]But immediately Elisha, the man of God, would warn the king of Israel, "Do not go near that place, for the Arameans are planning to mobilize their troops there." [10]So the king of Israel would send word to the place indicated by the man of God. Time and again Elisha warned the king, so that he would be on the alert there.

[11]The king of Aram became very upset over this. He called his officers together and demanded, "Which of you is the traitor? Who has been informing the king of Israel of my plans?"

[12]"It's not us, my lord the king," one of the officers replied. "Elisha, the prophet in Israel, tells the king of Israel even the words you speak in the privacy of your bedroom!"

[13]"Go and find out where he is," the king commanded, "so I can send troops to seize him."

And the report came back: "Elisha is at Dothan." [14]So one night the king of Aram sent a great army with many chariots and horses to surround the city.

[15]When the servant of the man of God got up early the next morning and went outside, there were troops, horses, and chariots everywhere. "Oh, sir, what will we do now?" the young man cried to Elisha.

[16]"Don't be afraid!" Elisha told him. "For there are more on our side than on theirs!" [17]Then Elisha prayed, "O LORD, open his eyes and let him see!" The LORD opened the young man's eyes, and when he looked up, he saw that the hillside around Elisha was filled with horses and chariots of fire.

[18]As the Aramean army advanced toward him, Elisha prayed, "O LORD, please make them blind." So the LORD struck them with blindness as Elisha had asked.

[19]Then Elisha went out and told them, "You have come the wrong way! This isn't the right city! Follow me, and I will take you to the man you are looking for." And he led them to the city of Samaria.

[20]As soon as they had entered Samaria, Elisha prayed, "O LORD, now open their eyes and let them see." So the LORD opened their eyes, and they discovered that they were in the middle of Samaria.

[21]When the king of Israel saw them, he shouted to Elisha, "My father, should I kill them? Should I kill them?"

[22]"Of course not!" Elisha replied. "Do we kill prisoners of war? Give them food and drink and send them home again to their master."

AMAZING FACTS

Elisha prayed, and the enemy army went blind . . . until he prayed again!
2 KINGS 6:18-23

[23]So the king made a great feast for them and then sent them home to their master. After that, the Aramean raiders stayed away from the land of Israel.

Ben-Hadad Besieges Samaria

[24]Some time later, however, King Ben-hadad of Aram mustered his entire army and besieged Samaria. [25]As a result, there was a great famine in the city. The siege lasted so long that a donkey's head sold for eighty pieces of silver, and a cup of dove's dung sold for five pieces* of silver.

[26]One day as the king of Israel was walking along the wall of the city, a woman called to him, "Please help me, my lord the king!"

[27]He answered, "If the LORD doesn't help you, what can I do? I have neither food from the threshing floor nor wine from the press to give you." [28]But then the king asked, "What is the matter?"

She replied, "This woman said to me: 'Come on, let's eat your son today, then we will eat my son tomorrow.' [29]So we cooked my son and ate him. Then the next day I said to her,

6:25 Hebrew *sold for 80 shekels* [2 pounds, or 0.9 kilograms] *of silver, and ¼ of a cab* [0.3 liters] *of dove's dung sold for 5 shekels* [2 ounces, or 57 grams]. *Dove's dung* may be a variety of wild vegetable.

'Kill your son so we can eat him,' but she has hidden her son."

30When the king heard this, he tore his clothes in despair. And as the king walked along the wall, the people could see that he was wearing burlap under his robe next to his skin. 31"May God strike me and even kill me if I don't separate Elisha's head from his shoulders this very day," the king vowed.

32Elisha was sitting in his house with the elders of Israel when the king sent a messenger to summon him. But before the messenger arrived, Elisha said to the elders, "A murderer has sent a man to cut off my head. When he arrives, shut the door and keep him out. We will soon hear his master's steps following him."

33While Elisha was still saying this, the messenger arrived. And the king* said, "All this misery is from the LORD! Why should I wait for the LORD any longer?"

CHAPTER 7

Elisha replied, "Listen to this message from the LORD! This is what the LORD says: By this time tomorrow in the markets of Samaria, five quarts of choice flour will cost only one piece of silver,* and ten quarts of barley grain will cost only one piece of silver.*"

2The officer assisting the king said to the man of God, "That couldn't happen even if the LORD opened the windows of heaven!"

But Elisha replied, "You will see it happen with your own eyes, but you won't be able to eat any of it!"

Lepers Visit the Enemy Camp

3Now there were four men with leprosy* sitting at the entrance of the city gates. "Why should we sit here waiting to die?" they asked each other. 4"We will starve if we stay here, but with the famine in the city, we will starve if we go back there. So we might as well go out and surrender to the Aramean army. If they let us live, so much the better. But if they kill us, we would have died anyway."

5So at twilight they set out for the camp of the Arameans. But when they came to the edge of the camp, no one was there! 6For the Lord had caused the Aramean army to hear the clatter of speeding chariots and the galloping of horses and the sounds of a great army approaching. "The king of Israel has hired the Hittites and Egyptians* to attack us!" they cried to one another. 7So they panicked and ran into the night, abandoning their tents, horses, donkeys, and everything else, as they fled for their lives.

8When the lepers arrived at the edge of the camp, they went into one tent after another, eating and drinking wine; and they carried off silver and gold and clothing and hid it. 9Finally, they said to each other, "This is not right. This is a day of good news, and we aren't sharing it with anyone! If we wait until morning, some calamity will certainly fall upon us. Come on, let's go back and tell the people at the palace."

10So they went back to the city and told the gatekeepers what had happened. "We went out to the Aramean camp," they said, "and no one was there! The horses and donkeys were tethered and the tents were all in order, but there wasn't a single person around!" 11Then the gatekeepers shouted the news to the people in the palace.

Israel Plunders the Camp

12The king got out of bed in the middle of the night and told his officers, "I know what has happened. The Arameans know we are starving, so they have left their camp and have hidden in the fields. They are expecting us to leave the city, and then they will take us alive and capture the city."

13One of his officers replied, "We had better send out scouts to check into this. Let them take five of the remaining horses. If something happens to them, it will be no worse than if they stay here and die with the rest of us."

14So two chariots with horses were prepared, and the king sent scouts to see what had happened to the Aramean army. 15They went all the way to the Jordan River, following a trail of clothing and equipment that the Arameans had thrown away in their mad rush to escape. The scouts returned and told the king about it. 16Then the people of Samaria rushed

6:33 Hebrew *he*. **7:1a** Hebrew *1 seah* [6 liters] *of choice flour will cost 1 shekel* [0.4 ounces, or 11 grams]; also in 7:16, 18. **7:1b** Hebrew *2 seahs* [12 liters] *of barley grain will cost 1 shekel* [0.4 ounces, or 11 grams]; also in 7:16, 18. **7:3** Or *with a contagious skin disease*. The Hebrew word used here and throughout this passage can describe various skin diseases. **7:6** Possibly *and the people of Muzur*, a district near Cilicia.

out and plundered the Aramean camp. So it was true that five quarts of choice flour were sold that day for one piece of silver, and ten quarts of barley grain were sold for one piece of silver, just as the LORD had promised. [17] The king appointed his officer to control the traffic at the gate, but he was knocked down and trampled to death as the people rushed out.

So everything happened exactly as the man of God had predicted when the king came to his house. [18] The man of God had said to the king, "By this time tomorrow in the markets of Samaria, five quarts of choice flour will cost one piece of silver, and ten quarts of barley grain will cost one piece of silver."

[19] The king's officer had replied, "That couldn't happen even if the LORD opened the windows of heaven!" And the man of God had said, "You will see it happen with your own eyes, but you won't be able to eat any of it!" [20] And so it was, for the people trampled him to death at the gate!

CHAPTER 8

The Woman from Shunem Returns Home

Elisha had told the woman whose son he had brought back to life, "Take your family and move to some other place, for the LORD has called for a famine on Israel that will last for seven years." [2] So the woman did as the man of God instructed. She took her family and settled in the land of the Philistines for seven years.

[3] After the famine ended she returned from the land of the Philistines, and she went to see the king about getting back her house and land. [4] As she came in, the king was talking with Gehazi, the servant of the man of God. The king had just said, "Tell me some stories about the great things Elisha has done." [5] And Gehazi was telling the king about the time Elisha had brought a boy back to life. At that very moment, the mother of the boy walked in to make her appeal to the king about her house and land.

"Look, my lord the king!" Gehazi exclaimed. "Here is the woman now, and this is her son—the very one Elisha brought back to life!"

[6] "Is this true?" the king asked her. And she told him the story. So he directed one of his officials to see that everything she had lost was restored to her, including the value of any crops that had been harvested during her absence.

Hazael Murders Ben-Hadad

[7] Elisha went to Damascus, the capital of Aram, where King Ben-hadad lay sick. When someone told the king that the man of God had come, [8] the king said to Hazael, "Take a gift to the man of God. Then tell him to ask the LORD, 'Will I recover from this illness?'"

[9] So Hazael loaded down forty camels with the finest products of Damascus as a gift for Elisha. He went to him and said, "Your servant Ben-hadad, the king of Aram, has sent me to ask, 'Will I recover from this illness?'"

[10] And Elisha replied, "Go and tell him, 'You will surely recover.' But actually the LORD has shown me that he will surely die!" [11] Elisha stared at Hazael* with a fixed gaze until Hazael became uneasy.* Then the man of God started weeping.

[12] "What's the matter, my lord?" Hazael asked him.

Elisha replied, "I know the terrible things you will do to the people of Israel. You will burn their fortified cities, kill their young men with the sword, dash their little children to the ground, and rip open their pregnant women!"

[13] Hazael responded, "How could a nobody like me* ever accomplish such great things?"

Elisha answered, "The LORD has shown me that you are going to be the king of Aram."

[14] When Hazael left Elisha and went back, the king asked him, "What did Elisha tell you?"

And Hazael replied, "He told me that you will surely recover."

[15] But the next day Hazael took a blanket, soaked it in water, and held it over the king's face until he died. Then Hazael became the next king of Aram.

Jehoram Rules in Judah

[16] Jehoram son of King Jehoshaphat of Judah began to rule over Judah in the fifth year of the reign of Joram son of Ahab, king of Israel. [17] Jehoram was thirty-two years old when he became king, and he reigned in Jerusalem eight years. [18] But Jehoram followed the example of

8:11a Hebrew *He stared at him.* **8:11b** The meaning of the Hebrew is uncertain. **8:13** Hebrew *a dog.*

the kings of Israel and was as wicked as King Ahab, for he had married one of Ahab's daughters. So Jehoram did what was evil in the LORD's sight. [19]But the LORD did not want to destroy Judah, for he had made a covenant with David and promised that his descendants would continue to rule, shining like a lamp forever.

[20]During Jehoram's reign, the Edomites revolted against Judah and crowned their own king. [21]So Jehoram* went with all his chariots to attack the town of Zair.* The Edomites surrounded him and his chariot commanders, but he went out at night and attacked them* under cover of darkness. But Jehoram's army deserted him and fled to their homes. [22]So Edom has been independent from Judah to this day. The town of Libnah also revolted about that same time.

[23]The rest of the events in Jehoram's reign and everything he did are recorded in *The Book of the History of the Kings of Judah.* [24]When Jehoram died, he was buried with his ancestors in the City of David. Then his son Ahaziah became the next king.

Ahaziah Rules in Judah

[25]Ahaziah son of Jehoram began to rule over Judah in the twelfth year of the reign of Joram son of Ahab, king of Israel.

[26]Ahaziah was twenty-two years old when he became king, and he reigned in Jerusalem one year. His mother was Athaliah, a granddaughter of King Omri of Israel. [27]Ahaziah followed the evil example of King Ahab's family. He did what was evil in the LORD's sight, just as Ahab's family had done, for he was related by marriage to the family of Ahab.

[28]Ahaziah joined Joram son of Ahab, the king of Israel, in his war against King Hazael of Aram at Ramoth-gilead. When the Arameans wounded King Joram in the battle, [29]he returned to Jezreel to recover from the wounds he had received at Ramoth.* Because Joram was wounded, King Ahaziah of Judah went to Jezreel to visit him.

CHAPTER 9

Jehu Anointed King of Israel

Meanwhile, Elisha the prophet had summoned a member of the group of prophets. "Get ready to travel,"* he told him, "and take this flask of olive oil with you. Go to Ramoth-gilead, [2]and find Jehu son of Jehoshaphat, son of Nimshi. Call him into a private room away from his friends, [3]and pour the oil over his head. Say to him, 'This is what the LORD says: I anoint you to be the king over Israel.' Then open the door and run for your life!"

[4]So the young prophet did as he was told and went to Ramoth-gilead. [5]When he arrived there, he found Jehu sitting around with the other army officers. "I have a message for you, Commander," he said.

"For which one of us?" Jehu asked.

"For you, Commander," he replied.

[6]So Jehu left the others and went into the house. Then the young prophet poured the oil over Jehu's head and said, "This is what the LORD, the God of Israel, says: I anoint you king over the LORD's people, Israel. [7]You are to destroy the family of Ahab, your master. In this way, I will avenge the murder of my prophets and all the LORD's servants who were killed by Jezebel. [8]The entire family of Ahab must be wiped out. I will destroy every one of his male descendants, slave and free alike, anywhere in Israel. [9]I will destroy the family of Ahab as I destroyed the families of Jeroboam son of Nebat and of Baasha son of Ahijah. [10]Dogs will eat Ahab's wife Jezebel at the plot of land in Jezreel, and no one will bury her." Then the young prophet opened the door and ran.

[11]Jehu went back to his fellow officers, and one of them asked him, "What did that madman want? Is everything all right?"

"You know how a man like that babbles on," Jehu replied.

[12]"You're hiding something," they said. "Tell us."

So Jehu told them, "He said to me, 'This is what the LORD says: I have anointed you to be king over Israel.'"

[13]Then they quickly spread out their cloaks on the bare steps and blew the ram's horn, shouting, "Jehu is king!"

Jehu Kills Joram and Ahaziah

[14]So Jehu son of Jehoshaphat, son of Nimshi, led a conspiracy against King Joram. (Now Joram had been with the army at Ramoth-gilead, defending Israel against the forces of

8:21a Hebrew *Joram*, a variant spelling of Jehoram; also in 8:23, 24. **8:21b** Greek version reads *Seir*. **8:21c** Or *he went out and escaped*. The meaning of the Hebrew is uncertain. **8:29** Hebrew *Ramah*, a variant spelling of Ramoth. **9:1** Hebrew *Bind up your loins*.

King Hazael of Aram. [15]But King Joram* was wounded in the fighting and returned to Jezreel to recover from his wounds.) So Jehu told the men with him, "If you want me to be king, don't let anyone leave town and go to Jezreel to report what we have done."

[16]Then Jehu got into a chariot and rode to Jezreel to find King Joram, who was lying there wounded. King Ahaziah of Judah was there, too, for he had gone to visit him. [17]The watchman on the tower of Jezreel saw Jehu and his company approaching, so he shouted to Joram, "I see a company of troops coming!"

"Send out a rider to ask if they are coming in peace," King Joram ordered.

[18]So a horseman went out to meet Jehu and said, "The king wants to know if you are coming in peace."

Jehu replied, "What do you know about peace? Fall in behind me!"

The watchman called out to the king, "The messenger has met them, but he's not returning."

[19]So the king sent out a second horseman. He rode up to them and said, "The king wants to know if you come in peace."

Again Jehu answered, "What do you know about peace? Fall in behind me!"

[20]The watchman exclaimed, "The messenger has met them, but he isn't returning either! It must be Jehu son of Nimshi, for he's driving like a madman."

[21]"Quick! Get my chariot ready!" King Joram commanded.

Then King Joram of Israel and King Ahaziah of Judah rode out in their chariots to meet Jehu. They met him at the plot of land that had belonged to Naboth of Jezreel. [22]King Joram demanded, "Do you come in peace, Jehu?"

Jehu replied, "How can there be peace as long as the idolatry and witchcraft of your mother, Jezebel, are all around us?"

[23]Then King Joram turned the horses around* and fled, shouting to King Ahaziah, "Treason, Ahaziah!" [24]But Jehu drew his bow and shot Joram between the shoulders. The arrow pierced his heart, and he sank down dead in his chariot.

[25]Jehu said to Bidkar, his officer, "Throw him into the plot of land that belonged to Naboth of Jezreel. Do you remember when you and I were riding along behind his father, Ahab? The LORD pronounced this message against him: [26]'I solemnly swear that I will repay him here on this plot of land, says the LORD, for the murder of Naboth and his sons that I saw yesterday.' So throw him out on Naboth's property, just as the LORD said."

[27]When King Ahaziah of Judah saw what was happening, he fled along the road to Beth-haggan. Jehu rode after him, shouting, "Shoot him, too!" So they shot Ahaziah in his chariot at the Ascent of Gur, near Ibleam. He was able to go on as far as Megiddo, but he died there. [28]His servants took him by chariot to Jerusalem, where they buried him with his ancestors in the City of David. [29]Ahaziah had become king over Judah in the eleventh year of the reign of Joram son of Ahab.

The Death of Jezebel

[30]When Jezebel, the queen mother, heard that Jehu had come to Jezreel, she painted her eyelids and fixed her hair and sat at a window. [31]When Jehu entered the gate of the palace, she shouted at him, "Have you come in peace, you murderer? You're just like Zimri, who murdered his master!"*

[32]Jehu looked up and saw her at the window and shouted, "Who is on my side?" And two or three eunuchs looked out at him. [33]"Throw her down!" Jehu yelled. So they threw her out the window, and her blood spattered against the wall and on the horses. And Jehu trampled her body under his horses' hooves.

[34]Then Jehu went into the palace and ate and drank. Afterward he said, "Someone go and bury this cursed woman, for she is the daughter of a king." [35]But when they went out to bury her, they found only her skull, her feet, and her hands.

[36]When they returned and told Jehu, he stated, "This fulfills the message from the LORD, which he spoke through his servant Elijah from Tishbe: 'At the plot of land in Jezreel, dogs will eat Jezebel's body. [37]Her remains will be scattered like dung on the plot of land in Jezreel, so that no one will be able to recognize her.'"

9:15 Hebrew *Jehoram*, a variant spelling of Joram; also in 9:17, 21, 22, 23, 24. **9:23** Hebrew *turned his hands*. **9:31** See 1 Kgs 16:9-10, where Zimri killed his master, King Elah.

CHAPTER 10

Jehu Kills Ahab's Family

Ahab had seventy sons living in the city of Samaria. So Jehu wrote letters and sent them to Samaria, to the elders and officials of the city,* and to the guardians of King Ahab's sons. He said, [2]"The king's sons are with you, and you have at your disposal chariots, horses, a fortified city, and weapons. As soon as you receive this letter, [3]select the best qualified of your master's sons to be your king, and prepare to fight for Ahab's dynasty."

[4]But they were paralyzed with fear and said, "We've seen that two kings couldn't stand against this man! What can we do?"

[5]So the palace and city administrators, together with the elders and the guardians of the king's sons, sent this message to Jehu: "We are your servants and will do anything you tell us. We will not make anyone king; do whatever you think is best."

[6]Jehu responded with a second letter: "If you are on my side and are going to obey me, bring the heads of your master's sons to me at Jezreel by this time tomorrow." Now the seventy sons of the king were being cared for by the leaders of Samaria, where they had been raised since childhood. [7]When the letter arrived, the leaders killed all seventy of the king's sons. They placed their heads in baskets and presented them to Jehu at Jezreel.

[8]A messenger went to Jehu and said, "They have brought the heads of the king's sons."

So Jehu ordered, "Pile them in two heaps at the entrance of the city gate, and leave them there until morning."

[9]In the morning he went out and spoke to the crowd that had gathered around them. "You are not to blame," he told them. "I am the one who conspired against my master and killed him. But who killed all these? [10]You can be sure that the message of the LORD that was spoken concerning Ahab's family will not fail. The LORD declared through his servant Elijah that this would happen." [11]Then Jehu killed all who were left of Ahab's relatives living in Jezreel and all his important officials, his personal friends, and his priests. So Ahab was left without a single survivor.

[12]Then Jehu set out for Samaria. Along the way, while he was at Beth-eked of the Shepherds, [13]he met some relatives of King Ahaziah of Judah. "Who are you?" he asked them.

And they replied, "We are relatives of King Ahaziah. We are going to visit the sons of King Ahab and the sons of the queen mother."

[14]"Take them alive!" Jehu shouted to his men. And they captured all forty-two of them and killed them at the well of Beth-eked. None of them escaped.

[15]When Jehu left there, he met Jehonadab son of Recab, who was coming to meet him. After they had greeted each other, Jehu said to him, "Are you as loyal to me as I am to you?"

"Yes, I am," Jehonadab replied.

"If you are," Jehu said, "then give me your hand." So Jehonadab put out his hand, and Jehu helped him into the chariot. [16]Then Jehu said, "Now come with me, and see how devoted I am to the LORD." So Jehonadab rode along with him.

[17]When Jehu arrived in Samaria, he killed everyone who was left there from Ahab's family, just as the LORD had promised through Elijah.

Jehu Kills the Priests of Baal

[18]Then Jehu called a meeting of all the people of the city and said to them, "Ahab's worship of Baal was nothing compared to the way I will worship him! [19]Therefore, summon all the prophets and worshipers of Baal, and call together all his priests. See to it that every one of them comes, for I am going to offer a great sacrifice to Baal. Anyone who fails to come will be put to death." But Jehu's cunning plan was to destroy all the worshipers of Baal.

[20]Then Jehu ordered, "Prepare a solemn assembly to worship Baal!" So they did. [21]He sent messengers throughout all Israel summoning those who worshiped Baal. They all came—not a single one remained behind—and they filled the temple of Baal from one end to the other. [22]And Jehu instructed the keeper of the wardrobe, "Be sure that every worshiper of Baal wears one of these robes." So robes were given to them.

[23]Then Jehu went into the temple of Baal with Jehonadab son of Recab. Jehu said to the worshipers of Baal, "Make sure no one who worships the LORD is here—only those who

10:1 As in some Greek manuscripts and Latin Vulgate (see also 10:6); Hebrew reads *of Jezreel.*

worship Baal." [24]So they were all inside the temple to offer sacrifices and burnt offerings. Now Jehu had stationed eighty of his men outside the building and had warned them, "If you let anyone escape, you will pay for it with your own life."

[25]As soon as Jehu had finished sacrificing the burnt offering, he commanded his guards and officers, "Go in and kill all of them. Don't let a single one escape!" So they killed them all with their swords, and the guards and officers dragged their bodies outside.* Then Jehu's men went into the innermost fortress* of the temple of Baal. [26]They dragged out the sacred pillar* used in the worship of Baal and burned it. [27]They smashed the sacred pillar and wrecked the temple of Baal, converting it into a public toilet, as it remains to this day.

[28]In this way, Jehu destroyed every trace of Baal worship from Israel. [29]He did not, however, destroy the gold calves at Bethel and Dan, with which Jeroboam son of Nebat had caused Israel to sin.

[30]Nonetheless the LORD said to Jehu, "You have done well in following my instructions to destroy the family of Ahab. Therefore, your descendants will be kings of Israel down to the fourth generation." [31]But Jehu did not obey the Law of the LORD, the God of Israel, with all his heart. He refused to turn from the sins that Jeroboam had led Israel to commit.

The Death of Jehu

[32]At about that time the LORD began to cut down the size of Israel's territory. King Hazael conquered several sections of the country [33]east of the Jordan River, including all of Gilead, Gad, Reuben, and Manasseh. He conquered the area from the town of Aroer by the Arnon Gorge to as far north as Gilead and Bashan.

[34]The rest of the events in Jehu's reign—everything he did and all his achievements—are recorded in *The Book of the History of the Kings of Israel.*

[35]When Jehu died, he was buried in Samaria. Then his son Jehoahaz became the next king. [36]In all, Jehu reigned over Israel from Samaria for twenty-eight years.

CHAPTER 11

Queen Athaliah Rules in Judah

When Athaliah, the mother of King Ahaziah of Judah, learned that her son was dead, she began to destroy the rest of the royal family.

10:25a Or *they left their bodies lying there;* or *they threw them out into the outermost court.* **10:25b** Hebrew *city.* **10:26** As in Greek and Syriac versions and Latin Vulgate; Hebrew reads *sacred pillars.*

IS IT OK?

IS IT OK TO WISH I HAD A DIFFERENT FAMILY?

If you think you have rough relatives, wait till you hear about Joash's rotten family! His grandmother, Athaliah, wanted to be queen, so she murdered her entire family. Joash's aunt rescued him, and he became king at age seven (see 2 Kings 11:1-3, 21). Don't you think Joash woke up every day wishing he had a "murder-free" family? Most of us dislike certain things about our families. But it's important to appreciate what's good about them. As much as Joash disliked Grandma Athaliah, he probably really appreciated his aunt. Keep your family problems in perspective by remembering Joash's story (your family isn't *that* bad). And as Joash did, you can do what's good, no matter what your family is like.

[2]But Ahaziah's sister Jehosheba, the daughter of King Jehoram,* took Ahaziah's infant son, Joash, and stole him away from among the rest of the king's children, who were about to be killed. She put Joash and his nurse in a bedroom to hide him from Athaliah, so the child was not murdered. [3]Joash remained hidden in the Temple of the LORD for six years while Athaliah ruled over the land.

Revolt against Athaliah

[4]In the seventh year of Athaliah's reign, Jehoiada the priest summoned the commanders, the Carite mercenaries, and the palace guards to come to the Temple of the LORD. He made a solemn pact with them and made them swear an oath of loyalty there in the LORD's Temple; then he showed them the king's son.

[5]Jehoiada told them, "This is what you must do. A third of you who are on duty on the Sabbath are to guard the royal palace itself. [6]Another third of you are to stand guard at the Sur Gate. And the final third must stand guard behind the palace guard. These three groups will all guard the palace. [7]The other two units who are off duty on the Sabbath must stand guard for the king at the LORD's Temple. [8]Form a bodyguard around the king and keep your weapons in hand. Kill anyone who tries to break through. Stay with the king wherever he goes."

[9]So the commanders did everything as Jehoiada the priest ordered. The commanders took charge of the men reporting for duty that Sabbath, as well as those who were going off duty. They brought them all to Jehoiada the priest, [10]and he supplied them with the spears and small shields that had once belonged to King David and were stored in the Temple of the LORD. [11]The palace guards stationed themselves around the king, with their weapons ready. They formed a line from the south side of the Temple around to the north side and all around the altar.

[12]Then Jehoiada brought out Joash, the king's son, placed the crown on his head, and presented him with a copy of God's laws.* They anointed him and proclaimed him king, and everyone clapped their hands and shouted, "Long live the king!"

The Death of Athaliah

[13]When Athaliah heard all the noise made by the palace guards and the people, she hurried to the LORD's Temple to see what was happening. [14]When she arrived, she saw the newly crowned king standing in his place of authority by the pillar, as was the custom at times of coronation. The commanders and trumpeters were surrounding him, and people from all over the land were rejoicing and blowing trumpets. When Athaliah saw all this, she tore her clothes in despair and shouted, "Treason! Treason!"

[15]Then Jehoiada the priest ordered the commanders who were in charge of the troops, "Take her to the soldiers in front of the Temple,* and kill anyone who tries to rescue her." For the priest had said, "She must not be killed in the Temple of the LORD." [16]So they seized her and led her out to the gate where horses enter the palace grounds, and she was killed there.

Jehoiada's Religious Reforms

[17]Then Jehoiada made a covenant between the LORD and the king and the people that they would be the LORD's people. He also made a covenant between the king and the people. [18]And all the people of the land went over to the temple of Baal and tore it down. They demolished the altars and smashed the idols to pieces, and they killed Mattan the priest of Baal in front of the altars.

Jehoiada the priest stationed guards at the Temple of the LORD. [19]Then the commanders, the Carite mercenaries, the palace guards, and all the people of the land escorted the king from the Temple of the LORD. They went through the gate of the guards and into the palace, and the king took his seat on the royal throne. [20]So all the people of the land rejoiced, and the city was peaceful because Athaliah had been killed at the king's palace.

[21]*Joash* was seven years old when he became king.

CHAPTER 12

Joash Repairs the Temple

[1]*Joash* began to rule over Judah in the seventh year of King Jehu's reign in Israel. He

11:2 Hebrew *Joram*, a variant spelling of Jehoram. **11:12** Or *a copy of the covenant*. **11:15** Or *Bring her out from between the ranks;* or *Take her out of the Temple precincts*. The meaning of the Hebrew is uncertain. **11:21a** Verse 11:21 is numbered 12:1 in Hebrew text. **11:21b** Hebrew *Jehoash*, a variant spelling of Joash. **12:1a** Verses 12:1-21 are numbered 12:2-22 in Hebrew text. **12:1b** Hebrew *Jehoash*, a variant spelling of Joash; also in 12:2, 4, 6, 7, 18.

reigned in Jerusalem forty years. His mother was Zibiah from Beersheba. [2]All his life Joash did what was pleasing in the LORD's sight because Jehoiada the priest instructed him. [3]Yet even so, he did not destroy the pagan shrines, and the people still offered sacrifices and burned incense there.

[4]One day King Joash said to the priests, "Collect all the money brought as a sacred offering to the LORD's Temple, whether it is a regular assessment, a payment of vows, or a voluntary gift. [5]Let the priests take some of that money to pay for whatever repairs are needed at the Temple."

[6]But by the twenty-third year of Joash's reign, the priests still had not repaired the Temple. [7]So King Joash called for Jehoiada and the other priests and asked them, "Why haven't you repaired the Temple? Don't use any more money for your own needs. From now on, it must all be spent on Temple repairs." [8]So the priests agreed not to accept any more money from the people, and they also agreed to let others take responsibility for repairing the Temple.

[9]Then Jehoiada the priest bored a hole in the lid of a large chest and set it on the right-hand side of the altar at the entrance of the Temple of the LORD. The priests guarding the entrance put all of the people's contributions into the chest. [10]Whenever the chest became full, the court secretary and the high priest counted the money that had been brought to the LORD's Temple and put it into bags. [11]Then they gave the money to the construction supervisors, who used it to pay the people working on the LORD's Temple—the carpenters, the builders, [12]the masons, and the stonecutters. They also used the money to buy the timber and the finished stone needed for repairing the LORD's Temple, and they paid any other expenses related to the Temple's restoration.

[13]The money brought to the Temple was not used for making silver bowls, lamp snuffers, basins, trumpets, or other articles of gold or silver for the Temple of the LORD. [14]It was paid to the workmen, who used it for the Temple repairs. [15]No accounting of this money was required from the construction supervisors, because they were honest and trustworthy men. [16]However, the money that was contributed for guilt offerings and sin offerings was not brought into the LORD's Temple. It was given to the priests for their own use.

The End of Joash's Reign

[17]About this time King Hazael of Aram went to war against Gath and captured it. Then he turned to attack Jerusalem. [18]King Joash collected all the sacred objects that Jehoshaphat, Jehoram, and Ahaziah, the previous kings of Judah, had dedicated, along with what he himself had dedicated. He sent them all to Hazael, along with all the gold in the treasuries of the LORD's Temple and the royal palace. So Hazael called off his attack on Jerusalem.

[19]The rest of the events in Joash's reign and everything he did are recorded in *The Book of the History of the Kings of Judah.*

[20]Joash's officers plotted against him and assassinated him at Beth-millo on the road to Silla. [21]The assassins were Jozacar* son of Shimeath and Jehozabad son of Shomer—both trusted advisers. Joash was buried with his ancestors in the City of David. Then his son Amaziah became the next king.

CHAPTER 13

Jehoahaz Rules in Israel

Jehoahaz son of Jehu began to rule over Israel in the twenty-third year of King Joash's reign in Judah. He reigned in Samaria seventeen years. [2]But he did what was evil in the LORD's sight. He followed the example of Jeroboam son of Nebat, continuing the sins that Jeroboam had led Israel to commit. [3]So the LORD was very angry with Israel, and he allowed King Hazael of Aram and his son Ben-hadad to defeat them repeatedly.

[4]Then Jehoahaz prayed for the LORD's help, and the LORD heard his prayer, for he could see how severely the king of Aram was oppressing Israel. [5]So the LORD provided someone to rescue the Israelites from the tyranny of the Arameans. Then Israel lived in safety again as they had in former days.

[6]But they continued to sin, following the evil example of Jeroboam. They also allowed the Asherah pole in Samaria to remain standing. [7]Finally, Jehoahaz's army was reduced to 50 charioteers, 10 chariots, and 10,000 foot

12:21 As in Greek and Syriac versions; Hebrew reads *Jozabad.*

soldiers. The king of Aram had killed the others, trampling them like dust under his feet.

[8]The rest of the events in Jehoahaz's reign—everything he did and the extent of his power—are recorded in *The Book of the History of the Kings of Israel.* [9]When Jehoahaz died, he was buried in Samaria. Then his son Jehoash* became the next king.

Jehoash Rules in Israel

[10]Jehoash son of Jehoahaz began to rule over Israel in the thirty-seventh year of King Joash's reign in Judah. He reigned in Samaria sixteen years. [11]But he did what was evil in the LORD's sight. He refused to turn from the sins that Jeroboam son of Nebat had led Israel to commit.

[12]The rest of the events in Jehoash's reign and everything he did, including the extent of his power and his war with King Amaziah of Judah, are recorded in *The Book of the History of the Kings of Israel.* [13]When Jehoash died, he was buried in Samaria with the kings of Israel. Then his son Jeroboam II became the next king.

Elisha's Final Prophecy

[14]When Elisha was in his last illness, King Jehoash of Israel visited him and wept over him. "My father! My father! I see the chariots and charioteers of Israel!" he cried.

[15]Elisha told him, "Get a bow and some arrows." And the king did as he was told. [16]Elisha told him, "Put your hand on the bow," and Elisha laid his own hands on the king's hands.

[17]Then he commanded, "Open that eastern window," and he opened it. Then he said, "Shoot!" So he shot an arrow. Elisha proclaimed, "This is the LORD's arrow, an arrow of victory over Aram, for you will completely conquer the Arameans at Aphek."

[18]Then he said, "Now pick up the other arrows and strike them against the ground." So the king picked them up and struck the ground three times. [19]But the man of God was angry with him. "You should have struck the ground five or six times!" he exclaimed. "Then you would have beaten Aram until it was entirely destroyed. Now you will be victorious only three times."

[20]Then Elisha died and was buried.

Groups of Moabite raiders used to invade the land each spring. [21]Once when some Israelites were burying a man, they spied a band of these raiders. So they hastily threw the corpse into the tomb of Elisha and fled. But as soon as the body touched Elisha's bones, the dead man revived and jumped to his feet!

[22]King Hazael of Aram had oppressed Israel during the entire reign of King Jehoahaz. [23]But the LORD was gracious and merciful to the people of Israel, and they were not totally destroyed. He pitied them because of his covenant with Abraham, Isaac, and Jacob. And to this day he still has not completely destroyed them or banished them from his presence.

[24]King Hazael of Aram died, and his son Ben-hadad became the next king. [25]Then Jehoash son of Jehoahaz recaptured from Ben-hadad son of Hazael the towns that had been

13:9 Hebrew *Joash*, a variant spelling of Jehoash; also in 13:10, 12, 13, 14, 25.

taken from Jehoash's father, Jehoahaz. Jehoash defeated Ben-hadad on three occasions, and he recovered the Israelite towns.

CHAPTER 14

Amaziah Rules in Judah

Amaziah son of Joash began to rule over Judah in the second year of the reign of King Jehoash* of Israel. [2]Amaziah was twenty-five years old when he became king, and he reigned in Jerusalem twenty-nine years. His mother was Jehoaddin from Jerusalem. [3]Amaziah did what was pleasing in the LORD's sight, but not like his ancestor David. Instead, he followed the example of his father, Joash. [4]Amaziah did not destroy the pagan shrines, and the people still offered sacrifices and burned incense there.

[5]When Amaziah was well established as king, he executed the officials who had assassinated his father. [6]However, he did not kill the children of the assassins, for he obeyed the command of the LORD as written by Moses in the Book of the Law: "Parents must not be put to death for the sins of their children, nor children for the sins of their parents. Those deserving to die must be put to death for their own crimes."*

[7]Amaziah also killed 10,000 Edomites in the Valley of Salt. He also conquered Sela and changed its name to Joktheel, as it is called to this day.

[8]One day Amaziah sent messengers with this challenge to Israel's king Jehoash, the son of Jehoahaz and grandson of Jehu: "Come and meet me in battle!"*

[9]But King Jehoash of Israel replied to King Amaziah of Judah with this story: "Out in the Lebanon mountains, a thistle sent a message to a mighty cedar tree: 'Give your daughter in marriage to my son.' But just then a wild animal of Lebanon came by and stepped on the thistle, crushing it!

[10]"You have indeed defeated Edom, and you are very proud of it. But be content with your victory and stay at home! Why stir up trouble that will only bring disaster on you and the people of Judah?"

[11]But Amaziah refused to listen, so King Jehoash of Israel mobilized his army against King Amaziah of Judah. The two armies drew up their battle lines at Beth-shemesh in Judah. [12]Judah was routed by the army of Israel, and its army scattered and fled for home. [13]King Jehoash of Israel captured Judah's king, Amaziah son of Joash and grandson of Ahaziah, at Beth-shemesh. Then he marched to Jerusalem, where he demolished 600 feet* of Jerusalem's wall, from the Ephraim Gate to the Corner Gate. [14]He carried off all the gold and silver and all the articles from the Temple of the LORD. He also seized the treasures from the royal palace, along with hostages, and then returned to Samaria.

[15]The rest of the events in Jehoash's reign and everything he did, including the extent of his power and his war with King Amaziah of Judah, are recorded in *The Book of the History of the Kings of Israel.* [16]When Jehoash died, he was buried in Samaria with the kings of Israel. And his son Jeroboam II became the next king.

[17]King Amaziah of Judah lived for fifteen years after the death of King Jehoash of Israel. [18]The rest of the events in Amaziah's reign are recorded in *The Book of the History of the Kings of Judah.*

[19]There was a conspiracy against Amaziah's life in Jerusalem, and he fled to Lachish. But his enemies sent assassins after him, and they killed him there. [20]They brought his body back to Jerusalem on a horse, and he was buried with his ancestors in the City of David.

[21]All the people of Judah had crowned Amaziah's sixteen-year-old son, Uzziah,* as king in place of his father, Amaziah. [22]After his father's death, Uzziah rebuilt the town of Elath and restored it to Judah.

Jeroboam II Rules in Israel

[23]Jeroboam II, the son of Jehoash, began to rule over Israel in the fifteenth year of King Amaziah's reign in Judah. Jeroboam reigned in Samaria forty-one years. [24]He did what was evil in the LORD's sight. He refused to turn from the sins that Jeroboam son of Nebat had led Israel to commit. [25]Jeroboam II recovered the territories of Israel between Lebo-hamath and the Dead Sea,* just as the LORD, the God of Israel, had promised through

14:1 Hebrew *Joash*, a variant spelling of Jehoash; also in 14:13, 23, 27. **14:6** Deut 24:16. **14:8** Hebrew *Come, let us look one another in the face.* **14:13** Hebrew *400 cubits* (180 meters). **14:21** Hebrew *Azariah*, a variant spelling of Uzziah. **14:25** Hebrew *the sea of the Arabah.*

Jonah son of Amittai, the prophet from Gath-hepher.

[26]For the LORD saw the bitter suffering of everyone in Israel, and that there was no one in Israel, slave or free, to help them. [27]And because the LORD had not said he would blot out the name of Israel completely, he used Jeroboam II, the son of Jehoash, to save them.

[28]The rest of the events in the reign of Jeroboam II and everything he did—including the extent of his power, his wars, and how he recovered for Israel both Damascus and Hamath, which had belonged to Judah*—are recorded in *The Book of the History of the Kings of Israel.* [29]When Jeroboam II died, he was buried in Samaria* with the kings of Israel. Then his son Zechariah became the next king.

CHAPTER 15

Uzziah Rules in Judah

Uzziah* son of Amaziah began to rule over Judah in the twenty-seventh year of the reign of King Jeroboam II of Israel. [2]He was sixteen years old when he became king, and he reigned in Jerusalem fifty-two years. His mother was Jecoliah from Jerusalem.

[3]He did what was pleasing in the LORD's sight, just as his father, Amaziah, had done. [4]But he did not destroy the pagan shrines, and the people still offered sacrifices and burned incense there. [5]The LORD struck the king with leprosy,* which lasted until the day he died. He lived in isolation in a separate house. The king's son Jotham was put in charge of the royal palace, and he governed the people of the land.

[6]The rest of the events in Uzziah's reign and everything he did are recorded in *The Book of the History of the Kings of Judah.* [7]When Uzziah died, he was buried with his ancestors in the City of David. And his son Jotham became the next king.

Zechariah Rules in Israel

[8]Zechariah son of Jeroboam II began to rule over Israel in the thirty-eighth year of King Uzziah's reign in Judah. He reigned in Samaria six months. [9]Zechariah did what was evil in the LORD's sight, as his ancestors had done. He refused to turn from the sins that Jeroboam son of Nebat had led Israel to commit. [10]Then Shallum son of Jabesh conspired against Zechariah, assassinated him in public,* and became the next king.

[11]The rest of the events in Zechariah's reign are recorded in *The Book of the History of the Kings of Israel.* [12]So the LORD's message to Jehu came true: "Your descendants will be kings of Israel down to the fourth generation."

Shallum Rules in Israel

[13]Shallum son of Jabesh began to rule over Israel in the thirty-ninth year of King Uzziah's reign in Judah. Shallum reigned in Samaria only one month. [14]Then Menahem son of Gadi went to Samaria from Tirzah and assassinated him, and he became the next king.

[15]The rest of the events in Shallum's reign, including his conspiracy, are recorded in *The Book of the History of the Kings of Israel.*

Menahem Rules in Israel

[16]At that time Menahem destroyed the town of Tappuah* and all the surrounding countryside as far as Tirzah, because its citizens refused to surrender the town. He killed the entire population and ripped open the pregnant women.

[17]Menahem son of Gadi began to rule over Israel in the thirty-ninth year of King Uzziah's reign in Judah. He reigned in Samaria ten years. [18]But Menahem did what was evil in the LORD's sight. During his entire reign, he refused to turn from the sins that Jeroboam son of Nebat had led Israel to commit.

[19]Then King Tiglath-pileser* of Assyria invaded the land. But Menahem paid him thirty-seven tons* of silver to gain his support in tightening his grip on royal power. [20]Menahem extorted the money from the rich of Israel, demanding that each of them pay fifty pieces* of silver to the king of Assyria. So the king of Assyria turned from attacking Israel and did not stay in the land.

[21]The rest of the events in Menahem's reign and everything he did are recorded in

14:28 Or *to Yaudi.* The meaning of the Hebrew is uncertain. **14:29** As in some Greek manuscripts; Hebrew lacks *he was buried in Samaria.* **15:1** Hebrew *Azariah,* a variant spelling of Uzziah; also in 15:6, 7, 8, 17, 23, 27. **15:5** Or *with a contagious skin disease.* The Hebrew word used here and throughout this passage can describe various skin diseases. **15:10** Or *at Ibleam.* **15:16** As in some Greek manuscripts; other Greek manuscripts read *at Ibleam.* Hebrew reads *Tiphsah.* **15:19a** Hebrew *Pul,* another name for Tiglath-pileser. **15:19b** Hebrew *1,000 talents* [34 metric tons]. **15:20** Hebrew *50 shekels* [20 ounces, or 570 grams].

The Book of the History of the Kings of Israel.
22 When Menahem died, his son Pekahiah became the next king.

Pekahiah Rules in Israel

23 Pekahiah son of Menahem began to rule over Israel in the fiftieth year of King Uzziah's reign in Judah. He reigned in Samaria two years. 24 But Pekahiah did what was evil in the LORD's sight. He refused to turn from the sins that Jeroboam son of Nebat had led Israel to commit.

25 Then Pekah son of Remaliah, the commander of Pekahiah's army, conspired against him. With fifty men from Gilead, Pekah assassinated the king, along with Argob and Arieh, in the citadel of the palace at Samaria. And Pekah reigned in his place.

26 The rest of the events in Pekahiah's reign and everything he did are recorded in *The Book of the History of the Kings of Israel.*

Pekah Rules in Israel

27 Pekah son of Remaliah began to rule over Israel in the fifty-second year of King Uzziah's reign in Judah. He reigned in Samaria twenty years. 28 But Pekah did what was evil in the LORD's sight. He refused to turn from the sins that Jeroboam son of Nebat had led Israel to commit.

29 During Pekah's reign, King Tiglath-pileser of Assyria attacked Israel again, and he captured the towns of Ijon, Abel-beth-maacah, Janoah, Kedesh, and Hazor. He also conquered the regions of Gilead, Galilee, and all of Naphtali, and he took the people to Assyria as captives. 30 Then Hoshea son of Elah conspired against Pekah and assassinated him. He began to rule over Israel in the twentieth year of Jotham son of Uzziah.

31 The rest of the events in Pekah's reign and everything he did are recorded in *The Book of the History of the Kings of Israel.*

Jotham Rules in Judah

32 Jotham son of Uzziah began to rule over Judah in the second year of King Pekah's reign in Israel. 33 He was twenty-five years old when he became king, and he reigned in Jerusalem sixteen years. His mother was Jerusha, the daughter of Zadok.

34 Jotham did what was pleasing in the LORD's sight. He did everything his father, Uzziah, had done. 35 But he did not destroy the pagan shrines, and the people still offered sacrifices and burned incense there. He rebuilt the upper gate of the Temple of the LORD.

36 The rest of the events in Jotham's reign and everything he did are recorded in *The Book of the History of the Kings of Judah.* 37 In those days the LORD began to send King Rezin of Aram and King Pekah of Israel to attack Judah. 38 When Jotham died, he was buried with his ancestors in the City of David. And his son Ahaz became the next king.

CHAPTER 16

Ahaz Rules in Judah

Ahaz son of Jotham began to rule over Judah in the seventeenth year of King Pekah's reign in Israel. 2 Ahaz was twenty years old when he became king, and he reigned in Jerusalem sixteen years. He did not do what was pleasing in the sight of the LORD his God, as his ancestor David had done. 3 Instead, he followed the example of the kings of Israel, even sacrificing his own son in the fire.* In this way, he followed the detestable practices of the pagan nations the LORD had driven from the land ahead of the Israelites. 4 He offered sacrifices and burned incense at the pagan shrines and on the hills and under every green tree.

5 Then King Rezin of Aram and King Pekah of Israel came up to attack Jerusalem. They besieged Ahaz but could not conquer him. 6 At that time the king of Edom* recovered the town of Elath for Edom.* He drove out the people of Judah and sent Edomites* to live there, as they do to this day.

7 King Ahaz sent messengers to King Tiglath-pileser of Assyria with this message: "I am your servant and your vassal.* Come up and rescue me from the attacking armies of Aram and Israel." 8 Then Ahaz took the silver and gold from the Temple of the LORD and the palace treasury and sent it as a payment to the Assyrian king. 9 So the king of Assyria attacked the Aramean capital of Damascus and led its population away as captives, resettling them in Kir. He also killed King Rezin.

16:3 Or *even making his son pass through the fire.* **16:6a** As in Latin Vulgate; Hebrew reads *Rezin king of Aram.* **16:6b** As in Latin Vulgate; Hebrew reads *Aram.* **16:6c** As in Greek version, Latin Vulgate, and an alternate reading of the Masoretic Text; the other alternate reads *Arameans.* **16:7** Hebrew *your son.*

[10]King Ahaz then went to Damascus to meet with King Tiglath-pileser of Assyria. While he was there, he took special note of the altar. Then he sent a model of the altar to Uriah the priest, along with its design in full detail. [11]Uriah followed the king's instructions and built an altar just like it, and it was ready before the king returned from Damascus. [12]When the king returned, he inspected the altar and made offerings on it. [13]He presented a burnt offering and a grain offering, he poured out a liquid offering, and he sprinkled the blood of peace offerings on the altar.

[14]Then King Ahaz removed the old bronze altar from its place in front of the LORD's Temple, between the entrance and the new altar, and placed it on the north side of the new altar. [15]He told Uriah the priest, "Use the new altar* for the morning sacrifices of burnt offering, the evening grain offering, the king's burnt offering and grain offering, and the burnt offerings of all the people, as well as their grain offerings and liquid offerings. Sprinkle the blood from all the burnt offerings and sacrifices on the new altar. The bronze altar will be for my personal use only." [16]Uriah the priest did just as King Ahaz commanded him.

[17]Then the king removed the side panels and basins from the portable water carts. He also removed the great bronze basin called the Sea from the backs of the bronze oxen and placed it on the stone pavement. [18]In deference to the king of Assyria, he also removed the canopy that had been constructed inside the palace for use on the Sabbath day,* as well as the king's outer entrance to the Temple of the LORD.

[19]The rest of the events in Ahaz's reign and everything he did are recorded in *The Book of the History of the Kings of Judah.* [20]When Ahaz died, he was buried with his ancestors in the City of David. Then his son Hezekiah became the next king.

CHAPTER 17

Hoshea Rules in Israel

Hoshea son of Elah began to rule over Israel in the twelfth year of King Ahaz's reign in Judah. He reigned in Samaria nine years. [2]He did what was evil in the LORD's sight, but not to the same extent as the kings of Israel who ruled before him.

[3]King Shalmaneser of Assyria attacked King Hoshea, so Hoshea was forced to pay heavy tribute to Assyria. [4]But Hoshea stopped paying the annual tribute and conspired against the king of Assyria by asking King So of Egypt* to help him shake free of Assyria's power. When the king of Assyria discovered this treachery, he seized Hoshea and put him in prison.

Samaria Falls to Assyria

[5]Then the king of Assyria invaded the entire land, and for three years he besieged the city of Samaria. [6]Finally, in the ninth year of King Hoshea's reign, Samaria fell, and the people of Israel were exiled to Assyria. They were settled in colonies in Halah, along the banks of the Habor River in Gozan, and in the cities of the Medes.

[7]This disaster came upon the people of Israel because they worshiped other gods. They sinned against the LORD their God, who had brought them safely out of Egypt and had rescued them from the power of Pharaoh, the king of Egypt. [8]They had followed the practices of the pagan nations the LORD had driven from the land ahead of them, as well as the practices the kings of Israel had introduced. [9]The people of Israel had also secretly done many things that were not pleasing to the LORD their God. They built pagan shrines for themselves in all their towns, from the smallest outpost to the largest walled city. [10]They set up sacred pillars and Asherah poles at the top of every hill and under every green tree. [11]They offered sacrifices on all the hilltops, just like the nations the LORD had driven from the land ahead of them. So the people of Israel had done many evil things, arousing the LORD's anger. [12]Yes, they worshiped idols,* despite the LORD's specific and repeated warnings.

[13]Again and again the LORD had sent his prophets and seers to warn both Israel and Judah: "Turn from all your evil ways. Obey my commands and decrees—the entire law that I commanded your ancestors to obey, and that I gave you through my servants the prophets."

[14]But the Israelites would not listen. They

16:15 Hebrew *the great altar.* **16:18** The meaning of the Hebrew is uncertain. **17:4** Or *by asking the king of Egypt at Sais.*
17:12 The Hebrew term (literally *round things*) probably alludes to dung.

It wasn't necessarily peer pressure. After all, no one dared me to do it. I came up with the idea on my own: How cool would it be to go inside the boys' locker room? True, it wasn't a totally original thought. Stacy had already gone in moments earlier . . . fearlessly twirling her school uniform skirt as she marched toward the locker room door. And everyone thought she was so cool. So, without hesitating, I went in after her, hoping to win my own share of points with the other girls.

Only things didn't turn out like I planned. After all, this was at a Christian school—on chapel day, no less.

After running around the boys' locker room and being chased out by some embarrassed guys, including my two older brothers, we went on to chapel to await our fate. They called Stacy into the principal's office first. I nervously waited my turn. But no one called my name. I had gotten away with it! However, the story spread quickly around school, so I eventually turned myself in. I knew I was just as guilty as Stacy. But the principal wasn't all that impressed with my honesty. I received in-school suspension, and I know my parents were ashamed.

I learned two lessons that day. One had to do with the importance of taking responsibility for my actions—no matter how painful the punishment. The other lesson was how stupid it is to try outdoing or topping one another's outrageous actions in junior high. I learned that is a good way to get in trouble and a bad way to earn others' approval.

Read about King Ahaz in 2 Kings 16. Rather than doing right and obeying God, King Ahaz chose to follow what the other nations did and seek their approval. Check out these verses on seeking the approval of others: Proverbs 3:1, 4; and John 5:41-42.

were as stubborn as their ancestors who had refused to believe in the LORD their God. [15]They rejected his decrees and the covenant he had made with their ancestors, and they despised all his warnings. They worshiped worthless idols, so they became worthless themselves. They followed the example of the nations around them, disobeying the LORD's command not to imitate them.

[16]They rejected all the commands of the LORD their God and made two calves from metal. They set up an Asherah pole and worshiped Baal and all the forces of heaven. [17]They even sacrificed their own sons and daughters in the fire.* They consulted fortune-tellers and practiced sorcery and sold themselves to evil, arousing the LORD's anger.

[18]Because the LORD was very angry with Israel, he swept them away from his presence. Only the tribe of Judah remained in the land. [19]But even the people of Judah refused to obey the commands of the LORD their God, for they followed the evil practices that Israel had introduced. [20]The LORD rejected all the descendants of Israel. He punished them by handing them over to their attackers until he had banished Israel from his presence.

[21]For when the LORD* tore Israel away from the kingdom of David, they chose Jeroboam son of Nebat as their king. But Jeroboam drew Israel away from following the LORD and made them commit a great sin. [22]And the people of Israel persisted in all the evil ways of Jeroboam. They did not turn from these sins [23]until the LORD finally swept them away from his presence, just as all his prophets had warned. So Israel was exiled from their land to Assyria, where they remain to this day.

Foreigners Settle in Israel

[24]The king of Assyria transported groups of people from Babylon, Cuthah, Avva, Hamath, and Sepharvaim and resettled them in the towns of Samaria, replacing the people of Israel. They took possession of Samaria and lived in its towns. [25]But since these foreign settlers did not worship the LORD when they first arrived, the LORD sent lions among them, which killed some of them.

[26]So a message was sent to the king of Assyria: "The people you have sent to live in the towns of Samaria do not know the religious customs of the God of the land. He has sent lions among them to destroy them because they have not worshiped him correctly."

[27]The king of Assyria then commanded, "Send one of the exiled priests back to Samaria. Let him live there and teach the new residents the religious customs of the God of the land." [28]So one of the priests who had been exiled from Samaria returned to Bethel and taught the new residents how to worship the LORD.

[29]But these various groups of foreigners also continued to worship their own gods. In town after town where they lived, they placed their idols at the pagan shrines that the people of Samaria had built. [30]Those from Babylon worshiped idols of their god Succoth-benoth. Those from Cuthah worshiped their god Nergal. And those from Hamath worshiped Ashima. [31]The Avvites worshiped their gods Nibhaz and Tartak. And the people from Sepharvaim even burned their own children as sacrifices to their gods Adrammelech and Anammelech.

[32]These new residents worshiped the LORD, but they also appointed from among themselves all sorts of people as priests to offer sacrifices at their places of worship. [33]And though they worshiped the LORD, they continued to follow their own gods according to the religious customs of the nations from which they came. [34]And this is still going on today. They continue to follow their former practices instead of truly worshiping the LORD and obeying the decrees, regulations, instructions, and commands he gave the descendants of Jacob, whose name he changed to Israel.

[35]For the LORD had made a covenant with the descendants of Jacob and commanded them: "Do not worship any other gods or bow before them or serve them or offer sacrifices to them. [36]But worship only the LORD, who brought you out of Egypt with great strength and a powerful arm. Bow down to him alone, and offer sacrifices only to him. [37]Be careful at all times to obey the decrees, regulations, instructions, and commands that he wrote for you. You must not worship other gods. [38]Do not forget the covenant I made with you,

17:17 Or *They even made their sons and daughters pass through the fire.* **17:21** Hebrew *he;* compare 1 Kgs 11:31-32.

and do not worship other gods. [39]You must worship only the LORD your God. He is the one who will rescue you from all your enemies."

[40]But the people would not listen and continued to follow their former practices. [41]So while these new residents worshiped the LORD, they also worshiped their idols. And to this day their descendants do the same.

CHAPTER 18

Hezekiah Rules in Judah

Hezekiah son of Ahaz began to rule over Judah in the third year of King Hoshea's reign in Israel. [2]He was twenty-five years old when he became king, and he reigned in Jerusalem twenty-nine years. His mother was Abijah,* the daughter of Zechariah. [3]He did what was pleasing in the LORD's sight, just as his ancestor David had done. [4]He removed the pagan shrines, smashed the sacred pillars, and cut down the Asherah poles. He broke up the bronze serpent that Moses had made, because the people of Israel had been offering sacrifices to it. The bronze serpent was called Nehushtan.*

[5]Hezekiah trusted in the LORD, the God of Israel. There was no one like him among all the kings of Judah, either before or after his time. [6]He remained faithful to the LORD in everything, and he carefully obeyed all the commands the LORD had given Moses. [7]So the LORD was with him, and Hezekiah was successful in everything he did. He revolted against the king of Assyria and refused to pay him tribute. [8]He also conquered the Philistines as far distant as Gaza and its territory, from their smallest outpost to their largest walled city.

[9]During the fourth year of Hezekiah's reign, which was the seventh year of King Hoshea's reign in Israel, King Shalmaneser of Assyria attacked the city of Samaria and began a siege against it. [10]Three years later, during the sixth year of King Hezekiah's reign and the ninth year of King Hoshea's reign in Israel, Samaria fell. [11]At that time the king of Assyria exiled the Israelites to Assyria and placed them in colonies in Halah, along the banks of the Habor River in Gozan, and in the cities of the Medes. [12]For they refused to listen to the LORD their God and obey him. Instead, they violated his covenant—all the laws that Moses the LORD's servant had commanded them to obey.

Assyria Invades Judah

[13]In the fourteenth year of King Hezekiah's reign,* King Sennacherib of Assyria came to attack the fortified towns of Judah and conquered them. [14]King Hezekiah sent this message to the king of Assyria at Lachish: "I have done wrong. I will pay whatever tribute money you demand if you will only withdraw." The king of Assyria then demanded a settlement of more than eleven tons of silver and one ton of gold.* [15]To gather this amount, King Hezekiah used all the silver stored in the Temple of the LORD and in the palace treasury. [16]Hezekiah even stripped the gold from the doors of the LORD's Temple and from the doorposts he had overlaid with gold, and he gave it all to the Assyrian king.

[17]Nevertheless, the king of Assyria sent his commander in chief, his field commander, and his chief of staff* from Lachish with a huge army to confront King Hezekiah in Jerusalem. The Assyrians took up a position beside the aqueduct that feeds water into the upper pool, near the road leading to the field where cloth is washed.* [18]They summoned King Hezekiah, but the king sent these officials to meet with them: Eliakim son of Hilkiah, the palace administrator; Shebna the court secretary; and Joah son of Asaph, the royal historian.

Sennacherib Threatens Jerusalem

[19]Then the Assyrian king's chief of staff told them to give this message to Hezekiah:

> "This is what the great king of Assyria says: What are you trusting in that makes you so confident? [20]Do you think that mere words can substitute for military skill and strength? Who are you counting on, that you have rebelled against me? [21]On Egypt? If you lean on Egypt, it will be like a reed that splinters beneath your weight and pierces your hand. Pharaoh, the king of Egypt, is completely unreliable!

18:2 As in parallel text at 2 Chr 29:1; Hebrew reads *Abi*, a variant spelling of Abijah. **18:4** *Nehushtan* sounds like the Hebrew terms that mean "snake," "bronze," and "unclean thing." **18:13** The fourteenth year of Hezekiah's reign was 701 B.C. **18:14** Hebrew *300 talents* [10 metric tons] *of silver and 30 talents* [1 metric ton] *of gold.* **18:17a** Or *the rabshakeh;* also in 18:19, 26, 27, 28, 37. **18:17b** Or *bleached.*

22"But perhaps you will say to me, 'We
are trusting in the LORD our God!' But
isn't he the one who was insulted by
Hezekiah? Didn't Hezekiah tear down
his shrines and altars and make everyone
in Judah and Jerusalem worship
only at the altar here in Jerusalem?
23"I'll tell you what! Strike a bargain
with my master, the king of Assyria.
I will give you 2,000 horses if you can
find that many men to ride on them!
24With your tiny army, how can you
think of challenging even the weakest
contingent of my master's troops, even
with the help of Egypt's chariots and
charioteers? 25What's more, do you think
we have invaded your land without
the LORD's direction? The LORD
himself told us, 'Attack this land and
destroy it!'"

26Then Eliakim son of Hilkiah, Shebna, and Joah said to the Assyrian chief of staff, "Please speak to us in Aramaic, for we understand it well. Don't speak in Hebrew,* for the people on the wall will hear."

27But Sennacherib's chief of staff replied, "Do you think my master sent this message only to you and your master? He wants all the people to hear it, for when we put this city under siege, they will suffer along with you. They will be so hungry and thirsty that they will eat their own dung and drink their own urine."

28Then the chief of staff stood and shouted in Hebrew to the people on the wall, "Listen to this message from the great king of Assyria! 29This is what the king says: Don't let Hezekiah deceive you. He will never be able to rescue you from my power. 30Don't let him fool you into trusting in the LORD by saying, 'The LORD will surely rescue us. This city will never fall into the hands of the Assyrian king!'

31"Don't listen to Hezekiah! These are the terms the king of Assyria is offering: Make peace with me—open the gates and come out. Then each of you can continue eating from your own grapevine and fig tree and drinking from your own well. 32Then I will arrange to take you to another land like this one—a land of grain and new wine, bread and vineyards, olive groves and honey. Choose life instead of death!

"Don't listen to Hezekiah when he tries to mislead you by saying, 'The LORD will rescue us!' 33Have the gods of any other nations ever saved their people from the king of Assyria? 34What happened to the gods of Hamath and Arpad? And what about the gods of Sepharvaim, Hena, and Ivvah? Did any god rescue Samaria from my power? 35What god of any nation has ever been able to save its people from my power? So what makes you think that the LORD can rescue Jerusalem from me?"

36But the people were silent and did not utter a word because Hezekiah had commanded them, "Do not answer him."

37Then Eliakim son of Hilkiah, the palace administrator; Shebna the court secretary; and Joah son of Asaph, the royal historian, went back to Hezekiah. They tore their clothes in despair, and they went in to see the king and told him what the Assyrian chief of staff had said.

CHAPTER 19

Hezekiah Seeks the LORD's Help

When King Hezekiah heard their report, he tore his clothes and put on burlap and went into the Temple of the LORD. 2And he sent Eliakim the palace administrator, Shebna the court secretary, and the leading priests, all dressed in burlap, to the prophet Isaiah son of Amoz. 3They told him, "This is what King Hezekiah says: Today is a day of trouble, insults, and disgrace. It is like when a child is ready to be born, but the mother has no strength to deliver the baby. 4But perhaps the LORD your God has heard the Assyrian chief of staff,* sent by the king to defy the living God, and will punish him for his words. Oh, pray for those of us who are left!"

5After King Hezekiah's officials delivered the king's message to Isaiah, 6the prophet replied, "Say to your master, 'This is what the LORD says: Do not be disturbed by this blasphemous speech against me from the Assyrian king's messengers. 7Listen! I myself will move against him,* and the king will receive a message that he is needed at home. So he will

18:26 Hebrew *in the dialect of Judah;* also in 18:28. **19:4** Or *the rabshakeh;* also in 19:8. **19:7** Hebrew *I will put a spirit in him.*

return to his land, where I will have him killed with a sword.'"

8 Meanwhile, the Assyrian chief of staff left Jerusalem and went to consult the king of Assyria, who had left Lachish and was attacking Libnah.

9 Soon afterward King Sennacherib received word that King Tirhakah of Ethiopia* was leading an army to fight against him. Before leaving to meet the attack, he sent messengers back to Hezekiah in Jerusalem with this message:

10 "This message is for King Hezekiah of Judah. Don't let your God, in whom you trust, deceive you with promises that Jerusalem will not be captured by the king of Assyria. 11 You know perfectly well what the kings of Assyria have done wherever they have gone. They have completely destroyed everyone who stood in their way! Why should you be any different? 12 Have the gods of other nations rescued them—such nations as Gozan, Haran, Rezeph, and the people of Eden who were in Tel-assar? My predecessors destroyed them all! 13 What happened to the king of Hamath and the king of Arpad? What happened to the kings of Sepharvaim, Hena, and Ivvah?"

14 After Hezekiah received the letter from the messengers and read it, he went up to the LORD's Temple and spread it out before the LORD. 15 And Hezekiah prayed this prayer before the LORD: "O LORD, God of Israel, you are enthroned between the mighty cherubim! You alone are God of all the kingdoms of the earth. You alone created the heavens and the earth. 16 Bend down, O LORD, and listen! Open your eyes, O LORD, and see! Listen to Sennacherib's words of defiance against the living God.

17 "It is true, LORD, that the kings of Assyria have destroyed all these nations. 18 And they have thrown the gods of these nations into the fire and burned them. But of course the Assyrians could destroy them! They were not gods at all—only idols of wood and stone shaped by human hands. 19 Now, O LORD our God, rescue us from his power; then all the kingdoms of the earth will know that you alone, O LORD, are God."

19:9 Hebrew *of Cush.*

Isaiah Predicts Judah's Deliverance

20 Then Isaiah son of Amoz sent this message to Hezekiah: "This is what the LORD, the God of Israel, says: I have heard your prayer about King Sennacherib of Assyria. 21 And the LORD has spoken this word against him:

"The virgin daughter of Zion
despises you and laughs at you.
The daughter of Jerusalem
shakes her head in derision as you flee.

22 "Whom have you been defying and ridiculing?
Against whom did you raise your voice?
At whom did you look with such haughty eyes?
It was the Holy One of Israel!
23 By your messengers you have defied the Lord.
You have said, 'With my many chariots
I have conquered the highest mountains—
yes, the remotest peaks of Lebanon.
I have cut down its tallest cedars
and its finest cypress trees.
I have reached its farthest corners
and explored its deepest forests.
24 I have dug wells in many foreign lands
and refreshed myself with their water.
With the sole of my foot
I stopped up all the rivers of Egypt!'

25 "But have you not heard?
I decided this long ago.
Long ago I planned it,
and now I am making it happen.
I planned for you to crush fortified cities
into heaps of rubble.
26 That is why their people have so little power
and are so frightened and confused.
They are as weak as grass,
as easily trampled as tender green shoots.
They are like grass sprouting on a housetop,
scorched before it can grow lush and tall.

27 "But I know you well—
where you stay
and when you come and go.
I know the way you have raged against me.

28 And because of your raging against me
and your arrogance, which I have heard
for myself,
I will put my hook in your nose
and my bit in your mouth.
I will make you return
by the same road on which you came."

Does God mind if I brag about myself?

Because of your raging against me and your arrogance . . . I will put my hook in your nose and my bit in your mouth. 2 KINGS 19:28

29 Then Isaiah said to Hezekiah, "Here is the proof that what I say is true:

"This year you will eat only what grows up
by itself,
and next year you will eat what springs
up from that.
But in the third year you will plant crops
and harvest them;
you will tend vineyards and eat their
fruit.
30 And you who are left in Judah,
who have escaped the ravages of the
siege,
will put roots down in your own soil
and will grow up and flourish.
31 For a remnant of my people will spread
out from Jerusalem,
a group of survivors from Mount Zion.
The passionate commitment of the LORD
of Heaven's Armies*
will make this happen!

32 "And this is what the LORD says about the king of Assyria:

"His armies will not enter Jerusalem.
They will not even shoot an arrow
at it.
They will not march outside its gates with
their shields
nor build banks of earth against its
walls.
33 The king will return to his own country
by the same road on which he came.
He will not enter this city,
says the LORD.
34 For my own honor and for the sake of my
servant David,
I will defend this city and protect it."

35 That night the angel of the LORD went out to the Assyrian camp and killed 185,000 Assyrian soldiers. When the surviving Assyrians* woke up the next morning, they found corpses everywhere. 36 Then King Sennacherib of Assyria broke camp and returned to his own land. He went home to his capital of Nineveh and stayed there.

37 One day while he was worshiping in the temple of his god Nisroch, his sons* Adrammelech and Sharezer killed him with their swords. They then escaped to the land of Ararat, and another son, Esarhaddon, became the next king of Assyria.

CHAPTER 20

Hezekiah's Sickness and Recovery

About that time Hezekiah became deathly ill, and the prophet Isaiah son of Amoz went to visit him. He gave the king this message: "This is what the LORD says: Set your affairs in order, for you are going to die. You will not recover from this illness."

2 When Hezekiah heard this, he turned his face to the wall and prayed to the LORD, 3 "Remember, O LORD, how I have always been faithful to you and have served you single-mindedly, always doing what pleases you." Then he broke down and wept bitterly.

4 But before Isaiah had left the middle courtyard,* this message came to him from the LORD: 5 "Go back to Hezekiah, the leader of my people. Tell him, 'This is what the LORD, the God of your ancestor David, says: I have heard your prayer and seen your tears. I will heal you, and three days from now you will get out of bed and go to the Temple of the LORD. 6 I will add fifteen years to your life, and I will rescue you and this city from the king of Assyria. I will

19:31 As in Greek and Syriac versions, Latin Vulgate, and an alternate reading of the Masoretic Text (see also Isa 37:32); the other alternate reads *the LORD*. **19:35** Hebrew *When they*. **19:37** As in Greek version and an alternate reading of the Masoretic Text (see also Isa 37:38); the other alternate reading lacks *his sons*. **20:4** As in Greek version and an alternate reading in the Masoretic Text; the other alternate reads *the middle of the city*.

defend this city for my own honor and for the sake of my servant David.'"

7 Then Isaiah said, "Make an ointment from figs." So Hezekiah's servants spread the ointment over the boil, and Hezekiah recovered!

8 Meanwhile, Hezekiah had said to Isaiah, "What sign will the LORD give to prove that he will heal me and that I will go to the Temple of the LORD three days from now?"

9 Isaiah replied, "This is the sign from the LORD to prove that he will do as he promised. Would you like the shadow on the sundial to go forward ten steps or backward ten steps?*"

10 "The shadow always moves forward," Hezekiah replied, "so that would be easy. Make it go ten steps backward instead." 11 So Isaiah the prophet asked the LORD to do this, and he caused the shadow to move ten steps backward on the sundial* of Ahaz!

Envoys from Babylon

12 Soon after this, Merodach-baladan son of Baladan, king of Babylon, sent Hezekiah his best wishes and a gift, for he had heard that Hezekiah had been very sick. 13 Hezekiah received the Babylonian envoys and showed them everything in his treasure-houses—the silver, the gold, the spices, and the aromatic oils. He also took them to see his armory and showed them everything in his royal treasuries! There was nothing in his palace or kingdom that Hezekiah did not show them.

14 Then Isaiah the prophet went to King Hezekiah and asked him, "What did those men want? Where were they from?"

Hezekiah replied, "They came from the distant land of Babylon."

15 "What did they see in your palace?" Isaiah asked.

"They saw everything," Hezekiah replied. "I showed them everything I own—all my royal treasuries."

16 Then Isaiah said to Hezekiah, "Listen to this message from the LORD: 17 The time is coming when everything in your palace—all the treasures stored up by your ancestors until now—will be carried off to Babylon. Nothing will be left, says the LORD. 18 Some of your very own sons will be taken away into exile. They will become eunuchs who will serve in the palace of Babylon's king."

19 Then Hezekiah said to Isaiah, "This message you have given me from the LORD is good." For the king was thinking, "At least there will be peace and security during my lifetime."

20 The rest of the events in Hezekiah's reign, including the extent of his power and how he

WHO HEARS? WHO CARES?

Mario always prayed—at bedtime, before meals, in church, on trips, and at special times. He never thought too much about it, he just prayed because he liked to talk to God and believed he was happy to hear and answer him. But Dean, a friend at church, said he didn't think prayer was very important. "After all," he said, "God knows what we're going to say and what he is going to do, so why should we pray?" What do you think? Does prayer make a difference? Should you bother praying every day? Read 2 Kings 20:1-6 for a great example.

20:9 Or *The shadow on the sundial has gone forward ten steps; do you want it to go backward ten steps?* **20:11** Hebrew *the steps.*

built a pool and dug a tunnel* to bring water into the city, are recorded in *The Book of the History of the Kings of Judah.* [21]Hezekiah died, and his son Manasseh became the next king.

CHAPTER 21

Manasseh Rules in Judah

Manasseh was twelve years old when he became king, and he reigned in Jerusalem fifty-five years. His mother was Hephzibah. [2]He did what was evil in the LORD's sight, following the detestable practices of the pagan nations that the LORD had driven from the land ahead of the Israelites. [3]He rebuilt the pagan shrines his father, Hezekiah, had destroyed. He constructed altars for Baal and set up an Asherah pole, just as King Ahab of Israel had done. He also bowed before all the powers of the heavens and worshiped them.

AMAZING FACTS

For many years, God's people no longer worshiped him at the Temple. And God's Word—written on a scroll—actually got lost in there!

2 KINGS 22:8-13

[4]He built pagan altars in the Temple of the LORD, the place where the LORD had said, "My name will remain in Jerusalem forever." [5]He built these altars for all the powers of the heavens in both courtyards of the LORD's Temple. [6]Manasseh also sacrificed his own son in the fire.* He practiced sorcery and divination, and he consulted with mediums and psychics. He did much that was evil in the LORD's sight, arousing his anger.

[7]Manasseh even made a carved image of Asherah and set it up in the Temple, the very place where the LORD had told David and his son Solomon: "My name will be honored forever in this Temple and in Jerusalem—the city I have chosen from among all the tribes of Israel. [8]If the Israelites will be careful to obey my commands—all the laws my servant Moses gave them—I will not send them into exile from this land that I gave their ancestors." [9]But the people refused to listen, and Manasseh led them to do even more evil than the pagan nations that the LORD had destroyed when the people of Israel entered the land.

[10]Then the LORD said through his servants the prophets: [11]"King Manasseh of Judah has done many detestable things. He is even more wicked than the Amorites, who lived in this land before Israel. He has caused the people of Judah to sin with his idols.* [12]So this is what the LORD, the God of Israel, says: I will bring such disaster on Jerusalem and Judah that the ears of those who hear about it will tingle with horror. [13]I will judge Jerusalem by the same standard I used for Samaria and the same measure* I used for the family of Ahab. I will wipe away the people of Jerusalem as one wipes a dish and turns it upside down. [14]Then I will reject even the remnant of my own people who are left, and I will hand them over as plunder for their enemies. [15]For they have done great evil in my sight and have angered me ever since their ancestors came out of Egypt."

[16]Manasseh also murdered many innocent people until Jerusalem was filled from one end to the other with innocent blood. This was in addition to the sin that he caused the people of Judah to commit, leading them to do evil in the LORD's sight.

[17]The rest of the events in Manasseh's reign and everything he did, including the sins he committed, are recorded in *The Book of the History of the Kings of Judah.* [18]When Manasseh died, he was buried in the palace garden, the garden of Uzza. Then his son Amon became the next king.

Amon Rules in Judah

[19]Amon was twenty-two years old when he became king, and he reigned in Jerusalem two years. His mother was Meshullemeth, the

20:20 Hebrew *watercourse.* **21:6** Or *also made his son pass through the fire.* **21:11** The Hebrew term (literally *round things*) probably alludes to dung; also in 21:21. **21:13** Hebrew *the same plumb line I used for Samaria and the same plumb bob.*

daughter of Haruz from Jotbah. [20]He did what
was evil in the LORD's sight, just as his father,
Manasseh, had done. [21]He followed the ex-
ample of his father, worshiping the same
idols his father had worshiped. [22]He aban-
doned the LORD, the God of his ancestors, and
he refused to follow the LORD's ways.

[23]Then Amon's own officials conspired
against him and assassinated him in his pal-
ace. [24]But the people of the land killed all
those who had conspired against King Amon,
and they made his son Josiah the next king.

[25]The rest of the events in Amon's reign
and what he did are recorded in *The Book of
the History of the Kings of Judah.* [26]He was
buried in his tomb in the garden of Uzza.
Then his son Josiah became the next king.

CHAPTER 22

Josiah Rules in Judah

Josiah was eight years old when he became
king, and he reigned in Jerusalem thirty-one
years. His mother was Jedidah, the daughter
of Adaiah from Bozkath. [2]He did what was
pleasing in the LORD's sight and followed the
example of his ancestor David. He did not
turn away from doing what was right.

[3]In the eighteenth year of his reign, King
Josiah sent Shaphan son of Azaliah and
grandson of Meshullam, the court secretary,
to the Temple of the LORD. He told him, [4]"Go
to Hilkiah the high priest and have him count
the money the gatekeepers have collected
from the people at the LORD's Temple.
[5]Entrust this money to the men assigned to
supervise the Temple's restoration. Then
they can use it to pay workers to repair the
Temple of the LORD. [6]They will need to hire
carpenters, builders, and masons. Also have
them buy the timber and the finished stone
needed to repair the Temple. [7]But don't re-
quire the construction supervisors to keep
account of the money they receive, for they
are honest and trustworthy men."

Hilkiah Discovers God's Law

[8]Hilkiah the high priest said to Shaphan the
court secretary, "I have found the Book of the
Law in the LORD's Temple!" Then Hilkiah gave
the scroll to Shaphan, and he read it.

[9]Shaphan went to the king and reported,
"Your officials have turned over the money
collected at the Temple of the LORD to the
workers and supervisors at the Temple."
[10]Shaphan also told the king, "Hilkiah the
priest has given me a scroll." So Shaphan read
it to the king.

[11]When the king heard what was written in
the Book of the Law, he tore his clothes in de-
spair. [12]Then he gave these orders to Hilkiah
the priest, Ahikam son of Shaphan, Acbor son
of Micaiah, Shaphan the court secretary, and
Asaiah the king's personal adviser: [13]"Go to
the Temple and speak to the LORD for me and
for the people and for all Judah. Inquire about
the words written in this scroll that has been
found. For the LORD's great anger is burning
against us because our ancestors have not
obeyed the words in this scroll. We have not
been doing everything it says we must do."

[14]So Hilkiah the priest, Ahikam, Acbor,
Shaphan, and Asaiah went to the New Quar-
ter* of Jerusalem to consult with the prophet
Huldah. She was the wife of Shallum son of
Tikvah, son of Harhas, the keeper of the Tem-
ple wardrobe.

[15]She said to them, "The LORD, the God of
Israel, has spoken! Go back and tell the man
who sent you, [16]'This is what the LORD says: I
am going to bring disaster on this city* and its
people. All the words written in the scroll that
the king of Judah has read will come true.
[17]For my people have abandoned me and
offered sacrifices to pagan gods, and I am
very angry with them for everything they have
done. My anger will burn against this place,
and it will not be quenched.'

[18]"But go to the king of Judah who sent you
to seek the LORD and tell him: 'This is what
the LORD, the God of Israel, says concerning
the message you have just heard: [19]You were
sorry and humbled yourself before the LORD
when you heard what I said against this city
and its people—that this land would be
cursed and become desolate. You tore your
clothing in despair and wept before me in re-
pentance. And I have indeed heard you, says
the LORD. [20]So I will not send the promised di-
saster until after you have died and been bur-
ied in peace. You will not see the disaster I am
going to bring on this city.'"

So they took her message back to the king.

22:14 Or *the Second Quarter*, a newer section of Jerusalem. Hebrew reads *the Mishneh.* **22:16** Hebrew *this place;* also in 22:19, 20.

CHAPTER 23

Josiah's Religious Reforms

Then the king summoned all the elders of Judah and Jerusalem. [2]And the king went up to the Temple of the LORD with all the people of Judah and Jerusalem, along with the priests and the prophets—all the people from the least to the greatest. There the king read to them the entire Book of the Covenant that had been found in the LORD's Temple. [3]The king took his place of authority beside the pillar and renewed the covenant in the LORD's presence. He pledged to obey the LORD by keeping all his commands, laws, and decrees with all his heart and soul. In this way, he confirmed all the terms of the covenant that were written in the scroll, and all the people pledged themselves to the covenant.

What makes a really good leader?

The king . . . pledged to obey the LORD by keeping all his commands, laws, and decrees with all his heart and soul.

2 KINGS 23:3

[4]Then the king instructed Hilkiah the high priest and the priests of the second rank and the Temple gatekeepers to remove from the LORD's Temple all the articles that were used to worship Baal, Asherah, and all the powers of the heavens. The king had all these things burned outside Jerusalem on the terraces of the Kidron Valley, and he carried the ashes away to Bethel. [5]He did away with the idolatrous priests, who had been appointed by the previous kings of Judah, for they had offered sacrifices at the pagan shrines throughout Judah and even in the vicinity of Jerusalem. They had also offered sacrifices to Baal, and to the sun, the moon, the constellations, and to all the powers of the heavens. [6]The king removed the Asherah pole from the LORD's Temple and took it outside Jerusalem to the Kidron Valley, where he burned it. Then he ground the ashes of the pole to dust and threw the dust over the graves of the people. [7]He also tore down the living quarters of the male and female shrine prostitutes that were inside the Temple of the LORD, where the women wove coverings for the Asherah pole.

[8]Josiah brought to Jerusalem all the priests who were living in other towns of Judah. He also defiled the pagan shrines, where they had offered sacrifices—all the way from Geba to Beersheba. He destroyed the shrines at the entrance to the gate of Joshua, the governor of Jerusalem. This gate was located to the left of the city gate as one enters the city. [9]The priests who had served at the pagan shrines were not allowed* to serve at the LORD's altar in Jerusalem, but they were allowed to eat unleavened bread with the other priests.

[10]Then the king defiled the altar of Topheth in the valley of Ben-Hinnom, so no one could ever again use it to sacrifice a son or daughter in the fire* as an offering to Molech. [11]He removed from the entrance of the LORD's Temple the horse statues that the former kings of Judah had dedicated to the sun. They were near the quarters of Nathan-melech the eunuch, an officer of the court.* The king also burned the chariots dedicated to the sun.

[12]Josiah tore down the altars that the kings of Judah had built on the palace roof above the upper room of Ahaz. The king destroyed the altars that Manasseh had built in the two courtyards of the LORD's Temple. He smashed them to bits* and scattered the pieces in the Kidron Valley. [13]The king also desecrated the pagan shrines east of Jerusalem, to the south of the Mount of Corruption, where King Solomon of Israel had built shrines for Ashtoreth, the detestable goddess of the Sidonians; and for Chemosh, the detestable god of the Moabites; and for Molech,* the vile god of the Ammonites. [14]He smashed the sacred pillars and cut down the Asherah poles. Then he desecrated these places by scattering human bones over them.

23:9 Hebrew *did not come up.* **23:10** Or *to make a son or daughter pass through the fire.* **23:11** The meaning of the Hebrew is uncertain. **23:12** Or *He quickly removed them.* **23:13** Hebrew *Milcom,* a variant spelling of Molech.

15 The king also tore down the altar at Bethel—the pagan shrine that Jeroboam son of
Nebat had made when he caused Israel to sin.
He burned down the shrine and ground it to
dust, and he burned the Asherah pole. 16 Then
Josiah turned around and noticed several
tombs in the side of the hill. He ordered that
the bones be brought out, and he burned
them on the altar at Bethel to desecrate it.
(This happened just as the LORD had promised through the man of God when Jeroboam
stood beside the altar at the festival.)

Then Josiah turned and looked up at the
tomb of the man of God* who had predicted
these things. 17 "What is that monument over
there?" Josiah asked.

And the people of the town told him, "It is
the tomb of the man of God who came from
Judah and predicted the very things that you
have just done to the altar at Bethel!"

18 Josiah replied, "Leave it alone. Don't disturb his bones." So they did not burn his
bones or those of the old prophet from Samaria.

19 Then Josiah demolished all the buildings
at the pagan shrines in the towns of Samaria,
just as he had done at Bethel. They had been
built by the various kings of Israel and had
made the LORD* very angry. 20 He executed
the priests of the pagan shrines on their own
altars, and he burned human bones on the altars to desecrate them. Finally, he returned to
Jerusalem.

Josiah Celebrates Passover

21 King Josiah then issued this order to all the
people: "You must celebrate the Passover to
the LORD your God, as required in this Book of
the Covenant." 22 There had not been a Passover celebration like that since the time when
the judges ruled in Israel, nor throughout all
the years of the kings of Israel and Judah.
23 This Passover was celebrated to the LORD in
Jerusalem in the eighteenth year of King Josiah's reign.

24 Josiah also got rid of the mediums and
psychics, the household gods, the idols,* and
every other kind of detestable practice, both
in Jerusalem and throughout the land of Judah. He did this in obedience to the laws written in the scroll that Hilkiah the priest had
found in the LORD's Temple. 25 Never before
had there been a king like Josiah, who turned
to the LORD with all his heart and soul and
strength, obeying all the laws of Moses. And
there has never been a king like him since.

26 Even so, the LORD was very angry with Judah because of all the wicked things Manasseh had done to provoke him. 27 For the LORD
said, "I will also banish Judah from my presence just as I have banished Israel. And I will
reject my chosen city of Jerusalem and the
Temple where my name was to be honored."

28 The rest of the events in Josiah's reign
and all his deeds are recorded in *The Book of the History of the Kings of Judah*.

29 While Josiah was king, Pharaoh Neco,
king of Egypt, went to the Euphrates River to
help the king of Assyria. King Josiah and his
army marched out to fight him,* but King
Neco* killed him when they met at Megiddo.
30 Josiah's officers took his body back in a
chariot from Megiddo to Jerusalem and buried him in his own tomb. Then the people of
the land anointed Josiah's son Jehoahaz and
made him the next king.

Jehoahaz Rules in Judah

31 Jehoahaz was twenty-three years old when
he became king, and he reigned in Jerusalem
three months. His mother was Hamutal, the
daughter of Jeremiah from Libnah. 32 He did
what was evil in the LORD's sight, just as his
ancestors had done.

33 Pharaoh Neco put Jehoahaz in prison at
Riblah in the land of Hamath to prevent him
from ruling* in Jerusalem. He also demanded
that Judah pay 7,500 pounds of silver and
75 pounds of gold* as tribute.

Jehoiakim Rules in Judah

34 Pharaoh Neco then installed Eliakim, another of Josiah's sons, to reign in place of his
father, and he changed Eliakim's name to Jehoiakim. Jehoahaz was taken to Egypt as a
prisoner, where he died.

35 In order to get the silver and gold demanded as tribute by Pharaoh Neco, Jehoiakim collected a tax from the people of Judah,

23:16 As in Greek version; Hebrew lacks *when Jeroboam stood beside the altar at the festival. Then Josiah turned and looked up at the tomb of the man of God.* **23:19** As in Greek and Syriac versions and Latin Vulgate; Hebrew lacks *the LORD*. **23:24** The Hebrew term (literally *round things*) probably alludes to dung. **23:29a** Or *Josiah went out to meet him.* **23:29b** Hebrew *he*. **23:33a** The meaning of the Hebrew is uncertain. **23:33b** Hebrew *100 talents* [3,400 kilograms] *of silver and 1 talent* [34 kilograms] *of gold*.

requiring them to pay in proportion to their wealth.

[36]Jehoiakim was twenty-five years old when he became king, and he reigned in Jerusalem eleven years. His mother was Zebidah, the daughter of Pedaiah from Rumah. [37]He did what was evil in the LORD's sight, just as his ancestors had done.

CHAPTER 24

During Jehoiakim's reign, King Nebuchadnezzar of Babylon invaded the land of Judah. Jehoiakim surrendered and paid him tribute for three years but then rebelled. [2]Then the LORD sent bands of Babylonian,* Aramean, Moabite, and Ammonite raiders against Judah to destroy it, just as the LORD had promised through his prophets. [3]These disasters happened to Judah because of the LORD's command. He had decided to banish Judah from his presence because of the many sins of Manasseh, [4]who had filled Jerusalem with innocent blood. The LORD would not forgive this.

[5]The rest of the events in Jehoiakim's reign and all his deeds are recorded in *The Book of the History of the Kings of Judah*. [6]When Jehoiakim died, his son Jehoiachin became the next king.

[7]The king of Egypt did not venture out of his country after that, for the king of Babylon captured the entire area formerly claimed by Egypt—from the Brook of Egypt to the Euphrates River.

Jehoiachin Rules in Judah

[8]Jehoiachin was eighteen years old when he became king, and he reigned in Jerusalem three months. His mother was Nehushta, the daughter of Elnathan from Jerusalem. [9]Jehoiachin did what was evil in the LORD's sight, just as his father had done.

[10]During Jehoiachin's reign, the officers of King Nebuchadnezzar of Babylon came up against Jerusalem and besieged it. [11]Nebuchadnezzar himself arrived at the city during the siege. [12]Then King Jehoiachin, along with the queen mother, his advisers, his commanders, and his officials, surrendered to the Babylonians.

In the eighth year of Nebuchadnezzar's reign, he took Jehoiachin prisoner. [13]As the LORD had said beforehand, Nebuchadnezzar carried away all the treasures from the LORD's Temple and the royal palace. He stripped away* all the gold objects that King Solomon of Israel had placed in the Temple. [14]King Nebuchadnezzar took all of Jerusalem captive, including all the commanders and the best of the soldiers, craftsmen, and artisans—10,000 in all. Only the poorest people were left in the land.

[15]Nebuchadnezzar led King Jehoiachin away as a captive to Babylon, along with the queen mother, his wives and officials, and all Jerusalem's elite. [16]He also exiled 7,000 of the best troops and 1,000 craftsmen and artisans, all of whom were strong and fit for war. [17]Then the king of Babylon installed Mattaniah, Jehoiachin's* uncle, as the next king, and he changed Mattaniah's name to Zedekiah.

Zedekiah Rules in Judah

[18]Zedekiah was twenty-one years old when he became king, and he reigned in Jerusalem eleven years. His mother was Hamutal, the daughter of Jeremiah from Libnah. [19]But Zedekiah did what was evil in the LORD's sight, just as Jehoiakim had done. [20]These things happened because of the LORD's anger against the people of Jerusalem and Judah, until he finally banished them from his presence and sent them into exile.

The Fall of Jerusalem

Zedekiah rebelled against the king of Babylon.

CHAPTER 25

So on January 15,* during the ninth year of Zedekiah's reign, King Nebuchadnezzar of Babylon led his entire army against Jerusalem. They surrounded the city and built siege ramps against its walls. [2]Jerusalem was kept under siege until the eleventh year of King Zedekiah's reign.

[3]By July 18 in the eleventh year of Zedekiah's reign,* the famine in the city had become very severe, and the last of the food was en-

24:2 Or *Chaldean*. **24:13** Or *He cut apart*. **24:17** Hebrew *his*. **25:1** Hebrew *on the tenth day of the tenth month*, of the ancient Hebrew lunar calendar. A number of events in 2 Kings can be cross-checked with dates in surviving Babylonian records and related accurately to our modern calendar. This day was January 15, 588 B.C. **25:3** Hebrew *By the ninth day of the [fourth] month* [in the eleventh year of Zedekiah's reign] (compare Jer 52:6 and the note there). This day was July 18, 586 B.C.; also see note on 25:1.

tirely gone. [4]Then a section of the city wall was broken down, and all the soldiers fled. Since the city was surrounded by the Babylonians,* they waited for nightfall. Then they slipped through the gate between the two walls behind the king's garden and headed toward the Jordan Valley.*

[5]But the Babylonian* troops chased the king and caught him on the plains of Jericho, for his men had all deserted him and scattered. [6]They took him to the king of Babylon at Riblah, where they pronounced judgment upon Zedekiah. [7]They made Zedekiah watch as they slaughtered his sons. Then they gouged out Zedekiah's eyes, bound him in bronze chains, and led him away to Babylon.

The Temple Destroyed

[8]On August 14 of that year,* which was the nineteenth year of King Nebuchadnezzar's reign, Nebuzaradan, the captain of the guard and an official of the Babylonian king, arrived in Jerusalem. [9]He burned down the Temple of the LORD, the royal palace, and all the houses of Jerusalem. He destroyed all the important buildings* in the city. [10]Then he supervised the entire Babylonian army as they tore down the walls of Jerusalem on every side. [11]Nebuzaradan, the captain of the guard, then took as exiles the rest of the people who remained in the city, the defectors who had declared their allegiance to the king of Babylon, and the rest of the population. [12]But the captain of the guard allowed some of the poorest people to stay behind in Judah to care for the vineyards and fields.

[13]The Babylonians broke up the bronze pillars in front of the LORD's Temple, the bronze water carts, and the great bronze basin called the Sea, and they carried all the bronze away to Babylon. [14]They also took all the ash buckets, shovels, lamp snuffers, dishes, and all the other bronze articles used for making sacrifices at the Temple. [15]Nebuzaradan, the captain of the guard, also took the incense burners and basins, and all the other articles made of pure gold or silver.

[16]The weight of the bronze from the two pillars, the Sea, and the water carts was too great to be measured. These things had been made for the LORD's Temple in the days of King Solomon. [17]Each of the pillars was 27 feet* tall. The bronze capital on top of each pillar was 7½ feet* high and was decorated with a network of bronze pomegranates all the way around.

[18]Nebuzaradan, the captain of the guard, took with him as prisoners Seraiah the high priest, Zephaniah the priest of the second rank, and the three chief gatekeepers. [19]And from among the people still hiding in the city, he took an officer who had been in charge of the Judean army; five of the king's personal advisers; the army commander's chief secretary, who was in charge of recruitment; and sixty other citizens. [20]Nebuzaradan, the captain of the guard, took them all to the king of Babylon at Riblah. [21]And there at Riblah, in the land of Hamath, the king of Babylon had them all put to death. So the people of Judah were sent into exile from their land.

Gedaliah Governs in Judah

[22]Then King Nebuchadnezzar appointed Gedaliah son of Ahikam and grandson of Shaphan as governor over the people he had left in Judah. [23]When all the army commanders and their men learned that the king of Babylon had appointed Gedaliah as governor, they went to see him at Mizpah. These included Ishmael son of Nethaniah, Johanan son of Kareah, Seraiah son of Tanhumeth the Netophathite, and Jezaniah* son of the Maacathite, and all their men.

[24]Gedaliah vowed to them that the Babylonian officials meant them no harm. "Don't be afraid of them. Live in the land and serve the king of Babylon, and all will go well for you," he promised.

[25]But in midautumn of that year,* Ishmael son of Nethaniah and grandson of Elishama, who was of the royal family, went to Mizpah with ten men and killed Gedaliah. He also killed all the Judeans and Babylonians who were with Gedaliah at Mizpah.

[26]Then all the people of Judah, from the

25:4a Or *the Chaldeans;* also in 25:13, 25, 26. **25:4b** Hebrew *the Arabah*. **25:5** Or *Chaldean;* also in 25:10, 24. **25:8** Hebrew *On the seventh day of the fifth month,* of the ancient Hebrew lunar calendar. This day was August 14, 586 B.C.; also see note on 25:1. **25:9** Or *destroyed the houses of all the important people.* **25:17a** Hebrew *18 cubits* [8.1 meters]. **25:17b** As in parallel texts at 1 Kgs 7:16, 2 Chr 3:15, and Jer 52:22, all of which read *5 cubits* [2.3 meters]; Hebrew reads *3 cubits,* which is 4.5 feet or 1.4 meters. **25:23** As in parallel text at Jer 40:8; Hebrew reads *Jaazaniah,* a variant spelling of Jezaniah. **25:25** Hebrew *in the seventh month,* of the ancient Hebrew lunar calendar. This month occurred within the months of October and November 586 B.C.; also see note on 25:1.

least to the greatest, as well as the army commanders, fled in panic to Egypt, for they were afraid of what the Babylonians would do to them.

Hope for Israel's Royal Line

[27]In the thirty-seventh year of the exile of King Jehoiachin of Judah, Evil-merodach ascended to the Babylonian throne. He was kind to* Jehoiachin and released him from prison on April 2 of that year.* [28]He spoke kindly to Jehoiachin and gave him a higher place than all the other exiled kings in Babylon. [29]He supplied Jehoiachin with new clothes to replace his prison garb and allowed him to dine in the king's presence for the rest of his life. [30]So the Babylonian king gave him a regular food allowance as long as he lived.

25:27a Hebrew *He raised the head of.* **25:27b** Hebrew *on the twenty-seventh day of the twelfth month,* of the ancient Hebrew lunar calendar. This day was April 2, 561 B.C.; also see note on 25:1.

1 Chronicles

WHO
David and Solomon.

WHERE
In ancient Israel.

WHEN
This book was written around 430 BC, but it describes events that happened at the same time as those in 1 Samuel.

WHY
To trace the ancestry of King David and to teach that worshiping God is the most important task of a person and a nation.

David realized that the LORD had confirmed him as king over Israel and had greatly blessed his kingdom for the sake of his people Israel. 1 CHRONICLES 14:2

Knowing your "family tree"—who you come from—helps you know who you are. First Chronicles, like a family tree, lists important people in the history of Israel—all of whom descended from Abraham. As you read, remember this is your family too.

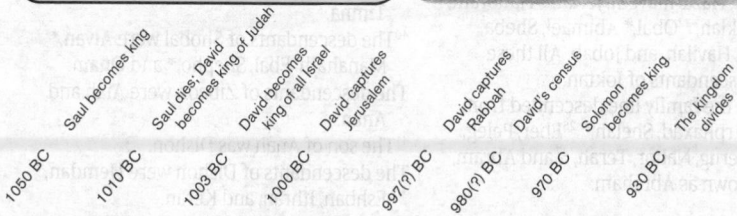

Thank you, God, for my family tree!

CHAPTER 1

From Adam to Noah's Sons

The descendants of Adam were Seth, Enosh,
[2]Kenan, Mahalalel, Jared,
[3]Enoch, Methuselah, Lamech, [4]and
Noah.
The sons of Noah were* Shem, Ham, and
Japheth.

Descendants of Japheth

[5]The descendants of Japheth were Gomer,
Magog, Madai, Javan, Tubal, Meshech,
and Tiras.
[6]The descendants of Gomer were Ashkenaz,
Riphath,* and Togarmah.
[7]The descendants of Javan were Elishah,
Tarshish, Kittim, and Rodanim.

1:4 As in Greek version (see also Gen 5:3-32); Hebrew lacks *The sons of Noah were*. **1:6** As in some Hebrew manuscripts and Greek version (see also Gen 10:3); most Hebrew manuscripts read *Diphath*.

Descendants of Ham

8 The descendants of Ham were Cush,
Mizraim,* Put, and Canaan.
9 The descendants of Cush were Seba,
Havilah, Sabtah, Raamah, and Sabteca.
The descendants of Raamah were Sheba
and Dedan. 10 Cush was also the ancestor
of Nimrod, who was the first heroic
warrior on earth.
11 Mizraim was the ancestor of the Ludites,
Anamites, Lehabites, Naphtuhites, 12 Path-
rusites, Casluhites, and the Caphtorites,
from whom the Philistines came.*
13 Canaan's oldest son was Sidon, the
ancestor of the Sidonians. Canaan was
also the ancestor of the Hittites,*
14 Jebusites, Amorites, Girgashites,
15 Hivites, Arkites, Sinites, 16 Arvadites,
Zemarites, and Hamathites.

Descendants of Shem

17 The descendants of Shem were Elam,
Asshur, Arphaxad, Lud, and Aram.
The descendants of Aram were* Uz, Hul,
Gether, and Mash.*
18 Arphaxad was the father of Shelah.
Shelah was the father of Eber.
19 Eber had two sons. The first was named
Peleg (which means "division"), for during
his lifetime the people of the world were
divided into different language groups.
His brother's name was Joktan.
20 Joktan was the ancestor of Almodad,
Sheleph, Hazarmaveth, Jerah, 21 Hadoram,
Uzal, Diklah, 22 Obal,* Abimael, Sheba,
23 Ophir, Havilah, and Jobab. All these
were descendants of Joktan.
24 So this is the family line descended from
Shem: Arphaxad, Shelah,* 25 Eber, Peleg,
Reu, 26 Serug, Nahor, Terah, 27 and Abram,
later known as Abraham.

Descendants of Abraham

28 The sons of Abraham were Isaac and
Ishmael. 29 These are their genealogical
records:
The sons of Ishmael were Nebaioth (the
oldest), Kedar, Adbeel, Mibsam, 30 Mishma,
Dumah, Massa, Hadad, Tema, 31 Jetur,
Naphish, and Kedemah. These were the
sons of Ishmael.
32 The sons of Keturah, Abraham's concubine,
were Zimran, Jokshan, Medan, Midian,
Ishbak, and Shuah.
The sons of Jokshan were Sheba and Dedan.
33 The sons of Midian were Ephah, Epher,
Hanoch, Abida, and Eldaah.
All these were descendants of Abraham
through his concubine Keturah.

Descendants of Isaac

34 Abraham was the father of Isaac. The sons
of Isaac were Esau and Israel.*

Descendants of Esau

35 The sons of Esau were Eliphaz, Reuel,
Jeush, Jalam, and Korah.
36 The descendants of Eliphaz were Teman,
Omar, Zepho,* Gatam, Kenaz, and
Amalek, who was born to Timna.*
37 The descendants of Reuel were Nahath,
Zerah, Shammah, and Mizzah.

Original Peoples of Edom

38 The descendants of Seir were Lotan,
Shobal, Zibeon, Anah, Dishon, Ezer, and
Dishan.
39 The descendants of Lotan were Hori and
Hemam.* Lotan's sister was named
Timna.
40 The descendants of Shobal were Alvan,*
Manahath, Ebal, Shepho,* and Onam.
The descendants of Zibeon were Aiah and
Anah.
41 The son of Anah was Dishon.
The descendants of Dishon were Hemdan,*
Eshban, Ithran, and Keran.
42 The descendants of Ezer were Bilhan,
Zaavan, and Akan.*
The descendants of Dishan* were Uz and
Aran.

1:8 Or *Egypt;* also in 1:11. **1:12** Hebrew *Casluhites, from whom the Philistines came, Caphtorites.* See Jer 47:4; Amos 9:7. **1:13** Hebrew *ancestor of Heth.* **1:17a** As in one Hebrew manuscript and some Greek manuscripts (see also Gen 10:23); most Hebrew manuscripts lack *The descendants of Aram were.* **1:17b** As in parallel text at Gen 10:23; Hebrew reads *and Meshech.* **1:22** As in some Hebrew manuscripts and Syriac version (see also Gen 10:28); most Hebrew manuscripts read *Ebal.* **1:24** Some Greek manuscripts read *Arphaxad, Cainan, Shelah.* See notes on Gen 10:24; 11:12-13. **1:34** *Israel* is the name that God gave to Jacob. **1:36a** As in many Hebrew manuscripts and a few Greek manuscripts (see also Gen 36:11); most Hebrew manuscripts read *Zephi.* **1:36b** As in some Greek manuscripts (see also Gen 36:12); Hebrew reads *Kenaz, Timna, and Amalek.* **1:39** As in parallel text at Gen 36:22; Hebrew reads *and Homam.* **1:40a** As in many Hebrew manuscripts and a few Greek manuscripts (see also Gen 36:23); most Hebrew manuscripts read *Alian.* **1:40b** As in some Hebrew manuscripts (see also Gen 36:23); most Hebrew manuscripts read *Shephi.* **1:41** As in many Hebrew manuscripts and some Greek manuscripts (see also Gen 36:26); most Hebrew manuscripts read *Hamran.* **1:42a** As in many Hebrew and Greek manuscripts (see also Gen 36:27); most Hebrew manuscripts read *Jaakan.* **1:42b** Hebrew *Dishon;* compare 1:38 and parallel text at Gen 36:28.

Rulers of Edom

43 These are the kings who ruled in the land
of Edom before any king ruled over the
Israelites*:

Bela son of Beor, who ruled from his city of
Dinhabah.
44 When Bela died, Jobab son of Zerah from
Bozrah became king in his place.
45 When Jobab died, Husham from the land
of the Temanites became king in his
place.
46 When Husham died, Hadad son of Bedad
became king in his place and ruled from
the city of Avith. He was the one who
destroyed the Midianite army in the land
of Moab.
47 When Hadad died, Samlah from the city
of Masrekah became king in his place.
48 When Samlah died, Shaul from the city
of Rehoboth-on-the-River became king
in his place.
49 When Shaul died, Baal-hanan son of Acbor
became king in his place.
50 When Baal-hanan died, Hadad became
king in his place and ruled from the city
of Pau.* His wife was Mehetabel, the
daughter of Matred and granddaughter
of Me-zahab. 51 Then Hadad died.

The clan leaders of Edom were Timna,
Alvah,* Jetheth, 52 Oholibamah, Elah, Pinon,
53 Kenaz, Teman, Mibzar, 54 Magdiel, and
Iram. These are the clan leaders of Edom.

CHAPTER 2

Descendants of Israel

The sons of Israel* were Reuben, Simeon,
Levi, Judah, Issachar, Zebulun, 2 Dan,
Joseph, Benjamin, Naphtali, Gad, and
Asher.

Descendants of Judah

3 Judah had three sons from Bathshua, a
Canaanite woman. Their names were Er,
Onan, and Shelah. But the LORD saw that
the oldest son, Er, was a wicked man, so he
killed him. 4 Later Judah had twin sons
from Tamar, his widowed daughter-in-
law. Their names were Perez and Zerah.
So Judah had five sons in all.
5 The sons of Perez were Hezron and Hamul.
6 The sons of Zerah were Zimri, Ethan,
Heman, Calcol, and Darda*—five in all.
7 The son of Carmi (a descendant of Zimri)
was Achan,* who brought disaster on
Israel by taking plunder that had been set
apart for the LORD.*
8 The son of Ethan was Azariah.

From Judah's Grandson Hezron to David

9 The sons of Hezron were Jerahmeel, Ram,
and Caleb.*
10 Ram was the father of Amminadab.
Amminadab was the father of Nahshon,
a leader of Judah.
11 Nahshon was the father of Salmon.*
Salmon was the father of Boaz.
12 Boaz was the father of Obed.
Obed was the father of Jesse.
13 Jesse's first son was Eliab, his second was
Abinadab, his third was Shimea, 14 his
fourth was Nethanel, his fifth was Raddai,
15 his sixth was Ozem, and his seventh was
David.
16 Their sisters were named Zeruiah and
Abigail. Zeruiah had three sons named
Abishai, Joab, and Asahel. 17 Abigail married
a man named Jether, an Ishmaelite, and
they had a son named Amasa.

Other Descendants of Hezron

18 Hezron's son Caleb had sons from his wife
Azubah and from Jerioth.* Her sons were
named Jesher, Shobab, and Ardon. 19 After
Azubah died, Caleb married Ephrathah,*
and they had a son named Hur. 20 Hur was
the father of Uri. Uri was the father of
Bezalel.
21 When Hezron was sixty years old, he
married Gilead's sister, the daughter of
Makir. They had a son named Segub.
22 Segub was the father of Jair, who ruled
twenty-three towns in the land of Gilead.
23 (But Geshur and Aram captured the
Towns of Jair* and also took Kenath and
its sixty surrounding villages.) All these

1:43 Or *before an Israelite king ruled over them.* **1:50** As in many Hebrew manuscripts, some Greek manuscripts, Syriac version, and Latin Vulgate (see also Gen 36:39); most Hebrew manuscripts read *Pai.* **1:51** As in parallel text at Gen 36:40; Hebrew reads *Aliah.* **2:1** *Israel* is the name that God gave to Jacob. **2:6** As in many Hebrew manuscripts, some Greek manuscripts, and Syriac version (see also 1 Kgs 4:31); Hebrew reads *Dara.* **2:7a** Hebrew *Achar;* compare Josh 7:1. *Achar* means "disaster." **2:7b** The Hebrew term used here refers to the complete consecration of things or people to the LORD, either by destroying them or by giving them as an offering. **2:9** Hebrew *Kelubai,* a variant spelling of Caleb; compare 2:18. **2:11** As in Greek version (see also Ruth 4:21); Hebrew reads *Salma.* **2:18** Or *Caleb had a daughter named Jerioth from his wife, Azubah.* The meaning of the Hebrew is uncertain. **2:19** Hebrew *Ephrath,* a variant spelling of Ephrathah; compare 2:50 and 4:4. **2:23** Or *captured Havvoth-jair.*

were descendants of Makir, the father of
Gilead.
24 Soon after Hezron died in the town of
Caleb-ephrathah, his wife Abijah gave
birth to a son named Ashhur (the father
of* Tekoa).

Descendants of Hezron's Son Jerahmeel

25 The sons of Jerahmeel, the oldest son of
Hezron, were Ram (the firstborn), Bunah,
Oren, Ozem, and Ahijah. 26 Jerahmeel had
a second wife named Atarah. She was the
mother of Onam.
27 The sons of Ram, the oldest son of
Jerahmeel, were Maaz, Jamin, and Eker.
28 The sons of Onam were Shammai and
Jada.
The sons of Shammai were Nadab and
Abishur.
29 The sons of Abishur and his wife Abihail
were Ahban and Molid.
30 The sons of Nadab were Seled and
Appaim. Seled died without children,
31 but Appaim had a son named Ishi. The
son of Ishi was Sheshan. Sheshan had a
descendant named Ahlai.
32 The sons of Jada, Shammai's brother, were
Jether and Jonathan. Jether died without
children, 33 but Jonathan had two sons
named Peleth and Zaza.
These were all descendants of Jerahmeel.
34 Sheshan had no sons, though he did have
daughters. He also had an Egyptian
servant named Jarha. 35 Sheshan gave one
of his daughters to be the wife of Jarha,
and they had a son named Attai.
36 Attai was the father of Nathan.
Nathan was the father of Zabad.
37 Zabad was the father of Ephlal.
Ephlal was the father of Obed.
38 Obed was the father of Jehu.
Jehu was the father of Azariah.
39 Azariah was the father of Helez.
Helez was the father of Eleasah.
40 Eleasah was the father of Sismai.
Sismai was the father of Shallum.
41 Shallum was the father of Jekamiah.
Jekamiah was the father of Elishama.

Descendants of Hezron's Son Caleb

42 The descendants of Caleb, the brother of
Jerahmeel, included Mesha (the
firstborn), who became the father of
Ziph. Caleb's descendants also included
the sons of Mareshah, the father of
Hebron.*
43 The sons of Hebron were Korah, Tappuah,
Rekem, and Shema. 44 Shema was the
father of Raham. Raham was the father
of Jorkeam. Rekem was the father of
Shammai. 45 The son of Shammai was
Maon. Maon was the father of Beth-zur.
46 Caleb's concubine Ephah gave birth to
Haran, Moza, and Gazez. Haran was the
father of Gazez.
47 The sons of Jahdai were Regem, Jotham,
Geshan, Pelet, Ephah, and Shaaph.
48 Another of Caleb's concubines, Maacah,
gave birth to Sheber and Tirhanah. 49 She
also gave birth to Shaaph (the father
of Madmannah) and Sheva (the father
of Macbenah and Gibea). Caleb also had
a daughter named Acsah.
50 These were all descendants of Caleb.

Descendants of Caleb's Son Hur

The sons of Hur, the oldest son of Caleb's
wife Ephrathah, were Shobal (the founder
of Kiriath-jearim), 51 Salma (the founder
of Bethlehem), and Hareph (the founder
of Beth-gader).
52 The descendants of Shobal (the founder
of Kiriath-jearim) were Haroeh, half the
Manahathites, 53 and the families of
Kiriath-jearim—the Ithrites, Puthites,
Shumathites, and Mishraites, from
whom came the people of Zorah and
Eshtaol.
54 The descendants of Salma were the people
of Bethlehem, the Netophathites, Atroth-
beth-joab, the other half of the Manahath-
ites, the Zorites, 55 and the families of scribes
living at Jabez—the Tirathites, Shimeathites,
and Sucathites. All these were Kenites who
descended from Hammath, the father of the
family of Recab.*

CHAPTER 3

Descendants of David

These are the sons of David who were born in
Hebron:

The oldest was Amnon, whose mother
was Ahinoam from Jezreel.

2:24 Or *the founder of;* also in 2:42, 45, 49. **2:42** Or *who founded Hebron.* The meaning of the Hebrew is uncertain. **2:55** Or *the founder of Beth-recab.*

The second was Daniel, whose mother was Abigail from Carmel.
2 The third was Absalom, whose mother was Maacah, the daughter of Talmai, king of Geshur.
The fourth was Adonijah, whose mother was Haggith.
3 The fifth was Shephatiah, whose mother was Abital.
The sixth was Ithream, whose mother was Eglah, David's wife.
4 These six sons were born to David in Hebron, where he reigned seven and a half years.

Then David reigned another thirty-three years in Jerusalem. 5 The sons born to David in Jerusalem included Shammua,* Shobab, Nathan, and Solomon. Their mother was Bathsheba,* the daughter of Ammiel. 6 David also had nine other sons: Ibhar, Elishua,* Elpelet,* 7 Nogah, Nepheg, Japhia, 8 Elishama, Eliada, and Eliphelet.

9 These were the sons of David, not including his sons born to his concubines. Their sister was named Tamar.

Descendants of Solomon

10 The descendants of Solomon were Rehoboam, Abijah, Asa, Jehoshaphat, 11 Jehoram,* Ahaziah, Joash, 12 Amaziah, Uzziah,* Jotham, 13 Ahaz, Hezekiah, Manasseh, 14 Amon, and Josiah.
15 The sons of Josiah were Johanan (the oldest), Jehoiakim (the second), Zedekiah (the third), and Jehoahaz* (the fourth).
16 The successors of Jehoiakim were his son Jehoiachin and his brother Zedekiah.*

Descendants of Jehoiachin

17 The sons of Jehoiachin,* who was taken prisoner by the Babylonians, were Shealtiel, 18 Malkiram, Pedaiah, Shenazzar, Jekamiah, Hoshama, and Nedabiah.
19 The sons of Pedaiah were Zerubbabel and Shimei.
The sons of Zerubbabel were Meshullam and Hananiah. (Their sister was Shelomith.)
20 His five other sons were Hashubah, Ohel, Berekiah, Hasadiah, and Jushab-hesed.
21 The sons of Hananiah were Pelatiah and Jeshaiah. Jeshaiah's son was Rephaiah. Rephaiah's son was Arnan. Arnan's son was Obadiah. Obadiah's son was Shecaniah.
22 The descendants of Shecaniah were Shemaiah and his sons, Hattush, Igal, Bariah, Neariah, and Shaphat—six in all.
23 The sons of Neariah were Elioenai, Hizkiah, and Azrikam—three in all.
24 The sons of Elioenai were Hodaviah, Eliashib, Pelaiah, Akkub, Johanan, Delaiah, and Anani—seven in all.

CHAPTER 4

Other Descendants of Judah

The descendants of Judah were Perez, Hezron, Carmi, Hur, and Shobal.
2 Shobal's son Reaiah was the father of Jahath. Jahath was the father of Ahumai and Lahad. These were the families of the Zorathites.
3 The descendants of* Etam were Jezreel, Ishma, Idbash, their sister Hazzelelponi, 4 Penuel (the father of* Gedor), and Ezer (the father of Hushah). These were the descendants of Hur (the firstborn of Ephrathah), the ancestor of Bethlehem.
5 Ashhur (the father of Tekoa) had two wives, named Helah and Naarah. 6 Naarah gave birth to Ahuzzam, Hepher, Temeni, and Haahashtari. 7 Helah gave birth to Zereth, Izhar,* Ethnan, 8 and Koz, who became the ancestor of Anub, Zobebah, and all the families of Aharhel son of Harum.
9 There was a man named Jabez who was more honorable than any of his brothers. His mother named him Jabez* because his birth had been so painful. 10 He was the one who prayed to the God of Israel, "Oh, that you would bless me and expand my territory! Please be with me in all that I do, and keep me from all trouble and pain!" And God granted him his request.
11 Kelub (the brother of Shuhah) was the father of Mehir. Mehir was the father of

3:5a As in Syriac version (see also 14:4; 2 Sam 5:14); Hebrew reads *Shimea*. **3:5b** Hebrew *Bathshua*, a variant spelling of Bathsheba. **3:6a** As in some Hebrew and Greek manuscripts (see also 14:5-7 and 2 Sam 5:15); most Hebrew manuscripts read *Elishama*. **3:6b** Hebrew *Eliphelet;* compare parallel text at 14:5-7. **3:11** Hebrew *Joram*, a variant spelling of Jehoram. **3:12** Hebrew *Azariah*, a variant spelling of Uzziah. **3:15** Hebrew *Shallum*, another name for Jehoahaz. **3:16** Hebrew *The sons of Jehoiakim were his son Jeconiah* [a variant spelling of Jehoiachin] *and his son Zedekiah*. **3:17** Hebrew *Jeconiah*, a variant spelling of Jehoiachin. **4:3** As in Greek version; Hebrew reads *father of*. The meaning of the Hebrew is uncertain. **4:4** Or *the founder of;* also in 4:5, 12, 14, 17, 18, and perhaps other instances where the text reads *the father of*. **4:7** As in an alternate reading in the Masoretic Text (see also Latin Vulgate); the other alternate and the Greek version read *Zohar*. **4:9** *Jabez* sounds like a Hebrew word meaning "distress" or "pain."

Eshton. [12]Eshton was the father of Beth-rapha, Paseah, and Tehinnah. Tehinnah was the father of Ir-nahash. These were the descendants of Recah.

[13]The sons of Kenaz were Othniel and Seraiah. Othniel's sons were Hathath and Meonothai.* [14]Meonothai was the father of Ophrah. Seraiah was the father of Joab, the founder of the Valley of Craftsmen,* so called because they were craftsmen.

[15]The sons of Caleb son of Jephunneh were Iru, Elah, and Naam. The son of Elah was Kenaz.

[16]The sons of Jehallelel were Ziph, Ziphah, Tiria, and Asarel.

[17]The sons of Ezrah were Jether, Mered, Epher, and Jalon. One of Mered's wives became* the mother of Miriam, Shammai, and Ishbah (the father of Eshtemoa). [18]He married a woman from Judah, who became the mother of Jered (the father of Gedor), Heber (the father of Soco), and Jekuthiel (the father of Zanoah). Mered also married Bithia, a daughter of Pharaoh, and she bore him children.

[19]Hodiah's wife was the sister of Naham. One of her sons was the father of Keilah the Garmite, and another was the father of Eshtemoa the Maacathite.

[20]The sons of Shimon were Amnon, Rinnah, Ben-hanan, and Tilon.

The descendants of Ishi were Zoheth and Ben-zoheth.

Descendants of Judah's Son Shelah

[21]Shelah was one of Judah's sons. The descendants of Shelah were Er (the father of Lecah); Laadah (the father of Mareshah); the families of linen workers at Beth-ashbea; [22]Jokim; the men of Cozeba; and Joash and Saraph, who ruled over Moab and Jashubi-lehem. These names all come from ancient records. [23]They were the pottery makers who lived in Netaim and Gederah. They lived there and worked for the king.

Descendants of Simeon

[24]The sons of Simeon were Jemuel,* Jamin, Jarib, Zohar,* and Shaul.

[25]The descendants of Shaul were Shallum, Mibsam, and Mishma.

[26]The descendants of Mishma were Hammuel, Zaccur, and Shimei.

[27]Shimei had sixteen sons and six daughters, but none of his brothers had large families. So Simeon's tribe never grew as large as the tribe of Judah.

[28]They lived in Beersheba, Moladah, Hazar-shual, [29]Bilhah, Ezem, Tolad, [30]Bethuel, Hormah, Ziklag, [31]Beth-marcaboth, Hazar-susim, Beth-biri, and Shaaraim. These towns were under their control until the time of King David. [32]Their descendants also lived in Etam, Ain, Rimmon, Token,

4:13 As in some Greek manuscripts and Latin Vulgate; Hebrew lacks *and Meonothai*. **4:14** Or *Joab, the father of Ge-harashim*. **4:17** Or *Jether's wife became;* Hebrew reads *She became*. **4:24a** As in Syriac version (see also Gen 46:10; Exod 6:15); Hebrew reads *Nemuel*. **4:24b** As in parallel texts at Gen 46:10 and Exod 6:15; Hebrew reads *Zerah*.

and Ashan—five towns [33]and their
surrounding villages as far away as
Baalath.* This was their territory, and
these names are listed in their
genealogical records.
[34]Other descendants of Simeon included
Meshobab, Jamlech, Joshah son of
Amaziah, [35]Joel, Jehu son of Joshibiah,
son of Seraiah, son of Asiel, [36]Elioenai,
Jaakobah, Jeshohaiah, Asaiah, Adiel,
Jesimiel, Benaiah, [37]and Ziza son of
Shiphi, son of Allon, son of Jedaiah, son
of Shimri, son of Shemaiah.

[38]These were the names of some of the leaders of Simeon's wealthy clans. Their families grew, [39]and they traveled to the region of Gerar,* in the east part of the valley, seeking pastureland for their flocks. [40]They found lush pastures there, and the land was quiet and peaceful.

Some of Ham's descendants had been living in that region. [41]But during the reign of King Hezekiah of Judah, these leaders of Simeon invaded the region and completely destroyed* the homes of the descendants of Ham and of the Meunites. No trace of them remains today. They killed everyone who lived there and took the land for themselves, because they wanted its good pastureland for their flocks. [42]Five hundred of these invaders from the tribe of Simeon went to Mount Seir, led by Pelatiah, Neariah, Rephaiah, and Uzziel—all sons of Ishi. [43]They destroyed the few Amalekites who had survived, and they have lived there ever since.

CHAPTER 5

Descendants of Reuben

The oldest son of Israel* was Reuben. But since he dishonored his father by sleeping with one of his father's concubines, his birthright was given to the sons of his brother Joseph. For this reason, Reuben is not listed in the genealogical records as the firstborn son. [2]The descendants of Judah became the most powerful tribe and provided a ruler for the nation,* but the birthright belonged to Joseph.

[3]The sons of Reuben, the oldest son of Israel,
were Hanoch, Pallu, Hezron, and Carmi.
[4]The descendants of Joel were Shemaiah,
Gog, Shimei, [5]Micah, Reaiah, Baal, [6]and
Beerah. Beerah was the leader of the
Reubenites when they were taken into
captivity by King Tiglath-pileser* of
Assyria.
[7]Beerah's* relatives are listed in their
genealogical records by their clans: Jeiel
(the leader), Zechariah, [8]and Bela son of
Azaz, son of Shema, son of Joel.
The Reubenites lived in the area that
stretches from Aroer to Nebo and Baal-
meon. [9]And since they had so many
livestock in the land of Gilead, they spread
east toward the edge of the desert that
stretches to the Euphrates River.
[10]During the reign of Saul, the Reubenites
defeated the Hagrites in battle. Then they
moved into the Hagrite settlements all
along the eastern edge of Gilead.

Descendants of Gad

[11]Next to the Reubenites, the descendants of
Gad lived in the land of Bashan as far east
as Salecah. [12]Joel was the leader in the
land of Bashan, and Shapham was second-
in-command, followed by Janai and
Shaphat.
[13]Their relatives, the leaders of seven other
clans, were Michael, Meshullam, Sheba,
Jorai, Jacan, Zia, and Eber. [14]These were all
descendants of Abihail son of Huri, son of
Jaroah, son of Gilead, son of Michael, son
of Jeshishai, son of Jahdo, son of Buz.
[15]Ahi son of Abdiel, son of Guni, was the
leader of their clans.

[16]The Gadite lived in the land of Gilead, in Bashan and its villages, and throughout all the pasturelands of Sharon. [17]All of these were listed in the genealogical records during the days of King Jotham of Judah and King Jeroboam of Israel.

The Tribes East of the Jordan

[18]There were 44,760 capable warriors in the armies of Reuben, Gad, and the half-tribe of Manasseh. They were all skilled in combat and armed with shields, swords, and bows. [19]They waged war against the Hagrites, the Jeturites,

4:33 As in some Greek manuscripts (see also Josh 19:8); Hebrew reads *Baal*. **4:39** As in Greek version; Hebrew reads *Gedor*. **4:41** The Hebrew term used here refers to the complete consecration of things or people to the LORD, either by destroying them or by giving them as an offering. **5:1** *Israel* is the name that God gave to Jacob. **5:2** Or *and from Judah came a prince*. **5:6** Hebrew *Tilgath-pilneser*, a variant spelling of Tiglath-pileser; also in 5:26. **5:7** Hebrew *His*.

the Naphishites, and the Nodabites. [20]They cried out to God during the battle, and he answered their prayer because they trusted in him. So the Hagrites and all their allies were defeated. [21]The plunder taken from the Hagrites included 50,000 camels, 250,000 sheep and goats, 2,000 donkeys, and 100,000 captives. [22]Many of the Hagrites were killed in the battle because God was fighting against them. The people of Reuben, Gad, and Manasseh lived in their land until they were taken into exile.

[23]The half-tribe of Manasseh was very large and spread through the land from Bashan to Baal-hermon, Senir, and Mount Hermon. [24]These were the leaders of their clans: Epher,* Ishi, Eliel, Azriel, Jeremiah, Hodaviah, and Jahdiel. These men had a great reputation as mighty warriors and leaders of their clans.

[25]But these tribes were unfaithful to the God of their ancestors. They worshiped the gods of the nations that God had destroyed. [26]So the God of Israel caused King Pul of Assyria (also known as Tiglath-pileser) to invade the land and take away the people of Reuben, Gad, and the half-tribe of Manasseh as captives. The Assyrians exiled them to Halah, Habor, Hara, and the Gozan River, where they remain to this day.

CHAPTER 6

The Priestly Line

[1]*The sons of Levi were Gershon, Kohath, and Merari.
[2]The descendants of Kohath included Amram, Izhar, Hebron, and Uzziel.
[3]The children of Amram were Aaron, Moses, and Miriam.
The sons of Aaron were Nadab, Abihu, Eleazar, and Ithamar.
[4] Eleazar was the father of Phinehas.
Phinehas was the father of Abishua.
[5] Abishua was the father of Bukki.
Bukki was the father of Uzzi.
[6] Uzzi was the father of Zerahiah.
Zerahiah was the father of Meraioth.
[7] Meraioth was the father of Amariah.
Amariah was the father of Ahitub.
[8] Ahitub was the father of Zadok.
Zadok was the father of Ahimaaz.
[9] Ahimaaz was the father of Azariah.
Azariah was the father of Johanan.
[10] Johanan was the father of Azariah, the high priest at the Temple* built by Solomon in Jerusalem.
[11] Azariah was the father of Amariah.
Amariah was the father of Ahitub.
[12] Ahitub was the father of Zadok.
Zadok was the father of Shallum.
[13] Shallum was the father of Hilkiah.
Hilkiah was the father of Azariah.
[14] Azariah was the father of Seraiah.
Seraiah was the father of Jehozadak,
[15]who went into exile when the LORD sent the people of Judah and Jerusalem into captivity under Nebuchadnezzar.

The Levite Clans

[16]*The sons of Levi were Gershon,* Kohath, and Merari.
[17]The descendants of Gershon included Libni and Shimei.
[18]The descendants of Kohath included Amram, Izhar, Hebron, and Uzziel.
[19]The descendants of Merari included Mahli and Mushi.

The following were the Levite clans, listed according to their ancestral descent:

[20]The descendants of Gershon included Libni, Jahath, Zimmah, [21]Joah, Iddo, Zerah, and Jeatherai.
[22]The descendants of Kohath included Amminadab, Korah, Assir, [23]Elkanah, Abiasaph,* Assir, [24]Tahath, Uriel, Uzziah, and Shaul.
[25]The descendants of Elkanah included Amasai, Ahimoth, [26]Elkanah, Zophai, Nahath, [27]Eliab, Jeroham, Elkanah, and Samuel.*
[28]The sons of Samuel were Joel* (the older) and Abijah (the second).
[29]The descendants of Merari included Mahli, Libni, Shimei, Uzzah, [30]Shimea, Haggiah, and Asaiah.

5:24 As in Greek version and Latin Vulgate; Hebrew reads *and Epher*. **6:1** Verses 6:1-15 are numbered 5:27-41 in Hebrew text. **6:10** Hebrew *the house*. **6:16a** Verses 6:16-81 are numbered 6:1-66 in Hebrew text. **6:16b** Hebrew *Gershom*, a variant spelling of Gershon (see 6:1); also in 6:17, 20, 43, 62, 71. **6:23** Hebrew *Ebiasaph*, a variant spelling of Abiasaph (also in 6:37); compare parallel text at Exod 6:24. **6:27** As in some Greek manuscripts (see also 6:33-34); Hebrew lacks *and Samuel*. **6:28** As in some Greek manuscripts and the Syriac version (see also 6:33 and 1 Sam 8:2); Hebrew lacks *Joel*.

The Temple Musicians

31David assigned the following men to lead
the music at the house of the LORD after the
Ark was placed there. 32They ministered with
music at the Tabernacle* until Solomon built
the Temple of the LORD in Jerusalem. They
carried out their work, following all the regu-
lations handed down to them. 33These are the
men who served, along with their sons:

Heman the musician was from the clan of
Kohath. His genealogy was traced back
through Joel, Samuel, 34Elkanah, Jeroham,
Eliel, Toah, 35Zuph, Elkanah, Mahath,
Amasai, 36Elkanah, Joel, Azariah,
Zephaniah, 37Tahath, Assir, Abiasaph,
Korah, 38Izhar, Kohath, Levi, and Israel.*
39Heman's first assistant was Asaph from the
clan of Gershon.* Asaph's genealogy was
traced back through Berekiah, Shimea,
40Michael, Baaseiah, Malkijah, 41Ethni,
Zerah, Adaiah, 42Ethan, Zimmah, Shimei,
43Jahath, Gershon, and Levi.
44Heman's second assistant was Ethan from
the clan of Merari. Ethan's genealogy was
traced back through Kishi, Abdi, Malluch,
45Hashabiah, Amaziah, Hilkiah, 46Amzi,
Bani, Shemer, 47Mahli, Mushi, Merari,
and Levi.

48Their fellow Levites were appointed to vari-
ous other tasks in the Tabernacle, the house
of God.

Aaron's Descendants

49Only Aaron and his descendants served as
priests. They presented the offerings on the al-
tar of burnt offering and the altar of incense,
and they performed all the other duties related
to the Most Holy Place. They made atonement
for Israel by doing everything that Moses, the
servant of God, had commanded them.

50The descendants of Aaron were Eleazar,
Phinehas, Abishua, 51Bukki, Uzzi, Zerahiah,
52Meraioth, Amariah, Ahitub, 53Zadok, and
Ahimaaz.

Territory for the Levites

54This is a record of the towns and territory
assigned by means of sacred lots to the de-
scendants of Aaron, who were from the clan
of Kohath. 55This territory included Hebron
and its surrounding pasturelands in Judah,
56but the fields and outlying areas belonging
to the city were given to Caleb son of Jephun-
neh. 57So the descendants of Aaron were
given the following towns, each with its
pasturelands: Hebron (a city of refuge),* Lib-
nah, Jattir, Eshtemoa, 58Holon,* Debir, 59Ain,*
Juttah,* and Beth-shemesh. 60And from the
territory of Benjamin they were given Gibe-
on,* Geba, Alemeth, and Anathoth, each with
its pasturelands. So thirteen towns were
given to the descendants of Aaron. 61The re-
maining descendants of Kohath received ten
towns from the territory of the half-tribe of
Manasseh by means of sacred lots.

62The descendants of Gershon received by
sacred lots thirteen towns from the territo-
ries of Issachar, Asher, Naphtali, and from the
Bashan area of Manasseh, east of the Jordan.

63The descendants of Merari received by
sacred lots twelve towns from the territories
of Reuben, Gad, and Zebulun.

64So the people of Israel assigned all these
towns and pasturelands to the Levites. 65The
towns in the territories of Judah, Simeon, and
Benjamin, mentioned above, were assigned to
them by means of sacred lots.

66The descendants of Kohath were given
the following towns from the territory of
Ephraim, each with its pasturelands: 67She-
chem (a city of refuge in the hill country of
Ephraim),* Gezer, 68Jokmeam, Beth-horon,
69Aijalon, and Gath-rimmon. 70The remaining
descendants of Kohath were assigned the
towns of Aner and Bileam from the territory
of the half-tribe of Manasseh, each with its
pasturelands.

71The descendants of Gershon received the
towns of Golan (in Bashan) and Ashtaroth
from the territory of the half-tribe of Manas-
seh, each with its pasturelands. 72From the
territory of Issachar, they were given Kedesh,
Daberath, 73Ramoth, and Anem, each with its
pasturelands. 74From the territory of Asher,
they received Mashal, Abdon, 75Hukok, and
Rehob, each with its pasturelands. 76From the

6:32 Hebrew *the Tabernacle, the Tent of Meeting.* **6:38** *Israel* is the name that God gave to Jacob. **6:39** Hebrew lacks *from the clan of Gershon;* see 6:43. **6:57** As in parallel text at Josh 21:13; Hebrew reads *were given the cities of refuge: Hebron, and the following towns, each with its pasturelands.* **6:58** As in parallel text at Josh 21:15; Masoretic Text reads *Hilez;* other manuscripts read *Hilen.* **6:59a** As in parallel text at Josh 21:16; Hebrew reads *Ashan.* **6:59b** As in Syriac version (see also Josh 21:16); Hebrew lacks *Juttah.* **6:60** As in parallel text at Josh 21:17; Hebrew lacks *Gibeon.* **6:66-67** As in parallel text at Josh 21:21. Hebrew text reads *were given the cities of refuge: Shechem in the hill country of Ephraim, and the following towns, each with its pasturelands.*

territory of Naphtali, they were given Kedesh in Galilee, Hammon, and Kiriathaim, each with its pasturelands.

77 The remaining descendants of Merari received the towns of Jokneam, Kartah,* Rimmon,* and Tabor from the territory of Zebulun, each with its pasturelands. 78 From the territory of Reuben, east of the Jordan River opposite Jericho, they received Bezer (a desert town), Jahaz,* 79 Kedemoth, and Mephaath, each with its pasturelands. 80 And from the territory of Gad, they received Ramoth in Gilead, Mahanaim, 81 Heshbon, and Jazer, each with its pasturelands.

CHAPTER 7

Descendants of Issachar

The four sons of Issachar were Tola, Puah, Jashub, and Shimron.

2 The sons of Tola were Uzzi, Rephaiah, Jeriel, Jahmai, Ibsam, and Shemuel. Each of them was the leader of an ancestral clan. At the time of King David, the total number of mighty warriors listed in the records of these clans was 22,600.

3 The son of Uzzi was Izrahiah. The sons of Izrahiah were Michael, Obadiah, Joel, and Isshiah. These five became the leaders of clans. 4 All of them had many wives and many sons, so the total number of men available for military service among their descendants was 36,000.

5 The total number of mighty warriors from all the clans of the tribe of Issachar was 87,000. All of them were listed in their genealogical records.

Descendants of Benjamin

6 Three of Benjamin's sons were Bela, Beker, and Jediael.

7 The five sons of Bela were Ezbon, Uzzi, Uzziel, Jerimoth, and Iri. Each of them was the leader of an ancestral clan. The total number of mighty warriors from these clans was 22,034, as listed in their genealogical records.

8 The sons of Beker were Zemirah, Joash, Eliezer, Elioenai, Omri, Jeremoth, Abijah, Anathoth, and Alemeth. 9 Each of them was the leader of an ancestral clan. The total number of mighty warriors and leaders from these clans was 20,200, as listed in their genealogical records.

10 The son of Jediael was Bilhan. The sons of Bilhan were Jeush, Benjamin, Ehud, Kenaanah, Zethan, Tarshish, and Ahishahar. 11 Each of them was the leader of an ancestral clan. From these clans the total number of mighty warriors ready for war was 17,200.

12 The sons of Ir were Shuppim and Huppim. Hushim was the son of Aher.

Descendants of Naphtali

13 The sons of Naphtali were Jahzeel,* Guni, Jezer, and Shillem.* They were all descendants of Jacob's concubine Bilhah.

Descendants of Manasseh

14 The descendants of Manasseh through his Aramean concubine included Asriel. She also bore Makir, the father of Gilead. 15 Makir found wives for* Huppim and Shuppim. Makir had a sister named Maacah. One of his descendants was Zelophehad, who had only daughters.

16 Makir's wife, Maacah, gave birth to a son whom she named Peresh. His brother's name was Sheresh. The sons of Peresh were Ulam and Rakem. 17 The son of Ulam was Bedan. All these were considered Gileadites, descendants of Makir son of Manasseh.

18 Makir's sister Hammoleketh gave birth to Ishhod, Abiezer, and Mahlah.

19 The sons of Shemida were Ahian, Shechem, Likhi, and Aniam.

Descendants of Ephraim

20 The descendants of Ephraim were Shuthelah, Bered, Tahath, Eleadah, Tahath, 21 Zabad, Shuthelah, Ezer, and Elead. These two were killed trying to steal livestock from the local farmers near Gath. 22 Their father, Ephraim, mourned for them a long time, and his relatives came to comfort him. 23 Afterward Ephraim slept with his

6:77a As in Greek version (see also Josh 21:34); Hebrew lacks *Jokneam, Kartah.* **6:77b** As in Greek version (see also Josh 19:13); Hebrew reads *Rimmono.* **6:78** Hebrew *Jahzah,* a variant spelling of Jahaz. **7:13a** As in parallel text at Gen 46:24; Hebrew reads *Jahziel,* a variant spelling of Jahzeel. **7:13b** As in some Hebrew and Greek manuscripts (see also Gen 46:24; Num 26:49); most Hebrew manuscripts read *Shallum.* **7:15** Or *Makir took a wife from.* The meaning of the Hebrew is uncertain.

wife, and she became pregnant and gave
birth to a son. Ephraim named him
Beriah* because of the tragedy his family
had suffered. [24]He had a daughter named
Sheerah. She built the towns of Lower
and Upper Beth-horon and Uzzen-
sheerah.
[25]The descendants of Ephraim included
Rephah, Resheph, Telah, Tahan,
[26]Ladan, Ammihud, Elishama, [27]Nun,
and Joshua.

[28]The descendants of Ephraim lived in the territory that included Bethel and its surrounding towns to the south, Naaran to the east, Gezer and its villages to the west, and Shechem and its surrounding villages to the north as far as Ayyah and its towns. [29]Along the border of Manasseh were the towns of Beth-shan,* Taanach, Megiddo, Dor, and their surrounding villages. The descendants of Joseph son of Israel* lived in these towns.

Descendants of Asher

[30]The sons of Asher were Imnah, Ishvah,
Ishvi, and Beriah. They had a sister named
Serah.
[31]The sons of Beriah were Heber and Malkiel
(the father of Birzaith).
[32]The sons of Heber were Japhlet, Shomer,
and Hotham. They had a sister named
Shua.
[33]The sons of Japhlet were Pasach, Bimhal,
and Ashvath.
[34]The sons of Shomer were Ahi,* Rohgah,
Hubbah, and Aram.
[35]The sons of his brother Helem* were
Zophah, Imna, Shelesh, and Amal.
[36]The sons of Zophah were Suah, Harnepher,
Shual, Beri, Imrah, [37]Bezer, Hod, Shamma,
Shilshah, Ithran,* and Beera.
[38]The sons of Jether were Jephunneh,
Pispah, and Ara.
[39]The sons of Ulla were Arah, Hanniel, and
Rizia.
[40]Each of these descendants of Asher was the head of an ancestral clan. They were all select men—mighty warriors and outstanding leaders. The total number of men available for military service was 26,000, as listed in their genealogical records.

CHAPTER 8

Descendants of Benjamin

Benjamin's first son was Bela, the second was
Ashbel, the third was Aharah, [2]the fourth
was Nohah, and the fifth was Rapha.
[3]The sons of Bela were Addar, Gera,
Abihud,* [4]Abishua, Naaman, Ahoah,
[5]Gera, Shephuphan, and Huram.
[6]The sons of Ehud, leaders of the clans
living at Geba, were exiled to Manahath.
[7]Ehud's sons were Naaman, Ahijah, and
Gera. Gera, who led them into exile, was
the father of Uzza and Ahihud.*
[8]After Shaharaim divorced his wives Hushim
and Baara, he had children in the land of
Moab. [9]His wife Hodesh gave birth to
Jobab, Zibia, Mesha, Malcam, [10]Jeuz, Sakia,
and Mirmah. These sons all became the
leaders of clans.
[11]Shaharaim's wife Hushim had already
given birth to Abitub and Elpaal. [12]The
sons of Elpaal were Eber, Misham,
Shemed (who built the towns of Ono and
Lod and their nearby villages), [13]Beriah,
and Shema. They were the leaders of the
clans living in Aijalon, and they drove out
the inhabitants of Gath.
[14]Ahio, Shashak, Jeremoth, [15]Zebadiah, Arad,
Eder, [16]Michael, Ishpah, and Joha were the
sons of Beriah.
[17]Zebadiah, Meshullam, Hizki, Heber,
[18]Ishmerai, Izliah, and Jobab were the
sons of Elpaal.
[19]Jakim, Zicri, Zabdi, [20]Elienai, Zillethai, Eliel,
[21]Adaiah, Beraiah, and Shimrath were the
sons of Shimei.
[22]Ishpan, Eber, Eliel, [23]Abdon, Zicri, Hanan,
[24]Hananiah, Elam, Anthothijah,
[25]Iphdeiah, and Penuel were the sons
of Shashak.
[26]Shamsherai, Shehariah, Athaliah,
[27]Jaareshiah, Elijah, and Zicri were the
sons of Jeroham.
[28]These were the leaders of the ancestral clans; they were listed in their genealogical records, and they all lived in Jerusalem.

7:23 *Beriah* sounds like a Hebrew term meaning "tragedy" or "misfortune." **7:29a** Hebrew *Beth-shean,* a variant spelling of Beth-shan. **7:29b** *Israel* is the name that God gave to Jacob. **7:34** Or *The sons of Shomer, his brother, were.* **7:35** Possibly another name for *Hotham;* compare 7:32. **7:37** Possibly another name for *Jether;* compare 7:38. **8:3** Possibly *Gera the father of Ehud;* compare 8:6. **8:7** Or *Gera, that is Heglam, was the father of Uzza and Ahihud.*

The Family of Saul

29 Jeiel* (the father of* Gibeon) lived in the
town of Gibeon. His wife's name was
Maacah, 30 and his oldest son was named
Abdon. Jeiel's other sons were Zur, Kish,
Baal, Ner,* Nadab, 31 Gedor, Ahio,
Zechariah,* 32 and Mikloth, who was the
father of Shimeam.* All these families
lived near each other in Jerusalem.
33 Ner was the father of Kish.
Kish was the father of Saul.
Saul was the father of Jonathan,
Malkishua, Abinadab, and Esh-baal.
34 Jonathan was the father of Merib-baal.
Merib-baal was the father of Micah.
35 Micah was the father of Pithon, Melech,
Tahrea,* and Ahaz.
36 Ahaz was the father of Jadah.*
Jadah was the father of Alemeth,
Azmaveth, and Zimri.
Zimri was the father of Moza.
37 Moza was the father of Binea.
Binea was the father of Rephaiah.*
Rephaiah was the father of Eleasah.
Eleasah was the father of Azel.
38 Azel had six sons: Azrikam, Bokeru,
Ishmael, Shearіah, Obadiah, and Hanan.
These were the sons of Azel.
39 Azel's brother Eshek had three sons: the
first was Ulam, the second was Jeush, and
the third was Eliphelet. 40 Ulam's sons
were all mighty warriors and expert
archers. They had many sons and
grandsons—150 in all.

All these were descendants of Benjamin.

CHAPTER 9

So all Israel was listed in the genealogical records in *The Book of the Kings of Israel.*

The Returning Exiles

The people of Judah were exiled to Babylon because they were unfaithful to the LORD.
2 The first of the exiles to return to their property in their former towns were priests, Levites, Temple servants, and other Israelites.
3 Some of the people from the tribes of Judah, Benjamin, Ephraim, and Manasseh came and settled in Jerusalem.

4 One family that returned was that of Uthai
son of Ammihud, son of Omri, son of Imri,
son of Bani, a descendant of Perez son of
Judah.
5 Others returned from the Shilonite clan,
including Asaiah (the oldest) and his sons.
6 From the Zerahite clan, Jeuel returned with
his relatives.
In all, 690 families from the tribe of Judah returned.

7 From the tribe of Benjamin came Sallu son
of Meshullam, son of Hodaviah, son of
Hassenuah; 8 Ibneiah son of Jeroham; Elah
son of Uzzi, son of Micri; and Meshullam
son of Shephatiah, son of Reuel, son of
Ibnijah.
9 These men were all leaders of clans, and they were listed in their genealogical records. In all, 956 families from the tribe of Benjamin returned.

The Returning Priests

10 Among the priests who returned were
Jedaiah, Jehoiarib, Jakin, 11 Azariah son of
Hilkiah, son of Meshullam, son of Zadok,
son of Meraioth, son of Ahitub. Azariah
was the chief officer of the house of God.
12 Other returning priests were Adaiah son of
Jeroham, son of Pashhur, son of Malkijah,
and Maasai son of Adiel, son of Jahzerah,
son of Meshullam, son of Meshillemith,
son of Immer.
13 In all, 1,760 priests returned. They were heads of clans and very able men. They were responsible for ministering at the house of God.

The Returning Levites

14 The Levites who returned were Shemaiah
son of Hasshub, son of Azrikam, son of
Hashabiah, a descendant of Merari;
15 Bakbakkar; Heresh; Galal; Mattaniah son
of Mica, son of Zicri, son of Asaph;
16 Obadiah son of Shemaiah, son of Galal,
son of Jeduthun; and Berekiah son of Asa,
son of Elkanah, who lived in the area of
Netophah.

8:29a As in some Greek manuscripts (see also 9:35); Hebrew lacks *Jeiel*. **8:29b** Or *the founder of*. **8:30** As in some Greek manuscripts (see also 9:36); Hebrew lacks *Ner*. **8:31** As in parallel text at 9:37; Hebrew reads *Zeker*, a variant spelling of Zechariah. **8:32** As in parallel text at 9:38; Hebrew reads *Shimeah*, a variant spelling of Shimeam. **8:35** As in parallel text at 9:41; Hebrew reads *Tarea*, a variant spelling of Tahrea. **8:36** As in parallel text at 9:42; Hebrew reads *Jehoaddah*, a variant spelling of Jadah. **8:37** As in parallel text at 9:43; Hebrew reads *Raphah*, a variant spelling of Rephaiah.

[17]The gatekeepers who returned were
Shallum, Akkub, Talmon, Ahiman, and
their relatives. Shallum was the chief
gatekeeper. [18]Prior to this time, they were
responsible for the King's Gate on the east
side. These men served as gatekeepers for
the camps of the Levites. [19]Shallum was
the son of Kore, a descendant of
Abiasaph,* from the clan of Korah. He
and his relatives, the Korahites, were
responsible for guarding the entrance to
the sanctuary, just as their ancestors had
guarded the Tabernacle in the camp of
the LORD.
[20]Phinehas son of Eleazar had been in
charge of the gatekeepers in earlier times,
and the LORD had been with him. [21]And
later Zechariah son of Meshelemiah was
responsible for guarding the entrance to
the Tabernacle.*

[22]In all, there were 212 gatekeepers in those days, and they were listed according to the genealogies in their villages. David and Samuel the seer had appointed their ancestors because they were reliable men. [23]These gatekeepers and their descendants, by their divisions, were responsible for guarding the entrance to the house of the LORD when that house was a tent. [24]The gatekeepers were stationed on all four sides—east, west, north, and south. [25]Their relatives in the villages came regularly to share their duties for seven-day periods.

[26]The four chief gatekeepers, all Levites, were trusted officials, for they were responsible for the rooms and treasuries at the house of God. [27]They would spend the night around the house of God, since it was their duty to guard it and to open the gates every morning.

[28]Some of the gatekeepers were assigned to care for the various articles used in worship. They checked them in and out to avoid any loss. [29]Others were responsible for the furnishings, the items in the sanctuary, and the supplies, such as choice flour, wine, olive oil, frankincense, and spices. [30]But it was the priests who blended the spices. [31]Mattithiah, a Levite and the oldest son of Shallum the Korahite, was entrusted with baking the bread used in the offerings. [32]And some members of the clan of Kohath were in charge of preparing the bread to be set on the table each Sabbath day.

[33]The musicians, all prominent Levites, lived at the Temple. They were exempt from other responsibilities since they were on duty at all hours. [34]All these men lived in Jerusalem. They were the heads of Levite families and were listed as prominent leaders in their genealogical records.

King Saul's Family Tree

[35]Jeiel (the father of* Gibeon) lived in the
town of Gibeon. His wife's name was
Maacah, [36]and his oldest son was named
Abdon. Jeiel's other sons were Zur,
Kish, Baal, Ner, Nadab, [37]Gedor, Ahio,
Zechariah, and Mikloth. [38]Mikloth was the
father of Shimeam. All these families
lived near each other in Jerusalem.
[39] Ner was the father of Kish.
Kish was the father of Saul.
Saul was the father of Jonathan,
Malkishua, Abinadab, and Esh-baal.
[40] Jonathan was the father of Merib-baal.
Merib-baal was the father of Micah.
[41] The sons of Micah were Pithon, Melech,
Tahrea, and Ahaz.*
[42] Ahaz was the father of Jadah.*
Jadah was the father of Alemeth,
Azmaveth, and Zimri.
Zimri was the father of Moza.
[43] Moza was the father of Binea.
Binea's son was Rephaiah.
Rephaiah's son was Eleasah.
Eleasah's son was Azel.
[44]Azel had six sons, whose names were
Azrikam, Bokeru, Ishmael, Shearіah,
Obadiah, and Hanan. These were the sons
of Azel.

CHAPTER 10

The Death of King Saul

Now the Philistines attacked Israel, and the men of Israel fled before them. Many were slaughtered on the slopes of Mount Gilboa. [2]The Philistines closed in on Saul and his sons, and they killed three of his sons—Jonathan, Abinadab, and Malkishua. [3]The fighting grew

9:19 Hebrew *Ebiasaph*, a variant spelling of Abiasaph; compare Exod 6:24. **9:21** Hebrew *Tent of Meeting*. **9:35** Or *the founder of*. **9:41** As in Syriac version and Latin Vulgate (see also 8:35); Hebrew lacks *and Ahaz*. **9:42** As in some Hebrew manuscripts and Greek version (see also 8:36); Hebrew reads *Jarah*.

very fierce around Saul, and the Philistine archers caught up with him and wounded him.

[4]Saul groaned to his armor bearer, "Take your sword and kill me before these pagan Philistines come to taunt and torture me."

But his armor bearer was afraid and would not do it. So Saul took his own sword and fell on it. [5]When his armor bearer realized that Saul was dead, he fell on his own sword and died. [6]So Saul and his three sons died there together, bringing his dynasty to an end.

[7]When all the Israelites in the Jezreel Valley saw that their army had fled and that Saul and his sons were dead, they abandoned their towns and fled. So the Philistines moved in and occupied their towns.

[8]The next day, when the Philistines went out to strip the dead, they found the bodies of Saul and his sons on Mount Gilboa. [9]So they stripped off Saul's armor and cut off his head. Then they proclaimed the good news of Saul's death before their idols and to the people throughout the land of Philistia. [10]They placed his armor in the temple of their gods, and they fastened his head to the temple of Dagon.

[11]But when everyone in Jabesh-gilead heard about everything the Philistines had done to Saul, [12]all their mighty warriors brought the bodies of Saul and his sons back to Jabesh. Then they buried their bones beneath the great tree at Jabesh, and they fasted for seven days.

[13]So Saul died because he was unfaithful to the LORD. He failed to obey the LORD's command, and he even consulted a medium [14]instead of asking the LORD for guidance. So the LORD killed him and turned the kingdom over to David son of Jesse.

CHAPTER 11

David Becomes King of All Israel

Then all Israel gathered before David at Hebron and told him, "We are your own flesh and blood. [2]In the past,* even when Saul was king, you were the one who really led the forces of Israel. And the LORD your God told you, 'You will be the shepherd of my people Israel. You will be the leader of my people Israel.'"

[3]So there at Hebron, David made a covenant before the LORD with all the elders of Israel. And they anointed him king of Israel, just as the LORD had promised through Samuel.

David Captures Jerusalem

[4]Then David and all Israel went to Jerusalem (or Jebus, as it used to be called), where the Jebusites, the original inhabitants of the land, were living. [5]The people of Jebus taunted David, saying, "You'll never get in here!" But David captured the fortress of Zion, which is now called the City of David.

[6]David had said to his troops, "Whoever is first to attack the Jebusites will become the commander of my armies!" And Joab, the son of David's sister Zeruiah, was first to attack, so he became the commander of David's armies.

[7]David made the fortress his home, and that is why it is called the City of David. [8]He extended the city from the supporting terraces* to the surrounding area, while Joab rebuilt the rest of Jerusalem. [9]And David became more and more powerful, because the LORD of Heaven's Armies was with him.

David's Mightiest Warriors

[10]These are the leaders of David's mighty warriors. Together with all Israel, they decided to make David their king, just as the LORD had promised concerning Israel.

[11]Here is the record of David's mightiest warriors: The first was Jashobeam the Hacmonite, who was leader of the Three—the mightiest warriors among David's men.* He once used his spear to kill 300 enemy warriors in a single battle.

[12]Next in rank among the Three was Eleazar son of Dodai,* a descendant of Ahoah. [13]He was with David in the battle against the Philistines at Pas-dammim. The battle took place in a field full of barley, and the Israelite army fled. [14]But Eleazar and David* held their ground in the middle of the field and beat back the Philistines. So the LORD saved them by giving them a great victory.

[15]Once when David was at the rock near the cave of Adullam, the Philistine army was camped in the valley of Rephaim. The Three (who were among the Thirty—an elite group among David's fighting men) went down to

11:2 Or *For some time.* **11:8** Hebrew *the millo.* The meaning of the Hebrew is uncertain. **11:11** As in some Greek manuscripts (see also 2 Sam 23:8); Hebrew reads *leader of the Thirty,* or *leader of the captains.* **11:12** As in parallel text at 2 Sam 23:9 (see also 1 Chr 27:4); Hebrew reads *Dodo,* a variant spelling of Dodai. **11:14** Hebrew *they.*

meet him there. [16]David was staying in the stronghold at the time, and a Philistine detachment had occupied the town of Bethlehem.

Can I really count on God for success?

Eleazar and David held their ground. . . . So the LORD saved them by giving them a great victory.
1 CHRONICLES 11:14

[17]David remarked longingly to his men, "Oh, how I would love some of that good water from the well by the gate in Bethlehem." [18]So the Three broke through the Philistine lines, drew some water from the well by the gate in Bethlehem, and brought it back to David. But David refused to drink it. Instead, he poured it out as an offering to the LORD. [19]"God forbid that I should drink this!" he exclaimed. "This water is as precious as the blood of these men* who risked their lives to bring it to me." So David did not drink it. These are examples of the exploits of the Three.

David's Thirty Mighty Men

[20]Abishai, the brother of Joab, was the leader of the Thirty.* He once used his spear to kill 300 enemy warriors in a single battle. It was by such feats that he became as famous as the Three. [21]Abishai was the most famous of the Thirty and was their commander, though he was not one of the Three.

[22]There was also Benaiah son of Jehoiada, a valiant warrior from Kabzeel. He did many heroic deeds, which included killing two champions* of Moab. Another time, on a snowy day, he chased a lion down into a pit and killed it. [23]Once, armed only with a club, he killed an Egyptian warrior who was 7½ feet* tall and whose spear was as thick as a weaver's beam. Benaiah wrenched the spear from the Egyptian's hand and killed him with it. [24]Deeds like these made Benaiah as famous as the three mightiest warriors. [25]He was more honored than the other members of the Thirty, though he was not one of the Three. And David made him captain of his bodyguard.

[26]David's mighty warriors also included:

Asahel, Joab's brother;
Elhanan son of Dodo from Bethlehem;
[27] Shammah from Harod;*
Helez from Pelon;
[28] Ira son of Ikkesh from Tekoa;
Abiezer from Anathoth;
[29] Sibbecai from Hushah;
Zalmon* from Ahoah;
[30] Maharai from Netophah;
Heled son of Baanah from Netophah;
[31] Ithai son of Ribai from Gibeah
(in the land of Benjamin);
Benaiah from Pirathon;
[32] Hurai from near Nahale-gaash*;
Abi-albon* from Arabah;
[33] Azmaveth from Bahurim*;
Eliahba from Shaalbon;
[34] the sons of Jashen* from Gizon;
Jonathan son of Shagee from Harar;
[35] Ahiam son of Sharar* from Harar;
Eliphal son of Ur;
[36] Hepher from Mekerah;
Ahijah from Pelon;
[37] Hezro from Carmel;
Paarai* son of Ezbai;
[38] Joel, the brother of Nathan;
Mibhar son of Hagri;
[39] Zelek from Ammon;
Naharai from Beeroth, Joab's armor
bearer;
[40] Ira from Jattir;
Gareb from Jattir;
[41] Uriah the Hittite;
Zabad son of Ahlai;
[42] Adina son of Shiza, the Reubenite
leader who had thirty men with him;

11:19 Hebrew *Shall I drink the lifeblood of these men?* **11:20** As in Syriac version; Hebrew reads *the Three;* also in 11:21. **11:22** Or *two sons of Ariel.* **11:23** Hebrew *5 cubits* [2.3 meters]. **11:27** As in parallel text at 2 Sam 23:25; Hebrew reads *Shammoth from Haror.* **11:29** As in parallel text at 2 Sam 23:28; Hebrew reads *Ilai.* **11:32a** Or *from the ravines of Gaash.* **11:32b** As in parallel text at 2 Sam 23:31; Hebrew reads *Abiel.* **11:33** As in parallel text at 2 Sam 23:31; Hebrew reads *Baharum.* **11:34** As in parallel text at 2 Sam 23:32; Hebrew reads *sons of Hashem.* **11:35** As in parallel text at 2 Sam 23:33; Hebrew reads *son of Sacar.* **11:37** As in parallel text at 2 Sam 23:35; Hebrew reads *Naarai.*

43 Hanan son of Maacah;
Joshaphat from Mithna;
44 Uzzia from Ashtaroth;
Shama and Jeiel, the sons of Hotham,
from Aroer;
45 Jediael son of Shimri;
Joha, his brother, from Tiz;
46 Eliel from Mahavah;
Jeribai and Joshaviah, the sons of Elnaam;
Ithmah from Moab;
47 Eliel and Obed;
Jaasiel from Zobah.*

CHAPTER 12

Warriors Join David's Army

The following men joined David at Ziklag while he was hiding from Saul son of Kish. They were among the warriors who fought beside David in battle. 2 All of them were expert archers, and they could shoot arrows or sling stones with their left hand as well as their right. They were all relatives of Saul from the tribe of Benjamin. 3 Their leader was Ahiezer son of Shemaah from Gibeah; his brother Joash was second-in-command. These were the other warriors:

Jeziel and Pelet, sons of Azmaveth;
Beracah;
Jehu from Anathoth;
4 Ishmaiah from Gibeon, a famous warrior
and leader among the Thirty;
*Jeremiah, Jahaziel, Johanan, and Jozabad
from Gederah;
5 Eluzai, Jerimoth, Bealiah, Shemariah, and
Shephatiah from Haruph;
6 Elkanah, Isshiah, Azarel, Joezer, and
Jashobeam, who were Korahites;
7 Joelah and Zebadiah, sons of Jeroham
from Gedor.

8 Some brave and experienced warriors from the tribe of Gad also defected to David while he was at the stronghold in the wilderness. They were expert with both shield and spear, as fierce as lions and as swift as deer on the mountains.

9 Ezer was their leader.
Obadiah was second.
Eliab was third.
10 Mishmannah was fourth.
Jeremiah was fifth.
11 Attai was sixth.
Eliel was seventh.
12 Johanan was eighth.
Elzabad was ninth.
13 Jeremiah was tenth.
Macbannai was eleventh.

14 These warriors from Gad were army commanders. The weakest among them could take on a hundred regular troops, and the strongest could take on a thousand! 15 These were the men who crossed the Jordan River during its seasonal flooding at the beginning of the year and drove out all the people living in the lowlands on both the east and west banks.

16 Others from Benjamin and Judah came to David at the stronghold. 17 David went out to meet them and said, "If you have come in peace to help me, we are friends. But if you have come to betray me to my enemies when I am innocent, then may the God of our ancestors see it and punish you."

18 Then the Spirit came upon Amasai, the leader of the Thirty, and he said,

"We are yours, David!
We are on your side, son of Jesse.
Peace and prosperity be with you,
and success to all who help you,
for your God is the one who helps you."

So David let them join him, and he made them officers over his troops.

19 Some men from Manasseh defected from the Israelite army and joined David when he set out with the Philistines to fight against Saul. But as it turned out, the Philistine rulers refused to let David and his men go with them. After much discussion, they sent them back, for they said, "It will cost us our heads if David switches loyalties to Saul and turns against us."

20 Here is a list of the men from Manasseh who defected to David as he was returning to Ziklag: Adnah, Jozabad, Jediael, Michael, Jozabad, Elihu, and Zillethai. Each commanded 1,000 troops from the tribe of Manasseh. 21 They helped David chase down bands of raiders, for they were all brave and able warriors who became commanders in his army. 22 Day after day more men joined David until he had a great army, like the army of God.

23 These are the numbers of armed war-

11:47 Or *the Mezobaite.* **12:4** Verses 12:4b-40 are numbered 12:5-41 in Hebrew text.

riors who joined David at Hebron. They were all eager to see David become king instead of Saul, just as the LORD had promised.

[24]From the tribe of Judah, there were 6,800 warriors armed with shields and spears.
[25]From the tribe of Simeon, there were 7,100 brave warriors.
[26]From the tribe of Levi, there were 4,600 warriors. [27]This included Jehoiada, leader of the family of Aaron, who had 3,700 under his command. [28]This also included Zadok, a brave young warrior, with 22 members of his family who were all officers.
[29]From the tribe of Benjamin, Saul's relatives, there were 3,000 warriors. Most of the men from Benjamin had remained loyal to Saul until this time.
[30]From the tribe of Ephraim, there were 20,800 brave warriors, each highly respected in his own clan.
[31]From the half-tribe of Manasseh west of the Jordan, 18,000 men were designated by name to help David become king.
[32]From the tribe of Issachar, there were 200 leaders of the tribe with their relatives. All these men understood the signs of the times and knew the best course for Israel to take.
[33]From the tribe of Zebulun, there were 50,000 skilled warriors. They were fully armed and prepared for battle and completely loyal to David.
[34]From the tribe of Naphtali, there were 1,000 officers and 37,000 warriors armed with shields and spears.
[35]From the tribe of Dan, there were 28,600 warriors, all prepared for battle.
[36]From the tribe of Asher, there were 40,000 trained warriors, all prepared for battle.
[37]From the east side of the Jordan River—where the tribes of Reuben and Gad and the half-tribe of Manasseh lived—there were 120,000 troops armed with every kind of weapon.

[38]All these men came in battle array to Hebron with the single purpose of making David the king over all Israel. In fact, everyone in Israel agreed that David should be their king. [39]They feasted and drank with David for three days, for preparations had been made by their relatives for their arrival. [40]And people from as far away as Issachar, Zebulun, and Naphtali brought food on donkeys, camels, mules, and oxen. Vast supplies of flour, fig cakes, clusters of raisins, wine, olive oil, cattle, sheep, and goats were brought to the celebration. There was great joy throughout the land of Israel.

CHAPTER 13

David Attempts to Move the Ark

David consulted with all his officials, including the generals and captains of his army.* [2]Then he addressed the entire assembly of Israel as follows: "If you approve and if it is the will of the LORD our God, let us send messages to all the Israelites throughout the land, including the priests and Levites in their towns and pasturelands. Let us invite them to come and join us. [3]It is time to bring back the Ark of our God, for we neglected it during the reign of Saul."

[4]The whole assembly agreed to this, for the people could see it was the right thing to do. [5]So David summoned all Israel, from the Shihor Brook of Egypt in the south all the way to the town of Lebo-hamath in the north, to join in bringing the Ark of God from Kiriath-jearim. [6]Then David and all Israel went to Baalah of Judah (also called Kiriath-jearim) to bring back the Ark of God, which bears the name* of the LORD who is enthroned between the cherubim. [7]They placed the Ark of God on a new cart and brought it from Abinadab's house. Uzzah and Ahio were guiding the cart. [8]David and all Israel were celebrating before God with all their might, singing songs and playing all kinds of musical instruments—lyres, harps, tambourines, cymbals, and trumpets.

[9]But when they arrived at the threshing floor of Nacon,* the oxen stumbled, and Uzzah reached out his hand to steady the Ark. [10]Then the LORD's anger was aroused against Uzzah, and he struck him dead because he had laid his hand on the Ark. So Uzzah died there in the presence of God.

[11]David was angry because the LORD's anger had burst out against Uzzah. He named that place Perez-uzzah (which means "to

13:1 Hebrew *the commanders of thousands and of hundreds.* **13:6** Or *the Ark of God, where the Name is proclaimed—the name.*
13:9 As in parallel text at 2 Sam 6:6; Hebrew reads *Kidon.*

burst out against Uzzah"), as it is still called today.

12David was now afraid of God, and he asked, "How can I ever bring the Ark of God back into my care?" 13So David did not move the Ark into the City of David. Instead, he took it to the house of Obed-edom of Gath. 14The Ark of God remained there in Obed-edom's house for three months, and the LORD blessed the household of Obed-edom and everything he owned.

CHAPTER 14

David's Palace and Family

Then King Hiram of Tyre sent messengers to David, along with cedar timber, and stonemasons and carpenters to build him a palace. 2And David realized that the LORD had confirmed him as king over Israel and had greatly blessed his kingdom for the sake of his people Israel.

3Then David married more wives in Jerusalem, and they had more sons and daughters. 4These are the names of David's sons who were born in Jerusalem: Shammua, Shobab, Nathan, Solomon, 5Ibhar, Elishua, Elpelet, 6Nogah, Nepheg, Japhia, 7Elishama, Eliada,* and Eliphelet.

David Conquers the Philistines

8When the Philistines heard that David had been anointed king over all Israel, they mobilized all their forces to capture him. But David was told they were coming, so he marched out to meet them. 9The Philistines arrived and made a raid in the valley of Rephaim. 10So David asked God, "Should I go out to fight the Philistines? Will you hand them over to me?"

The LORD replied, "Yes, go ahead. I will hand them over to you."

11So David and his troops went up to Baal-perazim and defeated the Philistines there. "God did it!" David exclaimed. "He used me to burst through my enemies like a raging flood!" So they named that place Baal-perazim (which means "the Lord who bursts through"). 12The Philistines had abandoned their gods there, so David gave orders to burn them.

13But after a while the Philistines returned and raided the valley again. 14And once again David asked God what to do. "Do not attack them straight on," God replied. "Instead, circle around behind and attack them near the poplar* trees. 15When you hear a sound like marching feet in the tops of the poplar trees, go out and attack! That will be the signal that God is moving ahead of you to strike down the Philistine army." 16So David did what God commanded, and they struck down the Philistine army all the way from Gibeon to Gezer.

17So David's fame spread everywhere, and the LORD caused all the nations to fear David.

CHAPTER 15

Preparing to Move the Ark

David now built several buildings for himself in the City of David. He also prepared a place for the Ark of God and set up a special tent for it. 2Then he commanded, "No one except the Levites may carry the Ark of God. The LORD has chosen them to carry the Ark of the LORD and to serve him forever."

3Then David summoned all Israel to Jerusalem to bring the Ark of the LORD to the place he had prepared for it. 4This is the number of the descendants of Aaron (the priests) and the Levites who were called together:

5From the clan of Kohath, 120, with Uriel as their leader.
6From the clan of Merari, 220, with Asaiah as their leader.
7From the clan of Gershon,* 130, with Joel as their leader.
8From the descendants of Elizaphan, 200, with Shemaiah as their leader.
9From the descendants of Hebron, 80, with Eliel as their leader.
10From the descendants of Uzziel, 112, with Amminadab as their leader.

11Then David summoned the priests, Zadok and Abiathar, and these Levite leaders: Uriel, Asaiah, Joel, Shemaiah, Eliel, and Amminadab. 12He said to them, "You are the leaders of the Levite families. You must purify yourselves and all your fellow Levites, so you can bring the Ark of the LORD, the God of Israel, to the place I have prepared for it. 13Because you Levites did not carry the Ark the first time, the anger of the LORD our God burst out against us. We failed to ask God how

14:7 Hebrew *Beeliada*, a variant spelling of Eliada; compare 3:8 and parallel text at 2 Sam 5:16. **14:14** Or *aspen*, or *balsam*; also in 14:15. The exact identification of this tree is uncertain. **15:7** Hebrew *Gershom*, a variant spelling of Gershon.

to move it properly." [14]So the priests and the Levites purified themselves in order to bring the Ark of the LORD, the God of Israel, to Jerusalem. [15]Then the Levites carried the Ark of God on their shoulders with its carrying poles, just as the LORD had instructed Moses.

[16]David also ordered the Levite leaders to appoint a choir of Levites who were singers and musicians to sing joyful songs to the accompaniment of harps, lyres, and cymbals. [17]So the Levites appointed Heman son of Joel along with his fellow Levites: Asaph son of Berekiah, and Ethan son of Kushaiah from the clan of Merari. [18]The following men were chosen as their assistants: Zechariah, Jaaziel,* Shemiramoth, Jehiel, Unni, Eliab, Benaiah, Maaseiah, Mattithiah, Eliphelehu, Mikneiah, and the gatekeepers—Obed-edom and Jeiel.

[19]The musicians Heman, Asaph, and Ethan were chosen to sound the bronze cymbals. [20]Zechariah, Aziel, Shemiramoth, Jehiel, Unni, Eliab, Maaseiah, and Benaiah were chosen to play the harps.* [21]Mattithiah, Eliphelehu, Mikneiah, Obed-edom, Jeiel, and Azaziah were chosen to play the lyres.* [22]Kenaniah, the head Levite, was chosen as the choir leader because of his skill.

[23]Berekiah and Elkanah were chosen to guard* the Ark. [24]Shebaniah, Joshaphat, Nethanel, Amasai, Zechariah, Benaiah, and Eliezer—all of whom were priests—were chosen to blow the trumpets as they marched in front of the Ark of God. Obed-edom and Jehiah were chosen to guard the Ark.

Moving the Ark to Jerusalem

[25]Then David and the elders of Israel and the generals of the army* went to the house of Obed-edom to bring the Ark of the LORD's Covenant up to Jerusalem with a great celebration. [26]And because God was clearly helping the Levites as they carried the Ark of the LORD's Covenant, they sacrificed seven bulls and seven rams.

[27]David was dressed in a robe of fine linen, as were all the Levites who carried the Ark, and also the singers, and Kenaniah the choir leader. David was also wearing a priestly garment.* [28]So all Israel brought up the Ark of the LORD's Covenant with shouts of joy, the blowing of rams' horns and trumpets, the crashing of cymbals, and loud playing on harps and lyres.

[29]But as the Ark of the LORD's Covenant entered the City of David, Michal, the daughter of Saul, looked down from her window. When she saw King David skipping about and laughing with joy, she was filled with contempt for him.

CHAPTER 16

They brought the Ark of God and placed it inside the special tent David had prepared for it. And they presented burnt offerings and peace offerings to God. [2]When he had finished his sacrifices, David blessed the people in the name of the LORD. [3]Then he gave to every man and woman in all Israel a loaf of bread, a cake of dates,* and a cake of raisins.

[4]David appointed the following Levites to lead the people in worship before the Ark of the LORD—to invoke his blessings, to give thanks, and to praise the LORD, the God of Israel. [5]Asaph, the leader of this group, sounded the cymbals. Second to him was Zechariah, followed by Jeiel, Shemiramoth, Jehiel, Mattithiah, Eliab, Benaiah, Obed-edom, and Jeiel. They played the harps and lyres. [6]The priests, Benaiah and Jahaziel, played the trumpets regularly before the Ark of God's Covenant.

David's Song of Praise

[7]On that day David gave to Asaph and his fellow Levites this song of thanksgiving to the LORD:

[8] Give thanks to the LORD and proclaim
his greatness.
Let the whole world know what he
has done.
[9] Sing to him; yes, sing his praises.
Tell everyone about his wonderful
deeds.
[10] Exult in his holy name;
rejoice, you who worship the LORD.
[11] Search for the LORD and for his strength;
continually seek him.
[12] Remember the wonders he has performed,
his miracles, and the rulings he has
given,

15:18 As in several Hebrew manuscripts and Greek version (see also parallel lists in 15:20; 16:5); Masoretic Text reads *Zechariah ben Jaaziel.* **15:20** Hebrew adds *according to Alamoth,* which is probably a musical term. The meaning of the Hebrew is uncertain. **15:21** Hebrew adds *according to the Sheminith,* which is probably a musical term. The meaning of the Hebrew is uncertain. **15:23** Hebrew *chosen as gatekeepers for;* also in 15:24. **15:25** Hebrew *the commanders of thousands.* **15:27** Hebrew *a linen ephod.* **16:3** Or *a portion of meat.* The meaning of the Hebrew is uncertain.

It's a miracle!

A few months ago, the doctors thought that Tony's baby brother would die. Tony and his family and lots of friends from church prayed for the baby all the time. Amazingly, Tony's baby brother began getting better. After a few weeks he was completely cured. What do you think God would like to hear Tony say?

To see how King David responded after God had done so much for him, read 1 Chronicles 16:7-36.

(Sometimes when we ask for a miracle, God says no. We can tell God we're sad and upset, but even then we can thank him for caring about how we feel and for knowing what's best.)

13 you children of his servant Israel,
you descendants of Jacob, his
chosen ones.

14 He is the LORD our God.
His justice is seen throughout the land.

15 Remember his covenant forever—
the commitment he made to a
thousand generations.

16 This is the covenant he made with
Abraham
and the oath he swore to Isaac.

17 He confirmed it to Jacob as a decree,
and to the people of Israel as a never-
ending covenant:

18 "I will give you the land of Canaan
as your special possession."

19 He said this when you were few in
number,
a tiny group of strangers in Canaan.

20 They wandered from nation to nation,
from one kingdom to another.

21 Yet he did not let anyone oppress them.
He warned kings on their behalf:

22 "Do not touch my chosen people,
and do not hurt my prophets."

23 Let the whole earth sing to the LORD!
Each day proclaim the good news that
he saves.

24 Publish his glorious deeds among the
nations.
Tell everyone about the amazing things
he does.

25 Great is the LORD! He is most worthy of
praise!
He is to be feared above all gods.

26 The gods of other nations are mere idols,
but the LORD made the heavens!

27 Honor and majesty surround him;
strength and joy fill his dwelling.

28 O nations of the world, recognize the
LORD,
recognize that the LORD is glorious
and strong.

29 Give to the LORD the glory he deserves!
Bring your offering and come into his
presence.
Worship the LORD in all his holy splendor.

30 Let all the earth tremble before him.
The world stands firm and cannot be
shaken.

31 Let the heavens be glad, and the earth
rejoice!
Tell all the nations, "The LORD reigns!"

32 Let the sea and everything in it shout his
praise!

Let the fields and their crops burst out
with joy!
33 Let the trees of the forest rustle with
praise,
for the LORD is coming to judge the
earth.

34 Give thanks to the LORD, for he is good!
His faithful love endures forever.
35 Cry out, "Save us, O God of our salvation!
Gather and rescue us from among the
nations,
so we can thank your holy name
and rejoice and praise you."
36 Praise the LORD, the God of Israel,
who lives from everlasting to
everlasting!

And all the people shouted "Amen!" and praised the LORD.

Worship at Jerusalem and Gibeon

37 David arranged for Asaph and his fellow Levites to serve regularly before the Ark of the LORD's Covenant, doing whatever needed to be done each day. 38 This group included Obed-edom (son of Jeduthun), Hosah, and sixty-eight other Levites as gatekeepers.

39 Meanwhile, David stationed Zadok the priest and his fellow priests at the Tabernacle of the LORD at the place of worship in Gibeon, where they continued to minister before the LORD. 40 They sacrificed the regular burnt offerings to the LORD each morning and evening on the altar set aside for that purpose, obeying everything written in the Law of the LORD, as he had commanded Israel. 41 David also appointed Heman, Jeduthun, and the others chosen by name to give thanks to the LORD, for "his faithful love endures forever." 42 They used their trumpets, cymbals, and other instruments to accompany their songs of praise to God.* And the sons of Jeduthun were appointed as gatekeepers.

43 Then all the people returned to their homes, and David turned and went home to bless his own family.

CHAPTER 17

The LORD's Covenant Promise to David

When David was settled in his palace, he summoned Nathan the prophet. "Look," David said, "I am living in a beautiful cedar palace,* but the Ark of the LORD's Covenant is out there under a tent!"

2 Nathan replied to David, "Do whatever you have in mind, for God is with you."

3 But that same night God said to Nathan,

4 "Go and tell my servant David, 'This is what the LORD has declared: You are not the one to build a house for me to live in. 5 I have never lived in a house, from the day I brought the Israelites out of Egypt until this very day. My home has always been a tent, moving from one place to another in a Tabernacle. 6 Yet no matter where I have gone with the Israelites, I have never once complained to Israel's leaders,* the shepherds of my people. I have never asked them, "Why haven't you built me a beautiful cedar house?"'

7 "Now go and say to my servant David, 'This is what the LORD of Heaven's Armies has declared: I took you from tending sheep in the pasture and selected you to be the leader of my people Israel. 8 I have been with you wherever you have gone, and I have destroyed all your enemies before your eyes. Now I will make your name as famous as anyone who has ever lived on the earth! 9 And I will provide a homeland for my people Israel, planting them in a secure place where they will never be disturbed. Evil nations won't oppress them as they've done in the past, 10 starting from the time I appointed judges to rule my people Israel. And I will defeat all your enemies.

"'Furthermore, I declare that the LORD will build a house for you—a dynasty of kings! 11 For when you die and join your ancestors, I will raise up one of your descendants, one of your sons, and I will make his kingdom strong. 12 He is the one who will build a house—a temple—for me. And I will secure his throne forever. 13 I will be his father, and he will be my son. I will never take my favor from him as I took it from the one who ruled before you. 14 I will confirm him as king over my house and my kingdom for all time, and his throne will be secure forever.'"

16:42 Or *to accompany the sacred music;* or *to accompany singing to God.* 17:1 Hebrew *a house of cedar.* 17:6 As in Greek version (see also 2 Sam 7:7); Hebrew reads *judges.*

15 So Nathan went back to David and told him
everything the LORD had said in this vision.

David's Prayer of Thanks

16 Then King David went in and sat before the
LORD and prayed,

"Who am I, O LORD God, and what is my
family, that you have brought me this far?
17 And now, O God, in addition to
everything else, you speak of giving your
servant a lasting dynasty! You speak as
though I were someone very great,*
O LORD God!

18 "What more can I say to you about
the way you have honored me? You know
what your servant is really like. 19 For the
sake of your servant, O LORD, and
according to your will, you have done all
these great things and have made them
known.

20 "O LORD, there is no one like you. We
have never even heard of another God like
you! 21 What other nation on earth is like
your people Israel? What other nation,
O God, have you redeemed from slavery
to be your own people? You made a great
name for yourself when you redeemed
your people from Egypt. You performed
awesome miracles and drove out the
nations that stood in their way. 22 You
chose Israel to be your very own people
forever, and you, O LORD, became their
God.

23 "And now, O LORD, I am your servant;
do as you have promised concerning me
and my family. May it be a promise that
will last forever. 24 And may your name be
established and honored forever so that
everyone will say, 'The LORD of Heaven's
Armies, the God of Israel, is Israel's God!'
And may the house of your servant David
continue before you forever.

25 "O my God, I have been bold enough
to pray to you because you have revealed
to your servant that you will build a house
for him—a dynasty of kings! 26 For you are
God, O LORD. And you have promised
these good things to your servant. 27 And
now, it has pleased you to bless the house
of your servant, so that it will continue
forever before you. For when you grant
a blessing, O LORD, it is an eternal
blessing!"

CHAPTER 18

David's Military Victories

After this, David defeated and subdued the
Philistines by conquering Gath and its sur-
rounding towns. 2 David also conquered the
land of Moab, and the Moabites who were
spared became David's subjects and paid him
tribute money.

3 David also destroyed the forces of Had-
adezer, king of Zobah, as far as Hamath,*
when Hadadezer marched out to strengthen
his control along the Euphrates River. 4 David
captured 1,000 chariots, 7,000 charioteers,
and 20,000 foot soldiers. He crippled all
the chariot horses except enough for 100
chariots.

5 When Arameans from Damascus arrived
to help King Hadadezer, David killed 22,000
of them. 6 Then he placed several army garri-
sons* in Damascus, the Aramean capital, and
the Arameans became David's subjects and
paid him tribute money. So the LORD made
David victorious wherever he went.

7 David brought the gold shields of Hadade-
zer's officers to Jerusalem, 8 along with a large
amount of bronze from Hadadezer's towns of
Tebah* and Cun. Later Solomon melted the
bronze and molded it into the great bronze
basin called the Sea, the pillars, and the vari-
ous bronze articles used at the Temple.

9 When King Toi* of Hamath heard that
David had destroyed the entire army of King
Hadadezer of Zobah, 10 he sent his son Joram*
to congratulate King David for his successful
campaign. Hadadezer and Toi had been ene-
mies and were often at war. Joram presented
David with many gifts of gold, silver, and
bronze.

11 King David dedicated all these gifts to the
LORD, along with the silver and gold he had
taken from the other nations—from Edom,
Moab, Ammon, Philistia, and Amalek.

12 Abishai son of Zeruiah destroyed 18,000
Edomites in the Valley of Salt. 13 He placed
army garrisons in Edom, and all the Edomites

17:17 The meaning of the Hebrew is uncertain. **18:3** The meaning of the Hebrew is uncertain. **18:6** As in Greek version and Latin Vulgate (see also 2 Sam 8:6); Hebrew lacks *several army garrisons.* **18:8** Hebrew reads *Tibhath,* a variant spelling of Tebah; compare parallel text at 2 Sam 8:8. **18:9** As in parallel text at 2 Sam 8:9; Hebrew reads *Tou;* also in 18:10. **18:10** As in parallel text at 2 Sam 8:10; Hebrew reads *Hadoram,* a variant spelling of Joram.

became David's subjects. In fact, the LORD made David victorious wherever he went.

[14]So David reigned over all Israel and did what was just and right for all his people. [15]Joab son of Zeruiah was commander of the army. Jehoshaphat son of Ahilud was the royal historian. [16]Zadok son of Ahitub and Ahimelech* son of Abiathar were the priests. Seraiah* was the court secretary. [17]Benaiah son of Jehoiada was captain of the king's bodyguard.* And David's sons served as the king's chief assistants.

CHAPTER 19

David Defeats the Ammonites

Some time after this, King Nahash of the Ammonites died, and his son Hanun* became king. [2]David said, "I am going to show loyalty to Hanun because his father, Nahash, was always loyal to me." So David sent messengers to express sympathy to Hanun about his father's death.

But when David's ambassadors arrived in the land of Ammon, [3]the Ammonite commanders said to Hanun, "Do you really think these men are coming here to honor your father? No! David has sent them to spy out the land so they can come in and conquer it!" [4]So Hanun seized David's ambassadors and shaved them, cut off their robes at the buttocks, and sent them back to David in shame.

[5]When David heard what had happened to the men, he sent messengers to tell them, "Stay at Jericho until your beards grow out, and then come back." For they felt deep shame because of their appearance.

[6]When the people of Ammon realized how seriously they had angered David, Hanun and the Ammonites sent 75,000 pounds* of silver to hire chariots and charioteers from Aram-naharaim, Aram-maacah, and Zobah. [7]They also hired 32,000 chariots and secured the support of the king of Maacah and his army. These forces camped at Medeba, where they were joined by the Ammonite troops that Hanun had recruited from his own towns. [8]When David heard about this, he sent Joab and all his warriors to fight them. [9]The Ammonite troops came out and drew up their battle lines at the entrance of the city, while the other kings positioned themselves to fight in the open fields.

AMAZING FACTS

King Hanun made a big diplomatic boo-boo when he snubbed King David. And it cost him tons of silver—worth several million dollars.

1 CHRONICLES 19:6

[10]When Joab saw that he would have to fight on both the front and the rear, he chose some of Israel's elite troops and placed them under his personal command to fight the Arameans in the fields. [11]He left the rest of the army under the command of his brother Abishai, who was to attack the Ammonites. [12]"If the Arameans are too strong for me, then come over and help me," Joab told his brother. "And if the Ammonites are too strong for you, I will help you. [13]Be courageous! Let us fight bravely for our people and the cities of our God. May the LORD's will be done."

[14]When Joab and his troops attacked, the Arameans began to run away. [15]And when the Ammonites saw the Arameans running, they also ran from Abishai and retreated into the city. Then Joab returned to Jerusalem.

[16]The Arameans now realized that they were no match for Israel, so they sent messengers and summoned additional Aramean troops from the other side of the Euphrates River.* These troops were under the command of Shobach,* the commander of Hadadezer's forces.

[17]When David heard what was happening,

18:16a As in some Hebrew manuscripts, Syriac version, and Latin Vulgate (see also 2 Sam 8:17); most Hebrew manuscripts read *Abimelech.* **18:16b** As in parallel text at 2 Sam 8:17; Hebrew reads *Shavsha.* **18:17** Hebrew *of the Kerethites and Pelethites.* **19:1** As in parallel text at 2 Sam 10:1; Hebrew lacks *Hanun.* **19:6** Hebrew *1,000 talents* [34,000 kilograms]. **19:16a** Hebrew *the river.* **19:16b** As in parallel text at 2 Sam 10:16; Hebrew reads *Shophach;* also in 19:18.

he mobilized all Israel, crossed the Jordan River, and positioned his troops in battle formation. Then David engaged the Arameans in battle, and they fought against him. [18]But again the Arameans fled from the Israelites. This time David's forces killed 7,000 charioteers and 40,000 foot soldiers, including Shobach, the commander of their army. [19]When Hadadezer's allies saw that they had been defeated by Israel, they surrendered to David and became his subjects. After that, the Arameans were no longer willing to help the Ammonites.

CHAPTER 20

David Captures Rabbah

In the spring of the year,* when kings normally go out to war, Joab led the Israelite army in successful attacks against the land of the Ammonites. In the process he laid siege to the city of Rabbah. However, David stayed behind in Jerusalem.

[2]When David arrived at Rabbah, he removed the crown from the king's head,* and it was placed on his own head. The crown was made of gold and set with gems, and he found that it weighed seventy-five pounds.* David took a vast amount of plunder from the city. [3]He also made slaves of the people of Rabbah and forced them to labor with saws, iron picks, and iron axes.* That is how David dealt with the people of all the Ammonite towns. Then David and all the army returned to Jerusalem.

Battles against Philistine Giants

[4]After this, war broke out with the Philistines at Gezer. As they fought, Sibbecai from Hushah killed Saph,* a descendant of the giants,* and so the Philistines were subdued.

[5]During another battle with the Philistines, Elhanan son of Jair killed Lahmi, the brother of Goliath of Gath. The handle of Lahmi's spear was as thick as a weaver's beam!

[6]In another battle with the Philistines at Gath, they encountered a huge man with six fingers on each hand and six toes on each foot, twenty-four in all, who was also a descendant of the giants. [7]But when he defied and taunted Israel, he was killed by Jonathan, the son of David's brother Shimea.

[8]These Philistines were descendants of the giants of Gath, but David and his warriors killed them.

CHAPTER 21

David Takes a Census

Satan rose up against Israel and caused David to take a census of the people of Israel. [2]So David said to Joab and the commanders of the army, "Take a census of all the people of Israel—from Beersheba in the south to Dan in the north—and bring me a report so I may know how many there are."

[3]But Joab replied, "May the LORD increase the number of his people a hundred times over! But why, my lord the king, do you want to do this? Are they not all your servants? Why must you cause Israel to sin?"

[4]But the king insisted that they take the census, so Joab traveled throughout all Israel to count the people. Then he returned to Jerusalem [5]and reported the number of people to David. There were 1,100,000 warriors in all Israel who could handle a sword, and 470,000 in Judah. [6]But Joab did not include the tribes of Levi and Benjamin in the census because he was so distressed at what the king had made him do.

Judgment for David's Sin

[7]God was very displeased with the census, and he punished Israel for it. [8]Then David said to God, "I have sinned greatly by taking this census. Please forgive my guilt for doing this foolish thing."

[9]Then the LORD spoke to Gad, David's seer. This was the message: [10]"Go and say to David, 'This is what the LORD says: I will give you three choices. Choose one of these punishments, and I will inflict it on you.'"

[11]So Gad came to David and said, "These are the choices the LORD has given you. [12]You may choose three years of famine, three months of destruction by the sword of your enemies, or three days of severe plague as the angel of the LORD brings devastation throughout the land

20:1 Hebrew *At the turn of the year*. The first day of the year in the ancient Hebrew lunar calendar occurred in March or April. **20:2a** Or *from the head of Milcom* (as in Greek version and Latin Vulgate). Milcom, also called Molech, was the god of the Ammonites. **20:2b** Hebrew *1 talent* [34 kilograms]. **20:3** As in parallel text at 2 Sam 12:31; Hebrew reads *and cut them with saws, iron picks, and saws*. **20:4a** As in parallel text at 2 Sam 21:18; Hebrew reads *Sippai*. **20:4b** Hebrew *descendant of the Rephaites;* also in 20:6, 8.

of Israel. Decide what answer I should give the LORD who sent me."

[13]"I'm in a desperate situation!" David replied to Gad. "But let me fall into the hands of the LORD, for his mercy is very great. Do not let me fall into human hands."

[14]So the LORD sent a plague upon Israel, and 70,000 people died as a result. [15]And God sent an angel to destroy Jerusalem. But just as the angel was preparing to destroy it, the LORD relented and said to the death angel, "Stop! That is enough!" At that moment the angel of the LORD was standing by the threshing floor of Araunah* the Jebusite.

[16]David looked up and saw the angel of the LORD standing between heaven and earth with his sword drawn, reaching out over Jerusalem. So David and the leaders of Israel put on burlap to show their deep distress and fell face down on the ground. [17]And David said to God, "I am the one who called for the census! I am the one who has sinned and done wrong! But these people are as innocent as sheep—what have they done? O LORD my God, let your anger fall against me and my family, but do not destroy your people."

David Builds an Altar

[18]Then the angel of the LORD told Gad to instruct David to go up and build an altar to the LORD on the threshing floor of Araunah the Jebusite. [19]So David went up to do what the LORD had commanded him through Gad. [20]Araunah, who was busy threshing wheat at the time, turned and saw the angel there. His four sons, who were with him, ran away and hid. [21]When Araunah saw David approaching, he left his threshing floor and bowed before David with his face to the ground.

[22]David said to Araunah, "Let me buy this threshing floor from you at its full price. Then I will build an altar to the LORD there, so that he will stop the plague."

[23]"Take it, my lord the king, and use it as you wish," Araunah said to David. "I will give the oxen for the burnt offerings, and the threshing boards for wood to build a fire on the altar, and the wheat for the grain offering. I will give it all to you."

[24]But King David replied to Araunah, "No, I insist on buying it for the full price. I will not take what is yours and give it to the LORD. I will not present burnt offerings that have cost me nothing!" [25]So David gave Araunah 600 pieces of gold* in payment for the threshing floor.

[26]David built an altar there to the LORD and sacrificed burnt offerings and peace offerings. And when David prayed, the LORD answered him by sending fire from heaven to burn up the offering on the altar. [27]Then the LORD spoke to the angel, who put the sword back into its sheath.

[28]When David saw that the LORD had answered his prayer, he offered sacrifices there at Araunah's threshing floor. [29]At that time the Tabernacle of the LORD and the altar of burnt offering that Moses had made in the wilderness were located at the place of worship in Gibeon. [30]But David was not able to go there to inquire of God, because he was terrified by the drawn sword of the angel of the LORD.

CHAPTER 22

Then David said, "This will be the location for the Temple of the LORD God and the place of the altar for Israel's burnt offerings!"

AMAZING FACTS

Once it was a place to thresh wheat. But God chose it as the place for his Temple.

1 CHRONICLES 21:18; 22:1

Preparations for the Temple

[2]So David gave orders to call together the foreigners living in Israel, and he assigned them the task of preparing finished stone for building the Temple of God. [3]David provided

21:15 As in parallel text at 2 Sam 24:16; Hebrew reads *Ornan*, another name for Araunah; also in 21:18-28. **21:25** Hebrew *600 shekels of gold*, about 15 pounds or 6.8 kilograms in weight.

large amounts of iron for the nails that would be needed for the doors in the gates and for the clamps, and he gave more bronze than could be weighed. [4]He also provided innumerable cedar logs, for the men of Tyre and Sidon had brought vast amounts of cedar to David.

[5]David said, "My son Solomon is still young and inexperienced. And since the Temple to be built for the LORD must be a magnificent structure, famous and glorious throughout the world, I will begin making preparations for it now." So David collected vast amounts of building materials before his death.

[6]Then David sent for his son Solomon and instructed him to build a Temple for the LORD, the God of Israel. [7]"My son, I wanted to build a Temple to honor the name of the LORD my God," David told him. [8]"But the LORD said to me, 'You have killed many men in the battles you have fought. And since you have shed so much blood in my sight, you will not be the one to build a Temple to honor my name. [9]But you will have a son who will be a man of peace. I will give him peace with his enemies in all the surrounding lands. His name will be Solomon,* and I will give peace and quiet to Israel during his reign. [10]He is the one who will build a Temple to honor my name. He will be my son, and I will be his father. And I will secure the throne of his kingdom over Israel forever.'

[11]"Now, my son, may the LORD be with you and give you success as you follow his directions in building the Temple of the LORD your God. [12]And may the LORD give you wisdom and understanding, that you may obey the Law of the LORD your God as you rule over Israel. [13]For you will be successful if you carefully obey the decrees and regulations that the LORD gave to Israel through Moses. Be strong and courageous; do not be afraid or lose heart!

[14]"I have worked hard to provide materials for building the Temple of the LORD—nearly 4,000 tons of gold, 40,000 tons of silver,* and so much iron and bronze that it cannot be weighed. I have also gathered timber and stone for the walls, though you may need to add more. [15]You have a large number of skilled stonemasons and carpenters and craftsmen of every kind. [16]You have expert goldsmiths and silversmiths and workers of bronze and iron. Now begin the work, and may the LORD be with you!"

[17]Then David ordered all the leaders of Israel to assist Solomon in this project. [18]"The LORD your God is with you," he declared. "He has given you peace with the surrounding nations. He has handed them over to me, and they are now subject to the LORD and his people. [19]Now seek the LORD your God with all your heart and soul. Build the sanctuary of the LORD God so that you can bring the Ark of the LORD's Covenant and the holy vessels of God into the Temple built to honor the LORD's name."

CHAPTER 23

Duties of the Levites

When David was an old man, he appointed his son Solomon to be king over Israel. [2]David summoned all the leaders of Israel, together with the priests and Levites. [3]All the Levites who were thirty years old or older were counted, and the total came to 38,000. [4]Then David said, "From all the Levites, 24,000 will supervise the work at the Temple of the LORD. Another 6,000 will serve as officials and judges. [5]Another 4,000 will work as gatekeepers, and 4,000 will praise the LORD with the musical instruments I have made." [6]Then David divided the Levites into divisions named after the clans descended from the three sons of Levi—Gershon, Kohath, and Merari.

The Gershonites

[7]The Gershonite family units were defined by their lines of descent from Libni* and Shimei, the sons of Gershon. [8]Three of the descendants of Libni were Jehiel (the family leader), Zetham, and Joel. [9]These were the leaders of the family of Libni.

Three of the descendants of Shimei were Shelomoth, Haziel, and Haran. [10]Four other descendants of Shimei were Jahath, Ziza,* Jeush, and Beriah. [11]Jahath was the family leader, and Ziza was next. Jeush and Beriah were counted as a single family because neither had many sons.

22:9 *Solomon* sounds like and is probably derived from the Hebrew word for "peace." **22:14** Hebrew *100,000 talents* [3,400 metric tons] *of gold, 1,000,000 talents* [34,000 metric tons] *of silver*. **23:7** Hebrew *Ladan* (also in 23:8, 9), a variant spelling of Libni; compare 6:17. **23:10** As in Greek version and Latin Vulgate (see also 23:11); Hebrew reads *Zina*.

The Kohathites

12 Four of the descendants of Kohath were
Amram, Izhar, Hebron, and Uzziel.
13 The sons of Amram were Aaron and
Moses. Aaron and his descendants were
set apart to dedicate the most holy things,
to offer sacrifices in the LORD's presence,
to serve the LORD, and to pronounce
blessings in his name forever.
14 As for Moses, the man of God, his
sons were included with the tribe of Levi.
15 The sons of Moses were Gershom and
Eliezer. 16 The descendants of Gershom
included Shebuel, the family leader.
17 Eliezer had only one son, Rehabiah, the
family leader. Rehabiah had numerous
descendants.
18 The descendants of Izhar included
Shelomith, the family leader.
19 The descendants of Hebron included
Jeriah (the family leader), Amariah (the
second), Jahaziel (the third), and
Jekameam (the fourth).
20 The descendants of Uzziel included Micah
(the family leader) and Isshiah (the
second).

The Merarites

21 The descendants of Merari included Mahli
and Mushi.
The sons of Mahli were Eleazar and Kish.
22 Eleazar died with no sons, only
daughters. His daughters married their
cousins, the sons of Kish.
23 Three of the descendants of Mushi were
Mahli, Eder, and Jerimoth.

24 These were the descendants of Levi by clans, the leaders of their family groups, registered carefully by name. Each had to be twenty years old or older to qualify for service in the house of the LORD. 25 For David said, "The LORD, the God of Israel, has given us peace, and he will always live in Jerusalem. 26 Now the Levites will no longer need to carry the Tabernacle and its furnishings from place to place." 27 In accordance with David's final instructions, all the Levites twenty years old or older were registered for service.

28 The work of the Levites was to assist the priests, the descendants of Aaron, as they served at the house of the LORD. They also took care of the courtyards and side rooms, helped perform the ceremonies of purification, and served in many other ways in the house of God. 29 They were in charge of the sacred bread that was set out on the table, the choice flour for the grain offerings, the wafers made without yeast, the cakes cooked in olive oil, and the other mixed breads. They were also responsible to check all the weights and measures. 30 And each morning and evening they stood before the LORD to sing songs of thanks and praise to him. 31 They assisted with the burnt offerings that were presented to the LORD on Sabbath days, at new moon celebrations, and at all the appointed festivals. The required number of Levites served in the LORD's presence at all times, following all the procedures they had been given.

32 And so, under the supervision of the priests, the Levites watched over the Tabernacle and the Temple* and faithfully carried out their duties of service at the house of the LORD.

CHAPTER 24

Duties of the Priests

This is how Aaron's descendants, the priests, were divided into groups for service. The sons of Aaron were Nadab, Abihu, Eleazar, and Ithamar. 2 But Nadab and Abihu died before their father, and they had no sons. So only Eleazar and Ithamar were left to carry on as priests.

3 With the help of Zadok, who was a descendant of Eleazar, and of Ahimelech, who was a descendant of Ithamar, David divided Aaron's descendants into groups according to their various duties. 4 Eleazar's descendants were divided into sixteen groups and Ithamar's into eight, for there were more family leaders among the descendants of Eleazar.

5 All tasks were assigned to the various groups by means of sacred lots so that no preference would be shown, for there were many qualified officials serving God in the sanctuary from among the descendants of both Eleazar and Ithamar. 6 Shemaiah son of Nethanel, a Levite, acted as secretary and wrote down the names and assignments in the presence of the king, the officials, Zadok the priest, Ahimelech son of Abiathar, and the family leaders of the priests and Levites. The

23:32 Hebrew *the Tent of Meeting and the sanctuary.*

descendants of Eleazar and Ithamar took turns casting lots.

7 The first lot fell to Jehoiarib.
The second lot fell to Jedaiah.
8 The third lot fell to Harim.
The fourth lot fell to Seorim.
9 The fifth lot fell to Malkijah.
The sixth lot fell to Mijamin.
10 The seventh lot fell to Hakkoz.
The eighth lot fell to Abijah.
11 The ninth lot fell to Jeshua.
The tenth lot fell to Shecaniah.
12 The eleventh lot fell to Eliashib.
The twelfth lot fell to Jakim.
13 The thirteenth lot fell to Huppah.
The fourteenth lot fell to Jeshebeab.
14 The fifteenth lot fell to Bilgah.
The sixteenth lot fell to Immer.
15 The seventeenth lot fell to Hezir.
The eighteenth lot fell to Happizzez.
16 The nineteenth lot fell to Pethahiah.
The twentieth lot fell to Jehezkel.
17 The twenty-first lot fell to Jakin.
The twenty-second lot fell to Gamul.
18 The twenty-third lot fell to Delaiah.
The twenty-fourth lot fell to Maaziah.

19 Each group carried out its appointed duties in the house of the LORD according to the procedures established by their ancestor Aaron in obedience to the commands of the LORD, the God of Israel.

Family Leaders among the Levites

20 These were the other family leaders descended from Levi:

From the descendants of Amram, the leader was Shebuel.*
From the descendants of Shebuel, the leader was Jehdeiah.
21 From the descendants of Rehabiah, the leader was Isshiah.
22 From the descendants of Izhar, the leader was Shelomith.*
From the descendants of Shelomith, the leader was Jahath.
23 From the descendants of Hebron, Jeriah was the leader,* Amariah was second, Jahaziel was third, and Jekameam was fourth.
24 From the descendants of Uzziel, the leader was Micah.
From the descendants of Micah, the leader was Shamir, 25 along with Isshiah, the brother of Micah.
From the descendants of Isshiah, the leader was Zechariah.
26 From the descendants of Merari, the leaders were Mahli and Mushi.
From the descendants of Jaaziah, the leader was Beno.
27 From the descendants of Merari through Jaaziah, the leaders were Beno, Shoham, Zaccur, and Ibri.
28 From the descendants of Mahli, the leader was Eleazar, though he had no sons.
29 From the descendants of Kish, the leader was Jerahmeel.
30 From the descendants of Mushi, the leaders were Mahli, Eder, and Jerimoth.

These were the descendants of Levi in their various families. 31 Like the descendants of Aaron, they were assigned to their duties by means of sacred lots, without regard to age or rank. Lots were drawn in the presence of King

24:20 Hebrew *Shubael* (also in 24:20b), a variant spelling of Shebuel; compare 23:16 and 26:24. **24:22** Hebrew *Shelomoth* (also in 24:22b), a variant spelling of Shelomith; compare 23:18. **24:23** Hebrew *From the descendants of Jeriah;* compare 23:19.

IDEAS TO LIVE BY King David gave his son Solomon some good ideas to guide him through life (see 1 Chronicles 28:9-10). These same ideas are ones that any Christian can learn and follow.

1. Get to know God personally.
2. Learn God's commands and discover what he wants you to do.
3. Worship God with your whole heart.
4. Serve God with a willing mind.
5. Be faithful.
6. Don't become discouraged.

David, Zadok, Ahimelech, and the family leaders of the priests and the Levites.

CHAPTER 25

Duties of the Musicians

David and the army commanders then appointed men from the families of Asaph, Heman, and Jeduthun to proclaim God's messages to the accompaniment of lyres, harps, and cymbals. Here is a list of their names and their work:

2 From the sons of Asaph, there were Zaccur, Joseph, Nethaniah, and Asarelah. They worked under the direction of their father, Asaph, who proclaimed God's messages by the king's orders.

3 From the sons of Jeduthun, there were Gedaliah, Zeri, Jeshaiah, Shimei,* Hashabiah, and Mattithiah, six in all. They worked under the direction of their father, Jeduthun, who proclaimed God's messages to the accompaniment of the lyre, offering thanks and praise to the LORD.

4 From the sons of Heman, there were Bukkiah, Mattaniah, Uzziel, Shubael,* Jerimoth, Hananiah, Hanani, Eliathah, Giddalti, Romamti-ezer, Joshbekashah, Mallothi, Hothir, and Mahazioth. 5 All these were the sons of Heman, the king's seer, for God had honored him with fourteen sons and three daughters.

6 All these men were under the direction of their fathers as they made music at the house of the LORD. Their responsibilities included the playing of cymbals, harps, and lyres at the house of God. Asaph, Jeduthun, and Heman reported directly to the king. 7 They and their families were all trained in making music before the LORD, and each of them—288 in all—was an accomplished musician. 8 The musicians were appointed to their term of service by means of sacred lots, without regard to whether they were young or old, teacher or student.

9 The first lot fell to Joseph of the Asaph clan and twelve of his sons and relatives.*
The second lot fell to Gedaliah and twelve of his sons and relatives.
10 The third lot fell to Zaccur and twelve of his sons and relatives.
11 The fourth lot fell to Zeri* and twelve of his sons and relatives.
12 The fifth lot fell to Nethaniah and twelve of his sons and relatives.
13 The sixth lot fell to Bukkiah and twelve of his sons and relatives.
14 The seventh lot fell to Asarelah* and twelve of his sons and relatives.
15 The eighth lot fell to Jeshaiah and twelve of his sons and relatives.
16 The ninth lot fell to Mattaniah and twelve of his sons and relatives.
17 The tenth lot fell to Shimei and twelve of his sons and relatives.
18 The eleventh lot fell to Uzziel* and twelve of his sons and relatives.
19 The twelfth lot fell to Hashabiah and twelve of his sons and relatives.
20 The thirteenth lot fell to Shubael and twelve of his sons and relatives.
21 The fourteenth lot fell to Mattithiah and twelve of his sons and relatives.
22 The fifteenth lot fell to Jerimoth* and twelve of his sons and relatives.
23 The sixteenth lot fell to Hananiah and twelve of his sons and relatives.
24 The seventeenth lot fell to Joshbekashah* and twelve of his sons and relatives.
25 The eighteenth lot fell to Hanani and twelve of his sons and relatives.
26 The nineteenth lot fell to Mallothi and twelve of his sons and relatives.
27 The twentieth lot fell to Eliathah and twelve of his sons and relatives.
28 The twenty-first lot fell to Hothir and twelve of his sons and relatives.
29 The twenty-second lot fell to Giddalti and twelve of his sons and relatives.
30 The twenty-third lot fell to Mahazioth and twelve of his sons and relatives.
31 The twenty-fourth lot fell to Romamti-ezer and twelve of his sons and relatives.

25:3 As in one Hebrew manuscript and some Greek manuscripts (see also 25:17); most Hebrew manuscripts lack *Shimei*. **25:4** Hebrew *Shebuel*, a variant spelling of Shubael; compare 25:20. **25:9** As in Greek version; Hebrew lacks *and twelve of his sons and relatives*. **25:11** Hebrew *Izri*, a variant spelling of Zeri; compare 25:3. **25:14** Hebrew *Jesarelah*, a variant spelling of Asarelah; compare 25:2. **25:18** Hebrew *Azarel*, a variant spelling of Uzziel; compare 25:4. **25:22** Hebrew *Jeremoth*, a variant spelling of Jerimoth; compare 25:4. **25:24** Hebrew *Joshbekasha*, a variant spelling of Joshbekashah; compare 25:4.

CHAPTER 26

Duties of the Gatekeepers

These are the divisions of the gatekeepers:

From the Korahites, there was Meshelemiah
son of Kore, of the family of Abiasaph.*
2 The sons of Meshelemiah were Zechariah
(the oldest), Jediael (the second), Zebadiah
(the third), Jathniel (the fourth), 3 Elam (the
fifth), Jehohanan (the sixth), and Eliehoenai
(the seventh).
4 The sons of Obed-edom, also gatekeepers,
were Shemaiah (the oldest), Jehozabad
(the second), Joah (the third), Sacar (the
fourth), Nethanel (the fifth), 5 Ammiel (the
sixth), Issachar (the seventh), and
Peullethai (the eighth). God had richly
blessed Obed-edom.
6 Obed-edom's son Shemaiah had sons
with great ability who earned positions of
great authority in the clan. 7 Their names
were Othni, Rephael, Obed, and Elzabad.
Their relatives, Elihu and Semakiah, were
also very capable men.
8 All of these descendants of Obed-
edom, including their sons and
grandsons—sixty-two of them in all—
were very capable men, well qualified for
their work.
9 Meshelemiah's eighteen sons and relatives
were also very capable men.

10 Hosah, of the Merari clan, appointed
Shimri as the leader among his sons,
though he was not the oldest. 11 His other
sons included Hilkiah (the second),
Tebaliah (the third), and Zechariah (the
fourth). Hosah's sons and relatives, who
served as gatekeepers, numbered thirteen
in all.

12 These divisions of the gatekeepers were named for their family leaders, and like the other Levites, they served at the house of the LORD. 13 They were assigned by families for guard duty at the various gates, without regard to age or training, for it was all decided by means of sacred lots.

14 The responsibility for the east gate went to Meshelemiah* and his group. The north gate was assigned to his son Zechariah, a man of unusual wisdom. 15 The south gate went to Obed-edom, and his sons were put in charge of the storehouse. 16 Shuppim and Hosah were assigned the west gate and the gateway leading up to the Temple.* Guard duties were divided evenly. 17 Six Levites were assigned each day to the east gate, four to the north gate, four to the south gate, and two pairs at the storehouse. 18 Six were assigned each day to the west gate, four to the gateway leading up to the Temple, and two to the courtyard.*

19 These were the divisions of the gatekeepers from the clans of Korah and Merari.

Treasurers and Other Officials

20 Other Levites, led by Ahijah, were in charge of the treasuries of the house of God and the treasuries of the gifts dedicated to the LORD. 21 From the family of Libni* in the clan of Gershon, Jehiel* was the leader. 22 The sons of Jehiel, Zetham and his brother Joel, were in charge of the treasuries of the house of the LORD.

23 These are the leaders that descended from Amram, Izhar, Hebron, and Uzziel:

24 From the clan of Amram, Shebuel was a
descendant of Gershom son of Moses. He
was the chief officer of the treasuries.
25 His relatives through Eliezer were
Rehabiah, Jeshaiah, Joram, Zicri, and
Shelomoth.
26 Shelomoth and his relatives were in
charge of the treasuries containing the
gifts that King David, the family leaders,
and the generals and captains* and other
officers of the army had dedicated to the
LORD. 27 These men dedicated some of the
plunder they had gained in battle to
maintain the house of the LORD.
28 Shelomoth* and his relatives also cared
for the gifts dedicated to the LORD by
Samuel the seer, Saul son of Kish, Abner
son of Ner, and Joab son of Zeruiah. All
the other dedicated gifts were in their
care, too.
29 From the clan of Izhar came Kenaniah. He
and his sons were given administrative

26:1 As in Greek version (see also Exod 6:24); Hebrew reads *Asaph*. **26:14** Hebrew *Shelemiah*, a variant spelling of Meshelemiah; compare 26:2. **26:16** Or *the gate of Shalleketh on the upper road* (also in 26:18). The meaning of the Hebrew is uncertain. **26:18** Or *the colonnade*. The meaning of the Hebrew is uncertain. **26:21a** Hebrew *Ladan*, a variant spelling of Libni; compare 6:17. **26:21b** Hebrew *Jehieli* (also in 26:22), a variant spelling of Jehiel; compare 23:8. **26:26** Hebrew *the commanders of thousands and of hundreds*. **26:28** Hebrew *Shelomith*, a variant spelling of Shelomoth.

responsibilities* over Israel as officials
and judges.
30 From the clan of Hebron came Hashabiah.
He and his relatives—1,700 capable
men—were put in charge of the Israelite
lands west of the Jordan River. They were
responsible for all matters related to the
things of the LORD and the service of the
king in that area.
31 Also from the clan of Hebron came
Jeriah,* who was the leader of the
Hebronites according to the genealogical
records. (In the fortieth year of David's
reign, a search was made in the records,
and capable men from the clan of Hebron
were found at Jazer in the land of Gilead.)
32 There were 2,700 capable men among
the relatives of Jeriah. King David sent
them to the east side of the Jordan River
and put them in charge of the tribes of
Reuben and Gad and the half-tribe of
Manasseh. They were responsible for all
matters related to God and to the king.

CHAPTER 27

Military Commanders and Divisions

This is the list of Israelite generals and captains,* and their officers, who served the king by supervising the army divisions that were on duty each month of the year. Each division served for one month and had 24,000 troops.

2 Jashobeam son of Zabdiel was commander
of the first division of 24,000 troops,
which was on duty during the first month.
3 He was a descendant of Perez and was in
charge of all the army officers for the first
month.
4 Dodai, a descendant of Ahoah, was
commander of the second division of
24,000 troops, which was on duty during
the second month. Mikloth was his chief
officer.
5 Benaiah son of Jehoiada the priest was
commander of the third division of
24,000 troops, which was on duty during
the third month. 6 This was the Benaiah
who commanded David's elite military
group known as the Thirty. His son
Ammizabad was his chief officer.
7 Asahel, the brother of Joab, was
commander of the fourth division of
24,000 troops, which was on duty during
the fourth month. Asahel was succeeded
by his son Zebadiah.
8 Shammah* the Izrahite was commander of
the fifth division of 24,000 troops, which
was on duty during the fifth month.
9 Ira son of Ikkesh from Tekoa was
commander of the sixth division of
24,000 troops, which was on duty during
the sixth month.
10 Helez, a descendant of Ephraim from
Pelon, was commander of the seventh
division of 24,000 troops, which was on
duty during the seventh month.
11 Sibbecai, a descendant of Zerah from
Hushah, was commander of the eighth
division of 24,000 troops, which was on
duty during the eighth month.
12 Abiezer from Anathoth in the territory of
Benjamin was commander of the ninth
division of 24,000 troops, which was on
duty during the ninth month.
13 Maharai, a descendant of Zerah from
Netophah, was commander of the tenth
division of 24,000 troops, which was on
duty during the tenth month.
14 Benaiah from Pirathon in Ephraim was
commander of the eleventh division of
24,000 troops, which was on duty during
the eleventh month.
15 Heled,* a descendant of Othniel from
Netophah, was commander of the twelfth
division of 24,000 troops, which was on
duty during the twelfth month.

Leaders of the Tribes

16 The following were the tribes of Israel and
their leaders:

Tribe	*Leader*
Reuben	Eliezer son of Zicri
Simeon	Shephatiah son of Maacah
17 Levi	Hashabiah son of Kemuel
Aaron (the priests)	Zadok
18 Judah	Elihu (a brother of David)
Issachar	Omri son of Michael
19 Zebulun	Ishmaiah son of Obadiah
Naphtali	Jeremoth son of Azriel
20 Ephraim	Hoshea son of Azaziah
Manasseh (west)	Joel son of Pedaiah

26:29 Or *were given outside work;* or *were given work away from the Temple area.* **26:31** Hebrew *Jerijah,* a variant spelling of Jeriah; compare 23:19. **27:1** Hebrew *commanders of thousands and of hundreds.* **27:8** Hebrew *Shamhuth,* a variant spelling of Shammah; compare 11:27 and 2 Sam 23:25. **27:15** Hebrew *Heldai,* a variant spelling of Heled; compare 11:30 and 2 Sam 23:29.

21 Manasseh in Gilead (east) . . . . . Iddo son of Zechariah
Benjamin . . . . . Jaasiel son of Abner
22 Dan . . . . . Azarel son of Jeroham

These were the leaders of the tribes of Israel.

23 When David took his census, he did not count those who were younger than twenty years of age, because the LORD had promised to make the Israelites as numerous as the stars in heaven. 24 Joab son of Zeruiah began the census but never finished it because* the anger of God fell on Israel. The total number was never recorded in King David's official records.

Officials of David's Kingdom

25 Azmaveth son of Adiel was in charge of the palace treasuries.
Jonathan son of Uzziah was in charge of the regional treasuries throughout the towns, villages, and fortresses of Israel.
26 Ezri son of Kelub was in charge of the field workers who farmed the king's lands.
27 Shimei from Ramah was in charge of the king's vineyards.
Zabdi from Shepham was responsible for the grapes and the supplies of wine.
28 Baal-hanan from Geder was in charge of the king's olive groves and sycamore-fig trees in the foothills of Judah.*
Joash was responsible for the supplies of olive oil.
29 Shitrai from Sharon was in charge of the cattle on the Sharon Plain.
Shaphat son of Adlai was responsible for the cattle in the valleys.
30 Obil the Ishmaelite was in charge of the camels.
Jehdeiah from Meronoth was in charge of the donkeys.
31 Jaziz the Hagrite was in charge of the king's flocks of sheep and goats.
All these officials were overseers of King David's property.

32 Jonathan, David's uncle, was a wise counselor to the king, a man of great insight, and a scribe. Jehiel the Hacmonite was responsible for teaching the king's sons. 33 Ahithophel was the royal adviser. Hushai the Arkite was the king's friend. 34 Ahithophel was succeeded by Jehoiada son of Benaiah and by Abiathar. Joab was commander of the king's army.

NO ONE WILL EVER KNOW!

Walking home from the park one day, Jeremy saw a wallet lying by the sidewalk. The street was empty and quiet. When Jeremy picked up the wallet and looked inside, he was surprised to see lots of ten- and twenty-dollar bills! He thought about taking some or all of the money and then putting the wallet back on the ground. *After all,* Jeremy thought, *it's "finders—keepers, losers—weepers," and I really need the money. No one will ever know!*

What do you think Jeremy should do? Why? Read 1 Chronicles 28:9.

CHAPTER 28

David's Instructions to Solomon

David summoned all the officials of Israel to Jerusalem—the leaders of the tribes, the

27:24 Or *never finished it, and yet.* **27:28** Hebrew *the Shephelah.*

I grew up in a Christian home. In fact, I don't remember life apart from doing things like going to church, praying with my parents, and attending VBS.

As I got into middle school and high school, I used to worry sometimes that my beliefs weren't really my own. I thought, *Am I really a Christian, or am I just blindly following whatever my parents believe?* Even though I felt like I knew Christianity inside and out, I was beginning to have a lot of questions that needed answers.

I think some of my Christian friends started to rebel because they felt the same way. I could easily have gone that way, too. Instead, I decided to take action. I was determined to learn exactly what God's Word says so that I'd know what I believed and why.

The first decision I made was to attend a Bible study instead of going to youth group. That was *my* choice, not my parents'. They let me decide for myself, and I really appreciated that. I saw that being independent from my parents didn't mean forgetting about God.

You know, that was David's advice to his son Solomon. He told him, "Get to know God yourself." All of us have to own our faith—and not just borrow the beliefs of our parents or grandparents or friends. I figured if that was what David had to say (and God made sure it was recorded in the Bible), then I had better pay attention!

I guess it's all a part of growing up—spiritually. If I want to grow up and not have my parents be so strict, I need to show them I can make good decisions on my own. It's the same with God. As I learn to trust him and depend on him, he will give me more responsibilities.

Check out what David said to his son Solomon in 1 Chronicles 28:9-10 regarding his faith. Take a look at 1 John 2:12-14 to see how we can grow in faith as we grow in our relationship with Jesus.

commanders of the army divisions, the other generals and captains,* the overseers of the royal property and livestock, the palace officials, the mighty men, and all the other brave warriors in the kingdom. [2]David rose to his feet and said: "My brothers and my people! It was my desire to build a temple where the Ark of the LORD's Covenant, God's footstool, could rest permanently. I made the necessary preparations for building it, [3]but God said to me, 'You must not build a temple to honor my name, for you are a warrior and have shed much blood.'

[4]"Yet the LORD, the God of Israel, has chosen me from among all my father's family to be king over Israel forever. For he has chosen the tribe of Judah to rule, and from among the families of Judah he chose my father's family. And from among my father's sons the LORD was pleased to make me king over all Israel. [5]And from among my sons—for the LORD has given me many—he chose Solomon to succeed me on the throne of Israel and to rule over the LORD's kingdom. [6]He said to me, 'Your son Solomon will build my Temple and its courtyards, for I have chosen him as my son, and I will be his father. [7]And if he continues to obey my commands and regulations as he does now, I will make his kingdom last forever.'

[8]"So now, with God as our witness, and in the sight of all Israel—the LORD's assembly—I give you this charge. Be careful to obey all the commands of the LORD your God, so that you may continue to possess this good land and leave it to your children as a permanent inheritance.

[9]"And Solomon, my son, learn to know the God of your ancestors intimately. Worship and serve him with your whole heart and a willing mind. For the LORD sees every heart and knows every plan and thought. If you seek him, you will find him. But if you forsake him, he will reject you forever. [10]So take this seriously. The LORD has chosen you to build a Temple as his sanctuary. Be strong, and do the work."

[11]Then David gave Solomon the plans for the Temple and its surroundings, including the entry room, the storerooms, the upstairs rooms, the inner rooms, and the inner sanctuary—which was the place of atonement. [12]David also gave Solomon all the plans he had in mind* for the courtyards of the LORD's Temple, the outside rooms, the treasuries, and the rooms for the gifts dedicated to the LORD. [13]The king also gave Solomon the instructions concerning the work of the various divisions of priests and Levites in the Temple of the LORD. And he gave specifications for the items in the Temple that were to be used for worship.

[14]David gave instructions regarding how much gold and silver should be used to make the items needed for service. [15]He told Solomon the amount of gold needed for the gold lampstands and lamps, and the amount of silver for the silver lampstands and lamps, depending on how each would be used. [16]He designated the amount of gold for the table on which the Bread of the Presence would be placed and the amount of silver for other tables.

[17]David also designated the amount of gold for the solid gold meat hooks used to handle the sacrificial meat and for the basins, pitchers, and dishes, as well as the amount of silver for every dish. [18]He designated the amount of refined gold for the altar of incense. Finally, he gave him a plan for the LORD's "chariot"—the gold cherubim* whose wings were stretched out over the Ark of the LORD's Covenant. [19]"Every part of this plan," David told Solomon, "was given to me in writing from the hand of the LORD.*"

[20]Then David continued, "Be strong and courageous, and do the work. Don't be afraid or discouraged, for the LORD God, my God, is with you. He will not fail you or forsake you. He will see to it that all the work related to the Temple of the LORD is finished correctly. [21]The various divisions of priests and Levites will serve in the Temple of God. Others with skills of every kind will volunteer, and the officials and the entire nation are at your command."

CHAPTER 29

Gifts for Building the Temple

Then King David turned to the entire assembly and said, "My son Solomon, whom God has clearly chosen as the next king of Israel, is still young and inexperienced. The work

28:1 Hebrew *the commanders of thousands and commanders of hundreds.* **28:12** Or *the plans of the spirit that was with him.*
28:18 Hebrew *for the gold cherub chariot.* **28:19** Or *was written under the direction of the LORD.*

ahead of him is enormous, for the Temple he will build is not for mere mortals—it is for the LORD God himself! [2]Using every resource at my command, I have gathered as much as I could for building the Temple of my God. Now there is enough gold, silver, bronze, iron, and wood, as well as great quantities of onyx, other precious stones, costly jewels, and all kinds of fine stone and marble.

When I face a tough situation, where can I find strength?

Power and might are in your hand, and at your discretion people are made great and given strength.
1 CHRONICLES 29:12

[3]"And now, because of my devotion to the Temple of my God, I am giving all of my own private treasures of gold and silver to help in the construction. This is in addition to the building materials I have already collected for his holy Temple. [4]I am donating more than 112 tons of gold* from Ophir and 262 tons of refined silver* to be used for overlaying the walls of the buildings [5]and for the other gold and silver work to be done by the craftsmen. Now then, who will follow my example and give offerings to the LORD today?"

[6]Then the family leaders, the leaders of the tribes of Israel, the generals and captains of the army,* and the king's administrative officers all gave willingly. [7]For the construction of the Temple of God, they gave about 188 tons of gold,* 10,000 gold coins,* 375 tons of silver,* 675 tons of bronze,* and 3,750 tons of iron.* [8]They also contributed numerous precious stones, which were deposited in the treasury of the house of the LORD under the care of Jehiel, a descendant of Gershon. [9]The people rejoiced over the offerings, for they had given freely and wholeheartedly to the LORD, and King David was filled with joy.

David's Prayer of Praise

[10]Then David praised the LORD in the presence of the whole assembly:

"O LORD, the God of our ancestor Israel,*
may you be praised forever and ever!
[11]Yours, O LORD, is the greatness, the power, the glory, the victory, and the majesty. Everything in the heavens and on earth is yours, O LORD, and this is your kingdom. We adore you as the one who is over all things. [12]Wealth and honor come from you alone, for you rule over everything. Power and might are in your hand, and at your discretion people are made great and given strength.

[13]"O our God, we thank you and praise your glorious name! [14]But who am I, and who are my people, that we could give anything to you? Everything we have has come from you, and we give you only what you first gave us! [15]We are here for only a moment, visitors and strangers in the land as our ancestors were before us. Our days on earth are like a passing shadow, gone so soon without a trace.

[16]"O LORD our God, even this material we have gathered to build a Temple to honor your holy name comes from you! It all belongs to you! [17]I know, my God, that you examine our hearts and rejoice when you find integrity there. You know I have done all this with good motives, and I have watched your people offer their gifts willingly and joyously.

[18]"O LORD, the God of our ancestors Abraham, Isaac, and Israel, make your people always want to obey you. See to it that their love for you never changes. [19]Give my son Solomon the wholehearted desire to obey all your commands, laws, and decrees, and to do everything necessary to build this Temple, for which I have made these preparations."

[20]Then David said to the whole assembly, "Give praise to the LORD your God!" And the entire assembly praised the LORD, the God of

29:4a Hebrew *3,000 talents* [102 metric tons] *of gold*. **29:4b** Hebrew *7,000 talents* [238 metric tons] *of silver*. **29:6** Hebrew *the commanders of thousands and commanders of hundreds*. **29:7a** Hebrew *5,000 talents* [170 metric tons] *of gold*. **29:7b** Hebrew *10,000 darics* [a Persian coin] *of gold*, about 185 pounds or 84 kilograms in weight. **29:7c** Hebrew *10,000 talents* [340 metric tons] *of silver*. **29:7d** Hebrew *18,000 talents* [612 metric tons] *of bronze*. **29:7e** Hebrew *100,000 talents* [3,400 metric tons] *of iron*. **29:10** *Israel* is the name that God gave to Jacob.

their ancestors, and they bowed low and knelt before the LORD and the king.

Solomon Named as King

[21]The next day they brought 1,000 bulls, 1,000 rams, and 1,000 male lambs as burnt offerings to the LORD. They also brought liquid offerings and many other sacrifices on behalf of all Israel. [22]They feasted and drank in the LORD's presence with great joy that day.

And again they crowned David's son Solomon as their new king. They anointed him before the LORD as their leader, and they anointed Zadok as priest. [23]So Solomon took the throne of the LORD in place of his father, David, and he succeeded in everything, and all Israel obeyed him. [24]All the officials, the warriors, and the sons of King David pledged their loyalty to King Solomon. [25]And the LORD exalted Solomon in the sight of all Israel, and he gave Solomon greater royal splendor than any king in Israel before him.

Summary of David's Reign

[26]So David son of Jesse reigned over all Israel. [27]He reigned over Israel for forty years, seven of them in Hebron and thirty-three in Jerusalem. [28]He died at a ripe old age, having enjoyed long life, wealth, and honor. Then his son Solomon ruled in his place.

[29]All the events of King David's reign, from beginning to end, are written in *The Record of Samuel the Seer*, *The Record of Nathan the Prophet*, and *The Record of Gad the Seer*. [30]These accounts include the mighty deeds of his reign and everything that happened to him and to Israel and to all the surrounding kingdoms.

2 CHRONICLES

WHO
Solomon, the queen of Sheba, Rehoboam, Asa, Jehoshaphat, Jehoram, Joash, Uzziah, Ahaz, Hezekiah, Manasseh, Josiah, and Huldah.

WHERE
In Israel and Judah.

WHEN
This book was written about 430 BC, but it describes events that happened around the same time as those in 1 and 2 Kings.

WHY
To unify Judah by showing the way God wants his people to live.

If my people . . . will humble themselves and pray . . . and turn from their wicked ways, I will hear from heaven and will forgive their sins. 2 CHRONICLES 7:14

Parents discipline their children so they learn right from wrong. God also disciplined his children. God's prophets warned them if they didn't change, God would punish them. The people didn't listen, so God sent armies to conquer Israel.

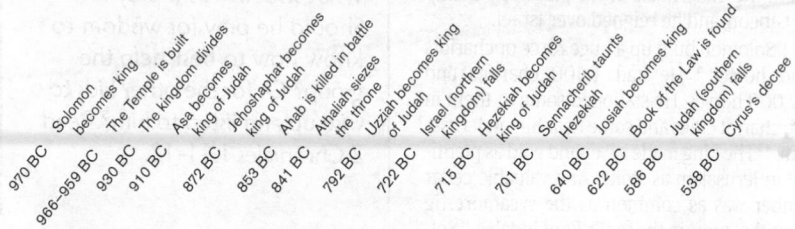

LEARN THE LESSON GOD WAS TEACHING ISRAEL: LISTEN TO AND OBEY GOD.

CHAPTER 1

Solomon Asks for Wisdom

Solomon son of David took firm control of his kingdom, for the LORD his God was with him and made him very powerful.

[2]Solomon called together all the leaders of Israel—the generals and captains of the army,* the judges, and all the political and clan leaders. [3]Then he led the entire assembly to the place of worship in Gibeon, for God's Tabernacle* was located there. (This was the Tabernacle that Moses, the LORD's servant, had made in the wilderness.)

[4]David had already moved the Ark of God from Kiriath-jearim to the tent he had prepared for it in Jerusalem. [5]But the bronze altar

1:2 Hebrew *the commanders of thousands and of hundreds.* 1:3 Hebrew *Tent of Meeting;* also in 1:6, 13.

made by Bezalel son of Uri and grandson of Hur was there* at Gibeon in front of the Tabernacle of the LORD. So Solomon and the people gathered in front of it to consult the LORD.* 6There in front of the Tabernacle, Solomon went up to the bronze altar in the LORD's presence and sacrificed 1,000 burnt offerings on it.

7That night God appeared to Solomon and said, "What do you want? Ask, and I will give it to you!"

8Solomon replied to God, "You showed faithful love to David, my father, and now you have made me king in his place. 9O LORD God, please continue to keep your promise to David my father, for you have made me king over a people as numerous as the dust of the earth! 10Give me the wisdom and knowledge to lead them properly,* for who could possibly govern this great people of yours?"

11God said to Solomon, "Because your greatest desire is to help your people, and you did not ask for wealth, riches, fame, or even the death of your enemies or a long life, but rather you asked for wisdom and knowledge to properly govern my people—12I will certainly give you the wisdom and knowledge you requested. But I will also give you wealth, riches, and fame such as no other king has had before you or will ever have in the future!"

13Then Solomon returned to Jerusalem from the Tabernacle at the place of worship in Gibeon, and he reigned over Israel.

14Solomon built up a huge force of chariots and horses.* He had 1,400 chariots and 12,000 horses. He stationed some of them in the chariot cities and some near him in Jerusalem. 15The king made silver and gold as plentiful in Jerusalem as stone. And valuable cedar timber was as common as the sycamore-fig trees that grow in the foothills of Judah.* 16Solomon's horses were imported from Egypt* and from Cilicia*; the king's traders acquired them from Cilicia at the standard price. 17At that time chariots from Egypt could be purchased for 600 pieces of silver,* and horses for 150 pieces of silver.* They were then exported to the kings of the Hittites and the kings of Aram.

PRAY FOR WHAT?

For weeks, Yoshi had been working on a social studies project with a group of kids. He had a really good idea for presenting the information they had collected, but the other kids thought it meant too much work. One kid even called Yoshi a stuck-up bully! That evening Yoshi told his dad about what happened. Dad said, "Let's pray about it." What should Yoshi pray for? Should he pray for wisdom to know how to best help the group? Or for the other kids to wise up and listen to him? Read 2 Chronicles 1:11-12.

CHAPTER 2

Preparations for Building the Temple

1*Solomon decided to build a Temple to honor the name of the LORD, and also a royal palace for himself. 2*He enlisted a force of 70,000 laborers, 80,000 men to quarry stone in the hill country, and 3,600 foremen.

1:5a As in Greek version and Latin Vulgate, and some Hebrew manuscripts. Masoretic Text reads *he placed*. **1:5b** Hebrew *to consult him*. **1:10** Hebrew *to go out and come in before this people*. **1:14** Or *charioteers;* also in 1:14b. **1:15** Hebrew *the Shephelah*. **1:16a** Possibly *Muzur*, a district near Cilicia; also in 1:17. **1:16b** Hebrew *Kue*, probably another name for Cilicia. **1:17a** Hebrew *600 [shekels] of silver*, about 15 pounds or 6.8 kilograms in weight. **1:17b** Hebrew *150 [shekels]*, about 3.8 pounds or 1.7 kilograms in weight. **2:1** Verse 2:1 is numbered 1:18 in Hebrew text. **2:2** Verses 2:2-18 are numbered 2:1-17 in Hebrew text.

[3]Solomon also sent this message to King Hiram* at Tyre:

"Send me cedar logs as you did for my father, David, when he was building his palace. [4]I am about to build a Temple to honor the name of the LORD my God. It will be a place set apart to burn fragrant incense before him, to display the special sacrificial bread, and to sacrifice burnt offerings each morning and evening, on the Sabbaths, at new moon celebrations, and at the other appointed festivals of the LORD our God. He has commanded Israel to do these things forever.

[5]"This must be a magnificent Temple because our God is greater than all other gods. [6]But who can really build him a worthy home? Not even the highest heavens can contain him! So who am I to consider building a Temple for him, except as a place to burn sacrifices to him?

[7]"So send me a master craftsman who can work with gold, silver, bronze, and iron, as well as with purple, scarlet, and blue cloth. He must be a skilled engraver who can work with the craftsmen of Judah and Jerusalem who were selected by my father, David.

[8]"Also send me cedar, cypress, and red sandalwood* logs from Lebanon, for I know that your men are without equal at cutting timber in Lebanon. I will send my men to help them. [9]An immense amount of timber will be needed, for the Temple I am going to build will be very large and magnificent. [10]In payment for your woodcutters, I will send 100,000 bushels of crushed wheat, 100,000 bushels of barley,* 110,000 gallons of wine, and 110,000 gallons of olive oil.*"

[11]King Hiram sent this letter of reply to Solomon:

"It is because the LORD loves his people that he has made you their king! [12]Praise the LORD, the God of Israel, who made the heavens and the earth! He has given King David a wise son, gifted with skill and understanding, who will build a Temple for the LORD and a royal palace for himself.

[13]"I am sending you a master craftsman named Huram-abi, who is extremely talented. [14]His mother is from the tribe of Dan in Israel, and his father is from Tyre. He is skillful at making things from gold, silver, bronze, and iron, and he also works with stone and wood. He can work with purple, blue, and scarlet cloth and fine linen. He is also an engraver and can follow any design given to him. He will work with your craftsmen and those appointed by my lord David, your father.

[15]"Send along the wheat, barley, olive oil, and wine that my lord has mentioned. [16]We will cut whatever timber you need from the Lebanon mountains and will float the logs in rafts down the coast of the Mediterranean Sea* to Joppa. From there you can transport the logs up to Jerusalem."

[17]Solomon took a census of all foreigners in the land of Israel, like the census his father had taken, and he counted 153,600. [18]He assigned 70,000 of them as common laborers, 80,000 as quarry workers in the hill country, and 3,600 as foremen.

CHAPTER 3

Solomon Builds the Temple

So Solomon began to build the Temple of the LORD in Jerusalem on Mount Moriah, where the LORD had appeared to David, his father. The Temple was built on the threshing floor of Araunah* the Jebusite, the site that David had selected. [2]The construction began in midspring,* during the fourth year of Solomon's reign.

[3]These are the dimensions Solomon used for the foundation of the Temple of God (using the old standard of measurement).* It was 90 feet long and 30 feet wide.* [4]The entry room at the front of the Temple was

2:3 Hebrew *Huram,* a variant spelling of Hiram; also in 2:11. **2:8** Or *juniper;* Hebrew reads *algum,* perhaps a variant spelling of *almug;* compare 9:10-11 and parallel text at 1 Kgs 10:11-12. **2:10a** Hebrew *20,000 cors* [3,640 kiloliters] *of crushed wheat, 20,000 cors of barley.* **2:10b** Hebrew *20,000 baths* [420 kiloliters] *of wine, and 20,000 baths of olive oil.* **2:16** Hebrew *the sea.* **3:1** Hebrew reads *Ornan,* a variant spelling of Araunah; compare 2 Sam 24:16. **3:2** Hebrew *on the second day of the second month.* This day of the ancient Hebrew lunar calendar occurred in April or May. **3:3a** The "old standard of measurement" was a cubit equal to 18 inches [46 centimeters]. The new standard was a cubit of approximately 21 inches [53 centimeters]. **3:3b** Hebrew *60 cubits* [27.6 meters] *long and 20 cubits* [9.2 meters] *wide.*

30 feet* wide, running across the entire width of the Temple, and 30 feet* high. He overlaid the inside with pure gold.

5He paneled the main room of the Temple with cypress wood, overlaid it with fine gold, and decorated it with carvings of palm trees and chains. 6He decorated the walls of the Temple with beautiful jewels and with gold from the land of Parvaim. 7He overlaid the beams, thresholds, walls, and doors throughout the Temple with gold, and he carved figures of cherubim on the walls.

8He made the Most Holy Place 30 feet wide, corresponding to the width of the Temple, and 30 feet deep. He overlaid its interior with 23 tons* of fine gold. 9The gold nails that were used weighed 20 ounces* each. He also overlaid the walls of the upper rooms with gold.

10He made two figures shaped like cherubim, overlaid them with gold, and placed them in the Most Holy Place. 11The total wingspan of the two cherubim standing side by side was 30 feet. One wing of the first figure was 7½ feet* long, and it touched the Temple wall. The other wing, also 7½ feet long, touched one of the wings of the second figure. 12In the same way, the second figure had one wing 7½ feet long that touched the opposite wall. The other wing, also 7½ feet long, touched the wing of the first figure. 13So the wingspan of the two cherubim side by side was 30 feet. They stood on their feet and faced out toward the main room of the Temple.

14Across the entrance of the Most Holy Place he hung a curtain made of fine linen, decorated with blue, purple, and scarlet thread and embroidered with figures of cherubim.

15For the front of the Temple, he made two pillars that were 27 feet* tall, each topped by a capital extending upward another 7½ feet. 16He made a network of interwoven chains and used them to decorate the tops of the pillars. He also made 100 decorative pomegranates and attached them to the chains. 17Then he set up the two pillars at the entrance of the Temple, one to the south of the entrance and the other to the north. He named the one on the south Jakin, and the one on the north Boaz.*

CHAPTER 4

Furnishings for the Temple

Solomon* also made a bronze altar 30 feet long, 30 feet wide, and 15 feet high.* 2Then he cast a great round basin, 15 feet across from rim to rim, called the Sea. It was 7½ feet deep and about 45 feet in circumference.* 3It was encircled just below its rim by two rows of figures that resembled oxen. There were about six oxen per foot* all the way around, and they were cast as part of the basin.

4The Sea was placed on a base of twelve bronze oxen, all facing outward. Three faced north, three faced west, three faced south, and three faced east, and the Sea rested on them. 5The walls of the Sea were about three inches* thick, and its rim flared out like a cup and resembled a water lily blossom. It could hold about 16,500 gallons* of water.

6He also made ten smaller basins for washing the utensils for the burnt offerings. He set five on the south side and five on the north. But the priests washed themselves in the Sea.

7He then cast ten gold lampstands according to the specifications that had been given, and he put them in the Temple. Five were placed against the south wall, and five were placed against the north wall.

8He also built ten tables and placed them in the Temple, five along the south wall and five along the north wall. Then he molded 100 gold basins.

9He then built a courtyard for the priests, and also the large outer courtyard. He made doors for the courtyard entrances and overlaid them with bronze. 10The great bronze basin called the Sea was placed near the southeast corner of the Temple.

11Huram-abi also made the necessary washbasins, shovels, and bowls.

So at last Huram-abi completed everything

3:4a Hebrew *20 cubits* [9.2 meters]; also in 3:8, 11, 13. **3:4b** As in some Greek and Syriac manuscripts, which read *20 cubits* [9.2 meters]; Hebrew reads *120 [cubits]*, which is 180 feet or 55 meters. **3:8** Hebrew *600 talents* [20.4 metric tons]. **3:9** Hebrew *50 shekels* [570 grams]. **3:11** Hebrew *5 cubits* [2.3 meters]; also in 3:11b, 12, 15. **3:15** As in Syriac version (see also 1 Kgs 7:15; 2 Kgs 25:17; Jer 52:21), which reads *18 cubits* [8.3 meters]; Hebrew reads *35 cubits*, which is 52.5 feet or 16.5 meters. **3:17** *Jakin* probably means "he establishes"; *Boaz* probably means "in him is strength." **4:1a** Or *Huram-abi*; Hebrew reads *He*. **4:1b** Hebrew *20 cubits* [9.2 meters] *long, 20 cubits wide, and 10 cubits* [4.6 meters] *high*. **4:2** Hebrew *10 cubits* [4.6 meters] *across . . . 5 cubits* [2.3 meters] *deep and 30 cubits* [13.8 meters] *in circumference*. **4:3** Or *20 oxen per meter*; Hebrew reads *10 per cubit*. **4:5a** Hebrew *a handbreadth* [8 centimeters]. **4:5b** Hebrew *3,000 baths* [63 kiloliters].

King Solomon had assigned him to make for
the Temple of God:

12 the two pillars;
the two bowl-shaped capitals on top of
the pillars;
the two networks of interwoven chains
that decorated the capitals;
13 the 400 pomegranates that hung from
the chains on the capitals (two rows of
pomegranates for each of the chain
networks that decorated the capitals
on top of the pillars);
14 the water carts holding the basins;
15 the Sea and the twelve oxen under it;
16 the ash buckets, the shovels, the meat
hooks, and all the related articles.

Huram-abi made all these things of burnished bronze for the Temple of the LORD, just as King Solomon had directed. 17 The king had them cast in clay molds in the Jordan Valley between Succoth and Zarethan.* 18 Solomon used such great quantities of bronze that its weight could not be determined.

19 Solomon also made all the furnishings for the Temple of God:

the gold altar;
the tables for the Bread of the Presence;
20 the lampstands and their lamps of solid
gold, to burn in front of the Most Holy
Place as prescribed;
21 the flower decorations, lamps, and
tongs—all of the purest gold;
22 the lamp snuffers, bowls, dishes, and
incense burners—all of solid gold;
the doors for the entrances to the Most
Holy Place and the main room of the
Temple, overlaid with gold.

CHAPTER 5

So Solomon finished all his work on the Temple of the LORD. Then he brought all the gifts his father, David, had dedicated—the silver, the gold, and the various articles—and he stored them in the treasuries of the Temple of God.

The Ark Brought to the Temple

2 Solomon then summoned to Jerusalem the elders of Israel and all the heads of tribes—the leaders of the ancestral families of Israel. They were to bring the Ark of the LORD's Covenant to the Temple from its location in the City of David, also known as Zion. 3 So all the men of Israel assembled before the king at the annual Festival of Shelters, which is held in early autumn.*

4 When all the elders of Israel arrived, the Levites picked up the Ark. 5 The priests and Levites brought up the Ark along with the special tent* and all the sacred items that had been in it. 6 There, before the Ark, King Solomon and the entire community of Israel sacrificed so many sheep, goats, and cattle that no one could keep count!

7 Then the priests carried the Ark of the LORD's Covenant into the inner sanctuary of the Temple—the Most Holy Place—and placed it beneath the wings of the cherubim. 8 The cherubim spread their wings over the Ark, forming a canopy over the Ark and its carrying poles. 9 These poles were so long that their ends could be seen from the Temple's main room—the Holy Place*—but not from the outside. They are still there to this day. 10 Nothing was in the Ark except the two stone tablets that Moses had placed in it at Mount Sinai,* where the LORD made a covenant with the people of Israel when they left Egypt.

11 Then the priests left the Holy Place. All the priests who were present had purified themselves, whether or not they were on duty that day. 12 And the Levites who were musicians—Asaph, Heman, Jeduthun, and all their sons and brothers—were dressed in fine linen robes and stood at the east side of the altar playing cymbals, lyres, and harps. They were joined by 120 priests who were playing trumpets. 13 The trumpeters and singers performed together in unison to praise and give thanks to the LORD. Accompanied by trumpets, cymbals, and other instruments, they raised their voices and praised the LORD with these words:

"He is good!
His faithful love endures forever!"

At that moment a thick cloud filled the Temple of the LORD. 14 The priests could not continue their service because of the cloud,

4:17 As in parallel text at 1 Kgs 7:46; Hebrew reads *Zeredah*. **5:3** Hebrew *at the festival that is in the seventh month*. The Festival of Shelters began on the fifteenth day of the seventh month of the ancient Hebrew lunar calendar. This day occurred in late September, October, or early November. **5:5** Hebrew *the Tent of Meeting*; i.e., the tent mentioned in 2 Sam 6:17 and 1 Chr 16:1. **5:9** As in some Hebrew manuscripts and Greek version (see also 1 Kgs 8:8); Masoretic Text reads *from the Ark in front of the Most Holy Place*. **5:10** Hebrew *Horeb*, another name for Sinai.

for the glorious presence of the LORD filled the Temple of God.

CHAPTER 6

Solomon Praises the LORD

Then Solomon prayed, "O LORD, you have said that you would live in a thick cloud of darkness. [2]Now I have built a glorious Temple for you, a place where you can live forever!"

[3]Then the king turned around to the entire community of Israel standing before him and gave this blessing: [4]"Praise the LORD, the God of Israel, who has kept the promise he made to my father, David. For he told my father, [5]'From the day I brought my people out of the land of Egypt, I have never chosen a city among any of the tribes of Israel as the place where a Temple should be built to honor my name. Nor have I chosen a king to lead my people Israel. [6]But now I have chosen Jerusalem as the place for my name to be honored, and I have chosen David to be king over my people Israel.'"

[7]Then Solomon said, "My father, David, wanted to build this Temple to honor the name of the LORD, the God of Israel. [8]But the LORD told him, 'You wanted to build the Temple to honor my name. Your intention is good, [9]but you are not the one to do it. One of your own sons will build the Temple to honor me.'

[10]"And now the LORD has fulfilled the promise he made, for I have become king in my father's place, and now I sit on the throne of Israel, just as the LORD promised. I have built this Temple to honor the name of the LORD, the God of Israel. [11]There I have placed the Ark, which contains the covenant that the LORD made with the people of Israel."

Solomon's Prayer of Dedication

[12]Then Solomon stood before the altar of the LORD in front of the entire community of Israel, and he lifted his hands in prayer. [13]Now Solomon had made a bronze platform 7½ feet long, 7½ feet wide, and 4½ feet high* and had placed it at the center of the Temple's outer courtyard. He stood on the platform, and then he knelt in front of the entire community of Israel and lifted his hands toward heaven. [14]He prayed,

"O LORD, God of Israel, there is no God like you in all of heaven and earth. You keep your covenant and show unfailing love to all who walk before you in wholehearted devotion. [15]You have kept your promise to your servant David, my father. You made that promise with your own mouth, and with your own hands you have fulfilled it today.

[16]"And now, O LORD, God of Israel, carry out the additional promise you made to your servant David, my father. For you said to him, 'If your descendants guard their behavior and faithfully follow my Law as you have done, one of them will always sit on the throne of Israel.' [17]Now, O LORD, God of Israel, fulfill this promise to your servant David.

[18]"But will God really live on earth among people? Why, even the highest heavens cannot contain you. How much less this Temple I have built! [19]Nevertheless, listen to my prayer and my plea, O LORD my God. Hear the cry and the prayer that your servant is making to you. [20]May you watch over this Temple day and night, this place where you have said you would put your name. May you always hear the prayers I make toward this place. [21]May you hear the humble and earnest requests from me and your people Israel when we pray toward this place. Yes, hear us from heaven where you live, and when you hear, forgive.

[22]"If someone wrongs another person and is required to take an oath of innocence in front of your altar at this Temple, [23]then hear from heaven and judge between your servants—the accuser and the accused. Pay back the guilty as they deserve. Acquit the innocent because of their innocence.

[24]"If your people Israel are defeated by their enemies because they have sinned against you, and if they turn back and acknowledge your name and pray to you here in this Temple, [25]then hear from heaven and forgive the sin of your people Israel and return them to this land you gave to them and to their ancestors.

[26]"If the skies are shut up and there is

6:13 Hebrew *5 cubits* [2.3 meters] *long, 5 cubits wide, and 3 cubits* [1.4 meters] *high.*

no rain because your people have sinned
against you, and if they pray toward this
Temple and acknowledge your name and
turn from their sins because you have
punished them, [27] then hear from heaven
and forgive the sins of your servants, your
people Israel. Teach them to follow the
right path, and send rain on your land that
you have given to your people as their
special possession.

[28] "If there is a famine in the land or a
plague or crop disease or attacks of
locusts or caterpillars, or if your people's
enemies are in the land besieging their
towns—whatever disaster or disease there
is—[29] and if your people Israel pray about
their troubles or sorrow, raising their
hands toward this Temple, [30] then hear
from heaven where you live, and forgive.
Give your people what their actions
deserve, for you alone know each human
heart. [31] Then they will fear you and walk
in your ways as long as they live in the
land you gave to our ancestors.

[32] "In the future, foreigners who do not
belong to your people Israel will hear of
you. They will come from distant lands
when they hear of your great name and
your strong hand and your powerful arm.
And when they pray toward this Temple,
[33] then hear from heaven where you live,
and grant what they ask of you. In this
way, all the people of the earth will come
to know and fear you, just as your own
people Israel do. They, too, will know that
this Temple I have built honors your
name.

[34] "If your people go out where you send
them to fight their enemies, and if they
pray to you by turning toward this city you
have chosen and toward this Temple I
have built to honor your name, [35] then
hear their prayers from heaven and
uphold their cause.

[36] "If they sin against you—and who has
never sinned?—you might become angry
with them and let their enemies conquer
them and take them captive to a foreign
land far away or near. [37] But in that land
of exile, they might turn to you in
repentance and pray, 'We have sinned,
done evil, and acted wickedly.' [38] If they
turn to you with their whole heart and
soul in the land of their captivity and
pray toward the land you gave to their
ancestors—toward this city you have
chosen, and toward this Temple I have
built to honor your name—[39] then hear
their prayers and their petitions from
heaven where you live, and uphold their
cause. Forgive your people who have
sinned against you.

[40] "O my God, may your eyes be open
and your ears attentive to all the prayers
made to you in this place.

[41] "And now arise, O LORD God, and enter
your resting place,
along with the Ark, the symbol of
your power.
May your priests, O LORD God, be
clothed with salvation;
may your loyal servants rejoice in
your goodness.
[42] O LORD God, do not reject the king you
have anointed.
Remember your unfailing love for
your servant David."

CHAPTER 7

The Dedication of the Temple

When Solomon finished praying, fire flashed
down from heaven and burned up the burnt
offerings and sacrifices, and the glorious pres-
ence of the LORD filled the Temple. [2] The
priests could not enter the Temple of the LORD
because the glorious presence of the LORD
filled it. [3] When all the people of Israel saw the
fire coming down and the glorious presence
of the LORD filling the Temple, they fell face
down on the ground and worshiped and
praised the LORD, saying,

"He is good!
His faithful love endures forever!"

[4] Then the king and all the people offered
sacrifices to the LORD. [5] King Solomon offered
a sacrifice of 22,000 cattle and 120,000
sheep and goats. And so the king and all the
people dedicated the Temple of God. [6] The
priests took their assigned positions, and so
did the Levites who were singing, "His faithful
love endures forever!" They accompanied the
singing with music from the instruments
King David had made for praising the LORD.

Across from the Levites, the priests blew the trumpets, while all Israel stood.

7 Solomon then consecrated the central area of the courtyard in front of the LORD's Temple. He offered burnt offerings and the fat of peace offerings there, because the bronze altar he had built could not hold all the burnt offerings, grain offerings, and sacrificial fat.

8 For the next seven days Solomon and all Israel celebrated the Festival of Shelters.* A large congregation had gathered from as far away as Lebo-hamath in the north and the Brook of Egypt in the south. 9 On the eighth day they had a closing ceremony, for they had celebrated the dedication of the altar for seven days and the Festival of Shelters for seven days. 10 Then at the end of the celebration,* Solomon sent the people home. They were all joyful and glad because the LORD had been so good to David and to Solomon and to his people Israel.

The LORD's Response to Solomon

11 So Solomon finished the Temple of the LORD, as well as the royal palace. He completed everything he had planned to do in the construction of the Temple and the palace. 12 Then one night the LORD appeared to Solomon and said,

"I have heard your prayer and have chosen this Temple as the place for making sacrifices. 13 At times I might shut up the heavens so that no rain falls, or command grasshoppers to devour your crops, or send plagues among you. 14 Then if my people who are called by my name will humble themselves and pray and seek my face and turn from their wicked ways, I will hear from heaven and will forgive their sins and restore their land. 15 My eyes will be open and my ears attentive to every prayer made in this place. 16 For I have chosen this Temple and set it apart to be holy—a place where my name will be honored forever. I will always watch over it, for it is dear to my heart.

17 "As for you, if you faithfully follow me as David your father did, obeying all my commands, decrees, and regulations, 18 then I will establish the throne of your dynasty. For I made this covenant with your father, David, when I said, 'One of your descendants will always rule over Israel.'

19 "But if you or your descendants abandon me and disobey the decrees and commands I have given you, and if you serve and worship other gods, 20 then I will uproot the people from this land that I have given them. I will reject this Temple that I have made holy to honor my name. I will make it an object of mockery and ridicule among the nations. 21 And though this Temple is impressive now, all who pass by will be appalled. They will ask, 'Why did the LORD do such terrible things to this land and to this Temple?'

22 "And the answer will be, 'Because his people abandoned the LORD, the God of their ancestors, who brought them out of Egypt, and they worshiped other gods instead and bowed down to them. That is why he has brought all these disasters on them.'"

Why should I confess my sins to God?

If my people . . . will humble themselves and pray . . . I will hear from heaven and will forgive their sins.

2 CHRONICLES 7:14

CHAPTER 8

Solomon's Many Achievements

It took Solomon twenty years to build the LORD's Temple and his own royal palace. At the end of that time, 2 Solomon turned his attention to rebuilding the towns that King Hiram* had given him, and he settled Israelites in them.

3 Solomon also fought against the town of Hamath-zobah and conquered it. 4 He rebuilt Tadmor in the wilderness and built towns in the region of Hamath as supply centers. 5 He fortified the towns of Upper Beth-horon and Lower Beth-horon, rebuilding their walls and installing barred gates. 6 He also rebuilt Baal-

7:8 Hebrew *the festival* (also in 7:9); see note on 5:3. **7:10** Hebrew *Then on the twenty-third day of the seventh month.* This day of the ancient Hebrew lunar calendar occurred in October or early November. **8:2** Hebrew *Huram,* a variant spelling of Hiram; also in 8:18.

ath and other supply centers and constructed towns where his chariots and horses* could be stationed. He built everything he desired in Jerusalem and Lebanon and throughout his entire realm.

[7]There were still some people living in the land who were not Israelites, including the Hittites, Amorites, Perizzites, Hivites, and Jebusites. [8]These were descendants of the nations whom the people of Israel had not destroyed. So Solomon conscripted them for his labor force, and they serve in the labor force to this day. [9]But Solomon did not conscript any of the Israelites for his labor force. Instead, he assigned them to serve as fighting men, officers in his army, commanders of his chariots, and charioteers. [10]King Solomon appointed 250 of them to supervise the people.

[11]Solomon moved his wife, Pharaoh's daughter, from the City of David to the new palace he had built for her. He said, "My wife must not live in King David's palace, for the Ark of the LORD has been there, and it is holy ground."

[12]Then Solomon presented burnt offerings to the LORD on the altar he had built for him in front of the entry room of the Temple. [13]He offered the sacrifices for the Sabbaths, the new moon festivals, and the three annual festivals—the Passover celebration, the Festival of Harvest,* and the Festival of Shelters—as Moses had commanded.

[14]In assigning the priests to their duties, Solomon followed the regulations of his father, David. He also assigned the Levites to lead the people in praise and to assist the priests in their daily duties. And he assigned the gatekeepers to their gates by their divisions, following the commands of David, the man of God. [15]Solomon did not deviate in any way from David's commands concerning the priests and Levites and the treasuries.

[16]So Solomon made sure that all the work related to building the Temple of the LORD was carried out, from the day its foundation was laid to the day of its completion.

[17]Later Solomon went to Ezion-geber and Elath,* ports along the shore of the Red Sea* in the land of Edom. [18]Hiram sent him ships commanded by his own officers and manned by experienced crews of sailors. These ships sailed to Ophir with Solomon's men and brought back to Solomon almost seventeen tons* of gold.

CHAPTER 9

Visit of the Queen of Sheba

When the queen of Sheba heard of Solomon's fame, she came to Jerusalem to test him with hard questions. She arrived with a large group of attendants and a great caravan of camels loaded with spices, large quantities of gold, and precious jewels. When she met with Solomon, she talked with him about everything she had on her mind. [2]Solomon had answers for all her questions; nothing was too hard for him to explain to her. [3]When the queen of Sheba realized how wise Solomon was, and when she saw the palace he had built, [4]she was overwhelmed. She was also amazed at the food on his tables, the organization of his officials and their splendid clothing, the cup-bearers and their robes, and the burnt offerings Solomon made at the Temple of the LORD.

[5]She exclaimed to the king, "Everything I heard in my country about your achievements* and wisdom is true! [6]I didn't believe what was said until I arrived here and saw it with my own eyes. In fact, I had not heard the half of your great wisdom! It is far beyond what I was told. [7]How happy your people must be! What a privilege for your officials to stand here day after day, listening to your wisdom! [8]Praise the LORD your God, who delights in you and has placed you on the throne as king to rule for him. Because God loves Israel and desires this kingdom to last forever, he has made you king over them so you can rule with justice and righteousness."

[9]Then she gave the king a gift of 9,000 pounds* of gold, great quantities of spices, and precious jewels. Never before had there been spices as fine as those the queen of Sheba gave to King Solomon.

[10](In addition, the crews of Hiram and Solomon brought gold from Ophir, and they also brought red sandalwood* and precious jewels. [11]The king used the sandalwood to make steps* for the Temple of the LORD and the royal palace, and to construct lyres and

8:6 Or *and charioteers*. **8:13** Or *Festival of Weeks*. **8:17a** As in Greek version (see also 2 Kgs 14:22; 16:6); Hebrew reads *Eloth*, a variant spelling of Elath. **8:17b** As in parallel text at 1 Kgs 9:26; Hebrew reads *the sea*. **8:18** Hebrew *450 talents* [15.3 metric tons]. **9:5** Hebrew *your words*. **9:9** Hebrew *120 talents* [4,000 kilograms]. **9:10** Hebrew *algum wood* (also in 9:11); perhaps a variant spelling of *almug*. Compare parallel text at 1 Kgs 10:11-12. **9:11** Or *gateways*. The meaning of the Hebrew is uncertain.

harps for the musicians. Never before had such beautiful things been seen in Judah.)

12 King Solomon gave the queen of Sheba whatever she asked for—gifts of greater value than the gifts she had given him. Then she and all her attendants returned to their own land.

AMAZING FACTS

King Solomon was incredibly rich. How rich? His income was 25 tons of gold a year!

2 CHRONICLES 9:13

Solomon's Wealth and Splendor

13 Each year Solomon received about 25 tons* of gold. 14 This did not include the additional revenue he received from merchants and traders. All the kings of Arabia and the governors of the provinces also brought gold and silver to Solomon.

15 King Solomon made 200 large shields of hammered gold, each weighing more than 15 pounds.* 16 He also made 300 smaller shields of hammered gold, each weighing more than 7½ pounds.* The king placed these shields in the Palace of the Forest of Lebanon.

17 Then the king made a huge throne, decorated with ivory and overlaid with pure gold. 18 The throne had six steps, with a footstool of gold. There were armrests on both sides of the seat, and the figure of a lion stood on each side of the throne. 19 There were also twelve other lions, one standing on each end of the six steps. No other throne in all the world could be compared with it!

20 All of King Solomon's drinking cups were solid gold, as were all the utensils in the Palace of the Forest of Lebanon. They were not made of silver, for silver was considered worthless in Solomon's day!

21 The king had a fleet of trading ships* manned by the sailors sent by Hiram.* Once every three years the ships returned, loaded with gold, silver, ivory, apes, and peacocks.*

22 So King Solomon became richer and wiser than any other king on earth. 23 Kings from every nation came to consult him and to hear the wisdom God had given him. 24 Year after year everyone who visited brought him gifts of silver and gold, clothing, weapons, spices, horses, and mules.

25 Solomon had 4,000 stalls for his horses and chariots, and he had 12,000 horses.* He stationed some of them in the chariot cities, and some near him in Jerusalem. 26 He ruled over all the kings from the Euphrates River* in the north to the land of the Philistines and the border of Egypt in the south. 27 The king made silver as plentiful in Jerusalem as stone. And valuable cedar timber was as common as the sycamore-fig trees that grow in the foothills of Judah.* 28 Solomon's horses were imported from Egypt* and many other countries.

Summary of Solomon's Reign

29 The rest of the events of Solomon's reign, from beginning to end, are recorded in *The Record of Nathan the Prophet,* and *The Prophecy of Ahijah from Shiloh,* and also in *The Visions of Iddo the Seer,* concerning Jeroboam son of Nebat. 30 Solomon ruled in Jerusalem over all Israel for forty years. 31 When he died, he was buried in the City of David, named for his father. Then his son Rehoboam became the next king.

CHAPTER 10

The Northern Tribes Revolt

Rehoboam went to Shechem, where all Israel had gathered to make him king. 2 When Jeroboam son of Nebat heard of this, he returned from Egypt, for he had fled to Egypt to escape from King Solomon. 3 The leaders of Israel summoned him, and Jeroboam and all Israel went to speak with Rehoboam. 4 "Your father was a hard master," they said. "Lighten the harsh labor demands and heavy taxes that

9:13 Hebrew *666 talents* [23 metric tons]. **9:15** Hebrew *600 [shekels] of hammered gold* [6.8 kilograms]. **9:16** Hebrew *300 [shekels] of gold* [3.4 kilograms]. **9:21a** Hebrew *fleet of ships that could sail to Tarshish.* **9:21b** Hebrew *Huram,* a variant spelling of Hiram. **9:21c** Or *and baboons.* **9:25** Or *12,000 charioteers.* **9:26** Hebrew *the river.* **9:27** Hebrew *the Shephelah.* **9:28** Possibly *Muzur,* a district near Cilicia.

your father imposed on us. Then we will be your loyal subjects."

5Rehoboam replied, "Come back in three days for my answer." So the people went away.

6Then King Rehoboam discussed the matter with the older men who had counseled his father, Solomon. "What is your advice?" he asked. "How should I answer these people?"

7The older counselors replied, "If you are good to these people and do your best to please them and give them a favorable answer, they will always be your loyal subjects."

8But Rehoboam rejected the advice of the older men and instead asked the opinion of the young men who had grown up with him and were now his advisers. 9"What is your advice?" he asked them. "How should I answer these people who want me to lighten the burdens imposed by my father?"

10The young men replied, "This is what you should tell those complainers who want a lighter burden: 'My little finger is thicker than my father's waist! 11Yes, my father laid heavy burdens on you, but I'm going to make them even heavier! My father beat you with whips, but I will beat you with scorpions!'"

12Three days later Jeroboam and all the people returned to hear Rehoboam's decision, just as the king had ordered. 13But Rehoboam spoke harshly to them, for he rejected the advice of the older counselors 14and followed the counsel of his younger advisers. He told the people, "My father laid* heavy burdens on you, but I'm going to make them even heavier! My father beat you with whips, but I will beat you with scorpions!"

15So the king paid no attention to the people. This turn of events was the will of God, for it fulfilled the LORD's message to Jeroboam son of Nebat through the prophet Ahijah from Shiloh.

16When all Israel realized* that the king had refused to listen to them, they responded,

"Down with the dynasty of David!
We have no interest in the son of Jesse.
Back to your homes, O Israel!
Look out for your own house,
O David!"

So all the people of Israel returned home. 17But Rehoboam continued to rule over the Israelites who lived in the towns of Judah.

18King Rehoboam sent Adoniram,* who was in charge of the labor force, to restore order, but the people of Israel stoned him to death. When this news reached King Rehoboam, he quickly jumped into his chariot and fled to Jerusalem. 19And to this day the northern tribes of Israel have refused to be ruled by a descendant of David.

CHAPTER 11

Shemaiah's Prophecy

When Rehoboam arrived at Jerusalem, he mobilized the men of Judah and Benjamin—180,000 select troops—to fight against Israel and to restore the kingdom to himself.

2But the LORD said to Shemaiah, the man of God, 3"Say to Rehoboam son of Solomon, king of Judah, and to all the Israelites in Judah and Benjamin: 4'This is what the LORD says: Do not fight against your relatives. Go back home, for what has happened is my doing!'" So they obeyed the message of the LORD and did not fight against Jeroboam.

Rehoboam Fortifies Judah

5Rehoboam remained in Jerusalem and fortified various towns for the defense of Judah. 6He built up Bethlehem, Etam, Tekoa, 7Bethzur, Soco, Adullam, 8Gath, Mareshah, Ziph, 9Adoraim, Lachish, Azekah, 10Zorah, Aijalon, and Hebron. These became the fortified towns of Judah and Benjamin. 11Rehoboam strengthened their defenses and stationed commanders in them, and he stored supplies of food, olive oil, and wine. 12He also put shields and spears in these towns as a further safety measure. So only Judah and Benjamin remained under his control.

13But all the priests and Levites living among the northern tribes of Israel sided with Rehoboam. 14The Levites even abandoned their pasturelands and property and moved to Judah and Jerusalem, because Jeroboam and his sons would not allow them to serve the LORD as priests. 15Jeroboam appointed his own priests to serve at the pagan shrines, where they worshiped the goat and

10:14 As in Greek version and many Hebrew manuscripts (see also 1 Kgs 12:14); Masoretic Text reads *I will lay*. **10:16** As in Syriac version, Latin Vulgate, and many Hebrew manuscripts (see also 1 Kgs 12:16); Masoretic Text lacks *realized*. **10:18** Hebrew *Hadoram*, a variant spelling of Adoniram; compare 1 Kgs 4:6; 5:14; 12:18.

I'M NOT THE ONLY ONE!

I WAS ON A park-district baseball team that was playing against a team on which two of my best friends were playing. I got knocked out at home plate, and the paramedics had to carry me off the field on a stretcher. I was devastated. And the catcher who knocked me out (another good friend of mine) apologized to me for weeks afterward. I'm not sure who was more embarrassed!

Lighten Up!

calf idols he had made. [16]From all the tribes of Israel, those who sincerely wanted to worship the LORD, the God of Israel, followed the Levites to Jerusalem, where they could offer sacrifices to the LORD, the God of their ancestors. [17]This strengthened the kingdom of Judah, and for three years they supported Rehoboam son of Solomon, for during those years they faithfully followed in the footsteps of David and Solomon.

Rehoboam's Family

[18]Rehoboam married his cousin Mahalath, the daughter of David's son Jerimoth and of Abihail, the daughter of Eliab son of Jesse. [19]Mahalath had three sons—Jeush, Shemariah, and Zaham.

[20]Later Rehoboam married another cousin, Maacah, the daughter of Absalom. Maacah gave birth to Abijah, Attai, Ziza, and Shelomith. [21]Rehoboam loved Maacah more than any of his other wives and concubines. In all, he had eighteen wives and sixty concubines, and they gave birth to twenty-eight sons and sixty daughters.

[22]Rehoboam appointed Maacah's son Abijah as leader among the princes, making it clear that he would be the next king. [23]Rehoboam also wisely gave responsibilities to his other sons and stationed some of them in the fortified towns throughout the land of Judah and Benjamin. He provided them with generous provisions, and he found many wives for them.

CHAPTER 12

Egypt Invades Judah

But when Rehoboam was firmly established and strong, he abandoned the Law of the LORD, and all Israel followed him in this sin. [2]Because they were unfaithful to the LORD, King Shishak of Egypt came up and attacked Jerusalem in the fifth year of King Rehoboam's reign. [3]He came with 1,200 chariots, 60,000 horses,* and a countless army of foot soldiers, including Libyans, Sukkites, and Ethiopians.* [4]Shishak conquered Judah's fortified towns and then advanced to attack Jerusalem.

[5]The prophet Shemaiah then met with Rehoboam and Judah's leaders, who had all fled to Jerusalem because of Shishak. Shemaiah told them, "This is what the LORD says: You have abandoned me, so I am abandoning you to Shishak."

[6]Then the leaders of Israel and the king humbled themselves and said, "The LORD is right in doing this to us!"

[7]When the LORD saw their change of heart, he gave this message to Shemaiah: "Since the people have humbled themselves, I will not completely destroy them and will soon give them some relief. I will not use Shishak to pour out my anger on Jerusalem. [8]But they will become his subjects, so they will know the difference between serving me and serving earthly rulers."

[9]So King Shishak of Egypt came up and attacked Jerusalem. He ransacked the treasur-

12:3a Or *charioteers*, or *horsemen*. **12:3b** Hebrew *and Cushites*.

ies of the LORD's Temple and the royal palace;
he stole everything, including all the gold
shields Solomon had made. [10]King Rehoboam later replaced them with bronze shields
as substitutes, and he entrusted them to the
care of the commanders of the guard who
protected the entrance to the royal palace.
[11]Whenever the king went to the Temple of
the LORD, the guards would also take the
shields and then return them to the guardroom. [12]Because Rehoboam humbled himself, the LORD's anger was turned away, and he
did not destroy him completely. There were
still some good things in the land of Judah.

Summary of Rehoboam's Reign

[13]King Rehoboam firmly established himself
in Jerusalem and continued to rule. He was
forty-one years old when he became king, and
he reigned seventeen years in Jerusalem, the
city the LORD had chosen from among all the
tribes of Israel as the place to honor his name.
Rehoboam's mother was Naamah, a woman
from Ammon. [14]But he was an evil king, for he
did not seek the LORD with all his heart.

[15]The rest of the events of Rehoboam's
reign, from beginning to end, are recorded in
The Record of Shemaiah the Prophet and *The
Record of Iddo the Seer*, which are part of the
genealogical record. Rehoboam and Jeroboam were continually at war with each other.
[16]When Rehoboam died, he was buried in the
City of David. Then his son Abijah became the
next king.

CHAPTER 13

Abijah's War with Jeroboam

Abijah began to rule over Judah in the eighteenth year of Jeroboam's reign in Israel. [2]He
reigned in Jerusalem three years. His mother
was Maacah,* the daughter of Uriel from Gibeah.

Then war broke out between Abijah and
Jeroboam. [3]Judah, led by King Abijah, fielded
400,000 select warriors, while Jeroboam
mustered 800,000 select troops from Israel.

[4]When the army of Judah arrived in the hill
country of Ephraim, Abijah stood on Mount
Zemaraim and shouted to Jeroboam and all
Israel: "Listen to me! [5]Don't you realize that
the LORD, the God of Israel, made a lasting
covenant* with David, giving him and his descendants the throne of Israel forever? [6]Yet
Jeroboam son of Nebat, a mere servant of David's son Solomon, rebelled against his master. [7]Then a whole gang of scoundrels joined
him, defying Solomon's son Rehoboam when
he was young and inexperienced and could
not stand up to them.

[8]"Do you really think you can stand against
the kingdom of the LORD that is led by the descendants of David? You may have a vast army,
and you have those gold calves that Jeroboam
made as your gods. [9]But you have chased away
the priests of the LORD (the descendants of
Aaron) and the Levites, and you have appointed your own priests, just like the pagan
nations. You let anyone become a priest these
days! Whoever comes to be dedicated with a
young bull and seven rams can become a
priest of these so-called gods of yours!

[10]"But as for us, the LORD is our God, and we
have not abandoned him. Only the descendants of Aaron serve the LORD as priests, and
the Levites alone may help them in their work.
[11]They present burnt offerings and fragrant
incense to the LORD every morning and evening. They place the Bread of the Presence on
the holy table, and they light the gold lampstand every evening. We are following the instructions of the LORD our God, but you have
abandoned him. [12]So you see, God is with us.
He is our leader. His priests blow their trumpets and lead us into battle against you. O people of Israel, do not fight against the LORD, the
God of your ancestors, for you will not succeed!"

[13]Meanwhile, Jeroboam had secretly sent
part of his army around behind the men of Judah to ambush them. [14]When Judah realized
that they were being attacked from the front
and the rear, they cried out to the LORD for
help. Then the priests blew the trumpets,
[15]and the men of Judah began to shout. At the
sound of their battle cry, God defeated Jeroboam and all Israel and routed them before
Abijah and the army of Judah.

[16]The Israelite army fled from Judah, and
God handed them over to Judah in defeat.
[17]Abijah and his army inflicted heavy losses on
them; 500,000 of Israel's select troops were
killed that day. [18]So Judah defeated Israel on

13:2 As in most Greek manuscripts and Syriac version (see also 2 Chr 11:20-21; 1 Kgs 15:2); Hebrew reads *Micaiah*, a variant spelling of Maacah. **13:5** Hebrew *a covenant of salt*.

that occasion because they trusted in the LORD, the God of their ancestors. [19]Abijah and his army pursued Jeroboam's troops and captured some of his towns, including Bethel, Jeshanah, and Ephron, along with their surrounding villages.

[20]So Jeroboam of Israel never regained his power during Abijah's lifetime, and finally the LORD struck him down and he died. [21]Meanwhile, Abijah of Judah grew more and more powerful. He married fourteen wives and had twenty-two sons and sixteen daughters.

[22]The rest of the events of Abijah's reign, including his words and deeds, are recorded in *The Commentary of Iddo the Prophet*.

CHAPTER 14

Early Years of Asa's Reign

[1]*When Abijah died, he was buried in the City of David. Then his son Asa became the next king. There was peace in the land for ten years. [2]*Asa did what was pleasing and good in the sight of the LORD his God. [3]He removed the foreign altars and the pagan shrines. He smashed the sacred pillars and cut down the Asherah poles. [4]He commanded the people of Judah to seek the LORD, the God of their ancestors, and to obey his law and his commands. [5]Asa also removed the pagan shrines, as well as the incense altars from every one of Judah's towns. So Asa's kingdom enjoyed a period of peace. [6]During those peaceful years, he was able to build up the fortified towns throughout Judah. No one tried to make war against him at this time, for the LORD was giving him rest from his enemies.

[7]Asa told the people of Judah, "Let us build towns and fortify them with walls, towers, gates, and bars. The land is still ours because we sought the LORD our God, and he has given us peace on every side." So they went ahead with these projects and brought them to completion.

[8]King Asa had an army of 300,000 warriors from the tribe of Judah, armed with large shields and spears. He also had an army of 280,000 warriors from the tribe of Benjamin, armed with small shields and bows. Both armies were composed of well-trained fighting men.

[9]Once an Ethiopian* named Zerah attacked Judah with an army of 1,000,000 men* and 300 chariots. They advanced to the town of Mareshah, [10]so Asa deployed his armies for battle in the valley north of Mareshah.* [11]Then Asa cried out to the LORD his God, "O LORD, no one but you can help the powerless against the mighty! Help us, O LORD our God, for we trust in you alone. It is in your name that we have come against this vast horde. O LORD, you are our God; do not let mere men prevail against you!"

[12]So the LORD defeated the Ethiopians* in the presence of Asa and the army of Judah, and the enemy fled. [13]Asa and his army pursued them as far as Gerar, and so many Ethiopians fell that they were unable to rally. They were destroyed by the LORD and his army, and the army of Judah carried off a vast amount of plunder.

[14]While they were at Gerar, they attacked all the towns in that area, and terror from the LORD came upon the people there. As a result, a vast amount of plunder was taken from these towns, too. [15]They also attacked the camps of herdsmen and captured many sheep, goats, and camels before finally returning to Jerusalem.

CHAPTER 15

Asa's Religious Reforms

Then the Spirit of God came upon Azariah son of Oded, [2]and he went out to meet King Asa as he was returning from the battle. "Listen to me, Asa!" he shouted. "Listen, all you people of Judah and Benjamin! The LORD will stay with you as long as you stay with him! Whenever you seek him, you will find him. But if you abandon him, he will abandon you. [3]For a long time Israel was without the true God, without a priest to teach them, and without the Law to instruct them. [4]But whenever they were in trouble and turned to the LORD, the God of Israel, and sought him out, they found him.

[5]"During those dark times, it was not safe to travel. Problems troubled the people of every land. [6]Nation fought against nation, and

14:1 Verse 14:1 is numbered 13:23 in the Hebrew text. **14:2** Verses 14:2-15 are numbered 14:1-14 in Hebrew text. **14:9a** Hebrew *a Cushite*. **14:9b** Or *an army of thousands and thousands;* Hebrew reads *an army of a thousand thousands*. **14:10** Or *in the Zephathah Valley near Mareshah*. **14:12** Hebrew *Cushites;* also in 14:13.

I started my own business earlier this year. While designing a greeting card for a friend one day, it occurred to me that I could possibly reach two goals of mine—becoming an illustrator and a businesswoman—right now, even before finishing high school.

First, I typed a list of services I'd offer and the cost for each. Then I created a flyer about my business and rode my bike to the print shop in my neighborhood to make copies of both documents. Although I'd received permission from my mom—who started her own business two years ago—to go ahead with my plans, I never asked her for advice. I thought, "I'm smart. I can do this alone." I was wrong.

Calls from customers began pouring in. So did the stress of fitting the jobs into my already busy schedule. Desperate for advice, I talked with my mom. She suggested I talk with one of her friends, another successful business person. The friend came over that evening and, basically, kept me from losing my business . . . and my mind.

During our conversation, she shared tips on how to better manage my time and how to handle difficult clients. She also gave me a list of Bible verses she wanted me to read. One verse in particular—Proverbs 15:22—got my attention. It now guides how I handle my growing business: *Plans go wrong for lack of advice; many advisers bring success.*

You probably have set some goals for yourself. Don't do what I did and wait until you're stuck to ask for help. Keep in mind that seeking the counsel of others won't necessarily interfere with your goals. It may even help you achieve them.

Check out 2 Chronicles 15:1-4 to see that even the kings of Israel realized they needed good counsel—and to learn where the best counsel came from.

city against city, for God was troubling them
with every kind of problem. 7 But as for you,
be strong and courageous, for your work will
be rewarded."

8 When Asa heard this message from Azariah the prophet,* he took courage and removed all the detestable idols from the land of Judah and Benjamin and in the towns he had captured in the hill country of Ephraim. And he repaired the altar of the LORD, which stood in front of the entry room of the LORD's Temple.

9 Then Asa called together all the people of Judah and Benjamin, along with the people of Ephraim, Manasseh, and Simeon who had settled among them. For many from Israel had moved to Judah during Asa's reign when they saw that the LORD his God was with him. 10 The people gathered at Jerusalem in late spring,* during the fifteenth year of Asa's reign.

11 On that day they sacrificed to the LORD 700 cattle and 7,000 sheep and goats from the plunder they had taken in the battle. 12 Then they entered into a covenant to seek the LORD, the God of their ancestors, with all their heart and soul. 13 They agreed that anyone who refused to seek the LORD, the God of Israel, would be put to death—whether young or old, man or woman. 14 They shouted out their oath of loyalty to the LORD with trumpets blaring and rams' horns sounding. 15 All in Judah were happy about this covenant, for they had entered into it with all their heart. They earnestly sought after God, and they found him. And the LORD gave them rest from their enemies on every side.

16 King Asa even deposed his grandmother* Maacah from her position as queen mother because she had made an obscene Asherah pole. He cut down her obscene pole, broke it up, and burned it in the Kidron Valley. 17 Although the pagan shrines were not removed from Israel, Asa's heart remained completely faithful throughout his life. 18 He brought into the Temple of God the silver and gold and the various items that he and his father had dedicated.

19 So there was no more war until the thirty-fifth year of Asa's reign.

CHAPTER 16

Final Years of Asa's Reign

In the thirty-sixth year of Asa's reign, King Baasha of Israel invaded Judah and fortified Ramah in order to prevent anyone from entering or leaving King Asa's territory in Judah.

2 Asa responded by removing the silver and gold from the treasuries of the Temple of the LORD and the royal palace. He sent it to King Ben-hadad of Aram, who was ruling in Damascus, along with this message:

> 3 "Let there be a treaty* between you and me like the one between your father and my father. See, I am sending you silver and gold. Break your treaty with King Baasha of Israel so that he will leave me alone."

4 Ben-hadad agreed to King Asa's request and sent the commanders of his army to attack the towns of Israel. They conquered the towns of Ijon, Dan, Abel-beth-maacah,* and all the store cities in Naphtali. 5 As soon as Baasha of Israel heard what was happening, he abandoned his project of fortifying Ramah and stopped all work on it. 6 Then King Asa called out all the men of Judah to carry away the building stones and timbers that Baasha had been using to fortify Ramah. Asa used these materials to fortify the towns of Geba and Mizpah.

7 At that time Hanani the seer came to King Asa and told him, "Because you have put your trust in the king of Aram instead of in the LORD your God, you missed your chance to destroy the army of the king of Aram. 8 Don't you remember what happened to the Ethiopians* and Libyans and their vast army, with all of their chariots and charioteers?* At that time you relied on the LORD, and he handed them over to you. 9 The eyes of the LORD search the whole earth in order to strengthen those whose hearts are fully committed to him. What a fool you have been! From now on you will be at war."

10 Asa became so angry with Hanani for saying this that he threw him into prison and put him in stocks. At that time Asa also began to oppress some of his people.

15:8 As in Syriac version and Latin Vulgate (see also 15:1); Hebrew reads *from Oded the prophet*. **15:10** Hebrew *in the third month*. This month of the ancient Hebrew lunar calendar usually occurs within the months of May and June. **15:16** Hebrew *his mother*. **16:3** As in Greek version; Hebrew reads *There is a treaty*. **16:4** As in parallel text at 1 Kgs 15:20; Hebrew reads *Abel-maim*, another name for Abel-beth-maacah. **16:8a** Hebrew *Cushites*. **16:8b** Or *and horsemen?*

Summary of Asa's Reign

11 The rest of the events of Asa's reign, from
beginning to end, are recorded in *The Book of*
the Kings of Judah and Israel. 12 In the thirty-
ninth year of his reign, Asa developed a seri-
ous foot disease. Yet even with the severity of
his disease, he did not seek the LORD's help
but turned only to his physicians. 13 So he died
in the forty-first year of his reign. 14 He was
buried in the tomb he had carved out for him-
self in the City of David. He was laid on a bed
perfumed with sweet spices and fragrant
ointments, and the people built a huge fu-
neral fire in his honor.

Does God really know that I try to obey him?

The eyes of the LORD search the whole earth in order to strengthen those whose hearts are fully committed to him. 2 CHRONICLES 16:9

CHAPTER 17

Jehoshaphat Rules in Judah

Then Jehoshaphat, Asa's son, became the
next king. He strengthened Judah to stand
against any attack from Israel. 2 He stationed
troops in all the fortified towns of Judah, and
he assigned additional garrisons to the land
of Judah and to the towns of Ephraim that his
father, Asa, had captured.

3 The LORD was with Jehoshaphat because
he followed the example of his father's early
years* and did not worship the images of
Baal. 4 He sought his father's God and obeyed
his commands instead of following the evil
practices of the kingdom of Israel. 5 So the
LORD established Jehoshaphat's control over
the kingdom of Judah. All the people of Judah
brought gifts to Jehoshaphat, so he became
very wealthy and highly esteemed. 6 He was
deeply committed to* the ways of the LORD.
He removed the pagan shrines and Asherah
poles from Judah.

7 In the third year of his reign Jehoshaphat
sent his officials to teach in all the towns of
Judah. These officials included Ben-hail,
Obadiah, Zechariah, Nethanel, and Micaiah.
8 He sent Levites along with them, including
Shemaiah, Nethaniah, Zebadiah, Asahel, She-
miramoth, Jehonathan, Adonijah, Tobijah,
and Tob-adonijah. He also sent out the priests
Elishama and Jehoram. 9 They took copies of
the Book of the Law of the LORD and traveled
around through all the towns of Judah, teach-
ing the people.

10 Then the fear of the LORD fell over all
the surrounding kingdoms so that none of
them wanted to declare war on Jehoshaphat.
11 Some of the Philistines brought him gifts
and silver as tribute, and the Arabs brought
7,700 rams and 7,700 male goats.

12 So Jehoshaphat became more and more
powerful and built fortresses and storage cit-
ies throughout Judah. 13 He stored numerous
supplies in Judah's towns and stationed an
army of seasoned troops at Jerusalem. 14 His
army was enrolled according to ancestral
clans.

From Judah there were 300,000 troops
organized in units of 1,000, under the
command of Adnah. 15 Next in command
was Jehohanan, who commanded
280,000 troops. 16 Next was Amasiah son
of Zicri, who volunteered for the LORD's
service, with 200,000 troops under his
command.

17 From Benjamin there were 200,000
troops equipped with bows and shields.
They were under the command of Eliada,
a veteran soldier. 18 Next in command was
Jehozabad, who commanded 180,000
armed men.

19 These were the troops stationed in Jerusa-
lem to serve the king, besides those Jehosha-
phat stationed in the fortified towns
throughout Judah.

CHAPTER 18

Jehoshaphat and Ahab

Jehoshaphat enjoyed great riches and high
esteem, and he made an alliance with Ahab of
Israel by having his son marry Ahab's daugh-
ter. 2 A few years later he went to Samaria to

17:3 Some Hebrew manuscripts read *the example of his father, David.* **17:6** Hebrew *His heart was courageous in.*

visit Ahab, who prepared a great banquet for him and his officials. They butchered great numbers of sheep, goats, and cattle for the feast. Then Ahab enticed Jehoshaphat to join forces with him to recover Ramoth-gilead.

[3]"Will you go with me to Ramoth-gilead?" King Ahab of Israel asked King Jehoshaphat of Judah.

Jehoshaphat replied, "Why, of course! You and I are as one, and my troops are your troops. We will certainly join you in battle." [4]Then Jehoshaphat added, "But first let's find out what the LORD says."

[5]So the king of Israel summoned the prophets, 400 of them, and asked them, "Should we go to war against Ramoth-gilead, or should I hold back?"

They all replied, "Yes, go right ahead! God will give the king victory."

[6]But Jehoshaphat asked, "Is there not also a prophet of the LORD here? We should ask him the same question."

[7]The king of Israel replied to Jehoshaphat, "There is one more man who could consult the LORD for us, but I hate him. He never prophesies anything but trouble for me! His name is Micaiah son of Imlah."

Jehoshaphat replied, "That's not the way a king should talk! Let's hear what he has to say."

[8]So the king of Israel called one of his officials and said, "Quick! Bring Micaiah son of Imlah."

Micaiah Prophesies against Ahab

[9]King Ahab of Israel and King Jehoshaphat of Judah, dressed in their royal robes, were sitting on thrones at the threshing floor near the gate of Samaria. All of Ahab's prophets were prophesying there in front of them. [10]One of them, Zedekiah son of Kenaanah, made some iron horns and proclaimed, "This is what the LORD says: With these horns you will gore the Arameans to death!"

[11]All the other prophets agreed. "Yes," they said, "go up to Ramoth-gilead and be victorious, for the LORD will give the king victory!"

[12]Meanwhile, the messenger who went to get Micaiah said to him, "Look, all the prophets are promising victory for the king. Be sure that you agree with them and promise success."

[13]But Micaiah replied, "As surely as the LORD lives, I will say only what my God says."

[14]When Micaiah arrived before the king, Ahab asked him, "Micaiah, should we go to war against Ramoth-gilead, or should I hold back?"

Micaiah replied sarcastically, "Yes, go up and be victorious, for you will have victory over them!"

[15]But the king replied sharply, "How many

IS IT OK?

IS IT OK TO LIE TO HELP SOMEONE?

Say you're a prophet. The king wants *your* advice on his battle plan. All 400 of the other prophets are saying, "Go for it, King!" But you know he shouldn't go. It would be so easy to lie and tell the king what he wants to hear. However, Micaiah chose to tell the truth, even though he knew it was wildly unpopular (see 2 Chronicles 18:13). As a "reward" for his honesty, he got slapped, arrested, and imprisoned! But he did the right thing, so God was happy with him. When everyone else says it's OK to cheat, swear, gossip, etc., and someone asks *your* opinion, will you choose to tell the easy lie or the hard truth?

times must I demand that you speak only the truth to me when you speak for the LORD?"

[16]Then Micaiah told him, "In a vision I saw all Israel scattered on the mountains, like sheep without a shepherd. And the LORD said, 'Their master has been killed.* Send them home in peace.'"

[17]"Didn't I tell you?" the king of Israel exclaimed to Jehoshaphat. "He never prophesies anything but trouble for me."

[18]Then Micaiah continued, "Listen to what the LORD says! I saw the LORD sitting on his throne with all the armies of heaven around him, on his right and on his left. [19]And the LORD said, 'Who can entice King Ahab of Israel to go into battle against Ramoth-gilead so he can be killed?'

"There were many suggestions, [20]and finally a spirit approached the LORD and said, 'I can do it!'

"'How will you do this?' the LORD asked.

[21]"And the spirit replied, 'I will go out and inspire all of Ahab's prophets to speak lies.'

" 'You will succeed,' said the LORD. 'Go ahead and do it.'

[22]"So you see, the LORD has put a lying spirit in the mouths of your prophets. For the LORD has pronounced your doom."

[23]Then Zedekiah son of Kenaanah walked up to Micaiah and slapped him across the face. "Since when did the Spirit of the LORD leave me to speak to you?" he demanded.

[24]And Micaiah replied, "You will find out soon enough when you are trying to hide in some secret room!"

[25]"Arrest him!" the king of Israel ordered. "Take him back to Amon, the governor of the city, and to my son Joash. [26]Give them this order from the king: 'Put this man in prison, and feed him nothing but bread and water until I return safely from the battle!'"

[27]But Micaiah replied, "If you return safely, it will mean that the LORD has not spoken through me!" Then he added to those standing around, "Everyone mark my words!"

The Death of Ahab

[28]So King Ahab of Israel and King Jehoshaphat of Judah led their armies against Ramoth-gilead. [29]The king of Israel said to Jehoshaphat, "As we go into battle, I will disguise myself so no one will recognize me, but you wear your royal robes." So the king of Israel disguised himself, and they went into battle.

[30]Meanwhile, the king of Aram had issued these orders to his chariot commanders: "Attack only the king of Israel! Don't bother with anyone else." [31]So when the Aramean chariot commanders saw Jehoshaphat in his royal robes, they went after him. "There is the king of Israel!" they shouted. But Jehoshaphat called out, and the LORD saved him. God helped him by turning the attackers away from him. [32]As soon as the chariot commanders realized he was not the king of Israel, they stopped chasing him.

[33]An Aramean soldier, however, randomly shot an arrow at the Israelite troops and hit the king of Israel between the joints of his armor. "Turn the horses* and get me out of here!" Ahab groaned to the driver of the chariot. "I'm badly wounded!"

[34]The battle raged all that day, and the king of Israel propped himself up in his chariot facing the Arameans. In the evening, just as the sun was setting, he died.

CHAPTER 19

Jehoshaphat Appoints Judges

When King Jehoshaphat of Judah arrived safely home in Jerusalem, [2]Jehu son of Hanani the seer went out to meet him. "Why should you help the wicked and love those who hate the LORD?" he asked the king. "Because of what you have done, the LORD is very angry with you. [3]Even so, there is some good in you, for you have removed the Asherah poles throughout the land, and you have committed yourself to seeking God."

[4]Jehoshaphat lived in Jerusalem, but he went out among the people, traveling from Beersheba to the hill country of Ephraim, encouraging the people to return to the LORD, the God of their ancestors. [5]He appointed judges throughout the nation in all the fortified towns, [6]and he said to them, "Always think carefully before pronouncing judgment. Remember that you do not judge to please people but to please the LORD. He will be with you when you render the verdict in each case. [7]Fear the LORD and judge with

18:16 Hebrew *These people have no master.* **18:33** Hebrew *Turn your hand.*

Leader of the Pack

When Gil's Sunday school teacher asked him to stay after class, he thought, *I wasn't the only rowdy one.* He hadn't crumpled his paper and thrown it at the ceiling—only suggested it. Gil had just "improved" the teacher's picture drawn on the board. "Gil, the others often go along with whatever you do or suggest," the teacher said. "You can be a good or bad influence in class. I'd like your help in being a positive leader." How should Gil respond? Read 2 Chronicles 19:4-7 to find out what God expects from *his* leaders.

integrity, for the LORD our God does not tolerate perverted justice, partiality, or the taking of bribes."

[8]In Jerusalem, Jehoshaphat appointed some of the Levites and priests and clan leaders in Israel to serve as judges for cases involving the LORD's regulations and for civil disputes. [9]These were his instructions to them: "You must always act in the fear of the LORD, with faithfulness and an undivided heart. [10]Whenever a case comes to you from fellow citizens in an outlying town, whether a murder case or some other violation of God's laws, commands, decrees, or regulations, you must warn them not to sin against the LORD, so that he will not be angry with you and them. Do this and you will not be guilty.

[11]"Amariah the high priest will have final say in all cases involving the LORD. Zebadiah son of Ishmael, a leader from the tribe of Judah, will have final say in all civil cases. The Levites will assist you in making sure that justice is served. Take courage as you fulfill your duties, and may the LORD be with those who do what is right."

CHAPTER 20

War with Surrounding Nations

After this, the armies of the Moabites, Ammonites, and some of the Meunites* declared war on Jehoshaphat. [2]Messengers came and told Jehoshaphat, "A vast army from Edom* is marching against you from beyond the Dead Sea.* They are already at Hazazon-tamar." (This was another name for En-gedi.)

[3]Jehoshaphat was terrified by this news and begged the LORD for guidance. He also ordered everyone in Judah to begin fasting. [4]So people from all the towns of Judah came to Jerusalem to seek the LORD's help.

[5]Jehoshaphat stood before the community of Judah and Jerusalem in front of the new courtyard at the Temple of the LORD. [6]He prayed, "O LORD, God of our ancestors, you alone are the God who is in heaven. You are ruler of all the kingdoms of the earth. You are powerful and mighty; no one can stand against you! [7]O our God, did you not drive out those who lived in this land when your people Israel arrived? And did you not give this land forever to the descendants of your friend Abraham? [8]Your people settled here and built this Temple to honor your name. [9]They said, 'Whenever we are faced with any calamity such as war,* plague, or famine, we can come to stand in your presence before this Temple where your name is honored. We can cry out

20:1 As in some Greek manuscripts (see also 26:7); Hebrew repeats *Ammonites.* **20:2a** As in one Hebrew manuscript; most Hebrew manuscripts and ancient versions read *Aram.* **20:2b** Hebrew *the sea.* **20:9** Or *sword of judgment;* or *sword, judgment.*

to you to save us, and you will hear us and rescue us.'

[10]"And now see what the armies of Ammon, Moab, and Mount Seir are doing. You would not let our ancestors invade those nations when Israel left Egypt, so they went around them and did not destroy them. [11]Now see how they reward us! For they have come to throw us out of your land, which you gave us as an inheritance. [12]O our God, won't you stop them? We are powerless against this mighty army that is about to attack us. We do not know what to do, but we are looking to you for help."

[13]As all the men of Judah stood before the LORD with their little ones, wives, and children, [14]the Spirit of the LORD came upon one of the men standing there. His name was Jahaziel son of Zechariah, son of Benaiah, son of Jeiel, son of Mattaniah, a Levite who was a descendant of Asaph.

[15]He said, "Listen, all you people of Judah and Jerusalem! Listen, King Jehoshaphat! This is what the LORD says: Do not be afraid! Don't be discouraged by this mighty army, for the battle is not yours, but God's. [16]Tomorrow, march out against them. You will find them coming up through the ascent of Ziz at the end of the valley that opens into the wilderness of Jeruel. [17]But you will not even need to fight. Take your positions; then stand still and watch the LORD's victory. He is with you, O people of Judah and Jerusalem. Do not be afraid or discouraged. Go out against them tomorrow, for the LORD is with you!"

[18]Then King Jehoshaphat bowed low with his face to the ground. And all the people of Judah and Jerusalem did the same, worshiping the LORD. [19]Then the Levites from the clans of Kohath and Korah stood to praise the LORD, the God of Israel, with a very loud shout.

[20]Early the next morning the army of Judah went out into the wilderness of Tekoa. On the way Jehoshaphat stopped and said, "Listen to me, all you people of Judah and Jerusalem! Believe in the LORD your God, and you will be able to stand firm. Believe in his prophets, and you will succeed."

[21]After consulting the people, the king appointed singers to walk ahead of the army, singing to the LORD and praising him for his holy splendor. This is what they sang:

"Give thanks to the LORD;
his faithful love endures forever!"

AMAZING FACTS

King Jehoshaphat once won a battle with . . . a sword? . . . a bomb? Nope. A marching choir!

2 CHRONICLES 20:20-24

[22]At the very moment they began to sing and give praise, the LORD caused the armies of Ammon, Moab, and Mount Seir to start fighting among themselves. [23]The armies of Moab and Ammon turned against their allies from Mount Seir and killed every one of them. After they had destroyed the army of Seir, they began attacking each other. [24]So when the army of Judah arrived at the lookout point in the wilderness, all they saw were dead bodies lying on the ground as far as they could see. Not a single one of the enemy had escaped.

[25]King Jehoshaphat and his men went out to gather the plunder. They found vast amounts of equipment, clothing,* and other valuables— more than they could carry. There was so much plunder that it took them three days just to collect it all! [26]On the fourth day they gathered in the Valley of Blessing,* which got its name that day because the people praised and thanked the LORD there. It is still called the Valley of Blessing today.

[27]Then all the men returned to Jerusalem, with Jehoshaphat leading them, overjoyed that the LORD had given them victory over their enemies. [28]They marched into Jerusalem to the music of harps, lyres, and trumpets, and they proceeded to the Temple of the LORD.

[29]When all the surrounding kingdoms heard that the LORD himself had fought

20:25 As in some Hebrew manuscripts and Latin Vulgate; most Hebrew manuscripts read *corpses*. **20:26** Hebrew *valley of Beracah*.

against the enemies of Israel, the fear of God came over them. [30]So Jehoshaphat's kingdom was at peace, for his God had given him rest on every side.

Summary of Jehoshaphat's Reign

[31]So Jehoshaphat ruled over the land of Judah. He was thirty-five years old when he became king, and he reigned in Jerusalem twenty-five years. His mother was Azubah, the daughter of Shilhi.

[32]Jehoshaphat was a good king, following the ways of his father, Asa. He did what was pleasing in the LORD's sight. [33]During his reign, however, he failed to remove all the pagan shrines, and the people never fully committed themselves to follow the God of their ancestors.

[34]The rest of the events of Jehoshaphat's reign, from beginning to end, are recorded in *The Record of Jehu Son of Hanani*, which is included in *The Book of the Kings of Israel*.

[35]Some time later King Jehoshaphat of Judah made an alliance with King Ahaziah of Israel, who was very wicked.* [36]Together they built a fleet of trading ships* at the port of Ezion-geber. [37]Then Eliezer son of Dodavahu from Mareshah prophesied against Jehoshaphat. He said, "Because you have allied yourself with King Ahaziah, the LORD will destroy your work." So the ships met with disaster and never put out to sea.*

CHAPTER 21

Jehoram Rules in Judah

When Jehoshaphat died, he was buried with his ancestors in the City of David. Then his son Jehoram became the next king.

[2]Jehoram's brothers—the other sons of Jehoshaphat—were Azariah, Jehiel, Zechariah, Azariahu, Michael, and Shephatiah; all these were the sons of Jehoshaphat king of Judah.* [3]Their father had given each of them valuable gifts of silver, gold, and costly items, and also some of Judah's fortified towns. However, he designated Jehoram as the next king because he was the oldest. [4]But when Jehoram had become solidly established as king, he killed all his brothers and some of the other leaders of Judah.

[5]Jehoram was thirty-two years old when he became king, and he reigned in Jerusalem eight years. [6]But Jehoram followed the example of the kings of Israel and was as wicked as King Ahab, for he had married one of Ahab's daughters. So Jehoram did what was evil in the LORD's sight. [7]But the LORD did not want to destroy David's dynasty, for he had made a covenant with David and promised that his descendants would continue to rule, shining like a lamp forever.

[8]During Jehoram's reign, the Edomites revolted against Judah and crowned their own king. [9]So Jehoram went out with his full army and all his chariots. The Edomites surrounded him and his chariot commanders, but he went out at night and attacked them* under cover of darkness. [10]Even so, Edom has been independent from Judah to this day. The town of Libnah also revolted about that same time. All this happened because Jehoram had abandoned the LORD, the God of his ancestors. [11]He had built pagan shrines in the hill country of Judah and had led the people of Jerusalem and Judah to give themselves to pagan gods and to go astray.

[12]Then Elijah the prophet wrote Jehoram this letter:

> "This is what the LORD, the God of your ancestor David, says: You have not followed the good example of your father, Jehoshaphat, or your grandfather King Asa of Judah. [13]Instead, you have been as evil as the kings of Israel. You have led the people of Jerusalem and Judah to worship idols, just as King Ahab did in Israel. And you have even killed your own brothers, men who were better than you. [14]So now the LORD is about to strike you, your people, your children, your wives, and all that is yours with a heavy blow. [15]You yourself will suffer with a severe intestinal disease that will get worse each day until your bowels come out."

[16]Then the LORD stirred up the Philistines and the Arabs, who lived near the Ethiopians,* to attack Jehoram. [17]They marched against Judah, broke down its defenses, and

20:35 Or *who made him do what was wicked.* **20:36** Hebrew *fleet of ships that could go to Tarshish.* **20:37** Hebrew *never set sail for Tarshish.* **21:2** Masoretic Text reads *of Israel;* also in 21:4. The author of Chronicles sees Judah as representative of the true Israel. (Some Hebrew manuscripts, Greek and Syriac versions, and Latin Vulgate read *of Judah.*) **21:9** Or *he went out and escaped.* The meaning of the Hebrew is uncertain. **21:16** Hebrew *the Cushites.*

carried away everything of value in the royal palace, including the king's sons and his wives. Only his youngest son, Ahaziah,* was spared.

[18]After all this, the LORD struck Jehoram with the severe intestinal disease. [19]The disease grew worse and worse, and at the end of two years it caused his bowels to come out, and he died in agony. His people did not build a great funeral fire to honor him as they had done for his ancestors.

[20]Jehoram was thirty-two years old when he became king, and he reigned in Jerusalem eight years. No one was sorry when he died. They buried him in the City of David, but not in the royal cemetery.

CHAPTER 22

Ahaziah Rules in Judah

Then the people of Jerusalem made Ahaziah, Jehoram's youngest son, their next king, since the marauding bands who came with the Arabs* had killed all the older sons. So Ahaziah son of Jehoram reigned as king of Judah.

[2]Ahaziah was twenty-two* years old when he became king, and he reigned in Jerusalem one year. His mother was Athaliah, a granddaughter of King Omri. [3]Ahaziah also followed the evil example of King Ahab's family, for his mother encouraged him in doing wrong. [4]He did what was evil in the LORD's sight, just as Ahab's family had done. They even became his advisers after the death of his father, and they led him to ruin.

[5]Following their evil advice, Ahaziah joined King Joram,* the son of King Ahab of Israel, in his war against King Hazael of Aram at Ramoth-gilead. When the Arameans wounded Joram in the battle, [6]he returned to Jezreel to recover from the wounds he had received at Ramoth.* Because Joram was wounded, King Ahaziah* of Judah went to Jezreel to visit him.

[7]But God had decided that this visit would be Ahaziah's downfall. While he was there, Ahaziah went out with Joram to meet Jehu grandson of Nimshi,* whom the LORD had appointed to destroy the dynasty of Ahab.

[8]While Jehu was executing judgment against the family of Ahab, he happened to meet some of Judah's officials and Ahaziah's relatives* who were traveling with Ahaziah. So Jehu killed them all. [9]Then Jehu's men searched for Ahaziah, and they found him hiding in the city of Samaria. They brought him to Jehu, who killed him. Ahaziah was given a decent burial because the people said, "He was the grandson of Jehoshaphat—a man who sought the LORD with all his heart." But none of the surviving members of Ahaziah's family was capable of ruling the kingdom.

Queen Athaliah Rules in Judah

[10]When Athaliah, the mother of King Ahaziah of Judah, learned that her son was dead, she began to destroy the rest of Judah's royal family. [11]But Ahaziah's sister Jehosheba,* the daughter of King Jehoram, took Ahaziah's infant son, Joash, and stole him away from among the rest of the king's children, who were about to be killed. She put Joash and his nurse in a bedroom. In this way, Jehosheba, wife of Jehoiada the priest and sister of Ahaziah, hid the child so that Athaliah could not murder him. [12]Joash remained hidden in the Temple of God for six years while Athaliah ruled over the land.

CHAPTER 23

Revolt against Athaliah

In the seventh year of Athaliah's reign, Jehoiada the priest decided to act. He summoned his courage and made a pact with five army commanders: Azariah son of Jeroham, Ishmael son of Jehohanan, Azariah son of Obed, Maaseiah son of Adaiah, and Elishaphat son of Zicri. [2]These men traveled secretly throughout Judah and summoned the Levites and clan leaders in all the towns to come to Jerusalem. [3]They all gathered at the Temple of God, where they made a solemn pact with Joash, the young king.

Jehoiada said to them, "Here is the king's son! The time has come for him to reign! The LORD has promised that a descendant of David will be our king. [4]This is what you must do.

21:17 Hebrew *Jehoahaz*, a variant spelling of Ahaziah; compare 22:1. **22:1** Or *marauding bands of Arabs*. **22:2** As in some Greek manuscripts and Syriac version (see also 2 Kgs 8:26); Hebrew reads *forty-two*. **22:5** Hebrew *Jehoram*, a variant spelling of Joram; also in 22:6, 7. **22:6a** Hebrew *Ramah*, a variant spelling of Ramoth. **22:6b** As in some Hebrew manuscripts, Greek and Syriac versions, and Latin Vulgate (see also 2 Kgs 8:29); most Hebrew manuscripts read *Azariah*. **22:7** Hebrew *descendant of Nimshi*; compare 2 Kgs 9:2, 14. **22:8** As in Greek version (see also 2 Kgs 10:13); Hebrew reads *and sons of the brothers of Ahaziah*. **22:11** As in parallel text at 2 Kgs 11:2; Hebrew lacks *Ahaziah's sister* and reads *Jehoshabeath* [a variant spelling of Jehosheba].

When you priests and Levites come on duty
on the Sabbath, a third of you will serve as
gatekeepers. [5]Another third will go over to
the royal palace, and the final third will be at
the Foundation Gate. Everyone else should
stay in the courtyards of the LORD's Temple.
[6]Remember, only the priests and Levites on
duty may enter the Temple of the LORD, for
they are set apart as holy. The rest of the people must obey the LORD's instructions and
stay outside. [7]You Levites, form a bodyguard
around the king and keep your weapons in
hand. Kill anyone who tries to enter the Temple. Stay with the king wherever he goes."

[8]So the Levites and all the people of Judah
did everything as Jehoiada the priest ordered.
The commanders took charge of the men reporting for duty that Sabbath, as well as those
who were going off duty. Jehoiada the priest
did not let anyone go home after their shift
ended. [9]Then Jehoiada supplied the commanders with the spears and the large and
small shields that had once belonged to King
David and were stored in the Temple of God.
[10]He stationed all the people around the king,
with their weapons ready. They formed a line
from the south side of the Temple around to
the north side and all around the altar.

[11]Then Jehoiada and his sons brought out
Joash, the king's son, placed the crown on his
head, and presented him with a copy of God's
laws.* They anointed him and proclaimed
him king, and everyone shouted, "Long live
the king!"

The Death of Athaliah

[12]When Athaliah heard the noise of the people running and the shouts of praise to the
king, she hurried to the LORD's Temple to see
what was happening. [13]When she arrived,
she saw the newly crowned king standing in
his place of authority by the pillar at the
Temple entrance. The commanders and
trumpeters were surrounding him, and people from all over the land were rejoicing and
blowing trumpets. Singers with musical instruments were leading the people in a great
celebration. When Athaliah saw all this, she
tore her clothes in despair and shouted,
"Treason! Treason!"

[14]Then Jehoiada the priest ordered the
commanders who were in charge of the
troops, "Take her to the soldiers in front of
the Temple,* and kill anyone who tries to rescue her." For the priest had said, "She must
not be killed in the Temple of the LORD." [15]So
they seized her and led her out to the entrance of the Horse Gate on the palace
grounds, and they killed her there.

Jehoiada's Religious Reforms

[16]Then Jehoiada made a covenant between
himself and the king and the people that they
would be the LORD's people. [17]And all the people went over to the temple of Baal and tore
it down. They demolished the altars and
smashed the idols, and they killed Mattan the
priest of Baal in front of the altars.

[18]Jehoiada now put the priests and Levites
in charge of the Temple of the LORD, following all the directions given by David. He also
commanded them to present burnt offerings
to the LORD, as prescribed by the Law of
Moses, and to sing and rejoice as David had
instructed. [19]He also stationed gatekeepers
at the gates of the LORD's Temple to keep out
those who for any reason were ceremonially
unclean.

[20]Then the commanders, nobles, rulers,
and all the people of the land escorted the
king from the Temple of the LORD. They went
through the upper gate and into the palace,
and they seated the king on the royal throne.
[21]So all the people of the land rejoiced, and
the city was peaceful because Athaliah had
been killed.

CHAPTER 24

Joash Repairs the Temple

Joash was seven years old when he became
king, and he reigned in Jerusalem forty years.
His mother was Zibiah from Beersheba. [2]Joash did what was pleasing in the LORD's sight
throughout the lifetime of Jehoiada the
priest. [3]Jehoiada chose two wives for Joash,
and he had sons and daughters.

[4]At one point Joash decided to repair and
restore the Temple of the LORD. [5]He summoned the priests and Levites and gave them
these instructions: "Go to all the towns of Judah and collect the required annual offerings,
so that we can repair the Temple of your God.

23:11 Or *a copy of the covenant.* **23:14** Or *Bring her out from between the ranks;* or *Take her out of the Temple precincts.* The meaning of the Hebrew is uncertain.

Do not delay!" But the Levites did not act immediately.

[6]So the king called for Jehoiada the high priest and asked him, "Why haven't you demanded that the Levites go out and collect the Temple taxes from the towns of Judah and from Jerusalem? Moses, the servant of the LORD, levied this tax on the community of Israel in order to maintain the Tabernacle of the Covenant.*"

[7]Over the years the followers of wicked Athaliah had broken into the Temple of God, and they had used all the dedicated things from the Temple of the LORD to worship the images of Baal.

[8]So now the king ordered a chest to be made and set outside the gate leading to the Temple of the LORD. [9]Then a proclamation was sent throughout Judah and Jerusalem, telling the people to bring to the LORD the tax that Moses, the servant of God, had required of the Israelites in the wilderness. [10]This pleased all the leaders and the people, and they gladly brought their money and filled the chest with it.

[11]Whenever the chest became full, the Levites would carry it to the king's officials. Then the court secretary and an officer of the high priest would come and empty the chest and take it back to the Temple again. This went on day after day, and a large amount of money was collected. [12]The king and Jehoiada gave the money to the construction supervisors, who hired masons and carpenters to restore the Temple of the LORD. They also hired metalworkers, who made articles of iron and bronze for the LORD's Temple.

[13]The men in charge of the renovation worked hard and made steady progress. They restored the Temple of God according to its original design and strengthened it. [14]When all the repairs were finished, they brought the remaining money to the king and Jehoiada. It was used to make various articles for the Temple of the LORD—articles for worship services and for burnt offerings, including ladles and other articles made of gold and silver. And the burnt offerings were sacrificed continually in the Temple of the LORD during the lifetime of Jehoiada the priest.

[15]Jehoiada lived to a very old age, finally dying at 130. [16]He was buried among the kings in the City of David, because he had done so much good in Israel for God and his Temple.

Jehoiada's Reforms Reversed

[17]But after Jehoiada's death, the leaders of Judah came and bowed before King Joash and persuaded him to listen to their advice. [18]They decided to abandon the Temple of the LORD, the God of their ancestors, and they worshiped Asherah poles and idols instead! Because of this sin, divine anger fell on Judah and Jerusalem. [19]Yet the LORD sent prophets to bring them back to him. The prophets warned them, but still the people would not listen.

[20]Then the Spirit of God came upon Zechariah son of Jehoiada the priest. He stood before the people and said, "This is what God says: Why do you disobey the LORD's commands and keep yourselves from prospering? You have abandoned the LORD, and now he has abandoned you!"

[21]Then the leaders plotted to kill Zechariah, and King Joash ordered that they stone him to death in the courtyard of the LORD's Temple. [22]That was how King Joash repaid Jehoiada for his loyalty—by killing his son. Zechariah's last words as he died were, "May the LORD see what they are doing and avenge my death!"

The End of Joash's Reign

[23]In the spring of the year* the Aramean army marched against Joash. They invaded Judah and Jerusalem and killed all the leaders of the nation. Then they sent all the plunder back to their king in Damascus. [24]Although the Arameans attacked with only a small army, the LORD helped them conquer the much larger army of Judah. The people of Judah had abandoned the LORD, the God of their ancestors, so judgment was carried out against Joash.

[25]The Arameans withdrew, leaving Joash severely wounded. But his own officials plotted to kill him for murdering the son* of Jehoiada the priest. They assassinated him as he lay in bed. Then he was buried in the City of David, but not in the royal cemetery. [26]The assassins were Jozacar,* the son of an

24:6 Hebrew *Tent of the Testimony*. **24:23** Hebrew *At the turn of the year*. The first day of the year in the ancient Hebrew lunar calendar occurred in March or April. **24:25** As in Greek version and Latin Vulgate; Hebrew reads *sons*. **24:26a** As in parallel text at 2 Kgs 12:21; Hebrew reads *Zabad*.

Ammonite woman named Shimeath, and Jehozabad, the son of a Moabite woman named Shomer.*

[27]The account of the sons of Joash, the prophecies about him, and the record of his restoration of the Temple of God are written in *The Commentary on the Book of the Kings*. His son Amaziah became the next king.

CHAPTER 25

Amaziah Rules in Judah

Amaziah was twenty-five years old when he became king, and he reigned in Jerusalem twenty-nine years. His mother was Jehoaddin* from Jerusalem. [2]Amaziah did what was pleasing in the LORD's sight, but not wholeheartedly.

[3]When Amaziah was well established as king, he executed the officials who had assassinated his father. [4]However, he did not kill the children of the assassins, for he obeyed the command of the LORD as written by Moses in the Book of the Law: "Parents must not be put to death for the sins of their children, nor children for the sins of their parents. Those deserving to die must be put to death for their own crimes."*

[5]Then Amaziah organized the army, assigning generals and captains* for all Judah and Benjamin. He took a census and found that he had an army of 300,000 select troops, twenty years old and older, all trained in the use of spear and shield. [6]He also paid about 7,500 pounds* of silver to hire 100,000 experienced fighting men from Israel.

[7]But a man of God came to him and said, "Your Majesty, do not hire troops from Israel, for the LORD is not with Israel. He will not help those people of Ephraim! [8]If you let them go with your troops into battle, you will be defeated by the enemy no matter how well you fight. God will overthrow you, for he has the power to help you or to trip you up."

[9]Amaziah asked the man of God, "But what about all that silver I paid to hire the army of Israel?"

The man of God replied, "The LORD is able to give you much more than this!" [10]So Amaziah discharged the hired troops and sent them back to Ephraim. This made them very angry with Judah, and they returned home in a great rage.

[11]Then Amaziah summoned his courage and led his army to the Valley of Salt, where they killed 10,000 Edomite troops from Seir. [12]They captured another 10,000 and took them to the top of a cliff and threw them off, dashing them to pieces on the rocks below.

[13]Meanwhile, the hired troops that Amaziah had sent home raided several of the towns of Judah between Samaria and Bethhoron. They killed 3,000 people and carried off great quantities of plunder.

[14]When King Amaziah returned from slaughtering the Edomites, he brought with him idols taken from the people of Seir. He set them up as his own gods, bowed down in front of them, and offered sacrifices to them! [15]This made the LORD very angry, and he sent a prophet to ask, "Why do you turn to gods who could not even save their own people from you?"

[16]But the king interrupted him and said, "Since when have I made you the king's counselor? Be quiet now before I have you killed!"

So the prophet stopped with this warning: "I know that God has determined to destroy you because you have done this and have refused to accept my counsel."

[17]After consulting with his advisers, King Amaziah of Judah sent this challenge to Israel's king Jehoash,* the son of Jehoahaz and grandson of Jehu: "Come and meet me in battle!"*

[18]But King Jehoash of Israel replied to King Amaziah of Judah with this story: "Out in the Lebanon mountains, a thistle sent a message to a mighty cedar tree: 'Give your daughter in marriage to my son.' But just then a wild animal of Lebanon came by and stepped on the thistle, crushing it!

[19]"You are saying, 'I have defeated Edom,' and you are very proud of it. But my advice is to stay at home. Why stir up trouble that will only bring disaster on you and the people of Judah?"

[20]But Amaziah refused to listen, for God was determined to destroy him for turning to the gods of Edom. [21]So King Jehoash of Israel mobilized his army against King Amaziah of

24:26b As in parallel text at 2 Kgs 12:21; Hebrew reads *Shimrith*, a variant spelling of Shomer. **25:1** As in parallel text at 2 Kgs 14:2; Hebrew reads *Jehoaddan*, a variant spelling of Jehoaddin. **25:4** Deut 24:16. **25:5** Hebrew *commanders of thousands and commanders of hundreds*. **25:6** Hebrew *100 talents* [3,400 kilograms]. **25:17a** Hebrew *Joash*, a variant spelling of Jehoash; also in 25:18, 21, 23, 25. **25:17b** Hebrew *Come, let us look one another in the face*.

Judah. The two armies drew up their battle lines at Beth-shemesh in Judah. [22]Judah was routed by the army of Israel, and its army scattered and fled for home. [23]King Jehoash of Israel captured Judah's king, Amaziah son of Joash and grandson of Ahaziah, at Beth-shemesh. Then he brought him to Jerusalem, where he demolished 600 feet* of Jerusalem's wall, from the Ephraim Gate to the Corner Gate. [24]He carried off all the gold and silver and all the articles from the Temple of God that had been in the care of Obed-edom. He also seized the treasures of the royal palace, along with hostages, and then returned to Samaria.

[25]King Amaziah of Judah lived on for fifteen years after the death of King Jehoash of Israel. [26]The rest of the events in Amaziah's reign, from beginning to end, are recorded in *The Book of the Kings of Judah and Israel.*

[27]After Amaziah turned away from the LORD, there was a conspiracy against his life in Jerusalem, and he fled to Lachish. But his enemies sent assassins after him, and they killed him there. [28]They brought his body back on a horse, and he was buried with his ancestors in the City of David.*

CHAPTER 26

Uzziah Rules in Judah

All the people of Judah had crowned Amaziah's sixteen-year-old son, Uzziah, as king in place of his father. [2]After his father's death, Uzziah rebuilt the town of Elath* and restored it to Judah.

Why is it so important to obey God?

[Uzziah] did what was pleasing in the LORD's sight. . . . As long as the king sought guidance from the LORD, God gave him success.

2 CHRONICLES 26:4-5

[3]Uzziah was sixteen years old when he became king, and he reigned in Jerusalem fifty-two years. His mother was Jecoliah from Jerusalem. [4]He did what was pleasing in the LORD's sight, just as his father, Amaziah, had done. [5]Uzziah sought God during the days of Zechariah, who taught him to fear God.* And as long as the king sought guidance from the LORD, God gave him success.

[6]Uzziah declared war on the Philistines and broke down the walls of Gath, Jabneh, and Ashdod. Then he built new towns in the Ashdod area and in other parts of Philistia. [7]God helped him in his wars against the Philistines, his battles with the Arabs of Gur,* and his wars with the Meunites. [8]The Meunites* paid annual tribute to him, and his fame spread even to Egypt, for he had become very powerful.

[9]Uzziah built fortified towers in Jerusalem at the Corner Gate, at the Valley Gate, and at the angle in the wall. [10]He also constructed forts in the wilderness and dug many water cisterns, because he kept great herds of livestock in the foothills of Judah* and on the plains. He was also a man who loved the soil. He had many workers who cared for his farms and vineyards, both on the hillsides and in the fertile valleys.

[11]Uzziah had an army of well-trained warriors, ready to march into battle, unit by unit. This army had been mustered and organized by Jeiel, the secretary of the army, and his assistant, Maaseiah. They were under the direction of Hananiah, one of the king's officials. [12]These regiments of mighty warriors were commanded by 2,600 clan leaders. [13]The army consisted of 307,500 men, all elite troops. They were prepared to assist the king against any enemy.

[14]Uzziah provided the entire army with shields, spears, helmets, coats of mail, bows, and sling stones. [15]And he built structures on the walls of Jerusalem, designed by experts to protect those who shot arrows and hurled large stones* from the towers and the corners of the wall. His fame spread far and wide, for

25:23 Hebrew *400 cubits* [180 meters]. **25:28** As in some Hebrew manuscripts and other ancient versions (see also 2 Kgs 14:20); most Hebrew manuscripts read *the city of Judah.* **26:2** As in Greek version (see also 2 Kgs 14:22; 16:6); Hebrew reads *Eloth,* a variant spelling of Elath. **26:5** As in Syriac and Greek versions; Hebrew reads *who instructed him in divine visions.* **26:7** As in Greek version; Hebrew reads *Gur-baal.* **26:8** As in Greek version; Hebrew reads *Ammonites.* Compare 26:7. **26:10** Hebrew *the Shephelah.* **26:15** Or *to shoot arrows and hurl large stones.*

the LORD gave him marvelous help, and he became very powerful.

Uzziah's Sin and Punishment

[16]But when he had become powerful, he also became proud, which led to his downfall. He sinned against the LORD his God by entering the sanctuary of the LORD's Temple and personally burning incense on the incense altar. [17]Azariah the high priest went in after him with eighty other priests of the LORD, all brave men. [18]They confronted King Uzziah and said, "It is not for you, Uzziah, to burn incense to the LORD. That is the work of the priests alone, the descendants of Aaron who are set apart for this work. Get out of the sanctuary, for you have sinned. The LORD God will not honor you for this!"

AMAZING FACTS

Uzziah's pride instantly turned him from a king to a leper who lived alone for the rest of his life.

2 CHRONICLES 26:16-21

[19]Uzziah, who was holding an incense burner, became furious. But as he was standing there raging at the priests before the incense altar in the LORD's Temple, leprosy* suddenly broke out on his forehead. [20]When Azariah the high priest and all the other priests saw the leprosy, they rushed him out. And the king himself was eager to get out because the LORD had struck him. [21]So King Uzziah had leprosy until the day he died. He lived in isolation in a separate house, for he was excluded from the Temple of the LORD. His son Jotham was put in charge of the royal palace, and he governed the people of the land.

[22]The rest of the events of Uzziah's reign, from beginning to end, are recorded by the prophet Isaiah son of Amoz. [23]When Uzziah died, he was buried with his ancestors; his grave was in a nearby burial field belonging to the kings, for the people said, "He had leprosy." And his son Jotham became the next king.

CHAPTER 27

Jotham Rules in Judah

Jotham was twenty-five years old when he became king, and he reigned in Jerusalem sixteen years. His mother was Jerusha, the daughter of Zadok.

[2]Jotham did what was pleasing in the LORD's sight. He did everything his father, Uzziah, had done, except that Jotham did not sin by entering the Temple of the LORD. But the people continued in their corrupt ways.

[3]Jotham rebuilt the upper gate of the Temple of the LORD. He also did extensive rebuilding on the wall at the hill of Ophel. [4]He built towns in the hill country of Judah and constructed fortresses and towers in the wooded areas. [5]Jotham went to war against the Ammonites and conquered them. Over the next three years he received from them an annual tribute of 7,500 pounds* of silver, 50,000 bushels of wheat, and 50,000 bushels of barley.*

[6]King Jotham became powerful because he was careful to live in obedience to the LORD his God.

[7]The rest of the events of Jotham's reign, including all his wars and other activities, are recorded in *The Book of the Kings of Israel and Judah.* [8]He was twenty-five years old when he became king, and he reigned in Jerusalem sixteen years. [9]When Jotham died, he was buried in the City of David. And his son Ahaz became the next king.

CHAPTER 28

Ahaz Rules in Judah

Ahaz was twenty years old when he became king, and he reigned in Jerusalem sixteen years. He did not do what was pleasing in the sight of the LORD, as his ancestor David had done. [2]Instead, he followed the example of the kings of Israel. He cast metal images for

26:19 Or *a contagious skin disease.* The Hebrew word used here and throughout this passage can describe various skin diseases.
27:5a Hebrew *100 talents* [3,400 kilograms]. **27:5b** Hebrew *10,000 cors* [1,820 kiloliters] *of wheat, and 10,000 cors of barley.*

the worship of Baal. [3]He offered sacrifices in the valley of Ben-Hinnom, even sacrificing his own sons in the fire.* In this way, he followed the detestable practices of the pagan nations the LORD had driven from the land ahead of the Israelites. [4]He offered sacrifices and burned incense at the pagan shrines and on the hills and under every green tree.

[5]Because of all this, the LORD his God allowed the king of Aram to defeat Ahaz and to exile large numbers of his people to Damascus. The armies of the king of Israel also defeated Ahaz and inflicted many casualties on his army. [6]In a single day Pekah son of Remaliah, Israel's king, killed 120,000 of Judah's troops, all of them experienced warriors, because they had abandoned the LORD, the God of their ancestors. [7]Then Zicri, a warrior from Ephraim, killed Maaseiah, the king's son; Azrikam, the king's palace commander; and Elkanah, the king's second-in-command. [8]The armies of Israel captured 200,000 women and children from Judah and seized tremendous amounts of plunder, which they took back to Samaria.

[9]But a prophet of the LORD named Oded was there in Samaria when the army of Israel returned home. He went out to meet them and said, "The LORD, the God of your ancestors, was angry with Judah and let you defeat them. But you have gone too far, killing them without mercy, and all heaven is disturbed. [10]And now you are planning to make slaves of these people from Judah and Jerusalem. What about your own sins against the LORD your God? [11]Listen to me and return these prisoners you have taken, for they are your own relatives. Watch out, because now the LORD's fierce anger has been turned against you!"

[12]Then some of the leaders of Israel*—Azariah son of Jehohanan, Berekiah son of Meshillemoth, Jehizkiah son of Shallum, and Amasa son of Hadlai—agreed with this and confronted the men returning from battle. [13]"You must not bring the prisoners here!" they declared. "We cannot afford to add to our sins and guilt. Our guilt is already great, and the LORD's fierce anger is already turned against Israel."

[14]So the warriors released the prisoners and handed over the plunder in the sight of the leaders and all the people. [15]Then the four men just mentioned by name came forward and distributed clothes from the plunder to the prisoners who were naked. They provided clothing and sandals to wear, gave them enough food and drink, and dressed their wounds with olive oil. They put those who were weak on donkeys and took all the prisoners back to their own people in Jericho, the city of palms. Then they returned to Samaria.

Ahaz Closes the Temple

[16]At that time King Ahaz of Judah asked the king of Assyria for help. [17]The armies of Edom had again invaded Judah and taken captives. [18]And the Philistines had raided towns located in the foothills of Judah* and in the Negev of Judah. They had already captured and occupied Beth-shemesh, Aijalon, Gederoth, Soco with its villages, Timnah with its villages, and Gimzo with its villages. [19]The LORD was humbling Judah because of King Ahaz of Judah,* for he had encouraged his people to sin and had been utterly unfaithful to the LORD.

[20]So when King Tiglath-pileser* of Assyria arrived, he attacked Ahaz instead of helping him. [21]Ahaz took valuable items from the LORD's Temple, the royal palace, and from the homes of his officials and gave them to the king of Assyria as tribute. But this did not help him.

[22]Even during this time of trouble, King Ahaz continued to reject the LORD. [23]He offered sacrifices to the gods of Damascus who had defeated him, for he said, "Since these gods helped the kings of Aram, they will help me, too, if I sacrifice to them." But instead, they led to his ruin and the ruin of all Judah.

[24]The king took the various articles from the Temple of God and broke them into pieces. He shut the doors of the LORD's Temple so that no one could worship there, and he set up altars to pagan gods in every corner of Jerusalem. [25]He made pagan shrines in all the towns of Judah for offering sacrifices to other

28:3 Or *even making his sons pass through the fire.* **28:12** Hebrew *Ephraim,* referring to the northern kingdom of Israel. **28:18** Hebrew *the Shephelah.* **28:19** Masoretic Text reads *of Israel;* also in 28:23, 27. The author of Chronicles sees Judah as representative of the true Israel. (Some Hebrew manuscripts and Greek version read *of Judah.*) **28:20** Hebrew *Tilgath-pilneser,* a variant spelling of Tiglath-pileser.

gods. In this way, he aroused the anger of the LORD, the God of his ancestors.

[26]The rest of the events of Ahaz's reign and everything he did, from beginning to end, are recorded in *The Book of the Kings of Judah and Israel*. [27]When Ahaz died, he was buried in Jerusalem but not in the royal cemetery of the kings of Judah. Then his son Hezekiah became the next king.

CHAPTER 29

Hezekiah Rules in Judah

Hezekiah was twenty-five years old when he became the king of Judah, and he reigned in Jerusalem twenty-nine years. His mother was Abijah, the daughter of Zechariah. [2]He did what was pleasing in the LORD's sight, just as his ancestor David had done.

Hezekiah Reopens the Temple

[3]In the very first month of the first year of his reign, Hezekiah reopened the doors of the Temple of the LORD and repaired them. [4]He summoned the priests and Levites to meet him at the courtyard east of the Temple. [5]He said to them, "Listen to me, you Levites! Purify yourselves, and purify the Temple of the LORD, the God of your ancestors. Remove all the defiled things from the sanctuary. [6]Our ancestors were unfaithful and did what was evil in the sight of the LORD our God. They abandoned the LORD and his dwelling place; they turned their backs on him. [7]They also shut the doors to the Temple's entry room, and they snuffed out the lamps. They stopped burning incense and presenting burnt offerings at the sanctuary of the God of Israel.

[8]"That is why the LORD's anger has fallen upon Judah and Jerusalem. He has made them an object of dread, horror, and ridicule, as you can see with your own eyes. [9]Because of this, our fathers have been killed in battle, and our sons and daughters and wives have been captured. [10]But now I will make a covenant with the LORD, the God of Israel, so that his fierce anger will turn away from us. [11]My sons, do not neglect your duties any longer! The LORD has chosen you to stand in his presence, to minister to him, and to lead the people in worship and present offerings to him."

[12]Then these Levites got right to work:

From the clan of Kohath: Mahath son of Amasai and Joel son of Azariah.
From the clan of Merari: Kish son of Abdi and Azariah son of Jehallelel.
From the clan of Gershon: Joah son of Zimmah and Eden son of Joah.
[13] From the family of Elizaphan: Shimri and Jeiel.
From the family of Asaph: Zechariah and Mattaniah.
[14] From the family of Heman: Jehiel and Shimei.
From the family of Jeduthun: Shemaiah and Uzziel.

[15]These men called together their fellow Levites, and they all purified themselves. Then they began to cleanse the Temple of the LORD, just as the king had commanded. They were careful to follow all the LORD's instructions in their work. [16]The priests went into the sanctuary of the Temple of the LORD to cleanse it, and they took out to the Temple courtyard all the defiled things they found. From there the Levites carted it all out to the Kidron Valley.

[17]They began the work in early spring, on the first day of the new year,* and in eight days they had reached the entry room of the LORD's Temple. Then they purified the Temple of the LORD itself, which took another eight days. So the entire task was completed in sixteen days.

The Temple Rededication

[18]Then the Levites went to King Hezekiah and gave him this report: "We have cleansed the entire Temple of the LORD, the altar of burnt offering with all its utensils, and the table of the Bread of the Presence with all its utensils. [19]We have also recovered all the items discarded by King Ahaz when he was unfaithful and closed the Temple. They are now in front of the altar of the LORD, purified and ready for use."

[20]Early the next morning King Hezekiah gathered the city officials and went to the Temple of the LORD. [21]They brought seven bulls, seven rams, and seven male lambs as a burnt offering, together with seven male goats as a sin offering for the kingdom, for

29:17 Hebrew *on the first day of the first month.* This day in the ancient Hebrew lunar calendar occurred in March or early April, 715 B.C.

the Temple, and for Judah. The king commanded the priests, who were descendants of Aaron, to sacrifice the animals on the altar of the LORD.

22 So they killed the bulls, and the priests took the blood and sprinkled it on the altar. Next they killed the rams and sprinkled their blood on the altar. And finally, they did the same with the male lambs. 23 The male goats for the sin offering were then brought before the king and the assembly of people, who laid their hands on them. 24 The priests then killed the goats as a sin offering and sprinkled their blood on the altar to make atonement for the sins of all Israel. The king had specifically commanded that this burnt offering and sin offering should be made for all Israel.

25 King Hezekiah then stationed the Levites at the Temple of the LORD with cymbals, lyres, and harps. He obeyed all the commands that the LORD had given to King David through Gad, the king's seer, and the prophet Nathan. 26 The Levites then took their positions around the Temple with the instruments of David, and the priests took their positions with the trumpets.

27 Then Hezekiah ordered that the burnt offering be placed on the altar. As the burnt offering was presented, songs of praise to the LORD were begun, accompanied by the trumpets and other instruments of David, the former king of Israel. 28 The entire assembly worshiped the LORD as the singers sang and the trumpets blew, until all the burnt offerings were finished. 29 Then the king and everyone with him bowed down in worship. 30 King Hezekiah and the officials ordered the Levites to praise the LORD with the psalms written by David and by Asaph the seer. So they offered joyous praise and bowed down in worship.

31 Then Hezekiah declared, "Now that you have consecrated yourselves to the LORD, bring your sacrifices and thanksgiving offerings to the Temple of the LORD." So the people brought their sacrifices and thanksgiving offerings, and all whose hearts were willing brought burnt offerings, too. 32 The people brought to the LORD 70 bulls, 100 rams, and 200 male lambs for burnt offerings. 33 They also brought 600 cattle and 3,000 sheep and goats as sacred offerings.

34 But there were too few priests to prepare all the burnt offerings. So their relatives the Levites helped them until the work was finished and more priests had been purified, for the Levites had been more conscientious about purifying themselves than the priests had been. 35 There was an abundance of burnt offerings, along with the usual liquid offerings, and a great deal of fat from the many peace offerings.

So the Temple of the LORD was restored to service. 36 And Hezekiah and all the people rejoiced because of what God had done for the people, for everything had been accomplished so quickly.

CHAPTER 30

Preparations for Passover

King Hezekiah now sent word to all Israel and Judah, and he wrote letters of invitation to the people of Ephraim and Manasseh. He asked everyone to come to the Temple of the LORD at Jerusalem to celebrate the Passover of the LORD, the God of Israel. 2 The king, his officials, and all the community of Jerusalem decided to celebrate Passover a month later than usual.* 3 They were unable to celebrate it at the prescribed time because not enough priests could be purified by then, and the people had not yet assembled at Jerusalem.

4 This plan for keeping the Passover seemed right to the king and all the people. 5 So they sent a proclamation throughout all Israel, from Beersheba in the south to Dan in the north, inviting everyone to come to Jerusalem to celebrate the Passover of the LORD, the God of Israel. The people had not been celebrating it in great numbers as required in the Law.

6 At the king's command, runners were sent throughout Israel and Judah. They carried letters that said:

> "O people of Israel, return to the LORD, the God of Abraham, Isaac, and Israel,* so that he will return to the few of us who have survived the conquest of the Assyrian kings. 7 Do not be like your ancestors and relatives who abandoned the LORD, the God of their ancestors, and became an

30:2 Hebrew *in the second month*. Passover was normally observed in the first month (of the ancient Hebrew lunar calendar).
30:6 *Israel* is the name that God gave to Jacob.

King Josiah

All I really wanted to do was play. But some men told me that I was to become King of Judah. Imagine—me only eight and already a king! It was tough, but from the beginning I decided to worship God like King David did. So I tore down all the images of false gods. I ground the statues to dust. Then I smashed their altars to bits. I wanted our people to follow the one true God. That was the right thing to do. Years later we found the Book of the Law hidden in the Temple. My people didn't know what it said, which made me sad. I made sure that we heard God's Word and obeyed.

Read more about young King Josiah in 2 Chronicles 33:25–35:26. His story also can be found in 2 Kings 21:24–23:30.

object of derision, as you yourselves can
see. [8]Do not be stubborn, as they were, but
submit yourselves to the LORD. Come to
his Temple, which he has set apart as holy
forever. Worship the LORD your God so
that his fierce anger will turn away from
you.
[9]"For if you return to the LORD, your
relatives and your children will be treated
mercifully by their captors, and they will
be able to return to this land. For the LORD
your God is gracious and merciful. If you
return to him, he will not continue to turn
his face from you."

Celebration of Passover

[10]The runners went from town to town
throughout Ephraim and Manasseh and as
far as the territory of Zebulun. But most of the
people just laughed at the runners and made
fun of them. [11]However, some people from
Asher, Manasseh, and Zebulun humbled
themselves and went to Jerusalem.
[12]At the same time, God's hand was on the
people in the land of Judah, giving them all
one heart to obey the orders of the king and
his officials, who were following the word of
the LORD. [13]So a huge crowd assembled at Je-
rusalem in midspring* to celebrate the Festi-
val of Unleavened Bread. [14]They set to work
and removed the pagan altars from Jerusa-
lem. They took away all the incense altars and
threw them into the Kidron Valley.
[15]On the fourteenth day of the second
month, one month later than usual,* the peo-
ple slaughtered the Passover lamb. This
shamed the priests and Levites, so they puri-
fied themselves and brought burnt offerings
to the Temple of the LORD. [16]Then they took
their places at the Temple as prescribed in the
Law of Moses, the man of God. The Levites
brought the sacrificial blood to the priests,
who then sprinkled it on the altar.
[17]Since many of the people had not puri-
fied themselves, the Levites had to slaughter
their Passover lamb for them, to set them
apart for the LORD. [18]Most of those who came
from Ephraim, Manasseh, Issachar, and Zeb-
ulun had not purified themselves. But King
Hezekiah prayed for them, and they were al-
lowed to eat the Passover meal anyway, even
though this was contrary to the requirements
of the Law. For Hezekiah said, "May the LORD,

30:13 Hebrew *in the second month*. The second month of the ancient Hebrew lunar calendar usually occurs within the months of April and May. **30:15** Hebrew *On the fourteenth day of the second month*. Passover normally began on the fourteenth day of the first month (see Lev 23:5).

who is good, pardon those [19]who decide to
follow the LORD, the God of their ancestors,
even though they are not properly cleansed
for the ceremony." [20]And the LORD listened to
Hezekiah's prayer and healed the people.

[21]So the people of Israel who were present
in Jerusalem joyously celebrated the Festival
of Unleavened Bread for seven days. Each day
the Levites and priests sang to the LORD, ac-
companied by loud instruments.* [22]Hezekiah
encouraged all the Levites regarding the skill
they displayed as they served the LORD. The
celebration continued for seven days. Peace
offerings were sacrificed, and the people
gave thanks to the LORD, the God of their an-
cestors.

[23]The entire assembly then decided to con-
tinue the festival another seven days, so they
celebrated joyfully for another week. [24]King
Hezekiah gave the people 1,000 bulls and
7,000 sheep and goats for offerings, and the
officials donated 1,000 bulls and 10,000
sheep and goats. Meanwhile, many more
priests purified themselves.

[25]The entire assembly of Judah rejoiced,
including the priests, the Levites, all who
came from the land of Israel, the foreigners
who came to the festival, and all those who
lived in Judah. [26]There was great joy in the
city, for Jerusalem had not seen a celebration
like this one since the days of Solomon, King
David's son. [27]Then the priests and Levites
stood and blessed the people, and God heard
their prayer from his holy dwelling in heaven.

CHAPTER 31

Hezekiah's Religious Reforms

When the festival ended, the Israelites who
attended went to all the towns of Judah, Ben-
jamin, Ephraim, and Manasseh, and they
smashed all the sacred pillars, cut down the
Asherah poles, and removed the pagan
shrines and altars. After this, the Israelites re-
turned to their own towns and homes.

[2]Hezekiah then organized the priests and
Levites into divisions to offer the burnt offer-
ings and peace offerings, and to worship and
give thanks and praise to the LORD at the gates
of the Temple. [3]The king also made a per-
sonal contribution of animals for the daily
morning and evening burnt offerings, the
weekly Sabbath festivals, the monthly new
moon festivals, and the annual festivals as
prescribed in the Law of the LORD. [4]In addi-
tion, he required the people in Jerusalem to
bring a portion of their goods to the priests
and Levites, so they could devote themselves
fully to the Law of the LORD.

[5]When the people of Israel heard these re-
quirements, they responded generously by
bringing the first share of their grain, new
wine, olive oil, honey, and all the produce of
their fields. They brought a large quantity—a
tithe of all they produced. [6]The people who
had moved to Judah from Israel, and the peo-
ple of Judah themselves, brought in the tithes
of their cattle, sheep, and goats and a tithe of
the things that had been dedicated to the
LORD their God, and they piled them up in
great heaps. [7]They began piling them up in
late spring, and the heaps continued to grow
until early autumn.* [8]When Hezekiah and his
officials came and saw these huge piles, they
thanked the LORD and his people Israel!

[9]"Where did all this come from?" Hezeki-
ah asked the priests and Levites.

[10]And Azariah the high priest, from the
family of Zadok, replied, "Since the people
began bringing their gifts to the LORD's Tem-
ple, we have had enough to eat and plenty to
spare. The LORD has blessed his people, and
all this is left over."

[11]Hezekiah ordered that storerooms be pre-
pared in the Temple of the LORD. When this
was done, [12]the people faithfully brought all
the tithes and gifts to the Temple. Conaniah
the Levite was put in charge, assisted by his
brother Shimei. [13]The supervisors under them
were Jehiel, Azaziah, Nahath, Asahel, Jerimoth,
Jozabad, Eliel, Ismakiah, Mahath, and Benaiah.
These appointments were made by King Hez-
ekiah and Azariah, the chief official in the
Temple of God.

[14]Kore son of Imnah the Levite, who was
the gatekeeper at the East Gate, was put in
charge of distributing the voluntary offer-
ings given to God, the gifts, and the things
that had been dedicated to the LORD. [15]His
faithful assistants were Eden, Miniamin,
Jeshua, Shemaiah, Amariah, and Shecaniah.

30:21 Or *sang to the LORD with all their strength.* **31:7** Hebrew *in the third month . . . until the seventh month.* The third month of the ancient Hebrew lunar calendar usually occurs within the months of May and June; the seventh month usually occurs within September and October.

They distributed the gifts among the families of priests in their towns by their divisions, dividing the gifts fairly among old and young alike. [16]They distributed the gifts to all males three years old or older, regardless of their place in the genealogical records. The distribution went to all who would come to the LORD's Temple to perform their daily duties according to their divisions. [17]They distributed gifts to the priests who were listed by their families in the genealogical records, and to the Levites twenty years old or older who were listed according to their jobs and their divisions. [18]Food allotments were also given to the families of all those listed in the genealogical records, including their little babies, wives, sons, and daughters. For they had all been faithful in purifying themselves.

[19]As for the priests, the descendants of Aaron, who were living in the open villages around the towns, men were appointed by name to distribute portions to every male among the priests and to all the Levites listed in the genealogical records.

[20]In this way, King Hezekiah handled the distribution throughout all Judah, doing what was pleasing and good in the sight of the LORD his God. [21]In all that he did in the service of the Temple of God and in his efforts to follow God's laws and commands, Hezekiah sought his God wholeheartedly. As a result, he was very successful.

CHAPTER 32

Assyria Invades Judah

After Hezekiah had faithfully carried out this work, King Sennacherib of Assyria invaded Judah. He laid siege to the fortified towns, giving orders for his army to break through their walls. [2]When Hezekiah realized that Sennacherib also intended to attack Jerusalem, [3]he consulted with his officials and military advisers, and they decided to stop the flow of the springs outside the city. [4]They organized a huge work crew to stop the flow of the springs, cutting off the brook that ran through the fields. For they said, "Why should the kings of Assyria come here and find plenty of water?"

[5]Then Hezekiah worked hard at repairing all the broken sections of the wall, erecting towers, and constructing a second wall outside the first. He also reinforced the supporting terraces* in the City of David and manu-factured large numbers of weapons and shields. [6]He appointed military officers over the people and assembled them before him in the square at the city gate. Then Hezekiah encouraged them by saying: [7]"Be strong and courageous! Don't be afraid or discouraged because of the king of Assyria or his mighty army, for there is a power far greater on our side! [8]He may have a great army, but they are merely men. We have the LORD our God to help us and to fight our battles for us!" Hezekiah's words greatly encouraged the people.

Sennacherib Threatens Jerusalem

[9]While King Sennacherib of Assyria was still besieging the town of Lachish, he sent his officers to Jerusalem with this message for Hezekiah and all the people in the city:

> [10]"This is what King Sennacherib of Assyria says: What are you trusting in that makes you think you can survive my siege of Jerusalem? [11]Hezekiah has said, 'The LORD our God will rescue us from the king of Assyria.' Surely Hezekiah is misleading you, sentencing you to death by famine and thirst! [12]Don't you realize that Hezekiah is the very person who destroyed all the LORD's shrines and altars? He commanded Judah and Jerusalem to worship only at the altar at the Temple and to offer sacrifices on it alone.
>
> [13]"Surely you must realize what I and the other kings of Assyria before me have done to all the people of the earth! Were any of the gods of those nations able to rescue their people from my power? [14]Which of their gods was able to rescue its people from the destructive power of my predecessors? What makes you think your God can rescue you from me? [15]Don't let Hezekiah deceive you! Don't let him fool you like this! I say it again—no god of any nation or kingdom has ever yet been able to rescue his people from me or my ancestors. How much less will your God rescue you from my power!"

32:5 Hebrew *the millo*. The meaning of the Hebrew is uncertain.

[16]And Sennacherib's officers further mocked the LORD God and his servant Hezekiah, heaping insult upon insult. [17]The king also sent letters scorning the LORD, the God of Israel. He wrote, "Just as the gods of all the other nations failed to rescue their people from my power, so the God of Hezekiah will also fail." [18]The Assyrian officials who brought the letters shouted this in Hebrew* to the people gathered on the walls of the city, trying to terrify them so it would be easier to capture the city. [19]These officers talked about the God of Jerusalem as though he were one of the pagan gods, made by human hands.

[20]Then King Hezekiah and the prophet Isaiah son of Amoz cried out in prayer to God in heaven. [21]And the LORD sent an angel who destroyed the Assyrian army with all its commanders and officers. So Sennacherib was forced to return home in disgrace to his own land. And when he entered the temple of his god, some of his own sons killed him there with a sword.

[22]That is how the LORD rescued Hezekiah and the people of Jerusalem from King Sennacherib of Assyria and from all the others who threatened them. So there was peace throughout the land. [23]From then on King Hezekiah became highly respected among all the surrounding nations, and many gifts for the LORD arrived at Jerusalem, with valuable presents for King Hezekiah, too.

Hezekiah's Sickness and Recovery

[24]About that time Hezekiah became deathly ill. He prayed to the LORD, who healed him and gave him a miraculous sign. [25]But Hezekiah did not respond appropriately to the kindness shown him, and he became proud. So the LORD's anger came against him and against Judah and Jerusalem. [26]Then Hezekiah humbled himself and repented of his pride, as did the people of Jerusalem. So the LORD's anger did not fall on them during Hezekiah's lifetime.

[27]Hezekiah was very wealthy and highly honored. He built special treasury buildings for his silver, gold, precious stones, and spices, and for his shields and other valuable items. [28]He also constructed many storehouses for his grain, new wine, and olive oil; and he made many stalls for his cattle and pens for his flocks of sheep and goats. [29]He built many towns and acquired vast flocks and herds, for God had given him great wealth. [30]He blocked up the upper spring of Gihon and brought the water down through a tunnel to the west side of the City of David. And so he succeeded in everything he did.

AMAZING FACTS

Get this. After King Hezekiah prayed with the prophet Isaiah, one angel defeated the entire Assyrian army.

2 CHRONICLES 32:20-21

[31]However, when ambassadors arrived from Babylon to ask about the remarkable events that had taken place in the land, God withdrew from Hezekiah in order to test him and to see what was really in his heart.

Summary of Hezekiah's Reign

[32]The rest of the events in Hezekiah's reign and his acts of devotion are recorded in *The Vision of the Prophet Isaiah Son of Amoz,* which is included in *The Book of the Kings of Judah and Israel.* [33]When Hezekiah died, he was buried in the upper area of the royal cemetery, and all Judah and Jerusalem honored him at his death. And his son Manasseh became the next king.

CHAPTER 33

Manasseh Rules in Judah

Manasseh was twelve years old when he became king, and he reigned in Jerusalem fifty-five years. [2]He did what was evil in the LORD's sight, following the detestable practices of

32:18 Hebrew *in the dialect of Judah.*

the pagan nations that the LORD had driven from the land ahead of the Israelites. [3]He rebuilt the pagan shrines his father, Hezekiah, had broken down. He constructed altars for the images of Baal and set up Asherah poles. He also bowed before all the powers of the heavens and worshiped them.

[4]He built pagan altars in the Temple of the LORD, the place where the LORD had said, "My name will remain in Jerusalem forever." [5]He built these altars for all the powers of the heavens in both courtyards of the LORD's Temple. [6]Manasseh also sacrificed his own sons in the fire* in the valley of Ben-Hinnom. He practiced sorcery, divination, and witchcraft, and he consulted with mediums and psychics. He did much that was evil in the LORD's sight, arousing his anger.

AMAZING FACTS

God got a king's attention by sending an army to capture him, bind him in chains, and put a ring through his nose!

2 CHRONICLES 33:10-13

[7]Manasseh even took a carved idol he had made and set it up in God's Temple, the very place where God had told David and his son Solomon: "My name will be honored forever in this Temple and in Jerusalem—the city I have chosen from among all the tribes of Israel. [8]If the Israelites will be careful to obey my commands—all the laws, decrees, and regulations given through Moses—I will not send them into exile from this land that I set aside for your ancestors." [9]But Manasseh led the people of Judah and Jerusalem to do even more evil than the pagan nations that the LORD had destroyed when the people of Israel entered the land.

[10]The LORD spoke to Manasseh and his people, but they ignored all his warnings. [11]So the LORD sent the commanders of the Assyrian armies, and they took Manasseh prisoner. They put a ring through his nose, bound him in bronze chains, and led him away to Babylon. [12]But while in deep distress, Manasseh sought the LORD his God and sincerely humbled himself before the God of his ancestors. [13]And when he prayed, the LORD listened to him and was moved by his request. So the LORD brought Manasseh back to Jerusalem and to his kingdom. Then Manasseh finally realized that the LORD alone is God!

[14]After this Manasseh rebuilt the outer wall of the City of David, from west of the Gihon Spring in the Kidron Valley to the Fish Gate, and continuing around the hill of Ophel. He built the wall very high. And he stationed his military officers in all of the fortified towns of Judah. [15]Manasseh also removed the foreign gods and the idol from the LORD's Temple. He tore down all the altars he had built on the hill where the Temple stood and all the altars that were in Jerusalem, and he dumped them outside the city. [16]Then he restored the altar of the LORD and sacrificed peace offerings and thanksgiving offerings on it. He also encouraged the people of Judah to worship the LORD, the God of Israel. [17]However, the people still sacrificed at the pagan shrines, though only to the LORD their God.

[18]The rest of the events of Manasseh's reign, his prayer to God, and the words the seers spoke to him in the name of the LORD, the God of Israel, are recorded in *The Book of the Kings of Israel.* [19]Manasseh's prayer, the account of the way God answered him, and an account of all his sins and unfaithfulness are recorded in *The Record of the Seers.** It includes a list of the locations where he built pagan shrines and set up Asherah poles and idols before he humbled himself and repented. [20]When Manasseh died, he was buried in his palace. Then his son Amon became the next king.

Amon Rules in Judah

[21]Amon was twenty-two years old when he became king, and he reigned in Jerusalem two

33:6 Or *also made his sons pass through the fire.* 33:19 Or *The Record of Hozai.*

years. [22]He did what was evil in the LORD's
sight, just as his father, Manasseh, had done.
He worshiped and sacrificed to all the idols
his father had made. [23]But unlike his father,
he did not humble himself before the LORD.
Instead, Amon sinned even more.

[24]Then Amon's own officials conspired
against him and assassinated him in his pal-
ace. [25]But the people of the land killed all those
who had conspired against King Amon, and
they made his son Josiah the next king.

CHAPTER 34

Josiah Rules in Judah

Josiah was eight years old when he became
king, and he reigned in Jerusalem thirty-one
years. [2]He did what was pleasing in the LORD's
sight and followed the example of his ances-
tor David. He did not turn away from doing
what was right.

[3]During the eighth year of his reign, while
he was still young, Josiah began to seek the
God of his ancestor David. Then in the twelfth
year he began to purify Judah and Jerusalem,
destroying all the pagan shrines, the Asherah
poles, and the carved idols and cast images.
[4]He ordered that the altars of Baal be demol-
ished and that the incense altars which stood
above them be broken down. He also made
sure that the Asherah poles, the carved idols,
and the cast images were smashed and scat-
tered over the graves of those who had sacri-
ficed to them. [5]He burned the bones of the
pagan priests on their own altars, and so he
purified Judah and Jerusalem.

[6]He did the same thing in the towns of
Manasseh, Ephraim, and Simeon, even as far
as Naphtali, and in the regions* all around
them. [7]He destroyed the pagan altars and the
Asherah poles, and he crushed the idols into
dust. He cut down all the incense altars
throughout the land of Israel. Finally, he re-
turned to Jerusalem.

[8]In the eighteenth year of his reign, after he
had purified the land and the Temple, Josiah
appointed Shaphan son of Azaliah, Maaseiah
the governor of Jerusalem, and Joah son of Jo-
ahaz, the royal historian, to repair the Temple
of the LORD his God. [9]They gave Hilkiah the
high priest the money that had been collected
by the Levites who served as gatekeepers at
the Temple of God. The gifts were brought by
people from Manasseh, Ephraim, and from
all the remnant of Israel, as well as from all Ju-
dah, Benjamin, and the people of Jerusalem.

JUST KICK IT

Jose's soccer team practiced on Saturday mornings right after the beginner soccer team. Jose and a teammate would often come early to stretch and warm up. Sometimes they watched the young team practice. Noah was a clumsy little boy who often looked lost on the field. One morning he tried to kick the ball but missed and fell down. The other boys on the team started laughing—Jose's teammate laughed too. Jose felt sorry for Noah. How can Jose encourage the little boy to keep practicing?

Read 2 Chronicles 34:3 to see how long it took young King Josiah to complete a job he had to do.

34:6 As in Syriac version. Hebrew reads *in their temples,* or *in their ruins.* The meaning of the Hebrew is uncertain.

[10]He entrusted the money to the men assigned to supervise the restoration of the LORD's Temple. Then they paid the workers who did the repairs and renovation of the Temple. [11]They hired carpenters and builders, who purchased finished stone for the walls and timber for the rafters and beams. They restored what earlier kings of Judah had allowed to fall into ruin.

[12]The workers served faithfully under the leadership of Jahath and Obadiah, Levites of the Merarite clan, and Zechariah and Meshullam, Levites of the Kohathite clan. Other Levites, all of whom were skilled musicians, [13]were put in charge of the laborers of the various trades. Still others assisted as secretaries, officials, and gatekeepers.

Hilkiah Discovers God's Law

[14]While they were bringing out the money collected at the LORD's Temple, Hilkiah the priest found the Book of the Law of the LORD that was written by Moses. [15]Hilkiah said to Shaphan the court secretary, "I have found the Book of the Law in the LORD's Temple!" Then Hilkiah gave the scroll to Shaphan.

[16]Shaphan took the scroll to the king and reported, "Your officials are doing everything they were assigned to do. [17]The money that was collected at the Temple of the LORD has been turned over to the supervisors and workmen." [18]Shaphan also told the king, "Hilkiah the priest has given me a scroll." So Shaphan read it to the king.

[19]When the king heard what was written in the Law, he tore his clothes in despair. [20]Then he gave these orders to Hilkiah, Ahikam son of Shaphan, Acbor son of Micaiah,* Shaphan the court secretary, and Asaiah the king's personal adviser: [21]"Go to the Temple and speak to the LORD for me and for all the remnant of Israel and Judah. Inquire about the words written in the scroll that has been found. For the LORD's great anger has been poured out on us because our ancestors have not obeyed the word of the LORD. We have not been doing everything this scroll says we must do."

[22]So Hilkiah and the other men went to the New Quarter* of Jerusalem to consult with the prophet Huldah. She was the wife of Shallum son of Tikvah, son of Harhas,* the keeper of the Temple wardrobe.

[23]She said to them, "The LORD, the God of Israel, has spoken! Go back and tell the man who sent you, [24]'This is what the LORD says: I am going to bring disaster on this city* and its people. All the curses written in the scroll that was read to the king of Judah will come true. [25]For my people have abandoned me and offered sacrifices to pagan gods, and I am very angry with them for everything they have done. My anger will be poured out on this place, and it will not be quenched.'

[26]"But go to the king of Judah who sent you to seek the LORD and tell him: 'This is what the LORD, the God of Israel, says concerning the message you have just heard: [27]You were sorry and humbled yourself before God when you heard his words against this city and its people. You humbled yourself and tore your clothing in despair and wept before me in repentance. And I have indeed heard you, says the LORD. [28]So I will not send the promised disaster until after you have died and been buried in peace. You yourself will not see the disaster I am going to bring on this city and its people.'"

So they took her message back to the king.

Josiah's Religious Reforms

[29]Then the king summoned all the elders of Judah and Jerusalem. [30]And the king went up to the Temple of the LORD with all the people of Judah and Jerusalem, along with the priests and the Levites—all the people from the greatest to the least. There the king read to them the entire Book of the Covenant that had been found in the LORD's Temple. [31]The king took his place of authority beside the pillar and renewed the covenant in the LORD's presence. He pledged to obey the LORD by keeping all his commands, laws, and decrees with all his heart and soul. He promised to obey all the terms of the covenant that were written in the scroll. [32]And he required everyone in Jerusalem and the people of Benjamin to make a similar pledge. The people of Jerusalem did so, renewing their covenant with God, the God of their ancestors.

[33]So Josiah removed all detestable idols

34:20 As in parallel text at 2 Kgs 22:12; Hebrew reads *Abdon son of Micah*. **34:22a** Or *the Second Quarter*, a newer section of Jerusalem. Hebrew reads *the Mishneh*. **34:22b** As in parallel text at 2 Kgs 22:14; Hebrew reads *son of Tokhath, son of Hasrah*. **34:24** Hebrew *this place;* also in 34:27, 28.

I SURVIVED

A while back, my biggest struggle in my spiritual life was devotions. Now, devos are something that every Christian is supposed to do. You know . . . we always hear about those great saints who spent hours with God, starting at four in the morning. With school and work and everything else I was involved in, I just couldn't seem to find the time. Thinking about doing devotions only made me feel guilty.

My problem was that I honestly didn't know what devotions were. I never was taught exactly *how* to do them. I just kept hearing I was supposed to "spend time with God in the Word" each day. A lot of times I would just flip open the Bible and read whatever my finger landed on. Definitely not a good method.

At a Christian bookstore one day, I decided to buy a devotional book. The one I chose tells stories of historical figures who believed in God and how they found faith in their hard times. It gives different Bible verses and shows how these people lived out the directions found in God's Word. Having this devotional book—something I'm really interested in—helps me *want* to sit down and learn about God each day.

My advice? First, make a set time each night (or morning) to sit down and do it. Don't leave your time for devotions to chance. Next, go out and buy a devotional book. I like to think of these books as guidebooks filled with good directions. Navigating through the Bible becomes so much easier when you know where to go. Finally, make a commitment to spend time in God's Word, like King Josiah did.

The Bible is "alive and powerful" (Hebrews 4:12) only if you use it!

Check out King Josiah's response upon discovering the lost scrolls containing God's Word in 2 Chronicles 34:30-32. Psalm 119 also gives awesome examples of someone who yearned to be devoted to God.

from the entire land of Israel and required everyone to worship the LORD their God. And throughout the rest of his lifetime, they did not turn away from the LORD, the God of their ancestors.

CHAPTER 35

Josiah Celebrates Passover

Then Josiah announced that the Passover of the LORD would be celebrated in Jerusalem, and so the Passover lamb was slaughtered on the fourteenth day of the first month.* [2]Josiah also assigned the priests to their duties and encouraged them in their work at the Temple of the LORD. [3]He issued this order to the Levites, who were to teach all Israel and who had been set apart to serve the LORD: "Put the holy Ark in the Temple that was built by Solomon son of David, the king of Israel. You no longer need to carry it back and forth on your shoulders. Now spend your time serving the LORD your God and his people Israel. [4]Report for duty according to the family divisions of your ancestors, following the directions of King David of Israel and the directions of his son Solomon.

[5]"Then stand in the sanctuary at the place appointed for your family division and help the families assigned to you as they bring their offerings to the Temple. [6]Slaughter the Passover lambs, purify yourselves, and prepare to help those who come. Follow all the directions that the LORD gave through Moses."

[7]Then Josiah provided 30,000 lambs and young goats for the people's Passover offerings, along with 3,000 cattle, all from the king's own flocks and herds. [8]The king's officials also made willing contributions to the people, priests, and Levites. Hilkiah, Zechariah, and Jehiel, the administrators of God's Temple, gave the priests 2,600 lambs and young goats and 300 cattle as Passover offerings. [9]The Levite leaders—Conaniah and his brothers Shemaiah and Nethanel, as well as Hashabiah, Jeiel, and Jozabad—gave 5,000 lambs and young goats and 500 cattle to the Levites for their Passover offerings.

[10]When everything was ready for the Passover celebration, the priests and the Levites took their places, organized by their divisions, as the king had commanded. [11]The Levites then slaughtered the Passover lambs and presented the blood to the priests, who sprinkled the blood on the altar while the Levites prepared the animals. [12]They divided the burnt offerings among the people by their family groups, so they could offer them to the LORD as prescribed in the Book of Moses. They did the same with the cattle. [13]Then they roasted the Passover lambs as prescribed; and they boiled the holy offerings in pots, kettles, and pans, and brought them out quickly so the people could eat them.

[14]Afterward the Levites prepared Passover offerings for themselves and for the priests—the descendants of Aaron—because the priests had been busy from morning till night offering the burnt offerings and the fat portions. The Levites took responsibility for all these preparations.

[15]The musicians, descendants of Asaph, were in their assigned places, following the commands that had been given by David, Asaph, Heman, and Jeduthun, the king's seer. The gatekeepers guarded the gates and did not need to leave their posts of duty, for their Passover offerings were prepared for them by their fellow Levites.

[16]The entire ceremony for the LORD's Passover was completed that day. All the burnt offerings were sacrificed on the altar of the LORD, as King Josiah had commanded. [17]All the Israelites present in Jerusalem celebrated Passover and the Festival of Unleavened Bread for seven days. [18]Never since the time of the prophet Samuel had there been such a Passover. None of the kings of Israel had ever kept a Passover as Josiah did, involving all the priests and Levites, all the people of Jerusalem, and people from all over Judah and Israel. [19]This Passover celebration took place in the eighteenth year of Josiah's reign.

Josiah Dies in Battle

[20]After Josiah had finished restoring the Temple, King Neco of Egypt led his army up from Egypt to do battle at Carchemish on the Euphrates River, and Josiah and his army marched out to fight him.* [21]But King Neco sent messengers to Josiah with this message:

> "What do you want with me, king of Judah? I have no quarrel with you today! I am on my way to fight another nation, and

35:1 This day in the ancient Hebrew lunar calendar was April 5, 622 B.C. **35:20** Or *Josiah went out to meet him.*

God has told me to hurry! Do not interfere
with God, who is with me, or he will
destroy you."

22But Josiah refused to listen to Neco, to whom God had indeed spoken, and he would not turn back. Instead, he disguised himself and led his army into battle on the plain of Megiddo. 23But the enemy archers hit King Josiah with their arrows and wounded him. He cried out to his men, "Take me from the battle, for I am badly wounded!"

24So they lifted Josiah out of his chariot and placed him in another chariot. Then they brought him back to Jerusalem, where he died. He was buried there in the royal cemetery. And all Judah and Jerusalem mourned for him. 25The prophet Jeremiah composed funeral songs for Josiah, and to this day choirs still sing these sad songs about his death. These songs of sorrow have become a tradition and are recorded in *The Book of Laments*.

26The rest of the events of Josiah's reign and his acts of devotion (carried out according to what was written in the Law of the LORD), 27from beginning to end—all are recorded in *The Book of the Kings of Israel and Judah*.

CHAPTER 36

Jehoahaz Rules in Judah

Then the people of the land took Josiah's son Jehoahaz and made him the next king in Jerusalem.

2Jehoahaz* was twenty-three years old when he became king, and he reigned in Jerusalem three months.

3Then he was deposed by the king of Egypt, who demanded that Judah pay 7,500 pounds of silver and 75 pounds of gold* as tribute.

Jehoiakim Rules in Judah

4The king of Egypt then installed Eliakim, the brother of Jehoahaz, as the next king of Judah and Jerusalem, and he changed Eliakim's name to Jehoiakim. Then Neco took Jehoahaz to Egypt as a prisoner.

5Jehoiakim was twenty-five years old when he became king, and he reigned in Jerusalem eleven years. He did what was evil in the sight of the LORD his God.

6Then King Nebuchadnezzar of Babylon came to Jerusalem and captured it, and he bound Jehoiakim in bronze chains and led him away to Babylon. 7Nebuchadnezzar also took some of the treasures from the Temple of the LORD, and he placed them in his palace* in Babylon.

8The rest of the events in Jehoiakim's reign, including all the evil things he did and everything found against him, are recorded in *The Book of the Kings of Israel and Judah*. Then his son Jehoiachin became the next king.

Jehoiachin Rules in Judah

9Jehoiachin was eighteen* years old when he became king, and he reigned in Jerusalem three months and ten days. Jehoiachin did what was evil in the LORD's sight.

10In the spring of the year* King Nebuchadnezzar took Jehoiachin to Babylon. Many treasures from the Temple of the LORD were also taken to Babylon at that time. And Nebuchadnezzar installed Jehoiachin's uncle,* Zedekiah, as the next king in Judah and Jerusalem.

Zedekiah Rules in Judah

11Zedekiah was twenty-one years old when he became king, and he reigned in Jerusalem eleven years. 12He did what was evil in the sight of the LORD his God, and he refused to humble himself when the prophet Jeremiah spoke to him directly from the LORD. 13He also rebelled against King Nebuchadnezzar, even though he had taken an oath of loyalty in God's name. Zedekiah was a hard and stubborn man, refusing to turn to the LORD, the God of Israel.

14Likewise, all the leaders of the priests and the people became more and more unfaithful. They followed all the pagan practices of the surrounding nations, desecrating the Temple of the LORD that had been consecrated in Jerusalem.

15The LORD, the God of their ancestors, repeatedly sent his prophets to warn them, for he had compassion on his people and his Temple. 16But the people mocked these messengers of God and despised their words. They scoffed at the prophets until the

36:2 Hebrew *Joahaz*, a variant spelling of Jehoahaz; also in 36:4. **36:3** Hebrew *100 talents* [3,400 kilograms] *of silver and 1 talent* [34 kilograms] *of gold*. **36:7** Or *temple*. **36:9** As in one Hebrew manuscript, some Greek manuscripts, and Syriac version (see also 2 Kgs 24:8); most Hebrew manuscripts read *eight*. **36:10a** Hebrew *At the turn of the year*. The first day of this year in the ancient Hebrew lunar calendar was April 13, 597 B.C. **36:10b** As in parallel text at 2 Kgs 24:17; Hebrew reads *brother*, or *relative*.

LORD's anger could no longer be restrained
and nothing could be done.

The Fall of Jerusalem

17So the LORD brought the king of Babylon
against them. The Babylonians* killed Judah's
young men, even chasing after them into the
Temple. They had no pity on the people, killing
both young men and young women, the old and
the infirm. God handed all of them over to
Nebuchadnezzar. 18The king took home to Bab-
ylon all the articles, large and small, used in the
Temple of God, and the treasures from both
the LORD's Temple and from the palace of the
king and his officials. 19Then his army burned
the Temple of God, tore down the walls of Je-
rusalem, burned all the palaces, and completely
destroyed everything of value.* 20The few who
survived were taken as exiles to Babylon, and
they became servants to the king and his sons
until the kingdom of Persia came to power.

21So the message of the LORD spoken
through Jeremiah was fulfilled. The land fi-
nally enjoyed its Sabbath rest, lying desolate
until the seventy years were fulfilled, just as
the prophet had said.

Cyrus Allows the Exiles to Return

22In the first year of King Cyrus of Persia,*
the LORD fulfilled the prophecy he had given
through Jeremiah.* He stirred the heart of
Cyrus to put this proclamation in writing
and to send it throughout his kingdom:

23"This is what King Cyrus of Persia says:
"The LORD, the God of heaven, has
given me all the kingdoms of the earth.
He has appointed me to build him a
Temple at Jerusalem, which is in Judah.
Any of you who are the LORD's people may
go there for this task. And may the LORD
your God be with you!"

36:17 Or *Chaldeans.* **36:19** Or *destroyed all the valuable articles from the Temple.* **36:22a** The first year of Cyrus's reign over Babylon was 538 B.C. **36:22b** See Jer 25:11-12; 29:10.

EZRA

WHO
Cyrus, Zerubbabel, Haggai, Zechariah, Darius, Artaxerxes I, and Ezra.

WHERE
In Babylon and back home in Jerusalem, the capital of Judah.

WHEN
This book was written around 450 BC, probably starting in Babylon and ending in Jerusalem.

WHY
To show God's faithfulness in bringing his people back to their land.

The gracious hand of his God was on him. This was because Ezra had determined to study and obey the Law of the LORD.
EZRA 7:9-10

What is a "great" person like? We usually think of someone rich and famous. But God thinks someone is great when that person serves him faithfully and courageously—obeying him no matter what! Ezra was such a man. His whole life was dedicated to serving God by helping God's people. Ezra was a great man!

586 BC — Jerusalem destroyed; exiles go to Babylon
539 BC — Babylon overthrown by Cyrus
538 BC — Cyrus's decree to return
537 BC — Exiles return to Jerusalem
536 BC — Temple construction begins
530 BC — Temple work halted
522 BC — Darius becomes king of Persia
520 BC — Temple work resumed; messages of Haggai, Zechariah given
516 BC — Temple completed
458 BC — Ezra comes to Jerusalem
445 BC — Nehemiah comes to Jerusalem

THINK OF WAYS YOU CAN SERVE GOD AND BE GREAT IN GOD'S EYES.

CHAPTER 1

Cyrus Allows the Exiles to Return

In the first year of King Cyrus of Persia,* the LORD fulfilled the prophecy he had given through Jeremiah.* He stirred the heart of Cyrus to put this proclamation in writing and to send it throughout his kingdom:

2 "This is what King Cyrus of Persia says:
"The LORD, the God of heaven, has given me all the kingdoms of the earth. He has appointed me to build him a Temple at Jerusalem, which is in Judah.
3 Any of you who are his people may go to Jerusalem in Judah to rebuild this Temple

1:1a The first year of Cyrus's reign over Babylon was 538 B.C. **1:1b** See Jer 25:11-12; 29:10.

of the LORD, the God of Israel, who lives in
Jerusalem. And may your God be with you!
4 Wherever this Jewish remnant is found,
let their neighbors contribute toward
their expenses by giving them silver and
gold, supplies for the journey, and
livestock, as well as a voluntary offering
for the Temple of God in Jerusalem."

5 Then God stirred the hearts of the priests and Levites and the leaders of the tribes of Judah and Benjamin to go to Jerusalem to rebuild the Temple of the LORD. 6 And all their neighbors assisted by giving them articles of silver and gold, supplies for the journey, and livestock. They gave them many valuable gifts in addition to all the voluntary offerings.

7 King Cyrus himself brought out the articles that King Nebuchadnezzar had taken from the LORD's Temple in Jerusalem and had placed in the temple of his own gods. 8 Cyrus directed Mithredath, the treasurer of Persia, to count these items and present them to Sheshbazzar, the leader of the exiles returning to Judah.* 9 This is a list of the items that were returned:

	gold basins	30
	silver basins	1,000
	silver incense burners*	29
10	gold bowls	30
	silver bowls	410
	other items	1,000

11 In all, there were 5,400 articles of gold and silver. Sheshbazzar brought all of these along when the exiles went from Babylon to Jerusalem.

CHAPTER 2

Exiles Who Returned with Zerubbabel

Here is the list of the Jewish exiles of the provinces who returned from their captivity. King Nebuchadnezzar had deported them to Babylon, but now they returned to Jerusalem and the other towns in Judah where they originally lived. 2 Their leaders were Zerubbabel, Jeshua, Nehemiah, Seraiah, Reelaiah, Mordecai, Bilshan, Mispar, Bigvai, Rehum, and Baanah.

This is the number of the men of Israel who returned from exile:

3	The family of Parosh	2,172
4	The family of Shephatiah	372
5	The family of Arah	775
6	The family of Pahath-moab (descendants of Jeshua and Joab)	2,812
7	The family of Elam	1,254
8	The family of Zattu	945
9	The family of Zaccai	760
10	The family of Bani	642
11	The family of Bebai	623
12	The family of Azgad	1,222
13	The family of Adonikam	666
14	The family of Bigvai	2,056
15	The family of Adin	454
16	The family of Ater (descendants of Hezekiah)	98
17	The family of Bezai	323
18	The family of Jorah	112
19	The family of Hashum	223
20	The family of Gibbar	95
21	The people of Bethlehem	123
22	The people of Netophah	56
23	The people of Anathoth	128
24	The people of Beth-azmaveth*	42
25	The people of Kiriath-jearim,* Kephirah, and Beeroth	743
26	The people of Ramah and Geba	621
27	The people of Micmash	122
28	The people of Bethel and Ai	223
29	The citizens of Nebo	52
30	The citizens of Magbish	156
31	The citizens of West Elam*	1,254
32	The citizens of Harim	320
33	The citizens of Lod, Hadid, and Ono	725
34	The citizens of Jericho	345
35	The citizens of Senaah	3,630

36 These are the priests who returned from exile:

	The family of Jedaiah (through the line of Jeshua)	973
37	The family of Immer	1,052
38	The family of Pashhur	1,247
39	The family of Harim	1,017

40 These are the Levites who returned from exile:

	The families of Jeshua and Kadmiel (descendants of Hodaviah)	74
41	The singers of the family of Asaph	128
42	The gatekeepers of the families of Shallum, Ater, Talmon, Akkub, Hatita, and Shobai	139

1:8 Hebrew *Sheshbazzar, the prince of Judah.* **1:9** The meaning of this Hebrew word is uncertain. **2:24** As in parallel text at Neh 7:28; Hebrew reads *Azmaveth.* **2:25** As in some Hebrew manuscripts and Greek version (see also Neh 7:29); Hebrew reads *Kiriath-arim.* **2:31** Or *of the other Elam.*

43 The descendants of the following Temple
servants returned from exile:
Ziha, Hasupha, Tabbaoth,
44 Keros, Siaha, Padon,
45 Lebanah, Hagabah, Akkub,
46 Hagab, Shalmai,* Hanan,
47 Giddel, Gahar, Reaiah,
48 Rezin, Nekoda, Gazzam,
49 Uzza, Paseah, Besai,
50 Asnah, Meunim, Nephusim,
51 Bakbuk, Hakupha, Harhur,
52 Bazluth, Mehida, Harsha,
53 Barkos, Sisera, Temah,
54 Neziah, and Hatipha.

55 The descendants of these servants of King
Solomon returned from exile:
Sotai, Hassophereth, Peruda,
56 Jaalah, Darkon, Giddel,
57 Shephatiah, Hattil, Pokereth-hazzebaim,
and Ami.

58 In all, the Temple servants and the descendants of Solomon's servants numbered 392.

59 Another group returned at this time from the towns of Tel-melah, Tel-harsha, Kerub, Addan, and Immer. However, they could not prove that they or their families were descendants of Israel. 60 This group included the families of Delaiah, Tobiah, and Nekoda—a total of 652 people.

61 Three families of priests—Hobaiah, Hakkoz, and Barzillai—also returned. (This Barzillai had married a woman who was a descendant of Barzillai of Gilead, and he had taken her family name.) 62 They searched for their names in the genealogical records, but they were not found, so they were disqualified from serving as priests. 63 The governor told them not to eat the priests' share of food from the sacrifices until a priest could consult the LORD about the matter by using the Urim and Thummim—the sacred lots.

64 So a total of 42,360 people returned to Judah, 65 in addition to 7,337 servants and 200 singers, both men and women. 66 They took with them 736 horses, 245 mules, 67 435 camels, and 6,720 donkeys.

68 When they arrived at the Temple of the LORD in Jerusalem, some of the family leaders made voluntary offerings toward the rebuilding of God's Temple on its original site, 69 and each leader gave as much as he could. The total of their gifts came to 61,000 gold coins,* 6,250 pounds* of silver, and 100 robes for the priests.

70 So the priests, the Levites, the singers, the gatekeepers, the Temple servants, and some of the common people settled in villages near Jerusalem. The rest of the people returned to their own towns throughout Israel.

CHAPTER 3

The Altar Is Rebuilt

In early autumn,* when the Israelites had settled in their towns, all the people assembled in Jerusalem with a unified purpose. 2 Then Jeshua son of Jehozadak* joined his fellow priests and Zerubbabel son of Shealtiel with his family in rebuilding the altar of the God of Israel. They wanted to sacrifice burnt offerings on it, as instructed in the Law of Moses, the man of God. 3 Even though the people were afraid of the local residents, they rebuilt the altar at its old site. Then they began to sacrifice burnt offerings on the altar to the LORD each morning and evening.

4 They celebrated the Festival of Shelters as prescribed in the Law, sacrificing the number of burnt offerings specified for each day of the festival. 5 They also offered the regular burnt offerings and the offerings required for the new moon celebrations and the annual festivals as prescribed by the LORD. The people also gave voluntary offerings to the LORD. 6 Fifteen days before the Festival of Shelters began,* the priests had begun to sacrifice burnt offerings to the LORD. This was even before they had started to lay the foundation of the LORD's Temple.

The People Begin to Rebuild the Temple

7 Then the people hired masons and carpenters and bought cedar logs from the people of Tyre and Sidon, paying them with food, wine, and olive oil. The logs were brought down

2:46 As in an alternate reading of the Masoretic Text (see also Neh 7:48); the other alternate reads *Shamlai*. **2:69a** Hebrew *61,000 darics of gold*, about 1,100 pounds or 500 kilograms in weight. **2:69b** Hebrew *5,000 minas* [3,000 kilograms]. **3:1** Hebrew *In the seventh month*. The year is not specified, so it may have been during Cyrus's first year (538 B.C.) or second year (537 B.C.). The seventh month of the ancient Hebrew lunar calendar occurred within the months of September/October 538 B.C. and October/November 537 B.C. **3:2** Hebrew *Jozadak*, a variant spelling of Jehozadak; also in 3:8. **3:6** Hebrew *On the first day of the seventh month*. This day in the ancient Hebrew lunar calendar occurred in September or October. The Festival of Shelters began on the fifteenth day of the seventh month.

from the Lebanon mountains and floated along the coast of the Mediterranean Sea* to Joppa, for King Cyrus had given permission for this.

[8]The construction of the Temple of God began in midspring,* during the second year after they arrived in Jerusalem. The work force was made up of everyone who had returned from exile, including Zerubbabel son of Shealtiel, Jeshua son of Jehozadak and his fellow priests, and all the Levites. The Levites who were twenty years old or older were put in charge of rebuilding the LORD's Temple. [9]The workers at the Temple of God were supervised by Jeshua with his sons and relatives, and Kadmiel and his sons, all descendants of Hodaviah.* They were helped in this task by the Levites of the family of Henadad.

Will God ever stop loving me? * **He is so good! His faithful love . . . endures forever!** EZRA 3:11

[10]When the builders completed the foundation of the LORD's Temple, the priests put on their robes and took their places to blow their trumpets. And the Levites, descendants of Asaph, clashed their cymbals to praise the LORD, just as King David had prescribed. [11]With praise and thanks, they sang this song to the LORD:

"He is so good!
His faithful love for Israel endures
forever!"

Then all the people gave a great shout, praising the LORD because the foundation of the LORD's Temple had been laid.

[12]But many of the older priests, Levites, and other leaders who had seen the first Temple wept aloud when they saw the new Temple's foundation. The others, however, were shouting for joy. [13]The joyful shouting and weeping mingled together in a loud noise that could be heard far in the distance.

CHAPTER 4

Enemies Oppose the Rebuilding

The enemies of Judah and Benjamin heard that the exiles were rebuilding a Temple to the LORD, the God of Israel. [2]So they approached Zerubbabel and the other leaders and said, "Let us build with you, for we worship your God just as you do. We have sacrificed to him ever since King Esarhaddon of Assyria brought us here."

[3]But Zerubbabel, Jeshua, and the other leaders of Israel replied, "You may have no part in this work. We alone will build the Temple for the LORD, the God of Israel, just as King Cyrus of Persia commanded us."

[4]Then the local residents tried to discourage and frighten the people of Judah to keep them from their work. [5]They bribed agents to work against them and to frustrate their plans. This went on during the entire reign of King Cyrus of Persia and lasted until King Darius of Persia took the throne.*

Later Opposition under Xerxes and Artaxerxes

[6]Years later when Xerxes* began his reign, the enemies of Judah wrote a letter of accusation against the people of Judah and Jerusalem.

[7]Even later, during the reign of King Artaxerxes of Persia,* the enemies of Judah, led by Bishlam, Mithredath, and Tabeel, sent a letter to Artaxerxes in the Aramaic language, and it was translated for the king.

[8]*Rehum the governor and Shimshai the court secretary wrote the letter, telling King Artaxerxes about the situation in Jerusalem. [9]They greeted the king for all their colleagues—the judges and local leaders, the people of Tarpel, the Persians, the Babylonians, and the people of Erech and Susa (that is, Elam). [10]They also sent greetings from the rest of the people whom the great and noble Ashurbanipal* had deported and relocated in Samaria and throughout the neighboring lands of the province west of the Euphrates River.* [11]This is a copy of their letter:

"To King Artaxerxes, from your loyal subjects in the province west of the Euphrates River.

3:7 Hebrew *the sea*. **3:8** Hebrew *in the second month*. This month in the ancient Hebrew lunar calendar occurred within the months of April and May 536 B.C. **3:9** Hebrew *sons of Judah* (i.e., *bene Yehudah*). *Bene* might also be read here as the proper name Binnui; *Yehudah* is probably another name for Hodaviah. Compare 2:40; Neh 7:43; 1 Esdras 5:58. **4:5** Darius reigned 521–486 B.C. **4:6** Hebrew *Ahasuerus*, another name for Xerxes. He reigned 486–465 B.C. **4:7** Artaxerxes reigned 465–424 B.C. **4:8** The original text of 4:8–6:18 is in Aramaic. **4:10a** Aramaic *Osnappar*, another name for Ashurbanipal. **4:10b** Aramaic *the province beyond the river;* also in 4:11, 16, 17, 20.

[12]"The king should know that the Jews
who came here to Jerusalem from
Babylon are rebuilding this rebellious and
evil city. They have already laid the
foundation and will soon finish its walls.
[13]And the king should know that if this
city is rebuilt and its walls are completed,
it will be much to your disadvantage, for
the Jews will then refuse to pay their
tribute, customs, and tolls to you.

[14]"Since we are your loyal subjects* and
do not want to see the king dishonored in
this way, we have sent the king this
information. [15]We suggest that a search
be made in your ancestors' records, where
you will discover what a rebellious city
this has been in the past. In fact, it was
destroyed because of its long and
troublesome history of revolt against the
kings and countries who controlled it.
[16]We declare to the king that if this city is
rebuilt and its walls are completed, the
province west of the Euphrates River will
be lost to you."

[17]Then King Artaxerxes sent this reply:

"To Rehum the governor, Shimshai the
court secretary, and their colleagues
living in Samaria and throughout the
province west of the Euphrates River.
Greetings.

[18]"The letter you sent has been
translated and read to me. [19]I ordered
a search of the records and have found
that Jerusalem has indeed been a hotbed
of insurrection against many kings. In
fact, rebellion and revolt are normal
there! [20]Powerful kings have ruled over
Jerusalem and the entire province west
of the Euphrates River, receiving tribute,
customs, and tolls. [21]Therefore, issue
orders to have these men stop their work.
That city must not be rebuilt except at
my express command. [22]Be diligent, and
don't neglect this matter, for we must not
permit the situation to harm the king's
interests."

[23]When this letter from King Artaxerxes
was read to Rehum, Shimshai, and their col-
leagues, they hurried to Jerusalem. Then, with
a show of strength, they forced the Jews to
stop building.

The Rebuilding Resumes

[24]So the work on the Temple of God in Jerusa-
lem had stopped, and it remained at a stand-
still until the second year of the reign of King
Darius of Persia.*

CHAPTER 5

At that time the prophets Haggai and Zecha-
riah son of Iddo prophesied to the Jews in Ju-
dah and Jerusalem. They prophesied in the
name of the God of Israel who was over them.
[2]Zerubbabel son of Shealtiel and Jeshua son
of Jehozadak* responded by starting again to
rebuild the Temple of God in Jerusalem. And
the prophets of God were with them and
helped them.

[3]But Tattenai, governor of the province
west of the Euphrates River,* and Shethar-
bozenai and their colleagues soon arrived in
Jerusalem and asked, "Who gave you permis-
sion to rebuild this Temple and restore this
structure?" [4]They also asked for the names of
all the men working on the Temple. [5]But be-
cause their God was watching over them, the
leaders of the Jews were not prevented from
building until a report was sent to Darius and
he returned his decision.

Tattenai's Letter to King Darius

[6]This is a copy of the letter that Tattenai the
governor, Shethar-bozenai, and the other of-
ficials of the province west of the Euphrates
River sent to King Darius:

[7]"To King Darius. Greetings.

[8]"The king should know that we went
to the construction site of the Temple of
the great God in the province of Judah. It
is being rebuilt with specially prepared
stones, and timber is being laid in its
walls. The work is going forward with
great energy and success.

[9]"We asked the leaders, 'Who gave
you permission to rebuild this Temple
and restore this structure?' [10]And we
demanded their names so that we could
tell you who the leaders were.

[11]"This was their answer: 'We are the

4:14 Aramaic *Since we eat the salt of the palace.* **4:24** The second year of Darius's reign was 520 B.C. The narrative started in 4:1-5 is resumed at verse 24. **5:2** Aramaic *Jozadak,* a variant spelling of Jehozadak. **5:3** Aramaic *the province beyond the river;* also in 5:6.

servants of the God of heaven and earth, and we are rebuilding the Temple that was built here many years ago by a great king of Israel. [12]But because our ancestors angered the God of heaven, he abandoned them to King Nebuchadnezzar of Babylon,* who destroyed this Temple and exiled the people to Babylonia. [13]However, King Cyrus of Babylon,* during the first year of his reign, issued a decree that the Temple of God should be rebuilt. [14]King Cyrus returned the gold and silver cups that Nebuchadnezzar had taken from the Temple of God in Jerusalem and had placed in the temple of Babylon. These cups were taken from that temple and presented to a man named Sheshbazzar, whom King Cyrus appointed as governor of Judah. [15]The king instructed him to return the cups to their place in Jerusalem and to rebuild the Temple of God there on its original site. [16]So this Sheshbazzar came and laid the foundations of the Temple of God in Jerusalem. The people have been working on it ever since, though it is not yet completed.'

[17]"Therefore, if it pleases the king, we request that a search be made in the royal archives of Babylon to discover whether King Cyrus ever issued a decree to rebuild God's Temple in Jerusalem. And then let the king send us his decision in this matter."

CHAPTER 6

Darius Approves the Rebuilding

So King Darius issued orders that a search be made in the Babylonian archives, which were stored in the treasury. [2]But it was at the fortress at Ecbatana in the province of Media that a scroll was found. This is what it said:

"Memorandum:

[3]"In the first year of King Cyrus's reign, a decree was sent out concerning the Temple of God at Jerusalem.

"Let the Temple be rebuilt on the site where Jews used to offer their sacrifices, using the original foundations. Its height will be ninety feet, and its width will be ninety feet.* [4]Every three layers of specially prepared stones will be topped by a layer of timber. All expenses will be paid by the royal treasury. [5]Furthermore, the gold and silver cups, which were taken to Babylon by Nebuchadnezzar from the Temple of God in Jerusalem, must be returned to Jerusalem and put back where they belong. Let them be taken back to the Temple of God."

[6]So King Darius sent this message:

"Now therefore, Tattenai, governor of the province west of the Euphrates River,*

5:12 Aramaic *Nebuchadnezzar the Chaldean.* **5:13** King Cyrus of Persia is here identified as the king of Babylon because Persia had conquered the Babylonian Empire. **6:3** Aramaic *Its height will be 60 cubits* [27.6 meters], *and its width will be 60 cubits.* It is commonly held that this verse should be emended to read: "Its height will be 30 cubits [45 feet, or 13.8 meters], its length will be 60 cubits [90 feet, or 27.6 meters], and its width will be 20 cubits [30 feet, or 9.2 meters]"; compare 1 Kgs 6:2. The emendation regarding the width is supported by the Syriac version. **6:6** Aramaic *the province beyond the river;* also in 6:6b, 8, 13.

and Shethar-bozenai, and your colleagues
and other officials west of the Euphrates
River—stay away from there! 7Do not
disturb the construction of the Temple of
God. Let it be rebuilt on its original site,
and do not hinder the governor of Judah
and the elders of the Jews in their work.

8"Moreover, I hereby decree that you
are to help these elders of the Jews as they
rebuild this Temple of God. You must pay
the full construction costs, without delay,
from my taxes collected in the province
west of the Euphrates River so that the
work will not be interrupted.

9"Give the priests in Jerusalem
whatever is needed in the way of young
bulls, rams, and male lambs for the burnt
offerings presented to the God of heaven.
And without fail, provide them with as
much wheat, salt, wine, and olive oil as
they need each day. 10Then they will be
able to offer acceptable sacrifices to the
God of heaven and pray for the welfare of
the king and his sons.

11"Those who violate this decree in any
way will have a beam pulled from their
house. Then they will be tied to it and
flogged, and their house will be reduced
to a pile of rubble.* 12May the God who
has chosen the city of Jerusalem as the
place to honor his name destroy any king
or nation that violates this command and
destroys this Temple.

"I, Darius, have issued this decree. Let it
be obeyed with all diligence."

The Temple's Dedication

13Tattenai, governor of the province west of
the Euphrates River, and Shethar-bozenai
and their colleagues complied at once with
the command of King Darius. 14So the Jewish
elders continued their work, and they were
greatly encouraged by the preaching of the
prophets Haggai and Zechariah son of Iddo.
The Temple was finally finished, as had been
commanded by the God of Israel and decreed
by Cyrus, Darius, and Artaxerxes, the kings
of Persia. 15The Temple was completed on
March 12,* during the sixth year of King Da-
rius's reign.

16The Temple of God was then dedicated
with great joy by the people of Israel, the
priests, the Levites, and the rest of the people
who had returned from exile. 17During the
dedication ceremony for the Temple of God,
100 young bulls, 200 rams, and 400 male
lambs were sacrificed. And 12 male goats
were presented as a sin offering for the
twelve tribes of Israel. 18Then the priests and
Levites were divided into their various divi-
sions to serve at the Temple of God in Jerusa-
lem, as prescribed in the Book of Moses.

Celebration of Passover

19On April 21* the returned exiles celebrated
Passover. 20The priests and Levites had puri-
fied themselves and were ceremonially clean.
So they slaughtered the Passover lamb for all
the returned exiles, for their fellow priests,
and for themselves. 21The Passover meal was
eaten by the people of Israel who had re-
turned from exile and by the others in the
land who had turned from their immoral cus-
toms to worship the LORD, the God of Israel.
22Then they celebrated the Festival of Unleav-
ened Bread for seven days. There was great
joy throughout the land because the LORD
had caused the king of Assyria* to be favor-
able to them, so that he helped them to re-
build the Temple of God, the God of Israel.

CHAPTER 7

Ezra Arrives in Jerusalem

Many years later, during the reign of King Ar-
taxerxes of Persia,* there was a man named
Ezra. He was the son* of Seraiah, son of Azari-
ah, son of Hilkiah, 2son of Shallum, son of Za-
dok, son of Ahitub, 3son of Amariah, son of
Azariah, son* of Meraioth, 4son of Zerahiah,
son of Uzzi, son of Bukki, 5son of Abishua, son
of Phinehas, son of Eleazar, son of Aaron the
high priest.* 6This Ezra was a scribe who was
well versed in the Law of Moses, which the
LORD, the God of Israel, had given to the peo-
ple of Israel. He came up to Jerusalem from
Babylon, and the king gave him everything he

6:11 Aramaic *a dunghill.* **6:15** Aramaic *on the third day of the month Adar,* of the ancient Hebrew lunar calendar. A number of events in Ezra can be cross-checked with dates in surviving Persian records and related accurately to our modern calendar. This day was March 12, 515 B.C. **6:19** Hebrew *On the fourteenth day of the first month,* of the ancient Hebrew lunar calendar. This day was April 21, 515 B.C.; also see note on 6:15. **6:22** King Darius of Persia is here identified as the king of Assyria because Persia had conquered the Babylonian Empire, which included the earlier Assyrian Empire. **7:1a** Artaxerxes reigned 465–424 B.C. **7:1b** Or *descendant;* see 1 Chr 6:14. **7:3** Or *descendant;* see 1 Chr 6:6-10. **7:5** Or *the first priest.*

asked for, because the gracious hand of the LORD his God was on him. [7]Some of the people of Israel, as well as some of the priests, Levites, singers, gatekeepers, and Temple servants, traveled up to Jerusalem with him in the seventh year of King Artaxerxes' reign.

[8]Ezra arrived in Jerusalem in August* of that year. [9]He had arranged to leave Babylon on April 8, the first day of the new year,* and he arrived at Jerusalem on August 4,* for the gracious hand of his God was on him. [10]This was because Ezra had determined to study and obey the Law of the LORD and to teach those decrees and regulations to the people of Israel.

Artaxerxes' Letter to Ezra

[11]King Artaxerxes had given a copy of the following letter to Ezra, the priest and scribe who studied and taught the commands and decrees of the LORD to Israel:

[12]*"From Artaxerxes, the king of kings, to Ezra the priest, the teacher of the law of the God of heaven. Greetings.

[13]"I decree that any of the people of Israel in my kingdom, including the priests and Levites, may volunteer to return to Jerusalem with you. [14]I and my council of seven hereby instruct you to conduct an inquiry into the situation in Judah and Jerusalem, based on your God's law, which is in your hand. [15]We also commission you to take with you silver and gold, which we are freely presenting as an offering to the God of Israel who lives in Jerusalem.

[16]"Furthermore, you are to take any silver and gold that you may obtain from the province of Babylon, as well as the voluntary offerings of the people and the priests that are presented for the Temple of their God in Jerusalem. [17]These donations are to be used specifically for the purchase of bulls, rams, male lambs, and the appropriate grain offerings and liquid offerings, all of which will be offered on the altar of the Temple of your God in Jerusalem. [18]Any silver and gold that is left over may be used in whatever way you and your colleagues feel is the will of your God.

[19]"But as for the cups we are entrusting to you for the service of the Temple of your God, deliver them all to the God of Jerusalem. [20]If you need anything else for your God's Temple or for any similar needs, you may take it from the royal treasury.

[21]"I, Artaxerxes the king, hereby send this decree to all the treasurers in the province west of the Euphrates River*: 'You are to give Ezra, the priest and teacher of the law of the God of heaven, whatever he requests of you. [22]You are to give him up to 7,500 pounds* of silver, 500 bushels* of wheat, 550 gallons of wine, 550 gallons of olive oil,* and an unlimited supply of salt. [23]Be careful to provide whatever the God of heaven demands for his Temple, for why should we risk bringing God's anger against the realm of the king and his sons? [24]I also decree that no priest, Levite, singer, gatekeeper, Temple servant, or other worker in this Temple of God will be required to pay tribute, customs, or tolls of any kind.'

[25]"And you, Ezra, are to use the wisdom your God has given you to appoint magistrates and judges who know your God's laws to govern all the people in the province west of the Euphrates River. Teach the law to anyone who does not know it. [26]Anyone who refuses to obey the law of your God and the law of the king will be punished immediately, either by death, banishment, confiscation of goods, or imprisonment."

Ezra Praises the LORD

[27]Praise the LORD, the God of our ancestors, who made the king want to beautify the Temple of the LORD in Jerusalem! [28]And praise him for demonstrating such unfailing love to me by honoring me before the king, his council, and all his mighty nobles! I felt encour-

7:8 Hebrew *in the fifth month*. This month in the ancient Hebrew lunar calendar occurred within the months of August and September 458 B.C. **7:9a** Hebrew *on the first day of the first month*, of the ancient Hebrew lunar calendar. This day was April 8, 458 B.C.; also see note on 6:15. **7:9b** Hebrew *on the first day of the fifth month*, of the ancient Hebrew lunar calendar. This day was August 4, 458 B.C.; also see note on 6:15. **7:12** The original text of 7:12-26 is in Aramaic. **7:21** Aramaic *the province beyond the river*; also in 7:25. **7:22a** Aramaic *100 talents* [3,400 kilograms]. **7:22b** Aramaic *100 cors* [18.2 kiloliters]. **7:22c** Aramaic *100 baths* [2.1 kiloliters] *of wine, 100 baths of olive oil.*

aged because the gracious hand of the LORD my God was on me. And I gathered some of the leaders of Israel to return with me to Jerusalem.

CHAPTER 8

Exiles Who Returned with Ezra

Here is a list of the family leaders and the genealogies of those who came with me from Babylon during the reign of King Artaxerxes:

2 From the family of Phinehas: Gershom.
From the family of Ithamar: Daniel.
From the family of David: Hattush, 3 a descendant of Shecaniah.
From the family of Parosh: Zechariah and 150 other men were registered.
4 From the family of Pahath-moab: Eliehoenai son of Zerahiah and 200 other men.
5 From the family of Zattu*: Shecaniah son of Jahaziel and 300 other men.
6 From the family of Adin: Ebed son of Jonathan and 50 other men.
7 From the family of Elam: Jeshaiah son of Athaliah and 70 other men.
8 From the family of Shephatiah: Zebadiah son of Michael and 80 other men.
9 From the family of Joab: Obadiah son of Jehiel and 218 other men.
10 From the family of Bani*: Shelomith son of Josiphiah and 160 other men.
11 From the family of Bebai: Zechariah son of Bebai and 28 other men.
12 From the family of Azgad: Johanan son of Hakkatan and 110 other men.
13 From the family of Adonikam, who came later*: Eliphelet, Jeuel, Shemaiah, and 60 other men.
14 From the family of Bigvai: Uthai, Zaccur,* and 70 other men.

Ezra's Journey to Jerusalem

15 I assembled the exiles at the Ahava Canal, and we camped there for three days while I went over the lists of the people and the priests who had arrived. I found that not one Levite had volunteered to come along. 16 So I sent for Eliezer, Ariel, Shemaiah, Elnathan, Jarib, Elnathan, Nathan, Zechariah, and Meshullam, who were leaders of the people. I also sent for Joiarib and Elnathan, who were men of discernment. 17 I sent them to Iddo, the leader of the Levites at Casiphia, to ask him and his relatives and the Temple servants to send us ministers for the Temple of God at Jerusalem.

18 Since the gracious hand of our God was on us, they sent us a man named Sherebiah, along with eighteen of his sons and brothers. He was a very astute man and a descendant of Mahli, who was a descendant of Levi son of Israel.* 19 They also sent Hashabiah, together with Jeshaiah from the descendants of Merari, and twenty of his sons and brothers, 20 and 220 Temple servants. The Temple servants were assistants to the Levites—a group of Temple workers first instituted by King David and his officials. They were all listed by name.

21 And there by the Ahava Canal, I gave orders for all of us to fast and humble ourselves before our God. We prayed that he would give us a safe journey and protect us, our children, and our goods as we traveled. 22 For I was ashamed to ask the king for soldiers and horsemen* to accompany us and protect us from enemies along the way. After all, we had told the king, "Our God's hand of protection is on all who worship him, but his fierce anger rages against those who abandon him." 23 So we fasted and earnestly prayed that our God would take care of us, and he heard our prayer.

24 I appointed twelve leaders of the priests—Sherebiah, Hashabiah, and ten other priests—25 to be in charge of transporting the silver, the gold, the gold bowls, and the other items that the king, his council, his officials, and all the people of Israel had presented for the Temple of God. 26 I weighed the treasure as I gave it to them and found the totals to be as follows:

24 tons* of silver,
7,500 pounds* of silver articles,
7,500 pounds of gold,
27 20 gold bowls, equal in value to 1,000 gold coins,*
2 fine articles of polished bronze, as precious as gold.

28 And I said to these priests, "You and these treasures have been set apart as holy to the

8:5 As in some Greek manuscripts (see also 1 Esdras 8:32); Hebrew lacks *Zattu*. **8:10** As in some Greek manuscripts (see also 1 Esdras 8:36); Hebrew lacks *Bani*. **8:13** Or *who were the last of his family*. **8:14** As in Greek and Syriac versions and an alternate reading of the Masoretic Text; the other alternate reads *Zabbud*. **8:18** *Israel* is the name that God gave to Jacob. **8:22** Or *charioteers*. **8:26a** Hebrew *650 talents* [22 metric tons]. **8:26b** Hebrew *100 talents* [3,400 kilograms]; also in 8:26c. **8:27** Hebrew *1,000 darics*, about 19 pounds or 8.6 kilograms in weight.

LORD. This silver and gold is a voluntary offering to the LORD, the God of our ancestors. [29]Guard these treasures well until you present them to the leading priests, the Levites, and the leaders of Israel, who will weigh them at the storerooms of the LORD's Temple in Jerusalem." [30]So the priests and the Levites accepted the task of transporting these treasures of silver and gold to the Temple of our God in Jerusalem.

[31]We broke camp at the Ahava Canal on April 19* and started off to Jerusalem. And the gracious hand of our God protected us and saved us from enemies and bandits along the way. [32]So we arrived safely in Jerusalem, where we rested for three days.

AMAZING FACTS

Ezra was so upset and sorry for the people's sins that he tore his clothes and pulled hair from his head and beard. Ouch!

EZRA 9:3

[33]On the fourth day after our arrival, the silver, gold, and other valuables were weighed at the Temple of our God and entrusted to Meremoth son of Uriah the priest and to Eleazar son of Phinehas, along with Jozabad son of Jeshua and Noadiah son of Binnui—both of whom were Levites. [34]Everything was accounted for by number and weight, and the total weight was officially recorded.

[35]Then the exiles who had come out of captivity sacrificed burnt offerings to the God of Israel. They presented twelve bulls for all the people of Israel, as well as ninety-six rams and seventy-seven male lambs. They also offered twelve male goats as a sin offering. All this was given as a burnt offering to the LORD. [36]The king's decrees were delivered to his highest officers and the governors of the province west of the Euphrates River,* who then cooperated by supporting the people and the Temple of God.

CHAPTER 9

Ezra's Prayer concerning Intermarriage

When these things had been done, the Jewish leaders came to me and said, "Many of the people of Israel, and even some of the priests and Levites, have not kept themselves separate from the other peoples living in the land. They have taken up the detestable practices of the Canaanites, Hittites, Perizzites, Jebusites, Ammonites, Moabites, Egyptians, and Amorites. [2]For the men of Israel have married women from these people and have taken them as wives for their sons. So the holy race has become polluted by these mixed marriages. Worse yet, the leaders and officials have led the way in this outrage."

[3]When I heard this, I tore my cloak and my shirt, pulled hair from my head and beard, and sat down utterly shocked. [4]Then all who trembled at the words of the God of Israel came and sat with me because of this outrage committed by the returned exiles. And I sat there utterly appalled until the time of the evening sacrifice.

[5]At the time of the sacrifice, I stood up from where I had sat in mourning with my clothes torn. I fell to my knees and lifted my hands to the LORD my God. [6]I prayed,

> "O my God, I am utterly ashamed; I blush to lift up my face to you. For our sins are piled higher than our heads, and our guilt has reached to the heavens. [7]From the days of our ancestors until now, we have been steeped in sin. That is why we and our kings and our priests have been at the mercy of the pagan kings of the land. We have been killed, captured, robbed, and disgraced, just as we are today.
>
> [8]"But now we have been given a brief moment of grace, for the LORD our God has allowed a few of us to survive as a remnant. He has given us security in this holy place. Our God has brightened our

8:31 Hebrew *on the twelfth day of the first month,* of the ancient Hebrew lunar calendar. This day was April 19, 458 B.C.; also see note on 6:15. **8:36** Hebrew *the province beyond the river.*

NO BIG DEAL?

Todd and Jake played together for a couple hours. Then Jake said, "If my mom asks, tell her I was with you the whole afternoon." Todd figured that Jake had been someplace where he shouldn't have been earlier in the afternoon. Todd told his friend, "If I said that, I would be lying."

"It's only a little lie," Jake said. "I didn't do anything wrong. I just don't want to get into trouble. It's no big deal."

Really? Is telling a small lie "no big deal"? Read Ezra 9:5-15 to see how Ezra felt about any kind of sin.

eyes and granted us some relief from our slavery. [9]For we were slaves, but in his unfailing love our God did not abandon us in our slavery. Instead, he caused the kings of Persia to treat us favorably. He revived us so we could rebuild the Temple of our God and repair its ruins. He has given us a protective wall in Judah and Jerusalem.

[10]"And now, O our God, what can we say after all of this? For once again we have abandoned your commands! [11]Your servants the prophets warned us when they said, 'The land you are entering to possess is totally defiled by the detestable practices of the people living there. From one end to the other, the land is filled with corruption. [12]Don't let your daughters marry their sons! Don't take their daughters as wives for your sons. Don't ever promote the peace and prosperity of those nations. If you follow these instructions, you will be strong and will enjoy the good things the land produces, and you will leave this prosperity to your children forever.'

[13]"Now we are being punished because of our wickedness and our great guilt. But we have actually been punished far less than we deserve, for you, our God, have allowed some of us to survive as a remnant. [14]But even so, we are again breaking your commands and intermarrying with people who do these detestable things. Won't your anger be enough to destroy us, so that even this little remnant no longer survives? [15]O LORD, God of Israel, you are just. We come before you in our guilt as nothing but an escaped remnant, though in such a condition none of us can stand in your presence."

CHAPTER 10

The People Confess Their Sin

While Ezra prayed and made this confession, weeping and lying face down on the ground in front of the Temple of God, a very large crowd of people from Israel—men, women, and children—gathered and wept bitterly with him. [2]Then Shecaniah son of Jehiel, a descendant of Elam, said to Ezra, "We have been unfaithful to our God, for we have married these pagan women of the land. But in spite of this there is hope for Israel. [3]Let us now make a covenant with our God to divorce our pagan wives and to send them away with their children. We will follow the advice given by you and by the others who respect the commands of our God. Let it be done according to the Law of God. [4]Get up, for it is your duty to tell us how to proceed in setting things straight. We are behind you, so be strong and take action."

5 So Ezra stood up and demanded that the leaders of the priests and the Levites and all the people of Israel swear that they would do as Shecaniah had said. And they all swore a solemn oath. 6 Then Ezra left the front of the Temple of God and went to the room of Jehohanan son of Eliashib. He spent the night* there without eating or drinking anything. He was still in mourning because of the unfaithfulness of the returned exiles.

7 Then a proclamation was made throughout Judah and Jerusalem that all the exiles should come to Jerusalem. 8 Those who failed to come within three days would, if the leaders and elders so decided, forfeit all their property and be expelled from the assembly of the exiles.

9 Within three days, all the people of Judah and Benjamin had gathered in Jerusalem. This took place on December 19,* and all the people were sitting in the square before the Temple of God. They were trembling both because of the seriousness of the matter and because it was raining. 10 Then Ezra the priest stood and said to them: "You have committed a terrible sin. By marrying pagan women, you have increased Israel's guilt. 11 So now confess your sin to the LORD, the God of your ancestors, and do what he demands. Separate yourselves from the people of the land and from these pagan women."

12 Then the whole assembly raised their voices and answered, "Yes, you are right; we must do as you say!" 13 Then they added, "This isn't something that can be done in a day or two, for many of us are involved in this extremely sinful affair. And this is the rainy season, so we cannot stay out here much longer. 14 Let our leaders act on behalf of us all. Let everyone who has a pagan wife come at a scheduled time, accompanied by the leaders and judges of his city, so that the fierce anger of our God concerning this affair may be turned away from us."

15 Only Jonathan son of Asahel and Jahzeiah son of Tikvah opposed this course of action, and they were supported by Meshullam and Shabbethai the Levite.

16 So this was the plan they followed. Ezra selected leaders to represent their families, designating each of the representatives by name. On December 29,* the leaders sat down to investigate the matter. 17 By March 27, the first day of the new year,* they had finished dealing with all the men who had married pagan wives.

Those Guilty of Intermarriage

18 These are the priests who had married pagan wives:

From the family of Jeshua son of Jehozadak* and his brothers: Maaseiah, Eliezer, Jarib, and Gedaliah. 19 They vowed to divorce their wives, and they each acknowledged their guilt by offering a ram as a guilt offering.

20 From the family of Immer: Hanani and Zebadiah.

21 From the family of Harim: Maaseiah, Elijah, Shemaiah, Jehiel, and Uzziah.

22 From the family of Pashhur: Elioenai, Maaseiah, Ishmael, Nethanel, Jozabad, and Elasah.

23 These are the Levites who were guilty: Jozabad, Shimei, Kelaiah (also called Kelita), Pethahiah, Judah, and Eliezer.

24 This is the singer who was guilty: Eliashib.

These are the gatekeepers who were guilty: Shallum, Telem, and Uri.

25 These are the other people of Israel who were guilty:

From the family of Parosh: Ramiah, Izziah, Malkijah, Mijamin, Eleazar, Hashabiah,* and Benaiah.

26 From the family of Elam: Mattaniah, Zechariah, Jehiel, Abdi, Jeremoth, and Elijah.

27 From the family of Zattu: Elioenai, Eliashib, Mattaniah, Jeremoth, Zabad, and Aziza.

28 From the family of Bebai: Jehohanan, Hananiah, Zabbai, and Athlai.

29 From the family of Bani: Meshullam, Malluch, Adaiah, Jashub, Sheal, and Jeremoth.

10:6 As in parallel text at 1 Esdras 9:2; Hebrew reads *He went.* **10:9** Hebrew *on the twentieth day of the ninth month,* of the ancient Hebrew lunar calendar. This day was December 19, 458 B.C.; also see note on 6:15. **10:16** Hebrew *On the first day of the tenth month,* of the ancient Hebrew lunar calendar. This day was December 29, 458 B.C.; also see note on 6:15. **10:17** Hebrew *By the first day of the first month,* of the ancient Hebrew lunar calendar. This day was March 27, 457 B.C.; also see note on 6:15. **10:18** Hebrew *Jozadak,* a variant spelling of Jehozadak. **10:25** As in parallel text at 1 Esdras 9:26; Hebrew reads *Malkijah.*

[30]From the family of Pahath-moab: Adna,
Kelal, Benaiah, Maaseiah, Mattaniah,
Bezalel, Binnui, and Manasseh.
[31]From the family of Harim: Eliezer,
Ishijah, Malkijah, Shemaiah,
Shimeon, [32]Benjamin, Malluch, and
Shemariah.
[33]From the family of Hashum: Mattenai,
Mattattah, Zabad, Eliphelet, Jeremai,
Manasseh, and Shimei.
[34]From the family of Bani: Maadai, Amram,
Uel, [35]Benaiah, Bedeiah, Keluhi, [36]Vaniah,
Meremoth, Eliashib, [37]Mattaniah,
Mattenai, and Jaasu.
[38]From the family of Binnui*: Shimei,
[39]Shelemiah, Nathan, Adaiah,
[40]Macnadebai, Shashai, Sharai, [41]Azarel,
Shelemiah, Shemariah, [42]Shallum,
Amariah, and Joseph.
[43]From the family of Nebo: Jeiel, Mattithiah,
Zabad, Zebina, Jaddai, Joel, and Benaiah.

[44]Each of these men had a pagan wife, and
some even had children by these wives.*

10:37-38 As in Greek version; Hebrew reads *Jaasu,* [38]*Bani, Binnui.* meaning of the Hebrew is uncertain.

10:44 Or *and they sent them away with their children.* The

Nehemiah

WHO
Nehemiah, Ezra, Sanballat, and Tobiah.

WHERE
Jerusalem, the capital of Judah.

WHEN
Around 445–432 BC, after the third group of Jews returned to their homeland.

WHY
To tell how the walls of Jerusalem were rebuilt and the people renewed their faith.

The wall was finished. . . .
[Our enemies] realized this
work had been done with
the help of our God.
NEHEMIAH 6:15-16

Imagine trying to do something very important but someone keeps stopping you. That happened to Nehemiah. It was discouraging, but Nehemiah knew God wanted him to help rebuild the walls of Jerusalem. Nehemiah set a good example of courage and determination for everyone to follow.

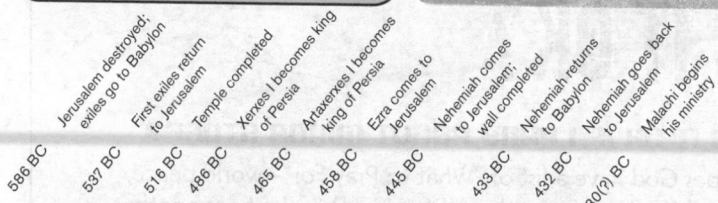

DO WHATEVER GOD WANTS YOU TO DO, NO MATTER WHAT THE OBSTACLES.

CHAPTER **1**

These are the memoirs of Nehemiah son of Hacaliah.

Nehemiah's Concern for Jerusalem

In late autumn, in the month of Kislev, in the twentieth year of King Artaxerxes' reign,* I was at the fortress of Susa. [2]Hanani, one of my brothers, came to visit me with some other men who had just arrived from Judah. I asked them about the Jews who had returned there from captivity and about how things were going in Jerusalem.

[3]They said to me, "Things are not going

1:1 Hebrew *In the month of Kislev of the twentieth year*. A number of dates in the book of Nehemiah can be cross-checked with dates in surviving Persian records and related accurately to our modern calendar. This month of the ancient Hebrew lunar calendar occurred within the months of November and December 446 B.C. The *twentieth year* probably refers to the reign of King Artaxerxes I; compare 2:1; 5:14.

well for those who returned to the province of Judah. They are in great trouble and disgrace. The wall of Jerusalem has been torn down, and the gates have been destroyed by fire."

4 When I heard this, I sat down and wept. In fact, for days I mourned, fasted, and prayed to the God of heaven. 5 Then I said,

"O LORD, God of heaven, the great and awesome God who keeps his covenant of unfailing love with those who love him and obey his commands, 6 listen to my prayer! Look down and see me praying night and day for your people Israel. I confess that we have sinned against you. Yes, even my own family and I have sinned! 7 We have sinned terribly by not obeying the commands, decrees, and regulations that you gave us through your servant Moses.

8 "Please remember what you told your servant Moses: 'If you are unfaithful to me, I will scatter you among the nations. 9 But if you return to me and obey my commands and live by them, then even if you are exiled to the ends of the earth, I will bring you back to the place I have chosen for my name to be honored.'

10 "The people you rescued by your great power and strong hand are your servants. 11 O Lord, please hear my prayer! Listen to the prayers of those of us who delight in honoring you. Please grant me success today by making the king favorable to me.* Put it into his heart to be kind to me."

In those days I was the king's cup-bearer.

CHAPTER 2

Nehemiah Goes to Jerusalem

Early the following spring, in the month of Nisan,* during the twentieth year of King Artaxerxes' reign, I was serving the king his wine. I had never before appeared sad in his presence. 2 So the king asked me, "Why are you looking so sad? You don't look sick to me. You must be deeply troubled."

Then I was terrified, 3 but I replied, "Long live the king! How can I not be sad? For the city where my ancestors are buried is in ruins, and the gates have been destroyed by fire."

4 The king asked, "Well, how can I help you?"

With a prayer to the God of heaven, 5 I replied, "If it please the king, and if you are

1:11 Hebrew *today in the sight of this man.* **2:1** Hebrew *In the month of Nisan.* This month of the ancient Hebrew lunar calendar occurred within the months of April and May 445 B.C.

IS IT OK?

IS IT OK IF I PRAY ABOUT MINOR STUFF?

Does God have a list of "What to Pray For"—world peace, food for the hungry, the AIDS crisis? Does he have another list of "What Not to Pray For"—spelling tests, fights with parents, fear of flying? Nope! God does *not* have a limited list of legitimate prayer requests. And he does *not* have a list of issues that are too minor for his attention. Nehemiah's prayers are a good example (see Nehemiah 1:11). He had this habit of talking to God about *everything*. We should do the same. Here's great news: Anything you care about, God cares about. Anything that worries you is something you can pray about. You can bet that God wants to hear about everything that matters to you.

pleased with me, your servant, send me to Judah to rebuild the city where my ancestors are buried."

[6]The king, with the queen sitting beside him, asked, "How long will you be gone? When will you return?" After I told him how long I would be gone, the king agreed to my request.

[7]I also said to the king, "If it please the king, let me have letters addressed to the governors of the province west of the Euphrates River,* instructing them to let me travel safely through their territories on my way to Judah. [8]And please give me a letter addressed to Asaph, the manager of the king's forest, instructing him to give me timber. I will need it to make beams for the gates of the Temple fortress, for the city walls, and for a house for myself." And the king granted these requests, because the gracious hand of God was on me.

[9]When I came to the governors of the province west of the Euphrates River, I delivered the king's letters to them. The king, I should add, had sent along army officers and horsemen* to protect me. [10]But when Sanballat the Horonite and Tobiah the Ammonite official heard of my arrival, they were very displeased that someone had come to help the people of Israel.

Nehemiah Inspects Jerusalem's Wall

[11]So I arrived in Jerusalem. Three days later, [12]I slipped out during the night, taking only a few others with me. I had not told anyone about the plans God had put in my heart for Jerusalem. We took no pack animals with us except the donkey I was riding. [13]After dark I went out through the Valley Gate, past the Jackal's Well,* and over to the Dung Gate to inspect the broken walls and burned gates. [14]Then I went to the Fountain Gate and to the King's Pool, but my donkey couldn't get through the rubble. [15]So, though it was still dark, I went up the Kidron Valley* instead, inspecting the wall before I turned back and entered again at the Valley Gate.

[16]The city officials did not know I had been out there or what I was doing, for I had not yet said anything to anyone about my plans. I had not yet spoken to the Jewish leaders—the priests, the nobles, the officials, or anyone else in the administration. [17]But now I said to them, "You know very well what trouble we are in. Jerusalem lies in ruins, and its gates have been destroyed by fire. Let us rebuild the wall of Jerusalem and end this disgrace!" [18]Then I told them about how the gracious hand of God had been on me, and about my conversation with the king.

They replied at once, "Yes, let's rebuild the wall!" So they began the good work.

[19]But when Sanballat, Tobiah, and Geshem the Arab heard of our plan, they scoffed contemptuously. "What are you doing? Are you rebelling against the king?" they asked.

[20]I replied, "The God of heaven will help us succeed. We, his servants, will start rebuilding this wall. But you have no share, legal right, or historic claim in Jerusalem."

CHAPTER 3

Rebuilding the Wall of Jerusalem

Then Eliashib the high priest and the other priests started to rebuild at the Sheep Gate. They dedicated it and set up its doors, building the wall as far as the Tower of the Hundred, which they dedicated, and the Tower of Hananel. [2]People from the town of Jericho worked next to them, and beyond them was Zaccur son of Imri.

[3]The Fish Gate was built by the sons of Hassenaah. They laid the beams, set up its doors, and installed its bolts and bars. [4]Meremoth son of Uriah and grandson of Hakkoz repaired the next section of wall. Beside him were Meshullam son of Berekiah and grandson of Meshezabel, and then Zadok son of Baana. [5]Next were the people from Tekoa, though their leaders refused to work with the construction supervisors.

[6]The Old City Gate* was repaired by Joiada son of Paseah and Meshullam son of Besodeiah. They laid the beams, set up its doors, and installed its bolts and bars. [7]Next to them were Melatiah from Gibeon, Jadon from Meronoth, people from Gibeon, and people from Mizpah, the headquarters of the governor of the province west of the Euphrates River.* [8]Next was Uzziel son of Harhaiah, a goldsmith by trade, who also worked on the wall. Beyond him was Hananiah, a manufacturer of perfumes. They

2:7 Hebrew *the province beyond the river;* also in 2:9. **2:9** Or *charioteers.* **2:13** Or *Serpent's Well.* **2:15** Hebrew *the valley.* **3:6** Or *The Mishneh Gate,* or *The Jeshanah Gate.* **3:7** Hebrew *the province beyond the river.*

left out a section of Jerusalem as they built the Broad Wall.*

[9]Rephaiah son of Hur, the leader of half the district of Jerusalem, was next to them on the wall. [10]Next Jedaiah son of Harumaph repaired the wall across from his own house, and next to him was Hattush son of Hashabneiah. [11]Then came Malkijah son of Harim and Hasshub son of Pahath-moab, who repaired another section of the wall and the Tower of the Ovens. [12]Shallum son of Hallohesh and his daughters repaired the next section. He was the leader of the other half of the district of Jerusalem.

[13]The Valley Gate was repaired by the people from Zanoah, led by Hanun. They set up its doors and installed its bolts and bars. They also repaired the 1,500 feet* of wall to the Dung Gate.

[14]The Dung Gate was repaired by Malkijah son of Recab, the leader of the Beth-hakkerem district. He rebuilt it, set up its doors, and installed its bolts and bars.

[15]The Fountain Gate was repaired by Shallum* son of Col-hozeh, the leader of the Mizpah district. He rebuilt it, roofed it, set up its doors, and installed its bolts and bars. Then he repaired the wall of the pool of Siloam* near the king's garden, and he rebuilt the wall as far as the stairs that descend from the City of David. [16]Next to him was Nehemiah son of Azbuk, the leader of half the district of Beth-zur. He rebuilt the wall from a place across from the tombs of David's family as far as the water reservoir and the House of the Warriors.

[17]Next to him, repairs were made by a group of Levites working under the supervision of Rehum son of Bani. Then came Hashabiah, the leader of half the district of Keilah, who supervised the building of the wall on behalf of his own district. [18]Next down the line were his countrymen led by Binnui* son of Henadad, the leader of the other half of the district of Keilah.

[19]Next to them, Ezer son of Jeshua, the leader of Mizpah, repaired another section of wall across from the ascent to the armory near the angle in the wall. [20]Next to him was Baruch son of Zabbai, who zealously repaired an additional section from the angle to the door of the house of Eliashib the high priest. [21]Meremoth son of Uriah and grandson of Hakkoz rebuilt another section of the wall extending from the door of Eliashib's house to the end of the house.

[22]The next repairs were made by the priests from the surrounding region. [23]After them, Benjamin and Hasshub repaired the section across from their house, and Azariah son of Maaseiah and grandson of Ananiah repaired the section across from his house. [24]Next was Binnui son of Henadad, who rebuilt another section of the wall from Azariah's house to the angle and the corner. [25]Palal son of Uzai carried on the work from a point opposite the angle and the tower that projects up from the king's upper house beside the court of the guard. Next to him were Pedaiah son of Parosh, [26]with the Temple servants living on the hill of Ophel, who repaired the wall as far as a point across from the Water Gate to the east and the projecting tower. [27]Then came the people of Tekoa, who repaired another section across from the great projecting tower and over to the wall of Ophel.

[28]Above the Horse Gate, the priests repaired the wall. Each one repaired the section immediately across from his own house. [29]Next Zadok son of Immer also rebuilt the wall across from his own house, and beyond him was Shemaiah son of Shecaniah, the gatekeeper of the East Gate. [30]Next Hananiah son of Shelemiah and Hanun, the sixth son of Zalaph, repaired another section, while Meshullam son of Berekiah rebuilt the wall across from where he lived. [31]Malkijah, one of the goldsmiths, repaired the wall as far as the housing for the Temple servants and merchants, across from the Inspection Gate. Then he continued as far as the upper room at the corner. [32]The other goldsmiths and merchants repaired the wall from that corner to the Sheep Gate.

CHAPTER 4

Enemies Oppose the Rebuilding

[1]*Sanballat was very angry when he learned that we were rebuilding the wall. He flew into a rage and mocked the Jews, [2]saying in front

3:8 Or *They fortified Jerusalem up to the Broad Wall.* **3:13** Hebrew *1,000 cubits* [450 meters]. **3:15a** As in Syriac version; Hebrew reads *Shallun.* **3:15b** Hebrew *pool of Shelah*, another name for the pool of Siloam. **3:18** As in a few Hebrew manuscripts, some Greek manuscripts, and Syriac version (see also 3:24; 10:9); most Hebrew manuscripts read *Bavvai.* **4:1** Verses 4:1-6 are numbered 3:33-38 in Hebrew text.

of his friends and the Samarian army officers, "What does this bunch of poor, feeble Jews think they're doing? Do they think they can build the wall in a single day by just offering a few sacrifices?* Do they actually think they can make something of stones from a rubbish heap—and charred ones at that?"

3 Tobiah the Ammonite, who was standing beside him, remarked, "That stone wall would collapse if even a fox walked along the top of it!"

4 Then I prayed, "Hear us, our God, for we are being mocked. May their scoffing fall back on their own heads, and may they themselves become captives in a foreign land! 5 Do not ignore their guilt. Do not blot out their sins, for they have provoked you to anger here in front of* the builders."

6 At last the wall was completed to half its height around the entire city, for the people had worked with enthusiasm.

7 *But when Sanballat and Tobiah and the Arabs, Ammonites, and Ashdodites heard that the work was going ahead and that the gaps in the wall of Jerusalem were being repaired, they were furious. 8 They all made plans to come and fight against Jerusalem and throw us into confusion. 9 But we prayed to our God and guarded the city day and night to protect ourselves.

10 Then the people of Judah began to complain, "The workers are getting tired, and there is so much rubble to be moved. We will never be able to build the wall by ourselves."

11 Meanwhile, our enemies were saying, "Before they know what's happening, we will swoop down on them and kill them and end their work."

12 The Jews who lived near the enemy came and told us again and again, "They will come from all directions and attack us!"* 13 So I placed armed guards behind the lowest parts of the wall in the exposed areas. I stationed the people to stand guard by families, armed with swords, spears, and bows.

14 Then as I looked over the situation, I called together the nobles and the rest of the people and said to them, "Don't be afraid of the enemy! Remember the Lord, who is great and glorious, and fight for your brothers, your sons, your daughters, your wives, and your homes!"

15 When our enemies heard that we knew of their plans and that God had frustrated them, we all returned to our work on the wall. 16 But from then on, only half my men worked while the other half stood guard with spears, shields, bows, and coats of mail. The leaders stationed themselves behind the people of Judah 17 who were building the wall. The laborers carried on their work with one hand supporting their load and one hand holding a weapon. 18 All the builders had a sword belted to their side. The trumpeter stayed with me to sound the alarm.

19 Then I explained to the nobles and officials and all the people, "The work is very spread out, and we are widely separated from each other along the wall. 20 When you hear the blast of the trumpet, rush to wherever it is sounding. Then our God will fight for us!"

21 We worked early and late, from sunrise to sunset. And half the men were always on guard. 22 I also told everyone living outside the walls to stay in Jerusalem. That way they and their servants could help with guard duty at night and work during the day. 23 During this time, none of us—not I, nor my relatives, nor my servants, nor the guards who were with me—ever took off our clothes. We carried our weapons with us at all times, even when we went for water.*

CHAPTER 5

Nehemiah Defends the Oppressed

About this time some of the men and their wives raised a cry of protest against their fellow Jews. 2 They were saying, "We have such large families. We need more food to survive."

3 Others said, "We have mortgaged our fields, vineyards, and homes to get food during the famine."

4 And others said, "We have had to borrow money on our fields and vineyards to pay our taxes. 5 We belong to the same family as those who are wealthy, and our children are just like theirs. Yet we must sell our children into slavery just to get enough money to live. We have already sold some of our daughters, and we

4:2 The meaning of the Hebrew is uncertain. **4:5** Or *for they have thrown insults in the face of.* **4:7** Verses 4:7-23 are numbered 4:1-17 in Hebrew text. **4:12** The meaning of the Hebrew is uncertain. **4:23** Or *Each carried his weapon in his right hand.* Hebrew reads *Each his weapon the water.* The meaning of the Hebrew is uncertain.

are helpless to do anything about it, for our fields and vineyards are already mortgaged to others."

[6]When I heard their complaints, I was very angry. [7]After thinking it over, I spoke out against these nobles and officials. I told them, "You are hurting your own relatives by charging interest when they borrow money!" Then I called a public meeting to deal with the problem.

[8]At the meeting I said to them, "We are doing all we can to redeem our Jewish relatives who have had to sell themselves to pagan foreigners, but you are selling them back into slavery again. How often must we redeem them?" And they had nothing to say in their defense.

[9]Then I pressed further, "What you are doing is not right! Should you not walk in the fear of our God in order to avoid being mocked by enemy nations? [10]I myself, as well as my brothers and my workers, have been lending the people money and grain, but now let us stop this business of charging interest. [11]You must restore their fields, vineyards, olive groves, and homes to them this very day. And repay the interest you charged when you lent them money, grain, new wine, and olive oil."

[12]They replied, "We will give back everything and demand nothing more from the people. We will do as you say." Then I called the priests and made the nobles and officials swear to do what they had promised.

[13]I shook out the folds of my robe and said, "If you fail to keep your promise, may God shake you like this from your homes and from your property!"

The whole assembly responded, "Amen," and they praised the LORD. And the people did as they had promised.

[14]For the entire twelve years that I was governor of Judah—from the twentieth year to the thirty-second year of the reign of King Artaxerxes*—neither I nor my officials drew on our official food allowance. [15]The former governors, in contrast, had laid heavy burdens on the people, demanding a daily ration of food and wine, besides forty pieces* of silver. Even their assistants took advantage of the people. But because I feared God, I did not act that way.

[16]I also devoted myself to working on the wall and refused to acquire any land. And I required all my servants to spend time working on the wall. [17]I asked for nothing, even though I regularly fed 150 Jewish officials at my table, besides all the visitors from other lands! [18]The provisions I paid for each day included one ox, six choice sheep or goats, and a large number of poultry. And every ten days we needed a large supply of all kinds of wine. Yet I refused to claim the governor's food allowance because the people already carried a heavy burden.

[19]Remember, O my God, all that I have done for these people, and bless me for it.

CHAPTER 6

Continued Opposition to Rebuilding

Sanballat, Tobiah, Geshem the Arab, and the rest of our enemies found out that I had finished rebuilding the wall and that no gaps remained—though we had not yet set up the doors in the gates. [2]So Sanballat and Geshem sent a message asking me to meet them at one of the villages* in the plain of Ono.

But I realized they were plotting to harm me, [3]so I replied by sending this message to them: "I am engaged in a great work, so I can't come. Why should I stop working to come and meet with you?"

[4]Four times they sent the same message, and each time I gave the same reply. [5]The fifth time, Sanballat's servant came with an open letter in his hand, [6]and this is what it said:

"There is a rumor among the surrounding nations, and Geshem* tells me it is true, that you and the Jews are planning to rebel and that is why you are building the wall. According to his reports, you plan to be their king. [7]He also reports that you have appointed prophets in Jerusalem to proclaim about you, 'Look! There is a king in Judah!'

"You can be very sure that this report will get back to the king, so I suggest that you come and talk it over with me."

5:14 That is, 445–433 B.C. **5:15** Hebrew *40 shekels* [1 pound, or 456 grams]. **6:2** As in Greek version; Hebrew reads *at Kephirim*. **6:6** Hebrew *Gashmu*, a variant spelling of Geshem.

Call me crazy, but I always wanted to do something big for God. Even when I was in middle school, I wanted to start a Christian club at my school. When I got to high school, I joined a Christian club that met weekly.

I was thrilled when they gave me (just a tiny, little freshman with a squeaky voice) two big jobs in the club—bringing the snacks and sharing the salvation message once a month.

My high hopes for doing something big for God came crashing down several weeks later. We prepared a fun club meeting with cool-looking snacks, hoping a lot of new people would attend and hear my story about Jesus living in me. But nobody new came . . . that's right . . . nobody. That hit me hard. I wanted to quit. A little voice in my head told me that all my hard work was for nothing.

It was then that I remembered what I had read in Nehemiah 6:8-9. Some people told Nehemiah that his plan to rebuild the walls of Jerusalem would never succeed. What did Nehemiah do? He didn't believe the others, and he didn't quit. Instead, he prayed and continued working.

Many times during the past couple of years I thought about quitting. Being involved with a Christian club at our school is discouraging because many kids are afraid to attend. They are afraid their friends might make fun of them. But just like Nehemiah, I haven't given up. I know God gave me what I wanted—the big job of telling my school friends about him. Now I'm leading the club, and I keep inviting my friends, because God is faithful and powerful. He would never give up on me. Why should I give up on him?

Check out Nehemiah's response to opposition in Nehemiah 6:8-9. For more encouragement in facing opposition, read Psalm 3:1-3; 25:2; and Revelation 1:17-18.

[8]I replied, "There is no truth in any part of your story. You are making up the whole thing."

[9]They were just trying to intimidate us, imagining that they could discourage us and stop the work. So I continued the work with even greater determination.*

[10]Later I went to visit Shemaiah son of Delaiah and grandson of Mehetabel, who was confined to his home. He said, "Let us meet together inside the Temple of God and bolt the doors shut. Your enemies are coming to kill you tonight."

[11]But I replied, "Should someone in my position run from danger? Should someone in my position enter the Temple to save his life? No, I won't do it!" [12]I realized that God had not spoken to him, but that he had uttered this prophecy against me because Tobiah and Sanballat had hired him. [13]They were hoping to intimidate me and make me sin. Then they would be able to accuse and discredit me.

[14]Remember, O my God, all the evil things that Tobiah and Sanballat have done. And remember Noadiah the prophet and all the prophets like her who have tried to intimidate me.

AMAZING FACTS

It took less than two months—52 days—to rebuild the wall around the whole city of Jerusalem. That's a fast-track project!

NEHEMIAH 6:15

The Builders Complete the Wall

[15]So on October 2* the wall was finished—just fifty-two days after we had begun. [16]When our enemies and the surrounding nations heard about it, they were frightened and humiliated. They realized this work had been done with the help of our God.

[17]During those fifty-two days, many letters went back and forth between Tobiah and the nobles of Judah. [18]For many in Judah had sworn allegiance to him because his father-in-law was Shecaniah son of Arah, and his son Jehohanan was married to the daughter of Meshullam son of Berekiah. [19]They kept telling me about Tobiah's good deeds, and then they told him everything I said. And Tobiah kept sending threatening letters to intimidate me.

CHAPTER 7

After the wall was finished and I had set up the doors in the gates, the gatekeepers, singers, and Levites were appointed. [2]I gave the responsibility of governing Jerusalem to my brother Hanani, along with Hananiah, the commander of the fortress, for he was a faithful man who feared God more than most. [3]I said to them, "Do not leave the gates open during the hottest part of the day.* And even while the gatekeepers are on duty, have them shut and bar the doors. Appoint the residents of Jerusalem to act as guards, everyone on a regular watch. Some will serve at sentry posts and some in front of their own homes."

Nehemiah Registers the People

[4]At that time the city was large and spacious, but the population was small, and none of the houses had been rebuilt. [5]So my God gave me the idea to call together all the nobles and leaders of the city, along with the ordinary citizens, for registration. I had found the genealogical record of those who had first returned to Judah. This is what was written there:

[6]Here is the list of the Jewish exiles of the provinces who returned from their captivity. King Nebuchadnezzar had deported them to Babylon, but now they returned to Jerusalem and the other towns in Judah where they originally lived. [7]Their leaders were Zerubbabel, Jeshua, Nehemiah, Seraiah,* Reelaiah,* Nahamani, Mordecai, Bilshan, Mispar,* Bigvai, Rehum,* and Baanah.

6:9 As in Greek version; Hebrew reads *But now to strengthen my hands.* **6:15** Hebrew *on the twenty-fifth day of the month Elul,* of the ancient Hebrew lunar calendar. This day was October 2, 445 B.C.; also see note on 1:1. **7:3** Or *Keep the gates of Jerusalem closed until the sun is hot.* **7:7a** As in parallel text at Ezra 2:2; Hebrew reads *Azariah.* **7:7b** As in parallel text at Ezra 2:2; Hebrew reads *Raamiah.* **7:7c** As in parallel text at Ezra 2:2; Hebrew reads *Mispereth.* **7:7d** As in parallel text at Ezra 2:2; Hebrew reads *Nehum.*

This is the number of the men of Israel who returned from exile:

8 The family of Parosh 2,172
9 The family of Shephatiah 372
10 The family of Arah. 652
11 The family of Pahath-moab (descendants of Jeshua and Joab) . 2,818
12 The family of Elam 1,254
13 The family of Zattu 845
14 The family of Zaccai. 760
15 The family of Bani* 648
16 The family of Bebai 628
17 The family of Azgad. 2,322
18 The family of Adonikam 667
19 The family of Bigvai. 2,067
20 The family of Adin. 655
21 The family of Ater (descendants of Hezekiah). 98
22 The family of Hashum 328
23 The family of Bezai 324
24 The family of Jorah*. 112
25 The family of Gibbar* 95
26 The people of Bethlehem and Netophah 188
27 The people of Anathoth 128
28 The people of Beth-azmaveth. 42
29 The people of Kiriath-jearim, Kephirah, and Beeroth 743
30 The people of Ramah and Geba. 621
31 The people of Micmash. 122
32 The people of Bethel and Ai 123
33 The people of West Nebo* 52
34 The citizens of West Elam* 1,254
35 The citizens of Harim. 320
36 The citizens of Jericho 345
37 The citizens of Lod, Hadid, and Ono . . . 721
38 The citizens of Senaah 3,930

39 These are the priests who returned from exile:

The family of Jedaiah (through the line of Jeshua). 973
40 The family of Immer 1,052
41 The family of Pashhur 1,247
42 The family of Harim 1,017

43 These are the Levites who returned from exile:

The families of Jeshua and Kadmiel (descendants of Hodaviah*) 74
44 The singers of the family of Asaph 148
45 The gatekeepers of the families of Shallum, Ater, Talmon, Akkub, Hatita, and Shobai 138

46 The descendants of the following Temple servants returned from exile:
Ziha, Hasupha, Tabbaoth,
47 Keros, Siaha,* Padon,
48 Lebanah, Hagabah, Shalmai,
49 Hanan, Giddel, Gahar,
50 Reaiah, Rezin, Nekoda,
51 Gazzam, Uzza, Paseah,
52 Besai, Meunim, Nephusim,*
53 Bakbuk, Hakupha, Harhur,
54 Bazluth,* Mehida, Harsha,
55 Barkos, Sisera, Temah,
56 Neziah, and Hatipha.

57 The descendants of these servants of King Solomon returned from exile:
Sotai, Hassophereth, Peruda,*
58 Jaalah,* Darkon, Giddel,
59 Shephatiah, Hattil, Pokereth-hazzebaim, and Ami.*

60 In all, the Temple servants and the descendants of Solomon's servants numbered 392.

61 Another group returned at this time from the towns of Tel-melah, Tel-harsha, Kerub, Addan,* and Immer. However, they could not prove that they or their families were descendants of Israel. 62 This group included the families of Delaiah, Tobiah, and Nekoda—a total of 642 people.

63 Three families of priests—Hobaiah, Hakkoz, and Barzillai—also returned. (This Barzillai had married a woman who was a descendant of Barzillai of Gilead, and he had taken her family name.) 64 They searched for their names in the genealogical records, but they were not found, so they were disqualified from serving as priests. 65 The governor told them not to eat the priests' share of food

7:15 As in parallel text at Ezra 2:10; Hebrew reads *Binnui*. **7:24** As in parallel text at Ezra 2:18; Hebrew reads *Hariph*. **7:25** As in parallel text at Ezra 2:20; Hebrew reads *Gibeon*. **7:33** Or *of the other Nebo*. **7:34** Or *of the other Elam*. **7:43** As in parallel text at Ezra 2:40; Hebrew reads *Hodevah*. **7:47** As in parallel text at Ezra 2:44; Hebrew reads *Sia*. **7:52** As in parallel text at Ezra 2:50; Hebrew reads *Nephushesim*. **7:54** As in parallel text at Ezra 2:52; Hebrew reads *Bazlith*. **7:57** As in parallel text at Ezra 2:55; Hebrew reads *Sotai, Sophereth, Perida*. **7:58** As in parallel text at Ezra 2:56; Hebrew reads *Jaala*. **7:59** As in parallel text at Ezra 2:57; Hebrew reads *Amon*. **7:61** As in parallel text at Ezra 2:59; Hebrew reads *Addon*.

from the sacrifices until a priest could consult the LORD about the matter by using the Urim and Thummim—the sacred lots.

66So a total of 42,360 people returned to Judah, 67in addition to 7,337 servants and 245 singers, both men and women. 68They took with them 736 horses, 245 mules,* 69435 camels, and 6,720 donkeys.

70Some of the family leaders gave gifts for the work. The governor gave to the treasury 1,000 gold coins,* 50 gold basins, and 530 robes for the priests. 71The other leaders gave to the treasury a total of 20,000 gold coins* and some 2,750 pounds* of silver for the work. 72The rest of the people gave 20,000 gold coins, about 2,500 pounds* of silver, and 67 robes for the priests.

73So the priests, the Levites, the gatekeepers, the singers, the Temple servants, and some of the common people settled near Jerusalem. The rest of the people returned to their own towns throughout Israel.

CHAPTER 8

Ezra Reads the Law

In October,* when the Israelites had settled in their towns, 8:1all the people assembled with a unified purpose at the square just inside the Water Gate. They asked Ezra the scribe to bring out the Book of the Law of Moses, which the LORD had given for Israel to obey.

2So on October 8* Ezra the priest brought the Book of the Law before the assembly, which included the men and women and all the children old enough to understand. 3He faced the square just inside the Water Gate from early morning until noon and read aloud to everyone who could understand. All the people listened closely to the Book of the Law.

4Ezra the scribe stood on a high wooden platform that had been made for the occasion. To his right stood Mattithiah, Shema, Anaiah, Uriah, Hilkiah, and Maaseiah. To his left stood Pedaiah, Mishael, Malkijah, Hashum, Hashbaddanah, Zechariah, and Meshullam. 5Ezra stood on the platform in full view of all the people. When they saw him open the book, they all rose to their feet.

6Then Ezra praised the LORD, the great God, and all the people chanted, "Amen! Amen!" as they lifted their hands. Then they bowed down and worshiped the LORD with their faces to the ground.

7The Levites—Jeshua, Bani, Sherebiah, Jamin, Akkub, Shabbethai, Hodiah, Maaseiah, Kelita, Azariah, Jozabad, Hanan, and Pelaiah—then instructed the people in the Law while everyone remained in their places. 8They read from the Book of the Law of God and clearly explained the meaning of what was being read, helping the people understand each passage.

9Then Nehemiah the governor, Ezra the priest and scribe, and the Levites who were interpreting for the people said to them, "Don't mourn or weep on such a day as this! For today is a sacred day before the LORD your God." For the people had all been weeping as they listened to the words of the Law.

When I'm feeling weak, how can I keep going?

The joy of the LORD is your strength!
NEHEMIAH 8:10

10And Nehemiah* continued, "Go and celebrate with a feast of rich foods and sweet drinks, and share gifts of food with people who have nothing prepared. This is a sacred day before our Lord. Don't be dejected and sad, for the joy of the LORD is your strength!"

11And the Levites, too, quieted the people, telling them, "Hush! Don't weep! For this is a sacred day." 12So the people went away to eat and drink at a festive meal, to share gifts of food, and to celebrate with great joy because they had heard God's words and understood them.

7:68 As in some Hebrew manuscripts (see also Ezra 2:66); most Hebrew manuscripts lack this verse. Verses 7:69-73 are numbered 7:68-72 in Hebrew text. **7:70** Hebrew *1,000 darics of gold*, about 19 pounds or 8.6 kilograms in weight. **7:71a** Hebrew *20,000 darics of gold*, about 375 pounds or 170 kilograms in weight; also in 7:72. **7:71b** Hebrew *2,200 minas* [1,300 kilograms]. **7:72** Hebrew *2,000 minas* [1,200 kilograms]. **7:73** Hebrew *in the seventh month*. This month of the ancient Hebrew lunar calendar occurred within the months of October and November 445 B.C. **8:2** Hebrew *on the first day of the seventh month*, of the ancient Hebrew lunar calendar. This day was October 8, 445 B.C.; also see note on 1:1. **8:10** Hebrew *he*.

The Festival of Shelters

13On October 9* the family leaders of all the people, together with the priests and Levites, met with Ezra the scribe to go over the Law in greater detail. 14As they studied the Law, they discovered that the LORD had commanded through Moses that the Israelites should live in shelters during the festival to be held that month.* 15He had said that a proclamation should be made throughout their towns and in Jerusalem, telling the people to go to the hills to get branches from olive, wild olive,* myrtle, palm, and other leafy trees. They were to use these branches to make shelters in which they would live during the festival, as prescribed in the Law.

16So the people went out and cut branches and used them to build shelters on the roofs of their houses, in their courtyards, in the courtyards of God's Temple, or in the squares just inside the Water Gate and the Ephraim Gate. 17So everyone who had returned from captivity lived in these shelters during the festival, and they were all filled with great joy! The Israelites had not celebrated like this since the days of Joshua* son of Nun.

18Ezra read from the Book of the Law of God on each of the seven days of the festival. Then on the eighth day they held a solemn assembly, as was required by law.

CHAPTER 9

The People Confess Their Sins

On October 31* the people assembled again, and this time they fasted and dressed in burlap and sprinkled dust on their heads. 2Those of Israelite descent separated themselves from all foreigners as they confessed their own sins and the sins of their ancestors. 3They remained standing in place for three hours* while the Book of the Law of the LORD their God was read aloud to them. Then for three more hours they confessed their sins and worshiped the LORD their God. 4The Levites—Jeshua, Bani, Kadmiel, Shebaniah, Bunni, Sherebiah, Bani, and Kenani—stood on the stairway of the Levites and cried out to the LORD their God with loud voices.

5Then the leaders of the Levites—Jeshua, Kadmiel, Bani, Hashabneiah, Sherebiah, Hodiah, Shebaniah, and Pethahiah—called out to the people: "Stand up and praise the LORD your God, for he lives from everlasting to everlasting!" Then they prayed:

"May your glorious name be praised! May it be exalted above all blessing and praise!

6"You alone are the LORD. You made the skies and the heavens and all the stars. You made the earth and the seas and everything in them. You preserve them all, and the angels of heaven worship you.

7"You are the LORD God, who chose Abram and brought him from Ur of the Chaldeans and renamed him Abraham. 8When he had proved himself faithful, you made a covenant with him to give him and his descendants the land of the Canaanites, Hittites, Amorites, Perizzites, Jebusites, and Girgashites. And you have done what you promised, for you are always true to your word.

9"You saw the misery of our ancestors in Egypt, and you heard their cries from beside the Red Sea.* 10You displayed miraculous signs and wonders against Pharaoh, his officials, and all his people, for you knew how arrogantly they were treating our ancestors. You have a glorious reputation that has never been forgotten. 11You divided the sea for your people so they could walk through on dry land! And then you hurled their enemies into the depths of the sea. They sank like stones beneath the mighty waters. 12You led our ancestors by a pillar of cloud during the day and a pillar of fire at night so that they could find their way.

13"You came down at Mount Sinai and spoke to them from heaven. You gave them regulations and instructions that were just, and decrees and commands that were good. 14You instructed them concerning your holy Sabbath. And you commanded them, through Moses your servant, to obey all your commands, decrees, and instructions.

15"You gave them bread from heaven

8:13 Hebrew *On the second day,* of the seventh month of the ancient Hebrew lunar calendar. This day was October 9, 445 B.C.; also see notes on 1:1 and 8:2. **8:14** Hebrew *in the seventh month.* This month of the ancient Hebrew lunar calendar usually occurs within the months of September and October. See Lev 23:39-43. **8:15** Or *pine;* Hebrew reads *oil tree.* **8:17** Hebrew *Jeshua,* a variant spelling of Joshua. **9:1** Hebrew *On the twenty-fourth day of that same month,* the seventh month of the ancient Hebrew lunar calendar. This day was October 31, 445 B.C.; also see notes on 1:1 and 8:2. **9:3** Hebrew *for a quarter of a day.* **9:9** Hebrew *sea of reeds.*

when they were hungry and water from
the rock when they were thirsty. You
commanded them to go and take
possession of the land you had sworn to
give them.

16"But our ancestors were proud and
stubborn, and they paid no attention to
your commands. 17They refused to obey
and did not remember the miracles you
had done for them. Instead, they became
stubborn and appointed a leader to take
them back to their slavery in Egypt! But
you are a God of forgiveness, gracious and
merciful, slow to become angry, and rich
in unfailing love. You did not abandon
them, 18even when they made an idol
shaped like a calf and said, 'This is your
god who brought you out of Egypt!' They
committed terrible blasphemies.

19"But in your great mercy you did not
abandon them to die in the wilderness.
The pillar of cloud still led them forward
by day, and the pillar of fire showed
them the way through the night. 20You
sent your good Spirit to instruct them,
and you did not stop giving them manna
from heaven or water for their thirst.
21For forty years you sustained them in
the wilderness, and they lacked nothing.
Their clothes did not wear out, and their
feet did not swell!

22"Then you helped our ancestors
conquer kingdoms and nations, and you
placed your people in every corner of the
land.* They took over the land of King
Sihon of Heshbon and the land of King
Og of Bashan. 23You made their
descendants as numerous as the stars in
the sky and brought them into the land
you had promised to their ancestors.

24"They went in and took possession of
the land. You subdued whole nations
before them. Even the Canaanites, who
inhabited the land, were powerless! Your
people could deal with these nations and
their kings as they pleased. 25Our
ancestors captured fortified cities and
fertile land. They took over houses full of
good things, with cisterns already dug and
vineyards and olive groves and fruit trees
in abundance. So they ate until they were
full and grew fat and enjoyed themselves
in all your blessings.

26"But despite all this, they were
disobedient and rebelled against you.
They turned their backs on your Law, they
killed your prophets who warned them to
return to you, and they committed terrible
blasphemies. 27So you handed them over
to their enemies, who made them suffer.
But in their time of trouble they cried to
you, and you heard them from heaven. In
your great mercy, you sent them liberators
who rescued them from their enemies.

28"But as soon as they were at peace,
your people again committed evil in your
sight, and once more you let their
enemies conquer them. Yet whenever
your people turned and cried to you again
for help, you listened once more from
heaven. In your wonderful mercy, you
rescued them many times!

29"You warned them to return to your
Law, but they became proud and
obstinate and disobeyed your commands.
They did not follow your regulations, by
which people will find life if only they
obey. They stubbornly turned their backs
on you and refused to listen. 30In your
love, you were patient with them for many
years. You sent your Spirit, who warned
them through the prophets. But still they
wouldn't listen! So once again you allowed
the peoples of the land to conquer them.
31But in your great mercy, you did not
destroy them completely or abandon
them forever. What a gracious and
merciful God you are!

32"And now, our God, the great and
mighty and awesome God, who keeps his
covenant of unfailing love, do not let all
the hardships we have suffered seem
insignificant to you. Great trouble has
come upon us and upon our kings and
leaders and priests and prophets and
ancestors—all of your people—from the
days when the kings of Assyria first
triumphed over us until now. 33Every time
you punished us you were being just. We
have sinned greatly, and you gave us only
what we deserved. 34Our kings, leaders,
priests, and ancestors did not obey your

9:22 The meaning of the Hebrew is uncertain.

Law or listen to the warnings in your commands and laws. [35]Even while they had their own kingdom, they did not serve you, though you showered your goodness on them. You gave them a large, fertile land, but they refused to turn from their wickedness.

[36]"So now today we are slaves in the land of plenty that you gave our ancestors for their enjoyment! We are slaves here in this good land. [37]The lush produce of this land piles up in the hands of the kings whom you have set over us because of our sins. They have power over us and our livestock. We serve them at their pleasure, and we are in great misery."

The People Agree to Obey

[38]*The people responded, "In view of all this,* we are making a solemn promise and putting it in writing. On this sealed document are the names of our leaders and Levites and priests."

CHAPTER 10

[1]*The document was ratified and sealed with the following names:

The governor:
Nehemiah son of Hacaliah, and also Zedekiah.

[2]The following priests:
Seraiah, Azariah, Jeremiah, [3]Pashhur, Amariah, Malkijah, [4]Hattush, Shebaniah, Malluch, [5]Harim, Meremoth, Obadiah, [6]Daniel, Ginnethon, Baruch, [7]Meshullam, Abijah, Mijamin, [8]Maaziah, Bilgai, and Shemaiah. These were the priests.

[9]The following Levites:
Jeshua son of Azaniah, Binnui from the family of Henadad, Kadmiel, [10]and their fellow Levites: Shebaniah, Hodiah, Kelita, Pelaiah, Hanan, [11]Mica, Rehob, Hashabiah, [12]Zaccur, Sherebiah, Shebaniah, [13]Hodiah, Bani, and Beninu.

[14]The following leaders:
Parosh, Pahath-moab, Elam, Zattu, Bani, [15]Bunni, Azgad, Bebai, [16]Adonijah, Bigvai, Adin, [17]Ater, Hezekiah, Azzur, [18]Hodiah, Hashum, Bezai, [19]Hariph, Anathoth, Nebai, [20]Magpiash, Meshullam, Hezir, [21]Meshezabel, Zadok, Jaddua, [22]Pelatiah, Hanan, Anaiah, [23]Hoshea, Hananiah, Hasshub, [24]Hallohesh, Pilha, Shobek, [25]Rehum, Hashabnah, Maaseiah, [26]Ahiah, Hanan, Anan, [27]Malluch, Harim, and Baanah.

The Vow of the People

[28]Then the rest of the people—the priests, Levites, gatekeepers, singers, Temple servants, and all who had separated themselves from the pagan people of the land in order to obey the Law of God, together with their wives, sons, daughters, and all who were old enough to understand—[29]joined their leaders and bound themselves with an oath. They swore a curse on themselves if they failed to obey the Law of God as issued by his servant Moses. They solemnly promised to carefully follow all the commands, regulations, and decrees of the LORD our Lord:

[30]"We promise not to let our daughters marry the pagan people of the land, and not to let our sons marry their daughters.

[31]"We also promise that if the people of the land should bring any merchandise or grain to be sold on the Sabbath or on any other holy day, we will refuse to buy it. Every seventh year we will let our land rest, and we will cancel all debts owed to us.

[32]"In addition, we promise to obey the command to pay the annual Temple tax of one-eighth of an ounce of silver* for the care of the Temple of our God. [33]This will provide for the Bread of the Presence; for the regular grain offerings and burnt offerings; for the offerings on the Sabbaths, the new moon celebrations, and the annual festivals; for the holy offerings; and for the sin offerings to make atonement for Israel. It will provide for everything necessary for the work of the Temple of our God.

[34]"We have cast sacred lots to determine when—at regular times each year—the families of the priests, Levites, and the common people should bring wood to God's Temple to be burned on the altar of the LORD our God, as is written in the Law.

[35]"We promise to bring the first part of every harvest to the LORD's Temple year

9:38a Verse 9:38 is numbered 10:1 in Hebrew text. **9:38b** Or *In spite of all this.* **10:1** Verses 10:1-39 are numbered 10:2-40 in Hebrew text. **10:32** Hebrew *tax of ⅓ of a shekel* [4 grams].

WHOSE MONEY?

Jonathan got a weekly allowance, and sometimes he made extra money from mowing lawns. Jonathan believed that he should give ten percent to church, so he set aside that money every time he was paid. On his birthday, Jonathan received almost fifty dollars from relatives. His mom asked, "Are you putting some of your birthday money in the church offering?" Jonathan was confused. He thought of those gifts as *his* money. After all, ten percent of fifty dollars would be five dollars—a lot of money to give. What should Jonathan do? Nehemiah 10:35-39 tells what the Israelites did with their gifts.

after year—whether it be a crop from the soil or from our fruit trees. [36]We agree to give God our oldest sons and the firstborn of all our herds and flocks, as prescribed in the Law. We will present them to the priests who minister in the Temple of our God. [37]We will store the produce in the storerooms of the Temple of our God. We will bring the best of our flour and other grain offerings, the best of our fruit, and the best of our new wine and olive oil. And we promise to bring to the Levites a tenth of everything our land produces, for it is the Levites who collect the tithes in all our rural towns.

[38]"A priest—a descendant of Aaron—will be with the Levites as they receive these tithes. And a tenth of all that is collected as tithes will be delivered by the Levites to the Temple of our God and placed in the storerooms. [39]The people and the Levites must bring these offerings of grain, new wine, and olive oil to the storerooms and place them in the sacred containers near the ministering priests, the gatekeepers, and the singers.

"We promise together not to neglect the Temple of our God."

CHAPTER 11

The People Occupy Jerusalem

The leaders of the people were living in Jerusalem, the holy city. A tenth of the people from the other towns of Judah and Benjamin were chosen by sacred lots to live there, too, while the rest stayed where they were. [2]And the people commended everyone who volunteered to resettle in Jerusalem.

[3]Here is a list of the names of the provincial officials who came to live in Jerusalem. (Most of the people, priests, Levites, Temple servants, and descendants of Solomon's servants continued to live in their own homes in the various towns of Judah, [4]but some of the people from Judah and Benjamin resettled in Jerusalem.)

From the tribe of Judah:

Athaiah son of Uzziah, son of Zechariah, son of Amariah, son of Shephatiah, son of Mahalalel, of the family of Perez. [5]Also Maaseiah son of Baruch, son of Col-hozeh, son of Hazaiah, son of Adaiah, son of Joiarib, son of Zechariah, of the family of Shelah.* [6]There were 468 descendants of Perez who lived in Jerusalem—all outstanding men.

11:5 Hebrew *son of the Shilonite.*

7 From the tribe of Benjamin:
Sallu son of Meshullam, son of Joed, son
of Pedaiah, son of Kolaiah, son of
Maaseiah, son of Ithiel, son of Jeshaiah.
8 After him were Gabbai and Sallai and a
total of 928 relatives. 9 Their chief officer
was Joel son of Zicri, who was assisted by
Judah son of Hassenuah, second-in-
command over the city.
10 From the priests:
Jedaiah son of Joiarib; Jakin; 11 and Seraiah
son of Hilkiah, son of Meshullam, son of
Zadok, son of Meraioth, son of Ahitub, the
supervisor of the Temple of God. 12 Also
822 of their associates, who worked at
the Temple. Also Adaiah son of Jeroham,
son of Pelaliah, son of Amzi, son of
Zechariah, son of Pashhur, son of
Malkijah, 13 along with 242 of his
associates, who were heads of their
families. Also Amashsai son of Azarel,
son of Ahzai, son of Meshillemoth, son of
Immer, 14 and 128 of his* outstanding
associates. Their chief officer was Zabdiel
son of Haggedolim.
15 From the Levites:
Shemaiah son of Hasshub, son of
Azrikam, son of Hashabiah, son of Bunni.
16 Also Shabbethai and Jozabad, who were
in charge of the work outside the Temple
of God. 17 Also Mattaniah son of Mica, son
of Zabdi, a descendant of Asaph, who
led in thanksgiving and prayer. Also
Bakbukiah, who was Mattaniah's assistant,
and Abda son of Shammua, son of Galal,
son of Jeduthun. 18 In all, there were
284 Levites in the holy city.
19 From the gatekeepers:
Akkub, Talmon, and 172 of their
associates, who guarded the gates.

20 The other priests, Levites, and the rest of the Israelites lived wherever their family inheritance was located in any of the towns of Judah. 21 The Temple servants, however, whose leaders were Ziha and Gishpa, all lived on the hill of Ophel.

22 The chief officer of the Levites in Jerusalem was Uzzi son of Bani, son of Hashabiah, son of Mattaniah, son of Mica, a descendant of Asaph, whose family served as singers at God's Temple. 23 Their daily responsibilities were carried out according to the terms of a royal command.

24 Pethahiah son of Meshezabel, a descendant of Zerah son of Judah, was the royal adviser in all matters of public administration.

25 As for the surrounding villages with their open fields, some of the people of Judah lived in Kiriath-arba with its settlements, Dibon with its settlements, and Jekabzeel with its villages. 26 They also lived in Jeshua, Moladah, Beth-pelet, 27 Hazar-shual, Beersheba with its settlements, 28 Ziklag, and Meconah with its settlements. 29 They also lived in En-rimmon, Zorah, Jarmuth, 30 Zanoah, and Adullam with their surrounding villages. They also lived in Lachish with its nearby fields and Azekah with its surrounding villages. So the people of Judah were living all the way from Beersheba in the south to the valley of Hinnom.

31 Some of the people of Benjamin lived at Geba, Micmash, Aija, and Bethel with its settlements. 32 They also lived in Anathoth, Nob, Ananiah, 33 Hazor, Ramah, Gittaim, 34 Hadid, Zeboim, Neballat, 35 Lod, Ono, and the Valley of Craftsmen.* 36 Some of the Levites who lived in Judah were sent to live with the tribe of Benjamin.

CHAPTER 12

A History of the Priests and Levites

Here is the list of the priests and Levites who returned with Zerubbabel son of Shealtiel and Jeshua the high priest:

Seraiah, Jeremiah, Ezra,
2 Amariah, Malluch, Hattush,
3 Shecaniah, Harim,* Meremoth,
4 Iddo, Ginnethon,* Abijah,
5 Miniamin, Moadiah,* Bilgah,
6 Shemaiah, Joiarib, Jedaiah,
7 Sallu, Amok, Hilkiah, and Jedaiah.
These were the leaders of the priests and their associates in the days of Jeshua.

8 The Levites who returned with them were Jeshua, Binnui, Kadmiel, Sherebiah, Judah, and Mattaniah, who with his associates was in charge of the songs of thanksgiving. 9 Their associates, Bakbukiah and Unni, stood opposite them during the service.

11:14 As in Greek version; Hebrew reads *their*. **11:35** Or *and Ge-harashim*. **12:3** Hebrew *Rehum*; compare 7:42; 12:15; Ezra 2:39. **12:4** As in some Hebrew manuscripts and Latin Vulgate (see also 12:16); most Hebrew manuscripts read *Ginnethoi*. **12:5** Hebrew *Mijamin, Maadiah*; compare 12:17.

10 Jeshua the high priest was the father of
Joiakim.
Joiakim was the father of Eliashib.
Eliashib was the father of Joiada.
11 Joiada was the father of Johanan.*
Johanan was the father of Jaddua.

12 Now when Joiakim was high priest, the family leaders of the priests were as follows:

Meraiah was leader of the family of
Seraiah.
Hananiah was leader of the family of
Jeremiah.
13 Meshullam was leader of the family of
Ezra.
Jehohanan was leader of the family of
Amariah.
14 Jonathan was leader of the family of
Malluch.*
Joseph was leader of the family of
Shecaniah.*
15 Adna was leader of the family of Harim.
Helkai was leader of the family of
Meremoth.*
16 Zechariah was leader of the family of
Iddo.
Meshullam was leader of the family of
Ginnethon.
17 Zicri was leader of the family of Abijah.
There was also a* leader of the family of
Miniamin.
Piltai was leader of the family of Moadiah.
18 Shammua was leader of the family of
Bilgah.
Jehonathan was leader of the family of
Shemaiah.
19 Mattenai was leader of the family of
Joiarib.
Uzzi was leader of the family of Jedaiah.
20 Kallai was leader of the family of Sallu.*
Eber was leader of the family of Amok.
21 Hashabiah was leader of the family of
Hilkiah.
Nethanel was leader of the family of
Jedaiah.

22 A record of the Levite families was kept during the years when Eliashib, Joiada, Johanan, and Jaddua served as high priest. Another record of the priests was kept during the reign of Darius the Persian.* 23 A record of the heads of the Levite families was kept in *The Book of History* down to the days of Johanan, the grandson* of Eliashib.

24 These were the family leaders of the Levites: Hashabiah, Sherebiah, Jeshua, Binnui,* Kadmiel, and other associates, who stood opposite them during the ceremonies of praise and thanksgiving, one section responding to the other, as commanded by David, the man of God. 25 This included Mattaniah, Bakbukiah, and Obadiah.

Meshullam, Talmon, and Akkub were the gatekeepers in charge of the storerooms at the gates. 26 These all served in the days of Joiakim son of Jeshua, son of Jehozadak,* and in the days of Nehemiah the governor and of Ezra the priest and scribe.

Dedication of Jerusalem's Wall

27 For the dedication of the new wall of Jerusalem, the Levites throughout the land were asked to come to Jerusalem to assist in the ceremonies. They were to take part in the joyous occasion with their songs of thanksgiving and with the music of cymbals, harps, and lyres. 28 The singers were brought together from the region around Jerusalem and from the villages of the Netophathites. 29 They also came from Beth-gilgal and the rural areas near Geba and Azmaveth, for the singers had built their own settlements around Jerusalem. 30 The priests and Levites first purified themselves; then they purified the people, the gates, and the wall.

31 I led the leaders of Judah to the top of the wall and organized two large choirs to give thanks. One of the choirs proceeded southward* along the top of the wall to the Dung Gate. 32 Hoshaiah and half the leaders of Judah followed them, 33 along with Azariah, Ezra, Meshullam, 34 Judah, Benjamin, Shemaiah, and Jeremiah. 35 Then came some priests who played trumpets, including Zechariah son of Jonathan, son of Shemaiah, son of Mattaniah, son of Micaiah, son of Zaccur, a de-

12:11 Hebrew *Jonathan;* compare 12:22. **12:14a** As in Greek version (see also 10:4; 12:2); Hebrew reads *Malluchi*. **12:14b** As in many Hebrew manuscripts, some Greek manuscripts, and Syriac version (see also 12:3); most Hebrew manuscripts read *Shebaniah*. **12:15** As in some Greek manuscripts (see also 12:3); Hebrew reads *Meraioth*. **12:17** Hebrew lacks the name of this family leader. **12:20** Hebrew *Sallai;* compare 12:7. **12:22** *Darius the Persian* is probably Darius II, who reigned 423–404 B.C., or possibly Darius III, who reigned 336–331 B.C. **12:23** Hebrew *descendant;* compare 12:10-11. **12:24** Hebrew *son of* (i.e., *ben*), which should probably be read here as the proper name Binnui; compare Ezra 3:9 and the note there. **12:26** Hebrew *Jozadak*, a variant spelling of Jehozadak. **12:31** Hebrew *to the right*.

scendant of Asaph. 36And Zechariah's colleagues were Shemaiah, Azarel, Milalai, Gilalai, Maai, Nethanel, Judah, and Hanani. They used the musical instruments prescribed by David, the man of God. Ezra the scribe led this procession. 37At the Fountain Gate they went straight up the steps on the ascent of the city wall toward the City of David. They passed the house of David and then proceeded to the Water Gate on the east.

38The second choir giving thanks went northward* around the other way to meet them. I followed them, together with the other half of the people, along the top of the wall past the Tower of the Ovens to the Broad Wall, 39then past the Ephraim Gate to the Old City Gate,* past the Fish Gate and the Tower of Hananel, and on to the Tower of the Hundred. Then we continued on to the Sheep Gate and stopped at the Guard Gate.

40The two choirs that were giving thanks then proceeded to the Temple of God, where they took their places. So did I, together with the group of leaders who were with me. 41We went together with the trumpet-playing priests—Eliakim, Maaseiah, Miniamin, Micaiah, Elioenai, Zechariah, and Hananiah—42and the singers—Maaseiah, Shemaiah, Eleazar, Uzzi, Jehohanan, Malkijah, Elam, and Ezer. They played and sang loudly under the direction of Jezrahiah the choir director.

43Many sacrifices were offered on that joyous day, for God had given the people cause for great joy. The women and children also participated in the celebration, and the joy of the people of Jerusalem could be heard far away.

Provisions for Temple Worship

44On that day men were appointed to be in charge of the storerooms for the offerings, the first part of the harvest, and the tithes. They were responsible to collect from the fields outside the towns the portions required by the Law for the priests and Levites. For all the people of Judah took joy in the priests and Levites and their work. 45They performed the service of their God and the service of purification, as commanded by David and his son Solomon, and so did the singers and the gatekeepers. 46The custom of having choir directors to lead the choirs in hymns of praise and thanksgiving to God began long ago in the days of David and Asaph. 47So now, in the days of Zerubbabel and of Nehemiah, all Israel brought a daily supply of food for the singers, the gatekeepers, and the Levites. The Levites, in turn, gave a portion of what they received to the priests, the descendants of Aaron.

CHAPTER 13

Nehemiah's Various Reforms

On that same day, as the Book of Moses was being read to the people, the passage was found that said no Ammonite or Moabite should ever be permitted to enter the assembly of God.* 2For they had not provided the Israelites with food and water in the wilderness. Instead, they hired Balaam to curse them, though our God turned the curse into a blessing. 3When this passage of the Law was read, all those of foreign descent were immediately excluded from the assembly.

4Before this had happened, Eliashib the priest, who had been appointed as supervisor of the storerooms of the Temple of our God and who was also a relative of Tobiah, 5had converted a large storage room and placed it at Tobiah's disposal. The room had previously been used for storing the grain offerings, the frankincense, various articles for the Temple, and the tithes of grain, new wine, and olive oil (which were prescribed for the Levites, the singers, and the gatekeepers), as well as the offerings for the priests.

6I was not in Jerusalem at that time, for I had returned to King Artaxerxes of Babylon in the thirty-second year of his reign,* though I later asked his permission to return. 7When I arrived back in Jerusalem, I learned about Eliashib's evil deed in providing Tobiah with a room in the courtyards of the Temple of God. 8I became very upset and threw all of Tobiah's belongings out of the room. 9Then I demanded that the rooms be purified, and I brought back the articles for God's Temple, the grain offerings, and the frankincense.

10I also discovered that the Levites had not

12:38 Hebrew *to the left*. **12:39** Or *the Mishneh Gate*, or *the Jeshanah Gate*. **13:1** See Deut 23:3-6. **13:6** King Artaxerxes of Persia is here identified as the king of Babylon because Persia had conquered the Babylonian Empire. The thirty-second year of Artaxerxes was 433 B.C.

NEHEMIAH

When I heard that the city walls of Jerusalem were in ruins, I cried. My people were not safe—they were open to attack. Something needed to be done. So I prayed to God. Then I asked the king to let me return home and help the people rebuild the walls. And so it happened. Once we started building, our enemies attacked and mocked us. But again I prayed. We came up with a plan. While half of us worked, the others guarded the workers using spears, shields, and bows. We finished building the huge wall in 52 days. Record time! Our enemies couldn't stop us because God was with us, helping us complete this project. Jerusalem was safe again.

Check out Nehemiah's story in the book that is named for him.

been given their prescribed portions of food, so they and the singers who were to conduct the worship services had all returned to work their fields. [11]I immediately confronted the leaders and demanded, "Why has the Temple of God been neglected?" Then I called all the Levites back again and restored them to their proper duties. [12]And once more all the people of Judah began bringing their tithes of grain, new wine, and olive oil to the Temple storerooms.

[13]I assigned supervisors for the storerooms: Shelemiah the priest, Zadok the scribe, and Pedaiah, one of the Levites. And I appointed Hanan son of Zaccur and grandson of Mattaniah as their assistant. These men had an excellent reputation, and it was their job to make honest distributions to their fellow Levites.

[14]Remember this good deed, O my God, and do not forget all that I have faithfully done for the Temple of my God and its services.

[15]In those days I saw men of Judah treading out their winepresses on the Sabbath. They were also bringing in grain, loading it on donkeys, and bringing their wine, grapes, figs, and all sorts of produce to Jerusalem to sell on the Sabbath. So I rebuked them for selling their produce on that day. [16]Some men from Tyre, who lived in Jerusalem, were bringing in fish and all kinds of merchandise. They were selling it on the Sabbath to the people of Judah—and in Jerusalem at that!

[17]So I confronted the nobles of Judah. "Why are you profaning the Sabbath in this evil way?" I asked. [18]"Wasn't it just this sort of thing that your ancestors did that caused our God to bring all this trouble upon us and our city? Now you are bringing even more wrath upon Israel by permitting the Sabbath to be desecrated in this way!"

[19]Then I commanded that the gates of Jerusalem should be shut as darkness fell every Friday evening,* not to be opened until the Sabbath ended. I sent some of my own servants to guard the gates so that no merchandise could be brought in on the Sabbath day. [20]The merchants and tradesmen with a variety of wares camped outside Jerusalem once or twice. [21]But I spoke sharply to them and said, "What are you doing out here, camping around the wall? If you do this again, I will arrest you!" And that was the last time they came on the Sabbath. [22]Then I commanded the Levites to purify themselves and to guard the gates in order to preserve the holiness of the Sabbath.

13:19 Hebrew *on the day before the Sabbath.*

Remember this good deed also, O my God!
Have compassion on me according to
your great and unfailing love.

[23]About the same time I realized that some of the men of Judah had married women from Ashdod, Ammon, and Moab. [24]Furthermore, half their children spoke the language of Ashdod or of some other people and could not speak the language of Judah at all. [25]So I confronted them and called down curses on them. I beat some of them and pulled out their hair. I made them swear in the name of God that they would not let their children intermarry with the pagan people of the land.

[26]"Wasn't this exactly what led King Solomon of Israel into sin?" I demanded. "There was no king from any nation who could compare to him, and God loved him and made him king over all Israel. But even he was led into sin by his foreign wives. [27]How could you even think of committing this sinful deed and acting unfaithfully toward God by marrying foreign women?"

[28]One of the sons of Joiada son of Eliashib the high priest had married a daughter of Sanballat the Horonite, so I banished him from my presence.

[29]Remember them, O my God, for they
have defiled the priesthood and the
solemn vows of the priests and Levites.

[30]So I purged out everything foreign and assigned tasks to the priests and Levites, making certain that each knew his work. [31]I also made sure that the supply of wood for the altar and the first portions of the harvest were brought at the proper times.

Remember this in my favor, O my God.

Esther

Who

Esther, Mordecai, King Xerxes, and Haman.

Where

Persia, particularly the capital city of Susa.

When

Around 483–471 BC.

Why

To show that God is in control and to let everyone know how much he loves and cares for his people.

Who knows if perhaps you were made queen for just such a time as this?
ESTHER 4:14

Timing is important when it comes to asking for a favor, when baking, or when participating in a sports activity. Esther, a Jewish girl who became the queen of Persia, knew about timing. She asked the king an important question at just the right moment. God gave her the opportunity at that time to save her Jewish people from death.

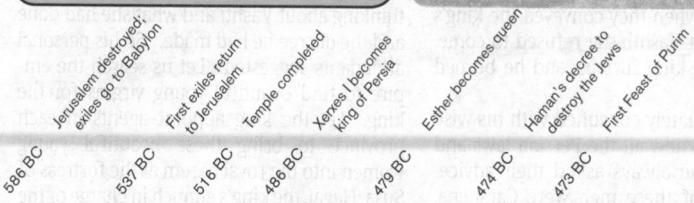

Don't miss your chance to serve God. Timing is everything!

CHAPTER 1

The King's Banquet

These events happened in the days of King Xerxes,* who reigned over 127 provinces stretching from India to Ethiopia.* [2]At that time Xerxes ruled his empire from his royal throne at the fortress of Susa. [3]In the third year of his reign, he gave a banquet for all his nobles and officials. He invited all the military officers of Persia and Media as well as the princes and nobles of the provinces. [4]The celebration lasted 180 days—a tremendous display of the opulent wealth of his empire and the pomp and splendor of his majesty.

1:1a Hebrew *Ahasuerus*, another name for Xerxes; also throughout the book of Esther. Xerxes reigned 486–465 B.C. **1:1b** Hebrew *to Cush*.

[5]When it was all over, the king gave a banquet for all the people, from the greatest to the least, who were in the fortress of Susa. It lasted for seven days and was held in the courtyard of the palace garden. [6]The courtyard was beautifully decorated with white cotton curtains and blue hangings, which were fastened with white linen cords and purple ribbons to silver rings embedded in marble pillars. Gold and silver couches stood on a mosaic pavement of porphyry, marble, mother-of-pearl, and other costly stones.

[7]Drinks were served in gold goblets of many designs, and there was an abundance of royal wine, reflecting the king's generosity. [8]By edict of the king, no limits were placed on the drinking, for the king had instructed all his palace officials to serve each man as much as he wanted.

[9]At the same time, Queen Vashti gave a banquet for the women in the royal palace of King Xerxes.

Queen Vashti Deposed

[10]On the seventh day of the feast, when King Xerxes was in high spirits because of the wine, he told the seven eunuchs who attended him—Mehuman, Biztha, Harbona, Bigtha, Abagtha, Zethar, and Carcas—[11]to bring Queen Vashti to him with the royal crown on her head. He wanted the nobles and all the other men to gaze on her beauty, for she was a very beautiful woman. [12]But when they conveyed the king's order to Queen Vashti, she refused to come. This made the king furious, and he burned with anger.

[13]He immediately consulted with his wise advisers, who knew all the Persian laws and customs, for he always asked their advice. [14]The names of these men were Carshena, Shethar, Admatha, Tarshish, Meres, Marsena, and Memucan—seven nobles of Persia and Media. They met with the king regularly and held the highest positions in the empire.

[15]"What must be done to Queen Vashti?" the king demanded. "What penalty does the law provide for a queen who refuses to obey the king's orders, properly sent through his eunuchs?"

[16]Memucan answered the king and his nobles, "Queen Vashti has wronged not only the king but also every noble and citizen throughout your empire. [17]Women everywhere will begin to despise their husbands when they learn that Queen Vashti has refused to appear before the king. [18]Before this day is out, the wives of all the king's nobles throughout Persia and Media will hear what the queen did and will start treating their husbands the same way. There will be no end to their contempt and anger.

[19]"So if it please the king, we suggest that you issue a written decree, a law of the Persians and Medes that cannot be revoked. It should order that Queen Vashti be forever banished from the presence of King Xerxes, and that the king should choose another queen more worthy than she. [20]When this decree is published throughout the king's vast empire, husbands everywhere, whatever their rank, will receive proper respect from their wives!"

[21]The king and his nobles thought this made good sense, so he followed Memucan's counsel. [22]He sent letters to all parts of the empire, to each province in its own script and language, proclaiming that every man should be the ruler of his own home and should say whatever he pleases.*

CHAPTER 2

Esther Becomes Queen

But after Xerxes' anger had subsided, he began thinking about Vashti and what she had done and the decree he had made. [2]So his personal attendants suggested, "Let us search the empire to find beautiful young virgins for the king. [3]Let the king appoint agents in each province to bring these beautiful young women into the royal harem at the fortress of Susa. Hegai, the king's eunuch in charge of the harem, will see that they are all given beauty treatments. [4]After that, the young woman who most pleases the king will be made queen instead of Vashti." This advice was very appealing to the king, so he put the plan into effect.

[5]At that time there was a Jewish man in the fortress of Susa whose name was Mordecai son of Jair. He was from the tribe of Benjamin and was a descendant of Kish and Shimei. [6]His family* had been among those who, with King Jehoiachin* of Judah, had been exiled

1:22 Or *and should speak in the language of his own people.* **2:6a** Hebrew *He.* **2:6b** Hebrew *Jeconiah,* a variant spelling of Jehoiachin.

from Jerusalem to Babylon by King Nebuchadnezzar. [7]This man had a very beautiful and lovely young cousin, Hadassah, who was also called Esther. When her father and mother died, Mordecai adopted her into his family and raised her as his own daughter.

[8]As a result of the king's decree, Esther, along with many other young women, was brought to the king's harem at the fortress of Susa and placed in Hegai's care. [9]Hegai was very impressed with Esther and treated her kindly. He quickly ordered a special menu for her and provided her with beauty treatments. He also assigned her seven maids specially chosen from the king's palace, and he moved her and her maids into the best place in the harem.

[10]Esther had not told anyone of her nationality and family background, because Mordecai had directed her not to do so. [11]Every day Mordecai would take a walk near the courtyard of the harem to find out about Esther and what was happening to her.

[12]Before each young woman was taken to the king's bed, she was given the prescribed twelve months of beauty treatments—six months with oil of myrrh, followed by six months with special perfumes and ointments. [13]When it was time for her to go to the king's palace, she was given her choice of whatever clothing or jewelry she wanted to take from the harem. [14]That evening she was taken to the king's private rooms, and the next morning she was brought to the second harem,* where the king's wives lived. There she would be under the care of Shaashgaz, the king's eunuch in charge of the concubines. She would never go to the king again unless he had especially enjoyed her and requested her by name.

[15]Esther was the daughter of Abihail, who was Mordecai's uncle. (Mordecai had adopted his younger cousin Esther.) When it was Esther's turn to go to the king, she accepted the advice of Hegai, the eunuch in charge of the harem. She asked for nothing except what he suggested, and she was admired by everyone who saw her.

[16]Esther was taken to King Xerxes at the royal palace in early winter* of the seventh year of his reign. [17]And the king loved Esther more than any of the other young women. He was so delighted with her that he set the royal crown on her head and declared her queen instead of Vashti. [18]To celebrate the occasion, he gave a great banquet in Esther's honor for

2:14 Or *to another part of the harem.* **2:16** Hebrew *in the tenth month, the month of Tebeth.* A number of dates in the book of Esther can be cross-checked with dates in surviving Persian records and related accurately to our modern calendar. This month of the ancient Hebrew lunar calendar occurred within the months of December 479 B.C. and January 478 B.C.

IS IT OK?

IS IT OK TO WANT TO LOOK GOOD?

Esther was beautiful (see Esther 2:7). Plus she had twelve straight months of spa treatments (verse 12)—what a life! Then she won the Miss Persia contest and became queen. She had a lot of pressure to look good all the time. But outer beauty must be balanced with inner beauty, and Esther won the crown in that contest too. She risked everything—being queen, her cushy lifestyle, even her life—in order to defend her people (Esther 4:16). That girl had character! It's OK to want to look good, as long as our main focus is on what's truly important—loving God and loving others. Esther was obsessed with doing what was right, not with how she looked. What about you?

all his nobles and officials, declaring a public holiday for the provinces and giving generous gifts to everyone.

[19]Even after all the young women had been transferred to the second harem* and Mordecai had become a palace official,* [20]Esther continued to keep her family background and nationality a secret. She was still following Mordecai's directions, just as she did when she lived in his home.

Mordecai's Loyalty to the King

[21]One day as Mordecai was on duty at the king's gate, two of the king's eunuchs, Bigthana* and Teresh—who were guards at the door of the king's private quarters—became angry at King Xerxes and plotted to assassinate him. [22]But Mordecai heard about the plot and gave the information to Queen Esther. She then told the king about it and gave Mordecai credit for the report. [23]When an investigation was made and Mordecai's story was found to be true, the two men were impaled on a sharpened pole. This was all recorded in *The Book of the History of King Xerxes' Reign.*

CHAPTER 3

Haman's Plot against the Jews

Some time later King Xerxes promoted Haman son of Hammedatha the Agagite over all the other nobles, making him the most powerful official in the empire. [2]All the king's officials would bow down before Haman to show him respect whenever he passed by, for so the king had commanded. But Mordecai refused to bow down or show him respect.

[3]Then the palace officials at the king's gate asked Mordecai, "Why are you disobeying the king's command?" [4]They spoke to him day after day, but still he refused to comply with the order. So they spoke to Haman about this to see if he would tolerate Mordecai's conduct, since Mordecai had told them he was a Jew.

[5]When Haman saw that Mordecai would not bow down or show him respect, he was filled with rage. [6]He had learned of Mordecai's nationality, so he decided it was not enough to lay hands on Mordecai alone. Instead, he looked for a way to destroy all the Jews throughout the entire empire of Xerxes.

[7]So in the month of April,* during the twelfth year of King Xerxes' reign, lots were

Taking a Stand

The vocabulary test was really hard, but James thought he did all right. James's friend Dallas was absent that day. When Dallas came back to school, he had to make up the test. Dallas told James, "I'm really struggling in that class. Can you help me out by just telling me what words are on the test?" James knew that this would be cheating and that cheating is wrong, but he wanted to help his friend. What should James do? Read Esther 3 and 4 to see how God feels about taking a stand for what's right.

2:19a The meaning of the Hebrew is uncertain. **2:19b** Hebrew *and Mordecai was sitting in the gate of the king.* **2:21** Hebrew *Bigthan;* compare 6:2. **3:7a** Hebrew *in the first month, the month of Nisan.* This month of the ancient Hebrew lunar calendar occurred within the months of April and May 474 B.C.; also see note on 2:16.

Baseball was my life! Every day I had practice; every weekend I had games or tournaments. Sometimes we traveled for days at a time to regional games or state championships. My whole life—even my friends—revolved around baseball.

I never got to hang out with other school friends and church friends. I never got to do other fun activities. My whole identity was "Jade the baseball player."

One day my wrist started hurting. I tried to ignore it, but eventually I had to go to the doctor. My life changed when I heard these words: "Your ligaments are torn. You'll need surgery. You won't be able to play baseball for a year, maybe more."

That was the worst thing that could have happened to me. No more baseball, no more scholarship . . . all I ever knew and wanted was gone!

But that year I gained friendships I had never been able to enjoy before. I started attending my youth group at church and going on fun outings with my new church friends. I began helping little kids at an inner-city mission that my church was involved with. I had never felt happier in my life!

A year later my wrist got better. All of a sudden I realized that if I went back to the life of baseball, I would slowly be removing myself from the church family that I had grown to love.

My decision was clear. I wasn't going to be "Jade the baseball player" anymore. Church, my Christian friends, and my service at the mission were far too important.

What I thought was the worst tragedy of my life ended up being the biggest blessing. God puts us in certain situations for a reason. We just need to take advantage of those "opportunities."

Read Esther 4 to see how the young queen responded to the "opportunity" that God placed before her.

cast in Haman's presence (the lots were called *purim*) to determine the best day and month to take action. And the day selected was March 7, nearly a year later.*

[8]Then Haman approached King Xerxes and said, "There is a certain race of people scattered through all the provinces of your empire who keep themselves separate from everyone else. Their laws are different from those of any other people, and they refuse to obey the laws of the king. So it is not in the king's interest to let them live. [9]If it please the king, issue a decree that they be destroyed, and I will give 10,000 large sacks* of silver to the government administrators to be deposited in the royal treasury."

[10]The king agreed, confirming his decision by removing his signet ring from his finger and giving it to Haman son of Hammedatha the Agagite, the enemy of the Jews. [11]The king said, "The money and the people are both yours to do with as you see fit."

[12]So on April 17* the king's secretaries were summoned, and a decree was written exactly as Haman dictated. It was sent to the king's highest officers, the governors of the respective provinces, and the nobles of each province in their own scripts and languages. The decree was written in the name of King Xerxes and sealed with the king's signet ring. [13]Dispatches were sent by swift messengers into all the provinces of the empire, giving the order that all Jews—young and old, including women and children—must be killed, slaughtered, and annihilated on a single day. This was scheduled to happen on March 7 of the next year.* The property of the Jews would be given to those who killed them.

[14]A copy of this decree was to be issued as law in every province and proclaimed to all peoples, so that they would be ready to do their duty on the appointed day. [15]At the king's command, the decree went out by swift messengers, and it was also proclaimed in the fortress of Susa. Then the king and Haman sat down to drink, but the city of Susa fell into confusion.

CHAPTER 4

Mordecai Requests Esther's Help

When Mordecai learned about all that had been done, he tore his clothes, put on burlap and ashes, and went out into the city, crying with a loud and bitter wail. [2]He went as far as the gate of the palace, for no one was allowed to enter the palace gate while wearing clothes of mourning. [3]And as news of the king's decree reached all the provinces, there was great mourning among the Jews. They fasted, wept, and wailed, and many people lay in burlap and ashes.

[4]When Queen Esther's maids and eunuchs came and told her about Mordecai, she was deeply distressed. She sent clothing to him to replace the burlap, but he refused it. [5]Then Esther sent for Hathach, one of the king's eunuchs who had been appointed as her attendant. She ordered him to go to Mordecai and find out what was troubling him and why he was in mourning. [6]So Hathach went out to Mordecai in the square in front of the palace gate.

[7]Mordecai told him the whole story, including the exact amount of money Haman had promised to pay into the royal treasury for the destruction of the Jews. [8]Mordecai gave Hathach a copy of the decree issued in Susa that called for the death of all Jews. He asked Hathach to show it to Esther and explain the situation to her. He also asked Hathach to direct her to go to the king to beg for mercy and plead for her people. [9]So Hathach returned to Esther with Mordecai's message.

[10]Then Esther told Hathach to go back and relay this message to Mordecai: [11]"All the king's officials and even the people in the provinces know that anyone who appears before the king in his inner court without being invited is doomed to die unless the king holds out his gold scepter. And the king has not called for me to come to him for thirty days." [12]So Hathach* gave Esther's message to Mordecai.

[13]Mordecai sent this reply to Esther: "Don't think for a moment that because you're in the palace you will escape when all other Jews are

3:7b As in 3:13, which reads *the thirteenth day of the twelfth month, the month of Adar*; Hebrew reads *in the twelfth month*, of the ancient Hebrew lunar calendar. The date selected was March 7, 473 B.C.; also see note on 2:16. **3:9** Hebrew *10,000 talents*, about 375 tons or 340 metric tons in weight. **3:12** Hebrew *On the thirteenth day of the first month*, of the ancient Hebrew lunar calendar. This day was April 17, 474 B.C.; also see note on 2:16. **3:13** Hebrew *on the thirteenth day of the twelfth month, the month of Adar*, of the ancient Hebrew lunar calendar. The date selected was March 7, 473 B.C.; also see note on 2:16. **4:12** As in Greek version; Hebrew reads *they*.

killed. [14]If you keep quiet at a time like this, deliverance and relief for the Jews will arise from some other place, but you and your relatives will die. Who knows if perhaps you were made queen for just such a time as this?"

I don't understand why God puts me in certain situations.

Who knows if perhaps you were made queen for just such a time as this? ESTHER 4:14

[15]Then Esther sent this reply to Mordecai: [16]"Go and gather together all the Jews of Susa and fast for me. Do not eat or drink for three days, night or day. My maids and I will do the same. And then, though it is against the law, I will go in to see the king. If I must die, I must die." [17]So Mordecai went away and did everything as Esther had ordered him.

CHAPTER 5

Esther's Request to the King

On the third day of the fast, Esther put on her royal robes and entered the inner court of the palace, just across from the king's hall. The king was sitting on his royal throne, facing the entrance. [2]When he saw Queen Esther standing there in the inner court, he welcomed her and held out the gold scepter to her. So Esther approached and touched the end of the scepter.

[3]Then the king asked her, "What do you want, Queen Esther? What is your request? I will give it to you, even if it is half the kingdom!"

[4]And Esther replied, "If it please the king, let the king and Haman come today to a banquet I have prepared for the king."

[5]The king turned to his attendants and said, "Tell Haman to come quickly to a banquet, as Esther has requested." So the king and Haman went to Esther's banquet.

[6]And while they were drinking wine, the king said to Esther, "Now tell me what you really want. What is your request? I will give it to you, even if it is half the kingdom!"

[7]Esther replied, "This is my request and deepest wish. [8]If I have found favor with the king, and if it pleases the king to grant my request and do what I ask, please come with Haman tomorrow to the banquet I will prepare for you. Then I will explain what this is all about."

Haman's Plan to Kill Mordecai

[9]Haman was a happy man as he left the banquet! But when he saw Mordecai sitting at the palace gate, not standing up or trembling nervously before him, Haman became furious. [10]However, he restrained himself and went on home.

Then Haman gathered together his friends and Zeresh, his wife, [11]and boasted to them about his great wealth and his many children. He bragged about the honors the king had given him and how he had been promoted over all the other nobles and officials.

[12]Then Haman added, "And that's not all! Queen Esther invited only me and the king himself to the banquet she prepared for us. And she has invited me to dine with her and the king again tomorrow!" [13]Then he added, "But this is all worth nothing as long as I see Mordecai the Jew just sitting there at the palace gate."

[14]So Haman's wife, Zeresh, and all his friends suggested, "Set up a sharpened pole that stands seventy-five feet* tall, and in the morning ask the king to impale Mordecai on it. When this is done, you can go on your merry way to the banquet with the king." This pleased Haman, and he ordered the pole set up.

CHAPTER 6

The King Honors Mordecai

That night the king had trouble sleeping, so he ordered an attendant to bring the book of the history of his reign so it could be read to him. [2]In those records he discovered an account of how Mordecai had exposed the plot

5:14 Hebrew *50 cubits* [22.5 meters].

of Bigthana and Teresh, two of the eunuchs who guarded the door to the king's private quarters. They had plotted to assassinate King Xerxes.

[3]"What reward or recognition did we ever give Mordecai for this?" the king asked.

His attendants replied, "Nothing has been done for him."

[4]"Who is that in the outer court?" the king inquired. As it happened, Haman had just arrived in the outer court of the palace to ask the king to impale Mordecai on the pole he had prepared.

[5]So the attendants replied to the king, "Haman is out in the court."

"Bring him in," the king ordered. [6]So Haman came in, and the king said, "What should I do to honor a man who truly pleases me?"

Haman thought to himself, "Whom would the king wish to honor more than me?" [7]So he replied, "If the king wishes to honor someone, [8]he should bring out one of the king's own royal robes, as well as a horse that the king himself has ridden—one with a royal emblem on its head. [9]Let the robes and the horse be handed over to one of the king's most noble officials. And let him see that the man whom the king wishes to honor is dressed in the king's robes and led through the city square on the king's horse. Have the official shout as they go, 'This is what the king does for someone he wishes to honor!'"

[10]"Excellent!" the king said to Haman. "Quick! Take the robes and my horse, and do just as you have said for Mordecai the Jew, who sits at the gate of the palace. Leave out nothing you have suggested!"

[11]So Haman took the robes and put them on Mordecai, placed him on the king's own horse, and led him through the city square, shouting, "This is what the king does for someone he wishes to honor!" [12]Afterward Mordecai returned to the palace gate, but Haman hurried home dejected and completely humiliated.

[13]When Haman told his wife, Zeresh, and all his friends what had happened, his wise advisers and his wife said, "Since Mordecai—this man who has humiliated you—is of Jewish birth, you will never succeed in your plans against him. It will be fatal to continue opposing him."

[14]While they were still talking, the king's eunuchs arrived and quickly took Haman to the banquet Esther had prepared.

CHAPTER 7

The King Executes Haman

So the king and Haman went to Queen Esther's banquet. [2]On this second occasion, while they were drinking wine, the king again said to Esther, "Tell me what you want, Queen Esther. What is your request? I will give it to you, even if it is half the kingdom!"

[3]Queen Esther replied, "If I have found favor with the king, and if it pleases the king to grant my request, I ask that my life and the lives of my people will be spared. [4]For my people and I have been sold to those who would kill, slaughter, and annihilate us. If we had merely been sold as slaves, I could remain quiet, for that would be too trivial a matter to warrant disturbing the king."

[5]"Who would do such a thing?" King Xerxes demanded. "Who would be so presumptuous as to touch you?"

[6]Esther replied, "This wicked Haman is our adversary and our enemy." Haman grew pale with fright before the king and queen. [7]Then the king jumped to his feet in a rage and went out into the palace garden.

Haman, however, stayed behind to plead for his life with Queen Esther, for he knew that the king intended to kill him. [8]In despair he fell on the couch where Queen Esther was reclining, just as the king was returning from the palace garden.

The king exclaimed, "Will he even assault the queen right here in the palace, before my very eyes?" And as soon as the king spoke, his attendants covered Haman's face, signaling his doom.

[9]Then Harbona, one of the king's eunuchs, said, "Haman has set up a sharpened pole that stands seventy-five feet* tall in his own courtyard. He intended to use it to impale Mordecai, the man who saved the king from assassination."

"Then impale Haman on it!" the king ordered. [10]So they impaled Haman on the pole

7:9 Hebrew *50 cubits* [22.5 meters].

he had set up for Mordecai, and the king's anger subsided.

CHAPTER 8

A Decree to Help the Jews

On that same day King Xerxes gave the property of Haman, the enemy of the Jews, to Queen Esther. Then Mordecai was brought before the king, for Esther had told the king how they were related. [2]The king took off his signet ring—which he had taken back from Haman—and gave it to Mordecai. And Esther appointed Mordecai to be in charge of Haman's property.

[3]Then Esther went again before the king, falling down at his feet and begging him with tears to stop the evil plot devised by Haman the Agagite against the Jews. [4]Again the king held out the gold scepter to Esther. So she rose and stood before him.

[5]Esther said, "If it please the king, and if I have found favor with him, and if he thinks it is right, and if I am pleasing to him, let there be a decree that reverses the orders of Haman son of Hammedatha the Agagite, who ordered that Jews throughout all the king's provinces should be destroyed. [6]For how can I endure to see my people and my family slaughtered and destroyed?"

[7]Then King Xerxes said to Queen Esther and Mordecai the Jew, "I have given Esther the property of Haman, and he has been impaled on a pole because he tried to destroy the Jews. [8]Now go ahead and send a message to the Jews in the king's name, telling them whatever you want, and seal it with the king's signet ring. But remember that whatever has already been written in the king's name and sealed with his signet ring can never be revoked."

[9]So on June 25* the king's secretaries were summoned, and a decree was written exactly as Mordecai dictated. It was sent to the Jews and to the highest officers, the governors, and the nobles of all the 127 provinces stretching from India to Ethiopia.* The decree was written in the scripts and languages of all the peoples of the empire, including that of the Jews. [10]The decree was written in the name of King Xerxes and sealed with the king's signet ring. Mordecai sent the dispatches by swift messengers, who rode fast horses especially bred for the king's service.

AMAZING FACTS

Who rescued the Jewish people from total destruction? It was none other than a beautiful young queen!

ESTHER 8:3-6, 16

[11]The king's decree gave the Jews in every city authority to unite to defend their lives. They were allowed to kill, slaughter, and annihilate anyone of any nationality or province who might attack them or their children and wives, and to take the property of their enemies. [12]The day chosen for this event throughout all the provinces of King Xerxes was March 7 of the next year.*

[13]A copy of this decree was to be issued as law in every province and proclaimed to all peoples, so that the Jews would be ready to take revenge on their enemies on the appointed day. [14]So urged on by the king's command, the messengers rode out swiftly on fast horses bred for the king's service. The same decree was also proclaimed in the fortress of Susa.

[15]Then Mordecai left the king's presence, wearing the royal robe of blue and white, the great crown of gold, and an outer cloak of fine linen and purple. And the people of Susa celebrated the new decree. [16]The Jews were filled with joy and gladness and were honored everywhere. [17]In every province and city, wherever the king's decree arrived, the Jews rejoiced and had a great celebration and declared a public festival and holiday. And

8:9a Hebrew *on the twenty-third day of the third month, the month of Sivan,* of the ancient Hebrew lunar calendar. This day was June 25, 474 B.C.; also see note on 2:16. **8:9b** Hebrew *to Cush.* **8:12** Hebrew *the thirteenth day of the twelfth month, the month of Adar,* of the ancient Hebrew lunar calendar. The date selected was March 7, 473 B.C.; also see note on 2:16.

many of the people of the land became Jews themselves, for they feared what the Jews might do to them.

CHAPTER 9

The Victory of the Jews

So on March 7* the two decrees of the king were put into effect. On that day, the enemies of the Jews had hoped to overpower them, but quite the opposite happened. It was the Jews who overpowered their enemies. [2]The Jews gathered in their cities throughout all the king's provinces to attack anyone who tried to harm them. But no one could make a stand against them, for everyone was afraid of them. [3]And all the nobles of the provinces, the highest officers, the governors, and the royal officials helped the Jews for fear of Mordecai. [4]For Mordecai had been promoted in the king's palace, and his fame spread throughout all the provinces as he became more and more powerful.

[5]So the Jews went ahead on the appointed day and struck down their enemies with the sword. They killed and annihilated their enemies and did as they pleased with those who hated them. [6]In the fortress of Susa itself, the Jews killed 500 men. [7]They also killed Parshandatha, Dalphon, Aspatha, [8]Poratha, Adalia, Aridatha, [9]Parmashta, Arisai, Aridai, and Vaizatha—[10]the ten sons of Haman son of Hammedatha, the enemy of the Jews. But they did not take any plunder.

[11]That very day, when the king was informed of the number of people killed in the fortress of Susa, [12]he called for Queen Esther. He said, "The Jews have killed 500 men in the fortress of Susa alone, as well as Haman's ten sons. If they have done that here, what has happened in the rest of the provinces? But now, what more do you want? It will be granted to you; tell me and I will do it."

[13]Esther responded, "If it please the king, give the Jews in Susa permission to do again tomorrow as they have done today, and let the bodies of Haman's ten sons be impaled on a pole."

[14]So the king agreed, and the decree was announced in Susa. And they impaled the bodies of Haman's ten sons. [15]Then the Jews at Susa gathered together on March 8* and killed 300 more men, and again they took no plunder.

[16]Meanwhile, the other Jews throughout the king's provinces had gathered together to defend their lives. They gained relief from all their enemies, killing 75,000 of those who hated them. But they did not take any plunder. [17]This was done throughout the provinces on March 7, and on March 8 they rested,* celebrating their victory with a day of feasting and gladness. [18](The Jews at Susa killed their enemies on March 7 and again on March 8, then rested on March 9,* making that their day of feasting and gladness.) [19]So to this day, rural Jews living in remote villages celebrate an annual festival and holiday on the appointed day in late winter,* when they rejoice and send gifts of food to each other.

The Festival of Purim

[20]Mordecai recorded these events and sent letters to the Jews near and far, throughout all the provinces of King Xerxes, [21]calling on them to celebrate an annual festival on these two days.* [22]He told them to celebrate these days with feasting and gladness and by giving gifts of food to each other and presents to the poor. This would commemorate a time when the Jews gained relief from their enemies, when their sorrow was turned into gladness and their mourning into joy.

[23]So the Jews accepted Mordecai's proposal and adopted this annual custom. [24]Haman son of Hammedatha the Agagite, the enemy of the Jews, had plotted to crush and destroy them on the date determined by casting lots (the lots were called *purim*). [25]But when Esther came before the king, he issued a decree causing Haman's evil plot to backfire, and Haman and his sons were impaled on a sharpened pole. [26]That is why this celebration is called Purim, because it is the ancient word for casting lots.

So because of Mordecai's letter and because of what they had experienced, [27]the Jews

9:1 Hebrew *on the thirteenth day of the twelfth month, the month of Adar,* of the ancient Hebrew lunar calendar. This day was March 7, 473 B.C.; also see note on 2:16. **9:15** Hebrew *the fourteenth day of the month of Adar,* of the Hebrew lunar calendar. This day was March 8, 473 B.C.; also see note on 2:16. **9:17** Hebrew *on the thirteenth day of the month of Adar, and on the fourteenth day they rested.* These days were March 7 and 8, 473 B.C.; also see note on 2:16. **9:18** Hebrew *killed their enemies on the thirteenth day and the fourteenth day, and then rested on the fifteenth day,* of the Hebrew month of Adar. **9:19** Hebrew *on the fourteenth day of the month of Adar.* This day of the Hebrew lunar calendar occurs in February or March. **9:21** Hebrew *on the fourteenth and fifteenth days of Adar,* of the Hebrew lunar calendar.

throughout the realm agreed to inaugurate this tradition and to pass it on to their descendants and to all who became Jews. They declared they would never fail to celebrate these two prescribed days at the appointed time each year. [28]These days would be remembered and kept from generation to generation and celebrated by every family throughout the provinces and cities of the empire. This Festival of Purim would never cease to be celebrated among the Jews, nor would the memory of what happened ever die out among their descendants.

[29]Then Queen Esther, the daughter of Abihail, along with Mordecai the Jew, wrote another letter putting the queen's full authority behind Mordecai's letter to establish the Festival of Purim. [30]Letters wishing peace and security were sent to the Jews throughout the 127 provinces of the empire of Xerxes. [31]These letters established the Festival of Purim—an annual celebration of these days at the appointed time, decreed by both Mordecai the Jew and Queen Esther. (The people decided to observe this festival, just as they had decided for themselves and their descendants to establish the times of fasting and mourning.) [32]So the command of Esther confirmed the practices of Purim, and it was all written down in the records.

CHAPTER 10

The Greatness of Xerxes and Mordecai

King Xerxes imposed a tribute throughout his empire, even to the distant coastlands. [2]His great achievements and the full account of the greatness of Mordecai, whom the king had promoted, are recorded in *The Book of the History of the Kings of Media and Persia.* [3]Mordecai the Jew became the prime minister, with authority next to that of King Xerxes himself. He was very great among the Jews, who held him in high esteem, because he continued to work for the good of his people and to speak up for the welfare of all their descendants.

JOB

WHO
Job, Eliphaz the Temanite, Bildad the Shuhite, Zophar the Naamathite, and Elihu the Buzite.

WHERE
In heaven and in the land of Uz.

WHEN
We don't know for sure, but it describes life around 2000–1800 BC during the time of Abraham.

WHY
To show that God is in control and to explain the meaning of true faith.

[Job] is the finest man in all the earth . . . a man of complete integrity. He fears God and stays away from evil.
JOB 2:3

If you think you have it tough, think about Job. He lost his home, animals, workers, and even his children. Then he got sick, his wife yelled at him, and his friends gave him a hard time. But he didn't give up. His faith in God stayed strong even when *everything* went wrong. That's true faith.

STAY CLOSE TO GOD, EVEN IN THE TOUGH TIMES.

CHAPTER 1

Prologue

There once was a man named Job who lived in the land of Uz. He was blameless—a man of complete integrity. He feared God and stayed away from evil. [2]He had seven sons and three daughters. [3]He owned 7,000 sheep, 3,000 camels, 500 teams of oxen, and 500 female donkeys. He also had many servants. He was, in fact, the richest person in that entire area.

[4]Job's sons would take turns preparing feasts in their homes, and they would also invite their three sisters to celebrate with them. [5]When these celebrations ended—sometimes after several days—Job would purify his

children. He would get up early in the morning and offer a burnt offering for each of them. For Job said to himself, "Perhaps my children have sinned and have cursed God in their hearts." This was Job's regular practice.

Job's First Test

[6]One day the members of the heavenly court* came to present themselves before the LORD, and the Accuser, Satan,* came with them. [7]"Where have you come from?" the LORD asked Satan.

Satan answered the LORD, "I have been patrolling the earth, watching everything that's going on."

[8]Then the LORD asked Satan, "Have you noticed my servant Job? He is the finest man in all the earth. He is blameless—a man of complete integrity. He fears God and stays away from evil."

[9]Satan replied to the LORD, "Yes, but Job has good reason to fear God. [10]You have always put a wall of protection around him and his home and his property. You have made him prosper in everything he does. Look how rich he is! [11]But reach out and take away everything he has, and he will surely curse you to your face!"

AMAZING FACTS

Enemies, fire, and wind took all of Job's children, farm workers, and animals . . . in just *one* day.

JOB 1:13-20

[12]"All right, you may test him," the LORD said to Satan. "Do whatever you want with everything he possesses, but don't harm him physically." So Satan left the LORD's presence.

[13]One day when Job's sons and daughters were feasting at the oldest brother's house, [14]a messenger arrived at Job's home with this news: "Your oxen were plowing, with the donkeys feeding beside them, [15]when the Sabeans raided us. They stole all the animals and killed all the farmhands. I am the only one who escaped to tell you."

[16]While he was still speaking, another messenger arrived with this news: "The fire of God has fallen from heaven and burned up your sheep and all the shepherds. I am the only one who escaped to tell you."

[17]While he was still speaking, a third messenger arrived with this news: "Three bands of Chaldean raiders have stolen your camels and killed your servants. I am the only one who escaped to tell you."

[18]While he was still speaking, another messenger arrived with this news: "Your sons and daughters were feasting in their oldest brother's home. [19]Suddenly, a powerful wind swept in from the wilderness and hit the house on all sides. The house collapsed, and all your children are dead. I am the only one who escaped to tell you."

[20]Job stood up and tore his robe in grief. Then he shaved his head and fell to the ground to worship. [21]He said,

"I came naked from my mother's womb,
and I will be naked when I leave.
The LORD gave me what I had,
and the LORD has taken it away.
Praise the name of the LORD!"

[22]In all of this, Job did not sin by blaming God.

CHAPTER 2

Job's Second Test

One day the members of the heavenly court* came again to present themselves before the LORD, and the Accuser, Satan,* came with them. [2]"Where have you come from?" the LORD asked Satan.

Satan answered the LORD, "I have been patrolling the earth, watching everything that's going on."

[3]Then the LORD asked Satan, "Have you noticed my servant Job? He is the finest man in all the earth. He is blameless—a man of complete integrity. He fears God and stays away

1:6a Hebrew *the sons of God.* **1:6b** Hebrew *and the satan;* similarly throughout this chapter. **2:1a** Hebrew *the sons of God.* **2:1b** Hebrew *and the satan;* similarly throughout this chapter.

from evil. And he has maintained his integrity, even though you urged me to harm him without cause."

[4]Satan replied to the LORD, "Skin for skin! A man will give up everything he has to save his life. [5]But reach out and take away his health, and he will surely curse you to your face!"

[6]"All right, do with him as you please," the LORD said to Satan. "But spare his life." [7]So Satan left the LORD's presence, and he struck Job with terrible boils from head to foot.

[8]Job scraped his skin with a piece of broken pottery as he sat among the ashes. [9]His wife said to him, "Are you still trying to maintain your integrity? Curse God and die."

[10]But Job replied, "You talk like a foolish woman. Should we accept only good things from the hand of God and never anything bad?" So in all this, Job said nothing wrong.

Job's Three Friends Share His Anguish

[11]When three of Job's friends heard of the tragedy he had suffered, they got together and traveled from their homes to comfort and console him. Their names were Eliphaz the Temanite, Bildad the Shuhite, and Zophar the Naamathite. [12]When they saw Job from a distance, they scarcely recognized him. Wailing loudly, they tore their robes and threw dust into the air over their heads to show their grief. [13]Then they sat on the ground with him for seven days and nights. No one said a word to Job, for they saw that his suffering was too great for words.

CHAPTER 3

Job's First Speech

At last Job spoke, and he cursed the day of his birth. [2]He said:

[3] "Let the day of my birth be erased,
and the night I was conceived.
[4] Let that day be turned to darkness.
Let it be lost even to God on high,
and let no light shine on it.
[5] Let the darkness and utter gloom claim
that day for its own.
Let a black cloud overshadow it,
and let the darkness terrify it.
[6] Let that night be blotted off the
calendar,
never again to be counted among the
days of the year,
never again to appear among the
months.
[7] Let that night be childless.
Let it have no joy.

IS IT OK?

IS IT OK IF I'M MAD AT GOD BECAUSE SOMETHING BAD HAPPENED?

Did you catch all those terrible, horrible, no-good, very bad things that happened to Job? What a rotten day! Can you imagine how he must have felt? We can see from Job's reaction that he was very upset over these events, and he didn't hold back from telling God just how he felt. (He gave God an earful!) But notice that Job never crossed over from upset-about-what-happened into upset-with-God territory. See, it's OK if you're angry about something that happened to you. But it's not OK if you blame God for it. When bad events happen, tell God exactly how you feel, but follow Job's example—not Mrs. Job's bad advice (see Job 2:9-10). Trust God even when you're hurting.

Listen!

Kyle's friend Charlie was going through a very tough time at home. Charlie's parents had been fighting a lot, and it looked like they were going to get divorced. Charlie wanted to talk with Kyle about his problems, so Kyle arranged a time when they could get together. Kyle was nervous about meeting with Charlie, though, because he didn't know what to say. What should Kyle do? Read Job 2:13 to see how Job's friends responded when he was wiped out by tragedy.

8 Let those who are experts at cursing—
whose cursing could rouse Leviathan*—
curse that day.
9 Let its morning stars remain dark.
Let it hope for light, but in vain;
may it never see the morning light.
10 Curse that day for failing to shut my
mother's womb,
for letting me be born to see all this
trouble.
11 "Why wasn't I born dead?
Why didn't I die as I came from
the womb?
12 Why was I laid on my mother's lap?
Why did she nurse me at her breasts?
13 Had I died at birth, I would now be
at peace.
I would be asleep and at rest.
14 I would rest with the world's kings and
prime ministers,
whose great buildings now lie in ruins.
15 I would rest with princes, rich in gold,
whose palaces were filled with silver.
16 Why wasn't I buried like a stillborn child,
like a baby who never lives to see
the light?
17 For in death the wicked cause no trouble,
and the weary are at rest.
18 Even captives are at ease in death,
with no guards to curse them.
19 Rich and poor are both there,
and the slave is free from his master.
20 "Oh, why give light to those in misery,
and life to those who are bitter?
21 They long for death, and it won't come.
They search for death more eagerly
than for hidden treasure.
22 They're filled with joy when they
finally die,
and rejoice when they find the grave.
23 Why is life given to those with no future,
those God has surrounded with
difficulties?
24 I cannot eat for sighing;
my groans pour out like water.
25 What I always feared has happened to me.
What I dreaded has come true.
26 I have no peace, no quietness.
I have no rest; only trouble comes."

CHAPTER 4

Eliphaz's First Response to Job

Then Eliphaz the Temanite replied to Job:

2 "Will you be patient and let me say
a word?
For who could keep from speaking out?
3 "In the past you have encouraged many
people;
you have strengthened those who
were weak.

3:8 The identification of Leviathan is disputed, ranging from an earthly creature to a mythical sea monster in ancient literature.

JOB

I hurt. Scraping away at my sores with broken pieces of pottery brings me no relief. It seems that God hates me. Once I had a happy home and everything I could want. Then one day thieves stole my donkeys and camels. They killed my servants. Fire killed my sheep. Worst of all, while my children were having a party, a storm knocked their house down and killed them all. Even my wife thinks I should give up on God. Why is this happening to me? Maybe someday I'll learn that God, my Creator, has the answers, not me. But I wonder what it will take for me to learn to trust him—no matter what.

You can read more about Job in the book of Job.

4 Your words have supported those who were falling;
you encouraged those with shaky knees.
5 But now when trouble strikes, you lose heart.
You are terrified when it touches you.
6 Doesn't your reverence for God give you confidence?
Doesn't your life of integrity give you hope?
7 "Stop and think! Do the innocent die?
When have the upright been destroyed?
8 My experience shows that those who plant trouble
and cultivate evil will harvest the same.
9 A breath from God destroys them.
They vanish in a blast of his anger.
10 The lion roars and the wildcat snarls,
but the teeth of strong lions will be broken.
11 The fierce lion will starve for lack of prey,
and the cubs of the lioness will be scattered.
12 "This truth was given to me in secret,
as though whispered in my ear.
13 It came to me in a disturbing vision at night,
when people are in a deep sleep.
14 Fear gripped me,
and my bones trembled.
15 A spirit* swept past my face,
and my hair stood on end.*
16 The spirit stopped, but I couldn't see its shape.
There was a form before my eyes.
In the silence I heard a voice say,
17 'Can a mortal be innocent before God?
Can anyone be pure before the Creator?'
18 "If God does not trust his own angels
and has charged his messengers with foolishness,
19 how much less will he trust people made of clay!
They are made of dust, crushed as easily as a moth.
20 They are alive in the morning but dead by evening,
gone forever without a trace.
21 Their tent-cords are pulled and the tent collapses,
and they die in ignorance.

CHAPTER 5

Eliphaz's Response Continues

1 "Cry for help, but will anyone answer you?
Which of the angels* will help you?
2 Surely resentment destroys the fool,

4:15a Or *wind;* also in 4:16. **4:15b** Or *its wind sent shivers up my spine.* **5:1** Hebrew *the holy ones.*

and jealousy kills the simple.
3 I have seen that fools may be successful
for the moment,
but then comes sudden disaster.
4 Their children are abandoned far from
help;
they are crushed in court with no one
to defend them.
5 The hungry devour their harvest,
even when it is guarded by brambles.*
The thirsty pant after their wealth.
6 But evil does not spring from the soil,
and trouble does not sprout from the
earth.
7 People are born for trouble
as readily as sparks fly up from a fire.

8 "If I were you, I would go to God
and present my case to him.
9 He does great things too marvelous to
understand.
He performs countless miracles.
10 He gives rain for the earth
and water for the fields.
11 He gives prosperity to the poor
and protects those who suffer.
12 He frustrates the plans of schemers
so the work of their hands will not
succeed.

Isn't it bad if God corrects me?

Consider the joy of those corrected by God! Do not despise the discipline of the Almighty when you sin. JOB 5:17

13 He traps the wise in their own cleverness
so their cunning schemes are thwarted.
14 They find it is dark in the daytime,
and they grope at noon as if it were
night.
15 He rescues the poor from the cutting
words of the strong,
and rescues them from the clutches of
the powerful.
16 And so at last the poor have hope,
and the snapping jaws of the wicked
are shut.

17 "But consider the joy of those corrected
by God!
Do not despise the discipline of the
Almighty when you sin.
18 For though he wounds, he also bandages.
He strikes, but his hands also heal.
19 From six disasters he will rescue you;
even in the seventh, he will keep you
from evil.
20 He will save you from death in time of
famine,
from the power of the sword in time
of war.
21 You will be safe from slander
and have no fear when destruction
comes.
22 You will laugh at destruction and
famine;
wild animals will not terrify you.
23 You will be at peace with the stones
of the field,
and its wild animals will be at peace
with you.
24 You will know that your home is
safe.
When you survey your possessions,
nothing will be missing.
25 You will have many children;
your descendants will be as plentiful
as grass!
26 You will go to the grave at a ripe
old age,
like a sheaf of grain harvested at the
proper time!

27 "We have studied life and found all this
to be true.
Listen to my counsel, and apply it to
yourself."

CHAPTER 6

Job's Second Speech: A Response to Eliphaz

Then Job spoke again:

2 "If my misery could be weighed
and my troubles be put on the scales,
3 they would outweigh all the sands
of the sea.

5:5 The meaning of the Hebrew for this phrase is uncertain.

That is why I spoke impulsively.
4 For the Almighty has struck me down
with his arrows.
Their poison infects my spirit.
God's terrors are lined up against me.
5 Don't I have a right to complain?
Don't wild donkeys bray when they find
no grass,
and oxen bellow when they have
no food?
6 Don't people complain about unsalted
food?
Does anyone want the tasteless white
of an egg?*
7 My appetite disappears when I look at it;
I gag at the thought of eating it!

8 "Oh, that I might have my request,
that God would grant my desire.
9 I wish he would crush me.
I wish he would reach out his hand
and kill me.
10 At least I can take comfort in this:
Despite the pain,
I have not denied the words of the
Holy One.
11 But I don't have the strength to endure.
I have nothing to live for.
12 Do I have the strength of a stone?
Is my body made of bronze?
13 No, I am utterly helpless,
without any chance of success.

14 "One should be kind to a fainting friend,
but you accuse me without any fear of
the Almighty.*
15 My brothers, you have proved as
unreliable as a seasonal brook
that overflows its banks in the spring
16 when it is swollen with ice and melting
snow.
17 But when the hot weather arrives, the
water disappears.
The brook vanishes in the heat.
18 The caravans turn aside to be refreshed,
but there is nothing to drink, so
they die.
19 The caravans from Tema search for this
water;
the travelers from Sheba hope to
find it.
20 They count on it but are disappointed.
When they arrive, their hopes are
dashed.
21 You, too, have given no help.
You have seen my calamity, and you
are afraid.
22 But why? Have I ever asked you for a gift?
Have I begged for anything of yours for
myself?
23 Have I asked you to rescue me from my
enemies,
or to save me from ruthless people?
24 Teach me, and I will keep quiet.
Show me what I have done wrong.
25 Honest words can be painful,
but what do your criticisms amount to?
26 Do you think your words are convincing
when you disregard my cry of
desperation?
27 You would even send an orphan into
slavery*
or sell a friend.
28 Look at me!
Would I lie to your face?
29 Stop assuming my guilt,
for I have done no wrong.
30 Do you think I am lying?
Don't I know the difference between
right and wrong?

CHAPTER 7

1 "Is not all human life a struggle?
Our lives are like that of a hired hand,
2 like a worker who longs for the shade,
like a servant waiting to be paid.
3 I, too, have been assigned months of
futility,
long and weary nights of misery.
4 Lying in bed, I think, 'When will it be
morning?'
But the night drags on, and I toss till
dawn.
5 My body is covered with maggots and
scabs.
My skin breaks open, oozing with pus.

Job Cries Out to God

6 "My days fly faster than a weaver's shuttle.
They end without hope.
7 O God, remember that my life is but
a breath,
and I will never again feel happiness.

6:6 Or *the tasteless juice of the mallow plant?* **6:14** Or *friend, / or he might lose his fear of the Almighty.* **6:27** Hebrew *even gamble over an orphan.*

8 You see me now, but not for long.
You will look for me, but I will be gone.
9 Just as a cloud dissipates and vanishes,
those who die* will not come back.
10 They are gone forever from their home—
never to be seen again.

11 "I cannot keep from speaking.
I must express my anguish.
My bitter soul must complain.
12 Am I a sea monster or a dragon
that you must place me under guard?
13 I think, 'My bed will comfort me,
and sleep will ease my misery,'
14 but then you shatter me with dreams
and terrify me with visions.
15 I would rather be strangled—
rather die than suffer like this.
16 I hate my life and don't want to go
on living.
Oh, leave me alone for my few
remaining days.

17 "What are people, that you should make
so much of us,
that you should think of us so often?
18 For you examine us every morning
and test us every moment.
19 Why won't you leave me alone,
at least long enough for me to swallow!
20 If I have sinned, what have I done to you,
O watcher of all humanity?
Why make me your target?
Am I a burden to you?
21 Why not just forgive my sin
and take away my guilt?
For soon I will lie down in the dust
and die.
When you look for me, I will be gone."

CHAPTER 8

Bildad's First Response to Job

Then Bildad the Shuhite replied to Job:

2 "How long will you go on like this?
You sound like a blustering wind.
3 Does God twist justice?
Does the Almighty twist what is right?
4 Your children must have sinned against
him,
so their punishment was well deserved.
5 But if you pray to God
and seek the favor of the Almighty,
6 and if you are pure and live with integrity,
he will surely rise up and restore your
happy home.
7 And though you started with little,
you will end with much.

8 "Just ask the previous generation.
Pay attention to the experience of our
ancestors.
9 For we were born but yesterday and know
nothing.
Our days on earth are as fleeting as
a shadow.
10 But those who came before us will
teach you.
They will teach you the wisdom of old.

11 "Can papyrus reeds grow tall without
a marsh?
Can marsh grass flourish without
water?
12 While they are still flowering, not ready
to be cut,
they begin to wither more quickly than
grass.
13 The same happens to all who forget God.
The hopes of the godless evaporate.
14 Their confidence hangs by a thread.
They are leaning on a spider's web.
15 They cling to their home for security, but
it won't last.
They try to hold it tight, but it will
not endure.
16 The godless seem like a lush plant
growing in the sunshine,
its branches spreading across the
garden.
17 Its roots grow down through a pile
of stones;
it takes hold on a bed of rocks.
18 But when it is uprooted,
it's as though it never existed!
19 That's the end of its life,
and others spring up from the earth
to replace it.

20 "But look, God will not reject a person
of integrity,
nor will he lend a hand to the
wicked.
21 He will once again fill your mouth with
laughter
and your lips with shouts of joy.

7:9 Hebrew *who go down to Sheol.*

22 Those who hate you will be clothed with shame,
and the home of the wicked will be destroyed."

CHAPTER 9

Job's Third Speech: A Response to Bildad

Then Job spoke again:

2 "Yes, I know all this is true in principle.
But how can a person be declared innocent in God's sight?
3 If someone wanted to take God to court,*
would it be possible to answer him even once in a thousand times?
4 For God is so wise and so mighty.
Who has ever challenged him successfully?

5 "Without warning, he moves the mountains,
overturning them in his anger.
6 He shakes the earth from its place,
and its foundations tremble.
7 If he commands it, the sun won't rise
and the stars won't shine.
8 He alone has spread out the heavens
and marches on the waves of the sea.
9 He made all the stars—the Bear and Orion,
the Pleiades and the constellations of the southern sky.
10 He does great things too marvelous to understand.
He performs countless miracles.

11 "Yet when he comes near, I cannot see him.
When he moves by, I do not see him go.
12 If he snatches someone in death, who can stop him?
Who dares to ask, 'What are you doing?'
13 And God does not restrain his anger.
Even the monsters of the sea* are crushed beneath his feet.

14 "So who am I, that I should try to answer God
or even reason with him?
15 Even if I were right, I would have no defense.
I could only plead for mercy.
16 And even if I summoned him and he responded,
I'm not sure he would listen to me.
17 For he attacks me with a storm
and repeatedly wounds me without cause.
18 He will not let me catch my breath,
but fills me instead with bitter sorrows.
19 If it's a question of strength, he's the strong one.
If it's a matter of justice, who dares to summon him to court?
20 Though I am innocent, my own mouth would pronounce me guilty.
Though I am blameless, it* would prove me wicked.

21 "I am innocent,
but it makes no difference to me—
I despise my life.
22 Innocent or wicked, it is all the same to God.
That's why I say, 'He destroys both the blameless and the wicked.'
23 When a plague* sweeps through,
he laughs at the death of the innocent.
24 The whole earth is in the hands of the wicked,
and God blinds the eyes of the judges.
If he's not the one who does it, who is?

25 "My life passes more swiftly than a runner.
It flees away without a glimpse of happiness.
26 It disappears like a swift papyrus boat,
like an eagle swooping down on its prey.
27 If I decided to forget my complaints,
to put away my sad face and be cheerful,
28 I would still dread all the pain,
for I know you will not find me innocent, O God.
29 Whatever happens, I will be found guilty.
So what's the use of trying?
30 Even if I were to wash myself with soap
and clean my hands with lye,
31 you would plunge me into a muddy ditch,
and my own filthy clothing would hate me.

9:3 Or *If God wanted to take someone to court.* **9:13** Hebrew *the helpers of Rahab,* the name of a mythical sea monster that represents chaos in ancient literature. **9:20** Or *he.* **9:23** Or *disaster.*

32 "God is not a mortal like me,
so I cannot argue with him or take him to trial.
33 If only there were a mediator between us,
someone who could bring us together.
34 The mediator could make God stop beating me,
and I would no longer live in terror of his punishment.
35 Then I could speak to him without fear,
but I cannot do that in my own strength.

CHAPTER 10

Job Frames His Plea to God

1 "I am disgusted with my life.
Let me complain freely.
My bitter soul must complain.
2 I will say to God, 'Don't simply condemn me—
tell me the charge you are bringing against me.
3 What do you gain by oppressing me?
Why do you reject me, the work of your own hands,
while smiling on the schemes of the wicked?
4 Are your eyes like those of a human?
Do you see things only as people see them?
5 Is your lifetime only as long as ours?
Is your life so short
6 that you must quickly probe for my guilt
and search for my sin?
7 Although you know I am not guilty,
no one can rescue me from your hands.
8 "'You formed me with your hands; you made me,
yet now you completely destroy me.
9 Remember that you made me from dust—
will you turn me back to dust so soon?
10 You guided my conception
and formed me in the womb.*
11 You clothed me with skin and flesh,
and you knit my bones and sinews together.
12 You gave me life and showed me your unfailing love.
My life was preserved by your care.
13 "'Yet your real motive—
your true intent—
14 was to watch me, and if I sinned,
you would not forgive my guilt.
15 If I am guilty, too bad for me;
and even if I'm innocent, I can't hold my head high,
because I am filled with shame and misery.
16 And if I hold my head high, you hunt me like a lion
and display your awesome power against me.
17 Again and again you witness against me.
You pour out your growing anger on me
and bring fresh armies against me.
18 "'Why, then, did you deliver me from my mother's womb?
Why didn't you let me die at birth?
19 It would be as though I had never existed,
going directly from the womb to the grave.
20 I have only a few days left, so leave me alone,
that I may have a moment of comfort
21 before I leave—never to return—
for the land of darkness and utter gloom.
22 It is a land as dark as midnight,
a land of gloom and confusion,
where even the light is dark as midnight.'"

CHAPTER 11

Zophar's First Response to Job

Then Zophar the Naamathite replied to Job:

2 "Shouldn't someone answer this torrent of words?
Is a person proved innocent just by a lot of talking?
3 Should I remain silent while you babble on?
When you mock God, shouldn't someone make you ashamed?
4 You claim, 'My beliefs are pure,'
and 'I am clean in the sight of God.'
5 If only God would speak;
if only he would tell you what he thinks!

10:10 Hebrew *You poured me out like milk / and curdled me like cheese.*

When I was in junior high, I always compared myself to other people, especially if they were "popular." I wanted to be just like them, so I let them influence just about everything in my life. If a pretty girl bought a cool shirt, I would talk my mom into buying me that exact same shirt. I bought Doc Martens (really clunky, expensive shoes) just because everyone else had them. I even let people influence what I brought in my lunch! It was that bad!

My self-esteem started to drop. My closest "friends" always found pleasure in playing mean practical jokes on me (which usually had something to do with my clothes or figure). I didn't like anything about myself. Compared to other girls, I thought I was ugly, fat, and boring.

Fortunately, in high school my friendships started to change. I began to realize that God made me unique. Even though I might never look like a model in a magazine, God loved me. Anything on the outside—my clothes, my make-up, my hair—didn't really make me who I was. I didn't have to compare myself to anyone anymore. I was beautiful on the inside since Jesus was in my heart.

Today, my new friends encourage me instead of criticize me. I still care about what other people think of me, but I don't let them influence everything I do. Trust me. When you get to high school, much of what seemed so important in junior high will seem ridiculous. If I had just realized how special I was to God and how pleased he was with me, I probably wouldn't have experienced so much emotional pain.

Check out Job 10:8-10 to see the truth about how you were uniquely created and how valued you are.

6 If only he would tell you the secrets
of wisdom,
for true wisdom is not a simple matter.
Listen! God is doubtless punishing you
far less than you deserve!

7 "Can you solve the mysteries of God?
Can you discover everything about
the Almighty?
8 Such knowledge is higher than the heavens—
and who are you?
It is deeper than the underworld*—
what do you know?
9 It is broader than the earth
and wider than the sea.
10 If God comes and puts a person in prison
or calls the court to order, who can
stop him?
11 For he knows those who are false,
and he takes note of all their sins.
12 An empty-headed person won't become
wise
any more than a wild donkey can bear
a human child.*

13 "If only you would prepare your heart
and lift up your hands to him in prayer!
14 Get rid of your sins,
and leave all iniquity behind you.
15 Then your face will brighten with
innocence.
You will be strong and free of fear.
16 You will forget your misery;
it will be like water flowing away.
17 Your life will be brighter than the noonday.
Even darkness will be as bright as
morning.
18 Having hope will give you courage.
You will be protected and will rest in
safety.
19 You will lie down unafraid,
and many will look to you for help.
20 But the wicked will be blinded.
They will have no escape.
Their only hope is death."

CHAPTER 12

Job's Fourth Speech: A Response to Zophar

Then Job spoke again:

2 "You people really know everything,
don't you?
And when you die, wisdom will die
with you!
3 Well, I know a few things myself—
and you're no better than I am.
Who doesn't know these things you've
been saying?
4 Yet my friends laugh at me,
for I call on God and expect an
answer.
I am a just and blameless man,
yet they laugh at me.
5 People who are at ease mock those in
trouble.
They give a push to people who are
stumbling.
6 But robbers are left in peace,
and those who provoke God live in
safety—
though God keeps them in his power.

7 "Just ask the animals, and they will teach
you.
Ask the birds of the sky, and they will
tell you.
8 Speak to the earth, and it will instruct you.
Let the fish in the sea speak to you.
9 For they all know
that my disaster* has come from the
hand of the LORD.
10 For the life of every living thing is in his
hand,
and the breath of every human
being.
11 The ear tests the words it hears
just as the mouth distinguishes
between foods.
12 Wisdom belongs to the aged,
and understanding to the old.

13 "But true wisdom and power are found
in God;
counsel and understanding are his.
14 What he destroys cannot be rebuilt.
When he puts someone in prison, there
is no escape.
15 If he holds back the rain, the earth
becomes a desert.
If he releases the waters, they flood
the earth.
16 Yes, strength and wisdom are his;
deceivers and deceived are both in
his power.

11:8 Hebrew *than Sheol.* **11:12** Or *than a wild male donkey can bear a tame colt.* **12:9** Hebrew *that this.*

17 He leads counselors away, stripped of
good judgment;
wise judges become fools.
18 He removes the royal robe of kings.
They are led away with ropes around
their waist.
19 He leads priests away, stripped of status;
he overthrows those with long years
in power.
20 He silences the trusted adviser
and removes the insight of the elders.
21 He pours disgrace upon princes
and disarms the strong.

22 "He uncovers mysteries hidden in darkness;
he brings light to the deepest gloom.
23 He builds up nations, and he destroys
them.
He expands nations, and he abandons
them.
24 He strips kings of understanding
and leaves them wandering in
a pathless wasteland.
25 They grope in the darkness without
a light.
He makes them stagger like drunkards.

CHAPTER 13

Job Wants to Argue His Case with God

1 "Look, I have seen all this with my own eyes
and heard it with my own ears, and
now I understand.
2 I know as much as you do.
You are no better than I am.
3 As for me, I would speak directly to the
Almighty.
I want to argue my case with God
himself.
4 As for you, you smear me with lies.
As physicians, you are worthless quacks.
5 If only you could be silent!
That's the wisest thing you could do.
6 Listen to my charge;
pay attention to my arguments.

7 "Are you defending God with lies?
Do you make your dishonest arguments
for his sake?
8 Will you slant your testimony in his favor?
Will you argue God's case for him?
9 What will happen when he finds out what
you are doing?

Can you fool him as easily as you fool
people?
10 No, you will be in trouble with him
if you secretly slant your testimony
in his favor.
11 Doesn't his majesty terrify you?
Doesn't your fear of him overwhelm
you?
12 Your platitudes are as valuable as ashes.
Your defense is as fragile as a clay pot.

13 "Be silent now and leave me alone.
Let me speak, and I will face the
consequences.
14 Yes, I will take my life in my hands
and say what I really think.
15 God might kill me, but I have no other
hope.*
I am going to argue my case with him.

13:15 An alternate reading in the Masoretic Text reads *God might kill me, but I hope in him.*

16 But this is what will save me—I am not godless.
If I were, I could not stand before him.

17 "Listen closely to what I am about to say.
Hear me out.
18 I have prepared my case;
I will be proved innocent.
19 Who can argue with me over this?
And if you prove me wrong, I will remain silent and die.

Job Asks How He Has Sinned

20 "O God, grant me these two things,
and then I will be able to face you.
21 Remove your heavy hand from me,
and don't terrify me with your awesome presence.
22 Now summon me, and I will answer!
Or let me speak to you, and you reply.
23 Tell me, what have I done wrong?
Show me my rebellion and my sin.
24 Why do you turn away from me?
Why do you treat me as your enemy?
25 Would you terrify a leaf blown by the wind?
Would you chase dry straw?

26 "You write bitter accusations against me
and bring up all the sins of my youth.
27 You put my feet in stocks.
You examine all my paths.
You trace all my footprints.
28 I waste away like rotting wood,
like a moth-eaten coat.

CHAPTER 14

1 "How frail is humanity!
How short is life, how full of trouble!
2 We blossom like a flower and then wither.
Like a passing shadow, we quickly disappear.
3 Must you keep an eye on such a frail creature
and demand an accounting from me?
4 Who can bring purity out of an impure person?
No one!
5 You have decided the length of our lives.
You know how many months we will live,
and we are not given a minute longer.
6 So leave us alone and let us rest!
We are like hired hands, so let us finish our work in peace.

7 "Even a tree has more hope!
If it is cut down, it will sprout again
and grow new branches.
8 Though its roots have grown old in the earth
and its stump decays,
9 at the scent of water it will bud
and sprout again like a new seedling.

10 "But when people die, their strength is gone.
They breathe their last, and then where are they?
11 As water evaporates from a lake
and a river disappears in drought,
12 people are laid to rest and do not rise again.
Until the heavens are no more, they will not wake up
nor be roused from their sleep.

13 "I wish you would hide me in the grave*
and forget me there until your anger has passed.
But mark your calendar to think of me again!
14 Can the dead live again?
If so, this would give me hope through all my years of struggle,
and I would eagerly await the release of death.
15 You would call and I would answer,
and you would yearn for me, your handiwork.
16 For then you would guard my steps,
instead of watching for my sins.
17 My sins would be sealed in a pouch,
and you would cover my guilt.

18 "But instead, as mountains fall and crumble
and as rocks fall from a cliff,
19 as water wears away the stones
and floods wash away the soil,
so you destroy people's hope.
20 You always overpower them, and they pass from the scene.
You disfigure them in death and send them away.

14:13 Hebrew *in Sheol.*

21 They never know if their children grow up in honor
or sink to insignificance.
22 They suffer painfully;
their life is full of trouble."

CHAPTER 15

Eliphaz's Second Response to Job

Then Eliphaz the Temanite replied:

2 "A wise man wouldn't answer with such empty talk!
You are nothing but a windbag.
3 The wise don't engage in empty chatter.
What good are such words?
4 Have you no fear of God,
no reverence for him?
5 Your sins are telling your mouth what to say.
Your words are based on clever deception.
6 Your own mouth condemns you, not I.
Your own lips testify against you.

7 "Were you the first person ever born?
Were you born before the hills were made?
8 Were you listening at God's secret council?
Do you have a monopoly on wisdom?
9 What do you know that we don't?
What do you understand that we do not?
10 On our side are aged, gray-haired men
much older than your father!

11 "Is God's comfort too little for you?
Is his gentle word not enough?
12 What has taken away your reason?
What has weakened your vision,*
13 that you turn against God
and say all these evil things?
14 Can any mortal be pure?
Can anyone born of a woman be just?
15 Look, God does not even trust the angels.*
Even the heavens are not absolutely pure in his sight.
16 How much less pure is a corrupt and sinful person
with a thirst for wickedness!

17 "If you will listen, I will show you.
I will answer you from my own experience.
18 And it is confirmed by the reports of wise men
who have heard the same thing from their fathers—
19 from those to whom the land was given
long before any foreigners arrived.

20 "The wicked writhe in pain throughout their lives.
Years of trouble are stored up for the ruthless.
21 The sound of terror rings in their ears,
and even on good days they fear the attack of the destroyer.
22 They dare not go out into the darkness
for fear they will be murdered.
23 They wander around, saying, 'Where can I find bread?'*
They know their day of destruction is near.
24 That dark day terrifies them.
They live in distress and anguish,
like a king preparing for battle.
25 For they shake their fists at God,
defying the Almighty.
26 Holding their strong shields,
they defiantly charge against him.

27 "These wicked people are heavy and prosperous;
their waists bulge with fat.
28 But their cities will be ruined.
They will live in abandoned houses
that are ready to tumble down.
29 Their riches will not last,
and their wealth will not endure.
Their possessions will no longer spread across the horizon.

30 "They will not escape the darkness.
The burning sun will wither their shoots,
and the breath of God will destroy them.
31 Let them no longer fool themselves by trusting in empty riches,
for emptiness will be their only reward.
32 Like trees, they will be cut down in the prime of life;

15:12 Or *Why do your eyes flash with anger;* Hebrew reads *Why do your eyes blink.* **15:15** Hebrew *the holy ones.* **15:23** Greek version reads *He is appointed to be food for a vulture.*

their branches will never again be
green.
33 They will be like a vine whose grapes are
harvested too early,
like an olive tree that loses its blossoms
before the fruit can form.
34 For the godless are barren.
Their homes, enriched through bribery,
will burn.
35 They conceive trouble and give birth
to evil.
Their womb produces deceit."

CHAPTER 16

Job's Fifth Speech: A Response to Eliphaz

Then Job spoke again:

2 "I have heard all this before.
What miserable comforters you are!
3 Won't you ever stop blowing hot air?
What makes you keep on talking?
4 I could say the same things if you were in
my place.
I could spout off criticism and shake
my head at you.
5 But if it were me, I would encourage you.
I would try to take away your grief.
6 Instead, I suffer if I defend myself,
and I suffer no less if I refuse
to speak.

7 "O God, you have ground me down
and devastated my family.
8 As if to prove I have sinned, you've
reduced me to skin and bones.
My gaunt flesh testifies against me.
9 God hates me and angrily tears me
apart.
He snaps his teeth at me
and pierces me with his eyes.
10 People jeer and laugh at me.
They slap my cheek in contempt.
A mob gathers against me.
11 God has handed me over to sinners.
He has tossed me into the hands
of the wicked.

12 "I was living quietly until he shattered
me.
He took me by the neck and broke me
in pieces.
Then he set me up as his target,
13 and now his archers surround me.
His arrows pierce me without mercy.
The ground is wet with my blood.*
14 Again and again he smashes against me,
charging at me like a warrior.
15 I wear burlap to show my grief.
My pride lies in the dust.
16 My eyes are red with weeping;
dark shadows circle my eyes.
17 Yet I have done no wrong,
and my prayer is pure.

18 "O earth, do not conceal my blood.
Let it cry out on my behalf.
19 Even now my witness is in heaven.
My advocate is there on high.
20 My friends scorn me,
but I pour out my tears to God.
21 I need someone to mediate between
God and me,
as a person mediates between
friends.
22 For soon I must go down that road
from which I will never return.

CHAPTER 17

Job Continues to Defend His Innocence

1 "My spirit is crushed,
and my life is nearly snuffed out.
The grave is ready to receive me.
2 I am surrounded by mockers.
I watch how bitterly they taunt me.

3 "You must defend my innocence,
O God,
since no one else will stand up for me.
4 You have closed their minds to
understanding,
but do not let them triumph.
5 They betray their friends for their own
advantage,
so let their children faint with hunger.

6 "God has made a mockery of me among
the people;
they spit in my face.
7 My eyes are swollen with weeping,
and I am but a shadow of my former
self.
8 The virtuous are horrified when they
see me.
The innocent rise up against the
ungodly.

16:13 Hebrew *my gall.*

9 The righteous keep moving forward,
and those with clean hands become
stronger and stronger.

Why should I keep doing the right thing, especially if it's difficult?

10 "As for all of you, come back with
a better argument,
though I still won't find a wise man
among you.
11 My days are over.
My hopes have disappeared.
My heart's desires are broken.
12 These men say that night is day;
they claim that the darkness is light.
13 What if I go to the grave*
and make my bed in darkness?
14 What if I call the grave my father,
and the maggot my mother or my
sister?
15 Where then is my hope?
Can anyone find it?
16 No, my hope will go down with me
to the grave.
We will rest together in the dust!"

CHAPTER 18

Bildad's Second Response to Job

Then Bildad the Shuhite replied:

2 "How long before you stop talking?
Speak sense if you want us to
answer!
3 Do you think we are mere animals?
Do you think we are stupid?
4 You may tear out your hair in anger,
but will that destroy the earth?
Will it make the rocks tremble?

5 "Surely the light of the wicked will be
snuffed out.
The sparks of their fire will not glow.
6 The light in their tent will grow dark.
The lamp hanging above them will be
quenched.
7 The confident stride of the wicked will
be shortened.
Their own schemes will be their
downfall.
8 The wicked walk into a net.

The righteous keep moving forward, and those with clean hands become stronger and stronger. JOB 17:9

They fall into a pit.
9 A trap grabs them by the heel.
A snare holds them tight.
10 A noose lies hidden on the ground.
A rope is stretched across their
path.

11 "Terrors surround the wicked
and trouble them at every step.
12 Hunger depletes their strength,
and calamity waits for them to
stumble.
13 Disease eats their skin;
death devours their limbs.
14 They are torn from the security of their
homes
and are brought down to the king
of terrors.
15 The homes of the wicked will burn
down;
burning sulfur rains on their
houses.
16 Their roots will dry up,
and their branches will wither.
17 All memory of their existence will fade
from the earth;
no one will remember their names.
18 They will be thrust from light into
darkness,
driven from the world.
19 They will have neither children nor
grandchildren,
nor any survivor in the place where
they lived.
20 People in the west are appalled at their
fate;
people in the east are horrified.
21 They will say, 'This was the home of
a wicked person,
the place of one who rejected God.'"

17:13 Hebrew *to Sheol;* also in 17:16.

CHAPTER 19

Job's Sixth Speech: A Response to Bildad

Then Job spoke again:

2 "How long will you torture me?
How long will you try to crush me with your words?
3 You have already insulted me ten times.
You should be ashamed of treating me so badly.
4 Even if I have sinned,
that is my concern, not yours.
5 You think you're better than I am,
using my humiliation as evidence of my sin.
6 But it is God who has wronged me,
capturing me in his net.*

7 "I cry out, 'Help!' but no one answers me.
I protest, but there is no justice.
8 God has blocked my way so I cannot move.
He has plunged my path into darkness.
9 He has stripped me of my honor
and removed the crown from my head.
10 He has demolished me on every side, and I am finished.
He has uprooted my hope like a fallen tree.
11 His fury burns against me;
he counts me as an enemy.
12 His troops advance.
They build up roads to attack me.
They camp all around my tent.

13 "My relatives stay far away,
and my friends have turned against me.
14 My family is gone,
and my close friends have forgotten me.
15 My servants and maids consider me a stranger.
I am like a foreigner to them.
16 When I call my servant, he doesn't come;
I have to plead with him!
17 My breath is repulsive to my wife.
I am rejected by my own family.
18 Even young children despise me.
When I stand to speak, they turn their backs on me.
19 My close friends detest me.
Those I loved have turned against me.
20 I have been reduced to skin and bones
and have escaped death by the skin of my teeth.

21 "Have mercy on me, my friends, have mercy,
for the hand of God has struck me.
22 Must you also persecute me, like God does?
Haven't you chewed me up enough?

23 "Oh, that my words could be recorded.
Oh, that they could be inscribed on a monument,
24 carved with an iron chisel and filled with lead,
engraved forever in the rock.

25 "But as for me, I know that my Redeemer lives,
and he will stand upon the earth at last.
26 And after my body has decayed,
yet in my body I will see God*!
27 I will see him for myself.
Yes, I will see him with my own eyes.
I am overwhelmed at the thought!

28 "How dare you go on persecuting me,
saying, 'It's his own fault'?
29 You should fear punishment yourselves,
for your attitude deserves punishment.
Then you will know that there is indeed a judgment."

CHAPTER 20

Zophar's Second Response to Job

Then Zophar the Naamathite replied:

2 "I must reply
because I am greatly disturbed.
3 I've had to endure your insults,
but now my spirit prompts me to reply.

4 "Don't you realize that from the beginning of time,
ever since people were first placed on the earth,
5 the triumph of the wicked has been short lived
and the joy of the godless has been only temporary?
6 Though the pride of the godless reaches to the heavens
and their heads touch the clouds,
7 yet they will vanish forever,

19:6 Or *for I am like a city under siege.* **19:26** Or *without my body I will see God.* The meaning of the Hebrew is uncertain.

thrown away like their own dung.
Those who knew them will ask,
'Where are they?'
8 They will fade like a dream and not be found.
They will vanish like a vision in the night.
9 Those who once saw them will see them no more.
Their families will never see them again.
10 Their children will beg from the poor,
for they must give back their stolen riches.
11 Though they are young,
their bones will lie in the dust.

12 "They enjoyed the sweet taste of wickedness,
letting it melt under their tongue.
13 They savored it,
holding it long in their mouths.
14 But suddenly the food in their bellies turns sour,
a poisonous venom in their stomach.
15 They will vomit the wealth they swallowed.
God won't let them keep it down.
16 They will suck the poison of cobras.
The viper will kill them.
17 They will never again enjoy streams of olive oil
or rivers of milk and honey.
18 They will give back everything they worked for.
Their wealth will bring them no joy.
19 For they oppressed the poor and left them destitute.
They foreclosed on their homes.
20 They were always greedy and never satisfied.
Nothing remains of all the things they dreamed about.
21 Nothing is left after they finish gorging themselves.
Therefore, their prosperity will not endure.

22 "In the midst of plenty, they will run into trouble
and be overcome by misery.
23 May God give them a bellyful of trouble.
May God rain down his anger upon them.
24 When they try to escape an iron weapon,
a bronze-tipped arrow will pierce them.
25 The arrow is pulled from their back,
and the arrowhead glistens with blood.*
The terrors of death are upon them.
26 Their treasures will be thrown into deepest darkness.
A wildfire will devour their goods,
consuming all they have left.
27 The heavens will reveal their guilt,
and the earth will testify against them.
28 A flood will sweep away their house.
God's anger will descend on them in torrents.
29 This is the reward that God gives the wicked.
It is the inheritance decreed by God."

CHAPTER 21

Job's Seventh Speech: A Response to Zophar

Then Job spoke again:

2 "Listen closely to what I am saying.
That's one consolation you can give me.
3 Bear with me, and let me speak.
After I have spoken, you may resume mocking me.

4 "My complaint is with God, not with people.
I have good reason to be so impatient.
5 Look at me and be stunned.
Put your hand over your mouth in shock.
6 When I think about what I am saying,
I shudder.
My body trembles.

7 "Why do the wicked prosper,
growing old and powerful?
8 They live to see their children grow up and settle down,
and they enjoy their grandchildren.
9 Their homes are safe from every fear,
and God does not punish them.
10 Their bulls never fail to breed.
Their cows bear calves and never miscarry.

20:25 Hebrew *with gall.*

11 They let their children frisk about like lambs.
Their little ones skip and dance.
12 They sing with tambourine and harp.
They celebrate to the sound of the flute.
13 They spend their days in prosperity,
then go down to the grave* in peace.
14 And yet they say to God, 'Go away.
We want no part of you and your ways.
15 Who is the Almighty, and why should we obey him?
What good will it do us to pray?'
16 (They think their prosperity is of their own doing,
but I will have nothing to do with that kind of thinking.)

17 "Yet the light of the wicked never seems to be extinguished.
Do they ever have trouble?
Does God distribute sorrows to them in anger?
18 Are they driven before the wind like straw?
Are they carried away by the storm like chaff?
Not at all!

19 "'Well,' you say, 'at least God will punish their children!'
But I say he should punish the ones who sin,
so that they understand his judgment.
20 Let them see their destruction with their own eyes.
Let them drink deeply of the anger of the Almighty.
21 For they will not care what happens to their family
after they are dead.

22 "But who can teach a lesson to God,
since he judges even the most powerful?
23 One person dies in prosperity,
completely comfortable and secure,
24 the picture of good health,
vigorous and fit.
25 Another person dies in bitter poverty,
never having tasted the good life.
26 But both are buried in the same dust,
both eaten by the same maggots.

21:13 Hebrew *to Sheol.*

27 "Look, I know what you're thinking.
I know the schemes you plot against me.
28 You will tell me of rich and wicked people
whose houses have vanished because of their sins.
29 But ask those who have been around,
and they will tell you the truth.
30 Evil people are spared in times of calamity
and are allowed to escape disaster.
31 No one criticizes them openly
or pays them back for what they have done.
32 When they are carried to the grave,
an honor guard keeps watch at their tomb.
33 A great funeral procession goes to the cemetery.
Many pay their respects as the body is laid to rest,
and the earth gives sweet repose.

34 "How can your empty clichés comfort me?
All your explanations are lies!"

CHAPTER 22

Eliphaz's Third Response to Job

Then Eliphaz the Temanite replied:

2 "Can a person do anything to help God?
Can even a wise person be helpful to him?
3 Is it any advantage to the Almighty if you are righteous?
Would it be any gain to him if you were perfect?
4 Is it because you're so pious that he accuses you
and brings judgment against you?
5 No, it's because of your wickedness!
There's no limit to your sins.

6 "For example, you must have lent money to your friend
and demanded clothing as security.
Yes, you stripped him to the bone.
7 You must have refused water for the thirsty
and food for the hungry.
8 You probably think the land belongs to the powerful

and only the privileged have a right
to it!
9 You must have sent widows away empty-
handed
and crushed the hopes of orphans.
10 That is why you are surrounded by traps
and tremble from sudden fears.
11 That is why you cannot see in the
darkness,
and waves of water cover you.

12 "God is so great—higher than the
heavens,
higher than the farthest stars.
13 But you reply, 'That's why God can't see
what I am doing!
How can he judge through the thick
darkness?
14 For thick clouds swirl about him, and he
cannot see us.
He is way up there, walking on the vault
of heaven.'

15 "Will you continue on the old paths
where evil people have walked?
16 They were snatched away in the prime
of life,
the foundations of their lives washed
away.
17 For they said to God, 'Leave us alone!
What can the Almighty do to us?'
18 Yet he was the one who filled their homes
with good things,
so I will have nothing to do with that
kind of thinking.

19 "The righteous will be happy to see the
wicked destroyed,
and the innocent will laugh in
contempt.
20 They will say, 'See how our enemies have
been destroyed.
The last of them have been consumed
in the fire.'

21 "Submit to God, and you will have peace;
then things will go well for you.
22 Listen to his instructions,
and store them in your heart.
23 If you return to the Almighty, you will be
restored—
so clean up your life.
24 If you give up your lust for money
and throw your precious gold into
the river,
25 the Almighty himself will be your
treasure.
He will be your precious silver!

26 "Then you will take delight in the
Almighty
and look up to God.
27 You will pray to him, and he will hear
you,
and you will fulfill your vows to him.
28 You will succeed in whatever you choose
to do,
and light will shine on the road ahead
of you.
29 If people are in trouble and you say,
'Help them,'
God will save them.
30 Even sinners will be rescued;
they will be rescued because your
hands are pure."

CHAPTER 23

Job's Eighth Speech: A Response to Eliphaz

Then Job spoke again:

2 "My complaint today is still a bitter
one,
and I try hard not to groan aloud.
3 If only I knew where to find God,
I would go to his court.
4 I would lay out my case
and present my arguments.
5 Then I would listen to his reply
and understand what he says to me.
6 Would he use his great power to argue
with me?
No, he would give me a fair hearing.
7 Honest people can reason with him,
so I would be forever acquitted by my
judge.
8 I go east, but he is not there.
I go west, but I cannot find him.
9 I do not see him in the north, for he is
hidden.
I look to the south, but he is
concealed.

10 "But he knows where I am going.
And when he tests me, I will come out
as pure as gold.
11 For I have stayed on God's paths;

I have followed his ways and not turned aside.
12 I have not departed from his commands,
but have treasured his words more than daily food.
13 But once he has made his decision, who can change his mind?
Whatever he wants to do, he does.
14 So he will do to me whatever he has planned.
He controls my destiny.
15 No wonder I am so terrified in his presence.
When I think of it, terror grips me.
16 God has made me sick at heart;
the Almighty has terrified me.
17 Darkness is all around me;
thick, impenetrable darkness is everywhere.

CHAPTER 24

Job Asks Why the Wicked Are Not Punished

1 "Why doesn't the Almighty bring the wicked to judgment?
Why must the godly wait for him in vain?
2 Evil people steal land by moving the boundary markers.
They steal livestock and put them in their own pastures.
3 They take the orphan's donkey
and demand the widow's ox as security for a loan.
4 The poor are pushed off the path;
the needy must hide together for safety.
5 Like wild donkeys in the wilderness,
the poor must spend all their time looking for food,
searching even in the desert for food for their children.
6 They harvest a field they do not own,
and they glean in the vineyards of the wicked.
7 All night they lie naked in the cold,
without clothing or covering.
8 They are soaked by mountain showers,
and they huddle against the rocks for want of a home.
9 "The wicked snatch a widow's child from her breast,
taking the baby as security for a loan.
10 The poor must go about naked, without any clothing.
They harvest food for others while they themselves are starving.
11 They press out olive oil without being allowed to taste it,
and they tread in the winepress as they suffer from thirst.
12 The groans of the dying rise from the city,
and the wounded cry for help,
yet God ignores their moaning.
13 "Wicked people rebel against the light.
They refuse to acknowledge its ways or stay in its paths.
14 The murderer rises in the early dawn
to kill the poor and needy;
at night he is a thief.
15 The adulterer waits for the twilight,

saying, 'No one will see me then.'
He hides his face so no one will know him.

16 Thieves break into houses at night
and sleep in the daytime.
They are not acquainted with the light.
17 The black night is their morning.
They ally themselves with the terrors of the darkness.

18 "But they disappear like foam down a river.
Everything they own is cursed,
and they are afraid to enter their own vineyards.
19 The grave* consumes sinners
just as drought and heat consume snow.
20 Their own mothers will forget them.
Maggots will find them sweet to eat.
No one will remember them.
Wicked people are broken like a tree in the storm.
21 They cheat the woman who has no son to help her.
They refuse to help the needy widow.

22 "God, in his power, drags away the rich.
They may rise high, but they have no assurance of life.
23 They may be allowed to live in security,
but God is always watching them.
24 And though they are great now,
in a moment they will be gone like all others,
cut off like heads of grain.
25 Can anyone claim otherwise?
Who can prove me wrong?"

CHAPTER 25

Bildad's Third Response to Job

Then Bildad the Shuhite replied:

2 "God is powerful and dreadful.
He enforces peace in the heavens.
3 Who is able to count his heavenly army?
Doesn't his light shine on all the earth?
4 How can a mortal be innocent before God?
Can anyone born of a woman be pure?
5 God is more glorious than the moon;
he shines brighter than the stars.
6 In comparison, people are maggots;
we mortals are mere worms."

CHAPTER 26

Job's Ninth Speech: A Response to Bildad

Then Job spoke again:

2 "How you have helped the powerless!
How you have saved the weak!
3 How you have enlightened my stupidity!
What wise advice you have offered!
4 Where have you gotten all these wise sayings?
Whose spirit speaks through you?

5 "The dead tremble—
those who live beneath the waters.
6 The underworld* is naked in God's presence.
The place of destruction* is uncovered.
7 God stretches the northern sky over empty space
and hangs the earth on nothing.
8 He wraps the rain in his thick clouds,
and the clouds don't burst with the weight.
9 He covers the face of the moon,*
shrouding it with his clouds.
10 He created the horizon when he separated the waters;
he set the boundary between day and night.
11 The foundations of heaven tremble;
they shudder at his rebuke.
12 By his power the sea grew calm.
By his skill he crushed the great sea monster.*
13 His Spirit made the heavens beautiful,
and his power pierced the gliding serpent.
14 These are just the beginning of all that he does,
merely a whisper of his power.
Who, then, can comprehend the thunder of his power?"

CHAPTER 27

Job's Final Speech

Job continued speaking:

2 "I vow by the living God, who has taken away my rights,
by the Almighty who has embittered my soul—
3 As long as I live,

24:19 Hebrew *Sheol*. **26:6a** Hebrew *Sheol*. **26:6b** Hebrew *Abaddon*. **26:9** Or *covers his throne*. **26:12** Hebrew *Rahab*, the name of a mythical sea monster that represents chaos in ancient literature.

while I have breath from God,
4 my lips will speak no evil,
and my tongue will speak no lies.
5 I will never concede that you are right;
I will defend my integrity until I die.
6 I will maintain my innocence without wavering.
My conscience is clear for as long as I live.

7 "May my enemy be punished like the wicked,
my adversary like those who do evil.
8 For what hope do the godless have when God cuts them off
and takes away their life?
9 Will God listen to their cry
when trouble comes upon them?
10 Can they take delight in the Almighty?
Can they call to God at any time?
11 I will teach you about God's power.
I will not conceal anything concerning the Almighty.
12 But you have seen all this,
yet you say all these useless things to me.

13 "This is what the wicked will receive from God;
this is their inheritance from the Almighty.
14 They may have many children,
but the children will die in war or starve to death.
15 Those who survive will die of a plague,
and not even their widows will mourn them.

16 "Evil people may have piles of money
and may store away mounds of clothing.
17 But the righteous will wear that clothing,
and the innocent will divide that money.
18 The wicked build houses as fragile as a spider's web,*
as flimsy as a shelter made of branches.
19 The wicked go to bed rich
but wake to find that all their wealth is gone.
20 Terror overwhelms them like a flood,
and they are blown away in the storms of the night.
21 The east wind carries them away, and they are gone.
It sweeps them away.
22 It whirls down on them without mercy.
They struggle to flee from its power.
23 But everyone jeers at them
and mocks them.

CHAPTER 28

Job Speaks of Wisdom and Understanding

1 "People know where to mine silver
and how to refine gold.
2 They know where to dig iron from the earth
and how to smelt copper from rock.
3 They know how to shine light in the darkness
and explore the farthest regions of the earth
as they search in the dark for ore.
4 They sink a mine shaft into the earth
far from where anyone lives.
They descend on ropes, swinging back and forth.
5 Food is grown on the earth above,
but down below, the earth is melted as by fire.
6 Here the rocks contain precious lapis lazuli,
and the dust contains gold.
7 These are treasures no bird of prey can see,
no falcon's eye observe.
8 No wild animal has walked upon these treasures;
no lion has ever set his paw there.
9 People know how to tear apart flinty rocks
and overturn the roots of mountains.
10 They cut tunnels in the rocks
and uncover precious stones.
11 They dam up the trickling streams
and bring to light the hidden treasures.

12 "But do people know where to find wisdom?
Where can they find understanding?
13 No one knows where to find it,
for it is not found among the living.
14 'It is not here,' says the ocean.
'Nor is it here,' says the sea.
15 It cannot be bought with gold.

27:18 As in Greek and Syriac versions (see also 8:14); Hebrew reads *a moth.*

It cannot be purchased with silver.
16 It's worth more than all the gold
of Ophir,
greater than precious onyx or lapis
lazuli.
17 Wisdom is more valuable than gold and
crystal.
It cannot be purchased with jewels
mounted in fine gold.
18 Coral and jasper are worthless in trying
to get it.
The price of wisdom is far above rubies.
19 Precious peridot from Ethiopia* cannot
be exchanged for it.
It's worth more than the purest gold.

20 "But do people know where to find
wisdom?
Where can they find understanding?
21 It is hidden from the eyes of all humanity.
Even the sharp-eyed birds in the sky
cannot discover it.
22 Destruction* and Death say,
'We've heard only rumors of where
wisdom can be found.'

23 "God alone understands the way to wisdom;
he knows where it can be found,
24 for he looks throughout the whole earth
and sees everything under the heavens.
25 He decided how hard the winds should
blow
and how much rain should fall.
26 He made the laws for the rain
and laid out a path for the lightning.
27 Then he saw wisdom and evaluated it.
He set it in place and examined it
thoroughly.
28 And this is what he says to all humanity:
'The fear of the Lord is true wisdom;
to forsake evil is real understanding.'"

CHAPTER 29

Job Speaks of His Former Blessings

Job continued speaking:

2 "I long for the years gone by
when God took care of me,
3 when he lit up the way before me
and I walked safely through the
darkness.
4 When I was in my prime,
God's friendship was felt in my home.
5 The Almighty was still with me,
and my children were around me.
6 My cows produced milk in abundance,
and my groves poured out streams of
olive oil.

7 "Those were the days when I went to the
city gate
and took my place among the honored
leaders.
8 The young stepped aside when they
saw me,
and even the aged rose in respect at my
coming.
9 The princes stood in silence
and put their hands over their
mouths.
10 The highest officials of the city stood
quietly,
holding their tongues in respect.

11 "All who heard me praised me.
All who saw me spoke well of me.
12 For I assisted the poor in their need
and the orphans who required help.
13 I helped those without hope, and they
blessed me.
And I caused the widows' hearts to sing
for joy.
14 Everything I did was honest.
Righteousness covered me like a robe,
and I wore justice like a turban.
15 I served as eyes for the blind
and feet for the lame.
16 I was a father to the poor
and assisted strangers who needed
help.
17 I broke the jaws of godless oppressors
and plucked their victims from their
teeth.

18 "I thought, 'Surely I will die surrounded by
my family
after a long, good life.*
19 For I am like a tree whose roots reach
the water,
whose branches are refreshed with
the dew.
20 New honors are constantly bestowed
on me,
and my strength is continually
renewed.'

28:19 Hebrew *from Cush.* 28:22 Hebrew *Abaddon.* 29:18 Hebrew *after I have counted my days like sand.*

21 "Everyone listened to my advice.
They were silent as they waited for me to speak.
22 And after I spoke, they had nothing to add,
for my counsel satisfied them.
23 They longed for me to speak as people long for rain.
They drank my words like a refreshing spring rain.
24 When they were discouraged, I smiled at them.
My look of approval was precious to them.
25 Like a chief, I told them what to do.
I lived like a king among his troops
and comforted those who mourned.

CHAPTER 30

Job Speaks of His Anguish

1 "But now I am mocked by people younger than I,
by young men whose fathers are not worthy to run with my sheepdogs.
2 A lot of good they are to me—
those worn-out wretches!
3 They are gaunt with hunger
and flee to the deserts,
to desolate and gloomy wastelands.
4 They pluck wild greens from among the bushes
and eat from the roots of broom trees.
5 They are driven from human society,
and people shout at them as if they were thieves.
6 So now they live in frightening ravines,
in caves and among the rocks.
7 They sound like animals howling among the bushes,
huddled together beneath the nettles.
8 They are nameless fools,
outcasts from society.

9 "And now they mock me with vulgar songs!
They taunt me!
10 They despise me and won't come near me,
except to spit in my face.
11 For God has cut my bowstring.
He has humbled me,
so they have thrown off all restraint.
12 These outcasts oppose me to my face.
They send me sprawling
and lay traps in my path.
13 They block my road
and do everything they can to destroy me.
They know I have no one to help me.
14 They come at me from all directions.
They jump on me when I am down.
15 I live in terror now.
My honor has blown away in the wind,
and my prosperity has vanished like a cloud.

16 "And now my life seeps away.
Depression haunts my days.
17 At night my bones are filled with pain,
which gnaws at me relentlessly.
18 With a strong hand, God grabs my shirt.
He grips me by the collar of my coat.
19 He has thrown me into the mud.
I'm nothing more than dust and ashes.

20 "I cry to you, O God, but you don't answer.
I stand before you, but you don't even look.
21 You have become cruel toward me.
You use your power to persecute me.
22 You throw me into the whirlwind
and destroy me in the storm.
23 And I know you are sending me to my death—
the destination of all who live.

24 "Surely no one would turn against the needy
when they cry for help in their trouble.
25 Did I not weep for those in trouble?
Was I not deeply grieved for the needy?
26 So I looked for good, but evil came instead.
I waited for the light, but darkness fell.
27 My heart is troubled and restless.
Days of suffering torment me.
28 I walk in gloom, without sunlight.
I stand in the public square and cry for help.
29 Instead, I am considered a brother to jackals
and a companion to owls.
30 My skin has turned dark,
and my bones burn with fever.
31 My harp plays sad music,
and my flute accompanies those who weep.

The Hidden Magazines

Earl had a baseball game, but he couldn't find his mitt. He looked in all the usual places—but no mitt. Then Earl remembered that his older brother had used it. His brother wasn't home, so Earl searched his brother's room. Earl finally found the mitt under his brother's bed on top of a pile of magazines. When Earl grabbed the mitt, the top magazine caught his eye. He couldn't believe it. He looked through the stack and saw that all of the magazines had pictures of naked women! Should he tell Mom? talk to his brother? just ignore it? Read Job 31:1.

CHAPTER 31

Job's Final Protest of Innocence

1 "I made a covenant with my eyes
not to look with lust at a young woman.
2 For what has God above chosen for us?
What is our inheritance from the Almighty on high?
3 Isn't it calamity for the wicked
and misfortune for those who do evil?
4 Doesn't he see everything I do
and every step I take?

5 "Have I lied to anyone
or deceived anyone?
6 Let God weigh me on the scales of justice,
for he knows my integrity.
7 If I have strayed from his pathway,
or if my heart has lusted for what my eyes have seen,
or if I am guilty of any other sin,
8 then let someone else eat the crops I have planted.
Let all that I have planted be uprooted.

9 "If my heart has been seduced by a woman,
or if I have lusted for my neighbor's wife,
10 then let my wife belong to* another man;
let other men sleep with her.
11 For lust is a shameful sin,
a crime that should be punished.
12 It is a fire that burns all the way to hell.*
It would wipe out everything I own.

13 "If I have been unfair to my male or female servants
when they brought their complaints to me,
14 how could I face God?
What could I say when he questioned me?
15 For God created both me and my servants.
He created us both in the womb.

16 "Have I refused to help the poor,
or crushed the hopes of widows?
17 Have I been stingy with my food
and refused to share it with orphans?
18 No, from childhood I have cared for orphans like a father,
and all my life I have cared for widows.
19 Whenever I saw the homeless without clothes
and the needy with nothing to wear,
20 did they not praise me
for providing wool clothing to keep them warm?

31:10 Hebrew *grind for*. 31:12 Hebrew *to Abaddon*.

21 "If I raised my hand against an orphan,
knowing the judges would take
my side,
22 then let my shoulder be wrenched out
of place!
Let my arm be torn from its socket!
23 That would be better than facing God's
judgment.
For if the majesty of God opposes me,
what hope is there?

24 "Have I put my trust in money
or felt secure because of my gold?
25 Have I gloated about my wealth
and all that I own?

26 "Have I looked at the sun shining in the
skies,
or the moon walking down its silver
pathway,
27 and been secretly enticed in my heart
to throw kisses at them in worship?
28 If so, I should be punished by
the judges,
for it would mean I had denied the
God of heaven.

29 "Have I ever rejoiced when disaster struck
my enemies,
or become excited when harm came
their way?
30 No, I have never sinned by cursing anyone
or by asking for revenge.

31 "My servants have never said,
'He let others go hungry.'
32 I have never turned away a stranger
but have opened my doors to
everyone.

33 "Have I tried to hide my sins like other
people do,
concealing my guilt in my heart?
34 Have I feared the crowd
or the contempt of the masses,
so that I kept quiet and stayed
indoors?

35 "If only someone would listen to me!
Look, I will sign my name to my
defense.
Let the Almighty answer me.
Let my accuser write out the charges
against me.
36 I would face the accusation proudly.
I would wear it like a crown.
37 For I would tell him exactly what I have
done.
I would come before him like a prince.

38 "If my land accuses me
and all its furrows cry out together,
39 or if I have stolen its crops
or murdered its owners,
40 then let thistles grow on that land instead
of wheat,
and weeds instead of barley."

Job's words are ended.

CHAPTER 32

Elihu Responds to Job's Friends

Job's three friends refused to reply further to him because he kept insisting on his innocence.

2 Then Elihu son of Barakel the Buzite, of the clan of Ram, became angry. He was angry because Job refused to admit that he had sinned and that God was right in punishing him. 3 He was also angry with Job's three friends, for they made God* appear to be wrong by their inability to answer Job's arguments. 4 Elihu had waited for the others to speak to Job because they were older than he. 5 But when he saw that they had no further reply, he spoke out angrily. 6 Elihu son of Barakel the Buzite said,

"I am young and you are old,
so I held back from telling you what
I think.
7 I thought, 'Those who are older should
speak,
for wisdom comes with age.'
8 But there is a spirit* within people,
the breath of the Almighty within
them,
that makes them intelligent.
9 Sometimes the elders are not wise.
Sometimes the aged do not understand
justice.
10 So listen to me,
and let me tell you what I think.

11 "I have waited all this time,
listening very carefully to your
arguments,
listening to you grope for words.

32:3 As in ancient Hebrew scribal tradition; the Masoretic Text reads *Job*. **32:8** Or *Spirit;* also in 32:18.

12 I have listened,
but not one of you has refuted Job
or answered his arguments.
13 And don't tell me, 'He is too wise for us.
Only God can convince him.'
14 If Job had been arguing with me,
I would not answer with your kind
of logic!
15 You sit there baffled,
with nothing more to say.
16 Should I continue to wait, now that you
are silent?
Must I also remain silent?
17 No, I will say my piece.
I will speak my mind.
18 For I am full of pent-up words,
and the spirit within me urges me on.
19 I am like a cask of wine without a vent,
like a new wineskin ready to burst!
20 I must speak to find relief,
so let me give my answers.
21 I won't play favorites
or try to flatter anyone.
22 For if I tried flattery,
my Creator would soon destroy me.

CHAPTER 33

Elihu Presents His Case against Job

1 "Listen to my words, Job;
pay attention to what I have to say.
2 Now that I have begun to speak,
let me continue.
3 I speak with all sincerity;
I speak the truth.
4 For the Spirit of God has made me,
and the breath of the Almighty gives
me life.
5 Answer me, if you can;
make your case and take your stand.
6 Look, you and I both belong to God.
I, too, was formed from clay.
7 So you don't need to be afraid of me.
I won't come down hard on you.

8 "You have spoken in my hearing,
and I have heard your very words.
9 You said, 'I am pure; I am without sin;
I am innocent; I have no guilt.
10 God is picking a quarrel with me,
and he considers me his enemy.
11 He puts my feet in the stocks
and watches my every move.'

12 "But you are wrong, and I will show
you why.
For God is greater than any human
being.
13 So why are you bringing a charge against
him?
Why say he does not respond to
people's complaints?
14 For God speaks again and again,
though people do not recognize it.
15 He speaks in dreams, in visions of the
night,
when deep sleep falls on people
as they lie in their beds.
16 He whispers in their ears
and terrifies them with warnings.
17 He makes them turn from doing wrong;
he keeps them from pride.
18 He protects them from the grave,
from crossing over the river of death.

19 "Or God disciplines people with pain on
their sickbeds,
with ceaseless aching in their bones.
20 They lose their appetite
for even the most delicious food.
21 Their flesh wastes away,
and their bones stick out.
22 They are at death's door;
the angels of death wait for them.

23 "But if an angel from heaven appears—
a special messenger to intercede for a
person
and declare that he is upright—
24 he will be gracious and say,
'Rescue him from the grave,
for I have found a ransom for his life.'
25 Then his body will become as healthy
as a child's,
firm and youthful again.
26 When he prays to God,
he will be accepted.
And God will receive him with joy
and restore him to good standing.
27 He will declare to his friends,
'I sinned and twisted the truth,
but it was not worth it.*
28 God rescued me from the grave,
and now my life is filled with light.'

29 "Yes, God does these things
again and again for people.

33:27 Greek version reads *but he* [God] *did not punish me as my sin deserved.*

30 He rescues them from the grave
so they may enjoy the light of life.
31 Mark this well, Job. Listen to me,
for I have more to say.
32 But if you have anything to say, go ahead.
Speak, for I am anxious to see you
justified.
33 But if not, then listen to me.
Keep silent and I will teach you
wisdom!"

CHAPTER 34

Elihu Accuses Job of Arrogance

Then Elihu said:

2 "Listen to me, you wise men.
Pay attention, you who have
knowledge.
3 Job said, 'The ear tests the words it hears
just as the mouth distinguishes
between foods.'
4 So let us discern for ourselves what
is right;
let us learn together what is good.
5 For Job also said, 'I am innocent,
but God has taken away my rights.
6 I am innocent, but they call me a liar.
My suffering is incurable, though
I have not sinned.'

7 "Tell me, has there ever been a man like
Job,
with his thirst for irreverent talk?
8 He chooses evil people as companions.
He spends his time with wicked men.
9 He has even said, 'Why waste time
trying to please God?'

10 "Listen to me, you who have
understanding.
Everyone knows that God doesn't sin!
The Almighty can do no wrong.
11 He repays people according to their
deeds.
He treats people as they deserve.
12 Truly, God will not do wrong.
The Almighty will not twist justice.
13 Did someone else put the world in
his care?
Who set the whole world in place?
14 If God were to take back his spirit
and withdraw his breath,
15 all life would cease,
and humanity would turn again to dust.

16 "Now listen to me if you are wise.
Pay attention to what I say.
17 Could God govern if he hated justice?
Are you going to condemn the almighty
judge?
18 For he says to kings, 'You are wicked,'
and to nobles, 'You are unjust.'
19 He doesn't care how great a person
may be,
and he pays no more attention to the
rich than to the poor.
He made them all.
20 In a moment they die.
In the middle of the night they pass
away;
the mighty are removed without
human hand.

21 "For God watches how people live;
he sees everything they do.
22 No darkness is thick enough
to hide the wicked from his eyes.
23 We don't set the time
when we will come before God in
judgment.
24 He brings the mighty to ruin without
asking anyone,
and he sets up others in their place.
25 He knows what they do,
and in the night he overturns and
destroys them.
26 He strikes them down because they
are wicked,
doing it openly for all to see.
27 For they turned away from following
him.
They have no respect for any of his
ways.
28 They cause the poor to cry out, catching
God's attention.
He hears the cries of the needy.
29 But if he chooses to remain quiet,
who can criticize him?
When he hides his face, no one can find
him,
whether an individual or a nation.
30 He prevents the godless from ruling
so they cannot be a snare to the
people.

31 "Why don't people say to God, 'I have
sinned,
but I will sin no more'?

Battles and Weapons

Throughout history men have defended themselves, and the people they love, against their enemies. They always used whatever was available to them at their time in history: city walls, shields, wooden arrows, flint knives, armor. Before guns, they used spears. Before metal, they used stone. Before stone, they used wood. Ancient weapons, just like tools, reveal the technology of each era.

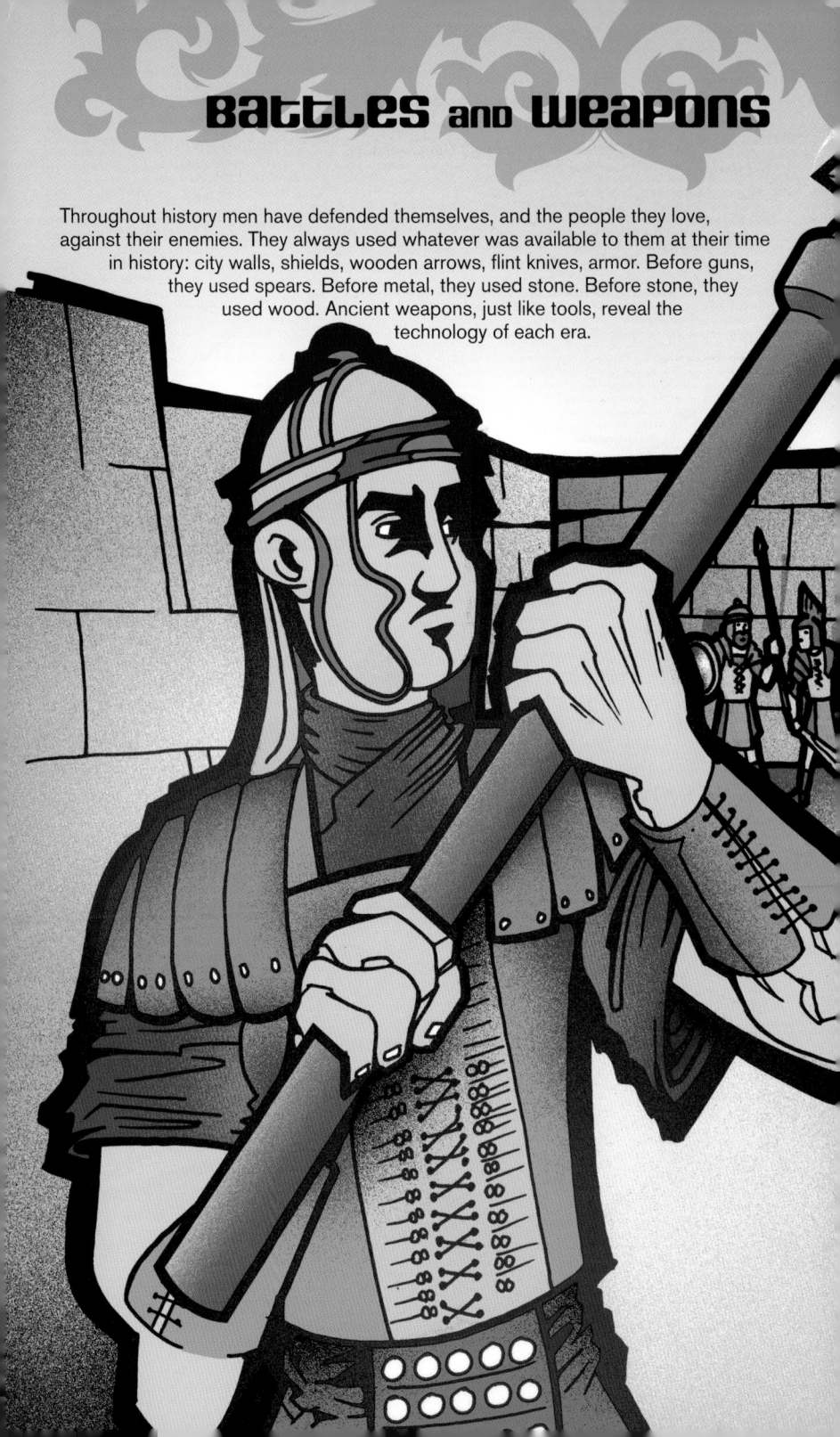

At the time when the Old Testament was written, war was all around. During the New Testament, Judea was ruled by the Romans. With Roman soldiers around, there was a forced peace. And there weren't as many attacks as you read about in the Old Testament.

WEAPONS

Walls and gates were a city's main defense. A *battering ram* was a long heavy log the soldiers used to break open a gate or even crash through a wall. There was one battle, though, where a ram was not necessary. Remember Jericho? The people just shouted and the wall fell down!

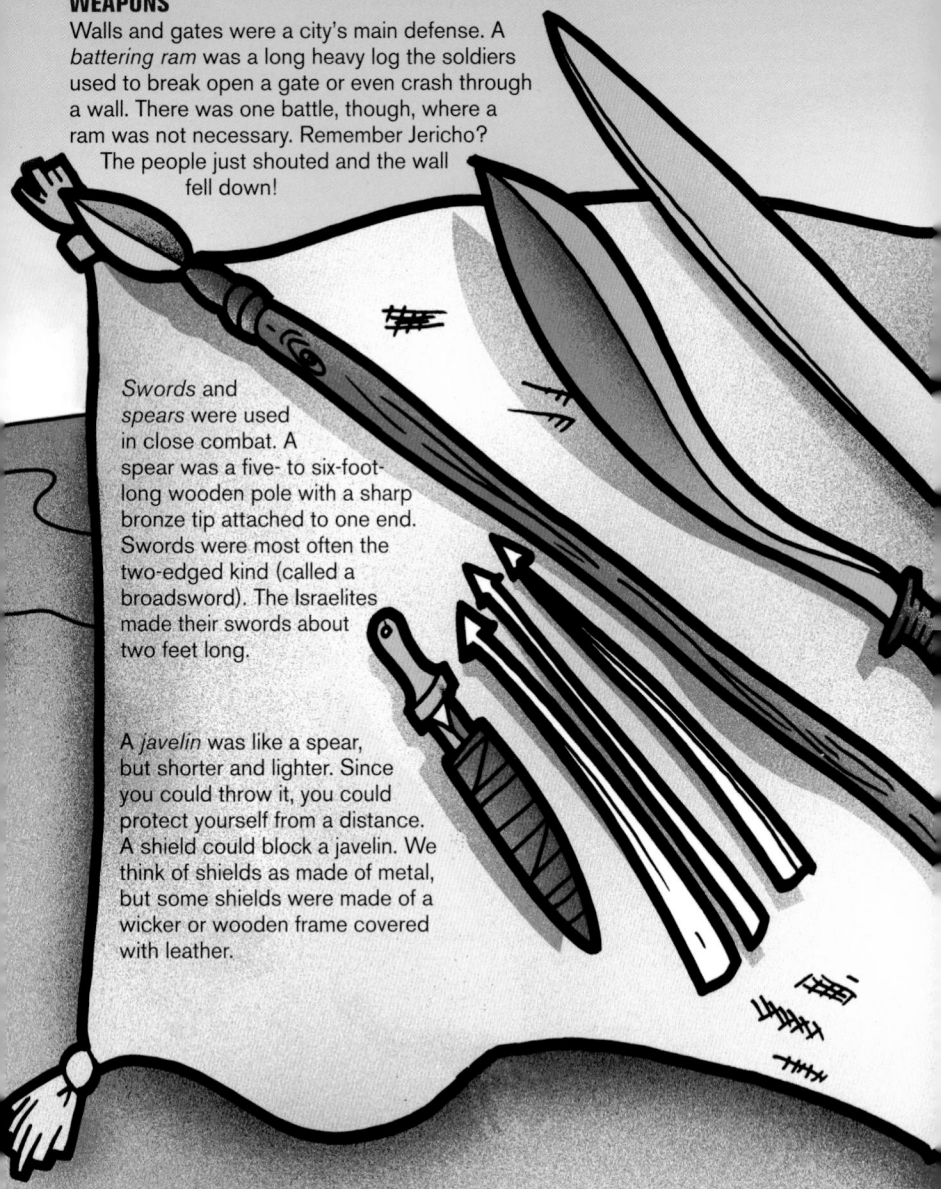

Swords and *spears* were used in close combat. A spear was a five- to six-foot-long wooden pole with a sharp bronze tip attached to one end. Swords were most often the two-edged kind (called a broadsword). The Israelites made their swords about two feet long.

A *javelin* was like a spear, but shorter and lighter. Since you could throw it, you could protect yourself from a distance. A shield could block a javelin. We think of shields as made of metal, but some shields were made of a wicker or wooden frame covered with leather.

The *sling* was a leather pouch with a strap attached to each side. The slinger would whirl the sling around his head and then release one of the straps. For a good slinger, the stone could shoot out of the pouch like a speeding bullet.

Long before people knew how to work with metal, they made their knives and spears out of *flint*. Flint is a kind of stone that can be split into small sharp pieces. Depending on their shape, those sharp pieces could be used to stab, cut, scrape, and even perform surgery.

BATTLES

When the Israelites resettled the Promised Land, they defeated one enemy after another. Why was it necessary to destroy all the cities and their people? Because they wouldn't give up their idols to worship only God. If this idol worship continued in the land, the people of Israel would be tempted to join in—which they did.

PRISONERS

In the New Testament time period, the Roman guards used stocks to control their prisoners. The prisoners' legs would be spread wide and "feet-cuffed" between two boards with holes just big enough for their ankles. The boards were locked together with iron clamps.

THE DEATH PENALTY

Today in some places people are sentenced to death for their crimes. In the last century this has been done through an overdose of poison or electric shock. In both the Old and New Testaments, stoning was a form of the death penalty. Another form was crucifixion.

Crucifixion—death by hanging on a cross—was reserved for people who were not Roman citizens. It involved nailing the prisoner's ankles to a wooden pole and his wrists to a cross-beam. The prisoner would die by starvation, suffocation, or dehydration. Death often did not come for two or three days. Sometimes it took up to nine days. This was considered the worst possible way to die.

In the ancient world, lions were sometimes used as weapons to carry out the death penalty. The lions' den in the book of Daniel was a pit where criminals could be executed by lions. The doorway would be blocked with a large stone to keep the animals and the people from escaping.

32 Or 'I don't know what evil I have done—
tell me.
If I have done wrong, I will stop at
once'?

33 "Must God tailor his justice to your
demands?
But you have rejected him!
The choice is yours, not mine.
Go ahead, share your wisdom with us.
34 After all, bright people will tell me,
and wise people will hear me say,
35 'Job speaks out of ignorance;
his words lack insight.'
36 Job, you deserve the maximum penalty
for the wicked way you have talked.
37 For you have added rebellion to your sin;
you show no respect,
and you speak many angry words
against God."

CHAPTER 35

Elihu Reminds Job of God's Justice

Then Elihu said:

2 "Do you think it is right for you to claim,
'I am righteous before God'?
3 For you also ask, 'What's in it for me?
What's the use of living a righteous
life?'

4 "I will answer you
and all your friends, too.
5 Look up into the sky,
and see the clouds high above you.
6 If you sin, how does that affect God?
Even if you sin again and again,
what effect will it have on him?
7 If you are good, is this some great gift
to him?
What could you possibly give him?
8 No, your sins affect only people like
yourself,
and your good deeds also affect only
humans.

9 "People cry out when they are oppressed.
They groan beneath the power of the
mighty.
10 Yet they don't ask, 'Where is God my
Creator,
the one who gives songs in the night?
11 Where is the one who makes us smarter
than the animals
and wiser than the birds of the sky?'
12 And when they cry out, God does not
answer
because of their pride.
13 But it is wrong to say God doesn't listen,
to say the Almighty isn't concerned.
14 You say you can't see him,
but he will bring justice if you will only
wait.*
15 You say he does not respond to sinners
with anger
and is not greatly concerned about
wickedness.*
16 But you are talking nonsense, Job.
You have spoken like a fool."

CHAPTER 36

Elihu continued speaking:

2 "Let me go on, and I will show you
the truth.
For I have not finished defending God!
3 I will present profound arguments
for the righteousness of my Creator.
4 I am telling you nothing but the truth,
for I am a man of great knowledge.

5 "God is mighty, but he does not despise
anyone!
He is mighty in both power and
understanding.
6 He does not let the wicked live
but gives justice to the afflicted.
7 He never takes his eyes off the innocent,
but he sets them on thrones with kings
and exalts them forever.
8 If they are bound in chains
and caught up in a web of trouble,
9 he shows them the reason.
He shows them their sins of pride.
10 He gets their attention
and commands that they turn
from evil.

11 "If they listen and obey God,
they will be blessed with prosperity
throughout their lives.
All their years will be pleasant.
12 But if they refuse to listen to him,

35:13-14 These verses can also be translated as follows: 13*Indeed, God doesn't listen to their empty plea; / the Almighty is not concerned. /* 14*How much less will he listen when you say you don't see him, / and that your case is before him and you're waiting for justice.* **35:15** As in Greek and Latin versions; the meaning of this Hebrew word is uncertain.

they will be killed by the sword*
and die from lack of understanding.
13 For the godless are full of resentment.
Even when he punishes them,
they refuse to cry out to him for help.
14 They die when they are young,
after wasting their lives in immoral living.
15 But by means of their suffering, he rescues those who suffer.
For he gets their attention through adversity.

16 "God is leading you away from danger, Job,
to a place free from distress.
He is setting your table with the best food.
17 But you are obsessed with whether the godless will be judged.
Don't worry, judgment and justice will be upheld.
18 But watch out, or you may be seduced by wealth.*
Don't let yourself be bribed into sin.
19 Could all your wealth*
or all your mighty efforts
keep you from distress?
20 Do not long for the cover of night,
for that is when people will be destroyed.*
21 Be on guard! Turn back from evil,
for God sent this suffering
to keep you from a life of evil.

Elihu Reminds Job of God's Power

22 "Look, God is all-powerful.
Who is a teacher like him?
23 No one can tell him what to do,
or say to him, 'You have done wrong.'
24 Instead, glorify his mighty works,
singing songs of praise.
25 Everyone has seen these things,
though only from a distance.

26 "Look, God is greater than we can understand.
His years cannot be counted.
27 He draws up the water vapor
and then distills it into rain.
28 The rain pours down from the clouds,
and everyone benefits.
29 Who can understand the spreading of the clouds
and the thunder that rolls forth from heaven?
30 See how he spreads the lightning around him
and how it lights up the depths of the sea.
31 By these mighty acts he nourishes* the people,
giving them food in abundance.
32 He fills his hands with lightning bolts
and hurls each at its target.
33 The thunder announces his presence;
the storm announces his indignant anger.*

CHAPTER 37

1 "My heart pounds as I think of this.
It trembles within me.
2 Listen carefully to the thunder of God's voice
as it rolls from his mouth.
3 It rolls across the heavens,
and his lightning flashes in every direction.
4 Then comes the roaring of the thunder—
the tremendous voice of his majesty.
He does not restrain it when he speaks.
5 God's voice is glorious in the thunder.
We can't even imagine the greatness of his power.

6 "He directs the snow to fall on the earth
and tells the rain to pour down.
7 Then everyone stops working
so they can watch his power.
8 The wild animals take cover
and stay inside their dens.
9 The stormy wind comes from its chamber,
and the driving winds bring the cold.
10 God's breath sends the ice,
freezing wide expanses of water.
11 He loads the clouds with moisture,
and they flash with his lightning.
12 The clouds churn about at his direction.
They do whatever he commands throughout the earth.

36:12 Or *they will cross the river* [of death]. **36:18** Or *But don't let your anger lead you to mockery.* **36:19** Or *Could all your cries for help.* **36:16-20** The meaning of the Hebrew in this passage is uncertain. **36:31** Or *he governs.* **36:33** Or *even the cattle know when a storm is coming.* The meaning of the Hebrew is uncertain.

13 He makes these things happen either to
punish people
or to show his unfailing love.

14 "Pay attention to this, Job.
Stop and consider the wonderful
miracles of God!
15 Do you know how God controls the storm
and causes the lightning to flash from
his clouds?
16 Do you understand how he moves the
clouds
with wonderful perfection and skill?
17 When you are sweltering in your clothes
and the south wind dies down and
everything is still,
18 he makes the skies reflect the heat like
a bronze mirror.
Can you do that?

19 "So teach the rest of us what to say to God.
We are too ignorant to make our own
arguments.
20 Should God be notified that I want to speak?
Can people even speak when they are
confused?*
21 We cannot look at the sun,
for it shines brightly in the sky
when the wind clears away the clouds.
22 So also, golden splendor comes from the
mountain of God.*
He is clothed in dazzling splendor.
23 We cannot imagine the power of the
Almighty;
but even though he is just and
righteous,
he does not destroy us.
24 No wonder people everywhere fear him.
All who are wise show him reverence."

CHAPTER 38

The LORD Challenges Job

Then the LORD answered Job from the whirlwind:

2 "Who is this that questions my wisdom
with such ignorant words?
3 Brace yourself like a man,
because I have some questions for you,
and you must answer them.

4 "Where were you when I laid the
foundations of the earth?
Tell me, if you know so much.
5 Who determined its dimensions
and stretched out the surveying line?
6 What supports its foundations,
and who laid its cornerstone
7 as the morning stars sang together
and all the angels* shouted for joy?

8 "Who kept the sea inside its boundaries
as it burst from the womb,

37:20 Or *speak without being swallowed up?* **37:22** Or *from the north;* or *from the abode.* **38:7** Hebrew *the sons of God.*

HOW SUFFERING AFFECTS US

Suffering helps us when:	Suffering hurts us when:
We turn to God for help and strength	We become hardened and reject God
We ask important questions we might not take time to think about normally	We refuse to ask any questions and miss some lessons that might be good for us
We let it get us ready to help others who suffer	We let it make us self-centered and selfish
We are open to be helped by others who are obeying God	We don't let others help us
It helps us think about what Christ suffered on the cross for us	We think God is being unjust and perhaps lead others to reject him
It helps us think about the amount of suffering in the world	We refuse to think about making any changes in our life

9 and as I clothed it with clouds
and wrapped it in thick darkness?
10 For I locked it behind barred gates,
limiting its shores.
11 I said, 'This far and no farther will you come.
Here your proud waves must stop!'

12 "Have you ever commanded the morning to appear
and caused the dawn to rise in the east?
13 Have you made daylight spread to the ends of the earth,
to bring an end to the night's wickedness?
14 As the light approaches,
the earth takes shape like clay pressed beneath a seal;
it is robed in brilliant colors.*
15 The light disturbs the wicked
and stops the arm that is raised in violence.

16 "Have you explored the springs from which the seas come?
Have you explored their depths?
17 Do you know where the gates of death are located?
Have you seen the gates of utter gloom?
18 Do you realize the extent of the earth?
Tell me about it if you know!

19 "Where does light come from,
and where does darkness go?
20 Can you take each to its home?
Do you know how to get there?
21 But of course you know all this!
For you were born before it was all created,
and you are so very experienced!

22 "Have you visited the storehouses of the snow
or seen the storehouses of hail?
23 (I have reserved them as weapons for the time of trouble,
for the day of battle and war.)
24 Where is the path to the source of light?
Where is the home of the east wind?

25 "Who created a channel for the torrents of rain?
Who laid out the path for the lightning?
26 Who makes the rain fall on barren land,
in a desert where no one lives?
27 Who sends rain to satisfy the parched ground
and make the tender grass spring up?

28 "Does the rain have a father?
Who gives birth to the dew?
29 Who is the mother of the ice?
Who gives birth to the frost from the heavens?
30 For the water turns to ice as hard as rock,
and the surface of the water freezes.

31 "Can you direct the movement of the stars—
binding the cluster of the Pleiades
or loosening the cords of Orion?
32 Can you direct the sequence of the seasons
or guide the Bear with her cubs across the heavens?
33 Do you know the laws of the universe?
Can you use them to regulate the earth?

34 "Can you shout to the clouds
and make it rain?
35 Can you make lightning appear
and cause it to strike as you direct?
36 Who gives intuition to the heart
and instinct to the mind?
37 Who is wise enough to count all the clouds?
Who can tilt the water jars of heaven
38 when the parched ground is dry
and the soil has hardened into clods?

39 "Can you stalk prey for a lioness
and satisfy the young lions' appetites
40 as they lie in their dens
or crouch in the thicket?
41 Who provides food for the ravens
when their young cry out to God
and wander about in hunger?

CHAPTER 39

The Lord's Challenge Continues

1 "Do you know when the wild goats give birth?
Have you watched as deer are born in the wild?
2 Do you know how many months they carry their young?
Are you aware of the time of their delivery?

38:14 Or *its features stand out like folds in a robe.*

3 They crouch down to give birth to their young
and deliver their offspring.
4 Their young grow up in the open fields,
then leave home and never return.

5 "Who gives the wild donkey its freedom?
Who untied its ropes?
6 I have placed it in the wilderness;
its home is the wasteland.
7 It hates the noise of the city
and has no driver to shout at it.
8 The mountains are its pastureland,
where it searches for every blade of grass.

9 "Will the wild ox consent to being tamed?
Will it spend the night in your stall?
10 Can you hitch a wild ox to a plow?
Will it plow a field for you?
11 Given its strength, can you trust it?
Can you leave and trust the ox to do your work?
12 Can you rely on it to bring home your grain
and deliver it to your threshing floor?

13 "The ostrich flaps her wings grandly,
but they are no match for the feathers of the stork.
14 She lays her eggs on top of the earth,
letting them be warmed in the dust.
15 She doesn't worry that a foot might crush them
or a wild animal might destroy them.
16 She is harsh toward her young,
as if they were not her own.
She doesn't care if they die.
17 For God has deprived her of wisdom.
He has given her no understanding.
18 But whenever she jumps up to run,
she passes the swiftest horse with its rider.

19 "Have you given the horse its strength
or clothed its neck with a flowing mane?
20 Did you give it the ability to leap like a locust?
Its majestic snorting is terrifying!
21 It paws the earth and rejoices in its strength
when it charges out to battle.
22 It laughs at fear and is unafraid.
It does not run from the sword.
23 The arrows rattle against it,
and the spear and javelin flash.
24 It paws the ground fiercely
and rushes forward into battle when the ram's horn blows.
25 It snorts at the sound of the horn.
It senses the battle in the distance.
It quivers at the captain's commands and the noise of battle.

26 "Is it your wisdom that makes the hawk soar
and spread its wings toward the south?
27 Is it at your command that the eagle rises
to the heights to make its nest?
28 It lives on the cliffs,
making its home on a distant, rocky crag.
29 From there it hunts its prey,
keeping watch with piercing eyes.
30 Its young gulp down blood.
Where there's a carcass, there you'll find it."

CHAPTER 40

Then the LORD said to Job,

2 "Do you still want to argue with the Almighty?
You are God's critic, but do you have the answers?"

Job Responds to the LORD

3 Then Job replied to the LORD,

4 "I am nothing—how could I ever find the answers?
I will cover my mouth with my hand.
5 I have said too much already.
I have nothing more to say."

The LORD Challenges Job Again

6 Then the LORD answered Job from the whirlwind:

7 "Brace yourself like a man,
because I have some questions for you,
and you must answer them.

8 "Will you discredit my justice
and condemn me just to prove you are right?
9 Are you as strong as God?
Can you thunder with a voice like his?
10 All right, put on your glory and splendor,
your honor and majesty.

11 Give vent to your anger.
Let it overflow against the proud.
12 Humiliate the proud with a glance;
walk on the wicked where they stand.
13 Bury them in the dust.
Imprison them in the world of the dead.
14 Then even I would praise you,
for your own strength would save you.

15 "Take a look at Behemoth,*
which I made, just as I made you.
It eats grass like an ox.
16 See its powerful loins
and the muscles of its belly.
17 Its tail is as strong as a cedar.
The sinews of its thighs are knit tightly together.
18 Its bones are tubes of bronze.
Its limbs are bars of iron.
19 It is a prime example of God's handiwork,
and only its Creator can threaten it.
20 The mountains offer it their best food,
where all the wild animals play.
21 It lies under the lotus plants,*
hidden by the reeds in the marsh.
22 The lotus plants give it shade
among the willows beside the stream.
23 It is not disturbed by the raging river,
not concerned when the swelling Jordan rushes around it.
24 No one can catch it off guard
or put a ring in its nose and lead it away.

CHAPTER 41

The Lord's Challenge Continues

1* "Can you catch Leviathan* with a hook
or put a noose around its jaw?
2 Can you tie it with a rope through the nose
or pierce its jaw with a spike?
3 Will it beg you for mercy
or implore you for pity?
4 Will it agree to work for you,
to be your slave for life?
5 Can you make it a pet like a bird,
or give it to your little girls to play with?
6 Will merchants try to buy it
to sell it in their shops?
7 Will its hide be hurt by spears
or its head by a harpoon?
8 If you lay a hand on it,
you will certainly remember the battle that follows.
You won't try that again!
9* No, it is useless to try to capture it.
The hunter who attempts it will be knocked down.
10 And since no one dares to disturb it,
who then can stand up to me?
11 Who has given me anything that I need to pay back?
Everything under heaven is mine.

12 "I want to emphasize Leviathan's limbs
and its enormous strength and graceful form.
13 Who can strip off its hide,
and who can penetrate its double layer of armor?*
14 Who could pry open its jaws?
For its teeth are terrible!
15 Its scales are like rows of shields
tightly sealed together.
16 They are so close together
that no air can get between them.
17 Each scale sticks tight to the next.
They interlock and cannot be penetrated.

18 "When it sneezes, it flashes light!
Its eyes are like the red of dawn.
19 Lightning leaps from its mouth;
flames of fire flash out.
20 Smoke streams from its nostrils
like steam from a pot heated over burning rushes.
21 Its breath would kindle coals,
for flames shoot from its mouth.

22 "The tremendous strength in Leviathan's neck
strikes terror wherever it goes.
23 Its flesh is hard and firm
and cannot be penetrated.
24 Its heart is hard as rock,
hard as a millstone.
25 When it rises, the mighty are afraid,
gripped by terror.
26 No sword can stop it,
no spear, dart, or javelin.

40:15 The identification of Behemoth is disputed, ranging from an earthly creature to a mythical sea monster in ancient literature. **40:21** Or *bramble bushes;* also in 40:22. **41:1a** Verses 41:1-8 are numbered 40:25-32 in Hebrew text. **41:1b** The identification of Leviathan is disputed, ranging from an earthly creature to a mythical sea monster in ancient literature. **41:9** Verses 41:9-34 are numbered 41:1-26 in Hebrew text. **41:13** As in Greek version; Hebrew reads *its bridle?*

27 Iron is nothing but straw to that creature,
and bronze is like rotten wood.
28 Arrows cannot make it flee.
Stones shot from a sling are like bits
of grass.
29 Clubs are like a blade of grass,
and it laughs at the swish of javelins.
30 Its belly is covered with scales as sharp
as glass.
It plows up the ground as it drags
through the mud.

31 "Leviathan makes the water boil with its
commotion.
It stirs the depths like a pot of
ointment.
32 The water glistens in its wake,
making the sea look white.
33 Nothing on earth is its equal,
no other creature so fearless.
34 Of all the creatures, it is the proudest.
It is the king of beasts."

CHAPTER 42

Job Responds to the Lord

Then Job replied to the Lord:

2 "I know that you can do anything,
and no one can stop you.
3 You asked, 'Who is this that questions my
wisdom with such ignorance?'
It is I—and I was talking about things I
knew nothing about,
things far too wonderful for me.
4 You said, 'Listen and I will speak!
I have some questions for you,
and you must answer them.'
5 I had only heard about you before,
but now I have seen you with my
own eyes.
6 I take back everything I said,
and I sit in dust and ashes to show my
repentance."

Conclusion: The Lord Blesses Job

7 After the Lord had finished speaking to Job, he said to Eliphaz the Temanite: "I am angry with you and your two friends, for you have not spoken accurately about me, as my servant Job has. 8 So take seven bulls and seven rams and go to my servant Job and offer a burnt offering for yourselves. My servant Job will pray for you, and I will accept his prayer on your behalf. I will not treat you as you deserve, for you have not spoken accurately about me, as my servant Job has." 9 So Eliphaz the Temanite, Bildad the Shuhite, and Zophar the Naamathite did as the Lord commanded them, and the Lord accepted Job's prayer.

10 When Job prayed for his friends, the Lord restored his fortunes. In fact, the Lord gave him twice as much as before! 11 Then all his brothers, sisters, and former friends came and feasted with him in his home. And they consoled him and comforted him because of all the trials the Lord had brought against him. And each of them brought him a gift of money* and a gold ring.

AMAZING FACTS

After Job had lost everything, God gave him twice as much as before. Now, that's a happy ending.

JOB 42:10-17

12 So the Lord blessed Job in the second half of his life even more than in the beginning. For now he had 14,000 sheep, 6,000 camels, 1,000 teams of oxen, and 1,000 female donkeys. 13 He also gave Job seven more sons and three more daughters. 14 He named his first daughter Jemimah, the second Keziah, and the third Keren-happuch. 15 In all the land no women were as lovely as the daughters of Job. And their father put them into his will along with their brothers.

16 Job lived 140 years after that, living to see four generations of his children and grandchildren. 17 Then he died, an old man who had lived a long, full life.

42:11 Hebrew *a kesitah;* the value or weight of the kesitah is no longer known.

PSALMS

WHO
David, king of Israel.

WHERE
Most of the psalms were written in Israel, and many were written by David in response to events in his life.

WHEN
Between the time of Moses (around 1440 BC) and the Babylonian captivity (586 BC).

WHY
For praising and worshiping God and confessing sin to him.

Let everything that breathes
sing praises to the LORD!
Praise the LORD!
PSALM 150:6

When you're upset and feeling bad, do you still pray? King David did. He talked to God all the time. David told God exactly how he felt. When he was honest with God, his friendship with God became stronger. David wrote many of the psalms. They are songs, poems, and prayers that express the writers' feelings.

YOU CAN TALK TO GOD ABOUT ANYTHING, ANYTIME, NO MATTER WHAT.

BOOK ONE (Psalms 1–41)

PSALM 1

1 Oh, the joys of those who do not
follow the advice of the wicked,
or stand around with sinners,
or join in with mockers.
2 But they delight in the law of
the LORD,
meditating on it day and night.
3 They are like trees planted along the
riverbank,
bearing fruit each season.

Friends

Jesse had to move to a new town, where he began attending a new school. This was a lonely time for Jesse because he didn't know anyone at this school. But recently he has become friends with a group of kids who hang around at a corner of the playground. They are rough—sometimes they swear and make fun of church—but they are nice to Jesse. He is happy that he finally has some friends. Should Jesse stick with these friends or keep looking for others? Read Psalm 1:1 to help find the answer.

Their leaves never wither,
and they prosper in all they do.

4 But not the wicked!
They are like worthless chaff, scattered
by the wind.
5 They will be condemned at the time
of judgment.
Sinners will have no place among
the godly.

6 For the LORD watches over the path
of the godly,
but the path of the wicked leads
to destruction.

PSALM 2

1 Why are the nations so angry?
Why do they waste their time with
futile plans?
2 The kings of the earth prepare for
battle;
the rulers plot together
against the LORD
and against his anointed one.
3 "Let us break their chains," they cry,
"and free ourselves from slavery
to God."

4 But the one who rules in heaven laughs.
The Lord scoffs at them.
5 Then in anger he rebukes them,
terrifying them with his fierce fury.
6 For the Lord declares, "I have placed my
chosen king on the throne
in Jerusalem,* on my holy mountain."

7 The king proclaims the LORD's decree:
"The LORD said to me, 'You are my son.*
Today I have become your Father.*
8 Only ask, and I will give you the nations
as your inheritance,
the whole earth as your possession.
9 You will break* them with an iron rod
and smash them like clay pots.'"

10 Now then, you kings, act wisely!
Be warned, you rulers of the earth!
11 Serve the LORD with reverent fear,
and rejoice with trembling.
12 Submit to God's royal son,* or he will
become angry,
and you will be destroyed in the midst
of all your activities—
for his anger flares up in an instant.
But what joy for all who take refuge
in him!

PSALM 3

A psalm of David, regarding the time David fled from his son Absalom.

1 O LORD, I have so many enemies;
so many are against me.

2:6 Hebrew *on Zion.* **2:7a** Or *Son;* also in 2:12. **2:7b** Or *Today I reveal you as my son.* **2:9** Greek version reads *rule.* Compare Rev 2:27. **2:12** The meaning of the Hebrew is uncertain.

2 So many are saying,
"God will never rescue him!"
*Interlude**

3 But you, O LORD, are a shield around me;
you are my glory, the one who holds my head high.
4 I cried out to the LORD,
and he answered me from his holy mountain. *Interlude*

5 I lay down and slept,
yet I woke up in safety,
for the LORD was watching over me.
6 I am not afraid of ten thousand enemies
who surround me on every side.

7 Arise, O LORD!
Rescue me, my God!
Slap all my enemies in the face!
Shatter the teeth of the wicked!
8 Victory comes from you, O LORD.
May you bless your people.
Interlude

PSALM 4

For the choir director: A psalm of David, to be accompanied by stringed instruments.

1 Answer me when I call to you,
O God who declares me innocent.
Free me from my troubles.
Have mercy on me and hear my prayer.

2 How long will you people ruin my reputation?
How long will you make groundless accusations?
How long will you continue your lies?
Interlude
3 You can be sure of this:
The LORD set apart the godly for himself.
The LORD will answer when I call to him.

4 Don't sin by letting anger control you.
Think about it overnight and remain silent. *Interlude*
5 Offer sacrifices in the right spirit,
and trust the LORD.

6 Many people say, "Who will show us better times?"
Let your face smile on us, LORD.
7 You have given me greater joy
than those who have abundant harvests of grain and new wine.
8 In peace I will lie down and sleep,
for you alone, O LORD, will keep me safe.

PSALM 5

For the choir director: A psalm of David, to be accompanied by the flute.

1 O LORD, hear me as I pray;
pay attention to my groaning.
2 Listen to my cry for help, my King and my God,
for I pray to no one but you.
3 Listen to my voice in the morning, LORD.
Each morning I bring my requests to you and wait expectantly.

4 O God, you take no pleasure in wickedness;
you cannot tolerate the sins of the wicked.
5 Therefore, the proud may not stand in your presence,
for you hate all who do evil.
6 You will destroy those who tell lies.
The LORD detests murderers and deceivers.

7 Because of your unfailing love, I can enter your house;
I will worship at your Temple with deepest awe.
8 Lead me in the right path, O LORD,
or my enemies will conquer me.
Make your way plain for me to follow.

9 My enemies cannot speak a truthful word.
Their deepest desire is to destroy others.
Their talk is foul, like the stench from an open grave.
Their tongues are filled with flattery.*
10 O God, declare them guilty.
Let them be caught in their own traps.
Drive them away because of their many sins,
for they have rebelled against you.

3:2 Hebrew *Selah*. The meaning of this word is uncertain, though it is probably a musical or literary term. It is rendered *Interlude* throughout the Psalms. **5:9** Greek version reads *with lies*. Compare Rom 3:13.

11 But let all who take refuge in you rejoice;
let them sing joyful praises forever.
Spread your protection over them,
that all who love your name may be
filled with joy.
12 For you bless the godly, O LORD;
you surround them with your shield
of love.

What kind of people does God bless? * **You bless the godly, O LORD; you surround them with your shield of love.** PSALM 5:12

PSALM 6

*For the choir director: A psalm of David, to be accompanied by an eight-stringed instrument.**

1 O LORD, don't rebuke me in your anger
or discipline me in your rage.
2 Have compassion on me, LORD, for
I am weak.
Heal me, LORD, for my bones are
in agony.
3 I am sick at heart.
How long, O LORD, until you
restore me?

4 Return, O LORD, and rescue me.
Save me because of your unfailing love.
5 For the dead do not remember you.
Who can praise you from the grave?*

6 I am worn out from sobbing.
All night I flood my bed with weeping,
drenching it with my tears.
7 My vision is blurred by grief;
my eyes are worn out because of all my
enemies.

8 Go away, all you who do evil,
for the LORD has heard my weeping.
9 The LORD has heard my plea;
the LORD will answer my prayer.
10 May all my enemies be disgraced and
terrified.
May they suddenly turn back in shame.

PSALM 7

A psalm of David, which he sang to the LORD concerning Cush of the tribe of Benjamin.

1 I come to you for protection, O LORD
my God.
Save me from my persecutors—rescue
me!
2 If you don't, they will maul me like
a lion,
tearing me to pieces with no one to
rescue me.
3 O LORD my God, if I have done wrong
or am guilty of injustice,

4 if I have betrayed a friend
or plundered my enemy without cause,
5 then let my enemies capture me.
Let them trample me into the ground
and drag my honor in the dust.
Interlude

6 Arise, O LORD, in anger!
Stand up against the fury of my
enemies!
Wake up, my God, and bring justice!
7 Gather the nations before you.
Rule over them from on high.
8 The LORD judges the nations.
Declare me righteous, O LORD,
for I am innocent, O Most High!
9 End the evil of those who are
wicked,
and defend the righteous.
For you look deep within the mind
and heart,
O righteous God.

10 God is my shield,
saving those whose hearts are true
and right.
11 God is an honest judge.
He is angry with the wicked every day.

12 If a person does not repent,
God* will sharpen his sword;
he will bend and string his bow.
13 He will prepare his deadly weapons
and shoot his flaming arrows.

14 The wicked conceive evil;
they are pregnant with trouble
and give birth to lies.
15 They dig a deep pit to trap others,
then fall into it themselves.

6:TITLE Hebrew *with stringed instruments; according to the sheminith.* 6:5 Hebrew *from Sheol?* 7:12 Hebrew *he.*

16 The trouble they make for others
backfires on them.
The violence they plan falls on their
own heads.

17 I will thank the LORD because he is just;
I will sing praise to the name of the
LORD Most High.

PSALM 8

*For the choir director: A psalm of David, to be accompanied by a stringed instrument.**

1 O LORD, our Lord, your majestic name
fills the earth!
Your glory is higher than the heavens.
2 You have taught children and infants
to tell of your strength,*
silencing your enemies
and all who oppose you.

3 When I look at the night sky and see the
work of your fingers—
the moon and the stars you set
in place—
4 what are mere mortals that you should
think about them,
human beings that you should care for
them?*
5 Yet you made them only a little lower than
God*
and crowned them* with glory and
honor.
6 You gave them charge of everything
you made,
putting all things under their
authority—
7 the flocks and the herds
and all the wild animals,
8 the birds in the sky, the fish in the sea,
and everything that swims the ocean
currents.

9 O LORD, our Lord, your majestic name fills
the earth!

PSALM 9

For the choir director: A psalm of David, to be sung to the tune "Death of the Son."

1 I will praise you, LORD, with all my heart;
I will tell of all the marvelous things
you have done.
2 I will be filled with joy because of you.
I will sing praises to your name,
O Most High.

3 My enemies retreated;
they staggered and died when you
appeared.
4 For you have judged in my favor;
from your throne you have judged
with fairness.
5 You have rebuked the nations and
destroyed the wicked;
you have erased their names forever.
6 The enemy is finished, in endless ruins;
the cities you uprooted are now
forgotten.

7 But the LORD reigns forever,
executing judgment from his throne.
8 He will judge the world with justice
and rule the nations with fairness.
9 The LORD is a shelter for the oppressed,
a refuge in times of trouble.
10 Those who know your name trust in you,
for you, O LORD, do not abandon those
who search for you.

11 Sing praises to the LORD who reigns in
Jerusalem.*
Tell the world about his unforgettable
deeds.
12 For he who avenges murder cares for
the helpless.
He does not ignore the cries of those
who suffer.

13 LORD, have mercy on me.
See how my enemies torment me.
Snatch me back from the jaws of death.

Should I really bother God with my problems?

The LORD is a shelter for the oppressed, a refuge in times of trouble. PSALM 9:9

8:TITLE Hebrew *according to the gittith.* **8:2** Greek version reads *to give you praise.* Compare Matt 21:16. **8:4** Hebrew *what is man that you should think of him, / the son of man that you should care for him?* **8:5a** Or *Yet you made them only a little lower than the angels;* Hebrew reads *Yet you made him* [i.e., man] *a little lower than Elohim.* **8:5b** Hebrew *him* [i.e., man]; similarly in 8:6. **9:11** Hebrew *Zion;* also in 9:14.

14 Save me so I can praise you publicly at
Jerusalem's gates,
so I can rejoice that you have
rescued me.
15 The nations have fallen into the pit they
dug for others.
Their own feet have been caught in the
trap they set.
16 The LORD is known for his justice.
The wicked are trapped by their own
deeds. *Quiet Interlude**
17 The wicked will go down to the grave.*
This is the fate of all the nations who
ignore God.
18 But the needy will not be ignored forever;
the hopes of the poor will not always be
crushed.
19 Arise, O LORD!
Do not let mere mortals defy you!
Judge the nations!
20 Make them tremble in fear, O LORD.
Let the nations know they are merely
human. *Interlude*

PSALM 10

1 O LORD, why do you stand so far away?
Why do you hide when I am in
trouble?
2 The wicked arrogantly hunt down the
poor.
Let them be caught in the evil they
plan for others.
3 For they brag about their evil desires;
they praise the greedy and curse
the LORD.
4 The wicked are too proud to seek God.
They seem to think that God is dead.
5 Yet they succeed in everything they do.
They do not see your punishment
awaiting them.
They sneer at all their enemies.
6 They think, "Nothing bad will ever
happen to us!
We will be free of trouble forever!"
7 Their mouths are full of cursing, lies, and
threats.*
Trouble and evil are on the tips of their
tongues.
8 They lurk in ambush in the villages,
waiting to murder innocent people.
They are always searching for helpless
victims.
9 Like lions crouched in hiding,
they wait to pounce on the
helpless.
Like hunters they capture the helpless
and drag them away in nets.
10 Their helpless victims are crushed;
they fall beneath the strength of the
wicked.
11 The wicked think, "God isn't watching us!
He has closed his eyes and won't even
see what we do!"
12 Arise, O LORD!
Punish the wicked, O God!
Do not ignore the helpless!
13 Why do the wicked get away with
despising God?
They think, "God will never call
us to account."
14 But you see the trouble and grief they
cause.
You take note of it and punish them.
The helpless put their trust in you.
You defend the orphans.
15 Break the arms of these wicked, evil
people!
Go after them until the last one is
destroyed.
16 The LORD is king forever and ever!
The godless nations will vanish from
the land.
17 LORD, you know the hopes of the
helpless.
Surely you will hear their cries and
comfort them.
18 You will bring justice to the orphans and
the oppressed,
so mere people can no longer terrify
them.

PSALM 11

For the choir director: A psalm of David.

1 I trust in the LORD for protection.
So why do you say to me,
"Fly like a bird to the mountains
for safety!

9:16 Hebrew *Higgaion Selah*. The meaning of this phrase is uncertain. **9:17** Hebrew *to Sheol*. **10:7** Greek version reads *cursing and bitterness*. Compare Rom 3:14.

2 The wicked are stringing their bows
and fitting their arrows on the
bowstrings.
They shoot from the shadows
at those whose hearts are right.
3 The foundations of law and order have
collapsed.
What can the righteous do?"

4 But the LORD is in his holy Temple;
the LORD still rules from heaven.
He watches everyone closely,
examining every person on earth.
5 The LORD examines both the righteous
and the wicked.
He hates those who love violence.
6 He will rain down blazing coals and
burning sulfur on the wicked,
punishing them with scorching winds.
7 For the righteous LORD loves justice.
The virtuous will see his face.

PSALM 12

*For the choir director: A psalm of David, to be accompanied by an eight-stringed instrument.**

1 Help, O LORD, for the godly are fast
disappearing!
The faithful have vanished from the
earth!
2 Neighbors lie to each other,
speaking with flattering lips and
deceitful hearts.
3 May the LORD cut off their flattering lips
and silence their boastful tongues.
4 They say, "We will lie to our hearts'
content.
Our lips are our own—who can
stop us?"

5 The LORD replies, "I have seen violence
done to the helpless,
and I have heard the groans
of the poor.
Now I will rise up to rescue them,
as they have longed for me to do."
6 The LORD's promises are pure,
like silver refined in a furnace,
purified seven times over.
7 Therefore, LORD, we know you will protect
the oppressed,
preserving them forever from this lying
generation,

12:TITLE Hebrew *according to the sheminith.*

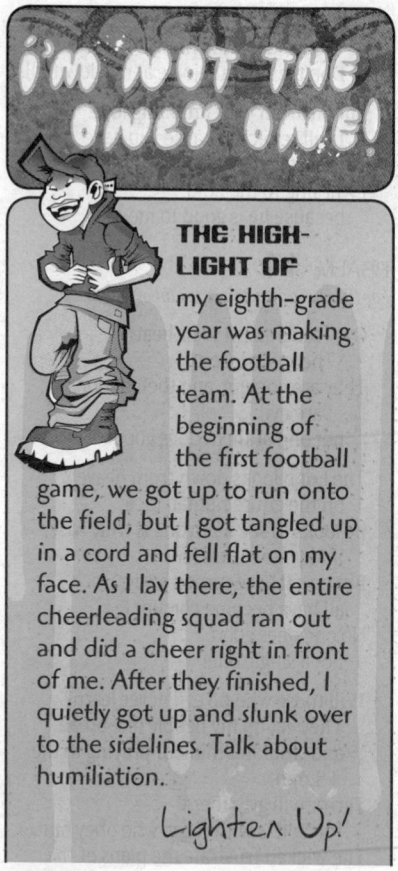

8 even though the wicked strut about,
and evil is praised throughout the land.

PSALM 13

For the choir director: A psalm of David.

1 O LORD, how long will you forget me?
Forever?
How long will you look the other way?
2 How long must I struggle with anguish
in my soul,
with sorrow in my heart every day?
How long will my enemy have the
upper hand?

3 Turn and answer me, O LORD my God!
Restore the sparkle to my eyes, or
I will die.

4 Don't let my enemies gloat, saying, "We
have defeated him!"
Don't let them rejoice at my downfall.

5 But I trust in your unfailing love.
I will rejoice because you have
rescued me.
6 I will sing to the LORD
because he is good to me.

PSALM 14

For the choir director: A psalm of David.

1 Only fools say in their hearts,
"There is no God."
They are corrupt, and their actions
are evil;
not one of them does good!

2 The LORD looks down from heaven
on the entire human race;
he looks to see if anyone is truly wise,
if anyone seeks God.
3 But no, all have turned away;
all have become corrupt.*
No one does good,
not a single one!

4 Will those who do evil never learn?
They eat up my people like bread
and wouldn't think of praying to the
LORD.
5 Terror will grip them,
for God is with those who obey him.
6 The wicked frustrate the plans of the
oppressed,
but the LORD will protect his people.

7 Who will come from Mount Zion to
rescue Israel?
When the LORD restores his people,
Jacob will shout with joy, and Israel
will rejoice.

PSALM 15

A psalm of David.

1 Who may worship in your sanctuary,
LORD?
Who may enter your presence on your
holy hill?
2 Those who lead blameless lives and do
what is right,
speaking the truth from sincere hearts.
3 Those who refuse to gossip
or harm their neighbors
or speak evil of their friends.
4 Those who despise flagrant sinners,
and honor the faithful followers
of the LORD,
and keep their promises even when it
hurts.
5 Those who lend money without charging
interest,
and who cannot be bribed to lie about
the innocent.
Such people will stand firm forever.

PSALM 16

A psalm of David.*

1 Keep me safe, O God,
for I have come to you for refuge.

2 I said to the LORD, "You are my Master!
Every good thing I have comes from
you."
3 The godly people in the land
are my true heroes!
I take pleasure in them!
4 Troubles multiply for those who chase
after other gods.
I will not take part in their sacrifices
of blood
or even speak the names of their
gods.

5 LORD, you alone are my inheritance, my
cup of blessing.
You guard all that is mine.
6 The land you have given me is a pleasant
land.
What a wonderful inheritance!

7 I will bless the LORD who guides me;
even at night my heart instructs me.
8 I know the LORD is always with me.
I will not be shaken, for he is right
beside me.

9 No wonder my heart is glad, and
I rejoice.*
My body rests in safety.
10 For you will not leave my soul among
the dead*
or allow your holy one* to rot
in the grave.

14:3 Greek version reads *have become useless*. Compare Rom 3:12. **16:TITLE** Hebrew *miktam*. This may be a literary or musical term. **16:9** Greek version reads *and my tongue shouts his praises*. Compare Acts 2:26. **16:10a** Hebrew *in Sheol*. **16:10b** Or *your Holy One*.

11 You will show me the way of life,
granting me the joy of your presence
and the pleasures of living with you
forever.*

PSALM 17

A prayer of David.

1 O LORD, hear my plea for justice.
Listen to my cry for help.
Pay attention to my prayer,
for it comes from honest lips.
2 Declare me innocent,
for you see those who do right.

3 You have tested my thoughts and
examined my heart in the
night.
You have scrutinized me and found
nothing wrong.

16:11 Greek version reads *You have shown me the way of life, / and you will fill me with the joy of your presence.* Compare Acts 2:28.

FINDING CHRIST IN THE PSALMS

Many parts of the Psalms seem to describe details from Christ's life and death. Jesus himself often quoted from this book. Here are some of the references to Christ in the Psalms.

Reference in Psalms	Reference to Christ	Fulfillment in the New Testament
2:7	The Messiah will be God's Son	Hebrews 1:5-6
16:8-10	He will rise from the dead	Luke 24:5-7
22:1-21	He will be crucified	Matthew 26–27
22:18	Soldiers will gamble for his clothing	Matthew 27:35; John 19:23-24
22:15	He will thirst while on the cross	John 19:28
22:22	He will speak of his Father	Hebrews 2:12
34:20	His bones will not be broken	John 19:36-37
40:6-8	He will come to do God's will	Hebrews 10:5-7
41:9	One close to him will betray him	Luke 22:48
45:6-7	His Kingdom will last forever	Hebrews 1:8-9
68:18	He will ascend into heaven	Ephesians 4:8-10
69:9	He will be zealous for God	John 2:17
69:21	He will be offered sour wine for his thirst on the cross	Matthew 27:48
89:3-4, 35-36	He will be a descendant of David	Luke 1:31-33
96:13	He will return to judge the world	1 Thessalonians 1:10
102:25-28	His words are eternal	Matthew 24:35
110:1	He is David's son and God's son	Matthew 22:44
110:4	He is the eternal priest-king	Hebrews 6:20
118:22	He will be rejected by many but accepted by God	1 Peter 2:7-8

I am determined not to sin in what
I say.
4 I have followed your commands,
which keep me from following cruel
and evil people.
5 My steps have stayed on your path;
I have not wavered from following
you.
6 I am praying to you because I know you
will answer, O God.
Bend down and listen as I pray.
7 Show me your unfailing love in wonderful
ways.
By your mighty power you rescue
those who seek refuge from their
enemies.
8 Guard me as you would guard your own
eyes.*
Hide me in the shadow of your
wings.
9 Protect me from wicked people who
attack me,
from murderous enemies who
surround me.
10 They are without pity.
Listen to their boasting!
11 They track me down and surround me,
watching for the chance to throw
me to the ground.
12 They are like hungry lions, eager to tear
me apart—
like young lions hiding in ambush.

13 Arise, O LORD!
Stand against them, and bring them
to their knees!
Rescue me from the wicked with your
sword!
14 By the power of your hand, O LORD,
destroy those who look to this world
for their reward.
But satisfy the hunger of your treasured
ones.
May their children have plenty,
leaving an inheritance for their
descendants.
15 Because I am righteous, I will see
you.
When I awake, I will see you face to
face and be satisfied.

PSALM 18

For the choir director: A psalm of David, the servant of the LORD. He sang this song to the LORD on the day the LORD rescued him from all his enemies and from Saul. He sang:

1 I love you, LORD;
you are my strength.
2 The LORD is my rock, my fortress,
and my savior;
my God is my rock, in whom I find
protection.
He is my shield, the power that saves me,
and my place of safety.
3 I called on the LORD, who is worthy
of praise,
and he saved me from my enemies.

4 The ropes of death entangled me;
floods of destruction swept over me.
5 The grave* wrapped its ropes around me;
death laid a trap in my path.
6 But in my distress I cried out to the LORD;
yes, I prayed to my God for help.
He heard me from his sanctuary;
my cry to him reached his ears.

7 Then the earth quaked and trembled.
The foundations of the mountains
shook;
they quaked because of his anger.
8 Smoke poured from his nostrils;
fierce flames leaped from his mouth.
Glowing coals blazed forth from him.
9 He opened the heavens and came down;
dark storm clouds were beneath his
feet.
10 Mounted on a mighty angelic being,*
he flew,
soaring on the wings of the wind.
11 He shrouded himself in darkness,
veiling his approach with dark rain
clouds.
12 Thick clouds shielded the brightness
around him
and rained down hail and burning
coals.*
13 The LORD thundered from heaven;
the voice of the Most High resounded
amid the hail and burning coals.
14 He shot his arrows and scattered his
enemies;

17:8 Hebrew *as the pupil of your eye.* **18:5** Hebrew *Sheol.* **18:10** Hebrew *a cherub.* **18:12** Or *and lightning bolts;* also in 18:13.

his lightning flashed, and they were
greatly confused.
15 Then at your command, O LORD,
at the blast of your breath,
the bottom of the sea could be seen,
and the foundations of the earth were
laid bare.
16 He reached down from heaven and
rescued me;
he drew me out of deep waters.
17 He rescued me from my powerful
enemies,
from those who hated me and were too
strong for me.
18 They attacked me at a moment when
I was in distress,
but the LORD supported me.
19 He led me to a place of safety;
he rescued me because he delights
in me.
20 The LORD rewarded me for doing right;
he restored me because of my
innocence.
21 For I have kept the ways of the LORD;
I have not turned from my God to
follow evil.
22 I have followed all his regulations;
I have never abandoned his decrees.
23 I am blameless before God;
I have kept myself from sin.
24 The LORD rewarded me for doing right.
He has seen my innocence.
25 To the faithful you show yourself faithful;
to those with integrity you show
integrity.
26 To the pure you show yourself pure,
but to the wicked you show yourself
hostile.
27 You rescue the humble,
but you humiliate the proud.
28 You light a lamp for me.
The LORD, my God, lights up my
darkness.
29 In your strength I can crush an army;
with my God I can scale any wall.
30 God's way is perfect.
All the LORD's promises prove true.
He is a shield for all who look to him
for protection.
31 For who is God except the LORD?
Who but our God is a solid rock?
32 God arms me with strength,
and he makes my way perfect.
33 He makes me as surefooted as a deer,
enabling me to stand on mountain
heights.
34 He trains my hands for battle;
he strengthens my arm to draw a
bronze bow.
35 You have given me your shield of victory.
Your right hand supports me;
your help has made me great.
36 You have made a wide path for my feet
to keep them from slipping.
37 I chased my enemies and caught them;
I did not stop until they were
conquered.
38 I struck them down so they could not
get up;
they fell beneath my feet.
39 You have armed me with strength for
the battle;
you have subdued my enemies under
my feet.
40 You placed my foot on their necks.
I have destroyed all who hated me.
41 They called for help, but no one came
to their rescue.
They even cried to the LORD, but he
refused to answer.
42 I ground them as fine as dust in the wind.
I swept them into the gutter like dirt.
43 You gave me victory over my accusers.
You appointed me ruler over nations;
people I don't even know now
serve me.
44 As soon as they hear of me, they submit;
foreign nations cringe before me.
45 They all lose their courage
and come trembling from their
strongholds.
46 The LORD lives! Praise to my Rock!
May the God of my salvation be exalted!
47 He is the God who pays back those who
harm me;
he subdues the nations under me
48 and rescues me from my enemies.
You hold me safe beyond the reach of my
enemies;
you save me from violent opponents.
49 For this, O LORD, I will praise you among
the nations;

I will sing praises to your name.
50 You give great victories to your king;
you show unfailing love to your anointed,
to David and all his descendants forever.

PSALM 19

For the choir director: A psalm of David.

1 The heavens proclaim the glory of God.
The skies display his craftsmanship.
2 Day after day they continue to speak;
night after night they make him known.
3 They speak without a sound or word;
their voice is never heard.*
4 Yet their message has gone throughout the earth,
and their words to all the world.
God has made a home in the heavens for the sun.
5 It bursts forth like a radiant bridegroom after his wedding.
It rejoices like a great athlete eager to run the race.
6 The sun rises at one end of the heavens
and follows its course to the other end.
Nothing can hide from its heat.

7 The instructions of the LORD are perfect,
reviving the soul.
The decrees of the LORD are trustworthy,
making wise the simple.
8 The commandments of the LORD are right,
bringing joy to the heart.
The commands of the LORD are clear,
giving insight for living.
9 Reverence for the LORD is pure,
lasting forever.
The laws of the LORD are true;
each one is fair.
10 They are more desirable than gold,
even the finest gold.
They are sweeter than honey,
even honey dripping from the comb.
11 They are a warning to your servant,
a great reward for those who obey them.

12 How can I know all the sins lurking in my heart?
Cleanse me from these hidden faults.
13 Keep your servant from deliberate sins!
Don't let them control me.
Then I will be free of guilt
and innocent of great sin.

14 May the words of my mouth
and the meditation of my heart
be pleasing to you,
O LORD, my rock and my redeemer.

PSALM 20

For the choir director: A psalm of David.

1 In times of trouble, may the LORD answer your cry.
May the name of the God of Jacob keep you safe from all harm.
2 May he send you help from his sanctuary
and strengthen you from Jerusalem.*
3 May he remember all your gifts
and look favorably on your burnt offerings. *Interlude*

4 May he grant your heart's desires
and make all your plans succeed.
5 May we shout for joy when we hear of your victory
and raise a victory banner in the name of our God.
May the LORD answer all your prayers.

6 Now I know that the LORD rescues his anointed king.
He will answer him from his holy heaven
and rescue him by his great power.
7 Some nations boast of their chariots and horses,
but we boast in the name of the LORD our God.
8 Those nations will fall down and collapse,
but we will rise up and stand firm.

9 Give victory to our king, O LORD!
Answer our cry for help.

19:3 Or *There is no speech or language where their voice is not heard.* **20:2** Hebrew *Zion.*

PSALM 21

For the choir director: A psalm of David.

1 How the king rejoices in your strength,
O LORD!
He shouts with joy because you give
him victory.
2 For you have given him his heart's desire;
you have withheld nothing he
requested. *Interlude*

What do some people brag about?

Some nations boast of their chariots and horses, but we boast in the name of the LORD our God.

PSALM 20:7

3 You welcomed him back with success and
prosperity.
You placed a crown of finest gold on
his head.
4 He asked you to preserve his life,
and you granted his request.
The days of his life stretch on forever.
5 Your victory brings him great honor,
and you have clothed him with
splendor and majesty.
6 You have endowed him with eternal
blessings
and given him the joy of your presence.
7 For the king trusts in the LORD.
The unfailing love of the Most High will
keep him from stumbling.

8 You will capture all your enemies.
Your strong right hand will seize all
who hate you.
9 You will throw them in a flaming furnace
when you appear.
The LORD will consume them in
his anger;
fire will devour them.
10 You will wipe their children from the face
of the earth;
they will never have descendants.
11 Although they plot against you,
their evil schemes will never succeed.
12 For they will turn and run
when they see your arrows aimed at
them.
13 Rise up, O LORD, in all your power.
With music and singing we celebrate
your mighty acts.

PSALM 22

For the choir director: A psalm of David, to be sung to the tune "Doe of the Dawn."

1 My God, my God, why have you
abandoned me?
Why are you so far away when I groan
for help?
2 Every day I call to you, my God, but you do
not answer.
Every night you hear my voice, but I
find no relief.

3 Yet you are holy,
enthroned on the praises of Israel.
4 Our ancestors trusted in you,
and you rescued them.
5 They cried out to you and were saved.
They trusted in you and were never
disgraced.

6 But I am a worm and not a man.
I am scorned and despised by all!
7 Everyone who sees me mocks me.
They sneer and shake their heads,
saying,
8 "Is this the one who relies on the LORD?
Then let the LORD save him!
If the LORD loves him so much,
let the LORD rescue him!"

9 Yet you brought me safely from my
mother's womb
and led me to trust you at my mother's
breast.
10 I was thrust into your arms at my birth.
You have been my God from the
moment I was born.

11 Do not stay so far from me,
for trouble is near,
and no one else can help me.
12 My enemies surround me like a herd of
bulls;
fierce bulls of Bashan have hemmed
me in!
13 Like lions they open their jaws against me,
roaring and tearing into their prey.

14 My life is poured out like water,
and all my bones are out of joint.
My heart is like wax,
melting within me.
15 My strength has dried up like sunbaked clay.
My tongue sticks to the roof of my mouth.
You have laid me in the dust and left me for dead.
16 My enemies surround me like a pack of dogs;
an evil gang closes in on me.
They have pierced my hands and feet.
17 I can count all my bones.
My enemies stare at me and gloat.
18 They divide my garments among themselves
and throw dice* for my clothing.

19 O LORD, do not stay far away!
You are my strength; come quickly to my aid!
20 Save me from the sword;
spare my precious life from these dogs.
21 Snatch me from the lion's jaws
and from the horns of these wild oxen.

22 I will proclaim your name to my brothers and sisters.*
I will praise you among your assembled people.
23 Praise the LORD, all you who fear him!
Honor him, all you descendants of Jacob!
Show him reverence, all you descendants of Israel!
24 For he has not ignored or belittled the suffering of the needy.
He has not turned his back on them,
but has listened to their cries for help.

25 I will praise you in the great assembly.
I will fulfill my vows in the presence of those who worship you.
26 The poor will eat and be satisfied.
All who seek the LORD will praise him.
Their hearts will rejoice with everlasting joy.
27 The whole earth will acknowledge the LORD and return to him.
All the families of the nations will bow down before him.
28 For royal power belongs to the LORD.
He rules all the nations.

29 Let the rich of the earth feast and worship.
Bow before him, all who are mortal,
all whose lives will end as dust.
30 Our children will also serve him.
Future generations will hear about the wonders of the Lord.
31 His righteous acts will be told to those not yet born.
They will hear about everything he has done.

PSALM 23

A psalm of David.

1 The LORD is my shepherd;
I have all that I need.
2 He lets me rest in green meadows;
he leads me beside peaceful streams.
3 He renews my strength.
He guides me along right paths,
bringing honor to his name.
4 Even when I walk
through the darkest valley,*
I will not be afraid,
for you are close beside me.
Your rod and your staff
protect and comfort me.
5 You prepare a feast for me
in the presence of my enemies.
You honor me by anointing my head with oil.
My cup overflows with blessings.
6 Surely your goodness and unfailing love will pursue me
all the days of my life,
and I will live in the house of the LORD forever.

PSALM 24

A psalm of David.

1 The earth is the LORD's, and everything in it.
The world and all its people belong to him.
2 For he laid the earth's foundation on the seas
and built it on the ocean depths.

22:18 Hebrew *cast lots.* **22:22** Hebrew *my brothers.* **23:4** Or *the dark valley of death.*

ADMIT ONE

Ricardo and his friends look forward to the county fair every summer, and they make plans to go on opening day. Ricardo has been saving his money so he can play the carnival games and win lots of prizes. When they get to the fair, Ricardo notices that there is a lower admission price for kids ten and younger. Ricardo is eleven, but he looks younger. If he says he is ten, he will have more money for playing games and buying cotton candy. What should Ricardo do? For help, read Psalm 24:3-4.

3 Who may climb the mountain
of the LORD?
Who may stand in his holy place?
4 Only those whose hands and hearts
are pure,
who do not worship idols
and never tell lies.
5 They will receive the LORD's blessing
and have a right relationship with God
their savior.

6 Such people may seek you
and worship in your presence,
O God of Jacob. *Interlude*

7 Open up, ancient gates!
Open up, ancient doors,
and let the King of glory enter.
8 Who is the King of glory?
The LORD, strong and mighty;
the LORD, invincible in battle.
9 Open up, ancient gates!
Open up, ancient doors,
and let the King of glory enter.
10 Who is the King of glory?
The LORD of Heaven's Armies—
he is the King of glory. *Interlude*

PSALM 25*

A psalm of David.

1 O LORD, I give my life to you.
2 I trust in you, my God!
Do not let me be disgraced,
or let my enemies rejoice in my defeat.
3 No one who trusts in you will ever be
disgraced,
but disgrace comes to those who try
to deceive others.

4 Show me the right path, O LORD;
point out the road for me to follow.
5 Lead me by your truth and teach me,
for you are the God who saves me.
All day long I put my hope in you.
6 Remember, O LORD, your compassion
and unfailing love,
which you have shown from long
ages past.
7 Do not remember the rebellious sins
of my youth.
Remember me in the light of your
unfailing love,
for you are merciful, O LORD.

8 The LORD is good and does what is right;
he shows the proper path to those who
go astray.
9 He leads the humble in doing right,
teaching them his way.
10 The LORD leads with unfailing love and
faithfulness
all who keep his covenant and obey
his demands.

25 This psalm is a Hebrew acrostic poem; each verse begins with a successive letter of the Hebrew alphabet.

11 For the honor of your name, O LORD,
forgive my many, many sins.
12 Who are those who fear the LORD?
He will show them the path they
should choose.
13 They will live in prosperity,
and their children will inherit the land.
14 The LORD is a friend to those who
fear him.
He teaches them his covenant.
15 My eyes are always on the LORD,
for he rescues me from the traps
of my enemies.

16 Turn to me and have mercy,
for I am alone and in deep distress.
17 My problems go from bad to worse.
Oh, save me from them all!
18 Feel my pain and see my trouble.
Forgive all my sins.
19 See how many enemies I have
and how viciously they hate me!
20 Protect me! Rescue my life from them!
Do not let me be disgraced, for in you I
take refuge.
21 May integrity and honesty protect me,
for I put my hope in you.

22 O God, ransom Israel
from all its troubles.

PSALM 26

A psalm of David.

1 Declare me innocent, O LORD,
for I have acted with integrity;
I have trusted in the LORD without
wavering.
2 Put me on trial, LORD, and cross-
examine me.
Test my motives and my heart.
3 For I am always aware of your unfailing
love,
and I have lived according to your
truth.
4 I do not spend time with liars
or go along with hypocrites.
5 I hate the gatherings of those who
do evil,
and I refuse to join in with the wicked.
6 I wash my hands to declare my innocence.
I come to your altar, O LORD,
7 singing a song of thanksgiving
and telling of all your wonders.
8 I love your sanctuary, LORD,
the place where your glorious presence
dwells.

9 Don't let me suffer the fate of sinners.
Don't condemn me along with
murderers.
10 Their hands are dirty with evil schemes,
and they constantly take bribes.
11 But I am not like that; I live with integrity.
So redeem me and show me mercy.
12 Now I stand on solid ground,
and I will publicly praise the LORD.

PSALM 27

A psalm of David.

1 The LORD is my light and my salvation—
so why should I be afraid?
The LORD is my fortress, protecting me
from danger,
so why should I tremble?
2 When evil people come to devour me,
when my enemies and foes attack me,
they will stumble and fall.
3 Though a mighty army surrounds me,
my heart will not be afraid.
Even if I am attacked,
I will remain confident.

4 The one thing I ask of the LORD—
the thing I seek most—
is to live in the house of the LORD all the
days of my life,
delighting in the LORD's perfections
and meditating in his Temple.
5 For he will conceal me there when
troubles come;
he will hide me in his sanctuary.
He will place me out of reach on
a high rock.
6 Then I will hold my head high
above my enemies who surround me.
At his sanctuary I will offer sacrifices with
shouts of joy,
singing and praising the LORD with
music.

7 Hear me as I pray, O LORD.
Be merciful and answer me!
8 My heart has heard you say, "Come and
talk with me."
And my heart responds, "LORD, I am
coming."

9 Do not turn your back on me.
Do not reject your servant in anger.
You have always been my helper.
Don't leave me now; don't abandon me,
O God of my salvation!
10 Even if my father and mother abandon me,
the LORD will hold me close.

11 Teach me how to live, O LORD.
Lead me along the right path,
for my enemies are waiting for me.
12 Do not let me fall into their hands.
For they accuse me of things I've never done;
with every breath they threaten me with violence.
13 Yet I am confident I will see the LORD's goodness
while I am here in the land of the living.

14 Wait patiently for the LORD.
Be brave and courageous.
Yes, wait patiently for the LORD.

PSALM 28

A psalm of David.

1 I pray to you, O LORD, my rock.
Do not turn a deaf ear to me.
For if you are silent,
I might as well give up and die.
2 Listen to my prayer for mercy
as I cry out to you for help,
as I lift my hands toward your holy sanctuary.

3 Do not drag me away with the wicked—
with those who do evil—
those who speak friendly words to their neighbors
while planning evil in their hearts.
4 Give them the punishment they so richly deserve!
Measure it out in proportion to their wickedness.
Pay them back for all their evil deeds!
Give them a taste of what they have done to others.
5 They care nothing for what the LORD has done
or for what his hands have made.
So he will tear them down,
and they will never be rebuilt!

6 Praise the LORD!
For he has heard my cry for mercy.
7 The LORD is my strength and shield.
I trust him with all my heart.
He helps me, and my heart is filled with joy.
I burst out in songs of thanksgiving.

8 The LORD gives his people strength.
He is a safe fortress for his anointed king.
9 Save your people!
Bless Israel, your special possession.*
Lead them like a shepherd,
and carry them in your arms forever.

PSALM 29

A psalm of David.

1 Honor the LORD, you heavenly beings*;
honor the LORD for his glory and strength.

AMAZING FACTS

Ever hear a voice so powerful that one word could completely shatter a 100-foot-tall cedar tree? That's how powerful God's voice is!

PSALM 29:4-5

2 Honor the LORD for the glory of his name.
Worship the LORD in the splendor of his holiness.

3 The voice of the LORD echoes above the sea.
The God of glory thunders.
The LORD thunders over the mighty sea.
4 The voice of the LORD is powerful;
the voice of the LORD is majestic.

28:9 Hebrew *Bless your inheritance.* **29:1** Hebrew *you sons of God.*

5 The voice of the LORD splits the mighty cedars;
the LORD shatters the cedars of Lebanon.
6 He makes Lebanon's mountains skip like a calf;
he makes Mount Hermon* leap like a young wild ox.
7 The voice of the LORD strikes with bolts of lightning.
8 The voice of the LORD makes the barren wilderness quake;
the LORD shakes the wilderness of Kadesh.
9 The voice of the LORD twists mighty oaks* and strips the forests bare.
In his Temple everyone shouts, "Glory!"
10 The LORD rules over the floodwaters.
The LORD reigns as king forever.
11 The LORD gives his people strength.
The LORD blesses them with peace.

PSALM 30

A psalm of David. A song for the dedication of the Temple.

1 I will exalt you, LORD, for you rescued me.
You refused to let my enemies triumph over me.
2 O LORD my God, I cried to you for help,
and you restored my health.
3 You brought me up from the grave,* O LORD.
You kept me from falling into the pit of death.
4 Sing to the LORD, all you godly ones!
Praise his holy name.
5 For his anger lasts only a moment,
but his favor lasts a lifetime!
Weeping may last through the night,
but joy comes with the morning.
6 When I was prosperous, I said,
"Nothing can stop me now!"
7 Your favor, O LORD, made me as secure as a mountain.
Then you turned away from me, and I was shattered.
8 I cried out to you, O LORD.
I begged the Lord for mercy, saying,
9 "What will you gain if I die,
if I sink into the grave?
Can my dust praise you?
Can it tell of your faithfulness?
10 Hear me, LORD, and have mercy on me.
Help me, O LORD."
11 You have turned my mourning into joyful dancing.
You have taken away my clothes of mourning and clothed me with joy,
12 that I might sing praises to you and not be silent.
O LORD my God, I will give you thanks forever!

PSALM 31

For the choir director: A psalm of David.

1 O LORD, I have come to you for protection;
don't let me be disgraced.
Save me, for you do what is right.
2 Turn your ear to listen to me;
rescue me quickly.
Be my rock of protection,
a fortress where I will be safe.
3 You are my rock and my fortress.
For the honor of your name, lead me out of this danger.
4 Pull me from the trap my enemies set for me,
for I find protection in you alone.
5 I entrust my spirit into your hand.
Rescue me, LORD, for you are a faithful God.
6 I hate those who worship worthless idols.
I trust in the LORD.
7 I will be glad and rejoice in your unfailing love,
for you have seen my troubles,
and you care about the anguish of my soul.
8 You have not handed me over to my enemies
but have set me in a safe place.
9 Have mercy on me, LORD, for I am in distress.
Tears blur my eyes.
My body and soul are withering away.
10 I am dying from grief;
my years are shortened by sadness.

29:6 Hebrew *Sirion*, another name for Mount Hermon. **29:9** Or *causes the deer to writhe in labor*. **30:3** Hebrew *from Sheol*.

I SURVIVED

Last year I stumbled into a "chat room" for teens and started chatting with other kids across the country. It was interesting talking with people I had never met before . . . people I couldn't see.

One day I met a guy in a chat room who seemed just like me. We had the same interests and really understood one another. He was even cool about the fact that I was a Christian and went to church. He said he was "Christian" too.

After a few months, he was all I thought about. I was in love with a boy I had never seen. That's probably why I started doing the things I did. He talked to me about things I knew I shouldn't be talking about. I had to be careful that my parents never walked in when we were chatting, because he would describe things to me that weren't exactly "PG." If this guy was "Christian" like he said he was, he didn't talk like any Christian I knew.

This really began to bother me. As much as I liked him, I felt SOOO guilty every time I was done chatting with him. I felt dirty and ashamed.

Finally, I couldn't bear it any longer. I had to tell someone. I'll never forget the day I walked into my older sister's room and told her. When she heard what was going on, she immediately told my mom. I was so relieved that someone finally knew.

When my mom came to my room, I burst into tears. At first she just hugged me. Then she said, "We're going to get through this."

I can't describe to you how FREE I felt once my family knew. Confessing my deep, dark secret was the best thing I had ever done.

Take a look at Psalm 32:1-5 to learn how David felt when he confessed his sins. Also read Psalms 40:11 and 51:2-4.

Sin has drained my strength;
I am wasting away from within.
11 I am scorned by all my enemies
and despised by my neighbors—
even my friends are afraid to come near me.
When they see me on the street,
they run the other way.
12 I am ignored as if I were dead,
as if I were a broken pot.
13 I have heard the many rumors about me,
and I am surrounded by terror.
My enemies conspire against me,
plotting to take my life.

14 But I am trusting you, O LORD,
saying, "You are my God!"
15 My future is in your hands.
Rescue me from those who hunt me down relentlessly.
16 Let your favor shine on your servant.
In your unfailing love, rescue me.
17 Don't let me be disgraced, O LORD,
for I call out to you for help.
Let the wicked be disgraced;
let them lie silent in the grave.*
18 Silence their lying lips—
those proud and arrogant lips that accuse the godly.

19 How great is the goodness
you have stored up for those who fear you.
You lavish it on those who come to you for protection,
blessing them before the watching world.
20 You hide them in the shelter of your presence,
safe from those who conspire against them.
You shelter them in your presence,
far from accusing tongues.

21 Praise the LORD,
for he has shown me the wonders of his unfailing love.
He kept me safe when my city was under attack.
22 In panic I cried out,
"I am cut off from the LORD!"
But you heard my cry for mercy
and answered my call for help.

23 Love the LORD, all you godly ones!
For the LORD protects those who are loyal to him,
but he harshly punishes the arrogant.
24 So be strong and courageous,
all you who put your hope in the LORD!

PSALM 32

A psalm of David.*

1 Oh, what joy for those
whose disobedience is forgiven,
whose sin is put out of sight!
2 Yes, what joy for those
whose record the LORD has cleared of guilt,*
whose lives are lived in complete honesty!
3 When I refused to confess my sin,
my body wasted away,
and I groaned all day long.
4 Day and night your hand of discipline was heavy on me.
My strength evaporated like water in the summer heat. *Interlude*

5 Finally, I confessed all my sins to you
and stopped trying to hide my guilt.
I said to myself, "I will confess my rebellion to the LORD."
And you forgave me! All my guilt is gone. *Interlude*

6 Therefore, let all the godly pray to you while there is still time,
that they may not drown in the floodwaters of judgment.
7 For you are my hiding place;
you protect me from trouble.
You surround me with songs of victory. *Interlude*

8 The LORD says, "I will guide you along the best pathway for your life.
I will advise you and watch over you.
9 Do not be like a senseless horse or mule
that needs a bit and bridle to keep it under control."

31:17 Hebrew *in Sheol*. **32:TITLE** Hebrew *maskil*. This may be a literary or musical term. **32:2** Greek version reads *of sin*. Compare Rom 4:7.

10 Many sorrows come to the wicked,
but unfailing love surrounds those who
trust the LORD.
11 So rejoice in the LORD and be glad, all you
who obey him!
Shout for joy, all you whose hearts
are pure!

PSALM 33

1 Let the godly sing for joy to the LORD;
it is fitting for the pure to praise him.
2 Praise the LORD with melodies on the lyre;
make music for him on the ten-
stringed harp.
3 Sing a new song of praise to him;
play skillfully on the harp, and sing
with joy.
4 For the word of the LORD holds true,
and we can trust everything he does.

Does God really watch over me? * **The LORD watches over those who fear him, those who rely on his unfailing love.** PSALM 33:18

5 He loves whatever is just and good;
the unfailing love of the LORD fills
the earth.

6 The LORD merely spoke,
and the heavens were created.
He breathed the word,
and all the stars were born.
7 He assigned the sea its boundaries
and locked the oceans in vast
reservoirs.
8 Let the whole world fear the LORD,
and let everyone stand in awe of him.
9 For when he spoke, the world began!
It appeared at his command.

10 The LORD frustrates the plans
of the nations
and thwarts all their schemes.
11 But the LORD's plans stand firm
forever;
his intentions can never be shaken.

12 What joy for the nation whose God
is the LORD,
whose people he has chosen as his
inheritance.
13 The LORD looks down from heaven
and sees the whole human race.
14 From his throne he observes
all who live on the earth.
15 He made their hearts,
so he understands everything they do.
16 The best-equipped army cannot save
a king,
nor is great strength enough to save
a warrior.
17 Don't count on your warhorse to give you
victory—
for all its strength, it cannot save you.
18 But the LORD watches over those who
fear him,
those who rely on his unfailing love.
19 He rescues them from death
and keeps them alive in times of
famine.

20 We put our hope in the LORD.
He is our help and our shield.
21 In him our hearts rejoice,
for we trust in his holy name.
22 Let your unfailing love surround us, LORD,
for our hope is in you alone.

PSALM 34*

A psalm of David, regarding the time he pretended to be insane in front of Abimelech, who sent him away.

1 I will praise the LORD at all times.
I will constantly speak his praises.
2 I will boast only in the LORD;
let all who are helpless take heart.
3 Come, let us tell of the LORD's greatness;
let us exalt his name together.

4 I prayed to the LORD, and he answered me.
He freed me from all my fears.
5 Those who look to him for help will be
radiant with joy;
no shadow of shame will darken
their faces.
6 In my desperation I prayed, and the LORD
listened;

34 This psalm is a Hebrew acrostic poem; each verse begins with a successive letter of the Hebrew alphabet.

he saved me from all my troubles.
7 For the angel of the LORD is a guard;
he surrounds and defends all who
fear him.

8 Taste and see that the LORD is good.
Oh, the joys of those who take refuge
in him!
9 Fear the LORD, you his godly people,
for those who fear him will have all
they need.
10 Even strong young lions sometimes go
hungry,
but those who trust in the LORD will
lack no good thing.

11 Come, my children, and listen to me,
and I will teach you to fear the LORD.
12 Does anyone want to live a life
that is long and prosperous?
13 Then keep your tongue from speaking
evil
and your lips from telling lies!
14 Turn away from evil and do good.
Search for peace, and work to
maintain it.

15 The eyes of the LORD watch over those
who do right;
his ears are open to their cries
for help.
16 But the LORD turns his face against those
who do evil;
he will erase their memory from the
earth.

17 The LORD hears his people when they call
to him for help.
He rescues them from all their troubles.
18 The LORD is close to the brokenhearted;
he rescues those whose spirits are
crushed.

19 The righteous person faces many
troubles,
but the LORD comes to the rescue
each time.
20 For the LORD protects the bones of the
righteous;
not one of them is broken!

21 Calamity will surely overtake the wicked,
and those who hate the righteous will
be punished.
22 But the LORD will redeem those who
serve him.
No one who takes refuge in him will
be condemned.

PSALM 35

A psalm of David.

1 O LORD, oppose those who oppose me.
Fight those who fight against me.
2 Put on your armor, and take up your
shield.
Prepare for battle, and come to my aid.
3 Lift up your spear and javelin
against those who pursue me.
Let me hear you say,
"I will give you victory!"

PSALMS TO LEARN AND LOVE

Almost everyone, whether religious or not, has heard Psalm 23 because it is quoted so often. Many other psalms are also familiar because they are quoted in music, in books, or in the words of the worship service.

Psalms about goodness	1; 19; 24; 133; 136; 139
Psalms of praise	8; 97; 103; 107; 113; 145; 150
Psalms of repentance and forgiveness	32:1-5; 51; 103
Psalms for times of trouble	3; 14; 22; 37:1-11; 42; 46; 53; 116:1-7
Psalms of confidence and trust	23; 40:1-4; 91; 119:11; 121; 127

I ♥ PSALMS

4 Bring shame and disgrace on those trying
to kill me;
turn them back and humiliate those
who want to harm me.
5 Blow them away like chaff in the wind—
a wind sent by the angel of the LORD.
6 Make their path dark and slippery,
with the angel of the LORD pursuing
them.
7 I did them no wrong, but they laid a trap
for me.
I did them no wrong, but they dug a pit
to catch me.
8 So let sudden ruin come upon them!
Let them be caught in the trap they set
for me!
Let them be destroyed in the pit they
dug for me.

9 Then I will rejoice in the LORD.
I will be glad because he rescues me.
10 With every bone in my body I will praise
him:
"LORD, who can compare with you?
Who else rescues the helpless from the
strong?
Who else protects the helpless and
poor from those who rob them?"

11 Malicious witnesses testify against me.
They accuse me of crimes I know
nothing about.
12 They repay me evil for good.
I am sick with despair.
13 Yet when they were ill, I grieved
for them.
I denied myself by fasting for them,
but my prayers returned unanswered.
14 I was sad, as though they were my friends
or family,
as if I were grieving for my own
mother.
15 But they are glad now that I am in trouble;
they gleefully join together against me.
I am attacked by people I don't even
know;
they slander me constantly.
16 They mock me and call me names;
they snarl at me.

17 How long, O Lord, will you look on and
do nothing?
Rescue me from their fierce attacks.
Protect my life from these lions!

18 Then I will thank you in front of the great
assembly.
I will praise you before all the people.
19 Don't let my treacherous enemies rejoice
over my defeat.
Don't let those who hate me without
cause gloat over my sorrow.
20 They don't talk of peace;
they plot against innocent people who
mind their own business.
21 They shout, "Aha! Aha!
With our own eyes we saw him do it!"

22 O LORD, you know all about this.
Do not stay silent.
Do not abandon me now, O Lord.
23 Wake up! Rise to my defense!
Take up my case, my God and my Lord.
24 Declare me not guilty, O LORD my God, for
you give justice.
Don't let my enemies laugh about me in
my troubles.
25 Don't let them say, "Look, we got what we
wanted!
Now we will eat him alive!"

26 May those who rejoice at my troubles
be humiliated and disgraced.
May those who triumph over me
be covered with shame and dishonor.
27 But give great joy to those who came to
my defense.
Let them continually say, "Great is the
LORD,
who delights in blessing his servant
with peace!"
28 Then I will proclaim your justice,
and I will praise you all day long.

PSALM 36

For the choir director: A psalm of David, the servant of the LORD.

1 Sin whispers to the wicked, deep within
their hearts.
They have no fear of God at all.
2 In their blind conceit,
they cannot see how wicked they really
are.
3 Everything they say is crooked and
deceitful.
They refuse to act wisely or do good.
4 They lie awake at night, hatching sinful
plots.

Their actions are never good.
They make no attempt to turn
from evil.

5 Your unfailing love, O LORD, is as vast
as the heavens;
your faithfulness reaches beyond the
clouds.
6 Your righteousness is like the mighty
mountains,
your justice like the ocean depths.
You care for people and animals alike,
O LORD.
7 How precious is your unfailing love,
O God!
All humanity finds shelter
in the shadow of your wings.
8 You feed them from the abundance of
your own house,
letting them drink from your river of
delights.
9 For you are the fountain of life,
the light by which we see.

10 Pour out your unfailing love on those
who love you;
give justice to those with honest hearts.
11 Don't let the proud trample me
or the wicked push me around.
12 Look! Those who do evil have fallen!
They are thrown down, never to rise
again.

PSALM 37*

A psalm of David.

1 Don't worry about the wicked
or envy those who do wrong.
2 For like grass, they soon fade away.
Like spring flowers, they soon wither.

3 Trust in the LORD and do good.
Then you will live safely in the land
and prosper.
4 Take delight in the LORD,
and he will give you your heart's
desires.

5 Commit everything you do to the LORD.
Trust him, and he will help you.
6 He will make your innocence radiate
like the dawn,
and the justice of your cause will shine
like the noonday sun.

7 Be still in the presence of the LORD,
and wait patiently for him to act.

37 This psalm is a Hebrew acrostic poem; each stanza begins with a successive letter of the Hebrew alphabet.

IS IT OK?

IS IT OK TO WORRY ABOUT THE FUTURE?

It's natural to feel nervous when you think about all the things that *could* go wrong in life (having to move and leave your friends, family problems, job loss, terrorist attacks, and so on). But that doesn't give us a free pass to worry. While it's OK to dislike bad things in life, it's not OK to sit around worrying about whether or not they'll happen. In Psalm 37:9, God tells us the wicked *will* be destroyed, and those who trust God *will* be rewarded. There's no question about how things will work out—God *will* take care of us! And if you're still worrying about this worry question, remember Jesus' clear instructions in Matthew 6:25: "Don't worry!"

Don't worry about evil people who prosper
or fret about their wicked schemes.
8 Stop being angry!
Turn from your rage!
Do not lose your temper—
it only leads to harm.
9 For the wicked will be destroyed,
but those who trust in the LORD will possess the land.

10 Soon the wicked will disappear.
Though you look for them, they will be gone.
11 The lowly will possess the land
and will live in peace and prosperity.

12 The wicked plot against the godly;
they snarl at them in defiance.
13 But the Lord just laughs,
for he sees their day of judgment coming.

14 The wicked draw their swords
and string their bows
to kill the poor and the oppressed,
to slaughter those who do right.
15 But their swords will stab their own hearts,
and their bows will be broken.

16 It is better to be godly and have little
than to be evil and rich.
17 For the strength of the wicked will be shattered,
but the LORD takes care of the godly.

18 Day by day the LORD takes care of the innocent,
and they will receive an inheritance that lasts forever.
19 They will not be disgraced in hard times;
even in famine they will have more than enough.

20 But the wicked will die.
The LORD's enemies are like flowers in a field—
they will disappear like smoke.

21 The wicked borrow and never repay,
but the godly are generous givers.
22 Those the LORD blesses will possess the land,
but those he curses will die.

23 The LORD directs the steps of the godly.
He delights in every detail of their lives.
24 Though they stumble, they will never fall,
for the LORD holds them by the hand.

25 Once I was young, and now I am old.
Yet I have never seen the godly abandoned
or their children begging for bread.
26 The godly always give generous loans to others,
and their children are a blessing.

27 Turn from evil and do good,
and you will live in the land forever.
28 For the LORD loves justice,
and he will never abandon the godly.

He will keep them safe forever,
but the children of the wicked will die.
29 The godly will possess the land
and will live there forever.

30 The godly offer good counsel;
they teach right from wrong.
31 They have made God's law their own,
so they will never slip from his path.

32 The wicked wait in ambush for the godly,
looking for an excuse to kill them.
33 But the LORD will not let the wicked succeed
or let the godly be condemned when they are put on trial.

34 Put your hope in the LORD.
Travel steadily along his path.
He will honor you by giving you the land.
You will see the wicked destroyed.

35 I have seen wicked and ruthless people
flourishing like a tree in its native soil.
36 But when I looked again, they were gone!
Though I searched for them, I could not find them!

37 Look at those who are honest and good,
for a wonderful future awaits those who love peace.
38 But the rebellious will be destroyed;
they have no future.

39 The LORD rescues the godly;
he is their fortress in times of trouble.

40 The LORD helps them,
rescuing them from the wicked.
He saves them,
and they find shelter in him.

PSALM 38

A psalm of David, asking God to remember him.

1 O LORD, don't rebuke me in your anger
or discipline me in your rage!
2 Your arrows have struck deep,
and your blows are crushing me.
3 Because of your anger, my whole body
is sick;
my health is broken because
of my sins.
4 My guilt overwhelms me—
it is a burden too heavy to bear.
5 My wounds fester and stink
because of my foolish sins.
6 I am bent over and racked with pain.
All day long I walk around filled with
grief.
7 A raging fever burns within me,
and my health is broken.
8 I am exhausted and completely crushed.
My groans come from an anguished
heart.

9 You know what I long for, Lord;
you hear my every sigh.
10 My heart beats wildly, my strength fails,
and I am going blind.
11 My loved ones and friends stay away,
fearing my disease.
Even my own family stands at
a distance.
12 Meanwhile, my enemies lay traps
to kill me.
Those who wish me harm make plans
to ruin me.
All day long they plan their treachery.

13 But I am deaf to all their threats.
I am silent before them as one who
cannot speak.
14 I choose to hear nothing,
and I make no reply.
15 For I am waiting for you, O LORD.
You must answer for me, O Lord
my God.
16 I prayed, "Don't let my enemies gloat
over me
or rejoice at my downfall."
17 I am on the verge of collapse,
facing constant pain.
18 But I confess my sins;
I am deeply sorry for what I have done.
19 I have many aggressive enemies;
they hate me without reason.
20 They repay me evil for good
and oppose me for pursuing good.
21 Do not abandon me, O LORD.
Do not stand at a distance, my God.
22 Come quickly to help me,
O Lord my savior.

PSALM 39

For Jeduthun, the choir director: A psalm of David.

1 I said to myself, "I will watch what I do
and not sin in what I say.
I will hold my tongue
when the ungodly are around me."
2 But as I stood there in silence—
not even speaking of good things—
the turmoil within me grew worse.
3 The more I thought about it,
the hotter I got,
igniting a fire of words:
4 "LORD, remind me how brief my time
on earth will be.
Remind me that my days are
numbered—
how fleeting my life is.
5 You have made my life no longer than
the width of my hand.
My entire lifetime is just a moment
to you;
at best, each of us is but a breath."
Interlude

6 We are merely moving shadows,
and all our busy rushing ends
in nothing.
We heap up wealth,
not knowing who will spend it.
7 And so, Lord, where do I put my hope?
My only hope is in you.
8 Rescue me from my rebellion.
Do not let fools mock me.
9 I am silent before you; I won't say
a word,
for my punishment is from you.
10 But please stop striking me!
I am exhausted by the blows from
your hand.

11 When you discipline us for our sins,
you consume like a moth what is
precious to us.
Each of us is but a breath. *Interlude*

12 Hear my prayer, O LORD!
Listen to my cries for help!
Don't ignore my tears.
For I am your guest—
a traveler passing through,
as my ancestors were before me.
13 Leave me alone so I can smile again
before I am gone and exist no more.

PSALM 40

For the choir director: A psalm of David.

1 I waited patiently for the LORD to help me,
and he turned to me and heard my cry.
2 He lifted me out of the pit of despair,
out of the mud and the mire.
He set my feet on solid ground
and steadied me as I walked along.
3 He has given me a new song to sing,
a hymn of praise to our God.
Many will see what he has done and
be amazed.
They will put their trust in the LORD.

4 Oh, the joys of those who trust the LORD,
who have no confidence in the proud
or in those who worship idols.
5 O LORD my God, you have performed
many wonders for us.
Your plans for us are too numerous
to list.
You have no equal.
If I tried to recite all your wonderful
deeds,
I would never come to the end of them.

6 You take no delight in sacrifices or
offerings.
Now that you have made me listen,
I finally understand*—
you don't require burnt offerings
or sin offerings.
7 Then I said, "Look, I have come.
As is written about me in the
Scriptures:
8 I take joy in doing your will, my God,
for your instructions are written on my
heart."

9 I have told all your people about your
justice.
I have not been afraid to speak out,
as you, O LORD, well know.
10 I have not kept the good news of your
justice hidden in my heart;
I have talked about your faithfulness
and saving power.
I have told everyone in the great assembly
of your unfailing love and faithfulness.

11 LORD, don't hold back your tender
mercies from me.
Let your unfailing love and faithfulness
always protect me.
12 For troubles surround me—
too many to count!
My sins pile up so high
I can't see my way out.
They outnumber the hairs on my head.
I have lost all courage.

13 Please, LORD, rescue me!
Come quickly, LORD, and help me.
14 May those who try to destroy me
be humiliated and put to shame.
May those who take delight in my trouble
be turned back in disgrace.
15 Let them be horrified by their shame,
for they said, "Aha! We've got him
now!"

16 But may all who search for you
be filled with joy and gladness in you.
May those who love your salvation
repeatedly shout, "The LORD is great!"
17 As for me, since I am poor and needy,
let the Lord keep me in his thoughts.
You are my helper and my savior.
O my God, do not delay.

PSALM 41

For the choir director: A psalm of David.

1 Oh, the joys of those who are kind to the
poor!
The LORD rescues them when they are
in trouble.
2 The LORD protects them
and keeps them alive.
He gives them prosperity in the land
and rescues them from their
enemies.

40:6 Greek text reads *You have given me a body*. Compare Heb 10:5.

3 The LORD nurses them when they are sick
and restores them to health.

4 "O LORD," I prayed, "have mercy on me.
Heal me, for I have sinned against you."
5 But my enemies say nothing but evil about me.
"How soon will he die and be forgotten?" they ask.
6 They visit me as if they were my friends,
but all the while they gather gossip,
and when they leave, they spread it everywhere.
7 All who hate me whisper about me,
imagining the worst.
8 "He has some fatal disease," they say.
"He will never get out of that bed!"
9 Even my best friend, the one I trusted completely,
the one who shared my food, has turned against me.

10 LORD, have mercy on me.
Make me well again, so I can pay them back!
11 I know you are pleased with me,
for you have not let my enemies triumph over me.
12 You have preserved my life because I am innocent;
you have brought me into your presence forever.

13 Praise the LORD, the God of Israel,
who lives from everlasting to everlasting.
Amen and amen!

BOOK TWO (Psalms 42–72)

PSALM 42

For the choir director: A psalm of the descendants of Korah.*

1 As the deer longs for streams of water,
so I long for you, O God.
2 I thirst for God, the living God.
When can I go and stand before him?
3 Day and night I have only tears for food,
while my enemies continually taunt me, saying,
"Where is this God of yours?"

42:TITLE Hebrew *maskil*. This may be a literary or musical term.

THIRD CHAIR

It just doesn't matter, Ian thought. *It just doesn't matter.* Ian couldn't remember a time when he felt so discouraged. He had done everything he could think of to improve his trumpet playing—extra practice and private lessons. Recently, the band instructor complimented Ian on his playing. So why did the band instructor put him back on third chair again? Ian was so upset; he hardly knew what to do. Should he talk to the instructor? Or quit? Or continue working hard? Read Psalm 42:11.

4 My heart is breaking
as I remember how it used to be:
I walked among the crowds of worshipers,
leading a great procession to the house of God,
singing for joy and giving thanks
amid the sound of a great celebration!

5 Why am I discouraged?
Why is my heart so sad?
I will put my hope in God!
I will praise him again—
my Savior and 6 my God!

Now I am deeply discouraged,
but I will remember you—
even from distant Mount Hermon, the
source of the Jordan,
from the land of Mount Mizar.
7 I hear the tumult of the raging seas
as your waves and surging tides
sweep over me.
8 But each day the LORD pours his unfailing
love upon me,
and through each night I sing his
songs,
praying to God who gives me life.

9 "O God my rock," I cry,
"Why have you forgotten me?
Why must I wander around in grief,
oppressed by my enemies?"
10 Their taunts break my bones.
They scoff, "Where is this God of
yours?"

11 Why am I discouraged?
Why is my heart so sad?
I will put my hope in God!
I will praise him again—
my Savior and my God!

PSALM 43

1 Declare me innocent, O God!
Defend me against these ungodly
people.
Rescue me from these unjust liars.
2 For you are God, my only safe haven.
Why have you tossed me aside?
Why must I wander around in grief,
oppressed by my enemies?
3 Send out your light and your truth;
let them guide me.
Let them lead me to your holy
mountain,
to the place where you live.
4 There I will go to the altar of God,
to God—the source of all my joy.
I will praise you with my harp,
O God, my God!

5 Why am I discouraged?
Why is my heart so sad?
I will put my hope in God!
I will praise him again—
my Savior and my God!

PSALM 44

For the choir director: A psalm of the descendants of Korah.*

1 O God, we have heard it with our
own ears—
our ancestors have told us
of all you did in their day,
in days long ago:
2 You drove out the pagan nations by
your power
and gave all the land to our
ancestors.
You crushed their enemies
and set our ancestors free.
3 They did not conquer the land with their
swords;
it was not their own strong arm that
gave them victory.
It was your right hand and strong arm
and the blinding light from your face
that helped them,
for you loved them.

4 You are my King and my God.
You command victories for Israel.*
5 Only by your power can we push back
our enemies;
only in your name can we trample
our foes.
6 I do not trust in my bow;
I do not count on my sword to save me.
7 You are the one who gives us victory over
our enemies;
you disgrace those who hate us.
8 O God, we give glory to you all day long
and constantly praise your name.
Interlude

9 But now you have tossed us aside in
dishonor.
You no longer lead our armies to
battle.
10 You make us retreat from our enemies
and allow those who hate us to plunder
our land.

44:TITLE Hebrew *maskil*. This may be a literary or musical term. **44:4** Hebrew *for Jacob*. The names "Jacob" and "Israel" are often interchanged throughout the Old Testament, referring sometimes to the individual patriarch and sometimes to the nation.

11 You have butchered us like sheep
and scattered us among the nations.
12 You sold your precious people for a pittance,
making nothing on the sale.
13 You let our neighbors mock us.
We are an object of scorn and derision to those around us.
14 You have made us the butt of their jokes;
they shake their heads at us in scorn.
15 We can't escape the constant humiliation;
shame is written across our faces.
16 All we hear are the taunts of our mockers.
All we see are our vengeful enemies.

17 All this has happened though we have not forgotten you.
We have not violated your covenant.
18 Our hearts have not deserted you.
We have not strayed from your path.
19 Yet you have crushed us in the jackal's desert home.
You have covered us with darkness and death.
20 If we had forgotten the name of our God
or spread our hands in prayer to foreign gods,
21 God would surely have known it,
for he knows the secrets of every heart.
22 But for your sake we are killed every day;
we are being slaughtered like sheep.

23 Wake up, O Lord! Why do you sleep?
Get up! Do not reject us forever.
24 Why do you look the other way?
Why do you ignore our suffering and oppression?
25 We collapse in the dust,
lying face down in the dirt.
26 Rise up! Help us!
Ransom us because of your unfailing love.

PSALM 45

For the choir director: A love song to be sung to the tune "Lilies." A psalm of the descendants of Korah.*

1 Beautiful words stir my heart.
I will recite a lovely poem about the king,
for my tongue is like the pen of a skillful poet.

2 You are the most handsome of all.
Gracious words stream from your lips.
God himself has blessed you forever.
3 Put on your sword, O mighty warrior!
You are so glorious, so majestic!
4 In your majesty, ride out to victory,
defending truth, humility, and justice.
Go forth to perform awe-inspiring deeds!
5 Your arrows are sharp, piercing your enemies' hearts.
The nations fall beneath your feet.

6 Your throne, O God,* endures forever and ever.
You rule with a scepter of justice.
7 You love justice and hate evil.
Therefore God, your God, has anointed you,
pouring out the oil of joy on you more than on anyone else.
8 Myrrh, aloes, and cassia perfume your robes.
In ivory palaces the music of strings entertains you.
9 Kings' daughters are among your noble women.
At your right side stands the queen,
wearing jewelry of finest gold from Ophir!

10 Listen to me, O royal daughter; take to heart what I say.
Forget your people and your family far away.
11 For your royal husband delights in your beauty;
honor him, for he is your lord.
12 The princess of Tyre* will shower you with gifts.
The wealthy will beg your favor.
13 The bride, a princess, looks glorious in her golden gown.
14 In her beautiful robes, she is led to the king,
accompanied by her bridesmaids.
15 What a joyful and enthusiastic procession
as they enter the king's palace!

45:TITLE Hebrew *maskil*. This may be a literary or musical term. **45:6** Or *Your divine throne*. **45:12** Hebrew *The daughter of Tyre*.

16 Your sons will become kings like their
father.
You will make them rulers over many
lands.
17 I will bring honor to your name in every
generation.
Therefore, the nations will praise you
forever and ever.

PSALM 46

*For the choir director: A song of the descendants of Korah, to be sung by soprano voices.**

1 God is our refuge and strength,
always ready to help in times of trouble.
2 So we will not fear when earthquakes
come
and the mountains crumble into the
sea.
3 Let the oceans roar and foam.
Let the mountains tremble as the
waters surge! *Interlude*

4 A river brings joy to the city of our God,
the sacred home of the Most High.
5 God dwells in that city; it cannot be
destroyed.
From the very break of day, God will
protect it.
6 The nations are in chaos,
and their kingdoms crumble!
God's voice thunders,
and the earth melts!
7 The LORD of Heaven's Armies is here
among us;
the God of Israel* is our fortress.
Interlude

8 Come, see the glorious works of the LORD:
See how he brings destruction upon
the world.
9 He causes wars to end throughout the
earth.
He breaks the bow and snaps the spear;
he burns the shields with fire.

10 "Be still, and know that I am God!
I will be honored by every nation.
I will be honored throughout the world."

11 The LORD of Heaven's Armies is here
among us;
the God of Israel is our fortress.
Interlude

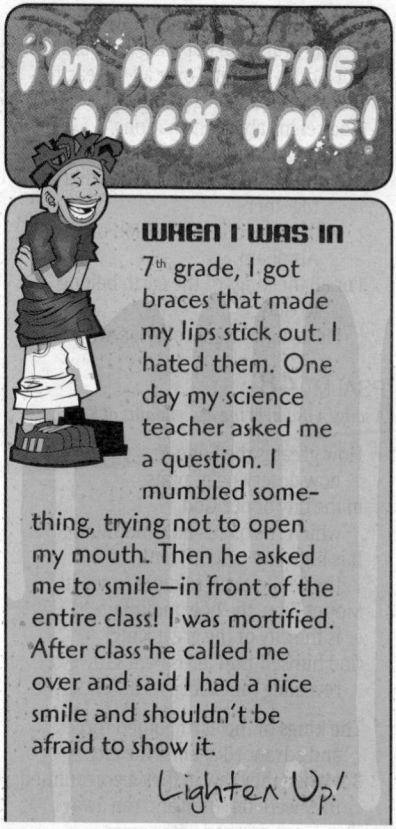

PSALM 47

For the choir director: A psalm of the descendants of Korah.

1 Come, everyone! Clap your hands!
Shout to God with joyful praise!
2 For the LORD Most High is awesome.
He is the great King of all the earth.
3 He subdues the nations before us,
putting our enemies beneath our feet.
4 He chose the Promised Land as our
inheritance,
the proud possession of Jacob's
descendants, whom he loves.
Interlude

5 God has ascended with a mighty shout.
The LORD has ascended with trumpets
blaring.

46:TITLE Hebrew *according to alamoth.* **46:7** Hebrew *of Jacob;* also in 46:11. See note on 44:4.

6 Sing praises to God, sing praises;
sing praises to our King, sing praises!
7 For God is the King over all the earth.
Praise him with a psalm.*
8 God reigns above the nations,
sitting on his holy throne.
9 The rulers of the world have gathered together
with the people of the God of Abraham.
For all the kings of the earth belong to God.
He is highly honored everywhere.

PSALM 48

A song. A psalm of the descendants of Korah.

1 How great is the LORD,
how deserving of praise,
in the city of our God,
which sits on his holy mountain!
2 It is high and magnificent;
the whole earth rejoices to see it!
Mount Zion, the holy mountain,*
is the city of the great King!
3 God himself is in Jerusalem's towers,
revealing himself as its defender.

4 The kings of the earth joined forces
and advanced against the city.
5 But when they saw it, they were stunned;
they were terrified and ran away.
6 They were gripped with terror
and writhed in pain like a woman in labor.
7 You destroyed them like the mighty ships of Tarshish
shattered by a powerful east wind.

8 We had heard of the city's glory,
but now we have seen it ourselves—
the city of the LORD of Heaven's Armies.
It is the city of our God;
he will make it safe forever.

Interlude

9 O God, we meditate on your unfailing love
as we worship in your Temple.
10 As your name deserves, O God,
you will be praised to the ends of the earth.
Your strong right hand is filled with victory.
11 Let the people on Mount Zion rejoice.
Let all the towns of Judah be glad
because of your justice.

12 Go, inspect the city of Jerusalem.*
Walk around and count the many towers.
13 Take note of the fortified walls,
and tour all the citadels,
that you may describe them
to future generations.
14 For that is what God is like.
He is our God forever and ever,
and he will guide us until we die.

PSALM 49

For the choir director: A psalm of the descendants of Korah.

1 Listen to this, all you people!
Pay attention, everyone in the world!
2 High and low,
rich and poor—listen!
3 For my words are wise,
and my thoughts are filled with insight.
4 I listen carefully to many proverbs
and solve riddles with inspiration from a harp.

5 Why should I fear when trouble comes,
when enemies surround me?
6 They trust in their wealth
and boast of great riches.
7 Yet they cannot redeem themselves from death*
by paying a ransom to God.
8 Redemption does not come so easily,
for no one can ever pay enough
9 to live forever
and never see the grave.

10 Those who are wise must finally die,
just like the foolish and senseless,
leaving all their wealth behind.
11 The grave is their eternal home,
where they will stay forever.
They may name their estates after themselves,
12 but their fame will not last.
They will die, just like animals.
13 This is the fate of fools,

47:7 Hebrew *maskil;* This may be a literary or musical term. **48:2** Or *Mount Zion, in the far north;* Hebrew reads *Mount Zion, the heights of Zaphon.* **48:12** Hebrew *Zion.* **49:7** Or *no one can redeem the life of another.*

though they are remembered
as being wise.* *Interlude*

14 Like sheep, they are led to the grave,*
where death will be their shepherd.
In the morning the godly will rule over them.
Their bodies will rot in the grave,
far from their grand estates.
15 But as for me, God will redeem my life.
He will snatch me from the power
of the grave. *Interlude*

16 So don't be dismayed when the wicked grow rich
and their homes become ever more splendid.
17 For when they die, they take nothing with them.
Their wealth will not follow them into the grave.
18 In this life they consider themselves fortunate
and are applauded for their success.
19 But they will die like all before them
and never again see the light of day.
20 People who boast of their wealth don't understand;
they will die, just like animals.

PSALM 50

A psalm of Asaph.

1 The LORD, the Mighty One, is God,
and he has spoken;
he has summoned all humanity
from where the sun rises to where it sets.
2 From Mount Zion, the perfection of beauty,
God shines in glorious radiance.
3 Our God approaches,
and he is not silent.
Fire devours everything in his way,
and a great storm rages around him.
4 He calls on the heavens above and earth below
to witness the judgment of his people.
5 "Bring my faithful people to me—
those who made a covenant with me by giving sacrifices."
6 Then let the heavens proclaim his justice,
for God himself will be the judge.
Interlude
7 "O my people, listen as I speak.
Here are my charges against you,
O Israel:
I am God, your God!
8 I have no complaint about your sacrifices
or the burnt offerings you constantly offer.
9 But I do not need the bulls from your barns
or the goats from your pens.
10 For all the animals of the forest are mine,
and I own the cattle on a thousand hills.
11 I know every bird on the mountains,
and all the animals of the field are mine.
12 If I were hungry, I would not tell you,
for all the world is mine and everything in it.
13 Do I eat the meat of bulls?
Do I drink the blood of goats?
14 Make thankfulness your sacrifice to God,
and keep the vows you made to the Most High.
15 Then call on me when you are in trouble,
and I will rescue you,
and you will give me glory."

16 But God says to the wicked:
"Why bother reciting my decrees
and pretending to obey my covenant?
17 For you refuse my discipline
and treat my words like trash.
18 When you see thieves, you approve of them,
and you spend your time with adulterers.
19 Your mouth is filled with wickedness,
and your tongue is full of lies.
20 You sit around and slander your brother—
your own mother's son.
21 While you did all this, I remained silent,
and you thought I didn't care.
But now I will rebuke you,
listing all my charges against you.
22 Repent, all of you who forget me,
or I will tear you apart,
and no one will help you.
23 But giving thanks is a sacrifice that truly honors me.

49:13 The meaning of the Hebrew is uncertain. **49:14** Hebrew *Sheol;* also in 49:14b, 15.

If you keep to my path,
I will reveal to you the salvation
of God."

PSALM 51

For the choir director: A psalm of David, regarding the time Nathan the prophet came to him after David had committed adultery with Bathsheba.

1 Have mercy on me, O God,
because of your unfailing love.
Because of your great compassion,
blot out the stain of my sins.
2 Wash me clean from my guilt.
Purify me from my sin.
3 For I recognize my rebellion;
it haunts me day and night.
4 Against you, and you alone, have
I sinned;
I have done what is evil in your sight.
You will be proved right in what you say,
and your judgment against me is
just.*
5 For I was born a sinner—
yes, from the moment my mother
conceived me.
6 But you desire honesty from the womb,*
teaching me wisdom even there.
7 Purify me from my sins,* and I will
be clean;

51:4 Greek version reads *and you will win your case in court.* Compare Rom 3:4. **51:6** Or *from the heart;* Hebrew reads *in the inward parts.* **51:7** Hebrew *Purify me with the hyssop branch.*

REASONS TO READ PSALMS

to know how to come to God each day	Psalm 5
to understand yourself more clearly	Psalm 8
to please God	Psalm 15
to find comfort	Psalm 23
to be forgiven for your sins	Psalm 51
to learn a new song	Psalm 92
to feel God's love	Psalm 103
to know why you should worship God	Psalm 104
to understand why you should read the Bible	Psalm 119
to learn a new prayer	Psalm 136
to give thanks to God	Psalm 136
to feel worthwhile	Psalm 139
to give praise to God	Psalm 145
to know that God is in control	Psalm 146

The Psalms put our deepest hurts, longings, thoughts, and prayers into words. They gently push us toward being what God wants us to be—people who love him and live for him.

wash me, and I will be whiter than
snow.
8 Oh, give me back my joy again;
you have broken me—
now let me rejoice.
9 Don't keep looking at my sins.
Remove the stain of my guilt.
10 Create in me a clean heart, O God.
Renew a loyal spirit within me.
11 Do not banish me from your
presence,
and don't take your Holy Spirit*
from me.
12 Restore to me the joy of your
salvation,
and make me willing to obey you.
13 Then I will teach your ways to rebels,
and they will return to you.
14 Forgive me for shedding blood, O God
who saves;
then I will joyfully sing of your
forgiveness.
15 Unseal my lips, O Lord,
that my mouth may praise you.
16 You do not desire a sacrifice, or I would
offer one.
You do not want a burnt offering.
17 The sacrifice you desire is a broken
spirit.
You will not reject a broken and
repentant heart, O God.
18 Look with favor on Zion and help her;
rebuild the walls of Jerusalem.
19 Then you will be pleased with sacrifices
offered in the right spirit—
with burnt offerings and whole burnt
offerings.
Then bulls will again be sacrificed
on your altar.

PSALM 52

For the choir director: A psalm of David, regarding the time Doeg the Edomite said to Saul, "David has gone to see Ahimelech."*

1 Why do you boast about your crimes,
great warrior?
Don't you realize God's justice
continues forever?
2 All day long you plot destruction.
Your tongue cuts like a sharp razor;
you're an expert at telling lies.
3 You love evil more than good
and lies more than truth. *Interlude*
4 You love to destroy others with your
words,
you liar!
5 But God will strike you down once and
for all.
He will pull you from your home
and uproot you from the land of the
living. *Interlude*
6 The righteous will see it and be amazed.
They will laugh and say,
7 "Look what happens to mighty warriors
who do not trust in God.
They trust their wealth instead
and grow more and more bold in their
wickedness."
8 But I am like an olive tree, thriving in the
house of God.
I will always trust in God's unfailing
love.
9 I will praise you forever, O God,
for what you have done.
I will trust in your good name
in the presence of your faithful people.

PSALM 53

For the choir director: A meditation; a psalm of David.*

1 Only fools say in their hearts,
"There is no God."
They are corrupt, and their actions are
evil;
not one of them does good!
2 God looks down from heaven
on the entire human race;
he looks to see if anyone is truly wise,
if anyone seeks God.
3 But no, all have turned away;
all have become corrupt.*
No one does good,
not a single one!
4 Will those who do evil never learn?
They eat up my people like bread
and wouldn't think of praying to God.
5 Terror will grip them,

51:11 Or *your spirit of holiness*. **52:TITLE** Hebrew *maskil*. This may be a literary or musical term. **53:TITLE** Hebrew *According to mahalath; a maskil*. These may be literary or musical terms. **53:3** Greek version reads *have become useless*. Compare Rom 3:12.

terror like they have never known
before.
God will scatter the bones of your
enemies.
You will put them to shame, for God
has rejected them.

6 Who will come from Mount Zion to
rescue Israel?
When God restores his people,
Jacob will shout with joy, and Israel
will rejoice.

PSALM 54

For the choir director: A psalm of David, regarding the time the Ziphites came and said to Saul, "We know where David is hiding." To be accompanied by stringed instruments.*

1 Come with great power, O God, and
rescue me!
Defend me with your might.
2 Listen to my prayer, O God.
Pay attention to my plea.
3 For strangers are attacking me;
violent people are trying to kill me.
They care nothing for God.

Interlude

4 But God is my helper.
The Lord keeps me alive!
5 May the evil plans of my enemies be
turned against them.
Do as you promised and put an end
to them.

6 I will sacrifice a voluntary offering to you;
I will praise your name, O LORD,
for it is good.
7 For you have rescued me from my
troubles
and helped me to triumph over my
enemies.

PSALM 55

For the choir director: A psalm of David, to be accompanied by stringed instruments.*

1 Listen to my prayer, O God.
Do not ignore my cry for help!
2 Please listen and answer me,
for I am overwhelmed by my troubles.
3 My enemies shout at me,
making loud and wicked threats.
They bring trouble on me
and angrily hunt me down.

4 My heart pounds in my chest.
The terror of death assaults me.
5 Fear and trembling overwhelm me,
and I can't stop shaking.
6 Oh, that I had wings like a dove;
then I would fly away and rest!
7 I would fly far away
to the quiet of the wilderness.

Interlude

8 How quickly I would escape—
far from this wild storm of hatred.

9 Confuse them, Lord, and frustrate their
plans,
for I see violence and conflict
in the city.
10 Its walls are patrolled day and night
against invaders,
but the real danger is wickedness
within the city.
11 Everything is falling apart;
threats and cheating are rampant
in the streets.

12 It is not an enemy who taunts me—
I could bear that.
It is not my foes who so arrogantly insult
me—
I could have hidden from them.
13 Instead, it is you—my equal,
my companion and close friend.
14 What good fellowship we once enjoyed
as we walked together to the house
of God.

15 Let death stalk my enemies;
let the grave* swallow them alive,
for evil makes its home within
them.

16 But I will call on God,
and the LORD will rescue me.
17 Morning, noon, and night
I cry out in my distress,
and the LORD hears my voice.
18 He ransoms me and keeps me
safe
from the battle waged against me,
though many still oppose me.

54:TITLE Hebrew *maskil*. This may be a literary or musical term. 55:TITLE Hebrew *maskil*. This may be a literary or musical term.
55:15 Hebrew *let Sheol*.

It started out so great. My close friend was interested in this girl. And I was interested in this girl's best friend. Perfect, right? Only as time went on, they began dating, and I saw my friend less and less. I never seemed to be able to hang out with him or even get him on the phone anymore.

Turns out, he felt threatened by me and thought I was trying to take away his girlfriend (which was totally untrue). I not only had no interest in his girlfriend, but he also knew that I liked a completely different girl. Even so, he still didn't trust me and purposefully distanced himself from me. This also hurt my relationship with the girl I liked (because she always ended up hanging out with her best friend . . . who was with my friend . . . who didn't want me around). Get it?

As confusing as it was, I'm glad God helped me handle it the right way. I'm not sure exactly why, but I never grew overly upset with my friend after we talked. Of course, it hurt me and I didn't necessarily feel like inviting him over to hang at my house. But I never rejected an invitation to be with him. I just stepped back and waited until he was ready to hang out again. Eventually, he came around. With time, he even apologized for treating me the way he did.

My advice would be to think of a fight with a friend as a chance to grow closer to God. In the meantime, consider doing what I did. Choose to rely on God to be your close friend, and let him help you patiently work things out with your friend.

Check out these verses on handling conflict with a friend: Psalm 55:12-13, 22 and Romans 8:31.

19 God, who has ruled forever,
will hear me and humble them.
Interlude
For my enemies refuse to change their ways;
they do not fear God.

20 As for my companion, he betrayed his friends;
he broke his promises.
21 His words are as smooth as butter,
but in his heart is war.
His words are as soothing as lotion,
but underneath are daggers!

22 Give your burdens to the LORD,
and he will take care of you.
He will not permit the godly to slip and fall.

23 But you, O God, will send the wicked
down to the pit of destruction.
Murderers and liars will die young,
but I am trusting you to save me.

PSALM 56

For the choir director: A psalm of David, regarding the time the Philistines seized him in Gath. To be sung to the tune "Dove on Distant Oaks."*

1 O God, have mercy on me,
for people are hounding me.
My foes attack me all day long.
2 I am constantly hounded by those who slander me,
and many are boldly attacking me.
3 But when I am afraid,
I will put my trust in you.
4 I praise God for what he has promised.
I trust in God, so why should I be afraid?
What can mere mortals do to me?

5 They are always twisting what I say;
they spend their days plotting to harm me.
6 They come together to spy on me—
watching my every step, eager to kill me.
7 Don't let them get away with their wickedness;
in your anger, O God, bring them down.

8 You keep track of all my sorrows.*
You have collected all my tears in your bottle.
You have recorded each one in your book.

9 My enemies will retreat when I call to you for help.
This I know: God is on my side!
10 I praise God for what he has promised;
yes, I praise the LORD for what he has promised.
11 I trust in God, so why should I be afraid?
What can mere mortals do to me?

12 I will fulfill my vows to you, O God,
and will offer a sacrifice of thanks for your help.
13 For you have rescued me from death;
you have kept my feet from slipping.
So now I can walk in your presence, O God,
in your life-giving light.

PSALM 57

For the choir director: A psalm of David, regarding the time he fled from Saul and went into the cave. To be sung to the tune "Do Not Destroy!"*

1 Have mercy on me, O God, have mercy!
I look to you for protection.
I will hide beneath the shadow of your wings
until the danger passes by.
2 I cry out to God Most High,*
to God who will fulfill his purpose for me.
3 He will send help from heaven to rescue me,
disgracing those who hound me.
Interlude
My God will send forth his unfailing love and faithfulness.

4 I am surrounded by fierce lions
who greedily devour human prey—
whose teeth pierce like spears and arrows,
and whose tongues cut like swords.

5 Be exalted, O God, above the highest heavens!
May your glory shine over all the earth.

56:TITLE Hebrew *miktam*. This may be a literary or musical term. **56:8** Or *my wanderings*. **57:TITLE** Hebrew *miktam*. This may be a literary or musical term. **57:2** Hebrew *Elohim-Elyon*.

6 My enemies have set a trap for me.
I am weary from distress.
They have dug a deep pit in my path,
but they themselves have fallen into it.
Interlude

7 My heart is confident in you, O God;
my heart is confident.
No wonder I can sing your praises!
8 Wake up, my heart!
Wake up, O lyre and harp!
I will wake the dawn with my song.
9 I will thank you, Lord, among all the people.
I will sing your praises among the nations.
10 For your unfailing love is as high as the heavens.
Your faithfulness reaches to the clouds.
11 Be exalted, O God, above the highest heavens.
May your glory shine over all the earth.

PSALM 58

For the choir director: A psalm of David, to be sung to the tune "Do Not Destroy!"*

1 Justice—do you rulers* know the meaning of the word?
Do you judge the people fairly?
2 No! You plot injustice in your hearts.
You spread violence throughout the land.
3 These wicked people are born sinners;
even from birth they have lied and gone their own way.
4 They spit venom like deadly snakes;
they are like cobras that refuse to listen,
5 ignoring the tunes of the snake charmers,
no matter how skillfully they play.

6 Break off their fangs, O God!
Smash the jaws of these lions, O LORD!
7 May they disappear like water into thirsty ground.
Make their weapons useless in their hands.*
8 May they be like snails that dissolve into slime,
like a stillborn child who will never see the sun.
9 God will sweep them away, both young and old,
faster than a pot heats over burning thorns.

10 The godly will rejoice when they see injustice avenged.
They will wash their feet in the blood of the wicked.
11 Then at last everyone will say,
"There truly is a reward for those who live for God;
surely there is a God who judges justly here on earth."

PSALM 59

For the choir director: A psalm of David, regarding the time Saul sent soldiers to watch David's house in order to kill him. To be sung to the tune "Do Not Destroy!"*

1 Rescue me from my enemies, O God.
Protect me from those who have come to destroy me.
2 Rescue me from these criminals;
save me from these murderers.
3 They have set an ambush for me.
Fierce enemies are out there waiting, LORD,
though I have not sinned or offended them.
4 I have done nothing wrong,
yet they prepare to attack me.
Wake up! See what is happening and help me!
5 O LORD God of Heaven's Armies, the God of Israel,
wake up and punish those hostile nations.
Show no mercy to wicked traitors.
Interlude

6 They come out at night,
snarling like vicious dogs
as they prowl the streets.
7 Listen to the filth that comes from their mouths;
their words cut like swords.
"After all, who can hear us?" they sneer.
8 But LORD, you laugh at them.
You scoff at all the hostile nations.

58:TITLE Hebrew *miktam*. This may be a literary or musical term. **58:1** Or *you gods*. **58:7** Or *Let them be trodden down and wither like grass*. The meaning of the Hebrew is uncertain. **59:TITLE** Hebrew *miktam*. This may be a literary or musical term.

9 You are my strength; I wait for you to
rescue me,
for you, O God, are my fortress.
10 In his unfailing love, my God will stand
with me.
He will let me look down in triumph on
all my enemies.
11 Don't kill them, for my people soon forget
such lessons;
stagger them with your power, and
bring them to their knees,
O Lord our shield.
12 Because of the sinful things they say,
because of the evil that is on their lips,
let them be captured by their pride,
their curses, and their lies.
13 Destroy them in your anger!
Wipe them out completely!
Then the whole world will know
that God reigns in Israel.* *Interlude*
14 My enemies come out at night,
snarling like vicious dogs
as they prowl the streets.
15 They scavenge for food
but go to sleep unsatisfied.*
16 But as for me, I will sing about your
power.
Each morning I will sing with joy about
your unfailing love.
For you have been my refuge,
a place of safety when I am in distress.
17 O my Strength, to you I sing praises,
for you, O God, are my refuge,
the God who shows me unfailing
love.

AMAZING FACTS

When David asked God to defeat his enemies, he knew that God would *stomp* 'em!
PSALM 60:11-12

PSALM 60

For the choir director: A psalm of David useful for teaching, regarding the time David fought Aram-naharaim and Aram-zobah, and Joab returned and killed 12,000 Edomites in the Valley of Salt. To be sung to the tune "Lily of the Testimony."*

1 You have rejected us, O God, and broken
our defenses.
You have been angry with us; now
restore us to your favor.
2 You have shaken our land and split
it open.
Seal the cracks, for the land trembles.
3 You have been very hard on us,
making us drink wine that sent us
reeling.
4 But you have raised a banner for those
who fear you—
a rallying point in the face of attack.
Interlude
5 Now rescue your beloved people.
Answer and save us by your power.
6 God has promised this by his holiness*:
"I will divide up Shechem with joy.
I will measure out the valley of Succoth.
7 Gilead is mine,
and Manasseh, too.
Ephraim, my helmet, will produce my
warriors,
and Judah, my scepter, will produce my
kings.
8 But Moab, my washbasin, will become my
servant,
and I will wipe my feet on Edom
and shout in triumph over Philistia."
9 Who will bring me into the fortified city?
Who will bring me victory over Edom?
10 Have you rejected us, O God?
Will you no longer march with our
armies?
11 Oh, please help us against our enemies,
for all human help is useless.
12 With God's help we will do mighty things,
for he will trample down our foes.

59:13 Hebrew *in Jacob*. See note on 44:4. **59:15** Or *and growl if they don't get enough*. **60:TITLE** Hebrew *miktam*. This may be a literary or musical term. **60:6** Or *in his sanctuary*.

PSALM 61

For the choir director: A psalm of David, to be accompanied by stringed instruments.

1 O God, listen to my cry!
Hear my prayer!
2 From the ends of the earth,
I cry to you for help
when my heart is overwhelmed.
Lead me to the towering rock of safety,
3 for you are my safe refuge,
a fortress where my enemies cannot reach me.
4 Let me live forever in your sanctuary,
safe beneath the shelter of your wings!
Interlude
5 For you have heard my vows, O God.
You have given me an inheritance reserved for those who fear your name.
6 Add many years to the life of the king!
May his years span the generations!
7 May he reign under God's protection forever.
May your unfailing love and faithfulness watch over him.
8 Then I will sing praises to your name forever
as I fulfill my vows each day.

PSALM 62

For Jeduthun, the choir director: A psalm of David.

1 I wait quietly before God,
for my victory comes from him.
2 He alone is my rock and my salvation,
my fortress where I will never be shaken.

3 So many enemies against one man—
all of them trying to kill me.
To them I'm just a broken-down wall
or a tottering fence.
4 They plan to topple me from my high position.
They delight in telling lies about me.
They praise me to my face
but curse me in their hearts.
Interlude
5 Let all that I am wait quietly before God,
for my hope is in him.
6 He alone is my rock and my salvation,
my fortress where I will not be shaken.
7 My victory and honor come from God alone.
He is my refuge, a rock where no enemy can reach me.
8 O my people, trust in him at all times.
Pour out your heart to him,
for God is our refuge. *Interlude*

9 Common people are as worthless as a puff of wind,
and the powerful are not what they appear to be.
If you weigh them on the scales,
together they are lighter than a breath of air.

10 Don't make your living by extortion
or put your hope in stealing.
And if your wealth increases,
don't make it the center of your life.

11 God has spoken plainly,
and I have heard it many times:
Power, O God, belongs to you;
12 unfailing love, O Lord, is yours.
Surely you repay all people
according to what they have done.

PSALM 63

A psalm of David, regarding a time when David was in the wilderness of Judah.

1 O God, you are my God;
I earnestly search for you.
My soul thirsts for you;
my whole body longs for you
in this parched and weary land
where there is no water.
2 I have seen you in your sanctuary
and gazed upon your power and glory.
3 Your unfailing love is better than life itself;
how I praise you!
4 I will praise you as long as I live,
lifting up my hands to you in prayer.
5 You satisfy me more than the richest feast.
I will praise you with songs of joy.

6 I lie awake thinking of you,
meditating on you through the night.
7 Because you are my helper,
I sing for joy in the shadow of your wings.

8 I cling to you;
your strong right hand holds me securely.

9 But those plotting to destroy me will come to ruin.
They will go down into the depths of the earth.
10 They will die by the sword
and become the food of jackals.
11 But the king will rejoice in God.
All who trust in him will praise him,
while liars will be silenced.

PSALM 64

For the choir director: A psalm of David.

1 O God, listen to my complaint.
Protect my life from my enemies' threats.
2 Hide me from the plots of this evil mob,
from this gang of wrongdoers.
3 They sharpen their tongues like swords
and aim their bitter words like arrows.
4 They shoot from ambush at the innocent,
attacking suddenly and fearlessly.
5 They encourage each other to do evil
and plan how to set their traps in secret.
"Who will ever notice?" they ask.
6 As they plot their crimes, they say,
"We have devised the perfect plan!"
Yes, the human heart and mind are cunning.

7 But God himself will shoot them with his arrows,
suddenly striking them down.
8 Their own tongues will ruin them,
and all who see them will shake their heads in scorn.
9 Then everyone will be afraid;
they will proclaim the mighty acts of God
and realize all the amazing things he does.
10 The godly will rejoice in the LORD
and find shelter in him.
And those who do what is right
will praise him.

PSALM 65

For the choir director: A song. A psalm of David.

1 What mighty praise, O God,
belongs to you in Zion.
We will fulfill our vows to you,
2 for you answer our prayers.
All of us must come to you.
3 Though we are overwhelmed by our sins,
you forgive them all.
4 What joy for those you choose to bring near,
those who live in your holy courts.
What festivities await us
inside your holy Temple.

5 You faithfully answer our prayers with awesome deeds,
O God our savior.
You are the hope of everyone on earth,
even those who sail on distant seas.
6 You formed the mountains by your power
and armed yourself with mighty strength.
7 You quieted the raging oceans
with their pounding waves
and silenced the shouting of the nations.
8 Those who live at the ends of the earth
stand in awe of your wonders.
From where the sun rises to where it sets,
you inspire shouts of joy.

9 You take care of the earth and water it,
making it rich and fertile.
The river of God has plenty of water;
it provides a bountiful harvest of grain,
for you have ordered it so.
10 You drench the plowed ground with rain,
melting the clods and leveling the ridges.
You soften the earth with showers
and bless its abundant crops.
11 You crown the year with a bountiful harvest;
even the hard pathways overflow with abundance.
12 The grasslands of the wilderness become a lush pasture,
and the hillsides blossom with joy.
13 The meadows are clothed with flocks of sheep,
and the valleys are carpeted with grain.
They all shout and sing for joy!

PSALM 66

For the choir director: A song. A psalm.

1 Shout joyful praises to God, all the earth!
2 Sing about the glory of his name!
Tell the world how glorious he is.
3 Say to God, "How awesome are your deeds!
Your enemies cringe before your mighty power.
4 Everything on earth will worship you;
they will sing your praises,
shouting your name in glorious songs."
Interlude

5 Come and see what our God has done,
what awesome miracles he performs for people!
6 He made a dry path through the Red Sea,*
and his people went across on foot.
There we rejoiced in him.
7 For by his great power he rules forever.
He watches every movement of the nations;
let no rebel rise in defiance. *Interlude*

8 Let the whole world bless our God
and loudly sing his praises.
9 Our lives are in his hands,
and he keeps our feet from stumbling.
10 You have tested us, O God;
you have purified us like silver.
11 You captured us in your net
and laid the burden of slavery on our backs.
12 Then you put a leader over us.*
We went through fire and flood,
but you brought us to a place of great abundance.

13 Now I come to your Temple with burnt offerings
to fulfill the vows I made to you—
14 yes, the sacred vows that I made
when I was in deep trouble.
15 That is why I am sacrificing burnt offerings to you—
the best of my rams as a pleasing aroma,
and a sacrifice of bulls and male goats.
Interlude

16 Come and listen, all you who fear God,
and I will tell you what he did for me.
17 For I cried out to him for help,
praising him as I spoke.
18 If I had not confessed the sin in my heart,
the Lord would not have listened.
19 But God did listen!
He paid attention to my prayer.
20 Praise God, who did not ignore my prayer
or withdraw his unfailing love from me.

PSALM 67

For the choir director: A song. A psalm, to be accompanied by stringed instruments.

1 May God be merciful and bless us.
May his face smile with favor on us.
Interlude

2 May your ways be known throughout the earth,
your saving power among people everywhere.
3 May the nations praise you, O God.
Yes, may all the nations praise you.
4 Let the whole world sing for joy,
because you govern the nations with justice
and guide the people of the whole world. *Interlude*

5 May the nations praise you, O God.
Yes, may all the nations praise you.
6 Then the earth will yield its harvests,
and God, our God, will richly bless us.
7 Yes, God will bless us,
and people all over the world will fear him.

PSALM 68

For the choir director: A song. A psalm of David.

1 Rise up, O God, and scatter your enemies.
Let those who hate God run for their lives.
2 Blow them away like smoke.
Melt them like wax in a fire.
Let the wicked perish in the presence of God.
3 But let the godly rejoice.
Let them be glad in God's presence.
Let them be filled with joy.
4 Sing praises to God and to his name!

66:6 Hebrew *the sea.* **66:12** Or *You made people ride over our heads.*

Sing loud praises to him who rides the clouds.
His name is the LORD—
rejoice in his presence!

5 Father to the fatherless, defender of widows—
this is God, whose dwelling is holy.
6 God places the lonely in families;
he sets the prisoners free and gives them joy.
But he makes the rebellious live in a sun-scorched land.

7 O God, when you led your people out from Egypt,
when you marched through the dry wasteland, *Interlude*
8 the earth trembled, and the heavens poured down rain
before you, the God of Sinai,
before God, the God of Israel.
9 You sent abundant rain, O God,
to refresh the weary land.
10 There your people finally settled,
and with a bountiful harvest, O God,
you provided for your needy people.

11 The Lord gives the word,
and a great army* brings the good news.
12 Enemy kings and their armies flee,
while the women of Israel divide the plunder.
13 Even those who lived among the sheepfolds found treasures—
doves with wings of silver
and feathers of gold.
14 The Almighty scattered the enemy kings
like a blowing snowstorm on Mount Zalmon.

15 The mountains of Bashan are majestic,
with many peaks stretching high into the sky.
16 Why do you look with envy, O rugged mountains,
at Mount Zion, where God has chosen to live,
where the LORD himself will live forever?

17 Surrounded by unnumbered thousands of chariots,
the Lord came from Mount Sinai into his sanctuary.
18 When you ascended to the heights,
you led a crowd of captives.
You received gifts from the people,
even from those who rebelled against you.
Now the LORD God will live among us there.

19 Praise the Lord; praise God our savior!
For each day he carries us in his arms. *Interlude*
20 Our God is a God who saves!
The Sovereign LORD rescues us from death.

21 But God will smash the heads of his enemies,
crushing the skulls of those who love their guilty ways.
22 The Lord says, "I will bring my enemies down from Bashan;
I will bring them up from the depths of the sea.
23 You, my people, will wash your feet in their blood,
and even your dogs will get their share!"

24 Your procession has come into view, O God—
the procession of my God and King as he goes into the sanctuary.
25 Singers are in front, musicians behind;
between them are young women playing tambourines.
26 Praise God, all you people of Israel;
praise the LORD, the source of Israel's life.
27 Look, the little tribe of Benjamin leads the way.
Then comes a great throng of rulers from Judah
and all the rulers of Zebulun and Naphtali.

28 Summon your might, O God.
Display your power, O God, as you have in the past.
29 The kings of the earth are bringing tribute to your Temple in Jerusalem.
30 Rebuke these enemy nations—

68:11 Or *a host of women.*

these wild animals lurking in the reeds,
this herd of bulls among the weaker calves.
Make them bring bars of silver in humble tribute.
Scatter the nations that delight in war.
31 Let Egypt come with gifts of precious metals*;
let Ethiopia* bow in submission to God.
32 Sing to God, you kingdoms of the earth.
Sing praises to the Lord. *Interlude*
33 Sing to the one who rides across the ancient heavens,
his mighty voice thundering from the sky.
34 Tell everyone about God's power.
His majesty shines down on Israel;
his strength is mighty in the heavens.
35 God is awesome in his sanctuary.
The God of Israel gives power and strength to his people.

Praise be to God!

PSALM 69

For the choir director: A psalm of David, to be sung to the tune "Lilies."

1 Save me, O God,
for the floodwaters are up to my neck.
2 Deeper and deeper I sink into the mire;
I can't find a foothold.
I am in deep water,
and the floods overwhelm me.
3 I am exhausted from crying for help;
my throat is parched.
My eyes are swollen with weeping,
waiting for my God to help me.
4 Those who hate me without cause
outnumber the hairs on my head.
Many enemies try to destroy me with lies,
demanding that I give back what I didn't steal.

5 O God, you know how foolish I am;
my sins cannot be hidden from you.
6 Don't let those who trust in you be ashamed because of me,
O Sovereign LORD of Heaven's Armies.
Don't let me cause them to be humiliated,
O God of Israel.

Activity Overload

Richard loved to be busy and couldn't stand an afternoon with nothing to do. Richard was in four school clubs, played an instrument, sang in the choir, *and* played football. He just didn't know how to say no! When the youth leader asked him to hand out flyers on a Saturday, Richard immediately agreed. Later he realized that he had activities morning, afternoon, and evening on the same day. The only time he could pass out flyers would be at 6 A.M. Finally Richard is beginning to feel overwhelmed. What should he do? Look at Psalm 69:15-17.

7 For I endure insults for your sake;
humiliation is written all over my face.
8 Even my own brothers pretend they don't know me;
they treat me like a stranger.

68:31a Or *of rich cloth.* **68:31b** Hebrew *Cush.*

9 Passion for your house has consumed me,
and the insults of those who insult you
have fallen on me.
10 When I weep and fast,
they scoff at me.
11 When I dress in burlap to show sorrow,
they make fun of me.
12 I am the favorite topic of town gossip,
and all the drunks sing about me.

13 But I keep praying to you, LORD,
hoping this time you will show me
favor.
In your unfailing love, O God,
answer my prayer with your sure
salvation.
14 Rescue me from the mud;
don't let me sink any deeper!
Save me from those who hate me,
and pull me from these deep waters.
15 Don't let the floods overwhelm me,
or the deep waters swallow me,
or the pit of death devour me.

16 Answer my prayers, O LORD,
for your unfailing love is wonderful.
Take care of me,
for your mercy is so plentiful.
17 Don't hide from your servant;
answer me quickly, for I am in deep
trouble!
18 Come and redeem me;
free me from my enemies.

19 You know of my shame, scorn, and disgrace.
You see all that my enemies are doing.
20 Their insults have broken my heart,
and I am in despair.
If only one person would show some pity;
if only one would turn and comfort me.
21 But instead, they give me poison* for
food;
they offer me sour wine for my thirst.

22 Let the bountiful table set before them
become a snare
and their prosperity become a trap.*
23 Let their eyes go blind so they cannot see,
and make their bodies shake
continually.*
24 Pour out your fury on them;
consume them with your burning
anger.
25 Let their homes become desolate
and their tents be deserted.
26 To the one you have punished, they add
insult to injury;
they add to the pain of those you have
hurt.
27 Pile their sins up high,
and don't let them go free.
28 Erase their names from the Book of Life;
don't let them be counted among the
righteous.

29 I am suffering and in pain.
Rescue me, O God, by your saving
power.

30 Then I will praise God's name with
singing,
and I will honor him with thanksgiving.
31 For this will please the LORD more than
sacrificing cattle,
more than presenting a bull with its
horns and hooves.
32 The humble will see their God at work
and be glad.
Let all who seek God's help be
encouraged.
33 For the LORD hears the cries of the needy;
he does not despise his imprisoned
people.

34 Praise him, O heaven and earth,
the seas and all that move in them.
35 For God will save Jerusalem*
and rebuild the towns of Judah.
His people will live there
and settle in their own land.
36 The descendants of those who obey him
will inherit the land,
and those who love him will live there
in safety.

PSALM 70

For the choir director: A psalm of David, asking God to remember him.

1 Please, God, rescue me!
Come quickly, LORD, and help me.
2 May those who try to kill me
be humiliated and put to shame.

69:21 Or *gall*. **69:22** Greek version reads *Let their bountiful table set before them become a snare, / a trap that makes them think all is well. / Let their blessings cause them to stumble, / and let them get what they deserve*. Compare Rom 11:9. **69:23** Greek version reads *and let their backs be bent forever*. Compare Rom 11:10. **69:35** Hebrew *Zion*.

May those who take delight in my trouble
be turned back in disgrace.
3 Let them be horrified by their shame,
for they said, "Aha! We've got him
now!"
4 But may all who search for you
be filled with joy and gladness in you.
May those who love your salvation
repeatedly shout, "God is great!"
5 But as for me, I am poor and needy;
please hurry to my aid, O God.
You are my helper and my savior;
O LORD, do not delay.

PSALM 71

1 O LORD, I have come to you for protection;
don't let me be disgraced.
2 Save me and rescue me,
for you do what is right.
Turn your ear to listen to me,
and set me free.
3 Be my rock of safety
where I can always hide.
Give the order to save me,
for you are my rock and my fortress.
4 My God, rescue me from the power of the
wicked,
from the clutches of cruel oppressors.
5 O Lord, you alone are my hope.
I've trusted you, O LORD, from
childhood.
6 Yes, you have been with me from birth;
from my mother's womb you have
cared for me.
No wonder I am always praising you!
7 My life is an example to many,
because you have been my strength and
protection.
8 That is why I can never stop praising you;
I declare your glory all day long.
9 And now, in my old age, don't set me
aside.
Don't abandon me when my strength
is failing.
10 For my enemies are whispering
against me.
They are plotting together to kill me.
11 They say, "God has abandoned him.
Let's go and get him,
for no one will help him now."
12 O God, don't stay away.
My God, please hurry to help me.
13 Bring disgrace and destruction on my
accusers.
Humiliate and shame those who want
to harm me.
14 But I will keep on hoping for your help;
I will praise you more and more.
15 I will tell everyone about your
righteousness.
All day long I will proclaim your saving
power,
though I am not skilled with words.*
16 I will praise your mighty deeds,
O Sovereign LORD.
I will tell everyone that you alone
are just.
17 O God, you have taught me from my
earliest childhood,
and I constantly tell others about the
wonderful things you do.
18 Now that I am old and gray,
do not abandon me, O God.
Let me proclaim your power to this new
generation,
your mighty miracles to all who come
after me.
19 Your righteousness, O God, reaches to the
highest heavens.
You have done such wonderful things.
Who can compare with you, O God?
20 You have allowed me to suffer much
hardship,
but you will restore me to life again
and lift me up from the depths of the
earth.
21 You will restore me to even greater honor
and comfort me once again.
22 Then I will praise you with music on the
harp,
because you are faithful to your
promises, O my God.
I will sing praises to you with a lyre,
O Holy One of Israel.
23 I will shout for joy and sing your praises,
for you have ransomed me.
24 I will tell about your righteous deeds
all day long,
for everyone who tried to hurt me
has been shamed and humiliated.

71:15 Or *though I cannot count it.*

PSALM 72

A psalm of Solomon.

1 Give your love of justice to the king,
O God,
and righteousness to the king's son.
2 Help him judge your people in the right
way;
let the poor always be treated fairly.
3 May the mountains yield prosperity
for all,
and may the hills be fruitful.
4 Help him to defend the poor,
to rescue the children of the needy,
and to crush their oppressors.
5 May they fear you* as long as the sun
shines,
as long as the moon remains in the sky.
Yes, forever!
6 May the king's rule be refreshing like
spring rain on freshly cut grass,
like the showers that water the earth.
7 May all the godly flourish during his
reign.
May there be abundant prosperity until
the moon is no more.
8 May he reign from sea to sea,
and from the Euphrates River* to the
ends of the earth.
9 Desert nomads will bow before him;
his enemies will fall before him in
the dust.
10 The western kings of Tarshish and other
distant lands
will bring him tribute.
The eastern kings of Sheba and Seba
will bring him gifts.
11 All kings will bow before him,
and all nations will serve him.
12 He will rescue the poor when they cry
to him;
he will help the oppressed, who have
no one to defend them.
13 He feels pity for the weak and the needy,
and he will rescue them.
14 He will redeem them from oppression
and violence,
for their lives are precious to him.
15 Long live the king!
May the gold of Sheba be given to him.
May the people always pray for him
and bless him all day long.
16 May there be abundant grain throughout
the land,
flourishing even on the hilltops.
May the fruit trees flourish like the trees
of Lebanon,
and may the people thrive like grass
in a field.
17 May the king's name endure forever;
may it continue as long as the sun
shines.
May all nations be blessed through him
and bring him praise.
18 Praise the LORD God, the God of Israel,
who alone does such wonderful
things.
19 Praise his glorious name forever!
Let the whole earth be filled with
his glory.
Amen and amen!
20 (This ends the prayers of David son
of Jesse.)

BOOK THREE (Psalms 73–89)

PSALM 73

A psalm of Asaph.

1 Truly God is good to Israel,
to those whose hearts are pure.
2 But as for me, I almost lost my footing.
My feet were slipping, and I was
almost gone.
3 For I envied the proud
when I saw them prosper despite their
wickedness.
4 They seem to live such painless lives;
their bodies are so healthy and strong.
5 They don't have troubles like other
people;
they're not plagued with problems like
everyone else.
6 They wear pride like a jeweled necklace
and clothe themselves with cruelty.
7 These fat cats have everything
their hearts could ever wish for!
8 They scoff and speak only evil;
in their pride they seek to crush others.
9 They boast against the very heavens,
and their words strut throughout
the earth.

72:5 Greek version reads *May they endure.* 72:8 Hebrew *the river.*

10 And so the people are dismayed and
confused,
drinking in all their words.
11 "What does God know?" they ask.
"Does the Most High even know what's
happening?"
12 Look at these wicked people—
enjoying a life of ease while their riches
multiply.

13 Did I keep my heart pure for nothing?
Did I keep myself innocent for no
reason?
14 I get nothing but trouble all day long;
every morning brings me pain.

What can I count on when I'm feeling weak?

My health may fail, and my spirit may grow weak, but God remains the strength of my heart; he is mine forever. PSALM 73:26

15 If I had really spoken this way to others,
I would have been a traitor to your
people.
16 So I tried to understand why the wicked
prosper.
But what a difficult task it is!
17 Then I went into your sanctuary, O God,
and I finally understood the destiny of
the wicked.
18 Truly, you put them on a slippery path
and send them sliding over the cliff to
destruction.
19 In an instant they are destroyed,
completely swept away by terrors.
20 When you arise, O Lord,
you will laugh at their silly ideas
as a person laughs at dreams in the
morning.

21 Then I realized that my heart was bitter,
and I was all torn up inside.
22 I was so foolish and ignorant—
I must have seemed like a senseless
animal to you.
23 Yet I still belong to you;
you hold my right hand.
24 You guide me with your counsel,
leading me to a glorious destiny.
25 Whom have I in heaven but you?
I desire you more than anything
on earth.
26 My health may fail, and my spirit may
grow weak,
but God remains the strength
of my heart;
he is mine forever.

27 Those who desert him will perish,
for you destroy those who
abandon you.
28 But as for me, how good it is to be
near God!
I have made the Sovereign LORD
my shelter,
and I will tell everyone about the
wonderful things you do.

PSALM 74

A psalm of Asaph.*

1 O God, why have you rejected us so long?
Why is your anger so intense against
the sheep of your own pasture?
2 Remember that we are the people you
chose long ago,
the tribe you redeemed as your own
special possession!
And remember Jerusalem,* your home
here on earth.
3 Walk through the awful ruins of the city;
see how the enemy has destroyed your
sanctuary.

4 There your enemies shouted their
victorious battle cries;
there they set up their battle standards.
5 They swung their axes
like woodcutters in a forest.
6 With axes and picks,
they smashed the carved paneling.
7 They burned your sanctuary to the
ground.
They defiled the place that bears
your name.

74:TITLE Hebrew *maskil*. This may be a literary or musical term. **74:2** Hebrew *Mount Zion*.

8 Then they thought, "Let's destroy
everything!"
So they burned down all the places
where God was worshiped.

9 We no longer see your miraculous signs.
All the prophets are gone,
and no one can tell us when it will end.
10 How long, O God, will you allow our
enemies to insult you?
Will you let them dishonor your name
forever?
11 Why do you hold back your strong right
hand?
Unleash your powerful fist and
destroy them.

12 You, O God, are my king from ages past,
bringing salvation to the earth.
13 You split the sea by your strength
and smashed the heads of the sea
monsters.
14 You crushed the heads of Leviathan*
and let the desert animals eat him.
15 You caused the springs and streams to
gush forth,
and you dried up rivers that never
run dry.
16 Both day and night belong to you;
you made the starlight* and the sun.
17 You set the boundaries of the earth,
and you made both summer and
winter.

18 See how these enemies insult you, LORD.
A foolish nation has dishonored your
name.
19 Don't let these wild beasts destroy your
turtledoves.
Don't forget your suffering people
forever.

20 Remember your covenant promises,
for the land is full of darkness and
violence!
21 Don't let the downtrodden be humiliated
again.
Instead, let the poor and needy praise
your name.

22 Arise, O God, and defend your cause.
Remember how these fools insult you
all day long.
23 Don't overlook what your enemies
have said
or their growing uproar.

PSALM 75

For the choir director: A psalm of Asaph. A song to be sung to the tune "Do Not Destroy!"

1 We thank you, O God!
We give thanks because you are near.
People everywhere tell of your
wonderful deeds.

2 God says, "At the time I have planned,
I will bring justice against the wicked.
3 When the earth quakes and its people live
in turmoil,
I am the one who keeps its foundations
firm. *Interlude*

4 "I warned the proud, 'Stop your boasting!'
I told the wicked, 'Don't raise your
fists!
5 Don't raise your fists in defiance at the
heavens
or speak with such arrogance.'"
6 For no one on earth—from east or west,
or even from the wilderness—
should raise a defiant fist.*
7 It is God alone who judges;
he decides who will rise and who will
fall.
8 For the LORD holds a cup in his hand
that is full of foaming wine mixed with
spices.
He pours out the wine in judgment,
and all the wicked must drink it,
draining it to the dregs.

9 But as for me, I will always proclaim what
God has done;
I will sing praises to the God of Jacob.
10 For God says, "I will break the strength
of the wicked,
but I will increase the power of the
godly."

PSALM 76

For the choir director: A psalm of Asaph. A song to be accompanied by stringed instruments.

1 God is honored in Judah;
his name is great in Israel.

74:14 The identification of Leviathan is disputed, ranging from an earthly creature to a mythical sea monster in ancient literature.
74:16 Or *moon;* Hebrew reads *light.* **75:6** Hebrew *should lift.*

2 Jerusalem* is where he lives;
Mount Zion is his home.
3 There he has broken the fiery arrows
of the enemy,
the shields and swords and weapons
of war. *Interlude*

4 You are glorious and more majestic
than the everlasting mountains.*
5 Our boldest enemies have been
plundered.
They lie before us in the sleep of death.
No warrior could lift a hand against us.
6 At the blast of your breath, O God of
Jacob,
their horses and chariots lay still.

7 No wonder you are greatly feared!
Who can stand before you when your
anger explodes?
8 From heaven you sentenced your enemies;
the earth trembled and stood silent
before you.
9 You stand up to judge those who do evil,
O God,
and to rescue the oppressed of the
earth. *Interlude*
10 Human defiance only enhances your glory,
for you use it as a weapon.*

11 Make vows to the LORD your God, and
keep them.
Let everyone bring tribute to the
Awesome One.
12 For he breaks the pride of princes,
and the kings of the earth fear him.

PSALM 77

For Jeduthun, the choir director: A psalm of Asaph.

1 I cry out to God; yes, I shout.
Oh, that God would listen to me!
2 When I was in deep trouble,
I searched for the Lord.
All night long I prayed, with hands lifted
toward heaven,
but my soul was not comforted.
3 I think of God, and I moan,
overwhelmed with longing for his help.
Interlude

4 You don't let me sleep.
I am too distressed even to pray!
5 I think of the good old days,
long since ended,
6 when my nights were filled with joyful
songs.
I search my soul and ponder the
difference now.
7 Has the Lord rejected me forever?
Will he never again be kind to me?
8 Is his unfailing love gone forever?
Have his promises permanently failed?
9 Has God forgotten to be gracious?
Has he slammed the door on his
compassion? *Interlude*

10 And I said, "This is my fate;
the Most High has turned his hand
against me."
11 But then I recall all you have done,
O LORD;
I remember your wonderful deeds of
long ago.
12 They are constantly in my thoughts.
I cannot stop thinking about your
mighty works.

13 O God, your ways are holy.
Is there any god as mighty as you?
14 You are the God of great wonders!
You demonstrate your awesome power
among the nations.
15 By your strong arm, you redeemed your
people,
the descendants of Jacob and Joseph.
Interlude

16 When the Red Sea* saw you, O God,
its waters looked and trembled!
The sea quaked to its very depths.
17 The clouds poured down rain;
the thunder rumbled in the sky.
Your arrows of lightning flashed.
18 Your thunder roared from the whirlwind;
the lightning lit up the world!
The earth trembled and shook.
19 Your road led through the sea,
your pathway through the mighty
waters—
a pathway no one knew was there!
20 You led your people along that road like a
flock of sheep,
with Moses and Aaron as their
shepherds.

76:2 Hebrew *Salem*, another name for Jerusalem. **76:4** As in Greek version; Hebrew reads *than mountains filled with beasts of prey*. **76:10** The meaning of the Hebrew is uncertain. **77:16** Hebrew *the waters*.

PSALM 78

A psalm of Asaph.*

1 O my people, listen to my instructions.
Open your ears to what I am saying,
2 for I will speak to you in a parable.
I will teach you hidden lessons from our past—
3 stories we have heard and known,
stories our ancestors handed down to us.
4 We will not hide these truths from our children;
we will tell the next generation
about the glorious deeds of the LORD,
about his power and his mighty wonders.
5 For he issued his laws to Jacob;
he gave his instructions to Israel.
He commanded our ancestors
to teach them to their children,
6 so the next generation might know them—
even the children not yet born—
and they in turn will teach their own children.
7 So each generation should set its hope anew on God,
not forgetting his glorious miracles
and obeying his commands.
8 Then they will not be like their ancestors—
stubborn, rebellious, and unfaithful,
refusing to give their hearts to God.

9 The warriors of Ephraim, though armed with bows,
turned their backs and fled on the day of battle.
10 They did not keep God's covenant
and refused to live by his instructions.
11 They forgot what he had done—
the great wonders he had shown them,
12 the miracles he did for their ancestors
on the plain of Zoan in the land of Egypt.
13 For he divided the sea and led them through,
making the water stand up like walls!
14 In the daytime he led them by a cloud,
and all night by a pillar of fire.
15 He split open the rocks in the wilderness
to give them water, as from a gushing spring.
16 He made streams pour from the rock,
making the waters flow down like a river!

17 Yet they kept on sinning against him,
rebelling against the Most High in the desert.
18 They stubbornly tested God in their hearts,
demanding the foods they craved.
19 They even spoke against God himself, saying,
"God can't give us food in the wilderness.
20 Yes, he can strike a rock so water gushes out,
but he can't give his people bread and meat."
21 When the LORD heard them, he was furious.
The fire of his wrath burned against Jacob.
Yes, his anger rose against Israel,
22 for they did not believe God
or trust him to care for them.
23 But he commanded the skies to open;
he opened the doors of heaven.
24 He rained down manna for them to eat;
he gave them bread from heaven.
25 They ate the food of angels!
God gave them all they could hold.
26 He released the east wind in the heavens
and guided the south wind by his mighty power.
27 He rained down meat as thick as dust—
birds as plentiful as the sand on the seashore!
28 He caused the birds to fall within their camp
and all around their tents.
29 The people ate their fill.
He gave them what they craved.
30 But before they satisfied their craving,
while the meat was yet in their mouths,
31 the anger of God rose against them,
and he killed their strongest men.
He struck down the finest of Israel's young men.

78:TITLE Hebrew *maskil*. This may be a literary or musical term.

32 But in spite of this, the people kept
sinning.
Despite his wonders, they refused
to trust him.
33 So he ended their lives in failure,
their years in terror.
34 When God began killing them,
they finally sought him.
They repented and took God seriously.
35 Then they remembered that God was
their rock,
that God Most High* was their
redeemer.
36 But all they gave him was lip service;
they lied to him with their tongues.
37 Their hearts were not loyal to him.
They did not keep his covenant.
38 Yet he was merciful and forgave their sins
and did not destroy them all.
Many times he held back his anger
and did not unleash his fury!
39 For he remembered that they were merely
mortal,
gone like a breath of wind that never
returns.
40 Oh, how often they rebelled against him
in the wilderness
and grieved his heart in that dry
wasteland.
41 Again and again they tested God's
patience
and provoked the Holy One of Israel.
42 They did not remember his power
and how he rescued them from their
enemies.
43 They did not remember his miraculous
signs in Egypt,
his wonders on the plain of Zoan.
44 For he turned their rivers into blood,
so no one could drink from the
streams.
45 He sent vast swarms of flies to consume
them
and hordes of frogs to ruin them.
46 He gave their crops to caterpillars;
their harvest was consumed by locusts.
47 He destroyed their grapevines with hail
and shattered their sycamore-figs with
sleet.
48 He abandoned their cattle to the hail,
their livestock to bolts of lightning.

78:35 Hebrew *El-Elyon*. **78:51** Hebrew *in the tents of Ham*.

49 He loosed on them his fierce anger—
all his fury, rage, and hostility.
He dispatched against them
a band of destroying angels.
50 He turned his anger against them;
he did not spare the Egyptians' lives
but ravaged them with the plague.
51 He killed the oldest son in each Egyptian
family,
the flower of youth throughout the
land of Egypt.*
52 But he led his own people like a flock
of sheep,
guiding them safely through the
wilderness.
53 He kept them safe so they were not afraid;
but the sea covered their enemies.
54 He brought them to the border of his
holy land,

to this land of hills he had won for them.
55 He drove out the nations before them;
he gave them their inheritance by lot.
He settled the tribes of Israel into their homes.
56 But they kept testing and rebelling against God Most High.
They did not obey his laws.
57 They turned back and were as faithless as their parents.
They were as undependable as a crooked bow.
58 They angered God by building shrines to other gods;
they made him jealous with their idols.
59 When God heard them, he was very angry,
and he completely rejected Israel.
60 Then he abandoned his dwelling at Shiloh,
the Tabernacle where he had lived among the people.
61 He allowed the Ark of his might to be captured;
he surrendered his glory into enemy hands.
62 He gave his people over to be butchered by the sword,
because he was so angry with his own people—his special possession.
63 Their young men were killed by fire;
their young women died before singing their wedding songs.
64 Their priests were slaughtered,
and their widows could not mourn their deaths.
65 Then the Lord rose up as though waking from sleep,
like a warrior aroused from a drunken stupor.
66 He routed his enemies
and sent them to eternal shame.
67 But he rejected Joseph's descendants;
he did not choose the tribe of Ephraim.
68 He chose instead the tribe of Judah,
and Mount Zion, which he loved.
69 There he built his sanctuary as high as the heavens,
as solid and enduring as the earth.
70 He chose his servant David,
calling him from the sheep pens.
71 He took David from tending the ewes and lambs
and made him the shepherd of Jacob's descendants—
God's own people, Israel.
72 He cared for them with a true heart
and led them with skillful hands.

PSALM 79

A psalm of Asaph.

1 O God, pagan nations have conquered your land,
your special possession.
They have defiled your holy Temple
and made Jerusalem a heap of ruins.
2 They have left the bodies of your servants
as food for the birds of heaven.
The flesh of your godly ones
has become food for the wild animals.
3 Blood has flowed like water all around Jerusalem;
no one is left to bury the dead.
4 We are mocked by our neighbors,
an object of scorn and derision to those around us.
5 O LORD, how long will you be angry with us? Forever?
How long will your jealousy burn like fire?
6 Pour out your wrath on the nations that refuse to acknowledge you—
on kingdoms that do not call upon your name.
7 For they have devoured your people Israel,*
making the land a desolate wilderness.
8 Do not hold us guilty for the sins of our ancestors!
Let your compassion quickly meet our needs,
for we are on the brink of despair.
9 Help us, O God of our salvation!
Help us for the glory of your name.
Save us and forgive our sins
for the honor of your name.
10 Why should pagan nations be allowed to scoff,
asking, "Where is their God?"

79:7 Hebrew *devoured Jacob*. See note on 44:4.

Show us your vengeance against the nations,
for they have spilled the blood of your servants.
11 Listen to the moaning of the prisoners.
Demonstrate your great power by saving those condemned to die.

12 O Lord, pay back our neighbors seven times
for the scorn they have hurled at you.
13 Then we your people, the sheep of your pasture,
will thank you forever and ever,
praising your greatness from generation to generation.

PSALM 80

For the choir director: A psalm of Asaph, to be sung to the tune "Lilies of the Covenant."

1 Please listen, O Shepherd of Israel,
you who lead Joseph's descendants like a flock.
O God, enthroned above the cherubim,
display your radiant glory
2 to Ephraim, Benjamin, and Manasseh.
Show us your mighty power.
Come to rescue us!

3 Turn us again to yourself, O God.
Make your face shine down upon us.
Only then will we be saved.
4 O LORD God of Heaven's Armies,
how long will you be angry with our prayers?
5 You have fed us with sorrow
and made us drink tears by the bucketful.
6 You have made us the scorn* of neighboring nations.
Our enemies treat us as a joke.

7 Turn us again to yourself, O God of Heaven's Armies.
Make your face shine down upon us.
Only then will we be saved.
8 You brought us from Egypt like a grapevine;
you drove away the pagan nations and transplanted us into your land.
9 You cleared the ground for us,
and we took root and filled the land.
10 Our shade covered the mountains;
our branches covered the mighty cedars.
11 We spread our branches west to the Mediterranean Sea;
our shoots spread east to the Euphrates River.*
12 But now, why have you broken down our walls
so that all who pass by may steal our fruit?
13 The wild boar from the forest devours it,
and the wild animals feed on it.

14 Come back, we beg you, O God of Heaven's Armies.
Look down from heaven and see our plight.
Take care of this grapevine
15 that you yourself have planted,
this son you have raised for yourself.
16 For we are chopped up and burned by our enemies.
May they perish at the sight of your frown.
17 Strengthen the man you love,
the son of your choice.
18 Then we will never abandon you again.
Revive us so we can call on your name once more.

19 Turn us again to yourself, O LORD God of Heaven's Armies.
Make your face shine down upon us.
Only then will we be saved.

PSALM 81

*For the choir director: A psalm of Asaph, to be accompanied by a stringed instrument.**

1 Sing praises to God, our strength.
Sing to the God of Jacob.
2 Sing! Beat the tambourine.
Play the sweet lyre and the harp.
3 Blow the ram's horn at new moon,
and again at full moon to call a festival!
4 For this is required by the decrees of Israel;
it is a regulation of the God of Jacob.
5 He made it a law for Israel*
when he attacked Egypt to set us free.

80:6 As in Syriac version; Hebrew reads *the strife*. **80:11** Hebrew *west to the sea, . . . east to the river*. **81:TITLE** Hebrew *according to the gittith*. **81:5** Hebrew *for Joseph*.

I heard an unknown voice say,
6 "Now I will take the load from your shoulders;
I will free your hands from their heavy tasks.
7 You cried to me in trouble, and I saved you;
I answered out of the thundercloud
and tested your faith when there was no water at Meribah. *Interlude*

8 "Listen to me, O my people, while I give you stern warnings.
O Israel, if you would only listen to me!
9 You must never have a foreign god;
you must not bow down before a false god.
10 For it was I, the LORD your God,
who rescued you from the land of Egypt.
Open your mouth wide, and I will fill it with good things.

11 "But no, my people wouldn't listen.
Israel did not want me around.
12 So I let them follow their own stubborn desires,
living according to their own ideas.
13 Oh, that my people would listen to me!
Oh, that Israel would follow me, walking in my paths!
14 How quickly I would then subdue their enemies!
How soon my hands would be upon their foes!
15 Those who hate the LORD would cringe before him;
they would be doomed forever.
16 But I would feed you with the finest wheat.
I would satisfy you with wild honey from the rock."

MAKING FUN

Travis and his friends are the oldest kids in school. They always sit at the same lunch table. They spend their lunch-time goofing around, telling jokes, and sometimes eating. Recently, some of Travis's friends have been picking on a younger student. They seem to enjoy making fun of him and calling him names. "What a little wimp," Karl said. "He never talks. No wonder he sits by himself." Travis knows this made the boy embarrassed and unhappy, but these are his friends. For help in knowing what Travis should do, read Psalm 82:4.

PSALM 82

A psalm of Asaph.

1 God presides over heaven's court;
he pronounces judgment on the heavenly beings:
2 "How long will you hand down unjust decisions
by favoring the wicked? *Interlude*
3 "Give justice to the poor and the orphan;
uphold the rights of the oppressed and the destitute.
4 Rescue the poor and helpless;
deliver them from the grasp of evil people.
5 But these oppressors know nothing;
they are so ignorant!
They wander about in darkness,

while the whole world is shaken
to the core.
6 I say, 'You are gods;
you are all children of the Most High.
7 But you will die like mere mortals
and fall like every other ruler.'"

8 Rise up, O God, and judge the earth,
for all the nations belong to you.

PSALM 83

A song. A psalm of Asaph.

1 O God, do not be silent!
Do not be deaf.
Do not be quiet, O God.
2 Don't you hear the uproar of your
enemies?
Don't you see that your arrogant
enemies are rising up?
3 They devise crafty schemes against your
people;
they conspire against your precious
ones.
4 "Come," they say, "let us wipe out Israel as
a nation.
We will destroy the very memory of its
existence."
5 Yes, this was their unanimous decision.
They signed a treaty as allies against
you—
6 these Edomites and Ishmaelites;
Moabites and Hagrites;
7 Gebalites, Ammonites, and Amalekites;
and people from Philistia and Tyre.
8 Assyria has joined them, too,
and is allied with the descendants
of Lot. *Interlude*

9 Do to them as you did to the Midianites
and as you did to Sisera and Jabin at the
Kishon River.
10 They were destroyed at Endor,
and their decaying corpses fertilized
the soil.
11 Let their mighty nobles die as Oreb and
Zeeb did.
Let all their princes die like Zebah and
Zalmunna,
12 for they said, "Let us seize for our own use
these pasturelands of God!"
13 O my God, scatter them like tumbleweed,
like chaff before the wind!
14 As a fire burns a forest
and as a flame sets mountains
ablaze,
15 chase them with your fierce storm;
terrify them with your tempest.
16 Utterly disgrace them
until they submit to your name,
O LORD.
17 Let them be ashamed and terrified
forever.
Let them die in disgrace.
18 Then they will learn that you alone are
called the LORD,
that you alone are the Most High,
supreme over all the earth.

PSALM 84

*For the choir director: A psalm of the descendants of Korah, to be accompanied by a stringed instrument.**

1 How lovely is your dwelling place,
O LORD of Heaven's Armies.
2 I long, yes, I faint with longing
to enter the courts of the LORD.
With my whole being, body and soul,
I will shout joyfully to the living
God.
3 Even the sparrow finds a home,
and the swallow builds her nest and
raises her young
at a place near your altar,
O LORD of Heaven's Armies, my King
and my God!
4 What joy for those who can live in your
house,
always singing your praises.
Interlude

5 What joy for those whose strength comes
from the LORD,
who have set their minds on a
pilgrimage to Jerusalem.
6 When they walk through the Valley
of Weeping,*
it will become a place of refreshing
springs.
The autumn rains will clothe it with
blessings.
7 They will continue to grow stronger,
and each of them will appear before
God in Jerusalem.*

84:TITLE Hebrew *according to the gittith.* **84:6** Or *Valley of Poplars;* Hebrew reads *valley of Baca.* **84:7** Hebrew *Zion.*

8 O LORD God of Heaven's Armies, hear my prayer.
Listen, O God of Jacob. *Interlude*

9 O God, look with favor upon the king, our shield!
Show favor to the one you have anointed.

10 A single day in your courts
is better than a thousand anywhere else!
I would rather be a gatekeeper in the house of my God
than live the good life in the homes of the wicked.

11 For the LORD God is our sun and our shield.
He gives us grace and glory.
The LORD will withhold no good thing from those who do what is right.

12 O LORD of Heaven's Armies,
what joy for those who trust in you.

PSALM 85

For the choir director: A psalm of the descendants of Korah.

1 LORD, you poured out blessings on your land!
You restored the fortunes of Israel.*

2 You forgave the guilt of your people—
yes, you covered all their sins. *Interlude*

3 You held back your fury.
You kept back your blazing anger.

4 Now restore us again, O God of our salvation.
Put aside your anger against us once more.

5 Will you be angry with us always?
Will you prolong your wrath to all generations?

6 Won't you revive us again,
so your people can rejoice in you?

7 Show us your unfailing love, O LORD,
and grant us your salvation.

8 I listen carefully to what God the LORD is saying,
for he speaks peace to his faithful people.
But let them not return to their foolish ways.

9 Surely his salvation is near to those who fear him,
so our land will be filled with his glory.

10 Unfailing love and truth have met together.
Righteousness and peace have kissed!

11 Truth springs up from the earth,
and righteousness smiles down from heaven.

12 Yes, the LORD pours down his blessings.
Our land will yield its bountiful harvest.

13 Righteousness goes as a herald before him,
preparing the way for his steps.

PSALM 86

A prayer of David.

1 Bend down, O LORD, and hear my prayer;
answer me, for I need your help.

2 Protect me, for I am devoted to you.
Save me, for I serve you and trust you.
You are my God.

3 Be merciful to me, O Lord,
for I am calling on you constantly.

4 Give me happiness, O Lord,
for I give myself to you.

5 O Lord, you are so good, so ready to forgive,
so full of unfailing love for all who ask for your help.

6 Listen closely to my prayer, O LORD;
hear my urgent cry.

7 I will call to you whenever I'm in trouble,
and you will answer me.

8 No pagan god is like you, O Lord.
None can do what you do!

9 All the nations you made
will come and bow before you, Lord;
they will praise your holy name.

10 For you are great and perform wonderful deeds.
You alone are God.

11 Teach me your ways, O LORD,
that I may live according to your truth!
Grant me purity of heart,
so that I may honor you.

85:1 Hebrew *of Jacob*. See note on 44:4.

12 With all my heart I will praise you, O Lord
my God.
I will give glory to your name forever,
13 for your love for me is very great.
You have rescued me from the depths
of death.*
14 O God, insolent people rise up against me;
a violent gang is trying to kill me.
You mean nothing to them.
15 But you, O Lord,
are a God of compassion and mercy,
slow to get angry
and filled with unfailing love and
faithfulness.
16 Look down and have mercy on me.
Give your strength to your servant;
save me, the son of your servant.
17 Send me a sign of your favor.
Then those who hate me will be put
to shame,
for you, O LORD, help and comfort me.

PSALM 87

A song. A psalm of the descendants of Korah.

1 On the holy mountain
stands the city founded by the LORD.
2 He loves the city of Jerusalem
more than any other city in Israel.*
3 O city of God,
what glorious things are said of you!
Interlude
4 I will count Egypt* and Babylon among
those who know me—
also Philistia and Tyre, and even distant
Ethiopia.*
They have all become citizens of
Jerusalem!
5 Regarding Jerusalem* it will be said,
"Everyone enjoys the rights of
citizenship there."
And the Most High will personally bless
this city.
6 When the LORD registers the nations, he
will say,
"They have all become citizens of
Jerusalem." *Interlude*
7 The people will play flutes* and sing,
"The source of my life springs from
Jerusalem!"

PSALM 88

For the choir director: A psalm of the descendants of Korah. A song to be sung to the tune "The Suffering of Affliction." A psalm of Heman the Ezrahite.*

1 O LORD, God of my salvation,
I cry out to you by day.
I come to you at night.
2 Now hear my prayer;
listen to my cry.
3 For my life is full of troubles,
and death* draws near.
4 I am as good as dead,
like a strong man with no strength left.
5 They have left me among the dead,
and I lie like a corpse in a grave.
I am forgotten,
cut off from your care.
6 You have thrown me into the lowest pit,
into the darkest depths.
7 Your anger weighs me down;
with wave after wave you have
engulfed me. *Interlude*
8 You have driven my friends away
by making me repulsive to them.
I am in a trap with no way of escape.
9 My eyes are blinded by my tears.
Each day I beg for your help, O LORD;
I lift my hands to you for mercy.
10 Are your wonderful deeds of any use to
the dead?
Do the dead rise up and praise you?
Interlude
11 Can those in the grave declare your
unfailing love?
Can they proclaim your faithfulness in
the place of destruction?*
12 Can the darkness speak of your wonderful
deeds?
Can anyone in the land of forgetfulness
talk about your righteousness?
13 O LORD, I cry out to you.
I will keep on pleading day by day.
14 O LORD, why do you reject me?
Why do you turn your face from me?

86:13 Hebrew *of Sheol.* **87:2** Hebrew *He loves the gates of Zion more than all the dwellings of Jacob.* See note on 44:4. **87:4a** Hebrew *Rahab,* the name of a mythical sea monster that represents chaos in ancient literature. The name is used here as a poetic name for Egypt. **87:4b** Hebrew *Cush.* **87:5** Hebrew *Zion.* **87:7** Or *will dance.* **88:TITLE** Hebrew *maskil.* This may be a literary or musical term. **88:3** Hebrew *Sheol.* **88:11** Hebrew *in Abaddon?*

15 I have been sick and close to death since
my youth.
I stand helpless and desperate before
your terrors.
16 Your fierce anger has overwhelmed me.
Your terrors have paralyzed me.
17 They swirl around me like floodwaters all
day long.
They have engulfed me completely.
18 You have taken away my companions and
loved ones.
Darkness is my closest friend.

PSALM 89

A psalm of Ethan the Ezrahite.*

1 I will sing of the LORD's unfailing love
forever!
Young and old will hear of your
faithfulness.
2 Your unfailing love will last forever.
Your faithfulness is as enduring as the
heavens.

3 The LORD said, "I have made a covenant
with David, my chosen servant.
I have sworn this oath to him:
4 'I will establish your descendants as kings
forever;
they will sit on your throne from now
until eternity.'" *Interlude*
5 All heaven will praise your great wonders,
LORD;
myriads of angels will praise you for
your faithfulness.
6 For who in all of heaven can compare
with the LORD?
What mightiest angel is anything like
the LORD?
7 The highest angelic powers stand in awe
of God.
He is far more awesome than all who
surround his throne.
8 O LORD God of Heaven's Armies!
Where is there anyone as mighty as
you, O LORD?
You are entirely faithful.

9 You rule the oceans.
You subdue their storm-tossed waves.
10 You crushed the great sea monster.*
You scattered your enemies with your
mighty arm.
11 The heavens are yours, and the earth
is yours;
everything in the world is yours—you
created it all.
12 You created north and south.
Mount Tabor and Mount Hermon
praise your name.
13 Powerful is your arm!
Strong is your hand!
Your right hand is lifted high in
glorious strength.
14 Righteousness and justice are the
foundation of your throne.
Unfailing love and truth walk before
you as attendants.
15 Happy are those who hear the joyful call
to worship,
for they will walk in the light of your
presence, LORD.
16 They rejoice all day long in your
wonderful reputation.
They exult in your righteousness.
17 You are their glorious strength.
It pleases you to make us strong.
18 Yes, our protection comes from
the LORD,
and he, the Holy One of Israel, has
given us our king.

19 Long ago you spoke in a vision to your
faithful people.
You said, "I have raised up a warrior.
I have selected him from the common
people to be king.
20 I have found my servant David.
I have anointed him with my
holy oil.
21 I will steady him with my hand;
with my powerful arm I will make
him strong.
22 His enemies will not defeat him,
nor will the wicked overpower him.
23 I will beat down his adversaries before
him
and destroy those who hate him.
24 My faithfulness and unfailing love will be
with him,
and by my authority he will grow in
power.

89:TITLE Hebrew *maskil*. This may be a literary or musical term. **89:10** Hebrew *Rahab*, the name of a mythical sea monster that represents chaos in ancient literature.

25 I will extend his rule over the sea,
his dominion over the rivers.
26 And he will call out to me, 'You are my Father,
my God, and the Rock of my salvation.'
27 I will make him my firstborn son,
the mightiest king on earth.
28 I will love him and be kind to him forever;
my covenant with him will never end.
29 I will preserve an heir for him;
his throne will be as endless as the days of heaven.
30 But if his descendants forsake my instructions
and fail to obey my regulations,
31 if they do not obey my decrees
and fail to keep my commands,
32 then I will punish their sin with the rod,
and their disobedience with beating.
33 But I will never stop loving him
nor fail to keep my promise to him.
34 No, I will not break my covenant;
I will not take back a single word I said.
35 I have sworn an oath to David,
and in my holiness I cannot lie:
36 His dynasty will go on forever;
his kingdom will endure as the sun.
37 It will be as eternal as the moon,
my faithful witness in the sky!"
Interlude
38 But now you have rejected him and cast him off.
You are angry with your anointed king.
39 You have renounced your covenant with him;
you have thrown his crown in the dust.
40 You have broken down the walls protecting him
and ruined every fort defending him.
41 Everyone who comes along has robbed him,
and he has become a joke to his neighbors.
42 You have strengthened his enemies
and made them all rejoice.
43 You have made his sword useless
and refused to help him in battle.
44 You have ended his splendor
and overturned his throne.
45 You have made him old before his time
and publicly disgraced him. *Interlude*

89:48 Hebrew *of Sheol.*

46 O LORD, how long will this go on?
Will you hide yourself forever?
How long will your anger burn like fire?
47 Remember how short my life is,
how empty and futile this human existence!
48 No one can live forever; all will die.
No one can escape the power of the grave.* *Interlude*
49 Lord, where is your unfailing love?
You promised it to David with a faithful pledge.
50 Consider, Lord, how your servants are disgraced!
I carry in my heart the insults of so many people.
51 Your enemies have mocked me, O LORD;
they mock your anointed king wherever he goes.
52 Praise the LORD forever!
Amen and amen!

BOOK FOUR (Psalms 90–106)

PSALM 90

A prayer of Moses, the man of God.

1 Lord, through all the generations
you have been our home!
2 Before the mountains were born,
before you gave birth to the earth and the world,
from beginning to end, you are God.
3 You turn people back to dust, saying,
"Return to dust, you mortals!"
4 For you, a thousand years are as a passing day,
as brief as a few night hours.
5 You sweep people away like dreams that disappear.
They are like grass that springs up in the morning.
6 In the morning it blooms and flourishes,
but by evening it is dry and withered.
7 We wither beneath your anger;
we are overwhelmed by your fury.
8 You spread out our sins before you—
our secret sins—and you see them all.
9 We live our lives beneath your wrath,
ending our years with a groan.

10 Seventy years are given to us!
Some even live to eighty.
But even the best years are filled with pain and trouble;
soon they disappear, and we fly away.
11 Who can comprehend the power of your anger?
Your wrath is as awesome as the fear you deserve.
12 Teach us to realize the brevity of life,
so that we may grow in wisdom.
13 O LORD, come back to us!
How long will you delay?
Take pity on your servants!
14 Satisfy us each morning with your unfailing love,
so we may sing for joy to the end of our lives.
15 Give us gladness in proportion to our former misery!
Replace the evil years with good.
16 Let us, your servants, see you work again;
let our children see your glory.
17 And may the Lord our God show us his approval
and make our efforts successful.
Yes, make our efforts successful!

PSALM 91

1 Those who live in the shelter of the Most High
will find rest in the shadow of the Almighty.

What should I say when I talk to God?

It is good to give thanks to the LORD, to sing praises to the Most High. It is good to proclaim your unfailing love in the morning, your faithfulness in the evening.

PSALM 92:1-2

2 This I declare about the LORD:
He alone is my refuge, my place of safety;
he is my God, and I trust him.
3 For he will rescue you from every trap
and protect you from deadly disease.
4 He will cover you with his feathers.
He will shelter you with his wings.
His faithful promises are your armor and protection.
5 Do not be afraid of the terrors of the night,
nor the arrow that flies in the day.
6 Do not dread the disease that stalks in darkness,
nor the disaster that strikes at midday.
7 Though a thousand fall at your side,
though ten thousand are dying around you,
these evils will not touch you.
8 Just open your eyes,
and see how the wicked are punished.
9 If you make the LORD your refuge,
if you make the Most High your shelter,
10 no evil will conquer you;
no plague will come near your home.
11 For he will order his angels
to protect you wherever you go.
12 They will hold you up with their hands
so you won't even hurt your foot on a stone.
13 You will trample upon lions and cobras;
you will crush fierce lions and serpents under your feet!
14 The LORD says, "I will rescue those who love me.
I will protect those who trust in my name.
15 When they call on me, I will answer;
I will be with them in trouble.
I will rescue and honor them.
16 I will reward them with a long life
and give them my salvation."

PSALM 92

A psalm. A song to be sung on the Sabbath Day.

1 It is good to give thanks to the LORD,
to sing praises to the Most High.

2 It is good to proclaim your unfailing love
in the morning,
your faithfulness in the evening,
3 accompanied by the ten-stringed harp
and the melody of the lyre.

4 You thrill me, LORD, with all you have
done for me!
I sing for joy because of what you have
done.
5 O LORD, what great works you do!
And how deep are your thoughts.
6 Only a simpleton would not know,
and only a fool would not understand
this:
7 Though the wicked sprout like weeds
and evildoers flourish,
they will be destroyed forever.

8 But you, O LORD, will be exalted forever.
9 Your enemies, LORD, will surely perish;
all evildoers will be scattered.
10 But you have made me as strong as
a wild ox.
You have anointed me with the finest
oil.
11 My eyes have seen the downfall of my
enemies;
my ears have heard the defeat of my
wicked opponents.
12 But the godly will flourish like palm trees
and grow strong like the cedars of
Lebanon.
13 For they are transplanted to the LORD's
own house.
They flourish in the courts of our God.
14 Even in old age they will still produce
fruit;
they will remain vital and green.
15 They will declare, "The LORD is just!
He is my rock!
There is no evil in him!"

PSALM 93

1 The LORD is king! He is robed in majesty.
Indeed, the LORD is robed in majesty
and armed with strength.
The world stands firm
and cannot be shaken.

2 Your throne, O LORD, has stood from time
immemorial.
You yourself are from the everlasting
past.
3 The floods have risen up, O LORD.
The floods have roared like thunder;
the floods have lifted their pounding
waves.
4 But mightier than the violent raging of the
seas,
mightier than the breakers on the
shore—
the LORD above is mightier than these!
5 Your royal laws cannot be changed.
Your reign, O LORD, is holy forever
and ever.

PSALM 94

1 O LORD, the God of vengeance,
O God of vengeance, let your glorious
justice shine forth!
2 Arise, O judge of the earth.
Give the proud what they deserve.
3 How long, O LORD?
How long will the wicked be allowed
to gloat?
4 How long will they speak with arrogance?
How long will these evil people boast?
5 They crush your people, LORD,
hurting those you claim as your own.
6 They kill widows and foreigners
and murder orphans.
7 "The LORD isn't looking," they say,
"and besides, the God of Israel* doesn't
care."

8 Think again, you fools!
When will you finally catch on?
9 Is he deaf—the one who made your
ears?
Is he blind—the one who formed
your eyes?
10 He punishes the nations—won't he also
punish you?
He knows everything—doesn't he also
know what you are doing?
11 The LORD knows people's thoughts;
he knows they are worthless!

12 Joyful are those you discipline, LORD,
those you teach with your instructions.
13 You give them relief from troubled
times

94:7 Hebrew *of Jacob*. See note on 44:4.

until a pit is dug to capture the
wicked.
14 The LORD will not reject his people;
he will not abandon his special
possession.
15 Judgment will again be founded on
justice,
and those with virtuous hearts will
pursue it.

16 Who will protect me from the wicked?
Who will stand up for me against
evildoers?
17 Unless the LORD had helped me,
I would soon have settled in the silence
of the grave.
18 I cried out, "I am slipping!"
but your unfailing love, O LORD,
supported me.
19 When doubts filled my mind,
your comfort gave me renewed hope
and cheer.

20 Can unjust leaders claim that God is on
their side—
leaders whose decrees permit
injustice?
21 They gang up against the righteous
and condemn the innocent to death.
22 But the LORD is my fortress;
my God is the mighty rock where I hide.
23 God will turn the sins of evil people back
on them.
He will destroy them for their sins.
The LORD our God will destroy them.

PSALM 95

1 Come, let us sing to the LORD!
Let us shout joyfully to the Rock of our
salvation.
2 Let us come to him with thanksgiving.
Let us sing psalms of praise to him.
3 For the LORD is a great God,
a great King above all gods.
4 He holds in his hands the depths of
the earth
and the mightiest mountains.
5 The sea belongs to him, for he made it.
His hands formed the dry land, too.

6 Come, let us worship and bow down.
Let us kneel before the LORD our
maker,
7 for he is our God.
We are the people he watches over,
the flock under his care.

If only you would listen to his voice today!
8 The LORD says, "Don't harden your hearts
as Israel did at Meribah,
as they did at Massah in the wilderness.
9 For there your ancestors tested and tried
my patience,
even though they saw everything I did.
10 For forty years I was angry with them, and
I said,
'They are a people whose hearts turn away
from me.
They refuse to do what I tell them.'
11 So in my anger I took an oath:
'They will never enter my place of
rest.'"

PSALM 96

1 Sing a new song to the LORD!
Let the whole earth sing to the LORD!
2 Sing to the LORD; praise his name.
Each day proclaim the good news that
he saves.
3 Publish his glorious deeds among the
nations.
Tell everyone about the amazing things
he does.
4 Great is the LORD! He is most worthy of
praise!
He is to be feared above all gods.
5 The gods of other nations are mere idols,
but the LORD made the heavens!
6 Honor and majesty surround him;
strength and beauty fill his sanctuary.

7 O nations of the world, recognize the LORD;
recognize that the LORD is glorious and
strong.
8 Give to the LORD the glory he deserves!
Bring your offering and come into
his courts.
9 Worship the LORD in all his holy splendor.
Let all the earth tremble before him.
10 Tell all the nations, "The LORD reigns!"
The world stands firm and cannot
be shaken.
He will judge all peoples fairly.

11 Let the heavens be glad, and the earth
rejoice!
Let the sea and everything in it shout
his praise!

I SURVIVED

Isn't it funny how you can hear a word, even use it a thousand times, and still not quite know what it means? Take the word *worship*. Ask any of my friends and they'd probably tell you that worship is my big thing. I'm always singing some song I've learned at camp and youth group. I'm also the drummer on several worship teams at my church. You'd think I'd be an expert on what the word *worship* really means! But God keeps surprising me.

To me, worship has always been fun. The time came for me to go deeper, though. Was the way I "did" worship at my church the only way? How did the people in the Bible worship God? I looked up words like *worship*, *sing*, and *praise* in the index of my Bible.

These verses gave me a pretty good picture of the way Bible-time people worshiped God: *Sing to the Lord; praise his name. Each day proclaim the good news that he saves. Publish his glorious deeds among the nations. Tell everyone about the amazing things he does (Psalm 96:2-3).* For people in the Bible, worship wasn't just singing songs. They worshiped God in tons of ways—they did sing, but they also danced, told other people about God, wrote about God's blessings, and prayed together. Worship was their way of life.

It's the same for us today. Our worship is the whole way we choose to love God with our lives. So basically that means anything I do, if I do it with a heart of thankfulness, can be a kind of worship! When I hear the word *worship* now, I don't just think of singing—I think about loving God with all that I am.

You can use Psalm 96 as a starting point for your worship time with God. Also see Psalms 9; 24; 84; and 103.

12 Let the fields and their crops burst out
with joy!
Let the trees of the forest rustle with
praise
13 before the LORD, for he is coming!
He is coming to judge the earth.
He will judge the world with justice,
and the nations with his truth.

PSALM 97

1 The LORD is king!
Let the earth rejoice!
Let the farthest coastlands be glad.
2 Dark clouds surround him.
Righteousness and justice are the
foundation of his throne.
3 Fire spreads ahead of him
and burns up all his foes.
4 His lightning flashes out across the world.
The earth sees and trembles.
5 The mountains melt like wax before the
LORD,
before the Lord of all the earth.
6 The heavens proclaim his righteousness;
every nation sees his glory.
7 Those who worship idols are disgraced—
all who brag about their worthless gods—
for every god must bow to him.
8 Jerusalem* has heard and rejoiced,
and all the towns of Judah are glad
because of your justice, O LORD!
9 For you, O LORD, are supreme over all the
earth;
you are exalted far above all gods.

10 You who love the LORD, hate evil!
He protects the lives of his godly
people
and rescues them from the power of
the wicked.
11 Light shines on the godly,
and joy on those whose hearts are right.
12 May all who are godly rejoice in the LORD
and praise his holy name!

PSALM 98

A psalm.

1 Sing a new song to the LORD,
for he has done wonderful deeds.
His right hand has won a mighty victory;
his holy arm has shown his saving
power!
2 The LORD has announced his victory
and has revealed his righteousness
to every nation!
3 He has remembered his promise to love
and be faithful to Israel.
The ends of the earth have seen the
victory of our God.

4 Shout to the LORD, all the earth;
break out in praise and sing for joy!
5 Sing your praise to the LORD with the
harp,
with the harp and melodious song,
6 with trumpets and the sound of the
ram's horn.
Make a joyful symphony before the
LORD, the King!

7 Let the sea and everything in it shout his
praise!
Let the earth and all living things
join in.
8 Let the rivers clap their hands in glee!
Let the hills sing out their songs of joy
9 before the LORD.
For the LORD is coming to judge the
earth.
He will judge the world with justice,
and the nations with fairness.

PSALM 99

1 The LORD is king!
Let the nations tremble!
He sits on his throne between the
cherubim.
Let the whole earth quake!
2 The LORD sits in majesty in Jerusalem,*
exalted above all the nations.
3 Let them praise your great and awesome
name.
Your name is holy!
4 Mighty King, lover of justice,
you have established fairness.
You have acted with justice
and righteousness throughout Israel.*
5 Exalt the LORD our God!
Bow low before his feet, for he is holy!

6 Moses and Aaron were among his
priests;
Samuel also called on his name.
They cried to the LORD for help,
and he answered them.

97:8 Hebrew *Zion*. **99:2** Hebrew *Zion*. **99:4** Hebrew *Jacob*. See note on 44:4.

7 He spoke to Israel from the pillar of cloud,
and they followed the laws and decrees
he gave them.
8 O LORD our God, you answered them.
You were a forgiving God to them,
but you punished them when they went
wrong.

9 Exalt the LORD our God,
and worship at his holy mountain in
Jerusalem,
for the LORD our God is holy!

PSALM 100

A psalm of thanksgiving.

1 Shout with joy to the LORD, all the earth!
2 Worship the LORD with gladness.
Come before him, singing with joy.
3 Acknowledge that the LORD is God!
He made us, and we are his.*
We are his people, the sheep of his
pasture.
4 Enter his gates with thanksgiving;
go into his courts with praise.
Give thanks to him and praise his
name.
5 For the LORD is good.
His unfailing love continues forever,
and his faithfulness continues to each
generation.

PSALM 101

A psalm of David.

1 I will sing of your love and justice, LORD.
I will praise you with songs.
2 I will be careful to live a blameless life—
when will you come to help me?
I will lead a life of integrity
in my own home.
3 I will refuse to look at
anything vile and vulgar.
I hate all who deal crookedly;
I will have nothing to do with them.
4 I will reject perverse ideas
and stay away from every evil.
5 I will not tolerate people who slander
their neighbors.
I will not endure conceit and pride.

6 I will search for faithful people
to be my companions.
Only those who are above reproach
will be allowed to serve me.
7 I will not allow deceivers to serve
in my house,
and liars will not stay in my presence.
8 My daily task will be to ferret out the
wicked
and free the city of the LORD from
their grip.

THE FINAL EXAM

Jordan had studied until bedtime for his math final, and he planned to finish studying in the morning. But he overslept! Jordan panicked. *How will I pass the test if I can't look over the last chapters?* he wondered. During third period, Mrs. Bogue asked Jordan to take a note to Mr. Simpson, Jordan's math teacher. Nobody was in the room, so Jordan put the note on Mr. Simpson's desk. Then Jordan noticed the math exam—with answers—sitting right there! No one was around. What should he do? Read Psalm 101:7.

100:3 As in an alternate reading in the Masoretic Text; the other alternate and some ancient versions read *and not we ourselves.*

PSALM 102

A prayer of one overwhelmed with trouble, pouring out problems before the LORD.

1 LORD, hear my prayer!
Listen to my plea!
2 Don't turn away from me
in my time of distress.
Bend down to listen,
and answer me quickly when I call to you.
3 For my days disappear like smoke,
and my bones burn like red-hot coals.
4 My heart is sick, withered like grass,
and I have lost my appetite.
5 Because of my groaning,
I am reduced to skin and bones.
6 I am like an owl in the desert,
like a little owl in a far-off wilderness.
7 I lie awake,
lonely as a solitary bird on the roof.
8 My enemies taunt me day after day.
They mock and curse me.
9 I eat ashes for food.
My tears run down into my drink
10 because of your anger and wrath.
For you have picked me up and thrown me out.
11 My life passes as swiftly as the evening shadows.
I am withering away like grass.

12 But you, O LORD, will sit on your throne forever.
Your fame will endure to every generation.
13 You will arise and have mercy on Jerusalem*—
and now is the time to pity her,
now is the time you promised to help.
14 For your people love every stone in her walls
and cherish even the dust in her streets.
15 Then the nations will tremble before the LORD.
The kings of the earth will tremble before his glory.
16 For the LORD will rebuild Jerusalem.
He will appear in his glory.
17 He will listen to the prayers of the destitute.
He will not reject their pleas.

18 Let this be recorded for future generations,
so that a people not yet born will praise the LORD.
19 Tell them the LORD looked down from his heavenly sanctuary.
He looked down to earth from heaven
20 to hear the groans of the prisoners,
to release those condemned to die.
21 And so the LORD's fame will be celebrated in Zion,
his praises in Jerusalem,
22 when multitudes gather together
and kingdoms come to worship the LORD.

23 He broke my strength in midlife,
cutting short my days.
24 But I cried to him, "O my God, who lives forever,
don't take my life while I am so young!
25 Long ago you laid the foundation of the earth
and made the heavens with your hands.
26 They will perish, but you remain forever;
they will wear out like old clothing.
You will change them like a garment
and discard them.
27 But you are always the same;
you will live forever.
28 The children of your people
will live in security.
Their children's children
will thrive in your presence."

PSALM 103

A psalm of David.

1 Let all that I am praise the LORD;
with my whole heart, I will praise his holy name.
2 Let all that I am praise the LORD;
may I never forget the good things he does for me.
3 He forgives all my sins
and heals all my diseases.

102:13 Hebrew *Zion;* also in 102:16.

4 He redeems me from death
and crowns me with love and tender mercies.
5 He fills my life with good things.
My youth is renewed like the eagle's!

6 The LORD gives righteousness
and justice to all who are treated unfairly.

7 He revealed his character to Moses
and his deeds to the people of Israel.
8 The LORD is compassionate and merciful,
slow to get angry and filled with unfailing love.
9 He will not constantly accuse us,
nor remain angry forever.
10 He does not punish us for all our sins;
he does not deal harshly with us, as we deserve.
11 For his unfailing love toward those who fear him
is as great as the height of the heavens above the earth.
12 He has removed our sins as far from us
as the east is from the west.
13 The LORD is like a father to his children,
tender and compassionate to those who fear him.
14 For he knows how weak we are;
he remembers we are only dust.
15 Our days on earth are like grass;
like wildflowers, we bloom and die.
16 The wind blows, and we are gone—
as though we had never been here.
17 But the love of the LORD remains forever
with those who fear him.
His salvation extends to the children's children
18 of those who are faithful to his covenant,
of those who obey his commandments!

19 The LORD has made the heavens his throne;
from there he rules over everything.

20 Praise the LORD, you angels,
you mighty ones who carry out his plans,
listening for each of his commands.
21 Yes, praise the LORD, you armies of angels
who serve him and do his will!
22 Praise the LORD, everything he has created,
everything in all his kingdom.

Let all that I am praise the LORD.

PSALM 104

1 Let all that I am praise the LORD.

O LORD my God, how great you are!
You are robed with honor and majesty.
2 You are dressed in a robe of light.
You stretch out the starry curtain of the heavens;
3 you lay out the rafters of your home in the rain clouds.
You make the clouds your chariot;
you ride upon the wings of the wind.

AMAZING FACTS

Want to know how God uses the clouds he created? They make a great wind-powered chariot!

PSALM 104:3

4 The winds are your messengers;
flames of fire are your servants.*

5 You placed the world on its foundation
so it would never be moved.
6 You clothed the earth with floods of water,
water that covered even the mountains.
7 At your command, the water fled;
at the sound of your thunder, it hurried away.
8 Mountains rose and valleys sank
to the levels you decreed.

104:4 Greek version reads *He sends his angels like the winds, / his servants like flames of fire.* Compare Heb 1:7.

9 Then you set a firm boundary for the seas,
so they would never again cover
the earth.

10 You make springs pour water into the
ravines,
so streams gush down from the
mountains.

11 They provide water for all the animals,
and the wild donkeys quench their
thirst.

12 The birds nest beside the streams
and sing among the branches of the
trees.

13 You send rain on the mountains from
your heavenly home,
and you fill the earth with the fruit
of your labor.

14 You cause grass to grow for the livestock
and plants for people to use.
You allow them to produce food from
the earth—

15 wine to make them glad,
olive oil to soothe their skin,
and bread to give them strength.

16 The trees of the LORD are well cared for—
the cedars of Lebanon that he planted.

17 There the birds make their nests,
and the storks make their homes
in the cypresses.

18 High in the mountains live the wild
goats,
and the rocks form a refuge for the
hyraxes.*

19 You made the moon to mark the seasons,
and the sun knows when to set.

20 You send the darkness, and it becomes
night,
when all the forest animals prowl
about.

21 Then the young lions roar for
their prey,
stalking the food provided by God.

22 At dawn they slink back
into their dens to rest.

23 Then people go off to their work,
where they labor until evening.

24 O LORD, what a variety of things you
have made!
In wisdom you have made them all.
The earth is full of your creatures.

25 Here is the ocean, vast and wide,
teeming with life of every kind,
both large and small.

26 See the ships sailing along,
and Leviathan,* which you made to
play in the sea.

27 They all depend on you
to give them food as they need it.

28 When you supply it, they gather it.
You open your hand to feed them,
and they are richly satisfied.

29 But if you turn away from them, they
panic.
When you take away their breath,
they die and turn again to dust.

30 When you give them your breath,* life
is created,
and you renew the face of the earth.

31 May the glory of the LORD continue
forever!
The LORD takes pleasure in all he has
made!

32 The earth trembles at his glance;
the mountains smoke at his touch.

33 I will sing to the LORD as long as I live.
I will praise my God to my last
breath!

34 May all my thoughts be pleasing to him,
for I rejoice in the LORD.

35 Let all sinners vanish from the face
of the earth;
let the wicked disappear forever.

Let all that I am praise the LORD.

Praise the LORD!

PSALM 105

1 Give thanks to the LORD and proclaim his
greatness.
Let the whole world know what he has
done.

2 Sing to him; yes, sing his praises.
Tell everyone about his wonderful
deeds.

3 Exult in his holy name;
rejoice, you who worship the LORD.

4 Search for the LORD and for his strength;
continually seek him.

104:18 Or *coneys*, or *rock badgers*. **104:26** The identification of Leviathan is disputed, ranging from an earthly creature to a mythical sea monster in ancient literature. **104:30** Or *When you send your Spirit*.

5 Remember the wonders he has performed,
his miracles, and the rulings he has given,
6 you children of his servant Abraham,
you descendants of Jacob, his chosen ones.

7 He is the LORD our God.
His justice is seen throughout the land.
8 He always stands by his covenant—
the commitment he made to a thousand generations.
9 This is the covenant he made with Abraham
and the oath he swore to Isaac.
10 He confirmed it to Jacob as a decree,
and to the people of Israel as a never-ending covenant:
11 "I will give you the land of Canaan
as your special possession."

12 He said this when they were few in number,
a tiny group of strangers in Canaan.
13 They wandered from nation to nation,
from one kingdom to another.
14 Yet he did not let anyone oppress them.
He warned kings on their behalf:
15 "Do not touch my chosen people,
and do not hurt my prophets."

16 He called for a famine on the land of Canaan,
cutting off its food supply.
17 Then he sent someone to Egypt ahead of them—
Joseph, who was sold as a slave.
18 They bruised his feet with fetters
and placed his neck in an iron collar.
19 Until the time came to fulfill his dreams,*
the LORD tested Joseph's character.
20 Then Pharaoh sent for him and set him free;
the ruler of the nation opened his prison door.
21 Joseph was put in charge of all the king's household;
he became ruler over all the king's possessions.
22 He could instruct the king's aides as he pleased
and teach the king's advisers.

23 Then Israel arrived in Egypt;
Jacob lived as a foreigner in the land of Ham.
24 And the LORD multiplied the people of Israel
until they became too mighty for their enemies.
25 Then he turned the Egyptians against the Israelites,
and they plotted against the LORD's servants.

26 But the LORD sent his servant Moses,
along with Aaron, whom he had chosen.
27 They performed miraculous signs among the Egyptians,
and wonders in the land of Ham.
28 The LORD blanketed Egypt in darkness,
for they had defied his commands to let his people go.
29 He turned their water into blood,
poisoning all the fish.
30 Then frogs overran the land
and even invaded the king's bedrooms.
31 When the LORD spoke, flies descended on the Egyptians,
and gnats swarmed across Egypt.
32 He sent them hail instead of rain,
and lightning flashed over the land.
33 He ruined their grapevines and fig trees
and shattered all the trees.
34 He spoke, and hordes of locusts came—
young locusts beyond number.
35 They ate up everything green in the land,
destroying all the crops in their fields.
36 Then he killed the oldest son in each Egyptian home,
the pride and joy of each family.

37 The LORD brought his people out of Egypt, loaded with silver and gold;
and not one among the tribes of Israel even stumbled.
38 Egypt was glad when they were gone,
for they feared them greatly.
39 The LORD spread a cloud above them as a covering
and gave them a great fire to light the darkness.
40 They asked for meat, and he sent them quail;

105:19 Hebrew *his word*.

he satisfied their hunger with manna—
bread from heaven.
41 He split open a rock, and water gushed out
to form a river through the dry wasteland.
42 For he remembered his sacred promise
to his servant Abraham.
43 So he brought his people out of Egypt with joy,
his chosen ones with rejoicing.
44 He gave his people the lands of pagan nations,
and they harvested crops that others had planted.
45 All this happened so they would follow his decrees
and obey his instructions.

Praise the LORD!

PSALM 106

1 Praise the LORD!

Give thanks to the LORD, for he is good!
His faithful love endures forever.
2 Who can list the glorious miracles of the LORD?
Who can ever praise him enough?
3 There is joy for those who deal justly with others
and always do what is right.

4 Remember me, LORD, when you show favor to your people;
come near and rescue me.
5 Let me share in the prosperity of your chosen ones.
Let me rejoice in the joy of your people;
let me praise you with those who are your heritage.

6 Like our ancestors, we have sinned.
We have done wrong! We have acted wickedly!
7 Our ancestors in Egypt
were not impressed by the LORD's miraculous deeds.
They soon forgot his many acts of kindness to them.
Instead, they rebelled against him at the Red Sea.*
8 Even so, he saved them—
to defend the honor of his name
and to demonstrate his mighty power.
9 He commanded the Red Sea* to dry up.
He led Israel across the sea as if it were a desert.
10 So he rescued them from their enemies
and redeemed them from their foes.
11 Then the water returned and covered their enemies;
not one of them survived.
12 Then his people believed his promises.
Then they sang his praise.

13 Yet how quickly they forgot what he had done!
They wouldn't wait for his counsel!
14 In the wilderness their desires ran wild,
testing God's patience in that dry wasteland.
15 So he gave them what they asked for,
but he sent a plague along with it.
16 The people in the camp were jealous of Moses
and envious of Aaron, the LORD's holy priest.
17 Because of this, the earth opened up;
it swallowed Dathan
and buried Abiram and the other rebels.
18 Fire fell upon their followers;
a flame consumed the wicked.

19 The people made a calf at Mount Sinai*;
they bowed before an image made of gold.
20 They traded their glorious God
for a statue of a grass-eating bull.
21 They forgot God, their savior,
who had done such great things in Egypt—
22 such wonderful things in the land of Ham,
such awesome deeds at the Red Sea.
23 So he declared he would destroy them.
But Moses, his chosen one, stepped between the LORD and the people.
He begged him to turn from his anger and not destroy them.

24 The people refused to enter the pleasant land,
for they wouldn't believe his promise to care for them.

106:7 Hebrew *at the sea, the sea of reeds.* **106:9** Hebrew *sea of reeds;* also in 106:22. **106:19** Hebrew *at Horeb,* another name for Sinai.

25 Instead, they grumbled in their tents
and refused to obey the LORD.
26 Therefore, he solemnly swore
that he would kill them in the wilderness,
27 that he would scatter their descendants among the nations,
exiling them to distant lands.

28 Then our ancestors joined in the worship of Baal at Peor;
they even ate sacrifices offered to the dead!
29 They angered the LORD with all these things,
so a plague broke out among them.
30 But Phinehas had the courage to intervene,
and the plague was stopped.
31 So he has been regarded as a righteous man
ever since that time.

32 At Meribah, too, they angered the LORD,
causing Moses serious trouble.
33 They made Moses angry,*
and he spoke foolishly.

34 Israel failed to destroy the nations in the land,
as the LORD had commanded them.
35 Instead, they mingled among the pagans
and adopted their evil customs.
36 They worshiped their idols,
which led to their downfall.
37 They even sacrificed their sons
and their daughters to the demons.
38 They shed innocent blood,
the blood of their sons and daughters.
By sacrificing them to the idols of Canaan,
they polluted the land with murder.
39 They defiled themselves by their evil deeds,
and their love of idols was adultery in the LORD's sight.

40 That is why the LORD's anger burned against his people,
and he abhorred his own special possession.
41 He handed them over to pagan nations,
and they were ruled by those who hated them.
42 Their enemies crushed them
and brought them under their cruel power.
43 Again and again he rescued them,
but they chose to rebel against him,
and they were finally destroyed by their sin.
44 Even so, he pitied them in their distress
and listened to their cries.
45 He remembered his covenant with them
and relented because of his unfailing love.
46 He even caused their captors
to treat them with kindness.

47 Save us, O LORD our God!
Gather us back from among the nations,
so we can thank your holy name
and rejoice and praise you.

48 Praise the LORD, the God of Israel,
who lives from everlasting to everlasting!
Let all the people say, "Amen!"

Praise the LORD!

BOOK FIVE (Psalms 107–150)

PSALM 107

1 Give thanks to the LORD, for he is good!
His faithful love endures forever.
2 Has the LORD redeemed you? Then speak out!
Tell others he has redeemed you from your enemies.
3 For he has gathered the exiles from many lands,
from east and west,
from north and south.

4 Some wandered in the wilderness,
lost and homeless.
5 Hungry and thirsty,
they nearly died.
6 "LORD, help!" they cried in their trouble,
and he rescued them from their distress.
7 He led them straight to safety,
to a city where they could live.
8 Let them praise the LORD for his great love

106:33 Hebrew *They embittered his spirit.*

and for the wonderful things he has
done for them.
9 For he satisfies the thirsty
and fills the hungry with good things.

10 Some sat in darkness and deepest gloom,
imprisoned in iron chains of misery.
11 They rebelled against the words of God,
scorning the counsel of the Most High.
12 That is why he broke them with hard
labor;
they fell, and no one was there to help
them.
13 "LORD, help!" they cried in their trouble,
and he saved them from their distress.
14 He led them from the darkness and
deepest gloom;
he snapped their chains.
15 Let them praise the LORD for his great love
and for the wonderful things he has
done for them.
16 For he broke down their prison gates of
bronze;
he cut apart their bars of iron.

17 Some were fools; they rebelled
and suffered for their sins.
18 They couldn't stand the thought of food,
and they were knocking on death's
door.
19 "LORD, help!" they cried in their trouble,
and he saved them from their distress.
20 He sent out his word and healed them,
snatching them from the door of death.
21 Let them praise the LORD for his great love
and for the wonderful things he has
done for them.
22 Let them offer sacrifices of thanksgiving
and sing joyfully about his glorious
acts.

23 Some went off to sea in ships,
plying the trade routes of the world.
24 They, too, observed the LORD's power in
action,
his impressive works on the deepest
seas.
25 He spoke, and the winds rose,
stirring up the waves.
26 Their ships were tossed to the heavens
and plunged again to the depths;
the sailors cringed in terror.
27 They reeled and staggered like drunkards
and were at their wits' end.
28 "LORD, help!" they cried in their trouble,
and he saved them from their distress.
29 He calmed the storm to a whisper
and stilled the waves.
30 What a blessing was that stillness
as he brought them safely into
harbor!
31 Let them praise the LORD for his
great love
and for the wonderful things he has
done for them.
32 Let them exalt him publicly before the
congregation
and before the leaders of the nation.

33 He changes rivers into deserts,
and springs of water into dry, thirsty
land.
34 He turns the fruitful land into salty
wastelands,
because of the wickedness of those
who live there.
35 But he also turns deserts into pools
of water,
the dry land into springs of water.
36 He brings the hungry to settle there
and to build their cities.
37 They sow their fields, plant their
vineyards,
and harvest their bumper crops.
38 How he blesses them!
They raise large families there,
and their herds of livestock increase.

39 When they decrease in number and
become impoverished
through oppression, trouble, and
sorrow,
40 the LORD pours contempt on their
princes,
causing them to wander in trackless
wastelands.
41 But he rescues the poor from trouble
and increases their families like flocks
of sheep.
42 The godly will see these things and
be glad,
while the wicked are struck silent.
43 Those who are wise will take all this
to heart;
they will see in our history the faithful
love of the LORD.

PSALM 108

A song. A psalm of David.

1 My heart is confident in you, O God;
no wonder I can sing your praises with all my heart!
2 Wake up, lyre and harp!
I will wake the dawn with my song.
3 I will thank you, LORD, among all the people.
I will sing your praises among the nations.
4 For your unfailing love is higher than the heavens.
Your faithfulness reaches to the clouds.
5 Be exalted, O God, above the highest heavens.
May your glory shine over all the earth.

6 Now rescue your beloved people.
Answer and save us by your power.
7 God has promised this by his holiness*:
"I will divide up Shechem with joy.
I will measure out the valley of Succoth.
8 Gilead is mine,
and Manasseh, too.
Ephraim, my helmet, will produce my warriors,
and Judah, my scepter, will produce my kings.
9 But Moab, my washbasin, will become my servant,
and I will wipe my feet on Edom
and shout in triumph over Philistia."

10 Who will bring me into the fortified city?
Who will bring me victory over Edom?
11 Have you rejected us, O God?
Will you no longer march with our armies?
12 Oh, please help us against our enemies,
for all human help is useless.
13 With God's help we will do mighty things,
for he will trample down our foes.

PSALM 109

For the choir director: A psalm of David.

1 O God, whom I praise,
don't stand silent and aloof
2 while the wicked slander me
and tell lies about me.
3 They surround me with hateful words
and fight against me for no reason.
4 I love them, but they try to destroy me with accusations
even as I am praying for them!
5 They repay evil for good,
and hatred for my love.

6 They say,* "Get an evil person to turn against him.
Send an accuser to bring him to trial.
7 When his case comes up for judgment,
let him be pronounced guilty.
Count his prayers as sins.
8 Let his years be few;
let someone else take his position.
9 May his children become fatherless,
and his wife a widow.
10 May his children wander as beggars
and be driven from their ruined homes.
11 May creditors seize his entire estate,
and strangers take all he has earned.
12 Let no one be kind to him;
let no one pity his fatherless children.
13 May all his offspring die.
May his family name be blotted out in a single generation.
14 May the LORD never forget the sins of his fathers;
may his mother's sins never be erased from the record.
15 May the LORD always remember these sins,
and may his name disappear from human memory.
16 For he refused all kindness to others;
he persecuted the poor and needy,
and he hounded the brokenhearted to death.
17 He loved to curse others;
now you curse him.
He never blessed others;
now don't you bless him.
18 Cursing is as natural to him as his clothing,
or the water he drinks,
or the rich food he eats.
19 Now may his curses return and cling to him like clothing;
may they be tied around him like a belt."

108:7 Or *in his sanctuary*. **109:6** Hebrew lacks *They say*.

20 May those curses become the LORD's punishment
for my accusers who speak evil of me.
21 But deal well with me, O Sovereign LORD,
for the sake of your own reputation!
Rescue me
because you are so faithful and good.
22 For I am poor and needy,
and my heart is full of pain.
23 I am fading like a shadow at dusk;
I am brushed off like a locust.
24 My knees are weak from fasting,
and I am skin and bones.
25 I am a joke to people everywhere;
when they see me, they shake their heads in scorn.

26 Help me, O LORD my God!
Save me because of your unfailing love.
27 Let them see that this is your doing,
that you yourself have done it, LORD.
28 Then let them curse me if they like,
but you will bless me!
When they attack me, they will be disgraced!
But I, your servant, will go right on rejoicing!
29 May my accusers be clothed with disgrace;
may their humiliation cover them like a cloak.
30 But I will give repeated thanks to the LORD,
praising him to everyone.
31 For he stands beside the needy,
ready to save them from those who condemn them.

PSALM 110

A psalm of David.

1 The LORD said to my Lord,
"Sit in the place of honor at my right hand
until I humble your enemies,
making them a footstool under your feet."

2 The LORD will extend your powerful kingdom from Jerusalem*;
you will rule over your enemies.
3 When you go to war,
your people will serve you willingly.
You are arrayed in holy garments,
and your strength will be renewed each day like the morning dew.

4 The LORD has taken an oath and will not break his vow:
"You are a priest forever in the order of Melchizedek."

5 The Lord stands at your right hand to protect you.
He will strike down many kings when his anger erupts.
6 He will punish the nations
and fill their lands with corpses;
he will shatter heads over the whole earth.
7 But he himself will be refreshed from brooks along the way.
He will be victorious.

PSALM 111*

1 Praise the LORD!

I will thank the LORD with all my heart
as I meet with his godly people.
2 How amazing are the deeds of the LORD!
All who delight in him should ponder them.
3 Everything he does reveals his glory and majesty.
His righteousness never fails.
4 He causes us to remember his wonderful works.
How gracious and merciful is our LORD!
5 He gives food to those who fear him;
he always remembers his covenant.
6 He has shown his great power to his people
by giving them the lands of other nations.
7 All he does is just and good,
and all his commandments are trustworthy.
8 They are forever true,
to be obeyed faithfully and with integrity.
9 He has paid a full ransom for his people.
He has guaranteed his covenant with them forever.

110:2 Hebrew *Zion*. **111** This psalm is a Hebrew acrostic poem; after the introductory note of praise, each line begins with a successive letter of the Hebrew alphabet.

What a holy, awe-inspiring name
he has!
10 Fear of the LORD is the foundation of true
wisdom.
All who obey his commandments will
grow in wisdom.

Praise him forever!

PSALM 112*

1 Praise the LORD!

How joyful are those who fear the LORD
and delight in obeying his commands.
2 Their children will be successful
everywhere;
an entire generation of godly people
will be blessed.
3 They themselves will be wealthy,
and their good deeds will last forever.
4 Light shines in the darkness for the
godly.
They are generous, compassionate, and
righteous.
5 Good comes to those who lend money
generously
and conduct their business fairly.
6 Such people will not be overcome
by evil.
Those who are righteous will be long
remembered.
7 They do not fear bad news;
they confidently trust the LORD to care
for them.

How should I react to bad news?

Those who are righteous . . . do not fear bad news; they confidently trust the LORD to care for them. PSALM 112:6–7

8 They are confident and fearless
and can face their foes triumphantly.
9 They share freely and give generously to
those in need.
Their good deeds will be remembered
forever.
They will have influence and honor.
10 The wicked will see this and be infuriated.
They will grind their teeth in anger;
they will slink away, their hopes
thwarted.

PSALM 113

1 Praise the LORD!

Yes, give praise, O servants of the LORD.
Praise the name of the LORD!
2 Blessed be the name of the LORD
now and forever.
3 Everywhere—from east to west—
praise the name of the LORD.
4 For the LORD is high above the nations;
his glory is higher than the heavens.

5 Who can be compared with the LORD
our God,
who is enthroned on high?
6 He stoops to look down
on heaven and on earth.
7 He lifts the poor from the dust
and the needy from the garbage dump.
8 He sets them among princes,
even the princes of his own people!
9 He gives the childless woman a family,
making her a happy mother.

Praise the LORD!

PSALM 114

1 When the Israelites escaped from Egypt—
when the family of Jacob left that
foreign land—
2 the land of Judah became God's sanctuary,
and Israel became his kingdom.

3 The Red Sea* saw them coming and
hurried out of their way!
The water of the Jordan River turned
away.
4 The mountains skipped like rams,
the hills like lambs!
5 What's wrong, Red Sea, that made you
hurry out of their way?
What happened, Jordan River, that you
turned away?
6 Why, mountains, did you skip like
rams?
Why, hills, like lambs?

112 This psalm is a Hebrew acrostic poem; after the introductory note of praise, each line begins with a successive letter of the Hebrew alphabet. **114:3** Hebrew *the sea;* also in 114:5.

7 Tremble, O earth, at the presence
of the Lord,
at the presence of the God of Jacob.
8 He turned the rock into a pool of water;
yes, a spring of water flowed from
solid rock.

PSALM 115

1 Not to us, O LORD, not to us,
but to your name goes all the glory
for your unfailing love and
faithfulness.
2 Why let the nations say,
"Where is their God?"
3 Our God is in the heavens,
and he does as he wishes.
4 Their idols are merely things of silver
and gold,
shaped by human hands.
5 They have mouths but cannot speak,
and eyes but cannot see.
6 They have ears but cannot hear,
and noses but cannot smell.
7 They have hands but cannot feel,
and feet but cannot walk,
and throats but cannot make a sound.
8 And those who make idols are just like
them,
as are all who trust in them.

9 O Israel, trust the LORD!
He is your helper and your shield.
10 O priests, descendants of Aaron, trust
the LORD!
He is your helper and your shield.
11 All you who fear the LORD, trust
the LORD!
He is your helper and your shield.

12 The LORD remembers us and will bless us.
He will bless the people of Israel
and bless the priests, the descendants
of Aaron.
13 He will bless those who fear the LORD,
both great and lowly.
14 May the LORD richly bless
both you and your children.
15 May you be blessed by the LORD,
who made heaven and earth.
16 The heavens belong to the LORD,
but he has given the earth to all
humanity.

116:3 Hebrew *of Sheol.*

17 The dead cannot sing praises to
the LORD,
for they have gone into the silence
of the grave.
18 But we can praise the LORD
both now and forever!

Praise the LORD!

PSALM 116

1 I love the LORD because he hears my voice
and my prayer for mercy.
2 Because he bends down to listen,
I will pray as long as I have breath!
3 Death wrapped its ropes around me;
the terrors of the grave* overtook me.
I saw only trouble and sorrow.
4 Then I called on the name of the LORD:
"Please, LORD, save me!"
5 How kind the LORD is! How good he is!
So merciful, this God of ours!
6 The LORD protects those of childlike faith;
I was facing death, and he saved me.
7 Let my soul be at rest again,
for the LORD has been good to me.
8 He has saved me from death,
my eyes from tears,
my feet from stumbling.
9 And so I walk in the LORD's presence
as I live here on earth!
10 I believed in you, so I said,
"I am deeply troubled, LORD."
11 In my anxiety I cried out to you,
"These people are all liars!"
12 What can I offer the LORD
for all he has done for me?
13 I will lift up the cup of salvation
and praise the LORD's name for
saving me.
14 I will keep my promises to the LORD
in the presence of all his people.
15 The LORD cares deeply
when his loved ones die.
16 O LORD, I am your servant;
yes, I am your servant, born into your
household;
you have freed me from my chains.
17 I will offer you a sacrifice of thanksgiving
and call on the name of the LORD.
18 I will fulfill my vows to the LORD
in the presence of all his people—

19 in the house of the LORD
in the heart of Jerusalem.

Praise the LORD!

PSALM 117

1 Praise the LORD, all you nations.
Praise him, all you people of the earth.
2 For he loves us with unfailing love;
the LORD's faithfulness endures
forever.

Praise the LORD!

PSALM 118

1 Give thanks to the LORD, for he is good!
His faithful love endures forever.

2 Let all Israel repeat:
"His faithful love endures forever."
3 Let Aaron's descendants, the priests,
repeat:
"His faithful love endures forever."
4 Let all who fear the LORD repeat:
"His faithful love endures forever."

5 In my distress I prayed to the LORD,
and the LORD answered me and set
me free.
6 The LORD is for me, so I will have no fear.
What can mere people do to me?
7 Yes, the LORD is for me; he will help me.
I will look in triumph at those who
hate me.
8 It is better to take refuge in the LORD
than to trust in people.
9 It is better to take refuge in the LORD
than to trust in princes.

10 Though hostile nations surrounded me,
I destroyed them all with the authority
of the LORD.
11 Yes, they surrounded and attacked me,
but I destroyed them all with the
authority of the LORD.
12 They swarmed around me like bees;
they blazed against me like a crackling
fire.
But I destroyed them all with the
authority of the LORD.
13 My enemies did their best to kill me,
but the LORD rescued me.
14 The LORD is my strength and my song;
he has given me victory.

15 Songs of joy and victory are sung in the
camp of the godly.
The strong right arm of the LORD has
done glorious things!
16 The strong right arm of the LORD is raised
in triumph.
The strong right arm of the LORD has
done glorious things!
17 I will not die; instead, I will live
to tell what the LORD has done.
18 The LORD has punished me severely,
but he did not let me die.

19 Open for me the gates where the
righteous enter,
and I will go in and thank the LORD.
20 These gates lead to the presence
of the LORD,
and the godly enter there.
21 I thank you for answering my prayer
and giving me victory!

22 The stone that the builders rejected
has now become the cornerstone.
23 This is the LORD's doing,
and it is wonderful to see.
24 This is the day the LORD has made.
We will rejoice and be glad in it.
25 Please, LORD, please save us.
Please, LORD, please give us success.
26 Bless the one who comes in the name
of the LORD.
We bless you from the house
of the LORD.
27 The LORD is God, shining upon us.
Take the sacrifice and bind it with
cords on the altar.
28 You are my God, and I will praise you!
You are my God, and I will exalt you!

29 Give thanks to the LORD, for he is good!
His faithful love endures forever.

PSALM 119*

Aleph

1 Joyful are people of integrity,
who follow the instructions of the
LORD.
2 Joyful are those who obey his laws
and search for him with all their
hearts.
3 They do not compromise with evil,

119 This psalm is a Hebrew acrostic poem; there are twenty-two stanzas, one for each successive letter of the Hebrew alphabet. Each of the eight verses within each stanza begins with the Hebrew letter named in its heading.

and they walk only in his paths.
4 You have charged us
to keep your commandments
carefully.
5 Oh, that my actions would consistently
reflect your decrees!
6 Then I will not be ashamed
when I compare my life with your
commands.
7 As I learn your righteous regulations,
I will thank you by living as I should!
8 I will obey your decrees.
Please don't give up on me!

Beth

9 How can a young person stay pure?
By obeying your word.
10 I have tried hard to find you—
don't let me wander from your
commands.
11 I have hidden your word in my heart,
that I might not sin against you.
12 I praise you, O LORD;
teach me your decrees.
13 I have recited aloud
all the regulations you have given us.
14 I have rejoiced in your laws
as much as in riches.
15 I will study your commandments
and reflect on your ways.
16 I will delight in your decrees
and not forget your word.

Gimel

17 Be good to your servant,
that I may live and obey your word.
18 Open my eyes to see
the wonderful truths in your instructions.
19 I am only a foreigner in the land.
Don't hide your commands from me!
20 I am always overwhelmed
with a desire for your regulations.
21 You rebuke the arrogant;
those who wander from your
commands are cursed.
22 Don't let them scorn and insult me,
for I have obeyed your laws.
23 Even princes sit and speak against me,
but I will meditate on your decrees.
24 Your laws please me;
they give me wise advice.

Daleth

25 I lie in the dust;
revive me by your word.
26 I told you my plans, and you answered.
Now teach me your decrees.
27 Help me understand the meaning of your
commandments,
and I will meditate on your wonderful
deeds.

IS IT OK?

IS IT OK TO WATCH A SHOW WITH BAD STUFF IN IT IF IT'S MOSTLY GOOD?

Would you drink a tall, creamy Oreo milkshake if it had just a *little* poison in it? What if the milkshake looked delicious? What if it was just a *tiny* drop of poison (not enough to kill you, just enough to make you sick)? Would you drink it? You have the same choice about what to feed your mind. A show might look good . . . but the bad parts are poison to your mind. One of your goals, according to Psalm 119:9, should be to stay pure, which you do by keeping your mind pure. If you can't cut out the bad parts of a show, or if you're wondering if you should really be watching it—then turn it off.

28 I weep with sorrow;
encourage me by your word.
29 Keep me from lying to myself;
give me the privilege of knowing your instructions.
30 I have chosen to be faithful;
I have determined to live by your regulations.
31 I cling to your laws.
LORD, don't let me be put to shame!
32 I will pursue your commands,
for you expand my understanding.

He

33 Teach me your decrees, O LORD;
I will keep them to the end.
34 Give me understanding and I will obey your instructions;
I will put them into practice with all my heart.
35 Make me walk along the path of your commands,
for that is where my happiness is found.
36 Give me an eagerness for your laws
rather than a love for money!
37 Turn my eyes from worthless things,
and give me life through your word.*
38 Reassure me of your promise,
made to those who fear you.
39 Help me abandon my shameful ways;
for your regulations are good.
40 I long to obey your commandments!
Renew my life with your goodness.

Waw

41 LORD, give me your unfailing love,
the salvation that you promised me.
42 Then I can answer those who taunt me,
for I trust in your word.
43 Do not snatch your word of truth from me,
for your regulations are my only hope.
44 I will keep on obeying your instructions
forever and ever.
45 I will walk in freedom,
for I have devoted myself to your commandments.
46 I will speak to kings about your laws,
and I will not be ashamed.
47 How I delight in your commands!
How I love them!
48 I honor and love your commands.
I meditate on your decrees.

Zayin

49 Remember your promise to me;
it is my only hope.
50 Your promise revives me;
it comforts me in all my troubles.
51 The proud hold me in utter contempt,
but I do not turn away from your instructions.
52 I meditate on your age-old regulations;
O LORD, they comfort me.
53 I become furious with the wicked,
because they reject your instructions.
54 Your decrees have been the theme of my songs
wherever I have lived.
55 I reflect at night on who you are, O LORD;
therefore, I obey your instructions.
56 This is how I spend my life:
obeying your commandments.

Heth

57 LORD, you are mine!
I promise to obey your words!
58 With all my heart I want your blessings.
Be merciful as you promised.
59 I pondered the direction of my life,
and I turned to follow your laws.
60 I will hurry, without delay,
to obey your commands.
61 Evil people try to drag me into sin,
but I am firmly anchored to your instructions.
62 I rise at midnight to thank you
for your just regulations.
63 I am a friend to anyone who fears you—
anyone who obeys your commandments.
64 O LORD, your unfailing love fills the earth;
teach me your decrees.

Teth

65 You have done many good things for me, LORD,
just as you promised.
66 I believe in your commands;
now teach me good judgment and knowledge.

119:37 Some manuscripts read *in your ways.*

ON TOP OF THE WORLD

Colin had a super teacher, and his best friends were in his classroom. His grades were good, and he was on the basketball team. Life couldn't be better! Recently, Colin and his best friend planned a weekend camp-out—just the two of them. But Colin's dad reminded him that the youth retreat was the same weekend. Colin wanted to go on the camp-out. *I don't need that God stuff,* Colin thought. *My life is great. Church is only for when you're in trouble.* What do you think Colin should do? Read Psalm 119:65-66.

67 I used to wander off until you
disciplined me;
but now I closely follow your word.
68 You are good and do only good;
teach me your decrees.
69 Arrogant people smear me with lies,
but in truth I obey your
commandments with all my heart.
70 Their hearts are dull and stupid,
but I delight in your instructions.
71 My suffering was good for me,
for it taught me to pay attention to your
decrees.
72 Your instructions are more valuable to me
than millions in gold and silver.

Yodh

73 You made me; you created me.
Now give me the sense to follow your
commands.
74 May all who fear you find in me a cause
for joy,
for I have put my hope in your word.
75 I know, O LORD, that your regulations are
fair;
you disciplined me because I needed it.
76 Now let your unfailing love comfort me,
just as you promised me, your servant.
77 Surround me with your tender mercies so
I may live,
for your instructions are my delight.
78 Bring disgrace upon the arrogant people
who lied about me;
meanwhile, I will concentrate on your
commandments.
79 Let me be united with all who fear you,
with those who know your laws.
80 May I be blameless in keeping your
decrees;
then I will never be ashamed.

Kaph

81 I am worn out waiting for your rescue,
but I have put my hope in your word.
82 My eyes are straining to see your promises
come true.
When will you comfort me?
83 I am shriveled like a wineskin in the
smoke,
but I have not forgotten to obey your
decrees.
84 How long must I wait?
When will you punish those who
persecute me?
85 These arrogant people who hate your
instructions
have dug deep pits to trap me.
86 All your commands are trustworthy.
Protect me from those who hunt me
down without cause.
87 They almost finished me off,
but I refused to abandon your
commandments.

88 In your unfailing love, spare my life;
then I can continue to obey your laws.

Lamedh

89 Your eternal word, O LORD,
stands firm in heaven.
90 Your faithfulness extends to every generation,
as enduring as the earth you created.
91 Your regulations remain true to this day,
for everything serves your plans.
92 If your instructions hadn't sustained me with joy,
I would have died in my misery.
93 I will never forget your commandments,
for by them you give me life.
94 I am yours; rescue me!
For I have worked hard at obeying your commandments.
95 Though the wicked hide along the way to kill me,
I will quietly keep my mind on your laws.
96 Even perfection has its limits,
but your commands have no limit.

Mem

97 Oh, how I love your instructions!
I think about them all day long.
98 Your commands make me wiser than my enemies,
for they are my constant guide.
99 Yes, I have more insight than my teachers,
for I am always thinking of your laws.

AMAZING FACTS

Congratulations! You are at the very center of the Bible in the middle of the longest psalm, which has 176 verses!
PSALM 119:88

Nun

105 Your word is a lamp to guide my feet
and a light for my path.
106 I've promised it once, and I'll promise it again:
I will obey your righteous regulations.
107 I have suffered much, O LORD;
restore my life again as you promised.
108 LORD, accept my offering of praise,
and teach me your regulations.
109 My life constantly hangs in the balance,
but I will not stop obeying your instructions.
110 The wicked have set their traps for me,

Why is it important to read the Bible?

Your commands make me wiser than my enemies. . . . I have more insight than my teachers. PSALM 119:98-99

100 I am even wiser than my elders,
for I have kept your commandments.
101 I have refused to walk on any evil path,
so that I may remain obedient to your word.
102 I haven't turned away from your regulations,
for you have taught me well.
103 How sweet your words taste to me;
they are sweeter than honey.
104 Your commandments give me understanding;
no wonder I hate every false way of life.

but I will not turn from your commandments.
111 Your laws are my treasure;
they are my heart's delight.
112 I am determined to keep your decrees to the very end.

Samekh

113 I hate those with divided loyalties,
but I love your instructions.
114 You are my refuge and my shield;
your word is my source of hope.
115 Get out of my life, you evil-minded people,

for I intend to obey the commands of
my God.
116 LORD, sustain me as you promised, that
I may live!
Do not let my hope be crushed.
117 Sustain me, and I will be rescued;
then I will meditate continually on your
decrees.
118 But you have rejected all who stray from
your decrees.
They are only fooling themselves.
119 You skim off the wicked of the earth like
scum;
no wonder I love to obey your laws!
120 I tremble in fear of you;
I stand in awe of your regulations.

Ayin

121 Don't leave me to the mercy of my
enemies,
for I have done what is just and right.
122 Please guarantee a blessing for me.
Don't let the arrogant oppress me!
123 My eyes strain to see your rescue,
to see the truth of your promise
fulfilled.
124 I am your servant; deal with me in
unfailing love,
and teach me your decrees.
125 Give discernment to me, your servant;
then I will understand your laws.
126 LORD, it is time for you to act,
for these evil people have violated your
instructions.
127 Truly, I love your commands
more than gold, even the finest gold.
128 Each of your commandments is right.
That is why I hate every false way.

Pe

129 Your laws are wonderful.
No wonder I obey them!
130 The teaching of your word gives light,
so even the simple can understand.
131 I pant with expectation,
longing for your commands.
132 Come and show me your mercy,
as you do for all who love your name.
133 Guide my steps by your word,
so I will not be overcome by evil.
134 Ransom me from the oppression of evil
people;
then I can obey your commandments.
135 Look upon me with love;
teach me your decrees.
136 Rivers of tears gush from my eyes
because people disobey your instructions.

Tsadhe

137 O LORD, you are righteous,
and your regulations are fair.
138 Your laws are perfect
and completely trustworthy.
139 I am overwhelmed with indignation,
for my enemies have disregarded your
words.
140 Your promises have been thoroughly
tested;
that is why I love them so much.
141 I am insignificant and despised,
but I don't forget your commandments.
142 Your justice is eternal,
and your instructions are perfectly
true.
143 As pressure and stress bear down on me,
I find joy in your commands.
144 Your laws are always right;
help me to understand them so I may
live.

Qoph

145 I pray with all my heart; answer me, LORD!
I will obey your decrees.
146 I cry out to you; rescue me,
that I may obey your laws.
147 I rise early, before the sun is up;
I cry out for help and put my hope in
your words.
148 I stay awake through the night,
thinking about your promise.
149 In your faithful love, O LORD, hear my cry;
let me be revived by following your
regulations.
150 Lawless people are coming to attack me;
they live far from your instructions.
151 But you are near, O LORD,
and all your commands are true.
152 I have known from my earliest days
that your laws will last forever.

Resh

153 Look upon my suffering and rescue me,
for I have not forgotten your
instructions.
154 Argue my case; take my side!
Protect my life as you promised.
155 The wicked are far from rescue,

for they do not bother with your decrees.
156 LORD, how great is your mercy;
let me be revived by following your regulations.
157 Many persecute and trouble me,
yet I have not swerved from your laws.
158 Seeing these traitors makes me sick at heart,
because they care nothing for your word.
159 See how I love your commandments, LORD.
Give back my life because of your unfailing love.
160 The very essence of your words is truth;
all your just regulations will stand forever.

Shin

161 Powerful people harass me without cause,
but my heart trembles only at your word.
162 I rejoice in your word
like one who discovers a great treasure.
163 I hate and abhor all falsehood,
but I love your instructions.
164 I will praise you seven times a day
because all your regulations are just.
165 Those who love your instructions have great peace
and do not stumble.
166 I long for your rescue, LORD,
so I have obeyed your commands.
167 I have obeyed your laws,
for I love them very much.
168 Yes, I obey your commandments and laws
because you know everything I do.

Taw

169 O LORD, listen to my cry;
give me the discerning mind you promised.
170 Listen to my prayer;
rescue me as you promised.
171 Let praise flow from my lips,
for you have taught me your decrees.
172 Let my tongue sing about your word,
for all your commands are right.
173 Give me a helping hand,
for I have chosen to follow your commandments.
174 O LORD, I have longed for your rescue,
and your instructions are my delight.
175 Let me live so I can praise you,
and may your regulations help me.
176 I have wandered away like a lost sheep;
come and find me,
for I have not forgotten your commands.

PSALM 120

A song for pilgrims ascending to Jerusalem.

1 I took my troubles to the LORD;
I cried out to him, and he answered my prayer.
2 Rescue me, O LORD, from liars
and from all deceitful people.
3 O deceptive tongue, what will God do to you?
How will he increase your punishment?
4 You will be pierced with sharp arrows
and burned with glowing coals.
5 How I suffer in far-off Meshech.
It pains me to live in distant Kedar.
6 I am tired of living
among people who hate peace.
7 I search for peace;
but when I speak of peace, they want war!

PSALM 121

A song for pilgrims ascending to Jerusalem.

1 I look up to the mountains—
does my help come from there?
2 My help comes from the LORD,
who made heaven and earth!
3 He will not let you stumble;
the one who watches over you will not slumber.
4 Indeed, he who watches over Israel
never slumbers or sleeps.
5 The LORD himself watches over you!
The LORD stands beside you as your protective shade.
6 The sun will not harm you by day,
nor the moon at night.
7 The LORD keeps you from all harm
and watches over your life.

8 The LORD keeps watch over you as you
come and go,
both now and forever.

PSALM 122

A song for pilgrims ascending to Jerusalem.
A psalm of David.

1 I was glad when they said to me,
"Let us go to the house of the LORD."
2 And now here we are,
standing inside your gates,
O Jerusalem.
3 Jerusalem is a well-built city;
its seamless walls cannot be breached.
4 All the tribes of Israel—the LORD's people—
make their pilgrimage here.
They come to give thanks to the name of
the LORD,
as the law requires of Israel.
5 Here stand the thrones where judgment
is given,
the thrones of the dynasty of David.

6 Pray for peace in Jerusalem.
May all who love this city prosper.
7 O Jerusalem, may there be peace within
your walls
and prosperity in your palaces.
8 For the sake of my family and friends,
I will say,
"May you have peace."
9 For the sake of the house of the LORD
our God,
I will seek what is best for you,
O Jerusalem.

PSALM 123

A song for pilgrims ascending to Jerusalem.

1 I lift my eyes to you,
O God, enthroned in heaven.
2 We keep looking to the LORD our God for
his mercy,
just as servants keep their eyes on their
master,
as a slave girl watches her mistress for
the slightest signal.
3 Have mercy on us, LORD, have mercy,
for we have had our fill of contempt.
4 We have had more than our fill of the
scoffing of the proud
and the contempt of the arrogant.

126:1 Hebrew *Zion*.

PSALM 124

A song for pilgrims ascending to Jerusalem.
A psalm of David.

1 What if the LORD had not been on
our side?
Let all Israel repeat:
2 What if the LORD had not been on
our side
when people attacked us?
3 They would have swallowed us alive
in their burning anger.
4 The waters would have engulfed us;
a torrent would have overwhelmed us.
5 Yes, the raging waters of their fury
would have overwhelmed our very lives.

6 Praise the LORD,
who did not let their teeth tear us apart!
7 We escaped like a bird from a hunter's
trap.
The trap is broken, and we are free!
8 Our help is from the LORD,
who made heaven and earth.

PSALM 125

A song for pilgrims ascending to Jerusalem.

1 Those who trust in the LORD are as secure
as Mount Zion;
they will not be defeated but will
endure forever.
2 Just as the mountains surround Jerusalem,
so the LORD surrounds his people, both
now and forever.
3 The wicked will not rule the land of the
godly,
for then the godly might be tempted to
do wrong.
4 O LORD, do good to those who are good,
whose hearts are in tune with you.
5 But banish those who turn to crooked
ways, O LORD.
Take them away with those who do
evil.

May Israel have peace!

PSALM 126

A song for pilgrims ascending to Jerusalem.

1 When the LORD brought back his exiles
to Jerusalem,*
it was like a dream!

[2] We were filled with laughter,
and we sang for joy.
And the other nations said,
"What amazing things the LORD has done for them."
[3] Yes, the LORD has done amazing things for us!
What joy!

[4] Restore our fortunes, LORD,
as streams renew the desert.
[5] Those who plant in tears
will harvest with shouts of joy.
[6] They weep as they go to plant their seed,
but they sing as they return with the harvest.

PSALM 127

A song for pilgrims ascending to Jerusalem.
A psalm of Solomon.

[1] Unless the LORD builds a house,
the work of the builders is wasted.
Unless the LORD protects a city,
guarding it with sentries will do no good.
[2] It is useless for you to work so hard
from early morning until late at night,
anxiously working for food to eat;
for God gives rest to his loved ones.

[3] Children are a gift from the LORD;
they are a reward from him.
[4] Children born to a young man
are like arrows in a warrior's hands.
[5] How joyful is the man whose quiver is full of them!
He will not be put to shame when he confronts his accusers at the city gates.

PSALM 128

A song for pilgrims ascending to Jerusalem.

[1] How joyful are those who fear the LORD—
all who follow his ways!

HOW GOD IS DESCRIBED IN PSALMS

Most of the psalms speak to God or about God. Here is a sample of how the psalm writers describe God.

God is . . .	References
All-knowing and ever-present	Psalm 139
Beautiful and desirable	Psalms 27; 36; 45
Creator	Psalms 8; 104; 148
Good and generous	Psalms 34; 81; 107
Great and sovereign	Psalms 33; 89; 96
Holy	Psalms 66; 99; 145
Loving and faithful	Psalms 23; 42; 51
Merciful and forgiving	Psalms 32; 111; 130
Powerful	Psalms 76; 89; 93
Willing to reveal his will, law, and direction	Psalms 1; 19; 119
Righteous and just	Psalms 71; 97; 113
Spirit	Psalms 104; 139; 143

2 You will enjoy the fruit of your labor.
How joyful and prosperous you will be!
3 Your wife will be like a fruitful grapevine,
flourishing within your home.
Your children will be like vigorous young olive trees
as they sit around your table.
4 That is the LORD's blessing
for those who fear him.

5 May the LORD continually bless you from Zion.
May you see Jerusalem prosper as long as you live.
6 May you live to enjoy your grandchildren.
May Israel have peace!

PSALM 129

A song for pilgrims ascending to Jerusalem.

1 From my earliest youth my enemies have persecuted me.
Let all Israel repeat this:
2 From my earliest youth my enemies have persecuted me,
but they have never defeated me.
3 My back is covered with cuts,
as if a farmer had plowed long furrows.
4 But the LORD is good;
he has cut me free from the ropes of the ungodly.

5 May all who hate Jerusalem*
be turned back in shameful defeat.
6 May they be as useless as grass on a rooftop,
turning yellow when only half grown,
7 ignored by the harvester,
despised by the binder.
8 And may those who pass by
refuse to give them this blessing:
"The LORD bless you;
we bless you in the LORD's name."

PSALM 130

A song for pilgrims ascending to Jerusalem.

1 From the depths of despair, O LORD,
I call for your help.
2 Hear my cry, O Lord.
Pay attention to my prayer.

3 LORD, if you kept a record of our sins,
who, O Lord, could ever survive?
4 But you offer forgiveness,
that we might learn to fear you.

5 I am counting on the LORD;
yes, I am counting on him.
I have put my hope in his word.
6 I long for the Lord
more than sentries long for the dawn,
yes, more than sentries long for the dawn.

7 O Israel, hope in the LORD;
for with the LORD there is unfailing love.
His redemption overflows.
8 He himself will redeem Israel
from every kind of sin.

PSALM 131

A song for pilgrims ascending to Jerusalem.
A psalm of David.

1 LORD, my heart is not proud;
my eyes are not haughty.
I don't concern myself with matters too great
or too awesome for me to grasp.
2 Instead, I have calmed and quieted myself,
like a weaned child who no longer cries for its mother's milk.
Yes, like a weaned child is my soul within me.

3 O Israel, put your hope in the LORD—
now and always.

PSALM 132

A song for pilgrims ascending to Jerusalem.

1 LORD, remember David
and all that he suffered.
2 He made a solemn promise to the LORD.
He vowed to the Mighty One of Israel,*
3 "I will not go home;
I will not let myself rest.
4 I will not let my eyes sleep
nor close my eyelids in slumber
5 until I find a place to build a house for the LORD,
a sanctuary for the Mighty One of Israel."

129:5 Hebrew *Zion.* **132:2** Hebrew *of Jacob;* also in 132:5. See note on 44:4.

The thing about brothers and sisters is that even though you love them to death, they can also drive you crazy. Sometimes you want to be with them, but sometimes you can't wait to get away from them. Unless you're an only child, you probably know what I mean.

I have an older sister—she's two years older than I am—and even though we're really different, we've always been close. When we were kids, we shared a room, and I always looked up to her. When she went away to college a year and a half ago, it was really strange. It was a hard time for our whole family. We were all excited for her, though, because she was able to go to the school she wanted to attend. She has experienced a whole new life there and really loves it. But her leaving home has left a big hole in our lives. Especially mine.

I basically lost a great friend. She and I still talk on the phone, and we catch up whenever she comes home, but it's different now. I guess that's normal.

On the good side, I have become much closer to the rest of my family. Plus I now have a role model for my life when I go to college next year.

Meanwhile, I'm trying not to take for granted the little everyday things of life. I try to remember to laugh with my brother and to cry and spend time with my little sister. Life changes, but as Romans 8:28 says, "God causes everything to work together for the good of those who love God." I can tell you that through these experiences, my family has gotten a lot closer.

Check out Psalm 133 and see the importance of unity and harmony among family members. Read also Psalm 34:14; Psalm 120:6; Proverbs 15:17; and Matthew 5:9.

6 We heard that the Ark was in Ephrathah;
then we found it in the distant
countryside of Jaar.
7 Let us go to the sanctuary of the LORD;
let us worship at the footstool of his
throne.
8 Arise, O LORD, and enter your resting
place,
along with the Ark, the symbol of your
power.
9 May your priests be clothed in godliness;
may your loyal servants sing for joy.
10 For the sake of your servant David,
do not reject the king you have
anointed.
11 The LORD swore an oath to David
with a promise he will never take back:
"I will place one of your descendants
on your throne.
12 If your descendants obey the terms of my
covenant
and the laws that I teach them,
then your royal line
will continue forever and ever."

13 For the LORD has chosen Jerusalem*;
he has desired it for his home.
14 "This is my resting place forever," he said.
"I will live here, for this is the home I
desired.
15 I will bless this city and make it
prosperous;
I will satisfy its poor with food.
16 I will clothe its priests with godliness;
its faithful servants will sing for joy.
17 Here I will increase the power of David;
my anointed one will be a light for my
people.
18 I will clothe his enemies with shame,
but he will be a glorious king."

PSALM 133

A song for pilgrims ascending to Jerusalem.
A psalm of David.

1 How wonderful and pleasant it is
when brothers live together in
harmony!
2 For harmony is as precious as the
anointing oil
that was poured over Aaron's head,
that ran down his beard
and onto the border of his robe.
3 Harmony is as refreshing as the dew from
Mount Hermon
that falls on the mountains of Zion.
And there the LORD has pronounced his
blessing,
even life everlasting.

PSALM 134

A song for pilgrims ascending to Jerusalem.

1 Oh, praise the LORD, all you servants
of the LORD,
you who serve at night in the house
of the LORD.
2 Lift up holy hands in prayer,
and praise the LORD.
3 May the LORD, who made heaven and
earth,
bless you from Jerusalem.*

PSALM 135

1 Praise the LORD!

Praise the name of the LORD!
Praise him, you who serve the LORD,
2 you who serve in the house of the LORD,
in the courts of the house of our God.
3 Praise the LORD, for the LORD is good;
celebrate his lovely name with music.
4 For the LORD has chosen Jacob for
himself,
Israel for his own special treasure.

5 I know the greatness of the LORD—
that our Lord is greater than any
other god.
6 The LORD does whatever pleases him
throughout all heaven and earth,
and on the seas and in their depths.
7 He causes the clouds to rise over the
whole earth.
He sends the lightning with the rain
and releases the wind from his
storehouses.

8 He destroyed the firstborn in each
Egyptian home,
both people and animals.
9 He performed miraculous signs and
wonders in Egypt
against Pharaoh and all his people.

132:13 Hebrew *Zion*. **134:3** Hebrew *Zion*.

10 He struck down great nations
and slaughtered mighty kings—
11 Sihon king of the Amorites,
Og king of Bashan,
and all the kings of Canaan.
12 He gave their land as an inheritance,
a special possession to his people
Israel.

13 Your name, O LORD, endures forever;
your fame, O LORD, is known to every
generation.
14 For the LORD will give justice to his people
and have compassion on his servants.

15 The idols of the nations are merely things
of silver and gold,
shaped by human hands.
16 They have mouths but cannot speak,
and eyes but cannot see.
17 They have ears but cannot hear,
and noses but cannot smell.
18 And those who make idols are just like
them,
as are all who trust in them.

19 O Israel, praise the LORD!
O priests—descendants of Aaron—
praise the LORD!
20 O Levites, praise the LORD!
All you who fear the LORD, praise the
LORD!
21 The LORD be praised from Zion,
for he lives here in Jerusalem.

Praise the LORD!

PSALM 136

1 Give thanks to the LORD, for he is good!
His faithful love endures forever.
2 Give thanks to the God of gods.
His faithful love endures forever.
3 Give thanks to the Lord of lords.
His faithful love endures forever.

4 Give thanks to him who alone does
mighty miracles.
His faithful love endures forever.
5 Give thanks to him who made the heavens
so skillfully.
His faithful love endures forever.
6 Give thanks to him who placed the earth
among the waters.
His faithful love endures forever.

7 Give thanks to him who made the
heavenly lights—
His faithful love endures forever.
8 the sun to rule the day,
His faithful love endures forever.
9 and the moon and stars to rule the
night.
His faithful love endures forever.

10 Give thanks to him who killed the
firstborn of Egypt.
His faithful love endures forever.
11 He brought Israel out of Egypt.
His faithful love endures forever.
12 He acted with a strong hand and powerful
arm.
His faithful love endures forever.
13 Give thanks to him who parted the Red
Sea.*
His faithful love endures forever.
14 He led Israel safely through,
His faithful love endures forever.
15 but he hurled Pharaoh and his army into
the Red Sea.
His faithful love endures forever.
16 Give thanks to him who led his people
through the wilderness.
His faithful love endures forever.

17 Give thanks to him who struck down
mighty kings.
His faithful love endures forever.
18 He killed powerful kings—
His faithful love endures forever.
19 Sihon king of the Amorites,
His faithful love endures forever.
20 and Og king of Bashan.
His faithful love endures forever.
21 God gave the land of these kings as an
inheritance—
His faithful love endures forever.
22 a special possession to his servant Israel.
His faithful love endures forever.

23 He remembered us in our weakness.
His faithful love endures forever.
24 He saved us from our enemies.
His faithful love endures forever.
25 He gives food to every living thing.
His faithful love endures forever.
26 Give thanks to the God of heaven.
His faithful love endures forever.

136:13 Hebrew *sea of reeds;* also in 136:15.

PSALM 137

1 Beside the rivers of Babylon, we sat and wept
as we thought of Jerusalem.*
2 We put away our harps,
hanging them on the branches of poplar trees.
3 For our captors demanded a song from us.
Our tormentors insisted on a joyful hymn:
"Sing us one of those songs of Jerusalem!"
4 But how can we sing the songs of the LORD
while in a pagan land?
5 If I forget you, O Jerusalem,
let my right hand forget how to play the harp.
6 May my tongue stick to the roof of my mouth
if I fail to remember you,
if I don't make Jerusalem my greatest joy.
7 O LORD, remember what the Edomites did
on the day the armies of Babylon captured Jerusalem.
"Destroy it!" they yelled.
"Level it to the ground!"
8 O Babylon, you will be destroyed.
Happy is the one who pays you back
for what you have done to us.
9 Happy is the one who takes your babies
and smashes them against the rocks!

137:1 Hebrew *Zion;* also in 137:3.

PSALM 138

A psalm of David.

1 I give you thanks, O LORD, with all my heart;
I will sing your praises before the gods.
2 I bow before your holy Temple as I worship.
I praise your name for your unfailing love and faithfulness;
for your promises are backed
by all the honor of your name.
3 As soon as I pray, you answer me;
you encourage me by giving me strength.
4 Every king in all the earth will thank you, LORD,
for all of them will hear your words.
5 Yes, they will sing about the LORD's ways,
for the glory of the LORD is very great.
6 Though the LORD is great, he cares for the humble,
but he keeps his distance from the proud.

IS IT OK?

IS IT OK IF I WANT TO BUILD THE PERFECT BODY?

It's OK to want to be healthy and take care of your body. But our culture is obsessed with looking good, considering big muscles a requirement for being popular. It's *not* OK to be obsessed with being muscular—to go crazy with working out—because then you get distracted from stuff that matters in life by something that truly doesn't matter. Whether you're naturally muscular or not, *you* are God's workmanship, and he considers you "marvelous" (see Psalm 139:14). What a compliment from your Maker! If God respects you and likes you the way you are, shouldn't you accept yourself too?

7 Though I am surrounded by troubles,
you will protect me from the anger
of my enemies.
You reach out your hand,
and the power of your right hand
saves me.
8 The LORD will work out his plans for
my life—
for your faithful love, O LORD, endures
forever.
Don't abandon me, for you made me.

PSALM 139

For the choir director: A psalm of David.

1 O LORD, you have examined my heart
and know everything about me.
2 You know when I sit down or stand up.
You know my thoughts even when I'm
far away.
3 You see me when I travel
and when I rest at home.
You know everything I do.
4 You know what I am going to say
even before I say it, LORD.
5 You go before me and follow me.
You place your hand of blessing on my
head.
6 Such knowledge is too wonderful for me,
too great for me to understand!
7 I can never escape from your Spirit!
I can never get away from your presence!
8 If I go up to heaven, you are there;
if I go down to the grave,* you are there.
9 If I ride the wings of the morning,
if I dwell by the farthest oceans,
10 even there your hand will guide me,
and your strength will support me.
11 I could ask the darkness to hide me
and the light around me to become
night—
12 but even in darkness I cannot hide
from you.
To you the night shines as bright as day.
Darkness and light are the same to you.
13 You made all the delicate, inner parts of
my body
and knit me together in my mother's
womb.
14 Thank you for making me so wonderfully
complex!
Your workmanship is marvelous—how
well I know it.
15 You watched me as I was being formed in
utter seclusion,
as I was woven together in the dark of
the womb.
16 You saw me before I was born.

139:8 Hebrew *to Sheol.*

Meet My Brother

Phillip had a leading role at his school's winter play, and his family came to see him. Phillip wanted his friends to meet his family and his younger brother, Ellis. Ellis was born with a nerve disorder that caused him to make sudden loud noises. Phillip loved Ellis and was sure his friends would too. Just before he went onstage, Phillip heard Ellis making noises. His friends started giggling. One guy said, "Who brought that dorky little kid? What a weirdo." Phillip turned red with embarrassment. What should he do? Look at Psalm 139:15-17.

Every day of my life was recorded in
your book.
Every moment was laid out
before a single day had passed.

17 How precious are your thoughts about
me,* O God.
They cannot be numbered!

Does God really spend time thinking about me?

How precious are your thoughts about me, O God. They cannot be numbered! PSALM 139:17

18 I can't even count them;
they outnumber the grains of sand!
And when I wake up,
you are still with me!

19 O God, if only you would destroy the
wicked!
Get out of my life, you murderers!
20 They blaspheme you;
your enemies misuse your name.
21 O LORD, shouldn't I hate those who hate
you?
Shouldn't I despise those who oppose
you?
22 Yes, I hate them with total hatred,
for your enemies are my enemies.

23 Search me, O God, and know my heart;
test me and know my anxious thoughts.
24 Point out anything in me that offends you,
and lead me along the path of
everlasting life.

PSALM 140

For the choir director: A psalm of David.

1 O LORD, rescue me from evil people.
Protect me from those who are violent,
2 those who plot evil in their hearts
and stir up trouble all day long.
3 Their tongues sting like a snake;
the venom of a viper drips from their
lips. *Interlude*

4 O LORD, keep me out of the hands of the
wicked.
Protect me from those who are violent,
for they are plotting against me.
5 The proud have set a trap to catch me;
they have stretched out a net;
they have placed traps all along
the way. *Interlude*

6 I said to the LORD, "You are my God!"
Listen, O LORD, to my cries for mercy!
7 O Sovereign LORD, the strong one who
rescued me,
you protected me on the day of battle.
8 LORD, do not let evil people have their
way.
Do not let their evil schemes succeed,
or they will become proud.
Interlude

9 Let my enemies be destroyed
by the very evil they have planned
for me.
10 Let burning coals fall down on their
heads.
Let them be thrown into the fire
or into watery pits from which they
can't escape.
11 Don't let liars prosper here in our land.
Cause great disasters to fall on the
violent.

12 But I know the LORD will help those they
persecute;
he will give justice to the poor.
13 Surely righteous people are praising your
name;
the godly will live in your presence.

PSALM 141

A psalm of David.

1 O LORD, I am calling to you. Please hurry!
Listen when I cry to you for help!
2 Accept my prayer as incense offered
to you,
and my upraised hands as an evening
offering.

3 Take control of what I say, O LORD,
and guard my lips.
4 Don't let me drift toward evil

139:17 Or *How precious to me are your thoughts.*

or take part in acts of wickedness.
Don't let me share in the delicacies
of those who do wrong.
5 Let the godly strike me!
It will be a kindness!
If they correct me, it is soothing medicine.
Don't let me refuse it.
But I pray constantly
against the wicked and their deeds.
6 When their leaders are thrown down
from a cliff,
the wicked will listen to my words and
find them true.
7 Like rocks brought up by a plow,
the bones of the wicked will lie
scattered without burial.*
8 I look to you for help, O Sovereign LORD.
You are my refuge; don't let them
kill me.
9 Keep me from the traps they have set
for me,
from the snares of those who do
wrong.
10 Let the wicked fall into their own nets,
but let me escape.

PSALM 142

A psalm of David, regarding his experience in the cave. A prayer.*

1 I cry out to the LORD;
I plead for the LORD's mercy.
2 I pour out my complaints before him
and tell him all my troubles.
3 When I am overwhelmed,
you alone know the way I should turn.
Wherever I go,
my enemies have set traps for me.
4 I look for someone to come and
help me,
but no one gives me a passing
thought!
No one will help me;
no one cares a bit what happens to me.
5 Then I pray to you, O LORD.
I say, "You are my place of refuge.
You are all I really want in life.
6 Hear my cry,
for I am very low.
Rescue me from my persecutors,
for they are too strong for me.
7 Bring me out of prison
so I can thank you.
The godly will crowd around me,
for you are good to me."

PSALM 143

A psalm of David.

1 Hear my prayer, O LORD;
listen to my plea!
Answer me because you are faithful
and righteous.
2 Don't put your servant on trial,
for no one is innocent before you.
3 My enemy has chased me.
He has knocked me to the ground
and forces me to live in darkness like
those in the grave.
4 I am losing all hope;
I am paralyzed with fear.
5 I remember the days of old.
I ponder all your great works
and think about what you have
done.
6 I lift my hands to you in prayer.
I thirst for you as parched land thirsts
for rain. *Interlude*
7 Come quickly, LORD, and answer me,
for my depression deepens.
Don't turn away from me,
or I will die.
8 Let me hear of your unfailing love each
morning,
for I am trusting you.
Show me where to walk,
for I give myself to you.
9 Rescue me from my enemies, LORD;
I run to you to hide me.
10 Teach me to do your will,
for you are my God.
May your gracious Spirit lead me forward
on a firm footing.
11 For the glory of your name, O LORD,
preserve my life.
Because of your faithfulness, bring me
out of this distress.
12 In your unfailing love, silence all my
enemies
and destroy all my foes,
for I am your servant.

141:7 Hebrew *scattered at the mouth of Sheol.* 142:TITLE Hebrew *maskil.* This may be a literary or musical term.

PSALM 144

A psalm of David.

1 Praise the LORD, who is my rock.
He trains my hands for war
and gives my fingers skill for battle.
2 He is my loving ally and my fortress,
my tower of safety, my rescuer.
He is my shield, and I take refuge in him.
He makes the nations* submit to me.

3 O LORD, what are human beings that you
should notice them,
mere mortals that you should think
about them?
4 For they are like a breath of air;
their days are like a passing shadow.

5 Open the heavens, LORD, and come down.
Touch the mountains so they billow
smoke.
6 Hurl your lightning bolts and scatter your
enemies!
Shoot your arrows and confuse them!
7 Reach down from heaven and rescue me;
rescue me from deep waters,
from the power of my enemies.
8 Their mouths are full of lies;
they swear to tell the truth, but they lie
instead.

9 I will sing a new song to you, O God!
I will sing your praises with a ten-
stringed harp.
10 For you grant victory to kings!
You rescued your servant David from
the fatal sword.
11 Save me!
Rescue me from the power of my
enemies.
Their mouths are full of lies;
they swear to tell the truth, but they lie
instead.

12 May our sons flourish in their youth
like well-nurtured plants.
May our daughters be like graceful pillars,
carved to beautify a palace.
13 May our barns be filled
with crops of every kind.
May the flocks in our fields multiply by
the thousands,
even tens of thousands,
14 and may our oxen be loaded down
with produce.
May there be no enemy breaking through
our walls,
no going into captivity,
no cries of alarm in our town squares.
15 Yes, joyful are those who live like this!
Joyful indeed are those whose God is
the LORD.

PSALM 145*

A psalm of praise of David.

1 I will exalt you, my God and King,
and praise your name forever and ever.
2 I will praise you every day;
yes, I will praise you forever.
3 Great is the LORD! He is most worthy
of praise!
No one can measure his greatness.

4 Let each generation tell its children
of your mighty acts;
let them proclaim your power.
5 I will meditate* on your majestic, glorious
splendor
and your wonderful miracles.
6 Your awe-inspiring deeds will be on every
tongue;
I will proclaim your greatness.
7 Everyone will share the story of your
wonderful goodness;
they will sing with joy about your
righteousness.

8 The LORD is merciful and compassionate,
slow to get angry and filled with
unfailing love.
9 The LORD is good to everyone.
He showers compassion on all his
creation.
10 All of your works will thank you, LORD,
and your faithful followers will praise
you.
11 They will speak of the glory of your
kingdom;
they will give examples of your power.
12 They will tell about your mighty deeds
and about the majesty and glory of your
reign.
13 For your kingdom is an everlasting
kingdom.
You rule throughout all generations.

144:2 Some manuscripts read *my people*. **145** This psalm is a Hebrew acrostic poem; each verse (including 13b) begins with a successive letter of the Hebrew alphabet. **145:5** Some manuscripts read *They will speak*.

The LORD always keeps his promises;
he is gracious in all he does.*
14 The LORD helps the fallen
and lifts those bent beneath their loads.
15 The eyes of all look to you in hope;
you give them their food as they need it.
16 When you open your hand,
you satisfy the hunger and thirst of every living thing.
17 The LORD is righteous in everything he does;
he is filled with kindness.
18 The LORD is close to all who call on him,
yes, to all who call on him in truth.
19 He grants the desires of those who fear him;
he hears their cries for help and rescues them.
20 The LORD protects all those who love him,
but he destroys the wicked.

21 I will praise the LORD,
and may everyone on earth bless his holy name
forever and ever.

PSALM 146

1 Praise the LORD!

Let all that I am praise the LORD.
2 I will praise the LORD as long as I live.
I will sing praises to my God with my dying breath.

3 Don't put your confidence in powerful people;
there is no help for you there.
4 When they breathe their last, they return to the earth,
and all their plans die with them.
5 But joyful are those who have the God of Israel* as their helper,
whose hope is in the LORD their God.
6 He made heaven and earth,
the sea, and everything in them.
He keeps every promise forever.
7 He gives justice to the oppressed
and food to the hungry.
The LORD frees the prisoners.
8 The LORD opens the eyes of the blind.

The LORD lifts up those who are weighed down.
The LORD loves the godly.
9 The LORD protects the foreigners among us.
He cares for the orphans and widows,
but he frustrates the plans of the wicked.

10 The LORD will reign forever.
He will be your God, O Jerusalem,* throughout the generations.

Praise the LORD!

PSALM 147

1 Praise the LORD!

How good to sing praises to our God!
How delightful and how fitting!

145:13 The last two lines of 145:13 are not found in many of the ancient manuscripts. **146:5** Hebrew *of Jacob*. See note on 44:4. **146:10** Hebrew *Zion*.

2 The LORD is rebuilding Jerusalem
and bringing the exiles back to Israel.
3 He heals the brokenhearted
and bandages their wounds.
4 He counts the stars
and calls them all by name.
5 How great is our Lord! His power
is absolute!
His understanding is beyond
comprehension!
6 The LORD supports the humble,
but he brings the wicked down into
the dust.

7 Sing out your thanks to the LORD;
sing praises to our God with a harp.
8 He covers the heavens with clouds,
provides rain for the earth,
and makes the grass grow in mountain
pastures.
9 He gives food to the wild animals
and feeds the young ravens when
they cry.
10 He takes no pleasure in the strength
of a horse
or in human might.
11 No, the LORD's delight is in those who
fear him,
those who put their hope in his
unfailing love.

12 Glorify the LORD, O Jerusalem!
Praise your God, O Zion!
13 For he has strengthened the bars of your
gates
and blessed your children within your
walls.
14 He sends peace across your nation
and satisfies your hunger with the
finest wheat.
15 He sends his orders to the world—
how swiftly his word flies!
16 He sends the snow like white wool;
he scatters frost upon the ground like
ashes.
17 He hurls the hail like stones.*
Who can stand against his freezing
cold?
18 Then, at his command, it all melts.
He sends his winds, and the ice thaws.
19 He has revealed his words to Jacob,
his decrees and regulations to Israel.
20 He has not done this for any other nation;
they do not know his regulations.

Praise the LORD!

PSALM 148

1 Praise the LORD!

Praise the LORD from the heavens!
Praise him from the skies!
2 Praise him, all his angels!
Praise him, all the armies of heaven!
3 Praise him, sun and moon!
Praise him, all you twinkling stars!
4 Praise him, skies above!
Praise him, vapors high above the
clouds!
5 Let every created thing give praise to
the LORD,
for he issued his command, and they
came into being.
6 He set them in place forever and ever.
His decree will never be revoked.

7 Praise the LORD from the earth,
you creatures of the ocean depths,
8 fire and hail, snow and clouds,*
wind and weather that obey him,
9 mountains and all hills,
fruit trees and all cedars,
10 wild animals and all livestock,
small scurrying animals and birds,
11 kings of the earth and all people,
rulers and judges of the earth,
12 young men and young women,
old men and children.

13 Let them all praise the name of the LORD.
For his name is very great;
his glory towers over the earth and
heaven!
14 He has made his people strong,
honoring his faithful ones—
the people of Israel who are close
to him.

Praise the LORD!

PSALM 149

1 Praise the LORD!

Sing to the LORD a new song.
Sing his praises in the assembly of the
faithful.

147:17 Hebrew *like bread crumbs.* **148:8** Or *mist,* or *smoke.*

2 O Israel, rejoice in your Maker.
O people of Jerusalem,* exult in your King.
3 Praise his name with dancing,
accompanied by tambourine and harp.
4 For the LORD delights in his people;
he crowns the humble with victory.
5 Let the faithful rejoice that he honors them.
Let them sing for joy as they lie on their beds.

6 Let the praises of God be in their mouths,
and a sharp sword in their hands—
7 to execute vengeance on the nations
and punishment on the peoples,
8 to bind their kings with shackles
and their leaders with iron chains,
9 to execute the judgment written against them.
This is the glorious privilege of his faithful ones.

Praise the LORD!

149:2 Hebrew *Zion*.

PSALM 150

1 Praise the LORD!

Praise God in his sanctuary;
praise him in his mighty heaven!
2 Praise him for his mighty works;
praise his unequaled greatness!
3 Praise him with a blast of the ram's horn;
praise him with the lyre and harp!
4 Praise him with the tambourine and dancing;
praise him with strings and flutes!
5 Praise him with a clash of cymbals;
praise him with loud clanging cymbals.
6 Let everything that breathes sing praises to the LORD!

Praise the LORD!

PROVERBS

WHO
Solomon.

WHERE
Most were written by Solomon in Jerusalem while he was king of Israel.

WHEN
Early in Solomon's reign, just after 970 BC.

WHY
To help people apply God's wisdom and moral instruction to their lives.

My child, never forget the things I have taught you.
PROVERBS 3:1

There's a difference between having knowledge and having wisdom. *Wisdom* means understanding how to use our knowledge so we can live our lives well and make good choices. Even the smartest people can be failures if they aren't wise. Solomon was smart *and* wise. He wrote Ecclesiastes, Song of Songs, and most of Proverbs, a collection of short, wise statements.

LOOK FOR PROVERBS THAT WILL HELP YOU LIVE WELL. ASK GOD TO GIVE YOU WISDOM.

CHAPTER 1

The Purpose of Proverbs

These are the proverbs of Solomon, David's
son, king of Israel.
2 Their purpose is to teach people wisdom
and discipline,
to help them understand the insights
of the wise.
3 Their purpose is to teach people to live
disciplined and successful lives,
to help them do what is right, just,
and fair.
4 These proverbs will give insight to the
simple,
knowledge and discernment to the
young.

5 Let the wise listen to these proverbs and
become even wiser.
Let those with understanding receive
guidance
6 by exploring the meaning in these
proverbs and parables,
the words of the wise and their riddles.

7 Fear of the LORD is the foundation of true
knowledge,
but fools despise wisdom and
discipline.

A Father's Exhortation: Acquire Wisdom

8 My child,* listen when your father
corrects you.
Don't neglect your mother's
instruction.
9 What you learn from them will crown
you with grace
and be a chain of honor around your
neck.

Why should I listen to my parents?

Listen when your father corrects you. Don't neglect your mother's instruction. What you learn from them will crown you with grace and be a chain of honor.

PROVERBS 1:8-9

10 My child, if sinners entice you,
turn your back on them!
11 They may say, "Come and join us.
Let's hide and kill someone!
Just for fun, let's ambush the
innocent!
12 Let's swallow them alive, like the grave*;
let's swallow them whole, like those
who go down to the pit of death.
13 Think of the great things we'll get!
We'll fill our houses with all the stuff
we take.
14 Come, throw in your lot with us;
we'll all share the loot."

15 My child, don't go along with them!
Stay far away from their paths.
16 They rush to commit evil deeds.
They hurry to commit murder.
17 If a bird sees a trap being set,
it knows to stay away.
18 But these people set an ambush for
themselves;
they are trying to get themselves
killed.
19 Such is the fate of all who are greedy
for money;
it robs them of life.

Wisdom Shouts in the Streets

20 Wisdom shouts in the streets.
She cries out in the public square.
21 She calls to the crowds along the main
street,
to those gathered in front of the
city gate:
22 "How long, you simpletons,
will you insist on being simpleminded?
How long will you mockers relish your
mocking?
How long will you fools hate
knowledge?

23 Come and listen to my counsel.
I'll share my heart with you
and make you wise.

24 "I called you so often, but you wouldn't
come.
I reached out to you, but you paid
no attention.
25 You ignored my advice
and rejected the correction I offered.
26 So I will laugh when you are in trouble!
I will mock you when disaster
overtakes you—
27 when calamity overtakes you like a storm,
when disaster engulfs you like a cyclone,
and anguish and distress overwhelm
you.

28 "When they cry for help, I will not answer.
Though they anxiously search for me,
they will not find me.

1:8 Hebrew *My son;* also in 1:10, 15. **1:12** Hebrew *like Sheol.*

29 For they hated knowledge
and chose not to fear the LORD.
30 They rejected my advice
and paid no attention when I corrected them.
31 Therefore, they must eat the bitter fruit of living their own way,
choking on their own schemes.
32 For simpletons turn away from me—to death.
Fools are destroyed by their own complacency.
33 But all who listen to me will live in peace,
untroubled by fear of harm."

CHAPTER 2

The Benefits of Wisdom

1 My child,* listen to what I say,
and treasure my commands.
2 Tune your ears to wisdom,
and concentrate on understanding.
3 Cry out for insight,
and ask for understanding.
4 Search for them as you would for silver;
seek them like hidden treasures.
5 Then you will understand what it means to fear the LORD,
and you will gain knowledge of God.
6 For the LORD grants wisdom!
From his mouth come knowledge and understanding.
7 He grants a treasure of common sense to the honest.
He is a shield to those who walk with integrity.
8 He guards the paths of the just
and protects those who are faithful to him.
9 Then you will understand what is right, just, and fair,
and you will find the right way to go.
10 For wisdom will enter your heart,
and knowledge will fill you with joy.
11 Wise choices will watch over you.
Understanding will keep you safe.
12 Wisdom will save you from evil people,
from those whose words are twisted.
13 These men turn from the right way
to walk down dark paths.
14 They take pleasure in doing wrong,

and they enjoy the twisted ways of evil.
15 Their actions are crooked,
and their ways are wrong.
16 Wisdom will save you from the immoral woman,
from the seductive words of the promiscuous woman.
17 She has abandoned her husband
and ignores the covenant she made before God.
18 Entering her house leads to death;
it is the road to the grave.*
19 The man who visits her is doomed.
He will never reach the paths of life.
20 Follow the steps of good men instead,
and stay on the paths of the righteous.
21 For only the godly will live in the land,

2:1 Hebrew *My son.* 2:18 Hebrew *to the spirits of the dead.*

and those with integrity will remain
in it.
22 But the wicked will be removed from
the land,
and the treacherous will be uprooted.

CHAPTER 3

Trusting in the Lord

1 My child,* never forget the things I have
taught you.
Store my commands in your heart.
2 If you do this, you will live many years,
and your life will be satisfying.
3 Never let loyalty and kindness leave you!
Tie them around your neck as a
reminder.
Write them deep within your heart.
4 Then you will find favor with both God
and people,
and you will earn a good reputation.

5 Trust in the Lord with all your heart;
do not depend on your own
understanding.
6 Seek his will in all you do,
and he will show you which path
to take.

7 Don't be impressed with your own
wisdom.
Instead, fear the Lord and turn away
from evil.
8 Then you will have healing for your body
and strength for your bones.

9 Honor the Lord with your wealth
and with the best part of everything
you produce.
10 Then he will fill your barns with grain,
and your vats will overflow with good
wine.

11 My child, don't reject the Lord's
discipline,
and don't be upset when he
corrects you.
12 For the Lord corrects those he loves,
just as a father corrects a child in
whom he delights.*

13 Joyful is the person who finds wisdom,
the one who gains understanding.
14 For wisdom is more profitable than silver,
and her wages are better than gold.
15 Wisdom is more precious than rubies;
nothing you desire can compare
with her.
16 She offers you long life in her right hand,
and riches and honor in her left.
17 She will guide you down delightful paths;
all her ways are satisfying.
18 Wisdom is a tree of life to those who
embrace her;
happy are those who hold her tightly.

19 By wisdom the Lord founded the earth;
by understanding he created the
heavens.
20 By his knowledge the deep fountains
of the earth burst forth,
and the dew settles beneath the night
sky.

21 My child, don't lose sight of common
sense and discernment.
Hang on to them,
22 for they will refresh your soul.
They are like jewels on a necklace.
23 They keep you safe on your way,
and your feet will not stumble.
24 You can go to bed without fear;
you will lie down and sleep soundly.
25 You need not be afraid of sudden disaster
or the destruction that comes upon the
wicked,
26 for the Lord is your security.
He will keep your foot from being
caught in a trap.

27 Do not withhold good from those who
deserve it
when it's in your power to help them.
28 If you can help your neighbor now,
don't say,
"Come back tomorrow, and then I'll
help you."

29 Don't plot harm against your neighbor,
for those who live nearby trust you.
30 Don't pick a fight without reason,
when no one has done you harm.

31 Don't envy violent people
or copy their ways.
32 Such wicked people are detestable
to the Lord,
but he offers his friendship to the
godly.

3:1 Hebrew *My son;* also in 3:11, 21. **3:12** Greek version reads *And he punishes those he accepts as his children.* Compare Heb 12:6.

Who doesn't get in arguments with parents, right? One of the biggest conflicts between my parents and me for a while was grades. Sound familiar?

I made good grades all the way up to sixth grade; then, for some reason, I stopped caring. Maybe it was because my older brother and sister were such good students and I was trying to be different. Anyway, my mom said I had better straighten up, but I didn't. I just didn't try hard in school. Finally, in eleventh grade, I got into serious trouble for getting bad grades. My dad explained that if I didn't start making good grades, I would never get into college.

I waited way too long to get serious, but once I started making good grades, I did okay. Now when I do a poor job on a test, I actually get mad at myself!

As I look back at the years when I didn't care about school—sixth grade through tenth—I see that my attitude affected other areas of my life too. I didn't even have a good relationship with God. Since then, though, I've been more focused on him. I am in a great small group and am growing closer to God. I don't know what I will end up doing, but I'm sure I will do my best at whatever that ends up being.

I really appreciate my mom and dad for hanging in there with me. I'm actually glad they stayed on me. I see now that they weren't trying to make my life miserable. Instead, they were trying to help me have a better life down the road.

You might want to remember that fact the next time your parents are on your case to do your best.

Check out these amazing passages on the importance of listening to your parents—Proverbs 4 and Proverbs 6:20-23.

33 The LORD curses the house of the wicked,
but he blesses the home of the upright.

34 The LORD mocks the mockers
but is gracious to the humble.*

35 The wise inherit honor,
but fools are put to shame!

CHAPTER 4

A Father's Wise Advice

1 My children,* listen when your father
corrects you.
Pay attention and learn good judgment,
2 for I am giving you good guidance.
Don't turn away from my instructions.
3 For I, too, was once my father's son,
tenderly loved as my mother's only
child.

4 My father taught me,
"Take my words to heart.
Follow my commands, and you will live.
5 Get wisdom; develop good judgment.
Don't forget my words or turn away
from them.
6 Don't turn your back on wisdom, for she
will protect you.
Love her, and she will guard you.
7 Getting wisdom is the wisest thing you
can do!
And whatever else you do, develop
good judgment.
8 If you prize wisdom, she will make you
great.
Embrace her, and she will honor you.
9 She will place a lovely wreath on your
head;
she will present you with a beautiful
crown."

10 My child,* listen to me and do as I say,
and you will have a long, good life.
11 I will teach you wisdom's ways
and lead you in straight paths.
12 When you walk, you won't be held back;
when you run, you won't stumble.
13 Take hold of my instructions; don't let
them go.
Guard them, for they are the key to life.

14 Don't do as the wicked do,
and don't follow the path of evildoers.
15 Don't even think about it; don't go that
way.
Turn away and keep moving.
16 For evil people can't sleep until they've
done their evil deed for the day.
They can't rest until they've caused
someone to stumble.
17 They eat the food of wickedness
and drink the wine of violence!

18 The way of the righteous is like the first
gleam of dawn,
which shines ever brighter until the full
light of day.
19 But the way of the wicked is like total
darkness.
They have no idea what they are
stumbling over.

20 My child, pay attention to what I say.
Listen carefully to my words.
21 Don't lose sight of them.
Let them penetrate deep into your
heart,
22 for they bring life to those who find them,
and healing to their whole body.

23 Guard your heart above all else,
for it determines the course of
your life.

24 Avoid all perverse talk;
stay away from corrupt speech.

25 Look straight ahead,
and fix your eyes on what lies before
you.
26 Mark out a straight path for your feet;
stay on the safe path.
27 Don't get sidetracked;
keep your feet from following evil.

CHAPTER 5

Avoid Immoral Women

1 My son, pay attention to my wisdom;
listen carefully to my wise counsel.
2 Then you will show discernment,
and your lips will express what you've
learned.
3 For the lips of an immoral woman are as
sweet as honey,
and her mouth is smoother than oil.
4 But in the end she is as bitter as poison,

3:34 Greek version reads *The LORD opposes the proud / but favors the humble.* Compare Jas 4:6; 1 Pet 5:5. **4:1** Hebrew *My sons.* **4:10** Hebrew *My son;* also in 4:20.

as dangerous as a double-edged sword.
5 Her feet go down to death;
her steps lead straight to the grave.*
6 For she cares nothing about the path
to life.
She staggers down a crooked trail and
doesn't realize it.
7 So now, my sons, listen to me.
Never stray from what I am about
to say:
8 Stay away from her!
Don't go near the door of her house!
9 If you do, you will lose your honor
and will lose to merciless people all you
have achieved.
10 Strangers will consume your wealth,
and someone else will enjoy the fruit of
your labor.
11 In the end you will groan in anguish
when disease consumes your body.
12 You will say, "How I hated discipline!
If only I had not ignored all the
warnings!
13 Oh, why didn't I listen to my teachers?
Why didn't I pay attention to my
instructors?
14 I have come to the brink of utter ruin,
and now I must face public disgrace."
15 Drink water from your own well—
share your love only with your wife.*
16 Why spill the water of your springs in the
streets,
having sex with just anyone?*
17 You should reserve it for yourselves.
Never share it with strangers.
18 Let your wife be a fountain of blessing
for you.
Rejoice in the wife of your youth.
19 She is a loving deer, a graceful doe.
Let her breasts satisfy you always.
May you always be captivated by her
love.
20 Why be captivated, my son, by an immoral
woman,
or fondle the breasts of a promiscuous
woman?
21 For the LORD sees clearly what a man
does,
examining every path he takes.
22 An evil man is held captive by his own
sins;
they are ropes that catch and hold him.
23 He will die for lack of self-control;
he will be lost because of his great
foolishness.

CHAPTER 6

Lessons for Daily Life

1 My child,* if you have put up security for
a friend's debt
or agreed to guarantee the debt of a
stranger—
2 if you have trapped yourself by your
agreement
and are caught by what you said—
3 follow my advice and save yourself,
for you have placed yourself at your
friend's mercy.
Now swallow your pride;
go and beg to have your name erased.
4 Don't put it off; do it now!
Don't rest until you do.
5 Save yourself like a gazelle escaping from
a hunter,
like a bird fleeing from a net.
6 Take a lesson from the ants, you
lazybones.
Learn from their ways and become
wise!
7 Though they have no prince
or governor or ruler to make them
work,
8 they labor hard all summer,
gathering food for the winter.
9 But you, lazybones, how long will you
sleep?
When will you wake up?
10 A little extra sleep, a little more slumber,
a little folding of the hands to rest—
11 then poverty will pounce on you like
a bandit;
scarcity will attack you like an armed
robber.
12 What are worthless and wicked people
like?
They are constant liars,
13 signaling their deceit with a wink of the
eye,

5:5 Hebrew *to Sheol.* **5:15** Hebrew *Drink water from your own cistern, / flowing water from your own well.* **5:16** Hebrew *Why spill your springs in the streets, / your streams in the city squares?* **6:1** Hebrew *My son.*

a nudge of the foot, or the wiggle
of fingers.
14 Their perverted hearts plot evil,
and they constantly stir up trouble.
15 But they will be destroyed suddenly,
broken in an instant beyond all hope
of healing.

16 There are six things the LORD hates—
no, seven things he detests:
17 haughty eyes,
a lying tongue,
hands that kill the innocent,
18 a heart that plots evil,
feet that race to do wrong,
19 a false witness who pours out lies,
a person who sows discord in a family.

20 My son, obey your father's commands,
and don't neglect your mother's
instruction.
21 Keep their words always in your heart.
Tie them around your neck.
22 When you walk, their counsel will lead
you.
When you sleep, they will protect you.
When you wake up, they will advise
you.
23 For their command is a lamp
and their instruction a light;
their corrective discipline
is the way to life.
24 It will keep you from the immoral woman,
from the smooth tongue of a
promiscuous woman.
25 Don't lust for her beauty.
Don't let her coy glances seduce you.
26 For a prostitute will bring you to poverty,*
but sleeping with another man's wife
will cost you your life.
27 Can a man scoop a flame into his lap
and not have his clothes catch on fire?
28 Can he walk on hot coals
and not blister his feet?
29 So it is with the man who sleeps with
another man's wife.
He who embraces her will not go
unpunished.

30 Excuses might be found for a thief
who steals because he is starving.
31 But if he is caught, he must pay back
seven times what he stole,
even if he has to sell everything in his
house.
32 But the man who commits adultery is an
utter fool,
for he destroys himself.
33 He will be wounded and disgraced.

6:26 Hebrew *to a loaf of bread.*

PEOPLE CALLED "WISE" IN THE BIBLE

Twelve significant people in the Bible were called "wise." We can look up to these people.

Who	What	Where
Joseph	Wise leader	Acts 7:10
Moses	Wise leader	Acts 7:20-22
Bezalel	Wise artist	Exodus 31:1-5
Joshua	Wise leader	Deuteronomy 34:9
Samuel	Wise leader	1 Samuel 3:19
David	Wise leader	2 Samuel 14:20
Abigail	Wise wife	1 Samuel 25:3, 32-33
Solomon	Wise counselor	1 Kings 3:5-14; 4:29-34
Daniel	Wise leader	Daniel 5:11-12
Wise men	Wise learners	Matthew 2:1-10
Paul	Wise messenger	2 Peter 3:15
Christ	Wise youth	Luke 2:40, 52
	Wise Savior	1 Corinthians 1:20-25
	Wisdom of God	

His shame will never be erased.
34 For the woman's jealous husband will be furious,
and he will show no mercy when he takes revenge.
35 He will accept no compensation,
nor be satisfied with a payoff of any size.

CHAPTER 7

Another Warning about Immoral Women

1 Follow my advice, my son;
always treasure my commands.
2 Obey my commands and live!
Guard my instructions as you guard your own eyes.*
3 Tie them on your fingers as a reminder.
Write them deep within your heart.

4 Love wisdom like a sister;
make insight a beloved member of your family.
5 Let them protect you from an affair with an immoral woman,
from listening to the flattery of a promiscuous woman.

6 While I was at the window of my house,
looking through the curtain,
7 I saw some naive young men,
and one in particular who lacked common sense.
8 He was crossing the street near the house of an immoral woman,
strolling down the path by her house.
9 It was at twilight, in the evening,
as deep darkness fell.
10 The woman approached him,
seductively dressed and sly of heart.
11 She was the brash, rebellious type,
never content to stay at home.
12 She is often in the streets and markets,
soliciting at every corner.
13 She threw her arms around him and kissed him,
and with a brazen look she said,
14 "I've just made my peace offerings
and fulfilled my vows.
15 You're the one I was looking for!
I came out to find you, and here you are!
16 My bed is spread with beautiful blankets,
with colored sheets of Egyptian linen.
17 I've perfumed my bed
with myrrh, aloes, and cinnamon.
18 Come, let's drink our fill of love until morning.
Let's enjoy each other's caresses,
19 for my husband is not home.
He's away on a long trip.
20 He has taken a wallet full of money with him
and won't return until later this month.*"

21 So she seduced him with her pretty speech
and enticed him with her flattery.
22 He followed her at once,
like an ox going to the slaughter.
He was like a stag caught in a trap,
23 awaiting the arrow that would pierce its heart.
He was like a bird flying into a snare,
little knowing it would cost him his life.

24 So listen to me, my sons,
and pay attention to my words.
25 Don't let your hearts stray away toward her.
Don't wander down her wayward path.
26 For she has been the ruin of many;
many men have been her victims.
27 Her house is the road to the grave.*
Her bedroom is the den of death.

CHAPTER 8

Wisdom Calls for a Hearing

1 Listen as Wisdom calls out!
Hear as understanding raises her voice!
2 On the hilltop along the road,
she takes her stand at the crossroads.
3 By the gates at the entrance to the town,
on the road leading in, she cries aloud,
4 "I call to you, to all of you!
I raise my voice to all people.
5 You simple people, use good judgment.
You foolish people, show some understanding.
6 Listen to me! For I have important things to tell you.
Everything I say is right,
7 for I speak the truth
and detest every kind of deception.
8 My advice is wholesome.

7:2 Hebrew *as the pupil of your eye.* **7:20** Hebrew *until the moon is full.* **7:27** Hebrew *to Sheol.*

There is nothing devious or crooked
in it.
9 My words are plain to anyone with
understanding,
clear to those with knowledge.
10 Choose my instruction rather than silver,
and knowledge rather than pure gold.
11 For wisdom is far more valuable than
rubies.
Nothing you desire can compare
with it.

AMAZING FACTS

What's worth more than rubies, doesn't come in a box, and you can't see or hold it? Nothing other than wisdom!

PROVERBS 8:11

12 "I, Wisdom, live together with good
judgment.
I know where to discover knowledge
and discernment.
13 All who fear the LORD will hate evil.
Therefore, I hate pride and arrogance,
corruption and perverse speech.
14 Common sense and success belong
to me.
Insight and strength are mine.
15 Because of me, kings reign,
and rulers make just decrees.
16 Rulers lead with my help,
and nobles make righteous judgments.*
17 "I love all who love me.
Those who search will surely find me.
18 I have riches and honor,
as well as enduring wealth and justice.
19 My gifts are better than gold, even the
purest gold,
my wages better than sterling silver!
20 I walk in righteousness,
in paths of justice.
21 Those who love me inherit wealth.
I will fill their treasuries.
22 "The LORD formed me from the
beginning,
before he created anything else.
23 I was appointed in ages past,
at the very first, before the earth began.
24 I was born before the oceans were
created,
before the springs bubbled forth their
waters.
25 Before the mountains were formed,
before the hills, I was born—
26 before he had made the earth and fields
and the first handfuls of soil.
27 I was there when he established the
heavens,
when he drew the horizon on the
oceans.
28 I was there when he set the clouds above,
when he established springs deep in
the earth.
29 I was there when he set the limits of the
seas,
so they would not spread beyond their
boundaries.
And when he marked off the earth's
foundations,
30 I was the architect at his side.
I was his constant delight,
rejoicing always in his presence.
31 And how happy I was with the world he
created;
how I rejoiced with the human
family!
32 "And so, my children,* listen to me,
for all who follow my ways are joyful.
33 Listen to my instruction and be wise.
Don't ignore it.
34 Joyful are those who listen to me,
watching for me daily at my gates,
waiting for me outside my home!
35 For whoever finds me finds life
and receives favor from the LORD.
36 But those who miss me injure
themselves.
All who hate me love death."

8:16 Some Hebrew manuscripts and Greek version read *and nobles are judges over the earth.* **8:32** Hebrew *my sons.*

CHAPTER 9

1 Wisdom has built her house;
she has carved its seven columns.
2 She has prepared a great banquet,
mixed the wines, and set the table.
3 She has sent her servants to invite
everyone to come.
She calls out from the heights
overlooking the city.
4 "Come in with me," she urges the
simple.
To those who lack good judgment,
she says,
5 "Come, eat my food,
and drink the wine I have mixed.
6 Leave your simple ways behind, and
begin to live;
learn to use good judgment."

7 Anyone who rebukes a mocker will get
an insult in return.
Anyone who corrects the wicked will
get hurt.
8 So don't bother correcting mockers;
they will only hate you.
But correct the wise,
and they will love you.
9 Instruct the wise,
and they will be even wiser.
Teach the righteous,
and they will learn even more.

10 Fear of the LORD is the foundation
of wisdom.
Knowledge of the Holy One results
in good judgment.

11 Wisdom will multiply your days
and add years to your life.
12 If you become wise, you will be the one
to benefit.
If you scorn wisdom, you will be the
one to suffer.

Folly Calls for a Hearing

13 The woman named Folly is brash.
She is ignorant and doesn't know it.
14 She sits in her doorway
on the heights overlooking the city.
15 She calls out to men going by
who are minding their own
business.
16 "Come in with me," she urges the simple.
To those who lack good judgment,
she says,
17 "Stolen water is refreshing;
food eaten in secret tastes the best!"
18 But little do they know that the dead
are there.
Her guests are in the depths of the grave.*

CHAPTER 10

The Proverbs of Solomon

The proverbs of Solomon:

A wise child* brings joy to a father;
a foolish child brings grief to a mother.

2 Tainted wealth has no lasting value,
but right living can save your life.

3 The LORD will not let the godly go hungry,
but he refuses to satisfy the craving of
the wicked.

4 Lazy people are soon poor;
hard workers get rich.

5 A wise youth harvests in the summer,
but one who sleeps during harvest
is a disgrace.

6 The godly are showered with blessings;
the words of the wicked conceal violent
intentions.

7 We have happy memories of the godly,
but the name of a wicked person
rots away.

8 The wise are glad to be instructed,
but babbling fools fall flat on their
faces.

9 People with integrity walk safely,
but those who follow crooked paths
will slip and fall.

10 People who wink at wrong cause trouble,
but a bold reproof promotes peace.*

11 The words of the godly are a life-giving
fountain;
the words of the wicked conceal violent
intentions.

12 Hatred stirs up quarrels,
but love makes up for all offenses.

9:18 Hebrew *in Sheol.* **10:1** Hebrew *son;* also in 10:1b. **10:10** As in Greek version; Hebrew reads *but babbling fools fall flat on their faces.*

13 Wise words come from the lips of people
with understanding,
but those lacking sense will be beaten
with a rod.

14 Wise people treasure knowledge,
but the babbling of a fool invites
disaster.

15 The wealth of the rich is their fortress;
the poverty of the poor is their
destruction.

16 The earnings of the godly enhance their
lives,
but evil people squander their money
on sin.

17 People who accept discipline are on the
pathway to life,
but those who ignore correction will
go astray.

18 Hiding hatred makes you a liar;
slandering others makes you a fool.

19 Too much talk leads to sin.
Be sensible and keep your mouth shut.

20 The words of the godly are like sterling
silver;
the heart of a fool is worthless.

21 The words of the godly encourage many,
but fools are destroyed by their lack of
common sense.

22 The blessing of the LORD makes a person
rich,
and he adds no sorrow with it.

23 Doing wrong is fun for a fool,
but living wisely brings pleasure to the
sensible.

24 The fears of the wicked will be fulfilled;
the hopes of the godly will be granted.

25 When the storms of life come, the wicked
are whirled away,
but the godly have a lasting foundation.

26 Lazy people irritate their employers,
like vinegar to the teeth or smoke in
the eyes.

27 Fear of the LORD lengthens one's life,
but the years of the wicked are cut
short.

WHAT A TREAT!

Pedro was stuffing treat bags for the youth group's Christmas party. Every year, his church invited kids from the local homeless shelter to a big party. They played games, ate cookies, sang songs, and then handed out treat bags to each kid. Pedro's job was to put a handful of candy into each bag. While he was working, Pedro got a bit hungry—especially for a piece of chocolate candy! If a bag or two had a few less pieces of candy, no one would notice, would they? What do you think Pedro should do? Read Proverbs 11:1 for the answer.

28 The hopes of the godly result in happiness,
but the expectations of the wicked
come to nothing.

29 The way of the LORD is a stronghold to
those with integrity,
but it destroys the wicked.

30 The godly will never be disturbed,
but the wicked will be removed from
the land.

31 The mouth of the godly person gives wise advice,
but the tongue that deceives will be cut off.

32 The lips of the godly speak helpful words,
but the mouth of the wicked speaks perverse words.

CHAPTER 11

1 The LORD detests the use of dishonest scales,
but he delights in accurate weights.

Why is it so bad to peek at my friend's test paper?

Honesty guides good people; dishonesty destroys treacherous people. PROVERBS 11:3

2 Pride leads to disgrace,
but with humility comes wisdom.

3 Honesty guides good people;
dishonesty destroys treacherous people.

4 Riches won't help on the day of judgment,
but right living can save you from death.

5 The godly are directed by honesty;
the wicked fall beneath their load of sin.

6 The godliness of good people rescues them;
the ambition of treacherous people traps them.

7 When the wicked die, their hopes die with them,
for they rely on their own feeble strength.

8 The godly are rescued from trouble,
and it falls on the wicked instead.

9 With their words, the godless destroy their friends,
but knowledge will rescue the righteous.

10 The whole city celebrates when the godly succeed;
they shout for joy when the wicked die.

11 Upright citizens are good for a city and make it prosper,
but the talk of the wicked tears it apart.

12 It is foolish to belittle one's neighbor;
a sensible person keeps quiet.

13 A gossip goes around telling secrets,
but those who are trustworthy can keep a confidence.

14 Without wise leadership, a nation falls;
there is safety in having many advisers.

15 There's danger in putting up security for a stranger's debt;
it's safer not to guarantee another person's debt.

16 A gracious woman gains respect,
but ruthless men gain only wealth.

17 Your kindness will reward you,
but your cruelty will destroy you.

18 Evil people get rich for the moment,
but the reward of the godly will last.

19 Godly people find life;
evil people find death.

20 The LORD detests people with crooked hearts,
but he delights in those with integrity.

21 Evil people will surely be punished,
but the children of the godly will go free.

22 A beautiful woman who lacks discretion
is like a gold ring in a pig's snout.

23 The godly can look forward to a reward,
while the wicked can expect only judgment.

24 Give freely and become more wealthy;
be stingy and lose everything.

25 The generous will prosper;
those who refresh others will themselves be refreshed.

WHAT AN ANIMAL!
It was Joel's turn to feed and walk the dog, but he put off doing it. It became later and later. When Joel realized what time it was, he thought, *What should I do? I have a ton of stuff to do to get ready for Jerry's birthday party*. If Joel takes time to care for the dog, he will be late for the party. What would you tell Joel to do? For help with an answer, read Proverbs 12:10.

26 People curse those who hoard their grain,
but they bless the one who sells in time of need.

27 If you search for good, you will find favor;
but if you search for evil, it will find you!

28 Trust in your money and down you go!
But the godly flourish like leaves in spring.

29 Those who bring trouble on their families inherit the wind.
The fool will be a servant to the wise.

30 The seeds of good deeds become a tree of life;
a wise person wins friends.*

31 If the righteous are rewarded here on earth,
what will happen to wicked sinners?*

CHAPTER 12

1 To learn, you must love discipline;
it is stupid to hate correction.

2 The LORD approves of those who are good,
but he condemns those who plan wickedness.

3 Wickedness never brings stability,
but the godly have deep roots.

4 A worthy wife is a crown for her husband,
but a disgraceful woman is like cancer in his bones.

5 The plans of the godly are just;
the advice of the wicked is treacherous.

6 The words of the wicked are like a murderous ambush,
but the words of the godly save lives.

7 The wicked die and disappear,
but the family of the godly stands firm.

8 A sensible person wins admiration,
but a warped mind is despised.

9 Better to be an ordinary person with a servant
than to be self-important but have no food.

10 The godly care for their animals,
but the wicked are always cruel.

11 A hard worker has plenty of food,
but a person who chases fantasies has no sense.

12 Thieves are jealous of each other's loot,
but the godly are well rooted and bear their own fruit.

13 The wicked are trapped by their own words,
but the godly escape such trouble.

11:30 Or *and those who win souls are wise.* **11:31** Greek version reads *If the righteous are barely saved, / what will happen to godless sinners?* Compare 1 Pet 4:18.

14 Wise words bring many benefits,
and hard work brings rewards.

15 Fools think their own way is right,
but the wise listen to others.

16 A fool is quick-tempered,
but a wise person stays calm when
insulted.

17 An honest witness tells the truth;
a false witness tells lies.

18 Some people make cutting remarks,
but the words of the wise bring healing.

19 Truthful words stand the test of time,
but lies are soon exposed.

20 Deceit fills hearts that are plotting evil;
joy fills hearts that are planning
peace!

21 No harm comes to the godly,
but the wicked have their fill of
trouble.

What's so wrong about telling a little white lie?

The Lord detests lying lips, but he delights in those who tell the truth.

PROVERBS 12:22

22 The LORD detests lying lips,
but he delights in those who tell
the truth.

23 The wise don't make a show of their
knowledge,
but fools broadcast their foolishness.

24 Work hard and become a leader;
be lazy and become a slave.

25 Worry weighs a person down;
an encouraging word cheers
a person up.

26 The godly give good advice to their
friends;*
the wicked lead them astray.

27 Lazy people don't even cook the game
they catch,
but the diligent make use of everything
they find.

28 The way of the godly leads to life;
that path does not lead to death.

CHAPTER 13

1 A wise child accepts a parent's
discipline;*
a mocker refuses to listen to
correction.

2 Wise words will win you a good meal,
but treacherous people have an
appetite for violence.

3 Those who control their tongue will have
a long life;
opening your mouth can ruin
everything.

4 Lazy people want much but get little,
but those who work hard will
prosper.

5 The godly hate lies;
the wicked cause shame and disgrace.

6 Godliness guards the path of the
blameless,
but the evil are misled by sin.

7 Some who are poor pretend to be rich;
others who are rich pretend to
be poor.

8 The rich can pay a ransom for their lives,
but the poor won't even get threatened.

9 The life of the godly is full of light
and joy,
but the light of the wicked will be
snuffed out.

10 Pride leads to conflict;
those who take advice are wise.

11 Wealth from get-rich-quick schemes
quickly disappears;
wealth from hard work grows over
time.

12:26 Or *The godly are cautious in friendship;* or *The godly are freed from evil.* The meaning of the Hebrew is uncertain.
13:1 Hebrew *A wise son accepts his father's discipline.*

12 Hope deferred makes the heart sick,
but a dream fulfilled is a tree of life.

13 People who despise advice are asking for trouble;
those who respect a command will succeed.

14 The instruction of the wise is like a life-giving fountain;
those who accept it avoid the snares of death.

15 A person with good sense is respected;
a treacherous person is headed for destruction.*

16 Wise people think before they act;
fools don't—and even brag about their foolishness.

17 An unreliable messenger stumbles into trouble,
but a reliable messenger brings healing.

18 If you ignore criticism, you will end in poverty and disgrace;
if you accept correction, you will be honored.

19 It is pleasant to see dreams come true,
but fools refuse to turn from evil to attain them.

20 Walk with the wise and become wise;
associate with fools and get in trouble.

21 Trouble chases sinners,
while blessings reward the righteous.

22 Good people leave an inheritance to their grandchildren,
but the sinner's wealth passes to the godly.

23 A poor person's farm may produce much food,
but injustice sweeps it all away.

24 Those who spare the rod of discipline hate their children.
Those who love their children care enough to discipline them.

25 The godly eat to their hearts' content,
but the belly of the wicked goes hungry.

CHAPTER 14

1 A wise woman builds her home,
but a foolish woman tears it down with her own hands.

2 Those who follow the right path fear the LORD;
those who take the wrong path despise him.

3 A fool's proud talk becomes a rod that beats him,
but the words of the wise keep them safe.

4 Without oxen a stable stays clean,
but you need a strong ox for a large harvest.

5 An honest witness does not lie;
a false witness breathes lies.

6 A mocker seeks wisdom and never finds it,
but knowledge comes easily to those with understanding.

7 Stay away from fools,
for you won't find knowledge on their lips.

8 The prudent understand where they are going,
but fools deceive themselves.

9 Fools make fun of guilt,
but the godly acknowledge it and seek reconciliation.

10 Each heart knows its own bitterness,
and no one else can fully share its joy.

11 The house of the wicked will be destroyed,
but the tent of the godly will flourish.

12 There is a path before each person that seems right,
but it ends in death.

13 Laughter can conceal a heavy heart,
but when the laughter ends, the grief remains.

14 Backsliders get what they deserve;
good people receive their reward.

13:15 As in Greek version; Hebrew reads *the way of the treacherous is lasting.*

15 Only simpletons believe everything
they're told!
The prudent carefully consider their
steps.

What can I do about my bad temper?

People with understanding control their anger; a hot temper shows great foolishness. PROVERBS 14:29

16 The wise are cautious* and avoid
danger;
fools plunge ahead with reckless
confidence.

17 Short-tempered people do foolish
things,
and schemers are hated.

18 Simpletons are clothed with foolishness,*
but the prudent are crowned with
knowledge.

19 Evil people will bow before good people;
the wicked will bow at the gates of
the godly.

20 The poor are despised even by their
neighbors,
while the rich have many "friends."

21 It is a sin to belittle one's neighbor;
blessed are those who help the poor.

22 If you plan to do evil, you will be lost;
if you plan to do good, you will receive
unfailing love and faithfulness.

23 Work brings profit,
but mere talk leads to poverty!

24 Wealth is a crown for the wise;
the effort of fools yields only
foolishness.

25 A truthful witness saves lives,
but a false witness is a traitor.

26 Those who fear the LORD are secure;
he will be a refuge for their children.

27 Fear of the LORD is a life-giving fountain;
it offers escape from the snares
of death.

28 A growing population is a king's glory;
a prince without subjects has nothing.

29 People with understanding control their
anger;
a hot temper shows great
foolishness.

30 A peaceful heart leads to a healthy body;
jealousy is like cancer in the bones.

31 Those who oppress the poor insult their
Maker,
but helping the poor honors him.

32 The wicked are crushed by disaster,
but the godly have a refuge when
they die.

33 Wisdom is enshrined in an understanding
heart;
wisdom is not* found among fools.

34 Godliness makes a nation great,
but sin is a disgrace to any people.

35 A king rejoices in wise servants
but is angry with those who disgrace
him.

CHAPTER 15

1 A gentle answer deflects anger,
but harsh words make tempers flare.

2 The tongue of the wise makes knowledge
appealing,
but the mouth of a fool belches out
foolishness.

3 The LORD is watching everywhere,
keeping his eye on both the evil and
the good.

4 Gentle words are a tree of life;
a deceitful tongue crushes the spirit.

5 Only a fool despises a parent's*
discipline;
whoever learns from correction is wise.

6 There is treasure in the house of the
godly,
but the earnings of the wicked bring
trouble.

14:16 Hebrew *The wise fear.* **14:18** Or *inherit foolishness.* **14:33** As in Greek and Syriac versions; Hebrew lacks *not.*
15:5 Hebrew *father's.*

7 The lips of the wise give good advice;
the heart of a fool has none to give.

8 The LORD detests the sacrifice of the wicked,
but he delights in the prayers of the upright.

9 The LORD detests the way of the wicked,
but he loves those who pursue godliness.

10 Whoever abandons the right path will be severely disciplined;
whoever hates correction will die.

11 Even Death and Destruction* hold no secrets from the LORD.
How much more does he know the human heart!

12 Mockers hate to be corrected,
so they stay away from the wise.

13 A glad heart makes a happy face;
a broken heart crushes the spirit.

14 A wise person is hungry for knowledge,
while the fool feeds on trash.

15 For the despondent, every day brings trouble;
for the happy heart, life is a continual feast.

16 Better to have little, with fear for the LORD,
than to have great treasure and inner turmoil.

17 A bowl of vegetables with someone you love
is better than steak with someone you hate.

18 A hot-tempered person starts fights;
a cool-tempered person stops them.

19 A lazy person's way is blocked with briers,
but the path of the upright is an open highway.

20 Sensible children bring joy to their father;
foolish children despise their mother.

21 Foolishness brings joy to those with no sense;
a sensible person stays on the right path.

22 Plans go wrong for lack of advice;
many advisers bring success.

23 Everyone enjoys a fitting reply;
it is wonderful to say the right thing at the right time!

24 The path of life leads upward for the wise;
they leave the grave* behind.

25 The LORD tears down the house of the proud,
but he protects the property of widows.

26 The LORD detests evil plans,
but he delights in pure words.

27 Greed brings grief to the whole family,
but those who hate bribes will live.

28 The heart of the godly thinks carefully before speaking;
the mouth of the wicked overflows with evil words.

29 The LORD is far from the wicked,
but he hears the prayers of the righteous.

30 A cheerful look brings joy to the heart;
good news makes for good health.

31 If you listen to constructive criticism,
you will be at home among the wise.

32 If you reject discipline, you only harm yourself;
but if you listen to correction, you grow in understanding.

33 Fear of the LORD teaches wisdom;
humility precedes honor.

CHAPTER 16

1 We can make our own plans,
but the LORD gives the right answer.

2 People may be pure in their own eyes,
but the LORD examines their motives.

3 Commit your actions to the LORD,
and your plans will succeed.

15:11 Hebrew *Sheol and Abaddon.* **15:24** Hebrew *Sheol.*

If you had come to my house a few years ago, chances are you would have found me on the couch, staring at the TV. I spent most of my time doing these things: eating, going to school, watching TV, eating some more, watching more TV, and sleeping. Next day . . . more of the same.

TV was my life.

Come to think of it, I had no life. I did nothing but watch TV.

One day, between TV shows, I actually picked up my Bible and started flipping through the pages. (Really, I did this!) Something caught my eye. There were big words on the side of one of the pages that asked, "What are you doing with your time?" I thought about it for a moment and immediately felt embarrassed.

"Nothing," I said out loud. I knew I had been doing nothing but shutting my mind off from reality for hours at a time as I stared at a television screen.

My eyes focused on the passage at the top of the page: *A lazy person's way is blocked with briers, but the path of the upright is an open highway (Proverbs 15:19)*. I didn't want to grow up and be known as "lazy."

For me, the change was immediate. I began doing other things. I got involved in more activities at church, I talked to my friends more, and I even hung out with my family more. Sometimes, we actually watch TV together—but not all day long.

Now when I get home after school and walk toward the family room, I see that the TV is still there. But I don't even miss it. I just pass right by the TV. After all, I've got better things to do. So do you!

Read Proverbs 15:19 and these other verses about the dangers of being lazy: Proverbs 10:4-5; 24:30-34; 2 Thessalonians 3:6-15.

4 The LORD has made everything for his own purposes,
even the wicked for a day of disaster.

5 The LORD detests the proud;
they will surely be punished.

6 Unfailing love and faithfulness make atonement for sin.
By fearing the LORD, people avoid evil.

7 When people's lives please the LORD,
even their enemies are at peace with them.

8 Better to have little, with godliness,
than to be rich and dishonest.

9 We can make our plans,
but the LORD determines our steps.

10 The king speaks with divine wisdom;
he must never judge unfairly.

11 The LORD demands accurate scales and balances;
he sets the standards for fairness.

12 A king detests wrongdoing,
for his rule is built on justice.

13 The king is pleased with words from righteous lips;
he loves those who speak honestly.

14 The anger of the king is a deadly threat;
the wise will try to appease it.

15 When the king smiles, there is life;
his favor refreshes like a spring rain.

16 How much better to get wisdom than gold,
and good judgment than silver!

17 The path of the virtuous leads away from evil;
whoever follows that path is safe.

I think I'm really "cool." Is there anything wrong with that?

Pride goes before destruction, and haughtiness before a fall.
PROVERBS 16:18

18 Pride goes before destruction,
and haughtiness before a fall.

19 Better to live humbly with the poor
than to share plunder with the proud.

20 Those who listen to instruction will prosper;
those who trust the LORD will be joyful.

21 The wise are known for their understanding,
and pleasant words are persuasive.

22 Discretion is a life-giving fountain to those who possess it,
but discipline is wasted on fools.

23 From a wise mind comes wise speech;
the words of the wise are persuasive.

24 Kind words are like honey—
sweet to the soul and healthy for the body.

25 There is a path before each person that seems right,
but it ends in death.

26 It is good for workers to have an appetite;
an empty stomach drives them on.

27 Scoundrels create trouble;
their words are a destructive blaze.

28 A troublemaker plants seeds of strife;
gossip separates the best of friends.

29 Violent people mislead their companions,
leading them down a harmful path.

30 With narrowed eyes, people plot evil;
with a smirk, they plan their mischief.

31 Gray hair is a crown of glory;
it is gained by living a godly life.

32 Better to be patient than powerful;
better to have self-control than to conquer a city.

33 We may throw the dice,*
but the LORD determines how they fall.

16:33 Hebrew *We may cast lots.*

CHAPTER 17

1 Better a dry crust eaten in peace
than a house filled with feasting—and conflict.

2 A wise servant will rule over the master's disgraceful son
and will share the inheritance of the master's children.

3 Fire tests the purity of silver and gold,
but the LORD tests the heart.

4 Wrongdoers eagerly listen to gossip;
liars pay close attention to slander.

5 Those who mock the poor insult their Maker;
those who rejoice at the misfortune of others will be punished.

6 Grandchildren are the crowning glory of the aged;
parents* are the pride of their children.

7 Eloquent words are not fitting for a fool;
even less are lies fitting for a ruler.

8 A bribe is like a lucky charm;
whoever gives one will prosper!

9 Love prospers when a fault is forgiven,
but dwelling on it separates close friends.

10 A single rebuke does more for a person of understanding
than a hundred lashes on the back of a fool.

11 Evil people are eager for rebellion,
but they will be severely punished.

12 It is safer to meet a bear robbed of her cubs
than to confront a fool caught in foolishness.

13 If you repay good with evil,
evil will never leave your house.

14 Starting a quarrel is like opening a floodgate,
so stop before a dispute breaks out.

15 Acquitting the guilty and condemning the innocent—
both are detestable to the LORD.

16 It is senseless to pay tuition to educate a fool,
since he has no heart for learning.

17 A friend is always loyal,
and a brother is born to help in time of need.

18 It's poor judgment to guarantee another person's debt
or put up security for a friend.

19 Anyone who loves to quarrel loves sin;
anyone who trusts in high walls invites disaster.

20 The crooked heart will not prosper;
the lying tongue tumbles into trouble.

21 It is painful to be the parent of a fool;
there is no joy for the father of a rebel.

22 A cheerful heart is good medicine,
but a broken spirit saps a person's strength.

23 The wicked take secret bribes
to pervert the course of justice.

24 Sensible people keep their eyes glued on wisdom,
but a fool's eyes wander to the ends of the earth.

25 Foolish children* bring grief to their father
and bitterness to the one who gave them birth.

26 It is wrong to punish the godly for being good
or to flog leaders for being honest.

27 A truly wise person uses few words;
a person with understanding is even-tempered.

28 Even fools are thought wise when they keep silent;
with their mouths shut, they seem intelligent.

CHAPTER 18

1 Unfriendly people care only about themselves;
they lash out at common sense.

17:6 Hebrew *fathers.* **17:25** Hebrew *A foolish son.*

2 Fools have no interest in understanding;
they only want to air their own opinions.

3 Doing wrong leads to disgrace,
and scandalous behavior brings contempt.

4 Wise words are like deep waters;
wisdom flows from the wise like a bubbling brook.

5 It is not right to acquit the guilty
or deny justice to the innocent.

6 Fools' words get them into constant quarrels;
they are asking for a beating.

7 The mouths of fools are their ruin;
they trap themselves with their lips.

8 Rumors are dainty morsels
that sink deep into one's heart.

9 A lazy person is as bad as
someone who destroys things.

10 The name of the LORD is a strong fortress;
the godly run to him and are safe.

11 The rich think of their wealth as a strong defense;
they imagine it to be a high wall of safety.

12 Haughtiness goes before destruction;
humility precedes honor.

13 Spouting off before listening to the facts
is both shameful and foolish.

14 The human spirit can endure a sick body,
but who can bear a crushed spirit?

15 Intelligent people are always ready to learn.
Their ears are open for knowledge.

16 Giving a gift can open doors;
it gives access to important people!

17 The first to speak in court sounds right—
until the cross-examination begins.

18 Flipping a coin* can end arguments;
it settles disputes between powerful opponents.

19 An offended friend is harder to win back
than a fortified city.
Arguments separate friends like a gate locked with bars.

20 Wise words satisfy like a good meal;
the right words bring satisfaction.

21 The tongue can bring death or life;
those who love to talk will reap the consequences.

22 The man who finds a wife finds a treasure,
and he receives favor from the LORD.

23 The poor plead for mercy;
the rich answer with insults.

24 There are "friends" who destroy each other,
but a real friend sticks closer than a brother.

CHAPTER 19

1 Better to be poor and honest
than to be dishonest and a fool.

2 Enthusiasm without knowledge is no good;
haste makes mistakes.

3 People ruin their lives by their own foolishness
and then are angry at the LORD.

4 Wealth makes many "friends";
poverty drives them all away.

5 A false witness will not go unpunished,
nor will a liar escape.

6 Many seek favors from a ruler;
everyone is the friend of a person who gives gifts!

7 The relatives of the poor despise them;
how much more will their friends avoid them!
Though the poor plead with them,
their friends are gone.

8 To acquire wisdom is to love oneself;
people who cherish understanding will prosper.

9 A false witness will not go unpunished,
and a liar will be destroyed.

10 It isn't right for a fool to live in luxury
or for a slave to rule over princes!

18:18 Hebrew *Casting lots.*

11 Sensible people control their temper;
they earn respect by overlooking
wrongs.

12 The king's anger is like a lion's roar,
but his favor is like dew on the grass.

13 A foolish child* is a calamity to a father;
a quarrelsome wife is as annoying as
constant dripping.

14 Fathers can give their sons an inheritance
of houses and wealth,
but only the LORD can give an
understanding wife.

15 Lazy people sleep soundly,
but idleness leaves them hungry.

16 Keep the commandments and keep
your life;
despising them leads to death.

17 If you help the poor, you are lending to
the LORD—
and he will repay you!

18 Discipline your children while there is
hope.
Otherwise you will ruin their lives.

19 Hot-tempered people must pay the
penalty.
If you rescue them once, you will have
to do it again.

20 Get all the advice and instruction
you can,
so you will be wise the rest of your life.

21 You can make many plans,
but the LORD's purpose will prevail.

22 Loyalty makes a person attractive.
It is better to be poor than dishonest.

23 Fear of the LORD leads to life,
bringing security and protection from
harm.

24 Lazy people take food in their hand
but don't even lift it to their mouth.

25 If you punish a mocker, the
simpleminded will learn a lesson;
if you correct the wise, they will be all
the wiser.

26 Children who mistreat their father or
chase away their mother
are an embarrassment and a public
disgrace.

27 If you stop listening to instruction,
my child,
you will turn your back on knowledge.

19:13 Hebrew *son;* also in 19:27.

IS IT OK?

IS IT OK TO CHEAT?

Some people take "shortcuts" in life. They cheat on their math quizzes, their taxes, and their spouses. While they may seem to be winning in the short run, guess who's losing big-time in the long run? God tells us it's better to be poor and honest than to win by being dishonest (see Proverbs 19:1). *Translation:* It's better to be honest and fail a test than to pass it by cheating. It's better to be honest and pay your taxes than to save money by cheating. It's better to be honest and have fewer friends than to make friends by lying about yourself or someone else. Why? If you're honest, God will reward you. In the end, cheaters never win.

28 A corrupt witness makes a mockery
of justice;
the mouth of the wicked gulps down
evil.

29 Punishment is made for mockers,
and the backs of fools are made to be
beaten.

CHAPTER 20

1 Wine produces mockers; alcohol leads to
brawls.
Those led astray by drink cannot be
wise.

2 The king's fury is like a lion's roar;
to rouse his anger is to risk your life.

3 Avoiding a fight is a mark of honor;
only fools insist on quarreling.

4 Those too lazy to plow in the right season
will have no food at the harvest.

5 Though good advice lies deep within the
heart,
a person with understanding will draw
it out.

6 Many will say they are loyal friends,
but who can find one who is truly
reliable?

7 The godly walk with integrity;
blessed are their children who follow
them.

8 When a king sits in judgment, he weighs
all the evidence,
distinguishing the bad from the good.

9 Who can say, "I have cleansed my heart;
I am pure and free from sin"?

10 False weights and unequal measures*—
the LORD detests double standards of
every kind.

11 Even children are known by the way
they act,
whether their conduct is pure, and
whether it is right.

12 Ears to hear and eyes to see—
both are gifts from the LORD.

13 If you love sleep, you will end in poverty.
Keep your eyes open, and there will be
plenty to eat!

14 The buyer haggles over the price, saying,
"It's worthless,"
then brags about getting a bargain!

15 Wise words are more valuable
than much gold and many rubies.

16 Get security from someone who
guarantees a stranger's debt.
Get a deposit if he does it for
foreigners.*

17 Stolen bread tastes sweet,
but it turns to gravel in the mouth.

18 Plans succeed through good counsel;
don't go to war without wise advice.

19 A gossip goes around telling secrets,
so don't hang around with chatterers.

20 If you insult your father or mother,
your light will be snuffed out in total
darkness.

21 An inheritance obtained too early in life
is not a blessing in the end.

22 Don't say, "I will get even for this wrong."
Wait for the LORD to handle the matter.

23 The LORD detests double standards;
he is not pleased by dishonest scales.

24 The LORD directs our steps,
so why try to understand everything
along the way?

25 Don't trap yourself by making a rash
promise to God
and only later counting the cost.

26 A wise king scatters the wicked like
wheat,
then runs his threshing wheel over
them.

27 The LORD's light penetrates the human
spirit,*
exposing every hidden motive.

28 Unfailing love and faithfulness protect
the king;
his throne is made secure through love.

29 The glory of the young is their strength;

20:10 Hebrew *A stone and a stone, an ephah and an ephah.* **20:16** An alternate reading in the Masoretic Text is *for a promiscuous woman.* **20:27** Or *The human spirit is the LORD's light.*

Passing Notes

Riley wrote a nasty note about a girl in class and passed it to his friend, three seats ahead. The note reached the second person when the teacher snatched it and read it aloud. He thought the guy holding the note had written it and gave him an after-school detention. Riley had escaped! Later, he heard some of his friends discussing the mean guy whom they thought had written the note. "What a cruel thing to do! Who would want to be his friend?" said one. Riley felt awful. Check out Proverbs 21:3 to see what Riley should do.

the gray hair of experience is the
splendor of the old.

30 Physical punishment cleanses
away evil;*
such discipline purifies the
heart.

CHAPTER 21

1 The king's heart is like a stream of water
directed by the LORD;
he guides it wherever he pleases.

2 People may be right in their own eyes,
but the LORD examines their heart.

3 The LORD is more pleased when we do
what is right and just
than when we offer him sacrifices.

4 Haughty eyes, a proud heart,
and evil actions are all sin.

5 Good planning and hard work lead to
prosperity,
but hasty shortcuts lead to poverty.

6 Wealth created by a lying tongue
is a vanishing mist and a deadly trap.*

7 The violence of the wicked sweeps
them away,
because they refuse to do what is just.

8 The guilty walk a crooked path;
the innocent travel a straight road.

9 It's better to live alone in the corner
of an attic
than with a quarrelsome wife in
a lovely home.

10 Evil people desire evil;
their neighbors get no mercy from
them.

11 If you punish a mocker, the
simpleminded become wise;
if you instruct the wise, they will be all
the wiser.

12 The Righteous One* knows what is going
on in the homes of the wicked;
he will bring disaster on them.

13 Those who shut their ears to the cries
of the poor
will be ignored in their own time
of need.

14 A secret gift calms anger;
a bribe under the table pacifies fury.

15 Justice is a joy to the godly,
but it terrifies evildoers.

20:30 The meaning of the Hebrew is uncertain. **21:6** As in Greek version; Hebrew reads *mist for those who seek death.* **21:12** Or *The righteous man.*

16 The person who strays from common sense
will end up in the company of the dead.

17 Those who love pleasure become poor;
those who love wine and luxury will never be rich.

18 The wicked are punished in place of the godly,
and traitors in place of the honest.

19 It's better to live alone in the desert
than with a quarrelsome, complaining wife.

20 The wise have wealth and luxury,
but fools spend whatever they get.

21 Whoever pursues righteousness and unfailing love
will find life, righteousness, and honor.

22 The wise conquer the city of the strong
and level the fortress in which they trust.

23 Watch your tongue and keep your mouth shut,
and you will stay out of trouble.

24 Mockers are proud and haughty;
they act with boundless arrogance.

25 Despite their desires, the lazy will come to ruin,
for their hands refuse to work.

26 Some people are always greedy for more,
but the godly love to give!

27 The sacrifice of an evil person is detestable,
especially when it is offered with wrong motives.

28 A false witness will be cut off,
but a credible witness will be allowed to speak.

29 The wicked bluff their way through,
but the virtuous think before they act.

30 No human wisdom or understanding or plan
can stand against the LORD.

31 The horse is prepared for the day of battle,
but the victory belongs to the LORD.

CHAPTER 22

1 Choose a good reputation over great riches;
being held in high esteem is better than silver or gold.

2 The rich and poor have this in common:
The LORD made them both.

3 A prudent person foresees danger and takes precautions.
The simpleton goes blindly on and suffers the consequences.

4 True humility and fear of the LORD
lead to riches, honor, and long life.

5 Corrupt people walk a thorny, treacherous road;
whoever values life will avoid it.

6 Direct your children onto the right path,
and when they are older, they will not leave it.

7 Just as the rich rule the poor,
so the borrower is servant to the lender.

8 Those who plant injustice will harvest disaster,
and their reign of terror will come to an end.*

9 Blessed are those who are generous,
because they feed the poor.

10 Throw out the mocker, and fighting goes, too.
Quarrels and insults will disappear.

11 Whoever loves a pure heart and gracious speech
will have the king as a friend.

12 The LORD preserves those with knowledge,
but he ruins the plans of the treacherous.

13 The lazy person claims, "There's a lion out there!
If I go outside, I might be killed!"

22:8 The Greek version includes an additional proverb: *God blesses a man who gives cheerfully, / but his worthless deeds will come to an end.* Compare 2 Cor 9:7.

14 The mouth of an immoral woman is a
dangerous trap;
those who make the LORD angry will
fall into it.

15 A youngster's heart is filled with
foolishness,
but physical discipline will drive it far
away.

16 A person who gets ahead by oppressing
the poor
or by showering gifts on the rich will
end in poverty.

Sayings of the Wise

17 Listen to the words of the wise;
apply your heart to my instruction.
18 For it is good to keep these sayings in your
heart
and always ready on your lips.
19 I am teaching you today—yes, you—
so you will trust in the LORD.
20 I have written thirty sayings* for you,
filled with advice and knowledge.
21 In this way, you may know the truth
and take an accurate report to those
who sent you.

22 Don't rob the poor just because you can,
or exploit the needy in court.
23 For the LORD is their defender.
He will ruin anyone who ruins them.

24 Don't befriend angry people
or associate with hot-tempered people,
25 or you will learn to be like them
and endanger your soul.

26 Don't agree to guarantee another
person's debt
or put up security for someone else.
27 If you can't pay it,
even your bed will be snatched from
under you.

28 Don't cheat your neighbor by moving the
ancient boundary markers
set up by previous generations.

29 Do you see any truly competent workers?
They will serve kings
rather than working for ordinary
people.

CHAPTER 23

1 While dining with a ruler,
pay attention to what is put before you.
2 If you are a big eater,
put a knife to your throat;
3 don't desire all the delicacies,
for he might be trying to trick you.

4 Don't wear yourself out trying to get rich.
Be wise enough to know when to quit.
5 In the blink of an eye wealth disappears,
for it will sprout wings
and fly away like an eagle.

6 Don't eat with people who are stingy;
don't desire their delicacies.
7 They are always thinking about how much
it costs.*
"Eat and drink," they say, but they don't
mean it.
8 You will throw up what little you've eaten,
and your compliments will be wasted.

9 Don't waste your breath on fools,
for they will despise the wisest advice.

10 Don't cheat your neighbor by moving the
ancient boundary markers;
don't take the land of defenseless
orphans.
11 For their Redeemer* is strong;
he himself will bring their charges
against you.

12 Commit yourself to instruction;
listen carefully to words of
knowledge.

13 Don't fail to discipline your children.
They won't die if you spank them.
14 Physical discipline
may well save them from death.*

15 My child,* if your heart is wise,
my own heart will rejoice!
16 Everything in me will celebrate
when you speak what is right.

17 Don't envy sinners,
but always continue to fear the LORD.
18 You will be rewarded for this;
your hope will not be disappointed.

19 My child, listen and be wise:
Keep your heart on the right course.

22:20 Or *excellent sayings;* the meaning of the Hebrew is uncertain. **23:7** The meaning of the Hebrew is uncertain. **23:11** Or *redeemer.* **23:14** Hebrew *from Sheol.* **23:15** Hebrew *My son;* also in 23:19.

20 Do not carouse with drunkards
or feast with gluttons,
21 for they are on their way to poverty,
and too much sleep clothes them
in rags.

22 Listen to your father, who gave you life,
and don't despise your mother when
she is old.
23 Get the truth and never sell it;
also get wisdom, discipline, and good
judgment.
24 The father of godly children has cause
for joy.
What a pleasure to have children who
are wise.*
25 So give your father and mother joy!
May she who gave you birth be happy.

26 O my son, give me your heart.
May your eyes take delight in following
my ways.
27 A prostitute is a dangerous trap;
a promiscuous woman is as dangerous
as falling into a narrow well.
28 She hides and waits like a robber,
eager to make more men unfaithful.

29 Who has anguish? Who has sorrow?
Who is always fighting? Who is always
complaining?
Who has unnecessary bruises? Who
has bloodshot eyes?
30 It is the one who spends long hours in the
taverns,
trying out new drinks.
31 Don't gaze at the wine, seeing how
red it is,
how it sparkles in the cup, how
smoothly it goes down.
32 For in the end it bites like a poisonous
snake;
it stings like a viper.
33 You will see hallucinations,
and you will say crazy things.
34 You will stagger like a sailor tossed
at sea,
clinging to a swaying mast.
35 And you will say, "They hit me, but I didn't
feel it.
I didn't even know it when they beat
me up.
When will I wake up
so I can look for another drink?"

CHAPTER 24

1 Don't envy evil people
or desire their company.
2 For their hearts plot violence,
and their words always stir up trouble.

3 A house is built by wisdom
and becomes strong through good
sense.
4 Through knowledge its rooms are filled
with all sorts of precious riches and
valuables.

5 The wise are mightier than the strong,*
and those with knowledge grow
stronger and stronger.
6 So don't go to war without wise guidance;
victory depends on having many
advisers.

7 Wisdom is too lofty for fools.
Among leaders at the city gate, they
have nothing to say.

8 A person who plans evil
will get a reputation as a troublemaker.
9 The schemes of a fool are sinful;
everyone detests a mocker.

10 If you fail under pressure,
your strength is too small.

11 Rescue those who are unjustly sentenced
to die;
save them as they stagger to their
death.
12 Don't excuse yourself by saying, "Look,
we didn't know."
For God understands all hearts, and he
sees you.
He who guards your soul knows you
knew.
He will repay all people as their actions
deserve.

13 My child,* eat honey, for it is good,
and the honeycomb is sweet to the
taste.
14 In the same way, wisdom is sweet to your
soul.

23:24 Hebrew *to have a wise son.* **24:5** As in Greek version; Hebrew reads *A wise man is strength.* **24:13** Hebrew *My son;* also in 24:21.

If you find it, you will have a bright
future,
and your hopes will not be cut
short.

15 Don't wait in ambush at the home of
the godly,
and don't raid the house where the
godly live.
16 The godly may trip seven times, but they
will get up again.
But one disaster is enough to overthrow
the wicked.

17 Don't rejoice when your enemies fall;
don't be happy when they
stumble.
18 For the LORD will be displeased with you
and will turn his anger away from
them.

19 Don't fret because of evildoers;
don't envy the wicked.
20 For evil people have no future;
the light of the wicked will be snuffed
out.

21 My child, fear the LORD and the king.
Don't associate with rebels,
22 for disaster will hit them suddenly.
Who knows what punishment
will come
from the LORD and the king?

More Sayings of the Wise

23 Here are some further sayings of the wise:

It is wrong to show favoritism when
passing judgment.
24 A judge who says to the wicked, "You are
innocent,"
will be cursed by many people and
denounced by the nations.
25 But it will go well for those who convict
the guilty;
rich blessings will be showered on
them.

26 An honest answer
is like a kiss of friendship.

27 Do your planning and prepare your fields
before building your house.

28 Don't testify against your neighbors
without cause;
don't lie about them.
29 And don't say, "Now I can pay them back
for what they've done to me!
I'll get even with them!"

30 I walked by the field of a lazy person,
the vineyard of one with no common
sense.
31 I saw that it was overgrown with nettles.
It was covered with weeds,
and its walls were broken down.
32 Then, as I looked and thought about it,

IS IT OK?

IS IT OK TO LOVE TO COMPETE?

Some of us have this wild competitive streak. In any kind of contest—soccer games, cross-country meets, spelling bees, science fairs—we love to compete! Competition can be fun; healthy competition helps us reach our potential and do our best in life. But it's also up to us to make sure that competition stays fun. If we get so caught up in competing that we're willing to hurt other people in order to win, that's not okay. Proverbs 24:17 warns us that while we might like to win, we shouldn't gloat over someone else who falls. If you love to compete, make sure you know how to keep it fun.

I learned this lesson:
33 A little extra sleep, a little more slumber,
a little folding of the hands to rest—
34 then poverty will pounce on you like a bandit;
scarcity will attack you like an armed robber.

CHAPTER 25

More Proverbs of Solomon

These are more proverbs of Solomon, collected by the advisers of King Hezekiah of Judah.

2 It is God's privilege to conceal things
and the king's privilege to discover them.

3 No one can comprehend the height of heaven, the depth of the earth,
or all that goes on in the king's mind!

4 Remove the impurities from silver,
and the sterling will be ready for the silversmith.

5 Remove the wicked from the king's court,
and his reign will be made secure by justice.

6 Don't demand an audience with the king
or push for a place among the great.

7 It's better to wait for an invitation to the head table
than to be sent away in public disgrace.

Just because you've seen something,
8 don't be in a hurry to go to court.
For what will you do in the end
if your neighbor deals you a shameful defeat?

9 When arguing with your neighbor,
don't betray another person's secret.

10 Others may accuse you of gossip,
and you will never regain your good reputation.

11 Timely advice is lovely,
like golden apples in a silver basket.

12 To one who listens, valid criticism
is like a gold earring or other gold jewelry.

13 Trustworthy messengers refresh like snow in summer.
They revive the spirit of their employer.

14 A person who promises a gift but doesn't give it
is like clouds and wind that bring no rain.

15 Patience can persuade a prince,
and soft speech can break bones.

16 Do you like honey?
Don't eat too much, or it will make you sick!

17 Don't visit your neighbors too often,
or you will wear out your welcome.

18 Telling lies about others
is as harmful as hitting them with an ax,
wounding them with a sword,
or shooting them with a sharp arrow.

19 Putting confidence in an unreliable person in times of trouble
is like chewing with a broken tooth or walking on a lame foot.

20 Singing cheerful songs to a person with a heavy heart
is like taking someone's coat in cold weather
or pouring vinegar in a wound.*

21 If your enemies are hungry, give them food to eat.
If they are thirsty, give them water to drink.

22 You will heap burning coals of shame on their heads,
and the LORD will reward you.

23 As surely as a north wind brings rain,
so a gossiping tongue causes anger!

24 It's better to live alone in the corner of an attic
than with a quarrelsome wife in a lovely home.

25 Good news from far away
is like cold water to the thirsty.

26 If the godly give in to the wicked,
it's like polluting a fountain or muddying a spring.

27 It's not good to eat too much honey,
and it's not good to seek honors for yourself.

25:20 As in Greek version; Hebrew reads *pouring vinegar on soda.*

28 A person without self-control
is like a city with broken-down walls.

CHAPTER 26

1 Honor is no more associated with fools
than snow with summer or rain with
harvest.

2 Like a fluttering sparrow or a darting
swallow,
an undeserved curse will not land on its
intended victim.

3 Guide a horse with a whip, a donkey with
a bridle,
and a fool with a rod to his back!

4 Don't answer the foolish arguments
of fools,
or you will become as foolish as
they are.

5 Be sure to answer the foolish arguments
of fools,
or they will become wise in their own
estimation.

6 Trusting a fool to convey a message
is like cutting off one's feet or drinking
poison!

7 A proverb in the mouth of a fool
is as useless as a paralyzed leg.

8 Honoring a fool
is as foolish as tying a stone to a
slingshot.

9 A proverb in the mouth of a fool
is like a thorny branch brandished by a
drunk.

10 An employer who hires a fool or
a bystander
is like an archer who shoots at random.

11 As a dog returns to its vomit,
so a fool repeats his foolishness.

12 There is more hope for fools
than for people who think they are wise.

13 The lazy person claims, "There's a lion on
the road!
Yes, I'm sure there's a lion out there!"

14 As a door swings back and forth on its
hinges,
so the lazy person turns over in bed.

15 Lazy people take food in their hand
but don't even lift it to their mouth.

16 Lazy people consider themselves smarter
than seven wise counselors.

17 Interfering in someone else's argument
is as foolish as yanking a dog's ears.

IS IT OK?

IS IT OK TO JUST LISTEN TO GOSSIP?

Imagine these scenarios. **Scene 1:** Your best friend is gossiping about you. (That would hurt, wouldn't it?) **Scene 2:** Someone else is gossiping about you, and your best friend is standing there listening, not defending you at all. (That would also hurt, right?) **Scene 3:** Someone starts gossiping about you to your best friend, but your best friend walks away. The conversation stops cold. (Wow, wouldn't that make you feel good?) See, gossip is harmful. It fuels fights and sinks deep into people's hearts (see Proverbs 26:20, 22). It's a terrible, hurtful thing; and even if you aren't the one actually *saying* anything, just *listening* is being part of the problem. Are you a gossip-fueler or a gossip-fighter?

18 Just as damaging
as a madman shooting a deadly weapon
19 is someone who lies to a friend
and then says, "I was only joking."

20 Fire goes out without wood,
and quarrels disappear when gossip stops.

21 A quarrelsome person starts fights
as easily as hot embers light charcoal or fire lights wood.

22 Rumors are dainty morsels
that sink deep into one's heart.

23 Smooth* words may hide a wicked heart,
just as a pretty glaze covers a clay pot.

24 People may cover their hatred with pleasant words,
but they're deceiving you.
25 They pretend to be kind, but don't believe them.
Their hearts are full of many evils.*
26 While their hatred may be concealed by trickery,
their wrongdoing will be exposed in public.

27 If you set a trap for others,
you will get caught in it yourself.
If you roll a boulder down on others,
it will crush you instead.

28 A lying tongue hates its victims,
and flattering words cause ruin.

CHAPTER 27

1 Don't brag about tomorrow,
since you don't know what the day will bring.

2 Let someone else praise you, not your own mouth—
a stranger, not your own lips.

3 A stone is heavy and sand is weighty,
but the resentment caused by a fool is even heavier.

4 Anger is cruel, and wrath is like a flood,
but jealousy is even more dangerous.

5 An open rebuke
is better than hidden love!

6 Wounds from a sincere friend
are better than many kisses from an enemy.

7 A person who is full refuses honey,
but even bitter food tastes sweet to the hungry.

8 A person who strays from home
is like a bird that strays from its nest.

9 The heartfelt counsel of a friend
is as sweet as perfume and incense.

10 Never abandon a friend—
either yours or your father's.
When disaster strikes, you won't have to ask your brother for assistance.
It's better to go to a neighbor than to a brother who lives far away.

11 Be wise, my child,* and make my heart glad.
Then I will be able to answer my critics.

12 A prudent person foresees danger and takes precautions.
The simpleton goes blindly on and suffers the consequences.

13 Get security from someone who guarantees a stranger's debt.
Get a deposit if he does it for foreigners.*

14 A loud and cheerful greeting early in the morning
will be taken as a curse!

15 A quarrelsome wife is as annoying
as constant dripping on a rainy day.
16 Stopping her complaints is like trying to stop the wind
or trying to hold something with greased hands.

17 As iron sharpens iron,
so a friend sharpens a friend.

18 As workers who tend a fig tree are allowed to eat the fruit,
so workers who protect their employer's interests will be rewarded.

19 As a face is reflected in water,
so the heart reflects the real person.

26:23 As in Greek version; Hebrew reads *Burning*. **26:25** Hebrew *seven evils*. **27:11** Hebrew *my son*. **27:13** As in Greek and Latin versions (see also 20:16); Hebrew reads *for a promiscuous woman*.

20 Just as Death and Destruction* are never satisfied,
so human desire is never satisfied.

21 Fire tests the purity of silver and gold,
but a person is tested by being praised.*

22 You cannot separate fools from their foolishness,
even though you grind them like grain with mortar and pestle.

23 Know the state of your flocks,
and put your heart into caring for your herds,
24 for riches don't last forever,
and the crown might not be passed to the next generation.
25 After the hay is harvested and the new crop appears
and the mountain grasses are gathered in,
26 your sheep will provide wool for clothing,
and your goats will provide the price of a field.
27 And you will have enough goats' milk for yourself,
your family, and your servant girls.

CHAPTER 28

1 The wicked run away when no one is chasing them,
but the godly are as bold as lions.

2 When there is moral rot within a nation, its government topples easily.
But wise and knowledgeable leaders bring stability.

3 A poor person who oppresses the poor is like a pounding rain that destroys the crops.

4 To reject the law is to praise the wicked;
to obey the law is to fight them.

5 Evil people don't understand justice,
but those who follow the LORD understand completely.

6 Better to be poor and honest than to be dishonest and rich.

7 Young people who obey the law are wise;
those with wild friends bring shame to their parents.*

8 Income from charging high interest rates will end up in the pocket of someone who is kind to the poor.

9 God detests the prayers of a person who ignores the law.

10 Those who lead good people along an evil path
will fall into their own trap,
but the honest will inherit good things.

11 Rich people may think they are wise,
but a poor person with discernment can see right through them.

12 When the godly succeed, everyone is glad.
When the wicked take charge, people go into hiding.

13 People who conceal their sins will not prosper,
but if they confess and turn from them, they will receive mercy.

14 Blessed are those who fear to do wrong,*
but the stubborn are headed for serious trouble.

15 A wicked ruler is as dangerous to the poor as a roaring lion or an attacking bear.

16 A ruler with no understanding will oppress his people,
but one who hates corruption will have a long life.

17 A murderer's tormented conscience will drive him into the grave.
Don't protect him!

18 The blameless will be rescued from harm,
but the crooked will be suddenly destroyed.

19 A hard worker has plenty of food,
but a person who chases fantasies ends up in poverty.

20 The trustworthy person will get a rich reward,
but a person who wants quick riches will get into trouble.

27:20 Hebrew *Sheol and Abaddon*. **27:21** Or *by flattery*. **28:7** Hebrew *their father*. **28:14** Or *those who fear the LORD*; Hebrew reads *those who fear*.

21 Showing partiality is never good,
yet some will do wrong for a mere
piece of bread.

22 Greedy people try to get rich quick
but don't realize they're headed for
poverty.

23 In the end, people appreciate honest
criticism
far more than flattery.

24 Anyone who steals from his father and
mother
and says, "What's wrong with that?"
is no better than a murderer.

25 Greed causes fighting;
trusting the LORD leads to
prosperity.

26 Those who trust their own insight are
foolish,
but anyone who walks in wisdom
is safe.

27 Whoever gives to the poor will lack
nothing,
but those who close their eyes to
poverty will be cursed.

28 When the wicked take charge, people go
into hiding.
When the wicked meet disaster, the
godly flourish.

CHAPTER 29

1 Whoever stubbornly refuses to accept
criticism
will suddenly be destroyed beyond
recovery.

2 When the godly are in authority, the
people rejoice.
But when the wicked are in power,
they groan.

3 The man who loves wisdom brings joy to
his father,
but if he hangs around with prostitutes,
his wealth is wasted.

4 A just king gives stability to his nation,
but one who demands bribes
destroys it.

5 To flatter friends
is to lay a trap for their feet.

6 Evil people are trapped by sin,
but the righteous escape, shouting for
joy.

7 The godly care about the rights of the
poor;
the wicked don't care at all.

8 Mockers can get a whole town agitated,
but the wise will calm anger.

9 If a wise person takes a fool to court,
there will be ranting and ridicule but
no satisfaction.

10 The bloodthirsty hate blameless people,
but the upright seek to help them.*

11 Fools vent their anger,
but the wise quietly hold it back.

12 If a ruler pays attention to liars,
all his advisers will be wicked.

13 The poor and the oppressor have this in
common—
the LORD gives sight to the eyes of both.

14 If a king judges the poor fairly,
his throne will last forever.

15 To discipline a child produces wisdom,
but a mother is disgraced by an
undisciplined child.

16 When the wicked are in authority, sin
flourishes,
but the godly will live to see their
downfall.

17 Discipline your children, and they will
give you peace of mind
and will make your heart glad.

18 When people do not accept divine
guidance, they run wild.
But whoever obeys the law is joyful.

19 Words alone will not discipline a servant;
the words may be understood, but they
are not heeded.

20 There is more hope for a fool
than for someone who speaks without
thinking.

29:10 Or *The bloodthirsty hate blameless people, / and they seek to kill the upright;* Hebrew reads *The bloodthirsty hate blameless people; / as for the upright, they seek their life.*

21 A servant pampered from childhood
will become a rebel.

22 An angry person starts fights;
a hot-tempered person commits all
kinds of sin.

23 Pride ends in humiliation,
while humility brings honor.

24 If you assist a thief, you only hurt yourself.
You are sworn to tell the truth, but you
dare not testify.

25 Fearing people is a dangerous trap,
but trusting the LORD means safety.

26 Many seek the ruler's favor,
but justice comes from the LORD.

27 The righteous despise the unjust;
the wicked despise the godly.

CHAPTER 30

The Sayings of Agur

The sayings of Agur son of Jakeh contain this message.*

I am weary, O God;
I am weary and worn out, O God.*
2 I am too stupid to be human,
and I lack common sense.
3 I have not mastered human wisdom,
nor do I know the Holy One.

4 Who but God goes up to heaven and
comes back down?
Who holds the wind in his fists?
Who wraps up the oceans in his cloak?
Who has created the whole wide
world?
What is his name—and his son's name?
Tell me if you know!

5 Every word of God proves true.
He is a shield to all who come to him
for protection.
6 Do not add to his words,
or he may rebuke you and expose you
as a liar.

7 O God, I beg two favors from you;
let me have them before I die.
8 First, help me never to tell a lie.
Second, give me neither poverty nor
riches!
Give me just enough to satisfy my
needs.
9 For if I grow rich, I may deny you and say,
"Who is the LORD?"
And if I am too poor, I may steal and
thus insult God's holy name.

10 Never slander a worker to the employer,
or the person will curse you, and you
will pay for it.

11 Some people curse their father
and do not thank their mother.
12 They are pure in their own eyes,
but they are filthy and unwashed.
13 They look proudly around,
casting disdainful glances.
14 They have teeth like swords
and fangs like knives.
They devour the poor from the earth
and the needy from among humanity.

15 The leech has two suckers
that cry out, "More, more!"*

There are three things that are never
satisfied—
no, four that never say, "Enough!":
16 the grave,*
the barren womb,
the thirsty desert,
the blazing fire.

17 The eye that mocks a father
and despises a mother's instructions

AMAZING FACTS

An eagle flies, a snake slithers, a ship sails the seas, men and women fall in love—amazing!

PROVERBS 30:18-19

30:1a Or *son of Jakeh from Massa;* or *son of Jakeh, an oracle.* **30:1b** The Hebrew can also be translated *The man declares this to Ithiel, / to Ithiel and to Ucal.* **30:15** Hebrew *two daughters who cry out, "Give, give!"* **30:16** Hebrew *Sheol.*

will be plucked out by ravens of the valley
and eaten by vultures.

18 There are three things that amaze me—
no, four things that I don't understand:
19 how an eagle glides through the sky,
how a snake slithers on a rock,
how a ship navigates the ocean,
how a man loves a woman.

20 An adulterous woman consumes a man,
then wipes her mouth and says,
"What's wrong with that?"

21 There are three things that make the earth tremble—
no, four it cannot endure:
22 a slave who becomes a king,
an overbearing fool who prospers,
23 a bitter woman who finally gets a husband,
a servant girl who supplants her mistress.

24 There are four things on earth that are small but unusually wise:
25 Ants—they aren't strong,
but they store up food all summer.
26 Hyraxes*—they aren't powerful,
but they make their homes among the rocks.
27 Locusts—they have no king,
but they march in formation.
28 Lizards—they are easy to catch,
but they are found even in kings' palaces.

29 There are three things that walk with stately stride—
no, four that strut about:
30 the lion, king of animals, who won't turn aside for anything,
31 the strutting rooster,
the male goat,
a king as he leads his army.

32 If you have been a fool by being proud or plotting evil,
cover your mouth in shame.

33 As the beating of cream yields butter
and striking the nose causes bleeding,
so stirring up anger causes quarrels.

Hezekiah

As King of Judah I've done both good and bad. I tore down stone images of false gods and ripped down pagan temples. That was right. But when God saved my people from the Assyrians, I took the credit. I boasted about our armies, about cutting down tall trees, and about digging deep wells. That was wrong.

One day I became very sick. Isaiah, God's prophet, said I would die. I begged God for a few more years. I reminded him of the times I had served him. Finally God agreed. He caused the sun's shadow to move backward as a sign that he would do what he promised.

You can read more about Hezekiah in 2 Kings 16:20–20:21; 2 Chronicles 28:27–32:33; and Isaiah 36:1–39:8.

CHAPTER 31

The Sayings of King Lemuel

The sayings of King Lemuel contain this message,* which his mother taught him.

2 O my son, O son of my womb,
O son of my vows,

30:26 Or *Coneys*, or *Rock badgers*. **31:1** Or *of Lemuel, king of Massa*; or *of King Lemuel, an oracle*.

3 do not waste your strength on women,
on those who ruin kings.

4 It is not for kings, O Lemuel, to guzzle wine.
Rulers should not crave alcohol.
5 For if they drink, they may forget the law
and not give justice to the oppressed.
6 Alcohol is for the dying,
and wine for those in bitter distress.
7 Let them drink to forget their poverty
and remember their troubles no more.

8 Speak up for those who cannot speak for themselves;
ensure justice for those being crushed.
9 Yes, speak up for the poor and helpless,
and see that they get justice.

A Wife of Noble Character

10 *Who can find a virtuous and capable wife?
She is more precious than rubies.
11 Her husband can trust her,
and she will greatly enrich his life.
12 She brings him good, not harm,
all the days of her life.

13 She finds wool and flax
and busily spins it.
14 She is like a merchant's ship,
bringing her food from afar.
15 She gets up before dawn to prepare breakfast for her household
and plan the day's work for her servant girls.

16 She goes to inspect a field and buys it;
with her earnings she plants a vineyard.
17 She is energetic and strong,
a hard worker.
18 She makes sure her dealings are profitable;
her lamp burns late into the night.

19 Her hands are busy spinning thread,
her fingers twisting fiber.
20 She extends a helping hand to the poor
and opens her arms to the needy.
21 She has no fear of winter for her household,
for everyone has warm* clothes.

22 She makes her own bedspreads.
She dresses in fine linen and purple gowns.
23 Her husband is well known at the city gates,
where he sits with the other civic leaders.
24 She makes belted linen garments
and sashes to sell to the merchants.

25 She is clothed with strength and dignity,
and she laughs without fear of the future.
26 When she speaks, her words are wise,
and she gives instructions with kindness.
27 She carefully watches everything in her household
and suffers nothing from laziness.

28 Her children stand and bless her.
Her husband praises her:
29 "There are many virtuous and capable women in the world,
but you surpass them all!"

30 Charm is deceptive, and beauty does not last;
but a woman who fears the LORD will be greatly praised.
31 Reward her for all she has done.
Let her deeds publicly declare her praise.

31:10 Verses 10-31 comprise a Hebrew acrostic poem; each verse begins with a successive letter of the Hebrew alphabet. **31:21** As in Greek and Latin versions; Hebrew reads *scarlet*.

ECCLESIASTES

WHO
Solomon.

WHERE
The royal palace in Jerusalem.

WHEN
It was probably around 935 BC, toward the end of his reign, when Solomon wrote this book.

WHY
To help future generations avoid the mistakes Solomon made and to teach that life has no meaning without God.

Don't let the excitement of youth cause you to forget your Creator. Honor him in your youth.
ECCLESIASTES 12:1

It's great to be young. Kids get to learn and have fun while adults work to pay for stuff and take care of the house. Solomon had everything when he was young, but he stopped listening to God as he grew up. He wrote the book of Ecclesiastes when he was older and wiser.

Remember Solomon and Listen to His Advice.

CHAPTER 1

These are the words of the Teacher,* King David's son, who ruled in Jerusalem.

Everything Is Meaningless

2 "Everything is meaningless," says the Teacher,
"completely meaningless!"
3 What do people get for all their hard work
under the sun? 4 Generations come and generations go, but the earth never changes. 5 The sun rises and the sun sets, then hurries around to rise again. 6 The wind blows south, and then turns north. Around and around it goes, blowing in circles. 7 Rivers run into the sea, but the sea is never full. Then the water returns again to the rivers and flows out again

1:1 Hebrew *Qoheleth;* this term is rendered "the Teacher" throughout this book.

to the sea. [8]Everything is wearisome beyond description. No matter how much we see, we are never satisfied. No matter how much we hear, we are not content.

[9]History merely repeats itself. It has all been done before. Nothing under the sun is truly new. [10]Sometimes people say, "Here is something new!" But actually it is old; nothing is ever truly new. [11]We don't remember what happened in the past, and in future generations, no one will remember what we are doing now.

The Teacher Speaks: The Futility of Wisdom

[12]I, the Teacher, was king of Israel, and I lived in Jerusalem. [13]I devoted myself to search for understanding and to explore by wisdom everything being done under heaven. I soon discovered that God has dealt a tragic existence to the human race. [14]I observed everything going on under the sun, and really, it is all meaningless—like chasing the wind.

[15] What is wrong cannot be made right.
What is missing cannot be recovered.

[16]I said to myself, "Look, I am wiser than any of the kings who ruled in Jerusalem before me. I have greater wisdom and knowledge than any of them." [17]So I set out to learn everything from wisdom to madness and folly. But I learned firsthand that pursuing all this is like chasing the wind.

[18] The greater my wisdom, the greater my grief.
To increase knowledge only increases sorrow.

CHAPTER 2

The Futility of Pleasure

I said to myself, "Come on, let's try pleasure. Let's look for the 'good things' in life." But I found that this, too, was meaningless. [2]So I said, "Laughter is silly. What good does it do to seek pleasure?" [3]After much thought, I decided to cheer myself with wine. And while still seeking wisdom, I clutched at foolishness. In this way, I tried to experience the only happiness most people find during their brief life in this world.

[4]I also tried to find meaning by building huge homes for myself and by planting beautiful vineyards. [5]I made gardens and parks, filling them with all kinds of fruit trees. [6]I built reservoirs to collect the water to irrigate my many flourishing groves. [7]I bought slaves, both men and women, and others were born into my household. I also owned large herds and flocks, more than any of the kings who had lived in Jerusalem before me. [8]I collected great sums of silver and gold, the treasure of many kings and provinces. I hired wonderful singers, both men and women, and had many beautiful concubines. I had everything a man could desire!

[9]So I became greater than all who had lived in Jerusalem before me, and my wisdom never failed me. [10]Anything I wanted, I would take. I denied myself no pleasure. I even found great pleasure in hard work, a reward for all my labors. [11]But as I looked at everything I had worked so hard to accomplish, it

was all so meaningless—like chasing the wind. There was nothing really worthwhile anywhere.

The Wise and the Foolish

[12]So I decided to compare wisdom with foolishness and madness (for who can do this better than I, the king?*). [13]I thought, "Wisdom is better than foolishness, just as light is better than darkness. [14]For the wise can see where they are going, but fools walk in the dark." Yet I saw that the wise and the foolish share the same fate. [15]Both will die. So I said to myself, "Since I will end up the same as the fool, what's the value of all my wisdom? This is all so meaningless!" [16]For the wise and the foolish both die. The wise will not be remembered any longer than the fool. In the days to come, both will be forgotten.

[17]So I came to hate life because everything done here under the sun is so troubling. Everything is meaningless—like chasing the wind.

The Futility of Work

[18]I came to hate all my hard work here on earth, for I must leave to others everything I have earned. [19]And who can tell whether my successors will be wise or foolish? Yet they will control everything I have gained by my skill and hard work under the sun. How meaningless! [20]So I gave up in despair, questioning the value of all my hard work in this world.

[21]Some people work wisely with knowledge and skill, then must leave the fruit of their efforts to someone who hasn't worked for it. This, too, is meaningless, a great tragedy. [22]So what do people get in this life for all their hard work and anxiety? [23]Their days of labor are filled with pain and grief; even at night their minds cannot rest. It is all meaningless.

[24]So I decided there is nothing better than to enjoy food and drink and to find satisfaction in work. Then I realized that these pleasures are from the hand of God. [25]For who can eat or enjoy anything apart from him?* [26]God gives wisdom, knowledge, and joy to those who please him. But if a sinner becomes wealthy, God takes the wealth away and gives it to those who please him. This, too, is meaningless—like chasing the wind.

CHAPTER 3

A Time for Everything

[1] For everything there is a season,
a time for every activity under heaven.
[2] A time to be born and a time to die.
A time to plant and a time to harvest.
[3] A time to kill and a time to heal.
A time to tear down and a time to build up.
[4] A time to cry and a time to laugh.
A time to grieve and a time to dance.
[5] A time to scatter stones and a time to gather stones.
A time to embrace and a time to turn away.
[6] A time to search and a time to quit searching.
A time to keep and a time to throw away.
[7] A time to tear and a time to mend.
A time to be quiet and a time to speak.
[8] A time to love and a time to hate.
A time for war and a time for peace.

[9]What do people really get for all their hard work? [10]I have seen the burden God has placed on us all. [11]Yet God has made everything beautiful for its own time. He has planted eternity in the human heart, but even so, people cannot see the whole scope of God's work from beginning to end. [12]So I concluded there is nothing better than to be happy and enjoy ourselves as long as we can. [13]And people should eat and drink and enjoy the fruits of their labor, for these are gifts from God.

[14]And I know that whatever God does is final. Nothing can be added to it or taken from it. God's purpose is that people should fear him. [15]What is happening now has happened before, and what will happen in the future has happened before, because God makes the same things happen over and over again.

The Injustices of Life

[16]I also noticed that under the sun there is evil in the courtroom. Yes, even the courts of law are corrupt! [17]I said to myself, "In due season

2:12 The meaning of the Hebrew is uncertain. **2:25** As in Greek and Syriac versions; Hebrew reads *apart from me?*

God will judge everyone, both good and bad, for all their deeds."

[18]I also thought about the human condition—how God proves to people that they are like animals. [19]For people and animals share the same fate—both breathe* and both must die. So people have no real advantage over the animals. How meaningless! [20]Both go to the same place—they came from dust and they return to dust. [21]For who can prove that the human spirit goes up and the spirit of animals goes down into the earth? [22]So I saw that there is nothing better for people than to be happy in their work. That is why we are here! No one will bring us back from death to enjoy life after we die.

CHAPTER 4

Again, I observed all the oppression that takes place under the sun. I saw the tears of the oppressed, with no one to comfort them. The oppressors have great power, and their victims are helpless. [2]So I concluded that the dead are better off than the living. [3]But most fortunate of all are those who are not yet born. For they have not seen all the evil that is done under the sun.

[4]Then I observed that most people are motivated to success because they envy their neighbors. But this, too, is meaningless—like chasing the wind.

[5] "Fools fold their idle hands,
leading them to ruin."

[6]And yet,

"Better to have one handful with quietness
than two handfuls with hard work
and chasing the wind."

The Advantages of Companionship

[7]I observed yet another example of something meaningless under the sun. [8]This is the case of a man who is all alone, without a child or a brother, yet who works hard to gain as much wealth as he can. But then he asks himself, "Who am I working for? Why am I giving up so much pleasure now?" It is all so meaningless and depressing.

[9]Two people are better off than one, for they can help each other succeed. [10]If one person falls, the other can reach out and help. But someone who falls alone is in real trouble. [11]Likewise, two people lying close together can keep each other warm. But how can one be warm alone? [12]A person standing alone can be attacked and defeated, but two can

3:19 Or *both have the same spirit.*

IS IT OK?

IS IT OK IF I DON'T HAVE MANY FRIENDS?

Ecclesiastes 4:9-12 talks about the benefits of close friendships. Friends stand up for you and help you out. Friends make you a stronger, better person. Friends help you not feel lonely. If you don't have many friends, maybe it's because you're unfriendly or stay distant from people. We all need others in our lives, and that means we have to let them get close to us. There are times when you might not have a lot of friends, even though you want them. That doesn't mean you aren't a fun or likeable person. It just means you need to keep working at being friendly—you *will* make friends in time. Till then, remember that God is always your friend.

While surfing the Net one day, I came across some pictures that I knew I shouldn't be looking at. But no one was around. So I kept looking. And looking. And looking. I couldn't help myself.

After I looked at all the free pictures, I discovered I could look at even *more* pictures for money. So I grabbed my mom's credit card and began charging it up.

One day when my mom picked me up from school, she was furious. Her credit card bill had come. I was in big trouble.

One of my youth sponsors, Greg, talked with me about it the next day. My mom had called him and told him we needed to talk. He didn't know any of the details—he just knew I had been having problems with something at home. I was really embarrassed to talk about it. I just told him that I had been doing something really bad and couldn't quit. Greg was cool. He told me that sometimes two people can beat something that one person can't. So I told Greg the whole story. I cried when I told him the details.

He asked me if I wanted to quit for good. I told him the truth. I wanted to quit.

That's the day we started our accountability group. Three of my friends from church and Greg and I meet every Thursday night before youth group. We share our struggles and victories, and we help each other in areas where we are weak. Thanks to my friends, I don't struggle with looking at those pictures anymore.

It's true! Two (or more) are better than one.

Find Ecclesiastes 4:9-10 and read about the value of helping each other out. Read Nehemiah 4 also to see how the Israelites worked together to rebuild the wall. Check out Mark 6:7 and Ephesians 4:2 for other examples of teamwork.

stand back-to-back and conquer. Three are even better, for a triple-braided cord is not easily broken.

The Futility of Political Power

[13]It is better to be a poor but wise youth than an old and foolish king who refuses all advice. [14]Such a youth could rise from poverty and succeed. He might even become king, though he has been in prison. [15]But then everyone rushes to the side of yet another youth* who replaces him. [16]Endless crowds stand around him,* but then another generation grows up and rejects him, too. So it is all meaningless—like chasing the wind.

CHAPTER 5

Approaching God with Care

[1]*As you enter the house of God, keep your ears open and your mouth shut. It is evil to make mindless offerings to God. [2]*Don't make rash promises, and don't be hasty in bringing matters before God. After all, God is in heaven, and you are here on earth. So let your words be few.

[3]Too much activity gives you restless dreams; too many words make you a fool.

[4]When you make a promise to God, don't delay in following through, for God takes no pleasure in fools. Keep all the promises you make to him. [5]It is better to say nothing than to make a promise and not keep it. [6]Don't let your mouth make you sin. And don't defend yourself by telling the Temple messenger that the promise you made was a mistake. That would make God angry, and he might wipe out everything you have achieved.

[7]Talk is cheap, like daydreams and other useless activities. Fear God instead.

The Futility of Wealth

[8]Don't be surprised if you see a poor person being oppressed by the powerful and if justice is being miscarried throughout the land. For every official is under orders from higher up, and matters of justice get lost in red tape and bureaucracy. [9]Even the king milks the land for his own profit!*

[10]Those who love money will never have enough. How meaningless to think that wealth brings true happiness! [11]The more you have, the more people come to help you spend it. So what good is wealth—except perhaps to watch it slip through your fingers!

[12]People who work hard sleep well, whether they eat little or much. But the rich seldom get a good night's sleep.

[13]There is another serious problem I have seen under the sun. Hoarding riches harms the saver. [14]Money is put into risky investments that turn sour, and everything is lost. In the end, there is nothing left to pass on to one's children. [15]We all come to the end of our lives as naked and empty-handed as on the day we were born. We can't take our riches with us.

[16]And this, too, is a very serious problem. People leave this world no better off than when they came. All their hard work is for nothing—like working for the wind. [17]Throughout their lives, they live under a cloud—frustrated, discouraged, and angry.

[18]Even so, I have noticed one thing, at least, that is good. It is good for people to eat, drink, and enjoy their work under the sun during the short life God has given them, and to accept their lot in life. [19]And it is a good thing to receive wealth from God and the good health to enjoy it. To enjoy your work and accept your lot in life—this is indeed a gift from God. [20]God keeps such people so busy enjoying life that they take no time to brood over the past.

CHAPTER 6

There is another serious tragedy I have seen under the sun, and it weighs heavily on humanity. [2]God gives some people great wealth and honor and everything they could ever want, but then he doesn't give them the chance to enjoy these things. They die, and someone else, even a stranger, ends up enjoying their wealth! This is meaningless—a sickening tragedy.

[3]A man might have a hundred children and live to be very old. But if he finds no satisfaction in life and doesn't even get a decent burial, it would have been better for him to be born dead. [4]His birth would have been meaningless, and he would have ended in darkness. He wouldn't even have had a name, [5]and he would never have seen the sun or known of its existence. Yet he would have had more peace

4:15 Hebrew *the second youth.* **4:16** Hebrew *There is no end to all the people, to all those who are before them.* **5:1** Verse 5:1 is numbered 4:17 in Hebrew text. **5:2** Verses 5:2-20 are numbered 5:1-19 in Hebrew text. **5:9** The meaning of the Hebrew in verses 8 and 9 is uncertain.

than in growing up to be an unhappy man. [6]He might live a thousand years twice over but still not find contentment. And since he must die like everyone else—well, what's the use?

[7]All people spend their lives scratching for food, but they never seem to have enough. [8]So are wise people really better off than fools? Do poor people gain anything by being wise and knowing how to act in front of others?

[9]Enjoy what you have rather than desiring what you don't have. Just dreaming about nice things is meaningless—like chasing the wind.

The Future—Determined and Unknown

[10]Everything has already been decided. It was known long ago what each person would be. So there's no use arguing with God about your destiny.

[11]The more words you speak, the less they mean. So what good are they?

[12]In the few days of our meaningless lives, who knows how our days can best be spent? Our lives are like a shadow. Who can tell what will happen on this earth after we are gone?

CHAPTER 7

Wisdom for Life

1 A good reputation is more valuable than costly perfume.
And the day you die is better than the day you are born.
2 Better to spend your time at funerals than at parties.
After all, everyone dies—
so the living should take this to heart.
3 Sorrow is better than laughter,
for sadness has a refining influence on us.
4 A wise person thinks a lot about death,
while a fool thinks only about having a good time.
5 Better to be criticized by a wise person than to be praised by a fool.
6 A fool's laughter is quickly gone,
like thorns crackling in a fire.
This also is meaningless.
7 Extortion turns wise people into fools,
and bribes corrupt the heart.
8 Finishing is better than starting.
Patience is better than pride.
9 Control your temper,
for anger labels you a fool.
10 Don't long for "the good old days."
This is not wise.
11 Wisdom is even better when you have money.
Both are a benefit as you go through life.
12 Wisdom and money can get you almost anything,
but only wisdom can save your life.

AMAZING FACTS

What could be better than money? Wisdom, that's what. It can save your life!
ECCLESIASTES 7:11-12

13 Accept the way God does things,
for who can straighten what he has made crooked?
14 Enjoy prosperity while you can,
but when hard times strike, realize that both come from God.
Remember that nothing is certain in this life.

The Limits of Human Wisdom

[15]I have seen everything in this meaningless life, including the death of good young people and the long life of wicked people. [16]So don't be too good or too wise! Why destroy yourself? [17]On the other hand, don't be too wicked either. Don't be a fool! Why die before your time? [18]Pay attention to these instructions, for anyone who fears God will avoid both extremes.*

7:18 Or *will follow them both.*

[19]One wise person is stronger than ten
leading citizens of a town!
[20]Not a single person on earth is always
good and never sins.
[21]Don't eavesdrop on others—you may
hear your servant curse you. [22]For you know
how often you yourself have cursed others.
[23]I have always tried my best to let wisdom
guide my thoughts and actions. I said to my-
self, "I am determined to be wise." But it
didn't work. [24]Wisdom is always distant and
difficult to find. [25]I searched everywhere, de-
termined to find wisdom and to understand
the reason for things. I was determined to
prove to myself that wickedness is stupid and
that foolishness is madness.
[26]I discovered that a seductive woman* is a
trap more bitter than death. Her passion is a
snare, and her soft hands are chains. Those
who are pleasing to God will escape her, but
sinners will be caught in her snare.
[27]"This is my conclusion," says the Teacher.
"I discovered this after looking at the matter
from every possible angle. [28]Though I have
searched repeatedly, I have not found what I
was looking for. Only one out of a thousand
men is virtuous, but not one woman! [29]But I
did find this: God created people to be virtu-
ous, but they have each turned to follow their
own downward path."

CHAPTER 8

[1] How wonderful to be wise,
to analyze and interpret things.
Wisdom lights up a person's face,
softening its harshness.

Obedience to the King

[2]Obey the king since you vowed to God that
you would. [3]Don't try to avoid doing your
duty, and don't stand with those who plot evil,
for the king can do whatever he wants. [4]His
command is backed by great power. No one
can resist or question it. [5]Those who obey
him will not be punished. Those who are wise
will find a time and a way to do what is right,
[6]for there is a time and a way for everything,
even when a person is in trouble.
[7]Indeed, how can people avoid what they
don't know is going to happen? [8]None of us
can hold back our spirit from departing. None
of us has the power to prevent the day of our
death. There is no escaping that obligation,
that dark battle. And in the face of death, wick-
edness will certainly not rescue the wicked.

The Wicked and the Righteous

[9]I have thought deeply about all that goes on
here under the sun, where people have the
power to hurt each other. [10]I have seen
wicked people buried with honor. Yet they
were the very ones who frequented the Tem-
ple and are now praised* in the same city
where they committed their crimes! This, too,
is meaningless. [11]When a crime is not pun-
ished quickly, people feel it is safe to do
wrong. [12]But even though a person sins a hun-
dred times and still lives a long time, I know
that those who fear God will be better off.
[13]The wicked will not prosper, for they do not
fear God. Their days will never grow long like
the evening shadows.
[14]And this is not all that is meaningless in
our world. In this life, good people are often
treated as though they were wicked, and
wicked people are often treated as though
they were good. This is so meaningless!
[15]So I recommend having fun, because
there is nothing better for people in this world
than to eat, drink, and enjoy life. That way they
will experience some happiness along with all
the hard work God gives them under the sun.
[16]In my search for wisdom and in my ob-
servation of people's burdens here on earth, I
discovered that there is ceaseless activity, day
and night. [17]I realized that no one can dis-
cover everything God is doing under the sun.
Not even the wisest people discover every-
thing, no matter what they claim.

CHAPTER 9

Death Comes to All

This, too, I carefully explored: Even though
the actions of godly and wise people are in
God's hands, no one knows whether God will
show them favor. [2]The same destiny ulti-
mately awaits everyone, whether righteous or
wicked, good or bad,* ceremonially clean or
unclean, religious or irreligious. Good people
receive the same treatment as sinners, and
people who make promises to God are
treated like people who don't.

7:26 Hebrew *a woman*. **8:10** As in some Hebrew manuscripts and Greek version; many Hebrew manuscripts read *and are forgotten*.
9:2 As in Greek and Syriac versions and Latin Vulgate; Hebrew lacks *or bad*.

[3]It seems so tragic that everyone under the sun suffers the same fate. That is why people are not more careful to be good. Instead, they choose their own mad course, for they have no hope. There is nothing ahead but death anyway. [4]There is hope only for the living. As they say, "It's better to be a live dog than a dead lion!"

[5]The living at least know they will die, but the dead know nothing. They have no further reward, nor are they remembered. [6]Whatever they did in their lifetime—loving, hating, envying—is all long gone. They no longer play a part in anything here on earth. [7]So go ahead. Eat your food with joy, and drink your wine with a happy heart, for God approves of this! [8]Wear fine clothes, with a splash of cologne!

[9]Live happily with the woman you love through all the meaningless days of life that God has given you under the sun. The wife God gives you is your reward for all your earthly toil. [10]Whatever you do, do well. For when you go to the grave,* there will be no work or planning or knowledge or wisdom.

[11]I have observed something else under the sun. The fastest runner doesn't always win the race, and the strongest warrior doesn't always win the battle. The wise sometimes go hungry, and the skillful are not necessarily wealthy. And those who are educated don't always lead successful lives. It is all decided by chance, by being in the right place at the right time.

[12]People can never predict when hard times might come. Like fish in a net or birds in a trap, people are caught by sudden tragedy.

Thoughts on Wisdom and Folly

[13]Here is another bit of wisdom that has impressed me as I have watched the way our world works. [14]There was a small town with only a few people, and a great king came with his army and besieged it. [15]A poor, wise man knew how to save the town, and so it was rescued. But afterward no one thought to thank him. [16]So even though wisdom is better than strength, those who are wise will be despised if they are poor. What they say will not be appreciated for long.

[17] Better to hear the quiet words of a wise person
than the shouts of a foolish king.
[18] Better to have wisdom than weapons of war,
but one sinner can destroy much that is good.

CHAPTER 10

[1] As dead flies cause even a bottle of perfume to stink,
so a little foolishness spoils great wisdom and honor.

[2] A wise person chooses the right road;
a fool takes the wrong one.

[3] You can identify fools
just by the way they walk down the street!

[4] If your boss is angry at you, don't quit!
A quiet spirit can overcome even great mistakes.

The Ironies of Life

[5]There is another evil I have seen under the sun. Kings and rulers make a grave mistake [6]when they give great authority to foolish people and low positions to people of proven worth. [7]I have even seen servants riding horseback like princes—and princes walking like servants!

[8] When you dig a well,
you might fall in.
When you demolish an old wall,
you could be bitten by a snake.
[9] When you work in a quarry,
stones might fall and crush you.
When you chop wood,
there is danger with each stroke of your ax.

[10] Using a dull ax requires great strength,
so sharpen the blade.
That's the value of wisdom;
it helps you succeed.

[11] If a snake bites before you charm it,
what's the use of being a snake charmer?

[12] Wise words bring approval,
but fools are destroyed by their own words.

9:10 Hebrew *to Sheol.*

13 Fools base their thoughts on foolish assumptions,
so their conclusions will be wicked madness;
14 they chatter on and on.

No one really knows what is going to happen;
no one can predict the future.

15 Fools are so exhausted by a little work
that they can't even find their way home.

16 What sorrow for the land ruled by a servant,*
the land whose leaders feast in the morning.
17 Happy is the land whose king is a noble leader
and whose leaders feast at the proper time
to gain strength for their work, not to get drunk.

18 Laziness leads to a sagging roof;
idleness leads to a leaky house.

19 A party gives laughter,
wine gives happiness,
and money gives everything!

20 Never make light of the king, even in your thoughts.
And don't make fun of the powerful, even in your own bedroom.
For a little bird might deliver your message and tell them what you said.

CHAPTER 11

The Uncertainties of Life

1 Send your grain across the seas,
and in time, profits will flow back to you.*
2 But divide your investments among many places,*
for you do not know what risks might lie ahead.

3 When clouds are heavy, the rains come down.
Whether a tree falls north or south, it stays where it falls.

4 Farmers who wait for perfect weather never plant.
If they watch every cloud, they never harvest.

5 Just as you cannot understand the path of the wind or the mystery of a tiny baby growing in its mother's womb,* so you cannot understand the activity of God, who does all things.
6 Plant your seed in the morning and keep busy all afternoon, for you don't know if profit will come from one activity or another—or maybe both.

Advice for Young and Old

7 Light is sweet; how pleasant to see a new day dawning.
8 When people live to be very old, let them rejoice in every day of life. But let them also remember there will be many dark days. Everything still to come is meaningless.
9 Young people,* it's wonderful to be young! Enjoy every minute of it. Do everything you want to do; take it all in. But remember that you must give an account to God for everything you do. 10 So refuse to worry, and keep your body healthy. But remember that youth, with a whole life before you, is meaningless.

God will be important to me someday, but I'm busy now.

Don't let the excitement of youth cause you to forget your Creator. Honor him in your youth before you grow old. ECCLESIASTES 12:1

CHAPTER 12

Don't let the excitement of youth cause you to forget your Creator. Honor him in your youth before you grow old and say, "Life is not pleasant anymore." 2 Remember him before the light of the sun, moon, and stars is dim to your old eyes, and rain clouds continually darken

10:16 Or *a child.* **11:1** Or *Give generously, / for your gifts will return to you later.* Hebrew reads *Throw your bread on the waters, / for after many days you will find it again.* **11:2** Hebrew *among seven or even eight.* **11:5** Some manuscripts read *Just as you cannot understand how breath comes to a tiny baby in its mother's womb.* **11:9** Hebrew *Young man.*

Party On!

Jackson was really into movies and was a big fan of a famous movie star. The superstar was Jackson's hero. During a TV interview the star was questioned about rumors of his drinking too much. He said, "I figure I'm here just a short time, so I'd better have all the fun I can. My motto is: 'Party!' " Some of Jackson's friends said that was their motto too. Were they right? Is that what life is all about? Read Ecclesiastes 12:1, 13-14 to see how King Solomon might have answered that question. How would you answer?

your sky. [3]Remember him before your legs—
the guards of your house—start to tremble;
and before your shoulders—the strong men—
stoop. Remember him before your teeth—
your few remaining servants—stop grinding;
and before your eyes—the women looking
through the windows—see dimly.

[4]Remember him before the door to life's
opportunities is closed and the sound of work
fades. Now you rise at the first chirping of the
birds, but then all their sounds will grow faint.

[5]Remember him before you become fear-
ful of falling and worry about danger in the
streets; before your hair turns white like an
almond tree in bloom, and you drag along
without energy like a dying grasshopper, and
the caperberry no longer inspires sexual de-
sire. Remember him before you near the
grave, your everlasting home, when the
mourners will weep at your funeral.

[6]Yes, remember your Creator now while
you are young, before the silver cord of life
snaps and the golden bowl is broken. Don't
wait until the water jar is smashed at the
spring and the pulley is broken at the well.
[7]For then the dust will return to the earth, and
the spirit will return to God who gave it.

Concluding Thoughts about the Teacher

[8]"Everything is meaningless," says the Teacher,
"completely meaningless."

[9]Keep this in mind: The Teacher was con-
sidered wise, and he taught the people every-
thing he knew. He listened carefully to many
proverbs, studying and classifying them.
[10]The Teacher sought to find just the right
words to express truths clearly.*

[11]The words of the wise are like cattle
prods—painful but helpful. Their collected
sayings are like a nail-studded stick with
which a shepherd* drives the sheep.

[12]But, my child,* let me give you some fur-
ther advice: Be careful, for writing books is
endless, and much study wears you out.

[13]That's the whole story. Here now is my fi-
nal conclusion: Fear God and obey his com-
mands, for this is everyone's duty. [14]God will
judge us for everything we do, including every
secret thing, whether good or bad.

12:10 Or *sought to write what was upright and true.* **12:11** Or *one shepherd.* **12:12** Hebrew *my son.*

SONG OF SONGS

WHO

King Solomon, the young woman from Shulam, and the young women of Jerusalem.

WHERE

The royal palace in Jerusalem.

WHEN

It was probably not long after 970 BC, when Solomon became king, that he wrote this book.

WHY

To describe the love between a bridegroom and his bride so we can understand God's love.

Like a lily among thistles is my darling among young women.
SONG OF SONGS 2:2

"Ooooh baby, I want you, I need you, I love you. . . ." Love songs don't always tell us the truth. In fact, sometimes they tell us the opposite of God's truth. Song of Songs is a book about the way *God* looks at love, sex, and marriage. God thinks all three are pretty special.

WHEN IT COMES TO LOVE, DON'T SETTLE FOR ANYTHING LESS THAN GOD'S BEST.

CHAPTER 1

This is Solomon's song of songs, more wonderful than any other.

Young Woman*

2 Kiss me and kiss me again,
for your love is sweeter than wine.
3 How fragrant your cologne;
your name is like its spreading fragrance.
No wonder all the young women love you!
4 Take me with you; come, let's run!
The king has brought me into his bedroom.

1:1 The headings identifying the speakers are not in the original text, though the Hebrew usually gives clues by means of the gender of the person speaking.

Young Women of Jerusalem
How happy we are for you, O king.
We praise your love even more than wine.

Young Woman
How right they are to adore you.

5 I am dark but beautiful,
O women of Jerusalem—
dark as the tents of Kedar,
dark as the curtains of Solomon's tents.
6 Don't stare at me because I am dark—
the sun has darkened my skin.
My brothers were angry with me;
they forced me to care for their vineyards,
so I couldn't care for myself—my own vineyard.

7 Tell me, my love, where are you leading your flock today?
Where will you rest your sheep at noon?
For why should I wander like a prostitute*
among your friends and their flocks?

Young Man
8 If you don't know, O most beautiful woman,
follow the trail of my flock,
and graze your young goats by the shepherds' tents.
9 You are as exciting, my darling,
as a mare among Pharaoh's stallions.
10 How lovely are your cheeks;
your earrings set them afire!
How lovely is your neck,
enhanced by a string of jewels.
11 We will make for you earrings of gold
and beads of silver.

Young Woman
12 The king is lying on his couch,
enchanted by the fragrance of my perfume.
13 My lover is like a sachet of myrrh
lying between my breasts.
14 He is like a bouquet of sweet henna blossoms
from the vineyards of En-gedi.

Young Man
15 How beautiful you are, my darling,
how beautiful!
Your eyes are like doves.

Young Woman
16 You are so handsome, my love,
pleasing beyond words!
The soft grass is our bed;
17 fragrant cedar branches are the beams of our house,
and pleasant smelling firs are the rafters.

CHAPTER 2

Young Woman
1 I am the spring crocus blooming on the Sharon Plain,*
the lily of the valley.

Young Man
2 Like a lily among thistles
is my darling among young women.

Young Woman
3 Like the finest apple tree in the orchard
is my lover among other young men.
I sit in his delightful shade
and taste his delicious fruit.
4 He escorts me to the banquet hall;
it's obvious how much he loves me.
5 Strengthen me with raisin cakes,
refresh me with apples,
for I am weak with love.
6 His left arm is under my head,
and his right arm embraces me.

7 Promise me, O women of Jerusalem,
by the gazelles and wild deer,
not to awaken love until the time is right.*

8 Ah, I hear my lover coming!
He is leaping over the mountains,
bounding over the hills.
9 My lover is like a swift gazelle
or a young stag.
Look, there he is behind the wall,
looking through the window,
peering into the room.

10 My lover said to me,
"Rise up, my darling!
Come away with me, my fair one!

1:7 Hebrew *like a veiled woman.* **2:1** Traditionally rendered *I am the rose of Sharon.* Sharon Plain is a region in the coastal plain of Palestine. **2:7** Or *not to awaken love until it is ready.*

When I was in junior high, my parents imposed very strict dating rules on my life. In short, I was not allowed to date at all until I turned 16—I couldn't even go on group dates or to dances. That's no dates. *Nada.* None.

At the time, I really wanted to have someone to hold hands with at basketball games and movies. I guess I just wanted to be known as a girl who could get a date. Looking back, I see how shallow that was and how my parents spared me pain by helping me choose not to date. That's not to say the decision to follow my parents' rules was easy. I liked a couple of boys, and several of them liked me back. I still remember how difficult it was to look at a boy I really liked and tell him I was not allowed to date him.

That memory is extremely painful, but I can see the benefits of my decision. Now I have no past regrets about relationships. For one thing, I'm lucky that I did not experience the traumatic breakups and heartaches that many of my friends did.

Another thing is that—except for the few that moved away since junior high—those "potential date" guys are now my closest friends. If I had dated them, I wouldn't still have them as friends. And they would not have been there to pull me through the hard times in my life. They have been by my side through everything, and I would not recommend sacrificing that for the memory of a boyfriend in junior high.

The best part is that we can all sit around now and laugh about our "almost relationships" and how glad we are they never happened.

Check out these verses on waiting for the right time for dating and love: Song of Songs 2:7 and 1 Corinthians 13:4.

11 Look, the winter is past,
and the rains are over and gone.
12 The flowers are springing up,
the season of singing birds* has come,
and the cooing of turtledoves fills
the air.
13 The fig trees are forming young fruit,
and the fragrant grapevines are
blossoming.
Rise up, my darling!
Come away with me, my fair one!"

Young Man

14 My dove is hiding behind the rocks,
behind an outcrop on the cliff.
Let me see your face;
let me hear your voice.
For your voice is pleasant,
and your face is lovely.

Young Women of Jerusalem

15 Catch all the foxes,
those little foxes,
before they ruin the vineyard of love,
for the grapevines are blossoming!

Young Woman

16 My lover is mine, and I am his.
He browses among the lilies.
17 Before the dawn breezes blow
and the night shadows flee,
return to me, my love, like a gazelle
or a young stag on the rugged
mountains.*

CHAPTER 3

Young Woman

1 One night as I lay in bed, I yearned
for my lover.
I yearned for him, but he did not
come.
2 So I said to myself, "I will get up and roam
the city,
searching in all its streets and squares.
I will search for the one I love."
So I searched everywhere but did not
find him.
3 The watchmen stopped me as they made
their rounds,
and I asked, "Have you seen the one I
love?"
4 Then scarcely had I left them
when I found my love!
I caught and held him tightly,
then I brought him to my mother's
house,
into my mother's bed, where I had
been conceived.

5 Promise me, O women of Jerusalem,
by the gazelles and wild deer,
not to awaken love until the time
is right.*

Young Women of Jerusalem

6 Who is this sweeping in from the
wilderness
like a cloud of smoke?
Who is it, fragrant with myrrh and
frankincense
and every kind of spice?
7 Look, it is Solomon's carriage,
surrounded by sixty heroic men,
the best of Israel's soldiers.
8 They are all skilled swordsmen,
experienced warriors.
Each wears a sword on his thigh,
ready to defend the king against an
attack in the night.
9 King Solomon's carriage is built
of wood imported from Lebanon.
10 Its posts are silver,
its canopy gold;
its cushions are purple.
It was decorated with love
by the young women of Jerusalem.

Young Woman

11 Come out to see King Solomon,
young women of Jerusalem.*
He wears the crown his mother
gave him on his wedding day,
his most joyous day.

CHAPTER 4

Young Man

1 You are beautiful, my darling,
beautiful beyond words.
Your eyes are like doves
behind your veil.
Your hair falls in waves,
like a flock of goats winding down
the slopes of Gilead.
2 Your teeth are as white as sheep,
recently shorn and freshly
washed.

2:12 Or *the season of pruning vines.* **2:17** Or *on the hills of Bether.* **3:5** Or *not to awaken love until it is ready.* **3:11** Hebrew *of Zion.*

A Bride in a Garden

The DJs on Randy's favorite radio station had started talking about sex a lot, and they played songs about it all the time. He couldn't believe some of the lyrics! At school some guys were talking about sex too. Nolan said, "Anything is OK as long as you're careful."

Song of Songs is a love poem that will help you know how Randy should respond. Song of Songs 4:12 describes how a groom treasures his bride. How should Randy live so that someday he and his wife will be able to treasure each other?

Your smile is flawless,
each tooth matched with its twin.*
3 Your lips are like scarlet ribbon;
your mouth is inviting.
Your cheeks are like rosy pomegranates
behind your veil.
4 Your neck is as beautiful as the tower
of David,
jeweled with the shields of a thousand
heroes.
5 Your breasts are like two fawns,
twin fawns of a gazelle grazing among
the lilies.
6 Before the dawn breezes blow
and the night shadows flee,
I will hurry to the mountain of myrrh
and to the hill of frankincense.
7 You are altogether beautiful,
my darling,
beautiful in every way.

8 Come with me from Lebanon, my bride,
come with me from Lebanon.
Come down* from Mount Amana,
from the peaks of Senir and
Hermon,
where the lions have their dens
and leopards live among the hills.

9 You have captured my heart,
my treasure,* my bride.
You hold it hostage with one glance
of your eyes,
with a single jewel of your necklace.
10 Your love delights me,
my treasure, my bride.
Your love is better than wine,
your perfume more fragrant than
spices.
11 Your lips are as sweet as nectar, my bride.
Honey and milk are under your tongue.
Your clothes are scented
like the cedars of Lebanon.

12 You are my private garden, my treasure,
my bride,
a secluded spring, a hidden fountain.
13 Your thighs shelter a paradise of
pomegranates
with rare spices—
henna with nard,
14 nard and saffron,
fragrant calamus and cinnamon,
with all the trees of frankincense,
myrrh, and aloes,
and every other lovely spice.
15 You are a garden fountain,
a well of fresh water
streaming down from Lebanon's
mountains.

4:2 Hebrew *Not one is missing; each has a twin.* **4:8** Or *Look down.* **4:9** Hebrew *my sister;* also in 4:10, 12.

Young Woman

16 Awake, north wind!
Rise up, south wind!
Blow on my garden
and spread its fragrance all around.
Come into your garden, my love;
taste its finest fruits.

CHAPTER 5

Young Man

1 I have entered my garden, my treasure,*
my bride!
I gather myrrh with my spices
and eat honeycomb with my honey.
I drink wine with my milk.

Young Women of Jerusalem

Oh, lover and beloved, eat and drink!
Yes, drink deeply of your love!

Young Woman

2 I slept, but my heart was awake,
when I heard my lover knocking and calling:
"Open to me, my treasure, my darling,
my dove, my perfect one.
My head is drenched with dew,
my hair with the dampness of the night."

3 But I responded,
"I have taken off my robe.
Should I get dressed again?
I have washed my feet.
Should I get them soiled?"

4 My lover tried to unlatch the door,
and my heart thrilled within me.
5 I jumped up to open the door for my love,
and my hands dripped with perfume.
My fingers dripped with lovely myrrh
as I pulled back the bolt.
6 I opened to my lover,
but he was gone!
My heart sank.
I searched for him
but could not find him anywhere.
I called to him,
but there was no reply.
7 The night watchmen found me
as they made their rounds.
They beat and bruised me
and stripped off my veil,
those watchmen on the walls.

8 Make this promise, O women of Jerusalem—
If you find my lover,
tell him I am weak with love.

Young Women of Jerusalem

9 Why is your lover better than all others,
O woman of rare beauty?
What makes your lover so special
that we must promise this?

Young Woman

10 My lover is dark and dazzling,
better than ten thousand others!
11 His head is finest gold,
his wavy hair is black as a raven.
12 His eyes sparkle like doves
beside springs of water;
they are set like jewels
washed in milk.
13 His cheeks are like gardens of spices
giving off fragrance.
His lips are like lilies,
perfumed with myrrh.
14 His arms are like rounded bars of gold,
set with beryl.
His body is like bright ivory,
glowing with lapis lazuli.
15 His legs are like marble pillars
set in sockets of finest gold.
His posture is stately,
like the noble cedars of Lebanon.
16 His mouth is sweetness itself;
he is desirable in every way.
Such, O women of Jerusalem,
is my lover, my friend.

CHAPTER 6

Young Women of Jerusalem

1 Where has your lover gone,
O woman of rare beauty?
Which way did he turn
so we can help you find him?

Young Woman

2 My lover has gone down to his garden,
to his spice beds,
to browse in the gardens
and gather the lilies.
3 I am my lover's, and my lover is mine.
He browses among the lilies.

5:1 Hebrew *my sister;* also in 5:2.

Young Man

4 You are beautiful, my darling,
like the lovely city of Tirzah.
Yes, as beautiful as Jerusalem,
as majestic as an army with billowing banners.
5 Turn your eyes away,
for they overpower me.
Your hair falls in waves,
like a flock of goats winding down the slopes of Gilead.
6 Your teeth are as white as sheep
that are freshly washed.
Your smile is flawless,
each tooth matched with its twin.*
7 Your cheeks are like rosy pomegranates
behind your veil.
8 Even among sixty queens
and eighty concubines
and countless young women,
9 I would still choose my dove, my perfect one—
the favorite of her mother,
dearly loved by the one who bore her.
The young women see her and praise her;
even queens and royal concubines sing her praises:
10 "Who is this, arising like the dawn,
as fair as the moon,
as bright as the sun,
as majestic as an army with billowing banners?"

Young Woman

11 I went down to the grove of walnut trees
and out to the valley to see the new spring growth,
to see whether the grapevines had budded
or the pomegranates were in bloom.
12 Before I realized it,
my strong desires had taken me to the chariot of a noble man.*

Young Women of Jerusalem

13* Return, return to us, O maid of Shulam.
Come back, come back, that we may see you again.

Young Man

Why do you stare at this young woman of Shulam,
as she moves so gracefully between two lines of dancers?*

CHAPTER 7

1* How beautiful are your sandaled feet,
O queenly maiden.
Your rounded thighs are like jewels,
the work of a skilled craftsman.
2 Your navel is perfectly formed
like a goblet filled with mixed wine.
Between your thighs lies a mound of wheat
bordered with lilies.
3 Your breasts are like two fawns,
twin fawns of a gazelle.
4 Your neck is as beautiful as an ivory tower.
Your eyes are like the sparkling pools in Heshbon
by the gate of Bath-rabbim.
Your nose is as fine as the tower of Lebanon
overlooking Damascus.
5 Your head is as majestic as Mount Carmel,
and the sheen of your hair radiates royalty.
The king is held captive by its tresses.
6 Oh, how beautiful you are!
How pleasing, my love, how full of delights!
7 You are slender like a palm tree,
and your breasts are like its clusters of fruit.
8 I said, "I will climb the palm tree
and take hold of its fruit."
May your breasts be like grape clusters,
and the fragrance of your breath like apples.
9 May your kisses be as exciting as the best wine,
flowing gently over lips and teeth.*

Young Woman

10 I am my lover's,
and he claims me as his own.
11 Come, my love, let us go out to the fields
and spend the night among the wildflowers.*

6:6 Hebrew *Not one is missing; each has a twin.* **6:12** Or *to the royal chariots of my people,* or *to the chariots of Amminadab.* The meaning of the Hebrew is uncertain. **6:13a** Verse 6:13 is numbered 7:1 in Hebrew text. **6:13b** Or *as you would at the movements of two armies?* or *as you would at the dance of Mahanaim?* The meaning of the Hebrew is uncertain. **7:1** Verses 7:1-13 are numbered 7:2-14 in Hebrew text. **7:9** As in Greek and Syriac versions and Latin Vulgate; Hebrew reads *over lips of sleepers.* **7:11** Or *in the villages.*

12 Let us get up early and go to the vineyards
to see if the grapevines have budded,
if the blossoms have opened,
and if the pomegranates have bloomed.
There I will give you my love.
13 There the mandrakes give off their fragrance,
and the finest fruits are at our door,
new delights as well as old,
which I have saved for you, my lover.

CHAPTER 8

Young Woman

1 Oh, I wish you were my brother,
who nursed at my mother's breasts.
Then I could kiss you no matter who was watching,
and no one would criticize me.
2 I would bring you to my childhood home,
and there you would teach me.*
I would give you spiced wine to drink,
my sweet pomegranate wine.
3 Your left arm would be under my head,
and your right arm would embrace me.

4 Promise me, O women of Jerusalem,
not to awaken love until the time is right.*

Young Women of Jerusalem

5 Who is this sweeping in from the desert,
leaning on her lover?

Young Woman

I aroused you under the apple tree,
where your mother gave you birth,
where in great pain she delivered you.
6 Place me like a seal over your heart,
like a seal on your arm.
For love is as strong as death,
its jealousy* as enduring as the grave.*
Love flashes like fire,
the brightest kind of flame.
7 Many waters cannot quench love,
nor can rivers drown it.
If a man tried to buy love
with all his wealth,
his offer would be utterly scorned.

The Young Woman's Brothers

8 We have a little sister
too young to have breasts.
What will we do for our sister
if someone asks to marry her?
9 If she is a virgin, like a wall,

8:2 Or *there she will teach me;* or *there she bore me.* **8:4** Or *not to awaken love until it is ready.* **8:6a** Or *its passion.* **8:6b** Hebrew *as Sheol.*

IS IT OK?

IS IT OK TO KISS SOMEONE OR MAKE OUT?

The Bible doesn't say, "Thou shalt not kiss." But in Song of Songs 8:4, God warns us "not to awaken love until the time is right." What does *that* mean? It means you need to be cautious and not rush into a romantic relationship. Why? You're nowhere near the point of being ready for a committed relationship like marriage. So you don't want to put yourself in a sexually tempting situation. When God says no, what he means is, "I love you and don't want you to hurt yourself." Kids who go too far sexually regret what they've lost. Don't let that be you. Talk with your parents about what your standards will be, and stick to 'em!

Isaiah

Ever wonder what it would be like to hear God whisper in your ear? One time I saw a vision of God on his throne and heard angels singing, "Holy, Holy, Holy!" I'll never forget the beauty or the fear. Then I heard him tell me to be his messenger.

Over the years God has told me many things. Often it's been bad news to pass on to my people when they weren't following God's ways. Now they hate me because I've told them the truth about their sins. I must give them God's message, though. I didn't ask to be a prophet, and I'm certainly not perfect. But I will keep encouraging people to obey God.

Read more about the prophet Isaiah in 2 Kings 19–20 and the book of Isaiah.

we will protect her with a
silver tower.
But if she is promiscuous, like a
swinging door,
we will block her door with a cedar bar.

Young Woman

10 I was a virgin, like a wall;
now my breasts are like towers.
When my lover looks at me,
he is delighted with what he sees.

11 Solomon has a vineyard at Baal-hamon,
which he leases out to tenant farmers.
Each of them pays a thousand pieces
of silver*
for harvesting its fruit.
12 But my vineyard is mine to give,
and Solomon need not pay a
thousand pieces of silver.
But I will give two hundred pieces
to those who care for its vines.

Young Man

13 O my darling, lingering in the gardens,
your companions are fortunate to hear
your voice.
Let me hear it, too!

Young Woman

14 Come away, my love! Be like a gazelle
or a young stag on the mountains
of spices.

8:11 Hebrew *1,000 shekels of silver.*

Isaiah

WHO
Isaiah and his two sons, Shear-jashub and Maher-shalal-hash-baz.

WHERE
Mainly in Jerusalem.

WHEN
Chapters 1–39 were probably written around 700 BC, during Isaiah's ministry; but chapters 40–66 may have been written near the end of his life, about 681 BC.

WHY
To call the nation back to God and tell of the Messiah.

Though your sins are like scarlet,
I will make them as white as snow.
ISAIAH 1:18

Sometimes we're afraid of what others might say if we tell them what we *really* think. In Bible times, a *prophet* was someone who told people what God really was thinking, even when the people didn't want to hear it. Isaiah was one of those prophets. It wasn't an easy job. This book is filled with his messages.

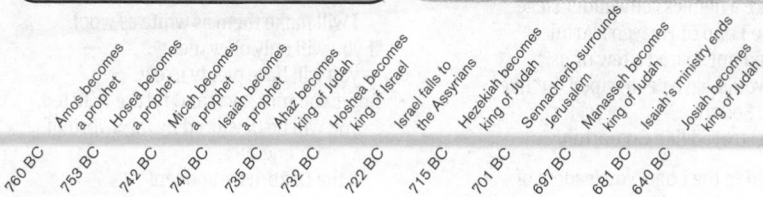

ASK GOD TO GIVE YOU COURAGE TO SPEAK OUT FOR HIM.

CHAPTER 1

These are the visions that Isaiah son of Amoz saw concerning Judah and Jerusalem. He saw these visions during the years when Uzziah, Jotham, Ahaz, and Hezekiah were kings of Judah.*

1:1 These kings reigned from 792 to 686 B.C.

A Message for Rebellious Judah

2 Listen, O heavens! Pay attention, earth!
This is what the LORD says:
"The children I raised and cared for have rebelled against me.

3 Even an ox knows its owner,
and a donkey recognizes its master's care—
but Israel doesn't know its master.
My people don't recognize my care for them."
4 Oh, what a sinful nation they are—
loaded down with a burden of guilt.
They are evil people,
corrupt children who have rejected the LORD.
They have despised the Holy One of Israel
and turned their backs on him.

5 Why do you continue to invite punishment?
Must you rebel forever?
Your head is injured,
and your heart is sick.
6 You are battered from head to foot—
covered with bruises, welts, and infected wounds—
without any soothing ointments or bandages.
7 Your country lies in ruins,
and your towns are burned.
Foreigners plunder your fields before your eyes
and destroy everything they see.
8 Beautiful Jerusalem* stands abandoned
like a watchman's shelter in a vineyard,
like a lean-to in a cucumber field after the harvest,
like a helpless city under siege.
9 If the LORD of Heaven's Armies
had not spared a few of us,*
we would have been wiped out like Sodom,
destroyed like Gomorrah.

10 Listen to the LORD, you leaders of "Sodom."
Listen to the law of our God, people of "Gomorrah."
11 "What makes you think I want all your sacrifices?"
says the LORD.
"I am sick of your burnt offerings of rams
and the fat of fattened cattle.
I get no pleasure from the blood
of bulls and lambs and goats.
12 When you come to worship me,
who asked you to parade through my courts with all your ceremony?
13 Stop bringing me your meaningless gifts;
the incense of your offerings disgusts me!
As for your celebrations of the new moon and the Sabbath
and your special days for fasting—
they are all sinful and false.
I want no more of your pious meetings.
14 I hate your new moon celebrations and your annual festivals.
They are a burden to me. I cannot stand them!
15 When you lift up your hands in prayer,
I will not look.
Though you offer many prayers, I will not listen,
for your hands are covered with the blood of innocent victims.
16 Wash yourselves and be clean!
Get your sins out of my sight.
Give up your evil ways.
17 Learn to do good.
Seek justice.
Help the oppressed.
Defend the cause of orphans.
Fight for the rights of widows.

18 "Come now, let's settle this,"
says the LORD.
"Though your sins are like scarlet,
I will make them as white as snow.
Though they are red like crimson,
I will make them as white as wool.
19 If you will only obey me,
you will have plenty to eat.
20 But if you turn away and refuse to listen,
you will be devoured by the sword of your enemies.
I, the LORD, have spoken!"

Unfaithful Jerusalem

21 See how Jerusalem, once so faithful,
has become a prostitute.
Once the home of justice and righteousness,
she is now filled with murderers.
22 Once like pure silver,
you have become like worthless slag.
Once so pure,
you are now like watered-down wine.

1:8 Hebrew *The daughter of Zion.* **1:9** Greek version reads *a few of our children.* Compare Rom 9:29.

23 Your leaders are rebels,
the companions of thieves.
All of them love bribes
and demand payoffs,
but they refuse to defend the cause
of orphans
or fight for the rights of widows.

24 Therefore, the Lord, the LORD of Heaven's
Armies,
the Mighty One of Israel, says,
"I will take revenge on my enemies
and pay back my foes!
25 I will raise my fist against you.
I will melt you down and skim off
your slag.
I will remove all your impurities.
26 Then I will give you good judges again
and wise counselors like you used
to have.
Then Jerusalem will again be called the
Home of Justice
and the Faithful City."

27 Zion will be restored by justice;
those who repent will be revived by
righteousness.
28 But rebels and sinners will be completely
destroyed,
and those who desert the LORD will be
consumed.

29 You will be ashamed of your idol
worship
in groves of sacred oaks.
You will blush because you worshiped
in gardens dedicated to idols.
30 You will be like a great tree with withered
leaves,
like a garden without water.
31 The strongest among you will disappear
like straw;
their evil deeds will be the spark that
sets it on fire.
They and their evil works will burn up
together,
and no one will be able to put out
the fire.

CHAPTER 2

The LORD's Future Reign

This is a vision that Isaiah son of Amoz saw concerning Judah and Jerusalem:

2 In the last days, the mountain of the
LORD's house
will be the highest of all—
the most important place on earth.
It will be raised above the other hills,
and people from all over the world will
stream there to worship.
3 People from many nations will come
and say,
"Come, let us go up to the mountain
of the LORD,
to the house of Jacob's God.
There he will teach us his ways,
and we will walk in his paths."
For the LORD's teaching will go out from
Zion;
his word will go out from Jerusalem.
4 The LORD will mediate between nations
and will settle international disputes.
They will hammer their swords into
plowshares
and their spears into pruning hooks.
Nation will no longer fight against nation,
nor train for war anymore.

A Warning of Judgment

5 Come, descendants of Jacob,
let us walk in the light of the LORD!
6 For the LORD has rejected his people,
the descendants of Jacob,
because they have filled their land with
practices from the East
and with sorcerers, as the Philistines
do.
They have made alliances with pagans.
7 Israel is full of silver and gold;
there is no end to its treasures.
Their land is full of warhorses;
there is no end to its chariots.
8 Their land is full of idols;
the people worship things they have
made
with their own hands.
9 So now they will be humbled,
and all will be brought low—
do not forgive them.
10 Crawl into caves in the rocks.
Hide in the dust
from the terror of the LORD
and the glory of his majesty.
11 Human pride will be brought down,
and human arrogance will be humbled.

Only the LORD will be exalted
on that day of judgment.

12 For the LORD of Heaven's Armies
has a day of reckoning.
He will punish the proud and mighty
and bring down everything that is exalted.
13 He will cut down the tall cedars of Lebanon
and all the mighty oaks of Bashan.
14 He will level all the high mountains
and all the lofty hills.
15 He will break down every high tower
and every fortified wall.
16 He will destroy all the great trading ships*
and every magnificent vessel.
17 Human pride will be humbled,
and human arrogance will be brought down.
Only the LORD will be exalted
on that day of judgment.

18 Idols will completely disappear.
19 When the LORD rises to shake the earth,
his enemies will crawl into holes in the ground.
They will hide in caves in the rocks
from the terror of the LORD
and the glory of his majesty.
20 On that day of judgment they will abandon the gold and silver idols
they made for themselves to worship.
They will leave their gods to the rodents and bats,
21 while they crawl away into caverns
and hide among the jagged rocks in the cliffs.
They will try to escape the terror of the LORD
and the glory of his majesty
as he rises to shake the earth.
22 Don't put your trust in mere humans.
They are as frail as breath.
What good are they?

CHAPTER 3

Judgment against Judah

1 The Lord, the LORD of Heaven's Armies,
will take away from Jerusalem and Judah
everything they depend on:
every bit of bread
and every drop of water,
2 all their heroes and soldiers,
judges and prophets,
fortune-tellers and elders,
3 army officers and high officials,
advisers, skilled craftsmen, and astrologers.

4 I will make boys their leaders,
and toddlers their rulers.
5 People will oppress each other—
man against man,
neighbor against neighbor.
Young people will insult their elders,
and vulgar people will sneer at the honorable.

6 In those days a man will say to his brother,
"Since you have a coat, you be our leader!
Take charge of this heap of ruins!"
7 But he will reply,
"No! I can't help.
I don't have any extra food or clothes.
Don't put me in charge!"

8 For Jerusalem will stumble,
and Judah will fall,
because they speak out against the LORD
and refuse to obey him.
They provoke him to his face.
9 The very look on their faces gives them away.
They display their sin like the people of Sodom
and don't even try to hide it.
They are doomed!
They have brought destruction upon themselves.

10 Tell the godly that all will be well for them.
They will enjoy the rich reward they have earned!
11 But the wicked are doomed,
for they will get exactly what they deserve.

12 Childish leaders oppress my people,
and women rule over them.
O my people, your leaders mislead you;
they send you down the wrong road.

2:16 Hebrew *every ship of Tarshish.*

13 The LORD takes his place in court
and presents his case against his people!
14 The LORD comes forward to pronounce judgment
on the elders and rulers of his people:
"You have ruined Israel, my vineyard.
Your houses are filled with things stolen from the poor.
15 How dare you crush my people,
grinding the faces of the poor into the dust?"
demands the Lord, the LORD of Heaven's Armies.

A Warning to Jerusalem

16 The LORD says, "Beautiful Zion* is haughty:
craning her elegant neck,
flirting with her eyes,
walking with dainty steps,
tinkling her ankle bracelets.
17 So the Lord will send scabs on her head;
the LORD will make beautiful Zion bald."
18 On that day of judgment
the Lord will strip away everything that makes her beautiful:
ornaments, headbands, crescent necklaces,
19 earrings, bracelets, and veils;
20 scarves, ankle bracelets, sashes,
perfumes, and charms;
21 rings, jewels,
22 party clothes, gowns, capes, and purses;
23 mirrors, fine linen garments,
head ornaments, and shawls.

24 Instead of smelling of sweet perfume, she will stink.
She will wear a rope for a sash,
and her elegant hair will fall out.
She will wear rough burlap instead of rich robes.
Shame will replace her beauty.*
25 The men of the city will be killed with the sword,
and her warriors will die in battle.
26 The gates of Zion will weep and mourn.
The city will be like a ravaged woman,
huddled on the ground.

3:16 Or *The women of Zion* (with corresponding changes to plural forms through verse 24); Hebrew reads *The daughters of Zion;* also in 3:17. **3:24** As in Dead Sea Scrolls; Masoretic Text reads *robes / because instead of beauty.*

IS IT OK?

IS IT OK TO WEAR REVEALING CLOTHING?

This is mostly a girls' question, but guys are affected by the answer. Let's get right to the heart of this issue. If girls wear skimpy clothes, *what's their motive?* Are they trying to get noticed? Do they want guys to stare at them? While it's flattering to get attention, the kind of attention they get from wearing revealing clothes isn't good attention; it's degrading attention. Guys who like girls because they wear a low-cut top are liking them for the wrong reason. God wants you to notice a girl's heart, not just her great bod. What's your focus? Are you obsessing about the wrong things, like what someone's wearing? (Check out Isaiah 3:16-17 and 1 Timothy 2:9-10 for God's thoughts on modesty.)

COOL WARDROBE

Victor longed to be more popular at school, but he didn't know how. He noticed that all the really popular guys wore cool jeans and had the "in" haircuts. They looked like people in the movies or on TV shows. Victor thought these students were snobby. They seemed to look down on others. But he was tired of being uncool. Should Victor bug his parents to buy him a cool wardrobe? Read Isaiah 3:16-26 to see what God says about people who think only of themselves and how they look.

CHAPTER 4

In that day so few men will be left that seven
women will fight for each man, saying, "Let us
all marry you! We will provide our own food
and clothing. Only let us take your name so
we won't be mocked as old maids."

A Promise of Restoration

2 But in that day, the branch* of the LORD
will be beautiful and glorious;
the fruit of the land will be the pride and glory
of all who survive in Israel.
3 All who remain in Zion
will be a holy people—
those who survive the destruction of Jerusalem
and are recorded among the living.
4 The Lord will wash the filth from beautiful Zion*
and cleanse Jerusalem of its bloodstains
with the hot breath of fiery judgment.
5 Then the LORD will provide shade for Mount Zion
and all who assemble there.
He will provide a canopy of cloud during the day
and smoke and flaming fire at night,
covering the glorious land.
6 It will be a shelter from daytime heat
and a hiding place from storms and rain.

CHAPTER 5

A Song about the LORD's Vineyard

1 Now I will sing for the one I love
a song about his vineyard:
My beloved had a vineyard
on a rich and fertile hill.
2 He plowed the land, cleared its stones,
and planted it with the best vines.
In the middle he built a watchtower
and carved a winepress in the nearby rocks.
Then he waited for a harvest of sweet grapes,
but the grapes that grew were bitter.
3 Now, you people of Jerusalem and Judah,
you judge between me and my vineyard.
4 What more could I have done for my vineyard
that I have not already done?
When I expected sweet grapes,
why did my vineyard give me bitter grapes?
5 Now let me tell you
what I will do to my vineyard:

4:2 Or *the Branch.* 4:4 Or *from the women of Zion;* Hebrew reads *from the daughters of Zion.*

I will tear down its hedges
and let it be destroyed.
I will break down its walls
and let the animals trample it.
6 I will make it a wild place
where the vines are not pruned and
the ground is not hoed,
a place overgrown with briers and
thorns.
I will command the clouds
to drop no rain on it.
7 The nation of Israel is the vineyard of the
LORD of Heaven's Armies.
The people of Judah are his pleasant
garden.
He expected a crop of justice,
but instead he found oppression.
He expected to find righteousness,
but instead he heard cries of violence.

Judah's Guilt and Judgment

8 What sorrow for you who buy up house
after house and field after field,
until everyone is evicted and you live
alone in the land.
9 But I have heard the LORD of Heaven's
Armies
swear a solemn oath:
"Many houses will stand deserted;
even beautiful mansions will be empty.
10 Ten acres* of vineyard will not produce
even six gallons* of wine.
Ten baskets of seed will yield only one
basket* of grain."
11 What sorrow for those who get up early in
the morning
looking for a drink of alcohol
and spend long evenings drinking wine
to make themselves flaming drunk.
12 They furnish wine and lovely music at
their grand parties—
lyre and harp, tambourine and flute—
but they never think about the LORD
or notice what he is doing.
13 So my people will go into exile far away
because they do not know me.
Those who are great and honored will
starve,
and the common people will die
of thirst.
14 The grave* is licking its lips in
anticipation,
opening its mouth wide.
The great and the lowly
and all the drunken mob will be
swallowed up.
15 Humanity will be destroyed, and people
brought down;
even the arrogant will lower their eyes
in humiliation.
16 But the LORD of Heaven's Armies will be
exalted by his justice.
The holiness of God will be displayed
by his righteousness.
17 In that day lambs will find good pastures,
and fattened sheep and young goats*
will feed among the ruins.
18 What sorrow for those who drag their
sins behind them
with ropes made of lies,
who drag wickedness behind them
like a cart!
19 They even mock God and say,
"Hurry up and do something!
We want to see what you can do.
Let the Holy One of Israel carry out
his plan,
for we want to know what it is."
20 What sorrow for those who say
that evil is good and good is evil,
that dark is light and light is dark,
that bitter is sweet and sweet is bitter.
21 What sorrow for those who are wise in
their own eyes
and think themselves so clever.
22 What sorrow for those who are heroes
at drinking wine
and boast about all the alcohol they
can hold.
23 They take bribes to let the wicked go free,
and they punish the innocent.
24 Therefore, just as fire licks up stubble
and dry grass shrivels in the flame,
so their roots will rot
and their flowers wither.
For they have rejected the law of the LORD
of Heaven's Armies;

5:10a Hebrew *A ten yoke*, that is, the area of land plowed by ten teams of oxen in one day. **5:10b** Hebrew *a bath* [21 liters]. **5:10c** Hebrew *A homer* [5 bushels or 182 liters] *of seed will yield only an ephah* [20 quarts or 22 liters]. **5:14** Hebrew *Sheol*. **5:17** As in Greek version; Hebrew reads *and strangers*.

they have despised the word of the
Holy One of Israel.
25 That is why the LORD's anger burns
against his people,
and why he has raised his fist to crush
them.
The mountains tremble,
and the corpses of his people litter the
streets like garbage.
But even then the LORD's anger is not
satisfied.
His fist is still poised to strike!
26 He will send a signal to distant nations far
away
and whistle to those at the ends
of the earth.
They will come racing toward
Jerusalem.
27 They will not get tired or stumble.
They will not stop for rest or sleep.
Not a belt will be loose,
not a sandal strap broken.

AMAZING FACTS

In Isaiah's heavenly vision, an angel touched his lips with a burning coal to "clean" Isaiah from sin so he could speak God's words. Ouch!

ISAIAH 6:6-7

28 Their arrows will be sharp
and their bows ready for battle.
Sparks will fly from their horses' hooves,
and the wheels of their chariots will
spin like a whirlwind.
29 They will roar like lions,
like the strongest of lions.
Growling, they will pounce on their
victims and carry them off,
and no one will be there to rescue
them.
30 They will roar over their victims on that
day of destruction
like the roaring of the sea.
If someone looks across the land,
only darkness and distress will
be seen;
even the light will be darkened by
clouds.

CHAPTER 6

Isaiah's Cleansing and Call

It was in the year King Uzziah died* that I saw the Lord. He was sitting on a lofty throne, and the train of his robe filled the Temple. 2 Attending him were mighty seraphim, each having six wings. With two wings they covered their faces, with two they covered their feet, and with two they flew. 3 They were calling out to each other,

"Holy, holy, holy is the LORD of Heaven's
Armies!
The whole earth is filled with his
glory!"

4 Their voices shook the Temple to its foundations, and the entire building was filled with smoke.

5 Then I said, "It's all over! I am doomed, for I am a sinful man. I have filthy lips, and I live among a people with filthy lips. Yet I have seen the King, the LORD of Heaven's Armies."

6 Then one of the seraphim flew to me with a burning coal he had taken from the altar with a pair of tongs. 7 He touched my lips with it and said, "See, this coal has touched your lips. Now your guilt is removed, and your sins are forgiven."

8 Then I heard the Lord asking, "Whom should I send as a messenger to this people? Who will go for us?"

I said, "Here I am. Send me."

9 And he said, "Yes, go, and say to this people,

'Listen carefully, but do not understand.
Watch closely, but learn nothing.'
10 Harden the hearts of these people.
Plug their ears and shut their eyes.
That way, they will not see with
their eyes,
nor hear with their ears,

6:1 King Uzziah died in 740 B.C.

nor understand with their hearts
and turn to me for healing."*

11 Then I said, "Lord, how long will this
go on?"
And he replied,

"Until their towns are empty,
their houses are deserted,
and the whole country is a wasteland;
12 until the LORD has sent everyone away,
and the entire land of Israel lies
deserted.
13 If even a tenth—a remnant—survive,
it will be invaded again and burned.
But as a terebinth or oak tree leaves a
stump when it is cut down,
so Israel's stump will be a holy seed."

CHAPTER 7

A Message for Ahaz

When Ahaz, son of Jotham and grandson of Uzziah, was king of Judah, King Rezin of Syria* and Pekah son of Remaliah, the king of Israel, set out to attack Jerusalem. However, they were unable to carry out their plan.

2 The news had come to the royal court of Judah: "Syria is allied with Israel* against us!" So the hearts of the king and his people trembled with fear, like trees shaking in a storm.

3 Then the LORD said to Isaiah, "Take your son Shear-jashub* and go out to meet King Ahaz. You will find him at the end of the aqueduct that feeds water into the upper pool, near the road leading to the field where cloth is washed.* 4 Tell him to stop worrying. Tell him he doesn't need to fear the fierce anger of those two burned-out embers, King Rezin of Syria and Pekah son of Remaliah. 5 Yes, the kings of Syria and Israel are plotting against him, saying, 6 'We will attack Judah and capture it for ourselves. Then we will install the son of Tabeel as Judah's king.' 7 But this is what the Sovereign LORD says:

"This invasion will never happen;
it will never take place;
8 for Syria is no stronger than its capital,
Damascus,
and Damascus is no stronger than its
king, Rezin.
As for Israel, within sixty-five years
it will be crushed and completely
destroyed.
9 Israel is no stronger than its capital,
Samaria,
and Samaria is no stronger than its
king, Pekah son of Remaliah.
Unless your faith is firm,
I cannot make you stand firm."

The Sign of Immanuel

10 Later, the LORD sent this message to King Ahaz: 11 "Ask the LORD your God for a sign of confirmation, Ahaz. Make it as difficult as you want—as high as heaven or as deep as the place of the dead.*"

12 But the king refused. "No," he said, "I will not test the LORD like that."

13 Then Isaiah said, "Listen well, you royal family of David! Isn't it enough to exhaust human patience? Must you exhaust the patience of my God as well? 14 All right then, the Lord himself will give you the sign. Look! The virgin* will conceive a child! She will give birth to a son and will call him Immanuel (which means 'God is with us'). 15 By the time this child is old enough to choose what is right and reject what is wrong, he will be eating yogurt* and honey. 16 For before the child is that old, the lands of the two kings you fear so much will both be deserted.

17 "Then the LORD will bring things on you, your nation, and your family unlike anything since Israel broke away from Judah. He will bring the king of Assyria upon you!"

18 In that day the LORD will whistle for the army of southern Egypt and for the army of Assyria. They will swarm around you like flies and bees. 19 They will come in vast hordes and settle in the fertile areas and also in the desolate valleys, caves, and thorny places. 20 In that day the Lord will hire a "razor" from beyond the Euphrates River*—the king of Assyria—and use it to shave off everything: your land, your crops, and your people.*

21 In that day a farmer will be fortunate to

6:9-10 Greek version reads *And he said, "Go and say to this people, / 'When you hear what I say, you will not understand. / When you see what I do, you will not comprehend.' / For the hearts of these people are hardened, / and their ears cannot hear, and they have closed their eyes— / so their eyes cannot see, / and their ears cannot hear, / and their hearts cannot understand, / and they cannot turn to me and let me heal them."* Compare Matt 13:14-15; Mark 4:12; Luke 8:10; Acts 28:26-27. **7:1** Hebrew *Aram;* also in 7:2, 4, 5, 8. **7:2** Hebrew *Ephraim,* referring to the northern kingdom of Israel; also in 7:5, 8, 9, 17. **7:3a** *Shear-jashub* means "A remnant will return." **7:3b** Or *bleached.* **7:11** Hebrew *as deep as Sheol.* **7:14** Or *young woman.* **7:15** Or *curds;* also in 7:22. **7:20a** Hebrew *the river.* **7:20b** Hebrew *shave off the head, the hair of the legs, and the beard.*

have a cow and two sheep or goats left.
22 Nevertheless, there will be enough milk for
everyone because so few people will be left in
the land. They will eat their fill of yogurt and
honey. 23 In that day the lush vineyards, now
worth 1,000 pieces of silver,* will become
patches of briers and thorns. 24 The entire land
will become a vast expanse of briers and thorns,
a hunting ground overrun by wildlife. 25 No one
will go to the fertile hillsides where the gardens
once grew, for briers and thorns will cover
them. Cattle, sheep, and goats will graze there.

CHAPTER 8

The Coming Assyrian Invasion

Then the LORD said to me, "Make a large sign-
board and clearly write this name on it: Maher-
shalal-hash-baz.*" 2 I asked Uriah the priest
and Zechariah son of Jeberekiah, both known
as honest men, to witness my doing this.
3 Then I slept with my wife, and she became
pregnant and gave birth to a son. And the
LORD said, "Call him Maher-shalal-hash-baz.
4 For before this child is old enough to say
'Papa' or 'Mama,' the king of Assyria will carry
away both the abundance of Damascus and
the riches of Samaria."

AMAZING FACTS

Isaiah named his son Maher-shalal-hash-baz—the longest name in the Bible. Try saying that three times fast!

ISAIAH 8:1-3

5 Then the LORD spoke to me again and
said, 6 "My care for the people of Judah is like
the gently flowing waters of Shiloah, but they
have rejected it. They are rejoicing over what
will happen to* King Rezin and King Pekah.*
7 Therefore, the Lord will overwhelm them
with a mighty flood from the Euphrates
River*—the king of Assyria and all his glory.
This flood will overflow all its channels 8 and
sweep into Judah until it is chin deep. It will
spread its wings, submerging your land from
one end to the other, O Immanuel.

9 "Huddle together, you nations, and be
terrified.
Listen, all you distant lands.
Prepare for battle, but you will be
crushed!
Yes, prepare for battle, but you will be
crushed!
10 Call your councils of war, but they will be
worthless.
Develop your strategies, but they will
not succeed.
For God is with us!*"

A Call to Trust the LORD

11 The LORD has given me a strong warning not
to think like everyone else does. He said,

12 "Don't call everything a conspiracy, like
they do,
and don't live in dread of what
frightens them.
13 Make the LORD of Heaven's Armies holy in
your life.
He is the one you should fear.
He is the one who should make you
tremble.
14 He will keep you safe.
But to Israel and Judah
he will be a stone that makes people
stumble,
a rock that makes them fall.
And for the people of Jerusalem
he will be a trap and a snare.
15 Many will stumble and fall,
never to rise again.
They will be snared and captured."

16 Preserve the teaching of God;
entrust his instructions to those who
follow me.
17 I will wait for the LORD,
who has turned away from the
descendants of Jacob.
I will put my hope in him.

7:23 Hebrew *1,000 shekels of silver*, about 25 pounds or 11.4 kilograms in weight. **8:1** *Maher-shalal-hash-baz* means "Swift to plunder and quick to carry away." **8:6a** Or *They are rejoicing because of*. **8:6b** Hebrew *and the son of Remaliah*. **8:7** Hebrew *the river*. **8:10** Hebrew *Immanuel!*

[18]I and the children the LORD has given me
serve as signs and warnings to Israel from the
LORD of Heaven's Armies who dwells in his
Temple on Mount Zion.
[19]Someone may say to you, "Let's ask the
mediums and those who consult the spirits of
the dead. With their whisperings and mutter-
ings, they will tell us what to do." But shouldn't
people ask God for guidance? Should the liv-
ing seek guidance from the dead?
[20]Look to God's instructions and teachings!
People who contradict his word are com-
pletely in the dark. [21]They will go from one
place to another, weary and hungry. And be-
cause they are hungry, they will rage and curse
their king and their God. They will look up to
heaven [22]and down at the earth, but wherever
they look, there will be trouble and anguish
and dark despair. They will be thrown out into
the darkness.

CHAPTER 9

Hope in the Messiah

[1]*Nevertheless, that time of darkness and de-
spair will not go on forever. The land of Zebu-
lun and Naphtali will be humbled, but there
will be a time in the future when Galilee of the
Gentiles, which lies along the road that runs
between the Jordan and the sea, will be filled
with glory.

[2]*The people who walk in darkness
will see a great light.
For those who live in a land of deep
darkness,*
a light will shine.
[3] You will enlarge the nation of Israel,
and its people will rejoice.
They will rejoice before you
as people rejoice at the harvest
and like warriors dividing the plunder.
[4] For you will break the yoke of their
slavery
and lift the heavy burden from their
shoulders.
You will break the oppressor's rod,
just as you did when you destroyed the
army of Midian.
[5] The boots of the warrior
and the uniforms bloodstained by war
will all be burned.
They will be fuel for the fire.

9:1 Verse 9:1 is numbered 8:23 in Hebrew text. **9:2a** Verses 9:2-21 are numbered 9:1-20 in Hebrew text. **9:2b** Greek version reads *a land where death casts its shadow*. Compare Matt 4:16.

IS IT OK?

IS IT OK TO PLAY WITH HOROSCOPES AND OUIJA BOARDS?

There's a simple answer to this one: *No!* And no exceptions, loopholes, get-out-of-jail-free cards, or "but if" clauses. Isaiah 8:19 says that God forbids us to experiment with the supernatural—no mediums, psychics, Ouija boards, horoscopes, and the like. Some people say it's just for fun, but dabbling in the supernatural always has a dangerous side to it—evil is real, and evil is more powerful than you. If you want to know the future, guess who you should ask instead? (Hint: He's a three-in-one deity who knows everything past, present, and future, and he wrote the book you're reading. From the beginning of time, he knew exactly when you would read this passage . . . cool, huh?)

6 For a child is born to us,
a son is given to us.
The government will rest on his shoulders.
And he will be called:
Wonderful Counselor,* Mighty God,
Everlasting Father, Prince of Peace.
7 His government and its peace will never end.
He will rule with fairness and justice from the throne of his ancestor David
for all eternity.
The passionate commitment of the LORD of Heaven's Armies
will make this happen!

The LORD's Anger against Israel

8 The Lord has spoken out against Jacob;
his judgment has fallen upon Israel.
9 And the people of Israel* and Samaria,
who spoke with such pride and arrogance,
will soon know it.
10 They said, "We will replace the broken bricks of our ruins with finished stone,
and replant the felled sycamore-fig trees with cedars."
11 But the LORD will bring Rezin's enemies against Israel
and stir up all their foes.
12 The Syrians* from the east and the Philistines from the west
will bare their fangs and devour Israel.
But even then the LORD's anger will not be satisfied.
His fist is still poised to strike.
13 For after all this punishment, the people will still not repent.
They will not seek the LORD of Heaven's Armies.
14 Therefore, in a single day the LORD will destroy both the head and the tail,
the noble palm branch and the lowly reed.
15 The leaders of Israel are the head,
and the lying prophets are the tail.
16 For the leaders of the people have misled them.
They have led them down the path of destruction.
17 That is why the Lord takes no pleasure in the young men
and shows no mercy even to the widows and orphans.
For they are all wicked hypocrites,
and they all speak foolishness.
But even then the LORD's anger will not be satisfied.
His fist is still poised to strike.
18 This wickedness is like a brushfire.
It burns not only briers and thorns
but also sets the forests ablaze.
Its burning sends up clouds of smoke.
19 The land will be blackened
by the fury of the LORD of Heaven's Armies.
The people will be fuel for the fire,
and no one will spare even his own brother.
20 They will attack their neighbor on the right
but will still be hungry.
They will devour their neighbor on the left
but will not be satisfied.
In the end they will even eat their own children.*
21 Manasseh will feed on Ephraim,
Ephraim will feed on Manasseh,
and both will devour Judah.
But even then the LORD's anger will not be satisfied.
His fist is still poised to strike.

CHAPTER 10

1 What sorrow awaits the unjust judges
and those who issue unfair laws.
2 They deprive the poor of justice
and deny the rights of the needy among my people.
They prey on widows
and take advantage of orphans.
3 What will you do when I punish you,
when I send disaster upon you from a distant land?
To whom will you turn for help?
Where will your treasures be safe?

9:6 Or *Wonderful, Counselor.* **9:9** Hebrew *of Ephraim,* referring to the northern kingdom of Israel. **9:12** Hebrew *Arameans.* **9:20** Or *eat their own arms.*

4 You will stumble along as prisoners
or lie among the dead.
But even then the LORD's anger will not be
satisfied.
His fist is still poised to strike.

Judgment against Assyria

5 "What sorrow awaits Assyria, the rod of
my anger.
I use it as a club to express my anger.
6 I am sending Assyria against a godless
nation,
against a people with whom I am angry.
Assyria will plunder them,
trampling them like dirt beneath its
feet.
7 But the king of Assyria will not
understand that he is my tool;
his mind does not work that way.
His plan is simply to destroy,
to cut down nation after nation.
8 He will say,
'Each of my princes will soon be a king.
9 We destroyed Calno just as we did
Carchemish.
Hamath fell before us as Arpad did.
And we destroyed Samaria just as we
did Damascus.
10 Yes, we have finished off many a kingdom
whose gods were greater than those in
Jerusalem and Samaria.
11 So we will defeat Jerusalem and her gods,
just as we destroyed Samaria with hers.'"

12 After the Lord has used the king of Assyria to accomplish his purposes on Mount Zion and in Jerusalem, he will turn against the king of Assyria and punish him—for he is proud and arrogant. 13 He boasts,

"By my own powerful arm I have done
this.
With my own shrewd wisdom I
planned it.
I have broken down the defenses of nations
and carried off their treasures.
I have knocked down their kings like a
bull.
14 I have robbed their nests of riches
and gathered up kingdoms as a farmer
gathers eggs.
No one can even flap a wing against me
or utter a peep of protest."
15 But can the ax boast greater power than
the person who uses it?
Is the saw greater than the person who
saws?
Can a rod strike unless a hand moves it?
Can a wooden cane walk by itself?
16 Therefore, the Lord, the LORD of Heaven's
Armies,
will send a plague among Assyria's
proud troops,
and a flaming fire will consume its glory.
17 The LORD, the Light of Israel, will be a fire;
the Holy One will be a flame.
He will devour the thorns and briers
with fire,
burning up the enemy in a single night.
18 The LORD will consume Assyria's glory
like a fire consumes a forest in a
fruitful land;
it will waste away like sick people in a
plague.
19 Of all that glorious forest, only a few trees
will survive—
so few that a child could count them!

Hope for the LORD's People

20 In that day the remnant left in Israel,
the survivors in the house of Jacob,
will no longer depend on allies
who seek to destroy them.
But they will faithfully trust the LORD,
the Holy One of Israel.
21 A remnant will return;*
yes, the remnant of Jacob will return to
the Mighty God.
22 But though the people of Israel are as
numerous
as the sand of the seashore,
only a remnant of them will return.
The LORD has rightly decided to destroy
his people.
23 Yes, the Lord, the LORD of Heaven's
Armies,
has already decided to destroy the
entire land.*

24 So this is what the Lord, the LORD of Heaven's Armies, says: "O my people in Zion,

10:21 Hebrew *Shear-jashub;* see 7:3; 8:18. **10:22-23** Greek version reads *only a remnant of them will be saved. / For he will carry out his sentence quickly and with finality and righteousness; / for God will carry out his sentence upon all the world with finality.* Compare Rom 9:27-28.

do not be afraid of the Assyrians when they oppress you with rod and club as the Egyptians did long ago. [25] In a little while my anger against you will end, and then my anger will rise up to destroy them." [26] The LORD of Heaven's Armies will lash them with his whip, as he did when Gideon triumphed over the Midianites at the rock of Oreb, or when the LORD's staff was raised to drown the Egyptian army in the sea.

[27] In that day the LORD will end the bondage
of his people.
He will break the yoke of slavery
and lift it from their shoulders.*

[28] Look, the Assyrians are now at Aiath.
They are passing through Migron
and are storing their equipment at
Micmash.

[29] They are crossing the pass
and are camping at Geba.
Fear strikes the town of Ramah.
All the people of Gibeah, the
hometown of Saul,
are running for their lives.

AMAZING FACTS

Imagine. One day the world will be so peaceful that babies will play around poisonous snakes and not get hurt.

ISAIAH 11:6-9

[30] Scream in terror,
you people of Gallim!
Shout out a warning to Laishah.
Oh, poor Anathoth!

[31] There go the people of Madmenah,
all fleeing.
The citizens of Gebim are trying
to hide.

[32] The enemy stops at Nob for the rest
of that day.
He shakes his fist at beautiful
Mount Zion, the mountain of
Jerusalem.

[33] But look! The Lord, the LORD of Heaven's
Armies,
will chop down the mighty tree of
Assyria with great power!
He will cut down the proud.
That lofty tree will be brought
down.

[34] He will cut down the forest trees
with an ax.
Lebanon will fall to the Mighty One.*

CHAPTER 11

A Branch from David's Line

[1] Out of the stump of David's family* will
grow a shoot—
yes, a new Branch bearing fruit from
the old root.

[2] And the Spirit of the LORD will rest on
him—
the Spirit of wisdom and
understanding,
the Spirit of counsel and might,
the Spirit of knowledge and the fear
of the LORD.

[3] He will delight in obeying the LORD.
He will not judge by appearance
nor make a decision based
on hearsay.

[4] He will give justice to the poor
and make fair decisions for the
exploited.
The earth will shake at the force of his
word,
and one breath from his mouth will
destroy the wicked.

[5] He will wear righteousness like a belt
and truth like an undergarment.

[6] In that day the wolf and the lamb will live
together;
the leopard will lie down with the baby
goat.
The calf and the yearling will be safe with
the lion,
and a little child will lead them all.

[7] The cow will graze near the bear.

10:27 As in Greek version; Hebrew reads *The yoke will be broken, / for you have grown so fat.* **10:34** Or *with an ax / as even the mighty trees of Lebanon fall.* **11:1** Hebrew *the stump of the line of Jesse.* Jesse was King David's father.

The cub and the calf will lie down
together.
The lion will eat hay like a cow.
8 The baby will play safely near the hole of
a cobra.
Yes, a little child will put its hand in a
nest of deadly snakes without harm.
9 Nothing will hurt or destroy in all my holy
mountain,
for as the waters fill the sea,
so the earth will be filled with people
who know the LORD.

10 In that day the heir to David's throne*
will be a banner of salvation to all the
world.
The nations will rally to him,
and the land where he lives will be a
glorious place.*
11 In that day the Lord will reach out his
hand a second time
to bring back the remnant of his
people—
those who remain in Assyria and northern
Egypt;
in southern Egypt, Ethiopia,* and Elam;
in Babylonia,* Hamath, and all the
distant coastlands.
12 He will raise a flag among the nations
and assemble the exiles of Israel.
He will gather the scattered people of
Judah
from the ends of the earth.

13 Then at last the jealousy between Israel*
and Judah will end.
They will not be rivals anymore.
14 They will join forces to swoop down on
Philistia to the west.
Together they will attack and plunder
the nations to the east.
They will occupy the lands of Edom and
Moab,
and Ammon will obey them.
15 The LORD will make a dry path through
the gulf of the Red Sea.*
He will wave his hand over the
Euphrates River,*
sending a mighty wind to divide it into
seven streams
so it can easily be crossed on foot.
16 He will make a highway for the remnant
of his people,
the remnant coming from Assyria,
just as he did for Israel long ago
when they returned from Egypt.

CHAPTER 12

Songs of Praise for Salvation

1 In that day you will sing:
"I will praise you, O LORD!
You were angry with me, but not
any more.
Now you comfort me.
2 See, God has come to save me.
I will trust in him and not be afraid.
The LORD GOD is my strength and my
song;
he has given me victory."

3 With joy you will drink deeply
from the fountain of salvation!
4 In that wonderful day you will sing:
"Thank the LORD! Praise his name!
Tell the nations what he has done.
Let them know how mighty he is!
5 Sing to the LORD, for he has done
wonderful things.
Make known his praise around the
world.
6 Let all the people of Jerusalem* shout his
praise with joy!
For great is the Holy One of Israel who
lives among you."

CHAPTER 13

A Message about Babylon

Isaiah son of Amoz received this message concerning the destruction of Babylon:

2 "Raise a signal flag on a bare hilltop.
Call up an army against Babylon.
Wave your hand to encourage them
as they march into the palaces of the
high and mighty.
3 I, the LORD, have dedicated these soldiers
for this task.
Yes, I have called mighty warriors to
express my anger,
and they will rejoice when I am
exalted."

11:10a Hebrew *the root of Jesse.* **11:10b** Greek version reads *In that day the heir to David's throne* [literally *the root of Jesse*] *will come, / and he will rule over the Gentiles. / They will place their hopes on him.* Compare Rom 15:12. **11:11a** Hebrew *in Pathros, Cush.* **11:11b** Hebrew *in Shinar.* **11:13** Hebrew *Ephraim,* referring to the northern kingdom of Israel. **11:15a** Hebrew *will destroy the tongue of the sea of Egypt.* **11:15b** Hebrew *the river.* **12:6** Hebrew *Zion.*

4 Hear the noise on the mountains!
Listen, as the vast armies march!
It is the noise and shouting of many nations.
The LORD of Heaven's Armies has called this army together.
5 They come from distant countries,
from beyond the farthest horizons.
They are the LORD's weapons to carry out his anger.
With them he will destroy the whole land.

6 Scream in terror, for the day of the LORD has arrived—
the time for the Almighty to destroy.
7 Every arm is paralyzed with fear.
Every heart melts,
8 and people are terrified.
Pangs of anguish grip them,
like those of a woman in labor.
They look helplessly at one another,
their faces aflame with fear.

9 For see, the day of the LORD is coming—
the terrible day of his fury and fierce anger.
The land will be made desolate,
and all the sinners destroyed with it.
10 The heavens will be black above them;
the stars will give no light.
The sun will be dark when it rises,
and the moon will provide no light.

11 "I, the LORD, will punish the world for its evil
and the wicked for their sin.
I will crush the arrogance of the proud
and humble the pride of the mighty.
12 I will make people scarcer than gold—
more rare than the fine gold of Ophir.
13 For I will shake the heavens.
The earth will move from its place
when the LORD of Heaven's Armies displays his wrath
in the day of his fierce anger."

14 Everyone in Babylon will run about like a hunted gazelle,
like sheep without a shepherd.
They will try to find their own people
and flee to their own land.
15 Anyone who is captured will be cut down—
run through with a sword.
16 Their little children will be dashed to death before their eyes.
Their homes will be sacked, and their wives will be raped.

17 "Look, I will stir up the Medes against Babylon.
They cannot be tempted by silver
or bribed with gold.
18 The attacking armies will shoot down the young men with arrows.
They will have no mercy on helpless babies
and will show no compassion for children."

19 Babylon, the most glorious of kingdoms,
the flower of Chaldean pride,
will be devastated like Sodom and Gomorrah
when God destroyed them.
20 Babylon will never be inhabited again.
It will remain empty for generation after generation.
Nomads will refuse to camp there,
and shepherds will not bed down their sheep.
21 Desert animals will move into the ruined city,
and the houses will be haunted by howling creatures.
Owls will live among the ruins,
and wild goats will go there to dance.
22 Hyenas will howl in its fortresses,
and jackals will make dens in its luxurious palaces.
Babylon's days are numbered;
its time of destruction will soon arrive.

CHAPTER 14

A Taunt for Babylon's King

But the LORD will have mercy on the descendants of Jacob. He will choose Israel as his special people once again. He will bring them back to settle once again in their own land. And people from many different nations will come and join them there and unite with the people of Israel.* 2 The nations of the world will help the LORD's people to return, and those who come to live in their land will serve

14:1 Hebrew *the house of Jacob*. The names "Jacob" and "Israel" are often interchanged throughout the Old Testament, referring sometimes to the individual patriarch and sometimes to the nation.

them. Those who captured Israel will themselves be captured, and Israel will rule over its enemies.

3 In that wonderful day when the LORD gives his people rest from sorrow and fear, from slavery and chains, 4 you will taunt the king of Babylon. You will say,

"The mighty man has been destroyed.
Yes, your insolence* is ended.
5 For the LORD has crushed your wicked power
and broken your evil rule.
6 You struck the people with endless blows of rage
and held the nations in your angry grip with unrelenting tyranny.
7 But finally the earth is at rest and quiet.
Now it can sing again!
8 Even the trees of the forest—
the cypress trees and the cedars of Lebanon—
sing out this joyous song:
'Since you have been cut down,
no one will come now to cut us down!'

9 "In the place of the dead* there is excitement
over your arrival.
The spirits of world leaders and mighty kings long dead
stand up to see you.
10 With one voice they all cry out,
'Now you are as weak as we are!
11 Your might and power were buried with you.*
The sound of the harp in your palace has ceased.
Now maggots are your sheet,
and worms your blanket.'

12 "How you are fallen from heaven,
O shining star, son of the morning!
You have been thrown down to the earth,
you who destroyed the nations of the world.
13 For you said to yourself,
'I will ascend to heaven and set my throne above God's stars.
I will preside on the mountain of the gods
far away in the north.*
14 I will climb to the highest heavens
and be like the Most High.'
15 Instead, you will be brought down to the place of the dead,
down to its lowest depths.
16 Everyone there will stare at you and ask,
'Can this be the one who shook the earth
and made the kingdoms of the world tremble?
17 Is this the one who destroyed the world
and made it into a wasteland?
Is this the king who demolished the world's greatest cities
and had no mercy on his prisoners?'

18 "The kings of the nations lie in stately glory,
each in his own tomb,
19 but you will be thrown out of your grave
like a worthless branch.
Like a corpse trampled underfoot,
you will be dumped into a mass grave
with those killed in battle.
You will descend to the pit.
20 You will not be given a proper burial,
for you have destroyed your nation
and slaughtered your people.
The descendants of such an evil person
will never again receive honor.
21 Kill this man's children!
Let them die because of their father's sins!
They must not rise and conquer the earth,
filling the world with their cities."

22 This is what the LORD of Heaven's Armies says:
"I, myself, have risen against Babylon!
I will destroy its children and its children's children,"
says the LORD.
23 "I will make Babylon a desolate place of owls,
filled with swamps and marshes.
I will sweep the land with the broom of destruction.
I, the LORD of Heaven's Armies, have spoken!"

A Message about Assyria

24 The LORD of Heaven's Armies has sworn this oath:

14:4 As in Dead Sea Scrolls; the meaning of the Masoretic Text is uncertain. **14:9** Hebrew *Sheol;* also in 14:15. **14:11** Hebrew *were brought down to Sheol.* **14:13** Or *on the heights of Zaphon.*

A FEW DAYS before my eighth-grade graduation, I was riding my bike along the sidewalk. Some girls were walking toward me and refused to move, so I swerved to avoid them. My front bicycle tire jammed between the concrete and the dirt, sending me flying across the sidewalk. At my graduation, I was covered with bruises and bandages from head to toe!

Lighten Up!

"It will all happen as I have planned.
It will be as I have decided.
25 I will break the Assyrians when they are in Israel;
I will trample them on my mountains.
My people will no longer be their slaves
nor bow down under their heavy loads.
26 I have a plan for the whole earth,
a hand of judgment upon all the nations.
27 The LORD of Heaven's Armies has spoken—
who can change his plans?
When his hand is raised,
who can stop him?"

A Message about Philistia

28 This message came to me the year King Ahaz died:*
29 Do not rejoice, you Philistines,
that the rod that struck you is broken—
that the king who attacked you is dead.
For from that snake a more poisonous snake will be born,
a fiery serpent to destroy you!
30 I will feed the poor in my pasture;
the needy will lie down in peace.
But as for you, I will wipe you out with famine
and destroy the few who remain.
31 Wail at the gates! Weep in the cities!
Melt with fear, you Philistines!
A powerful army comes like smoke from the north.
Each soldier rushes forward eager to fight.
32 What should we tell the Philistine messengers? Tell them,

"The LORD has built Jerusalem*;
its walls will give refuge to his oppressed people."

CHAPTER 15

A Message about Moab

This message came to me concerning Moab:

In one night the town of Ar will be leveled,
and the city of Kir will be destroyed.
2 Your people will go to their temple in Dibon to mourn.
They will go to their sacred shrines to weep.
They will wail for the fate of Nebo and Medeba,
shaving their heads in sorrow and cutting off their beards.
3 They will wear burlap as they wander the streets.
From every home and public square will come the sound of wailing.
4 The people of Heshbon and Elealeh will cry out;
their voices will be heard as far away as Jahaz!
The bravest warriors of Moab will cry out in utter terror.
They will be helpless with fear.

14:28 King Ahaz died in 715 B.C. **14:32** Hebrew *Zion*.

5 My heart weeps for Moab.
Its people flee to Zoar and Eglath-shelishiyah.
Weeping, they climb the road to Luhith.
Their cries of distress can be heard all along the road to Horonaim.
6 Even the waters of Nimrim are dried up!
The grassy banks are scorched.
The tender plants are gone;
nothing green remains.
7 The people grab their possessions
and carry them across the Ravine of Willows.
8 A cry of distress echoes through the land of Moab
from one end to the other—
from Eglaim to Beer-elim.
9 The stream near Dibon* runs red with blood,
but I am still not finished with Dibon!
Lions will hunt down the survivors—
both those who try to escape
and those who remain behind.

CHAPTER 16

1 Send lambs from Sela as tribute
to the ruler of the land.
Send them through the desert
to the mountain of beautiful Zion.
2 The women of Moab are left like homeless birds
at the shallow crossings of the Arnon River.
3 "Help us," they cry.
"Defend us against our enemies.
Protect us from their relentless attack.
Do not betray us now that we have escaped.
4 Let our refugees stay among you.
Hide them from our enemies until the terror is past."

When oppression and destruction have ended
and enemy raiders have disappeared,
5 then God will establish one of David's descendants as king.
He will rule with mercy and truth.
He will always do what is just
and be eager to do what is right.
6 We have heard about proud Moab—
about its pride and arrogance and rage.
But all that boasting has disappeared.
7 The entire land of Moab weeps.
Yes, everyone in Moab mourns
for the cakes of raisins from Kir-hareseth.
They are all gone now.
8 The farms of Heshbon are abandoned;
the vineyards at Sibmah are deserted.
The rulers of the nations have broken down Moab—
that beautiful grapevine.
Its tendrils spread north as far as the town of Jazer
and trailed eastward into the wilderness.
Its shoots reached so far west
that they crossed over the Dead Sea.*

9 So now I weep for Jazer and the vineyards of Sibmah;
my tears will flow for Heshbon and Elealeh.
There are no more shouts of joy
over your summer fruits and harvest.
10 Gone now is the gladness,
gone the joy of harvest.
There will be no singing in the vineyards,
no more happy shouts,
no treading of grapes in the winepresses.
I have ended all their harvest joys.
11 My heart's cry for Moab is like a lament on a harp.
I am filled with anguish for Kir-hareseth.*
12 The people of Moab will worship at their pagan shrines,
but it will do them no good.
They will cry to the gods in their temples,
but no one will be able to save them.

13 The LORD has already said these things about Moab in the past. 14 But now the LORD says, "Within three years, counting each day,* the glory of Moab will be ended. From its great population, only a few of its people will be left alive."

15:9 As in Dead Sea Scrolls, some Greek manuscripts, and Latin Vulgate; Masoretic Text reads *Dimon;* also in 15:9b. **16:8** Hebrew *the sea.* **16:11** Hebrew *Kir-heres,* a variant spelling of Kir-hareseth. **16:14** Hebrew *Within three years, as a servant bound by contract would count them.*

CHAPTER 17

A Message about Damascus and Israel

This message came to me concerning Damascus:

"Look, the city of Damascus will disappear!
It will become a heap of ruins.
2 The towns of Aroer will be deserted.
Flocks will graze in the streets and lie down undisturbed,
with no one to chase them away.
3 The fortified towns of Israel* will also be destroyed,
and the royal power of Damascus will end.
All that remains of Syria*
will share the fate of Israel's departed glory,"
declares the LORD of Heaven's Armies.
4 "In that day Israel's* glory will grow dim;
its robust body will waste away.
5 The whole land will look like a grainfield
after the harvesters have gathered the grain.
It will be desolate,
like the fields in the valley of Rephaim after the harvest.
6 Only a few of its people will be left,
like stray olives left on a tree after the harvest.
Only two or three remain in the highest branches,
four or five scattered here and there on the limbs,"
declares the LORD, the God of Israel.
7 Then at last the people will look to their Creator
and turn their eyes to the Holy One of Israel.
8 They will no longer look to their idols for help
or worship what their own hands have made.
They will never again bow down to their Asherah poles
or worship at the pagan shrines they have built.
9 Their largest cities will be like a deserted forest,
like the land the Hivites and Amorites abandoned*
when the Israelites came here so long ago.
It will be utterly desolate.
10 Why? Because you have turned from the God who can save you.
You have forgotten the Rock who can hide you.
So you may plant the finest grapevines
and import the most expensive seedlings.
11 They may sprout on the day you set them out;
yes, they may blossom on the very morning you plant them,
but you will never pick any grapes from them.
Your only harvest will be a load of grief and unrelieved pain.
12 Listen! The armies of many nations
roar like the roaring of the sea.
Hear the thunder of the mighty forces
as they rush forward like thundering waves.
13 But though they thunder like breakers on a beach,
God will silence them, and they will run away.
They will flee like chaff scattered by the wind,
like a tumbleweed whirling before a storm.

What happens if I have given all my attention to the other stuff in my life?

You have turned from the God who can save you. You have forgotten the Rock who can hide you.
ISAIAH 17:10

17:3a Hebrew *of Ephraim*, referring to the northern kingdom of Israel. **17:3b** Hebrew *Aram*. **17:4** Hebrew *Jacob's*. See note on 14:1.
17:9 As in Greek version; Hebrew reads *like places of the wood and the highest bough*.

14 In the evening Israel waits in terror,
but by dawn its enemies are dead.
This is the just reward of those who plunder us,
a fitting end for those who destroy us.

CHAPTER 18

A Message about Ethiopia

1 Listen, Ethiopia*—land of fluttering sails*
that lies at the headwaters of the Nile,
2 that sends ambassadors
in swift boats down the river.
Go, swift messengers!
Take a message to a tall, smooth-skinned people,
who are feared far and wide
for their conquests and destruction,
and whose land is divided by rivers.

3 All you people of the world,
everyone who lives on the earth—
when I raise my battle flag on the mountain, look!
When I blow the ram's horn, listen!
4 For the LORD has told me this:
"I will watch quietly from my dwelling place—
as quietly as the heat rises on a summer day,
or as the morning dew forms during the harvest."
5 Even before you begin your attack,
while your plans are ripening like grapes,
the LORD will cut off your new growth with pruning shears.
He will snip off and discard your spreading branches.
6 Your mighty army will be left dead in the fields
for the mountain vultures and wild animals.
The vultures will tear at the corpses all summer.
The wild animals will gnaw at the bones all winter.

7 At that time the LORD of Heaven's Armies will receive gifts
from this land divided by rivers,
from this tall, smooth-skinned people,
who are feared far and wide for their conquests and destruction.
They will bring the gifts to Jerusalem,*
where the LORD of Heaven's Armies dwells.

CHAPTER 19

A Message about Egypt

This message came to me concerning Egypt:

Look! The LORD is advancing against Egypt,
riding on a swift cloud.
The idols of Egypt tremble.
The hearts of the Egyptians melt with fear.

2 "I will make Egyptian fight against Egyptian—
brother against brother,
neighbor against neighbor,
city against city,
province against province.
3 The Egyptians will lose heart,
and I will confuse their plans.
They will plead with their idols for wisdom
and call on spirits, mediums, and those who consult the spirits of the dead.
4 I will hand Egypt over
to a hard, cruel master.
A fierce king will rule them,"
says the Lord, the LORD of Heaven's Armies.

5 The waters of the Nile will fail to rise and flood the fields.
The riverbed will be parched and dry.
6 The canals of the Nile will dry up,
and the streams of Egypt will stink with rotting reeds and rushes.
7 All the greenery along the riverbank
and all the crops along the river
will dry up and blow away.
8 The fishermen will lament for lack of work.
Those who cast hooks into the Nile will groan,
and those who use nets will lose heart.
9 There will be no flax for the harvesters,
no thread for the weavers.
10 They will be in despair,
and all the workers will be sick at heart.

18:1a Hebrew *Cush*. **18:1b** Or *land of many locusts;* Hebrew reads *land of whirring wings*. **18:7** Hebrew *to Mount Zion*.

11 What fools are the officials of Zoan!
Their best counsel to the king of Egypt
is stupid and wrong.
Will they still boast to Pharaoh of their
wisdom?
Will they dare brag about all their wise
ancestors?
12 Where are your wise counselors,
Pharaoh?
Let them tell you what God plans,
what the LORD of Heaven's Armies is
going to do to Egypt.
13 The officials of Zoan are fools,
and the officials of Memphis* are
deluded.
The leaders of the people
have led Egypt astray.
14 The LORD has sent a spirit of foolishness
on them,
so all their suggestions are wrong.
They cause Egypt to stagger
like a drunk in his vomit.
15 There is nothing Egypt can do.
All are helpless—
the head and the tail,
the noble palm branch and the lowly
reed.

AMAZING FACTS

Isaiah walked around completely naked for three years because God told him to do it. Now *that's* obedience!

ISAIAH 20:1-3

16 In that day the Egyptians will be as weak as women. They will cower in fear beneath the upraised fist of the LORD of Heaven's Armies. 17 Just to speak the name of Israel will terrorize them, for the LORD of Heaven's Armies has laid out his plans against them.

18 In that day five of Egypt's cities will follow the LORD of Heaven's Armies. They will even begin to speak Hebrew, the language of Canaan. One of these cities will be Heliopolis, the City of the Sun.*

19 In that day there will be an altar to the LORD in the heart of Egypt, and there will be a monument to the LORD at its border. 20 It will be a sign and a witness that the LORD of Heaven's Armies is worshiped in the land of Egypt. When the people cry to the LORD for help against those who oppress them, he will send them a savior who will rescue them. 21 The LORD will make himself known to the Egyptians. Yes, they will know the LORD and will give their sacrifices and offerings to him. They will make a vow to the LORD and will keep it. 22 The LORD will strike Egypt, and then he will bring healing. For the Egyptians will turn to the LORD, and he will listen to their pleas and heal them.

23 In that day Egypt and Assyria will be connected by a highway. The Egyptians and Assyrians will move freely between their lands, and they will both worship God. 24 And Israel will be their ally. The three will be together, and Israel will be a blessing to them. 25 For the LORD of Heaven's Armies will say, "Blessed be Egypt, my people. Blessed be Assyria, the land I have made. Blessed be Israel, my special possession!"

CHAPTER 20

A Message about Egypt and Ethiopia

In the year when King Sargon of Assyria sent his commander in chief to capture the Philistine city of Ashdod,* 2 the LORD told Isaiah son of Amoz, "Take off the burlap you have been wearing, and remove your sandals." Isaiah did as he was told and walked around naked and barefoot.

3 Then the LORD said, "My servant Isaiah has been walking around naked and barefoot for the last three years. This is a sign—a symbol of the terrible troubles I will bring upon Egypt and Ethiopia.* 4 For the king of Assyria will take away the Egyptians and Ethiopians* as prisoners. He will make them walk naked and barefoot, both young and old, their buttocks bared, to the shame of Egypt. 5 Then the Philistines will be thrown into panic, for they

19:13 Hebrew *Noph*. **19:18** Or *will be the City of Destruction*. **20:1** Ashdod was captured by Assyria in 711 B.C. **20:3** Hebrew *Cush*; also in 20:5. **20:4** Hebrew *Cushites*.

counted on the power of Ethiopia and boasted of their allies in Egypt! 6 They will say, 'If this can happen to Egypt, what chance do we have? We were counting on Egypt to protect us from the king of Assyria.'"

CHAPTER 21

A Message about Babylon

This message came to me concerning Babylon—the desert by the sea*:

Disaster is roaring down on you from
the desert,
like a whirlwind sweeping in from
the Negev.
2 I see a terrifying vision:
I see the betrayer betraying,
the destroyer destroying.
Go ahead, you Elamites and Medes,
attack and lay siege.
I will make an end
to all the groaning Babylon caused.
3 My stomach aches and burns with
pain.
Sharp pangs of anguish are
upon me,
like those of a woman in labor.
I grow faint when I hear what God is
planning;
I am too afraid to look.
4 My mind reels and my heart races.
I longed for evening to come,
but now I am terrified of the dark.

5 Look! They are preparing a great
feast.
They are spreading rugs for people
to sit on.
Everyone is eating and drinking.
But quick! Grab your shields and prepare
for battle.
You are being attacked!

6 Meanwhile, the Lord said to me,
"Put a watchman on the city wall.
Let him shout out what he sees.
7 He should look for chariots
drawn by pairs of horses,
and for riders on donkeys and
camels.
Let the watchman be fully alert."

8 Then the watchman* called out,
"Day after day I have stood on the
watchtower, my lord.
Night after night I have remained
at my post.
9 Now at last—look!
Here comes a man in a chariot
with a pair of horses!"
Then the watchman said,
"Babylon is fallen, fallen!
All the idols of Babylon
lie broken on the ground!"
10 O my people, threshed and winnowed,
I have told you everything the LORD
of Heaven's Armies has said,
everything the God of Israel has
told me.

A Message about Edom

11 This message came to me concerning Edom*:

Someone from Edom* keeps calling
to me,
"Watchman, how much longer until
morning?
When will the night be over?"
12 The watchman replies,
"Morning is coming, but night will soon
return.
If you wish to ask again, then come
back and ask."

A Message about Arabia

13 This message came to me concerning Arabia:

O caravans from Dedan,
hide in the deserts of Arabia.
14 O people of Tema,
bring water to these thirsty people,
food to these weary refugees.
15 They have fled from the sword,
from the drawn sword,
from the bent bow
and the terrors of battle.

16 The Lord said to me, "Within a year, counting each day,* all the glory of Kedar will come to an end. 17 Only a few of its courageous

21:1 Hebrew *concerning the desert by the sea.* **21:8** As in Dead Sea Scrolls and Syriac version; Masoretic Text reads *a lion.* **21:11a** Hebrew *Dumah,* which means "silence" or "stillness." It is a wordplay on the word *Edom.* **21:11b** Hebrew *Seir,* another name for Edom. **21:16** Hebrew *Within a year, as a servant bound by contract would count it.* Some ancient manuscripts read *Within three years,* as in 16:14.

archers will survive. I, the LORD, the God of Israel, have spoken!"

CHAPTER 22

A Message about Jerusalem

This message came to me concerning Jerusalem—the Valley of Vision*:

What is happening?
Why is everyone running to the rooftops?
2 The whole city is in a terrible uproar.
What do I see in this reveling city?
Bodies are lying everywhere,
killed not in battle but by famine and disease.
3 All your leaders have fled.
They surrendered without resistance.
The people tried to slip away,
but they were captured, too.
4 That's why I said, "Leave me alone to weep;
do not try to comfort me.
Let me cry for my people
as I watch them being destroyed."

5 Oh, what a day of crushing defeat!
What a day of confusion and terror
brought by the Lord, the LORD of Heaven's Armies,
upon the Valley of Vision!
The walls of Jerusalem have been broken,
and cries of death echo from the mountainsides.
6 Elamites are the archers,
with their chariots and charioteers.
The men of Kir hold up the shields.
7 Chariots fill your beautiful valleys,
and charioteers storm your gates.
8 Judah's defenses have been stripped away.
You run to the armory* for your weapons.
9 You inspect the breaks in the walls of Jerusalem.*
You store up water in the lower pool.
10 You survey the houses and tear some down
for stone to strengthen the walls.
11 Between the city walls, you build a reservoir
for water from the old pool.
But you never ask for help from the One who did all this.
You never considered the One who planned this long ago.

12 At that time the Lord, the LORD of Heaven's Armies,
called you to weep and mourn.
He told you to shave your heads in sorrow for your sins
and to wear clothes of burlap to show your remorse.
13 But instead, you dance and play;
you slaughter cattle and kill sheep.
You feast on meat and drink wine.
You say, "Let's feast and drink,
for tomorrow we die!"

14 The LORD of Heaven's Armies has revealed this to me: "Till the day you die, you will never be forgiven for this sin." That is the judgment of the Lord, the LORD of Heaven's Armies.

A Message for Shebna

15 This is what the Lord, the LORD of Heaven's Armies, said to me: "Confront Shebna, the palace administrator, and give him this message:

16 "Who do you think you are,
and what are you doing here,
building a beautiful tomb for yourself—
a monument high up in the rock?
17 For the LORD is about to hurl you away, mighty man.
He is going to grab you,
18 crumple you into a ball,
and toss you away into a distant, barren land.
There you will die,
and your glorious chariots will be broken and useless.
You are a disgrace to your master!

19 "Yes, I will drive you out of office," says the LORD. "I will pull you down from your high position. 20 And then I will call my servant Eliakim son of Hilkiah to replace you. 21 I will dress him in your royal robes and will give him your title and your authority. And he will be a father to the people of Jerusalem and Judah. 22 I will give him the key to the house of David—the highest position in the royal

22:1 Hebrew *concerning the Valley of Vision.* **22:8** Hebrew *to the House of the Forest;* see 1 Kgs 7:2-5. **22:9** Hebrew *the city of David.*

court. When he opens doors, no one will be
able to close them; when he closes doors, no
one will be able to open them. [23]He will bring
honor to his family name, for I will drive him
firmly in place like a nail in the wall. [24]They
will give him great responsibility, and he will
bring honor to even the lowliest members of
his family.*"

[25]But the LORD of Heaven's Armies also
says: "The time will come when I will pull out
the nail that seemed so firm. It will come out
and fall to the ground. Everything it supports
will fall with it. I, the LORD, have spoken!"

CHAPTER 23

A Message about Tyre

This message came to me concerning Tyre:

Weep, O ships of Tarshish,
for the harbor and houses of Tyre are gone!
The rumors you heard in Cyprus*
are all true.
2 Mourn in silence, you people of the coast
and you merchants of Sidon.
Your traders crossed the sea,
3 sailing over deep waters.
They brought you grain from Egypt*
and harvests from along the Nile.
You were the marketplace of the world.

4 But now you are put to shame, city of Sidon,
for Tyre, the fortress of the sea, says,
"Now I am childless;
I have no sons or daughters."
5 When Egypt hears the news about Tyre,
there will be great sorrow.
6 Send word now to Tarshish!
Wail, you people who live in distant lands!
7 Is this silent ruin all that is left of your once joyous city?
What a long history was yours!
Think of all the colonists you sent to distant places.

8 Who has brought this disaster on Tyre,
that great creator of kingdoms?
Her traders were all princes,
her merchants were nobles.
9 The LORD of Heaven's Armies has done it
to destroy your pride
and bring low all earth's nobility.
10 Come, people of Tarshish,
sweep over the land like the flooding Nile,
for Tyre is defenseless.*
11 The LORD held out his hand over the sea
and shook the kingdoms of the earth.
He has spoken out against Phoenicia,*
ordering that her fortresses be destroyed.
12 He says, "Never again will you rejoice,
O daughter of Sidon, for you have been crushed.
Even if you flee to Cyprus,
you will find no rest."

13 Look at the land of Babylonia*—
the people of that land are gone!
The Assyrians have handed Babylon over
to the wild animals of the desert.
They have built siege ramps against its walls,
torn down its palaces,
and turned it to a heap of rubble.

14 Wail, O ships of Tarshish,
for your harbor is destroyed!

[15]For seventy years, the length of a king's
life, Tyre will be forgotten. But then the city
will come back to life as in the song about the
prostitute:

16 Take a harp and walk the streets,
you forgotten harlot.
Make sweet melody and sing your songs
so you will be remembered again.

[17]Yes, after seventy years the LORD will re-
vive Tyre. But she will be no different than
she was before. She will again be a prostitute
to all kingdoms around the world. [18]But in the
end her profits will be given to the LORD. Her
wealth will not be hoarded but will provide
good food and fine clothing for the LORD's
priests.

CHAPTER 24

Destruction of the Earth

[1]Look! The LORD is about to destroy
the earth
and make it a vast wasteland.

22:24 Hebrew *They will hang on him all the glory of his father's house: its offspring and offshoots, all its lesser vessels, from the bowls to all the jars.* **23:1** Hebrew *Kittim;* also in 23:12. **23:3** Hebrew *from Shihor,* a branch of the Nile River. **23:10** The meaning of the Hebrew in this verse is uncertain. **23:11** Hebrew *Canaan.* **23:13** Or *Chaldea.*

He devastates the surface of the earth
and scatters the people.
2 Priests and laypeople,
servants and masters,
maids and mistresses,
buyers and sellers,
lenders and borrowers,
bankers and debtors—none will be spared.
3 The earth will be completely emptied and looted.
The LORD has spoken!
4 The earth mourns and dries up,
and the crops waste away and wither.
Even the greatest people on earth waste away.
5 The earth suffers for the sins of its people,
for they have twisted God's instructions,
violated his laws,
and broken his everlasting covenant.
6 Therefore, a curse consumes the earth.
Its people must pay the price for their sin.
They are destroyed by fire,
and only a few are left alive.
7 The grapevines waste away,
and there is no new wine.
All the merrymakers sigh and mourn.
8 The cheerful sound of tambourines is stilled;
the happy cries of celebration are heard no more.
The melodious chords of the harp are silent.
9 Gone are the joys of wine and song;
alcoholic drink turns bitter in the mouth.
10 The city writhes in chaos;
every home is locked to keep out intruders.
11 Mobs gather in the streets, crying out for wine.
Joy has turned to gloom.
Gladness has been banished from the land.
12 The city is left in ruins,
its gates battered down.
13 Throughout the earth the story is the same—
only a remnant is left,
like the stray olives left on the tree
or the few grapes left on the vine after harvest.
14 But all who are left shout and sing for joy.
Those in the west praise the LORD's majesty.
15 In eastern lands, give glory to the LORD.
In the lands beyond the sea, praise the name of the LORD, the God of Israel.
16 We hear songs of praise from the ends of the earth,
songs that give glory to the Righteous One!

But my heart is heavy with grief.
Weep for me, for I wither away.
Deceit still prevails,
and treachery is everywhere.
17 Terror and traps and snares will be your lot,
you people of the earth.
18 Those who flee in terror will fall into a trap,
and those who escape the trap will be caught in a snare.

Destruction falls like rain from the heavens;
the foundations of the earth shake.
19 The earth has broken up.
It has utterly collapsed;
it is violently shaken.
20 The earth staggers like a drunk.
It trembles like a tent in a storm.
It falls and will not rise again,
for the guilt of its rebellion is very heavy.

21 In that day the LORD will punish the gods in the heavens
and the proud rulers of the nations on earth.
22 They will be rounded up and put in prison.
They will be shut up in prison
and will finally be punished.
23 Then the glory of the moon will wane,
and the brightness of the sun will fade,
for the LORD of Heaven's Armies will rule on Mount Zion.
He will rule in great glory in Jerusalem,
in the sight of all the leaders of his people.

CHAPTER 25

Praise for Judgment and Salvation

1 O LORD, I will honor and praise your name,
for you are my God.
You do such wonderful things!
You planned them long ago,
and now you have accomplished them.
2 You turn mighty cities into heaps of ruins.
Cities with strong walls are turned to rubble.
Beautiful palaces in distant lands disappear
and will never be rebuilt.
3 Therefore, strong nations will declare your glory;
ruthless nations will fear you.

4 But you are a tower of refuge to the poor, O LORD,
a tower of refuge to the needy in distress.
You are a refuge from the storm
and a shelter from the heat.
For the oppressive acts of ruthless people
are like a storm beating against a wall,
5 or like the relentless heat of the desert.
But you silence the roar of foreign nations.
As the shade of a cloud cools relentless heat,
so the boastful songs of ruthless people are stilled.

6 In Jerusalem,* the LORD of Heaven's Armies
will spread a wonderful feast
for all the people of the world.
It will be a delicious banquet
with clear, well-aged wine and choice meat.
7 There he will remove the cloud of gloom,
the shadow of death that hangs over the earth.
8 He will swallow up death forever!*
The Sovereign LORD will wipe away all tears.
He will remove forever all insults and mockery
against his land and people.
The LORD has spoken!

9 In that day the people will proclaim,
"This is our God!
We trusted in him, and he saved us!
This is the LORD, in whom we trusted.
Let us rejoice in the salvation he brings!"
10 For the LORD's hand of blessing will rest on Jerusalem.
But Moab will be crushed.
It will be like straw trampled down and left to rot.
11 God will push down Moab's people
as a swimmer pushes down water with his hands.
He will end their pride
and all their evil works.
12 The high walls of Moab will be demolished.
They will be brought down to the ground,
down into the dust.

CHAPTER 26

A Song of Praise to the LORD

In that day, everyone in the land of Judah will sing this song:

Our city is strong!
We are surrounded by the walls of God's salvation.
2 Open the gates to all who are righteous;
allow the faithful to enter.
3 You will keep in perfect peace
all who trust in you,
all whose thoughts are fixed on you!
4 Trust in the LORD always,
for the LORD GOD is the eternal Rock.
5 He humbles the proud
and brings down the arrogant city.

How can I stop worrying all the time?

Trust in the LORD always, for the LORD GOD is the eternal Rock.
ISAIAH 26:4

25:6 Hebrew *On this mountain;* also in 25:10. **25:8** Greek version reads *Death is swallowed up in victory.* Compare 1 Cor 15:54.

TROUBLED THOUGHTS

Things were falling apart for Mike. He had a hard time with his schoolwork, his grandpa was very sick, and his parents fought a lot. Because Mike worried so much, he couldn't sleep at night and found it hard to pay attention in class. Nothing seemed to help. Mike tried playing with the dog, watching TV, and spending time with his friends. But all Mike could think about were his problems. What do you think Mike should do? Isaiah 26:3 gives a promise from God that will help.

He brings it down to the dust.
6 The poor and oppressed trample it underfoot,
and the needy walk all over it.

7 But for those who are righteous,
the way is not steep and rough.
You are a God who does what is right,
and you smooth out the path ahead of them.
8 LORD, we show our trust in you by obeying your laws;
our heart's desire is to glorify your name.
9 All night long I search for you;
in the morning I earnestly seek for God.
For only when you come to judge the earth
will people learn what is right.
10 Your kindness to the wicked does not make them do good.
Although others do right, the wicked keep doing wrong
and take no notice of the LORD's majesty.
11 O LORD, they pay no attention to your upraised fist.
Show them your eagerness to defend your people.
Then they will be ashamed.
Let your fire consume your enemies.

12 LORD, you will grant us peace;
all we have accomplished is really from you.
13 O LORD our God, others have ruled us,
but you alone are the one we worship.
14 Those we served before are dead and gone.
Their departed spirits will never return!
You attacked them and destroyed them,
and they are long forgotten.
15 O LORD, you have made our nation great;
yes, you have made us great.
You have extended our borders,
and we give you the glory!

16 LORD, in distress we searched for you.
We prayed beneath the burden of your discipline.
17 Just as a pregnant woman
writhes and cries out in pain as she gives birth,
so were we in your presence, LORD.
18 We, too, writhe in agony,
but nothing comes of our suffering.
We have not given salvation to the earth,
nor brought life into the world.
19 But those who die in the LORD will live;
their bodies will rise again!
Those who sleep in the earth
will rise up and sing for joy!
For your life-giving light will fall like dew
on your people in the place of the dead!

Restoration for Israel

20 Go home, my people,
and lock your doors!
Hide yourselves for a little while
until the LORD's anger has passed.
21 Look! The LORD is coming from heaven
to punish the people of the earth for
their sins.
The earth will no longer hide those who
have been killed.
They will be brought out for all to see.

CHAPTER 27

In that day the LORD will take his terrible, swift sword and punish Leviathan,* the swiftly moving serpent, the coiling, writhing serpent. He will kill the dragon of the sea.

2 "In that day,
sing about the fruitful vineyard.
3 I, the LORD, will watch over it,
watering it carefully.
Day and night I will watch so no one can
harm it.
4 My anger will be gone.
If I find briers and thorns growing,
I will attack them;
I will burn them up—
5 unless they turn to me for help.
Let them make peace with me;
yes, let them make peace with me."
6 The time is coming when Jacob's
descendants will take root.
Israel will bud and blossom
and fill the whole earth with fruit!

7 Has the LORD struck Israel
as he struck her enemies?
Has he punished her
as he punished them?
8 No, but he exiled Israel to call her to
account.
She was exiled from her land
as though blown away in a storm from
the east.
9 The LORD did this to purge Israel's*
wickedness,
to take away all her sin.
As a result, all the pagan altars will be
crushed to dust.
No Asherah pole or pagan shrine will
be left standing.
10 The fortified towns will be silent and
empty,
the houses abandoned, the streets
overgrown with weeds.
Calves will graze there,
chewing on twigs and branches.
11 The people are like the dead branches of
a tree,
broken off and used for kindling
beneath the cooking pots.
Israel is a foolish and stupid nation,
for its people have turned away from
God.
Therefore, the one who made them
will show them no pity or mercy.

12 Yet the time will come when the LORD will gather them together like handpicked grain. One by one he will gather them—from the Euphrates River* in the east to the Brook of Egypt in the west. 13 In that day the great trumpet will sound. Many who were dying in exile in Assyria and Egypt will return to Jerusalem to worship the LORD on his holy mountain.

CHAPTER 28

A Message about Samaria

1 What sorrow awaits the proud city of
Samaria—
the glorious crown of the drunks of
Israel.*
It sits at the head of a fertile valley,
but its glorious beauty will fade like a
flower.
It is the pride of a people
brought down by wine.
2 For the Lord will send a mighty army
against it.
Like a mighty hailstorm and a torrential
rain,
they will burst upon it like a surging flood
and smash it to the ground.
3 The proud city of Samaria—
the glorious crown of the drunks of
Israel*—
will be trampled beneath its enemies'
feet.
4 It sits at the head of a fertile valley,

27:1 The identification of Leviathan is disputed, ranging from an earthly creature to a mythical sea monster in ancient literature. **27:9** Hebrew *Jacob's*. See note on 14:1. **27:12** Hebrew *the river*. **28:1** Hebrew *What sorrow awaits the crowning glory of the drunks of Ephraim*, referring to Samaria, capital of the northern kingdom of Israel. **28:3** Hebrew *The crowning glory of the drunks of Ephraim*; see note on 28:1.

but its glorious beauty will fade like a flower.
Whoever sees it will snatch it up,
as an early fig is quickly picked and eaten.

5 Then at last the LORD of Heaven's Armies will himself be Israel's glorious crown.
He will be the pride and joy of the remnant of his people.
6 He will give a longing for justice to their judges.
He will give great courage to their warriors who stand at the gates.

7 Now, however, Israel is led by drunks who reel with wine and stagger with alcohol.
The priests and prophets stagger with alcohol
and lose themselves in wine.
They reel when they see visions and stagger as they render decisions.
8 Their tables are covered with vomit; filth is everywhere.
9 "Who does the LORD think we are?" they ask.
"Why does he speak to us like this?
Are we little children, just recently weaned?
10 He tells us everything over and over—
one line at a time, one line at a time,
a little here, and a little there!"

11 So now God will have to speak to his people
through foreign oppressors who speak a strange language!
12 God has told his people,
"Here is a place of rest; let the weary rest here.
This is a place of quiet rest."
But they would not listen.
13 So the LORD will spell out his message for them again,
one line at a time, one line at a time,
a little here, and a little there,
so that they will stumble and fall.
They will be injured, trapped, and captured.

14 Therefore, listen to this message from the LORD,
you scoffing rulers in Jerusalem.
15 You boast, "We have struck a bargain to cheat death
and have made a deal to dodge the grave.*
The coming destruction can never touch us,
for we have built a strong refuge made of lies and deception."

16 Therefore, this is what the Sovereign LORD says:
"Look! I am placing a foundation stone in Jerusalem,*
a firm and tested stone.
It is a precious cornerstone that is safe to build on.
Whoever believes need never be shaken.*
17 I will test you with the measuring line of justice
and the plumb line of righteousness.
Since your refuge is made of lies, a hailstorm will knock it down.
Since it is made of deception, a flood will sweep it away.
18 I will cancel the bargain you made to cheat death,
and I will overturn your deal to dodge the grave.
When the terrible enemy sweeps through,
you will be trampled into the ground.
19 Again and again that flood will come, morning after morning,
day and night, until you are carried away."

This message will bring terror to your people.
20 The bed you have made is too short to lie on.
The blankets are too narrow to cover you.
21 The LORD will come as he did against the Philistines at Mount Perazim
and against the Amorites at Gibeon.

28:15 Hebrew *Sheol;* also in 28:18. **28:16a** Hebrew *in Zion.* **28:16b** Greek version reads *Look! I am placing a stone in the foundation of Jerusalem* [literally *Zion*], */ a precious cornerstone for its foundation, chosen for great honor. / Anyone who trusts in him will never be disgraced.* Compare Rom 9:33; 1 Pet 2:6.

He will come to do a strange thing;
he will come to do an unusual deed:
22 For the Lord, the LORD of Heaven's Armies,
has plainly said that he is determined to crush the whole land.
So scoff no more,
or your punishment will be even greater.

23 Listen to me;
listen, and pay close attention.
24 Does a farmer always plow and never sow?
Is he forever cultivating the soil and never planting?
25 Does he not finally plant his seeds—
black cumin, cumin, wheat, barley, and emmer wheat—
each in its proper way,
and each in its proper place?
26 The farmer knows just what to do,
for God has given him understanding.
27 A heavy sledge is never used to thresh black cumin;
rather, it is beaten with a light stick.
A threshing wheel is never rolled on cumin;
instead, it is beaten lightly with a flail.
28 Grain for bread is easily crushed,
so he doesn't keep on pounding it.
He threshes it under the wheels of a cart,
but he doesn't pulverize it.
29 The LORD of Heaven's Armies is a wonderful teacher,
and he gives the farmer great wisdom.

CHAPTER 29

A Message about Jerusalem

1 "What sorrow awaits Ariel,* the City of David.
Year after year you celebrate your feasts.
2 Yet I will bring disaster upon you,
and there will be much weeping and sorrow.
For Jerusalem will become what her name Ariel means—
an altar covered with blood.
3 I will be your enemy,
surrounding Jerusalem and attacking its walls.
I will build siege towers
and destroy it.
4 Then deep from the earth you will speak;
from low in the dust your words will come.
Your voice will whisper from the ground
like a ghost conjured up from the grave.
5 "But suddenly, your ruthless enemies will be crushed
like the finest of dust.
Your many attackers will be driven away
like chaff before the wind.
Suddenly, in an instant,
6 I, the LORD of Heaven's Armies, will act for you
with thunder and earthquake and great noise,
with whirlwind and storm and consuming fire.
7 All the nations fighting against Jerusalem*
will vanish like a dream!
Those who are attacking her walls
will vanish like a vision in the night.
8 A hungry person dreams of eating
but wakes up still hungry.
A thirsty person dreams of drinking
but is still faint from thirst when morning comes.
So it will be with your enemies,
with those who attack Mount Zion."

9 Are you amazed and incredulous?
Don't you believe it?
Then go ahead and be blind.
You are stupid, but not from wine!
You stagger, but not from liquor!
10 For the LORD has poured out on you a spirit of deep sleep.
He has closed the eyes of your prophets and visionaries.

11 All the future events in this vision are like a sealed book to them. When you give it to those who can read, they will say, "We can't read it because it is sealed." 12 When you give it to those who cannot read, they will say, "We don't know how to read."

29:1 *Ariel* sounds like a Hebrew term that means "hearth" or "altar." **29:7** Hebrew *Ariel*.

13 And so the Lord says,
"These people say they are mine.
They honor me with their lips,
but their hearts are far from me.
And their worship of me
is nothing but man-made rules learned by rote.*
14 Because of this, I will once again astound these hypocrites
with amazing wonders.
The wisdom of the wise will pass away,
and the intelligence of the intelligent will disappear."

15 What sorrow awaits those who try to hide their plans from the LORD,
who do their evil deeds in the dark!
"The LORD can't see us," they say.
"He doesn't know what's going on!"
16 How foolish can you be?
He is the Potter, and he is certainly greater than you, the clay!
Should the created thing say of the one who made it,
"He didn't make me"?
Does a jar ever say,
"The potter who made me is stupid"?

17 Soon—and it will not be very long—
the forests of Lebanon will become a fertile field,
and the fertile field will yield bountiful crops.
18 In that day the deaf will hear words read from a book,
and the blind will see through the gloom and darkness.
19 The humble will be filled with fresh joy from the LORD.
The poor will rejoice in the Holy One of Israel.
20 The scoffer will be gone,
the arrogant will disappear,
and those who plot evil will be killed.
21 Those who convict the innocent
by their false testimony will disappear.
A similar fate awaits those who use trickery to pervert justice
and who tell lies to destroy the innocent.

22 That is why the LORD, who redeemed Abraham, says to the people of Israel,*

"My people will no longer be ashamed
or turn pale with fear.
23 For when they see their many children
and all the blessings I have given them,
they will recognize the holiness of the Holy One of Israel.
They will stand in awe of the God of Jacob.
24 Then the wayward will gain understanding,
and complainers will accept instruction.

CHAPTER 30

Judah's Worthless Treaty with Egypt

1 "What sorrow awaits my rebellious children,"
says the LORD.
"You make plans that are contrary to mine.
You make alliances not directed by my Spirit,
thus piling up your sins.
2 For without consulting me,
you have gone down to Egypt for help.
You have put your trust in Pharaoh's protection.
You have tried to hide in his shade.
3 But by trusting Pharaoh, you will be humiliated,
and by depending on him, you will be disgraced.
4 For though his power extends to Zoan
and his officials have arrived in Hanes,
5 all who trust in him will be ashamed.
He will not help you.
Instead, he will disgrace you."

6 This message came to me concerning the animals in the Negev:

The caravan moves slowly
across the terrible desert to Egypt—
donkeys weighed down with riches
and camels loaded with treasure—
all to pay for Egypt's protection.
They travel through the wilderness,
a place of lionesses and lions,
a place where vipers and poisonous snakes live.

29:13 Greek version reads *Their worship is a farce, / for they teach man-made ideas as commands from God.* Compare Mark 7:7.
29:22 Hebrew *of Jacob.* See note on 14:1.

All this, and Egypt will give you nothing in
return.
7 Egypt's promises are worthless!
Therefore, I call her Rahab—
the Harmless Dragon.*

A Warning for Rebellious Judah

8 Now go and write down these words.
Write them in a book.
They will stand until the end of time
as a witness
9 that these people are stubborn rebels
who refuse to pay attention to the
LORD's instructions.
10 They tell the seers,
"Stop seeing visions!"
They tell the prophets,
"Don't tell us what is right.
Tell us nice things.
Tell us lies.
11 Forget all this gloom.
Get off your narrow path.
Stop telling us about your
'Holy One of Israel.'"

12 This is the reply of the Holy One of Israel:

"Because you despise what I tell you
and trust instead in oppression and
lies,
13 calamity will come upon you suddenly—
like a bulging wall that bursts and falls.
In an instant it will collapse
and come crashing down.
14 You will be smashed like a piece of
pottery—
shattered so completely that
there won't be a piece big enough
to carry coals from a fireplace
or a little water from the well."

15 This is what the Sovereign LORD,
the Holy One of Israel, says:
"Only in returning to me
and resting in me will you be saved.
In quietness and confidence is your
strength.
But you would have none of it.
16 You said, 'No, we will get our help from
Egypt.
They will give us swift horses for riding
into battle.'

The Star Player

Howard was the best male basketball player in school and maybe in the state. Unfortunately, Howard frequently exhibited poor sportsmanship. He often embarrassed his own team with his trash talk and other antics. Right before a super-important game, the team captain told Howard, "If you try to show off or trash-talk against the other team, all of the guys on our team will do whatever we can to keep the ball away from you—even if we lose the game." Howard was astonished. What do you think he should do? Read Isaiah 30:15 to see a way Howard could respond.

But the only swiftness you are going to see
is the swiftness of your enemies
chasing you!
17 One of them will chase a thousand of you.
Five of them will make all of you flee.

30:7 Hebrew *Rahab who sits still.* Rahab is the name of a mythical sea monster that represents chaos in ancient literature. The name is used here as a poetic name for Egypt.

You will be left like a lonely flagpole
on a hill
or a tattered banner on a distant
mountaintop."

Blessings for the Lord's People

18 So the Lord must wait for you to come to
him
so he can show you his love and
compassion.
For the Lord is a faithful God.
Blessed are those who wait for his help.

19 O people of Zion, who live in Jerusalem,
you will weep no more.
He will be gracious if you ask for help.
He will surely respond to the sound of
your cries.
20 Though the Lord gave you adversity
for food
and suffering for drink,
he will still be with you to teach you.
You will see your teacher with your
own eyes.
21 Your own ears will hear him.
Right behind you a voice will say,
"This is the way you should go,"
whether to the right or to the left.
22 Then you will destroy all your silver idols
and your precious gold images.
You will throw them out like filthy rags,
saying to them, "Good riddance!"

23 Then the Lord will bless you with rain at planting time. There will be wonderful harvests and plenty of pastureland for your livestock. 24 The oxen and donkeys that till the ground will eat good grain, its chaff blown away by the wind. 25 In that day, when your enemies are slaughtered and the towers fall, there will be streams of water flowing down every mountain and hill. 26 The moon will be as bright as the sun, and the sun will be seven times brighter—like the light of seven days in one! So it will be when the Lord begins to heal his people and cure the wounds he gave them.

27 Look! The Lord is coming from far away,
burning with anger,
surrounded by thick, rising smoke.
His lips are filled with fury;
his words consume like fire.
28 His hot breath pours out like a flood
up to the neck of his enemies.
He will sift out the proud nations for
destruction.
He will bridle them and lead them away
to ruin.

29 But the people of God will sing a song
of joy,
like the songs at the holy festivals.
You will be filled with joy,
as when a flutist leads a group of
pilgrims
to Jerusalem, the mountain of the Lord—
to the Rock of Israel.
30 And the Lord will make his majestic voice
heard.
He will display the strength of his
mighty arm.
It will descend with devouring flames,
with cloudbursts, thunderstorms, and
huge hailstones.
31 At the Lord's command, the Assyrians will
be shattered.
He will strike them down with his royal
scepter.
32 And as the Lord strikes them with his rod
of punishment,
his people will celebrate with
tambourines and harps.
Lifting his mighty arm, he will fight the
Assyrians.
33 Topheth—the place of burning—
has long been ready for the Assyrian
king;
the pyre is piled high with wood.
The breath of the Lord, like fire from a
volcano,
will set it ablaze.

CHAPTER 31

The Futility of Relying on Egypt

1 What sorrow awaits those who look to
Egypt for help,
trusting their horses, chariots, and
charioteers
and depending on the strength of human
armies
instead of looking to the Lord,
the Holy One of Israel.
2 In his wisdom, the Lord will send great
disaster;
he will not change his mind.
He will rise against the wicked
and against their helpers.

3 For these Egyptians are mere humans, not God!
Their horses are puny flesh, not mighty spirits!
When the LORD raises his fist against them,
those who help will stumble,
and those being helped will fall.
They will all fall down and die together.

4 But this is what the LORD has told me:

"When a strong young lion
stands growling over a sheep it has killed,
it is not frightened by the shouts and noise
of a whole crowd of shepherds.
In the same way, the LORD of Heaven's Armies
will come down and fight on Mount Zion.
5 The LORD of Heaven's Armies will hover over Jerusalem
and protect it like a bird protecting its nest.
He will defend and save the city;
he will pass over it and rescue it."

6 Though you are such wicked rebels, my people, come and return to the LORD. 7 I know the glorious day will come when each of you will throw away the gold idols and silver images your sinful hands have made.

8 "The Assyrians will be destroyed,
but not by the swords of men.
The sword of God will strike them,
and they will panic and flee.
The strong young Assyrians
will be taken away as captives.
9 Even the strongest will quake with terror,
and princes will flee when they see your battle flags,"
says the LORD, whose fire burns in Zion,
whose flame blazes from Jerusalem.

CHAPTER 32

Israel's Ultimate Deliverance

1 Look, a righteous king is coming!
And honest princes will rule under him.
2 Each one will be like a shelter from the wind
and a refuge from the storm,
like streams of water in the desert
and the shadow of a great rock in a parched land.
3 Then everyone who has eyes will be able to see the truth,
and everyone who has ears will be able to hear it.
4 Even the hotheads will be full of sense and understanding.
Those who stammer will speak out plainly.
5 In that day ungodly fools will not be heroes.
Scoundrels will not be respected.
6 For fools speak foolishness
and make evil plans.
They practice ungodliness
and spread false teachings about the LORD.
They deprive the hungry of food
and give no water to the thirsty.
7 The smooth tricks of scoundrels are evil.
They plot crooked schemes.
They lie to convict the poor,
even when the cause of the poor is just.
8 But generous people plan to do what is generous,
and they stand firm in their generosity.
9 Listen, you women who lie around in ease.
Listen to me, you who are so smug.
10 In a short time—just a little more than a year—
you careless ones will suddenly begin to care.
For your fruit crops will fail,
and the harvest will never take place.
11 Tremble, you women of ease;
throw off your complacency.
Strip off your pretty clothes,
and put on burlap to show your grief.
12 Beat your breasts in sorrow for your bountiful farms
and your fruitful grapevines.
13 For your land will be overgrown with thorns and briers.
Your joyful homes and happy towns will be gone.

14 The palace and the city will be deserted,
and busy towns will be empty.
Wild donkeys will frolic and flocks will graze
in the empty forts* and watchtowers
15 until at last the Spirit is poured out
on us from heaven.
Then the wilderness will become a fertile field,
and the fertile field will yield bountiful crops.
16 Justice will rule in the wilderness
and righteousness in the fertile field.
17 And this righteousness will bring peace.
Yes, it will bring quietness and confidence forever.
18 My people will live in safety, quietly at home.
They will be at rest.
19 Even if the forest should be destroyed
and the city torn down,
20 the LORD will greatly bless his people.
Wherever they plant seed, bountiful crops will spring up.
Their cattle and donkeys will graze freely.

CHAPTER 33

A Message about Assyria

1 What sorrow awaits you Assyrians, who have destroyed others*
but have never been destroyed yourselves.
You betray others,
but you have never been betrayed.
When you are done destroying,
you will be destroyed.
When you are done betraying,
you will be betrayed.
2 But LORD, be merciful to us,
for we have waited for you.
Be our strong arm each day
and our salvation in times of trouble.
3 The enemy runs at the sound of your voice.
When you stand up, the nations flee!
4 Just as caterpillars and locusts strip the fields and vines,
so the fallen army of Assyria will be stripped!
5 Though the LORD is very great and lives in heaven,
he will make Jerusalem* his home of justice and righteousness.
6 In that day he will be your sure foundation,
providing a rich store of salvation, wisdom, and knowledge.
The fear of the LORD will be your treasure.
7 But now your brave warriors weep in public.
Your ambassadors of peace cry in bitter disappointment.
8 Your roads are deserted;
no one travels them anymore.
The Assyrians have broken their peace treaty
and care nothing for the promises they made before witnesses.*
They have no respect for anyone.
9 The land of Israel wilts in mourning.
Lebanon withers with shame.
The plain of Sharon is now a wilderness.
Bashan and Carmel have been plundered.
10 But the LORD says: "Now I will stand up.
Now I will show my power and might.
11 You Assyrians produce nothing but dry grass and stubble.
Your own breath will turn to fire and consume you.
12 Your people will be burned up completely,
like thornbushes cut down and tossed in a fire.
13 Listen to what I have done, you nations far away!
And you that are near, acknowledge my might!"
14 The sinners in Jerusalem shake with fear.
Terror seizes the godless.
"Who can live with this devouring fire?" they cry.
"Who can survive this all-consuming fire?"
15 Those who are honest and fair,
who refuse to profit by fraud,
who stay far away from bribes,

32:14 Hebrew *the Ophel*. **33:1** Hebrew *What sorrow awaits you, O destroyer*. The Hebrew text does not specifically name Assyria as the object of the prophecy in this chapter. **33:5** Hebrew *Zion;* also in 33:14. **33:8** As in Dead Sea Scrolls; Masoretic Text reads *care nothing for the cities*.

who refuse to listen to those who plot
murder,
who shut their eyes to all enticement to
do wrong—
16 these are the ones who will dwell on high.
The rocks of the mountains will be
their fortress.
Food will be supplied to them,
and they will have water in abundance.

17 Your eyes will see the king in all his
splendor,
and you will see a land that stretches
into the distance.
18 You will think back to this time of terror,
asking,
"Where are the Assyrian officers
who counted our towers?
Where are the bookkeepers
who recorded the plunder taken from
our fallen city?"
19 You will no longer see these fierce, violent
people
with their strange, unknown language.

20 Instead, you will see Zion as a place of
holy festivals.
You will see Jerusalem, a city quiet and
secure.
It will be like a tent whose ropes are taut
and whose stakes are firmly fixed.
21 The LORD will be our Mighty One.
He will be like a wide river of
protection
that no enemy can cross,
that no enemy ship can sail upon.
22 For the LORD is our judge,
our lawgiver, and our king.
He will care for us and save us.
23 The enemies' sails hang loose
on broken masts with useless tackle.
Their treasure will be divided by the
people of God.
Even the lame will take their share!
24 The people of Israel will no longer say,
"We are sick and helpless,"
for the LORD will forgive their sins.

CHAPTER 34

A Message for the Nations

1 Come here and listen, O nations of the
earth.
Let the world and everything in it hear
my words.
2 For the LORD is enraged against the
nations.
His fury is against all their armies.
He will completely destroy* them,
dooming them to slaughter.
3 Their dead will be left unburied,
and the stench of rotting bodies will
fill the land.
The mountains will flow with their
blood.
4 The heavens above will melt away
and disappear like a rolled-up scroll.
The stars will fall from the sky
like withered leaves from a grapevine,

34:2 The Hebrew term used here refers to the complete consecration of things or people to the LORD, either by destroying them or by giving them as an offering; similarly in 34:5.

or shriveled figs from a
fig tree.

5 And when my sword has finished
its work in the heavens,
it will fall upon Edom,
the nation I have marked for
destruction.
6 The sword of the LORD is drenched with
blood
and covered with fat—
with the blood of lambs and goats,
with the fat of rams prepared for
sacrifice.
Yes, the LORD will offer a sacrifice in the
city of Bozrah.
He will make a mighty slaughter
in Edom.
7 Even men as strong as wild oxen will die—
the young men alongside the veterans.
The land will be soaked with blood
and the soil enriched with fat.

8 For it is the day of the LORD's revenge,
the year when Edom will be paid back
for all it did to Israel.*
9 The streams of Edom will be filled with
burning pitch,
and the ground will be covered with
fire.
10 This judgment on Edom will never end;
the smoke of its burning will rise
forever.
The land will lie deserted from generation
to generation.
No one will live there anymore.
11 It will be haunted by the desert owl and
the screech owl,
the great owl and the raven.*
For God will measure that land carefully;
he will measure it for chaos and
destruction.
12 It will be called the Land of Nothing,
and all its nobles will soon be gone.*
13 Thorns will overrun its palaces;
nettles and thistles will grow in its
forts.
The ruins will become a haunt for jackals
and a home for owls.
14 Desert animals will mingle there with
hyenas,
their howls filling the night.
Wild goats will bleat at one another
among the ruins,
and night creatures* will come there to
rest.
15 There the owl will make her nest and lay
her eggs.
She will hatch her young and cover
them with her wings.
And the buzzards will come,
each one with its mate.

16 Search the book of the LORD,
and see what he will do.
Not one of these birds and animals will
be missing,
and none will lack a mate,
for the LORD has promised this.
His Spirit will make it all come true.
17 He has surveyed and divided the land
and deeded it over to those creatures.
They will possess it forever,
from generation to generation.

CHAPTER 35

Hope for Restoration

1 Even the wilderness and desert will be
glad in those days.
The wasteland will rejoice and blossom
with spring crocuses.
2 Yes, there will be an abundance
of flowers
and singing and joy!
The deserts will become as green as the
mountains of Lebanon,
as lovely as Mount Carmel or the plain
of Sharon.
There the LORD will display his
glory,
the splendor of our God.
3 With this news, strengthen those who
have tired hands,
and encourage those who have weak
knees.
4 Say to those with fearful hearts,
"Be strong, and do not fear,
for your God is coming to destroy your
enemies.
He is coming to save you."

5 And when he comes, he will open the
eyes of the blind
and unplug the ears of the deaf.

34:8 Hebrew *to Zion*. **34:11** The identification of some of these birds is uncertain. **34:12** The meaning of the Hebrew is uncertain. **34:14** Hebrew *Lilith*, possibly a reference to a mythical demon of the night.

6 The lame will leap like a deer,
and those who cannot speak will sing for joy!
Springs will gush forth in the wilderness,
and streams will water the wasteland.
7 The parched ground will become a pool,
and springs of water will satisfy the thirsty land.
Marsh grass and reeds and rushes will flourish
where desert jackals once lived.
8 And a great road will go through that once deserted land.
It will be named the Highway of Holiness.
Evil-minded people will never travel on it.
It will be only for those who walk in God's ways;
fools will never walk there.
9 Lions will not lurk along its course,
nor any other ferocious beasts.
There will be no other dangers.
Only the redeemed will walk on it.
10 Those who have been ransomed by the LORD will return.
They will enter Jerusalem* singing,
crowned with everlasting joy.
Sorrow and mourning will disappear,
and they will be filled with joy and gladness.

CHAPTER 36

Assyria Invades Judah

In the fourteenth year of King Hezekiah's reign,* King Sennacherib of Assyria came to attack the fortified towns of Judah and conquered them. 2 Then the king of Assyria sent his chief of staff* from Lachish with a huge army to confront King Hezekiah in Jerusalem. The Assyrians took up a position beside the aqueduct that feeds water into the upper pool, near the road leading to the field where cloth is washed.*

3 These are the officials who went out to meet with them: Eliakim son of Hilkiah, the palace administrator; Shebna the court secretary; and Joah son of Asaph, the royal historian.

Sennacherib Threatens Jerusalem

4 Then the Assyrian king's chief of staff told them to give this message to Hezekiah:

"This is what the great king of Assyria says: What are you trusting in that makes you so confident? 5 Do you think that mere words can substitute for military skill and strength? Who are you counting on, that you have rebelled against me? 6 On Egypt? If you lean on Egypt, it will be like a reed that splinters beneath your weight and pierces your hand. Pharaoh, the king of Egypt, is completely unreliable!

7 "But perhaps you will say to me, 'We are trusting in the LORD our God!' But isn't he the one who was insulted by Hezekiah? Didn't Hezekiah tear down his shrines and altars and make everyone in Judah and Jerusalem worship only at the altar here in Jerusalem?

8 "I'll tell you what! Strike a bargain with my master, the king of Assyria. I will give you 2,000 horses if you can find that many men to ride on them! 9 With your tiny army, how can you think of challenging even the weakest contingent of my master's troops, even with the help of Egypt's chariots and charioteers? 10 What's more, do you think we have invaded your land without the LORD's direction? The LORD himself told us, 'Attack this land and destroy it!'"

11 Then Eliakim, Shebna, and Joah said to the Assyrian chief of staff, "Please speak to us in Aramaic, for we understand it well. Don't speak in Hebrew,* for the people on the wall will hear."

12 But Sennacherib's chief of staff replied, "Do you think my master sent this message only to you and your master? He wants all the people to hear it, for when we put this city under siege, they will suffer along with you. They will be so hungry and thirsty that they will eat their own dung and drink their own urine."

13 Then the chief of staff stood and shouted in Hebrew to the people on the wall, "Listen to this message from the great king of Assyria! 14 This is what the king says: Don't let Hezekiah deceive you. He will never be able to rescue

35:10 Hebrew *Zion*. **36:1** The fourteenth year of Hezekiah's reign was 701 B.C. **36:2a** Or *the rabshakeh;* also in 36:4, 11, 12, 22. **36:2b** Or *bleached*. **36:11** Hebrew *in the dialect of Judah;* also in 36:13.

you. [15]Don't let him fool you into trusting in the LORD by saying, 'The LORD will surely rescue us. This city will never fall into the hands of the Assyrian king!'

[16]"Don't listen to Hezekiah! These are the terms the king of Assyria is offering: Make peace with me—open the gates and come out. Then each of you can continue eating from your own grapevine and fig tree and drinking from your own well. [17]Then I will arrange to take you to another land like this one—a land of grain and new wine, bread and vineyards.

[18]"Don't let Hezekiah mislead you by saying, 'The LORD will rescue us!' Have the gods of any other nations ever saved their people from the king of Assyria? [19]What happened to the gods of Hamath and Arpad? And what about the gods of Sepharvaim? Did any god rescue Samaria from my power? [20]What god of any nation has ever been able to save its people from my power? So what makes you think that the LORD can rescue Jerusalem from me?"

[21]But the people were silent and did not utter a word because Hezekiah had commanded them, "Do not answer him."

[22]Then Eliakim son of Hilkiah, the palace administrator; Shebna the court secretary; and Joah son of Asaph, the royal historian, went back to Hezekiah. They tore their clothes in despair, and they went in to see the king and told him what the Assyrian chief of staff had said.

CHAPTER 37

Hezekiah Seeks the LORD's Help

When King Hezekiah heard their report, he tore his clothes and put on burlap and went into the Temple of the LORD. [2]And he sent Eliakim the palace administrator, Shebna the court secretary, and the leading priests, all dressed in burlap, to the prophet Isaiah son of Amoz. [3]They told him, "This is what King Hezekiah says: Today is a day of trouble, insults, and disgrace. It is like when a child is ready to be born, but the mother has no strength to deliver the baby. [4]But perhaps the LORD your God has heard the Assyrian chief of staff,* sent by the king to defy the living God, and will punish him for his words. Oh, pray for those of us who are left!"

[5]After King Hezekiah's officials delivered the king's message to Isaiah, [6]the prophet replied, "Say to your master, 'This is what the LORD says: Do not be disturbed by this blasphemous speech against me from the Assyrian king's messengers. [7]Listen! I myself will move against him,* and the king will receive a message that he is needed at home. So he will return to his land, where I will have him killed with a sword.'"

[8]Meanwhile, the Assyrian chief of staff left Jerusalem and went to consult the king of Assyria, who had left Lachish and was attacking Libnah.

[9]Soon afterward King Sennacherib received word that King Tirhakah of Ethiopia* was leading an army to fight against him. Before leaving to meet the attack, he sent messengers back to Hezekiah in Jerusalem with this message:

> [10]"This message is for King Hezekiah of Judah. Don't let your God, in whom you trust, deceive you with promises that Jerusalem will not be captured by the king of Assyria. [11]You know perfectly well what the kings of Assyria have done wherever they have gone. They have completely destroyed everyone who stood in their way! Why should you be any different? [12]Have the gods of other nations rescued them—such nations as Gozan, Haran, Rezeph, and the people of Eden who were in Tel-assar? My predecessors destroyed them all! [13]What happened to the king of Hamath and the king of Arpad? What happened to the kings of Sepharvaim, Hena, and Ivvah?"

[14]After Hezekiah received the letter from the messengers and read it, he went up to the LORD's Temple and spread it out before the LORD. [15]And Hezekiah prayed this prayer before the LORD: [16]"O LORD of Heaven's Armies, God of Israel, you are enthroned between the mighty cherubim! You alone are God of all the kingdoms of the earth. You alone created the heavens and the earth. [17]Bend down, O LORD, and listen! Open your eyes, O LORD, and see! Listen to Sennacherib's words of defiance against the living God.

[18]"It is true, LORD, that the kings of Assyria

37:4 Or *the rabshakeh;* also in 37:8. **37:7** Hebrew *I will put a spirit in him.* **37:9** Hebrew *of Cush.*

have destroyed all these nations. [19]And they
have thrown the gods of these nations into
the fire and burned them. But of course the
Assyrians could destroy them! They were not
gods at all—only idols of wood and stone
shaped by human hands. [20]Now, O LORD our
God, rescue us from his power; then all the
kingdoms of the earth will know that you
alone, O LORD, are God.*"

Isaiah Predicts Judah's Deliverance

[21]Then Isaiah son of Amoz sent this message
to Hezekiah: "This is what the LORD, the God
of Israel, says: Because you prayed about King
Sennacherib of Assyria, [22]the LORD has spo-
ken this word against him:

"The virgin daughter of Zion
despises you and laughs at you.
The daughter of Jerusalem
shakes her head in derision as you
flee.

[23] "Whom have you been defying and
ridiculing?
Against whom did you raise your voice?
At whom did you look with such haughty
eyes?
It was the Holy One of Israel!
[24] By your messengers you have defied the
Lord.
You have said, 'With my many chariots
I have conquered the highest mountains—
yes, the remotest peaks of Lebanon.
I have cut down its tallest cedars
and its finest cypress trees.
I have reached its farthest heights
and explored its deepest forests.
[25] I have dug wells in many foreign lands*
and refreshed myself with their water.
With the sole of my foot,
I stopped up all the rivers of Egypt!'

[26] "But have you not heard?
I decided this long ago.
Long ago I planned it,
and now I am making it happen.
I planned for you to crush fortified cities
into heaps of rubble.
[27] That is why their people have so little
power
and are so frightened and confused.
They are as weak as grass,
as easily trampled as tender green
shoots.
They are like grass sprouting on a
housetop,
scorched* before it can grow lush
and tall.

[28] "But I know you well—
where you stay
and when you come and go.
I know the way you have raged
against me.
[29] And because of your raging against me
and your arrogance, which I have heard
for myself,
I will put my hook in your nose
and my bit in your mouth.
I will make you return
by the same road on which you came."

[30]Then Isaiah said to Hezekiah, "Here is the
proof that what I say is true:

"This year you will eat only what grows
up by itself,
and next year you will eat what springs
up from that.
But in the third year you will plant crops
and harvest them;
you will tend vineyards and eat their
fruit.
[31] And you who are left in Judah,
who have escaped the ravages of the
siege,
will put roots down in your own soil
and grow up and flourish.
[32] For a remnant of my people will spread
out from Jerusalem,
a group of survivors from Mount Zion.
The passionate commitment of the LORD
of Heaven's Armies
will make this happen!

[33]"And this is what the LORD says about the
king of Assyria:

"'His armies will not enter Jerusalem.
They will not even shoot an arrow at it.
They will not march outside its gates with
their shields
nor build banks of earth against
its walls.

37:20 As in Dead Sea Scrolls (see also 2 Kgs 19:19); Masoretic Text reads *you alone are the LORD.* **37:25** As in Dead Sea Scrolls (see also 2 Kgs 19:24); Masoretic Text lacks *in many foreign lands.* **37:27** As in Dead Sea Scrolls and some Greek manuscripts (see also 2 Kgs 19:26); most Hebrew manuscripts read *like a terraced field.*

34 The king will return to his own country
by the same road on which he came.
He will not enter this city,'
says the LORD.
35 'For my own honor and for the sake of my
servant David,
I will defend this city and protect it.'"

36 That night the angel of the LORD went out to the Assyrian camp and killed 185,000 Assyrian soldiers. When the surviving Assyrians* woke up the next morning, they found corpses everywhere. 37 Then King Sennacherib of Assyria broke camp and returned to his own land. He went home to his capital of Nineveh and stayed there.

38 One day while he was worshiping in the temple of his god Nisroch, his sons Adrammelech and Sharezer killed him with their swords. They then escaped to the land of Ararat, and another son, Esarhaddon, became the next king of Assyria.

CHAPTER 38

Hezekiah's Sickness and Recovery

About that time Hezekiah became deathly ill, and the prophet Isaiah son of Amoz went to visit him. He gave the king this message: "This is what the LORD says: 'Set your affairs in order, for you are going to die. You will not recover from this illness.'"

AMAZING FACTS

Because of one man's prayer, time actually went *backwards*. That's powerful praying!

ISAIAH 38:1-8

2 When Hezekiah heard this, he turned his face to the wall and prayed to the LORD, 3 "Remember, O LORD, how I have always been faithful to you and have served you single-mindedly, always doing what pleases you." Then he broke down and wept bitterly.

4 Then this message came to Isaiah from the LORD: 5 "Go back to Hezekiah and tell him, 'This is what the LORD, the God of your ancestor David, says: I have heard your prayer and seen your tears. I will add fifteen years to your life, 6 and I will rescue you and this city from the king of Assyria. Yes, I will defend this city.

7 "'And this is the sign from the LORD to prove that he will do as he promised: 8 I will cause the sun's shadow to move ten steps backward on the sundial* of Ahaz!'" So the shadow on the sundial moved backward ten steps.

Hezekiah's Poem of Praise

9 When King Hezekiah was well again, he wrote this poem:

10 I said, "In the prime of my life,
must I now enter the place of the
dead?*
Am I to be robbed of the rest of my
years?"
11 I said, "Never again will I see the LORD
GOD
while still in the land of the living.
Never again will I see my friends
or be with those who live in this
world.
12 My life has been blown away
like a shepherd's tent in a storm.
It has been cut short,
as when a weaver cuts cloth from
a loom.
Suddenly, my life was over.
13 I waited patiently all night,
but I was torn apart as though
by lions.
Suddenly, my life was over.
14 Delirious, I chattered like a swallow
or a crane,
and then I moaned like a mourning
dove.
My eyes grew tired of looking to heaven
for help.
I am in trouble, Lord. Help me!"
15 But what could I say?
For he himself sent this sickness.

37:36 Hebrew *When they.* 38:8 Hebrew *the steps.* 38:10 Hebrew *enter the gates of Sheol?*

Now I will walk humbly throughout
my years
because of this anguish I have felt.
16 Lord, your discipline is good,
for it leads to life and health.
You restore my health
and allow me to live!
17 Yes, this anguish was good for me,
for you have rescued me from death
and forgiven all my sins.
18 For the dead* cannot praise you;
they cannot raise their voices in praise.
Those who go down to the grave
can no longer hope in your
faithfulness.
19 Only the living can praise you as I do
today.
Each generation tells of your
faithfulness to the next.
20 Think of it—the LORD is ready to heal me!
I will sing his praises with instruments
every day of my life
in the Temple of the LORD.

21 Isaiah had said to Hezekiah's servants, "Make an ointment from figs and spread it over the boil, and Hezekiah will recover."

22 And Hezekiah had asked, "What sign will prove that I will go to the Temple of the LORD?"

CHAPTER 39

Envoys from Babylon

Soon after this, Merodach-baladan son of Baladan, king of Babylon, sent Hezekiah his best wishes and a gift. He had heard that Hezekiah had been very sick and that he had recovered. 2 Hezekiah was delighted with the Babylonian envoys and showed them everything in his treasure-houses—the silver, the gold, the spices, and the aromatic oils. He also took them to see his armory and showed them everything in his royal treasuries! There was nothing in his palace or kingdom that Hezekiah did not show them.

3 Then Isaiah the prophet went to King Hezekiah and asked him, "What did those men want? Where were they from?"

Hezekiah replied, "They came from the distant land of Babylon."

4 "What did they see in your palace?" asked Isaiah.

"They saw everything," Hezekiah replied. "I showed them everything I own—all my royal treasuries."

5 Then Isaiah said to Hezekiah, "Listen to this message from the LORD of Heaven's Armies: 6 'The time is coming when everything in your palace—all the treasures stored up by your ancestors until now—will be carried off to Babylon. Nothing will be left,' says the LORD. 7 'Some of your very own sons will be taken away into exile. They will become eunuchs who will serve in the palace of Babylon's king.'"

8 Then Hezekiah said to Isaiah, "This message you have given me from the LORD is good." For the king was thinking, "At least there will be peace and security during my lifetime."

CHAPTER 40

Comfort for God's People

1 "Comfort, comfort my people,"
says your God.
2 "Speak tenderly to Jerusalem.
Tell her that her sad days are gone
and her sins are pardoned.
Yes, the LORD has punished her twice over
for all her sins."

3 Listen! It's the voice of someone shouting,
"Clear the way through the wilderness
for the LORD!
Make a straight highway through the
wasteland
for our God!
4 Fill in the valleys,
and level the mountains and hills.
Straighten the curves,
and smooth out the rough places.
5 Then the glory of the LORD will be
revealed,
and all people will see it together.
The LORD has spoken!"*

6 A voice said, "Shout!"
I asked, "What should I shout?"

"Shout that people are like the grass.
Their beauty fades as quickly
as the flowers in a field.

38:18 Hebrew *Sheol*. **40:3-5** Greek version reads *He is a voice shouting in the wilderness, / "Prepare the way for the LORD's coming! / Clear a road for our God! / Fill in the valleys, / and level the mountains and hills. / And then the glory of the LORD will be revealed, / and all people will see the salvation sent from God. / The LORD has spoken!"* Compare Matt 3:3; Mark 1:3; Luke 3:4-6.

7 The grass withers and the flowers fade
beneath the breath of the LORD.
And so it is with people.
8 The grass withers and the flowers fade,
but the word of our God stands
forever."

9 O Zion, messenger of good news,
shout from the mountaintops!
Shout it louder, O Jerusalem.*
Shout, and do not be afraid.
Tell the towns of Judah,
"Your God is coming!"
10 Yes, the Sovereign LORD is coming in
power.
He will rule with a powerful arm.
See, he brings his reward with him as
he comes.
11 He will feed his flock like a shepherd.
He will carry the lambs in his arms,
holding them close to his heart.
He will gently lead the mother sheep
with their young.

The LORD Has No Equal

12 Who else has held the oceans in
his hand?
Who has measured off the heavens
with his fingers?
Who else knows the weight of the earth
or has weighed the mountains and hills
on a scale?
13 Who is able to advise the Spirit of the
LORD?*
Who knows enough to give him advice
or teach him?
14 Has the LORD ever needed anyone's
advice?
Does he need instruction about what is
good?
Did someone teach him what is right
or show him the path of justice?

15 No, for all the nations of the world
are but a drop in the bucket.
They are nothing more
than dust on the scales.
He picks up the whole earth
as though it were a grain of sand.
16 All the wood in Lebanon's forests
and all Lebanon's animals would
not be enough
to make a burnt offering worthy
of our God.
17 The nations of the world are worth
nothing to him.
In his eyes they count for less than
nothing—
mere emptiness and froth.

The Paper Chase

Miguel had a humongous term paper to write that counted for half of his final grade in his English class. He had been working on it for weeks—researching, reading, and making an outline. After his teacher approved the outline, Miguel started writing. He was doing great and had only two sections left to complete when he became overwhelmed. He can't think of anything more to write. Miguel is exhausted. How is he going to get it all done? What do you think he should do? Read Isaiah 40:29-31 for some good advice.

40:9 Or *O messenger of good news, shout to Zion from the mountaintops! Shout it louder to Jerusalem.* **40:13** Greek version reads *Who can know the LORD's thoughts?* Compare Rom 11:34; 1 Cor 2:16.

18 To whom can you compare God?
What image can you find to resemble him?
19 Can he be compared to an idol formed in a mold,
overlaid with gold, and decorated with silver chains?
20 Or if people are too poor for that,
they might at least choose wood that won't decay
and a skilled craftsman
to carve an image that won't fall down!
21 Haven't you heard? Don't you understand?
Are you deaf to the words of God—
the words he gave before the world began?

Where can I find the strength to keep on doing what's right?

Those who trust in the LORD will find new strength. They will soar high on wings like eagles. They will run and not grow weary. They will walk and not faint. ISAIAH 40:31

Are you so ignorant?
22 God sits above the circle of the earth.
The people below seem like grasshoppers to him!
He spreads out the heavens like a curtain
and makes his tent from them.
23 He judges the great people of the world
and brings them all to nothing.
24 They hardly get started, barely taking root,
when he blows on them and they wither.
The wind carries them off like chaff.
25 "To whom will you compare me?
Who is my equal?" asks the Holy One.
26 Look up into the heavens.
Who created all the stars?
He brings them out like an army, one after another,
calling each by its name.
Because of his great power and incomparable strength,
not a single one is missing.
27 O Jacob, how can you say the LORD does not see your troubles?
O Israel, how can you say God ignores your rights?
28 Have you never heard?
Have you never understood?
The LORD is the everlasting God,
the Creator of all the earth.
He never grows weak or weary.
No one can measure the depths of his understanding.
29 He gives power to the weak
and strength to the powerless.
30 Even youths will become weak and tired,
and young men will fall in exhaustion.
31 But those who trust in the LORD will find new strength.
They will soar high on wings like eagles.
They will run and not grow weary.
They will walk and not faint.

CHAPTER 41

God's Help for Israel

1 "Listen in silence before me, you lands beyond the sea.
Bring your strongest arguments.
Come now and speak.
The court is ready for your case.
2 "Who has stirred up this king from the east,
rightly calling him to God's service?
Who gives this man victory over many nations
and permits him to trample their kings underfoot?
With his sword, he reduces armies to dust.
With his bow, he scatters them like chaff before the wind.
3 He chases them away and goes on safely,
though he is walking over unfamiliar ground.
4 Who has done such mighty deeds,
summoning each new generation from the beginning of time?
It is I, the LORD, the First and the Last.
I alone am he."

5 The lands beyond the sea watch in fear.
Remote lands tremble and mobilize for war.
6 The idol makers encourage one another,
saying to each other, "Be strong!"
7 The carver encourages the goldsmith,
and the molder helps at the anvil.
"Good," they say. "It's coming along fine."
Carefully they join the parts together,
then fasten the thing in place so it won't fall over.

8 "But as for you, Israel my servant,
Jacob my chosen one,
descended from Abraham my friend,
9 I have called you back from the ends of the earth,
saying, 'You are my servant.'
For I have chosen you
and will not throw you away.
10 Don't be afraid, for I am with you.
Don't be discouraged, for I am your God.
I will strengthen you and help you.
I will hold you up with my victorious right hand.

11 "See, all your angry enemies lie there,
confused and humiliated.
Anyone who opposes you will die
and come to nothing.
12 You will look in vain
for those who tried to conquer you.
Those who attack you
will come to nothing.
13 For I hold you by your right hand—
I, the LORD your God.
And I say to you,
'Don't be afraid. I am here to help you.
14 Though you are a lowly worm, O Jacob,
don't be afraid, people of Israel, for I will help you.
I am the LORD, your Redeemer.
I am the Holy One of Israel.'
15 You will be a new threshing instrument
with many sharp teeth.
You will tear your enemies apart,
making chaff of mountains.
16 You will toss them into the air,
and the wind will blow them all away;
a whirlwind will scatter them.
Then you will rejoice in the LORD.
You will glory in the Holy One of Israel.

17 "When the poor and needy search for water and there is none,
and their tongues are parched from thirst,
then I, the LORD, will answer them.
I, the God of Israel, will never abandon them.
18 I will open up rivers for them on the high plateaus.
I will give them fountains of water in the valleys.
I will fill the desert with pools of water.
Rivers fed by springs will flow across the parched ground.
19 I will plant trees in the barren desert—
cedar, acacia, myrtle, olive, cypress, fir, and pine.
20 I am doing this so all who see this miracle will understand what it means—
that it is the LORD who has done this,
the Holy One of Israel who created it.

21 "Present the case for your idols," says the LORD.
"Let them show what they can do," says the King of Israel.*
22 "Let them try to tell us what happened long ago
so that we may consider the evidence.
Or let them tell us what the future holds,
so we can know what's going to happen.
23 Yes, tell us what will occur in the days ahead.
Then we will know you are gods.
In fact, do anything—good or bad!
Do something that will amaze and frighten us.
24 But no! You are less than nothing and can do nothing at all.
Those who choose you pollute themselves.
25 "But I have stirred up a leader who will come from the north.
I have called him by name from the east.
I will give him victory over kings and princes.
He will trample them as a potter treads on clay.

41:21 Hebrew *the King of Jacob*. See note on 14:1.

26 "Who told you from the beginning
that this would happen?
Who predicted this,
making you admit that he was right?
No one said a word!
27 I was the first to tell Zion,
'Look! Help is on the way!'*
I will send Jerusalem a messenger with
good news.
28 Not one of your idols told you this.
Not one gave any answer when I asked.
29 See, they are all foolish, worthless things.
All your idols are as empty as the wind.

CHAPTER 42

The Lord's Chosen Servant

1 "Look at my servant, whom I strengthen.
He is my chosen one, who pleases me.
I have put my Spirit upon him.
He will bring justice to the nations.
2 He will not shout
or raise his voice in public.
3 He will not crush the weakest reed
or put out a flickering candle.
He will bring justice to all who have
been wronged.
4 He will not falter or lose heart
until justice prevails throughout the
earth.
Even distant lands beyond the sea will
wait for his instruction.*"

5 God, the Lord, created the heavens and
stretched them out.
He created the earth and everything
in it.
He gives breath to everyone,
life to everyone who walks the earth.
And it is he who says,
6 "I, the Lord, have called you to
demonstrate my righteousness.
I will take you by the hand and guard
you,
and I will give you to my people, Israel,
as a symbol of my covenant with them.
And you will be a light to guide the
nations.
7 You will open the eyes of the blind.
You will free the captives from prison,
releasing those who sit in dark
dungeons.
8 "I am the Lord; that is my name!
I will not give my glory to anyone else,
nor share my praise with carved idols.
9 Everything I prophesied has come true,
and now I will prophesy again.
I will tell you the future before it
happens."

A Song of Praise to the Lord

10 Sing a new song to the Lord!
Sing his praises from the ends of the
earth!
Sing, all you who sail the seas,
all you who live in distant coastlands.
11 Join in the chorus, you desert towns;
let the villages of Kedar rejoice!
Let the people of Sela sing for joy;
shout praises from the mountaintops!
12 Let the whole world glorify the Lord;
let it sing his praise.
13 The Lord will march forth like a mighty
hero;
he will come out like a warrior, full of
fury.
He will shout his battle cry
and crush all his enemies.

14 He will say, "I have long been silent;
yes, I have restrained myself.
But now, like a woman in labor,
I will cry and groan and pant.
15 I will level the mountains and hills
and blight all their greenery.
I will turn the rivers into dry land
and will dry up all the pools.
16 I will lead blind Israel down a new path,
guiding them along an unfamiliar
way.
I will brighten the darkness before them
and smooth out the road ahead of
them.
Yes, I will indeed do these things;
I will not forsake them.
17 But those who trust in idols,
who say, 'You are our gods,'
will be turned away in shame.

Israel's Failure to Listen and See

18 "Listen, you who are deaf!
Look and see, you blind!
19 Who is as blind as my own people, my
servant?

41:27 Or *'Look! They are coming home.'* **42:4** Greek version reads *And his name will be the hope of all the world.* Compare Matt 12:21.

Who is as deaf as my messenger?
Who is as blind as my chosen people,
the servant of the LORD?
20 You see and recognize what is right
but refuse to act on it.
You hear with your ears,
but you don't really listen."

21 Because he is righteous,
the LORD has exalted his glorious law.
22 But his own people have been robbed and plundered,
enslaved, imprisoned, and trapped.
They are fair game for anyone
and have no one to protect them,
no one to take them back home.

23 Who will hear these lessons from the past
and see the ruin that awaits you in the future?
24 Who allowed Israel to be robbed and hurt?
It was the LORD, against whom we sinned,
for the people would not walk in his path,
nor would they obey his law.
25 Therefore, he poured out his fury on them
and destroyed them in battle.
They were enveloped in flames,
but they still refused to understand.
They were consumed by fire,
but they did not learn their lesson.

CHAPTER 43

The Savior of Israel

1 But now, O Jacob, listen to the LORD who created you.
O Israel, the one who formed you says,
"Do not be afraid, for I have ransomed you.
I have called you by name; you are mine.
2 When you go through deep waters,
I will be with you.
When you go through rivers of difficulty,
you will not drown.
When you walk through the fire of oppression,
you will not be burned up;
the flames will not consume you.
3 For I am the LORD, your God,
the Holy One of Israel, your Savior.
I gave Egypt as a ransom for your freedom;
I gave Ethiopia* and Seba in your place.
4 Others were given in exchange for you.
I traded their lives for yours
because you are precious to me.
You are honored, and I love you.

5 "Do not be afraid, for I am with you.
I will gather you and your children from east and west.
6 I will say to the north and south,
'Bring my sons and daughters back to Israel
from the distant corners of the earth.
7 Bring all who claim me as their God,
for I have made them for my glory.
It was I who created them.'"

8 Bring out the people who have eyes but are blind,
who have ears but are deaf.
9 Gather the nations together!
Assemble the peoples of the world!
Which of their idols has ever foretold such things?
Which can predict what will happen tomorrow?
Where are the witnesses of such predictions?
Who can verify that they spoke the truth?

10 "But you are my witnesses, O Israel!" says the LORD.
"You are my servant.
You have been chosen to know me, believe in me,
and understand that I alone am God.
There is no other God—
there never has been, and there never will be.
11 I, yes I, am the LORD,
and there is no other Savior.
12 First I predicted your rescue,
then I saved you and proclaimed it to the world.
No foreign god has ever done this.
You are witnesses that I am the only God,"
says the LORD.

43:3 Hebrew *Cush.*

I SURVIVED

Nobody likes to think about it, but if you live long enough, you eventually *will* have to say good-bye to people you love.

I was five when my mom was diagnosed with cancer. At first, life just kind of went on like normal. Then, after my brother, Ben, was born, my mom's health took a turn for the worse. We thought for sure she was going to die, but God spared her life. Somehow, miraculously, it was almost like the cancer was completely gone!

A couple of years later, at the same time we found out my mom was pregnant again, the cancer came back. Because of the baby, Mom didn't feel she should take the cancer treatments. There was so much praying. People came over to our house all day long every day and prayed that the baby would be fine and that my mom would be healed.

My sister, Hannah, was fine after she was born—and today she is a very healthy, smart girl. But about one year after her birth, my mom passed away.

Through that experience of losing a parent, I realized that you really have to lean on the rest of your family. It's amazing how close you can get to your family during and after an event like that. You also learn who your real friends are. They are the ones who are there when you need them. Most of all, you realize how much you need God. Even good families and close friends will make mistakes, but God will never fail us. He will always be there. I'm constantly amazed to see how he is able to bring good things out of bad times.

Read Isaiah 43:2 to learn how God comforts us in our troubles. See also Romans 8:28 and Hebrews 13:5 for more encouragement.

13 "From eternity to eternity I am God.
No one can snatch anyone out
of my hand.
No one can undo what I have done."

The Lord's Promise of Victory

14 This is what the Lord says—your Redeemer,
the Holy One of Israel:

"For your sakes I will send an army against
Babylon,
forcing the Babylonians* to flee in
those ships they are so proud of.
15 I am the Lord, your Holy One,
Israel's Creator and King.
16 I am the Lord, who opened a way through
the waters,
making a dry path through the sea.
17 I called forth the mighty army of Egypt
with all its chariots and horses.
I drew them beneath the waves, and they
drowned,
their lives snuffed out like a
smoldering candlewick.

18 "But forget all that—
it is nothing compared to what I am
going to do.
19 For I am about to do something new.
See, I have already begun! Do you not
see it?
I will make a pathway through the
wilderness.
I will create rivers in the dry wasteland.
20 The wild animals in the fields will thank
me,
the jackals and owls, too,
for giving them water in the desert.
Yes, I will make rivers in the dry wasteland
so my chosen people can be refreshed.
21 I have made Israel for myself,
and they will someday honor me before
the whole world.

22 "But, dear family of Jacob, you refuse to
ask for my help.
You have grown tired of me, O Israel!
23 You have not brought me sheep or goats
for burnt offerings.
You have not honored me with
sacrifices,
though I have not burdened and wearied
you
with requests for grain offerings and
frankincense.
24 You have not brought me fragrant
calamus
or pleased me with the fat from
sacrifices.
Instead, you have burdened me with
your sins
and wearied me with your faults.

25 "I—yes, I alone—will blot out your sins for
my own sake
and will never think of them again.
26 Let us review the situation together,
and you can present your case to prove
your innocence.
27 From the very beginning, your first
ancestor sinned against me;
all your leaders broke my laws.
28 That is why I have disgraced your priests;
I have decreed complete destruction*
for Jacob
and shame for Israel.

CHAPTER 44

1 "But now, listen to me, Jacob my
servant,
Israel my chosen one.
2 The Lord who made you and helps you
says:
Do not be afraid, O Jacob, my servant,
O dear Israel,* my chosen one.
3 For I will pour out water to quench your
thirst
and to irrigate your parched fields.
And I will pour out my Spirit on your
descendants,
and my blessing on your children.
4 They will thrive like watered grass,
like willows on a riverbank.
5 Some will proudly claim, 'I belong to the
Lord.'
Others will say, 'I am a descendant of
Jacob.'
Some will write the Lord's name on their
hands
and will take the name of Israel as their
own."

43:14 Or *Chaldeans*. **43:28** The Hebrew term used here refers to the complete consecration of things or people to the Lord, either by destroying them or by giving them as an offering. **44:2** Hebrew *Jeshurun*, a term of endearment for Israel.

The Foolishness of Idols

6 This is what the LORD says—Israel's King and
Redeemer, the LORD of Heaven's Armies:
"I am the First and the Last;
there is no other God.
7 Who is like me?
Let him step forward and prove to you
his power.
Let him do as I have done since ancient
times
when I established a people and
explained its future.
8 Do not tremble; do not be afraid.
Did I not proclaim my purposes for you
long ago?
You are my witnesses—is there any other
God?
No! There is no other Rock—not one!"

9 How foolish are those who manufacture
idols.
These prized objects are really
worthless.
The people who worship idols don't
know this,
so they are all put to shame.
10 Who but a fool would make his
own god—
an idol that cannot help him one bit?
11 All who worship idols will be disgraced
along with all these craftsmen—mere
humans—
who claim they can make a god.
They may all stand together,
but they will stand in terror and shame.

12 The blacksmith stands at his forge to
make a sharp tool,
pounding and shaping it with all his
might.
His work makes him hungry and weak.
It makes him thirsty and faint.
13 Then the wood-carver measures a block
of wood
and draws a pattern on it.
He works with chisel and plane
and carves it into a human figure.
He gives it human beauty
and puts it in a little shrine.
14 He cuts down cedars;
he selects the cypress and the oak;
he plants the pine in the forest
to be nourished by the rain.

15 Then he uses part of the wood to make a
fire.
With it he warms himself and bakes his
bread.
Then—yes, it's true—he takes the rest of it
and makes himself a god to worship!
He makes an idol
and bows down in front of it!
16 He burns part of the tree to roast his meat
and to keep himself warm.
He says, "Ah, that fire feels good."
17 Then he takes what's left
and makes his god: a carved idol!
He falls down in front of it,
worshiping and praying to it.
"Rescue me!" he says.
"You are my god!"

18 Such stupidity and ignorance!
Their eyes are closed, and they cannot
see.
Their minds are shut, and they cannot
think.
19 The person who made the idol never
stops to reflect,
"Why, it's just a block of wood!
I burned half of it for heat
and used it to bake my bread and roast
my meat.
How can the rest of it be a god?
Should I bow down to worship a piece
of wood?"
20 The poor, deluded fool feeds on ashes.
He trusts something that can't help
him at all.
Yet he cannot bring himself to ask,
"Is this idol that I'm holding in my hand
a lie?"

Restoration for Jerusalem

21 "Pay attention, O Jacob,
for you are my servant, O Israel.
I, the LORD, made you,
and I will not forget you.
22 I have swept away your sins like a cloud.
I have scattered your offenses like the
morning mist.
Oh, return to me,
for I have paid the price to set you
free."

23 Sing, O heavens, for the LORD has done
this wondrous thing.

Shout for joy, O depths of the earth!
Break into song,
O mountains and forests and every tree!
For the LORD has redeemed Jacob
and is glorified in Israel.

24 This is what the LORD says—
your Redeemer and Creator:
"I am the LORD, who made all things.
I alone stretched out the heavens.
Who was with me
when I made the earth?
25 I expose the false prophets as liars
and make fools of fortune-tellers.
I cause the wise to give bad advice,
thus proving them to be fools.
26 But I carry out the predictions of my prophets!
By them I say to Jerusalem, 'People will live here again,'
and to the towns of Judah, 'You will be rebuilt;
I will restore all your ruins!'
27 When I speak to the rivers and say, 'Dry up!'
they will be dry.
28 When I say of Cyrus, 'He is my shepherd,'
he will certainly do as I say.
He will command, 'Rebuild Jerusalem';
he will say, 'Restore the Temple.'"

CHAPTER 45

Cyrus, the LORD's Chosen One

1 This is what the LORD says to Cyrus, his anointed one,
whose right hand he will empower.
Before him, mighty kings will be paralyzed with fear.
Their fortress gates will be opened,
never to shut again.
2 This is what the LORD says:

"I will go before you, Cyrus,
and level the mountains.*
I will smash down gates of bronze
and cut through bars of iron.
3 And I will give you treasures hidden in the darkness—
secret riches.
I will do this so you may know that I am the LORD,
the God of Israel, the one who calls you by name.

4 "And why have I called you for this work?
Why did I call you by name when you did not know me?
It is for the sake of Jacob my servant,
Israel my chosen one.
5 I am the LORD;
there is no other God.
I have equipped you for battle,
though you don't even know me,
6 so all the world from east to west
will know there is no other God.
I am the LORD, and there is no other.
7 I create the light and make the darkness.
I send good times and bad times.
I, the LORD, am the one who does these things.

8 "Open up, O heavens,
and pour out your righteousness.
Let the earth open wide
so salvation and righteousness can sprout up together.
I, the LORD, created them.

9 "What sorrow awaits those who argue with their Creator.
Does a clay pot argue with its maker?
Does the clay dispute with the one who shapes it, saying,
'Stop, you're doing it wrong!'
Does the pot exclaim,
'How clumsy can you be?'
10 How terrible it would be if a newborn baby said to its father,
'Why was I born?'
or if it said to its mother,
'Why did you make me this way?'"

11 This is what the LORD says—
the Holy One of Israel and your Creator:
"Do you question what I do for my children?
Do you give me orders about the work of my hands?
12 I am the one who made the earth
and created people to live on it.
With my hands I stretched out the heavens.

45:2 As in Dead Sea Scrolls and Greek version; Masoretic Text reads *the swellings.*

All the stars are at my command.
13 I will raise up Cyrus to fulfill my righteous purpose,
and I will guide his actions.
He will restore my city and free my captive people—
without seeking a reward!
I, the LORD of Heaven's Armies, have spoken!"

Future Conversion of Gentiles

14 This is what the LORD says:

"You will rule the Egyptians,
the Ethiopians,* and the Sabeans.
They will come to you with all their merchandise,
and it will all be yours.
They will follow you as prisoners in chains.
They will fall to their knees in front of you and say,
'God is with you, and he is the only God.
There is no other.'"

15 Truly, O God of Israel, our Savior,
you work in mysterious ways.
16 All craftsmen who make idols will be humiliated.
They will all be disgraced together.
17 But the LORD will save the people of Israel with eternal salvation.
Throughout everlasting ages,
they will never again be humiliated and disgraced.

18 For the LORD is God,
and he created the heavens and earth and put everything in place.
He made the world to be lived in,
not to be a place of empty chaos.
"I am the LORD," he says,
"and there is no other.
19 I publicly proclaim bold promises.
I do not whisper obscurities in some dark corner.
I would not have told the people of Israel* to seek me
if I could not be found.
I, the LORD, speak only what is true
and declare only what is right.

20 "Gather together and come,
you fugitives from surrounding nations.
What fools they are who carry around their wooden idols
and pray to gods that cannot save!
21 Consult together, argue your case.
Get together and decide what to say.
Who made these things known so long ago?
What idol ever told you they would happen?
Was it not I, the LORD?
For there is no other God but me,
a righteous God and Savior.
There is none but me.
22 Let all the world look to me for salvation!
For I am God; there is no other.
23 I have sworn by my own name;
I have spoken the truth,
and I will never go back on my word:
Every knee will bend to me,
and every tongue will confess allegiance to me.*"
24 The people will declare,
"The LORD is the source of all my righteousness and strength."
And all who were angry with him
will come to him and be ashamed.
25 In the LORD all the generations of Israel will be justified,
and in him they will boast.

CHAPTER 46

Babylon's False Gods

1 Bel and Nebo, the gods of Babylon,
bow as they are lowered to the ground.
They are being hauled away on ox carts.
The poor beasts stagger under the weight.
2 Both the idols and their owners are bowed down.
The gods cannot protect the people,
and the people cannot protect the gods.
They go off into captivity together.

3 "Listen to me, descendants of Jacob,
all you who remain in Israel.
I have cared for you since you were born.
Yes, I carried you before you were born.

45:14 Hebrew *Cushites*. **45:19** Hebrew *of Jacob*. See note on 14:1. **45:23** Hebrew *will confess;* Greek version reads *will confess and give praise to God*. Compare Rom 14:11.

4 I will be your God throughout your lifetime—
until your hair is white with age.
I made you, and I will care for you.
I will carry you along and save you.

5 "To whom will you compare me?
Who is my equal?
6 Some people pour out their silver and gold
and hire a craftsman to make a god from it.
Then they bow down and worship it!
7 They carry it around on their shoulders,
and when they set it down, it stays there.
It can't even move!
And when someone prays to it, there is no answer.
It can't rescue anyone from trouble.

8 "Do not forget this! Keep it in mind!
Remember this, you guilty ones.
9 Remember the things I have done in the past.
For I alone am God!
I am God, and there is none like me.
10 Only I can tell you the future
before it even happens.
Everything I plan will come to pass,
for I do whatever I wish.
11 I will call a swift bird of prey from the east—
a leader from a distant land to come and do my bidding.
I have said what I would do,
and I will do it.

12 "Listen to me, you stubborn people
who are so far from doing right.
13 For I am ready to set things right,
not in the distant future, but right now!
I am ready to save Jerusalem*
and show my glory to Israel.

CHAPTER 47

Prediction of Babylon's Fall

1 "Come down, virgin daughter of Babylon,
and sit in the dust.
For your days of sitting on a throne have ended.
O daughter of Babylonia,* never again will you be
the lovely princess, tender and delicate.
2 Take heavy millstones and grind flour.
Remove your veil, and strip off your robe.
Expose yourself to public view.
3 You will be naked and burdened with shame.
I will take vengeance against you without pity."

4 Our Redeemer, whose name is the LORD of Heaven's Armies,
is the Holy One of Israel.

5 "O beautiful Babylon, sit now in darkness and silence.
Never again will you be known as the queen of kingdoms.
6 For I was angry with my chosen people
and punished them by letting them fall into your hands.
But you, Babylon, showed them no mercy.
You oppressed even the elderly.
7 You said, 'I will reign forever as queen of the world!'
You did not reflect on your actions
or think about their consequences.

8 "Listen to this, you pleasure-loving kingdom,
living at ease and feeling secure.
You say, 'I am the only one, and there is no other.
I will never be a widow or lose my children.'
9 Well, both these things will come upon you in a moment:
widowhood and the loss of your children.
Yes, these calamities will come upon you,
despite all your witchcraft and magic.

10 "You felt secure in your wickedness.
'No one sees me,' you said.
But your 'wisdom' and 'knowledge' have led you astray,
and you said, 'I am the only one, and there is no other.'
11 So disaster will overtake you,
and you won't be able to charm it away.
Calamity will fall upon you,
and you won't be able to buy your way out.

46:13 Hebrew *Zion.* **47:1** Or *Chaldea;* also in 47:5.

A catastrophe will strike you suddenly,
one for which you are not prepared.

12 "Now use your magical charms!
Use the spells you have worked at all
these years!
Maybe they will do you some good.
Maybe they can make someone afraid
of you.
13 All the advice you receive has made you
tired.
Where are all your astrologers,
those stargazers who make predictions
each month?
Let them stand up and save you from
what the future holds.
14 But they are like straw burning in
a fire;
they cannot save themselves from the
flame.
You will get no help from them
at all;
their hearth is no place to sit for
warmth.
15 And all your friends,
those with whom you've done business
since childhood,
will go their own ways,
turning a deaf ear to your cries.

CHAPTER 48

God's Stubborn People

1 "Listen to me, O family of Jacob,
you who are called by the name
of Israel
and born into the family
of Judah.
Listen, you who take oaths in the name
of the LORD
and call on the God of Israel.
You don't keep your promises,
2 even though you call yourself the
holy city
and talk about depending on the God
of Israel,
whose name is the LORD of Heaven's
Armies.

TODAY'S IDOLATRY

Isaiah tells us, "How foolish are those who manufacture idols" (44:9). We read about people who worshiped idols of wood and stone in Bible times. But an idol can be anything or anyone we trust in more than God. How would you answer these questions?

Who created me?

To whom do I look to make me feel safe?

Who do I trust most in the world?

To whom do I look to find out what is true?

Who is in charge of what will happen to me?

3 Long ago I told you what was going to happen.
Then suddenly I took action,
and all my predictions came true.
4 For I know how stubborn and obstinate you are.
Your necks are as unbending as iron.
Your heads are as hard as bronze.
5 That is why I told you what would happen;
I told you beforehand what I was going to do.
Then you could never say, 'My idols did it.
My wooden image and metal god commanded it to happen!'
6 You have heard my predictions and seen them fulfilled,
but you refuse to admit it.
Now I will tell you new things,
secrets you have not yet heard.
7 They are brand new, not things from the past.
So you cannot say, 'We knew that all the time!'

8 "Yes, I will tell you of things that are entirely new,
things you never heard of before.
For I know so well what traitors you are.
You have been rebels from birth.
9 Yet for my own sake and for the honor of my name,
I will hold back my anger and not wipe you out.
10 I have refined you, but not as silver is refined.
Rather, I have refined you in the furnace of suffering.
11 I will rescue you for my sake—
yes, for my own sake!
I will not let my reputation be tarnished,
and I will not share my glory with idols!

Freedom from Babylon

12 "Listen to me, O family of Jacob,
Israel my chosen one!
I alone am God,
the First and the Last.
13 It was my hand that laid the foundations of the earth,
my right hand that spread out the heavens above.
When I call out the stars,
they all appear in order."

14 Have any of your idols ever told you this?
Come, all of you, and listen:
The LORD has chosen Cyrus as his ally.
He will use him to put an end to the empire of Babylon
and to destroy the Babylonian* armies.

15 "I have said it: I am calling Cyrus!
I will send him on this errand and will help him succeed.
16 Come closer, and listen to this.
From the beginning I have told you plainly what would happen."

And now the Sovereign LORD and his Spirit
have sent me with this message.
17 This is what the LORD says—
your Redeemer, the Holy One of Israel:
"I am the LORD your God,
who teaches you what is good for you
and leads you along the paths you should follow.
18 Oh, that you had listened to my commands!
Then you would have had peace flowing like a gentle river
and righteousness rolling over you like waves in the sea.
19 Your descendants would have been like the sands along the seashore—
too many to count!
There would have been no need for your destruction,
or for cutting off your family name."

20 Yet even now, be free from your captivity!
Leave Babylon and the Babylonians.*
Sing out this message!
Shout it to the ends of the earth!
The LORD has redeemed his servants,
the people of Israel.*
21 They were not thirsty
when he led them through the desert.
He divided the rock,
and water gushed out for them to drink.
22 "But there is no peace for the wicked,"
says the LORD.

48:14 Or *Chaldean*. **48:20a** Or *the Chaldeans*. **48:20b** Hebrew *his servant, Jacob*. See note on 14:1.

CHAPTER 49

The LORD's Servant Commissioned

1 Listen to me, all you in distant lands!
Pay attention, you who are far away!
The LORD called me before my birth;
from within the womb he called me by name.
2 He made my words of judgment as sharp as a sword.
He has hidden me in the shadow of his hand.
I am like a sharp arrow in his quiver.

3 He said to me, "You are my servant, Israel,
and you will bring me glory."

4 I replied, "But my work seems so useless!
I have spent my strength for nothing and to no purpose.
Yet I leave it all in the LORD's hand;
I will trust God for my reward."

5 And now the LORD speaks—
the one who formed me in my mother's womb to be his servant,
who commissioned me to bring Israel back to him.
The LORD has honored me,
and my God has given me strength.
6 He says, "You will do more than restore the people of Israel to me.
I will make you a light to the Gentiles,
and you will bring my salvation to the ends of the earth."

7 The LORD, the Redeemer
and Holy One of Israel,
says to the one who is despised and rejected by the nations,
to the one who is the servant of rulers:
"Kings will stand at attention when you pass by.
Princes will also bow low
because of the LORD, the faithful one,
the Holy One of Israel, who has chosen you."

Promises of Israel's Restoration

8 This is what the LORD says:

"At just the right time, I will respond to you.*
On the day of salvation I will help you.
I will protect you and give you to the people
as my covenant with them.
Through you I will reestablish the land of Israel
and assign it to its own people again.
9 I will say to the prisoners, 'Come out in freedom,'
and to those in darkness, 'Come into the light.'
They will be my sheep, grazing in green pastures
and on hills that were previously bare.
10 They will neither hunger nor thirst.
The searing sun will not reach them anymore.
For the LORD in his mercy will lead them;
he will lead them beside cool waters.
11 And I will make my mountains into level paths for them.
The highways will be raised above the valleys.
12 See, my people will return from far away,
from lands to the north and west,
and from as far south as Egypt.*"

13 Sing for joy, O heavens!
Rejoice, O earth!
Burst into song, O mountains!
For the LORD has comforted his people
and will have compassion on them in their suffering.

14 Yet Jerusalem* says, "The LORD has deserted us;
the Lord has forgotten us."

15 "Never! Can a mother forget her nursing child?
Can she feel no love for the child she has borne?
But even if that were possible,
I would not forget you!
16 See, I have written your name on the palms of my hands.
Always in my mind is a picture of Jerusalem's walls in ruins.
17 Soon your descendants will come back,
and all who are trying to destroy you will go away.
18 Look around you and see,

49:8 Greek version reads *I heard you*. Compare 2 Cor 6:2. **49:12** As in Dead Sea Scrolls, which read *from the region of Aswan*, which is in southern Egypt. Masoretic Text reads *from the region of Sinim*. **49:14** Hebrew *Zion*.

for all your children will come back to you.
As surely as I live," says the LORD,
"they will be like jewels or bridal ornaments for you to display.

19 "Even the most desolate parts of your abandoned land
will soon be crowded with your people.
Your enemies who enslaved you
will be far away.
20 The generations born in exile will return and say,
'We need more room! It's crowded here!'
21 Then you will think to yourself,
'Who has given me all these descendants?
For most of my children were killed,
and the rest were carried away into exile.
I was left here all alone.
Where did all these people come from?
Who bore these children?
Who raised them for me?'"

22 This is what the Sovereign LORD says:
"See, I will give a signal to the godless nations.
They will carry your little sons back to you in their arms;
they will bring your daughters on their shoulders.
23 Kings and queens will serve you
and care for all your needs.
They will bow to the earth before you
and lick the dust from your feet.
Then you will know that I am the LORD.
Those who trust in me will never be put to shame."

24 Who can snatch the plunder of war from the hands of a warrior?
Who can demand that a tyrant* let his captives go?
25 But the LORD says,
"The captives of warriors will be released,
and the plunder of tyrants will be retrieved.
For I will fight those who fight you,
and I will save your children.
26 I will feed your enemies with their own flesh.
They will be drunk with rivers of their own blood.
All the world will know that I, the LORD,
am your Savior and your Redeemer,
the Mighty One of Israel.*"

CHAPTER 50

This is what the LORD says:

"Was your mother sent away because I divorced her?
Did I sell you as slaves to my creditors?
No, you were sold because of your sins.
And your mother, too, was taken because of your sins.
2 Why was no one there when I came?
Why didn't anyone answer when I called?
Is it because I have no power to rescue?
No, that is not the reason!
For I can speak to the sea and make it dry up!
I can turn rivers into deserts covered with dying fish.
3 I dress the skies in darkness,
covering them with clothes of mourning."

The LORD's Obedient Servant

4 The Sovereign LORD has given me his words of wisdom,
so that I know how to comfort the weary.
Morning by morning he wakens me
and opens my understanding to his will.
5 The Sovereign LORD has spoken to me,
and I have listened.
I have not rebelled or turned away.
6 I offered my back to those who beat me
and my cheeks to those who pulled out my beard.
I did not hide my face
from mockery and spitting.

7 Because the Sovereign LORD helps me,
I will not be disgraced.
Therefore, I have set my face like a stone,
determined to do his will.

49:24 As in Dead Sea Scrolls, Syriac version, and Latin Vulgate (also see 49:25); Masoretic Text reads *a righteous person*.
49:26 Hebrew *of Jacob*. See note on 14:1.

And I know that I will not be put to shame.
8 He who gives me justice is near.
Who will dare to bring charges against me now?
Where are my accusers?
Let them appear!
9 See, the Sovereign LORD is on my side!
Who will declare me guilty?
All my enemies will be destroyed
like old clothes that have been eaten by moths!

10 Who among you fears the LORD
and obeys his servant?
If you are walking in darkness,
without a ray of light,
trust in the LORD
and rely on your God.
11 But watch out, you who live in your own light
and warm yourselves by your own fires.
This is the reward you will receive from me:
You will soon fall down in great torment.

CHAPTER 51

A Call to Trust the LORD

1 "Listen to me, all who hope for deliverance—
all who seek the LORD!
Consider the rock from which you were cut,
the quarry from which you were mined.
2 Yes, think about Abraham, your ancestor,
and Sarah, who gave birth to your nation.
Abraham was only one man when I called him.
But when I blessed him, he became a great nation."

3 The LORD will comfort Israel* again
and have pity on her ruins.
Her desert will blossom like Eden,
her barren wilderness like the garden of the LORD.
Joy and gladness will be found there.
Songs of thanksgiving will fill the air.

4 "Listen to me, my people.
Hear me, Israel,
for my law will be proclaimed,
and my justice will become a light to the nations.
5 My mercy and justice are coming soon.
My salvation is on the way.
My strong arm will bring justice to the nations.
All distant lands will look to me
and wait in hope for my powerful arm.
6 Look up to the skies above,
and gaze down on the earth below.
For the skies will disappear like smoke,
and the earth will wear out like a piece of clothing.
The people of the earth will die like flies,
but my salvation lasts forever.
My righteous rule will never end!

7 "Listen to me, you who know right from wrong,
you who cherish my law in your hearts.
Do not be afraid of people's scorn,
nor fear their insults.
8 For the moth will devour them as it devours clothing.
The worm will eat at them as it eats wool.
But my righteousness will last forever.
My salvation will continue from generation to generation."

9 Wake up, wake up, O LORD! Clothe yourself with strength!
Flex your mighty right arm!
Rouse yourself as in the days of old
when you slew Egypt, the dragon of the Nile.*
10 Are you not the same today,
the one who dried up the sea,
making a path of escape through the depths
so that your people could cross over?
11 Those who have been ransomed by the LORD will return.
They will enter Jerusalem* singing,
crowned with everlasting joy.
Sorrow and mourning will disappear,
and they will be filled with joy and gladness.

51:3 Hebrew *Zion;* also in 51:16. **51:9** Hebrew *You slew Rahab; you pierced the dragon.* Rahab is the name of a mythical sea monster that represents chaos in ancient literature. The name is used here as a poetic name for Egypt. **51:11** Hebrew *Zion.*

12 "I, yes I, am the one who comforts you.
So why are you afraid of mere humans,
who wither like the grass and
disappear?

Why shouldn't I fear what other people might say about me?

"I, yes I, am the one who comforts you. So why are you afraid of mere humans, who wither like the grass and disappear?" ISAIAH 51:12

13 Yet you have forgotten the LORD, your
Creator,
the one who stretched out the sky
like a canopy
and laid the foundations of the earth.
Will you remain in constant dread of
human oppressors?
Will you continue to fear the anger of
your enemies?
Where is their fury and anger now?
It is gone!
14 Soon all you captives will be released!
Imprisonment, starvation, and death
will not be your fate!
15 For I am the LORD your God,
who stirs up the sea, causing its waves
to roar.
My name is the LORD of Heaven's
Armies.
16 And I have put my words in your mouth
and hidden you safely in my hand.
I stretched out* the sky like a canopy
and laid the foundations of the earth.
I am the one who says to Israel,
'You are my people!'"

17 Wake up, wake up, O Jerusalem!
You have drunk the cup of the LORD's
fury.
You have drunk the cup of terror,
tipping out its last drops.
18 Not one of your children is left alive
to take your hand and guide you.
19 These two calamities have fallen on you:
desolation and destruction, famine
and war.
And who is left to sympathize with
you?
Who is left to comfort you?*
20 For your children have fainted and lie in
the streets,
helpless as antelopes caught in
a net.
The LORD has poured out his fury;
God has rebuked them.
21 But now listen to this, you afflicted ones
who sit in a drunken stupor,
though not from drinking wine.
22 This is what the Sovereign LORD,
your God and Defender, says:
"See, I have taken the terrible cup from
your hands.
You will drink no more of my fury.
23 Instead, I will hand that cup to your
tormentors,
those who said, 'We will trample you
into the dust
and walk on your backs.'"

CHAPTER 52

Deliverance for Jerusalem

1 Wake up, wake up, O Zion!
Clothe yourself with strength.
Put on your beautiful clothes, O holy city
of Jerusalem,
for unclean and godless people will
enter your gates no longer.
2 Rise from the dust, O Jerusalem.
Sit in a place of honor.
Remove the chains of slavery from your
neck,
O captive daughter of Zion.
3 For this is what the LORD says:
"When I sold you into exile,
I received no payment.
Now I can redeem you
without having to pay for you."

4 This is what the Sovereign LORD says:
"Long ago my people chose to live in Egypt.
Now they are oppressed by Assyria. 5 What is

51:16 As in Syriac version (see also 51:13); Hebrew reads *planted.* Masoretic Text reads *How can I comfort you?*

51:19 As in Dead Sea Scrolls and Greek, Latin, and Syriac versions;

this?" asks the LORD. "Why are my people enslaved again? Those who rule them shout in exultation. My name is blasphemed all day long.* [6] But I will reveal my name to my people, and they will come to know its power. Then at last they will recognize that I am the one who speaks to them."

[7] How beautiful on the mountains
are the feet of the messenger who brings good news,
the good news of peace and salvation,
the news that the God of Israel* reigns!
[8] The watchmen shout and sing with joy,
for before their very eyes
they see the LORD returning to Jerusalem.*
[9] Let the ruins of Jerusalem break into joyful song,
for the LORD has comforted his people.
He has redeemed Jerusalem.
[10] The LORD has demonstrated his holy power
before the eyes of all the nations.
All the ends of the earth will see
the victory of our God.

[11] Get out! Get out and leave your captivity,
where everything you touch is unclean.
Get out of there and purify yourselves,
you who carry home the sacred objects of the LORD.
[12] You will not leave in a hurry,
running for your lives.
For the LORD will go ahead of you;
yes, the God of Israel will protect you from behind.

The LORD's Suffering Servant

[13] See, my servant will prosper;
he will be highly exalted.
[14] But many were amazed when they saw him.*
His face was so disfigured he seemed hardly human,
and from his appearance, one would scarcely know he was a man.
[15] And he will startle* many nations.
Kings will stand speechless in his presence.
For they will see what they had not been told;
they will understand what they had not heard about.*

CHAPTER 53

[1] Who has believed our message?
To whom has the LORD revealed his powerful arm?
[2] My servant grew up in the LORD's presence like a tender green shoot,
like a root in dry ground.
There was nothing beautiful or majestic about his appearance,
nothing to attract us to him.

AMAZING FACTS

Isaiah described Jesus' death about seven hundred years before it happened!

ISAIAH 53:2-12

[3] He was despised and rejected—
a man of sorrows, acquainted with deepest grief.
We turned our backs on him and looked the other way.
He was despised, and we did not care.

[4] Yet it was our weaknesses he carried;
it was our sorrows* that weighed him down.
And we thought his troubles were a punishment from God,
a punishment for his own sins!
[5] But he was pierced for our rebellion,
crushed for our sins.

52:5 Greek version reads *The Gentiles continually blaspheme my name because of you.* Compare Rom 2:24. **52:7** Hebrew *of Zion.* **52:8** Hebrew *to Zion.* **52:14** As in Syriac version; Hebrew reads *you.* **52:15a** Or *cleanse.* **52:15b** Greek version reads *Those who have never been told about him will see, / and those who have never heard of him will understand.* Compare Rom 15:21. **53:4** Or *Yet it was our sicknesses he carried; / it was our diseases.*

He was beaten so we could be whole.
He was whipped so we could be healed.
6 All of us, like sheep, have strayed away.
We have left God's paths to follow our own.
Yet the LORD laid on him
the sins of us all.

7 He was oppressed and treated harshly,
yet he never said a word.
He was led like a lamb to the slaughter.
And as a sheep is silent before the shearers,
he did not open his mouth.
8 Unjustly condemned,
he was led away.*
No one cared that he died without descendants,
that his life was cut short in midstream.*
But he was struck down
for the rebellion of my people.
9 He had done no wrong
and had never deceived anyone.
But he was buried like a criminal;
he was put in a rich man's grave.

10 But it was the LORD's good plan to crush him
and cause him grief.
Yet when his life is made an offering for sin,
he will have many descendants.
He will enjoy a long life,
and the LORD's good plan will prosper in his hands.
11 When he sees all that is accomplished by his anguish,
he will be satisfied.
And because of his experience,
my righteous servant will make it possible
for many to be counted righteous,
for he will bear all their sins.
12 I will give him the honors of a victorious soldier,
because he exposed himself to death.
He was counted among the rebels.
He bore the sins of many and interceded for rebels.

CHAPTER 54

Future Glory for Jerusalem

1 "Sing, O childless woman,
you who have never given birth!
Break into loud and joyful song, O Jerusalem,
you who have never been in labor.
For the desolate woman now has more children
than the woman who lives with her husband,"
says the LORD.
2 "Enlarge your house; build an addition.
Spread out your home, and spare no expense!
3 For you will soon be bursting at the seams.
Your descendants will occupy other nations
and resettle the ruined cities.

4 "Fear not; you will no longer live in shame.
Don't be afraid; there is no more disgrace for you.
You will no longer remember the shame of your youth
and the sorrows of widowhood.
5 For your Creator will be your husband;
the LORD of Heaven's Armies is his name!
He is your Redeemer, the Holy One of Israel,
the God of all the earth.
6 For the LORD has called you back from your grief—
as though you were a young wife abandoned by her husband,"
says your God.
7 "For a brief moment I abandoned you,
but with great compassion I will take you back.
8 In a burst of anger I turned my face away for a little while.
But with everlasting love I will have compassion on you,"
says the LORD, your Redeemer.

9 "Just as I swore in the time of Noah
that I would never again let a flood cover the earth,

53:8a Greek version reads *He was humiliated and received no justice.* Compare Acts 8:33. **53:8b** Or *As for his contemporaries, / who cared that his life was cut short in midstream?* Greek version reads *Who can speak of his descendants? / For his life was taken from the earth.* Compare Acts 8:33.

I can't believe they left me behind! Do they hate me or what?
I couldn't help but wonder as I watched the bus pull away, loaded with all my friends on their way to David's paintball birthday party. His father had rented a huge charter bus to pick up kids from school and take them out to the party. The guys had brought their overnight bags to class with them, and they were talking it up all day. It was obvious who was going to spend the night at David's that night. And equally obvious who wasn't.

David told me he didn't invite me because they didn't have enough paintball guns. But I knew the truth. He had left me out. As the bus turned the corner and drove out of sight, my parents pulled up in our minivan to take me home. I fought back the tears until I tumbled into the backseat.

At first, I thought about how I could get back at David. I could have a gigantic party and not invite him or his friends. But then I realized that it's not right to leave others out, no matter what they do to me. I talked to my mom about how I felt, and she reminded me that I wasn't the only one who was left out. In fact, I started to notice that some pretty cool people had not been invited. I could hang out with them.

If you've ever been left out, I know how you feel. It hurts. But maybe—like me—after you think about it, you'll realize that missing the party isn't the huge deal you once thought it was. And there are other people to whom you can be a friend.

Check out these verses on rejection: Isaiah 53:3; Matthew 5:4; and Romans 12:17.

DOWN, BUT NOT OUT

Caleb had a great day at school and was in a good mood when he walked up his driveway. But when Caleb walked in the door, he immediately thought, *Something's not right.* His parents were sitting together, and they looked very serious. Dad said, "I have some bad news. I lost my job today." Caleb couldn't think of a thing to say, but a thousand worries filled his brain. *What will Dad do? Why did this have to happen to us?* What might help Caleb feel better? Read Isaiah 54:10 for some comforting things you could tell him.

so now I swear
that I will never again be angry and punish you.
10 For the mountains may move
and the hills disappear,
but even then my faithful love for you will remain.
My covenant of blessing will never be broken,"
says the LORD, who has mercy on you.

11 "O storm-battered city,
troubled and desolate!
I will rebuild you with precious jewels
and make your foundations from lapis lazuli.
12 I will make your towers of sparkling rubies,
your gates of shining gems,
and your walls of precious stones.
13 I will teach all your children,
and they will enjoy great peace.
14 You will be secure under a government that is just and fair.
Your enemies will stay far away.
You will live in peace,
and terror will not come near.
15 If any nation comes to fight you,
it is not because I sent them.
Whoever attacks you will go down in defeat.

16 "I have created the blacksmith
who fans the coals beneath the forge
and makes the weapons of destruction.
And I have created the armies that destroy.
17 But in that coming day
no weapon turned against you will succeed.
You will silence every voice
raised up to accuse you.
These benefits are enjoyed by the servants of the LORD;
their vindication will come from me.
I, the LORD, have spoken!

CHAPTER 55

Invitation to the LORD's Salvation

1 "Is anyone thirsty?
Come and drink—
even if you have no money!
Come, take your choice of wine or milk—
it's all free!
2 Why spend your money on food that does not give you strength?
Why pay for food that does you no good?

Listen to me, and you will eat what
is good.
You will enjoy the finest food.

3 "Come to me with your ears wide open.
Listen, and you will find life.
I will make an everlasting covenant with
you.
I will give you all the unfailing love I
promised to David.
4 See how I used him to display my power
among the peoples.
I made him a leader among the nations.
5 You also will command nations you do
not know,
and peoples unknown to you will come
running to obey,
because I, the LORD your God,
the Holy One of Israel, have made you
glorious."

6 Seek the LORD while you can find him.
Call on him now while he is near.
7 Let the wicked change their ways
and banish the very thought of doing
wrong.
Let them turn to the LORD that he may
have mercy on them.
Yes, turn to our God, for he will forgive
generously.

8 "My thoughts are nothing like your
thoughts," says the LORD.
"And my ways are far beyond anything
you could imagine.
9 For just as the heavens are higher than the
earth,
so my ways are higher than your ways
and my thoughts higher than your
thoughts.

10 "The rain and snow come down from the
heavens
and stay on the ground to water the
earth.
They cause the grain to grow,
producing seed for the farmer
and bread for the hungry.
11 It is the same with my word.
I send it out, and it always produces
fruit.
It will accomplish all I want it to,
and it will prosper everywhere I send it.
12 You will live in joy and peace.
The mountains and hills will burst into
song,
and the trees of the field will clap their
hands!
13 Where once there were thorns, cypress
trees will grow.
Where nettles grew, myrtles will sprout
up.
These events will bring great honor to the
LORD's name;
they will be an everlasting sign of his
power and love."

CHAPTER 56

Blessings for All Nations

This is what the LORD says:

"Be just and fair to all.
Do what is right and good,
for I am coming soon to rescue you
and to display my righteousness among
you.
2 Blessed are all those
who are careful to do this.
Blessed are those who honor my Sabbath
days of rest
and keep themselves from doing
wrong.

3 "Don't let foreigners who commit
themselves to the LORD say,
'The LORD will never let me be part of
his people.'
And don't let the eunuchs say,
'I'm a dried-up tree with no children
and no future.'
4 For this is what the LORD says:
I will bless those eunuchs
who keep my Sabbath days holy
and who choose to do what pleases me
and commit their lives to me.
5 I will give them—within the walls of my
house—
a memorial and a name
far greater than sons and daughters
could give.
For the name I give them is an everlasting
one.
It will never disappear!

6 "I will also bless the foreigners who
commit themselves to the LORD,
who serve him and love his name,

who worship him and do not desecrate
the Sabbath day of rest,
and who hold fast to my covenant.
7 I will bring them to my holy mountain
of Jerusalem
and will fill them with joy in my house
of prayer.
I will accept their burnt offerings and
sacrifices,
because my Temple will be called a
house of prayer for all nations.
8 For the Sovereign LORD,
who brings back the outcasts of Israel,
says:
I will bring others, too,
besides my people Israel."

Sinful Leaders Condemned

9 Come, wild animals of the field!
Come, wild animals of the forest!
Come and devour my people!
10 For the leaders of my people—
the LORD's watchmen, his shepherds—
are blind and ignorant.
They are like silent watchdogs
that give no warning when danger
comes.
They love to lie around, sleeping and
dreaming.
11 Like greedy dogs, they are never
satisfied.
They are ignorant shepherds,
all following their own path
and intent on personal gain.
12 "Come," they say, "let's get some wine and
have a party.
Let's all get drunk.
Then tomorrow we'll do it again
and have an even bigger party!"

CHAPTER 57

1 Good people pass away;
the godly often die before their time.
But no one seems to care or wonder
why.
No one seems to understand
that God is protecting them from the
evil to come.
2 For those who follow godly paths
will rest in peace when they die.

Idolatrous Worship Condemned

3 "But you—come here, you witches'
children,
you offspring of adulterers and
prostitutes!
4 Whom do you mock,
making faces and sticking out your
tongues?
You children of sinners and liars!
5 You worship your idols with great passion

IS IT OK?

IS IT OK IF I'M SCARED TO DIE?

No one looks forward to dying. Since we've never been through it before, it's natural to feel afraid and to wonder if dying might hurt. If we're smart, we take care of ourselves and try to avoid dying as long as we can. But when our time comes, God doesn't want us to be scared. God gives us two very cool verses in Isaiah 57:1-2 that say death isn't as bad as we might think. They remind us that God is always in control and working out his purpose—even in death. God also promises that when Christians die, we will rest in peace. Though it may seem hard to imagine, life with God will be much better than life right now!

beneath the oaks and under every
green tree.
You sacrifice your children down in the
valleys,
among the jagged rocks in the cliffs.
6 Your gods are the smooth stones in the
valleys.
You worship them with liquid offerings
and grain offerings.
They, not I, are your inheritance.
Do you think all this makes me happy?
7 You have committed adultery on every
high mountain.
There you have worshiped idols
and have been unfaithful to me.
8 You have put pagan symbols
on your doorposts and behind your
doors.
You have left me
and climbed into bed with these
detestable gods.
You have committed yourselves to them.
You love to look at their naked bodies.
9 You have given olive oil to Molech*
with many gifts of perfume.
You have traveled far,
even into the world of the dead,*
to find new gods to love.
10 You grew weary in your search,
but you never gave up.
Desire gave you renewed strength,
and you did not grow weary.

11 "Are you afraid of these idols?
Do they terrify you?
Is that why you have lied to me
and forgotten me and my words?
Is it because of my long silence
that you no longer fear me?
12 Now I will expose your so-called good
deeds.
None of them will help you.
13 Let's see if your idols can save you
when you cry to them for help.
Why, a puff of wind can knock them
down!
If you just breathe on them, they fall
over!
But whoever trusts in me will inherit the
land
and possess my holy mountain."

God Forgives the Repentant

14 God says, "Rebuild the road!
Clear away the rocks and stones
so my people can return from
captivity."
15 The high and lofty one who lives in
eternity,
the Holy One, says this:
"I live in the high and holy place
with those whose spirits are contrite
and humble.
I restore the crushed spirit of the humble
and revive the courage of those with
repentant hearts.
16 For I will not fight against you forever;
I will not always be angry.
If I were, all people would pass away—
all the souls I have made.
17 I was angry,
so I punished these greedy people.
I withdrew from them,
but they kept going on their own
stubborn way.
18 I have seen what they do,
but I will heal them anyway!
I will lead them.
I will comfort those who mourn,
19 bringing words of praise to their lips.
May they have abundant peace, both near
and far,"
says the LORD, who heals them.
20 "But those who still reject me are like the
restless sea,
which is never still
but continually churns up mud and
dirt.
21 There is no peace for the wicked,"
says my God.

CHAPTER 58

True and False Worship

1 "Shout with the voice of a trumpet blast.
Shout aloud! Don't be timid.
Tell my people Israel* of their sins!
2 Yet they act so pious!
They come to the Temple every day
and seem delighted to learn all
about me.
They act like a righteous nation
that would never abandon the laws of
its God.

57:9a Or *to the king*. **57:9b** Hebrew *into Sheol*. **58:1** Hebrew *Jacob*. See note on 14:1.

They ask me to take action on their behalf,
pretending they want to be near me.
3 'We have fasted before you!' they say.
'Why aren't you impressed?
We have been very hard on ourselves,
and you don't even notice it!'

"I will tell you why!" I respond.
"It's because you are fasting to please yourselves.
Even while you fast,
you keep oppressing your workers.
4 What good is fasting
when you keep on fighting and quarreling?
This kind of fasting
will never get you anywhere with me.
5 You humble yourselves
by going through the motions of penance,
bowing your heads
like reeds bending in the wind.
You dress in burlap
and cover yourselves with ashes.
Is this what you call fasting?
Do you really think this will please the LORD?

6 "No, this is the kind of fasting I want:
Free those who are wrongly imprisoned;
lighten the burden of those who work for you.
Let the oppressed go free,
and remove the chains that bind people.
7 Share your food with the hungry,
and give shelter to the homeless.
Give clothes to those who need them,
and do not hide from relatives who need your help.

8 "Then your salvation will come like the dawn,
and your wounds will quickly heal.
Your godliness will lead you forward,
and the glory of the LORD will protect you from behind.
9 Then when you call, the LORD will answer.
'Yes, I am here,' he will quickly reply.

"Remove the heavy yoke of oppression.
Stop pointing your finger and spreading vicious rumors!
10 Feed the hungry,
and help those in trouble.
Then your light will shine out from the darkness,
and the darkness around you will be as bright as noon.
11 The LORD will guide you continually,
giving you water when you are dry
and restoring your strength.
You will be like a well-watered garden,
like an ever-flowing spring.
12 Some of you will rebuild the deserted ruins of your cities.
Then you will be known as a rebuilder of walls
and a restorer of homes.

13 "Keep the Sabbath day holy.
Don't pursue your own interests on that day,
but enjoy the Sabbath
and speak of it with delight as the LORD's holy day.
Honor the Sabbath in everything you do on that day,
and don't follow your own desires or talk idly.
14 Then the LORD will be your delight.
I will give you great honor
and satisfy you with the inheritance I promised to your ancestor Jacob.
I, the LORD, have spoken!"

CHAPTER 59

Warnings against Sin

1 Listen! The LORD's arm is not too weak to save you,
nor is his ear too deaf to hear you call.
2 It's your sins that have cut you off from God.
Because of your sins, he has turned away
and will not listen anymore.
3 Your hands are the hands of murderers,
and your fingers are filthy with sin.
Your lips are full of lies,
and your mouth spews corruption.

4 No one cares about being fair and honest.
The people's lawsuits are based on lies.
They conceive evil deeds
and then give birth to sin.

Nobody in my school is homeless, hungry, or lacking clothes. I read in Isaiah 58:5-7 that God says true worship is meeting these needs. So what am I supposed to do to show God's love to other kids?

My friends at school aren't very religious. They dislike people who try to preach to them or act superior and more holy than they are. Bible thumping turns my friends off to God. But they aren't turned off by someone who takes time to be there for them, listens to their problems, and helps them. That's who I am trying to be.

Last week a friend came to me really upset and in tears. Her parents are divorced, and neither of them seems able to find time for her right now. She's got a house to live in, but in reality she is "homeless" because her parents are never there. I'm learning that God shines through me when I "give shelter" to my hurting friends by answering their phone calls in the middle of the night or when I cancel my plans with other friends to help them. My listening gives them a safe, secure place where they can be honest about how they feel.

Hurting friends may have plenty of food in their refrigerator, but they are still hungry for love. I share "food with the hungry" when they see that I care for them. When they are upset, I try to calm them down. When they feel hopeless and unloved, I share Bible verses with them and pray for them. They tell me it gives them a more positive outlook on life.

I'm not doing this by myself. God is helping me show his love to my friends when they need it most.

Read Isaiah 58:5-7 on showing God's love. Then check out Matthew 25:35-40; Luke 3:11; and Hebrews 13:1-2 for other thoughts on sharing God's love.

5 They hatch deadly snakes
and weave spiders' webs.
Whoever falls into their webs will die,
and there's danger even in getting near them.
6 Their webs can't be made into clothing,
and nothing they do is productive.
All their activity is filled with sin,
and violence is their trademark.
7 Their feet run to do evil,
and they rush to commit murder.
They think only about sinning.
Misery and destruction always follow them.
8 They don't know where to find peace
or what it means to be just and good.
They have mapped out crooked roads,
and no one who follows them knows a moment's peace.

9 So there is no justice among us,
and we know nothing about right living.
We look for light but find only darkness.
We look for bright skies but walk in gloom.
10 We grope like the blind along a wall,
feeling our way like people without eyes.
Even at brightest noontime,
we stumble as though it were dark.
Among the living,
we are like the dead.
11 We growl like hungry bears;
we moan like mournful doves.
We look for justice, but it never comes.
We look for rescue, but it is far away from us.
12 For our sins are piled up before God
and testify against us.
Yes, we know what sinners we are.
13 We know we have rebelled and have denied the LORD.
We have turned our backs on our God.
We know how unfair and oppressive we have been,
carefully planning our deceitful lies.
14 Our courts oppose the righteous,
and justice is nowhere to be found.
Truth stumbles in the streets,
and honesty has been outlawed.
15 Yes, truth is gone,
and anyone who renounces evil is attacked.

The LORD looked and was displeased
to find there was no justice.
16 He was amazed to see that no one intervened
to help the oppressed.
So he himself stepped in to save them with his strong arm,
and his justice sustained him.
17 He put on righteousness as his body armor
and placed the helmet of salvation on his head.
He clothed himself with a robe of vengeance
and wrapped himself in a cloak of divine passion.
18 He will repay his enemies for their evil deeds.
His fury will fall on his foes.
He will pay them back even to the ends of the earth.
19 In the west, people will respect the name of the LORD;
in the east, they will glorify him.
For he will come like a raging flood tide
driven by the breath of the LORD.*

20 "The Redeemer will come to Jerusalem
to buy back those in Israel
who have turned from their sins,"*
says the LORD.

21 "And this is my covenant with them," says the LORD. "My Spirit will not leave them, and neither will these words I have given you. They will be on your lips and on the lips of your children and your children's children forever. I, the LORD, have spoken!

CHAPTER 60

Future Glory for Jerusalem

1 "Arise, Jerusalem! Let your light shine for all to see.
For the glory of the LORD rises to shine on you.
2 Darkness as black as night covers all the nations of the earth,

59:19 Or *When the enemy comes like a raging flood tide, / the Spirit of the LORD will drive him back.* **59:20** Hebrew *The Redeemer will come to Zion / to buy back those in Jacob / who have turned from their sins.* Greek version reads *The one who rescues will come on behalf of Zion, / and he will turn Jacob away from ungodliness.* Compare Rom 11:26.

but the glory of the LORD rises and
appears over you.
3 All nations will come to your light;
mighty kings will come to see your
radiance.

4 "Look and see, for everyone is coming
home!
Your sons are coming from distant
lands;
your little daughters will be carried
home.
5 Your eyes will shine,
and your heart will thrill with joy,
for merchants from around the world will
come to you.
They will bring you the wealth of many
lands.
6 Vast caravans of camels will converge on
you,
the camels of Midian and Ephah.
The people of Sheba will bring gold and
frankincense
and will come worshiping the LORD.
7 The flocks of Kedar will be given
to you,
and the rams of Nebaioth will be
brought for my altars.
I will accept their offerings,
and I will make my Temple glorious.

8 "And what do I see flying like clouds to
Israel,
like doves to their nests?
9 They are ships from the ends of the earth,
from lands that trust in me,
led by the great ships of Tarshish.
They are bringing the people of Israel
home from far away,
carrying their silver and gold.
They will honor the LORD your God,
the Holy One of Israel,
for he has filled you with splendor.

10 "Foreigners will come to rebuild your
towns,
and their kings will serve you.
For though I have destroyed you in my
anger,
I will now have mercy on you through
my grace.
11 Your gates will stay open day and night
to receive the wealth of many lands.
The kings of the world will be led as
captives
in a victory procession.
12 For the nations that refuse to serve you
will be destroyed.

13 "The glory of Lebanon will be yours—
the forests of cypress, fir, and pine—
to beautify my sanctuary.
My Temple will be glorious!
14 The descendants of your tormentors
will come and bow before you.
Those who despised you
will kiss your feet.
They will call you the City of the LORD,
and Zion of the Holy One of Israel.

15 "Though you were once despised and
hated,
with no one traveling through you,
I will make you beautiful forever,
a joy to all generations.
16 Powerful kings and mighty nations
will satisfy your every need,
as though you were a child
nursing at the breast of a queen.
You will know at last that I, the LORD,
am your Savior and your Redeemer,
the Mighty One of Israel.*
17 I will exchange your bronze for gold,
your iron for silver,
your wood for bronze,
and your stones for iron.
I will make peace your leader
and righteousness your ruler.
18 Violence will disappear from your land;
the desolation and destruction of war
will end.
Salvation will surround you like city walls,
and praise will be on the lips of all who
enter there.

19 "No longer will you need the sun to shine
by day,
nor the moon to give its light by night,
for the LORD your God will be your
everlasting light,
and your God will be your glory.
20 Your sun will never set;
your moon will not go down.
For the LORD will be your everlasting
light.

60:16 Hebrew *of Jacob*. See note on 14:1.

Your days of mourning will come
to an end.
21 All your people will be righteous.
They will possess their land forever,
for I will plant them there with my own hands
in order to bring myself glory.
22 The smallest family will become a thousand people,
and the tiniest group will become a mighty nation.
At the right time, I, the LORD, will make it happen."

CHAPTER 61

Good News for the Oppressed

1 The Spirit of the Sovereign LORD is upon me,
for the LORD has anointed me
to bring good news to the poor.
He has sent me to comfort the brokenhearted
and to proclaim that captives will be released
and prisoners will be freed.*
2 He has sent me to tell those who mourn
that the time of the LORD's favor has come,*
and with it, the day of God's anger against their enemies.

What can make me glad when things aren't going so well?

I am overwhelmed with joy in the LORD my God! For he has dressed me with the clothing of salvation and draped me in a robe of righteousness. ISAIAH 61:10

3 To all who mourn in Israel,*
he will give a crown of beauty for ashes,
a joyous blessing instead of mourning,
festive praise instead of despair.
In their righteousness, they will be like great oaks
that the LORD has planted for his own glory.
4 They will rebuild the ancient ruins,
repairing cities destroyed long ago.
They will revive them,
though they have been deserted for many generations.
5 Foreigners will be your servants.
They will feed your flocks
and plow your fields
and tend your vineyards.
6 You will be called priests of the LORD,
ministers of our God.
You will feed on the treasures of the nations
and boast in their riches.
7 Instead of shame and dishonor,
you will enjoy a double share of honor.
You will possess a double portion of prosperity in your land,
and everlasting joy will be yours.
8 "For I, the LORD, love justice.
I hate robbery and wrongdoing.
I will faithfully reward my people for their suffering
and make an everlasting covenant with them.
9 Their descendants will be recognized
and honored among the nations.
Everyone will realize that they are a people
the LORD has blessed."
10 I am overwhelmed with joy in the LORD my God!
For he has dressed me with the clothing of salvation
and draped me in a robe of righteousness.
I am like a bridegroom in his wedding suit
or a bride with her jewels.
11 The Sovereign LORD will show his justice to the nations of the world.
Everyone will praise him!
His righteousness will be like a garden in early spring,

61:1 Greek version reads *and the blind will see.* Compare Luke 4:18. **61:2** Or *to proclaim the acceptable year of the LORD.*
61:3 Hebrew *in Zion.*

with plants springing up
everywhere.

CHAPTER 62

Isaiah's Prayer for Jerusalem

1 Because I love Zion,
I will not keep still.
Because my heart yearns for Jerusalem,
I cannot remain silent.
I will not stop praying for her
until her righteousness shines like the dawn,
and her salvation blazes like a burning torch.
2 The nations will see your righteousness.
World leaders will be blinded by your glory.
And you will be given a new name
by the LORD's own mouth.
3 The LORD will hold you in his hand
for all to see—
a splendid crown in the hand of God.
4 Never again will you be called "The Forsaken City"*
or "The Desolate Land."*
Your new name will be "The City of God's Delight"*
and "The Bride of God,"*
for the LORD delights in you
and will claim you as his bride.
5 Your children will commit themselves to you, O Jerusalem,
just as a young man commits himself to his bride.
Then God will rejoice over you
as a bridegroom rejoices over his bride.
6 O Jerusalem, I have posted watchmen on your walls;
they will pray day and night, continually.
Take no rest, all you who pray to the LORD.
7 Give the LORD no rest until he completes his work,
until he makes Jerusalem the pride of the earth.
8 The LORD has sworn to Jerusalem by his own strength:
"I will never again hand you over to your enemies.
Never again will foreign warriors come
and take away your grain and new wine.
9 You raised the grain, and you will eat it, praising the LORD.
Within the courtyards of the Temple,
you yourselves will drink the wine you have pressed."
10 Go out through the gates!
Prepare the highway for my people to return!
Smooth out the road; pull out the boulders;
raise a flag for all the nations to see.
11 The LORD has sent this message to every land:
"Tell the people of Israel,*
'Look, your Savior is coming.
See, he brings his reward with him as he comes.'"
12 They will be called "The Holy People"
and "The People Redeemed by the LORD."
And Jerusalem will be known as "The Desirable Place"
and "The City No Longer Forsaken."

CHAPTER 63

Judgment against the LORD's Enemies

1 Who is this who comes from Edom,
from the city of Bozrah,
with his clothing stained red?
Who is this in royal robes,
marching in his great strength?
"It is I, the LORD, announcing your salvation!
It is I, the LORD, who has the power to save!"
2 Why are your clothes so red,
as if you have been treading out grapes?
3 "I have been treading the winepress alone;
no one was there to help me.
In my anger I have trampled my enemies
as if they were grapes.
In my fury I have trampled my foes.
Their blood has stained my clothes.

62:4a Hebrew *Azubah*, which means "forsaken." **62:4b** Hebrew *Shemamah*, which means "desolate." **62:4c** Hebrew *Hephzibah*, which means "my delight is in her." **62:4d** Hebrew *Beulah*, which means "married." **62:11** Hebrew *Tell the daughter of Zion*.

4 For the time has come for me to avenge
my people,
to ransom them from their oppressors.
5 I was amazed to see that no one
intervened
to help the oppressed.
So I myself stepped in to save them with
my strong arm,
and my wrath sustained me.
6 I crushed the nations in my anger
and made them stagger and fall to the
ground,
spilling their blood upon the earth."

Praise for Deliverance

7 I will tell of the LORD's unfailing love.
I will praise the LORD for all he has
done.
I will rejoice in his great goodness to
Israel,
which he has granted according to his
mercy and love.
8 He said, "They are my very own people.
Surely they will not betray me again."
And he became their Savior.
9 In all their suffering he also suffered,
and he personally* rescued them.
In his love and mercy he redeemed them.
He lifted them up and carried them
through all the years.
10 But they rebelled against him
and grieved his Holy Spirit.
So he became their enemy
and fought against them.

11 Then they remembered those days of old
when Moses led his people out of
Egypt.
They cried out, "Where is the one who
brought Israel through the sea,
with Moses as their shepherd?
Where is the one who sent his Holy Spirit
to be among his people?
12 Where is the one whose power was
displayed
when Moses lifted up his hand—
the one who divided the sea before them,
making himself famous forever?
13 Where is the one who led them through
the bottom of the sea?
They were like fine stallions
racing through the desert, never
stumbling.
14 As with cattle going down into a peaceful
valley,
the Spirit of the LORD gave them rest.
You led your people, LORD,
and gained a magnificent reputation."

Prayer for Mercy and Pardon

15 LORD, look down from heaven;
look from your holy, glorious home,
and see us.
Where is the passion and the might
you used to show on our behalf?
Where are your mercy and compassion
now?
16 Surely you are still our Father!
Even if Abraham and Jacob* would
disown us,
LORD, you would still be our Father.
You are our Redeemer from ages past.
17 LORD, why have you allowed us to turn
from your path?
Why have you given us stubborn hearts
so we no longer fear you?
Return and help us, for we are your
servants,
the tribes that are your special
possession.
18 How briefly your holy people possessed
your holy place,
and now our enemies have destroyed it.
19 Sometimes it seems as though we never
belonged to you,
as though we had never been known as
your people.

CHAPTER 64

1 *Oh, that you would burst from the
heavens and come down!
How the mountains would quake in
your presence!
2 *As fire causes wood to burn
and water to boil,
your coming would make the nations
tremble.
Then your enemies would learn the
reason for your fame!
3 When you came down long ago,
you did awesome deeds beyond our
highest expectations.

63:9 Hebrew *and the angel of his presence.* **63:16** Hebrew *Israel.* See note on 14:1. **64:1** In the Hebrew text this verse is included in 63:19. **64:2** Verses 64:2-12 are numbered 64:1-11 in Hebrew text.

And oh, how the mountains quaked!
4 For since the world began,
no ear has heard
and no eye has seen a God like you,
who works for those who wait for him!
5 You welcome those who gladly do good,
who follow godly ways.
But you have been very angry with us,
for we are not godly.
We are constant sinners;
how can people like us be saved?
6 We are all infected and impure with sin.
When we display our righteous deeds,
they are nothing but filthy rags.
Like autumn leaves, we wither and fall,
and our sins sweep us away like the wind.
7 Yet no one calls on your name
or pleads with you for mercy.
Therefore, you have turned away from us
and turned us over* to our sins.

8 And yet, O LORD, you are our Father.
We are the clay, and you are the potter.
We all are formed by your hand.
9 Don't be so angry with us, LORD.
Please don't remember our sins forever.
Look at us, we pray,
and see that we are all your people.
10 Your holy cities are destroyed.
Zion is a wilderness;
yes, Jerusalem is a desolate ruin.
11 The holy and beautiful Temple
where our ancestors praised you
has been burned down,
and all the things of beauty are destroyed.
12 After all this, LORD, must you still refuse to help us?
Will you continue to be silent and punish us?

CHAPTER 65

Judgment and Final Salvation

The LORD says,

"I was ready to respond, but no one asked for help.

I was ready to be found, but no one was looking for me.
I said, 'Here I am, here I am!'
to a nation that did not call on my name.*
2 All day long I opened my arms to a rebellious people.*
But they follow their own evil paths
and their own crooked schemes.
3 All day long they insult me to my face
by worshiping idols in their sacred gardens.
They burn incense on pagan altars.
4 At night they go out among the graves,
worshiping the dead.
They eat the flesh of pigs

64:7 As in Greek, Syriac, and Aramaic versions; Hebrew reads *melted us*. **65:1** Or *to a nation that did not bear my name*.
65:1-2 Greek version reads *I was found by people who were not looking for me. / I showed myself to those who were not asking for me. / All day long I opened my arms to them, / but they were disobedient and rebellious*. Compare Rom 10:20-21.

and make stews with other forbidden foods.
5 Yet they say to each other,
'Don't come too close or you will defile me!
I am holier than you!'
These people are a stench in my nostrils,
an acrid smell that never goes away.
6 "Look, my decree is written out* in front of me:
I will not stand silent;
I will repay them in full!
Yes, I will repay them—
7 both for their own sins
and for those of their ancestors,"
says the LORD.
"For they also burned incense on the mountains
and insulted me on the hills.
I will pay them back in full!
8 "But I will not destroy them all,"
says the LORD.
"For just as good grapes are found among a cluster of bad ones
(and someone will say, 'Don't throw them all away—
some of those grapes are good!'),
so I will not destroy all Israel.
For I still have true servants there.
9 I will preserve a remnant of the people of Israel*
and of Judah to possess my land.
Those I choose will inherit it,
and my servants will live there.
10 The plain of Sharon will again be filled with flocks
for my people who have searched for me,
and the valley of Achor will be a place to pasture herds.
11 "But because the rest of you have forsaken the LORD
and have forgotten his Temple,
and because you have prepared feasts to honor the god of Fate
and have offered mixed wine to the god of Destiny,
12 now I will 'destine' you for the sword.
All of you will bow down before the executioner.
For when I called, you did not answer.
When I spoke, you did not listen.
You deliberately sinned—before my very eyes—
and chose to do what you know I despise."
13 Therefore, this is what the Sovereign LORD says:
"My servants will eat,
but you will starve.
My servants will drink,
but you will be thirsty.
My servants will rejoice,
but you will be sad and ashamed.
14 My servants will sing for joy,
but you will cry in sorrow and despair.
15 Your name will be a curse word among my people,
for the Sovereign LORD will destroy you
and will call his true servants by another name.
16 All who invoke a blessing or take an oath will do so by the God of truth.
For I will put aside my anger
and forget the evil of earlier days.
17 "Look! I am creating new heavens and a new earth,
and no one will even think about the old ones anymore.
18 Be glad; rejoice forever in my creation!
And look! I will create Jerusalem as a place of happiness.
Her people will be a source of joy.
19 I will rejoice over Jerusalem
and delight in my people.
And the sound of weeping and crying will be heard in it no more.
20 "No longer will babies die when only a few days old.
No longer will adults die before they have lived a full life.
No longer will people be considered old at one hundred!
Only the cursed will die that young!
21 In those days people will live in the houses they build
and eat the fruit of their own vineyards.
22 Unlike the past, invaders will not take their houses

65:6 Or *their sins are written out;* Hebrew reads *it stands written.* **65:9** Hebrew *remnant of Jacob.* See note on 14:1.

and confiscate their vineyards.
For my people will live as long as trees,
and my chosen ones will have time to enjoy their hard-won gains.
23 They will not work in vain,
and their children will not be doomed to misfortune.
For they are people blessed by the LORD,
and their children, too, will be blessed.
24 I will answer them before they even call to me.
While they are still talking about their needs,
I will go ahead and answer their prayers!
25 The wolf and the lamb will feed together.
The lion will eat hay like a cow.
But the snakes will eat dust.
In those days no one will be hurt or destroyed on my holy mountain.
I, the LORD, have spoken!"

CHAPTER 66

This is what the LORD says:

"Heaven is my throne,
and the earth is my footstool.
Could you build me a temple as good as that?
Could you build me such a resting place?
2 My hands have made both heaven and earth;
they and everything in them are mine.*
I, the LORD, have spoken!

"I will bless those who have humble and contrite hearts,
who tremble at my word.
3 But those who choose their own ways—
delighting in their detestable sins—
will not have their offerings accepted.
When such people sacrifice a bull,
it is no more acceptable than a human sacrifice.
When they sacrifice a lamb,
it's as though they had sacrificed a dog!
When they bring an offering of grain,
they might as well offer the blood of a pig.
When they burn frankincense,
it's as if they had blessed an idol.
4 I will send them great trouble—
all the things they feared.
For when I called, they did not answer.
When I spoke, they did not listen.
They deliberately sinned before my very eyes
and chose to do what they know I despise."

5 Hear this message from the LORD,
all you who tremble at his words:
"Your own people hate you
and throw you out for being loyal to my name.
'Let the LORD be honored!' they scoff.
'Be joyful in him!'
But they will be put to shame.
6 What is all the commotion in the city?
What is that terrible noise from the Temple?
It is the voice of the LORD
taking vengeance against his enemies.

7 "Before the birth pains even begin,
Jerusalem gives birth to a son.
8 Who has ever seen anything as strange as this?
Who ever heard of such a thing?
Has a nation ever been born in a single day?
Has a country ever come forth in a mere moment?
But by the time Jerusalem's* birth pains begin,
her children will be born.
9 Would I ever bring this nation to the point of birth
and then not deliver it?" asks the LORD.
"No! I would never keep this nation from being born,"
says your God.

10 "Rejoice with Jerusalem!
Be glad with her, all you who love her
and all you who mourn for her.
11 Drink deeply of her glory
even as an infant drinks at its mother's comforting breasts."

12 This is what the LORD says:
"I will give Jerusalem a river of peace and prosperity.

66:2 As in Greek, Latin, and Syriac versions; Hebrew reads *these things are*. **66:8** Hebrew *Zion's*.

The wealth of the nations will flow
to her.
Her children will be nursed at her breasts,
carried in her arms, and held on her
lap.
13 I will comfort you there in Jerusalem
as a mother comforts her child."

14 When you see these things, your heart
will rejoice.
You will flourish like the grass!
Everyone will see the LORD's hand of
blessing on his servants—
and his anger against his enemies.
15 See, the LORD is coming with fire,
and his swift chariots roar like a
whirlwind.
He will bring punishment with the fury
of his anger
and the flaming fire of his hot rebuke.
16 The LORD will punish the world by fire
and by his sword.
He will judge the earth,
and many will be killed by him.

17 "Those who 'consecrate' and 'purify' themselves in a sacred garden with its idol in the center—feasting on pork and rats and other detestable meats—will come to a terrible end," says the LORD.

18 "I can see what they are doing, and I know what they are thinking. So I will gather all nations and peoples together, and they will see my glory. 19 I will perform a sign among them. And I will send those who survive to be messengers to the nations—to Tarshish, to the Libyans* and Lydians* (who are famous as archers), to Tubal and Greece,* and to all the lands beyond the sea that have not heard of my fame or seen my glory. There they will declare my glory to the nations. 20 They will bring the remnant of your people back from every nation. They will bring them to my holy mountain in Jerusalem as an offering to the LORD. They will ride on horses, in chariots and wagons, and on mules and camels," says the LORD. 21 "And I will appoint some of them to be my priests and Levites. I, the LORD, have spoken!

22 "As surely as my new heavens and earth
will remain,
so will you always be my people,
with a name that will never disappear,"
says the LORD.
23 "All humanity will come to worship me
from week to week
and from month to month.
24 And as they go out, they will see
the dead bodies of those who have
rebelled against me.
For the worms that devour them will
never die,
and the fire that burns them will
never go out.
All who pass by
will view them with utter horror."

66:19a As in some Greek manuscripts, which read *Put* (that is, *Libya*); Hebrew reads *Pul*. **66:19b** Hebrew *Lud*. **66:19c** Hebrew *Javan*.

Jeremiah

WHO
Jeremiah, Judah's kings, Baruch, Ebed-melech, King Nebuchadnezzar, and the Recabites.

WHERE
Judah, and particularly its capital city, Jerusalem.

WHEN
Around 627–586 BC, during Jeremiah's ministry—up to the time when Judah was taken captive by Babylon.

WHY
To show God's people the need to turn away from their sins and turn back to God.

I know, LORD, that our lives are not our own. We are not able to plan our own course. So correct me, LORD.
JEREMIAH 10:23-24

It's fun to win trophies and get compliments for doing a good job. The prophet Jeremiah never got that kind of attention. He was often hurt and frustrated. But he kept on doing his job of telling the truth to God's people. Jeremiah knew that this pleased God.

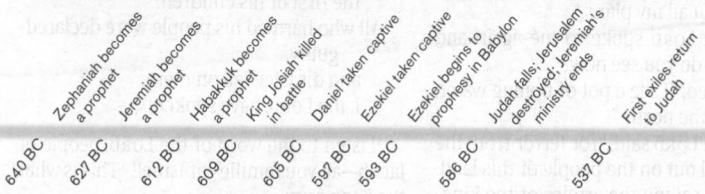

REMEMBER JEREMIAH. GOD IS THE MOST IMPORTANT ONE FOR YOU TO PLEASE.

CHAPTER 1

These are the words of Jeremiah son of Hilkiah, one of the priests from the town of Anathoth in the land of Benjamin. [2]The LORD first gave messages to Jeremiah during the thirteenth year of the reign of Josiah son of Amon, king of Judah.* [3]The LORD's messages continued throughout the reign of King Jehoiakim, Josiah's son, until the eleventh year of the reign of King Zedekiah, another of Josiah's sons. In August* of that eleventh year the people of Jerusalem were taken away as captives.

1:2 The thirteenth year of Josiah's reign was 627 B.C. **1:3** Hebrew *In the fifth month,* of the ancient Hebrew lunar calendar. A number of events in Jeremiah can be cross-checked with dates in surviving Babylonian records and related accurately to our modern calendar. The fifth month in the eleventh year of Zedekiah's reign occurred within the months of August and September 586 B.C. Also see 52:12 and the note there.

Jeremiah's Call and First Visions

4 The LORD gave me this message:

5 "I knew you before I formed you in your mother's womb.
Before you were born I set you apart
and appointed you as my prophet to the nations."

6 "O Sovereign LORD," I said, "I can't speak for you! I'm too young!"

7 The LORD replied, "Don't say, 'I'm too young,' for you must go wherever I send you and say whatever I tell you. 8 And don't be afraid of the people, for I will be with you and will protect you. I, the LORD, have spoken!"

9 Then the LORD reached out and touched my mouth and said,

"Look, I have put my words in your mouth!
10 Today I appoint you to stand up against nations and kingdoms.
Some you must uproot and tear down, destroy and overthrow.
Others you must build up and plant."

11 Then the LORD said to me, "Look, Jeremiah! What do you see?"

And I replied, "I see a branch from an almond tree."

12 And the LORD said, "That's right, and it means that I am watching,* and I will certainly carry out all my plans."

13 Then the LORD spoke to me again and asked, "What do you see now?"

And I replied, "I see a pot of boiling water, spilling from the north."

14 "Yes," the LORD said, "for terror from the north will boil out on the people of this land. 15 Listen! I am calling the armies of the kingdoms of the north to come to Jerusalem. I, the LORD, have spoken!

"They will set their thrones at the gates of the city.
They will attack its walls and all the other towns of Judah.
16 I will pronounce judgment on my people for all their evil—
for deserting me and burning incense to other gods.
Yes, they worship idols made with their own hands!

17 "Get up and prepare for action.
Go out and tell them everything I tell you to say.
Do not be afraid of them,
or I will make you look foolish in front of them.
18 For see, today I have made you strong like a fortified city that cannot be captured,
like an iron pillar or a bronze wall.
You will stand against the whole land—
the kings, officials, priests, and people of Judah.
19 They will fight you, but they will fail.
For I am with you, and I will take care of you.
I, the LORD, have spoken!"

CHAPTER 2

The LORD's Case against His People

The LORD gave me another message. He said, 2 "Go and shout this message to Jerusalem. This is what the LORD says:

"I remember how eager you were to please me
as a young bride long ago,
how you loved me and followed me
even through the barren wilderness.
3 In those days Israel was holy to the LORD,
the first of his children.*
All who harmed his people were declared guilty,
and disaster fell on them.
I, the LORD, have spoken!"

4 Listen to the word of the LORD, people of Jacob—all you families of Israel! 5 This is what the LORD says:

"What did your ancestors find wrong with me
that led them to stray so far from me?
They worshiped worthless idols,
only to become worthless themselves.
6 They did not ask, 'Where is the LORD
who brought us safely out of Egypt
and led us through the barren wilderness—
a land of deserts and pits,

1:12 The Hebrew word for "watching" *(shoqed)* sounds like the word for "almond tree" *(shaqed)*. **2:3** Hebrew *the firstfruits of his harvest.*

a land of drought and death,
where no one lives or even travels?'

7 "And when I brought you into a fruitful land
to enjoy its bounty and goodness,
you defiled my land and
corrupted the possession I had promised you.
8 The priests did not ask,
'Where is the LORD?'
Those who taught my word ignored me,
the rulers turned against me,
and the prophets spoke in the name of Baal,
wasting their time on worthless idols.
9 Therefore, I will bring my case against you,"
says the LORD.
"I will even bring charges against your children's children
in the years to come.

10 "Go west and look in the land of Cyprus*;
go east and search through the land of Kedar.
Has anyone ever heard of anything
as strange as this?
11 Has any nation ever traded its gods for new ones,
even though they are not gods at all?
Yet my people have exchanged their glorious God*
for worthless idols!
12 The heavens are shocked at such a thing
and shrink back in horror and dismay,"
says the LORD.
13 "For my people have done two evil things:
They have abandoned me—
the fountain of living water.
And they have dug for themselves cracked cisterns
that can hold no water at all!

The Results of Israel's Sin

14 "Why has Israel become a slave?
Why has he been carried away as plunder?
15 Strong lions have roared against him,
and the land has been destroyed.
The towns are now in ruins,
and no one lives in them anymore.
16 Egyptians, marching from their cities of Memphis* and Tahpanhes,
have destroyed Israel's glory and power.
17 And you have brought this upon yourselves
by rebelling against the LORD your God,
even though he was leading you on the way!

18 "What have you gained by your alliances with Egypt
and your covenants with Assyria?
What good to you are the streams of the Nile*
or the waters of the Euphrates River?*
19 Your wickedness will bring its own punishment.
Your turning from me will shame you.
You will see what an evil, bitter thing it is
to abandon the LORD your God and not to fear him.
I, the Lord, the LORD of Heaven's Armies, have spoken!

20 "Long ago I broke the yoke that oppressed you
and tore away the chains of your slavery,
but still you said,
'I will not serve you.'
On every hill and under every green tree,
you have prostituted yourselves by bowing down to idols.

AMAZING FACTS

There's a stain you can't clean no matter how hard you scrub or how strong your soap is—only God can get it clean!

JEREMIAH 2:22

2:10 Hebrew *Kittim*. **2:11** Hebrew *their glory*. **2:16** Hebrew *Noph*. **2:18a** Hebrew *of Shihor*, a branch of the Nile River. **2:18b** Hebrew *the river*?

21 But I was the one who planted you,
choosing a vine of the purest stock—
the very best.
How did you grow into this corrupt
wild vine?
22 No amount of soap or lye can make you
clean.
I still see the stain of your guilt.
I, the Sovereign LORD, have spoken!

Israel, an Unfaithful Wife

23 "You say, 'That's not true!
I haven't worshiped the images of Baal!'
But how can you say that?
Go and look in any valley in the land!
Face the awful sins you have done.
You are like a restless female camel
desperately searching for a mate.
24 You are like a wild donkey,
sniffing the wind at mating time.
Who can restrain her lust?
Those who desire her don't need to
search,
for she goes running to them!
25 When will you stop running?
When will you stop panting after other
gods?
But you say, 'Save your breath.
I'm in love with these foreign gods,
and I can't stop loving them now!'
26 "Israel is like a thief
who feels shame only when he gets
caught.
They, their kings, officials, priests, and
prophets—
all are alike in this.
27 To an image carved from a piece of wood
they say,
'You are my father.'
To an idol chiseled from a block of stone
they say,
'You are my mother.'
They turn their backs on me,
but in times of trouble they cry out
to me,
'Come and save us!'
28 But why not call on these gods you have
made?
When trouble comes, let them save you
if they can!
For you have as many gods
as there are towns in Judah.
29 Why do you accuse me of doing wrong?
You are the ones who have rebelled,"
says the LORD.
30 "I have punished your children,
but they did not respond to my
discipline.
You yourselves have killed your prophets
as a lion kills its prey.
31 "O my people, listen to the words of the
LORD!
Have I been like a desert to Israel?
Have I been to them a land of
darkness?
Why then do my people say, 'At last we
are free from God!
We don't need him anymore!'
32 Does a young woman forget her jewelry?
Does a bride hide her wedding dress?
Yet for years on end
my people have forgotten me.
33 "How you plot and scheme to win your
lovers.
Even an experienced prostitute could
learn from you!
34 Your clothing is stained with the blood of
the innocent and the poor,
though you didn't catch them breaking
into your houses!
35 And yet you say,
'I have done nothing wrong.
Surely God isn't angry with me!'
But now I will punish you severely
because you claim you have not sinned.
36 First here, then there—
you flit from one ally to another asking
for help.
But your new friends in Egypt will let you
down,
just as Assyria did before.
37 In despair, you will be led into exile
with your hands on your heads,
for the LORD has rejected the nations you
trust.
They will not help you at all.

CHAPTER 3

1 "If a man divorces a woman
and she goes and marries someone
else,
he will not take her back again,
for that would surely corrupt the land.

But you have prostituted yourself with
many lovers,
so why are you trying to come back
to me?"
says the LORD.
2 "Look at the shrines on every hilltop.
Is there any place you have not been
defiled
by your adultery with other gods?
You sit like a prostitute beside the road
waiting for a customer.
You sit alone like a nomad in the desert.
You have polluted the land with your
prostitution
and your wickedness.
3 That's why even the spring rains have
failed.
For you are a brazen prostitute and
completely shameless.
4 Yet you say to me,
'Father, you have been my guide since
my youth.
5 Surely you won't be angry forever!
Surely you can forget about it!'
So you talk,
but you keep on doing all the evil
you can."

Judah Follows Israel's Example

6 During the reign of King Josiah, the LORD said to me, "Have you seen what fickle Israel has done? Like a wife who commits adultery, Israel has worshiped other gods on every hill and under every green tree. 7 I thought, 'After she has done all this, she will return to me.' But she did not return, and her faithless sister Judah saw this. 8 She saw that I divorced faithless Israel because of her adultery. But that treacherous sister Judah had no fear, and now she, too, has left me and given herself to prostitution. 9 Israel treated it all so lightly—she thought nothing of committing adultery by worshiping idols made of wood and stone. So now the land has been polluted. 10 But despite all this, her faithless sister Judah has never sincerely returned to me. She has only pretended to be sorry. I, the LORD, have spoken!"

Hope for Wayward Israel

11 Then the LORD said to me, "Even faithless Israel is less guilty than treacherous Judah!
12 Therefore, go and give this message to Israel.* This is what the LORD says:

"O Israel, my faithless people,
come home to me again,
for I am merciful.
I will not be angry with you forever.
13 Only acknowledge your guilt.
Admit that you rebelled against the
LORD your God
and committed adultery against him
by worshiping idols under every green
tree.
Confess that you refused to listen
to my voice.
I, the LORD, have spoken!
14 "Return home, you wayward children,"
says the LORD,
"for I am your master.
I will bring you back to the land of
Israel*—
one from this town and two from
that family—
from wherever you are scattered.
15 And I will give you shepherds after my
own heart,
who will guide you with knowledge and
understanding.

16 "And when your land is once more filled with people," says the LORD, "you will no longer wish for 'the good old days' when you possessed the Ark of the LORD's Covenant. You will not miss those days or even remember them, and there will be no need to rebuild the Ark. 17 In that day Jerusalem will be known as 'The Throne of the LORD.' All nations will come there to honor the LORD. They will no longer stubbornly follow their own evil desires. 18 In those days the people of Judah and Israel will return together from exile in the north. They will return to the land I gave their ancestors as an inheritance forever.

19 "I thought to myself,
'I would love to treat you as my own
children!'
I wanted nothing more than to give you
this beautiful land—
the finest possession in the world.
I looked forward to your calling me
'Father,'

3:12 Hebrew *toward the north.* 3:14 Hebrew *to Zion.*

and I wanted you never to turn
from me.
20 But you have been unfaithful to me, you
people of Israel!
You have been like a faithless wife who
leaves her husband.
I, the LORD, have spoken."

21 Voices are heard high on the windswept
mountains,
the weeping and pleading of Israel's
people.
For they have chosen crooked paths
and have forgotten the LORD their God.

22 "My wayward children," says the LORD,
"come back to me, and I will heal your
wayward hearts."

"Yes, we're coming," the people reply,
"for you are the LORD our God.
23 Our worship of idols on the hills
and our religious orgies on the
mountains
are a delusion.
Only in the LORD our God
will Israel ever find salvation.
24 From childhood we have watched
as everything our ancestors worked
for—
their flocks and herds, their sons and
daughters—
was squandered on a delusion.
25 Let us now lie down in shame
and cover ourselves with dishonor,
for we and our ancestors have sinned
against the LORD our God.
From our childhood to this day
we have never obeyed him."

CHAPTER 4

1 "O Israel," says the LORD,
"if you wanted to return to me, you
could.
You could throw away your detestable
idols
and stray away no more.
2 Then when you swear by my name,
saying,
'As surely as the LORD lives,'
you could do so
with truth, justice, and righteousness.
Then you would be a blessing to the
nations of the world,
and all people would come and praise
my name."

Coming Judgment against Judah

3 This is what the LORD says to the people of
Judah and Jerusalem:

"Plow up the hard ground of your hearts!
Do not waste your good seed among
thorns.
4 O people of Judah and Jerusalem,
surrender your pride and power.
Change your hearts before the LORD,*
or my anger will burn like an
unquenchable fire
because of all your sins.

5 "Shout to Judah, and broadcast to
Jerusalem!
Tell them to sound the alarm
throughout the land:
'Run for your lives!
Flee to the fortified cities!'
6 Raise a signal flag as a warning for
Jerusalem*:
'Flee now! Do not delay!'
For I am bringing terrible destruction
upon you
from the north."

7 A lion stalks from its den,
a destroyer of nations.
It has left its lair and is headed your way.
It's going to devastate your land!
Your towns will lie in ruins,
with no one living in them anymore.
8 So put on clothes of mourning
and weep with broken hearts,
for the fierce anger of the LORD
is still upon us.

9 "In that day," says the LORD,
"the king and the officials will tremble
in fear.
The priests will be struck with horror,
and the prophets will be appalled."

10 Then I said, "O Sovereign LORD,
the people have been deceived by what
you said,
for you promised peace for Jerusalem.
But the sword is held at their throats!"

4:4 Hebrew *Circumcise yourselves to the LORD, and take away the foreskins of your heart.* **4:6** Hebrew *Zion.*

11 The time is coming when the LORD will say
to the people of Jerusalem,
"My dear people, a burning wind is blowing in from the desert,
and it's not a gentle breeze useful for winnowing grain.
12 It is a roaring blast sent by me!
Now I will pronounce your destruction!"

13 Our enemy rushes down on us like storm clouds!
His chariots are like whirlwinds.
His horses are swifter than eagles.
How terrible it will be, for we are doomed!
14 O Jerusalem, cleanse your heart
that you may be saved.
How long will you harbor
your evil thoughts?
15 Your destruction has been announced
from Dan and the hill country of Ephraim.

16 "Warn the surrounding nations
and announce this to Jerusalem:
The enemy is coming from a distant land,
raising a battle cry against the towns of Judah.
17 They surround Jerusalem like watchmen around a field,
for my people have rebelled against me," says the LORD.
18 "Your own actions have brought this upon you.
This punishment is bitter, piercing you to the heart!"

Jeremiah Weeps for His People

19 My heart, my heart—I writhe in pain!
My heart pounds within me! I cannot be still.
For I have heard the blast of enemy trumpets
and the roar of their battle cries.
20 Waves of destruction roll over the land,
until it lies in complete desolation.
Suddenly my tents are destroyed;
in a moment my shelters are crushed.
21 How long must I see the battle flags
and hear the trumpets of war?

22 "My people are foolish
and do not know me," says the LORD.
"They are stupid children
who have no understanding.
They are clever enough at doing wrong,
but they have no idea how to do right!"

Jeremiah's Vision of Coming Disaster

23 I looked at the earth, and it was empty and formless.
I looked at the heavens, and there was no light.
24 I looked at the mountains and hills,
and they trembled and shook.
25 I looked, and all the people were gone.
All the birds of the sky had flown away.
26 I looked, and the fertile fields had become a wilderness.
The towns lay in ruins,
crushed by the LORD's fierce anger.

27 This is what the LORD says:
"The whole land will be ruined,
but I will not destroy it completely.
28 The earth will mourn
and the heavens will be draped in black
because of my decree against my people.
I have made up my mind and will not change it."

29 At the noise of charioteers and archers,
the people flee in terror.
They hide in the bushes
and run for the mountains.
All the towns have been abandoned—
not a person remains!
30 What are you doing,
you who have been plundered?
Why do you dress up in beautiful clothing
and put on gold jewelry?
Why do you brighten your eyes with mascara?
Your primping will do you no good!
The allies who were your lovers
despise you and seek to kill you.

31 I hear a cry, like that of a woman in labor,
the groans of a woman giving birth to her first child.
It is beautiful Jerusalem*
gasping for breath and crying out,
"Help! I'm being murdered!"

4:31 Hebrew *the daughter of Zion.*

CHAPTER 5

The Sins of Judah

1 "Run up and down every street in
Jerusalem," says the LORD.
"Look high and low; search throughout
the city!
If you can find even one just and honest
person,
I will not destroy the city.
2 But even when they are under oath,
saying, 'As surely as the LORD lives,'
they are still telling lies!"

3 LORD, you are searching for honesty.
You struck your people,
but they paid no attention.
You crushed them,
but they refused to be corrected.
They are determined, with faces set like
stone;
they have refused to repent.

4 Then I said, "But what can we expect from
the poor?
They are ignorant.
They don't know the ways of the LORD.
They don't understand God's laws.
5 So I will go and speak to their leaders.
Surely they know the ways of the LORD
and understand God's laws."
But the leaders, too, as one man,
had thrown off God's yoke
and broken his chains.
6 So now a lion from the forest will attack
them;
a wolf from the desert will pounce on
them.
A leopard will lurk near their towns,
tearing apart any who dare to venture
out.
For their rebellion is great,
and their sins are many.

7 "How can I pardon you?
For even your children have turned
from me.
They have sworn by gods that are not gods
at all!
I fed my people until they were full.
But they thanked me by committing
adultery
and lining up at the brothels.
8 They are well-fed, lusty stallions,
each neighing for his neighbor's wife.
9 Should I not punish them for this?" says
the LORD.
"Should I not avenge myself against
such a nation?

10 "Go down the rows of the vineyards and
destroy the grapevines,
leaving a scattered few alive.
Strip the branches from the vines,
for these people do not belong to the
LORD.
11 The people of Israel and Judah
are full of treachery against me,"
says the LORD.
12 "They have lied about the LORD
and said, 'He won't bother us!
No disasters will come upon us.
There will be no war or famine.
13 God's prophets are all windbags
who don't really speak for him.
Let their predictions of disaster fall on
themselves!'"

14 Therefore, this is what the LORD God of
Heaven's Armies says:

"Because the people are talking like this,
my messages will flame out of your
mouth
and burn the people like kindling
wood.
15 O Israel, I will bring a distant nation
against you,"
says the LORD.
"It is a mighty nation,
an ancient nation,
a people whose language you do not
know,
whose speech you cannot understand.
16 Their weapons are deadly;
their warriors are mighty.
17 They will devour the food of your harvest;
they will devour your sons and
daughters.
They will devour your flocks and herds;
they will devour your grapes and figs.
And they will destroy your fortified towns,
which you think are so safe.

18 "Yet even in those days I will not blot you
out completely," says the LORD. 19 "And when
your people ask, 'Why did the LORD our God
do all this to us?' you must reply, 'You rejected
him and gave yourselves to foreign gods in

your own land. Now you will serve foreigners
in a land that is not your own.'

A Warning for God's People

20 "Make this announcement to Israel,*
and say this to Judah:
21 Listen, you foolish and senseless people,
with eyes that do not see
and ears that do not hear.
22 Have you no respect for me?
Why don't you tremble in my
presence?
I, the LORD, define the ocean's sandy
shoreline
as an everlasting boundary that the
waters cannot cross.
The waves may toss and roar,
but they can never pass the boundaries
I set.
23 But my people have stubborn and
rebellious hearts.
They have turned away and abandoned
me.
24 They do not say from the heart,
'Let us live in awe of the LORD our God,
for he gives us rain each spring and fall,
assuring us of a harvest when the time
is right.'
25 Your wickedness has deprived you of
these wonderful blessings.
Your sin has robbed you of all these
good things.
26 "Among my people are wicked men
who lie in wait for victims like a hunter
hiding in a blind.
They continually set traps
to catch people.
27 Like a cage filled with birds,
their homes are filled with evil plots.
And now they are great and rich.
28 They are fat and sleek,
and there is no limit to their wicked
deeds.
They refuse to provide justice to orphans
and deny the rights of the poor.
29 Should I not punish them for this?" says
the LORD.
"Should I not avenge myself against
such a nation?
30 A horrible and shocking thing
has happened in this land—
31 the prophets give false prophecies,
and the priests rule with an iron hand.
Worse yet, my people like it that way!
But what will you do when the end
comes?

CHAPTER 6

Jerusalem's Last Warning

1 "Run for your lives, you people of
Benjamin!
Get out of Jerusalem!
Sound the alarm in Tekoa!
Send up a signal at Beth-hakkerem!
A powerful army is coming from the
north,
coming with disaster and destruction.
2 O Jerusalem,* you are my beautiful and
delicate daughter—
but I will destroy you!
3 Enemies will surround you, like
shepherds camped around the city.
Each chooses a place for his troops to
devour.
4 They shout, 'Prepare for battle!
Attack at noon!'
'No, it's too late; the day is fading,
and the evening shadows are falling.'
5 'Well then, let's attack at night
and destroy her palaces!'"
6 This is what the LORD of Heaven's Armies
says:
"Cut down the trees for battering rams.
Build siege ramps against the walls of
Jerusalem.
This is the city to be punished,
for she is wicked through and through.
7 She spouts evil like a fountain.
Her streets echo with the sounds of
violence and destruction.
I always see her sickness and sores.
8 Listen to this warning, Jerusalem,
or I will turn from you in disgust.
Listen, or I will turn you into a heap of
ruins,
a land where no one lives."
9 This is what the LORD of Heaven's Armies
says:
"Even the few who remain in Israel
will be picked over again,

5:20 Hebrew *to the house of Jacob*. The names "Jacob" and "Israel" are often interchanged throughout the Old Testament, referring sometimes to the individual patriarch and sometimes to the nation. **6:2** Hebrew *Daughter of Zion*.

as when a harvester checks each vine a second time
to pick the grapes that were missed."

Judah's Constant Rebellion

10 To whom can I give warning?
Who will listen when I speak?
Their ears are closed,
and they cannot hear.
They scorn the word of the LORD.
They don't want to listen at all.
11 So now I am filled with the LORD's fury.
Yes, I am tired of holding it in!

"I will pour out my fury on children playing in the streets
and on gatherings of young men,
on husbands and wives
and on those who are old and gray.
12 Their homes will be turned over to their enemies,
as will their fields and their wives.
For I will raise my powerful fist
against the people of this land,"
says the LORD.
13 "From the least to the greatest,
their lives are ruled by greed.
From prophets to priests,
they are all frauds.
14 They offer superficial treatments
for my people's mortal wound.
They give assurances of peace
when there is no peace.
15 Are they ashamed of their disgusting actions?
Not at all—they don't even know how to blush!
Therefore, they will lie among the slaughtered.
They will be brought down when I punish them,"
says the LORD.

Judah Rejects the LORD's Way

16 This is what the LORD says:
"Stop at the crossroads and look around.
Ask for the old, godly way, and walk in it.
Travel its path, and you will find rest for your souls.
But you reply, 'No, that's not the road we want!'
17 I posted watchmen over you who said,
'Listen for the sound of the alarm.'
But you replied,
'No! We won't pay attention!'

18 "Therefore, listen to this, all you nations.
Take note of my people's situation.
19 Listen, all the earth!
I will bring disaster on my people.
It is the fruit of their own schemes,
because they refuse to listen to me.
They have rejected my word.
20 There's no use offering me sweet frankincense from Sheba.
Keep your fragrant calamus imported from distant lands!
I will not accept your burnt offerings.
Your sacrifices have no pleasing aroma for me."

21 Therefore, this is what the LORD says:
"I will put obstacles in my people's path.
Fathers and sons will both fall over them.
Neighbors and friends will die together."

An Invasion from the North

22 This is what the LORD says:
"Look! A great army coming from the north!
A great nation is rising against you from far-off lands.
23 They are armed with bows and spears.
They are cruel and show no mercy.
They sound like a roaring sea
as they ride forward on horses.
They are coming in battle formation,
planning to destroy you, beautiful Jerusalem.*"

24 We have heard reports about the enemy,
and we wring our hands in fright.
Pangs of anguish have gripped us,
like those of a woman in labor.
25 Don't go out to the fields!
Don't travel on the roads!
The enemy's sword is everywhere
and terrorizes us at every turn!
26 Oh, my people, dress yourselves in burlap
and sit among the ashes.
Mourn and weep bitterly, as for the loss of an only son.

6:23 Hebrew *daughter of Zion.*

For suddenly the destroying armies will
be upon you!

27 "Jeremiah, I have made you a tester of
metals,*
that you may determine the quality of
my people.
28 They are the worst kind of rebel,
full of slander.
They are as hard as bronze and iron,
and they lead others into corruption.
29 The bellows fiercely fan the flames
to burn out the corruption.
But it does not purify them,
for the wickedness remains.
30 I will label them 'Rejected Silver,'
for I, the LORD, am discarding them."

CHAPTER 7

Jeremiah Speaks at the Temple

The LORD gave another message to Jeremiah. He said, 2"Go to the entrance of the LORD's Temple, and give this message to the people: 'O Judah, listen to this message from the LORD! Listen to it, all of you who worship here! 3This is what the LORD of Heaven's Armies, the God of Israel, says:

"'Even now, if you quit your evil ways, I will let you stay in your own land. 4But don't be fooled by those who promise you safety simply because the LORD's Temple is here. They chant, "The LORD's Temple is here! The LORD's Temple is here!" 5But I will be merciful only if you stop your evil thoughts and deeds and start treating each other with justice; 6only if you stop exploiting foreigners, orphans, and widows; only if you stop your murdering; and only if you stop harming yourselves by worshiping idols. 7Then I will let you stay in this land that I gave to your ancestors to keep forever.

Why is it so important to treat others nicely?

I will be merciful only if you stop your evil thoughts and deeds and start treating each other with justice.

JEREMIAH 7:5

8"'Don't be fooled into thinking that you will never suffer because the Temple is here. It's a lie! 9Do you really think you can steal, murder, commit adultery, lie, and burn incense to Baal and all those other new gods of yours, 10and then come here and stand before me in my Temple and chant, "We are safe!"—only to go right back to all those evils again? 11Don't you yourselves admit that this Temple, which bears my name, has become a den of thieves? Surely I see all the evil going on there. I, the LORD, have spoken!

12"'Go now to the place at Shiloh where I once put the Tabernacle that bore my name. See what I did there because of all the wickedness of my people, the Israelites. 13While you were doing these wicked things, says the LORD, I spoke to you about it repeatedly, but you would not listen. I called out to you, but you refused to answer. 14So just as I destroyed Shiloh, I will now destroy this Temple that bears my name, this Temple that you trust in for help, this place that I gave to you and your ancestors. 15And I will send you out of my sight into exile, just as I did your relatives, the people of Israel.*'

Judah's Persistent Idolatry

16"Pray no more for these people, Jeremiah. Do not weep or pray for them, and don't beg me to help them, for I will not listen to you. 17Don't you see what they are doing throughout the towns of Judah and in the streets of Jerusalem? 18No wonder I am so angry! Watch how the children gather wood and the fathers build sacrificial fires. See how the women knead dough and make cakes to offer to the Queen of Heaven. And they pour out liquid offerings to their other idol gods! 19Am I the one they are hurting?" asks the LORD. "Most of all, they hurt themselves, to their own shame."

20So this is what the Sovereign LORD says: "I will pour out my terrible fury on this place. Its people, animals, trees, and crops will be consumed by the unquenchable fire of my anger."

6:27 As in Greek version; Hebrew reads *a tester of my people a fortress.* **7:15** Hebrew *of Ephraim*, referring to the northern kingdom of Israel.

21 This is what the LORD of Heaven's Armies,
the God of Israel, says: "Take your burnt
offerings and your other sacrifices and eat
them yourselves! 22 When I led your ancestors
out of Egypt, it was not burnt offerings and
sacrifices I wanted from them. 23 This is what
I told them: 'Obey me, and I will be your God,
and you will be my people. Do everything as I
say, and all will be well!'

24 "But my people would not listen to me.
They kept doing whatever they wanted, fol-
lowing the stubborn desires of their evil
hearts. They went backward instead of for-
ward. 25 From the day your ancestors left
Egypt until now, I have continued to send my
servants, the prophets—day in and day out.
26 But my people have not listened to me or
even tried to hear. They have been stubborn
and sinful—even worse than their ancestors.

27 "Tell them all this, but do not expect them
to listen. Shout out your warnings, but do not
expect them to respond. 28 Say to them, 'This is
the nation whose people will not obey the
LORD their God and who refuse to be taught.
Truth has vanished from among them; it is no
longer heard on their lips. 29 Shave your head in
mourning, and weep alone on the mountains.
For the LORD has rejected and forsaken this
generation that has provoked his fury.'

The Valley of Slaughter

30 "The people of Judah have sinned before my
very eyes," says the LORD. "They have set up
their abominable idols right in the Temple
that bears my name, defiling it. 31 They have
built pagan shrines at Topheth, the garbage
dump in the valley of Ben-Hinnom, and there
they burn their sons and daughters in the fire. I
have never commanded such a horrible deed;
it never even crossed my mind to command
such a thing! 32 So beware, for the time is com-
ing," says the LORD, "when that garbage dump
will no longer be called Topheth or the valley
of Ben-Hinnom, but the Valley of Slaughter.
They will bury the bodies in Topheth until
there is no more room for them. 33 The bodies
of my people will be food for the vultures and
wild animals, and no one will be left to scare
them away. 34 I will put an end to the happy
singing and laughter in the streets of Jerusa-
lem. The joyful voices of bridegrooms and
brides will no longer be heard in the towns of
Judah. The land will lie in complete desolation.

CHAPTER 8

"In that day," says the LORD, "the enemy will
break open the graves of the kings and offi-
cials of Judah, and the graves of the priests,
prophets, and common people of Jerusalem.
2 They will spread out their bones on the
ground before the sun, moon, and stars—the
gods my people have loved, served, and wor-
shiped. Their bones will not be gathered up
again or buried but will be scattered on the
ground like manure. 3 And the people of this
evil nation who survive will wish to die rather
than live where I will send them. I, the LORD of
Heaven's Armies, have spoken!

Deception by False Prophets

4 "Jeremiah, say to the people, 'This is what the
LORD says:

"'When people fall down, don't they get
up again?
When they discover they're on the
wrong road, don't they turn back?
5 Then why do these people stay on their
self-destructive path?
Why do the people of Jerusalem refuse
to turn back?
They cling tightly to their lies
and will not turn around.
6 I listen to their conversations
and don't hear a word of truth.
Is anyone sorry for doing wrong?
Does anyone say, "What a terrible thing
I have done"?
No! All are running down the path of sin
as swiftly as a horse galloping into
battle!
7 Even the stork that flies across the sky
knows the time of her migration,
as do the turtledove, the swallow, and the
crane.*
They all return at the proper time
each year.
But not my people!
They do not know the LORD's laws.
8 "'How can you say, "We are wise because
we have the word of the LORD,"
when your teachers have twisted it by
writing lies?

8:7 The identification of some of these birds is uncertain.

9 These wise teachers will fall
into the trap of their own foolishness,
for they have rejected the word of the LORD.
Are they so wise after all?
10 I will give their wives to others
and their farms to strangers.
From the least to the greatest,
their lives are ruled by greed.
Yes, even my prophets and priests are like that.
They are all frauds.
11 They offer superficial treatments
for my people's mortal wound.
They give assurances of peace
when there is no peace.
12 Are they ashamed of these disgusting actions?
Not at all—they don't even know how to blush!
Therefore, they will lie among the slaughtered.
They will be brought down when I punish them,
says the LORD.
13 I will surely consume them.
There will be no more harvests of figs and grapes.
Their fruit trees will all die.
Whatever I gave them will soon be gone.
I, the LORD, have spoken!'

14 "Then the people will say,
'Why should we wait here to die?
Come, let's go to the fortified towns and die there.
For the LORD our God has decreed our destruction
and has given us a cup of poison to drink
because we sinned against the LORD.
15 We hoped for peace, but no peace came.
We hoped for a time of healing, but found only terror.'

16 "The snorting of the enemies' warhorses can be heard
all the way from the land of Dan in the north!
The neighing of their stallions makes the whole land tremble.
They are coming to devour the land
and everything in it—
cities and people alike.
17 I will send these enemy troops among you
like poisonous snakes you cannot charm.
They will bite you, and you will die.
I, the LORD, have spoken!"

Jeremiah Weeps for Sinful Judah

18 My grief is beyond healing;
my heart is broken.
19 Listen to the weeping of my people;
it can be heard all across the land.
"Has the LORD abandoned Jerusalem?*"
the people ask.
"Is her King no longer there?"

"Oh, why have they provoked my anger
with their carved idols
and their worthless foreign gods?" says the LORD.

20 "The harvest is finished,
and the summer is gone," the people cry,
"yet we are not saved!"

21 I hurt with the hurt of my people.
I mourn and am overcome with grief.
22 Is there no medicine in Gilead?
Is there no physician there?
Why is there no healing
for the wounds of my people?

CHAPTER 9

1*If only my head were a pool of water
and my eyes a fountain of tears,
I would weep day and night
for all my people who have been slaughtered.
2*Oh, that I could go away and forget my people
and live in a travelers' shack in the desert.
For they are all adulterers—
a pack of treacherous liars.

Judgment for Disobedience

3 "My people bend their tongues like bows
to shoot out lies.
They refuse to stand up for the truth.
They only go from bad to worse.

8:19 Hebrew *Zion?* **9:1** Verse 9:1 is numbered 8:23 in Hebrew text. **9:2** Verses 9:2-26 are numbered 9:1-25 in Hebrew text.

They do not know me,"
says the LORD.

4 "Beware of your neighbor!
Don't even trust your brother!
For brother takes advantage of brother,
and friend slanders friend.
5 They all fool and defraud each other;
no one tells the truth.
With practiced tongues they tell lies;
they wear themselves out with all their sinning.
6 They pile lie upon lie
and utterly refuse to acknowledge me,"
says the LORD.

7 Therefore, this is what the LORD of Heaven's Armies says:
"See, I will melt them down in a crucible
and test them like metal.
What else can I do with my people?*
8 For their tongues shoot lies like poisoned arrows.
They speak friendly words to their neighbors
while scheming in their heart to kill them.
9 Should I not punish them for this?" says the LORD.
"Should I not avenge myself against such a nation?"

10 I will weep for the mountains
and wail for the wilderness pastures.
For they are desolate and empty of life;
the lowing of cattle is heard no more;
the birds and wild animals have all fled.

11 "I will make Jerusalem into a heap of ruins," says the LORD.
"It will be a place haunted by jackals.
The towns of Judah will be ghost towns,
with no one living in them."

12 Who is wise enough to understand all this? Who has been instructed by the LORD and can explain it to others? Why has the land been so ruined that no one dares to travel through it?

13 The LORD replies, "This has happened because my people have abandoned my instructions; they have refused to obey what I said. 14 Instead, they have stubbornly followed their own desires and worshiped the images of Baal, as their ancestors taught them. 15 So now, this is what the LORD of Heaven's Armies, the God of Israel, says: Look! I will feed them with bitterness and give them poison to drink. 16 I will scatter them around the world, in places they and their ancestors never heard of, and even there I will chase them with the sword until I have destroyed them completely."

Weeping in Jerusalem

17 This is what the LORD of Heaven's Armies says:
"Consider all this, and call for the mourners.
Send for the women who mourn at funerals.
18 Quick! Begin your weeping!
Let the tears flow from your eyes.
19 Hear the people of Jerusalem* crying in despair,
'We are ruined! We are completely humiliated!
We must leave our land,
because our homes have been torn down.'"

20 Listen, you women, to the words of the LORD;
open your ears to what he has to say.
Teach your daughters to wail;
teach one another how to lament.
21 For death has crept in through our windows
and has entered our mansions.
It has killed off the flower of our youth:
Children no longer play in the streets,
and young men no longer gather in the squares.

22 This is what the LORD says:
"Bodies will be scattered across the fields like clumps of manure,
like bundles of grain after the harvest.
No one will be left to bury them."

23 This is what the LORD says:
"Don't let the wise boast in their wisdom,
or the powerful boast in their power,
or the rich boast in their riches.
24 But those who wish to boast
should boast in this alone:

9:7 Hebrew *with the daughter of my people?* Greek version reads *with the evil daughter of my people?* **9:19** Hebrew *Zion.*

The Greatest!

Darius really enjoyed spending time with a certain group of kids because they were nice, lots of fun, and they liked him. Lately, however, everyone seemed to be bragging about how good they were—in sports, in school, and in everything! Darius didn't want to be left out, and he knew he could brag about all his accomplishments too. But Darius didn't like to brag. What do you think he should do? Read Jeremiah 9:23-24 for help in finding an answer.

that they truly know me and understand
that I am the LORD
who demonstrates unfailing love
and who brings justice and
righteousness to the earth,
and that I delight in these things.
I, the LORD, have spoken!

25 "A time is coming," says the LORD, "when
I will punish all those who are circumcised in
body but not in spirit—26 the Egyptians,
Edomites, Ammonites, Moabites, the people
who live in the desert in remote places,* and
yes, even the people of Judah. And like all
these pagan nations, the people of Israel also
have uncircumcised hearts."

CHAPTER 10

Idolatry Brings Destruction

Hear the word that the LORD speaks to you,
O Israel! 2 This is what the LORD says:

"Do not act like the other nations,
who try to read their future in the stars.
Do not be afraid of their predictions,
even though other nations are terrified
by them.
3 Their ways are futile and foolish.
They cut down a tree, and a craftsman
carves an idol.
4 They decorate it with gold and silver
and then fasten it securely with
hammer and nails
so it won't fall over.
5 Their gods are like
helpless scarecrows in a cucumber
field!
They cannot speak,
and they need to be carried because
they cannot walk.
Do not be afraid of such gods,
for they can neither harm you nor do
you any good."

6 LORD, there is no one like you!
For you are great, and your name is full
of power.
7 Who would not fear you, O King of
nations?
That title belongs to you alone!
Among all the wise people of the earth
and in all the kingdoms of the world,
there is no one like you.

8 People who worship idols are stupid and
foolish.
The things they worship are made
of wood!
9 They bring beaten sheets of silver from
Tarshish
and gold from Uphaz,
and they give these materials to skillful
craftsmen
who make their idols.
Then they dress these gods in royal blue
and purple robes

9:26 Or *in the desert and clip the corners of their hair.*

made by expert tailors.
10 But the LORD is the only true God.
He is the living God and the everlasting King!
The whole earth trembles at his anger.
The nations cannot stand up to his wrath.

11 Say this to those who worship other gods: "Your so-called gods, who did not make the heavens and earth, will vanish from the earth and from under the heavens."*

12 But God made the earth by his power,
and he preserves it by his wisdom.
With his own understanding
he stretched out the heavens.
13 When he speaks in the thunder,
the heavens roar with rain.
He causes the clouds to rise over the earth.
He sends the lightning with the rain
and releases the wind from his storehouses.
14 The whole human race is foolish and has no knowledge!
The craftsmen are disgraced by the idols they make,
for their carefully shaped works are a fraud.
These idols have no breath or power.
15 Idols are worthless; they are ridiculous lies!
On the day of reckoning they will all be destroyed.
16 But the God of Israel* is no idol!
He is the Creator of everything that exists,
including Israel, his own special possession.
The LORD of Heaven's Armies is his name!

The Coming Destruction

17 Pack your bags and prepare to leave;
the siege is about to begin.
18 For this is what the LORD says:
"Suddenly, I will fling out
all you who live in this land.
I will pour great troubles upon you,
and at last you will feel my anger."

19 My wound is severe,
and my grief is great.
My sickness is incurable,
but I must bear it.
20 My home is gone,
and no one is left to help me rebuild it.

10:11 The original text of this verse is in Aramaic. **10:16** Hebrew *the Portion of Jacob*. See note on 5:20.

IS IT OK?

IS IT OK TO TRY OTHER RELIGIONS?

Comparing the Lord God, Creator of the universe, to the gods of other religions is like comparing a human to a scarecrow (see Jeremiah 10:5-6). The human and scarecrow might wear the same outfit. They could be the same height and go by the same name. But one can walk away, and the other is helpless even to reach down and tie his shoe. That's what other religions are like—helpless scarecrows. Other religions are a major waste of your time, because the gods of other religions can't walk, talk, or do you any good, let alone get you to heaven (see John 14:6). Trying other religions is an insult to the one true God, who is great and powerful.

My children have been taken away,
and I will never see them again.
21 The shepherds of my people have lost their senses.
They no longer seek wisdom from the LORD.
Therefore, they fail completely,
and their flocks are scattered.
22 Listen! Hear the terrifying roar of great armies
as they roll down from the north.
The towns of Judah will be destroyed
and become a haunt for jackals.

Jeremiah's Prayer

23 I know, LORD, that our lives are not our own.
We are not able to plan our own course.
24 So correct me, LORD, but please be gentle.
Do not correct me in anger, for I would die.
25 Pour out your wrath on the nations that refuse to acknowledge you—
on the peoples that do not call upon your name.
For they have devoured your people Israel*;
they have devoured and consumed them,
making the land a desolate wilderness.

CHAPTER 11

Judah's Broken Covenant

The LORD gave another message to Jeremiah. He said, 2"Remind the people of Judah and Jerusalem about the terms of my covenant with them. 3Say to them, 'This is what the LORD, the God of Israel, says: Cursed is anyone who does not obey the terms of my covenant! 4For I said to your ancestors when I brought them out of the iron-smelting furnace of Egypt, "If you obey me and do whatever I command you, then you will be my people, and I will be your God." 5I said this so I could keep my promise to your ancestors to give you a land flowing with milk and honey—the land you live in today.'"

Then I replied, "Amen, LORD! May it be so."

6Then the LORD said, "Broadcast this message in the streets of Jerusalem. Go from town to town throughout the land and say, 'Remember the ancient covenant, and do everything it requires. 7For I solemnly warned your ancestors when I brought them out of Egypt, "Obey me!" I have repeated this warning over and over to this day, 8but your ancestors did not listen or even pay attention. Instead, they stubbornly followed their own evil desires. And because they refused to obey, I brought upon them all the curses described in this covenant.'"

9Again the LORD spoke to me and said, "I have discovered a conspiracy against me among the people of Judah and Jerusalem. 10They have returned to the sins of their forefathers. They have refused to listen to me and are worshiping other gods. Israel and Judah have both broken the covenant I made with their ancestors. 11Therefore, this is what the LORD says: I am going to bring calamity upon them, and they will not escape. Though they beg for mercy, I will not listen to their cries. 12Then the people of Judah and Jerusalem will pray to their idols and burn incense before them. But the idols will not save them when disaster strikes! 13Look now, people of Judah; you have as many gods as you have towns. You have as many altars of shame—altars for burning incense to your god Baal—as there are streets in Jerusalem.

14"Pray no more for these people, Jeremiah. Do not weep or pray for them, for I will not listen to them when they cry out to me in distress.

15 "What right do my beloved people have to come to my Temple,
when they have done so many immoral things?
Can their vows and sacrifices prevent their destruction?
They actually rejoice in doing evil!
16 I, the LORD, once called them a thriving olive tree,
beautiful to see and full of good fruit.
But now I have sent the fury of their enemies
to burn them with fire,
leaving them charred and broken.

17"I, the LORD of Heaven's Armies, who planted this olive tree, have ordered it

10:25 Hebrew *devoured Jacob*. See note on 5:20.

destroyed. For the people of Israel and Judah
have done evil, arousing my anger by burning
incense to Baal."

A Plot against Jeremiah

18 Then the LORD told me about the plots my
enemies were making against me. 19 I was like
a lamb being led to the slaughter. I had no
idea that they were planning to kill me! "Let's
destroy this man and all his words," they said.
"Let's cut him down, so his name will be for-
gotten forever."

20 O LORD of Heaven's Armies,
you make righteous judgments,
and you examine the deepest thoughts
and secrets.
Let me see your vengeance against them,
for I have committed my cause to you.

21 This is what the LORD says about the men
of Anathoth who wanted me dead. They had
said, "We will kill you if you do not stop
prophesying in the LORD's name." 22 So this is
what the LORD of Heaven's Armies says about
them: "I will punish them! Their young men
will die in battle, and their boys and girls will
starve to death. 23 Not one of these plotters
from Anathoth will survive, for I will bring di-
saster upon them when their time of punish-
ment comes."

CHAPTER 12

Jeremiah Questions the LORD's Justice

1 LORD, you always give me justice
when I bring a case before you.
So let me bring you this complaint:
Why are the wicked so prosperous?
Why are evil people so happy?
2 You have planted them,
and they have taken root and
prospered.
Your name is on their lips,
but you are far from their hearts.
3 But as for me, LORD, you know my heart.
You see me and test my thoughts.
Drag these people away like sheep to be
butchered!
Set them aside to be slaughtered!

4 How long must this land mourn?
Even the grass in the fields has
withered.
The wild animals and birds have
disappeared
because of the evil in the land.
For the people have said,
"The LORD doesn't see what's ahead
for us!"

The LORD's Reply to Jeremiah

5 "If racing against mere men makes you
tired,
how will you race against horses?
If you stumble and fall on open ground,
what will you do in the thickets near
the Jordan?
6 Even your brothers, members of your own
family,
have turned against you.
They plot and raise complaints against
you.
Do not trust them,
no matter how pleasantly they speak.

7 "I have abandoned my people, my special
possession.
I have surrendered my dearest ones to
their enemies.
8 My chosen people have roared at me like
a lion of the forest,
so I have treated them with contempt.
9 My chosen people act like speckled
vultures,*
but they themselves are surrounded
by vultures.
Bring on the wild animals to pick their
corpses clean!

10 "Many rulers have ravaged my vineyard,
trampling down the vines
and turning all its beauty into a barren
wilderness.
11 They have made it an empty wasteland;
I hear its mournful cry.
The whole land is desolate,
and no one even cares.
12 On all the bare hilltops,
destroying armies can be seen.
The sword of the LORD devours people
from one end of the nation to the
other.
No one will escape!
13 My people have planted wheat
but are harvesting thorns.

12:9 Or *speckled hyenas.*

They have worn themselves out,
but it has done them no good.
They will harvest a crop of shame
because of the fierce anger of the
LORD."

A Message for Israel's Neighbors

[14]Now this is what the LORD says: "I will uproot from their land all the evil nations reaching out for the possession I gave my people Israel. And I will uproot Judah from among them. [15]But afterward I will return and have compassion on all of them. I will bring them home to their own lands again, each nation to its own possession. [16]And if these nations truly learn the ways of my people, and if they learn to swear by my name, saying, 'As surely as the LORD lives' (just as they taught my people to swear by the name of Baal), then they will be given a place among my people. [17]But any nation who refuses to obey me will be uprooted and destroyed. I, the LORD, have spoken!"

CHAPTER 13

Jeremiah's Linen Loincloth

This is what the LORD said to me: "Go and buy a linen loincloth and put it on, but do not wash it." [2]So I bought the loincloth as the LORD directed me, and I put it on.

[3]Then the LORD gave me another message: [4]"Take the linen loincloth you are wearing, and go to the Euphrates River.* Hide it there in a hole in the rocks." [5]So I went and hid it by the Euphrates as the LORD had instructed me.

[6]A long time afterward the LORD said to me, "Go back to the Euphrates and get the loincloth I told you to hide there." [7]So I went to the Euphrates and dug it out of the hole where I had hidden it. But now it was rotting and falling apart. The loincloth was good for nothing.

[8]Then I received this message from the LORD: [9]"This is what the LORD says: This shows how I will rot away the pride of Judah and Jerusalem. [10]These wicked people refuse to listen to me. They stubbornly follow their own desires and worship other gods. Therefore, they will become like this loincloth—good for nothing! [11]As a loincloth clings to a man's waist, so I created Judah and Israel to cling to me, says the LORD. They were to be

13:4 Hebrew *Perath;* also in 13:5, 6, 7.

my people, my pride, my glory—an honor to my name. But they would not listen to me.

[12]"So tell them, 'This is what the LORD, the God of Israel, says: May all your jars be filled with wine.' And they will reply, 'Of course! Jars are made to be filled with wine!'

[13]"Then tell them, 'No, this is what the LORD means: I will fill everyone in this land with drunkenness—from the king sitting on David's throne to the priests and the prophets, right down to the common people of Jerusalem. [14]I will smash them against each other, even parents against children, says the LORD. I will not let my pity or mercy or compassion keep me from destroying them.'"

A Warning against Pride

[15] Listen and pay attention!
Do not be arrogant, for the LORD
has spoken.

16 Give glory to the LORD your God
before it is too late.
Acknowledge him before he brings
darkness upon you,
causing you to stumble and fall on the
darkening mountains.
For then, when you look for light,
you will find only terrible darkness and
gloom.
17 And if you still refuse to listen,
I will weep alone because of your pride.
My eyes will overflow with tears,
because the LORD's flock will be led
away into exile.

18 Say to the king and his mother,
"Come down from your thrones
and sit in the dust,
for your glorious crowns
will soon be snatched from your
heads."
19 The towns of the Negev will close their
gates,
and no one will be able to open them.
The people of Judah will be taken away as
captives.
All will be carried into exile.

20 Open up your eyes and see
the armies marching down from the
north!
Where is your flock—
your beautiful flock—
that he gave you to care for?
21 What will you say when the LORD takes
the allies you have cultivated
and appoints them as your rulers?
Pangs of anguish will grip you,
like those of a woman in labor!
22 You may ask yourself,
"Why is all this happening to me?"
It is because of your many sins!
That is why you have been stripped
and raped by invading armies.
23 Can an Ethiopian* change the color
of his skin?
Can a leopard take away its spots?
Neither can you start doing good,
for you have always done evil.

24 "I will scatter you like chaff
that is blown away by the desert
winds.
25 This is your allotment,
the portion I have assigned to you,"
says the LORD,
"for you have forgotten me,
putting your trust in false gods.
26 I myself will strip you
and expose you to shame.
27 I have seen your adultery and lust,
and your disgusting idol worship out in
the fields and on the hills.
What sorrow awaits you, Jerusalem!
How long before you are pure?"

CHAPTER 14

Judah's Terrible Drought

This message came to Jeremiah from the LORD, explaining why he was holding back the rain:

2 "Judah wilts;
commerce at the city gates grinds to a
halt.
All the people sit on the ground in
mourning,
and a great cry rises from Jerusalem.
3 The nobles send servants to get water,
but all the wells are dry.
The servants return with empty pitchers,
confused and desperate,
covering their heads in grief.
4 The ground is parched
and cracked for lack of rain.
The farmers are deeply troubled;
they, too, cover their heads.
5 Even the doe abandons her newborn fawn
because there is no grass in the field.
6 The wild donkeys stand on the bare hills
panting like thirsty jackals.
They strain their eyes looking for grass,
but there is none to be found."
7 The people say, "Our wickedness has
caught up with us, LORD,
but help us for the sake of your own
reputation.
We have turned away from you
and sinned against you again and again.
8 O Hope of Israel, our Savior in times of
trouble,
why are you like a stranger to us?
Why are you like a traveler passing
through the land,
stopping only for the night?

13:23 Hebrew *a Cushite.*

9 Are you also confused?
Is our champion helpless to save us?
You are right here among us, LORD.
We are known as your people.
Please don't abandon us now!"

10 So this is what the LORD says to his people:
"You love to wander far from me
and do not restrain yourselves.
Therefore, I will no longer accept you as my people.
Now I will remember all your wickedness
and will punish you for your sins."

The LORD Forbids Jeremiah to Intercede

11 Then the LORD said to me, "Do not pray for these people anymore. 12 When they fast, I will pay no attention. When they present their burnt offerings and grain offerings to me, I will not accept them. Instead, I will devour them with war, famine, and disease."

13 Then I said, "O Sovereign LORD, their prophets are telling them, 'All is well—no war or famine will come. The LORD will surely send you peace.'"

14 Then the LORD said, "These prophets are telling lies in my name. I did not send them or tell them to speak. I did not give them any messages. They prophesy of visions and revelations they have never seen or heard. They speak foolishness made up in their own lying hearts. 15 Therefore, this is what the LORD says: I will punish these lying prophets, for they have spoken in my name even though I never sent them. They say that no war or famine will come, but they themselves will die by war and famine! 16 As for the people to whom they prophesy—their bodies will be thrown out into the streets of Jerusalem, victims of famine and war. There will be no one left to bury them. Husbands, wives, sons, and daughters—all will be gone. For I will pour out their own wickedness on them. 17 Now, Jeremiah, say this to them:

"Night and day my eyes overflow with tears.
I cannot stop weeping,
for my virgin daughter—my precious people—
has been struck down
and lies mortally wounded.
18 If I go out into the fields,
I see the bodies of people slaughtered by the enemy.
If I walk the city streets,
I see people who have died of starvation.
The prophets and priests continue with their work,
but they don't know what they're doing."

A Prayer for Healing

19 LORD, have you completely rejected Judah?
Do you really hate Jerusalem?*
Why have you wounded us past all hope of healing?
We hoped for peace, but no peace came.
We hoped for a time of healing, but found only terror.
20 LORD, we confess our wickedness
and that of our ancestors, too.
We all have sinned against you.
21 For the sake of your reputation, LORD, do not abandon us.
Do not disgrace your own glorious throne.
Please remember us,
and do not break your covenant with us.
22 Can any of the worthless foreign gods send us rain?
Does it fall from the sky by itself?
No, you are the one, O LORD our God!
Only you can do such things.
So we will wait for you to help us.

CHAPTER 15

Judah's Inevitable Doom

Then the LORD said to me, "Even if Moses and Samuel stood before me pleading for these people, I wouldn't help them. Away with them! Get them out of my sight! 2 And if they say to you, 'But where can we go?' tell them, 'This is what the LORD says:

"'Those who are destined for death, to death;
those who are destined for war, to war;
those who are destined for famine, to famine;
those who are destined for captivity, to captivity.'

14:19 Hebrew *Zion?*

3"I will send four kinds of destroyers
against them," says the LORD. "I will send the
sword to kill, the dogs to drag away, the vul-
tures to devour, and the wild animals to finish
up what is left. 4Because of the wicked things
Manasseh son of Hezekiah, king of Judah, did
in Jerusalem, I will make my people an object
of horror to all the kingdoms of the earth.

5 "Who will feel sorry for you, Jerusalem?
Who will weep for you?
Who will even bother to ask how you
are?
6 You have abandoned me
and turned your back on me,"
says the LORD.
"Therefore, I will raise my fist to destroy
you.
I am tired of always giving you another
chance.
7 I will winnow you like grain at the gates
of your cities
and take away the children you hold dear.
I will destroy my own people,
because they refuse to change their evil
ways.
8 There will be more widows
than the grains of sand on the seashore.
At noontime I will bring a destroyer
against the mothers of young men.
I will cause anguish and terror
to come upon them suddenly.
9 The mother of seven grows faint and
gasps for breath;
her sun has gone down while it is still
day.
She sits childless now,
disgraced and humiliated.
And I will hand over those who are left
to be killed by the enemy.
I, the LORD, have spoken!"

Jeremiah's Complaint

10Then I said,

"What sorrow is mine, my mother.
Oh, that I had died at birth!
I am hated everywhere I go.
I am neither a lender who threatens to
foreclose
nor a borrower who refuses to pay—
yet they all curse me."

11The LORD replied,

"I will take care of you, Jeremiah.
Your enemies will ask you to plead on
their behalf
in times of trouble and distress.
12 Can a man break a bar of iron from
the north,
or a bar of bronze?
13 At no cost to them,
I will hand over your wealth and
treasures
as plunder to your enemies,
for sin runs rampant in your land.
14 I will tell your enemies to take you
as captives to a foreign land.
For my anger blazes like a fire
that will burn forever.*"

15Then I said,

"LORD, you know what's happening to me.
Please step in and help me. Punish my
persecutors!
Please give me time; don't let me die
young.
It's for your sake that I am suffering.
16 When I discovered your words, I
devoured them.
They are my joy and my heart's delight,
for I bear your name,
O LORD God of Heaven's Armies.
17 I never joined the people in their merry
feasts.
I sat alone because your hand was on me.
I was filled with indignation at their
sins.
18 Why then does my suffering continue?
Why is my wound so incurable?
Your help seems as uncertain as a
seasonal brook,
like a spring that has gone dry."

19This is how the LORD responds:

"If you return to me, I will restore you
so you can continue to serve me.
If you speak good words rather than
worthless ones,
you will be my spokesman.
You must influence them;
do not let them influence you!
20 They will fight against you like an
attacking army,

15:14 As in some Hebrew manuscripts (see also 17:4); most Hebrew manuscripts read *will burn against you.*

but I will make you as secure as a
fortified wall of bronze.
They will not conquer you,
for I am with you to protect and
rescue you.
I, the LORD, have spoken!
21 Yes, I will certainly keep you safe from
these wicked men.
I will rescue you from their cruel hands."

CHAPTER 16

Jeremiah Forbidden to Marry

The LORD gave me another message. He said,
2"Do not get married or have children in this
place. 3For this is what the LORD says about
the children born here in this city and about
their mothers and fathers: 4They will die from
terrible diseases. No one will mourn for them
or bury them, and they will lie scattered on
the ground like manure. They will die from
war and famine, and their bodies will be food
for the vultures and wild animals."

Judah's Coming Punishment

5This is what the LORD says: "Do not go to fu-
nerals to mourn and show sympathy for these
people, for I have removed my protection and
peace from them. I have taken away my un-
failing love and my mercy. 6Both the great and
the lowly will die in this land. No one will bury
them or mourn for them. Their friends will
not cut themselves in sorrow or shave their
heads in sadness. 7No one will offer a meal to
comfort those who mourn for the dead—not
even at the death of a mother or father. No
one will send a cup of wine to console them.

8"And do not go to their feasts and parties.
Do not eat and drink with them at all. 9For this
is what the LORD of Heaven's Armies, the God
of Israel, says: In your own lifetime, before
your very eyes, I will put an end to the happy
singing and laughter in this land. The joyful
voices of bridegrooms and brides will no lon-
ger be heard.

10"When you tell the people all these things,
they will ask, 'Why has the LORD decreed such
terrible things against us? What have we done
to deserve such treatment? What is our sin
against the LORD our God?'

11"Then you will give them the LORD's reply:
'It is because your ancestors were unfaithful to
me. They worshiped other gods and served
them. They abandoned me and did not obey
my word. 12And you are even worse than your
ancestors! You stubbornly follow your own evil
desires and refuse to listen to me. 13So I will
throw you out of this land and send you into a
foreign land where you and your ancestors
have never been. There you can worship idols
day and night—and I will grant you no favors!'

Hope despite the Disaster

14"But the time is coming," says the LORD,
"when people who are taking an oath will no
longer say, 'As surely as the LORD lives, who
rescued the people of Israel from the land of
Egypt.' 15Instead, they will say, 'As surely as
the LORD lives, who brought the people of Is-
rael back to their own land from the land of
the north and from all the countries to which
he had exiled them.' For I will bring them
back to this land that I gave their ancestors.

16"But now I am sending for many fisher-
men who will catch them," says the LORD. "I am
sending for hunters who will hunt them down
in the mountains, hills, and caves. 17I am
watching them closely, and I see every sin.
They cannot hope to hide from me. 18I will
double their punishment for all their sins, be-
cause they have defiled my land with lifeless
images of their detestable gods and have filled
my territory with their evil deeds."

Jeremiah's Prayer of Confidence

19 LORD, you are my strength and fortress,
my refuge in the day of trouble!
Nations from around the world
will come to you and say,
"Our ancestors left us a foolish heritage,
for they worshiped worthless idols.
20 Can people make their own gods?
These are not real gods at all!"

21 The LORD says,
"Now I will show them my power;
now I will show them my might.
At last they will know and understand
that I am the LORD.

CHAPTER 17

Judah's Sin and Punishment

1 "The sin of Judah
is inscribed with an iron chisel—
engraved with a diamond point on their
stony hearts

and on the corners of their altars.
2 Even their children go to worship
at their pagan altars and Asherah poles,
beneath every green tree
and on every high hill.
3 So I will hand over my holy mountain—
along with all your wealth and treasures
and your pagan shrines—
as plunder to your enemies,
for sin runs rampant in your land.
4 The wonderful possession I have reserved for you
will slip from your hands.
I will tell your enemies to take you
as captives to a foreign land.
For my anger blazes like a fire
that will burn forever."

Wisdom from the Lord

5 This is what the Lord says:
"Cursed are those who put their trust in mere humans,
who rely on human strength
and turn their hearts away from the Lord.
6 They are like stunted shrubs in the desert,
with no hope for the future.
They will live in the barren wilderness,
in an uninhabited salty land.

7 "But blessed are those who trust in the Lord
and have made the Lord their hope and confidence.
8 They are like trees planted along a riverbank,
with roots that reach deep into the water.
Such trees are not bothered by the heat
or worried by long months of drought.
Their leaves stay green,
and they never stop producing fruit.

9 "The human heart is the most deceitful of all things,
and desperately wicked.
Who really knows how bad it is?
10 But I, the Lord, search all hearts
and examine secret motives.
I give all people their due rewards,
according to what their actions deserve."

THE GUILTY GOALIE

Grant's soccer team was in the last minute of the state tournament, and they were leading 2 to 1. Grant, the goalie, was ready for the final shot. He leaped into the air, but the ball sailed overhead into the goal and went through a hole in back. The referee didn't see what happened and whistled the ball out of bounds—not a goal! The other team protested the call while Grant's team erupted in victory. Grant knew the other team was right. But if he told the ref, the score would be tied and his team might lose. What should he do? Read Jeremiah 17:11.

Jeremiah's Trust in the Lord

11 Like a partridge that hatches eggs she has not laid,
so are those who get their wealth by unjust means.
At midlife they will lose their riches;
in the end, they will become poor old fools.
12 But we worship at your throne—
eternal, high, and glorious!

13 O LORD, the hope of Israel,
all who turn away from you will be disgraced.
They will be buried in the dust of the earth,
for they have abandoned the LORD, the fountain of living water.

14 O LORD, if you heal me, I will be truly healed;
if you save me, I will be truly saved.
My praises are for you alone!
15 People scoff at me and say,
"What is this 'message from the LORD' you talk about?
Why don't your predictions come true?"

16 LORD, I have not abandoned my job as a shepherd for your people.
I have not urged you to send disaster.
You have heard everything I've said.
17 LORD, don't terrorize me!
You alone are my hope in the day of disaster.
18 Bring shame and dismay on all who persecute me,
but don't let me experience shame and dismay.
Bring a day of terror on them.
Yes, bring double destruction upon them!

Observing the Sabbath

19 This is what the LORD said to me: "Go and stand in the gates of Jerusalem, first in the gate where the king goes in and out, and then in each of the other gates. 20 Say to all the people, 'Listen to this message from the LORD, you kings of Judah and all you people of Judah and everyone living in Jerusalem. 21 This is what the LORD says: Listen to my warning! Stop carrying on your trade at Jerusalem's gates on the Sabbath day. 22 Do not do your work on the Sabbath, but make it a holy day. I gave this command to your ancestors, 23 but they did not listen or obey. They stubbornly refused to pay attention or accept my discipline.

24 "'But if you obey me, says the LORD, and do not carry on your trade at the gates or work on the Sabbath day, and if you keep it holy, 25 then kings and their officials will go in and out of these gates forever. There will always be a descendant of David sitting on the throne here in Jerusalem. Kings and their officials will always ride in and out among the people of Judah in chariots and on horses, and this city will remain forever. 26 And from all around Jerusalem, from the towns of Judah and Benjamin, from the western foothills* and the hill country and the Negev, the people will come with their burnt offerings and sacrifices. They will bring their grain offerings, frankincense, and thanksgiving offerings to the LORD's Temple.

27 "'But if you do not listen to me and refuse to keep the Sabbath holy, and if on the Sabbath day you bring loads of merchandise through the gates of Jerusalem just as on other days, then I will set fire to these gates. The fire will spread to the palaces, and no one will be able to put out the roaring flames.'"

CHAPTER 18

The Potter and the Clay

The LORD gave another message to Jeremiah. He said, 2 "Go down to the potter's shop, and I will speak to you there." 3 So I did as he told me and found the potter working at his wheel. 4 But the jar he was making did not turn out as he had hoped, so he crushed it into a lump of clay again and started over.

5 Then the LORD gave me this message: 6 "O Israel, can I not do to you as this potter has done to his clay? As the clay is in the potter's hand, so are you in my hand. 7 If I announce that a certain nation or kingdom is to be uprooted, torn down, and destroyed, 8 but then that nation renounces its evil ways, I will not destroy it as I had planned. 9 And if I announce that I will plant and build up a certain nation or kingdom, 10 but then that nation turns to evil and refuses to obey me, I will not bless it as I said I would.

11 "Therefore, Jeremiah, go and warn all Judah and Jerusalem. Say to them, 'This is what the LORD says: I am planning disaster for you instead of good. So turn from your evil ways, each of you, and do what is right.'"

12 But the people replied, "Don't waste your breath. We will continue to live as we want to, stubbornly following our own evil desires."

13 So this is what the LORD says:

"Has anyone ever heard of such a thing,
even among the pagan nations?

17:26 Hebrew *the Shephelah.*

My virgin daughter Israel
has done something terrible!
14 Does the snow ever disappear from the mountaintops of Lebanon?
Do the cold streams flowing from those distant mountains ever run dry?
15 But my people are not so reliable, for they have deserted me;
they burn incense to worthless idols.
They have stumbled off the ancient highways
and walk in muddy paths.
16 Therefore, their land will become desolate,
a monument to their stupidity.
All who pass by will be astonished
and will shake their heads in amazement.
17 I will scatter my people before their enemies
as the east wind scatters dust.
And in all their trouble I will turn my back on them
and refuse to notice their distress."

A Plot against Jeremiah

18 Then the people said, "Come on, let's plot a way to stop Jeremiah. We have plenty of priests and wise men and prophets. We don't need him to teach the word and give us advice and prophecies. Let's spread rumors about him and ignore what he says."

19 LORD, hear me and help me!
Listen to what my enemies are saying.
20 Should they repay evil for good?
They have dug a pit to kill me,
though I pleaded for them
and tried to protect them from your anger.
21 So let their children starve!
Let them die by the sword!
Let their wives become childless widows.
Let their old men die in a plague,
and let their young men be killed in battle!
22 Let screaming be heard from their homes
as warriors come suddenly upon them.
For they have dug a pit for me
and have hidden traps along my path.
23 LORD, you know all about their murderous plots against me.
Don't forgive their crimes and blot out their sins.
Let them die before you.
Deal with them in your anger.

CHAPTER 19

Jeremiah's Shattered Jar

This is what the LORD said to me: "Go and buy a clay jar. Then ask some of the leaders of the people and of the priests to follow you. 2 Go out through the Gate of Broken Pots to the garbage dump in the valley of Ben-Hinnom, and give them this message. 3 Say to them, 'Listen to this message from the LORD, you kings of Judah and citizens of Jerusalem! This is what the LORD of Heaven's Armies, the God of Israel, says: I will bring a terrible disaster on this place, and the ears of those who hear about it will ring!

4 "'For Israel has forsaken me and turned this valley into a place of wickedness. The people burn incense to foreign gods—idols never before acknowledged by this generation, by their ancestors, or by the kings of Judah. And they have filled this place with the blood of innocent children. 5 They have built pagan shrines to Baal, and there they burn their sons as sacrifices to Baal. I have never commanded such a horrible deed; it never even crossed my mind to command such a thing! 6 So beware, for the time is coming, says the LORD, when this garbage dump will no longer be called Topheth or the valley of Ben-Hinnom, but the Valley of Slaughter.

7 "'For I will upset the careful plans of Judah and Jerusalem. I will allow the people to be slaughtered by invading armies, and I will leave their dead bodies as food for the vultures and wild animals. 8 I will reduce Jerusalem to ruins, making it a monument to their stupidity. All who pass by will be astonished and will gasp at the destruction they see there. 9 I will see to it that your enemies lay siege to the city until all the food is gone. Then those trapped inside will eat their own sons and daughters and friends. They will be driven to utter despair.'

10 "As these men watch you, Jeremiah, smash the jar you brought. 11 Then say to them, 'This is what the LORD of Heaven's Armies says: As this jar lies shattered, so I will shatter the people of Judah and Jerusalem beyond all hope of repair. They will bury the bodies here in Topheth, the garbage dump, until there is no more room for them. 12 This is what I will do to this place and its people, says the LORD. I will cause this city to become defiled like Topheth. 13 Yes, all the

houses in Jerusalem, including the palace of Judah's kings, will become like Topheth—all the houses where you burned incense on the rooftops to your star gods, and where liquid offerings were poured out to your idols.'"

[14]Then Jeremiah returned from Topheth, the garbage dump where he had delivered this message, and he stopped in front of the Temple of the LORD. He said to the people there, [15]"This is what the LORD of Heaven's Armies, the God of Israel, says: 'I will bring disaster upon this city and its surrounding towns as I promised, because you have stubbornly refused to listen to me.'"

CHAPTER 20

Jeremiah and Pashhur

Now Pashhur son of Immer, the priest in charge of the Temple of the LORD, heard what Jeremiah was prophesying. [2]So he arrested Jeremiah the prophet and had him whipped and put in stocks at the Benjamin Gate of the LORD's Temple.

[3]The next day, when Pashhur finally released him, Jeremiah said, "Pashhur, the LORD has changed your name. From now on you are to be called 'The Man Who Lives in Terror.'* [4]For this is what the LORD says: 'I will send terror upon you and all your friends, and you will watch as they are slaughtered by the swords of the enemy. I will hand the people of Judah over to the king of Babylon. He will take them captive to Babylon or run them through with the sword. [5]And I will let your enemies plunder Jerusalem. All the famed treasures of the city—the precious jewels and gold and silver of your kings—will be carried off to Babylon. [6]As for you, Pashhur, you and all your household will go as captives to Babylon. There you will die and be buried, you and all your friends to whom you prophesied that everything would be all right.'"

Jeremiah's Complaint

[7] O LORD, you misled me,
and I allowed myself to be misled.
You are stronger than I am,
and you overpowered me.
Now I am mocked every day;
everyone laughs at me.
[8] When I speak, the words burst out.
"Violence and destruction!" I shout.
So these messages from the LORD
have made me a household joke.
[9] But if I say I'll never mention the LORD
or speak in his name,
his word burns in my heart like a fire.
It's like a fire in my bones!
I am worn out trying to hold it in!
I can't do it!
[10] I have heard the many rumors about me.
They call me "The Man Who Lives in Terror."
They threaten, "If you say anything, we will report it."
Even my old friends are watching me,
waiting for a fatal slip.
"He will trap himself," they say,
"and then we will get our revenge on him."
[11] But the LORD stands beside me like a great warrior.
Before him my persecutors will stumble.
They cannot defeat me.
They will fail and be thoroughly humiliated.
Their dishonor will never be forgotten.
[12] O LORD of Heaven's Armies,
you test those who are righteous,
and you examine the deepest thoughts and secrets.
Let me see your vengeance against them,
for I have committed my cause to you.
[13] Sing to the LORD!
Praise the LORD!
For though I was poor and needy,
he rescued me from my oppressors.
[14] Yet I curse the day I was born!
May no one celebrate the day of my birth.
[15] I curse the messenger who told my father,
"Good news—you have a son!"
[16] Let him be destroyed like the cities of old
that the LORD overthrew without mercy.
Terrify him all day long with battle shouts,
[17] because he did not kill me at birth.
Oh, that I had died in my mother's womb,
that her body had been my grave!
[18] Why was I ever born?
My entire life has been filled
with trouble, sorrow, and shame.

20:3 Hebrew *Magor-missabib*, which means "surrounded by terror"; also in 20:10.

CHAPTER 21

No Deliverance from Babylon

The LORD spoke through Jeremiah when King Zedekiah sent Pashhur son of Malkijah and Zephaniah son of Maaseiah, the priest, to speak with him. They begged Jeremiah, [2]"Please speak to the LORD for us and ask him to help us. King Nebuchadnezzar* of Babylon is attacking Judah. Perhaps the LORD will be gracious and do a mighty miracle as he has done in the past. Perhaps he will force Nebuchadnezzar to withdraw his armies."

[3]Jeremiah replied, "Go back to King Zedekiah and tell him, [4]'This is what the LORD, the God of Israel, says: I will make your weapons useless against the king of Babylon and the Babylonians* who are outside your walls attacking you. In fact, I will bring your enemies right into the heart of this city. [5]I myself will fight against you with a strong hand and a powerful arm, for I am very angry. You have made me furious! [6]I will send a terrible plague upon this city, and both people and animals will die. [7]And after all that, says the LORD, I will hand over King Zedekiah, his staff, and everyone else in the city who survives the disease, war, and famine. I will hand them over to King Nebuchadnezzar of Babylon and to their other enemies. He will slaughter them and show them no mercy, pity, or compassion.'

[8]"Tell all the people, 'This is what the LORD says: Take your choice of life or death! [9]Everyone who stays in Jerusalem will die from war, famine, or disease, but those who go out and surrender to the Babylonians will live. Their reward will be life! [10]For I have decided to bring disaster and not good upon this city, says the LORD. It will be handed over to the king of Babylon, and he will reduce it to ashes.'

Judgment on Judah's Kings

[11]"Say to the royal family of Judah, 'Listen to this message from the LORD! [12]This is what the LORD says to the dynasty of David:

"'Give justice each morning to the people you judge!
Help those who have been robbed;
rescue them from their oppressors.
Otherwise, my anger will burn like an unquenchable fire
because of all your sins.
[13] I will personally fight against the people in Jerusalem,
that mighty fortress—
the people who boast, "No one can touch us here.
No one can break in here."
[14] And I myself will punish you for your sinfulness,
says the LORD.
I will light a fire in your forests
that will burn up everything around you.'"

CHAPTER 22

A Message for Judah's Kings

This is what the LORD said to me: "Go over and speak directly to the king of Judah. Say to him, [2]'Listen to this message from the LORD, you king of Judah, sitting on David's throne. Let your attendants and your people listen, too. [3]This is what the LORD says: Be fair-minded and just. Do what is right! Help those who have been robbed; rescue them from their oppressors. Quit your evil deeds! Do not mistreat foreigners, orphans, and widows. Stop murdering the innocent! [4]If you obey me, there will always be a descendant of David sitting on the throne here in Jerusalem. The king will ride through the palace gates in chariots and on horses, with his parade of attendants and subjects. [5]But if you refuse to pay attention to this warning, I swear by my own name, says the LORD, that this palace will become a pile of rubble.'"

A Message about the Palace

[6]Now this is what the LORD says concerning Judah's royal palace:

"I love you as much as fruitful Gilead
and the green forests of Lebanon.
But I will turn you into a desert,
with no one living within your walls.
[7] I will call for wreckers,
who will bring out their tools to dismantle you.
They will tear out all your fine cedar beams
and throw them on the fire.

[8]"People from many nations will pass by the ruins of this city and say to one another,

21:2 Hebrew *Nebuchadrezzar*, a variant spelling of Nebuchadnezzar; also in 21:7. **21:4** Or *Chaldeans*; also in 21:9.

'Why did the LORD destroy such a great city?'
9And the answer will be, 'Because they violated their covenant with the LORD their God
by worshiping other gods.'"

A Message about Jehoahaz

10 Do not weep for the dead king or mourn
his loss.
Instead, weep for the captive king
being led away!
For he will never return to see his
native land again.

11For this is what the LORD says about Jehoahaz,* who succeeded his father, King Josiah,
and was taken away as a captive: "He will
never return. 12He will die in a distant land
and will never again see his own country."

A Message about Jehoiakim

13 And the LORD says, "What sorrow awaits
Jehoiakim,*
who builds his palace with forced
labor.*
He builds injustice into its walls,
for he makes his neighbors work for
nothing.
He does not pay them for their labor.
14 He says, 'I will build a magnificent palace
with huge rooms and many windows.
I will panel it throughout with fragrant
cedar
and paint it a lovely red.'
15 But a beautiful cedar palace does not
make a great king!
Your father, Josiah, also had plenty to
eat and drink.
But he was just and right in all his
dealings.
That is why God blessed him.
16 He gave justice and help to the poor and
needy,
and everything went well for him.
Isn't that what it means to know me?"
says the LORD.
17 "But you! You have eyes only for greed
and dishonesty!
You murder the innocent,
oppress the poor, and reign
ruthlessly."
18Therefore, this is what the LORD says about
Jehoiakim, son of King Josiah:
"The people will not mourn for him,
crying to one another,
'Alas, my brother! Alas, my sister!'
His subjects will not mourn for him,
crying,
'Alas, our master is dead! Alas, his
splendor is gone!'
19 He will be buried like a dead donkey—
dragged out of Jerusalem and dumped
outside the gates!
20 Weep for your allies in Lebanon.
Shout for them in Bashan.
Search for them in the regions east of the
river.*
See, they are all destroyed.
Not one is left to help you.
21 I warned you when you were prosperous,
but you replied, 'Don't bother me.'
You have been that way since
childhood—
you simply will not obey me!
22 And now the wind will blow away your
allies.
All your friends will be taken away as
captives.
Surely then you will see your
wickedness and be ashamed.
23 It may be nice to live in a beautiful
palace
paneled with wood from the cedars of
Lebanon,
but soon you will groan with pangs of
anguish—
anguish like that of a woman in labor.

A Message for Jehoiachin

24"As surely as I live," says the LORD, "I will
abandon you, Jehoiachin* son of Jehoiakim,
king of Judah. Even if you were the signet ring
on my right hand, I would pull you off. 25I will
hand you over to those who seek to kill you,
those you so desperately fear—to King Nebuchadnezzar* of Babylon and the mighty Babylonian* army. 26I will expel you and your
mother from this land, and you will die in a
foreign country, not in your native land.
27You will never again return to the land you
yearn for.

22:11 Hebrew *Shallum*, another name for Jehoahaz. **22:13a** The brother and successor of the exiled Jehoahaz. See 22:18.
22:13b Hebrew *by unrighteousness*. **22:20** Or *in Abarim*. **22:24** Hebrew *Coniah*, a variant spelling of Jehoiachin; also 22:28.
22:25a Hebrew *Nebuchadrezzar*, a variant spelling of Nebuchadnezzar. **22:25b** Or *Chaldean*.

28 "Why is this man Jehoiachin like a
discarded, broken jar?
Why are he and his children to be
exiled to a foreign land?
29 O earth, earth, earth!
Listen to this message from the LORD!
30 This is what the LORD says:
'Let the record show that this man
Jehoiachin was childless.
He is a failure,
for none of his children will succeed him
on the throne of David
to rule over Judah.'

CHAPTER 23

The Righteous Descendant

"What sorrow awaits the leaders of my people—the shepherds of my sheep—for they have destroyed and scattered the very ones they were expected to care for," says the LORD.

2 Therefore, this is what the LORD, the God of Israel, says to these shepherds: "Instead of caring for my flock and leading them to safety, you have deserted them and driven them to destruction. Now I will pour out judgment on you for the evil you have done to them. 3 But I will gather together the remnant of my flock from the countries where I have driven them. I will bring them back to their own sheepfold, and they will be fruitful and increase in number. 4 Then I will appoint responsible shepherds who will care for them, and they will never be afraid again. Not a single one will be lost or missing. I, the LORD, have spoken!

5 "For the time is coming,"
says the LORD,
"when I will raise up a righteous
descendant*
from King David's line.
He will be a King who rules with wisdom.
He will do what is just and right
throughout the land.
6 And this will be his name:
'The LORD Is Our Righteousness.'*
In that day Judah will be saved,
and Israel will live in safety.

7 "In that day," says the LORD, "when people are taking an oath, they will no longer say, 'As surely as the LORD lives, who rescued the people of Israel from the land of Egypt.' 8 Instead, they will say, 'As surely as the LORD lives, who brought the people of Israel back to their own land from the land of the north and from all the countries to which he had exiled them.' Then they will live in their own land."

Judgment on False Prophets

9 My heart is broken because of the false
prophets,
and my bones tremble.
I stagger like a drunkard,
like someone overcome by wine,
because of the holy words
the LORD has spoken against them.
10 For the land is full of adultery,
and it lies under a curse.
The land itself is in mourning—
its wilderness pastures are dried up.
For they all do evil
and abuse what power they have.

11 "Even the priests and prophets
are ungodly, wicked men.
I have seen their despicable acts
right here in my own Temple,"
says the LORD.
12 "Therefore, the paths they take
will become slippery.
They will be chased through the dark,
and there they will fall.
For I will bring disaster upon them
at the time fixed for their punishment.
I, the LORD, have spoken!

13 "I saw that the prophets of Samaria were
terribly evil,
for they prophesied in the name of Baal
and led my people of Israel into sin.
14 But now I see that the prophets of
Jerusalem are even worse!
They commit adultery and love
dishonesty.
They encourage those who are doing evil
so that no one turns away from their
sins.
These prophets are as wicked
as the people of Sodom and Gomorrah
once were."

15 Therefore, this is what the LORD of Heaven's Armies says concerning the prophets:

"I will feed them with bitterness
and give them poison to drink.

23:5 Hebrew *a righteous branch.* 23:6 Hebrew *Yahweh Tsidqenu.*

For it is because of Jerusalem's prophets
that wickedness has filled this
land."

16 This is what the LORD of Heaven's Armies
says to his people:

"Do not listen to these prophets when
they prophesy to you,
filling you with futile hopes.
They are making up everything they
say.
They do not speak for the LORD!
17 They keep saying to those who despise my
word,
'Don't worry! The LORD says you will
have peace!'
And to those who stubbornly follow their
own desires,
they say, 'No harm will come your way!'
18 "Have any of these prophets been in the
LORD's presence
to hear what he is really saying?
Has even one of them cared enough
to listen?
19 Look! The LORD's anger bursts out like a
storm,
a whirlwind that swirls down on the
heads of the wicked.
20 The anger of the LORD will not diminish
until it has finished all he has planned.
In the days to come
you will understand all this very clearly.
21 "I have not sent these prophets,
yet they run around claiming to speak
for me.
I have given them no message,
yet they go on prophesying.
22 If they had stood before me and listened
to me,
they would have spoken my words,
and they would have turned my
people
from their evil ways and deeds.
23 Am I a God who is only close at hand?"
says the LORD.
"No, I am far away at the same time.
24 Can anyone hide from me in a secret
place?
Am I not everywhere in all the heavens
and earth?"
says the LORD.

Is God really here with me and in heaven at the same time?

"Can anyone hide from me in a secret place? Am I not everywhere in all the heavens and earth?" says the LORD.

JEREMIAH 23:24

25 "I have heard these prophets say, 'Listen to
the dream I had from God last night.' And then
they proceed to tell lies in my name. 26 How
long will this go on? If they are prophets, they
are prophets of deceit, inventing everything
they say. 27 By telling these false dreams, they
are trying to get my people to forget me, just as
their ancestors did by worshiping the idols of
Baal.

28 "Let these false prophets tell their
dreams,
but let my true messengers faithfully
proclaim my every word.
There is a difference between straw
and grain!
29 Does not my word burn like fire?"
says the LORD.
"Is it not like a mighty hammer
that smashes a rock to pieces?

30 "Therefore," says the LORD, "I am against
these prophets who steal messages from each
other and claim they are from me. 31 I am
against these smooth-tongued prophets who
say, 'This prophecy is from the LORD!' 32 I am
against these false prophets. Their imaginary
dreams are flagrant lies that lead my people
into sin. I did not send or appoint them, and
they have no message at all for my people. I,
the LORD, have spoken!

False Prophecies and False Prophets

33 "Suppose one of the people or one of the
prophets or priests asks you, 'What prophecy
has the LORD burdened you with now?' You

must reply, 'You are the burden!* The LORD
says he will abandon you!'
34"If any prophet, priest, or anyone else
says, 'I have a prophecy from the LORD,' I will
punish that person along with his entire
family. 35 You should keep asking each other,
'What is the LORD's answer?' or 'What is the
LORD saying?' 36 But stop using this phrase,
'prophecy from the LORD.' For people are us-
ing it to give authority to their own ideas,
turning upside down the words of our God,
the living God, the LORD of Heaven's Armies.
37"This is what you should say to the
prophets: 'What is the LORD's answer?' or
'What is the LORD saying?' 38 But suppose they
respond, 'This is a prophecy from the LORD!'
Then you should say, 'This is what the LORD
says: Because you have used this phrase,
"prophecy from the LORD," even though I
warned you not to use it, 39 I will forget you
completely.* I will expel you from my pres-
ence, along with this city that I gave to you and
your ancestors. 40 And I will make you an ob-
ject of ridicule, and your name will be infa-
mous throughout the ages.'"

CHAPTER 24

Good and Bad Figs

After King Nebuchadnezzar* of Babylon ex-
iled Jehoiachin* son of Jehoiakim, king of Ju-
dah, to Babylon along with the officials of
Judah and all the craftsmen and artisans, the
LORD gave me this vision. I saw two baskets of
figs placed in front of the LORD's Temple in
Jerusalem. 2 One basket was filled with fresh,
ripe figs, while the other was filled with bad
figs that were too rotten to eat.
3 Then the LORD said to me, "What do you
see, Jeremiah?"
I replied, "Figs, some very good and some
very bad, too rotten to eat."
4 Then the LORD gave me this message:
5 "This is what the LORD, the God of Israel,
says: The good figs represent the exiles I sent
from Judah to the land of the Babylonians.* 6 I
will watch over and care for them, and I will
bring them back here again. I will build them
up and not tear them down. I will plant them
and not uproot them. 7 I will give them hearts
that recognize me as the LORD. They will be
my people, and I will be their God, for they
will return to me wholeheartedly.
8 "But the bad figs," the LORD said, "repre-
sent King Zedekiah of Judah, his officials, all
the people left in Jerusalem, and those who
live in Egypt. I will treat them like bad figs, too
rotten to eat. 9 I will make them an object of
horror and a symbol of evil to every nation on
earth. They will be disgraced and mocked,
taunted and cursed, wherever I scatter them.
10 And I will send war, famine, and disease un-
til they have vanished from the land of Israel,
which I gave to them and their ancestors."

CHAPTER 25

Seventy Years of Captivity

This message for all the people of Judah came
to Jeremiah from the LORD during the fourth
year of Jehoiakim's reign over Judah.* This
was the year when King Nebuchadnezzar* of
Babylon began his reign.
2 Jeremiah the prophet said to all the peo-
ple in Judah and Jerusalem, 3 "For the past
twenty-three years—from the thirteenth year
of the reign of Josiah son of Amon,* king of
Judah, until now—the LORD has been giving
me his messages. I have faithfully passed
them on to you, but you have not listened.
4 "Again and again the LORD has sent you his
servants, the prophets, but you have not lis-
tened or even paid attention. 5 Each time the
message was this: 'Turn from the evil road
you are traveling and from the evil things you
are doing. Only then will I let you live in this
land that the LORD gave to you and your an-
cestors forever. 6 Do not provoke my anger by
worshiping idols you made with your own
hands. Then I will not harm you.'
7 "But you would not listen to me," says the
LORD. "You made me furious by worshiping
idols you made with your own hands, bring-
ing on yourselves all the disasters you now
suffer. 8 And now the LORD of Heaven's
Armies says: Because you have not listened to
me, 9 I will gather together all the armies of
the north under King Nebuchadnezzar of
Babylon, whom I have appointed as my dep-
uty. I will bring them all against this land and

23:33 As in Greek version and Latin Vulgate; Hebrew reads *What burden?* **23:39** Some Hebrew manuscripts and Greek version read *I will surely lift you up.* **24:1a** Hebrew *Nebuchadrezzar*, a variant spelling of Nebuchadnezzar. **24:1b** Hebrew *Jeconiah*, a variant spelling of Jehoiachin. **24:5** Or *Chaldeans.* **25:1a** The fourth year of Jehoiakim's reign and the accession year of Nebuchadnezzar's reign was 605 B.C. **25:1b** Hebrew *Nebuchadrezzar*, a variant spelling of Nebuchadnezzar; also in 25:9. **25:3** The thirteenth year of Josiah's reign was 627 B.C.

its people and against the surrounding nations. I will completely destroy* you and
make you an object of horror and contempt
and a ruin forever. [10]I will take away your
happy singing and laughter. The joyful voices
of bridegrooms and brides will no longer be
heard. Your millstones will fall silent, and the
lights in your homes will go out. [11]This entire
land will become a desolate wasteland. Israel
and her neighboring lands will serve the king
of Babylon for seventy years.

[12]"Then, after the seventy years of captivity are over, I will punish the king of Babylon
and his people for their sins," says the LORD.
"I will make the country of the Babylonians*
a wasteland forever. [13]I will bring upon them
all the terrors I have promised in this book—
all the penalties announced by Jeremiah
against the nations. [14]Many nations and great
kings will enslave the Babylonians, just as
they enslaved my people. I will punish them
in proportion to the suffering they cause my
people."

The Cup of the LORD's Anger

[15]This is what the LORD, the God of Israel, said
to me: "Take from my hand this cup filled to
the brim with my anger, and make all the nations to whom I send you drink from it.
[16]When they drink from it, they will stagger,
crazed by the warfare I will send against them."

[17]So I took the cup of anger from the LORD
and made all the nations drink from it—every
nation to which the LORD sent me. [18]I went to
Jerusalem and the other towns of Judah, and
their kings and officials drank from the cup.
From that day until this, they have been a desolate ruin, an object of horror, contempt, and
cursing. [19]I gave the cup to Pharaoh, king of
Egypt, his attendants, his officials, and all his
people, [20]along with all the foreigners living
in that land. I also gave it to all the kings of the
land of Uz and the kings of the Philistine cities of Ashkelon, Gaza, Ekron, and what remains of Ashdod. [21]Then I gave the cup to the
nations of Edom, Moab, and Ammon, [22]and
the kings of Tyre and Sidon, and the kings of
the regions across the sea. [23]I gave it to Dedan,
Tema, and Buz, and to the people who live in
distant places.* [24]I gave it to the kings of Arabia, the kings of the nomadic tribes of the
desert, [25]and to the kings of Zimri, Elam, and
Media. [26]And I gave it to the kings of the
northern countries, far and near, one after
the other—all the kingdoms of the world. And
finally, the king of Babylon* himself drank
from the cup of the LORD's anger.

[27]Then the LORD said to me, "Now tell them,
'This is what the LORD of Heaven's Armies, the
God of Israel, says: Drink from this cup of my
anger. Get drunk and vomit; fall to rise no
more, for I am sending terrible wars against
you.' [28]And if they refuse to accept the cup, tell
them, 'The LORD of Heaven's Armies says: You
have no choice but to drink from it. [29]I have
begun to punish Jerusalem, the city that bears
my name. Now should I let you go unpunished? No, you will not escape disaster. I will
call for war against all the nations of the earth.
I, the LORD of Heaven's Armies, have spoken!'

[30]"Now prophesy all these things, and say
to them,

"'The LORD will roar against his own land
from his holy dwelling in heaven.
He will shout like those who tread grapes;
he will shout against everyone on earth.
[31] His cry of judgment will reach the ends of
the earth,
for the LORD will bring his case against
all the nations.
He will judge all the people of the earth,
slaughtering the wicked with the
sword.
I, the LORD, have spoken!'"

[32] This is what the LORD of Heaven's Armies
says:
"Look! Disaster will fall upon nation
after nation!
A great whirlwind of fury is rising
from the most distant corners of the
earth!"

[33]In that day those the LORD has slaughtered will fill the earth from one end to the
other. No one will mourn for them or gather
up their bodies to bury them. They will be
scattered on the ground like manure.

[34] Weep and moan, you evil shepherds!
Roll in the dust, you leaders of the flock!

25:9 The Hebrew term used here refers to the complete consecration of things or people to the LORD, either by destroying them or by giving them as an offering. **25:12** Or *Chaldeans*. **25:23** Or *who clip the corners of their hair*. **25:26** Hebrew *of Sheshach*, a code name for Babylon.

The time of your slaughter has arrived;
you will fall and shatter like a fragile vase.
35 You will find no place to hide;
there will be no way to escape.
36 Listen to the frantic cries of the shepherds.
The leaders of the flock are wailing in despair,
for the LORD is ruining their pastures.
37 Peaceful meadows will be turned into a wasteland
by the LORD's fierce anger.
38 He has left his den like a strong lion seeking its prey,
and their land will be made desolate
by the sword of the enemy
and the LORD's fierce anger.

CHAPTER 26

Jeremiah's Escape from Death

This message came to Jeremiah from the LORD early in the reign of Jehoiakim son of Josiah,* king of Judah. 2"This is what the LORD says: Stand in the courtyard in front of the Temple of the LORD, and make an announcement to the people who have come there to worship from all over Judah. Give them my entire message; include every word. 3Perhaps they will listen and turn from their evil ways. Then I will change my mind about the disaster I am ready to pour out on them because of their sins.

4"Say to them, 'This is what the LORD says: If you will not listen to me and obey my word I have given you, 5and if you will not listen to my servants, the prophets—for I sent them again and again to warn you, but you would not listen to them—6then I will destroy this Temple as I destroyed Shiloh, the place where the Tabernacle was located. And I will make Jerusalem an object of cursing in every nation on earth.'"

7The priests, the prophets, and all the people listened to Jeremiah as he spoke in front of the LORD's Temple. 8But when Jeremiah had finished his message, saying everything the LORD had told him to say, the priests and prophets and all the people at the Temple mobbed him. "Kill him!" they shouted. 9"What right do you have to prophesy in the LORD's name that this Temple will be destroyed like Shiloh? What do you mean, saying that Jerusalem will be destroyed and left with no inhabitants?" And all the people threatened him as he stood in front of the Temple.

10When the officials of Judah heard what was happening, they rushed over from the palace and sat down at the New Gate of the Temple to hold court. 11The priests and prophets presented their accusations to the officials and the people. "This man should die!" they said. "You have heard with your own ears what a traitor he is, for he has prophesied against this city."

12Then Jeremiah spoke to the officials and the people in his own defense. "The LORD sent me to prophesy against this Temple and this city," he said. "The LORD gave me every word that I have spoken. 13But if you stop your sinning and begin to obey the LORD your God, he will change his mind about this disaster that he has announced against you. 14As for me, I am in your hands—do with me as you think best. 15But if you kill me, rest assured that you will be killing an innocent man! The responsibility for such a deed will lie on you, on this city, and on every person living in it. For it is absolutely true that the LORD sent me to speak every word you have heard."

16Then the officials and the people said to the priests and prophets, "This man does not deserve the death sentence, for he has spoken to us in the name of the LORD our God."

17Then some of the wise old men stood and spoke to all the people assembled there. 18They said, "Remember when Micah of Moresheth prophesied during the reign of King Hezekiah of Judah. He told the people of Judah,

'This is what the LORD of Heaven's Armies says:
Mount Zion will be plowed like an open field;
Jerusalem will be reduced to ruins!
A thicket will grow on the heights
where the Temple now stands.'*

19But did King Hezekiah and the people kill him for saying this? No, they turned from their sins and worshiped the LORD. They

26:1 The first year of Jehoiakim's reign was 608 B.C. **26:18** Mic 3:12.

begged him for mercy. Then the LORD changed his mind about the terrible disaster he had pronounced against them. So we are about to do ourselves great harm."

[20]At this time Uriah son of Shemaiah from Kiriath-jearim was also prophesying for the LORD. And he predicted the same terrible disaster against the city and nation as Jeremiah did. [21]When King Jehoiakim and the army officers and officials heard what he was saying, the king sent someone to kill him. But Uriah heard about the plan and escaped in fear to Egypt. [22]Then King Jehoiakim sent Elnathan son of Acbor to Egypt along with several other men to capture Uriah. [23]They took him prisoner and brought him back to King Jehoiakim. The king then killed Uriah with a sword and had him buried in an unmarked grave.

[24]Nevertheless, Ahikam son of Shaphan stood up for Jeremiah and persuaded the court not to turn him over to the mob to be killed.

CHAPTER 27

Jeremiah Wears an Ox Yoke

This message came to Jeremiah from the LORD early in the reign of Zedekiah* son of Josiah, king of Judah.

[2]This is what the LORD said to me: "Make a yoke, and fasten it on your neck with leather straps. [3]Then send messages to the kings of Edom, Moab, Ammon, Tyre, and Sidon through their ambassadors who have come to see King Zedekiah in Jerusalem. [4]Give them this message for their masters: 'This is what the LORD of Heaven's Armies, the God of Israel, says: [5]With my great strength and powerful arm I made the earth and all its people and every animal. I can give these things of mine to anyone I choose. [6]Now I will give your countries to King Nebuchadnezzar of Babylon, who is my servant. I have put everything, even the wild animals, under his control. [7]All the nations will serve him, his son, and his grandson until his time is up. Then many nations and great kings will conquer and rule over Babylon. [8]So you must submit to Babylon's king and serve him; put your neck under Babylon's yoke! I will punish any nation that refuses to be his slave, says the LORD. I will send war, famine, and disease upon that nation until Babylon has conquered it.

AMAZING FACTS

God told Jeremiah to wear a yoke around his neck—like an ox—for a BIG object lesson!

JEREMIAH 27:1-2, 5-8

[9]"'Do not listen to your false prophets, fortune-tellers, interpreters of dreams, mediums, and sorcerers who say, "The king of Babylon will not conquer you." [10]They are all liars, and their lies will lead to your being driven out of your land. I will drive you out and send you far away to die. [11]But the people of any nation that submits to the king of Babylon will be allowed to stay in their own country to farm the land as usual. I, the LORD, have spoken!'"

[12]Then I repeated this same message to King Zedekiah of Judah. "If you want to live, submit to the yoke of the king of Babylon and his people. [13]Why do you insist on dying—you and your people? Why should you choose war, famine, and disease, which the LORD will bring against every nation that refuses to submit to Babylon's king? [14]Do not listen to the false prophets who keep telling you, 'The king of Babylon will not conquer you.' They are liars. [15]This is what the LORD says: 'I have not sent these prophets! They are telling you lies in my name, so I will drive you from this land. You will all die—you and all these prophets, too.'"

[16]Then I spoke to the priests and the people and said, "This is what the LORD says: 'Do not listen to your prophets who claim that soon the gold articles taken from my Temple will be returned from Babylon. It is all a lie! [17]Do not listen to them. Surrender to the king of Babylon, and you will live. Why should this whole city be destroyed? [18]If they really are prophets and speak the LORD's messages, let them pray to the LORD of Heaven's Armies.

27:1 As in some Hebrew manuscripts and Syriac version (see also 27:3, 12); most Hebrew manuscripts read *Jehoiakim*.

Let them pray that the articles remaining in the LORD's Temple and in the king's palace and in the palaces of Jerusalem will not be carried away to Babylon!'

19"For the LORD of Heaven's Armies has spoken about the pillars in front of the Temple, the great bronze basin called the Sea, the water carts, and all the other ceremonial articles. 20King Nebuchadnezzar of Babylon left them here when he exiled Jehoiachin* son of Jehoiakim, king of Judah, to Babylon, along with all the other nobles of Judah and Jerusalem. 21Yes, this is what the LORD of Heaven's Armies, the God of Israel, says about the precious things still in the Temple and in the palace of Judah's king: 22'They will all be carried away to Babylon and will stay there until I send for them,' says the LORD. 'Then I will bring them back to Jerusalem again.'"

CHAPTER 28

Jeremiah Condemns Hananiah

One day in late summer* of that same year—the fourth year of the reign of Zedekiah, king of Judah—Hananiah son of Azzur, a prophet from Gibeon, addressed me publicly in the Temple while all the priests and people listened. He said, 2"This is what the LORD of Heaven's Armies, the God of Israel, says: 'I will remove the yoke of the king of Babylon from your necks. 3Within two years I will bring back all the Temple treasures that King Nebuchadnezzar carried off to Babylon. 4And I will bring back Jehoiachin* son of Jehoiakim, king of Judah, and all the other captives that were taken to Babylon. I will surely break the yoke that the king of Babylon has put on your necks. I, the LORD, have spoken!'"

5Jeremiah responded to Hananiah as they stood in front of all the priests and people at the Temple. 6He said, "Amen! May your prophecies come true! I hope the LORD does everything you say. I hope he does bring back from Babylon the treasures of this Temple and all the captives. 7But listen now to the solemn words I speak to you in the presence of all these people. 8The ancient prophets who preceded you and me spoke against many nations, always warning of war, disaster, and disease. 9So a prophet who predicts peace must show he is right. Only when his predictions come true can we know that he is really from the LORD."

10Then Hananiah the prophet took the yoke off Jeremiah's neck and broke it in pieces. 11And Hananiah said again to the crowd that had gathered, "This is what the LORD says: 'Just as this yoke has been broken, within two years I will break the yoke of oppression from all the nations now subject to King Nebuchadnezzar of Babylon.' " With that, Jeremiah left the Temple area.

12Soon after this confrontation with Hananiah, the LORD gave this message to Jeremiah: 13"Go and tell Hananiah, 'This is what the LORD says: You have broken a wooden yoke, but you have replaced it with a yoke of iron. 14The LORD of Heaven's Armies, the God of Israel, says: I have put a yoke of iron on the necks of all these nations, forcing them into slavery under King Nebuchadnezzar of Babylon. I have put everything, even the wild animals, under his control.'"

15Then Jeremiah the prophet said to Hananiah, "Listen, Hananiah! The LORD has not sent you, but the people believe your lies. 16Therefore, this is what the LORD says: 'You must die. Your life will end this very year because you have rebelled against the LORD.'"

17Two months later* the prophet Hananiah died.

CHAPTER 29

A Letter to the Exiles

Jeremiah wrote a letter from Jerusalem to the elders, priests, prophets, and all the people who had been exiled to Babylon by King Nebuchadnezzar. 2This was after King Jehoiachin,* the queen mother, the court officials, the other officials of Judah, and all the craftsmen and artisans had been deported from Jerusalem. 3He sent the letter with Elasah son of Shaphan and Gemariah son of Hilkiah when they went to Babylon as King Zedekiah's ambassadors to Nebuchadnezzar. This is what Jeremiah's letter said:

4This is what the LORD of Heaven's Armies, the God of Israel, says to all the captives he has exiled to Babylon from

27:20 Hebrew *Jeconiah*, a variant spelling of Jehoiachin. **28:1** Hebrew *In the fifth month*, of the ancient Hebrew lunar calendar. The fifth month in the fourth year of Zedekiah's reign occurred within the months of August and September 593 B.C. Also see note on 1:3. **28:4** Hebrew *Jeconiah*, a variant spelling of Jehoiachin. **28:17** Hebrew *In the seventh month of that same year*. See 28:1 and the note there. **29:2** Hebrew *Jeconiah*, a variant spelling of Jehoiachin.

Future Plans

As part of a series on careers involving science, Sam's science class had heard several speakers—an oceanographer, a meteorologist, and a doctor. All these careers sounded exciting to Sam. But he had also heard an awesome missionary speak at church about her medical work at an orphanage overseas. The more Sam thought about his future, the more confused and discouraged he became. He kept wondering, *What am I going to do when I grow up?* What do you think might help Sam feel better about his future? For help, read Jeremiah 29:11.

Jerusalem: 5"Build homes, and plan to stay. Plant gardens, and eat the food they produce. 6Marry and have children. Then find spouses for them so that you may have many grandchildren. Multiply! Do not dwindle away! 7And work for the peace and prosperity of the city where I sent you into exile. Pray to the LORD for it, for its welfare will determine your welfare."

8This is what the LORD of Heaven's Armies, the God of Israel, says: "Do not let your prophets and fortune-tellers who are with you in the land of Babylon trick you. Do not listen to their dreams, 9because they are telling you lies in my name. I have not sent them," says the LORD.

10This is what the LORD says: "You will be in Babylon for seventy years. But then I will come and do for you all the good things I have promised, and I will bring you home again. 11For I know the plans I have for you," says the LORD. "They are plans for good and not for disaster, to give you a future and a hope. 12In those days when you pray, I will listen. 13If you look for me wholeheartedly, you will find me. 14I will be found by you," says the LORD. "I will end your captivity and restore your fortunes. I will gather you out of the nations where I sent you and will bring you home again to your own land."

15You claim that the LORD has raised up prophets for you in Babylon. 16But this is what the LORD says about the king who sits on David's throne and all those still living here in Jerusalem—your relatives who were not exiled to Babylon. 17This is what the LORD of Heaven's Armies says: "I will send war, famine, and disease upon them and make them like bad figs, too rotten to eat. 18Yes, I will pursue them with war, famine, and disease, and I will scatter them around the world. In every nation where I send them, I will make them an object of damnation, horror, contempt, and mockery. 19For they refuse to listen to me, though I have spoken to them repeatedly through the prophets I sent. And you who are in exile have not listened either," says the LORD.

20Therefore, listen to this message from the LORD, all you captives there in Babylon. 21This is what the LORD of Heaven's Armies, the God of Israel, says about your prophets—Ahab son of Kolaiah and Zedekiah son of Maaseiah—who are telling you lies in my name: "I will turn them over to Nebuchadnezzar* for execution before your eyes. 22Their

29:21 Hebrew *Nebuchadrezzar*, a variant spelling of Nebuchadnezzar.

terrible fate will become proverbial, so
that the Judean exiles will curse someone
by saying, 'May the LORD make you like
Zedekiah and Ahab, whom the king of
Babylon burned alive!' [23]For these men
have done terrible things among my
people. They have committed adultery
with their neighbors' wives and have lied
in my name, saying things I did not
command. I am a witness to this. I, the
LORD, have spoken."

A Message for Shemaiah

[24]The LORD sent this message to Shemaiah the Nehelamite in Babylon: [25]"This is what the LORD of Heaven's Armies, the God of Israel, says: You wrote a letter on your own authority to Zephaniah son of Maaseiah, the priest, and you sent copies to the other priests and people in Jerusalem. You wrote to Zephaniah,

[26]"The LORD has appointed you to replace
Jehoiada as the priest in charge of the
house of the LORD. You are responsible to
put into stocks and neck irons any crazy
man who claims to be a prophet. [27]So why
have you done nothing to stop Jeremiah
from Anathoth, who pretends to be a
prophet among you? [28]Jeremiah sent a
letter here to Babylon, predicting that our
captivity will be a long one. He said, 'Build
homes, and plan to stay. Plant gardens,
and eat the food they produce.'"

[29]But when Zephaniah the priest received Shemaiah's letter, he took it to Jeremiah and read it to him. [30]Then the LORD gave this message to Jeremiah: [31]"Send an open letter to all the exiles in Babylon. Tell them, 'This is what the LORD says concerning Shemaiah the Nehelamite: Since he has prophesied to you when I did not send him and has tricked you into believing his lies, [32]I will punish him and his family. None of his descendants will see the good things I will do for my people, for he has incited you to rebel against me. I, the LORD, have spoken!'"

CHAPTER 30

Promises of Deliverance

The LORD gave another message to Jeremiah. He said, [2]"This is what the LORD, the God of Israel, says: Write down for the record everything I have said to you, Jeremiah. [3]For the time is coming when I will restore the fortunes of my people of Israel and Judah. I will bring them home to this land that I gave to their ancestors, and they will possess it again. I, the LORD, have spoken!"

[4]This is the message the LORD gave concerning Israel and Judah. [5]This is what the LORD says:

"I hear cries of fear;
there is terror and no peace.
[6] Now let me ask you a question:
Do men give birth to babies?
Then why do they stand there,
ashen-faced,
hands pressed against their sides
like a woman in labor?
[7] In all history there has never been such
a time of terror.
It will be a time of trouble for my
people Israel.*
Yet in the end they will be saved!
[8] For in that day,"
says the LORD of Heaven's Armies,
"I will break the yoke from their necks
and snap their chains.
Foreigners will no longer be their
masters.
[9] For my people will serve the LORD
their God
and their king descended from David—
the king I will raise up for them.

[10] "So do not be afraid, Jacob, my servant;
do not be dismayed, Israel,"
says the LORD.
"For I will bring you home again from
distant lands,
and your children will return from
their exile.
Israel will return to a life of peace
and quiet,
and no one will terrorize them.
[11] For I am with you and will save you,"
says the LORD.
"I will completely destroy the nations
where I have scattered you,
but I will not completely destroy
you.
I will discipline you, but with justice;
I cannot let you go unpunished."

30:7 Hebrew *Jacob;* also in 30:10b, 18. See note on 5:20.

12 This is what the LORD says:
"Your injury is incurable—
a terrible wound.
13 There is no one to help you
or to bind up your injury.
No medicine can heal you.
14 All your lovers—your allies—have left you
and do not care about you anymore.
I have wounded you cruelly,
as though I were your enemy.
For your sins are many,
and your guilt is great.
15 Why do you protest your punishment—
this wound that has no cure?
I have had to punish you
because your sins are many
and your guilt is great.

16 "But all who devour you will be devoured,
and all your enemies will be sent into exile.
All who plunder you will be plundered,
and all who attack you will be attacked.
17 I will give you back your health
and heal your wounds," says the LORD.
"For you are called an outcast—
'Jerusalem* for whom no one cares.'"

18 This is what the LORD says:
"When I bring Israel home again from captivity
and restore their fortunes,
Jerusalem will be rebuilt on its ruins,
and the palace reconstructed as before.
19 There will be joy and songs of thanksgiving,
and I will multiply my people, not diminish them;
I will honor them, not despise them.
20 Their children will prosper as they did long ago.
I will establish them as a nation before me,
and I will punish anyone who hurts them.
21 They will have their own ruler again,
and he will come from their own people.
I will invite him to approach me," says the LORD,
"for who would dare to come unless invited?
22 You will be my people,
and I will be your God."

23 Look! The LORD's anger bursts out like a storm,
a driving wind that swirls down on the heads of the wicked.
24 The fierce anger of the LORD will not diminish
until it has finished all he has planned.
In the days to come
you will understand all this.

CHAPTER 31

Hope for Restoration

"In that day," says the LORD, "I will be the God of all the families of Israel, and they will be my people. 2 This is what the LORD says:

"Those who survive the coming destruction
will find blessings even in the barren land,
for I will give rest to the people of Israel."

3 Long ago the LORD said to Israel:
"I have loved you, my people, with an everlasting love.
With unfailing love I have drawn you to myself.
4 I will rebuild you, my virgin Israel.
You will again be happy
and dance merrily with your tambourines.
5 Again you will plant your vineyards on the mountains of Samaria
and eat from your own gardens there.
6 The day will come when watchmen will shout
from the hill country of Ephraim,
'Come, let us go up to Jerusalem*
to worship the LORD our God.'"

7 Now this is what the LORD says:
"Sing with joy for Israel.*
Shout for the greatest of nations!
Shout out with praise and joy:
'Save your people, O LORD,
the remnant of Israel!'
8 For I will bring them from the north
and from the distant corners of the earth.

30:17 Hebrew *Zion*. **31:6** Hebrew *Zion*; also in 31:12. **31:7** Hebrew *Jacob*; also in 31:11. See note on 5:20.

I will not forget the blind and lame,
the expectant mothers and women in labor.
A great company will return!
9 Tears of joy will stream down their faces,
and I will lead them home with great care.
They will walk beside quiet streams
and on smooth paths where they will not stumble.
For I am Israel's father,
and Ephraim is my oldest child.

10 "Listen to this message from the LORD,
you nations of the world;
proclaim it in distant coastlands:
The LORD, who scattered his people,
will gather them and watch over them
as a shepherd does his flock.
11 For the LORD has redeemed Israel
from those too strong for them.
12 They will come home and sing songs of joy on the heights of Jerusalem.
They will be radiant because of the LORD's good gifts—
the abundant crops of grain, new wine, and olive oil,
and the healthy flocks and herds.
Their life will be like a watered garden,
and all their sorrows will be gone.
13 The young women will dance for joy,
and the men—old and young—will join in the celebration.
I will turn their mourning into joy.
I will comfort them and exchange their sorrow for rejoicing.
14 The priests will enjoy abundance,
and my people will feast on my good gifts.
I, the LORD, have spoken!"

Rachel's Sadness Turns to Joy

15 This is what the LORD says:

"A cry is heard in Ramah—
deep anguish and bitter weeping.
Rachel weeps for her children,
refusing to be comforted—
for her children are gone."

16 But now this is what the LORD says:
"Do not weep any longer,
for I will reward you," says the LORD.
"Your children will come back to you
from the distant land of the enemy.
17 There is hope for your future," says the LORD.
"Your children will come again to their own land.
18 I have heard Israel* saying,
'You disciplined me severely,
like a calf that needs training for the yoke.
Turn me again to you and restore me,
for you alone are the LORD my God.
19 I turned away from God,
but then I was sorry.
I kicked myself for my stupidity!
I was thoroughly ashamed of all I did in my younger days.'

20 "Is not Israel still my son,
my darling child?" says the LORD.
"I often have to punish him,
but I still love him.
That's why I long for him
and surely will have mercy on him.
21 Set up road signs;
put up guideposts.
Mark well the path
by which you came.
Come back again, my virgin Israel;
return to your towns here.
22 How long will you wander,
my wayward daughter?
For the LORD will cause something new to happen—
Israel will embrace her God.*"

23 This is what the LORD of Heaven's Armies, the God of Israel, says: "When I bring them back from captivity, the people of Judah and its towns will again say, 'The LORD bless you, O righteous home, O holy mountain!' 24 Townspeople and farmers and shepherds alike will live together in peace and happiness. 25 For I have given rest to the weary and joy to the sorrowing."

26 At this, I woke up and looked around. My sleep had been very sweet.

27 "The day is coming," says the LORD, "when I will greatly increase the human population and the number of animals here in Israel and Judah. 28 In the past I deliberately uprooted and tore down this nation. I overthrew it, destroyed

31:18 Hebrew *Ephraim*, referring to the northern kingdom of Israel; also in 31:20. **31:22** Hebrew *a woman will surround a man.*

it, and brought disaster upon it. But in the future I will just as deliberately plant it and build it up. I, the LORD, have spoken!

29"The people will no longer quote this proverb:

'The parents have eaten sour grapes,
but their children's mouths pucker at
the taste.'

30All people will die for their own sins—those who eat the sour grapes will be the ones whose mouths will pucker.

31"The day is coming," says the LORD, "when I will make a new covenant with the people of Israel and Judah. 32This covenant will not be like the one I made with their ancestors when I took them by the hand and brought them out of the land of Egypt. They broke that covenant, though I loved them as a husband loves his wife," says the LORD.

33"But this is the new covenant I will make with the people of Israel on that day," says the LORD. "I will put my instructions deep within them, and I will write them on their hearts. I will be their God, and they will be my people. 34And they will not need to teach their neighbors, nor will they need to teach their relatives, saying, 'You should know the LORD.' For everyone, from the least to the greatest, will know me already," says the LORD. "And I will forgive their wickedness, and I will never again remember their sins."

35 It is the LORD who provides the sun to
light the day
and the moon and stars to light the
night,
and who stirs the sea into roaring
waves.
His name is the LORD of Heaven's Armies,
and this is what he says:
36 "I am as likely to reject my people Israel
as I am to abolish the laws of nature!"
37 This is what the LORD says:
"Just as the heavens cannot be measured
and the foundations of the earth
cannot be explored,
so I will not consider casting them away
for the evil they have done.
I, the LORD, have spoken!

38"The day is coming," says the LORD, "when all Jerusalem will be rebuilt for me, from the Tower of Hananel to the Corner Gate. 39A measuring line will be stretched out over the hill of Gareb and across to Goah. 40And the entire area—including the graveyard and ash dump in the valley, and all the fields out to the Kidron Valley on the east as far as the Horse Gate—will be holy to the LORD. The city will never again be captured or destroyed."

CHAPTER 32

Jeremiah's Land Purchase

The following message came to Jeremiah from the LORD in the tenth year of the reign of Zedekiah,* king of Judah. This was also the eighteenth year of the reign of King Nebuchadnezzar.* 2Jerusalem was then under siege from the Babylonian army, and Jeremiah was imprisoned in the courtyard of the guard in the royal palace. 3King Zedekiah had put him there, asking why he kept giving this prophecy: "This is what the LORD says: 'I am about to hand this city over to the king of Babylon, and he will take it. 4King Zedekiah will be captured by the Babylonians* and taken to meet the king of Babylon face to face. 5He will take Zedekiah to Babylon, and I will deal with him there,' says the LORD. 'If you fight against the Babylonians, you will never succeed.'"

6At that time the LORD sent me a message. He said, 7"Your cousin Hanamel son of Shallum will come and say to you, 'Buy my field at Anathoth. By law you have the right to buy it before it is offered to anyone else.'"

8Then, just as the LORD had said he would, my cousin Hanamel came and visited me in the prison. He said, "Please buy my field at Anathoth in the land of Benjamin. By law you have the right to buy it before it is offered to anyone else, so buy it for yourself." Then I knew that the message I had heard was from the LORD.

9So I bought the field at Anathoth, paying Hanamel seventeen pieces* of silver for it. 10I signed and sealed the deed of purchase before witnesses, weighed out the silver, and paid him. 11Then I took the sealed deed and an unsealed copy of the deed, which contained the terms and conditions of the purchase, 12and I handed them to Baruch son of Neriah and

32:1a The tenth year of Zedekiah's reign and the eighteenth year of Nebuchadnezzar's reign was 587 B.C. **32:1b** Hebrew *Nebuchadrezzar*, a variant spelling of Nebuchadnezzar; also in 32:28. **32:4** Or *Chaldeans*; also in 32:5, 24, 25, 28, 29, 43. **32:9** Hebrew *17 shekels*, about 7 ounces or 194 grams in weight.

grandson of Mahseiah. I did all this in the presence of my cousin Hanamel, the witnesses who had signed the deed, and all the men of Judah who were there in the courtyard of the guardhouse.

[13]Then I said to Baruch as they all listened, [14]"This is what the LORD of Heaven's Armies, the God of Israel, says: 'Take both this sealed deed and the unsealed copy, and put them into a pottery jar to preserve them for a long time.' [15]For this is what the LORD of Heaven's Armies, the God of Israel, says: 'Someday people will again own property here in this land and will buy and sell houses and vineyards and fields.'"

Jeremiah's Prayer

[16]Then after I had given the papers to Baruch, I prayed to the LORD:

[17]"O Sovereign LORD! You made the heavens and earth by your strong hand and powerful arm. Nothing is too hard for you! [18]You show unfailing love to thousands, but you also bring the consequences of one generation's sin upon the next. You are the great and powerful God, the LORD of Heaven's Armies. [19]You have all wisdom and do great and mighty miracles. You see the conduct of all people, and you give them what they deserve. [20]You performed miraculous signs and wonders in the land of Egypt—things still remembered to this day! And you have continued to do great miracles in Israel and all around the world. You have made your name famous to this day.

[21]"You brought Israel out of Egypt with mighty signs and wonders, with a strong hand and powerful arm, and with overwhelming terror. [22]You gave the people of Israel this land that you had promised their ancestors long before—a land flowing with milk and honey. [23]Our ancestors came and conquered it and lived in it, but they refused to obey you or follow your word. They have not done anything you commanded. That is why you have sent this terrible disaster upon them.

[24]"See how the siege ramps have been built against the city walls! Through war, famine, and disease, the city will be handed over to the Babylonians, who will conquer it. Everything has happened just as you said. [25]And yet, O Sovereign LORD, you have told me to buy the field—paying good money for it before these witnesses—even though the city will soon be handed over to the Babylonians."

TOO HARD TO HANDLE?

Christopher's parents seemed to fight all the time. He was worried they might separate or get divorced. He thought about his home situation all the time and wanted to talk to someone about it. Christopher's best friend wouldn't understand; he had a perfect family. Christopher knew his church youth leader would say, "Take your problems to God; he will help you." But Christopher didn't think even God was big enough to help him deal with the huge problems he was facing at home. What do you think Christopher should do? See Jeremiah 32:27 for a reminder about what God can do.

A Prediction of Jerusalem's Fall

26Then this message came to Jeremiah from
the LORD: 27"I am the LORD, the God of all the
peoples of the world. Is anything too hard for
me? 28Therefore, this is what the LORD says: I
will hand this city over to the Babylonians and
to Nebuchadnezzar, king of Babylon, and he
will capture it. 29The Babylonians outside the
walls will come in and set fire to the city. They
will burn down all these houses where the
people provoked my anger by burning in-
cense to Baal on the rooftops and by pouring
out liquid offerings to other gods. 30Israel and
Judah have done nothing but wrong since
their earliest days. They have infuriated me
with all their evil deeds," says the LORD.
31"From the time this city was built until now,
it has done nothing but anger me, so I am de-
termined to get rid of it.

I have a problem that I don't think even God can fix!

I am the LORD, the God of all the peoples of the world. Is anything too hard for me? JEREMIAH 32:27

32"The sins of Israel and Judah—the sins of
the people of Jerusalem, the kings, the officials,
the priests, and the prophets—have stirred up
my anger. 33My people have turned their backs
on me and have refused to return. Even though
I diligently taught them, they would not receive
instruction or obey. 34They have set up their
abominable idols right in my own Temple, de-
filing it. 35They have built pagan shrines to Baal
in the valley of Ben-Hinnom, and there they sac-
rifice their sons and daughters to Molech. I
have never commanded such a horrible deed; it
never even crossed my mind to command such
a thing. What an incredible evil, causing Judah
to sin so greatly!

A Promise of Restoration

36"Now I want to say something more about
this city. You have been saying, 'It will fall to
the king of Babylon through war, famine, and
disease.' But this is what the LORD, the God of
Israel, says: 37I will certainly bring my people
back again from all the countries where I will
scatter them in my fury. I will bring them back
to this very city and let them live in peace and
safety. 38They will be my people, and I will be
their God. 39And I will give them one heart and
one purpose: to worship me forever, for their
own good and for the good of all their descen-
dants. 40And I will make an everlasting cov-
enant with them: I will never stop doing good
for them. I will put a desire in their hearts to
worship me, and they will never leave me. 41I
will find joy doing good for them and will
faithfully and wholeheartedly replant them in
this land.

42"This is what the LORD says: Just as I have
brought all these calamities on them, so I will
do all the good I have promised them. 43Fields
will again be bought and sold in this land about
which you now say, 'It has been ravaged by the
Babylonians, a desolate land where people and
animals have all disappeared.' 44Yes, fields will
once again be bought and sold—deeds signed
and sealed and witnessed—in the land of Ben-
jamin and here in Jerusalem, in the towns of
Judah and in the hill country, in the foothills of
Judah* and in the Negev, too. For someday I
will restore prosperity to them. I, the LORD,
have spoken!"

CHAPTER 33

Promises of Peace and Prosperity

While Jeremiah was still confined in the court-
yard of the guard, the LORD gave him this sec-
ond message: 2"This is what the LORD says—the
LORD who made the earth, who formed and es-
tablished it, whose name is the LORD: 3Ask me
and I will tell you remarkable secrets you do
not know about things to come. 4For this is
what the LORD, the God of Israel, says: You have
torn down the houses of this city and even the
king's palace to get materials to strengthen
the walls against the siege ramps and swords of
the enemy. 5You expect to fight the Babylo-
nians,* but the men of this city are already as
good as dead, for I have determined to destroy
them in my terrible anger. I have abandoned
them because of all their wickedness.

6"Nevertheless, the time will come when I

32:44 Hebrew *the Shephelah.* **33:5** Or *Chaldeans.*

will heal Jerusalem's wounds and give it prosperity and true peace. [7]I will restore the fortunes of Judah and Israel and rebuild their towns. [8]I will cleanse them of their sins against me and forgive all their sins of rebellion. [9]Then this city will bring me joy, glory, and honor before all the nations of the earth! The people of the world will see all the good I do for my people, and they will tremble with awe at the peace and prosperity I provide for them.

[10]"This is what the LORD says: You have said, 'This is a desolate land where people and animals have all disappeared.' Yet in the empty streets of Jerusalem and Judah's other towns, there will be heard once more [11]the sounds of joy and laughter. The joyful voices of bridegrooms and brides will be heard again, along with the joyous songs of people bringing thanksgiving offerings to the LORD. They will sing,

'Give thanks to the LORD of Heaven's Armies,
for the LORD is good.
His faithful love endures forever!'

For I will restore the prosperity of this land to what it was in the past, says the LORD.

[12]"This is what the LORD of Heaven's Armies says: This land—though it is now desolate and has no people and animals—will once more have pastures where shepherds can lead their flocks. [13]Once again shepherds will count their flocks in the towns of the hill country, the foothills of Judah,* the Negev, the land of Benjamin, the vicinity of Jerusalem, and all the towns of Judah. I, the LORD, have spoken!

[14]"The day will come, says the LORD, when I will do for Israel and Judah all the good things I have promised them.

[15] "In those days and at that time
I will raise up a righteous descendant*
from King David's line.
He will do what is just and right
throughout the land.
[16] In that day Judah will be saved,
and Jerusalem will live in safety.
And this will be its name:
'The LORD Is Our Righteousness.'*

[17]For this is what the LORD says: David will have a descendant sitting on the throne of Israel forever. [18]And there will always be Levitical priests to offer burnt offerings and grain offerings and sacrifices to me."

[19]Then this message came to Jeremiah from the LORD: [20]"This is what the LORD says: If you can break my covenant with the day and the night so that one does not follow the other, [21]only then will my covenant with my servant David be broken. Only then will he no longer have a descendant to reign on his throne. The same is true for my covenant with the Levitical priests who minister before me. [22]And as the stars of the sky cannot be counted and the sand on the seashore cannot be measured, so I will multiply the descendants of my servant David and the Levites who minister before me."

[23]The LORD gave another message to Jeremiah. He said, [24]"Have you noticed what people are saying?—'The LORD chose Judah and Israel and then abandoned them!' They are sneering and saying that Israel is not worthy to be counted as a nation. [25]But this is what the LORD says: I would no more reject my people than I would change my laws that govern night and day, earth and sky. [26]I will never abandon the descendants of Jacob or David, my servant, or change the plan that David's descendants will rule the descendants of Abraham, Isaac, and Jacob. Instead, I will restore them to their land and have mercy on them."

CHAPTER 34

A Warning for Zedekiah

King Nebuchadnezzar of Babylon came with all the armies from the kingdoms he ruled, and he fought against Jerusalem and the towns of Judah. At that time this message came to Jeremiah from the LORD: [2]"Go to King Zedekiah of Judah, and tell him, 'This is what the LORD, the God of Israel, says: I am about to hand this city over to the king of Babylon, and he will burn it down. [3]You will not escape his grasp but will be captured and taken to meet the king of Babylon face to face. Then you will be exiled to Babylon.

[4]"'But listen to this promise from the LORD, O Zedekiah, king of Judah. This is what the LORD says: You will not be killed in war [5]but will die peacefully. People will burn incense in your memory, just as they did for your ancestors, the kings who preceded you. They

33:13 Hebrew *the Shephelah.* 33:15 Hebrew *a righteous branch.* 33:16 Hebrew *Yahweh Tsidqenu.*

will mourn for you, crying, "Alas, our master is dead!" This I have decreed, says the LORD.'"

[6]So Jeremiah the prophet delivered the message to King Zedekiah of Judah. [7]At this time the Babylonian army was besieging Jerusalem, Lachish, and Azekah—the only fortified cities of Judah not yet captured.

Freedom for Hebrew Slaves

[8]This message came to Jeremiah from the LORD after King Zedekiah made a covenant with the people, proclaiming freedom for the slaves. [9]He had ordered all the people to free their Hebrew slaves—both men and women. No one was to keep a fellow Judean in bondage. [10]The officials and all the people had obeyed the king's command, [11]but later they changed their minds. They took back the men and women they had freed, forcing them to be slaves again.

[12]So the LORD gave them this message through Jeremiah: [13]"This is what the LORD, the God of Israel, says: I made a covenant with your ancestors long ago when I rescued them from their slavery in Egypt. [14]I told them that every Hebrew slave must be freed after serving six years. But your ancestors paid no attention to me. [15]Recently you repented and did what was right, following my command. You freed your slaves and made a solemn covenant with me in the Temple that bears my name. [16]But now you have shrugged off your oath and defiled my name by taking back the men and women you had freed, forcing them to be slaves once again.

[17]"Therefore, this is what the LORD says: Since you have not obeyed me by setting your countrymen free, I will set you free to be destroyed by war, disease, and famine. You will be an object of horror to all the nations of the earth. [18]Because you have broken the terms of our covenant, I will cut you apart just as you cut apart the calf when you walked between its halves to solemnize your vows. [19]Yes, I will cut you apart, whether you are officials of Judah or Jerusalem, court officials, priests, or common people—for you have broken your oath. [20]I will give you to your enemies, and they will kill you. Your bodies will be food for the vultures and wild animals.

[21]"I will hand over King Zedekiah of Judah and his officials to the army of the king of Babylon. And although Babylon's king has left Jerusalem for a while, [22]I will call the Babylonian armies back again. They will fight against this city and will capture it and burn it down. I will see to it that all the towns of Judah are destroyed, with no one living there."

CHAPTER 35

The Faithful Recabites

This is the message the LORD gave Jeremiah when Jehoiakim son of Josiah was king of Judah: [2]"Go to the settlement where the families of the Recabites live, and invite them to the LORD's Temple. Take them into one of the inner rooms, and offer them some wine."

[3]So I went to see Jaazaniah son of Jeremiah and grandson of Habazziniah and all his brothers and sons—representing all the Recabite families. [4]I took them to the Temple, and we went into the room assigned to the sons of Hanan son of Igdaliah, a man of God. This room was located next to the one used by the Temple officials, directly above the room of Maaseiah son of Shallum, the Temple gatekeeper.

[5]I set cups and jugs of wine before them and invited them to have a drink, [6]but they refused. "No," they said, "we don't drink wine, because our ancestor Jehonadab* son of Recab gave us this command: 'You and your descendants must never drink wine. [7]And do not build houses or plant crops or vineyards, but always live in tents. If you follow these commands, you will live long, good lives in the land.' [8]So we have obeyed him in all these things. We have never had a drink of wine to this day, nor have our wives, our sons, or our daughters. [9]We haven't built houses or owned vineyards or farms or planted crops. [10]We have lived in tents and have fully obeyed all the commands of Jehonadab, our ancestor. [11]But when King Nebuchadnezzar* of Babylon attacked this country, we were afraid of the Babylonian and Syrian* armies. So we decided to move to Jerusalem. That is why we are here."

[12]Then the LORD gave this message to Jeremiah: [13]"This is what the LORD of Heaven's Armies, the God of Israel, says: Go and say to the people in Judah and Jerusalem, 'Come and learn a lesson about how to obey me. [14]The

35:6 Hebrew *Jonadab*, a variant spelling of Jehonadab; also in 35:10, 14, 16, 18, 19. See 2 Kgs 10:15. **35:11a** Hebrew *Nebuchadrezzar*, a variant spelling of Nebuchadnezzar. **35:11b** Or *Chaldean and Aramean.*

AMAZING FACTS

Some people in the Bible were commanded to live in tents for their entire lives. It was a nonstop campout!

JEREMIAH 35:5-7

Recabites do not drink wine to this day because their ancestor Jehonadab told them not to. But I have spoken to you again and again, and you refuse to obey me. [15]Time after time I sent you prophets, who told you, "Turn from your wicked ways, and start doing things right. Stop worshiping other gods so that you might live in peace here in the land I have given to you and your ancestors." But you would not listen to me or obey me. [16]The descendants of Jehonadab son of Recab have obeyed their ancestor completely, but you have refused to listen to me.'

[17]"Therefore, this is what the LORD God of Heaven's Armies, the God of Israel, says: 'Because you refuse to listen or answer when I call, I will send upon Judah and Jerusalem all the disasters I have threatened.'"

[18]Then Jeremiah turned to the Recabites and said, "This is what the LORD of Heaven's Armies, the God of Israel, says: 'You have obeyed your ancestor Jehonadab in every respect, following all his instructions.' [19]Therefore, this is what the LORD of Heaven's Armies, the God of Israel, says: 'Jehonadab son of Recab will always have descendants who serve me.'"

CHAPTER 36

Baruch Reads the LORD's Messages

During the fourth year that Jehoiakim son of Josiah was king in Judah,* the LORD gave this message to Jeremiah: [2]"Get a scroll, and write down all my messages against Israel, Judah, and the other nations. Begin with the first message back in the days of Josiah, and write down every message, right up to the present time. [3]Perhaps the people of Judah will repent when they hear again all the terrible things I have planned for them. Then I will be able to forgive their sins and wrongdoings."

[4]So Jeremiah sent for Baruch son of Neriah, and as Jeremiah dictated all the prophecies that the LORD had given him, Baruch wrote them on a scroll. [5]Then Jeremiah said to Baruch, "I am a prisoner here and unable to go to the Temple. [6]So you go to the Temple on the next day of fasting, and read the messages from the LORD that I have had you write on this scroll. Read them so the people who are there from all over Judah will hear them. [7]Perhaps even yet they will turn from their evil ways and ask the LORD's forgiveness before it is too late. For the LORD has threatened them with his terrible anger."

[8]Baruch did as Jeremiah told him and read these messages from the LORD to the people at the Temple. [9]He did this on a day of sacred fasting held in late autumn,* during the fifth year of the reign of Jehoiakim son of Josiah. People from all over Judah had come to Jerusalem to attend the services at the Temple on that day. [10]Baruch read Jeremiah's words on the scroll to all the people. He stood in front of the Temple room of Gemariah, son of Shaphan the secretary. This room was just off the upper courtyard of the Temple, near the New Gate entrance.

[11]When Micaiah son of Gemariah and grandson of Shaphan heard the messages from the LORD, [12]he went down to the secretary's room in the palace where the administrative officials were meeting. Elishama the secretary was there, along with Delaiah son of Shemaiah, Elnathan son of Acbor, Gemariah son of Shaphan, Zedekiah son of Hananiah, and all the other officials. [13]When Micaiah told them about the messages Baruch was reading to the people, [14]the officials sent Jehudi son of Nethaniah, grandson of Shelemiah and great-grandson of Cushi, to ask Baruch to come and read the messages to them, too. So Baruch took the scroll and went to them. [15]"Sit down and read the scroll to us,"

36:1 The fourth year of Jehoiakim's reign was 605 B.C. **36:9** Hebrew *in the ninth month*, of the ancient Hebrew lunar calendar (also in 36:22). The ninth month in the fifth year of Jehoiakim's reign occurred within the months of November and December 604 B.C. Also see note on 1:3.

the officials said, and Baruch did as they requested.

16When they heard all the messages, they looked at one another in alarm. "We must tell the king what we have heard," they said to Baruch. 17"But first, tell us how you got these messages. Did they come directly from Jeremiah?"

18So Baruch explained, "Jeremiah dictated them, and I wrote them down in ink, word for word, on this scroll."

19"You and Jeremiah should both hide," the officials told Baruch. "Don't tell anyone where you are!" 20Then the officials left the scroll for safekeeping in the room of Elishama the secretary and went to tell the king what had happened.

King Jehoiakim Burns the Scroll

21The king sent Jehudi to get the scroll. Jehudi brought it from Elishama's room and read it to the king as all his officials stood by. 22It was late autumn, and the king was in a winterized part of the palace, sitting in front of a fire to keep warm. 23Each time Jehudi finished reading three or four columns, the king took a knife and cut off that section of the scroll. He then threw it into the fire, section by section, until the whole scroll was burned up. 24Neither the king nor his attendants showed any signs of fear or repentance at what they heard. 25Even when Elnathan, Delaiah, and Gemariah begged the king not to burn the scroll, he wouldn't listen.

26Then the king commanded his son Jerahmeel, Seraiah son of Azriel, and Shelemiah son of Abdeel to arrest Baruch and Jeremiah. But the LORD had hidden them.

Jeremiah Rewrites the Scroll

27After the king had burned the scroll on which Baruch had written Jeremiah's words, the LORD gave Jeremiah another message. He said, 28"Get another scroll, and write everything again just as you did on the scroll King Jehoiakim burned. 29Then say to the king, 'This is what the LORD says: You burned the scroll because it said the king of Babylon would destroy this land and empty it of people and animals. 30Now this is what the LORD says about King Jehoiakim of Judah: He will have no heirs to sit on the throne of David. His dead body will be thrown out to lie unburied—exposed to the heat of the day and the frost of the night. 31I will punish him and his family and his attendants for their sins. I will pour out on them and on all the people of Jerusalem and Judah all the disasters I promised, for they would not listen to my warnings.'"

32So Jeremiah took another scroll and dictated again to his secretary, Baruch. He wrote everything that had been on the scroll King Jehoiakim had burned in the fire. Only this time he added much more!

CHAPTER 37

Zedekiah Calls for Jeremiah

Zedekiah son of Josiah succeeded Jehoiachin* son of Jehoiakim as the king of Judah. He was appointed by King Nebuchadnezzar* of Babylon. 2But neither King Zedekiah nor his attendants nor the people who were left in the land listened to what the LORD said through Jeremiah.

3Nevertheless, King Zedekiah sent Jehucal son of Shelemiah, and Zephaniah the priest, son of Maaseiah, to ask Jeremiah, "Please pray to the LORD our God for us." 4Jeremiah had not yet been imprisoned, so he could come and go among the people as he pleased.

5At this time the army of Pharaoh Hophra* of Egypt appeared at the southern border of Judah. When the Babylonian* army heard about it, they withdrew from their siege of Jerusalem.

6Then the LORD gave this message to Jeremiah: 7"This is what the LORD, the God of Israel, says: The king of Judah sent you to ask me what is going to happen. Tell him, 'Pharaoh's army is about to return to Egypt, though he came here to help you. 8Then the Babylonians* will come back and capture this city and burn it to the ground.'

9"This is what the LORD says: Do not fool yourselves into thinking that the Babylonians are gone for good. They aren't! 10Even if you were to destroy the entire Babylonian army, leaving only a handful of wounded survivors, they would still stagger from their tents and burn this city to the ground!"

37:1a Hebrew *Coniah*, a variant spelling of Jehoiachin. **37:1b** Hebrew *Nebuchadrezzar*, a variant spelling of Nebuchadnezzar. **37:5a** Hebrew *army of Pharaoh;* see 44:30. **37:5b** Or *Chaldean;* also in 37:10, 11. **37:8** Or *Chaldeans;* also in 37:9, 13.

AMAZING FACTS

The king's officers didn't like Jeremiah's message, so they threw him into a deep, muddy well. It took 30 men to pull him out!

JEREMIAH 38:4-6, 10

Jeremiah Is Imprisoned

[11]When the Babylonian army left Jerusalem because of Pharaoh's approaching army, [12]Jeremiah started to leave the city on his way to the territory of Benjamin, to claim his share of the property among his relatives there.* [13]But as he was walking through the Benjamin Gate, a sentry arrested him and said, "You are defecting to the Babylonians!" The sentry making the arrest was Irijah son of Shelemiah, grandson of Hananiah.

[14]"That's not true!" Jeremiah protested. "I had no intention of doing any such thing." But Irijah wouldn't listen, and he took Jeremiah before the officials. [15]They were furious with Jeremiah and had him flogged and imprisoned in the house of Jonathan the secretary. Jonathan's house had been converted into a prison. [16]Jeremiah was put into a dungeon cell, where he remained for many days.

[17]Later King Zedekiah secretly requested that Jeremiah come to the palace, where the king asked him, "Do you have any messages from the LORD?"

"Yes, I do!" said Jeremiah. "You will be defeated by the king of Babylon."

[18]Then Jeremiah asked the king, "What crime have I committed? What have I done against you, your attendants, or the people that I should be imprisoned like this? [19]Where are your prophets now who told you the king of Babylon would not attack you or this land? [20]Listen, my lord the king, I beg you. Don't send me back to the dungeon in the house of Jonathan the secretary, for I will die there."

[21]So King Zedekiah commanded that Jeremiah not be returned to the dungeon. Instead, he was imprisoned in the courtyard of the guard in the royal palace. The king also commanded that Jeremiah be given a loaf of fresh bread every day as long as there was any left in the city. So Jeremiah was put in the palace prison.

CHAPTER 38

Jeremiah in a Cistern

Now Shephatiah son of Mattan, Gedaliah son of Pashhur, Jehucal* son of Shelemiah, and Pashhur son of Malkijah heard what Jeremiah had been telling the people. He had been saying, [2]"This is what the LORD says: 'Everyone who stays in Jerusalem will die from war, famine, or disease, but those who surrender to the Babylonians* will live. Their reward will be life. They will live!' [3]The LORD also says: 'The city of Jerusalem will certainly be handed over to the army of the king of Babylon, who will capture it.'"

[4]So these officials went to the king and said, "Sir, this man must die! That kind of talk will undermine the morale of the few fighting men we have left, as well as that of all the people. This man is a traitor!"

[5]King Zedekiah agreed. "All right," he said. "Do as you like. I can't stop you."

[6]So the officials took Jeremiah from his cell and lowered him by ropes into an empty cistern in the prison yard. It belonged to Malkijah, a member of the royal family. There was no water in the cistern, but there was a thick layer of mud at the bottom, and Jeremiah sank down into it.

[7]But Ebed-melech the Ethiopian,* an important court official, heard that Jeremiah was in the cistern. At that time the king was holding court at the Benjamin Gate, [8]so Ebed-melech rushed from the palace to speak with him. [9]"My lord the king," he said, "these men have done a very evil thing in putting Jeremiah the prophet into the cistern. He will soon die of hunger, for almost all the bread in the city is gone."

[10]So the king told Ebed-melech, "Take

37:12 Hebrew *to separate from there in the midst of the people.* **38:1** Hebrew *Jucal,* a variant spelling of Jehucal; see 37:3. **38:2** Or *Chaldeans;* also in 38:18, 19, 23. **38:7** Hebrew *the Cushite.*

thirty of my men with you, and pull Jeremiah out of the cistern before he dies."

[11]So Ebed-melech took the men with him and went to a room in the palace beneath the treasury, where he found some old rags and discarded clothing. He carried these to the cistern and lowered them to Jeremiah on a rope. [12]Ebed-melech called down to Jeremiah, "Put these rags under your armpits to protect you from the ropes." Then when Jeremiah was ready, [13]they pulled him out. So Jeremiah was returned to the courtyard of the guard—the palace prison—where he remained.

Zedekiah Questions Jeremiah

[14]One day King Zedekiah sent for Jeremiah and had him brought to the third entrance of the LORD's Temple. "I want to ask you something," the king said. "And don't try to hide the truth."

[15]Jeremiah said, "If I tell you the truth, you will kill me. And if I give you advice, you won't listen to me anyway."

[16]So King Zedekiah secretly promised him, "As surely as the LORD our Creator lives, I will not kill you or hand you over to the men who want you dead."

[17]Then Jeremiah said to Zedekiah, "This is what the LORD God of Heaven's Armies, the God of Israel, says: 'If you surrender to the Babylonian officers, you and your family will live, and the city will not be burned down. [18]But if you refuse to surrender, you will not escape! This city will be handed over to the Babylonians, and they will burn it to the ground.'"

[19]"But I am afraid to surrender," the king said, "for the Babylonians may hand me over to the Judeans who have defected to them. And who knows what they will do to me!"

[20]Jeremiah replied, "You won't be handed over to them if you choose to obey the LORD. Your life will be spared, and all will go well for you. [21]But if you refuse to surrender, this is what the LORD has revealed to me: [22]All the women left in your palace will be brought out and given to the officers of the Babylonian army. Then the women will taunt you, saying,

'What fine friends you have!
They have betrayed and misled you.
When your feet sank in the mud,
they left you to your fate!'

[23]All your wives and children will be led out to the Babylonians, and you will not escape. You will be seized by the king of Babylon, and this city will be burned down."

[24]Then Zedekiah said to Jeremiah, "Don't tell anyone you told me this, or you will die! [25]My officials may hear that I spoke to you, and they may say, 'Tell us what you and the king were talking about. If you don't tell us, we will kill you.' [26]If this happens, just tell them you begged me not to send you back to Jonathan's dungeon, for fear you would die there."

[27]Sure enough, it wasn't long before the king's officials came to Jeremiah and asked him why the king had called for him. But Jeremiah followed the king's instructions, and they left without finding out the truth. No one had overheard the conversation between Jeremiah and the king. [28]And Jeremiah remained a prisoner in the courtyard of the guard until the day Jerusalem was captured.

CHAPTER 39

The Fall of Jerusalem

In January* of the ninth year of King Zedekiah's reign, King Nebuchadnezzar* came with his army to besiege Jerusalem. [2]Two and a half years later, on July 18* in the eleventh year of Zedekiah's reign, the Babylonians broke through the wall, and the city fell. [3]All the officers of the Babylonian army came in and sat in triumph at the Middle Gate: Nergal-sharezer of Samgar, and Nebo-sarsekim,* a chief officer, and Nergal-sharezer, the king's adviser, and all the other officers.

[4]When King Zedekiah and all the soldiers saw that the Babylonians had broken into the city, they fled. They waited for nightfall and then slipped through the gate between the two walls behind the king's garden and headed toward the Jordan Valley.*

[5]But the Babylonian* troops chased the king and caught him on the plains of Jericho.

39:1a Hebrew *in the tenth month,* of the ancient Hebrew lunar calendar. A number of events in Jeremiah can be cross-checked with dates in surviving Babylonian records and related accurately to our modern calendar. This event occurred on January 15, 588 B.C.; see 52:4a and the note there. **39:1b** Hebrew *Nebuchadrezzar,* a variant spelling of Nebuchadnezzar; also in 39:11. **39:2** Hebrew *On the ninth day of the fourth month.* This day was July 18, 586 B.C.; also see note on 39:1a. **39:3** Or *Nergal-sharezer, Samgar-nebo, Sarsekim.* **39:4** Hebrew *the Arabah.* **39:5** Or *Chaldean;* similarly in 39:8.

They took him to King Nebuchadnezzar of Babylon, who was at Riblah in the land of Hamath. There the king of Babylon pronounced judgment upon Zedekiah. [6]He made Zedekiah watch as they slaughtered his sons and all the nobles of Judah. [7]Then they gouged out Zedekiah's eyes, bound him in bronze chains, and led him away to Babylon.

[8]Meanwhile, the Babylonians burned Jerusalem, including the palace, and tore down the walls of the city. [9]Then Nebuzaradan, the captain of the guard, sent to Babylon the rest of the people who remained in the city as well as those who had defected to him. [10]But Nebuzaradan left a few of the poorest people in Judah, and he assigned them vineyards and fields to care for.

Jeremiah Remains in Judah

[11]King Nebuchadnezzar had told Nebuzaradan, the captain of the guard, to find Jeremiah. [12]"See that he isn't hurt," he said. "Look after him well, and give him anything he wants." [13]So Nebuzaradan, the captain of the guard; Nebushazban, a chief officer; Nergal-sharezer, the king's adviser; and the other officers of Babylon's king [14]sent messengers to bring Jeremiah out of the prison. They put him under the care of Gedaliah son of Ahikam and grandson of Shaphan, who took him back to his home. So Jeremiah stayed in Judah among his own people.

[15]The LORD had given the following message to Jeremiah while he was still in prison: [16]"Say to Ebed-melech the Ethiopian,* 'This is what the LORD of Heaven's Armies, the God of Israel, says: I will do to this city everything I have threatened. I will send disaster, not prosperity. You will see its destruction, [17]but I will rescue you from those you fear so much. [18]Because you trusted me, I will give you your life as a reward. I will rescue you and keep you safe. I, the LORD, have spoken!'"

CHAPTER 40

The LORD gave a message to Jeremiah after Nebuzaradan, the captain of the guard, had released him at Ramah. He had found Jeremiah bound in chains among all the other captives of Jerusalem and Judah who were being sent to exile in Babylon.

[2]The captain of the guard called for Jeremiah and said, "The LORD your God has brought this disaster on this land, [3]just as he said he would. For these people have sinned against the LORD and disobeyed him. That is why it happened. [4]But I am going to take off your chains and let you go. If you want to come with me to Babylon, you are welcome. I will see that you are well cared for. But if you don't want to come, you may stay here. The whole land is before you—go wherever you like. [5]If you decide to stay, then return to Gedaliah son of Ahikam and grandson of Shaphan. He has been appointed governor of Judah by the king of Babylon. Stay there with the people he rules. But it's up to you; go wherever you like."

Then Nebuzaradan, the captain of the guard, gave Jeremiah some food and money and let him go. [6]So Jeremiah returned to Gedaliah son of Ahikam at Mizpah, and he lived in Judah with the few who were still left in the land.

Gedaliah Governs in Judah

[7]The leaders of the Judean guerrilla bands in the countryside heard that the king of Babylon had appointed Gedaliah son of Ahikam as governor over the poor people who were left behind in Judah—the men, women, and children who hadn't been exiled to Babylon. [8]So they went to see Gedaliah at Mizpah. These included: Ishmael son of Nethaniah, Johanan and Jonathan sons of Kareah, Seraiah son of Tanhumeth, the sons of Ephai the Netophathite, Jezaniah son of the Maacathite, and all their men.

[9]Gedaliah vowed to them that the Babylonians* meant them no harm. "Don't be afraid to serve them. Live in the land and serve the king of Babylon, and all will go well for you," he promised. [10]"As for me, I will stay at Mizpah to represent you before the Babylonians who come to meet with us. Settle in the towns you have taken, and live off the land. Harvest the grapes and summer fruits and olives, and store them away."

[11]When the Judeans in Moab, Ammon, Edom, and the other nearby countries heard that the king of Babylon had left a few people in Judah and that Gedaliah was the governor, [12]they began to return to Judah from the

39:16 Hebrew *the Cushite*. **40:9** Or *Chaldeans;* also in 40:10.

places to which they had fled. They stopped at Mizpah to meet with Gedaliah and then went into the Judean countryside to gather a great harvest of grapes and other crops.

A Plot against Gedaliah

[13]Soon after this, Johanan son of Kareah and the other guerrilla leaders came to Gedaliah at Mizpah. [14]They said to him, "Did you know that Baalis, king of Ammon, has sent Ishmael son of Nethaniah to assassinate you?" But Gedaliah refused to believe them.

[15]Later Johanan had a private conference with Gedaliah and volunteered to kill Ishmael secretly. "Why should we let him come and murder you?" Johanan asked. "What will happen then to the Judeans who have returned? Why should the few of us who are still left be scattered and lost?"

[16]But Gedaliah said to Johanan, "I forbid you to do any such thing, for you are lying about Ishmael."

CHAPTER 41

The Murder of Gedaliah

But in midautumn,* Ishmael son of Nethaniah and grandson of Elishama, who was a member of the royal family and had been one of the king's high officials, went to Mizpah with ten men to meet Gedaliah. While they were eating together, [2]Ishmael and his ten men suddenly jumped up, drew their swords, and killed Gedaliah, whom the king of Babylon had appointed governor. [3]Ishmael also killed all the Judeans and the Babylonian* soldiers who were with Gedaliah at Mizpah.

[4]The next day, before anyone had heard about Gedaliah's murder, [5]eighty men arrived from Shechem, Shiloh, and Samaria to worship at the Temple of the LORD. They had shaved off their beards, torn their clothes, and cut themselves, and had brought along grain offerings and frankincense. [6]Ishmael left Mizpah to meet them, weeping as he went. When he reached them, he said, "Oh, come and see what has happened to Gedaliah!"

[7]But as soon as they were all inside the town, Ishmael and his men killed all but ten of them and threw their bodies into a cistern. [8]The other ten had talked Ishmael into letting them go by promising to bring him their stores of wheat, barley, olive oil, and honey that they had hidden away. [9]The cistern where Ishmael dumped the bodies of the men he murdered was the large one dug by King Asa when he fortified Mizpah to protect himself against King Baasha of Israel. Ishmael son of Nethaniah filled it with corpses.

[10]Then Ishmael made captives of the king's daughters and the other people who had been left under Gedaliah's care in Mizpah by Nebuzaradan, the captain of the guard. Taking them with him, he started back toward the land of Ammon.

[11]But when Johanan son of Kareah and the other guerrilla leaders heard about Ishmael's crimes, [12]they took all their men and set out to stop him. They caught up with him at the large pool near Gibeon. [13]The people Ishmael had captured shouted for joy when they saw Johanan and the other guerrilla leaders. [14]And all the captives from Mizpah escaped and began to help Johanan. [15]Meanwhile, Ishmael and eight of his men escaped from Johanan into the land of Ammon.

[16]Then Johanan son of Kareah and the other guerrilla leaders took all the people they had rescued in Gibeon—the soldiers, women, children, and court officials* whom Ishmael had captured after he killed Gedaliah. [17]They took them all to the village of Geruth-kimham near Bethlehem, where they prepared to leave for Egypt. [18]They were afraid of what the Babylonians* would do when they heard that Ishmael had killed Gedaliah, the governor appointed by the Babylonian king.

CHAPTER 42

Warning to Stay in Judah

Then all the guerrilla leaders, including Johanan son of Kareah and Jezaniah* son of Hoshaiah, and all the people, from the least to the greatest, approached [2]Jeremiah the prophet. They said, "Please pray to the LORD your God for us. As you can see, we are only a tiny remnant compared to what we were before. [3]Pray that the LORD your God will show us what to do and where to go."

[4]"All right," Jeremiah replied. "I will pray to

41:1 Hebrew *in the seventh month*, of the ancient Hebrew lunar calendar. This month occurred within the months of October and November 586 B.C.; also see note on 39:1a. **41:3** Or *Chaldean*. **41:16** Or *eunuchs*. **41:18** Or *Chaldeans*. **42:1** Greek version reads *Azariah*; compare 43:2.

the LORD your God, as you have asked, and I will tell you everything he says. I will hide nothing from you."

5 Then they said to Jeremiah, "May the LORD your God be a faithful witness against us if we refuse to obey whatever he tells us to do! 6 Whether we like it or not, we will obey the LORD our God to whom we are sending you with our plea. For if we obey him, everything will turn out well for us."

What if I don't want to do what God says?

Whether we like it or not, we will obey the LORD our God. . . . For if we obey him, everything will turn out well for us. JEREMIAH 42:6

7 Ten days later the LORD gave his reply to Jeremiah. 8 So he called for Johanan son of Kareah and the other guerrilla leaders, and for all the people, from the least to the greatest. 9 He said to them, "You sent me to the LORD, the God of Israel, with your request, and this is his reply: 10 "Stay here in this land. If you do, I will build you up and not tear you down; I will plant you and not uproot you. For I am sorry about all the punishment I have had to bring upon you. 11 Do not fear the king of Babylon anymore,' says the LORD. 'For I am with you and will save you and rescue you from his power. 12 I will be merciful to you by making him kind, so he will let you stay here in your land.'

13 "But if you refuse to obey the LORD your God, and if you say, 'We will not stay here; 14 instead, we will go to Egypt where we will be free from war, the call to arms, and hunger,' 15 then hear the LORD's message to the remnant of Judah. This is what the LORD of Heaven's Armies, the God of Israel, says: 'If you are determined to go to Egypt and live there, 16 the very war and famine you fear will catch up to you, and you will die there. 17 That is the fate awaiting every one of you who insists on going to live in Egypt. Yes, you will die from war, famine, and disease. None of you will escape the disaster I will bring upon you there.'

18 "This is what the LORD of Heaven's Armies, the God of Israel, says: 'Just as my anger and fury have been poured out on the people of Jerusalem, so they will be poured out on you when you enter Egypt. You will be an object of damnation, horror, cursing, and mockery. And you will never see your homeland again.'

19 "Listen, you remnant of Judah. The LORD has told you: 'Do not go to Egypt!' Don't forget this warning I have given you today. 20 For you were not being honest when you sent me to pray to the LORD your God for you. You said, 'Just tell us what the LORD our God says, and we will do it!' 21 And today I have told you exactly what he said, but you will not obey the LORD your God any better now than you have in the past. 22 So you can be sure that you will die from war, famine, and disease in Egypt, where you insist on going."

CHAPTER 43

Jeremiah Taken to Egypt

When Jeremiah had finished giving this message from the LORD their God to all the people, 2 Azariah son of Hoshaiah and Johanan son of Kareah and all the other proud men said to Jeremiah, "You lie! The LORD our God hasn't forbidden us to go to Egypt! 3 Baruch son of Neriah has convinced you to say this, because he wants us to stay here and be killed by the Babylonians* or be carried off into exile."

4 So Johanan and the other guerrilla leaders and all the people refused to obey the LORD's command to stay in Judah. 5 Johanan and the other leaders took with them all the people who had returned from the nearby countries to which they had fled. 6 In the crowd were men, women, and children, the king's daughters, and all those whom Nebuzaradan, the captain of the guard, had left with Gedaliah. The prophet Jeremiah and Baruch were also included. 7 The people refused to obey the voice of the LORD and went to Egypt, going as far as the city of Tahpanhes.

8 Then at Tahpanhes, the LORD gave another message to Jeremiah. He said, 9 "While the people of Judah are watching, take some large rocks and bury them under the pavement

43:3 Or *Chaldeans.*

stones at the entrance of Pharaoh's palace here in Tahpanhes. [10]Then say to the people of Judah, 'This is what the LORD of Heaven's Armies, the God of Israel, says: I will certainly bring my servant Nebuchadnezzar,* king of Babylon, here to Egypt. I will set his throne over these stones that I have hidden. He will spread his royal canopy over them. [11]And when he comes, he will destroy the land of Egypt. He will bring death to those destined for death, captivity to those destined for captivity, and war to those destined for war. [12]He will set fire to the temples of Egypt's gods; he will burn the temples and carry the idols away as plunder. He will pick clean the land of Egypt as a shepherd picks fleas from his cloak. And he himself will leave unharmed. [13]He will break down the sacred pillars standing in the temple of the sun* in Egypt, and he will burn down the temples of Egypt's gods.'"

CHAPTER 44

Judgment for Idolatry

This is the message Jeremiah received concerning the Judeans living in northern Egypt in the cities of Migdol, Tahpanhes, and Memphis,* and in southern Egypt* as well: [2]"This is what the LORD of Heaven's Armies, the God of Israel, says: You saw the calamity I brought on Jerusalem and all the towns of Judah. They now lie deserted and in ruins. [3]They provoked my anger with all their wickedness. They burned incense and worshiped other gods—gods that neither they nor you nor any of your ancestors had ever even known.

[4]"Again and again I sent my servants, the prophets, to plead with them, 'Don't do these horrible things that I hate so much.' [5]But my people would not listen or turn back from their wicked ways. They kept on burning incense to these gods. [6]And so my fury boiled over and fell like fire on the towns of Judah and into the streets of Jerusalem, and they are still a desolate ruin today.

[7]"And now the LORD God of Heaven's Armies, the God of Israel, asks you: Why are you destroying yourselves? For not one of you will survive—not a man, woman, or child among you who has come here from Judah, not even the babies in your arms. [8]Why provoke my anger by burning incense to the idols you have made here in Egypt? You will only destroy yourselves and make yourselves an object of cursing and mockery for all the nations of the earth. [9]Have you forgotten the sins of your ancestors, the sins of the kings and queens of Judah, and the sins you and your wives committed in Judah and Jerusalem? [10]To this very hour you have shown no remorse or reverence. No one has chosen to follow my word and the decrees I gave to you and your ancestors before you.

[11]"Therefore, this is what the LORD of Heaven's Armies, the God of Israel, says: I am determined to destroy every one of you! [12]I will take this remnant of Judah—those who were determined to come here and live in Egypt—and I will consume them. They will

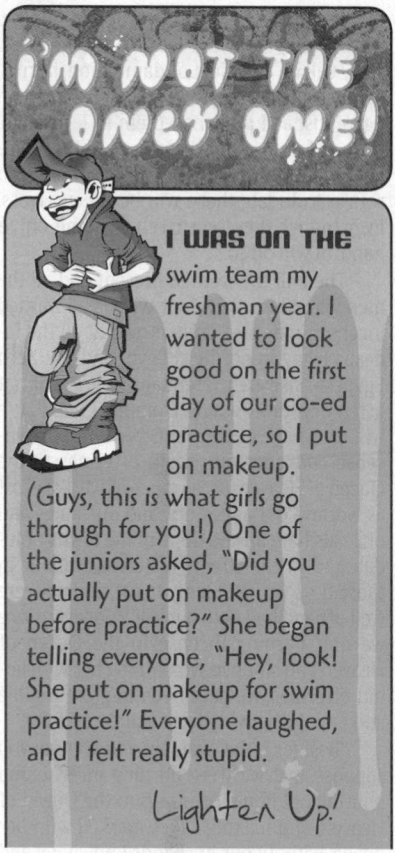

43:10 Hebrew *Nebuchadrezzar*, a variant spelling of Nebuchadnezzar. **43:13** Or *in Heliopolis*. **44:1a** Hebrew *Noph*. **44:1b** Hebrew *in Pathros*.

fall here in Egypt, killed by war and famine.
All will die, from the least to the greatest.
They will be an object of damnation, horror,
cursing, and mockery. [13]I will punish them in
Egypt just as I punished them in Jerusalem,
by war, famine, and disease. [14]Of that rem-
nant who fled to Egypt, hoping someday to
return to Judah, there will be no survivors.
Even though they long to return home, only a
handful will do so."

[15]Then all the women present and all the
men who knew that their wives had burned
incense to idols—a great crowd of all the Ju-
deans living in northern Egypt and southern
Egypt*—answered Jeremiah, [16]"We will not
listen to your messages from the LORD! [17]We
will do whatever we want. We will burn in-
cense and pour out liquid offerings to the
Queen of Heaven just as much as we like—just
as we, and our ancestors, and our kings and
officials have always done in the towns of Ju-
dah and in the streets of Jerusalem. For in
those days we had plenty to eat, and we were
well off and had no troubles! [18]But ever since
we quit burning incense to the Queen of
Heaven and stopped worshiping her with liq-
uid offerings, we have been in great trouble
and have been dying from war and famine."

[19]"Besides," the women added, "do you
suppose that we were burning incense and
pouring out liquid offerings to the Queen of
Heaven, and making cakes marked with her
image, without our husbands knowing it and
helping us? Of course not!"

[20]Then Jeremiah said to all of them, men
and women alike, who had given him that an-
swer, [21]"Do you think the LORD did not know
that you and your ancestors, your kings and
officials, and all the people were burning in-
cense to idols in the towns of Judah and in the
streets of Jerusalem? [22]It was because the
LORD could no longer bear all the disgusting
things you were doing that he made your land
an object of cursing—a desolate ruin without
inhabitants—as it is today. [23]All these terrible
things happened to you because you have
burned incense to idols and sinned against
the LORD. You have refused to obey him and
have not followed his instructions, his de-
crees, and his laws."

[24]Then Jeremiah said to them all, including
the women, "Listen to this message from the
LORD, all you citizens of Judah who live in
Egypt. [25]This is what the LORD of Heaven's Ar-
mies, the God of Israel, says: 'You and your
wives have said, "We will keep our promises
to burn incense and pour out liquid offerings
to the Queen of Heaven," and you have proved
by your actions that you meant it. So go ahead
and carry out your promises and vows to her!'

[26]"But listen to this message from the
LORD, all you Judeans now living in Egypt: 'I
have sworn by my great name,' says the LORD,
'that my name will no longer be spoken by any
of the Judeans in the land of Egypt. None of
you may invoke my name or use this oath: "As
surely as the Sovereign LORD lives." [27]For I will
watch over you to bring you disaster and not
good. Everyone from Judah who is now living
in Egypt will suffer war and famine until all of
you are dead. [28]Only a small number will es-
cape death and return to Judah from Egypt.
Then all those who came to Egypt will find out
whose words are true—mine or theirs!

[29]"'And this is the proof I give you,' says the
LORD, 'that all I have threatened will happen
to you and that I will punish you here.' [30]This
is what the LORD says: 'I will turn Pharaoh
Hophra, king of Egypt, over to his enemies
who want to kill him, just as I turned King
Zedekiah of Judah over to King Nebuchad-
nezzar* of Babylon.'"

CHAPTER 45

A Message for Baruch

The prophet Jeremiah gave a message to Ba-
ruch son of Neriah in the fourth year of the
reign of Jehoiakim son of Josiah,* after Ba-
ruch had written down everything Jeremiah
had dictated to him. He said, [2]"This is what
the LORD, the God of Israel, says to you, Ba-
ruch: [3]You have said, 'I am overwhelmed with
trouble! Haven't I had enough pain already?
And now the LORD has added more! I am worn
out from sighing and can find no rest.'

[4]"Baruch, this is what the LORD says: 'I will
destroy this nation that I built. I will uproot
what I planted. [5]Are you seeking great things
for yourself? Don't do it! I will bring great di-
saster upon all these people; but I will give you
your life as a reward wherever you go. I, the
LORD, have spoken!'"

44:15 Hebrew *in Egypt, in Pathros.* **44:30** Hebrew *Nebuchadrezzar,* a variant spelling of Nebuchadnezzar. **45:1** The fourth year of Jehoiakim's reign was 605 B.C.

CHAPTER 46

Messages for the Nations

The following messages were given to Jeremiah the prophet from the LORD concerning foreign nations.

Messages about Egypt

2 This message concerning Egypt was given in the fourth year of the reign of Jehoiakim son of Josiah, the king of Judah, on the occasion of the battle of Carchemish* when Pharaoh Neco, king of Egypt, and his army were defeated beside the Euphrates River by King Nebuchadnezzar* of Babylon.

3 "Prepare your shields,
and advance into battle!
4 Harness the horses,
and mount the stallions.
Take your positions.
Put on your helmets.
Sharpen your spears,
and prepare your armor.
5 But what do I see?
The Egyptian army flees in terror.
The bravest of its fighting men run
without a backward glance.
They are terrorized at every turn,"
says the LORD.
6 "The swiftest runners cannot flee;
the mightiest warriors cannot escape.
By the Euphrates River to the north,
they stumble and fall.

7 "Who is this, rising like the Nile at floodtime,
overflowing all the land?
8 It is the Egyptian army,
overflowing all the land,
boasting that it will cover the earth like a flood,
destroying cities and their people.
9 Charge, you horses and chariots;
attack, you mighty warriors of Egypt!
Come, all you allies from Ethiopia, Libya, and Lydia*
who are skilled with the shield and bow!
10 For this is the day of the Lord, the LORD of Heaven's Armies,
a day of vengeance on his enemies.
The sword will devour until it is satisfied,
yes, until it is drunk with your blood!
The Lord, the LORD of Heaven's Armies,
will receive a sacrifice today
in the north country beside the Euphrates River.

11 "Go up to Gilead to get medicine,
O virgin daughter of Egypt!
But your many treatments
will bring you no healing.
12 The nations have heard of your shame.
The earth is filled with your cries of despair.
Your mightiest warriors will run into each other
and fall down together."

13 Then the LORD gave the prophet Jeremiah this message about King Nebuchadnezzar's plans to attack Egypt.

14 "Shout it out in Egypt!
Publish it in the cities of Migdol, Memphis,* and Tahpanhes!
Mobilize for battle,
for the sword will devour everyone around you.
15 Why have your warriors fallen?
They cannot stand, for the LORD has knocked them down.
16 They stumble and fall over each other
and say among themselves,
'Come, let's go back to our people,
to the land of our birth.
Let's get away from the sword of the enemy!'
17 There they will say,
'Pharaoh, the king of Egypt, is a loudmouth
who missed his opportunity!'

18 "As surely as I live," says the King,
whose name is the LORD of Heaven's Armies,
"one is coming against Egypt
who is as tall as Mount Tabor,
or as Mount Carmel by the sea!
19 Pack up! Get ready to leave for exile,
you citizens of Egypt!
The city of Memphis will be destroyed,
without a single inhabitant.

46:2a This event occurred in 605 B.C., during the fourth year of Jehoiakim's reign (according to the calendar system in which the new year begins in the spring). **46:2b** Hebrew *Nebuchadrezzar*, a variant spelling of Nebuchadnezzar; also in 46:13, 26. **46:9** Hebrew *from Cush, Put, and Lud*. **46:14** Hebrew *Noph*; also in 46:19.

20 Egypt is as sleek as a beautiful young cow,
but a horsefly from the north is on its way!
21 Egypt's mercenaries have become like fattened calves.
They, too, will turn and run,
for it is a day of great disaster for Egypt,
a time of great punishment.
22 Egypt flees, silent as a serpent gliding away.
The invading army marches in;
they come against her with axes like woodsmen.
23 They will cut down her people like trees," says the LORD,
"for they are more numerous than locusts.
24 Egypt will be humiliated;
she will be handed over to people from the north."

25 The LORD of Heaven's Armies, the God of Israel, says: "I will punish Amon, the god of Thebes,* and all the other gods of Egypt. I will punish its rulers and Pharaoh, too, and all who trust in him. 26 I will hand them over to those who want them killed—to King Nebuchadnezzar of Babylon and his army. But afterward the land will recover from the ravages of war. I, the LORD, have spoken!

27 "But do not be afraid, Jacob, my servant;
do not be dismayed, Israel.
For I will bring you home again from distant lands,
and your children will return from their exile.
Israel* will return to a life of peace and quiet,
and no one will terrorize them.
28 Do not be afraid, Jacob, my servant,
for I am with you," says the LORD.
"I will completely destroy the nations to which I have exiled you,
but I will not completely destroy you.
I will discipline you, but with justice;
I cannot let you go unpunished."

CHAPTER 47

A Message about Philistia

This is the LORD's message to the prophet Jeremiah concerning the Philistines of Gaza, before it was captured by the Egyptian army.
2 This is what the LORD says:

"A flood is coming from the north
to overflow the land.
It will destroy the land and everything in it—
cities and people alike.
People will scream in terror,
and everyone in the land will wail.
3 Hear the clatter of stallions' hooves
and the rumble of wheels as the chariots rush by.
Terrified fathers run madly,
without a backward glance at their helpless children.
4 "The time has come for the Philistines to be destroyed,
along with their allies from Tyre and Sidon.
Yes, the LORD is destroying the remnant of the Philistines,
those colonists from the island of Crete.*
5 Gaza will be humiliated, its head shaved bald;
Ashkelon will lie silent.
You remnant from the Mediterranean coast,*
how long will you lament and mourn?
6 "Now, O sword of the LORD,
when will you be at rest again?
Go back into your sheath;
rest and be still.
7 "But how can it be still
when the LORD has sent it on a mission?
For the city of Ashkelon
and the people living along the sea
must be destroyed."

CHAPTER 48

A Message about Moab

This message was given concerning Moab. This is what the LORD of Heaven's Armies, the God of Israel, says:

"What sorrow awaits the city of Nebo;
it will soon lie in ruins.
The city of Kiriathaim will be humiliated and captured;

46:25 Hebrew *of No*. **46:27** Hebrew *Jacob*. See note on 5:20. **47:4** Hebrew *from Caphtor*. **47:5** Hebrew *the plain*.

the fortress will be humiliated and
broken down.
2 No one will ever brag about Moab again,
for in Heshbon there is a plot to
destroy her.
'Come,' they say, 'we will cut her off from
being a nation.'
The town of Madmen,* too, will be
silenced;
the sword will follow you there.
3 Listen to the cries from Horonaim,
cries of devastation and great
destruction.
4 All Moab is destroyed.
Her little ones will cry out.*
5 Her refugees weep bitterly,
climbing the slope to Luhith.
They cry out in terror,
descending the slope to Horonaim.
6 Flee for your lives!
Hide* in the wilderness!
7 Because you have trusted in your wealth
and skill,
you will be taken captive.
Your god Chemosh, with his priests
and officials,
will be hauled off to distant lands!

8 "All the towns will be destroyed,
and no one will escape—
either on the plateaus or in the valleys,
for the LORD has spoken.
9 Oh, that Moab had wings
so she could fly away,*
for her towns will be left empty,
with no one living in them.
10 Cursed are those who refuse to do the
LORD's work,
who hold back their swords from
shedding blood!

11 "From his earliest history, Moab has lived
in peace,
never going into exile.
He is like wine that has been allowed
to settle.
He has not been poured from flask to
flask,
and he is now fragrant and smooth.
12 But the time is coming soon," says the
LORD,
"when I will send men to pour him
from his jar.
They will pour him out,
then shatter the jar!
13 At last Moab will be ashamed of his idol
Chemosh,
as the people of Israel were ashamed
of their gold calf at Bethel.*

14 "You used to boast, 'We are heroes,
mighty men of war.'
15 But now Moab and his towns will be
destroyed.
His most promising youth are doomed
to slaughter,"
says the King, whose name is the LORD
of Heaven's Armies.
16 "Destruction is coming fast for Moab;
calamity threatens ominously.
17 You friends of Moab,
weep for him and cry!
See how the strong scepter is broken,
how the beautiful staff is shattered!

18 "Come down from your glory
and sit in the dust, you people
of Dibon,
for those who destroy Moab will shatter
Dibon, too.
They will tear down all your towers.
19 You people of Aroer,
stand beside the road and watch.
Shout to those who flee from Moab,
'What has happened there?'

20 "And the reply comes back,
'Moab lies in ruins, disgraced;
weep and wail!
Tell it by the banks of the Arnon River:
Moab has been destroyed!'
21 Judgment has been poured out on the
towns of the plateau—
on Holon and Jahaz* and Mephaath,
22 on Dibon and Nebo and Beth-diblathaim,
23 on Kiriathaim and Beth-gamul and
Beth-meon,
24 on Kerioth and Bozrah—
all the towns of Moab, far and near.

25 "The strength of Moab has ended.
His arm has been broken," says the
LORD.

48:2 *Madmen* sounds like the Hebrew word for "silence"; it should not be confused with the English word *madmen*. **48:4** Greek version reads *Her cries are heard as far away as Zoar*. **48:6** Or *Hide like a wild donkey;* or *Hide like a juniper shrub;* or *Be like* [the town of] *Aroer*. The meaning of the Hebrew is uncertain. **48:9** Or *Put salt on Moab, / for she will be laid waste*. **48:13** Hebrew *ashamed when they trusted in Bethel*. **48:21** Hebrew *Jahzah*, a variant spelling of Jahaz.

26 "Let him stagger and fall like a drunkard,
for he has rebelled against the LORD.
Moab will wallow in his own vomit,
ridiculed by all.
27 Did you not ridicule the people of Israel?
Were they caught in the company of thieves
that you should despise them as you do?

28 "You people of Moab,
flee from your towns and live in the caves.
Hide like doves that nest
in the clefts of the rocks.
29 We have all heard of the pride of Moab,
for his pride is very great.
We know of his lofty pride,
his arrogance, and his haughty heart.
30 I know about his insolence,"
says the LORD,
"but his boasts are empty—
as empty as his deeds.
31 So now I wail for Moab;
yes, I will mourn for Moab.
My heart is broken for the men of Kir-hareseth.*

32 "You people of Sibmah, rich in vineyards,
I will weep for you even more than I did for Jazer.
Your spreading vines once reached as far as the Dead Sea,*
but the destroyer has stripped you bare!
He has harvested your grapes and summer fruits.
33 Joy and gladness are gone from fruitful Moab.
The presses yield no wine.
No one treads the grapes with shouts of joy.
There is shouting, yes, but not of joy.

34"Instead, their awful cries of terror can be heard from Heshbon clear across to Elealeh and Jahaz; from Zoar all the way to Horonaim and Eglath-shelishiyah. Even the waters of Nimrim are dried up now.
35"I will put an end to Moab," says the LORD, "for the people offer sacrifices at the pagan shrines and burn incense to their false gods.
36My heart moans like a flute for Moab and Kir-hareseth, for all their wealth has disappeared. 37The people shave their heads and beards in mourning. They slash their hands and put on clothes made of burlap. 38There is crying and sorrow in every Moabite home and on every street. For I have smashed Moab like an old, unwanted jar. 39How it is shattered! Hear the wailing! See the shame of Moab! It has become an object of ridicule, an example of ruin to all its neighbors."
40This is what the LORD says:

"Look! The enemy swoops down like an eagle,
spreading his wings over Moab.
41 Its cities will fall,
and its strongholds will be seized.
Even the mightiest warriors will be in anguish
like a woman in labor.
42 Moab will no longer be a nation,
for it has boasted against the LORD.

43 "Terror and traps and snares will be your lot,
O Moab," says the LORD.
44 "Those who flee in terror will fall into a trap,
and those who escape the trap will step into a snare.
I will see to it that you do not get away,
for the time of your judgment has come,"
says the LORD.
45 "The people flee as far as Heshbon
but are unable to go on.
For a fire comes from Heshbon,
King Sihon's ancient home,
to devour the entire land
with all its rebellious people.

46 "O Moab, they weep for you!
The people of the god Chemosh are destroyed!
Your sons and your daughters
have been taken away as captives.
47 But I will restore the fortunes of Moab
in days to come.
I, the LORD, have spoken!"

This is the end of Jeremiah's prophecy concerning Moab.

48:31 Hebrew *Kir-heres*, a variant spelling of Kir-hareseth; also in 48:36. **48:32** Hebrew *the sea of Jazer*.

CHAPTER 49

A Message about Ammon

This message was given concerning the Ammonites. This is what the LORD says:

"Are there no descendants of Israel
to inherit the land of Gad?
Why are you, who worship Molech,*
living in its towns?
2 In the days to come," says the LORD,
"I will sound the battle cry against your
city of Rabbah.
It will become a desolate heap of ruins,
and the neighboring towns will be
burned.
Then Israel will take back the land
you took from her," says the LORD.

3 "Cry out, O Heshbon,
for the town of Ai is destroyed.
Weep, O people of Rabbah!
Put on your clothes of mourning.
Weep and wail, hiding in the hedges,
for your god Molech, with his priests
and officials,
will be hauled off to distant lands.
4 You are proud of your fertile valleys,
but they will soon be ruined.
You trusted in your wealth,
you rebellious daughter,
and thought no one could ever
harm you.
5 But look! I will bring terror upon you,"
says the Lord, the LORD of Heaven's
Armies.
"Your neighbors will chase you from your
land,
and no one will help your exiles as they
flee.
6 But I will restore the fortunes of the
Ammonites
in days to come.
I, the LORD, have spoken."

Messages about Edom

7 This message was given concerning Edom. This is what the LORD of Heaven's Armies says:

"Is there no wisdom in Teman?
Is no one left to give wise counsel?
8 Turn and flee!
Hide in deep caves, you people of
Dedan!
For when I bring disaster on Edom,*
I will punish you, too!
9 Those who harvest grapes
always leave a few for the poor.
If thieves came at night,
they would not take everything.
10 But I will strip bare the land of Edom,
and there will be no place left
to hide.
Its children, its brothers, and its neighbors
will all be destroyed,
and Edom itself will be no more.
11 But I will protect the orphans who remain
among you.
Your widows, too, can depend on me
for help."

12 And this is what the LORD says: "If the innocent must suffer, how much more must you! You will not go unpunished! You must drink this cup of judgment! 13 For I have sworn by my own name," says the LORD, "that Bozrah will become an object of horror and a heap of ruins; it will be mocked and cursed. All its towns and villages will be desolate forever."

14 I have heard a message from the LORD
that an ambassador was sent to the
nations to say,
"Form a coalition against Edom,
and prepare for battle!"

15 The LORD says to Edom,
"I will cut you down to size among the
nations.
You will be despised by all.
16 You have been deceived
by the fear you inspire in others
and by your own pride.
You live in a rock fortress
and control the mountain heights.
But even if you make your nest among
the peaks with the eagles,
I will bring you crashing down,"
says the LORD.

17 "Edom will be an object of horror.
All who pass by will be appalled
and will gasp at the destruction they
see there.

49:1 Hebrew *Malcam*, a variant spelling of Molech; also in 49:3. **49:8** Hebrew *Esau*; also in 49:10.

I'LL DO IT MYSELF

Fifth graders got special privileges at Juan's school, and they were proud to be the only kids who would have second-floor classrooms. Juan was also proud that he had flown on an airplane alone and spent a week with his grandparents. When Juan's mom helped his little sister gather her school supplies, she offered to help him, too. Juan said, "No, thanks." He really didn't have a clue where his things were, but it just wasn't cool to admit he needed as much help as his sister! Do you think Juan should let his mom help him? Check out Jeremiah 49:16 for some clues.

18 It will be like the destruction of Sodom
and Gomorrah
and their neighboring towns," says the
LORD.
"No one will live there;
no one will inhabit it.

49:21 Hebrew *sea of reeds.*

19 I will come like a lion from the thickets of
the Jordan,
leaping on the sheep in the pasture.
I will chase Edom from its land,
and I will appoint the leader of my
choice.
For who is like me, and who can challenge
me?
What ruler can oppose my will?"
20 Listen to the LORD's plans against Edom
and the people of Teman.
Even the little children will be dragged
off like sheep,
and their homes will be destroyed.
21 The earth will shake with the noise of
Edom's fall,
and its cry of despair will be heard all
the way to the Red Sea.*
22 Look! The enemy swoops down like an
eagle,
spreading his wings over Bozrah.
Even the mightiest warriors will be in
anguish
like a woman in labor.

A Message about Damascus

23 This message was given concerning Damascus. This is what the LORD says:

"The towns of Hamath and Arpad are
struck with fear,
for they have heard the news of their
destruction.
Their hearts are troubled
like a wild sea in a raging storm.
24 Damascus has become feeble,
and all her people turn to flee.
Fear, anguish, and pain have gripped her
as they grip a woman in labor.
25 That famous city, a city of joy,
will be forsaken!
26 Her young men will fall in the streets
and die.
Her soldiers will all be killed,"
says the LORD of Heaven's Armies.
27 "And I will set fire to the walls of Damascus
that will burn up the palaces of
Ben-hadad."

A Message about Kedar and Hazor

28 This message was given concerning Kedar and the kingdoms of Hazor, which were at-

tacked by King Nebuchadnezzar* of Babylon.
This is what the LORD says:

"Advance against Kedar!
Destroy the warriors from the East!
29 Their flocks and tents will be captured,
and their household goods and camels
will be taken away.
Everywhere shouts of panic will be heard:
'We are terrorized at every turn!'
30 Run for your lives," says the LORD.
"Hide yourselves in deep caves, you
people of Hazor,
for King Nebuchadnezzar of Babylon has
plotted against you
and is preparing to destroy you.

31 "Go up and attack that complacent
nation,"
says the LORD.
"Its people live alone in the desert
without walls or gates.
32 Their camels and other livestock will all
be yours.
I will scatter to the winds these people
who live in remote places.*
I will bring calamity upon them
from every direction," says the LORD.
33 "Hazor will be inhabited by jackals,
and it will be desolate forever.
No one will live there;
no one will inhabit it."

A Message about Elam

34 This message concerning Elam came to the
prophet Jeremiah from the LORD at the begin-
ning of the reign of King Zedekiah of Judah.
35 This is what the LORD of Heaven's Armies
says:

"I will destroy the archers of Elam—
the best of their forces.
36 I will bring enemies from all directions,
and I will scatter the people of Elam to
the four winds.
They will be exiled to countries around
the world.
37 I myself will go with Elam's enemies to
shatter it.
In my fierce anger, I will bring great
disaster
upon the people of Elam," says the
LORD.
"Their enemies will chase them with the
sword
until I have destroyed them completely.
38 I will set my throne in Elam," says the
LORD,
"and I will destroy its king and officials.
39 But I will restore the fortunes of Elam
in days to come.
I, the LORD, have spoken!"

CHAPTER 50

A Message about Babylon

The LORD gave Jeremiah the prophet this
message concerning Babylon and the land of
the Babylonians.* 2 This is what the LORD says:

"Tell the whole world,
and keep nothing back.
Raise a signal flag
to tell everyone that Babylon will fall!
Her images and idols* will be shattered.
Her gods Bel and Marduk will be utterly
disgraced.
3 For a nation will attack her from the north
and bring such destruction that no one
will live there again.
Everything will be gone;
both people and animals will flee.

Hope for Israel and Judah

4 "In those coming days,"
says the LORD,
"the people of Israel will return home
together with the people of Judah.
They will come weeping
and seeking the LORD their God.
5 They will ask the way to Jerusalem*
and will start back home again.
They will bind themselves to the LORD
with an eternal covenant that will never
be forgotten.

6 "My people have been lost sheep.
Their shepherds have led them astray
and turned them loose in the
mountains.
They have lost their way
and can't remember how to get back to
the sheepfold.

49:28 Hebrew *Nebuchadrezzar*, a variant spelling of Nebuchadnezzar; also in 49:30. **49:32** Or *who clip the corners of their hair*. **50:1** Or *Chaldeans;* also in 50:8, 25, 35, 45. **50:2** The Hebrew term (literally *round things*) probably alludes to dung. **50:5** Hebrew *Zion;* also in 50:28.

7 All who found them devoured them.
Their enemies said,
'We did nothing wrong in attacking them,
for they sinned against the LORD,
their true place of rest,
and the hope of their ancestors.'

8 "But now, flee from Babylon!
Leave the land of the Babylonians.
Like male goats at the head of the flock,
lead my people home again.
9 For I am raising up an army
of great nations from the north.
They will join forces to attack Babylon,
and she will be captured.
The enemies' arrows will go straight to the mark;
they will not miss!
10 Babylonia* will be looted
until the attackers are glutted with loot.
I, the LORD, have spoken!

Babylon's Sure Fall

11 "You rejoice and are glad,
you who plundered my chosen people.
You frisk about like a calf in a meadow
and neigh like a stallion.
12 But your homeland* will be overwhelmed
with shame and disgrace.
You will become the least of nations—
a wilderness, a dry and desolate land.
13 Because of the LORD's anger,
Babylon will become a deserted wasteland.
All who pass by will be horrified
and will gasp at the destruction they see there.

14 "Yes, prepare to attack Babylon,
all you surrounding nations.
Let your archers shoot at her; spare no arrows.
For she has sinned against the LORD.
15 Shout war cries against her from every side.
Look! She surrenders!
Her walls have fallen.
It is the LORD's vengeance,
so take vengeance on her.
Do to her as she has done to others!
16 Take from Babylon all those who plant crops;
send all the harvesters away.
Because of the sword of the enemy,
everyone will run away and rush back to their own lands.

Hope for God's People

17 "The Israelites are like sheep
that have been scattered by lions.
First the king of Assyria ate them up.
Then King Nebuchadnezzar* of Babylon cracked their bones."
18 Therefore, this is what the LORD of Heaven's Armies,
the God of Israel, says:
"Now I will punish the king of Babylon and his land,
just as I punished the king of Assyria.
19 And I will bring Israel home again to its own land,
to feed in the fields of Carmel and Bashan,
and to be satisfied once more
in the hill country of Ephraim and Gilead.
20 In those days," says the LORD,
"no sin will be found in Israel or in Judah,
for I will forgive the remnant I preserve.

The LORD's Judgment on Babylon

21 "Go up, my warriors, against the land of Merathaim
and against the people of Pekod.
Pursue, kill, and completely destroy* them,
as I have commanded you," says the LORD.
22 "Let the battle cry be heard in the land,
a shout of great destruction.
23 Babylon, the mightiest hammer in all the earth,
lies broken and shattered.
Babylon is desolate among the nations!
24 Listen, Babylon, for I have set a trap for you.
You are caught, for you have fought against the LORD.

50:10 Or *Chaldea*. **50:12** Hebrew *your mother*. **50:17** Hebrew *Nebuchadrezzar*, a variant spelling of Nebuchadnezzar. **50:21** The Hebrew term used here refers to the complete consecration of things or people to the LORD, either by destroying them or by giving them as an offering.

25 The LORD has opened his armory
and brought out weapons to vent his fury.
The terror that falls upon the Babylonians
will be the work of the Sovereign LORD
of Heaven's Armies.
26 Yes, come against her from distant lands.
Break open her granaries.
Crush her walls and houses into heaps of rubble.
Destroy her completely, and leave nothing!
27 Destroy even her young bulls—
it will be terrible for them, too!
Slaughter them all!
For Babylon's day of reckoning has come.
28 Listen to the people who have escaped from Babylon,
as they tell in Jerusalem
how the LORD our God has taken vengeance
against those who destroyed his Temple.
29 "Send out a call for archers to come to Babylon.
Surround the city so none can escape.
Do to her as she has done to others,
for she has defied the LORD, the Holy One of Israel.
30 Her young men will fall in the streets and die.
Her soldiers will all be killed,"
says the LORD.

31 "See, I am your enemy, you arrogant people,"
says the Lord, the LORD of Heaven's Armies.
"Your day of reckoning has arrived—
the day when I will punish you.
32 O land of arrogance, you will stumble and fall,
and no one will raise you up.
For I will light a fire in the cities of Babylon
that will burn up everything around them."

33 This is what the LORD of Heaven's Armies says:
"The people of Israel and Judah have been wronged.

AMAZING FACTS

Babylon was known as "the mightiest hammer in all the earth." But even that nation couldn't stand against God's power.
JEREMIAH 50:22-25

Their captors hold them and refuse to let them go.
34 But the one who redeems them is strong.
His name is the LORD of Heaven's Armies.
He will defend them
and give them rest again in Israel.
But for the people of Babylon
there will be no rest!

35 "The sword of destruction will strike the Babylonians,"
says the LORD.
"It will strike the people of Babylon—
her officials and wise men, too.
36 The sword will strike her wise counselors,
and they will become fools.
The sword will strike her mightiest warriors,
and panic will seize them.
37 The sword will strike her horses and chariots
and her allies from other lands,
and they will all become like women.
The sword will strike her treasures,
and they all will be plundered.
38 The sword will even strike her water supply,
causing it to dry up.
And why? Because the whole land is filled with idols,
and the people are madly in love with them.

39 "Soon Babylon will be inhabited by desert animals and hyenas.

It will be a home for owls.
Never again will people live there;
it will lie desolate forever.
40 I will destroy it as I* destroyed Sodom and Gomorrah
and their neighboring towns," says the LORD.
"No one will live there;
no one will inhabit it.

41 "Look! A great army is coming from the north.
A great nation and many kings
are rising against you from far-off lands.
42 They are armed with bows and spears.
They are cruel and show no mercy.
As they ride forward on horses,
they sound like a roaring sea.
They are coming in battle formation,
planning to destroy you, Babylon.
43 The king of Babylon has heard reports about the enemy,
and he is weak with fright.
Pangs of anguish have gripped him,
like those of a woman in labor.

44 "I will come like a lion from the thickets of the Jordan,
leaping on the sheep in the pasture.
I will chase Babylon from its land,
and I will appoint the leader of my choice.
For who is like me, and who can challenge me?
What ruler can oppose my will?"

45 Listen to the LORD's plans against Babylon
and the land of the Babylonians.
Even the little children will be dragged off like sheep,
and their homes will be destroyed.
46 The earth will shake with the shout,
"Babylon has been taken!"
and its cry of despair will be heard around the world.

CHAPTER 51

1 This is what the LORD says:
"I will stir up a destroyer against Babylon
and the people of Babylonia.*
2 Foreigners will come and winnow her,
blowing her away as chaff.
They will come from every side
to rise against her in her day of trouble.
3 Don't let the archers put on their armor
or draw their bows.
Don't spare even her best soldiers!
Let her army be completely destroyed.*
4 They will fall dead in the land of the Babylonians,*
slashed to death in her streets.
5 For the LORD of Heaven's Armies
has not abandoned Israel and Judah.
He is still their God,
even though their land was filled with sin
against the Holy One of Israel."

6 Flee from Babylon! Save yourselves!
Don't get trapped in her punishment!
It is the LORD's time for vengeance;
he will repay her in full.
7 Babylon has been a gold cup in the LORD's hands,
a cup that made the whole earth drunk.
The nations drank Babylon's wine,
and it drove them all mad.
8 But suddenly Babylon, too, has fallen.
Weep for her.
Give her medicine.
Perhaps she can yet be healed.
9 We would have helped her if we could,
but nothing can save her now.
Let her go; abandon her.
Return now to your own land.
For her punishment reaches to the heavens;
it is so great it cannot be measured.
10 The LORD has vindicated us.
Come, let us announce in Jerusalem*
everything the LORD our God has done.

11 Sharpen the arrows!
Lift up the shields!*
For the LORD has inspired the kings of the Medes
to march against Babylon and destroy her.
This is his vengeance against those
who desecrated his Temple.

50:40 Hebrew *as God*. **51:1** Hebrew *of Leb-kamai*, a code name for Babylonia. **51:3** The Hebrew term used here refers to the complete consecration of things or people to the LORD, either by destroying them or by giving them as an offering. **51:4** Or *Chaldeans;* also in 51:54. **51:10** Hebrew *Zion;* also in 51:24. **51:11** Greek version reads *Fill up the quivers*.

12 Raise the battle flag against Babylon!
Reinforce the guard and station the watchmen.
Prepare an ambush,
for the LORD will fulfill all his plans against Babylon.
13 You are a city by a great river,
a great center of commerce,
but your end has come.
The thread of your life is cut.
14 The LORD of Heaven's Armies has taken this vow
and has sworn to it by his own name:
"Your cities will be filled with enemies,
like fields swarming with locusts,
and they will shout in triumph over you."

A Hymn of Praise to the LORD

15 The LORD made the earth by his power,
and he preserves it by his wisdom.
With his own understanding
he stretched out the heavens.
16 When he speaks in the thunder,
the heavens are filled with water.
He causes the clouds to rise over the earth.
He sends the lightning with the rain
and releases the wind from his storehouses.
17 The whole human race is foolish and has no knowledge!
The craftsmen are disgraced by the idols they make,
for their carefully shaped works are a fraud.
These idols have no breath or power.
18 Idols are worthless; they are ridiculous lies!
On the day of reckoning they will all be destroyed.
19 But the God of Israel* is no idol!
He is the Creator of everything that exists,
including his people, his own special possession.
The LORD of Heaven's Armies is his name!

Babylon's Great Punishment

20 "You* are my battle-ax and sword,"
says the LORD.
"With you I will shatter nations
and destroy many kingdoms.
21 With you I will shatter armies—
destroying the horse and rider,
the chariot and charioteer.
22 With you I will shatter men and women,
old people and children,
young men and maidens.
23 With you I will shatter shepherds and flocks,
farmers and oxen,
captains and officers.
24 "I will repay Babylon
and the people of Babylonia*
for all the wrong they have done
to my people in Jerusalem," says the LORD.
25 "Look, O mighty mountain, destroyer of the earth!
I am your enemy," says the LORD.
"I will raise my fist against you,
to knock you down from the heights.
When I am finished,
you will be nothing but a heap of burnt rubble.
26 You will be desolate forever.
Even your stones will never again be used for building.
You will be completely wiped out,"
says the LORD.
27 Raise a signal flag to the nations.
Sound the battle cry!
Mobilize them all against Babylon.
Prepare them to fight against her!
Bring out the armies of Ararat, Minni, and Ashkenaz.
Appoint a commander,
and bring a multitude of horses like swarming locusts!
28 Bring against her the armies of the nations—
led by the kings of the Medes
and all their captains and officers.
29 The earth trembles and writhes in pain,
for everything the LORD has planned against Babylon stands unchanged.

51:19 Hebrew *the Portion of Jacob*. See note on 5:20. **51:20** Possibly Cyrus, whom God used to conquer Babylon. Compare Isa 44:28; 45:1. **51:24** Or *Chaldea;* also in 51:35.

Babylon will be left desolate without a
single inhabitant.
30 Her mightiest warriors no longer fight.
They stay in their barracks, their courage
gone.
They have become like women.
The invaders have burned the houses
and broken down the city gates.
31 The news is passed from one runner to
the next
as the messengers hurry to tell the king
that his city has been captured.
32 All the escape routes are blocked.
The marshes have been set aflame,
and the army is in a panic.

33 This is what the LORD of Heaven's Armies,
the God of Israel, says:
"Babylon is like wheat on a threshing
floor,
about to be trampled.
In just a little while
her harvest will begin."

34 "King Nebuchadnezzar* of Babylon has
eaten and crushed us
and drained us of strength.
He has swallowed us like a great
monster
and filled his belly with our riches.
He has thrown us out of our own
country.
35 Make Babylon suffer as she made us
suffer,"
say the people of Zion.
"Make the people of Babylonia pay for
spilling our blood,"
says Jerusalem.

The LORD's Vengeance on Babylon

36 This is what the LORD says to Jerusalem:

"I will be your lawyer to plead your case,
and I will avenge you.
I will dry up her river,
as well as her springs,
37 and Babylon will become a heap of ruins,
haunted by jackals.
She will be an object of horror and
contempt,
a place where no one lives.
38 Her people will roar together like strong
lions.
They will growl like lion cubs.
39 And while they lie inflamed with all their
wine,
I will prepare a different kind of feast
for them.
I will make them drink until they fall
asleep,
and they will never wake up again,"
says the LORD.
40 "I will bring them down
like lambs to the slaughter,
like rams and goats to be sacrificed.

41 "How Babylon* is fallen—
great Babylon, praised throughout the
earth!
Now she has become an object of horror
among the nations.
42 The sea has risen over Babylon;
she is covered by its crashing waves.
43 Her cities now lie in ruins;
she is a dry wasteland
where no one lives or even passes by.
44 And I will punish Bel, the god of Babylon,
and make him vomit up all he has
eaten.
The nations will no longer come and
worship him.
The wall of Babylon has fallen!

A Message for the Exiles

45 "Come out, my people, flee from Babylon.
Save yourselves! Run from the LORD's
fierce anger.
46 But do not panic; don't be afraid
when you hear the first rumor of
approaching forces.
For rumors will keep coming year by
year.
Violence will erupt in the land
as the leaders fight against each other.
47 For the time is surely coming
when I will punish this great city and all
her idols.
Her whole land will be disgraced,
and her dead will lie in the streets.
48 Then the heavens and earth will rejoice,
for out of the north will come
destroying armies
against Babylon," says the LORD.
49 "Just as Babylon killed the people of Israel
and others throughout the world,

51:34 Hebrew *Nebuchadrezzar*, a variant spelling of Nebuchadnezzar. **51:41** Hebrew *Sheshach*, a code name for Babylon.

so must her people be killed.
50 Get out, all you who have escaped the sword!
Do not stand and watch—flee while you can!
Remember the LORD, though you are in a far-off land,
and think about your home in Jerusalem."

51 "We are ashamed," the people say.
"We are insulted and disgraced
because the LORD's Temple
has been defiled by foreigners."

52 "Yes," says the LORD, "but the time is coming
when I will destroy Babylon's idols.
The groans of her wounded people
will be heard throughout the land.
53 Though Babylon reaches as high as the heavens
and makes her fortifications incredibly strong,
I will still send enemies to plunder her.
I, the LORD, have spoken!

Babylon's Complete Destruction

54 "Listen! Hear the cry of Babylon,
the sound of great destruction from the land of the Babylonians.
55 For the LORD is destroying Babylon.
He will silence her loud voice.
Waves of enemies pound against her;
the noise of battle rings through the city.
56 Destroying armies come against Babylon.
Her mighty men are captured,
and their weapons break in their hands.
For the LORD is a God who gives just punishment;
he always repays in full.
57 I will make her officials and wise men drunk,
along with her captains, officers, and warriors.
They will fall asleep
and never wake up again!"
says the King, whose name is
the LORD of Heaven's Armies.
58 This is what the LORD of Heaven's Armies says:
"The thick walls of Babylon will be leveled to the ground,
and her massive gates will be burned.
The builders from many lands have worked in vain,
for their work will be destroyed by fire!"

Jeremiah's Message Sent to Babylon

59 The prophet Jeremiah gave this message to Seraiah son of Neriah and grandson of Mahseiah, a staff officer, when Seraiah went to Babylon with King Zedekiah of Judah. This was during the fourth year of Zedekiah's reign.* 60 Jeremiah had recorded on a scroll all the terrible disasters that would soon come upon Babylon—all the words written here. 61 He said to Seraiah, "When you get to Babylon, read aloud everything on this scroll. 62 Then say, 'LORD, you have said that you will destroy Babylon so that neither people nor animals will remain here. She will lie empty and abandoned forever.' 63 When you have finished reading the scroll, tie it to a stone and throw it into the Euphrates River. 64 Then say, 'In this same way Babylon and her people will sink, never again to rise, because of the disasters I will bring upon her.'"

This is the end of Jeremiah's messages.

CHAPTER 52

The Fall of Jerusalem

Zedekiah was twenty-one years old when he became king, and he reigned in Jerusalem eleven years. His mother was Hamutal, the daughter of Jeremiah from Libnah. 2 But Zedekiah did what was evil in the LORD's sight, just as Jehoiakim had done. 3 These things happened because of the LORD's anger against the people of Jerusalem and Judah, until he finally banished them from his presence and sent them into exile.

Zedekiah rebelled against the king of Babylon. 4 So on January 15,* during the ninth year of Zedekiah's reign, King Nebuchadnezzar* of Babylon led his entire army against Jerusalem. They surrounded the city and built siege ramps against its walls. 5 Jerusalem was

51:59 The fourth year of Zedekiah's reign was 593 B.C. **52:4a** Hebrew *on the tenth day of the tenth month*, of the ancient Hebrew lunar calendar. A number of events in Jeremiah can be cross-checked with dates in surviving Babylonian records and related accurately to our modern calendar. This day was January 15, 588 B.C. **52:4b** Hebrew *Nebuchadrezzar*, a variant spelling of Nebuchadnezzar; also in 52:12, 28, 29, 30.

kept under siege until the eleventh year of King Zedekiah's reign.

6 By July 18 in the eleventh year of Zedekiah's reign,* the famine in the city had become very severe, and the last of the food was entirely gone. 7 Then a section of the city wall was broken down, and all the soldiers fled. Since the city was surrounded by the Babylonians,* they waited for nightfall. Then they slipped through the gate between the two walls behind the king's garden and headed toward the Jordan Valley.*

8 But the Babylonian troops chased King Zedekiah and caught him on the plains of Jericho, for his men had all deserted him and scattered. 9 They took him to the king of Babylon at Riblah in the land of Hamath. There the king of Babylon pronounced judgment upon Zedekiah. 10 He made Zedekiah watch as they slaughtered his sons and all the other officials of Judah. 11 Then they gouged out Zedekiah's eyes, bound him in bronze chains, and led him away to Babylon. Zedekiah remained there in prison until the day of his death.

The Temple Destroyed

12 On August 17 of that year,* which was the nineteenth year of King Nebuchadnezzar's reign, Nebuzaradan, the captain of the guard and an official of the Babylonian king, arrived in Jerusalem. 13 He burned down the Temple of the LORD, the royal palace, and all the houses of Jerusalem. He destroyed all the important buildings* in the city. 14 Then he supervised the entire Babylonian* army as they tore down the walls of Jerusalem on every side. 15 Nebuzaradan, the captain of the guard, then took as exiles some of the poorest of the people, the rest of the people who remained in the city, the defectors who had declared their allegiance to the king of Babylon, and the rest of the craftsmen. 16 But Nebuzaradan allowed some of the poorest people to stay behind in Judah to care for the vineyards and fields.

17 The Babylonians broke up the bronze pillars in front of the LORD's Temple, the bronze water carts, and the great bronze basin called the Sea, and they carried all the bronze away to Babylon. 18 They also took all the ash buckets, shovels, lamp snuffers, basins, dishes, and all the other bronze articles used for making sacrifices at the Temple. 19 Nebuzaradan, the captain of the guard, also took the small bowls, incense burners, basins, pots, lampstands, dishes, bowls used for liquid offerings, and all the other articles made of pure gold or silver.

20 The weight of the bronze from the two pillars, the Sea with the twelve bronze oxen beneath it, and the water carts was too great to be measured. These things had been made for the LORD's Temple in the days of King Solomon. 21 Each of the pillars was 27 feet tall and 18 feet in circumference.* They were hollow, with walls 3 inches thick.* 22 The bronze capital on top of each pillar was 7½ feet* high and was decorated with a network of bronze pomegranates all the way around. 23 There were 96 pomegranates on the sides, and a total of 100 on the network around the top.

24 Nebuzaradan, the captain of the guard, took with him as prisoners Seraiah the high priest, Zephaniah the priest of the second rank, and the three chief gatekeepers. 25 And from among the people still hiding in the city, he took an officer who had been in charge of the Judean army; seven of the king's personal advisers; the army commander's chief secretary, who was in charge of recruitment; and sixty other citizens. 26 Nebuzaradan, the captain of the guard, took them all to the king of Babylon at Riblah. 27 And there at Riblah, in the land of Hamath, the king of Babylon had them all put to death. So the people of Judah were sent into exile from their land.

28 The number of captives taken to Babylon in the seventh year of Nebuchadnezzar's reign* was 3,023. 29 Then in Nebuchadnezzar's eighteenth year* he took 832 more. 30 In Nebuchadnezzar's twenty-third year* he sent Nebuzaradan, the captain of the guard, who took 745 more—a total of 4,600 captives in all.

Hope for Israel's Royal Line

31 In the thirty-seventh year of the exile of King Jehoiachin of Judah, Evil-merodach as-

52:6 Hebrew *By the ninth day of the fourth month* [in the eleventh year of Zedekiah's reign]. This day was July 18, 586 B.C.; also see note on 52:4a. **52:7a** Or *the Chaldeans;* similarly in 52:8, 17. **52:7b** Hebrew *the Arabah.* **52:12** Hebrew *On the tenth day of the fifth month,* of the ancient Hebrew lunar calendar. This day was August 17, 586 B.C.; also see note on 52:4a. **52:13** Or *destroyed the houses of all the important people.* **52:14** Or *Chaldean.* **52:21a** Hebrew *18 cubits* [8.1 meters] *tall and 12 cubits* [5.4 meters] *in circumference.* **52:21b** Hebrew *4 fingers thick* [8 centimeters]. **52:22** Hebrew *5 cubits* [2.3 meters]. **52:28** This exile in the seventh year of Nebuchadnezzar's reign occurred in 597 B.C. **52:29** This exile in the eighteenth year of Nebuchadnezzar's reign occurred in 586 B.C. **52:30** This exile in the twenty-third year of Nebuchadnezzar's reign occurred in 581 B.C.

cended to the Babylonian throne. He was kind to* Jehoiachin and released him from prison on March 31 of that year.* [32]He spoke kindly to Jehoiachin and gave him a higher place than all the other exiled kings in Babylon. [33]He supplied Jehoiachin with new clothes to replace his prison garb and allowed him to dine in the king's presence for the rest of his life. [34]So the Babylonian king gave him a regular food allowance as long as he lived. This continued until the day of his death.

52:31a Hebrew *He raised the head of.* **52:31b** Hebrew *on the twenty-fifth day of the twelfth month,* of the ancient Hebrew lunar calendar. This day was March 31, 561 B.C.; also see note on 52:4a.

Lamentations

WHO
Jeremiah and the people of Jerusalem.

WHERE
In Judah.

WHEN
Soon after 586 BC when Jerusalem was conquered by Babylon.

WHY
To show that God suffers when his people suffer.

Great is his faithfulness; his mercies begin afresh each morning.
LAMENTATIONS 3:23

Jeremiah has been called the "weeping prophet." He cried a lot, but not for himself. Jeremiah cried because his people were lost without God. Many people are lost today, too. When people don't know and follow God, they will suffer. That should make us sad, and maybe even make us cry sometimes.

ASK GOD TO HELP YOU CARE ABOUT THE PEOPLE AROUND YOU WHO DON'T KNOW HIM.

CHAPTER 1*

Sorrow in Jerusalem

1 Jerusalem, once so full of people,
is now deserted.
She who was once great among the nations
now sits alone like a widow.
Once the queen of all the earth,
she is now a slave.

1 Each of the first four chapters of this book is an acrostic, laid out in the order of the Hebrew alphabet. The first word of each verse begins with a successive Hebrew letter. Chapters 1, 2, and 4 have one verse for each of the 22 Hebrew letters. Chapter 3 contains 22 stanzas of three verses each. Though chapter 5 has 22 verses, it is not an acrostic.

2 She sobs through the night;
tears stream down her cheeks.
Among all her lovers,
there is no one left to comfort her.
All her friends have betrayed her
and become her enemies.

3 Judah has been led away into captivity,
oppressed with cruel slavery.
She lives among foreign nations
and has no place of rest.
Her enemies have chased her down,
and she has nowhere to turn.

4 The roads to Jerusalem* are in mourning,
for crowds no longer come to celebrate
the festivals.
The city gates are silent,
her priests groan,
her young women are crying—
how bitter is her fate!

5 Her oppressors have become her masters,
and her enemies prosper,
for the LORD has punished Jerusalem
for her many sins.
Her children have been captured
and taken away to distant lands.

6 All the majesty of beautiful Jerusalem*
has been stripped away.
Her princes are like starving deer
searching for pasture.
They are too weak to run
from the pursuing enemy.

7 In the midst of her sadness and
wandering,
Jerusalem remembers her ancient
splendor.
But now she has fallen to her enemy,
and there is no one to help her.
Her enemy struck her down
and laughed as she fell.

8 Jerusalem has sinned greatly,
so she has been tossed away like a
filthy rag.
All who once honored her now despise
her,
for they have seen her stripped naked
and humiliated.
All she can do is groan
and hide her face.

9 She defiled herself with immorality
and gave no thought to her future.
Now she lies in the gutter
with no one to lift her out.
"LORD, see my misery," she cries.
"The enemy has triumphed."

10 The enemy has plundered her completely,
taking every precious thing she owns.
She has seen foreigners violate her sacred
Temple,
the place the LORD had forbidden them
to enter.

11 Her people groan as they search for
bread.
They have sold their treasures for food
to stay alive.
"O LORD, look," she mourns,
"and see how I am despised.

12 "Does it mean nothing to you, all you who
pass by?
Look around and see if there is any
suffering like mine,
which the LORD brought on me
when he erupted in fierce anger.

13 "He has sent fire from heaven that burns
in my bones.
He has placed a trap in my path and
turned me back.
He has left me devastated,
racked with sickness all day long.

14 "He wove my sins into ropes
to hitch me to a yoke of captivity.
The Lord sapped my strength and turned
me over to my enemies;
I am helpless in their hands.

15 "The Lord has treated my mighty men
with contempt.
At his command a great army has come
to crush my young warriors.
The Lord has trampled his beloved city*
like grapes are trampled in a winepress.

16 "For all these things I weep;
tears flow down my cheeks.
No one is here to comfort me;
any who might encourage me are
far away.
My children have no future,
for the enemy has conquered us."

1:4 Hebrew *Zion;* also in 1:17. **1:6** Hebrew *of the daughter of Zion.* **1:15** Hebrew *the virgin daughter of Judah.*

17 Jerusalem reaches out for help,
but no one comforts her.
Regarding his people Israel,*
the LORD has said,
"Let their neighbors be their enemies!
Let them be thrown away like a filthy rag!"

18 "The LORD is right," Jerusalem says,
"for I rebelled against him.
Listen, people everywhere;
look upon my anguish and despair,
for my sons and daughters
have been taken captive to distant lands.

19 "I begged my allies for help,
but they betrayed me.
My priests and leaders
starved to death in the city,
even as they searched for food
to save their lives.

20 "LORD, see my anguish!
My heart is broken
and my soul despairs,
for I have rebelled against you.
In the streets the sword kills,
and at home there is only death.

21 "Others heard my groans,
but no one turned to comfort me.
When my enemies heard about my troubles,
they were happy to see what you had done.
Oh, bring the day you promised,
when they will suffer as I have suffered.

22 "Look at all their evil deeds, LORD.
Punish them,
as you have punished me
for all my sins.
My groans are many,
and I am sick at heart."

CHAPTER 2

God's Anger at Sin

1 The Lord in his anger
has cast a dark shadow over beautiful Jerusalem.*
The fairest of Israel's cities lies in the dust,
thrown down from the heights of heaven.
In his day of great anger,
the Lord has shown no mercy even to his Temple.*

2 Without mercy the Lord has destroyed
every home in Israel.*
In his anger he has broken down
the fortress walls of beautiful Jerusalem.*
He has brought them to the ground,
dishonoring the kingdom and its rulers.

3 All the strength of Israel
vanishes beneath his fierce anger.
The Lord has withdrawn his protection
as the enemy attacks.
He consumes the whole land of Israel
like a raging fire.

4 He bends his bow against his people,
as though he were their enemy.
His strength is used against them
to kill their finest youth.
His fury is poured out like fire
on beautiful Jerusalem.*

5 Yes, the Lord has vanquished Israel
like an enemy.
He has destroyed her palaces
and demolished her fortresses.
He has brought unending sorrow and tears
upon beautiful Jerusalem.

6 He has broken down his Temple
as though it were merely a garden shelter.
The LORD has blotted out all memory
of the holy festivals and Sabbath days.
Kings and priests fall together
before his fierce anger.

7 The Lord has rejected his own altar;
he despises his own sanctuary.
He has given Jerusalem's palaces
to her enemies.

1:17 Hebrew *Jacob*. The names "Jacob" and "Israel" are often interchanged throughout the Old Testament, referring sometimes to the individual patriarch and sometimes to the nation. **2:1a** Hebrew *the daughter of Zion;* also in 2:8, 10, 18. **2:1b** Hebrew *his footstool*. **2:2a** Hebrew *Jacob;* also in 2:3b. See note on 1:17. **2:2b** Hebrew *the daughter of Judah;* also in 2:5. **2:4** Hebrew *on the tent of the daughter of Zion*.

They shout in the LORD's Temple
as though it were a day of celebration.

8 The LORD was determined
to destroy the walls of beautiful Jerusalem.
He made careful plans for their destruction,
then did what he had planned.
Therefore, the ramparts and walls
have fallen down before him.

9 Jerusalem's gates have sunk into the ground.
He has smashed their locks and bars.
Her kings and princes have been exiled to distant lands;
her law has ceased to exist.
Her prophets receive
no more visions from the LORD.

10 The leaders of beautiful Jerusalem
sit on the ground in silence.
They are clothed in burlap
and throw dust on their heads.
The young women of Jerusalem
hang their heads in shame.

11 I have cried until the tears no longer come;
my heart is broken.
My spirit is poured out in agony
as I see the desperate plight of my people.
Little children and tiny babies
are fainting and dying in the streets.

12 They cry out to their mothers,
"We need food and drink!"
Their lives ebb away in the streets
like the life of a warrior wounded in battle.
They gasp for life
as they collapse in their mothers' arms.

13 What can I say about you?
Who has ever seen such sorrow?
O daughter of Jerusalem,
to what can I compare your anguish?
O virgin daughter of Zion,
how can I comfort you?
For your wound is as deep as the sea.
Who can heal you?

14 Your prophets have said
so many foolish things, false to the core.
They did not save you from exile
by pointing out your sins.
Instead, they painted false pictures,
filling you with false hope.

15 All who pass by jeer at you.
They scoff and insult beautiful Jerusalem,* saying,
"Is this the city called 'Most Beautiful in All the World'
and 'Joy of All the Earth'?"

16 All your enemies mock you.
They scoff and snarl and say,
"We have destroyed her at last!
We have long waited for this day,
and it is finally here!"

17 But it is the LORD who did just as he planned.
He has fulfilled the promises of disaster
he made long ago.
He has destroyed Jerusalem without mercy.
He has caused her enemies to gloat over her
and has given them power over her.

18 Cry aloud* before the Lord,
O walls of beautiful Jerusalem!
Let your tears flow like a river
day and night.
Give yourselves no rest;
give your eyes no relief.

19 Rise during the night and cry out.
Pour out your hearts like water to the Lord.
Lift up your hands to him in prayer,
pleading for your children,
for in every street
they are faint with hunger.

20 "O LORD, think about this!
Should you treat your own people this way?
Should mothers eat their own children,
those they once bounced on their knees?

2:15 Hebrew *the daughter of Jerusalem.* **2:18** Hebrew *Their heart cried.*

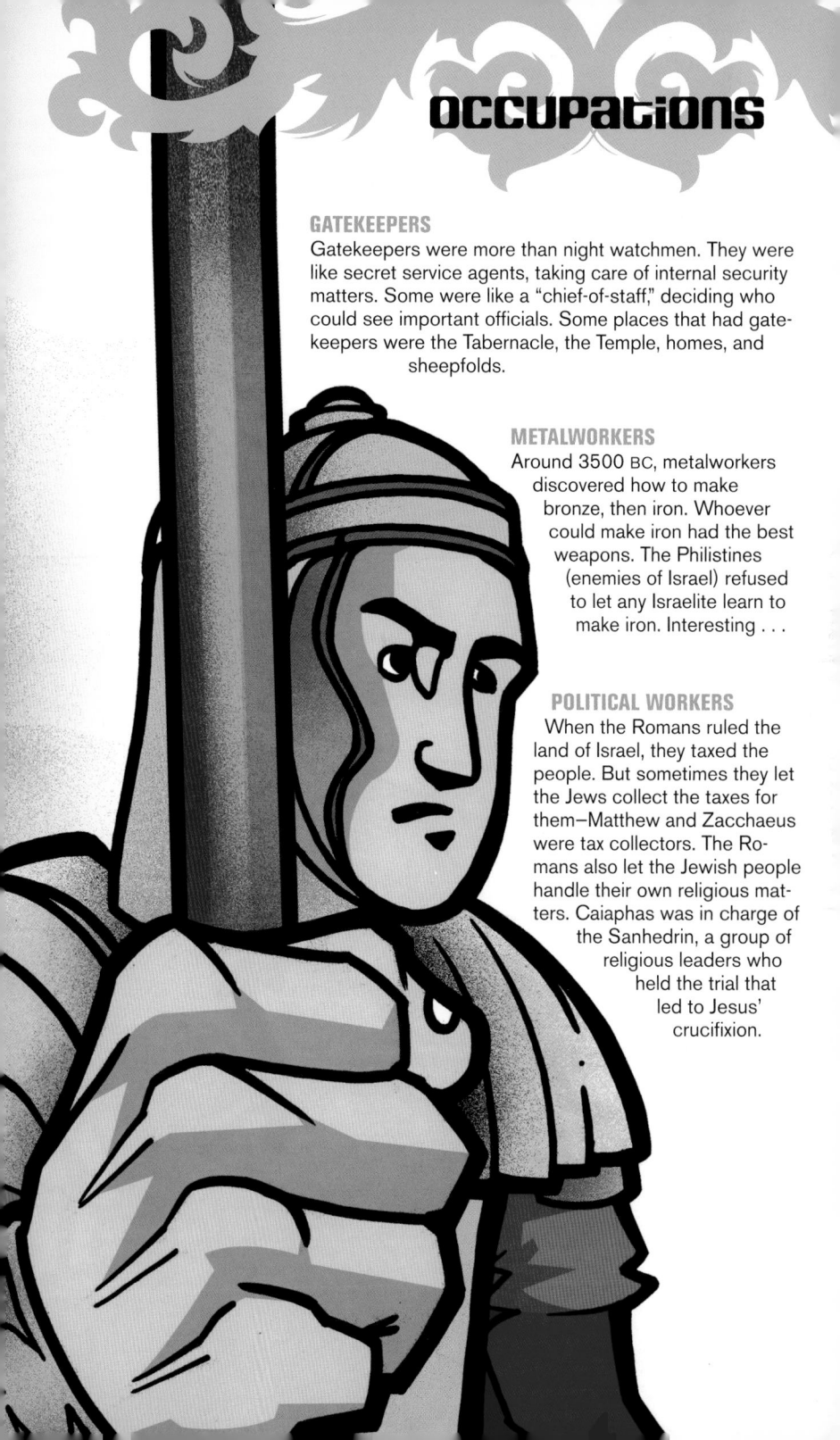

occupations

GATEKEEPERS

Gatekeepers were more than night watchmen. They were like secret service agents, taking care of internal security matters. Some were like a "chief-of-staff," deciding who could see important officials. Some places that had gatekeepers were the Tabernacle, the Temple, homes, and sheepfolds.

METALWORKERS

Around 3500 BC, metalworkers discovered how to make bronze, then iron. Whoever could make iron had the best weapons. The Philistines (enemies of Israel) refused to let any Israelite learn to make iron. Interesting . . .

POLITICAL WORKERS

When the Romans ruled the land of Israel, they taxed the people. But sometimes they let the Jews collect the taxes for them—Matthew and Zacchaeus were tax collectors. The Romans also let the Jewish people handle their own religious matters. Caiaphas was in charge of the Sanhedrin, a group of religious leaders who held the trial that led to Jesus' crucifixion.

SLAVES

Slavery was widely practiced in Bible times. People became slaves for many different reasons. Some were born into it, and some were abandoned by their parents. Some were war captives, others sold themselves in order to pay off debts. Still others were sentenced to it for crimes they had committed.

MUSICIANS

Ancient musicians? You bet! King David was a great musician—a singer, harpist, and songwriter who set up a worship choir. Many of the Levites were musicians as well as priests. They played instruments such as trumpets and cymbals.

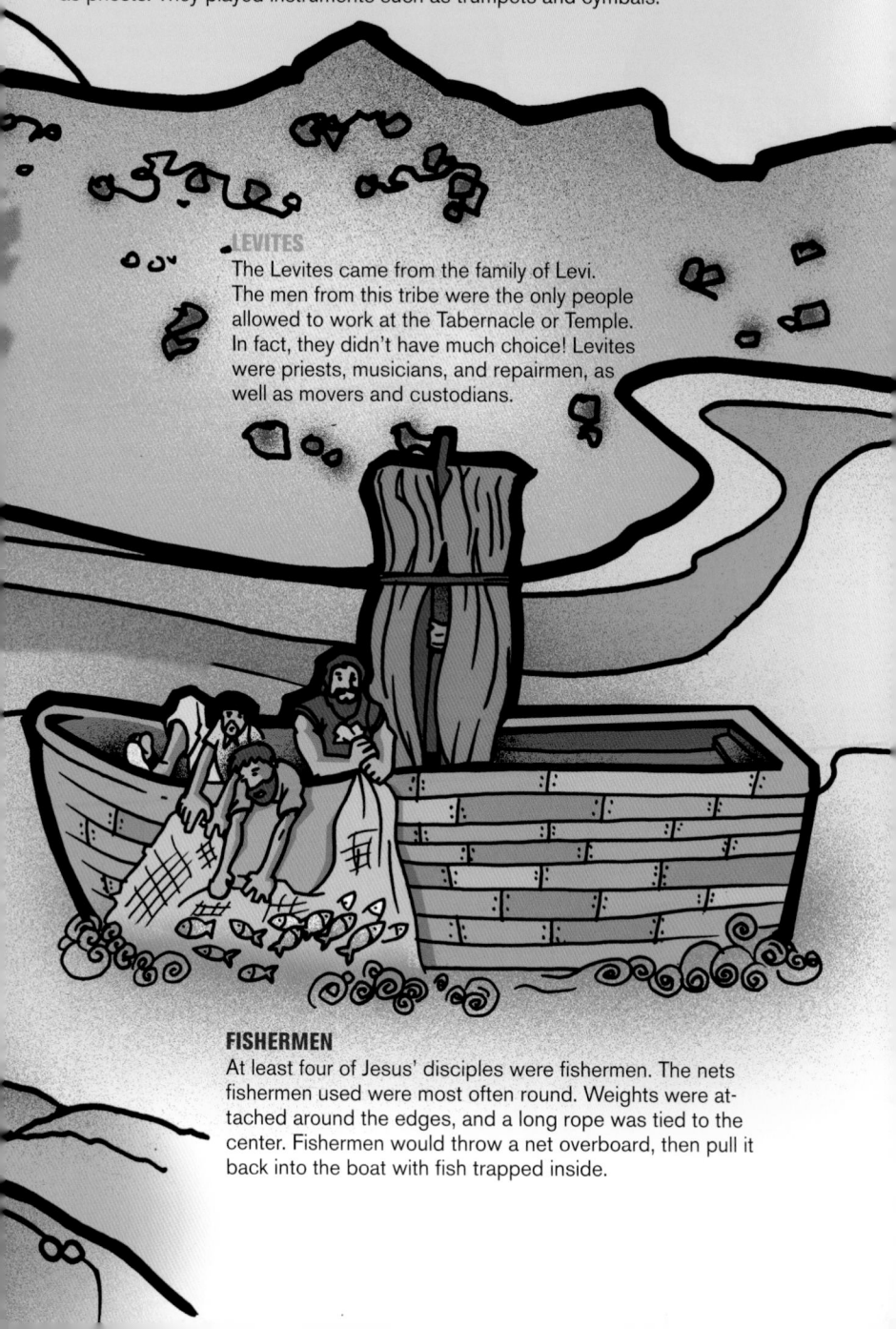

LEVITES

The Levites came from the family of Levi. The men from this tribe were the only people allowed to work at the Tabernacle or Temple. In fact, they didn't have much choice! Levites were priests, musicians, and repairmen, as well as movers and custodians.

FISHERMEN

At least four of Jesus' disciples were fishermen. The nets fishermen used were most often round. Weights were attached around the edges, and a long rope was tied to the center. Fishermen would throw a net overboard, then pull it back into the boat with fish trapped inside.

In some Bible-time cities there were whole streets that focused on one trade (Street of Weavers or Street of Sandalmakers, for example). Today we have the same kind of thing (the garment district or the banking district, for example).

TRADESMEN

A trade is a business or job that usually requires special skills. Solomon hired goldsmiths, silversmiths, brass makers, ironworkers, stonecutters, carpenters, weavers, dyers, and engravers to build the Temple. Some of them had become famous for their good work.

TANNERS

Tanners prepared animal skins, turning the hides into leather. The leather was used to make shoes, tents, shields, and floor coverings. Jews looked down on tanners because they worked with dead animals, which were considered unclean.

FARMERS

The main farm crops were wheat and barley. Following the autumn rains, the farmer sowed (planted) the grain by hand. If there were winter rains, he could harvest the crop in April or May.

OLYMPIC ATHLETES

Did you know the Olympics were named after Olympia, a plain west of Corinth (where Paul started a church)? Even in the first century you could be an Olympic athlete.

CARPENTERS

Ancient carpenters did all kinds of work. They used many of the same tools as modern carpenters to make doors, furniture, boats, farm equipment, cabinets, and sculptures.

POTTERS

Potters formed objects from clay. They stayed very busy because pottery was affordable and everyone used it. A potter's shop included space for a lot of tools and a lot of pots. There also were furnaces for baking the pottery and wheels for shaping the wet clay into pots.

Should priests and prophets be killed
within the Lord's Temple?

21 "See them lying in the streets—
young and old,
boys and girls,
killed by the swords of the enemy.
You have killed them in your anger,
slaughtering them without mercy.

22 "You have invited terrors from all around,
as though you were calling them to a
day of feasting.
In the day of the LORD's anger,
no one has escaped or survived.
The enemy has killed all the children
whom I carried and raised."

CHAPTER 3

Hope in the LORD's Faithfulness

1 I am the one who has seen the afflictions
that come from the rod of the LORD's
anger.
2 He has led me into darkness,
shutting out all light.
3 He has turned his hand against me
again and again, all day long.

4 He has made my skin and flesh grow old.
He has broken my bones.
5 He has besieged and surrounded me
with anguish and distress.
6 He has buried me in a dark place,
like those long dead.

7 He has walled me in, and I cannot
escape.
He has bound me in heavy chains.
8 And though I cry and shout,
he has shut out my prayers.
9 He has blocked my way with a high stone
wall;
he has made my road crooked.

10 He has hidden like a bear or a lion,
waiting to attack me.
11 He has dragged me off the path and torn
me in pieces,
leaving me helpless and devastated.
12 He has drawn his bow
and made me the target for his
arrows.

13 He shot his arrows
deep into my heart.

Sticks and Stones . . .
Drew and Heather are good spellers, and they have studied hard for the school spelling bee. On the day of the contest, Drew is nervous. But as he goes on, he gains confidence. Finally, it's down to him and Heather. The word is given, and Heather goes first. She misses the word by one letter. Now it's up to Drew. He spells it right and wins! Later, as Drew is walking home, Heather follows him and taunts him: "Hey, it's the walking dictionary. Wait until next year, Mr. Know-It-All." How do you think Drew should respond? Check out Lamentations 3:30.

14 My own people laugh at me.
All day long they sing their mocking
songs.
15 He has filled me with bitterness
and given me a bitter cup of sorrow to
drink.

16 He has made me chew on gravel.
He has rolled me in the dust.

17 Peace has been stripped away,
and I have forgotten what prosperity is.
18 I cry out, "My splendor is gone!
Everything I had hoped for from the
LORD is lost!"

19 The thought of my suffering and
homelessness
is bitter beyond words.*
20 I will never forget this awful time,
as I grieve over my loss.
21 Yet I still dare to hope
when I remember this:

22 The faithful love of the LORD never
ends!*
His mercies never cease.
23 Great is his faithfulness;
his mercies begin afresh each morning.
24 I say to myself, "The LORD is my
inheritance;
therefore, I will hope in him!"

25 The LORD is good to those who depend
on him,
to those who search for him.
26 So it is good to wait quietly
for salvation from the LORD.
27 And it is good for people to submit at an
early age
to the yoke of his discipline:

28 Let them sit alone in silence
beneath the LORD's demands.
29 Let them lie face down in the dust,
for there may be hope at last.
30 Let them turn the other cheek to those
who strike them
and accept the insults of their
enemies.

Does God sit in heaven waiting to zap people for doing things that are wrong?

Though he brings grief, he also shows compassion because of the greatness of his unfailing love. For he does not enjoy hurting people or causing them sorrow. LAMENTATIONS 3:32-33

31 For no one is abandoned
by the Lord forever.
32 Though he brings grief, he also shows
compassion
because of the greatness of his
unfailing love.
33 For he does not enjoy hurting people
or causing them sorrow.

34 If people crush underfoot
all the prisoners of the land,
35 if they deprive others of their rights
in defiance of the Most High,
36 if they twist justice in the courts—
doesn't the Lord see all these things?

37 Who can command things to happen
without the Lord's permission?
38 Does not the Most High
send both calamity and good?
39 Then why should we, mere humans,
complain
when we are punished for our
sins?

40 Instead, let us test and examine
our ways.
Let us turn back to the LORD.
41 Let us lift our hearts and hands
to God in heaven and say,
42 "We have sinned and rebelled,
and you have not forgiven us.

43 "You have engulfed us with your anger,
chased us down,
and slaughtered us without
mercy.
44 You have hidden yourself in a cloud
so our prayers cannot reach you.
45 You have discarded us as refuse and
garbage
among the nations.

46 "All our enemies
have spoken out against us.

47 We are filled with fear,
for we are trapped, devastated, and
ruined."
48 Tears stream from my eyes

3:19 Or *is wormwood and gall.* **3:22** As in Syriac version; Hebrew reads *of the LORD keeps us from destruction.*

because of the destruction of my
people!

49 My tears flow endlessly;
they will not stop
50 until the LORD looks down
from heaven and sees.
51 My heart is breaking
over the fate of all the women of
Jerusalem.

52 My enemies, whom I have never
harmed,
hunted me down like a bird.
53 They threw me into a pit
and dropped stones on me.
54 The water rose over my head,
and I cried out, "This is the end!"

55 But I called on your name, LORD,
from deep within the pit.
56 You heard me when I cried, "Listen to my
pleading!
Hear my cry for help!"
57 Yes, you came when I called;
you told me, "Do not fear."

58 Lord, you are my lawyer! Plead
my case!
For you have redeemed my life.
59 You have seen the wrong they have done
to me, LORD.
Be my judge, and prove me right.
60 You have seen the vengeful plots
my enemies have laid against me.

61 LORD, you have heard the vile names they
call me.
You know all about the plans they have
made.
62 My enemies whisper and mutter
as they plot against me all day long.
63 Look at them! Whether they sit or
stand,
I am the object of their mocking
songs.

64 Pay them back, LORD,
for all the evil they have done.
65 Give them hard and stubborn hearts,
and then let your curse fall on them!
66 Chase them down in your anger,
destroying them beneath the LORD's
heavens.

CHAPTER 4

God's Anger Satisfied

1 How the gold has lost its luster!
Even the finest gold has become dull.
The sacred gemstones
lie scattered in the streets!

2 See how the precious children of
Jerusalem,*
worth their weight in fine gold,
are now treated like pots of clay
made by a common potter.

3 Even the jackals feed their young,
but not my people Israel.
They ignore their children's cries,
like ostriches in the desert.

4 The parched tongues of their little ones
stick to the roofs of their mouths in
thirst.
The children cry for bread,
but no one has any to give them.

5 The people who once ate the richest
foods
now beg in the streets for anything they
can get.
Those who once wore the finest clothes
now search the garbage dumps for
food.

6 The guilt* of my people
is greater than that of Sodom,
where utter disaster struck in a moment
and no hand offered help.

7 Our princes once glowed with health—
brighter than snow, whiter than milk.
Their faces were as ruddy as rubies,
their appearance like fine jewels.*

8 But now their faces are blacker than soot.
No one recognizes them in the streets.
Their skin sticks to their bones;
it is as dry and hard as wood.

9 Those killed by the sword are better off
than those who die of hunger.
Starving, they waste away
for lack of food from the fields.

10 Tenderhearted women
have cooked their own children.
They have eaten them
to survive the siege.

4:2 Hebrew *precious sons of Zion.* **4:6** Or *punishment.* **4:7** Hebrew *like lapis lazuli.*

11 But now the anger of the LORD is satisfied.
His fierce anger has been poured out.
He started a fire in Jerusalem*
that burned the city to its foundations.

12 Not a king in all the earth—
no one in all the world—
would have believed that an enemy
could march through the gates of
Jerusalem.

13 Yet it happened because of the sins of her
prophets
and the sins of her priests,
who defiled the city
by shedding innocent blood.

14 They wandered blindly
through the streets,
so defiled by blood
that no one dared touch them.

15 "Get away!" the people shouted at them.
"You're defiled! Don't touch us!"
So they fled to distant lands
and wandered among foreign nations,
but none would let them stay.

16 The LORD himself has scattered them,
and he no longer helps them.
People show no respect for the priests
and no longer honor the leaders.

17 We looked in vain for our allies
to come and save us,
but we were looking to nations
that could not help us.

18 We couldn't go into the streets
without danger to our lives.
Our end was near; our days were
numbered.
We were doomed!

19 Our enemies were swifter than eagles
in flight.
If we fled to the mountains, they found
us.
If we hid in the wilderness,
they were waiting for us there.

20 Our king—the LORD's anointed, the very
life of our nation—
was caught in their snares.
We had thought that his shadow
would protect us against any nation on
earth!

21 Are you rejoicing in the land of Uz,
O people of Edom?
But you, too, must drink from the cup of
the LORD's anger.
You, too, will be stripped naked in your
drunkenness.

22 O beautiful Jerusalem,* your punishment
will end;
you will soon return from exile.
But Edom, your punishment is just
beginning;
soon your many sins will be exposed.

CHAPTER 5

Prayer for Restoration

1 LORD, remember what has happened
to us.
See how we have been disgraced!
2 Our inheritance has been turned over
to strangers,
our homes to foreigners.
3 We are orphaned and fatherless.
Our mothers are widowed.
4 We have to pay for water to drink,
and even firewood is expensive.
5 Those who pursue us are at our heels;
we are exhausted but are given
no rest.
6 We submitted to Egypt and Assyria
to get enough food to survive.
7 Our ancestors sinned, but they have
died—
and we are suffering the punishment
they deserved!

8 Slaves have now become our masters;
there is no one left to rescue us.
9 We hunt for food at the risk of our lives,
for violence rules the countryside.
10 The famine has blackened our skin
as though baked in an oven.
11 Our enemies rape the women in
Jerusalem*
and the young girls in all the towns
of Judah.
12 Our princes are being hanged by their
thumbs,
and our elders are treated with
contempt.

4:11 Hebrew *in Zion.* **4:22** Hebrew *O daughter of Zion.* **5:11** Hebrew *in Zion.*

13 Young men are led away to work at
millstones,
and boys stagger under heavy loads of
wood.
14 The elders no longer sit in the city gates;
the young men no longer dance and
sing.
15 Joy has left our hearts;
our dancing has turned to mourning.
16 The garlands have* fallen from our
heads.
Weep for us because we have sinned.
17 Our hearts are sick and weary,
and our eyes grow dim with tears.
18 For Jerusalem* is empty and desolate,
a place haunted by jackals.
19 But LORD, you remain the same
forever!
Your throne continues from generation
to generation.
20 Why do you continue to forget us?
Why have you abandoned us for so
long?
21 Restore us, O LORD, and bring us back to
you again!
Give us back the joys we once had!
22 Or have you utterly rejected us?
Are you angry with us still?

5:16 Or *The crown has.* **5:18** Hebrew *Mount Zion.*

EZEKIEL

WHO
Ezekiel, Israel's leaders, Ezekiel's wife, King Nebuchadnezzar, and "the Prince."

WHERE
In Babylon.

WHEN
Around 571 BC while many Jews were captive in Babylon.

WHY
To announce God's judgment and his coming salvation.

I will put a new spirit in you.
EZEKIEL 36:26

God created people with the ability to make choices. The most important choice we make is whether we will obey God. Ezekiel chose to obey God even when it was hard. He became a street preacher, warning people about God's judgment and telling them to turn away from their sins and back to God.

627 BC — Jeremiah becomes a prophet to Judah
605 BC — Daniel taken captive to Babylon
597 BC — Ezekiel taken captive to Babylon
593 BC — Ezekiel becomes a prophet to exiles
586 BC — Judah falls; Jerusalem destroyed
571 BC — Ezekiel's ministry ends
539 BC — Babylon overthrown by Cyrus
537 BC — First exiles return to Judah

THINK ABOUT WHAT GOD HAS ASKED YOU TO DO. WILL YOU OBEY?

CHAPTER 1

A Vision of Living Beings

On July 31* of my thirtieth year,* while I was with the Judean exiles beside the Kebar River in Babylon, the heavens were opened and I saw visions of God. [2]This happened during the fifth year of King Jehoiachin's captivity. [3](The LORD gave this message to Ezekiel son of Buzi, a priest, beside the Kebar River in the land of the Babylonians,* and he felt the hand of the LORD take hold of him.)

[4]As I looked, I saw a great storm coming

1:1a Hebrew *On the fifth day of the fourth month,* of the ancient Hebrew lunar calendar. A number of dates in Ezekiel can be cross-checked with dates in surviving Babylonian records and related accurately to our modern calendar. This event occurred on July 31, 593 B.C. **1:1b** Or *in the thirtieth year.* **1:3** Or *Chaldeans.*

from the north, driving before it a huge cloud
that flashed with lightning and shone with
brilliant light. There was fire inside the cloud,
and in the middle of the fire glowed some-
thing like gleaming amber.* 5From the center
of the cloud came four living beings that
looked human, 6except that each had four
faces and four wings. 7Their legs were straight,
and their feet had hooves like those of a calf
and shone like burnished bronze. 8Under each
of their four wings I could see human hands.
So each of the four beings had four faces and
four wings. 9The wings of each living being
touched the wings of the beings beside it. Each
one moved straight forward in any direction
without turning around.

10Each had a human face in the front, the
face of a lion on the right side, the face of an
ox on the left side, and the face of an eagle at
the back. 11Each had two pairs of outstretched
wings—one pair stretched out to touch the
wings of the living beings on either side of it,
and the other pair covered its body. 12They
went in whatever direction the spirit chose,
and they moved straight forward in any direc-
tion without turning around.

13The living beings looked like bright coals
of fire or brilliant torches, and lightning
seemed to flash back and forth among them.
14And the living beings darted to and fro like
flashes of lightning.

15As I looked at these beings, I saw four
wheels touching the ground beside them, one
wheel belonging to each. 16The wheels spar-
kled as if made of beryl. All four wheels looked
alike and were made the same; each wheel had
a second wheel turning crosswise within it.
17The beings could move in any of the four di-
rections they faced, without turning as they
moved. 18The rims of the four wheels were tall
and frightening, and they were covered with
eyes all around.

19When the living beings moved, the
wheels moved with them. When they flew up-
ward, the wheels went up, too. 20The spirit of
the living beings was in the wheels. So wher-
ever the spirit went, the wheels and the living
beings also went. 21When the beings moved,
the wheels moved. When the beings stopped,
the wheels stopped. When the beings flew
upward, the wheels rose up, for the spirit of
the living beings was in the wheels.

22Spread out above them was a surface like

1:4 Or *like burnished metal;* also in 1:27.

YOU'VE GOT A FRIEND

Wyatt and Craig did lots of fun things together. They were good friends. Then someone told Craig, "I saw Wyatt drinking a beer behind the school." Craig didn't want to believe it, but something Wyatt said later made Craig think maybe the story was true. Should Craig keep quiet and pretend nothing happened? Or should he confront Wyatt about what he heard?

In Ezekiel 2:3-7, you can read how God gave Ezekiel the job of confronting his nation with their wrongdoing—whether they listened or not. Sometimes being a good friend isn't all fun; sometimes it means telling the truth.

the sky, glittering like crystal. [23]Beneath this surface the wings of each living being stretched out to touch the others' wings, and each had two wings covering its body. [24]As they flew, their wings sounded to me like waves crashing against the shore or like the voice of the Almighty* or like the shouting of a mighty army. When they stopped, they let down their wings. [25]As they stood with wings lowered, a voice spoke from beyond the crystal surface above them.

[26]Above this surface was something that looked like a throne made of blue lapis lazuli. And on this throne high above was a figure whose appearance resembled a man. [27]From what appeared to be his waist up, he looked like gleaming amber, flickering like a fire. And from his waist down, he looked like a burning flame, shining with splendor. [28]All around him was a glowing halo, like a rainbow shining in the clouds on a rainy day. This is what the glory of the LORD looked like to me. When I saw it, I fell face down on the ground, and I heard someone's voice speaking to me.

CHAPTER 2

Ezekiel's Call and Commission

"Stand up, son of man," said the voice. "I want to speak with you." [2]The Spirit came into me as he spoke, and he set me on my feet. I listened carefully to his words. [3]"Son of man," he said, "I am sending you to the nation of Israel, a rebellious nation that has rebelled against me. They and their ancestors have been rebelling against me to this very day. [4]They are a stubborn and hard-hearted people. But I am sending you to say to them, 'This is what the Sovereign LORD says!' [5]And whether they listen or refuse to listen—for remember, they are rebels—at least they will know they have had a prophet among them.

[6]"Son of man, do not fear them or their words. Don't be afraid even though their threats surround you like nettles and briers and stinging scorpions. Do not be dismayed by their dark scowls, even though they are rebels. [7]You must give them my messages whether they listen or not. But they won't listen, for they are completely rebellious! [8]Son of man, listen to what I say to you. Do not join them in their rebellion. Open your mouth, and eat what I give you."

[9]Then I looked and saw a hand reaching out to me. It held a scroll, [10]which he unrolled. And I saw that both sides were covered with funeral songs, words of sorrow, and pronouncements of doom.

CHAPTER 3

The voice said to me, "Son of man, eat what I am giving you—eat this scroll! Then go and give its message to the people of Israel." [2]So I opened my mouth, and he fed me the scroll. [3]"Fill your stomach with this," he said. And when I ate it, it tasted as sweet as honey in my mouth.

AMAZING FACTS

Ezekiel was told to eat a scroll—like several pieces of notebook paper—and it tasted like honey!

EZEKIEL 3:1-3

[4]Then he said, "Son of man, go to the people of Israel and give them my messages. [5]I am not sending you to a foreign people whose language you cannot understand. [6]No, I am not sending you to people with strange and difficult speech. If I did, they would listen! [7]But the people of Israel won't listen to you any more than they listen to me! For the whole lot of them are hard-hearted and stubborn. [8]But look, I have made you as obstinate and hard-hearted as they are. [9]I have made your forehead as hard as the hardest rock! So don't be afraid of them or fear their angry looks, even though they are rebels."

[10]Then he added, "Son of man, let all my words sink deep into your own heart first. Listen to them carefully for yourself. [11]Then

1:24 Hebrew *Shaddai*.

go to your people in exile and say to them, 'This is what the Sovereign LORD says!' Do this whether they listen to you or not."

12 Then the Spirit lifted me up, and I heard a loud rumbling sound behind me. (May the glory of the LORD be praised in his place!)* 13 It was the sound of the wings of the living beings as they brushed against each other and the rumbling of their wheels beneath them.

14 The Spirit lifted me up and took me away. I went in bitterness and turmoil, but the LORD's hold on me was strong. 15 Then I came to the colony of Judean exiles in Tel-abib, beside the Kebar River. I was overwhelmed and sat among them for seven days.

A Watchman for Israel

16 After seven days the LORD gave me a message. He said, 17 "Son of man, I have appointed you as a watchman for Israel. Whenever you receive a message from me, warn people immediately. 18 If I warn the wicked, saying, 'You are under the penalty of death,' but you fail to deliver the warning, they will die in their sins. And I will hold you responsible for their deaths. 19 If you warn them and they refuse to repent and keep on sinning, they will die in their sins. But you will have saved yourself because you obeyed me.

20 "If righteous people turn away from their righteous behavior and ignore the obstacles I put in their way, they will die. And if you do not warn them, they will die in their sins. None of their righteous acts will be remembered, and I will hold you responsible for their deaths. 21 But if you warn righteous people not to sin and they listen to you and do not sin, they will live, and you will have saved yourself, too."

22 Then the LORD took hold of me and said, "Get up and go out into the valley, and I will speak to you there." 23 So I got up and went, and there I saw the glory of the LORD, just as I had seen in my first vision by the Kebar River. And I fell face down on the ground.

24 Then the Spirit came into me and set me on my feet. He spoke to me and said, "Go to your house and shut yourself in. 25 There, son of man, you will be tied with ropes so you cannot go out among the people. 26 And I will make your tongue stick to the roof of your mouth so that you will be speechless and unable to rebuke them, for they are rebels. 27 But when I give you a message, I will loosen your tongue and let you speak. Then you will say to them, 'This is what the Sovereign LORD says!' Those who choose to listen will listen, but those who refuse will refuse, for they are rebels.

CHAPTER 4

A Sign of the Coming Siege

"And now, son of man, take a large clay brick and set it down in front of you. Then draw a map of the city of Jerusalem on it. 2 Show the city under siege. Build a wall around it so no one can escape. Set up the enemy camp, and surround the city with siege ramps and battering rams. 3 Then take an iron griddle and place it between you and the city. Turn toward the city and demonstrate how harsh the siege will be against Jerusalem. This will be a warning to the people of Israel.

4 "Now lie on your left side and place the sins of Israel on yourself. You are to bear their sins for the number of days you lie there on your side. 5 I am requiring you to bear Israel's sins for 390 days—one day for each year of their sin. 6 After that, turn over and lie on your right side for 40 days—one day for each year of Judah's sin.

7 "Meanwhile, keep staring at the siege of Jerusalem. Lie there with your arm bared and prophesy her destruction. 8 I will tie you up with ropes so you won't be able to turn from side to side until the days of your siege have been completed.

9 "Now go and get some wheat, barley, beans, lentils, millet, and emmer wheat, and mix them together in a storage jar. Use them to make bread for yourself during the 390 days you will be lying on your side. 10 Ration this out to yourself, eight ounces* of food for each day, and eat it at set times. 11 Then measure out a jar* of water for each day, and drink it at set times. 12 Prepare and eat this food as you would barley cakes. While all the people are watching, bake it over a fire using dried human dung as fuel and then eat the bread." 13 Then the LORD said, "This is how Israel will eat defiled bread in the Gentile lands to which I will banish them!"

14 Then I said, "O Sovereign LORD, must I be defiled by using human dung? For I have

3:12 A possible reading for this verse is *Then the Spirit lifted me up, and as the glory of the LORD rose from its place, I heard a loud rumbling sound behind me.* **4:10** Hebrew *20 shekels* [228 grams]. **4:11** Hebrew *⅙ of a hin* [about 1 pint or 0.6 liters].

never been defiled before. From the time I was a child until now I have never eaten any animal that died of sickness or was killed by other animals. I have never eaten any meat forbidden by the law."

[15]"All right," the LORD said. "You may bake your bread with cow dung instead of human dung." [16]Then he told me, "Son of man, I will make food very scarce in Jerusalem. It will be weighed out with great care and eaten fearfully. The water will be rationed out drop by drop, and the people will drink it with dismay. [17]Lacking food and water, people will look at one another in terror, and they will waste away under their punishment.

CHAPTER 5

A Sign of the Coming Judgment

"Son of man, take a sharp sword and use it as a razor to shave your head and beard. Use a scale to weigh the hair into three equal parts. [2]Place a third of it at the center of your map of Jerusalem. After acting out the siege, burn it there. Scatter another third across your map and chop it with a sword. Scatter the last third to the wind, for I will scatter my people with the sword. [3]Keep just a bit of the hair and tie it up in your robe. [4]Then take some of these hairs out and throw them into the fire, burning them up. A fire will then spread from this remnant and destroy all of Israel.

[5]"This is what the Sovereign LORD says: This is an illustration of what will happen to Jerusalem. I placed her at the center of the nations, [6]but she has rebelled against my regulations and decrees and has been even more wicked than the surrounding nations. She has refused to obey the regulations and decrees I gave her to follow.

[7]"Therefore, this is what the Sovereign LORD says: You people have behaved worse than your neighbors and have refused to obey my decrees and regulations. You have not even lived up to the standards of the nations around you. [8]Therefore, I myself, the Sovereign LORD, am now your enemy. I will punish you publicly while all the nations watch. [9]Because of your detestable idols, I will punish you like I have never punished anyone before or ever will again. [10]Parents will eat their own children, and children will eat their parents. I will punish you and scatter to the winds the few who survive.

AMAZING FACTS

Talk about weird drama! Ezekiel used shaved-off hairs from his head to act out what was coming up for Jerusalem.

EZEKIEL 5:1-4

[11]"As surely as I live, says the Sovereign LORD, I will cut you off completely. I will show you no pity at all because you have defiled my Temple with your vile images and detestable sins. [12]A third of your people will die in the city from disease and famine. A third of them will be slaughtered by the enemy outside the city walls. And I will scatter a third to the winds, chasing them with my sword. [13]Then at last my anger will be spent, and I will be satisfied. And when my fury against them has subsided, all Israel will know that I, the LORD, have spoken to them in my jealous anger.

[14]"So I will turn you into a ruin, a mockery in the eyes of the surrounding nations and to all who pass by. [15]You will become an object of mockery and taunting and horror. You will be a warning to all the nations around you. They will see what happens when the LORD punishes a nation in anger and rebukes it, says the LORD.

[16]"I will shower you with the deadly arrows of famine to destroy you. The famine will become more and more severe until every crumb of food is gone. [17]And along with the famine, wild animals will attack you and rob you of your children. Disease and war will stalk your land, and I will bring the sword of the enemy against you. I, the LORD, have spoken!"

CHAPTER 6

Judgment against Israel's Mountains

Again a message came to me from the LORD: [2]"Son of man, turn and face the mountains of Israel and prophesy against them. [3]Proclaim

Living in a Bible-time House

If you lived in a Bible-time house, your life would be much different from what it is today. Most houses had only two or three rooms. Rooftops were used like a deck or patio are today. On a hot evening, people sat on the flat roof to do their chores. There was very little furniture and no carpeting. A mat or two might be on the floor. People had no electricity in those days. Think of all the things you have that use electricity. There was no running water, so there were no bathtubs or showers and no toilets. Think about all the ways your day would be different in a Bible-time house.

this message from the Sovereign LORD against the mountains of Israel. This is what the Sovereign LORD says to the mountains and hills and to the ravines and valleys: I am about to bring war upon you, and I will smash your pagan shrines. [4]All your altars will be demolished, and your places of worship will be destroyed. I will kill your people in front of your idols.* [5]I will lay your corpses in front of your idols and scatter your bones around your altars. [6]Wherever you live there will be desolation, and I will destroy your pagan shrines. Your altars will be demolished, your idols will be smashed, your places of worship will be torn down, and all the religious objects you have made will be destroyed. [7]The place will be littered with corpses, and you will know that I alone am the LORD.

[8]"But I will let a few of my people escape destruction, and they will be scattered among the nations of the world. [9]Then when they are exiled among the nations, they will remember me. They will recognize how hurt I am by their unfaithful hearts and lustful eyes that long for their idols. Then at last they will hate themselves for all their detestable sins.

Does it really matter if I don't obey God?

I will call you to account for all your detestable sins. I will turn my eyes away and show no pity. . . . Then you will know that I am the LORD. EZEKIEL 7:3-4

[10]They will know that I alone am the LORD and that I was serious when I said I would bring this calamity on them.

[11]"This is what the Sovereign LORD says: Clap your hands in horror, and stamp your feet. Cry out because of all the detestable sins the people of Israel have committed. Now they are going to die from war and famine and disease. [12]Disease will strike down those who are far away in exile. War will destroy those who are nearby. And anyone who survives will be killed by famine. So at last I will spend my fury on them. [13]They will know that I am the LORD when their dead lie scattered among their idols and altars on every hill and mountain and under every green tree and every great shade tree—the places where they offered sacrifices to their idols. [14]I will crush them and make their cities desolate from the wilderness in the south to Riblah* in the north. Then they will know that I am the LORD."

CHAPTER 7

The Coming of the End

Then this message came to me from the LORD: [2]"Son of man, this is what the Sovereign LORD says to Israel:

"The end is here!
Wherever you look—
east, west, north, or south—
your land is finished.
[3] No hope remains,
for I will unleash my anger against you.
I will call you to account
for all your detestable sins.
[4] I will turn my eyes away and show no pity.
I will repay you for all your detestable sins.
Then you will know that I am the LORD.

[5] "This is what the Sovereign LORD says:
Disaster after disaster
is coming your way!
[6] The end has come.
It has finally arrived.
Your final doom is waiting!
[7] O people of Israel, the day of your destruction is dawning.
The time has come; the day of trouble is near.
Shouts of anguish will be heard on the mountains,
not shouts of joy.
[8] Soon I will pour out my fury on you
and unleash my anger against you.

6:4 The Hebrew term (literally *round things*) probably alludes to dung; also in 6:5, 6, 9, 13. **6:14** As in some Hebrew manuscripts; most Hebrew manuscripts read *Diblah*.

I SURVIVED

At one time, I thought I wanted to be a supermodel. I never really liked getting all dolled up, though. I just liked seeing all the trendy clothes and wanted to have a supermodel's salary.

For two years, I received miscellaneous jobs through a local modeling agency. Then I started getting a lot of weekend gigs—all of which paid a lot of money. My mom was always pessimistic about my career choice, and she really disliked hearing that I would now be working Saturdays *and* Sundays (even though it would only be after church). She said she was sure I would later regret working so much while in school.

She was right. My busy schedule prevented me from finishing my college entrance exam prep course. So I got low scores on the exam. I also botched important assignments for some of my classes. Consequently, my GPA took a dive . . . so did my chance of getting college scholarships.

But I wasn't worried. I thought, *I'll just pay for college with my modeling salary.* I was wrong. Because I was always exhausted, I arrived late to a couple of assignments. The result was that I was fired from the agency.

At that point, I had no other choice but to trust that God would provide for me. I needed his help, not just with finding money for college, but also with getting my grades back up. I'm happy to say that God took care of both areas. I received an academic scholarship for a local college and will enter the school this fall to begin pursuing a career I'm sure I'll like even more than modeling—fashion design.

Check out Ezekiel 7:19 to see how God views money. Read also 1 Timothy 6:17 for more on what the Bible says about money and how we should trust God more than money to provide for our every need.

I will call you to account
for all your detestable sins.
9 I will turn my eyes away and show no pity.
I will repay you for all your detestable sins.
Then you will know that it is I, the LORD,
who is striking the blow.

10 "The day of judgment is here;
your destruction awaits!
The people's wickedness and pride
have blossomed to full flower.
11 Their violence has grown into a rod
that will beat them for their wickedness.
None of these proud and wicked people will survive.
All their wealth and prestige will be swept away.
12 Yes, the time has come;
the day is here!
Buyers should not rejoice over bargains,
nor sellers grieve over losses,
for all of them will fall
under my terrible anger.
13 Even if the merchants survive,
they will never return to their business.
For what God has said applies to everyone—
it will not be changed!
Not one person whose life is twisted by sin
will ever recover.

The Desolation of Israel

14 "The trumpet calls Israel's army to mobilize,
but no one listens,
for my fury is against them all.
15 There is war outside the city
and disease and famine within.
Those outside the city walls
will be killed by enemy swords.
Those inside the city
will die of famine and disease.
16 The survivors who escape to the mountains
will moan like doves, weeping for their sins.
17 Their hands will hang limp,
their knees will be weak as water.
18 They will dress themselves in burlap;
horror and shame will cover them.
They will shave their heads
in sorrow and remorse.

19 "They will throw their money in the streets,
tossing it out like worthless trash.
Their silver and gold won't save them
on that day of the LORD's anger.
It will neither satisfy nor feed them,
for their greed can only trip them up.
20 They were proud of their beautiful jewelry
and used it to make detestable idols and vile images.
Therefore, I will make all their wealth
disgusting to them.
21 I will give it as plunder to foreigners,
to the most wicked of nations,
and they will defile it.
22 I will turn my eyes from them
as these robbers invade and defile my treasured land.

23 "Prepare chains for my people,
for the land is bloodied by terrible crimes.
Jerusalem is filled with violence.
24 I will bring the most ruthless of nations
to occupy their homes.
I will break down their proud fortresses
and defile their sanctuaries.
25 Terror and trembling will overcome my people.
They will look for peace but not find it.
26 Calamity will follow calamity;
rumor will follow rumor.
They will look in vain
for a vision from the prophets.
They will receive no teaching from the priests
and no counsel from the leaders.
27 The king and the prince will stand helpless,
weeping in despair,
and the people's hands
will tremble with fear.
I will bring on them
the evil they have done to others,
and they will receive the punishment
they so richly deserve.
Then they will know that I am the LORD."

CHAPTER 8

Idolatry in the Temple

Then on September 17,* during the sixth year of King Jehoiachin's captivity, while the leaders of Judah were in my home, the Sovereign LORD took hold of me. [2]I saw a figure that appeared to be a man. From what appeared to be his waist down, he looked like a burning flame. From the waist up he looked like gleaming amber.* [3]He reached out what seemed to be a hand and took me by the hair. Then the Spirit lifted me up into the sky and transported me to Jerusalem in a vision from God. I was taken to the north gate of the inner courtyard of the Temple, where there is a large idol that has made the LORD very jealous. [4]Suddenly, the glory of the God of Israel was there, just as I had seen it before in the valley.

[5]Then the LORD said to me, "Son of man, look toward the north." So I looked, and there to the north, beside the entrance to the gate near the altar, stood the idol that had made the LORD so jealous.

[6]"Son of man," he said, "do you see what they are doing? Do you see the detestable sins the people of Israel are committing to drive me from my Temple? But come, and you will see even more detestable sins than these!" [7]Then he brought me to the door of the Temple courtyard, where I could see a hole in the wall. [8]He said to me, "Now, son of man, dig into the wall." So I dug into the wall and found a hidden doorway.

[9]"Go in," he said, "and see the wicked and detestable sins they are committing in there!" [10]So I went in and saw the walls engraved with all kinds of crawling animals and detestable creatures. I also saw the various idols* worshiped by the people of Israel. [11]Seventy leaders of Israel were standing there with Jaazaniah son of Shaphan in the center. Each of them held an incense burner, from which a cloud of incense rose above their heads.

[12]Then the LORD said to me, "Son of man, have you seen what the leaders of Israel are doing with their idols in dark rooms? They are saying, 'The LORD doesn't see us; he has deserted our land!'" [13]Then the LORD added, "Come, and I will show you even more detestable sins than these!"

[14]He brought me to the north gate of the LORD's Temple, and some women were sitting there, weeping for the god Tammuz. [15]"Have you seen this?" he asked. "But I will show you even more detestable sins than these!"

[16]Then he brought me into the inner courtyard of the LORD's Temple. At the entrance to the sanctuary, between the entry room and the bronze altar, there were about twenty-five men with their backs to the sanctuary of the LORD. They were facing east, bowing low to the ground, worshiping the sun!

[17]"Have you seen this, son of man?" he asked. "Is it nothing to the people of Judah that they commit these detestable sins, leading the whole nation into violence, thumbing their noses at me, and provoking my anger? [18]Therefore, I will respond in fury. I will neither pity nor spare them. And though they cry for mercy, I will not listen."

CHAPTER 9

The Slaughter of Idolaters

Then the LORD thundered, "Bring on the men appointed to punish the city! Tell them to bring their weapons with them!" [2]Six men soon appeared from the upper gate that faces north, each carrying a deadly weapon in his hand. With them was a man dressed in linen, who carried a writer's case at his side. They all went into the Temple courtyard and stood beside the bronze altar.

[3]Then the glory of the God of Israel rose up from between the cherubim, where it had rested, and moved to the entrance of the Temple. And the LORD called to the man dressed in linen who was carrying the writer's case. [4]He said to him, "Walk through the streets of Jerusalem and put a mark on the foreheads of all who weep and sigh because of the detestable sins being committed in their city."

[5]Then I heard the LORD say to the other men, "Follow him through the city and kill everyone whose forehead is not marked. Show no mercy; have no pity! [6]Kill them all—old and young, girls and women and little children. But do not touch anyone with the mark. Begin right here at the Temple." So they began by killing the seventy leaders.

[7]"Defile the Temple!" the LORD commanded. "Fill its courtyards with corpses.

8:1 Hebrew *on the fifth day of the sixth month*, of the ancient Hebrew lunar calendar. This event occurred on September 17, 592 B.C.; also see note on 1:1. **8:2** Or *like burnished metal*. **8:10** The Hebrew term (literally *round things*) probably alludes to dung.

Go!" So they went and began killing throughout the city.

[8]While they were out killing, I was all alone. I fell face down on the ground and cried out, "O Sovereign LORD! Will your fury against Jerusalem wipe out everyone left in Israel?"

[9]Then he said to me, "The sins of the people of Israel and Judah are very, very great. The entire land is full of murder; the city is filled with injustice. They are saying, 'The LORD doesn't see it! The LORD has abandoned the land!' [10]So I will not spare them or have any pity on them. I will fully repay them for all they have done."

[11]Then the man in linen clothing, who carried the writer's case, reported back and said, "I have done as you commanded."

CHAPTER 10

The LORD's Glory Leaves the Temple

In my vision I saw what appeared to be a throne of blue lapis lazuli above the crystal surface over the heads of the cherubim. [2]Then the LORD spoke to the man in linen clothing and said, "Go between the whirling wheels beneath the cherubim, and take a handful of burning coals and scatter them over the city." He did this as I watched.

AMAZING FACTS

God once told a man to scatter burning coals over a whole city. That created a real "HOT spot"!

EZEKIEL 10:2

[3]The cherubim were standing at the south end of the Temple when the man went in, and the cloud of glory filled the inner courtyard. [4]Then the glory of the LORD rose up from above the cherubim and went over to the door of the Temple. The Temple was filled with this cloud of glory, and the courtyard glowed brightly with the glory of the LORD. [5]The moving wings of the cherubim sounded like the voice of God Almighty* and could be heard even in the outer courtyard.

[6]The LORD said to the man in linen clothing, "Go between the cherubim and take some burning coals from between the wheels." So the man went in and stood beside one of the wheels. [7]Then one of the cherubim reached out his hand and took some live coals from the fire burning among them. He put the coals into the hands of the man in linen clothing, and the man took them and went out. [8](All the cherubim had what looked like human hands under their wings.)

[9]I looked, and each of the four cherubim had a wheel beside him, and the wheels sparkled like beryl. [10]All four wheels looked alike and were made the same; each wheel had a second wheel turning crosswise within it. [11]The cherubim could move in any of the four directions they faced, without turning as they moved. They went straight in the direction they faced, never turning aside. [12]Both the cherubim and the wheels were covered with eyes. The cherubim had eyes all over their bodies, including their hands, their backs, and their wings. [13]I heard someone refer to the wheels as "the whirling wheels." [14]Each of the four cherubim had four faces: the first was the face of an ox,* the second was a human face, the third was the face of a lion, and the fourth was the face of an eagle.

[15]Then the cherubim rose upward. These were the same living beings I had seen beside the Kebar River. [16]When the cherubim moved, the wheels moved with them. When they lifted their wings to fly, the wheels stayed beside them. [17]When the cherubim stopped, the wheels stopped. When they flew upward, the wheels rose up, for the spirit of the living beings was in the wheels.

[18]Then the glory of the LORD moved out from the door of the Temple and hovered above the cherubim. [19]And as I watched, the cherubim flew with their wheels to the east gate of the LORD's Temple. And the glory of the God of Israel hovered above them.

[20]These were the same living beings I had seen beneath the God of Israel when I was by

10:5 Hebrew *El-Shaddai.* **10:14** Hebrew *the face of a cherub;* compare 1:10.

I grew up in a home where my parents and I never went to church. I never learned about God or read the Bible, although I figured there probably was a god out there somewhere. I just didn't know who or what that god might be.

My friends and I always used to play violent video games. I didn't think they were so bad. After all, everyone I knew seemed to be playing them. We liked the shooting and all the action, even if they were a little gross sometimes.

One Easter a good friend invited me to church. The pastor explained who God is and said that God wanted a relationship with me. Maybe I was just ready to hear it, but that very Sunday I gave my life to Christ and began a relationship with him.

Over the next year God began to work on many of the areas of my life. Before long I realized that the video games I had been playing were not only an incredible waste of time; they were also filling my mind with garbage. So I just found other things to do with my time. I got involved in my youth group at church. I even invited some of the friends who I used to play those games with to come with me to church. A few of them actually started coming.

Living my life for God has totally changed my life. I'm a better person because of him. He has given me a new outlook, a new purpose, and a new life. The good news is that if God can change me, he can change anyone.

Read Ezekiel 11:19 to see what God promises to do for those who come to him. Take a look at Ezekiel 36:26 and Colossians 3:3-15 to discover more about this new life in Christ.

the Kebar River. I knew they were cherubim,
[21] for each had four faces and four wings and
what looked like human hands under their
wings. [22] And their faces were just like the
faces of the beings I had seen at the Kebar,
and they traveled straight ahead, just as the
others had.

CHAPTER 11

Judgment on Israel's Leaders

Then the Spirit lifted me and brought me to
the east gateway of the LORD's Temple, where
I saw twenty-five prominent men of the city.
Among them were Jaazaniah son of Azzur
and Pelatiah son of Benaiah, who were lead-
ers among the people.

[2] The Spirit said to me, "Son of man, these
are the men who are planning evil and giving
wicked counsel in this city. [3] They say to the
people, 'Is it not a good time to build houses?
This city is like an iron pot. We are safe inside
it like meat in a pot.*' [4] Therefore, son of man,
prophesy against them loudly and clearly."

[5] Then the Spirit of the LORD came upon
me, and he told me to say, "This is what the
LORD says to the people of Israel: I know what
you are saying, for I know every thought that
comes into your minds. [6] You have murdered
many in this city and filled its streets with the
dead.

[7] "Therefore, this is what the Sovereign
LORD says: This city is an iron pot all right, but
the pieces of meat are the victims of your in-
justice. As for you, I will soon drag you from
this pot. [8] I will bring on you the sword of war
you so greatly fear, says the Sovereign LORD. [9] I
will drive you out of Jerusalem and hand you
over to foreigners, who will carry out my judg-
ments against you. [10] You will be slaughtered
all the way to the borders of Israel. I will exe-
cute judgment on you, and you will know that
I am the LORD. [11] No, this city will not be an
iron pot for you, and you will not be like meat
safe inside it. I will judge you even to the bor-
ders of Israel, [12] and you will know that I am
the LORD. For you have refused to obey my de-
crees and regulations; instead, you have cop-
ied the standards of the nations around you."

[13] While I was still prophesying, Pelatiah
son of Benaiah suddenly died. Then I fell face
down on the ground and cried out, "O Sover-
eign LORD, are you going to kill everyone in
Israel?"

Hope for Exiled Israel

[14] Then this message came to me from the
LORD: [15] "Son of man, the people still left in Je-
rusalem are talking about you and your rela-
tives and all the people of Israel who are in
exile. They are saying, 'Those people are far
away from the LORD, so now he has given their
land to us!'

[16] "Therefore, tell the exiles, 'This is what
the Sovereign LORD says: Although I have
scattered you in the countries of the world, I
will be a sanctuary to you during your time in
exile. [17] I, the Sovereign LORD, will gather you
back from the nations where you have been
scattered, and I will give you the land of Israel
once again.'

[18] "When the people return to their home-
land, they will remove every trace of their vile
images and detestable idols. [19] And I will give
them singleness of heart and put a new spirit
within them. I will take away their stony, stub-
born heart and give them a tender, responsive
heart,* [20] so they will obey my decrees and
regulations. Then they will truly be my peo-
ple, and I will be their God. [21] But as for those
who long for vile images and detestable idols,
I will repay them fully for their sins. I, the Sov-
ereign LORD, have spoken!"

The LORD's Glory Leaves Jerusalem

[22] Then the cherubim lifted their wings and
rose into the air with their wheels beside
them, and the glory of the God of Israel hov-
ered above them. [23] Then the glory of the
LORD went up from the city and stopped
above the mountain to the east.

[24] Afterward the Spirit of God carried me
back again to Babylonia,* to the people in ex-
ile there. And so ended the vision of my visit
to Jerusalem. [25] And I told the exiles every-
thing the LORD had shown me.

CHAPTER 12

Signs of the Coming Exile

Again a message came to me from the LORD:
[2] "Son of man, you live among rebels who have
eyes but refuse to see. They have ears but re-
fuse to hear. For they are a rebellious people.

11:3 Hebrew *This city is the pot, and we are the meat.* **11:19** Hebrew *a heart of flesh.* **11:24** Or *Chaldea.*

[3]"So now, son of man, pretend you are being sent into exile. Pack the few items an exile could carry, and leave your home to go somewhere else. Do this right in front of the people so they can see you. For perhaps they will pay attention to this, even though they are such rebels. [4]Bring your baggage outside during the day so they can watch you. Then in the evening, as they are watching, leave your house as captives do when they begin a long march to distant lands. [5]Dig a hole through the wall while they are watching and go out through it. [6]As they watch, lift your pack to your shoulders and walk away into the night. Cover your face so you cannot see the land you are leaving. For I have made you a sign for the people of Israel."

[7]So I did as I was told. In broad daylight I brought my pack outside, filled with the things I might carry into exile. Then in the evening while the people looked on, I dug through the wall with my hands and went out into the night with my pack on my shoulder.

[8]The next morning this message came to me from the LORD: [9]"Son of man, these rebels, the people of Israel, have asked you what all this means. [10]Say to them, 'This is what the Sovereign LORD says: These actions contain a message for King Zedekiah in Jerusalem* and for all the people of Israel.' [11]Explain that your actions are a sign to show what will soon happen to them, for they will be driven into exile as captives.

[12]"Even Zedekiah will leave Jerusalem at night through a hole in the wall, taking only what he can carry with him. He will cover his face, and his eyes will not see the land he is leaving. [13]Then I will throw my net over him and capture him in my snare. I will bring him to Babylon, the land of the Babylonians,* though he will never see it, and he will die there. [14]I will scatter his servants and warriors to the four winds and send the sword after them. [15]And when I scatter them among the nations, they will know that I am the LORD. [16]But I will spare a few of them from death by war, famine, or disease, so they can confess all their detestable sins to their captors. Then they will know that I am the LORD."

[17]Then this message came to me from the LORD: [18]"Son of man, tremble as you eat your food. Shake with fear as you drink your water. [19]Tell the people, 'This is what the Sovereign LORD says concerning those living in Israel and Jerusalem: They will eat their food with trembling and sip their water in despair, for their land will be stripped bare because of their violence. [20]The cities will be destroyed and the farmland made desolate. Then you will know that I am the LORD.'"

A New Proverb for Israel

[21]Again a message came to me from the LORD: [22]"Son of man, you've heard that proverb they quote in Israel: 'Time passes, and prophecies come to nothing.' [23]Tell the people, 'This is what the Sovereign LORD says: I will put an end to this proverb, and you will soon stop quoting it.' Now give them this new proverb to replace the old one: 'The time has come for every prophecy to be fulfilled!'

[24]"There will be no more false visions and flattering predictions in Israel. [25]For I am the LORD! If I say it, it will happen. There will be no more delays, you rebels of Israel. I will fulfill my threat of destruction in your own lifetime. I, the Sovereign LORD, have spoken!"

[26]Then this message came to me from the LORD: [27]"Son of man, the people of Israel are saying, 'He's talking about the distant future. His visions won't come true for a long, long time.' [28]Therefore, tell them, 'This is what the Sovereign LORD says: No more delay! I will now do everything I have threatened. I, the Sovereign LORD, have spoken!'"

CHAPTER 13

Judgment against False Prophets

Then this message came to me from the LORD: [2]"Son of man, prophesy against the false prophets of Israel who are inventing their own prophecies. Say to them, 'Listen to the word of the LORD. [3]This is what the Sovereign LORD says: What sorrow awaits the false prophets who are following their own imaginations and have seen nothing at all!'

[4]"O people of Israel, these prophets of yours are like jackals digging in the ruins. [5]They have done nothing to repair the breaks in the walls around the nation. They have not helped it to stand firm in battle on the day of the LORD. [6]Instead, they have told lies and made false

12:10 Hebrew *the prince in Jerusalem;* similarly in 12:12. **12:13** Or *Chaldeans.*

predictions. They say, 'This message is from the LORD,' even though the LORD never sent them. And yet they expect him to fulfill their prophecies! [7]Can your visions be anything but false if you claim, 'This message is from the LORD,' when I have not even spoken to you?

[8]"Therefore, this is what the Sovereign LORD says: Because what you say is false and your visions are a lie, I will stand against you, says the Sovereign LORD. [9]I will raise my fist against all the prophets who see false visions and make lying predictions, and they will be banished from the community of Israel. I will blot their names from Israel's record books, and they will never again set foot in their own land. Then you will know that I am the Sovereign LORD.

[10]"This will happen because these evil prophets deceive my people by saying, 'All is peaceful' when there is no peace at all! It's as if the people have built a flimsy wall, and these prophets are trying to reinforce it by covering it with whitewash! [11]Tell these whitewashers that their wall will soon fall down. A heavy rainstorm will undermine it; great hailstones and mighty winds will knock it down. [12]And when the wall falls, the people will cry out, 'What happened to your whitewash?'

[13]"Therefore, this is what the Sovereign LORD says: I will sweep away your whitewashed wall with a storm of indignation, with a great flood of anger, and with hailstones of fury. [14]I will break down your wall right to its foundation, and when it falls, it will crush you. Then you will know that I am the LORD. [15]At last my anger against the wall and those who covered it with whitewash will be satisfied. Then I will say to you: 'The wall and those who whitewashed it are both gone. [16]They were lying prophets who claimed peace would come to Jerusalem when there was no peace. I, the Sovereign LORD, have spoken!'

Judgment against False Women Prophets

[17]"Now, son of man, speak out against the women who prophesy from their own imaginations. [18]This is what the Sovereign LORD says: What sorrow awaits you women who are ensnaring the souls of my people, young and old alike. You tie magic charms on their wrists and furnish them with magic veils. Do you think you can trap others without bringing destruction on yourselves? [19]You bring shame on me among my people for a few handfuls of barley or a piece of bread. By lying to my people who love to listen to lies, you kill those who should not die, and you promise life to those who should not live.

[20]"This is what the Sovereign LORD says: I am against all your magic charms, which you use to ensnare my people like birds. I will tear them from your arms, setting my people free like birds set free from a cage. [21]I will tear off the magic veils and save my people from your grasp. They will no longer be your victims. Then you will know that I am the LORD. [22]You have discouraged the righteous with your lies, but I didn't want them to be sad. And you have encouraged the wicked by promising them life, even though they continue in their sins. [23]Because of all this, you will no longer talk of seeing visions that you never saw, nor will you make predictions. For I will rescue my people from your grasp. Then you will know that I am the LORD."

CHAPTER 14

The Idolatry of Israel's Leaders

Then some of the leaders of Israel visited me, and while they were sitting with me, [2]this message came to me from the LORD: [3]"Son of man, these leaders have set up idols* in their hearts. They have embraced things that will make them fall into sin. Why should I listen to their requests? [4]Tell them, 'This is what the Sovereign LORD says: The people of Israel have set up idols in their hearts and fallen into sin, and then they go to a prophet asking for a message. So I, the LORD, will give them the kind of answer their great idolatry deserves. [5]I will do this to capture the minds and hearts of all my people who have turned from me to worship their detestable idols.'

[6]"Therefore, tell the people of Israel, 'This is what the Sovereign LORD says: Repent and turn away from your idols, and stop all your detestable sins. [7]I, the LORD, will answer all those, both Israelites and foreigners, who reject me and set up idols in their hearts and so fall into sin, and who then come to a prophet asking for my advice. [8]I will turn against such people and make a terrible example of them, eliminating them from among my people. Then you will know that I am the LORD.

14:3 The Hebrew term (literally *round things*) probably alludes to dung; also in 14:4, 5, 6, 7.

9"'And if a prophet is deceived into giving a message, it is because I, the LORD, have deceived that prophet. I will lift my fist against such prophets and cut them off from the community of Israel. 10False prophets and those who seek their guidance will all be punished for their sins. 11In this way, the people of Israel will learn not to stray from me, polluting themselves with sin. They will be my people, and I will be their God. I, the Sovereign LORD, have spoken!'"

The Certainty of the LORD's Judgment

12Then this message came to me from the LORD: 13"Son of man, suppose the people of a country were to sin against me, and I lifted my fist to crush them, cutting off their food supply and sending a famine to destroy both people and animals. 14Even if Noah, Daniel, and Job were there, their righteousness would save no one but themselves, says the Sovereign LORD.

15"Or suppose I were to send wild animals to invade the country, kill the people, and make the land too desolate and dangerous to pass through. 16As surely as I live, says the Sovereign LORD, even if those three men were there, they wouldn't be able to save their own sons or daughters. They alone would be saved, but the land would be made desolate.

17"Or suppose I were to bring war against the land, and I sent enemy armies to destroy both people and animals. 18As surely as I live, says the Sovereign LORD, even if those three men were there, they wouldn't be able to save their own sons or daughters. They alone would be saved.

19"Or suppose I were to pour out my fury by sending an epidemic into the land, and the disease killed people and animals alike. 20As surely as I live, says the Sovereign LORD, even if Noah, Daniel, and Job were there, they wouldn't be able to save their own sons or daughters. They alone would be saved by their righteousness.

21"Now this is what the Sovereign LORD says: How terrible it will be when all four of these dreadful punishments fall upon Jerusalem—war, famine, wild animals, and disease—destroying all her people and animals. 22Yet there will be survivors, and they will come here to join you as exiles in Babylon.

You will see with your own eyes how wicked they are, and then you will feel better about what I have done to Jerusalem. 23When you meet them and see their behavior, you will understand that these things are not being done to Israel without cause. I, the Sovereign LORD, have spoken!"

CHAPTER 15

Jerusalem—a Useless Vine

Then this message came to me from the LORD: 2"Son of man, how does a grapevine compare to a tree? Is a vine's wood as useful as the wood of a tree? 3Can its wood be used for making things, like pegs to hang up pots and pans? 4No, it can only be used for fuel, and even as fuel, it burns too quickly. 5Vines are useless both before and after being put into the fire!

[6]"And this is what the Sovereign LORD says: The people of Jerusalem are like grapevines growing among the trees of the forest. Since they are useless, I have thrown them on the fire to be burned. [7]And I will see to it that if they escape from one fire, they will fall into another. When I turn against them, you will know that I am the LORD. [8]And I will make the land desolate because my people have been unfaithful to me. I, the Sovereign LORD, have spoken!"

CHAPTER 16

Jerusalem—an Unfaithful Wife

Then another message came to me from the LORD: [2]"Son of man, confront Jerusalem with her detestable sins. [3]Give her this message from the Sovereign LORD: You are nothing but a Canaanite! Your father was an Amorite and your mother a Hittite. [4]On the day you were born, no one cared about you. Your umbilical cord was not cut, and you were never washed, rubbed with salt, and wrapped in cloth. [5]No one had the slightest interest in you; no one pitied you or cared for you. On the day you were born, you were unwanted, dumped in a field and left to die.

[6]"But I came by and saw you there, helplessly kicking about in your own blood. As you lay there, I said, 'Live!' [7]And I helped you to thrive like a plant in the field. You grew up and became a beautiful jewel. Your breasts became full, and your body hair grew, but you were still naked. [8]And when I passed by again, I saw that you were old enough for love. So I wrapped my cloak around you to cover your nakedness and declared my marriage vows. I made a covenant with you, says the Sovereign LORD, and you became mine.

[9]"Then I bathed you and washed off your blood, and I rubbed fragrant oils into your skin. [10]I gave you expensive clothing of fine linen and silk, beautifully embroidered, and sandals made of fine goatskin leather. [11]I gave you lovely jewelry, bracelets, beautiful necklaces, [12]a ring for your nose, earrings for your ears, and a lovely crown for your head. [13]And so you were adorned with gold and silver. Your clothes were made of fine linen and were beautifully embroidered. You ate the finest foods—choice flour, honey, and olive oil—and became more beautiful than ever. You looked like a queen, and so you were! [14]Your fame soon spread throughout the world because of your beauty. I dressed you in my splendor and perfected your beauty, says the Sovereign LORD.

[15]"But you thought your fame and beauty were your own. So you gave yourself as a prostitute to every man who came along. Your beauty was theirs for the asking. [16]You used the lovely things I gave you to make shrines for idols, where you played the prostitute. Unbelievable! How could such a thing ever happen? [17]You took the very jewels and gold and silver ornaments I had given you and made statues of men and worshiped them. This is adultery against me! [18]You used the beautifully embroidered clothes I gave you to dress your idols. Then you used my special oil and my incense to worship them. [19]Imagine it! You set before them as a sacrifice the choice flour, olive oil, and honey I had given you, says the Sovereign LORD.

[20]"Then you took your sons and daughters—the children you had borne to me—and sacrificed them to your gods. Was your prostitution not enough? [21]Must you also slaughter my children by sacrificing them to idols? [22]In all your years of adultery and detestable sin, you have not once remembered the days long ago when you lay naked in a field, kicking about in your own blood.

[23]"What sorrow awaits you, says the Sovereign LORD. In addition to all your other wickedness, [24]you built a pagan shrine and put altars to idols in every town square. [25]On every street corner you defiled your beauty, offering your body to every passerby in an endless stream of prostitution. [26]Then you added lustful Egypt to your lovers, provoking my anger with your increasing promiscuity. [27]That is why I struck you with my fist and reduced your boundaries. I handed you over to your enemies, the Philistines, and even they were shocked by your lewd conduct. [28]You have prostituted yourself with the Assyrians, too. It seems you can never find enough new lovers! And after your prostitution there, you still were not satisfied. [29]You added to your lovers by embracing Babylonia,* the land of merchants, but you still weren't satisfied.

16:29 Or *Chaldea.*

30"What a sick heart you have, says the Sovereign LORD, to do such things as these, acting
like a shameless prostitute. 31You build your
pagan shrines on every street corner and your
altars to idols in every square. In fact, you
have been worse than a prostitute, so eager
for sin that you have not even demanded pay-
ment. 32Yes, you are an adulterous wife who
takes in strangers instead of her own hus-
band. 33Prostitutes charge for their services—
but not you! You give gifts to your lovers, brib-
ing them to come and have sex with you. 34So
you are the opposite of other prostitutes. You
pay your lovers instead of their paying you!

Judgment on Jerusalem's Prostitution

35"Therefore, you prostitute, listen to this
message from the LORD! 36This is what the
Sovereign LORD says: Because you have
poured out your lust and exposed yourself in
prostitution to all your lovers, and because
you have worshiped detestable idols,* and
because you have slaughtered your children
as sacrifices to your gods, 37this is what I am
going to do. I will gather together all your al-
lies—the lovers with whom you have sinned,
both those you loved and those you hated—
and I will strip you naked in front of them so
they can stare at you. 38I will punish you for
your murder and adultery. I will cover you
with blood in my jealous fury. 39Then I will
give you to these many nations who are your
lovers, and they will destroy you. They will
knock down your pagan shrines and the al-
tars to your idols. They will strip you and take
your beautiful jewels, leaving you stark na-
ked. 40They will band together in a mob to
stone you and cut you up with swords. 41They
will burn your homes and punish you in front
of many women. I will stop your prostitution
and end your payments to your many lovers.

42"Then at last my fury against you will be
spent, and my jealous anger will subside. I will
be calm and will not be angry with you any-
more. 43But first, because you have not re-
membered your youth but have angered me
by doing all these evil things, I will fully repay
you for all of your sins, says the Sovereign
LORD. For you have added lewd acts to all your
detestable sins. 44Everyone who makes up
proverbs will say of you, 'Like mother, like
daughter.' 45For your mother loathed her hus-
band and her children, and so do you. And
you are exactly like your sisters, for they de-
spised their husbands and their children.
Truly your mother was a Hittite and your fa-
ther an Amorite.

46"Your older sister was Samaria, who lived
with her daughters in the north. Your youn-
ger sister was Sodom, who lived with her
daughters in the south. 47But you have not
merely sinned as they did. You quickly sur-
passed them in corruption. 48As surely as I
live, says the Sovereign LORD, Sodom and her
daughters were never as wicked as you and
your daughters. 49Sodom's sins were pride,
gluttony, and laziness, while the poor and
needy suffered outside her door. 50She was
proud and committed detestable sins, so I
wiped her out, as you have seen.*

51"Even Samaria did not commit half your
sins. You have done far more detestable
things than your sisters ever did. They seem
righteous compared to you. 52Shame on you!
Your sins are so terrible that you make your
sisters seem righteous, even virtuous.

53"But someday I will restore the fortunes
of Sodom and Samaria, and I will restore you,
too. 54Then you will be truly ashamed of
everything you have done, for your sins make
them feel good in comparison. 55Yes, your sis-
ters, Sodom and Samaria, and all their people
will be restored, and at that time you also will
be restored. 56In your proud days you held
Sodom in contempt. 57But now your greater
wickedness has been exposed to all the world,
and you are the one who is scorned—by
Edom* and all her neighbors and by Philistia.
58This is your punishment for all your lewd-
ness and detestable sins, says the LORD.

59"Now this is what the Sovereign LORD
says: I will give you what you deserve, for you
have taken your solemn vows lightly by
breaking your covenant. 60Yet I will remem-
ber the covenant I made with you when you
were young, and I will establish an everlasting
covenant with you. 61Then you will remember
with shame all the evil you have done. I will
make your sisters, Samaria and Sodom, to be
your daughters, even though they are not part
of our covenant. 62And I will reaffirm my cov-
enant with you, and you will know that I am

16:36 The Hebrew term (literally *round things*) probably alludes to dung. **16:50** As in a few Hebrew manuscripts and Greek version; Masoretic Text reads *as I have seen*. **16:57** As in many Hebrew manuscripts and Syriac version; Masoretic Text reads *Aram*.

the LORD. 63 You will remember your sins and
cover your mouth in silent shame when I for-
give you of all that you have done. I, the Sover-
eign LORD, have spoken!"

CHAPTER 17

A Story of Two Eagles

Then this message came to me from the
LORD: 2 "Son of man, give this riddle, and tell
this story to the people of Israel. 3 Give them
this message from the Sovereign LORD:

"A great eagle with broad wings and long
feathers,
covered with many-colored plumage,
came to Lebanon.
He seized the top of a cedar tree
4 and plucked off its highest branch.
He carried it away to a city filled with
merchants.
He planted it in a city of traders.
5 He also took a seedling from the land
and planted it in fertile soil.
He placed it beside a broad river,
where it could grow like a willow tree.
6 It took root there and
grew into a low, spreading vine.
Its branches turned up toward the eagle,
and its roots grew down into the
ground.
It produced strong branches
and put out shoots.
7 But then another great eagle came
with broad wings and full plumage.
So the vine now sent its roots and
branches
toward him for water,
8 even though it was already planted in
good soil
and had plenty of water
so it could grow into a splendid vine
and produce rich leaves and luscious
fruit.

9 "So now the Sovereign LORD asks:
Will this vine grow and prosper?
No! I will pull it up, roots and all!
I will cut off its fruit
and let its leaves wither and die.
I will pull it up easily
without a strong arm or a large
army.
10 But when the vine is transplanted,
will it thrive?
No, it will wither away
when the east wind blows against it.
It will die in the same good soil
where it had grown so well."

The Riddle Explained

11 Then this message came to me from the
LORD: 12 "Say to these rebels of Israel: Don't
you understand the meaning of this riddle of
the eagles? The king of Babylon came to Jeru-
salem, took away her king and princes, and
brought them to Babylon. 13 He made a treaty
with a member of the royal family and forced
him to take an oath of loyalty. He also exiled
Israel's most influential leaders, 14 so Israel
would not become strong again and revolt.
Only by keeping her treaty with Babylon
could Israel survive.

15 "Nevertheless, this man of Israel's royal
family rebelled against Babylon, sending am-
bassadors to Egypt to request a great army
and many horses. Can Israel break her sworn
treaties like that and get away with it? 16 No!
For as surely as I live, says the Sovereign LORD,
the king of Israel will die in Babylon, the land
of the king who put him in power and whose
treaty he disregarded and broke. 17 Pharaoh
and all his mighty army will fail to help Israel
when the king of Babylon lays siege to Jerusa-
lem again and destroys many lives. 18 For the
king of Israel disregarded his treaty and
broke it after swearing to obey; therefore, he
will not escape.

19 "So this is what the Sovereign LORD says:
As surely as I live, I will punish him for break-
ing my covenant and disregarding the solemn
oath he made in my name. 20 I will throw my
net over him and capture him in my snare. I
will bring him to Babylon and put him on trial
for this treason against me. 21 And all his best
warriors* will be killed in battle, and those
who survive will be scattered to the four
winds. Then you will know that I, the LORD,
have spoken.

22 "This is what the Sovereign LORD says: I
will take a branch from the top of a tall cedar,
and I will plant it on the top of Israel's highest
mountain. 23 It will become a majestic cedar,
sending forth its branches and producing

17:21 Or *his fleeing warriors*. The meaning of the Hebrew is uncertain.

seed. Birds of every sort will nest in it, finding shelter in the shade of its branches. [24]And all the trees will know that it is I, the LORD, who cuts the tall tree down and makes the short tree grow tall. It is I who makes the green tree wither and gives the dead tree new life. I, the LORD, have spoken, and I will do what I said!"

CHAPTER 18

The Justice of a Righteous God

Then another message came to me from the LORD: [2]"Why do you quote this proverb concerning the land of Israel: 'The parents have eaten sour grapes, but their children's mouths pucker at the taste'? [3]As surely as I live, says the Sovereign LORD, you will not quote this proverb anymore in Israel. [4]For all people are mine to judge—both parents and children alike. And this is my rule: The person who sins is the one who will die.

[5]"Suppose a certain man is righteous and does what is just and right. [6]He does not feast in the mountains before Israel's idols* or worship them. He does not commit adultery or have intercourse with a woman during her menstrual period. [7]He is a merciful creditor, not keeping the items given as security by poor debtors. He does not rob the poor but instead gives food to the hungry and provides clothes for the needy. [8]He grants loans without interest, stays away from injustice, is honest and fair when judging others, [9]and faithfully obeys my decrees and regulations. Anyone who does these things is just and will surely live, says the Sovereign LORD.

[10]"But suppose that man has a son who grows up to be a robber or murderer and refuses to do what is right. [11]And that son does all the evil things his father would never do—he worships idols on the mountains, commits adultery, [12]oppresses the poor and helpless, steals from debtors by refusing to let them redeem their security, worships idols, commits detestable sins, [13]and lends money at excessive interest. Should such a sinful person live? No! He must die and must take full blame.

[14]"But suppose that sinful son, in turn, has a son who sees his father's wickedness and decides against that kind of life. [15]This son refuses to worship idols on the mountains and does not commit adultery. [16]He does not exploit the poor, but instead is fair to debtors

18:6 The Hebrew term (literally *round things*) probably alludes to dung; also in 18:12, 15.

IS IT OK?

IS IT OK TO BELIEVE SOMETHING DIFFERENT FROM WHAT MY PARENTS BELIEVE?

Drum roll, please . . . Ezekiel's big news is that God says *you are responsible for your own beliefs and actions*. (Check out God's message in Ezekiel 18:19-22.) You pay for your own sins—if you don't seek God's forgiveness—and you are rewarded for your own good deeds. No "get into heaven free" passes because your mother is a saint. And no automatic punishment for you if your parents don't believe in God. *You* are responsible for what you believe. As you sort through your beliefs, remember: (1) No matter what your parents believe, you must respect and obey them even if you don't agree with them. (2) Let the Bible guide you—it is the only 100 percent trustworthy source of truth.

and does not rob them. He gives food to the hungry and provides clothes for the needy. [17]He helps the poor,* does not lend money at interest, and obeys all my regulations and decrees. Such a person will not die because of his father's sins; he will surely live. [18]But the father will die for his many sins—for being cruel, robbing people, and doing what was clearly wrong among his people.

[19]"'What?' you ask. 'Doesn't the child pay for the parent's sins?' No! For if the child does what is just and right and keeps my decrees, that child will surely live. [20]The person who sins is the one who will die. The child will not be punished for the parent's sins, and the parent will not be punished for the child's sins. Righteous people will be rewarded for their own righteous behavior, and wicked people will be punished for their own wickedness. [21]But if wicked people turn away from all their sins and begin to obey my decrees and do what is just and right, they will surely live and not die. [22]All their past sins will be forgotten, and they will live because of the righteous things they have done.

[23]"Do you think that I like to see wicked people die? says the Sovereign Lord. Of course not! I want them to turn from their wicked ways and live. [24]However, if righteous people turn from their righteous behavior and start doing sinful things and act like other sinners, should they be allowed to live? No, of course not! All their righteous acts will be forgotten, and they will die for their sins.

[25]"Yet you say, 'The Lord isn't doing what's right!' Listen to me, O people of Israel. Am I the one not doing what's right, or is it you? [26]When righteous people turn from their righteous behavior and start doing sinful things, they will die for it. Yes, they will die because of their sinful deeds. [27]And if wicked people turn from their wickedness, obey the law, and do what is just and right, they will save their lives. [28]They will live because they thought it over and decided to turn from their sins. Such people will not die. [29]And yet the people of Israel keep saying, 'The Lord isn't doing what's right!' O people of Israel, it is you who are not doing what's right, not I.

[30]"Therefore, I will judge each of you, O people of Israel, according to your actions, says the Sovereign Lord. Repent, and turn from your sins. Don't let them destroy you! [31]Put all your rebellion behind you, and find yourselves a new heart and a new spirit. For why should you die, O people of Israel? [32]I don't want you to die, says the Sovereign Lord. Turn back and live!

CHAPTER 19

A Funeral Song for Israel's Kings

"Sing this funeral song for the princes of Israel:

[2] "What is your mother?
A lioness among lions!
She lay down among the young lions
and reared her cubs.
[3] She raised one of her cubs
to become a strong young lion.
He learned to hunt and devour prey,
and he became a man-eater.
[4] Then the nations heard about him,
and he was trapped in their pit.
They led him away with hooks
to the land of Egypt.

[5] "When the lioness saw
that her hopes for him were gone,
she took another of her cubs
and taught him to be a strong young lion.
[6] He prowled among the other lions
and stood out among them in his strength.
He learned to hunt and devour prey,
and he, too, became a man-eater.
[7] He demolished fortresses*
and destroyed their towns and cities.
Their farms were desolated,
and their crops were destroyed.
The land and its people trembled in fear
when they heard him roar.
[8] Then the armies of the nations attacked him,
surrounding him from every direction.
They threw a net over him
and captured him in their pit.
[9] With hooks, they dragged him into a cage
and brought him before the king of Babylon.

18:17 Greek version reads *He refuses to do evil.* **19:7** As in Greek version; Hebrew reads *He knew widows.*

They held him in captivity,
so his voice could never again be heard
on the mountains of Israel.

10 "Your mother was like a vine
planted by the water's edge.
It had lush, green foliage
because of the abundant water.
11 Its branches became strong—
strong enough to be a ruler's scepter.
It grew very tall,
towering above all others.
It stood out because of its height
and its many lush branches.
12 But the vine was uprooted in fury
and thrown down to the ground.
The desert wind dried up its fruit
and tore off its strong branches,
so that it withered
and was destroyed by fire.
13 Now the vine is transplanted to the
wilderness,
where the ground is hard and dry.
14 A fire has burst out from its branches
and devoured its fruit.
Its remaining limbs are not
strong enough to be a ruler's scepter.

"This is a funeral song, and it will be used in a funeral."

CHAPTER 20

The Rebellion of Israel

On August 14,* during the seventh year of King Jehoiachin's captivity, some of the leaders of Israel came to request a message from the LORD. They sat down in front of me to wait for his reply. 2 Then this message came to me from the LORD: 3 "Son of man, tell the leaders of Israel, 'This is what the Sovereign LORD says: How dare you come to ask me for a message? As surely as I live, says the Sovereign LORD, I will tell you nothing!'

4 "Son of man, bring charges against them and condemn them. Make them realize how detestable the sins of their ancestors really were. 5 Give them this message from the Sovereign LORD: When I chose Israel—when I revealed myself to the descendants of Jacob in Egypt—I took a solemn oath that I, the LORD, would be their God. 6 I took a solemn oath that day that I would bring them out of Egypt to a land I had discovered and explored for them—a good land, a land flowing with milk and honey, the best of all lands anywhere. 7 Then I said to them, 'Each of you, get rid of the vile images you are so obsessed with. Do not defile yourselves with the idols* of Egypt, for I am the LORD your God.'

8 "But they rebelled against me and would not listen. They did not get rid of the vile images they were obsessed with, or forsake the idols of Egypt. Then I threatened to pour out my fury on them to satisfy my anger while they were still in Egypt. 9 But I didn't do it, for I acted to protect the honor of my name. I would not allow shame to be brought on my name among the surrounding nations who saw me reveal myself by bringing the Israelites out of Egypt. 10 So I brought them out of Egypt and led them into the wilderness. 11 There I gave them my decrees and regulations so they could find life by keeping them. 12 And I gave them my Sabbath days of rest as a sign between them and me. It was to remind them that I am the LORD, who had set them apart to be holy.

13 "But the people of Israel rebelled against me, and they refused to obey my decrees there in the wilderness. They wouldn't obey my regulations even though obedience would have given them life. They also violated my Sabbath days. So I threatened to pour out my fury on them, and I made plans to utterly consume them in the wilderness. 14 But again I held back in order to protect the honor of my name before the nations who had seen my power in bringing Israel out of Egypt. 15 But I took a solemn oath against them in the wilderness. I swore I would not bring them into the land I had given them, a land flowing with milk and honey, the most beautiful place on earth. 16 For they had rejected my regulations, refused to follow my decrees, and violated my Sabbath days. Their hearts were given to their idols. 17 Nevertheless, I took pity on them and held back from destroying them in the wilderness.

18 "Then I warned their children not to follow in their parents' footsteps, defiling themselves with their idols. 19 'I am the LORD your God,' I told them. 'Follow my decrees, pay attention to my regulations, 20 and keep my

20:1 Hebrew *In the fifth month, on the tenth day,* of the ancient Hebrew lunar calendar. This day was August 14, 591 B.C.; also see note on 1:1. **20:7** The Hebrew term (literally *round things*) probably alludes to dung; also in 20:8, 16, 18, 24, 31, 39.

Sabbath days holy, for they are a sign to remind you that I am the LORD your God.'

21"But their children, too, rebelled against me. They refused to keep my decrees and follow my regulations, even though obedience would have given them life. And they also violated my Sabbath days. So again I threatened to pour out my fury on them in the wilderness. 22Nevertheless, I withdrew my judgment against them to protect the honor of my name before the nations that had seen my power in bringing them out of Egypt. 23But I took a solemn oath against them in the wilderness. I swore I would scatter them among all the nations 24because they did not obey my regulations. They scorned my decrees by violating my Sabbath days and longing for the idols of their ancestors. 25I gave them over to worthless decrees and regulations that would not lead to life. 26I let them pollute themselves* with the very gifts I had given them, and I allowed them to give their firstborn children as offerings to their gods—so I might devastate them and remind them that I alone am the LORD.

Judgment and Restoration

27"Therefore, son of man, give the people of Israel this message from the Sovereign LORD: Your ancestors continued to blaspheme and betray me, 28for when I brought them into the land I had promised them, they offered sacrifices on every high hill and under every green tree they saw! They roused my fury as they offered up sacrifices to their gods. They brought their perfumes and incense and poured out their liquid offerings to them. 29I said to them, 'What is this high place where you are going?' (This kind of pagan shrine has been called Bamah—'high place'—ever since.)

30"Therefore, give the people of Israel this message from the Sovereign LORD: Do you plan to pollute yourselves just as your ancestors did? Do you intend to keep prostituting yourselves by worshiping vile images? 31For when you offer gifts to them and give your little children to be burned as sacrifices,* you continue to pollute yourselves with idols to this day. Should I allow you to ask for a message from me, O people of Israel? As surely as I live, says the Sovereign LORD, I will tell you nothing.

32"You say, 'We want to be like the nations all around us, who serve idols of wood and stone.' But what you have in mind will never happen. 33As surely as I live, says the Sovereign LORD, I will rule over you with an iron fist in great anger and with awesome power. 34And in anger I will reach out with my strong hand and powerful arm, and I will bring you back* from the lands where you are scattered. 35I will bring you into the wilderness of the nations, and there I will judge you face to face. 36I will judge you there just as I did your ancestors in the wilderness after bringing them out of Egypt, says the Sovereign LORD. 37I will examine you carefully and hold you to the terms of the covenant. 38I will purge you of all those who rebel and revolt against me. I will bring them out of the countries where they are in exile, but they will never enter the land of Israel. Then you will know that I am the LORD.

39"As for you, O people of Israel, this is what the Sovereign LORD says: Go right ahead and worship your idols, but sooner or later you will obey me and will stop bringing shame on my holy name by worshiping idols. 40For on my holy mountain, the great mountain of Israel, says the Sovereign LORD, the people of Israel will someday worship me, and I will accept them. There I will require that you bring me all your offerings and choice gifts and sacrifices. 41When I bring you home from exile, you will be like a pleasing sacrifice to me. And I will display my holiness through you as all the nations watch. 42Then when I have brought you home to the land I promised with a solemn oath to give to your ancestors, you will know that I am the LORD. 43You will look back on all the ways you defiled yourselves and will hate yourselves because of the evil you have done. 44You will know that I am the LORD, O people of Israel, when I have honored my name by treating you mercifully in spite of your wickedness. I, the Sovereign LORD, have spoken!"

Judgment against the Negev

45*Then this message came to me from the LORD: 46"Son of man, turn and face the south*

20:25-26 Or *I gave them worthless decrees and regulations. . . . I polluted them.* **20:31** Or *and make your little children pass through the fire.* **20:34** Greek version reads *I will welcome you.* Compare 2 Cor 6:17. **20:45** Verses 20:45-49 are numbered 21:1-5 in Hebrew text. **20:46** Hebrew *toward Teman.*

and speak out against it; prophesy against the brushlands of the Negev. 47 Tell the southern wilderness, 'This is what the Sovereign LORD says: Hear the word of the LORD! I will set you on fire, and every tree, both green and dry, will be burned. The terrible flames will not be quenched and will scorch everything from south to north. 48 And everyone in the world will see that I, the LORD, have set this fire. It will not be put out.'"

49 Then I said, "O Sovereign LORD, they are saying of me, 'He only talks in riddles!'"

CHAPTER 21

The LORD's Sword of Judgment

1 *Then this message came to me from the LORD: 2 "Son of man, turn and face Jerusalem and prophesy against Israel and her sanctuaries. 3 Tell her, 'This is what the LORD says: I am your enemy, O Israel, and I am about to unsheath my sword to destroy your people—the righteous and the wicked alike. 4 Yes, I will cut off both the righteous and the wicked! I will draw my sword against everyone in the land from south to north. 5 Everyone in the world will know that I am the LORD. My sword is in my hand, and it will not return to its sheath until its work is finished.'

6 "Son of man, groan before the people! Groan before them with bitter anguish and a broken heart. 7 When they ask why you are groaning, tell them, 'I groan because of the terrifying news I have heard. When it comes true, the boldest heart will melt with fear; all strength will disappear. Every spirit will faint; strong knees will become as weak as water. And the Sovereign LORD says: It is coming! It's on its way!'"

8 Then the LORD said to me, 9 "Son of man, give the people this message from the Lord:

"A sword, a sword
is being sharpened and polished.
10 It is sharpened for terrible slaughter
and polished to flash like lightning!
Now will you laugh?
Those far stronger than you have fallen
beneath its power!*
11 Yes, the sword is now being sharpened
and polished;
it is being prepared for the
executioner.
12 "Son of man, cry out and wail;
pound your thighs in anguish,
for that sword will slaughter my people
and their leaders—
everyone will die!
13 It will put them all to the test.
What chance do they have?*
says the Sovereign LORD.
14 "Son of man, prophesy to them
and clap your hands.
Then take the sword and brandish it
twice,
even three times,
to symbolize the great massacre,
the great massacre facing them on
every side.
15 Let their hearts melt with terror,
for the sword glitters at every gate.
It flashes like lightning
and is polished for slaughter!
16 O sword, slash to the right,
then slash to the left,
wherever you will,
wherever you want.
17 I, too, will clap my hands,
and I will satisfy my fury.
I, the LORD, have spoken!"

Omens for Babylon's King

18 Then this message came to me from the LORD: 19 "Son of man, make a map and trace two routes on it for the sword of Babylon's king to follow. Put a signpost on the road that comes out of Babylon where the road forks into two—20 one road going to Ammon and its capital, Rabbah, and the other to Judah and fortified Jerusalem. 21 The king of Babylon now stands at the fork, uncertain whether to attack Jerusalem or Rabbah. He calls his magicians to look for omens. They cast lots by shaking arrows from the quiver. They inspect the livers of animal sacrifices. 22 The omen in his right hand says, 'Jerusalem!' With battering rams his soldiers will go against the gates, shouting for the kill. They will put up siege towers and build ramps against the walls. 23 The people of Jerusalem will think it is a false omen, because of their treaty with the

21:1 Verses 21:1-32 are numbered 21:6-37 in Hebrew text. **21:10** The meaning of the Hebrew is uncertain. **21:13** The meaning of the Hebrew is uncertain.

Babylonians. But the king of Babylon will remind the people of their rebellion. Then he will attack and capture them.

24"Therefore, this is what the Sovereign LORD says: Again and again you remind me of your sin and your guilt. You don't even try to hide it! In everything you do, your sins are obvious for all to see. So now the time of your punishment has come!

25"O you corrupt and wicked prince of Israel, your final day of reckoning is here! 26This is what the Sovereign LORD says:

"Take off your jeweled crown,
for the old order changes.
Now the lowly will be exalted,
and the mighty will be brought down.

Will God shake things up someday?

[God] says: "Take off your jeweled crown, for the old order changes. Now the lowly will be exalted, and the mighty will be brought down."
EZEKIEL 21:26

27 Destruction! Destruction!
I will surely destroy the kingdom.
And it will not be restored until the one appears
who has the right to judge it.
Then I will hand it over to him.

A Message for the Ammonites

28"And now, son of man, prophesy concerning the Ammonites and their mockery. Give them this message from the Sovereign LORD:

"A sword, a sword
is drawn for your slaughter.
It is polished to destroy,
flashing like lightning!
29 Your prophets have given false visions,
and your fortune-tellers have told lies.
The sword will fall on the necks of the wicked
for whom the day of final reckoning has come.
30 "Now return the sword to its sheath,
for in your own country,
the land of your birth,
I will pass judgment upon you.
31 I will pour out my fury on you
and blow on you with the fire of my anger.
I will hand you over to cruel men
who are skilled in destruction.
32 You will be fuel for the fire,
and your blood will be spilled in your own land.
You will be utterly wiped out,
your memory lost to history,
for I, the LORD, have spoken!"

CHAPTER 22

The Sins of Jerusalem

Now this message came to me from the LORD: 2"Son of man, are you ready to judge Jerusalem? Are you ready to judge this city of murderers? Publicly denounce her detestable sins, 3and give her this message from the Sovereign LORD: O city of murderers, doomed and damned—city of idols,* filthy and foul—4you are guilty because of the blood you have shed. You are defiled because of the idols you have made. Your day of destruction has come! You have reached the end of your years. I will make you an object of mockery throughout the world. 5O infamous city, filled with confusion, you will be mocked by people far and near.

6"Every leader in Israel who lives within your walls is bent on murder. 7Fathers and mothers are treated with contempt. Foreigners are forced to pay for protection. Orphans and widows are wronged and oppressed among you. 8You despise my holy things and violate my Sabbath days of rest. 9People accuse others falsely and send them to their death. You are filled with idol worshipers and people who do obscene things. 10Men sleep with their fathers' wives and have intercourse with women who are menstruating. 11Within your walls live men who commit adultery with their neighbors' wives, who de-

22:3 The Hebrew term (literally *round things*) probably alludes to dung; also in 22:4.

file their daughters-in-law, or who rape their own sisters. [12]There are hired murderers, loan racketeers, and extortioners everywhere. They never even think of me and my commands, says the Sovereign LORD.

[13]"But now I clap my hands in indignation over your dishonest gain and bloodshed. [14]How strong and courageous will you be in my day of reckoning? I, the LORD, have spoken, and I will do what I said. [15]I will scatter you among the nations and purge you of your wickedness. [16]And when I have been dishonored among the nations because of you,* you will know that I am the LORD."

The LORD's Refining Furnace

[17]Then this message came to me from the LORD: [18]"Son of man, the people of Israel are the worthless slag that remains after silver is smelted. They are the dross that is left over—a useless mixture of copper, tin, iron, and lead. [19]So tell them, 'This is what the Sovereign LORD says: Because you are all worthless slag, I will bring you to my crucible in Jerusalem. [20]Just as copper, iron, lead, and tin are melted down in a furnace, I will melt you down in the heat of my fury. [21]I will gather you together and blow the fire of my anger upon you, [22]and you will melt like silver in fierce heat. Then you will know that I, the LORD, have poured out my fury on you.'"

The Sins of Israel's Leaders

[23]Again a message came to me from the LORD: [24]"Son of man, give the people of Israel this message: In the day of my indignation, you will be like a polluted land, a land without rain. [25]Your princes* plot conspiracies just as lions stalk their prey. They devour innocent people, seizing treasures and extorting wealth. They make many widows in the land. [26]Your priests have violated my instructions and defiled my holy things. They make no distinction between what is holy and what is not. And they do not teach my people the difference between what is ceremonially clean and unclear. They disregard my Sabbath days so that I am dishonored among them. [27]Your leaders are like wolves who tear apart their victims. They actually destroy people's lives for money! [28]And your prophets cover up for them by announcing false visions and making lying predictions. They say, 'My message is from the Sovereign LORD,' when the LORD hasn't spoken a single word to them. [29]Even common people oppress the poor, rob the needy, and deprive foreigners of justice.

[30]"I looked for someone who might rebuild the wall of righteousness that guards the land. I searched for someone to stand in the gap in the wall so I wouldn't have to destroy the land, but I found no one. [31]So now I will pour out my fury on them, consuming them with the fire of my anger. I will heap on their heads the full penalty for all their sins. I, the Sovereign LORD, have spoken!"

CHAPTER 23

The Adultery of Two Sisters

This message came to me from the LORD: [2]"Son of man, once there were two sisters who were daughters of the same mother. [3]They became prostitutes in Egypt. Even as young girls, they allowed men to fondle their breasts. [4]The older girl was named Oholah, and her sister was Oholibah. I married them, and they bore me sons and daughters. I am speaking of Samaria and Jerusalem, for Oholah is Samaria and Oholibah is Jerusalem.

[5]"Then Oholah lusted after other lovers instead of me, and she gave her love to the Assyrian officers. [6]They were all attractive young men, captains and commanders dressed in handsome blue, charioteers driving their horses. [7]And so she prostituted herself with the most desirable men of Assyria, worshiping their idols* and defiling herself. [8]For when she left Egypt, she did not leave her spirit of prostitution behind. She was still as lewd as in her youth, when the Egyptians slept with her, fondled her breasts, and used her as a prostitute.

[9]"And so I handed her over to her Assyrian lovers, whom she desired so much. [10]They stripped her, took away her children as their slaves, and then killed her. After she received her punishment, her reputation was known to every woman in the land.

[11]"Yet even though Oholibah saw what had happened to Oholah, her sister, she followed right in her footsteps. And she was even more depraved, abandoning herself to her lust and

22:16 Or *when you have been dishonored among the nations.* **22:25** As in Greek version; Hebrew reads *prophets.* **23:7** The Hebrew term (literally *round things*) probably alludes to dung; also in 23:30, 37, 39, 49.

prostitution. [12]She fawned over all the Assyrian officers—those captains and commanders in handsome uniforms, those charioteers driving their horses—all of them attractive young men. [13]I saw the way she was going, defiling herself just like her older sister.

[14]"Then she carried her prostitution even further. She fell in love with pictures that were painted on a wall—pictures of Babylonian* military officers, outfitted in striking red uniforms. [15]Handsome belts encircled their waists, and flowing turbans crowned their heads. They were dressed like chariot officers from the land of Babylonia.* [16]When she saw these paintings, she longed to give herself to them, so she sent messengers to Babylonia to invite them to come to her. [17]So they came and committed adultery with her, defiling her in the bed of love. After being defiled, however, she rejected them in disgust.

[18]"In the same way, I became disgusted with Oholibah and rejected her, just as I had rejected her sister, because she flaunted herself before them and gave herself to satisfy their lusts. [19]Yet she turned to even greater prostitution, remembering her youth when she was a prostitute in Egypt. [20]She lusted after lovers with genitals as large as a donkey's and emissions like those of a horse. [21]And so, Oholibah, you relived your former days as a young girl in Egypt, when you first allowed your breasts to be fondled.

The Lord's Judgment of Oholibah

[22]"Therefore, Oholibah, this is what the Sovereign Lord says: I will send your lovers against you from every direction—those very nations from which you turned away in disgust. [23]For the Babylonians will come with all the Chaldeans from Pekod and Shoa and Koa. And all the Assyrians will come with them—handsome young captains, commanders, chariot officers, and other high-ranking officers, all riding their horses. [24]They will all come against you from the north* with chariots, wagons, and a great army prepared for attack. They will take up positions on every side, surrounding you with men armed with shields and helmets. And I will hand you over to them for punishment so they can do with you as they please. [25]I will turn my jealous anger against you, and they will deal harshly with you. They will cut off your nose and ears, and any survivors will then be slaughtered by the sword. Your children will be taken away as captives, and everything that is left will be burned. [26]They will strip you of your beautiful clothes and jewels. [27]In this way, I will put a stop to the lewdness and prostitution you brought from Egypt. You will never again cast longing eyes on those things or fondly remember your time in Egypt.

[28]"For this is what the Sovereign Lord says: I will surely hand you over to your enemies, to those you loathe, those you rejected. [29]They will treat you with hatred and rob you of all you own, leaving you stark naked. The shame of your prostitution will be exposed to all the world. [30]You brought all this on yourself by prostituting yourself to other nations, defiling yourself with all their idols. [31]Because you have followed in your sister's footsteps, I will force you to drink the same cup of terror she drank.

[32]"Yes, this is what the Sovereign Lord says:

"You will drink from your sister's cup of terror,
a cup that is large and deep.
It is filled to the brim
with scorn and derision.
[33] Drunkenness and anguish will fill you,
for your cup is filled to the brim with distress and desolation,
the same cup your sister Samaria drank.
[34] You will drain that cup of terror
to the very bottom.
Then you will smash it to pieces
and beat your breast in anguish.
I, the Sovereign Lord, have spoken!

[35]"And because you have forgotten me and turned your back on me, this is what the Sovereign Lord says: You must bear the consequences of all your lewdness and prostitution."

The Lord's Judgment on Both Sisters

[36]The Lord said to me, "Son of man, you must accuse Oholah and Oholibah of all their detestable sins. [37]They have committed both adultery and murder—adultery by worship-

23:14 Or *Chaldean.* **23:15** Or *Chaldea;* also in 23:16. **23:24** As in Greek version; the meaning of the Hebrew is uncertain.

ing idols and murder by burning as sacrifices the children they bore to me. [38]Furthermore, they have defiled my Temple and violated my Sabbath day! [39]On the very day that they sacrificed their children to their idols, they boldly came into my Temple to worship! They came in and defiled my house.

[40]"You sisters sent messengers to distant lands to get men. Then when they arrived, you bathed yourselves, painted your eyelids, and put on your finest jewels for them. [41]You sat with them on a beautifully embroidered couch and put my incense and my special oil on a table that was spread before you. [42]From your room came the sound of many men carousing. They were lustful men and drunkards* from the wilderness, who put bracelets on your wrists and beautiful crowns on your heads. [43]Then I said, 'If they really want to have sex with old worn-out prostitutes like these, let them!' [44]And that is what they did. They had sex with Oholah and Oholibah, these shameless prostitutes. [45]But righteous people will judge these sister cities for what they really are—adulterers and murderers.

[46]"Now this is what the Sovereign LORD says: Bring an army against them and hand them over to be terrorized and plundered. [47]For their enemies will stone them and kill them with swords. They will butcher their sons and daughters and burn their homes. [48]In this way, I will put an end to lewdness and idolatry in the land, and my judgment will be a warning to others not to follow their wicked example. [49]You will be fully repaid for all your prostitution—your worship of idols. Yes, you will suffer the full penalty. Then you will know that I am the Sovereign LORD."

CHAPTER 24

The Sign of the Cooking Pot

On January 15,* during the ninth year of King Jehoiachin's captivity, this message came to me from the LORD: [2]"Son of man, write down today's date, because on this very day the king of Babylon is beginning his attack against Jerusalem. [3]Then give these rebels an illustration with this message from the Sovereign LORD:

"Put a pot on the fire,
and pour in some water.
[4] Fill it with choice pieces of meat—
the rump and the shoulder
and all the most tender cuts.
[5] Use only the best sheep from the flock,
and heap fuel on the fire beneath the pot.
Bring the pot to a boil,
and cook the bones along with the meat.
[6] "Now this is what the Sovereign LORD says:
What sorrow awaits Jerusalem,
the city of murderers!
She is a cooking pot
whose corruption can't be cleaned out.
Take the meat out in random order,
for no piece is better than another.
[7] For the blood of her murders
is splashed on the rocks.
It isn't even spilled on the ground,
where the dust could cover it!
[8] So I will splash her blood on a rock
for all to see,
an expression of my anger
and vengeance against her.
[9] "This is what the Sovereign LORD says:
What sorrow awaits Jerusalem,
the city of murderers!
I myself will pile up the fuel beneath her.
[10] Yes, heap on the wood!
Let the fire roar to make the pot boil.
Cook the meat with many spices,
and afterward burn the bones.
[11] Now set the empty pot on the coals.
Heat it red hot!
Burn away the filth and corruption.
[12] But it's hopeless;
the corruption can't be cleaned out.
So throw it into the fire.
[13] Your impurity is your lewdness
and the corruption of your idolatry.
I tried to cleanse you,
but you refused.
So now you will remain in your filth
until my fury against you has been satisfied.

[14]"I, the LORD, have spoken! The time has come, and I won't hold back. I will not change my mind, and I will have no pity on you. You

23:42 Or *Sabeans*. 24:1 Hebrew *On the tenth day of the tenth month*, of the ancient Hebrew lunar calendar. This event occurred on January 15, 588 B.C.; also see note on 1:1.

will be judged on the basis of all your wicked actions, says the Sovereign LORD."

The Death of Ezekiel's Wife

15 Then this message came to me from the LORD: 16 "Son of man, with one blow I will take away your dearest treasure. Yet you must not show any sorrow at her death. Do not weep; let there be no tears. 17 Groan silently, but let there be no wailing at her grave. Do not uncover your head or take off your sandals. Do not perform the usual rituals of mourning or accept any food brought to you by consoling friends."

18 So I proclaimed this to the people the next morning, and in the evening my wife died. The next morning I did everything I had been told to do. 19 Then the people asked, "What does all this mean? What are you trying to tell us?"

20 So I said to them, "A message came to me from the LORD, 21 and I was told to give this message to the people of Israel. This is what the Sovereign LORD says: I will defile my Temple, the source of your security and pride, the place your heart delights in. Your sons and daughters whom you left behind in Judea will be slaughtered by the sword. 22 Then you will do as Ezekiel has done. You will not mourn in public or console yourselves by eating the food brought by friends. 23 Your heads will remain covered, and your sandals will not be taken off. You will not mourn or weep, but you will waste away because of your sins. You will mourn privately for all the evil you have done. 24 Ezekiel is an example for you; you will do just as he has done. And when that time comes, you will know that I am the Sovereign LORD."

25 Then the LORD said to me, "Son of man, on the day I take away their stronghold—their joy and glory, their heart's desire, their dearest treasure—I will also take away their sons and daughters. 26 And on that day a survivor from Jerusalem will come to you in Babylon and tell you what has happened. 27 And when he arrives, your voice will suddenly return so you can talk to him, and you will be a symbol for these people. Then they will know that I am the LORD."

CHAPTER 25

A Message for Ammon

Then this message came to me from the LORD: 2 "Son of man, turn and face the land of Ammon and prophesy against its people. 3 Give the Ammonites this message from the Sovereign LORD: Hear the word of the Sovereign LORD! Because you cheered when my Temple was defiled, mocked Israel in her desolation, and laughed at Judah as she went away into exile, 4 I will allow nomads from the eastern deserts to overrun your country. They will set up their camps among you and pitch their tents on your land. They will harvest all your fruit and drink the milk from your livestock. 5 And I will turn the city of Rabbah into a pasture for camels, and all the land of the Ammonites into a resting place for sheep and goats. Then you will know that I am the LORD.

6 "This is what the Sovereign LORD says: Because you clapped and danced and cheered with glee at the destruction of my people, 7 I will raise my fist of judgment against you. I will give you as plunder to many nations. I will cut you off from being a nation and destroy you completely. Then you will know that I am the LORD.

A Message for Moab

8 "This is what the Sovereign LORD says: Because the people of Moab have said that Judah is just like all the other nations, 9 I will open up their eastern flank and wipe out their glorious frontier towns—Beth-jeshimoth, Baal-meon, and Kiriathaim. 10 And I will hand Moab over to nomads from the eastern deserts, just as I handed over Ammon. Yes, the Ammonites will no longer be counted among the nations. 11 In the same way, I will bring my judgment down on the Moabites. Then they will know that I am the LORD.

A Message for Edom

12 "This is what the Sovereign LORD says: The people of Edom have sinned greatly by avenging themselves against the people of Judah. 13 Therefore, says the Sovereign LORD, I will raise my fist of judgment against Edom. I will wipe out its people and animals with the sword. I will make a wasteland of everything from Teman to Dedan. 14 I will accomplish this by the hand of my people of Israel. They will carry out my vengeance with anger, and Edom will know that this vengeance is from me. I, the Sovereign LORD, have spoken!

A Message for Philistia

15"This is what the Sovereign LORD says: The people of Philistia have acted against Judah out of bitter revenge and long-standing contempt. 16Therefore, this is what the Sovereign LORD says: I will raise my fist of judgment against the land of the Philistines. I will wipe out the Kerethites and utterly destroy the people who live by the sea. 17I will execute terrible vengeance against them to punish them for what they have done. And when I have inflicted my revenge, they will know that I am the LORD."

CHAPTER 26

A Message for Tyre

On February 3, during the twelfth year of King Jehoiachin's captivity,* this message came to me from the LORD: 2"Son of man, Tyre has rejoiced over the fall of Jerusalem, saying, 'Ha! She who was the gateway to the rich trade routes to the east has been broken, and I am the heir! Because she has been made desolate, I will become wealthy!'

3"Therefore, this is what the Sovereign LORD says: I am your enemy, O Tyre, and I will bring many nations against you, like the waves of the sea crashing against your shoreline. 4They will destroy the walls of Tyre and tear down its towers. I will scrape away its soil and make it a bare rock! 5It will be just a rock in the sea, a place for fishermen to spread their nets, for I have spoken, says the Sovereign LORD. Tyre will become the prey of many nations, 6and its mainland villages will be destroyed by the sword. Then they will know that I am the LORD.

7"This is what the Sovereign LORD says: From the north I will bring King Nebuchadnezzar* of Babylon against Tyre. He is king of kings and brings his horses, chariots, charioteers, and great army. 8First he will destroy your mainland villages. Then he will attack you by building a siege wall, constructing a ramp, and raising a roof of shields against you. 9He will pound your walls with battering rams and demolish your towers with sledgehammers. 10The hooves of his horses will choke the city with dust, and the noise of the charioteers and chariot wheels will shake your walls as they storm through your broken gates. 11His horsemen will trample through every street in the city. They will butcher your people, and your strong pillars will topple.

12"They will plunder all your riches and merchandise and break down your walls. They will destroy your lovely homes and dump your stones and timbers and even your dust into the sea. 13I will stop the music of your songs. No more will the sound of harps be heard among your people. 14I will make your island a bare rock, a place for fishermen to spread their nets. You will never be rebuilt, for I, the LORD, have spoken. Yes, the Sovereign LORD has spoken!

The Effect of Tyre's Destruction

15"This is what the Sovereign LORD says to Tyre: The whole coastline will tremble at the sound of your fall, as the screams of the wounded echo in the continuing slaughter. 16All the seaport rulers will step down from their thrones and take off their royal robes and beautiful clothing. They will sit on the ground trembling with horror at your destruction. 17Then they will wail for you, singing this funeral song:

"O famous island city,
once ruler of the sea,
how you have been destroyed!
Your people, with their naval power,
once spread fear around the world.
18 Now the coastlands tremble at your
fall.
The islands are dismayed as you
disappear.

19"This is what the Sovereign LORD says: I will make Tyre an uninhabited ruin, like many others. I will bury you beneath the terrible waves of enemy attack. Great seas will swallow you. 20I will send you to the pit to join those who descended there long ago. Your city will lie in ruins, buried beneath the earth, like those in the pit who have entered the world of the dead. You will have no place of respect here in the land of the living. 21I will bring you to a terrible end, and you will exist no more. You will be looked for, but you will never again be found. I, the Sovereign LORD, have spoken!"

26:1 Hebrew *In the eleventh year, on the first day of the month,* of the ancient Hebrew lunar calendar year. Since an element is missing in the date formula here, scholars have reconstructed this probable reading: *In the eleventh [month of the twelfth] year, on the first day of the month.* This reading would put this message on February 3, 585 B.C.; also see note on 1:1. **26:7** Hebrew *Nebuchadrezzar,* a variant spelling of Nebuchadnezzar.

CHAPTER 27

The End of Tyre's Glory

Then this message came to me from the LORD: [2]"Son of man, sing a funeral song for Tyre, [3]that mighty gateway to the sea, the trading center of the world. Give Tyre this message from the Sovereign LORD:

"You boasted, O Tyre,
'My beauty is perfect!'
[4] You extended your boundaries into the sea.
Your builders made your beauty perfect.
[5] You were like a great ship
built of the finest cypress from Senir.*
They took a cedar from Lebanon
to make a mast for you.
[6] They carved your oars
from the oaks of Bashan.
Your deck of pine from the coasts of Cyprus*
was inlaid with ivory.
[7] Your sails were made of Egypt's finest linen,
and they flew as a banner above you.
You stood beneath blue and purple awnings
made bright with dyes from the coasts of Elishah.
[8] Your oarsmen came from Sidon and Arvad;
your helmsmen were skilled men from Tyre itself.
[9] Wise old craftsmen from Gebal did the caulking.
Ships from every land came with goods to barter for your trade.

[10]"Men from distant Persia, Lydia, and Libya* served in your great army. They hung their shields and helmets on your walls, giving you great honor. [11]Men from Arvad and Helech stood on your walls. Your towers were manned by men from Gammad. Their shields hung on your walls, completing your beauty.

[12]"Tarshish sent merchants to buy your wares in exchange for silver, iron, tin, and lead. [13]Merchants from Greece,* Tubal, and Meshech brought slaves and articles of bronze to trade with you.

[14]"From Beth-togarmah came riding horses, chariot horses, and mules, all in exchange for your goods. [15]Merchants came to you from Dedan.* Numerous coastlands were your captive markets; they brought payment in ivory tusks and ebony wood.

[16]"Syria* sent merchants to buy your rich variety of goods. They traded turquoise, purple dyes, embroidery, fine linen, and jewelry of coral and rubies. [17]Judah and Israel traded for your wares, offering wheat from Minnith, figs,* honey, olive oil, and balm.

[18]"Damascus sent merchants to buy your rich variety of goods, bringing wine from Helbon and white wool from Zahar. [19]Greeks from Uzal* came to trade for your merchandise. Wrought iron, cassia, and fragrant calamus were bartered for your wares.

[20]"Dedan sent merchants to trade their expensive saddle blankets with you. [21]The Arabians and the princes of Kedar sent merchants to trade lambs and rams and male goats in exchange for your goods. [22]The merchants of Sheba and Raamah came with all kinds of spices, jewels, and gold in exchange for your wares.

[23]"Haran, Canneh, Eden, Sheba, Asshur, and Kilmad came with their merchandise, too. [24]They brought choice fabrics to trade—blue cloth, embroidery, and multicolored carpets rolled up and bound with cords. [25]The ships of Tarshish were your ocean caravans. Your island warehouse was filled to the brim!

The Destruction of Tyre

[26] "But look! Your oarsmen
have taken you into stormy seas!
A mighty eastern gale
has wrecked you in the heart of the sea!
[27] Everything is lost—
your riches and wares,
your sailors and pilots,
your ship builders, merchants, and warriors.
On the day of your ruin,
everyone on board sinks into the depths of the sea.
[28] Your cities by the sea tremble
as your pilots cry out in terror.

27:5 Or *Hermon*. **27:6** Hebrew *Kittim*. **27:10** Hebrew *Paras, Lud, and Put*. **27:13** Hebrew *Javan*. **27:15** Greek version reads *Rhodes*. **27:16** Hebrew *Aram;* some manuscripts read *Edom*. **27:17** The meaning of the Hebrew is uncertain. **27:19** Hebrew *Vedan and Javan from Uzal*. The meaning of the Hebrew is uncertain.

29 All the oarsmen abandon their ships;
the sailors and pilots on shore come to stand on the beach.
30 They cry aloud over you
and weep bitterly.
They throw dust on their heads
and roll in ashes.
31 They shave their heads in grief for you
and dress themselves in burlap.
They weep for you with bitter anguish
and deep mourning.
32 As they wail and mourn over you,
they sing this sad funeral song:
'Was there ever such a city as Tyre,
now silent at the bottom of the sea?
33 The merchandise you traded
satisfied the desires of many nations.
Kings at the ends of the earth
were enriched by your trade.
34 Now you are a wrecked ship,
broken at the bottom of the sea.
All your merchandise and crew
have gone down with you.
35 All who live along the coastlands
are appalled at your terrible fate.
Their kings are filled with horror
and look on with twisted faces.
36 The merchants among the nations
shake their heads at the sight of you,*
for you have come to a horrible end
and will exist no more.'"

CHAPTER 28

A Message for Tyre's King

Then this message came to me from the LORD: 2"Son of man, give the prince of Tyre this message from the Sovereign LORD:

"In your great pride you claim, 'I am a god!
I sit on a divine throne in the heart of the sea.'
But you are only a man and not a god,
though you boast that you are a god.
3 You regard yourself as wiser than Daniel
and think no secret is hidden from you.
4 With your wisdom and understanding
you have amassed great wealth—
gold and silver for your treasuries.
5 Yes, your wisdom has made you very rich,
and your riches have made you very proud.

AMAZING FACTS

Ezekiel had visions with special effects—an entire city sank into the sea!

EZEKIEL 27:26-32

6 "Therefore, this is what the Sovereign LORD says:
Because you think you are as wise as a god,
7 I will now bring against you a foreign army,
the terror of the nations.
They will draw their swords against your marvelous wisdom
and defile your splendor!
8 They will bring you down to the pit,
and you will die in the heart of the sea,
pierced with many wounds.
9 Will you then boast, 'I am a god!'
to those who kill you?
To them you will be no god
but merely a man!
10 You will die like an outcast*
at the hands of foreigners.
I, the Sovereign LORD, have spoken!"

11Then this further message came to me from the LORD: 12"Son of man, sing this funeral song for the king of Tyre. Give him this message from the Sovereign LORD:

"You were the model of perfection,
full of wisdom and exquisite in beauty.
13 You were in Eden,
the garden of God.
Your clothing was adorned with every precious stone*—
red carnelian, pale-green peridot, white moonstone,

27:36 Hebrew *hiss at you.* **28:10** Hebrew *will die the death of the uncircumcised.* **28:13** The identification of some of these gemstones is uncertain.

blue-green beryl, onyx, green jasper,
blue lapis lazuli, turquoise, and emerald—
all beautifully crafted for you
and set in the finest gold.
They were given to you
on the day you were created.
14 I ordained and anointed you
as the mighty angelic guardian.*
You had access to the holy mountain of God
and walked among the stones of fire.
15 "You were blameless in all you did
from the day you were created
until the day evil was found in you.
16 Your rich commerce led you to violence,
and you sinned.
So I banished you in disgrace
from the mountain of God.
I expelled you, O mighty guardian,
from your place among the stones of fire.
17 Your heart was filled with pride
because of all your beauty.
Your wisdom was corrupted
by your love of splendor.
So I threw you to the ground
and exposed you to the curious gaze of kings.
18 You defiled your sanctuaries
with your many sins and your dishonest trade.
So I brought fire out from within you,
and it consumed you.
I reduced you to ashes on the ground
in the sight of all who were watching.
19 All who knew you are appalled at your fate.
You have come to a terrible end,
and you will exist no more."

A Message for Sidon

20 Then another message came to me from the LORD: 21 "Son of man, turn and face the city of Sidon and prophesy against it. 22 Give the people of Sidon this message from the Sovereign LORD:

"I am your enemy, O Sidon,
and I will reveal my glory by what I do to you.
When I bring judgment against you
and reveal my holiness among you,
everyone watching will know
that I am the LORD.
23 I will send a plague against you,
and blood will be spilled in your streets.
The attack will come from every direction,
and your people will lie slaughtered within your walls.
Then everyone will know
that I am the LORD.
24 No longer will Israel's scornful neighbors
prick and tear at her like briers and thorns.
For then they will know
that I am the Sovereign LORD.

Restoration for Israel

25 "This is what the Sovereign LORD says: The people of Israel will again live in their own land, the land I gave my servant Jacob. For I will gather them from the distant lands where I have scattered them. I will reveal to the nations of the world my holiness among my people. 26 They will live safely in Israel and build homes and plant vineyards. And when I punish the neighboring nations that treated them with contempt, they will know that I am the LORD their God."

CHAPTER 29

A Message for Egypt

On January 7,* during the tenth year of King Jehoiachin's captivity, this message came to me from the LORD: 2 "Son of man, turn and face Egypt and prophesy against Pharaoh the king and all the people of Egypt. 3 Give them this message from the Sovereign LORD:

"I am your enemy, O Pharaoh, king of Egypt—
you great monster, lurking in the streams of the Nile.
For you have said, 'The Nile River is mine;
I made it for myself.'
4 I will put hooks in your jaws
and drag you out on the land
with fish sticking to your scales.
5 I will leave you and all your fish
stranded in the wilderness to die.

28:14 Hebrew *guardian cherub;* similarly in 28:16. **29:1** Hebrew *On the twelfth day of the tenth month,* of the ancient Hebrew lunar calendar. This event occurred on January 7, 587 B.C.; also see note on 1:1.

You will lie unburied on the open ground,
for I have given you as food to the wild animals and birds.
6 All the people of Egypt will know that I am the LORD,
for to Israel you were just a staff made of reeds.
7 When Israel leaned on you,
you splintered and broke
and stabbed her in the armpit.
When she put her weight on you, you gave way,
and her back was thrown out of joint.

8"Therefore, this is what the Sovereign LORD says: I will bring an army against you, O Egypt, and destroy both people and animals. 9The land of Egypt will become a desolate wasteland, and the Egyptians will know that I am the LORD.

"Because you said, 'The Nile River is mine; I made it,' 10I am now the enemy of both you and your river. I will make the land of Egypt a totally desolate wasteland, from Migdol to Aswan, as far south as the border of Ethiopia.* 11For forty years not a soul will pass that way, neither people nor animals. It will be completely uninhabited. 12I will make Egypt desolate, and it will be surrounded by other desolate nations. Its cities will be empty and desolate for forty years, surrounded by other ruined cities. I will scatter the Egyptians to distant lands.

13"But this is what the Sovereign LORD also says: At the end of the forty years I will bring the Egyptians home again from the nations to which they have been scattered. 14I will restore the prosperity of Egypt and bring its people back to the land of Pathros in southern Egypt from which they came. But Egypt will remain an unimportant, minor kingdom. 15It will be the lowliest of all the nations, never again great enough to rise above its neighbors.

16"Then Israel will no longer be tempted to trust in Egypt for help. Egypt's shattered condition will remind Israel of how sinful she was to trust Egypt in earlier days. Then Israel will know that I am the Sovereign LORD."

Nebuchadnezzar to Conquer Egypt

17On April 26, the first day of the new year,* during the twenty-seventh year of King Jehoiachin's captivity, this message came to me from the LORD: 18"Son of man, the army of King Nebuchadnezzar* of Babylon fought so hard against Tyre that the warriors' heads were rubbed bare and their shoulders were raw and blistered. Yet Nebuchadnezzar and his army won no plunder to compensate them for all their work. 19Therefore, this is what the Sovereign LORD says: I will give the land of Egypt to Nebuchadnezzar, king of Babylon. He will carry off its wealth, plundering everything it has so he can pay his army. 20Yes, I have given him the land of Egypt as a reward for his work, says the Sovereign LORD, because he was working for me when he destroyed Tyre.

21"And the day will come when I will cause the ancient glory of Israel to revive,* and then, Ezekiel, your words will be respected. Then they will know that I am the LORD."

CHAPTER 30

A Sad Day for Egypt

This is another message that came to me from the LORD: 2"Son of man, prophesy and give this message from the Sovereign LORD:

"Weep and wail
for that day,
3 for the terrible day is almost here—
the day of the LORD!
It is a day of clouds and gloom,
a day of despair for the nations.
4 A sword will come against Egypt,
and those who are slaughtered will cover the ground.
Its wealth will be carried away
and its foundations destroyed.
The land of Ethiopia* will be ravished.
5 Ethiopia, Libya, Lydia, all Arabia,*
and all their other allies
will be destroyed in that war.

6 "For this is what the LORD says:
All of Egypt's allies will fall,
and the pride of her power will end.

29:10 Hebrew *from Migdol to Syene as far as the border of Cush.* **29:17** Hebrew *On the first day of the first month,* of the ancient Hebrew lunar calendar. This event occurred on April 26, 571 B.C.; also see note on 1:1. **29:18** Hebrew *Nebuchadrezzar,* a variant spelling of Nebuchadnezzar; also in 29:19. **29:21** Hebrew *I will cause a horn to sprout for the house of Israel.* **30:4** Hebrew *Cush;* similarly in 30:9. **30:5** Hebrew *Cush, Put, Lud, all Arabia, Cub. Cub* is otherwise unknown and may be another spelling for *Lub* (Libya).

From Migdol to Aswan*
they will be slaughtered by the sword,
says the Sovereign LORD.
7 Egypt will be desolate,
surrounded by desolate nations,
and its cities will be in ruins,
surrounded by other ruined cities.
8 And the people of Egypt will know that I am the LORD
when I have set Egypt on fire
and destroyed all their allies.
9 At that time I will send swift messengers in ships
to terrify the complacent Ethiopians.
Great panic will come upon them
on that day of Egypt's certain destruction.
Watch for it!
It is sure to come!

10 "For this is what the Sovereign LORD says:
By the power of King Nebuchadnezzar* of Babylon,
I will destroy the hordes of Egypt.
11 He and his armies—the most ruthless of all—
will be sent to demolish the land.
They will make war against Egypt
until slaughtered Egyptians cover the ground.
12 I will dry up the Nile River
and sell the land to wicked men.
I will destroy the land of Egypt and everything in it
by the hands of foreigners.
I, the LORD, have spoken!

13 "This is what the Sovereign LORD says:
I will smash the idols* of Egypt
and the images at Memphis.*
There will be no rulers left in Egypt;
terror will sweep the land.
14 I will destroy southern Egypt,*
set fire to Zoan,
and bring judgment against Thebes.*
15 I will pour out my fury on Pelusium,*
the strongest fortress of Egypt,
and I will stamp out
the hordes of Thebes.
16 Yes, I will set fire to all Egypt!
Pelusium will be racked with pain;
Thebes will be torn apart;
Memphis will live in constant terror.
17 The young men of Heliopolis and Bubastis* will die in battle,
and the women* will be taken away as slaves.
18 When I come to break the proud strength of Egypt,
it will be a dark day for Tahpanhes, too.
A dark cloud will cover Tahpanhes,
and its daughters will be led away as captives.
19 And so I will greatly punish Egypt,
and they will know that I am the LORD."

The Broken Arms of Pharaoh

20 On April 29,* during the eleventh year of King Jehoiachin's captivity, this message came to me from the LORD: 21 "Son of man, I have broken the arm of Pharaoh, the king of Egypt. His arm has not been put in a cast so that it may heal. Neither has it been bound up with a splint to make it strong enough to hold a sword. 22 Therefore, this is what the Sovereign LORD says: I am the enemy of Pharaoh, the king of Egypt! I will break both of his arms—the good arm along with the broken one—and I will make his sword clatter to the ground. 23 I will scatter the Egyptians to many lands throughout the world. 24 I will strengthen the arms of Babylon's king and put my sword in his hand. But I will break the arms of Pharaoh, king of Egypt, and he will lie there mortally wounded, groaning in pain. 25 I will strengthen the arms of the king of Babylon, while the arms of Pharaoh fall useless to his sides. And when I put my sword in the hand of Babylon's king and he brings it against the land of Egypt, Egypt will know that I am the LORD. 26 I will scatter the Egyptians among the nations, dispersing them throughout the earth. Then they will know that I am the LORD."

30:6 Hebrew *to Syene*. **30:10** Hebrew *Nebuchadrezzar*, a variant spelling of Nebuchadnezzar. **30:13a** The Hebrew term (literally *round things*) probably alludes to dung. **30:13b** Hebrew *Noph;* also in 30:16. **30:14a** Hebrew *Pathros*. **30:14b** Hebrew *No;* also in 30:15, 16. **30:15** Hebrew *Sin;* also in 30:16. **30:17a** Hebrew *of Awen and Pi-beseth*. **30:17b** Or *and her cities*. **30:20** Hebrew *On the seventh day of the first month*, of the ancient Hebrew lunar calendar. This event occurred on April 29, 587 B.C.; also see note on 1:1.

CHAPTER 31

Egypt Compared to Fallen Assyria

On June 21,* during the eleventh year of King Jehoiachin's captivity, this message came to me from the LORD: 2"Son of man, give this message to Pharaoh, king of Egypt, and all his hordes:

"To whom would you compare your greatness?
3 You are like mighty Assyria,
which was once like a cedar of Lebanon,
with beautiful branches that cast deep forest shade
and with its top high among the clouds.
4 Deep springs watered it
and helped it to grow tall and luxuriant.
The water flowed around it like a river,
streaming to all the trees nearby.
5 This great tree towered high,
higher than all the other trees around it.
It prospered and grew long thick branches
because of all the water at its roots.
6 The birds nested in its branches,
and in its shade all the wild animals gave birth.
All the great nations of the world lived in its shadow.
7 It was strong and beautiful,
with wide-spreading branches,
for its roots went deep into abundant water.
8 No other cedar in the garden of God could rival it.
No cypress had branches to equal it;
no plane tree had boughs to compare.
No tree in the garden of God came close to it in beauty.
9 Because I made this tree so beautiful,
and gave it such magnificent foliage,
it was the envy of all the other trees of Eden,
the garden of God.

10"Therefore, this is what the Sovereign LORD says: Because Egypt* became proud and arrogant, and because it set itself so high above the others, with its top reaching to the clouds, 11I will hand it over to a mighty nation that will destroy it as its wickedness deserves. I have already discarded it. 12A foreign army—the terror of the nations—has cut it down and left it fallen on the ground. Its branches are scattered across the mountains and valleys and ravines of the land. All those who lived in its shadow have gone away and left it lying there.

13 "The birds roost on its fallen trunk,
and the wild animals lie among its branches.
14 Let the tree of no other nation
proudly exult in its own prosperity,
though it be higher than the clouds
and it be watered from the depths.
For all are doomed to die,
to go down to the depths of the earth.
They will land in the pit
along with everyone else on earth.

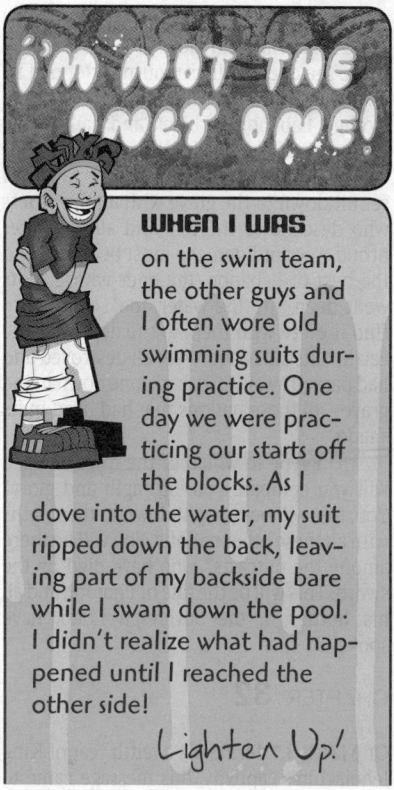

31:1 Hebrew *On the first day of the third month*, of the ancient Hebrew lunar calendar. This event occurred on June 21, 587 B.C.; also see note on 1:1. 31:10 Hebrew *you*.

[15]"This is what the Sovereign LORD says:
When Assyria went down to the grave,* I
made the deep springs mourn. I stopped its
rivers and dried up its abundant water. I
clothed Lebanon in black and caused the
trees of the field to wilt. [16]I made the nations
shake with fear at the sound of its fall, for I
sent it down to the grave with all the others
who descend to the pit. And all the other
proud trees of Eden, the most beautiful and
the best of Lebanon, the ones whose roots
went deep into the water, took comfort to
find it there with them in the depths of the
earth. [17]Its allies, too, were all destroyed and
had passed away. They had gone down to the
grave—all those nations that had lived in its
shade.

[18]"O Egypt, to which of the trees of Eden
will you compare your strength and glory?
You, too, will be brought down to the depths
with all these other nations. You will lie there
among the outcasts* who have died by the
sword. This will be the fate of Pharaoh and all
his hordes. I, the Sovereign LORD, have
spoken!"

CHAPTER 32

A Warning for Pharaoh

On March 3,* during the twelfth year of King
Jehoiachin's captivity, this message came to
me from the LORD: [2]"Son of man, mourn for
Pharaoh, king of Egypt, and give him this mes-
sage:

"You think of yourself as a strong
young lion among the nations,
but you are really just a sea monster,
heaving around in your own rivers,
stirring up mud with your feet.
[3] Therefore, this is what the Sovereign LORD
says:
I will send many people
to catch you in my net
and haul you out of the water.
[4] I will leave you stranded on the land
to die.
All the birds of the heavens will land
on you,
and the wild animals of the whole
earth
will gorge themselves on you.
[5] I will scatter your flesh on the hills
and fill the valleys with your bones.
[6] I will drench the earth with your gushing
blood
all the way to the mountains,
filling the ravines to the brim.
[7] When I blot you out,
I will veil the heavens and darken the
stars.
I will cover the sun with a cloud,
and the moon will not give you
its light.
[8] I will darken the bright stars overhead
and cover your land in darkness.
I, the Sovereign LORD, have spoken!

[9]"I will disturb many hearts when I bring
news of your downfall to distant nations you
have never seen. [10]Yes, I will shock many
lands, and their kings will be terrified at your
fate. They will shudder in fear for their lives
as I brandish my sword before them on the
day of your fall. [11]For this is what the Sover-
eign LORD says:

"The sword of the king of Babylon
will come against you.
[12] I will destroy your hordes with the swords
of mighty warriors—
the terror of the nations.
They will shatter the pride of Egypt,
and all its hordes will be destroyed.
[13] I will destroy all your flocks and herds
that graze beside the streams.
Never again will people or animals
muddy those waters with their feet.
[14] Then I will let the waters of Egypt become
calm again,
and they will flow as smoothly as
olive oil,
says the Sovereign LORD.
[15] And when I destroy Egypt
and strip you of everything you own
and strike down all your people,
then you will know that I am the LORD.
[16] Yes, this is the funeral song
they will sing for Egypt.
Let all the nations mourn.
Let them mourn for Egypt and its
hordes.
I, the Sovereign LORD, have spoken!"

31:15 Hebrew *to Sheol;* also in 31:16, 17. **31:18** Hebrew *among the uncircumcised.* **32:1** Hebrew *On the first day of the twelfth month,* of the ancient Hebrew lunar calendar. This event occurred on March 3, 585 B.C.; also see note on 1:1.

Egypt Falls into the Pit

17On March 17,* during the twelfth year, another message came to me from the LORD: 18"Son of man, weep for the hordes of Egypt and for the other mighty nations.* For I will send them down to the world below in company with those who descend to the pit. 19Say to them,

'O Egypt, are you lovelier than the other nations?
No! So go down to the pit and lie there among the outcasts.*'

20The Egyptians will fall with the many who have died by the sword, for the sword is drawn against them. Egypt and its hordes will be dragged away to their judgment. 21Down in the grave* mighty leaders will mockingly welcome Egypt and its allies, saying, 'They have come down; they lie among the outcasts, hordes slaughtered by the sword.'

22"Assyria lies there surrounded by the graves of its army, those who were slaughtered by the sword. 23Their graves are in the depths of the pit, and they are surrounded by their allies. They struck terror in the hearts of people everywhere, but now they have been slaughtered by the sword.

24"Elam lies there surrounded by the graves of all its hordes, those who were slaughtered by the sword. They struck terror in the hearts of people everywhere, but now they have descended as outcasts to the world below. Now they lie in the pit and share the shame of those who have gone before them. 25They have a resting place among the slaughtered, surrounded by the graves of all their hordes. Yes, they terrorized the nations while they lived, but now they lie in shame with others in the pit, all of them outcasts, slaughtered by the sword.

26"Meshech and Tubal are there, surrounded by the graves of all their hordes. They once struck terror in the hearts of people everywhere. But now they are outcasts, all slaughtered by the sword. 27They are not buried in honor like their fallen heroes, who went down to the grave* with their weapons—their shields covering their bodies* and their swords beneath their heads. Their guilt rests upon them because they brought terror to everyone while they were still alive.

28"You too, Egypt, will lie crushed and broken among the outcasts, all slaughtered by the sword.

29"Edom is there with its kings and princes. Mighty as they were, they also lie among those slaughtered by the sword, with the outcasts who have gone down to the pit.

30"All the princes of the north and the Sidonians are there with others who have died. Once a terror, they have been put to shame. They lie there as outcasts with others who were slaughtered by the sword. They share the shame of all who have descended to the pit.

31"When Pharaoh and his entire army arrive, he will take comfort that he is not alone in having his hordes killed, says the Sovereign LORD. 32Although I have caused his terror to fall upon all the living, Pharaoh and his hordes will lie there among the outcasts who were slaughtered by the sword. I, the Sovereign LORD, have spoken!"

CHAPTER 33

Ezekiel as Israel's Watchman

Once again a message came to me from the LORD: 2"Son of man, give your people this message: 'When I bring an army against a country, the people of that land choose one of their own to be a watchman. 3When the watchman sees the enemy coming, he sounds the alarm to warn the people. 4Then if those who hear the alarm refuse to take action, it is their own fault if they die. 5They heard the alarm but ignored it, so the responsibility is theirs. If they had listened to the warning, they could have saved their lives. 6But if the watchman sees the enemy coming and doesn't sound the alarm to warn the people, he is responsible for their captivity. They will die in their sins, but I will hold the watchman responsible for their deaths.'

7"Now, son of man, I am making you a watchman for the people of Israel. Therefore, listen to what I say and warn them for me. 8If I announce that some wicked people are sure

32:17 Hebrew *On the fifteenth day of the month,* presumably in the twelfth month of the ancient Hebrew lunar calendar (see 32:1). This would put this message at the end of King Jehoiachin's twelfth year of captivity, on March 17, 585 B.C.; also see note on 1:1. Greek version reads *On the fifteenth day of the first month,* which would put this message on April 27, 586 B.C., at the beginning of Jehoiachin's twelfth year. **32:18** The meaning of the Hebrew is uncertain. **32:19** Hebrew *the uncircumcised;* also in 32:21, 24, 25, 26, 28, 29, 30, 32. **32:21** Hebrew *in Sheol.* **32:27a** Hebrew *to Sheol.* **32:27b** The meaning of the Hebrew is uncertain.

to die and you fail to tell them to change their ways, then they will die in their sins, and I will hold you responsible for their deaths. [9]But if you warn them to repent and they don't repent, they will die in their sins, but you will have saved yourself.

The Watchman's Message

[10]"Son of man, give the people of Israel this message: You are saying, 'Our sins are heavy upon us; we are wasting away! How can we survive?' [11]As surely as I live, says the Sovereign LORD, I take no pleasure in the death of wicked people. I only want them to turn from their wicked ways so they can live. Turn! Turn from your wickedness, O people of Israel! Why should you die?

[12]"Son of man, give your people this message: The righteous behavior of righteous people will not save them if they turn to sin, nor will the wicked behavior of wicked people destroy them if they repent and turn from their sins. [13]When I tell righteous people that they will live, but then they sin, expecting their past righteousness to save them, then none of their righteous acts will be remembered. I will destroy them for their sins. [14]And suppose I tell some wicked people that they will surely die, but then they turn from their sins and do what is just and right. [15]For instance, they might give back a debtor's security, return what they have stolen, and obey my life-giving laws, no longer doing what is evil. If they do this, then they will surely live and not die. [16]None of their past sins will be brought up again, for they have done what is just and right, and they will surely live.

[17]"Your people are saying, 'The Lord isn't doing what's right,' but it is they who are not doing what's right. [18]For again I say, when righteous people turn away from their righteous behavior and turn to evil, they will die. [19]But if wicked people turn from their wickedness and do what is just and right, they will live. [20]O people of Israel, you are saying, 'The Lord isn't doing what's right.' But I judge each of you according to your deeds."

Explanation of Jerusalem's Fall

[21]On January 8,* during the twelfth year of our captivity, a survivor from Jerusalem came to me and said, "The city has fallen!" [22]The previous evening the LORD had taken hold of me and given me back my voice. So I was able to speak when this man arrived the next morning.

[23]Then this message came to me from the LORD: [24]"Son of man, the scattered remnants of Judah living among the ruined cities keep saying, 'Abraham was only one man, yet he gained possession of the entire land. We are many; surely the land has been given to us as a possession.' [25]So tell these people, 'This is what the Sovereign LORD says: You eat meat with blood in it, you worship idols,* and you murder the innocent. Do you really think the land should be yours? [26]Murderers! Idolaters! Adulterers! Should the land belong to you?'

[27]"Say to them, 'This is what the Sovereign LORD says: As surely as I live, those living in the ruins will die by the sword. And I will send wild animals to eat those living in the open fields. Those hiding in the forts and caves will die of disease. [28]I will completely destroy the land and demolish her pride. Her arrogant power will come to an end. The mountains of Israel will be so desolate that no one will even travel through them. [29]When I have completely destroyed the land because of their detestable sins, then they will know that I am the LORD.'

[30]"Son of man, your people talk about you in their houses and whisper about you at the doors. They say to each other, 'Come on, let's go hear the prophet tell us what the LORD is saying!' [31]So my people come pretending to be

Why doesn't God just kill off all the evil people?

"I take no pleasure in the death of wicked people. I only want them to turn from their wicked ways so they can live." EZEKIEL 33:11

33:21 Hebrew *On the fifth day of the tenth month*, of the ancient Hebrew lunar calendar. This event occurred on January 8, 585 B.C.; also see note on 1:1. 33:25 The Hebrew term (literally *round things*) probably alludes to dung.

sincere and sit before you. They listen to your words, but they have no intention of doing what you say. Their mouths are full of lustful words, and their hearts seek only after money. [32]You are very entertaining to them, like someone who sings love songs with a beautiful voice or plays fine music on an instrument. They hear what you say, but they don't act on it! [33]But when all these terrible things happen to them—as they certainly will—then they will know a prophet has been among them."

CHAPTER 34

The Shepherds of Israel

Then this message came to me from the LORD: [2]"Son of man, prophesy against the shepherds, the leaders of Israel. Give them this message from the Sovereign LORD: What sorrow awaits you shepherds who feed yourselves instead of your flocks. Shouldn't shepherds feed their sheep? [3]You drink the milk, wear the wool, and butcher the best animals, but you let your flocks starve. [4]You have not taken care of the weak. You have not tended the sick or bound up the injured. You have not gone looking for those who have wandered away and are lost. Instead, you have ruled them with harshness and cruelty. [5]So my sheep have been scattered without a shepherd, and they are easy prey for any wild animal. [6]They have wandered through all the mountains and all the hills, across the face of the earth, yet no one has gone to search for them.

[7]"Therefore, you shepherds, hear the word of the LORD: [8]As surely as I live, says the Sovereign LORD, you abandoned my flock and left them to be attacked by every wild animal. And though you were my shepherds, you didn't search for my sheep when they were lost. You took care of yourselves and left the sheep to starve. [9]Therefore, you shepherds, hear the word of the LORD. [10]This is what the Sovereign LORD says: I now consider these shepherds my enemies, and I will hold them responsible for what has happened to my flock. I will take away their right to feed the flock, and I will stop them from feeding themselves. I will rescue my flock from their mouths; the sheep will no longer be their prey.

The Good Shepherd

[11]"For this is what the Sovereign LORD says: I myself will search and find my sheep. [12]I will be like a shepherd looking for his scattered flock. I will find my sheep and rescue them from all the places where they were scattered on that dark and cloudy day. [13]I will bring them back home to their own land of Israel from among the peoples and nations. I will feed them on the mountains of Israel and by the rivers and in all the places where people live. [14]Yes, I will give them good pastureland on the high hills of Israel. There they will lie down in pleasant places and feed in the lush pastures of the hills. [15]I myself will tend my sheep and give them a place to lie down in peace, says the Sovereign LORD. [16]I will search for my lost ones who strayed away, and I will bring them safely home again. I will bandage the injured and strengthen the weak. But I will destroy those who are fat and powerful. I will feed them, yes—feed them justice!

[17]"And as for you, my flock, this is what the Sovereign LORD says to his people: I will judge between one animal of the flock and another, separating the sheep from the goats. [18]Isn't it enough for you to keep the best of the pastures for yourselves? Must you also trample down the rest? Isn't it enough for you to drink clear water for yourselves? Must you also muddy the rest with your feet? [19]Why must my flock eat what you have trampled down and drink water you have fouled?

[20]"Therefore, this is what the Sovereign LORD says: I will surely judge between the fat sheep and the scrawny sheep. [21]For you fat sheep pushed and butted and crowded my sick and hungry flock until you scattered them to distant lands. [22]So I will rescue my flock, and they will no longer be abused. I will judge between one animal of the flock and another. [23]And I will set over them one shepherd, my servant David. He will feed them and be a shepherd to them. [24]And I, the LORD, will be their God, and my servant David will be a prince among my people. I, the LORD, have spoken!

The LORD's Covenant of Peace

[25]"I will make a covenant of peace with my people and drive away the dangerous animals from the land. Then they will be able to camp safely in the wildest places and sleep in the woods without fear. [26]I will bless my people and their homes around my holy hill. And in

the proper season I will send the showers they need. There will be showers of blessing. [27]The orchards and fields of my people will yield bumper crops, and everyone will live in safety. When I have broken their chains of slavery and rescued them from those who enslaved them, then they will know that I am the LORD. [28]They will no longer be prey for other nations, and wild animals will no longer devour them. They will live in safety, and no one will frighten them.

[29]"And I will make their land famous for its crops, so my people will never again suffer from famines or the insults of foreign nations. [30]In this way, they will know that I, the LORD their God, am with them. And they will know that they, the people of Israel, are my people, says the Sovereign LORD. [31]You are my flock, the sheep of my pasture. You are my people, and I am your God. I, the Sovereign LORD, have spoken!"

CHAPTER 35

A Message for Edom

Again a message came to me from the LORD: [2]"Son of man, turn and face Mount Seir, and prophesy against its people. [3]Give them this message from the Sovereign LORD:

"I am your enemy, O Mount Seir,
and I will raise my fist against you
to destroy you completely.
[4] I will demolish your cities
and make you desolate.
Then you will know that I am the LORD.

[5]"Your eternal hatred for the people of Israel led you to butcher them when they were helpless, when I had already punished them for all their sins. [6]As surely as I live, says the Sovereign LORD, since you show no distaste for blood, I will give you a bloodbath of your own. Your turn has come! [7]I will make Mount Seir utterly desolate, killing off all who try to escape and any who return. [8]I will fill your mountains with the dead. Your hills, your valleys, and your ravines will be filled with people slaughtered by the sword. [9]I will make you desolate forever. Your cities will never be rebuilt. Then you will know that I am the LORD.

[10]"For you said, 'The lands of Israel and Judah will be ours. We will take possession of them. What do we care that the LORD is there!' [11]Therefore, as surely as I live, says the Sovereign LORD, I will pay back your angry deeds with my own. I will punish you for all your acts of anger, envy, and hatred. And I will make myself known to Israel* by what I do to you. [12]Then you will know that I, the LORD, have heard every contemptuous word you spoke against the mountains of Israel. For you said, 'They are desolate; they have been given to us as food to eat!' [13]In saying that, you boasted proudly against me, and I have heard it all!

[14]"This is what the Sovereign LORD says: The whole world will rejoice when I make you desolate. [15]You rejoiced at the desolation of Israel's territory. Now I will rejoice at yours! You will be wiped out, you people of Mount Seir and all who live in Edom! Then you will know that I am the LORD.

CHAPTER 36

Restoration for Israel

"Son of man, prophesy to Israel's mountains. Give them this message: O mountains of Israel, hear the word of the LORD! [2]This is what the Sovereign LORD says: Your enemies have taunted you, saying, 'Aha! Now the ancient heights belong to us!' [3]Therefore, son of man, give the mountains of Israel this message from the Sovereign LORD: Your enemies have attacked you from all directions, making you the property of many nations and the object of much mocking and slander. [4]Therefore, O mountains of Israel, hear the word of the Sovereign LORD. He speaks to the hills and mountains, ravines and valleys, and to ruined wastes and long-deserted cities that have been destroyed and mocked by the surrounding nations. [5]This is what the Sovereign LORD says: My jealous anger burns against these nations, especially Edom, because they have shown utter contempt for me by gleefully taking my land for themselves as plunder.

[6]"Therefore, prophesy to the hills and mountains, the ravines and valleys of Israel. This is what the Sovereign LORD says: I am furious that you have suffered shame before the surrounding nations. [7]Therefore, this is what the Sovereign LORD says: I have taken a solemn oath that those nations will soon have their own shame to endure.

35:11 Hebrew *to them;* Greek version reads *to you.*

[8]"But the mountains of Israel will produce heavy crops of fruit for my people—for they will be coming home again soon! [9]See, I care about you, and I will pay attention to you. Your ground will be plowed and your crops planted. [10]I will greatly increase the population of Israel, and the ruined cities will be rebuilt and filled with people. [11]I will increase not only the people, but also your animals. O mountains of Israel, I will bring people to live on you once again. I will make you even more prosperous than you were before. Then you will know that I am the LORD. [12]I will cause my people to walk on you once again, and you will be their territory. You will never again rob them of their children.

[13]"This is what the Sovereign LORD says: The other nations taunt you, saying, 'Israel is a land that devours its own people and robs them of their children!' [14]But you will never again devour your people or rob them of their children, says the Sovereign LORD. [15]I will not let you hear those other nations insult you, and you will no longer be mocked by them. You will not be a land that causes its nation to fall, says the Sovereign LORD."

[16]Then this further message came to me from the LORD: [17]"Son of man, when the people of Israel were living in their own land, they defiled it by the evil way they lived. To me their conduct was as unclean as a woman's menstrual cloth. [18]They polluted the land with murder and the worship of idols,* so I poured out my fury on them. [19]I scattered them to many lands to punish them for the evil way they had lived. [20]But when they were scattered among the nations, they brought shame on my holy name. For the nations said, 'These are the people of the LORD, but he couldn't keep them safe in his own land!' [21]Then I was concerned for my holy name, on which my people brought shame among the nations.

[22]"Therefore, give the people of Israel this message from the Sovereign LORD: I am bringing you back, but not because you deserve it. I am doing it to protect my holy name, on which you brought shame while you were scattered among the nations. [23]I will show how holy my great name is—the name on which you brought shame among the nations. And when I reveal my holiness through you before their very eyes, says the Sovereign LORD, then the nations will know that I am the LORD. [24]For I will gather you up from all the nations and bring you home again to your land.

[25]"Then I will sprinkle clean water on you, and you will be clean. Your filth will be washed away, and you will no longer worship idols. [26]And I will give you a new heart, and I will put a new spirit in you. I will take out your stony, stubborn heart and give you a tender, responsive heart.* [27]And I will put my Spirit in you so that you will follow my decrees and be careful to obey my regulations.

[28]"And you will live in Israel, the land I gave your ancestors long ago. You will be my people, and I will be your God. [29]I will cleanse you of your filthy behavior. I will give you good crops of grain, and I will send no more famines on the land. [30]I will give you great harvests from your fruit trees and fields, and never again will the surrounding nations be

36:18 The Hebrew term (literally *round things*) probably alludes to dung; also in 36:25. **36:26** Hebrew *a heart of flesh.*

OLD AND NEW COVENANTS

OLD COVENANT	NEW COVENANT
Written on stone	Written on people's hearts
Based on the Law	Based on desire to love and serve God
Must be taught	Known by all
Legal relationship with God	Personal relationship with God

AMAZING FACTS

Ezekiel spoke words from God that turned a valley of dry bones into living, breathing people again.

EZEKIEL 37:1-14

able to scoff at your land for its famines. 31Then you will remember your past sins and despise yourselves for all the detestable things you did. 32But remember, says the Sovereign LORD, I am not doing this because you deserve it. O my people of Israel, you should be utterly ashamed of all you have done!

33"This is what the Sovereign LORD says: When I cleanse you from your sins, I will repopulate your cities, and the ruins will be rebuilt. 34The fields that used to lie empty and desolate in plain view of everyone will again be farmed. 35And when I bring you back, people will say, 'This former wasteland is now like the Garden of Eden! The abandoned and ruined cities now have strong walls and are filled with people!' 36Then the surrounding nations that survive will know that I, the LORD, have rebuilt the ruins and replanted the wasteland. For I, the LORD, have spoken, and I will do what I say.

37"This is what the Sovereign LORD says: I am ready to hear Israel's prayers and to increase their numbers like a flock. 38They will be as numerous as the sacred flocks that fill Jerusalem's streets at the time of her festivals. The ruined cities will be crowded with people once more, and everyone will know that I am the LORD."

CHAPTER 37

A Valley of Dry Bones

The LORD took hold of me, and I was carried away by the Spirit of the LORD to a valley filled with bones. 2He led me all around among the bones that covered the valley floor. They were scattered everywhere across the ground and were completely dried out. 3Then he asked me, "Son of man, can these bones become living people again?"

"O Sovereign LORD," I replied, "you alone know the answer to that."

4Then he said to me, "Speak a prophetic message to these bones and say, 'Dry bones, listen to the word of the LORD! 5This is what the Sovereign LORD says: Look! I am going to put breath into you and make you live again! 6I will put flesh and muscles on you and cover you with skin. I will put breath into you, and you will come to life. Then you will know that I am the LORD.'"

7So I spoke this message, just as he told me. Suddenly as I spoke, there was a rattling noise all across the valley. The bones of each body came together and attached themselves as complete skeletons. 8Then as I watched, muscles and flesh formed over the bones. Then skin formed to cover their bodies, but they still had no breath in them.

9Then he said to me, "Speak a prophetic message to the winds, son of man. Speak a prophetic message and say, 'This is what the Sovereign LORD says: Come, O breath, from the four winds! Breathe into these dead bodies so they may live again.'"

10So I spoke the message as he commanded me, and breath came into their bodies. They all came to life and stood up on their feet—a great army.

11Then he said to me, "Son of man, these bones represent the people of Israel. They are saying, 'We have become old, dry bones—all hope is gone. Our nation is finished.' 12Therefore, prophesy to them and say, 'This is what the Sovereign LORD says: O my people, I will open your graves of exile and cause you to rise again. Then I will bring you back to the land of Israel. 13When this happens, O my people, you will know that I am the LORD. 14I will put my Spirit in you, and you will live again and return home to your own land. Then you will know that I, the LORD, have spoken, and I have done what I said. Yes, the LORD has spoken!'"

Reunion of Israel and Judah

15Again a message came to me from the LORD: 16"Son of man, take a piece of wood and carve on it these words: 'This represents Judah and its allied tribes.' Then take another piece and carve these words on it: 'This represents Ephraim and the northern tribes of Israel.'* [17]Now hold them together in your hand as if they were one piece of wood. [18]When your people ask you what your actions mean, [19]say to them, 'This is what the Sovereign LORD says: I will take Ephraim and the northern tribes and join them to Judah. I will make them one piece of wood in my hand.'

[20]"Then hold out the pieces of wood you have inscribed, so the people can see them. [21]And give them this message from the Sovereign LORD: I will gather the people of Israel from among the nations. I will bring them home to their own land from the places where they have been scattered. [22]I will unify them into one nation on the mountains of Israel. One king will rule them all; no longer will they be divided into two nations or into two kingdoms. [23]They will never again pollute themselves with their idols* and vile images and rebellion, for I will save them from their sinful backsliding. I will cleanse them. Then they will truly be my people, and I will be their God.

[24]"My servant David will be their king, and they will have only one shepherd. They will obey my regulations and be careful to keep my decrees. [25]They will live in the land I gave my servant Jacob, the land where their ancestors lived. They and their children and their grandchildren after them will live there forever, generation after generation. And my servant David will be their prince forever. [26]And I will make a covenant of peace with them, an everlasting covenant. I will give them their land and increase their numbers,* and I will put my Temple among them forever. [27]I will make my home among them. I will be their God, and they will be my people. [28]And when my Temple is among them forever, the nations will know that I am the LORD, who makes Israel holy."

CHAPTER 38

A Message for Gog

This is another message that came to me from the LORD: [2]"Son of man, turn and face Gog of the land of Magog, the prince who rules over the nations of Meshech and Tubal, and prophesy against him. [3]Give him this message from the Sovereign LORD: Gog, I am your enemy! [4]I will turn you around and put hooks in your jaws to lead you out with your whole army—your horses and charioteers in full armor and a great horde armed with shields and swords. [5]Persia, Ethiopia, and Libya* will join you, too, with all their weapons. [6]Gomer and all its armies will also join you, along with the armies of Beth-togarmah from the distant north, and many others.

[7]"Get ready; be prepared! Keep all the armies around you mobilized, and take command of them. [8]A long time from now you will be called into action. In the distant future you will swoop down on the land of Israel, which will be enjoying peace after recovering from war and after its people have returned from many lands to the mountains of Israel. [9]You and all your allies—a vast and awesome army—will roll down on them like a storm and cover the land like a cloud.

[10]"This is what the Sovereign LORD says: At that time evil thoughts will come to your mind, and you will devise a wicked scheme. [11]You will say, 'Israel is an unprotected land filled with unwalled villages! I will march against her and destroy these people who live in such confidence! [12]I will go to those formerly desolate cities that are now filled with people who have returned from exile in many nations. I will capture vast amounts of plunder, for the people are rich with livestock and other possessions now. They think the whole world revolves around them!' [13]But Sheba and Dedan and the merchants of Tarshish will ask, 'Do you really think the armies you have gathered can rob them of silver and gold? Do you think you can drive away their livestock and seize their goods and carry off plunder?'

[14]"Therefore, son of man, prophesy against Gog. Give him this message from the Sovereign LORD: When my people are living in peace in their land, then you will rouse yourself.* [15]You will come from your homeland in the distant north with your vast cavalry and your mighty army, [16]and you will attack my people Israel, covering their land like a cloud. At that time in the distant future, I will bring you against my land as everyone watches, and

37:16 Hebrew *This is Ephraim's wood, representing Joseph and all the house of Israel.* **37:23** The Hebrew term (literally *round things*) probably alludes to dung. **37:26** Hebrew reads *I will give them and increase their numbers;* Greek version lacks the entire phrase. **38:5** Hebrew *Paras, Cush, and Put.* **38:14** As in Greek version; Hebrew reads *then you will know.*

my holiness will be displayed by what happens to you, Gog. Then all the nations will know that I am the LORD.

17"This is what the Sovereign LORD asks: Are you the one I was talking about long ago, when I announced through Israel's prophets that in the future I would bring you against my people? 18But this is what the Sovereign LORD says: When Gog invades the land of Israel, my fury will boil over! 19In my jealousy and blazing anger, I promise a mighty shaking in the land of Israel on that day. 20All living things—the fish in the sea, the birds of the sky, the animals of the field, the small animals that scurry along the ground, and all the people on earth—will quake in terror at my presence. Mountains will be thrown down; cliffs will crumble; walls will fall to the earth. 21I will summon the sword against you on all the hills of Israel, says the Sovereign LORD. Your men will turn their swords against each other. 22I will punish you and your armies with disease and bloodshed; I will send torrential rain, hailstones, fire, and burning sulfur! 23In this way, I will show my greatness and holiness, and I will make myself known to all the nations of the world. Then they will know that I am the LORD.

CHAPTER 39

The Slaughter of Gog's Hordes

"Son of man, prophesy against Gog. Give him this message from the Sovereign LORD: I am your enemy, O Gog, ruler of the nations of Meshech and Tubal. 2I will turn you around and drive you toward the mountains of Israel, bringing you from the distant north. 3I will knock the bow from your left hand and the arrows from your right hand, and I will leave you helpless. 4You and your army and your allies will all die on the mountains. I will feed you to the vultures and wild animals. 5You will fall in the open fields, for I have spoken, says the Sovereign LORD. 6And I will rain down fire on Magog and on all your allies who live safely on the coasts. Then they will know that I am the LORD.

7"In this way, I will make known my holy name among my people of Israel. I will not let anyone bring shame on it. And the nations, too, will know that I am the LORD, the Holy One of Israel. 8That day of judgment will come, says the Sovereign LORD. Everything will happen just as I have declared it.

9"Then the people in the towns of Israel will go out and pick up your small and large shields, bows and arrows, javelins and spears, and they will use them for fuel. There will be enough to last them seven years! 10They won't need to cut wood from the fields or forests, for these weapons will give them all the fuel they need. They will plunder those who planned to plunder them, and they will rob those who planned to rob them, says the Sovereign LORD.

11"And I will make a vast graveyard for Gog and his hordes in the Valley of the Travelers, east of the Dead Sea.* It will block the way of those who travel there, and they will change the name of the place to the Valley of Gog's Hordes. 12It will take seven months for the people of Israel to bury the bodies and cleanse the land. 13Everyone in Israel will help, for it will be a glorious victory for Israel when I demonstrate my glory on that day, says the Sovereign LORD.

14"After seven months, teams of men will be appointed to search the land for skeletons to bury, so the land will be made clean again. 15Whenever bones are found, a marker will be set up so the burial crews will take them to be buried in the Valley of Gog's Hordes. 16(There will be a town there named Hamonah, which means 'horde.') And so the land will finally be cleansed.

17"And now, son of man, this is what the Sovereign LORD says: Call all the birds and wild animals. Say to them: Gather together for my great sacrificial feast. Come from far and near to the mountains of Israel, and there eat flesh and drink blood! 18Eat the flesh of mighty men and drink the blood of princes as though they were rams, lambs, goats, and bulls—all fattened animals from Bashan! 19Gorge yourselves with flesh until you are glutted; drink blood until you are drunk. This is the sacrificial feast I have prepared for you. 20Feast at my banquet table—feast on horses and charioteers, on mighty men and all kinds of valiant warriors, says the Sovereign LORD.

21"In this way, I will demonstrate my glory to the nations. Everyone will see the punish-

39:11 Hebrew *the sea.*

ment I have inflicted on them and the power
of my fist when I strike. 22And from that time
on the people of Israel will know that I am the
LORD their God. 23The nations will then know
why Israel was sent away to exile—it was pun-
ishment for sin, for they were unfaithful to
their God. Therefore, I turned away from
them and let their enemies destroy them. 24I
turned my face away and punished them be-
cause of their defilement and their sins.

Restoration for God's People

25"So now, this is what the Sovereign LORD
says: I will end the captivity of my people*; I
will have mercy on all Israel, for I jealously
guard my holy reputation! 26They will accept
responsibility for* their past shame and un-
faithfulness after they come home to live in
peace in their own land, with no one to bother
them. 27When I bring them home from the
lands of their enemies, I will display my holi-
ness among them for all the nations to see.
28Then my people will know that I am the
LORD their God, because I sent them away
to exile and brought them home again. I will
leave none of my people behind. 29And I
will never again turn my face from them, for I
will pour out my Spirit upon the people of Is-
rael. I, the Sovereign LORD, have spoken!"

CHAPTER 40

The New Temple Area

On April 28,* during the twenty-fifth year of
our captivity—fourteen years after the fall of
Jerusalem—the LORD took hold of me. 2In a vi-
sion from God he took me to the land of Israel
and set me down on a very high mountain.
From there I could see toward the south what
appeared to be a city. 3As he brought me
nearer, I saw a man whose face shone like
bronze standing beside a gateway entrance.
He was holding in his hand a linen measuring
cord and a measuring rod.

4He said to me, "Son of man, watch and lis-
ten. Pay close attention to everything I show
you. You have been brought here so I can
show you many things. Then you will return
to the people of Israel and tell them every-
thing you have seen."

The East Gateway

5I could see a wall completely surrounding
the Temple area. The man took a measuring
rod that was 10½ feet* long and measured
the wall, and the wall was 10½ feet* thick and
10½ feet high.

6Then he went over to the eastern gateway.
He climbed the steps and measured the
threshold of the gateway; it was 10½ feet
front to back.* 7There were guard alcoves on
each side built into the gateway passage. Each
of these alcoves was 10½ feet square, with a
distance between them of 8¾ feet* along the
passage wall. The gateway's inner threshold,
which led to the entry room at the inner end
of the gateway passage, was 10½ feet front to
back. 8He also measured the entry room of
the gateway.* 9It was 14 feet* across, with
supporting columns 3½ feet* thick. This en-
try room was at the inner end of the gateway
structure, facing toward the Temple.

10There were three guard alcoves on each
side of the gateway passage. Each had the
same measurements, and the dividing walls
separating them were also identical. 11The
man measured the gateway entrance, which
was 17½ feet* wide at the opening and 22¾
feet* wide in the gateway passage. 12In front
of each of the guard alcoves was a 21-inch*
curb. The alcoves themselves were 10½ feet*
on each side.

13Then he measured the entire width of
the gateway, measuring the distance between
the back walls of facing guard alcoves; this
distance was 43¾ feet.* 14He measured the
dividing walls all along the inside of the gate-
way up to the entry room of the gateway; this
distance was 105 feet.* 15The full length of
the gateway passage was 87½ feet* from one
end to the other. 16There were recessed win-
dows that narrowed inward through the walls
of the guard alcoves and their dividing walls.

39:25 Hebrew *of Jacob*. **39:26** A few Hebrew manuscripts read *They will forget*. **40:1** Hebrew *At the beginning of the year, on the tenth day of the month*, of the ancient Hebrew lunar calendar. This event occurred on April 28, 573 B.C.; also see note on 1:1. **40:5a** Hebrew *6 long cubits* [3.2 meters], *each being a cubit* [18 inches or 45 centimeters] *and a handbreadth* [3 inches or 8 centimeters] *in length*. **40:5b** Hebrew *1 rod* [3.2 meters]; also in 40:5c, 7. **40:6** As in Greek version, which reads *1 rod* [3.2 meters] *deep;* Hebrew reads *1 rod deep, and 1 threshold, 1 rod deep*. **40:7** Hebrew *5 cubits* [2.7 meters]; also in 40:48. **40:8** Many Hebrew manuscripts add *which faced inward toward the Temple; it was 1 rod* [10.5 feet or 3.2 meters] *deep. 9Then he measured the entry room of the gateway*. **40:9a** Hebrew *8 cubits* [4.2 meters]. **40:9b** Hebrew *2 cubits* [1.1 meters]. **40:11a** Hebrew *10 cubits* [5.3 meters]. **40:11b** Hebrew *13 cubits* [6.9 meters]. **40:12a** Hebrew *1 cubit* [53 centimeters]. **40:12b** Hebrew *6 cubits* [3.2 meters]. **40:13** Hebrew *25 cubits* [13.3 meters]; also in 40:21, 25, 29, 30, 33, 36. **40:14** Hebrew *60 cubits* [31.8 meters]. Greek version reads *20 cubits* [35 feet or 10.6 meters]. The meaning of the Hebrew in this verse is uncertain. **40:15** Hebrew *50 cubits* [26.5 meters]; also in 40:21, 25, 29, 33, 36.

There were also windows in the entry room. The surfaces of the dividing walls were decorated with carved palm trees.

The Outer Courtyard

[17]Then the man brought me through the gateway into the outer courtyard of the Temple. A stone pavement ran along the walls of the courtyard, and thirty rooms were built against the walls, opening onto the pavement. [18]This pavement flanked the gates and extended out from the walls into the courtyard the same distance as the gateway entrance. This was the lower pavement. [19]Then the man measured across the Temple's outer courtyard between the outer and inner gateways; the distance was 175 feet.*

The North Gateway

[20]The man measured the gateway on the north just like the one on the east. [21]Here, too, there were three guard alcoves on each side, with dividing walls and an entry room. All the measurements matched those of the east gateway. The gateway passage was 87½ feet long and 43¾ feet wide between the back walls of facing guard alcoves. [22]The windows, the entry room, and the palm tree decorations were identical to those in the east gateway. There were seven steps leading up to the gateway entrance, and the entry room was at the inner end of the gateway passage. [23]Here on the north side, just as on the east, there was another gateway leading to the Temple's inner courtyard directly opposite this outer gateway. The distance between the two gateways was 175 feet.

The South Gateway

[24]Then the man took me around to the south gateway and measured its various parts, and they were exactly the same as in the others. [25]It had windows along the walls as the others did, and there was an entry room where the gateway passage opened into the outer courtyard. And like the others, the gateway passage was 87½ feet long and 43¾ feet wide between the back walls of facing guard alcoves. [26]This gateway also had a stairway of seven steps leading up to it, and an entry room at the inner end, and palm tree decorations along the dividing walls. [27]And here again, directly opposite the outer gateway, was another gateway that led into the inner courtyard. The distance between the two gateways was 175 feet.

Gateways to the Inner Courtyard

[28]Then the man took me to the south gateway leading into the inner courtyard. He measured it, and it had the same measurements as the other gateways. [29]Its guard alcoves, dividing walls, and entry room were the same size as those in the others. It also had windows along its walls and in the entry room. And like the others, the gateway passage was 87½ feet long and 43¾ feet wide. [30](The entry rooms of the gateways leading into the inner courtyard were 14 feet* across and 43¾ feet wide.) [31]The entry room to the south gateway faced into the outer courtyard. It had palm tree decorations on its columns, and there were eight steps leading to its entrance.

[32]Then he took me to the east gateway leading to the inner courtyard. He measured it, and it had the same measurements as the other gateways. [33]Its guard alcoves, dividing walls, and entry room were the same size as those of the others, and there were windows along the walls and in the entry room. The gateway passage measured 87½ feet long and 43¾ feet wide. [34]Its entry room faced into the outer courtyard. It had palm tree decorations on its columns, and there were eight steps leading to its entrance.

[35]Then he took me around to the north gateway leading to the inner courtyard. He measured it, and it had the same measurements as the other gateways. [36]The guard alcoves, dividing walls, and entry room of this gateway had the same measurements as in the others and the same window arrangements. The gateway passage measured 87½ feet long and 43¾ feet wide. [37]Its entry room faced into the outer courtyard, and it had palm tree decorations on the columns. There were eight steps leading to its entrance.

Rooms for Preparing Sacrifices

[38]A door led from the entry room of one of the inner gateways into a side room, where the meat for sacrifices was washed. [39]On each side of this entry room were two tables, where the

40:19 Hebrew *100 cubits* [53 meters]; also in 40:23, 27, 47. **40:30** As in 40:9, which reads *8 cubits* [14 feet or 4.2 meters]; here the Hebrew reads *5 cubits* [8¾ feet or 2.7 meters]. Some Hebrew manuscripts and the Greek version lack this entire verse.

sacrificial animals were slaughtered for the burnt offerings, sin offerings, and guilt offerings. [40]Outside the entry room, on each side of the stairs going up to the north entrance, were two more tables. [41]So there were eight tables in all—four inside and four outside—where the sacrifices were cut up and prepared. [42]There were also four tables of finished stone for preparation of the burnt offerings, each 31½ inches square and 21 inches high.* On these tables were placed the butchering knives and other implements for slaughtering the sacrificial animals. [43]There were hooks, each 3 inches* long, fastened to the foyer walls. The sacrificial meat was laid on the tables.

Rooms for the Priests

[44]Inside the inner courtyard were two rooms,* one beside the north gateway, facing south, and the other beside the south* gateway, facing north. [45]And the man said to me, "The room beside the north inner gate is for the priests who supervise the Temple maintenance. [46]The room beside the south inner gate is for the priests in charge of the altar—the descendants of Zadok—for they alone of all the Levites may approach the LORD to minister to him."

The Inner Courtyard and Temple

[47]Then the man measured the inner courtyard, and it was a square, 175 feet wide and 175 feet across. The altar stood in the courtyard in front of the Temple. [48]Then he brought me to the entry room of the Temple. He measured the walls on either side of the opening to the entry room, and they were 8¾ feet thick. The entrance itself was 24½ feet wide, and the walls on each side of the entrance were an additional 5¼ feet long.* [49]The entry room was 35 feet* wide and 21 feet* deep. There were ten steps leading up to it, with a column on each side.

CHAPTER 41

After that, the man brought me into the sanctuary of the Temple. He measured the walls on either side of its doorway, and they were 10½ feet* thick. [2]The doorway was 17½ feet* wide, and the walls on each side of it were 8¾ feet* long. The sanctuary itself was 70 feet long and 35 feet wide.*

[3]Then he went beyond the sanctuary into the inner room. He measured the walls on either side of its entrance, and they were 3½ feet* thick. The entrance was 10½ feet wide, and the walls on each side of the entrance were 12¼ feet* long. [4]The inner room of the sanctuary was 35 feet* long and 35 feet wide. "This," he told me, "is the Most Holy Place."

[5]Then he measured the wall of the Temple, and it was 10½ feet thick. There was a row of rooms along the outside wall; each room was 7 feet* wide. [6]These side rooms were built in three levels, one above the other, with thirty rooms on each level. The supports for these side rooms rested on exterior ledges on the Temple wall; they did not extend into the wall. [7]Each level was wider than the one below it, corresponding to the narrowing of the Temple wall as it rose higher. A stairway led up from the bottom level through the middle level to the top level.

[8]I saw that the Temple was built on a terrace, which provided a foundation for the side rooms. This terrace was 10½ feet* high. [9]The outer wall of the Temple's side rooms was 8¾ feet thick. This left an open area between these side rooms [10]and the row of rooms along the outer wall of the inner courtyard. This open area was 35 feet wide, and it went all the way around the Temple. [11]Two doors opened from the side rooms into the terrace yard, which was 8¾ feet wide. One door faced north and the other south.

[12]A large building stood on the west, facing the Temple courtyard. It was 122½ feet wide and 157½ feet long, and its walls were 8¾ feet* thick. [13]Then the man measured the Temple, and it was 175 feet* long. The courtyard around the building, including its walls, was an additional 175 feet in length. [14]The inner courtyard to the east of the Temple was also 175 feet wide. [15]The building to the west, including its two walls, was also 175 feet wide.

40:42 Hebrew *1½ cubits* [80 centimeters] *long and 1½ cubits wide and 1 cubit* [53 centimeters] *high*. **40:43** Hebrew *a handbreadth* [8 centimeters]. **40:44a** As in Greek version; Hebrew reads *rooms for singers*. **40:44b** As in Greek version; Hebrew reads *east*. **40:48** As in Greek version, which reads *The entrance was 14 cubits* [7.4 meters] *wide, and the walls of the entrance were 3 cubits* [1.6 meters] *on each side;* Hebrew lacks *14 cubits wide, and the walls of the entrance were*. **40:49a** Hebrew *20 cubits* [10.6 meters]. **40:49b** As in Greek version, which reads *12 cubits* [21 feet or 6.4 meters]; Hebrew reads *11 cubits* [19¼ feet or 5.8 meters]. **41:1** Hebrew *6 cubits* [3.2 meters]; also in 41:3, 5. **41:2a** Hebrew *10 cubits* [5.3 meters]. **41:2b** Hebrew *5 cubits* [2.7 meters]; also in 41:9, 11. **41:2c** Hebrew *40 cubits* [21.2 meters] *long and 20 cubits* [10.6 meters] *wide*. **41:3a** Hebrew *2 cubits* [1.1 meters]. **41:3b** Hebrew *7 cubits* [3.7 meters]. **41:4** Hebrew *20 cubits* [10.6 meters]; also in 41:4b, 10. **41:5** Hebrew *4 cubits* [2.1 meters]. **41:8** Hebrew *1 rod, 6 cubits* [3.2 meters]. **41:12** Hebrew *70 cubits* [37.1 meters] *wide and 90 cubits* [47.7 meters] *long, and its walls were 5 cubits* [2.7 meters] *thick*. **41:13** Hebrew *100 cubits* [53 meters]; also in 41:13b, 14, 15.

The sanctuary, the inner room, and the entry room of the Temple [16]were all paneled with wood, as were the frames of the recessed windows. The inner walls of the Temple were paneled with wood above and below the windows. [17]The space above the door leading into the inner room, and its walls inside and out, were also paneled. [18]All the walls were decorated with carvings of cherubim, each with two faces, and there was a carving of a palm tree between each of the cherubim. [19]One face—that of a man—looked toward the palm tree on one side. The other face—that of a young lion—looked toward the palm tree on the other side. The figures were carved all along the inside of the Temple, [20]from the floor to the top of the walls, including the outer wall of the sanctuary.

[21]There were square columns at the entrance to the sanctuary, and the ones at the entrance of the Most Holy Place were similar. [22]There was an altar made of wood, 5¼ feet high and 3½ feet across.* Its corners, base, and sides were all made of wood. "This," the man told me, "is the table that stands in the LORD's presence."

[23]Both the sanctuary and the Most Holy Place had double doorways, [24]each with two swinging doors. [25]The doors leading into the sanctuary were decorated with carved cherubim and palm trees, just as on the walls. And there was a wooden roof at the front of the entry room to the Temple. [26]On both sides of the entry room were recessed windows decorated with carved palm trees. The side rooms along the outside wall also had roofs.

CHAPTER 42

Rooms for the Priests

Then the man led me out of the Temple courtyard by way of the north gateway. We entered the outer courtyard and came to a group of rooms against the north wall of the inner courtyard. [2]This structure, whose entrance opened toward the north, was 175 feet* long and 87½ feet* wide. [3]One block of rooms overlooked the 35-foot* width of the inner courtyard. Another block of rooms looked out onto the pavement of the outer courtyard. The two blocks were built three levels high and stood across from each other. [4]Between the two blocks of rooms ran a walkway 17½ feet* wide. It extended the entire 175 feet of the complex,* and all the doors faced north. [5]Each of the two upper levels of rooms was narrower than the one beneath it because the upper levels had to allow space for walkways in front of them. [6]Since there were three levels and they did not have supporting columns as in the courtyards, each of the upper levels was set back from the level beneath it. [7]There was an outer wall that separated the rooms from the outer courtyard; it was 87½ feet long. [8]This wall added length to the outer block of rooms, which extended for only 87½ feet, while the inner block—the rooms toward the Temple—extended for 175 feet. [9]There was an eastern entrance from the outer courtyard to these rooms.

[10]On the south* side of the Temple there were two blocks of rooms just south of the inner courtyard between the Temple and the outer courtyard. These rooms were arranged just like the rooms on the north. [11]There was a walkway between the two blocks of rooms just like the complex on the north side of the Temple. This complex of rooms was the same length and width as the other one, and it had the same entrances and doors. The dimensions of each were identical. [12]So there was an entrance in the wall facing the doors of the inner block of rooms, and another on the east at the end of the interior walkway.

[13]Then the man told me, "These rooms that overlook the Temple from the north and south are holy. Here the priests who offer sacrifices to the LORD will eat the most holy offerings. And because these rooms are holy, they will be used to store the sacred offerings—the grain offerings, sin offerings, and guilt offerings. [14]When the priests leave the sanctuary, they must not go directly to the outer courtyard. They must first take off the clothes they wore while ministering, because these clothes are holy. They must put on other clothes before entering the parts of the building complex open to the public."

[15]When the man had finished measuring the inside of the Temple area, he led me out through the east gateway to measure the en-

41:22 Hebrew *3 cubits* [1.6 meters] *high and 2 cubits* [1.1 meters] *across*. **42:2a** Hebrew *100 cubits* [53 meters]; also in 42:8.
42:2b Hebrew *50 cubits* [26.5 meters]; also in 42:7, 8. **42:3** Hebrew *20-cubit* [10.6-meter]. **42:4a** Hebrew *10 cubits* [5.3 meters].
42:4b As in Greek and Syriac versions, which read *Its length was 100 cubits* [53 meters]; Hebrew reads *and a passage 1 cubit* [18 inches or 53 centimeters] *wide*. **42:10** As in Greek version; Hebrew reads *east*.

tire perimeter. [16]He measured the east side with his measuring rod, and it was 875 feet long.* [17]Then he measured the north side, and it was also 875 feet. [18]The south side was also 875 feet, [19]and the west side was also 875 feet. [20]So the area was 875 feet on each side with a wall all around it to separate what was holy from what was common.

CHAPTER 43

The Lord's Glory Returns

After this, the man brought me back around to the east gateway. [2]Suddenly, the glory of the God of Israel appeared from the east. The sound of his coming was like the roar of rushing waters, and the whole landscape shone with his glory. [3]This vision was just like the others I had seen, first by the Kebar River and then when he came to destroy Jerusalem. I fell face down on the ground. [4]And the glory of the Lord came into the Temple through the east gateway.

[5]Then the Spirit took me up and brought me into the inner courtyard, and the glory of the Lord filled the Temple. [6]And I heard someone speaking to me from within the Temple, while the man who had been measuring stood beside me. [7]The Lord said to me, "Son of man, this is the place of my throne and the place where I will rest my feet. I will live here forever among the people of Israel. They and their kings will not defile my holy name any longer by their adulterous worship of other gods or by honoring the relics of their kings who have died. [8]They put their idol altars right next to mine with only a wall between them and me. They defiled my holy name by such detestable sin, so I consumed them in my anger. [9]Now let them stop worshiping other gods and honoring the relics of their kings, and I will live among them forever.

[10]"Son of man, describe to the people of Israel the Temple I have shown you, so they will be ashamed of all their sins. Let them study its plan, [11]and they will be ashamed* of what they have done. Describe to them all the specifications of the Temple—including its entrances and exits—and everything else about it. Tell them about its decrees and laws. Write down all these specifications and decrees as they watch so they will be sure to remember and follow them. [12]And this is the basic law of the Temple: absolute holiness! The entire top of the mountain where the Temple is built is holy. Yes, this is the basic law of the Temple.

The Altar

[13]"These are the measurements of the altar*: There is a gutter all around the altar 21 inches deep and 21 inches wide,* with a curb 9 inches* wide around its edge. And this is the height* of the altar: [14]From the gutter the altar rises 3½ feet* to a lower ledge that surrounds the altar and is 21 inches* wide. From the lower ledge the altar rises 7 feet* to the upper ledge that is also 21 inches wide. [15]The top of the altar, the hearth, rises another 7 feet higher, with a horn rising up from each of the four corners. [16]The top of the altar is square, measuring 21 feet by 21 feet.* [17]The upper ledge also forms a square, measuring 24½ feet by 24½ feet,* with a 21-inch gutter and a 10½-inch curb* all around the edge. There are steps going up the east side of the altar."

[18]Then he said to me, "Son of man, this is what the Sovereign Lord says: These will be the regulations for the burning of offerings and the sprinkling of blood when the altar is built. [19]At that time, the Levitical priests of the family of Zadok, who minister before me, are to be given a young bull for a sin offering, says the Sovereign Lord. [20]You will take some of its blood and smear it on the four horns of the altar, the four corners of the upper ledge, and the curb that runs around that ledge. This will cleanse and make atonement for the altar. [21]Then take the young bull for the sin offering and burn it at the appointed place outside the Temple area.

[22]"On the second day, sacrifice as a sin offering a young male goat that has no physical defects. Then cleanse and make atonement for the altar again, just as you did with the young bull. [23]When you have finished the

42:16 As in 45:2 and in Greek version at 42:17, which reads *500 cubits* [265 meters]; Hebrew reads *500 rods* [5,250 feet or 1,590 meters]; similarly in 42:17, 18, 19, 20. **43:11** As in Greek version; Hebrew reads *if they are ashamed*. **43:13a** Hebrew *measurements of the altar in long cubits, each being a cubit* [18 inches or 45 centimeters] *and a handbreadth* [3 inches or 8 centimeters] *in length*. **43:13b** Hebrew *a cubit* [53 centimeters] *deep and a cubit wide*. **43:13c** Hebrew *1 span* [23 centimeters]. **43:13d** As in Greek version; Hebrew reads *base*. **43:14a** Hebrew *2 cubits* [1.1 meters]. **43:14b** Hebrew *1 cubit* [53 centimeters]; also in 43:14d. **43:14c** Hebrew *4 cubits* [2.1 meters]; also in 43:15. **43:16** Hebrew *12 cubits* [6.4 meters] *long and 12 cubits wide*. **43:17a** Hebrew *14 cubits* [7.4 meters] *long and 14 cubits wide*. **43:17b** Hebrew *a gutter of 1 cubit* [53 centimeters] *and a curb of ½ a cubit* [27 centimeters].

cleansing ceremony, offer another young bull that has no defects and a perfect ram from the flock. [24]You are to present them to the LORD, and the priests are to sprinkle salt on them and offer them as a burnt offering to the LORD.

[25]"Every day for seven days a male goat, a young bull, and a ram from the flock will be sacrificed as a sin offering. None of these animals may have physical defects of any kind. [26]Do this each day for seven days to cleanse and make atonement for the altar, thus setting it apart for holy use. [27]On the eighth day, and on each day afterward, the priests will sacrifice on the altar the burnt offerings and peace offerings of the people. Then I will accept you. I, the Sovereign LORD, have spoken!"

CHAPTER 44

The Prince, Levites, and Priests

Then the man brought me back to the east gateway in the outer wall of the Temple area, but it was closed. [2]And the LORD said to me, "This gate must remain closed; it will never again be opened. No one will ever open it and pass through, for the LORD, the God of Israel, has entered here. Therefore, it must always remain shut. [3]Only the prince himself may sit inside this gateway to feast in the LORD's presence. But he may come and go only through the entry room of the gateway."

[4]Then the man brought me through the north gateway to the front of the Temple. I looked and saw that the glory of the LORD filled the Temple of the LORD, and I fell face down on the ground.

[5]And the LORD said to me, "Son of man, take careful notice. Use your eyes and ears, and listen to everything I tell you about the regulations concerning the LORD's Temple. Take careful note of the procedures for using the Temple's entrances and exits. [6]And give these rebels, the people of Israel, this message from the Sovereign LORD: O people of Israel, enough of your detestable sins! [7]You have brought uncircumcised foreigners into my sanctuary—people who have no heart for God. In this way, you defiled my Temple even as you offered me my food, the fat and blood of sacrifices. In addition to all your other detestable sins, you have broken my covenant. [8]Instead of safeguarding my sacred rituals, you have hired foreigners to take charge of my sanctuary.

[9]"So this is what the Sovereign LORD says: No foreigners, including those who live among the people of Israel, will enter my sanctuary if they have not been circumcised and have not surrendered themselves to the LORD. [10]And the men of the tribe of Levi who abandoned me when Israel strayed away from me to worship idols* must bear the consequences of their unfaithfulness. [11]They may still be Temple guards and gatekeepers, and they may slaughter the animals brought for burnt offerings and be present to help the people. [12]But they encouraged my people to worship idols, causing Israel to fall into deep sin. So I have taken a solemn oath that they must bear the consequences for their sins, says the Sovereign LORD. [13]They may not approach me to minister as priests. They may not touch any of my holy things or the holy offerings, for they must bear the shame of all the detestable sins they have committed. [14]They are to serve as the Temple caretakers, taking charge of the maintenance work and performing general duties.

[15]"However, the Levitical priests of the family of Zadok continued to minister faithfully in the Temple when Israel abandoned me for idols. These men will serve as my ministers. They will stand in my presence and offer the fat and blood of the sacrifices, says the Sovereign LORD. [16]They alone will enter my sanctuary and approach my table to serve me. They will fulfill all my requirements.

[17]"When they enter the gateway to the inner courtyard, they must wear only linen clothing. They must wear no wool while on duty in the inner courtyard or in the Temple itself. [18]They must wear linen turbans and linen undergarments. They must not wear anything that would cause them to perspire. [19]When they return to the outer courtyard where the people are, they must take off the clothes they wear while ministering to me. They must leave them in the sacred rooms and put on other clothes so they do not endanger anyone by transmitting holiness to them through this clothing.

[20]"They must neither shave their heads nor

44:10 The Hebrew term (literally *round things*) probably alludes to dung; also in 44:12.

let their hair grow too long. Instead, they must trim it regularly. [21]The priests must not drink wine before entering the inner courtyard. [22]They may choose their wives only from among the virgins of Israel or the widows of the priests. They may not marry other widows or divorced women. [23]They will teach my people the difference between what is holy and what is common, what is ceremonially clean and unclean.

[24]"They will serve as judges to resolve any disagreements among my people. Their decisions must be based on my regulations. And the priests themselves must obey my instructions and decrees at all the sacred festivals, and see to it that the Sabbaths are set apart as holy days.

[25]"A priest must not defile himself by being in the presence of a dead person unless it is his father, mother, child, brother, or unmarried sister. In such cases it is permitted. [26]Even then, he can return to his Temple duties only after being ceremonially cleansed and then waiting for seven days. [27]The first day he returns to work and enters the inner courtyard and the sanctuary, he must offer a sin offering for himself, says the Sovereign LORD.

[28]"The priests will not have any property or possession of land, for I alone am their special possession. [29]Their food will come from the gifts and sacrifices brought to the Temple by the people—the grain offerings, the sin offerings, and the guilt offerings. Whatever anyone sets apart* for the LORD will belong to the priests. [30]The first of the ripe fruits and all the gifts brought to the LORD will go to the priests. The first samples of each grain harvest and the first of your flour must also be given to the priests so the LORD will bless your homes. [31]The priests may not eat meat from any bird or animal that dies a natural death or that dies after being attacked by another animal.

CHAPTER 45

Division of the Land

"When you divide the land among the tribes of Israel, you must set aside a section for the LORD as his holy portion. This piece of land will be 8⅓ miles long and 6⅔ miles wide.* The entire area will be holy. [2]A section of this land, measuring 875 feet by 875 feet,* will be set aside for the Temple. An additional strip of land 87½ feet* wide is to be left empty all around it. [3]Within the larger sacred area, measure out a portion of land 8⅓ miles long and 3⅓ miles wide.* Within it the sanctuary of the Most Holy Place will be located. [4]This area will be holy, set aside for the priests who minister to the LORD in the sanctuary. They will use it for their homes, and my Temple will be located within it. [5]The strip of sacred land next to it, also 8⅓ miles long and 3⅓ miles wide, will be a living area for the Levites who work at the Temple. It will be their possession and a place for their towns.*

[6]"Adjacent to the larger sacred area will be a section of land 8⅓ miles long and 1⅔ miles wide.* This will be set aside for a city where anyone in Israel can live.

[7]"Two special sections of land will be set apart for the prince. One section will share a border with the east side of the sacred lands and city, and the second section will share a border on the west side. Then the far eastern and western borders of the prince's lands will line up with the eastern and western boundaries of the tribal areas. [8]These sections of land will be the prince's allotment. Then my princes will no longer oppress and rob my people; they will assign the rest of the land to the people, giving an allotment to each tribe.

Rules for the Princes

[9]"For this is what the Sovereign LORD says: Enough, you princes of Israel! Stop your violence and oppression and do what is just and right. Quit robbing and cheating my people out of their land. Stop expelling them from their homes, says the Sovereign LORD. [10]Use only honest weights and scales and honest measures, both dry and liquid.* [11]The homer* will be your standard unit for measuring volume. The ephah and the bath* will each measure one-tenth of a homer. [12]The

44:29 The Hebrew term used here refers to the complete consecration of things or people to the LORD, either by destroying them or by giving them as an offering. **45:1** As in Greek version, which reads *25,000 cubits* [13.3 kilometers] *long and 20,000 cubits* [10.6 kilometers] *wide;* Hebrew reads *25,000 cubits long and 10,000 cubits* [3⅓ miles or 5.3 kilometers] *wide*. Compare 45:3, 5; 48:9. **45:2a** Hebrew *500 cubits* [265 meters] *by 500 cubits, a square*. **45:2b** Hebrew *50 cubits* [26.5 meters]. **45:3** Hebrew *25,000 cubits* [13.3 kilometers] *long and 10,000 cubits* [5.3 kilometers] *wide;* also in 45:5. **45:5** As in Greek version; Hebrew reads *They will have as their possession 20 rooms*. **45:6** Hebrew *25,000 cubits* [13.3 kilometers] *long and 5,000 cubits* [2.65 kilometers] *wide*. **45:10** Hebrew *use honest scales, an honest ephah, and an honest bath*. **45:11a** The *homer* measures about 40 gallons or 182 liters. **45:11b** The *ephah* is a dry measure; the *bath* is a liquid measure.

Buyer Beware?

Colton had a pile of stuff to sell at his family's garage sale. His mom said, "You can keep the money you earn." Colton wanted to get enough money to buy a new skateboard. So he pulled out his old ten-speed bike. He knew that the chain always fell off after he rode it for a while, and the brakes squealed and stuck. But Colton figured no one would test ride the bike, and he could probably get twenty dollars for it. He would clean it up, too, so what did it matter? What do you think Colton should do? Read Ezekiel 45:9-10 to see what God values.

standard unit for weight will be the silver shekel.* One shekel will consist of twenty gerahs, and sixty shekels will be equal to one mina.*

Special Offerings and Celebrations

13"You must give this tax to the prince: one bushel of wheat or barley for every 60* you harvest, 14one percent of your olive oil,* 15and one sheep or goat for every 200 in your flocks in Israel. These will be the grain offerings, burnt offerings, and peace offerings that will make atonement for the people who bring them, says the Sovereign Lord. 16All the people of Israel must join in bringing these offerings to the prince. 17The prince will be required to provide offerings that are given at the religious festivals, the new moon celebrations, the Sabbath days, and all other similar occasions. He will provide the sin offerings, burnt offerings, grain offerings, liquid offerings, and peace offerings to purify the people of Israel, making them right with the Lord.*

18"This is what the Sovereign Lord says: In early spring, on the first day of each new year,* sacrifice a young bull with no defects to purify the Temple. 19The priest will take blood from this sin offering and put it on the doorposts of the Temple, the four corners of the upper ledge of the altar, and the gateposts at the entrance to the inner courtyard. 20Do this also on the seventh day of the new year for anyone who has sinned through error or ignorance. In this way, you will purify* the Temple.

21"On the fourteenth day of the first month,* you must celebrate the Passover. This festival will last for seven days. The bread you eat during that time must be made without yeast. 22On the day of Passover the prince will provide a young bull as a sin offering for himself and the people of Israel. 23On each of the seven days of the feast he will prepare a burnt offering to the Lord, consisting of seven young bulls and seven rams without defects. A male goat will also be given each day for a sin offering. 24The prince will provide a basket of flour as a grain offering and a gallon of olive oil* with each young bull and ram.

25"During the seven days of the Festival of Shelters, which occurs every year in early au-

45:12a The *shekel* weighs about 0.4 ounces or 11 grams. **45:12b** Elsewhere the *mina* is equated to 50 shekels. **45:13** Hebrew *⅙ of an ephah from each homer of wheat and ⅙ of an ephah from each homer of barley.* **45:14** Hebrew *the portion of oil, measured by the bath, is 1/10 of a bath from each cor, which consists of 10 baths or 1 homer, for 10 baths are equivalent to a homer.* **45:17** Or *to make atonement for the people of Israel.* **45:18** Hebrew *On the first day of the first month,* of the Hebrew calendar. This day in the ancient Hebrew lunar calendar occurred in March or April. **45:20** Or *will make atonement for.* **45:21** This day in the ancient Hebrew lunar calendar occurred in late March, April, or early May. **45:24** Hebrew *an ephah* [20 quarts or 22 liters] *of flour . . . and a hin* [3.8 liters] *of olive oil.*

tumn,* the prince will provide these same sacrifices for the sin offering, the burnt offering, and the grain offering, along with the required olive oil.

CHAPTER 46

"This is what the Sovereign LORD says: The east gateway of the inner courtyard will be closed during the six workdays each week, but it will be open on Sabbath days and the days of new moon celebrations. [2]The prince will enter the entry room of the gateway from the outside. Then he will stand by the gatepost while the priest offers his burnt offering and peace offering. He will bow down in worship inside the gateway passage and then go back out the way he came. The gateway will not be closed until evening. [3]The common people will bow down and worship the LORD in front of this gateway on Sabbath days and the days of new moon celebrations.

[4]"Each Sabbath day the prince will present to the LORD a burnt offering of six lambs and one ram, all with no defects. [5]He will present a grain offering of a basket of choice flour to go with the ram and whatever amount of flour he chooses to go with each lamb, and he is to offer one gallon of olive oil* for each basket of flour. [6]At the new moon celebrations, he will bring one young bull, six lambs, and one ram, all with no defects. [7]With the young bull he must bring a basket of choice flour for a grain offering. With the ram he must bring another basket of flour. And with each lamb he is to bring whatever amount of flour he chooses to give. With each basket of flour he must offer one gallon of olive oil.

[8]"The prince must enter the gateway through the entry room, and he must leave the same way. [9]But when the people come in through the north gateway to worship the LORD during the religious festivals, they must leave by the south gateway. And those who entered through the south gateway must leave by the north gateway. They must never leave by the same gateway they came in, but must always use the opposite gateway. [10]The prince will enter and leave with the people on these occasions.

[11]"So at the special feasts and sacred festivals, the grain offering will be a basket of choice flour with each young bull, another basket of flour with each ram, and as much flour as the prince chooses to give with each lamb. Give one gallon of olive oil with each basket of flour. [12]When the prince offers a voluntary burnt offering or peace offering to the LORD, the east gateway to the inner courtyard will be opened for him, and he will offer his sacrifices as he does on Sabbath days. Then he will leave, and the gateway will be shut behind him.

[13]"Each morning you must sacrifice a one-year-old lamb with no defects as a burnt offering to the LORD. [14]With the lamb, a grain offering must also be given to the LORD—about three quarts of flour with a third of a gallon of olive oil* to moisten the choice flour. This will be a permanent law for you. [15]The lamb, the grain offering, and the olive oil must be given as a daily sacrifice every morning without fail.

[16]"This is what the Sovereign LORD says: If the prince gives a gift of land to one of his sons as his inheritance, it will belong to him and his descendants forever. [17]But if the prince gives a gift of land from his inheritance to one of his servants, the servant may keep it only until the Year of Jubilee, which comes every fiftieth year.* At that time the land will return to the prince. But when the prince gives gifts to his sons, those gifts will be permanent. [18]And the prince may never take anyone's property by force. If he gives property to his sons, it must be from his own land, for I do not want any of my people unjustly evicted from their property."

The Temple Kitchens

[19]In my vision, the man brought me through the entrance beside the gateway and led me to the sacred rooms assigned to the priests, which faced toward the north. He showed me a place at the extreme west end of these rooms. [20]He explained, "This is where the priests will cook the meat from the guilt offerings and sin offerings and bake the flour from the grain offerings into bread. They will

45:25 Hebrew *the festival which begins on the fifteenth day of the seventh month* (see Lev 23:34). This day in the ancient Hebrew lunar calendar occurred in late September, October, or early November. **46:5** Hebrew *an ephah* (20 quarts or 22 liters) *of choice flour . . . a hin* (3.8 liters) *of olive oil;* similarly in 46:7, 11. **46:14** Hebrew *⅙ of an ephah* (3.7 liters) *of flour with ⅓ of a hin* (1.3 liters) *of olive oil.* **46:17** Hebrew *until the Year of Release;* see Lev 25:8-17.

do it here to avoid carrying the sacrifices through the outer courtyard and endangering the people by transmitting holiness to them."

21Then he brought me back to the outer courtyard and led me to each of its four corners. In each corner I saw an enclosure. 22Each of these enclosures was 70 feet long and 52½ feet wide,* surrounded by walls. 23Along the inside of these walls was a ledge of stone with fireplaces under the ledge all the way around. 24The man said to me, "These are the kitchens to be used by the Temple assistants to boil the sacrifices offered by the people."

CHAPTER 47

The River of Healing

In my vision, the man brought me back to the entrance of the Temple. There I saw a stream flowing east from beneath the door of the Temple and passing to the right of the altar on its south side. 2The man brought me outside the wall through the north gateway and led me around to the eastern entrance. There I could see the water flowing out through the south side of the east gateway.

3Measuring as he went, he took me along the stream for 1,750 feet* and then led me across. The water was up to my ankles. 4He measured off another 1,750 feet and led me across again. This time the water was up to my knees. After another 1,750 feet, it was up to my waist. 5Then he measured another 1,750 feet, and the river was too deep to walk across. It was deep enough to swim in, but too deep to walk through.

6He asked me, "Have you been watching, son of man?" Then he led me back along the riverbank. 7When I returned, I was surprised by the sight of many trees growing on both sides of the river. 8Then he said to me, "This river flows east through the desert into the valley of the Dead Sea.* The waters of this stream will make the salty waters of the Dead Sea fresh and pure. 9There will be swarms of living things wherever the water of this river flows. Fish will abound in the Dead Sea, for its waters will become fresh. Life will flourish wherever this water flows. 10Fishermen will stand along the shores of the Dead Sea. All the way from En-gedi to En-eglaim, the shores will be covered with nets drying in the sun. Fish of every kind will fill the Dead Sea, just as they fill the Mediterranean.* 11But the marshes and swamps will not be purified; they will still be salty. 12Fruit trees of all kinds will grow along both sides of the river. The leaves of these trees will never turn brown and fall, and there will always be fruit on their branches. There will be a new crop every month, for they are watered by the river flowing from the Temple. The fruit will be for food and the leaves for healing."

Boundaries for the Land

13This is what the Sovereign LORD says: "Divide the land in this way for the twelve tribes of Israel: The descendants of Joseph will be given two shares of land.* 14Otherwise each tribe will receive an equal share. I took a solemn oath and swore that I would give this land to your ancestors, and it will now come to you as your possession.

15"These are the boundaries of the land: The northern border will run from the Mediterranean toward Hethlon, then on through Lebo-hamath to Zedad; 16then it will run to Berothah and Sibraim, which are on the border between Damascus and Hamath, and finally to Hazer-hatticon, on the border of Hauran. 17So the northern border will run from the Mediterranean to Hazar-enan, on the border between Hamath to the north and Damascus to the south.

18"The eastern border starts at a point between Hauran and Damascus and runs south along the Jordan River between Israel and Gilead, past the Dead Sea* and as far south as Tamar.* This will be the eastern border.

19"The southern border will go west from Tamar to the waters of Meribah at Kadesh* and then follow the course of the Brook of Egypt to the Mediterranean. This will be the southern border.

20"On the west side, the Mediterranean itself will be your border from the southern border to the point where the

46:22 Hebrew *40 cubits* [21.2 meters] *long and 30 cubits* [15.9 meters] *wide.* **47:3** Hebrew *1,000 cubits* [530 meters]; also in 47:4, 5. **47:8** Hebrew *the sea.* **47:10** Hebrew *the great sea;* also in 47:15, 17, 19, 20. **47:13** It was important to retain twelve portions of land. Since Levi had no portion, the descendants of Joseph's sons, Ephraim and Manasseh, received land as two tribes. **47:18a** Hebrew *the eastern sea.* **47:18b** As in Greek version; Hebrew reads *you will measure.* **47:19** Hebrew *waters of Meribath-kadesh.*

northern border begins, opposite Lebo-hamath.

21"Divide the land within these boundaries among the tribes of Israel. 22Distribute the land as an allotment for yourselves and for the foreigners who have joined you and are raising their families among you. They will be like native-born Israelites to you and will receive an allotment among the tribes. 23These foreigners are to be given land within the territory of the tribe with whom they now live. I, the Sovereign LORD, have spoken!

How should we treat people who are different from us?

Distribute the land . . . for yourselves and for the foreigners who have joined you and are raising their families among you. They will be like native-born Israelites.

EZEKIEL 47:22

CHAPTER 48

Division of the Land

"Here is the list of the tribes of Israel and the territory each is to receive. The territory of Dan is in the extreme north. Its boundary line follows the Hethlon road to Lebo-hamath and then runs on to Hazar-enan on the border of Damascus, with Hamath to the north. Dan's territory extends all the way across the land of Israel from east to west.

2"Asher's territory lies south of Dan's and also extends from east to west. 3Naphtali's land lies south of Asher's, also extending from east to west. 4Then comes Manasseh south of Naphtali, and its territory also extends from east to west. 5South of Manasseh is Ephraim, 6and then Reuben, 7and then Judah, all of whose boundaries extend from east to west.

8"South of Judah is the land set aside for a special purpose. It will be 8⅓ miles* wide and will extend as far east and west as the tribal territories, with the Temple at the center.

9"The area set aside for the LORD's Temple will be 8⅓ miles long and 6⅔ miles wide.* 10For the priests there will be a strip of land measuring 8⅓ miles long by 3⅓ miles wide,* with the LORD's Temple at the center. 11This area is set aside for the ordained priests, the descendants of Zadok who served me faithfully and did not go astray with the people of Israel and the rest of the Levites. 12It will be their special portion when the land is distributed, the most sacred land of all. Next to the priests' territory will lie the land where the other Levites will live.

13"The land allotted to the Levites will be the same size and shape as that belonging to the priests—8⅓ miles long and 3⅓ miles wide. Together these portions of land will measure 8⅓ miles long by 6⅔ miles wide.* 14None of this special land may ever be sold or traded or used by others, for it belongs to the LORD; it is set apart as holy.

15"An additional strip of land 8⅓ miles long by 1⅔ miles wide,* south of the sacred Temple area, will be allotted for public use—homes, pasturelands, and common lands, with a city at the center. 16The city will measure 1½ miles* on each side—north, south, east, and west. 17Open lands will surround the city for 150 yards* in every direction. 18Outside the city there will be a farming area that stretches 3⅓ miles to the east and 3⅓ miles to the west* along the border of the sacred area. This farmland will produce food for the people working in the city. 19Those who come from the various tribes to work in the city may farm it. 20This entire area—including the sacred lands and the city—is a square that measures 8⅓ miles* on each side.

21"The areas that remain, to the east and to the west of the sacred lands and the city, will

48:8 Hebrew *25,000 cubits* [13.3 kilometers]. **48:9** As in one Greek manuscript and the Greek reading in 45:1: *25,000 cubits* [13.3 kilometers] *long and 20,000 cubits* [10.6 kilometers] *wide*; Hebrew reads *25,000 cubits long and 10,000 cubits* [3⅓ miles or 5.3 kilometers] *wide*. Similarly in 48:13b. Compare 45:1-5; 48:10-13. **48:10** Hebrew *25,000 cubits* [13.3 kilometers] *long by 10,000 cubits* [5.3 kilometers] *wide*; also in 48:13a. **48:13** See note on 48:9. **48:15** Hebrew *25,000 cubits* [13.3 kilometers] *long by 5,000 cubits* [2.65 kilometers] *wide*. **48:16** Hebrew *4,500 cubits* [2.4 kilometers]; also in 48:30, 32, 33, 34. **48:17** Hebrew *250 cubits* [133 meters]. **48:18** Hebrew *10,000 cubits* [5.3 kilometers] *to the east and 10,000 cubits to the west*. **48:20** Hebrew *25,000 cubits* [13.3 kilometers]; also in 48:21.

belong to the prince. Each of these areas will be 8⅓ miles wide, extending in opposite directions to the eastern and western borders of Israel, with the sacred lands and the sanctuary of the Temple in the center. [22]So the prince's land will include everything between the territories allotted to Judah and Benjamin, except for the areas set aside for the sacred lands and the city.

[23]"These are the territories allotted to the rest of the tribes. Benjamin's territory lies just south of the prince's lands, and it extends across the entire land of Israel from east to west. [24]South of Benjamin's territory lies that of Simeon, also extending across the land from east to west. [25]Next is the territory of Issachar with the same eastern and western boundaries.

[26]"Then comes the territory of Zebulun, which also extends across the land from east to west. [27]The territory of Gad is just south of Zebulun with the same borders to the east and west. [28]The southern border of Gad runs from Tamar to the waters of Meribah at Kadesh* and then follows the Brook of Egypt to the Mediterranean.*

[29]"These are the allotments that will be set aside for each tribe's exclusive possession. I, the Sovereign LORD, have spoken!

The Gates of the City

[30]"These will be the exits to the city: On the north wall, which is 1½ miles long, [31]there will be three gates, each one named after a tribe of Israel. The first will be named for Reuben, the second for Judah, and the third for Levi. [32]On the east wall, also 1½ miles long, the gates will be named for Joseph, Benjamin, and Dan. [33]The south wall, also 1½ miles long, will have gates named for Simeon, Issachar, and Zebulun. [34]And on the west wall, also 1½ miles long, the gates will be named for Gad, Asher, and Naphtali.

[35]"The distance around the entire city will be 6 miles.* And from that day the name of the city will be 'The LORD Is There.'*"

48:28a Hebrew *waters of Meribath-kadesh.* **48:28b** Hebrew *the great sea.* **48:35a** Hebrew *18,000 cubits* [9.6 kilometers]. **48:35b** Hebrew *Yahweh Shammah.*

Daniel

WHO
Daniel, King Nebuchadnezzar, Shadrach, Meshach, Abednego, Belshazzar, and Darius.

WHERE
In Babylon.

WHEN
Around 535 BC while some of the Jews were captive in Babylon.

WHY
To tell about Jews who stayed faithful, and to show that God is in control.

Those who lead many to righteousness will shine like the stars forever.
DANIEL 12:3

Daniel, a foreigner in Babylon, served in a high government position. He always did what was right, though people pressured him to do wrong things. He even prayed to God when it was against the law. Because Daniel obeyed God, he was able to do some amazing things. He made God look good to those around him.

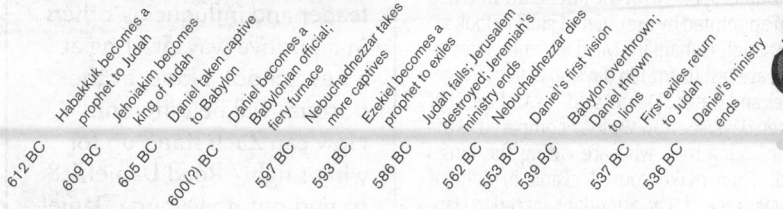

ASK GOD TO GIVE YOU COURAGEOUS FAITH LIKE DANIEL HAD.

CHAPTER 1

Daniel in Nebuchadnezzar's Court

During the third year of King Jehoiakim's reign in Judah,* King Nebuchadnezzar of Babylon came to Jerusalem and besieged it. [2]The Lord gave him victory over King Jehoiakim of Judah and permitted him to take some of the sacred objects from the Temple of God. So Nebuchadnezzar took them back to the land of Babylonia* and placed them in the treasure-house of his god.

[3]Then the king ordered Ashpenaz, his chief of staff, to bring to the palace some of the young men of Judah's royal family and

1:1 This event occurred in 605 B.C., during the third year of Jehoiakim's reign (according to the calendar system in which the new year begins in the spring). **1:2** Hebrew *the land of Shinar*.

other noble families, who had been brought to Babylon as captives. 4"Select only strong, healthy, and good-looking young men," he said. "Make sure they are well versed in every branch of learning, are gifted with knowledge and good judgment, and are suited to serve in the royal palace. Train these young men in the language and literature of Babylon.*" 5The king assigned them a daily ration of food and wine from his own kitchens. They were to be trained for three years, and then they would enter the royal service.

6Daniel, Hananiah, Mishael, and Azariah were four of the young men chosen, all from the tribe of Judah. 7The chief of staff renamed them with these Babylonian names:

Daniel was called Belteshazzar.
Hananiah was called Shadrach.
Mishael was called Meshach.
Azariah was called Abednego.

8But Daniel was determined not to defile himself by eating the food and wine given to them by the king. He asked the chief of staff for permission not to eat these unacceptable foods. 9Now God had given the chief of staff both respect and affection for Daniel. 10But he responded, "I am afraid of my lord the king, who has ordered that you eat this food and wine. If you become pale and thin compared to the other youths your age, I am afraid the king will have me beheaded."

11Daniel spoke with the attendant who had been appointed by the chief of staff to look after Daniel, Hananiah, Mishael, and Azariah. 12"Please test us for ten days on a diet of vegetables and water," Daniel said. 13"At the end of the ten days, see how we look compared to the other young men who are eating the king's food. Then make your decision in light of what you see." 14The attendant agreed to Daniel's suggestion and tested them for ten days.

15At the end of the ten days, Daniel and his three friends looked healthier and better nourished than the young men who had been eating the food assigned by the king. 16So after that, the attendant fed them only vegetables instead of the food and wine provided for the others.

17God gave these four young men an unusual aptitude for understanding every aspect of literature and wisdom. And God gave Daniel the special ability to interpret the meanings of visions and dreams.

18When the training period ordered by the king was completed, the chief of staff brought all the young men to King Nebuchadnezzar. 19The king talked with them, and no

MAKE UP YOUR MIND

Next year Zach will go to a new school much larger than his old one. He has heard stories about kids at that school—how smoking and drinking are common and how swearing is acceptable. Zach knows that the pressure to fit in and do what the other kids do will be great. He has never experienced that. Zach is used to being a leader and influencing others in a positive way. Starting at a new school, alone, at the bottom, will be different. How can Zach stand up for what's right? Read Daniel 1:8 to find out how young Daniel handled a similar situation.

1:4 Or *of the Chaldeans.*

one impressed him as much as Daniel, Hananiah, Mishael, and Azariah. So they entered the royal service. [20]Whenever the king consulted them in any matter requiring wisdom and balanced judgment, he found them ten times more capable than any of the magicians and enchanters in his entire kingdom.

[21]Daniel remained in the royal service until the first year of the reign of King Cyrus.*

CHAPTER 2

Nebuchadnezzar's Dream

One night during the second year of his reign,* Nebuchadnezzar had such disturbing dreams that he couldn't sleep. [2]He called in his magicians, enchanters, sorcerers, and astrologers,* and he demanded that they tell him what he had dreamed. As they stood before the king, [3]he said, "I have had a dream that deeply troubles me, and I must know what it means."

[4]Then the astrologers answered the king in Aramaic,* "Long live the king! Tell us the dream, and we will tell you what it means."

[5]But the king said to the astrologers, "I am serious about this. If you don't tell me what my dream was and what it means, you will be torn limb from limb, and your houses will be turned into heaps of rubble! [6]But if you tell me what I dreamed and what the dream means, I will give you many wonderful gifts and honors. Just tell me the dream and what it means!"

[7]They said again, "Please, Your Majesty. Tell us the dream, and we will tell you what it means."

[8]The king replied, "I know what you are doing! You're stalling for time because you know I am serious when I say, [9]'If you don't tell me the dream, you are doomed.' So you have conspired to tell me lies, hoping I will change my mind. But tell me the dream, and then I'll know that you can tell me what it means."

[10]The astrologers replied to the king, "No one on earth can tell the king his dream! And no king, however great and powerful, has ever asked such a thing of any magician, enchanter, or astrologer! [11]The king's demand is impossible. No one except the gods can tell you your dream, and they do not live here among people."

[12]The king was furious when he heard this, and he ordered that all the wise men of Babylon be executed. [13]And because of the king's decree, men were sent to find and kill Daniel and his friends.

[14]When Arioch, the commander of the king's guard, came to kill them, Daniel handled the situation with wisdom and discretion. [15]He asked Arioch, "Why has the king issued such a harsh decree?" So Arioch told him all that had happened. [16]Daniel went at once to see the king and requested more time to tell the king what the dream meant.

[17]Then Daniel went home and told his friends Hananiah, Mishael, and Azariah what had happened. [18]He urged them to ask the God of heaven to show them his mercy by telling them the secret, so they would not be executed along with the other wise men of Babylon. [19]That night the secret was revealed to Daniel in a vision. Then Daniel praised the God of heaven. [20]He said,

"Praise the name of God forever and ever,
for he has all wisdom and power.
[21] He controls the course of world events;
he removes kings and sets up other kings.
He gives wisdom to the wise
and knowledge to the scholars.
[22] He reveals deep and mysterious things
and knows what lies hidden in darkness,
though he is surrounded by light.
[23] I thank and praise you, God of my ancestors,
for you have given me wisdom and strength.
You have told me what we asked of you
and revealed to us what the king demanded."

Daniel Interprets the Dream

[24]Then Daniel went in to see Arioch, whom the king had ordered to execute the wise men of Babylon. Daniel said to him, "Don't kill the wise men. Take me to the king, and I will tell him the meaning of his dream."

[25]Arioch quickly took Daniel to the king

1:21 Cyrus began his reign (over Babylon) in 539 B.C. **2:1** The second year of Nebuchadnezzar's reign was 603 B.C. **2:2** Or *Chaldeans;* also in 2:4, 5, 10. **2:4** The original text from this point through chapter 7 is in Aramaic.

and said, "I have found one of the captives
from Judah who will tell the king the meaning
of his dream!"
[26]The king said to Daniel (also known as
Belteshazzar), "Is this true? Can you tell me
what my dream was and what it means?"
[27]Daniel replied, "There are no wise men,
enchanters, magicians, or fortune-tellers who
can reveal the king's secret. [28]But there is a
God in heaven who reveals secrets, and he has
shown King Nebuchadnezzar what will hap-
pen in the future. Now I will tell you your
dream and the visions you saw as you lay on
your bed.
[29]"While Your Majesty was sleeping, you
dreamed about coming events. He who re-
veals secrets has shown you what is going to
happen. [30]And it is not because I am wiser
than anyone else that I know the secret of
your dream, but because God wants you to
understand what was in your heart.
[31]"In your vision, Your Majesty, you saw
standing before you a huge, shining statue of
a man. It was a frightening sight. [32]The head
of the statue was made of fine gold. Its chest
and arms were silver, its belly and thighs were
bronze, [33]its legs were iron, and its feet were a
combination of iron and baked clay. [34]As you
watched, a rock was cut from a mountain, but
not by human hands. It struck the feet of iron
and clay, smashing them to bits. [35]The whole
statue was crushed into small pieces of iron,
clay, bronze, silver, and gold. Then the wind
blew them away without a trace, like chaff on
a threshing floor. But the rock that knocked
the statue down became a great mountain
that covered the whole earth.
[36]"That was the dream. Now we will tell the
king what it means. [37]Your Majesty, you are
the greatest of kings. The God of heaven has
given you sovereignty, power, strength, and
honor. [38]He has made you the ruler over all
the inhabited world and has put even the wild
animals and birds under your control. You
are the head of gold.
[39]"But after your kingdom comes to an end,
another kingdom, inferior to yours, will rise
to take your place. After that kingdom has
fallen, yet a third kingdom, represented by
bronze, will rise to rule the world. [40]Following
that kingdom, there will be a fourth one, as
strong as iron. That kingdom will smash and
crush all previous empires, just as iron
smashes and crushes everything it strikes.
[41]The feet and toes you saw were a combina-
tion of iron and baked clay, showing that this
kingdom will be divided. Like iron mixed
with clay, it will have some of the strength of
iron. [42]But while some parts of it will be as
strong as iron, other parts will be as weak as
clay. [43]This mixture of iron and clay also
shows that these kingdoms will try to
strengthen themselves by forming alliances
with each other through intermarriage. But
they will not hold together, just as iron and
clay do not mix.
[44]"During the reigns of those kings, the
God of heaven will set up a kingdom that will
never be destroyed or conquered. It will crush
all these kingdoms into nothingness, and it
will stand forever. [45]That is the meaning of
the rock cut from the mountain, though not
by human hands, that crushed to pieces the
statue of iron, bronze, clay, silver, and gold.
The great God was showing the king what will
happen in the future. The dream is true, and
its meaning is certain."

Nebuchadnezzar Rewards Daniel

[46]Then King Nebuchadnezzar threw himself
down before Daniel and worshiped him, and
he commanded his people to offer sacrifices
and burn sweet incense before him. [47]The
king said to Daniel, "Truly, your God is the
greatest of gods, the Lord over kings, a
revealer of mysteries, for you have been able
to reveal this secret."
[48]Then the king appointed Daniel to a high
position and gave him many valuable gifts. He
made Daniel ruler over the whole province of
Babylon, as well as chief over all his wise men.
[49]At Daniel's request, the king appointed Sha-
drach, Meshach, and Abednego to be in
charge of all the affairs of the province of
Babylon, while Daniel remained in the king's
court.

CHAPTER 3

Nebuchadnezzar's Gold Statue

King Nebuchadnezzar made a gold statue
ninety feet tall and nine feet wide* and set it
up on the plain of Dura in the province of

3:1 Aramaic *60 cubits* [27 meters] *tall and 6 cubits* [2.7 meters] *wide.*

I never seemed to have trouble making friends . . . until junior high. All of a sudden, everything changed. I didn't have much in common with most of the kids at school anymore. They always talked about movies that I didn't watch and video games that I wasn't allowed to play. And once they found out that I didn't do that stuff, I was an easy target. Even my two or three remaining friends from elementary school started avoiding me.

I started to wonder why it was so hard to make friends. I began to think, *Maybe if I start doing what the other kids do and talking the way they do, they might accept me.* But I knew that a lot of what they did was wrong. I had to decide. Was I going to change to be like them or continue to live the way I knew I should?

That's when I noticed Anthony, a guy from my school who just started going to church this year. He used to hang out with a bunch of jerks at my school, but recently he began making new friends. It was pretty amazing, actually. At lunch I would see him go over and sit next to someone sitting all alone. I know firsthand . . . because once he sat with me.

Anthony was all the inspiration I needed. I decided not to try to get others to like me by doing wrong things. Instead, I went out on a limb and started making new friends. I made more friends without going against what I believed. And some of those guys are my best friends today.

Read how Daniel's three friends refused to go with the crowd in Daniel 3. For more on what the Bible has to say about standing up for what you know is right, look up Romans 12:2.

Babylon. [2]Then he sent messages to the high officers, officials, governors, advisers, treasurers, judges, magistrates, and all the provincial officials to come to the dedication of the statue he had set up. [3]So all these officials* came and stood before the statue King Nebuchadnezzar had set up.

[4]Then a herald shouted out, "People of all races and nations and languages, listen to the king's command! [5]When you hear the sound of the horn, flute, zither, lyre, harp, pipes, and other musical instruments,* bow to the ground to worship King Nebuchadnezzar's gold statue. [6]Anyone who refuses to obey will immediately be thrown into a blazing furnace."

[7]So at the sound of the musical instruments,* all the people, whatever their race or nation or language, bowed to the ground and worshiped the gold statue that King Nebuchadnezzar had set up.

[8]But some of the astrologers* went to the king and informed on the Jews. [9]They said to King Nebuchadnezzar, "Long live the king! [10]You issued a decree requiring all the people to bow down and worship the gold statue when they hear the sound of the horn, flute, zither, lyre, harp, pipes, and other musical instruments. [11]That decree also states that those who refuse to obey must be thrown into a blazing furnace. [12]But there are some Jews—Shadrach, Meshach, and Abednego—whom you have put in charge of the province of Babylon. They pay no attention to you, Your Majesty. They refuse to serve your gods and do not worship the gold statue you have set up."

[13]Then Nebuchadnezzar flew into a rage and ordered that Shadrach, Meshach, and Abednego be brought before him. When they were brought in, [14]Nebuchadnezzar said to them, "Is it true, Shadrach, Meshach, and Abednego, that you refuse to serve my gods or to worship the gold statue I have set up? [15]I will give you one more chance to bow down and worship the statue I have made when you hear the sound of the musical instruments.* But if you refuse, you will be thrown immediately into the blazing furnace. And then what god will be able to rescue you from my power?"

[16]Shadrach, Meshach, and Abednego replied, "O Nebuchadnezzar, we do not need to

3:3 Aramaic *the high officers, officials, governors, advisers, treasurers, judges, magistrates, and all the provincial officials.* **3:5** The identification of some of these musical instruments is uncertain. **3:7** Aramaic *the horn, flute, zither, lyre, harp, and other musical instruments.* **3:8** Aramaic *Chaldeans.* **3:15** Aramaic *the horn, flute, zither, lyre, harp, pipes, and other musical instruments.*

IS IT OK?

IS IT OK TO CHANGE WHO I AM TO FIT IN?

A chameleon is a sneaky little lizard that changes its color to match its background. Nice trick, huh? For a *lizard!* But blending in is not always the best choice. Some people act one way when they're at church or home, but then they act totally different when they try to blend in with their friends. Daniel's three buddies had an easy opportunity to be chameleons. They were ordered to bow down to the king's gold statue . . . or die. They didn't do it, though. Instead, they did what was risky but right—and God protected them for it (see Daniel 3:13-28). The next time you're tempted to just blend in, choose instead to stand out for God.

defend ourselves before you. [17]If we are thrown into the blazing furnace, the God whom we serve is able to save us. He will rescue us from your power, Your Majesty. [18]But even if he doesn't, we want to make it clear to you, Your Majesty, that we will never serve your gods or worship the gold statue you have set up."

The Blazing Furnace

[19]Nebuchadnezzar was so furious with Shadrach, Meshach, and Abednego that his face became distorted with rage. He commanded that the furnace be heated seven times hotter than usual. [20]Then he ordered some of the strongest men of his army to bind Shadrach, Meshach, and Abednego and throw them into the blazing furnace. [21]So they tied them up and threw them into the furnace, fully dressed in their pants, turbans, robes, and other garments. [22]And because the king, in his anger, had demanded such a hot fire in the furnace, the flames killed the soldiers as they threw the three men in. [23]So Shadrach, Meshach, and Abednego, securely tied, fell into the roaring flames.

[24]But suddenly, Nebuchadnezzar jumped up in amazement and exclaimed to his advisers, "Didn't we tie up three men and throw them into the furnace?"

"Yes, Your Majesty, we certainly did," they replied.

[25]"Look!" Nebuchadnezzar shouted. "I see four men, unbound, walking around in the fire unharmed! And the fourth looks like a god*!"

[26]Then Nebuchadnezzar came as close as he could to the door of the flaming furnace and shouted: "Shadrach, Meshach, and Abednego, servants of the Most High God, come out! Come here!"

So Shadrach, Meshach, and Abednego stepped out of the fire. [27]Then the high officers, officials, governors, and advisers crowded around them and saw that the fire had not touched them. Not a hair on their heads was singed, and their clothing was not scorched. They didn't even smell of smoke!

[28]Then Nebuchadnezzar said, "Praise to the God of Shadrach, Meshach, and Abednego! He sent his angel to rescue his servants who trusted in him. They defied the king's command and were willing to die rather than serve or worship any god except their own God. [29]Therefore, I make this decree: If any people, whatever their race or nation or language, speak a word against the God of Shadrach, Meshach, and Abednego, they will be torn limb from limb, and their houses will be turned into heaps of rubble. There is no other god who can rescue like this!"

AMAZING FACTS

Strong soldiers threw three men into a furnace so hot that it killed the soldiers. But the three inside survived without a scorch!

DANIEL 3:19-27

[30]Then the king promoted Shadrach, Meshach, and Abednego to even higher positions in the province of Babylon.

CHAPTER 4

Nebuchadnezzar's Dream about a Tree

[1]*King Nebuchadnezzar sent this message to the people of every race and nation and language throughout the world:

"Peace and prosperity to you!

[2]"I want you all to know about the miraculous signs and wonders the Most High God has performed for me.

[3] How great are his signs,
how powerful his wonders!
His kingdom will last forever,
his rule through all generations.

[4]*"I, Nebuchadnezzar, was living in my palace in comfort and prosperity. [5]But one night I had a dream that frightened

3:25 Aramaic *like a son of the gods.* **4:1** Verses 4:1-3 are numbered 3:31-33 in Aramaic text. **4:4** Verses 4:4-37 are numbered 4:1-34 in Aramaic text.

me; I saw visions that terrified me as I lay
in my bed. [6]So I issued an order calling in
all the wise men of Babylon, so they could
tell me what my dream meant. [7]When all
the magicians, enchanters, astrologers,*
and fortune-tellers came in, I told them
the dream, but they could not tell me what
it meant. [8]At last Daniel came in before
me, and I told him the dream. (He was
named Belteshazzar after my god, and the
spirit of the holy gods is in him.)

[9]"I said to him, 'Belteshazzar, chief of
the magicians, I know that the spirit of the
holy gods is in you and that no mystery is
too great for you to solve. Now tell me
what my dream means.

[10]" 'While I was lying in my bed, this is
what I dreamed. I saw a large tree in the
middle of the earth. [11]The tree grew very
tall and strong, reaching high into the
heavens for all the world to see. [12]It had
fresh green leaves, and it was loaded with
fruit for all to eat. Wild animals lived in
its shade, and birds nested in its branches.
All the world was fed from this tree.

[13]" 'Then as I lay there dreaming, I saw
a messenger,* a holy one, coming down
from heaven. [14]The messenger shouted,

"Cut down the tree and lop off its
branches!
Shake off its leaves and scatter its
fruit!
Chase the wild animals from its shade
and the birds from its branches.
[15] But leave the stump and the roots in the
ground,
bound with a band of iron and
bronze
and surrounded by tender grass.
Now let him be drenched with the dew
of heaven,
and let him live with the wild animals
among the plants of the field.
[16] For seven periods of time,
let him have the mind of a wild
animal
instead of the mind of a human.
[17] For this has been decreed by the mes-
sengers*;
it is commanded by the holy ones,
so that everyone may know
that the Most High rules over the
kingdoms of the world.
He gives them to anyone he chooses—
even to the lowliest of people."

[18]" 'Belteshazzar, that was the dream
that I, King Nebuchadnezzar, had. Now
tell me what it means, for none of the
wise men of my kingdom can do so. But
you can tell me because the spirit of the
holy gods is in you.'

Daniel Explains the Dream

[19]"Upon hearing this, Daniel (also known
as Belteshazzar) was overcome for a time,
frightened by the meaning of the dream.
Then the king said to him, 'Belteshazzar,
don't be alarmed by the dream and what it
means.'

"Belteshazzar replied, 'I wish the events
foreshadowed in this dream would
happen to your enemies, my lord, and not
to you! [20]The tree you saw was growing
very tall and strong, reaching high into the
heavens for all the world to see. [21]It had
fresh green leaves and was loaded with
fruit for all to eat. Wild animals lived in
its shade, and birds nested in its branches.
[22]That tree, Your Majesty, is you. For you
have grown strong and great; your
greatness reaches up to heaven, and your
rule to the ends of the earth.

[23]" 'Then you saw a messenger, a holy
one, coming down from heaven and
saying, "Cut down the tree and destroy it.
But leave the stump and the roots in the
ground, bound with a band of iron and
bronze and surrounded by tender grass.
Let him be drenched with the dew of
heaven. Let him live with the animals of
the field for seven periods of time."

[24]" 'This is what the dream means, Your
Majesty, and what the Most High has
declared will happen to my lord the king.
[25]You will be driven from human society,
and you will live in the fields with the wild
animals. You will eat grass like a cow, and
you will be drenched with the dew of
heaven. Seven periods of time will pass
while you live this way, until you learn that
the Most High rules over the kingdoms of
the world and gives them to anyone he

4:7 Or *Chaldeans*. **4:13** Aramaic *a watcher;* also in 4:23. **4:17** Aramaic *the watchers*.

chooses. [26]But the stump and roots of the tree were left in the ground. This means that you will receive your kingdom back again when you have learned that heaven rules.

[27]" 'King Nebuchadnezzar, please accept my advice. Stop sinning and do what is right. Break from your wicked past and be merciful to the poor. Perhaps then you will continue to prosper.'

The Dream's Fulfillment

[28]"But all these things did happen to King Nebuchadnezzar. [29]Twelve months later he was taking a walk on the flat roof of the royal palace in Babylon. [30]As he looked out across the city, he said, 'Look at this great city of Babylon! By my own mighty power, I have built this beautiful city as my royal residence to display my majestic splendor.'

[31]"While these words were still in his mouth, a voice called down from heaven, 'O King Nebuchadnezzar, this message is for you! You are no longer ruler of this kingdom. [32]You will be driven from human society. You will live in the fields with the wild animals, and you will eat grass like a cow. Seven periods of time will pass while you live this way, until you learn that the Most High rules over the kingdoms of the world and gives them to anyone he chooses.'

[33]"That same hour the judgment was fulfilled, and Nebuchadnezzar was driven from human society. He ate grass like a cow, and he was drenched with the dew of heaven. He lived this way until his hair was as long as eagles' feathers and his nails were like birds' claws.

Nebuchadnezzar Praises God

[34]"After this time had passed, I, Nebuchadnezzar, looked up to heaven. My sanity returned, and I praised and worshiped the Most High and honored the one who lives forever.

His rule is everlasting,
and his kingdom is eternal.
[35] All the people of the earth
are nothing compared to him.
He does as he pleases
among the angels of heaven
and among the people of the earth.
No one can stop him or say to him,
'What do you mean by doing these things?'

[36]"When my sanity returned to me, so did my honor and glory and kingdom. My advisers and nobles sought me out, and I was restored as head of my kingdom, with even greater honor than before.

AMAZING FACTS

As punishment for his pride, King Nebuchadnezzar had to live like a cow for seven years, eating nothing but grass.

DANIEL 4:28-33

[37]"Now I, Nebuchadnezzar, praise and glorify and honor the King of heaven. All his acts are just and true, and he is able to humble the proud."

CHAPTER 5

The Writing on the Wall

Many years later King Belshazzar gave a great feast for 1,000 of his nobles, and he drank wine with them. [2]While Belshazzar was drinking the wine, he gave orders to bring in the gold and silver cups that his predecessor,* Nebuchadnezzar, had taken from the Temple in Jerusalem. He wanted to drink from them with his nobles, his wives, and his concubines. [3]So they brought these gold cups taken from the Temple, the house of God in Jerusalem, and the king and his nobles, his wives, and his concubines drank from them. [4]While they drank from them they praised their idols made of gold, silver, bronze, iron, wood, and stone.

5:2 Aramaic *father;* also in 5:11, 13, 18.

[5]Suddenly, they saw the fingers of a human hand writing on the plaster wall of the king's palace, near the lampstand. The king himself saw the hand as it wrote, [6]and his face turned pale with fright. His knees knocked together in fear and his legs gave way beneath him.

[7]The king shouted for the enchanters, astrologers,* and fortune-tellers to be brought before him. He said to these wise men of Babylon, "Whoever can read this writing and tell me what it means will be dressed in purple robes of royal honor and will have a gold chain placed around his neck. He will become the third highest ruler in the kingdom!"

[8]But when all the king's wise men had come in, none of them could read the writing or tell him what it meant. [9]So the king grew even more alarmed, and his face turned pale. His nobles, too, were shaken.

[10]But when the queen mother heard what was happening, she hurried to the banquet hall. She said to Belshazzar, "Long live the king! Don't be so pale and frightened. [11]There is a man in your kingdom who has within him the spirit of the holy gods. During Nebuchadnezzar's reign, this man was found to have insight, understanding, and wisdom like that of the gods. Your predecessor, the king—your predecessor King Nebuchadnezzar—made him chief over all the magicians, enchanters, astrologers, and fortune-tellers of Babylon. [12]This man Daniel, whom the king named Belteshazzar, has exceptional ability and is filled with divine knowledge and understanding. He can interpret dreams, explain riddles, and solve difficult problems. Call for Daniel, and he will tell you what the writing means."

Daniel Explains the Writing

[13]So Daniel was brought in before the king. The king asked him, "Are you Daniel, one of the exiles brought from Judah by my predecessor, King Nebuchadnezzar? [14]I have heard that you have the spirit of the gods within you and that you are filled with insight, understanding, and wisdom. [15]My wise men and enchanters have tried to read the words on the wall and tell me their meaning, but they cannot do it. [16]I am told that you can give interpretations and solve difficult problems. If you can read these words and tell me their meaning, you will be clothed in purple robes of royal honor, and you will have a gold chain placed around your neck. You will become the third highest ruler in the kingdom."

[17]Daniel answered the king, "Keep your gifts or give them to someone else, but I will tell you what the writing means. [18]Your Majesty, the Most High God gave sovereignty, majesty, glory, and honor to your predecessor, Nebuchadnezzar. [19]He made him so great that people of all races and nations and languages trembled before him in fear. He killed those he wanted to kill and spared those he wanted to spare. He honored those he wanted to honor and disgraced those he wanted to disgrace. [20]But when his heart and mind were puffed up with arrogance, he was brought down from his royal throne and stripped of his glory. [21]He was driven from human society. He was given the mind of a wild animal, and he lived among the wild donkeys. He ate grass like a cow, and he was drenched with the dew of heaven, until he learned that the Most High God rules over the kingdoms of the world and appoints anyone he desires to rule over them.

[22]"You are his successor,* O Belshazzar, and you knew all this, yet you have not humbled yourself. [23]For you have proudly defied the Lord of heaven and have had these cups from his Temple brought before you. You and your nobles and your wives and concubines have been drinking wine from them while praising gods of silver, gold, bronze, iron, wood, and stone—gods that neither see nor hear nor know anything at all. But you have not honored the God who gives you the breath of life and controls your destiny! [24]So God has sent this hand to write this message.

[25]"This is the message that was written: MENE, MENE, TEKEL, and PARSIN. [26]This is what these words mean:

Mene means 'numbered'—God has numbered the days of your reign and has brought it to an end.

[27] *Tekel* means 'weighed'—you have been weighed on the balances and have not measured up.

[28] *Parsin** means 'divided'—your kingdom has been divided and given to the Medes and Persians."

5:7 Or *Chaldeans;* also in 5:11. **5:22** Aramaic *son*. **5:28** Aramaic *Peres*, the singular of *Parsin*.

[29]Then at Belshazzar's command, Daniel was dressed in purple robes, a gold chain was hung around his neck, and he was proclaimed the third highest ruler in the kingdom.

[30]That very night Belshazzar, the Babylonian* king, was killed.*

[31]*And Darius the Mede took over the kingdom at the age of sixty-two.

CHAPTER 6

Daniel in the Lions' Den

[1]*Darius the Mede decided to divide the kingdom into 120 provinces, and he appointed a high officer to rule over each province. [2]The king also chose Daniel and two others as administrators to supervise the high officers and protect the king's interests. [3]Daniel soon proved himself more capable than all the other administrators and high officers. Because of Daniel's great ability, the king made plans to place him over the entire empire.

[4]Then the other administrators and high officers began searching for some fault in the way Daniel was handling government affairs, but they couldn't find anything to criticize or condemn. He was faithful, always responsible, and completely trustworthy. [5]So they concluded, "Our only chance of finding grounds for accusing Daniel will be in connection with the rules of his religion."

[6]So the administrators and high officers went to the king and said, "Long live King Darius! [7]We are all in agreement—we administrators, officials, high officers, advisers, and governors—that the king should make a law that will be strictly enforced. Give orders that for the next thirty days any person who prays to anyone, divine or human—except to you, Your Majesty—will be thrown into the den of lions. [8]And now, Your Majesty, issue and sign this law so it cannot be changed, an official law of the Medes and Persians that cannot be revoked." [9]So King Darius signed the law.

[10]But when Daniel learned that the law had been signed, he went home and knelt down as usual in his upstairs room, with its windows open toward Jerusalem. He prayed three times a day, just as he had always done, giving thanks to his God. [11]Then the officials went together to Daniel's house and found him praying and asking for God's help. [12]So they went straight to the king and reminded him about his law. "Did you not sign a law that for the next thirty days any person who prays to anyone, divine or human—except to you, Your Majesty—will be thrown into the den of lions?"

The Prayer Habit

Vincent is extremely busy—and he loves it. He is on the swim team, plays in the band, and works on the school newspaper. Vincent also volunteers at the hospital and sings in the church choir. Not to mention doing homework. Vincent is *busy*. So when Vincent's best friend, who was having a rough time, came and asked Vincent to pray for him, Vincent said sure. But it just seemed that Vincent could never find the time to fit prayer into his schedule. What would you do? Read Daniel 6:10-23 to learn about Daniel's prayer habits.

5:30a Or *Chaldean*. **5:30b** The Persians and Medes conquered Babylon in October 539 B.C. **5:31** Verse 5:31 is numbered 6:1 in Aramaic text. **6:1** Verses 6:1-28 are numbered 6:2-29 in Aramaic text.

"Yes," the king replied, "that decision stands; it is an official law of the Medes and Persians that cannot be revoked."

13 Then they told the king, "That man Daniel, one of the captives from Judah, is ignoring you and your law. He still prays to his God three times a day."

14 Hearing this, the king was deeply troubled, and he tried to think of a way to save Daniel. He spent the rest of the day looking for a way to get Daniel out of this predicament.

15 In the evening the men went together to the king and said, "Your Majesty, you know that according to the law of the Medes and the Persians, no law that the king signs can be changed."

AMAZING FACTS

Daniel once spent the night with wild, hungry lions that didn't take even one little nibble. He came out without a scratch!

DANIEL 6:16-23

16 So at last the king gave orders for Daniel to be arrested and thrown into the den of lions. The king said to him, "May your God, whom you serve so faithfully, rescue you."

17 A stone was brought and placed over the mouth of the den. The king sealed the stone with his own royal seal and the seals of his nobles, so that no one could rescue Daniel. 18 Then the king returned to his palace and spent the night fasting. He refused his usual entertainment and couldn't sleep at all that night.

19 Very early the next morning, the king got up and hurried out to the lions' den. 20 When he got there, he called out in anguish, "Daniel, servant of the living God! Was your God, whom you serve so faithfully, able to rescue you from the lions?"

21 Daniel answered, "Long live the king! 22 My God sent his angel to shut the lions' mouths so that they would not hurt me; for I have been found innocent in his sight. And I have not wronged you, Your Majesty."

23 The king was overjoyed and ordered that Daniel be lifted from the den. Not a scratch was found on him, for he had trusted in his God.

24 Then the king gave orders to arrest the men who had maliciously accused Daniel. He had them thrown into the lions' den, along with their wives and children. The lions leaped on them and tore them apart before they even hit the floor of the den.

25 Then King Darius sent this message to the people of every race and nation and language throughout the world:

"Peace and prosperity to you!
26 "I decree that everyone throughout
my kingdom should tremble with fear
before the God of Daniel.

For he is the living God,
and he will endure forever.
His kingdom will never be destroyed,
and his rule will never end.
27 He rescues and saves his people;
he performs miraculous signs and wonders
in the heavens and on earth.
He has rescued Daniel
from the power of the lions."

28 So Daniel prospered during the reign of Darius and the reign of Cyrus the Persian.*

CHAPTER 7

Daniel's Vision of Four Beasts

Earlier, during the first year of King Belshazzar's reign in Babylon,* Daniel had a dream and saw visions as he lay in his bed. He wrote down the dream, and this is what he saw.

2 In my vision that night, I, Daniel, saw a great storm churning the surface of a great sea, with strong winds blowing from every direction. 3 Then four huge beasts came up out of the water, each different from the others.

4 The first beast was like a lion with eagles'

6:28 Or *of Darius, that is, the reign of Cyrus the Persian.* **7:1** The first year of Belshazzar's reign (who was co-regent with his father, Nabonidus) was 556 B.C. (or perhaps as late as 553 B.C.).

wings. As I watched, its wings were pulled off,
and it was left standing with its two hind feet
on the ground, like a human being. And it was
given a human mind.

5 Then I saw a second beast, and it looked
like a bear. It was rearing up on one side, and
it had three ribs in its mouth between its
teeth. And I heard a voice saying to it, "Get up!
Devour the flesh of many people!"

6 Then the third of these strange beasts ap-
peared, and it looked like a leopard. It had
four bird's wings on its back, and it had four
heads. Great authority was given to this beast.

7 Then in my vision that night, I saw a
fourth beast—terrifying, dreadful, and very
strong. It devoured and crushed its victims
with huge iron teeth and trampled their re-
mains beneath its feet. It was different from
any of the other beasts, and it had ten horns.

8 As I was looking at the horns, suddenly
another small horn appeared among them.
Three of the first horns were torn out by the
roots to make room for it. This little horn had
eyes like human eyes and a mouth that was
boasting arrogantly.

9 I watched as thrones were put in place
and the Ancient One* sat down
to judge.
His clothing was as white as snow,
his hair like purest wool.
He sat on a fiery throne
with wheels of blazing fire,
10 and a river of fire was pouring out,
flowing from his presence.
Millions of angels ministered to him;
many millions stood to attend him.
Then the court began its session,
and the books were opened.

11 I continued to watch because I could hear
the little horn's boastful speech. I kept watch-
ing until the fourth beast was killed and its
body was destroyed by fire. 12 The other three
beasts had their authority taken from them,
but they were allowed to live a while longer.*

13 As my vision continued that night, I saw
someone like a son of man* coming with the
clouds of heaven. He approached the Ancient
One and was led into his presence. 14 He was
given authority, honor, and sovereignty over
all the nations of the world, so that people of
every race and nation and language would
obey him. His rule is eternal—it will never
end. His kingdom will never be destroyed.

The Vision Is Explained

15 I, Daniel, was troubled by all I had seen, and
my visions terrified me. 16 So I approached
one of those standing beside the throne and
asked him what it all meant. He explained it
to me like this: 17 "These four huge beasts
represent four kingdoms that will arise from
the earth. 18 But in the end, the holy people of
the Most High will be given the kingdom, and
they will rule forever and ever."

19 Then I wanted to know the true meaning
of the fourth beast, the one so different from
the others and so terrifying. It had devoured
and crushed its victims with iron teeth and
bronze claws, trampling their remains be-
neath its feet. 20 I also asked about the ten
horns on the fourth beast's head and the little
horn that came up afterward and destroyed
three of the other horns. This horn had
seemed greater than the others, and it had
human eyes and a mouth that was boasting
arrogantly. 21 As I watched, this horn was wag-
ing war against God's holy people and was de-
feating them, 22 until the Ancient One—the
Most High—came and judged in favor of his
holy people. Then the time arrived for the
holy people to take over the kingdom.

23 Then he said to me, "This fourth beast is
the fourth world power that will rule the
earth. It will be different from all the others.
It will devour the whole world, trampling and
crushing everything in its path. 24 Its ten horns
are ten kings who will rule that empire. Then
another king will arise, different from the
other ten, who will subdue three of them.
25 He will defy the Most High and oppress the
holy people of the Most High. He will try to
change their sacred festivals and laws, and
they will be placed under his control for a
time, times, and half a time.

26 "But then the court will pass judgment,
and all his power will be taken away and com-
pletely destroyed. 27 Then the sovereignty,
power, and greatness of all the kingdoms
under heaven will be given to the holy people
of the Most High. His kingdom will last for-
ever, and all rulers will serve and obey him."

7:9 Aramaic *an Ancient of Days;* also in 7:13, 22. **7:12** Aramaic *for a season and a time.* **7:13** Or *like a Son of Man.*

[28]That was the end of the vision. I, Daniel, was terrified by my thoughts and my face was pale with fear, but I kept these things to myself.

CHAPTER 8

Daniel's Vision of a Ram and Goat

[1]*During the third year of King Belshazzar's reign, I, Daniel, saw another vision, following the one that had already appeared to me. [2]In this vision I was at the fortress of Susa, in the province of Elam, standing beside the Ulai River.*

[3]As I looked up, I saw a ram with two long horns standing beside the river.* One of the horns was longer than the other, even though it had grown later than the other one. [4]The ram butted everything out of his way to the west, to the north, and to the south, and no one could stand against him or help his victims. He did as he pleased and became very great.

[5]While I was watching, suddenly a male goat appeared from the west, crossing the land so swiftly that he didn't even touch the ground. This goat, which had one very large horn between its eyes, [6]headed toward the two-horned ram that I had seen standing beside the river, rushing at him in a rage. [7]The goat charged furiously at the ram and struck him, breaking off both his horns. Now the ram was helpless, and the goat knocked him down and trampled him. No one could rescue the ram from the goat's power.

[8]The goat became very powerful. But at the height of his power, his large horn was broken off. In the large horn's place grew four prominent horns pointing in the four directions of the earth. [9]Then from one of the prominent horns came a small horn whose power grew very great. It extended toward the south and the east and toward the glorious land of Israel. [10]Its power reached to the heavens, where it attacked the heavenly army, throwing some of the heavenly beings and some of the stars to the ground and trampling them. [11]It even challenged the Commander of heaven's army by canceling the daily sacrifices offered to him and by destroying his Temple. [12]The army of heaven was restrained from responding to this rebellion. So the daily sacrifice was halted, and truth was overthrown. The horn succeeded in everything it did.*

[13]Then I heard two holy ones talking to each other. One of them asked, "How long will the events of this vision last? How long will the rebellion that causes desecration stop the daily sacrifices? How long will the Temple and heaven's army be trampled on?"

8:1 The original text from this point through chapter 12 is in Hebrew. See note at 2:4. **8:2** Or *the Ulai Gate;* also in 8:16. **8:3** Or *the gate;* also in 8:6. **8:11-12** The meaning of the Hebrew for these verses is uncertain.

NEBUCHADNEZZAR'S DREAM

Scholars believe that the large statue Nebuchadnezzar dreamed about (2:24-45) stood for four world kingdoms that would come in the future: the Babylonian Empire, the Medo-Persian Empire, the Grecian Empire, and the Roman Empire. Daniel said all of these would be crushed and brought to an end by the Kingdom of God, which will continue forever.

Part	Made of	Empire	Time it was in control
Head	Gold	Babylonian	606 BC–539 BC
Chest and Arms	Silver	Medo-Persian	539 BC–331 BC
Belly and Thighs	Bronze	Grecian	331 BC–146 BC
Legs and Feet	Iron and Clay	Roman	146 BC–AD 476

[14]The other replied, "It will take 2,300 evenings and mornings; then the Temple will be made right again."

Gabriel Explains the Vision

[15]As I, Daniel, was trying to understand the meaning of this vision, someone who looked like a man stood in front of me. [16]And I heard a human voice calling out from the Ulai River, "Gabriel, tell this man the meaning of his vision."

[17]As Gabriel approached the place where I was standing, I became so terrified that I fell with my face to the ground. "Son of man," he said, "you must understand that the events you have seen in your vision relate to the time of the end."

[18]While he was speaking, I fainted and lay there with my face to the ground. But Gabriel roused me with a touch and helped me to my feet.

[19]Then he said, "I am here to tell you what will happen later in the time of wrath. What you have seen pertains to the very end of time. [20]The two-horned ram represents the kings of Media and Persia. [21]The shaggy male goat represents the king of Greece,* and the large horn between his eyes represents the first king of the Greek Empire. [22]The four prominent horns that replaced the one large horn show that the Greek Empire will break into four kingdoms, but none as great as the first.

[23]"At the end of their rule, when their sin is at its height, a fierce king, a master of intrigue, will rise to power. [24]He will become very strong, but not by his own power. He will cause a shocking amount of destruction and succeed in everything he does. He will destroy powerful leaders and devastate the holy people. [25]He will be a master of deception and will become arrogant; he will destroy many without warning. He will even take on the Prince of princes in battle, but he will be broken, though not by human power.

[26]"This vision about the 2,300 evenings and mornings* is true. But none of these things will happen for a long time, so keep this vision a secret."

[27]Then I, Daniel, was overcome and lay sick for several days. Afterward I got up and performed my duties for the king, but I was greatly troubled by the vision and could not understand it.

CHAPTER 9

Daniel's Prayer for His People

It was the first year of the reign of Darius the Mede, the son of Ahasuerus, who became king of the Babylonians.* [2]During the first year of his reign, I, Daniel, learned from reading the word of the LORD, as revealed to Jeremiah the prophet, that Jerusalem must lie desolate for seventy years.* [3]So I turned to the Lord God and pleaded with him in prayer and fasting. I also wore rough burlap and sprinkled myself with ashes.

[4]I prayed to the LORD my God and confessed:

"O Lord, you are a great and awesome God! You always fulfill your covenant and keep your promises of unfailing love to those who love you and obey your commands. [5]But we have sinned and done wrong. We have rebelled against you and scorned your commands and regulations. [6]We have refused to listen to your servants the prophets, who spoke on your authority to our kings and princes and ancestors and to all the people of the land.

[7]"Lord, you are in the right; but as you see, our faces are covered with shame. This is true of all of us, including the people of Judah and Jerusalem and all Israel, scattered near and far, wherever you have driven us because of our disloyalty to you. [8]O LORD, we and our kings, princes, and ancestors are covered with shame because we have sinned against you. [9]But the Lord our God is merciful and forgiving, even though we have rebelled against him. [10]We have not obeyed the LORD our God, for we have not followed the instructions he gave us through his servants the prophets. [11]All Israel has disobeyed your instruction and turned away, refusing to listen to your voice.

"So now the solemn curses and judgments written in the Law of Moses, the servant of God, have been poured

8:21 Hebrew *of Javan*. **8:26** Hebrew *about the evenings and mornings;* compare 8:14. **9:1** Or *the Chaldeans*. **9:2** See Jer 25:11-12; 29:10.

down on us because of our sin. [12]You have kept your word and done to us and our rulers exactly as you warned. Never has there been such a disaster as happened in Jerusalem. [13]Every curse written against us in the Law of Moses has come true. Yet we have refused to seek mercy from the LORD our God by turning from our sins and recognizing his truth. [14]Therefore, the LORD has brought upon us the disaster he prepared. The LORD our God was right to do all of these things, for we did not obey him.

[15]"O Lord our God, you brought lasting honor to your name by rescuing your people from Egypt in a great display of power. But we have sinned and are full of wickedness. [16]In view of all your faithful mercies, Lord, please turn your furious anger away from your city Jerusalem, your holy mountain. All the neighboring nations mock Jerusalem and your people because of our sins and the sins of our ancestors.

[17]"O our God, hear your servant's prayer! Listen as I plead. For your own sake, Lord, smile again on your desolate sanctuary.

[18]"O my God, lean down and listen to me. Open your eyes and see our despair. See how your city—the city that bears your name—lies in ruins. We make this plea, not because we deserve help, but because of your mercy.

[19]"O Lord, hear. O Lord, forgive. O Lord, listen and act! For your own sake, do not delay, O my God, for your people and your city bear your name."

Gabriel's Message about the Anointed One

[20]I went on praying and confessing my sin and the sin of my people, pleading with the LORD my God for Jerusalem, his holy mountain. [21]As I was praying, Gabriel, whom I had seen in the earlier vision, came swiftly to me at the time of the evening sacrifice. [22]He explained to me, "Daniel, I have come here to give you insight and understanding. [23]The moment you began praying, a command was given. And now I am here to tell you what it was, for you are very precious to God. Listen carefully so that you can understand the meaning of your vision.

[24]"A period of seventy sets of seven* has been decreed for your people and your holy city to finish their rebellion, to put an end to their sin, to atone for their guilt, to bring in everlasting righteousness, to confirm the prophetic vision, and to anoint the Most Holy Place.* [25]Now listen and understand! Seven sets of seven plus sixty-two sets of seven* will pass from the time the command is given to rebuild Jerusalem until a ruler—the Anointed One*—comes. Jerusalem will be rebuilt with streets and strong defenses,* despite the perilous times.

[26]"After this period of sixty-two sets of seven,* the Anointed One will be killed, appearing to have accomplished nothing, and a ruler will arise whose armies will destroy the city and the Temple. The end will come with a flood, and war and its miseries are decreed from that time to the very end. [27]The ruler will make a treaty with the people for a period of one set of seven,* but after half this time, he will put an end to the sacrifices and offerings. And as a climax to all his terrible deeds,* he will set up a sacrilegious object that causes desecration,* until the fate decreed for this defiler is finally poured out on him."

CHAPTER 10

Daniel's Vision of a Messenger

In the third year of the reign of King Cyrus of Persia,* Daniel (also known as Belteshazzar) had another vision. He understood that the vision concerned events certain to happen in the future—times of war and great hardship.

[2]When this vision came to me, I, Daniel, had been in mourning for three whole weeks. [3]All that time I had eaten no rich food. No meat or wine crossed my lips, and I used no fragrant lotions until those three weeks had passed.

[4]On April 23,* as I was standing on the

9:24a Hebrew *seventy sevens.* **9:24b** Or *the Most Holy One.* **9:25a** Hebrew *Seven sevens plus sixty-two sevens.* **9:25b** Or *an anointed one;* similarly in 9:26. Hebrew reads *a messiah.* **9:25c** Or *and a moat,* or *and trenches.* **9:26** Hebrew *After sixty-two sevens.* **9:27a** Hebrew *for one seven.* **9:27b** Hebrew *And on the wing of abominations;* the meaning of the Hebrew is uncertain. **9:27c** Hebrew *an abomination of desolation.* **10:1** The third year of Cyrus's reign was 536 B.C. **10:4** Hebrew *On the twenty-fourth day of the first month,* of the ancient Hebrew lunar calendar. This date in the book of Daniel can be cross-checked with dates in surviving Persian records and can be related accurately to our modern calendar. This event occurred on April 23, 536 B.C.

bank of the great Tigris River, [5]I looked up
and saw a man dressed in linen clothing, with
a belt of pure gold around his waist. [6]His body
looked like a precious gem. His face flashed
like lightning, and his eyes flamed like
torches. His arms and feet shone like pol-
ished bronze, and his voice roared like a vast
multitude of people.

[7]Only I, Daniel, saw this vision. The men
with me saw nothing, but they were suddenly
terrified and ran away to hide. [8]So I was left
there all alone to see this amazing vision. My
strength left me, my face grew deathly pale,
and I felt very weak. [9]Then I heard the man
speak, and when I heard the sound of his
voice, I fainted and lay there with my face to
the ground.

[10]Just then a hand touched me and lifted
me, still trembling, to my hands and knees.
[11]And the man said to me, "Daniel, you are
very precious to God, so listen carefully to
what I have to say to you. Stand up, for I have
been sent to you." When he said this to me, I
stood up, still trembling.

[12]Then he said, "Don't be afraid, Daniel.
Since the first day you began to pray for
understanding and to humble yourself be-
fore your God, your request has been heard in
heaven. I have come in answer to your prayer.
[13]But for twenty-one days the spirit prince* of
the kingdom of Persia blocked my way. Then
Michael, one of the archangels,* came to help
me, and I left him there with the spirit prince
of the kingdom of Persia.* [14]Now I am here to
explain what will happen to your people in
the future, for this vision concerns a time yet
to come."

[15]While he was speaking to me, I looked
down at the ground, unable to say a word.
[16]Then the one who looked like a man*
touched my lips, and I opened my mouth and
began to speak. I said to the one standing in
front of me, "I am filled with anguish because
of the vision I have seen, my lord, and I am
very weak. [17]How can someone like me, your
servant, talk to you, my lord? My strength is
gone, and I can hardly breathe."

[18]Then the one who looked like a man
touched me again, and I felt my strength re-
turning. [19]"Don't be afraid," he said, "for you
are very precious to God. Peace! Be encour-
aged! Be strong!"

As he spoke these words to me, I suddenly
felt stronger and said to him, "Please speak to
me, my lord, for you have strengthened me."

[20]He replied, "Do you know why I have
come? Soon I must return to fight against the
spirit prince of the kingdom of Persia, and af-
ter that the spirit prince of the kingdom of
Greece* will come. [21]Meanwhile, I will tell you
what is written in the Book of Truth. (No one
helps me against these spirit princes except
Michael, your spirit prince.* [11:1]I have been
standing beside Michael* to support and
strengthen him since the first year of the
reign of Darius the Mede.)

CHAPTER 11

Kings of the South and North

[2]"Now then, I will reveal the truth to you.
Three more Persian kings will reign, to be
succeeded by a fourth, far richer than the
others. He will use his wealth to stir up every-
one to fight against the kingdom of Greece.*

[3]"Then a mighty king will rise to power
who will rule with great authority and accom-
plish everything he sets out to do. [4]But at the
height of his power, his kingdom will be bro-
ken apart and divided into four parts. It will
not be ruled by the king's descendants, nor
will the kingdom hold the authority it once
had. For his empire will be uprooted and
given to others.

[5]"The king of the south will increase in
power, but one of his own officials will be-
come more powerful than he and will rule his
kingdom with great strength.

[6]"Some years later an alliance will be
formed between the king of the north and the
king of the south. The daughter of the king of
the south will be given in marriage to the king
of the north to secure the alliance, but she will
lose her influence over him, and so will her fa-
ther. She will be abandoned along with her
supporters. [7]But when one of her relatives*
becomes king of the south, he will raise an
army and enter the fortress of the king of the
north and defeat him. [8]When he returns to

10:13a Hebrew *the prince;* also in 10:13c, 20. **10:13b** Hebrew *the chief princes.* **10:13c** As in one Greek version; Hebrew reads *and I was left there with the kings of Persia.* The meaning of the Hebrew is uncertain. **10:16** As in most manuscripts of the Masoretic Text; one manuscript of the Masoretic Text and one Greek version read *Then something that looked like a human hand.* **10:20** Hebrew *of Javan.* **10:21** Hebrew *against these except Michael, your prince.* **11:1** Hebrew *him.* **11:2** Hebrew *of Javan.* **11:7** Hebrew *a branch from her roots.*

DANIEL

The king was planning to make me one of his top men. But his other officers didn't like that. So they got him to sign a new law that said people could pray only to the king. When I heard about it, I couldn't believe it. Pray to a man? Never. Because I worship the true God, I continued to pray to him three times a day. The king's officers knew they'd find me praying to God. When they did, they reported it, of course. The king looked sad when he sent me to the hungry lions. But they were really just big house cats, thanks to the angels God sent to hold their mouths shut. God protects me even during dark times!

Read Daniel 6:1-28 to discover more about Daniel's strong faith.

Egypt, he will carry back their idols with him, along with priceless articles of gold and silver. For some years afterward he will leave the king of the north alone.

9"Later the king of the north will invade the realm of the king of the south but will soon return to his own land. 10However, the sons of the king of the north will assemble a mighty army that will advance like a flood and carry the battle as far as the enemy's fortress.

11"Then, in a rage, the king of the south will rally against the vast forces assembled by the king of the north and will defeat them. 12After the enemy army is swept away, the king of the south will be filled with pride and will execute many thousands of his enemies. But his success will be short lived.

13"A few years later the king of the north will return with a fully equipped army far greater than before. 14At that time there will be a general uprising against the king of the south. Violent men among your own people will join them in fulfillment of this vision, but they will not succeed. 15Then the king of the north will come and lay siege to a fortified city and capture it. The best troops of the south will not be able to stand in the face of the onslaught.

16"The king of the north will march onward unopposed; none will be able to stop him. He will pause in the glorious land of Israel,* intent on destroying it. 17He will make plans to come with the might of his entire kingdom and will form an alliance with the king of the south. He will give him a daughter in marriage in order to overthrow the kingdom from within, but his plan will fail.

18"After this, he will turn his attention to the coastland and conquer many cities. But a commander from another land will put an end to his insolence and cause him to retreat in shame. 19He will take refuge in his own fortresses but will stumble and fall and be seen no more.

20"His successor will send out a tax collector to maintain the royal splendor. But after a very brief reign, he will die, though not from anger or in battle.

21"The next to come to power will be a despicable man who is not in line for royal succession. He will slip in when least expected and take over the kingdom by flattery and intrigue. 22Before him great armies will be swept away, including a covenant prince. 23With deceitful promises, he will make various alliances. He will become strong despite having only a handful of followers. 24Without

11:16 Hebrew *the glorious land.*

warning he will enter the richest areas of the land. Then he will distribute among his followers the plunder and wealth of the rich—something his predecessors had never done. He will plot the overthrow of strongholds, but this will last for only a short while.

[25]"Then he will stir up his courage and raise a great army against the king of the south. The king of the south will go to battle with a mighty army, but to no avail, for there will be plots against him. [26]His own household will cause his downfall. His army will be swept away, and many will be killed. [27]Seeking nothing but each other's harm, these kings will plot against each other at the conference table, attempting to deceive each other. But it will make no difference, for the end will come at the appointed time.

[28]"The king of the north will then return home with great riches. On the way he will set himself against the people of the holy covenant, doing much damage before continuing his journey.

[29]"Then at the appointed time he will once again invade the south, but this time the result will be different. [30]For warships from western coastlands* will scare him off, and he will withdraw and return home. But he will vent his anger against the people of the holy covenant and reward those who forsake the covenant.

[31]"His army will take over the Temple fortress, pollute the sanctuary, put a stop to the daily sacrifices, and set up the sacrilegious object that causes desecration.* [32]He will flatter and win over those who have violated the covenant. But the people who know their God will be strong and will resist him.

[33]"Wise leaders will give instruction to many, but these teachers will die by fire and sword, or they will be jailed and robbed. [34]During these persecutions, little help will arrive, and many who join them will not be sincere. [35]And some of the wise will fall victim to persecution. In this way, they will be refined and cleansed and made pure until the time of the end, for the appointed time is still to come.

[36]"The king will do as he pleases, exalting himself and claiming to be greater than every god, even blaspheming the God of gods. He will succeed, but only until the time of wrath is completed. For what has been determined will surely take place. [37]He will have no respect for the gods of his ancestors, or for the god loved by women, or for any other god, for he will boast that he is greater than them all. [38]Instead of these, he will worship the god of fortresses—a god his ancestors never knew—and lavish on him gold, silver, precious stones, and expensive gifts. [39]Claiming this foreign god's help, he will attack the strongest fortresses. He will honor those who submit to him, appointing them to positions of authority and dividing the land among them as their reward.*

[40]"Then at the time of the end, the king of the south will attack the king of the north. The king of the north will storm out with chariots, charioteers, and a vast navy. He will invade various lands and sweep through them like a flood. [41]He will enter the glorious land of Israel,* and many nations will fall, but Moab, Edom, and the best part of Ammon will escape. [42]He will conquer many countries, and even Egypt will not escape. [43]He will gain control over the gold, silver, and treasures of Egypt, and the Libyans and Ethiopians* will be his servants.

[44]"But then news from the east and the north will alarm him, and he will set out in great anger to destroy and obliterate many. [45]He will stop between the glorious holy mountain and the sea and will pitch his royal tents. But while he is there, his time will suddenly run out, and no one will help him.

CHAPTER 12

The Time of the End

"At that time Michael, the archangel* who stands guard over your nation, will arise. Then there will be a time of anguish greater than any since nations first came into existence. But at that time every one of your people whose name is written in the book will be rescued. [2]Many of those whose bodies lie dead and buried will rise up, some to everlasting life and some to shame and everlasting disgrace. [3]Those who are wise will shine as bright as the sky, and those who lead many to righteousness will shine like the stars forever. [4]But you, Daniel, keep this prophecy a secret; seal up the book until the time of the end, when many will

11:30 Hebrew *from Kittim*. **11:31** Hebrew *the abomination of desolation*. **11:39** Or *at a price*. **11:41** Hebrew *the glorious land*. **11:43** Hebrew *Cushites*. **12:1** Hebrew *the great prince*.

rush here and there, and knowledge will increase."

[5]Then I, Daniel, looked and saw two others standing on opposite banks of the river. [6]One of them asked the man dressed in linen, who was now standing above the river, "How long will it be until these shocking events are over?"

[7]The man dressed in linen, who was standing above the river, raised both his hands toward heaven and took a solemn oath by the One who lives forever, saying, "It will go on for a time, times, and half a time. When the shattering of the holy people has finally come to an end, all these things will have happened."

[8]I heard what he said, but I did not understand what he meant. So I asked, "How will all this finally end, my lord?"

[9]But he said, "Go now, Daniel, for what I have said is kept secret and sealed until the time of the end. [10]Many will be purified, cleansed, and refined by these trials. But the wicked will continue in their wickedness, and none of them will understand. Only those who are wise will know what it means.

[11]"From the time the daily sacrifice is stopped and the sacrilegious object that causes desecration* is set up to be worshiped, there will be 1,290 days. [12]And blessed are those who wait and remain until the end of the 1,335 days!

[13]"As for you, go your way until the end. You will rest, and then at the end of the days, you will rise again to receive the inheritance set aside for you."

12:11 Hebrew *the abomination of desolation.*

HOSEA

WHO
Hosea, Gomer, their children, and the people of Israel.

WHERE
In the northern kingdom of Israel.

WHEN
Around 715 BC when Jeroboam was king.

WHY
To show how much God loves his people in spite of their sin.

Come back to your God.
Act with love and justice.
HOSEA 12:6

Hosea's job as a prophet was to *show* God's message to his people. God told Hosea to marry Gomer, who would be unfaithful to him. He told Hosea to love Gomer no matter what. This would show the people of Israel that even though they were unfaithful to God, he would love them no matter what.

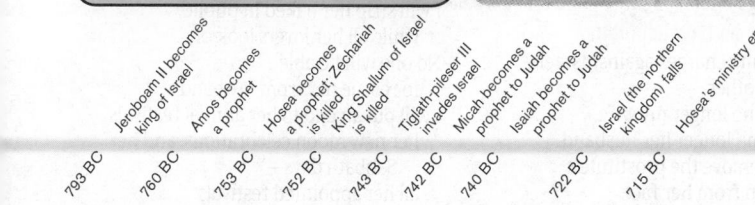

REMEMBER THAT GOD LOVES YOU NO MATTER WHAT.

CHAPTER 1

The LORD gave this message to Hosea son of Beeri during the years when Uzziah, Jotham, Ahaz, and Hezekiah were kings of Judah, and Jeroboam son of Jehoash* was king of Israel.

Hosea's Wife and Children

[2]When the LORD first began speaking to Israel through Hosea, he said to him, "Go and marry a prostitute,* so that some of her children will be conceived in prostitution. This will illustrate how Israel has acted like a prostitute by turning against the LORD and worshiping other gods."

[3]So Hosea married Gomer, the daughter of Diblaim, and she became pregnant and gave Hosea a son. [4]And the LORD said, "Name the child Jezreel, for I am about to punish King

1:1 Hebrew *Joash*, a variant spelling of Jehoash. **1:2** Or *a promiscuous woman*.

Jehu's dynasty to avenge the murders he committed at Jezreel. In fact, I will bring an end to Israel's independence. [5]I will break its military power in the Jezreel Valley."

[6]Soon Gomer became pregnant again and gave birth to a daughter. And the LORD said to Hosea, "Name your daughter Lo-ruhamah—'Not loved'—for I will no longer show love to the people of Israel or forgive them. [7]But I will show love to the people of Judah. I will free them from their enemies—not with weapons and armies or horses and charioteers, but by my power as the LORD their God."

[8]After Gomer had weaned Lo-ruhamah, she again became pregnant and gave birth to a second son. [9]And the LORD said, "Name him Lo-ammi—'Not my people'—for Israel is not my people, and I am not their God.

[10]*"Yet the time will come when Israel's people will be like the sands of the seashore—too many to count! Then, at the place where they were told, 'You are not my people,' it will be said, 'You are children of the living God.' [11]Then the people of Judah and Israel will unite together. They will choose one leader for themselves, and they will return from exile together. What a day that will be—the day of Jezreel*—when God will again plant his people in his land.

[2:1]*"In that day you will call your brothers Ammi—'My people.' And you will call your sisters Ruhamah—'The ones I love.'

CHAPTER 2

Charges against an Unfaithful Wife

[2] "But now bring charges against Israel—your mother—
for she is no longer my wife,
and I am no longer her husband.
Tell her to remove the prostitute's makeup from her face
and the clothing that exposes her breasts.
[3] Otherwise, I will strip her as naked
as she was on the day she was born.
I will leave her to die of thirst,
as in a dry and barren wilderness.
[4] And I will not love her children,
for they were conceived in prostitution.
[5] Their mother is a shameless prostitute
and became pregnant in a shameful way.
She said, 'I'll run after other lovers
and sell myself to them for food and water,
for clothing of wool and linen,
and for olive oil and drinks.'
[6] "For this reason I will fence her in with thornbushes.
I will block her path with a wall
to make her lose her way.
[7] When she runs after her lovers,
she won't be able to catch them.
She will search for them
but not find them.
Then she will think,
'I might as well return to my husband,
for I was better off with him than I am now.'
[8] She doesn't realize it was I who gave her everything she has—
the grain, the new wine, the olive oil;
I even gave her silver and gold.
But she gave all my gifts to Baal.
[9] "But now I will take back the ripened grain and new wine
I generously provided each harvest season.
I will take away the wool and linen clothing
I gave her to cover her nakedness.
[10] I will strip her naked in public,
while all her lovers look on.
No one will be able
to rescue her from my hands.
[11] I will put an end to her annual festivals,
her new moon celebrations, and her Sabbath days—
all her appointed festivals.
[12] I will destroy her grapevines and fig trees,
things she claims her lovers gave her.
I will let them grow into tangled thickets,
where only wild animals will eat the fruit.
[13] I will punish her for all those times
when she burned incense to her images of Baal,

1:10 Verses 1:10-11 are numbered 2:1-2 in Hebrew text. **1:11** *Jezreel* means "God plants." **2:1** Verses 2:1-23 are numbered 2:3-25 in Hebrew text.

when she put on her earrings and jewels
and went out to look for her lovers
but forgot all about me,"
says the LORD.

The LORD's Love for Unfaithful Israel

14 "But then I will win her back once again.
I will lead her into the desert
and speak tenderly to her there.
15 I will return her vineyards to her
and transform the Valley of Trouble*
into a gateway of hope.
She will give herself to me there,
as she did long ago when she was young,
when I freed her from her captivity in Egypt.
16 When that day comes," says the LORD,
"you will call me 'my husband'
instead of 'my master.'*
17 O Israel, I will wipe the many names of Baal from your lips,
and you will never mention them again.
18 On that day I will make a covenant
with all the wild animals and the birds of the sky
and the animals that scurry along the ground
so they will not harm you.
I will remove all weapons of war from the land,
all swords and bows,
so you can live unafraid
in peace and safety.
19 I will make you my wife forever,
showing you righteousness and justice,
unfailing love and compassion.
20 I will be faithful to you and make you mine,
and you will finally know me as the LORD.
21 "In that day, I will answer,"
says the LORD.
"I will answer the sky as it pleads for clouds.
And the sky will answer the earth with rain.
22 Then the earth will answer the thirsty cries
of the grain, the grapevines, and the olive trees.
And they in turn will answer,
'Jezreel'—'God plants!'
23 At that time I will plant a crop of Israelites
and raise them for myself.
I will show love
to those I called 'Not loved.'*
And to those I called 'Not my people,'*
I will say, 'Now you are my people.'
And they will reply, 'You are our God!'"

CHAPTER 3

Hosea's Wife Is Redeemed

Then the LORD said to me, "Go and love your wife again, even though she* commits adultery with another lover. This will illustrate that the LORD still loves Israel, even though the people have turned to other gods and love to worship them.*"

2 So I bought her back for fifteen pieces of silver* and five bushels of barley and a measure of wine.* 3 Then I said to her, "You must live in my house for many days and stop your prostitution. During this time, you will not have sexual relations with anyone, not even with me.*"

4 This shows that Israel will go a long time without a king or prince, and without sacrifices, sacred pillars, priests,* or even idols! 5 But afterward the people will return and devote themselves to the LORD their God and to David's descendant, their king.* In the last days, they will tremble in awe of the LORD and of his goodness.

CHAPTER 4

The LORD's Case against Israel

1 Hear the word of the LORD, O people of Israel!
The LORD has brought charges against you, saying:
"There is no faithfulness, no kindness,
no knowledge of God in your land.
2 You make vows and break them;
you kill and steal and commit adultery.

2:15 Hebrew *valley of Achor*. **2:16** Hebrew *'my baal.'* **2:23a** Hebrew *Lo-ruhamah;* see 1:6. **2:23b** Hebrew *Lo-ammi;* see 1:9. **3:1a** Or *Go and love a woman who*. **3:1b** Hebrew *love their raisin cakes*. **3:2a** Hebrew *15 shekels of silver*, about 6 ounces or 171 grams in weight. **3:2b** As in Greek version, which reads *a homer of barley and a wineskin full of wine;* Hebrew reads *a homer* [5 bushels or 182 liters] *of barley and a lethech* [2.5 bushels or 91 liters] *of barley*. **3:3** Or *and I will live with you*. **3:4** Hebrew *ephod*, the vest worn by the priest. **3:5** Hebrew *to David their king*.

There is violence everywhere—
one murder after another.
3 That is why your land is in mourning,
and everyone is wasting away.
Even the wild animals, the birds of the sky,
and the fish of the sea are disappearing.

4 "Don't point your finger at someone else
and try to pass the blame!
My complaint, you priests,
is with you.*
5 So you will stumble in broad daylight,
and your false prophets will fall with you in the night.
And I will destroy Israel, your mother.

AMAZING FACTS

Would you ask a piece of wood for advice? The people of Israel did.
HOSEA 4:12

6 My people are being destroyed
because they don't know me.
Since you priests refuse to know me,
I refuse to recognize you as my priests.
Since you have forgotten the laws of your God,
I will forget to bless your children.
7 The more priests there are,
the more they sin against me.
They have exchanged the glory of God
for the shame of idols.*

8 "When the people bring their sin offerings, the priests get fed.
So the priests are glad when the people sin!
9 'And what the priests do, the people also do.'
So now I will punish both priests and people
for their wicked deeds.
10 They will eat and still be hungry.
They will play the prostitute and gain nothing from it,
for they have deserted the LORD
11 to worship other gods.

"Wine has robbed my people
of their understanding.
12 They ask a piece of wood for advice!
They think a stick can tell them the future!
Longing after idols
has made them foolish.
They have played the prostitute,
serving other gods and deserting their God.
13 They offer sacrifices to idols on the mountaintops.
They go up into the hills to burn incense
in the pleasant shade of oaks, poplars, and terebinth trees.

"That is why your daughters turn to prostitution,
and your daughters-in-law commit adultery.
14 But why should I punish them
for their prostitution and adultery?
For your men are doing the same thing,
sinning with whores and shrine prostitutes.
O foolish people! You refuse to understand,
so you will be destroyed.

15 "Though you, Israel, are a prostitute,
may Judah avoid such guilt.
Do not join the false worship at Gilgal or Beth-aven,*
even though they take oaths there in the LORD's name.
16 Israel is stubborn,
like a stubborn heifer.
So should the LORD feed her
like a lamb in a lush pasture?
17 Leave Israel* alone,
because she is married to idolatry.

4:4 Hebrew *Your people are like those with a complaint against the priests.* **4:7** As in Syriac version and an ancient Hebrew tradition; Masoretic Text reads *I will turn their glory into shame.* **4:15** *Beth-aven* means "house of wickedness"; it is being used as another name for Bethel, which means "house of God." **4:17** Hebrew *Ephraim,* referring to the northern kingdom of Israel.

18 When the rulers of Israel finish their drinking,
off they go to find some prostitutes.
They love shame more than honor.*
19 So a mighty wind will sweep them away.
Their sacrifices to idols will bring them shame.

CHAPTER 5

The Failure of Israel's Leaders

1 "Hear this, you priests.
Pay attention, you leaders of Israel.
Listen, you members of the royal family.
Judgment has been handed down against you.
For you have led the people into a snare
by worshiping the idols at Mizpah and Tabor.
2 You have dug a deep pit to trap them at Acacia Grove.*
But I will settle with you for what you have done.
3 I know what you are like, O Ephraim.
You cannot hide yourself from me, O Israel.
You have left me as a prostitute leaves her husband;
you are utterly defiled.
4 Your deeds won't let you return to your God.
You are a prostitute through and through,
and you do not know the LORD.

5 "The arrogance of Israel testifies against her;
Israel and Ephraim will stumble under their load of guilt.
Judah, too, will fall with them.
6 When they come with their flocks and herds
to offer sacrifices to the LORD,
they will not find him,
because he has withdrawn from them.
7 They have betrayed the honor of the LORD,
bearing children that are not his.
Now their false religion will devour them along with their wealth.*

8 "Sound the alarm in Gibeah!
Blow the trumpet in Ramah!
Raise the battle cry in Beth-aven*!
Lead on into battle, O warriors of Benjamin!
9 One thing is certain, Israel*:
On your day of punishment,
you will become a heap of rubble.

10 "The leaders of Judah have become like thieves.*
So I will pour my anger on them like a waterfall.
11 The people of Israel will be crushed and broken by my judgment
because they are determined to worship idols.*
12 I will destroy Israel as a moth consumes wool.
I will make Judah as weak as rotten wood.

13 "When Israel and Judah saw how sick they were,
Israel turned to Assyria—
to the great king there—
but he could neither help nor cure them.
14 I will be like a lion to Israel,
like a strong young lion to Judah.
I will tear them to pieces!
I will carry them off,
and no one will be left to rescue them.
15 Then I will return to my place
until they admit their guilt and turn to me.
For as soon as trouble comes,
they will earnestly search for me."

CHAPTER 6

A Call to Repentance

1 "Come, let us return to the LORD.
He has torn us to pieces;
now he will heal us.
He has injured us;
now he will bandage our wounds.
2 In just a short time he will restore us,
so that we may live in his presence.
3 Oh, that we might know the LORD!
Let us press on to know him.

4:18 As in Greek version; the meaning of the Hebrew is uncertain. **5:2** Hebrew *at Shittim*. The meaning of the Hebrew for this sentence is uncertain. **5:7** The meaning of the Hebrew is uncertain. **5:8** *Beth-aven* means "house of wickedness"; it is being used as another name for Bethel, which means "house of God." **5:9** Hebrew *Ephraim*, referring to the northern kingdom of Israel; also in 5:11, 12, 13, 14. **5:10** Hebrew *like those who move a boundary marker*. **5:11** Or *determined to follow human commands*. The meaning of the Hebrew is uncertain.

Sometimes I forget to talk to God until I'm in trouble.

As soon as trouble comes, they will earnestly search for me. HOSEA 5:15

He will respond to us as surely as the
arrival of dawn
or the coming of rains in early spring."

4 "O Israel* and Judah,
what should I do with you?" asks the
LORD.
"For your love vanishes like the morning
mist
and disappears like dew in the sunlight.
5 I sent my prophets to cut you to pieces—
to slaughter you with my words,
with judgments as inescapable
as light.
6 I want you to show love,*
not offer sacrifices.
I want you to know me*
more than I want burnt offerings.
7 But like Adam,* you broke my covenant
and betrayed my trust.

8 "Gilead is a city of sinners,
tracked with footprints of blood.
9 Priests form bands of robbers,
waiting in ambush for their victims.
They murder travelers along the road to
Shechem
and practice every kind of sin.
10 Yes, I have seen something horrible in
Ephraim and Israel:
My people are defiled by prostituting
themselves with other gods!

11 "O Judah, a harvest of punishment is also
waiting for you,
though I wanted to restore the fortunes
of my people.

CHAPTER 7

Israel's Love for Wickedness

1 "I want to heal Israel,* but its sins are too
great.
Samaria is filled with liars.
Thieves are on the inside
and bandits on the outside!
2 Its people don't realize
that I am watching them.
Their sinful deeds are all around them,
and I see them all.

3 "The people entertain the king with their
wickedness,
and the princes laugh at their lies.
4 They are all adulterers,
always aflame with lust.
They are like an oven that is kept hot
while the baker is kneading the dough.
5 On royal holidays, the princes get drunk
with wine,
carousing with those who mock them.
6 Their hearts are like an oven
blazing with intrigue.
Their plot smolders* through the night,
and in the morning it breaks out like a
raging fire.
7 Burning like an oven,
they consume their leaders.
They kill their kings one after another,
and no one cries to me for help.

8 "The people of Israel mingle with godless
foreigners,
making themselves as worthless as a
half-baked cake!
9 Worshiping foreign gods has sapped their
strength,
but they don't even know it.
Their hair is gray,
but they don't realize they're old and
weak.
10 Their arrogance testifies against them,
yet they don't return to the LORD their
God
or even try to find him.

11 "The people of Israel have become like
silly, witless doves,
first calling to Egypt, then flying to
Assyria for help.
12 But as they fly about,

6:4 Hebrew *Ephraim*, referring to the northern kingdom of Israel. **6:6a** Greek version translates this Hebrew term as *to show mercy*. Compare Matt 9:13; 12:7. **6:6b** Hebrew *to know God*. **6:7** Or *But at Adam*. **7:1** Hebrew *Ephraim*, referring to the northern kingdom of Israel; also in 7:8, 11. **7:6** Hebrew *Their baker sleeps*.

I will throw my net over them
and bring them down like a bird from the sky.
I will punish them for all the evil they do.*

13 "What sorrow awaits those who have deserted me!
Let them die, for they have rebelled against me.
I wanted to redeem them,
but they have told lies about me.
14 They do not cry out to me with sincere hearts.
Instead, they sit on their couches and wail.
They cut themselves,* begging foreign gods for grain and new wine,
and they turn away from me.
15 I trained them and made them strong,
yet now they plot evil against me.
16 They look everywhere except to the Most High.
They are as useless as a crooked bow.
Their leaders will be killed by their enemies
because of their insolence toward me.
Then the people of Egypt will laugh at them.

CHAPTER 8

Israel Harvests the Whirlwind

1 "Sound the alarm!
The enemy descends like an eagle on the people of the LORD,
for they have broken my covenant and revolted against my law.
2 Now Israel pleads with me,
'Help us, for you are our God!'
3 But it is too late.
The people of Israel have rejected what is good,
and now their enemies will chase after them.
4 The people have appointed kings without my consent,
and princes without my knowledge.
By making idols for themselves from their silver and gold,
they have brought about their own destruction.

5 "O Samaria, I reject this calf—this idol you have made.
My fury burns against you.
How long will you be incapable of innocence?
6 This calf you worship, O Israel,
was crafted by your own hands!
It is not God!
Therefore, it must be smashed to bits.
7 "They have planted the wind
and will harvest the whirlwind.
The stalks of grain wither
and produce nothing to eat.
And even if there is any grain,
foreigners will eat it.

7:12 Hebrew *I will punish them because of what was reported against them in the assembly.* **7:14** As in Greek version; Hebrew reads *They gather together.*

8 The people of Israel have been swallowed up;
they lie among the nations like an old discarded pot.
9 Like a wild donkey looking for a mate,
they have gone up to Assyria.
The people of Israel* have sold themselves—
sold themselves to many lovers.
10 But though they have sold themselves to many allies,
I will now gather them together for judgment.
Then they will writhe
under the burden of the great king.

11 "Israel has built many altars to take away sin,
but these very altars became places for sinning!
12 Even though I gave them all my laws,
they act as if those laws don't apply to them.
13 The people of Israel love their rituals of sacrifice,
but to me their sacrifices are all meaningless.
I will hold my people accountable for their sins,
and I will punish them.
They will return to Egypt.
14 Israel has forgotten its Maker and built great palaces,
and Judah has fortified its cities.
Therefore, I will send down fire on their cities
and will burn up their fortresses."

CHAPTER 9

Hosea Announces Israel's Punishment

1 O people of Israel,
do not rejoice as other nations do.
For you have been unfaithful to your God,
hiring yourselves out like prostitutes,
worshiping other gods on every threshing floor.
2 So now your harvests will be too small to feed you.
There will be no grapes for making new wine.
3 You may no longer stay here in the LORD's land.
Instead, you will return to Egypt,
and in Assyria you will eat food
that is ceremonially unclean.
4 There you will make no offerings of wine to the LORD.
None of your sacrifices there will please him.
They will be unclean, like food touched by a person in mourning.
All who present such sacrifices will be defiled.
They may eat this food themselves,
but they may not offer it to the LORD.
5 What then will you do on festival days?
How will you observe the LORD's festivals?
6 Even if you escape destruction from Assyria,
Egypt will conquer you, and Memphis* will bury you.
Nettles will take over your treasures of silver;
thistles will invade your ruined homes.

7 The time of Israel's punishment has come;
the day of payment is here.
Soon Israel will know this all too well.
Because of your great sin and hostility,
you say, "The prophets are crazy
and the inspired men are fools!"
8 The prophet is a watchman over Israel* for my God,
yet traps are laid for him wherever he goes.
He faces hostility even in the house of God.
9 The things my people do are as depraved as what they did in Gibeah long ago.
God will not forget.
He will surely punish them for their sins.

10 The LORD says, "O Israel, when I first found you,
it was like finding fresh grapes in the desert.
When I saw your ancestors,
it was like seeing the first ripe figs of the season.

8:9 Hebrew *Ephraim*, referring to the northern kingdom of Israel; also in 8:11. **9:6** Memphis was the capital of northern Egypt.
9:8 Hebrew *Ephraim*, referring to the northern kingdom of Israel; also in 9:11, 13, 16.

But then they deserted me for Baal-peor,
giving themselves to that shameful idol.
Soon they became vile,
as vile as the god they worshiped.
11 The glory of Israel will fly away like a bird,
for your children will not be born
or grow in the womb
or even be conceived.
12 Even if you do have children who grow up,
I will take them from you.
It will be a terrible day when I turn away
and leave you alone.
13 I have watched Israel become as beautiful
as Tyre.
But now Israel will bring out her
children for slaughter."

14 O LORD, what should I request for your
people?
I will ask for wombs that don't give
birth
and breasts that give no milk.

15 The LORD says, "All their wickedness
began at Gilgal;
there I began to hate them.
I will drive them from my land
because of their evil actions.
I will love them no more
because all their leaders are rebels.
16 The people of Israel are struck down.
Their roots are dried up,
and they will bear no more fruit.
And if they give birth,
I will slaughter their beloved children."

17 My God will reject the people of Israel
because they will not listen or obey.
They will be wanderers,
homeless among the nations.

CHAPTER 10

The LORD's Judgment against Israel

1 How prosperous Israel is—
a luxuriant vine loaded with fruit.
But the richer the people get,
the more pagan altars they build.
The more bountiful their harvests,
the more beautiful their sacred pillars.
2 The hearts of the people are fickle;
they are guilty and must be punished.
The LORD will break down their altars
and smash their sacred pillars.
3 Then they will say, "We have no king
because we didn't fear the LORD.
But even if we had a king,
what could he do for us anyway?"
4 They spout empty words
and make covenants they don't intend
to keep.
So injustice springs up among them
like poisonous weeds in a farmer's
field.

5 The people of Samaria tremble in fear
for what might happen to their calf idol
at Beth-aven.*
The people mourn and the priests wail,
because its glory will be stripped
away.*
6 This idol will be carted away to Assyria,
a gift to the great king there.
Ephraim will be ridiculed and Israel will
be shamed,
because its people have trusted in this
idol.
7 Samaria and its king will be cut off;
they will float away like driftwood on
an ocean wave.
8 And the pagan shrines of Aven,* the place
of Israel's sin, will crumble.
Thorns and thistles will grow up
around their altars.
They will beg the mountains, "Bury us!"
and plead with the hills, "Fall on us!"

9 The LORD says, "O Israel, ever since
Gibeah,
there has been only sin and more
sin!
You have made no progress whatsoever.
Was it not right that the wicked men of
Gibeah were attacked?
10 Now whenever it fits my plan,
I will attack you, too.
I will call out the armies of the nations
to punish you for your multiplied
sins.

11 "Israel* is like a trained heifer treading
out the grain—
an easy job she loves.
But I will put a heavy yoke on her
tender neck.

10:5a *Beth-aven* means "house of wickedness"; it is being used as another name for Bethel, which means "house of God." **10:5b** Or *will be taken away into exile*. **10:8** *Aven* is a reference to Beth-aven; see 10:5a and the note there. **10:11a** Hebrew *Ephraim*, referring to the northern kingdom of Israel.

I will force Judah to pull the plow
and Israel* to break up the hard ground.
12 I said, 'Plant the good seeds of
righteousness,
and you will harvest a crop of love.
Plow up the hard ground of your hearts,
for now is the time to seek the LORD,
that he may come
and shower righteousness upon you.'

13 "But you have cultivated wickedness
and harvested a thriving crop of sins.
You have eaten the fruit of lies—
trusting in your military might,
believing that great armies
could make your nation safe.
14 Now the terrors of war
will rise among your people.
All your fortifications will fall,
just as when Shalman destroyed Beth-arbel.
Even mothers and children
were dashed to death there.
15 You will share that fate, Bethel,
because of your great wickedness.
When the day of judgment dawns,
the king of Israel will be completely destroyed.

CHAPTER 11

The LORD's Love for Israel

1 "When Israel was a child, I loved him,
and I called my son out of Egypt.
2 But the more I* called to him,
the farther he moved from me,
offering sacrifices to the images of Baal
and burning incense to idols.
3 I myself taught Israel* how to walk,
leading him along by the hand.
But he doesn't know or even care
that it was I who took care of him.
4 I led Israel along
with my ropes of kindness and love.
I lifted the yoke from his neck,
and I myself stooped to feed him.
5 "But since my people refuse to return to me,
they will return to Egypt
and will be forced to serve Assyria.
6 War will swirl through their cities;
their enemies will crash through their gates.
They will destroy them,
trapping them in their own evil plans.
7 For my people are determined to desert me.
They call me the Most High,
but they don't truly honor me.

8 "Oh, how can I give you up, Israel?
How can I let you go?
How can I destroy you like Admah
or demolish you like Zeboiim?
My heart is torn within me,
and my compassion overflows.
9 No, I will not unleash my fierce anger.
I will not completely destroy Israel,
for I am God and not a mere mortal.
I am the Holy One living among you,
and I will not come to destroy.
10 For someday the people will follow me.
I, the LORD, will roar like a lion.
And when I roar,
my people will return trembling from the west.
11 Like a flock of birds, they will come from Egypt.
Trembling like doves, they will return from Assyria.
And I will bring them home again,"
says the LORD.

Charges against Israel and Judah

12*Israel surrounds me with lies and deceit,
but Judah still obeys God
and is faithful to the Holy One.*

CHAPTER 12

1*The people of Israel* feed on the wind;
they chase after the east wind all day long.

10:11b Hebrew *Jacob*. The names "Jacob" and "Israel" are often interchanged throughout the Old Testament, referring sometimes to the individual patriarch and sometimes to the nation. **11:2** As in Greek version; Hebrew reads *they*. **11:3** Hebrew *Ephraim*, referring to the northern kingdom of Israel; also in 11:8, 9, 12. **11:12a** Verse 11:12 is numbered 12:1 in Hebrew text. **11:12b** Or *and Judah is unruly against God, the faithful Holy One*. The meaning of the Hebrew is uncertain. **12:1a** Verses 12:1-14 are numbered 12:2-15 in Hebrew text. **12:1b** Hebrew *Ephraim*, referring to the northern kingdom of Israel; also in 12:8, 14.

RULES ARE RULES?
William and his friends had club meetings in his basement. The number one club rule was that if anyone missed a meeting, he would be kicked out. Last week Alex said, "Mom told me I had to go shopping with her next Saturday." William reminded Alex that Saturday was a meeting day. Alex answered, "I'm sorry. I can't come." But what about the rule? If William lets Alex miss a meeting, he thinks the other guys might eventually do the same thing—and then maybe nobody will come. What do you think William should do? Hosea 12:6 has a clue for how William can respond.

They pile up lies and violence;
they are making an alliance with Assyria
while sending olive oil to buy support
from Egypt.

2 Now the LORD is bringing charges against
Judah.
He is about to punish Jacob* for all his
deceitful ways,
and pay him back for all he has done.
3 Even in the womb,
Jacob struggled with his brother;
when he became a man,
he even fought with God.
4 Yes, he wrestled with the angel and won.
He wept and pleaded for a blessing
from him.
There at Bethel he met God face to face,
and God spoke to him*—
5 the LORD God of Heaven's Armies,
the LORD is his name!
6 So now, come back to your God.
Act with love and justice,
and always depend on him.

7 But no, the people are like crafty
merchants
selling from dishonest scales—
they love to cheat.
8 Israel boasts, "I am rich!
I've made a fortune all by myself!
No one has caught me cheating!
My record is spotless!"

9 "But I am the LORD your God,
who rescued you from slavery
in Egypt.
And I will make you live in tents again,
as you do each year at the Festival of
Shelters.*
10 I sent my prophets to warn you
with many visions and parables."

11 But the people of Gilead are worthless
because of their idol worship.
And in Gilgal, too, they sacrifice bulls;
their altars are lined up like the heaps
of stone
along the edges of a plowed field.
12 Jacob fled to the land of Aram,
and there he* earned a wife by tending
sheep.
13 Then by a prophet
the LORD brought Jacob's descendants*
out of Egypt;
and by that prophet
they were protected.

12:2 *Jacob* sounds like the Hebrew word for "deceiver." **12:4** As in Greek and Syriac versions; Hebrew reads *to us*. **12:9** Hebrew *as in the days of your appointed feast*. **12:12** Hebrew *Israel*. See note on 10:11b. **12:13** Hebrew *brought Israel*. See note on 10:11b.

14 But the people of Israel
have bitterly provoked the LORD,
so their Lord will now sentence them to death
in payment for their sins.

CHAPTER 13

The LORD's Anger against Israel

1 When the tribe of Ephraim spoke,
the people shook with fear,
for that tribe was important in Israel.
But the people of Ephraim sinned by worshiping Baal
and thus sealed their destruction.
2 Now they continue to sin by making silver idols,
images shaped skillfully with human hands.
"Sacrifice to these," they cry,
"and kiss the calf idols!"
3 Therefore, they will disappear like the morning mist,
like dew in the morning sun,
like chaff blown by the wind,
like smoke from a chimney.

4 "I have been the LORD your God
ever since I brought you out of Egypt.
You must acknowledge no God but me,
for there is no other savior.
5 I took care of you in the wilderness,
in that dry and thirsty land.
6 But when you had eaten and were satisfied,
you became proud and forgot me.
7 So now I will attack you like a lion,
like a leopard that lurks along the road.
8 Like a bear whose cubs have been taken away,
I will tear out your heart.
I will devour you like a hungry lioness
and mangle you like a wild animal.

9 "You are about to be destroyed, O Israel—
yes, by me, your only helper.
10 Now where is* your king?
Let him save you!
Where are all the leaders of the land,
the king and the officials you demanded of me?
11 In my anger I gave you kings,
and in my fury I took them away.

12 "Ephraim's guilt has been collected,
and his sin has been stored up for punishment.
13 Pain has come to the people
like the pain of childbirth,
but they are like a child
who resists being born.
The moment of birth has arrived,
but they stay in the womb!

14 "Should I ransom them from the grave*?
Should I redeem them from death?
O death, bring on your terrors!
O grave, bring on your plagues!*
For I will not take pity on them.
15 Ephraim was the most fruitful of all his brothers,
but the east wind—a blast from the LORD—
will arise in the desert.
All their flowing springs will run dry,
and all their wells will disappear.
Every precious thing they own
will be plundered and carried away.
16 *The people of Samaria
must bear the consequences of their guilt
because they rebelled against their God.
They will be killed by an invading army,
their little ones dashed to death against the ground,
their pregnant women ripped open by swords."

CHAPTER 14

Healing for the Repentant

1 *Return, O Israel, to the LORD your God,
for your sins have brought you down.
2 Bring your confessions, and return to the LORD.
Say to him,
"Forgive all our sins and graciously receive us,
so that we may offer you our praises.*
3 Assyria cannot save us,
nor can our warhorses.

13:10 As in Greek and Syriac versions and Latin Vulgate; Hebrew reads *I will be.* **13:14a** Hebrew *Sheol;* also in 13:14b. **13:14b** Greek version reads *O death, where is your punishment? / O grave* [Hades], *where is your sting?* Compare 1 Cor 15:55. **13:16** Verse 16 is numbered 14:1 in Hebrew text. **14:1** Verses 14:1-9 are numbered 14:2-10 in Hebrew text. **14:2** As in Greek and Syriac versions, which read *may repay the fruit of our lips;* Hebrew reads *may repay the bulls of our lips.*

Never again will we say to the idols we
have made,
'You are our gods.'
No, in you alone
do the orphans find mercy."

4 The LORD says,
"Then I will heal you of your
faithlessness;
my love will know no bounds,
for my anger will be gone forever.
5 I will be to Israel
like a refreshing dew from heaven.
Israel will blossom like the lily;
it will send roots deep into the soil
like the cedars in Lebanon.
6 Its branches will spread out like beautiful
olive trees,
as fragrant as the cedars of Lebanon.
7 My people will again live under my shade.
They will flourish like grain and
blossom like grapevines.
They will be as fragrant as the wines of
Lebanon.

8 "O Israel,* stay away from idols!
I am the one who answers your prayers
and cares for you.
I am like a tree that is always green;
all your fruit comes from me."

9 Let those who are wise understand these
things.
Let those with discernment listen
carefully.
The paths of the LORD are true and right,
and righteous people live by walking in
them.
But in those paths sinners stumble and
fall.

14:8 Hebrew *Ephraim*, referring to the northern kingdom of Israel.

JOEL

WHO
Joel and the people of Judah.

WHERE
In the southern kingdom of Judah.

WHEN
During Joel's ministry, which occurred somewhere around 835 to 796 BC.

WHY
To warn Judah about God's judgment on their sins.

The LORD says, "Turn to me now, while there is time. Give me your hearts."
JOEL 2:12

When your teacher says, "It's time for the test," study time is over. You had better be ready. Joel preached about the Day of the Lord—God's deadline. He warned the people that God's judgment was coming, so they should stop sinning. When judgment did come, there would be no more time to get ready.

853 BC — King Ahab dies in battle
848 BC — Elisha becomes a prophet
841 BC — Jehu becomes king of Israel; Athaliah seizes Judah's throne
835 BC — Joel becomes a prophet; Joash becomes king of Judah
814 BC — Jehoahaz becomes king of Israel
798 BC — Jehoash becomes king of Israel
796? BC — Joel's ministry ends
793 BC — Jonah becomes a prophet; Jeroboam II becomes king of Israel

LET GOD SHOW YOU HOW HE WANTS YOU TO CHANGE.

CHAPTER 1

The LORD gave this message to Joel son Pethuel.

Mourning over the Locust Plague

2 Hear this, you leaders of the people.
Listen, all who live in the land.
In all your history,
has anything like this happened before?
3 Tell your children about it in the years to come,
and let your children tell their children.
Pass the story down from generation to generation.
4 After the cutting locusts finished eating the crops,
the swarming locusts took what was left!

After them came the hopping locusts,
and then the stripping locusts,* too!

5 Wake up, you drunkards, and weep!
Wail, all you wine-drinkers!
All the grapes are ruined,
and all your sweet wine is gone.
6 A vast army of locusts* has invaded my land,
a terrible army too numerous to count.
Its teeth are like lions' teeth,
its fangs like those of a lioness.
7 It has destroyed my grapevines
and ruined my fig trees,
stripping their bark and destroying it,
leaving the branches white and bare.

8 Weep like a bride dressed in black,
mourning the death of her husband.
9 For there is no grain or wine
to offer at the Temple of the LORD.
So the priests are in mourning.
The ministers of the LORD are weeping.
10 The fields are ruined,
the land is stripped bare.
The grain is destroyed,
the grapes have shriveled,
and the olive oil is gone.

11 Despair, all you farmers!
Wail, all you vine growers!
Weep, because the wheat and barley—
all the crops of the field—are ruined.
12 The grapevines have dried up,
and the fig trees have withered.
The pomegranate trees, palm trees, and apple trees—
all the fruit trees—have dried up.
And the people's joy has dried up with them.

13 Dress yourselves in burlap and weep, you priests!
Wail, you who serve before the altar!
Come, spend the night in burlap,
you ministers of my God.
For there is no grain or wine
to offer at the Temple of your God.
14 Announce a time of fasting;
call the people together for a solemn meeting.
Bring the leaders
and all the people of the land
into the Temple of the LORD your God,
and cry out to him there.
15 The day of the LORD is near,
the day when destruction comes from the Almighty.
How terrible that day will be!

16 Our food disappears before our very eyes.
No joyful celebrations are held in the house of our God.
17 The seeds die in the parched ground,
and the grain crops fail.
The barns stand empty,
and granaries are abandoned.
18 How the animals moan with hunger!
The herds of cattle wander about confused,
because they have no pasture.
The flocks of sheep and goats bleat in misery.

19 LORD, help us!
The fire has consumed the wilderness pastures,
and flames have burned up all the trees.
20 Even the wild animals cry out to you
because the streams have dried up,
and fire has consumed the wilderness pastures.

CHAPTER 2

Locusts Invade like an Army

1 Sound the alarm in Jerusalem*!
Raise the battle cry on my holy mountain!
Let everyone tremble in fear
because the day of the LORD is upon us.
2 It is a day of darkness and gloom,
a day of thick clouds and deep blackness.
Suddenly, like dawn spreading across the mountains,
a great and mighty army appears.
Nothing like it has been seen before
or will ever be seen again.

3 Fire burns in front of them,
and flames follow after them.
Ahead of them the land lies
as beautiful as the Garden of Eden.

1:4 The precise identification of the four kinds of locusts mentioned here is uncertain. **1:6** Hebrew *A nation.* **2:1** Hebrew *Zion;* also in 2:15, 23.

Behind them is nothing but desolation;
not one thing escapes.
4 They look like horses;
they charge forward like warhorses.*
5 Look at them as they leap along the
mountaintops.
Listen to the noise they make—like the
rumbling of chariots,
like the roar of fire sweeping across a
field of stubble,
or like a mighty army moving into
battle.

6 Fear grips all the people;
every face grows pale with terror.
7 The attackers march like warriors
and scale city walls like soldiers.
Straight forward they march,
never breaking rank.
8 They never jostle each other;
each moves in exactly the right
position.
They break through defenses
without missing a step.
9 They swarm over the city
and run along its walls.
They enter all the houses,
climbing like thieves through the
windows.
10 The earth quakes as they advance,
and the heavens tremble.
The sun and moon grow dark,
and the stars no longer shine.

11 The LORD is at the head of the column.
He leads them with a shout.
This is his mighty army,
and they follow his orders.
The day of the LORD is an awesome,
terrible thing.
Who can possibly survive?

A Call to Repentance

12 That is why the LORD says,
"Turn to me now, while there
is time.
Give me your hearts.
Come with fasting, weeping, and
mourning.
13 Don't tear your clothing in your grief,
but tear your hearts instead."
Return to the LORD your God,
for he is merciful and compassionate,
slow to get angry and filled with
unfailing love.
He is eager to relent and not punish.
14 Who knows? Perhaps he will give you
a reprieve,
sending you a blessing instead of this
curse.

2:4 Or *like charioteers.*

CLEAN!

Francisco got a call from his friend Marc. "I really need to talk, Francisco. Something happened and I'm really struggling. . . ." Francisco just listened and tried to understand what his friend was going through. After the phone call, he thought a lot about what Marc had told him. Marc had done something very wrong and felt terribly guilty about it. Francisco knew Marc felt really bad, and he wanted to help his friend. But what could he say to Marc? Check out Joel 2:12-13 for a wonderful promise from God that Francisco can share with his friend.

Perhaps you will be able to offer grain and wine
to the LORD your God as before.

15 Blow the ram's horn in Jerusalem!
Announce a time of fasting;
call the people together
for a solemn meeting.
16 Gather all the people—
the elders, the children, and even the babies.
Call the bridegroom from his quarters
and the bride from her private room.
17 Let the priests, who minister in the LORD's presence,
stand and weep between the entry room to the Temple and the altar.
Let them pray, "Spare your people, LORD!
Don't let your special possession become an object of mockery.
Don't let them become a joke for unbelieving foreigners who say,
'Has the God of Israel left them?'"

The LORD's Promise of Restoration

18 Then the LORD will pity his people
and jealously guard the honor of his land.
19 The LORD will reply,
"Look! I am sending you grain and new wine and olive oil,
enough to satisfy your needs.
You will no longer be an object of mockery
among the surrounding nations.
20 I will drive away these armies from the north.
I will send them into the parched wastelands.
Those in the front will be driven into the Dead Sea,
and those at the rear into the Mediterranean.*
The stench of their rotting bodies will rise over the land."

Surely the LORD has done great things!
21 Don't be afraid, my people.
Be glad now and rejoice,
for the LORD has done great things.
22 Don't be afraid, you animals of the field,
for the wilderness pastures will soon be green.
The trees will again be filled with fruit;
fig trees and grapevines will be loaded down once more.
23 Rejoice, you people of Jerusalem!
Rejoice in the LORD your God!
For the rain he sends demonstrates his faithfulness.
Once more the autumn rains will come,
as well as the rains of spring.
24 The threshing floors will again be piled high with grain,
and the presses will overflow with new wine and olive oil.
25 The LORD says, "I will give you back what you lost
to the swarming locusts, the hopping locusts,
the stripping locusts, and the cutting locusts.*
It was I who sent this great destroying army against you.
26 Once again you will have all the food you want,
and you will praise the LORD your God,
who does these miracles for you.
Never again will my people be disgraced.
27 Then you will know that I am among my people Israel,
that I am the LORD your God, and there is no other.
Never again will my people be disgraced.

The LORD's Promise of His Spirit

28* "Then, after doing all those things,
I will pour out my Spirit upon all people.
Your sons and daughters will prophesy.
Your old men will dream dreams,
and your young men will see visions.
29 In those days I will pour out my Spirit
even on servants—men and women alike.
30 And I will cause wonders in the heavens and on the earth—
blood and fire and columns of smoke.

2:20 Hebrew *into the eastern sea, . . . into the western sea.* **2:25** The precise identification of the four kinds of locusts mentioned here is uncertain. **2:28** Verses 2:28-32 are numbered 3:1-5 in Hebrew text.

31 The sun will become dark,
and the moon will turn blood red
before that great and terrible* day of
the LORD arrives.
32 But everyone who calls on the name
of the LORD
will be saved,
for some on Mount Zion in Jerusalem
will escape,
just as the LORD has said.
These will be among the survivors
whom the LORD has called.

Who can be saved? * **Everyone who calls on the name of the LORD will be saved.** JOEL 2:32

CHAPTER 3

Judgment against Enemy Nations

1* "At the time of those events," says the
LORD,
"when I restore the prosperity of Judah
and Jerusalem,
2 I will gather the armies of the world
into the valley of Jehoshaphat.*
There I will judge them
for harming my people, my special
possession,
for scattering my people among the
nations,
and for dividing up my land.
3 They threw dice* to decide which
of my people
would be their slaves.
They traded boys to obtain prostitutes
and sold girls for enough wine to get
drunk.

4 "What do you have against me, Tyre and Sidon and you cities of Philistia? Are you trying to take revenge on me? If you are, then watch out! I will strike swiftly and pay you back for everything you have done. 5 You have taken my silver and gold and all my precious treasures, and have carried them off to your pagan temples. 6 You have sold the people of Judah and Jerusalem to the Greeks,* so they could take them far from their homeland.

7 "But I will bring them back from all the places to which you sold them, and I will pay you back for everything you have done. 8 I will sell your sons and daughters to the people of Judah, and they will sell them to the people of Arabia,* a nation far away. I, the LORD, have spoken!"

9 Say to the nations far and wide:
"Get ready for war!
Call out your best warriors.
Let all your fighting men advance for
the attack.
10 Hammer your plowshares into swords
and your pruning hooks into spears.
Train even your weaklings to be
warriors.
11 Come quickly, all you nations
everywhere.
Gather together in the valley."

And now, O LORD, call out your warriors!

12 "Let the nations be called to arms.
Let them march to the valley of
Jehoshaphat.
There I, the LORD, will sit
to pronounce judgment on them all.
13 Swing the sickle,
for the harvest is ripe.*
Come, tread the grapes,
for the winepress is full.
The storage vats are overflowing
with the wickedness of these
people."

14 Thousands upon thousands are waiting
in the valley of decision.
There the day of the LORD will soon
arrive.
15 The sun and moon will grow dark,
and the stars will no longer shine.
16 The LORD's voice will roar from Zion
and thunder from Jerusalem,
and the heavens and the earth will
shake.
But the LORD will be a refuge for
his people,
a strong fortress for the people
of Israel.

2:31 Greek version reads *glorious*. **3:1** Verses 3:1-21 are numbered 4:1-21 in Hebrew text. **3:2** *Jehoshaphat* means "the LORD judges." **3:3** Hebrew *They cast lots*. **3:6** Hebrew *to the peoples of Javan*. **3:8** Hebrew *to the Sabeans*. **3:13** Greek version reads *for the harvest time has come*. Compare Mark 4:29.

Blessings for God's People

17 "Then you will know that I, the LORD your God,
live in Zion, my holy mountain.
Jerusalem will be holy forever,
and foreign armies will never conquer her again.
18 In that day the mountains will drip with sweet wine,
and the hills will flow with milk.
Water will fill the streambeds of Judah,
and a fountain will burst forth from the LORD's Temple,
watering the arid valley of acacias.*
19 But Egypt will become a wasteland
and Edom will become a wilderness,
because they attacked the people of Judah
and killed innocent people in their land.
20 "But Judah will be filled with people forever,
and Jerusalem will endure through all generations.
21 I will pardon my people's crimes,
which I have not yet pardoned;
and I, the LORD, will make my home in Jerusalem* with my people."

3:18 Hebrew *valley of Shittim*. 3:21 Hebrew *Zion*.

AMOS

WHO
Amos, Amaziah the priest, and King Jeroboam II.

WHERE
The northern kingdom of Israel.

WHEN
Around 760–750 BC when Jeroboam II was king of Israel.

WHY
To tell Israel about the judgment that was coming because they worshiped idols, ignored God's laws, and mistreated the poor.

[The Lord says,] "I want to see a mighty flood of justice, an endless river of righteous living."
AMOS 5:24

God wants to use *all* kinds of people to do his work. Amos was an ordinary person who took care of sheep and fig trees. He was not a prophet or a priest, but God gave him a message. Amos didn't make excuses or complain. He just did what God asked him to do.

793 BC — Jeroboam II becomes king of Israel
760 BC — Amos becomes a prophet to Israel
753 BC — Hosea becomes a prophet to Israel
752 BC — King Shallum of Israel is killed
740 BC — Isaiah becomes a prophet to Judah

Be ready to serve God anywhere, anytime, like Amos.

CHAPTER 1

This message was given to Amos, a shepherd from the town of Tekoa in Judah. He received this message in visions two years before the earthquake, when Uzziah was king of Judah and Jeroboam II, the son of Jehoash,* was king of Israel.

1:1 Hebrew *Joash*, a variant spelling of Jehoash.

2 This is what he saw and heard:

"The LORD's voice will roar from Zion
and thunder from Jerusalem!
The lush pastures of the shepherds
will dry up;
the grass on Mount Carmel will wither
and die."

God's Judgment on Israel's Neighbors

3 This is what the LORD says:

"The people of Damascus have sinned
again and again,*
and I will not let them go unpunished!
They beat down my people in Gilead
as grain is threshed with iron sledges.
4 So I will send down fire on King Hazael's
palace,
and the fortresses of King Ben-hadad
will be destroyed.
5 I will break down the gates of Damascus
and slaughter the people in the valley
of Aven.
I will destroy the ruler in Beth-eden,
and the people of Aram will go as
captives to Kir,"
says the LORD.

6 This is what the LORD says:

"The people of Gaza have sinned again
and again,
and I will not let them go unpunished!
They sent whole villages into exile,
selling them as slaves to Edom.
7 So I will send down fire on the walls of
Gaza,
and all its fortresses will be destroyed.
8 I will slaughter the people of Ashdod
and destroy the king of Ashkelon.
Then I will turn to attack Ekron,
and the few Philistines still left will be
killed,"
says the Sovereign LORD.

9 This is what the LORD says:

"The people of Tyre have sinned again
and again,
and I will not let them go unpunished!
They broke their treaty of brotherhood
with Israel,
selling whole villages as slaves
to Edom.
10 So I will send down fire on the walls
of Tyre,
and all its fortresses will be destroyed."

11 This is what the LORD says:

"The people of Edom have sinned again
and again,
and I will not let them go unpunished!
They chased down their relatives, the
Israelites, with swords,
showing them no mercy.
In their rage, they slashed them
continually
and were unrelenting in their anger.
12 So I will send down fire on Teman,
and the fortresses of Bozrah will be
destroyed."

13 This is what the LORD says:

"The people of Ammon have sinned again
and again,
and I will not let them go unpunished!
When they attacked Gilead to extend
their borders,
they ripped open pregnant women with
their swords.
14 So I will send down fire on the walls of
Rabbah,
and all its fortresses will be destroyed.
The battle will come upon them with
shouts,
like a whirlwind in a mighty storm.
15 And their king* and his princes will go
into exile together,"
says the LORD.

CHAPTER 2

This is what the LORD says:

"The people of Moab have sinned again
and again,*
and I will not let them go unpunished!
They desecrated the bones of Edom's king,
burning them to ashes.
2 So I will send down fire on the land of Moab,
and all the fortresses in Kerioth will be
destroyed.
The people will fall in the noise of battle,
as the warriors shout and the ram's
horn sounds.
3 And I will destroy their king
and slaughter all their princes,"
says the LORD.

God's Judgment on Judah and Israel

4 This is what the LORD says:

"The people of Judah have sinned again
and again,

1:3 Hebrew *have committed three sins, even four;* also in 1:6, 9, 11, 13. **1:15** Hebrew *malcam,* possibly referring to their god Molech.
2:1 Hebrew *have committed three sins, even four;* also in 2:4, 6.

and I will not let them go unpunished!
They have rejected the instruction of the LORD,
refusing to obey his decrees.
They have been led astray by the same lies
that deceived their ancestors.
5 So I will send down fire on Judah,
and all the fortresses of Jerusalem will
be destroyed."

6 This is what the LORD says:

"The people of Israel have sinned again
and again,
and I will not let them go unpunished!
They sell honorable people for silver
and poor people for a pair of sandals.
7 They trample helpless people in the dust
and shove the oppressed out of the way.
Both father and son sleep with the same
woman,
corrupting my holy name.
8 At their religious festivals,
they lounge in clothing their debtors
put up as security.
In the house of their gods,*
they drink wine bought with unjust fines.

9 "But as my people watched,
I destroyed the Amorites,
though they were as tall as cedars
and as strong as oaks.
I destroyed the fruit on their branches
and dug out their roots.
10 It was I who rescued you from Egypt
and led you through the desert for
forty years,
so you could possess the land of the
Amorites.
11 I chose some of your sons to be prophets
and others to be Nazirites.
Can you deny this, my people of Israel?"
asks the LORD.
12 "But you caused the Nazirites to sin by
making them drink wine,
and you commanded the prophets,
'Shut up!'

13 "So I will make you groan
like a wagon loaded down with sheaves
of grain.
14 Your fastest runners will not get away.
The strongest among you will become
weak.
Even mighty warriors will be unable to
save themselves.
15 The archers will not stand their ground.
The swiftest runners won't be fast enough
to escape.
Even those riding horses won't be able
to save themselves.

AMAZING FACTS

The people of Israel were so wicked that they would trade poor people for a pair of sandals.

AMOS 2:6

16 On that day the most courageous of your
fighting men
will drop their weapons and run for
their lives,"
says the LORD.

CHAPTER 3

Listen to this message that the LORD has spoken against you, O people of Israel and Judah—against the entire family I rescued from Egypt:

2 "From among all the families on the earth,
I have been intimate with you alone.
That is why I must punish you
for all your sins."

Witnesses against Guilty Israel

3 Can two people walk together
without agreeing on the direction?
4 Does a lion ever roar in a thicket
without first finding a victim?
Does a young lion growl in its den
without first catching its prey?
5 Does a bird ever get caught in a trap
that has no bait?
Does a trap spring shut
when there's nothing to catch?

2:8 Or *their God.*

6 When the ram's horn blows a warning,
shouldn't the people be alarmed?
Does disaster come to a city
unless the LORD has planned it?

7 Indeed, the Sovereign LORD never does anything
until he reveals his plans to his servants the prophets.

8 The lion has roared—
so who isn't frightened?
The Sovereign LORD has spoken—
so who can refuse to proclaim his message?

9 Announce this to the leaders of Philistia*
and to the great ones of Egypt:
"Take your seats now on the hills around Samaria,
and witness the chaos and oppression in Israel."

10 "My people have forgotten how to do right,"
says the LORD.
"Their fortresses are filled with wealth taken by theft and violence.

11 Therefore," says the Sovereign LORD,
"an enemy is coming!
He will surround them and shatter their defenses.
Then he will plunder all their fortresses."

12 This is what the LORD says:

"A shepherd who tries to rescue a sheep from a lion's mouth
will recover only two legs or a piece of an ear.
So it will be for the Israelites in Samaria lying on luxurious beds,
and for the people of Damascus reclining on couches.*

13 "Now listen to this, and announce it throughout all Israel,*" says the Lord, the LORD God of Heaven's Armies.

14 "On the very day I punish Israel for its sins,
I will destroy the pagan altars at Bethel.
The horns of the altar will be cut off
and fall to the ground.

15 And I will destroy the beautiful homes of the wealthy—
their winter mansions and their summer houses, too—
all their palaces filled with ivory,"
says the LORD.

CHAPTER 4

Israel's Failure to Learn

1 Listen to me, you fat cows*
living in Samaria,
you women who oppress the poor
and crush the needy,
and who are always calling to your husbands,
"Bring us another drink!"

2 The Sovereign LORD has sworn this by his holiness:
"The time will come when you will be led away
with hooks in your noses.
Every last one of you will be dragged away
like a fish on a hook!

3 You will be led out through the ruins of the wall;
you will be thrown from your fortresses,*"
says the LORD.

4 "Go ahead and offer sacrifices to the idols at Bethel.
Keep on disobeying at Gilgal.
Offer sacrifices each morning,
and bring your tithes every three days.

5 Present your bread made with yeast
as an offering of thanksgiving.
Then give your extra voluntary offerings
so you can brag about it everywhere!
This is the kind of thing you Israelites love to do,"
says the Sovereign LORD.

6 "I brought hunger to every city
and famine to every town.
But still you would not return to me,"
says the LORD.

7 "I kept the rain from falling
when your crops needed it the most.
I sent rain on one town

3:9 Hebrew *Ashdod*. **3:12** The meaning of the Hebrew in this sentence is uncertain. **3:13** Hebrew *the house of Jacob*. The names "Jacob" and "Israel" are often interchanged throughout the Old Testament, referring sometimes to the individual patriarch and sometimes to the nation. **4:1** Hebrew *you cows of Bashan*. **4:3** Or *thrown out toward Harmon*, possibly a reference to Mount Hermon.

but withheld it from another.
Rain fell on one field,
while another field withered away.
8 People staggered from town to town
looking for water,
but there was never enough.
But still you would not return to me,"
says the LORD.

9 "I struck your farms and vineyards with
blight and mildew.
Locusts devoured all your fig and olive
trees.
But still you would not return to me,"
says the LORD.

10 "I sent plagues on you
like the plagues I sent on Egypt long
ago.
I killed your young men in war
and led all your horses away.*
The stench of death filled the air!
But still you would not return to me,"
says the LORD.

11 "I destroyed some of your cities,
as I destroyed* Sodom and Gomorrah.
Those of you who survived
were like charred sticks pulled from
a fire.
But still you would not return to me,"
says the LORD.

12 "Therefore, I will bring upon you all the
disasters I have announced.
Prepare to meet your God in judgment,
you people of Israel!"

13 For the LORD is the one who shaped the
mountains,
stirs up the winds, and reveals his
thoughts to mankind.
He turns the light of dawn into darkness
and treads on the heights of the earth.
The LORD God of Heaven's Armies
is his name!

CHAPTER 5

A Call to Repentance

Listen, you people of Israel! Listen to this funeral song I am singing:

2 "The virgin Israel has fallen,
never to rise again!
She lies abandoned on the ground,
with no one to help her up."

3 The Sovereign LORD says:

"When a city sends a thousand men to
battle,
only a hundred will return.
When a town sends a hundred,
only ten will come back alive."

4 Now this is what the LORD says to the family of Israel:

"Come back to me and live!
5 Don't worship at the pagan altars at Bethel;
don't go to the shrines at Gilgal or
Beersheba.
For the people of Gilgal will be dragged
off into exile,
and the people of Bethel will be
reduced to nothing."
6 Come back to the LORD and live!
Otherwise, he will roar through Israel*
like a fire,
devouring you completely.
Your gods in Bethel
won't be able to quench the flames.
7 You twist justice, making it a bitter pill for
the oppressed.
You treat the righteous like dirt.

8 It is the LORD who created the stars,
the Pleiades and Orion.
He turns darkness into morning
and day into night.
He draws up water from the oceans
and pours it down as rain on the land.
The LORD is his name!
9 With blinding speed and power he
destroys the strong,
crushing all their defenses.

10 How you hate honest judges!
How you despise people who
tell the truth!
11 You trample the poor,
stealing their grain through taxes and
unfair rent.
Therefore, though you build beautiful
stone houses,
you will never live in them.
Though you plant lush vineyards,

4:10 Or *and slaughtered your captured horses.* **4:11** Hebrew *as when God destroyed.* **5:6** Hebrew *the house of Joseph.*

you will never drink wine from
them.
12 For I know the vast number of
your sins
and the depth of your rebellions.
You oppress good people by taking bribes
and deprive the poor of justice
in the courts.
13 So those who are smart keep their mouths
shut,
for it is an evil time.

14 Do what is good and run from evil
so that you may live!
Then the LORD God of Heaven's
Armies will be your helper,
just as you have claimed.
15 Hate evil and love what is good;
turn your courts into true halls of
justice.

Who cares if I'm always fair and try to do what's right?

[The LORD says,] "I want to see a mighty flood of justice, an endless river of righteous living." AMOS 5:24

Perhaps even yet the LORD God of
Heaven's Armies
will have mercy on the remnant of his
people.*

16 Therefore, this is what the Lord, the LORD
God of Heaven's Armies, says:

"There will be crying in all the public
squares
and mourning in every street.
Call for the farmers to weep with you,
and summon professional mourners
to wail.
17 There will be wailing in every vineyard,
for I will destroy them all,"
says the LORD.

Warning of Coming Judgment

18 What sorrow awaits you who say,
"If only the day of the LORD were here!"
You have no idea what you are wishing
for.
That day will bring darkness, not light.
19 In that day you will be like a man who
runs from a lion—
only to meet a bear.
Escaping from the bear, he leans his hand
against a wall in his house—
and he's bitten by a snake.
20 Yes, the day of the LORD will be dark and
hopeless,
without a ray of joy or hope.

21 "I hate all your show and pretense—
the hypocrisy of your religious festivals
and solemn assemblies.
22 I will not accept your burnt offerings and
grain offerings.
I won't even notice all your choice
peace offerings.
23 Away with your noisy hymns of praise!
I will not listen to the music of your
harps.

24 Instead, I want to see a mighty flood of
justice,
an endless river of righteous living.

25 "Was it to me you were bringing sacrifices and offerings during the forty years in the wilderness, Israel? 26 No, you served your pagan gods—Sakkuth your king god and Kaiwan your star god—the images you made for yourselves. 27 So I will send you into exile, to a land east of Damascus,*" says the LORD, whose name is the God of Heaven's Armies.

CHAPTER 6

1 What sorrow awaits you who lounge in
luxury in Jerusalem,*
and you who feel secure in Samaria!
You are famous and popular in Israel,
and people go to you for help.
2 But go over to Calneh
and see what happened there.
Then go to the great city of Hamath
and down to the Philistine city of Gath.
You are no better than they were,

5:15 Hebrew *the remnant of Joseph.* **5:26-27** Greek version reads *No, you carried your pagan gods—the shrine of Molech, the star of your god Rephan, and the images you made for yourselves. So I will send you into exile, to a land east of Damascus.* Compare Acts 7:43. **6:1** Hebrew *in Zion.*

and look at how they were destroyed.
3 You push away every thought of coming disaster,
but your actions only bring the day of judgment closer.
4 How terrible for you who sprawl on ivory beds
and lounge on your couches,
eating the meat of tender lambs from the flock
and of choice calves fattened in the stall.
5 You sing trivial songs to the sound of the harp
and fancy yourselves to be great musicians like David.
6 You drink wine by the bowlful
and perfume yourselves with fragrant lotions.
You care nothing about the ruin of your nation.*
7 Therefore, you will be the first to be led away as captives.
Suddenly, all your parties will end.

8 The Sovereign LORD has sworn by his own name, and this is what he, the LORD God of Heaven's Armies, says:

"I despise the arrogance of Israel,*
and I hate their fortresses.
I will give this city
and everything in it to their enemies."

9 (If there are ten men left in one house, they will all die. 10 And when a relative who is responsible to dispose of the dead* goes into the house to carry out the bodies, he will ask the last survivor, "Is anyone else with you?" When the person begins to swear, "No, by . . . ," he will interrupt and say, "Stop! Don't even mention the name of the LORD.")

11 When the LORD gives the command,
homes both great and small will be smashed to pieces.

12 Can horses gallop over boulders?
Can oxen be used to plow them?
But that's how foolish you are when you turn justice into poison
and the sweet fruit of righteousness into bitterness.

13 And you brag about your conquest of Lo-debar.*
You boast, "Didn't we take Karnaim* by our own strength?"

14 "O people of Israel, I am about to bring an enemy nation against you,"
says the LORD God of Heaven's Armies.
"They will oppress you throughout your land—
from Lebo-hamath in the north
to the Arabah Valley in the south."

CHAPTER 7

A Vision of Locusts

The Sovereign LORD showed me a vision. I saw him preparing to send a vast swarm of locusts over the land. This was after the king's share had been harvested from the fields and as the main crop was coming up. 2 In my vision the locusts ate every green plant in sight. Then I said, "O Sovereign LORD, please forgive us or we will not survive, for Israel* is so small."

3 So the LORD relented from this plan. "I will not do it," he said.

A Vision of Fire

4 Then the Sovereign LORD showed me another vision. I saw him preparing to punish his people with a great fire. The fire had burned up the depths of the sea and was devouring the entire land. 5 Then I said, "O Sovereign LORD, please stop or we will not survive, for Israel is so small."

6 Then the LORD relented from this plan, too. "I will not do that either," said the Sovereign LORD.

A Vision of a Plumb Line

7 Then he showed me another vision. I saw the Lord standing beside a wall that had been built using a plumb line. He was using a plumb line to see if it was still straight. 8 And the LORD said to me, "Amos, what do you see?"

I answered, "A plumb line."

And the Lord replied, "I will test my people with this plumb line. I will no longer ignore all their sins. 9 The pagan shrines of your ancestors* will be ruined, and the temples of Israel will be destroyed; I will bring the dynasty of King Jeroboam to a sudden end."

6:6 Hebrew *of Joseph*. **6:8** Hebrew *Jacob*. See note on 3:13. **6:10** Or *to burn the dead*. The meaning of the Hebrew is uncertain. **6:13a** *Lo-debar* means "nothing." **6:13b** *Karnaim* means "horns," a term that symbolizes strength. **7:2** Hebrew *Jacob*; also in 7:5. See note on 3:13. **7:9** Hebrew *of Isaac*.

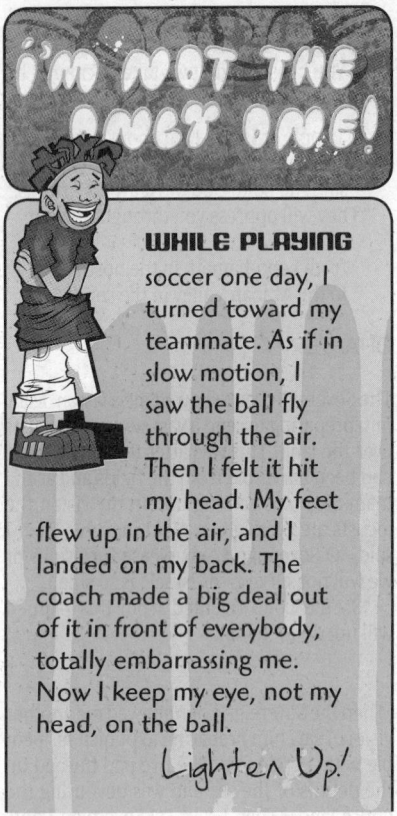

Amos and Amaziah

[10]Then Amaziah, the priest of Bethel, sent a message to Jeroboam, king of Israel: "Amos is hatching a plot against you right here on your very doorstep! What he is saying is intolerable. [11]He is saying, 'Jeroboam will soon be killed, and the people of Israel will be sent away into exile.'"

[12]Then Amaziah sent orders to Amos: "Get out of here, you prophet! Go on back to the land of Judah, and earn your living by prophesying there! [13]Don't bother us with your prophecies here in Bethel. This is the king's sanctuary and the national place of worship!"

[14]But Amos replied, "I'm not a professional prophet, and I was never trained to be one.* I'm just a shepherd, and I take care of sycamore-fig trees. [15]But the LORD called me away from my flock and told me, 'Go and prophesy to my people in Israel.' [16]Now then, listen to this message from the LORD:

"You say,
'Don't prophesy against Israel.
Stop preaching against my people.*'
[17] But this is what the LORD says:
'Your wife will become a prostitute in this city,
and your sons and daughters will be killed.
Your land will be divided up,
and you yourself will die in a foreign land.
And the people of Israel will certainly become captives in exile,
far from their homeland.'"

CHAPTER 8

A Vision of Ripe Fruit

Then the Sovereign LORD showed me another vision. In it I saw a basket filled with ripe fruit. [2]"What do you see, Amos?" he asked.

I replied, "A basket full of ripe fruit."

Then the LORD said, "Like this fruit, Israel is ripe for punishment! I will not delay their punishment again. [3]In that day the singing in the Temple will turn to wailing. Dead bodies will be scattered everywhere. They will be carried out of the city in silence. I, the Sovereign LORD, have spoken!"

[4] Listen to this, you who rob the poor and trample down the needy!
[5] You can't wait for the Sabbath day to be over
and the religious festivals to end
so you can get back to cheating the helpless.
You measure out grain with dishonest measures
and cheat the buyer with dishonest scales.*
[6] And you mix the grain you sell with chaff swept from the floor.
Then you enslave poor people for one piece of silver or a pair of sandals.

[7] Now the LORD has sworn this oath by his own name, the Pride of Israel*:

7:14 Or *I'm not a prophet nor the son of a prophet.* **7:16** Hebrew *against the house of Isaac.* **8:5** Hebrew *You make the ephah* [a unit for measuring grain] *small and the shekel* [a unit of weight] *great, and you deal falsely by using deceitful balances.* **8:7** Hebrew *the pride of Jacob.* See note on 3:13.

"I will never forget
the wicked things you have done!
8 The earth will tremble for your deeds,
and everyone will mourn.
The ground will rise like the Nile River at floodtime;
it will heave up, then sink again.

9 "In that day," says the Sovereign LORD,
"I will make the sun go down at noon
and darken the earth while it is still day.
10 I will turn your celebrations into times of mourning
and your singing into weeping.
You will wear funeral clothes
and shave your heads to show your sorrow—
as if your only son had died.
How very bitter that day will be!

11 "The time is surely coming," says the Sovereign LORD,
"when I will send a famine on the land—
not a famine of bread or water
but of hearing the words of the LORD.
12 People will stagger from sea to sea
and wander from border to border*
searching for the word of the LORD,
but they will not find it.
13 Beautiful girls and strong young men
will grow faint in that day,
thirsting for the LORD's word.
14 And those who swear by the shameful idols of Samaria—
who take oaths in the name of the god of Dan
and make vows in the name of the god of Beersheba*—
they will all fall down,
never to rise again."

CHAPTER 9

A Vision of God at the Altar

Then I saw a vision of the Lord standing beside the altar. He said,

"Strike the tops of the Temple columns,
so that the foundation will shake.
Bring down the roof
on the heads of the people below.
I will kill with the sword those who survive.
No one will escape!

2 "Even if they dig down to the place of the dead,*
I will reach down and pull them up.
Even if they climb up into the heavens,
I will bring them down.
3 Even if they hide at the very top of Mount Carmel,
I will search them out and capture them.
Even if they hide at the bottom of the ocean,
I will send the sea serpent after them to bite them.
4 Even if their enemies drive them into exile,
I will command the sword to kill them there.
I am determined to bring disaster upon them
and not to help them."

5 The Lord, the LORD of Heaven's Armies,
touches the land and it melts,
and all its people mourn.
The ground rises like the Nile River at floodtime,
and then it sinks again.
6 The LORD's home reaches up to the heavens,
while its foundation is on the earth.
He draws up water from the oceans
and pours it down as rain on the land.
The LORD is his name!

7 "Are you Israelites more important to me than the Ethiopians?*" asks the LORD.
"I brought Israel out of Egypt,
but I also brought the Philistines from Crete*
and led the Arameans out of Kir.

8 "I, the Sovereign LORD,
am watching this sinful nation of Israel.
I will destroy it
from the face of the earth.
But I will never completely destroy the family of Israel,*"
says the LORD.

8:12 Hebrew *from north to east.* **8:14** Hebrew *the way of Beersheba.* **9:2** Hebrew *to Sheol.* **9:7a** Hebrew *the Cushites?* **9:7b** Hebrew *Caphtor.* **9:8** Hebrew *the house of Jacob.* See note on 3:13.

9 "For I will give the command
and will shake Israel along with the other nations
as grain is shaken in a sieve,
yet not one true kernel will be lost.
10 But all the sinners will die by the sword—
all those who say, 'Nothing bad will happen to us.'

A Promise of Restoration

11 "In that day I will restore the fallen house* of David.
I will repair its damaged walls.
From the ruins I will rebuild it
and restore its former glory.
12 And Israel will possess what is left of Edom
and all the nations I have called to be mine.*"
The LORD has spoken,
and he will do these things.

13 "The time will come," says the LORD,
"when the grain and grapes will grow faster
than they can be harvested.
Then the terraced vineyards on the hills of Israel
will drip with sweet wine!
14 I will bring my exiled people of Israel
back from distant lands,
and they will rebuild their ruined cities
and live in them again.
They will plant vineyards and gardens;
they will eat their crops and drink their wine.
15 I will firmly plant them there
in their own land.
They will never again be uprooted
from the land I have given them,"
says the LORD your God.

9:11a Or *kingdom;* Hebrew reads *tent.* **9:11b-12** Greek version reads *and restore its former glory, / so that the rest of humanity, including the Gentiles— / all those I have called to be mine—might seek me.* Compare Acts 15:16-17.

OBADIAH

WHO
Obadiah and the people of Edom.

WHERE
The southern kingdom of Judah.

WHEN
Possibly during the reign of Jehoram in Judah around 853–841 BC.

WHY
To show that God judges those who have harmed his people.

I, the LORD, will judge all godless nations! . . . All your evil deeds will fall back on your own heads.
OBADIAH 1:15

Good parents defend their children and stand against anyone who wants to harm them. Parents do this even when their children are not perfect. That's what God does for his people. He protects them from bullies. Obadiah describes how God would respond to any nation that tried to hurt his children, Israel.

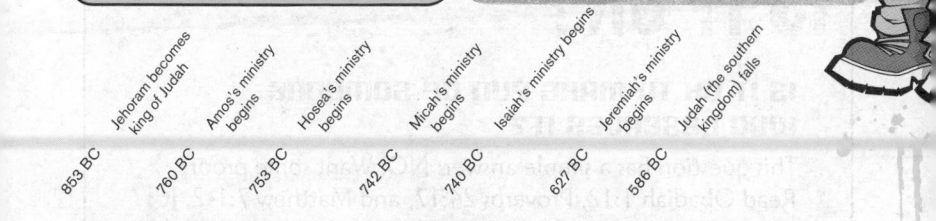

READ OBADIAH'S MESSAGE AND THINK ABOUT HOW MUCH GOD CARES FOR YOU.

This is the vision that the Sovereign LORD revealed to Obadiah concerning the land of Edom.

Edom's Judgment Announced

We have heard a message from the LORD
that an ambassador was sent to the nations to say,
"Get ready, everyone!
Let's assemble our armies and attack Edom!"

2 The LORD says to Edom,
"I will cut you down to size among the nations;
you will be greatly despised.

3 You have been deceived by your own pride
because you live in a rock fortress
and make your home high in the mountains.
'Who can ever reach us way up here?'
you ask boastfully.
4 But even if you soar as high as eagles
and build your nest among the stars,
I will bring you crashing down,"
says the LORD.

5 "If thieves came at night and robbed you
(what a disaster awaits you!),
they would not take everything.
Those who harvest grapes
always leave a few for the poor.
But your enemies will wipe you out completely!
6 Every nook and cranny of Edom*
will be searched and looted.
Every treasure will be found and taken.

7 "All your allies will turn against you.
They will help to chase you from your land.
They will promise you peace
while plotting to deceive and destroy you.
Your trusted friends will set traps for you,
and you won't even know about it.
8 At that time not a single wise person
will be left in the whole land of Edom,"
says the LORD.
"For on the mountains of Edom
I will destroy everyone who has understanding.
9 The mightiest warriors of Teman
will be terrified,
and everyone on the mountains of Edom
will be cut down in the slaughter.

Reasons for Edom's Punishment

10 "Because of the violence you did
to your close relatives in Israel,*
you will be filled with shame
and destroyed forever.
11 When they were invaded,
you stood aloof, refusing to help them.
Foreign invaders carried off their wealth
and cast lots to divide up Jerusalem,

6 Hebrew *Esau;* also in 8b, 9, 18, 19, 21. **10** Hebrew *your brother Jacob.* The names "Jacob" and "Israel" are often interchanged throughout the Old Testament, referring sometimes to the individual patriarch and sometimes to the nation.

IS IT OK?

IS IT OK TO MAKE FUN OF SOMEONE WHO DESERVES IT?

This question has a simple answer: NO. Want some proof? Read Obadiah 1:12, Proverbs 24:17, and Matthew 7:1-2. It's so easy to make fun of others—to gloat over someone who's been mean to you and to laugh when someone you don't like gets embarrassed or hurt. But in Obadiah, verse 12, God rebuked the people of Edom for laughing when his people were in trouble. God didn't laugh with them. In fact, God punished the Edomites for laughing at his people. When you're tempted to make fun of someone else, first imagine yourself in that person's shoes. Think about how it would feel if people were laughing at you. Then choose to be quiet and kind.

but you acted like one of Israel's
enemies.

12 "You should not have gloated
when they exiled your relatives to
distant lands.
You should not have rejoiced
when the people of Judah suffered
such misfortune.
You should not have spoken arrogantly
in that terrible time of trouble.
13 You should not have plundered the land
of Israel
when they were suffering such
calamity.
You should not have gloated over their
destruction
when they were suffering such
calamity.
You should not have seized their wealth
when they were suffering such
calamity.
14 You should not have stood at the
crossroads,
killing those who tried to escape.
You should not have captured the
survivors
and handed them over in their terrible
time of trouble.

Edom Destroyed, Israel Restored

15 "The day is near when I, the LORD,
will judge all godless nations!
As you have done to Israel,
so it will be done to you.
All your evil deeds
will fall back on your own heads.
16 Just as you swallowed up my people
on my holy mountain,
so you and the surrounding nations
will swallow the punishment I pour out
on you.
Yes, all you nations will drink and stagger
and disappear from history.

17 "But Jerusalem* will become a refuge for
those who escape;
it will be a holy place.
And the people of Israel* will come back
to reclaim their inheritance.
18 The people of Israel will be a raging fire,
and Edom a field of dry stubble.
The descendants of Joseph will be a flame
roaring across the field, devouring
everything.
There will be no survivors in Edom.
I, the LORD, have spoken!

19 "Then my people living in the Negev
will occupy the mountains of Edom.
Those living in the foothills of Judah*
will possess the Philistine plains
and take over the fields of Ephraim and
Samaria.
And the people of Benjamin
will occupy the land of Gilead.
20 The exiles of Israel will return to their
land
and occupy the Phoenician coast as far
north as Zarephath.
The captives from Jerusalem exiled in the
north*
will return home and resettle the towns
of the Negev.
21 Those who have been rescued* will go up
to* Mount Zion in Jerusalem
to rule over the mountains of Edom.
And the LORD himself will be king!"

17a Hebrew *Mount Zion*. **17b** Hebrew *house of Jacob;* also in 18. See note on 10. **19** Hebrew *the Shephelah*. **20** Hebrew *in Sepharad*. **21a** As in Greek and Syriac versions; Hebrew reads *Rescuers*. **21b** Or *from*.

JONAH

WHO
Jonah, the ship's captain and crew, and the people of Nineveh.

WHERE
In Joppa and in Nineveh.

WHEN
Around 785–760 BC, before Israel was conquered by Assyria.

WHY
To show that God's message is for all people.

[The LORD said,] "Nineveh has more than 120,000 people living in spiritual darkness. . . . Shouldn't I feel sorry for such a great city?"
JONAH 4:11

At first Jonah refused to preach in Nineveh. It was the capital city of Assyria, a hated enemy of the people of Israel. Jonah didn't want these enemies to repent and receive mercy and forgiveness. But after a run-in with a big fish, he did what God asked.

793 BC — Jeroboam II becomes king of Israel; Jonah becomes a prophet
792 BC — Uzziah becomes king of Judah
783 BC — Shalmaneser IV becomes king of Assyria
772 BC — Ashur-dan III becomes king of Assyria
760 BC — Amos becomes a prophet
759? BC — Jonah preaches to Nineveh
754 BC — Ashur-nirari V becomes king of Assyria
753 BC — Jonah's ministry ends
722 BC — Israel falls to Assyria

DON'T RUN THE OTHER WAY. PRAY FOR YOUR ENEMIES. TELL THEM ABOUT GOD'S LOVE.

CHAPTER 1

Jonah Runs from the LORD

The LORD gave this message to Jonah son of Amittai: [2]"Get up and go to the great city of Nineveh. Announce my judgment against it because I have seen how wicked its people are."

[3]But Jonah got up and went in the opposite direction to get away from the LORD. He went down to the port of Joppa, where he found a ship leaving for Tarshish. He bought a ticket and went on board, hoping to escape from the LORD by sailing to Tarshish.

[4]But the LORD hurled a powerful wind over

BUT I DON'T WANT TO!

Robert spent all morning cleaning up his room. Everything was finally in order. If Mom gave the okay, he still could hang out with his friends before his grandparents arrived. Mom looked around his room and said, "Okay, I have one more thing for you to do. Please help your little sister clean her room." *What?* Robert thought. *It's not fair! Nobody helped me.* Robert felt like saying, "No way, Mom!" What might happen if Robert says no? Look up Jonah 1:1-17 to see what happened to Jonah when he said "no way" to God. What might happen if Robert stays to help?

the sea, causing a violent storm that threatened to break the ship apart. [5]Fearing for their lives, the desperate sailors shouted to their gods for help and threw the cargo overboard to lighten the ship.

But all this time Jonah was sound asleep down in the hold. [6]So the captain went down after him. "How can you sleep at a time like this?" he shouted. "Get up and pray to your god! Maybe he will pay attention to us and spare our lives."

[7]Then the crew cast lots to see which of them had offended the gods and caused the terrible storm. When they did this, the lots identified Jonah as the culprit. [8]"Why has this awful storm come down on us?" they demanded. "Who are you? What is your line of work? What country are you from? What is your nationality?"

[9]Jonah answered, "I am a Hebrew, and I worship the LORD, the God of heaven, who made the sea and the land."

[10]The sailors were terrified when they heard this, for he had already told them he was running away from the LORD. "Oh, why did you do it?" they groaned. [11]And since the storm was getting worse all the time, they asked him, "What should we do to you to stop this storm?"

[12]"Throw me into the sea," Jonah said, "and it will become calm again. I know that this terrible storm is all my fault."

[13]Instead, the sailors rowed even harder to get the ship to the land. But the stormy sea was too violent for them, and they couldn't make it. [14]Then they cried out to the LORD, Jonah's God. "O LORD," they pleaded, "don't make us die for this man's sin. And don't hold us responsible for his death. O LORD, you have sent this storm upon him for your own good reasons."

[15]Then the sailors picked Jonah up and threw him into the raging sea, and the storm stopped at once! [16]The sailors were awestruck by the LORD's great power, and they offered him a sacrifice and vowed to serve him.

[17]*Now the LORD had arranged for a great fish to swallow Jonah. And Jonah was inside the fish for three days and three nights.

CHAPTER 2

Jonah's Prayer

[1]*Then Jonah prayed to the LORD his God from inside the fish. [2]He said,

"I cried out to the LORD in my great trouble,
and he answered me.

1:17 Verse 1:17 is numbered 2:1 in Hebrew text. **2:1** Verses 2:1-10 are numbered 2:2-11 in Hebrew text.

I called to you from the land of
the dead,*
and LORD, you heard me!
3 You threw me into the ocean depths,
and I sank down to the heart of
the sea.
The mighty waters engulfed me;
I was buried beneath your wild and
stormy waves.
4 Then I said, 'O LORD, you have driven me
from your presence.
Yet I will look once more toward your
holy Temple.'

5 "I sank beneath the waves,
and the waters closed over me.
Seaweed wrapped itself around my
head.
6 I sank down to the very roots of the
mountains.
I was imprisoned in the earth,
whose gates lock shut forever.
But you, O LORD my God,
snatched me from the jaws of
death!
7 As my life was slipping away,
I remembered the LORD.
And my earnest prayer went out to you
in your holy Temple.
8 Those who worship false gods
turn their backs on all God's mercies.
9 But I will offer sacrifices to you with
songs of praise,
and I will fulfill all my vows.
For my salvation comes from the LORD
alone."

10 Then the LORD ordered the fish to spit Jonah out onto the beach.

CHAPTER 3

Jonah Goes to Nineveh

Then the LORD spoke to Jonah a second time:
2 "Get up and go to the great city of Nineveh,
and deliver the message I have given you."

3 This time Jonah obeyed the LORD's command and went to Nineveh, a city so large that it took three days to see it all.* 4 On the day Jonah entered the city, he shouted to the crowds: "Forty days from now Nineveh will be destroyed!" 5 The people of Nineveh believed God's message, and from the greatest to the least, they declared a fast and put on burlap to show their sorrow.

6 When the king of Nineveh heard what Jonah was saying, he stepped down from his throne and took off his royal robes. He dressed himself in burlap and sat on a heap of ashes.

2:2 Hebrew *from Sheol.* 3:3 Hebrew *a great city to God, of three days' journey.*

MIRACLES IN THE BOOK OF JONAH

God caused a great storm. 1:4

God had a great fish swallow Jonah. 1:17

God made the fish spit up Jonah. 2:10

God made a vine to shade Jonah. 4:6

God made a worm to eat the vine. 4:7

God made a scorching wind blow on Jonah. 4:8

7 Then the king and his nobles sent this decree
throughout the city:

"No one, not even the animals from your
herds and flocks, may eat or drink
anything at all. 8 People and animals alike
must wear garments of mourning, and
everyone must pray earnestly to God.
They must turn from their evil ways and
stop all their violence. 9 Who can tell?
Perhaps even yet God will change his
mind and hold back his fierce anger from
destroying us."

AMAZING FACTS

Jonah preached in Nineveh, telling the people to turn from evil—and they did! So what did Jonah do? Got mad and pouted!

JONAH 3:1-5, 10; 4:1-3

10 When God saw what they had done and
how they had put a stop to their evil ways, he
changed his mind and did not carry out the
destruction he had threatened.

CHAPTER 4

Jonah's Anger at the LORD's Mercy

This change of plans greatly upset Jonah,
and he became very angry. 2 So he com-
plained to the LORD about it: "Didn't I say be-
fore I left home that you would do this,
LORD? That is why I ran away to Tarshish! I
knew that you are a merciful and compas-
sionate God, slow to get angry and filled with
unfailing love. You are eager to turn back
from destroying people. 3 Just kill me now,
LORD! I'd rather be dead than alive if what I
predicted will not happen."

4 The LORD replied, "Is it right for you to be
angry about this?"

5 Then Jonah went out to the east side of the
city and made a shelter to sit under as he
waited to see what would happen to the city.
6 And the LORD God arranged for a leafy plant
to grow there, and soon it spread its broad
leaves over Jonah's head, shading him from
the sun. This eased his discomfort, and Jonah
was very grateful for the plant.

7 But God also arranged for a worm! The
next morning at dawn the worm ate through
the stem of the plant so that it withered
away. 8 And as the sun grew hot, God ar-
ranged for a scorching east wind to blow on
Jonah. The sun beat down on his head until
he grew faint and wished to die. "Death is
certainly better than living like this!" he ex-
claimed.

9 Then God said to Jonah, "Is it right for you
to be angry because the plant died?"

"Yes," Jonah retorted, "even angry enough
to die!"

10 Then the LORD said, "You feel sorry about
the plant, though you did nothing to put it
there. It came quickly and died quickly. 11 But
Nineveh has more than 120,000 people liv-
ing in spiritual darkness,* not to mention all
the animals. Shouldn't I feel sorry for such a
great city?"

4:11 Hebrew *people who don't know their right hand from their left.*

MICAH

WHO
Micah and the citizens of Samaria, Jerusalem, and Bethlehem.

WHERE
In Samaria (to the north) and in Jerusalem (to the south).

WHEN
Possibly during the reigns of Jotham, Ahaz, and Hezekiah, around 742–687 BC.

WHY
To warn God's people that judgment would be coming and to offer forgiveness to them.

This is what [God] requires of you: to do what is right, to love mercy, and to walk humbly with your God.
MICAH 6:8

"This is for your own good." Ever hear an adult say that? It usually comes right before something unpleasant, like medicine or punishment. Micah's message was like that. God was about to punish his people because he loved them. You can see God's anger—and his love—in action.

753 BC — Hosea becomes a prophet
750 BC — Jotham becomes king of Judah
743 BC — Tiglath-pileser III invades Israel
742 BC — Micah becomes a prophet; Pekahiah becomes king
740 BC — Isaiah becomes a prophet
735 BC — Ahaz becomes king of Judah
722 BC — Israel (the northern kingdom) falls
715 BC — Hosea's ministry ends; Hezekiah becomes king of Judah
701 BC — Sennacherib surrounds Jerusalem
687 BC — Micah's ministry ends

DECIDE TO BE A PERSON WHO LIVES THE WAY GOD WANTS.

CHAPTER 1

The LORD gave this message to Micah of Moresheth during the years when Jotham, Ahaz, and Hezekiah were kings of Judah. The visions he saw concerned both Samaria and Jerusalem.

Grief over Samaria and Jerusalem

2 Attention! Let all the people of the world
listen!
Let the earth and everything in it hear.
The Sovereign LORD is making
accusations against you;
the Lord speaks from his holy
Temple.
3 Look! The LORD is coming!
He leaves his throne in heaven
and tramples the heights of the earth.
4 The mountains melt beneath his feet
and flow into the valleys

like wax in a fire,
like water pouring down a hill.
5 And why is this happening?
Because of the rebellion of Israel*—
yes, the sins of the whole nation.
Who is to blame for Israel's rebellion?
Samaria, its capital city!
Where is the center of idolatry in Judah?
In Jerusalem, its capital!

6 "So I, the LORD, will make the city of Samaria
a heap of ruins.
Her streets will be plowed up
for planting vineyards.
I will roll the stones of her walls into the valley below,
exposing her foundations.
7 All her carved images will be smashed.
All her sacred treasures will be burned.
These things were bought with the money earned by her prostitution,
and they will now be carried away
to pay prostitutes elsewhere."

8 Therefore, I will mourn and lament.
I will walk around barefoot and naked.
I will howl like a jackal
and moan like an owl.
9 For my people's wound
is too deep to heal.
It has reached into Judah,
even to the gates of Jerusalem.

10 Don't tell our enemies in Gath*;
don't weep at all.
You people in Beth-leaphrah,*
roll in the dust to show your despair.
11 You people in Shaphir,*
go as captives into exile—naked and ashamed.
The people of Zaanan*
dare not come outside their walls.
The people of Beth-ezel* mourn,
for their house has no support.
12 The people of Maroth* anxiously wait for relief,
but only bitterness awaits them
as the LORD's judgment reaches
even to the gates of Jerusalem.

13 Harness your chariot horses and flee,
you people of Lachish.*
You were the first city in Judah
to follow Israel in her rebellion,
and you led Jerusalem* into sin.
14 Send farewell gifts to Moresheth-gath*;
there is no hope of saving it.
The town of Aczib*
has deceived the kings of Israel.
15 O people of Mareshah,*
I will bring a conqueror to capture your town.
And the leaders* of Israel
will go to Adullam.

16 Oh, people of Judah, shave your heads in sorrow,
for the children you love will be snatched away.
Make yourselves as bald as a vulture,
for your little ones will be exiled to distant lands.

CHAPTER 2

Judgment against Wealthy Oppressors

1 What sorrow awaits you who lie awake at night,
thinking up evil plans.
You rise at dawn and hurry to carry them out,
simply because you have the power to do so.
2 When you want a piece of land,
you find a way to seize it.
When you want someone's house,
you take it by fraud and violence.
You cheat a man of his property,
stealing his family's inheritance.

3 But this is what the LORD says:
"I will reward your evil with evil;
you won't be able to pull your neck out of the noose.
You will no longer walk around proudly,
for it will be a terrible time."

4 In that day your enemies will make fun of you
by singing this song of despair about you:

1:5 Hebrew *Jacob;* also in 1:5b. The names "Jacob" and "Israel" are often interchanged throughout the Old Testament, referring sometimes to the individual patriarch and sometimes to the nation. **1:10a** *Gath* sounds like the Hebrew term for "tell." **1:10b** *Beth-leaphrah* means "house of dust." **1:11a** *Shaphir* means "pleasant." **1:11b** *Zaanan* sounds like the Hebrew term for "come out." **1:11c** *Beth-ezel* means "adjoining house." **1:12** *Maroth* sounds like the Hebrew term for "bitter." **1:13a** *Lachish* sounds like the Hebrew term for "team of horses." **1:13b** Hebrew *the daughter of Zion.* **1:14a** *Moresheth* sounds like the Hebrew term for "gift" or "dowry." **1:14b** *Aczib* means "deception." **1:15a** *Mareshah* sounds like the Hebrew term for "conqueror." **1:15b** Hebrew *the glory.*

"We are finished,
completely ruined!
God has confiscated our land,
taking it from us.
He has given our fields
to those who betrayed us.*"
5 Others will set your boundaries then,
and the LORD's people will have no say
in how the land is divided.

True and False Prophets

6 "Don't say such things,"
the people respond.*
"Don't prophesy like that.
Such disasters will never come
our way!"

7 Should you talk that way, O family of
Israel?*
Will the LORD's Spirit have patience
with such behavior?
If you would do what is right,
you would find my words comforting.
8 Yet to this very hour
my people rise against me like an
enemy!
You steal the shirts right off the backs
of those who trusted you,
making them as ragged as men
returning from battle.
9 You have evicted women from their
pleasant homes
and forever stripped their children of
all that God would give them.
10 Up! Begone!
This is no longer your land and home,
for you have filled it with sin
and ruined it completely.

11 Suppose a prophet full of lies would
say to you,
"I'll preach to you the joys of wine and
alcohol!"
That's just the kind of prophet you
would like!

Hope for Restoration

12 "Someday, O Israel, I will gather you;
I will gather the remnant who are left.
I will bring you together again like sheep
in a pen,
like a flock in its pasture.
Yes, your land will again
be filled with noisy crowds!
13 Your leader will break out
and lead you out of exile,
out through the gates of the enemy
cities,
back to your own land.
Your king will lead you;
the LORD himself will guide you."

CHAPTER 3

Judgment against Israel's Leaders

1 I said, "Listen, you leaders of Israel!
You are supposed to know right from
wrong,
2 but you are the very ones
who hate good and love evil.
You skin my people alive
and tear the flesh from their bones.
3 Yes, you eat my people's flesh,
strip off their skin,
and break their bones.
You chop them up
like meat for the cooking pot.
4 Then you beg the LORD for help in times
of trouble!
Do you really expect him to answer?
After all the evil you have done,
he won't even look at you!"

5 This is what the LORD says:
"You false prophets are leading my
people astray!
You promise peace for those who
give you food,
but you declare war on those who
refuse to feed you.
6 Now the night will close around you,
cutting off all your visions.
Darkness will cover you,
putting an end to your predictions.
The sun will set for you prophets,
and your day will come to an end.
7 Then you seers will be put to shame,
and you fortune-tellers will be
disgraced.
And you will cover your faces
because there is no answer
from God."

8 But as for me, I am filled with power—
with the Spirit of the LORD.

2:4 Or *to those who took us captive.* **2:6** Or *the prophets respond;* Hebrew reads *they prophesy.* **2:7** Hebrew *O house of Jacob?* See note on 1:5a.

I am filled with justice and strength
to boldly declare Israel's sin and
rebellion.
9 Listen to me, you leaders of Israel!
You hate justice and twist all that is
right.
10 You are building Jerusalem
on a foundation of murder and
corruption.
11 You rulers make decisions based on
bribes;
you priests teach God's laws only
for a price;
you prophets won't prophesy unless you
are paid.
Yet all of you claim to depend on the
LORD.
"No harm can come to us," you say,
"for the LORD is here among us."
12 Because of you, Mount Zion will be
plowed like an open field;
Jerusalem will be reduced to ruins!
A thicket will grow on the heights
where the Temple now stands.

CHAPTER 4

The LORD's Future Reign

1 In the last days, the mountain of the
LORD's house
will be the highest of all—
the most important place on earth.
It will be raised above the other hills,
and people from all over the world will
stream there to worship.
2 People from many nations will come and
say,
"Come, let us go up to the mountain of the
LORD,
to the house of Jacob's God.
There he will teach us his ways,
and we will walk in his paths."
For the LORD's teaching will go out from
Zion;
his word will go out from Jerusalem.
3 The LORD will mediate between peoples
and will settle disputes between strong
nations far away.
They will hammer their swords into
plowshares
and their spears into pruning hooks.
Nation will no longer fight against nation,
nor train for war anymore.
4 Everyone will live in peace and prosperity,
enjoying their own grapevines and fig
trees,
for there will be nothing to fear.
The LORD of Heaven's Armies
has made this promise!
5 Though the nations around us follow
their idols,
we will follow the LORD our God forever
and ever.

Israel's Return from Exile

6 "In that coming day," says the LORD,
"I will gather together those who are lame,
those who have been exiles,
and those whom I have filled with grief.
7 Those who are weak will survive as a
remnant;
those who were exiles will become a
strong nation.
Then I, the LORD, will rule from
Jerusalem*
as their king forever."
8 As for you, Jerusalem,
the citadel of God's people,*
your royal might and power
will come back to you again.
The kingship will be restored
to my precious Jerusalem.
9 But why are you now screaming
in terror?
Have you no king to lead you?
Have your wise people all died?
Pain has gripped you like a woman in
childbirth.
10 Writhe and groan like a woman in labor,
you people of Jerusalem,*
for now you must leave this city
to live in the open country.
You will soon be sent in exile
to distant Babylon.
But the LORD will rescue you there;
he will redeem you from the grip of
your enemies.
11 Now many nations have gathered against
you.
"Let her be desecrated," they say.
"Let us see the destruction of
Jerusalem.*"

4:7 Hebrew *Mount Zion.* **4:8** Hebrew *As for you, Migdal-eder, / the Ophel of the daughter of Zion.* **4:10** Hebrew *O daughter of Zion.* **4:11** Hebrew *of Zion.*

12 But they do not know the LORD's thoughts
or understand his plan.
These nations don't know
that he is gathering them together
to be beaten and trampled
like sheaves of grain on a threshing floor.
13 "Rise up and crush the nations, O Jerusalem!"*
says the LORD.
"For I will give you iron horns and bronze hooves,
so you can trample many nations to pieces.
You will present their stolen riches to the LORD,
their wealth to the LORD of all the earth."

CHAPTER 5

1*Mobilize! Marshal your troops!
The enemy is laying siege to Jerusalem.
They will strike Israel's leader
in the face with a rod.

A Ruler from Bethlehem

2*But you, O Bethlehem Ephrathah,
are only a small village among all the people of Judah.
Yet a ruler of Israel will come from you,
one whose origins are from the distant past.
3 The people of Israel will be abandoned to their enemies
until the woman in labor gives birth.
Then at last his fellow countrymen
will return from exile to their own land.
4 And he will stand to lead his flock with the LORD's strength,
in the majesty of the name of the LORD his God.
Then his people will live there undisturbed,
for he will be highly honored around the world.
5 And he will be the source of peace.

When the Assyrians invade our land
and break through our defenses,
we will appoint seven rulers to watch over us,
eight princes to lead us.
6 They will rule Assyria with drawn swords
and enter the gates of the land of Nimrod.
He will rescue us from the Assyrians
when they pour over the borders to invade our land.

The Remnant Purified

7 Then the remnant left in Israel*
will take their place among the nations.
They will be like dew sent by the LORD
or like rain falling on the grass,
which no one can hold back
and no one can restrain.
8 The remnant left in Israel
will take their place among the nations.
They will be like a lion among the animals of the forest,
like a strong young lion among flocks of sheep and goats,
pouncing and tearing as they go
with no rescuer in sight.
9 The people of Israel will stand up to their foes,
and all their enemies will be wiped out.

AMAZING FACTS

Around 700 years before Jesus was born, Micah knew the exact name of the village that would be Jesus' birthplace.

MICAH 5:2

10 "In that day," says the LORD,
"I will slaughter your horses
and destroy your chariots.
11 I will tear down your walls
and demolish your defenses.
12 I will put an end to all witchcraft,

4:13 Hebrew *"Rise up and thresh, O daughter of Zion."* **5:1** Verse 5:1 is numbered 4:14 in Hebrew text. **5:2** Verses 5:2-15 are numbered 5:1-14 in Hebrew text. **5:7** Hebrew *in Jacob;* also in 5:8. See note on 1:5a.

and there will be no more fortune-tellers.
13 I will destroy all your idols and sacred pillars,
so you will never again worship the work of your own hands.
14 I will abolish your idol shrines with their Asherah poles
and destroy your pagan cities.
15 I will pour out my vengeance
on all the nations that refuse to obey me."

CHAPTER 6

The LORD's Case against Israel

Listen to what the LORD is saying:

"Stand up and state your case against me.
Let the mountains and hills be called to witness your complaints.
2 And now, O mountains,
listen to the LORD's complaint!
He has a case against his people.
He will bring charges against Israel.

3 "O my people, what have I done to you?
What have I done to make you tired of me?
Answer me!
4 For I brought you out of Egypt
and redeemed you from slavery.
I sent Moses, Aaron, and Miriam to help you.
5 Don't you remember, my people,
how King Balak of Moab tried to have you cursed
and how Balaam son of Beor blessed you instead?
And remember your journey from Acacia Grove* to Gilgal,
when I, the LORD, did everything I could to teach you about my faithfulness."

6 What can we bring to the LORD?
What kind of offerings should we give him?
Should we bow before God
with offerings of yearling calves?
7 Should we offer him thousands of rams
and ten thousand rivers of olive oil?
Should we sacrifice our firstborn children
to pay for our sins?
8 No, O people, the LORD has told you what is good,
and this is what he requires of you:
to do what is right, to love mercy,
and to walk humbly with your God.

Israel's Guilt and Punishment

9 Fear the LORD if you are wise!
His voice calls to everyone in Jerusalem:
"The armies of destruction are coming;
the LORD is sending them.*
10 What shall I say about the homes of the wicked
filled with treasures gained by cheating?
What about the disgusting practice
of measuring out grain with dishonest measures?*
11 How can I tolerate your merchants
who use dishonest scales and weights?
12 The rich among you have become wealthy
through extortion and violence.
Your citizens are so used to lying
that their tongues can no longer tell the truth.

13 "Therefore, I will wound you!
I will bring you to ruin for all your sins.
14 You will eat but never have enough.
Your hunger pangs and emptiness will remain.
And though you try to save your money,
it will come to nothing in the end.
You will save a little,
but I will give it to those who conquer you.
15 You will plant crops
but not harvest them.
You will press your olives
but not get enough oil to anoint yourselves.
You will trample the grapes
but get no juice to make your wine.
16 You keep only the laws of evil King Omri;
you follow only the example of wicked King Ahab!
Therefore, I will make an example of you,
bringing you to complete ruin.
You will be treated with contempt,
mocked by all who see you."

6:5 Hebrew *Shittim*. **6:9** Hebrew *"Listen to the rod. / Who appointed it?"* **6:10** Hebrew *of using the short ephah?* The ephah was a unit for measuring grain.

CHAPTER 7

Misery Turned to Hope

1 How miserable I am!
I feel like the fruit picker after the harvest
who can find nothing to eat.
Not a cluster of grapes or a single
early fig
can be found to satisfy my hunger.
2 The godly people have all disappeared;
not one honest person is left on the
earth.
They are all murderers,
setting traps even for their own
brothers.
3 Both their hands are equally skilled at
doing evil!
Officials and judges alike demand
bribes.
The people with influence get what they
want,
and together they scheme to twist
justice.
4 Even the best of them is like a brier;
the most honest is as dangerous as a
hedge of thorns.
But your judgment day is coming swiftly
now.
Your time of punishment is here,
a time of confusion.
5 Don't trust anyone—
not your best friend or even your
wife!
6 For the son despises his father.
The daughter defies her mother.
The daughter-in-law defies her
mother-in-law.
Your enemies are right in your own
household!

7 As for me, I look to the LORD for help.
I wait confidently for God to save me,
and my God will certainly hear me.
8 Do not gloat over me, my enemies!
For though I fall, I will rise again.
Though I sit in darkness,
the LORD will be my light.
9 I will be patient as the LORD punishes me,
for I have sinned against him.
But after that, he will take up my case
and give me justice for all I have
suffered from my enemies.
The LORD will bring me into the light,
and I will see his righteousness.

Stolen Fun

Some of Jason's friends were laughing about their shopping-mall adventure. Some of them had distracted a drugstore clerk while one guy stole a handful of candy bars. It was so easy! They talked about what they would take next weekend. Someone suggested trying to shoplift a basketball! Jason quietly listened until someone asked, "Hey, Jas, you gonna come with us this time?" Jason said he'd think about it. On Saturday morning, Jason was nervous and didn't know what to do about the mall trip that afternoon. What do you think he should do? Read Micah 7:1-4 to see how Micah would have felt about that trip.

10 Then my enemies will see that the LORD
is on my side.
They will be ashamed that they
taunted me, saying,

"So where is the LORD—
that God of yours?"
With my own eyes I will see their downfall;
they will be trampled like mud in the streets.

11 In that day, Israel, your cities will be rebuilt,
and your borders will be extended.
12 People from many lands will come and honor you—
from Assyria all the way to the towns of Egypt,
from Egypt all the way to the Euphrates River,*
and from distant seas and mountains.
13 But the land* will become empty and desolate
because of the wickedness of those who live there.

The LORD's Compassion on Israel

14 O LORD, protect your people with your shepherd's staff;
lead your flock, your special possession.
Though they live alone in a thicket
on the heights of Mount Carmel,*
let them graze in the fertile pastures of Bashan and Gilead
as they did long ago.

15 "Yes," says the LORD,
"I will do mighty miracles for you,
like those I did when I rescued you
from slavery in Egypt."

16 All the nations of the world will stand amazed
at what the LORD will do for you.
They will be embarrassed
at their feeble power.
They will cover their mouths in silent awe,
deaf to everything around them.
17 Like snakes crawling from their holes,
they will come out to meet the LORD our God.
They will fear him greatly,
trembling in terror at his presence.

18 Where is another God like you,
who pardons the guilt of the remnant,
overlooking the sins of his special people?
You will not stay angry with your people forever,
because you delight in showing unfailing love.
19 Once again you will have compassion on us.
You will trample our sins under your feet
and throw them into the depths of the ocean!
20 You will show us your faithfulness and unfailing love
as you promised to our ancestors Abraham and Jacob long ago.

7:12 Hebrew *the river*. **7:13** Or *earth*. **7:14** Or *surrounded by a fruitful land*.

nahum

WHO
Nahum, the people of Nineveh, and the people of Judah.

WHERE
The southern kingdom of Judah.

WHEN
During Nahum's ministry between 663 and 654 BC.

WHY
To pronounce God's judgment on Assyria and to comfort Judah.

The LORD is good, a strong refuge when trouble comes. He is close to those who trust in him.
NAHUM 1:7

At one time, Assyria was the most powerful nation on earth and would do *anything* to win. God had sent Jonah to warn the people that Nineveh would be destroyed if they didn't change. They did change. But after a while they became evil again. Nahum came to warn the Assyrians one more time.

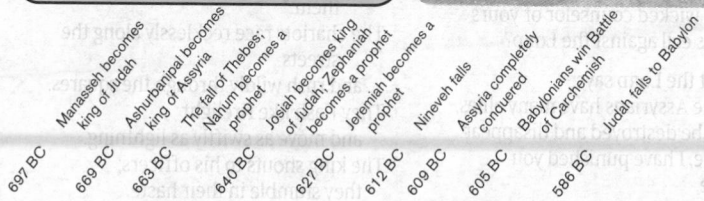

Let the words of Nahum warn you to obey God completely.

CHAPTER 1

This message concerning Nineveh came as a vision to Nahum, who lived in Elkosh.

The LORD's Anger against Nineveh

2 The LORD is a jealous God,
filled with vengeance and rage.
He takes revenge on all who oppose him
and continues to rage against his enemies!
3 The LORD is slow to get angry, but his power is great,
and he never lets the guilty go unpunished.
He displays his power in the whirlwind and the storm.

The billowing clouds are the dust
beneath his feet.
4 At his command the oceans dry up,
and the rivers disappear.
The lush pastures of Bashan and
Carmel fade,
and the green forests of Lebanon
wither.
5 In his presence the mountains quake,
and the hills melt away;
the earth trembles,
and its people are destroyed.
6 Who can stand before his fierce anger?
Who can survive his burning fury?
His rage blazes forth like fire,
and the mountains crumble to dust in
his presence.

7 The LORD is good,
a strong refuge when trouble comes.
He is close to those who trust in him.
8 But he will sweep away his enemies
in an overwhelming flood.
He will pursue his foes
into the darkness of night.

9 Why are you scheming against the LORD?
He will destroy you with one blow;
he won't need to strike twice!
10 His enemies, tangled like thornbushes
and staggering like drunks,
will be burned up like dry stubble
in a field.
11 Who is this wicked counselor of yours
who plots evil against the LORD?

12 This is what the LORD says:
"Though the Assyrians have many allies,
they will be destroyed and disappear.
O my people, I have punished you
before,
but I will not punish you again.
13 Now I will break the yoke of bondage
from your neck
and tear off the chains of Assyrian
oppression."

14 And this is what the LORD says concerning
the Assyrians in Nineveh:
"You will have no more children to carry
on your name.
I will destroy all the idols in the temples
of your gods.
I am preparing a grave for you
because you are despicable!"

15*Look! A messenger is coming over the
mountains with good news!
He is bringing a message of peace.
Celebrate your festivals, O people of Judah,
and fulfill all your vows,
for your wicked enemies will never invade
your land again.
They will be completely destroyed!

CHAPTER 2

The Fall of Nineveh

1*Your enemy is coming to crush you,
Nineveh.
Man the ramparts! Watch the roads!
Prepare your defenses! Call out your
forces!

2 Even though the destroyer has destroyed
Judah,
the LORD will restore its honor.
Israel's vine has been stripped of
branches,
but he will restore its splendor.

3 Shields flash red in the sunlight!
See the scarlet uniforms of the valiant
troops!
Watch as their glittering chariots move
into position,
with a forest of spears waving above
them.*
4 The chariots race recklessly along the
streets
and rush wildly through the squares.
They flash like firelight
and move as swiftly as lightning.
5 The king shouts to his officers;
they stumble in their haste,
rushing to the walls to set up their
defenses.
6 The river gates have been torn open!
The palace is about to collapse!
7 Nineveh's exile has been decreed,
and all the servant girls mourn its
capture.
They moan like doves
and beat their breasts in sorrow.
8 Nineveh is like a leaking water reservoir!
The people are slipping away.

1:15 Verse 1:15 is numbered 2:1 in Hebrew text. **2:1** Verses 2:1-13 are numbered 2:2-14 in Hebrew text. **2:3** Greek and Syriac versions read *into position, / the horses whipped into a frenzy.*

"Stop, stop!" someone shouts,
but no one even looks back.
9 Loot the silver!
Plunder the gold!
There's no end to Nineveh's treasures—
its vast, uncounted wealth.
10 Soon the city is plundered, empty, and ruined.
Hearts melt and knees shake.
The people stand aghast,
their faces pale and trembling.

11 Where now is that great Nineveh,
that den filled with young lions?
It was a place where people—like lions and their cubs—
walked freely and without fear.
12 The lion tore up meat for his cubs
and strangled prey for his mate.
He filled his den with prey,
his caverns with his plunder.

13 "I am your enemy!"
says the LORD of Heaven's Armies.
"Your chariots will soon go up in smoke.
Your young men* will be killed in battle.
Never again will you plunder conquered nations.
The voices of your proud messengers will be heard no more."

CHAPTER 3

The LORD's Judgment against Nineveh

1 What sorrow awaits Nineveh,
the city of murder and lies!
She is crammed with wealth
and is never without victims.
2 Hear the crack of whips,
the rumble of wheels!
Horses' hooves pound,
and chariots clatter wildly.
3 See the flashing swords and glittering spears
as the charioteers charge past!
There are countless casualties,
heaps of bodies—
so many bodies that
people stumble over them.
4 All this because Nineveh,
the beautiful and faithless city,
mistress of deadly charms,
enticed the nations with her beauty.
She taught them all her magic,
enchanting people everywhere.

5 "I am your enemy!"
says the LORD of Heaven's Armies.
"And now I will lift your skirts
and show all the earth your nakedness and shame.
6 I will cover you with filth
and show the world how vile you really are.
7 All who see you will shrink back and say,
'Nineveh lies in ruins.
Where are the mourners?'
Does anyone regret your destruction?"

2:13 Hebrew *young lions.*

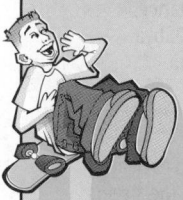

I WAS MEETING some friends in our church parking lot to go play laser tag. While one friend and I waited, we decided to slide around on the icy spots. As we were sliding, my friend lost control and knocked me to the ground. My rear end and back got covered with mud and snow. I had no way to get home, so I was stuck with a muddy backside all day!

Lighten Up!

8 Are you any better than the city
of Thebes,*
situated on the Nile River, surrounded
by water?
She was protected by the river on all
sides,
walled in by water.
9 Ethiopia* and the land of Egypt
gave unlimited assistance.
The nations of Put and Libya
were among her allies.
10 Yet Thebes fell,
and her people were led away as
captives.
Her babies were dashed to death
against the stones of the streets.
Soldiers threw dice* to get Egyptian
officers as servants.
All their leaders were bound in chains.

11 And you, Nineveh, will also stagger like a
drunkard.
You will hide for fear of the attacking
enemy.
12 All your fortresses will fall.
They will be devoured like the ripe figs
that fall into the mouths
of those who shake the trees.
13 Your troops will be as weak
and helpless as women.
The gates of your land will be opened
wide to the enemy
and set on fire and burned.
14 Get ready for the siege!
Store up water!
Strengthen the defenses!
Go into the pits to trample clay,
and pack it into molds,
making bricks to repair the walls.

15 But the fire will devour you;
the sword will cut you down.
The enemy will consume you like locusts,
devouring everything they see.
There will be no escape,
even if you multiply like swarming
locusts.
16 Your merchants have multiplied
until they outnumber the stars.
But like a swarm of locusts,
they strip the land and fly away.
17 Your guards* and officials are also like
swarming locusts
that crowd together in the hedges
on a cold day.
But like locusts that fly away when the
sun comes up,
all of them will fly away and disappear.

18 Your shepherds are asleep, O Assyrian
king;
your princes lie dead in the dust.
Your people are scattered across the
mountains
with no one to gather them together.
19 There is no healing for your wound;
your injury is fatal.
All who hear of your destruction
will clap their hands for joy.
Where can anyone be found
who has not suffered from your
continual cruelty?

3:8 Hebrew *No-amon;* also in 3:10. **3:9** Hebrew *Cush.* **3:10** Hebrew *They cast lots.* **3:17** Or *princes.*

HABAKKUK

WHO
Habakkuk and the Babylonians.

WHERE
The southern kingdom of Judah.

WHEN
Between 612 and 589 BC.

WHY
To show that God is in control even when evil seems to be winning.

The Sovereign LORD is my strength! He makes me as surefooted as a deer.
HABAKKUK 3:19

Life is filled with questions. Some are so difficult that only God can answer them. Habakkuk had many questions. He asked God why bad things happened and why people got away with doing bad things. God didn't get angry with Habakkuk for asking. Instead, God explained the big picture that Habakkuk couldn't see.

Jeremiah becomes a prophet	Habakkuk becomes a prophet	King Josiah dies in battle	Daniel taken captive to Babylon	Ezekiel a captive in Babylon; Zedekiah becomes king	Habakkuk's ministry ends	Fall of Judah; Jerusalem destroyed
627 BC	612 BC	609 BC	605 BC	597 BC	589 BC	586 BC

ASK GOD ANY QUESTION YOU WANT; THEN LISTEN FOR HIS ANSWER.

CHAPTER 1

This is the message that the prophet Habakkuk received in a vision.

Habakkuk's Complaint

2 How long, O LORD, must I call for help?
But you do not listen!
"Violence is everywhere!" I cry,
but you do not come to save.

3 Must I forever see these evil deeds?
Why must I watch all this misery?
Wherever I look,
I see destruction and violence.
I am surrounded by people
who love to argue and fight.

4 The law has become paralyzed,
and there is no justice in the courts.

The wicked far outnumber the righteous,
so that justice has become perverted.

The Lord's Reply

5 The Lord replied,

"Look around at the nations;
look and be amazed!*
For I am doing something in your own day,
something you wouldn't believe
even if someone told you about it.
6 I am raising up the Babylonians,*
a cruel and violent people.
They will march across the world
and conquer other lands.
7 They are notorious for their cruelty
and do whatever they like.
8 Their horses are swifter than cheetahs*
and fiercer than wolves at dusk.
Their charioteers charge from far away.
Like eagles, they swoop down to devour their prey.

9 "On they come, all bent on violence.
Their hordes advance like a desert wind,
sweeping captives ahead of them like sand.
10 They scoff at kings and princes
and scorn all their fortresses.
They simply pile ramps of earth
against their walls and capture them!
11 They sweep past like the wind
and are gone.
But they are deeply guilty,
for their own strength is their god."

Habakkuk's Second Complaint

12 O Lord my God, my Holy One, you who are eternal—
surely you do not plan to wipe us out?
O Lord, our Rock, you have sent these Babylonians to correct us,
to punish us for our many sins.
13 But you are pure and cannot stand the sight of evil.
Will you wink at their treachery?
Should you be silent while the wicked
swallow up people more righteous than they?
14 Are we only fish to be caught and killed?
Are we only sea creatures that have no leader?
15 Must we be strung up on their hooks
and caught in their nets while they rejoice and celebrate?
16 Then they will worship their nets
and burn incense in front of them.
"These nets are the gods who have made us rich!"
they will claim.
17 Will you let them get away with this forever?
Will they succeed forever in their heartless conquests?

CHAPTER 2

1 I will climb up to my watchtower
and stand at my guardpost.
There I will wait to see what the Lord says
and how he* will answer my complaint.

The Lord's Second Reply

2 Then the Lord said to me,

"Write my answer plainly on tablets,
so that a runner can carry the correct message to others.
3 This vision is for a future time.
It describes the end, and it will be fulfilled.
If it seems slow in coming, wait patiently,
for it will surely take place.
It will not be delayed.

4 "Look at the proud!
They trust in themselves, and their lives are crooked.
But the righteous will live by their faithfulness to God.*
5 Wealth* is treacherous,
and the arrogant are never at rest.
They open their mouths as wide as the grave,*
and like death, they are never satisfied.
In their greed they have gathered up many nations
and swallowed many peoples.

6 "But soon their captives will taunt them.
They will mock them, saying,

1:5 Greek version reads *Look, you mockers; / look and be amazed and die.* Compare Acts 13:41. **1:6** Or *Chaldeans.* **1:8** Or *leopards.* **2:1** As in Syriac version; Hebrew reads *I.* **2:3b-4** Greek version reads *If the vision is delayed, wait patiently, / for it will surely come and not delay. / 4I will take no pleasure in anyone who turns away. / But the righteous person will live by my faith.* Compare Rom 1:17; Gal 3:11; Heb 10:37-38. **2:5a** As in Dead Sea Scroll 1QpHab; other Hebrew manuscripts read *Wine.* **2:5b** Hebrew *as Sheol.*

'What sorrow awaits you thieves!
Now you will get what you deserve!
You've become rich by extortion,
but how much longer can this go on?'
7 Suddenly, your debtors will take action.
They will turn on you and take all you have,
while you stand trembling and helpless.
8 Because you have plundered many nations,
now all the survivors will plunder you.
You committed murder throughout the countryside
and filled the towns with violence.

9 "What sorrow awaits you who build big houses
with money gained dishonestly!
You believe your wealth will buy security,
putting your family's nest beyond the reach of danger.
10 But by the murders you committed,
you have shamed your name and forfeited your lives.
11 The very stones in the walls cry out against you,
and the beams in the ceilings echo the complaint.

12 "What sorrow awaits you who build cities
with money gained through murder and corruption!
13 Has not the LORD of Heaven's Armies promised
that the wealth of nations will turn to ashes?
They work so hard,
but all in vain!
14 For as the waters fill the sea,
the earth will be filled with an awareness
of the glory of the LORD.

15 "What sorrow awaits you who make your neighbors drunk!
You force your cup on them
so you can gloat over their shameful nakedness.
16 But soon it will be your turn to be disgraced.
Come, drink and be exposed!*
Drink from the cup of the LORD's judgment,
and all your glory will be turned to shame.
17 You cut down the forests of Lebanon.
Now you will be cut down.
You destroyed the wild animals,
so now their terror will be yours.
You committed murder throughout the countryside
and filled the towns with violence.

18 "What good is an idol carved by man,
or a cast image that deceives you?
How foolish to trust in your own creation—
a god that can't even talk!
19 What sorrow awaits you who say to wooden idols,
'Wake up and save us!'
To speechless stone images you say,
'Rise up and teach us!'
Can an idol tell you what to do?
They may be overlaid with gold and silver,
but they are lifeless inside.
20 But the LORD is in his holy Temple.
Let all the earth be silent before him."

CHAPTER 3

Habakkuk's Prayer

This prayer was sung by the prophet Habakkuk*:

2 I have heard all about you, LORD.
I am filled with awe by your amazing works.
In this time of our deep need,
help us again as you did in years gone by.
And in your anger,
remember your mercy.

3 I see God moving across the deserts from Edom,*
the Holy One coming from Mount Paran.*
His brilliant splendor fills the heavens,
and the earth is filled with his praise.
4 His coming is as brilliant as the sunrise.
Rays of light flash from his hands,
where his awesome power is hidden.

2:16 Dead Sea Scrolls and Greek and Syriac versions read *and stagger!* **3:1** Hebrew adds *according to shigionoth,* probably indicating the musical setting for the prayer. **3:3a** Hebrew *Teman.* **3:3b** Hebrew adds *selah;* also in 3:9, 13. The meaning of this Hebrew term is uncertain; it is probably a musical or literary term.

5 Pestilence marches before him;
plague follows close behind.
6 When he stops, the earth shakes.
When he looks, the nations tremble.
He shatters the everlasting mountains
and levels the eternal hills.
He is the Eternal One!
7 I see the people of Cushan in distress,
and the nation of Midian trembling
in terror.

8 Was it in anger, LORD, that you struck
the rivers
and parted the sea?
Were you displeased with them?
No, you were sending your chariots
of salvation!

When things aren't going well for me, how should I react?

Even though the fig trees have no blossoms . . . and the cattle barns are empty, yet I will rejoice in the LORD! I will be joyful in the God of my salvation! HABAKKUK 3:17–18

9 You brandished your bow
and your quiver of arrows.
You split open the earth with flowing
rivers.
10 The mountains watched and trembled.
Onward swept the raging waters.
The mighty deep cried out,
lifting its hands to the LORD.
11 The sun and moon stood still in the sky
as your brilliant arrows flew
and your glittering spear flashed.

12 You marched across the land in anger
and trampled the nations in your fury.
13 You went out to rescue your chosen
people,
to save your anointed ones.
You crushed the heads of the wicked
and stripped their bones from head
to toe.
14 With his own weapons,
you destroyed the chief of those
who rushed out like a whirlwind,
thinking Israel would be easy prey.
15 You trampled the sea with your horses,
and the mighty waters piled high.

16 I trembled inside when I heard this;
my lips quivered with fear.
My legs gave way beneath me,*
and I shook in terror.
I will wait quietly for the coming
day
when disaster will strike the
people who invade us.
17 Even though the fig trees have no
blossoms,
and there are no grapes on the vines;
even though the olive crop fails,
and the fields lie empty and barren;
even though the flocks die in the fields,
and the cattle barns are empty,
18 yet I will rejoice in the LORD!
I will be joyful in the God of my
salvation!
19 The Sovereign LORD is my strength!
He makes me as surefooted as a deer,*
able to tread upon the heights.

(For the choir director: This prayer is to be accompanied by stringed instruments.)

3:16 Hebrew *Decay entered my bones.* 3:19 Or *He gives me the speed of a deer.*

Zephaniah

WHO
Zephaniah and the people of Judah.

WHERE
The southern kingdom of Judah.

WHEN
Probably near the end of Zephaniah's ministry, around 640–621 BC.

WHY
To wake up the people of Judah so they would turn back to God.

Gather together, you shameless nation. Gather before judgment begins.
ZEPHANIAH 2:1-2

Ever gotten into trouble and then had to wait in your room for the dreaded "talk"? It's hard waiting for something unpleasant. Part of Zephaniah's message left the people of Judah waiting for their punishment for disobeying God's laws. Other parts of his message reminded them that God would also forgive.

640 BC — Zephaniah becomes a prophet; Josiah becomes king of Judah
627 BC — Jeremiah becomes a prophet
622 BC — Book of the Law found in the Temple
621 BC — Zephaniah's ministry ends
609 BC — Josiah dies in battle
605 BC — First captives taken to Babylon
597 BC — Babylon's second attack on Judah
586 BC — Judah (the southern kingdom) falls

Remember, you can receive God's forgiveness by confessing your sin and trusting in Him.

CHAPTER 1

The LORD gave this message to Zephaniah when Josiah son of Amon was king of Judah. Zephaniah was the son of Cushi, son of Gedaliah, son of Amariah, son of Hezekiah.

Coming Judgment against Judah

2 "I will sweep away everything
from the face of the earth," says the LORD.
3 "I will sweep away people and animals
alike.

I will sweep away the birds of
the sky and the fish in the sea.
I will reduce the wicked to heaps
of rubble,*
and I will wipe humanity from
the face of the earth," says the
LORD.
4 "I will crush Judah and Jerusalem with my
fist
and destroy every last trace of their
Baal worship.
I will put an end to all the idolatrous
priests,
so that even the memory of them will
disappear.
5 For they go up to their roofs
and bow down to the sun, moon, and
stars.
They claim to follow the LORD,
but then they worship Molech,* too.
6 And I will destroy those who used to
worship me
but now no longer do.
They no longer ask for the LORD's
guidance
or seek my blessings."

7 Stand in silence in the presence of the
Sovereign LORD,
for the awesome day of the LORD's
judgment is near.
The LORD has prepared his people for a
great slaughter
and has chosen their executioners.*
8 "On that day of judgment,"
says the LORD,
"I will punish the leaders and princes of
Judah
and all those following pagan customs.
9 Yes, I will punish those who participate in
pagan worship ceremonies,
and those who fill their masters' houses
with violence and deceit.

10 "On that day," says the LORD,
"a cry of alarm will come from the Fish
Gate
and echo throughout the New Quarter of
the city.*
And a great crash will sound from the
hills.
11 Wail in sorrow, all you who live in the
market area,
for all the merchants and traders will
be destroyed.

12 "I will search with lanterns in Jerusalem's
darkest corners
to punish those who sit complacent in
their sins.
They think the LORD will do nothing to
them,
either good or bad.
13 So their property will be plundered,
their homes will be ransacked.
They will build new homes
but never live in them.
They will plant vineyards
but never drink wine from them.

14 "That terrible day of the LORD is near.
Swiftly it comes—
a day of bitter tears,
a day when even strong men will cry
out.
15 It will be a day when the LORD's anger is
poured out—
a day of terrible distress and anguish,
a day of ruin and desolation,
a day of darkness and gloom,
a day of clouds and blackness,
16 a day of trumpet calls and battle cries.
Down go the walled cities
and the strongest battlements!

17 "Because you have sinned against the LORD,
I will make you grope around like the
blind.
Your blood will be poured into the dust,
and your bodies will lie rotting on the
ground."

18 Your silver and gold will not save you
on that day of the LORD's anger.
For the whole land will be devoured
by the fire of his jealousy.
He will make a terrifying end
of all the people on earth.*

CHAPTER 2

A Call to Repentance

1 Gather together—yes, gather together,
you shameless nation.

1:3 The meaning of the Hebrew is uncertain. **1:5** Hebrew *Malcam*, a variant spelling of Molech; or it could possibly mean *their king*. **1:7** Hebrew *has prepared a sacrifice and sanctified his guests*. **1:10** Or *the Second Quarter*, a newer section of Jerusalem. Hebrew reads *the Mishneh*. **1:18** Or *the people living in the land*.

2 Gather before judgment begins,
before your time to repent is blown
away like chaff.
Act now, before the fierce fury of the
LORD falls
and the terrible day of the LORD's anger
begins.
3 Seek the LORD, all who are humble,
and follow his commands.
Seek to do what is right
and to live humbly.
Perhaps even yet the LORD will protect
you—
protect you from his anger on that day
of destruction.

Judgment against Philistia

4 Gaza and Ashkelon will be abandoned,
Ashdod and Ekron torn down.
5 And what sorrow awaits you Philistines*
who live along the coast and in the land
of Canaan,
for this judgment is against you, too!
The LORD will destroy you
until not one of you is left.
6 The Philistine coast will become a
wilderness pasture,
a place of shepherd camps
and enclosures for sheep and goats.
7 The remnant of the tribe of Judah will
pasture there.
They will rest at night in the abandoned
houses in Ashkelon.
For the LORD their God will visit his
people in kindness
and restore their prosperity again.

Judgment against Moab and Ammon

8 "I have heard the taunts of the Moabites
and the insults of the Ammonites,
mocking my people
and invading their borders.
9 Now, as surely as I live,"
says the LORD of Heaven's Armies, the
God of Israel,
"Moab and Ammon will be destroyed—
destroyed as completely as Sodom and
Gomorrah.
Their land will become a place of stinging
nettles,
salt pits, and eternal desolation.
The remnant of my people will plunder
them
and take their land."
10 They will receive the wages of their pride,
for they have scoffed at the people of
the LORD of Heaven's Armies.
11 The LORD will terrify them
as he destroys all the gods in the land.
Then nations around the world will
worship the LORD,
each in their own land.

Judgment against Ethiopia and Assyria

12 "You Ethiopians* will also be slaughtered
by my sword," says the LORD.
13 And the LORD will strike the lands of the
north with his fist,
destroying the land of Assyria.
He will make its great capital, Nineveh, a
desolate wasteland,
parched like a desert.
14 The proud city will become a pasture
for flocks and herds,
and all sorts of wild animals will settle
there.
The desert owl and screech owl will roost
on its ruined columns,
their calls echoing through the gaping
windows.
Rubble will block all the doorways,
and the cedar paneling will be exposed
to the weather.
15 This is the boisterous city,
once so secure.
"I am the greatest!" it boasted.
"No other city can compare with me!"
But now, look how it has become
an utter ruin,
a haven for wild animals.
Everyone passing by will laugh in
derision
and shake a defiant fist.

CHAPTER 3

Jerusalem's Rebellion and Redemption

1 What sorrow awaits rebellious, polluted
Jerusalem,
the city of violence and crime!
2 No one can tell it anything;
it refuses all correction.

2:5 Hebrew *Kerethites*. 2:12 Hebrew *Cushites*.

It does not trust in the LORD
or draw near to its God.
3 Its leaders are like roaring lions
hunting for their victims.
Its judges are like ravenous wolves at
evening time,
who by dawn have left no trace
of their prey.
4 Its prophets are arrogant liars seeking
their own gain.
Its priests defile the Temple by
disobeying God's instructions.
5 But the LORD is still there in the city,
and he does no wrong.
Day by day he hands down justice,
and he does not fail.
But the wicked know no shame.

6 "I have wiped out many nations,
devastating their fortress walls and
towers.
Their streets are now deserted;
their cities lie in silent ruin.
There are no survivors—
none at all.
7 I thought, 'Surely they will have reverence
for me now!
Surely they will listen to my warnings.
Then I won't need to strike again,
destroying their homes.'
But no, they get up early
to continue their evil deeds.
8 Therefore, be patient," says the LORD.
"Soon I will stand and accuse these
evil nations.
For I have decided to gather the kingdoms
of the earth
and pour out my fiercest anger and
fury on them.
All the earth will be devoured
by the fire of my jealousy.

9 "Then I will purify the speech of all
people,
so that everyone can worship the LORD
together.
10 My scattered people who live beyond the
rivers of Ethiopia*
will come to present their offerings.
11 On that day you will no longer need to be
ashamed,
for you will no longer be rebels against
me.
I will remove all proud and arrogant
people from among you.
There will be no more haughtiness on
my holy mountain.
12 Those who are left will be the lowly and
humble,
for it is they who trust in the name of
the LORD.
13 The remnant of Israel will do no wrong;
they will never tell lies or deceive one
another.
They will eat and sleep in safety,
and no one will make them afraid."

14 Sing, O daughter of Zion;
shout aloud, O Israel!
Be glad and rejoice with all your heart,
O daughter of Jerusalem!
15 For the LORD will remove his hand of
judgment
and will disperse the armies of your
enemy.
And the LORD himself, the King of Israel,
will live among you!
At last your troubles will be over,
and you will never again fear disaster.
16 On that day the announcement to
Jerusalem will be,
"Cheer up, Zion! Don't be
afraid!
17 For the LORD your God is living among
you.
He is a mighty savior.
He will take delight in you with
gladness.

Does God really like me? * **The LORD your God . . . will take delight in you with gladness. With his love, he will calm all your fears. He will rejoice over you with joyful songs.** ZEPHANIAH 3:17

3:10 Hebrew *Cush.*

With his love, he will calm all your fears.*
He will rejoice over you with joyful songs."
18 "I will gather you who mourn for the appointed festivals;
you will be disgraced no more.*
19 And I will deal severely with all who have oppressed you.
I will save the weak and helpless ones;
I will bring together
those who were chased away.
I will give glory and fame to my former exiles,
wherever they have been mocked and shamed.
20 On that day I will gather you together
and bring you home again.
I will give you a good name, a name of distinction,
among all the nations of the earth,
as I restore your fortunes before their very eyes.
I, the LORD, have spoken!"

3:17 Or *He will be silent in his love*. Greek and Syriac versions read *He will renew you with his love*. **3:18** The meaning of the Hebrew for this verse is uncertain.

Haggai

WHO
Haggai, Zerubbabel, Jeshua, and the people of Jerusalem.

WHERE
In the city of Jerusalem.

WHEN
Around 520 BC, the time when the temple in Jerusalem was being rebuilt.

WHY
To call the people to honor God by rebuilding the temple in Jerusalem.

Go up into the hills, bring down timber, and rebuild my house.
HAGGAI 1:8

If you were stranded on a desert island, what would you list as your couldn't-live-without items? DVDs? TV? Video game player? Would God be on the list? The people of Jerusalem had deleted God from their priority lists. They had let him slip from their lives. Haggai reminded the people what—or who—was really important in life.

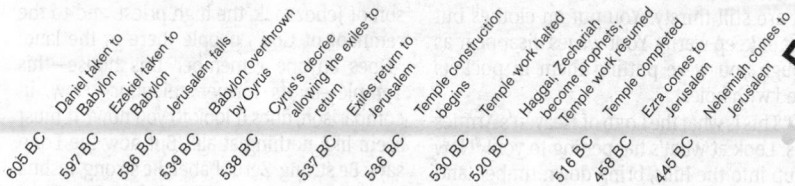

REMEMBER TO MAKE GOD NUMBER ONE IN YOUR LIFE.

CHAPTER 1

A Call to Rebuild the Temple

On August 29* of the second year of King Darius's reign, the LORD gave a message through the prophet Haggai to Zerubbabel son of Shealtiel, governor of Judah, and to Jeshua* son of Jehozadak, the high priest.

[2] "This is what the LORD of Heaven's Armies says: The people are saying, 'The time has not yet come to rebuild the house of the LORD.'"

[3] Then the LORD sent this message through the prophet Haggai: [4] "Why are you living in luxurious houses while my house lies in ruins? [5] This is what the LORD of Heaven's

1:1a Hebrew *On the first day of the sixth month*, of the ancient Hebrew lunar calendar. A number of dates in Haggai can be cross-checked with dates in surviving Persian records and related accurately to our modern calendar. This event occurred on August 29, 520 B.C. **1:1b** Hebrew *Joshua*, a variant spelling of Jeshua; also in 1:12, 14.

Armies says: Look at what's happening to you! [6]You have planted much but harvest little. You eat but are not satisfied. You drink but are still thirsty. You put on clothes but cannot keep warm. Your wages disappear as though you were putting them in pockets filled with holes!

[7]"This is what the LORD of Heaven's Armies says: Look at what's happening to you! [8]Now go up into the hills, bring down timber, and rebuild my house. Then I will take pleasure in it and be honored, says the LORD. [9]You hoped for rich harvests, but they were poor. And when you brought your harvest home, I blew it away. Why? Because my house lies in ruins, says the LORD of Heaven's Armies, while all of you are busy building your own fine houses. [10]It's because of you that the heavens withhold the dew and the earth produces no crops. [11]I have called for a drought on your fields and hills—a drought to wither the grain and grapes and olive trees and all your other crops, a drought to starve you and your livestock and to ruin everything you have worked so hard to get."

Obedience to God's Call

[12]Then Zerubbabel son of Shealtiel, and Jeshua son of Jehozadak, the high priest, and the whole remnant of God's people began to obey the message from the LORD their God. When they heard the words of the prophet Haggai, whom the LORD their God had sent, the people feared the LORD. [13]Then Haggai, the LORD's messenger, gave the people this message from the LORD: "I am with you, says the LORD!"

[14]So the LORD sparked the enthusiasm of Zerubbabel son of Shealtiel, governor of Judah, and the enthusiasm of Jeshua son of Jehozadak, the high priest, and the enthusiasm of the whole remnant of God's people. They began to work on the house of their God, the LORD of Heaven's Armies, [15]on September 21* of the second year of King Darius's reign.

CHAPTER 2

The New Temple's Diminished Splendor

Then on October 17 of that same year,* the LORD sent another message through the prophet Haggai. [2]"Say this to Zerubbabel son of Shealtiel, governor of Judah, and to Jeshua* son of Jehozadak, the high priest, and to the remnant of God's people there in the land: [3]'Does anyone remember this house—this Temple—in its former splendor? How, in comparison, does it look to you now? It must seem like nothing at all! [4]But now the LORD says: Be strong, Zerubbabel. Be strong, Jeshua son of Jehozadak, the high priest. Be strong, all you people still left in the land. And now get to work, for I am with you, says the LORD of Heaven's Armies. [5]My Spirit remains among you, just as I promised when you came out of Egypt. So do not be afraid.'

[6]"For this is what the LORD of Heaven's Armies says: In just a little while I will again shake the heavens and the earth, the oceans and the dry land. [7]I will shake all the nations,

1:15 Hebrew *on the twenty-fourth day of the sixth month*, of the ancient Hebrew lunar calendar. This event occurred on September 21, 520 B.C.; also see note on 1:1a. **2:1** Hebrew *on the twenty-first day of the seventh month*, of the ancient Hebrew lunar calendar. This event (in the second year of Darius's reign) occurred on October 17, 520 B.C.; also see note on 1:1a. **2:2** Hebrew *Joshua*, a variant spelling of Jeshua; also in 2:4.

Several years ago, my parents experienced a rough period in their marriage. They were always arguing about something—my mom's drinking, my dad's late hours, you name it.

One evening, as I was watching TV in our living room, my dad came in and sat down on the couch. Since he was rarely home before I went to bed, I jumped at the chance to talk with him.

We talked about all kinds of things. Then I brought up the subject of college. I said I looked forward to going someday and asked him why he never finished. He didn't want to talk about it, but I kept asking him.

His response was a total shock to me. "It's actually because of you," he said. He explained he was in school and working full time when my mom unexpectedly got pregnant. After I was born, my mom didn't go back to work, so he got a second job—and dropped out of school.

When he finished talking, I excused myself and went to my room. I began to wonder, *Did I cause their problems? Do they love me—or do they regret having me?* Too upset to do my homework, I pulled some devotional booklets from my bookshelf and started flipping through them.

One of them contained an article on self-worth. Since I had little, I decided to read it. The article's main points still speak to me: I'm alive because God wants me to be alive. . . . God chose me. . . . I am his child. . . . Nothing can separate me from his love. Because of his love, my life has meaning and worth. Because God also loves you, your life has meaning and worth too.

Check out Haggai 2:23 to see God's tremendous affirmation to Zerubbabel and to us. Check out Romans 8:38–39 and Ephesians 1:4 for more on our special worth to God.

and the treasures of all the nations will be
brought to this Temple. I will fill this place
with glory, says the LORD of Heaven's Armies.
[8]The silver is mine, and the gold is mine, says
the LORD of Heaven's Armies. [9]The future
glory of this Temple will be greater than its
past glory, says the LORD of Heaven's Armies.
And in this place I will bring peace. I, the LORD
of Heaven's Armies, have spoken!"

Blessings Promised for Obedience

[10]On December 18* of the second year of King
Darius's reign, the LORD sent this message to
the prophet Haggai: [11]"This is what the LORD
of Heaven's Armies says. Ask the priests this
question about the law: [12]'If one of you is carry-
ing some meat from a holy sacrifice in his
robes and his robe happens to brush against
some bread or stew, wine or olive oil, or any
other kind of food, will it also become holy?'"

The priests replied, "No."

[13]Then Haggai asked, "If someone be-
comes ceremonially unclean by touching a
dead person and then touches any of these
foods, will the food be defiled?"

And the priests answered, "Yes."

[14]Then Haggai responded, "That is how it is
with this people and this nation, says the
LORD. Everything they do and everything they
offer is defiled by their sin. [15]Look at what
was happening to you before you began to lay
the foundation of the LORD's Temple. [16]When
you hoped for a twenty-bushel crop, you har-
vested only ten. When you expected to draw
fifty gallons from the winepress, you found
only twenty. [17]I sent blight and mildew and
hail to destroy everything you worked so hard
to produce. Even so, you refused to return to
me, says the LORD.

[18]"Think about this eighteenth day of De-
cember, the day* when the foundation of the
LORD's Temple was laid. Think carefully. [19]I
am giving you a promise now while the seed is
still in the barn.* You have not yet harvested
your grain, and your grapevines, fig trees,
pomegranates, and olive trees have not yet
produced their crops. But from this day on-
ward I will bless you."

Promises for Zerubbabel

[20]On that same day, December 18,* the LORD
sent this second message to Haggai: [21]"Tell
Zerubbabel, the governor of Judah, that I am
about to shake the heavens and the earth. [22]I
will overthrow royal thrones and destroy the
power of foreign kingdoms. I will overturn
their chariots and riders. The horses will fall,
and their riders will kill each other.

[23]"But when this happens, says the LORD of
Heaven's Armies, I will honor you, Zerubba-
bel son of Shealtiel, my servant. I will make
you like a signet ring on my finger, says the
LORD, for I have chosen you. I, the LORD of
Heaven's Armies, have spoken!"

2:10 Hebrew *On the twenty-fourth day of the ninth month,* of the ancient Hebrew lunar calendar (similarly in 2:18). This event occurred on December 18, 520 B.C.; also see note on 1:1a. **2:18** Or *On this eighteenth day of December, think about the day.* **2:19** Hebrew *Is the seed yet in the barn?* **2:20** Hebrew *On the twenty-fourth day of the [ninth] month;* see note on 2:10.

Zechariah

WHO
Zechariah, Zerubbabel, Jeshua, and the Jews rebuilding the temple.

WHERE
In the city of Jerusalem.

WHEN
Chapters 1–8 were written about 520–518 BC, while chapters 9–14 were written around 480 BC.

WHY
To give God's people hope of future deliverance by promising to send a king to be their Messiah (Savior).

Rejoice, O people of Zion! Shout in triumph . . . ! Look, your king is coming.
ZECHARIAH 9:9

Some people try to learn about the future from astrologers, fortune-tellers, and even fortune cookies! But only God knows the future. He told the prophet Zechariah that he would send the Messiah—a king—to rescue his people and to make the world a new place. What great news! (In John 4:26, Jesus says he is the Messiah.)

538 BC — Cyrus's decree allowing exiles to return
537 BC — Exiles return to Jerusalem
536 BC — Temple construction begins
530 BC — Temple work halted
520 BC — Haggai, Zechariah become prophets; Temple work resumed
516 BC — Temple completed
458 BC — Ezra comes to Jerusalem
445 BC — Nehemiah comes to Jerusalem

TRUST GOD WITH YOUR FUTURE.

CHAPTER 1

A Call to Return to the LORD

In November* of the second year of King Darius's reign, the LORD gave this message to the prophet Zechariah son of Berekiah and grandson of Iddo:

2"I, the LORD, was very angry with your ancestors. 3Therefore, say to the people, 'This is what the LORD of Heaven's Armies says: Return to me, and I will return to you, says the LORD of Heaven's Armies.' 4Don't be like your ancestors who would not listen or pay attention

1:1 Hebrew *In the eighth month.* A number of dates in Zechariah can be cross-checked with dates in surviving Persian records and related accurately to our modern calendar. This month of the ancient Hebrew lunar calendar occurred within the months of October and November 520 B.C.

when the earlier prophets said to them, 'This is what the LORD of Heaven's Armies says: Turn from your evil ways, and stop all your evil practices.'

5"Where are your ancestors now? They and the prophets are long dead. 6But everything I said through my servants the prophets happened to your ancestors, just as I said. As a result, they repented and said, 'We have received what we deserved from the LORD of Heaven's Armies. He has done what he said he would do.'"

A Man among the Myrtle Trees

7Three months later, on February 15,* the LORD sent another message to the prophet Zechariah son of Berekiah and grandson of Iddo.

8In a vision during the night, I saw a man sitting on a red horse that was standing among some myrtle trees in a small valley. Behind him were riders on red, brown, and white horses. 9I asked the angel who was talking with me, "My lord, what do these horses mean?"

AMAZING FACTS

Zechariah had a vision of a man measuring the width and length of the entire city of Jerusalem—with a tape measure!

ZECHARIAH 2:1-2

"I will show you," the angel replied.

10The rider standing among the myrtle trees then explained, "They are the ones the LORD has sent out to patrol the earth."

11Then the other riders reported to the angel of the LORD, who was standing among the myrtle trees, "We have been patrolling the earth, and the whole earth is at peace."

12Upon hearing this, the angel of the LORD prayed this prayer: "O LORD of Heaven's Armies, for seventy years now you have been angry with Jerusalem and the towns of Judah. How long until you again show mercy to them?" 13And the LORD spoke kind and comforting words to the angel who talked with me.

14Then the angel said to me, "Shout this message for all to hear: 'This is what the LORD of Heaven's Armies says: My love for Jerusalem and Mount Zion is passionate and strong. 15But I am very angry with the other nations that are now enjoying peace and security. I was only a little angry with my people, but the nations inflicted harm on them far beyond my intentions.

16"'Therefore, this is what the LORD says: I have returned to show mercy to Jerusalem. My Temple will be rebuilt, says the LORD of Heaven's Armies, and measurements will be taken for the reconstruction of Jerusalem.*'

17"Say this also: 'This is what the LORD of Heaven's Armies says: The towns of Israel will again overflow with prosperity, and the LORD will again comfort Zion and choose Jerusalem as his own.'"

Four Horns and Four Blacksmiths

18*Then I looked up and saw four animal horns. 19"What are these?" I asked the angel who was talking with me.

He replied, "These horns represent the nations that scattered Judah, Israel, and Jerusalem."

20Then the LORD showed me four blacksmiths. 21"What are these men coming to do?" I asked.

The angel replied, "These four horns—these nations—scattered and humbled Judah. Now these blacksmiths have come to terrify those nations and throw them down and destroy them."

CHAPTER 2

Future Prosperity of Jerusalem

1*When I looked again, I saw a man with a measuring line in his hand. 2"Where are you going?" I asked.

He replied, "I am going to measure Jerusalem, to see how wide and how long it is."

1:7 Hebrew *On the twenty-fourth day of the eleventh month, the month of Shebat, in the second year of Darius.* This event occurred on February 15, 519 B.C.; also see note on 1:1. **1:16** Hebrew *and the measuring line will be stretched out over Jerusalem.* **1:18** Verses 1:18-21 are numbered 2:1-4 in Hebrew text. **2:1** Verses 2:1-13 are numbered 2:5-17 in Hebrew text.

[3]Then the angel who was with me went to meet a second angel who was coming toward him. [4]The other angel said, "Hurry, and say to that young man, 'Jerusalem will someday be so full of people and livestock that there won't be room enough for everyone! Many will live outside the city walls. [5]Then I, myself, will be a protective wall of fire around Jerusalem, says the LORD. And I will be the glory inside the city!'"

The Exiles Are Called Home

[6]The LORD says, "Come away! Flee from Babylon in the land of the north, for I have scattered you to the four winds. [7]Come away, people of Zion, you who are exiled in Babylon!"

[8]After a period of glory, the LORD of Heaven's Armies sent me* against the nations who plundered you. For he said, "Anyone who harms you harms my most precious possession.* [9]I will raise my fist to crush them, and their own slaves will plunder them." Then you will know that the LORD of Heaven's Armies has sent me.

[10]The LORD says, "Shout and rejoice, O beautiful Jerusalem,* for I am coming to live among you. [11]Many nations will join themselves to the LORD on that day, and they, too, will be my people. I will live among you, and you will know that the LORD of Heaven's Armies sent me to you. [12]The land of Judah will be the LORD's special possession in the holy land, and he will once again choose Jerusalem to be his own city. [13]Be silent before the LORD, all humanity, for he is springing into action from his holy dwelling."

CHAPTER 3

Cleansing for the High Priest

Then the angel showed me Jeshua* the high priest standing before the angel of the LORD. The Accuser, Satan,* was there at the angel's right hand, making accusations against Jeshua. [2]And the LORD said to Satan, "I, the LORD, reject your accusations, Satan. Yes, the LORD, who has chosen Jerusalem, rebukes you. This man is like a burning stick that has been snatched from the fire."

[3]Jeshua's clothing was filthy as he stood there before the angel. [4]So the angel said to the others standing there, "Take off his filthy clothes." And turning to Jeshua he said, "See, I have taken away your sins, and now I am giving you these fine new clothes."

[5]Then I said, "They should also place a clean turban on his head." So they put a clean priestly turban on his head and dressed him in new clothes while the angel of the LORD stood by.

[6]Then the angel of the LORD spoke very solemnly to Jeshua and said, [7]"This is what the LORD of Heaven's Armies says: If you follow my ways and carefully serve me, then you will be given authority over my Temple and its courtyards. I will let you walk among these others standing here.

[8]"Listen to me, O Jeshua the high priest, and all you other priests. You are symbols of things to come. Soon I am going to bring my servant, the Branch. [9]Now look at the jewel I have set before Jeshua, a single stone with seven facets.* I will engrave an inscription on it, says the LORD of Heaven's Armies, and I will remove the sins of this land in a single day.

[10]"And on that day, says the LORD of Heaven's Armies, each of you will invite your neighbor to sit with you peacefully under your own grapevine and fig tree."

CHAPTER 4

A Lampstand and Two Olive Trees

Then the angel who had been talking with me returned and woke me, as though I had been asleep. [2]"What do you see now?" he asked.

I answered, "I see a solid gold lampstand with a bowl of oil on top of it. Around the bowl are seven lamps, each having seven spouts with wicks. [3]And I see two olive trees, one on each side of the bowl." [4]Then I asked the angel, "What are these, my lord? What do they mean?"

[5]"Don't you know?" the angel asked.

"No, my lord," I replied.

[6]Then he said to me, "This is what the LORD says to Zerubbabel: It is not by force nor by strength, but by my Spirit, says the LORD of Heaven's Armies. [7]Nothing, not even a mighty mountain, will stand in Zerubbabel's way; it will become a level plain before him! And

2:8a The meaning of the Hebrew is uncertain. **2:8b** Hebrew *Anyone who touches you touches the pupil of his eye.* **2:10** Hebrew *O daughter of Zion.* **3:1a** Hebrew *Joshua,* a variant spelling of Jeshua; also in 3:3, 4, 6, 8, 9. **3:1b** Hebrew *The satan;* similarly in 3:2. **3:9** Hebrew *seven eyes.*

when Zerubbabel sets the final stone of the Temple in place, the people will shout: 'May God bless it! May God bless it!'*"

[8]Then another message came to me from the LORD: [9]"Zerubbabel is the one who laid the foundation of this Temple, and he will complete it. Then you will know that the LORD of Heaven's Armies has sent me. [10]Do not despise these small beginnings, for the LORD rejoices to see the work begin, to see the plumb line in Zerubbabel's hand."

(The seven lamps* represent the eyes of the LORD that search all around the world.)

[11]Then I asked the angel, "What are these two olive trees on each side of the lampstand, [12]and what are the two olive branches that pour out golden oil through two gold tubes?"

[13]"Don't you know?" he asked.

"No, my lord," I replied.

[14]Then he said to me, "They represent the two heavenly beings who stand in the court of the Lord of all the earth."

CHAPTER 5

A Flying Scroll

I looked up again and saw a scroll flying through the air.

[2]"What do you see?" the angel asked.

"I see a flying scroll," I replied. "It appears to be about 30 feet long and 15 feet wide.*"

[3]Then he said to me, "This scroll contains the curse that is going out over the entire land. One side of the scroll says that those who steal will be banished from the land; the other side says that those who swear falsely will be banished from the land. [4]And this is what the LORD of Heaven's Armies says: I am sending this curse into the house of every thief and into the house of everyone who swears falsely using my name. And my curse will remain in that house and completely destroy it—even its timbers and stones."

A Woman in a Basket

[5]Then the angel who was talking with me came forward and said, "Look up and see what's coming."

[6]"What is it?" I asked.

He replied, "It is a basket for measuring grain,* and it's filled with the sins* of everyone throughout the land."

[7]Then the heavy lead cover was lifted off the basket, and there was a woman sitting inside it. [8]The angel said, "The woman's name is Wickedness," and he pushed her back into the basket and closed the heavy lid again.

[9]Then I looked up and saw two women flying toward us, gliding on the wind. They had wings like a stork, and they picked up the basket and flew into the sky.

[10]"Where are they taking the basket?" I asked the angel.

[11]He replied, "To the land of Babylonia,* where they will build a temple for the basket. And when the temple is ready, they will set the basket there on its pedestal."

4:7 Hebrew *'Grace, grace to it.'* **4:10** Or *The seven facets* (see 3:9); Hebrew reads *These seven.* **5:2** Hebrew *20 cubits* [9 meters] *long and 10 cubits* [4.5 meters] *wide.* **5:6a** Hebrew *an ephah* [20 quarts or 22 liters]; also in 5:7, 8, 9, 10, 11. **5:6b** As in Greek version; Hebrew reads *the appearance.* **5:11** Hebrew *the land of Shinar.*

CHAPTER 6

Four Chariots

Then I looked up again and saw four chariots coming from between two bronze mountains. [2]The first chariot was pulled by red horses, the second by black horses, [3]the third by white horses, and the fourth by powerful dappled-gray horses. [4]"And what are these, my lord?" I asked the angel who was talking with me.

[5]The angel replied, "These are the four spirits* of heaven who stand before the Lord of all the earth. They are going out to do his work. [6]The chariot with black horses is going north, the chariot with white horses is going west,* and the chariot with dappled-gray horses is going south."

[7]The powerful horses were eager to set out to patrol the earth. And the LORD said, "Go and patrol the earth!" So they left at once on their patrol.

[8]Then the LORD summoned me and said, "Look, those who went north have vented the anger of my Spirit* there in the land of the north."

The Crowning of Jeshua

[9]Then I received another message from the LORD: [10]"Heldai, Tobijah, and Jedaiah will bring gifts of silver and gold from the Jews exiled in Babylon. As soon as they arrive, meet them at the home of Josiah son of Zephaniah. [11]Accept their gifts, and make a crown* from the silver and gold. Then put the crown on the head of Jeshua* son of Jehozadak, the high priest. [12]Tell him, 'This is what the LORD of Heaven's Armies says: Here is the man called the Branch. He will branch out from where he is and build the Temple of the LORD. [13]Yes, he will build the Temple of the LORD. Then he will receive royal honor and will rule as king from his throne. He will also serve as priest from his throne,* and there will be perfect harmony between his two roles.'

[14]"The crown will be a memorial in the Temple of the LORD to honor those who gave it—Heldai,* Tobijah, Jedaiah, and Josiah* son of Zephaniah."

[15]People will come from distant lands to rebuild the Temple of the LORD. And when this happens, you will know that my messages have been from the LORD of Heaven's Armies. All this will happen if you carefully obey what the LORD your God says.

CHAPTER 7

A Call to Justice and Mercy

On December 7* of the fourth year of King Darius's reign, another message came to Zechariah from the LORD. [2]The people of Bethel had sent Sharezer and Regemmelech,* along with their attendants, to seek the LORD's favor. [3]They were to ask this question of the prophets and the priests at the Temple of the LORD of Heaven's Armies: "Should we continue to mourn and fast each summer on the anniversary of the Temple's destruction,* as we have done for so many years?"

[4]The LORD of Heaven's Armies sent me this message in reply: [5]"Say to all your people and your priests, 'During these seventy years of exile, when you fasted and mourned in the summer and in early autumn,* was it really for me that you were fasting? [6]And even now in your holy festivals, aren't you eating and drinking just to please yourselves? [7]Isn't this the same message the LORD proclaimed through the prophets in years past when Jerusalem and the towns of Judah were bustling with people, and the Negev and the foothills of Judah* were well populated?'"

[8]Then this message came to Zechariah from the LORD: [9]"This is what the LORD of Heaven's Armies says: Judge fairly, and show mercy and kindness to one another. [10]Do not oppress widows, orphans, foreigners, and the poor. And do not scheme against each other.

[11]"Your ancestors refused to listen to this message. They stubbornly turned away and put their fingers in their ears to keep from hearing. [12]They made their hearts as hard as

6:5 Or *the four winds*. **6:6** Hebrew *is going after them*. **6:8** Hebrew *have given my Spirit rest*. **6:11a** As in Greek and Syriac versions; Hebrew reads *crowns*. **6:11b** Hebrew *Joshua*, a variant spelling of Jeshua. **6:13** Or *There will be a priest by his throne*. **6:14a** As in Syriac version (compare 6:10); Hebrew reads *Helem*. **6:14b** As in Syriac version (compare 6:10); Hebrew reads *Hen*. **7:1** Hebrew *On the fourth day of the ninth month, the month of Kislev*, of the ancient Hebrew lunar calendar. This event occurred on December 7, 518 B.C.; also see note on 1:1. **7:2** Or *Bethel-sharezer had sent Regemmelech*. **7:3** Hebrew *mourn and fast in the fifth month*. The Temple had been destroyed in the fifth month of the ancient Hebrew lunar calendar (August 586 B.C.); see 2 Kgs 25:8. **7:5** Hebrew *fasted and mourned in the fifth and seventh months*. The fifth month of the ancient Hebrew lunar calendar usually occurs within the months of July and August. The seventh month usually occurs within the months of September and October; both the Day of Atonement and the Festival of Shelters were celebrated in the seventh month. **7:7** Hebrew *the Shephelah*.

stone, so they could not hear the instructions
or the messages that the LORD of Heaven's
Armies had sent them by his Spirit through
the earlier prophets. That is why the LORD of
Heaven's Armies was so angry with them.
13"Since they refused to listen when I
called to them, I would not listen when they
called to me, says the LORD of Heaven's Ar-
mies. 14As with a whirlwind, I scattered them
among the distant nations, where they lived
as strangers. Their land became so desolate
that no one even traveled through it. They
turned their pleasant land into a desert."

CHAPTER 8

Promised Blessings for Jerusalem

Then another message came to me from the
LORD of Heaven's Armies: 2"This is what the
LORD of Heaven's Armies says: My love for
Mount Zion is passionate and strong; I am
consumed with passion for Jerusalem!
3"And now the LORD says: I am returning to
Mount Zion, and I will live in Jerusalem. Then
Jerusalem will be called the Faithful City; the
mountain of the LORD of Heaven's Armies will
be called the Holy Mountain.
4"This is what the LORD of Heaven's Armies
says: Once again old men and women will
walk Jerusalem's streets with their canes and
will sit together in the city squares. 5And the
streets of the city will be filled with boys and
girls at play.
6"This is what the LORD of Heaven's Armies
says: All this may seem impossible to you now,
a small remnant of God's people. But is it im-
possible for me? says the LORD of Heaven's
Armies.
7"This is what the LORD of Heaven's Ar-
mies says: You can be sure that I will rescue
my people from the east and from the west. 8I
will bring them home again to live safely in
Jerusalem. They will be my people, and I will
be faithful and just toward them as their God.
9"This is what the LORD of Heaven's Ar-
mies says: Be strong and finish the task! Ever
since the laying of the foundation of the
Temple of the LORD of Heaven's Armies, you
have heard what the prophets have been say-
ing about completing the building. 10Before
the work on the Temple began, there were no
jobs and no money to hire people or animals.
No traveler was safe from the enemy, for

KEEPING SECRETS

Ryan was going to have a friend stay over on Friday night so they could leave early for the football game on Saturday. Ryan usually asked Tucker to do special things with him; but this time he invited a new guy in his class, and the new kid enthusiastically accepted. Then Tucker called. "I thought you weren't going to the game tomorrow, but I heard you and the new guy are going. Is that true?" he blurted out. Ryan didn't know how Tucker found out, but he could hear the hurt in his friend's voice. What should Ryan say? Take a look at Zechariah 8:16-17.

there were enemies on all sides. I had turned
everyone against each other.
11"But now I will not treat the remnant of
my people as I treated them before, says the
LORD of Heaven's Armies. 12For I am planting
seeds of peace and prosperity among you.
The grapevines will be heavy with fruit. The
earth will produce its crops, and the heavens

will release the dew. Once more I will cause the remnant in Judah and Israel to inherit these blessings. [13]Among the other nations, Judah and Israel became symbols of a cursed nation. But no longer! Now I will rescue you and make you both a symbol and a source of blessing. So don't be afraid. Be strong, and get on with rebuilding the Temple!

[14]"For this is what the LORD of Heaven's Armies says: I was determined to punish you when your ancestors angered me, and I did not change my mind, says the LORD of Heaven's Armies. [15]But now I am determined to bless Jerusalem and the people of Judah. So don't be afraid. [16]But this is what you must do: Tell the truth to each other. Render verdicts in your courts that are just and that lead to peace. [17]Don't scheme against each other. Stop your love of telling lies that you swear are the truth. I hate all these things, says the LORD."

[18]Here is another message that came to me from the LORD of Heaven's Armies. [19]"This is what the LORD of Heaven's Armies says: The traditional fasts and times of mourning you have kept in early summer, midsummer, autumn, and winter* are now ended. They will become festivals of joy and celebration for the people of Judah. So love truth and peace.

[20]"This is what the LORD of Heaven's Armies says: People from nations and cities around the world will travel to Jerusalem. [21]The people of one city will say to the people of another, 'Come with us to Jerusalem to ask the LORD to bless us. Let's worship the LORD of Heaven's Armies. I'm determined to go.' [22]Many peoples and powerful nations will come to Jerusalem to seek the LORD of Heaven's Armies and to ask for his blessing.

[23]"This is what the LORD of Heaven's Armies says: In those days ten men from different nations and languages of the world will clutch at the sleeve of one Jew. And they will say, 'Please let us walk with you, for we have heard that God is with you.'"

CHAPTER 9

Judgment against Israel's Enemies

This is the message* from the LORD against the land of Aram* and the city of Damascus, for the eyes of humanity, including all the tribes of Israel, are on the LORD.

[2] Doom is certain for Hamath,
near Damascus,
and for the cities of Tyre and Sidon,
though they are so clever.
[3] Tyre has built a strong fortress
and has made silver and gold
as plentiful as dust in the streets!
[4] But now the Lord will strip away Tyre's possessions
and hurl its fortifications into the sea,
and it will be burned to the ground.
[5] The city of Ashkelon will see Tyre fall
and will be filled with fear.
Gaza will shake with terror,
as will Ekron, for their hopes will be dashed.
Gaza's king will be killed,
and Ashkelon will be deserted.
[6] Foreigners will occupy the city of Ashdod.
I will destroy the pride of the Philistines.
[7] I will grab the bloody meat from their mouths
and snatch the detestable sacrifices from their teeth.
Then the surviving Philistines will worship our God
and become like a clan in Judah.*
The Philistines of Ekron will join my people,
as the ancient Jebusites once did.
[8] I will guard my Temple
and protect it from invading armies.
I am watching closely to ensure
that no more foreign oppressors overrun my people's land.

Zion's Coming King

[9] Rejoice, O people of Zion!*
Shout in triumph, O people of Jerusalem!
Look, your king is coming to you.
He is righteous and victorious,*
yet he is humble, riding on a donkey—
riding on a donkey's colt.

8:19 Hebrew *in the fourth, fifth, seventh, and tenth months.* The fourth month of the ancient Hebrew lunar calendar usually occurs within the months of June and July. The fifth month usually occurs within the months of July and August. The seventh month usually occurs within the months of September and October. The tenth month usually occurs within the months of December and January. **9:1a** Hebrew *An Oracle: The message.* **9:1b** Hebrew *land of Hadrach.* **9:7** Hebrew *and will become a leader in Judah.* **9:9a** Hebrew *O daughter of Zion!* **9:9b** Hebrew *and is being vindicated.*

10 I will remove the battle chariots from Israel*
and the warhorses from Jerusalem.
I will destroy all the weapons used in battle,
and your king will bring peace to the nations.
His realm will stretch from sea to sea
and from the Euphrates River* to the ends of the earth.*
11 Because of the covenant I made with you, sealed with blood,
I will free your prisoners
from death in a waterless dungeon.
12 Come back to the place of safety,
all you prisoners who still have hope!
I promise this very day
that I will repay two blessings for each of your troubles.
13 Judah is my bow,
and Israel is my arrow.
Jerusalem* is my sword,
and like a warrior, I will brandish it against the Greeks.*

Is it OK to look for answers anywhere that looks good to you?

Household gods give worthless advice, fortune-tellers predict only lies, and interpreters of dreams pronounce falsehoods.
ZECHARIAH 10:2

14 The LORD will appear above his people;
his arrows will fly like lightning!
The Sovereign LORD will sound the ram's horn
and attack like a whirlwind from the southern desert.
15 The LORD of Heaven's Armies will protect his people,
and they will defeat their enemies by hurling great stones.
They will shout in battle as though drunk with wine.
They will be filled with blood like a bowl,
drenched with blood like the corners of the altar.
16 On that day the LORD their God will rescue his people,
just as a shepherd rescues his sheep.
They will sparkle in his land
like jewels in a crown.
17 How wonderful and beautiful they will be!
The young men will thrive on abundant grain,
and the young women will flourish on new wine.

CHAPTER 10

The LORD Will Restore His People

1 Ask the LORD for rain in the spring,
for he makes the storm clouds.
And he will send showers of rain
so every field becomes a lush pasture.
2 Household gods give worthless advice,
fortune-tellers predict only lies,
and interpreters of dreams pronounce falsehoods that give no comfort.
So my people are wandering like lost sheep;
they are attacked because they have no shepherd.
3 "My anger burns against your shepherds,
and I will punish these leaders.*
For the LORD of Heaven's Armies has arrived
to look after Judah, his flock.
He will make them strong and glorious,
like a proud warhorse in battle.
4 From Judah will come the cornerstone,
the tent peg,
the bow for battle,
and all the rulers.
5 They will be like mighty warriors in battle,
trampling their enemies in the mud under their feet.
Since the LORD is with them as they fight,
they will overthrow even the enemy's horsemen.

9:10a Hebrew *Ephraim*, referring to the northern kingdom of Israel; also in 9:13. **9:10b** Hebrew *the river*. **9:10c** Or *the end of the land*. **9:13a** Hebrew *Zion*. **9:13b** Hebrew *the sons of Javan*. **10:3** Or *these male goats*.

6 "I will strengthen Judah and save Israel*;
I will restore them because of my compassion.
It will be as though I had never rejected them,
for I am the LORD their God, who will hear their cries.
7 The people of Israel* will become like mighty warriors,
and their hearts will be made happy as if by wine.
Their children, too, will see it and be glad;
their hearts will rejoice in the LORD.
8 When I whistle to them, they will come running,
for I have redeemed them.
From the few who are left,
they will grow as numerous as they were before.
9 Though I have scattered them like seeds among the nations,
they will still remember me in distant lands.
They and their children will survive and return again to Israel.
10 I will bring them back from Egypt and gather them from Assyria.
I will resettle them in Gilead and Lebanon until there is no more room for them all.
11 They will pass safely through the sea of distress,*
for the waves of the sea will be held back,
and the waters of the Nile will dry up.
The pride of Assyria will be crushed,
and the rule of Egypt will end.
12 By my power* I will make my people strong,
and by my authority they will go wherever they wish.
I, the LORD, have spoken!"

CHAPTER 11

1 Open your doors, Lebanon,
so that fire may devour your cedar forests.
2 Weep, you cypress trees, for all the ruined cedars;
the most majestic ones have fallen.
Weep, you oaks of Bashan,
for the thick forests have been cut down.
3 Listen to the wailing of the shepherds,
for their rich pastures are destroyed.
Hear the young lions roaring,
for their thickets in the Jordan Valley are ruined.

The Good and Evil Shepherds

4 This is what the LORD my God says: "Go and care for the flock that is intended for slaughter. 5 The buyers slaughter their sheep without remorse. The sellers say, 'Praise the LORD! Now I'm rich!' Even the shepherds have no compassion for them. 6 Likewise, I will no longer have pity on the people of the land," says the LORD. "I will let them fall into each other's hands and into the hands of their king. They will turn the land into a wilderness, and I will not rescue them."

7 So I cared for the flock intended for slaughter—the flock that was oppressed. Then I took two shepherd's staffs and named one Favor and the other Union. 8 I got rid of their three evil shepherds in a single month.

But I became impatient with these sheep, and they hated me, too. 9 So I told them, "I won't be your shepherd any longer. If you die, you die. If you are killed, you are killed. And let those who remain devour each other!"

10 Then I took my staff called Favor and cut it in two, showing that I had revoked the covenant I had made with all the nations. 11 That was the end of my covenant with them. The suffering flock was watching me, and they knew that the LORD was speaking through my actions.

12 And I said to them, "If you like, give me my wages, whatever I am worth; but only if you want to." So they counted out for my wages thirty pieces of silver.

13 And the LORD said to me, "Throw it to the potter*"—this magnificent sum at which they valued me! So I took the thirty coins and threw them to the potter in the Temple of the LORD.

14 Then I took my other staff, Union, and cut it in two, showing that the bond of unity between Judah and Israel was broken.

15 Then the LORD said to me, "Go again and play the part of a worthless shepherd. 16 This

10:6 Hebrew *save the house of Joseph.* **10:7** Hebrew *of Ephraim.* **10:11** Or *the sea of Egypt,* referring to the Red Sea. **10:12** Hebrew *In the LORD.* **11:13** Syriac version reads *into the treasury;* also in 11:13b. Compare Matt 27:6-10.

illustrates how I will give this nation a shepherd who will not care for those who are dying, nor look after the young,* nor heal the injured, nor feed the healthy. Instead, this shepherd will eat the meat of the fattest sheep and tear off their hooves.

17 "What sorrow awaits this worthless
shepherd
who abandons the flock!
The sword will cut his arm
and pierce his right eye.
His arm will become useless,
and his right eye completely blind."

CHAPTER 12

Future Deliverance for Jerusalem

This* message concerning the fate of Israel came from the LORD: "This message is from the LORD, who stretched out the heavens, laid the foundations of the earth, and formed the human spirit. 2 I will make Jerusalem like an intoxicating drink that makes the nearby nations stagger when they send their armies to besiege Jerusalem and Judah. 3 On that day I will make Jerusalem an immovable rock. All the nations will gather against it to try to move it, but they will only hurt themselves.

4 "On that day," says the LORD, "I will cause every horse to panic and every rider to lose his nerve. I will watch over the people of Judah, but I will blind all the horses of their enemies. 5 And the clans of Judah will say to themselves, 'The people of Jerusalem have found strength in the LORD of Heaven's Armies, their God.'

6 "On that day I will make the clans of Judah like a flame that sets a woodpile ablaze or like a burning torch among sheaves of grain. They will burn up all the neighboring nations right and left, while the people living in Jerusalem remain secure.

7 "The LORD will give victory to the rest of Judah first, before Jerusalem, so that the people of Jerusalem and the royal line of David will not have greater honor than the rest of Judah. 8 On that day the LORD will defend the people of Jerusalem; the weakest among them will be as mighty as King David! And the royal descendants will be like God, like the angel of the LORD who goes before them! 9 For on that day I will begin to destroy all the nations that come against Jerusalem.

10 "Then I will pour out a spirit* of grace and prayer on the family of David and on the people of Jerusalem. They will look on me whom they have pierced and mourn for him as for an only son. They will grieve bitterly for him as for a firstborn son who has died. 11 The sorrow and mourning in Jerusalem on that day will be like the great mourning for Hadad-rimmon in the valley of Megiddo.

12 "All Israel will mourn, each clan by itself, and with the husbands separate from their wives. The clan of David will mourn alone, as will the clan of Nathan, 13 the clan of Levi, and the clan of Shimei. 14 Each of the surviving clans from Judah will mourn separately, and with the husbands separate from their wives.

CHAPTER 13

A Fountain of Cleansing

"On that day a fountain will be opened for the dynasty of David and for the people of Jerusalem, a fountain to cleanse them from all their sins and impurity.

2 "And on that day," says the LORD of Heaven's Armies, "I will erase idol worship throughout the land, so that even the names of the idols will be forgotten. I will remove from the land both the false prophets and the spirit of impurity that came with them. 3 If anyone continues to prophesy, his own father and mother will tell him, 'You must die, for you have prophesied lies in the name of the LORD.' And as he prophesies, his own father and mother will stab him.

4 "On that day people will be ashamed to claim the prophetic gift. No one will pretend to be a prophet by wearing prophet's clothes. 5 He will say, 'I'm no prophet; I'm a farmer. I began working for a farmer as a boy.' 6 And if someone asks, 'Then what about those wounds on your chest?*' he will say, 'I was wounded at my friends' house!'

The Scattering of the Sheep

7 "Awake, O sword, against my
shepherd,
the man who is my partner,"
says the LORD of Heaven's
Armies.

11:16 Or *the scattered.* 12:1 Hebrew *An Oracle: This.* 12:10 Or *the Spirit.* 13:6 Hebrew *wounds between your hands?*

"Strike down the shepherd,
and the sheep will be scattered,
and I will turn against the lambs.
8 Two-thirds of the people in the land
will be cut off and die," says the LORD.
"But one-third will be left in the land.
9 I will bring that group through the fire
and make them pure.
I will refine them like silver
and purify them like gold.
They will call on my name,
and I will answer them.
I will say, 'These are my people,'
and they will say, 'The LORD is our
God.'"

CHAPTER 14

The LORD Will Rule the Earth

Watch, for the day of the LORD is coming when your possessions will be plundered right in front of you! 2 I will gather all the nations to fight against Jerusalem. The city will be taken, the houses looted, and the women raped. Half the population will be taken into captivity, and the rest will be left among the ruins of the city.

3 Then the LORD will go out to fight against those nations, as he has fought in times past. 4 On that day his feet will stand on the Mount of Olives, east of Jerusalem. And the Mount of Olives will split apart, making a wide valley running from east to west. Half the mountain will move toward the north and half toward the south. 5 You will flee through this valley, for it will reach across to Azal.* Yes, you will flee as you did from the earthquake in the days of King Uzziah of Judah. Then the LORD my God will come, and all his holy ones with him.*

6 On that day the sources of light will no longer shine,* 7 yet there will be continuous day! Only the LORD knows how this could happen. There will be no normal day and night, for at evening time it will still be light.

8 On that day life-giving waters will flow out from Jerusalem, half toward the Dead Sea and half toward the Mediterranean,* flowing continuously in both summer and winter.

9 And the LORD will be king over all the earth. On that day there will be one LORD—his name alone will be worshiped.

10 All the land from Geba, north of Judah, to Rimmon, south of Jerusalem, will become one vast plain. But Jerusalem will be raised up in its original place and will be inhabited all the way from the Benjamin Gate over to the site of the old gate, then to the Corner Gate, and from the Tower of Hananel to the king's winepresses. 11 And Jerusalem will be filled, safe at last, never again to be cursed and destroyed.

12 And the LORD will send a plague on all the nations that fought against Jerusalem. Their people will become like walking corpses, their flesh rotting away. Their eyes will rot in their sockets, and their tongues will rot in their mouths. 13 On that day they will be terrified, stricken by the LORD with great panic. They will fight their neighbors hand to hand. 14 Judah, too, will be fighting at Jerusalem. The wealth of all the neighboring nations will be captured—great quantities of gold and silver and fine clothing. 15 This same plague will strike the horses, mules, camels, donkeys, and all the other animals in the enemy camps.

AMAZING FACTS

Zechariah had a vision of the Lord standing on a mountain that split in two, forming a valley that many people could walk through!

ZECHARIAH 14:4

16 In the end, the enemies of Jerusalem who survive the plague will go up to Jerusalem each year to worship the King, the LORD of Heaven's Armies, and to celebrate the Festival of Shelters. 17 Any nation in the world that refuses to come to Jerusalem to worship the King, the LORD of Heaven's Armies, will have no rain. 18 If the people of Egypt refuse to attend the festival, the LORD will punish them with the same plague that he sends on the other nations who

14:5a The meaning of the Hebrew is uncertain. **14:5b** As in Greek version; Hebrew reads *with you.* **14:6** Hebrew *there will be no light, no cold or frost.* The meaning of the Hebrew is uncertain. **14:8** Hebrew *half toward the eastern sea and half toward the western sea.*

refuse to go. [19]Egypt and the other nations will
all be punished if they don't go to celebrate the
Festival of Shelters.

[20]On that day even the harness bells of the
horses will be inscribed with these words:
HOLY TO THE LORD. And the cooking pots in
the Temple of the LORD will be as sacred as
the basins used beside the altar. [21]In fact,
every cooking pot in Jerusalem and Judah will
be holy to the LORD of Heaven's Armies. All
who come to worship will be free to use any of
these pots to boil their sacrifices. And on that
day there will no longer be traders* in the
Temple of the LORD of Heaven's Armies.

14:21 Hebrew *Canaanites.*

Malachi

WHO
Malachi, the priests, and the people of Judah.

WHERE
In Jerusalem, the capital of Judah.

WHEN
Around 430 BC, after the Jews had returned to Jerusalem from Babylon.

WHY
To confront the people with their sins and challenge them to restore their relationship with God.

For you who fear my name . . .
you will go free, leaping with joy
like calves let out to pasture.
MALACHI 4:2

Many kids go to church only because their parents make them go. Some of the ancient Jews also worshiped God just because they had to—going through the motions, giving their second-best. Malachi warned them that worshiping because you *have to* isn't really worship. God wants your best, and he wants it to come from the heart.

586 BC	537 BC	536 BC	520 BC	516 BC	479 BC	465 BC	458 BC	445 BC	430 BC
Jerusalem is destroyed	Exiles return to Jerusalem	Temple construction begins	Haggai, Zechariah become prophets; Temple work resumed	Temple completed	Esther becomes queen of Persia	Artaxerxes I becomes king of Persia	Ezra comes to Jerusalem	Nehemiah comes to Jerusalem	Malachi becomes a prophet

Get serious about your relationship with God.

CHAPTER 1

This is the message* that the LORD gave to Israel through the prophet Malachi.*

The LORD's Love for Israel

2 "I have always loved you," says the LORD.

But you retort, "Really? How have you loved us?"

And the LORD replies, "This is how I showed my love for you: I loved your ancestor Jacob, 3 but I rejected his brother, Esau, and devastated his hill country. I turned Esau's inheritance into a desert for jackals."

4 Esau's descendants in Edom may say, "We have been shattered, but we will rebuild the ruins."

1:1a Hebrew *An Oracle: The message.* **1:1b** *Malachi* means "my messenger."

IS THAT YOUR BEST?
Greg's Sunday school class had taken on a service project to help collect canned goods for the local food pantry. Greg was in charge of making posters for the project. He had lots of good ideas. But every time he planned to work on the posters, something came up. Now it was Saturday night, and Greg suddenly remembered the posters! Should he quickly throw something together, figuring it's only Sunday school? Or should he take the time to do a good job and bring the posters in later? Read Malachi 1:6-8 to see how God feels when we give him less than our best.

But the LORD of Heaven's Armies replies, "They may try to rebuild, but I will demolish them again. Their country will be known as 'The Land of Wickedness,' and their people will be called 'The People with Whom the LORD Is Forever Angry.' [5]When you see the destruction for yourselves, you will say, 'Truly, the LORD's greatness reaches far beyond Israel's borders!'"

Unworthy Sacrifices

[6]The LORD of Heaven's Armies says to the priests: "A son honors his father, and a servant respects his master. If I am your father and master, where are the honor and respect I deserve? You have shown contempt for my name!

"But you ask, 'How have we ever shown contempt for your name?'

[7]"You have shown contempt by offering defiled sacrifices on my altar.

"Then you ask, 'How have we defiled the sacrifices?*'

"You defile them by saying the altar of the LORD deserves no respect. [8]When you give blind animals as sacrifices, isn't that wrong? And isn't it wrong to offer animals that are crippled and diseased? Try giving gifts like that to your governor, and see how pleased he is!" says the LORD of Heaven's Armies.

[9]"Go ahead, beg God to be merciful to you! But when you bring that kind of offering, why should he show you any favor at all?" asks the LORD of Heaven's Armies.

[10]"How I wish one of you would shut the Temple doors so that these worthless sacrifices could not be offered! I am not pleased with you," says the LORD of Heaven's Armies, "and I will not accept your offerings. [11]But my name is honored* by people of other nations from morning till night. All around the world they offer* sweet incense and pure offerings in honor of my name. For my name is great among the nations," says the LORD of Heaven's Armies.

[12]"But you dishonor my name with your actions. By bringing contemptible food, you are saying it's all right to defile the Lord's table. [13]You say, 'It's too hard to serve the LORD,' and you turn up your noses at my commands," says the LORD of Heaven's Armies. "Think of it! Animals that are stolen and crippled and sick are being presented as offerings! Should I accept from you such offerings as these?" asks the LORD.

[14]"Cursed is the cheat who promises to give

1:7 As in Greek version; Hebrew reads *defiled you?* **1:11a** Or *will be honored.* **1:11b** Or *will offer.*

Like you, I have a lot of friends whose parents are separated or divorced. I don't know why so many married couples split up—even Christian couples.

Personally, I feel blessed. Growing up, I could always tell that my parents had a strong marriage. They've always tried to follow the God-given principles set out for marriage in the Bible—serving, listening, giving, forgiving. My mom would always do special little things for my dad, like having his favorite snack for him, and my dad would do similar things for my mom. They will tell you that they have had plenty of hard times, but God has always brought them through the tough stuff.

I will probably get married in a few years, so it has been awesome to see what a good marriage looks like. It is just incredible to see God work in a marriage when two people actually become one.

Like I said, a lot of my friends don't have that positive example. They've had bad home lives, watching their parents fight and be selfish and get divorced. From what I've been reading in the Bible, I know that it breaks God's heart to see people treat their marriage so lightly and divorce.

The older I get, the more I realize that if your parents have a good marriage, that doesn't guarantee you will too. And if your parents had a bad marriage, that doesn't mean you are doomed. You can still one day have an awesome marriage. All things are possible with God. The most important relationship in a marriage is with God. Both the husband and wife have to put him first. Seriously, without God at the center, I'm not sure a good marriage is even possible.

Take a look at Malachi 2:14-16 to see how God truly views marriage and how he truly views divorce. Then read more about marriage in Ephesians 5:21-33.

a fine ram from his flock but then sacrifices a defective one to the Lord. For I am a great king," says the LORD of Heaven's Armies, "and my name is feared among the nations!

CHAPTER 2

A Warning to the Priests

"Listen, you priests—this command is for you! [2]Listen to me and make up your minds to honor my name," says the LORD of Heaven's Armies, "or I will bring a terrible curse against you. I will curse even the blessings you receive. Indeed, I have already cursed them, because you have not taken my warning to heart. [3]I will punish your descendants and splatter your faces with the manure from your festival sacrifices, and I will throw you on the manure pile. [4]Then at last you will know it was I who sent you this warning so that my covenant with the Levites can continue," says the LORD of Heaven's Armies.

[5]"The purpose of my covenant with the Levites was to bring life and peace, and that is what I gave them. This required reverence from them, and they greatly revered me and stood in awe of my name. [6]They passed on to the people the truth of the instructions they received from me. They did not lie or cheat; they walked with me, living good and righteous lives, and they turned many from lives of sin.

[7]"The words of a priest's lips should preserve knowledge of God, and people should go to him for instruction, for the priest is the messenger of the LORD of Heaven's Armies. [8]But you priests have left God's paths. Your instructions have caused many to stumble into sin. You have corrupted the covenant I made with the Levites," says the LORD of Heaven's Armies. [9]"So I have made you despised and humiliated in the eyes of all the people. For you have not obeyed me but have shown favoritism in the way you carry out my instructions."

A Call to Faithfulness

[10]Are we not all children of the same Father? Are we not all created by the same God? Then why do we betray each other, violating the covenant of our ancestors?

[11]Judah has been unfaithful, and a detestable thing has been done in Israel and in Jerusalem. The men of Judah have defiled the LORD's beloved sanctuary by marrying women who worship idols. [12]May the LORD cut off from the nation of Israel* every last man who has done this and yet brings an offering to the LORD of Heaven's Armies.

2:12 Hebrew *from the tents of Jacob*. The names "Jacob" and "Israel" are often interchanged throughout the Old Testament, referring sometimes to the individual patriarch and sometimes to the nation.

IS IT OK?

IS IT OK IF I WANT MY PARENTS TO GET BACK TOGETHER?

Divorce hurts—it rips two people apart. They (and their children) always get injured in the process. That's why God says he *hates* divorce (see Malachi 2:16). If your parents are divorced, it's totally natural to want them to get back together. It's OK to wish for that and even to pray for it. At the same time, you have to try to live with what has happened. It wasn't your fault that your parents got divorced, and it's not your job to get them back together. Talk to your parents about your feelings. And remember that if you just ask, God is right there to help you face whatever happens in your life.

[13]Here is another thing you do. You cover the LORD's altar with tears, weeping and groaning because he pays no attention to your offerings and doesn't accept them with pleasure. [14]You cry out, "Why doesn't the LORD accept my worship?" I'll tell you why! Because the LORD witnessed the vows you and your wife made when you were young. But you have been unfaithful to her, though she remained your faithful partner, the wife of your marriage vows.

[15]Didn't the LORD make you one with your wife? In body and spirit you are his.* And what does he want? Godly children from your union. So guard your heart; remain loyal to the wife of your youth. [16]"For I hate divorce!" says the LORD, the God of Israel. "To divorce your wife is to overwhelm her with cruelty,*" says the LORD of Heaven's Armies. "So guard your heart; do not be unfaithful to your wife."

[17]You have wearied the LORD with your words.

"How have we wearied him?" you ask.

You have wearied him by saying that all who do evil are good in the LORD's sight, and he is pleased with them. You have wearied him by asking, "Where is the God of justice?"

CHAPTER 3

The Coming Day of Judgment

"Look! I am sending my messenger, and he will prepare the way before me. Then the Lord you are seeking will suddenly come to his Temple. The messenger of the covenant, whom you look for so eagerly, is surely coming," says the LORD of Heaven's Armies.

[2]"But who will be able to endure it when he comes? Who will be able to stand and face him when he appears? For he will be like a blazing fire that refines metal, or like a strong soap that bleaches clothes. [3]He will sit like a refiner of silver, burning away the dross. He will purify the Levites, refining them like gold and silver, so that they may once again offer acceptable sacrifices to the LORD. [4]Then once more the LORD will accept the offerings brought to him by the people of Judah and Jerusalem, as he did in the past.

[5]"At that time I will put you on trial. I am eager to witness against all sorcerers and adulterers and liars. I will speak against those who cheat employees of their wages, who oppress widows and orphans, or who deprive the foreigners living among you of justice, for these people do not fear me," says the LORD of Heaven's Armies.

A Call to Repentance

[6]"I am the LORD, and I do not change. That is why you descendants of Jacob are not already destroyed. [7]Ever since the days of your ancestors, you have scorned my decrees and failed to obey them. Now return to me, and I will return to you," says the LORD of Heaven's Armies.

"But you ask, 'How can we return when we have never gone away?'

[8]"Should people cheat God? Yet you have cheated me!

"But you ask, 'What do you mean? When did we ever cheat you?'

"You have cheated me of the tithes and offerings due to me. [9]You are under a curse, for your whole nation has been cheating me. [10]Bring all the tithes into the storehouse so there will be enough food in my Temple. If you do," says the LORD of Heaven's Armies, "I will open the windows of heaven for you. I will pour out a blessing so great you won't have enough room to take it in! Try it! Put me to the test! [11]Your crops will be abundant, for I will guard them from insects and disease.* Your grapes will not fall from the vine before they are ripe," says the LORD of Heaven's Armies. [12]"Then all nations will call you blessed, for your land will be such a delight," says the LORD of Heaven's Armies.

[13]"You have said terrible things about me," says the LORD.

"But you say, 'What do you mean? What have we said against you?'

[14]"You have said, 'What's the use of serving God? What have we gained by obeying his commands or by trying to show the LORD of Heaven's Armies that we are sorry for our sins? [15]From now on we will call the arrogant blessed. For those who do evil get rich, and those who dare God to punish them suffer no harm.'"

The LORD's Promise of Mercy

[16]Then those who feared the LORD spoke with each other, and the LORD listened to what they

2:15 Or *Didn't the one LORD make us and preserve our life and breath?* or *Didn't the one LORD make her, both flesh and spirit?* The meaning of the Hebrew is uncertain. **2:16** Hebrew *to cover one's garment with violence.* **3:11** Hebrew *from the devourer.*

said. In his presence, a scroll of remembrance was written to record the names of those who feared him and always thought about the honor of his name.

17"They will be my people," says the LORD of Heaven's Armies. "On the day when I act in judgment, they will be my own special treasure. I will spare them as a father spares an obedient child. 18Then you will again see the difference between the righteous and the wicked, between those who serve God and those who do not."

CHAPTER 4

The Coming Day of Judgment

1*The LORD of Heaven's Armies says, "The day of judgment is coming, burning like a furnace. On that day the arrogant and the wicked will be burned up like straw. They will be consumed—roots, branches, and all.

2"But for you who fear my name, the Sun of Righteousness will rise with healing in his wings.* And you will go free, leaping with joy like calves let out to pasture. 3On the day when I act, you will tread upon the wicked as if they were dust under your feet," says the LORD of Heaven's Armies.

4"Remember to obey the Law of Moses, my servant—all the decrees and regulations that I gave him on Mount Sinai* for all Israel.

5"Look, I am sending you the prophet Elijah before the great and dreadful day of the LORD arrives. 6His preaching will turn the hearts of fathers to their children, and the hearts of children to their fathers. Otherwise I will come and strike the land with a curse."

4:1 Verses 4:1-6 are numbered 3:19-24 in Hebrew text. **4:2** Or *the sun of righteousness will rise with healing in its wings.*
4:4 Hebrew *Horeb*, another name for Sinai.

NEW TESTAMENT

matthew

WHO

Jesus, Mary, Joseph, John the Baptist, disciples (including Peter, James, and John), suffering woman, Gentile woman, religious leaders, Caiaphas, Pilate, and Mary Magdalene.

WHERE

In Jerusalem.

WHEN

Probably between AD 60 and 65.

WHY

To prove that Jesus is the Messiah, the eternal King.

She will have a son, and you are to name him Jesus, for he will save his people from their sins.
MATTHEW 1:21

Matthew wrote about Jesus' whole life: his birth, death, resurrection. Of all the famous people who ever lived—Napoleon, George Washington, and Martin Luther King, Jr. to name a few—the one who changed the most lives is Jesus Christ. Two thousand years ago he started a spiritual revolution that is still going strong.

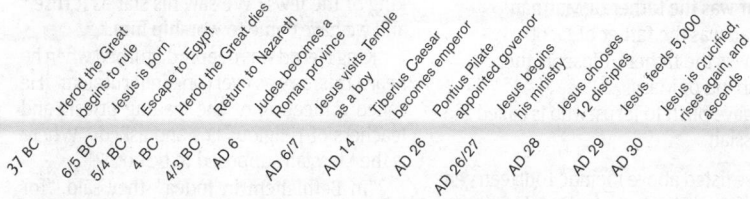

CHECK IT OUT—JESUS CAN CHANGE YOUR LIFE, TOO.

CHAPTER 1

The Ancestors of Jesus the Messiah

This is a record of the ancestors of Jesus the Messiah, a descendant of David* and of Abraham:

2 Abraham was the father of Isaac.
Isaac was the father of Jacob.
Jacob was the father of Judah and his brothers.
3 Judah was the father of Perez and Zerah (whose mother was Tamar).
Perez was the father of Hezron.
Hezron was the father of Ram.*
4 Ram was the father of Amminadab.
Amminadab was the father of Nahshon.
Nahshon was the father of Salmon.
5 Salmon was the father of Boaz (whose mother was Rahab).

1:1 Greek *Jesus the Messiah, son of David.* **1:3** Greek *Aram,* a variant spelling of Ram; also in 1:4. See 1 Chr 2:9-10.

Boaz was the father of Obed (whose
mother was Ruth).
Obed was the father of Jesse.
6 Jesse was the father of King David.
David was the father of Solomon (whose
mother was Bathsheba, the widow
of Uriah).
7 Solomon was the father of Rehoboam.
Rehoboam was the father of Abijah.
Abijah was the father of Asa.*
8 Asa was the father of Jehoshaphat.
Jehoshaphat was the father of Jehoram.*
Jehoram was the father* of Uzziah.
9 Uzziah was the father of Jotham.
Jotham was the father of Ahaz.
Ahaz was the father of Hezekiah.
10 Hezekiah was the father of Manasseh.
Manasseh was the father of Amon.*
Amon was the father of Josiah.
11 Josiah was the father of Jehoiachin* and
his brothers (born at the time of the
exile to Babylon).
12 After the Babylonian exile:
Jehoiachin was the father of Shealtiel.
Shealtiel was the father of Zerubbabel.
13 Zerubbabel was the father of Abiud.
Abiud was the father of Eliakim.
Eliakim was the father of Azor.
14 Azor was the father of Zadok.
Zadok was the father of Akim.
Akim was the father of Eliud.
15 Eliud was the father of Eleazar.
Eleazar was the father of Matthan.
Matthan was the father of Jacob.
16 Jacob was the father of Joseph, the
husband of Mary.
Mary gave birth to Jesus, who is called the
Messiah.

17 All those listed above include fourteen generations from Abraham to David, fourteen from David to the Babylonian exile, and fourteen from the Babylonian exile to the Messiah.

The Birth of Jesus the Messiah

18 This is how Jesus the Messiah was born. His mother, Mary, was engaged to be married to Joseph. But before the marriage took place, while she was still a virgin, she became pregnant through the power of the Holy Spirit. 19 Joseph, her fiancé, was a good man and did not want to disgrace her publicly, so he decided to break the engagement* quietly.

20 As he considered this, an angel of the Lord appeared to him in a dream. "Joseph, son of David," the angel said, "do not be afraid to take Mary as your wife. For the child within her was conceived by the Holy Spirit. 21 And she will have a son, and you are to name him Jesus,* for he will save his people from their sins."

22 All of this occurred to fulfill the Lord's message through his prophet:

23 "Look! The virgin will conceive a child!
She will give birth to a son,
and they will call him Immanuel,*
which means 'God is with us.'"

24 When Joseph woke up, he did as the angel of the Lord commanded and took Mary as his wife. 25 But he did not have sexual relations with her until her son was born. And Joseph named him Jesus.

CHAPTER 2

Visitors from the East

Jesus was born in Bethlehem in Judea, during the reign of King Herod. About that time some wise men* from eastern lands arrived in Jerusalem, asking, 2 "Where is the newborn king of the Jews? We saw his star as it rose,* and we have come to worship him."

3 King Herod was deeply disturbed when he heard this, as was everyone in Jerusalem. 4 He called a meeting of the leading priests and teachers of religious law and asked, "Where is the Messiah supposed to be born?"

5 "In Bethlehem in Judea," they said, "for this is what the prophet wrote:

6 'And you, O Bethlehem in the land of
Judah,
are not least among the ruling cities*
of Judah,
for a ruler will come from you
who will be the shepherd for my people
Israel.'*"

1:7 Greek *Asaph*, a variant spelling of Asa; also in 1:8. See 1 Chr 3:10. **1:8a** Greek *Joram*, a variant spelling of Jehoram; also in 1:8b. See 1 Kgs 22:50 and note at 1 Chr 3:11. **1:8b** Or *ancestor;* also in 1:11. **1:10** Greek *Amos*, a variant spelling of Amon; also in 1:10b. See 1 Chr 3:14. **1:11** Greek *Jeconiah*, a variant spelling of Jehoiachin; also in 1:12. See 2 Kgs 24:6 and note at 1 Chr 3:16. **1:19** Greek *to divorce her*. **1:21** *Jesus* means "The LORD saves." **1:23** Isa 7:14; 8:8, 10 (Greek version). **2:1** Or *royal astrologers;* Greek reads *magi;* also in 2:7, 16. **2:2** Or *star in the east*. **2:6a** Greek *the rulers*. **2:6b** Mic 5:2; 2 Sam 5:2.

[7]Then Herod called for a private meeting
with the wise men, and he learned from them
the time when the star first appeared. [8]Then
he told them, "Go to Bethlehem and search
carefully for the child. And when you find
him, come back and tell me so that I can go
and worship him, too!"

[9]After this interview the wise men went
their way. And the star they had seen in the
east guided them to Bethlehem. It went ahead
of them and stopped over the place where the
child was. [10]When they saw the star, they were
filled with joy! [11]They entered the house and
saw the child with his mother, Mary, and they
bowed down and worshiped him. Then they
opened their treasure chests and gave him
gifts of gold, frankincense, and myrrh.

[12]When it was time to leave, they returned
to their own country by another route, for
God had warned them in a dream not to re-
turn to Herod.

The Escape to Egypt

[13]After the wise men were gone, an angel of
the Lord appeared to Joseph in a dream. "Get
up! Flee to Egypt with the child and his
mother," the angel said. "Stay there until I tell
you to return, because Herod is going to
search for the child to kill him."

[14]That night Joseph left for Egypt with the
child and Mary, his mother, [15]and they stayed
there until Herod's death. This fulfilled what
the Lord had spoken through the prophet: "I
called my Son out of Egypt."*

[16]Herod was furious when he realized that
the wise men had outwitted him. He sent sol-
diers to kill all the boys in and around Bethle-
hem who were two years old and under, based
on the wise men's report of the star's first ap-
pearance. [17]Herod's brutal action fulfilled
what God had spoken through the prophet
Jeremiah:

[18] "A cry was heard in Ramah—
weeping and great mourning.
Rachel weeps for her children,
refusing to be comforted,
for they are dead."*

The Return to Nazareth

[19]When Herod died, an angel of the Lord ap-
peared in a dream to Joseph in Egypt. [20]"Get
up!" the angel said. "Take the child and his
mother back to the land of Israel, because those
who were trying to kill the child are dead."

[21]So Joseph got up and returned to the land
of Israel with Jesus and his mother. [22]But
when he learned that the new ruler of Judea
was Herod's son Archelaus, he was afraid to go
there. Then, after being warned in a dream, he
left for the region of Galilee. [23]So the family
went and lived in a town called Nazareth. This
fulfilled what the prophets had said: "He will
be called a Nazarene."

CHAPTER 3

John the Baptist Prepares the Way

In those days John the Baptist came to the Ju-
dean wilderness and began preaching. His
message was, [2]"Repent of your sins and turn
to God, for the Kingdom of Heaven is near.*"
[3]The prophet Isaiah was speaking about John
when he said,

"He is a voice shouting in the wilderness,
'Prepare the way for the LORD's coming!
Clear the road for him!'"*

[4]John's clothes were woven from coarse
camel hair, and he wore a leather belt around
his waist. For food he ate locusts and wild
honey. [5]People from Jerusalem and from all
of Judea and all over the Jordan Valley went
out to see and hear John. [6]And when they con-
fessed their sins, he baptized them in the Jor-
dan River.

[7]But when he saw many Pharisees and Sad-
ducees coming to watch him baptize,* he de-
nounced them. "You brood of snakes!" he
exclaimed. "Who warned you to flee God's
coming wrath? [8]Prove by the way you live that
you have repented of your sins and turned to
God. [9]Don't just say to each other, 'We're safe,
for we are descendants of Abraham.' That
means nothing, for I tell you, God can create
children of Abraham from these very stones.
[10]Even now the ax of God's judgment is poised,
ready to sever the roots of the trees. Yes, every
tree that does not produce good fruit will be
chopped down and thrown into the fire.

[11]"I baptize with* water those who repent
of their sins and turn to God. But someone is
coming soon who is greater than I am—so
much greater that I'm not worthy even to be

2:15 Hos 11:1. **2:18** Jer 31:15. **3:2** Or *has come*, or *is coming soon*. **3:3** Isa 40:3 (Greek version). **3:7** Or *coming to be baptized*. **3:11a** Or *in*.

JOSEPH

An angel told me that Mary, the woman who was to be my wife, would have a baby and we should name him *Jesus*. Well, Mary had a son, and we called the boy *Jesus*. You don't argue with angels.

We took Jesus with us to Jerusalem when he was twelve, and we lost him. Finally, we found him talking with the priests and teachers in the Temple. At first I was angry that Jesus hadn't told us where he was going, but then Jesus told us an amazing thing: He was doing his Father's business. But I never told him to go to the Temple. I knew he wasn't talking about me. But I also knew he was a special young man who would do great things someday.

Read more about Joseph in Matthew 1:18-25; 2:13-23; and Luke 2:1-52.

his slave and carry his sandals. He will baptize you with the Holy Spirit and with fire.* [12]He is ready to separate the chaff from the wheat with his winnowing fork. Then he will clean up the threshing area, gathering the wheat into his barn but burning the chaff with never-ending fire."

The Baptism of Jesus

[13]Then Jesus went from Galilee to the Jordan River to be baptized by John. [14]But John tried to talk him out of it. "I am the one who needs to be baptized by you," he said, "so why are you coming to me?"

[15]But Jesus said, "It should be done, for we must carry out all that God requires.*" So John agreed to baptize him.

[16]After his baptism, as Jesus came up out of the water, the heavens were opened* and he saw the Spirit of God descending like a dove and settling on him. [17]And a voice from heaven said, "This is my dearly loved Son, who brings me great joy."

CHAPTER 4

The Temptation of Jesus

Then Jesus was led by the Spirit into the wilderness to be tempted there by the devil. [2]For forty days and forty nights he fasted and became very hungry.

[3]During that time the devil* came and said to him, "If you are the Son of God, tell these stones to become loaves of bread."

[4]But Jesus told him, "No! The Scriptures say,

'People do not live by bread alone,
but by every word that comes from the mouth of God.'*"

[5]Then the devil took him to the holy city, Jerusalem, to the highest point of the Temple, [6]and said, "If you are the Son of God, jump off! For the Scriptures say,

'He will order his angels to protect you.
And they will hold you up with their hands
so you won't even hurt your foot on a stone.'*"

[7]Jesus responded, "The Scriptures also say, 'You must not test the LORD your God.'*"

[8]Next the devil took him to the peak of a very high mountain and showed him all the kingdoms of the world and their glory. [9]"I will give it all to you," he said, "if you will kneel down and worship me."

3:11b Or *in the Holy Spirit and in fire.* **3:15** Or *for we must fulfill all righteousness.* **3:16** Some manuscripts read *opened to him.* **4:3** Greek *the tempter.* **4:4** Deut 8:3. **4:6** Ps 91:11-12. **4:7** Deut 6:16.

[10]"Get out of here, Satan," Jesus told him. "For the Scriptures say,

'You must worship the LORD your God
and serve only him.'*"

[11]Then the devil went away, and angels came and took care of Jesus.

The Ministry of Jesus Begins

[12]When Jesus heard that John had been arrested, he left Judea and returned to Galilee. [13]He went first to Nazareth, then left there and moved to Capernaum, beside the Sea of Galilee, in the region of Zebulun and Naphtali. [14]This fulfilled what God said through the prophet Isaiah:

[15] "In the land of Zebulun and of Naphtali,
beside the sea, beyond the Jordan River,
in Galilee where so many Gentiles live,
[16] the people who sat in darkness
have seen a great light.
And for those who lived in the land where
death casts its shadow,
a light has shined."*

[17]From then on Jesus began to preach, "Repent of your sins and turn to God, for the Kingdom of Heaven is near.*"

The First Disciples

[18]One day as Jesus was walking along the shore of the Sea of Galilee, he saw two brothers—Simon, also called Peter, and Andrew—throwing a net into the water, for they fished for a living. [19]Jesus called out to them, "Come, follow me, and I will show you how to fish for people!" [20]And they left their nets at once and followed him.

[21]A little farther up the shore he saw two other brothers, James and John, sitting in a boat with their father, Zebedee, repairing their nets. And he called them to come, too. [22]They immediately followed him, leaving the boat and their father behind.

Crowds Follow Jesus

[23]Jesus traveled throughout the region of Galilee, teaching in the synagogues and announcing the Good News about the Kingdom. And he healed every kind of disease and illness. [24]News about him spread as far as Syria, and people soon began bringing to him all who were sick. And whatever their sickness or disease, or if they were demon possessed or epileptic or paralyzed—he healed them all. [25]Large crowds followed him wherever he went—people from Galilee, the Ten Towns,* Jerusalem, from all over Judea, and from east of the Jordan River.

CHAPTER 5

The Sermon on the Mount

One day as he saw the crowds gathering, Jesus went up on the mountainside and sat down. His disciples gathered around him, [2]and he began to teach them.

The Beatitudes

[3] "God blesses those who are poor and
realize their need for him,*
for the Kingdom of Heaven is theirs.
[4] God blesses those who mourn,
for they will be comforted.
[5] God blesses those who are humble,
for they will inherit the whole earth.
[6] God blesses those who hunger and thirst
for justice,*
for they will be satisfied.
[7] God blesses those who are merciful,
for they will be shown mercy.
[8] God blesses those whose hearts are
pure,
for they will see God.
[9] God blesses those who work for peace,
for they will be called the children
of God.
[10] God blesses those who are persecuted
for doing right,
for the Kingdom of Heaven is theirs.

What's a good reason for being nice to my sister and brother?

God blesses those who are merciful, for they will be shown mercy.
MATTHEW 5:7

4:10 Deut 6:13. **4:15-16** Isa 9:1-2 (Greek version). **4:17** Or *has come*, or *is coming soon*. **4:25** Greek *Decapolis*. **5:3** Greek *poor in spirit*. **5:6** Or *for righteousness*.

MEDITERRANEAN SEA
GALILEE
Cana
Nazareth
Sychar
Caesarea
SAMARIA
JUDEA
Jerusalem
To EGYPT
Bethlehem

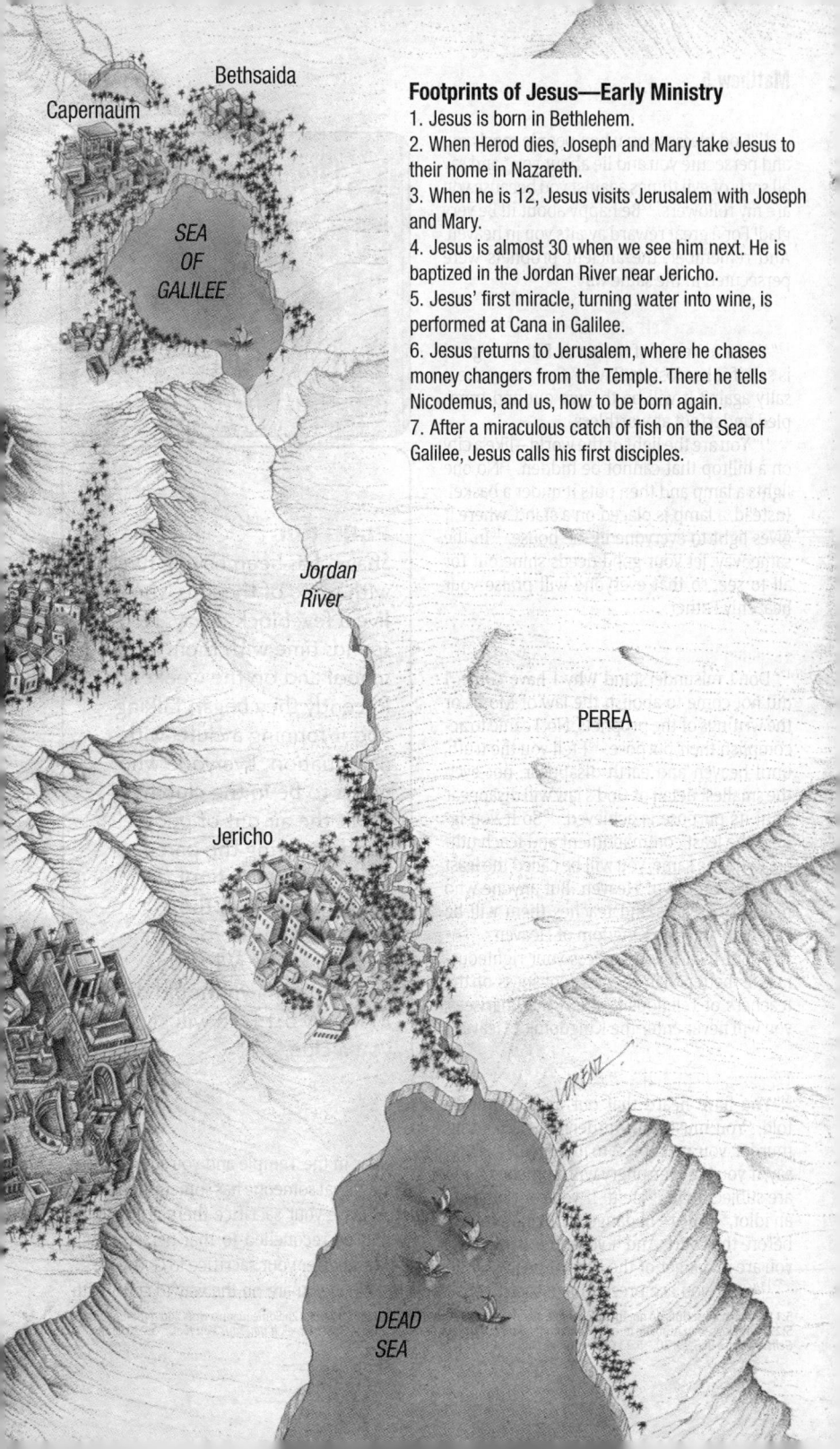

Footprints of Jesus—Early Ministry

1. Jesus is born in Bethlehem.
2. When Herod dies, Joseph and Mary take Jesus to their home in Nazareth.
3. When he is 12, Jesus visits Jerusalem with Joseph and Mary.
4. Jesus is almost 30 when we see him next. He is baptized in the Jordan River near Jericho.
5. Jesus' first miracle, turning water into wine, is performed at Cana in Galilee.
6. Jesus returns to Jerusalem, where he chases money changers from the Temple. There he tells Nicodemus, and us, how to be born again.
7. After a miraculous catch of fish on the Sea of Galilee, Jesus calls his first disciples.

[11]"God blesses you when people mock you and persecute you and lie about you* and say all sorts of evil things against you because you are my followers. [12]Be happy about it! Be very glad! For a great reward awaits you in heaven. And remember, the ancient prophets were persecuted in the same way.

Teaching about Salt and Light

[13]"You are the salt of the earth. But what good is salt if it has lost its flavor? Can you make it salty again? It will be thrown out and trampled underfoot as worthless.

[14]"You are the light of the world—like a city on a hilltop that cannot be hidden. [15]No one lights a lamp and then puts it under a basket. Instead, a lamp is placed on a stand, where it gives light to everyone in the house. [16]In the same way, let your good deeds shine out for all to see, so that everyone will praise your heavenly Father.

Teaching about the Law

[17]"Don't misunderstand why I have come. I did not come to abolish the law of Moses or the writings of the prophets. No, I came to accomplish their purpose. [18]I tell you the truth, until heaven and earth disappear, not even the smallest detail of God's law will disappear until its purpose is achieved. [19]So if you ignore the least commandment and teach others to do the same, you will be called the least in the Kingdom of Heaven. But anyone who obeys God's laws and teaches them will be called great in the Kingdom of Heaven.

[20]"But I warn you—unless your righteousness is better than the righteousness of the teachers of religious law and the Pharisees, you will never enter the Kingdom of Heaven!

Teaching about Anger

[21]"You have heard that our ancestors were told, 'You must not murder. If you commit murder, you are subject to judgment.'* [22]But I say, if you are even angry with someone,* you are subject to judgment! If you call someone an idiot,* you are in danger of being brought before the court. And if you curse someone,* you are in danger of the fires of hell.*

[23]"So if you are presenting a sacrifice* at the altar in the Temple and you suddenly remember that someone has something against you, [24]leave your sacrifice there at the altar. Go and be reconciled to that person. Then come and offer your sacrifice to God.

[25]"When you are on the way to court with

FLAT OUT

Shawn has been having fun with some of the kids who live a few blocks away. He spends time with them after school and on the weekends. Recently they began talking about forming a club—with an initiation. Everyone who wants to be in the club has to let the air out of people's car tires during the parent open house at school. Shawn really likes those kids and wants to be part of their group. What do you think Shawn should do? Matthew 5:14-16 will give you a clue.

5:11 Some manuscripts do not include *and lie about you.* **5:21** Exod 20:13; Deut 5:17. **5:22a** Some manuscripts add *without cause.* **5:22b** Greek uses an Aramaic term of contempt: *If you say to your brother, 'Raca.'* **5:22c** Greek *if you say, 'You fool.'* **5:22d** Greek *Gehenna;* also in 5:29, 30. **5:23** Greek *gift;* also in 5:24.

I was angry and ready to fight. I had just broken up with my girlfriend. Then I found out she was planning to go out with one of my closest friends. He was the friend who for the past couple months had been telling me that I shouldn't be wasting my time with this girl.

Now the truth was out. He had wanted to go out with my girlfriend the whole time he was advising me to break up with her.

I wanted to give him a good pounding. But I never did fight him. I knew that fighting would have hurt my relationship with God. Jesus told his disciples in Matthew 5:38-42 that revenge is not the way to settle a problem. God helped me see that even though I was hurt and angry about what my friend and ex-girlfriend had done, what was done to me was over. I couldn't go back and change what had happened. The only choice I had was how I would respond to what they had done. I chose not to make it worse by starting a fight with this guy, who had been my close friend.

I sent him an IM one day and told him how angry I was about what he had done. But I said that I didn't want to fight about it. He understood and said he would feel the same way. We decided that this was a great opportunity for both of us to get our focus back on God.

One more thing . . . my friend never did go out with my ex-girlfriend. And I saved my friendship with this guy by forgiving him for what he had planned to do.

Check out what God has to say about revenge in Matthew 5:38-42. Also check out Leviticus 19:18; Psalm 37:8; Proverbs 29:22; and Romans 12:18-21.

your adversary, settle your differences quickly.
Otherwise, your accuser may hand you over to
the judge, who will hand you over to an officer,
and you will be thrown into prison. 26And if
that happens, you surely won't be free again
until you have paid the last penny.*

Teaching about Adultery

27"You have heard the commandment that
says, 'You must not commit adultery.'* 28But I
say, anyone who even looks at a woman with
lust has already committed adultery with her
in his heart. 29So if your eye—even your good
eye*—causes you to lust, gouge it out and
throw it away. It is better for you to lose one
part of your body than for your whole body to
be thrown into hell. 30And if your hand—even
your stronger hand*—causes you to sin, cut it
off and throw it away. It is better for you to
lose one part of your body than for your
whole body to be thrown into hell.

Teaching about Divorce

31"You have heard the law that says, 'A man
can divorce his wife by merely giving her a
written notice of divorce.'* 32But I say that a
man who divorces his wife, unless she has
been unfaithful, causes her to commit adul-
tery. And anyone who marries a divorced
woman also commits adultery.

Teaching about Vows

33"You have also heard that our ancestors
were told, 'You must not break your vows; you
must carry out the vows you make to the
LORD.'* 34But I say, do not make any vows! Do
not say, 'By heaven!' because heaven is God's
throne. 35And do not say, 'By the earth!' be-
cause the earth is his footstool. And do not
say, 'By Jerusalem!' for Jerusalem is the city of
the great King. 36Do not even say, 'By my
head!' for you can't turn one hair white or
black. 37Just say a simple, 'Yes, I will,' or 'No, I
won't.' Anything beyond this is from the evil
one.

Teaching about Revenge

38"You have heard the law that says the pun-
ishment must match the injury: 'An eye for an
eye, and a tooth for a tooth.'* 39But I say, do
not resist an evil person! If someone slaps you
on the right cheek, offer the other cheek also.
40If you are sued in court and your shirt is
taken from you, give your coat, too. 41If a sol-
dier demands that you carry his gear for a
mile,* carry it two miles. 42Give to those who
ask, and don't turn away from those who want
to borrow.

Teaching about Love for Enemies

43"You have heard the law that says, 'Love
your neighbor'* and hate your enemy. 44But I
say, love your enemies!* Pray for those who
persecute you! 45In that way, you will be act-
ing as true children of your Father in heaven.
For he gives his sunlight to both the evil and
the good, and he sends rain on the just and the
unjust alike. 46If you love only those who love
you, what reward is there for that? Even cor-
rupt tax collectors do that much. 47If you are
kind only to your friends,* how are you dif-
ferent from anyone else? Even pagans do
that. 48But you are to be perfect, even as your
Father in heaven is perfect.

CHAPTER 6

Teaching about Giving to the Needy

"Watch out! Don't do your good deeds pub-
licly, to be admired by others, for you will
lose the reward from your Father in heaven.
2When you give to someone in need, don't
do as the hypocrites do—blowing trumpets
in the synagogues and streets to call atten-
tion to their acts of charity! I tell you the
truth, they have received all the reward they
will ever get. 3But when you give to someone
in need, don't let your left hand know what
your right hand is doing. 4Give your gifts in
private, and your Father, who sees every-
thing, will reward you.

Teaching about Prayer and Fasting

5"When you pray, don't be like the hypocrites
who love to pray publicly on street corners
and in the synagogues where everyone can see
them. I tell you the truth, that is all the reward
they will ever get. 6But when you pray, go
away by yourself, shut the door behind you,

5:26 Greek *the last kodrantes* [i.e., quadrans]. **5:27** Exod 20:14; Deut 5:18. **5:29** Greek *your right eye*. **5:30** Greek *your right hand*. **5:31** Deut 24:1. **5:33** Num 30:2. **5:38** Greek *the law that says: 'An eye for an eye and a tooth for a tooth.'* Exod 21:24; Lev 24:20; Deut 19:21. **5:41** Greek *milion* [4,854 feet or 1,478 meters]. **5:43** Lev 19:18. **5:44** Some manuscripts add *Bless those who curse you. Do good to those who hate you.* Compare Luke 6:27-28. **5:47** Greek *your brothers*.

and pray to your Father in private. Then your Father, who sees everything, will reward you.

7"When you pray, don't babble on and on as people of other religions do. They think their prayers are answered merely by repeating their words again and again. 8Don't be like them, for your Father knows exactly what you need even before you ask him! 9Pray like this:

Our Father in heaven,
may your name be kept holy.
10 May your Kingdom come soon.
May your will be done on earth,
as it is in heaven.
11 Give us today the food we need,*
12 and forgive us our sins,
as we have forgiven those who sin
against us.
13 And don't let us yield to temptation,*
but rescue us from the evil one.*

14"If you forgive those who sin against you, your heavenly Father will forgive you. 15But if you refuse to forgive others, your Father will not forgive your sins.

16"And when you fast, don't make it obvious, as the hypocrites do, for they try to look miserable and disheveled so people will admire them for their fasting. I tell you the truth, that is the only reward they will ever get. 17But when you fast, comb your hair and wash your face. 18Then no one will notice that you are fasting, except your Father, who knows what you do in private. And your Father, who sees everything, will reward you.

Teaching about Money and Possessions

19"Don't store up treasures here on earth, where moths eat them and rust destroys them, and where thieves break in and steal. 20Store your treasures in heaven, where moths and rust cannot destroy, and thieves do not break in and steal. 21Wherever your treasure is, there the desires of your heart will also be.

22"Your eye is a lamp that provides light for your body. When your eye is good, your whole body is filled with light. 23But when your eye is bad, your whole body is filled with darkness. And if the light you think you have is actually darkness, how deep that darkness is!

24"No one can serve two masters. For you will hate one and love the other; you will be devoted to one and despise the other. You cannot serve both God and money.

25"That is why I tell you not to worry about everyday life—whether you have enough food and drink, or enough clothes to wear. Isn't life more than food, and your body more than clothing? 26Look at the birds. They don't plant or harvest or store food in barns, for your heavenly Father feeds them. And aren't you far more valuable to him than they are? 27Can all your worries add a single moment to your life?

28"And why worry about your clothing? Look at the lilies of the field and how they grow. They don't work or make their clothing, 29yet Solomon in all his glory was not dressed as beautifully as they are. 30And if God cares so wonderfully for wildflowers that are here today and thrown into the fire tomorrow, he will certainly care for you. Why do you have so little faith?

31"So don't worry about these things, saying, 'What will we eat? What will we drink? What will we wear?' 32These things dominate the thoughts of unbelievers, but your heavenly Father already knows all your needs. 33Seek the Kingdom of God* above all else, and live righteously, and he will give you everything you need.

34"So don't worry about tomorrow, for tomorrow will bring its own worries. Today's trouble is enough for today.

CHAPTER 7

Do Not Judge Others

"Do not judge others, and you will not be judged. 2For you will be treated as you treat others.* The standard you use in judging is the standard by which you will be judged.*

3"And why worry about a speck in your friend's eye* when you have a log in your own? 4How can you think of saying to your friend,* 'Let me help you get rid of that speck in your eye,' when you can't see past the log in your own eye? 5Hypocrite! First get rid of the log in your own eye; then you will see well enough to deal with the speck in your friend's eye.

6:11 Or *Give us today our food for the day;* or *Give us today our food for tomorrow.* **6:13a** Or *And keep us from being tested.* **6:13b** Or *from evil.* Some manuscripts add *For yours is the kingdom and the power and the glory forever. Amen.* **6:33** Some manuscripts do not include *of God.* **7:2a** Or *For God will judge you as you judge others.* **7:2b** Or *The measure you give will be the measure you get back.* **7:3** Greek *your brother's eye;* also in 7:5. **7:4** Greek *your brother.*

[6]"Don't waste what is holy on people who are unholy.* Don't throw your pearls to pigs! They will trample the pearls, then turn and attack you.

Effective Prayer

[7]"Keep on asking, and you will receive what you ask for. Keep on seeking, and you will find. Keep on knocking, and the door will be opened to you. [8]For everyone who asks, receives. Everyone who seeks, finds. And to everyone who knocks, the door will be opened.

[9]"You parents—if your children ask for a loaf of bread, do you give them a stone instead? [10]Or if they ask for a fish, do you give them a snake? Of course not! [11]So if you sinful people know how to give good gifts to your children, how much more will your heavenly Father give good gifts to those who ask him.

The Golden Rule

[12]"Do to others whatever you would like them to do to you. This is the essence of all that is taught in the law and the prophets.

The Narrow Gate

[13]"You can enter God's Kingdom only through the narrow gate. The highway to hell* is broad, and its gate is wide for the many who choose that way. [14]But the gateway to life is very narrow and the road is difficult, and only a few ever find it.

The Tree and Its Fruit

[15]"Beware of false prophets who come disguised as harmless sheep but are really vicious wolves. [16]You can identify them by their fruit, that is, by the way they act. Can you pick grapes from thornbushes, or figs from thistles? [17]A good tree produces good fruit, and a bad tree produces bad fruit. [18]A good tree can't produce bad fruit, and a bad tree can't produce good fruit. [19]So every tree that does not produce good fruit is chopped down and thrown into the fire. [20]Yes, just as you can identify a tree by its fruit, so you can identify people by their actions.

True Disciples

[21]"Not everyone who calls out to me, 'Lord! Lord!' will enter the Kingdom of Heaven.

7:6 Greek *Don't give the sacred to dogs.* **7:13** Greek *The road that leads to destruction.*

THE BEATITUDES

In his longest recorded sermon, Jesus began by describing the traits he looks for in his followers. He called those who live out those traits fortunate because God has something special in store for them. The best example of each trait is found in Jesus himself. If our goal is to become like him, the beatitudes will challenge the way we live each day.

Verse	Characteristic	How to develop this attitude
5:3	Humility	James 4:7-10
5:4	Mourning	Psalm 51; James 4:7-10
5:5	Meekness and lowliness	Matthew 11:28-30
5:6	Justice and goodness	John 16:10-11; Philippians 3:8-9
5:7	Kindness and mercy	Ephesians 5:1-2
5:8	Hearts that are pure	1 John 3:1-3
5:9	Peace	Romans 12:9-21; Hebrews 12:10-11
5:10	Faithfulness	2 Timothy 3:12

Only those who actually do the will of my
Father in heaven will enter. 22On judgment
day many will say to me, 'Lord! Lord! We
prophesied in your name and cast out de-
mons in your name and performed many
miracles in your name.' 23But I will reply, 'I
never knew you. Get away from me, you who
break God's laws.'

Building on a Solid Foundation

24"Anyone who listens to my teaching and fol-
lows it is wise, like a person who builds a
house on solid rock. 25Though the rain comes
in torrents and the floodwaters rise and the
winds beat against that house, it won't col-
lapse because it is built on bedrock. 26But
anyone who hears my teaching and doesn't
obey it is foolish, like a person who builds a
house on sand. 27When the rains and floods
come and the winds beat against that house, it
will collapse with a mighty crash."

28When Jesus had finished saying these
things, the crowds were amazed at his teach-
ing, 29for he taught with real authority—quite
unlike their teachers of religious law.

CHAPTER 8

Jesus Heals a Man with Leprosy

Large crowds followed Jesus as he came down
the mountainside. 2Suddenly, a man with lep-
rosy approached him and knelt before him.
"Lord," the man said, "if you are willing, you
can heal me and make me clean."

3Jesus reached out and touched him. "I am
willing," he said. "Be healed!" And instantly
the leprosy disappeared. 4Then Jesus said to
him, "Don't tell anyone about this. Instead, go
to the priest and let him examine you. Take
along the offering required in the law of
Moses for those who have been healed of lep-
rosy.* This will be a public testimony that you
have been cleansed."

The Faith of a Roman Officer

5When Jesus returned to Capernaum, a Ro-
man officer* came and pleaded with him,
6"Lord, my young servant* lies in bed, para-
lyzed and in terrible pain."

7Jesus said, "I will come and heal him."

8But the officer said, "Lord, I am not worthy
to have you come into my home. Just say the
word from where you are, and my servant will
be healed. 9I know this because I am under
the authority of my superior officers, and I
have authority over my soldiers. I only need to
say, 'Go,' and they go, or 'Come,' and they
come. And if I say to my slaves, 'Do this,' they
do it."

10When Jesus heard this, he was amazed.
Turning to those who were following him, he
said, "I tell you the truth, I haven't seen faith
like this in all Israel! 11And I tell you this, that
many Gentiles will come from all over the
world—from east and west—and sit down
with Abraham, Isaac, and Jacob at the feast in
the Kingdom of Heaven. 12But many Israel-
ites—those for whom the Kingdom was pre-
pared—will be thrown into outer darkness,
where there will be weeping and gnashing of
teeth."

13Then Jesus said to the Roman officer, "Go
back home. Because you believed, it has hap-
pened." And the young servant was healed
that same hour.

Jesus Heals Many People

14When Jesus arrived at Peter's house, Peter's
mother-in-law was sick in bed with a high fe-
ver. 15But when Jesus touched her hand, the
fever left her. Then she got up and prepared a
meal for him.

16That evening many demon-possessed
people were brought to Jesus. He cast out the
evil spirits with a simple command, and he
healed all the sick. 17This fulfilled the word of
the Lord through the prophet Isaiah, who
said,

"He took our sicknesses
and removed our diseases."*

The Cost of Following Jesus

18When Jesus saw the crowd around him, he
instructed his disciples to cross to the other
side of the lake.

19Then one of the teachers of religious law
said to him, "Teacher, I will follow you wher-
ever you go."

20But Jesus replied, "Foxes have dens to live
in, and birds have nests, but the Son of Man*
has no place even to lay his head."

8:4 See Lev 14:2-32. **8:5** Greek *a centurion;* similarly in 8:8, 13. **8:6** Or *child;* also in 8:13. **8:17** Isa 53:4. **8:20** "Son of Man" is a title Jesus used for himself.

[21]Another of his disciples said, "Lord, first
let me return home and bury my father."
[22]But Jesus told him, "Follow me now. Let
the spiritually dead bury their own dead.*"

Jesus Calms the Storm

[23]Then Jesus got into the boat and started
across the lake with his disciples. [24]Suddenly, a
fierce storm struck the lake, with waves break-
ing into the boat. But Jesus was sleeping. [25]The
disciples went and woke him up, shouting,
"Lord, save us! We're going to drown!"
[26]Jesus responded, "Why are you afraid?
You have so little faith!" Then he got up and
rebuked the wind and waves, and suddenly
there was a great calm.
[27]The disciples were amazed. "Who is this
man?" they asked. "Even the winds and waves
obey him!"

Jesus Heals Two Demon-Possessed Men

[28]When Jesus arrived on the other side of the
lake, in the region of the Gadarenes,* two
men who were possessed by demons met
him. They lived in a cemetery and were so vio-
lent that no one could go through that area.
[29]They began screaming at him, "Why are
you interfering with us, Son of God? Have you
come here to torture us before God's ap-
pointed time?"
[30]There happened to be a large herd of pigs
feeding in the distance. [31]So the demons
begged, "If you cast us out, send us into that
herd of pigs."
[32]"All right, go!" Jesus commanded them.
So the demons came out of the men and en-
tered the pigs, and the whole herd plunged
down the steep hillside into the lake and
drowned in the water.
[33]The herdsmen fled to the nearby town,
telling everyone what happened to the
demon-possessed men. [34]Then the entire
town came out to meet Jesus, but they begged
him to go away and leave them alone.

CHAPTER 9

Jesus Heals a Paralyzed Man

Jesus climbed into a boat and went back
across the lake to his own town. [2]Some peo-
ple brought to him a paralyzed man on a mat.
Seeing their faith, Jesus said to the paralyzed
man, "Be encouraged, my child! Your sins are
forgiven."
[3]But some of the teachers of religious law
said to themselves, "That's blasphemy! Does
he think he's God?"
[4]Jesus knew* what they were thinking, so he
asked them, "Why do you have such evil
thoughts in your hearts? [5]Is it easier to say
'Your sins are forgiven,' or 'Stand up and walk'?
[6]So I will prove to you that the Son of Man* has
the authority on earth to forgive sins." Then
Jesus turned to the paralyzed man and said,
"Stand up, pick up your mat, and go home!"
[7]And the man jumped up and went home!
[8]Fear swept through the crowd as they saw
this happen. And they praised God for send-
ing a man with such great authority.*

Jesus Calls Matthew

[9]As Jesus was walking along, he saw a man
named Matthew sitting at his tax collector's
booth. "Follow me and be my disciple," Jesus
said to him. So Matthew got up and followed
him.
[10]Later, Matthew invited Jesus and his dis-
ciples to his home as dinner guests, along
with many tax collectors and other disreputa-
ble sinners. [11]But when the Pharisees saw this,
they asked his disciples, "Why does your
teacher eat with such scum?*"
[12]When Jesus heard this, he said, "Healthy
people don't need a doctor—sick people do."
[13]Then he added, "Now go and learn the
meaning of this Scripture: 'I want you to show
mercy, not offer sacrifices.'* For I have come
to call not those who think they are righteous,
but those who know they are sinners."

A Discussion about Fasting

[14]One day the disciples of John the Baptist
came to Jesus and asked him, "Why don't
your disciples fast* like we do and the Phari-
sees do?"
[15]Jesus replied, "Do wedding guests mourn
while celebrating with the groom? Of course
not. But someday the groom will be taken
away from them, and then they will fast.
[16]"Besides, who would patch old clothing

8:22 Greek *Let the dead bury their own dead.* **8:28** Other manuscripts read *Gerasenes;* still others read *Gergesenes.* Compare Mark 5:1; Luke 8:26. **9:4** Some manuscripts read *saw.* **9:6** "Son of Man" is a title Jesus used for himself. **9:8** Greek *for giving such authority to human beings.* **9:11** Greek *with tax collectors and sinners?* **9:13** Hos 6:6 (Greek version). **9:14** Some manuscripts read *fast often.*

with new cloth? For the new patch would shrink and rip away from the old cloth, leaving an even bigger tear than before.

17"And no one puts new wine into old wineskins. For the old skins would burst from the pressure, spilling the wine and ruining the skins. New wine is stored in new wineskins so that both are preserved."

Jesus Heals in Response to Faith

18As Jesus was saying this, the leader of a synagogue came and knelt before him. "My daughter has just died," he said, "but you can bring her back to life again if you just come and lay your hand on her."

19So Jesus and his disciples got up and went with him. 20Just then a woman who had suffered for twelve years with constant bleeding came up behind him. She touched the fringe of his robe, 21for she thought, "If I can just touch his robe, I will be healed."

22Jesus turned around, and when he saw her he said, "Daughter, be encouraged! Your faith has made you well." And the woman was healed at that moment.

23When Jesus arrived at the official's home, he saw the noisy crowd and heard the funeral music. 24"Get out!" he told them. "The girl isn't dead; she's only asleep." But the crowd laughed at him. 25After the crowd was put outside, however, Jesus went in and took the girl by the hand, and she stood up! 26The resport of this miracle swept through the entire countryside.

Jesus Heals the Blind

27After Jesus left the girl's home, two blind men followed along behind him, shouting, "Son of David, have mercy on us!"

28They went right into the house where he was staying, and Jesus asked them, "Do you believe I can make you see?"

"Yes, Lord," they told him, "we do."

29Then he touched their eyes and said, "Because of your faith, it will happen." 30Then their eyes were opened, and they could see! Jesus sternly warned them, "Don't tell anyone about this." 31But instead, they went out and spread his fame all over the region.

32When they left, a demon-possessed man who couldn't speak was brought to Jesus. 33So Jesus cast out the demon, and then the man

SEVEN REASONS NOT TO WORRY

1 The same God who created life in you can be trusted with the details of your life. 6:25

2 Worrying about the future keeps you from doing your best today. 6:26

3 Worrying is more harmful than helpful. 6:27

4 God does not ignore those who depend on him. 6:28-30

5 Worry shows a lack of faith and of understanding of God. 6:32

6 There are real challenges God wants us to pursue, and worrying keeps us from them. 6:33

7 Living one day at a time keeps us from worrying too much. 6:34

began to speak. The crowds were amazed. "Nothing like this has ever happened in Israel!" they exclaimed.

34But the Pharisees said, "He can cast out demons because he is empowered by the prince of demons."

The Need for Workers

35Jesus traveled through all the towns and villages of that area, teaching in the synagogues and announcing the Good News about the Kingdom. And he healed every kind of disease and illness. 36When he saw the crowds, he had compassion on them because they were confused and helpless, like sheep without a shepherd. 37He said to his disciples, "The harvest is great, but the workers are few. 38So pray to the Lord who is in charge of the harvest; ask him to send more workers into his fields."

CHAPTER 10

Jesus Sends Out the Twelve Apostles

Jesus called his twelve disciples together and gave them authority to cast out evil* spirits and to heal every kind of disease and illness. 2Here are the names of the twelve apostles:

first, Simon (also called Peter),
then Andrew (Peter's brother),
James (son of Zebedee),
John (James's brother),
3 Philip,
Bartholomew,
Thomas,
Matthew (the tax collector),
James (son of Alphaeus),
Thaddaeus,*
4 Simon (the zealot*),
Judas Iscariot (who later betrayed him).

5Jesus sent out the twelve apostles with these instructions: "Don't go to the Gentiles or the Samaritans, 6but only to the people of Israel—God's lost sheep. 7Go and announce to them that the Kingdom of Heaven is near.* 8Heal the sick, raise the dead, cure those with leprosy, and cast out demons. Give as freely as you have received!

9"Don't take any money in your money belts—no gold, silver, or even copper coins. 10Don't carry a traveler's bag with a change of clothes and sandals or even a walking stick. Don't hesitate to accept hospitality, because those who work deserve to be fed.

11"Whenever you enter a city or village, search for a worthy person and stay in his home until you leave town. 12When you enter the home, give it your blessing. 13If it turns out to be a worthy home, let your blessing stand; if it is not, take back the blessing. 14If any household or town refuses to welcome you or listen to your message, shake its dust from your feet as you leave. 15I tell you the truth, the wicked cities of Sodom and Gomorrah will be better off than such a town on the judgment day.

16"Look, I am sending you out as sheep among wolves. So be as shrewd as snakes and harmless as doves. 17But beware! For you will be handed over to the courts and will be flogged with whips in the synagogues. 18You will stand trial before governors and kings because you are my followers. But this will be your opportunity to tell the rulers and other unbelievers about me.* 19When you are arrested, don't worry about how to respond or what to say. God will give you the right words at the right time. 20For it is not you who will be speaking—it will be the Spirit of your Father speaking through you.

21"A brother will betray his brother to death, a father will betray his own child, and children will rebel against their parents and cause them to be killed. 22And all nations will hate you because you are my followers.* But everyone who endures to the end will be saved. 23When you are persecuted in one town, flee to the next. I tell you the truth, the Son of Man* will return before you have reached all the towns of Israel.

24"Students* are not greater than their teacher, and slaves are not greater than their master. 25Students are to be like their teacher, and slaves are to be like their master. And since I, the master of the household, have been called the prince of demons,* the members of my household will be called by even worse names!

26"But don't be afraid of those who

10:1 Greek *unclean.* **10:3** Other manuscripts read *Lebbaeus;* still others read *Lebbaeus who is called Thaddaeus.* **10:4** Greek *the Cananean,* an Aramaic term for Jewish nationalists. **10:7** Or *has come,* or *is coming soon.* **10:18** Or *But this will be your testimony against the rulers and other unbelievers.* **10:22** Greek *on account of my name.* **10:23** "Son of Man" is a title Jesus used for himself. **10:24** Or *Disciples.* **10:25** Greek *Beelzeboul;* other manuscripts read *Beezeboul;* Latin version reads *Beelzebub.*

James and John

We are more than brothers—we're friends. For years we've been catching fish in nets and bringing them into this boat. We work with our father. Every morning we head out for a long day in the hot sun. Our skin is tanned and wrinkled, but we're used to it. James and I like working together, but sometimes not much happens. To pass the time we mend our nets and tell stories.

One day a man named Jesus asked us if we'd like to be fishers of men and women. We had never caught people in our nets. But when Jesus said, "Follow me," we did. Jesus showed us how to fish for people and bring them into God's kingdom.

Find out more about James and John in Matthew 4:19-22; Mark 3:17; and Luke 9:51-55.

threaten you. For the time is coming when everything that is covered will be revealed, and all that is secret will be made known to all. 27 What I tell you now in the darkness, shout abroad when daybreak comes. What I whisper in your ear, shout from the housetops for all to hear!

28 "Don't be afraid of those who want to kill your body; they cannot touch your soul. Fear only God, who can destroy both soul and body in hell.* 29 What is the price of two sparrows—one copper coin*? But not a single sparrow can fall to the ground without your Father knowing it. 30 And the very hairs on your head are all numbered. 31 So don't be afraid; you are more valuable to God than a whole flock of sparrows.

32 "Everyone who acknowledges me publicly here on earth, I will also acknowledge before my Father in heaven. 33 But everyone who denies me here on earth, I will also deny before my Father in heaven.

34 "Don't imagine that I came to bring peace to the earth! I came not to bring peace, but a sword.

35 'I have come to set a man against
his father,
a daughter against her mother,
and a daughter-in-law against her
mother-in-law.
36 Your enemies will be right in your
own household!'*

37 "If you love your father or mother more than you love me, you are not worthy of being mine; or if you love your son or daughter more than me, you are not worthy of being mine. 38 If you refuse to take up your cross and follow me, you are not worthy of being mine. 39 If you cling to your life, you will lose it; but if you give up your life for me, you will find it.

40 "Anyone who receives you receives me, and anyone who receives me receives the Father who sent me. 41 If you receive a prophet as one who speaks for God,* you will be given the same reward as a prophet. And if you receive righteous people because of their righteousness, you will be given a reward like theirs. 42 And if you give even a cup of cold water to one of the least of my followers, you will surely be rewarded."

CHAPTER 11

Jesus and John the Baptist

When Jesus had finished giving these instructions to his twelve disciples, he went out to teach and preach in towns throughout the region.

10:28 Greek *Gehenna*. **10:29** Greek *one assarion* [i.e., one "as," a Roman coin equal to 1/16 of a denarius]. **10:35-36** Mic 7:6.
10:41 Greek *receive a prophet in the name of a prophet*.

[2]John the Baptist, who was in prison, heard
about all the things the Messiah was doing. So
he sent his disciples to ask Jesus, [3]"Are you
the Messiah we've been expecting,* or should
we keep looking for someone else?"

[4]Jesus told them, "Go back to John and tell
him what you have heard and seen—[5]the
blind see, the lame walk, the lepers are cured,
the deaf hear, the dead are raised to life, and
the Good News is being preached to the poor.
[6]And tell him, 'God blesses those who do not
turn away because of me.*'"

[7]As John's disciples were leaving, Jesus began talking about him to the crowds. "What
kind of man did you go into the wilderness to
see? Was he a weak reed, swayed by every
breath of wind? [8]Or were you expecting to see
a man dressed in expensive clothes? No, people with expensive clothes live in palaces.
[9]Were you looking for a prophet? Yes, and he
is more than a prophet. [10]John is the man to
whom the Scriptures refer when they say,

'Look, I am sending my messenger ahead
of you,
and he will prepare your way before
you.'*

[11]"I tell you the truth, of all who have ever
lived, none is greater than John the Baptist.
Yet even the least person in the Kingdom of
Heaven is greater than he is! [12]And from the
time John the Baptist began preaching until
now, the Kingdom of Heaven has been
forcefully advancing,* and violent people
are attacking it. [13]For before John came, all
the prophets and the law of Moses looked
forward to this present time. [14]And if you are
willing to accept what I say, he is Elijah, the
one the prophets said would come.* [15]Anyone with ears to hear should listen and
understand!

[16]"To what can I compare this generation?
It is like children playing a game in the public
square. They complain to their friends,

[17] 'We played wedding songs,
and you didn't dance,
so we played funeral songs,
and you didn't mourn.'

[18]For John didn't spend his time eating and
drinking, and you say, 'He's possessed by a
demon.' [19]The Son of Man,* on the other
hand, feasts and drinks, and you say, 'He's a
glutton and a drunkard, and a friend of tax
collectors and other sinners!' But wisdom is
shown to be right by its results."

Judgment for the Unbelievers

[20]Then Jesus began to denounce the towns
where he had done so many of his miracles,
because they hadn't repented of their sins
and turned to God. [21]"What sorrow awaits
you, Korazin and Bethsaida! For if the miracles I did in you had been done in wicked
Tyre and Sidon, their people would have repented of their sins long ago, clothing themselves in burlap and throwing ashes on their
heads to show their remorse. [22]I tell you, Tyre
and Sidon will be better off on judgment day
than you.

[23]"And you people of Capernaum, will you
be honored in heaven? No, you will go down
to the place of the dead.* For if the miracles I
did for you had been done in wicked Sodom,
it would still be here today. [24]I tell you, even
Sodom will be better off on judgment day
than you."

Jesus' Prayer of Thanksgiving

[25]At that time Jesus prayed this prayer: "O Father, Lord of heaven and earth, thank you for
hiding these things from those who think
themselves wise and clever, and for revealing
them to the childlike. [26]Yes, Father, it pleased
you to do it this way!

[27]"My Father has entrusted everything to
me. No one truly knows the Son except the
Father, and no one truly knows the Father except the Son and those to whom the Son
chooses to reveal him."

[28]Then Jesus said, "Come to me, all of you
who are weary and carry heavy burdens, and I
will give you rest. [29]Take my yoke upon you.
Let me teach you, because I am humble and
gentle at heart, and you will find rest for your
souls. [30]For my yoke is easy to bear, and the
burden I give you is light."

CHAPTER 12

A Discussion about the Sabbath

At about that time Jesus was walking through
some grainfields on the Sabbath. His disci-

11:3 Greek *Are you the one who is coming?* **11:6** Or *who are not offended by me.* **11:10** Mal 3:1. **11:12** Or *the Kingdom of Heaven has suffered from violence.* **11:14** See Mal 4:5. **11:19** "Son of Man" is a title Jesus used for himself. **11:23** Greek *to Hades.*

ples were hungry, so they began breaking off
some heads of grain and eating them. [2]But
some Pharisees saw them do it and protested,
"Look, your disciples are breaking the law by
harvesting grain on the Sabbath."

[3]Jesus said to them, "Haven't you read in
the Scriptures what David did when he and
his companions were hungry? [4]He went into
the house of God, and he and his companions
broke the law by eating the sacred loaves of
bread that only the priests are allowed to eat.
[5]And haven't you read in the law of Moses that
the priests on duty in the Temple may work
on the Sabbath? [6]I tell you, there is one here
who is even greater than the Temple! [7]But
you would not have condemned my innocent
disciples if you knew the meaning of this
Scripture: 'I want to show mercy, not
offer sacrifices.'* [8]For the Son of Man* is
Lord, even over the Sabbath!"

Jesus Heals on the Sabbath

[9]Then Jesus went over to their synagogue,
[10]where he noticed a man with a deformed
hand. The Pharisees asked Jesus, "Does the
law permit a person to work by healing on the
Sabbath?" (They were hoping he would say
yes, so they could bring charges against him.)

[11]And he answered, "If you had a sheep that
fell into a well on the Sabbath, wouldn't you
work to pull it out? Of course you would.
[12]And how much more valuable is a person
than a sheep! Yes, the law permits a person to
do good on the Sabbath."

[13]Then he said to the man, "Hold out your
hand." So the man held out his hand, and it
was restored, just like the other one! [14]Then
the Pharisees called a meeting to plot how to
kill Jesus.

Jesus, God's Chosen Servant

[15]But Jesus knew what they were planning. So
he left that area, and many people followed
him. He healed all the sick among them, [16]but
he warned them not to reveal who he was.
[17]This fulfilled the prophecy of Isaiah con-
cerning him:

[18] "Look at my Servant, whom I have chosen.
He is my Beloved, who pleases me.
I will put my Spirit upon him,
and he will proclaim justice to the
nations.
[19] He will not fight or shout
or raise his voice in public.
[20] He will not crush the weakest reed
or put out a flickering candle.
Finally he will cause justice to be
victorious.
[21] And his name will be the hope
of all the world."*

Jesus and the Prince of Demons

[22]Then a demon-possessed man, who was
blind and couldn't speak, was brought to
Jesus. He healed the man so that he could
both speak and see. [23]The crowd was amazed
and asked, "Could it be that Jesus is the Son of
David, the Messiah?"

[24]But when the Pharisees heard about the
miracle, they said, "No wonder he can cast out
demons. He gets his power from Satan,* the
prince of demons."

[25]Jesus knew their thoughts and replied,
"Any kingdom divided by civil war is doomed.
A town or family splintered by feuding will
fall apart. [26]And if Satan is casting out Satan,
he is divided and fighting against himself. His
own kingdom will not survive. [27]And if I am
empowered by Satan, what about your own
exorcists? They cast out demons, too, so they
will condemn you for what you have said.
[28]But if I am casting out demons by the Spirit
of God, then the Kingdom of God has arrived
among you. [29]For who is powerful enough to
enter the house of a strong man like Satan
and plunder his goods? Only someone even
stronger—someone who could tie him up and
then plunder his house.

[30]"Anyone who isn't with me opposes me,
and anyone who isn't working with me is ac-
tually working against me.

[31]"So I tell you, every sin and blasphemy
can be forgiven—except blasphemy against
the Holy Spirit, which will never be forgiven.
[32]Anyone who speaks against the Son of Man
can be forgiven, but anyone who speaks
against the Holy Spirit will never be forgiven,
either in this world or in the world to come.

[33]"A tree is identified by its fruit. If a tree is
good, its fruit will be good. If a tree is bad, its
fruit will be bad. [34]You brood of snakes! How

12:7 Hos 6:6 (Greek version). **12:8** "Son of Man" is a title Jesus used for himself. **12:18-21** Isa 42:1-4 (Greek version for 42:4).
12:24 Greek *Beelzeboul;* also in 12:27. Other manuscripts read *Beezeboul;* Latin version reads *Beelzebub*.

could evil men like you speak what is good
and right? For whatever is in your heart deter-
mines what you say. 35A good person pro-
duces good things from the treasury of a good
heart, and an evil person produces evil things
from the treasury of an evil heart. 36And I tell
you this, you must give an account on judg-
ment day for every idle word you speak. 37The
words you say will either acquit you or con-
demn you."

The Sign of Jonah

38One day some teachers of religious law and
Pharisees came to Jesus and said, "Teacher,
we want you to show us a miraculous sign to
prove your authority."

39But Jesus replied, "Only an evil, adulter-
ous generation would demand a miraculous
sign; but the only sign I will give them is the
sign of the prophet Jonah. 40For as Jonah was
in the belly of the great fish for three days and
three nights, so will the Son of Man be in the
heart of the earth for three days and three
nights.

41"The people of Nineveh will stand up
against this generation on judgment day and
condemn it, for they repented of their sins at
the preaching of Jonah. Now someone
greater than Jonah is here—but you refuse to
repent. 42The queen of Sheba* will also stand
up against this generation on judgment day
and condemn it, for she came from a distant
land to hear the wisdom of Solomon. Now
someone greater than Solomon is here—but
you refuse to listen.

43"When an evil* spirit leaves a person, it
goes into the desert, seeking rest but finding
none. 44Then it says, 'I will return to the per-
son I came from.' So it returns and finds its
former home empty, swept, and in order.
45Then the spirit finds seven other spirits
more evil than itself, and they all enter the
person and live there. And so that person is
worse off than before. That will be the expe-
rience of this evil generation."

The True Family of Jesus

46As Jesus was speaking to the crowd, his
mother and brothers stood outside, asking to
speak to him. 47Someone told Jesus, "Your
mother and your brothers are outside, and
they want to speak to you."*

48Jesus asked, "Who is my mother? Who
are my brothers?" 49Then he pointed to his
disciples and said, "Look, these are my
mother and brothers. 50Anyone who does the
will of my Father in heaven is my brother and
sister and mother!"

12:42 Greek *The queen of the south.* **12:43** Greek *unclean.* **12:47** Some manuscripts do not include verse 47. Compare Mark 3:32 and Luke 8:20.

IS IT OK?

IS IT OK TO SWEAR?

God isn't like an uptight, grouchy grown-up who is listening to see if you slip up and swear. What God cares about is your *heart*. And the best test of what's in your heart is—your *language*! If you go around swearing, that might mean your heart contains bitterness or anger or pride. If you go around saying good things, your heart probably is filled with joy or compassion or love. Plus, Jesus said that you'll have to explain your words to God someday (see Matthew 12:36-37). That's a scary thought if you've been saying not-so-good stuff! The next time you think about swearing, swallow those words and speak the good things that are in your heart.

CHAPTER 13

Parable of the Farmer Scattering Seed

Later that same day Jesus left the house and
sat beside the lake. [2]A large crowd soon gath-
ered around him, so he got into a boat. Then
he sat there and taught as the people stood on
the shore. [3]He told many stories in the form
of parables, such as this one:

"Listen! A farmer went out to plant some
seeds. [4]As he scattered them across his field,
some seeds fell on a footpath, and the birds
came and ate them. [5]Other seeds fell on shal-
low soil with underlying rock. The seeds
sprouted quickly because the soil was shal-
low. [6]But the plants soon wilted under the hot
sun, and since they didn't have deep roots,
they died. [7]Other seeds fell among thorns that
grew up and choked out the tender plants.
[8]Still other seeds fell on fertile soil, and they
produced a crop that was thirty, sixty, and
even a hundred times as much as had been
planted! [9]Anyone with ears to hear should lis-
ten and understand."

[10]His disciples came and asked him, "Why
do you use parables when you talk to the peo-
ple?"

[11]He replied, "You are permitted to under-
stand the secrets* of the Kingdom of Heaven,
but others are not. [12]To those who listen to
my teaching, more understanding will be
given, and they will have an abundance of
knowledge. But for those who are not listen-
ing, even what little understanding they have
will be taken away from them. [13]That is why I
use these parables,

For they look, but they don't really see.
They hear, but they don't really listen or
understand.

[14]This fulfills the prophecy of Isaiah that says,

'When you hear what I say,
you will not understand.
When you see what I do,
you will not comprehend.
[15] For the hearts of these people are
hardened,
and their ears cannot hear,
and they have closed their eyes—
so their eyes cannot see,
and their ears cannot hear,
and their hearts cannot understand,
and they cannot turn to me
and let me heal them.'*

[16]"But blessed are your eyes, because they
see; and your ears, because they hear. [17]I tell
you the truth, many prophets and righteous
people longed to see what you see, but they
didn't see it. And they longed to hear what you
hear, but they didn't hear it.

[18]"Now listen to the explanation of the par-
able about the farmer planting seeds: [19]The
seed that fell on the footpath represents
those who hear the message about the King-
dom and don't understand it. Then the evil
one comes and snatches away the seed that
was planted in their hearts. [20]The seed on the
rocky soil represents those who hear the mes-
sage and immediately receive it with joy. [21]But
since they don't have deep roots, they don't
last long. They fall away as soon as they have
problems or are persecuted for believing
God's word. [22]The seed that fell among the
thorns represents those who hear God's word,
but all too quickly the message is crowded out
by the worries of this life and the lure of
wealth, so no fruit is produced. [23]The seed
that fell on good soil represents those who
truly hear and understand God's word and
produce a harvest of thirty, sixty, or even a
hundred times as much as had been planted!"

Parable of the Wheat and Weeds

[24]Here is another story Jesus told: "The King-
dom of Heaven is like a farmer who planted
good seed in his field. [25]But that night as the
workers slept, his enemy came and planted
weeds among the wheat, then slipped away.
[26]When the crop began to grow and produce
grain, the weeds also grew.

[27]"The farmer's workers went to him and
said, 'Sir, the field where you planted that
good seed is full of weeds! Where did they
come from?'

[28]"'An enemy has done this!' the farmer ex-
claimed.

" 'Should we pull out the weeds?' they
asked.

[29]"'No,' he replied, 'you'll uproot the wheat
if you do. [30]Let both grow together until the
harvest. Then I will tell the harvesters to sort
out the weeds, tie them into bundles, and
burn them, and to put the wheat in the barn.'"

13:11 Greek *the mysteries*. **13:14-15** Isa 6:9-10 (Greek version).

Parable of the Mustard Seed

31Here is another illustration Jesus used: "The
Kingdom of Heaven is like a mustard seed
planted in a field. 32It is the smallest of all
seeds, but it becomes the largest of garden
plants; it grows into a tree, and birds come
and make nests in its branches."

Parable of the Yeast

33Jesus also used this illustration: "The King-
dom of Heaven is like the yeast a woman used
in making bread. Even though she put only a
little yeast in three measures of flour, it per-
meated every part of the dough."

34Jesus always used stories and illustra-
tions like these when speaking to the crowds.
In fact, he never spoke to them without using
such parables. 35This fulfilled what God had
spoken through the prophet:

"I will speak to you in parables.
I will explain things hidden since the
creation of the world.*"

Parable of the Wheat and Weeds Explained

36Then, leaving the crowds outside, Jesus went
into the house. His disciples said, "Please ex-
plain to us the story of the weeds in the field."

37Jesus replied, "The Son of Man* is the
farmer who plants the good seed. 38The field
is the world, and the good seed represents the
people of the Kingdom. The weeds are the
people who belong to the evil one. 39The en-
emy who planted the weeds among the wheat
is the devil. The harvest is the end of the
world,* and the harvesters are the angels.

40"Just as the weeds are sorted out and
burned in the fire, so it will be at the end of the
world. 41The Son of Man will send his angels,
and they will remove from his Kingdom every-
thing that causes sin and all who do evil. 42And
the angels will throw them into the fiery fur-
nace, where there will be weeping and gnash-
ing of teeth. 43Then the righteous will shine
like the sun in their Father's Kingdom. Anyone
with ears to hear should listen and understand!

Parables of the Hidden Treasure and the Pearl

44"The Kingdom of Heaven is like a treasure
that a man discovered hidden in a field. In his
excitement, he hid it again and sold everything
he owned to get enough money to buy the field.

45"Again, the Kingdom of Heaven is like a
merchant on the lookout for choice pearls.
46When he discovered a pearl of great value,
he sold everything he owned and bought it!

Parable of the Fishing Net

47"Again, the Kingdom of Heaven is like a fish-
ing net that was thrown into the water and
caught fish of every kind. 48When the net was
full, they dragged it up onto the shore, sat
down, and sorted the good fish into crates, but
threw the bad ones away. 49That is the way it
will be at the end of the world. The angels will
come and separate the wicked people from
the righteous, 50throwing the wicked into the
fiery furnace, where there will be weeping and
gnashing of teeth. 51Do you understand all
these things?"

"Yes," they said, "we do."

52Then he added, "Every teacher of religious
law who becomes a disciple in the Kingdom of
Heaven is like a homeowner who brings from
his storeroom new gems of truth as well as
old."

Jesus Rejected at Nazareth

53When Jesus had finished telling these sto-
ries and illustrations, he left that part of the
country. 54He returned to Nazareth, his home-
town. When he taught there in the synagogue,
everyone was amazed and said, "Where does
he get this wisdom and the power to do mira-
cles?" 55Then they scoffed, "He's just the car-
penter's son, and we know Mary, his mother,
and his brothers—James, Joseph,* Simon, and
Judas. 56All his sisters live right here among us.
Where did he learn all these things?" 57And
they were deeply offended and refused to be-
lieve in him.

Then Jesus told them, "A prophet is hon-
ored everywhere except in his own hometown
and among his own family." 58And so he did
only a few miracles there because of their un-
belief.

CHAPTER 14

The Death of John the Baptist

When Herod Antipas, the ruler of Galilee,*
heard about Jesus, 2he said to his advisers,

13:35 Some manuscripts do not include *of the world*. Ps 78:2. **13:37** "Son of Man" is a title Jesus used for himself. **13:39** Or *the age;* also in 13:40, 49. **13:55** Other manuscripts read *Joses;* still others read *John*. **14:1** Greek *Herod the tetrarch*. Herod Antipas was a son of King Herod and was ruler over Galilee.

"This must be John the Baptist raised from the dead! That is why he can do such miracles."

[3]For Herod had arrested and imprisoned John as a favor to his wife Herodias (the former wife of Herod's brother Philip). [4]John had been telling Herod, "It is against God's law for you to marry her." [5]Herod wanted to kill John, but he was afraid of a riot, because all the people believed John was a prophet.

[6]But at a birthday party for Herod, Herodias's daughter performed a dance that greatly pleased him, [7]so he promised with a vow to give her anything she wanted. [8]At her mother's urging, the girl said, "I want the head of John the Baptist on a tray!" [9]Then the king regretted what he had said; but because of the vow he had made in front of his guests, he issued the necessary orders. [10]So John was beheaded in the prison, [11]and his head was brought on a tray and given to the girl, who took it to her mother. [12]Later, John's disciples came for his body and buried it. Then they went and told Jesus what had happened.

Jesus Feeds Five Thousand

[13]As soon as Jesus heard the news, he left in a boat to a remote area to be alone. But the crowds heard where he was headed and followed on foot from many towns. [14]Jesus saw the huge crowd as he stepped from the boat, and he had compassion on them and healed their sick.

[15]That evening the disciples came to him and said, "This is a remote place, and it's already getting late. Send the crowds away so they can go to the villages and buy food for themselves."

[16]But Jesus said, "That isn't necessary—you feed them."

[17]"But we have only five loaves of bread and two fish!" they answered.

[18]"Bring them here," he said. [19]Then he told the people to sit down on the grass. Jesus took the five loaves and two fish, looked up toward heaven, and blessed them. Then, breaking the loaves into pieces, he gave the bread to the disciples, who distributed it to the people. [20]They all ate as much as they wanted, and afterward, the disciples picked up twelve baskets of leftovers. [21]About 5,000 men were fed that day, in addition to all the women and children!

Jesus Walks on Water

[22]Immediately after this, Jesus insisted that his disciples get back into the boat and cross to the other side of the lake, while he sent the people home. [23]After sending them home, he went up into the hills by himself to pray. Night fell while he was there alone.

AMAZING FACTS

A strong wind, big waves, a little boat—and now a ghost? No. It was Jesus, walking on *top* of the water!

MATTHEW 14:22-27

[24]Meanwhile, the disciples were in trouble far away from land, for a strong wind had risen, and they were fighting heavy waves. [25]About three o'clock in the morning* Jesus came toward them, walking on the water. [26]When the disciples saw him walking on the water, they were terrified. In their fear, they cried out, "It's a ghost!"

[27]But Jesus spoke to them at once. "Don't be afraid," he said. "Take courage. I am here!*"

[28]Then Peter called to him, "Lord, if it's really you, tell me to come to you, walking on the water."

[29]"Yes, come," Jesus said.

So Peter went over the side of the boat and walked on the water toward Jesus. [30]But when he saw the strong* wind and the waves, he was terrified and began to sink. "Save me, Lord!" he shouted.

[31]Jesus immediately reached out and grabbed him. "You have so little faith," Jesus said. "Why did you doubt me?"

[32]When they climbed back into the boat, the wind stopped. [33]Then the disciples worshiped him. "You really are the Son of God!" they exclaimed.

14:25 Greek *In the fourth watch of the night.* **14:27** Or *The 'I AM' is here;* Greek reads *I am.* See Exod 3:14. **14:30** Some manuscripts do not include *strong.*

34After they had crossed the lake, they
landed at Gennesaret. 35When the people
recognized Jesus, the news of his arrival
spread quickly throughout the whole area,
and soon people were bringing all their sick
to be healed. 36They begged him to let the sick
touch at least the fringe of his robe, and all
who touched him were healed.

CHAPTER 15

Jesus Teaches about Inner Purity

Some Pharisees and teachers of religious law
now arrived from Jerusalem to see Jesus. They
asked him, 2"Why do your disciples disobey
our age-old tradition? For they ignore our tra-
dition of ceremonial hand washing before
they eat."

3Jesus replied, "And why do you, by your
traditions, violate the direct commandments
of God? 4For instance, God says, 'Honor your
father and mother,'* and 'Anyone who speaks
disrespectfully of father or mother must be
put to death.'* 5But you say it is all right for
people to say to their parents, 'Sorry, I can't
help you. For I have vowed to give to God what
I would have given to you.' 6In this way, you
say they don't need to honor their parents.*
And so you cancel the word of God for the
sake of your own tradition. 7You hypocrites!
Isaiah was right when he prophesied about
you, for he wrote,

8 'These people honor me with their lips,
but their hearts are far from me.
9 Their worship is a farce,
for they teach man-made ideas as
commands from God.'*"

10Then Jesus called to the crowd to come
and hear. "Listen," he said, "and try to under-
stand. 11It's not what goes into your mouth
that defiles you; you are defiled by the words
that come out of your mouth."

12Then the disciples came to him and
asked, "Do you realize you offended the Phar-
isees by what you just said?"

13Jesus replied, "Every plant not planted by
my heavenly Father will be uprooted, 14so ig-
nore them. They are blind guides leading the
blind, and if one blind person guides another,
they will both fall into a ditch."

15Then Peter said to Jesus, "Explain to us
the parable that says people aren't defiled by
what they eat."

16"Don't you understand yet?" Jesus asked.
17"Anything you eat passes through the stom-
ach and then goes into the sewer. 18But the
words you speak come from the heart—that's
what defiles you. 19For from the heart come
evil thoughts, murder, adultery, all sexual im-
morality, theft, lying, and slander. 20These are
what defile you. Eating with unwashed hands
will never defile you."

What's so wrong about using a few bad words once in a while?

The words you speak come from the heart—that's what defiles you. MATTHEW 15:18

The Faith of a Gentile Woman

21Then Jesus left Galilee and went north to the
region of Tyre and Sidon. 22A Gentile* woman
who lived there came to him, pleading, "Have
mercy on me, O Lord, Son of David! For my
daughter is possessed by a demon that tor-
ments her severely."

23But Jesus gave her no reply, not even a
word. Then his disciples urged him to send
her away. "Tell her to go away," they said. "She
is bothering us with all her begging."

24Then Jesus said to the woman, "I was sent
only to help God's lost sheep—the people of
Israel."

25But she came and worshiped him, plead-
ing again, "Lord, help me!"

26Jesus responded, "It isn't right to take
food from the children and throw it to the
dogs."

27She replied, "That's true, Lord, but even
dogs are allowed to eat the scraps that fall be-
neath their masters' table."

15:4a Exod 20:12; Deut 5:16. **15:4b** Exod 21:17 (Greek version); Lev 20:9 (Greek version). **15:6** Greek *their father;* other manuscripts read *their father or their mother.* **15:8-9** Isa 29:13 (Greek version). **15:22** Greek *Canaanite.*

[28]"Dear woman," Jesus said to her, "your faith is great. Your request is granted." And her daughter was instantly healed.

Jesus Heals Many People

[29]Jesus returned to the Sea of Galilee and climbed a hill and sat down. [30]A vast crowd brought to him people who were lame, blind, crippled, those who couldn't speak, and many others. They laid them before Jesus, and he healed them all. [31]The crowd was amazed! Those who hadn't been able to speak were talking, the crippled were made well, the lame were walking, and the blind could see again! And they praised the God of Israel.

Jesus Feeds Four Thousand

[32]Then Jesus called his disciples and told them, "I feel sorry for these people. They have been here with me for three days, and they have nothing left to eat. I don't want to send them away hungry, or they will faint along the way."

[33]The disciples replied, "Where would we get enough food here in the wilderness for such a huge crowd?"

[34]Jesus asked, "How much bread do you have?"

They replied, "Seven loaves, and a few small fish."

[35]So Jesus told all the people to sit down on the ground. [36]Then he took the seven loaves and the fish, thanked God for them, and broke them into pieces. He gave them to the disciples, who distributed the food to the crowd.

[37]They all ate as much as they wanted. Afterward, the disciples picked up seven large baskets of leftover food. [38]There were 4,000 men who were fed that day, in addition to all the women and children. [39]Then Jesus sent the people home, and he got into a boat and crossed over to the region of Magadan.

CHAPTER 16

Leaders Demand a Miraculous Sign

One day the Pharisees and Sadducees came to test Jesus, demanding that he show them a miraculous sign from heaven to prove his authority.

[2]He replied, "You know the saying, 'Red sky at night means fair weather tomorrow; [3]red sky in the morning means foul weather all day.' You know how to interpret the weather signs in the sky, but you don't know how to interpret the signs of the times!* [4]Only an evil, adulterous generation would demand a miraculous sign, but the only sign I will give them is the sign of the prophet Jonah.*" Then Jesus left them and went away.

Yeast of the Pharisees and Sadducees

[5]Later, after they crossed to the other side of the lake, the disciples discovered they had forgotten to bring any bread. [6]"Watch out!" Jesus warned them. "Beware of the yeast of the Pharisees and Sadducees."

[7]At this they began to argue with each other because they hadn't brought any bread. [8]Jesus knew what they were saying, so he said, "You have so little faith! Why are you arguing with each other about having no bread? [9]Don't you understand even yet? Don't you remember the 5,000 I fed with five loaves, and the baskets of leftovers you picked up? [10]Or the 4,000 I fed with seven loaves, and the large baskets of leftovers you picked up? [11]Why can't you understand that I'm not talking about bread? So again I say, 'Beware of the yeast of the Pharisees and Sadducees.'"

[12]Then at last they understood that he wasn't speaking about the yeast in bread, but about the deceptive teaching of the Pharisees and Sadducees.

Peter's Declaration about Jesus

[13]When Jesus came to the region of Caesarea Philippi, he asked his disciples, "Who do people say that the Son of Man is?"*

[14]"Well," they replied, "some say John the Baptist, some say Elijah, and others say Jeremiah or one of the other prophets."

[15]Then he asked them, "But who do you say I am?"

[16]Simon Peter answered, "You are the Messiah,* the Son of the living God."

[17]Jesus replied, "You are blessed, Simon son of John,* because my Father in heaven has revealed this to you. You did not learn this from any human being. [18]Now I say to you that you are Peter (which means 'rock'),* and upon this

16:2-3 Several manuscripts do not include any of the words in 16:2-3 after *He replied.* **16:4** Greek *the sign of Jonah.* **16:13** "Son of Man" is a title Jesus used for himself. **16:16** Or *the Christ. Messiah* (a Hebrew term) and *Christ* (a Greek term) both mean "the anointed one." **16:17** Greek *Simon bar-Jonah;* see John 1:42; 21:15-17. **16:18a** Greek *that you are Peter.*

rock I will build my church, and all the powers of hell* will not conquer it. [19]And I will give you the keys of the Kingdom of Heaven. Whatever you forbid* on earth will be forbidden in heaven, and whatever you permit* on earth will be permitted in heaven."

[20]Then he sternly warned the disciples not to tell anyone that he was the Messiah.

Jesus Predicts His Death

[21]From then on Jesus* began to tell his disciples plainly that it was necessary for him to go to Jerusalem, and that he would suffer many terrible things at the hands of the elders, the leading priests, and the teachers of religious law. He would be killed, but on the third day he would be raised from the dead.

AMAZING FACTS

On a mountaintop, the brilliant light of God the Father shone through Jesus—God the Son. It was a holy transformation!

MATTHEW 17:1-8

[22]But Peter took him aside and began to reprimand him* for saying such things. "Heaven forbid, Lord," he said. "This will never happen to you!"

[23]Jesus turned to Peter and said, "Get away from me, Satan! You are a dangerous trap to me. You are seeing things merely from a human point of view, not from God's."

[24]Then Jesus said to his disciples, "If any of you wants to be my follower, you must turn from your selfish ways, take up your cross, and follow me. [25]If you try to hang on to your life, you will lose it. But if you give up your life for my sake, you will save it. [26]And what do you benefit if you gain the whole world but lose your own soul?* Is anything worth more than your soul? [27]For the Son of Man will come with his angels in the glory of his Father and will judge all people according to their deeds. [28]And I tell you the truth, some standing here right now will not die before they see the Son of Man coming in his Kingdom."

CHAPTER 17

The Transfiguration

Six days later Jesus took Peter and the two brothers, James and John, and led them up a high mountain to be alone. [2]As the men watched, Jesus' appearance was transformed so that his face shone like the sun, and his clothes became as white as light. [3]Suddenly, Moses and Elijah appeared and began talking with Jesus.

[4]Peter exclaimed, "Lord, it's wonderful for us to be here! If you want, I'll make three shelters as memorials*—one for you, one for Moses, and one for Elijah."

[5]But even as he spoke, a bright cloud overshadowed them, and a voice from the cloud said, "This is my dearly loved Son, who brings me great joy. Listen to him." [6]The disciples were terrified and fell face down on the ground.

[7]Then Jesus came over and touched them. "Get up," he said. "Don't be afraid." [8]And when they looked up, Moses and Elijah were gone, and they saw only Jesus.

[9]As they went back down the mountain, Jesus commanded them, "Don't tell anyone what you have seen until the Son of Man* has been raised from the dead."

[10]Then his disciples asked him, "Why do the teachers of religious law insist that Elijah must return before the Messiah comes?*"

[11]Jesus replied, "Elijah is indeed coming first to get everything ready. [12]But I tell you, Elijah has already come, but he wasn't recognized, and they chose to abuse him. And in the same way they will also make the Son of Man suffer." [13]Then the disciples realized he was talking about John the Baptist.

Jesus Heals a Demon-Possessed Boy

[14]At the foot of the mountain, a large crowd was waiting for them. A man came and knelt before Jesus and said, [15]"Lord, have mercy on my son. He has seizures and suffers terribly.

16:18b Greek *and the gates of Hades.* **16:19a** Or *bind,* or *lock.* **16:19b** Or *loose,* or *open.* **16:21** Some manuscripts read *Jesus the Messiah.* **16:22** Or *began to correct him.* **16:26** Or *your self?* also in 16:26b. **17:4** Greek *three tabernacles.* **17:9** "Son of Man" is a title Jesus used for himself. **17:10** Greek *that Elijah must come first?*

He often falls into the fire or into the water.
16So I brought him to your disciples, but they
couldn't heal him."
17Jesus said, "You faithless and corrupt
people! How long must I be with you? How
long must I put up with you? Bring the boy
here to me." 18Then Jesus rebuked the demon
in the boy, and it left him. From that moment
the boy was well.
19Afterward the disciples asked Jesus pri-
vately, "Why couldn't we cast out that demon?"
20"You don't have enough faith," Jesus told
them. "I tell you the truth, if you had faith even
as small as a mustard seed, you could say to this
mountain, 'Move from here to there,' and it
would move. Nothing would be impossible.*"

Jesus Again Predicts His Death

22After they gathered again in Galilee, Jesus
told them, "The Son of Man is going to be be-
trayed into the hands of his enemies. 23He will
be killed, but on the third day he will be raised
from the dead." And the disciples were filled
with grief.

Payment of the Temple Tax

24On their arrival in Capernaum, the collectors
of the Temple tax* came to Peter and asked
him, "Doesn't your teacher pay the Temple tax?"
25"Yes, he does," Peter replied. Then he
went into the house.
But before he had a chance to speak, Jesus
asked him, "What do you think, Peter?* Do
kings tax their own people or the people they
have conquered?*"
26"They tax the people they have con-
quered," Peter replied.
"Well, then," Jesus said, "the citizens are
free! 27However, we don't want to offend
them, so go down to the lake and throw in a
line. Open the mouth of the first fish you
catch, and you will find a large silver coin.*
Take it and pay the tax for both of us."

CHAPTER 18

The Greatest in the Kingdom

About that time the disciples came to Jesus
and asked, "Who is greatest in the Kingdom
of Heaven?"
2Jesus called a little child to him and put
the child among them. 3Then he said, "I tell
you the truth, unless you turn from your sins
and become like little children, you will never
get into the Kingdom of Heaven. 4So anyone
who becomes as humble as this little child is
the greatest in the Kingdom of Heaven.
5"And anyone who welcomes a little child
like this on my behalf* is welcoming me. 6But
if you cause one of these little ones who trusts
in me to fall into sin, it would be better for you
to have a large millstone tied around your
neck and be drowned in the depths of the sea.
7"What sorrow awaits the world, because it
tempts people to sin. Temptations are inevi-
table, but what sorrow awaits the person who
does the tempting. 8So if your hand or foot
causes you to sin, cut it off and throw it away.
It's better to enter eternal life with only one
hand or one foot than to be thrown into eter-
nal fire with both of your hands and feet.
9And if your eye causes you to sin, gouge it out
and throw it away. It's better to enter eternal
life with only one eye than to have two eyes
and be thrown into the fire of hell.*
10"Beware that you don't look down on any
of these little ones. For I tell you that in
heaven their angels are always in the pres-
ence of my heavenly Father.*

Parable of the Lost Sheep

12"If a man has a hundred sheep and one of
them wanders away, what will he do? Won't
he leave the ninety-nine others on the hills
and go out to search for the one that is lost?
13And if he finds it, I tell you the truth, he will
rejoice over it more than over the ninety-nine
that didn't wander away! 14In the same way, it
is not my heavenly Father's will that even one
of these little ones should perish.

Correcting Another Believer

15"If another believer* sins against you,* go
privately and point out the offense. If the
other person listens and confesses it, you
have won that person back. 16But if you are
unsuccessful, take one or two others with you
and go back again, so that everything you say
may be confirmed by two or three witnesses.

17:20 Some manuscripts add verse 21, *But this kind of demon won't leave except by prayer and fasting*. Compare Mark 9:29. **17:24** Greek *the two-drachma [tax]*; also in 17:24b. See Exod 30:13-16; Neh 10:32-33. **17:25a** Greek *Simon?* **17:25b** Greek *their sons or others?* **17:27** Greek *a stater* [a Greek coin equivalent to four drachmas]. **18:5** Greek *in my name*. **18:9** Greek *the Gehenna of fire*. **18:10** Some manuscripts add verse 11, *And the Son of Man came to save those who are lost*. Compare Luke 19:10. **18:15a** Greek *If your brother*. **18:15b** Some manuscripts do not include *against you*.

A LOAN AGAIN?

Elliot borrowed a dollar from Dylan and promised to pay it back as soon as he could. But two weeks later Elliot said he still couldn't pay back the dollar. Dylan began to think that Elliot never intended to pay him back. It wasn't a lot of money, but he could use it. Besides, it was the principle of the thing. Just when Dylan was thinking about the money, he saw Elliot coming. What should he do? How do you think he should treat Elliot? Read Matthew 18:21-35 for some ideas.

17 If the person still refuses to listen, take your case to the church. Then if he or she won't accept the church's decision, treat that person as a pagan or a corrupt tax collector.

18 "I tell you the truth, whatever you forbid* on earth will be forbidden in heaven, and whatever you permit* on earth will be permitted in heaven.

19 "I also tell you this: If two of you agree here on earth concerning anything you ask, my Father in heaven will do it for you. 20 For where two or three gather together as my followers,* I am there among them."

Parable of the Unforgiving Debtor

21 Then Peter came to him and asked, "Lord, how often should I forgive someone* who sins against me? Seven times?"

22 "No, not seven times," Jesus replied, "but seventy times seven!*

23 "Therefore, the Kingdom of Heaven can be compared to a king who decided to bring his accounts up to date with servants who had borrowed money from him. 24 In the process, one of his debtors was brought in who owed him millions of dollars.* 25 He couldn't pay, so his master ordered that he be sold—along with his wife, his children, and everything he owned—to pay the debt.

26 "But the man fell down before his master and begged him, 'Please, be patient with me, and I will pay it all.' 27 Then his master was filled with pity for him, and he released him and forgave his debt.

28 "But when the man left the king, he went to a fellow servant who owed him a few thousand dollars.* He grabbed him by the throat and demanded instant payment.

29 "His fellow servant fell down before him and begged for a little more time. 'Be patient with me, and I will pay it,' he pleaded. 30 But his creditor wouldn't wait. He had the man arrested and put in prison until the debt could be paid in full.

31 "When some of the other servants saw this, they were very upset. They went to the king and told him everything that had happened. 32 Then the king called in the man he had forgiven and said, 'You evil servant! I forgave you that tremendous debt because you pleaded with me. 33 Shouldn't you have mercy on your fellow servant, just as I had mercy on you?' 34 Then the angry king sent the man to prison to be tortured until he had paid his entire debt.

35 "That's what my heavenly Father will do to you if you refuse to forgive your brothers and sisters* from your heart."

18:18a Or *bind*, or *lock*. **18:18b** Or *loose*, or *open*. **18:20** Greek *gather together in my name*. **18:21** Greek *my brother*. **18:22** Or *seventy-seven times*. **18:24** Greek *10,000 talents* [375 tons or 340 metric tons of silver]. **18:28** Greek *100 denarii*. A denarius was equivalent to a laborer's full day's wage. **18:35** Greek *your brother*.

CHAPTER 19

Discussion about Divorce and Marriage

When Jesus had finished saying these things, he left Galilee and went down to the region of Judea east of the Jordan River. [2]Large crowds followed him there, and he healed their sick.

[3]Some Pharisees came and tried to trap him with this question: "Should a man be allowed to divorce his wife for just any reason?"

[4]"Haven't you read the Scriptures?" Jesus replied. "They record that from the beginning 'God made them male and female.'*" [5]And he said, "'This explains why a man leaves his father and mother and is joined to his wife, and the two are united into one.'* [6]Since they are no longer two but one, let no one split apart what God has joined together."

[7]"Then why did Moses say in the law that a man could give his wife a written notice of divorce and send her away?"* they asked.

[8]Jesus replied, "Moses permitted divorce only as a concession to your hard hearts, but it was not what God had originally intended. [9]And I tell you this, whoever divorces his wife and marries someone else commits adultery—unless his wife has been unfaithful.*"

[10]Jesus' disciples then said to him, "If this is the case, it is better not to marry!"

[11]"Not everyone can accept this statement," Jesus said. "Only those whom God helps. [12]Some are born as eunuchs, some have been made eunuchs by others, and some choose not to marry* for the sake of the Kingdom of Heaven. Let anyone accept this who can."

Jesus Blesses the Children

[13]One day some parents brought their children to Jesus so he could lay his hands on them and pray for them. But the disciples scolded the parents for bothering him.

[14]But Jesus said, "Let the children come to me. Don't stop them! For the Kingdom of Heaven belongs to those who are like these children." [15]And he placed his hands on their heads and blessed them before he left.

The Rich Man

[16]Someone came to Jesus with this question: "Teacher,* what good deed must I do to have eternal life?"

[17]"Why ask me about what is good?" Jesus replied. "There is only One who is good. But to answer your question—if you want to receive eternal life, keep* the commandments."

[18]"Which ones?" the man asked.

Peter

I remember the night I denied knowing Jesus, my Savior and friend.

Let me explain. Soldiers had taken Jesus to the high priest's house. I hid in the courtyard there to see what would happen. A servant girl pointed at me and said, "You were with Jesus!" I should have proudly said, "Yes, I was." Instead, I lied. I told her she was all wrong. Two other people said I knew Jesus. Again I said, "No! I don't know the man!"

Just then a rooster crowed, and I remembered Jesus saying that I would deny him. What a coward I am. Will I ever have another chance to tell the truth about Jesus?

Read about Peter at Jesus' trial in Matthew 26:69-75, and check out Peter's conversation with Jesus in John 21.

19:4 Gen 1:27; 5:2. **19:5** Gen 2:24. **19:7** See Deut 24:1. **19:9** Some manuscripts add *And anyone who marries a divorced woman commits adultery.* Compare Matt 5:32. **19:12** Greek *and some make themselves eunuchs.* **19:16** Some manuscripts read *Good Teacher.* **19:17** Some manuscripts read *continue to keep.*

And Jesus replied: "'You must not murder. You must not commit adultery. You must not steal. You must not testify falsely. [19]Honor your father and mother. Love your neighbor as yourself.'*"

[20]"I've obeyed all these commandments," the young man replied. "What else must I do?"

[21]Jesus told him, "If you want to be perfect, go and sell all your possessions and give the money to the poor, and you will have treasure in heaven. Then come, follow me."

[22]But when the young man heard this, he went away sad, for he had many possessions.

[23]Then Jesus said to his disciples, "I tell you the truth, it is very hard for a rich person to enter the Kingdom of Heaven. [24]I'll say it again—it is easier for a camel to go through the eye of a needle than for a rich person to enter the Kingdom of God!"

[25]The disciples were astounded. "Then who in the world can be saved?" they asked.

[26]Jesus looked at them intently and said, "Humanly speaking, it is impossible. But with God everything is possible."

[27]Then Peter said to him, "We've given up everything to follow you. What will we get?"

[28]Jesus replied, "I assure you that when the world is made new* and the Son of Man* sits upon his glorious throne, you who have been my followers will also sit on twelve thrones, judging the twelve tribes of Israel. [29]And everyone who has given up houses or brothers or sisters or father or mother or children or property, for my sake, will receive a hundred times as much in return and will inherit eternal life. [30]But many who are the greatest now will be least important then, and those who seem least important now will be the greatest then.*

CHAPTER 20

Parable of the Vineyard Workers

"For the Kingdom of Heaven is like the landowner who went out early one morning to hire workers for his vineyard. [2]He agreed to pay the normal daily wage* and sent them out to work.

[3]"At nine o'clock in the morning he was passing through the marketplace and saw some people standing around doing nothing. [4]So he hired them, telling them he would pay them whatever was right at the end of the day. [5]So they went to work in the vineyard. At noon and again at three o'clock he did the same thing.

[6]"At five o'clock that afternoon he was in town again and saw some more people standing around. He asked them, 'Why haven't you been working today?'

[7]"They replied, 'Because no one hired us.'

"The landowner told them, 'Then go out and join the others in my vineyard.'

[8]"That evening he told the foreman to call the workers in and pay them, beginning with the last workers first. [9]When those hired at five o'clock were paid, each received a full day's wage. [10]When those hired first came to get their pay, they assumed they would receive more. But they, too, were paid a day's wage. [11]When they received their pay, they protested to the owner, [12]'Those people worked only one hour, and yet you've paid them just as much as you paid us who worked all day in the scorching heat.'

[13]"He answered one of them, 'Friend, I haven't been unfair! Didn't you agree to work all day for the usual wage? [14]Take your money and go. I wanted to pay this last worker the same as you. [15]Is it against the law for me to do what I want with my money? Should you be jealous because I am kind to others?'

[16]"So those who are last now will be first then, and those who are first will be last."

Jesus Again Predicts His Death

[17]As Jesus was going up to Jerusalem, he took the twelve disciples aside privately and told them what was going to happen to him. [18]"Listen," he said, "we're going up to Jerusalem, where the Son of Man* will be betrayed to the leading priests and the teachers of religious law. They will sentence him to die. [19]Then they will hand him over to the Romans* to be mocked, flogged with a whip, and crucified. But on the third day he will be raised from the dead."

19:18-19 Exod 20:12-16; Deut 5:16-20; Lev 19:18. **19:28a** Or *in the regeneration.* **19:28b** "Son of Man" is a title Jesus used for himself. **19:30** Greek *But many who are first will be last; and the last, first.* **20:2** Greek *a denarius,* the payment for a full day's labor; similarly in 20:9, 10, 13. **20:18** "Son of Man" is a title Jesus used for himself. **20:19** Greek *the Gentiles.*

Jesus Teaches about Serving Others

20Then the mother of James and John, the
sons of Zebedee, came to Jesus with her sons.
She knelt respectfully to ask a favor. 21"What
is your request?" he asked.

She replied, "In your Kingdom, please let
my two sons sit in places of honor next to you,
one on your right and the other on your left."

22But Jesus answered by saying to them,
"You don't know what you are asking! Are you
able to drink from the bitter cup of suffering
I am about to drink?"

"Oh yes," they replied, "we are able!"

23Jesus told them, "You will indeed drink
from my bitter cup. But I have no right to say
who will sit on my right or my left. My Father
has prepared those places for the ones he has
chosen."

24When the ten other disciples heard what
James and John had asked, they were indig-
nant. 25But Jesus called them together and
said, "You know that the rulers in this world
lord it over their people, and officials flaunt
their authority over those under them. 26But
among you it will be different. Whoever wants
to be a leader among you must be your servant,
27and whoever wants to be first among you
must become your slave. 28For even the Son of
Man came not to be served but to serve others
and to give his life as a ransom for many."

Jesus Heals Two Blind Men

29As Jesus and the disciples left the town of Je-
richo, a large crowd followed behind. 30Two
blind men were sitting beside the road. When
they heard that Jesus was coming that way,
they began shouting, "Lord, Son of David, have
mercy on us!"

31"Be quiet!" the crowd yelled at them.

But they only shouted louder, "Lord, Son of
David, have mercy on us!"

32When Jesus heard them, he stopped and
called, "What do you want me to do for you?"

33"Lord," they said, "we want to see!" 34Jesus
felt sorry for them and touched their eyes. In-
stantly they could see! Then they followed him.

CHAPTER 21

Jesus' Triumphant Entry

As Jesus and the disciples approached Jerusa-
lem, they came to the town of Bethphage on
the Mount of Olives. Jesus sent two of them
on ahead. 2"Go into the village over there," he
said. "As soon as you enter it, you will see a
donkey tied there, with its colt beside it. Untie
them and bring them to me. 3If anyone asks
what you are doing, just say, 'The Lord needs
them,' and he will immediately let you take
them."

4This took place to fulfill the prophecy that
said,

5 "Tell the people of Jerusalem,*
'Look, your King is coming to you.
He is humble, riding on a donkey—
riding on a donkey's colt.'"*

6The two disciples did as Jesus com-
manded. 7They brought the donkey and the
colt to him and threw their garments over the
colt, and he sat on it.*

8Most of the crowd spread their garments
on the road ahead of him, and others cut
branches from the trees and spread them on
the road. 9Jesus was in the center of the pro-
cession, and the people all around him were
shouting,

"Praise God* for the Son of David!
Blessings on the one who comes in the
name of the LORD!
Praise God in highest heaven!"*

10The entire city of Jerusalem was in an up-
roar as he entered. "Who is this?" they asked.

11And the crowds replied, "It's Jesus, the
prophet from Nazareth in Galilee."

Jesus Clears the Temple

12Jesus entered the Temple and began to
drive out all the people buying and selling an-
imals for sacrifice. He knocked over the ta-
bles of the money changers and the chairs of
those selling doves. 13He said to them, "The
Scriptures declare, 'My Temple will be called
a house of prayer,' but you have turned it into
a den of thieves!"*

14The blind and the lame came to him in the
Temple, and he healed them. 15The leading
priests and the teachers of religious law saw
these wonderful miracles and heard even the
children in the Temple shouting, "Praise God
for the Son of David."

But the leaders were indignant. 16They

21:5a Greek *Tell the daughter of Zion.* Isa 62:11. **21:5b** Zech 9:9. **21:7** Greek *over them, and he sat on them.* **21:9a** Greek *Hosanna,* an exclamation of praise that literally means "save now"; also in 21:9b, 15. **21:9b** Pss 118:25-26; 148:1. **21:13** Isa 56:7; Jer 7:11.

asked Jesus, "Do you hear what these children are saying?"

"Yes," Jesus replied. "Haven't you ever read the Scriptures? For they say, 'You have taught children and infants to give you praise.'* "
17 Then he returned to Bethany, where he stayed overnight.

Jesus Curses the Fig Tree

18 In the morning, as Jesus was returning to Jerusalem, he was hungry, 19 and he noticed a fig tree beside the road. He went over to see if there were any figs, but there were only leaves. Then he said to it, "May you never bear fruit again!" And immediately the fig tree withered up.

20 The disciples were amazed when they saw this and asked, "How did the fig tree wither so quickly?"

21 Then Jesus told them, "I tell you the truth, if you have faith and don't doubt, you can do things like this and much more. You can even say to this mountain, 'May you be lifted up and thrown into the sea,' and it will happen. 22 You can pray for anything, and if you have faith, you will receive it."

The Authority of Jesus Challenged

23 When Jesus returned to the Temple and began teaching, the leading priests and elders came up to him. They demanded, "By what authority are you doing all these things? Who gave you the right?"

24 "I'll tell you by what authority I do these things if you answer one question," Jesus replied. 25 "Did John's authority to baptize come from heaven, or was it merely human?"

They talked it over among themselves. "If we say it was from heaven, he will ask us why we didn't believe John. 26 But if we say it was merely human, we'll be mobbed because the people believe John was a prophet." 27 So they finally replied, "We don't know."

And Jesus responded, "Then I won't tell you by what authority I do these things.

Parable of the Two Sons

28 "But what do you think about this? A man with two sons told the older boy, 'Son, go out and work in the vineyard today.' 29 The son answered, 'No, I won't go,' but later he changed his mind and went anyway. 30 Then the father told the other son, 'You go,' and he said, 'Yes, sir, I will.' But he didn't go.

31 "Which of the two obeyed his father?"

They replied, "The first."*

Then Jesus explained his meaning: "I tell you the truth, corrupt tax collectors and prostitutes will get into the Kingdom of God before you do. 32 For John the Baptist came and showed you the right way to live, but you didn't believe him, while tax collectors and prostitutes did. And even when you saw this happening, you refused to believe him and repent of your sins.

Parable of the Evil Farmers

33 "Now listen to another story. A certain landowner planted a vineyard, built a wall around it, dug a pit for pressing out the grape juice, and built a lookout tower. Then he leased the vineyard to tenant farmers and moved to another country. 34 At the time of the grape harvest, he sent his servants to collect his share of the crop. 35 But the farmers grabbed his servants, beat one, killed one, and stoned another. 36 So the landowner sent a larger group of his servants to collect for him, but the results were the same.

37 "Finally, the owner sent his son, thinking, 'Surely they will respect my son.'

38 "But when the tenant farmers saw his son coming, they said to one another, 'Here comes the heir to this estate. Come on, let's kill him and get the estate for ourselves!' 39 So they grabbed him, dragged him out of the vineyard, and murdered him.

40 "When the owner of the vineyard returns," Jesus asked, "what do you think he will do to those farmers?"

41 The religious leaders replied, "He will put the wicked men to a horrible death and lease the vineyard to others who will give him his share of the crop after each harvest."

42 Then Jesus asked them, "Didn't you ever read this in the Scriptures?

'The stone that the builders rejected
has now become the cornerstone.
This is the LORD's doing,
and it is wonderful to see.'*

21:16 Ps 8:2. **21:29-31** Other manuscripts read *"The second."* In still other manuscripts the first son says "Yes" but does nothing, the second son says "No" but then repents and goes, and the answer to Jesus' question is that the second son obeyed his father. **21:42** Ps 118:22-23.

43 I tell you, the Kingdom of God will be taken
away from you and given to a nation that will
produce the proper fruit. 44 Anyone who
stumbles over that stone will be broken to
pieces, and it will crush anyone it falls on.*"

45 When the leading priests and Pharisees
heard this parable, they realized he was tell-
ing the story against them—they were the
wicked farmers. 46 They wanted to arrest him,
but they were afraid of the crowds, who con-
sidered Jesus to be a prophet.

CHAPTER 22

Parable of the Great Feast

Jesus also told them other parables. He said,
2 "The Kingdom of Heaven can be illustrated
by the story of a king who prepared a great
wedding feast for his son. 3 When the banquet
was ready, he sent his servants to notify those
who were invited. But they all refused to come!

4 "So he sent other servants to tell them,
'The feast has been prepared. The bulls and
fattened cattle have been killed, and every-
thing is ready. Come to the banquet!' 5 But the
guests he had invited ignored them and went
their own way, one to his farm, another to his
business. 6 Others seized his messengers and
insulted them and killed them.

7 "The king was furious, and he sent out his
army to destroy the murderers and burn their
town. 8 And he said to his servants, 'The wed-
ding feast is ready, and the guests I invited
aren't worthy of the honor. 9 Now go out to the
street corners and invite everyone you see.'
10 So the servants brought in everyone they
could find, good and bad alike, and the ban-
quet hall was filled with guests.

11 "But when the king came in to meet the
guests, he noticed a man who wasn't wearing
the proper clothes for a wedding. 12 'Friend,'
he asked, 'how is it that you are here without
wedding clothes?' But the man had no reply.
13 Then the king said to his aides, 'Bind his
hands and feet and throw him into the outer
darkness, where there will be weeping and
gnashing of teeth.'

14 "For many are called, but few are chosen."

Taxes for Caesar

15 Then the Pharisees met together to plot
how to trap Jesus into saying something for
which he could be arrested. 16 They sent some
of their disciples, along with the supporters
of Herod, to meet with him. "Teacher," they
said, "we know how honest you are. You teach
the way of God truthfully. You are impartial
and don't play favorites. 17 Now tell us what
you think about this: Is it right to pay taxes to
Caesar or not?"

18 But Jesus knew their evil motives. "You
hypocrites!" he said. "Why are you trying to
trap me? 19 Here, show me the coin used for
the tax." When they handed him a Roman
coin,* 20 he asked, "Whose picture and title
are stamped on it?"

21 "Caesar's," they replied.

"Well, then," he said, "give to Caesar what

21:44 This verse is not included in some early manuscripts. Compare Luke 20:18. **22:19** Greek *a denarius.*

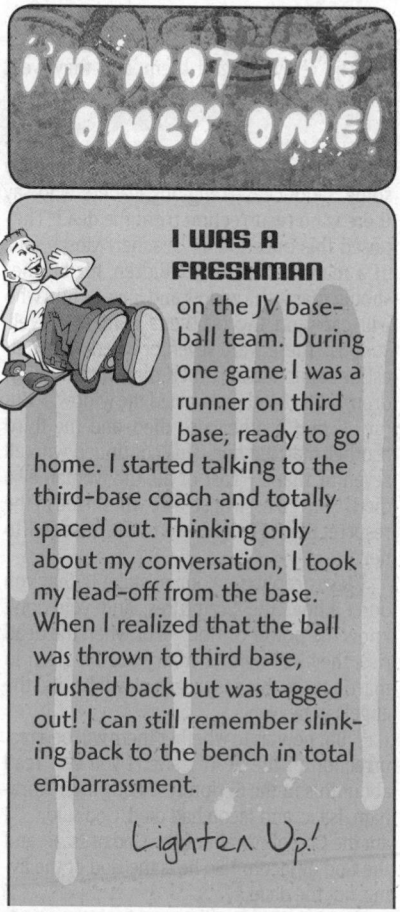

belongs to Caesar, and give to God what belongs to God."

22His reply amazed them, and they went away.

Discussion about Resurrection

23That same day Jesus was approached by some Sadducees—religious leaders who say there is no resurrection from the dead. They posed this question: 24"Teacher, Moses said, 'If a man dies without children, his brother should marry the widow and have a child who will carry on the brother's name.'* 25Well, suppose there were seven brothers. The oldest one married and then died without children, so his brother married the widow. 26But the second brother also died, and the third brother married her. This continued with all seven of them. 27Last of all, the woman also died. 28So tell us, whose wife will she be in the resurrection? For all seven were married to her."

29Jesus replied, "Your mistake is that you don't know the Scriptures, and you don't know the power of God. 30For when the dead rise, they will neither marry nor be given in marriage. In this respect they will be like the angels in heaven.

31"But now, as to whether there will be a resurrection of the dead—haven't you ever read about this in the Scriptures? Long after Abraham, Isaac, and Jacob had died, God said,* 32'I am the God of Abraham, the God of Isaac, and the God of Jacob.'* So he is the God of the living, not the dead."

33When the crowds heard him, they were astounded at his teaching.

The Most Important Commandment

34But when the Pharisees heard that he had silenced the Sadducees with his reply, they met together to question him again. 35One of them, an expert in religious law, tried to trap him with this question: 36"Teacher, which is the most important commandment in the law of Moses?"

37Jesus replied, "'You must love the LORD your God with all your heart, all your soul, and all your mind.'* 38This is the first and greatest commandment. 39A second is equally important: 'Love your neighbor as yourself.'* 40The entire law and all the demands of the prophets are based on these two commandments."

Whose Son Is the Messiah?

41Then, surrounded by the Pharisees, Jesus asked them a question: 42"What do you think about the Messiah? Whose son is he?"

They replied, "He is the son of David."

43Jesus responded, "Then why does David, speaking under the inspiration of the Spirit, call the Messiah 'my Lord'? For David said,

44 'The LORD said to my Lord,
Sit in the place of honor at my right hand
until I humble your enemies beneath
your feet.'*

45Since David called the Messiah 'my Lord,' how can the Messiah be his son?"

46No one could answer him. And after that, no one dared to ask him any more questions.

CHAPTER 23

Jesus Criticizes the Religious Leaders

Then Jesus said to the crowds and to his disciples, 2"The teachers of religious law and the Pharisees are the official interpreters of the law of Moses.* 3So practice and obey whatever they tell you, but don't follow their example. For they don't practice what they teach. 4They crush people with unbearable religious demands and never lift a finger to ease the burden.

5"Everything they do is for show. On their arms they wear extra wide prayer boxes with Scripture verses inside, and they wear robes with extra long tassels.* 6And they love to sit at the head table at banquets and in the seats of honor in the synagogues. 7They love to receive respectful greetings as they walk in the marketplaces, and to be called 'Rabbi.'*

8"Don't let anyone call you 'Rabbi,' for you have only one teacher, and all of you are equal as brothers and sisters.* 9And don't address anyone here on earth as 'Father,' for only God in heaven is your spiritual Father. 10And don't let anyone call you 'Teacher,' for you have only one teacher, the Messiah. 11The greatest among you must be a servant. 12But those who exalt themselves will be humbled, and those who humble themselves will be exalted.

22:24 Deut 25:5-6. **22:31** Greek *read about this? God said.* **22:32** Exod 3:6. **22:37** Deut 6:5. **22:39** Lev 19:18. **22:44** Ps 110:1. **23:2** Greek *and the Pharisees sit in the seat of Moses.* **23:5** Greek *They enlarge their phylacteries and lengthen their tassels.* **23:7** *Rabbi,* from Aramaic, means "master" or "teacher." **23:8** Greek *brothers.*

[13]"What sorrow awaits you teachers of religious law and you Pharisees. Hypocrites! For you shut the door of the Kingdom of Heaven in people's faces. You won't go in yourselves, and you don't let others enter either.*

[15]"What sorrow awaits you teachers of religious law and you Pharisees. Hypocrites! For you cross land and sea to make one convert, and then you turn that person into twice the child of hell* you yourselves are!

[16]"Blind guides! What sorrow awaits you! For you say that it means nothing to swear 'by God's Temple,' but that it is binding to swear 'by the gold in the Temple.' [17]Blind fools! Which is more important—the gold or the Temple that makes the gold sacred? [18]And you say that to swear 'by the altar' is not binding, but to swear 'by the gifts on the altar' is binding. [19]How blind! For which is more important—the gift on the altar or the altar that makes the gift sacred? [20]When you swear 'by the altar,' you are swearing by it and by everything on it. [21]And when you swear 'by the Temple,' you are swearing by it and by God, who lives in it. [22]And when you swear 'by heaven,' you are swearing by the throne of God and by God, who sits on the throne.

[23]"What sorrow awaits you teachers of religious law and you Pharisees. Hypocrites! For you are careful to tithe even the tiniest income from your herb gardens,* but you ignore the more important aspects of the law—justice, mercy, and faith. You should tithe, yes, but do not neglect the more important things. [24]Blind guides! You strain your water so you won't accidentally swallow a gnat, but you swallow a camel!*

[25]"What sorrow awaits you teachers of religious law and you Pharisees. Hypocrites! For you are so careful to clean the outside of the cup and the dish, but inside you are filthy—full of greed and self-indulgence! [26]You blind Pharisee! First wash the inside of the cup and the dish,* and then the outside will become clean, too.

[27]"What sorrow awaits you teachers of religious law and you Pharisees. Hypocrites! For you are like whitewashed tombs—beautiful on the outside but filled on the inside with dead people's bones and all sorts of impurity. [28]Outwardly you look like righteous people, but inwardly your hearts are filled with hypocrisy and lawlessness.

[29]"What sorrow awaits you teachers of religious law and you Pharisees. Hypocrites! For you build tombs for the prophets your ancestors killed, and you decorate the monuments of the godly people your ancestors destroyed. [30]Then you say, 'If we had lived in the days of our ancestors, we would never have joined them in killing the prophets.'

[31]"But in saying that, you testify against yourselves that you are indeed the descendants of those who murdered the prophets. [32]Go ahead and finish what your ancestors started. [33]Snakes! Sons of vipers! How will you escape the judgment of hell?

[34]"Therefore, I am sending you prophets and wise men and teachers of religious law. But you will kill some by crucifixion, and you will flog others with whips in your synagogues, chasing them from city to city. [35]As a result, you will be held responsible for the murder of all godly people of all time—from the murder of righteous Abel to the murder of Zechariah son of Berekiah, whom you killed in the Temple between the sanctuary and the altar. [36]I tell you the truth, this judgment will fall on this very generation.

Jesus Grieves over Jerusalem

[37]"O Jerusalem, Jerusalem, the city that kills the prophets and stones God's messengers! How often I have wanted to gather your children together as a hen protects her chicks beneath her wings, but you wouldn't let me. [38]And now, look, your house is abandoned and desolate.* [39]For I tell you this, you will never see me again until you say, 'Blessings on the one who comes in the name of the LORD!'*"

CHAPTER 24

Jesus Foretells the Future

As Jesus was leaving the Temple grounds, his disciples pointed out to him the various Temple buildings. [2]But he responded, "Do you see

23:13 Some manuscripts add verse 14, *What sorrow awaits you teachers of religious law and you Pharisees. Hypocrites! You shamelessly cheat widows out of their property and then pretend to be pious by making long prayers in public. Because of this, you will be severely punished.* Compare Mark 12:40 and Luke 20:47. **23:15** Greek *of Gehenna;* also in 23:33. **23:23** Greek *tithe the mint, the dill, and the cumin.* **23:24** See Lev 11:4, 23, where gnats and camels are both forbidden as food. **23:26** Some manuscripts do not include *and the dish.* **23:38** Some manuscripts do not include *and desolate.* **23:39** Ps 118:26.

all these buildings? I tell you the truth, they will be completely demolished. Not one stone will be left on top of another!"

3Later, Jesus sat on the Mount of Olives. His disciples came to him privately and said, "Tell us, when will all this happen? What sign will signal your return and the end of the world?*"

4Jesus told them, "Don't let anyone mislead you, 5for many will come in my name, claiming, 'I am the Messiah.' They will deceive many. 6And you will hear of wars and threats of wars, but don't panic. Yes, these things must take place, but the end won't follow immediately. 7Nation will go to war against nation, and kingdom against kingdom. There will be famines and earthquakes in many parts of the world. 8But all this is only the first of the birth pains, with more to come.

9"Then you will be arrested, persecuted, and killed. You will be hated all over the world because you are my followers.* 10And many will turn away from me and betray and hate each other. 11And many false prophets will appear and will deceive many people. 12Sin will be rampant everywhere, and the love of many will grow cold. 13But the one who endures to the end will be saved. 14And the Good News about the Kingdom will be preached throughout the whole world, so that all nations* will hear it; and then the end will come.

15"The day is coming when you will see what Daniel the prophet spoke about—the sacrilegious object that causes desecration* standing in the Holy Place." (Reader, pay attention!) 16"Then those in Judea must flee to the hills. 17A person out on the deck of a roof must not go down into the house to pack. 18A person out in the field must not return even to get a coat. 19How terrible it will be for pregnant women and for nursing mothers in those days. 20And pray that your flight will not be in winter or on the Sabbath. 21For there will be greater anguish than at any time since the world began. And it will never be so great again. 22In fact, unless that time of calamity is shortened, not a single person will survive. But it will be shortened for the sake of God's chosen ones.

23"Then if anyone tells you, 'Look, here is the Messiah,' or 'There he is,' don't believe it. 24For false messiahs and false prophets will rise up and perform great signs and wonders so as to deceive, if possible, even God's chosen ones. 25See, I have warned you about this ahead of time.

26"So if someone tells you, 'Look, the Messiah is out in the desert,' don't bother to go and look. Or, 'Look, he is hiding here,' don't believe it! 27For as the lightning flashes in the east and shines to the west, so it will be when the Son of Man* comes. 28Just as the gathering of vultures shows there is a carcass nearby, so these signs indicate that the end is near.*

29"Immediately after the anguish of those days,

the sun will be darkened,
the moon will give no light,
the stars will fall from the sky,
and the powers in the heavens will be shaken.*

30And then at last, the sign that the Son of Man is coming will appear in the heavens, and there will be deep mourning among all the peoples of the earth. And they will see the Son of Man coming on the clouds of heaven with power and great glory.* 31And he will send out his angels with the mighty blast of a trumpet, and they will gather his chosen ones from all over the world*—from the farthest ends of the earth and heaven.

32"Now learn a lesson from the fig tree. When its branches bud and its leaves begin to sprout, you know that summer is near. 33In the same way, when you see all these things, you can know his return is very near, right at the door. 34I tell you the truth, this generation* will not pass from the scene until all these things take place. 35Heaven and earth will disappear, but my words will never disappear.

36"However, no one knows the day or hour when these things will happen, not even the angels in heaven or the Son himself.* Only the Father knows.

37"When the Son of Man returns, it will be like it was in Noah's day. 38In those days before the flood, the people were enjoying banquets and parties and weddings right up to the time Noah entered his boat. 39People

24:3 Or *the age?* **24:9** Greek *on account of my name.* **24:14** Or *all peoples.* **24:15** Greek *the abomination of desolation.* See Dan 9:27; 11:31; 12:11. **24:27** "Son of Man" is a title Jesus used for himself. **24:28** Greek *Wherever the carcass is, the vultures gather.* **24:29** See Isa 13:10; 34:4; Joel 2:10. **24:30** See Dan 7:13. **24:31** Greek *from the four winds.* **24:34** Or *this age,* or *this nation.* **24:36** Some manuscripts do not include *or the Son himself.*

didn't realize what was going to happen until the flood came and swept them all away. That is the way it will be when the Son of Man comes.

40"Two men will be working together in the field; one will be taken, the other left. 41Two women will be grinding flour at the mill; one will be taken, the other left.

42"So you, too, must keep watch! For you don't know what day your Lord is coming. 43Understand this: If a homeowner knew exactly when a burglar was coming, he would keep watch and not permit his house to be broken into. 44You also must be ready all the time, for the Son of Man will come when least expected.

45"A faithful, sensible servant is one to whom the master can give the responsibility of managing his other household servants and feeding them. 46If the master returns and finds that the servant has done a good job, there will be a reward. 47I tell you the truth, the master will put that servant in charge of all he owns. 48But what if the servant is evil and thinks, 'My master won't be back for a while,' 49and he begins beating the other servants, partying, and getting drunk? 50The master will return unannounced and unexpected, 51and he will cut the servant to pieces and assign him a place with the hypocrites. In that place there will be weeping and gnashing of teeth.

CHAPTER 25

Parable of the Ten Bridesmaids

"Then the Kingdom of Heaven will be like ten bridesmaids* who took their lamps and went to meet the bridegroom. 2Five of them were foolish, and five were wise. 3The five who were foolish didn't take enough olive oil for their lamps, 4but the other five were wise enough to take along extra oil. 5When the bridegroom was delayed, they all became drowsy and fell asleep.

6"At midnight they were roused by the shout, 'Look, the bridegroom is coming! Come out and meet him!'

7"All the bridesmaids got up and prepared their lamps. 8Then the five foolish ones asked the others, 'Please give us some of your oil because our lamps are going out.'

9"But the others replied, 'We don't have enough for all of us. Go to a shop and buy some for yourselves.'

10"But while they were gone to buy oil, the bridegroom came. Then those who were ready went in with him to the marriage feast, and the door was locked. 11Later, when the other five bridesmaids returned, they stood outside, calling, 'Lord! Lord! Open the door for us!'

12"But he called back, 'Believe me, I don't know you!'

13"So you, too, must keep watch! For you do not know the day or hour of my return.

Parable of the Three Servants

14"Again, the Kingdom of Heaven can be illustrated by the story of a man going on a long trip. He called together his servants and entrusted his money to them while he was gone. 15He gave five bags of silver* to one, two bags of silver to another, and one bag of silver to the last—dividing it in proportion to their abilities. He then left on his trip.

16"The servant who received the five bags of silver began to invest the money and earned five more. 17The servant with two bags of silver also went to work and earned two more. 18But the servant who received the one bag of silver dug a hole in the ground and hid the master's money.

19"After a long time their master returned from his trip and called them to give an account of how they had used his money. 20The servant to whom he had entrusted the five bags of silver came forward with five more and said, 'Master, you gave me five bags of silver to invest, and I have earned five more.'

21"The master was full of praise. 'Well done, my good and faithful servant. You have been faithful in handling this small amount, so now I will give you many more responsibilities. Let's celebrate together!*'

22"The servant who had received the two bags of silver came forward and said, 'Master, you gave me two bags of silver to invest, and I have earned two more.'

23"The master said, 'Well done, my good and faithful servant. You have been faithful in handling this small amount, so now I will give

25:1 Or *virgins;* also in 25:7, 11. **25:15** Greek *talents;* also throughout the story. A talent is equal to 75 pounds or 34 kilograms.
25:21 Greek *Enter into the joy of your master* [or *your Lord*]; also in 25:23.

SOMETHING BORROWED, SOMETHING NEW

Randall's mother, Mrs. Scott, and a single mom with three sons were good friends. Mrs. Scott often gave Randall's outgrown clothes to this family. One of the boys was in Randall's class, but he wasn't friendly to Randall. One day Randall overheard the boy talking about the sweater he was wearing. It was a sweater that Randall got from his grandma before she died. The boy said, "I hate this old sweater, but it's the only one I have to wear until my mom can buy me something else." Randall's feelings were really hurt. How can he look at this situation? Read Matthew 25:31-40 and see what you learn.

you many more responsibilities. Let's celebrate together!'

24"Then the servant with the one bag of silver came and said, 'Master, I knew you were a harsh man, harvesting crops you didn't plant and gathering crops you didn't cultivate. 25I was afraid I would lose your money, so I hid it in the earth. Look, here is your money back.'

26"But the master replied, 'You wicked and lazy servant! If you knew I harvested crops I didn't plant and gathered crops I didn't cultivate, 27why didn't you deposit my money in the bank? At least I could have gotten some interest on it.'

28"Then he ordered, 'Take the money from this servant, and give it to the one with the ten bags of silver. 29To those who use well what they are given, even more will be given, and they will have an abundance. But from those who do nothing, even what little they have will be taken away. 30Now throw this useless servant into outer darkness, where there will be weeping and gnashing of teeth.'

The Final Judgment

31"But when the Son of Man* comes in his glory, and all the angels with him, then he will sit upon his glorious throne. 32All the nations* will be gathered in his presence, and he will separate the people as a shepherd separates the sheep from the goats. 33He will place the sheep at his right hand and the goats at his left.

34"Then the King will say to those on his right, 'Come, you who are blessed by my Father, inherit the Kingdom prepared for you from the creation of the world. 35For I was hungry, and you fed me. I was thirsty, and you gave me a drink. I was a stranger, and you invited me into your home. 36I was naked, and you gave me clothing. I was sick, and you cared for me. I was in prison, and you visited me.'

37"Then these righteous ones will reply, 'Lord, when did we ever see you hungry and feed you? Or thirsty and give you something to drink? 38Or a stranger and show you hospitality? Or naked and give you clothing? 39When did we ever see you sick or in prison and visit you?'

40"And the King will say, 'I tell you the truth, when you did it to one of the least of these my brothers and sisters,* you were doing it to me!'

41"Then the King will turn to those on the left and say, 'Away with you, you cursed ones,

25:31 "Son of Man" is a title Jesus used for himself. **25:32** Or *peoples*. **25:40** Greek *my brothers*.

into the eternal fire prepared for the devil
and his demons.* 42For I was hungry, and you
didn't feed me. I was thirsty, and you didn't
give me a drink. 43I was a stranger, and you
didn't invite me into your home. I was naked,
and you didn't give me clothing. I was sick
and in prison, and you didn't visit me.'

44"Then they will reply, 'Lord, when did we
ever see you hungry or thirsty or a stranger or
naked or sick or in prison, and not help you?'

45"And he will answer, 'I tell you the truth,
when you refused to help the least of these
my brothers and sisters, you were refusing to
help me.'

46"And they will go away into eternal pun-
ishment, but the righteous will go into eter-
nal life."

CHAPTER 26

The Plot to Kill Jesus

When Jesus had finished saying all these
things, he said to his disciples, 2"As you know,
Passover begins in two days, and the Son of
Man* will be handed over to be crucified."

3At that same time the leading priests and
elders were meeting at the residence of Caia-
phas, the high priest, 4plotting how to capture
Jesus secretly and kill him. 5"But not during
the Passover celebration," they agreed, "or the
people may riot."

Jesus Anointed at Bethany

6Meanwhile, Jesus was in Bethany at the home
of Simon, a man who had previously had lep-
rosy. 7While he was eating,* a woman came in
with a beautiful alabaster jar of expensive
perfume and poured it over his head.

8The disciples were indignant when they
saw this. "What a waste!" they said. 9"It could
have been sold for a high price and the money
given to the poor."

10But Jesus, aware of this, replied, "Why
criticize this woman for doing such a good
thing to me? 11You will always have the poor
among you, but you will not always have me.
12She has poured this perfume on me to pre-
pare my body for burial. 13I tell you the truth,
wherever the Good News is preached
throughout the world, this woman's deed will
be remembered and discussed."

Judas Agrees to Betray Jesus

14Then Judas Iscariot, one of the twelve disci-
ples, went to the leading priests 15and asked,
"How much will you pay me to betray Jesus to
you?" And they gave him thirty pieces of sil-
ver. 16From that time on, Judas began looking
for an opportunity to betray Jesus.

The Last Supper

17On the first day of the Festival of Unleav-
ened Bread, the disciples came to Jesus and
asked, "Where do you want us to prepare the
Passover meal for you?"

18"As you go into the city," he told them,
"you will see a certain man. Tell him, 'The
Teacher says: My time has come, and I will eat
the Passover meal with my disciples at your
house.'" 19So the disciples did as Jesus told
them and prepared the Passover meal there.

20When it was evening, Jesus sat down at
the table* with the twelve disciples.* 21While
they were eating, he said, "I tell you the truth,
one of you will betray me."

22Greatly distressed, each one asked in
turn, "Am I the one, Lord?"

23He replied, "One of you who has just
eaten from this bowl with me will betray me.
24For the Son of Man must die, as the Scrip-
tures declared long ago. But how terrible it
will be for the one who betrays him. It would
be far better for that man if he had never
been born!"

25Judas, the one who would betray him,
also asked, "Rabbi, am I the one?"

And Jesus told him, "You have said it."

26As they were eating, Jesus took some
bread and blessed it. Then he broke it in
pieces and gave it to the disciples, saying,
"Take this and eat it, for this is my body."

27And he took a cup of wine and gave
thanks to God for it. He gave it to them and
said, "Each of you drink from it, 28for this is
my blood, which confirms the covenant* be-
tween God and his people. It is poured out as
a sacrifice to forgive the sins of many. 29Mark
my words—I will not drink wine again until
the day I drink it new with you in my Father's
Kingdom."

30Then they sang a hymn and went out to
the Mount of Olives.

25:41 Greek *his angels*. **26:2** "Son of Man" is a title Jesus used for himself. **26:7** Or *reclining*. **26:20a** Or *Jesus reclined*. **26:20b** Some manuscripts read *the Twelve*. **26:28** Some manuscripts read *the new covenant*.

Jesus Predicts Peter's Denial

31On the way, Jesus told them, "Tonight all of
you will desert me. For the Scriptures say,

'God will strike* the Shepherd,
and the sheep of the flock will be
scattered.'

32But after I have been raised from the dead, I
will go ahead of you to Galilee and meet you
there."

33Peter declared, "Even if everyone else
deserts you, I will never desert you."

34Jesus replied, "I tell you the truth, Peter—
this very night, before the rooster crows, you
will deny three times that you even know
me."

35"No!" Peter insisted. "Even if I have to die
with you, I will never deny you!" And all the
other disciples vowed the same.

Jesus Prays in Gethsemane

36Then Jesus went with them to the olive
grove called Gethsemane, and he said, "Sit
here while I go over there to pray." 37He took
Peter and Zebedee's two sons, James and
John, and he became anguished and dis-
tressed. 38He told them, "My soul is crushed
with grief to the point of death. Stay here and
keep watch with me."

39He went on a little farther and bowed
with his face to the ground, praying, "My Fa-
ther! If it is possible, let this cup of suffering
be taken away from me. Yet I want your will to
be done, not mine."

40Then he returned to the disciples and
found them asleep. He said to Peter, "Could-
n't you watch with me even one hour? 41Keep
watch and pray, so that you will not give in to
temptation. For the spirit is willing, but the
body is weak!"

42Then Jesus left them a second time and
prayed, "My Father! If this cup cannot be
taken away* unless I drink it, your will be
done." 43When he returned to them again,
he found them sleeping, for they couldn't
keep their eyes open.

44So he went to pray a third time, saying the
same things again. 45Then he came to the dis-
ciples and said, "Go ahead and sleep. Have
your rest. But look—the time has come. The
Son of Man is betrayed into the hands of sin-
ners. 46Up, let's be going. Look, my betrayer is
here!"

Jesus Is Betrayed and Arrested

47And even as Jesus said this, Judas, one of
the twelve disciples, arrived with a crowd of
men armed with swords and clubs. They had
been sent by the leading priests and elders of
the people. 48The traitor, Judas, had given
them a prearranged signal: "You will know
which one to arrest when I greet him with a
kiss." 49So Judas came straight to Jesus.
"Greetings, Rabbi!" he exclaimed and gave
him the kiss.

50Jesus said, "My friend, go ahead and do
what you have come for."

Then the others grabbed Jesus and ar-
rested him. 51But one of the men with Jesus
pulled out his sword and struck the high
priest's slave, slashing off his ear.

52"Put away your sword," Jesus told him.
"Those who use the sword will die by the
sword. 53Don't you realize that I could ask my
Father for thousands* of angels to protect us,
and he would send them instantly? 54But if I
did, how would the Scriptures be fulfilled
that describe what must happen now?"

55Then Jesus said to the crowd, "Am I some
dangerous revolutionary, that you come with
swords and clubs to arrest me? Why didn't
you arrest me in the Temple? I was there
teaching every day. 56But this is all happening
to fulfill the words of the prophets as re-
corded in the Scriptures." At that point, all the
disciples deserted him and fled.

Jesus before the Council

57Then the people who had arrested Jesus led
him to the home of Caiaphas, the high priest,
where the teachers of religious law and the el-
ders had gathered. 58Meanwhile, Peter fol-
lowed him at a distance and came to the high
priest's courtyard. He went in and sat with the
guards and waited to see how it would all end.

59Inside, the leading priests and the entire
high council* were trying to find witnesses
who would lie about Jesus, so they could put
him to death. 60But even though they found
many who agreed to give false witness, they
could not use anyone's testimony. Finally,
two men came forward 61who declared, "This

26:31 Greek *I will strike.* Zech 13:7. **26:42** Greek *If this cannot pass.* **26:53** Greek *twelve legions.* **26:59** Greek *the Sanhedrin.*

man said, 'I am able to destroy the Temple of God and rebuild it in three days.'"

62Then the high priest stood up and said to Jesus, "Well, aren't you going to answer these charges? What do you have to say for yourself?" 63But Jesus remained silent. Then the high priest said to him, "I demand in the name of the living God—tell us if you are the Messiah, the Son of God."

64Jesus replied, "You have said it. And in the future you will see the Son of Man seated in the place of power at God's right hand* and coming on the clouds of heaven."*

65Then the high priest tore his clothing to show his horror and said, "Blasphemy! Why do we need other witnesses? You have all heard his blasphemy. 66What is your verdict?"

"Guilty!" they shouted. "He deserves to die!"

67Then they began to spit in Jesus' face and beat him with their fists. And some slapped him, 68jeering, "Prophesy to us, you Messiah! Who hit you that time?"

Peter Denies Jesus

69Meanwhile, Peter was sitting outside in the courtyard. A servant girl came over and said to him, "You were one of those with Jesus the Galilean."

70But Peter denied it in front of everyone. "I don't know what you're talking about," he said.

71Later, out by the gate, another servant girl noticed him and said to those standing around, "This man was with Jesus of Nazareth.*"

72Again Peter denied it, this time with an oath. "I don't even know the man," he said.

73A little later some of the other bystanders came over to Peter and said, "You must be one of them; we can tell by your Galilean accent."

74Peter swore, "A curse on me if I'm lying—I don't know the man!" And immediately the rooster crowed.

75Suddenly, Jesus' words flashed through Peter's mind: "Before the rooster crows, you will deny three times that you even know me." And he went away, weeping bitterly.

CHAPTER 27

Judas Hangs Himself

Very early in the morning the leading priests and the elders of the people met again to lay plans for putting Jesus to death. 2Then they bound him, led him away, and took him to Pilate, the Roman governor.

3When Judas, who had betrayed him, realized that Jesus had been condemned to die, he was filled with remorse. So he took the thirty pieces of silver back to the leading priests and the elders. 4"I have sinned," he declared, "for I have betrayed an innocent man."

"What do we care?" they retorted. "That's your problem."

5Then Judas threw the silver coins down in the Temple and went out and hanged himself.

6The leading priests picked up the coins. "It wouldn't be right to put this money in the Temple treasury," they said, "since it was payment for murder."* 7After some discussion they finally decided to buy the potter's field, and they made it into a cemetery for foreigners. 8That is why the field is still called the Field of Blood. 9This fulfilled the prophecy of Jeremiah that says,

> "They took* the thirty pieces of silver—
> the price at which he was valued by the people of Israel,
> 10 and purchased the potter's field,
> as the LORD directed.*"

Jesus' Trial before Pilate

11Now Jesus was standing before Pilate, the Roman governor. "Are you the king of the Jews?" the governor asked him.

Jesus replied, "You have said it."

12But when the leading priests and the elders made their accusations against him, Jesus remained silent. 13"Don't you hear all these charges they are bringing against you?" Pilate demanded. 14But Jesus made no response to any of the charges, much to the governor's surprise.

15Now it was the governor's custom each year during the Passover celebration to release one prisoner to the crowd—anyone they wanted. 16This year there was a notorious prisoner, a man named Barabbas.* 17As the crowds gathered before Pilate's house that morning, he asked them, "Which one do you want me to release to you—Barabbas, or Jesus who is called the Messiah?" 18(He knew very

26:64a Greek *seated at the right hand of the power.* See Ps 110:1. **26:64b** See Dan 7:13. **26:71** Or *Jesus the Nazarene.* **27:6** Greek *since it is the price for blood.* **27:9** Or *I took.* **27:9-10** Greek *as the LORD directed me.* Zech 11:12-13; Jer 32:6-9. **27:16** Some manuscripts read *Jesus Barabbas;* also in 27:17.

well that the religious leaders had arrested Jesus out of envy.)

[19]Just then, as Pilate was sitting on the judgment seat, his wife sent him this message: "Leave that innocent man alone. I suffered through a terrible nightmare about him last night."

[20]Meanwhile, the leading priests and the elders persuaded the crowd to ask for Barabbas to be released and for Jesus to be put to death. [21]So the governor asked again, "Which of these two do you want me to release to you?"

The crowd shouted back, "Barabbas!"

[22]Pilate responded, "Then what should I do with Jesus who is called the Messiah?"

They shouted back, "Crucify him!"

[23]"Why?" Pilate demanded. "What crime has he committed?"

But the mob roared even louder, "Crucify him!"

[24]Pilate saw that he wasn't getting anywhere and that a riot was developing. So he sent for a bowl of water and washed his hands before the crowd, saying, "I am innocent of this man's blood. The responsibility is yours!"

[25]And all the people yelled back, "We will take responsibility for his death—we and our children!"*

[26]So Pilate released Barabbas to them. He ordered Jesus flogged with a lead-tipped whip, then turned him over to the Roman soldiers to be crucified.

The Soldiers Mock Jesus

[27]Some of the governor's soldiers took Jesus into their headquarters* and called out the entire regiment. [28]They stripped him and put a scarlet robe on him. [29]They wove thorn branches into a crown and put it on his head, and they placed a reed stick in his right hand as a scepter. Then they knelt before him in mockery and taunted, "Hail! King of the Jews!" [30]And they spit on him and grabbed the stick and struck him on the head with it. [31]When they were finally tired of mocking him, they took off the robe and put his own clothes on him again. Then they led him away to be crucified.

The Crucifixion

[32]Along the way, they came across a man named Simon, who was from Cyrene,* and the soldiers forced him to carry Jesus' cross. [33]And they went out to a place called Golgotha (which means "Place of the Skull"). [34]The soldiers gave him wine mixed with bitter gall, but when he had tasted it, he refused to drink it.

[35]After they had nailed him to the cross, the soldiers gambled for his clothes by throwing dice.* [36]Then they sat around and kept guard as he hung there. [37]A sign was fastened above Jesus' head, announcing the charge against him. It read: "This is Jesus, the King of the Jews." [38]Two revolutionaries* were crucified with him, one on his right and one on his left.

[39]The people passing by shouted abuse, shaking their heads in mockery. [40]"Look at you now!" they yelled at him. "You said you were going to destroy the Temple and rebuild it in three days. Well then, if you are the Son of God, save yourself and come down from the cross!"

[41]The leading priests, the teachers of religious law, and the elders also mocked Jesus. [42]"He saved others," they scoffed, "but he can't save himself! So he is the King of Israel, is he? Let him come down from the cross right now, and we will believe in him! [43]He trusted God, so let God rescue him now if he wants him! For he said, 'I am the Son of God.'" [44]Even the revolutionaries who were crucified with him ridiculed him in the same way.

The Death of Jesus

[45]At noon, darkness fell across the whole land until three o'clock. [46]At about three o'clock, Jesus called out with a loud voice, *"Eli, Eli,* lema sabachthani?"* which means "My God, my God, why have you abandoned me?"*

[47]Some of the bystanders misunderstood and thought he was calling for the prophet Elijah. [48]One of them ran and filled a sponge with sour wine, holding it up to him on a reed stick so he could drink. [49]But the rest said,

27:25 Greek *"His blood be on us and on our children."* **27:27** Or *into the Praetorium.* **27:32** *Cyrene* was a city in northern Africa. **27:35** Greek *by casting lots.* A few late manuscripts add *This fulfilled the word of the prophet: "They divided my garments among themselves and cast lots for my robe."* See Ps 22:18. **27:38** Or *criminals;* also in 27:44. **27:46a** Some manuscripts read *Eloi, Eloi.* **27:46b** Ps 22:1.

"Wait! Let's see whether Elijah comes to save him."*

50Then Jesus shouted out again, and he released his spirit. 51At that moment the curtain in the sanctuary of the Temple was torn in two, from top to bottom. The earth shook, rocks split apart, 52and tombs opened. The bodies of many godly men and women who had died were raised from the dead. 53They left the cemetery after Jesus' resurrection, went into the holy city of Jerusalem, and appeared to many people.

54The Roman officer* and the other soldiers at the crucifixion were terrified by the earthquake and all that had happened. They said, "This man truly was the Son of God!"

55And many women who had come from Galilee with Jesus to care for him were watching from a distance. 56Among them were Mary Magdalene, Mary (the mother of James and Joseph), and the mother of James and John, the sons of Zebedee.

The Burial of Jesus

57As evening approached, Joseph, a rich man from Arimathea who had become a follower of Jesus, 58went to Pilate and asked for Jesus' body. And Pilate issued an order to release it to him. 59Joseph took the body and wrapped it in a long sheet of clean linen cloth. 60He placed it in his own new tomb, which had been carved out of the rock. Then he rolled a great stone across the entrance and left. 61Both Mary Magdalene and the other Mary were sitting across from the tomb and watching.

The Guard at the Tomb

62The next day, on the Sabbath,* the leading priests and Pharisees went to see Pilate. 63They told him, "Sir, we remember what that deceiver once said while he was still alive: 'After three days I will rise from the dead.' 64So we request that you seal the tomb until the third day. This will prevent his disciples from coming and stealing his body and then telling everyone he was raised from the dead! If that happens, we'll be worse off than we were at first."

65Pilate replied, "Take guards and secure it the best you can." 66So they sealed the tomb and posted guards to protect it.

AMAZING FACTS

You know Jesus came back to life. But did you know many godly people did too? Their graves opened up and they walked away!

MATTHEW 27:50-53

CHAPTER 28

The Resurrection

Early on Sunday morning,* as the new day was dawning, Mary Magdalene and the other Mary went out to visit the tomb.

2Suddenly there was a great earthquake! For an angel of the Lord came down from heaven, rolled aside the stone, and sat on it. 3His face shone like lightning, and his clothing was as white as snow. 4The guards shook with fear when they saw him, and they fell into a dead faint.

5Then the angel spoke to the women. "Don't be afraid!" he said. "I know you are looking for Jesus, who was crucified. 6He isn't here! He is risen from the dead, just as he said would happen. Come, see where his body was lying. 7And now, go quickly and tell his disciples that he has risen from the dead, and he is going ahead of you to Galilee. You will see him there. Remember what I have told you."

8The women ran quickly from the tomb. They were very frightened but also filled with great joy, and they rushed to give the disciples the angel's message. 9And as they went, Jesus met them and greeted them. And they ran to him, grasped his feet, and worshiped him. 10Then Jesus said to them, "Don't be afraid! Go

27:49 Some manuscripts add *And another took a spear and pierced his side, and out flowed water and blood.* Compare John 19:34. **27:54** Greek *The centurion.* **27:62** Or *On the next day, which is after the Preparation.* **28:1** Greek *After the Sabbath, on the first day of the week.*

tell my brothers to leave for Galilee, and they will see me there."

The Report of the Guard

[11]As the women were on their way, some of the guards went into the city and told the leading priests what had happened. [12]A meeting with the elders was called, and they decided to give the soldiers a large bribe. [13]They told the soldiers, "You must say, 'Jesus' disciples came during the night while we were sleeping, and they stole his body.' [14]If the governor hears about it, we'll stand up for you so you won't get in trouble." [15]So the guards accepted the bribe and said what they were told to say. Their story spread widely among the Jews, and they still tell it today.

The Great Commission

[16]Then the eleven disciples left for Galilee, going to the mountain where Jesus had told them to go. [17]When they saw him, they worshiped him—but some of them doubted!

[18]Jesus came and told his disciples, "I have been given all authority in heaven and on earth. [19]Therefore, go and make disciples of all the nations,* baptizing them in the name of the Father and the Son and the Holy Spirit. [20]Teach these new disciples to obey all the commands I have given you. And be sure of this: I am with you always, even to the end of the age."

28:19 Or *all peoples.*

mark

WHO
Jesus, the disciples, Pilate, Mary Magdalene, and the Jewish religious leaders.

WHERE
In Rome.

WHEN
Between AD 55 and 65.

WHY
To present the person, work, and teachings of Jesus Christ.

"Come, follow me, and I will show you how to fish for people!"
MARK 1:17

Jesus surprised people. He turned their thinking upside down and inside out. He taught that whoever wanted to be great should be a servant. That's a different spin on being number one, isn't it? Jesus *is* the greatest—God himself and our Savior—but he entered history as a servant and gave his life for us.

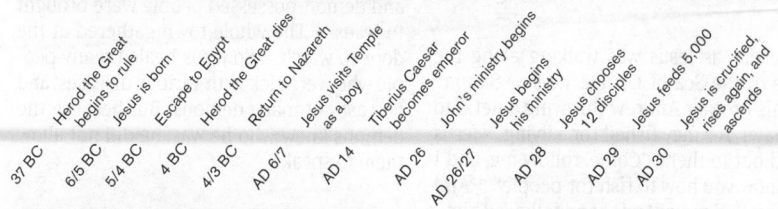

Watch Jesus in action and listen carefully to what he says.

CHAPTER 1

John the Baptist Prepares the Way

This is the Good News about Jesus the Messiah, the Son of God.* It began [2]just as the prophet Isaiah had written:

"Look, I am sending my messenger ahead
of you,
and he will prepare your way.*

[3] He is a voice shouting in the wilderness,
'Prepare the way for the LORD's coming!
Clear the road for him!'*"

[4]This messenger was John the Baptist. He was in the wilderness and preached that people should be baptized to show that they had repented of their sins and turned to God to be forgiven. [5]All of Judea, including all the people

1:1 Some manuscripts do not include *the Son of God*. **1:2** Mal 3:1. **1:3** Isa 40:3 (Greek version).

of Jerusalem, went out to see and hear John. And when they confessed their sins, he baptized them in the Jordan River. [6]His clothes were woven from coarse camel hair, and he wore a leather belt around his waist. For food he ate locusts and wild honey.

[7]John announced: "Someone is coming soon who is greater than I am—so much greater that I'm not even worthy to stoop down like a slave and untie the straps of his sandals. [8]I baptize you with* water, but he will baptize you with the Holy Spirit!"

The Baptism and Temptation of Jesus

[9]One day Jesus came from Nazareth in Galilee, and John baptized him in the Jordan River. [10]As Jesus came up out of the water, he saw the heavens splitting apart and the Holy Spirit descending on him* like a dove. [11]And a voice from heaven said, "You are my dearly loved Son, and you bring me great joy."

[12]The Spirit then compelled Jesus to go into the wilderness, [13]where he was tempted by Satan for forty days. He was out among the wild animals, and angels took care of him.

[14]Later on, after John was arrested, Jesus went into Galilee, where he preached God's Good News.* [15]"The time promised by God has come at last!" he announced. "The Kingdom of God is near! Repent of your sins and believe the Good News!"

The First Disciples

[16]One day as Jesus was walking along the shore of the Sea of Galilee, he saw Simon* and his brother Andrew throwing a net into the water, for they fished for a living. [17]Jesus called out to them, "Come, follow me, and I will show you how to fish for people!" [18]And they left their nets at once and followed him.

[19]A little farther up the shore Jesus saw Zebedee's sons, James and John, in a boat repairing their nets. [20]He called them at once, and they also followed him, leaving their father, Zebedee, in the boat with the hired men.

Jesus Casts Out an Evil Spirit

[21]Jesus and his companions went to the town of Capernaum. When the Sabbath day came, he went into the synagogue and began to teach. [22]The people were amazed at his teaching, for he taught with real authority—quite unlike the teachers of religious law.

[23]Suddenly, a man in the synagogue who was possessed by an evil* spirit began shouting, [24]"Why are you interfering with us, Jesus of Nazareth? Have you come to destroy us? I know who you are—the Holy One of God!"

[25]Jesus cut him short. "Be quiet! Come out of the man," he ordered. [26]At that, the evil spirit screamed, threw the man into a convulsion, and then came out of him.

[27]Amazement gripped the audience, and they began to discuss what had happened. "What sort of new teaching is this?" they asked excitedly. "It has such authority! Even evil spirits obey his orders!" [28]The news about Jesus spread quickly throughout the entire region of Galilee.

Jesus Heals Many People

[29]After Jesus left the synagogue with James and John, they went to Simon and Andrew's home. [30]Now Simon's mother-in-law was sick in bed with a high fever. They told Jesus about her right away. [31]So he went to her bedside, took her by the hand, and helped her sit up. Then the fever left her, and she prepared a meal for them.

[32]That evening after sunset, many sick and demon-possessed people were brought to Jesus. [33]The whole town gathered at the door to watch. [34]So Jesus healed many people who were sick with various diseases, and he cast out many demons. But because the demons knew who he was, he did not allow them to speak.

Jesus Preaches in Galilee

[35]Before daybreak the next morning, Jesus got up and went out to an isolated place to pray. [36]Later Simon and the others went out to find him. [37]When they found him, they said, "Everyone is looking for you."

[38]But Jesus replied, "We must go on to other towns as well, and I will preach to them, too. That is why I came." [39]So he traveled throughout the region of Galilee, preaching in the synagogues and casting out demons.

1:8 Or *in;* also in 1:8b. **1:10** Or *toward him,* or *into him.* **1:14** Some manuscripts read *the Good News of the Kingdom of God.* **1:16** *Simon* is called "Peter" in 3:16 and thereafter. **1:23** Greek *unclean;* also in 1:26, 27.

THE TWELVE DISCIPLES Jesus' disciples were ordinary men who became extraordinary because of Jesus Christ. Even though they didn't really understand who he was during his lifetime, they became powerful witnesses to his resurrection. Their lives were transformed by God's power. The story of Jesus' disciples in the Gospels continues in the book of Acts and many of the Epistles.

Name	A Key Lesson from His Life	Selected References
SIMON PETER (son of John)	Christians fail at times; but when they return to Jesus, he forgives them and strengthens their faith.	Matthew 4:18-20 Mark 8:29-33 Luke 22:31-34 John 21:15-19 Acts 2:14-41; 10:1–11:18
JAMES (son of Zebedee) He and his brother John were called the "Sons of Thunder."	Christians must be willing to die for Jesus.	Mark 3:17; 10:35-40 Luke 9:52-56 Acts 12:1-2
JOHN (son of Zebedee), James's brother, and "the disciple Jesus loved"	The transforming power of the love of Christ is available to all.	Mark 1:19; 10:35-40 Luke 9:52-56 John 19:26-27; 21:20-24
ANDREW (Peter's brother)	Christians are to tell other people about Jesus.	Matthew 4:18-20 John 1:35-42; 6:8-9; 12:20-22
PHILIP	God uses our questions to teach us.	Matthew 10:3 John 1:43-46; 6:2-7; 12:20-22; 14:8-11
BARTHOLOMEW (Nathanael)	Jesus respects honesty in people—even if they challenge him because of it.	Mark 3:18 John 1:45-51; 21:1-13
MATTHEW (Levi)	Christianity is not for people who think they're already good; it is for people who know they've failed and want help.	Matthew 9:9-13 Mark 2:15-17 Luke 5:27-32
THOMAS (the twin)	Even when Christians have serious doubts, Jesus reaches out to them to restore their faith.	Matthew 10:3 John 14:5; 20:24-29; 21:1-13
JAMES (son of Alphaeus)	Unknown.	Matthew 10:3 Mark 3:18 Luke 6:15
THADDAEUS (Judas, son of James)	Christians follow Jesus because they believe in him; they do not always understand the details of God's plan.	Matthew 10:3 Mark 3:18 John 14:22
SIMON THE ZEALOT	If we are willing to give up our plans for the future, we can participate in Jesus' plans.	Matthew 10:4 Mark 3:18 Luke 6:15
JUDAS ISCARIOT	It is not enough to be familiar with Jesus' teaching. Jesus' true followers love and obey him.	Matthew 26:20-25 Luke 22:47-48 John 12:4-8

Jesus Heals a Man with Leprosy

40A man with leprosy came and knelt in front
of Jesus, begging to be healed. "If you are will-
ing, you can heal me and make me clean," he
said.
41Moved with compassion,* Jesus reached
out and touched him. "I am willing," he said.
"Be healed!" 42Instantly the leprosy disap-
peared, and the man was healed. 43Then Jesus
sent him on his way with a stern warning:
44"Don't tell anyone about this. Instead, go to
the priest and let him examine you. Take along
the offering required in the law of Moses for
those who have been healed of leprosy.* This
will be a public testimony that you have been
cleansed."
45But the man went and spread the word,
proclaiming to everyone what had happened.
As a result, large crowds soon surrounded
Jesus, and he couldn't publicly enter a town
anywhere. He had to stay out in the secluded
places, but people from everywhere kept com-
ing to him.

CHAPTER 2

Jesus Heals a Paralyzed Man

When Jesus returned to Capernaum several
days later, the news spread quickly that he
was back home. 2Soon the house where he
was staying was so packed with visitors that
there was no more room, even outside the
door. While he was preaching God's word to
them, 3four men arrived carrying a para-
lyzed man on a mat. 4They couldn't bring
him to Jesus because of the crowd, so they
dug a hole through the roof above his head.
Then they lowered the man on his mat, right
down in front of Jesus. 5Seeing their faith,
Jesus said to the paralyzed man, "My child,
your sins are forgiven."
6But some of the teachers of religious law
who were sitting there thought to themselves,
7"What is he saying? This is blasphemy! Only
God can forgive sins!"
8Jesus knew immediately what they were
thinking, so he asked them, "Why do you
question this in your hearts? 9Is it easier to
say to the paralyzed man 'Your sins are for-
given,' or 'Stand up, pick up your mat, and
walk'? 10So I will prove to you that the Son of
Man* has the authority on earth to forgive
sins." Then Jesus turned to the paralyzed
man and said, 11"Stand up, pick up your mat,
and go home!"
12And the man jumped up, grabbed his
mat, and walked out through the stunned on-
lookers. They were all amazed and praised
God, exclaiming, "We've never seen anything
like this before!"

Jesus Calls Levi (Matthew)

13Then Jesus went out to the lakeshore again
and taught the crowds that were coming to
him. 14As he walked along, he saw Levi son of
Alphaeus sitting at his tax collector's booth.
"Follow me and be my disciple," Jesus said to
him. So Levi got up and followed him.
15Later, Levi invited Jesus and his disciples
to his home as dinner guests, along with many
tax collectors and other disreputable sinners.
(There were many people of this kind among
Jesus' followers.) 16But when the teachers of
religious law who were Pharisees* saw him
eating with tax collectors and other sinners,
they asked his disciples, "Why does he eat
with such scum?*"
17When Jesus heard this, he told them,
"Healthy people don't need a doctor—sick
people do. I have come to call not those who
think they are righteous, but those who know
they are sinners."

A Discussion about Fasting

18Once when John's disciples and the Phari-
sees were fasting, some people came to Jesus
and asked, "Why don't your disciples fast like
John's disciples and the Pharisees do?"
19Jesus replied, "Do wedding guests fast
while celebrating with the groom? Of course
not. They can't fast while the groom is with
them. 20But someday the groom will be taken
away from them, and then they will fast.
21"Besides, who would patch old clothing
with new cloth? For the new patch would
shrink and rip away from the old cloth, leav-
ing an even bigger tear than before.
22"And no one puts new wine into old
wineskins. For the wine would burst the
wineskins, and the wine and the skins would
both be lost. New wine calls for new wine-
skins."

1:41 Some manuscripts read *Moved with anger*. **1:44** See Lev 14:2-32. **2:10** "Son of Man" is a title Jesus used for himself.
2:16a Greek *the scribes of the Pharisees*. **2:16b** Greek *with tax collectors and sinners?*

Matthew

I was a tax collector. If someone owed me five gold coins, I said they owed six and kept the extra. That's how I got paid. What's wrong with that?

One day as people passed by I called out, "Pay your taxes or get in trouble!" One man who stopped didn't want to talk about money. He wanted to talk about *me*. He asked me to follow him and become his disciple, so I did.

I had a dinner for Jesus in my home. I invited friends to meet him. Many sat around the table listening. The Pharisees didn't like this because these religious leaders hated me. They couldn't believe Jesus would eat with a sinner like me. I'm sure glad he did.

Read about Matthew's dinner in Matthew 9:9-13 and Mark 2:13-17.

A Discussion about the Sabbath

[23]One Sabbath day as Jesus was walking through some grainfields, his disciples began breaking off heads of grain to eat. [24]But the Pharisees said to Jesus, "Look, why are they breaking the law by harvesting grain on the Sabbath?"

[25]Jesus said to them, "Haven't you ever read in the Scriptures what David did when he and his companions were hungry? [26]He went into the house of God (during the days when Abiathar was high priest) and broke the law by eating the sacred loaves of bread that only the priests are allowed to eat. He also gave some to his companions."

[27]Then Jesus said to them, "The Sabbath was made to meet the needs of people, and not people to meet the requirements of the Sabbath. [28]So the Son of Man is Lord, even over the Sabbath!"

CHAPTER 3

Jesus Heals on the Sabbath

Jesus went into the synagogue again and noticed a man with a deformed hand. [2]Since it was the Sabbath, Jesus' enemies watched him closely. If he healed the man's hand, they planned to accuse him of working on the Sabbath.

[3]Jesus said to the man with the deformed hand, "Come and stand in front of everyone." [4]Then he turned to his critics and asked, "Does the law permit good deeds on the Sabbath, or is it a day for doing evil? Is this a day to save life or to destroy it?" But they wouldn't answer him.

[5]He looked around at them angrily and was deeply saddened by their hard hearts. Then he said to the man, "Hold out your hand." So the man held out his hand, and it was restored! [6]At once the Pharisees went away and met with the supporters of Herod to plot how to kill Jesus.

Crowds Follow Jesus

[7]Jesus went out to the lake with his disciples, and a large crowd followed him. They came from all over Galilee, Judea, [8]Jerusalem, Idumea, from east of the Jordan River, and even from as far north as Tyre and Sidon. The news about his miracles had spread far and wide, and vast numbers of people came to see him.

[9]Jesus instructed his disciples to have a boat ready so the crowd would not crush him. [10]He had healed many people that day, so all the sick people eagerly pushed forward to touch him. [11]And whenever those possessed by evil*

3:11 Greek *unclean;* also in 3:30.

spirits caught sight of him, the spirits would
throw them to the ground in front of him
shrieking, "You are the Son of God!" [12]But
Jesus sternly commanded the spirits not to re-
veal who he was.

Jesus Chooses the Twelve Apostles

[13]Afterward Jesus went up on a mountain and
called out the ones he wanted to go with him.
And they came to him. [14]Then he appointed
twelve of them and called them his apostles.*
They were to accompany him, and he would
send them out to preach, [15]giving them au-
thority to cast out demons. [16]These are the
twelve he chose:

Simon (whom he named Peter),
[17] James and John (the sons of Zebedee, but
Jesus nicknamed them "Sons of
Thunder"*),
[18] Andrew,
Philip,
Bartholomew,
Matthew,
Thomas,
James (son of Alphaeus),
Thaddaeus,
Simon (the zealot*),
[19] Judas Iscariot (who later betrayed him).

Jesus and the Prince of Demons

[20]One time Jesus entered a house, and the
crowds began to gather again. Soon he and
his disciples couldn't even find time to eat.
[21]When his family heard what was happen-
ing, they tried to take him away. "He's out of
his mind," they said.

[22]But the teachers of religious law who had
arrived from Jerusalem said, "He's possessed
by Satan,* the prince of demons. That's
where he gets the power to cast out demons."

[23]Jesus called them over and responded
with an illustration. "How can Satan cast out
Satan?" he asked. [24]"A kingdom divided by
civil war will collapse. [25]Similarly, a family
splintered by feuding will fall apart. [26]And if
Satan is divided and fights against himself,
how can he stand? He would never survive.
[27]Let me illustrate this further. Who is power-
ful enough to enter the house of a strong man
like Satan and plunder his goods? Only some-
one even stronger—someone who could tie
him up and then plunder his house.

[28]"I tell you the truth, all sin and blasphemy
can be forgiven, [29]but anyone who blas-
phemes the Holy Spirit will never be forgiven.
This is a sin with eternal consequences." [30]He
told them this because they were saying, "He's
possessed by an evil spirit."

The True Family of Jesus

[31]Then Jesus' mother and brothers came to
see him. They stood outside and sent word
for him to come out and talk with them.
[32]There was a crowd sitting around Jesus, and
someone said, "Your mother and your broth-
ers* are outside asking for you."

[33]Jesus replied, "Who is my mother? Who
are my brothers?" [34]Then he looked at those
around him and said, "Look, these are my
mother and brothers. [35]Anyone who does
God's will is my brother and sister and
mother."

CHAPTER 4

Parable of the Farmer Scattering Seed

Once again Jesus began teaching by the
lakeshore. A very large crowd soon gathered
around him, so he got into a boat. Then he sat
in the boat while all the people remained on
the shore. [2]He taught them by telling many
stories in the form of parables, such as this
one:

[3]"Listen! A farmer went out to plant some
seed. [4]As he scattered it across his field, some
of the seed fell on a footpath, and the birds
came and ate it. [5]Other seed fell on shallow
soil with underlying rock. The seed sprouted
quickly because the soil was shallow. [6]But the
plant soon wilted under the hot sun, and since
it didn't have deep roots, it died. [7]Other seed
fell among thorns that grew up and choked
out the tender plants so they produced no
grain. [8]Still other seeds fell on fertile soil, and
they sprouted, grew, and produced a crop
that was thirty, sixty, and even a hundred
times as much as had been planted!" [9]Then
he said, "Anyone with ears to hear should lis-
ten and understand."

[10]Later, when Jesus was alone with the
twelve disciples and with the others who were

3:14 Some manuscripts do not include *and called them his apostles.* **3:17** Greek *whom he named Boanerges, which means Sons of Thunder.* **3:18** Greek *the Cananean,* an Aramaic term for Jewish nationalists. **3:22** Greek *Beelzeboul;* other manuscripts read *Beezeboul;* Latin version reads *Beelzebub.* **3:32** Some manuscripts add *and sisters.*

gathered around, they asked him what the parables meant.

[11]He replied, "You are permitted to understand the secret* of the Kingdom of God. But I use parables for everything I say to outsiders, [12]so that the Scriptures might be fulfilled:

'When they see what I do,
they will learn nothing.
When they hear what I say,
they will not understand.
Otherwise, they will turn to me
and be forgiven.'*"

[13]Then Jesus said to them, "If you can't understand the meaning of this parable, how will you understand all the other parables? [14]The farmer plants seed by taking God's word to others. [15]The seed that fell on the footpath represents those who hear the message, only to have Satan come at once and take it away. [16]The seed on the rocky soil represents those who hear the message and immediately receive it with joy. [17]But since they don't have deep roots, they don't last long. They fall away as soon as they have problems or are persecuted for believing God's word. [18]The seed that fell among the thorns represents others who hear God's word, [19]but all too quickly the message is crowded out by the worries of this life, the lure of wealth, and the desire for other things, so no fruit is produced. [20]And the seed that fell on good soil represents those who hear and accept God's word and produce a harvest of thirty, sixty, or even a hundred times as much as had been planted!"

Parable of the Lamp

[21]Then Jesus asked them, "Would anyone light a lamp and then put it under a basket or under a bed? Of course not! A lamp is placed on a stand, where its light will shine. [22]For everything that is hidden will eventually be brought into the open, and every secret will be brought to light. [23]Anyone with ears to hear should listen and understand."

[24]Then he added, "Pay close attention to what you hear. The closer you listen, the more understanding you will be given*—and you will receive even more. [25]To those who listen to my teaching, more understanding will be given. But for those who are not listening, even what little understanding they have will be taken away from them."

How can I understand what God wants me to do with my life?

[Jesus said,] "To those who listen to my teaching, more understanding will be given." MARK 4:25

Parable of the Growing Seed

[26]Jesus also said, "The Kingdom of God is like a farmer who scatters seed on the ground. [27]Night and day, while he's asleep or awake, the seed sprouts and grows, but he does not understand how it happens. [28]The earth produces the crops on its own. First a leaf blade pushes through, then the heads of wheat are formed, and finally the grain ripens. [29]And as soon as the grain is ready, the farmer comes and harvests it with a sickle, for the harvest time has come."

Parable of the Mustard Seed

[30]Jesus said, "How can I describe the Kingdom of God? What story should I use to illustrate it? [31]It is like a mustard seed planted in the ground. It is the smallest of all seeds, [32]but it becomes the largest of all garden plants; it grows long branches, and birds can make nests in its shade."

[33]Jesus used many similar stories and illustrations to teach the people as much as they could understand. [34]In fact, in his public ministry he never taught without using parables; but afterward, when he was alone with his disciples, he explained everything to them.

Jesus Calms the Storm

[35]As evening came, Jesus said to his disciples, "Let's cross to the other side of the lake." [36]So they took Jesus in the boat and started out,

4:11 Greek *mystery*. **4:12** Isa 6:9-10 (Greek version). **4:24** Or *The measure you give will be the measure you get back.*

leaving the crowds behind (although other boats followed). [37]But soon a fierce storm came up. High waves were breaking into the boat, and it began to fill with water.

[38]Jesus was sleeping at the back of the boat with his head on a cushion. The disciples woke him up, shouting, "Teacher, don't you care that we're going to drown?"

[39]When Jesus woke up, he rebuked the wind and said to the waves, "Silence! Be still!" Suddenly the wind stopped, and there was a great calm. [40]Then he asked them, "Why are you afraid? Do you still have no faith?"

[41]The disciples were absolutely terrified. "Who is this man?" they asked each other. "Even the wind and waves obey him!"

CHAPTER 5

Jesus Heals a Demon-Possessed Man

So they arrived at the other side of the lake, in the region of the Gerasenes.* [2]When Jesus climbed out of the boat, a man possessed by an evil* spirit came out from a cemetery to meet him. [3]This man lived among the burial caves and could no longer be restrained, even with a chain. [4]Whenever he was put into chains and shackles—as he often was—he snapped the chains from his wrists and smashed the shackles. No one was strong enough to subdue him. [5]Day and night he wandered among the burial caves and in the hills, howling and cutting himself with sharp stones.

[6]When Jesus was still some distance away, the man saw him, ran to meet him, and bowed low before him. [7]With a shriek, he screamed, "Why are you interfering with me, Jesus, Son of the Most High God? In the name of God, I beg you, don't torture me!" [8]For Jesus had already said to the spirit, "Come out of the man, you evil spirit."

[9]Then Jesus demanded, "What is your name?"

And he replied, "My name is Legion, because there are many of us inside this man." [10]Then the evil spirits begged him again and again not to send them to some distant place.

[11]There happened to be a large herd of pigs feeding on the hillside nearby. [12]"Send us into those pigs," the spirits begged. "Let us enter them."

[13]So Jesus gave them permission. The evil spirits came out of the man and entered the pigs, and the entire herd of about 2,000 pigs plunged down the steep hillside into the lake and drowned in the water.

[14]The herdsmen fled to the nearby town and the surrounding countryside, spreading the news as they ran. People rushed out to see what had happened. [15]A crowd soon gathered around Jesus, and they saw the man who had been possessed by the legion of demons. He was sitting there fully clothed and perfectly sane, and they were all afraid. [16]Then those who had seen what happened told the others about the demon-possessed man and the pigs. [17]And the crowd began pleading with Jesus to go away and leave them alone.

[18]As Jesus was getting into the boat, the man who had been demon possessed begged to go with him. [19]But Jesus said, "No, go home to your family, and tell them everything the Lord has done for you and how merciful he has been." [20]So the man started off to visit the Ten Towns* of that region and began to proclaim the great things Jesus had done for him; and everyone was amazed at what he told them.

Jesus Heals in Response to Faith

[21]Jesus got into the boat again and went back to the other side of the lake, where a large crowd gathered around him on the shore. [22]Then a leader of the local synagogue, whose name was Jairus, arrived. When he saw Jesus, he fell at his feet, [23]pleading fervently with him. "My little daughter is dying," he said. "Please come and lay your hands on her; heal her so she can live."

[24]Jesus went with him, and all the people followed, crowding around him. [25]A woman in the crowd had suffered for twelve years with constant bleeding. [26]She had suffered a great deal from many doctors, and over the years she had spent everything she had to pay them, but she had gotten no better. In fact, she had gotten worse. [27]She had heard about Jesus, so she came up behind him through the crowd and touched his robe. [28]For she thought to herself, "If I can just touch his robe, I will be healed." [29]Immediately the bleeding stopped, and she could feel in her

5:1 Other manuscripts read *Gadarenes;* still others read *Gergesenes*. See Matt 8:28; Luke 8:26. **5:2** Greek *unclean;* also in 5:8, 13. **5:20** Greek *Decapolis*.

body that she had been healed of her terrible condition.

30Jesus realized at once that healing power had gone out from him, so he turned around in the crowd and asked, "Who touched my robe?"

31His disciples said to him, "Look at this crowd pressing around you. How can you ask, 'Who touched me?'"

32But he kept on looking around to see who had done it. 33Then the frightened woman, trembling at the realization of what had happened to her, came and fell to her knees in front of him and told him what she had done. 34And he said to her, "Daughter, your faith has made you well. Go in peace. Your suffering is over."

35While he was still speaking to her, messengers arrived from the home of Jairus, the leader of the synagogue. They told him, "Your daughter is dead. There's no use troubling the Teacher now."

36But Jesus overheard* them and said to Jairus, "Don't be afraid. Just have faith."

37Then Jesus stopped the crowd and wouldn't let anyone go with him except Peter, James, and John (the brother of James). 38When they came to the home of the synagogue leader, Jesus saw much commotion and weeping and wailing. 39He went inside and asked, "Why all this commotion and weeping? The child isn't dead; she's only asleep."

40The crowd laughed at him. But he made them all leave, and he took the girl's father and mother and his three disciples into the room where the girl was lying. 41Holding her hand, he said to her, *"Talitha koum,"* which means "Little girl, get up!" 42And the girl, who was twelve years old, immediately stood up and walked around! They were overwhelmed and totally amazed. 43Jesus gave them strict orders not to tell anyone what had happened, and then he told them to give her something to eat.

CHAPTER 6

Jesus Rejected at Nazareth

Jesus left that part of the country and returned with his disciples to Nazareth, his hometown. 2The next Sabbath he began teaching in the synagogue, and many who heard him were amazed. They asked, "Where did he get all this wisdom and the power to perform such miracles?" 3Then they scoffed, "He's just a carpenter, the son of Mary* and the brother of James, Joseph,* Judas, and Simon. And his sisters live right here among us." They were deeply offended and refused to believe in him.

4Then Jesus told them, "A prophet is honored everywhere except in his own hometown and among his relatives and his own family." 5And because of their unbelief, he couldn't do any miracles among them except to place his hands on a few sick people and heal them. 6And he was amazed at their unbelief.

Jesus Sends Out the Twelve Disciples

Then Jesus went from village to village, teaching the people. 7And he called his twelve disciples together and began sending them out two by two, giving them authority to cast out evil* spirits. 8He told them to take nothing for their journey except a walking stick—no food, no traveler's bag, no money.* 9He allowed them to wear sandals but not to take a change of clothes.

10"Wherever you go," he said, "stay in the same house until you leave town. 11But if any place refuses to welcome you or listen to you, shake its dust from your feet as you leave to show that you have abandoned those people to their fate."

12So the disciples went out, telling everyone they met to repent of their sins and turn to God. 13And they cast out many demons and healed many sick people, anointing them with olive oil.

The Death of John the Baptist

14Herod Antipas, the king, soon heard about Jesus, because everyone was talking about him. Some were saying,* "This must be John the Baptist raised from the dead. That is why he can do such miracles." 15Others said, "He's the prophet Elijah." Still others said, "He's a prophet like the other great prophets of the past."

16When Herod heard about Jesus, he said, "John, the man I beheaded, has come back from the dead."

5:36 Or *ignored*. **6:3a** Some manuscripts read *He's just the son of the carpenter and of Mary*. **6:3b** Most manuscripts read *Joses*; see Matt 13:55. **6:7** Greek *unclean*. **6:8** Greek *no copper coins in their money belts*. **6:14** Some manuscripts read *He was saying*.

[17]For Herod had sent soldiers to arrest and imprison John as a favor to Herodias. She had been his brother Philip's wife, but Herod had married her. [18]John had been telling Herod, "It is against God's law for you to marry your brother's wife." [19]So Herodias bore a grudge against John and wanted to kill him. But without Herod's approval she was powerless, [20]for Herod respected John; and knowing that he was a good and holy man, he protected him. Herod was greatly disturbed whenever he talked with John, but even so, he liked to listen to him.

[21]Herodias's chance finally came on Herod's birthday. He gave a party for his high government officials, army officers, and the leading citizens of Galilee. [22]Then his daughter, also named Herodias,* came in and performed a dance that greatly pleased Herod and his guests. "Ask me for anything you like," the king said to the girl, "and I will give it to you." [23]He even vowed, "I will give you whatever you ask, up to half my kingdom!"

[24]She went out and asked her mother, "What should I ask for?"

Her mother told her, "Ask for the head of John the Baptist!"

[25]So the girl hurried back to the king and told him, "I want the head of John the Baptist, right now, on a tray!"

[26]Then the king deeply regretted what he had said; but because of the vows he had made in front of his guests, he couldn't refuse her. [27]So he immediately sent an executioner to the prison to cut off John's head and bring it to him. The soldier beheaded John in the prison, [28]brought his head on a tray, and gave it to the girl, who took it to her mother. [29]When John's disciples heard what had happened, they came to get his body and buried it in a tomb.

Jesus Feeds Five Thousand

[30]The apostles returned to Jesus from their ministry tour and told him all they had done and taught. [31]Then Jesus said, "Let's go off by ourselves to a quiet place and rest awhile." He said this because there were so many people coming and going that Jesus and his apostles didn't even have time to eat.

[32]So they left by boat for a quiet place, where they could be alone. [33]But many people recognized them and saw them leaving, and people from many towns ran ahead along the shore and got there ahead of them. [34]Jesus saw the huge crowd as he stepped from the boat, and he had compassion on them because they were like sheep without a shepherd. So he began teaching them many things.

[35]Late in the afternoon his disciples came to him and said, "This is a remote place, and it's already getting late. [36]Send the crowds away so they can go to the nearby farms and villages and buy something to eat."

[37]But Jesus said, "You feed them."

"With what?" they asked. "We'd have to work for months to earn enough money* to buy food for all these people!"

[38]"How much bread do you have?" he asked. "Go and find out."

They came back and reported, "We have five loaves of bread and two fish."

[39]Then Jesus told the disciples to have the people sit down in groups on the green grass. [40]So they sat down in groups of fifty or a hundred.

[41]Jesus took the five loaves and two fish, looked up toward heaven, and blessed them. Then, breaking the loaves into pieces, he kept giving the bread to the disciples so they could distribute it to the people. He also divided the fish for everyone to share. [42]They all ate as much as they wanted, [43]and afterward, the disciples picked up twelve baskets of leftover

AMAZING FACTS

How many people could you feed with two fish and five loaves of bread? Jesus fed not only 5,000 men, but their families, too!

MARK 6:30-44

6:22 Some manuscripts read *the daughter of Herodias herself*. **6:37** Greek *It would take 200 denarii*. A denarius was equivalent to a laborer's full day's wage.

bread and fish. 44A total of 5,000 men and their families were fed from those loaves!

Jesus Walks on Water

45Immediately after this, Jesus insisted that his disciples get back into the boat and head across the lake to Bethsaida, while he sent the people home. 46After telling everyone goodbye, he went up into the hills by himself to pray.

47Late that night, the disciples were in their boat in the middle of the lake, and Jesus was alone on land. 48He saw that they were in serious trouble, rowing hard and struggling against the wind and waves. About three o'clock in the morning* Jesus came toward them, walking on the water. He intended to go past them, 49but when they saw him walking on the water, they cried out in terror, thinking he was a ghost. 50They were all terrified when they saw him.

But Jesus spoke to them at once. "Don't be afraid," he said. "Take courage! I am here!*" 51Then he climbed into the boat, and the wind stopped. They were totally amazed, 52for they still didn't understand the significance of the miracle of the loaves. Their hearts were too hard to take it in.

53After they had crossed the lake, they landed at Gennesaret. They brought the boat to shore 54and climbed out. The people recognized Jesus at once, 55and they ran throughout the whole area, carrying sick people on mats to wherever they heard he was. 56Wherever he went—in villages, cities, or the countryside—they brought the sick out to the marketplaces. They begged him to let the sick touch at least the fringe of his robe, and all who touched him were healed.

CHAPTER 7

Jesus Teaches about Inner Purity

One day some Pharisees and teachers of religious law arrived from Jerusalem to see Jesus. 2They noticed that some of his disciples failed to follow the Jewish ritual of hand washing before eating. 3(The Jews, especially the Pharisees, do not eat until they have poured water over their cupped hands,* as required by their ancient traditions. 4Similarly, they don't eat anything from the market until they immerse their hands* in water. This is but one of many traditions they have clung to—such as their ceremonial washing of cups, pitchers, and kettles.*)

5So the Pharisees and teachers of religious law asked him, "Why don't your disciples follow our age-old tradition? They eat without first performing the hand-washing ceremony."

6Jesus replied, "You hypocrites! Isaiah was right when he prophesied about you, for he wrote,

> 'These people honor me with their lips,
> but their hearts are far from me.
> 7 Their worship is a farce,
> for they teach man-made ideas as
> commands from God.'*

8For you ignore God's law and substitute your own tradition."

9Then he said, "You skillfully sidestep God's law in order to hold on to your own tradition. 10For instance, Moses gave you this law from God: 'Honor your father and mother,'* and 'Anyone who speaks disrespectfully of father or mother must be put to death.'* 11But you say it is all right for people to say to their parents, 'Sorry, I can't help you. For I have vowed to give to God what I would have given to you.'* 12In this way, you let them disregard their needy parents. 13And so you cancel the word of God in order to hand down your own tradition. And this is only one example among many others."

14Then Jesus called to the crowd to come and hear. "All of you listen," he said, "and try to understand. 15It's not what goes into your body that defiles you; you are defiled by what comes from your heart.*"

17Then Jesus went into a house to get away from the crowd, and his disciples asked him what he meant by the parable he had just used. 18"Don't you understand either?" he asked. "Can't you see that the food you put into your body cannot defile you? 19Food doesn't go into your heart, but only passes through the stomach and then goes into the

6:48 Greek *About the fourth watch of the night.* **6:50** Or *The 'I AM' is here;* Greek reads *I am.* See Exod 3:14. **7:3** Greek *have washed with the fist.* **7:4a** Some manuscripts read *sprinkle themselves.* **7:4b** Some manuscripts add *and dining couches.* **7:7** Isa 29:13 (Greek version). **7:10a** Exod 20:12; Deut 5:16. **7:10b** Exod 21:17 (Greek version); Lev 20:9 (Greek version). **7:11** Greek *'What I would have given to you is Corban' (that is, a gift).* **7:15** Some manuscripts add verse 16, *Anyone with ears to hear should listen and understand.* Compare 4:9, 23.

sewer." (By saying this, he declared that every kind of food is acceptable in God's eyes.)

[20]And then he added, "It is what comes from inside that defiles you. [21]For from within, out of a person's heart, come evil thoughts, sexual immorality, theft, murder, [22]adultery, greed, wickedness, deceit, lustful desires, envy, slander, pride, and foolishness. [23]All these vile things come from within; they are what defile you."

The Faith of a Gentile Woman

[24]Then Jesus left Galilee and went north to the region of Tyre.* He didn't want anyone to know which house he was staying in, but he couldn't keep it a secret. [25]Right away a woman who had heard about him came and fell at his feet. Her little girl was possessed by an evil* spirit, [26]and she begged him to cast out the demon from her daughter.

Since she was a Gentile, born in Syrian Phoenicia, [27]Jesus told her, "First I should feed the children—my own family, the Jews.* It isn't right to take food from the children and throw it to the dogs."

[28]She replied, "That's true, Lord, but even the dogs under the table are allowed to eat the scraps from the children's plates."

[29]"Good answer!" he said. "Now go home, for the demon has left your daughter." [30]And when she arrived home, she found her little girl lying quietly in bed, and the demon was gone.

Jesus Heals a Deaf Man

[31]Jesus left Tyre and went up to Sidon before going back to the Sea of Galilee and the region of the Ten Towns.* [32]A deaf man with a speech impediment was brought to him, and the people begged Jesus to lay his hands on the man to heal him.

[33]Jesus led him away from the crowd so they could be alone. He put his fingers into the man's ears. Then, spitting on his own fingers, he touched the man's tongue. [34]Looking up to heaven, he sighed and said, *"Ephphatha,"* which means, "Be opened!" [35]Instantly the man could hear perfectly, and his tongue was freed so he could speak plainly!

[36]Jesus told the crowd not to tell anyone, but the more he told them not to, the more they spread the news. [37]They were completely amazed and said again and again, "Everything he does is wonderful. He even makes the deaf to hear and gives speech to those who cannot speak."

CHAPTER 8

Jesus Feeds Four Thousand

About this time another large crowd had gathered, and the people ran out of food again. Jesus called his disciples and told them, [2]"I feel sorry for these people. They have been here with me for three days, and they have nothing left to eat. [3]If I send them home hungry, they will faint along the way. For some of them have come a long distance."

[4]His disciples replied, "How are we supposed to find enough food to feed them out here in the wilderness?"

[5]Jesus asked, "How much bread do you have?"

"Seven loaves," they replied.

[6]So Jesus told all the people to sit down on the ground. Then he took the seven loaves, thanked God for them, and broke them into pieces. He gave them to his disciples, who distributed the bread to the crowd. [7]A few small fish were found, too, so Jesus also blessed these and told the disciples to distribute them.

[8]They ate as much as they wanted. Afterward, the disciples picked up seven large baskets of leftover food. [9]There were about 4,000 people in the crowd that day, and Jesus sent them home after they had eaten. [10]Immediately after this, he got into a boat with his disciples and crossed over to the region of Dalmanutha.

Pharisees Demand a Miraculous Sign

[11]When the Pharisees heard that Jesus had arrived, they came and started to argue with him. Testing him, they demanded that he show them a miraculous sign from heaven to prove his authority.

[12]When he heard this, he sighed deeply in his spirit and said, "Why do these people keep demanding a miraculous sign? I tell you the truth, I will not give this generation any such sign." [13]So he got back into the boat and left them, and he crossed to the other side of the lake.

7:24 Some manuscripts add *and Sidon.* **7:25** Greek *unclean.* **7:27** Greek *Let the children eat first.* **7:31** Greek *Decapolis.*

Yeast of the Pharisees and Herod

14 But the disciples had forgotten to bring any
food. They had only one loaf of bread with
them in the boat. 15 As they were crossing the
lake, Jesus warned them, "Watch out! Beware
of the yeast of the Pharisees and of Herod."

16 At this they began to argue with each
other because they hadn't brought any bread.
17 Jesus knew what they were saying, so he said,
"Why are you arguing about having no bread?
Don't you know or understand even yet? Are
your hearts too hard to take it in? 18 'You have
eyes—can't you see? You have ears—can't you
hear?'* Don't you remember anything at all?
19 When I fed the 5,000 with five loaves of
bread, how many baskets of leftovers did you
pick up afterward?"

"Twelve," they said.

20 "And when I fed the 4,000 with seven
loaves, how many large baskets of leftovers
did you pick up?"

"Seven," they said.

21 "Don't you understand yet?" he asked them.

Jesus Heals a Blind Man

22 When they arrived at Bethsaida, some people brought a blind man to Jesus, and they
begged him to touch the man and heal him.
23 Jesus took the blind man by the hand and
led him out of the village. Then, spitting on
the man's eyes, he laid his hands on him and
asked, "Can you see anything now?"

24 The man looked around. "Yes," he said, "I
see people, but I can't see them very clearly.
They look like trees walking around."

25 Then Jesus placed his hands on the man's
eyes again, and his eyes were opened. His sight
was completely restored, and he could see
everything clearly. 26 Jesus sent him away, saying, "Don't go back into the village on your way
home."

Peter's Declaration about Jesus

27 Jesus and his disciples left Galilee and went
up to the villages near Caesarea Philippi. As
they were walking along, he asked them,
"Who do people say I am?"

28 "Well," they replied, "some say John the
Baptist, some say Elijah, and others say you
are one of the other prophets."

SPEAK UP!

Adrian was a Christian, but he didn't talk much about Jesus, church, or the Bible with his friends. It never seemed necessary, and Adrian thought they might not understand. One day a good friend asked, "Adrian, you go to church. Can you explain why you believe in Jesus?" Adrian was kind of embarrassed. He felt like changing the subject or giving a quick answer, but he wasn't sure that would be right. How do you think Adrian should answer? In Mark 8:38, Jesus tells how he feels about someone who is ashamed of him. See what you think.

29 Then he asked them, "But who do you say
I am?"

Peter replied, "You are the Messiah.*"

30 But Jesus warned them not to tell anyone
about him.

8:18 Jer 5:21. **8:29** Or *the Christ*. *Messiah* (a Hebrew term) and *Christ* (a Greek term) both mean "the anointed one."

Jesus Predicts His Death

31Then Jesus began to tell them that the Son
of Man* must suffer many terrible things and
be rejected by the elders, the leading priests,
and the teachers of religious law. He would be
killed, but three days later he would rise from
the dead. 32As he talked about this openly
with his disciples, Peter took him aside and
began to reprimand him for saying such
things.*

33Jesus turned around and looked at his
disciples, then reprimanded Peter. "Get away
from me, Satan!" he said. "You are seeing
things merely from a human point of view,
not from God's."

34Then, calling the crowd to join his disci-
ples, he said, "If any of you wants to be my fol-
lower, you must turn from your selfish ways,
take up your cross, and follow me. 35If you try
to hang on to your life, you will lose it. But if
you give up your life for my sake and for the
sake of the Good News, you will save it. 36And
what do you benefit if you gain the whole
world but lose your own soul?* 37Is anything
worth more than your soul? 38If anyone is
ashamed of me and my message in these
adulterous and sinful days, the Son of Man
will be ashamed of that person when he re-
turns in the glory of his Father with the holy
angels."

CHAPTER 9

Jesus went on to say, "I tell you the truth, some
standing here right now will not die before
they see the Kingdom of God arrive in great
power!"

The Transfiguration

2Six days later Jesus took Peter, James, and
John, and led them up a high mountain to be
alone. As the men watched, Jesus' appearance
was transformed, 3and his clothes became
dazzling white, far whiter than any earthly
bleach could ever make them. 4Then Elijah
and Moses appeared and began talking with
Jesus.

5Peter exclaimed, "Rabbi, it's wonderful
for us to be here! Let's make three shelters as
memorials*—one for you, one for Moses, and
one for Elijah." 6He said this because he didn't
really know what else to say, for they were all
terrified.

7Then a cloud overshadowed them, and a
voice from the cloud said, "This is my dearly
loved Son. Listen to him." 8Suddenly, when
they looked around, Moses and Elijah were
gone, and they saw only Jesus with them.

9As they went back down the mountain, he
told them not to tell anyone what they had
seen until the Son of Man* had risen from the
dead. 10So they kept it to themselves, but they
often asked each other what he meant by "ris-
ing from the dead."

11Then they asked him, "Why do the teach-
ers of religious law insist that Elijah must re-
turn before the Messiah comes?*"

12Jesus responded, "Elijah is indeed com-
ing first to get everything ready. Yet why do
the Scriptures say that the Son of Man must
suffer greatly and be treated with utter con-
tempt? 13But I tell you, Elijah has already
come, and they chose to abuse him, just as the
Scriptures predicted."

Jesus Heals a Demon-Possessed Boy

14When they returned to the other disciples,
they saw a large crowd surrounding them,
and some teachers of religious law were argu-
ing with them. 15When the crowd saw Jesus,
they were overwhelmed with awe, and they
ran to greet him.

16"What is all this arguing about?" Jesus
asked.

17One of the men in the crowd spoke up
and said, "Teacher, I brought my son so you
could heal him. He is possessed by an evil
spirit that won't let him talk. 18And whenever
this spirit seizes him, it throws him violently
to the ground. Then he foams at the mouth
and grinds his teeth and becomes rigid.* So I
asked your disciples to cast out the evil spirit,
but they couldn't do it."

19Jesus said to them,* "You faithless peo-
ple! How long must I be with you? How long
must I put up with you? Bring the boy to me."

20So they brought the boy. But when the
evil spirit saw Jesus, it threw the child into a
violent convulsion, and he fell to the ground,
writhing and foaming at the mouth.

8:31 "Son of Man" is a title Jesus used for himself. **8:32** Or *began to correct him.* **8:36** Or *your self?* also in 8:37. **9:5** Greek *three tabernacles.* **9:9** "Son of Man" is a title Jesus used for himself. **9:11** Greek *that Elijah must come first?* **9:18** Or *becomes weak.* **9:19** Or *said to his disciples.*

Last week I was walking down the hallway to my social studies class, feeling sorry for myself. On most days it seems like everyone in my school has a special talent—except me. All my classmates can do something impressive that wins them awards and recognition. What can I do? Nothing. A big fat zero.

Whenever these thoughts get loose in my brain, they make me feel completely inferior to everyone else. Then one day I read what Jesus said about how to be a success in life. Jesus said that the way to be great is to be a servant to everyone else. He did, really. Look it up in Mark 9:35.

Now that's the one thing I can do—I like to help people. I try to help everyone. There are times when people take advantage of me, and I end up getting upset with myself for bothering to help. But most of the time I feel really good about the things I do.

I'm convinced that God created me for a reason. All I know so far is that God wants me to keep on helping people. I see people at my church who give time and energy to help others, and they do it with a cheerful, joyful spirit. I could do that as an adult someday too—that could be me.

I am going to see where helping people leads me. Being a helpful servant to others will be my hobby. That won't make me inferior to other people. Jesus says it will make me great—the best of all in his Kingdom.

Read Psalm 112:5-9; Isaiah 58:7-8; Matthew 20:25-28; and Philippians 2:1-8 for more about using your abilities to serve others.

[21]"How long has this been happening?"
Jesus asked the boy's father.
He replied, "Since he was a little boy. [22]The
spirit often throws him into the fire or into
water, trying to kill him. Have mercy on us
and help us, if you can."
[23]"What do you mean, 'If I can'?" Jesus
asked. "Anything is possible if a person be-
lieves."
[24]The father instantly cried out, "I do be-
lieve, but help me overcome my unbelief!"
[25]When Jesus saw that the crowd of on-
lookers was growing, he rebuked the evil*
spirit. "Listen, you spirit that makes this boy
unable to hear and speak," he said. "I com-
mand you to come out of this child and never
enter him again!"
[26]Then the spirit screamed and threw the
boy into another violent convulsion and left
him. The boy appeared to be dead. A murmur
ran through the crowd as people said, "He's
dead." [27]But Jesus took him by the hand and
helped him to his feet, and he stood up.
[28]Afterward, when Jesus was alone in the
house with his disciples, they asked him,
"Why couldn't we cast out that evil spirit?"
[29]Jesus replied, "This kind can be cast out
only by prayer.*"

Jesus Again Predicts His Death

[30]Leaving that region, they traveled through
Galilee. Jesus didn't want anyone to know he
was there, [31]for he wanted to spend more
time with his disciples and teach them. He
said to them, "The Son of Man is going to be
betrayed into the hands of his enemies. He
will be killed, but three days later he will rise
from the dead." [32]They didn't understand
what he was saying, however, and they were
afraid to ask him what he meant.

The Greatest in the Kingdom

[33]After they arrived at Capernaum and settled
in a house, Jesus asked his disciples, "What
were you discussing out on the road?" [34]But
they didn't answer, because they had been ar-
guing about which of them was the greatest.
[35]He sat down, called the twelve disciples over
to him, and said, "Whoever wants to be first
must take last place and be the servant of
everyone else."
[36]Then he put a little child among them.
Taking the child in his arms, he said to them,
[37]"Anyone who welcomes a little child like
this on my behalf* welcomes me, and anyone
who welcomes me welcomes not only me but
also my Father who sent me."

Using the Name of Jesus

[38]John said to Jesus, "Teacher, we saw some-
one using your name to cast out demons, but
we told him to stop because he wasn't in our
group."
[39]"Don't stop him!" Jesus said. "No one who
performs a miracle in my name will soon be
able to speak evil of me. [40]Anyone who is not
against us is for us. [41]If anyone gives you even
a cup of water because you belong to the Mes-
siah, I tell you the truth, that person will surely
be rewarded.
[42]"But if you cause one of these little ones
who trusts in me to fall into sin, it would be
better for you to be thrown into the sea with a
large millstone hung around your neck. [43]If
your hand causes you to sin, cut it off. It's
better to enter eternal life with only one hand
than to go into the unquenchable fires of
hell* with two hands.* [45]If your foot causes
you to sin, cut it off. It's better to enter eternal
life with only one foot than to be thrown into
hell with two feet.* [47]And if your eye causes
you to sin, gouge it out. It's better to enter the
Kingdom of God with only one eye than to
have two eyes and be thrown into hell,
[48]'where the maggots never die and the fire
never goes out.'*
[49]"For everyone will be tested with fire.*
[50]Salt is good for seasoning. But if it loses its
flavor, how do you make it salty again? You
must have the qualities of salt among your-
selves and live in peace with each other."

CHAPTER 10

Discussion about Divorce and Marriage

Then Jesus left Capernaum and went down to
the region of Judea and into the area east of
the Jordan River. Once again crowds gathered
around him, and as usual he was teaching
them.

9:25 Greek *unclean.* **9:29** Some manuscripts read *by prayer and fasting.* **9:37** Greek *in my name.* **9:43a** Greek *Gehenna;* also in 9:45, 47. **9:43b** Some manuscripts add verse 44, *'where the maggots never die and the fire never goes out.'* See 9:48. **9:45** Some manuscripts add verse 46, *'where the maggots never die and the fire never goes out.'* See 9:48. **9:48** Isa 66:24. **9:49** Greek *salted with fire;* other manuscripts add *and every sacrifice will be salted with salt.*

[2]Some Pharisees came and tried to trap him with this question: "Should a man be allowed to divorce his wife?"

[3]Jesus answered them with a question: "What did Moses say in the law about divorce?"

[4]"Well, he permitted it," they replied. "He said a man can give his wife a written notice of divorce and send her away."*

[5]But Jesus responded, "He wrote this commandment only as a concession to your hard hearts. [6]But 'God made them male and female'* from the beginning of creation. [7]'This explains why a man leaves his father and mother and is joined to his wife,* [8]and the two are united into one.'* Since they are no longer two but one, [9]let no one split apart what God has joined together."

[10]Later, when he was alone with his disciples in the house, they brought up the subject again. [11]He told them, "Whoever divorces his wife and marries someone else commits adultery against her. [12]And if a woman divorces her husband and marries someone else, she commits adultery."

Jesus Blesses the Children

[13]One day some parents brought their children to Jesus so he could touch and bless them. But the disciples scolded the parents for bothering him.

[14]When Jesus saw what was happening, he was angry with his disciples. He said to them, "Let the children come to me. Don't stop them! For the Kingdom of God belongs to those who are like these children. [15]I tell you the truth, anyone who doesn't receive the Kingdom of God like a child will never enter it." [16]Then he took the children in his arms and placed his hands on their heads and blessed them.

The Rich Man

[17]As Jesus was starting out on his way to Jerusalem, a man came running up to him, knelt down, and asked, "Good Teacher, what must I do to inherit eternal life?"

[18]"Why do you call me good?" Jesus asked. "Only God is truly good. [19]But to answer your question, you know the commandments: 'You must not murder. You must not commit adultery. You must not steal. You must not testify falsely. You must not cheat anyone. Honor your father and mother.'*"

[20]"Teacher," the man replied, "I've obeyed all these commandments since I was young."

[21]Looking at the man, Jesus felt genuine love for him. "There is still one thing you haven't done," he told him. "Go and sell all your possessions and give the money to the poor, and you will have treasure in heaven. Then come, follow me."

[22]At this the man's face fell, and he went away sad, for he had many possessions.

AMAZING FACTS

A rich man was really a poor man—he couldn't see why being Jesus' friend was more important than keeping his things.

MARK 10:17-22

[23]Jesus looked around and said to his disciples, "How hard it is for the rich to enter the Kingdom of God!" [24]This amazed them. But Jesus said again, "Dear children, it is very hard* to enter the Kingdom of God. [25]In fact, it is easier for a camel to go through the eye of a needle than for a rich person to enter the Kingdom of God!"

[26]The disciples were astounded. "Then who in the world can be saved?" they asked.

[27]Jesus looked at them intently and said, "Humanly speaking, it is impossible. But not with God. Everything is possible with God."

[28]Then Peter began to speak up. "We've given up everything to follow you," he said.

[29]"Yes," Jesus replied, "and I assure you that everyone who has given up house or brothers or sisters or mother or father or children or property, for my sake and for the Good News,

10:4 See Deut 24:1. **10:6** Gen 1:27; 5:2. **10:7** Some manuscripts do not include *and is joined to his wife*. **10:7-8** Gen 2:24. **10:19** Exod 20:12-16; Deut 5:16-20. **10:24** Some manuscripts read *very hard for those who trust in riches*.

[30]will receive now in return a hundred times as
many houses, brothers, sisters, mothers, chil-
dren, and property—along with persecution.
And in the world to come that person will have
eternal life. [31]But many who are the greatest
now will be least important then, and those
who seem least important now will be the
greatest then.*"

Jesus Again Predicts His Death

[32]They were now on the way up to Jerusalem,
and Jesus was walking ahead of them. The
disciples were filled with awe, and the people
following behind were overwhelmed with
fear. Taking the twelve disciples aside, Jesus
once more began to describe everything that
was about to happen to him. [33]"Listen," he
said, "we're going up to Jerusalem, where the
Son of Man* will be betrayed to the leading
priests and the teachers of religious law. They
will sentence him to die and hand him over to
the Romans.* [34]They will mock him, spit on
him, flog him with a whip, and kill him, but af-
ter three days he will rise again."

Jesus Teaches about Serving Others

[35]Then James and John, the sons of Zebedee,
came over and spoke to him. "Teacher," they
said, "we want you to do us a favor."

[36]"What is your request?" he asked.

[37]They replied, "When you sit on your glo-
rious throne, we want to sit in places of honor
next to you, one on your right and the other
on your left."

[38]But Jesus said to them, "You don't know
what you are asking! Are you able to drink
from the bitter cup of suffering I am about to
drink? Are you able to be baptized with the
baptism of suffering I must be baptized with?"

[39]"Oh yes," they replied, "we are able!"

Then Jesus told them, "You will indeed
drink from my bitter cup and be baptized
with my baptism of suffering. [40]But I have no
right to say who will sit on my right or my left.
God has prepared those places for the ones he
has chosen."

[41]When the ten other disciples heard what
James and John had asked, they were indig-
nant. [42]So Jesus called them together and
said, "You know that the rulers in this world
lord it over their people, and officials flaunt
their authority over those under them. [43]But
among you it will be different. Whoever
wants to be a leader among you must be your
servant, [44]and whoever wants to be first
among you must be the slave of everyone else.
[45]For even the Son of Man came not to be
served but to serve others and to give his life
as a ransom for many."

Jesus Heals Blind Bartimaeus

[46]Then they reached Jericho, and as Jesus and
his disciples left town, a large crowd followed
him. A blind beggar named Bartimaeus (son
of Timaeus) was sitting beside the road.
[47]When Bartimaeus heard that Jesus of Naza-
reth was nearby, he began to shout, "Jesus,
Son of David, have mercy on me!"

[48]"Be quiet!" many of the people yelled at
him.

But he only shouted louder, "Son of David,
have mercy on me!"

[49]When Jesus heard him, he stopped and
said, "Tell him to come here."

So they called the blind man. "Cheer up,"
they said. "Come on, he's calling you!" [50]Barti-
maeus threw aside his coat, jumped up, and
came to Jesus.

[51]"What do you want me to do for you?"
Jesus asked.

"My rabbi,*" the blind man said, "I want to
see!"

[52]And Jesus said to him, "Go, for your faith
has healed you." Instantly the man could see,
and he followed Jesus down the road.*

CHAPTER 11

Jesus' Triumphant Entry

As Jesus and his disciples approached Jerusa-
lem, they came to the towns of Bethphage and
Bethany on the Mount of Olives. Jesus sent
two of them on ahead. [2]"Go into that village
over there," he told them. "As soon as you en-
ter it, you will see a young donkey tied there
that no one has ever ridden. Untie it and bring
it here. [3]If anyone asks, 'What are you doing?'
just say, 'The Lord needs it and will return it
soon.'"

[4]The two disciples left and found the colt
standing in the street, tied outside the front
door. [5]As they were untying it, some bystand-
ers demanded, "What are you doing, untying

10:31 Greek *But many who are first will be last; and the last, first.* **10:33a** "Son of Man" is a title Jesus used for himself.
10:33b Greek *the Gentiles.* **10:51** Greek uses the Hebrew term *Rabboni.* **10:52** Or *on the way.*

that colt?" [6]They said what Jesus had told them to say, and they were permitted to take it. [7]Then they brought the colt to Jesus and threw their garments over it, and he sat on it.

[8]Many in the crowd spread their garments on the road ahead of him, and others spread leafy branches they had cut in the fields. [9]Jesus was in the center of the procession, and the people all around him were shouting,

"Praise God!*
Blessings on the one who comes in the name of the LORD!
[10] Blessings on the coming Kingdom of our ancestor David!
Praise God in highest heaven!"*

What if I don't feel like forgiving someone who has hurt me?

When you are praying, first forgive anyone you are holding a grudge against, so that your Father in heaven will forgive your sins, too. MARK 11:25

[11]So Jesus came to Jerusalem and went into the Temple. After looking around carefully at everything, he left because it was late in the afternoon. Then he returned to Bethany with the twelve disciples.

Jesus Curses the Fig Tree

[12]The next morning as they were leaving Bethany, Jesus was hungry. [13]He noticed a fig tree in full leaf a little way off, so he went over to see if he could find any figs. But there were only leaves because it was too early in the season for fruit. [14]Then Jesus said to the tree, "May no one ever eat your fruit again!" And the disciples heard him say it.

Jesus Clears the Temple

[15]When they arrived back in Jerusalem, Jesus entered the Temple and began to drive out the people buying and selling animals for sacrifices. He knocked over the tables of the money changers and the chairs of those selling doves, [16]and he stopped everyone from using the Temple as a marketplace.* [17]He said to them, "The Scriptures declare, 'My Temple will be called a house of prayer for all nations,' but you have turned it into a den of thieves."*

[18]When the leading priests and teachers of religious law heard what Jesus had done, they began planning how to kill him. But they were afraid of him because the people were so amazed at his teaching.

[19]That evening Jesus and the disciples left* the city.

[20]The next morning as they passed by the fig tree he had cursed, the disciples noticed it had withered from the roots up. [21]Peter remembered what Jesus had said to the tree on the previous day and exclaimed, "Look, Rabbi! The fig tree you cursed has withered and died!"

[22]Then Jesus said to the disciples, "Have faith in God. [23]I tell you the truth, you can say to this mountain, 'May you be lifted up and thrown into the sea,' and it will happen. But you must really believe it will happen and have no doubt in your heart. [24]I tell you, you can pray for anything, and if you believe that you've received it, it will be yours. [25]But when you are praying, first forgive anyone you are holding a grudge against, so that your Father in heaven will forgive your sins, too.*"

The Authority of Jesus Challenged

[27]Again they entered Jerusalem. As Jesus was walking through the Temple area, the leading priests, the teachers of religious law, and the elders came up to him. [28]They demanded, "By what authority are you doing all these things? Who gave you the right to do them?"

[29]"I'll tell you by what authority I do these things if you answer one question," Jesus replied. [30]"Did John's authority to baptize come from heaven, or was it merely human? Answer me!"

11:9 Greek *Hosanna*, an exclamation of praise that literally means "save now"; also in 11:10. **11:9-10** Pss 118:25-26; 148:1. **11:16** Or *from carrying merchandise through the Temple.* **11:17** Isa 56:7; Jer 7:11. **11:19** Greek *they left;* other manuscripts read *he left.* **11:25** Some manuscripts add verse 26, *But if you refuse to forgive, your Father in heaven will not forgive your sins.* Compare Matt 6:15.

31 They talked it over among themselves. "If
we say it was from heaven, he will ask why we
didn't believe John. 32 But do we dare say it was
merely human?" For they were afraid of what
the people would do, because everyone be-
lieved that John was a prophet. 33 So they fi-
nally replied, "We don't know."

And Jesus responded, "Then I won't tell
you by what authority I do these things."

CHAPTER 12

Parable of the Evil Farmers

Then Jesus began teaching them with sto-
ries: "A man planted a vineyard. He built
a wall around it, dug a pit for pressing out
the grape juice, and built a lookout tower.
Then he leased the vineyard to tenant
farmers and moved to another country. 2 At
the time of the grape harvest, he sent one
of his servants to collect his share of the
crop. 3 But the farmers grabbed the servant,
beat him up, and sent him back empty-
handed. 4 The owner then sent another ser-
vant, but they insulted him and beat him
over the head. 5 The next servant he sent
was killed. Others he sent were either
beaten or killed, 6 until there was only one
left—his son whom he loved dearly. The
owner finally sent him, thinking, 'Surely
they will respect my son.'

7 "But the tenant farmers said to one an-
other, 'Here comes the heir to this estate. Let's
kill him and get the estate for ourselves!' 8 So
they grabbed him and murdered him and
threw his body out of the vineyard.

9 "What do you suppose the owner of the
vineyard will do?" Jesus asked. "I'll tell you—
he will come and kill those farmers and lease
the vineyard to others. 10 Didn't you ever read
this in the Scriptures?

'The stone that the builders
rejected
has now become the cornerstone.
11 This is the LORD's doing,
and it is wonderful to see.'*"

12 The religious leaders* wanted to arrest
Jesus because they realized he was telling the
story against them—they were the wicked
farmers. But they were afraid of the crowd, so
they left him and went away.

Taxes for Caesar

13 Later the leaders sent some Pharisees and
supporters of Herod to trap Jesus into saying
something for which he could be arrested.
14 "Teacher," they said, "we know how honest
you are. You are impartial and don't play
favorites. You teach the way of God truth-
fully. Now tell us—is it right to pay taxes
to Caesar or not? 15 Should we pay them, or
shouldn't we?"

Jesus saw through their hypocrisy and said,
"Why are you trying to trap me? Show me a
Roman coin,* and I'll tell you." 16 When they
handed it to him, he asked, "Whose picture
and title are stamped on it?"

"Caesar's," they replied.

17 "Well, then," Jesus said, "give to Caesar
what belongs to Caesar, and give to God what
belongs to God."

His reply completely amazed them.

Discussion about Resurrection

18 Then Jesus was approached by some Sadd-
cees—religious leaders who say there is no
resurrection from the dead. They posed this
question: 19 "Teacher, Moses gave us a law that
if a man dies, leaving a wife without children,
his brother should marry the widow and have
a child who will carry on the brother's name.*
20 Well, suppose there were seven brothers.
The oldest one married and then died without
children. 21 So the second brother married the
widow, but he also died without children.
Then the third brother married her. 22 This
continued with all seven of them, and still
there were no children. Last of all, the woman
also died. 23 So tell us, whose wife will she be in
the resurrection? For all seven were married
to her."

24 Jesus replied, "Your mistake is that you
don't know the Scriptures, and you don't
know the power of God. 25 For when the dead
rise, they will neither marry nor be given in
marriage. In this respect they will be like the
angels in heaven.

26 "But now, as to whether the dead will be
raised—haven't you ever read about this in the
writings of Moses, in the story of the burning
bush? Long after Abraham, Isaac, and Jacob
had died, God said to Moses,* 'I am the God of
Abraham, the God of Isaac, and the God of Ja-

12:10-11 Ps 118:22-23. **12:12** Greek *They*. **12:15** Greek *a denarius*. **12:19** See Deut 25:5-6. **12:26a** Greek *in the story of the bush? God said to him*.

make a choice

Nathaniel couldn't concentrate in school. All he could think about was his new video game. He had started a game the night before and couldn't wait to try a secret move he had learned about at lunchtime. If he got enough points, he could move up a level! As Nathaniel rushed out the door after school, Joseph asked, "Want to come over and shoot some hoops?" Joseph was a new kid and pretty shy. Nathaniel was surprised at Joseph's invitation. He *really* wanted to finish his video game! What do you think Nathaniel should do? Read Mark 12:31 for some help.

cob.'* [27]So he is the God of the living, not the dead. You have made a serious error."

The Most Important Commandment

[28]One of the teachers of religious law was standing there listening to the debate. He realized that Jesus had answered well, so he asked, "Of all the commandments, which is the most important?"

[29]Jesus replied, "The most important commandment is this: 'Listen, O Israel! The LORD our God is the one and only LORD. [30]And you must love the LORD your God with all your heart, all your soul, all your mind, and all your strength.'* [31]The second is equally important: 'Love your neighbor as yourself.'* No other commandment is greater than these."

[32]The teacher of religious law replied, "Well said, Teacher. You have spoken the truth by saying that there is only one God and no other. [33]And I know it is important to love him with all my heart and all my understanding and all my strength, and to love my neighbor as myself. This is more important than to offer all of the burnt offerings and sacrifices required in the law."

[34]Realizing how much the man understood, Jesus said to him, "You are not far from the Kingdom of God." And after that, no one dared to ask him any more questions.

Whose Son Is the Messiah?

[35]Later, as Jesus was teaching the people in the Temple, he asked, "Why do the teachers of religious law claim that the Messiah is the son of David? [36]For David himself, speaking under the inspiration of the Holy Spirit, said,

> 'The LORD said to my Lord,
> Sit in the place of honor at my right hand
> until I humble your enemies beneath
> your feet.'*

[37]Since David himself called the Messiah 'my Lord,' how can the Messiah be his son?" The large crowd listened to him with great delight.

[38]Jesus also taught: "Beware of these teachers of religious law! For they like to parade around in flowing robes and receive respectful greetings as they walk in the marketplaces. [39]And how they love the seats of honor in the synagogues and the head table at banquets. [40]Yet they shamelessly cheat widows out of their property and then pretend to be pious by making long prayers in public. Because of this, they will be more severely punished."

12:26b Exod 3:6. **12:29-30** Deut 6:4-5. **12:31** Lev 19:18. **12:36** Ps 110:1.

JUDAS

I was having dinner with Jesus in Bethany. We were at the home of Simon, who had once been a leper. A woman there did something I thought was crazy. She broke open a costly jar of perfume and poured the whole thing over Jesus' head. What a waste! All that valuable perfume could have been sold and the money given to the poor.

Jesus looked at me sadly when I complained. He said, "This woman has done a good deed. There will always be poor people, and you can help them whenever you want. As for me, I won't be around much longer." Jesus always talks in riddles. I never understand him. Sometimes I don't even like him very much.

You can read more about Judas in Matthew 26:6-16, 47-49; 27:3-5.

The Widow's Offering

41 Jesus sat down near the collection box in the Temple and watched as the crowds dropped in their money. Many rich people put in large amounts. 42 Then a poor widow came and dropped in two small coins.*

43 Jesus called his disciples to him and said, "I tell you the truth, this poor widow has given more than all the others who are making contributions. 44 For they gave a tiny part of their surplus, but she, poor as she is, has given everything she had to live on."

CHAPTER 13

Jesus Foretells the Future

As Jesus was leaving the Temple that day, one of his disciples said, "Teacher, look at these magnificent buildings! Look at the impressive stones in the walls."

2 Jesus replied, "Yes, look at these great buildings. But they will be completely demolished. Not one stone will be left on top of another!"

3 Later, Jesus sat on the Mount of Olives across the valley from the Temple. Peter, James, John, and Andrew came to him privately and asked him, 4 "Tell us, when will all this happen? What sign will show us that these things are about to be fulfilled?"

5 Jesus replied, "Don't let anyone mislead you, 6 for many will come in my name, claiming, 'I am the Messiah.'* They will deceive many. 7 And you will hear of wars and threats of wars, but don't panic. Yes, these things must take place, but the end won't follow immediately. 8 Nation will go to war against nation, and kingdom against kingdom. There will be earthquakes in many parts of the world, as well as famines. But this is only the first of the birth pains, with more to come.

9 "When these things begin to happen, watch out! You will be handed over to the local councils and beaten in the synagogues. You will stand trial before governors and kings because you are my followers. But this will be your opportunity to tell them about me.* 10 For the Good News must first be preached to all nations.* 11 But when you are arrested and stand trial, don't worry in advance about what to say. Just say what God tells you at that time, for it is not you who will be speaking, but the Holy Spirit.

12 "A brother will betray his brother to death, a father will betray his own child, and children will rebel against their parents and

12:42 Greek *two lepta, which is a kodrantes* [i.e., a quadrans]. **13:6** Greek *claiming, 'I am.'* **13:9** Or *But this will be your testimony against them.* **13:10** Or *all peoples.*

cause them to be killed. 13And everyone will
hate you because you are my followers.* But
the one who endures to the end will be saved.

14"The day is coming when you will see the
sacrilegious object that causes desecration*
standing where he* should not be." (Reader,
pay attention!) "Then those in Judea must flee
to the hills. 15A person out on the deck of a
roof must not go down into the house to pack.
16A person out in the field must not return
even to get a coat. 17How terrible it will be for
pregnant women and for nursing mothers in
those days. 18And pray that your flight will not
be in winter. 19For there will be greater an-
guish in those days than at any time since God
created the world. And it will never be so
great again. 20In fact, unless the Lord shortens
that time of calamity, not a single person will
survive. But for the sake of his chosen ones he
has shortened those days.

21"Then if anyone tells you, 'Look, here is
the Messiah,' or 'There he is,' don't believe it.
22For false messiahs and false prophets will
rise up and perform signs and wonders so as
to deceive, if possible, even God's chosen
ones. 23Watch out! I have warned you about
this ahead of time!

24"At that time, after the anguish of those
days,

the sun will be darkened,
the moon will give no light,
25 the stars will fall from the sky,
and the powers in the heavens will be
shaken.*

26Then everyone will see the Son of Man*
coming on the clouds with great power and
glory.* 27And he will send out his angels to
gather his chosen ones from all over the
world*—from the farthest ends of the earth
and heaven.

28"Now learn a lesson from the fig tree.
When its branches bud and its leaves begin to
sprout, you know that summer is near. 29In
the same way, when you see all these things
taking place, you can know that his return is
very near, right at the door. 30I tell you the
truth, this generation* will not pass from the
scene before all these things take place.
31Heaven and earth will disappear, but my
words will never disappear.

32"However, no one knows the day or hour
when these things will happen, not even the
angels in heaven or the Son himself. Only the
Father knows. 33And since you don't know
when that time will come, be on guard! Stay
alert*!

34"The coming of the Son of Man can be il-
lustrated by the story of a man going on a long
trip. When he left home, he gave each of his
slaves instructions about the work they were
to do, and he told the gatekeeper to watch for
his return. 35You, too, must keep watch! For
you don't know when the master of the
household will return—in the evening, at
midnight, before dawn, or at daybreak.
36Don't let him find you sleeping when he ar-
rives without warning. 37I say to you what I say
to everyone: Watch for him!"

CHAPTER 14

Jesus Anointed at Bethany

It was now two days before Passover and the
Festival of Unleavened Bread. The leading
priests and the teachers of religious law were
still looking for an opportunity to capture
Jesus secretly and kill him. 2"But not during
the Passover celebration," they agreed, "or the
people may riot."

3Meanwhile, Jesus was in Bethany at the
home of Simon, a man who had previously
had leprosy. While he was eating,* a woman
came in with a beautiful alabaster jar of ex-
pensive perfume made from essence of nard.
She broke open the jar and poured the per-
fume over his head.

4Some of those at the table were indignant.
"Why waste such expensive perfume?" they
asked. 5"It could have been sold for a year's
wages* and the money given to the poor!" So
they scolded her harshly.

6But Jesus replied, "Leave her alone. Why
criticize her for doing such a good thing to
me? 7You will always have the poor among
you, and you can help them whenever you
want to. But you will not always have me. 8She
has done what she could and has anointed my
body for burial ahead of time. 9I tell you the
truth, wherever the Good News is preached

13:13 Greek *on account of my name*. **13:14a** Greek *the abomination of desolation*. See Dan 9:27; 11:31; 12:11. **13:14b** Or *it*. **13:24-25** See Isa 13:10; 34:4; Joel 2:10. **13:26a** "Son of Man" is a title Jesus used for himself. **13:26b** See Dan 7:13. **13:27** Greek *from the four winds*. **13:30** Or *this age*, or *this nation*. **13:33** Some manuscripts add *and pray*. **14:3** Or *reclining*. **14:5** Greek *for 300 denarii*. A denarius was equivalent to a laborer's full day's wage.

throughout the world, this woman's deed will be remembered and discussed."

Judas Agrees to Betray Jesus

[10]Then Judas Iscariot, one of the twelve disciples, went to the leading priests to arrange to betray Jesus to them. [11]They were delighted when they heard why he had come, and they promised to give him money. So he began looking for an opportunity to betray Jesus.

The Last Supper

[12]On the first day of the Festival of Unleavened Bread, when the Passover lamb is sacrificed, Jesus' disciples asked him, "Where do you want us to go to prepare the Passover meal for you?"

[13]So Jesus sent two of them into Jerusalem with these instructions: "As you go into the city, a man carrying a pitcher of water will meet you. Follow him. [14]At the house he enters, say to the owner, 'The Teacher asks: Where is the guest room where I can eat the Passover meal with my disciples?' [15]He will take you upstairs to a large room that is already set up. That is where you should prepare our meal." [16]So the two disciples went into the city and found everything just as Jesus had said, and they prepared the Passover meal there.

[17]In the evening Jesus arrived with the twelve disciples.* [18]As they were at the table* eating, Jesus said, "I tell you the truth, one of you eating with me here will betray me."

[19]Greatly distressed, each one asked in turn, "Am I the one?"

[20]He replied, "It is one of you twelve who is eating from this bowl with me. [21]For the Son of Man* must die, as the Scriptures declared long ago. But how terrible it will be for the one who betrays him. It would be far better for that man if he had never been born!"

[22]As they were eating, Jesus took some bread and blessed it. Then he broke it in pieces and gave it to the disciples, saying, "Take it, for this is my body."

[23]And he took a cup of wine and gave thanks to God for it. He gave it to them, and they all drank from it. [24]And he said to them, "This is my blood, which confirms the covenant* between God and his people. It is poured out as a sacrifice for many. [25]I tell you the truth, I will not drink wine again until the day I drink it new in the Kingdom of God."

[26]Then they sang a hymn and went out to the Mount of Olives.

Jesus Predicts Peter's Denial

[27]On the way, Jesus told them, "All of you will desert me. For the Scriptures say,

14:17 Greek *the Twelve*. **14:18** Or *As they reclined*. **14:21** "Son of Man" is a title Jesus used for himself. **14:24** Some manuscripts read *the new covenant*.

KEY CHARACTERISTICS OF CHRIST

Characteristic	References
Jesus is the Son of God	Matthew 16:15-16; Mark 1:1; Luke 22:70; John 8:24
Jesus is God who became human	John 1:1-2, 14; 20:28
Jesus is the Christ, the Messiah	Matthew 26:63-64; Mark 14:61-62; Luke 9:20; John 4:25-26
Jesus came to help sinners	Luke 5:32; Matthew 9:13
Jesus has the power to forgive sins	Mark 2:9-12; Luke 24:47
Jesus has authority over death	Mark 5:22-24, 35-42; John 11:1-44; Luke 24:5-6; Matthew 28:5-6
Jesus has power to give eternal life	John 10:28; 17:2
Jesus healed the sick	Matthew 8:5-13; Mark 1:32-34; Luke 5:12-15; John 9:1-7
Jesus taught with authority	Mark 1:21-22; Matthew 7:29
Jesus was compassionate	Mark 1:41; 8:3; Matthew 9:36
Jesus experienced sorrow	Matthew 26:38; John 11:35
Jesus never disobeyed God	Matthew 3:15; John 8:46

'God will strike* the Shepherd,
and the sheep will be scattered.'

[28]But after I am raised from the dead, I will go ahead of you to Galilee and meet you there."

[29]Peter said to him, "Even if everyone else deserts you, I never will."

[30]Jesus replied, "I tell you the truth, Peter—this very night, before the rooster crows twice, you will deny three times that you even know me."

[31]"No!" Peter declared emphatically. "Even if I have to die with you, I will never deny you!" And all the others vowed the same.

Jesus Prays in Gethsemane

[32]They went to the olive grove called Gethsemane, and Jesus said, "Sit here while I go and pray." [33]He took Peter, James, and John with him, and he became deeply troubled and distressed. [34]He told them, "My soul is crushed with grief to the point of death. Stay here and keep watch with me."

[35]He went on a little farther and fell to the ground. He prayed that, if it were possible, the awful hour awaiting him might pass him by. [36]"Abba, Father,"* he cried out, "everything is possible for you. Please take this cup of suffering away from me. Yet I want your will to be done, not mine."

[37]Then he returned and found the disciples asleep. He said to Peter, "Simon, are you asleep? Couldn't you watch with me even one hour? [38]Keep watch and pray, so that you will not give in to temptation. For the spirit is willing, but the body is weak."

[39]Then Jesus left them again and prayed the same prayer as before. [40]When he returned to them again, he found them sleeping, for they couldn't keep their eyes open. And they didn't know what to say.

[41]When he returned to them the third time, he said, "Go ahead and sleep. Have your rest. But no—the time has come. The Son of Man is betrayed into the hands of sinners. [42]Up, let's be going. Look, my betrayer is here!"

Jesus Is Betrayed and Arrested

[43]And immediately, even as Jesus said this, Judas, one of the twelve disciples, arrived with a crowd of men armed with swords and clubs. They had been sent by the leading priests, the teachers of religious law, and the elders. [44]The traitor, Judas, had given them a prearranged signal: "You will know which one to arrest when I greet him with a kiss. Then you can take him away under guard." [45]As soon as they arrived, Judas walked up to Jesus. "Rabbi!" he exclaimed, and gave him the kiss.

[46]Then the others grabbed Jesus and arrested him. [47]But one of the men with Jesus pulled out his sword and struck the high priest's slave, slashing off his ear.

[48]Jesus asked them, "Am I some dangerous revolutionary, that you come with swords and clubs to arrest me? [49]Why didn't you arrest me in the Temple? I was there among you teaching every day. But these things are happening to fulfill what the Scriptures say about me."

[50]Then all his disciples deserted him and ran away. [51]One young man following behind was clothed only in a long linen shirt. When the mob tried to grab him, [52]he slipped out of his shirt and ran away naked.

Jesus before the Council

[53]They took Jesus to the high priest's home where the leading priests, the elders, and the teachers of religious law had gathered. [54]Meanwhile, Peter followed him at a distance and went right into the high priest's courtyard. There he sat with the guards, warming himself by the fire.

[55]Inside, the leading priests and the entire high council* were trying to find evidence against Jesus, so they could put him to death. But they couldn't find any. [56]Many false witnesses spoke against him, but they contradicted each other. [57]Finally, some men stood up and gave this false testimony: [58]"We heard him say, 'I will destroy this Temple made with human hands, and in three days I will build another, made without human hands.'" [59]But even then they didn't get their stories straight!

[60]Then the high priest stood up before the others and asked Jesus, "Well, aren't you going to answer these charges? What do you have to say for yourself?" [61]But Jesus was silent and made no reply. Then the high priest asked him, "Are you the Messiah, the Son of the Blessed One?"

14:27 Greek *I will strike.* Zech 13:7. **14:36** *Abba* is an Aramaic term for "father." **14:55** Greek *the Sanhedrin.*

[62]Jesus said, "I AM.* And you will see the
Son of Man seated in the place of power at
God's right hand* and coming on the clouds
of heaven.*"
[63]Then the high priest tore his clothing to
show his horror and said, "Why do we need
other witnesses? [64]You have all heard his blas-
phemy. What is your verdict?"
"Guilty!" they all cried. "He deserves to die!"
[65]Then some of them began to spit at him,
and they blindfolded him and beat him with
their fists. "Prophesy to us," they jeered. And
the guards slapped him as they took him away.

Peter Denies Jesus

[66]Meanwhile, Peter was in the courtyard be-
low. One of the servant girls who worked for
the high priest came by [67]and noticed Peter
warming himself at the fire. She looked at
him closely and said, "You were one of those
with Jesus of Nazareth.*"
[68]But Peter denied it. "I don't know what
you're talking about," he said, and he went out
into the entryway. Just then, a rooster crowed.*
[69]When the servant girl saw him standing
there, she began telling the others, "This man
is definitely one of them!" [70]But Peter denied
it again.
A little later some of the other bystanders
confronted Peter and said, "You must be one
of them, because you are a Galilean."
[71]Peter swore, "A curse on me if I'm lying—I
don't know this man you're talking about!"
[72]And immediately the rooster crowed the
second time.
Suddenly, Jesus' words flashed through Pe-
ter's mind: "Before the rooster crows twice,
you will deny three times that you even know
me." And he broke down and wept.

CHAPTER 15

Jesus' Trial before Pilate

Very early in the morning the leading priests,
the elders, and the teachers of religious law—
the entire high council*—met to discuss their
next step. They bound Jesus, led him away,
and took him to Pilate, the Roman governor.
[2]Pilate asked Jesus, "Are you the king of the
Jews?"
Jesus replied, "You have said it."
[3]Then the leading priests kept accusing him
of many crimes, [4]and Pilate asked him, "Aren't
you going to answer them? What about all
these charges they are bringing against you?"
[5]But Jesus said nothing, much to Pilate's
surprise.

14:62a Or *The 'I AM' is here;* or *I am the LORD.* See Exod 3:14. **14:62b** Greek *at the right hand of the power.* See Ps 110:1. **14:62c** See Dan 7:13. **14:67** Or *Jesus the Nazarene.* **14:68** Some manuscripts do not include *Just then, a rooster crowed.* **15:1** Greek *the Sanhedrin;* also in 15:43.

IS IT OK?

IS IT OK TO WANT TO BE POPULAR?

Pilate wanted to be popular. He wanted the crowd to like him. What do you think might have happened if Pilate had ignored the crowd and had done what he knew was right (see Mark 15:15)? Perhaps Pilate would have been remembered as the Roman governor who defended Jesus. Instead he's remembered for having Jesus crucified. Wanting to be popular is not a bad thing. But wanting to be popular so desperately that you make wrong decisions is a very bad thing. You can be strong, knowing that Jesus loves you way more than the "cool crowd" does. When you have the choice either to do what's right or to be popular with the crowd, which will you choose?

[6]Now it was the governor's custom each year during the Passover celebration to release one prisoner—anyone the people requested. [7]One of the prisoners at that time was Barabbas, a revolutionary who had committed murder in an uprising. [8]The crowd went to Pilate and asked him to release a prisoner as usual.

[9]"Would you like me to release to you this 'King of the Jews'?" Pilate asked. [10](For he realized by now that the leading priests had arrested Jesus out of envy.) [11]But at this point the leading priests stirred up the crowd to demand the release of Barabbas instead of Jesus. [12]Pilate asked them, "Then what should I do with this man you call the king of the Jews?"

[13]They shouted back, "Crucify him!"

[14]"Why?" Pilate demanded. "What crime has he committed?"

But the mob roared even louder, "Crucify him!"

[15]So to pacify the crowd, Pilate released Barabbas to them. He ordered Jesus flogged with a lead-tipped whip, then turned him over to the Roman soldiers to be crucified.

The Soldiers Mock Jesus

[16]The soldiers took Jesus into the courtyard of the governor's headquarters (called the Praetorium) and called out the entire regiment. [17]They dressed him in a purple robe, and they wove thorn branches into a crown and put it on his head. [18]Then they saluted him and taunted, "Hail! King of the Jews!" [19]And they struck him on the head with a reed stick, spit on him, and dropped to their knees in mock worship. [20]When they were finally tired of mocking him, they took off the purple robe and put his own clothes on him again. Then they led him away to be crucified.

The Crucifixion

[21]A passerby named Simon, who was from Cyrene,* was coming in from the countryside just then, and the soldiers forced him to carry Jesus' cross. (Simon was the father of Alexander and Rufus.) [22]And they brought Jesus to a place called Golgotha (which means "Place of the Skull"). [23]They offered him wine drugged with myrrh, but he refused it.

[24]Then the soldiers nailed him to the cross. They divided his clothes and threw dice* to decide who would get each piece. [25]It was nine o'clock in the morning when they crucified him. [26]A sign announced the charge against him. It read, "The King of the Jews." [27]Two revolutionaries* were crucified with him, one on his right and one on his left.*

[29]The people passing by shouted abuse, shaking their heads in mockery. "Ha! Look at you now!" they yelled at him. "You said you were going to destroy the Temple and rebuild it in three days. [30]Well then, save yourself and come down from the cross!"

[31]The leading priests and teachers of religious law also mocked Jesus. "He saved others," they scoffed, "but he can't save himself! [32]Let this Messiah, this King of Israel, come down from the cross so we can see it and believe him!" Even the men who were crucified with Jesus ridiculed him.

The Death of Jesus

[33]At noon, darkness fell across the whole land until three o'clock. [34]Then at three o'clock Jesus called out with a loud voice, *"Eloi, Eloi, lema sabachthani?"* which means "My God, my God, why have you abandoned me?"*

[35]Some of the bystanders misunderstood and thought he was calling for the prophet Elijah. [36]One of them ran and filled a sponge with sour wine, holding it up to him on a reed stick so he could drink. "Wait!" he said. "Let's see whether Elijah comes to take him down!"

[37]Then Jesus uttered another loud cry and breathed his last. [38]And the curtain in the sanctuary of the Temple was torn in two, from top to bottom.

[39]When the Roman officer* who stood facing him* saw how he had died, he exclaimed, "This man truly was the Son of God!"

[40]Some women were there, watching from a distance, including Mary Magdalene, Mary (the mother of James the younger and of Joseph*), and Salome. [41]They had been followers of Jesus and had cared for him while he was in Galilee. Many other women who had come with him to Jerusalem were also there.

15:21 *Cyrene* was a city in northern Africa. **15:24** Greek *cast lots*. See Ps 22:18. **15:27a** Or *Two criminals*. **15:27b** Some manuscripts add verse 28, *And the Scripture was fulfilled that said, "He was counted among those who were rebels."* See Isa 53:12; also compare Luke 22:37. **15:34** Ps 22:1. **15:39a** Greek *the centurion;* similarly in 15:44, 45. **15:39b** Some manuscripts add *heard his cry and*. **15:40** Greek *Joses;* also in 15:47. See Matt 27:56.

The Burial of Jesus

42 This all happened on Friday, the day of prep-
aration,* the day before the Sabbath. As eve-
ning approached, 43 Joseph of Arimathea took
a risk and went to Pilate and asked for Jesus'
body. (Joseph was an honored member of the
high council, and he was waiting for the King-
dom of God to come.) 44 Pilate couldn't believe
that Jesus was already dead, so he called for the
Roman officer and asked if he had died yet.
45 The officer confirmed that Jesus was dead,
so Pilate told Joseph he could have the body.
46 Joseph bought a long sheet of linen cloth.
Then he took Jesus' body down from the cross,
wrapped it in the cloth, and laid it in a tomb
that had been carved out of the rock. Then he
rolled a stone in front of the entrance. 47 Mary
Magdalene and Mary the mother of Joseph
saw where Jesus' body was laid.

CHAPTER 16

The Resurrection

Saturday evening, when the Sabbath ended,
Mary Magdalene, Mary the mother of James,
and Salome went out and purchased burial
spices so they could anoint Jesus' body. 2 Very
early on Sunday morning,* just at sunrise,
they went to the tomb. 3 On the way they were
asking each other, "Who will roll away the
stone for us from the entrance to the tomb?"
4 But as they arrived, they looked up and saw
that the stone, which was very large, had al-
ready been rolled aside.

5 When they entered the tomb, they saw a
young man clothed in a white robe sitting on
the right side. The women were shocked, 6 but
the angel said, "Don't be alarmed. You are
looking for Jesus of Nazareth,* who was cruci-
fied. He isn't here! He is risen from the dead!
Look, this is where they laid his body. 7 Now go
and tell his disciples, including Peter, that
Jesus is going ahead of you to Galilee. You will
see him there, just as he told you before he
died."

8 The women fled from the tomb, trem-
bling and bewildered, and they said nothing
to anyone because they were too frightened.*

[*Shorter Ending of Mark*]

Then they briefly reported all this to Peter
and his companions. Afterward Jesus himself
sent them out from east to west with the sa-
cred and unfailing message of salvation that
gives eternal life. Amen.

[*Longer Ending of Mark*]

9 After Jesus rose from the dead early on
Sunday morning, the first person who saw
him was Mary Magdalene, the woman from
whom he had cast out seven demons. 10 She
went to the disciples, who were grieving and
weeping, and told them what had happened.
11 But when she told them that Jesus was alive
and she had seen him, they didn't believe her.

12 Afterward he appeared in a different
form to two of his followers who were walk-
ing from Jerusalem into the country. 13 They

15:42 Greek *It was the day of preparation.* **16:2** Greek *on the first day of the week;* also in 16:9. **16:6** Or *Jesus the Nazarene.*
16:8 The most reliable early manuscripts of the Gospel of Mark end at verse 8. Other manuscripts include various endings to the Gospel. A few include both the "shorter ending" and the "longer ending." The majority of manuscripts include the "longer ending" immediately after verse 8.

rushed back to tell the others, but no one believed them.

[14]Still later he appeared to the eleven disciples as they were eating together. He rebuked them for their stubborn unbelief because they refused to believe those who had seen him after he had been raised from the dead.*

[15]And then he told them, "Go into all the world and preach the Good News to everyone. [16]Anyone who believes and is baptized will be saved. But anyone who refuses to believe will be condemned. [17]These miraculous signs will accompany those who believe: They will cast out demons in my name, and they will speak in new languages.* [18]They will be able to handle snakes with safety, and if they drink anything poisonous, it won't hurt them. They will be able to place their hands on the sick, and they will be healed."

[19]When the Lord Jesus had finished talking with them, he was taken up into heaven and sat down in the place of honor at God's right hand. [20]And the disciples went everywhere and preached, and the Lord worked through them, confirming what they said by many miraculous signs.

16:14 Some early manuscripts add: *And they excused themselves, saying, "This age of lawlessness and unbelief is under Satan, who does not permit God's truth and power to conquer the evil [unclean] spirits. Therefore, reveal your justice now." This is what they said to Christ. And Christ replied to them, "The period of years of Satan's power has been fulfilled, but other dreadful things will happen soon. And I was handed over to death for those who have sinned, so that they may return to the truth and sin no more, and so they may inherit the spiritual, incorruptible, and righteous glory in heaven."* **16:17** Or *new tongues;* some manuscripts do not include *new.*

LUKE

WHO
Jesus, Elizabeth, Zechariah, John the Baptist, Anna, Simeon, Mary, the disciples, Zacchaeus, Herod the Great, Pilate, and Mary Magdalene.

WHERE
In Rome or Caesarea.

WHEN
About AD 60.

WHY
To present an accurate account of the life of Christ and to present Christ as the perfect human and Savior.

Who is this man? . . . When he gives a command, even the wind and waves obey him!
LUKE 8:25

Luke, one of Jesus' followers, was a doctor. When he wrote about Jesus' life, Luke recorded Jesus' birth through the eyes of a doctor—teaching us that Jesus entered this world as a helpless baby. Luke shows Jesus as God's Son and as a human being. Jesus was the Son of God and the Son of Man.

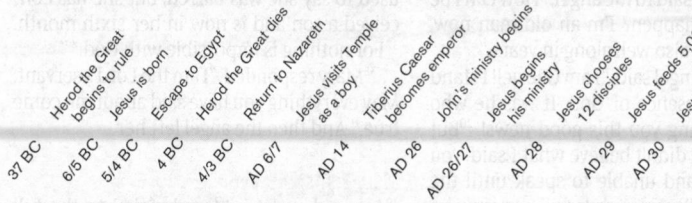

Praise God for sending His Son. Worship Him as Savior and Lord.

CHAPTER 1

Introduction

Many people have set out to write accounts
about the events that have been fulfilled
among us. [2]They used the eyewitness reports
circulating among us from the early disci-
ples.* [3]Having carefully investigated every-
thing from the beginning, I also have decided
to write a careful account for you, most hon-
orable Theophilus, [4]so you can be certain of
the truth of everything you were taught.

The Birth of John the Baptist Foretold

[5]When Herod was king of Judea, there was a
Jewish priest named Zechariah. He was a
member of the priestly order of Abijah, and his

1:2 Greek *from those who from the beginning were servants of the word.*

wife, Elizabeth, was also from the priestly line
of Aaron. [6]Zechariah and Elizabeth were righ-
teous in God's eyes, careful to obey all of the
Lord's commandments and regulations. [7]They
had no children because Elizabeth was unable
to conceive, and they were both very old.

[8]One day Zechariah was serving God in the
Temple, for his order was on duty that week.
[9]As was the custom of the priests, he was cho-
sen by lot to enter the sanctuary of the Lord
and burn incense. [10]While the incense was
being burned, a great crowd stood outside,
praying.

[11]While Zechariah was in the sanctuary, an
angel of the Lord appeared to him, standing to
the right of the incense altar. [12]Zechariah was
shaken and overwhelmed with fear when he
saw him. [13]But the angel said, "Don't be afraid,
Zechariah! God has heard your prayer. Your
wife, Elizabeth, will give you a son, and you are
to name him John. [14]You will have great joy and
gladness, and many will rejoice at his birth,
[15]for he will be great in the eyes of the Lord. He
must never touch wine or other alcoholic
drinks. He will be filled with the Holy Spirit,
even before his birth.* [16]And he will turn many
Israelites to the Lord their God. [17]He will be a
man with the spirit and power of Elijah. He will
prepare the people for the coming of the Lord.
He will turn the hearts of the fathers to their
children,* and he will cause those who are re-
bellious to accept the wisdom of the godly."

[18]Zechariah said to the angel, "How can I be
sure this will happen? I'm an old man now,
and my wife is also well along in years."

[19]Then the angel said, "I am Gabriel! I stand
in the very presence of God. It was he who
sent me to bring you this good news! [20]But
now, since you didn't believe what I said, you
will be silent and unable to speak until the
child is born. For my words will certainly be
fulfilled at the proper time."

[21]Meanwhile, the people were waiting for
Zechariah to come out of the sanctuary, won-
dering why he was taking so long. [22]When he
finally did come out, he couldn't speak to
them. Then they realized from his gestures
and his silence that he must have seen a vision
in the sanctuary.

[23]When Zechariah's week of service in the
Temple was over, he returned home. [24]Soon
afterward his wife, Elizabeth, became preg-
nant and went into seclusion for five months.
[25]"How kind the Lord is!" she exclaimed. "He
has taken away my disgrace of having no chil-
dren."

The Birth of Jesus Foretold

[26]In the sixth month of Elizabeth's pregnancy,
God sent the angel Gabriel to Nazareth, a vil-
lage in Galilee, [27]to a virgin named Mary. She
was engaged to be married to a man named
Joseph, a descendant of King David. [28]Gabriel
appeared to her and said, "Greetings, favored
woman! The Lord is with you!*"

[29]Confused and disturbed, Mary tried to
think what the angel could mean. [30]"Don't be
afraid, Mary," the angel told her, "for you have
found favor with God! [31]You will conceive and
give birth to a son, and you will name him
Jesus. [32]He will be very great and will be called
the Son of the Most High. The Lord God will
give him the throne of his ancestor David.
[33]And he will reign over Israel* forever; his
Kingdom will never end!"

[34]Mary asked the angel, "But how can this
happen? I am a virgin."

[35]The angel replied, "The Holy Spirit will
come upon you, and the power of the Most
High will overshadow you. So the baby to be
born will be holy, and he will be called the Son
of God. [36]What's more, your relative Elizabeth
has become pregnant in her old age! People
used to say she was barren, but she has con-
ceived a son and is now in her sixth month.
[37]For nothing is impossible with God.*"

[38]Mary responded, "I am the Lord's servant.
May everything you have said about me come
true." And then the angel left her.

Mary Visits Elizabeth

[39]A few days later Mary hurried to the hill
country of Judea, to the town [40]where Zecha-
riah lived. She entered the house and greeted
Elizabeth. [41]At the sound of Mary's greeting,
Elizabeth's child leaped within her, and Eliza-
beth was filled with the Holy Spirit.

[42]Elizabeth gave a glad cry and exclaimed to
Mary, "God has blessed you above all women,
and your child is blessed. [43]Why am I so hon-
ored, that the mother of my Lord should visit
me? [44]When I heard your greeting, the baby in

1:15 Or *even from birth.* **1:17** See Mal 4:5-6. **1:28** Some manuscripts add *Blessed are you among women.* **1:33** Greek *over the house of Jacob.* **1:37** Some manuscripts read *For the word of God will never fail.*

Zechariah

I should have listened, but it was such an unexpected visit. How often does an angel appear? He said my wife would have a baby. A son! I didn't believe him. After all, my wife and I were both old. So he took away my voice.

As we awaited the birth, everyone thought that I'd name the child after myself, as was our custom. "No, his name is *John*," Elizabeth said, after our boy was born. But our family and friends didn't believe her. So I took a tablet and scribbled a note. *Yes. His name is John!* Immediately I could speak again. Well, with my voice back and a new baby in the home, it was a joyful, noisy place!

Read Zechariah's story in Luke 1:5-25, 57-66.

my womb jumped for joy. 45 You are blessed because you believed that the Lord would do what he said."

The Magnificat: Mary's Song of Praise

46 Mary responded,

"Oh, how my soul praises the Lord.
47 How my spirit rejoices in God my Savior!
48 For he took notice of his lowly servant girl, and from now on all generations will call me blessed.
49 For the Mighty One is holy, and he has done great things for me.
50 He shows mercy from generation to generation to all who fear him.
51 His mighty arm has done tremendous things! He has scattered the proud and haughty ones.
52 He has brought down princes from their thrones and exalted the humble.
53 He has filled the hungry with good things and sent the rich away with empty hands.
54 He has helped his servant Israel and remembered to be merciful.
55 For he made this promise to our ancestors, to Abraham and his children forever."

56 Mary stayed with Elizabeth about three months and then went back to her own home.

The Birth of John the Baptist

57 When it was time for Elizabeth's baby to be born, she gave birth to a son. 58 And when her neighbors and relatives heard that the Lord had been very merciful to her, everyone rejoiced with her.

59 When the baby was eight days old, they all came for the circumcision ceremony. They wanted to name him Zechariah, after his father. 60 But Elizabeth said, "No! His name is John!"

61 "What?" they exclaimed. "There is no one in all your family by that name." 62 So they used gestures to ask the baby's father what he wanted to name him. 63 He motioned for a writing tablet, and to everyone's surprise he wrote, "His name is John." 64 Instantly Zechariah could speak again, and he began praising God.

65 Awe fell upon the whole neighborhood, and the news of what had happened spread throughout the Judean hills. 66 Everyone who heard about it reflected on these events and asked, "What will this child turn out to be?" For the hand of the Lord was surely upon him in a special way.

Zechariah's Prophecy

67 Then his father, Zechariah, was filled with
the Holy Spirit and gave this prophecy:

68 "Praise the Lord, the God of Israel,
because he has visited and redeemed
his people.
69 He has sent us a mighty Savior*
from the royal line of his servant David,
70 just as he promised
through his holy prophets long ago.
71 Now we will be saved from our enemies
and from all who hate us.
72 He has been merciful to our ancestors
by remembering his sacred covenant—
73 the covenant he swore with an oath
to our ancestor Abraham.
74 We have been rescued from our enemies
so we can serve God without fear,
75 in holiness and righteousness
for as long as we live.

76 "And you, my little son,
will be called the prophet of the Most
High,
because you will prepare the way for
the Lord.
77 You will tell his people how to find
salvation
through forgiveness of their sins.
78 Because of God's tender mercy,
the morning light from heaven is about
to break upon us,*
79 to give light to those who sit in darkness
and in the shadow of death,
and to guide us to the path of peace."

80 John grew up and became strong in spirit. And he lived in the wilderness until he began his public ministry to Israel.

CHAPTER 2

The Birth of Jesus

At that time the Roman emperor, Augustus, decreed that a census should be taken throughout the Roman Empire. 2 (This was the first census taken when Quirinius was governor of Syria.) 3 All returned to their own ancestral towns to register for this census. 4 And because Joseph was a descendant of King David, he had to go to Bethlehem in Judea, David's ancient home. He traveled there from the village of Nazareth in Galilee. 5 He took with him Mary, his fiancée, who was now obviously pregnant.

6 And while they were there, the time came for her baby to be born. 7 She gave birth to her first child, a son. She wrapped him snugly in strips of cloth and laid him in a manger, because there was no lodging available for them.

The Shepherds and Angels

8 That night there were shepherds staying in the fields nearby, guarding their flocks of sheep. 9 Suddenly, an angel of the Lord appeared among them, and the radiance of the Lord's glory surrounded them. They were terrified, 10 but the angel reassured them. "Don't be afraid!" he said. "I bring you good news that will bring great joy to all people. 11 The Savior—yes, the Messiah, the Lord—has been born today in Bethlehem, the city of David! 12 And you will recognize him by this sign: You will find a baby wrapped snugly in strips of cloth, lying in a manger."

13 Suddenly, the angel was joined by a vast host of others—the armies of heaven—praising God and saying,

14 "Glory to God in highest heaven,
and peace on earth to those with whom
God is pleased."

15 When the angels had returned to heaven, the shepherds said to each other, "Let's go to Bethlehem! Let's see this thing that has happened, which the Lord has told us about."

16 They hurried to the village and found Mary and Joseph. And there was the baby, lying in the manger. 17 After seeing him, the shepherds told everyone what had happened and what the angel had said to them about this child. 18 All who heard the shepherds' story were astonished, 19 but Mary kept all these things in her heart and thought about them often. 20 The shepherds went back to their flocks, glorifying and praising God for all they had heard and seen. It was just as the angel had told them.

Jesus Is Presented in the Temple

21 Eight days later, when the baby was circumcised, he was named Jesus, the name given him by the angel even before he was conceived.

1:69 Greek *has raised up a horn of salvation for us.* **1:78** Or *the Morning Light from Heaven is about to visit us.*

[22]Then it was time for their purification
offering, as required by the law of Moses after
the birth of a child; so his parents took him to
Jerusalem to present him to the Lord. [23]The
law of the Lord says, "If a woman's first child
is a boy, he must be dedicated to the LORD."*
[24]So they offered the sacrifice required in the
law of the Lord—"either a pair of turtledoves
or two young pigeons."*

The Prophecy of Simeon

[25]At that time there was a man in Jerusalem
named Simeon. He was righteous and devout
and was eagerly waiting for the Messiah to
come and rescue Israel. The Holy Spirit was
upon him [26]and had revealed to him that he
would not die until he had seen the Lord's
Messiah. [27]That day the Spirit led him to the
Temple. So when Mary and Joseph came to
present the baby Jesus to the Lord as the law
required, [28]Simeon was there. He took the
child in his arms and praised God, saying,

29 "Sovereign Lord, now let your servant die
in peace,
as you have promised.
30 I have seen your salvation,
31 which you have prepared for all people.
32 He is a light to reveal God to the nations,
and he is the glory of your people
Israel!"

[33]Jesus' parents were amazed at what was
being said about him. [34]Then Simeon blessed
them, and he said to Mary, the baby's mother,
"This child is destined to cause many in Israel
to fall, but he will be a joy to many others. He
has been sent as a sign from God, but many
will oppose him. [35]As a result, the deepest
thoughts of many hearts will be revealed. And
a sword will pierce your very soul."

The Prophecy of Anna

[36]Anna, a prophet, was also there in the Temple. She was the daughter of Phanuel from
the tribe of Asher, and she was very old. Her
husband died when they had been married
only seven years. [37]Then she lived as a widow
to the age of eighty-four.* She never left the
Temple but stayed there day and night, worshiping God with fasting and prayer. [38]She
came along just as Simeon was talking with
Mary and Joseph, and she began praising God.
She talked about the child to everyone who
had been waiting expectantly for God to rescue Jerusalem.

[39]When Jesus' parents had fulfilled all the
requirements of the law of the Lord, they returned home to Nazareth in Galilee. [40]There
the child grew up healthy and strong. He was
filled with wisdom, and God's favor was on
him.

Jesus Speaks with the Teachers

[41]Every year Jesus' parents went to Jerusalem
for the Passover festival. [42]When Jesus was
twelve years old, they attended the festival as
usual. [43]After the celebration was over, they
started home to Nazareth, but Jesus stayed

2:23 Exod 13:2. **2:24** Lev 12:8. **2:37** Or *She had been a widow for eighty-four years.*

DON'T BE AFRAID

When God or his angels spoke to Bible-time people, they all had the same response—fear. God always told them not to be afraid. As soon as they understood that God accepted them and wanted to communicate with them, they stopped being afraid. He had given them freedom to be his friends. You are free to be God's friend too. How are you using your freedom?

Person	Reference
Abraham	Genesis 15:1
Moses	Numbers 21:34; Deuteronomy 3:2
Joshua	Joshua 8:1
Jeremiah	Lamentations 3:57
Daniel	Daniel 10:12, 19
Zechariah	Luke 1:13
Mary	Luke 1:30
Shepherds	Luke 2:10
Peter	Luke 5:10
Paul	Acts 27:24
John	Revelation 1:17-18

DO NOT FEAR!

JOHN THE BAPTIST

One day Jesus came and asked me to baptize him. Me? I was not worthy even to untie his sandal. But he insisted, and I heard a voice from heaven say, "This is my Son." I trembled to be so near to God.

But later I began to wonder if I was right about who Jesus was. So I sent my followers to ask him, "Are you the Promised One?"

Jesus sent a clear answer. He said that many people were being healed. The blind could see and the deaf could hear. The lame were dancing. The poor were listening to the Good News. I had ears and eyes. I could see that Jesus was the long-awaited One.

Learn more about John the Baptist in Matthew 3:1-6; 11:2-6 and Luke 3:1-22.

behind in Jerusalem. His parents didn't miss him at first, 44because they assumed he was among the other travelers. But when he didn't show up that evening, they started looking for him among their relatives and friends.

45When they couldn't find him, they went back to Jerusalem to search for him there. 46Three days later they finally discovered him in the Temple, sitting among the religious teachers, listening to them and asking questions. 47All who heard him were amazed at his understanding and his answers.

48His parents didn't know what to think. "Son," his mother said to him, "why have you done this to us? Your father and I have been frantic, searching for you everywhere."

49"But why did you need to search?" he asked. "Didn't you know that I must be in my Father's house?"* 50But they didn't understand what he meant.

51Then he returned to Nazareth with them and was obedient to them. And his mother stored all these things in her heart.

52Jesus grew in wisdom and in stature and in favor with God and all the people.

CHAPTER 3

John the Baptist Prepares the Way

It was now the fifteenth year of the reign of Tiberius, the Roman emperor. Pontius Pilate was governor over Judea; Herod Antipas was ruler* over Galilee; his brother Philip was ruler* over Iturea and Traconitis; Lysanias was ruler over Abilene. 2Annas and Caiaphas were the high priests. At this time a message from God came to John son of Zechariah, who was living in the wilderness. 3Then John went from place to place on both sides of the Jordan River, preaching that people should be baptized to show that they had repented of their sins and turned to God to be forgiven. 4Isaiah had spoken of John when he said,

"He is a voice shouting in the wilderness,
'Prepare the way for the LORD's coming!
Clear the road for him!
5 The valleys will be filled,
and the mountains and hills made level.
The curves will be straightened,
and the rough places made smooth.
6 And then all people will see
the salvation sent from God.'"*

7When the crowds came to John for baptism, he said, "You brood of snakes! Who warned you to flee God's coming wrath? 8Prove by the way you live that you have repented of your sins and turned to God. Don't just say to each other, 'We're safe, for we are descendants of Abraham.' That means noth-

2:49 Or *"Didn't you realize that I should be involved with my Father's affairs?"* **3:1a** Greek *Herod was tetrarch.* Herod Antipas was a son of King Herod. **3:1b** Greek *tetrarch;* also in 3:1c. **3:4-6** Isa 40:3-5 (Greek version).

ing, for I tell you, God can create children of
Abraham from these very stones. 9Even now
the ax of God's judgment is poised, ready to
sever the roots of the trees. Yes, every tree
that does not produce good fruit will be
chopped down and thrown into the fire."
10The crowds asked, "What should we do?"
11John replied, "If you have two shirts, give
one to the poor. If you have food, share it with
those who are hungry."
12Even corrupt tax collectors came to be
baptized and asked, "Teacher, what should
we do?"
13He replied, "Collect no more taxes than
the government requires."
14"What should we do?" asked some sol-
diers.
John replied, "Don't extort money or make
false accusations. And be content with your
pay."
15Everyone was expecting the Messiah to
come soon, and they were eager to know
whether John might be the Messiah. 16John
answered their questions by saying, "I baptize
you with* water; but someone is coming soon
who is greater than I am—so much greater
that I'm not even worthy to be his slave and
untie the straps of his sandals. He will baptize
you with the Holy Spirit and with fire.* 17He is
ready to separate the chaff from the wheat
with his winnowing fork. Then he will clean
up the threshing area, gathering the wheat
into his barn but burning the chaff with
never-ending fire." 18John used many such
warnings as he announced the Good News to
the people.
19John also publicly criticized Herod Anti-
pas, the ruler of Galilee,* for marrying Hero-
dias, his brother's wife, and for many other
wrongs he had done. 20So Herod put John in
prison, adding this sin to his many others.

The Baptism of Jesus

21One day when the crowds were being bap-
tized, Jesus himself was baptized. As he was
praying, the heavens opened, 22and the Holy
Spirit, in bodily form, descended on him like
a dove. And a voice from heaven said, "You
are my dearly loved Son, and you bring me
great joy.*"

The Ancestors of Jesus

23Jesus was about thirty years old when he be-
gan his public ministry.

Jesus was known as the son of Joseph.
Joseph was the son of Heli.
24 Heli was the son of Matthat.
Matthat was the son of Levi.
Levi was the son of Melki.
Melki was the son of Jannai.
Jannai was the son of Joseph.
25 Joseph was the son of Mattathias.
Mattathias was the son of Amos.
Amos was the son of Nahum.
Nahum was the son of Esli.
Esli was the son of Naggai.
26 Naggai was the son of Maath.
Maath was the son of Mattathias.
Mattathias was the son of Semein.
Semein was the son of Josech.
Josech was the son of Joda.
27 Joda was the son of Joanan.
Joanan was the son of Rhesa.
Rhesa was the son of Zerubbabel.
Zerubbabel was the son of Shealtiel.
Shealtiel was the son of Neri.
28 Neri was the son of Melki.
Melki was the son of Addi.
Addi was the son of Cosam.
Cosam was the son of Elmadam.
Elmadam was the son of Er.
29 Er was the son of Joshua.
Joshua was the son of Eliezer.
Eliezer was the son of Jorim.
Jorim was the son of Matthat.
Matthat was the son of Levi.
30 Levi was the son of Simeon.
Simeon was the son of Judah.
Judah was the son of Joseph.
Joseph was the son of Jonam.
Jonam was the son of Eliakim.
31 Eliakim was the son of Melea.
Melea was the son of Menna.
Menna was the son of Mattatha.
Mattatha was the son of Nathan.
Nathan was the son of David.
32 David was the son of Jesse.
Jesse was the son of Obed.
Obed was the son of Boaz.
Boaz was the son of Salmon.*
Salmon was the son of Nahshon.

3:16a Or *in.* **3:16b** Or *in the Holy Spirit and in fire.* **3:19** Greek *Herod the tetrarch.* **3:22** Some manuscripts read *my Son, and today I have become your Father.* **3:32** Greek *Sala,* a variant spelling of Salmon; also in 3:32b. See Ruth 4:22.

33 Nahshon was the son of Amminadab.
Amminadab was the son of Admin.
Admin was the son of Arni.*
Arni was the son of Hezron.
Hezron was the son of Perez.
Perez was the son of Judah.
34 Judah was the son of Jacob.
Jacob was the son of Isaac.
Isaac was the son of Abraham.
Abraham was the son of Terah.
Terah was the son of Nahor.
35 Nahor was the son of Serug.
Serug was the son of Reu.
Reu was the son of Peleg.
Peleg was the son of Eber.
Eber was the son of Shelah.
36 Shelah was the son of Cainan.
Cainan was the son of Arphaxad.
Arphaxad was the son of Shem.
Shem was the son of Noah.
Noah was the son of Lamech.
37 Lamech was the son of Methuselah.
Methuselah was the son of Enoch.
Enoch was the son of Jared.
Jared was the son of Mahalalel.
Mahalalel was the son of Kenan.
38 Kenan was the son of Enosh.*
Enosh was the son of Seth.
Seth was the son of Adam.
Adam was the son of God.

CHAPTER 4

The Temptation of Jesus

Then Jesus, full of the Holy Spirit, returned from the Jordan River. He was led by the Spirit in the wilderness,* 2 where he was tempted by the devil for forty days. Jesus ate nothing all that time and became very hungry.

3 Then the devil said to him, "If you are the Son of God, tell this stone to become a loaf of bread."

4 But Jesus told him, "No! The Scriptures say, 'People do not live by bread alone.'*"

5 Then the devil took him up and revealed to him all the kingdoms of the world in a moment of time. 6 "I will give you the glory of these kingdoms and authority over them," the devil said, "because they are mine to give to anyone I please. 7 I will give it all to you if you will worship me."

8 Jesus replied, "The Scriptures say,

'You must worship the LORD your God
and serve only him.'*"

9 Then the devil took him to Jerusalem, to the highest point of the Temple, and said, "If you are the Son of God, jump off! 10 For the Scriptures say,

'He will order his angels to protect and
guard you.
11 And they will hold you up with their
hands
so you won't even hurt your foot on a
stone.'*"

12 Jesus responded, "The Scriptures also say, 'You must not test the LORD your God.'*"

13 When the devil had finished tempting Jesus, he left him until the next opportunity came.

Jesus Rejected at Nazareth

14 Then Jesus returned to Galilee, filled with the Holy Spirit's power. Reports about him spread quickly through the whole region. 15 He taught regularly in their synagogues and was praised by everyone.

16 When he came to the village of Nazareth, his boyhood home, he went as usual to the synagogue on the Sabbath and stood up to read the Scriptures. 17 The scroll of Isaiah the prophet was handed to him. He unrolled the scroll and found the place where this was written:

18 "The Spirit of the LORD is upon me,
for he has anointed me to bring Good
News to the poor.
He has sent me to proclaim that captives
will be released,
that the blind will see,
that the oppressed will be set free,
19 and that the time of the LORD's favor
has come.*"

20 He rolled up the scroll, handed it back to the attendant, and sat down. All eyes in the synagogue looked at him intently. 21 Then he began to speak to them. "The Scripture you've just heard has been fulfilled this very day!"

3:33 Some manuscripts read *Amminadab was the son of Aram*. *Arni* and *Aram* are alternate spellings of Ram. See 1 Chr 2:9-10. **3:38** Greek *Enos*, a variant spelling of Enosh; also in 3:38b. See Gen 5:6. **4:1** Some manuscripts read *into the wilderness*. **4:4** Deut 8:3. **4:8** Deut 6:13. **4:10-11** Ps 91:11-12. **4:12** Deut 6:16. **4:18-19** Or *and to proclaim the acceptable year of the LORD*. Isa 61:1-2 (Greek version); 58:6.

[22]Everyone spoke well of him and was amazed by the gracious words that came from his lips. "How can this be?" they asked. "Isn't this Joseph's son?"

[23]Then he said, "You will undoubtedly quote me this proverb: 'Physician, heal yourself'—meaning, 'Do miracles here in your hometown like those you did in Capernaum.' [24]But I tell you the truth, no prophet is accepted in his own hometown.

[25]"Certainly there were many needy widows in Israel in Elijah's time, when the heavens were closed for three and a half years, and a severe famine devastated the land. [26]Yet Elijah was not sent to any of them. He was sent instead to a foreigner—a widow of Zarephath in the land of Sidon. [27]And there were many lepers in Israel in the time of the prophet Elisha, but the only one healed was Naaman, a Syrian."

[28]When they heard this, the people in the synagogue were furious. [29]Jumping up, they mobbed him and forced him to the edge of the hill on which the town was built. They intended to push him over the cliff, [30]but he passed right through the crowd and went on his way.

Jesus Casts Out a Demon

[31]Then Jesus went to Capernaum, a town in Galilee, and taught there in the synagogue every Sabbath day. [32]There, too, the people were amazed at his teaching, for he spoke with authority.

[33]Once when he was in the synagogue, a man possessed by a demon—an evil* spirit—began shouting at Jesus, [34]"Go away! Why are you interfering with us, Jesus of Nazareth? Have you come to destroy us? I know who you are—the Holy One of God!"

[35]Jesus cut him short. "Be quiet! Come out of the man," he ordered. At that, the demon threw the man to the floor as the crowd watched; then it came out of him without hurting him further.

[36]Amazed, the people exclaimed, "What authority and power this man's words possess! Even evil spirits obey him, and they flee at his command!" [37]The news about Jesus spread through every village in the entire region.

Jesus Heals Many People

[38]After leaving the synagogue that day, Jesus went to Simon's home, where he found Simon's mother-in-law very sick with a high fever. "Please heal her," everyone begged. [39]Standing at her bedside, he rebuked the fever, and it left her. And she got up at once and prepared a meal for them.

[40]As the sun went down that evening, people throughout the village brought sick family members to Jesus. No matter what their diseases were, the touch of his hand healed every one. [41]Many were possessed by demons; and the demons came out at his command, shouting, "You are the Son of God!" But because they knew he was the Messiah, he rebuked them and refused to let them speak.

Jesus Continues to Preach

[42]Early the next morning Jesus went out to an isolated place. The crowds searched everywhere for him, and when they finally found him, they begged him not to leave them. [43]But he replied, "I must preach the Good News of the Kingdom of God in other towns, too, because that is why I was sent." [44]So he continued to travel around, preaching in synagogues throughout Judea.*

CHAPTER 5

The First Disciples

One day as Jesus was preaching on the shore of the Sea of Galilee,* great crowds pressed in on him to listen to the word of God. [2]He noticed two empty boats at the water's edge, for the fishermen had left them and were washing their nets. [3]Stepping into one of the boats, Jesus asked Simon,* its owner, to push it out into the water. So he sat in the boat and taught the crowds from there.

[4]When he had finished speaking, he said to Simon, "Now go out where it is deeper, and let down your nets to catch some fish."

[5]"Master," Simon replied, "we worked hard all last night and didn't catch a thing. But if you say so, I'll let the nets down again." [6]And this time their nets were so full of fish they began to tear! [7]A shout for help brought their partners in the other boat, and soon both boats were filled with fish and on the verge of sinking.

4:33 Greek *unclean;* also in 4:36. **4:44** Some manuscripts read *Galilee.* **5:1** Greek *Lake Gennesaret,* another name for the Sea of Galilee. **5:3** *Simon* is called "Peter" in 6:14 and thereafter.

[8]When Simon Peter realized what had happened, he fell to his knees before Jesus and said, "Oh, Lord, please leave me—I'm too much of a sinner to be around you." [9]For he was awestruck by the number of fish they had caught, as were the others with him. [10]His partners, James and John, the sons of Zebedee, were also amazed.

Jesus replied to Simon, "Don't be afraid! From now on you'll be fishing for people!" [11]And as soon as they landed, they left everything and followed Jesus.

AMAZING FACTS

Some fishermen were so excited about following Jesus that they didn't stop to pack anything!

LUKE 5:1-11

Jesus Heals a Man with Leprosy

[12]In one of the villages, Jesus met a man with an advanced case of leprosy. When the man saw Jesus, he bowed with his face to the ground, begging to be healed. "Lord," he said, "if you are willing, you can heal me and make me clean."

[13]Jesus reached out and touched him. "I am willing," he said. "Be healed!" And instantly the leprosy disappeared. [14]Then Jesus instructed him not to tell anyone what had happened. He said, "Go to the priest and let him examine you. Take along the offering required in the law of Moses for those who have been healed of leprosy.* This will be a public testimony that you have been cleansed."

[15]But despite Jesus' instructions, the report of his power spread even faster, and vast crowds came to hear him preach and to be healed of their diseases. [16]But Jesus often withdrew to the wilderness for prayer.

Jesus Heals a Paralyzed Man

[17]One day while Jesus was teaching, some Pharisees and teachers of religious law were sitting nearby. (It seemed that these men showed up from every village in all Galilee and Judea, as well as from Jerusalem.) And the Lord's healing power was strongly with Jesus.

[18]Some men came carrying a paralyzed man on a sleeping mat. They tried to take him inside to Jesus, [19]but they couldn't reach him because of the crowd. So they went up to the roof and took off some tiles. Then they lowered the sick man on his mat down into the crowd, right in front of Jesus. [20]Seeing their faith, Jesus said to the man, "Young man, your sins are forgiven."

[21]But the Pharisees and teachers of religious law said to themselves, "Who does he think he is? That's blasphemy! Only God can forgive sins!"

[22]Jesus knew what they were thinking, so he asked them, "Why do you question this in your hearts? [23]Is it easier to say 'Your sins are forgiven,' or 'Stand up and walk'? [24]So I will prove to you that the Son of Man* has the authority on earth to forgive sins." Then Jesus turned to the paralyzed man and said, "Stand up, pick up your mat, and go home!"

[25]And immediately, as everyone watched, the man jumped up, picked up his mat, and went home praising God. [26]Everyone was gripped with great wonder and awe, and they praised God, exclaiming, "We have seen amazing things today!"

Jesus Calls Levi (Matthew)

[27]Later, as Jesus left the town, he saw a tax collector named Levi sitting at his tax collector's booth. "Follow me and be my disciple," Jesus said to him. [28]So Levi got up, left everything, and followed him.

[29]Later, Levi held a banquet in his home with Jesus as the guest of honor. Many of Levi's fellow tax collectors and other guests also ate with them. [30]But the Pharisees and their teachers of religious law complained bitterly to Jesus' disciples, "Why do you eat and drink with such scum?*"

[31]Jesus answered them, "Healthy people don't need a doctor—sick people do. [32]I have come to call not those who think they are

5:14 See Lev 14:2-32. **5:24** "Son of Man" is a title Jesus used for himself. **5:30** Greek *with tax collectors and sinners?*

righteous, but those who know they are sinners and need to repent."

A Discussion about Fasting

33 One day some people said to Jesus, "John the
Baptist's disciples fast and pray regularly, and
so do the disciples of the Pharisees. Why are
your disciples always eating and drinking?"
34 Jesus responded, "Do wedding guests
fast while celebrating with the groom? Of
course not. 35 But someday the groom will be
taken away from them, and then they will
fast."
36 Then Jesus gave them this illustration:
"No one tears a piece of cloth from a new gar-
ment and uses it to patch an old garment. For
then the new garment would be ruined, and
the new patch wouldn't even match the old
garment.
37 "And no one puts new wine into old wine-
skins. For the new wine would burst the wine-
skins, spilling the wine and ruining the skins.
38 New wine must be stored in new wineskins.
39 But no one who drinks the old wine seems to
want the new wine. 'The old is just fine,' they
say."

CHAPTER 6

A Discussion about the Sabbath

One Sabbath day as Jesus was walking
through some grainfields, his disciples broke
off heads of grain, rubbed off the husks in
their hands, and ate the grain. 2 But some
Pharisees said, "Why are you breaking the
law by harvesting grain on the Sabbath?"
3 Jesus replied, "Haven't you read in the
Scriptures what David did when he and his
companions were hungry? 4 He went into the
house of God and broke the law by eating the
sacred loaves of bread that only the priests
can eat. He also gave some to his companions." 5 And Jesus added, "The Son of Man* is
Lord, even over the Sabbath."

Jesus Heals on the Sabbath

6 On another Sabbath day, a man with a de-
formed right hand was in the synagogue while
Jesus was teaching. 7 The teachers of religious
law and the Pharisees watched Jesus closely. If
he healed the man's hand, they planned to ac-
cuse him of working on the Sabbath.
8 But Jesus knew their thoughts. He said to
the man with the deformed hand, "Come and
stand in front of everyone." So the man came
forward. 9 Then Jesus said to his critics, "I have
a question for you. Does the law permit good
deeds on the Sabbath, or is it a day for doing
evil? Is this a day to save life or to destroy it?"
10 He looked around at them one by one and
then said to the man, "Hold out your hand."
So the man held out his hand, and it was re-
stored! 11 At this, the enemies of Jesus were
wild with rage and began to discuss what to
do with him.

Jesus Chooses the Twelve Apostles

12 One day soon afterward Jesus went up on a
mountain to pray, and he prayed to God all
night. 13 At daybreak he called together all of
his disciples and chose twelve of them to be
apostles. Here are their names:

14 Simon (whom he named Peter),
Andrew (Peter's brother),
James,
John,
Philip,
Bartholomew,
15 Matthew,
Thomas,
James (son of Alphaeus),
Simon (who was called the zealot),
16 Judas (son of James),
Judas Iscariot (who later betrayed him).

Crowds Follow Jesus

17 When they came down from the mountain,
the disciples stood with Jesus on a large, level
area, surrounded by many of his followers
and by the crowds. There were people from
all over Judea and from Jerusalem and from
as far north as the seacoasts of Tyre and Si-
don. 18 They had come to hear him and to be
healed of their diseases; and those troubled
by evil* spirits were healed. 19 Everyone tried
to touch him, because healing power went
out from him, and he healed everyone.

The Beatitudes

20 Then Jesus turned to his disciples and said,

"God blesses you who are poor,
for the Kingdom of God is yours.

6:5 "Son of Man" is a title Jesus used for himself. **6:18** Greek *unclean.*

CUT UP AND CUT DOWN

There was a girl in Seth's class who got on everyone's nerves. She had a high-pitched voice that almost sounded like a whine. Every time she talked, it was like fingernails scraping a chalkboard. Recently her name came up, and some kids started cutting her down. Later Seth thought of a joke about the girl to tell the group—he knew they'd love it. He tried to convince himself it would be OK. *Oh, it's harmless,* Seth thought. *It would get a laugh and the girl would never know, right?* Read Luke 6:37 to see what Jesus might tell Seth.

21 God blesses you who are hungry now,
for you will be satisfied.
God blesses you who weep now,
for in due time you will laugh.

22 What blessings await you when people hate
you and exclude you and mock you and curse
you as evil because you follow the Son of Man.
23 When that happens, be happy! Yes, leap for
joy! For a great reward awaits you in heaven.
And remember, their ancestors treated the
ancient prophets that same way.

Sorrows Foretold

24 "What sorrow awaits you who are rich,
for you have your only happiness now.
25 What sorrow awaits you who are fat and
prosperous now,
for a time of awful hunger awaits you.
What sorrow awaits you who laugh now,
for your laughing will turn to mourning
and sorrow.
26 What sorrow awaits you who are praised
by the crowds,
for their ancestors also praised false
prophets.

Love for Enemies

27 "But to you who are willing to listen, I say,
love your enemies! Do good to those who hate
you. 28 Bless those who curse you. Pray for
those who hurt you. 29 If someone slaps you
on one cheek, offer the other cheek also. If
someone demands your coat, offer your shirt
also. 30 Give to anyone who asks; and when
things are taken away from you, don't try to
get them back. 31 Do to others as you would
like them to do to you.

32 "If you love only those who love you, why
should you get credit for that? Even sinners
love those who love them! 33 And if you do
good only to those who do good to you, why
should you get credit? Even sinners do that
much! 34 And if you lend money only to those
who can repay you, why should you get
credit? Even sinners will lend to other sinners
for a full return.

35 "Love your enemies! Do good to them.
Lend to them without expecting to be repaid.
Then your reward from heaven will be very
great, and you will truly be acting as children
of the Most High, for he is kind to those who
are unthankful and wicked. 36 You must be
compassionate, just as your Father is compas-
sionate.

Do Not Judge Others

37 "Do not judge others, and you will not be
judged. Do not condemn others, or it will all
come back against you. Forgive others, and
you will be forgiven. 38 Give, and you will re-
ceive. Your gift will return to you in full—

pressed down, shaken together to make room
for more, running over, and poured into your
lap. The amount you give will determine the
amount you get back.*"
39 Then Jesus gave the following illustration:
"Can one blind person lead another? Won't
they both fall into a ditch? 40 Students* are not
greater than their teacher. But the student who
is fully trained will become like the teacher.
41 "And why worry about a speck in your
friend's eye* when you have a log in your
own? 42 How can you think of saying, 'Friend,*
let me help you get rid of that speck in your
eye,' when you can't see past the log in your
own eye? Hypocrite! First get rid of the log in
your own eye; then you will see well enough to
deal with the speck in your friend's eye.

The Tree and Its Fruit

43 "A good tree can't produce bad fruit, and a
bad tree can't produce good fruit. 44 A tree is
identified by its fruit. Figs are never gathered
from thornbushes, and grapes are not picked
from bramble bushes. 45 A good person pro-
duces good things from the treasury of a good
heart, and an evil person produces evil things
from the treasury of an evil heart. What you
say flows from what is in your heart.

Building on a Solid Foundation

46 "So why do you keep calling me 'Lord, Lord!'
when you don't do what I say? 47 I will show
you what it's like when someone comes to me,
listens to my teaching, and then follows it. 48 It
is like a person building a house who digs
deep and lays the foundation on solid rock.
When the floodwaters rise and break against
that house, it stands firm because it is well
built. 49 But anyone who hears and doesn't
obey is like a person who builds a house with-
out a foundation. When the floods sweep
down against that house, it will collapse into a
heap of ruins."

CHAPTER 7

The Faith of a Roman Officer

When Jesus had finished saying all this to
the people, he returned to Capernaum. 2 At
that time the highly valued slave of a Roman
officer* was sick and near death. 3 When the
officer heard about Jesus, he sent some re-
spected Jewish elders to ask him to come
and heal his slave. 4 So they earnestly begged
Jesus to help the man. "If anyone deserves
your help, he does," they said, 5 "for he loves
the Jewish people and even built a synagogue
for us."
6 So Jesus went with them. But just before
they arrived at the house, the officer sent
some friends to say, "Lord, don't trouble your-
self by coming to my home, for I am not wor-
thy of such an honor. 7 I am not even worthy to
come and meet you. Just say the word from
where you are, and my servant will be healed.
8 I know this because I am under the authority
of my superior officers, and I have authority
over my soldiers. I only need to say, 'Go,' and
they go, or 'Come,' and they come. And if I say
to my slaves, 'Do this,' they do it."
9 When Jesus heard this, he was amazed.
Turning to the crowd that was following him,
he said, "I tell you, I haven't seen faith like this
in all Israel!" 10 And when the officer's friends
returned to his house, they found the slave
completely healed.

Jesus Raises a Widow's Son

11 Soon afterward Jesus went with his disci-
ples to the village of Nain, and a large crowd
followed him. 12 A funeral procession was
coming out as he approached the village
gate. The young man who had died was a
widow's only son, and a large crowd from the
village was with her. 13 When the Lord saw
her, his heart overflowed with compassion.
"Don't cry!" he said. 14 Then he walked over to
the coffin and touched it, and the bearers
stopped. "Young man," he said, "I tell you,
get up." 15 Then the dead boy sat up and be-
gan to talk! And Jesus gave him back to his
mother.
16 Great fear swept the crowd, and they
praised God, saying, "A mighty prophet has
risen among us," and "God has visited his
people today." 17 And the news about Jesus
spread throughout Judea and the surround-
ing countryside.

Jesus and John the Baptist

18 The disciples of John the Baptist told John
about everything Jesus was doing. So John
called for two of his disciples, 19 and he sent

6:38 Or *The measure you give will be the measure you get back.* **6:40** Or *Disciples.* **6:41** Greek *your brother's eye;* also in 6:42.
6:42 Greek *Brother.* **7:2** Greek *a centurion;* similarly in 7:6.

them to the Lord to ask him, "Are you the Messiah we've been expecting,* or should we keep looking for someone else?"

[20]John's two disciples found Jesus and said to him, "John the Baptist sent us to ask, 'Are you the Messiah we've been expecting, or should we keep looking for someone else?'"

[21]At that very time, Jesus cured many people of their diseases, illnesses, and evil spirits, and he restored sight to many who were blind. [22]Then he told John's disciples, "Go back to John and tell him what you have seen and heard—the blind see, the lame walk, the lepers are cured, the deaf hear, the dead are raised to life, and the Good News is being preached to the poor. [23]And tell him, 'God blesses those who do not turn away because of me.*'"

[24]After John's disciples left, Jesus began talking about him to the crowds. "What kind of man did you go into the wilderness to see? Was he a weak reed, swayed by every breath of wind? [25]Or were you expecting to see a man dressed in expensive clothes? No, people who wear beautiful clothes and live in luxury are found in palaces. [26]Were you looking for a prophet? Yes, and he is more than a prophet. [27]John is the man to whom the Scriptures refer when they say,

'Look, I am sending my messenger ahead
of you,
and he will prepare your way before
you.'*

[28]I tell you, of all who have ever lived, none is greater than John. Yet even the least person in the Kingdom of God is greater than he is!"

[29]When they heard this, all the people—even the tax collectors—agreed that God's way was right,* for they had been baptized by John. [30]But the Pharisees and experts in religious law rejected God's plan for them, for they had refused John's baptism.

[31]"To what can I compare the people of this generation?" Jesus asked. "How can I describe them? [32]They are like children playing a game in the public square. They complain to their friends,

'We played wedding songs,
and you didn't dance,
so we played funeral songs,
and you didn't weep.'

[33]For John the Baptist didn't spend his time eating bread or drinking wine, and you say, 'He's possessed by a demon.' [34]The Son of Man,* on the other hand, feasts and drinks, and you say, 'He's a glutton and a drunkard, and a friend of tax collectors and other sinners!' [35]But wisdom is shown to be right by the lives of those who follow it.*"

Jesus Anointed by a Sinful Woman

[36]One of the Pharisees asked Jesus to have dinner with him, so Jesus went to his home and sat down to eat.* [37]When a certain immoral woman from that city heard he was eating there, she brought a beautiful alabaster jar filled with expensive perfume. [38]Then she knelt behind him at his feet, weeping. Her tears fell on his feet, and she wiped them off with her hair. Then she kept kissing his feet and putting perfume on them.

[39]When the Pharisee who had invited him saw this, he said to himself, "If this man were a prophet, he would know what kind of woman is touching him. She's a sinner!"

[40]Then Jesus answered his thoughts. "Simon," he said to the Pharisee, "I have something to say to you."

"Go ahead, Teacher," Simon replied.

[41]Then Jesus told him this story: "A man loaned money to two people—500 pieces of silver* to one and 50 pieces to the other. [42]But neither of them could repay him, so he kindly forgave them both, canceling their debts. Who do you suppose loved him more after that?"

[43]Simon answered, "I suppose the one for whom he canceled the larger debt."

"That's right," Jesus said. [44]Then he turned to the woman and said to Simon, "Look at this woman kneeling here. When I entered your home, you didn't offer me water to wash the dust from my feet, but she has washed them with her tears and wiped them with her hair. [45]You didn't greet me with a kiss, but from the time I first came in, she has not stopped kissing my feet. [46]You neglected the courtesy of olive oil to anoint my head, but she has anointed my feet with rare perfume.

7:19 Greek *Are you the one who is coming?* Also in 7:20. **7:23** Or *who are not offended by me.* **7:27** Mal 3:1. **7:29** Or *praised God for his justice.* **7:34** "Son of Man" is a title Jesus used for himself. **7:35** Or *But wisdom is justified by all her children.* **7:36** Or *and reclined.* **7:41** Greek *500 denarii.* A denarius was equivalent to a laborer's full day's wage.

47"I tell you, her sins—and they are many—
have been forgiven, so she has shown me
much love. But a person who is forgiven little
shows only little love." 48Then Jesus said to the
woman, "Your sins are forgiven."

49The men at the table said among them-
selves, "Who is this man, that he goes around
forgiving sins?"

50And Jesus said to the woman, "Your faith
has saved you; go in peace."

CHAPTER 8

Women Who Followed Jesus

Soon afterward Jesus began a tour of the
nearby towns and villages, preaching and an-
nouncing the Good News about the Kingdom
of God. He took his twelve disciples with him,
2along with some women who had been cured
of evil spirits and diseases. Among them were
Mary Magdalene, from whom he had cast
out seven demons; 3Joanna, the wife of Chuza,
Herod's business manager; Susanna; and
many others who were contributing from
their own resources to support Jesus and his
disciples.

Parable of the Farmer Scattering Seed

4One day Jesus told a story in the form of a par-
able to a large crowd that had gathered from
many towns to hear him: 5"A farmer went out
to plant his seed. As he scattered it across his
field, some seed fell on a footpath, where it was
stepped on, and the birds ate it. 6Other seed fell
among rocks. It began to grow, but the plant
soon wilted and died for lack of moisture.
7Other seed fell among thorns that grew up
with it and choked out the tender plants. 8Still
other seed fell on fertile soil. This seed grew
and produced a crop that was a hundred times
as much as had been planted!" When he had
said this, he called out, "Anyone with ears to
hear should listen and understand."

9His disciples asked him what this parable
meant. 10He replied, "You are permitted to
understand the secrets* of the Kingdom of
God. But I use parables to teach the others so
that the Scriptures might be fulfilled:

'When they look, they won't really see.
When they hear, they won't
understand.'*

11"This is the meaning of the parable: The
seed is God's word. 12The seeds that fell on
the footpath represent those who hear the
message, only to have the devil come and take
it away from their hearts and prevent them
from believing and being saved. 13The seeds
on the rocky soil represent those who hear
the message and receive it with joy. But since
they don't have deep roots, they believe for a
while, then they fall away when they face
temptation. 14The seeds that fell among the

8:10a Greek *mysteries*. **8:10b** Isa 6:9 (Greek version).

JESUS AND WOMEN

In first-century Jewish culture, women were usually treated as second-class citizens and had few of the rights men had. But Jesus crossed those barriers, and Luke showed the special care Jesus had for women. Jesus treated all people with equal respect. Here are some of his encounters with women.

Jesus raises a widow's son from the dead Luke 7:11-17
A sinful woman anoints Jesus' feet Luke 7:36-50
Jesus forgives an unfaithful wife John 8:1-11
A group of women travels with Jesus Luke 8:1-3
Jesus visits Mary and Martha Luke 10:38-42
Jesus heals a handicapped woman Luke 13:10-17
Jesus heals the daughter of a Gentile woman Mark 7:24-30
Weeping women follow Jesus on his way to the cross Luke 23:27-31
Jesus' mother and other women gather at the cross John 19:25-27
Jesus appears to Mary Magdalene Mark 16:9-11
Jesus appears to other women after his resurrection Matthew 28:8-10

thorns represent those who hear the message, but all too quickly the message is crowded out by the cares and riches and pleasures of this life. And so they never grow into maturity. [15]And the seeds that fell on the good soil represent honest, good-hearted people who hear God's word, cling to it, and patiently produce a huge harvest.

Parable of the Lamp

[16]"No one lights a lamp and then covers it with a bowl or hides it under a bed. A lamp is placed on a stand, where its light can be seen by all who enter the house. [17]For all that is secret will eventually be brought into the open, and everything that is concealed will be brought to light and made known to all.

[18]"So pay attention to how you hear. To those who listen to my teaching, more understanding will be given. But for those who are not listening, even what they think they understand will be taken away from them."

The True Family of Jesus

[19]Then Jesus' mother and brothers came to see him, but they couldn't get to him because of the crowd. [20]Someone told Jesus, "Your mother and your brothers are outside, and they want to see you."

[21]Jesus replied, "My mother and my brothers are all those who hear God's word and obey it."

Jesus Calms the Storm

[22]One day Jesus said to his disciples, "Let's cross to the other side of the lake." So they got into a boat and started out. [23]As they sailed across, Jesus settled down for a nap. But soon a fierce storm came down on the lake. The boat was filling with water, and they were in real danger.

[24]The disciples went and woke him up, shouting, "Master, Master, we're going to drown!"

When Jesus woke up, he rebuked the wind and the raging waves. Suddenly the storm stopped and all was calm. [25]Then he asked them, "Where is your faith?"

The disciples were terrified and amazed. "Who is this man?" they asked each other. "When he gives a command, even the wind and waves obey him!"

Jesus Heals a Demon-Possessed Man

[26]So they arrived in the region of the Gerasenes,* across the lake from Galilee. [27]As Jesus was climbing out of the boat, a man who was possessed by demons came out to meet him. For a long time he had been homeless and naked, living in a cemetery outside the town.

[28]As soon as he saw Jesus, he shrieked and fell down in front of him. Then he screamed, "Why are you interfering with me, Jesus, Son of the Most High God? Please, I beg you, don't torture me!" [29]For Jesus had already commanded the evil* spirit to come out of him. This spirit had often taken control of the man. Even when he was placed under guard and put in chains and shackles, he simply broke them and rushed out into the wilderness, completely under the demon's power.

[30]Jesus demanded, "What is your name?"

"Legion," he replied, for he was filled with many demons. [31]The demons kept begging Jesus not to send them into the bottomless pit.*

[32]There happened to be a large herd of pigs feeding on the hillside nearby, and the demons begged him to let them enter into the pigs.

So Jesus gave them permission. [33]Then the demons came out of the man and entered the pigs, and the entire herd plunged down the steep hillside into the lake and drowned.

[34]When the herdsmen saw it, they fled to the nearby town and the surrounding countryside, spreading the news as they ran. [35]People rushed out to see what had happened. A crowd soon gathered around Jesus, and they saw the man who had been freed from the demons. He was sitting at Jesus' feet, fully clothed and perfectly sane, and they were all afraid. [36]Then those who had seen what happened told the others how the demon-possessed man had been healed. [37]And all the people in the region of the Gerasenes begged Jesus to go away and leave them alone, for a great wave of fear swept over them.

So Jesus returned to the boat and left, crossing back to the other side of the lake.

8:26 Other manuscripts read *Gadarenes;* still others read *Gergesenes;* also in 8:37. See Matt 8:28; Mark 5:1. **8:29** Greek *unclean.*
8:31 Or *the abyss,* or *the underworld.*

38 The man who had been freed from the demons begged to go with him. But Jesus sent him home, saying, 39 "No, go back to your family, and tell them everything God has done for you." So he went all through the town proclaiming the great things Jesus had done for him.

Jesus Heals in Response to Faith

40 On the other side of the lake the crowds welcomed Jesus, because they had been waiting for him. 41 Then a man named Jairus, a leader of the local synagogue, came and fell at Jesus' feet, pleading with him to come home with him. 42 His only daughter,* who was about twelve years old, was dying.

As Jesus went with him, he was surrounded by the crowds. 43 A woman in the crowd had suffered for twelve years with constant bleeding,* and she could find no cure. 44 Coming up behind Jesus, she touched the fringe of his robe. Immediately, the bleeding stopped.

45 "Who touched me?" Jesus asked.

Everyone denied it, and Peter said, "Master, this whole crowd is pressing up against you."

46 But Jesus said, "Someone deliberately touched me, for I felt healing power go out from me." 47 When the woman realized that she could not stay hidden, she began to tremble and fell to her knees in front of him. The whole crowd heard her explain why she had touched him and that she had been immediately healed. 48 "Daughter," he said to her, "your faith has made you well. Go in peace."

49 While he was still speaking to her, a messenger arrived from the home of Jairus, the leader of the synagogue. He told him, "Your daughter is dead. There's no use troubling the Teacher now."

50 But when Jesus heard what had happened, he said to Jairus, "Don't be afraid. Just have faith, and she will be healed."

51 When they arrived at the house, Jesus wouldn't let anyone go in with him except Peter, John, James, and the little girl's father and mother. 52 The house was filled with people weeping and wailing, but he said, "Stop the weeping! She isn't dead; she's only asleep."

53 But the crowd laughed at him because they all knew she had died. 54 Then Jesus took her by the hand and said in a loud voice, "My child, get up!" 55 And at that moment her life* returned, and she immediately stood up! Then Jesus told them to give her something to eat. 56 Her parents were overwhelmed, but Jesus insisted that they not tell anyone what had happened.

CHAPTER 9

Jesus Sends Out the Twelve Disciples

One day Jesus called together his twelve disciples* and gave them power and authority to cast out all demons and to heal all diseases. 2 Then he sent them out to tell everyone about the Kingdom of God and to heal the sick. 3 "Take nothing for your journey," he instructed them. "Don't take a walking stick, a traveler's bag, food, money,* or even a change of clothes. 4 Wherever you go, stay in the same house until you leave town. 5 And if a town refuses to welcome you, shake its dust from your feet as you leave to show that you have abandoned those people to their fate."

6 So they began their circuit of the villages, preaching the Good News and healing the sick.

Herod's Confusion

7 When Herod Antipas, the ruler of Galilee,* heard about everything Jesus was doing, he was puzzled. Some were saying that John the Baptist had been raised from the dead. 8 Others thought Jesus was Elijah or one of the other prophets risen from the dead.

9 "I beheaded John," Herod said, "so who is this man about whom I hear such stories?" And he kept trying to see him.

Jesus Feeds Five Thousand

10 When the apostles returned, they told Jesus everything they had done. Then he slipped quietly away with them toward the town of Bethsaida. 11 But the crowds found out where he was going, and they followed him. He welcomed them and taught them about the Kingdom of God, and he healed those who were sick.

12 Late in the afternoon the twelve disciples came to him and said, "Send the crowds away

8:42 Or *His only child, a daughter.* **8:43** Some manuscripts add *having spent everything she had on doctors.* **8:55** Or *her spirit.* **9:1** Greek *the Twelve;* other manuscripts read *the twelve apostles.* **9:3** Or *silver coins.* **9:7** Greek *Herod the tetrarch.* Herod Antipas was a son of King Herod and was ruler over Galilee.

to the nearby villages and farms, so they can find food and lodging for the night. There is nothing to eat here in this remote place."

13 But Jesus said, "You feed them."

"But we have only five loaves of bread and two fish," they answered. "Or are you expecting us to go and buy enough food for this whole crowd?" 14 For there were about 5,000 men there.

Jesus replied, "Tell them to sit down in groups of about fifty each." 15 So the people all sat down. 16 Jesus took the five loaves and two fish, looked up toward heaven, and blessed them. Then, breaking the loaves into pieces, he kept giving the bread and fish to the disciples so they could distribute it to the people. 17 They all ate as much as they wanted, and afterward, the disciples picked up twelve baskets of leftovers!

Peter's Declaration about Jesus

18 One day Jesus left the crowds to pray alone. Only his disciples were with him, and he asked them, "Who do people say I am?"

19 "Well," they replied, "some say John the Baptist, some say Elijah, and others say you are one of the other ancient prophets risen from the dead."

20 Then he asked them, "But who do you say I am?"

Peter replied, "You are the Messiah* sent from God!"

Jesus Predicts His Death

21 Jesus warned his disciples not to tell anyone who he was. 22 "The Son of Man* must suffer many terrible things," he said. "He will be rejected by the elders, the leading priests, and the teachers of religious law. He will be killed, but on the third day he will be raised from the dead."

23 Then he said to the crowd, "If any of you wants to be my follower, you must turn from your selfish ways, take up your cross daily, and follow me. 24 If you try to hang on to your life, you will lose it. But if you give up your life for my sake, you will save it. 25 And what do you benefit if you gain the whole world but are yourself lost or destroyed? 26 If anyone is ashamed of me and my message, the Son of Man will be ashamed of that person when he returns in his glory and in the glory of the Father and the holy angels. 27 I tell you the truth, some standing here right now will not die before they see the Kingdom of God."

Zacchaeus

I collect taxes, and I've always liked money. So I've been known to cheat people sometimes . . . make them pay a little more than they need to and keep the difference. It's expected in this business.

One day I wanted to hear this new teacher named Jesus speak. I'm not a tall man, so I climbed up a tree to get a better view. I was surprised when Jesus looked up at me and smiled. "I'm going to visit you today," he said. I listened to his words and knew he spoke for God. I decided then and there to stop cheating people. I repaid those I had stolen from by giving them back four times what I'd taken. What a good feeling!

Read about Zacchaeus in Luke 19:1-10.

The Transfiguration

28 About eight days later Jesus took Peter, John, and James up on a mountain to pray.

9:20 Or *the Christ*. *Messiah* (a Hebrew term) and *Christ* (a Greek term) both mean "the anointed one." **9:22** "Son of Man" is a title Jesus used for himself.

[29]And as he was praying, the appearance of his face was transformed, and his clothes became dazzling white. [30]Suddenly, two men, Moses and Elijah, appeared and began talking with Jesus. [31]They were glorious to see. And they were speaking about his exodus from this world, which was about to be fulfilled in Jerusalem.

[32]Peter and the others had fallen asleep. When they woke up, they saw Jesus' glory and the two men standing with him. [33]As Moses and Elijah were starting to leave, Peter, not even knowing what he was saying, blurted out, "Master, it's wonderful for us to be here! Let's make three shelters as memorials*—one for you, one for Moses, and one for Elijah." [34]But even as he was saying this, a cloud overshadowed them, and terror gripped them as the cloud covered them.

[35]Then a voice from the cloud said, "This is my Son, my Chosen One.* Listen to him." [36]When the voice finished, Jesus was there alone. They didn't tell anyone at that time what they had seen.

Jesus Heals a Demon-Possessed Boy

[37]The next day, after they had come down the mountain, a large crowd met Jesus. [38]A man in the crowd called out to him, "Teacher, I beg you to look at my son, my only child. [39]An evil spirit keeps seizing him, making him scream. It throws him into convulsions so that he foams at the mouth. It batters him and hardly ever leaves him alone. [40]I begged your disciples to cast out the spirit, but they couldn't do it."

[41]Jesus said, "You faithless and corrupt people! How long must I be with you and put up with you?" Then he said to the man, "Bring your son here."

[42]As the boy came forward, the demon knocked him to the ground and threw him into a violent convulsion. But Jesus rebuked the evil* spirit and healed the boy. Then he gave him back to his father. [43]Awe gripped the people as they saw this majestic display of God's power.

Jesus Again Predicts His Death

While everyone was marveling at everything he was doing, Jesus said to his disciples, [44]"Listen to me and remember what I say. The Son of Man is going to be betrayed into the hands of his enemies." [45]But they didn't know what he meant. Its significance was hidden from them, so they couldn't understand it, and they were afraid to ask him about it.

The Greatest in the Kingdom

[46]Then his disciples began arguing about which of them was the greatest. [47]But Jesus knew their thoughts, so he brought a little child to his side. [48]Then he said to them, "Anyone who welcomes a little child like this on my behalf* welcomes me, and anyone who welcomes me also welcomes my Father who sent me. Whoever is the least among you is the greatest."

Using the Name of Jesus

[49]John said to Jesus, "Master, we saw someone using your name to cast out demons, but we told him to stop because he isn't in our group."

[50]But Jesus said, "Don't stop him! Anyone who is not against you is for you."

Opposition from Samaritans

[51]As the time drew near for him to ascend to heaven, Jesus resolutely set out for Jerusalem. [52]He sent messengers ahead to a Samaritan village to prepare for his arrival. [53]But the people of the village did not welcome Jesus because he was on his way to Jerusalem. [54]When James and John saw this, they said to Jesus, "Lord, should we call down fire from heaven to burn them up*?" [55]But Jesus turned and rebuked them.* [56]So they went on to another village.

The Cost of Following Jesus

[57]As they were walking along, someone said to Jesus, "I will follow you wherever you go."

[58]But Jesus replied, "Foxes have dens to live in, and birds have nests, but the Son of Man has no place even to lay his head."

[59]He said to another person, "Come, follow me."

The man agreed, but he said, "Lord, first let me return home and bury my father."

[60]But Jesus told him, "Let the spiritually

9:33 Greek *three tabernacles.* **9:35** Some manuscripts read *This is my dearly loved Son.* **9:42** Greek *unclean.* **9:48** Greek *in my name.* **9:54** Some manuscripts add *as Elijah did.* **9:55** Some manuscripts add an expanded conclusion to verse 55 and an additional sentence in verse 56: *And he said, "You don't realize what your hearts are like. [56]For the Son of Man has not come to destroy people's lives, but to save them."*

dead bury their own dead!* Your duty is to go
and preach about the Kingdom of God."
61 Another said, "Yes, Lord, I will follow you,
but first let me say good-bye to my family."
62 But Jesus told him, "Anyone who puts a
hand to the plow and then looks back is not fit
for the Kingdom of God."

CHAPTER 10

Jesus Sends Out His Disciples

The Lord now chose seventy-two* other dis-
ciples and sent them ahead in pairs to all the
towns and places he planned to visit. 2 These
were his instructions to them: "The harvest is
great, but the workers are few. So pray to the
Lord who is in charge of the harvest; ask him
to send more workers into his fields. 3 Now go,
and remember that I am sending you out as
lambs among wolves. 4 Don't take any money
with you, nor a traveler's bag, nor an extra pair
of sandals. And don't stop to greet anyone on
the road.
5 "Whenever you enter someone's home,
first say, 'May God's peace be on this house.'
6 If those who live there are peaceful, the
blessing will stand; if they are not, the bless-
ing will return to you. 7 Don't move around
from home to home. Stay in one place, eating
and drinking what they provide. Don't hesi-
tate to accept hospitality, because those who
work deserve their pay.
8 "If you enter a town and it welcomes you,
eat whatever is set before you. 9 Heal the sick,
and tell them, 'The Kingdom of God is near
you now.' 10 But if a town refuses to welcome
you, go out into its streets and say, 11 'We wipe
even the dust of your town from our feet to
show that we have abandoned you to your
fate. And know this—the Kingdom of God is
near!' 12 I assure you, even wicked Sodom will
be better off than such a town on judgment
day.
13 "What sorrow awaits you, Korazin and
Bethsaida! For if the miracles I did in you had
been done in wicked Tyre and Sidon, their
people would have repented of their sins long
ago, clothing themselves in burlap and throw-
ing ashes on their heads to show their re-
morse. 14 Yes, Tyre and Sidon will be better off
on judgment day than you. 15 And you people

9:60 Greek *Let the dead bury their own dead.* **10:1** Some manuscripts read *seventy;* also in 10:17.

A COLLECTION OF ATTITUDES

The needs of others bring out various attitudes in us. Jesus used the story of the good, but despised, Samaritan (Luke 10:25-37) to make clear what attitude was right. Note these different attitudes toward the wounded man.

To the **bandits**, the man was someone they could rob of his money.

To the **religious man**, the wounded man was a problem to be avoided.

To the **law expert**, the wounded man was something to talk about.

To the **Samaritan**, the wounded man was a human being worth being cared for and loved.

To the **innkeeper**, the wounded man was a customer to serve for a fee.

To **Jesus**, the wounded man—and everyone else—was worth dying for.

of Capernaum, will you be honored in heaven? No, you will go down to the place of the dead.*"

16 Then he said to the disciples, "Anyone who accepts your message is also accepting me. And anyone who rejects you is rejecting me. And anyone who rejects me is rejecting God, who sent me."

17 When the seventy-two disciples returned, they joyfully reported to him, "Lord, even the demons obey us when we use your name!"

18 "Yes," he told them, "I saw Satan fall from heaven like lightning! 19 Look, I have given you authority over all the power of the enemy, and you can walk among snakes and scorpions and crush them. Nothing will injure you. 20 But don't rejoice because evil spirits obey you; rejoice because your names are registered in heaven."

Jesus' Prayer of Thanksgiving

21 At that same time Jesus was filled with the joy of the Holy Spirit, and he said, "O Father, Lord of heaven and earth, thank you for hiding these things from those who think themselves wise and clever, and for revealing them to the childlike. Yes, Father, it pleased you to do it this way.

22 "My Father has entrusted everything to me. No one truly knows the Son except the Father, and no one truly knows the Father except the Son and those to whom the Son chooses to reveal him."

23 Then when they were alone, he turned to the disciples and said, "Blessed are the eyes that see what you have seen. 24 I tell you, many prophets and kings longed to see what you see, but they didn't see it. And they longed to hear what you hear, but they didn't hear it."

The Most Important Commandment

25 One day an expert in religious law stood up to test Jesus by asking him this question: "Teacher, what should I do to inherit eternal life?"

26 Jesus replied, "What does the law of Moses say? How do you read it?"

27 The man answered, "'You must love the LORD your God with all your heart, all your soul, all your strength, and all your mind.' And, 'Love your neighbor as yourself.'"*

28 "Right!" Jesus told him. "Do this and you will live!"

29 The man wanted to justify his actions, so he asked Jesus, "And who is my neighbor?"

Parable of the Good Samaritan

30 Jesus replied with a story: "A Jewish man was traveling from Jerusalem down to Jericho, and he was attacked by bandits. They stripped him of his clothes, beat him up, and left him half dead beside the road.

31 "By chance a priest came along. But when he saw the man lying there, he crossed to the other side of the road and passed him by. 32 A Temple assistant* walked over and looked at him lying there, but he also passed by on the other side.

33 "Then a despised Samaritan came along, and when he saw the man, he felt compassion for him. 34 Going over to him, the Samaritan soothed his wounds with olive oil and wine and bandaged them. Then he put the man on his own donkey and took him to an inn, where he took care of him. 35 The next day he handed the innkeeper two silver coins,* telling him, 'Take care of this man. If his bill runs higher than this, I'll pay you the next time I'm here.'

36 "Now which of these three would you say was a neighbor to the man who was attacked by bandits?" Jesus asked.

37 The man replied, "The one who showed him mercy."

Then Jesus said, "Yes, now go and do the same."

Jesus Visits Martha and Mary

38 As Jesus and the disciples continued on their way to Jerusalem, they came to a certain village where a woman named Martha welcomed him into her home. 39 Her sister, Mary, sat at the Lord's feet, listening to what he taught. 40 But Martha was distracted by the big dinner she was preparing. She came to Jesus and said, "Lord, doesn't it seem unfair to you that my sister just sits here while I do all the work? Tell her to come and help me."

41 But the Lord said to her, "My dear Martha, you are worried and upset over all these

10:15 Greek *to Hades*. **10:27** Deut 6:5; Lev 19:18. **10:32** Greek *A Levite*. **10:35** Greek *two denarii*. A denarius was equivalent to a laborer's full day's wage.

details! 42 There is only one thing worth being
concerned about. Mary has discovered it, and
it will not be taken away from her."

CHAPTER 11

Teaching about Prayer

Once Jesus was in a certain place praying. As
he finished, one of his disciples came to him
and said, "Lord, teach us to pray, just as John
taught his disciples."
2 Jesus said, "This is how you should pray:*

"Father, may your name be kept holy.
May your Kingdom come soon.
3 Give us each day the food we need,*
4 and forgive us our sins,
as we forgive those who sin against us.
And don't let us yield to temptation.*"

5 Then, teaching them more about prayer,
he used this story: "Suppose you went to a
friend's house at midnight, wanting to borrow
three loaves of bread. You say to him, 6 'A
friend of mine has just arrived for a visit, and I
have nothing for him to eat.' 7 And suppose he
calls out from his bedroom, 'Don't bother me.
The door is locked for the night, and my family
and I are all in bed. I can't help you.' 8 But I tell
you this—though he won't do it for friend-
ship's sake, if you keep knocking long enough,
he will get up and give you whatever you need
because of your shameless persistence.*
9 "And so I tell you, keep on asking, and you
will receive what you ask for. Keep on seek-
ing, and you will find. Keep on knocking, and
the door will be opened to you. 10 For everyone
who asks, receives. Everyone who seeks,
finds. And to everyone who knocks, the door
will be opened.
11 "You fathers—if your children ask* for a
fish, do you give them a snake instead? 12 Or if
they ask for an egg, do you give them a scor-
pion? Of course not! 13 So if you sinful people
know how to give good gifts to your children,
how much more will your heavenly Father
give the Holy Spirit to those who ask him."

Jesus and the Prince of Demons

14 One day Jesus cast out a demon from a man
who couldn't speak, and when the demon was
gone, the man began to speak. The crowds
were amazed, 15 but some of them said, "No
wonder he can cast out demons. He gets his
power from Satan,* the prince of demons."
16 Others, trying to test Jesus, demanded that
he show them a miraculous sign from heaven
to prove his authority.
17 He knew their thoughts, so he said, "Any
kingdom divided by civil war is doomed. A
family splintered by feuding will fall apart.
18 You say I am empowered by Satan. But if Sa-
tan is divided and fighting against himself,
how can his kingdom survive? 19 And if I am
empowered by Satan, what about your own
exorcists? They cast out demons, too, so they
will condemn you for what you have said.
20 But if I am casting out demons by the power
of God,* then the Kingdom of God has arrived
among you. 21 For when a strong man like Sa-
tan is fully armed and guards his palace, his
possessions are safe—22 until someone even
stronger attacks and overpowers him, strips
him of his weapons, and carries off his be-
longings.
23 "Anyone who isn't with me opposes me,
and anyone who isn't working with me is ac-
tually working against me.
24 "When an evil* spirit leaves a person, it
goes into the desert, searching for rest. But
when it finds none, it says, 'I will return to the
person I came from.' 25 So it returns and finds
that its former home is all swept and in order.
26 Then the spirit finds seven other spirits
more evil than itself, and they all enter the
person and live there. And so that person is
worse off than before."
27 As he was speaking, a woman in the
crowd called out, "God bless your mother—
the womb from which you came, and the
breasts that nursed you!"
28 Jesus replied, "But even more blessed are
all who hear the word of God and put it into
practice."

The Sign of Jonah

29 As the crowd pressed in on Jesus, he said,
"This evil generation keeps asking me to show
them a miraculous sign. But the only sign I will
give them is the sign of Jonah. 30 What hap-

11:2 Some manuscripts add additional phrases from the Lord's Prayer as it reads in Matt 6:9-13. **11:3** Or *Give us each day our food for the day;* or *Give us each day our food for tomorrow.* **11:4** Or *And keep us from being tested.* **11:8** Or *in order to avoid shame,* or *so his reputation won't be damaged.* **11:11** Some manuscripts add *for bread, do you give them a stone? Or (if they ask).* **11:15** Greek *Beelzeboul;* also in 11:18, 19. Other manuscripts read *Beezeboul;* Latin version reads *Beelzebub.* **11:20** Greek *by the finger of God.* **11:24** Greek *unclean.*

pened to him was a sign to the people of Nineveh that God had sent him. What happens to the Son of Man* will be a sign to these people that he was sent by God.

31"The queen of Sheba* will stand up against this generation on judgment day and condemn it, for she came from a distant land to hear the wisdom of Solomon. Now someone greater than Solomon is here—but you refuse to listen. 32The people of Nineveh will also stand up against this generation on judgment day and condemn it, for they repented of their sins at the preaching of Jonah. Now someone greater than Jonah is here—but you refuse to repent.

Receiving the Light

33"No one lights a lamp and then hides it or puts it under a basket.* Instead, a lamp is placed on a stand, where its light can be seen by all who enter the house.

34"Your eye is a lamp that provides light for your body. When your eye is good, your whole body is filled with light. But when it is bad, your body is filled with darkness. 35Make sure that the light you think you have is not actually darkness. 36If you are filled with light, with no dark corners, then your whole life will be radiant, as though a floodlight were filling you with light."

Jesus Criticizes the Religious Leaders

37As Jesus was speaking, one of the Pharisees invited him home for a meal. So he went in and took his place at the table.* 38His host was amazed to see that he sat down to eat without first performing the hand-washing ceremony required by Jewish custom. 39Then the Lord said to him, "You Pharisees are so careful to clean the outside of the cup and the dish, but inside you are filthy—full of greed and wickedness! 40Fools! Didn't God make the inside as well as the outside? 41So clean the inside by giving gifts to the poor, and you will be clean all over.

42"What sorrow awaits you Pharisees! For you are careful to tithe even the tiniest income from your herb gardens,* but you ignore justice and the love of God. You should tithe, yes, but do not neglect the more important things.

43"What sorrow awaits you Pharisees! For you love to sit in the seats of honor in the synagogues and receive respectful greetings as you walk in the marketplaces. 44Yes, what sorrow awaits you! For you are like hidden graves in a

11:30 "Son of Man" is a title Jesus used for himself. **11:31** Greek *The queen of the south.* **11:33** Some manuscripts do not include *or puts it under a basket.* **11:37** Or *and reclined.* **11:42** Greek *tithe the mint, the rue, and every herb.*

IS IT OK?

IS IT OK TO LOOK AT DIRTY PICTURES?

In Luke 11:34, Jesus says that your eyes are like lamps that shine into your heart. That means what you look at can either shine light into your life or stamp out the light. Jesus gives a clear choice. *Option 1: Light.* Look at what's good. This fills your mind with good, clean, pure thoughts. You don't feel guilty. You're free! *Option 2: Darkness.* Look at what's evil—dirty pictures, R-rated movies, or bad Web sites. This fills your mind with unclean thoughts, making you feel guilty and distant from God. Those dirty images can stay in your mind for years, causing all kinds of problems. So, with Jesus' words in mind, how would *you* answer this question?

field. People walk over them without knowing the corruption they are stepping on."

45"Teacher," said an expert in religious law, "you have insulted us, too, in what you just said."

46"Yes," said Jesus, "what sorrow also awaits you experts in religious law! For you crush people with unbearable religious demands, and you never lift a finger to ease the burden. 47What sorrow awaits you! For you build monuments for the prophets your own ancestors killed long ago. 48But in fact, you stand as witnesses who agree with what your ancestors did. They killed the prophets, and you join in their crime by building the monuments! 49This is what God in his wisdom said about you:* 'I will send prophets and apostles to them, but they will kill some and persecute the others.'

50"As a result, this generation will be held responsible for the murder of all God's prophets from the creation of the world—51from the murder of Abel to the murder of Zechariah, who was killed between the altar and the sanctuary. Yes, it will certainly be charged against this generation.

52"What sorrow awaits you experts in religious law! For you remove the key to knowledge from the people. You don't enter the Kingdom yourselves, and you prevent others from entering."

53As Jesus was leaving, the teachers of religious law and the Pharisees became hostile and tried to provoke him with many questions. 54They wanted to trap him into saying something they could use against him.

CHAPTER 12

A Warning against Hypocrisy

Meanwhile, the crowds grew until thousands were milling about and stepping on each other. Jesus turned first to his disciples and warned them, "Beware of the yeast of the Pharisees—their hypocrisy. 2The time is coming when everything that is covered up will be revealed, and all that is secret will be made known to all. 3Whatever you have said in the dark will be heard in the light, and what you have whispered behind closed doors will be shouted from the housetops for all to hear!

4"Dear friends, don't be afraid of those who want to kill your body; they cannot do any more to you after that. 5But I'll tell you whom to fear. Fear God, who has the power to kill you and then throw you into hell.* Yes, he's the one to fear.

6"What is the price of five sparrows—two copper coins*? Yet God does not forget a

WISHING WELL

Jackson's family wasn't poor, but they weren't rich either. His parents always talked about stretching the dollar, and it seemed his friends had more than he did. Recently Jackson went to the mall with a friend. His friend bought CDs and clothes; Jackson could only look, wishing he could buy some stuff. At home, everything looked drab and shabby. That's when Jackson started to wonder if getting rich might be a good goal for his life. Do you think having lots of money would make Jackson happy? Check out Luke 12:15.

11:49 Greek *Therefore, the wisdom of God said.* **12:5** Greek *Gehenna.* **12:6** Greek *two assaria* [Roman coins equal to 1/16 of a denarius].

single one of them. 7And the very hairs on your head are all numbered. So don't be afraid; you are more valuable to God than a whole flock of sparrows.

8"I tell you the truth, everyone who acknowledges me publicly here on earth, the Son of Man* will also acknowledge in the presence of God's angels. 9But anyone who denies me here on earth will be denied before God's angels. 10Anyone who speaks against the Son of Man can be forgiven, but anyone who blasphemes the Holy Spirit will not be forgiven.

11"And when you are brought to trial in the synagogues and before rulers and authorities, don't worry about how to defend yourself or what to say, 12for the Holy Spirit will teach you at that time what needs to be said."

Parable of the Rich Fool

13Then someone called from the crowd, "Teacher, please tell my brother to divide our father's estate with me."

14Jesus replied, "Friend, who made me a judge over you to decide such things as that?" 15Then he said, "Beware! Guard against every kind of greed. Life is not measured by how much you own."

If I could just get a new bike, I'd be happy, wouldn't I?

[Jesus said,] "Beware! Guard against every kind of greed. Life is not measured by how much you own."
LUKE 12:15

16Then he told them a story: "A rich man had a fertile farm that produced fine crops. 17He said to himself, 'What should I do? I don't have room for all my crops.' 18Then he said, 'I know! I'll tear down my barns and build bigger ones. Then I'll have room enough to store all my wheat and other goods. 19And I'll sit back and say to myself, "My friend, you have enough stored away for years to come. Now take it easy! Eat, drink, and be merry!"'

20"But God said to him, 'You fool! You will die this very night. Then who will get everything you worked for?'

21"Yes, a person is a fool to store up earthly wealth but not have a rich relationship with God."

Teaching about Money and Possessions

22Then, turning to his disciples, Jesus said, "That is why I tell you not to worry about everyday life—whether you have enough food to eat or enough clothes to wear. 23For life is more than food, and your body more than clothing. 24Look at the ravens. They don't plant or harvest or store food in barns, for God feeds them. And you are far more valuable to him than any birds! 25Can all your worries add a single moment to your life? 26And if worry can't accomplish a little thing like that, what's the use of worrying over bigger things?

27"Look at the lilies and how they grow. They don't work or make their clothing, yet Solomon in all his glory was not dressed as beautifully as they are. 28And if God cares so wonderfully for flowers that are here today and thrown into the fire tomorrow, he will certainly care for you. Why do you have so little faith?

29"And don't be concerned about what to eat and what to drink. Don't worry about such things. 30These things dominate the thoughts of unbelievers all over the world, but your Father already knows your needs. 31Seek the Kingdom of God above all else, and he will give you everything you need.

32"So don't be afraid, little flock. For it gives your Father great happiness to give you the Kingdom.

33"Sell your possessions and give to those in need. This will store up treasure for you in heaven! And the purses of heaven never get old or develop holes. Your treasure will be safe; no thief can steal it and no moth can destroy it. 34Wherever your treasure is, there the desires of your heart will also be.

Be Ready for the Lord's Coming

35"Be dressed for service and keep your lamps burning, 36as though you were waiting for your master to return from the wedding feast. Then you will be ready to open the door and

12:8 "Son of Man" is a title Jesus used for himself.

let him in the moment he arrives and knocks.
37 The servants who are ready and waiting for
his return will be rewarded. I tell you the truth,
he himself will seat them, put on an apron,
and serve them as they sit and eat! 38 He may
come in the middle of the night or just before
dawn.* But whenever he comes, he will re-
ward the servants who are ready.

39 "Understand this: If a homeowner knew
exactly when a burglar was coming, he would
not permit his house to be broken into. 40 You
also must be ready all the time, for the Son of
Man will come when least expected."

41 Peter asked, "Lord, is that illustration just
for us or for everyone?"

42 And the Lord replied, "A faithful, sensi-
ble servant is one to whom the master can
give the responsibility of managing his other
household servants and feeding them. 43 If
the master returns and finds that the servant
has done a good job, there will be a reward. 44 I
tell you the truth, the master will put that ser-
vant in charge of all he owns. 45 But what if
the servant thinks, 'My master won't be back
for a while,' and he begins beating the other
servants, partying, and getting drunk? 46 The
master will return unannounced and unex-
pected, and he will cut the servant in pieces
and banish him with the unfaithful.

47 "And a servant who knows what the mas-
ter wants, but isn't prepared and doesn't carry
out those instructions, will be severely pun-
ished. 48 But someone who does not know, and
then does something wrong, will be punished
only lightly. When someone has been given
much, much will be required in return; and
when someone has been entrusted with
much, even more will be required.

Jesus Causes Division

49 "I have come to set the world on fire, and I
wish it were already burning! 50 I have a terrible
baptism of suffering ahead of me, and I am
under a heavy burden until it is accomplished.
51 Do you think I have come to bring peace to
the earth? No, I have come to divide people
against each other! 52 From now on families
will be split apart, three in favor of me, and two
against—or two in favor and three against.

53 'Father will be divided against son
and son against father;
mother against daughter
and daughter against mother;
and mother-in-law against daughter-in-law
and daughter-in-law against mother-in-law.'*"

54 Then Jesus turned to the crowd and said,
"When you see clouds beginning to form in
the west, you say, 'Here comes a shower.' And
you are right. 55 When the south wind blows,
you say, 'Today will be a scorcher.' And it is.
56 You fools! You know how to interpret the
weather signs of the earth and sky, but you
don't know how to interpret the present
times.

57 "Why can't you decide for yourselves
what is right? 58 When you are on the way to
court with your accuser, try to settle the mat-
ter before you get there. Otherwise, your ac-
cuser may drag you before the judge, who will
hand you over to an officer, who will throw
you into prison. 59 And if that happens, you
won't be free again until you have paid the
very last penny.*"

CHAPTER 13

A Call to Repentance

About this time Jesus was informed that Pi-
late had murdered some people from Galilee
as they were offering sacrifices at the Tem-
ple. 2 "Do you think those Galileans were
worse sinners than all the other people from
Galilee?" Jesus asked. "Is that why they suf-
fered? 3 Not at all! And you will perish, too, un-
less you repent of your sins and turn to God.
4 And what about the eighteen people who
died when the tower in Siloam fell on them?
Were they the worst sinners in Jerusalem?
5 No, and I tell you again that unless you re-
pent, you will perish, too."

Parable of the Barren Fig Tree

6 Then Jesus told this story: "A man planted a
fig tree in his garden and came again and
again to see if there was any fruit on it, but he
was always disappointed. 7 Finally, he said to
his gardener, 'I've waited three years, and
there hasn't been a single fig! Cut it down. It's
just taking up space in the garden.'

8 "The gardener answered, 'Sir, give it one
more chance. Leave it another year, and I'll

12:38 Greek *in the second or third watch.* **12:53** Mic 7:6. **12:59** Greek *last lepton* [the smallest Jewish coin].

give it special attention and plenty of fertilizer. [9]If we get figs next year, fine. If not, then you can cut it down.'"

Jesus Heals on the Sabbath

[10]One Sabbath day as Jesus was teaching in a synagogue, [11]he saw a woman who had been crippled by an evil spirit. She had been bent double for eighteen years and was unable to stand up straight. [12]When Jesus saw her, he called her over and said, "Dear woman, you are healed of your sickness!" [13]Then he touched her, and instantly she could stand straight. How she praised God!

[14]But the leader in charge of the synagogue was indignant that Jesus had healed her on the Sabbath day. "There are six days of the week for working," he said to the crowd. "Come on those days to be healed, not on the Sabbath."

[15]But the Lord replied, "You hypocrites! Each of you works on the Sabbath day! Don't you untie your ox or your donkey from its stall on the Sabbath and lead it out for water? [16]This dear woman, a daughter of Abraham, has been held in bondage by Satan for eighteen years. Isn't it right that she be released, even on the Sabbath?"

[17]This shamed his enemies, but all the people rejoiced at the wonderful things he did.

Parable of the Mustard Seed

[18]Then Jesus said, "What is the Kingdom of God like? How can I illustrate it? [19]It is like a tiny mustard seed that a man planted in a garden; it grows and becomes a tree, and the birds make nests in its branches."

Parable of the Yeast

[20]He also asked, "What else is the Kingdom of God like? [21]It is like the yeast a woman used in making bread. Even though she put only a little yeast in three measures of flour, it permeated every part of the dough."

The Narrow Door

[22]Jesus went through the towns and villages, teaching as he went, always pressing on toward Jerusalem. [23]Someone asked him, "Lord, will only a few be saved?"

He replied, [24]"Work hard to enter the narrow door to God's Kingdom, for many will try to enter but will fail. [25]When the master of the house has locked the door, it will be too late. You will stand outside knocking and pleading, 'Lord, open the door for us!' But he will reply, 'I don't know you or where you come from.' [26]Then you will say, 'But we ate and drank with you, and you taught in our streets.' [27]And he will reply, 'I tell you, I don't know you or where you come from. Get away from me, all you who do evil.'

[28]"There will be weeping and gnashing of teeth, for you will see Abraham, Isaac, Jacob, and all the prophets in the Kingdom of God, but you will be thrown out. [29]And people will come from all over the world—from east and west, north and south—to take their places in the Kingdom of God. [30]And note this: Some who seem least important now will be the greatest then, and some who are the greatest now will be least important then.*"

Jesus Grieves over Jerusalem

[31]At that time some Pharisees said to him, "Get away from here if you want to live! Herod Antipas wants to kill you!"

[32]Jesus replied, "Go tell that fox that I will keep on casting out demons and healing people today and tomorrow; and the third day I will accomplish my purpose. [33]Yes, today, tomorrow, and the next day I must proceed on my way. For it wouldn't do for a prophet of God to be killed except in Jerusalem!

[34]"O Jerusalem, Jerusalem, the city that kills the prophets and stones God's messengers! How often I have wanted to gather your children together as a hen protects her chicks beneath her wings, but you wouldn't let me. [35]And now, look, your house is abandoned. And you will never see me again until you say, 'Blessings on the one who comes in the name of the LORD!'*"

CHAPTER 14

Jesus Heals on the Sabbath

One Sabbath day Jesus went to eat dinner in the home of a leader of the Pharisees, and the people were watching him closely. [2]There was a man there whose arms and legs were swollen.* [3]Jesus asked the Pharisees and experts in religious law, "Is it permitted in the

13:30 Greek *Some are last who will be first, and some are first who will be last.* **13:35** Ps 118:26. **14:2** Or *who had dropsy.*

law to heal people on the Sabbath day, or not?" [4]When they refused to answer, Jesus touched the sick man and healed him and sent him away. [5]Then he turned to them and said, "Which of you doesn't work on the Sabbath? If your son* or your cow falls into a pit, don't you rush to get him out?" [6]Again they could not answer.

Jesus Teaches about Humility

[7]When Jesus noticed that all who had come to the dinner were trying to sit in the seats of honor near the head of the table, he gave them this advice: [8]"When you are invited to a wedding feast, don't sit in the seat of honor. What if someone who is more distinguished than you has also been invited? [9]The host will come and say, 'Give this person your seat.' Then you will be embarrassed, and you will have to take whatever seat is left at the foot of the table!

Why is it bad to brag about all the cool things I can do?

[Jesus explained,] "Those who exalt themselves will be humbled, and those who humble themselves will be exalted." LUKE 14:11

[10]"Instead, take the lowest place at the foot of the table. Then when your host sees you, he will come and say, 'Friend, we have a better place for you!' Then you will be honored in front of all the other guests. [11]For those who exalt themselves will be humbled, and those who humble themselves will be exalted."

[12]Then he turned to his host. "When you put on a luncheon or a banquet," he said, "don't invite your friends, brothers, relatives, and rich neighbors. For they will invite you back, and that will be your only reward. [13]Instead, invite the poor, the crippled, the lame, and the blind. [14]Then at the resurrection of the righteous, God will reward you for inviting those who could not repay you."

Parable of the Great Feast

[15]Hearing this, a man sitting at the table with Jesus exclaimed, "What a blessing it will be to attend a banquet* in the Kingdom of God!"

[16]Jesus replied with this story: "A man prepared a great feast and sent out many invitations. [17]When the banquet was ready, he sent his servant to tell the guests, 'Come, the banquet is ready.' [18]But they all began making excuses. One said, 'I have just bought a field and must inspect it. Please excuse me.' [19]Another said, 'I have just bought five pairs of oxen, and I want to try them out. Please excuse me.' [20]Another said, 'I now have a wife, so I can't come.'

[21]"The servant returned and told his master what they had said. His master was furious and said, 'Go quickly into the streets and alleys of the town and invite the poor, the crippled, the blind, and the lame.' [22]After the servant had done this, he reported, 'There is still room for more.' [23]So his master said, 'Go out into the country lanes and behind the hedges and urge anyone you find to come, so that the house will be full. [24]For none of those I first invited will get even the smallest taste of my banquet.'"

The Cost of Being a Disciple

[25]A large crowd was following Jesus. He turned around and said to them, [26]"If you want to be my disciple, you must hate everyone else by comparison—your father and mother, wife and children, brothers and sisters—yes, even your own life. Otherwise, you cannot be my disciple. [27]And if you do not carry your own cross and follow me, you cannot be my disciple.

[28]"But don't begin until you count the cost. For who would begin construction of a building without first calculating the cost to see if there is enough money to finish it? [29]Otherwise, you might complete only the foundation before running out of money, and then everyone would laugh at you. [30]They would say, 'There's the person who started that building and couldn't afford to finish it!'

[31]"Or what king would go to war against another king without first sitting down with his counselors to discuss whether his army of 10,000 could defeat the 20,000 soldiers

14:5 Some manuscripts read *donkey*. **14:15** Greek *to eat bread*.

marching against him? [32]And if he can't, he will send a delegation to discuss terms of peace while the enemy is still far away. [33]So you cannot become my disciple without giving up everything you own.

[34]"Salt is good for seasoning. But if it loses its flavor, how do you make it salty again? [35]Flavorless salt is good neither for the soil nor for the manure pile. It is thrown away. Anyone with ears to hear should listen and understand!"

CHAPTER 15

Parable of the Lost Sheep

Tax collectors and other notorious sinners often came to listen to Jesus teach. [2]This made the Pharisees and teachers of religious law complain that he was associating with such sinful people—even eating with them!

[3]So Jesus told them this story: [4]"If a man has a hundred sheep and one of them gets lost, what will he do? Won't he leave the ninety-nine others in the wilderness and go to search for the one that is lost until he finds it? [5]And when he has found it, he will joyfully carry it home on his shoulders. [6]When he arrives, he will call together his friends and neighbors, saying, 'Rejoice with me because I have found my lost sheep.' [7]In the same way, there is more joy in heaven over one lost sinner who repents and returns to God than over ninety-nine others who are righteous and haven't strayed away!

Parable of the Lost Coin

[8]"Or suppose a woman has ten silver coins* and loses one. Won't she light a lamp and sweep the entire house and search carefully until she finds it? [9]And when she finds it, she will call in her friends and neighbors and say, 'Rejoice with me because I have found my lost coin.' [10]In the same way, there is joy in the presence of God's angels when even one sinner repents."

Parable of the Lost Son

[11]To illustrate the point further, Jesus told them this story: "A man had two sons. [12]The younger son told his father, 'I want my share of your estate now before you die.' So his father agreed to divide his wealth between his sons.

[13]"A few days later this younger son packed all his belongings and moved to a distant land, and there he wasted all his money in wild living. [14]About the time his money ran out, a great famine swept over the land, and he began to starve. [15]He persuaded a local farmer to hire him, and the man sent him into his fields to feed the pigs. [16]The young man became so hungry that even the pods he was feeding the pigs looked good to him. But no one gave him anything.

[17]"When he finally came to his senses, he said to himself, 'At home even the hired servants have food enough to spare, and here I am dying of hunger! [18]I will go home to my father and say, "Father, I have sinned against both heaven and you, [19]and I am no longer worthy of being called your son. Please take me on as a hired servant."'

[20]"So he returned home to his father. And while he was still a long way off, his father saw him coming. Filled with love and compassion, he ran to his son, embraced him, and kissed him. [21]His son said to him, 'Father, I have sinned against both heaven and you, and I am no longer worthy of being called your son.*'

[22]"But his father said to the servants, 'Quick! Bring the finest robe in the house and put it on him. Get a ring for his finger and sandals for his feet. [23]And kill the calf we have been fattening. We must celebrate with a feast, [24]for this son of mine was dead and has now returned to life. He was lost, but now he is found.' So the party began.

[25]"Meanwhile, the older son was in the fields working. When he returned home, he heard music and dancing in the house, [26]and he asked one of the servants what was going on. [27]'Your brother is back,' he was told, 'and your father has killed the fattened calf. We are celebrating because of his safe return.'

[28]"The older brother was angry and wouldn't go in. His father came out and begged him, [29]but he replied, 'All these years I've slaved for you and never once refused to do a single thing you told me to. And in all that time you never gave me even one young goat for a feast with my friends. [30]Yet when this son of yours comes back after squandering your money on prostitutes, you celebrate by killing the fattened calf!'

15:8 Greek *ten drachmas*. A drachma was the equivalent of a full day's wage. **15:21** Some manuscripts add *Please take me on as a hired servant.*

31"His father said to him, 'Look, dear son, you have always stayed by me, and everything I have is yours. 32We had to celebrate this happy day. For your brother was dead and has come back to life! He was lost, but now he is found!'"

CHAPTER 16

Parable of the Shrewd Manager

Jesus told this story to his disciples: "There was a certain rich man who had a manager handling his affairs. One day a report came that the manager was wasting his employer's money. 2So the employer called him in and said, 'What's this I hear about you? Get your report in order, because you are going to be fired.'

3"The manager thought to himself, 'Now what? My boss has fired me. I don't have the strength to dig ditches, and I'm too proud to beg. 4Ah, I know how to ensure that I'll have plenty of friends who will give me a home when I am fired.'

5"So he invited each person who owed money to his employer to come and discuss the situation. He asked the first one, 'How much do you owe him?' 6The man replied, 'I owe him 800 gallons of olive oil.' So the manager told him, 'Take the bill and quickly change it to 400 gallons.*'

7" 'And how much do you owe my employer?' he asked the next man. 'I owe him 1,000 bushels of wheat,' was the reply. 'Here,' the manager said, 'take the bill and change it to 800 bushels.*'

8"The rich man had to admire the dishonest rascal for being so shrewd. And it is true that the children of this world are more shrewd in dealing with the world around them than are the children of the light. 9Here's the lesson: Use your worldly resources to benefit others and make friends. Then, when your earthly possessions are gone, they will welcome you to an eternal home.*

10"If you are faithful in little things, you will be faithful in large ones. But if you are dishonest in little things, you won't be honest with greater responsibilities. 11And if you are untrustworthy about worldly wealth, who will trust you with the true riches of heaven? 12And if you are not faithful with other people's things, why should you be trusted with things of your own?

How can I get my parents to trust me more?

[Jesus taught,] "If you are faithful in little things, you will be faithful in large ones. But if you are dishonest in little things, you won't be honest with greater responsibilities."

LUKE 16:10

13"No one can serve two masters. For you will hate one and love the other; you will be devoted to one and despise the other. You cannot serve both God and money."

14The Pharisees, who dearly loved their money, heard all this and scoffed at him. 15Then he said to them, "You like to appear righteous in public, but God knows your hearts. What this world honors is detestable in the sight of God.

16"Until John the Baptist, the law of Moses and the messages of the prophets were your guides. But now the Good News of the Kingdom of God is preached, and everyone is eager to get in.* 17But that doesn't mean that the law has lost its force. It is easier for heaven and earth to disappear than for the smallest point of God's law to be overturned.

18"For example, a man who divorces his wife and marries someone else commits adultery. And anyone who marries a woman divorced from her husband commits adultery."

Parable of the Rich Man and Lazarus

19Jesus said, "There was a certain rich man who was splendidly clothed in purple and fine linen and who lived each day in luxury. 20At his gate lay a poor man named Lazarus who was covered with sores. 21As Lazarus lay

16:6 Greek *100 baths . . . 50 (baths).* **16:7** Greek *100 korous . . . 80 (korous).* **16:9** Or *you will be welcomed into eternal homes.* **16:16** Or *everyone is urged to enter in.*

Earning Trust

When George's mother started to work longer hours, George and his parents made an agreement that he'd always come right home after school, call his mom, have a snack, and start on his homework. He would clear any changes with his parents ahead of time. They agreed to a one-month trial period. By the third week George was comfortable with the routine. One day after school Leon said, "Come over and take a spin on my new 18-speed bike." George figured he could take a quick ride, run home, and still get everything done. Mom would never know. What should George do? Read Luke 16:10 for an idea.

there longing for scraps from the rich man's table, the dogs would come and lick his open sores.

22"Finally, the poor man died and was carried by the angels to be with Abraham.* The rich man also died and was buried, 23and his soul went to the place of the dead.* There, in torment, he saw Abraham in the far distance with Lazarus at his side.

24"The rich man shouted, 'Father Abraham, have some pity! Send Lazarus over here to dip the tip of his finger in water and cool my tongue. I am in anguish in these flames.'

25"But Abraham said to him, 'Son, remember that during your lifetime you had everything you wanted, and Lazarus had nothing. So now he is here being comforted, and you are in anguish. 26And besides, there is a great chasm separating us. No one can cross over to you from here, and no one can cross over to us from there.'

27"Then the rich man said, 'Please, Father Abraham, at least send him to my father's home. 28For I have five brothers, and I want him to warn them so they don't end up in this place of torment.'

29"But Abraham said, 'Moses and the prophets have warned them. Your brothers can read what they wrote.'

30"The rich man replied, 'No, Father Abraham! But if someone is sent to them from the dead, then they will repent of their sins and turn to God.'

31"But Abraham said, 'If they won't listen to Moses and the prophets, they won't listen even if someone rises from the dead.'"

CHAPTER 17

Teachings about Forgiveness and Faith

One day Jesus said to his disciples, "There will always be temptations to sin, but what sorrow awaits the person who does the tempting! 2It would be better to be thrown into the sea with a millstone hung around your neck than to cause one of these little ones to fall into sin. 3So watch yourselves!

"If another believer* sins, rebuke that person; then if there is repentance, forgive. 4Even if that person wrongs you seven times a day and each time turns again and asks forgiveness, you must forgive."

5The apostles said to the Lord, "Show us how to increase our faith."

6The Lord answered, "If you had faith even as small as a mustard seed, you could say to

16:22 Greek *into Abraham's bosom.* **16:23** Greek *to Hades.* **17:3** Greek *If your brother.*

this mulberry tree, 'May you be uprooted and thrown into the sea,' and it would obey you!

7"When a servant comes in from plowing or taking care of sheep, does his master say, 'Come in and eat with me'? 8No, he says, 'Prepare my meal, put on your apron, and serve me while I eat. Then you can eat later.' 9And does the master thank the servant for doing what he was told to do? Of course not. 10In the same way, when you obey me you should say, 'We are unworthy servants who have simply done our duty.'"

Ten Healed of Leprosy

11As Jesus continued on toward Jerusalem, he reached the border between Galilee and Samaria. 12As he entered a village there, ten lepers stood at a distance, 13crying out, "Jesus, Master, have mercy on us!"

14He looked at them and said, "Go show yourselves to the priests."* And as they went, they were cleansed of their leprosy.

15One of them, when he saw that he was healed, came back to Jesus, shouting, "Praise God!" 16He fell to the ground at Jesus' feet, thanking him for what he had done. This man was a Samaritan.

AMAZING FACTS

When ten men with leprosy asked for Jesus' help, he just looked at them and they were healed—all ten at the same time!

LUKE 17:11-19

17Jesus asked, "Didn't I heal ten men? Where are the other nine? 18Has no one returned to give glory to God except this foreigner?" 19And Jesus said to the man, "Stand up and go. Your faith has healed you.*"

The Coming of the Kingdom

20One day the Pharisees asked Jesus, "When will the Kingdom of God come?"

Jesus replied, "The Kingdom of God can't be detected by visible signs.* 21You won't be able to say, 'Here it is!' or 'It's over there!' For the Kingdom of God is already among you.*"

22Then he said to his disciples, "The time is coming when you will long to see the day when the Son of Man returns,* but you won't see it. 23People will tell you, 'Look, there is the Son of Man,' or 'Here he is,' but don't go out and follow them. 24For as the lightning flashes and lights up the sky from one end to the other, so it will be on the day when the Son of Man comes. 25But first the Son of Man must suffer terribly* and be rejected by this generation.

26"When the Son of Man returns, it will be like it was in Noah's day. 27In those days, the people enjoyed banquets and parties and weddings right up to the time Noah entered his boat and the flood came and destroyed them all.

28"And the world will be as it was in the days of Lot. People went about their daily business—eating and drinking, buying and selling, farming and building—29until the morning Lot left Sodom. Then fire and burning sulfur rained down from heaven and destroyed them all. 30Yes, it will be 'business as usual' right up to the day when the Son of Man is revealed. 31On that day a person out on the deck of a roof must not go down into the house to pack. A person out in the field must not return home. 32Remember what happened to Lot's wife! 33If you cling to your life, you will lose it, and if you let your life go, you will save it. 34That night two people will be asleep in one bed; one will be taken, the other left. 35Two women will be grinding flour together at the mill; one will be taken, the other left.*"

37"Where will this happen, Lord?"* the disciples asked.

Jesus replied, "Just as the gathering of vultures shows there is a carcass nearby, so these signs indicate that the end is near."*

CHAPTER 18

Parable of the Persistent Widow

One day Jesus told his disciples a story to show that they should always pray and never

17:14 See Lev 14:2-32. **17:19** Or *Your faith has saved you.* **17:20** Or *by your speculations.* **17:21** Or *is within you,* or *is in your grasp.* **17:22** Or *long for even one day with the Son of Man.* "Son of Man" is a title Jesus used for himself. **17:25** Or *suffer many things.* **17:35** Some manuscripts add verse 36, *Two men will be working in the field; one will be taken, the other left.* Compare Matt 24:40. **17:37a** Greek *"Where, Lord?"* **17:37b** Greek *"Wherever the carcass is, the vultures gather."*

give up. 2"There was a judge in a certain
city," he said, "who neither feared God nor
cared about people. 3A widow of that city
came to him repeatedly, saying, 'Give me justice in this dispute with my enemy.' 4The
judge ignored her for a while, but finally he
said to himself, 'I don't fear God or care
about people, 5but this woman is driving me
crazy. I'm going to see that she gets justice,
because she is wearing me out with her constant requests!'"

6Then the Lord said, "Learn a lesson from
this unjust judge. 7Even he rendered a just decision in the end. So don't you think God will
surely give justice to his chosen people who
cry out to him day and night? Will he keep
putting them off? 8I tell you, he will grant justice to them quickly! But when the Son of
Man* returns, how many will he find on the
earth who have faith?"

Does Jesus really care about me? I'm just a kid.

[Jesus said,] "Let the children come to me. Don't stop them! For the Kingdom of God belongs to those who are like these children."
LUKE 18:16

Parable of the Pharisee and Tax Collector

9Then Jesus told this story to some who had
great confidence in their own righteousness
and scorned everyone else: 10"Two men went
to the Temple to pray. One was a Pharisee,
and the other was a despised tax collector.
11The Pharisee stood by himself and prayed
this prayer*: 'I thank you, God, that I am not a
sinner like everyone else. For I don't cheat, I
don't sin, and I don't commit adultery. I'm
certainly not like that tax collector! 12I fast
twice a week, and I give you a tenth of my income.'

13"But the tax collector stood at a distance
and dared not even lift his eyes to heaven as
he prayed. Instead, he beat his chest in sorrow, saying, 'O God, be merciful to me, for I
am a sinner.' 14I tell you, this sinner, not the
Pharisee, returned home justified before
God. For those who exalt themselves will be
humbled, and those who humble themselves
will be exalted."

Jesus Blesses the Children

15One day some parents brought their little
children to Jesus so he could touch and bless
them. But when the disciples saw this, they
scolded the parents for bothering him.

16Then Jesus called for the children and
said to the disciples, "Let the children come to
me. Don't stop them! For the Kingdom of God
belongs to those who are like these children.
17I tell you the truth, anyone who doesn't receive the Kingdom of God like a child will
never enter it."

The Rich Man

18Once a religious leader asked Jesus this
question: "Good Teacher, what should I do to
inherit eternal life?"

19"Why do you call me good?" Jesus asked
him. "Only God is truly good. 20But to answer
your question, you know the commandments:
'You must not commit adultery. You must not
murder. You must not steal. You must not testify falsely. Honor your father and mother.'*"

21The man replied, "I've obeyed all these
commandments since I was young."

22When Jesus heard his answer, he said,
"There is still one thing you haven't done. Sell
all your possessions and give the money to the
poor, and you will have treasure in heaven.
Then come, follow me."

23But when the man heard this he became
very sad, for he was very rich.

24When Jesus saw this,* he said, "How hard
it is for the rich to enter the Kingdom of God!
25In fact, it is easier for a camel to go through
the eye of a needle than for a rich person to
enter the Kingdom of God!"

26Those who heard this said, "Then who in
the world can be saved?"

18:8 "Son of Man" is a title Jesus used for himself. **18:11** Some manuscripts read *stood and prayed this prayer to himself.*
18:20 Exod 20:12-16; Deut 5:16-20. **18:24** Some manuscripts read *When Jesus saw how sad the man was.*

[27]He replied, "What is impossible for people is possible with God."

[28]Peter said, "We've left our homes to follow you."

[29]"Yes," Jesus replied, "and I assure you that everyone who has given up house or wife or brothers or parents or children, for the sake of the Kingdom of God, [30]will be repaid many times over in this life, and will have eternal life in the world to come."

Jesus Again Predicts His Death

[31]Taking the twelve disciples aside, Jesus said, "Listen, we're going up to Jerusalem, where all the predictions of the prophets concerning the Son of Man will come true. [32]He will be handed over to the Romans,* and he will be mocked, treated shamefully, and spit upon. [33]They will flog him with a whip and kill him, but on the third day he will rise again."

[34]But they didn't understand any of this. The significance of his words was hidden from them, and they failed to grasp what he was talking about.

18:32 Greek *the Gentiles*. **18:37** Or *Jesus of Nazareth*.

Jesus Heals a Blind Beggar

[35]As Jesus approached Jericho, a blind beggar was sitting beside the road. [36]When he heard the noise of a crowd going past, he asked what was happening. [37]They told him that Jesus the Nazarene* was going by. [38]So he began shouting, "Jesus, Son of David, have mercy on me!"

[39]"Be quiet!" the people in front yelled at him.

But he only shouted louder, "Son of David, have mercy on me!"

[40]When Jesus heard him, he stopped and ordered that the man be brought to him. As the man came near, Jesus asked him, [41]"What do you want me to do for you?"

"Lord," he said, "I want to see!"

[42]And Jesus said, "All right, receive your sight! Your faith has healed you." [43]Instantly the man could see, and he followed Jesus, praising God. And all who saw it praised God, too.

CHAPTER 19

Jesus and Zacchaeus

Jesus entered Jericho and made his way through the town. [2]There was a man there

IS IT OK?

IS IT OK TO LEAVE OUT SOMEONE WHO'S NOT COOL?

Zacchaeus was *not cool*. He was super-short. He had no friends. He collected taxes for the Romans and then cheated his own people. Nobody wanted to hang out with him. What's surprising is that Jesus went out of his way to find Zacchaeus and go with him to his house. Zacchaeus changed into a pretty cool follower of Jesus after that. (You can read about it in Luke 19:1-10). Jesus did miracles, gave mind-boggling speeches, and had crowds following him everywhere—he was really *cool*. But he didn't let that stop him from hanging out with a guy who truly *needed* a friend. So be like Jesus and try to include others. You never know what might happen!

named Zacchaeus. He was the chief tax collector in the region, and he had become very rich.
3He tried to get a look at Jesus, but he was too
short to see over the crowd. 4So he ran ahead
and climbed a sycamore-fig tree beside the
road, for Jesus was going to pass that way.

5When Jesus came by, he looked up at Zacchaeus and called him by name. "Zacchaeus!" he said. "Quick, come down! I must be a guest in your home today."

6Zacchaeus quickly climbed down and took Jesus to his house in great excitement and joy. 7But the people were displeased. "He has gone to be the guest of a notorious sinner," they grumbled.

8Meanwhile, Zacchaeus stood before the Lord and said, "I will give half my wealth to the poor, Lord, and if I have cheated people on their taxes, I will give them back four times as much!"

9Jesus responded, "Salvation has come to this home today, for this man has shown himself to be a true son of Abraham. 10For the Son of Man* came to seek and save those who are lost."

Parable of the Ten Servants

11The crowd was listening to everything Jesus said. And because he was nearing Jerusalem, he told them a story to correct the impression that the Kingdom of God would begin right away. 12He said, "A nobleman was called away to a distant empire to be crowned king and then return. 13Before he left, he called together ten of his servants and divided among them ten pounds of silver,* saying, 'Invest this for me while I am gone.' 14But his people hated him and sent a delegation after him to say, 'We do not want him to be our king.'

15"After he was crowned king, he returned and called in the servants to whom he had given the money. He wanted to find out what their profits were. 16The first servant reported, 'Master, I invested your money and made ten times the original amount!'

17" 'Well done!' the king exclaimed. 'You are a good servant. You have been faithful with the little I entrusted to you, so you will be governor of ten cities as your reward.'

18"The next servant reported, 'Master, I invested your money and made five times the original amount.'

19" 'Well done!' the king said. 'You will be governor over five cities.'

20"But the third servant brought back only the original amount of money and said, 'Master, I hid your money and kept it safe. 21I was afraid because you are a hard man to deal with, taking what isn't yours and harvesting crops you didn't plant.'

22" 'You wicked servant!' the king roared. 'Your own words condemn you. If you knew that I'm a hard man who takes what isn't mine and harvests crops I didn't plant, 23why didn't you deposit my money in the bank? At least I could have gotten some interest on it.'

24"Then, turning to the others standing nearby, the king ordered, 'Take the money from this servant, and give it to the one who has ten pounds.'

25" 'But, master,' they said, 'he already has ten pounds!'

26" 'Yes,' the king replied, 'and to those who use well what they are given, even more will be given. But from those who do nothing, even what little they have will be taken away. 27And as for these enemies of mine who didn't want me to be their king—bring them in and execute them right here in front of me.'"

Jesus' Triumphant Entry

28After telling this story, Jesus went on toward Jerusalem, walking ahead of his disciples. 29As he came to the towns of Bethphage and Bethany on the Mount of Olives, he sent two disciples ahead. 30"Go into that village over there," he told them. "As you enter it, you will see a young donkey tied there that no one has ever ridden. Untie it and bring it here. 31If anyone asks, 'Why are you untying that colt?' just say, 'The Lord needs it.'"

32So they went and found the colt, just as Jesus had said. 33And sure enough, as they were untying it, the owners asked them, "Why are you untying that colt?"

34And the disciples simply replied, "The Lord needs it." 35So they brought the colt to Jesus and threw their garments over it for him to ride on.

36As he rode along, the crowds spread out their garments on the road ahead of him. 37When he reached the place where the road started down the Mount of Olives, all of his

19:10 "Son of Man" is a title Jesus used for himself. **19:13** Greek *ten minas;* one mina was worth about three months' wages.

followers began to shout and sing as they walked along, praising God for all the wonderful miracles they had seen.

38 "Blessings on the King who comes in the
name of the LORD!
Peace in heaven, and glory in highest
heaven!"*

39 But some of the Pharisees among the crowd said, "Teacher, rebuke your followers for saying things like that!"

40 He replied, "If they kept quiet, the stones along the road would burst into cheers!"

Jesus Weeps over Jerusalem

41 But as he came closer to Jerusalem and saw the city ahead, he began to weep. 42 "How I wish today that you of all people would understand the way to peace. But now it is too late, and peace is hidden from your eyes. 43 Before long your enemies will build ramparts against your walls and encircle you and close in on you from every side. 44 They will crush you into the ground, and your children with you. Your enemies will not leave a single stone in place, because you did not accept your opportunity for salvation."

Jesus Clears the Temple

45 Then Jesus entered the Temple and began to drive out the people selling animals for sacrifices. 46 He said to them, "The Scriptures declare, 'My Temple will be a house of prayer,' but you have turned it into a den of thieves."*

47 After that, he taught daily in the Temple, but the leading priests, the teachers of religious law, and the other leaders of the people began planning how to kill him. 48 But they could think of nothing, because all the people hung on every word he said.

CHAPTER 20

The Authority of Jesus Challenged

One day as Jesus was teaching the people and preaching the Good News in the Temple, the leading priests, the teachers of religious law, and the elders came up to him. 2 They demanded, "By what authority are you doing all these things? Who gave you the right?"

3 "Let me ask you a question first," he replied. 4 "Did John's authority to baptize come from heaven, or was it merely human?"

5 They talked it over among themselves. "If we say it was from heaven, he will ask why we didn't believe John. 6 But if we say it was merely human, the people will stone us because they are convinced John was a prophet." 7 So they finally replied that they didn't know.

8 And Jesus responded, "Then I won't tell you by what authority I do these things."

Parable of the Evil Farmers

9 Now Jesus turned to the people again and told them this story: "A man planted a vineyard, leased it to tenant farmers, and moved to another country to live for several years. 10 At the time of the grape harvest, he sent one of his servants to collect his share of the crop. But the farmers attacked the servant, beat him up, and sent him back empty-handed. 11 So the owner sent another servant, but they also insulted him, beat him up, and sent him away empty-handed. 12 A third man was sent, and they wounded him and chased him away.

13 "'What will I do?' the owner asked himself. 'I know! I'll send my cherished son. Surely they will respect him.'

14 "But when the tenant farmers saw his son, they said to each other, 'Here comes the heir to this estate. Let's kill him and get the estate for ourselves!' 15 So they dragged him out of the vineyard and murdered him.

"What do you suppose the owner of the vineyard will do to them?" Jesus asked. 16 "I'll tell you—he will come and kill those farmers and lease the vineyard to others."

"How terrible that such a thing should ever happen," his listeners protested.

17 Jesus looked at them and said, "Then what does this Scripture mean?

'The stone that the builders rejected
has now become the cornerstone.'*

18 Everyone who stumbles over that stone will be broken to pieces, and it will crush anyone it falls on."

19 The teachers of religious law and the leading priests wanted to arrest Jesus immediately because they realized he was telling the story against them—they were the wicked farmers. But they were afraid of the people's reaction.

19:38 Pss 118:26; 148:1. **19:46** Isa 56:7; Jer 7:11. **20:17** Ps 118:22.

Authority has never been my favorite word. For the longest time I hated doing anything that I was told to do just because I felt "forced" to do it. I would put off doing my homework; I would argue about doing chores; I would give my parents an attitude when they asked for my help. I figured the best way to get what I wanted was to ignore anyone who told me what to do.

The Bible has a different view on authority. Only one of the Ten Commandments comes with a promise. It's in Exodus 20:12: "Honor your father and mother. Then you will live a long, full life in the land the LORD your God is giving you." God is very clear about this—we should honor and obey our parents.

We may think that growing up and leaving home will free us from respecting and obeying authority. Not true. In Romans 13:1 Paul says that God commands adults to obey government leaders. Paul also says that God put these leaders in control and if we follow their laws, we have nothing to fear from them. However, if we break the laws, God has given them the authority to punish us. Jesus said to his followers that we are to "give to Caesar what belongs to Caesar, and give to God what belongs to God" (Luke 20:25). That means we have a duty to obey both government and God.

I've learned that when I obey God's law and submit to authorities (parents, teachers, and government leaders) even if their rules don't always make sense to me, I get what is best for me. And I know God will help me recognize those rare times when people in authority differ with God's authority, which always comes first.

For more on obeying the authorities in our life, read Luke 20:20–25 and Romans 13:1–7.

Taxes for Caesar

20 Watching for their opportunity, the leaders
sent spies pretending to be honest men. They
tried to get Jesus to say something that could
be reported to the Roman governor so he
would arrest Jesus. 21 "Teacher," they said, "we
know that you speak and teach what is right
and are not influenced by what others think.
You teach the way of God truthfully. 22 Now
tell us—is it right for us to pay taxes to Caesar
or not?"

23 He saw through their trickery and said,
24 "Show me a Roman coin.* Whose picture
and title are stamped on it?"

"Caesar's," they replied.

25 "Well then," he said, "give to Caesar what
belongs to Caesar, and give to God what belongs to God."

26 So they failed to trap him by what he said
in front of the people. Instead, they were
amazed by his answer, and they became silent.

Discussion about Resurrection

27 Then Jesus was approached by some Sad-
ducees—religious leaders who say there is
no resurrection from the dead. 28 They posed
this question: "Teacher, Moses gave us a law
that if a man dies, leaving a wife but no children, his brother should marry the widow
and have a child who will carry on the
brother's name.* 29 Well, suppose there were
seven brothers. The oldest one married and
then died without children. 30 So the second
brother married the widow, but he also died.
31 Then the third brother married her. This
continued with all seven of them, who died
without children. 32 Finally, the woman also
died. 33 So tell us, whose wife will she be in
the resurrection? For all seven were married
to her!"

34 Jesus replied, "Marriage is for people
here on earth. 35 But in the age to come, those
worthy of being raised from the dead will neither marry nor be given in marriage. 36 And
they will never die again. In this respect they
will be like angels. They are children of God
and children of the resurrection.

37 "But now, as to whether the dead will be
raised—even Moses proved this when he
wrote about the burning bush. Long after
Abraham, Isaac, and Jacob had died, he referred to the Lord* as 'the God of Abraham,
the God of Isaac, and the God of Jacob.'* 38 So
he is the God of the living, not the dead, for
they are all alive to him."

39 "Well said, Teacher!" remarked some of
the teachers of religious law who were standing there. 40 And then no one dared to ask him
any more questions.

Whose Son Is the Messiah?

41 Then Jesus presented them with a question.
"Why is it," he asked, "that the Messiah is said
to be the son of David? 42 For David himself
wrote in the book of Psalms:

'The LORD said to my Lord,
Sit in the place of honor at my
right hand

20:24 Greek *a denarius.* **20:28** See Deut 25:5-6. **20:37a** Greek *when he wrote about the bush. He referred to the Lord.* **20:37b** Exod 3:6.

43 until I humble your enemies,
making them a footstool under your
feet.'*

44Since David called the Messiah 'Lord,' how
can the Messiah be his son?"

45Then, with the crowds listening, he
turned to his disciples and said, 46"Beware of
these teachers of religious law! For they like
to parade around in flowing robes and love to
receive respectful greetings as they walk in
the marketplaces. And how they love the
seats of honor in the synagogues and the head
table at banquets. 47Yet they shamelessly
cheat widows out of their property and then
pretend to be pious by making long prayers in
public. Because of this, they will be severely
punished."

CHAPTER 21

The Widow's Offering

While Jesus was in the Temple, he watched
the rich people dropping their gifts in the col-
lection box. 2Then a poor widow came by and
dropped in two small coins.*

3"I tell you the truth," Jesus said, "this poor
widow has given more than all the rest of
them. 4For they have given a tiny part of their
surplus, but she, poor as she is, has given
everything she has."

Jesus Foretells the Future

5Some of his disciples began talking about
the majestic stonework of the Temple and the
memorial decorations on the walls. But Jesus
said, 6"The time is coming when all these
things will be completely demolished. Not
one stone will be left on top of another!"

7"Teacher," they asked, "when will all this
happen? What sign will show us that these
things are about to take place?"

8He replied, "Don't let anyone mislead you,
for many will come in my name, claiming, 'I
am the Messiah,'* and saying, 'The time has
come!' But don't believe them. 9And when you
hear of wars and insurrections, don't panic.
Yes, these things must take place first, but the
end won't follow immediately." 10Then he
added, "Nation will go to war against nation,
and kingdom against kingdom. 11There will
be great earthquakes, and there will be fam-
ines and plagues in many lands, and there will
be terrifying things and great miraculous
signs from heaven.

12"But before all this occurs, there will be a
time of great persecution. You will be
dragged into synagogues and prisons, and
you will stand trial before kings and gover-
nors because you are my followers. 13But this
will be your opportunity to tell them about
me.* 14So don't worry in advance about how
to answer the charges against you, 15for I will
give you the right words and such wisdom
that none of your opponents will be able to
reply or refute you! 16Even those closest to
you—your parents, brothers, relatives, and
friends—will betray you. They will even kill
some of you. 17And everyone will hate you be-
cause you are my followers.* 18But not a hair
of your head will perish! 19By standing firm,
you will win your souls.

20"And when you see Jerusalem sur-
rounded by armies, then you will know that
the time of its destruction has arrived. 21Then
those in Judea must flee to the hills. Those in
Jerusalem must get out, and those out in the
country should not return to the city. 22For
those will be days of God's vengeance, and the
prophetic words of the Scriptures will be ful-
filled. 23How terrible it will be for pregnant
women and for nursing mothers in those
days. For there will be disaster in the land and
great anger against this people. 24They will be
killed by the sword or sent away as captives to
all the nations of the world. And Jerusalem
will be trampled down by the Gentiles until
the period of the Gentiles comes to an end.

25"And there will be strange signs in the
sun, moon, and stars. And here on earth
the nations will be in turmoil, perplexed by
the roaring seas and strange tides. 26People
will be terrified at what they see coming
upon the earth, for the powers in the heavens
will be shaken. 27Then everyone will see the
Son of Man* coming on a cloud with power
and great glory.* 28So when all these things
begin to happen, stand and look up, for your
salvation is near!"

29Then he gave them this illustration: "No-
tice the fig tree, or any other tree. 30When the
leaves come out, you know without being told
that summer is near. 31In the same way, when

20:42-43 Ps 110:1. **21:2** Greek *two lepta* [the smallest of Jewish coins]. **21:8** Greek *claiming, 'I am.'* **21:13** Or *This will be your testimony against them.* **21:17** Greek *on account of my name.* **21:27a** "Son of Man" is a title Jesus used for himself. **21:27b** See Dan 7:13.

you see all these things taking place, you can
know that the Kingdom of God is near. 32I tell
you the truth, this generation will not pass
from the scene until all these things have
taken place. 33Heaven and earth will disap-
pear, but my words will never disappear.

34"Watch out! Don't let your hearts be
dulled by carousing and drunkenness, and by
the worries of this life. Don't let that day catch
you unaware, 35like a trap. For that day will
come upon everyone living on the earth.
36Keep alert at all times. And pray that you
might be strong enough to escape these com-
ing horrors and stand before the Son of Man."

37Every day Jesus went to the Temple to
teach, and each evening he returned to spend
the night on the Mount of Olives. 38The
crowds gathered at the Temple early each
morning to hear him.

CHAPTER 22

Judas Agrees to Betray Jesus

The Festival of Unleavened Bread, which is
also called Passover, was approaching. 2The
leading priests and teachers of religious law
were plotting how to kill Jesus, but they were
afraid of the people's reaction.

3Then Satan entered into Judas Iscariot,
who was one of the twelve disciples, 4and he
went to the leading priests and captains of the
Temple guard to discuss the best way to be-
tray Jesus to them. 5They were delighted, and
they promised to give him money. 6So he
agreed and began looking for an opportunity
to betray Jesus so they could arrest him when
the crowds weren't around.

The Last Supper

7Now the Festival of Unleavened Bread
arrived, when the Passover lamb is sacrificed.
8Jesus sent Peter and John ahead and said,
"Go and prepare the Passover meal, so we can
eat it together."

9"Where do you want us to prepare it?"
they asked him.

10He replied, "As soon as you enter Jerusa-
lem, a man carrying a pitcher of water will
meet you. Follow him. At the house he enters,
11say to the owner, 'The Teacher asks: Where
is the guest room where I can eat the Passover
meal with my disciples?' 12He will take you
upstairs to a large room that is already set up.
That is where you should prepare our meal."
13They went off to the city and found every-
thing just as Jesus had said, and they prepared
the Passover meal there.

14When the time came, Jesus and the apos-
tles sat down together at the table.* 15Jesus
said, "I have been very eager to eat this Pass-
over meal with you before my suffering be-
gins. 16For I tell you now that I won't eat this
meal again until its meaning is fulfilled in the
Kingdom of God."

17Then he took a cup of wine and gave
thanks to God for it. Then he said, "Take this
and share it among yourselves. 18For I will not
drink wine again until the Kingdom of God
has come."

19He took some bread and gave thanks to
God for it. Then he broke it in pieces and gave
it to the disciples, saying, "This is my body,
which is given for you. Do this to remember
me."

20After supper he took another cup of wine
and said, "This cup is the new covenant be-
tween God and his people—an agreement
confirmed with my blood, which is poured
out as a sacrifice for you.*

21"But here at this table, sitting among us as
a friend, is the man who will betray me. 22For
it has been determined that the Son of Man*
must die. But what sorrow awaits the one who
betrays him." 23The disciples began to ask
each other which of them would ever do such
a thing.

24Then they began to argue among them-
selves about who would be the greatest
among them. 25Jesus told them, "In this world
the kings and great men lord it over their peo-
ple, yet they are called 'friends of the people.'
26But among you it will be different. Those
who are the greatest among you should take
the lowest rank, and the leader should be like
a servant. 27Who is more important, the one
who sits at the table or the one who serves?
The one who sits at the table, of course. But
not here! For I am among you as one who
serves.

28"You have stayed with me in my time of
trial. 29And just as my Father has granted me a
Kingdom, I now grant you the right 30to eat
and drink at my table in my Kingdom. And

22:14 Or *reclined together*. **22:19-20** Some manuscripts do not include 22:19b-20, *which is given for you . . . which is poured out as a sacrifice for you.* **22:22** "Son of Man" is a title Jesus used for himself.

you will sit on thrones, judging the twelve tribes of Israel.

Jesus Predicts Peter's Denial

31"Simon, Simon, Satan has asked to sift each of you like wheat. 32But I have pleaded in prayer for you, Simon, that your faith should not fail. So when you have repented and turned to me again, strengthen your brothers."

33Peter said, "Lord, I am ready to go to prison with you, and even to die with you."

34But Jesus said, "Peter, let me tell you something. Before the rooster crows tomorrow morning, you will deny three times that you even know me."

35Then Jesus asked them, "When I sent you out to preach the Good News and you did not have money, a traveler's bag, or an extra pair of sandals, did you need anything?"

"No," they replied.

36"But now," he said, "take your money and a traveler's bag. And if you don't have a sword, sell your cloak and buy one! 37For the time has come for this prophecy about me to be fulfilled: 'He was counted among the rebels.'* Yes, everything written about me by the prophets will come true."

38"Look, Lord," they replied, "we have two swords among us."

"That's enough," he said.

Jesus Prays on the Mount of Olives

39Then, accompanied by the disciples, Jesus left the upstairs room and went as usual to the Mount of Olives. 40There he told them, "Pray that you will not give in to temptation."

41He walked away, about a stone's throw, and knelt down and prayed, 42"Father, if you are willing, please take this cup of suffering away from me. Yet I want your will to be done, not mine." 43Then an angel from heaven appeared and strengthened him. 44He prayed more fervently, and he was in such agony of spirit that his sweat fell to the ground like great drops of blood.*

45At last he stood up again and returned to the disciples, only to find them asleep, exhausted from grief. 46"Why are you sleeping?" he asked them. "Get up and pray, so that you will not give in to temptation."

Jesus Is Betrayed and Arrested

47But even as Jesus said this, a crowd approached, led by Judas, one of the twelve disciples. Judas walked over to Jesus to greet him with a kiss. 48But Jesus said, "Judas, would you betray the Son of Man with a kiss?"

49When the other disciples saw what was about to happen, they exclaimed, "Lord, should we fight? We brought the swords!" 50And one of them struck at the high priest's slave, slashing off his right ear.

51But Jesus said, "No more of this." And he touched the man's ear and healed him.

52Then Jesus spoke to the leading priests, the captains of the Temple guard, and the elders who had come for him. "Am I some dangerous revolutionary," he asked, "that you come with swords and clubs to arrest me? 53Why didn't you arrest me in the Temple? I was there every day. But this is your moment, the time when the power of darkness reigns."

Peter Denies Jesus

54So they arrested him and led him to the high priest's home. And Peter followed at a distance. 55The guards lit a fire in the middle of the courtyard and sat around it, and Peter joined them there. 56A servant girl noticed him in the firelight and began staring at him. Finally she said, "This man was one of Jesus' followers!"

57But Peter denied it. "Woman," he said, "I don't even know him!"

58After a while someone else looked at him and said, "You must be one of them!"

"No, man, I'm not!" Peter retorted.

59About an hour later someone else insisted, "This must be one of them, because he is a Galilean, too."

60But Peter said, "Man, I don't know what you are talking about." And immediately, while he was still speaking, the rooster crowed.

61At that moment the Lord turned and looked at Peter. Suddenly, the Lord's words flashed through Peter's mind: "Before the rooster crows tomorrow morning, you will deny three times that you even know me." 62And Peter left the courtyard, weeping bitterly.

63The guards in charge of Jesus began mocking and beating him. 64They blindfolded him and said, "Prophesy to us! Who hit

22:37 Isa 53:12. **22:43-44** Verses 43 and 44 are not included in many ancient manuscripts.

you that time?" 65And they hurled all sorts of terrible insults at him.

Jesus before the Council

66At daybreak all the elders of the people assembled, including the leading priests and the teachers of religious law. Jesus was led before this high council,* 67and they said, "Tell us, are you the Messiah?"

But he replied, "If I tell you, you won't believe me. 68And if I ask you a question, you won't answer. 69But from now on the Son of Man will be seated in the place of power at God's right hand.*"

70They all shouted, "So, are you claiming to be the Son of God?"

And he replied, "You say that I am."

71"Why do we need other witnesses?" they said. "We ourselves heard him say it."

CHAPTER 23

Jesus' Trial before Pilate

Then the entire council took Jesus to Pilate, the Roman governor. 2They began to state their case: "This man has been leading our people astray by telling them not to pay their taxes to the Roman government and by claiming he is the Messiah, a king."

3So Pilate asked him, "Are you the king of the Jews?"

Jesus replied, "You have said it."

4Pilate turned to the leading priests and to the crowd and said, "I find nothing wrong with this man!"

5Then they became insistent. "But he is causing riots by his teaching wherever he goes—all over Judea, from Galilee to Jerusalem!"

6"Oh, is he a Galilean?" Pilate asked. 7When they said that he was, Pilate sent him to Herod Antipas, because Galilee was under Herod's jurisdiction, and Herod happened to be in Jerusalem at the time.

8Herod was delighted at the opportunity to see Jesus, because he had heard about him and had been hoping for a long time to see him perform a miracle. 9He asked Jesus question after question, but Jesus refused to answer. 10Meanwhile, the leading priests and the teachers of religious law stood there shouting their accusations. 11Then Herod and his soldiers began mocking and ridiculing Jesus. Finally, they put a royal robe on him and sent him back to Pilate. 12(Herod and Pilate, who had been enemies before, became friends that day.)

13Then Pilate called together the leading priests and other religious leaders, along with the people, 14and he announced his verdict. "You brought this man to me, accusing him of leading a revolt. I have examined him thoroughly on this point in your presence and find him innocent. 15Herod came to the same conclusion and sent him back to us. Nothing this man has done calls for the death penalty. 16So I will have him flogged, and then I will release him."*

18Then a mighty roar rose from the crowd, and with one voice they shouted, "Kill him, and release Barabbas to us!" 19(Barabbas was in prison for taking part in an insurrection in Jerusalem against the government, and for murder.) 20Pilate argued with them, because he wanted to release Jesus. 21But they kept shouting, "Crucify him! Crucify him!"

22For the third time he demanded, "Why? What crime has he committed? I have found no reason to sentence him to death. So I will have him flogged, and then I will release him."

23But the mob shouted louder and louder, demanding that Jesus be crucified, and their voices prevailed. 24So Pilate sentenced Jesus to die as they demanded. 25As they had requested, he released Barabbas, the man in prison for insurrection and murder. But he turned Jesus over to them to do as they wished.

The Crucifixion

26As they led Jesus away, a man named Simon, who was from Cyrene,* happened to be coming in from the countryside. The soldiers seized him and put the cross on him and made him carry it behind Jesus. 27A large crowd trailed behind, including many grief-stricken women. 28But Jesus turned and said to them, "Daughters of Jerusalem, don't weep for me, but weep for yourselves and for your children. 29For the days are coming when they will say, 'Fortunate indeed are the women who are childless, the wombs that have not borne a

22:66 Greek *before their Sanhedrin.* **22:69** See Ps 110:1. **23:16** Some manuscripts add verse 17, *Now it was necessary for him to release one prisoner to them during the Passover celebration.* Compare Matt 27:15; Mark 15:6; John 18:39. **23:26** *Cyrene* was a city in northern Africa.

child and the breasts that have never nursed.'
30 People will beg the mountains, 'Fall on us,'
and plead with the hills, 'Bury us.'* 31 For if
these things are done when the tree is green,
what will happen when it is dry?*"

32 Two others, both criminals, were led out
to be executed with him. 33 When they came
to a place called The Skull,* they nailed him to
the cross. And the criminals were also crucified—one on his right and one on his left.

34 Jesus said, "Father, forgive them, for they
don't know what they are doing."* And the
soldiers gambled for his clothes by throwing
dice.*

35 The crowd watched and the leaders
scoffed. "He saved others," they said, "let him
save himself if he is really God's Messiah, the
Chosen One." 36 The soldiers mocked him, too,
by offering him a drink of sour wine. 37 They
called out to him, "If you are the King of the
Jews, save yourself!" 38 A sign was fastened
above him with these words: "This is the King
of the Jews."

39 One of the criminals hanging beside him
scoffed, "So you're the Messiah, are you?
Prove it by saving yourself—and us, too, while
you're at it!"

40 But the other criminal protested, "Don't
you fear God even when you have been sentenced to die? 41 We deserve to die for our
crimes, but this man hasn't done anything
wrong." 42 Then he said, "Jesus, remember me
when you come into your Kingdom."

43 And Jesus replied, "I assure you, today
you will be with me in paradise."

The Death of Jesus

44 By this time it was about noon, and darkness
fell across the whole land until three o'clock.
45 The light from the sun was gone. And suddenly, the curtain in the sanctuary of the Temple was torn down the middle. 46 Then Jesus
shouted, "Father, I entrust my spirit into your
hands!"* And with those words he breathed
his last.

47 When the Roman officer* overseeing the
execution saw what had happened, he worshiped God and said, "Surely this man was innocent.*" 48 And when all the crowd that came
to see the crucifixion saw what had happened,
they went home in deep sorrow.* 49 But Jesus'
friends, including the women who had followed him from Galilee, stood at a distance
watching.

AMAZING FACTS

From noon until Jesus died at three o'clock, there was no light from the sun. So darkness was everywhere.

LUKE 23:44-45

The Burial of Jesus

50 Now there was a good and righteous man
named Joseph. He was a member of the Jewish
high council, 51 but he had not agreed with the
decision and actions of the other religious
leaders. He was from the town of Arimathea in
Judea, and he was waiting for the Kingdom of
God to come. 52 He went to Pilate and asked for
Jesus' body. 53 Then he took the body down
from the cross and wrapped it in a long sheet
of linen cloth and laid it in a new tomb that had
been carved out of rock. 54 This was done late
on Friday afternoon, the day of preparation,*
as the Sabbath was about to begin.

55 As his body was taken away, the women
from Galilee followed and saw the tomb
where his body was placed. 56 Then they went
home and prepared spices and ointments to
anoint his body. But by the time they were finished the Sabbath had begun, so they rested
as required by the law.

CHAPTER 24

The Resurrection

But very early on Sunday morning* the
women went to the tomb, taking the spices

23:30 Hos 10:8. **23:31** Or *If these things are done to me, the living tree, what will happen to you, the dry tree?* **23:33** Sometimes rendered *Calvary*, which comes from the Latin word for "skull." **23:34a** This sentence is not included in many ancient manuscripts. **23:34b** Greek *by casting lots*. See Ps 22:18. **23:46** Ps 31:5. **23:47a** Greek *the centurion*. **23:47b** Or *righteous*. **23:48** Greek *went home beating their breasts*. **23:54** Greek *It was the day of preparation*. **24:1** Greek *But on the first day of the week, very early in the morning*.

they had prepared. [2]They found that the stone had been rolled away from the entrance. [3]So they went in, but they didn't find the body of the Lord Jesus. [4]As they stood there puzzled, two men suddenly appeared to them, clothed in dazzling robes.

[5]The women were terrified and bowed with their faces to the ground. Then the men asked, "Why are you looking among the dead for someone who is alive? [6]He isn't here! He is risen from the dead! Remember what he told you back in Galilee, [7]that the Son of Man* must be betrayed into the hands of sinful men and be crucified, and that he would rise again on the third day."

[8]Then they remembered that he had said this. [9]So they rushed back from the tomb to tell his eleven disciples—and everyone else—what had happened. [10]It was Mary Magdalene, Joanna, Mary the mother of James, and several other women who told the apostles what had happened. [11]But the story sounded like nonsense to the men, so they didn't believe it. [12]However, Peter jumped up and ran to the tomb to look. Stooping, he peered in and saw the empty linen wrappings; then he went home again, wondering what had happened.

The Walk to Emmaus

[13]That same day two of Jesus' followers were walking to the village of Emmaus, seven miles* from Jerusalem. [14]As they walked along they were talking about everything that had happened. [15]As they talked and discussed these things, Jesus himself suddenly came and began walking with them. [16]But God kept them from recognizing him.

[17]He asked them, "What are you discussing so intently as you walk along?"

They stopped short, sadness written across their faces. [18]Then one of them, Cleopas, replied, "You must be the only person in Jerusalem who hasn't heard about all the things that have happened there the last few days."

[19]"What things?" Jesus asked.

"The things that happened to Jesus, the man from Nazareth," they said. "He was a prophet who did powerful miracles, and he was a mighty teacher in the eyes of God and all the people. [20]But our leading priests and other religious leaders handed him over to be condemned to death, and they crucified him. [21]We had hoped he was the Messiah who had come to rescue Israel. This all happened three days ago.

[22]"Then some women from our group of his followers were at his tomb early this morning, and they came back with an amazing report. [23]They said his body was missing, and they had seen angels who told them Jesus is alive! [24]Some of our men ran out to see, and sure enough, his body was gone, just as the women had said."

[25]Then Jesus said to them, "You foolish people! You find it so hard to believe all that the prophets wrote in the Scriptures. [26]Wasn't it clearly predicted that the Messiah would have to suffer all these things before entering his glory?" [27]Then Jesus took them through the writings of Moses and all the prophets, explaining from all the Scriptures the things concerning himself.

[28]By this time they were nearing Emmaus and the end of their journey. Jesus acted as if he were going on, [29]but they begged him, "Stay the night with us, since it is getting late." So he went home with them. [30]As they sat down to eat,* he took the bread and blessed it. Then he broke it and gave it to them. [31]Suddenly, their eyes were opened, and they recognized him. And at that moment he disappeared!

[32]They said to each other, "Didn't our hearts burn within us as he talked with us on the road and explained the Scriptures to us?" [33]And within the hour they were on their way back to Jerusalem. There they found the eleven disciples and the others who had gathered with them, [34]who said, "The Lord has really risen! He appeared to Peter.*"

Jesus Appears to the Disciples

[35]Then the two from Emmaus told their story of how Jesus had appeared to them as they were walking along the road, and how they had recognized him as he was breaking the bread. [36]And just as they were telling about it, Jesus himself was suddenly standing there among them. "Peace be with you," he said. [37]But the whole group was startled and frightened, thinking they were seeing a ghost!

24:7 "Son of Man" is a title Jesus used for himself. **24:13** Greek *60 stadia* [11.1 kilometers]. **24:30** Or *As they reclined.* **24:34** Greek *Simon.*

[38]"Why are you frightened?" he asked. "Why are your hearts filled with doubt? [39]Look at my hands. Look at my feet. You can see that it's really me. Touch me and make sure that I am not a ghost, because ghosts don't have bodies, as you see that I do." [40]As he spoke, he showed them his hands and his feet.

[41]Still they stood there in disbelief, filled with joy and wonder. Then he asked them, "Do you have anything here to eat?" [42]They gave him a piece of broiled fish, [43]and he ate it as they watched.

[44]Then he said, "When I was with you before, I told you that everything written about me in the law of Moses and the prophets and in the Psalms must be fulfilled." [45]Then he opened their minds to understand the Scriptures. [46]And he said, "Yes, it was written long ago that the Messiah would suffer and die and rise from the dead on the third day. [47]It was also written that this message would be proclaimed in the authority of his name to all the nations,* beginning in Jerusalem: 'There is forgiveness of sins for all who repent.' [48]You are witnesses of all these things.

[49]"And now I will send the Holy Spirit, just as my Father promised. But stay here in the city until the Holy Spirit comes and fills you with power from heaven."

The Ascension

[50]Then Jesus led them to Bethany, and lifting his hands to heaven, he blessed them. [51]While he was blessing them, he left them and was taken up to heaven. [52]So they worshiped him and then returned to Jerusalem filled with great joy. [53]And they spent all of their time in the Temple, praising God.

24:47 Or *all peoples.*

JOHN

WHO

Jesus, John the Baptist, the disciples, Nicodemus, the Samaritan woman, Mary, Martha, Lazarus, Jesus' mother Mary, Pilate, and Mary Magdalene.

WHERE

The disciple John wrote the book in Ephesus before he was exiled to the island of Patmos.

WHEN

After the destruction of Jerusalem in AD 70.

WHY

To prove without a doubt that Jesus is the Son of God and that all who believe in him will have eternal life.

The Word gave life to everything that was created, and his life brought light to everyone.
JOHN 1:4

Imagine you see fish that will die from pollution if they keep swimming downriver. Your shouts to stop them scare them. If you could only become a fish, you could warn them. In a way, that's what God did for us. Jesus (God's Son, the Word) became a person to save us from sin and death.

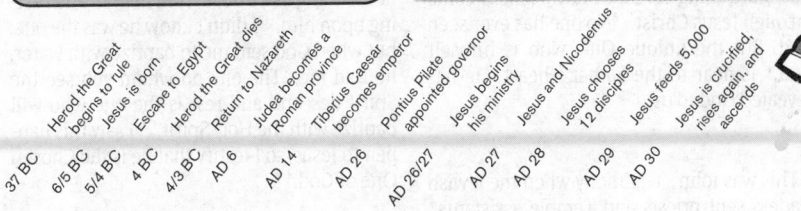

AS YOU READ THE BOOK OF JOHN, WATCH GOD IN ACTION, LIVING AND DYING FOR YOU.

CHAPTER 1

Prologue: Christ, the Eternal Word

1 In the beginning the Word already existed.
The Word was with God,
and the Word was God.
2 He existed in the beginning with God.
3 God created everything through him,
and nothing was created except through him.
4 The Word gave life to everything that was created,*

1:3-4 Or *and nothing that was created was created except through him. The Word gave life to everything.*

and his life brought light to everyone.
5 The light shines in the darkness,
and the darkness can never
extinguish it.*

6 God sent a man, John the Baptist,* 7 to tell
about the light so that everyone might believe
because of his testimony. 8 John himself was
not the light; he was simply a witness to tell
about the light. 9 The one who is the true light,
who gives light to everyone, was coming into
the world.

10 He came into the very world he created,
but the world didn't recognize him. 11 He
came to his own people, and even they re-
jected him. 12 But to all who believed him and
accepted him, he gave the right to become
children of God. 13 They are reborn—not with
a physical birth resulting from human pas-
sion or plan, but a birth that comes from God.

14 So the Word became human* and made
his home among us. He was full of unfailing
love and faithfulness.* And we have seen his
glory, the glory of the Father's one and only
Son.

15 John testified about him when he
shouted to the crowds, "This is the one I was
talking about when I said, 'Someone is com-
ing after me who is far greater than I am, for
he existed long before me.'"

16 From his abundance we have all re-
ceived one gracious blessing after another.*
17 For the law was given through Moses, but
God's unfailing love and faithfulness came
through Jesus Christ. 18 No one has ever seen
God. But the unique One, who is himself
God,* is near to the Father's heart. He has
revealed God to us.

The Testimony of John the Baptist

19 This was John's testimony when the Jewish
leaders sent priests and Temple assistants*
from Jerusalem to ask John, "Who are you?"
20 He came right out and said, "I am not the
Messiah."

21 "Well then, who are you?" they asked.
"Are you Elijah?"

"No," he replied.

"Are you the Prophet we are expecting?"*

"No."

22 "Then who are you? We need an answer
for those who sent us. What do you have to
say about yourself?"

23 John replied in the words of the prophet
Isaiah:

"I am a voice shouting in the wilderness,
'Clear the way for the LORD's coming!'"*

24 Then the Pharisees who had been sent
25 asked him, "If you aren't the Messiah or Eli-
jah or the Prophet, what right do you have to
baptize?"

26 John told them, "I baptize with* water,
but right here in the crowd is someone you do
not recognize. 27 Though his ministry follows
mine, I'm not even worthy to be his slave and
untie the straps of his sandal."

28 This encounter took place in Bethany, an
area east of the Jordan River, where John was
baptizing.

Jesus, the Lamb of God

29 The next day John saw Jesus coming toward
him and said, "Look! The Lamb of God who
takes away the sin of the world! 30 He is the
one I was talking about when I said, 'A man is
coming after me who is far greater than I am,
for he existed long before me.' 31 I did not rec-
ognize him as the Messiah, but I have been
baptizing with water so that he might be re-
vealed to Israel."

32 Then John testified, "I saw the Holy Spirit
descending like a dove from heaven and rest-
ing upon him. 33 I didn't know he was the one,
but when God sent me to baptize with water,
he told me, 'The one on whom you see the
Spirit descend and rest is the one who will
baptize with the Holy Spirit.' 34 I saw this hap-
pen to Jesus, so I testify that he is the Chosen
One of God.*"

The First Disciples

35 The following day John was again standing
with two of his disciples. 36 As Jesus walked by,
John looked at him and declared, "Look!
There is the Lamb of God!" 37 When John's
two disciples heard this, they followed Jesus.

38 Jesus looked around and saw them fol-
lowing. "What do you want?" he asked them.

1:5 Or *and the darkness has not understood it.* **1:6** Greek *a man named John.* **1:14a** Greek *became flesh.* **1:14b** Or *grace and truth;* also in 1:17. **1:16** Or *received the grace of Christ rather than the grace of the law;* Greek reads *received grace upon grace.* **1:18** Some manuscripts read *But the one and only Son.* **1:19** Greek *and Levites.* **1:21** Greek *Are you the Prophet?* See Deut 18:15, 18; Mal 4:5-6. **1:23** Isa 40:3. **1:26** Or *in;* also in 1:31, 33. **1:34** Some manuscripts read *the Son of God.*

They replied, "Rabbi" (which means "Teacher"), "where are you staying?"

39"Come and see," he said. It was about four o'clock in the afternoon when they went with him to the place where he was staying, and they remained with him the rest of the day.

40Andrew, Simon Peter's brother, was one of these men who heard what John said and then followed Jesus. 41Andrew went to find his brother, Simon, and told him, "We have found the Messiah" (which means "Christ"*).

42Then Andrew brought Simon to meet Jesus. Looking intently at Simon, Jesus said, "Your name is Simon, son of John—but you will be called Cephas" (which means "Peter"*).

43The next day Jesus decided to go to Galilee. He found Philip and said to him, "Come, follow me." 44Philip was from Bethsaida, Andrew and Peter's hometown.

45Philip went to look for Nathanael and told him, "We have found the very person Moses* and the prophets wrote about! His name is Jesus, the son of Joseph from Nazareth."

46"Nazareth!" exclaimed Nathanael. "Can anything good come from Nazareth?"

"Come and see for yourself," Philip replied.

47As they approached, Jesus said, "Now here is a genuine son of Israel—a man of complete integrity."

48"How do you know about me?" Nathanael asked.

Jesus replied, "I could see you under the fig tree before Philip found you."

49Then Nathanael exclaimed, "Rabbi, you are the Son of God—the King of Israel!"

50Jesus asked him, "Do you believe this just because I told you I had seen you under the fig tree? You will see greater things than this." 51Then he said, "I tell you the truth, you will all see heaven open and the angels of God going up and down on the Son of Man, the one who is the stairway between heaven and earth.*"

CHAPTER 2

The Wedding at Cana

The next day* there was a wedding celebration in the village of Cana in Galilee. Jesus' mother was there, 2and Jesus and his disciples were also invited to the celebration. 3The wine supply ran out during the festivities, so Jesus' mother told him, "They have no more wine."

4"Dear woman, that's not our problem," Jesus replied. "My time has not yet come."

5But his mother told the servants, "Do whatever he tells you."

6Standing nearby were six stone water jars, used for Jewish ceremonial washing. Each could hold twenty to thirty gallons.* 7Jesus told the servants, "Fill the jars with water." When the jars had been filled, 8he said, "Now dip some out, and take it to the master of ceremonies." So the servants followed his instructions.

9When the master of ceremonies tasted the water that was now wine, not knowing where it had come from (though, of course, the servants knew), he called the bridegroom over. 10"A host always serves the best wine first," he said. "Then, when everyone has had a lot to drink, he brings out the less expensive wine. But you have kept the best until now!"

11This miraculous sign at Cana in Galilee was the first time Jesus revealed his glory. And his disciples believed in him.

12After the wedding he went to Capernaum for a few days with his mother, his brothers, and his disciples.

Jesus Clears the Temple

13It was nearly time for the Jewish Passover celebration, so Jesus went to Jerusalem. 14In the Temple area he saw merchants selling cattle, sheep, and doves for sacrifices; he also saw dealers at tables exchanging foreign money. 15Jesus made a whip from some ropes and chased them all out of the Temple. He drove out the sheep and cattle, scattered the money changers' coins over the floor, and turned over their tables. 16Then, going over to the people who sold doves, he told them, "Get these things out of here. Stop turning my Father's house into a marketplace!"

17Then his disciples remembered this prophecy from the Scriptures: "Passion for God's house will consume me."*

18But the Jewish leaders demanded, "What

1:41 *Messiah* (a Hebrew term) and *Christ* (a Greek term) both mean "the anointed one." **1:42** The names *Cephas* (from Aramaic) and *Peter* (from Greek) both mean "rock." **1:45** Greek *Moses in the law.* **1:51** Greek *going up and down on the Son of Man;* see Gen 28:10-17. "Son of Man" is a title Jesus used for himself. **2:1** Greek *On the third day;* see 1:35, 43. **2:6** Greek *2 or 3 measures* [75 to 113 liters]. **2:17** Or *"Concern for God's house will be my undoing."* Ps 69:9.

are you doing? If God gave you authority to do this, show us a miraculous sign to prove it."

19"All right," Jesus replied. "Destroy this temple, and in three days I will raise it up."

How do I know that God loves me?

For God loved the world so much that he gave his one and only Son, so that everyone who believes in him will not perish but have eternal life.

JOHN 3:16

20"What!" they exclaimed. "It has taken forty-six years to build this Temple, and you can rebuild it in three days?" 21But when Jesus said "this temple," he meant his own body. 22After he was raised from the dead, his disciples remembered he had said this, and they believed both the Scriptures and what Jesus had said.

Jesus and Nicodemus

23Because of the miraculous signs Jesus did in Jerusalem at the Passover celebration, many began to trust in him. 24But Jesus didn't trust them, because he knew human nature. 25No one needed to tell him what mankind is really like.

CHAPTER 3

There was a man named Nicodemus, a Jewish religious leader who was a Pharisee. 2After dark one evening, he came to speak with Jesus. "Rabbi," he said, "we all know that God has sent you to teach us. Your miraculous signs are evidence that God is with you."

3Jesus replied, "I tell you the truth, unless you are born again,* you cannot see the Kingdom of God."

4"What do you mean?" exclaimed Nicodemus. "How can an old man go back into his mother's womb and be born again?"

5Jesus replied, "I assure you, no one can enter the Kingdom of God without being born of water and the Spirit.* 6Humans can reproduce only human life, but the Holy Spirit gives birth to spiritual life.* 7So don't be surprised when I say, 'You* must be born again.' 8The wind blows wherever it wants. Just as you can hear the wind but can't tell where it comes from or where it is going, so you can't explain how people are born of the Spirit."

9"How are these things possible?" Nicodemus asked.

10Jesus replied, "You are a respected Jewish teacher, and yet you don't understand these things? 11I assure you, we tell you what we know and have seen, and yet you won't believe our testimony. 12But if you don't believe me when I tell you about earthly things, how can you possibly believe if I tell you about heavenly things? 13No one has ever gone to heaven and returned. But the Son of Man* has come down from heaven. 14And as Moses lifted up the bronze snake on a pole in the wilderness, so the Son of Man must be lifted up, 15so that everyone who believes in him will have eternal life.*

16"For God loved the world so much that he gave his one and only Son, so that everyone who believes in him will not perish but have eternal life. 17God sent his Son into the world not to judge the world, but to save the world through him.

18"There is no judgment against anyone who believes in him. But anyone who does not believe in him has already been judged for not believing in God's one and only Son. 19And the judgment is based on this fact: God's light came into the world, but people loved the darkness more than the light, for their actions were evil. 20All who do evil hate the light and refuse to go near it for fear their sins will be exposed. 21But those who do what is right come to the light so others can see that they are doing what God wants.*"

John the Baptist Exalts Jesus

22Then Jesus and his disciples left Jerusalem and went into the Judean countryside. Jesus

3:3 Or *born from above;* also in 3:7. **3:5** Or *and spirit.* The Greek word for *Spirit* can also be translated *wind;* see 3:8. **3:6** Greek *what is born of the Spirit is spirit.* **3:7** The Greek word for *you* is plural; also in 3:12. **3:13** Some manuscripts add *who lives in heaven.* "Son of Man" is a title Jesus used for himself. **3:15** Or *everyone who believes will have eternal life in him.* **3:21** Or *can see God at work in what he is doing.*

spent some time with them there, baptizing people.

[23]At this time John the Baptist was baptizing at Aenon, near Salim, because there was plenty of water there; and people kept coming to him for baptism. [24](This was before John was thrown into prison.) [25]A debate broke out between John's disciples and a certain Jew* over ceremonial cleansing. [26]So John's disciples came to him and said, "Rabbi, the man you met on the other side of the Jordan River, the one you identified as the Messiah, is also baptizing people. And everybody is going to him instead of coming to us."

[27]John replied, "No one can receive anything unless God gives it from heaven. [28]You yourselves know how plainly I told you, 'I am not the Messiah. I am only here to prepare the way for him.' [29]It is the bridegroom who marries the bride, and the best man is simply glad to stand with him and hear his vows. Therefore, I am filled with joy at his success. [30]He must become greater and greater, and I must become less and less.

[31]"He has come from above and is greater than anyone else. We are of the earth, and we speak of earthly things, but he has come from heaven and is greater than anyone else.* [32]He testifies about what he has seen and heard, but how few believe what he tells them! [33]Anyone who accepts his testimony can affirm that God is true. [34]For he is sent by God. He speaks God's words, for God gives him the Spirit without limit. [35]The Father loves his Son and has put everything into his hands. [36]And anyone who believes in God's Son has eternal life. Anyone who doesn't obey the Son will never experience eternal life but remains under God's angry judgment."

CHAPTER 4

Jesus and the Samaritan Woman

Jesus* knew the Pharisees had heard that he was baptizing and making more disciples than John [2](though Jesus himself didn't baptize them—his disciples did). [3]So he left Judea and returned to Galilee.

[4]He had to go through Samaria on the way. [5]Eventually he came to the Samaritan village of Sychar, near the field that Jacob gave to his son Joseph. [6]Jacob's well was there; and Jesus, tired from the long walk, sat wearily beside the well about noontime. [7]Soon a Samaritan woman came to draw water, and Jesus said to her, "Please give me a drink." [8]He was alone at the time because his disciples had gone into the village to buy some food.

WHO'S DIFFERENT—YOU OR ME?

Recently some kids from another ethnic group called Derrick names as he walked home from school. Derrick got angry. He decided he didn't like "those kinds" of people. Then he got an invitation to a party. Derrick wanted to go to the party, but he knew that "those kinds" of kids would be there. What would you do if you were Derrick? How should you treat people whose skin is a different color from yours or whose cultural background is different? Read John 4:1-26 to see how Jesus related to a woman who was from a minority group—and wasn't even liked by her own people.

3:25 Some manuscripts read *some Jews*. **3:31** Some manuscripts do not include *and is greater than anyone else*. **4:1** Some manuscripts read *The Lord*.

[9]The woman was surprised, for Jews refuse
to have anything to do with Samaritans.* She
said to Jesus, "You are a Jew, and I am a Sa-
maritan woman. Why are you asking me for a
drink?"
[10]Jesus replied, "If you only knew the gift
God has for you and who you are speaking to,
you would ask me, and I would give you living
water."
[11]"But sir, you don't have a rope or a
bucket," she said, "and this well is very deep.
Where would you get this living water? [12]And
besides, do you think you're greater than our
ancestor Jacob, who gave us this well? How
can you offer better water than he and his
sons and his animals enjoyed?"
[13]Jesus replied, "Anyone who drinks this
water will soon become thirsty again. [14]But
those who drink the water I give will never be
thirsty again. It becomes a fresh, bubbling
spring within them, giving them eternal life."
[15]"Please, sir," the woman said, "give me
this water! Then I'll never be thirsty again, and
I won't have to come here to get water."
[16]"Go and get your husband," Jesus told
her.
[17]"I don't have a husband," the woman re-
plied.
Jesus said, "You're right! You don't have a
husband—[18]for you have had five husbands,
and you aren't even married to the man you're
living with now. You certainly spoke the
truth!"
[19]"Sir," the woman said, "you must be a
prophet. [20]So tell me, why is it that you Jews
insist that Jerusalem is the only place of wor-
ship, while we Samaritans claim it is here at
Mount Gerizim,* where our ancestors wor-
shiped?"
[21]Jesus replied, "Believe me, dear woman,
the time is coming when it will no longer mat-
ter whether you worship the Father on this
mountain or in Jerusalem. [22]You Samaritans
know very little about the one you worship,
while we Jews know all about him, for salva-
tion comes through the Jews. [23]But the time is
coming—indeed it's here now—when true
worshipers will worship the Father in spirit
and in truth. The Father is looking for those
who will worship him that way. [24]For God is
Spirit, so those who worship him must wor-
ship in spirit and in truth."
[25]The woman said, "I know the Messiah is
coming—the one who is called Christ. When
he comes, he will explain everything to us."
[26]Then Jesus told her, "I AM the Messiah!"*
[27]Just then his disciples came back. They
were shocked to find him talking to a woman,
but none of them had the nerve to ask, "What
do you want with her?" or "Why are you talk-
ing to her?" [28]The woman left her water jar
beside the well and ran back to the village,
telling everyone, [29]"Come and see a man who
told me everything I ever did! Could he possi-
bly be the Messiah?" [30]So the people came
streaming from the village to see him.
[31]Meanwhile, the disciples were urging
Jesus, "Rabbi, eat something."
[32]But Jesus replied, "I have a kind of food
you know nothing about."
[33]"Did someone bring him food while we
were gone?" the disciples asked each other.
[34]Then Jesus explained: "My nourishment
comes from doing the will of God, who sent
me, and from finishing his work. [35]You know
the saying, 'Four months between planting
and harvest.' But I say, wake up and look
around. The fields are already ripe* for har-
vest. [36]The harvesters are paid good wages,
and the fruit they harvest is people brought to
eternal life. What joy awaits both the planter
and the harvester alike! [37]You know the say-
ing, 'One plants and another harvests.' And
it's true. [38]I sent you to harvest where you
didn't plant; others had already done the
work, and now you will get to gather the har-
vest."

Many Samaritans Believe

[39]Many Samaritans from the village believed
in Jesus because the woman had said, "He told
me everything I ever did!" [40]When they came
out to see him, they begged him to stay in
their village. So he stayed for two days, [41]long
enough for many more to hear his message
and believe. [42]Then they said to the woman,
"Now we believe, not just because of what you
told us, but because we have heard him our-
selves. Now we know that he is indeed the
Savior of the world."

4:9 Some manuscripts do not include this sentence. **4:20** Greek *on this mountain.* **4:26** Or *"The 'I AM' is here"*; or *"I am the LORD"*; Greek reads *"I am, the one speaking to you."* See Exod 3:14. **4:35** Greek *white.*

Jesus Heals an Official's Son

43At the end of the two days, Jesus went on to
Galilee. 44He himself had said that a prophet
is not honored in his own hometown. 45Yet
the Galileans welcomed him, for they had
been in Jerusalem at the Passover celebration
and had seen everything he did there.

46As he traveled through Galilee, he came
to Cana, where he had turned the water into
wine. There was a government official in
nearby Capernaum whose son was very sick.
47When he heard that Jesus had come from
Judea to Galilee, he went and begged Jesus to
come to Capernaum to heal his son, who was
about to die.

48Jesus asked, "Will you never believe in
me unless you see miraculous signs and won-
ders?"

49The official pleaded, "Lord, please come
now before my little boy dies."

50Then Jesus told him, "Go back home.
Your son will live!" And the man believed
what Jesus said and started home.

51While the man was on his way, some of
his servants met him with the news that his
son was alive and well. 52He asked them when
the boy had begun to get better, and they re-
plied, "Yesterday afternoon at one o'clock his
fever suddenly disappeared!" 53Then the fa-
ther realized that that was the very time Jesus
had told him, "Your son will live." And he and
his entire household believed in Jesus. 54This
was the second miraculous sign Jesus did in
Galilee after coming from Judea.

CHAPTER 5

Jesus Heals a Lame Man

Afterward Jesus returned to Jerusalem for
one of the Jewish holy days. 2Inside the city,
near the Sheep Gate, was the pool of Bethes-
da,* with five covered porches. 3Crowds of
sick people—blind, lame, or paralyzed—lay
on the porches.* 5One of the men lying there
had been sick for thirty-eight years. 6When
Jesus saw him and knew he had been ill for a
long time, he asked him, "Would you like to
get well?"

7"I can't, sir," the sick man said, "for I have
no one to put me into the pool when the water
bubbles up. Someone else always gets there
ahead of me."

8Jesus told him, "Stand up, pick up your
mat, and walk!"

9Instantly, the man was healed! He rolled
up his sleeping mat and began walking! But
this miracle happened on the Sabbath, 10so
the Jewish leaders objected. They said to the
man who was cured, "You can't work on the
Sabbath! The law doesn't allow you to carry
that sleeping mat!"

11But he replied, "The man who healed me
told me, 'Pick up your mat and walk.'"

12"Who said such a thing as that?" they de-
manded.

13The man didn't know, for Jesus had dis-
appeared into the crowd. 14But afterward
Jesus found him in the Temple and told him,
"Now you are well; so stop sinning, or some-
thing even worse may happen to you." 15Then
the man went and told the Jewish leaders that
it was Jesus who had healed him.

Jesus Claims to Be the Son of God

16So the Jewish leaders began harassing*
Jesus for breaking the Sabbath rules. 17But
Jesus replied, "My Father is always working,
and so am I." 18So the Jewish leaders tried all
the harder to find a way to kill him. For he not
only broke the Sabbath, he called God his Fa-
ther, thereby making himself equal with God.

19So Jesus explained, "I tell you the truth,
the Son can do nothing by himself. He does
only what he sees the Father doing. Whatever
the Father does, the Son also does. 20For the
Father loves the Son and shows him every-
thing he is doing. In fact, the Father will show
him how to do even greater works than heal-
ing this man. Then you will truly be aston-
ished. 21For just as the Father gives life to
those he raises from the dead, so the Son
gives life to anyone he wants. 22In addition,
the Father judges no one. Instead, he has
given the Son absolute authority to judge, 23so
that everyone will honor the Son, just as they
honor the Father. Anyone who does not
honor the Son is certainly not honoring the
Father who sent him.

24"I tell you the truth, those who listen to
my message and believe in God who sent me

5:2 Other manuscripts read *Beth-zatha;* still others read *Bethsaida.* **5:3** Some manuscripts add an expanded conclusion to verse 3 and all of verse 4: *waiting for a certain movement of the water, 4for an angel of the Lord came from time to time and stirred up the water. And the first person to step in after the water was stirred was healed of whatever disease he had.* **5:16** Or *persecuting.*

have eternal life. They will never be condemned for their sins, but they have already passed from death into life.

[25]"And I assure you that the time is coming, indeed it's here now, when the dead will hear my voice—the voice of the Son of God. And those who listen will live. [26]The Father has life in himself, and he has granted that same life-giving power to his Son. [27]And he has given him authority to judge everyone because he is the Son of Man.* [28]Don't be so surprised! Indeed, the time is coming when all the dead in their graves will hear the voice of God's Son, [29]and they will rise again. Those who have done good will rise to experience eternal life, and those who have continued in evil will rise to experience judgment. [30]I can do nothing on my own. I judge as God tells me. Therefore, my judgment is just, because I carry out the will of the one who sent me, not my own will.

Witnesses to Jesus

[31]"If I were to testify on my own behalf, my testimony would not be valid. [32]But someone else is also testifying about me, and I assure you that everything he says about me is true. [33]In fact, you sent investigators to listen to John the Baptist, and his testimony about me was true. [34]Of course, I have no need of human witnesses, but I say these things so you might be saved. [35]John was like a burning and shining lamp, and you were excited for a while about his message. [36]But I have a greater witness than John—my teachings and my miracles. The Father gave me these works to accomplish, and they prove that he sent me. [37]And the Father who sent me has testified about me himself. You have never heard his voice or seen him face to face, [38]and you do not have his message in your hearts, because you do not believe me—the one he sent to you.

[39]"You search the Scriptures because you think they give you eternal life. But the Scriptures point to me! [40]Yet you refuse to come to me to receive this life.

[41]"Your approval means nothing to me, [42]because I know you don't have God's love within you. [43]For I have come to you in my Father's name, and you have rejected me. Yet if others come in their own name, you gladly welcome them. [44]No wonder you can't believe! For you gladly honor each other, but you don't care about the honor that comes from the one who alone is God.*

[45]"Yet it isn't I who will accuse you before the Father. Moses will accuse you! Yes, Moses, in whom you put your hopes. [46]If you really believed Moses, you would believe me, because he wrote about me. [47]But since you don't believe what he wrote, how will you believe what I say?"

CHAPTER 6

Jesus Feeds Five Thousand

After this, Jesus crossed over to the far side of the Sea of Galilee, also known as the Sea of Tiberias. [2]A huge crowd kept following him wherever he went, because they saw his miraculous signs as he healed the sick. [3]Then Jesus climbed a hill and sat down with his disciples around him. [4](It was nearly time for the Jewish Passover celebration.) [5]Jesus soon saw a huge crowd of people coming to look for him. Turning to Philip, he asked, "Where can we buy bread to feed all these people?" [6]He was testing Philip, for he already knew what he was going to do.

[7]Philip replied, "Even if we worked for months, we wouldn't have enough money* to feed them!"

[8]Then Andrew, Simon Peter's brother, spoke up. [9]"There's a young boy here with five barley loaves and two fish. But what good is that with this huge crowd?"

[10]"Tell everyone to sit down," Jesus said. So they all sat down on the grassy slopes. (The men alone numbered about 5,000.) [11]Then Jesus took the loaves, gave thanks to God, and distributed them to the people. Afterward he did the same with the fish. And they all ate as much as they wanted. [12]After everyone was full, Jesus told his disciples, "Now gather the leftovers, so that nothing is wasted." [13]So they picked up the pieces and filled twelve baskets with scraps left by the people who had eaten from the five barley loaves.

[14]When the people saw him* do this miraculous sign, they exclaimed, "Surely, he is the Prophet we have been expecting!"*

5:27 "Son of Man" is a title Jesus used for himself. **5:44** Some manuscripts read *from the only One*. **6:7** Greek *Two hundred denarii would not be enough*. A denarius was equivalent to a laborer's full day's wage. **6:14a** Some manuscripts read *Jesus*. **6:14b** See Deut 18:15, 18; Mal 4:5-6.

My sister and her friend were trying to fix me up. Their plan was to walk downtown with their boyfriends and me and "accidentally" meet this guy they had picked out for me.

When I realized what was happening, my mind started racing—thinking about what I could do and say to make this guy think I was cool. I wanted to make a good impression on him and get him to like me.

Then I changed my mind. Why should I pretend to be something that I'm not just to get him to find me attractive? I decided I was going to be myself and let him like me or not like me for who I really was—not someone I was pretending to be.

Jesus refused to play the approval game by trying to impress the religious leaders. Their approval meant nothing to him. His only goal was to please God (his Father in heaven) and do what God sent him to earth to do.

The real love that's most important to me comes from God, who accepts me even though he knows I'm not perfect. When I talk to him about my faults, he doesn't get upset. He helps me do better. I want his approval more than anything a boyfriend can give me.

Check out these verses from John 5:41-44 and John12:41-43 to see where we should and should not look for approval.

Nicodemus

One night I met Jesus in private. I knew that if I were seen with him, my reputation among the other religious leaders would be ruined. I had so many questions. I didn't understand the idea of being "born again." How could I become a baby now that I was an old man? But after talking to Jesus, I realized that by believing in him, I really could become a new person.

Jesus changed my life by listening to me as a friend and teaching me who he was. When he died, I wept. I brought myrrh and aloes for his burial. That's our tradition. It was my gift, but I wished I could have done more for him.

Read John 3:1-21 and 19:38-42 to learn more about Nicodemus.

[15]When Jesus saw that they were ready to force him to be their king, he slipped away into the hills by himself.

Jesus Walks on Water

[16]That evening Jesus' disciples went down to the shore to wait for him. [17]But as darkness fell and Jesus still hadn't come back, they got into the boat and headed across the lake toward Capernaum. [18]Soon a gale swept down upon them, and the sea grew very rough. [19]They had rowed three or four miles* when suddenly they saw Jesus walking on the water toward the boat. They were terrified, [20]but he called out to them, "Don't be afraid. I am here!*" [21]Then they were eager to let him in the boat, and immediately they arrived at their destination!

Jesus, the Bread of Life

[22]The next day the crowd that had stayed on the far shore saw that the disciples had taken the only boat, and they realized Jesus had not gone with them. [23]Several boats from Tiberias landed near the place where the Lord had blessed the bread and the people had eaten. [24]So when the crowd saw that neither Jesus nor his disciples were there, they got into the boats and went across to Capernaum to look for him. [25]They found him on the other side of the lake and asked, "Rabbi, when did you get here?"

[26]Jesus replied, "I tell you the truth, you want to be with me because I fed you, not because you understood the miraculous signs. [27]But don't be so concerned about perishable things like food. Spend your energy seeking the eternal life that the Son of Man* can give you. For God the Father has given me the seal of his approval."

[28]They replied, "We want to perform God's works, too. What should we do?"

[29]Jesus told them, "This is the only work God wants from you: Believe in the one he has sent."

[30]They answered, "Show us a miraculous sign if you want us to believe in you. What can you do? [31]After all, our ancestors ate manna while they journeyed through the wilderness! The Scriptures say, 'Moses gave them bread from heaven to eat.'*"

[32]Jesus said, "I tell you the truth, Moses didn't give you bread from heaven. My Father did. And now he offers you the true bread from heaven. [33]The true bread of God is the one who comes down from heaven and gives life to the world."

6:19 Greek *25 or 30 stadia* [4.6 or 5.5 kilometers]. **6:20** Or *The 'I AM' is here;* Greek reads *I am*. See Exod 3:14. **6:27** "Son of Man" is a title Jesus used for himself. **6:31** Exod 16:4; Ps 78:24.

[34]"Sir," they said, "give us that bread every day."

[35]Jesus replied, "I am the bread of life. Whoever comes to me will never be hungry again. Whoever believes in me will never be thirsty. [36]But you haven't believed in me even though you have seen me. [37]However, those the Father has given me will come to me, and I will never reject them. [38]For I have come down from heaven to do the will of God who sent me, not to do my own will. [39]And this is the will of God, that I should not lose even one of all those he has given me, but that I should raise them up at the last day. [40]For it is my Father's will that all who see his Son and believe in him should have eternal life. I will raise them up at the last day."

[41]Then the people* began to murmur in disagreement because he had said, "I am the bread that came down from heaven." [42]They said, "Isn't this Jesus, the son of Joseph? We know his father and mother. How can he say, 'I came down from heaven'?"

[43]But Jesus replied, "Stop complaining about what I said. [44]For no one can come to me unless the Father who sent me draws them to me, and at the last day I will raise them up. [45]As it is written in the Scriptures,* 'They will all be taught by God.' Everyone who listens to the Father and learns from him comes to me. [46](Not that anyone has ever seen the Father; only I, who was sent from God, have seen him.)

[47]"I tell you the truth, anyone who believes has eternal life. [48]Yes, I am the bread of life! [49]Your ancestors ate manna in the wilderness, but they all died. [50]Anyone who eats the bread from heaven, however, will never die. [51]I am the living bread that came down from heaven. Anyone who eats this bread will live forever; and this bread, which I will offer so the world may live, is my flesh."

[52]Then the people began arguing with each other about what he meant. "How can this man give us his flesh to eat?" they asked.

[53]So Jesus said again, "I tell you the truth, unless you eat the flesh of the Son of Man and drink his blood, you cannot have eternal life within you. [54]But anyone who eats my flesh and drinks my blood has eternal life, and I will raise that person at the last day. [55]For my flesh is true food, and my blood is true drink. [56]Anyone who eats my flesh and drinks my blood remains in me, and I in him. [57]I live because of the living Father who sent me; in the same way, anyone who feeds on me will live because of me. [58]I am the true bread that came down from heaven. Anyone who eats this bread will not die as your ancestors did (even though they ate the manna) but will live forever."

[59]He said these things while he was teaching in the synagogue in Capernaum.

Many Disciples Desert Jesus

[60]Many of his disciples said, "This is very hard to understand. How can anyone accept it?"

[61]Jesus was aware that his disciples were complaining, so he said to them, "Does this offend you? [62]Then what will you think if you see the Son of Man ascend to heaven again? [63]The Spirit alone gives eternal life. Human effort accomplishes nothing. And the very words I have spoken to you are spirit and life. [64]But some of you do not believe me." (For Jesus knew from the beginning which ones didn't believe, and he knew who would betray him.) [65]Then he said, "That is why I said that people can't come to me unless the Father gives them to me."

[66]At this point many of his disciples turned away and deserted him. [67]Then Jesus turned to the Twelve and asked, "Are you also going to leave?"

[68]Simon Peter replied, "Lord, to whom would we go? You have the words that give eternal life. [69]We believe, and we know you are the Holy One of God.*"

[70]Then Jesus said, "I chose the twelve of you, but one is a devil." [71]He was speaking of Judas, son of Simon Iscariot, one of the Twelve, who would later betray him.

CHAPTER 7

Jesus and His Brothers

After this, Jesus traveled around Galilee. He wanted to stay out of Judea, where the Jewish leaders were plotting his death. [2]But soon it was time for the Jewish Festival of Shelters, [3]and Jesus' brothers said to him, "Leave here and go to Judea, where your followers can see your miracles! [4]You can't become famous if

6:41 Greek *Jewish people;* also in 6:52. **6:45** Greek *in the prophets.* Isa 54:13. **6:69** Other manuscripts read *you are the Christ, the Holy One of God;* still others read *you are the Christ, the Son of God;* and still others read *you are the Christ, the Son of the living God.*

you hide like this! If you can do such wonderful things, show yourself to the world!" [5]For even his brothers didn't believe in him.

[6]Jesus replied, "Now is not the right time for me to go, but you can go anytime. [7]The world can't hate you, but it does hate me because I accuse it of doing evil. [8]You go on. I'm not going* to this festival, because my time has not yet come." [9]After saying these things, Jesus remained in Galilee.

Jesus Teaches Openly at the Temple

[10]But after his brothers left for the festival, Jesus also went, though secretly, staying out of public view. [11]The Jewish leaders tried to find him at the festival and kept asking if anyone had seen him. [12]There was a lot of grumbling about him among the crowds. Some argued, "He's a good man," but others said, "He's nothing but a fraud who deceives the people." [13]But no one had the courage to speak favorably about him in public, for they were afraid of getting in trouble with the Jewish leaders.

[14]Then, midway through the festival, Jesus went up to the Temple and began to teach. [15]The people* were surprised when they heard him. "How does he know so much when he hasn't been trained?" they asked.

[16]So Jesus told them, "My message is not my own; it comes from God who sent me. [17]Anyone who wants to do the will of God will know whether my teaching is from God or is merely my own. [18]Those who speak for themselves want glory only for themselves, but a person who seeks to honor the one who sent him speaks truth, not lies. [19]Moses gave you the law, but none of you obeys it! In fact, you are trying to kill me."

[20]The crowd replied, "You're demon possessed! Who's trying to kill you?"

[21]Jesus replied, "I did one miracle on the Sabbath, and you were amazed. [22]But you work on the Sabbath, too, when you obey Moses' law of circumcision. (Actually, this tradition of circumcision began with the patriarchs, long before the law of Moses.) [23]For if the correct time for circumcising your son falls on the Sabbath, you go ahead and do it so as not to break the law of Moses. So why should you be angry with me for healing a man on the Sabbath? [24]Look beneath the surface so you can judge correctly."

Is Jesus the Messiah?

[25]Some of the people who lived in Jerusalem started to ask each other, "Isn't this the man they are trying to kill? [26]But here he is, speaking in public, and they say nothing to him. Could our leaders possibly believe that he is the Messiah? [27]But how could he be? For we know where this man comes from. When the Messiah comes, he will simply appear; no one will know where he comes from."

[28]While Jesus was teaching in the Temple, he called out, "Yes, you know me, and you know where I come from. But I'm not here on my own. The one who sent me is true, and you don't know him. [29]But I know him because I come from him, and he sent me to you." [30]Then the leaders tried to arrest him; but no one laid a hand on him, because his time* had not yet come.

[31]Many among the crowds at the Temple believed in him. "After all," they said, "would you expect the Messiah to do more miraculous signs than this man has done?"

[32]When the Pharisees heard that the crowds were whispering such things, they and the leading priests sent Temple guards to arrest Jesus. [33]But Jesus told them, "I will be with you only a little longer. Then I will return to the one who sent me. [34]You will search for me but not find me. And you cannot go where I am going."

[35]The Jewish leaders were puzzled by this statement. "Where is he planning to go?" they asked. "Is he thinking of leaving the country and going to the Jews in other lands?* Maybe he will even teach the Greeks! [36]What does he mean when he says, 'You will search for me but not find me,' and 'You cannot go where I am going'?"

Jesus Promises Living Water

[37]On the last day, the climax of the festival, Jesus stood and shouted to the crowds, "Anyone who is thirsty may come to me! [38]Anyone who believes in me may come and drink! For the Scriptures declare, 'Rivers of living water will flow from his heart.' "* [39](When he said

7:8 Some manuscripts read *not yet going.* **7:15** Greek *Jewish people.* **7:30** Greek *his hour.* **7:35** Or *the Jews who live among the Greeks?* **7:37-38** Or *"Let anyone who is thirsty come to me and drink. [38]For the Scriptures declare, 'Rivers of living water will flow from the heart of anyone who believes in me.'"*

"living water," he was speaking of the Spirit, who would be given to everyone believing in him. But the Spirit had not yet been given,* because Jesus had not yet entered into his glory.)

Division and Unbelief

40 When the crowds heard him say this, some of them declared, "Surely this man is the Prophet we've been expecting."* 41 Others said, "He is the Messiah." Still others said, "But he can't be! Will the Messiah come from Galilee? 42 For the Scriptures clearly state that the Messiah will be born of the royal line of David, in Bethlehem, the village where King David was born."* 43 So the crowd was divided about him. 44 Some even wanted him arrested, but no one laid a hand on him.

45 When the Temple guards returned without having arrested Jesus, the leading priests and Pharisees demanded, "Why didn't you bring him in?"

46 "We have never heard anyone speak like this!" the guards responded.

47 "Have you been led astray, too?" the Pharisees mocked. 48 "Is there a single one of us rulers or Pharisees who believes in him? 49 This foolish crowd follows him, but they are ignorant of the law. God's curse is on them!"

50 Then Nicodemus, the leader who had met with Jesus earlier, spoke up. 51 "Is it legal to convict a man before he is given a hearing?" he asked.

52 They replied, "Are you from Galilee, too? Search the Scriptures and see for yourself—no prophet ever comes* from Galilee!"

[The most ancient Greek manuscripts do not include John 7:53–8:11.]

53 Then the meeting broke up, and everybody went home.

CHAPTER 8

A Woman Caught in Adultery

Jesus returned to the Mount of Olives, 2 but early the next morning he was back again at the Temple. A crowd soon gathered, and he sat down and taught them. 3 As he was speaking, the teachers of religious law and the Pharisees brought a woman who had been caught in the act of adultery. They put her in front of the crowd.

4 "Teacher," they said to Jesus, "this woman was caught in the act of adultery. 5 The law of Moses says to stone her. What do you say?"

6 They were trying to trap him into saying something they could use against him, but Jesus stooped down and wrote in the dust with his finger. 7 They kept demanding an answer, so he stood up again and said, "All right, but let the one who has never sinned throw the first stone!" 8 Then he stooped down again and wrote in the dust.

9 When the accusers heard this, they slipped away one by one, beginning with the oldest, until only Jesus was left in the middle of the crowd with the woman. 10 Then Jesus stood up again and said to the woman, "Where are your accusers? Didn't even one of them condemn you?"

11 "No, Lord," she said.

And Jesus said, "Neither do I. Go and sin no more."

Jesus, the Light of the World

12 Jesus spoke to the people once more and said, "I am the light of the world. If you follow me, you won't have to walk in darkness, because you will have the light that leads to life."

13 The Pharisees replied, "You are making those claims about yourself! Such testimony is not valid."

14 Jesus told them, "These claims are valid even though I make them about myself. For I know where I came from and where I am going, but you don't know this about me. 15 You judge me by human standards, but I do not judge anyone. 16 And if I did, my judgment would be correct in every respect because I am not alone. The Father* who sent me is with me. 17 Your own law says that if two people agree about something, their witness is accepted as fact.* 18 I am one witness, and my Father who sent me is the other."

19 "Where is your father?" they asked.

Jesus answered, "Since you don't know who I am, you don't know who my Father is. If you knew me, you would also know my Father." 20 Jesus made these statements while he was teaching in the section of the Temple

7:39 Some manuscripts read *But as yet there was no Spirit.* Still others read *But as yet there was no Holy Spirit* **7:40** See Deut 18:15, 18; Mal 4:5-6. **7:42** See Mic 5:2. **7:52** Some manuscripts read *the prophet does not come.* **8:16** Some manuscripts read *The One.* **8:17** See Deut 19:15.

known as the Treasury. But he was not arrested, because his time* had not yet come.

The Unbelieving People Warned

21 Later Jesus said to them again, "I am going
away. You will search for me but will die in
your sin. You cannot come where I am going."
22 The people* asked, "Is he planning to
commit suicide? What does he mean, 'You
cannot come where I am going'?"
23 Jesus continued, "You are from below; I
am from above. You belong to this world; I do
not. 24 That is why I said that you will die in
your sins; for unless you believe that I AM who
I claim to be,* you will die in your sins."
25 "Who are you?" they demanded.
Jesus replied, "The one I have always
claimed to be.* 26 I have much to say about
you and much to condemn, but I won't. For I
say only what I have heard from the one who
sent me, and he is completely truthful." 27 But
they still didn't understand that he was talking about his Father.
28 So Jesus said, "When you have lifted up
the Son of Man on the cross, then you will
understand that I AM he.* I do nothing on my
own but say only what the Father taught me.
29 And the one who sent me is with me—he has
not deserted me. For I always do what pleases
him." 30 Then many who heard him say these
things believed in him.

Jesus and Abraham

31 Jesus said to the people who believed in
him, "You are truly my disciples if you remain
faithful to my teachings. 32 And you will know
the truth, and the truth will set you free."
33 "But we are descendants of Abraham,"
they said. "We have never been slaves to anyone. What do you mean, 'You will be set
free'?"
34 Jesus replied, "I tell you the truth, everyone who sins is a slave of sin. 35 A slave is not a
permanent member of the family, but a son is
part of the family forever. 36 So if the Son sets
you free, you are truly free. 37 Yes, I realize that
you are descendants of Abraham. And yet
some of you are trying to kill me because
there's no room in your hearts for my message. 38 I am telling you what I saw when I was
with my Father. But you are following the advice of your father."
39 "Our father is Abraham!" they declared.
"No," Jesus replied, "for if you were really
the children of Abraham, you would follow
his example.* 40 Instead, you are trying to kill
me because I told you the truth, which I heard
from God. Abraham never did such a thing.
41 No, you are imitating your real father."
They replied, "We aren't illegitimate children! God himself is our true Father."
42 Jesus told them, "If God were your Father,
you would love me, because I have come to
you from God. I am not here on my own, but
he sent me. 43 Why can't you understand what
I am saying? It's because you can't even hear
me! 44 For you are the children of your father
the devil, and you love to do the evil things he
does. He was a murderer from the beginning.
He has always hated the truth, because there
is no truth in him. When he lies, it is consistent with his character; for he is a liar and the
father of lies. 45 So when I tell the truth, you
just naturally don't believe me! 46 Which of
you can truthfully accuse me of sin? And
since I am telling you the truth, why don't you
believe me? 47 Anyone who belongs to God listens gladly to the words of God. But you don't
listen because you don't belong to God."
48 The people retorted, "You Samaritan
devil! Didn't we say all along that you were
possessed by a demon?"
49 "No," Jesus said, "I have no demon in me.
For I honor my Father—and you dishonor me.
50 And though I have no wish to glorify myself,
God is going to glorify me. He is the true
judge. 51 I tell you the truth, anyone who obeys
my teaching will never die!"
52 The people said, "Now we know you are
possessed by a demon. Even Abraham and
the prophets died, but you say, 'Anyone who
obeys my teaching will never die!' 53 Are you
greater than our father Abraham? He died,
and so did the prophets. Who do you think
you are?"
54 Jesus answered, "If I want glory for myself, it doesn't count. But it is my Father who
will glorify me. You say, 'He is our God,*' 55 but
you don't even know him. I know him. If I said
otherwise, I would be as great a liar as you! But

8:20 Greek *his hour*. **8:22** Greek *Jewish people*; also in 8:31, 48, 52, 57. **8:24** Greek *unless you believe that I am*. See Exod 3:14. **8:25** Or *Why do I speak to you at all?* **8:28** Greek *When you have lifted up the Son of Man, then you will know that I am*. "Son of Man" is a title Jesus used for himself. **8:39** Some manuscripts read *if you are really the children of Abraham, follow his example*. **8:54** Some manuscripts read *your God*.

I do know him and obey him. [56]Your father Abraham rejoiced as he looked forward to my coming. He saw it and was glad."

[57]The people said, "You aren't even fifty years old. How can you say you have seen Abraham?*"

[58]Jesus answered, "I tell you the truth, before Abraham was even born, I AM!*" [59]At that point they picked up stones to throw at him. But Jesus was hidden from them and left the Temple.

CHAPTER 9

Jesus Heals a Man Born Blind

As Jesus was walking along, he saw a man who had been blind from birth. [2]"Rabbi," his disciples asked him, "why was this man born blind? Was it because of his own sins or his parents' sins?"

[3]"It was not because of his sins or his parents' sins," Jesus answered. "This happened so the power of God could be seen in him. [4]We must quickly carry out the tasks assigned us by the one who sent us.* The night is coming, and then no one can work. [5]But while I am here in the world, I am the light of the world."

[6]Then he spit on the ground, made mud with the saliva, and spread the mud over the blind man's eyes. [7]He told him, "Go wash yourself in the pool of Siloam" (Siloam means "sent"). So the man went and washed and came back seeing!

[8]His neighbors and others who knew him as a blind beggar asked each other, "Isn't this the man who used to sit and beg?" [9]Some said he was, and others said, "No, he just looks like him!"

But the beggar kept saying, "Yes, I am the same one!"

[10]They asked, "Who healed you? What happened?"

[11]He told them, "The man they call Jesus made mud and spread it over my eyes and told me, 'Go to the pool of Siloam and wash yourself.' So I went and washed, and now I can see!"

[12]"Where is he now?" they asked.

"I don't know," he replied.

[13]Then they took the man who had been blind to the Pharisees, [14]because it was on the Sabbath that Jesus had made the mud and healed him. [15]The Pharisees asked the man all about it. So he told them, "He put the mud over my eyes, and when I washed it away, I could see!"

[16]Some of the Pharisees said, "This man Jesus is not from God, for he is working on the Sabbath." Others said, "But how could an ordinary sinner do such miraculous signs?" So there was a deep division of opinion among them.

[17]Then the Pharisees again questioned the man who had been blind and demanded, "What's your opinion about this man who healed you?"

The man replied, "I think he must be a prophet."

8:57 Some manuscripts read *How can you say Abraham has seen you?* **8:58** Or *before Abraham was even born, I have always been alive;* Greek reads *before Abraham was, I am.* See Exod 3:14. **9:4** Other manuscripts read *I must quickly carry out the tasks assigned me by the one who sent me;* still others read *We must quickly carry out the tasks assigned us by the one who sent me.*

[18]The Jewish leaders still refused to believe
the man had been blind and could now see, so
they called in his parents. [19]They asked them,
"Is this your son? Was he born blind? If so,
how can he now see?"

[20]His parents replied, "We know this is our
son and that he was born blind, [21]but we don't
know how he can see or who healed him. Ask
him. He is old enough to speak for himself."
[22]His parents said this because they were
afraid of the Jewish leaders, who had an-
nounced that anyone saying Jesus was the
Messiah would be expelled from the syna-
gogue. [23]That's why they said, "He is old
enough. Ask him."

[24]So for the second time they called in the
man who had been blind and told him, "God
should get the glory for this,* because we
know this man Jesus is a sinner."

[25]"I don't know whether he is a sinner," the
man replied. "But I know this: I was blind, and
now I can see!"

[26]"But what did he do?" they asked. "How
did he heal you?"

[27]"Look!" the man exclaimed. "I told you
once. Didn't you listen? Why do you want to
hear it again? Do you want to become his dis-
ciples, too?"

[28]Then they cursed him and said, "You are
his disciple, but we are disciples of Moses!
[29]We know God spoke to Moses, but we don't
even know where this man comes from."

[30]"Why, that's very strange!" the man re-
plied. "He healed my eyes, and yet you don't
know where he comes from? [31]We know that
God doesn't listen to sinners, but he is ready
to hear those who worship him and do his
will. [32]Ever since the world began, no one has
been able to open the eyes of someone born
blind. [33]If this man were not from God, he
couldn't have done it."

[34]"You were born a total sinner!" they an-
swered. "Are you trying to teach us?" And they
threw him out of the synagogue.

Spiritual Blindness

[35]When Jesus heard what had happened, he
found the man and asked, "Do you believe in
the Son of Man?*"

[36]The man answered, "Who is he, sir? I
want to believe in him."

[37]"You have seen him," Jesus said, "and he
is speaking to you!"

[38]"Yes, Lord, I believe!" the man said. And
he worshiped Jesus.

[39]Then Jesus told him,* "I entered this
world to render judgment—to give sight to
the blind and to show those who think they
see* that they are blind."

[40]Some Pharisees who were standing
nearby heard him and asked, "Are you saying
we're blind?"

[41]"If you were blind, you wouldn't be
guilty," Jesus replied. "But you remain guilty
because you claim you can see.

CHAPTER 10

The Good Shepherd and His Sheep

"I tell you the truth, anyone who sneaks over
the wall of a sheepfold, rather than going
through the gate, must surely be a thief and a
robber! [2]But the one who enters through the
gate is the shepherd of the sheep. [3]The gate-
keeper opens the gate for him, and the sheep
recognize his voice and come to him. He calls
his own sheep by name and leads them out.
[4]After he has gathered his own flock, he walks
ahead of them, and they follow him because
they know his voice. [5]They won't follow a
stranger; they will run from him because they
don't know his voice."

[6]Those who heard Jesus use this illustra-
tion didn't understand what he meant, [7]so he
explained it to them: "I tell you the truth, I am
the gate for the sheep. [8]All who came before
me* were thieves and robbers. But the true
sheep did not listen to them. [9]Yes, I am the
gate. Those who come in through me will be
saved.* They will come and go freely and will
find good pastures. [10]The thief's purpose is to
steal and kill and destroy. My purpose is to
give them a rich and satisfying life.

[11]"I am the good shepherd. The good shep-
herd sacrifices his life for the sheep. [12]A hired
hand will run when he sees a wolf coming. He
will abandon the sheep because they don't
belong to him and he isn't their shepherd.
And so the wolf attacks them and scatters the
flock. [13]The hired hand runs away because

9:24 Or *Give glory to God, not to Jesus;* Greek reads *Give glory to God.* **9:35** Some manuscripts read *the Son of God?* "Son of Man" is a title Jesus used for himself. **9:38-39a** Some manuscripts do not include *"Yes, Lord, I believe!" the man said. And he worshiped Jesus. Then Jesus told him.* **9:39b** Greek *those who see.* **10:8** Some manuscripts do not include *before me.* **10:9** Or *will find safety.*

he's working only for the money and doesn't
really care about the sheep.
14"I am the good shepherd; I know my own
sheep, and they know me, 15just as my Father
knows me and I know the Father. So I sacri-
fice my life for the sheep. 16I have other
sheep, too, that are not in this sheepfold. I
must bring them also. They will listen to my
voice, and there will be one flock with one
shepherd.
17"The Father loves me because I sacrifice
my life so I may take it back again. 18No one
can take my life from me. I sacrifice it volun-
tarily. For I have the authority to lay it down
when I want to and also to take it up again. For
this is what my Father has commanded."
19When he said these things, the people*
were again divided in their opinions about
him. 20Some said, "He's demon possessed and
out of his mind. Why listen to a man like
that?" 21Others said, "This doesn't sound like
a man possessed by a demon! Can a demon
open the eyes of the blind?"

Jesus Claims to Be the Son of God

22It was now winter, and Jesus was in Jerusa-
lem at the time of Hanukkah, the Festival of
Dedication. 23He was in the Temple, walking
through the section known as Solomon's Col-
onnade. 24The people surrounded him and
asked, "How long are you going to keep us in
suspense? If you are the Messiah, tell us
plainly."
25Jesus replied, "I have already told you,
and you don't believe me. The proof is the
work I do in my Father's name. 26But you
don't believe me because you are not my
sheep. 27My sheep listen to my voice; I know
them, and they follow me. 28I give them eter-
nal life, and they will never perish. No one can
snatch them away from me, 29for my Father
has given them to me, and he is more power-
ful than anyone else.* No one can snatch
them from the Father's hand. 30The Father
and I are one."
31Once again the people picked up stones
to kill him. 32Jesus said, "At my Father's direc-
tion I have done many good works. For which
one are you going to stone me?"
33They replied, "We're stoning you not for
any good work, but for blasphemy! You, a
mere man, claim to be God."
34Jesus replied, "It is written in your own
Scriptures* that God said to certain leaders
of the people, 'I say, you are gods!'* 35And you
know that the Scriptures cannot be altered.
So if those people who received God's mes-
sage were called 'gods,' 36why do you call it
blasphemy when I say, 'I am the Son of God'?
After all, the Father set me apart and sent me
into the world. 37Don't believe me unless I
carry out my Father's work. 38But if I do his
work, believe in the evidence of the miracu-
lous works I have done, even if you don't be-
lieve me. Then you will know and understand
that the Father is in me, and I am in the
Father."
39Once again they tried to arrest him, but
he got away and left them. 40He went beyond
the Jordan River near the place where John
was first baptizing and stayed there awhile.
41And many followed him. "John didn't per-
form miraculous signs," they remarked to
one another, "but everything he said about
this man has come true." 42And many who
were there believed in Jesus.

CHAPTER 11

The Raising of Lazarus

A man named Lazarus was sick. He lived in
Bethany with his sisters, Mary and Martha.
2This is the Mary who later poured the expen-
sive perfume on the Lord's feet and wiped
them with her hair.* Her brother, Lazarus,
was sick. 3So the two sisters sent a message to
Jesus telling him, "Lord, your dear friend is
very sick."
4But when Jesus heard about it he said,
"Lazarus's sickness will not end in death. No,
it happened for the glory of God so that the
Son of God will receive glory from this." 5So
although Jesus loved Martha, Mary, and Laza-
rus, 6he stayed where he was for the next two
days. 7Finally, he said to his disciples, "Let's go
back to Judea."
8But his disciples objected. "Rabbi," they
said, "only a few days ago the people* in Judea
were trying to stone you. Are you going there
again?"
9Jesus replied, "There are twelve hours of

10:19 Greek *Jewish people;* also in 10:24, 31. **10:29** Other manuscripts read *for what my Father has given me is more powerful than anything;* still others read *for regarding that which my Father has given me, he is greater than all.* **10:34a** Greek *your own law.* **10:34b** Ps 82:6. **11:2** This incident is recorded in chapter 12. **11:8** Greek *Jewish people;* also in 11:19, 31, 33, 36, 45, 54.

daylight every day. During the day people can walk safely. They can see because they have the light of this world. [10]But at night there is danger of stumbling because they have no light." [11]Then he said, "Our friend Lazarus has fallen asleep, but now I will go and wake him up."

[12]The disciples said, "Lord, if he is sleeping, he will soon get better!" [13]They thought Jesus meant Lazarus was simply sleeping, but Jesus meant Lazarus had died.

[14]So he told them plainly, "Lazarus is dead. [15]And for your sakes, I'm glad I wasn't there, for now you will really believe. Come, let's go see him."

[16]Thomas, nicknamed the Twin,* said to his fellow disciples, "Let's go, too—and die with Jesus."

[17]When Jesus arrived at Bethany, he was told that Lazarus had already been in his grave for four days. [18]Bethany was only a few miles* down the road from Jerusalem, [19]and many of the people had come to console Martha and Mary in their loss. [20]When Martha got word that Jesus was coming, she went to meet him. But Mary stayed in the house. [21]Martha said to Jesus, "Lord, if only you had been here, my brother would not have died. [22]But even now I know that God will give you whatever you ask."

[23]Jesus told her, "Your brother will rise again."

[24]"Yes," Martha said, "he will rise when everyone else rises, at the last day."

AMAZING FACTS

Lazarus had been dead for *four days*. Jesus came, called him, and Lazarus walked out of the tomb!

JOHN 11:30-44

[25]Jesus told her, "I am the resurrection and the life.* Anyone who believes in me will live, even after dying. [26]Everyone who lives in me and believes in me will never ever die. Do you believe this, Martha?"

[27]"Yes, Lord," she told him. "I have always believed you are the Messiah, the Son of God, the one who has come into the world from God." [28]Then she returned to Mary. She called Mary aside from the mourners and told her, "The Teacher is here and wants to see you." [29]So Mary immediately went to him.

[30]Jesus had stayed outside the village, at the place where Martha met him. [31]When the people who were at the house consoling Mary saw her leave so hastily, they assumed she was going to Lazarus's grave to weep. So they followed her there. [32]When Mary arrived and saw Jesus, she fell at his feet and said, "Lord, if only you had been here, my brother would not have died."

[33]When Jesus saw her weeping and saw the other people wailing with her, a deep anger welled up within him,* and he was deeply troubled. [34]"Where have you put him?" he asked them.

They told him, "Lord, come and see." [35]Then Jesus wept. [36]The people who were standing nearby said, "See how much he loved him!" [37]But some said, "This man healed a blind man. Couldn't he have kept Lazarus from dying?"

[38]Jesus was still angry as he arrived at the tomb, a cave with a stone rolled across its entrance. [39]"Roll the stone aside," Jesus told them.

But Martha, the dead man's sister, protested, "Lord, he has been dead for four days. The smell will be terrible."

[40]Jesus responded, "Didn't I tell you that you would see God's glory if you believe?" [41]So they rolled the stone aside. Then Jesus looked up to heaven and said, "Father, thank you for hearing me. [42]You always hear me, but I said it out loud for the sake of all these people standing here, so that they will believe you sent me." [43]Then Jesus shouted, "Lazarus, come out!" [44]And the dead man came out, his hands and feet bound in graveclothes, his face wrapped in a headcloth. Jesus told them, "Unwrap him and let him go!"

11:16 Greek *Thomas, who was called Didymus.* **11:18** Greek *was about 15 stadia* (about 2.8 kilometers). **11:25** Some manuscripts do not include *and the life.* **11:33** Or *he was angry in his spirit.*

The Plot to Kill Jesus

45Many of the people who were with Mary be-
lieved in Jesus when they saw this happen.
46But some went to the Pharisees and told
them what Jesus had done. 47Then the lead-
ing priests and Pharisees called the high
council* together. "What are we going to
do?" they asked each other. "This man cer-
tainly performs many miraculous signs. 48If
we allow him to go on like this, soon everyone
will believe in him. Then the Roman army will
come and destroy both our Temple* and our
nation."

49Caiaphas, who was high priest at that
time,* said, "You don't know what you're talk-
ing about! 50You don't realize that it's better
for you that one man should die for the peo-
ple than for the whole nation to be de-
stroyed."

51He did not say this on his own; as high
priest at that time he was led to prophesy that
Jesus would die for the entire nation. 52And
not only for that nation, but to bring together
and unite all the children of God scattered
around the world.

53So from that time on, the Jewish leaders
began to plot Jesus' death. 54As a result, Jesus
stopped his public ministry among the peo-
ple and left Jerusalem. He went to a place near
the wilderness, to the village of Ephraim, and
stayed there with his disciples.

55It was now almost time for the Jewish
Passover celebration, and many people from
all over the country arrived in Jerusalem sev-
eral days early so they could go through the
purification ceremony before Passover be-
gan. 56They kept looking for Jesus, but as they
stood around in the Temple, they said to each
other, "What do you think? He won't come
for Passover, will he?" 57Meanwhile, the lead-
ing priests and Pharisees had publicly or-
dered that anyone seeing Jesus must report it
immediately so they could arrest him.

CHAPTER 12

Jesus Anointed at Bethany

Six days before the Passover celebration be-
gan, Jesus arrived in Bethany, the home of
Lazarus—the man he had raised from the
dead. 2A dinner was prepared in Jesus' honor.
Martha served, and Lazarus was among those
who ate* with him. 3Then Mary took a twelve-
ounce jar* of expensive perfume made from
essence of nard, and she anointed Jesus' feet
with it, wiping his feet with her hair. The
house was filled with the fragrance.

4But Judas Iscariot, the disciple who would
soon betray him, said, 5"That perfume was
worth a year's wages.* It should have been
sold and the money given to the poor." 6Not
that he cared for the poor—he was a thief, and
since he was in charge of the disciples'
money, he often stole some for himself.

7Jesus replied, "Leave her alone. She did
this in preparation for my burial. 8You will al-
ways have the poor among you, but you will
not always have me."

9When all the people* heard of Jesus' ar-
rival, they flocked to see him and also to see
Lazarus, the man Jesus had raised from the
dead. 10Then the leading priests decided to
kill Lazarus, too, 11for it was because of him
that many of the people had deserted them*
and believed in Jesus.

Jesus' Triumphant Entry

12The next day, the news that Jesus was on the
way to Jerusalem swept through the city. A
large crowd of Passover visitors 13took palm
branches and went down the road to meet
him. They shouted,

"Praise God!*
Blessings on the one who comes in the
name of the LORD!
Hail to the King of Israel!"*

14Jesus found a young donkey and rode on it,
fulfilling the prophecy that said:

15 "Don't be afraid, people of Jerusalem.*
Look, your King is coming,
riding on a donkey's colt."*

16His disciples didn't understand at the
time that this was a fulfillment of prophecy.
But after Jesus entered into his glory, they re-
membered what had happened and realized
that these things had been written about him.

17Many in the crowd had seen Jesus call

11:47 Greek *the Sanhedrin*. **11:48** Or *our position;* Greek reads *our place*. **11:49** Greek *that year;* also in 11:51. **12:2** Or *who reclined*. **12:3** Greek *took 1 litra* (327 grams). **12:5** Greek *worth 300 denarii*. A denarius was equivalent to a laborer's full day's wage. **12:9** Greek *Jewish people;* also in 12:11. **12:11** Or *had deserted their traditions;* Greek reads *had deserted*. **12:13a** Greek *Hosanna*, an exclamation of praise adapted from a Hebrew expression that means "save now." **12:13b** Ps 118:25-26; Zeph 3:15. **12:15a** Greek *daughter of Zion*. **12:15b** Zech 9:9.

Lazarus from the tomb, raising him from the dead, and they were telling others* about it. [18]That was the reason so many went out to meet him—because they had heard about this miraculous sign. [19]Then the Pharisees said to each other, "There's nothing we can do. Look, everyone* has gone after him!"

Jesus Predicts His Death

[20]Some Greeks who had come to Jerusalem for the Passover celebration [21]paid a visit to Philip, who was from Bethsaida in Galilee. They said, "Sir, we want to meet Jesus." [22]Philip told Andrew about it, and they went together to ask Jesus.

[23]Jesus replied, "Now the time has come for the Son of Man* to enter into his glory. [24]I tell you the truth, unless a kernel of wheat is planted in the soil and dies, it remains alone. But its death will produce many new kernels—a plentiful harvest of new lives. [25]Those who love their life in this world will lose it. Those who care nothing for their life in this world will keep it for eternity. [26]Anyone who wants to be my disciple must follow me, because my servants must be where I am. And the Father will honor anyone who serves me.

[27]"Now my soul is deeply troubled. Should I pray, 'Father, save me from this hour'? But this is the very reason I came! [28]Father, bring glory to your name."

Then a voice spoke from heaven, saying, "I have already brought glory to my name, and I will do so again." [29]When the crowd heard the voice, some thought it was thunder, while others declared an angel had spoken to him.

[30]Then Jesus told them, "The voice was for your benefit, not mine. [31]The time for judging this world has come, when Satan, the ruler of this world, will be cast out. [32]And when I am lifted up from the earth, I will draw everyone to myself." [33]He said this to indicate how he was going to die.

[34]The crowd responded, "We understood from Scripture* that the Messiah would live forever. How can you say the Son of Man will die? Just who is this Son of Man, anyway?"

[35]Jesus replied, "My light will shine for you just a little longer. Walk in the light while you can, so the darkness will not overtake you. Those who walk in the darkness cannot see where they are going. [36]Put your trust in the light while there is still time; then you will become children of the light."

After saying these things, Jesus went away and was hidden from them.

The Unbelief of the People

[37]But despite all the miraculous signs Jesus had done, most of the people still did not believe in him. [38]This is exactly what Isaiah the prophet had predicted:

"LORD, who has believed our message?
To whom has the LORD revealed his
powerful arm?"*

[39]But the people couldn't believe, for as Isaiah also said,

[40] "The Lord has blinded their eyes
and hardened their hearts—
so that their eyes cannot see,
and their hearts cannot understand,
and they cannot turn to me
and have me heal them."*

[41]Isaiah was referring to Jesus when he said this, because he saw the future and spoke of the Messiah's glory. [42]Many people did believe in him, however, including some of the Jewish leaders. But they wouldn't admit it for fear that the Pharisees would expel them from the synagogue. [43]For they loved human praise more than the praise of God.

[44]Jesus shouted to the crowds, "If you trust me, you are trusting not only me, but also God who sent me. [45]For when you see me, you are seeing the one who sent me. [46]I have come as a light to shine in this dark world, so that all who put their trust in me will no longer remain in the dark. [47]I will not judge those who hear me but don't obey me, for I have come to save the world and not to judge it. [48]But all who reject me and my message will be judged on the day of judgment by the truth I have spoken. [49]I don't speak on my own authority. The Father who sent me has commanded me what to say and how to say it. [50]And I know his commands lead to eternal life; so I say whatever the Father tells me to say."

12:17 Greek *were testifying*. **12:19** Greek *the world*. **12:23** "Son of Man" is a title Jesus used for himself. **12:34** Greek *from the law*. **12:38** Isa 53:1. **12:40** Isa 6:10.

CHAPTER 13

Jesus Washes His Disciples' Feet

Before the Passover celebration, Jesus knew
that his hour had come to leave this world and
return to his Father. He had loved his disci-
ples during his ministry on earth, and now he
loved them to the very end.* 2It was time for
supper, and the devil had already prompted
Judas,* son of Simon Iscariot, to betray Jesus.
3Jesus knew that the Father had given him au-
thority over everything and that he had come
from God and would return to God. 4So he got
up from the table, took off his robe, wrapped
a towel around his waist, 5and poured water
into a basin. Then he began to wash the disci-
ples' feet, drying them with the towel he had
around him.

6When Jesus came to Simon Peter, Peter
said to him, "Lord, are you going to wash my
feet?"

7Jesus replied, "You don't understand now
what I am doing, but someday you will."

8"No," Peter protested, "you will never ever
wash my feet!"

Jesus replied, "Unless I wash you, you won't
belong to me."

9Simon Peter exclaimed, "Then wash my
hands and head as well, Lord, not just my
feet!"

10Jesus replied, "A person who has bathed
all over does not need to wash, except for the
feet,* to be entirely clean. And you disciples
are clean, but not all of you." 11For Jesus knew
who would betray him. That is what he meant
when he said, "Not all of you are clean."

12After washing their feet, he put on his
robe again and sat down and asked, "Do
you understand what I was doing? 13You
call me 'Teacher' and 'Lord,' and you are
right, because that's what I am. 14And since
I, your Lord and Teacher, have washed your
feet, you ought to wash each other's feet.
15I have given you an example to follow.
Do as I have done to you. 16I tell you the truth,
slaves are not greater than their master. Nor
is the messenger more important than the
one who sends the message. 17Now that you
know these things, God will bless you for
doing them.

Jesus Predicts His Betrayal

18"I am not saying these things to all of you; I
know the ones I have chosen. But this fulfills
the Scripture that says, 'The one who eats my
food has turned against me.'* 19I tell you this
beforehand, so that when it happens you will
believe that I AM the Messiah.* 20I tell you the
truth, anyone who welcomes my messenger is
welcoming me, and anyone who welcomes
me is welcoming the Father who sent me."

21Now Jesus was deeply troubled,* and he
exclaimed, "I tell you the truth, one of you will
betray me!"

22The disciples looked at each other, won-
dering whom he could mean. 23The disciple
Jesus loved was sitting next to Jesus at the
table.* 24Simon Peter motioned to him to ask,
"Who's he talking about?" 25So that disciple
leaned over to Jesus and asked, "Lord, who
is it?"

26Jesus responded, "It is the one to whom I
give the bread I dip in the bowl." And when he
had dipped it, he gave it to Judas, son of Si-
mon Iscariot. 27When Judas had eaten the
bread, Satan entered into him. Then Jesus
told him, "Hurry and do what you're going to
do." 28None of the others at the table knew
what Jesus meant. 29Since Judas was their
treasurer, some thought Jesus was telling him
to go and pay for the food or to give some
money to the poor. 30So Judas left at once, go-
ing out into the night.

Jesus Predicts Peter's Denial

31As soon as Judas left the room, Jesus said,
"The time has come for the Son of Man* to
enter into his glory, and God will be glorified
because of him. 32And since God receives
glory because of the Son,* he will soon give
glory to the Son. 33Dear children, I will be with
you only a little longer. And as I told the Jew-
ish leaders, you will search for me, but you
can't come where I am going. 34So now I am
giving you a new commandment: Love each
other. Just as I have loved you, you should love
each other. 35Your love for one another will
prove to the world that you are my disciples."

36Simon Peter asked, "Lord, where are you
going?"

13:1 Or *he showed them the full extent of his love.* **13:2** Or *the devil had already intended for Judas.* **13:10** Some manuscripts do not include *except for the feet.* **13:18** Ps 41:9. **13:19** Or *that the 'I AM' has come;* or *that I am the* LORD; Greek reads *that I am.* See Exod 3:14. **13:21** Greek *was troubled in his spirit.* **13:23** Greek *was reclining on Jesus' bosom.* The "disciple Jesus loved" was probably John. **13:31** "Son of Man" is a title Jesus used for himself. **13:32** Some manuscripts do not include *And since God receives glory because of the Son.*

And Jesus replied, "You can't go with me now, but you will follow me later."

37"But why can't I come now, Lord?" he asked. "I'm ready to die for you."

38Jesus answered, "Die for me? I tell you the truth, Peter—before the rooster crows tomorrow morning, you will deny three times that you even know me.

CHAPTER 14

Jesus, the Way to the Father

"Don't let your hearts be troubled. Trust in God, and trust also in me. 2There is more than enough room in my Father's home.* If this were not so, would I have told you that I am going to prepare a place for you?* 3When everything is ready, I will come and get you, so that you will always be with me where I am. 4And you know the way to where I am going."

5"No, we don't know, Lord," Thomas said. "We have no idea where you are going, so how can we know the way?"

6Jesus told him, "I am the way, the truth, and the life. No one can come to the Father except through me. 7If you had really known me, you would know who my Father is.* From now on, you do know him and have seen him!"

8Philip said, "Lord, show us the Father, and we will be satisfied."

9Jesus replied, "Have I been with you all this time, Philip, and yet you still don't know who I am? Anyone who has seen me has seen the Father! So why are you asking me to show him to you? 10Don't you believe that I am in the Father and the Father is in me? The words I speak are not my own, but my Father who lives in me does his work through me. 11Just believe that I am in the Father and the Father is in me. Or at least believe because of the work you have seen me do.

12"I tell you the truth, anyone who believes in me will do the same works I have done, and even greater works, because I am going to be with the Father. 13You can ask for anything in my name, and I will do it, so that the Son can bring glory to the Father. 14Yes, ask me for anything in my name, and I will do it!

Jesus Promises the Holy Spirit

15"If you love me, obey* my commandments. 16And I will ask the Father, and he will give you another Advocate,* who will never leave you. 17He is the Holy Spirit, who leads into all truth. The world cannot receive him, because it isn't looking for him and doesn't recognize him. But you know him, because he lives with you now and later will be in you.* 18No, I will not abandon you as orphans—I will come to you. 19Soon the world will no longer see me, but you will see me. Since I live, you also will live. 20When I am raised to life again, you will know that I am in my Father, and you are in me, and I am in you. 21Those who accept my commandments and obey them are the ones who love me. And because they love me, my Father will love them. And I will love them and reveal myself to each of them."

22Judas (not Judas Iscariot, but the other disciple with that name) said to him, "Lord, why are you going to reveal yourself only to us and not to the world at large?"

23Jesus replied, "All who love me will do what I say. My Father will love them, and we will come and make our home with each of them. 24Anyone who doesn't love me will not obey me. And remember, my words are not my own. What I am telling you is from the Father who sent me. 25I am telling you these things now while I am still with you. 26But when the Father sends the Advocate as my representative—that is, the Holy Spirit—he will teach you everything and will remind you of everything I have told you.

27"I am leaving you with a gift—peace of mind and heart. And the peace I give is a gift the world cannot give. So don't be troubled or afraid. 28Remember what I told you: I am going away, but I will come back to you again. If you really loved me, you would be happy that I am going to the Father, who is greater than I am. 29I have told you these things before they happen so that when they do happen, you will believe.

30"I don't have much more time to talk to you, because the ruler of this world approaches. He has no power over me, 31but I will do what the Father requires of me, so that

14:2a Or *There are many rooms in my Father's house.* **14:2b** Or *If this were not so, I would have told you that I am going to prepare a place for you.* Some manuscripts read *If this were not so, I would have told you. I am going to prepare a place for you.* **14:7** Some manuscripts read *If you have really known me, you will know who my Father is.* **14:15** Other manuscripts read *you will obey;* still others read *you should obey.* **14:16** Or *Comforter,* or *Encourager,* or *Counselor.* Greek reads *Paraclete;* also in 14:26. **14:17** Some manuscripts read *and is in you.*

Dirt-Bike Racing

Jeff's best friend, Quinn, loved dirt-bike racing. He had spent a lot of time and money fixing up an old dirt bike and getting ready for the race on Saturday. Now he was ready to demonstrate his skills and really wanted Jeff to come watch. But Jeff wanted to be on time to his cousin's birthday party that afternoon. Quinn's family had been going through some tough times, and Jeff was trying to be an encouragement to him. But he really wasn't into dirt-bike racing! What do you think Jeff should do? Read John 15:9-13.

the world will know that I love the Father. Come, let's be going.

CHAPTER 15

Jesus, the True Vine

"I am the true grapevine, and my Father is the gardener. [2]He cuts off every branch of mine that doesn't produce fruit, and he prunes the branches that do bear fruit so they will produce even more. [3]You have already been pruned and purified by the message I have given you. [4]Remain in me, and I will remain in you. For a branch cannot produce fruit if it is severed from the vine, and you cannot be fruitful unless you remain in me.

[5]"Yes, I am the vine; you are the branches. Those who remain in me, and I in them, will produce much fruit. For apart from me you can do nothing. [6]Anyone who does not remain in me is thrown away like a useless branch and withers. Such branches are gathered into a pile to be burned. [7]But if you remain in me and my words remain in you, you may ask for anything you want, and it will be granted! [8]When you produce much fruit, you are my true disciples. This brings great glory to my Father.

[9]"I have loved you even as the Father has loved me. Remain in my love. [10]When you obey my commandments, you remain in my love, just as I obey my Father's commandments and remain in his love. [11]I have told you these things so that you will be filled with my joy. Yes, your joy will overflow! [12]This is my commandment: Love each other in the same way I have loved you. [13]There is no greater love than to lay down one's life for one's friends. [14]You are my friends if you do what I command. [15]I no longer call you slaves, because a master doesn't confide in his slaves. Now you are my friends, since I have told you everything the Father told me. [16]You didn't choose me. I chose you. I appointed you to go and produce lasting fruit, so that the Father will give you whatever you ask for, using my name. [17]This is my command: Love each other.

The World's Hatred

[18]"If the world hates you, remember that it hated me first. [19]The world would love you as one of its own if you belonged to it, but you are no longer part of the world. I chose you to come out of the world, so it hates you. [20]Do you remember what I told you? 'A slave is not greater than the master.' Since they persecuted me, naturally they will persecute you. And if they had listened to me, they would listen to you. [21]They will do all this to you because of me, for they have rejected the one who sent me. [22]They would not be guilty if I had not come and spoken to them. But now they have no excuse for their sin. [23]Anyone

who hates me also hates my Father. [24]If I hadn't done such miraculous signs among them that no one else could do, they would not be guilty. But as it is, they have seen everything I did, yet they still hate me and my Father. [25]This fulfills what is written in their Scriptures*: 'They hated me without cause.'

[26]"But I will send you the Advocate*—the Spirit of truth. He will come to you from the Father and will testify all about me. [27]And you must also testify about me because you have been with me from the beginning of my ministry.

CHAPTER 16

"I have told you these things so that you won't abandon your faith. [2]For you will be expelled from the synagogues, and the time is coming when those who kill you will think they are doing a holy service for God. [3]This is because they have never known the Father or me. [4]Yes, I'm telling you these things now, so that when they happen, you will remember my warning. I didn't tell you earlier because I was going to be with you for a while longer.

The Work of the Holy Spirit

[5]"But now I am going away to the one who sent me, and not one of you is asking where I am going. [6]Instead, you grieve because of what I've told you. [7]But in fact, it is best for you that I go away, because if I don't, the Advocate* won't come. If I do go away, then I will send him to you. [8]And when he comes, he will convict the world of its sin, and of God's righteousness, and of the coming judgment. [9]The world's sin is that it refuses to believe in me. [10]Righteousness is available because I go to the Father, and you will see me no more. [11]Judgment will come because the ruler of this world has already been judged.

[12]"There is so much more I want to tell you, but you can't bear it now. [13]When the Spirit of truth comes, he will guide you into all truth. He will not speak on his own but will tell you what he has heard. He will tell you about the future. [14]He will bring me glory by telling you whatever he receives from me. [15]All that belongs to the Father is mine; this is why I said, 'The Spirit will tell you whatever he receives from me.'

Sadness Will Be Turned to Joy

[16]"In a little while you won't see me anymore. But a little while after that, you will see me again."

[17]Some of the disciples asked each other, "What does he mean when he says, 'In a little while you won't see me, but then you will see me,' and 'I am going to the Father'? [18]And what does he mean by 'a little while'? We don't understand."

[19]Jesus realized they wanted to ask him about it, so he said, "Are you asking yourselves what I meant? I said in a little while you won't see me, but a little while after that you will see me again. [20]I tell you the truth, you will weep and mourn over what is going to happen to me, but the world will rejoice. You will grieve, but your grief will suddenly turn to wonderful joy. [21]It will be like a woman suffering the pains of labor. When her child is born, her anguish gives way to joy because she has brought a new baby into the world. [22]So you have sorrow now, but I will see you again; then you will rejoice, and no one can rob you of that joy. [23]At that time you won't need to ask me for anything. I tell you the truth, you will ask the Father directly, and he will grant your request because you use my name. [24]You haven't done this before. Ask, using my name, and you will receive, and you will have abundant joy.

[25]"I have spoken of these matters in figures of speech, but soon I will stop speaking figuratively and will tell you plainly all about the Father. [26]Then you will ask in my name. I'm not saying I will ask the Father on your behalf, [27]for the Father himself loves you dearly because you love me and believe that I came from God.* [28]Yes, I came from the Father into the world, and now I will leave the world and return to the Father."

[29]Then his disciples said, "At last you are speaking plainly and not figuratively. [30]Now we understand that you know everything, and there's no need to question you. From this we believe that you came from God."

[31]Jesus asked, "Do you finally believe? [32]But the time is coming—indeed it's here now—when you will be scattered, each one going his own way, leaving me alone. Yet I am not alone because the Father is with me. [33]I have told you all this so that you may have peace in me.

15:25 Greek *in their law*. Pss 35:19; 69:4. **15:26** Or *Comforter*, or *Encourager*, or *Counselor*. Greek reads *Paraclete*. **16:7** Or *Comforter*, or *Encourager*, or *Counselor*. Greek reads *Paraclete*. **16:27** Some manuscripts read *from the Father*.

I SURVIVED

It was the spring of my seventh-grade year, and my best friend's mom was dying of cancer. Mrs. Chapman was like a second mom to me, and she was also my mom's best friend. I will never forget the day she died. I woke up to a dark gloom that I can't fully describe, and I just knew. Dazed, I walked into my parents' room to find my mom still in bed, crying on the phone. Mrs. Chapman had passed away during the night.

In the next week, I was a part of many events in honor of Mrs. Chapman, including her funeral. It was so hard and so confusing. I wanted somehow to take all the pain away and put it on myself so that no one else would hurt. I was trying to be so strong, trying to carry everyone's burden, because I really believed that was my job.

Finally summer came and I went to church camp. That's where I realized I wasn't strong enough to hold it all in, and I finally let go. I let God be my strength and I cried, I hurt, and I allowed myself to grieve. It felt so good. Since that time, I have experienced other losses, and I still struggle with letting go and not trying to carry it all on my own. But I've learned it's okay to hurt, cry, and be sad when you lose someone close to you—as long as you also look for strength from God.

I survived a major crisis in my life because I learned that you can let go and let God carry everything on his shoulders—even the death of someone you love.

Check out John 16:33 and 1 Corinthians 15:57 for help on how to survive grief and pain.

Here on earth you will have many trials and sorrows. But take heart, because I have overcome the world."

CHAPTER 17

The Prayer of Jesus

After saying all these things, Jesus looked up to heaven and said, "Father, the hour has come. Glorify your Son so he can give glory back to you. [2]For you have given him authority over everyone. He gives eternal life to each one you have given him. [3]And this is the way to have eternal life—to know you, the only true God, and Jesus Christ, the one you sent to earth. [4]I brought glory to you here on earth by completing the work you gave me to do. [5]Now, Father, bring me into the glory we shared before the world began.

[6]"I have revealed you* to the ones you gave me from this world. They were always yours. You gave them to me, and they have kept your word. [7]Now they know that everything I have is a gift from you, [8]for I have passed on to them the message you gave me. They accepted it and know that I came from you, and they believe you sent me.

[9]"My prayer is not for the world, but for those you have given me, because they belong to you. [10]All who are mine belong to you, and you have given them to me, so they bring me glory. [11]Now I am departing from the world; they are staying in this world, but I am coming to you. Holy Father, you have given me your name;* now protect them by the power of your name so that they will be united just as we are. [12]During my time here, I protected them by the power of the name you gave me.* I guarded them so that not one was lost, except the one headed for destruction, as the Scriptures foretold.

[13]"Now I am coming to you. I told them many things while I was with them in this world so they would be filled with my joy. [14]I have given them your word. And the world hates them because they do not belong to the world, just as I do not belong to the world. [15]I'm not asking you to take them out of the world, but to keep them safe from the evil one. [16]They do not belong to this world any more than I do. [17]Make them holy by your truth; teach them your word, which is truth. [18]Just as you sent me into the world, I am sending them into the world. [19]And I give myself as a holy sacrifice for them so they can be made holy by your truth.

[20]"I am praying not only for these disciples but also for all who will ever believe in me through their message. [21]I pray that they will all be one, just as you and I are one—as you are in me, Father, and I am in you. And may they be in us so that the world will believe you sent me.

[22]"I have given them the glory you gave me, so they may be one as we are one. [23]I am in them and you are in me. May they experience such perfect unity that the world will know that you sent me and that you love them as much as you love me. [24]Father, I want these whom you have given me to be with me where I am. Then they can see all the glory you gave me because you loved me even before the world began!

[25]"O righteous Father, the world doesn't know you, but I do; and these disciples know you sent me. [26]I have revealed you to them, and I will continue to do so. Then your love for me will be in them, and I will be in them."

CHAPTER 18

Jesus Is Betrayed and Arrested

After saying these things, Jesus crossed the Kidron Valley with his disciples and entered a grove of olive trees. [2]Judas, the betrayer, knew this place, because Jesus had often gone there with his disciples. [3]The leading priests and Pharisees had given Judas a contingent of Roman soldiers and Temple guards to accompany him. Now with blazing torches, lanterns, and weapons, they arrived at the olive grove.

[4]Jesus fully realized all that was going to happen to him, so he stepped forward to meet them. "Who are you looking for?" he asked.

[5]"Jesus the Nazarene,"* they replied.

"I AM he,"* Jesus said. (Judas, who betrayed him, was standing with them.) [6]As Jesus said "I AM he," they all drew back and fell to the ground! [7]Once more he asked them, "Who are you looking for?"

And again they replied, "Jesus the Nazarene."

[8]"I told you that I AM he," Jesus said. "And since I am the one you want, let these others

17:6 Greek *have revealed your name;* also in 17:26. **17:11** Some manuscripts read *you have given me these [disciples].* **17:12** Some manuscripts read *I protected those you gave me, by the power of your name.* **18:5a** Or *Jesus of Nazareth;* also in 18:7. **18:5b** Or *"The 'I AM' is here";* or *"I am the LORD";* Greek reads *I am;* also in 18:6, 8. See Exod 3:14.

go." [9]He did this to fulfill his own statement: "I did not lose a single one of those you have given me."*

[10]Then Simon Peter drew a sword and slashed off the right ear of Malchus, the high priest's slave. [11]But Jesus said to Peter, "Put your sword back into its sheath. Shall I not drink from the cup of suffering the Father has given me?"

Jesus at the High Priest's House

[12]So the soldiers, their commanding officer, and the Temple guards arrested Jesus and tied him up. [13]First they took him to Annas, the father-in-law of Caiaphas, the high priest at that time.* [14]Caiaphas was the one who had told the other Jewish leaders, "It's better that one man should die for the people."

Peter's First Denial

[15]Simon Peter followed Jesus, as did another of the disciples. That other disciple was acquainted with the high priest, so he was allowed to enter the high priest's courtyard with Jesus. [16]Peter had to stay outside the gate. Then the disciple who knew the high priest spoke to the woman watching at the gate, and she let Peter in. [17]The woman asked Peter, "You're not one of that man's disciples, are you?"

"No," he said, "I am not."

[18]Because it was cold, the household servants and the guards had made a charcoal fire. They stood around it, warming themselves, and Peter stood with them, warming himself.

The High Priest Questions Jesus

[19]Inside, the high priest began asking Jesus about his followers and what he had been teaching them. [20]Jesus replied, "Everyone knows what I teach. I have preached regularly in the synagogues and the Temple, where the people* gather. I have not spoken in secret. [21]Why are you asking me this question? Ask those who heard me. They know what I said."

18:9 See John 6:39 and 17:12. **18:13** Greek *that year.* **18:20** Greek *Jewish people;* also in 18:38.

WHO SAW JESUS AFTER HIS RESURRECTION?

The truth of Christianity rests heavily on the Resurrection. If Jesus rose from the grave, who saw him? How trustworthy were the witnesses? Those who claimed to have seen the risen Jesus went on to turn the world upside down. Most of them also died for being followers of Christ. People rarely die for half-hearted belief. These are people who saw Jesus risen from the grave:

Mary Magdalene	Mark 16:9-11; John 20:10-18
The other women at the tomb	Matthew 28:8-10
Peter in Jerusalem	Luke 24:34; 1 Corinthians 15:5
The two travelers on the road	Mark 16:12-13; Luke 24:13-35
Ten disciples behind closed doors	Luke 24:36-43; John 20:19-25
All the disciples, with Thomas (excluding Judas Iscariot)	John 20:26-31; 1 Corinthians 15:5
Seven disciples while fishing	John 21:1-14
Eleven disciples on the mountain	Matthew 28:16-20
A crowd of more than 500	1 Corinthians 15:6
Jesus' brother James	1 Corinthians 15:7
Those who watched Jesus ascend into heaven	Luke 24:44-51; Acts 1:3-9

Footprints of Jesus—The Last Week

1. Jesus stays at Bethany. From there, he goes to the Mount of Olives.
2. Jesus throws the money changers out of the Temple, and then he teaches there.
3. On the way back to Bethany, Jesus teaches on the Mount of Olives. Later that evening at Bethany, Mary pours ointment on Jesus' feet.
4. Jesus and his disciples eat the Last Supper together in an upper room. After supper, they go to the Garden of Gethsemane.

5. Jesus is taken to Caiaphas's house to be tried.
6. Jesus is transferred to the Antonia Fortress to be tried by Pilate.
7. Jesus is taken to Herod's palace.
8. Herod returns Jesus to Pilate.
9. Jesus is condemned and carries his cross through the streets of Jerusalem to Golgotha. There he is crucified.

22 Then one of the Temple guards standing
nearby slapped Jesus across the face. "Is that
the way to answer the high priest?" he de-
manded.
23 Jesus replied, "If I said anything wrong,
you must prove it. But if I'm speaking the
truth, why are you beating me?"
24 Then Annas bound Jesus and sent him to
Caiaphas, the high priest.

Peter's Second and Third Denials

25 Meanwhile, as Simon Peter was standing by
the fire warming himself, they asked him
again, "You're not one of his disciples, are you?"
He denied it, saying, "No, I am not."
26 But one of the household slaves of the
high priest, a relative of the man whose ear
Peter had cut off, asked, "Didn't I see you out
there in the olive grove with Jesus?" 27 Again
Peter denied it. And immediately a rooster
crowed.

Jesus' Trial before Pilate

28 Jesus' trial before Caiaphas ended in the
early hours of the morning. Then he was
taken to the headquarters of the Roman gov-
ernor.* His accusers didn't go inside because
it would defile them, and they wouldn't be al-
lowed to celebrate the Passover. 29 So Pilate,
the governor, went out to them and asked,
"What is your charge against this man?"
30 "We wouldn't have handed him over to
you if he weren't a criminal!" they retorted.
31 "Then take him away and judge him by
your own law," Pilate told them.
"Only the Romans are permitted to exe-
cute someone," the Jewish leaders replied.
32 (This fulfilled Jesus' prediction about the
way he would die.*)
33 Then Pilate went back into his head-
quarters and called for Jesus to be brought to
him. "Are you the king of the Jews?" he asked
him.
34 Jesus replied, "Is this your own question,
or did others tell you about me?"
35 "Am I a Jew?" Pilate retorted. "Your own
people and their leading priests brought you
to me for trial. Why? What have you done?"
36 Jesus answered, "My Kingdom is not an
earthly kingdom. If it were, my followers
would fight to keep me from being handed
over to the Jewish leaders. But my Kingdom is
not of this world."
37 Pilate said, "So you are a king?"
Jesus responded, "You say I am a king.
Actually, I was born and came into the world
to testify to the truth. All who love the truth
recognize that what I say is true."
38 "What is truth?" Pilate asked. Then he
went out again to the people and told them,
"He is not guilty of any crime. 39 But you have a
custom of asking me to release one prisoner
each year at Passover. Would you like me to
release this 'King of the Jews'?"
40 But they shouted back, "No! Not this man.
We want Barabbas!" (Barabbas was a revolu-
tionary.)

CHAPTER 19

Jesus Sentenced to Death

Then Pilate had Jesus flogged with a lead-
tipped whip. 2 The soldiers wove a crown of
thorns and put it on his head, and they put a
purple robe on him. 3 "Hail! King of the Jews!"
they mocked, as they slapped him across the
face.
4 Pilate went outside again and said to the
people, "I am going to bring him out to you
now, but understand clearly that I find him
not guilty." 5 Then Jesus came out wearing the
crown of thorns and the purple robe. And Pi-
late said, "Look, here is the man!"
6 When they saw him, the leading priests
and Temple guards began shouting, "Crucify
him! Crucify him!"
"Take him yourselves and crucify him," Pi-
late said. "I find him not guilty."
7 The Jewish leaders replied, "By our law he
ought to die because he called himself the
Son of God."
8 When Pilate heard this, he was more
frightened than ever. 9 He took Jesus back into
the headquarters* again and asked him,
"Where are you from?" But Jesus gave no an-
swer. 10 "Why don't you talk to me?" Pilate de-
manded. "Don't you realize that I have the
power to release you or crucify you?"
11 Then Jesus said, "You would have no
power over me at all unless it were given to
you from above. So the one who handed me
over to you has the greater sin."
12 Then Pilate tried to release him, but the

18:28 Greek *to the Praetorium;* also in 18:33. **18:32** See John 12:32-33. **19:9** Greek *the Praetorium.*

Jewish leaders shouted, "If you release this man, you are no 'friend of Caesar.'* Anyone who declares himself a king is a rebel against Caesar."

[13]When they said this, Pilate brought Jesus out to them again. Then Pilate sat down on the judgment seat on the platform that is called the Stone Pavement (in Hebrew, *Gabbatha*). [14]It was now about noon on the day of preparation for the Passover. And Pilate said to the people,* "Look, here is your king!"

[15]"Away with him," they yelled. "Away with him! Crucify him!"

"What? Crucify your king?" Pilate asked.

"We have no king but Caesar," the leading priests shouted back.

[16]Then Pilate turned Jesus over to them to be crucified.

The Crucifixion

So they took Jesus away. [17]Carrying the cross by himself, he went to the place called Place of the Skull (in Hebrew, *Golgotha*). [18]There they nailed him to the cross. Two others were crucified with him, one on either side, with Jesus between them. [19]And Pilate posted a sign on the cross that read, "Jesus of Nazareth,* the King of the Jews." [20]The place where Jesus was crucified was near the city, and the sign was written in Hebrew, Latin, and Greek, so that many people could read it.

[21]Then the leading priests objected and said to Pilate, "Change it from 'The King of the Jews' to 'He said, I am King of the Jews.'"

[22]Pilate replied, "No, what I have written, I have written."

[23]When the soldiers had crucified Jesus, they divided his clothes among the four of them. They also took his robe, but it was seamless, woven in one piece from top to bottom. [24]So they said, "Rather than tearing it apart, let's throw dice* for it." This fulfilled the Scripture that says, "They divided my garments among themselves and threw dice for my clothing."* So that is what they did.

[25]Standing near the cross were Jesus' mother, and his mother's sister, Mary (the wife of Clopas), and Mary Magdalene. [26]When Jesus saw his mother standing there beside the disciple he loved, he said to her, "Dear woman, here is your son." [27]And he said to this disciple, "Here is your mother." And from then on this disciple took her into his home.

The Death of Jesus

[28]Jesus knew that his mission was now finished, and to fulfill Scripture he said, "I am thirsty."* [29]A jar of sour wine was sitting there, so they soaked a sponge in it, put it on a hyssop branch, and held it up to his lips. [30]When Jesus had tasted it, he said, "It is finished!" Then he bowed his head and released his spirit.

[31]It was the day of preparation, and the Jewish leaders didn't want the bodies hanging there the next day, which was the Sabbath (and a very special Sabbath, because it was the Passover). So they asked Pilate to hasten their deaths by ordering that their legs be broken. Then their bodies could be taken down. [32]So the soldiers came and broke the legs of the two men crucified with Jesus. [33]But when they came to Jesus, they saw that he was already dead, so they didn't break his legs. [34]One of the soldiers, however, pierced his side with a spear, and immediately blood and water flowed out. [35](This report is from an eyewitness giving an accurate account. He speaks the truth so that you also can believe.*) [36]These things happened in fulfillment of the Scriptures that say, "Not one of his bones will be broken,"* [37]and "They will look on the one they pierced."*

The Burial of Jesus

[38]Afterward Joseph of Arimathea, who had been a secret disciple of Jesus (because he feared the Jewish leaders), asked Pilate for permission to take down Jesus' body. When Pilate gave permission, Joseph came and took the body away. [39]With him came Nicodemus, the man who had come to Jesus at night. He brought about seventy-five pounds* of perfumed ointment made from myrrh and aloes. [40]Following Jewish burial custom, they wrapped Jesus' body with the spices in long sheets of linen cloth. [41]The place of crucifixion was near a garden, where there was a new tomb, never used before. [42]And so, because it was the day of preparation for the Jewish Passover* and since the tomb was close at hand, they laid Jesus there.

19:12 "Friend of Caesar" is a technical term that refers to an ally of the emperor. **19:14** Greek *Jewish people;* also in 19:20. **19:19** Or *Jesus the Nazarene.* **19:24a** Greek *cast lots.* **19:24b** Ps 22:18. **19:28** See Pss 22:15; 69:21. **19:35** Some manuscripts read *can continue to believe.* **19:36** Exod 12:46; Num 9:12; Ps 34:20. **19:37** Zech 12:10. **19:39** Greek *100 litras* [32.7 kilograms]. **19:42** Greek *because of the Jewish day of preparation.*

CHAPTER 20

The Resurrection

Early on Sunday morning,* while it was still dark, Mary Magdalene came to the tomb and found that the stone had been rolled away from the entrance. [2]She ran and found Simon Peter and the other disciple, the one whom Jesus loved. She said, "They have taken the Lord's body out of the tomb, and we don't know where they have put him!"

[3]Peter and the other disciple started out for the tomb. [4]They were both running, but the other disciple outran Peter and reached the tomb first. [5]He stooped and looked in and saw the linen wrappings lying there, but he didn't go in. [6]Then Simon Peter arrived and went inside. He also noticed the linen wrappings lying there, [7]while the cloth that had covered Jesus' head was folded up and lying apart from the other wrappings. [8]Then the disciple who had reached the tomb first also went in, and he saw and believed—[9]for until then they still hadn't understood the Scriptures that said Jesus must rise from the dead. [10]Then they went home.

AMAZING FACTS

After Jesus' death, his disciples were afraid and hid behind locked doors. Can you imagine their surprise when suddenly Jesus was standing there with them?

JOHN 20:19-20

Jesus Appears to Mary Magdalene

[11]Mary was standing outside the tomb crying, and as she wept, she stooped and looked in. [12]She saw two white-robed angels, one sitting at the head and the other at the foot of the place where the body of Jesus had been lying. [13]"Dear woman, why are you crying?" the angels asked her.

"Because they have taken away my Lord," she replied, "and I don't know where they have put him."

[14]She turned to leave and saw someone standing there. It was Jesus, but she didn't recognize him. [15]"Dear woman, why are you crying?" Jesus asked her. "Who are you looking for?"

She thought he was the gardener. "Sir," she said, "if you have taken him away, tell me where you have put him, and I will go and get him."

[16]"Mary!" Jesus said.

She turned to him and cried out, "Rabboni!" (which is Hebrew for "Teacher").

[17]"Don't cling to me," Jesus said, "for I haven't yet ascended to the Father. But go find my brothers and tell them, 'I am ascending to my Father and your Father, to my God and your God.'"

[18]Mary Magdalene found the disciples and told them, "I have seen the Lord!" Then she gave them his message.

Jesus Appears to His Disciples

[19]That Sunday evening* the disciples were meeting behind locked doors because they were afraid of the Jewish leaders. Suddenly, Jesus was standing there among them! "Peace be with you," he said. [20]As he spoke, he showed them the wounds in his hands and his side. They were filled with joy when they saw the Lord! [21]Again he said, "Peace be with you. As the Father has sent me, so I am sending you." [22]Then he breathed on them and said, "Receive the Holy Spirit. [23]If you forgive anyone's sins, they are forgiven. If you do not forgive them, they are not forgiven."

Jesus Appears to Thomas

[24]One of the twelve disciples, Thomas (nicknamed the Twin),* was not with the others when Jesus came. [25]They told him, "We have seen the Lord!"

But he replied, "I won't believe it unless I see the nail wounds in his hands, put my fingers into them, and place my hand into the wound in his side."

[26]Eight days later the disciples were together again, and this time Thomas was with them. The doors were locked; but suddenly,

20:1 Greek *On the first day of the week.* **20:19** Greek *In the evening of that day, the first day of the week.* **20:24** Greek *Thomas, who was called Didymus.*

Transportation and Places

CAVES

Caves sometimes provided family burial places. A shelf was carved in the stone wall of the cave. The body was placed there until it decayed. Then the bones would be moved to another part of the cave so the stone shelf would be ready when the next family member died.

Caves were also used as places of refuge. Lot and his daughters hid in caves when their home burned (Genesis 19:30). David spent a lot of his time hiding from King Saul in caves (1 Samuel 22:1; 24:1-3). Other uses for caves: as houses and storage places.

SHIPS

In New Testament times there were two kinds of ships: cargo ships and warships (all made of wood). To travel, you usually paid for a ride on a cargo ship. (Paul traveled in a grain ship that carried 276 people and wrecked.)

Cargo ships were wide and round. Roman warships were narrow and long (much faster).

ROADS

Many ancient "roads" were just dirt paths where the rocks and brush had been cleared away. Then the Romans came. They were great at making roads. They paved roads twenty feet wide with flat stones. They even sloped the roads for drainage and put markers every one thousand paces to check distances.

The first and most famous Roman paved road, which led to Rome, was called the Appian Way. Today you can still see parts of the Appian Way near Rome.

POWER WALKING

In Jesus' time, most people traveled on foot. Walkers could usually cover 15–18 miles per day. That means it would have taken Jesus a whole day to walk from his hometown, Nazareth, to the Sea of Galilee. To get to Jerusalem from Nazareth, he and his disciples would have had to walk for more than three days.

CALL A TAXI?

Sometimes kings and queens were carried in royal chairs between poles supported on slaves' shoulders. The rich also traveled in horse-drawn carriages, and merchants used heavy carts (pulled by oxen) to transport grain and other goods.

WIDE LOADS?

Donkeys and mules were the best animals in terms of carrying loads. A donkey could carry a load of up to 130 pounds, at about 2.5 mph. That's around 15 miles a day. A mule (part horse and part donkey) could carry 160 pounds at 3–4 mph. That's about 20–25 miles a day. Which u-haul-it would you rather use?

THE GARBAGE DUMP

In cities today, trucks pick up garbage and carry it to the dump. In the country, people sometimes have to take their own garbage to the dump. That's how it was in the ancient world. The people of Jerusalem carried their garbage in pots and threw it into the valley called Hinnom, where it was sometimes burned. The gate leading to this valley was called the Refuse Gate. Can you imagine how that place smelled?

HIGH-SPEED TRAVEL?

Donkey caravans could travel about 20 miles a day, and fully loaded camel caravans could cover 18–20 miles a day. Still, if speed was more important than anything else, someone riding a fast camel could travel much farther–up to 70 miles a day! That's express delivery!

PRISONS

The Bible describes many kinds of prisons. Joseph was thrown into a pit by his brothers. Samson had to grind grain in a Philistine prison. Jeremiah was threatened with stocks and shackles and was thrown into a cistern. Peter was chained between 2 soldiers in a prison with an iron gate by the street. And Paul was under house arrest (guarded at home) in Rome.

CITY WALLS

A walled city was a safe place to live. A city like Jericho could have walls up to 25 feet high and 20 feet thick! In fact, some cities had two walls with a narrow space between for extra protection. Soldiers on top of city walls could see an army that was still miles away. Most city walls had towers that were wider and sometimes taller than the walls. Residents could use the towers to watch other parts of the walls and to fight attackers trying to climb the walls.

THE PALACE

From Saul in the Old Testament to Herod in the New Testament, Bible-time kings lived in beautiful palaces. David built a palace of cedar wood. His son Solomon built a much more expensive palace of cedar wood and hand-cut stones. Ahab had an ivory palace. Herod, in the New Testament, lived in a palace in Jerusalem.

as before, Jesus was standing among them.
"Peace be with you," he said. [27] Then he said to
Thomas, "Put your finger here, and look at my
hands. Put your hand into the wound in my
side. Don't be faithless any longer. Believe!"
[28] "My Lord and my God!" Thomas ex-
claimed.
[29] Then Jesus told him, "You believe be-
cause you have seen me. Blessed are those
who believe without seeing me."

Purpose of the Book

[30] The disciples saw Jesus do many other mi-
raculous signs in addition to the ones re-
corded in this book. [31] But these are written so
that you may continue to believe* that Jesus is
the Messiah, the Son of God, and that by be-
lieving in him you will have life by the power
of his name.

CHAPTER 21

Epilogue: Jesus Appears to Seven Disciples

Later, Jesus appeared again to the disciples
beside the Sea of Galilee.* This is how it hap-
pened. [2] Several of the disciples were there—
Simon Peter, Thomas (nicknamed the Twin),*
Nathanael from Cana in Galilee, the sons of
Zebedee, and two other disciples.
[3] Simon Peter said, "I'm going fishing."
"We'll come, too," they all said. So they
went out in the boat, but they caught nothing
all night.
[4] At dawn Jesus was standing on the beach,
but the disciples couldn't see who he was. [5] He
called out, "Fellows,* have you caught any
fish?"
"No," they replied.
[6] Then he said, "Throw out your net on the
right-hand side of the boat, and you'll get
some!" So they did, and they couldn't haul in
the net because there were so many fish in it.
[7] Then the disciple Jesus loved said to Peter,
"It's the Lord!" When Simon Peter heard that
it was the Lord, he put on his tunic (for he had
stripped for work), jumped into the water,
and headed to shore. [8] The others stayed with
the boat and pulled the loaded net to the
shore, for they were only about a hundred
yards* from shore. [9] When they got there,

20:31 Some manuscripts read *that you may believe.* **21:1** Greek *Sea of Tiberias,* another name for the Sea of Galilee. **21:2** Greek *Thomas, who was called Didymus.* **21:5** Greek *Children.* **21:8** Greek *200 cubits* [90 meters].

IS IT OK?

IS IT OK TO WONDER IF JESUS IS REALLY GOD AND REALLY ALIVE?

When his friends told him that Jesus rose from the dead and was alive, Thomas said he wouldn't believe it unless he saw the proof with his own eyes—check it out in John 20:24-25. (That's bold, Tom!) It's OK to wonder if Jesus is God and if he's alive. Just ask him. God loves you and will send his Son, Jesus, to show up in your life as he did in Thomas's life. Because we can't see Jesus, we have to have faith that he's real. *Faith* means that we believe what Jesus tells us about himself. So if you have doubts, just keep asking God your questions as you pray in Jesus' name. Then look in the Bible—and in your heart—for the answers.

they found breakfast waiting for them—fish
cooking over a charcoal fire, and some bread.
10"Bring some of the fish you've just
caught," Jesus said. 11So Simon Peter went
aboard and dragged the net to the shore.
There were 153 large fish, and yet the net
hadn't torn.
12"Now come and have some breakfast!"
Jesus said. None of the disciples dared to ask
him, "Who are you?" They knew it was the
Lord. 13Then Jesus served them the bread and
the fish. 14This was the third time Jesus had
appeared to his disciples since he had been
raised from the dead.
15After breakfast Jesus asked Simon Peter,
"Simon son of John, do you love me more than
these?*"
"Yes, Lord," Peter replied, "you know I love
you."
"Then feed my lambs," Jesus told him.
16Jesus repeated the question: "Simon son
of John, do you love me?"
"Yes, Lord," Peter said, "you know I love
you."
"Then take care of my sheep," Jesus said.
17A third time he asked him, "Simon son of
John, do you love me?"
Peter was hurt that Jesus asked the ques-
tion a third time. He said, "Lord, you know
everything. You know that I love you."
Jesus said, "Then feed my sheep.
18"I tell you the truth, when you were
young, you were able to do as you liked; you
dressed yourself and went wherever you
wanted to go. But when you are old, you will
stretch out your hands, and others* will dress
you and take you where you don't want to go."
19Jesus said this to let him know by what kind
of death he would glorify God. Then Jesus
told him, "Follow me."
20Peter turned around and saw behind
them the disciple Jesus loved—the one who
had leaned over to Jesus during supper and
asked, "Lord, who will betray you?" 21Peter
asked Jesus, "What about him, Lord?"
22Jesus replied, "If I want him to remain
alive until I return, what is that to you? As for
you, follow me." 23So the rumor spread
among the community of believers* that this
disciple wouldn't die. But that isn't what Jesus
said at all. He only said, "If I want him to re-
main alive until I return, what is that to you?"
24This disciple is the one who testifies to
these events and has recorded them here.
And we know that his account of these things
is accurate.
25Jesus also did many other things. If they
were all written down, I suppose the whole
world could not contain the books that would
be written.

21:15 Or *more than these others do?* **21:18** Some manuscripts read *and another one.* **21:23** Greek *the brothers.*

Acts

WHO
Peter, John, James, Stephen, Philip, Paul, Barnabas, Dorcas, John Mark, Rhoda, Cornelius, James (Jesus' brother), Timothy, Lydia, Silas, and Luke.

WHERE
When Luke wrote this, he was probably in Rome.

WHEN
Between AD 63 and 70.

WHY
To give an accurate account of the birth and growth of the early Christian church.

You will receive power when the Holy Spirit comes upon you. And you will be my witnesses.
ACTS 1:8

Jesus left behind several hundred people from many different backgrounds with the job of taking the Good News about himself all over the world. How did they handle disagreements? What kept them going when tough times came? The book of Acts tells the exciting story of how the church began.

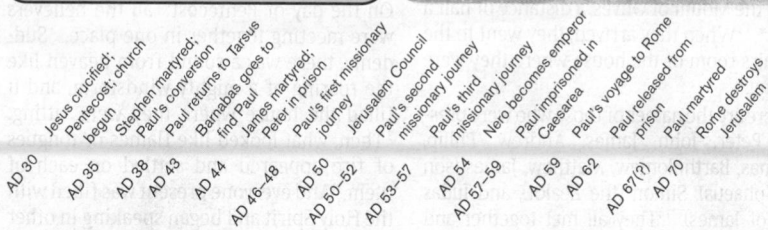

Remember that God will give you strength to tell your friends about Jesus.

CHAPTER 1

The Promise of the Holy Spirit

In my first book* I told you, Theophilus, about everything Jesus began to do and teach
2 until the day he was taken up to heaven after giving his chosen apostles further instructions through the Holy Spirit. 3 During the forty days after his crucifixion, he appeared to the apostles from time to time, and he proved to them in many ways that he was actually alive. And he talked to them about the Kingdom of God.

1:1 The reference is to the Gospel of Luke.

[4]Once when he was eating with them, he commanded them, "Do not leave Jerusalem until the Father sends you the gift he promised, as I told you before. [5]John baptized with* water, but in just a few days you will be baptized with the Holy Spirit."

The Ascension of Jesus

[6]So when the apostles were with Jesus, they kept asking him, "Lord, has the time come for you to free Israel and restore our kingdom?"

[7]He replied, "The Father alone has the authority to set those dates and times, and they are not for you to know. [8]But you will receive power when the Holy Spirit comes upon you. And you will be my witnesses, telling people about me everywhere—in Jerusalem, throughout Judea, in Samaria, and to the ends of the earth."

[9]After saying this, he was taken up into a cloud while they were watching, and they could no longer see him. [10]As they strained to see him rising into heaven, two white-robed men suddenly stood among them. [11]"Men of Galilee," they said, "why are you standing here staring into heaven? Jesus has been taken from you into heaven, but someday he will return from heaven in the same way you saw him go!"

Matthias Replaces Judas

[12]Then the apostles returned to Jerusalem from the Mount of Olives, a distance of half a mile.* [13]When they arrived, they went to the upstairs room of the house where they were staying.

Here are the names of those who were present: Peter, John, James, Andrew, Philip, Thomas, Bartholomew, Matthew, James (son of Alphaeus), Simon (the Zealot), and Judas (son of James). [14]They all met together and were constantly united in prayer, along with Mary the mother of Jesus, several other women, and the brothers of Jesus.

[15]During this time, when about 120 believers* were together in one place, Peter stood up and addressed them. [16]"Brothers," he said, "the Scriptures had to be fulfilled concerning Judas, who guided those who arrested Jesus. This was predicted long ago by the Holy Spirit, speaking through King David. [17]Judas was one of us and shared in the ministry with us."

[18](Judas had bought a field with the money he received for his treachery. Falling headfirst there, his body split open, spilling out all his intestines. [19]The news of his death spread to all the people of Jerusalem, and they gave the place the Aramaic name *Akeldama*, which means "Field of Blood.")

[20]Peter continued, "This was written in the book of Psalms, where it says, 'Let his home become desolate, with no one living in it.' It also says, 'Let someone else take his position.'*

[21]"So now we must choose a replacement for Judas from among the men who were with us the entire time we were traveling with the Lord Jesus—[22]from the time he was baptized by John until the day he was taken from us. Whoever is chosen will join us as a witness of Jesus' resurrection."

[23]So they nominated two men: Joseph called Barsabbas (also known as Justus) and Matthias. [24]Then they all prayed, "O Lord, you know every heart. Show us which of these men you have chosen [25]as an apostle to replace Judas in this ministry, for he has deserted us and gone where he belongs." [26]Then they cast lots, and Matthias was selected to become an apostle with the other eleven.

CHAPTER 2

The Holy Spirit Comes

On the day of Pentecost* all the believers were meeting together in one place. [2]Suddenly, there was a sound from heaven like the roaring of a mighty windstorm, and it filled the house where they were sitting. [3]Then, what looked like flames or tongues of fire appeared and settled on each of them. [4]And everyone present was filled with the Holy Spirit and began speaking in other languages,* as the Holy Spirit gave them this ability.

[5]At that time there were devout Jews from every nation living in Jerusalem. [6]When they heard the loud noise, everyone came running, and they were bewildered to hear their own languages being spoken by the believers.

[7]They were completely amazed. "How can this be?" they exclaimed. "These people are

1:5 Or *in;* also in 1:5b. **1:12** Greek *a Sabbath day's journey.* **1:15** Greek *brothers.* **1:20** Pss 69:25; 109:8. **2:1** The Festival of Pentecost came 50 days after Passover (when Jesus was crucified). **2:4** Or *in other tongues.*

all from Galilee, [8]and yet we hear them
speaking in our own native languages! [9]Here
we are—Parthians, Medes, Elamites, people
from Mesopotamia, Judea, Cappadocia,
Pontus, the province of Asia, [10]Phrygia,
Pamphylia, Egypt, and the areas of Libya
around Cyrene, visitors from Rome [11](both
Jews and converts to Judaism), Cretans, and
Arabs. And we all hear these people speaking
in our own languages about the wonderful
things God has done!" [12]They stood there
amazed and perplexed. "What can this
mean?" they asked each other.
[13]But others in the crowd ridiculed them,
saying, "They're just drunk, that's all!"

AMAZING FACTS

The disciples were suddenly able to speak in many different languages they hadn't spoken before. How? Holy Spirit power!
ACTS 2:1-4

Peter Preaches to the Crowd

[14]Then Peter stepped forward with the eleven
other apostles and shouted to the crowd, "Lis-
ten carefully, all of you, fellow Jews and resi-
dents of Jerusalem! Make no mistake about
this. [15]These people are not drunk, as some of
you are assuming. Nine o'clock in the morn-
ing is much too early for that. [16]No, what you
see was predicted long ago by the prophet
Joel:

[17] 'In the last days,' God says,
'I will pour out my Spirit upon all
people.
Your sons and daughters will prophesy.
Your young men will see visions,
and your old men will dream dreams.
[18] In those days I will pour out my
Spirit
even on my servants—men and women
alike—
and they will prophesy.
[19] And I will cause wonders in the heavens
above
and signs on the earth below—
blood and fire and clouds of smoke.
[20] The sun will become dark,
and the moon will turn blood red
before that great and glorious day of
the LORD arrives.
[21] But everyone who calls on the name
of the LORD
will be saved.'*

[22]"People of Israel, listen! God publicly en-
dorsed Jesus the Nazarene* by doing power-
ful miracles, wonders, and signs through him,
as you well know. [23]But God knew what would
happen, and his prearranged plan was carried
out when Jesus was betrayed. With the help
of lawless Gentiles, you nailed him to a cross
and killed him. [24]But God released him from
the horrors of death and raised him back to
life, for death could not keep him in its grip.
[25]King David said this about him:

'I see that the LORD is always
with me.
I will not be shaken, for he is right
beside me.
[26] No wonder my heart is glad,
and my tongue shouts his praises!
My body rests in hope.
[27] For you will not leave my soul among
the dead*
or allow your Holy One to rot in the
grave.
[28] You have shown me the way of life,
and you will fill me with the joy
of your presence.'*

[29]"Dear brothers, think about this! You can
be sure that the patriarch David wasn't refer-
ring to himself, for he died and was buried,
and his tomb is still here among us. [30]But he
was a prophet, and he knew God had prom-
ised with an oath that one of David's own de-
scendants would sit on his throne. [31]David
was looking into the future and speaking of
the Messiah's resurrection. He was saying

2:17-21 Joel 2:28-32. **2:22** Or *Jesus of Nazareth*. **2:27** Greek *in Hades*; also in 2:31. **2:25-28** Ps 16:8-11 (Greek version).

that God would not leave him among the dead
or allow his body to rot in the grave.
32"God raised Jesus from the dead, and we
are all witnesses of this. 33Now he is exalted to
the place of highest honor in heaven, at God's
right hand. And the Father, as he had prom-
ised, gave him the Holy Spirit to pour out
upon us, just as you see and hear today. 34For
David himself never ascended into heaven,
yet he said,

'The LORD said to my Lord,
"Sit in the place of honor at my right
hand
35 until I humble your enemies,
making them a footstool under your
feet."'*

36"So let everyone in Israel know for cer-
tain that God has made this Jesus, whom you
crucified, to be both Lord and Messiah!"
37Peter's words pierced their hearts, and
they said to him and to the other apostles,
"Brothers, what should we do?"
38Peter replied, "Each of you must repent
of your sins and turn to God, and be baptized
in the name of Jesus Christ for the forgive-
ness of your sins. Then you will receive
the gift of the Holy Spirit. 39This promise is
to you, and to your children, and even to
the Gentiles*—all who have been called by
the Lord our God." 40Then Peter continued
preaching for a long time, strongly urging
all his listeners, "Save yourselves from this
crooked generation!"
41Those who believed what Peter said were
baptized and added to the church that day—
about 3,000 in all.

The Believers Form a Community

42All the believers devoted themselves to the
apostles' teaching, and to fellowship, and to
sharing in meals (including the Lord's Sup-
per*), and to prayer.
43A deep sense of awe came over them all,
and the apostles performed many miraculous
signs and wonders. 44And all the believers
met together in one place and shared every-
thing they had. 45They sold their property and
possessions and shared the money with those
in need. 46They worshiped together at the
Temple each day, met in homes for the Lord's
Supper, and shared their meals with great joy
and generosity*—47all the while praising God
and enjoying the goodwill of all the people.
And each day the Lord added to their fellow-
ship those who were being saved.

CHAPTER 3

Peter Heals a Crippled Beggar

Peter and John went to the Temple one after-
noon to take part in the three o'clock prayer
service. 2As they approached the Temple, a
man lame from birth was being carried in.
Each day he was put beside the Temple gate,
the one called the Beautiful Gate, so he could
beg from the people going into the Temple.
3When he saw Peter and John about to enter,
he asked them for some money.
4Peter and John looked at him intently, and
Peter said, "Look at us!" 5The lame man
looked at them eagerly, expecting some
money. 6But Peter said, "I don't have any silver
or gold for you. But I'll give you what I have. In
the name of Jesus Christ the Nazarene,* get
up and* walk!"
7Then Peter took the lame man by the right
hand and helped him up. And as he did, the
man's feet and ankles were instantly healed
and strengthened. 8He jumped up, stood on
his feet, and began to walk! Then, walking,
leaping, and praising God, he went into the
Temple with them.
9All the people saw him walking and heard
him praising God. 10When they realized he
was the lame beggar they had seen so often at
the Beautiful Gate, they were absolutely as-
tounded! 11They all rushed out in amazement
to Solomon's Colonnade, where the man was
holding tightly to Peter and John.

Peter Preaches in the Temple

12Peter saw his opportunity and addressed
the crowd. "People of Israel," he said, "what is
so surprising about this? And why stare at us
as though we had made this man walk by our
own power or godliness? 13For it is the God of
Abraham, Isaac, and Jacob—the God of all our
ancestors—who has brought glory to his ser-
vant Jesus by doing this. This is the same Jesus
whom you handed over and rejected before
Pilate, despite Pilate's decision to release him.
14You rejected this holy, righteous one and in-

2:34-35 Ps 110:1. **2:39** Or *and to people far in the future;* Greek reads *and to those far away.* **2:42** Greek *the breaking of bread;* also in 2:46. **2:46** Or *and sincere hearts.* **3:6a** Or *Jesus Christ of Nazareth.* **3:6b** Some manuscripts do not include *get up and.*

stead demanded the release of a murderer.
15 You killed the author of life, but God raised
him from the dead. And we are witnesses of
this fact!

16 "Through faith in the name of Jesus, this
man was healed—and you know how crippled
he was before. Faith in Jesus' name has healed
him before your very eyes.

17 "Friends,* I realize that what you and
your leaders did to Jesus was done in igno-
rance. 18 But God was fulfilling what all the
prophets had foretold about the Messiah—
that he must suffer these things. 19 Now re-
pent of your sins and turn to God, so that your
sins may be wiped away. 20 Then times of re-
freshment will come from the presence of
the Lord, and he will again send you Jesus,
your appointed Messiah. 21 For he must re-
main in heaven until the time for the final
restoration of all things, as God promised
long ago through his holy prophets. 22 Moses
said, 'The LORD your God will raise up for you
a Prophet like me from among your own peo-
ple. Listen carefully to everything he tells
you.'* 23 Then Moses said, 'Anyone who will
not listen to that Prophet will be completely
cut off from God's people.'*

24 "Starting with Samuel, every prophet
spoke about what is happening today. 25 You
are the children of those prophets, and you
are included in the covenant God promised to
your ancestors. For God said to Abraham,
'Through your descendants* all the families
on earth will be blessed.' 26 When God raised
up his servant, Jesus, he sent him first to you
people of Israel, to bless you by turning each
of you back from your sinful ways."

CHAPTER 4

Peter and John before the Council

While Peter and John were speaking to the
people, they were confronted by the priests,
the captain of the Temple guard, and some
of the Sadducees. 2 These leaders were very
disturbed that Peter and John were teach-
ing the people that through Jesus there is a
resurrection of the dead. 3 They arrested
them and, since it was already evening, put
them in jail until morning. 4 But many of the
people who heard their message believed it,
so the number of believers now totaled
about 5,000 men, not counting women and
children.*

5 The next day the council of all the rulers
and elders and teachers of religious law met
in Jerusalem. 6 Annas the high priest was
there, along with Caiaphas, John, Alexander,
and other relatives of the high priest. 7 They
brought in the two disciples and demanded,
"By what power, or in whose name, have you
done this?"

8 Then Peter, filled with the Holy Spirit, said
to them, "Rulers and elders of our people,
9 are we being questioned today because
we've done a good deed for a crippled man?
Do you want to know how he was healed?
10 Let me clearly state to all of you and to all the
people of Israel that he was healed by the
powerful name of Jesus Christ the Nazarene,*
the man you crucified but whom God raised
from the dead. 11 For Jesus is the one referred
to in the Scriptures, where it says,

> 'The stone that you builders rejected
> has now become the cornerstone.'*

12 There is salvation in no one else! God has
given no other name under heaven by which
we must be saved."

13 The members of the council were
amazed when they saw the boldness of Peter
and John, for they could see that they were
ordinary men with no special training in the
Scriptures. They also recognized them as
men who had been with Jesus. 14 But since
they could see the man who had been healed
standing right there among them, there was
nothing the council could say. 15 So they or-
dered Peter and John out of the council
chamber* and conferred among them-
selves.

16 "What should we do with these men?"
they asked each other. "We can't deny that
they have performed a miraculous sign, and
everybody in Jerusalem knows about it. 17 But
to keep them from spreading their propa-
ganda any further, we must warn them not to
speak to anyone in Jesus' name again." 18 So
they called the apostles back in and com-
manded them never again to speak or teach
in the name of Jesus.

19 But Peter and John replied, "Do you think
God wants us to obey you rather than him?

3:17 Greek *Brothers.* **3:22** Deut 18:15. **3:23** Deut 18:19; Lev 23:29. **3:25** Greek *your seed;* see Gen 12:3; 22:18. **4:4** Greek *5,000 adult males.* **4:10** Or *Jesus Christ of Nazareth.* **4:11** Ps 118:22. **4:15** Greek *the Sanhedrin.*

The Phone Fib

"What a day! Everything went wrong at work and the boss is mad," Spencer's dad said at dinner. Spencer's mom mentioned that the pastor was going to call later to talk about the church budget. "Not tonight," said Dad. "No more problems today." As soon as Dad sat down, the phone rang. Spencer answered the phone, "Hello, Pastor Ted." In the background Spencer's dad shook his head no. "Dad? Well . . ." Spencer didn't know what to do. He didn't want to lie, but he didn't want to get his dad upset. What should Spencer do? Read Acts 5:29 for a clue.

[20]We cannot stop telling about everything we have seen and heard."

[21]The council then threatened them further, but they finally let them go because they didn't know how to punish them without starting a riot. For everyone was praising God [22]for this miraculous sign—the healing of a man who had been lame for more than forty years.

The Believers Pray for Courage

[23]As soon as they were freed, Peter and John returned to the other believers and told them what the leading priests and elders had said. [24]When they heard the report, all the believers lifted their voices together in prayer to God: "O Sovereign Lord, Creator of heaven and earth, the sea, and everything in them—[25]you spoke long ago by the Holy Spirit through our ancestor David, your servant, saying,

> 'Why were the nations so angry?
> Why did they waste their time with
> futile plans?
> [26] The kings of the earth prepared
> for battle;
> the rulers gathered together
> against the LORD
> and against his Messiah.'*

[27]"In fact, this has happened here in this very city! For Herod Antipas, Pontius Pilate the governor, the Gentiles, and the people of Israel were all united against Jesus, your holy servant, whom you anointed. [28]But everything they did was determined beforehand according to your will. [29]And now, O Lord, hear their threats, and give us, your servants, great boldness in preaching your word. [30]Stretch out your hand with healing power; may miraculous signs and wonders be done through the name of your holy servant Jesus."

[31]After this prayer, the meeting place shook, and they were all filled with the Holy Spirit. Then they preached the word of God with boldness.

The Believers Share Their Possessions

[32]All the believers were united in heart and mind. And they felt that what they owned was not their own, so they shared everything they had. [33]The apostles testified powerfully to the resurrection of the Lord Jesus, and God's great blessing was upon them all. [34]There were no needy people among them, because those who owned land or houses would sell them [35]and bring the money to the apostles to give to those in need.

4:25-26 Or *his anointed one;* or *his Christ*. Ps 2:1-2.

[36]For instance, there was Joseph, the one the apostles nicknamed Barnabas (which means "Son of Encouragement"). He was from the tribe of Levi and came from the island of Cyprus. [37]He sold a field he owned and brought the money to the apostles.

CHAPTER 5

Ananias and Sapphira

But there was a certain man named Ananias who, with his wife, Sapphira, sold some property. [2]He brought part of the money to the apostles, claiming it was the full amount. With his wife's consent, he kept the rest.

[3]Then Peter said, "Ananias, why have you let Satan fill your heart? You lied to the Holy Spirit, and you kept some of the money for yourself. [4]The property was yours to sell or not sell, as you wished. And after selling it, the money was also yours to give away. How could you do a thing like this? You weren't lying to us but to God!"

[5]As soon as Ananias heard these words, he fell to the floor and died. Everyone who heard about it was terrified. [6]Then some young men got up, wrapped him in a sheet, and took him out and buried him.

[7]About three hours later his wife came in, not knowing what had happened. [8]Peter asked her, "Was this the price you and your husband received for your land?"

"Yes," she replied, "that was the price."

[9]And Peter said, "How could the two of you even think of conspiring to test the Spirit of the Lord like this? The young men who buried your husband are just outside the door, and they will carry you out, too."

[10]Instantly, she fell to the floor and died. When the young men came in and saw that she was dead, they carried her out and buried her beside her husband. [11]Great fear gripped the entire church and everyone else who heard what had happened.

The Apostles Heal Many

[12]The apostles were performing many miraculous signs and wonders among the people. And all the believers were meeting regularly at the Temple in the area known as Solomon's Colonnade. [13]But no one else dared to join them, even though all the people had high regard for them. [14]Yet more and more people believed and were brought to the Lord—crowds of both men and women. [15]As a result of the apostles' work, sick people were brought out into the streets on beds and mats so that Peter's shadow might fall across some of them as he went by. [16]Crowds came from the villages around Jerusalem, bringing their sick and those possessed by evil* spirits, and they were all healed.

The Apostles Meet Opposition

[17]The high priest and his officials, who were Sadducees, were filled with jealousy. [18]They arrested the apostles and put them in the public jail. [19]But an angel of the Lord came at night, opened the gates of the jail, and brought them out. Then he told them, [20]"Go to the Temple and give the people this message of life!"

[21]So at daybreak the apostles entered the Temple, as they were told, and immediately began teaching.

When the high priest and his officials arrived, they convened the high council*—the full assembly of the elders of Israel. Then they sent for the apostles to be brought from the jail for trial. [22]But when the Temple guards went to the jail, the men were gone. So they returned to the council and reported, [23]"The jail was securely locked, with the guards standing outside, but when we opened the gates, no one was there!"

[24]When the captain of the Temple guard and the leading priests heard this, they were perplexed, wondering where it would all end. [25]Then someone arrived with startling news: "The men you put in jail are standing in the Temple, teaching the people!"

[26]The captain went with his Temple guards and arrested the apostles, but without violence, for they were afraid the people would stone them. [27]Then they brought the apostles before the high council, where the high priest confronted them. [28]"Didn't we tell you never again to teach in this man's name?" he demanded. "Instead, you have filled all Jerusalem with your teaching about him, and you want to make us responsible for his death!"

[29]But Peter and the apostles replied, "We

5:16 Greek *unclean.* **5:21** Greek *Sanhedrin;* also in 5:27, 41.

must obey God rather than any human authority. [30]The God of our ancestors raised Jesus from the dead after you killed him by hanging him on a cross.* [31]Then God put him in the place of honor at his right hand as Prince and Savior. He did this so the people of Israel would repent of their sins and be forgiven. [32]We are witnesses of these things and so is the Holy Spirit, who is given by God to those who obey him."

[33]When they heard this, the high council was furious and decided to kill them. [34]But one member, a Pharisee named Gamaliel, who was an expert in religious law and respected by all the people, stood up and ordered that the men be sent outside the council chamber for a while. [35]Then he said to his colleagues, "Men of Israel, take care what you are planning to do to these men! [36]Some time ago there was that fellow Theudas, who pretended to be someone great. About 400 others joined him, but he was killed, and all his followers went their various ways. The whole movement came to nothing. [37]After him, at the time of the census, there was Judas of Galilee. He got people to follow him, but he was killed, too, and all his followers were scattered.

[38]"So my advice is, leave these men alone. Let them go. If they are planning and doing these things merely on their own, it will soon be overthrown. [39]But if it is from God, you will not be able to overthrow them. You may even find yourselves fighting against God!"

[40]The others accepted his advice. They called in the apostles and had them flogged. Then they ordered them never again to speak in the name of Jesus, and they let them go.

[41]The apostles left the high council rejoicing that God had counted them worthy to suffer disgrace for the name of Jesus.* [42]And every day, in the Temple and from house to house, they continued to teach and preach this message: "Jesus is the Messiah."

What should I do if an adult tells me to do something I know is wrong?

We must obey God rather than any human authority. ACTS 5:29

CHAPTER 6

Seven Men Chosen to Serve

But as the believers* rapidly multiplied, there were rumblings of discontent. The Greek-speaking believers complained about the Herew-speaking believers, saying that their widows were being discriminated against in the daily distribution of food.

[2]So the Twelve called a meeting of all the believers. They said, "We apostles should spend our time teaching the word of God, not running a food program. [3]And so, brothers, select seven men who are well respected and are full of the Spirit and wisdom. We will give them this responsibility. [4]Then we apostles can spend our time in prayer and teaching the word."

[5]Everyone liked this idea, and they chose the following: Stephen (a man full of faith and the Holy Spirit), Philip, Procorus, Nicanor, Timon, Parmenas, and Nicolas of Antioch (an earlier convert to the Jewish faith). [6]These seven were presented to the apostles, who prayed for them as they laid their hands on them.

[7]So God's message continued to spread. The number of believers greatly increased in Jerusalem, and many of the Jewish priests were converted, too.

Stephen Is Arrested

[8]Stephen, a man full of God's grace and power, performed amazing miracles and signs among the people. [9]But one day some men from the Synagogue of Freed Slaves, as it was called, started to debate with him. They were Jews from Cyrene, Alexandria, Cilicia, and the province of Asia. [10]None of them could stand

5:30 Greek *on a tree.* **5:41** Greek *for the name.* **6:1** Greek *disciples;* also in 6:2, 7.

Stephen

When the disciples asked me to distribute food, I happily agreed. I wanted to help others, and that gave the disciples more time to tell people about Jesus. God worked wonders through me. I was surprised! But then some people told lies about me, accusing me of saying terrible things about God.

I'm in their power now. My life will be over soon. Yet I must speak the truth so they will understand why I trust Jesus and love him. I remind them about our ancestors, who saw God's miracles but disobeyed God over and over. The men are angry and throwing stones. But look . . . I see heaven opening! Jesus is standing there. Lord Jesus, receive me.

Read more about Stephen in Acts 6–7.

against the wisdom and the Spirit with which Stephen spoke.

11 So they persuaded some men to lie about Stephen, saying, "We heard him blaspheme Moses, and even God." 12 This roused the people, the elders, and the teachers of religious law. So they arrested Stephen and brought him before the high council.*

13 The lying witnesses said, "This man is always speaking against the holy Temple and against the law of Moses. 14 We have heard him say that this Jesus of Nazareth* will destroy the Temple and change the customs Moses handed down to us."

15 At this point everyone in the high council stared at Stephen, because his face became as bright as an angel's.

CHAPTER 7

Stephen Addresses the Council

Then the high priest asked Stephen, "Are these accusations true?"

2 This was Stephen's reply: "Brothers and fathers, listen to me. Our glorious God appeared to our ancestor Abraham in Mesopotamia before he settled in Haran.* 3 God told him, 'Leave your native land and your relatives, and come into the land that I will show you.'* 4 So Abraham left the land of the Chaldeans and lived in Haran until his father died. Then God brought him here to the land where you now live.

5 "But God gave him no inheritance here, not even one square foot of land. God did promise, however, that eventually the whole land would belong to Abraham and his descendants—even though he had no children yet. 6 God also told him that his descendants would live in a foreign land, where they would be oppressed as slaves for 400 years. 7 'But I will punish the nation that enslaves them,' God said, 'and in the end they will come out and worship me here in this place.'*

8 "God also gave Abraham the covenant of circumcision at that time. So when Abraham became the father of Isaac, he circumcised him on the eighth day. And the practice was continued when Isaac became the father of Jacob, and when Jacob became the father of the twelve patriarchs of the Israelite nation.

9 "These patriarchs were jealous of their brother Joseph, and they sold him to be a slave in Egypt. But God was with him 10 and rescued him from all his troubles. And God gave him favor before Pharaoh, king of Egypt. God also gave Joseph unusual wisdom, so that Pharaoh appointed him governor

6:12 Greek *Sanhedrin;* also in 6:15. **6:14** Or *Jesus the Nazarene.* **7:2** *Mesopotamia* was the region now called Iraq. *Haran* was a city in what is now called Syria. **7:3** Gen 12:1. **7:5-7** Gen 12:7; 15:13-14; Exod 3:12.

over all of Egypt and put him in charge of the palace.

11"But a famine came upon Egypt and Canaan. There was great misery, and our ancestors ran out of food. 12Jacob heard that there was still grain in Egypt, so he sent his sons—our ancestors—to buy some. 13The second time they went, Joseph revealed his identity to his brothers,* and they were introduced to Pharaoh. 14Then Joseph sent for his father, Jacob, and all his relatives to come to Egypt, seventy-five persons in all. 15So Jacob went to Egypt. He died there, as did our ancestors. 16Their bodies were taken to Shechem and buried in the tomb Abraham had bought for a certain price from Hamor's sons in Shechem.

17"As the time drew near when God would fulfill his promise to Abraham, the number of our people in Egypt greatly increased. 18But then a new king came to the throne of Egypt who knew nothing about Joseph. 19This king exploited our people and oppressed them, forcing parents to abandon their newborn babies so they would die.

20"At that time Moses was born—a beautiful child in God's eyes. His parents cared for him at home for three months. 21When they had to abandon him, Pharaoh's daughter adopted him and raised him as her own son. 22Moses was taught all the wisdom of the Egyptians, and he was powerful in both speech and action.

23"One day when Moses was forty years old, he decided to visit his relatives, the people of Israel. 24He saw an Egyptian mistreating an Israelite. So Moses came to the man's defense and avenged him, killing the Egyptian. 25Moses assumed his fellow Israelites would realize that God had sent him to rescue them, but they didn't.

26"The next day he visited them again and saw two men of Israel fighting. He tried to be a peacemaker. 'Men,' he said, 'you are brothers. Why are you fighting each other?'

27"But the man in the wrong pushed Moses aside. 'Who made you a ruler and judge over us?' he asked. 28'Are you going to kill me as you killed that Egyptian yesterday?' 29When Moses heard that, he fled the country and lived as a foreigner in the land of Midian. There his two sons were born.

30"Forty years later, in the desert near Mount Sinai, an angel appeared to Moses in the flame of a burning bush. 31When Moses saw it, he was amazed at the sight. As he went to take a closer look, the voice of the LORD called out to him, 32'I am the God of your ancestors—the God of Abraham, Isaac, and Jacob.' Moses shook with terror and did not dare to look.

33"Then the LORD said to him, 'Take off your sandals, for you are standing on holy ground. 34I have certainly seen the oppression of my people in Egypt. I have heard their groans and have come down to rescue them. Now go, for I am sending you back to Egypt.'*

35"So God sent back the same man his people had previously rejected when they demanded, 'Who made you a ruler and judge over us?' Through the angel who appeared to him in the burning bush, God sent Moses to be their ruler and savior. 36And by means of many wonders and miraculous signs, he led them out of Egypt, through the Red Sea, and through the wilderness for forty years.

37"Moses himself told the people of Israel, 'God will raise up for you a Prophet like me from among your own people.'* 38Moses was with our ancestors, the assembly of God's people in the wilderness, when the angel spoke to him at Mount Sinai. And there Moses received life-giving words to pass on to us.*

39"But our ancestors refused to listen to Moses. They rejected him and wanted to return to Egypt. 40They told Aaron, 'Make us some gods who can lead us, for we don't know what has become of this Moses, who brought us out of Egypt.' 41So they made an idol shaped like a calf, and they sacrificed to it and celebrated over this thing they had made. 42Then God turned away from them and abandoned them to serve the stars of heaven as their gods! In the book of the prophets it is written,

'Was it to me you were bringing sacrifices
and offerings
during those forty years in the
wilderness, Israel?
43 No, you carried your pagan gods—
the shrine of Molech,
the star of your god Rephan,

7:13 Other manuscripts read *Joseph was recognized by his brothers.* **7:31-34** Exod 3:5-10. **7:37** Deut 18:15. **7:38** Some manuscripts read *to you.*

Growing up in church I had always heard about Christians in other countries being persecuted and facing opposition because of their public witness for Christ. I never thought it would happen to me.

Last year my principal tried to stop our Christian club from meeting at our high school. He said our club was too controversial. He wanted us to either stop meeting or become an "interfaith club" where all religions were presented and discussed equally.

The student club leaders and I felt like Stephen must have felt when he stood before the Jewish leaders in Acts 7. At first we didn't know what to do, but we prayed and asked for help from a lawyer who explained our legal rights to express and practice our faith in school.

God gave us the same kind of courage Stephen had when he boldly told the story of Jesus. We met with our principal and stood up for our legal rights to start and lead a Christian club in our school.

Since that day our club has grown to be one of the largest clubs in the school. Every week we are talking with more and more of our classmates about Jesus. Our principal now supports us when other people criticize us. Sometimes he even attends the weekly meeting.

This has been a year of big changes for me. The Holy Spirit has given me courage and strength to stand up for what I believe. I go to school every day very proud to be a Christian.

For more on standing up to persecution, read Ezekiel 2:6; Acts 7:54-59; and Philippians 1:27-28.

and the images you made to worship
them.
So I will send you into exile
as far away as Babylon.'*

44"Our ancestors carried the Tabernacle* with them through the wilderness. It was constructed according to the plan God had shown to Moses. 45Years later, when Joshua led our ancestors in battle against the nations that God drove out of this land, the Tabernacle was taken with them into their new territory. And it stayed there until the time of King David.

46"David found favor with God and asked for the privilege of building a permanent Temple for the God of Jacob.* 47But it was Solomon who actually built it. 48However, the Most High doesn't live in temples made by human hands. As the prophet says,

49 'Heaven is my throne,
and the earth is my footstool.
Could you build me a temple as good
as that?'
asks the LORD.
'Could you build me such a resting place?
50 Didn't my hands make both heaven and
earth?'*

51"You stubborn people! You are heathen* at heart and deaf to the truth. Must you forever resist the Holy Spirit? That's what your ancestors did, and so do you! 52Name one prophet your ancestors didn't persecute! They even killed the ones who predicted the coming of the Righteous One—the Messiah whom you betrayed and murdered. 53You deliberately disobeyed God's law, even though you received it from the hands of angels."

54The Jewish leaders were infuriated by Stephen's accusation, and they shook their fists at him in rage.* 55But Stephen, full of the Holy Spirit, gazed steadily into heaven and saw the glory of God, and he saw Jesus standing in the place of honor at God's right hand. 56And he told them, "Look, I see the heavens opened and the Son of Man standing in the place of honor at God's right hand!"

57Then they put their hands over their ears and began shouting. They rushed at him 58and dragged him out of the city and began to stone him. His accusers took off their coats and laid them at the feet of a young man named Saul.*

59As they stoned him, Stephen prayed, "Lord Jesus, receive my spirit." 60He fell to his knees, shouting, "Lord, don't charge them with this sin!" And with that, he died.

CHAPTER 8

Saul was one of the witnesses, and he agreed completely with the killing of Stephen.

Persecution Scatters the Believers

A great wave of persecution began that day, sweeping over the church in Jerusalem; and all the believers except the apostles were scattered through the regions of Judea and Samaria. 2(Some devout men came and buried Stephen with great mourning.) 3But Saul was going everywhere to destroy the church. He went from house to house, dragging out both men and women to throw them into prison.

Philip Preaches in Samaria

4But the believers who were scattered preached the Good News about Jesus wherever they went. 5Philip, for example, went to the city of Samaria and told the people there about the Messiah. 6Crowds listened intently to Philip because they were eager to hear his message and see the miraculous signs he did. 7Many evil* spirits were cast out, screaming as they left their victims. And many who had been paralyzed or lame were healed. 8So there was great joy in that city.

9A man named Simon had been a sorcerer there for many years, amazing the people of Samaria and claiming to be someone great. 10Everyone, from the least to the greatest, often spoke of him as "the Great One—the Power of God." 11They listened closely to him because for a long time he had astounded them with his magic.

12But now the people believed Philip's message of Good News concerning the Kingdom of God and the name of Jesus Christ. As a result, many men and women were baptized. 13Then Simon himself believed and was baptized. He began following Philip wherever he went, and he was amazed by the signs and great miracles Philip performed.

7:42-43 Amos 5:25-27 (Greek version). **7:44** Greek *the tent of witness*. **7:46** Some manuscripts read *the house of Jacob*. **7:49-50** Isa 66:1-2. **7:51** Greek *uncircumcised*. **7:54** Greek *they were grinding their teeth against him*. **7:58** *Saul* is later called Paul; see 13:9. **8:7** Greek *unclean*.

[14]When the apostles in Jerusalem heard that the people of Samaria had accepted God's message, they sent Peter and John there. [15]As soon as they arrived, they prayed for these new believers to receive the Holy Spirit. [16]The Holy Spirit had not yet come upon any of them, for they had only been baptized in the name of the Lord Jesus. [17]Then Peter and John laid their hands upon these believers, and they received the Holy Spirit.

[18]When Simon saw that the Spirit was given when the apostles laid their hands on people, he offered them money to buy this power. [19]"Let me have this power, too," he exclaimed, "so that when I lay my hands on people, they will receive the Holy Spirit!"

[20]But Peter replied, "May your money be destroyed with you for thinking God's gift can be bought! [21]You can have no part in this, for your heart is not right with God. [22]Repent of your wickedness and pray to the Lord. Perhaps he will forgive your evil thoughts, [23]for I can see that you are full of bitter jealousy and are held captive by sin."

[24]"Pray to the Lord for me," Simon exclaimed, "that these terrible things you've said won't happen to me!"

[25]After testifying and preaching the word of the Lord in Samaria, Peter and John returned to Jerusalem. And they stopped in many Samaritan villages along the way to preach the Good News.

Philip and the Ethiopian Eunuch

[26]As for Philip, an angel of the Lord said to him, "Go south* down the desert road that runs from Jerusalem to Gaza." [27]So he started out, and he met the treasurer of Ethiopia, a eunuch of great authority under the Kandake, the queen of Ethiopia. The eunuch had gone to Jerusalem to worship, [28]and he was now returning. Seated in his carriage, he was reading aloud from the book of the prophet Isaiah.

[29]The Holy Spirit said to Philip, "Go over and walk along beside the carriage."

[30]Philip ran over and heard the man reading from the prophet Isaiah. Philip asked, "Do you understand what you are reading?"

[31]The man replied, "How can I, unless someone instructs me?" And he urged Philip to come up into the carriage and sit with him.

[32]The passage of Scripture he had been reading was this:

"He was led like a sheep to the slaughter.
And as a lamb is silent before the shearers,
he did not open his mouth.
[33] He was humiliated and received no justice.
Who can speak of his descendants?
For his life was taken from the earth."*

[34]The eunuch asked Philip, "Tell me, was the prophet talking about himself or someone else?" [35]So beginning with this same Scripture, Philip told him the Good News about Jesus.

[36]As they rode along, they came to some water, and the eunuch said, "Look! There's some water! Why can't I be baptized?"* [38]He ordered the carriage to stop, and they went down into the water, and Philip baptized him.

[39]When they came up out of the water, the Spirit of the Lord snatched Philip away. The eunuch never saw him again but went on his way rejoicing. [40]Meanwhile, Philip found himself farther north at the town of Azotus. He preached the Good News there and in every town along the way until he came to Caesarea.

CHAPTER 9

Saul's Conversion

Meanwhile, Saul was uttering threats with every breath and was eager to kill the Lord's followers.* So he went to the high priest. [2]He requested letters addressed to the synagogues in Damascus, asking for their cooperation in the arrest of any followers of the Way he found there. He wanted to bring them—both men and women—back to Jerusalem in chains.

[3]As he was approaching Damascus on this mission, a light from heaven suddenly shone down around him. [4]He fell to the ground and heard a voice saying to him, "Saul! Saul! Why are you persecuting me?"

[5]"Who are you, lord?" Saul asked.

And the voice replied, "I am Jesus, the one you are persecuting! [6]Now get up and go into the city, and you will be told what you must do."

[7]The men with Saul stood speechless, for they heard the sound of someone's voice but

8:26 Or *Go at noon.* **8:32-33** Isa 53:7-8 (Greek version). **8:36** Some manuscripts add verse 37, *"You can," Philip answered, "if you believe with all your heart." And the eunuch replied, "I believe that Jesus Christ is the Son of God."* **9:1** Greek *disciples.*

saw no one! [8]Saul picked himself up off the ground, but when he opened his eyes he was blind. So his companions led him by the hand to Damascus. [9]He remained there blind for three days and did not eat or drink.

[10]Now there was a believer* in Damascus named Ananias. The Lord spoke to him in a vision, calling, "Ananias!"

"Yes, Lord!" he replied.

[11]The Lord said, "Go over to Straight Street, to the house of Judas. When you get there, ask for a man from Tarsus named Saul. He is praying to me right now. [12]I have shown him a vision of a man named Ananias coming in and laying hands on him so he can see again."

[13]"But Lord," exclaimed Ananias, "I've heard many people talk about the terrible things this man has done to the believers* in Jerusalem! [14]And he is authorized by the leading priests to arrest everyone who calls upon your name."

[15]But the Lord said, "Go, for Saul is my chosen instrument to take my message to the Gentiles and to kings, as well as to the people of Israel. [16]And I will show him how much he must suffer for my name's sake."

[17]So Ananias went and found Saul. He laid his hands on him and said, "Brother Saul, the Lord Jesus, who appeared to you on the road, has sent me so that you might regain your sight and be filled with the Holy Spirit." [18]Instantly something like scales fell from Saul's eyes, and he regained his sight. Then he got up and was baptized. [19]Afterward he ate some food and regained his strength.

Saul in Damascus and Jerusalem

Saul stayed with the believers* in Damascus for a few days. [20]And immediately he began preaching about Jesus in the synagogues, saying, "He is indeed the Son of God!"

[21]All who heard him were amazed. "Isn't this the same man who caused such devastation among Jesus' followers in Jerusalem?" they asked. "And didn't he come here to arrest them and take them in chains to the leading priests?"

[22]Saul's preaching became more and more powerful, and the Jews in Damascus couldn't refute his proofs that Jesus was indeed the Messiah. [23]After a while some of the Jews plotted together to kill him. [24]They were watching for him day and night at the city gate so they could murder him, but Saul was told about their plot. [25]So during the night, some of the other believers* lowered him in a large basket through an opening in the city wall.

[26]When Saul arrived in Jerusalem, he tried to meet with the believers, but they were all afraid of him. They did not believe he had truly become a believer! [27]Then Barnabas brought him to the apostles and told them how Saul had seen the Lord on the way to Damascus and how the Lord had spoken to Saul. He also told them that Saul had preached boldly in the name of Jesus in Damascus.

[28]So Saul stayed with the apostles and went all around Jerusalem with them, preaching boldly in the name of the Lord. [29]He debated with some Greek-speaking Jews, but they tried to murder him. [30]When the believers* heard about this, they took him down to Caesarea and sent him away to Tarsus, his hometown.

[31]The church then had peace throughout Judea, Galilee, and Samaria, and it became stronger as the believers lived in the fear of the Lord. And with the encouragement of the Holy Spirit, it also grew in numbers.

Peter Heals Aeneas and Raises Dorcas

[32]Meanwhile, Peter traveled from place to place, and he came down to visit the believers in the town of Lydda. [33]There he met a man named Aeneas, who had been paralyzed and bedridden for eight years. [34]Peter said to him, "Aeneas, Jesus Christ heals you! Get up, and roll up your sleeping mat!" And he was healed instantly. [35]Then the whole population of Lydda and Sharon saw Aeneas walking around, and they turned to the Lord.

[36]There was a believer in Joppa named Tabitha (which in Greek is Dorcas*). She was always doing kind things for others and helping the poor. [37]About this time she became ill and died. Her body was washed for burial and laid in an upstairs room. [38]But the believers had heard that Peter was nearby at Lydda, so they sent two men to beg him, "Please come as soon as possible!"

[39]So Peter returned with them; and as soon

9:10 Greek *disciple;* also in 9:26, 36. **9:13** Greek *God's holy people;* also in 9:32, 41. **9:19** Greek *disciples;* also in 9:26, 38. **9:25** Greek *his disciples.* **9:30** Greek *brothers.* **9:36** The names *Tabitha* in Aramaic and *Dorcas* in Greek both mean "gazelle."

as he arrived, they took him to the upstairs room. The room was filled with widows who were weeping and showing him the coats and other clothes Dorcas had made for them. [40]But Peter asked them all to leave the room; then he knelt and prayed. Turning to the body he said, "Get up, Tabitha." And she opened her eyes! When she saw Peter, she sat up! [41]He gave her his hand and helped her up. Then he called in the widows and all the believers, and he presented her to them alive.

[42]The news spread through the whole town, and many believed in the Lord. [43]And Peter stayed a long time in Joppa, living with Simon, a tanner of hides.

CHAPTER 10

Cornelius Calls for Peter

In Caesarea there lived a Roman army officer* named Cornelius, who was a captain of the Italian Regiment. [2]He was a devout, God-fearing man, as was everyone in his household. He gave generously to the poor and prayed regularly to God. [3]One afternoon about three o'clock, he had a vision in which he saw an angel of God coming toward him. "Cornelius!" the angel said.

[4]Cornelius stared at him in terror. "What is it, sir?" he asked the angel.

And the angel replied, "Your prayers and gifts to the poor have been received by God as an offering! [5]Now send some men to Joppa, and summon a man named Simon Peter. [6]He is staying with Simon, a tanner who lives near the seashore."

[7]As soon as the angel was gone, Cornelius called two of his household servants and a devout soldier, one of his personal attendants. [8]He told them what had happened and sent them off to Joppa.

Peter Visits Cornelius

[9]The next day as Cornelius's messengers were nearing the town, Peter went up on the flat roof to pray. It was about noon, [10]and he was hungry. But while a meal was being prepared, he fell into a trance. [11]He saw the sky open, and something like a large sheet was let down by its four corners. [12]In the sheet were all sorts of animals, reptiles, and birds. [13]Then a

10:1 Greek *a centurion;* similarly in 10:22.

IS IT OK?

IS IT OK TO AVOID PEOPLE WHO ARE DIFFERENT FROM ME?

Back in Peter's day Jewish people were pretty exclusive. They didn't hang out with anyone except other Jews, and they were even picky about which of their own people they liked. But then God taught Peter a lesson that he wants us to learn too: We should never "think of anyone as impure" (see Acts 10:28). Sometimes we feel uncomfortable around people who are different from us. Maybe they dress differently, talk funny, and look a little weird to us. (They probably think we're weird too.) But God wants us to be friendly and accept them just as they are. When you befriend someone of a different background or race, you discover that you have more in common than you thought.

voice said to him, "Get up, Peter; kill and eat them."

[14]"No, Lord," Peter declared. "I have never eaten anything that our Jewish laws have declared impure and unclean.*"

[15]But the voice spoke again: "Do not call something unclean if God has made it clean." [16]The same vision was repeated three times. Then the sheet was suddenly pulled up to heaven.

[17]Peter was very perplexed. What could the vision mean? Just then the men sent by Cornelius found Simon's house. Standing outside the gate, [18]they asked if a man named Simon Peter was staying there.

[19]Meanwhile, as Peter was puzzling over the vision, the Holy Spirit said to him, "Three men have come looking for you. [20]Get up, go downstairs, and go with them without hesitation. Don't worry, for I have sent them."

[21]So Peter went down and said, "I'm the man you are looking for. Why have you come?"

[22]They said, "We were sent by Cornelius, a Roman officer. He is a devout and God-fearing man, well respected by all the Jews. A holy angel instructed him to summon you to his house so that he can hear your message." [23]So Peter invited the men to stay for the night. The next day he went with them, accompanied by some of the brothers from Joppa.

[24]They arrived in Caesarea the following day. Cornelius was waiting for them and had called together his relatives and close friends. [25]As Peter entered his home, Cornelius fell at his feet and worshiped him. [26]But Peter pulled him up and said, "Stand up! I'm a human being just like you!" [27]So they talked together and went inside, where many others were assembled.

[28]Peter told them, "You know it is against our laws for a Jewish man to enter a Gentile home like this or to associate with you. But God has shown me that I should no longer think of anyone as impure or unclean. [29]So I came without objection as soon as I was sent for. Now tell me why you sent for me."

[30]Cornelius replied, "Four days ago I was praying in my house about this same time, three o'clock in the afternoon. Suddenly, a man in dazzling clothes was standing in front of me. [31]He told me, 'Cornelius, your prayer has been heard, and your gifts to the poor have been noticed by God! [32]Now send messengers to Joppa, and summon a man named Simon Peter. He is staying in the home of Simon, a tanner who lives near the seashore.' [33]So I sent for you at once, and it was good of you to come. Now we are all here, waiting before God to hear the message the Lord has given you."

The Gentiles Hear the Good News

[34]Then Peter replied, "I see very clearly that God shows no favoritism. [35]In every nation he accepts those who fear him and do what is right. [36]This is the message of Good News for the people of Israel—that there is peace with God through Jesus Christ, who is Lord of all. [37]You know what happened throughout Judea, beginning in Galilee, after John began preaching his message of baptism. [38]And you know that God anointed Jesus of Nazareth with the Holy Spirit and with power. Then Jesus went around doing good and healing all who were oppressed by the devil, for God was with him.

[39]"And we apostles are witnesses of all he did throughout Judea and in Jerusalem. They put him to death by hanging him on a cross,* [40]but God raised him to life on the third day. Then God allowed him to appear, [41]not to the general public,* but to us whom God had chosen in advance to be his witnesses. We were those who ate and drank with him after he rose from the dead. [42]And he ordered us to preach everywhere and to testify that Jesus is the one appointed by God to be the judge of all—the living and the dead. [43]He is the one all the prophets testified about, saying that everyone who believes in him will have their sins forgiven through his name."

The Gentiles Receive the Holy Spirit

[44]Even as Peter was saying these things, the Holy Spirit fell upon all who were listening to the message. [45]The Jewish believers* who came with Peter were amazed that the gift of the Holy Spirit had been poured out on the Gentiles, too. [46]For they heard them speaking in other tongues* and praising God.

Then Peter asked, [47]"Can anyone object to their being baptized, now that they have received the Holy Spirit just as we did?" [48]So he

10:14 Greek *anything common and unclean.* **10:39** Greek *on a tree.* **10:41** Greek *the people.* **10:45** Greek *The faithful ones of the circumcision.* **10:46** Or *in other languages.*

gave orders for them to be baptized in the name of Jesus Christ. Afterward Cornelius asked him to stay with them for several days.

CHAPTER 11

Peter Explains His Actions

Soon the news reached the apostles and other
believers* in Judea that the Gentiles had re-
ceived the word of God. [2]But when Peter ar-
rived back in Jerusalem, the Jewish believers*
criticized him. [3]"You entered the home of
Gentiles* and even ate with them!" they said.

[4]Then Peter told them exactly what had
happened. [5]"I was in the town of Joppa," he
said, "and while I was praying, I went into a
trance and saw a vision. Something like a
large sheet was let down by its four corners
from the sky. And it came right down to me.
[6]When I looked inside the sheet, I saw all sorts
of tame and wild animals, reptiles, and birds.
[7]And I heard a voice say, 'Get up, Peter; kill and
eat them.'

[8]"'No, Lord,' I replied. 'I have never eaten
anything that our Jewish laws have declared
impure or unclean.*'

[9]"But the voice from heaven spoke again:
'Do not call something unclean if God has
made it clean.' [10]This happened three times
before the sheet and all it contained was
pulled back up to heaven.

[11]"Just then three men who had been sent
from Caesarea arrived at the house where we
were staying. [12]The Holy Spirit told me to go
with them and not to worry that they were
Gentiles. These six brothers here accompa-
nied me, and we soon entered the home of
the man who had sent for us. [13]He told us how
an angel had appeared to him in his home and
had told him, 'Send messengers to Joppa, and
summon a man named Simon Peter. [14]He will
tell you how you and everyone in your house-
hold can be saved!'

[15]"As I began to speak," Peter continued,
"the Holy Spirit fell on them, just as he fell on
us at the beginning. [16]Then I thought of the
Lord's words when he said, 'John baptized
with* water, but you will be baptized with the
Holy Spirit.' [17]And since God gave these
Gentiles the same gift he gave us when we be-
lieved in the Lord Jesus Christ, who was I to
stand in God's way?"

[18]When the others heard this, they stopped
objecting and began praising God. They said,
"We can see that God has also given the
Gentiles the privilege of repenting of their
sins and receiving eternal life."

The Church in Antioch of Syria

[19]Meanwhile, the believers who had been scat-
tered during the persecution after Stephen's
death traveled as far as Phoenicia, Cyprus, and
Antioch of Syria. They preached the word of
God, but only to Jews. [20]However, some of the
believers who went to Antioch from Cyprus
and Cyrene began preaching to the Gentiles*
about the Lord Jesus. [21]The power of the Lord
was with them, and a large number of these
Gentiles believed and turned to the Lord.

[22]When the church at Jerusalem heard
what had happened, they sent Barnabas to
Antioch. [23]When he arrived and saw this evi-
dence of God's blessing, he was filled with joy,
and he encouraged the believers to stay true
to the Lord. [24]Barnabas was a good man, full
of the Holy Spirit and strong in faith. And
many people were brought to the Lord.

[25]Then Barnabas went on to Tarsus to look
for Saul. [26]When he found him, he brought
him back to Antioch. Both of them stayed
there with the church for a full year, teaching
large crowds of people. (It was at Antioch that
the believers* were first called Christians.)

[27]During this time some prophets traveled
from Jerusalem to Antioch. [28]One of them
named Agabus stood up in one of the meet-
ings and predicted by the Spirit that a great
famine was coming upon the entire Roman
world. (This was fulfilled during the reign of
Claudius.) [29]So the believers in Antioch de-
cided to send relief to the brothers and sis-
ters* in Judea, everyone giving as much as
they could. [30]This they did, entrusting their
gifts to Barnabas and Saul to take to the elders
of the church in Jerusalem.

CHAPTER 12

James Is Killed and Peter Is Imprisoned

About that time King Herod Agrippa* began
to persecute some believers in the church.

11:1 Greek *brothers*. **11:2** Greek *those of the circumcision*. **11:3** Greek *of uncircumcised men*. **11:8** Greek *anything common or unclean*. **11:16** Or *in*; also in 11:16b. **11:20** Greek *the Hellenists* (i.e., those who speak Greek); other manuscripts read *the Greeks*. **11:26** Greek *disciples*; also in 11:29. **11:29** Greek *the brothers*. **12:1** Greek *Herod the king*. He was the nephew of Herod Antipas and a grandson of Herod the Great.

[2]He had the apostle James (John's brother) killed with a sword. [3]When Herod saw how much this pleased the Jewish people, he also arrested Peter. (This took place during the Passover celebration.*) [4]Then he imprisoned him, placing him under the guard of four squads of four soldiers each. Herod intended to bring Peter out for public trial after the Passover. [5]But while Peter was in prison, the church prayed very earnestly for him.

AMAZING FACTS

Could a chained prisoner guarded by soldiers break out of a locked Roman prison? Peter did—with a little help from an angel!

ACTS 12:6-19

Peter's Miraculous Escape from Prison

[6]The night before Peter was to be placed on trial, he was asleep, fastened with two chains between two soldiers. Others stood guard at the prison gate. [7]Suddenly, there was a bright light in the cell, and an angel of the Lord stood before Peter. The angel struck him on the side to awaken him and said, "Quick! Get up!" And the chains fell off his wrists. [8]Then the angel told him, "Get dressed and put on your sandals." And he did. "Now put on your coat and follow me," the angel ordered.

[9]So Peter left the cell, following the angel. But all the time he thought it was a vision. He didn't realize it was actually happening. [10]They passed the first and second guard posts and came to the iron gate leading to the city, and this opened for them all by itself. So they passed through and started walking down the street, and then the angel suddenly left him.

[11]Peter finally came to his senses. "It's really true!" he said. "The Lord has sent his angel and saved me from Herod and from what the Jewish leaders* had planned to do to me!"

[12]When he realized this, he went to the home of Mary, the mother of John Mark, where many were gathered for prayer. [13]He knocked at the door in the gate, and a servant girl named Rhoda came to open it. [14]When she recognized Peter's voice, she was so overjoyed that, instead of opening the door, she ran back inside and told everyone, "Peter is standing at the door!"

[15]"You're out of your mind!" they said. When she insisted, they decided, "It must be his angel."

[16]Meanwhile, Peter continued knocking. When they finally opened the door and saw him, they were amazed. [17]He motioned for them to quiet down and told them how the Lord had led him out of prison. "Tell James and the other brothers what happened," he said. And then he went to another place.

[18]At dawn there was a great commotion among the soldiers about what had happened to Peter. [19]Herod Agrippa ordered a thorough search for him. When he couldn't be found, Herod interrogated the guards and sentenced them to death. Afterward Herod left Judea to stay in Caesarea for a while.

The Death of Herod Agrippa

[20]Now Herod was very angry with the people of Tyre and Sidon. So they sent a delegation to make peace with him because their cities were dependent upon Herod's country for food. The delegates won the support of Blastus, Herod's personal assistant, [21]and an appointment with Herod was granted. When the day arrived, Herod put on his royal robes, sat on his throne, and made a speech to them. [22]The people gave him a great ovation, shouting, "It's the voice of a god, not of a man!"

[23]Instantly, an angel of the Lord struck Herod with a sickness, because he accepted the people's worship instead of giving the glory to God. So he was consumed with worms and died.

[24]Meanwhile, the word of God continued to spread, and there were many new believers.

[25]When Barnabas and Saul had finished their mission to Jerusalem, they returned,* taking John Mark with them.

12:3 Greek *the days of unleavened bread.* **12:11** Or *the Jewish people.* **12:25** Or *mission, they returned to Jerusalem.* Other manuscripts read *mission, they returned from Jerusalem;* still others read *mission, they returned from Jerusalem to Antioch.*

CHAPTER 13

Barnabas and Saul Are Commissioned

Among the prophets and teachers of the church at Antioch of Syria were Barnabas, Simeon (called "the black man"*), Lucius (from Cyrene), Manaen (the childhood companion of King Herod Antipas*), and Saul. [2]One day as these men were worshiping the Lord and fasting, the Holy Spirit said, "Dedicate Barnabas and Saul for the special work to which I have called them." [3]So after more fasting and prayer, the men laid their hands on them and sent them on their way.

Paul's First Missionary Journey

[4]So Barnabas and Saul were sent out by the Holy Spirit. They went down to the seaport of Seleucia and then sailed for the island of Cyprus. [5]There, in the town of Salamis, they went to the Jewish synagogues and preached the word of God. John Mark went with them as their assistant.

[6]Afterward they traveled from town to town across the entire island until finally they reached Paphos, where they met a Jewish sorcerer, a false prophet named Bar-Jesus. [7]He had attached himself to the governor, Sergius Paulus, who was an intelligent man. The governor invited Barnabas and Saul to visit him, for he wanted to hear the word of God. [8]But Elymas, the sorcerer (as his name means in Greek), interfered and urged the governor to pay no attention to what Barnabas and Saul said. He was trying to keep the governor from believing.

[9]Saul, also known as Paul, was filled with the Holy Spirit, and he looked the sorcerer in the eye. [10]Then he said, "You son of the devil, full of every sort of deceit and fraud, and enemy of all that is good! Will you never stop perverting the true ways of the Lord? [11]Watch now, for the Lord has laid his hand of punishment upon you, and you will be struck blind. You will not see the sunlight for some time." Instantly mist and darkness came over the man's eyes, and he began groping around begging for someone to take his hand and lead him.

[12]When the governor saw what had happened, he became a believer, for he was astonished at the teaching about the Lord.

JOHN MARK

I was a young man when I learned about Jesus. I wanted to tell others about him, so I went on a missionary trip with Paul and Barnabas. But I got homesick and left.

Later, Barnabas suggested that I go on another journey. Paul said he didn't want me along. So Barnabas and Paul split up. I went to Cyprus with Barnabas; Silas went to Macedonia with Paul. I caused a split between two friends. It's not what I wanted, though twice as many people learned about Jesus. So God brought something good from my mistake. And Paul forgave me, asking me to come to him later when he was in prison.

You can find out more about John Mark in Acts 12:25–13:13; 15:36-41; 2 Timothy 4:11.

Paul Preaches in Antioch of Pisidia

[13]Paul and his companions then left Paphos by ship for Pamphylia, landing at the port town of Perga. There John Mark left them and returned to Jerusalem. [14]But Paul and Barnabas traveled inland to Antioch of Pisidia.*

13:1a Greek *who was called Niger*. **13:1b** Greek *Herod the tetrarch*. **13:13-14** *Pamphylia* and *Pisidia* were districts in what is now Turkey.

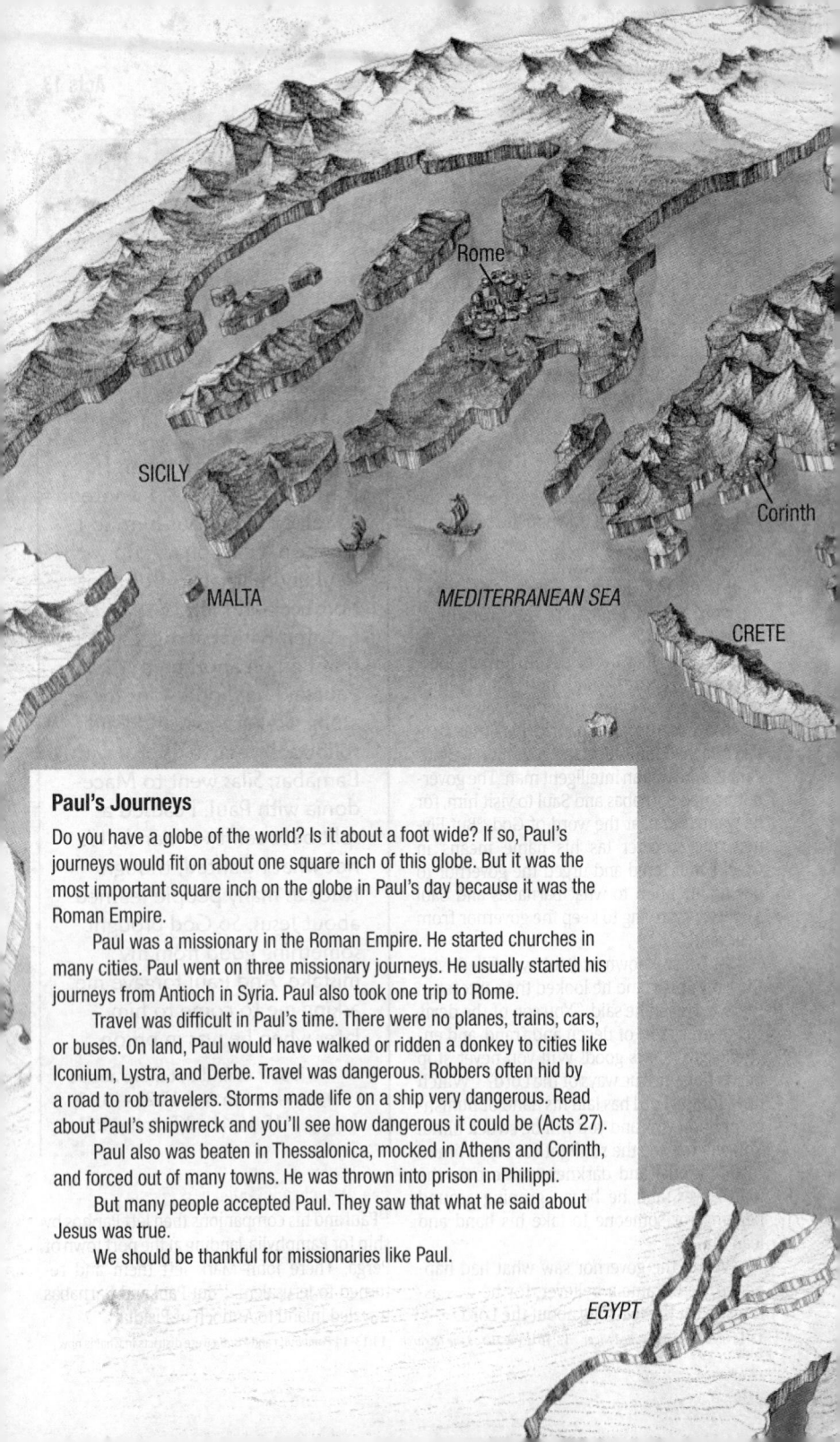

Paul's Journeys

Do you have a globe of the world? Is it about a foot wide? If so, Paul's journeys would fit on about one square inch of this globe. But it was the most important square inch on the globe in Paul's day because it was the Roman Empire.

Paul was a missionary in the Roman Empire. He started churches in many cities. Paul went on three missionary journeys. He usually started his journeys from Antioch in Syria. Paul also took one trip to Rome.

Travel was difficult in Paul's time. There were no planes, trains, cars, or buses. On land, Paul would have walked or ridden a donkey to cities like Iconium, Lystra, and Derbe. Travel was dangerous. Robbers often hid by a road to rob travelers. Storms made life on a ship very dangerous. Read about Paul's shipwreck and you'll see how dangerous it could be (Acts 27).

Paul also was beaten in Thessalonica, mocked in Athens and Corinth, and forced out of many towns. He was thrown into prison in Philippi.

But many people accepted Paul. They saw that what he said about Jesus was true.

We should be thankful for missionaries like Paul.

Philippi
Thessalonica
Troas
Athens
Iconium
Antioch in
PISIDIA
Lystra
Ephesus
Derbe
Perga
CYPRUS
Salamis
Antioch
Paphos
Ptolemais
Caesarea
ISRAEL

On the Sabbath they went to the synagogue for the services. [15]After the usual readings from the books of Moses* and the prophets, those in charge of the service sent them this message: "Brothers, if you have any word of encouragement for the people, come and give it."

[16]So Paul stood, lifted his hand to quiet them, and started speaking. "Men of Israel," he said, "and you God-fearing Gentiles, listen to me.

[17]"The God of this nation of Israel chose our ancestors and made them multiply and grow strong during their stay in Egypt. Then with a powerful arm he led them out of their slavery. [18]He put up with them* through forty years of wandering in the wilderness. [19]Then he destroyed seven nations in Canaan and gave their land to Israel as an inheritance. [20]All this took about 450 years.

"After that, God gave them judges to rule until the time of Samuel the prophet. [21]Then the people begged for a king, and God gave them Saul son of Kish, a man of the tribe of Benjamin, who reigned for forty years. [22]But God removed Saul and replaced him with David, a man about whom God said, 'I have found David son of Jesse, a man after my own heart. He will do everything I want him to do.'*

[23]"And it is one of King David's descendants, Jesus, who is God's promised Savior of Israel! [24]Before he came, John the Baptist preached that all the people of Israel needed to repent of their sins and turn to God and be baptized. [25]As John was finishing his ministry he asked, 'Do you think I am the Messiah? No, I am not! But he is coming soon—and I'm not even worthy to be his slave and untie the sandals on his feet.'

[26]"Brothers—you sons of Abraham, and also you God-fearing Gentiles—this message of salvation has been sent to us! [27]The people in Jerusalem and their leaders did not recognize Jesus as the one the prophets had spoken about. Instead, they condemned him, and in doing this they fulfilled the prophets' words that are read every Sabbath. [28]They found no legal reason to execute him, but they asked Pilate to have him killed anyway.

[29]"When they had done all that the prophecies said about him, they took him down from the cross* and placed him in a tomb. [30]But God raised him from the dead! [31]And over a period of many days he appeared to those who had gone with him from Galilee to Jerusalem. They are now his witnesses to the people of Israel.

[32]"And now we are here to bring you this Good News. The promise was made to our ancestors, [33]and God has now fulfilled it for us, their descendants, by raising Jesus. This is what the second psalm says about Jesus:

'You are my Son.
Today I have become your Father.*'

[34]For God had promised to raise him from the dead, not leaving him to rot in the grave. He said, 'I will give you the sacred blessings I promised to David.'* [35]Another psalm explains it more fully: 'You will not allow your Holy One to rot in the grave.'* [36]This is not a reference to David, for after David had done the will of God in his own generation, he died and was buried with his ancestors, and his body decayed. [37]No, it was a reference to someone else—someone whom God raised and whose body did not decay.

[38]*"Brothers, listen! We are here to proclaim that through this man Jesus there is forgiveness for your sins. [39]Everyone who believes in him is declared right with God—something the law of Moses could never do. [40]Be careful! Don't let the prophets' words apply to you. For they said,

[41] 'Look, you mockers,
be amazed and die!
For I am doing something in your
own day,
something you wouldn't believe
even if someone told you about it.'*"

[42]As Paul and Barnabas left the synagogue that day, the people begged them to speak about these things again the next week. [43]Many Jews and devout converts to Judaism followed Paul and Barnabas, and the two men urged them to continue to rely on the grace of God.

Paul Turns to the Gentiles

[44]The following week almost the entire city turned out to hear them preach the word of

13:15 Greek *from the law*. **13:18** Some manuscripts read *He cared for them*; compare Deut 1:31. **13:22** 1 Sam 13:14. **13:29** Greek *from the tree*. **13:33** Or *Today I reveal you as my Son*. Ps 2:7. **13:34** Isa 55:3. **13:35** Ps 16:10. **13:38** English translations divide verses 38 and 39 in various ways. **13:41** Hab 1:5 (Greek version).

the Lord. [45]But when some of the Jews saw the crowds, they were jealous; so they slandered Paul and argued against whatever he said.

[46]Then Paul and Barnabas spoke out boldly and declared, "It was necessary that we first preach the word of God to you Jews. But since you have rejected it and judged yourselves unworthy of eternal life, we will offer it to the Gentiles. [47]For the Lord gave us this command when he said,

> 'I have made you a light to the
> Gentiles,
> to bring salvation to the farthest
> corners of the earth.'*"

[48]When the Gentiles heard this, they were very glad and thanked the Lord for his message; and all who were chosen for eternal life became believers. [49]So the Lord's message spread throughout that region.

[50]Then the Jews stirred up the influential religious women and the leaders of the city, and they incited a mob against Paul and Barnabas and ran them out of town. [51]So they shook the dust from their feet as a sign of rejection and went to the town of Iconium. [52]And the believers* were filled with joy and with the Holy Spirit.

CHAPTER 14

Paul and Barnabas in Iconium

The same thing happened in Iconium.* Paul and Barnabas went to the Jewish synagogue and preached with such power that a great number of both Jews and Greeks became believers. [2]Some of the Jews, however, spurned God's message and poisoned the minds of the Gentiles against Paul and Barnabas. [3]But the apostles stayed there a long time, preaching boldly about the grace of the Lord. And the Lord proved their message was true by giving them power to do miraculous signs and wonders. [4]But the people of the town were divided in their opinion about them. Some sided with the Jews, and some with the apostles.

[5]Then a mob of Gentiles and Jews, along with their leaders, decided to attack and stone them. [6]When the apostles learned of it, they fled to the region of Lycaonia—to the towns of Lystra and Derbe and the surrounding area. [7]And there they preached the Good News.

Paul and Barnabas in Lystra and Derbe

[8]While they were at Lystra, Paul and Barnabas came upon a man with crippled feet. He had been that way from birth, so he had never walked. He was sitting [9]and listening as Paul preached. Looking straight at him, Paul realized he had faith to be healed. [10]So Paul called to him in a loud voice, "Stand up!" And the man jumped to his feet and started walking.

[11]When the crowd saw what Paul had done, they shouted in their local dialect, "These men are gods in human form!" [12]They decided that Barnabas was the Greek god Zeus and that Paul was Hermes, since he was the chief speaker. [13]Now the temple of Zeus was located just outside the town. So the priest of the temple and the crowd brought bulls and wreaths of flowers to the town gates, and they prepared to offer sacrifices to the apostles.

[14]But when the apostles Barnabas and Paul heard what was happening, they tore their clothing in dismay and ran out among the people, shouting, [15]"Friends,* why are you doing this? We are merely human beings—just like you! We have come to bring you the Good News that you should turn from these worthless things and turn to the living God, who made heaven and earth, the sea, and everything in them. [16]In the past he permitted all the nations to go their own ways, [17]but he never left them without evidence of himself and his goodness. For instance, he sends you rain and good crops and gives you food and joyful hearts." [18]But even with these words, Paul and Barnabas could scarcely restrain the people from sacrificing to them.

[19]Then some Jews arrived from Antioch and Iconium and won the crowds to their side. They stoned Paul and dragged him out of town, thinking he was dead. [20]But as the believers* gathered around him, he got up and went back into the town. The next day he left with Barnabas for Derbe.

Paul and Barnabas Return to Antioch of Syria

[21]After preaching the Good News in Derbe and making many disciples, Paul and Barnabas returned to Lystra, Iconium, and Antioch of Pisidia, [22]where they strengthened the believers. They encouraged them to continue in

13:47 Isa 49:6. **13:52** Greek *the disciples*. **14:1** *Iconium*, as well as *Lystra* and *Derbe* (14:6), were towns in what is now Turkey. **14:15** Greek *Men*. **14:20** Greek *disciples*; also in 14:22, 28.

the faith, reminding them that we must suffer many hardships to enter the Kingdom of God. [23]Paul and Barnabas also appointed elders in every church. With prayer and fasting, they turned the elders over to the care of the Lord, in whom they had put their trust. [24]Then they traveled back through Pisidia to Pamphylia. [25]They preached the word in Perga, then went down to Attalia.

[26]Finally, they returned by ship to Antioch of Syria, where their journey had begun. The believers there had entrusted them to the grace of God to do the work they had now completed. [27]Upon arriving in Antioch, they called the church together and reported everything God had done through them and how he had opened the door of faith to the Gentiles, too. [28]And they stayed there with the believers for a long time.

15:1 Greek *brothers;* also in 15:3, 23, 32, 33, 36, 40.

CHAPTER 15

The Council at Jerusalem

While Paul and Barnabas were at Antioch of Syria, some men from Judea arrived and began to teach the believers*: "Unless you are circumcised as required by the law of Moses, you cannot be saved." [2]Paul and Barnabas disagreed with them, arguing vehemently. Finally, the church decided to send Paul and Barnabas to Jerusalem, accompanied by some local believers, to talk to the apostles and elders about this question. [3]The church sent the delegates to Jerusalem, and they stopped along the way in Phoenicia and Samaria to visit the believers. They told them—much to everyone's joy—that the Gentiles, too, were being converted.

[4]When they arrived in Jerusalem, Barnabas and Paul were welcomed by the whole

GREAT ESCAPES IN THE BIBLE

Who escaped	Reference	What happened	Application
Moses	Exodus 2:11-15	Fled Egypt after killing an Egyptian to defend a fellow Israelite	God even fit this mistake into his plan for Moses. He can do the same for us.
Israelites	Exodus 12:28-42	Escaped Egypt after 430 years, mostly in slavery	God did not forget his promise to deliver the Israelites. He will not forget his promises to us, either.
Elijah	1 Kings 19:1-18	Fled into the desert out of fear of Queen Jezebel	Elijah was a great success, but he still got scared. Even when God is helping us, we may have personal weaknesses to deal with.
Paul	Acts 9:25	Lowered over the wall in a basket to get out of Damascus	God protected Paul because he had a special purpose for Paul's life. God has a special purpose for your life, too!
Peter	Acts 12:1-11	Freed from prison by an angel	God can use extraordinary means to carry out his plan–often when least expected.
Paul and Silas	Acts 16:22-39	Chains loosened and prison doors opened because of an earthquake	Paul and Silas chose not to leave the prison, and as a result, the jailer and his family came to know Christ. When we focus on God, he is able to work in unexpected ways.

church, including the apostles and elders. They reported everything God had done through them. [5]But then some of the believers who belonged to the sect of the Pharisees stood up and insisted, "The Gentile converts must be circumcised and required to follow the law of Moses."

[6]So the apostles and elders met together to resolve this issue. [7]At the meeting, after a long discussion, Peter stood and addressed them as follows: "Brothers, you all know that God chose me from among you some time ago to preach to the Gentiles so that they could hear the Good News and believe. [8]God knows people's hearts, and he confirmed that he accepts Gentiles by giving them the Holy Spirit, just as he did to us. [9]He made no distinction between us and them, for he cleansed their hearts through faith. [10]So why are you now challenging God by burdening the Gentile believers* with a yoke that neither we nor our ancestors were able to bear? [11]We believe that we are all saved the same way, by the undeserved grace of the Lord Jesus."

[12]Everyone listened quietly as Barnabas and Paul told about the miraculous signs and wonders God had done through them among the Gentiles.

[13]When they had finished, James stood and said, "Brothers, listen to me. [14]Peter* has told you about the time God first visited the Gentiles to take from them a people for himself. [15]And this conversion of Gentiles is exactly what the prophets predicted. As it is written:

[16] 'Afterward I will return
and restore the fallen house* of David.
I will rebuild its ruins
and restore it,
[17] so that the rest of humanity might seek
the LORD,
including the Gentiles—
all those I have called to be mine.
The LORD has spoken—
[18] he who made these things known so
long ago.'*

[19]"And so my judgment is that we should not make it difficult for the Gentiles who are turning to God. [20]Instead, we should write and tell them to abstain from eating food offered to idols, from sexual immorality, from eating the meat of strangled animals, and from consuming blood. [21]For these laws of Moses have been preached in Jewish synagogues in every city on every Sabbath for many generations."

The Letter for Gentile Believers

[22]Then the apostles and elders together with the whole church in Jerusalem chose delegates, and they sent them to Antioch of Syria with Paul and Barnabas to report on this decision. The men chosen were two of the church leaders*—Judas (also called Barsabbas) and Silas. [23]This is the letter they took with them:

"This letter is from the apostles and elders, your brothers in Jerusalem. It is written to the Gentile believers in Antioch, Syria, and Cilicia. Greetings!

[24]"We understand that some men from here have troubled you and upset you with their teaching, but we did not send them! [25]So we decided, having come to complete agreement, to send you official representatives, along with our beloved Barnabas and Paul, [26]who have risked their lives for the name of our Lord Jesus Christ. [27]We are sending Judas and Silas to confirm what we have decided concerning your question.

[28]"For it seemed good to the Holy Spirit and to us to lay no greater burden on you than these few requirements: [29]You must abstain from eating food offered to idols, from consuming blood or the meat of strangled animals, and from sexual immorality. If you do this, you will do well. Farewell."

[30]The messengers went at once to Antioch, where they called a general meeting of the believers and delivered the letter. [31]And there was great joy throughout the church that day as they read this encouraging message.

[32]Then Judas and Silas, both being prophets, spoke at length to the believers, encouraging and strengthening their faith. [33]They stayed for a while, and then the believers sent them back to the church in Jerusalem with a blessing of peace.* [35]Paul and Barnabas stayed in Antioch. They and many others taught and preached the word of the Lord there.

15:10 Greek *disciples*. **15:14** Greek *Symeon*. **15:16** Or *kingdom;* Greek reads *tent*. **15:16-18** Amos 9:11-12 (Greek version); Isa 45:21. **15:22** Greek *were leaders among the brothers*. **15:33** Some manuscripts add verse 34, *But Silas decided to stay there*.

Paul and Barnabas Separate

36 After some time Paul said to Barnabas, "Let's
go back and visit each city where we previ-
ously preached the word of the Lord, to see
how the new believers are doing." 37 Barnabas
agreed and wanted to take along John Mark.
38 But Paul disagreed strongly, since John Mark
had deserted them in Pamphylia and had not
continued with them in their work. 39 Their
disagreement was so sharp that they separated. Barnabas took John Mark with him and
sailed for Cyprus. 40 Paul chose Silas, and as he
left, the believers entrusted him to the Lord's
gracious care. 41 Then he traveled throughout
Syria and Cilicia, strengthening the churches
there.

CHAPTER 16

Paul's Second Missionary Journey

Paul went first to Derbe and then to Lystra,
where there was a young disciple named Timothy. His mother was a Jewish believer, but
his father was a Greek. 2 Timothy was well
thought of by the believers* in Lystra and
Iconium, 3 so Paul wanted him to join them on
their journey. In deference to the Jews of the
area, he arranged for Timothy to be circumcised before they left, for everyone knew that
his father was a Greek. 4 Then they went from
town to town, instructing the believers to follow the decisions made by the apostles and
elders in Jerusalem. 5 So the churches were
strengthened in their faith and grew larger
every day.

A Call from Macedonia

6 Next Paul and Silas traveled through the area
of Phrygia and Galatia, because the Holy
Spirit had prevented them from preaching
the word in the province of Asia at that time.
7 Then coming to the borders of Mysia, they
headed north for the province of Bithynia,*
but again the Spirit of Jesus did not allow
them to go there. 8 So instead, they went on
through Mysia to the seaport of Troas.

9 That night Paul had a vision: A man from
Macedonia in northern Greece was standing there, pleading with him, "Come over to
Macedonia and help us!" 10 So we* decided to
leave for Macedonia at once, having concluded that God was calling us to preach the
Good News there.

Lydia of Philippi Believes in Jesus

11 We boarded a boat at Troas and sailed
straight across to the island of Samothrace,
and the next day we landed at Neapolis.
12 From there we reached Philippi, a major city
of that district of Macedonia and a Roman
colony. And we stayed there several days.

13 On the Sabbath we went a little way outside the city to a riverbank, where we thought
people would be meeting for prayer, and we
sat down to speak with some women who had
gathered there. 14 One of them was Lydia from
Thyatira, a merchant of expensive purple
cloth, who worshiped God. As she listened to
us, the Lord opened her heart, and she accepted what Paul was saying. 15 She was baptized along with other members of her
household, and she asked us to be her guests.
"If you agree that I am a true believer in the
Lord," she said, "come and stay at my home."
And she urged us until we agreed.

Paul and Silas in Prison

16 One day as we were going down to the place
of prayer, we met a demon-possessed slave
girl. She was a fortune-teller who earned a lot
of money for her masters. 17 She followed Paul
and the rest of us, shouting, "These men are
servants of the Most High God, and they have
come to tell you how to be saved."

18 This went on day after day until Paul got
so exasperated that he turned and said to the
demon within her, "I command you in the
name of Jesus Christ to come out of her." And
instantly it left her.

19 Her masters' hopes of wealth were now
shattered, so they grabbed Paul and Silas and
dragged them before the authorities at the
marketplace. 20 "The whole city is in an uproar
because of these Jews!" they shouted to the city
officials. 21 "They are teaching customs that
are illegal for us Romans to practice."

22 A mob quickly formed against Paul and
Silas, and the city officials ordered them
stripped and beaten with wooden rods.
23 They were severely beaten, and then they
were thrown into prison. The jailer was ordered to make sure they didn't escape. 24 So

16:2 Greek *brothers;* also in 16:40. **16:6-7** *Phrygia, Galatia, Asia, Mysia,* and *Bithynia* were all districts in what is now Turkey.
16:10 Luke, the writer of this book, here joined Paul and accompanied him on his journey.

the jailer put them into the inner dungeon and clamped their feet in the stocks.

[25]Around midnight Paul and Silas were praying and singing hymns to God, and the other prisoners were listening. [26]Suddenly, there was a massive earthquake, and the prison was shaken to its foundations. All the doors immediately flew open, and the chains of every prisoner fell off! [27]The jailer woke up to see the prison doors wide open. He assumed the prisoners had escaped, so he drew his sword to kill himself. [28]But Paul shouted to him, "Stop! Don't kill yourself! We are all here!"

[29]The jailer called for lights and ran to the dungeon and fell down trembling before Paul and Silas. [30]Then he brought them out and asked, "Sirs, what must I do to be saved?"

How do I know for sure that I'll go to heaven when I die?

Believe in the Lord Jesus and you will be saved. ACTS 16:31

[31]They replied, "Believe in the Lord Jesus and you will be saved, along with everyone in your household." [32]And they shared the word of the Lord with him and with all who lived in his household. [33]Even at that hour of the night, the jailer cared for them and washed their wounds. Then he and everyone in his household were immediately baptized. [34]He brought them into his house and set a meal before them, and he and his entire household rejoiced because they all believed in God.

[35]The next morning the city officials sent the police to tell the jailer, "Let those men go!" [36]So the jailer told Paul, "The city officials have said you and Silas are free to leave. Go in peace."

[37]But Paul replied, "They have publicly beaten us without a trial and put us in prison—and we are Roman citizens. So now they want us to leave secretly? Certainly not! Let them come themselves to release us!"

[38]When the police reported this, the city officials were alarmed to learn that Paul and Silas were Roman citizens. [39]So they came to the jail and apologized to them. Then they brought them out and begged them to leave the city. [40]When Paul and Silas left the prison, they returned to the home of Lydia. There they met with the believers and encouraged them once more. Then they left town.

CHAPTER 17

Paul Preaches in Thessalonica

Paul and Silas then traveled through the towns of Amphipolis and Apollonia and came to Thessalonica, where there was a Jewish synagogue. [2]As was Paul's custom, he went to the synagogue service, and for three Sabbaths in a row he used the Scriptures to reason with the people. [3]He explained the prophecies and proved that the Messiah must suffer and rise from the dead. He said, "This Jesus I'm telling you about is the Messiah." [4]Some of the Jews who listened were persuaded and joined Paul and Silas, along with many God-fearing Greek men and quite a few prominent women.*

[5]But some of the Jews were jealous, so they gathered some troublemakers from the marketplace to form a mob and start a riot. They attacked the home of Jason, searching for Paul and Silas so they could drag them out to the crowd.* [6]Not finding them there, they dragged out Jason and some of the other believers* instead and took them before the city council. "Paul and Silas have caused trouble all over the world," they shouted, "and now they are here disturbing our city, too. [7]And Jason has welcomed them into his home. They are all guilty of treason against Caesar, for they profess allegiance to another king, named Jesus."

[8]The people of the city, as well as the city council, were thrown into turmoil by these reports. [9]So the officials forced Jason and the other believers to post bond, and then they released them.

Paul and Silas in Berea

[10]That very night the believers sent Paul and Silas to Berea. When they arrived there, they went to the Jewish synagogue. [11]And the

17:4 Some manuscripts read *quite a few of the wives of the leading men.* **17:5** Or *the city council.* **17:6** Greek *brothers;* also in 17:10, 14.

people of Berea were more open-minded than those in Thessalonica, and they listened eagerly to Paul's message. They searched the Scriptures day after day to see if Paul and Silas were teaching the truth. [12]As a result, many Jews believed, as did many of the prominent Greek women and men.

[13]But when some Jews in Thessalonica learned that Paul was preaching the word of God in Berea, they went there and stirred up trouble. [14]The believers acted at once, sending Paul on to the coast, while Silas and Timothy remained behind. [15]Those escorting Paul went with him all the way to Athens; then they returned to Berea with instructions for Silas and Timothy to hurry and join him.

Paul Preaches in Athens

[16]While Paul was waiting for them in Athens, he was deeply troubled by all the idols he saw everywhere in the city. [17]He went to the synagogue to reason with the Jews and the God-fearing Gentiles, and he spoke daily in the public square to all who happened to be there.

[18]He also had a debate with some of the Epicurean and Stoic philosophers. When he told them about Jesus and his resurrection, they said, "What's this babbler trying to say with these strange ideas he's picked up?" Others said, "He seems to be preaching about some foreign gods."

[19]Then they took him to the high council of the city.* "Come and tell us about this new teaching," they said. [20]"You are saying some rather strange things, and we want to know what it's all about." [21](It should be explained that all the Athenians as well as the foreigners in Athens seemed to spend all their time discussing the latest ideas.)

[22]So Paul, standing before the council,* addressed them as follows: "Men of Athens, I notice that you are very religious in every way, [23]for as I was walking along I saw your many shrines. And one of your altars had this inscription on it: 'To an Unknown God.' This God, whom you worship without knowing, is the one I'm telling you about.

[24]"He is the God who made the world and everything in it. Since he is Lord of heaven and earth, he doesn't live in man-made temples, [25]and human hands can't serve his needs—for he has no needs. He himself gives life and breath to everything, and he satisfies every need. [26]From one man* he created all the nations throughout the whole earth. He

17:19 Or *the most learned society of philosophers in the city.* Greek reads *the Areopagus.* **17:22** Traditionally rendered *standing in the middle of Mars Hill;* Greek reads *standing in the middle of the Areopagus.* **17:26** Greek *From one;* other manuscripts read *From one blood.*

IS IT OK?

IS IT OK TO BELIEVE IN EVOLUTION?

God doesn't tell us every detail of the origin of the universe. He didn't include special features on "The Making of the Universe" on a DVD for us. But he does tell us that he created the heavens and the earth (Genesis 1:1; Acts 17:24), and that he is Lord, King, and Master of the universe. If we believe God is real and his Word is true, then we believe that he created the world. Many Christians believe differently about just *how* or *when* God created everything. But the bottom line is that *God created;* and his Son, Jesus Christ, was there. God created everything through Christ (Colossians 1:15-16).

decided beforehand when they should rise
and fall, and he determined their boundaries.
27"His purpose was for the nations to seek
after God and perhaps feel their way toward
him and find him—though he is not far from
any one of us. 28For in him we live and move
and exist. As some of your* own poets have
said, 'We are his offspring.' 29And since this is
true, we shouldn't think of God as an idol de-
signed by craftsmen from gold or silver or
stone.
30"God overlooked people's ignorance
about these things in earlier times, but now
he commands everyone everywhere to repent
of their sins and turn to him. 31For he has set a
day for judging the world with justice by the
man he has appointed, and he proved to
everyone who this is by raising him from the
dead."
32When they heard Paul speak about the
resurrection of the dead, some laughed in
contempt, but others said, "We want to hear
more about this later." 33That ended Paul's
discussion with them, 34but some joined him
and became believers. Among them were Di-
onysius, a member of the council,* a woman
named Damaris, and others with them.

CHAPTER 18

Paul Meets Priscilla and Aquila in Corinth

Then Paul left Athens and went to Corinth.*
2There he became acquainted with a Jew
named Aquila, born in Pontus, who had re-
cently arrived from Italy with his wife,
Priscilla. They had left Italy when Claudius
Caesar deported all Jews from Rome. 3Paul
lived and worked with them, for they were
tentmakers* just as he was.
4Each Sabbath found Paul at the syna-
gogue, trying to convince the Jews and Greeks
alike. 5And after Silas and Timothy came
down from Macedonia, Paul spent all his time
preaching the word. He testified to the Jews
that Jesus was the Messiah. 6But when they
opposed and insulted him, Paul shook the
dust from his clothes and said, "Your blood is
upon your own heads—I am innocent. From
now on I will go preach to the Gentiles."
7Then he left and went to the home of
Titius Justus, a Gentile who worshiped God
and lived next door to the synagogue. 8Cris-
pus, the leader of the synagogue, and every-
one in his household believed in the Lord.
Many others in Corinth also heard Paul, be-
came believers, and were baptized.
9One night the Lord spoke to Paul in a vi-
sion and told him, "Don't be afraid! Speak out!
Don't be silent! 10For I am with you, and no
one will attack and harm you, for many peo-
ple in this city belong to me." 11So Paul stayed
there for the next year and a half, teaching the
word of God.
12But when Gallio became governor of
Achaia, some Jews rose up together against
Paul and brought him before the governor for
judgment. 13They accused Paul of "persuad-
ing people to worship God in ways that are
contrary to our law."
14But just as Paul started to make his de-
fense, Gallio turned to Paul's accusers and
said, "Listen, you Jews, if this were a case in-
volving some wrongdoing or a serious crime, I
would have a reason to accept your case. 15But
since it is merely a question of words and
names and your Jewish law, take care of it
yourselves. I refuse to judge such matters."
16And he threw them out of the courtroom.
17The crowd* then grabbed Sosthenes, the
leader of the synagogue, and beat him right
there in the courtroom. But Gallio paid no at-
tention.

Paul Returns to Antioch of Syria

18Paul stayed in Corinth for some time after
that, then said good-bye to the brothers and
sisters* and went to nearby Cenchrea. There
he shaved his head according to Jewish cus-
tom, marking the end of a vow. Then he set
sail for Syria, taking Priscilla and Aquila with
him.
19They stopped first at the port of Ephesus,
where Paul left the others behind. While he
was there, he went to the synagogue to reason
with the Jews. 20They asked him to stay lon-
ger, but he declined. 21As he left, however, he
said, "I will come back later,* God willing."
Then he set sail from Ephesus. 22The next

17:28 Some manuscripts read *our*. **17:34** Greek *an Areopagite*. **18:1** *Athens* and *Corinth* were major cities in Achaia, the region in the southern portion of the Greek peninsula. **18:3** Or *leatherworkers*. **18:17** Greek *Everyone;* other manuscripts read *All the Greeks*. **18:18** Greek *brothers;* also in 18:27. **18:21** Some manuscripts read *"I must by all means be at Jerusalem for the upcoming festival, but I will come back later."*

Barnabas

What's it like to look into the eyes of someone who has been a killer? I know. I saw Saul (now called Paul) shortly after he became a follower of Jesus. No one in the church trusted the man. You couldn't blame the people after the horrible things he had done to Jesus' followers. Still, there was something about Paul's story of hearing the Lord's voice that made me trust him. I introduced him to other believers, and they finally began to see the man had changed.

Paul became one of the world's best preachers. He and I became best friends, and together we told many people about Jesus.

Read about how Barnabas encouraged others in Acts 9:26-27 and 11:22-30.

stop was at the port of Caesarea. From there he went up and visited the church at Jerusalem* and then went back to Antioch.

23 After spending some time in Antioch, Paul went back through Galatia and Phrygia, visiting and strengthening all the believers.*

Apollos Instructed at Ephesus

24 Meanwhile, a Jew named Apollos, an eloquent speaker who knew the Scriptures well, had arrived in Ephesus from Alexandria in Egypt. 25 He had been taught the way of the Lord, and he taught others about Jesus with an enthusiastic spirit* and with accuracy. However, he knew only about John's baptism. 26 When Priscilla and Aquila heard him preaching boldly in the synagogue, they took him aside and explained the way of God even more accurately.

27 Apollos had been thinking about going to Achaia, and the brothers and sisters in Ephesus encouraged him to go. They wrote to the believers in Achaia, asking them to welcome him. When he arrived there, he proved to be of great benefit to those who, by God's grace, had believed. 28 He refuted the Jews with powerful arguments in public debate. Using the Scriptures, he explained to them that Jesus was the Messiah.

CHAPTER 19

Paul's Third Missionary Journey

While Apollos was in Corinth, Paul traveled through the interior regions until he reached Ephesus, on the coast, where he found several believers.* 2 "Did you receive the Holy Spirit when you believed?" he asked them.

"No," they replied, "we haven't even heard that there is a Holy Spirit."

3 "Then what baptism did you experience?" he asked.

And they replied, "The baptism of John."

4 Paul said, "John's baptism called for repentance from sin. But John himself told the people to believe in the one who would come later, meaning Jesus."

5 As soon as they heard this, they were baptized in the name of the Lord Jesus. 6 Then when Paul laid his hands on them, the Holy Spirit came on them, and they spoke in other tongues* and prophesied. 7 There were about twelve men in all.

Paul Ministers in Ephesus

8 Then Paul went to the synagogue and preached boldly for the next three months, arguing persuasively about the Kingdom of God. 9 But some became stubborn, rejecting

18:22 Greek *the church.* **18:23** Greek *disciples;* also in 18:27. **18:25** Or *with enthusiasm in the Spirit.* **19:1** Greek *disciples;* also in 19:9, 30. **19:6** Or *in other languages.*

his message and publicly speaking against the Way. So Paul left the synagogue and took the believers with him. Then he held daily discussions at the lecture hall of Tyrannus. [10]This went on for the next two years, so that people throughout the province of Asia—both Jews and Greeks—heard the word of the Lord.

[11]God gave Paul the power to perform unusual miracles. [12]When handkerchiefs or aprons that had merely touched his skin were placed on sick people, they were healed of their diseases, and evil spirits were expelled.

[13]A group of Jews was traveling from town to town casting out evil spirits. They tried to use the name of the Lord Jesus in their incantation, saying, "I command you in the name of Jesus, whom Paul preaches, to come out!" [14]Seven sons of Sceva, a leading priest, were doing this. [15]But one time when they tried it, the evil spirit replied, "I know Jesus, and I know Paul, but who are you?" [16]Then the man with the evil spirit leaped on them, overpowered them, and attacked them with such violence that they fled from the house, naked and battered.

[17]The story of what happened spread quickly all through Ephesus, to Jews and Greeks alike. A solemn fear descended on the city, and the name of the Lord Jesus was greatly honored. [18]Many who became believers confessed their sinful practices. [19]A number of them who had been practicing sorcery brought their incantation books and burned them at a public bonfire. The value of the books was several million dollars.* [20]So the message about the Lord spread widely and had a powerful effect.

[21]Afterward Paul felt compelled by the Spirit* to go over to Macedonia and Achaia before going to Jerusalem. "And after that," he said, "I must go on to Rome!" [22]He sent his two assistants, Timothy and Erastus, ahead to Macedonia while he stayed awhile longer in the province of Asia.

The Riot in Ephesus

[23]About that time, serious trouble developed in Ephesus concerning the Way. [24]It began with Demetrius, a silversmith who had a large business manufacturing silver shrines of the Greek goddess Artemis.* He kept many craftsmen busy. [25]He called them together, along with others employed in similar trades, and addressed them as follows:

"Gentlemen, you know that our wealth comes from this business. [26]But as you have seen and heard, this man Paul has persuaded many people that handmade gods aren't really gods at all. And he's done this not only here in Ephesus but throughout the entire province! [27]Of course, I'm not just talking about the loss of public respect for our business. I'm also concerned that the temple of the great goddess Artemis will lose its influence and that Artemis—this magnificent goddess worshiped throughout the province of Asia and all around the world—will be robbed of her great prestige!"

[28]At this their anger boiled, and they began shouting, "Great is Artemis of the Ephesians!" [29]Soon the whole city was filled with confusion. Everyone rushed to the amphitheater, dragging along Gaius and Aristarchus, who were Paul's traveling companions from Macedonia. [30]Paul wanted to go in, too, but the believers wouldn't let him. [31]Some of the officials of the province, friends of Paul, also sent a message to him, begging him not to risk his life by entering the amphitheater.

[32]Inside, the people were all shouting, some one thing and some another. Everything was in confusion. In fact, most of them didn't even know why they were there. [33]The Jews in the crowd pushed Alexander forward and told him to explain the situation. He motioned for silence and tried to speak. [34]But when the crowd realized he was a Jew, they started shouting again and kept it up for about two hours: "Great is Artemis of the Ephesians! Great is Artemis of the Ephesians!"

[35]At last the mayor was able to quiet them down enough to speak. "Citizens of Ephesus," he said. "Everyone knows that Ephesus is the official guardian of the temple of the great Artemis, whose image fell down to us from heaven. [36]Since this is an undeniable fact, you should stay calm and not do anything rash. [37]You have brought these men here, but they have stolen nothing from the temple and have not spoken against our goddess.

[38]"If Demetrius and the craftsmen have a case against them, the courts are in session and

19:19 Greek *50,000 pieces of silver*, each of which was the equivalent of a day's wage. **19:21** Or *decided in his spirit*. **19:24** *Artemis* is otherwise known as Diana.

the officials can hear the case at once. Let them make formal charges. [39]And if there are complaints about other matters, they can be settled in a legal assembly. [40]I am afraid we are in danger of being charged with rioting by the Roman government, since there is no cause for all this commotion. And if Rome demands an explanation, we won't know what to say." [41]*Then he dismissed them, and they dispersed.

CHAPTER 20

Paul Goes to Macedonia and Greece

When the uproar was over, Paul sent for the believers* and encouraged them. Then he said good-bye and left for Macedonia. [2]While there, he encouraged the believers in all the towns he passed through. Then he traveled down to Greece, [3]where he stayed for three months. He was preparing to sail back to Syria when he discovered a plot by some Jews against his life, so he decided to return through Macedonia.

[4]Several men were traveling with him. They were Sopater son of Pyrrhus from Berea; Aristarchus and Secundus from Thessalonica; Gaius from Derbe; Timothy; and Tychicus and Trophimus from the province of Asia. [5]They went on ahead and waited for us at Troas. [6]After the Passover* ended, we boarded a ship at Philippi in Macedonia and five days later joined them in Troas, where we stayed a week.

Paul's Final Visit to Troas

[7]On the first day of the week, we gathered with the local believers to share in the Lord's Supper.* Paul was preaching to them, and since he was leaving the next day, he kept talking until midnight. [8]The upstairs room where we met was lighted with many flickering lamps. [9]As Paul spoke on and on, a young man named Eutychus, sitting on the windowsill, became very drowsy. Finally, he fell sound asleep and dropped three stories to his death below. [10]Paul went down, bent over him, and took him into his arms. "Don't worry," he said, "he's alive!" [11]Then they all went back upstairs, shared in the Lord's Supper,* and ate together. Paul continued talking to them until dawn, and then he left. [12]Meanwhile, the young man was taken home unhurt, and everyone was greatly relieved.

SUCCESS?

Casey was very concerned about one of his friends. Casey had been praying for an opportunity to talk to him about Jesus. Casey tried to be a good friend and waited patiently for the right time. Then one afternoon at his friend's house, it seemed like the perfect time for Casey to tell him about Jesus. But his friend didn't seem interested. He even joked about what Casey said. Casey felt discouraged and wondered if all his prayers and witnessing were worth it. Read Acts 20:24 to see how Paul handled rejection and what made his life worthwhile.

Paul Meets the Ephesian Elders

[13]Paul went by land to Assos, where he had arranged for us to join him, while we traveled by ship. [14]He joined us there, and we sailed together to Mitylene. [15]The next day we sailed

19:41 Some translations include verse 41 as part of verse 40. **20:1** Greek *disciples*. **20:6** Greek *the days of unleavened bread*. **20:7** Greek *to break bread*. **20:11** Greek *broke the bread*.

past the island of Kios. The following day we crossed to the island of Samos, and* a day later we arrived at Miletus.

16Paul had decided to sail on past Ephesus, for he didn't want to spend any more time in the province of Asia. He was hurrying to get to Jerusalem, if possible, in time for the Festival of Pentecost. 17But when we landed at Miletus, he sent a message to the elders of the church at Ephesus, asking them to come and meet him.

18When they arrived he declared, "You know that from the day I set foot in the province of Asia until now 19I have done the Lord's work humbly and with many tears. I have endured the trials that came to me from the plots of the Jews. 20I never shrank back from telling you what you needed to hear, either publicly or in your homes. 21I have had one message for Jews and Greeks alike—the necessity of repenting from sin and turning to God, and of having faith in our Lord Jesus.

22"And now I am bound by the Spirit* to go to Jerusalem. I don't know what awaits me, 23except that the Holy Spirit tells me in city after city that jail and suffering lie ahead. 24But my life is worth nothing to me unless I use it for finishing the work assigned me by the Lord Jesus—the work of telling others the Good News about the wonderful grace of God.

25"And now I know that none of you to whom I have preached the Kingdom will ever see me again. 26I declare today that I have been faithful. If anyone suffers eternal death, it's not my fault,* 27for I didn't shrink from declaring all that God wants you to know.

28"So guard yourselves and God's people. Feed and shepherd God's flock—his church, purchased with his own blood*—over which the Holy Spirit has appointed you as elders.* 29I know that false teachers, like vicious wolves, will come in among you after I leave, not sparing the flock. 30Even some men from your own group will rise up and distort the truth in order to draw a following. 31Watch out! Remember the three years I was with you—my constant watch and care over you night and day, and my many tears for you.

32"And now I entrust you to God and the message of his grace that is able to build you up and give you an inheritance with all those he has set apart for himself.

33"I have never coveted anyone's silver or gold or fine clothes. 34You know that these hands of mine have worked to supply my own needs and even the needs of those who were with me. 35And I have been a constant example of how you can help those in need by working hard. You should remember the words of the Lord Jesus: 'It is more blessed to give than to receive.'"

36When he had finished speaking, he knelt and prayed with them. 37They all cried as they embraced and kissed him good-bye. 38They were sad most of all because he had said that they would never see him again. Then they escorted him down to the ship.

CHAPTER 21

Paul's Journey to Jerusalem

After saying farewell to the Ephesian elders, we sailed straight to the island of Cos. The next day we reached Rhodes and then went to Patara. 2There we boarded a ship sailing for Phoenicia. 3We sighted the island of Cyprus, passed it on our left, and landed at the harbor of Tyre, in Syria, where the ship was to unload its cargo.

4We went ashore, found the local believers,* and stayed with them a week. These believers prophesied through the Holy Spirit that Paul should not go on to Jerusalem. 5When we returned to the ship at the end of the week, the entire congregation, including women* and children, left the city and came down to the shore with us. There we knelt, prayed, 6and said our farewells. Then we went aboard, and they returned home.

7The next stop after leaving Tyre was Ptolemais, where we greeted the brothers and sisters* and stayed for one day. 8The next day we went on to Caesarea and stayed at the home of Philip the Evangelist, one of the seven men who had been chosen to distribute food. 9He had four unmarried daughters who had the gift of prophecy.

10Several days later a man named Agabus, who also had the gift of prophecy, arrived from Judea. 11He came over, took Paul's belt, and bound his own feet and hands with it.

20:15 Some manuscripts read *and having stayed at Trogyllium.* **20:22** Or *by my spirit,* or *by an inner compulsion;* Greek reads *by the spirit.* **20:26** Greek *I am innocent of the blood of all.* **20:28a** Or *with the blood of his own [Son].* **20:28b** Greek *overseers.* **21:4** Greek *disciples;* also in 21:16. **21:5** Or *wives.* **21:7** Greek *brothers;* also in 21:17.

Then he said, "The Holy Spirit declares, 'So shall the owner of this belt be bound by the Jewish leaders in Jerusalem and turned over to the Gentiles.'" [12]When we heard this, we and the local believers all begged Paul not to go on to Jerusalem.

[13]But he said, "Why all this weeping? You are breaking my heart! I am ready not only to be jailed at Jerusalem but even to die for the sake of the Lord Jesus." [14]When it was clear that we couldn't persuade him, we gave up and said, "The Lord's will be done."

Paul Arrives at Jerusalem

[15]After this we packed our things and left for Jerusalem. [16]Some believers from Caesarea accompanied us, and they took us to the home of Mnason, a man originally from Cyprus and one of the early believers. [17]When we arrived, the brothers and sisters in Jerusalem welcomed us warmly.

[18]The next day Paul went with us to meet with James, and all the elders of the Jerusalem church were present. [19]After greeting them, Paul gave a detailed account of the things God had accomplished among the Gentiles through his ministry.

[20]After hearing this, they praised God. And then they said, "You know, dear brother, how many thousands of Jews have also believed, and they all follow the law of Moses very seriously. [21]But the Jewish believers here in Jerusalem have been told that you are teaching all the Jews who live among the Gentiles to turn their backs on the laws of Moses. They've heard that you teach them not to circumcise their children or follow other Jewish customs. [22]What should we do? They will certainly hear that you have come.

[23]"Here's what we want you to do. We have four men here who have completed their vow. [24]Go with them to the Temple and join them in the purification ceremony, paying for them to have their heads ritually shaved. Then everyone will know that the rumors are all false and that you yourself observe the Jewish laws.

[25]"As for the Gentile believers, they should do what we already told them in a letter: They should abstain from eating food offered to idols, from consuming blood or the meat of strangled animals, and from sexual immorality."

LUKE

Paul was my good friend, so I went with him to Rome for his trial. We traveled by boat, and Roman soldiers guarded Paul and the other prisoners.

While at sea, a fierce storm arose. Paul assured the captain and the crew that God would keep everyone safe. I'm not sure if they believed Paul, but after fourteen long nights we finally saw land.

Then the ship hit a sandbar and was torn to pieces. The guards wanted to kill the prisoners so they couldn't escape. But the captain wanted to spare Paul, so he stopped them. All of us grabbed pieces of the broken ship and made it safely to shore. God indeed had saved us.

Check out the story of Luke and Paul's shipwreck in Acts 27.

Paul Is Arrested

[26]So Paul went to the Temple the next day with the other men. They had already started the purification ritual, so he publicly announced the date when their vows would end and sacrifices would be offered for each of them.

[27]The seven days were almost ended when
some Jews from the province of Asia saw Paul
in the Temple and roused a mob against him.
They grabbed him, [28]yelling, "Men of Israel,
help us! This is the man who preaches against
our people everywhere and tells everybody to
disobey the Jewish laws. He speaks against
the Temple—and even defiles this holy place
by bringing in Gentiles.*" [29](For earlier that
day they had seen him in the city with
Trophimus, a Gentile from Ephesus,* and
they assumed Paul had taken him into the
Temple.)

[30]The whole city was rocked by these accu-
sations, and a great riot followed. Paul was
grabbed and dragged out of the Temple, and
immediately the gates were closed behind
him. [31]As they were trying to kill him, word
reached the commander of the Roman regi-
ment that all Jerusalem was in an uproar. [32]He
immediately called out his soldiers and offi-
cers* and ran down among the crowd. When
the mob saw the commander and the troops
coming, they stopped beating Paul.

[33]Then the commander arrested him and
ordered him bound with two chains. He
asked the crowd who he was and what he had
done. [34]Some shouted one thing and some
another. Since he couldn't find out the truth
in all the uproar and confusion, he ordered
that Paul be taken to the fortress. [35]As Paul
reached the stairs, the mob grew so violent
the soldiers had to lift him to their shoulders
to protect him. [36]And the crowd followed be-
hind, shouting, "Kill him, kill him!"

Paul Speaks to the Crowd

[37]As Paul was about to be taken inside, he
said to the commander, "May I have a word
with you?"

"Do you know Greek?" the commander
asked, surprised. [38]"Aren't you the Egyptian
who led a rebellion some time ago and took
4,000 members of the Assassins out into the
desert?"

[39]"No," Paul replied, "I am a Jew and a citi-
zen of Tarsus in Cilicia, which is an important
city. Please, let me talk to these people." [40]The
commander agreed, so Paul stood on the
stairs and motioned to the people to be quiet.
Soon a deep silence enveloped the crowd, and
he addressed them in their own language,
Aramaic.*

CHAPTER 22

"Brothers and esteemed fathers," Paul said,
"listen to me as I offer my defense." [2]When
they heard him speaking in their own lan-
guage,* the silence was even greater.

[3]Then Paul said, "I am a Jew, born in Tarsus,
a city in Cilicia, and I was brought up and edu-
cated here in Jerusalem under Gamaliel. As
his student, I was carefully trained in our
Jewish laws and customs. I became very zeal-
ous to honor God in everything I did, just like
all of you today. [4]And I persecuted the follow-
ers of the Way, hounding some to death, ar-
resting both men and women and throwing
them in prison. [5]The high priest and the
whole council of elders can testify that this is
so. For I received letters from them to our
Jewish brothers in Damascus, authorizing me
to bring the Christians from there to Jerusa-
lem, in chains, to be punished.

[6]"As I was on the road, approaching Da-
mascus about noon, a very bright light from
heaven suddenly shone down around me. [7]I
fell to the ground and heard a voice saying to
me, 'Saul, Saul, why are you persecuting me?'

[8]"'Who are you, lord?' I asked.

"And the voice replied, 'I am Jesus the
Nazarene,* the one you are persecuting.'
[9]The people with me saw the light but didn't
understand the voice speaking to me.

[10]"I asked, 'What should I do, Lord?'

"And the Lord told me, 'Get up and go into
Damascus, and there you will be told every-
thing you are to do.'

[11]"I was blinded by the intense light and
had to be led by the hand to Damascus by my
companions. [12]A man named Ananias lived
there. He was a godly man, deeply devoted to
the law, and well regarded by all the Jews of
Damascus. [13]He came and stood beside me
and said, 'Brother Saul, regain your sight.' And
that very moment I could see him!

[14]"Then he told me, 'The God of our ances-
tors has chosen you to know his will and to
see the Righteous One and hear him speak.
[15]For you are to be his witness, telling every-
one what you have seen and heard. [16]What
are you waiting for? Get up and be baptized.

21:28 Greek *Greeks*. **21:29** Greek *Trophimus, the Ephesian*. **21:32** Greek *centurions*. **21:40** Or *Hebrew*. **22:2** Greek *in Aramaic*, or *in Hebrew*. **22:8** Or *Jesus of Nazareth*.

Have your sins washed away by calling on the name of the Lord.'

17"After I returned to Jerusalem, I was praying in the Temple and fell into a trance. 18I saw a vision of Jesus* saying to me, 'Hurry! Leave Jerusalem, for the people here won't accept your testimony about me.'

19"'But Lord,' I argued, 'they certainly know that in every synagogue I imprisoned and beat those who believed in you. 20And I was in complete agreement when your witness Stephen was killed. I stood by and kept the coats they took off when they stoned him.'

21"But the Lord said to me, 'Go, for I will send you far away to the Gentiles!'"

22The crowd listened until Paul said that word. Then they all began to shout, "Away with such a fellow! He isn't fit to live!" 23They yelled, threw off their coats, and tossed handfuls of dust into the air.

Paul Reveals His Roman Citizenship

24The commander brought Paul inside and ordered him lashed with whips to make him confess his crime. He wanted to find out why the crowd had become so furious. 25When they tied Paul down to lash him, Paul said to the officer* standing there, "Is it legal for you to whip a Roman citizen who hasn't even been tried?"

26When the officer heard this, he went to the commander and asked, "What are you doing? This man is a Roman citizen!"

27So the commander went over and asked Paul, "Tell me, are you a Roman citizen?"

"Yes, I certainly am," Paul replied.

28"I am, too," the commander muttered, "and it cost me plenty!"

Paul answered, "But I am a citizen by birth!"

29The soldiers who were about to interrogate Paul quickly withdrew when they heard he was a Roman citizen, and the commander was frightened because he had ordered him bound and whipped.

Paul before the High Council

30The next day the commander ordered the leading priests into session with the Jewish high council.* He wanted to find out what the trouble was all about, so he released Paul to have him stand before them.

CHAPTER 23

Gazing intently at the high council,* Paul began: "Brothers, I have always lived before God with a clear conscience!"

2Instantly Ananias the high priest commanded those close to Paul to slap him on the mouth. 3But Paul said to him, "God will slap you, you corrupt hypocrite!* What kind of judge are you to break the law yourself by ordering me struck like that?"

4Those standing near Paul said to him, "Do you dare to insult God's high priest?"

5"I'm sorry, brothers. I didn't realize he was the high priest," Paul replied, "for the Scriptures say, 'You must not speak evil of any of your rulers.'*"

6Paul realized that some members of the high council were Sadducees and some were Pharisees, so he shouted, "Brothers, I am a Pharisee, as were my ancestors! And I am on trial because my hope is in the resurrection of the dead!"

7This divided the council—the Pharisees against the Sadducees—8for the Sadducees say there is no resurrection or angels or spirits, but the Pharisees believe in all of these. 9So there was a great uproar. Some of the teachers of religious law who were Pharisees jumped up and began to argue forcefully. "We see nothing wrong with him," they shouted. "Perhaps a spirit or an angel spoke to him." 10As the conflict grew more violent, the commander was afraid they would tear Paul apart. So he ordered his soldiers to go and rescue him by force and take him back to the fortress.

11That night the Lord appeared to Paul and said, "Be encouraged, Paul. Just as you have been a witness to me here in Jerusalem, you must preach the Good News in Rome as well."

The Plan to Kill Paul

12The next morning a group of Jews* got together and bound themselves with an oath not to eat or drink until they had killed Paul. 13There were more than forty of them in the conspiracy. 14They went to the leading priests and elders and told them, "We have bound ourselves with an oath to eat nothing until we have killed Paul. 15So you and the high council should ask the commander to bring Paul back to the council again. Pretend you want to

22:18 Greek *him.* **22:25** Greek *the centurion;* also in 22:26. **22:30** Greek *Sanhedrin.* **23:1** Greek *Sanhedrin;* also in 23:6, 15, 20, 28. **23:3** Greek *you whitewashed wall.* **23:5** Exod 22:28. **23:12** Greek *the Jews.*

examine his case more fully. We will kill him on the way."

16But Paul's nephew—his sister's son—heard of their plan and went to the fortress and told Paul. 17Paul called for one of the Roman officers* and said, "Take this young man to the commander. He has something important to tell him."

18So the officer did, explaining, "Paul, the prisoner, called me over and asked me to bring this young man to you because he has something to tell you."

19The commander took his hand, led him aside, and asked, "What is it you want to tell me?"

20Paul's nephew told him, "Some Jews are going to ask you to bring Paul before the high council tomorrow, pretending they want to get some more information. 21But don't do it! There are more than forty men hiding along the way ready to ambush him. They have vowed not to eat or drink anything until they have killed him. They are ready now, just waiting for your consent."

22"Don't let anyone know you told me this," the commander warned the young man.

Paul Is Sent to Caesarea

23Then the commander called two of his officers and ordered, "Get 200 soldiers ready to leave for Caesarea at nine o'clock tonight. Also take 200 spearmen and 70 mounted troops. 24Provide horses for Paul to ride, and get him safely to Governor Felix." 25Then he wrote this letter to the governor:

> 26"From Claudius Lysias, to his Excellency, Governor Felix: Greetings!
>
> 27"This man was seized by some Jews, and they were about to kill him when I arrived with the troops. When I learned that he was a Roman citizen, I removed him to safety. 28Then I took him to their high council to try to learn the basis of the accusations against him. 29I soon discovered the charge was something regarding their religious law—certainly nothing worthy of imprisonment or death. 30But when I was informed of a plot to kill him, I immediately sent him on to you. I have told his accusers to bring their charges before you."

31So that night, as ordered, the soldiers took Paul as far as Antipatris. 32They returned to the fortress the next morning, while the mounted troops took him on to Caesarea. 33When they arrived in Caesarea, they presented Paul and the letter to Governor Felix. 34He read it and then asked Paul what province he was from. "Cilicia," Paul answered.

35"I will hear your case myself when your accusers arrive," the governor told him. Then the governor ordered him kept in the prison at Herod's headquarters.*

CHAPTER 24

Paul Appears before Felix

Five days later Ananias, the high priest, arrived with some of the Jewish elders and the lawyer* Tertullus, to present their case against Paul to the governor. 2When Paul was called in, Tertullus presented the charges against Paul in the following address to the governor:

"You have provided a long period of peace for us Jews and with foresight have enacted reforms for us. 3For all of this, Your Excellency, we are very grateful to you. 4But I don't want to bore you, so please give me your attention for only a moment. 5We have found this man to be a troublemaker who is constantly stirring up riots among the Jews all over the world. He is a ringleader of the cult known as the Nazarenes. 6Furthermore, he was trying to desecrate the Temple when we arrested him.* 8You can find out the truth of our accusations by examining him yourself." 9Then the other Jews chimed in, declaring that everything Tertullus said was true.

10The governor then motioned for Paul to speak. Paul said, "I know, sir, that you have been a judge of Jewish affairs for many years, so I gladly present my defense before you. 11You can quickly discover that I arrived in Jerusalem no more than twelve days ago to worship at the Temple. 12My accusers never found me arguing with anyone in the Temple, nor stirring up a riot in any synagogue or on the streets of the city. 13These men cannot prove the things they accuse me of doing.

23:17 Greek *centurions;* also in 23:23. **23:35** Greek *Herod's Praetorium.* **24:1** Greek *some elders and an orator.* **24:6** Some manuscripts add an expanded conclusion to verse 6, all of verse 7, and an additional phrase in verse 8: *We would have judged him by our law, 7but Lysias, the commander of the garrison, came and violently took him away from us, 8commanding his accusers to come before you.*

THE RIGHT CHOICE

Terry's baseball team had three practices and a game during the final week of the season. One of Terry's friends, who had moved away, was in town visiting. The old gang of friends decided to go to the early movie on Friday, but Terry had his baseball practice then. His friends said, "Just skip practice and come along." He really wanted to see his old friend. It wouldn't hurt to miss one practice, would it? But then he'd feel bad about letting his coach down. What do you think Terry should do? Check out Acts 24:16 for some guidance.

[14]"But I admit that I follow the Way, which they call a cult. I worship the God of our ancestors, and I firmly believe the Jewish law and everything written in the prophets. [15]I have the same hope in God that these men have, that he will raise both the righteous and the unrighteous. [16]Because of this, I always try to maintain a clear conscience before God and all people.

[17]"After several years away, I returned to Jerusalem with money to aid my people and to offer sacrifices to God. [18]My accusers saw me in the Temple as I was completing a purification ceremony. There was no crowd around me and no rioting. [19]But some Jews from the province of Asia were there—and they ought to be here to bring charges if they have anything against me! [20]Ask these men here what crime the Jewish high council* found me guilty of, [21]except for the one time I shouted out, 'I am on trial before you today because I believe in the resurrection of the dead!'"

[22]At that point Felix, who was quite familiar with the Way, adjourned the hearing and said, "Wait until Lysias, the garrison commander, arrives. Then I will decide the case." [23]He ordered an officer* to keep Paul in custody but to give him some freedom and allow his friends to visit him and take care of his needs.

[24]A few days later Felix came back with his wife, Drusilla, who was Jewish. Sending for Paul, they listened as he told them about faith in Christ Jesus. [25]As he reasoned with them about righteousness and self-control and the coming day of judgment, Felix became frightened. "Go away for now," he replied. "When it is more convenient, I'll call for you again." [26]He also hoped that Paul would bribe him, so he sent for him quite often and talked with him.

[27]After two years went by in this way, Felix was succeeded by Porcius Festus. And because Felix wanted to gain favor with the Jewish people, he left Paul in prison.

CHAPTER 25

Paul Appears before Festus

Three days after Festus arrived in Caesarea to take over his new responsibilities, he left for Jerusalem, [2]where the leading priests and other Jewish leaders met with him and made their accusations against Paul. [3]They asked Festus as a favor to transfer Paul to Jerusalem (planning to ambush and kill him on the way). [4]But Festus replied that Paul was at Caesarea and he himself would be returning there soon.

24:20 Greek *Sanhedrin*. **24:23** Greek *a centurion*.

[5]So he said, "Those of you in authority can return with me. If Paul has done anything wrong, you can make your accusations."

[6]About eight or ten days later Festus returned to Caesarea, and on the following day he took his seat in court and ordered that Paul be brought in. [7]When Paul arrived, the Jewish leaders from Jerusalem gathered around and made many serious accusations they couldn't prove.

[8]Paul denied the charges. "I am not guilty of any crime against the Jewish laws or the Temple or the Roman government," he said.

[9]Then Festus, wanting to please the Jews, asked him, "Are you willing to go to Jerusalem and stand trial before me there?"

[10]But Paul replied, "No! This is the official Roman court, so I ought to be tried right here. You know very well I am not guilty of harming the Jews. [11]If I have done something worthy of death, I don't refuse to die. But if I am innocent, no one has a right to turn me over to these men to kill me. I appeal to Caesar!"

[12]Festus conferred with his advisers and then replied, "Very well! You have appealed to Caesar, and to Caesar you will go!"

[13]A few days later King Agrippa arrived with his sister, Bernice,* to pay their respects to Festus. [14]During their stay of several days, Festus discussed Paul's case with the king. "There is a prisoner here," he told him, "whose case was left for me by Felix. [15]When I was in Jerusalem, the leading priests and Jewish elders pressed charges against him and asked me to condemn him. [16]I pointed out to them that Roman law does not convict people without a trial. They must be given an opportunity to confront their accusers and defend themselves.

[17]"When his accusers came here for the trial, I didn't delay. I called the case the very next day and ordered Paul brought in. [18]But the accusations made against him weren't any of the crimes I expected. [19]Instead, it was something about their religion and a dead man named Jesus, who Paul insists is alive. [20]I was at a loss to know how to investigate these things, so I asked him whether he would be willing to stand trial on these charges in Jerusalem. [21]But Paul appealed to have his case decided by the emperor. So I ordered that he be held in custody until I could arrange to send him to Caesar."

[22]"I'd like to hear the man myself," Agrippa said.

And Festus replied, "You will—tomorrow!"

Paul Speaks to Agrippa

[23]So the next day Agrippa and Bernice arrived at the auditorium with great pomp, accompanied by military officers and prominent men of the city. Festus ordered that Paul be brought in. [24]Then Festus said, "King Agrippa and all who are here, this is the man whose death is demanded by all the Jews, both here and in Jerusalem. [25]But in my opinion he has done nothing deserving death. However, since he appealed his case to the emperor, I have decided to send him to Rome.

[26]"But what shall I write the emperor? For there is no clear charge against him. So I have brought him before all of you, and especially you, King Agrippa, so that after we examine him, I might have something to write. [27]For it makes no sense to send a prisoner to the emperor without specifying the charges against him!"

CHAPTER 26

Then Agrippa said to Paul, "You may speak in your defense."

So Paul, gesturing with his hand, started his defense: [2]"I am fortunate, King Agrippa, that you are the one hearing my defense today against all these accusations made by the Jewish leaders, [3]for I know you are an expert on all Jewish customs and controversies. Now please listen to me patiently!

[4]"As the Jewish leaders are well aware, I was given a thorough Jewish training from my earliest childhood among my own people and in Jerusalem. [5]If they would admit it, they know that I have been a member of the Pharisees, the strictest sect of our religion. [6]Now I am on trial because of my hope in the fulfillment of God's promise made to our ancestors. [7]In fact, that is why the twelve tribes of Israel zealously worship God night and day, and they share the same hope I have. Yet, Your Majesty, they accuse me for having this hope! [8]Why does it seem incredible to any of you that God can raise the dead?

[9]"I used to believe that I ought to do everything I could to oppose the very name of Jesus the Nazarene.* [10]Indeed, I did just that

25:13 Greek *Agrippa the king and Bernice arrived.* **26:9** Or *Jesus of Nazareth.*

in Jerusalem. Authorized by the leading priests, I caused many believers* there to be sent to prison. And I cast my vote against them when they were condemned to death. [11]Many times I had them punished in the synagogues to get them to curse Jesus.* I was so violently opposed to them that I even chased them down in foreign cities.

[12]"One day I was on such a mission to Damascus, armed with the authority and commission of the leading priests. [13]About noon, Your Majesty, as I was on the road, a light from heaven brighter than the sun shone down on me and my companions. [14]We all fell down, and I heard a voice saying to me in Aramaic,* 'Saul, Saul, why are you persecuting me? It is useless for you to fight against my will.*'

[15]"'Who are you, lord?' I asked.

"And the Lord replied, 'I am Jesus, the one you are persecuting. [16]Now get to your feet! For I have appeared to you to appoint you as my servant and witness. You are to tell the world what you have seen and what I will show you in the future. [17]And I will rescue you from both your own people and the Gentiles. Yes, I am sending you to the Gentiles [18]to open their eyes, so they may turn from darkness to light and from the power of Satan to God. Then they will receive forgiveness for their sins and be given a place among God's people, who are set apart by faith in me.'

[19]"And so, King Agrippa, I obeyed that vision from heaven. [20]I preached first to those in Damascus, then in Jerusalem and throughout all Judea, and also to the Gentiles, that all must repent of their sins and turn to God—and prove they have changed by the good things they do. [21]Some Jews arrested me in the Temple for preaching this, and they tried to kill me. [22]But God has protected me right up to this present time so I can testify to everyone, from the least to the greatest. I teach nothing except what the prophets and Moses said would happen—[23]that the Messiah would suffer and be the first to rise from the dead, and in this way announce God's light to Jews and Gentiles alike."

[24]Suddenly, Festus shouted, "Paul, you are insane. Too much study has made you crazy!"

[25]But Paul replied, "I am not insane, Most Excellent Festus. What I am saying is the sober truth. [26]And King Agrippa knows about these things. I speak boldly, for I am sure these events are all familiar to him, for they were not done in a corner! [27]King Agrippa, do you believe the prophets? I know you do—"

[28]Agrippa interrupted him. "Do you think you can persuade me to become a Christian so quickly?"*

[29]Paul replied, "Whether quickly or not, I pray to God that both you and everyone here in this audience might become the same as I am, except for these chains."

[30]Then the king, the governor, Bernice, and all the others stood and left. [31]As they went out, they talked it over and agreed, "This man

26:10 Greek *many of God's holy people.* **26:11** Greek *to blaspheme.* **26:14a** Or *Hebrew.* **26:14b** Greek *It is hard for you to kick against the oxgoads.* **26:28** Or *"A little more, and your arguments would make me a Christian."*

hasn't done anything to deserve death or imprisonment."

32 And Agrippa said to Festus, "He could have been set free if he hadn't appealed to Caesar."

CHAPTER 27

Paul Sails for Rome

When the time came, we set sail for Italy. Paul and several other prisoners were placed in the custody of a Roman officer* named Julius, a captain of the Imperial Regiment. 2 Aristarchus, a Macedonian from Thessalonica, was also with us. We left on a ship whose home port was Adramyttium on the northwest coast of the province of Asia;* it was scheduled to make several stops at ports along the coast of the province.

3 The next day when we docked at Sidon, Julius was very kind to Paul and let him go ashore to visit with friends so they could provide for his needs. 4 Putting out to sea from there, we encountered strong headwinds that made it difficult to keep the ship on course, so we sailed north of Cyprus between the island and the mainland. 5 Keeping to the open sea, we passed along the coast of Cilicia and Pamphylia, landing at Myra, in the province of Lycia. 6 There the commanding officer found an Egyptian ship from Alexandria that was bound for Italy, and he put us on board.

7 We had several days of slow sailing, and after great difficulty we finally neared Cnidus. But the wind was against us, so we sailed across to Crete and along the sheltered coast of the island, past the cape of Salmone. 8 We struggled along the coast with great difficulty and finally arrived at Fair Havens, near the town of Lasea. 9 We had lost a lot of time. The weather was becoming dangerous for sea travel because it was so late in the fall,* and Paul spoke to the ship's officers about it.

10 "Men," he said, "I believe there is trouble ahead if we go on—shipwreck, loss of cargo, and danger to our lives as well." 11 But the officer in charge of the prisoners listened more to the ship's captain and the owner than to Paul. 12 And since Fair Havens was an exposed harbor—a poor place to spend the winter—most of the crew wanted to go on to Phoenix, farther up the coast of Crete, and spend the winter there. Phoenix was a good harbor with only a southwest and northwest exposure.

The Storm at Sea

13 When a light wind began blowing from the south, the sailors thought they could make it. So they pulled up anchor and sailed close to the shore of Crete. 14 But the weather changed abruptly, and a wind of typhoon strength (called a "northeaster") burst across the island and blew us out to sea. 15 The sailors couldn't turn the ship into the wind, so they gave up and let it run before the gale.

16 We sailed along the sheltered side of a small island named Cauda,* where with great difficulty we hoisted aboard the lifeboat being towed behind us. 17 Then the sailors bound ropes around the hull of the ship to strengthen it. They were afraid of being driven across to the sandbars of Syrtis off the African coast, so they lowered the sea anchor to slow the ship and were driven before the wind.

18 The next day, as gale-force winds continued to batter the ship, the crew began throwing the cargo overboard. 19 The following day they even took some of the ship's gear and threw it overboard. 20 The terrible storm raged for many days, blotting out the sun and the stars, until at last all hope was gone.

21 No one had eaten for a long time. Finally, Paul called the crew together and said, "Men, you should have listened to me in the first place and not left Crete. You would have avoided all this damage and loss. 22 But take courage! None of you will lose your lives, even though the ship will go down. 23 For last night an angel of the God to whom I belong and whom I serve stood beside me, 24 and he said, 'Don't be afraid, Paul, for you will surely stand trial before Caesar! What's more, God in his goodness has granted safety to everyone sailing with you.' 25 So take courage! For I believe God. It will be just as he said. 26 But we will be shipwrecked on an island."

27:1 Greek *centurion;* similarly in 27:6, 11, 31, 43. **27:2** *Asia* was a Roman province in what is now western Turkey. **27:9** Greek *because the fast was now already gone by.* This fast was associated with the Day of Atonement (*Yom Kippur*), which occurred in late September or early October. **27:16** Some manuscripts read *Clauda.*

The Shipwreck

27 About midnight on the fourteenth night of
the storm, as we were being driven across the
Sea of Adria,* the sailors sensed land was
near. 28 They dropped a weighted line and
found that the water was 120 feet deep. But
a little later they measured again and found
it was only 90 feet deep.* 29 At this rate they
were afraid we would soon be driven against
the rocks along the shore, so they threw out
four anchors from the back of the ship and
prayed for daylight.

AMAZING FACTS

When a deadly snake bit Paul's hand, everyone expected him to swell up or drop dead. Instead, Paul just shook it off, totally unharmed.

ACTS 28:3-5

30 Then the sailors tried to abandon the
ship; they lowered the lifeboat as though they
were going to put out anchors from the front
of the ship. 31 But Paul said to the command-
ing officer and the soldiers, "You will all die
unless the sailors stay aboard." 32 So the sol-
diers cut the ropes to the lifeboat and let it
drift away.

33 Just as day was dawning, Paul urged
everyone to eat. "You have been so worried
that you haven't touched food for two weeks,"
he said. 34 "Please eat something now for your
own good. For not a hair of your heads will
perish." 35 Then he took some bread, gave
thanks to God before them all, and broke off a
piece and ate it. 36 Then everyone was encour-
aged and began to eat— 37 all 276 of us who
were on board. 38 After eating, the crew light-
ened the ship further by throwing the cargo
of wheat overboard.

39 When morning dawned, they didn't rec-
ognize the coastline, but they saw a bay with a
beach and wondered if they could get to
shore by running the ship aground. 40 So they
cut off the anchors and left them in the sea.
Then they lowered the rudders, raised the
foresail, and headed toward shore. 41 But they
hit a shoal and ran the ship aground too soon.
The bow of the ship stuck fast, while the
stern was repeatedly smashed by the force of
the waves and began to break apart.

42 The soldiers wanted to kill the prisoners
to make sure they didn't swim ashore and es-
cape. 43 But the commanding officer wanted
to spare Paul, so he didn't let them carry out
their plan. Then he ordered all who could
swim to jump overboard first and make for
land. 44 The others held on to planks or debris
from the broken ship.* So everyone escaped
safely to shore.

CHAPTER 28

Paul on the Island of Malta

Once we were safe on shore, we learned that
we were on the island of Malta. 2 The people of
the island were very kind to us. It was cold and
rainy, so they built a fire on the shore to wel-
come us.

3 As Paul gathered an armful of sticks and
was laying them on the fire, a poisonous
snake, driven out by the heat, bit him on the
hand. 4 The people of the island saw it hang-
ing from his hand and said to each other, "A
murderer, no doubt! Though he escaped the
sea, justice will not permit him to live." 5 But
Paul shook off the snake into the fire and was
unharmed. 6 The people waited for him to
swell up or suddenly drop dead. But when they
had waited a long time and saw that he wasn't
harmed, they changed their minds and de-
cided he was a god.

7 Near the shore where we landed was an
estate belonging to Publius, the chief official
of the island. He welcomed us and treated us
kindly for three days. 8 As it happened,
Publius's father was ill with fever and dysen-
tery. Paul went in and prayed for him, and
laying his hands on him, he healed him.
9 Then all the other sick people on the island
came and were healed. 10 As a result we were
showered with honors, and when the time

27:27 The *Sea of Adria* includes the central portion of the Mediterranean. **27:28** Greek *20 fathoms . . . 15 fathoms* [37 meters . . . 27 meters]. **27:44** Or *or were helped by members of the ship's crew.*

came to sail, people supplied us with everything we would need for the trip.

Paul Arrives at Rome

[11]It was three months after the shipwreck that we set sail on another ship that had wintered at the island—an Alexandrian ship with the twin gods* as its figurehead. [12]Our first stop was Syracuse,* where we stayed three days. [13]From there we sailed across to Rhegium.* A day later a south wind began blowing, so the following day we sailed up the coast to Puteoli. [14]There we found some believers,* who invited us to spend a week with them. And so we came to Rome.

[15]The brothers and sisters* in Rome had heard we were coming, and they came to meet us at the Forum* on the Appian Way. Others joined us at The Three Taverns.* When Paul saw them, he was encouraged and thanked God.

[16]When we arrived in Rome, Paul was permitted to have his own private lodging, though he was guarded by a soldier.

Paul Preaches at Rome under Guard

[17]Three days after Paul's arrival, he called together the local Jewish leaders. He said to them, "Brothers, I was arrested in Jerusalem and handed over to the Roman government, even though I had done nothing against our people or the customs of our ancestors. [18]The Romans tried me and wanted to release me, because they found no cause for the death sentence. [19]But when the Jewish leaders protested the decision, I felt it necessary to appeal to Caesar, even though I had no desire to press charges against my own people. [20]I asked you to come here today so we could get acquainted and so I could explain to you that I am bound with this chain because I believe that the hope of Israel—the Messiah—has already come."

[21]They replied, "We have had no letters from Judea or reports against you from anyone who has come here. [22]But we want to hear what you believe, for the only thing we know about this movement is that it is denounced everywhere."

[23]So a time was set, and on that day a large number of people came to Paul's lodging. He explained and testified about the Kingdom of God and tried to persuade them about Jesus from the Scriptures. Using the law of Moses and the books of the prophets, he spoke to them from morning until evening. [24]Some were persuaded by the things he said, but others did not believe. [25]And after they had argued back and forth among themselves, they left with this final word from Paul: "The Holy Spirit was right when he said to your ancestors through Isaiah the prophet,

[26] 'Go and say to this people:
When you hear what I say,
you will not understand.
When you see what I do,
you will not comprehend.
[27] For the hearts of these people are
hardened,
and their ears cannot hear,
and they have closed their eyes—
so their eyes cannot see,
and their ears cannot hear,
and their hearts cannot understand,
and they cannot turn to me
and let me heal them.'*

[28]So I want you to know that this salvation from God has also been offered to the Gentiles, and they will accept it."*

[30]For the next two years, Paul lived in Rome at his own expense.* He welcomed all who visited him, [31]boldly proclaiming the Kingdom of God and teaching about the Lord Jesus Christ. And no one tried to stop him.

28:11 The *twin gods* were the Roman gods Castor and Pollux. **28:12** *Syracuse* was on the island of Sicily. **28:13** *Rhegium* was on the southern tip of Italy. **28:14** Greek *brothers*. **28:15a** Greek *brothers*. **28:15b** *The Forum* was about 43 miles (70 kilometers) from Rome. **28:15c** *The Three Taverns* was about 35 miles (57 kilometers) from Rome. **28:26-27** Isa 6:9-10 (Greek version). **28:28** Some manuscripts add verse 29, *And when he had said these words, the Jews departed, greatly disagreeing with each other*. **28:30** Or *in his own rented quarters*.

ROMANS

WHO
Paul and Phoebe.

WHERE
From Corinth, where Paul was starting a church.

WHEN
Around AD 57, before Paul visited Rome to teach the Roman Christians more about Christ.

WHY
To introduce Paul to the Christians in Rome and to explain clearly the Christian message.

For the wages of sin is death, but the free gift of God is eternal life through Christ Jesus our Lord.
ROMANS 6:23

Romans is a good news/bad news book. Paul began with the bad news: All people are sinners and stand condemned before God, their Judge. Then he shared the good news: People can be forgiven of their sins and saved because of God's grace, through their faith in Christ.

LOOK FOR YOURSELF IN THIS BOOK—A SINNER (ROMANS 6:23) AND A FORGIVEN CHILD OF GOD (ROMANS 5:1 AND 8:1)!

CHAPTER 1

Greetings from Paul

This letter is from Paul, a slave of Christ Jesus, chosen by God to be an apostle and sent out to preach his Good News. [2]God promised this Good News long ago through his prophets in the holy Scriptures. [3]The Good News is about his Son. In his earthly life he was born into King David's family line, [4]and he was shown to be* the Son of God when he was raised from the dead by the power of the Holy Spirit.* He is Jesus Christ our Lord. [5]Through

1:4a Or *and was designated.* **1:4b** Or *by the Spirit of holiness;* or *in the new realm of the Spirit.*

Christ, God has given us the privilege* and authority as apostles to tell Gentiles everywhere what God has done for them, so that they will believe and obey him, bringing glory to his name.

[6]And you are included among those Gentiles who have been called to belong to Jesus Christ. [7]I am writing to all of you in Rome who are loved by God and are called to be his own holy people.

May God our Father and the Lord Jesus Christ give you grace and peace.

God's Good News

[8]Let me say first that I thank my God through Jesus Christ for all of you, because your faith in him is being talked about all over the world. [9]God knows how often I pray for you. Day and night I bring you and your needs in prayer to God, whom I serve with all my heart* by spreading the Good News about his Son.

[10]One of the things I always pray for is the opportunity, God willing, to come at last to see you. [11]For I long to visit you so I can bring you some spiritual gift that will help you grow strong in the Lord. [12]When we get together, I want to encourage you in your faith, but I also want to be encouraged by yours.

[13]I want you to know, dear brothers and sisters,* that I planned many times to visit you, but I was prevented until now. I want to work among you and see spiritual fruit, just as I have seen among other Gentiles. [14]For I have a great sense of obligation to people in both the civilized world and the rest of the world,* to the educated and uneducated alike. [15]So I am eager to come to you in Rome, too, to preach the Good News.

[16]For I am not ashamed of this Good News about Christ. It is the power of God at work, saving everyone who believes—the Jew first and also the Gentile.* [17]This Good News tells us how God makes us right in his sight. This is accomplished from start to finish by faith. As the Scriptures say, "It is through faith that a righteous person has life."*

God's Anger at Sin

[18]But God shows his anger from heaven against all sinful, wicked people who suppress the truth by their wickedness.* [19]They know the truth about God because he has made it obvious to them. [20]For ever since the world was created, people have seen the earth and sky. Through everything God made, they can clearly see his invisible qualities—his eternal power and divine nature. So they have no excuse for not knowing God.

[21]Yes, they knew God, but they wouldn't worship him as God or even give him thanks. And they began to think up foolish ideas of what God was like. As a result, their minds became dark and confused. [22]Claiming to be wise, they instead became utter fools. [23]And instead of worshiping the glorious, ever-living God, they worshiped idols made to look like mere people and birds and animals and reptiles.

[24]So God abandoned them to do whatever shameful things their hearts desired. As a result, they did vile and degrading things with each other's bodies. [25]They traded the truth about God for a lie. So they worshiped and served the things God created instead of the Creator himself, who is worthy of eternal praise! Amen. [26]That is why God abandoned them to their shameful desires. Even the women turned against the natural way to have sex and instead indulged in sex with each other. [27]And the men, instead of having normal sexual relations with women, burned with lust for each other. Men did shameful things with other men, and as a result of this sin, they suffered within themselves the penalty they deserved.

[28]Since they thought it foolish to acknowledge God, he abandoned them to their foolish thinking and let them do things that should never be done. [29]Their lives became full of every kind of wickedness, sin, greed, hate, envy, murder, quarreling, deception, malicious behavior, and gossip. [30]They are backstabbers, haters of God, insolent, proud, and boastful. They invent new ways of sinning, and they disobey their parents. [31]They refuse to understand, break their promises, are heartless, and have no mercy. [32]They know God's justice requires that those who do these things deserve to die, yet they do them anyway. Worse yet, they encourage others to do them, too.

1:5 Or *the grace.* **1:9** Or *in my spirit.* **1:13** Greek *brothers.* **1:14** Greek *to Greeks and barbarians.* **1:16** Greek *also the Greek.* **1:17** Or *"The righteous will live by faith."* Hab 2:4. **1:18** Or *who, by their wickedness, prevent the truth from being known.*

CHAPTER 2

God's Judgment of Sin

You may think you can condemn such people,
but you are just as bad, and you have no ex-
cuse! When you say they are wicked and
should be punished, you are condemning
yourself, for you who judge others do these
very same things. [2]And we know that God, in
his justice, will punish anyone who does such
things. [3]Since you judge others for doing
these things, why do you think you can avoid
God's judgment when you do the same
things? [4]Don't you see how wonderfully kind,
tolerant, and patient God is with you? Does
this mean nothing to you? Can't you see that
his kindness is intended to turn you from
your sin?

[5]But because you are stubborn and refuse
to turn from your sin, you are storing up terri-
ble punishment for yourself. For a day of
anger is coming, when God's righteous judg-
ment will be revealed. [6]He will judge everyone
according to what they have done. [7]He will
give eternal life to those who keep on doing
good, seeking after the glory and honor and
immortality that God offers. [8]But he will pour
out his anger and wrath on those who live for
themselves, who refuse to obey the truth and
instead live lives of wickedness. [9]There will
be trouble and calamity for everyone who
keeps on doing what is evil—for the Jew first
and also for the Gentile.* [10]But there will be
glory and honor and peace from God for
all who do good—for the Jew first and also
for the Gentile. [11]For God does not show fa-
voritism.

[12]When the Gentiles sin, they will be de-
stroyed, even though they never had God's
written law. And the Jews, who do have God's
law, will be judged by that law when they fail
to obey it. [13]For merely listening to the law
doesn't make us right with God. It is obeying
the law that makes us right in his sight. [14]Even
Gentiles, who do not have God's written law,
show that they know his law when they in-
stinctively obey it, even without having heard
it. [15]They demonstrate that God's law is writ-
ten in their hearts, for their own conscience
and thoughts either accuse them or tell them
they are doing right. [16]And this is the message
I proclaim—that the day is coming when God,
through Christ Jesus, will judge everyone's se-
cret life.

The Jews and the Law

[17]You who call yourselves Jews are relying on
God's law, and you boast about your special
relationship with him. [18]You know what he
wants; you know what is right because you
have been taught his law. [19]You are convinced

2:9 Greek *also for the Greek;* also in 2:10.

SALVATION'S FREEWAY

Everyone has sinned. Romans 3:23

The wages of sin is death. Romans 6:23

Christ [died] for us while we were still sinners. Romans 5:8

If you confess with your mouth that Jesus is Lord and believe in your heart that God raised him from the dead, you will be saved. Romans 10:9

that you are a guide for the blind and a light
for people who are lost in darkness. [20]You
think you can instruct the ignorant and teach
children the ways of God. For you are certain
that God's law gives you complete knowledge
and truth.

[21]Well then, if you teach others, why don't
you teach yourself? You tell others not to
steal, but do you steal? [22]You say it is wrong to
commit adultery, but do you commit adul-
tery? You condemn idolatry, but do you use
items stolen from pagan temples?* [23]You are
so proud of knowing the law, but you dis-
honor God by breaking it. [24]No wonder the
Scriptures say, "The Gentiles blaspheme the
name of God because of you."*

[25]The Jewish ceremony of circumcision
has value only if you obey God's law. But if you
don't obey God's law, you are no better off
than an uncircumcised Gentile. [26]And if the
Gentiles obey God's law, won't God declare
them to be his own people? [27]In fact,
uncircumcised Gentiles who keep God's law
will condemn you Jews who are circumcised
and possess God's law but don't obey it.

[28]For you are not a true Jew just because you
were born of Jewish parents or because you
have gone through the ceremony of circumci-
sion. [29]No, a true Jew is one whose heart is right
with God. And true circumcision is not merely
obeying the letter of the law; rather, it is a
change of heart produced by God's Spirit. And
a person with a changed heart seeks praise*
from God, not from people.

CHAPTER 3

God Remains Faithful

Then what's the advantage of being a Jew? Is
there any value in the ceremony of circumci-
sion? [2]Yes, there are great benefits! First of
all, the Jews were entrusted with the whole
revelation of God.*

[3]True, some of them were unfaithful; but
just because they were unfaithful, does that
mean God will be unfaithful? [4]Of course not!
Even if everyone else is a liar, God is true. As
the Scriptures say about him,

"You will be proved right in what you say,
and you will win your case in court."*

[5]"But," some might say, "our sinfulness
serves a good purpose, for it helps people see
how righteous God is. Isn't it unfair, then, for
him to punish us?" (This is merely a human
point of view.) [6]Of course not! If God were
not entirely fair, how would he be qualified
to judge the world? [7]"But," someone might
still argue, "how can God condemn me as a
sinner if my dishonesty highlights his truth-
fulness and brings him more glory?" [8]And
some people even slander us by claiming
that we say, "The more we sin, the better it
is!" Those who say such things deserve to be
condemned.

All People Are Sinners

[9]Well then, should we conclude that we Jews
are better than others? No, not at all, for we
have already shown that all people, whether
Jews or Gentiles,* are under the power of sin.

My friends seem OK. Why do people say they're sinners?

No one is righteous—not even one.
ROMANS 3:10

[10]As the Scriptures say,

"No one is righteous—
not even one.
[11] No one is truly wise;
no one is seeking God.
[12] All have turned away;
all have become useless.
No one does good,
not a single one."*
[13] "Their talk is foul, like the stench from
an open grave.
Their tongues are filled with lies."
"Snake venom drips from their lips."*
[14] "Their mouths are full of cursing and
bitterness."*
[15] "They rush to commit murder.

2:22 Greek *do you steal from temples?* **2:24** Isa 52:5 (Greek version). **2:29** Or *receives praise.* **3:2** Greek *the oracles of God.* **3:4** Ps 51:4 (Greek version). **3:9** Greek *or Greeks.* **3:10-12** Pss 14:1-3; 53:1-3 (Greek version). **3:13** Pss 5:9 (Greek version); 140:3. **3:14** Ps 10:7 (Greek version).

16 Destruction and misery always follow
them.
17 They don't know where to find peace."*
18 "They have no fear of God at all."*

19 Obviously, the law applies to those to whom it was given, for its purpose is to keep people from having excuses, and to show that the entire world is guilty before God. 20 For no one can ever be made right with God by doing what the law commands. The law simply shows us how sinful we are.

Christ Took Our Punishment

21 But now God has shown us a way to be made right with him without keeping the requirements of the law, as was promised in the writings of Moses* and the prophets long ago. 22 We are made right with God by placing our faith in Jesus Christ. And this is true for everyone who believes, no matter who we are.

23 For everyone has sinned; we all fall short of God's glorious standard. 24 Yet God, with undeserved kindness, declares that we are righteous. He did this through Christ Jesus when he freed us from the penalty for our sins. 25 For God presented Jesus as the sacrifice for sin. People are made right with God when they believe that Jesus sacrificed his life, shedding his blood. This sacrifice shows that God was being fair when he held back and did not punish those who sinned in times past, 26 for he was looking ahead and including them in what he would do in this present time. God did this to demonstrate his righteousness, for he himself is fair and just, and he declares sinners to be right in his sight when they believe in Jesus.

27 Can we boast, then, that we have done anything to be accepted by God? No, because our acquittal is not based on obeying the law. It is based on faith. 28 So we are made right with God through faith and not by obeying the law.

29 After all, is God the God of the Jews only? Isn't he also the God of the Gentiles? Of course he is. 30 There is only one God, and he makes people right with himself only by faith, whether they are Jews or Gentiles.* 31 Well then, if we emphasize faith, does this mean that we can forget about the law? Of course not! In fact, only when we have faith do we truly fulfill the law.

CHAPTER 4

The Faith of Abraham

Abraham was, humanly speaking, the founder of our Jewish nation. What did he discover about being made right with God? 2 If his good deeds had made him acceptable to God, he would have had something to boast about. But that was not God's way. 3 For the Scriptures tell us, "Abraham believed God, and God counted him as righteous because of his faith."*

4 When people work, their wages are not a gift, but something they have earned. 5 But people are counted as righteous, not because of their work, but because of their faith in God who forgives sinners. 6 David also spoke of this when he described the happiness of those who are declared righteous without working for it:

7 "Oh, what joy for those
whose disobedience is forgiven,
whose sins are put out of sight.
8 Yes, what joy for those
whose record the LORD has cleared of
sin."*

9 Now, is this blessing only for the Jews, or is it also for uncircumcised Gentiles?* Well, we have been saying that Abraham was counted as righteous by God because of his faith. 10 But how did this happen? Was he counted as righteous only after he was circumcised, or was it before he was circumcised? Clearly, God accepted Abraham before he was circumcised!

11 Circumcision was a sign that Abraham already had faith and that God had already accepted him and declared him to be righteous—even before he was circumcised. So Abraham is the spiritual father of those who have faith but have not been circumcised. They are counted as righteous because of their faith. 12 And Abraham is also the spiritual father of those who have been circumcised, but only if they have the same kind of faith Abraham had before he was circumcised.

13 Clearly, God's promise to give the whole earth to Abraham and his descendants was

3:15-17 Isa 59:7-8. **3:18** Ps 36:1. **3:21** Greek *in the law*. **3:30** Greek *whether they are circumcised or uncircumcised*. **4:3** Gen 15:6. **4:7-8** Ps 32:1-2 (Greek version). **4:9** Greek *is this blessing only for the circumcised, or is it also for the uncircumcised?*

based not on his obedience to God's law, but on a right relationship with God that comes by faith. [14]If God's promise is only for those who obey the law, then faith is not necessary and the promise is pointless. [15]For the law always brings punishment on those who try to obey it. (The only way to avoid breaking the law is to have no law to break!)

[16]So the promise is received by faith. It is given as a free gift. And we are all certain to receive it, whether or not we live according to the law of Moses, if we have faith like Abraham's. For Abraham is the father of all who believe. [17]That is what the Scriptures mean when God told him, "I have made you the father of many nations."* This happened because Abraham believed in the God who brings the dead back to life and who creates new things out of nothing.

AMAZING FACTS

Know what the Bible says we should do in bad times? Celebrate! Check out why.

ROMANS 5:3-5

[18]Even when there was no reason for hope, Abraham kept hoping—believing that he would become the father of many nations. For God had said to him, "That's how many descendants you will have!"* [19]And Abraham's faith did not weaken, even though, at about 100 years of age, he figured his body was as good as dead—and so was Sarah's womb.

[20]Abraham never wavered in believing God's promise. In fact, his faith grew stronger, and in this he brought glory to God. [21]He was fully convinced that God is able to do whatever he promises. [22]And because of Abraham's faith, God counted him as righteous. [23]And when God counted him as righteous, it wasn't just for Abraham's benefit. It was recorded [24]for our benefit, too, assuring us that God will also count us as righteous if we believe in him, the one who raised Jesus our Lord from the dead. [25]He was handed over to die because of our sins, and he was raised to life to make us right with God.

CHAPTER 5

Faith Brings Joy

Therefore, since we have been made right in God's sight by faith, we have peace with God because of what Jesus Christ our Lord has done for us. [2]Because of our faith, Christ has brought us into this place of undeserved privilege where we now stand, and we confidently and joyfully look forward to sharing God's glory.

[3]We can rejoice, too, when we run into problems and trials, for we know that they help us develop endurance. [4]And endurance develops strength of character, and character strengthens our confident hope of salvation. [5]And this hope will not lead to disappointment. For we know how dearly God loves us, because he has given us the Holy Spirit to fill our hearts with his love.

[6]When we were utterly helpless, Christ came at just the right time and died for us sinners. [7]Now, most people would not be willing to die for an upright person, though someone might perhaps be willing to die for a person who is especially good. [8]But God showed his great love for us by sending Christ to die for us while we were still sinners. [9]And since we have been made right in God's sight by the blood of Christ, he will certainly save us from God's condemnation. [10]For since our friendship with God was restored by the death of his Son while we were still his enemies, we will certainly be saved through the life of his Son. [11]So now we can rejoice in our wonderful new relationship with God because our Lord Jesus Christ has made us friends of God.

Adam and Christ Contrasted

[12]When Adam sinned, sin entered the world. Adam's sin brought death, so death spread to everyone, for everyone sinned. [13]Yes, people

4:17 Gen 17:5. **4:18** Gen 15:5.

sinned even before the law was given. But it was not counted as sin because there was not yet any law to break. [14]Still, everyone died—from the time of Adam to the time of Moses—even those who did not disobey an explicit commandment of God, as Adam did. Now Adam is a symbol, a representation of Christ, who was yet to come. [15]But there is a great difference between Adam's sin and God's gracious gift. For the sin of this one man, Adam, brought death to many. But even greater is God's wonderful grace and his gift of forgiveness to many through this other man, Jesus Christ. [16]And the result of God's gracious gift is very different from the result of that one man's sin. For Adam's sin led to condemnation, but God's free gift leads to our being made right with God, even though we are guilty of many sins. [17]For the sin of this one man, Adam, caused death to rule over many. But even greater is God's wonderful grace and his gift of righteousness, for all who receive it will live in triumph over sin and death through this one man, Jesus Christ.

[18]Yes, Adam's one sin brings condemnation for everyone, but Christ's one act of righteousness brings a right relationship with God and new life for everyone. [19]Because one person disobeyed God, many became sinners. But because one other person obeyed God, many will be made righteous.

[20]God's law was given so that all people could see how sinful they were. But as people sinned more and more, God's wonderful grace became more abundant. [21]So just as sin ruled over all people and brought them to death, now God's wonderful grace rules instead, giving us right standing with God and resulting in eternal life through Jesus Christ our Lord.

CHAPTER 6

Sin's Power Is Broken

Well then, should we keep on sinning so that God can show us more and more of his wonderful grace? [2]Of course not! Since we have died to sin, how can we continue to live in it? [3]Or have you forgotten that when we were joined with Christ Jesus in baptism, we joined him in his death? [4]For we died and were buried with Christ by baptism. And just as Christ was raised from the dead by the glorious power of the Father, now we also may live new lives.

[5]Since we have been united with him in his death, we will also be raised to life as he was. [6]We know that our old sinful selves were crucified with Christ so that sin might lose its power in our lives. We are no longer slaves to sin. [7]For when we died with Christ we were set free from the power of sin. [8]And since we died with Christ, we know we will also live with him. [9]We are sure of this because Christ was raised from the dead, and he will never die again. Death no longer has any power over him. [10]When he died, he died once to break the power of sin. But now that he lives, he lives for the glory of God. [11]So you also should consider yourselves to be dead to the power of sin and alive to God through Christ Jesus.

[12]Do not let sin control the way you live;* do not give in to sinful desires. [13]Do not let any part of your body become an instrument of evil to serve sin. Instead, give yourselves completely to God, for you were dead, but now you have new life. So use your whole body as an instrument to do what is right for the glory of God. [14]Sin is no longer your master, for you no longer live under the requirements of the law. Instead, you live under the freedom of God's grace.

[15]Well then, since God's grace has set us free from the law, does that mean we can go on sinning? Of course not! [16]Don't you realize that you become the slave of whatever you choose to obey? You can be a slave to sin, which leads to death, or you can choose to obey God, which leads to righteous living. [17]Thank God! Once you were slaves of sin, but now you wholeheartedly obey this teaching we have given you. [18]Now you are free from your slavery to sin, and you have become slaves to righteous living.

[19]Because of the weakness of your human nature, I am using the illustration of slavery to help you understand all this. Previously, you let yourselves be slaves to impurity and lawlessness, which led ever deeper into sin. Now you must give yourselves to be slaves to righteous living so that you will become holy.

[20]When you were slaves to sin, you were free from the obligation to do right. [21]And

6:12 Or *Do not let sin reign in your body, which is subject to death.*

what was the result? You are now ashamed of the things you used to do, things that end in eternal doom. [22]But now you are free from the power of sin and have become slaves of God. Now you do those things that lead to holiness and result in eternal life. [23]For the wages of sin is death, but the free gift of God is eternal life through Christ Jesus our Lord.

CHAPTER 7

No Longer Bound to the Law

Now, dear brothers and sisters*—you who are familiar with the law—don't you know that the law applies only while a person is living? [2]For example, when a woman marries, the law binds her to her husband as long as he is alive. But if he dies, the laws of marriage no longer apply to her. [3]So while her husband is alive, she would be committing adultery if she married another man. But if her husband dies, she is free from that law and does not commit adultery when she remarries.

[4]So, my dear brothers and sisters, this is the point: You died to the power of the law when you died with Christ. And now you are united with the one who was raised from the dead. As a result, we can produce a harvest of good deeds for God. [5]When we were controlled by our old nature,* sinful desires were at work within us, and the law aroused these evil desires that produced a harvest of sinful deeds, resulting in death. [6]But now we have been released from the law, for we died to it and are no longer captive to its power. Now we can serve God, not in the old way of obeying the letter of the law, but in the new way of living in the Spirit.

God's Law Reveals Our Sin

[7]Well then, am I suggesting that the law of God is sinful? Of course not! In fact, it was the law that showed me my sin. I would never have known that coveting is wrong if the law had not said, "You must not covet."* [8]But sin used this command to arouse all kinds of covetous desires within me! If there were no law, sin would not have that power. [9]At one time I lived without understanding the law. But when I learned the command not to covet, for instance, the power of sin came to life, [10]and I died. So I discovered that the law's commands, which were supposed to bring life, brought spiritual death instead. [11]Sin took advantage of those commands and deceived me; it used the commands to kill me. [12]But still, the law itself is holy, and its commands are holy and right and good.

[13]But how can that be? Did the law, which is good, cause my death? Of course not! Sin used what was good to bring about my condemnation to death. So we can see how terrible sin really is. It uses God's good commands for its own evil purposes.

Struggling with Sin

[14]So the trouble is not with the law, for it is spiritual and good. The trouble is with me, for I am all too human, a slave to sin. [15]I don't really understand myself, for I want to do what is right, but I don't do it. Instead, I do what I hate. [16]But if I know that what I am doing is wrong, this shows that I agree that the law is good. [17]So I am not the one doing wrong; it is sin living in me that does it.

[18]And I know that nothing good lives in me, that is, in my sinful nature.* I want to do what is right, but I can't. [19]I want to do what is good, but I don't. I don't want to do what is wrong, but I do it anyway. [20]But if I do what I don't want to do, I am not really the one doing wrong; it is sin living in me that does it.

[21]I have discovered this principle of life—that when I want to do what is right, I inevitably do what is wrong. [22]I love God's law with all my heart. [23]But there is another power* within me that is at war with my mind. This power makes me a slave to the sin that is still within me. [24]Oh, what a miserable person I am! Who will free me from this life that is dominated by sin and death? [25]Thank God! The answer is in Jesus Christ our Lord. So you see how it is: In my mind I really want to obey God's law, but because of my sinful nature I am a slave to sin.

CHAPTER 8

Life in the Spirit

So now there is no condemnation for those who belong to Christ Jesus. [2]And because you belong to him, the power* of the life-giving Spirit has freed you* from the power of sin that leads to death. [3]The law of Moses was un-

7:1 Greek *brothers;* also in 7:4. **7:5** Greek *When we were in the flesh.* **7:7** Exod 20:17; Deut 5:21. **7:18** Greek *my flesh;* also in 7:25. **7:23** Greek *law;* also in 7:23b. **8:2a** Greek *the law;* also in 8:2b. **8:2b** Some manuscripts read *me.*

able to save us because of the weakness of our sinful nature.* So God did what the law could not do. He sent his own Son in a body like the bodies we sinners have. And in that body God declared an end to sin's control over us by giving his Son as a sacrifice for our sins. [4]He did this so that the just requirement of the law would be fully satisfied for us, who no longer follow our sinful nature but instead follow the Spirit.

[5]Those who are dominated by the sinful nature think about sinful things, but those who are controlled by the Holy Spirit think about things that please the Spirit. [6]So letting your sinful nature control your mind leads to death. But letting the Spirit control your mind leads to life and peace. [7]For the sinful nature is always hostile to God. It never did obey God's laws, and it never will. [8]That's why those who are still under the control of their sinful nature can never please God.

[9]But you are not controlled by your sinful nature. You are controlled by the Spirit if you have the Spirit of God living in you. (And remember that those who do not have the Spirit of Christ living in them do not belong to him at all.) [10]And Christ lives within you, so even though your body will die because of sin, the Spirit gives you life* because you have been made right with God. [11]The Spirit of God, who raised Jesus from the dead, lives in you. And just as God raised Christ Jesus from the dead, he will give life to your mortal bodies by this same Spirit living within you.

[12]Therefore, dear brothers and sisters,* you have no obligation to do what your sinful nature urges you to do. [13]For if you live by its dictates, you will die. But if through the power of the Spirit you put to death the deeds of your sinful nature,* you will live. [14]For all who are led by the Spirit of God are children* of God.

[15]So you have not received a spirit that makes you fearful slaves. Instead, you received God's Spirit when he adopted you as his own children.* Now we call him, "Abba, Father."* [16]For his Spirit joins with our spirit to affirm that we are God's children. [17]And since we are his children, we are his heirs. In fact, together with Christ we are heirs of God's glory. But if we are to share his glory, we must also share his suffering.

The Future Glory

[18]Yet what we suffer now is nothing compared to the glory he will reveal to us later. [19]For all creation is waiting eagerly for that future day when God will reveal who his children really are. [20]Against its will, all creation was subjected to God's curse. But with eager hope, [21]the creation looks forward to the day when it will join God's children in glorious freedom from death and decay. [22]For we know that all creation has been groaning as in the pains of childbirth right up to the present time. [23]And we believers also groan, even though we have the Holy Spirit within us as a foretaste of future glory, for we long for our bodies to be released from sin and suffering.

8:3 Greek *our flesh;* similarly in 8:4, 5, 6, 7, 8, 9, 12. **8:10** Or *your spirit is alive.* **8:12** Greek *brothers;* also in 8:29. **8:13** Greek *deeds of the body.* **8:14** Greek *sons;* also in 8:19. **8:15a** Greek *you received a spirit of sonship.* **8:15b** *Abba* is an Aramaic term for "father."

IMPORTANT IDEAS IN ROMANS

Important ideas	It's in	It's called
The price of sin is death. Jesus paid the price so we could go free.	Romans 3:24; 8:23	Redemption
God removes the punishment for sin through the perfect sacrifice of Jesus Christ.	Romans 3:25	Atonement
God declares us "not guilty" for our sins.	Romans 4:25; 5:18	Justification
The Holy Spirit helps us become more and more like Jesus.	Romans 5:2-5; 15:16	Sanctification
God will make us brand new in heaven.	Romans 8:18-19	Glorification
God chooses people for a specific purpose.	Romans 9:10-13	Election

We, too, wait with eager hope for the day when God will give us our full rights as his adopted children,* including the new bodies he has promised us. [24]We were given this hope when we were saved. (If we already have something, we don't need to hope* for it. [25]But if we look forward to something we don't yet have, we must wait patiently and confidently.)

[26]And the Holy Spirit helps us in our weakness. For example, we don't know what God wants us to pray for. But the Holy Spirit prays for us with groanings that cannot be expressed in words. [27]And the Father who knows all hearts knows what the Spirit is saying, for the Spirit pleads for us believers* in harmony with God's own will. [28]And we know that God causes everything to work together* for the good of those who love God and are called according to his purpose for them. [29]For God knew his people in advance, and he chose them to become like his Son, so that his Son would be the firstborn* among many brothers and sisters. [30]And having chosen them, he called them to come to him. And having called them, he gave them right standing with himself. And having given them right standing, he gave them his glory.

Nothing Can Separate Us from God's Love

[31]What shall we say about such wonderful things as these? If God is for us, who can ever be against us? [32]Since he did not spare even his own Son but gave him up for us all, won't he also give us everything else? [33]Who dares accuse us whom God has chosen for his own? No one—for God himself has given us right standing with himself. [34]Who then will condemn us? No one—for Christ Jesus died for us and was raised to life for us, and he is sitting in the place of honor at God's right hand, pleading for us.

[35]Can anything ever separate us from Christ's love? Does it mean he no longer loves us if we have trouble or calamity, or are persecuted, or hungry, or destitute, or in danger, or threatened with death? [36](As the Scriptures say, "For your sake we are killed every day; we are being slaughtered like sheep."*) [37]No, despite all these things, overwhelming victory is ours through Christ, who loved us.

[38]And I am convinced that nothing can ever separate us from God's love. Neither death nor life, neither angels nor demons,* neither our fears for today nor our worries about tomorrow—not even the powers of hell can separate us from God's love. [39]No power in the sky above or in the earth below—indeed, nothing in all creation will ever be able to separate us from the love of God that is revealed in Christ Jesus our Lord.

CHAPTER 9

God's Selection of Israel

With Christ as my witness, I speak with utter truthfulness. My conscience and the Holy Spirit confirm it. [2]My heart is filled with bitter sorrow and unending grief [3]for my people, my Jewish brothers and sisters.* I would be willing to be forever cursed—cut off from Christ!—if that would save them. [4]They are the people of Israel, chosen to be God's adopted children.* God revealed his glory to them. He made covenants with them and gave them his law. He gave them the privilege of worshiping him and receiving his wonderful promises. [5]Abraham, Isaac, and Jacob are their ancestors, and Christ himself was an Israelite as far as his human nature is concerned. And he is God, the one who rules over everything and is worthy of eternal praise! Amen.*

[6]Well then, has God failed to fulfill his promise to Israel? No, for not all who are born into the nation of Israel are truly members of God's people! [7]Being descendants of Abraham doesn't make them truly Abraham's children. For the Scriptures say, "Isaac is the son through whom your descendants will be counted,"* though Abraham had other children, too. [8]This means that Abraham's physical descendants are not necessarily children of God. Only the children of the promise are considered to be Abraham's children. [9]For God had promised, "I will return about this time next year, and Sarah will have a son."*

[10]This son was our ancestor Isaac. When he married Rebekah, she gave birth to twins.* [11]But before they were born, before they had

8:23 Greek *wait anxiously for sonship*. **8:24** Some manuscripts read *wait*. **8:27** Greek *for God's holy people*. **8:28** Some manuscripts read *And we know that everything works together*. **8:29** Or *would be supreme*. **8:36** Ps 44:22. **8:38** Greek *nor rulers*. **9:3** Greek *my brothers*. **9:4** Greek *chosen for sonship*. **9:5** Or *May God, the one who rules over everything, be praised forever. Amen*. **9:7** Gen 21:12. **9:9** Gen 18:10, 14. **9:10** Greek *she conceived children through this one man*.

done anything good or bad, she received a message from God. (This message shows that God chooses people according to his own purposes; [12]he calls people, but not according to their good or bad works.) She was told, "Your older son will serve your younger son."* [13]In the words of the Scriptures, "I loved Jacob, but I rejected Esau."*

[14]Are we saying, then, that God was unfair? Of course not! [15]For God said to Moses,

"I will show mercy to anyone I choose,
and I will show compassion to anyone
I choose."*

[16]So it is God who decides to show mercy. We can neither choose it nor work for it.

[17]For the Scriptures say that God told Pharaoh, "I have appointed you for the very purpose of displaying my power in you and to spread my fame throughout the earth."* [18]So you see, God chooses to show mercy to some, and he chooses to harden the hearts of others so they refuse to listen.

[19]Well then, you might say, "Why does God blame people for not responding? Haven't they simply done what he makes them do?"

[20]No, don't say that. Who are you, a mere human being, to argue with God? Should the thing that was created say to the one who created it, "Why have you made me like this?" [21]When a potter makes jars out of clay, doesn't he have a right to use the same lump of clay to make one jar for decoration and another to throw garbage into? [22]In the same way, even though God has the right to show his anger and his power, he is very patient with those on whom his anger falls, who are destined for destruction. [23]He does this to make the riches of his glory shine even brighter on those to whom he shows mercy, who were prepared in advance for glory. [24]And we are among those whom he selected, both from the Jews and from the Gentiles.

[25]Concerning the Gentiles, God says in the prophecy of Hosea,

"Those who were not my people,
I will now call my people.
And I will love those
whom I did not love before."*

[26]And,

"Then, at the place where they were told,
'You are not my people,'
there they will be called
'children of the living God.'"*

[27]And concerning Israel, Isaiah the prophet cried out,

"Though the people of Israel are as
numerous as the sand of the
seashore,
only a remnant will be saved.
[28] For the LORD will carry out his sentence
upon the earth
quickly and with finality."*

[29]And Isaiah said the same thing in another place:

"If the LORD of Heaven's Armies
had not spared a few of our children,
we would have been wiped out like
Sodom,
destroyed like Gomorrah."*

Israel's Unbelief

[30]What does all this mean? Even though the Gentiles were not trying to follow God's standards, they were made right with God. And it was by faith that this took place. [31]But the people of Israel, who tried so hard to get right with God by keeping the law, never succeeded. [32]Why not? Because they were trying to get right with God by keeping the law* instead of by trusting in him. They stumbled over the great rock in their path. [33]God warned them of this in the Scriptures when he said,

"I am placing a stone in Jerusalem* that
makes people stumble,
a rock that makes them fall.
But anyone who trusts in him
will never be disgraced."*

CHAPTER 10

Dear brothers and sisters,* the longing of my heart and my prayer to God is for the people of Israel to be saved. [2]I know what enthusiasm they have for God, but it is misdirected zeal. [3]For they don't understand God's way

9:12 Gen 25:23. **9:13** Mal 1:2-3. **9:15** Exod 33:19. **9:17** Exod 9:16 (Greek version). **9:25** Hos 2:23. **9:26** Greek *sons of the living God*. Hos 1:10. **9:27-28** Isa 10:22-23 (Greek version). **9:29** Isa 1:9. **9:32** Greek *by works*. **9:33a** Greek *in Zion*. **9:33b** Isa 8:14; 28:16 (Greek version). **10:1** Greek *Brothers*.

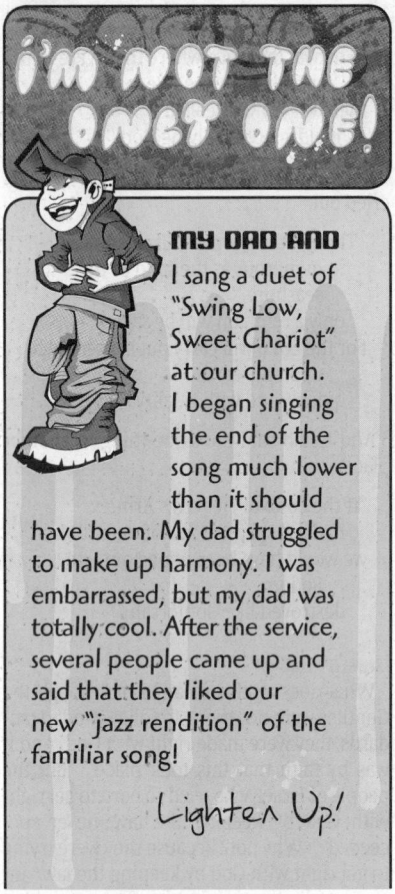

of making people right with himself. Refusing to accept God's way, they cling to their own way of getting right with God by trying to keep the law. [4]For Christ has already accomplished the purpose for which the law was given.* As a result, all who believe in him are made right with God.

Salvation Is for Everyone

[5]For Moses writes that the law's way of making a person right with God requires obedience to all of its commands.* [6]But faith's way of getting right with God says, "Don't say in your heart, 'Who will go up to heaven?' (to bring Christ down to earth). [7]And don't say, 'Who will go down to the place of the dead?' (to bring Christ back to life again)." [8]In fact, it says,

> "The message is very close at hand;
> it is on your lips and in your heart."*

And that message is the very message about faith that we preach: [9]If you confess with your mouth that Jesus is Lord and believe in your heart that God raised him from the dead, you will be saved. [10]For it is by believing in your heart that you are made right with God, and it is by confessing with your mouth that you are saved. [11]As the Scriptures tell us, "Anyone who trusts in him will never be disgraced."* [12]Jew and Gentile* are the same in this respect. They have the same Lord, who gives generously to all who call on him. [13]For "Everyone who calls on the name of the LORD will be saved."*

[14]But how can they call on him to save them unless they believe in him? And how can they believe in him if they have never heard about him? And how can they hear about him unless someone tells them? [15]And how will anyone go and tell them without being sent? That is why the Scriptures say, "How beautiful are the feet of messengers who bring good news!"*

[16]But not everyone welcomes the Good News, for Isaiah the prophet said, "LORD, who has believed our message?"* [17]So faith comes from hearing, that is, hearing the Good News about Christ. [18]But I ask, have the people of Israel actually heard the message? Yes, they have:

> "The message has gone throughout the earth,
> and the words to all the world."*

[19]But I ask, did the people of Israel really understand? Yes, they did, for even in the time of Moses, God said,

> "I will rouse your jealousy through people who are not even a nation.
> I will provoke your anger through the foolish Gentiles."*

[20]And later Isaiah spoke boldly for God, saying,

> "I was found by people who were not looking for me.

10:4 Or *For Christ is the end of the law.* **10:5** See Lev 18:5. **10:6-8** Deut 30:12-14. **10:11** Isa 28:16 (Greek version). **10:12** Greek *and Greek.* **10:13** Joel 2:32. **10:15** Isa 52:7. **10:16** Isa 53:1. **10:18** Ps 19:4. **10:19** Deut 32:21.

I showed myself to those who were not
asking for me.*"

21 But regarding Israel, God said,

"All day long I opened my arms to them,
but they were disobedient and
rebellious."*

CHAPTER 11

God's Mercy on Israel

I ask, then, has God rejected his own people,
the nation of Israel? Of course not! I myself
am an Israelite, a descendant of Abraham and
a member of the tribe of Benjamin.

2 No, God has not rejected his own people,
whom he chose from the very beginning. Do
you realize what the Scriptures say about
this? Elijah the prophet complained to God
about the people of Israel and said, 3 "LORD,
they have killed your prophets and torn down
your altars. I am the only one left, and now
they are trying to kill me, too."*

4 And do you remember God's reply? He
said, "No, I have 7,000 others who have never
bowed down to Baal!"*

5 It is the same today, for a few of the people
of Israel* have remained faithful because
of God's grace—his undeserved kindness in
choosing them. 6 And since it is through God's
kindness, then it is not by their good works.
For in that case, God's grace would not be
what it really is—free and undeserved.

7 So this is the situation: Most of the people
of Israel have not found the favor of God they
are looking for so earnestly. A few have—the
ones God has chosen—but the hearts of the
rest were hardened. 8 As the Scriptures say,

"God has put them into a deep sleep.
To this day he has shut their eyes so they
do not see,
and closed their ears so they do not
hear."*

9 Likewise, David said,

"Let their bountiful table become a snare,
a trap that makes them think all is well.
Let their blessings cause them to stumble,
and let them get what they deserve.
10 Let their eyes go blind so they cannot see,
and let their backs be bent forever."*

11 Did God's people stumble and fall beyond recovery? Of course not! They were disobedient, so God made salvation available to the Gentiles. But he wanted his own people to become jealous and claim it for themselves. 12 Now if the Gentiles were enriched because the people of Israel turned down God's offer of salvation, think how much greater a blessing the world will share when they finally accept it.

13 I am saying all this especially for you Gentiles. God has appointed me as the apostle to the Gentiles. I stress this, 14 for I want somehow to make the people of Israel jealous of what you Gentiles have, so I might save some of them. 15 For since their rejection meant that God offered salvation to the rest of the world, their acceptance will be even more wonderful. It will be life for those who were dead! 16 And since Abraham and the other patriarchs were holy, their descendants will also be holy—just as the entire batch of dough is holy because the portion given as an offering is holy. For if the roots of the tree are holy, the branches will be, too.

17 But some of these branches from Abraham's tree—some of the people of Israel—have been broken off. And you Gentiles, who were branches from a wild olive tree, have been grafted in. So now you also receive the blessing God has promised Abraham and his children, sharing in the rich nourishment from the root of God's special olive tree. 18 But you must not brag about being grafted in to replace the branches that were broken off. You are just a branch, not the root.

19 "Well," you may say, "those branches were broken off to make room for me." 20 Yes, but remember—those branches were broken off because they didn't believe in Christ, and you are there because you do believe. So don't think highly of yourself, but fear what could happen. 21 For if God did not spare the original branches, he won't* spare you either.

22 Notice how God is both kind and severe. He is severe toward those who disobeyed, but kind to you if you continue to trust in his kindness. But if you stop trusting, you also will be cut off. 23 And if the people of Israel turn from their unbelief, they will be grafted in again, for God has the power to graft them

10:20 Isa 65:1 (Greek version). **10:21** Isa 65:2 (Greek version). **11:3** 1 Kgs 19:10, 14. **11:4** 1 Kgs 19:18. **11:5** Greek *for a remnant.* **11:8** Isa 29:10; Deut 29:4. **11:9-10** Ps 69:22-23 (Greek version). **11:21** Some manuscripts read *perhaps he won't.*

new and different

Erik was not allowed to see PG–13 movies. When he asked his parents if he could go to a movie recently, they said OK because the movie was rated G. Erik's dad dropped him and his friends off at the theater, and they all bought their tickets. But once they got inside, Erik's friends walked past the G-rated movie and headed for one rated PG–13. Erik knew he was not supposed to go there, but he wanted to be with his friends. What do you think Erik should do? Read Romans 12:2 for God's advice in this situation.

back into the tree. [24]You, by nature, were a branch cut from a wild olive tree. So if God was willing to do something contrary to nature by grafting you into his cultivated tree, he will be far more eager to graft the original branches back into the tree where they belong.

God's Mercy Is for Everyone

[25]I want you to understand this mystery, dear brothers and sisters,* so that you will not feel proud about yourselves. Some of the people of Israel have hard hearts, but this will last only until the full number of Gentiles comes to Christ. [26]And so all Israel will be saved. As the Scriptures say,

"The one who rescues will come from Jerusalem,*
and he will turn Israel* away from ungodliness.
[27] And this is my covenant with them,
that I will take away their sins."*

[28]Many of the people of Israel are now enemies of the Good News, and this benefits you Gentiles. Yet they are still the people he loves because he chose their ancestors Abraham, Isaac, and Jacob. [29]For God's gifts and his call can never be withdrawn. [30]Once, you Gentiles were rebels against God, but when the people of Israel rebelled against him, God was merciful to you instead. [31]Now they are the rebels, and God's mercy has come to you so that they, too, will share* in God's mercy. [32]For God has imprisoned everyone in disobedience so he could have mercy on everyone.

[33]Oh, how great are God's riches and wisdom and knowledge! How impossible it is for us to understand his decisions and his ways!

[34] For who can know the LORD's thoughts?
Who knows enough to give him advice?*
[35] And who has given him so much
that he needs to pay it back?*

[36]For everything comes from him and exists by his power and is intended for his glory. All glory to him forever! Amen.

CHAPTER 12

A Living Sacrifice to God

And so, dear brothers and sisters,* I plead with you to give your bodies to God because of all he has done for you. Let them be a living and holy sacrifice—the kind he will find acceptable. This is truly the way to worship him.* [2]Don't copy the behavior and customs of this world, but let God transform you into a

11:25 Greek *brothers.* **11:26a** Greek *from Zion.* **11:26b** Greek *Jacob.* **11:26-27** Isa 59:20-21; 27:9 (Greek version). **11:31** Other manuscripts read *will now share;* still others read *will someday share.* **11:34** Isa 40:13 (Greek version). **11:35** See Job 41:11. **12:1a** Greek *brothers.* **12:1b** Or *This is your spiritual worship;* or *This is your reasonable service.*

new person by changing the way you think. Then you will learn to know God's will for you, which is good and pleasing and perfect.

[3]Because of the privilege and authority* God has given me, I give each of you this warning: Don't think you are better than you really are. Be honest in your evaluation of yourselves, measuring yourselves by the faith God has given us.* [4]Just as our bodies have many parts and each part has a special function, [5]so it is with Christ's body. We are many parts of one body, and we all belong to each other.

[6]In his grace, God has given us different gifts for doing certain things well. So if God has given you the ability to prophesy, speak out with as much faith as God has given you. [7]If your gift is serving others, serve them well. If you are a teacher, teach well. [8]If your gift is to encourage others, be encouraging. If it is giving, give generously. If God has given you leadership ability, take the responsibility seriously. And if you have a gift for showing kindness to others, do it gladly.

[9]Don't just pretend to love others. Really love them. Hate what is wrong. Hold tightly to what is good. [10]Love each other with genuine affection,* and take delight in honoring each other. [11]Never be lazy, but work hard and serve the Lord enthusiastically.* [12]Rejoice in our confident hope. Be patient in trouble, and keep on praying. [13]When God's people are in need, be ready to help them. Always be eager to practice hospitality.

[14]Bless those who persecute you. Don't curse them; pray that God will bless them. [15]Be happy with those who are happy, and weep with those who weep. [16]Live in harmony with each other. Don't be too proud to enjoy the company of ordinary people. And don't think you know it all!

[17]Never pay back evil with more evil. Do things in such a way that everyone can see you are honorable. [18]Do all that you can to live in peace with everyone.

[19]Dear friends, never take revenge. Leave that to the righteous anger of God. For the Scriptures say,

"I will take revenge;
I will pay them back,"*
says the LORD.

[20]Instead,

"If your enemies are hungry, feed them.
If they are thirsty, give them something to drink.
In doing this, you will heap
burning coals of shame on their heads."*

How can I keep from doing what's bad?

Don't let evil conquer you, but conquer evil by doing good.
ROMANS 12:21

[21]Don't let evil conquer you, but conquer evil by doing good.

CHAPTER 13

Respect for Authority

Everyone must submit to governing authorities. For all authority comes from God, and those in positions of authority have been placed there by God. [2]So anyone who rebels against authority is rebelling against what God has instituted, and they will be punished. [3]For the authorities do not strike fear in people who are doing right, but in those who are doing wrong. Would you like to live without fear of the authorities? Do what is right, and they will honor you. [4]The authorities are God's servants, sent for your good. But if you are doing wrong, of course you should be afraid, for they have the power to punish you. They are God's servants, sent for the very purpose of punishing those who do what is wrong. [5]So you must submit to them, not only to avoid punishment, but also to keep a clear conscience.

[6]Pay your taxes, too, for these same reasons. For government workers need to be paid. They are serving God in what they do. [7]Give to everyone what you owe them: Pay your taxes and government fees to those who

12:3a Or *Because of the grace;* compare 1:5. **12:3b** Or *by the faith God has given you;* or *by the standard of our God-given faith.* **12:10** Greek *with brotherly love.* **12:11** Or *but serve the Lord with a zealous spirit;* or *but let the Spirit excite you as you serve the Lord.* **12:19** Deut 32:35. **12:20** Prov 25:21-22.

collect them, and give respect and honor to those who are in authority.

Love Fulfills God's Requirements

[8]Owe nothing to anyone—except for your obligation to love one another. If you love your neighbor, you will fulfill the requirements of God's law. [9]For the commandments say, "You must not commit adultery. You must not murder. You must not steal. You must not covet."* These—and other such commandments—are summed up in this one commandment: "Love your neighbor as yourself."* [10]Love does no wrong to others, so love fulfills the requirements of God's law.

[11]This is all the more urgent, for you know how late it is; time is running out. Wake up, for our salvation is nearer now than when we first believed. [12]The night is almost gone; the day of salvation will soon be here. So remove your dark deeds like dirty clothes, and put on the shining armor of right living. [13]Because we belong to the day, we must live decent lives for all to see. Don't participate in the darkness of wild parties and drunkenness, or in sexual promiscuity and immoral living, or in quarreling and jealousy. [14]Instead, clothe yourself with the presence of the Lord Jesus Christ. And don't let yourself think about ways to indulge your evil desires.

CHAPTER 14

The Danger of Criticism

Accept other believers who are weak in faith, and don't argue with them about what they think is right or wrong. [2]For instance, one person believes it's all right to eat anything. But another believer with a sensitive conscience will eat only vegetables. [3]Those who feel free to eat anything must not look down on those who don't. And those who don't eat certain foods must not condemn those who do, for God has accepted them. [4]Who are you to condemn someone else's servants? Their own master will judge whether they stand or fall. And with the Lord's help, they will stand and receive his approval.

[5]In the same way, some think one day is more holy than another day, while others think every day is alike. You should each be fully convinced that whichever day you choose is acceptable. [6]Those who worship the Lord on a special day do it to honor him. Those who eat any kind of food do so to honor the Lord, since they give thanks to God before eating. And those who refuse to eat certain foods also want to please the Lord and give thanks to God. [7]For we don't live for ourselves or die for ourselves. [8]If we live, it's to honor the Lord. And if we die, it's to honor the Lord. So whether we live or die, we belong to the Lord. [9]Christ died and rose again for this very purpose—to be Lord both of the living and of the dead.

[10]So why do you condemn another believer*? Why do you look down on another believer? Remember, we will all stand before the judgment seat of God. [11]For the Scriptures say,

> "'As surely as I live,' says the LORD,
> 'every knee will bend to me,
> and every tongue will confess and give praise to God.*'"

[12]Yes, each of us will give a personal account to God. [13]So let's stop condemning each other. Decide instead to live in such a way that you will not cause another believer to stumble and fall.

[14]I know and am convinced on the authority of the Lord Jesus that no food, in and of itself, is wrong to eat. But if someone believes it is wrong, then for that person it is wrong. [15]And if another believer is distressed by what you eat, you are not acting in love if you eat it. Don't let your eating ruin someone for whom Christ died. [16]Then you will not be criticized for doing something you believe is good. [17]For the Kingdom of God is not a matter of what we eat or drink, but of living a life of goodness and peace and joy in the Holy Spirit. [18]If you serve Christ with this attitude, you will please God, and others will approve of you, too. [19]So then, let us aim for harmony in the church and try to build each other up.

[20]Don't tear apart the work of God over what you eat. Remember, all foods are acceptable, but it is wrong to eat something if it makes another person stumble. [21]It is better not to eat meat or drink wine or do anything

13:9a Exod 20:13-15, 17. **13:9b** Lev 19:18. **14:10** Greek *your brother;* also in 14:10b, 13, 15, 21. **14:11** Or *confess allegiance to God.* Isa 49:18; 45:23 (Greek version).

When I was younger, I'd often say to my friends at school that I couldn't wait until I was old enough to drink alcohol. So I didn't.

When I entered high school, I became friends with some older, unsaved kids who liked to party . . . a lot. They weren't old enough to drink either, but they somehow managed to show up at school dances and ball games with liquor.

I was excited about hanging around them at first. But, as time went on, I began to notice they were always yelling at—and complaining about—one another.

During one particularly rowdy dance, I decided I'd had enough. I called my dad and asked him to pick me up.

While getting ready for bed that night, I decided to do something I should've done months before—see if my Bible said anything about alcohol. It did.

One passage I read was Romans 13:13-14. It says, "Because we belong to the day, we must live decent lives for all to see. Don't participate in the darkness of wild parties and drunkenness, or in sexual promiscuity and immoral living, or in quarreling and jealousy. Instead, clothe yourself with the presence of the Lord Jesus Christ. And don't let yourself think about ways to indulge your evil desires."

I wrote that passage on an index card and taped it to my bedroom mirror. I hoped it would remind me whenever I headed out of the house that I don't have to behave the way the world does to have fun. Several years later, the verses are still there . . . and still doing their job.

For more on what the Bible has to say about alcohol use, look up Proverbs 20:1, Isaiah 5:11, and Ephesians 5:18.

else if it might cause another believer to stumble. [22]You may believe there's nothing wrong with what you are doing, but keep it between yourself and God. Blessed are those who don't feel guilty for doing something they have decided is right. [23]But if you have doubts about whether or not you should eat something, you are sinning if you go ahead and do it. For you are not following your convictions. If you do anything you believe is not right, you are sinning.

CHAPTER 15

Living to Please Others

We who are strong must be considerate of those who are sensitive about things like this. We must not just please ourselves. [2]We should help others do what is right and build them up in the Lord. [3]For even Christ didn't live to please himself. As the Scriptures say, "The insults of those who insult you, O God, have fallen on me."* [4]Such things were written in the Scriptures long ago to teach us. And the Scriptures give us hope and encouragement as we wait patiently for God's promises to be fulfilled.

[5]May God, who gives this patience and encouragement, help you live in complete harmony with each other, as is fitting for followers of Christ Jesus. [6]Then all of you can join together with one voice, giving praise and glory to God, the Father of our Lord Jesus Christ.

[7]Therefore, accept each other just as Christ has accepted you so that God will be given glory. [8]Remember that Christ came as a servant to the Jews* to show that God is true to the promises he made to their ancestors. [9]He also came so that the Gentiles might give glory to God for his mercies to them. That is what the psalmist meant when he wrote:

"For this, I will praise you among the Gentiles;
I will sing praises to your name."*

[10]And in another place it is written,

"Rejoice with his people,
you Gentiles."*

[11]And yet again,

"Praise the LORD, all you Gentiles.
Praise him, all you people of the earth."*

[12]And in another place Isaiah said,

"The heir to David's throne* will come,
and he will rule over the Gentiles.
They will place their hope on him."*

[13]I pray that God, the source of hope, will fill you completely with joy and peace because you trust in him. Then you will overflow with confident hope through the power of the Holy Spirit.

Paul's Reason for Writing

[14]I am fully convinced, my dear brothers and sisters,* that you are full of goodness. You know these things so well you can teach each other all about them. [15]Even so, I have been bold enough to write about some of these points, knowing that all you need is this reminder. For by God's grace, [16]I am a special messenger from Christ Jesus to you Gentiles. I bring you the Good News so that I might present you as an acceptable offering to God, made holy by the Holy Spirit. [17]So I have reason to be enthusiastic about all Christ Jesus has done through me in my service to God. [18]Yet I dare not boast about anything except what Christ has done through me, bringing the Gentiles to God by my message and by the way I worked among them. [19]They were convinced by the power of miraculous signs and wonders and by the power of God's Spirit.* In this way, I have fully presented the Good News of Christ from Jerusalem all the way to Illyricum.*

[20]My ambition has always been to preach the Good News where the name of Christ has never been heard, rather than where a church has already been started by someone else. [21]I have been following the plan spoken of in the Scriptures, where it says,

"Those who have never been told about him will see,
and those who have never heard of him will understand."*

15:3 Greek *who insult you have fallen on me*. Ps 69:9. **15:8** Greek *servant of circumcision*. **15:9** Ps 18:49. **15:10** Deut 32:43. **15:11** Ps 117:1. **15:12a** Greek *The root of Jesse*. David was the son of Jesse. **15:12b** Isa 11:10 (Greek version). **15:14** Greek *brothers;* also in 15:30. **15:19a** Other manuscripts read *the Spirit;* still others read *the Holy Spirit*. **15:19b** *Illyricum* was a region northeast of Italy. **15:21** Isa 52:15 (Greek version).

A while ago, my dad started going to a church of a different denomination. The new church was Christian—they just did things a little differently from what I was used to. I decided to keep going with my mom to the church our family has always attended.

I know my mom took it hard when my dad joined another church. I was worried that we couldn't be a family if we didn't all have the same beliefs. When I turned to my pastor for help, he told me to look at what Paul says about Christian differences in Romans chapter 14. So I flipped open my Bible and found exactly what I needed: "So why do you condemn another believer? Why do you look down on another believer? Remember, we will all stand before the judgment seat of God" (14:10). For Paul, it was *OK* that Christians had personal convictions about certain things—as long as they followed Christ's teachings. Paul reminded people to be loving and tolerant of the differences.

Sure, it would be easier if we all believed exactly alike. But Christians (and people in general!) aren't all the same. In fact, I've learned that our "differentness" actually makes the body of Christ *interesting*. I don't agree with my dad on everything now, but I sure learn a lot about what I do believe when we talk.

Whenever I start getting down about the things that divide my family, I try to remember that we all love Jesus. I know it would be another story if Dad wasn't a Christian at all—if he had decided to follow another faith like Hinduism. It helps me to know that my family will always be bound together by Jesus because we all love him. And that's what matters most.

Check out Romans 14 for more on appreciating Christian differences.

22 In fact, my visit to you has been delayed so
long because I have been preaching in these
places.

Paul's Travel Plans

23 But now I have finished my work in these re-
gions, and after all these long years of waiting,
I am eager to visit you. 24 I am planning to go to
Spain, and when I do, I will stop off in Rome.
And after I have enjoyed your fellowship for a
little while, you can provide for my journey.

25 But before I come, I must go to Jerusalem
to take a gift to the believers* there. 26 For you
see, the believers in Macedonia and Achaia*
have eagerly taken up an offering for the poor
among the believers in Jerusalem. 27 They
were glad to do this because they feel they
owe a real debt to them. Since the Gentiles re-
ceived the spiritual blessings of the Good
News from the believers in Jerusalem, they
feel the least they can do in return is to help
them financially. 28 As soon as I have delivered
this money and completed this good deed of
theirs, I will come to see you on my way to
Spain. 29 And I am sure that when I come,
Christ will richly bless our time together.

30 Dear brothers and sisters, I urge you in
the name of our Lord Jesus Christ to join in
my struggle by praying to God for me. Do this
because of your love for me, given to you by
the Holy Spirit. 31 Pray that I will be rescued
from those in Judea who refuse to obey God.
Pray also that the believers there will be will-
ing to accept the donation* I am taking to Je-
rusalem. 32 Then, by the will of God, I will be
able to come to you with a joyful heart, and we
will be an encouragement to each other.

33 And now may God, who gives us his
peace, be with you all. Amen.*

CHAPTER 16

Paul Greets His Friends

I commend to you our sister Phoebe, who is a
deacon in the church in Cenchrea. 2 Welcome
her in the Lord as one who is worthy of honor
among God's people. Help her in whatever
she needs, for she has been helpful to many,
and especially to me.

3 Give my greetings to Priscilla and Aquila,
my co-workers in the ministry of Christ Jesus.
4 In fact, they once risked their lives for me. I
am thankful to them, and so are all the Gentile
churches. 5 Also give my greetings to the
church that meets in their home.

Greet my dear friend Epenetus. He was the

PAUL (SAUL)

For a long time I was blind to truth. One day on my way to Damascus to arrest Christians, a bright light covered me. A voice from heaven came out of the light: Jesus asked me, "Why are you persecuting me?" Stunned, I asked him what to do. He sent me to Damascus. For three days I was blind. I didn't eat or drink. Then a believer came to tell me I would see and be filled with the Holy Spirit. Something like fish scales fell from my eyes. I could see again—physically and spiritually. After that I no longer had Christians arrested. I traveled and wrote letters, teaching people how to *become* Christians and live for Christ!

Read about Paul in Acts 7:58–28:31 and in his New Testament letters, including the one to the Roman church.

15:25 Greek *God's holy people;* also in 15:26, 31. **15:26** *Macedonia* and *Achaia* were the northern and southern regions of Greece. **15:31** Greek *the ministry;* other manuscripts read *the gift*. **15:33** Some manuscripts do not include *Amen*. One very early manuscript places 16:25-27 here.

first person from the province of Asia to become a follower of Christ. [6]Give my greetings to Mary, who has worked so hard for your benefit. [7]Greet Andronicus and Junia,* my fellow Jews,* who were in prison with me. They are highly respected among the apostles and became followers of Christ before I did. [8]Greet Ampliatus, my dear friend in the Lord. [9]Greet Urbanus, our co-worker in Christ, and my dear friend Stachys.

[10]Greet Apelles, a good man whom Christ approves. And give my greetings to the believers from the household of Aristobulus. [11]Greet Herodion, my fellow Jew.* Greet the Lord's people from the household of Narcissus. [12]Give my greetings to Tryphena and Tryphosa, the Lord's workers, and to dear Persis, who has worked so hard for the Lord. [13]Greet Rufus, whom the Lord picked out to be his very own; and also his dear mother, who has been a mother to me.

[14]Give my greetings to Asyncritus, Phlegon, Hermes, Patrobas, Hermas, and the brothers and sisters* who meet with them. [15]Give my greetings to Philologus, Julia, Nereus and his sister, and to Olympas and all the believers* who meet with them. [16]Greet each other in Christian love.* All the churches of Christ send you their greetings.

Paul's Final Instructions

[17]And now I make one more appeal, my dear brothers and sisters. Watch out for people who cause divisions and upset people's faith by teaching things contrary to what you have been taught. Stay away from them. [18]Such people are not serving Christ our Lord; they are serving their own personal interests. By smooth talk and glowing words they deceive innocent people. [19]But everyone knows that you are obedient to the Lord. This makes me very happy. I want you to be wise in doing right and to stay innocent of any wrong. [20]The God of peace will soon crush Satan under your feet. May the grace of our Lord Jesus* be with you.

[21]Timothy, my fellow worker, sends you his greetings, as do Lucius, Jason, and Sosipater, my fellow Jews.

[22]I, Tertius, the one writing this letter for Paul, send my greetings, too, as one of the Lord's followers.

[23]Gaius says hello to you. He is my host and also serves as host to the whole church. Erastus, the city treasurer, sends you his greetings, and so does our brother Quartus.*

[25]Now all glory to God, who is able to make you strong, just as my Good News says. This message about Jesus Christ has revealed his plan for you Gentiles, a plan kept secret from the beginning of time. [26]But now as the prophets* foretold and as the eternal God has commanded, this message is made known to all Gentiles everywhere, so that they too might believe and obey him. [27]All glory to the only wise God, through Jesus Christ, forever. Amen.

16:7a *Junia* is a feminine name. Some late manuscripts accent the word so it reads *Junias*, a masculine name; still others read *Julia* (feminine). **16:7b** Or *compatriots;* also in 16:21. **16:11** Or *compatriot*. **16:14** Greek *brothers;* also in 16:17. **16:15** Greek *all of God's holy people*. **16:16** Greek *with a sacred kiss*. **16:20** Some manuscripts read *Lord Jesus Christ*. **16:23** Some manuscripts add verse 24, *May the grace of our Lord Jesus Christ be with you all. Amen*. Still others add this sentence after verse 27. **16:26** Greek *the prophetic writings*.

1 Corinthians

WHO
Paul and Timothy.

WHERE
Paul wrote this letter from Ephesus near the end of his three-year stay.

WHEN
Around AD 55.

WHY
To point out problems in the church at Corinth, to offer solutions to those problems, and to teach the believers how to live for Christ in a godless society.

The temptations in your life are no different from what others experience. And God is faithful. He will not allow the temptation to be more than you can stand.
1 CORINTHIANS 10:13

Suppose you lived in a community where people believed in everything except the one true God. That's how it was for the Corinthians. Paul wrote to them to encourage them in their faith and to tell them how they should live.

Dig into Paul's letter to the church at Corinth; it was written for you, too.

CHAPTER **1**

Greetings from Paul

This letter is from Paul, chosen by the will of God to be an apostle of Christ Jesus, and from our brother Sosthenes.

[2]I am writing to God's church in Corinth,* to you who have been called by God to be his own holy people. He made you holy by means of Christ Jesus,* just as he did for all people everywhere who call on the name of our Lord Jesus Christ, their Lord and ours.

[3]May God our Father and the Lord Jesus Christ give you grace and peace.

1:2a *Corinth* was the capital city of Achaia, the southern region of the Greek peninsula. **1:2b** Or *because you belong to Christ Jesus.*

Paul Gives Thanks to God

4I always thank my God for you and for the
gracious gifts he has given you, now that you
belong to Christ Jesus. 5Through him, God
has enriched your church in every way—with
all of your eloquent words and all of your
knowledge. 6This confirms that what I told
you about Christ is true. 7Now you have every
spiritual gift you need as you eagerly wait for
the return of our Lord Jesus Christ. 8He will
keep you strong to the end so that you will be
free from all blame on the day when our Lord
Jesus Christ returns. 9God will do this, for he
is faithful to do what he says, and he has in-
vited you into partnership with his Son, Jesus
Christ our Lord.

Divisions in the Church

10I appeal to you, dear brothers and sisters,*
by the authority of our Lord Jesus Christ, to
live in harmony with each other. Let there be
no divisions in the church. Rather, be of one
mind, united in thought and purpose. 11For
some members of Chloe's household have
told me about your quarrels, my dear broth-
ers and sisters. 12Some of you are saying, "I
am a follower of Paul." Others are saying, "I
follow Apollos," or "I follow Peter,*" or "I fol-
low only Christ."

13Has Christ been divided into factions?
Was I, Paul, crucified for you? Were any of
you baptized in the name of Paul? Of course
not! 14I thank God that I did not baptize any of
you except Crispus and Gaius, 15for now no
one can say they were baptized in my name.
16(Oh yes, I also baptized the household of
Stephanas, but I don't remember baptizing
anyone else.) 17For Christ didn't send me to
baptize, but to preach the Good News—and
not with clever speech, for fear that the cross
of Christ would lose its power.

The Wisdom of God

18The message of the cross is foolish to those
who are headed for destruction! But we who
are being saved know it is the very power of
God. 19As the Scriptures say,

"I will destroy the wisdom of the wise
and discard the intelligence of the
intelligent."*

20So where does this leave the philoso-
phers, the scholars, and the world's brilliant
debaters? God has made the wisdom of this-
world look foolish. 21Since God in his wisdom
saw to it that the world would never know
him through human wisdom, he has used our
foolish preaching to save those who believe.
22It is foolish to the Jews, who ask for signs
from heaven. And it is foolish to the Greeks,
who seek human wisdom. 23So when we
preach that Christ was crucified, the Jews are
offended and the Gentiles say it's all non-
sense.

24But to those called by God to salvation,
both Jews and Gentiles,* Christ is the power
of God and the wisdom of God. 25This foolish
plan of God is wiser than the wisest of human
plans, and God's weakness is stronger than
the greatest of human strength.

26Remember, dear brothers and sisters,
that few of you were wise in the world's eyes
or powerful or wealthy* when God called you.
27Instead, God chose things the world consid-
ers foolish in order to shame those who think
they are wise. And he chose things that are
powerless to shame those who are powerful.
28God chose things despised by the world,*
things counted as nothing at all, and used
them to bring to nothing what the world con-
siders important. 29As a result, no one can
ever boast in the presence of God.

30God has united you with Christ Jesus. For
our benefit God made him to be wisdom it-
self. Christ made us right with God; he made
us pure and holy, and he freed us from sin.
31Therefore, as the Scriptures say, "If you
want to boast, boast only about the LORD."*

CHAPTER 2

Paul's Message of Wisdom

When I first came to you, dear brothers and
sisters,* I didn't use lofty words and impres-
sive wisdom to tell you God's secret plan.*
2For I decided that while I was with you I
would forget everything except Jesus Christ,
the one who was crucified. 3I came to you in
weakness—timid and trembling. 4And my
message and my preaching were very plain.
Rather than using clever and persuasive
speeches, I relied only on the power of the

1:10 Greek *brothers;* also in 1:11, 26. **1:12** Greek *Cephas.* **1:19** Isa 29:14. **1:24** Greek *and Greeks.* **1:26** Or *high born.* **1:28** Or *God chose those who are low born.* **1:31** Jer 9:24. **2:1a** Greek *brothers.* **2:1b** Greek *God's mystery;* other manuscripts read *God's testimony.*

Holy Spirit. [5]I did this so you would trust not in human wisdom but in the power of God.

[6]Yet when I am among mature believers, I do speak with words of wisdom, but not the kind of wisdom that belongs to this world or to the rulers of this world, who are soon forgotten. [7]No, the wisdom we speak of is the mystery of God*—his plan that was previously hidden, even though he made it for our ultimate glory before the world began. [8]But the rulers of this world have not understood it; if they had, they would not have crucified our glorious Lord. [9]That is what the Scriptures mean when they say,

"No eye has seen, no ear has heard,
and no mind has imagined
what God has prepared
for those who love him."*

[10]But* it was to us that God revealed these things by his Spirit. For his Spirit searches out everything and shows us God's deep secrets. [11]No one can know a person's thoughts except that person's own spirit, and no one can know God's thoughts except God's own Spirit. [12]And we have received God's Spirit (not the world's spirit), so we can know the wonderful things God has freely given us.

[13]When we tell you these things, we do not use words that come from human wisdom. Instead, we speak words given to us by the Spirit, using the Spirit's words to explain spiritual truths.* [14]But people who aren't spiritual* can't receive these truths from God's Spirit. It all sounds foolish to them and they can't understand it, for only those who are spiritual can understand what the Spirit means. [15]Those who are spiritual can evaluate all things, but they themselves cannot be evaluated by others. [16]For,

"Who can know the LORD's thoughts?
Who knows enough to teach him?"*

But we understand these things, for we have the mind of Christ.

CHAPTER 3

Paul and Apollos, Servants of Christ

Dear brothers and sisters,* when I was with you I couldn't talk to you as I would to spiritual people.* I had to talk as though you belonged to this world or as though you were infants in the Christian life.* [2]I had to feed you with milk, not with solid food, because you weren't ready for anything stronger. And you still aren't ready, [3]for you are still controlled by your sinful nature. You are jealous of one another and quarrel with each other. Doesn't that prove you are controlled by your sinful nature? Aren't you living like people of the world? [4]When one of you says, "I am a follower of Paul," and another says, "I follow Apollos," aren't you acting just like people of the world?

[5]After all, who is Apollos? Who is Paul? We are only God's servants through whom you believed the Good News. Each of us did the

ONE DAY I WAS LATE for football practice. The team always changed in the upper gym, which was the girls' gym. The other guys had already left, and I hurriedly undressed so I could catch up with them. To my dismay, I heard girls' voices coming. I struggled to get my uniform on quickly, but it was too late. They walked in on me in my underwear, and we were all equally embarrassed.

Lighten Up!

2:7 Greek *But we speak God's wisdom in a mystery.* 2:9 Isa 64:4. 2:10 Some manuscripts read *For.* 2:13 Or *explaining spiritual truths in spiritual language,* or *explaining spiritual truths to spiritual people.* 2:14 Or *who don't have the Spirit;* or *who have only physical life.* 2:16 Isa 40:13 (Greek version). 3:1a Greek *Brothers.* 3:1b Or *to people who have the Spirit.* 3:1c Greek *in Christ.*

work the Lord gave us. [6]I planted the seed in your hearts, and Apollos watered it, but it was God who made it grow. [7]It's not important who does the planting, or who does the watering. What's important is that God makes the seed grow. [8]The one who plants and the one who waters work together with the same purpose. And both will be rewarded for their own hard work. [9]For we are both God's workers. And you are God's field. You are God's building.

[10]Because of God's grace to me, I have laid the foundation like an expert builder. Now others are building on it. But whoever is building on this foundation must be very careful. [11]For no one can lay any foundation other than the one we already have—Jesus Christ.

[12]Anyone who builds on that foundation may use a variety of materials—gold, silver, jewels, wood, hay, or straw. [13]But on the judgment day, fire will reveal what kind of work each builder has done. The fire will show if a person's work has any value. [14]If the work survives, that builder will receive a reward. [15]But if the work is burned up, the builder will suffer great loss. The builder will be saved, but like someone barely escaping through a wall of flames.

[16]Don't you realize that all of you together are the temple of God and that the Spirit of God lives in* you? [17]God will destroy anyone who destroys this temple. For God's temple is holy, and you are that temple.

AMAZING FACTS

Think you've got a deep hidden secret? God knows all about it. He sees right through you!

1 CORINTHIANS 4:5

[18]Stop deceiving yourselves. If you think you are wise by this world's standards, you need to become a fool to be truly wise. [19]For the wisdom of this world is foolishness to God. As the Scriptures say,

"He traps the wise
in the snare of their own cleverness."*

[20]And again,

"The LORD knows the thoughts of the wise;
he knows they are worthless."*

[21]So don't boast about following a particular human leader. For everything belongs to you—[22]whether Paul or Apollos or Peter,* or the world, or life and death, or the present and the future. Everything belongs to you, [23]and you belong to Christ, and Christ belongs to God.

CHAPTER 4

Paul's Relationship with the Corinthians

So look at Apollos and me as mere servants of Christ who have been put in charge of explaining God's mysteries. [2]Now, a person who is put in charge as a manager must be faithful. [3]As for me, it matters very little how I might be evaluated by you or by any human authority. I don't even trust my own judgment on this point. [4]My conscience is clear, but that doesn't prove I'm right. It is the Lord himself who will examine me and decide.

[5]So don't make judgments about anyone ahead of time—before the Lord returns. For he will bring our darkest secrets to light and will reveal our private motives. Then God will give to each one whatever praise is due.

[6]Dear brothers and sisters,* I have used Apollos and myself to illustrate what I've been saying. If you pay attention to what I have quoted from the Scriptures,* you won't be proud of one of your leaders at the expense of another. [7]For what gives you the right to make such a judgment? What do you have that God hasn't given you? And if everything you have is from God, why boast as though it were not a gift?

[8]You think you already have everything you need. You think you are already rich. You have begun to reign in God's kingdom with-

3:16 Or *among*. **3:19** Job 5:13. **3:20** Ps 94:11. **3:22** Greek *Cephas*. **4:6a** Greek *Brothers*. **4:6b** Or *If you learn not to go beyond "what is written."*

out us! I wish you really were reigning already, for then we would be reigning with you. [9]Instead, I sometimes think God has put us apostles on display, like prisoners of war at the end of a victor's parade, condemned to die. We have become a spectacle to the entire world—to people and angels alike.

[10]Our dedication to Christ makes us look like fools, but you claim to be so wise in Christ! We are weak, but you are so powerful! You are honored, but we are ridiculed. [11]Even now we go hungry and thirsty, and we don't have enough clothes to keep warm. We are often beaten and have no home. [12]We work wearily with our own hands to earn our living. We bless those who curse us. We are patient with those who abuse us. [13]We appeal gently when evil things are said about us. Yet we are treated like the world's garbage, like everybody's trash—right up to the present moment.

[14]I am not writing these things to shame you, but to warn you as my beloved children. [15]For even if you had ten thousand others to teach you about Christ, you have only one spiritual father. For I became your father in Christ Jesus when I preached the Good News to you. [16]So I urge you to imitate me.

[17]That's why I have sent Timothy, my beloved and faithful child in the Lord. He will remind you of how I follow Christ Jesus, just as I teach in all the churches wherever I go.

[18]Some of you have become arrogant, thinking I will not visit you again. [19]But I will come—and soon—if the Lord lets me, and then I'll find out whether these arrogant people just give pretentious speeches or whether they really have God's power. [20]For the Kingdom of God is not just a lot of talk; it is living by God's power. [21]Which do you choose? Should I come with a rod to punish you, or should I come with love and a gentle spirit?

CHAPTER 5

Paul Condemns Spiritual Pride

I can hardly believe the report about the sexual immorality going on among you—something that even pagans don't do. I am told that a man in your church is living in sin with his stepmother.* [2]You are so proud of yourselves, but you should be mourning in sorrow and shame. And you should remove this man from your fellowship.

[3]Even though I am not with you in person, I am with you in the Spirit.* And as though I were there, I have already passed judgment on this man [4]in the name of the Lord Jesus. You must call a meeting of the church.* I will be present with you in spirit, and so will the power of our Lord Jesus. [5]Then you must throw this man out and hand him over to Satan so that his sinful nature will be destroyed* and he himself* will be saved on the day the Lord* returns.

[6]Your boasting about this is terrible. Don't you realize that this sin is like a little yeast that spreads through the whole batch of dough? [7]Get rid of the old "yeast" by removing this wicked person from among you. Then you will be like a fresh batch of dough made without yeast, which is what you really are. Christ, our Passover Lamb, has been sacrificed for us.* [8]So let us celebrate the festival, not with the old bread* of wickedness and evil, but with the new bread* of sincerity and truth.

[9]When I wrote to you before, I told you not to associate with people who indulge in sexual sin. [10]But I wasn't talking about unbelievers who indulge in sexual sin, or are greedy, or cheat people, or worship idols. You would have to leave this world to avoid people like that. [11]I meant that you are not to associate with anyone who claims to be a believer* yet indulges in sexual sin, or is greedy, or worships idols, or is abusive, or is a drunkard, or cheats people. Don't even eat with such people.

[12]It isn't my responsibility to judge outsiders, but it certainly is your responsibility to judge those inside the church who are sinning. [13]God will judge those on the outside; but as the Scriptures say, "You must remove the evil person from among you."*

CHAPTER 6

Avoiding Lawsuits with Christians

When one of you has a dispute with another believer, how dare you file a lawsuit and ask a secular court to decide the matter instead of taking it to other believers*! [2]Don't you realize that someday we believers will judge the world? And since you are going to judge the

5:1 Greek *his father's wife*. **5:3** Or *in spirit*. **5:4** Or *In the name of the Lord Jesus, you must call a meeting of the church*. **5:5a** Or *so that his body will be destroyed;* Greek reads *for the destruction of the flesh*. **5:5b** Greek *and the spirit*. **5:5c** Other manuscripts read *the Lord Jesus;* still others read *our Lord Jesus Christ*. **5:7** Greek *has been sacrificed*. **5:8a** Greek *not with old leaven*. **5:8b** Greek *but with unleavened [bread]*. **5:11** Greek *a brother*. **5:13** Deut 17:7. **6:1** Greek *God's holy people;* also in 6:2.

world, can't you decide even these little things among yourselves? [3]Don't you realize that we will judge angels? So you should surely be able to resolve ordinary disputes in this life. [4]If you have legal disputes about such matters, why go to outside judges who are not respected by the church? [5]I am saying this to shame you. Isn't there anyone in all the church who is wise enough to decide these issues? [6]But instead, one believer* sues another—right in front of unbelievers!

[7]Even to have such lawsuits with one another is a defeat for you. Why not just accept the injustice and leave it at that? Why not let yourselves be cheated? [8]Instead, you yourselves are the ones who do wrong and cheat even your fellow believers.*

[9]Don't you realize that those who do wrong will not inherit the Kingdom of God? Don't fool yourselves. Those who indulge in sexual sin, or who worship idols, or commit adultery, or are male prostitutes, or practice homosexuality, [10]or are thieves, or greedy people, or drunkards, or are abusive, or cheat people—none of these will inherit the Kingdom of God. [11]Some of you were once like that. But you were cleansed; you were made holy; you were made right with God by calling on the name of the Lord Jesus Christ and by the Spirit of our God.

Avoiding Sexual Sin

[12]You say, "I am allowed to do anything"—but not everything is good for you. And even though "I am allowed to do anything," I must not become a slave to anything. [13]You say, "Food was made for the stomach, and the stomach for food." (This is true, though someday God will do away with both of them.) But you can't say that our bodies were made for sexual immorality. They were made for the Lord, and the Lord cares about our bodies. [14]And God will raise us from the dead by his power, just as he raised our Lord from the dead.

[15]Don't you realize that your bodies are actually parts of Christ? Should a man take his body, which is part of Christ, and join it to a prostitute? Never! [16]And don't you realize that if a man joins himself to a prostitute, he becomes one body with her? For the Scriptures say, "The two are united into one."* [17]But the person who is joined to the Lord is one spirit with him.

[18]Run from sexual sin! No other sin so clearly affects the body as this one does. For sexual immorality is a sin against your own body. [19]Don't you realize that your body is the temple of the Holy Spirit, who lives in you and was given to you by God? You do not belong to yourself, [20]for God bought you with a high price. So you must honor God with your body.

What's so wrong with smoking and drinking?

You do not belong to yourself, for God bought you with a high price. So you must honor God with your body. 1 CORINTHIANS 6:19-20

CHAPTER 7

Instruction on Marriage

Now regarding the questions you asked in your letter. Yes, it is good to abstain from sexual relations.* [2]But because there is so much sexual immorality, each man should have his own wife, and each woman should have her own husband.

[3]The husband should fulfill his wife's sexual needs, and the wife should fulfill her husband's needs. [4]The wife gives authority over her body to her husband, and the husband gives authority over his body to his wife.

[5]Do not deprive each other of sexual relations, unless you both agree to refrain from sexual intimacy for a limited time so you can give yourselves more completely to prayer. Afterward, you should come together again so that Satan won't be able to tempt you because of your lack of self-control. [6]I say this as a concession, not as a command. [7]But I wish everyone were single, just as I am. Yet each person has a special gift from God, of one kind or another.

[8]So I say to those who aren't married and to widows—it's better to stay unmarried, just as I am. [9]But if they can't control themselves, they

6:6 Greek *one brother*. **6:8** Greek *even the brothers*. **6:16** Gen 2:24. **7:1** Or *to live a celibate life;* Greek reads *It is good for a man not to touch a woman.*

HOME SWEET HOME

At a party, when the host parents stepped out for a few minutes, someone brought out some cigarettes and passed them around. Everyone seemed to be taking a cigarette and lighting up. Then the pack was passed to Micah. Micah had never smoked before, so he wondered what it would be like. Micah didn't want the group to make fun of him if he didn't try smoking. Should Micah smoke or not? Check out 1 Corinthians 6:19-20 for help in making a decision.

should go ahead and marry. It's better to marry than to burn with lust.

[10]But for those who are married, I have a command that comes not from me, but from the Lord.* A wife must not leave her husband. [11]But if she does leave him, let her remain single or else be reconciled to him. And the husband must not leave his wife.

[12]Now, I will speak to the rest of you, though I do not have a direct command from the Lord. If a Christian man* has a wife who is not a believer and she is willing to continue living with him, he must not leave her. [13]And if a Christian woman has a husband who is not a believer and he is willing to continue living with her, she must not leave him. [14]For the Christian wife brings holiness to her marriage, and the Christian husband* brings holiness to his marriage. Otherwise, your children would not be holy, but now they are holy. [15](But if the husband or wife who isn't a believer insists on leaving, let them go. In such cases the Christian husband or wife* is no longer bound to the other, for God has called you* to live in peace.) [16]Don't you wives realize that your husbands might be saved because of you? And don't you husbands realize that your wives might be saved because of you?

[17]Each of you should continue to live in whatever situation the Lord has placed you, and remain as you were when God first called you. This is my rule for all the churches. [18]For instance, a man who was circumcised before he became a believer should not try to reverse it. And the man who was uncircumcised when he became a believer should not be circumcised now. [19]For it makes no difference whether or not a man has been circumcised. The important thing is to keep God's commandments.

[20]Yes, each of you should remain as you were when God called you. [21]Are you a slave? Don't let that worry you—but if you get a chance to be free, take it. [22]And remember, if you were a slave when the Lord called you, you are now free in the Lord. And if you were free when the Lord called you, you are now a slave of Christ. [23]God paid a high price for you, so don't be enslaved by the world.* [24]Each of you, dear brothers and sisters,* should remain as you were when God first called you.

[25]Now regarding your question about the young women who are not yet married. I do not have a command from the Lord for them. But the Lord in his mercy has given me wisdom that can be trusted, and I will share it with you. [26]Because of the present crisis,* I think it is best to remain as you are. [27]If you have a wife, do not seek to end the marriage. If you do not have a wife, do not seek to get

7:10 See Matt 5:32; 19:9; Mark 10:11-12; Luke 16:18. **7:12** Greek *a brother*. **7:14** Greek *the brother*. **7:15a** Greek *the brother or sister*. **7:15b** Some manuscripts read *us*. **7:23** Greek *don't become slaves of people*. **7:24** Greek *brothers*; also in 7:29. **7:26** Or *the pressures of life*.

married. [28]But if you do get married, it is not a sin. And if a young woman gets married, it is not a sin. However, those who get married at this time will have troubles, and I am trying to spare you those problems.

[29]But let me say this, dear brothers and sisters: The time that remains is very short. So from now on, those with wives should not focus only on their marriage. [30]Those who weep or who rejoice or who buy things should not be absorbed by their weeping or their joy or their possessions. [31]Those who use the things of the world should not become attached to them. For this world as we know it will soon pass away.

[32]I want you to be free from the concerns of this life. An unmarried man can spend his time doing the Lord's work and thinking how to please him. [33]But a married man has to think about his earthly responsibilities and how to please his wife. [34]His interests are divided. In the same way, a woman who is no longer married or has never been married can be devoted to the Lord and holy in body and in spirit. But a married woman has to think about her earthly responsibilities and how to please her husband. [35]I am saying this for your benefit, not to place restrictions on you. I want you to do whatever will help you serve the Lord best, with as few distractions as possible.

[36]But if a man thinks that he's treating his fiancée improperly and will inevitably give in to his passion, let him marry her as he wishes. It is not a sin. [37]But if he has decided firmly not to marry and there is no urgency and he can control his passion, he does well not to marry. [38]So the person who marries his fiancée does well, and the person who doesn't marry does even better.

[39]A wife is bound to her husband as long as he lives. If her husband dies, she is free to marry anyone she wishes, but only if he loves the Lord.* [40]But in my opinion it would be better for her to stay single, and I think I am giving you counsel from God's Spirit when I say this.

CHAPTER 8

Food Sacrificed to Idols

Now regarding your question about food that has been offered to idols. Yes, we know that "we all have knowledge" about this issue. But while knowledge makes us feel important, it is love that strengthens the church. [2]Anyone who claims to know all the answers doesn't really know very much. [3]But the person who loves God is the one whom God recognizes.*

[4]So, what about eating meat that has been offered to idols? Well, we all know that an idol is not really a god and that there is only one God. [5]There may be so-called gods both in heaven and on earth, and some people actually worship many gods and many lords. [6]But we know that there is only one God, the Father, who created everything, and we live for him. And there is only one Lord, Jesus Christ, through whom God made everything and through whom we have been given life.

[7]However, not all believers know this. Some are accustomed to thinking of idols as being real, so when they eat food that has been offered to idols, they think of it as the worship of real gods, and their weak consciences are violated. [8]It's true that we can't win God's approval by what we eat. We don't lose anything if we don't eat it, and we don't gain anything if we do.

[9]But you must be careful so that your freedom does not cause others with a weaker conscience to stumble. [10]For if others see you—with your "superior knowledge"—eating in the temple of an idol, won't they be encouraged to violate their conscience by eating food that has been offered to an idol? [11]So because of your superior knowledge, a weak believer* for whom Christ died will be destroyed. [12]And when you sin against other believers* by encouraging them to do something they believe is wrong, you are sinning against Christ. [13]So if what I eat causes another believer to sin, I will never eat meat again as long as I live—for I don't want to cause another believer to stumble.

CHAPTER 9

Paul Gives Up His Rights

Am I not as free as anyone else? Am I not an apostle? Haven't I seen Jesus our Lord with my own eyes? Isn't it because of my work that you belong to the Lord? [2]Even if others think I am

7:39 Greek *but only in the Lord.* **8:3** Some manuscripts read *the person who loves has full knowledge.* **8:11** Greek *brother;* also in 8:13. **8:12** Greek *brothers.*

not an apostle, I certainly am to you. You yourselves are proof that I am the Lord's apostle.

[3]This is my answer to those who question my authority.* [4]Don't we have the right to live in your homes and share your meals? [5]Don't we have the right to bring a Christian wife with us as the other apostles and the Lord's brothers do, and as Peter* does? [6]Or is it only Barnabas and I who have to work to support ourselves?

[7]What soldier has to pay his own expenses? What farmer plants a vineyard and doesn't have the right to eat some of its fruit? What shepherd cares for a flock of sheep and isn't allowed to drink some of the milk? [8]Am I expressing merely a human opinion, or does the law say the same thing? [9]For the law of Moses says, "You must not muzzle an ox to keep it from eating as it treads out the grain."* Was God thinking only about oxen when he said this? [10]Wasn't he actually speaking to us? Yes, it was written for us, so that the one who plows and the one who threshes the grain might both expect a share of the harvest.

[11]Since we have planted spiritual seed among you, aren't we entitled to a harvest of physical food and drink? [12]If you support others who preach to you, shouldn't we have an even greater right to be supported? But we have never used this right. We would rather put up with anything than be an obstacle to the Good News about Christ.

[13]Don't you realize that those who work in the temple get their meals from the offerings brought to the temple? And those who serve at the altar get a share of the sacrificial offerings. [14]In the same way, the Lord ordered that those who preach the Good News should be supported by those who benefit from it. [15]Yet I have never used any of these rights. And I am not writing this to suggest that I want to start now. In fact, I would rather die than lose my right to boast about preaching without charge. [16]Yet preaching the Good News is not something I can boast about. I am compelled by God to do it. How terrible for me if I didn't preach the Good News!

[17]If I were doing this on my own initiative, I would deserve payment. But I have no choice, for God has given me this sacred trust. [18]What then is my pay? It is the opportunity to preach the Good News without charging anyone.

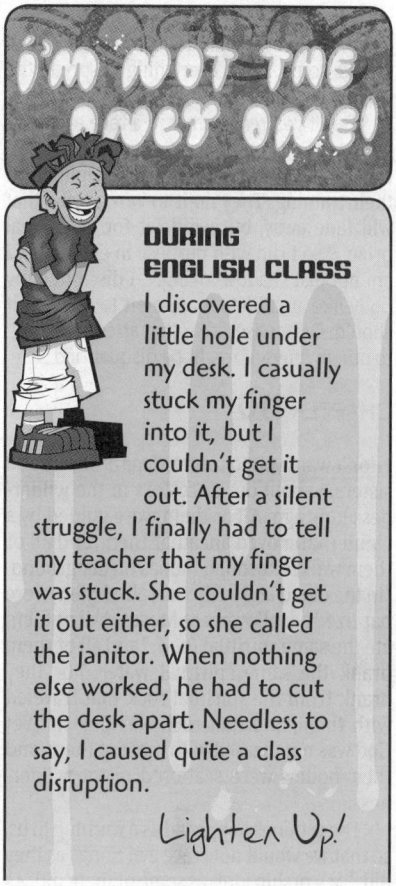

That's why I never demand my rights when I preach the Good News.

[19]Even though I am a free man with no master, I have become a slave to all people to bring many to Christ. [20]When I was with the Jews, I lived like a Jew to bring the Jews to Christ. When I was with those who follow the Jewish law, I too lived under that law. Even though I am not subject to the law, I did this so I could bring to Christ those who are under the law. [21]When I am with the Gentiles who do not follow the Jewish law,* I too live apart from that law so I can bring them to Christ. But I do not ignore the law of God; I obey the law of Christ.

[22]When I am with those who are weak, I share their weakness, for I want to bring the

9:3 Greek *those who examine me.* **9:5** Greek *Cephas.* **9:9** Deut 25:4. **9:21** Greek *those without the law.*

weak to Christ. Yes, I try to find common ground with everyone, doing everything I can to save some. [23]I do everything to spread the Good News and share in its blessings.

[24]Don't you realize that in a race everyone runs, but only one person gets the prize? So run to win! [25]All athletes are disciplined in their training. They do it to win a prize that will fade away, but we do it for an eternal prize. [26]So I run with purpose in every step. I am not just shadowboxing. [27]I discipline my body like an athlete, training it to do what it should. Otherwise, I fear that after preaching to others I myself might be disqualified.

CHAPTER 10

Lessons from Israel's Idolatry

I don't want you to forget, dear brothers and sisters,* about our ancestors in the wilderness long ago. All of them were guided by a cloud that moved ahead of them, and all of them walked through the sea on dry ground. [2]In the cloud and in the sea, all of them were baptized as followers of Moses. [3]All of them ate the same spiritual food, [4]and all of them drank the same spiritual water. For they drank from the spiritual rock that traveled with them, and that rock was Christ. [5]Yet God was not pleased with most of them, and their bodies were scattered in the wilderness.

[6]These things happened as a warning to us, so that we would not crave evil things as they did, [7]or worship idols as some of them did. As the Scriptures say, "The people celebrated with feasting and drinking, and they indulged in pagan revelry."* [8]And we must not engage in sexual immorality as some of them did, causing 23,000 of them to die in one day.

[9]Nor should we put Christ* to the test, as some of them did and then died from snakebites. [10]And don't grumble as some of them did, and then were destroyed by the angel of death. [11]These things happened to them as examples for us. They were written down to warn us who live at the end of the age.

[12]If you think you are standing strong, be careful not to fall. [13]The temptations in your life are no different from what others experience. And God is faithful. He will not allow the temptation to be more than you can stand. When you are tempted, he will show you a way out so that you can endure.

[14]So, my dear friends, flee from the worship of idols. [15]You are reasonable people. Decide for yourselves if what I am saying is true. [16]When we bless the cup at the Lord's Table, aren't we sharing in the blood of Christ? And when we break the bread, aren't we sharing in the body of Christ? [17]And though we are many, we all eat from one loaf of bread, showing that we are one body. [18]Think about the people of Israel. Weren't they united by eating the sacrifices at the altar?

[19]What am I trying to say? Am I saying that food offered to idols has some significance, or that idols are real gods? [20]No, not at all. I am saying that these sacrifices are offered to demons, not to God. And I don't want you to participate with demons. [21]You cannot drink from the cup of the Lord and from the cup of demons, too. You cannot eat at the Lord's Table and at the table of demons, too. [22]What? Do we dare to rouse the Lord's jealousy? Do you think we are stronger than he is?

[23]You say, "I am allowed to do anything"*—but not everything is good for you. You say, "I am allowed to do anything"—but not everything is beneficial. [24]Don't be concerned for your own good but for the good of others.

[25]So you may eat any meat that is sold in the marketplace without raising questions of conscience. [26]For "the earth is the LORD's, and everything in it."*

[27]If someone who isn't a believer asks you home for dinner, accept the invitation if you want to. Eat whatever is offered to you without raising questions of conscience. [28](But suppose someone tells you, "This meat was offered to an idol." Don't eat it, out of consideration for the conscience of the one who told you. [29]It might not be a matter of conscience for you, but it is for the other person.) For why should my freedom be limited by what someone else thinks? [30]If I can thank God for the food and enjoy it, why should I be condemned for eating it?

[31]So whether you eat or drink, or whatever you do, do it all for the glory of God. [32]Don't give offense to Jews or Gentiles* or the church of God. [33]I, too, try to please everyone

10:1 Greek *brothers*. **10:7** Exod 32:6. **10:9** Some manuscripts read *the Lord*. **10:23** Greek *All things are lawful;* also in 10:23b. **10:26** Ps 24:1. **10:32** Greek *or Greeks*.

in everything I do. I don't just do what is best
for me; I do what is best for others so that
many may be saved. [11:1]And you should imi-
tate me, just as I imitate Christ.

CHAPTER 11

Instructions for Public Worship

[2]I am so glad that you always keep me in
your thoughts, and that you are following
the teachings I passed on to you. [3]But there
is one thing I want you to know: The head
of every man is Christ, the head of woman
is man, and the head of Christ is God.* [4]A
man dishonors his head* if he covers his
head while praying or prophesying. [5]But a
woman dishonors her head* if she prays or
prophesies without a covering on her head,
for this is the same as shaving her head.
[6]Yes, if she refuses to wear a head covering,
she should cut off all her hair! But since it is
shameful for a woman to have her hair cut
or her head shaved, she should wear a cov-
ering.*

[7]A man should not wear anything on his
head when worshiping, for man is made in
God's image and reflects God's glory. And
woman reflects man's glory. [8]For the first
man didn't come from woman, but the first
woman came from man. [9]And man was not
made for woman, but woman was made for
man. [10]For this reason, and because the
angels are watching, a woman should wear a
covering on her head to show she is under au-
thority.*

[11]But among the Lord's people, women are
not independent of men, and men are not in-
dependent of women. [12]For although the first
woman came from man, every other man was
born from a woman, and everything comes
from God.

[13]Judge for yourselves. Is it right for a
woman to pray to God in public without cov-
ering her head? [14]Isn't it obvious that it's dis-
graceful for a man to have long hair? [15]And
isn't long hair a woman's pride and joy? For it
has been given to her as a covering. [16]But if
anyone wants to argue about this, I simply say
that we have no other custom than this, and
neither do God's other churches.

Order at the Lord's Supper

[17]But in the following instructions, I cannot
praise you. For it sounds as if more harm than
good is done when you meet together. [18]First,
I hear that there are divisions among you
when you meet as a church, and to some ex-
tent I believe it. [19]But, of course, there must
be divisions among you so that you who have
God's approval will be recognized!

[20]When you meet together, you are not
really interested in the Lord's Supper. [21]For
some of you hurry to eat your own meal with-
out sharing with others. As a result, some go
hungry while others get drunk. [22]What? Don't
you have your own homes for eating and
drinking? Or do you really want to disgrace
God's church and shame the poor? What am I
supposed to say? Do you want me to praise
you? Well, I certainly will not praise you for
this!

[23]For I pass on to you what I received from
the Lord himself. On the night when he was
betrayed, the Lord Jesus took some bread
[24]and gave thanks to God for it. Then he
broke it in pieces and said, "This is my body,
which is given for you.* Do this to remember
me." [25]In the same way, he took the cup of
wine after supper, saying, "This cup is the
new covenant between God and his people—
an agreement confirmed with my blood. Do
this to remember me as often as you drink it."
[26]For every time you eat this bread and drink
this cup, you are announcing the Lord's death
until he comes again.

[27]So anyone who eats this bread or drinks
this cup of the Lord unworthily is guilty of
sinning against* the body and blood of the
Lord. [28]That is why you should examine your-
self before eating the bread and drinking the
cup. [29]For if you eat the bread or drink the cup
without honoring the body of Christ,* you are
eating and drinking God's judgment upon
yourself. [30]That is why many of you are weak
and sick and some have even died.

[31]But if we would examine ourselves, we
would not be judged by God in this way. [32]Yet
when we are judged by the Lord, we are being
disciplined so that we will not be condemned
along with the world.

11:3 Or *to know: The source of every man is Christ, the source of woman is man, and the source of Christ is God.* Or *to know: Every man is responsible to Christ, a woman is responsible to her husband, and Christ is responsible to God.* **11:4** Or *dishonors Christ.* **11:5** Or *dishonors her husband.* **11:6** Or *should have long hair.* **11:10** Greek *should have an authority on her head.* **11:24** Greek *which is for you;* other manuscripts read *which is broken for you.* **11:27** Or *is responsible for.* **11:29** Greek *the body;* other manuscripts read *the Lord's body.*

[33]So, my dear brothers and sisters,* when you gather for the Lord's Supper, wait for each other. [34]If you are really hungry, eat at home so you won't bring judgment upon yourselves when you meet together. I'll give you instructions about the other matters after I arrive.

CHAPTER 12

Spiritual Gifts

Now, dear brothers and sisters,* regarding your question about the special abilities the Spirit gives us. I don't want you to misunderstand this. [2]You know that when you were still pagans, you were led astray and swept along in worshiping speechless idols. [3]So I want you to know that no one speaking by the Spirit of God will curse Jesus, and no one can say Jesus is Lord, except by the Holy Spirit.

[4]There are different kinds of spiritual gifts, but the same Spirit is the source of them all. [5]There are different kinds of service, but we serve the same Lord. [6]God works in different ways, but it is the same God who does the work in all of us.

[7]A spiritual gift is given to each of us so we can help each other. [8]To one person the Spirit gives the ability to give wise advice*; to another the same Spirit gives a message of special knowledge.* [9]The same Spirit gives great faith to another, and to someone else the one Spirit gives the gift of healing. [10]He gives one person the power to perform miracles, and another the ability to prophesy. He gives someone else the ability to discern whether a message is from the Spirit of God or from another spirit. Still another person is given the ability to speak in unknown languages,* while another is given the ability to interpret what is being said. [11]It is the one and only Spirit who distributes all these gifts. He alone decides which gift each person should have.

One Body with Many Parts

[12]The human body has many parts, but the many parts make up one whole body. So it is with the body of Christ. [13]Some of us are Jews, some are Gentiles,* some are slaves, and some are free. But we have all been baptized into one body by one Spirit, and we all share the same Spirit.*

[14]Yes, the body has many different parts, not just one part. [15]If the foot says, "I am not a part of the body because I am not a hand," that does not make it any less a part of the body. [16]And if the ear says, "I am not part of the body because I am not an eye," would that make it any less a part of the body? [17]If the whole body were an eye, how would you hear? Or if your whole body were an ear, how would you smell anything?

[18]But our bodies have many parts, and God has put each part just where he wants it. [19]How strange a body would be if it had only one part! [20]Yes, there are many parts, but only one body. [21]The eye can never say to the hand, "I don't need you." The head can't say to the feet, "I don't need you."

[22]In fact, some parts of the body that seem weakest and least important are actually the most necessary. [23]And the parts we regard as less honorable are those we clothe with the greatest care. So we carefully protect those parts that should not be seen, [24]while the more honorable parts do not require this special care. So God has put the body together such that extra honor and care are given to those parts that have less dignity. [25]This makes for harmony among the members, so that all the members care for each other. [26]If one part suffers, all the parts suffer with it, and if one part is honored, all the parts are glad.

[27]All of you together are Christ's body, and each of you is a part of it. [28]Here are some of the parts God has appointed for the church:

first are apostles,
second are prophets,
third are teachers,
then those who do miracles,
those who have the gift of healing,
those who can help others,
those who have the gift of leadership,
those who speak in unknown languages.

[29]Are we all apostles? Are we all prophets? Are we all teachers? Do we all have the power to do miracles? [30]Do we all have the gift of healing? Do we all have the ability to speak in unknown languages? Do we all have the ability to interpret unknown languages? Of

11:33 Greek *brothers.* **12:1** Greek *brothers.* **12:8a** Or *gives a word of wisdom.* **12:8b** Or *gives a word of knowledge.* **12:10** Or *in various tongues;* also in 12:28, 30. **12:13a** Greek *some are Greeks.* **12:13b** Greek *we were all given one Spirit to drink.*

I used to believe that since I wasn't really interested in becoming a pastor or a missionary, I couldn't really serve God. I'm the kind of guy who's mostly interested in computers, art, and music. I've always been that way. Now I can see that God has given me a lot of unique gifts—things I never thought I'd use.

A few years back I started getting into video games. Yeah, I know what you're thinking, "How could the ability to play video games be a gift from God?" Well, my friends and I were sick of having to wade through the garbage to find a good game. So we started actually designing our own video games.

Our games have interwoven story lines that are based on honor, courage, and godliness—themes that have real virtue and substance to them, where it's not all hack and slash and gore and chicks. We want to have a higher standard. In that way we give glory to the Lord.

It's amazing. Ever since we began making our games, the Lord's opened doors for us. I'm getting involved with some of my friends from youth group. We're planning on starting a Christian-based company that makes mainstream quality video games. We've been thinking about it for a few years. I know we'll make it happen.

Now I know the same Holy Spirit that has gifted a missionary in my church to serve God in another country has given me the ability to serve God right where I live, ministering to teens who end up playing the games I design. God has blessed me with the chance to use the things I'm best at to serve him.

Read 1 Corinthians 12:4-7 to find out more about God's gifts. Also check out Romans 12:6-8 and Ephesians 4:7-13.

SUB WAY

Ramón had a substitute teacher in science class who seemed confused about what to teach. In fact, she couldn't seem to find the lesson plans or the grade book in the huge pile of papers on the desk. Some of the kids gave her false information while others gave her a hard time and made fun of her. Ramón found himself laughing at the situation and thought about joining in. What should Ramón do? See 1 Corinthians 13:4-5, where Paul tells what a loving response would be.

course not! [31]So you should earnestly desire the most helpful gifts.

But now let me show you a way of life that is best of all.

CHAPTER 13

Love Is the Greatest

If I could speak all the languages of earth and of angels, but didn't love others, I would only be a noisy gong or a clanging cymbal. [2]If I had the gift of prophecy, and if I understood all of God's secret plans and possessed all knowledge, and if I had such faith that I could move mountains, but didn't love others, I would be nothing. [3]If I gave everything I have to the poor and even sacrificed my body, I could boast about it;* but if I didn't love others, I would have gained nothing.

[4]Love is patient and kind. Love is not jealous or boastful or proud [5]or rude. It does not demand its own way. It is not irritable, and it keeps no record of being wronged. [6]It does not rejoice about injustice but rejoices whenever the truth wins out. [7]Love never gives up, never loses faith, is always hopeful, and endures through every circumstance.

[8]Prophecy and speaking in unknown languages* and special knowledge will become useless. But love will last forever! [9]Now our knowledge is partial and incomplete, and even the gift of prophecy reveals only part of the whole picture! [10]But when the time of perfection comes, these partial things will become useless.

[11]When I was a child, I spoke and thought and reasoned as a child. But when I grew up, I put away childish things. [12]Now we see things imperfectly, like puzzling reflections in a mirror, but then we will see everything with perfect clarity.* All that I know now is partial and incomplete, but then I will know everything completely, just as God now knows me completely.

[13]Three things will last forever—faith, hope, and love—and the greatest of these is love.

CHAPTER 14

Tongues and Prophecy

Let love be your highest goal! But you should also desire the special abilities the Spirit gives—especially the ability to prophesy. [2]For if you have the ability to speak in tongues,* you will be talking only to God, since people won't be able to understand you. You will be speaking by the power of the Spirit,* but it will all be mysterious. [3]But one who prophesies strengthens others, encourages them, and comforts them. [4]A person who speaks in tongues is strengthened personally, but one who speaks a word of prophecy strengthens the entire church.

[5]I wish you could all speak in tongues, but

13:3 Some manuscripts read *sacrificed my body to be burned.* **13:8** Or *in tongues.* **13:12** Greek *see face to face.* **14:2a** Or *in unknown languages;* also in 14:4, 5, 13, 14, 18, 22, 26, 27, 28, 39. **14:2b** Or *speaking in your spirit.*

even more I wish you could all prophesy. For prophecy is greater than speaking in tongues, unless someone interprets what you are saying so that the whole church will be strengthened.

[6]Dear brothers and sisters,* if I should come to you speaking in an unknown language,* how would that help you? But if I bring you a revelation or some special knowledge or prophecy or teaching, that will be helpful. [7]Even lifeless instruments like the flute or the harp must play the notes clearly, or no one will recognize the melody. [8]And if the bugler doesn't sound a clear call, how will the soldiers know they are being called to battle?

[9]It's the same for you. If you speak to people in words they don't understand, how will they know what you are saying? You might as well be talking into empty space.

[10]There are many different languages in the world, and every language has meaning. [11]But if I don't understand a language, I will be a foreigner to someone who speaks it, and the one who speaks it will be a foreigner to me. [12]And the same is true for you. Since you are so eager to have the special abilities the Spirit gives, seek those that will strengthen the whole church.

[13]So anyone who speaks in tongues should pray also for the ability to interpret what has been said. [14]For if I pray in tongues, my spirit is praying, but I don't understand what I am saying.

[15]Well then, what shall I do? I will pray in the spirit,* and I will also pray in words I understand. I will sing in the spirit, and I will also sing in words I understand. [16]For if you praise God only in the spirit, how can those who don't understand you praise God along with you? How can they join you in giving thanks when they don't understand what you are saying? [17]You will be giving thanks very well, but it won't strengthen the people who hear you.

[18]I thank God that I speak in tongues more than any of you. [19]But in a church meeting I would rather speak five understandable words to help others than ten thousand words in an unknown language.

[20]Dear brothers and sisters, don't be childish in your understanding of these things. Be innocent as babies when it comes to evil, but be mature in understanding matters of this kind. [21]It is written in the Scriptures*:

"I will speak to my own people
through strange languages
and through the lips of foreigners.
But even then, they will not listen to me,"*
says the LORD.

[22]So you see that speaking in tongues is a sign, not for believers, but for unbelievers. Prophecy, however, is for the benefit of believers, not unbelievers. [23]Even so, if unbelievers or people who don't understand these things come into your church meeting and hear everyone speaking in an unknown language, they will think you are crazy. [24]But if all of you are prophesying, and unbelievers or people who don't understand these things come into your meeting, they will be convicted of sin and judged by what you say. [25]As they listen, their secret thoughts will be exposed, and they will fall to their knees and worship God, declaring, "God is truly here among you."

A Call to Orderly Worship

[26]Well, my brothers and sisters, let's summarize. When you meet together, one will sing, another will teach, another will tell some special revelation God has given, one will speak in tongues, and another will interpret what is said. But everything that is done must strengthen all of you.

[27]No more than two or three should speak in tongues. They must speak one at a time, and someone must interpret what they say. [28]But if no one is present who can interpret, they must be silent in your church meeting and speak in tongues to God privately.

[29]Let two or three people prophesy, and let the others evaluate what is said. [30]But if someone is prophesying and another person receives a revelation from the Lord, the one who is speaking must stop. [31]In this way, all who prophesy will have a turn to speak, one after the other, so that everyone will learn and be encouraged. [32]Remember that people who prophesy are in control of their spirit and can take turns. [33]For God is not a God of disorder

14:6a Greek *brothers;* also in 14:20, 26, 39. **14:6b** Or *in tongues;* also in 14:19, 23. **14:15** Or *in the Spirit;* also in 14:15b, 16. **14:21a** Greek *in the law.* **14:21b** Isa 28:11-12.

but of peace, as in all the meetings of God's holy people.*

[34]Women should be silent during the church meetings. It is not proper for them to speak. They should be submissive, just as the law says. [35]If they have any questions, they should ask their husbands at home, for it is improper for women to speak in church meetings.*

[36]Or do you think God's word originated with you Corinthians? Are you the only ones to whom it was given? [37]If you claim to be a prophet or think you are spiritual, you should recognize that what I am saying is a command from the Lord himself. [38]But if you do not recognize this, you yourself will not be recognized.*

[39]So, my dear brothers and sisters, be eager to prophesy, and don't forbid speaking in tongues. [40]But be sure that everything is done properly and in order.

CHAPTER 15

The Resurrection of Christ

Let me now remind you, dear brothers and sisters,* of the Good News I preached to you before. You welcomed it then, and you still stand firm in it. [2]It is this Good News that saves you if you continue to believe the message I told you—unless, of course, you believed something that was never true in the first place.*

[3]I passed on to you what was most important and what had also been passed on to me. Christ died for our sins, just as the Scriptures said. [4]He was buried, and he was raised from the dead on the third day, just as the Scriptures said. [5]He was seen by Peter* and then by the Twelve. [6]After that, he was seen by more than 500 of his followers* at one time, most of whom are still alive, though some have died. [7]Then he was seen by James and later by all the apostles. [8]Last of all, as though I had been born at the wrong time, I also saw him. [9]For I am the least of all the apostles. In fact, I'm not even worthy to be called an apostle after the way I persecuted God's church.

[10]But whatever I am now, it is all because God poured out his special favor on me—and not without results. For I have worked harder than any of the other apostles; yet it was not I but God who was working through me by his grace. [11]So it makes no difference whether I preach or they preach, for we all preach the same message you have already believed.

The Resurrection of the Dead

[12]But tell me this—since we preach that Christ rose from the dead, why are some of you saying there will be no resurrection of the dead? [13]For if there is no resurrection of the dead, then Christ has not been raised either. [14]And if Christ has not been raised, then all our preaching is useless, and your faith is useless. [15]And we apostles would all be lying about God—for we have said that God raised Christ from the grave. But that can't be true if there is no resurrection of the dead. [16]And if there is no resurrection of the dead, then Christ has not been raised. [17]And if Christ has not been raised, then your faith is useless and you are still guilty of your sins. [18]In that case, all who have died believing in Christ are lost! [19]And if our hope in Christ is only for this life, we are more to be pitied than anyone in the world.

[20]But in fact, Christ has been raised from the dead. He is the first of a great harvest of all who have died.

[21]So you see, just as death came into the world through a man, now the resurrection from the dead has begun through another man. [22]Just as everyone dies because we all belong to Adam, everyone who belongs to Christ will be given new life. [23]But there is an order to this resurrection: Christ was raised as the first of the harvest; then all who belong to Christ will be raised when he comes back.

[24]After that the end will come, when he will turn the Kingdom over to God the Father, having destroyed every ruler and authority and power. [25]For Christ must reign until he humbles all his enemies beneath his feet. [26]And the last enemy to be destroyed is death. [27]For the Scriptures say, "God has put all things under his authority."* (Of course, when it says "all things are under his authority," that does not include God himself, who gave Christ his authority.) [28]Then, when all things are under

14:33 The phrase *as in all the meetings of God's holy people* could instead be joined to the beginning of 14:34. **14:35** Some manuscripts place verses 34-35 after 14:40. **14:38** Some manuscripts read *If you are ignorant of this, stay in your ignorance.* **15:1** Greek *brothers;* also in 15:31, 50, 58. **15:2** Or *unless you never believed it in the first place.* **15:5** Greek *Cephas.* **15:6** Greek *the brothers.* **15:27** Ps 8:6.

his authority, the Son will put himself under God's authority, so that God, who gave his Son authority over all things, will be utterly supreme over everything everywhere.

[29]If the dead will not be raised, what point is there in people being baptized for those who are dead? Why do it unless the dead will someday rise again?

[30]And why should we ourselves risk our lives hour by hour? [31]For I swear, dear brothers and sisters, that I face death daily. This is as certain as my pride in what Christ Jesus our Lord has done in you. [32]And what value was there in fighting wild beasts—those people of Ephesus*—if there will be no resurrection from the dead? And if there is no resurrection, "Let's feast and drink, for tomorrow we die!"* [33]Don't be fooled by those who say such things, for "bad company corrupts good character." [34]Think carefully about what is right, and stop sinning. For to your shame I say that some of you don't know God at all.

The Resurrection Body

[35]But someone may ask, "How will the dead be raised? What kind of bodies will they have?" [36]What a foolish question! When you put a seed into the ground, it doesn't grow into a plant unless it dies first. [37]And what you put in the ground is not the plant that will grow, but only a bare seed of wheat or whatever you are planting. [38]Then God gives it the new body he wants it to have. A different plant grows from each kind of seed. [39]Similarly there are different kinds of flesh—one kind for humans, another for animals, another for birds, and another for fish.

[40]There are also bodies in the heavens and bodies on the earth. The glory of the heavenly bodies is different from the glory of the earthly bodies. [41]The sun has one kind of glory, while the moon and stars each have another kind. And even the stars differ from each other in their glory.

[42]It is the same way with the resurrection of the dead. Our earthly bodies are planted in the ground when we die, but they will be raised to live forever. [43]Our bodies are buried in brokenness, but they will be raised in glory. They are buried in weakness, but they will be raised in strength. [44]They are buried as natural human bodies, but they will be raised as spiritual bodies. For just as there are natural bodies, there are also spiritual bodies.

[45]The Scriptures tell us, "The first man, Adam, became a living person."* But the last Adam—that is, Christ—is a life-giving Spirit. [46]What comes first is the natural body, then the spiritual body comes later. [47]Adam, the first man, was made from the dust of the earth, while Christ, the second man, came from heaven. [48]Earthly people are like the earthly man, and heavenly people are like the heavenly man. [49]Just as we are now like the earthly man, we will someday be like* the heavenly man.

AMAZING FACTS

One day every follower of Jesus will get a totally new body just like his. Now, that makeover will be way beyond extreme!

1 CORINTHIANS 15:48

[50]What I am saying, dear brothers and sisters, is that our physical bodies cannot inherit the Kingdom of God. These dying bodies cannot inherit what will last forever.

[51]But let me reveal to you a wonderful secret. We will not all die, but we will all be transformed! [52]It will happen in a moment, in the blink of an eye, when the last trumpet is blown. For when the trumpet sounds, those who have died will be raised to live forever. And we who are living will also be transformed. [53]For our dying bodies must be transformed into bodies that will never die; our mortal bodies must be transformed into immortal bodies.

[54]Then, when our dying bodies have been transformed into bodies that will never die,* this Scripture will be fulfilled:

15:32a Greek *fighting wild beasts in Ephesus.* **15:32b** Isa 22:13. **15:45** Gen 2:7. **15:49** Some manuscripts read *let us be like.* **15:54a** Some manuscripts add *and our mortal bodies have been transformed into immortal bodies.*

"Death is swallowed up in victory.*
55 O death, where is your victory?
O death, where is your sting?*"

56 For sin is the sting that results in death, and the law gives sin its power. 57 But thank God! He gives us victory over sin and death through our Lord Jesus Christ.

58 So, my dear brothers and sisters, be strong and immovable. Always work enthusiastically for the Lord, for you know that nothing you do for the Lord is ever useless.

CHAPTER 16

The Collection for Jerusalem

Now regarding your question about the money being collected for God's people in Jerusalem. You should follow the same procedure I gave to the churches in Galatia. 2 On the first day of each week, you should each put aside a portion of the money you have earned. Don't wait until I get there and then try to collect it all at once. 3 When I come, I will write letters of recommendation for the messengers you choose to deliver your gift to Jerusalem. 4 And if it seems appropriate for me to go along, they can travel with me.

Paul's Final Instructions

5 I am coming to visit you after I have been to Macedonia,* for I am planning to travel through Macedonia. 6 Perhaps I will stay awhile with you, possibly all winter, and then you can send me on my way to my next destination. 7 This time I don't want to make just a short visit and then go right on. I want to come and stay awhile, if the Lord will let me. 8 In the meantime, I will be staying here at Ephesus until the Festival of Pentecost. 9 There is a wide-open door for a great work here, although many oppose me.

10 When Timothy comes, don't intimidate him. He is doing the Lord's work, just as I am. 11 Don't let anyone treat him with contempt. Send him on his way with your blessing when he returns to me. I expect him to come with the other believers.*

12 Now about our brother Apollos—I urged him to visit you with the other believers, but he was not willing to go right now. He will see you later when he has the opportunity.

13 Be on guard. Stand firm in the faith. Be courageous.* Be strong. 14 And do everything with love.

15 You know that Stephanas and his household were the first of the harvest of believers in Greece,* and they are spending their lives in service to God's people. I urge you, dear brothers and sisters,* 16 to submit to them and others like them who serve with such devotion. 17 I am very glad that Stephanas, Fortunatus, and Achaicus have come here. They have been providing the help you weren't here to give me. 18 They have been a wonderful encouragement to me, as they have been to you. You must show your appreciation to all who serve so well.

Paul's Final Greetings

19 The churches here in the province of Asia* send greetings in the Lord, as do Aquila and Priscilla* and all the others who gather in their home for church meetings. 20 All the brothers and sisters here send greetings to you. Greet each other with Christian love.*

21 HERE IS MY GREETING IN MY OWN HANDWRITING—PAUL.

22 If anyone does not love the Lord, that person is cursed. Our Lord, come!*

23 May the grace of the Lord Jesus be with you.

24 My love to all of you in Christ Jesus.*

15:54b Isa 25:8. **15:55** Hos 13:14 (Greek version). **16:5** *Macedonia* was in the northern region of Greece. **16:11** Greek *with the brothers;* also in 16:12. **16:13** Greek *Be men.* **16:15a** Greek *in Achaia,* the southern region of the Greek peninsula. **16:15b** Greek *brothers;* also in 16:20. **16:19a** *Asia* was a Roman province in what is now western Turkey. **16:19b** Greek *Prisca.* **16:20** Greek *with a sacred kiss.* **16:22** From Aramaic, *Marana tha.* Some manuscripts read *Maran atha,* "Our Lord has come." **16:24** Some manuscripts add *Amen.*

2 Corinthians

WHO
Paul, Timothy, Titus, and the false teachers.

WHERE
Written in Macedonia during Paul's third missionary journey.

WHEN
Around AD 55 to 57.

WHY
To challenge the believers in Corinth to live for Christ.

Anyone who belongs to Christ has become a new person. The old life is gone; a new life has begun!
2 CORINTHIANS 5:17

Best friends *always* tell you the truth. That's what Paul did. When he heard that a church was struggling with sin or listening to false teaching, Paul wrote to the people. He told them how to live. Paul wasn't afraid to tell the truth about the importance of staying close to Jesus.

PAUL COURAGEOUSLY TOLD HIS FRIENDS THE TRUTH ABOUT THEIR LIVES. BE THAT KIND OF PERSON WITH YOUR FRIENDS, TOO.

CHAPTER 1

Greetings from Paul

This letter is from Paul, chosen by the will of God to be an apostle of Christ Jesus, and from our brother Timothy.

I am writing to God's church in Corinth and to all of his holy people throughout Greece.*

[2]May God our Father and the Lord Jesus Christ give you grace and peace.

God Offers Comfort to All

[3]All praise to God, the Father of our Lord Jesus Christ. God is our merciful Father and the source of all comfort. [4]He comforts us in all

1:1 Greek *Achaia*, the southern region of the Greek peninsula.

our troubles so that we can comfort others. When they are troubled, we will be able to give them the same comfort God has given us. [5]For the more we suffer for Christ, the more God will shower us with his comfort through Christ. [6]Even when we are weighed down with troubles, it is for your comfort and salvation! For when we ourselves are comforted, we will certainly comfort you. Then you can patiently endure the same things we suffer. [7]We are confident that as you share in our sufferings, you will also share in the comfort God gives us.

[8]We think you ought to know, dear brothers and sisters,* about the trouble we went through in the province of Asia. We were crushed and overwhelmed beyond our ability to endure, and we thought we would never live through it. [9]In fact, we expected to die. But as a result, we stopped relying on ourselves and learned to rely only on God, who raises the dead. [10]And he did rescue us from mortal danger, and he will rescue us again. We have placed our confidence in him, and he will continue to rescue us. [11]And you are helping us by praying for us. Then many people will give thanks because God has graciously answered so many prayers for our safety.

Paul's Change of Plans

[12]We can say with confidence and a clear conscience that we have lived with a God-given holiness* and sincerity in all our dealings. We have depended on God's grace, not on our own human wisdom. That is how we have conducted ourselves before the world, and especially toward you. [13]Our letters have been straightforward, and there is nothing written between the lines and nothing you can't understand. I hope someday you will fully understand us, [14]even if you don't understand us now. Then on the day when the Lord Jesus* returns, you will be proud of us in the same way we are proud of you.

[15]Since I was so sure of your understanding and trust, I wanted to give you a double blessing by visiting you twice—[16]first on my way to Macedonia and again when I returned from Macedonia.* Then you could send me on my way to Judea.

[17]You may be asking why I changed my plan. Do you think I make my plans carelessly? Do you think I am like people of the world who say "Yes" when they really mean "No"? [18]As surely as God is faithful, our word to you does not waver between "Yes" and "No." [19]For Jesus Christ, the Son of God, does not waver between "Yes" and "No." He is the one whom Silas,* Timothy, and I preached to you, and as God's ultimate "Yes," he always does what he says. [20]For all of God's promises have been fulfilled in Christ with a resounding "Yes!" And through Christ, our "Amen" (which means "Yes") ascends to God for his glory.

[21]It is God who enables us, along with you, to stand firm for Christ. He has commissioned us, [22]and he has identified us as his own by placing the Holy Spirit in our hearts as the first installment that guarantees everything he has promised us.

[23]Now I call upon God as my witness that I am telling the truth. The reason I didn't return to Corinth was to spare you from a severe rebuke. [24]But that does not mean we want to dominate you by telling you how to put your faith into practice. We want to work together with you so you will be full of joy, for it is by your own faith that you stand firm.

CHAPTER 2

So I decided that I would not bring you grief with another painful visit. [2]For if I cause you grief, who will make me glad? Certainly not someone I have grieved. [3]That is why I wrote to you as I did, so that when I do come, I won't be grieved by the very ones who ought to give me the greatest joy. Surely you all know that my joy comes from your being joyful. [4]I wrote that letter in great anguish, with a troubled heart and many tears. I didn't want to grieve you, but I wanted to let you know how much love I have for you.

Forgiveness for the Sinner

[5]I am not overstating it when I say that the man who caused all the trouble hurt all of you more than he hurt me. [6]Most of you opposed him, and that was punishment enough. [7]Now, however, it is time to forgive and comfort him. Otherwise he may be overcome by dis-

1:8 Greek *brothers*. **1:12** Some manuscripts read *honesty*. **1:14** Some manuscripts read *our Lord Jesus*. **1:16** *Macedonia* was in the northern region of Greece. **1:19** Greek *Silvanus*.

couragement. [8]So I urge you now to reaffirm your love for him.

[9]I wrote to you as I did to test you and see if you would fully comply with my instructions. [10]When you forgive this man, I forgive him, too. And when I forgive whatever needs to be forgiven, I do so with Christ's authority for your benefit, [11]so that Satan will not outsmart us. For we are familiar with his evil schemes.

[12]When I came to the city of Troas to preach the Good News of Christ, the Lord opened a door of opportunity for me. [13]But I had no peace of mind because my dear brother Titus hadn't yet arrived with a report from you. So I said good-bye and went on to Macedonia to find him.

Ministers of the New Covenant

[14]But thank God! He has made us his captives and continues to lead us along in Christ's triumphal procession. Now he uses us to spread the knowledge of Christ everywhere, like a sweet perfume. [15]Our lives are a Christ-like fragrance rising up to God. But this fragrance is perceived differently by those who are being saved and by those who are perishing. [16]To those who are perishing, we are a dreadful smell of death and doom. But to those who are being saved, we are a life-giving perfume. And who is adequate for such a task as this?

[17]You see, we are not like the many hucksters* who preach for personal profit. We preach the word of God with sincerity and with Christ's authority, knowing that God is watching us.

CHAPTER 3

Are we beginning to praise ourselves again? Are we like others, who need to bring you letters of recommendation, or who ask you to write such letters on their behalf? Surely not! [2]The only letter of recommendation we need is you yourselves. Your lives are a letter written in our* hearts; everyone can read it and recognize our good work among you. [3]Clearly, you are a letter from Christ showing the result of our ministry among you. This "letter" is written not with pen and ink, but with the Spirit of the living God. It is carved not on tablets of stone, but on human hearts.

[4]We are confident of all this because of our great trust in God through Christ. [5]It is not that we think we are qualified to do anything on our own. Our qualification comes from God. [6]He has enabled us to be ministers of his new covenant. This is a covenant not of written laws, but of the Spirit. The old written covenant ends in death; but under the new covenant, the Spirit gives life.

The Glory of the New Covenant

[7]The old way,* with laws etched in stone, led to death, though it began with such glory that the people of Israel could not bear to look at Moses' face. For his face shone with the glory of God, even though the brightness was already fading away. [8]Shouldn't we expect far greater glory under the new way, now that the

2:17 Some manuscripts read *the rest of the hucksters.* **3:2** Some manuscripts read *your.* **3:7** Or *ministry;* also in 3:8, 9, 10, 11, 12.

Holy Spirit is giving life? [9]If the old way, which brings condemnation, was glorious, how much more glorious is the new way, which makes us right with God! [10]In fact, that first glory was not glorious at all compared with the overwhelming glory of the new way. [11]So if the old way, which has been replaced, was glorious, how much more glorious is the new, which remains forever!

[12]Since this new way gives us such confidence, we can be very bold. [13]We are not like Moses, who put a veil over his face so the people of Israel would not see the glory, even though it was destined to fade away. [14]But the people's minds were hardened, and to this day whenever the old covenant is being read, the same veil covers their minds so they cannot understand the truth. And this veil can be removed only by believing in Christ. [15]Yes, even today when they read Moses' writings, their hearts are covered with that veil, and they do not understand.

[16]But whenever someone turns to the Lord, the veil is taken away. [17]For the Lord is the Spirit, and wherever the Spirit of the Lord is, there is freedom. [18]So all of us who have had that veil removed can see and reflect the glory of the Lord. And the Lord—who is the Spirit—makes us more and more like him as we are changed into his glorious image.

CHAPTER 4

Treasure in Fragile Clay Jars

Therefore, since God in his mercy has given us this new way,* we never give up. [2]We reject all shameful deeds and underhanded methods. We don't try to trick anyone or distort the word of God. We tell the truth before God, and all who are honest know this.

[3]If the Good News we preach is hidden behind a veil, it is hidden only from people who are perishing. [4]Satan, who is the god of this world, has blinded the minds of those who don't believe. They are unable to see the glorious light of the Good News. They don't understand this message about the glory of Christ, who is the exact likeness of God.

[5]You see, we don't go around preaching about ourselves. We preach that Jesus Christ is Lord, and we ourselves are your servants for Jesus' sake. [6]For God, who said, "Let there be light in the darkness," has made this light shine in our hearts so we could know the glory of God that is seen in the face of Jesus Christ.

[7]We now have this light shining in our hearts, but we ourselves are like fragile clay jars containing this great treasure.* This makes it clear that our great power is from God, not from ourselves.

[8]We are pressed on every side by troubles, but we are not crushed. We are perplexed, but not driven to despair. [9]We are hunted down, but never abandoned by God. We get knocked down, but we are not destroyed. [10]Through suffering, our bodies continue to share in the death of Jesus so that the life of Jesus may also be seen in our bodies.

[11]Yes, we live under constant danger of death because we serve Jesus, so that the life of Jesus will be evident in our dying bodies. [12]So we live in the face of death, but this has resulted in eternal life for you.

[13]But we continue to preach because we have the same kind of faith the psalmist had when he said, "I believed in God, so I spoke."* [14]We know that God, who raised the Lord Jesus,* will also raise us with Jesus and present us to himself together with you. [15]All of this is for your benefit. And as God's grace reaches more and more people, there will be great thanksgiving, and God will receive more and more glory.

[16]That is why we never give up. Though our bodies are dying, our spirits are* being renewed every day. [17]For our present troubles are small and won't last very long. Yet they produce for us a glory that vastly outweighs them and will last forever! [18]So we don't look at the troubles we can see now; rather, we fix our gaze on things that cannot be seen. For the things we see now will soon be gone, but the things we cannot see will last forever.

CHAPTER 5

New Bodies

For we know that when this earthly tent we live in is taken down (that is, when we die and leave this earthly body), we will have a house in heaven, an eternal body made for us by God himself and not by human hands. [2]We grow weary in our present bodies, and we long to

4:1 Or *ministry*. **4:7** Greek *We now have this treasure in clay jars*. **4:13** Ps 116:10. **4:14** Some manuscripts read *who raised Jesus*. **4:16** Greek *our inner being is*.

put on our heavenly bodies like new clothing.
[3]For we will put on heavenly bodies; we will
not be spirits without bodies.* [4]While we live
in these earthly bodies, we groan and sigh, but
it's not that we want to die and get rid of these
bodies that clothe us. Rather, we want to put
on our new bodies so that these dying bodies
will be swallowed up by life. [5]God himself has
prepared us for this, and as a guarantee he has
given us his Holy Spirit.

[6]So we are always confident, even though
we know that as long as we live in these bodies
we are not at home with the Lord. [7]For we live
by believing and not by seeing. [8]Yes, we are
fully confident, and we would rather be away
from these earthly bodies, for then we will be
at home with the Lord. [9]So whether we are
here in this body or away from this body, our
goal is to please him. [10]For we must all stand
before Christ to be judged. We will each re-
ceive whatever we deserve for the good or evil
we have done in this earthly body.

Am I really any different now that I've become a Christian?

Anyone who belongs to Christ has become a new person. The old life is gone; a new life has begun!
2 CORINTHIANS 5:17

We Are God's Ambassadors

[11]Because we understand our fearful respon-
sibility to the Lord, we work hard to persuade
others. God knows we are sincere, and I hope
you know this, too. [12]Are we commending
ourselves to you again? No, we are giving you a
reason to be proud of us,* so you can answer
those who brag about having a spectacular
ministry rather than having a sincere heart.
[13]If it seems we are crazy, it is to bring glory to
God. And if we are in our right minds, it is for
your benefit. [14]Either way, Christ's love con-
trols us.* Since we believe that Christ died for
all, we also believe that we have all died to our
old life.* [15]He died for everyone so that those
who receive his new life will no longer live for
themselves. Instead, they will live for Christ,
who died and was raised for them.

[16]So we have stopped evaluating others
from a human point of view. At one time we
thought of Christ merely from a human point
of view. How differently we know him now!
[17]This means that anyone who belongs to
Christ has become a new person. The old life
is gone; a new life has begun!

[18]And all of this is a gift from God, who
brought us back to himself through Christ.
And God has given us this task of reconciling
people to him. [19]For God was in Christ, recon-
ciling the world to himself, no longer count-
ing people's sins against them. And he gave us
this wonderful message of reconciliation.
[20]So we are Christ's ambassadors; God is mak-
ing his appeal through us. We speak for
Christ when we plead, "Come back to God!"
[21]For God made Christ, who never sinned, to
be the offering for our sin,* so that we could
be made right with God through Christ.

CHAPTER 6

As God's partners,* we beg you not to accept
this marvelous gift of God's kindness and
then ignore it. [2]For God says,

"At just the right time, I heard you.
On the day of salvation, I helped you."*

Indeed, the "right time" is now. Today is the
day of salvation.

Paul's Hardships

[3]We live in such a way that no one will stum-
ble because of us, and no one will find fault
with our ministry. [4]In everything we do, we
show that we are true ministers of God. We
patiently endure troubles and hardships and
calamities of every kind. [5]We have been
beaten, been put in prison, faced angry mobs,
worked to exhaustion, endured sleepless
nights, and gone without food. [6]We prove our-
selves by our purity, our understanding, our
patience, our kindness, by the Holy Spirit
within us,* and by our sincere love. [7]We faith-
fully preach the truth. God's power is working
in us. We use the weapons of righteousness in

5:3 Greek *we will not be naked.* **5:12** Some manuscripts read *proud of yourselves.* **5:14a** Or *urges us on.* **5:14b** Greek *Since one died for all, then all died.* **5:21** Or *to become sin itself.* **6:1** Or *As we work together.* **6:2** Isa 49:8 (Greek version). **6:6** Or *by our holiness of spirit.*

the right hand for attack and the left hand for defense. [8]We serve God whether people honor us or despise us, whether they slander us or praise us. We are honest, but they call us impostors. [9]We are ignored, even though we are well known. We live close to death, but we are still alive. We have been beaten, but we have not been killed. [10]Our hearts ache, but we always have joy. We are poor, but we give spiritual riches to others. We own nothing, and yet we have everything.

[11]Oh, dear Corinthian friends! We have spoken honestly with you, and our hearts are open to you. [12]There is no lack of love on our part, but you have withheld your love from us. [13]I am asking you to respond as if you were my own children. Open your hearts to us!

The Temple of the Living God

[14]Don't team up with those who are unbelievers. How can righteousness be a partner with wickedness? How can light live with darkness? [15]What harmony can there be between Christ and the devil*? How can a believer be a partner with an unbeliever? [16]And what union can there be between God's temple and idols? For we are the temple of the living God. As God said:

"I will live in them
and walk among them.
I will be their God,
and they will be my people.*
[17] Therefore, come out from among
unbelievers,
and separate yourselves from them,
says the LORD.
Don't touch their filthy things,
and I will welcome you.*
[18] And I will be your Father,
and you will be my sons and
daughters,
says the LORD Almighty.*"

CHAPTER 7

Because we have these promises, dear friends, let us cleanse ourselves from everything that can defile our body or spirit. And let us work toward complete holiness because we fear God.

6:15 Greek *Beliar;* various other manuscripts render this proper name of the devil as *Belian, Beliab,* or *Belial.* **6:16** Lev 26:12; Ezek 37:27. **6:17** Isa 52:11; Ezek 20:34 (Greek version). **6:18** 2 Sam 7:14.

IS IT OK?

IS IT OK TO GO OUT WITH NON-CHRISTIANS?

God wants us to *influence* non-Christians, but he doesn't want us to *"team up"* with them (see 2 Corinthians 6:14-15). Where's the fine line between those two ideas? Let's look at some examples. Is it OK to play on the same sports team as a non-Christian? Absolutely. Do class projects together? Yup. Be friends? Definitely—what an awesome way to win someone to Christ! Be *best* friends? Not ideal. Date a non-Christian? Risky. Marry a non-Christian? Dangerous. *Why?* Because God should be the most important one in your life, and unbelievers can't relate to that. Even without meaning to do it, unbelievers can distract you from God and get you to compromise your standards. The best way to avoid that heartache is not to go out with non-Christians.

[2]Please open your hearts to us. We have not done wrong to anyone, nor led anyone astray, nor taken advantage of anyone. [3]I'm not saying this to condemn you. I said before that you are in our hearts, and we live or die together with you. [4]I have the highest confidence in you, and I take great pride in you. You have greatly encouraged me and made me happy despite all our troubles.

Paul's Joy at the Church's Repentance

[5]When we arrived in Macedonia, there was no rest for us. We faced conflict from every direction, with battles on the outside and fear on the inside. [6]But God, who encourages those who are discouraged, encouraged us by the arrival of Titus. [7]His presence was a joy, but so was the news he brought of the encouragement he received from you. When he told us how much you long to see me, and how sorry you are for what happened, and how loyal you are to me, I was filled with joy!

[8]I am not sorry that I sent that severe letter to you, though I was sorry at first, for I know it was painful to you for a little while. [9]Now I am glad I sent it, not because it hurt you, but because the pain caused you to repent and change your ways. It was the kind of sorrow God wants his people to have, so you were not harmed by us in any way. [10]For the kind of sorrow God wants us to experience leads us away from sin and results in salvation. There's no regret for that kind of sorrow. But worldly sorrow, which lacks repentance, results in spiritual death.

[11]Just see what this godly sorrow produced in you! Such earnestness, such concern to clear yourselves, such indignation, such alarm, such longing to see me, such zeal, and such a readiness to punish wrong. You showed that you have done everything necessary to make things right. [12]My purpose, then, was not to write about who did the wrong or who was wronged. I wrote to you so that in the sight of God you could see for yourselves how loyal you are to us. [13]We have been greatly encouraged by this.

In addition to our own encouragement, we were especially delighted to see how happy Titus was about the way all of you welcomed him and set his mind* at ease. [14]I had told him how proud I was of you—and you didn't disappoint me. I have always told you the truth, and now my boasting to Titus has also proved true! [15]Now he cares for you more than ever when he remembers the way all of you obeyed him and welcomed him with such fear and deep respect. [16]I am very happy now because I have complete confidence in you.

CHAPTER 8

A Call to Generous Giving

Now I want you to know, dear brothers and sisters,* what God in his kindness has done through the churches in Macedonia. [2]They are being tested by many troubles, and they are very poor. But they are also filled with abundant joy, which has overflowed in rich generosity.

[3]For I can testify that they gave not only what they could afford, but far more. And they did it of their own free will. [4]They begged us again and again for the privilege of sharing in the gift for the believers in Jerusalem.* [5]They even did more than we had hoped, for their first action was to give themselves to the Lord and to us, just as God wanted them to do.

[6]So we have urged Titus, who encouraged your giving in the first place, to return to you and encourage you to finish this ministry of giving. [7]Since you excel in so many ways—in your faith, your gifted speakers, your knowledge, your enthusiasm, and your love from us*—I want you to excel also in this gracious act of giving.

[8]I am not commanding you to do this. But I am testing how genuine your love is by comparing it with the eagerness of the other churches.

[9]You know the generous grace of our Lord Jesus Christ. Though he was rich, yet for your sakes he became poor, so that by his poverty he could make you rich.

[10]Here is my advice: It would be good for you to finish what you started a year ago. Last year you were the first who wanted to give, and you were the first to begin doing it. [11]Now you should finish what you started. Let the eagerness you showed in the beginning be matched now by your giving. Give in proportion to what you have. [12]Whatever you give is acceptable if you give it eagerly. And

7:13 Greek *his spirit*. **8:1** Greek *brothers*. **8:4** Greek *for God's holy people*. **8:7** Some manuscripts read *your love for us*.

give according to what you have, not what you don't have. [13]Of course, I don't mean your giving should make life easy for others and hard for yourselves. I only mean that there should be some equality. [14]Right now you have plenty and can help those who are in need. Later, they will have plenty and can share with you when you need it. In this way, things will be equal. [15]As the Scriptures say,

> "Those who gathered a lot had nothing left over,
> and those who gathered only a little had enough."*

Titus and His Companions

[16]But thank God! He has given Titus the same enthusiasm for you that I have. [17]Titus welcomed our request that he visit you again. In fact, he himself was very eager to go and see you. [18]We are also sending another brother with Titus. All the churches praise him as a preacher of the Good News. [19]He was appointed by the churches to accompany us as we take the offering to Jerusalem*—a service that glorifies the Lord and shows our eagerness to help.

[20]We are traveling together to guard against any criticism for the way we are handling this generous gift. [21]We are careful to be honorable before the Lord, but we also want everyone else to see that we are honorable.

[22]We are also sending with them another of our brothers who has proven himself many times and has shown on many occasions how eager he is. He is now even more enthusiastic because of his great confidence in you. [23]If anyone asks about Titus, say that he is my partner who works with me to help you. And the brothers with him have been sent by the churches,* and they bring honor to Christ. [24]So show them your love, and prove to all the churches that our boasting about you is justified.

CHAPTER 9

The Collection for Christians in Jerusalem

I really don't need to write to you about this ministry of giving for the believers in Jerusalem.* [2]For I know how eager you are to help, and I have been boasting to the churches in Macedonia that you in Greece* were ready to send an offering a year ago. In fact, it was your enthusiasm that stirred up many of the Macedonian believers to begin giving.

[3]But I am sending these brothers to be sure you really are ready, as I have been telling them, and that your money is all collected. I don't want to be wrong in my boasting about you. [4]We would be embarrassed—not to mention your own embarrassment—if some

Giving and Getting

Alex pulled out a pack of his favorite gum and noticed that he had only two sticks left. He decided to enjoy one right away and save the second stick for later in the day. The only problem was that Alex's best friend saw him take out one stick and put the other one back in his pocket. Alex really liked the gum and wanted to save it, but he also wanted to be a good friend. Read 2 Corinthians 9:6 for one of God's principles about giving.

8:15 Exod 16:18. **8:19** See 1 Cor 16:3-4. **8:23** Greek *are apostles of the churches*. **9:1** Greek *about the offering for God's holy people*. **9:2** Greek *in Achaia*, the southern region of the Greek peninsula. *Macedonia* was in the northern region of Greece.

Macedonian believers came with me and found that you weren't ready after all I had told them! [5]So I thought I should send these brothers ahead of me to make sure the gift you promised is ready. But I want it to be a willing gift, not one given grudgingly.

[6]Remember this—a farmer who plants only a few seeds will get a small crop. But the one who plants generously will get a generous crop. [7]You must each decide in your heart how much to give. And don't give reluctantly or in response to pressure. "For God loves a person who gives cheerfully."* [8]And God will generously provide all you need. Then you will always have everything you need and plenty left over to share with others. [9]As the Scriptures say,

"They share freely and give generously
to the poor.
Their good deeds will be remembered
forever."*

[10]For God is the one who provides seed for the farmer and then bread to eat. In the same way, he will provide and increase your resources and then produce a great harvest of generosity* in you.

[11]Yes, you will be enriched in every way so that you can always be generous. And when we take your gifts to those who need them, they will thank God. [12]So two good things will result from this ministry of giving—the needs of the believers in Jerusalem* will be met, and they will joyfully express their thanks to God.

[13]As a result of your ministry, they will give glory to God. For your generosity to them and to all believers will prove that you are obedient to the Good News of Christ. [14]And they will pray for you with deep affection because of the overflowing grace God has given to you. [15]Thank God for this gift* too wonderful for words!

CHAPTER 10

Paul Defends His Authority

Now I, Paul, appeal to you with the gentleness and kindness of Christ—though I realize you think I am timid in person and bold only when I write from far away. [2]Well, I am begging you now so that when I come I won't have to be bold with those who think we act from human motives.

[3]We are human, but we don't wage war as humans do. [4]*We use God's mighty weapons, not worldly weapons, to knock down the strongholds of human reasoning and to destroy false arguments. [5]We destroy every proud obstacle that keeps people from knowing God. We capture their rebellious thoughts and teach them to obey Christ. [6]And after you have become fully obedient, we will punish everyone who remains disobedient.

[7]Look at the obvious facts.* Those who say they belong to Christ must recognize that we belong to Christ as much as they do. [8]I may seem to be boasting too much about the authority given to us by the Lord. But our authority builds you up; it doesn't tear you down. So I will not be ashamed of using my authority.

[9]I'm not trying to frighten you by my letters. [10]For some say, "Paul's letters are demanding and forceful, but in person he is weak, and his speeches are worthless!" [11]Those people should realize that our actions when we arrive in person will be as forceful as what we say in our letters from far away.

[12]Oh, don't worry; we wouldn't dare say that we are as wonderful as these other men who tell you how important they are! But they are only comparing themselves with each other, using themselves as the standard of measurement. How ignorant!

[13]We will not boast about things done outside our area of authority. We will boast only about what has happened within the boundaries of the work God has given us, which includes our working with you. [14]We are not reaching beyond these boundaries when we claim authority over you, as if we had never visited you. For we were the first to travel all the way to Corinth with the Good News of Christ.

[15]Nor do we boast and claim credit for the work someone else has done. Instead, we hope that your faith will grow so that the boundaries of our work among you will be extended. [16]Then we will be able to go and preach the Good News in other places far beyond you, where no one else is working. Then there will be no question of our boasting about work

9:7 See footnote on Prov 22:8. **9:9** Ps 112:9. **9:10** Greek *righteousness*. **9:12** Greek *of God's holy people*. **9:15** Greek *his gift*. **10:4** English translations divide verses 4 and 5 in various ways. **10:7** Or *You look at things only on the basis of appearance*.

done in someone else's territory. [17]As the Scriptures say, "If you want to boast, boast only about the LORD."*

[18]When people commend themselves, it doesn't count for much. The important thing is for the Lord to commend them.

CHAPTER 11

Paul and the False Apostles

I hope you will put up with a little more of my foolishness. Please bear with me. [2]For I am jealous for you with the jealousy of God himself. I promised you as a pure bride* to one husband—Christ. [3]But I fear that somehow your pure and undivided devotion to Christ will be corrupted, just as Eve was deceived by the cunning ways of the serpent. [4]You happily put up with whatever anyone tells you, even if they preach a different Jesus than the one we preach, or a different kind of Spirit than the one you received, or a different kind of gospel than the one you believed.

AMAZING FACTS

Paul lived through five whippings, three beatings, a stoning, three shipwrecks, hunger, cold, prison, and more—all for doing what was right!

2 CORINTHIANS 11:23-27

[5]But I don't consider myself inferior in any way to these "super apostles" who teach such things. [6]I may be unskilled as a speaker, but I'm not lacking in knowledge. We have made this clear to you in every possible way.

[7]Was I wrong when I humbled myself and honored you by preaching God's Good News to you without expecting anything in return? [8]I "robbed" other churches by accepting their contributions so I could serve you at no cost. [9]And when I was with you and didn't have enough to live on, I did not become a financial burden to anyone. For the brothers who came from Macedonia brought me all that I needed. I have never been a burden to you, and I never will be. [10]As surely as the truth of Christ is in me, no one in all of Greece* will ever stop me from boasting about this. [11]Why? Because I don't love you? God knows that I do.

[12]But I will continue doing what I have always done. This will undercut those who are looking for an opportunity to boast that their work is just like ours. [13]These people are false apostles. They are deceitful workers who disguise themselves as apostles of Christ. [14]But I am not surprised! Even Satan disguises himself as an angel of light. [15]So it is no wonder that his servants also disguise themselves as servants of righteousness. In the end they will get the punishment their wicked deeds deserve.

Paul's Many Trials

[16]Again I say, don't think that I am a fool to talk like this. But even if you do, listen to me, as you would to a foolish person, while I also boast a little. [17]Such boasting is not from the Lord, but I am acting like a fool. [18]And since others boast about their human achievements, I will, too. [19]After all, you think you are so wise, but you enjoy putting up with fools! [20]You put up with it when someone enslaves you, takes everything you have, takes advantage of you, takes control of everything, and slaps you in the face. [21]I'm ashamed to say that we've been too "weak" to do that!

But whatever they dare to boast about—I'm talking like a fool again—I dare to boast about it, too. [22]Are they Hebrews? So am I. Are they Israelites? So am I. Are they descendants of Abraham? So am I. [23]Are they servants of Christ? I know I sound like a madman, but I have served him far more! I have worked harder, been put in prison more often, been whipped times without number, and faced death again and again. [24]Five different times the Jewish leaders gave me thirty-nine lashes. [25]Three times I was beaten with rods. Once I was stoned. Three times I was shipwrecked. Once I spent a whole night and a day adrift at sea. [26]I have traveled on many long journeys. I have faced danger from rivers and from

10:17 Jer 9:24. **11:2** Greek *a virgin*. **11:10** Greek *Achaia*, the southern region of the Greek peninsula.

It's kind of easy to talk about suffering until you actually go through it. Both my sister and I have dealt with pretty bad headaches throughout our lives. Last year, I even had to miss weeks of school because the pain was so bad. I was raised in a Christian home, and I truly love God. But I always felt that it wasn't fair that I should be stuck with this kind of illness when most of my non-Christian friends had life easy! Almost every day I asked God why.

Then, as I was reading my Bible, I came across 2 Corinthians 12:5-10, where Paul describes his own suffering. His words completely blew my mind. Although Paul didn't go into details about his physical problem, I could totally relate when he explained that he "begged the Lord to take it away." That was me! Still, what did Paul mean by saying he was glad to boast about his weaknesses? My headaches were nothing to be proud of!

The more I thought about the verses, the more I realized that my headaches *had* taught me to depend on God. When I'm really hurting, I'm more likely to pray for advice and ask for God's help to endure. Maybe I wouldn't give him that time if everything in my life were the way I wanted it.

I'm a pretty independent person. But having these headaches constantly reminds me that I need to rely on God's strength and not my own. Even though I go through some bad times, I know that God is in control in my life. No matter how awful my pain, God understands it because he came to earth and experienced it himself. That's one of the greatest comforts for me.

For more on how to handle suffering, read Psalm 41:3; Romans 5:1-5; 2 Corinthians 12:5-10; and James 5:14-16.

robbers. I have faced danger from my own people, the Jews, as well as from the Gentiles. I have faced danger in the cities, in the deserts, and on the seas. And I have faced danger from men who claim to be believers but are not.* [27] I have worked hard and long, enduring many sleepless nights. I have been hungry and thirsty and have often gone without food. I have shivered in the cold, without enough clothing to keep me warm.

[28] Then, besides all this, I have the daily burden of my concern for all the churches. [29] Who is weak without my feeling that weakness? Who is led astray, and I do not burn with anger?

[30] If I must boast, I would rather boast about the things that show how weak I am. [31] God, the Father of our Lord Jesus, who is worthy of eternal praise, knows I am not lying. [32] When I was in Damascus, the governor under King Aretas kept guards at the city gates to catch me. [33] I had to be lowered in a basket through a window in the city wall to escape from him.

CHAPTER 12

Paul's Vision and His Thorn in the Flesh

This boasting will do no good, but I must go on. I will reluctantly tell about visions and revelations from the Lord. [2] I* was caught up to the third heaven fourteen years ago. Whether I was in my body or out of my body, I don't know—only God knows. [3] Yes, only God knows whether I was in my body or outside my body. But I do know [4] that I was caught up* to paradise and heard things so astounding that they cannot be expressed in words, things no human is allowed to tell.

[5] That experience is worth boasting about, but I'm not going to do it. I will boast only about my weaknesses. [6] If I wanted to boast, I would be no fool in doing so, because I would be telling the truth. But I won't do it, because I don't want anyone to give me credit beyond what they can see in my life or hear in my message, [7] even though I have received such wonderful revelations from God. So to keep me from becoming proud, I was given a thorn in my flesh, a messenger from Satan to torment me and keep me from becoming proud.

[8] Three different times I begged the Lord to take it away. [9] Each time he said, "My grace is all you need. My power works best in weakness." So now I am glad to boast about my weaknesses, so that the power of Christ can work through me. [10] That's why I take pleasure in my weaknesses, and in the insults, hardships, persecutions, and troubles that I suffer for Christ. For when I am weak, then I am strong.

Paul's Concern for the Corinthians

[11] You have made me act like a fool—boasting like this.* You ought to be writing commendations for me, for I am not at all inferior to these "super apostles," even though I am nothing at all. [12] When I was with you, I certainly gave you proof that I am an apostle. For I patiently did many signs and wonders and miracles among you. [13] The only thing I failed to do, which I do in the other churches, was to become a financial burden to you. Please forgive me for this wrong!

[14] Now I am coming to you for the third time, and I will not be a burden to you. I don't want what you have—I want you. After all, children don't provide for their parents. Rather, parents provide for their children. [15] I will gladly spend myself and all I have for you, even though it seems that the more I love you, the less you love me.

[16] Some of you admit I was not a burden to you. But others still think I was sneaky and took advantage of you by trickery. [17] But how? Did any of the men I sent to you take advantage of you? [18] When I urged Titus to visit you and sent our other brother with him, did Titus take advantage of you? No! For we have the same spirit and walk in each other's steps, doing things the same way.

[19] Perhaps you think we're saying these things just to defend ourselves. No, we tell you this as Christ's servants, and with God as our witness. Everything we do, dear friends, is to strengthen you. [20] For I am afraid that when I come I won't like what I find, and you won't like my response. I am afraid that I will find quarreling, jealousy, anger, selfishness, slander, gossip, arrogance, and disorderly behavior. [21] Yes, I am afraid that when I come again, God will humble me in your presence. And I will be grieved because many of you have not given up your old sins. You have not repented

11:26 Greek *from false brothers.* **12:2** Greek *I know a man in Christ who.* **12:3-4** Greek *But I know such a man, 4 that he was caught up.* **12:11** Some manuscripts do not include *boasting like this.*

of your impurity, sexual immorality, and eagerness for lustful pleasure.

CHAPTER 13

Paul's Final Advice

This is the third time I am coming to visit you (and as the Scriptures say, "The facts of every case must be established by the testimony of two or three witnesses"*). [2]I have already warned those who had been sinning when I was there on my second visit. Now I again warn them and all others, just as I did before, that next time I will not spare them.

[3]I will give you all the proof you want that Christ speaks through me. Christ is not weak when he deals with you; he is powerful among you. [4]Although he was crucified in weakness, he now lives by the power of God. We, too, are weak, just as Christ was, but when we deal with you we will be alive with him and will have God's power.

[5]Examine yourselves to see if your faith is genuine. Test yourselves. Surely you know that Jesus Christ is among you*; if not, you have failed the test of genuine faith. [6]As you test yourselves, I hope you will recognize that we have not failed the test of apostolic authority.

[7]We pray to God that you will not do what is wrong by refusing our correction. I hope we won't need to demonstrate our authority when we arrive. Do the right thing before we come—even if that makes it look like we have failed to demonstrate our authority. [8]For we cannot oppose the truth, but must always stand for the truth. [9]We are glad to seem weak if it helps show that you are actually strong. We pray that you will become mature.

[10]I am writing this to you before I come, hoping that I won't need to deal severely with you when I do come. For I want to use the authority the Lord has given me to strengthen you, not to tear you down.

Paul's Final Greetings

[11]Dear brothers and sisters,* I close my letter with these last words: Be joyful. Grow to maturity. Encourage each other. Live in harmony and peace. Then the God of love and peace will be with you.

[12]Greet each other with Christian love.* [13]All of God's people here send you their greetings.

[14]*May the grace of the Lord Jesus Christ, the love of God, and the fellowship of the Holy Spirit be with you all.

13:1 Deut 19:15. **13:5** Or *in you*. **13:11** Greek *Brothers*. **13:12** Greek *with a sacred kiss*. **13:14** Some English translations include verse 13 as part of verse 12, and then verse 14 becomes verse 13.

Galatians

WHO
Paul, Peter, Barnabas, Titus, Abraham, and the Judaizers.

WHERE
Written and sent by Paul from Antioch.

WHEN
Around AD 49, before the Jerusalem Council in AD 50.

WHY
To challenge the Judaizers (who said Gentiles had to obey Jewish laws to be saved) and to call Christians to faith and freedom in Christ.

You have been called to live in freedom. . . . Use your freedom to serve one another in love.
GALATIANS 5:13

Remember how it feels to be free from school for the summer? We are free in Christ, too. But the Galatians thought they had to do a lot of religious stuff to please God. Paul told them that they only needed to trust Christ. Then his love would free them to enjoy doing good.

Paul tells the Galatians—and us—to enjoy being free in Christ!

CHAPTER 1

Greetings from Paul

This letter is from Paul, an apostle. I was not appointed by any group of people or any human authority, but by Jesus Christ himself and by God the Father, who raised Jesus from the dead.

[2]All the brothers and sisters* here join me in sending this letter to the churches of Galatia.

[3]May God our Father and the Lord Jesus Christ* give you grace and peace. [4]Jesus gave his life for our sins, just as God our Father planned, in order to rescue us from this evil

1:2 Greek *brothers;* also in 1:11. 1:3 Some manuscripts read *God the Father and our Lord Jesus Christ.*

world in which we live. [5]All glory to God forever and ever! Amen.

There Is Only One Good News

[6]I am shocked that you are turning away so soon from God, who called you to himself through the loving mercy of Christ.* You are following a different way that pretends to be the Good News [7]but is not the Good News at all. You are being fooled by those who deliberately twist the truth concerning Christ.

[8]Let God's curse fall on anyone, including us or even an angel from heaven, who preaches a different kind of Good News than the one we preached to you. [9]I say again what we have said before: If anyone preaches any other Good News than the one you welcomed, let that person be cursed.

[10]Obviously, I'm not trying to win the approval of people, but of God. If pleasing people were my goal, I would not be Christ's servant.

Paul's Message Comes from Christ

[11]Dear brothers and sisters, I want you to understand that the gospel message I preach is not based on mere human reasoning. [12]I received my message from no human source, and no one taught me. Instead, I received it by direct revelation from Jesus Christ.*

[13]You know what I was like when I followed the Jewish religion—how I violently persecuted God's church. I did my best to destroy it. [14]I was far ahead of my fellow Jews in my zeal for the traditions of my ancestors.

[15]But even before I was born, God chose me and called me by his marvelous grace. Then it pleased him [16]to reveal his Son to me* so that I would proclaim the Good News about Jesus to the Gentiles.

When this happened, I did not rush out to consult with any human being.* [17]Nor did I go up to Jerusalem to consult with those who were apostles before I was. Instead, I went away into Arabia, and later I returned to the city of Damascus.

[18]Then three years later I went to Jerusalem to get to know Peter,* and I stayed with him for fifteen days. [19]The only other apostle I met at that time was James, the Lord's brother. [20]I declare before God that what I am writing to you is not a lie.

[21]After that visit I went north into the provinces of Syria and Cilicia. [22]And still the Christians in the churches in Judea didn't know me personally. [23]All they knew was that people were saying, "The one who used to persecute us is now preaching the very faith he tried to destroy!" [24]And they praised God because of me.

CHAPTER 2

The Apostles Accept Paul

Then fourteen years later I went back to Jerusalem again, this time with Barnabas; and Titus came along, too. [2]I went there because God revealed to me that I should go. While I was there I met privately with those considered to be leaders of the church and shared with them the message I had been preaching to the Gentiles. I wanted to make sure that we were in agreement, for fear that all my efforts had been wasted and I was running the race for nothing. [3]And they supported me and did not even demand that my companion Titus be circumcised, though he was a Gentile.*

[4]Even that question came up only because of some so-called Christians there—false ones, really*—who were secretly brought in. They sneaked in to spy on us and take away the freedom we have in Christ Jesus. They wanted to enslave us and force us to follow their Jewish regulations. [5]But we refused to give in to them for a single moment. We wanted to preserve the truth of the gospel message for you.

[6]And the leaders of the church had nothing to add to what I was preaching. (By the way, their reputation as great leaders made no difference to me, for God has no favorites.) [7]Instead, they saw that God had given me the responsibility of preaching the gospel to the Gentiles, just as he had given Peter the responsibility of preaching to the Jews. [8]For the same God who worked through Peter as the apostle to the Jews also worked through me as the apostle to the Gentiles.

[9]In fact, James, Peter,* and John, who were known as pillars of the church, recognized the gift God had given me, and they accepted Bar-

1:6 Some manuscripts read *through loving mercy.* **1:12** Or *by the revelation of Jesus Christ.* **1:16a** Or *in me.* **1:16b** Greek *with flesh and blood.* **1:18** Greek *Cephas.* **2:3** Greek *a Greek.* **2:4** Greek *some false brothers.* **2:9** Greek *Cephas;* also in 2:11, 14.

nabas and me as their co-workers. They encouraged us to keep preaching to the Gentiles, while they continued their work with the Jews. [10]Their only suggestion was that we keep on helping the poor, which I have always been eager to do.

Paul Confronts Peter

[11]But when Peter came to Antioch, I had to oppose him to his face, for what he did was very wrong. [12]When he first arrived, he ate with the Gentile Christians, who were not circumcised. But afterward, when some friends of James came, Peter wouldn't eat with the Gentiles anymore. He was afraid of criticism from these people who insisted on the necessity of circumcision. [13]As a result, other Jewish Christians followed Peter's hypocrisy, and even Barnabas was led astray by their hypocrisy.

[14]When I saw that they were not following the truth of the gospel message, I said to Peter in front of all the others, "Since you, a Jew by birth, have discarded the Jewish laws and are living like a Gentile, why are you now trying to make these Gentiles follow the Jewish traditions?

[15]"You and I are Jews by birth, not 'sinners' like the Gentiles. [16]Yet we know that a person is made right with God by faith in Jesus Christ, not by obeying the law. And we have believed in Christ Jesus, so that we might be made right with God because of our faith in Christ, not because we have obeyed the law. For no one will ever be made right with God by obeying the law."*

[17]But suppose we seek to be made right with God through faith in Christ and then we are found guilty because we have abandoned the law. Would that mean Christ has led us into sin? Absolutely not! [18]Rather, I am a sinner if I rebuild the old system of law I already tore down. [19]For when I tried to keep the law, it condemned me. So I died to the law—I stopped trying to meet all its requirements—so that I might live for God. [20]My old self has been crucified with Christ.* It is no longer I who live, but Christ lives in me. So I live in this earthly body by trusting in the Son of God, who loved me and gave himself for me. [21]I do not treat the grace of God as meaningless. For if keeping the law could make us right with God, then there was no need for Christ to die.

AMAZING FACTS

Paul didn't like his old self, so he trusted Jesus and got a new life. You can get a new life too!

GALATIANS 2:20

CHAPTER 3

The Law and Faith in Christ

Oh, foolish Galatians! Who has cast an evil spell on you? For the meaning of Jesus Christ's death was made as clear to you as if you had seen a picture of his death on the cross. [2]Let me ask you this one question: Did you receive the Holy Spirit by obeying the law of Moses? Of course not! You received the Spirit because you believed the message you heard about Christ. [3]How foolish can you be? After starting your Christian lives in the Spirit, why are you now trying to become perfect by your own human effort? [4]Have you experienced* so much for nothing? Surely it was not in vain, was it?

[5]I ask you again, does God give you the Holy Spirit and work miracles among you because you obey the law? Of course not! It is because you believe the message you heard about Christ.

[6]In the same way, "Abraham believed God, and God counted him as righteous because of his faith."* [7]The real children of Abraham, then, are those who put their faith in God.

[8]What's more, the Scriptures looked forward to this time when God would declare the Gentiles to be righteous because of their faith. God proclaimed this good news to Abraham long ago when he said, "All nations

2:16 Some translators hold that the quotation extends through verse 14; others through verse 16; and still others through verse 21.
2:20 Some English translations put this sentence in verse 19. **3:4** Or *Have you suffered*. **3:6** Gen 15:6.

will be blessed through you."* [9]So all who put their faith in Christ share the same blessing Abraham received because of his faith.

[10]But those who depend on the law to make them right with God are under his curse, for the Scriptures say, "Cursed is everyone who does not observe and obey all the commands that are written in God's Book of the Law."* [11]So it is clear that no one can be made right with God by trying to keep the law. For the Scriptures say, "It is through faith that a righteous person has life."* [12]This way of faith is very different from the way of law, which says, "It is through obeying the law that a person has life."*

[13]But Christ has rescued us from the curse pronounced by the law. When he was hung on the cross, he took upon himself the curse for our wrongdoing. For it is written in the Scriptures, "Cursed is everyone who is hung on a tree."* [14]Through Christ Jesus, God has blessed the Gentiles with the same blessing he promised to Abraham, so that we who are believers might receive the promised* Holy Spirit through faith.

The Law and God's Promise

[15]Dear brothers and sisters,* here's an example from everyday life. Just as no one can set aside or amend an irrevocable agreement, so it is in this case. [16]God gave the promises to Abraham and his child.* And notice that the Scripture doesn't say "to his children,*" as if it meant many descendants. Rather, it says "to his child"—and that, of course, means Christ. [17]This is what I am trying to say: The agreement God made with Abraham could not be canceled 430 years later when God gave the law to Moses. God would be breaking his promise. [18]For if the inheritance could be received by keeping the law, then it would not be the result of accepting God's promise. But God graciously gave it to Abraham as a promise.

[19]Why, then, was the law given? It was given alongside the promise to show people their sins. But the law was designed to last only until the coming of the child who was promised. God gave his law through angels to Moses, who was the mediator between God and the people. [20]Now a mediator is helpful if more than one party must reach an agreement. But God, who is one, did not use a mediator when he gave his promise to Abraham.

[21]Is there a conflict, then, between God's law and God's promises?* Absolutely not! If the law could give us new life, we could be made right with God by obeying it. [22]But the Scriptures declare that we are all prisoners of sin, so we receive God's promise of freedom only by believing in Jesus Christ.

God's Children through Faith

[23]Before the way of faith in Christ was available to us, we were placed under guard by the law. We were kept in protective custody, so to speak, until the way of faith was revealed.

[24]Let me put it another way. The law was our guardian until Christ came; it protected us until we could be made right with God through faith. [25]And now that the way of faith has come, we no longer need the law as our guardian.

[26]For you are all children* of God through faith in Christ Jesus. [27]And all who have been united with Christ in baptism have put on Christ, like putting on new clothes.* [28]There is no longer Jew or Gentile,* slave or free, male and female. For you are all one in Christ Jesus. [29]And now that you belong to Christ, you are the true children* of Abraham. You are his heirs, and God's promise to Abraham belongs to you.

CHAPTER 4

Think of it this way. If a father dies and leaves an inheritance for his young children, those children are not much better off than slaves until they grow up, even though they actually own everything their father had. [2]They have to obey their guardians until they reach whatever age their father set. [3]And that's the way it was with us before Christ came. We were like children; we were slaves to the basic spiritual principles* of this world.

[4]But when the right time came, God sent his Son, born of a woman, subject to the law. [5]God sent him to buy freedom for us who were slaves to the law, so that he could adopt us as his very own children.* [6]And because

3:8 Gen 12:3; 18:18; 22:18. **3:10** Deut 27:26. **3:11** Hab 2:4. **3:12** Lev 18:5. **3:13** Deut 21:23 (Greek version). **3:14** Some manuscripts read *the blessing of the*. **3:15** Greek *Brothers*. **3:16a** Greek *seed;* also in 3:16c, 19. See notes on Gen 12:7 and 13:15. **3:16b** Greek *seeds*. **3:21** Some manuscripts read *and the promises?* **3:26** Greek *sons*. **3:27** Greek *have put on Christ*. **3:28** Greek *Jew or Greek*. **3:29** Greek *seed*. **4:3** Or *powers;* also in 4:9. **4:5** Greek *sons;* also in 4:6.

we* are his children, God has sent the Spirit of his Son into our hearts, prompting us to call out, "Abba, Father."* [7]Now you are no longer a slave but God's own child.* And since you are his child, God has made you his heir.

Paul's Concern for the Galatians

[8]Before you Gentiles knew God, you were slaves to so-called gods that do not even exist. [9]So now that you know God (or should I say, now that God knows you), why do you want to go back again and become slaves once more to the weak and useless spiritual principles of this world? [10]You are trying to earn favor with God by observing certain days or months or seasons or years. [11]I fear for you. Perhaps all my hard work with you was for nothing. [12]Dear brothers and sisters,* I plead with you to live as I do in freedom from these things, for I have become like you Gentiles—free from those laws.

You did not mistreat me when I first preached to you. [13]Surely you remember that I was sick when I first brought you the Good News. [14]But even though my condition tempted you to reject me, you did not despise me or turn me away. No, you took me in and cared for me as though I were an angel from God or even Christ Jesus himself. [15]Where is that joyful and grateful spirit you felt then? I am sure you would have taken out your own eyes and given them to me if it had been possible. [16]Have I now become your enemy because I am telling you the truth?

[17]Those false teachers are so eager to win your favor, but their intentions are not good. They are trying to shut you off from me so that you will pay attention only to them. [18]If someone is eager to do good things for you, that's all right; but let them do it all the time, not just when I'm with you.

[19]Oh, my dear children! I feel as if I'm going through labor pains for you again, and they will continue until Christ is fully developed in your lives. [20]I wish I were with you right now so I could change my tone. But at this distance I don't know how else to help you.

Abraham's Two Children

[21]Tell me, you who want to live under the law, do you know what the law actually says? [22]The Scriptures say that Abraham had two sons, one from his slave wife and one from his freeborn wife.* [23]The son of the slave wife was born in a human attempt to bring about the fulfillment of God's promise. But the son of the freeborn wife was born as God's own fulfillment of his promise.

[24]These two women serve as an illustration of God's two covenants. The first woman, Hagar, represents Mount Sinai where people received the law that enslaved them. [25]And

Freedom

Brandon was furious with his parents because they grounded him for breaking a family rule. *They are just too strict—I can't do anything!* Brandon thought to himself. Then he thought about how great it would be to be finished with school. He could move out and do whatever he wanted to do. *There would be no rules—I would be free!* Brandon said to himself. Would that really be freedom? Or does real freedom have certain limits? See Galatians 5:13 for the answer.

4:6a Greek *you.* **4:6b** *Abba* is an Aramaic term for "father." **4:7** Greek *son;* also in 4:7b. **4:12** Greek *brothers;* also in 4:28, 31. **4:22** See Gen 16:15; 21:2-3.

now Jerusalem is just like Mount Sinai in Arabia,* because she and her children live in slavery to the law. [26]But the other woman, Sarah, represents the heavenly Jerusalem. She is the free woman, and she is our mother. [27]As Isaiah said,

"Rejoice, O childless woman,
you who have never given birth!
Break into a joyful shout,
you who have never been in labor!
For the desolate woman now has more children
than the woman who lives with her husband!"*

[28]And you, dear brothers and sisters, are children of the promise, just like Isaac. [29]But you are now being persecuted by those who want you to keep the law, just as Ishmael, the child born by human effort, persecuted Isaac, the child born by the power of the Spirit.

[30]But what do the Scriptures say about that? "Get rid of the slave and her son, for the son of the slave woman will not share the inheritance with the free woman's son."* [31]So, dear brothers and sisters, we are not children of the slave woman; we are children of the free woman.

CHAPTER 5

Freedom in Christ

So Christ has truly set us free. Now make sure that you stay free, and don't get tied up again in slavery to the law.

[2]Listen! I, Paul, tell you this: If you are counting on circumcision to make you right with God, then Christ will be of no benefit to you. [3]I'll say it again. If you are trying to find favor with God by being circumcised, you must obey every regulation in the whole law of Moses. [4]For if you are trying to make yourselves right with God by keeping the law, you have been cut off from Christ! You have fallen away from God's grace.

[5]But we who live by the Spirit eagerly wait to receive by faith the righteousness God has promised to us. [6]For when we place our faith in Christ Jesus, there is no benefit in being circumcised or being uncircumcised. What is important is faith expressing itself in love.

[7]You were running the race so well. Who has held you back from following the truth? [8]It certainly isn't God, for he is the one who called you to freedom. [9]This false teaching is like a little yeast that spreads through the whole batch of dough! [10]I am trusting the Lord to keep you from believing false teachings. God will judge that person, whoever he is, who has been confusing you.

[11]Dear brothers and sisters,* if I were still preaching that you must be circumcised—as some say I do—why am I still being persecuted? If I were no longer preaching salvation through the cross of Christ, no one would be offended. [12]I just wish that those troublemakers who want to mutilate you by circumcision would mutilate themselves.*

[13]For you have been called to live in freedom, my brothers and sisters. But don't use your freedom to satisfy your sinful nature. Instead, use your freedom to serve one another in love. [14]For the whole law can be summed up in this one command: "Love your neighbor as yourself."* [15]But if you are always biting and devouring one another, watch out! Beware of destroying one another.

Living by the Spirit's Power

[16]So I say, let the Holy Spirit guide your lives. Then you won't be doing what your sinful nature craves. [17]The sinful nature wants to do

How does God help me become a better person?

The Holy Spirit produces this kind of fruit in our lives: love, joy, peace, patience, kindness, goodness, faithfulness, gentleness, and self-control. GALATIANS 5:22-23

4:25 Greek *And Hagar, which is Mount Sinai in Arabia, is now like Jerusalem;* other manuscripts read *And Mount Sinai in Arabia is now like Jerusalem.* **4:27** Isa 54:1. **4:30** Gen 21:10. **5:11** Greek *Brothers;* similarly in 5:13. **5:12** Or *castrate themselves,* or *cut themselves off from you;* Greek reads *cut themselves off.* **5:14** Lev 19:18.

When I entered high school, I tried out for our school's football team. After a series of intense practices, the coaches posted the names of the guys they had selected. I was the only freshman on the list! During the following weeks, I was on cloud nine. Then something happened that I never would have expected: I broke my right leg.

It was so bad I ended up needing surgery. I also had to stay home from school to recuperate. During that time I didn't do anything but lie in my bed and feel sorry for myself. I didn't do the homework that classmates brought to me. I even refused to do my therapy exercises.

Fortunately, two of my buddies snapped me out of my funk. One day they showed up at my house with a bag of funny movies they'd rented. Their visit really lifted my spirits . . . and changed my outlook on things. I even did some of my exercises after they left.

When I put the videos back into the bag the guys had brought, I noticed a handwritten note taped to the bag. It read, "A cheerful heart is good medicine, but a broken spirit saps a person's strength" (Proverbs 17:22).

My friends were trying to tell me that when life seems tough, there are often things we can do to help each other feel better. The visit from my buddies really cheered me up and made me appreciate God's gifts of friendship and laughter.

The next time you learn about someone who is sad, ask God to show you what to do to make that person happy again. You may be surprised to discover how helpful your gift of friendship and laughter can be.

For more on the importance of encouragement, take a look at 2 Corinthians 1:3-4, Galatians 6:2, and Philippians 2:25-30.

evil, which is just the opposite of what the Spirit wants. And the Spirit gives us desires that are the opposite of what the sinful nature desires. These two forces are constantly fighting each other, so you are not free to carry out your good intentions. [18]But when you are directed by the Spirit, you are not under obligation to the law of Moses.

[19]When you follow the desires of your sinful nature, the results are very clear: sexual immorality, impurity, lustful pleasures, [20]idolatry, sorcery, hostility, quarreling, jealousy, outbursts of anger, selfish ambition, dissension, division, [21]envy, drunkenness, wild parties, and other sins like these. Let me tell you again, as I have before, that anyone living that sort of life will not inherit the Kingdom of God.

[22]But the Holy Spirit produces this kind of fruit in our lives: love, joy, peace, patience, kindness, goodness, faithfulness, [23]gentleness, and self-control. There is no law against these things!

[24]Those who belong to Christ Jesus have nailed the passions and desires of their sinful nature to his cross and crucified them there. [25]Since we are living by the Spirit, let us follow the Spirit's leading in every part of our lives. [26]Let us not become conceited, or provoke one another, or be jealous of one another.

CHAPTER 6

We Harvest What We Plant

Dear brothers and sisters, if another believer* is overcome by some sin, you who are godly* should gently and humbly help that person back onto the right path. And be careful not to fall into the same temptation yourself. [2]Share each other's burdens, and in this way obey the law of Christ. [3]If you think you are too important to help someone, you are only fooling yourself. You are not that important.

[4]Pay careful attention to your own work, for then you will get the satisfaction of a job well done, and you won't need to compare yourself to anyone else. [5]For we are each responsible for our own conduct.

[6]Those who are taught the word of God should provide for their teachers, sharing all good things with them.

[7]Don't be misled—you cannot mock the justice of God. You will always harvest what you plant. [8]Those who live only to satisfy their own sinful nature will harvest decay and death from that sinful nature. But those

6:1a Greek *Brothers, if a man.* **6:1b** Greek *spiritual.*

IS IT OK?

IS IT OK TO KEEP SOMETHING IMPORTANT TO MYSELF?

Some things are OK to keep to yourself. Your crush. Your most embarrassing moment. Your favorite flavor of ice cream. Some things aren't OK to keep to yourself. An eating disorder. A sibling's lies. A friend in danger. A person you're afraid of. Some things just feel heavy, and you know they're important. Those are the things you need to make sure you tell an adult you trust, such as a parent, pastor, or teacher. God wants us to share our troubles and problems with other people (see Galatians 6:2). We're supposed to help *others* when they need it and let other people help *us* when we need it. Sharing a problem isn't a sign of weakness; it's a sign of wisdom.

who live to please the Spirit will harvest everlasting life from the Spirit. [9]So let's not get tired of doing what is good. At just the right time we will reap a harvest of blessing if we don't give up. [10]Therefore, whenever we have the opportunity, we should do good to everyone—especially to those in the family of faith.

Even though I try hard, I can't do anything as well as my big sister.

Pay careful attention to your own work, for then you will get the satisfaction of a job well done, and you won't need to compare yourself to anyone else. GALATIANS 6:4

Paul's Final Advice

[11]NOTICE WHAT LARGE LETTERS I USE AS I WRITE THESE CLOSING WORDS IN MY OWN HANDWRITING.

[12]Those who are trying to force you to be circumcised want to look good to others. They don't want to be persecuted for teaching that the cross of Christ alone can save. [13]And even those who advocate circumcision don't keep the whole law themselves. They only want you to be circumcised so they can boast about it and claim you as their disciples.

[14]As for me, may I never boast about anything except the cross of our Lord Jesus Christ. Because of that cross,* my interest in this world has been crucified, and the world's interest in me has also died. [15]It doesn't matter whether we have been circumcised or not. What counts is whether we have been transformed into a new creation. [16]May God's peace and mercy be upon all who live by this principle; they are the new people of God.*

[17]From now on, don't let anyone trouble me with these things. For I bear on my body the scars that show I belong to Jesus.

[18]Dear brothers and sisters,* may the grace of our Lord Jesus Christ be with your spirit. Amen.

6:14 Or *Because of him.* **6:16** Greek *this principle, and upon the Israel of God.* **6:18** Greek *Brothers.*

EPHESIANS

WHO
Paul and Tychicus.

WHERE
Written and sent by Paul from Rome.

WHEN
Around AD 60, when Paul was in prison for preaching.

WHY
To strengthen the faith of the believers in Ephesus by explaining the characteristics and purpose of the church.

There is one body and one Spirit, just as you have been called to one glorious hope for the future.
EPHESIANS 4:4

People come in all shapes, sizes, and personalities. Should we try to find people in the church who are just like us and keep away from the others? In Ephesians, Paul tells us to remove anything that separates us and reach out to all Christians, even those who are very different.

READ EPHESIANS AND FIND THE UNITY THAT GOD DESIRES IN HIS FAMILY.

CHAPTER **1**

Greetings from Paul

This letter is from Paul, chosen by the will of God to be an apostle of Christ Jesus.

I am writing to God's holy people in Ephesus,* who are faithful followers of Christ Jesus.

[2]May God our Father and the Lord Jesus Christ give you grace and peace.

Spiritual Blessings

[3]All praise to God, the Father of our Lord Jesus Christ, who has blessed us with every spiritual blessing in the heavenly realms because we

1:1 The most ancient manuscripts do not include *in Ephesus.*

are united with Christ. [4]Even before he made the world, God loved us and chose us in Christ to be holy and without fault in his eyes. [5]God decided in advance to adopt us into his own family by bringing us to himself through Jesus Christ. This is what he wanted to do, and it gave him great pleasure. [6]So we praise God for the glorious grace he has poured out on us who belong to his dear Son.* [7]He is so rich in kindness and grace that he purchased our freedom with the blood of his Son and forgave our sins. [8]He has showered his kindness on us, along with all wisdom and understanding.

[9]God has now revealed to us his mysterious plan regarding Christ, a plan to fulfill his own good pleasure. [10]And this is the plan: At the right time he will bring everything together under the authority of Christ—everything in heaven and on earth. [11]Furthermore, because we are united with Christ, we have received an inheritance from God,* for he chose us in advance, and he makes everything work out according to his plan.

[12]God's purpose was that we Jews who were the first to trust in Christ would bring praise and glory to God. [13]And now you Gentiles have also heard the truth, the Good News that God saves you. And when you believed in Christ, he identified you as his own* by giving you the Holy Spirit, whom he promised long ago. [14]The Spirit is God's guarantee that he will give us the inheritance he promised and that he has purchased us to be his own people. He did this so we would praise and glorify him.

Paul's Prayer for Spiritual Wisdom

[15]Ever since I first heard of your strong faith in the Lord Jesus and your love for God's people everywhere,* [16]I have not stopped thanking God for you. I pray for you constantly, [17]asking God, the glorious Father of our Lord Jesus Christ, to give you spiritual wisdom* and insight so that you might grow in your knowledge of God. [18]I pray that your hearts will be flooded with light so that you can understand the confident hope he has given to those he called—his holy people who are his rich and glorious inheritance.*

[19]I also pray that you will understand the incredible greatness of God's power for us who believe him. This is the same mighty power [20]that raised Christ from the dead and seated him in the place of honor at God's right hand in the heavenly realms. [21]Now he is far above any ruler or authority or power or leader or anything else—not only in this world but also in the world to come. [22]God has put all things under the authority of Christ and has made him head over all things for the benefit of the church. [23]And the church is his body; it is made full and complete by Christ, who fills all things everywhere with himself.

CHAPTER 2

Made Alive with Christ

Once you were dead because of your disobedience and your many sins. [2]You used to live in sin, just like the rest of the world, obeying the devil—the commander of the powers in the unseen world.* He is the spirit at work in the hearts of those who refuse to obey God. [3]All of us used to live that way, following the passionate desires and inclinations of our sinful nature. By our very nature we were subject to God's anger, just like everyone else.

[4]But God is so rich in mercy, and he loved us so much, [5]that even though we were dead because of our sins, he gave us life when he raised Christ from the dead. (It is only by God's grace that you have been saved!) [6]For he raised us from the dead along with Christ and seated us with him in the heavenly realms because we are united with Christ Jesus. [7]So God can point to us in all future ages as examples of the incredible wealth of his grace and kindness toward us, as shown in all he has done for us who are united with Christ Jesus.

[8]God saved you by his grace when you believed. And you can't take credit for this; it is a gift from God. [9]Salvation is not a reward for the good things we have done, so none of us can boast about it. [10]For we are God's masterpiece. He has created us anew in Christ Jesus, so we can do the good things he planned for us long ago.

Oneness and Peace in Christ

[11]Don't forget that you Gentiles used to be outsiders. You were called "uncircumcised heathens" by the Jews, who were proud of

1:6 Greek *to us in the beloved.* **1:11** Or *we have become God's inheritance.* **1:13** Or *he put his seal on you.* **1:15** Some manuscripts read *your faithfulness to the Lord Jesus and to God's people everywhere.* **1:17** Or *to give you the Spirit of wisdom.* **1:18** Or *called, and the rich and glorious inheritance he has given to his holy people.* **2:2** Greek *obeying the commander of the power of the air.*

their circumcision, even though it affected only their bodies and not their hearts. [12]In those days you were living apart from Christ. You were excluded from citizenship among the people of Israel, and you did not know the covenant promises God had made to them. You lived in this world without God and without hope. [13]But now you have been united with Christ Jesus. Once you were far away from God, but now you have been brought near to him through the blood of Christ.

[14]For Christ himself has brought peace to us. He united Jews and Gentiles into one people when, in his own body on the cross, he broke down the wall of hostility that separated us. [15]He did this by ending the system of law with its commandments and regulations. He made peace between Jews and Gentiles by creating in himself one new people from the two groups. [16]Together as one body, Christ reconciled both groups to God by means of his death on the cross, and our hostility toward each other was put to death.

[17]He brought this Good News of peace to you Gentiles who were far away from him, and peace to the Jews who were near. [18]Now

GOD'S ARMOR FOR US

Paul tells us to use every piece of God's armor to resist Satan's attacks.

Piece of Armor	Use	Application
BELT	Truth	Satan fights with lies, and sometimes his lies sound like the truth; but God's truth can defeat Satan's lies.
BODY ARMOR	God's righteousness	God approves of us because we have trusted Christ to save us and cleanse our hearts from sin. His approval, like body armor, protects our heart—our feelings and our self-worth.
SHOES	Peace that comes from the Good News	Satan tries to make us think that telling others the Good News is too big a task and too scary. But God helps us want to tell others about him and to feel confident doing it.
SHIELD	Faith	The shield of faith protects us from Satan's flaming arrows: insults, setbacks, and temptations.
HELMET	Salvation	Satan wants to make us doubt God, Jesus, and our salvation. The helmet protects our mind from doubting what God has done for us.
SWORD	The Word of God	The sword is the only weapon for attacking in this list of armor. We need to use God's Word against Satan when we face temptation to sin.

all of us can come to the Father through the same Holy Spirit because of what Christ has done for us.

A Temple for the Lord

[19]So now you Gentiles are no longer strangers and foreigners. You are citizens along with all of God's holy people. You are members of God's family. [20]Together, we are his house, built on the foundation of the apostles and the prophets. And the cornerstone is Christ Jesus himself. [21]We are carefully joined together in him, becoming a holy temple for the Lord. [22]Through him you Gentiles are also being made part of this dwelling where God lives by his Spirit.

CHAPTER 3

God's Mysterious Plan Revealed

When I think of all this, I, Paul, a prisoner of Christ Jesus for the benefit of you Gentiles*... [2]assuming, by the way, that you know God gave me the special responsibility of extending his grace to you Gentiles. [3]As I briefly wrote earlier, God himself revealed his mysterious plan to me. [4]As you read what I have written, you will understand my insight into this plan regarding Christ. [5]God did not reveal it to previous generations, but now by his Spirit he has revealed it to his holy apostles and prophets.

[6]And this is God's plan: Both Gentiles and Jews who believe the Good News share equally in the riches inherited by God's children. Both are part of the same body, and both enjoy the promise of blessings because they belong to Christ Jesus.* [7]By God's grace and mighty power, I have been given the privilege of serving him by spreading this Good News.

[8]Though I am the least deserving of all God's people, he graciously gave me the privilege of telling the Gentiles about the endless treasures available to them in Christ. [9]I was chosen to explain to everyone* this mysterious plan that God, the Creator of all things, had kept secret from the beginning.

[10]God's purpose in all this was to use the church to display his wisdom in its rich variety to all the unseen rulers and authorities in the heavenly places. [11]This was his eternal plan, which he carried out through Christ Jesus our Lord.

[12]Because of Christ and our faith in him,* we can now come boldly and confidently into God's presence. [13]So please don't lose heart because of my trials here. I am suffering for you, so you should feel honored.

Paul's Prayer for Spiritual Growth

[14]When I think of all this, I fall to my knees and pray to the Father,* [15]the Creator of everything in heaven and on earth.* [16]I pray that from his glorious, unlimited resources he will empower you with inner strength through his Spirit. [17]Then Christ will make his home in your hearts as you trust in him. Your roots will grow down into God's love and keep you strong. [18]And may you have the power to understand, as all God's people should, how wide, how long, how high, and how deep his love is. [19]May you experience the love of Christ, though it is too great to understand fully. Then you will be made complete with all the fullness of life and power that comes from God.

[20]Now all glory to God, who is able, through his mighty power at work within us, to accomplish infinitely more than we might ask or think. [21]Glory to him in the church and in Christ Jesus through all generations forever and ever! Amen.

CHAPTER 4

Unity in the Body

Therefore I, a prisoner for serving the Lord, beg you to lead a life worthy of your calling, for you have been called by God. [2]Always be humble and gentle. Be patient with each other, making allowance for each other's faults because of your love. [3]Make every effort to keep yourselves united in the Spirit, binding yourselves together with peace. [4]For there is one body and one Spirit, just as you have been called to one glorious hope for the future. [5]There is one Lord, one faith, one baptism, [6]and one God and Father, who is over all and in all and living through all.

[7]However, he has given each one of us a special gift* through the generosity of Christ. [8]That is why the Scriptures say,

3:1 Paul resumes this thought in verse 14: "When I think of all this, I fall to my knees and pray to the Father." **3:6** Or *because they are united with Christ Jesus.* **3:9** Some manuscripts do not include *to everyone.* **3:12** Or *Because of Christ's faithfulness.* **3:14** Some manuscripts read *the Father of our Lord Jesus Christ.* **3:15** Or *from whom every family in heaven and on earth takes its name.* **4:7** Greek *a grace.*

"When he ascended to the heights,
he led a crowd of captives
and gave gifts to his people."*

[9]Notice that it says "he ascended." This clearly means that Christ also descended to our lowly world.* [10]And the same one who descended is the one who ascended higher than all the heavens, so that he might fill the entire universe with himself.

[11]Now these are the gifts Christ gave to the church: the apostles, the prophets, the evangelists, and the pastors and teachers. [12]Their responsibility is to equip God's people to do his work and build up the church, the body of Christ. [13]This will continue until we all come to such unity in our faith and knowledge of God's Son that we will be mature in the Lord, measuring up to the full and complete standard of Christ.

How can my brother and I stop fighting all the time?

Be kind to each other, tenderhearted, forgiving one another, just as God through Christ has forgiven you.
EPHESIANS 4:32

[14]Then we will no longer be immature like children. We won't be tossed and blown about by every wind of new teaching. We will not be influenced when people try to trick us with lies so clever they sound like the truth. [15]Instead, we will speak the truth in love, growing in every way more and more like Christ, who is the head of his body, the church. [16]He makes the whole body fit together perfectly. As each part does its own special work, it helps the other parts grow, so that the whole body is healthy and growing and full of love.

Living as Children of Light

[17]With the Lord's authority I say this: Live no longer as the Gentiles do, for they are hopelessly confused. [18]Their minds are full of darkness; they wander far from the life God gives because they have closed their minds and hardened their hearts against him. [19]They have no sense of shame. They live for lustful pleasure and eagerly practice every kind of impurity.

[20]But that isn't what you learned about Christ. [21]Since you have heard about Jesus and have learned the truth that comes from him, [22]throw off your old sinful nature and your former way of life, which is corrupted by lust and deception. [23]Instead, let the Spirit renew your thoughts and attitudes. [24]Put on your new nature, created to be like God—truly righteous and holy.

[25]So stop telling lies. Let us tell our neighbors the truth, for we are all parts of the same body. [26]And "don't sin by letting anger control you."* Don't let the sun go down while you are still angry, [27]for anger gives a foothold to the devil.

[28]If you are a thief, quit stealing. Instead, use your hands for good hard work, and then give generously to others in need. [29]Don't use foul or abusive language. Let everything you say be good and helpful, so that your words will be an encouragement to those who hear them.

[30]And do not bring sorrow to God's Holy Spirit by the way you live. Remember, he has identified you as his own,* guaranteeing that you will be saved on the day of redemption.

[31]Get rid of all bitterness, rage, anger, harsh words, and slander, as well as all types of evil behavior. [32]Instead, be kind to each other, tenderhearted, forgiving one another, just as God through Christ has forgiven you.

CHAPTER 5

Living in the Light

Imitate God, therefore, in everything you do, because you are his dear children. [2]Live a life filled with love, following the example of Christ. He loved us* and offered himself as a sacrifice for us, a pleasing aroma to God.

[3]Let there be no sexual immorality, impurity, or greed among you. Such sins have no

4:8 Ps 68:18. **4:9** Or *to the lowest parts of the earth.* **4:26** Ps 4:4. **4:30** Or *has put his seal on you.* **5:2** Some manuscripts read *loved you.*

Write On?

While riding his bike late one afternoon, Julian thought he saw some kids spray-painting words on the back of the school building. The words were big and black and easily seen from the sidewalk. But Julian rode closer to get a better look. The kids who were doing the spraying saw him and yelled, "Hey, come over and help us decorate the school. It's lots of fun, man!" What do you think Julian should do? Read Ephesians 5:11 to find the answer.

place among God's people. [4]Obscene stories, foolish talk, and coarse jokes—these are not for you. Instead, let there be thankfulness to God. [5]You can be sure that no immoral, impure, or greedy person will inherit the Kingdom of Christ and of God. For a greedy person is an idolater, worshiping the things of this world.

[6]Don't be fooled by those who try to excuse these sins, for the anger of God will fall on all who disobey him. [7]Don't participate in the things these people do. [8]For once you were full of darkness, but now you have light from the Lord. So live as people of light! [9]For this light within you produces only what is good and right and true.

[10]Carefully determine what pleases the Lord. [11]Take no part in the worthless deeds of evil and darkness; instead, expose them. [12]It is shameful even to talk about the things that ungodly people do in secret. [13]But their evil intentions will be exposed when the light shines on them, [14]for the light makes everything visible. This is why it is said,

"Awake, O sleeper,
rise up from the dead,
and Christ will give you light."

Living by the Spirit's Power

[15]So be careful how you live. Don't live like fools, but like those who are wise. [16]Make the most of every opportunity in these evil days. [17]Don't act thoughtlessly, but understand what the Lord wants you to do. [18]Don't be drunk with wine, because that will ruin your life. Instead, be filled with the Holy Spirit, [19]singing psalms and hymns and spiritual songs among yourselves, and making music to the Lord in your hearts. [20]And give thanks for everything to God the Father in the name of our Lord Jesus Christ.

Spirit-Guided Relationships: Wives and Husbands

[21]And further, submit to one another out of reverence for Christ.

[22]For wives, this means submit to your husbands as to the Lord. [23]For a husband is the head of his wife as Christ is the head of the church. He is the Savior of his body, the church. [24]As the church submits to Christ, so you wives should submit to your husbands in everything.

[25]For husbands, this means love your wives, just as Christ loved the church. He gave up his life for her [26]to make her holy and clean, washed by the cleansing of God's word.* [27]He did this to present her to himself as a glorious church without a spot or wrinkle or any other blemish. Instead, she will be holy and without fault. [28]In the same way, husbands ought to love their wives as they love their own bodies.

5:26 Greek *washed by water with the word.*

For a man who loves his wife actually shows
love for himself. [29]No one hates his own body
but feeds and cares for it, just as Christ cares
for the church. [30]And we are members of his
body.
[31]As the Scriptures say, "A man leaves his father and mother and is joined to his wife, and the two are united into one."* [32]This is a great mystery, but it is an illustration of the way Christ and the church are one. [33]So again I say, each man must love his wife as he loves himself, and the wife must respect her husband.

CHAPTER 6

Children and Parents

Children, obey your parents because you belong to the Lord,* for this is the right thing to do. [2]"Honor your father and mother." This is the first commandment with a promise: [3]If you honor your father and mother, "things will go well for you, and you will have a long life on the earth."*

[4]Fathers, do not provoke your children to anger by the way you treat them. Rather, bring them up with the discipline and instruction that comes from the Lord.

Slaves and Masters

[5]Slaves, obey your earthly masters with deep respect and fear. Serve them sincerely as you would serve Christ. [6]Try to please them all the time, not just when they are watching you. As slaves of Christ, do the will of God with all your heart. [7]Work with enthusiasm, as though you were working for the Lord rather than for people. [8]Remember that the Lord will reward each one of us for the good we do, whether we are slaves or free.

[9]Masters, treat your slaves in the same way. Don't threaten them; remember, you both have the same Master in heaven, and he has no favorites.

The Whole Armor of God

[10]A final word: Be strong in the Lord and in his mighty power. [11]Put on all of God's armor so that you will be able to stand firm against all strategies of the devil. [12]For we* are not fighting against flesh-and-blood enemies, but against evil rulers and authorities of the unseen world, against mighty powers in this dark world, and against evil spirits in the heavenly places.

[13]Therefore, put on every piece of God's armor so you will be able to resist the enemy in the time of evil. Then after the battle you will still be standing firm. [14]Stand your ground, putting on the belt of truth and the body armor of God's righteousness. [15]For shoes, put on the peace that comes from the Good News

5:31 Gen 2:24. **6:1** Or *Children, obey your parents who belong to the Lord;* some manuscripts read simply *Children, obey your parents.* **6:2-3** Exod 20:12; Deut 5:16. **6:12** Some manuscripts read *you.*

IS IT OK?

IS IT OK IF I'M MAD AT MY PARENTS?

All parents have quirks. Maybe your parents are loud. Or maybe they like to embarrass you. Or maybe they get mad about the dumbest things. Or maybe they're super-nosy. It's a law of nature that you *will* get mad at your parents sometimes, just as they got mad at their parents sometimes. But even when your parents irritate or upset you, you still have to obey and respect them because you belong to the Lord, and it's the right thing to do (see Ephesians 6:1-3). Being mad isn't a sin, but how you react can be. Make sure you control your words and your actions, even when you're mad.

AMAZING FACTS

God's protection plan against evil includes truth, faith, salvation, and his Word—he hears our prayers, too. So evil doesn't stand a chance!

EPHESIANS 6:10-18

so that you will be fully prepared.* [16]In addition to all of these, hold up the shield of faith to stop the fiery arrows of the devil.* [17]Put on salvation as your helmet, and take the sword of the Spirit, which is the word of God.

[18]Pray in the Spirit at all times and on every occasion. Stay alert and be persistent in your prayers for all believers everywhere.*

[19]And pray for me, too. Ask God to give me the right words so I can boldly explain God's mysterious plan that the Good News is for Jews and Gentiles alike.* [20]I am in chains now, still preaching this message as God's ambassador. So pray that I will keep on speaking boldly for him, as I should.

Final Greetings

[21]To bring you up to date, Tychicus will give you a full report about what I am doing and how I am getting along. He is a beloved brother and faithful helper in the Lord's work. [22]I have sent him to you for this very purpose—to let you know how we are doing and to encourage you.

[23]Peace be with you, dear brothers and sisters,* and may God the Father and the Lord Jesus Christ give you love with faithfulness. [24]May God's grace be eternally upon all who love our Lord Jesus Christ.

6:15 Or *For shoes, put on the readiness to preach the Good News of peace with God.* **6:16** Greek *the evil one.* **6:18** Greek *all of God's holy people.* **6:19** Greek *explain the mystery of the Good News;* some manuscripts read simply *explain the mystery.* **6:23** Greek *brothers.*

PHILIPPIANS

WHO
Paul, Timothy, Euodia, Syntyche, and Epaphroditus.

WHERE
Written and sent by Paul from a prison in Rome.

WHEN
Around AD 61.

WHY
To thank the Christians in Philippi and show them that true joy comes from Jesus Christ.

Always be full of joy in the Lord.
I say it again—rejoice!
PHILIPPIANS 4:4

When good things happen, do you feel good? That's how it often works. When things are going great, people usually feel great. That's happiness. For most people, happiness depends on "happenings." Joy is different. It is deeper; it's an inner confidence that comes from knowing Jesus Christ. Paul wrote a lot about joy in Philippians.

DISCOVER HOW YOU CAN BE TRULY HAPPY AND CONTENT, EVEN WHEN LIFE SEEMS CRUMMY.

CHAPTER 1

Greetings from Paul

This letter is from Paul and Timothy, slaves of Christ Jesus.

I am writing to all of God's holy people in Philippi who belong to Christ Jesus, including the elders* and deacons.

[2]May God our Father and the Lord Jesus Christ give you grace and peace.

Paul's Thanksgiving and Prayer

[3]Every time I think of you, I give thanks to my God. [4]Whenever I pray, I make my requests for all of you with joy, [5]for you have been my

1:1 Or *overseers;* or *bishops.*

partners in spreading the Good News about Christ from the time you first heard it until now. [6]And I am certain that God, who began the good work within you, will continue his work until it is finally finished on the day when Christ Jesus returns.

[7]So it is right that I should feel as I do about all of you, for you have a special place in my heart. You share with me the special favor of God, both in my imprisonment and in defending and confirming the truth of the Good News. [8]God knows how much I love you and long for you with the tender compassion of Christ Jesus.

How can I be more popular?

Don't be selfish; don't try to impress others. Be humble, thinking of others as better than yourselves.

PHILIPPIANS 2:3

[9]I pray that your love will overflow more and more, and that you will keep on growing in knowledge and understanding. [10]For I want you to understand what really matters, so that you may live pure and blameless lives until the day of Christ's return. [11]May you always be filled with the fruit of your salvation—the righteous character produced in your life by Jesus Christ*—for this will bring much glory and praise to God.

Paul's Joy That Christ Is Preached

[12]And I want you to know, my dear brothers and sisters,* that everything that has happened to me here has helped to spread the Good News. [13]For everyone here, including the whole palace guard,* knows that I am in chains because of Christ. [14]And because of my imprisonment, most of the believers* here have gained confidence and boldly speak God's message* without fear.

[15]It's true that some are preaching out of jealousy and rivalry. But others preach about Christ with pure motives. [16]They preach because they love me, for they know I have been appointed to defend the Good News. [17]Those others do not have pure motives as they preach about Christ. They preach with selfish ambition, not sincerely, intending to make my chains more painful to me. [18]But that doesn't matter. Whether their motives are false or genuine, the message about Christ is being preached either way, so I rejoice. And I will continue to rejoice. [19]For I know that as you pray for me and the Spirit of Jesus Christ helps me, this will lead to my deliverance.

Paul's Life for Christ

[20]For I fully expect and hope that I will never be ashamed, but that I will continue to be bold for Christ, as I have been in the past. And I trust that my life will bring honor to Christ, whether I live or die. [21]For to me, living means living for Christ, and dying is even better. [22]But if I live, I can do more fruitful work for Christ. So I really don't know which is better. [23]I'm torn between two desires: I long to go and be with Christ, which would be far better for me. [24]But for your sakes, it is better that I continue to live.

[25]Knowing this, I am convinced that I will remain alive so I can continue to help all of you grow and experience the joy of your faith. [26]And when I come to you again, you will have even more reason to take pride in Christ Jesus because of what he is doing through me.

Live as Citizens of Heaven

[27]Above all, you must live as citizens of heaven, conducting yourselves in a manner worthy of the Good News about Christ. Then, whether I come and see you again or only hear about you, I will know that you are standing together with one spirit and one purpose, fighting together for the faith, which is the Good News. [28]Don't be intimidated in any way by your enemies. This will be a sign to them that they are going to be destroyed, but that you are going to be saved, even by God himself. [29]For you have been given not only the privilege of trusting in Christ but also the privilege of suffering for him. [30]We are in this struggle together.

1:11 Greek *with the fruit of righteousness through Jesus Christ.* **1:12** Greek *brothers.* **1:13** Greek *including all the Praetorium.* **1:14a** Greek *brothers in the Lord.* **1:14b** Some manuscripts read *speak the message.*

You have seen my struggle in the past, and you know that I am still in the midst of it.

CHAPTER 2

Have the Attitude of Christ

Is there any encouragement from belonging to Christ? Any comfort from his love? Any fellowship together in the Spirit? Are your hearts tender and compassionate? [2]Then make me truly happy by agreeing wholeheartedly with each other, loving one another, and working together with one mind and purpose.

[3]Don't be selfish; don't try to impress others. Be humble, thinking of others as better than yourselves. [4]Don't look out only for your own interests, but take an interest in others, too.

[5]You must have the same attitude that Christ Jesus had.

[6] Though he was God,*
he did not think of equality
with God
as something to cling to.
[7] Instead, he gave up his divine
privileges*;
he took the humble position of
a slave*
and was born as a human being.
When he appeared in human form,*
[8] he humbled himself in obedience
to God
and died a criminal's death on
a cross.

[9] Therefore, God elevated him to the place
of highest honor
and gave him the name above all other
names,
[10] that at the name of Jesus every knee
should bow,
in heaven and on earth and under
the earth,
[11] and every tongue confess that Jesus Christ
is Lord,
to the glory of God the Father.

Shine Brightly for Christ

[12]Dear friends, you always followed my instructions when I was with you. And now that I am away, it is even more important. Work hard to show the results of your salvation, obeying God with deep reverence and fear. [13]For God is working in you, giving you the desire and the power to do what pleases him.

[14]Do everything without complaining and arguing, [15]so that no one can criticize you. Live clean, innocent lives as children of God, shining like bright lights in a world full of crooked and perverse people. [16]Hold firmly to the word of life; then, on the day of Christ's return, I will be proud that I did not run the race in vain and that my work was not useless. [17]But I will rejoice even if I lose my life, pouring it out like a liquid offering to God,* just like your faithful service is an offering to God. And I want all of you to share that joy. [18]Yes, you should rejoice, and I will share your joy.

AMAZING FACTS

Someday *everyone* will bow down to Jesus—even people who don't believe in him will finally have to admit he is Lord over all.

PHILIPPIANS 2:9-11

Paul Commends Timothy

[19]If the Lord Jesus is willing, I hope to send Timothy to you soon for a visit. Then he can cheer me up by telling me how you are getting along. [20]I have no one else like Timothy, who genuinely cares about your welfare. [21]All the others care only for themselves and not for what matters to Jesus Christ. [22]But you know how Timothy has proved himself. Like a son with his father, he has served with me in preaching the Good News. [23]I hope to send him to you just as soon as I find out what is going to happen to me here. [24]And I have

2:6 Or *Being in the form of God.* **2:7a** Greek *he emptied himself.* **2:7b** Or *the form of a slave.* **2:7c** Some English translations put this phrase in verse 8. **2:17** Greek *I will rejoice even if I am to be poured out as a liquid offering.*

confidence from the Lord that I myself will come to see you soon.

Paul Commends Epaphroditus

[25]Meanwhile, I thought I should send Epaphroditus back to you. He is a true brother, co-worker, and fellow soldier. And he was your messenger to help me in my need. [26]I am sending him because he has been longing to see you, and he was very distressed that you heard he was ill. [27]And he certainly was ill; in fact, he almost died. But God had mercy on him—and also on me, so that I would not have one sorrow after another.

[28]So I am all the more anxious to send him back to you, for I know you will be glad to see him, and then I will not be so worried about you. [29]Welcome him with Christian love* and with great joy, and give him the honor that people like him deserve. [30]For he risked his life for the work of Christ, and he was at the point of death while doing for me what you couldn't do from far away.

CHAPTER 3

The Priceless Value of Knowing Christ

Whatever happens, my dear brothers and sisters,* rejoice in the Lord. I never get tired of telling you these things, and I do it to safeguard your faith.

[2]Watch out for those dogs, those people who do evil, those mutilators who say you must be circumcised to be saved. [3]For we who worship by the Spirit of God* are the ones who are truly circumcised. We rely on what Christ Jesus has done for us. We put no confidence in human effort, [4]though I could have confidence in my own effort if anyone could. Indeed, if others have reason for confidence in their own efforts, I have even more!

[5]I was circumcised when I was eight days old. I am a pure-blooded citizen of Israel and a member of the tribe of Benjamin—a real Hebrew if there ever was one! I was a member of the Pharisees, who demand the strictest obedience to the Jewish law. [6]I was so zealous that I harshly persecuted the

2:29 Greek *in the Lord.* **3:1** Greek *brothers;* also in 3:13, 17. **3:3** Some manuscripts read *worship God in spirit;* one early manuscript reads *worship in spirit.*

IS IT OK?

IS IT OK IF I HATE HELPING OUT AROUND THE HOUSE?

Who really enjoys vacuuming, shoveling snow, taking out the trash, cleaning the cat's litter box, and scrubbing the toilets? You don't have to *like* helping out around the house. You might even borderline *hate* it. But you still have to do it—and God wants you to do it without complaining and arguing (see Philippians 2:14-16). Try these survival tips when you're asked to help out at home: (1) Say yes and smile. (2) Start the most unwanted task right away and get it over with. Stalling only drags it out longer and makes it worse. (3) Think about something you do like. After you finish your chores, go have some fun to reward yourself.

Baseball Burnout

Aaron wearily got in the car after baseball practice. He grunted a one-word answer as his dad asked: "How was practice? Did you get any hits? How was your arm?" All Aaron wanted to do was go home, take a shower, put on his music, and forget about baseball. He has played baseball since he was on the T-ball team in kindergarten, and frankly, Aaron is burned out. The coaches demand so much, and his dad has such high expectations. Aaron wants to escape from it all! Should he just quit? Check out Philippians 3:13-14 to see what Paul did when he faced burnout.

church. And as for righteousness, I obeyed the law without fault.

[7]I once thought these things were valuable, but now I consider them worthless because of what Christ has done. [8]Yes, everything else is worthless when compared with the infinite value of knowing Christ Jesus my Lord. For his sake I have discarded everything else, counting it all as garbage, so that I could gain Christ [9]and become one with him. I no longer count on my own righteousness through obeying the law; rather, I become righteous through faith in Christ.* For God's way of making us right with himself depends on faith. [10]I want to know Christ and experience the mighty power that raised him from the dead. I want to suffer with him, sharing in his death, [11]so that one way or another I will experience the resurrection from the dead!

Pressing toward the Goal

[12]I don't mean to say that I have already achieved these things or that I have already reached perfection. But I press on to possess that perfection for which Christ Jesus first possessed me. [13]No, dear brothers and sisters, I have not achieved it,* but I focus on this one thing: Forgetting the past and looking forward to what lies ahead, [14]I press on to reach the end of the race and receive the heavenly prize for which God, through Christ Jesus, is calling us.

[15]Let all who are spiritually mature agree on these things. If you disagree on some point, I believe God will make it plain to you. [16]But we must hold on to the progress we have already made.

[17]Dear brothers and sisters, pattern your lives after mine, and learn from those who follow our example. [18]For I have told you often before, and I say it again with tears in my eyes, that there are many whose conduct shows they are really enemies of the cross of Christ. [19]They are headed for destruction. Their god is their appetite, they brag about shameful things, and they think only about this life here on earth. [20]But we are citizens of heaven, where the Lord Jesus Christ lives. And we are eagerly waiting for him to return as our Savior. [21]He will take our weak mortal bodies and change them into glorious bodies like his own, using the same power with which he will bring everything under his control.

3:9 Or *through the faithfulness of Christ.* 3:13 Some manuscripts read *not yet achieved it.*

CHAPTER 4

Therefore, my dear brothers and sisters,* stay true to the Lord. I love you and long to see you, dear friends, for you are my joy and the crown I receive for my work.

Words of Encouragement

[2]Now I appeal to Euodia and Syntyche. Please, because you belong to the Lord, settle your disagreement. [3]And I ask you, my true partner,* to help these two women, for they worked hard with me in telling others the Good News. They worked along with Clement and the rest of my co-workers, whose names are written in the Book of Life.

[4]Always be full of joy in the Lord. I say it again—rejoice! [5]Let everyone see that you are considerate in all you do. Remember, the Lord is coming soon.

[6]Don't worry about anything; instead, pray about everything. Tell God what you need, and thank him for all he has done. [7]Then you will experience God's peace, which exceeds anything we can understand. His peace will guard your hearts and minds as you live in Christ Jesus.

[8]And now, dear brothers and sisters, one final thing. Fix your thoughts on what is true, and honorable, and right, and pure, and lovely, and admirable. Think about things that are excellent and worthy of praise. [9]Keep putting into practice all you learned and received from me—everything you heard from me and saw me doing. Then the God of peace will be with you.

Paul's Thanks for Their Gifts

[10]How I praise the Lord that you are concerned about me again. I know you have always been concerned for me, but you didn't have the chance to help me. [11]Not that I was ever in need, for I have learned how to be content with whatever I have. [12]I know how to live on almost nothing or with everything. I have learned the secret of living in every situation, whether it is with a full stomach or empty, with plenty or little. [13]For I can do everything through Christ,* who gives me strength.

4:1 Greek *brothers;* also in 4:8. **4:3** Or *loyal Syzygus.* **4:13** Greek *through the one.*

IS IT OK?

IS IT OK TO LISTEN TO WHATEVER KIND OF MUSIC I WANT?

God is a creative God. As our Creator, he gave us creative abilities too—including the ability to create music. God's taste in music is guided by what's *good*. All kinds of music can be good—country, reggae, rap, pop, hymns, opera, blues, classical, techno—you name it! But music with bad, angry, or vulgar lyrics has a negative effect on you, even if you don't realize it. Those bad vibes fill your brain, and then throughout the day it's those bad voices and words that come to mind. If you fill your mind instead with what's true, pure, and admirable (see Philippians 4:8), then that plays through your head throughout the day . . . regardless of which kind of music it's set to!

[14]Even so, you have done well to share with me
in my present difficulty.
[15]As you know, you Philippians were the
only ones who gave me financial help when I
first brought you the Good News and then
traveled on from Macedonia. No other church
did this. [16]Even when I was in Thessalonica
you sent help more than once. [17]I don't say this
because I want a gift from you. Rather, I want
you to receive a reward for your kindness.
[18]At the moment I have all I need—and
more! I am generously supplied with the gifts
you sent me with Epaphroditus. They are a
sweet-smelling sacrifice that is acceptable and
pleasing to God. [19]And this same God who
takes care of me will supply all your needs
from his glorious riches, which have been
given to us in Christ Jesus.
[20]Now all glory to God our Father forever
and ever! Amen.

Paul's Final Greetings

[21]Give my greetings to each of God's holy people—all who belong to Christ Jesus. The brothers who are with me send you their greetings.
[22]And all the rest of God's people send you greetings, too, especially those in Caesar's household.
[23]May the grace of the Lord Jesus Christ be with your spirit.

COLOSSIANS

WHO
Paul, Timothy, Tychicus, Onesimus, Aristarchus, Mark, and Epaphras.

WHERE
Written and sent from a prison in Rome.

WHEN
Around AD 60 when Paul was in prison the first time.

WHY
To point out mistakes the Christians in Colosse were making and to show that believers have everything they need in Christ.

Whatever you do or say, do it as a representative of the Lord Jesus.
COLOSSIANS 3:17

Paul wrote this letter to people in Colosse who had turned from other religions and put their faith in Jesus. Some of them were combining their new faith with old beliefs in idols. Paul wrote to help the Colossians see the truth again. He reminded them that the Lord Jesus Christ was all they needed!

Read Colossians and listen to Paul's inspired advice.

CHAPTER **1**

Greetings from Paul

This letter is from Paul, chosen by the will of God to be an apostle of Christ Jesus, and from our brother Timothy.

[2]We are writing to God's holy people in the city of Colosse, who are faithful brothers and sisters* in Christ.

May God our Father give you grace and peace.

Paul's Thanksgiving and Prayer

[3]We always pray for you, and we give thanks to God, the Father of our Lord Jesus Christ. [4]For we have heard of your faith in Christ Jesus and your love for all of God's people,

1:2 Greek *faithful brothers.*

5which come from your confident hope of what God has reserved for you in heaven. You have had this expectation ever since you first heard the truth of the Good News.

6This same Good News that came to you is going out all over the world. It is bearing fruit everywhere by changing lives, just as it changed your lives from the day you first heard and understood the truth about God's wonderful grace.

7You learned about the Good News from Epaphras, our beloved co-worker. He is Christ's faithful servant, and he is helping us on your behalf.* 8He has told us about the love for others that the Holy Spirit has given you.

9So we have not stopped praying for you since we first heard about you. We ask God to give you complete knowledge of his will and to give you spiritual wisdom and understanding. 10Then the way you live will always honor and please the Lord, and your lives will produce every kind of good fruit. All the while, you will grow as you learn to know God better and better.

11We also pray that you will be strengthened with all his glorious power so you will have all the endurance and patience you need. May you be filled with joy,* 12always thanking the Father. He has enabled you to share in the inheritance that belongs to his people, who live in the light. 13For he has rescued us from the kingdom of darkness and transferred us into the Kingdom of his dear Son, 14who purchased our freedom* and forgave our sins.

Christ Is Supreme

15 Christ is the visible image of the invisible God.
He existed before anything was created and is supreme over all creation,*
16 for through him God created everything in the heavenly realms and on earth.
He made the things we can see and the things we can't see—
such as thrones, kingdoms, rulers, and authorities in the unseen world.
Everything was created through him and for him.
17 He existed before anything else, and he holds all creation together.
18 Christ is also the head of the church, which is his body.
He is the beginning, supreme over all who rise from the dead.*
So he is first in everything.
19 For God in all his fullness was pleased to live in Christ,
20 and through him God reconciled everything to himself.
He made peace with everything in heaven and on earth by means of Christ's blood on the cross.

21This includes you who were once far away from God. You were his enemies, separated from him by your evil thoughts and actions. 22Yet now he has reconciled you to himself through the death of Christ in his physical body. As a result, he has brought you into his own presence, and you are holy and blameless as you stand before him without a single fault.

23But you must continue to believe this truth and stand firmly in it. Don't drift away from the assurance you received when you heard the Good News. The Good News has been preached all over the world, and I, Paul, have been appointed as God's servant to proclaim it.

Paul's Work for the Church

24I am glad when I suffer for you in my body, for I am participating in the sufferings of Christ that continue for his body, the church. 25God has given me the responsibility of serving his church by proclaiming his entire message to you. 26This message was kept secret for centuries and generations past, but now it has been revealed to God's people. 27For God wanted them to know that the riches and glory of Christ are for you Gentiles, too. And this is the secret: Christ lives in you. This gives you assurance of sharing his glory.

28So we tell others about Christ, warning everyone and teaching everyone with all the wisdom God has given us. We want to present them to God, perfect* in their relationship to

1:7 Or *he is ministering on your behalf;* some manuscripts read *he is ministering on our behalf.* **1:11** Or *all the patience and endurance you need with joy.* **1:14** Some manuscripts add *with his blood.* **1:15** Or *He is the firstborn of all creation.* **1:18** Or *the firstborn from the dead.* **1:28** Or *mature.*

When I became a Christian, I started listening to the local Christian radio station. I really enjoyed the music—it's amazing how much it affected me. If I started off my day listening to it, I found myself praying and talking to God. If I was having a bad day, the encouraging words of the music helped because they reminded me to go to God for help.

A couple years ago I made some friends who didn't go to church. Every time I went to their houses or rode in their cars, they were listening to radio stations that didn't play Christian music. I noticed a couple things immediately that I had never noticed before I became a Christian: the DJs often used dirty language, and a lot of the songs were about sleeping around or doing drugs. The lyrics were loaded with filthy language too. But my friends seemed to like the music, so I listened along with them. After I got used to the stations everyone else enjoyed, I didn't even notice the language of the DJs or the lyrics of the songs anymore. I thought, *Maybe this is okay. It probably won't affect me.*

I was wrong. My language got bad, and my attitude was poor. Worse yet, when I got grumpy, I lost my temper. I didn't have the reminder that God cared about me and about my relationships—with him and with my friends. I was spending less time talking to God and thinking about God, and the result was unfortunate.

Now I'm back to Christian music. My mood is much better and so is my perspective. Beware of what you put into your head. Music affects us, whether we're willing to admit it or not.

To find out what God's Word has to say about getting rid of bad influences in our lives, read Colossians 3:5-8; also Romans 6:13 and Galatians 5:19-21.

Christ. [29]That's why I work and struggle so hard, depending on Christ's mighty power that works within me.

CHAPTER 2

I want you to know how much I have agonized for you and for the church at Laodicea, and for many other believers who have never met me personally. [2]I want them to be encouraged and knit together by strong ties of love. I want them to have complete confidence that they understand God's mysterious plan, which is Christ himself. [3]In him lie hidden all the treasures of wisdom and knowledge.

[4]I am telling you this so no one will deceive you with well-crafted arguments. [5]For though I am far away from you, my heart is with you. And I rejoice that you are living as you should and that your faith in Christ is strong.

Freedom from Rules and New Life in Christ

[6]And now, just as you accepted Christ Jesus as your Lord, you must continue to follow him. [7]Let your roots grow down into him, and let your lives be built on him. Then your faith will grow strong in the truth you were taught, and you will overflow with thankfulness.

[8]Don't let anyone capture you with empty philosophies and high-sounding nonsense that come from human thinking and from the spiritual powers* of this world, rather than from Christ. [9]For in Christ lives all the fullness of God in a human body.* [10]So you also are complete through your union with Christ, who is the head over every ruler and authority.

[11]When you came to Christ, you were "circumcised," but not by a physical procedure. Christ performed a spiritual circumcision—the cutting away of your sinful nature.* [12]For you were buried with Christ when you were baptized. And with him you were raised to new life because you trusted the mighty power of God, who raised Christ from the dead.

[13]You were dead because of your sins and because your sinful nature was not yet cut away. Then God made you alive with Christ, for he forgave all our sins. [14]He canceled the record of the charges against us and took it away by nailing it to the cross. [15]In this way, he disarmed* the spiritual rulers and authorities. He shamed them publicly by his victory over them on the cross.

[16]So don't let anyone condemn you for what you eat or drink, or for not celebrating

GYM DANDY

During gym class, Nicholas was chosen as one of the football captains. Nicholas and the other captain were to take turns picking kids for their teams. *Now's my chance to get a winning team,* Nicholas thought. There were two kids who usually got chosen last because no one wanted them on their team. Nicholas knew they felt terrible when they were passed by, but he really wanted to win. Should Nicholas ignore them and hope the other captain picks them, or should he choose them even though they won't help his team? Read Colossians 3:12-13 to find out what God says.

2:8 Or *the spiritual principles;* also in 2:20. **2:9** Or *in him dwells all the completeness of the Godhead bodily.* **2:11** Greek *the cutting away of the body of the flesh.* **2:15** Or *he stripped off.*

certain holy days or new moon ceremonies or Sabbaths. [17]For these rules are only shadows of the reality yet to come. And Christ himself is that reality. [18]Don't let anyone condemn you by insisting on pious self-denial or the worship of angels,* saying they have had visions about these things. Their sinful minds have made them proud, [19]and they are not connected to Christ, the head of the body. For he holds the whole body together with its joints and ligaments, and it grows as God nourishes it.

[20]You have died with Christ, and he has set you free from the spiritual powers of this world. So why do you keep on following the rules of the world, such as, [21]"Don't handle! Don't taste! Don't touch!"? [22]Such rules are mere human teachings about things that deteriorate as we use them. [23]These rules may seem wise because they require strong devotion, pious self-denial, and severe bodily discipline. But they provide no help in conquering a person's evil desires.

CHAPTER 3

Living the New Life

Since you have been raised to new life with Christ, set your sights on the realities of heaven, where Christ sits in the place of honor at God's right hand. [2]Think about the things of heaven, not the things of earth. [3]For you died to this life, and your real life is hidden with Christ in God. [4]And when Christ, who is your* life, is revealed to the whole world, you will share in all his glory.

[5]So put to death the sinful, earthly things lurking within you. Have nothing to do with sexual immorality, impurity, lust, and evil desires. Don't be greedy, for a greedy person is an idolater, worshiping the things of this world. [6]Because of these sins, the anger of God is coming.* [7]You used to do these things when your life was still part of this world. [8]But now is the time to get rid of anger, rage, malicious behavior, slander, and dirty language. [9]Don't lie to each other, for you have stripped off your old sinful nature and all its wicked deeds. [10]Put on your new nature, and be renewed as you learn to know your Creator and become like him. [11]In this new life, it doesn't matter if you are a Jew or a Gentile,* circumcised or uncircumcised, barbaric, uncivilized,* slave, or free. Christ is all that matters, and he lives in all of us.

[12]Since God chose you to be the holy people he loves, you must clothe yourselves with tenderhearted mercy, kindness, humility, gentleness, and patience. [13]Make allowance for each other's faults, and forgive anyone who offends you. Remember, the Lord forgave you, so you must forgive others. [14]Above all, clothe yourselves with love, which binds us all together in perfect harmony. [15]And let the peace that comes from Christ rule in your hearts. For as members of one body you are called to live in peace. And always be thankful.

[16]Let the message about Christ, in all its richness, fill your lives. Teach and counsel each other with all the wisdom he gives. Sing psalms and hymns and spiritual songs to God with thankful hearts. [17]And whatever you do or say, do it as a representative of the Lord Jesus, giving thanks through him to God the Father.

AMAZING FACTS

Guess who is pleased when you obey your mom and dad. God is!

COLOSSIANS 3:20

Instructions for Christian Households

[18]Wives, submit to your husbands, as is fitting for those who belong to the Lord.

[19]Husbands, love your wives and never treat them harshly.

[20]Children, always obey your parents, for this pleases the Lord. [21]Fathers, do not aggravate your children, or they will become discouraged.

2:18 Or *or worshiping with angels.* **3:4** Some manuscripts read *our.* **3:6** Some manuscripts read *is coming on all who disobey him.* **3:11a** Greek *a Greek.* **3:11b** Greek *Barbarian, Scythian.*

22 Slaves, obey your earthly masters in everything you do. Try to please them all the time, not just when they are watching you. Serve them sincerely because of your reverent fear of the Lord. 23 Work willingly at whatever you do, as though you were working for the Lord rather than for people. 24 Remember that the Lord will give you an inheritance as your reward, and that the Master you are serving is Christ.* 25 But if you do what is wrong, you will be paid back for the wrong you have done. For God has no favorites.

CHAPTER 4

Masters, be just and fair to your slaves. Remember that you also have a Master—in heaven.

An Encouragement for Prayer

2 Devote yourselves to prayer with an alert mind and a thankful heart. 3 Pray for us, too, that God will give us many opportunities to speak about his mysterious plan concerning Christ. That is why I am here in chains. 4 Pray that I will proclaim this message as clearly as I should.

5 Live wisely among those who are not believers, and make the most of every opportunity. 6 Let your conversation be gracious and attractive* so that you will have the right response for everyone.

Paul's Final Instructions and Greetings

7 Tychicus will give you a full report about how I am getting along. He is a beloved brother and faithful helper who serves with me in the Lord's work. 8 I have sent him to you for this very purpose—to let you know how we are doing and to encourage you. 9 I am also sending Onesimus, a faithful and beloved brother, one of your own people. He and Tychicus will tell you everything that's happening here.

10 Aristarchus, who is in prison with me, sends you his greetings, and so does Mark, Barnabas's cousin. As you were instructed before, make Mark welcome if he comes your way. 11 Jesus (the one we call Justus) also sends his greetings. These are the only Jewish believers among my co-workers; they are working with me here for the Kingdom of God. And what a comfort they have been!

12 Epaphras, a member of your own fellowship and a servant of Christ Jesus, sends you his greetings. He always prays earnestly for you, asking God to make you strong and perfect, fully confident that you are following the whole will of God. 13 I can assure you that he prays hard for you and also for the believers in Laodicea and Hierapolis.

14 Luke, the beloved doctor, sends his greetings, and so does Demas. 15 Please give my greetings to our brothers and sisters* at

3:24 Or *and serve Christ as your Master.* **4:6** Greek *and seasoned with salt.* **4:15** Greek *brothers.*

IS IT OK?

IS IT OK IF I DON'T WORK HARD?

God wants us to do our best, and to work *hard* and *cheerfully* at what we're doing—whether that's homework, chores, football practice, piano lessons, or babysitting a little brother. *Why,* you ask? Because if you're a Christian, God is the most important Boss in your life. He gave you all your talents and abilities, and he wants you to do a good job of using them. You're not working for your teacher, your parents, your coach, your piano teacher, or your siblings. You're working for God (see Colossians 3:23)—and he deserves your very best!

Laodicea, and to Nympha and the church that meets in her house.

[16]After you have read this letter, pass it on to the church at Laodicea so they can read it, too. And you should read the letter I wrote to them.

[17]And say to Archippus, "Be sure to carry out the ministry the Lord gave you."

[18]HERE IS MY GREETING IN MY OWN HANDWRITING—PAUL.

Remember my chains.

May God's grace be with you.

1 Thessalonians

WHO
Paul, Timothy, and Silas.

WHERE
Written and sent from Corinth.

WHEN
Around AD 51. It was one of the first letters Paul wrote.

WHY
To strengthen the Thessalonian Christians in their faith and to give them hope through the promise of Christ's return.

Always be joyful. Never stop praying. Be thankful in all circumstances.
1 THESSALONIANS 5:16-18

The believers in Thessalonica had many reasons to be afraid. When people became Christians, their families often turned against them or they suffered in other ways. Paul wrote to give the Thessalonians hope. He reminded them that what they believed was true and that Jesus would come back someday.

IF YOU'RE AFRAID OR WONDERING ABOUT THE FUTURE, THIS BOOK WILL GIVE YOU HOPE.

CHAPTER 1

Greetings from Paul

This letter is from Paul, Silas,* and Timothy.

We are writing to the church in Thessalonica, to you who belong to God the Father and the Lord Jesus Christ.

May God give you grace and peace.

The Faith of the Thessalonian Believers

2 We always thank God for all of you and pray for you constantly. 3 As we pray to our God and Father about you, we think of your faithful work, your loving deeds, and the enduring hope you have because of our Lord Jesus Christ.

4 We know, dear brothers and sisters,* that

1:1 Greek *Silvanus*, the Greek form of the name. 1:4 Greek *brothers*.

God loves you and has chosen you to be his own people. [5]For when we brought you the Good News, it was not only with words but also with power, for the Holy Spirit gave you full assurance* that what we said was true. And you know of our concern for you from the way we lived when we were with you. [6]So you received the message with joy from the Holy Spirit in spite of the severe suffering it brought you. In this way, you imitated both us and the Lord. [7]As a result, you have become an example to all the believers in Greece—throughout both Macedonia and Achaia.*

[8]And now the word of the Lord is ringing out from you to people everywhere, even beyond Macedonia and Achaia, for wherever we go we find people telling us about your faith in God. We don't need to tell them about it, [9]for they keep talking about the wonderful welcome you gave us and how you turned away from idols to serve the living and true God. [10]And they speak of how you are looking forward to the coming of God's Son from heaven—Jesus, whom God raised from the dead. He is the one who has rescued us from the terrors of the coming judgment.

CHAPTER 2

Paul Remembers His Visit

You yourselves know, dear brothers and sisters,* that our visit to you was not a failure. [2]You know how badly we had been treated at Philippi just before we came to you and how much we suffered there. Yet our God gave us the courage to declare his Good News to you boldly, in spite of great opposition. [3]So you can see we were not preaching with any deceit or impure motives or trickery.

[4]For we speak as messengers approved by God to be entrusted with the Good News. Our purpose is to please God, not people. He alone examines the motives of our hearts. [5]Never once did we try to win you with flattery, as you well know. And God is our witness that we were not pretending to be your friends just to get your money! [6]As for human praise, we have never sought it from you or anyone else.

[7]As apostles of Christ we certainly had a right to make some demands of you, but instead we were like children* among you. Or we were like a mother feeding and caring for her own children. [8]We loved you so much that we shared with you not only God's Good News but our own lives, too.

[9]Don't you remember, dear brothers and sisters, how hard we worked among you? Night and day we toiled to earn a living so that we would not be a burden to any of you as we preached God's Good News to you. [10]You yourselves are our witnesses—and so is God—that we were devout and honest and faultless toward all of you believers. [11]And you know that we treated each of you as a father treats his own children. [12]We pleaded with you, encouraged you, and urged you to live your lives in a way that God would consider worthy. For he called you to share in his Kingdom and glory.

[13]Therefore, we never stop thanking God that when you received his message from us, you didn't think of our words as mere human ideas. You accepted what we said as the very word of God—which, of course, it is. And this word continues to work in you who believe.

[14]And then, dear brothers and sisters, you suffered persecution from your own countrymen. In this way, you imitated the believers in God's churches in Judea who, because of their belief in Christ Jesus, suffered from their own people, the Jews. [15]For some of the Jews killed the prophets, and some even killed the Lord Jesus. Now they have persecuted us, too. They fail to please God and work against all humanity [16]as they try to keep us from preaching the Good News of salvation to the Gentiles. By doing this, they continue to pile up their sins. But the anger of God has caught up with them at last.

Timothy's Good Report about the Church

[17]Dear brothers and sisters, after we were separated from you for a little while (though our hearts never left you), we tried very hard to come back because of our intense longing to see you again. [18]We wanted very much to come to you, and I, Paul, tried again and again, but Satan prevented us. [19]After all, what gives us hope and joy, and what will be our proud reward and crown as we stand before our Lord Jesus when he returns? It is you! [20]Yes, you are our pride and joy.

1:5 Or *with the power of the Holy Spirit, so you can have full assurance.* **1:7** *Macedonia* and *Achaia* were the northern and southern regions of Greece. **2:1** Greek *brothers;* also in 2:9, 14, 17. **2:7** Some manuscripts read *we were gentle.*

About a year ago, I started spending a lot of time with a girl from my school. We'd go to the mall, the neighborhood pizza parlor, and even the library together. I was sure we were in love! As we spent more and more time together, even though we were both Christians, I started struggling with the temptation to have sex. I tried to tell myself, *Other couples are doing it, right?*

One night I invited my girlfriend over for pizza and a video after my parents left for a party. I told her they'd be home, so she got upset when she realized I'd tricked her. Although she considered calling her dad to pick her up, she changed her mind and stayed.

We enjoyed hanging out together . . . until I started kissing her. She then reminded me about her abstinence pledge. I complained, "Couples in the movies I watch and the songs I listen to don't wait for marriage to have sex." Her razor-edged response really helped me get back in focus: "They don't know the Lord . . . and I'm starting to think you don't either!"

After her dad picked her up, I looked for my Bible. I wanted to see how much it talked about sexuality. It said plenty.

First Thessalonians 4:3-5 told me what I most needed to hear. It says to "stay away from all sexual sin . . . and live in holiness and honor," not to act like "pagans who do not know God and his ways." No wonder my girlfriend thought I didn't know the Lord—I sure wasn't acting like I did.

I became a changed person that night. I no longer try to imitate what other people are doing. Instead, I aim to do what's right in God's eyes.

For other verses on keeping yourself pure from sexual sin, check out 1 Corinthians 6:18-20 and Hebrews 13:4.

CHAPTER **3**

Finally, when we could stand it no longer, we decided to stay alone in Athens, [2]and we sent Timothy to visit you. He is our brother and God's co-worker* in proclaiming the Good News of Christ. We sent him to strengthen you, to encourage you in your faith, [3]and to keep you from being shaken by the troubles you were going through. But you know that we are destined for such troubles. [4]Even while we were with you, we warned you that troubles would soon come—and they did, as you well know. [5]That is why, when I could bear it no longer, I sent Timothy to find out whether your faith was still strong. I was afraid that the tempter had gotten the best of you and that our work had been useless.

[6]But now Timothy has just returned, bringing us good news about your faith and love. He reports that you always remember our visit with joy and that you want to see us as much as we want to see you. [7]So we have been greatly encouraged in the midst of our troubles and suffering, dear brothers and sisters,* because you have remained strong in your faith. [8]It gives us new life to know that you are standing firm in the Lord.

A CALL FOR HELP

Carlos planned to rush through his evening routine and finish his homework so he would have time to work on his bookshelves before bed. He and his dad were making the bookshelves to donate to a local retirement home. As Carlos opened his math book, Wade called. Wade had eaten lunch with Carlos and his friends. Carlos knew that Wade was a gabber. Carlos also knew Wade had questions about his faith and needed some encouragement. Carlos wanted to help his friend, but he didn't have time to talk for thirty minutes. What should Carlos do? See 1 Thessalonians 4:18.

AMAZING FACTS

When Jesus returns, a trumpet will sound and Christians will rise from their graves. If we're alive, we'll join them and Jesus in the clouds!

1 THESSALONIANS 4:15-17

[9]How we thank God for you! Because of you we have great joy as we enter God's presence. [10]Night and day we pray earnestly for you, asking God to let us see you again to fill the gaps in your faith.

[11]May God our Father and our Lord Jesus bring us to you very soon. [12]And may the Lord make your love for one another and for all people grow and overflow, just as our love for you overflows. [13]May he, as a result, make your hearts strong, blameless, and holy as you stand

3:2 Other manuscripts read *and God's servant;* still others read *and a co-worker,* or *and a servant and co-worker for God,* or *and God's servant and our co-worker.* **3:7** Greek *brothers.*

before God our Father when our Lord Jesus comes again with all his holy people. Amen.

CHAPTER 4

Live to Please God

Finally, dear brothers and sisters,* we urge you in the name of the Lord Jesus to live in a way that pleases God, as we have taught you. You live this way already, and we encourage you to do so even more. [2]For you remember what we taught you by the authority of the Lord Jesus.

[3]God's will is for you to be holy, so stay away from all sexual sin. [4]Then each of you will control his own body* and live in holiness and honor—[5]not in lustful passion like the pagans who do not know God and his ways. [6]Never harm or cheat a Christian brother in this matter by violating his wife,* for the Lord avenges all such sins, as we have solemnly warned you before. [7]God has called us to live holy lives, not impure lives. [8]Therefore, anyone who refuses to live by these rules is not disobeying human teaching but is rejecting God, who gives his Holy Spirit to you.

[9]But we don't need to write to you about the importance of loving each other,* for God himself has taught you to love one another. [10]Indeed, you already show your love for all the believers* throughout Macedonia. Even so, dear brothers and sisters, we urge you to love them even more.

I would love to get back at that kid who makes fun of me.

See that no one pays back evil for evil, but always try to do good to each other and to all people.

1 THESSALONIANS 5:15

[11]Make it your goal to live a quiet life, minding your own business and working with your hands, just as we instructed you before. [12]Then people who are not Christians will respect the way you live, and you will not need to depend on others.

The Hope of the Resurrection

[13]And now, dear brothers and sisters, we want you to know what will happen to the believers who have died* so you will not grieve like people who have no hope. [14]For since we believe that Jesus died and was raised to life again, we also believe that when Jesus returns, God will bring back with him the believers who have died.

[15]We tell you this directly from the Lord: We who are still living when the Lord returns will not meet him ahead of those who have died.* [16]For the Lord himself will come down from heaven with a commanding shout, with the voice of the archangel, and with the trumpet call of God. First, the Christians who have died* will rise from their graves. [17]Then, together with them, we who are still alive and remain on the earth will be caught up in the clouds to meet the Lord in the air. Then we will be with the Lord forever. [18]So encourage each other with these words.

CHAPTER 5

Now concerning how and when all this will happen, dear brothers and sisters,* we don't really need to write you. [2]For you know quite well that the day of the Lord's return will come unexpectedly, like a thief in the night. [3]When people are saying, "Everything is peaceful and secure," then disaster will fall on them as suddenly as a pregnant woman's labor pains begin. And there will be no escape.

[4]But you aren't in the dark about these things, dear brothers and sisters, and you won't be surprised when the day of the Lord comes like a thief.* [5]For you are all children of the light and of the day; we don't belong to darkness and night. [6]So be on your guard, not asleep like the others. Stay alert and be clearheaded. [7]Night is the time when people sleep and drinkers get drunk. [8]But let us who live in the light be clearheaded, protected by the armor of faith and love, and wearing as our helmet the confidence of our salvation.

4:1 Greek *brothers;* also in 4:10, 13. **4:4** Or *will know how to take a wife for himself;* or *will learn to live with his own wife;* Greek reads *will know how to possess his own vessel.* **4:6** Greek *Never harm or cheat a brother in this matter.* **4:9** Greek *about brotherly love.* **4:10** Greek *the brothers.* **4:13** Greek *those who have fallen asleep;* also in 4:14. **4:15** Greek *those who have fallen asleep.* **4:16** Greek *the dead in Christ.* **5:1** Greek *brothers;* also in 5:4, 12, 14, 25, 26, 27. **5:4** Some manuscripts read *comes upon you as if you were thieves.*

[9]For God chose to save us through our Lord
Jesus Christ, not to pour out his anger on us.
[10]Christ died for us so that, whether we are
dead or alive when he returns, we can live
with him forever. [11]So encourage each other
and build each other up, just as you are al-
ready doing.

Paul's Final Advice

[12]Dear brothers and sisters, honor those who
are your leaders in the Lord's work. They work
hard among you and give you spiritual guid-
ance. [13]Show them great respect and whole-
hearted love because of their work. And live
peacefully with each other.

[14]Brothers and sisters, we urge you to warn
those who are lazy. Encourage those who are
timid. Take tender care of those who are
weak. Be patient with everyone.

[15]See that no one pays back evil for evil, but
always try to do good to each other and to all
people.

[16]Always be joyful. [17]Never stop praying.
[18]Be thankful in all circumstances, for this is
God's will for you who belong to Christ Jesus.

[19]Do not stifle the Holy Spirit. [20]Do not
scoff at prophecies, [21]but test everything that
is said. Hold on to what is good. [22]Stay away
from every kind of evil.

Paul's Final Greetings

[23]Now may the God of peace make you holy in
every way, and may your whole spirit and soul
and body be kept blameless until our Lord
Jesus Christ comes again. [24]God will make this
happen, for he who calls you is faithful.

[25]Dear brothers and sisters, pray for us.

[26]Greet all the brothers and sisters with
Christian love.*

[27]I command you in the name of the Lord
to read this letter to all the brothers and
sisters.

[28]May the grace of our Lord Jesus Christ be
with you.

5:26 Greek *with a holy kiss.*

IS IT OK?

IS IT OK NOT TO PRAY ALL THE TIME?

It would be tricky to pray *all* the time as 1 Thessalonians 5:17 instructs—especially if you close your eyes when you pray! So what does God mean when he has Paul write that we are to "never stop praying"? He means we can talk to him anytime, anywhere. God is *always listening.* If you have ten minutes and want to say a long prayer, he'll be listening! If you have ten seconds and need to get a message to him, he'll be listening! Keep on praying. Wherever you are and whatever you're doing—walking or sitting, eating or studying, playing ball or lying down—you can pray. In your mind or out loud, you can have a running conversation with God. He'll be listening.

2 Thessalonians

WHO
Paul, Silas, and Timothy.

WHERE
Written and sent from Corinth.

WHEN
In AD 51 or 52 a few months after 1 Thessalonians was written.

WHY
To clear up confusion about when Jesus is coming back.

Stand firm and keep a strong grip on the teaching we passed on to you both in person and by letter.
2 THESSALONIANS 2:15

The Christians in Thessalonica misunderstood what Paul meant in his first letter about Christ's return. So Paul wrote another letter explaining what will happen *before* Jesus returns. He encouraged the believers to be patient, to keep working, and to be ready.

See how Paul corrected a communication breakdown, and learn the signs of Christ's return.

CHAPTER 1

Greetings from Paul

This letter is from Paul, Silas,* and Timothy.

We are writing to the church in Thessalonica, to you who belong to God our Father and the Lord Jesus Christ.

[2]May God our Father* and the Lord Jesus Christ give you grace and peace.

Encouragement during Persecution

[3]Dear brothers and sisters,* we can't help but thank God for you, because your faith is flourishing and your love for one another is

1:1 Greek *Silvanus*, the Greek form of the name. 1:2 Some manuscripts read *God the Father*. 1:3 Greek *Brothers*.

growing. [4]We proudly tell God's other churches about your endurance and faithfulness in all the persecutions and hardships you are suffering. [5]And God will use this persecution to show his justice and to make you worthy of his Kingdom, for which you are suffering. [6]In his justice he will pay back those who persecute you.

[7]And God will provide rest for you who are being persecuted and also for us when the Lord Jesus appears from heaven. He will come with his mighty angels, [8]in flaming fire, bringing judgment on those who don't know God and on those who refuse to obey the Good News of our Lord Jesus. [9]They will be punished with eternal destruction, forever separated from the Lord and from his glorious power. [10]When he comes on that day, he will receive glory from his holy people—praise from all who believe. And this includes you, for you believed what we told you about him.

[11]So we keep on praying for you, asking our God to enable you to live a life worthy of his call. May he give you the power to accomplish all the good things your faith prompts you to do. [12]Then the name of our Lord Jesus will be honored because of the way you live, and you will be honored along with him. This is all made possible because of the grace of our God and Lord, Jesus Christ.*

CHAPTER 2

Events prior to the Lord's Second Coming

Now, dear brothers and sisters,* let us clarify some things about the coming of our Lord Jesus Christ and how we will be gathered to meet him. [2]Don't be so easily shaken or alarmed by those who say that the day of the Lord has already begun. Don't believe them, even if they claim to have had a spiritual vision, a revelation, or a letter supposedly from us. [3]Don't be fooled by what they say. For that day will not come until there is a great rebellion against God and the man of lawlessness* is revealed—the one who brings destruction.* [4]He will exalt himself and defy everything that people call god and every object of worship. He will even sit in the temple of God, claiming that he himself is God.

[5]Don't you remember that I told you about all this when I was with you? [6]And you know what is holding him back, for he can be revealed only when his time comes. [7]For this lawlessness is already at work secretly, and it will remain secret until the one who is holding it back steps out of the way. [8]Then the man of lawlessness will be revealed, but the Lord Jesus will kill him with the breath of his mouth and destroy him by the splendor of his coming.

[9]This man will come to do the work of Satan with counterfeit power and signs and miracles. [10]He will use every kind of evil deception to fool those on their way to destruc-

1:12 Or *of our God and our Lord Jesus Christ.* **2:1** Greek *brothers;* also in 2:13, 15. **2:3a** Some manuscripts read *the man of sin.* **2:3b** Greek *the son of destruction.*

tion, because they refuse to love and accept
the truth that would save them. [11]So God will
cause them to be greatly deceived, and they
will believe these lies. [12]Then they will be con-
demned for enjoying evil rather than believ-
ing the truth.

Believers Should Stand Firm

[13]As for us, we can't help but thank God for
you, dear brothers and sisters loved by the
Lord. We are always thankful that God chose
you to be among the first* to experience sal-
vation—a salvation that came through the
Spirit who makes you holy and through your
belief in the truth. [14]He called you to salvation
when we told you the Good News; now you can
share in the glory of our Lord Jesus Christ.

[15]With all these things in mind, dear broth-
ers and sisters, stand firm and keep a strong
grip on the teaching we passed on to you both
in person and by letter.

[16]Now may our Lord Jesus Christ himself
and God our Father, who loved us and by his
grace gave us eternal comfort and a wonder-
ful hope, [17]comfort you and strengthen you in
every good thing you do and say.

CHAPTER 3

Paul's Request for Prayer

Finally, dear brothers and sisters,* we ask you
to pray for us. Pray that the Lord's message
will spread rapidly and be honored wherever
it goes, just as when it came to you. [2]Pray, too,
that we will be rescued from wicked and evil
people, for not everyone is a believer. [3]But the
Lord is faithful; he will strengthen you and
guard you from the evil one.* [4]And we are
confident in the Lord that you are doing and
will continue to do the things we commanded
you. [5]May the Lord lead your hearts into a full
understanding and expression of the love of
God and the patient endurance that comes
from Christ.

An Exhortation to Proper Living

[6]And now, dear brothers and sisters, we give
you this command in the name of our Lord
Jesus Christ: Stay away from all believers* who
live idle lives and don't follow the tradition
they received* from us. [7]For you know that
you ought to imitate us. We were not idle
when we were with you. [8]We never accepted
food from anyone without paying for it. We
worked hard day and night so we would not be
a burden to any of you. [9]We certainly had the
right to ask you to feed us, but we wanted to
give you an example to follow. [10]Even while we
were with you, we gave you this command:
"Those unwilling to work will not get to eat."

[11]Yet we hear that some of you are living
idle lives, refusing to work and meddling in
other people's business. [12]We command
such people and urge them in the name of the
Lord Jesus Christ to settle down and work to
earn their own living. [13]As for the rest of you,
dear brothers and sisters, never get tired of
doing good.

[14]Take note of those who refuse to obey
what we say in this letter. Stay away from
them so they will be ashamed. [15]Don't think
of them as enemies, but warn them as you
would a brother or sister.*

Paul's Final Greetings

[16]Now may the Lord of peace himself give you
his peace at all times and in every situation.
The Lord be with you all.

[17]HERE IS MY GREETING IN MY OWN HAND-
WRITING—PAUL. I DO THIS IN ALL MY LETTERS TO
PROVE THEY ARE FROM ME.

[18]May the grace of our Lord Jesus Christ be
with you all.

2:13 Some manuscripts read *chose you from the very beginning*. **3:1** Greek *brothers;* also in 3:6, 13. **3:3** Or *from evil*. **3:6a** Greek *from every brother*. **3:6b** Some manuscripts read *you received*. **3:15** Greek *as a brother*.

1 Timothy

WHO
Paul and Timothy.

WHERE
Written and sent from Rome or Macedonia.

WHEN
Around AD 64 while Timothy was in Ephesus helping the believers there.

WHY
To encourage and instruct Timothy.

Don't let anyone think less of you because you are young. Be an example to all believers.
1 TIMOTHY 4:12

You can be a good leader at any age. Timothy was a young boy when he put his faith in Christ. Paul was like a father to Timothy, and they were close friends as Timothy grew to be a young man. Paul sent Timothy to Ephesus to solve some problems in that church. Then Paul wrote to help Timothy in his work.

DON'T FEEL UNIMPORTANT JUST BECAUSE YOU ARE YOUNG. WHATEVER YOUR AGE, YOU CAN BE A GOOD EXAMPLE OF HOW TO FOLLOW CHRIST.

CHAPTER 1

Greetings from Paul

This letter is from Paul, an apostle of Christ Jesus, appointed by the command of God our Savior and Christ Jesus, who gives us hope.

[2]I am writing to Timothy, my true son in the faith.

May God the Father and Christ Jesus our Lord give you grace, mercy, and peace.

Warnings against False Teachings

[3]When I left for Macedonia, I urged you to stay there in Ephesus and stop those whose teaching is contrary to the truth. [4]Don't let

them waste their time in endless discussion of myths and spiritual pedigrees. These things only lead to meaningless speculations,* which don't help people live a life of faith in God.*

5 The purpose of my instruction is that all believers would be filled with love that comes from a pure heart, a clear conscience, and genuine faith. 6 But some people have missed this whole point. They have turned away from these things and spend their time in meaningless discussions. 7 They want to be known as teachers of the law of Moses, but they don't know what they are talking about, even though they speak so confidently.

8 We know that the law is good when used correctly. 9 For the law was not intended for people who do what is right. It is for people who are lawless and rebellious, who are ungodly and sinful, who consider nothing sacred and defile what is holy, who kill their father or mother or commit other murders. 10 The law is for people who are sexually immoral, or who practice homosexuality, or are slave traders,* liars, promise breakers, or who do anything else that contradicts the wholesome teaching 11 that comes from the glorious Good News entrusted to me by our blessed God.

Paul's Gratitude for God's Mercy

12 I thank Christ Jesus our Lord, who has given me strength to do his work. He considered me trustworthy and appointed me to serve him, 13 even though I used to blaspheme the name of Christ. In my insolence, I persecuted his people. But God had mercy on me because I did it in ignorance and unbelief. 14 Oh, how generous and gracious our Lord was! He filled me with the faith and love that come from Christ Jesus.

15 This is a trustworthy saying, and everyone should accept it: "Christ Jesus came into the world to save sinners"—and I am the worst of them all. 16 But God had mercy on me so that Christ Jesus could use me as a prime example of his great patience with even the worst sinners. Then others will realize that they, too, can believe in him and receive eternal life. 17 All honor and glory to God forever and ever! He is the eternal King, the unseen one who never dies; he alone is God. Amen.

Timothy's Responsibility

18 Timothy, my son, here are my instructions for you, based on the prophetic words spoken about you earlier. May they help you fight well in the Lord's battles. 19 Cling to your faith in Christ, and keep your conscience clear. For some people have deliberately violated their consciences; as a result, their faith has been shipwrecked. 20 Hymenaeus and Alexander are two examples. I threw them out and handed them over to Satan so they might learn not to blaspheme God.

CHAPTER 2

Instructions about Worship

I urge you, first of all, to pray for all people. Ask God to help them; intercede on their behalf, and give thanks for them. 2 Pray this way for kings and all who are in authority so that we can live peaceful and quiet lives marked by godliness and dignity. 3 This is good and pleases God our Savior, 4 who wants everyone to be saved and to understand the truth. 5 For there is only one God and one Mediator who can reconcile God and humanity—the man Christ Jesus. 6 He gave his life to purchase freedom for everyone. This is the message God gave to the world at just the right time. 7 And I have been chosen as a preacher and apostle to teach the Gentiles this message about faith and truth. I'm not exaggerating—just telling the truth.

8 In every place of worship, I want men to pray with holy hands lifted up to God, free from anger and controversy.

9 And I want women to be modest in their appearance.* They should wear decent and appropriate clothing and not draw attention to themselves by the way they fix their hair or by wearing gold or pearls or expensive clothes. 10 For women who claim to be devoted to God should make themselves attractive by the good things they do.

11 Women should learn quietly and submissively. 12 I do not let women teach men or have authority over them.* Let them listen quietly. 13 For God made Adam first, and afterward he made Eve. 14 And it was not Adam who was de-

1:4a Greek *in myths and endless genealogies, which cause speculation.* **1:4b** Greek *a stewardship of God in faith.* **1:10** Or *kidnappers.* **2:9** Or *to pray in modest apparel.* **2:12** Or *teach men or usurp their authority.*

TO PRAY OR NOT TO PRAY

Corey and his friend Alec played soccer on the same team. They liked the same movies. And they both had a good time when they went to the mall together. But Corey and Alec also had strong opinions. Sometimes Corey had a hard time giving up his plans for Alec's plans. One Sunday during Corey's Sunday school class, his face turned red because he felt so angry just thinking about how bossy Alec could be. Then he heard his teacher asking him if he would lead the class in prayer. What do you think he should do? Check out 1 Timothy 2:8 for some help.

ceived by Satan. The woman was deceived, and sin was the result. 15But women will be saved through childbearing,* assuming they continue to live in faith, love, holiness, and modesty.

CHAPTER 3

Leaders in the Church

This is a trustworthy saying: "If someone aspires to be an elder,* he desires an honorable position." 2So an elder must be a man whose life is above reproach. He must be faithful to his wife.* He must exercise self-control, live wisely, and have a good reputation. He must enjoy having guests in his home, and he must be able to teach. 3He must not be a heavy drinker* or be violent. He must be gentle, not quarrelsome, and not love money. 4He must manage his own family well, having children who respect and obey him. 5For if a man cannot manage his own household, how can he take care of God's church?

6An elder must not be a new believer, because he might become proud, and the devil would cause him to fall.* 7Also, people outside the church must speak well of him so that he will not be disgraced and fall into the devil's trap.

8In the same way, deacons must be well respected and have integrity. They must not be heavy drinkers or dishonest with money. 9They must be committed to the mystery of the faith now revealed and must live with a clear conscience. 10Before they are appointed as deacons, let them be closely examined. If they pass the test, then let them serve as deacons.

11In the same way, their wives* must be respected and must not slander others. They must exercise self-control and be faithful in everything they do.

12A deacon must be faithful to his wife, and he must manage his children and household well. 13Those who do well as deacons will be rewarded with respect from others and will have increased confidence in their faith in Christ Jesus.

The Truths of Our Faith

14I am writing these things to you now, even though I hope to be with you soon, 15so that if I am delayed, you will know how people must conduct themselves in the household of God. This is the church of the living God, which is the pillar and foundation of the truth.

2:15 Or *will be saved by accepting their role as mothers,* or *will be saved by the birth of the Child.* **3:1** Or *an overseer,* or *a bishop;* also in 3:2, 6. **3:2** Or *must have only one wife,* or *must be married only once;* Greek reads *must be the husband of one wife;* also in 3:12. **3:3** Greek *must not drink too much wine;* similarly in 3:8. **3:6** Or *he might fall into the same judgment as the devil.* **3:11** Or *the women deacons.* The Greek word can be translated *women* or *wives.*

[16]Without question, this is the great mystery of our faith*:

Christ* was revealed in a human
body
and vindicated by the Spirit.*
He was seen by angels
and announced to the nations.
He was believed in throughout the world
and taken to heaven in glory.

the Savior of all people and particularly of all believers.

[11]Teach these things and insist that everyone learn them. [12]Don't let anyone think less of you because you are young. Be an example to all believers in what you say, in the way you live, in your love, your faith, and your purity. [13]Until I get there, focus on reading the Scriptures to the church, encouraging the believers, and teaching them.

I'm just a kid. How can I help older people know about God?

Don't let anyone think less of you because you are young. Be an example to all believers in what you say, in the way you live, in your love, your faith, and your purity.

1 TIMOTHY 4:12

CHAPTER 4

Warnings against False Teachers

Now the Holy Spirit tells us clearly that in the last times some will turn away from the true faith; they will follow deceptive spirits and teachings that come from demons. [2]These people are hypocrites and liars, and their consciences are dead.*

[3]They will say it is wrong to be married and wrong to eat certain foods. But God created those foods to be eaten with thanks by faithful people who know the truth. [4]Since everything God created is good, we should not reject any of it but receive it with thanks. [5]For we know it is made acceptable* by the word of God and prayer.

A Good Servant of Christ Jesus

[6]If you explain these things to the brothers and sisters,* Timothy, you will be a worthy servant of Christ Jesus, one who is nourished by the message of faith and the good teaching you have followed. [7]Do not waste time arguing over godless ideas and old wives' tales. Instead, train yourself to be godly. [8]"Physical training is good, but training for godliness is much better, promising benefits in this life and in the life to come." [9]This is a trustworthy saying, and everyone should accept it. [10]This is why we work hard and continue to struggle,* for our hope is in the living God, who is

[14]Do not neglect the spiritual gift you received through the prophecy spoken over you when the elders of the church laid their hands on you. [15]Give your complete attention to these matters. Throw yourself into your tasks so that everyone will see your progress. [16]Keep a close watch on how you live and on your teaching. Stay true to what is right for the sake of your own salvation and the salvation of those who hear you.

CHAPTER 5

Advice about Widows, Elders, and Slaves

Never speak harshly to an older man,* but appeal to him respectfully as you would to your own father. Talk to younger men as you would to your own brothers. [2]Treat older women as you would your mother, and treat younger women with all purity as you would your own sisters.

[3]Take care of* any widow who has no one else to care for her. [4]But if she has children or grandchildren, their first responsibility is to show godliness at home and repay their parents by taking care of them. This is something that pleases God.

[5]Now a true widow, a woman who is truly alone in this world, has placed her hope in God. She prays night and day, asking God for his help. [6]But the widow who lives only for

3:16a Or *of godliness.* **3:16b** Greek *He who;* other manuscripts read *God.* **3:16c** Or *in his spirit.* **4:2** Greek *are seared.* **4:5** Or *made holy.* **4:6** Greek *brothers.* **4:10** Some manuscripts read *continue to suffer.* **5:1** Or *an elder.* **5:3** Or *Honor.*

Wherever I go, people always tell me how young I look. "You're *how* old?" they ask, with shocked expressions. Adults sometimes guess my age as five or six years younger than I really am!

It used to bother me a lot. When someone made a comment, I would just feel myself start to burn. I wanted respect for what I *did* and who I *was*—not for what I looked like! I mean, I'm in high school now, not kindergarten!

That's why, when I read Paul's letters to Timothy, I immediately connected. Timothy was a young guy. He was also put in a pretty important position of leadership. Like me, he had to deal with older people who seemed to be looking down on him all the time.

Now I realize God has also called me to be a leader. I've been a Christian practically all my life. I may not be as old as some other people, but I know a lot about God. Jesus has been leading my life for years now. So whether I'm at my old Christian middle school or my new public high school, I'm still a Christian. That means people sometimes actually *look up* to me to show them Christ. That's a big responsibility.

I've even chosen 1 Timothy 4:12 as a kind of personal motto for my life. Whenever I read it, I'm reminded that, no matter what age I am, I'm called to be an example to those around me, even my teachers at school.

Every once in a while, people still make comments about my young appearance. But it doesn't bother me now. I think of Timothy. And I remember what's really important—the way we act as Christians—not the way we look.

Check out these verses on learning to serve God no matter how young you are: 2 Chronicles 34:1-3; Ecclesiastes 12:1; and 1 Timothy 4:12.

pleasure is spiritually dead even while she lives. 7Give these instructions to the church so that no one will be open to criticism.

8But those who won't care for their relatives, especially those in their own household, have denied the true faith. Such people are worse than unbelievers.

9A widow who is put on the list for support must be a woman who is at least sixty years old and was faithful to her husband.* 10She must be well respected by everyone because of the good she has done. Has she brought up her children well? Has she been kind to strangers and served other believers humbly?* Has she helped those who are in trouble? Has she always been ready to do good?

11The younger widows should not be on the list, because their physical desires will overpower their devotion to Christ and they will want to remarry. 12Then they would be guilty of breaking their previous pledge. 13And if they are on the list, they will learn to be lazy and will spend their time gossiping from house to house, meddling in other people's business and talking about things they shouldn't. 14So I advise these younger widows to marry again, have children, and take care of their own homes. Then the enemy will not be able to say anything against them. 15For I am afraid that some of them have already gone astray and now follow Satan.

16If a woman who is a believer has relatives who are widows, she must take care of them and not put the responsibility on the church. Then the church can care for the widows who are truly alone.

17Elders who do their work well should be respected and paid well,* especially those who work hard at both preaching and teaching. 18For the Scripture says, "You must not muzzle an ox to keep it from eating as it treads out the grain." And in another place, "Those who work deserve their pay!"*

19Do not listen to an accusation against an elder unless it is confirmed by two or three witnesses. 20Those who sin should be reprimanded in front of the whole church; this will serve as a strong warning to others.

21I solemnly command you in the presence of God and Christ Jesus and the highest angels to obey these instructions without taking sides or showing favoritism to anyone.

22Never be in a hurry about appointing a church leader.* Do not share in the sins of others. Keep yourself pure.

23Don't drink only water. You ought to drink a little wine for the sake of your stomach because you are sick so often.

24Remember, the sins of some people are obvious, leading them to certain judgment. But there are others whose sins will not be revealed until later. 25In the same way, the good deeds of some people are obvious. And the good deeds done in secret will someday come to light.

CHAPTER 6

All slaves should show full respect for their masters so they will not bring shame on the name of God and his teaching. 2If the masters are believers, that is no excuse for being disrespectful. Those slaves should work all the harder because their efforts are helping other believers* who are well loved.

False Teaching and True Riches

Teach these things, Timothy, and encourage everyone to obey them. 3Some people may contradict our teaching, but these are the wholesome teachings of the Lord Jesus Christ. These teachings promote a godly life. 4Anyone who teaches something different is arrogant and lacks understanding. Such a person has an unhealthy desire to quibble over the meaning of words. This stirs up arguments ending in jealousy, division, slander, and evil suspicions. 5These people always cause trouble. Their minds are corrupt, and they have turned their backs on the truth. To them, a show of godliness is just a way to become wealthy.

6Yet true godliness with contentment is itself great wealth. 7After all, we brought nothing with us when we came into the world, and we can't take anything with us when we leave it. 8So if we have enough food and clothing, let us be content.

9But people who long to be rich fall into temptation and are trapped by many foolish and harmful desires that plunge them into ruin and destruction. 10For the love of money

5:9 Greek *was the wife of one husband.* **5:10** Greek *and washed the feet of God's holy people?* **5:17** Greek *should be worthy of double honor.* **5:18** Deut 25:4; Luke 10:7. **5:22** Greek *about the laying on of hands.* **6:2** Greek *brothers.*

is the root of all kinds of evil. And some people, craving money, have wandered from the true faith and pierced themselves with many sorrows.

Paul's Final Instructions

[11]But you, Timothy, are a man of God; so run from all these evil things. Pursue righteousness and a godly life, along with faith, love, perseverance, and gentleness. [12]Fight the good fight for the true faith. Hold tightly to the eternal life to which God has called you, which you have confessed so well before many witnesses. [13]And I charge you before God, who gives life to all, and before Christ Jesus, who gave a good testimony before Pontius Pilate, [14]that you obey this command without wavering. Then no one can find fault with you from now until our Lord Jesus Christ comes again. [15]For at just the right time Christ will be revealed from heaven by the blessed and only almighty God, the King of all kings and Lord of all lords. [16]He alone can never die, and he lives in light so brilliant that no human can approach him. No human eye has ever seen him, nor ever will. All honor and power to him forever! Amen.

[17]Teach those who are rich in this world not to be proud and not to trust in their money, which is so unreliable. Their trust should be in God, who richly gives us all we need for our enjoyment. [18]Tell them to use their money to do good. They should be rich in good works and generous to those in need, always being ready to share with others. [19]By doing this they will be storing up their treasure as a good foundation for the future so that they may experience true life.

AMAZING FACTS

Loving money is costly—it can lead to evil actions and even the death of your faith.

1 TIMOTHY 6:9-10

[20]Timothy, guard what God has entrusted to you. Avoid godless, foolish discussions with those who oppose you with their so-called knowledge. [21]Some people have wandered from the faith by following such foolishness.

May God's grace be with you all.

2 TIMOTHY

WHO
Paul, Timothy, Luke, and Mark.

WHERE
Written and sent by Paul from prison in Rome.

WHEN
Around AD 66 or 67, while Timothy was still in Ephesus.

WHY
To encourage Timothy and give him final instructions.

Work hard so you can present yourself to God and receive his approval. Be a good worker, one who does not need to be ashamed.
2 TIMOTHY 2:15

If someone you loved was in prison and going to die, think about how important a letter from that person would be. This letter was the last one Timothy received from Paul, his mentor. Can you imagine how Timothy must have treasured it?

AS YOU READ 2 TIMOTHY, LISTEN FOR HIS WISE WORDS INSPIRED BY GOD—THEY ARE FOR YOU, TOO.

CHAPTER 1

Greetings from Paul

This letter is from Paul, chosen by the will of God to be an apostle of Christ Jesus. I have been sent out to tell others about the life he has promised through faith in Christ Jesus.

[2]I am writing to Timothy, my dear son.

May God the Father and Christ Jesus our Lord give you grace, mercy, and peace.

Encouragement to Be Faithful

[3]Timothy, I thank God for you—the God I serve with a clear conscience, just as my ancestors did. Night and day I constantly remember you in my prayers. [4]I long to see you again, for I remember your tears as we parted. And I will be filled with joy when we are together again.

[5]I remember your genuine faith, for you

TIMOTHY

Though I am only a young man, I know what God wants me to do. My father was not a believer, but my mother and grandmother taught me the way of faith when I was a boy, and I have followed Jesus ever since.

The most exciting moment of my life was when Paul asked me to join his missionary work. As we traveled from church to church, we encouraged the believers with our teaching. I learned so much from watching Paul at work! Now that I am leading my own church, I love to read and reread Paul's letters to me. Near the end of his first letter he reminded me to "fight the good fight for the true faith" and to be a man of God.

Read about Timothy's travels with Paul in Acts 16:1-5 and 20:1-6; 1 Corinthians 16:10-11; and Philippians 2:19-23.

share the faith that first filled your grandmother Lois and your mother, Eunice. And I know that same faith continues strong in you. [6]This is why I remind you to fan into flames the spiritual gift God gave you when I laid my hands on you. [7]For God has not given us a spirit of fear and timidity, but of power, love, and self-discipline.

[8]So never be ashamed to tell others about our Lord. And don't be ashamed of me, either, even though I'm in prison for him. With the strength God gives you, be ready to suffer with me for the sake of the Good News. [9]For God saved us and called us to live a holy life. He did this, not because we deserved it, but because that was his plan from before the beginning of time—to show us his grace through Christ Jesus. [10]And now he has made all of this plain to us by the appearing of Christ Jesus, our Savior. He broke the power of death and illuminated the way to life and immortality through the Good News. [11]And God chose me to be a preacher, an apostle, and a teacher of this Good News.

[12]That is why I am suffering here in prison. But I am not ashamed of it, for I know the one in whom I trust, and I am sure that he is able to guard what I have entrusted to him* until the day of his return.

[13]Hold on to the pattern of wholesome teaching you learned from me—a pattern shaped by the faith and love that you have in Christ Jesus. [14]Through the power of the Holy Spirit who lives within us, carefully guard the precious truth that has been entrusted to you.

[15]As you know, everyone from the province of Asia has deserted me—even Phygelus and Hermogenes.

[16]May the Lord show special kindness to Onesiphorus and all his family because he often visited and encouraged me. He was never ashamed of me because I was in chains. [17]When he came to Rome, he searched everywhere until he found me. [18]May the Lord show him special kindness on the day of Christ's return. And you know very well how helpful he was in Ephesus.

CHAPTER 2

A Good Soldier of Christ Jesus

Timothy, my dear son, be strong through the grace that God gives you in Christ Jesus. [2]You have heard me teach things that have been confirmed by many reliable witnesses. Now teach these truths to other trustworthy people who will be able to pass them on to others.

1:12 Or *what has been entrusted to me.*

We've always had cable TV in our house. None of the real bad stuff—just MTV and the basic channels. When I turned sixteen this year, I got cable in my room.

I started watching a lot of shows that I had never watched with my parents. All my friends talked about these shows. They were really funny and really . . . you know.

Two areas of my life started changing big-time: my language and my thoughts. Even though I wasn't watching anything R-rated, the language and sexual talk on cable was pretty bad. So my language changed for the worse, and I started to think about sex a lot. I found myself turning on some of the reality shows simply because they always showed girls in bikinis. I was addicted.

One night the youth pastor at my church told our youth group that many of us were "flirting with disaster." He told us if we allow something to creep into our life that doesn't belong there, before we even realize it, it changes us. He said the only way to escape is to get rid of the temptation. I knew cable had changed me, and I needed to get rid of it.

It was one of the hardest things I ever did, but I told my parents to take the cable channels out of my room. My dad and I ended up having a real good talk. He apologized for allowing it in the first place. Then he got rid of a few channels on the family TV that could be a temptation too. Now we just watch sports and a few family shows.

My friends still talk about the cable shows. But I just bring up sports. Before you know it, we're talking basketball. It worked for me, and it can work for you.

Check out 2 Timothy 2:22 on ways to handle temptation. Read also 1 Timothy 6:11.

[3]Endure suffering along with me, as a good soldier of Christ Jesus. [4]Soldiers don't get tied up in the affairs of civilian life, for then they cannot please the officer who enlisted them. [5]And athletes cannot win the prize unless they follow the rules. [6]And hardworking farmers should be the first to enjoy the fruit of their labor. [7]Think about what I am saying. The Lord will help you understand all these things.

[8]Always remember that Jesus Christ, a descendant of King David, was raised from the dead. This is the Good News I preach. [9]And because I preach this Good News, I am suffering and have been chained like a criminal. But the word of God cannot be chained. [10]So I am willing to endure anything if it will bring salvation and eternal glory in Christ Jesus to those God has chosen.

[11]This is a trustworthy saying:

If we die with him,
we will also live with him.
[12] If we endure hardship,
we will reign with him.
If we deny him,
he will deny us.
[13] If we are unfaithful,
he remains faithful,
for he cannot deny who he is.

[14]Remind everyone about these things, and command them in God's presence to stop fighting over words. Such arguments are useless, and they can ruin those who hear them.

An Approved Worker

[15]Work hard so you can present yourself to God and receive his approval. Be a good worker, one who does not need to be ashamed and who correctly explains the word of truth. [16]Avoid worthless, foolish talk that only leads to more godless behavior. [17]This kind of talk spreads like cancer,* as in the case of Hymenaeus and Philetus. [18]They have left the path of truth, claiming that the resurrection of the dead has already occurred; in this way, they have turned some people away from the faith.

[19]But God's truth stands firm like a foundation stone with this inscription: "The LORD knows those who are his,"* and "All who belong to the LORD must turn away from evil."*

[20]In a wealthy home some utensils are made of gold and silver, and some are made of wood and clay. The expensive utensils are used for special occasions, and the cheap ones are for everyday use. [21]If you keep yourself pure, you will be a special utensil for honorable use. Your life will be clean, and you will be ready for the Master to use you for every good work.

[22]Run from anything that stimulates youthful lusts. Instead, pursue righteous living, faithfulness, love, and peace. Enjoy the companionship of those who call on the Lord with pure hearts.

[23]Again I say, don't get involved in foolish, ignorant arguments that only start fights. [24]A servant of the Lord must not quarrel but must be kind to everyone, be able to teach, and be patient with difficult people. [25]Gently instruct those who oppose the truth. Perhaps God will change those people's hearts, and they will learn the truth. [26]Then they will come to their senses and escape from the devil's trap. For they have been held captive by him to do whatever he wants.

CHAPTER 3

The Dangers of the Last Days

You should know this, Timothy, that in the last days there will be very difficult times. [2]For people will love only themselves and their money. They will be boastful and proud, scoffing at God, disobedient to their parents, and ungrateful. They will consider nothing sacred. [3]They will be unloving and unforgiving; they will slander others and have no self-control. They will be cruel and hate what is good. [4]They will betray their friends, be reckless, be puffed up with pride, and love pleasure rather than God. [5]They will act religious, but they will reject the power that could make them godly. Stay away from people like that!

[6]They are the kind who work their way into people's homes and win the confidence of* vulnerable women who are burdened with the guilt of sin and controlled by various desires. [7](Such women are forever following new teachings, but they are never able to understand the truth.) [8]These teachers oppose the truth just as Jannes and Jambres opposed Moses. They have depraved minds and a counterfeit faith. [9]But they won't get away

2:17 Greek *gangrene*. **2:19a** Num 16:5. **2:19b** See Isa 52:11. **3:6** Greek *and take captive*.

THE BIRTHDAY PRESENT

It had been a wonderful birthday. Matthew had received some new DVDs, a couple of cool T-shirts for school, and a small digital camera. Still, his parents had another gift to give him. As Matthew waited in anticipation, his parents proudly presented him with a rectangular package. They told Matthew that this gift would become one of his most treasured possessions. Matthew opened the present to discover a beautiful leather-bound Bible. Matthew thanked his parents and took it to his room. As he leafed through the pages, he thought about his parents' words. Now that he had received this new Bible, what should he do with it? Take a look at 2 Timothy 3:15-17 for an idea.

with this for long. Someday everyone will recognize what fools they are, just as with Jannes and Jambres.

Paul's Charge to Timothy

[10]But you, Timothy, certainly know what I teach, and how I live, and what my purpose in life is. You know my faith, my patience, my love, and my endurance. [11]You know how much persecution and suffering I have endured. You know all about how I was persecuted in Antioch, Iconium, and Lystra—but the Lord rescued me from all of it. [12]Yes, and everyone who wants to live a godly life in Christ Jesus will suffer persecution. [13]But evil people and impostors will flourish. They will deceive others and will themselves be deceived.

[14]But you must remain faithful to the things you have been taught. You know they are true, for you know you can trust those who taught you. [15]You have been taught the holy Scriptures from childhood, and they have given you the wisdom to receive the salvation that comes by trusting in Christ Jesus. [16]All Scripture is inspired by God and is useful to teach us what is true and to make us realize what is wrong in our lives. It corrects us when we are wrong and teaches us to do what is right. [17]God uses it to prepare and equip his people to do every good work.

CHAPTER 4

I solemnly urge you in the presence of God and Christ Jesus, who will someday judge the living and the dead when he appears to set up his Kingdom: [2]Preach the word of God. Be prepared, whether the time is favorable or not. Patiently correct, rebuke, and encourage your people with good teaching.

[3]For a time is coming when people will no longer listen to sound and wholesome teaching. They will follow their own desires and will look for teachers who will tell them whatever their itching ears want to hear. [4]They will reject the truth and chase after myths.

[5]But you should keep a clear mind in every situation. Don't be afraid of suffering for the Lord. Work at telling others the Good News, and fully carry out the ministry God has given you.

[6]As for me, my life has already been poured out as an offering to God. The time of my death is near. [7]I have fought the good fight, I have finished the race, and I have remained faithful. [8]And now the prize awaits me—the

crown of righteousness, which the Lord, the
righteous Judge, will give me on the day of his
return. And the prize is not just for me but for
all who eagerly look forward to his appearing.

Paul's Final Words

[9]Timothy, please come as soon as you can.
[10]Demas has deserted me because he loves the
things of this life and has gone to Thes-
salonica. Crescens has gone to Galatia, and Ti-
tus has gone to Dalmatia. [11]Only Luke is with
me. Bring Mark with you when you come, for
he will be helpful to me in my ministry. [12]I sent
Tychicus to Ephesus. [13]When you come, be
sure to bring the coat I left with Carpus at
Troas. Also bring my books, and especially my
papers.*

[14]Alexander the coppersmith did me much
harm, but the Lord will judge him for what he
has done. [15]Be careful of him, for he fought
against everything we said.

[16]The first time I was brought before the
judge, no one came with me. Everyone aban-
doned me. May it not be counted against
them. [17]But the Lord stood with me and gave
me strength so that I might preach the Good
News in its entirety for all the Gentiles to hear.
And he rescued me from certain death.* [18]Yes,
and the Lord will deliver me from every evil
attack and will bring me safely into his heav-
enly Kingdom. All glory to God forever and
ever! Amen.

Paul's Final Greetings

[19]Give my greetings to Priscilla and Aquila
and those living in the household of On-
esiphorus. [20]Erastus stayed at Corinth, and I
left Trophimus sick at Miletus.

[21]Do your best to get here before winter. Eu-
bulus sends you greetings, and so do Pudens,
Linus, Claudia, and all the brothers and
sisters.*

[22]May the Lord be with your spirit. And
may his grace be with all of you.

4:13 Greek *especially the parchments.* **4:17** Greek *from the mouth of a lion.* **4:21** Greek *brothers.*

Titus

WHO
Paul and Titus.

WHERE
Probably written and sent by Paul from Macedonia.

WHEN
Around AD 64—at about the same time Paul wrote 1 Timothy.

WHY
To advise Titus in leading the churches on the island of Crete.

Promote the kind of living that reflects wholesome teaching.
TITUS 2:1

You probably receive instructions each day: *Don't stay out late. Don't smoke or drink.* Paul's letter to Titus is packed with practical advice like that. Titus was a new Christian who had become a leader in the church on the island of Crete. Paul gave Titus all kinds of advice on staying pure in an impure world.

Dive into this letter and discover for yourself God's perfect advice for how to live.

CHAPTER 1

Greetings from Paul

This letter is from Paul, a slave of God and an apostle of Jesus Christ. I have been sent to proclaim faith to* those God has chosen and to teach them to know the truth that shows them how to live godly lives. [2]This truth gives them confidence that they have eternal life, which God—who does not lie—promised them before the world began. [3]And now at just the right time he has revealed this message, which we announce to everyone. It is by the command of God our Savior that I have been entrusted with this work for him.

1:1 Or *to strengthen the faith of.*

[4]I am writing to Titus, my true son in the faith that we share.

May God the Father and Christ Jesus our Savior give you grace and peace.

Titus's Work in Crete

[5]I left you on the island of Crete so you could complete our work there and appoint elders in each town as I instructed you. [6]An elder must live a blameless life. He must be faithful to his wife,* and his children must be believers who don't have a reputation for being wild or rebellious. [7]An elder* is a manager of God's household, so he must live a blameless life. He must not be arrogant or quick-tempered; he must not be a heavy drinker,* violent, or dishonest with money.

[8]Rather, he must enjoy having guests in his home, and he must love what is good. He must live wisely and be just. He must live a devout and disciplined life. [9]He must have a strong belief in the trustworthy message he was taught; then he will be able to encourage others with wholesome teaching and show those who oppose it where they are wrong.

[10]For there are many rebellious people who engage in useless talk and deceive others. This is especially true of those who insist on circumcision for salvation. [11]They must be silenced, because they are turning whole families away from the truth by their false teaching. And they do it only for money. [12]Even one of their own men, a prophet from Crete, has said about them, "The people of Crete are all liars, cruel animals, and lazy gluttons."* [13]This is true. So reprimand them sternly to make them strong in the faith. [14]They must stop listening to Jewish myths and the commands of people who have turned away from the truth.

[15]Everything is pure to those whose hearts are pure. But nothing is pure to those who are corrupt and unbelieving, because their minds and consciences are corrupted. [16]Such people claim they know God, but they deny him by the way they live. They are detestable and disobedient, worthless for doing anything good.

CHAPTER 2

Promote Right Teaching

As for you, Titus, promote the kind of living that reflects wholesome teaching. [2]Teach the older men to exercise self-control, to be worthy of respect, and to live wisely. They must have sound faith and be filled with love and patience.

[3]Similarly, teach the older women to live in a way that honors God. They must not slander others or be heavy drinkers.* Instead, they should teach others what is good. [4]These older women must train the younger women to love their husbands and their children, [5]to live wisely and be pure, to work in their homes,* to do good, and to be submissive to their husbands. Then they will not bring shame on the word of God.

[6]In the same way, encourage the young men to live wisely. [7]And you yourself must be an example to them by doing good works of every kind. Let everything you do reflect the integrity and seriousness of your teaching. [8]Teach the truth so that your teaching can't be criticized. Then those who oppose us will be ashamed and have nothing bad to say about us.

[9]Slaves must always obey their masters and do their best to please them. They must not talk back [10]or steal, but must show themselves to be entirely trustworthy and good. Then they will make the teaching about God our Savior attractive in every way.

[11]For the grace of God has been revealed, bringing salvation to all people. [12]And we are instructed to turn from godless living and sinful pleasures. We should live in this evil world with wisdom, righteousness, and devotion to God, [13]while we look forward with hope to that wonderful day when the glory of our great God and Savior, Jesus Christ, will be revealed. [14]He gave his life to free us from every kind of sin, to cleanse us, and to make us his very own people, totally committed to doing good deeds.

[15]You must teach these things and encourage the believers to do them. You have the authority to correct them when necessary, so don't let anyone disregard what you say.

CHAPTER 3

Do What Is Good

Remind the believers to submit to the government and its officers. They should be obedient, always ready to do what is good. [2]They

1:6 Or *must have only one wife,* or *must be married only once;* Greek reads *must be the husband of one wife.* **1:7a** Or *An overseer,* or *A bishop.* **1:7b** Greek *must not drink too much wine.* **1:12** This quotation is from Epimenides of Knossos. **2:3** Greek *be enslaved to much wine.* **2:5** Some manuscripts read *to care for their homes.*

must not slander anyone and must avoid
quarreling. Instead, they should be gentle and
show true humility to everyone.
[3]Once we, too, were foolish and disobedi-
ent. We were misled and became slaves to
many lusts and pleasures. Our lives were full
of evil and envy, and we hated each other.
[4]But—"When God our Savior revealed his
kindness and love, [5]he saved us, not because
of the righteous things we had done, but be-
cause of his mercy. He washed away our sins,
giving us a new birth and new life through the
Holy Spirit.* [6]He generously poured out the
Spirit upon us through Jesus Christ our Sav-
ior. [7]Because of his grace he declared us righ-
teous and gave us confidence that we will
inherit eternal life." [8]This is a trustworthy
saying, and I want you to insist on these teach-
ings so that all who trust in God will devote
themselves to doing good. These teachings
are good and beneficial for everyone.
[9]Do not get involved in foolish discussions
about spiritual pedigrees* or in quarrels and
fights about obedience to Jewish laws. These
things are useless and a waste of time. [10]If peo-
ple are causing divisions among you, give a
first and second warning. After that, have
nothing more to do with them. [11]For people
like that have turned away from the truth, and
their own sins condemn them.

Paul's Final Remarks and Greetings

[12]I am planning to send either Artemas or
Tychicus to you. As soon as one of them ar-
rives, do your best to meet me at Nicopolis,
for I have decided to stay there for the win-
ter. [13]Do everything you can to help Zenas
the lawyer and Apollos with their trip. See
that they are given everything they need.
[14]Our people must learn to do good by meet-
ing the urgent needs of others; then they will
not be unproductive.
[15]Everybody here sends greetings. Please
give my greetings to the believers—all who
love us.
May God's grace be with you all.

3:5 Greek *He saved us through the washing of regeneration and renewing of the Holy Spirit.* **3:9** Or *spiritual genealogies.*

PHILEMON

WHO
Paul, Philemon, and Onesimus.

WHERE
Paul wrote this letter from prison in Rome.

WHEN
Around AD 60 during Paul's first imprisonment in Rome.

WHY
To convince Philemon to forgive his runaway slave.

I always thank my God when I pray for you . . . because I keep hearing about your faith in the Lord Jesus and your love for all of God's people. PHILEMON 1:4-5

Onesimus, a slave who belonged to Philemon, ran away to gain freedom. He met Paul and somewhere along the way believed in Jesus! Here Paul writes a personal letter to his friend Philemon, asking him to accept his former slave as a brother.

LEARN FROM THIS SHORT LETTER ABOUT THE AWESOME CHANGES JESUS CAN MAKE IN A PERSON'S LIFE.

Greetings from Paul

This letter is from Paul, a prisoner for preaching the Good News about Christ Jesus, and from our brother Timothy.

I am writing to Philemon, our beloved co-worker, [2]and to our sister Apphia, and to our fellow soldier Archippus, and to the church that meets in your* house.

[3]May God our Father and the Lord Jesus Christ give you grace and peace.

2 Throughout this letter, *you* and *your* are singular except in verses 3, 22, and 25.

I'M NOT THE ONLY ONE!

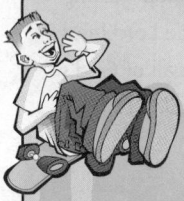

I WAS GETTING my hair cut one day. When the barber was finished, he wanted me to look at the back of my head to make sure I liked it. As I tried to look, I fell over—right out of the chair, onto the floor. I casually picked myself up and assured everyone in the shop that I was fine. I think the barber is still laughing about it.

Lighten Up!

Paul's Thanksgiving and Prayer

4 I always thank my God when I pray for you,
Philemon, 5 because I keep hearing about
your faith in the Lord Jesus and your love for
all of God's people. 6 And I am praying that you
will put into action the generosity that comes
from your faith as you understand and experience all the good things we have in Christ.
7 Your love has given me much joy and comfort, my brother, for your kindness has often
refreshed the hearts of God's people.

Paul's Appeal for Onesimus

8 That is why I am boldly asking a favor of you.
I could demand it in the name of Christ because it is the right thing for you to do. 9 But
because of our love, I prefer simply to ask you.
Consider this as a request from me—Paul, an
old man and now also a prisoner for the sake
of Christ Jesus.*

10 I appeal to you to show kindness to my
child, Onesimus. I became his father in the
faith while here in prison. 11 Onesimus*
hasn't been of much use to you in the past, but
now he is very useful to both of us. 12 I am
sending him back to you, and with him comes
my own heart.

13 I wanted to keep him here with me while
I am in these chains for preaching the Good
News, and he would have helped me on your
behalf. 14 But I didn't want to do anything
without your consent. I wanted you to help
because you were willing, not because you
were forced. 15 It seems you lost Onesimus
for a little while so that you could have him
back forever. 16 He is no longer like a slave to
you. He is more than a slave, for he is a beloved brother, especially to me. Now he will
mean much more to you, both as a man and as
a brother in the Lord.

17 So if you consider me your partner, welcome him as you would welcome me. 18 If he
has wronged you in any way or owes you anything, charge it to me. 19 I, PAUL, WRITE THIS
WITH MY OWN HAND: I WILL REPAY IT. AND I
WON'T MENTION THAT YOU OWE ME YOUR VERY
SOUL!

20 Yes, my brother, please do me this favor*
for the Lord's sake. Give me this encouragement in Christ.

21 I am confident as I write this letter that
you will do what I ask and even more! 22 One
more thing—please prepare a guest room for
me, for I am hoping that God will answer your
prayers and let me return to you soon.

Paul's Final Greetings

23 Epaphras, my fellow prisoner in Christ Jesus,
sends you his greetings. 24 So do Mark, Aristarchus, Demas, and Luke, my co-workers.

25 May the grace of the Lord Jesus Christ be
with your spirit.

9 Or *a prisoner of Christ Jesus.* **11** *Onesimus* means "useful." **20** Greek *onaimen,* a play on the name Onesimus.

Hebrews

WHO
The unknown author, Hebrew Christians, Old Testament men and women of faith mentioned in chapter 11.

WHERE
We don't know.

WHEN
Probably before the destruction of the Temple in Jerusalem in AD 70.

WHY
To explain that Jesus Christ was all the Jewish believers needed—faith in him was far superior to their old Jewish religion.

Let us run with endurance the race God has set before us.
HEBREWS 12:1

Seeing a grown-up act like a baby would seem strange, wouldn't it? But sometimes people act like babies in their spiritual lives. In the same way that little children need to grow up physically, new "baby" Christians need to grow up in their relationship with God. That's what the book of Hebrews is all about—growing up in Christ.

Whether you've been a Christian for a week or for years, you need to listen to the message in this book.

CHAPTER 1

Jesus Christ Is God's Son

Long ago God spoke many times and in many
ways to our ancestors through the prophets.
2 And now in these final days, he has spoken to
us through his Son. God promised everything
to the Son as an inheritance, and through the
Son he created the universe. 3 The Son radiates
God's own glory and expresses the very char-
acter of God, and he sustains everything by the
mighty power of his command. When he had
cleansed us from our sins, he sat down in the
place of honor at the right hand of the majestic
God in heaven. 4 This shows that the Son is far

greater than the angels, just as the name God gave him is greater than their names.

The Son Is Greater Than the Angels

5For God never said to any angel what he said to Jesus:

"You are my Son.
Today I have become your Father.*"

God also said,

"I will be his Father,
and he will be my Son."*

6And when he brought his supreme* Son into the world, God said,*

"Let all of God's angels worship him."*

7Regarding the angels, he says,

"He sends his angels like the winds,
his servants like flames of fire."*

8But to the Son he says,

"Your throne, O God, endures forever
and ever.
You rule with a scepter of justice.
9 You love justice and hate evil.
Therefore, O God, your God has
anointed you,
pouring out the oil of joy on you more
than on anyone else."*

10He also says to the Son,

"In the beginning, Lord, you laid the
foundation of the earth
and made the heavens with your
hands.
11 They will perish, but you remain
forever.
They will wear out like old clothing.
12 You will fold them up like a cloak
and discard them like old clothing.
But you are always the same;
you will live forever."*

13And God never said to any of the angels,

"Sit in the place of honor at my right hand
until I humble your enemies,
making them a footstool under your
feet."*

14Therefore, angels are only servants—spirits sent to care for people who will inherit salvation.

CHAPTER 2

A Warning against Drifting Away

So we must listen very carefully to the truth we have heard, or we may drift away from it. 2For the message God delivered through angels has always stood firm, and every violation of the law and every act of disobedience was punished. 3So what makes us think we can escape if we ignore this great salvation that was first announced by the Lord Jesus himself and then delivered to us by those who heard him speak? 4And God confirmed the message by giving signs and wonders and various miracles and gifts of the Holy Spirit whenever he chose.

Jesus, the Man

5And furthermore, it is not angels who will control the future world we are talking about. 6For in one place the Scriptures say,

"What are mere mortals that you should
think about them,
or a son of man* that you should care
for him?
7 Yet you made them only a little lower
than the angels
and crowned them with glory and
honor.*
8 You gave them authority over all
things."*

Now when it says "all things," it means nothing is left out. But we have not yet seen all things put under their authority. 9What we do see is Jesus, who was given a position "a little lower than the angels"; and because he suffered death for us, he is now "crowned with glory and honor." Yes, by God's grace, Jesus tasted death for everyone. 10God, for whom and through whom everything was made, chose to bring many children into glory. And it was only right that he should make Jesus, through his suffering, a perfect leader, fit to bring them into their salvation.

11So now Jesus and the ones he makes holy have the same Father. That is why Jesus is not

1:5a Or *Today I reveal you as my Son.* Ps 2:7. **1:5b** 2 Sam 7:14. **1:6a** Or *firstborn.* **1:6b** Or *when he again brings his supreme Son* [or *firstborn Son*] *into the world, God will say.* **1:6c** Deut 32:43. **1:7** Ps 104:4 (Greek version). **1:8-9** Ps 45:6-7. **1:10-12** Ps 102:25-27. **1:13** Ps 110:1. **2:6** Or *the Son of Man.* **2:7** Some manuscripts add *You gave them charge of everything you made.* **2:6-8** Ps 8:4-6 (Greek version).

ashamed to call them his brothers and sisters.* [12]For he said to God,

"I will proclaim your name to my brothers
and sisters.
I will praise you among your assembled
people."*

[13]He also said,

"I will put my trust in him,"
that is, "I and the children God has
given me."*

[14]Because God's children are human beings—made of flesh and blood—the Son also became flesh and blood. For only as a human being could he die, and only by dying could he break the power of the devil, who had* the power of death. [15]Only in this way could he set free all who have lived their lives as slaves to the fear of dying.

[16]We also know that the Son did not come to help angels; he came to help the descendants of Abraham. [17]Therefore, it was necessary for him to be made in every respect like us, his brothers and sisters,* so that he could be our merciful and faithful High Priest before God. Then he could offer a sacrifice that would take away the sins of the people. [18]Since he himself has gone through suffering and testing, he is able to help us when we are being tested.

CHAPTER 3

Jesus Is Greater Than Moses

And so, dear brothers and sisters who belong to God and* are partners with those called to heaven, think carefully about this Jesus whom we declare to be God's messenger* and High Priest. [2]For he was faithful to God, who appointed him, just as Moses served faithfully when he was entrusted with God's entire* house.

[3]But Jesus deserves far more glory than Moses, just as a person who builds a house deserves more praise than the house itself. [4]For every house has a builder, but the one who built everything is God.

[5]Moses was certainly faithful in God's house as a servant. His work was an illustration of the truths God would reveal later. [6]But Christ, as the Son, is in charge of God's entire house. And we are God's house, if we keep our courage and remain confident in our hope in Christ.*

[7]That is why the Holy Spirit says,

"Today when you hear his voice,
[8] don't harden your hearts
as Israel did when they rebelled,
when they tested me in the wilderness.
[9] There your ancestors tested and tried my
patience,
even though they saw my miracles for
forty years.
[10] So I was angry with them, and I said,
'Their hearts always turn away from me.
They refuse to do what I tell them.'
[11] So in my anger I took an oath:
'They will never enter my place of
rest.'"*

[12]Be careful then, dear brothers and sisters.* Make sure that your own hearts are not evil and unbelieving, turning you away from the living God. [13]You must warn each other every day, while it is still "today," so that none of you will be deceived by sin and hardened against God. [14]For if we are faithful to the end, trusting God just as firmly as when we first believed, we will share in all that belongs to Christ. [15]Remember what it says:

"Today when you hear his voice,
don't harden your hearts
as Israel did when they rebelled."*

[16]And who was it who rebelled against God, even though they heard his voice? Wasn't it the people Moses led out of Egypt? [17]And who made God angry for forty years? Wasn't it the people who sinned, whose corpses lay in the wilderness? [18]And to whom was God speaking when he took an oath that they would never enter his rest? Wasn't it the people who disobeyed him? [19]So we see that because of their unbelief they were not able to enter his rest.

CHAPTER 4

Promised Rest for God's People

God's promise of entering his rest still stands, so we ought to tremble with fear that some of

2:11 Greek *brothers;* also in 2:12. **2:12** Ps 22:22. **2:13** Isa 8:17-18. **2:14** Or *has.* **2:17** Greek *like the brothers.* **3:1a** Greek *And so, holy brothers who.* **3:1b** Greek *God's apostle.* **3:2** Some manuscripts do not include *entire.* **3:6** Some manuscripts add *faithful to the end.* **3:7-11** Ps 95:7-11. **3:12** Greek *brothers.* **3:15** Ps 95:7-8.

Living in a Bible-time Village

Can you count the houses in this Bible-time village? How many people can you find? What else do you see? If you lived in this village, your life would be much different. Do you see any stoplights? Do you see any cars or trucks? Are there any buses or trains or planes? You won't find any policemen or firemen either. You won't find a post office, bank, supermarket, or gas station. Streets are stone or dirt. Houses are made of stone with flat roofs. You won't find any blacktop or concrete. There are no sidewalks. The stores are not like ours. You'll see people selling things in little booths. Can you find the village well? People got water from it with a pot or bucket. They lowered the pot into the well and pulled the water out. You probably don't have many camels or donkeys in your town. But you'll find some here. Can you count them? What else do you see that is different from your town? Would you like to live in this Bible-time village?

you might fail to experience it. [2]For this good news—that God has prepared this rest—has been announced to us just as it was to them. But it did them no good because they didn't share the faith of those who listened to God.* [3]For only we who believe can enter his rest. As for the others, God said,

"In my anger I took an oath:
'They will never enter my place of rest,'"*

even though this rest has been ready since he made the world. [4]We know it is ready because of the place in the Scriptures where it mentions the seventh day: "On the seventh day God rested from all his work."* [5]But in the other passage God said, "They will never enter my place of rest."*

[6]So God's rest is there for people to enter, but those who first heard this good news failed to enter because they disobeyed God. [7]So God set another time for entering his rest, and that time is today. God announced this through David much later in the words already quoted:

"Today when you hear his voice,
don't harden your hearts."*

[8]Now if Joshua had succeeded in giving them this rest, God would not have spoken about another day of rest still to come. [9]So there is a special rest* still waiting for the people of God. [10]For all who have entered into God's rest have rested from their labors, just as God did after creating the world. [11]So let us do our best to enter that rest. But if we disobey God, as the people of Israel did, we will fall.

[12]For the word of God is alive and powerful. It is sharper than the sharpest two-edged sword, cutting between soul and spirit, between joint and marrow. It exposes our innermost thoughts and desires. [13]Nothing in all creation is hidden from God. Everything is naked and exposed before his eyes, and he is the one to whom we are accountable.

Christ Is Our High Priest

[14]So then, since we have a great High Priest who has entered heaven, Jesus the Son of God, let us hold firmly to what we believe. [15]This High Priest of ours understands our weaknesses, for he faced all of the same testings we do, yet he did not sin. [16]So let us come boldly to the throne of our gracious God. There we will receive his mercy, and we will find grace to help us when we need it most.

CHAPTER 5

Every high priest is a man chosen to represent other people in their dealings with God. He presents their gifts to God and offers sacrifices for their sins. [2]And he is able to deal gently with ignorant and wayward people because he himself is subject to the same weaknesses. [3]That is why he must offer sacrifices for his own sins as well as theirs.

[4]And no one can become a high priest simply because he wants such an honor. He must be called by God for this work, just as Aaron was. [5]That is why Christ did not honor himself by assuming he could become High Priest. No, he was chosen by God, who said to him,

"You are my Son.
Today I have become your Father.*"

[6]And in another passage God said to him,

"You are a priest forever in the order of Melchizedek."*

[7]While Jesus was here on earth, he offered prayers and pleadings, with a loud cry and tears, to the one who could rescue him from death. And God heard his prayers because of

I'm afraid to ask God for help. He may think my problems are dumb.

Let us come boldly to the throne of our gracious God. There we will receive his mercy, and we will find grace to help us when we need it most. HEBREWS 4:16

4:2 Some manuscripts read *they didn't combine what they heard with faith.* **4:3** Ps 95:11. **4:4** Gen 2:2. **4:5** Ps 95:11. **4:7** Ps 95:7-8. **4:9** Or *a Sabbath rest.* **5:5** Or *Today I reveal you as my Son.* Ps 2:7. **5:6** Ps 110:4.

NO ONE WILL KNOW

Joshua was with his big brother and some of his brother's friends at a video-game arcade. They were having a blast talking, listening to music, playing games, and devouring snacks. Then the group decided to lie about their ages and order some beer. They looked mature and thought they could get away with it. Joshua knew his parents would be furious. But he was having fun and decided to go along with the others. Joshua thought, *Mom and Dad aren't here, so no one will ever know.* Is Joshua right to think that it's OK because no one will ever know? Before you answer, check out Hebrews 4:13.

his deep reverence for God. [8]Even though Jesus was God's Son, he learned obedience from the things he suffered. [9]In this way, God qualified him as a perfect High Priest, and he became the source of eternal salvation for all those who obey him. [10]And God designated him to be a High Priest in the order of Melchizedek.

A Call to Spiritual Growth

[11]There is much more we would like to say about this, but it is difficult to explain, especially since you are spiritually dull and don't seem to listen. [12]You have been believers so long now that you ought to be teaching others. Instead, you need someone to teach you again the basic things about God's word.* You are like babies who need milk and cannot eat solid food. [13]For someone who lives on milk is still an infant and doesn't know how to do what is right. [14]Solid food is for those who are mature, who through training have the skill to recognize the difference between right and wrong.

CHAPTER 6

So let us stop going over the basic teachings about Christ again and again. Let us go on instead and become mature in our understanding. Surely we don't need to start again with the fundamental importance of repenting from evil deeds* and placing our faith in God. [2]You don't need further instruction about baptisms, the laying on of hands, the resurrection of the dead, and eternal judgment. [3]And so, God willing, we will move forward to further understanding.

[4]For it is impossible to bring back to repentance those who were once enlightened—those who have experienced the good things of heaven and shared in the Holy Spirit, [5]who have tasted the goodness of the word of God and the power of the age to come—[6]and who then turn away from God. It is impossible to bring such people back to repentance; by rejecting the Son of God, they themselves are nailing him to the cross once again and holding him up to public shame.

[7]When the ground soaks up the falling rain and bears a good crop for the farmer, it has God's blessing. [8]But if a field bears thorns and thistles, it is useless. The farmer will soon condemn that field and burn it.

[9]Dear friends, even though we are talking this way, we really don't believe it applies to you. We are confident that you are meant for

5:12 Or *about the oracles of God.* **6:1** Greek *from dead works.*

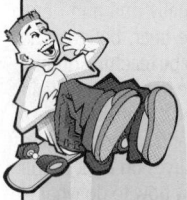

AT LUNCH ONE DAY some older girls were picking on a younger girl. So I went over and told them to stop. I think the younger girl had a crush on me. She acted thrilled that I had rescued her. My friends laughed when she kept smiling at me. I finally went back to her table and told her to stop looking at me and smiling. I guess I embarrassed her—and myself—even more when I said that!

Lighten Up!

better things, things that come with salvation. [10]For God is not unjust. He will not forget how hard you have worked for him and how you have shown your love to him by caring for other believers,* as you still do. [11]Our great desire is that you will keep on loving others as long as life lasts, in order to make certain that what you hope for will come true. [12]Then you will not become spiritually dull and indifferent. Instead, you will follow the example of those who are going to inherit God's promises because of their faith and endurance.

God's Promises Bring Hope

[13]For example, there was God's promise to Abraham. Since there was no one greater to swear by, God took an oath in his own name, saying:

[14] "I will certainly bless you,
and I will multiply your descendants
beyond number."*

[15]Then Abraham waited patiently, and he received what God had promised.

[16]Now when people take an oath, they call on someone greater than themselves to hold them to it. And without any question that oath is binding. [17]God also bound himself with an oath, so that those who received the promise could be perfectly sure that he would never change his mind. [18]So God has given both his promise and his oath. These two things are unchangeable because it is impossible for God to lie. Therefore, we who have fled to him for refuge can have great confidence as we hold to the hope that lies before us. [19]This hope is a strong and trustworthy anchor for our souls. It leads us through the curtain into God's inner sanctuary. [20]Jesus has already gone in there for us. He has become our eternal High Priest in the order of Melchizedek.

CHAPTER 7

Melchizedek Is Greater Than Abraham

This Melchizedek was king of the city of Salem and also a priest of God Most High. When Abraham was returning home after winning a great battle against the kings, Melchizedek met him and blessed him. [2]Then Abraham took a tenth of all he had captured in battle and gave it to Melchizedek. The name Melchizedek means "king of justice," and king of Salem means "king of peace." [3]There is no record of his father or mother or any of his ancestors—no beginning or end to his life. He remains a priest forever, resembling the Son of God.

[4]Consider then how great this Melchizedek was. Even Abraham, the great patriarch of Israel, recognized this by giving him a tenth of what he had taken in battle. [5]Now the law of Moses required that the priests, who are descendants of Levi, must collect a tithe from the rest of the people of Israel,* who are also descendants of Abraham. [6]But Melchizedek, who was not a descendant of Levi, collected a tenth from Abraham. And Melchizedek

6:10 Greek *for God's holy people.* **6:14** Gen 22:17. **7:5** Greek *from their brothers.*

placed a blessing upon Abraham, the one who had already received the promises of God. [7]And without question, the person who has the power to give a blessing is greater than the one who is blessed.

[8]The priests who collect tithes are men who die, so Melchizedek is greater than they are, because we are told that he lives on. [9]In addition, we might even say that these Levites—the ones who collect the tithe—paid a tithe to Melchizedek when their ancestor Abraham paid a tithe to him. [10]For although Levi wasn't born yet, the seed from which he came was in Abraham's body when Melchizedek collected the tithe from him.

[11]So if the priesthood of Levi, on which the law was based, could have achieved the perfection God intended, why did God need to establish a different priesthood, with a priest in the order of Melchizedek instead of the order of Levi and Aaron?*

[12]And if the priesthood is changed, the law must also be changed to permit it. [13]For the priest we are talking about belongs to a different tribe, whose members have never served at the altar as priests. [14]What I mean is, our Lord came from the tribe of Judah, and Moses never mentioned priests coming from that tribe.

Jesus Is like Melchizedek

[15]This change has been made very clear since a different priest, who is like Melchizedek, has appeared. [16]Jesus became a priest, not by meeting the physical requirement of belonging to the tribe of Levi, but by the power of a life that cannot be destroyed. [17]And the psalmist pointed this out when he prophesied,

> "You are a priest forever in the order of Melchizedek."*

[18]Yes, the old requirement about the priesthood was set aside because it was weak and useless. [19]For the law never made anything perfect. But now we have confidence in a better hope, through which we draw near to God.

[20]This new system was established with a solemn oath. Aaron's descendants became priests without such an oath, [21]but there was an oath regarding Jesus. For God said to him,

> "The LORD has taken an oath and will not break his vow:
> 'You are a priest forever.'"*

[22]Because of this oath, Jesus is the one who guarantees this better covenant with God.

[23]There were many priests under the old system, for death prevented them from remaining in office. [24]But because Jesus lives forever, his priesthood lasts forever. [25]Therefore he is able, once and forever, to save* those who come to God through him. He lives forever to intercede with God on their behalf.

[26]He is the kind of high priest we need because he is holy and blameless, unstained by sin. He has been set apart from sinners and has been given the highest place of honor in heaven.* [27]Unlike those other high priests, he does not need to offer sacrifices every day. They did this for their own sins first and then for the sins of the people. But Jesus did this once for all when he offered himself as the sacrifice for the people's sins. [28]The law appointed high priests who were limited by human weakness. But after the law was given, God appointed his Son with an oath, and his Son has been made the perfect High Priest forever.

CHAPTER 8

Christ Is Our High Priest

Here is the main point: We have a High Priest who sat down in the place of honor beside the throne of the majestic God in heaven. [2]There he ministers in the heavenly Tabernacle,* the true place of worship that was built by the Lord and not by human hands.

[3]And since every high priest is required to offer gifts and sacrifices, our High Priest must make an offering, too. [4]If he were here on earth, he would not even be a priest, since there already are priests who offer the gifts required by the law. [5]They serve in a system of worship that is only a copy, a shadow of the real one in heaven. For when Moses was getting ready to build the Tabernacle, God gave him this warning: "Be sure that you make everything according to the pattern I have shown you here on the mountain."*

[6]But now Jesus, our High Priest, has been given a ministry that is far superior to the old

7:11 Greek *the order of Aaron?* **7:17** Ps 110:4. **7:21** Ps 110:4. **7:25** Or *is able to save completely.* **7:26** Or *has been exalted higher than the heavens.* **8:2** Or *tent;* also in 8:5. **8:5** Exod 25:40; 26:30.

priesthood, for he is the one who mediates
for us a far better covenant with God, based
on better promises.

7 If the first covenant had been faultless,
there would have been no need for a second
covenant to replace it. 8 But when God found
fault with the people, he said:

"The day is coming, says the LORD,
when I will make a new covenant
with the people of Israel and Judah.
9 This covenant will not be like the one
I made with their ancestors
when I took them by the hand
and led them out of the land of Egypt.
They did not remain faithful to my
covenant,
so I turned my back on them, says the
LORD.
10 But this is the new covenant I will make
with the people of Israel on that day,*
says the LORD:
I will put my laws in their minds,
and I will write them on their hearts.
I will be their God,
and they will be my people.
11 And they will not need to teach their
neighbors,
nor will they need to teach their
relatives,*
saying, 'You should know the LORD.'
For everyone, from the least to the
greatest,
will know me already.
12 And I will forgive their wickedness,
and I will never again remember their
sins."*

13 When God speaks of a "new" covenant, it
means he has made the first one obsolete. It is
now out of date and will soon disappear.

CHAPTER 9

Old Rules about Worship

That first covenant between God and Israel
had regulations for worship and a place of
worship here on earth. 2 There were two
rooms in that Tabernacle.* In the first room
were a lampstand, a table, and sacred loaves
of bread on the table. This room was called
the Holy Place. 3 Then there was a curtain, and
behind the curtain was the second room*
called the Most Holy Place. 4 In that room
were a gold incense altar and a wooden chest
called the Ark of the Covenant, which was
covered with gold on all sides. Inside the Ark
were a gold jar containing manna, Aaron's
staff that sprouted leaves, and the stone tab-
lets of the covenant. 5 Above the Ark were the
cherubim of divine glory, whose wings
stretched out over the Ark's cover, the place
of atonement. But we cannot explain these
things in detail now.

6 When these things were all in place, the
priests regularly entered the first room* as
they performed their religious duties. 7 But
only the high priest ever entered the Most
Holy Place, and only once a year. And he al-
ways offered blood for his own sins and for
the sins the people had committed in igno-
rance. 8 By these regulations the Holy Spirit
revealed that the entrance to the Most Holy
Place was not freely open as long as the Tab-
ernacle* and the system it represented were
still in use.

9 This is an illustration pointing to the pres-
ent time. For the gifts and sacrifices that the
priests offer are not able to cleanse the con-
sciences of the people who bring them. 10 For
that old system deals only with food and
drink and various cleansing ceremonies—
physical regulations that were in effect only
until a better system could be established.

Christ Is the Perfect Sacrifice

11 So Christ has now become the High Priest
over all the good things that have come.* He
has entered that greater, more perfect Taber-
nacle in heaven, which was not made by hu-
man hands and is not part of this created
world. 12 With his own blood—not the blood
of goats and calves—he entered the Most
Holy Place once for all time and secured our
redemption forever.

13 Under the old system, the blood of goats
and bulls and the ashes of a young cow could
cleanse people's bodies from ceremonial im-
purity. 14 Just think how much more the blood
of Christ will purify our consciences from sin-
ful deeds* so that we can worship the living
God. For by the power of the eternal Spirit,

8:10 Greek *after those days.* **8:11** Greek *their brother.* **8:8-12** Jer 31:31-34. **9:2** Or *tent;* also in 9:11, 21. **9:3** Greek *second tent.* **9:6** Greek *first tent.* **9:8** Or *the first room;* Greek reads *the first tent.* **9:11** Some manuscripts read *that are about to come.* **9:14** Greek *from dead works.*

Christ offered himself to God as a perfect sacrifice for our sins. [15]That is why he is the one who mediates a new covenant between God and people, so that all who are called can receive the eternal inheritance God has promised them. For Christ died to set them free from the penalty of the sins they had committed under that first covenant.

[16]Now when someone leaves a will,* it is necessary to prove that the person who made it is dead.* [17]The will goes into effect only after the person's death. While the person who made it is still alive, the will cannot be put into effect.

[18]That is why even the first covenant was put into effect with the blood of an animal. [19]For after Moses had read each of God's commandments to all the people, he took the blood of calves and goats,* along with water, and sprinkled both the book of God's law and all the people, using hyssop branches and scarlet wool. [20]Then he said, "This blood confirms the covenant God has made with you."* [21]And in the same way, he sprinkled blood on the Tabernacle and on everything used for worship. [22]In fact, according to the law of Moses, nearly everything was purified with blood. For without the shedding of blood, there is no forgiveness.

[23]That is why the Tabernacle and everything in it, which were copies of things in heaven, had to be purified by the blood of animals. But the real things in heaven had to be purified with far better sacrifices than the blood of animals.

[24]For Christ did not enter into a holy place made with human hands, which was only a copy of the true one in heaven. He entered into heaven itself to appear now before God on our behalf. [25]And he did not enter heaven to offer himself again and again, like the high priest here on earth who enters the Most Holy Place year after year with the blood of an animal. [26]If that had been necessary, Christ would have had to die again and again, ever since the world began. But now, once for all time, he has appeared at the end of the age* to remove sin by his own death as a sacrifice.

[27]And just as each person is destined to die once and after that comes judgment, [28]so also Christ died once for all time as a sacrifice to take away the sins of many people. He will come again, not to deal with our sins, but to bring salvation to all who are eagerly waiting for him.

CHAPTER 10

Christ's Sacrifice Once for All

The old system under the law of Moses was only a shadow, a dim preview of the good things to come, not the good things themselves. The sacrifices under that system were repeated again and again, year after year, but they were never able to provide perfect cleansing for those who came to worship. [2]If they could have provided perfect cleansing, the sacrifices would have stopped, for the worshipers would have been purified once for all time, and their feelings of guilt would have disappeared.

[3]But instead, those sacrifices actually reminded them of their sins year after year. [4]For it is not possible for the blood of bulls and goats to take away sins. [5]That is why, when Christ* came into the world, he said to God,

"You did not want animal sacrifices or sin offerings.
But you have given me a body to offer.
[6] You were not pleased with burnt offerings
or other offerings for sin.
[7] Then I said, 'Look, I have come to do your
will, O God—
as is written about me in the
Scriptures.'"*

[8]First, Christ said, "You did not want animal sacrifices or sin offerings or burnt offerings or other offerings for sin, nor were you pleased with them" (though they are required by the law of Moses). [9]Then he said, "Look, I have come to do your will." He cancels the first covenant in order to put the second into effect. [10]For God's will was for us to be made holy by the sacrifice of the body of Jesus Christ, once for all time.

[11]Under the old covenant, the priest stands and ministers before the altar day after day, offering the same sacrifices again and again, which can never take away sins. [12]But our

9:16a Or *covenant;* also in 9:17. **9:16b** Or *Now when someone makes a covenant, it is necessary to ratify it with the death of a sacrifice.* **9:19** Some manuscripts do not include *and goats.* **9:20** Exod 24:8. **9:26** Greek *the ages.* **10:5** Greek *he;* also in 10:8. **10:5-7** Ps 40:6-8 (Greek version).

High Priest offered himself to God as a single sacrifice for sins, good for all time. Then he sat down in the place of honor at God's right hand. [13]There he waits until his enemies are humbled and made a footstool under his feet. [14]For by that one offering he forever made perfect those who are being made holy.

[15]And the Holy Spirit also testifies that this is so. For he says,

[16] "This is the new covenant I will make
with my people on that day,* says the LORD:
I will put my laws in their hearts,
and I will write them on their minds."*

[17]Then he says,

"I will never again remember
their sins and lawless deeds."*

[18]And when sins have been forgiven, there is no need to offer any more sacrifices.

A Call to Persevere

[19]And so, dear brothers and sisters,* we can boldly enter heaven's Most Holy Place because of the blood of Jesus. [20]By his death,* Jesus opened a new and life-giving way through the curtain into the Most Holy Place. [21]And since we have a great High Priest who rules over God's house, [22]let us go right into the presence of God with sincere hearts fully-trusting him. For our guilty consciences have been sprinkled with Christ's blood to make us clean, and our bodies have been washed with pure water.

[23]Let us hold tightly without wavering to the hope we affirm, for God can be trusted to keep his promise. [24]Let us think of ways to motivate one another to acts of love and good works. [25]And let us not neglect our meeting together, as some people do, but encourage one another, especially now that the day of his return is drawing near.

[26]Dear friends, if we deliberately continue sinning after we have received knowledge of the truth, there is no longer any sacrifice that will cover these sins. [27]There is only the terrible expectation of God's judgment and the raging fire that will consume his enemies. [28]For anyone who refused to obey the law of Moses was put to death without mercy on the testimony of two or three witnesses. [29]Just think how much worse the punishment will be for those who have trampled on the Son of God, and have treated the blood of the covenant, which made us holy, as if it were com-

10:16a Greek *after those days.* **10:16b** Jer 31:33a. **10:17** Jer 31:34b. **10:19** Greek *brothers.* **10:20** Greek *Through his flesh.*

IS IT OK?

IS IT OK IF I THINK CHURCH IS BORING?

Name one place in the world that's fun all the time. Disney World? Nope, not when they're cleaning gum off the rides. The beach? Not during a hurricane. Your friend's house? Not when your friend's mom is having a rotten day. Sometimes church is fun and exciting, and sometimes it may seem dull and boring. But even if you don't always *feel* like going, it's not OK to bail (read Hebrews 10:25). As imperfect as the church sometimes is, God loves it when his people gather to worship and learn about him. Since you are part of the church, do your part to make it fun. Obey God by going and having a good attitude about being in his house.

mon and unholy, and have insulted and disdained the Holy Spirit who brings God's mercy to us. [30]For we know the one who said,

"I will take revenge.
I will pay them back."*

He also said,

"The LORD will judge his own people."*

[31]It is a terrible thing to fall into the hands of the living God.

[32]Think back on those early days when you first learned about Christ.* Remember how you remained faithful even though it meant terrible suffering. [33]Sometimes you were exposed to public ridicule and were beaten, and sometimes you helped others who were suffering the same things. [34]You suffered along with those who were thrown into jail, and when all you owned was taken from you, you accepted it with joy. You knew there were better things waiting for you that will last forever.

[35]So do not throw away this confident trust in the Lord. Remember the great reward it brings you! [36]Patient endurance is what you need now, so that you will continue to do God's will. Then you will receive all that he has promised.

[37] "For in just a little while,
the Coming One will come and not delay.
[38] And my righteous ones will live by faith.*
But I will take no pleasure in anyone who turns away."*

[39]But we are not like those who turn away from God to their own destruction. We are the faithful ones, whose souls will be saved.

CHAPTER 11

Great Examples of Faith

Faith is the confidence that what we hope for will actually happen; it gives us assurance about things we cannot see. [2]Through their faith, the people in days of old earned a good reputation.

[3]By faith we understand that the entire universe was formed at God's command, that what we now see did not come from anything that can be seen.

[4]It was by faith that Abel brought a more acceptable offering to God than Cain did. Abel's offering gave evidence that he was a righteous man, and God showed his approval of his gifts. Although Abel is long dead, he still speaks to us by his example of faith.

AMAZING FACTS

To be a superhero in God's eyes, all it takes is FAITH—as long as it's God in whom we put our faith.

HEBREWS 10:35–11:40

[5]It was by faith that Enoch was taken up to heaven without dying—"he disappeared, because God took him."* For before he was taken up, he was known as a person who pleased God. [6]And it is impossible to please God without faith. Anyone who wants to come to him must believe that God exists and that he rewards those who sincerely seek him.

[7]It was by faith that Noah built a large boat to save his family from the flood. He obeyed God, who warned him about things that had never happened before. By his faith Noah condemned the rest of the world, and he received the righteousness that comes by faith.

[8]It was by faith that Abraham obeyed when God called him to leave home and go to another land that God would give him as his inheritance. He went without knowing where he was going. [9]And even when he reached the land God promised him, he lived there by faith—for he was like a foreigner, living in tents. And so did Isaac and Jacob, who inherited the same promise. [10]Abraham was confidently looking forward to a city with eternal foundations, a city designed and built by God.

[11]It was by faith that even Sarah was able to have a child, though she was barren and was

10:30a Deut 32:35. **10:30b** Deut 32:36. **10:32** Greek *when you were first enlightened.* **10:38** Or *my righteous ones will live by their faithfulness;* Greek reads *my righteous one will live by faith.* **10:37-38** Hab 2:3-4. **11:5** Gen 5:24.

too old. She believed* that God would keep
his promise. [12]And so a whole nation came
from this one man who was as good as dead—
a nation with so many people that, like the
stars in the sky and the sand on the seashore,
there is no way to count them.

[13]All these people died still believing what
God had promised them. They did not receive
what was promised, but they saw it all from a
distance and welcomed it. They agreed that
they were foreigners and nomads here on
earth. [14]Obviously people who say such things
are looking forward to a country they can call
their own. [15]If they had longed for the country they came from, they could have gone
back. [16]But they were looking for a better
place, a heavenly homeland. That is why God
is not ashamed to be called their God, for he
has prepared a city for them.

[17]It was by faith that Abraham offered
Isaac as a sacrifice when God was testing him.
Abraham, who had received God's promises,
was ready to sacrifice his only son, Isaac,
[18]even though God had told him, "Isaac is the
son through whom your descendants will be
counted."* [19]Abraham reasoned that if Isaac
died, God was able to bring him back to life
again. And in a sense, Abraham did receive
his son back from the dead.

[20]It was by faith that Isaac promised blessings for the future to his sons, Jacob and Esau.

[21]It was by faith that Jacob, when he was old
and dying, blessed each of Joseph's sons and
bowed in worship as he leaned on his staff.

[22]It was by faith that Joseph, when he was
about to die, said confidently that the people
of Israel would leave Egypt. He even commanded them to take his bones with them
when they left.

[23]It was by faith that Moses' parents hid
him for three months when he was born.
They saw that God had given them an unusual
child, and they were not afraid to disobey the
king's command.

[24]It was by faith that Moses, when he grew
up, refused to be called the son of Pharaoh's
daughter. [25]He chose to share the oppression
of God's people instead of enjoying the fleeting pleasures of sin. [26]He thought it was better
to suffer for the sake of Christ than to own the
treasures of Egypt, for he was looking ahead to
his great reward. [27]It was by faith that Moses
left the land of Egypt, not fearing the king's
anger. He kept right on going because he kept
his eyes on the one who is invisible. [28]It was by
faith that Moses commanded the people of Israel to keep the Passover and to sprinkle blood
on the doorposts so that the angel of death
would not kill their firstborn sons.

[29]It was by faith that the people of Israel
went right through the Red Sea as though
they were on dry ground. But when the Egyptians tried to follow, they were all drowned.

[30]It was by faith that the people of Israel
marched around Jericho for seven days, and
the walls came crashing down.

[31]It was by faith that Rahab the prostitute
was not destroyed with the people in her city
who refused to obey God. For she had given a
friendly welcome to the spies.

[32]How much more do I need to say? It
would take too long to recount the stories of
the faith of Gideon, Barak, Samson, Jephthah,
David, Samuel, and all the prophets. [33]By faith
these people overthrew kingdoms, ruled with
justice, and received what God had promised
them. They shut the mouths of lions,
[34]quenched the flames of fire, and escaped
death by the edge of the sword. Their weakness was turned to strength. They became
strong in battle and put whole armies to
flight. [35]Women received their loved ones
back again from death.

But others were tortured, refusing to turn
from God in order to be set free. They placed
their hope in a better life after the resurrection. [36]Some were jeered at, and their backs
were cut open with whips. Others were
chained in prisons. [37]Some died by stoning,
some were sawed in half,* and others were
killed with the sword. Some went about wearing skins of sheep and goats, destitute and oppressed and mistreated. [38]They were too good
for this world, wandering over deserts and
mountains, hiding in caves and holes in the
ground.

[39]All these people earned a good reputation because of their faith, yet none of them
received all that God had promised. [40]For God
had something better in mind for us, so that
they would not reach perfection without us.

11:11 Or *It was by faith that he [Abraham] was able to have a child, even though Sarah was barren and he was too old. He believed.*
11:18 Gen 21:12. **11:37** Some manuscripts add *some were tested.*

CHAPTER 12

God's Discipline Proves His Love

Therefore, since we are surrounded by such a huge crowd of witnesses to the life of faith, let us strip off every weight that slows us down, especially the sin that so easily trips us up. And let us run with endurance the race God has set before us. [2]We do this by keeping our eyes on Jesus, the champion who initiates and perfects our faith.* Because of the joy* awaiting him, he endured the cross, disregarding its shame. Now he is seated in the place of honor beside God's throne. [3]Think of all the hostility he endured from sinful people;* then you won't become weary and give up. [4]After all, you have not yet given your lives in your struggle against sin.

[5]And have you forgotten the encouraging words God spoke to you as his children?* He said,

"My child,* don't make light of the
LORD's discipline,
and don't give up when he
corrects you.
[6] For the LORD disciplines those he loves,
and he punishes each one he accepts
as his child."*

[7]As you endure this divine discipline, remember that God is treating you as his own children. Who ever heard of a child who is never disciplined by its father? [8]If God doesn't discipline you as he does all of his children, it means that you are illegitimate and are not really his children at all. [9]Since we respected our earthly fathers who disciplined us, shouldn't we submit even more to the discipline of the Father of our spirits, and live forever?*

[10]For our earthly fathers disciplined us for a few years, doing the best they knew how. But God's discipline is always good for us, so that we might share in his holiness. [11]No discipline is enjoyable while it is happening—it's painful! But afterward there will be a peaceful harvest of right living for those who are trained in this way.

[12]So take a new grip with your tired hands and strengthen your weak knees. [13]Mark out a straight path for your feet so that those who are weak and lame will not fall but become strong.

A Call to Listen to God

[14]Work at living in peace with everyone, and work at living a holy life, for those who are not holy will not see the Lord. [15]Look after each other so that none of you fails to receive the grace of God. Watch out that no poisonous root of bitterness grows up to trouble you, corrupting many. [16]Make sure that no one is immoral or godless like Esau, who traded his birthright as the firstborn son for a single meal. [17]You know that afterward, when he wanted his father's blessing, he was rejected. It was too late for repentance, even though he begged with bitter tears.

[18]You have not come to a physical mountain,* to a place of flaming fire, darkness, gloom, and whirlwind, as the Israelites did at Mount Sinai. [19]For they heard an awesome trumpet blast and a voice so terrible that they begged God to stop speaking. [20]They staggered back under God's command: "If even an animal touches the mountain, it must be stoned to death."* [21]Moses himself was so frightened at the sight that he said, "I am terrified and trembling."*

[22]No, you have come to Mount Zion, to the city of the living God, the heavenly Jerusalem, and to countless thousands of angels in a joyful gathering. [23]You have come to the assembly of God's firstborn children, whose names are written in heaven. You have come to God himself, who is the judge over all things. You have come to the spirits of the righteous ones in heaven who have now been made perfect. [24]You have come to Jesus, the one who mediates the new covenant between God and people, and to the sprinkled blood, which speaks of forgiveness instead of crying out for vengeance like the blood of Abel.

[25]Be careful that you do not refuse to listen to the One who is speaking. For if the people of Israel did not escape when they refused to listen to Moses, the earthly messenger, we will certainly not escape if we reject the One who speaks to us from heaven! [26]When God spoke from Mount Sinai his voice shook the earth, but now he makes another promise: "Once

12:2a Or *Jesus, the originator and perfecter of our faith.* **12:2b** Or *Instead of the joy.* **12:3** Some manuscripts read *Think of how people hurt themselves by opposing him.* **12:5a** Greek *sons;* also in 12:7, 8. **12:5b** Greek *son;* also in 12:6, 7. **12:5-6** Prov 3:11-12 (Greek version). **12:9** Or *and really live?* **12:18** Greek *to something that can be touched.* **12:20** Exod 19:13. **12:21** Deut 9:19.

again I will shake not only the earth but the heavens also."* [27]This means that all of creation will be shaken and removed, so that only unshakable things will remain.

[28]Since we are receiving a Kingdom that is unshakable, let us be thankful and please God by worshiping him with holy fear and awe. [29]For our God is a devouring fire.

CHAPTER 13

Concluding Words

Keep on loving each other as brothers and sisters.* [2]Don't forget to show hospitality to strangers, for some who have done this have entertained angels without realizing it! [3]Remember those in prison, as if you were there yourself. Remember also those being mistreated, as if you felt their pain in your own bodies.

[4]Give honor to marriage, and remain faithful to one another in marriage. God will surely judge people who are immoral and those who commit adultery.

[5]Don't love money; be satisfied with what you have. For God has said,

"I will never fail you.
I will never abandon you."*

[6]So we can say with confidence,

"The LORD is my helper,
so I will have no fear.
What can mere people do to me?"*

[7]Remember your leaders who taught you the word of God. Think of all the good that has come from their lives, and follow the example of their faith.

[8]Jesus Christ is the same yesterday, today, and forever. [9]So do not be attracted by strange, new ideas. Your strength comes from God's grace, not from rules about food, which don't help those who follow them.

[10]We have an altar from which the priests in the Tabernacle* have no right to eat. [11]Under the old system, the high priest brought the blood of animals into the Holy Place as a sacrifice for sin, and the bodies of the animals were burned outside the camp. [12]So also Jesus suffered and died outside the city gates to make his people holy by means of his own blood. [13]So let us go out to him, outside the camp, and bear the disgrace he bore. [14]For this world is not our permanent home; we are looking forward to a home yet to come.

[15]Therefore, let us offer through Jesus a continual sacrifice of praise to God, proclaiming our allegiance to his name. [16]And don't forget to do good and to share with those in need. These are the sacrifices that please God.

[17]Obey your spiritual leaders, and do what they say. Their work is to watch over your souls, and they are accountable to God. Give them reason to do this with joy and not with sorrow. That would certainly not be for your benefit.

[18]Pray for us, for our conscience is clear and we want to live honorably in everything we do. [19]And especially pray that I will be able to come back to you soon.

[20] Now may the God of peace—
who brought up from the dead our
Lord Jesus,
the great Shepherd of the sheep,
and ratified an eternal covenant with
his blood—
[21] may he equip you with all you need
for doing his will.
May he produce in you,*
through the power of Jesus Christ,
every good thing that is pleasing to him.
All glory to him forever and ever!
Amen.

[22]I urge you, dear brothers and sisters,* to pay attention to what I have written in this brief exhortation.

[23]I want you to know that our brother Timothy has been released from jail. If he comes here soon, I will bring him with me to see you.

[24]Greet all your leaders and all the believers there.* The believers from Italy send you their greetings.

[25]May God's grace be with you all.

12:26 Hag 2:6. **13:1** Greek *Continue in brotherly love*. **13:5** Deut 31:6, 8. **13:6** Ps 118:6. **13:10** Or *tent*. **13:21** Some manuscripts read *in us*. **13:22** Greek *brothers*. **13:24** Greek *all of God's holy people*.

James

WHO
James, the author, was Jesus' brother and a leader of the church of Jerusalem.

WHERE
Written to believers everywhere from Jerusalem.

WHEN
Probably in AD 49.

WHY
To teach that real faith makes a difference in how people live.

Don't just listen to God's word. You must do what it says. Otherwise, you are only fooling yourselves.
JAMES 1:22

Sometimes people say they believe in God and go to church, but they don't live the way true Christians should live. Their "walk" doesn't match their "talk." James speaks out against that kind of living and boldly tells Christians to shape up, watch what they say, and do good deeds.

ARE YOU A TALKER OR A DOER? FIND OUT HOW CHRISTIANS ARE REALLY SUPPOSED TO LIVE!

CHAPTER **1**

Greetings from James

This letter is from James, a slave of God and of the Lord Jesus Christ.

I am writing to the "twelve tribes"—Jewish believers scattered abroad.

Greetings!

Faith and Endurance

[2]Dear brothers and sisters,* when troubles come your way, consider it an opportunity for great joy. [3]For you know that when your faith

1:2 Greek *brothers;* also in 1:16, 19.

is tested, your endurance has a chance to grow. [4]So let it grow, for when your endurance is fully developed, you will be perfect and complete, needing nothing.

[5]If you need wisdom, ask our generous God, and he will give it to you. He will not rebuke you for asking. [6]But when you ask him, be sure that your faith is in God alone. Do not waver, for a person with divided loyalty is as unsettled as a wave of the sea that is blown and tossed by the wind. [7]Such people should not expect to receive anything from the Lord. [8]Their loyalty is divided between God and the world, and they are unstable in everything they do.

[9]Believers who are* poor have something to boast about, for God has honored them. [10]And those who are rich should boast that God has humbled them. They will fade away like a little flower in the field. [11]The hot sun rises and the grass withers; the little flower droops and falls, and its beauty fades away. In the same way, the rich will fade away with all of their achievements.

[12]God blesses those who patiently endure testing and temptation. Afterward they will receive the crown of life that God has promised to those who love him. [13]And remember, when you are being tempted, do not say, "God is tempting me." God is never tempted to do wrong,* and he never tempts anyone else. [14]Temptation comes from our own desires, which entice us and drag us away. [15]These desires give birth to sinful actions. And when sin is allowed to grow, it gives birth to death.

[16]So don't be misled, my dear brothers and sisters. [17]Whatever is good and perfect comes down to us from God our Father, who created all the lights in the heavens.* He never changes or casts a shifting shadow.* [18]He chose to give birth to us by giving us his true word. And we, out of all creation, became his prized possession.*

Listening and Doing

[19]Understand this, my dear brothers and sisters: You must all be quick to listen, slow to speak, and slow to get angry. [20]Human anger* does not produce the righteousness* God desires. [21]So get rid of all the filth and evil in your lives, and humbly accept the word God has planted in your hearts, for it has the power to save your souls.

[22]But don't just listen to God's word. You must do what it says. Otherwise, you are only fooling yourselves. [23]For if you listen to the word and don't obey, it is like glancing at your face in a mirror. [24]You see yourself, walk away, and forget what you look like. [25]But if you look carefully into the perfect law that sets you free, and if you do what it says and don't forget what you heard, then God will bless you for doing it.

[26]If you claim to be religious but don't control your tongue, you are fooling yourself, and your religion is worthless. [27]Pure and genuine religion in the sight of God the Father means caring for orphans and widows in their distress and refusing to let the world corrupt you.

CHAPTER 2

A Warning against Prejudice

My dear brothers and sisters,* how can you claim to have faith in our glorious Lord Jesus Christ if you favor some people over others?

[2]For example, suppose someone comes into your meeting* dressed in fancy clothes and expensive jewelry, and another comes in who is poor and dressed in dirty clothes. [3]If you give special attention and a good seat to the rich person, but you say to the poor one, "You can stand over there, or else sit on the floor"—well, [4]doesn't this discrimination show that your judgments are guided by evil motives?

[5]Listen to me, dear brothers and sisters. Hasn't God chosen the poor in this world to be rich in faith? Aren't they the ones who will inherit the Kingdom he promised to those who love him? [6]But you dishonor the poor! Isn't it the rich who oppress you and drag you into court? [7]Aren't they the ones who slander Jesus Christ, whose noble name* you bear?

[8]Yes indeed, it is good when you obey the royal law as found in the Scriptures: "Love your neighbor as yourself."* [9]But if you favor some people over others, you are committing a sin. You are guilty of breaking the law.

[10]For the person who keeps all of the laws except one is as guilty as a person who has

1:9 Greek *The brother who is.* **1:13** Or *God should not be put to a test by evil people.* **1:17a** Greek *from above, from the Father of lights.* **1:17b** Some manuscripts read *He never changes, as a shifting shadow does.* **1:18** Greek *we became a kind of firstfruit of his creatures.* **1:20a** Greek *A man's anger.* **1:20b** Or *the justice.* **2:1** Greek *brothers;* also in 2:5, 14. **2:2** Greek *your synagogue.* **2:7** Greek *slander the noble name.* **2:8** Lev 19:18.

broken all of God's laws. [11]For the same God who said, "You must not commit adultery," also said, "You must not murder."* So if you murder someone but do not commit adultery, you have still broken the law.

[12]So whatever you say or whatever you do, remember that you will be judged by the law that sets you free. [13]There will be no mercy for those who have not shown mercy to others. But if you have been merciful, God will be merciful when he judges you.

Faith without Good Deeds Is Dead

[14]What good is it, dear brothers and sisters, if you say you have faith but don't show it by your actions? Can that kind of faith save anyone? [15]Suppose you see a brother or sister who has no food or clothing, [16]and you say, "Good-bye and have a good day; stay warm and eat well"—but then you don't give that person any food or clothing. What good does that do?

[17]So you see, faith by itself isn't enough. Unless it produces good deeds, it is dead and useless.

Why do I have to be so careful about what I say?

A small rudder makes a huge ship turn. . . . In the same way, the tongue is a small thing that makes grand speeches. But a tiny spark can set a great forest on fire. JAMES 3:4-5

[18]Now someone may argue, "Some people have faith; others have good deeds." But I say, "How can you show me your faith if you don't have good deeds? I will show you my faith by my good deeds."

[19]You say you have faith, for you believe that there is one God.* Good for you! Even the demons believe this, and they tremble in terror. [20]How foolish! Can't you see that faith without good deeds is useless?

[21]Don't you remember that our ancestor Abraham was shown to be right with God by his actions when he offered his son Isaac on the altar? [22]You see, his faith and his actions worked together. His actions made his faith complete. [23]And so it happened just as the Scriptures say: "Abraham believed God, and God counted him as righteous because of his faith."* He was even called the friend of God.* [24]So you see, we are shown to be right with God by what we do, not by faith alone.

[25]Rahab the prostitute is another example. She was shown to be right with God by her actions when she hid those messengers and sent them safely away by a different road. [26]Just as the body is dead without breath,* so also faith is dead without good works.

CHAPTER 3

Controlling the Tongue

Dear brothers and sisters,* not many of you should become teachers in the church, for we who teach will be judged more strictly. [2]Indeed, we all make many mistakes. For if we could control our tongues, we would be perfect and could also control ourselves in every other way.

[3]We can make a large horse go wherever we want by means of a small bit in its mouth. [4]And a small rudder makes a huge ship turn wherever the pilot chooses to go, even though the winds are strong. [5]In the same way, the tongue is a small thing that makes grand speeches.

But a tiny spark can set a great forest on fire. [6]And the tongue is a flame of fire. It is a whole world of wickedness, corrupting your entire body. It can set your whole life on fire, for it is set on fire by hell itself.*

[7]People can tame all kinds of animals, birds, reptiles, and fish, [8]but no one can tame the tongue. It is restless and evil, full of deadly poison. [9]Sometimes it praises our Lord and Father, and sometimes it curses those who have been made in the image of God. [10]And so blessing and cursing come

2:11 Exod 20:13-14; Deut 5:17-18. **2:19** Some manuscripts read *that God is one;* see Deut 6:4. **2:23a** Gen 15:6. **2:23b** See Isa 41:8. **2:26** Or *without spirit.* **3:1** Greek *brothers;* also in 3:10. **3:6** Or *for it will burn in hell* (Greek *Gehenna*).

pouring out of the same mouth. Surely, my brothers and sisters, this is not right! [11]Does a spring of water bubble out with both fresh water and bitter water? [12]Does a fig tree produce olives, or a grapevine produce figs? No, and you can't draw fresh water from a salty spring.*

True Wisdom Comes from God

[13]If you are wise and understand God's ways, prove it by living an honorable life, doing good works with the humility that comes from wisdom. [14]But if you are bitterly jealous and there is selfish ambition in your heart, don't cover up the truth with boasting and lying. [15]For jealousy and selfishness are not God's kind of wisdom. Such things are earthly, unspiritual, and demonic. [16]For wherever there is jealousy and selfish ambition, there you will find disorder and evil of every kind.

[17]But the wisdom from above is first of all pure. It is also peace loving, gentle at all times, and willing to yield to others. It is full of mercy and good deeds. It shows no favoritism and is always sincere. [18]And those who are peacemakers will plant seeds of peace and reap a harvest of righteousness.*

CHAPTER 4

Drawing Close to God

What is causing the quarrels and fights among you? Don't they come from the evil desires at war within you? [2]You want what you don't have, so you scheme and kill to get it. You are jealous of what others have, but you can't get it, so you fight and wage war to take it away from them. Yet you don't have what you want because you don't ask God for it. [3]And even when you ask, you don't get it because your motives are all wrong—you want only what will give you pleasure.

[4]You adulterers!* Don't you realize that friendship with the world makes you an enemy of God? I say it again: If you want to be a friend of the world, you make yourself an enemy of God. [5]What do you think the Scriptures mean when they say that the spirit God has placed within us is filled with envy?* [6]But he gives us even more grace to stand against such evil desires. As the Scriptures say,

3:12 Greek *from salt.* **3:18** Or *of good things,* or *of justice.* **4:4** Greek *You adulteresses!* **4:5** Or *that God longs jealously for the human spirit he has placed within us?* or *that the Holy Spirit, whom God has placed within us, opposes our envy?*

IS IT OK?

IS IT OK TO LAUGH AT DIRTY JOKES?

Imagine an apple tree that grew delicious, sweet apples *and* poisonous, sour apples. Or imagine a mountain spring that sometimes gave you clean, refreshing water but other times gave you muddy, nasty water. Pretty awful, right? The same thing goes for our mouths. If we say we love God and sometimes praise him with our words, but other times say bad words or tell dirty jokes, we are being hypocrites. Even if *you* aren't telling the dirty jokes, by laughing at them you're joining in. When you hear a dirty joke, walk away or suggest talking about something else. Or tell a really good clean joke! God wants you to have fun, and he wants your words to be sweet and refreshing (see James 3:7-10).

Last year I went to a Friday night football game and was introduced to a guy five years older than me. He was in college, but he seemed really nice and somehow I ended up with his number. So I called him. Over the next couple of months we became good friends.

One night my parents met him when he stopped by my house. As soon as he left, my dad erupted, "I don't like his attitude." My mom added, "And he's much too old to be hanging around high school girls!"

At the time, I was upset that they were so negative. *Why were they acting this way?*

I had noticed that my college friend drank quite a bit and went to a lot of parties. But he admitted that he wasn't perfect and seemed to really want to get his life together. "Just because I do bad things," he would argue, "doesn't mean I'm a bad person."

Besides, he and I were just friends—that's what he told me.

Then one Friday night I saw him kissing a fifteen-year-old girl from my school. I couldn't believe it. This guy didn't have any boundaries at all. He thought everything he did was okay. Well . . . I didn't. This guy was bad news! He was part of a different world, and I had been too blind to see it.

Take it from me. I learned the hard way that you need to be smart about choosing your friends. The people we hang out with can really influence us—in a good way or a bad way. You may want to be friends with the coolest kid in your neighborhood, but if that person doesn't share the same values or beliefs that you do, you'd better proceed with caution. I know that now, and I'm much more careful about the people I choose to hang around with.

Read James 4:4 for more thoughts on worldly friends. Check out also John 15:19 and 1 John 2:15.

"God opposes the proud
but favors the humble."*

[7]So humble yourselves before God. Resist the devil, and he will flee from you. [8]Come close to God, and God will come close to you. Wash your hands, you sinners; purify your hearts, for your loyalty is divided between God and the world. [9]Let there be tears for what you have done. Let there be sorrow and deep grief. Let there be sadness instead of laughter, and gloom instead of joy. [10]Humble yourselves before the Lord, and he will lift you up in honor.

AMAZING FACTS

Did you know that God actually will give you the power to make the devil run away from you? Just don't give in to him!

JAMES 4:7

Warning against Judging Others

[11]Don't speak evil against each other, dear brothers and sisters.* If you criticize and judge each other, then you are criticizing and judging God's law. But your job is to obey the law, not to judge whether it applies to you. [12]God alone, who gave the law, is the Judge. He alone has the power to save or to destroy. So what right do you have to judge your neighbor?

Warning about Self-Confidence

[13]Look here, you who say, "Today or tomorrow we are going to a certain town and will stay there a year. We will do business there and make a profit." [14]How do you know what your life will be like tomorrow? Your life is like the morning fog—it's here a little while, then it's gone. [15]What you ought to say is, "If the Lord wants us to, we will live and do this or that." [16]Otherwise you are boasting about your own plans, and all such boasting is evil.

[17]Remember, it is sin to know what you ought to do and then not do it.

CHAPTER 5

Warning to the Rich

Look here, you rich people: Weep and groan with anguish because of all the terrible troubles ahead of you. [2]Your wealth is rotting away, and your fine clothes are moth-eaten rags. [3]Your gold and silver have become worthless. The very wealth you were counting on will eat away your flesh like fire. This treasure you have accumulated will stand as evidence against you on the day of judgment. [4]For listen! Hear the cries of the field workers whom you have cheated of their pay. The wages you held back cry out against you. The cries of those who harvest your fields have reached the ears of the LORD of Heaven's Armies.

[5]You have spent your years on earth in luxury, satisfying your every desire. You have fattened yourselves for the day of slaughter. [6]You have condemned and killed innocent people,* who do not resist you.*

Patience and Endurance

[7]Dear brothers and sisters,* be patient as you wait for the Lord's return. Consider the farmers who patiently wait for the rains in the fall and in the spring. They eagerly look for the valuable harvest to ripen. [8]You, too, must be patient. Take courage, for the coming of the Lord is near.

[9]Don't grumble about each other, brothers and sisters, or you will be judged. For look—the Judge is standing at the door!

[10]For examples of patience in suffering, dear brothers and sisters, look at the prophets who spoke in the name of the Lord. [11]We give great honor to those who endure under suffering. For instance, you know about Job, a man of great endurance. You can see how the Lord was kind to him at the end, for the Lord is full of tenderness and mercy.

[12]But most of all, my brothers and sisters, never take an oath, by heaven or earth or any-

4:6 Prov 3:34 (Greek version). **4:11** Greek *brothers.* **5:6a** Or *killed the Righteous One.* **5:6b** Or *Don't they resist you?* or *Doesn't God oppose you?* or *Aren't they now accusing you before God?* **5:7** Greek *brothers;* also in 5:9, 10, 12, 19.

thing else. Just say a simple yes or no, so that
you will not sin and be condemned.

The Power of Prayer

[13]Are any of you suffering hardships? You
should pray. Are any of you happy? You
should sing praises. [14]Are any of you sick?
You should call for the elders of the church to
come and pray over you, anointing you with
oil in the name of the Lord. [15]Such a prayer
offered in faith will heal the sick, and the
Lord will make you well. And if you have com-
mitted any sins, you will be forgiven.

[16]Confess your sins to each other and pray
for each other so that you may be healed. The
earnest prayer of a righteous person has great
power and produces wonderful results. [17]Eli-
jah was as human as we are, and yet when he
prayed earnestly that no rain would fall, none
fell for three and a half years! [18]Then, when he
prayed again, the sky sent down rain and the
earth began to yield its crops.

Restore Wandering Believers

[19]My dear brothers and sisters, if someone
among you wanders away from the truth and
is brought back, [20]you can be sure that who-
ever brings the sinner back will save that
person from death and bring about the for-
giveness of many sins.

1 Peter

WHO
Peter, Silas, and Mark.

WHERE
Peter wrote this letter from Rome.

WHEN
Around AD 62–64 during extreme persecution.

WHY
To offer encouragement to suffering believers in Rome and throughout the Mediterranean world.

You are living stones that God is building into his spiritual temple.
1 PETER 2:5

When Peter wrote this first letter, life already was hard for Christians everywhere. But soon it would be much worse. Peter wrote to encourage the believers who were suffering and to prepare them for what was to come. As you read, thank God for Christians who gave their lives for Christ.

Be ready to stand up for what you believe, even if others make fun of you.

CHAPTER **1**

Greetings from Peter

This letter is from Peter, an apostle of Jesus Christ.

I am writing to God's chosen people who are living as foreigners in the provinces of Pontus, Galatia, Cappadocia, Asia, and Bithynia.* [2]God the Father knew you and chose you long ago, and his Spirit has made you holy. As a result, you have obeyed him and have been cleansed by the blood of Jesus Christ.

May God give you more and more grace and peace.

1:1 *Pontus, Galatia, Cappadocia, Asia,* and *Bithynia* were Roman provinces in what is now Turkey.

The Hope of Eternal Life

3 All praise to God, the Father of our Lord Jesus
Christ. It is by his great mercy that we have
been born again, because God raised Jesus
Christ from the dead. Now we live with great
expectation, 4 and we have a priceless inheri-
tance—an inheritance that is kept in heaven
for you, pure and undefiled, beyond the reach
of change and decay. 5 And through your
faith, God is protecting you by his power until
you receive this salvation, which is ready to be
revealed on the last day for all to see.

6 So be truly glad.* There is wonderful joy
ahead, even though you have to endure many
trials for a little while. 7 These trials will show
that your faith is genuine. It is being tested as
fire tests and purifies gold—though your faith
is far more precious than mere gold. So when
your faith remains strong through many trials,
it will bring you much praise and glory and
honor on the day when Jesus Christ is revealed
to the whole world.

8 You love him even though you have never
seen him. Though you do not see him now,
you trust him; and you rejoice with a glori-
ous, inexpressible joy. 9 The reward for trust-
ing him will be the salvation of your souls.

10 This salvation was something even the
prophets wanted to know more about when
they prophesied about this gracious salva-
tion prepared for you. 11 They wondered
what time or situation the Spirit of Christ
within them was talking about when he told
them in advance about Christ's suffering
and his great glory afterward.

12 They were told that their messages were
not for themselves, but for you. And now this
Good News has been announced to you by
those who preached in the power of the Holy
Spirit sent from heaven. It is all so wonderful
that even the angels are eagerly watching
these things happen.

A Call to Holy Living

13 So think clearly and exercise self-control.
Look forward to the gracious salvation that
will come to you when Jesus Christ is revealed
to the world. 14 So you must live as God's obe-
dient children. Don't slip back into your old
ways of living to satisfy your own desires. You
didn't know any better then. 15 But now you
must be holy in everything you do, just as God
who chose you is holy. 16 For the Scriptures
say, "You must be holy because I am holy."*

17 And remember that the heavenly Father
to whom you pray has no favorites. He will
judge or reward you according to what you
do. So you must live in reverent fear of him
during your time as "foreigners in the land."
18 For you know that God paid a ransom to
save you from the empty life you inherited
from your ancestors. And the ransom he paid
was not mere gold or silver. 19 It was the pre-
cious blood of Christ, the sinless, spotless
Lamb of God. 20 God chose him as your ran-
som long before the world began, but he has
now revealed him to you in these last days.

21 Through Christ you have come to trust in
God. And you have placed your faith and hope
in God because he raised Christ from the
dead and gave him great glory.

22 You were cleansed from your sins when
you obeyed the truth, so now you must show
sincere love to each other as brothers and sis-
ters.* Love each other deeply with all your
heart.*

23 For you have been born again, but not to a
life that will quickly end. Your new life will
last forever because it comes from the eter-
nal, living word of God. 24 As the Scriptures
say,

"People are like grass;
their beauty is like a flower in the field.
The grass withers and the flower fades.
25 But the word of the Lord remains
forever."*

And that word is the Good News that was
preached to you.

CHAPTER 2

So get rid of all evil behavior. Be done with all
deceit, hypocrisy, jealousy, and all unkind
speech. 2 Like newborn babies, you must crave
pure spiritual milk so that you will grow into a
full experience of salvation. Cry out for this
nourishment, 3 now that you have had a taste
of the Lord's kindness.

Living Stones for God's House

4 You are coming to Christ, who is the living
cornerstone of God's temple. He was rejected

1:6 Or *So you are truly glad.* **1:16** Lev 11:44-45; 19:2; 20:7. **1:22a** Greek *must have brotherly love.* **1:22b** Some manuscripts read *with a pure heart.* **1:24-25** Isa 40:6-8.

by people, but he was chosen by God for great honor.

5And you are living stones that God is building into his spiritual temple. What's more, you are his holy priests.* Through the mediation of Jesus Christ, you offer spiritual sacrifices that please God. 6As the Scriptures say,

"I am placing a cornerstone in Jerusalem,*
chosen for great honor,
and anyone who trusts in him
will never be disgraced."*

7Yes, you who trust him recognize the honor God has given him. But for those who reject him,

"The stone that the builders rejected
has now become the cornerstone."*

8And,

"He is the stone that makes people
stumble,
the rock that makes them fall."*

They stumble because they do not obey God's word, and so they meet the fate that was planned for them.

9But you are not like that, for you are a chosen people. You are royal priests,* a holy nation, God's very own possession. As a result, you can show others the goodness of God, for he called you out of the darkness into his wonderful light.

10 "Once you had no identity as a people;
now you are God's people.
Once you received no mercy;
now you have received God's mercy."*

11Dear friends, I warn you as "temporary residents and foreigners" to keep away from worldly desires that wage war against your very souls. 12Be careful to live properly among your unbelieving neighbors. Then even if they accuse you of doing wrong, they will see your honorable behavior, and they will give honor to God when he judges the world.*

Respecting People in Authority

13For the Lord's sake, respect all human authority—whether the king as head of state, 14or the officials he has appointed. For the king has sent them to punish those who do wrong and to honor those who do right.

15It is God's will that your honorable lives should silence those ignorant people who make foolish accusations against you. 16For you are free, yet you are God's slaves, so don't use your freedom as an excuse to do evil. 17Respect everyone, and love your Christian brothers and sisters.* Fear God, and respect the king.

Slaves

18You who are slaves must accept the authority of your masters with all respect.* Do what they tell you—not only if they are kind and reasonable, but even if they are cruel. 19For God is pleased with you when you do what you know is right and patiently endure unfair treatment. 20Of course, you get no credit for being patient if you are beaten for doing wrong. But if you suffer for doing good and endure it patiently, God is pleased with you.

21For God called you to do good, even if it means suffering, just as Christ suffered* for you. He is your example, and you must follow in his steps.

AMAZING FACTS

As Jesus' followers, we are royal priests! We can talk to God on his throne and bring others to him.

1 PETER 2:9

22 He never sinned,
nor ever deceived anyone.*
23 He did not retaliate when he was insulted,
nor threaten revenge when he suffered.
He left his case in the hands of God,
who always judges fairly.

2:5 Greek *holy priesthood*. **2:6a** Greek *in Zion*. **2:6b** Isa 28:16 (Greek version). **2:7** Ps 118:22. **2:8** Isa 8:14. **2:9** Greek *a royal priesthood*. **2:10** Hos 1:6, 9; 2:23. **2:12** Or *on the day of visitation*. **2:17** Greek *love the brotherhood*. **2:18** Or *because you fear God*. **2:21** Some manuscripts read *died*. **2:22** Isa 53:9.

24 He personally carried our sins
in his body on the cross
so that we can be dead to sin
and live for what is right.
By his wounds
you are healed.
25 Once you were like sheep
who wandered away.
But now you have turned to your
Shepherd,
the Guardian of your souls.

CHAPTER 3

Wives

In the same way, you wives must accept the authority of your husbands. Then, even if some refuse to obey the Good News, your godly lives will speak to them without any words. They will be won over 2 by observing your pure and reverent lives.

3 Don't be concerned about the outward beauty of fancy hairstyles, expensive jewelry, or beautiful clothes. 4 You should clothe yourselves instead with the beauty that comes from within, the unfading beauty of a gentle and quiet spirit, which is so precious to God. 5 This is how the holy women of old made themselves beautiful. They trusted God and accepted the authority of their husbands. 6 For instance, Sarah obeyed her husband, Abraham, and called him her master. You are her daughters when you do what is right without fear of what your husbands might do.

Husbands

7 In the same way, you husbands must give honor to your wives. Treat your wife with understanding as you live together. She may be weaker than you are, but she is your equal partner in God's gift of new life. Treat her as you should so your prayers will not be hindered.

All Christians

8 Finally, all of you should be of one mind. Sympathize with each other. Love each other as brothers and sisters.* Be tenderhearted, and keep a humble attitude. 9 Don't repay evil for evil. Don't retaliate with insults when people insult you. Instead, pay them back with a blessing. That is what God has called you to do, and he will bless you for it. 10 For the Scriptures say,

"If you want to enjoy life
and see many happy days,
keep your tongue from speaking evil
and your lips from telling lies.
11 Turn away from evil and do good.
Search for peace, and work to
maintain it.
12 The eyes of the Lord watch over those
who do right,
and his ears are open to their prayers.
But the Lord turns his face
against those who do evil."*

Suffering for Doing Good

13 Now, who will want to harm you if you are eager to do good? 14 But even if you suffer for doing what is right, God will reward you for it. So don't worry or be afraid of their threats. 15 Instead, you must worship Christ as Lord of your life. And if someone asks about your Christian hope, always be ready to explain it. 16 But do this in a gentle and respectful way.* Keep your conscience clear. Then if people speak against you, they will be ashamed when they see what a good life you live because you belong to Christ. 17 Remember, it is better to suffer for doing good, if that is what God wants, than to suffer for doing wrong!

18 Christ suffered* for our sins once for all time. He never sinned, but he died for sinners to bring you safely home to God. He suffered physical death, but he was raised to life in the Spirit.*

19 So he went and preached to the spirits in prison— 20 those who disobeyed God long ago when God waited patiently while Noah was building his boat. Only eight people were saved from drowning in that terrible flood.* 21 And that water is a picture of baptism, which now saves you, not by removing dirt from your body, but as a response to God from* a clean conscience. It is effective because of the resurrection of Jesus Christ.

22 Now Christ has gone to heaven. He is seated in the place of honor next to God, and all the angels and authorities and powers accept his authority.

3:8 Greek *Show brotherly love.* **3:10-12** Ps 34:12-16. **3:16** Some English translations put this sentence in verse 15. **3:18a** Some manuscripts read *died.* **3:18b** Or *in spirit.* **3:20** Greek *saved through water.* **3:21** Or *as an appeal to God for.*

My girlfriend, Tatiana, became obsessed with her appearance the year she finished middle school. She told me that one Saturday she went with her mom to the mall. When she got bored, her mom let her go to the store next door and look around.

My girlfriend discovered that the clothes in that store looked like they'd jumped out of a magazine. Needless to say, she fell in love with the stuff!

She had her allowance in her jacket pocket, so she bought two outfits. When she went back to meet her mom, she found out that her mom wasn't pleased, to say the least.

Not long after that, Tatiana updated her hairstyle. Then she started doing her nails . . . every day. Every cent she earned or received as a gift went into things she thought would make her look beautiful. The truth is, she was more beautiful before she started working so hard at it.

Tatiana told me that she and her mom had many heated discussions about her new appearance. She even called her aunt to complain about how unfair her mom was being.

Rather than take sides, Tatiana's aunt told her to get her Bible and look up 1 Peter 3:3-4. It said that "beauty that comes from within" is what is "precious to God." That made sense to me, because I liked Tatiana better before she started all that beauty stuff.

I was really glad that my girlfriend changed after she talked to her aunt. She changed how she thought about clothing and how she treated her mom—and she had more time for me. External beauty shouldn't be that important—not even to a guy—especially when a girl is acting disrespectful and ugly.

For more on true beauty, check out Proverbs 31:30 and 1 Timothy 2:9-10.

ACCUSED!

During gym class Dennis asked to go into the locker room to use the bathroom. Dennis came back to class and thought nothing more about it. After class, however, three kids discovered that money had been stolen from their gym lockers. Though Dennis didn't steal it (and had no idea who did), the gym teacher called him in and accused him of being the thief. Dennis couldn't prove that he was innocent, of course, but he felt awful. What should Dennis do? Read 1 Peter 3:15-17 for God's helpful advice.

CHAPTER 4

Living for God

So then, since Christ suffered physical pain, you must arm yourselves with the same attitude he had, and be ready to suffer, too. For if you have suffered physically for Christ, you have finished with sin.* [2] You won't spend the rest of your lives chasing your own desires, but you will be anxious to do the will of God. [3] You have had enough in the past of the evil things that godless people enjoy—their immorality and lust, their feasting and drunkenness and wild parties, and their terrible worship of idols.

[4] Of course, your former friends are surprised when you no longer plunge into the flood of wild and destructive things they do. So they slander you. [5] But remember that they will have to face God, who will judge everyone, both the living and the dead. [6] That is why the Good News was preached to those who are now dead*—so although they were destined to die like all people,* they now live forever with God in the Spirit.*

[7] The end of the world is coming soon. Therefore, be earnest and disciplined in your prayers. [8] Most important of all, continue to show deep love for each other, for love covers a multitude of sins. [9] Cheerfully share your home with those who need a meal or a place to stay.

[10] God has given each of you a gift from his great variety of spiritual gifts. Use them well to serve one another. [11] Do you have the gift of speaking? Then speak as though God himself were speaking through you. Do you have the gift of helping others? Do it with all the strength and energy that God supplies. Then everything you do will bring glory to God through Jesus Christ. All glory and power to him forever and ever! Amen.

Suffering for Being a Christian

[12] Dear friends, don't be surprised at the fiery trials you are going through, as if something strange were happening to you. [13] Instead, be very glad—for these trials make you partners with Christ in his suffering, so that you will have the wonderful joy of seeing his glory when it is revealed to all the world.

[14] So be happy when you are insulted for being a Christian,* for then the glorious Spirit of God* rests upon you.* [15] If you suffer, however, it must not be for murder, stealing, making trouble, or prying into other people's affairs. [16] But it is no shame to suffer for being a Christian. Praise God for the privilege of being called by his name! [17] For the time has

4:1 Or *For the one* [or *One*] *who has suffered physically has finished with sin.* **4:6a** Greek *preached even to the dead.* **4:6b** Or *so although people had judged them worthy of death.* **4:6c** Or *in spirit.* **4:14a** Greek *for the name of Christ.* **4:14b** Or *for the glory of God, which is his Spirit.* **4:14c** Some manuscripts add *On their part he is blasphemed, but on your part he is glorified.*

come for judgment, and it must begin with God's household. And if judgment begins with us, what terrible fate awaits those who have never obeyed God's Good News? [18]And also,

"If the righteous are barely saved,
what will happen to godless sinners?"*

[19]So if you are suffering in a manner that pleases God, keep on doing what is right, and trust your lives to the God who created you, for he will never fail you.

CHAPTER 5

Advice for Elders and Young Men

And now, a word to you who are elders in the churches. I, too, am an elder and a witness to the sufferings of Christ. And I, too, will share in his glory when he is revealed to the whole world. As a fellow elder, I appeal to you: [2]Care for the flock that God has entrusted to you. Watch over it willingly, not grudgingly—not for what you will get out of it, but because you are eager to serve God. [3]Don't lord it over the people assigned to your care, but lead them by your own good example. [4]And when the Great Shepherd appears, you will receive a crown of never-ending glory and honor.

[5]In the same way, you younger men must accept the authority of the elders. And all of you, serve each other in humility, for

"God opposes the proud
but favors the humble."*

[6]So humble yourselves under the mighty power of God, and at the right time he will lift you up in honor. [7]Give all your worries and cares to God, for he cares about you.

[8]Stay alert! Watch out for your great enemy, the devil. He prowls around like a roaring lion, looking for someone to devour. [9]Stand firm against him, and be strong in your faith. Remember that your Christian brothers and sisters* all over the world are going through the same kind of suffering you are.

[10]In his kindness God called you to share in his eternal glory by means of Christ Jesus. So after you have suffered a little while, he will restore, support, and strengthen you, and he will place you on a firm foundation. [11]All power to him forever! Amen.

Peter's Final Greetings

[12]I have written and sent this short letter to you with the help of Silas,* whom I commend to you as a faithful brother. My purpose in writing is to encourage you and assure you that what you are experiencing is truly part of God's grace for you. Stand firm in this grace.

[13]Your sister church here in Babylon* sends you greetings, and so does my son Mark. [14]Greet each other with Christian love.*

Peace be with all of you who are in Christ.

4:18 Prov 11:31 (Greek version). **5:5** Prov 3:34 (Greek version). **5:9** Greek *your brothers*. **5:12** Greek *Silvanus*. **5:13** Greek *The elect one in Babylon*. Babylon was probably symbolic for Rome. **5:14** Greek *with a kiss of love*.

2 Peter

WHO
Peter and Paul.

WHERE
Peter wrote this letter from Rome.

WHEN
Around AD 67, just a few years before the Temple in Jerusalem was destroyed.

WHY
To warn Christians about false teachers and to encourage them to grow in their faith.

May God give you more and more grace and peace as you grow in your knowledge of God and Jesus our Lord.
2 PETER 1:2

Warning signs appear on billboards, TV commercials, and even medicine bottles. Peter's second letter is a big warning sign to the early Christians. He warns them not to listen to false teachers or become lazy in their faith. Peter reminds them that Jesus is coming back, just as he promised!

WE STILL NEED TO LISTEN TO PETER'S WARNINGS. AS YOU READ, THINK ABOUT WHAT GOD IS TELLING YOU TO DO.

CHAPTER 1

Greetings from Peter

This letter is from Simon* Peter, a slave and apostle of Jesus Christ.

I am writing to you who share the same precious faith we have. This faith was given to you because of the justice and fairness* of Jesus Christ, our God and Savior.

[2]May God give you more and more grace and peace as you grow in your knowledge of God and Jesus our Lord.

Growing in Faith

[3]By his divine power, God has given us everything we need for living a godly life. We have received all of this by coming to know him,

1:1a Greek *Symeon*. **1:1b** Or *to you in the righteousness.*

the one who called us to himself by means of his marvelous glory and excellence. [4]And because of his glory and excellence, he has given us great and precious promises. These are the promises that enable you to share his divine nature and escape the world's corruption caused by human desires.

[5]In view of all this, make every effort to respond to God's promises. Supplement your faith with a generous provision of moral excellence, and moral excellence with knowledge, [6]and knowledge with self-control, and self-control with patient endurance, and patient endurance with godliness, [7]and godliness with brotherly affection, and brotherly affection with love for everyone.

[8]The more you grow like this, the more productive and useful you will be in your knowledge of our Lord Jesus Christ. [9]But those who fail to develop in this way are shortsighted or blind, forgetting that they have been cleansed from their old sins.

[10]So, dear brothers and sisters,* work hard to prove that you really are among those God has called and chosen. Do these things, and you will never fall away. [11]Then God will give you a grand entrance into the eternal Kingdom of our Lord and Savior Jesus Christ.

Paying Attention to Scripture

[12]Therefore, I will always remind you about these things—even though you already know them and are standing firm in the truth you have been taught. [13]And it is only right that I should keep on reminding you as long as I live.* [14]For our Lord Jesus Christ has shown me that I must soon leave this earthly life,* [15]so I will work hard to make sure you always remember these things after I am gone.

[16]For we were not making up clever stories when we told you about the powerful coming of our Lord Jesus Christ. We saw his majestic splendor with our own eyes [17]when he received honor and glory from God the Father. The voice from the majestic glory of God said to him, "This is my dearly loved Son, who brings me great joy."* [18]We ourselves heard that voice from heaven when we were with him on the holy mountain.

[19]Because of that experience, we have even greater confidence in the message proclaimed by the prophets. You must pay close attention to what they wrote, for their words are like a lamp shining in a dark place—until the Day dawns, and Christ the Morning Star shines* in your hearts. [20]Above all, you must realize that no prophecy in Scripture ever came from the prophet's own understanding,* [21]or from human initiative. No, those prophets were moved by the Holy Spirit, and they spoke from God.

CHAPTER 2

The Danger of False Teachers

But there were also false prophets in Israel, just as there will be false teachers among you. They will cleverly teach destructive heresies and even deny the Master who bought them. In this way, they will bring sudden destruction on themselves. [2]Many will follow their evil teaching and shameful immorality. And because of these teachers, the way of truth will be slandered. [3]In their greed they will make up clever lies to get hold of your money. But God condemned them long ago, and their destruction will not be delayed.

[4]For God did not spare even the angels who sinned. He threw them into hell,* in gloomy pits of darkness,* where they are being held until the day of judgment. [5]And God did not spare the ancient world—except for Noah and the seven others in his family. Noah warned the world of God's righteous judgment. So God protected Noah when he destroyed the world of ungodly people with a vast flood. [6]Later, God condemned the cities of Sodom and Gomorrah and turned them into heaps of ashes. He made them an example of what will happen to ungodly people. [7]But God also rescued Lot out of Sodom because he was a righteous man who was sick of the shameful immorality of the wicked people around him. [8]Yes, Lot was a righteous man who was tormented in his soul by the wickedness he saw and heard day after day. [9]So you see, the Lord knows how to rescue godly people from their trials, even while keeping the wicked under punishment until the day of final judgment. [10]He is especially hard on those

1:10 Greek *brothers.* **1:13** Greek *as long as I am in this tent* [or *tabernacle*]. **1:14** Greek *I must soon put off my tent* [or *tabernacle*]. **1:17** Matt 17:5; Mark 9:7; Luke 9:35. **1:19** Or *rises.* **1:20** Or *is a matter of one's own interpretation.* **2:4a** Greek *Tartarus.* **2:4b** Some manuscripts read *in chains of gloom.*

who follow their own twisted sexual desire, and who despise authority.

These people are proud and arrogant, daring even to scoff at supernatural beings* without so much as trembling. [11]But the angels, who are far greater in power and strength, do not dare to bring from the Lord* a charge of blasphemy against those supernatural beings.

[12]These false teachers are like unthinking animals, creatures of instinct, born to be caught and destroyed. They scoff at things they do not understand, and like animals, they will be destroyed. [13]Their destruction is their reward for the harm they have done. They love to indulge in evil pleasures in broad daylight. They are a disgrace and a stain among you. They delight in deception* even as they eat with you in your fellowship meals. [14]They commit adultery with their eyes, and their desire for sin is never satisfied. They lure unstable people into sin, and they are well trained in greed. They live under God's curse. [15]They have wandered off the right road and followed the footsteps of Balaam son of Beor,* who loved to earn money by doing wrong. [16]But Balaam was stopped from his mad course when his donkey rebuked him with a human voice.

[17]These people are as useless as dried-up springs or as mist blown away by the wind. They are doomed to blackest darkness. [18]They brag about themselves with empty, foolish boasting. With an appeal to twisted sexual desires, they lure back into sin those who have barely escaped from a lifestyle of deception. [19]They promise freedom, but they themselves are slaves of sin and corruption. For you are a slave to whatever controls you. [20]And when people escape from the wickedness of the world by knowing our Lord and Savior Jesus Christ and then get tangled up and enslaved by sin again, they are worse off than before. [21]It would be better if they had never known the way to righteousness than to know it and then reject the command they were given to live a holy life. [22]They prove the truth of this proverb: "A dog returns to its vomit."* And another says, "A washed pig returns to the mud."

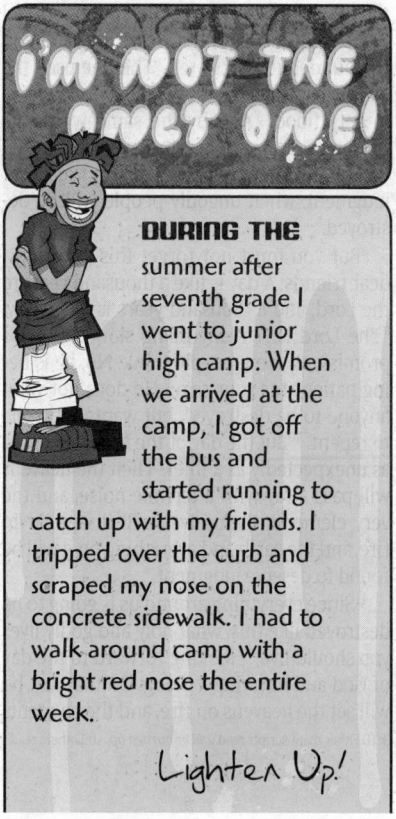

CHAPTER 3

The Day of the Lord Is Coming

This is my second letter to you, dear friends, and in both of them I have tried to stimulate your wholesome thinking and refresh your memory. [2]I want you to remember what the holy prophets said long ago and what our Lord and Savior commanded through your apostles.

[3]Most importantly, I want to remind you that in the last days scoffers will come, mocking the truth and following their own desires. [4]They will say, "What happened to the promise that Jesus is coming again? From before the times of our ancestors, everything has remained the same since the world was first created."

[5]They deliberately forget that God made

2:10 Greek *at glorious ones,* which are probably evil angels. **2:11** Other manuscripts read *to the Lord;* still others do not include this phrase at all. **2:13** Some manuscripts read *in fellowship meals.* **2:15** Some manuscripts read *Bosor.* **2:22** Prov 26:11.

the heavens by the word of his command, and
he brought the earth out from the water and
surrounded it with water. [6]Then he used the
water to destroy the ancient world with a
mighty flood. [7]And by the same word, the
present heavens and earth have been stored
up for fire. They are being kept for the day of
judgment, when ungodly people will be de-
stroyed.

[8]But you must not forget this one thing,
dear friends: A day is like a thousand years to
the Lord, and a thousand years is like a day.
[9]The Lord isn't really being slow about his
promise, as some people think. No, he is be-
ing patient for your sake. He does not want
anyone to be destroyed, but wants everyone
to repent. [10]But the day of the Lord will come
as unexpectedly as a thief. Then the heavens
will pass away with a terrible noise, and the
very elements themselves will disappear in
fire, and the earth and everything on it will be
found to deserve judgment.*

[11]Since everything around us is going to be
destroyed like this, what holy and godly lives
you should live, [12]looking forward to the day
of God and hurrying it along. On that day, he
will set the heavens on fire, and the elements
will melt away in the flames. [13]But we are
looking forward to the new heavens and new
earth he has promised, a world filled with
God's righteousness.

[14]And so, dear friends, while you are wait-
ing for these things to happen, make every ef-
fort to be found living peaceful lives that are
pure and blameless in his sight.

[15]And remember, our Lord's patience gives
people time to be saved. This is what our be-
loved brother Paul also wrote to you with the
wisdom God gave him—[16]speaking of these
things in all of his letters. Some of his com-
ments are hard to understand, and those who
are ignorant and unstable have twisted his
letters to mean something quite different,
just as they do with other parts of Scripture.
And this will result in their destruction.

Peter's Final Words

[17]I am warning you ahead of time, dear
friends. Be on guard so that you will not be car-
ried away by the errors of these wicked people
and lose your own secure footing. [18]Rather,
you must grow in the grace and knowledge of
our Lord and Savior Jesus Christ.

All glory to him, both now and forever!
Amen.

3:10 Other manuscripts read *will be burned up;* still others read *will be found destroyed.*

1 JOHN

WHO
Jesus' disciple John wrote this letter when he was an older man.

WHERE
John was in Ephesus when he wrote this letter.

WHEN
Between AD 85 and 90, before John was exiled to the island of Patmos.

WHY
To reassure Christians in their faith and to tell the truth about false teachings.

See how very much our Father loves us, for he calls us his children.
1 JOHN 3:1

Everyone talks about love, but there doesn't seem to be much of it around. Instead we hear more about hate, abuse, anger, revenge, violence, and fear. So what is *true love?* Where does it come from? How long does it last? To find the answers to these questions and many more, read 1 John.

DISCOVER THE SOURCE OF LOVE AND HOW YOU CAN PASS IT ON. IT'S WHAT THE WORLD NEEDS.

CHAPTER 1

Introduction

We proclaim to you the one who existed from
the beginning,* whom we have heard and
seen. We saw him with our own eyes and
touched him with our own hands. He is the
Word of life. [2]This one who is life itself was
revealed to us, and we have seen him. And
now we testify and proclaim to you that he is
the one who is eternal life. He was with the
Father, and then he was revealed to us. [3]We
proclaim to you what we ourselves have actu-
ally seen and heard so that you may have
fellowship with us. And our fellowship is with

1:1 Greek *What was from the beginning.*

the Father and with his Son, Jesus Christ. [4]We are writing these things so that you may fully share our joy.*

Living in the Light

[5]This is the message we heard from Jesus* and now declare to you: God is light, and there is no darkness in him at all. [6]So we are lying if we say we have fellowship with God but go on living in spiritual darkness; we are not practicing the truth. [7]But if we are living in the light, as God is in the light, then we have fellowship with each other, and the blood of Jesus, his Son, cleanses us from all sin.

[8]If we claim we have no sin, we are only fooling ourselves and not living in the truth. [9]But if we confess our sins to him, he is faithful and just to forgive us our sins and to cleanse us from all wickedness. [10]If we claim we have not sinned, we are calling God a liar and showing that his word has no place in our hearts.

CHAPTER 2

My dear children, I am writing this to you so that you will not sin. But if anyone does sin, we have an advocate who pleads our case before the Father. He is Jesus Christ, the one who is truly righteous. [2]He himself is the sacrifice that atones for our sins—and not only our sins but the sins of all the world.

[3]And we can be sure that we know him if we obey his commandments. [4]If someone claims, "I know God," but doesn't obey God's commandments, that person is a liar and is not living in the truth. [5]But those who obey God's word truly show how completely they love him. That is how we know we are living in him. [6]Those who say they live in God should live their lives as Jesus did.

A New Commandment

[7]Dear friends, I am not writing a new commandment for you; rather it is an old one you have had from the very beginning. This old commandment—to love one another—is the same message you heard before. [8]Yet it is also new. Jesus lived the truth of this commandment, and you also are living it. For the darkness is disappearing, and the true light is already shining.

[9]If anyone claims, "I am living in the light," but hates a Christian brother or sister,* that person is still living in darkness. [10]Anyone

1:4 Or *so that our joy may be complete;* some manuscripts read *your joy.* **1:5** Greek *from him.* **2:9** Greek *hates his brother;* similarly in 2:11.

IS IT OK?

IS IT OK TO CARE ABOUT OTHER THINGS MORE THAN GOD?

There are a lot of wonderful things in your life. Your family. Your stuff. Your dog. Your friends. It's good to care about all of those things. But God wants to be first in your life. Don't let the stuff of this world distract you and choke out your love for God (check out Matthew 22:36-38 and Luke 8:14). *Nothing* is supposed to compete with Jesus in your heart. Do you love anything more than him? Remember that other things are fading fast (see 1 John 2:15-17). In ten years your favorite sports team won't be good, your dog will be deaf, and your PlayStation will be broken. But God will be the same. Love him first and best always.

who loves another brother or sister* is living
in the light and does not cause others to stum-
ble. [11]But anyone who hates another brother
or sister is still living and walking in darkness.
Such a person does not know the way to go,
having been blinded by the darkness.

[12] I am writing to you who are God's
children
because your sins have been forgiven
through Jesus.*
[13] I am writing to you who are mature in the
faith*
because you know Christ, who existed
from the beginning.
I am writing to you who are young in the
faith
because you have won your battle with
the evil one.
[14] I have written to you who are God's
children
because you know the Father.
I have written to you who are mature in
the faith
because you know Christ, who existed
from the beginning.
I have written to you who are young in the
faith
because you are strong.
God's word lives in your hearts,
and you have won your battle with the
evil one.

Do Not Love This World

[15]Do not love this world nor the things it
offers you, for when you love the world, you
do not have the love of the Father in you. [16]For
the world offers only a craving for physical
pleasure, a craving for everything we see, and
pride in our achievements and possessions.
These are not from the Father, but are from
this world. [17]And this world is fading away,
along with everything that people crave. But
anyone who does what pleases God will live
forever.

Warning about Antichrists

[18]Dear children, the last hour is here. You
have heard that the Antichrist is coming, and
already many such antichrists have appeared.
From this we know that the last hour has
come. [19]These people left our churches, but
they never really belonged with us; otherwise
they would have stayed with us. When they
left, it proved that they did not belong with us.
[20]But you are not like that, for the Holy One
has given you his Spirit,* and all of you know
the truth. [21]So I am writing to you not because
you don't know the truth but because you
know the difference between truth and lies.
[22]And who is a liar? Anyone who says that
Jesus is not the Christ.* Anyone who denies
the Father and the Son is an antichrist.*
[23]Anyone who denies the Son doesn't have

2:10 Greek *loves his brother.* **2:12** Greek *through his name.* **2:13** Or *to you fathers;* also in 2:14. **2:20** Greek *But you have an anointing from the Holy One.* **2:22a** Or *not the Messiah.* **2:22b** Or *the antichrist.*

A BOOK OF CONTRASTS

John wrote to show the difference between real Christianity and anything else. Here are some of his favorite contrasts.

Contrast between	Passage
LIGHT *and* darkness	1:5
THE NEW COMMANDMENT *and* the old commandment	2:7-8
LOVING GOD *and* loving the world	2:15-16
CHRIST *and* Antichrist	2:18
TRUTH *and* lies	2:20-21
CHILDREN OF GOD *and* children of the devil	3:1-10
ETERNAL LIFE *and* eternal death	3:14
LOVE *and* hatred	3:15-16
TRUE PROPHECY *and* false prophecy	4:1-3
LOVE *and* fear	4:18-19
HAVING LIFE *and* not having life	5:11-12

the Father, either. But anyone who acknowledges the Son has the Father also.

[24]So you must remain faithful to what you have been taught from the beginning. If you do, you will remain in fellowship with the Son and with the Father. [25]And in this fellowship we enjoy the eternal life he promised us.

[26]I am writing these things to warn you about those who want to lead you astray. [27]But you have received the Holy Spirit,* and he lives within you, so you don't need anyone to teach you what is true. For the Spirit* teaches you everything you need to know, and what he teaches is true—it is not a lie. So just as he has taught you, remain in fellowship with Christ.

Living as Children of God

[28]And now, dear children, remain in fellowship with Christ so that when he returns, you will be full of courage and not shrink back from him in shame.

[29]Since we know that Christ is righteous, we also know that all who do what is right are God's children.

CHAPTER 3

See how very much our Father loves us, for he calls us his children, and that is what we are! But the people who belong to this world don't recognize that we are God's children because they don't know him. [2]Dear friends, we are already God's children, but he has not yet shown us what we will be like when Christ appears. But we do know that we will be like him, for we will see him as he really is. [3]And all who have this eager expectation will keep themselves pure, just as he is pure.

[4]Everyone who sins is breaking God's law, for all sin is contrary to the law of God. [5]And you know that Jesus came to take away our sins, and there is no sin in him. [6]Anyone who continues to live in him will not sin. But anyone who keeps on sinning does not know him or understand who he is.

[7]Dear children, don't let anyone deceive you about this: When people do what is right, it shows that they are righteous, even as Christ is righteous. [8]But when people keep on sinning, it shows that they belong to the devil, who has been sinning since the beginning. But the Son of God came to destroy the works of the devil. [9]Those who have been born into God's family do not make a practice of sinning, because God's life* is in them. So they can't keep on sinning, because they are children of God. [10]So now we can tell who are children of God and who are children of the devil. Anyone who does not live righteously and does not love other believers* does not belong to God.

Love One Another

[11]This is the message you have heard from the beginning: We should love one another. [12]We must not be like Cain, who belonged to the evil one and killed his brother. And why did he kill him? Because Cain had been doing what was evil, and his brother had been doing what was righteous. [13]So don't be surprised, dear brothers and sisters,* if the world hates you.

[14]If we love our Christian brothers and sisters,* it proves that we have passed from death to life. But a person who has no love is still dead. [15]Anyone who hates another brother or sister* is really a murderer at heart. And you know that murderers don't have eternal life within them.

[16]We know what real love is because Jesus gave up his life for us. So we also ought to give up our lives for our brothers and sisters. [17]If someone has enough money to live well and sees a brother or sister* in need but shows no compassion—how can God's love be in that person?

[18]Dear children, let's not merely say that we love each other; let us show the truth by our actions. [19]Our actions will show that we belong to the truth, so we will be confident when we stand before God. [20]Even if we feel guilty, God is greater than our feelings, and he knows everything.

[21]Dear friends, if we don't feel guilty, we can come to God with bold confidence. [22]And we will receive from him whatever we ask because we obey him and do the things that please him.

[23]And this is his commandment: We must believe in the name of his Son, Jesus Christ, and love one another, just as he commanded us. [24]Those who obey God's commandments

2:27a Greek *the anointing from him.* **2:27b** Greek *the anointing.* **3:9** Greek *because his seed.* **3:10** Greek *does not love his brother.* **3:13** Greek *brothers.* **3:14** Greek *the brothers;* similarly in 3:16. **3:15** Greek *hates his brother.* **3:17** Greek *sees his brother.*

remain in fellowship with him, and he with them. And we know he lives in us because the Spirit he gave us lives in us.

CHAPTER 4

Discerning False Prophets

Dear friends, do not believe everyone who claims to speak by the Spirit. You must test them to see if the spirit they have comes from God. For there are many false prophets in the world. [2]This is how we know if they have the Spirit of God: If a person claiming to be a prophet* acknowledges that Jesus Christ came in a real body, that person has the Spirit of God. [3]But if someone claims to be a prophet and does not acknowledge the truth about Jesus, that person is not from God. Such a person has the spirit of the Antichrist, which you heard is coming into the world and indeed is already here.

[4]But you belong to God, my dear children. You have already won a victory over those people, because the Spirit who lives in you is greater than the spirit who lives in the world. [5]Those people belong to this world, so they speak from the world's viewpoint, and the world listens to them. [6]But we belong to God, and those who know God listen to us. If they do not belong to God, they do not listen to us. That is how we know if someone has the Spirit of truth or the spirit of deception.

Loving One Another

[7]Dear friends, let us continue to love one another, for love comes from God. Anyone who loves is a child of God and knows God. [8]But anyone who does not love does not know God, for God is love.

[9]God showed how much he loved us by sending his one and only Son into the world so that we might have eternal life through him. [10]This is real love—not that we loved God, but that he loved us and sent his Son as a sacrifice to take away our sins.

[11]Dear friends, since God loved us that much, we surely ought to love each other. [12]No one has ever seen God. But if we love each other, God lives in us, and his love is brought to full expression in us.

[13]And God has given us his Spirit as proof that we live in him and he in us. [14]Furthermore, we have seen with our own eyes and now testify that the Father sent his Son to be the Savior of the world. [15]All who confess that Jesus is the Son of God have God living in them, and they live in God. [16]We know how much God loves us, and we have put our trust in his love.

God is love, and all who live in love live in God, and God lives in them. [17]And as we live in God, our love grows more perfect. So we will not be afraid on the day of judgment, but we can face him with confidence because we live like Jesus here in this world.

[18]Such love has no fear, because perfect love expels all fear. If we are afraid, it is for fear of punishment, and this shows that we have not fully experienced his perfect love. [19]We love each other* because he loved us first.

My brother makes me so mad. I just hate him!

If someone says, "I love God," but hates a Christian brother or sister, that person is a liar; for if we don't love people we can see, how can we love God, whom we cannot see? 1 JOHN 4:20

[20]If someone says, "I love God," but hates a Christian brother or sister,* that person is a liar; for if we don't love people we can see, how can we love God, whom we cannot see? [21]And he has given us this command: Those who love God must also love their Christian brothers and sisters.*

CHAPTER 5

Faith in the Son of God

Everyone who believes that Jesus is the Christ* has become a child of God. And everyone who

4:2 Greek *If a spirit;* similarly in 4:3. **4:19** Greek *We love.* Other manuscripts read *We love God;* still others read *We love him.* **4:20** Greek *hates his brother.* **4:21** Greek *The one who loves God must also love his brother.* **5:1** Or *the Messiah.*

loves the Father loves his children, too. [2]We
know we love God's children if we love God
and obey his commandments. [3]Loving God
means keeping his commandments, and his
commandments are not burdensome. [4]For
every child of God defeats this evil world, and
we achieve this victory through our faith.
[5]And who can win this battle against the
world? Only those who believe that Jesus is the
Son of God.

[6]And Jesus Christ was revealed as God's Son
by his baptism in water and by shedding his
blood on the cross*—not by water only, but by
water and blood. And the Spirit, who is truth,
confirms it with his testimony. [7]So we have
these three witnesses*—[8]the Spirit, the water,
and the blood—and all three agree. [9]Since we
believe human testimony, surely we can be-
lieve the greater testimony that comes from
God. And God has testified about his Son. [10]All
who believe in the Son of God know in their
hearts that this testimony is true. Those who
don't believe this are actually calling God a liar
because they don't believe what God has testi-
fied about his Son.

[11]And this is what God has testified: He
has given us eternal life, and this life is in his
Son. [12]Whoever has the Son has life; who-
ever does not have God's Son does not have
life.

Conclusion

[13]I have written this to you who believe in the
name of the Son of God, so that you may
know you have eternal life. [14]And we are con-
fident that he hears us whenever we ask for
anything that pleases him. [15]And since we
know he hears us when we make our re-
quests, we also know that he will give us what
we ask for.

[16]If you see a Christian brother or sister*
sinning in a way that does not lead to death,
you should pray, and God will give that person
life. But there is a sin that leads to death, and I
am not saying you should pray for those who
commit it. [17]All wicked actions are sin, but
not every sin leads to death.

[18]We know that God's children do not
make a practice of sinning, for God's Son
holds them securely, and the evil one cannot
touch them. [19]We know that we are children
of God and that the world around us is under
the control of the evil one.

[20]And we know that the Son of God has
come, and he has given us understanding so
that we can know the true God.* And now we
live in fellowship with the true God because we
live in fellowship with his Son, Jesus Christ. He
is the only true God, and he is eternal life.

[21]Dear children, keep away from anything
that might take God's place in your hearts.*

5:6 Greek *This is he who came by water and blood.* **5:7** A few very late manuscripts add *in heaven—the Father, the Word, and the Holy Spirit, and these three are one. And we have three witnesses on earth.* **5:16** Greek *a brother.* **5:20** Greek *the one who is true.* **5:21** Greek *keep yourselves from idols.*

2 JOHN

WHO
As an older man, Jesus' disciple John wrote to the chosen lady and her children.

WHERE
John wrote this letter from Ephesus.

WHEN
Around AD 90, about the same time as 1 John was written.

WHY
To emphasize the basic and most important points in following Christ—truth and love.

Love means doing what God has commanded us, and he has commanded us to love one another.
2 JOHN 1:6

When it comes to serious matters, no one likes to be fooled. In the early church, people were being fooled by false teachers who were leading believers away from God. John wrote this letter to bring Christians back to the truth and to steer them away from false teachers.

DON'T BE FOOLED BY PEOPLE WHO TRY TO GET YOU TO BELIEVE THAT JESUS ISN'T GOD'S SON OR THAT THE BIBLE ISN'T GOD'S WORD.

Greetings

This letter is from John, the elder.*

I am writing to the chosen lady and to her children,* whom I love in the truth—as does everyone else who knows the truth—[2]because the truth lives in us and will be with us forever.

[3]Grace, mercy, and peace, which come from

1a Greek *From the elder.* 1b Or *the church God has chosen and its members.*

God the Father and from Jesus Christ—the Son of the Father—will continue to be with us who live in truth and love.

Live in the Truth

[4]How happy I was to meet some of your children and find them living according to the truth, just as the Father commanded.

I can't see God, so what can I do to show my love for him?

Love means doing what God has commanded us, and he has commanded us to love one another, just as you heard from the beginning.
2 JOHN 1:6

[5]I am writing to remind you, dear friends,* that we should love one another. This is not a new commandment, but one we have had from the beginning. [6]Love means doing what God has commanded us, and he has commanded us to love one another, just as you heard from the beginning.

[7]I say this because many deceivers have gone out into the world. They deny that Jesus Christ came* in a real body. Such a person is a deceiver and an antichrist. [8]Watch out that you do not lose what we* have worked so hard to achieve. Be diligent so that you receive your full reward. [9]Anyone who wanders away from this teaching has no relationship with God. But anyone who remains in the teaching of Christ has a relationship with both the Father and the Son.

[10]If anyone comes to your meeting and does not teach the truth about Christ, don't invite that person into your home or give any kind of encouragement. [11]Anyone who encourages such people becomes a partner in their evil work.

Conclusion

[12]I have much more to say to you, but I don't want to do it with paper and ink. For I hope to visit you soon and talk with you face to face. Then our joy will be complete.

[13]Greetings from the children of your sister,* chosen by God.

5 Greek *I urge you, lady.* **7** Or *will come.* **8** Some manuscripts read *you.* **13** Or *from the members of your sister church.*

3 JOHN

WHO
Jesus' disciple John as an older man, Gaius, Diotrephes, and Demetrius.

WHERE
John wrote this letter from Ephesus.

WHEN
Around AD 90.

WHY
John wrote to praise Gaius for his hospitality and to encourage Gaius in his Christian life.

Dear friend, you are being faithful to God when you care for the traveling teachers who pass through. 3 JOHN 1:5

Hospitality means reaching out to others, even strangers. It means time, work, and money. For Gaius, it was a habit. He had gained a reputation for friendship and generosity to traveling teachers and missionaries. John wrote to thank Gaius for his love for others and to encourage him in his faith.

Read 3 John and decide to be like Gaius, someone who is loving, generous, and hospitable.

Greetings

This letter is from John, the elder.*

I am writing to Gaius, my dear friend, whom I love in the truth.

2 Dear friend, I hope all is well with you and that you are as healthy in body as you are strong in spirit. 3 Some of the traveling teachers* recently returned and made me very happy by telling me about your faithfulness and that you are living according to the truth. 4 I could have no greater joy than to hear that my children are following the truth.

1 Greek *From the elder.* 3 Greek *the brothers;* also in verses 5 and 10.

Caring for the Lord's Workers

5 Dear friend, you are being faithful to God when
you care for the traveling teachers who pass
through, even though they are strangers to you.
6 They have told the church here of your loving
friendship. Please continue providing for such
teachers in a manner that pleases God. 7 For they
are traveling for the Lord,* and they accept
nothing from people who are not believers.* 8 So
we ourselves should support them so that we
can be their partners as they teach the truth.

9 I wrote to the church about this, but Dio-
trephes, who loves to be the leader, refuses
to have anything to do with us. 10 When I
come, I will report some of the things he is
doing and the evil accusations he is making
against us. Not only does he refuse to wel-
come the traveling teachers, he also tells oth-
ers not to help them. And when they do help,
he puts them out of the church.

11 Dear friend, don't let this bad example
influence you. Follow only what is good.
Remember that those who do good prove
that they are God's children, and those
who do evil prove that they do not know
God.*

12 Everyone speaks highly of Demetrius, as
does the truth itself. We ourselves can say the
same for him, and you know we speak the
truth.

Conclusion

13 I have much more to say to you, but I don't
want to write it with pen and ink. 14 For I hope
to see you soon, and then we will talk face to
face.

15 *Peace be with you.

Your friends here send you their greetings.
Please give my personal greetings to each of
our friends there.

7a Greek *They went out on behalf of the Name.* **7b** Greek *from Gentiles.* **11** Greek *they have not seen God.* **15** Some English translations combine verses 14 and 15 into verse 14.

JUDE

WHO
Jude and James.

WHERE
We don't know.

WHEN
Around AD 65.

WHY
To remind the church to always be ready for opposition.

Await the mercy of our Lord Jesus Christ, who will bring you eternal life. In this way, you will keep yourselves safe in God's love.
JUDE 1:21

You're a Christian in AD 65. How do you prepare for people who oppose your faith? Jude wrote this letter to tell Christians to be ready to defend themselves against false teachers. He told them to be alert, to remember what God had done, and to focus on Jesus Christ.

GOD WILL HELP YOU STAND UP TO ANYONE WHO IS AGAINST YOU BECAUSE OF YOUR FAITH.

Greetings from Jude

This letter is from Jude, a slave of Jesus Christ and a brother of James.

I am writing to all who have been called by God the Father, who loves you and keeps you safe in the care of Jesus Christ.*

[2]May God give you more and more mercy, peace, and love.

1 Or *keeps you for Jesus Christ.*

The Danger of False Teachers

[3]Dear friends, I had been eagerly planning to write to you about the salvation we all share. But now I find that I must write about something else, urging you to defend the faith that God has entrusted once for all time to his holy people. [4]I say this because some ungodly people have wormed their way into your churches,

saying that God's marvelous grace allows us to live immoral lives. The condemnation of such people was recorded long ago, for they have denied our only Master and Lord, Jesus Christ.

5 So I want to remind you, though you already know these things, that Jesus* first rescued the nation of Israel from Egypt, but later he destroyed those who did not remain faithful. 6 And I remind you of the angels who did not stay within the limits of authority God gave them but left the place where they belonged. God has kept them securely chained in prisons of darkness, waiting for the great day of judgment. 7 And don't forget Sodom and Gomorrah and their neighboring towns, which were filled with immorality and every kind of sexual perversion. Those cities were destroyed by fire and serve as a warning of the eternal fire of God's judgment.

8 In the same way, these people—who claim authority from their dreams—live immoral lives, defy authority, and scoff at supernatural beings.* 9 But even Michael, one of the mightiest of the angels,* did not dare accuse the devil of blasphemy, but simply said, "The Lord rebuke you!" (This took place when Michael was arguing with the devil about Moses' body.) 10 But these people scoff at things they do not understand. Like unthinking animals, they do whatever their instincts tell them, and so they bring about their own destruction. 11 What sorrow awaits them! For they follow in the footsteps of Cain, who killed his brother. Like Balaam, they deceive people for money. And like Korah, they perish in their rebellion.

12 When these people eat with you in your fellowship meals commemorating the Lord's love, they are like dangerous reefs that can shipwreck you.* They are like shameless shepherds who care only for themselves. They are like clouds blowing over the land without giving any rain. They are like trees in autumn that are doubly dead, for they bear no fruit and have been pulled up by the roots. 13 They are like wild waves of the sea, churning up the foam of their shameful deeds. They are like wandering stars, doomed forever to blackest darkness.

14 Enoch, who lived in the seventh generation after Adam, prophesied about these people. He said, "Listen! The Lord is coming with countless thousands of his holy ones 15 to execute judgment on the people of the world. He will convict every person of all the ungodly things they have done and for all the insults that ungodly sinners have spoken against him."*

16 These people are grumblers and complainers, living only to satisfy their desires. They brag loudly about themselves, and they flatter others to get what they want.

A Call to Remain Faithful

17 But you, my dear friends, must remember what the apostles of our Lord Jesus Christ said. 18 They told you that in the last times there would be scoffers whose purpose in life is to satisfy their ungodly desires. 19 These people are the ones who are creating divisions among you. They follow their natural instincts because they do not have God's Spirit in them.

20 But you, dear friends, must build each other up in your most holy faith, pray in the power of the Holy Spirit,* 21 and await the mercy of our Lord Jesus Christ, who will bring you eternal life. In this way, you will keep yourselves safe in God's love.

22 And you must show mercy to* those whose faith is wavering. 23 Rescue others by snatching them from the flames of judgment. Show mercy to still others,* but do so with great caution, hating the sins that contaminate their lives.*

A Prayer of Praise

24 Now all glory to God, who is able to keep you from falling away and will bring you with great joy into his glorious presence without a single fault. 25 All glory to him who alone is God, our Savior through Jesus Christ our Lord. All glory, majesty, power, and authority are his before all time, and in the present, and beyond all time! Amen.

5 As in the best manuscripts; various other manuscripts read *[the] Lord*, or *God*, or *Christ*; one reads *God Christ*. **8** Greek *at glorious ones*, which are probably evil angels. **9** Greek *Michael, the archangel*. **12** Or *they are contaminants among you*; or *they are stains*. **14-15** The quotation comes from intertestamental literature: Enoch 1:9. **20** Greek *pray in the Holy Spirit*. **22** Some manuscripts read *must reprove*. **22-23a** Some manuscripts have only two categories of people: (1) those whose faith is wavering and therefore need to be snatched from the flames of judgment, and (2) those who need to be shown mercy. **23b** Greek *with fear, hating even the clothing stained by the flesh*.

Revelation

WHO
The disciple John as an older man and Jesus in heaven.

WHERE
John wrote this letter from the island of Patmos.

WHEN
Around AD 95 when Christians were under persecution.

WHY
To reveal the true and full identity of Christ and to give warning and hope to all believers.

The one sitting on the throne said . . . "To all who are thirsty I will give freely from the springs of the water of life."
REVELATION 21:5-6

Revelation, the last book in the Bible, tells about the last chapter in history. God will conquer all his enemies, and Jesus Christ will reign forever and ever. Even when we hear about all the problems in the world, the book of Revelation gives us hope for the future.

Read Revelation and celebrate. Our King is coming!

CHAPTER 1

Prologue

This is a revelation from* Jesus Christ, which God gave him to show his servants the events that must soon* take place. He sent an angel to present this revelation to his servant John, [2]who faithfully reported everything he saw. This is his report of the word of God and the testimony of Jesus Christ.

[3]God blesses the one who reads the words of this prophecy to the church, and he blesses all who listen to its message and obey what it says, for the time is near.

John's Greeting to the Seven Churches

[4]This letter is from John to the seven churches in the province of Asia.*

Grace and peace to you from the one who

1:1a Or *of*. **1:1b** Or *suddenly*, or *quickly*. **1:4a** *Asia* was a Roman province in what is now western Turkey.

is, who always was, and who is still to come;
from the sevenfold Spirit* before his throne;
5 and from Jesus Christ. He is the faithful wit-
ness to these things, the first to rise from the
dead, and the ruler of all the kings of the
world.

All glory to him who loves us and has freed
us from our sins by shedding his blood for us.
6 He has made us a Kingdom of priests for God
his Father. All glory and power to him forever
and ever! Amen.

7 Look! He comes with the clouds of
heaven.
And everyone will see him—
even those who pierced him.
And all the nations of the world
will mourn for him.
Yes! Amen!

8 "I am the Alpha and the Omega—the be-
ginning and the end,"* says the Lord God. "I
am the one who is, who always was, and who is
still to come—the Almighty One."

AMAZING FACTS

Want to know how Jesus looks in heaven? Catch John's vision of Jesus' hair, eyes, feet, voice, and face—then be amazed!

REVELATION 1:12-16

Vision of the Son of Man

9 I, John, am your brother and your partner in
suffering and in God's Kingdom and in the
patient endurance to which Jesus calls us. I
was exiled to the island of Patmos for preach-
ing the word of God and for my testimony
about Jesus. 10 It was the Lord's Day, and I was
worshiping in the Spirit.* Suddenly, I heard
behind me a loud voice like a trumpet blast.
11 It said, "Write in a book* everything you see,
and send it to the seven churches in the cities
of Ephesus, Smyrna, Pergamum, Thyatira,
Sardis, Philadelphia, and Laodicea."

12 When I turned to see who was speaking
to me, I saw seven gold lampstands. 13 And
standing in the middle of the lampstands
was someone like the Son of Man.* He was
wearing a long robe with a gold sash across
his chest. 14 His head and his hair were white
like wool, as white as snow. And his eyes
were like flames of fire. 15 His feet were like
polished bronze refined in a furnace, and his
voice thundered like mighty ocean waves.
16 He held seven stars in his right hand, and a
sharp two-edged sword came from his
mouth. And his face was like the sun in all its
brilliance.

17 When I saw him, I fell at his feet as if I
were dead. But he laid his right hand on me
and said, "Don't be afraid! I am the First and
the Last. 18 I am the living one. I died, but
look—I am alive forever and ever! And I hold
the keys of death and the grave.*

19 "Write down what you have seen—both
the things that are now happening and the
things that will happen.* 20 This is the mean-
ing of the mystery of the seven stars you saw
in my right hand and the seven gold
lampstands: The seven stars are the angels*
of the seven churches, and the seven
lampstands are the seven churches.

CHAPTER 2

The Message to the Church in Ephesus

"Write this letter to the angel* of the church
in Ephesus. This is the message from the one
who holds the seven stars in his right hand,
the one who walks among the seven gold
lampstands:

2 "I know all the things you do. I have seen
your hard work and your patient
endurance. I know you don't tolerate evil
people. You have examined the claims of
those who say they are apostles but are
not. You have discovered they are liars.
3 You have patiently suffered for me
without quitting.

1:4b Greek *the seven spirits.* 1:8 Greek *I am the Alpha and the Omega,* referring to the first and last letters of the Greek alphabet. 1:10 Or *in spirit.* 1:11 Or *on a scroll.* 1:13 Or *like a son of man.* See Dan 7:13. "Son of Man" is a title Jesus used for himself. 1:18 Greek *and Hades.* 1:19 Or *what you have seen and what they mean—the things that have already begun to happen.* 1:20 Or *the messengers.* 2:1 Or *the messenger;* also in 2:8, 12, 18.

4"But I have this complaint against you.
You don't love me or each other as you did
at first!* 5Look how far you have fallen!
Turn back to me and do the works you did
at first. If you don't repent, I will come
and remove your lampstand from its
place among the churches. 6But this is in
your favor: You hate the evil deeds of the
Nicolaitans, just as I do.

7"Anyone with ears to hear must listen
to the Spirit and understand what he is
saying to the churches. To everyone who
is victorious I will give fruit from the tree
of life in the paradise of God.

The Message to the Church in Smyrna

8"Write this letter to the angel of the church
in Smyrna. This is the message from the one
who is the First and the Last, who was dead
but is now alive:

9"I know about your suffering and your
poverty—but you are rich! I know the
blasphemy of those opposing you. They
say they are Jews, but they are not,
because their synagogue belongs to Satan.
10Don't be afraid of what you are about to
suffer. The devil will throw some of you
into prison to test you. You will suffer for
ten days. But if you remain faithful even
when facing death, I will give you the
crown of life.

11"Anyone with ears to hear must listen
to the Spirit and understand what he is
saying to the churches. Whoever is
victorious will not be harmed by the
second death.

The Message to the Church in Pergamum

12"Write this letter to the angel of the church
in Pergamum. This is the message from the
one with the sharp two-edged sword:

13"I know that you live in the city where
Satan has his throne, yet you have
remained loyal to me. You refused to deny
me even when Antipas, my faithful

2:4 Greek *You have lost your first love.*

THE BEGINNING AND THE END

The Bible records for us the beginning and the end of the world.

GENESIS	REVELATION
The sun is created	The sun is not needed
Satan is victorious	Satan is defeated
Sin enters the human race	Sin is banished
People run and hide from God	People are invited to live with God forever
People are cursed	The curse is removed
Tears are shed, with sorrow for sin	No more sin, no more tears or sorrow
The garden and the earth are cursed	God's city is glorified, the earth is made new
The fruit from the Tree of Life is not to be eaten	God's people may eat from the Tree of Life
Paradise is lost	Paradise is regained
People are doomed to death	Death is defeated, believers live forever with God

witness, was martyred among you there in
Satan's city.
14"But I have a few complaints against
you. You tolerate some among you whose
teaching is like that of Balaam, who
showed Balak how to trip up the people of
Israel. He taught them to sin by eating
food offered to idols and by committing
sexual sin. 15In a similar way, you have
some Nicolaitans among you who follow
the same teaching. 16Repent of your sin,
or I will come to you suddenly and fight
against them with the sword of my
mouth.
17"Anyone with ears to hear must listen
to the Spirit and understand what he is
saying to the churches. To everyone who
is victorious I will give some of the manna
that has been hidden away in heaven. And
I will give to each one a white stone, and
on the stone will be engraved a new name
that no one understands except the one
who receives it.

The Message to the Church in Thyatira

18"Write this letter to the angel of the church
in Thyatira. This is the message from the Son
of God, whose eyes are like flames of fire,
whose feet are like polished bronze:

19"I know all the things you do. I have
seen your love, your faith, your service,
and your patient endurance. And I can see
your constant improvement in all these
things.
20"But I have this complaint against
you. You are permitting that woman—
that Jezebel who calls herself a prophet—
to lead my servants astray. She teaches
them to commit sexual sin and to eat
food offered to idols. 21I gave her time
to repent, but she does not want to turn
away from her immorality.
22"Therefore, I will throw her on a bed
of suffering,* and those who commit
adultery with her will suffer greatly unless
they repent and turn away from her evil
deeds. 23I will strike her children dead.
Then all the churches will know that I am
the one who searches out the thoughts
and intentions of every person. And I will
give to each of you whatever you deserve.
24"But I also have a message for the rest
of you in Thyatira who have not followed
this false teaching ('deeper truths,' as they
call them—depths of Satan, actually). I will
ask nothing more of you 25except that you
hold tightly to what you have until I come.
26To all who are victorious, who obey me
to the very end,

To them I will give authority over all the
nations.
27 They will rule the nations with an iron
rod
and smash them like clay pots.*

28They will have the same authority I
received from my Father, and I will also
give them the morning star!
29"Anyone with ears to hear must listen
to the Spirit and understand what he is
saying to the churches.

CHAPTER 3

The Message to the Church in Sardis

"Write this letter to the angel* of the church
in Sardis. This is the message from the one
who has the sevenfold Spirit* of God and the
seven stars:

"I know all the things you do, and that you
have a reputation for being alive—but you
are dead. 2Wake up! Strengthen what
little remains, for even what is left is
almost dead. I find that your actions do
not meet the requirements of my God.
3Go back to what you heard and believed
at first; hold to it firmly. Repent and turn
to me again. If you don't wake up, I will
come to you suddenly, as unexpected as
a thief.
4"Yet there are some in the church
in Sardis who have not soiled their
clothes with evil. They will walk with
me in white, for they are worthy. 5All
who are victorious will be clothed in
white. I will never erase their names
from the Book of Life, but I will
announce before my Father and his
angels that they are mine.
6"Anyone with ears to hear must listen
to the Spirit and understand what he is
saying to the churches.

2:22 Greek *a bed*. **2:26-27** Ps 2:8-9 (Greek Version). **3:1a** Or *the messenger*; also in 3:7, 14. **3:1b** Greek *the seven spirits*.

I've Got It All!

Julio was having a great school year. His best friend was in his class, he made it into the advanced math program, and he had the best teacher in school. Julio also was doing well on the basketball team. One day Julio's mom mentioned that the library was having a reading buddy program for kids from needy families. She asked, "Would you like to be a buddy?" Julio didn't answer right away. Why should he waste his time with these kids? He had better things to do. What do you think Julio should do? Check out Revelation 3:17-19.

The Message to the Church in Philadelphia

7"Write this letter to the angel of the church in Philadelphia.

This is the message from the one who is
holy and true,
the one who has the key of David.
What he opens, no one can close;
and what he closes, no one can open:*

8"I know all the things you do, and I have opened a door for you that no one can close. You have little strength, yet you obeyed my word and did not deny me. 9Look, I will force those who belong to Satan's synagogue—those liars who say they are Jews but are not—to come and bow down at your feet. They will acknowledge that you are the ones I love.

10"Because you have obeyed my command to persevere, I will protect you from the great time of testing that will come upon the whole world to test those who belong to this world. 11I am coming soon.* Hold on to what you have, so that no one will take away your crown. 12All who are victorious will become pillars in the Temple of my God, and they will never have to leave it. And I will write on them the name of my God, and they will be citizens in the city of my God—the new Jerusalem that comes down from heaven from my God. And I will also write on them my new name.

13"Anyone with ears to hear must listen to the Spirit and understand what he is saying to the churches.

The Message to the Church in Laodicea

14"Write this letter to the angel of the church in Laodicea. This is the message from the one who is the Amen—the faithful and true witness, the beginning* of God's new creation:

15"I know all the things you do, that you are neither hot nor cold. I wish that you were one or the other! 16But since you are like lukewarm water, neither hot nor cold, I will spit you out of my mouth! 17You say, 'I am rich. I have everything I want. I don't need a thing!' And you don't realize that you are wretched and miserable and poor and blind and naked. 18So I advise you to buy gold from me—gold that has been purified by fire. Then you will be rich. Also buy white garments from me so you

3:7 Isa 22:22. 3:11 Or *suddenly*, or *quickly*. 3:14 Or *the ruler*, or *the source*.

will not be shamed by your nakedness,
and ointment for your eyes so you will be
able to see. [19] I correct and discipline
everyone I love. So be diligent and turn
from your indifference.

[20] "Look! I stand at the door and knock.
If you hear my voice and open the door,
I will come in, and we will share a meal
together as friends. [21] Those who are
victorious will sit with me on my throne,
just as I was victorious and sat with my
Father on his throne.

[22] "Anyone with ears to hear must listen
to the Spirit and understand what he is
saying to the churches."

CHAPTER 4

Worship in Heaven

Then as I looked, I saw a door standing open in heaven, and the same voice I had heard before spoke to me like a trumpet blast. The voice said, "Come up here, and I will show you what must happen after this." [2] And instantly I was in the Spirit,* and I saw a throne in heaven and someone sitting on it. [3] The one sitting on the throne was as brilliant as gemstones—like jasper and carnelian. And the glow of an emerald circled his throne like a rainbow. [4] Twenty-four thrones surrounded him, and twenty-four elders sat on them. They were all clothed in white and had gold crowns on their heads. [5] From the throne came flashes of lightning and the rumble of thunder. And in front of the throne were seven torches with burning flames. This is the sevenfold Spirit* of God. [6] In front of the throne was a shiny sea of glass, sparkling like crystal.

In the center and around the throne were four living beings, each covered with eyes, front and back. [7] The first of these living beings was like a lion; the second was like an ox; the third had a human face; and the fourth was like an eagle in flight. [8] Each of these living beings had six wings, and their wings were covered all over with eyes, inside and out. Day after day and night after night they keep on saying,

"Holy, holy, holy is the Lord God, the
Almighty—
the one who always was, who is, and
who is still to come."

[9] Whenever the living beings give glory and honor and thanks to the one sitting on the throne (the one who lives forever and ever), [10] the twenty-four elders fall down and worship the one sitting on the throne (the one who lives forever and ever). And they lay their crowns before the throne and say,

[11] "You are worthy, O Lord our God,
to receive glory and honor and power.
For you created all things,
and they exist because you created
what you pleased."

CHAPTER 5

The Lamb Opens the Scroll

Then I saw a scroll* in the right hand of the one who was sitting on the throne. There was writing on the inside and the outside of the scroll, and it was sealed with seven seals. [2] And I saw a strong angel, who shouted with a loud voice: "Who is worthy to break the seals on this scroll and open it?" [3] But no one in heaven or on earth or under the earth was able to open the scroll and read it.

[4] Then I began to weep bitterly because no one was found worthy to open the scroll and read it. [5] But one of the twenty-four elders said to me, "Stop weeping! Look, the Lion of the tribe of Judah, the heir to David's throne,* has won the victory. He is worthy to open the scroll and its seven seals."

[6] Then I saw a Lamb that looked as if it had been slaughtered, but it was now standing between the throne and the four living beings and among the twenty-four elders. He had seven horns and seven eyes, which represent the sevenfold Spirit* of God that is sent out into every part of the earth. [7] He stepped forward and took the scroll from the right hand of the one sitting on the throne. [8] And when he took the scroll, the four living beings and the twenty-four elders fell down before the Lamb. Each one had a harp, and they held gold bowls filled with incense, which are the prayers of God's people. [9] And they sang a new song with these words:

"You are worthy to take the scroll
and break its seals and open it.
For you were slaughtered, and your blood
has ransomed people for God

4:2 Or *in spirit*. **4:5** Greek *They are the seven spirits*. **5:1** Or *book;* also in 5:2, 3, 4, 5, 7, 8, 9. **5:5** Greek *the root of David*. See Isa 11:10. **5:6** Greek *which are the seven spirits*.

from every tribe and language and
people and nation.
10 And you have caused them to become
a Kingdom of priests for our God.
And they will reign* on the earth."

11 Then I looked again, and I heard the voices of thousands and millions of angels around the throne and of the living beings and the elders. 12 And they sang in a mighty chorus:

"Worthy is the Lamb who was
slaughtered—
to receive power and riches
and wisdom and strength
and honor and glory and blessing."

13 And then I heard every creature in heaven and on earth and under the earth and in the sea. They sang:

"Blessing and honor and glory and power
belong to the one sitting on the throne
and to the Lamb forever and ever."

14 And the four living beings said, "Amen!" And the twenty-four elders fell down and worshiped the Lamb.

AMAZING FACTS

Imagine a choir featuring millions of angels praising Jesus, the Lamb of God. That's one heavenly worship service!

REVELATION 5:11-12

CHAPTER 6

The Lamb Breaks the First Six Seals

As I watched, the Lamb broke the first of the seven seals on the scroll.* Then I heard one of the four living beings say with a voice like thunder, "Come!" 2 I looked up and saw a white horse standing there. Its rider carried a bow, and a crown was placed on his head. He rode out to win many battles and gain the victory.

3 When the Lamb broke the second seal, I heard the second living being say, "Come!" 4 Then another horse appeared, a red one. Its rider was given a mighty sword and the authority to take peace from the earth. And there was war and slaughter everywhere.

5 When the Lamb broke the third seal, I heard the third living being say, "Come!" I looked up and saw a black horse, and its rider was holding a pair of scales in his hand. 6 And I heard a voice from among the four living beings say, "A loaf of wheat bread or three loaves of barley will cost a day's pay.* And don't waste* the olive oil and wine."

7 When the Lamb broke the fourth seal, I heard the fourth living being say, "Come!" 8 I looked up and saw a horse whose color was pale green. Its rider was named Death, and his companion was the Grave.* These two were given authority over one-fourth of the earth, to kill with the sword and famine and disease* and wild animals.

9 When the Lamb broke the fifth seal, I saw under the altar the souls of all who had been martyred for the word of God and for being faithful in their testimony. 10 They shouted to the Lord and said, "O Sovereign Lord, holy and true, how long before you judge the people who belong to this world and avenge our blood for what they have done to us?" 11 Then a white robe was given to each of them. And they were told to rest a little longer until the full number of their brothers and sisters*—their fellow servants of Jesus who were to be martyred—had joined them.

12 I watched as the Lamb broke the sixth seal, and there was a great earthquake. The sun became as dark as black cloth, and the moon became as red as blood. 13 Then the stars of the sky fell to the earth like green figs falling from a tree shaken by a strong wind. 14 The sky was rolled up like a scroll, and all of the mountains and islands were moved from their places.

5:10 Some manuscripts read *they are reigning*. **6:1** Or *book*. **6:6a** Greek *A choinix* [1 quart or 1 liter] *of wheat for a denarius, and 3 choinix of barley for a denarius*. A denarius was equivalent to a laborer's full day's wage. **6:6b** Or *harm*. **6:8a** Greek *was Hades*. **6:8b** Greek *death*. **6:11** Greek *their brothers*.

15 Then everyone—the kings of the earth,
the rulers, the generals, the wealthy, the pow-
erful, and every slave and free person—all hid
themselves in the caves and among the rocks
of the mountains. 16 And they cried to the
mountains and the rocks, "Fall on us and hide
us from the face of the one who sits on the
throne and from the wrath of the Lamb. 17 For
the great day of their wrath has come, and
who is able to survive?"

CHAPTER 7

God's People Will Be Preserved

Then I saw four angels standing at the four
corners of the earth, holding back the four
winds so they did not blow on the earth or the
sea, or even on any tree. 2 And I saw another
angel coming up from the east, carrying the
seal of the living God. And he shouted to
those four angels, who had been given power
to harm land and sea, 3 "Wait! Don't harm the
land or the sea or the trees until we have
placed the seal of God on the foreheads of his
servants."

4 And I heard how many were marked with
the seal of God—144,000 were sealed from
all the tribes of Israel:

5	from Judah	12,000
	from Reuben	12,000
	from Gad	12,000
6	from Asher	12,000
	from Naphtali	12,000
	from Manasseh	12,000
7	from Simeon	12,000
	from Levi	12,000
	from Issachar	12,000
8	from Zebulun	12,000
	from Joseph	12,000
	from Benjamin	12,000

Praise from the Great Crowd

9 After this I saw a vast crowd, too great to
count, from every nation and tribe and people
and language, standing in front of the throne
and before the Lamb. They were clothed in
white robes and held palm branches in their
hands. 10 And they were shouting with a great
roar,

"Salvation comes from our God who sits
on the throne
and from the Lamb!"

11 And all the angels were standing around
the throne and around the elders and the four
living beings. And they fell before the throne
with their faces to the ground and worshiped
God. 12 They sang,

"Amen! Blessing and glory and wisdom
and thanksgiving and honor
and power and strength belong to our
God
forever and ever! Amen."

13 Then one of the twenty-four elders asked
me, "Who are these who are clothed in white?
Where did they come from?"

14 And I said to him, "Sir, you are the one
who knows."

Then he said to me, "These are the ones
who died in* the great tribulation.* They have
washed their robes in the blood of the Lamb
and made them white.

15 "That is why they stand in front of God's
throne
and serve him day and night in his
Temple.
And he who sits on the throne
will give them shelter.
16 They will never again be hungry or thirsty;
they will never be scorched by the heat
of the sun.
17 For the Lamb on the throne*
will be their Shepherd.
He will lead them to springs of life-giving
water.
And God will wipe every tear from their
eyes."

CHAPTER 8

The Lamb Breaks the Seventh Seal

When the Lamb broke the seventh seal on the
scroll,* there was silence throughout heaven
for about half an hour. 2 I saw the seven angels
who stand before God, and they were given
seven trumpets.

3 Then another angel with a gold incense
burner came and stood at the altar. And a
great amount of incense was given to him to
mix with the prayers of God's people as an
offering on the gold altar before the throne.
4 The smoke of the incense, mixed with the
prayers of God's holy people, ascended up
to God from the altar where the angel had

7:14a Greek *who came out of.* **7:14b** Or *the great suffering.* **7:17** Greek *on the center of the throne.* **8:1** Or *book.*

poured them out. [5]Then the angel filled the incense burner with fire from the altar and threw it down upon the earth; and thunder crashed, lightning flashed, and there was a terrible earthquake.

The First Four Trumpets

[6]Then the seven angels with the seven trumpets prepared to blow their mighty blasts.

[7]The first angel blew his trumpet, and hail and fire mixed with blood were thrown down on the earth. One-third of the earth was set on fire, one-third of the trees were burned, and all the green grass was burned.

[8]Then the second angel blew his trumpet, and a great mountain of fire was thrown into the sea. One-third of the water in the sea became blood, [9]one-third of all things living in the sea died, and one-third of all the ships on the sea were destroyed.

[10]Then the third angel blew his trumpet, and a great star fell from the sky, burning like a torch. It fell on one-third of the rivers and on the springs of water. [11]The name of the star was Bitterness.* It made one-third of the water bitter, and many people died from drinking the bitter water.

[12]Then the fourth angel blew his trumpet, and one-third of the sun was struck, and one-third of the moon, and one-third of the stars, and they became dark. And one-third of the day was dark, and also one-third of the night.

[13]Then I looked, and I heard a single eagle crying loudly as it flew through the air, "Terror, terror, terror to all who belong to this world because of what will happen when the last three angels blow their trumpets."

CHAPTER 9

The Fifth Trumpet Brings the First Terror

Then the fifth angel blew his trumpet, and I saw a star that had fallen to earth from the sky, and he was given the key to the shaft of the bottomless pit.* [2]When he opened it, smoke poured out as though from a huge furnace, and the sunlight and air turned dark from the smoke.

[3]Then locusts came from the smoke and descended on the earth, and they were given power to sting like scorpions. [4]They were told not to harm the grass or plants or trees, but only the people who did not have the seal of God on their foreheads. [5]They were told not to kill them but to torture them for five months with pain like the pain of a scorpion sting. [6]In those days people will seek death but will not find it. They will long to die, but death will flee from them!

[7]The locusts looked like horses prepared for battle. They had what looked like gold crowns on their heads, and their faces looked like human faces. [8]They had hair like women's hair and teeth like the teeth of a lion. [9]They wore armor made of iron, and their wings roared like an army of chariots rushing into battle. [10]They had tails that stung like scorpions, and for five months they had the

8:11 Greek *Wormwood.* **9:1** Or *the abyss,* or *the underworld;* also in 9:11.

power to torment people. [11]Their king is the angel from the bottomless pit; his name in Hebrew is *Abaddon*, and in Greek, *Apollyon*—the Destroyer.

[12]The first terror is past, but look, two more terrors are coming!

The Sixth Trumpet Brings the Second Terror

[13]Then the sixth angel blew his trumpet, and I heard a voice speaking from the four horns of the gold altar that stands in the presence of God. [14]And the voice said to the sixth angel who held the trumpet, "Release the four angels who are bound at the great Euphrates River." [15]Then the four angels who had been prepared for this hour and day and month and year were turned loose to kill one-third of all the people on earth. [16]I heard the size of their army, which was 200 million mounted troops.

[17]And in my vision, I saw the horses and the riders sitting on them. The riders wore armor that was fiery red and dark blue and yellow. The horses had heads like lions, and fire and smoke and burning sulfur billowed from their mouths. [18]One-third of all the people on earth were killed by these three plagues—by the fire and smoke and burning sulfur that came from the mouths of the horses. [19]Their power was in their mouths and in their tails. For their tails had heads like snakes, with the power to injure people.

[20]But the people who did not die in these plagues still refused to repent of their evil deeds and turn to God. They continued to worship demons and idols made of gold, silver, bronze, stone, and wood—idols that can neither see nor hear nor walk! [21]And they did not repent of their murders or their witchcraft or their sexual immorality or their thefts.

AMAZING FACTS

No wonder John's stomach hurt. He ate an entire scroll that was sweet to taste but then turned sour.

REVELATION 10:9-10

CHAPTER 10

The Angel and the Small Scroll

Then I saw another mighty angel coming down from heaven, surrounded by a cloud, with a rainbow over his head. His face shone like the sun, and his feet were like pillars of fire. [2]And in his hand was a small scroll* that had been opened. He stood with his right foot on the sea and his left foot on the land. [3]And he gave a great shout like the roar of a lion. And when he shouted, the seven thunders answered.

[4]When the seven thunders spoke, I was about to write. But I heard a voice from heaven saying, "Keep secret* what the seven thunders said, and do not write it down."

[5]Then the angel I saw standing on the sea and on the land raised his right hand toward heaven. [6]He swore an oath in the name of the one who lives forever and ever, who created the heavens and everything in them, the earth and everything in it, and the sea and everything in it. He said, "There will be no more delay. [7]When the seventh angel blows his trumpet, God's mysterious plan will be fulfilled. It will happen just as he announced it to his servants the prophets."

[8]Then the voice from heaven spoke to me again: "Go and take the open scroll from the hand of the angel who is standing on the sea and on the land."

[9]So I went to the angel and told him to give me the small scroll. "Yes, take it and eat it," he said. "It will be sweet as honey in your mouth, but it will turn sour in your stomach!" [10]So I took the small scroll from the hand of the angel, and I ate it! It was sweet in my mouth, but when I swallowed it, it turned sour in my stomach.

[11]Then I was told, "You must prophesy again about many peoples, nations, languages, and kings."

10:2 Or *book;* also in 10:8, 9, 10. **10:4** Greek *Seal up.*

CHAPTER 11

The Two Witnesses

Then I was given a measuring stick, and I was
told, "Go and measure the Temple of God and
the altar, and count the number of worship-
ers. [2]But do not measure the outer courtyard,
for it has been turned over to the nations.
They will trample the holy city for 42 months.
[3]And I will give power to my two witnesses,
and they will be clothed in burlap and will
prophesy during those 1,260 days."

[4]These two prophets are the two olive
trees and the two lampstands that stand be-
fore the Lord of all the earth. [5]If anyone tries
to harm them, fire flashes from their mouths
and consumes their enemies. This is how
anyone who tries to harm them must die.
[6]They have power to shut the sky so that no
rain will fall for as long as they prophesy. And
they have the power to turn the rivers and
oceans into blood, and to strike the earth
with every kind of plague as often as they
wish.

[7]When they complete their testimony, the
beast that comes up out of the bottomless
pit* will declare war against them, and he
will conquer them and kill them. [8]And their
bodies will lie in the main street of Jerusa-
lem,* the city that is figuratively called
"Sodom" and "Egypt," the city where their
Lord was crucified. [9]And for three and a half
days, all peoples, tribes, languages, and na-
tions will stare at their bodies. No one will be
allowed to bury them. [10]All the people who
belong to this world will gloat over them and
give presents to each other to celebrate the
death of the two prophets who had tor-
mented them.

[11]But after three and a half days, God
breathed life into them, and they stood up!
Terror struck all who were staring at them.
[12]Then a loud voice from heaven called to
the two prophets, "Come up here!" And they
rose to heaven in a cloud as their enemies
watched.

[13]At the same time there was a terrible
earthquake that destroyed a tenth of the city.
Seven thousand people died in that earth-
quake, and everyone else was terrified and
gave glory to the God of heaven.

[14]The second terror is past, but look, the
third terror is coming quickly.

The Seventh Trumpet Brings the Third Terror

[15]Then the seventh angel blew his trumpet,
and there were loud voices shouting in
heaven:

"The world has now become the
Kingdom of our Lord and of his
Christ,*
and he will reign forever and ever."

[16]The twenty-four elders sitting on their
thrones before God fell with their faces to the
ground and worshiped him. [17]And they said,

"We give thanks to you, Lord God, the
Almighty,
the one who is and who always was,
for now you have assumed your great
power
and have begun to reign.
[18] The nations were filled with wrath,
but now the time of your wrath has
come.
It is time to judge the dead
and reward your servants the
prophets,
as well as your holy people,
and all who fear your name,
from the least to the greatest.
It is time to destroy
all who have caused destruction on the
earth."

[19]Then, in heaven, the Temple of God was
opened and the Ark of his covenant could be
seen inside the Temple. Lightning flashed,
thunder crashed and roared, and there was an
earthquake and a terrible hailstorm.

CHAPTER 12

The Woman and the Dragon

Then I witnessed in heaven an event of great
significance. I saw a woman clothed with the
sun, with the moon beneath her feet, and a
crown of twelve stars on her head. [2]She was
pregnant, and she cried out because of her la-
bor pains and the agony of giving birth.

[3]Then I witnessed in heaven another sig-
nificant event. I saw a large red dragon with
seven heads and ten horns, with seven crowns
on his heads. [4]His tail swept away one-third of
the stars in the sky, and he threw them to the
earth. He stood in front of the woman as she

11:7 Or *the abyss*, or *the underworld*. **11:8** Greek *the great city*. **11:15** Or *his Messiah*.

was about to give birth, ready to devour her
baby as soon as it was born.
5 She gave birth to a son who was to rule all
nations with an iron rod. And her child was
snatched away from the dragon and was
caught up to God and to his throne. 6 And the
woman fled into the wilderness, where God
had prepared a place to care for her for 1,260
days.
7 Then there was war in heaven. Michael
and his angels fought against the dragon and
his angels. 8 And the dragon lost the battle,
and he and his angels were forced out of
heaven. 9 This great dragon—the ancient ser-
pent called the devil, or Satan, the one deceiv-
ing the whole world—was thrown down to the
earth with all his angels.
10 Then I heard a loud voice shouting across
the heavens,

"It has come at last—
salvation and power
and the Kingdom of our God,
and the authority of his Christ.*
For the accuser of our brothers and
sisters*
has been thrown down to earth—
the one who accuses them
before our God day and night.
11 And they have defeated him by the blood
of the Lamb
and by their testimony.
And they did not love their lives so much
that they were afraid to die.
12 Therefore, rejoice, O heavens!
And you who live in the heavens,
rejoice!
But terror will come on the earth and the
sea,
for the devil has come down to you in
great anger,
knowing that he has little time."

13 When the dragon realized that he had
been thrown down to the earth, he pursued
the woman who had given birth to the male
child. 14 But she was given two wings like those
of a great eagle so she could fly to the place
prepared for her in the wilderness. There she
would be cared for and protected from the
dragon* for a time, times, and half a time.
15 Then the dragon tried to drown the
woman with a flood of water that flowed from
his mouth. 16 But the earth helped her by open-
ing its mouth and swallowing the river that
gushed out from the mouth of the dragon.
17 And the dragon was angry at the woman and
declared war against the rest of her children—
all who keep God's commandments and main-
tain their testimony for Jesus.
18 Then the dragon took his stand* on the
shore beside the sea.

CHAPTER 13

The Beast out of the Sea

Then I saw a beast rising up out of the sea. It
had seven heads and ten horns, with ten
crowns on its horns. And written on each
head were names that blasphemed God.
2 This beast looked like a leopard, but it had
the feet of a bear and the mouth of a lion! And
the dragon gave the beast his own power and
throne and great authority.
3 I saw that one of the heads of the beast
seemed wounded beyond recovery—but the
fatal wound was healed! The whole world mar-
veled at this miracle and gave allegiance to the
beast. 4 They worshiped the dragon for giving
the beast such power, and they also worshiped
the beast. "Who is as great as the beast?" they
exclaimed. "Who is able to fight against him?"
5 Then the beast was allowed to speak great
blasphemies against God. And he was given
authority to do whatever he wanted for forty-
two months. 6 And he spoke terrible words of
blasphemy against God, slandering his name
and his dwelling—that is, those who dwell in
heaven.* 7 And the beast was allowed to wage
war against God's holy people and to conquer
them. And he was given authority to rule over
every tribe and people and language and na-
tion. 8 And all the people who belong to this
world worshiped the beast. They are the ones
whose names were not written in the Book of
Life before the world was made—the Book that
belongs to the Lamb who was slaughtered.*

9 Anyone with ears to hear
should listen and understand.
10 Anyone who is destined for prison
will be taken to prison.

12:10a Or *his Messiah.* **12:10b** Greek *brothers.* **12:14** Greek *the serpent;* also in 12:15. See 12:9. **12:18** Greek *Then he took his stand;* some manuscripts read *Then I took my stand.* Some translations put this entire sentence into 13:1. **13:6** Some manuscripts read *and his dwelling and all who dwell in heaven.* **13:8** Or *not written in the Book of Life that belongs to the Lamb who was slaughtered before the world was made.*

Anyone destined to die by the sword
will die by the sword.

This means that God's holy people must endure persecution patiently and remain faithful.

The Beast out of the Earth

11 Then I saw another beast come up out of the earth. He had two horns like those of a lamb, but he spoke with the voice of a dragon. 12 He exercised all the authority of the first beast. And he required all the earth and its people to worship the first beast, whose fatal wound had been healed. 13 He did astounding miracles, even making fire flash down to earth from the sky while everyone was watching. 14 And with all the miracles he was allowed to perform on behalf of the first beast, he

THE NAMES OF JESUS

The book of Revelation gives many different names for Jesus. Each one tells something special about him and his role in God's plan of salvation.

THE ALPHA AND THE OMEGA—THE BEGINNING AND THE END	1:8
LORD	1:8
ALMIGHTY ONE	1:8
SON OF MAN	1:13
THE FIRST AND THE LAST	1:17
THE LIVING ONE	1:18
SON OF GOD	2:18
WITNESS	3:14
CREATOR	4:11
LION OF THE TRIBE OF JUDAH	5:5
HEIR TO DAVID'S THRONE	5:5
LAMB	5:6
SHEPHERD	7:17
CHRIST	12:10
FAITHFUL AND TRUE	19:11
WORD OF GOD	19:13
KING OF ALL KINGS	19:16
LORD OF ALL LORDS	19:16
THE BRIGHT MORNING STAR	22:16

deceived all the people who belong to this world. He ordered the people to make a great statue of the first beast, who was fatally wounded and then came back to life. [15]He was then permitted to give life to this statue so that it could speak. Then the statue of the beast commanded that anyone refusing to worship it must die.

[16]He required everyone—small and great, rich and poor, free and slave—to be given a mark on the right hand or on the forehead. [17]And no one could buy or sell anything without that mark, which was either the name of the beast or the number representing his name. [18]Wisdom is needed here. Let the one with understanding solve the meaning of the number of the beast, for it is the number of a man.* His number is 666.*

CHAPTER 14

The Lamb and the 144,000

Then I saw the Lamb standing on Mount Zion, and with him were 144,000 who had his name and his Father's name written on their foreheads. [2]And I heard a sound from heaven like the roar of mighty ocean waves or the rolling of loud thunder. It was like the sound of many harpists playing together.

[3]This great choir sang a wonderful new song in front of the throne of God and before the four living beings and the twenty-four elders. No one could learn this song except the 144,000 who had been redeemed from the earth. [4]They have kept themselves as pure as virgins,* following the Lamb wherever he goes. They have been purchased from among the people on the earth as a special offering* to God and to the Lamb. [5]They have told no lies; they are without blame.

The Three Angels

[6]And I saw another angel flying through the sky, carrying the eternal Good News to proclaim to the people who belong to this world—to every nation, tribe, language, and people. [7]"Fear God," he shouted. "Give glory to him. For the time has come when he will sit as judge. Worship him who made the heavens, the earth, the sea, and all the springs of water."

[8]Then another angel followed him through the sky, shouting, "Babylon is fallen—that great city is fallen—because she made all the nations of the world drink the wine of her passionate immorality."

[9]Then a third angel followed them, shouting, "Anyone who worships the beast and his statue or who accepts his mark on the forehead or on the hand [10]must drink the wine of God's anger. It has been poured full strength into God's cup of wrath. And they will be tormented with fire and burning sulfur in the presence of the holy angels and the Lamb. [11]The smoke of their torment will rise forever and ever, and they will have no relief day or night, for they have worshiped the beast and his statue and have accepted the mark of his name."

[12]This means that God's holy people must endure persecution patiently, obeying his commands and maintaining their faith in Jesus.

[13]And I heard a voice from heaven saying, "Write this down: Blessed are those who die in the Lord from now on. Yes, says the Spirit, they are blessed indeed, for they will rest from their hard work; for their good deeds follow them!"

The Harvest of the Earth

[14]Then I saw a white cloud, and seated on the cloud was someone like the Son of Man.* He had a gold crown on his head and a sharp sickle in his hand.

[15]Then another angel came from the Temple and shouted to the one sitting on the cloud, "Swing the sickle, for the time of harvest has come; the crop on earth is ripe." [16]So the one sitting on the cloud swung his sickle over the earth, and the whole earth was harvested.

[17]After that, another angel came from the Temple in heaven, and he also had a sharp sickle. [18]Then another angel, who had power to destroy with fire, came from the altar. He shouted to the angel with the sharp sickle, "Swing your sickle now to gather the clusters of grapes from the vines of the earth, for they are ripe for judgment." [19]So the angel swung his sickle over the earth and loaded the grapes into the great winepress of God's wrath. [20]The grapes were trampled in the winepress out-

13:18a Or *of humanity.* **13:18b** Some manuscripts read *616.* **14:4a** Greek *They are virgins who have not defiled themselves with women.* **14:4b** Greek *as firstfruits.* **14:14** Or *like a son of man.* See Dan 7:13. "Son of Man" is a title Jesus used for himself.

side the city, and blood flowed from the wine-
press in a stream about 180 miles* long and
as high as a horse's bridle.

CHAPTER 15

The Song of Moses and of the Lamb

Then I saw in heaven another marvelous
event of great significance. Seven angels were
holding the seven last plagues, which would
bring God's wrath to completion. [2]I saw be-
fore me what seemed to be a glass sea mixed
with fire. And on it stood all the people who
had been victorious over the beast and his
statue and the number representing his
name. They were all holding harps that God
had given them. [3]And they were singing the
song of Moses, the servant of God, and the
song of the Lamb:

"Great and marvelous are your works,
O Lord God, the Almighty.
Just and true are your ways,
O King of the nations.*
[4] Who will not fear you, Lord,
and glorify your name?
For you alone are holy.
All nations will come and worship
before you,
for your righteous deeds have been
revealed."

The Seven Bowls of the Seven Plagues

[5]Then I looked and saw that the Temple in
heaven, God's Tabernacle, was thrown wide
open. [6]The seven angels who were holding
the seven plagues came out of the Temple.
They were clothed in spotless white linen*
with gold sashes across their chests. [7]Then
one of the four living beings handed each of
the seven angels a gold bowl filled with the
wrath of God, who lives forever and ever. [8]The
Temple was filled with smoke from God's
glory and power. No one could enter the Tem-
ple until the seven angels had completed
pouring out the seven plagues.

CHAPTER 16

Then I heard a mighty voice from the Temple
say to the seven angels, "Go your ways and
pour out on the earth the seven bowls con-
taining God's wrath."

[2]So the first angel left the Temple and
poured out his bowl on the earth, and horri-
ble, malignant sores broke out on everyone
who had the mark of the beast and who wor-
shiped his statue.

[3]Then the second angel poured out his
bowl on the sea, and it became like the blood
of a corpse. And everything in the sea died.

[4]Then the third angel poured out his bowl
on the rivers and springs, and they became
blood. [5]And I heard the angel who had au-
thority over all water saying,

"You are just, O Holy One, who is and who
always was,
because you have sent these
judgments.
[6] Since they shed the blood
of your holy people and your prophets,
you have given them blood to drink.
It is their just reward."

[7]And I heard a voice from the altar,* saying,

"Yes, O Lord God, the Almighty,
your judgments are true and just."

[8]Then the fourth angel poured out his bowl
on the sun, causing it to scorch everyone with
its fire. [9]Everyone was burned by this blast of
heat, and they cursed the name of God, who
had control over all these plagues. They did
not repent of their sins and turn to God and
give him glory.

[10]Then the fifth angel poured out his bowl
on the throne of the beast, and his kingdom
was plunged into darkness. His subjects
ground their teeth in anguish, [11]and they
cursed the God of heaven for their pains and
sores. But they did not repent of their evil
deeds and turn to God.

[12]Then the sixth angel poured out his
bowl on the great Euphrates River, and it
dried up so that the kings from the east
could march their armies toward the west
without hindrance. [13]And I saw three evil*
spirits that looked like frogs leap from the
mouths of the dragon, the beast, and the
false prophet. [14]They are demonic spirits
who work miracles and go out to all the rul-
ers of the world to gather them for battle
against the Lord on that great judgment day
of God the Almighty.

14:20 Greek *1,600 stadia* [296 kilometers]. **15:3** Some manuscripts read *King of the ages*. **15:6** Other manuscripts read *white stone;* still others read *white [garments] made of linen*. **16:7** Greek *I heard the altar*. **16:13** Greek *unclean*.

15"Look, I will come as unexpectedly as a thief! Blessed are all who are watching for me, who keep their clothing ready so they will not have to walk around naked and ashamed."

16And the demonic spirits gathered all the rulers and their armies to a place with the Hebrew name *Armageddon.**

17Then the seventh angel poured out his bowl into the air. And a mighty shout came from the throne in the Temple, saying, "It is finished!" 18Then the thunder crashed and rolled, and lightning flashed. And a great earthquake struck—the worst since people were placed on the earth. 19The great city of Babylon split into three sections, and the cities of many nations fell into heaps of rubble. So God remembered all of Babylon's sins, and he made her drink the cup that was filled with the wine of his fierce wrath. 20And every island disappeared, and all the mountains were leveled. 21There was a terrible hailstorm, and hailstones weighing as much as seventy-five pounds* fell from the sky onto the people below. They cursed God because of the terrible plague of the hailstorm.

CHAPTER 17

The Great Prostitute

One of the seven angels who had poured out the seven bowls came over and spoke to me. "Come with me," he said, "and I will show you the judgment that is going to come on the great prostitute, who rules over many waters. 2The kings of the world have committed adultery with her, and the people who belong to this world have been made drunk by the wine of her immorality."

3So the angel took me in the Spirit* into the wilderness. There I saw a woman sitting on a scarlet beast that had seven heads and ten horns, and blasphemies against God were written all over it. 4The woman wore purple and scarlet clothing and beautiful jewelry made of gold and precious gems and pearls. In her hand she held a gold goblet full of obscenities and the impurities of her immorality. 5A mysterious name was written on her forehead: "Babylon the Great, Mother of All Prostitutes and Obscenities in the World." 6I could see that she was drunk—drunk with the blood of God's holy people who were witnesses for Jesus. I stared at her in complete amazement.

7"Why are you so amazed?" the angel asked. "I will tell you the mystery of this woman and of the beast with seven heads and ten horns on which she sits. 8The beast you saw was once alive but isn't now. And yet he will soon come up out of the bottomless pit* and go to eternal destruction. And the people who belong to this world, whose names were not written in the Book of Life before the world was made, will be amazed at the reappearance of this beast who had died.

9"This calls for a mind with understanding: The seven heads of the beast represent the seven hills where the woman rules. They also represent seven kings. 10Five kings have already fallen, the sixth now reigns, and the seventh is yet to come, but his reign will be brief.

16:16 Or *Harmagedon.* **16:21** Greek *1 talent* [34 kilograms]. **17:3** Or *in spirit.* **17:8** Or *the abyss,* or *the underworld.*

[11]"The scarlet beast that was, but is no longer, is the eighth king. He is like the other seven, and he, too, is headed for destruction. [12]The ten horns of the beast are ten kings who have not yet risen to power. They will be appointed to their kingdoms for one brief moment to reign with the beast. [13]They will all agree to give him their power and authority. [14]Together they will go to war against the Lamb, but the Lamb will defeat them because he is Lord of all lords and King of all kings. And his called and chosen and faithful ones will be with him."

[15]Then the angel said to me, "The waters where the prostitute is ruling represent masses of people of every nation and language. [16]The scarlet beast and his ten horns all hate the prostitute. They will strip her naked, eat her flesh, and burn her remains with fire. [17]For God has put a plan into their minds, a plan that will carry out his purposes. They will agree to give their authority to the scarlet beast, and so the words of God will be fulfilled. [18]And this woman you saw in your vision represents the great city that rules over the kings of the world."

CHAPTER 18

The Fall of Babylon

After all this I saw another angel come down from heaven with great authority, and the earth grew bright with his splendor. [2]He gave a mighty shout:

"Babylon is fallen—that great city is fallen!
She has become a home for demons.
She is a hideout for every foul spirit,
a hideout for every foul* vulture
and every foul and dreadful animal.*
[3] For all the nations have fallen*
because of the wine of her passionate immorality.
The kings of the world
have committed adultery with her.
Because of her desires for extravagant luxury,
the merchants of the world have grown rich."

[4]Then I heard another voice calling from heaven,

"Come away from her, my people.
Do not take part in her sins,
or you will be punished with her.
[5] For her sins are piled as high as heaven,
and God remembers her evil deeds.
[6] Do to her as she has done to others.
Double her penalty* for all her evil deeds.
She brewed a cup of terror for others,
so brew twice as much* for her.
[7] She glorified herself and lived in luxury,
so match it now with torment and sorrow.
She boasted in her heart,
'I am queen on my throne.
I am no helpless widow,
and I have no reason to mourn.'
[8] Therefore, these plagues will overtake her in a single day—
death and mourning and famine.
She will be completely consumed by fire,
for the Lord God who judges her is mighty."

[9]And the kings of the world who committed adultery with her and enjoyed her great luxury will mourn for her as they see the smoke rising from her charred remains. [10]They will stand at a distance, terrified by her great torment. They will cry out,

"How terrible, how terrible for you,
O Babylon, you great city!
In a single moment
God's judgment came on you."

[11]The merchants of the world will weep and mourn for her, for there is no one left to buy their goods. [12]She bought great quantities of gold, silver, jewels, and pearls; fine linen, purple, silk, and scarlet cloth; things made of fragrant thyine wood, ivory goods, and objects made of expensive wood; and bronze, iron, and marble. [13]She also bought cinnamon, spice, incense, myrrh, frankincense, wine, olive oil, fine flour, wheat, cattle, sheep, horses, chariots, and bodies—that is, human slaves.

[14] "The fancy things you loved so much
are gone," they cry.
"All your luxuries and splendor
are gone forever,
never to be yours again."

18:2a Greek *unclean;* also in each of the two following phrases. **18:2b** Some manuscripts condense the last two lines to read *a hideout for every foul [unclean] and dreadful vulture.* **18:3** Some manuscripts read *have drunk.* **18:6a** Or *Give her an equal penalty.* **18:6b** Or *brew just as much.*

15 The merchants who became wealthy by
selling her these things will stand at a distance, terrified by her great torment. They
will weep and cry out,

16 "How terrible, how terrible for that great
city!
She was clothed in finest purple and
scarlet linens,
decked out with gold and precious
stones and pearls!
17 In a single moment
all the wealth of the city is gone!"

And all the captains of the merchant ships
and their passengers and sailors and crews
will stand at a distance. 18 They will cry out as
they watch the smoke ascend, and they will
say, "Where is there another city as great as
this?" 19 And they will weep and throw dust on
their heads to show their grief. And they will
cry out,

"How terrible, how terrible for that great
city!
The shipowners became wealthy
by transporting her great wealth on the
seas.
In a single moment it is all gone."

20 Rejoice over her fate, O heaven
and people of God and apostles and
prophets!
For at last God has judged her
for your sakes.

21 Then a mighty angel picked up a boulder
the size of a huge millstone. He threw it into
the ocean and shouted,

"Just like this, the great city Babylon
will be thrown down with violence
and will never be found again.
22 The sound of harps, singers, flutes, and
trumpets
will never be heard in you again.
No craftsmen and no trades
will ever be found in you again.
The sound of the mill
will never be heard in you again.
23 The light of a lamp
will never shine in you again.
The happy voices of brides and grooms
will never be heard in you again.
For your merchants were the greatest in
the world,
and you deceived the nations with your
sorceries.
24 In your* streets flowed the blood of the
prophets and of God's holy people
and the blood of people slaughtered all
over the world."

CHAPTER 19

Songs of Victory in Heaven

After this, I heard what sounded like a vast
crowd in heaven shouting,

"Praise the LORD!*
Salvation and glory and power belong
to our God.
2 His judgments are true and just.
He has punished the great prostitute
who corrupted the earth with her
immorality.
He has avenged the murder of his
servants."

3 And again their voices rang out:

"Praise the LORD!
The smoke from that city ascends
forever and ever!"

4 Then the twenty-four elders and the four
living beings fell down and worshiped God,
who was sitting on the throne. They cried out,
"Amen! Praise the LORD!"
5 And from the throne came a voice that
said,

"Praise our God,
all his servants,
all who fear him,
from the least to the greatest."

6 Then I heard again what sounded like the
shout of a vast crowd or the roar of mighty
ocean waves or the crash of loud thunder:

"Praise the LORD!
For the Lord our God,* the Almighty,
reigns.
7 Let us be glad and rejoice,
and let us give honor to him.
For the time has come for the wedding
feast of the Lamb,
and his bride has prepared herself.

18:24 Greek *her*. **19:1** Greek *Hallelujah*; also in 19:3, 4, 6. *Hallelujah* is the transliteration of a Hebrew term that means "Praise the LORD." **19:6** Some manuscripts read *the Lord God*.

[8] She has been given the finest of pure
white linen to wear."
For the fine linen represents the good
deeds of God's holy people.

[9]And the angel said to me, "Write this: Blessed are those who are invited to the wedding feast of the Lamb." And he added, "These are true words that come from God."

[10]Then I fell down at his feet to worship him, but he said, "No, don't worship me. I am a servant of God, just like you and your brothers and sisters* who testify about their faith in Jesus. Worship only God. For the essence of prophecy is to give a clear witness for Jesus.*"

The Rider on the White Horse

[11]Then I saw heaven opened, and a white horse was standing there. Its rider was named Faithful and True, for he judges fairly and wages a righteous war. [12]His eyes were like flames of fire, and on his head were many crowns. A name was written on him that no one understood except himself. [13]He wore a robe dipped in blood, and his title was the Word of God. [14]The armies of heaven, dressed in the finest of pure white linen, followed him on white horses. [15]From his mouth came a sharp sword to strike down the nations. He will rule them with an iron rod. He will release the fierce wrath of God, the Almighty, like juice flowing from a winepress. [16]On his robe at his thigh* was written this title: King of all kings and Lord of all lords.

[17]Then I saw an angel standing in the sun, shouting to the vultures flying high in the sky: "Come! Gather together for the great banquet God has prepared. [18]Come and eat the flesh of kings, generals, and strong warriors; of horses and their riders; and of all humanity, both free and slave, small and great."

[19]Then I saw the beast and the kings of the world and their armies gathered together to fight against the one sitting on the horse and his army. [20]And the beast was captured, and with him the false prophet who did mighty miracles on behalf of the beast—miracles that deceived all who had accepted the mark of the beast and who worshiped his statue. Both the beast and his false prophet were thrown alive into the fiery lake of burning sulfur. [21]Their entire army was killed by the sharp sword that came from the mouth of the one riding the white horse. And the vultures all gorged themselves on the dead bodies.

CHAPTER 20

The Thousand Years

Then I saw an angel coming down from heaven with the key to the bottomless pit* and a heavy chain in his hand. [2]He seized the dragon—that old serpent, who is the devil, Satan—and bound him in chains for a thousand

19:10a Greek *brothers.* **19:10b** Or *is the message confirmed by Jesus.* **19:16** Or *On his robe and thigh.* **20:1** Or *the abyss,* or *the underworld;* also in 20:3.

WHAT WE KNOW ABOUT ETERNITY

The Bible doesn't tell us a lot about heaven (eternity). It tells us more about how we can have eternal life as a free gift from God. But there are a few hints about what our future will be like if we have accepted Christ's gift of eternal life.

A place is prepared for us. (John 14:2-3)

We will be like Jesus. (1 John 3:2)

We will have new bodies. (1 Corinthians 15:42-44)

Our experience will be wonderful. (1 Corinthians 2:9)

We will enjoy a new earth. (Revelation 21:1)

We will know everything completely. (1 Corinthians 13:12)

We will have new emotions. (Revelation 21:4)

There will be no more death. (Revelation 21:4)

years. [3]The angel threw him into the bottomless pit, which he then shut and locked so Satan could not deceive the nations anymore until the thousand years were finished. Afterward he must be released for a little while.

[4]Then I saw thrones, and the people sitting on them had been given the authority to judge. And I saw the souls of those who had been beheaded for their testimony about Jesus and for proclaiming the word of God. They had not worshiped the beast or his statue, nor accepted his mark on their foreheads or their hands. They all came to life again, and they reigned with Christ for a thousand years.

[5]This is the first resurrection. (The rest of the dead did not come back to life until the thousand years had ended.) [6]Blessed and holy are those who share in the first resurrection. For them the second death holds no power, but they will be priests of God and of Christ and will reign with him a thousand years.

AMAZING FACTS

Did you know that the most awesome city in the universe will come down to earth right out of heaven someday? Check it out.

REVELATION 21:10-27

The Defeat of Satan

[7]When the thousand years come to an end, Satan will be let out of his prison. [8]He will go out to deceive the nations—called Gog and Magog—in every corner of the earth. He will gather them together for battle—a mighty army, as numberless as sand along the seashore. [9]And I saw them as they went up on the broad plain of the earth and surrounded God's people and the beloved city. But fire from heaven came down on the attacking armies and consumed them.

[10]Then the devil, who had deceived them, was thrown into the fiery lake of burning sulfur, joining the beast and the false prophet. There they will be tormented day and night forever and ever.

The Final Judgment

[11]And I saw a great white throne and the one sitting on it. The earth and sky fled from his presence, but they found no place to hide. [12]I saw the dead, both great and small, standing before God's throne. And the books were opened, including the Book of Life. And the dead were judged according to what they had done, as recorded in the books. [13]The sea gave up its dead, and death and the grave* gave up their dead. And all were judged according to their deeds. [14]Then death and the grave were thrown into the lake of fire. This lake of fire is the second death. [15]And anyone whose name was not found recorded in the Book of Life was thrown into the lake of fire.

CHAPTER 21

The New Jerusalem

Then I saw a new heaven and a new earth, for the old heaven and the old earth had disappeared. And the sea was also gone. [2]And I saw the holy city, the new Jerusalem, coming down from God out of heaven like a bride beautifully dressed for her husband.

[3]I heard a loud shout from the throne, saying, "Look, God's home is now among his people! He will live with them, and they will be his people. God himself will be with them.* [4]He will wipe every tear from their eyes, and there will be no more death or sorrow or crying or pain. All these things are gone forever."

[5]And the one sitting on the throne said, "Look, I am making everything new!" And then he said to me, "Write this down, for what I tell you is trustworthy and true." [6]And he also said, "It is finished! I am the Alpha and the Omega—the Beginning and the End. To all who are thirsty I will give freely from the springs of the water of life. [7]All who are victorious will inherit all these blessings, and I will be their God, and they will be my children.

[8]"But cowards, unbelievers, the corrupt, murderers, the immoral, those who practice witchcraft, idol worshipers, and all liars—

20:13 Greek *and Hades;* also in 20:14. **21:3** Some manuscripts read *God himself will be with them, their God.*

their fate is in the fiery lake of burning sulfur. This is the second death."

[9]Then one of the seven angels who held the seven bowls containing the seven last plagues came and said to me, "Come with me! I will show you the bride, the wife of the Lamb."

[10]So he took me in the Spirit* to a great, high mountain, and he showed me the holy city, Jerusalem, descending out of heaven from God. [11]It shone with the glory of God and sparkled like a precious stone—like jasper as clear as crystal. [12]The city wall was broad and high, with twelve gates guarded by twelve angels. And the names of the twelve tribes of Israel were written on the gates. [13]There were three gates on each side—east, north, south, and west. [14]The wall of the city had twelve foundation stones, and on them were written the names of the twelve apostles of the Lamb.

[15]The angel who talked to me held in his hand a gold measuring stick to measure the city, its gates, and its wall. [16]When he measured it, he found it was a square, as wide as it was long. In fact, its length and width and height were each 1,400 miles.* [17]Then he measured the walls and found them to be 216 feet thick* (according to the human standard used by the angel).

[18]The wall was made of jasper, and the city was pure gold, as clear as glass. [19]The wall of the city was built on foundation stones inlaid with twelve precious stones:* the first was jasper, the second sapphire, the third agate, the fourth emerald, [20]the fifth onyx, the sixth carnelian, the seventh chrysolite, the eighth beryl, the ninth topaz, the tenth chrysoprase, the eleventh jacinth, the twelfth amethyst.

[21]The twelve gates were made of pearls—each gate from a single pearl! And the main street was pure gold, as clear as glass.

[22]I saw no temple in the city, for the Lord God Almighty and the Lamb are its temple. [23]And the city has no need of sun or moon, for the glory of God illuminates the city, and the Lamb is its light. [24]The nations will walk in its light, and the kings of the world will enter the city in all their glory. [25]Its gates will never be closed at the end of day because there is no night there. [26]And all the nations will bring their glory and honor into the city. [27]Nothing evil* will be allowed to enter, nor anyone who practices shameful idolatry and dishonesty—but only those whose names are written in the Lamb's Book of Life.

CHAPTER 22

Then the angel showed me a river with the water of life, clear as crystal, flowing from the throne of God and of the Lamb. [2]It flowed down the center of the main street. On each side of the river grew a tree of life, bearing twelve crops of fruit,* with a fresh crop each month. The leaves were used for medicine to heal the nations.

[3]No longer will there be a curse upon anything. For the throne of God and of the Lamb will be there, and his servants will worship him. [4]And they will see his face, and his name will be written on their foreheads. [5]And there will be no night there—no need for lamps or sun—for the Lord God will shine on them. And they will reign forever and ever.

[6]Then the angel said to me, "Everything you have heard and seen is trustworthy and true. The Lord God, who inspires his prophets,* has sent his angel to tell his servants what will happen soon.*"

Jesus Is Coming

[7]"Look, I am coming soon! Blessed are those who obey the words of prophecy written in this book.*"

[8]I, John, am the one who heard and saw all these things. And when I heard and saw them, I fell down to worship at the feet of the angel who showed them to me. [9]But he said, "No, don't worship me. I am a servant of God, just like you and your brothers the prophets, as well as all who obey what is written in this book. Worship only God!"

[10]Then he instructed me, "Do not seal up the prophetic words in this book, for the time is near. [11]Let the one who is doing harm continue to do harm; let the one who is vile continue to be vile; let the one who is righteous continue to live righteously; let the one who is holy continue to be holy."

21:10 Or *in spirit*. **21:16** Greek *12,000 stadia* (2,220 kilometers). **21:17** Greek *144 cubits* (65 meters). **21:19** The identification of some of these gemstones is uncertain. **21:27** Or *ceremonially unclean*. **22:2** Or *twelve kinds of fruit*. **22:6a** Or *The Lord, the God of the spirits of the prophets*. **22:6b** Or *suddenly*, or *quickly*; also in 22:7, 12, 20. **22:7** Or *scroll*; also in 22:9, 10, 18, 19.

[12]"Look, I am coming soon, bringing my reward with me to repay all people according to their deeds. [13]I am the Alpha and the Omega, the First and the Last, the Beginning and the End."

[14]Blessed are those who wash their robes. They will be permitted to enter through the gates of the city and eat the fruit from the tree of life. [15]Outside the city are the dogs—the sorcerers, the sexually immoral, the murderers, the idol worshipers, and all who love to live a lie.

[16]"I, Jesus, have sent my angel to give you this message for the churches. I am both the source of David and the heir to his throne.* I am the bright morning star."

[17]The Spirit and the bride say, "Come." Let anyone who hears this say, "Come." Let anyone who is thirsty come. Let anyone who desires drink freely from the water of life. [18]And I solemnly declare to everyone who hears the words of prophecy written in this book: If anyone adds anything to what is written here, God will add to that person the plagues described in this book. [19]And if anyone removes any of the words from this book of prophecy, God will remove that person's share in the tree of life and in the holy city that are described in this book.

[20]He who is the faithful witness to all these things says, "Yes, I am coming soon!"

Amen! Come, Lord Jesus!

[21]May the grace of the Lord Jesus be with God's holy people.*

22:16 Greek *I am the root and offspring of David.* **22:21** Other manuscripts read *be with all;* still others read *be with all of God's holy people.* Some manuscripts add *Amen.*

The Greatest Stories Reading Plan

Now that you have this great new Bible, where do you start? You could open the Bible to just any old place and start reading. Or you could start at the beginning and keep going until you reach the end. But if these ideas sound a bit overwhelming, try this reading plan. It is designed to take you through the best of the Bible in one year. As you read each entry, check it off so you mark your progress throughout the year. You can start it at any time, so jump right in!

Old Testament

Genesis 1:1–2:3	How It All Started	pages 3–5	☐
Genesis 2:15–3:24	Adam and Eve	pages 5–7	☐
Genesis 4:1-16	Cain and Abel	pages 7–8	☐
Genesis 6:9-22	Noah Gets to Build a Boat	page 10	☐
Genesis 7:1-24	All Aboard!	pages 10–11	☐
Genesis 8:1-22	A Long Wait	page 11	☐
Genesis 9:1-17	Rules and Rainbows	pages 11–14	☐
Genesis 11:1-9	The Tower of Babel	page 15	☐
Genesis 12:1-9; 17:1-8	God's Promise to Abraham	pages 16; 20–21	☐
Genesis 18:1-15	Unusual Visitors	pages 21–22	☐
Genesis 19:15-29	Destruction of Sodom and Gomorrah	pages 23–24	☐
Genesis 21:8-21	Hagar and Ishmael	page 25	☐
Genesis 22:1-19	Abraham's Painful Decision	page 26	☐
Genesis 24:1-27	Search for a Bride	pages 27–28	☐
Genesis 24:28-67	Isaac and Rebekah	pages 28–29	☐
Genesis 25:19-34	Jacob and Esau	page 30	☐
Genesis 27:1-40	Jacob Tricks His Father	pages 32–33	☐
Genesis 28:10-22	Jacob Meets God	page 34	☐
Genesis 29:14-30	Jacob's Marriages	page 35	☐
Genesis 32:1–33:16	Jacob Returns Home	pages 40–41	☐
Genesis 37:1-36	Jacob's Children	pages 45–47	☐
Genesis 39:1-23	Joseph in Trouble	pages 48–49	☐
Genesis 40:1-23	Dreams in Prison	pages 49–50	☐
Genesis 41:1-36	Dreams in the Palace	pages 50–51	☐
Genesis 41:37-57	Joseph in Charge	pages 51–52	☐
Genesis 42:1-38	Joseph Sees His Brothers Again	pages 52–53	☐
Genesis 43:1-34	Back to Joseph	pages 53–55	☐
Genesis 44:1-34	Crisis in the Palace	pages 55–56	☐
Genesis 45:1-28	Finding a Lost Son	pages 56–57	☐
Genesis 49:1-33	Jacob's Final Words	pages 61–62	☐
Exodus 1:8–2:10	Moses Is Born	pages 65–66	☐
Exodus 2:11-25	Moses on the Run	pages 66–68	☐
Exodus 3:1-22	God's Burning Bush	pages 68–69	☐
Exodus 4:1-17	Moses Isn't Sure	pages 69–70	☐
Exodus 5:1-23	Resistance	page 71	☐
Exodus 6:1-13	Rejection	pages 71–72	☐
Exodus 7:1-14	A Stubborn Ruler	pages 72–73	☐

Exodus 7:15–9:7	Five out of Ten Plagues	pages 73–75	☐
Exodus 9:8–10:29	Four More Plagues	pages 75–78	☐
Exodus 11:1-10; 12:29-36	The Ultimate Plague	pages 78; 79	☐
Exodus 13:17–14:31	A Narrow Escape	pages 81–82	☐
Exodus 15:22-27; 17:1-7	God Provides Water	pages 83; 85	☐
Exodus 16:1-36	God's Unusual Food Supply	pages 83–85	☐
Exodus 18:1-27	Helpful Advice	pages 86–87	☐
Exodus 19:1-25	An Appointment with God	pages 87–88	☐
Exodus 20:1-22	The Ten Commandments	pages 88–89	☐
Exodus 32:1-29	The Golden Calf	pages 103–104	☐
Exodus 40	Instructions about God's Tent	pages 113–114	☐
Numbers 12:1-16	Moses under Fire	pages 167–168	☐
Numbers 13:1-33	Spying on the Promised Land	pages 168–169	☐
Numbers 14:1-45	A Majority That Was Wrong	pages 169–172	☐
Numbers 21:4-9	Another Hard Lesson	page 181	☐
Numbers 22:5-38	Balaam and His Donkey	pages 183–184	☐
Deuteronomy 29:1-29	Moses Reviews God's Actions	pages 235–237	☐
Deuteronomy 30:1-20	Moses Challenges the People	page 237	☐
Deuteronomy 31:1-8	Moses Appoints a New Leader	page 238	☐
Deuteronomy 34:1-12	The Death of Moses	page 244	☐
Joshua 1:1-18	God Takes Over	pages 245–246	☐
Joshua 2:1-24	Spies Visit Jericho	pages 246–247	☐
Joshua 3:1-17	The Invasion of Canaan	pages 247–248	☐
Joshua 5:13–6:27	The Battle of Jericho	pages 251–252	☐
Joshua 7:1-26	Ultimate Consequences	pages 252–253	☐
Joshua 10:1-15	The Longest Day	pages 256–257	☐
Joshua 23:1-16	Joshua Warns the Leaders	page 271	☐
Joshua 24:1-31	Joshua's Last Words	pages 272–273	☐
Judges 4:4-24	Judge Deborah	pages 279–280	☐
Judges 6:1-40	Gideon Becomes a Judge	pages 283–284	☐
Judges 7:1-25	Gideon and the Midianites	pages 284–286	☐
Judges 13:1-25	The Birth of Samson	pages 292–293	☐
Judges 14:1-20	Samson's Riddle	pages 293–294	☐
Judges 15:1-20	Samson and the Jawbone	pages 294–295	☐
Judges 16:1-21	Samson and Delilah	pages 295–297	☐
Judges 16:22-31	Samson's Death	page 297	☐
Ruth 1:1-22	Ruth and Naomi—A Friendship	pages 303–305	☐
Ruth 2:1-23	Ruth Meets Boaz	pages 305–306	☐
Ruth 3:1-18	Ruth Finds a Husband	page 306	☐
Ruth 4:1-22	A Happy Ending	pages 307–308	☐
1 Samuel 1:1-28	A Serious Prayer	pages 309–311	☐
1 Samuel 3:1-21	God Calls Samuel	pages 312–313	☐
1 Samuel 8:1-22	The People Want a King	pages 317–318	☐
1 Samuel 9:1-21	Saul and the Lost Donkeys	page 318	☐
1 Samuel 10:1-27	Saul Becomes King	pages 319–320	☐
1 Samuel 12:1-25	Samuel Says Good-bye	pages 321–322	☐
1 Samuel 14:1-23	A Son to Make a Father Proud	pages 323–324	☐
1 Samuel 16:1-13	Samuel Appoints David	pages 327–328	☐
1 Samuel 17:1-31	David and Goliath's Challenge	pages 328–330	☐
1 Samuel 17:32-58	David Kills Goliath	pages 330–331	☐
1 Samuel 18:1-30	Trouble between Saul and David	pages 331–332	☐

1 Samuel 20:1-42	David and Jonathan	pages 334–336	☐
1 Samuel 24:1-22	David Spares Saul's Life	pages 339–340	☐
1 Samuel 25:1-42	David and Abigail	pages 340–341	☐
1 Samuel 28:1-25	Saul and the Occult	pages 343–344	☐
2 Samuel 5:1-12	David Becomes King over All Israel	page 352	☐
2 Samuel 9:1-13	The King's Kindness	pages 355–356	☐
2 Samuel 11:1-27	David and Bathsheba	pages 357–358	☐
2 Samuel 12:1-25	David and Nathan	pages 358–359	☐
2 Samuel 13:1-19	Family Consequences of Sin	page 360	☐
2 Samuel 13:20-39	Family Revenge	pages 360–361	☐
2 Samuel 15:1-37	Family Betrayal	pages 363–364	☐
2 Samuel 18:1-18	The Death of Absalom	pages 366–367	☐
1 Kings 1:5-27	Conflict over the Throne	pages 377–380	☐
1 Kings 1:28-53	David Gives Solomon the Crown	pages 380–381	☐
1 Kings 3:1-15	Solomon's Wisdom	page 383	☐
1 Kings 3:16-28	Solomon Solves a Problem	page 383	☐
1 Kings 6:1-38	Solomon Builds the Temple	pages 385–387	☐
1 Kings 10:1-13	Solomon and the Queen of Sheba	pages 392–393	☐
1 Kings 12:1-24	Solomon's Unwise Son	pages 396–397	☐
1 Kings 17:1-24	God Takes Care of Elijah	page 403	☐
1 Kings 18:16-46	Elijah versus the Priests of Baal	pages 404–405	☐
1 Kings 19:1-21	Spiritual Burnout	pages 405–406	☐
1 Kings 21:1-29	The Stolen Vineyard	pages 408–409	☐
1 Kings 22:29-40	The Death of King Ahab	pages 410–411	☐
2 Kings 2:1-12	Elijah's Chariot	pages 414–415	☐
2 Kings 2:13-25	Elisha's Miracles	pages 415–416	☐
2 Kings 5:1-27	The Healing of Naaman	pages 419–420	☐
2 Kings 11:1-21	The King Who Was Seven Years Old	pages 427–428	☐
2 Kings 22:1–23:3	Discovery of the Lost Book	pages 443–444	☐
Ezra 3:7-13	Rebuilding the Temple	pages 529–530	☐
Nehemiah 2:1-20	Nehemiah Returns to Jerusalem	pages 542–543	☐
Nehemiah 5:1-19	Nehemiah's Concern for the Poor	pages 545–546	☐
Nehemiah 8:1-18	Reading God's Word	pages 550–551	☐
Esther 1:1-22	The Fall of a Queen	pages 561–562	☐
Esther 2:1-23	A Strange Way to Become Queen	pages 562–564	☐
Esther 3:1-15	The Jews in Danger	pages 564–566	☐
Esther 4:1-17	The Queen Decides to Help	pages 566–567	☐
Esther 5:1-14	Esther Risks Her Life	page 567	☐
Esther 6:1–7:10	God Protects His People	pages 567–569	☐
Job 1:1-22	The Testing of Job	pages 573–574	☐
Job 2:1-13	Job and His Friends	pages 574–575	☐
Job 38:1-41	God Speaks to Job	pages 605–606	☐
Job 42:1-17	The Rest of Job's Story	page 609	☐
Psalm1:1-6	Two Kinds of Lives	page 611-612	☐
Psalm 8:1-9	The Values of Humans	page 615	☐
Psalm 23:1-6	A Sheep's Song	page 624	☐
Psalm 51:1-19	A Confession	pages 644–645	☐

Psalm 103:1-22	What God Is Like	pages 678–679	☐
Psalm 139:1-24	How Well God Knows Us	pages 703–704	☐
Psalm 145:1-21	God for All People and Time	pages 706–707	☐
Proverbs 4:1-27	Wise Words about Life	page 716	☐
Proverbs 5:1-23	Wise Words about Sex	pages 716–717	☐
Ecclesiastes 12:1-14	A Summary of Life	pages 758–759	☐
Isaiah 6:1-13	God Chooses Isaiah	pages 778–779	☐
Isaiah 53	The Suffering Servant	pages 831–832	☐
Jeremiah 1:1-10	God Calls a Prophet	pages 849–850	☐
Jeremiah 36	The Book Burning	pages 894–895	☐
Jeremiah 38:1-13	Jeremiah in the Well	pages 896–897	☐
Ezekiel 37:1-14	A Valley of Dry Bones	page 972	☐
Daniel 1:1-21	Coping with Pressure to Conform	pages 987–989	☐
Daniel 2:1-24	A King's Dream	page 989	☐
Daniel 2:25-49	The Meaning of the Dream	pages 989–990	☐
Daniel 3:1-30	Three Friends in a Furnace	pages 990–993	☐
Daniel 5:1-30	The Writing on the Wall	pages 995–997	☐
Daniel 6:1-28	Daniel and the Lions' Den	pages 997–998	☐
Jonah 1:1–2:10	Bending God's Directions	pages 1041–1043	☐
Jonah 3:1–4:11	Wrong Motives	pages 1043–1044	☐
New Testament			
Luke 1:1-14; John 1:1-18	Beginnings	pages 1165–1166; 1211–1212	☐
Luke 1:5-25	The Angel and Zechariah	pages 1165–1166	☐
Luke 1:26-56	Mary and Elizabeth	pages 1166–1167	☐
Luke 1:57-80	John the Baptist Is Born	pages 1167–1168	☐
Matthew 1:1-25	A Family Tree	pages 1091–1092	☐
Luke 2:1-20	Jesus Is Born!	page 1168	☐
Luke 2:21-39	Jesus' First Trip to Church	pages 1168–1169	☐
Matthew 2:1-12	Foreign Visitors	pages 1092–1093	☐
Matthew 2:13-23	Escape and Return	page 1093	☐
Luke 2:41-52	Jesus in the Temple Again	pages 1169–1170	☐
Mark 1:1-13	Baptism and Temptation	pages 1135–1136	☐
John 1:19-34	John the Baptist and Jesus	page 1212	☐
John 1:35-51	Jesus' First Disciples	pages 1212–1213	☐
John 2:1-25	Jesus and Surprises	pages 1213–1214	☐
John 3:1-21	Jesus and Nicodemus	page 1214	☐
John 3:22-36; Luke 3:19-20	John Gets into Trouble	pages 1214–1215; 1171	☐
John 4:1-42	Jesus Changes a Town	pages 1215–1216	☐
John 4:43-54	Jesus Preaching and Healing	page 1217	☐
Luke 4:16-30	Jesus Rejected	page 1172-1173	☐
Mark 1:16-39	Jesus Calls People to Follow	page 1136	☐
Luke 5:1-36	Miracles and a Question	pages 1173–1175	☐
John 5:1-47	Jesus Demonstrates He Is God's Son	pages 1217–1218	☐
Mark 2:23–3:19	Jesus and Disciples	pages 1139–1140	☐
Matthew 5:1-16	Jesus Gives the Beatitudes	pages 1095–1098	☐
Matthew 5:17-30	Jesus on Law, Anger and Lust	pages 1098–1100	☐
Matthew 5:31-48	Jesus on Relationships	page 1100	☐

Matthew 6:1-18	Jesus on Doing Good Things	pages 1100–1101	☐
Matthew 6:19-34	Jesus on Money and Worry	page 1101	☐
Matthew 7:1-12	Jesus on Criticizing and Praying	pages 1101–1102	☐
Matthew 7:13-29	How Jesus Looks at Us	pages 1102–1103	☐
Luke 7:1-17	Jesus and Foreigners	page 1177	☐
Matthew 11:1-30	Jesus Describes John	pages 1107–1108	☐
Luke 7:36–8:3	Jesus and Women	pages 1178–1179	☐
Matthew 12:22-50	Troubles for Jesus	pages 1109–1110	☐
Mark 4:1-29	Jesus Teaches about Seeds	pages 1140–1141	☐
Matthew 13:24-43	More of Jesus' Parables	pages 1111–1112	☐
Matthew 13:44-52	Even More Parables	page 1112	☐
Luke 8:22-56	Jesus in Control	pages 1180–1181	☐
Matthew 9:27-38	The Concerns of Jesus	pages 1105–1106	☐
Mark 6:1-13	Some Don't Listen; Some Need to Hear	page 1143	☐
Matthew 10:16-42	Jesus Prepares His Disciples	pages 1106–1107	☐
Mark 6:14-29	Herod Kills John the Baptist	pages 1143–1144	☐
Matthew 14:13-36	Jesus: Cook, Water Walker, Healer	pages 1113–1114	☐
John 6:22-40	Jesus Is the Bread from Heaven	pages 1220-1221	☐
John 6:41-71	Jesus Criticized and Deserted	page 1221	☐
Mark 7:1-37	Jesus Teaches and Defines Purity	pages 1145–1146	☐
Matthew 15:32–16:12	Jesus Feeds and Warns	page 1115	☐
Mark 8:22–9:1	Peter Identifies Jesus	pages 1147–1148	☐
Luke 9:28-45	Jesus Is Transfigured	pages 1182–1183	☐
Matthew 17:24–18:6	Who's the Greatest?	page 1117	☐
Mark 9:38-50	Who's on Our Side?	page 1150	☐
Matthew 18:10-22	Jesus as He Teaches	pages 1117–1118	☐
John 7:1-31	Jesus Out in the Open	pages 1221–1222	☐
John 7:32-53	A Warrant for Jesus' Arrest	pages 1222–1223	☐
John 8:1-20	Jesus: Forgiveness and Light	pages 1223–1224	☐
John 8:21-59	Jesus: Giver of Freedom	pages 1224–1225	☐
Luke 10:1-24	Jesus Sends Seventy Messengers	pages 1184–1185	☐
Luke 10:25-42	Jesus Tells a Story and Visits Friends	pages 1185–1186	☐
Luke 11:1-13	Jesus Teaches about Prayer	page 1186	☐
Luke 11:14-32	Accusations and Unbelief	pages 1186–1187	☐
Luke 11:33-54	Real Spirituality versus Unreal	pages 1187–1188	☐
Luke 12:1-21	Religious and Rich Fools	pages 1188–1189	☐
Luke 12:22-48	Jesus Warns about Worry	pages 1189–1190	☐
Luke 12:49-59	Jesus Warns about Troubles	page 1190	☐
Luke 13:1-21	Jesus and the Kingdom of God	pages 1190–1191	☐
John 9:1-41	Jesus and a Blind Man	pages 1225–1226	☐
John 10:1-18	Jesus Is the Good Shepherd	pages 1226–1227	☐
Luke 13:22-35	Jesus: The King Who Grieves	page 1191	☐
Luke 14:1-14	Jesus on Seeking Honor	pages 1191–1192	☐
Luke 14:15-35	Jesus on Being His Disciple	pages 1192–1193	☐
Luke 15:1-10	Two Parables of Losing and Finding	page 1193	☐
Luke 15:11-32	A Son Who Was Found	pages 1193–1194	☐

Luke 16:1-18	The Parable of the Shrewd Accountant	page 1194	☐
Luke 16:19-31	The Rich Man and the Beggar	pages 1194–1195	☐
John 11:1-36	Lazarus Dies	pages 1227–1228	☐
John 11:37-57	Jesus Raises Lazarus	pages 1228–1229	☐
Luke 17:1-19	Jesus and Ten Lepers	pages 1195-1196	☐
Luke 17:20-37	Jesus and the Kingdom of God	page 1196	☐
Luke18:1-14	Jesus Teaches about Prayer	pages 1196–1197	☐
Mark 10:1-16	Jesus on Family Matters	pages 1150–1151	☐
Mark 10:17-31	Jesus and the Rich Man	pages 1151–1152	☐
Matthew 20:1-16	A Parable about Equal Pay	page 1120	☐
Mark 10:35-52	Jesus on Serving Others	page 1152	☐
Luke 19:1-27	Jesus and Zacchaeus	pages 1198–1199	☐
John 12:1-11	A Woman Anoints Jesus	page 1229	☐
Matthew 21:1-17	Jesus Rides into Jerusalem	pages 1121–1122	☐
John 12:20-36	Jesus Explains Why He Must Die	page 1230	☐
John 12:37-50	Jesus and His Message	page 1230	☐
Mark 11:20-33	Permission to Pray for Anything	pages 1153–1154	☐
Matthew 21:28-46	Two Parables	pages 1122–1123	☐
Matthew 22:1-14	Jesus Tells about the Wedding Feast	page 1123	☐
Luke 20:20-40	Jesus Answers Questions	page 1202	☐
Mark 12:28-37	Questions Given and Taken	page 1155	☐
Matthew 23:1-39	Jesus: Warnings and Grieving	pages 1124–1125	☐
Luke 21:1-24	Jesus Talks about the Future	page 1203	☐
Luke 21:25-38	Jesus on Being Prepared	pages 1203–1204	☐
Matthew 25:1-30	Parables and Being Prepared	pages 1127–1128	☐
Matthew 25:31-46	Jesus on the Final Judgment	pages 1128–1129	☐
Luke 22:1-13	Preparing the Last Supper	page 1204	☐
John 13:1-17	Jesus Washes His Disciples' Feet	page 1231	☐
John 13:18-38	A Sad Prediction	pages 1231–1232	☐
John 14:1-14	Jesus Is the Way	page 1232	☐
John 14:15-31	Jesus Promises the Comforter	pages 1232–1233	☐
John 15:1-16	Jesus Teaches about the Vine and the Branches	page 1233	☐
John 15:17–16:4	Jesus Warns about Troubles	pages 1233–1234	☐
John 16:5-33	Jesus on the Holy Spirit and Prayer	pages 1234-1236	☐
John 17:1-26	Jesus Prays	page 1236	☐
Mark 14:26-52	A Repeated Prediction	pages 1158–1159	☐
John 18:1-24	Jesus Betrayed and Abandoned	pages 1236–1240	☐
Matthew 26:57-75	Trial and Denial	pages 1130–1131	☐
Matthew 27:1-10	The Religious Trial and Judas's Death	page 1131	☐
Luke 23:1-12	Two Political Trials	page 1206	☐
Mark 15:6-24	Sentencing and Torture	page 1161	☐
Luke 23:32-49	Jesus Crucified	page 1207	☐
Matthew 27:57-66	Jesus' Body Laid in a Guarded Tomb	page 1133	☐

John 20:1-18	Jesus Is Alive!	page 1242	☐
Matthew 28:8-15	Reactions to the Resurrection	pages 1133–1134	☐
Luke 24:13-43	Appearances of Jesus	pages 1208–1209	☐
John 20:24–21:14	More Appearances of Jesus	pages 1242–1244	☐
John 21:15-25	Jesus Talks with Peter	page 1244	☐
Matthew 28:16-20	Jesus Gives the Great Commission	page 1134	☐
Luke 24:44-53	Jesus Says Farewell	page 1209	☐
Acts 1:1-11	The Departure of Jesus	pages 1245–1246	☐
Acts 1:12-26	First Things First	page 1246	☐
Acts 2:1-13	An Amazing Gift	pages 1246–1247	☐
Acts 2:14-40	Peter's First Sermon	pages 1247–1248	☐
Acts 2:41–3:11	Daily Life in the Early Church	page 1248	☐
Acts 3:12–4:4	Peter's Second Sermon	pages 1248–1249	☐
Acts 4:5-22	Hostile Reactions	pages 1249–1250	☐
Acts 4:23-37	Praying and Sharing	pages 1250–1251	☐
Acts 5:1-16	Strange Events	page 1251	☐
Acts 5:17-42	Arrested!	pages 1251–1252	☐
Acts 6:1-15	Stephen: Special Servant	pages 1252–1253	☐
Acts 7:1-29	History Review I	pages 1253–1254	☐
Acts 7:30-60	History Review II	pages 1254–1256	☐
Acts 8:1-25	Benefits of Persecution	pages 1256–1257	☐
Acts 8:26-40	Unexpected Appointment	page 1257	☐
Acts 9:1-19	Paul Meets Jesus	pages 1257–1258	☐
Acts 9:20-31	Paul's New Life	page 1258	☐
Acts 9:32-42	God Uses Peter	pages 1258–1259	☐
Acts 10:1-23	Peter Sees a Lesson	pages 1259–1260	☐
Acts 10:24-48	Peter Learns a Lesson	pages 1260-1261	☐
Acts 11:1-18	Gentiles Get a Chance	page 1261	☐
Acts 11:19-29	Christians Helping One Another	page 1261	☐
Acts 12:1-25	A Great Escape and Capital Punishment	pages 1261–1262	☐
Acts 13:1-12	Paul and Barnabas: Travel and Preaching	page 1263	☐
Acts 14:1-28	Response and Reaction	pages 1267–1268	☐
Acts 15:1-21	A Church Conference	pages 1268–1269	☐
Acts 15:22-41	The Gentiles Are Accepted	pages 1269–1270	☐
Acts 16:1-15	Paul, Silas, and Timothy	page 1270	☐
Acts 16:16-40	Adventures in Jail	pages 1270–1271	☐
Acts 17:1-15	Different Responses in Two Cities	pages 1271–1272	☐
Acts 17:16-34	Paul in Athens	pages 1272–1273	☐
Acts 19:1-20	Paul in Ephesus	pages 1274–1275	☐
Acts 19:21-41	The Riot	pages 1275–1276	☐
Acts 20:1-12	Sleeping in Church	page 1276	☐
Acts 20:13-38	Saying Good-bye in Ephesus	pages 1276–1277	☐
Acts 21:1-17	Difficult Decision	pages 1277–1278	☐
Acts 21:18-36	Paul in Jerusalem	pages 1278–1279	☐
Acts 21:37–22:29	Paul Speaks	pages 1279–1280	☐
Acts 22:30–23:22	A Plan to Kill Paul	pages 1280–1281	☐
Acts 23:23–24:27	Paul in Prison	pages 1281–1282	☐

Acts 25:1-27	Paul Speaks to Festus	pages 1282–1283	☐
Acts 26:1-32	Paul Speaks to Agrippa	pages 1283–1285	☐
Acts 27:1-26	The Storm at Sea	page 1285	☐
Acts 27:27-44	The Shipwreck	page 1286	☐
Acts 28:1-14	The Winter on Malta	pages 1286–1287	☐
Acts 28:15-31	Paul in Rome	page 1287	☐
Romans 5:1-11	Faith Brings Joy	page 1294	☐
Romans 8:1-8	Truly Free from Sin	pages 1296–1297	☐
Romans 8:19-39	How God Loves	pages 1297–1298	☐
Romans 12:1-21	Living Sacrifice	pages 1302–1303	☐
1 Corinthians 13:1-13	Real Love	page 1324	☐
1 Corinthians 15:1-20	The Basic Gospel	page 1326	☐
1 Corinthians 15:42-58	Destiny!	pages 1327–1328	☐
2 Corinthians 4:1-18	Weak Containers: Strong Content	page 1332	☐
Galatians 5:13-26	Two Radically Different Lives	pages 1348–1350	☐
Ephesians 1:3-23	God's Action	pages 1353–1354	☐
Ephesians 2:1-22	God's Plan	pages 1354–1356	☐
Ephesians 4:1-16	Picture of the Church	pages 1356–1357	☐
Ephesians 6:10-20	Armor of God	pages 1359–1360	☐
Philippians 2:1-18	The Mind of Jesus	page 1363	☐
Philippians 3:1-21	Learning Joy	pages 1364–1365	☐
Colossians 2:1-15	What We Have in Christ	page 1372	☐
Colossians 3:1-17	Christian Relationships	page 1373	☐
1 Thessalonians 1:1-10	Spiritual Reputation	pages 1377–1378	☐
1 Thessalonians 4:1-18	Living for God	page 1381	☐
2 Thessalonians 1:1-12	Encouragement	pages 1383–1384	☐
2 Thessalonians 3:1-18	Final Requests	page 1385	☐
1 Timothy 4:1-16	Always Going Forward	page 1390	☐
1 Timothy 6:3-21	A Friend's Final Words	pages 1392–1393	☐
2 Timothy 1:1-18	The Importance of Examples	pages 1395–1396	☐
2 Timothy 3:1-17	Last Days	pages 1398–1399	☐
Titus 3:1-11; Philemon 1:4-7	Good Counsel	pages 1402-1403; 1406	☐
Hebrews 10:19-39	The New Life	pages 1418–1419	☐
Hebrews 11:1-40	A Review of Faith	pages 1419–1420	☐
Hebrews 12:1-13	Our Turn	page 1421	☐
James 1:2-27	Tough Times, Happy People	pages 1423–1424	☐
James 2:1-13	Valuing Other People	pages 1424–1425	☐
James 3:1-12	Words as Weapons	pages 1425–1426	☐
1 Peter 2:1-25	Living Stones	pages 1432–1434	☐
1 Peter 3:1-22	Relationships and Pain	page 1434	☐
2 Peter 1:2-21	Knowing God	pages 1439–1440	☐
1 John 1:1-10	The Way of Forgiveness	pages 1443–1444	☐
1 John 3:1-24	God Is Love	pages 1446–1447	☐
2 John 1:4-6; 3 John 1:5-8; Jude 1:17-25	Family Matters	pages 1450; 1452; 1454	☐
Revelation 1:1-20	Jesus the King	pages 1455–1456	☐
Revelation 21:1-27	Everything Made New	pages 1474–1475	☐
Revelation 22:1-21	Life in the New City	pages 1475–1476	☐

GOD'S GIFT TO YOU

Be honest. What's the best part about Christmas, birthdays, and other special occasions? The gifts, right? (We said be honest!) Who can resist a huge box with a big red bow, or a tiny package wrapped in shimmering, shiny paper? We all like to receive gifts, and we even *expect* to get gifts on those special days, like our birthday or Christmas.

But how about getting a gift when you least expect it? You come home from school, and there it sits on the table—a brightly wrapped package with your name on it. That's a real bonus! Well, here's some good news for you. Today you are eligible to receive the greatest, most unexpected gift ever.

What is the gift?

"For God loved the world so much that he gave his one and only Son, so that everyone who believes in him will not perish but have eternal life" (John 3:16). Did you catch that? God loves *you* so much that he sent his Son, Jesus, to the earth for *you*. Through faith in Jesus, you can receive eternal life and have a relationship with the Creator of the universe (John 17:3). That's the greatest gift ever given to anyone in all history.

Why do we need it?

So what's the big deal about this gift? Good question. In a word, the answer is sin. According to the Bible, everyone who is breathing sins (Romans 3:23). What is sin? Basically, it's doing what God says is wrong (1 John 3:4) and not doing what is right (James 4:17). Sin includes lying, stealing, and murdering, but it also includes anything we say, think, or do that goes against what God commands. The bottom line is that *everyone* sins every day. No exceptions.

So, you say, what's the big problem with that? Sin separates us from God. Because God is perfect, he can't allow anyone sinful to come into his presence. So unless something happens to change our situation and get rid of our sin problem, we all are lost, cut off, doomed. "It's your sins that have cut you off from God. Because of your sins, he has turned away and will not listen anymore" (Isaiah 59:2). That's really bad news.

The good news is that God does not leave us there. Through Jesus, God's unexpected and perfect gift, we now can have a relationship with him. (See John 14:6.) By offering himself as the perfect sacrifice, Jesus took care of our sin problem on the cross—forever. "Christ suffered for our sins once for all time. He never sinned, but he died for sinners to bring you safely home to God" (1 Peter 3:18).

So how do we get this gift?

You just need to accept it. And you do this by taking these three important steps:

1) *Turn from your sin.* "Now repent of your sins and turn to God, so that your sins may be wiped away" (Acts 3:19). This means telling God you are sorry for doing, saying, or thinking whatever is not pleasing to him.

2) *Trust in Jesus.* "We are made right with God by placing our faith in Jesus Christ. And this is true for everyone who believes, no matter who we are" (Romans 3:22). In this step, you thank God for sending his Son to die on the cross in your place, taking the penalty for your sins.

3) *Receive Christ as your Savior.* "But to all who believed him and accepted him, he gave the right to become children of God" (John 1:12). This means asking God to come into your life and to take control. You commit yourself to God.

What's next?

By accepting this gift, you become God's very own child (1 John 3:1). So here's what to do next. These steps will help your relationship with God grow deeper.

1) *Tell someone!* Tell a parent, a Sunday school teacher, or a friend about the gift and how you received it. This person should be someone who can help you along this exciting new faith journey.

2) *Begin reading God's Word (the Bible).* This will help you learn more about God and his plan for you. A reading plan is included in this Bible to help you get started.

3) *Talk daily to God through prayer.* There is no issue too big or too small for God to handle. Bring all your concerns to him in prayer, and he will listen. "Don't worry about anything; instead, pray about everything. Tell God what you need, and thank him for all he has done" (Philippians 4:6).

4) *Finally, celebrate!* You have just received a gift that will never fade, break down, or wear out; it's a gift that will last forever. "So now we can rejoice in our wonderful new relationship with God because our Lord Jesus Christ has made us friends of God" (Romans 5:11).

How to Read the Bible

Now that you have your new Bible and a plan for reading it (check out "The Greatest Stories Reading Plan" on page 1477 of this Bible), you probably are wondering: *How can I ever really understand what I'm reading?* After all, the Bible isn't just *any* book. It is God's Word, written to you, to help you grow closer to him and become more like Jesus. As Paul reminds us, "All Scripture is inspired by God and is useful to teach us what is true and to make us realize what is wrong in our lives. It corrects us when we are wrong and teaches us to do what is right. God uses it to prepare and equip his people to do every good work" (2 Timothy 3:16-17).

When you get a handle on the fact that every word in the Bible was inspired by God (meaning that God revealed his thoughts and his plan to certain believers, who wrote it down) and that every word is there to help direct you to do what is right, you realize how important it is to understand what God is saying to you. To *understand* the Bible, you need to do more than just read it. You need to think about what you have read by asking questions and then putting into practice what God is telling you to do or think or say or change.

So how do you do that? First, select a story or passage and read through it once to get the overall picture of what is going on. Then read it a second time, asking yourself these questions: *Who? Where? When? Why?* and *What now?* The first four questions help you understand the facts about the story and what is happening. The last question helps you think about what to do now that you have read God's Word. Let's consider each question.

- **Who?** As you read the passage, check out the people in the story. What are they like? If these people were living in our world today, who would they be like? Put yourself in the story. Who would you be?
- **Where?** Take note of where the story takes place. Is it in the desert, in a city, or on a battlefield? How does the place make a difference in the story?
- **When?** Look at the context of the story by briefly looking at the verses surrounding the passage. What happened right before the story? What happened right after? For example, if you are reading a passage about Jesus' life, did this event happen at the beginning of his ministry or toward the end of his life? A passage is easier to understand if you know the circumstances under which it took place.
- **Why?** Remember the point that God inspired every single word in the Bible? It's important to think about why God put this particular passage or story in the Bible. What is God telling you through this story or passage? What is the main point?
- **What now?** This final question is your opportunity to reflect on what you should do as a result of what you have learned. This is the place where you ask yourself: *What is God saying to me or about me? What is it I should do because of what God is saying? What should I change?* This process is called application—where you are taking what you learned from a particular Bible passage and making it a part of your life. As James tells us in his book, "Don't just listen to God's word. You must do what it says. Otherwise, you are only fooling yourselves" (James 1:22).

As you begin your journey with God's Word, you may want to get a notebook to jot down your thoughts and your answers to these questions. It doesn't have to be fancy—any kind of notebook will do. Use your notebook to write down questions you may have as you read a particular passage that might spur further study. This will be helpful in developing a habit of Bible study that will last a lifetime.

Studying and reading God's Word *is* a lifelong process. You can read the Bible over and over again and always find something new and fresh to learn about yourself and about God. "For the word of God is alive and powerful" (Hebrews 4:12).

I survived! index

Topic	Page
Accountability	753
Advice	499
Alcohol	1305
Approval from God	1219
Approval from others	435
Authority	1201
Beauty	1435
Comparing yourself to others	583
Complaining	165
Confessing your sins	629
Conflict with friends	647
Dating	763
Differences	1307
Discipline	379
Encouraging others	1349
Faith	481
Family	699
Fears	249
Friends who are worldly	1427
Friendships to avoid	135
God's care and comfort	819
God's love showing through us	839
God's Word	523
Grief and loss	1235
Humility	333
Influences that are good	1371
Laziness	729
Life: new	941
Marriage and divorce	1085
Opportunities: making the most of them	67
Opportunities: using them	565
Opposition	1255
Parents: listening to them	213
Parents: lying to them	325
Parents: wisdom from them	715
Peer pressure	991
Positives: focusing on them	173
Quitting: not doing it	547
Rejection	833
Revenge	1099
Self-worth	1069
Serving God by using your gifts	1323
Serving others	1149
Serving while you're young	1391
Sexual purity	1379

Suffering 1339
Temptation 1397
Trusting in the right thing 937
Worship that is true 675

Topic **Page**
Anger at God 575
Anger at your parents 1359
Appearance 563
Attitude 8
Beliefs 949
Body building 702
Cheating 733
Chores 1364
Church attendance 1418
Clothing 775
Competition 739
Conforming 992
Contentment 211
Dating and kissing 768
Dating non-Christians 1334
Death 836
Divorce 1086
Doubts about God 1243
Evolution 1272
Family 427
Friends 752
Goals 280
Gossip 741
Hating life 367
Homosexuality 137
Jokes to avoid 1426
Laughing at others 1038
Love for God 1444
Love for those who aren't "cool" 1198
Lying to help someone 502
Messiness 129
Music 1366
Occult 781
Parents 332
People who are different 1259
Popularity 1160
Pornography 1187

Praying about little stuff 542
Praying anytime, anywhere 1382
Relaxing. 38
Religions 864
Revenge 241
Secrets. 1350
Self-doubt 320
Sibling rivalry 167
Smoking. 126
Step-parents 88
Strangers online 255
Swearing 1110
Television 690
Working hard 1374
Worrying 634

Bible Character **Page**
Aaron 175
Abraham 20
Ahab 407
Barak. 282
Baranabas 1274
Boaz 307
Daniel 1004
David. 357
Elisha 417
Esau 43
Gideon. 285
Hezekiah 746
Isaac 31
Isaiah 769
Jacob. 36
James and John 1107
Job 577
John the Baptist 1170
John Mark. 1263
Jonathan 335
Joseph (N. T.) 1094
Joseph (O. T.). 49
Joshua 250
Judas 1156

King Josiah 516
Luke 1278
Matthew 1139
Moses 68
Nehemiah 558
Nicodemus 1220
Paul (Saul) 1308
Peter 1119
Samson 296
Samuel 313
Saul 343
Solomon 393
Stephen 1253
Timothy 1396
Zacchaeus 1182
Zechariah 1167

Title **Page**
Accused! 1436
Activity Overload 655
Admit One 625
All Alone 34
Baseball Burnout 1365
Best Friends? 278
Birthday Present, The 1399
Bride in a Garden 765
But I Don't Want To! 1042
Buyer Beware? 982
Call for Help 1380
Class Picnic, The 204
Clean! 1023
Cool Wardrobe 776
Cut Up and Cut Down 1176
Dirt-Bike Racing 1233
Down, but Not Out 834
Earning Trust 1195
Final Exam, The 677
Flat Out 1098
Freedom 1347
Friends 612
Fun at the Water Park 93
Future Plans 885
Giving and Getting 1336

Good Advice? 396
Greatest, The 863
Guilty Goalie, The 872
Gym Dandy 1372
Hidden Magazines, The 599
Home Sweet Home 1317
"I Spy" 270
I'll Do it Myself 908
I've Got It All! 1459
Is That Your Best? 1084
It's a Miracle! 468
Just Kick It 521
Keeping Secrets 1076
Ketchup Caper, The 90
Leader of the Pack 504
Listen! 576
Loan Again? 1118
Looking Good 329
Make a Choice 1155
Make Up Your Mind 988
Making a Good Impression 17
Making Fun 666
Meet My Brother 703
Moving Up 338
New and Different 1302
No Big Deal? 537
No One Will Ever Know! 480
No One Will Know 1413
Old and Funny 415
On Top of the World 692
Paper Chase, The 814
Party On! 759
Party Poopers, The 183
Passing Notes 735
Pet Project 378
Phone Fib, The 1250
Pool Party, The 86
Pray for What? 486
Prayer Habit, The 997
Quitting Time 196
Revenge? 57
Right Choice, The 1282
Rules Are Rules? 1017
Scared Silly 246
Science Fair? 240
Serves Him Right! 119
Setbacks 48
Something Borrowed, Something New 1128
Speak Up! 1147
Star Player, The 803
Sticking Close 304
Sticks and Stones 923

Stolen Fun 1051
Stolen Goods 138
Sub Way 1324
Success? 1276
Taking a Stand 564
Third Chair 638
To Pray or Not to Pray 1389
Too Hard to Handle? 890
Trading Cards 294
Troubled Thoughts 798
Truth Hurts, The 359
Unjust Criticism 310
Unknown Future, The 225
Video Game, The 6
What a Treat! 722
What an Animal! 724
Who Hears? Who Cares? 441
Who's Different—You or Me? 1215
Whose Money? 554
Wishing Well 1188
Write On? 1358
You've Got a Friend 930

Topic **Page**
Babysitting disaster 585
Backing into a ditch 1074
Bringing down a dance partner 594
Candle, a girl's ponytail, and a fire 145
Driving into a neighbor's mailbox 867
Embarrassed by the rescuer 1414
Embarrassed in the locker room 1313
Falling down two flights of stairs 1202
Falling out of the barber's chair 1406
Finishing last in every race 362
Football player on the ground 617
French class 54
Getting hit with a soccer ball 1034
Graduation with bruises 788
Gum and hair create disaster 305
Janitor has to cut a desk apart 1319
Jazzed-up duet 1300
Kick that broke a toe 1470
Kiss that never was 289

Knocked out playing baseball 496
Lost retainers 228
Makeup for swim practice 901
Messed up band solo 399
Muddy backside 845
Nervous driver's ed student 750
New driver gets lost 945
Off base and tagged out 1123
On the ground in underwear 807
Only ones standing 430
Out of control on a skateboard 707
Play a game or listen to the sermon? 713
Playing the piano with swollen hands 1013
Problem sweatpants 1225
Red nose at camp 1441
Ruined DustBuster 1384
Running into a pole 262
Scheming guys try to meet a girl 199
School concert and a hiccup 1463
Sick in front of a hundred people 1331
Sick on a carnival ride 532
Sidewalk sprawl 1284
Sleeve caught as car drives away 1162
Spinach between front teeth 1068
Split swimming suit 965
Stuck under a desk 219
Stuck with a muddy back 1055
Too shy to call 454
Wearing braces and smiling 641
Which girl asked me to a dance? 663
Wrong class 315

Topic	Reference	Page
Angel-led escape	Acts 12:6-19	1262
Angel that destroyed an army	2 Chronicles 32:20-21	519
Babies playing with snakes	Isaiah 11:6-9	784
Balaam's donkey	Numbers 22:21-41	184
Behind closed doors	John 20:19-20	1242
Being a superhero	Hebrews 10:35–11:40	1419
Biggest bed	Deuteronomy 3:11	207
Blind army	2 Kings 6:18-23	421
Book John ate	Revelation 10:9-10	1464
Bronze snake	Numbers 21:4-9	181
Celebrating problems	Romans 5:3-5	1294

Choir of millions	Revelation 5:11-12	1461
Choir that won a battle	2 Chronicles 20:20-24	505
City that sank into the sea	Ezekiel 27:26-32	961
Cost of loving money	1 Timothy 6:9-10	1393
Cursing church leaders	Deuteronomy 27:11-26	233
Daniel in the lions' den	Daniel 6:16-23	998
Day the sun stood still	Joshua 10:12-13	257
Dead man walking	John 11:30-44	1228
Deadly snake bite	Acts 28:3-5	1286
Dinner for 5,000	Mark 6:30-44	1144
Dry bones that came to life	Ezekiel 37:1-14	972
Elijah raises the dead	1 Kings 17:17-22	403
Elijah taken to heaven	2 Kings 2:11	414
Ezekiel eats a scroll	Ezekiel 3:1-3	931
Ezekiel's strange haircut	Ezekiel 5:1-4	933
Face that shone like the sun	Matthew 17:1-8	1116
Fiery furnace	Daniel 3:19-27	993
Fire from heaven	Leviticus 9:24	124
First skyscraper	Genesis 11:1-9	15
Fishermen have no time to pack	Luke 5:1-11	1174
Four amazing things	Proverbs 30:18-19	745
Gideon's fleece	Judges 6:36-40	284
God's place for the Temple	1 Chronicles 21:18; 22:1	473
God's protection plan	Ephesians 6:10-18	1360
God's weather weapon	1 Samuel 7:10	317
Golden calf	Exodus 32:1-20	103
Head tossed over a wall	2 Samuel 20:20-22	371
How God gets around	Psalm 104:3	679
How Jesus looks in heaven	Revelation 1:12-16	1456
How to get a king's attention	2 Chronicles 33:10-13	520
Isaiah's heavenly vision	Isaiah 6:6-7	778
Jacob's wrestling match	Genesis 32:24-32	41
Jeremiah and the well	Jeremiah 38:4-6, 10	896
Jeremiah and the yoke	Jeremiah 27:1-2, 5-8	883
Jesus walks on water	Matthew 14:22-27	1113
Jesus' birthplace prophesied	Micah 5:2	1049
Job's bad day	Job 1:13-20	574
Job's happy ending	Job 42:10-17	609
Joining Jesus in the clouds	1 Thessalonians 4:15-17	1380
Jonathan and the honey	1 Samuel 14:24-29, 42-45	324
Joseph	Genesis 41:1-46	50
Just like grasshoppers	Numbers 13:33	169
King Hanun's bad mistake	1 Chronicles 19:6	471
King Solomon's wealth	2 Chronicles 9:13	494
Longest name in the Bible	Isaiah 8:1-3	780
Longest Psalm	Psalm 119:88	693
Long-lasting shoes	Deuteronomy 29:5	236
Long-lost scroll	2 Kings 22:8-13	442
Lot's wife	Genesis 19:26	23
Mad cow king	Daniel 4:28-33	995
Man who dropped coals on city	Ezekiel 10:2	940
Man who measured a city	Zechariah 2:1-2	1072

Many graves open up	Matthew 27:50-53	1133
Most awesome city in the universe	Revelation 21:10-27	1474
Mountain split in two	Zechariah 14:4	1081
Naked prophet	Isaiah 20:1-3	792
Nation God stepped on	Psalm 60:11-12	650
New bodies—extreme makeovers	1 Corinthians 15:48	1327
No secrets from God	1 Corinthians 4:5	1314
Old age	Genesis 5:27; 9:29	9
Our new life in Jesus	Galatians 2:20	1345
Poor trade	Amos 2:6	1029
Prophecy of Jesus' death	Isaiah 53:2-12	831
Queen who saved her people	Esther 8:3-6, 16	569
Record wall-rebuilding	Nehemiah 6:15	548
Rich man who was poor	Mark 10:17-22	1151
Samson and the lion	Judges 14:6	293
Scapegoat	Leviticus 16:9-10, 20-22	133
Sending the devil on the run	James 4:7	1428
Sound that defeated the enemy	2 Samuel 5:22-25	352
Speaking many languages	Acts 2:1-4	1247
Stain no soap can wash	Jeremiah 2:22	851
Success followed by a pout	Jonah 3:1-5, 10; 4:1-3	1044
Temple built without a sound	1 Kings 6:7	386
Ten lepers healed with one look	Luke 17:11-19	1196
Ten plagues	Exodus 7:15–11:10	73
Tent-dwellers	Jeremiah 35:5-7	894
Three hours of daytime darkness	Luke 23:44-45	1207
Time moved backwards	Isaiah 38:1-8	812
Torn clothing	Ezra 9:3	536
Trusting wood more than God	Hosea 4:12	1010
12-fingered giant	2 Samuel 21:20-21	372
Uzziah becomes a leper	2 Chronicles 26:16-21	512
Value of wisdom	Proverbs 8:11	720
Voice that can shatter a tree	Psalm 29:4-5	627
Water from a rock	Exodus 17:1-7	85
We are royal priests	1 Peter 2:9	1433
What makes God happy	Colossians 3:20	1373
What's better than being rich	Ecclesiastes 7:11-12	755
Whippings, beatings, and stonings	2 Corinthians 11:23-27	1338
World at Jesus' feet	Philippians 2:9-11	1363
World's biggest hammer	Jeremiah 50:22-25	911
Yell that brought down walls	Joshua 6:20	252

memory verse index

Reference	*Question*	Page
Genesis 1:27	*Why should I treat people with respect if they don't deserve it?*	4
Genesis 15:1	*What should I do when I'm feeling afraid and insecure?*	19
Genesis 28:15	*Sometimes I feel that nobody cares and that I'm all alone*	35
Genesis 41:16	*Some days I feel like I can't do anything right*	51
Genesis 49:25	*I am feeling overwhelmed. Where can I get some help?*	62
Exodus 3:5	*Who is worthy of my respect?*	69
Exodus 20:12	*Do I have to do everything my parents tell me?*	89
Exodus 34:6	*Does God ever get angry at us?*	106
Leviticus 11:44	*Why is it so important to live a clean life?*	127
Leviticus 19:11	*Is it OK to tell just a little lie if it won't hurt anyone?*	139
Numbers 6:26	*How can I calm myself down when I'm nervous?*	159
Numbers 18:29	*Is it OK to give God what's left over of my money and my time?*	179
Numbers 27:17	*Why do we need leaders?*	191
Deuteronomy 6:6-7	*How can I keep from doing wrong things?*	212
Deuteronomy 16:17	*How much do I need to give to God?*	223
Deuteronomy 30:19-20	*What's the most important decision I'll ever have to make?*	238
Joshua 1:9	*What should I do when I'm afraid to try something new?*	247
Joshua 6:27	*How can I be successful in what I do?*	253
Judges 5:3	*Who deserves our worship and praise?*	281
Judges 17:6	*What happens when we live without God?*	297
1 Samuel 2:6-7	*Sometimes life seems crazy and out of control. Is anyone really in control?*	311
1 Samuel 12:24	*How can I stop feeling sorry for myself?*	322
1 Samuel 16:7	*I'm tired of other kids making fun of the way I look*	328
1 Samuel 20:42	*How can I be a good friend?*	336
2 Samuel 7:22	*Is there anyone else like God?*	354
2 Samuel 23:5	*Can I really trust God to keep his promises?*	374
1 Kings 2:7	*How can you repay those who have been kind to you?*	381
1 Kings 8:27	*Does God live in one place?*	390
2 Kings 19:28	*Does God mind if I brag about myself?*	440
2 Kings 23:3	*What makes a really good leader?*	444
1 Chronicles 11:14	*Can I really count on God for success?*	463
1 Chronicles 29:12	*When I face a tough situation, where can I find strength?*	483

2 Chronicles 7:14	*Why should I confess my sins to God?*	492
2 Chronicles 16:9	*Does God really know that I try to obey him?*	501
2 Chronicles 26:4-5	*Why is it so important to obey God?*	511
Ezra 3:11	*Will God ever stop loving me?*	530
Nehemiah 8:10	*When I'm feeling weak, how can I keep going?*	550
Esther 4:14	*I don't understand why God puts me in certain situations*	567
Job 5:17	*Isn't it bad if God corrects me?*	578
Job 17:9	*Why should I keep doing the right thing, especially if it's difficult?*	589
Psalm 5:12	*What kind of people does God bless?*	614
Psalm 9:9	*Should I really bother God with my problems?*	615
Psalm 20:7	*What do some people brag about?*	623
Psalm 33:18	*Does God really watch over me?*	631
Psalm 73:26	*What can I count on when I'm feeling weak?*	659
Psalm 92:1-2	*What should I say when I talk to God?*	672
Psalm 112:6-7	*How should I react to bad news?*	687
Psalm 119:98-99	*Why is it important to read the Bible?*	693
Psalm 139:17	*Does God really spend time thinking about me?*	704
Proverbs 1:8-9	*Why should I listen to my parents?*	712
Proverbs 11:3	*Why is it so bad to peek at my friend's test paper?*	723
Proverbs 12:22	*What's so wrong about telling a little white lie?*	725
Proverbs 14:29	*What can I do about my bad temper?*	727
Proverbs 16:18	*I think I'm really "cool." Is there anything wrong with that?*	730
Ecclesiastes 12:1	*God will be important to me someday, but I'm busy now*	758
Isaiah 17:10	*What happens if I have given all my attention to the other stuff in my life?*	790
Isaiah 26:4	*How can I stop worrying all the time?*	797
Isaiah 40:31	*Where can I find the strength to keep on doing what's right?*	815
Isaiah 51:12	*Why shouldn't I fear what other people might say about me?*	830
Isaiah 61:10	*What can make me glad when things aren't going so well?*	842
Jeremiah 7:5	*Why is it so important to treat others nicely?*	859
Jeremiah 23:24	*Is God really here with me and in heaven at the same time?*	879
Jeremiah 32:27	*I have a problem that I don't think even God can fix!*	891
Jeremiah 42:6	*What if I don't want to do what God says?*	900
Lamentations 3:32-33	*Does God sit in heaven waiting to zap people for doing things that are wrong?*	924
Ezekiel 7:3-4	*Does it really matter if I don't obey God?*	936
Ezekiel 21:26	*Will God shake things up someday?*	954
Ezekiel 33:11	*Why doesn't God just kill off all the evil people?*	968
Ezekiel 47:22	*How should we treat people who are different from us?*	985
Hosea 5:15	*Sometimes I forget to talk to God until I'm in trouble*	1012

Joel 2:32	*Who can be saved?*	1025
Amos 5:24	*Who cares if I'm always fair and try to do what's right?*	1032
Habakkuk 3:17-18	*When things aren't going well for me, how should I react?*	1060
Zephaniah 3:17	*Does God really like me?*	1064
Zechariah 10:2	*Is it OK to look for answers anywhere that looks good to you?*	1078
Matthew 5:7	*What's a good reason for being nice to my sister and brother?*	1095
Matthew 15:18	*What's so wrong about using a few bad words once in a while?*	1114
Mark 4:25	*How can I understand what God wants me to do with my life?*	1141
Mark 11:25	*What if I don't feel like forgiving someone who has hurt me?*	1153
Luke 12:15	*If I could just get a new bike, I'd be happy, wouldn't I?*	1189
Luke 14:11	*Why is it bad to brag about all the cool things I can do?*	1192
Luke 16:10	*How can I get my parents to trust me more?*	1194
Luke 18:16	*Does Jesus really care about me? I'm just a kid*	1197
John 3:16	*How do I know that God loves me?*	1214
Acts 5:29	*What should I do if an adult tells me to do something I know is wrong?*	1252
Acts 16:31	*How do I know for sure that I'll go to heaven when I die?*	1271
Romans 3:10	*My friends seem OK. Why do people say they're sinners?*	1292
Romans 12:21	*How can I keep from doing what's bad?*	1303
1 Corinthians 6:19-20	*What's so wrong with smoking and drinking?*	1316
2 Corinthians 5:17	*Am I really any different now that I've become a Christian?*	1333
Galatians 5:22-23	*How does God help me become a better person?*	1348
Galatians 6:4	*Even though I try hard, I can't do anything as well as my big sister*	1351
Ephesians 4:32	*How can my brother and I stop fighting all the time?*	1357
Philippians 2:3	*How can I be more popular?*	1362
1 Thessalonians 5:15	*I would love to get back at that kid who makes fun of me*	1381
1 Timothy 4:12	*I'm just a kid. How can I help older people know about God?*	1390
Hebrews 4:16	*I'm afraid to ask God for help. He may think my problems are dumb*	1412
James 3:4-5	*Why do I have to be so careful about what I say?*	1425

1 John 4:20	*My brother makes me so mad. I just hate him!*	1447
2 John 1:6	*I can't see God, so what can I do to show my love for him?*	1450

Reference	Title	Page
Genesis 1–2	*Days of Creation*	5
Genesis11–13	*Abram's Journey from Ur to Canaan*	12–13
Exodus 7–12	*The Plagues*	77
Exodus 14	*Doubters in the Bible*	81
Exodus 20	*Jesus and the Ten Commandments*	97
Numbers 2	*Arrangement of Tribes around the Tabernacle While in the Wilderness*	153
Numbers 14	*The Exodus and 40 Years in the Wilderness*	170–171
Deuteronomy 8	*Obedience*	215
1 Samuel 28	*Simple Objects*	344
1 Chronicles 28	*Ideas to Live By*	476
Job 38	*How Suffering Affects Us*	605
Psalm 17	*Finding Christ in the Psalms*	619
Psalm 35	*Psalms to Learn and Love*	632
Psalm 51	*Reasons to Read Psalms*	644
Psalm 128	*How God Is Described in Psalms*	697
Proverbs 6	*People Called "Wise" in the Bible*	718
Isaiah 44	*Today's Idolatry*	825
Ezekiel 6	*Living in a Bible-time House*	934–935
Ezekiel 36	*Old and New Covenants*	971
Daniel 2	*Nebuchadnezzar's Dream*	1000
Jonah 1–4	*Miracles in the Book of Jonah*	1043
Matthew 5	*Footprints of Jesus—Early Ministry*	1096–1097
Matthew 5	*The Beatitudes*	1102
Matthew 6	*Seven Reasons Not to Worry*	1105
Mark 1	*The Twelve Disciples*	1137
Mark 14	*Key Characteristics of Christ*	1158
Luke 2	*Don't Be Afraid*	1169
Luke 8	*Jesus and Women*	1179
Luke 10	*A Collection of Attitudes*	1184
John 18	*Who Saw Jesus After His Resurrection?*	1237
John 18	*Footprints of Jesus—The Last Week*	1238–1239
Acts 13	*Paul's Journeys*	1264–1265
Acts 15	*Great Escapes in the Bible*	1268
Romans 2	*Salvation's Freeway*	1291
Romans 8	*Important Ideas in Romans*	1297

Ephesians 2	*God's Armor for Us*	1355
Hebrews 4	*Living in a Bible-time Village*	1410–1411
1 John	*A Book of Contrasts*	1445
Revelation 2	*The Beginning and the End*	1457
Revelation 13	*The Names of Jesus*	1467
Revelation 20	*What We Know about Eternity*	1473

Story

Adam and Eve, Genesis 2:4–4:25 5–8
Balaam's donkey speaks, Numbers 22:21-35 184
Beatitudes, Matthew 5:1-12 1095–1098
Bronze snake, Numbers 21:4-9 181
Burning bush, Exodus 3 68–69
Cain kills Abel, Genesis 4 7–8
Creation, Genesis 1:1–2:7 3–5
Daniel in the lions' den, Daniel 6 997–998
David and Bathsheba, 2 Samuel 11:1–12:25 357–359
David and Goliath, 1 Samuel 17 328–331
Elijah on Mt. Carmel, 1 Kings 18:16-46 404–405
Elijah's chariot of fire, 2 Kings 2:1-12 414–415
Esau sells his birthright, Genesis 25:27-34 30
Esther becomes queen and saves her people, Esther 1–10 561–571
Exodus from Egypt, Exodus 12:31-51 79–80
Faith chapter, Hebrews 11 1419–1420
Fiery furnace, Daniel 3 990–993
First sin, Genesis 3 6–7
Fruit of the Spirit, Galatians 5:22-23 1350
Garden of Eden, Genesis 2:4–3:24 5–7
Gideon and the fleece, Judges 6:33-40 284
Gideon battles the Midianites, Judges 7:1-22 284–286
Golden calf, Exodus 32 103–105
Golden rule, Matthew 7:12 1102
Great Commission, Matthew 28:18-20 1134
Holy Spirit comes at Pentecost, Acts 2:1-21 1246–1247
Isaac almost sacrificed, Genesis 22 26
Jacob wrestles the angel, Genesis 32:22-32 41
Jericho (battle of), Joshua 6 251–252
Jesus, Bread of Life, John 6:35 1221
Jesus, Gate for the sheep, John 10:7 1226
Jesus, Good Shepherd, John 10:11-16 1226–1227
Jesus, Light of the World, John 8:12 1223
Jesus, Vine, John 15:1 1233
Jesus, Way Truth, and the Life, John 14:6 1232
Jesus' baptism, Matthew 3:13-17 1094

Jesus' birth, Luke 2:1-20 1168
Jesus' death on the cross, Matthew 27:32-66 1132–1133
Jesus' resurrection, Matthew 28:1-10 1133-1134
Jesus' temptation by Satan, Matthew 4:1-11 1094–1095
Jesus' transfiguration, Matthew 17:1-13 1116
John the Baptist killed, Mark 6:14-29 1143–1144
Jonah and the fish, Jonah 1:1–2:10 1041–1043
Jordan River parts, Joshua 3 247–248
Joseph sent to Egypt, Genesis 37 45–47
Lazarus raised from the dead, John 11:1-44 1227–1228
Lord's Prayer, Matthew 6:9-13 1101
Lot's wife turns to salt, Genesis 19:12-26 23
Love chapter, 1 Corinthians 13 1324
Moses protected as a baby, Exodus 2:1-10 66
Naaman is healed of leprosy, 2 Kings 5 419–420
Nicodemus talks with Jesus, John 3:1-21 1214
Noah and the ark, Genesis 6:9–9:17 10–14
Passover in Egypt, Exodus 12:1-30 78–79
Paul and Silas sing in prison, Acts 16:16-40 1270–1271
Paul's conversion, Acts 9:1-19 1257–1258
Paul's shipwreck, Acts 27:1–28:10 1285–1287
Pentecost, Acts 2:1-13 1246–1247
Peter's escape from prison, Acts 12:1-19 1261–1262
Plagues on Egypt, Exodus 7–11 72–78
Rainbow after the flood, Genesis 9:8-17 11–14
Red Sea parts, Exodus 14:5-31 81–82
Samson and Delilah, Judges 16:4-22 295–297
Sermon on the Mount, Matthew 5–7 1095–1103
Sodom and Gomorrah, Genesis 19:1-29 22–24
Stoning of Stephen, Acts 6:8–7:60 1252–1256
Sun stands still, Joshua 10:1-15 256–257
Ten Commandments, Exodus 20:1-17 88–89
Tower of Babel, Genesis 11:1-9 15
Wise men visit Jesus, Matthew 2:1-12 1092–1093
Zacchaeus meets Jesus, Luke 19:1-10 1198–1199

Jesus' Teaching Parables

About the Kingdom of God

Fishing Net, Matthew 13:47-50 1112
Growing Seed, Mark 4:26-29 1141
Mustard Seed, Luke 13:18-19 1191
Pearl, Matthew 13:45-46 1112
Soils, Luke 8:5-8, 11-15 1179–1180
Treasure, Matthew 13:44 1112
Weeds, Matthew 13:24-30, 36-43 1111–1112
Yeast (Leaven), Luke 13:20-21 1191

About Service and Obedience

Loaned Money, Matthew 25:14-30 1127–1128
Servant's Role, Luke 17:7-10 1196
Workers in the Vineyard, Matthew 20:1-16 1120

About Prayer
Friend at Midnight, Luke 11:5-8 1186
Persistent Widow/Unjust Judge, Luke 18:1-8 1196–1197

About Neighbors
The Good Samaritan, Luke 10:30-37 1185

About Humility
Lowest Seat, Luke 14:7-14 1192
Proud Pharisee and the Corrupt Tax Collector, Luke 18:9-14 1197

About Wealth
Wealthy Fool, Luke 12:16-21 1189
Great Feast, Luke 14:16-24 1192
Shrewd Manager, Luke 16:1-9 1194

Jesus' Gospel Parables

About God's Love
Lost Coin, Luke 15:8-10 1193
Lost Sheep, Luke 15:3-7 1193
Lost Son, Luke 15:11-32 1193–1194

About Thankfulness
The Forgiven Loans, Luke 7:41-43 1178

Jesus' Parables of Judgment and the Future

About Christ's Return
Ten Virgins, Matthew 25:1-13 1127
Traveling Boss, Mark 13:34-37 1157
Wise and Faithful Servant, Luke 12:42-48 1190

About God's Values
Evil Tenants, Matthew 21:33-44 1122–1123
Marriage Feast, Matthew 22:1-14 1123
Two Sons, Matthew 21:28-32 1122
Unforgiving Servant, Matthew 18:23-35. 1118
Unproductive Fig Tree, Luke 13:6-9 1190–1191

Jesus' Miracles

Blind Bartimaeus receives sight, Mark 10:46-52 1152
Blind man sees at Bethsaida, Mark 8:22-26 1147
Centurion's servant is healed, Luke 7:1-10 1177
Coin in a fish's mouth, Matthew 17:24-27. 1117
Cursing the fig tree, Matthew 21:18-22 1122
Deaf and dumb man is healed, Mark 7:31-37. 1146
Demon is sent out of a man, Luke 4:33-37 1173
Demon-possessed boy is cured, Mark 9:14-29 1148–1150
Demons sent into the pigs, Luke 8:26-39 1180-1181
Diseased woman healed, Mark 5:25-34 1142–1143
Fish are caught miraculously (first time), Luke 5:1-11 1173–1174
Fish are caught miraculously (second time), John 21:1-14 1243–1244
Five thousand people are fed, John 6:5-14. 1218
Four thousand are fed, Matthew 15:29-38 1115

Girl is freed from a demon, Mark 7:24-30 1146
Handicapped woman is healed, Luke 13:10-17 1191
Jairus's daughter is raised from the dead, Luke 8:41-42, 49-56 1181
Jesus cures a sick man, Luke 14:1-6 1191–1192
Jesus heals a man born blind, John 9:1-34 1225–1226
Jesus heals a paralyzed man, Mark 2:1-12 1138
Jesus heals the mute man, Matthew 9:32-34 1105–1106
Jesus restores a man's ear, Luke 22:49-51 1205
Jesus turns water into wine, John 2:1-11 1213
Jesus walks on the sea, Matthew 14:22-33. 1113
Lame man is cured, John 5:1-15 1217
Lazarus is raised from the dead, John 11 1227–1229
Leper is healed, Matthew 8:1-4. 1103
Mute demon-possessed man is healed, Matthew 12:22-23 1109
Nobleman's son is healed at Cana, John 4:46-54 1217
Peter's mother-in-law healed, Matthew 8:14-15 1103
Stilling the storm, Mark 4:35-41 1141–1142
Ten lepers are cured, Luke 17:11-19 1196
Two blind men find sight, Matthew 9:27-31 1105
Widow of Nain's son is raised from the dead, Luke 7:11-17. 1177
Withered hand is restored, Matthew 12:9-14. 1109